PROPERTY:
PRINCIPLES AND POLICIES

by

THOMAS W. MERRILL
Charles Keller Beekman Professor of Law
Columbia Law School

HENRY E. SMITH
Fred A. Johnston Professor of Property and Environmental Law
Yale Law School

FOUNDATION PRESS
2007

© 2007 By FOUNDATION PRESS

      195 Broadway, 9th Floor
      New York, NY 10007
      Phone Toll Free 1–877–888–1330
      Fax (212) 367–6799
      foundation–press.com
Printed in the United States of America

ISBN 978–1–59941–011–1

 TEXT IS PRINTED ON 10% POST CONSUMER RECYCLED PAPER

1st Reprint—2008

To Bob Ellickson and Carol Rose

teachers, colleagues, and friends

*

PREFACE

This casebook differs from others in that it regards property law as a single subject unified by core principles. There are many important differences between real property (land and buildings), personal property (movable things), intellectual property (original inventions, expressions, and marks), and natural resources (public lands, water, wildlife). Nevertheless, we believe there are certain basic principles that unite these different manifestations of property, and that these principles can and should be the focus of an introductory course.

The most basic principle is that property at its core entails the right to exclude others from some discrete thing. This right gives rise to a general duty on the part of others to abstain from interfering with the thing. This structure of rights and duties leads to characteristic bundles of rights, unites the various institutional forms we call property, and differentiates property rights from personal rights and contract rights. The basic exclusion strategy also serves as the starting point for further elaborations, refinements, exceptions, and overlays, which govern the use of resources with greater particularity. Together these rights to exclude and governance rules collectively make up the law of property and connect property to adjacent areas of contracts, torts, regulation, and public law.

We do not present our foundational principles as dogma. They serve as organizing devices for the casebook. The materials are designed to challenge each student to decide for him or herself whether property is defined by common principles such as the right to exclude others, or whether any such principle is so riddled with qualifications that property can only be regarded as an ad hoc "bundle of rights" without any distinguishing features.

In keeping with our perspective that property law is a unified subject, the casebook does not focus on one type of property such as land, nor does it organize materials into traditional subfields such as real, personal, intellectual, and natural resources. Instead, we draw on cases and materials from each of these areas throughout the book. No attempt is made to provide comprehensive coverage of any subfield; comprehensiveness is not possible, even in real estate law, the traditional focus. Rather our focus is on design principles common to all subfields of property. This reorientation is also appropriate, we believe, given that intellectual property and environmental issues loom much larger in the law school curriculum – and the practice of law – than was true in earlier generations when real estate law was paramount. An introduction to property law should provide a grounding that students can build upon whatever direction their future studies and practice may take.

Although our organizing principles are innovative, the selection of materials is deliberately conventional, as befits a field where stability of expectations plays such a large role. Judicial opinions serve as the primary vehicle for instruction, and we have tried to retain a high proportion of the chestnuts that have traditionally featured in property law materials. The cases are punctuated at intervals with short excerpts from the secondary literature or (in some instances) our own short summary of the secondary literature. These excerpts are designed to supply institutional or historical context, or to raise philosophical or policy questions not expressly addressed by the opinions. The secondary-source excerpts can serve as jumping off points for class discussion, or can be assigned as background reading, as the teacher sees fit.

In editing opinions, we have tried to strike a compromise between, on the one hand, burdening the student with extraneous issues and boilerplate and, on the other hand, reducing opinions to squibs lacking any context. We believe it is important, particularly in an introductory course like property law, to see how the characterization of facts in opinions influences legal conclusions, and how procedural and remedial issues interact with substantive issues. We have tried to leave in enough contextual detail to permit these connections to be explored in class. With respect to secondary materials, the editing is much more drastic, and is designed to capture one or two key points rather than the full nuanced argument. Deletions of text in all materials are indicated by three stars (* * *), but citations have often been omitted without any indication. We have frequently modified the citation form in opinions to conform to modern style. Footnotes have generally been deleted, but where they are retained, we have used their original number. Editor footnotes are indicated by symbols (*, †, etc.).

We have many people to thank for their generous contributions to this book. For their insightful comments on drafts, we would like to thank Richard Briffault, Robert Ellickson, Richard Epstein, Cynthia Estlund, Lance Liebman, Jonathan Nash, Claire Priest, Carol Rose, Sun-Joo Shin, Bruce Smith, Joshua Tate, and the anonymous reviewers for Foundation Press. A special debt of gratitude goes to our students at Columbia, Harvard, and Yale, who participated enthusiastically in our experiments with the earlier versions of this book. For their invaluable assistance tracking down permissions and helping with production, we thank Bradford Connor, P.J. Gach, Monika Piotrowicz, and Sarah Sladen. Our illustrator, Leslie Evans of Seadog Press, provided extensive assistance with illustrations and figures. We have also benefited greatly from the efforts of our research assistants at Columbia and Yale: Mina Farbood, Benjamin Gould, Michael Grisolia, Valerie Jaffee, David Olasky, Matteo Rizzolli, and Mainon Schwartz. Vic Khanna, Alan Schwartz, and the staffs at the Columbia, Harvard, and Yale Law Libraries have also been very kind and helpful in tracking down various materials. We are also deeply appreciative of the many people who assisted us with their advice and permission in connection with the material listed in the acknowledgments. For their excellent work on the book in all stages of its development, we thank John Bloomquist, Jim Coates, Steve Errick, Tim Payne, and the staff at Foundation Press. Finally, we most of all would like to thank our families for their crucial support in this project.

*

ACKNOWLEDGMENTS

The authors gratefully acknowledge the permission kindly granted to reproduce the textual excerpts and illustrations indicated below.

Books and Articles

Adler, Jonathan H., *Legal Obstacles to Private Ordering In Marine Fisheries*, 8 Roger Williams U. L. Rev. 9 (2002). Reprinted with permission.

Arruñada, Benito, *Property Enforcement as Organized Consent*, Journal of Law, Economics & Organization (2003), Vol. 19, pp. 401-44 by permission of Oxford University Press.

Baird, Douglas, and Thomas Jackson, *Information, Uncertainty and the Transfer of Property*, 13 Journal of Legal Studies 299 (1984). Copyright 1984 by The University of Chicago. All rights reserved.

Gerry W. Beyer, 19A *West's Legal Forms, Real Estate Transactions, Residential* § 48.3 (3d ed. 2002), West Publishing Co. Reprinted with permission.

Calabresi, Guido, and A. Douglas Melamed, *Property Rules, Liability Rules, and Inalienability: One View of the Cathedral*, 85 Harvard Law Review 1089 (1972). Reprinted by permission of the Harvard Law Review Association and William S. Hein Company for *The Harvard Law Review*, Vol. 85, pages 1089, 1090, 1092, and 1093.

Chafee, Jr., Zechariah, and Sidney Post Simpson, *Cases on Equity, Jurisdiction and Specific Performance* (1934), pages 704-06, 710-11. West Publishing Co. Reprinted with permission.

Coase, Ronald, *The Federal Communications Commission*, 2 Journal of Law & Economics 1 (1959). Copyright © 1959 by the University of Chicago. All rights reserved.

Coase, Ronald, *The Problem of Social Cost*, 3 Journal of Law & Economics 1 (1960). Copyright © 1960 by the University of Chicago. All rights reserved.

Craswell, Richard, *Passing on the Costs of Legal Rules: Efficiency and Distribution in Buyer-Seller Relationships*, 43 Stanford Law Review 361 (1991), pages 378-79. Reprinted with permission.

Dagan, Hanoch, *Property and the Public Domain*, 18 Yale Journal of Law & the Humanities 84 (2006) (Special Issue). Reprinted by permission of *The Yale Journal of Law & the Humanities*, Vol.18, pages 84-86, 87, 92-93.

Demsetz, Harold, *Toward a Theory of Property Rights*, 57 American Economic Review 347-48, 350-58 (1967) (Papers & Proceedings). The American Economic Review. Reprinted with permission.

Eggertsson, Thráinn, *Open Access versus Common Property*, in Terry L. Anderson and Fred S. McChesney, *Property Rights: Cooperation, Conflict, and Law* (2003), pages 74-82, 84-85. Princeton University Press. Reprinted with permission.

Ellickson, Robert, *Property in Land*, 102 Yale Law Journal 1315 (1993). Reprinted by permission of The Yale Law Journal Company and William C. Hein Company from *The Yale Law Journal*, Vol. 102, pages 1315-1400.

Grey, Tom, *The Disintegration of Property*, NYU Press. Copyright 1980 by New York University. Reprinted with the permission of New York University Press.

Haar, Charles M., and Lance Liebman, *Property and Law* (1985), Little Brown & Co. Reprinted with permission.

Hansmann, Henry, *Condominium and Cooperative Housing: Transactional Efficiency, Tax Subsidies, and Tenure Choice*, 20 Journal of Legal Studies 25 (1991). Copyright 1991 by The University of Chicago. All rights reserved.

LaFave, Wayne R., *Criminal Law*, West Publishing Co. Reprinted with permission.

Landes, William M., and Richard A. Posner, *Indefinitely Renewable Copyright*, 70 University of Chicago Law Review 471 (2003). Reprinted with permission.

Leach, W. Barton, and James K. Logan, *Perpetuities: A Standard Saving Clause to Avoid Violations of the Rule*, 74 Harvard Law Review 1141 (1961). Reprinted by permission of the Harvard Law Review Association and William S. Hein Company from *The Harvard Law Review*, Vol. 74, pages 1141-42.

Lee, Thomas R., *Stare Decisions in Historical Perspective*, 52 Vanderbilt Law Review 645 (1999). Reprinted with permission.

Lessig, Lawrence, *Free Culture*, Penguin Books. "Law: Duration," from FREE CULTURE by Lawrence Lessig, copyright © 2004 by Lawrence Lessig. Used by permission of The Penguin Press, a division of Penguin Group (USA) Inc.

Libecap, Gary, *Contracting for Property Rights*, © Cambridge University Press 1989. Reprinted with the permission of Cambridge University Press.

Penner, J.E., *The Idea of Property* (1997), Oxford University Press. Reprinted with permission.

Radin, Margaret, *Property and Personhood*, 34 Stanford Law Review 957 (1982). Reprinted with permission.

Radin, Margaret Jane, *Market-Inalienability*, 100 Harvard Law Review 1849 (1987), pages 1849, 1909-10, 1912-13, 1915-17. Reprinted with permission.

Rose, Carol, *The Comedy of the Commons: Custom, Commerce, and Inherently Public Property*, 53 University of Chicago Law Review 711 (1986). Reprinted with permission.

Rose, Carol, *Crystals and Mud in Property Law*, 40 Stanford Law Review 577 (1988). Reprinted with permission.

Rose, Carol, *Energy and Efficiency in the Realignment of Common-Law Water Rights*, 19 Journal of Legal Studies 261 (1990). Reprinted with permission.

Skilton, Robert, *Developments in Mortgage Law*, 17 Temple Law Review (1943). Reproduced with the permission of *Temple Law Review*, Vol. 17 © 1943 Temple University of the Commonwealth System of Higher Education.

Sugden, Robert, *The Economics of Rights, Co-operation and Welfare* (2d ed. 2004), Palgrave Macmillan. Reprinted with permission.

Wyman, Katrina, *From Fur to Fish*, 80 New York University Law Review 117 (2005). Reprinted with permission.

Illustrations

An Alaskan Fishing Boat, National Geographic photograph courtesy of Getty Images.

Bertaud, Alain, and Bertrand Renaud, graph, Socialist Cities without Land Markets, 41 Journal of Urban Economics 137, 141 (1997).

The Brokaw Mansion, 1 East 79th Street, New York City, photograph, *The Irving Brokaw Mansion Fifth Avenue & 79th Street.* Glass Plate Negative. Undated. Museum of the City of New York. The Underhill Collection. B.1642

The Chrisman Sisters in Front of Lizzie Chrisman's Homestead, Custer County, Nebraska, 1886, photograph, Courtesy Nebraska State Historical Society Photograph Collection.

Clifton Terrace, Washington, D.C., photograph, Courtesy Richard Chused.

Craswell, Richard, *Passing on the Costs of Legal Rules: Efficiency and Distribution in Buyer-Seller Relationships*, 43 Stanford Law Review 361 (1991), page 378. Figure 5—Low- and high-valuing marginal customers. Reprinted with permission.

Eads and Nelson's Steam Wreck Boat Sub-Marine No. 7, 1858, photograph, Courtesy Missouri Historical Society, St. Louis.

The Empire Mine Today, Courtesy Cleveland-Cliffs Corporation.

The Fontainebleau and Eden Roc Hotels, Miami Beach, Florida (2 images), Courtesy The Bramson Archive, Miami, FL. The top image shows the hotels before the wall, the bottom image after its construction.

Great Onyx Cave, Postcard published by the Great Onyx Cave Hotel (L.P. Edwards, Proprietor). Courtesy Kentucky Library, Western Kentucky University.

Gwernhaylod House, Overton: West Elevation, 1956, photograph, © Crown copyright: Royal Commission on the Ancient and Historical Monuments of Wales.

Hamidi, left, and a supporter delivering a message to Intel employees on a floppy disk after the Superior Court had enjoined his emails, photograph, Don Preisler/New York Times.

A Holdout, photograph, © 2006, The Washington Post. Photo by Bill O'Leary. Reprinted with Permission.

House in *Shelley v. Kraemer* with Commemorative Marker, Saint Louis Post-Dispatch.

The Howard County Hunt Club, photograph, Courtesy Howard County Historical Society.

Jenkins, Elliott and Thorne Donnelley, Founders of WDAP, Forerunner of WGN, photograph, Reprinted with permission from WGN Radio, Chicago, Illinois.

Kelo, Susette in Front of Her House, Photo by Isaac Reese, 2004 © Institute for Justice.

The Kelo House and Its Surroundings, Photograph by Tim Martin. Courtesy The Day Publishing Co., New London, Connecticut.

Klamath Falls City Library, ca. 1960, Courtesy Klamath County Museums.

Lakeside Village, Culver City, California, Courtesy Jack and Ginny Sher.

Lucas's Two Lots, November 1994, Courtesy William A. Fischel, Department of Economics, Dartmouth College.

Map of the Area Involved in Lucas, Douglas R. Porter, The *Lucas* Case, Urban Land, Sept. 1992, at 27, 29.

Map of Boston and Environs, *Source*: Octavius Pickering, Case of the proprietors of Charles River bridge against the proprietors of Warren bridge: argued and determined in the Supreme Judicial Court of Massachusetts, 54 & plate (Boston, Hilliard, Gray, Little, and Wilkins 1830). Courtesy of Special Collections Department, Harvard Law School Library.

Map of Land Claims in *Johnson v. M'Intosh*, From the Law and History Review. Copyright 2001 by the Board of Trustees of the University of Illinois. Used with permission of the University of Illinois Press.

Map of Land at Issue in *Delfino v. Vealencis*, Manel Baucells and Steven A. Lippman, Justice Delayed is Justice Denied: A Cooperative Game Theoretic Analysis of Hold-Up in Co-Ownership, 22 Cardozo L. Rev. 1191, 1222 (2001).

Mayor Ed J. Howard, Ann E. Hodges, and Chief W.D. Ashcraft, the afternoon of the fall, Courtesy Alabama Museum of Natural History, The University of Alabama.

The *Mexican*, Marischal Murray, Ships and South Africa (1933).

The Moakley Mural and the Grace Bible Church, East Bridgewater, Massachusetts, photograph by Craig Murray. Courtesy Craig Murray.

The Mobile Home at Its Final Resting Place after Being Dragged across the Jacques' Field, photograph, Courtesy Patrick A. Dewane, Jr., attorney for Harvey and Lois Jacque.

Myatt, John in His Studio, Photo: Jean-Philippe Defaut/The New York Times/Redux.

Nowlin Jewelry Website, *Source*: http://www.nowlinjewelry.com/body-pageintro2.htm Courtesy John Nowlin.

One of the Former Lucas Lots after Construction, March 2000, Courtesy William A. Fischel, Department of Economics, Dartmouth College.

Organ Donor Card, Courtesy New York Organ Donor Network.

Pennsylvania Railroad Station, New York City, Museum of the City of New York.

PETA Bumper Sticker, Courtesy PETA.

Plaque and Bicycle Path at the Site Involved in *Dolan v. City of Tigard*, Courtesy Dan Dolan.

Professor Longhair, 1977, photograph by Leni Sinclair. Courtesy Leni Sinclair.

Rothko, Mark in his 69th Street Studio, Photograph by Hans Namuth. Courtesy Center for Creative Photography, University of Arizona ©1991 Hans Namuth Estate.

Sanborn Fire Insurance Map of Area in *Sanborn v. McLean, Source*: 9 Sanborn Map Co., Insurance Maps of Detroit, Michigan, No. 12 (1925).

The St. Vrain Creek, photograph by Susan Thomas, Courtesy Susan Thomas.

Timetable for Pacific Air Transport, February 1, 1928, photograph, From the Collection of Craig Morris.

Title Page of the First of the Bamford Manuscripts, Courtesy Princeton University Library.

A View of Navy Pier from the Shoreline in Chicago, photograph, David Bjorgen. This image is licensed under the Creative Commons Attribution ShareAlike License v. 2.5: http://creativecommons.org/licenses/by-sa/2.5/

Zoning of Properties near the Ambler Realty Tract, Timothy Alan Fluck, *Euclid v. Ambler*: A Retrospective, 52 J. Am. Planning Ass'n 326, Map 2 (Summer 1986).

*

SUMMARY OF CONTENTS

xvii

TABLE OF CONTENTS

Feb 3d

*

TABLE OF CASES

Principal cases are in bold type. Non-principal cases are in roman type. References are to Pages.

*

PROPERTY:

Principles and Policies

*

CHAPTER I

WHAT IS PROPERTY?

A.   TWO CONCEPTIONS OF PROPERTY

What is property? There is a surprisingly wide range of answers to this basic question. We start with two conceptions of property. One may be familiar to you already: property as a right to a thing good against the world. In contrast to this traditional everyday view, many theorists adopt a competing conception of property as a collection ("bundle") of rights, with content that varies according to context and policy choices. As a way into these conceptions and the study of property law, we present in this Chapter a series of cases about interferences with interests in land. The cases provide an introduction to some basic legal concepts important to the study of property, including trespass and nuisance, the conditions for awarding injunctions rather than damages for violations of property rights, and the action for restitution for unjust enrichment. We also use the cases to raise more fundamental issues about the nature of property.

1.   TRESPASS TO LAND

Jacque v. Steenberg Homes, Inc.
Supreme Court of Wisconsin, 1997.
563 N.W.2d 154.

■ WILLIAM A. BABLITCH, JUSTICE. Steenberg Homes had a mobile home to deliver. Unfortunately for Harvey and Lois Jacque (the Jacques), the easiest route of delivery was across their land. Despite adamant protests by the Jacques, Steenberg plowed a path through the Jacques' snow-covered field and via that path, delivered the mobile home. Consequently, the Jacques sued Steenberg Homes for intentional trespass. At trial, Steenberg Homes conceded the intentional trespass, but argued that no compensatory damages had been proved, and that punitive damages could not be awarded without compensatory damages. Although the jury awarded the Jacques $1 in nominal damages and $100,000 in punitive damages, the circuit court set aside the jury's award of $100,000. The court of appeals affirmed, reluctantly concluding that it could not reinstate the punitive damages because it was bound by precedent establishing that an award of nominal damages will not sustain a punitive damage award. * * *

I.

The relevant facts follow. Plaintiffs, Lois and Harvey Jacques, are an elderly couple, now retired from farming, who own roughly 170 acres near

1

Wilke's Lake in the town of Schleswig. The defendant, Steenberg Homes, Inc. (Steenberg), is in the business of selling mobile homes. In the fall of 1993, a neighbor of the Jacques purchased a mobile home from Steenberg. Delivery of the mobile home was included in the sales price.

Steenberg determined that the easiest route to deliver the mobile home was across the Jacques' land. Steenberg preferred transporting the home across the Jacques' land because the only alternative was a private road which was covered in up to seven feet of snow and contained a sharp curve which would require sets of "rollers" to be used when maneuvering the home around the curve. Steenberg asked the Jacques on several separate occasions whether it could move the home across the Jacques' farm field. The Jacques refused. The Jacques were sensitive about allowing others on their land because they had lost property valued at over $10,000 to other neighbors in an adverse possession action in the mid–1980's. Despite repeated refusals from the Jacques, Steenberg decided to sell the mobile home, which was to be used as a summer cottage, and delivered it on February 15, 1994.

On the morning of delivery, Mr. Jacque observed the mobile home parked on the corner of the town road adjacent to his property. He decided to find out where the movers planned to take the home. The movers, who were Steenberg employees, showed Mr. Jacque the path they planned to take with the mobile home to reach the neighbor's lot. The path cut across the Jacques' land. Mr. Jacque informed the movers that it was the Jacques' land they were planning to cross and that Steenberg did not have permission to cross their land. He told them that Steenberg had been refused permission to cross the Jacques' land.

One of Steenberg's employees called the assistant manager, who then came out to the Jacques' home. In the meantime, the Jacques called and asked some of their neighbors and the town chairman to come over immediately. Once everyone was present, the Jacques showed the assistant manager an aerial map and plat book of the township to prove their ownership of the land, and reiterated their demand that the home not be moved across their land.

At that point, the assistant manager asked Mr. Jacque how much money it would take to get permission. Mr. Jacque responded that it was not a question of money; the Jacques just did not want Steenberg to cross their land. Mr. Jacque testified that he told Steenberg to "[F]ollow the road, that is what the road is for." Steenberg employees left the meeting without permission to cross the land.

At trial, one of Steenberg's employees testified that, upon coming out of the Jacques' home, the assistant manager stated: "I don't give a —— what [Mr. Jacque] said, just get the home in there any way you can." The other Steenberg employee confirmed this testimony and further testified that the assistant manager told him to park the company truck in such a way that no one could get down the town road to see the route the employees were taking with the home. The assistant manager denied giving these instructions, and Steenberg argued that the road was blocked for safety reasons.

The employees, after beginning down the private road, ultimately used a "bobcat" to cut a path through the Jacques' snow-covered field and hauled the home across the Jacques' land to the neighbor's lot. One employee testified that upon returning to the office and informing the assistant manager that they had gone across the field, the assistant manager reacted by giggling and laughing. The other employee confirmed this testimony. The assistant manager disputed this testimony.

When a neighbor informed the Jacques that Steenberg had, in fact, moved the mobile home across the Jacques' land, Mr. Jacque called the Manitowoc County Sheriff's Department. After interviewing the parties and observing the scene, an officer from the sheriff's department issued a $30 citation to Steenberg's assistant manager. * * *

This case presents three issues: (1) whether an award of nominal damages for intentional trespass to land may support a punitive damage award and, if so; (2) whether the law should apply to Steenberg or should only be applied prospectively and, if we apply the law to Steenberg; (3) whether the $100,000 in punitive damages awarded by the jury is excessive. * * *

Figure 1–1
The Mobile Home at Its Final Resting Place after Being Dragged Across the Jacques' Field

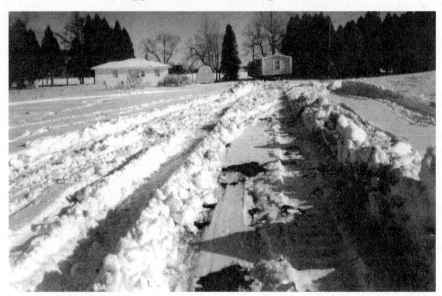

Courtesy Patrick A. Dewane, Jr., attorney for Harvey and Lois Jacque.

II.

* * * Steenberg argues that, as a matter of law, punitive damages could not be awarded by the jury because punitive damages must be supported by an award of compensatory damages and here the jury awarded only nominal and punitive damages. The Jacques contend that the rationale supporting the compensatory damage award requirement is inapposite when the wrongful act is an intentional trespass to land. We agree with the Jacques. * * *

The general rule was stated in *Barnard v. Cohen*, 162 N.W. 480 (Wis. 1917), where the question presented was: "In an action for libel, can there be a recovery of punitory damages if only nominal compensatory damages are found?" With the bare assertion that authority and better reason supported its conclusion, the *Barnard* court said no. *Barnard* continues to state the general rule of punitive damages in Wisconsin. See Tucker v. Marcus, 418 N.W.2d 818, 823–24 (Wis. 1988). The rationale for the compensatory damage requirement is that if the individual cannot show actual harm, he or she has but a nominal interest, hence, society has little interest in having the unlawful, but otherwise harmless, conduct deterred, therefore, punitive damages are inappropriate. Jacque v. Steenberg Homes, Inc., 548 N.W.2d 80 (Wis. Ct. App. 1996); Maxwell v. Kennedy, 7 N.W. 657, 658–59 (Wis. 1880).

However, whether nominal damages can support a punitive damage award in the case of an intentional trespass to land has never been squarely addressed by this court. Nonetheless, Wisconsin law is not without reference to this situation. In 1854 the court established punitive damages, allowing the assessment of "damages as a punishment to the defendant for the purpose of making an example." McWilliams v. Bragg, 3 Wis. 424, 425 (1854).[3] The *McWilliams* court related the facts and an illustrative tale from the English case of *Merest v. Harvey,* 128 Eng. Rep. 761 (C.P. 1814), to explain the rationale underlying punitive damages.

In *Merest,* a landowner was shooting birds in his field when he was approached by the local magistrate who wanted to hunt with him. Although the landowner refused, the magistrate proceeded to hunt. When the landowner continued to object, the magistrate threatened to have him jailed and dared him to file suit. Although little actual harm had been caused, the English court upheld damages of 500 pounds, explaining "in a case where a man disregards every principle which actuates the conduct of gentlemen, what is to restrain him except large damages?" McWilliams, 3 Wis. 424 at 428.

To explain the need for punitive damages, even where actual harm is slight, *McWilliams* related the hypothetical tale from *Merest* of an intentional trespasser:

> Suppose a gentleman has a paved walk in his paddock, before his
> window, and that a man intrudes and walks up and down before the

---

3. Because *McWilliams* was an action of trespass for assault and battery, we cite it not for its precedential value, but for its reasoning.

window of his house, and looks in while the owner is at dinner, is the trespasser permitted to say "here is a halfpenny for you which is the full extent of the mischief I have done." Would that be a compensation? I cannot say that it would be....

McWilliams, 3 Wis. at 428. Thus, in the case establishing punitive damages in this state, this court recognized that in certain situations of trespass, the actual harm is not in the damage done to the land, which may be minimal, but in the loss of the individual's right to exclude others from his or her property and, the court implied that this right may be punished by a large damage award despite the lack of measurable harm.

* * * The Jacques argue that both the individual and society have significant interests in deterring intentional trespass to land, regardless of the lack of measurable harm that results. We agree with the Jacques. An examination of the individual interests invaded by an intentional trespass to land, and society's interests in preventing intentional trespass to land, leads us to the conclusion that the *Barnard* rule should not apply when the tort supporting the award is intentional trespass to land.

We turn first to the individual landowner's interest in protecting his or her land from trespass. The United States Supreme Court has recognized that the private landowner's right to exclude others from his or her land is "one of the most essential sticks in the bundle of rights that are commonly characterized as property." Dolan v. City of Tigard, 512 U.S. 374, 384 (1994). This court has long recognized "[e]very person['s] constitutional right to the exclusive enjoyment of his own property for any purpose which does not invade the rights of another person." Diana Shooting Club v. Lamoreaux, 89 N.W. 880, 886 (Wis. 1902) (holding that the victim of an intentional trespass should have been allowed to take judgment for nominal damages and costs). Thus, both this court and the Supreme Court recognize the individual's legal right to exclude others from private property.

Yet a right is hollow if the legal system provides insufficient means to protect it. Felix Cohen offers the following analysis summarizing the relationship between the individual and the state regarding property rights:

[T]hat is property to which the following label can be attached:

> To the world:

> Keep off X unless you have my permission, which I may grant or withhold.

>> Signed: Private Citizen

>> Endorsed: The state

Felix S. Cohen, Dialogue on Private Property, 9 Rutgers Law Review 357, 374 (1954). Harvey and Lois Jacque have the right to tell Steenberg Homes and any other trespasser, "No, you cannot cross our land." But that right has no practical meaning unless protected by the State. And, as this court recognized as early as 1854, a "halfpenny" award does not constitute state protection.

The nature of the nominal damage award in an intentional trespass to land case further supports an exception to *Barnard*. Because a legal right is involved, the law recognizes that actual harm occurs in every trespass. The action for intentional trespass to land is directed at vindication of the legal right. W. Page Keeton, Prosser and Keeton on Torts, § 13 (5th ed. 1984). The law infers some damage from every direct entry upon the land of another. Id. The law recognizes actual harm in every trespass to land whether or not compensatory damages are awarded. Id. Thus, in the case of intentional trespass to land, the nominal damage award represents the recognition that, although immeasurable in mere dollars, actual harm has occurred.

The potential for harm resulting from intentional trespass also supports an exception to *Barnard*. A series of intentional trespasses, as the Jacques had the misfortune to discover in an unrelated action, can threaten the individual's very ownership of the land. The conduct of an intentional trespasser, if repeated, might ripen into prescription or adverse possession and, as a consequence, the individual landowner can lose his or her property rights to the trespasser. See Wis. Stat. § 893.28.

In sum, the individual has a strong interest in excluding trespassers from his or her land. Although only nominal damages were awarded to the Jacques, Steenberg's intentional trespass caused actual harm. We turn next to society's interest in protecting private property from the intentional trespasser.

Society has an interest in punishing and deterring intentional trespassers beyond that of protecting the interests of the individual landowner. Society has an interest in preserving the integrity of the legal system. Private landowners should feel confident that wrongdoers who trespass upon their land will be appropriately punished. When landowners have confidence in the legal system, they are less likely to resort to "self-help" remedies. In *McWilliams,* the court recognized the importance of " 'prevent[ing] the practice of dueling, [by permitting] juries [ ] to *punish* insult by exemplary damages.' " McWilliams, 3 Wis. at 428. Although dueling is rarely a modern form of self-help, one can easily imagine a frustrated landowner taking the law into his or her own hands when faced with a brazen trespasser, like Steenberg, who refuses to heed no trespass warnings.

People expect wrongdoers to be appropriately punished. Punitive damages have the effect of bringing to punishment types of conduct that, though oppressive and hurtful to the individual, almost invariably go unpunished by the public prosecutor. Kink v. Combs, 135 N.W.2d 789 (Wis. 1965). The $30 forfeiture was certainly not an appropriate punishment for Steenberg's egregious trespass in the eyes of the Jacques. It was more akin to Merest's "halfpenny." If punitive damages are not allowed in a situation like this, what punishment will prohibit the intentional trespass to land? Moreover, what is to stop Steenberg Homes from concluding, in the future, that delivering its mobile homes via an intentional trespass and paying the resulting Class B forfeiture, is not more profitable than obeying the law?

Steenberg Homes plowed a path across the Jacques' land and dragged the mobile home across that path, in the face of the Jacques' adamant refusal. A $30 forfeiture and a $1 nominal damage award are unlikely to restrain Steenberg Homes from similar conduct in the future. An appropriate punitive damage award probably will.

In sum, as the court of appeals noted, the *Barnard* rule sends the wrong message to Steenberg Homes and any others who contemplate trespassing on the land of another. It implicitly tells them that they are free to go where they please, regardless of the landowner's wishes. As long as they cause no compensable harm, the only deterrent intentional trespassers face is the nominal damage award of $1, the modern equivalent of *Merest's* halfpenny, and the possibility of a Class B forfeiture under Wis. Stat. § 943.13. We conclude that both the private landowner and society have much more than a nominal interest in excluding others from private land. Intentional trespass to land causes actual harm to the individual, regardless of whether that harm can be measured in mere dollars. Consequently, the *Barnard* rationale will not support a refusal to allow punitive damages when the tort involved is an intentional trespass to land. Accordingly, assuming that the other requirements for punitive damages have been met, we hold that nominal damages may support a punitive damage award in an action for intentional trespass to land. * * *

In conclusion, we hold that when nominal damages are awarded for an intentional trespass to land, punitive damages may, in the discretion of the jury, be awarded. Our decision today shall apply to Steenberg Homes. Finally, we hold that the $100,000 punitive damages awarded by the jury is not excessive. Accordingly, we reverse and remand to the circuit court for reinstatement of the punitive damage award.

NOTES AND QUESTIONS

1. There is no dispute in this case that Steenberg Homes committed an intentional trespass by moving the mobile home across the Jacques' farm field. The law of intentional trespass is "exceptionally simple and exceptionally rigorous." William L. Prosser, Torts 63 (4th ed. 1971). Any intentional intrusion that deprives another of possession of land, even if only temporarily, is considered a trespass. Restatement (Second) of Torts § 158. Intentional trespass is a strict liability tort: There is no inquiry into the balance of interests between the plaintiff and defendant or whether the intrusion was reasonable. Perhaps most strikingly, someone who commits an intentional trespass is subject to liability "irrespective of whether he thereby causes *any* harm to any legally protected interest of the other." Id. (emphasis added). In this sense, trespass to land is like the tort of battery. As one English judge put it: "If a man gives another a cuff on the ear, though it cost him nothing, no not so much as a little diachylon, yet he shall have his action; for it is a personal injury. So a man shall have an action against another for driving over his ground, though it do him no damage; for it is an invasion of his property, and the other has no right to

come there." Ashby v. White, 92 Eng. Rep. 126, 137 (K.B. 1703) (Lord Holt). Does this suggest that a person's land is seen as an extension of her body, and that the law protects both in order to vindicate fundamental rights of personal autonomy? As we will see in Chapter IV, the law is not so protective of personal property, or chattels (movable things). The *Restatement of Torts* says that a trespass to chattels will result in liability only if it causes harm to the owner of the thing. Restatement (Second) of Torts § 218 cmt. e. What might account for this difference?

2.   One historical explanation for the absence of any harm requirement is that the action for trespass to land was often used to resolve disputes over title to land. Suppose A and B are neighbors and they disagree about the location of the boundary between their properties. Even though neither has done anything to harm the other, A can sue B (or vice versa) for trespass, and the court in the course of deciding the dispute will determine where in fact the boundary lies between their two parcels. If a showing of harm were required, then either A or B would have to take some action—like erecting a fence or trampling a flower bed—in order to get the boundary dispute resolved, but it is obviously undesirable to require harmful acts from persons who would not otherwise undertake them, simply in order to resolve their respective rights to land. With the twentieth-century development of so-called quiet title actions (in which any interested person can seek a declaratory judgment resolving a dispute over title to land), however, this rationale has lost most of its force. Does this reform suggest that the action for trespass should now be limited to intrusions that cause actual harm?

3.   Did the Jacques have a sound reason for refusing permission to Steenberg Homes to move the mobile home across their field? The Jacques testified that they were sensitive about intrusions on their land because they had lost some of their property in an adverse possession lawsuit. Adverse possession, which we take up in Chapter II, is a transfer of ownership that takes place when someone occupies land *without permission*, and the statute of limitations runs before the owner challenges the occupation. If the Jacques had given their permission to Steenberg employees to cut across their land, there would have been no basis to assert a claim for adverse possession. In any event, the statute of limitations for challenging trespass to land in Wisconsin is 20 years, Wis. Stat. § 893.25, and the Steenberg moving operation would last only a few hours. So the Jacques' stated reason for objecting to the shortcut had no objective basis in law. Should this make a difference in deciding whether they should be allowed to sue for trespass, or to whether they should be allowed to recover $100,000 in punitive damages?

4.   Even if the Jacques had no sound reason for objecting to Steenberg Homes cutting across their land, why might the legal system want a rule that always (or nearly always) requires permission of the owner before people are allowed to intrude? Most of the Wisconsin Supreme Court's discussion of this point seems to assume the conclusion: The right to exclude must be enforced because it is an important right. The court suggests two reasons for strictly enforcing such a right: to avoid potential

violence and protect privacy rights. But is either concern implicated in the facts of this case? Should that matter in deciding whether to apply the strict rule? Are these arguments ultimately circular? People might not resort to violence to repel intruders if they understood that they did not have the right to exclude trespasses that do no injury to their land. And people might not be so sensitive about their privacy rights if these trespasses were tolerated. Can you think of other reasons for giving owners a near-absolute right to exclude others?

5.   Maneuvering a mobile home around a sharp curve in a country road with seven feet of snow on the ground sounds like it might be quite dangerous, and could risk bodily injury to Steenberg employees or physical damage to the mobile home. Do you think the court should have taken this into account? Courts in some circumstances have recognized a defense of necessity to an action for trespass (see Chapter IV). Should Steenberg Homes be able to claim necessity here? If not, why not?

6.   The U.S. Supreme Court has held that "grossly excessive or arbitrary" punitive damages awards violate due process, State Farm Mutual Automobile Ins. Co. v. Campbell, 538 U.S. 408, 416 (2003), and has indicated that ratios of punitive to compensatory damages exceeding nine to one are presumptively suspect as a matter of constitutional law. The punitive damages in *Jacque* are 100,000 times the compensatory damages. The Court also has instructed that one factor in determining whether an award is excessive is the relationship between the award and the maximum civil or criminal penalty the state authorizes for similar conduct. State Farm, 583 U.S. at 428; BMW of North America, Inc. v. Gore, 517 U.S. 559, 583 (1996). According to an omitted portion of the opinion in *Jacque,* the maximum fine under Wisconsin law for misdemeanor trespass was $1,000. The award in *Jacque* is 100 times this amount. On both measures, therefore, the punitive damages award seems suspect. On the other hand, the Court has also noted that an award in excess of nine times compensatory damages "may comport with due process where a particularly egregious act has resulted in only a small amount of economic damages." State Farm, supra, at 426 (internal quotations marks omitted); citing BMW at 582 (noting that a higher ratio might be necessary where "the injury is hard to detect or the monetary value of noneconomic harm might have been difficult to determine"). Does this exception apply here? Is the $1,000 ceiling set by the legislature for misdemeanor trespass an accurate benchmark of the social consequences of intentional trespass to unenclosed land? Is it possible that the purpose of the criminal trespass provision is not really to deter trespasses, so much as to provide a mechanism for the sheriff's department to mediate disputes like the one between the Jacques and Steenberg Homes? See Chapter IV.A.

Hinman v. Pacific Air Transport

United States Court of Appeals, Ninth Circuit, 1936.
84 F.2d 755.

■ HANEY, CIRCUIT JUDGE. From decrees sustaining motions to dismiss filed by defendants in two suits, appellants appeal and bring for review by this court the rights of a landowner in connection with the flight of aircraft above his land. Appellant filed one bill against Pacific Air Transport, an Oregon corporation, and another bill against United Air Lines Transport Corporation, a Delaware corporation, in each of which the allegations are nearly identical. Although two appeals are before the court, briefs filed discuss both cases, and therefore we will consider them together. * * *

It is * * * alleged that defendants are engaged in the business of operating a commercial air line, and that at all times "after the month of May, 1929, defendants daily, repeatedly and upon numerous occasions have disturbed, invaded and trespassed upon the ownership and possession of plaintiffs' tract"; that at said times defendants have operated aircraft in, across, and through said airspace at altitudes less than 100 feet above the surface; that plaintiffs notified defendants to desist from trespassing on said airspace; and that defendants have disregarded said notice, unlawfully and against the will of plaintiffs, and continue and threaten to continue such trespasses. * * *

The prayer asks an injunction restraining the operation of the aircraft through the airspace over plaintiffs' property and for $90,000 damages in each of the cases.

Figure 1–2
Timetable for Pacific Air Transport, February 1, 1928

From the Collection of Craig Morris.

Appellees contend that it is settled law in California that the owner of land has no property rights in superjacent airspace, either by code enactments or by judicial decrees and that the ad coelum doctrine* does not

---

* [*Ad coelum* is short for *cuius est solum eius usque ad coelum et ad inferos*, which means "whoever owns the soil owns also to the sky and to the depths."—eds.]

apply in California. We have examined the statutes of California, particularly California Civil Code, § 659 and § 829, as well as Grandona v. Lovdal, 21 P. 366; Wood v. Moulton, 80 P. 92; and Kafka v. Bozio, 218 P. 753, but we find nothing therein to negative the ad coelum formula. Furthermore, if we should adopt this formula as being the law, there might be serious doubt as to whether a state statute could change it without running counter to the Fourteenth amendment to the Constitution of the United States. If we could accept and literally construe the ad coelum doctrine, it would simplify the solution of this case; however, we reject that doctrine. We think it is not the law, and that it never was the law.

This formula "from the center of the earth to the sky" was invented at some remote time in the past when the use of space above land actual or conceivable was confined to narrow limits, and simply meant that the owner of the land could use the overlying space to such an extent as he was able, and that no one could ever interfere with that use.

This formula was never taken literally, but was a figurative phrase to express the full and complete ownership of land and the right to whatever superjacent airspace was necessary or convenient to the enjoyment of the land.

In applying a rule of law, or construing a statute or constitutional provision, we cannot shut our eyes to common knowledge, the progress of civilization, or the experience of mankind. A literal construction of this formula will bring about an absurdity. The sky has no definite location. It is that which presents itself to the eye when looking upward; as we approach it, it recedes. There can be no ownership of infinity, nor can equity prevent a supposed violation of an abstract conception.

The appellants' case, then, rests upon the assumption that as owners of the soil they have an absolute and present title to all the space above the earth's surface, owned by them, to such a height as is, or may become, useful to the enjoyment of their land. This height, the appellants assert in the bill, is of indefinite distance, but not less than 150 feet. * * * This, then, is appellants' premise, and upon this proposition they rest their case. Such an inquiry was never pursued in the history of jurisprudence until the occasion is furnished by the common use of vehicles of the air.

We believe, and hold, that appellants' premise is unsound. The question presented is applied to a new status and little aid can be found in actual precedent. The solution is found in the application of elementary legal principles. The first and foremost of these principles is that the very essence and origin of the legal right of property is dominion over it. Property must have been reclaimed from the general mass of the earth, and it must be capable by its nature of exclusive possession. Without possession, no right in it can be maintained.

The air, like the sea, is by its nature incapable of private ownership, except in so far as one may actually use it. This principle was announced long ago by Justinian. It is in fact the basis upon which practically all of our so-called water codes are based.

We own so much of the space above the ground as we can occupy or make use of, in connection with the enjoyment of our land. This right is not fixed. It varies with our varying needs and is coextensive with them. The owner of land owns as much of the space above him as he uses, but only so long as he uses it. All that lies beyond belongs to the world.

When it is said that man owns, or may own, to the heavens, that merely means that no one can acquire a right to the space above him that will limit him in whatever use he can make of it as a part of his enjoyment of the land. To this extent his title to the air is paramount. No other person can acquire any title or exclusive right to any space above him.

Any use of such air or space by others which is injurious to his land, or which constitutes an actual interference with his possession or his beneficial use thereof, would be a trespass for which he would have remedy. But any claim of the landowner beyond this cannot find a precedent in law, nor support in reason.

It would be, and is, utterly impracticable and would lead to endless confusion, if the law should uphold attempts of landowners to stake out, or assert claims to definite, unused spaces in the air in order to protect some contemplated future use of it. Such a rule, if adopted, would constitute a departure never before attempted by mankind, and utterly at variance with the reason of the law. If such a rule were conceivable, how will courts protect the various landowners in their varying claims of portions of the sky? How enforce a right of ejectment or restitution? Such a rule is not necessary for the protection of the landowner in any right guaranteed him by the Constitution in the enjoyment of his property. If a right like this were recognized and upheld by the courts, it would cause confusion worse confounded. It is opposed to common sense and to all human experience.

We cannot shut our eyes to the practical result of legal recognition of the asserted claims of appellants herein, for it leads to a legal implication to the effect that any use of airspace above the surface owner of land, without his consent would be a trespass either by the operator of an airplane or a radio operator. We will not foist any such chimerical concept of property rights upon the jurisprudence of this country.

We now consider the allegation of the bill that appellees' airplanes, in landing, glide through the air, within a distance of less than 100 feet to the surface of appellants' land, or possibly to a distance within five feet thereof, at one end of his tract. This presents another question for discussion. Whether such close proximity to appellants' land may constitute an impairment of his full enjoyment of the same is a question of fact. If it does, he may be entitled to relief in a proper case.

Appellants are not entitled to injunctive relief upon the bill filed here, because no facts are alleged with respect to circumstances of appellants' use of the premises which will enable this court to infer that any actual or substantial damage will accrue from the acts of the appellees complained of.

The case differs from the usual case of enjoining a trespass. Ordinarily, if a trespass is committed upon land, the plaintiff is entitled to at least nominal damages without proving or alleging any actual damage. In the instant case, traversing the airspace above appellants' land is not, of itself, a trespass at all, but it is a lawful act unless it is done under circumstances which will cause injury to appellants' possession.

Appellants do not, therefore, in their bill state a case of trespass, unless they allege a case of actual and substantial damage. The bill fails to do this. It merely draws a naked conclusion as to damages without facts or circumstances to support it. It follows that the complaint does not state a case for injunctive relief. * * *

The decree of the District Court is affirmed.

■ MATHEWS, CIRCUIT JUDGE, dissents.

NOTES AND QUESTIONS

1.   Some version of the *ad coelum* rule (see n. * supra) is followed in nearly all legal systems for purposes of defining the right to exclude others from land. See Andrea B. Carroll, Examining a Comparative Law Myth: Two Hundred Years of Riparian Misconception, 80 Tul. L. Rev. 901 (2006). As Professor Carroll recounts, the rule was extracted from Roman law, and given its Latin name, by medieval monks known as Glossators working in Italy in the twelfth and thirteenth centuries. One of these Glossators, Franciscus, was brought to England by King Edward I in 1273, which led to the introduction of the concept to English law. Lord Coke invoked the concept by its Latin name in some cases in the seventeenth century, and also noted it in his *Institutes*. See 1 Edwardo Coke, The First Part of the Institutes of the Laws of England; Or, A Commentary upon Littleton, § 4a (Francis Hargrave & Charles Butler eds., 16th ed. 1809) (1628). All this, of course, was well before airplanes were invented.

2.   The *ad coelum* rule is fundamental to property in land. Deeds to land nearly always are stated in terms of some measurement of the surface area. But under the *ad coelum* rule, the owner of the surface is also entitled to dig below the surface (for example to construct a basement for a house) and to build above the surface (for example to construct a two-story house). Without such an understanding, obviously, the bare right to the surface would be largely worthless. Rights to the column of space above the surface are often referred to as "air rights." Absent some zoning restriction or covenant restricting the height of buildings, the *ad coelum* rule means that the owner of the surface can construct a building as tall as engineering prowess will allow. Thus, a farmer in an unzoned area of rural Illinois could replicate the Sears Tower on his land, provided he could obtain financing for the project. Height restrictions are common in zoning ordinances, however, and these have been held to be a legitimate exercise of the police power, not requiring any payment of compensation. See Welch v. Swasey, 214 U.S. 91 (1909); see also Penn Central Transp. Co. v. City of New York, 438 U.S. 104 (1978), reproduced in Chapter XII. We take up some of the issues presented by the *ad coelum* rule's application to subsurface rights in Chapter II.

3.   The question whether airplane overflights are trespasses under the *ad coelum* rule was always more theoretically interesting than practically important. No court (as far as we are aware) ever held that airplanes could be held liable in trespass for flying at cruise altitudes over land below. The injury to each surface owner is small or nonexistent, and the transaction costs of negotiating permissions with each owner would be so large that they would make it impossible to fly airplanes. Courts are far too pragmatic to take such an extreme assertion of rights seriously. The puzzle in *Hinman* (and similar cases involving airplane overflights) is how to carve out an exception for overflights from the *ad coelum* rule without otherwise damaging the rule's general utility. Four different doctrinal moves have been suggested at various times to accomplish this excision.

(1) The action for trespass is available only to persons who are in possession of land. See Restatement (Second) of Torts § 158(a). One argument, therefore, is that as long as the owner of the surface has not asserted dominion and control over the portion of the column of space in which airplanes fly, the owner cannot sue in trespass. The problem with this argument is that the owner of land is generally regarded as being in "constructive" possession of the land sufficient to maintain trespass, even if the owner is not in actual possession. 87 C.J.S. Trespass § 25 (2000). For example, although the Jacques do not appear to have been in active control of the portion of their farm where Steenberg Homes trespassed, this did not defeat their right to sue for trespass.

(2) One could argue that airplane overflights are actionable as trespasses only if they cause actual harm to the surface owner. The problem with this argument is, as we have seen, that actual injury or harm is not a traditional element of trespass to land. Again, even though the Jacques did not suffer any actual harm because of the trespass by Steenberg Homes, they were allowed to recover in an action for trespass.

(3) Richard Epstein has argued that airplane overflights are technically trespasses, but the surface owner is not entitled to any damages or other relief because she obtains "implicit in kind compensation" from being able to take advantage of the benefits that airplane travel has to offer—that is, from being able to commit similar trespasses over other people's property. See Richard A. Epstein, *Intel v. Hamidi*: The Role of Self–Help in Cyberspace?, 1 J.L. Econ. & Pol'y 147, 154–55 (2005). In effect, every surface owner has implicitly granted a license to every other person to trespass over her property, since this makes everyone in society better off. There are various problems with this argument, one of which is that when airplane travel first developed and challenges were brought based on trespass, no one could be sure air travel would work out to the benefit of all. Today we can say this is undoubtedly true, but it may not have been obvious at the dawn of air travel.

(4) One could reclassify the airspace in which airplanes travel as a type of public property—public navigable airspace—in which no surface owner has any claim of private property rights. The analogy would be to navigable rivers or public highways, which are considered public property open to all.

A problem with this theory is that the declaration of public ownership of the navigable airspace might be regarded as a taking of private property, given the previous understanding that the surface owner owns "to the heavens." But even if it were a taking, the compensation might be small or nothing, given the absence of harm and the "implicit compensation" emphasized by Epstein.

4. Which of these legal arguments is embraced by the Court in *Hinman*? The U.S. Supreme Court eventually embraced the fourth theory in *United States v. Causby*, 328 U.S. 256 (1946). The Court concluded that Congress had effectively asserted federal government control over navigable airspace. The Court also concluded that the legislative declaration of federal ownership was not a taking of property, unless the flights come in so low over the property as to destroy the use and enjoyment of the surface area and improvements. For more on *Causby*, see Chapter III. Which solution to the problem of overflights do you find the most appealing?

5. The problem of airplane overflights has recently reemerged in debates about the assembly of digital databases. In particular, Google has developed a new product called GooglePrint (also known as Google Library) which consists of the full text of millions of published books, both copyrighted and noncopyrighted. The program allows users to search for particular words, phrases, authors, etc. in all the books in the database. For copyrighted works, the user can only access small spans of about 25 words with each search. The Authors Guild has sued Google on behalf of copyright owners, claiming that Google has infringed their copyrights by making a digital copy of their works without their consent. Some of Google's supporters such as Larry Lessig have responded that the problem is essentially the same as that of airplane overflights: The injury to each author is small or nonexistent, and the transaction costs of negotiating consents with each copyright owner would be so large as to make the project of creating such a database infeasible. They argue that just as the courts carved out an exception to the law of trespass for overflights, so they should carve out an exception from copyright law for use of copyrighted books in large searchable databases. Compare http://www.lessig.org/blog/archives/003140.shtml (Lessig analogizing GooglePrint to airplane overflights) with http://weblog.ipcentral.info/archives/2005/11/google_print_th.html (James DeLong criticizing the aptness of the analogy). (The controversy continues at http://www.lessig.org/blog/archives/003202.shtml and http://weblog.ipcentral.info/archives/2005/11/wednesday_morni_1.html.) Does Lessig's argument suggest that there may be other circumstances in which exceptions to trespass law should be recognized based on small injury to the landowner and high transaction costs of negotiating permissions? See generally Chapter IV.B (considering various other exceptions to the landowner's right to exclude).

2. Conceptions of Property—Philosophical Perspectives

Scholars who seek to identify the meaning of property tend to fall into two camps. On the one hand, there are the essentialists, who seek to uncover the single true definition of property as a legal concept. Essential-ist efforts can be more or less complex. In an often-quoted passage, William Blackstone, with a bit of self-conscious drama, wrote: "There is nothing which so generally strikes the imagination, and engages the affections of mankind, as the right of property; or that sole and despotic dominion which one man claims and exercises over the external things of the world, in total exclusion of the right of any other individual in the universe." 2 William Blackstone, Commentaries on the Laws of England *2 (1766). This reflects a relatively simple essentialist conception: Property confers a kind of exclusive sovereign control over some "external thing." Others have come up with more complex characterizations of property that are still essential-ist, in that they are premised on the understanding that there is one correct meaning of property. For example, Tony Honoré, an English analyt-ical philosopher, has developed a conception of what "full ownership" means in a mature liberal legal system that features no less than eleven elements. See Tony Honoré, Ownership, in Making Law Bind 161 (1987).

On the other hand, there are the skeptics, who believe that it is fruitless to try to come up with a single canonical conception of what property means in a legal system. For the skeptics, "property" is just a word that means nothing until we spell out—using different words—exactly what we are talking about in any given context. The skeptical view is reflected in the common metaphor that property is a "bundle of rights" or "bundle of sticks." The metaphor was apparently first used in a nineteenth century treatise, see John Lewis, Treatise on the Law of Eminent Domain in the United States 43 (1888), and gained wider currency in the 1920s and 1930s. See, e.g., Benjamin N. Cardozo, the Paradoxes of Legal Science 129 (1928). The metaphor implies that one can add to or subtract from the bundle more or less without limit, and still talk about the bundle as property. Many of the Legal Realists who came to the fore in the 1930s shared this view of the plasticity of property. The skeptical perspective is also reflected in the First Edition of the American Law Institute's *Restate-ment of Property*. See Restatement of Property § 10 (1936) ("The word 'owner,' as it is used in this Restatement, means the person who has one or more interests.").

Although the skeptical tradition has the widest following among Amer-ican law professors today, essentialism is making something of a comeback. We start with an excerpt from James Penner, a legal philosopher at King's College London who defends the essentialist view, and then an excerpt from Tom Grey, a Professor of Law at Stanford who reflects the skeptical tradition that dominates in America.

J.E. Penner, *The Idea of Property in Law* 23, 26–27, 68, 70–71, 75–76 (1997)

A right *in rem* is, roughly, a right in respect of a *res*, a thing. The classic example is a property right. Rights *in rem* are characterized as those rights which bind "all the world," that is, rights which must be respected by all, or virtually all, of the subjects of the legal system; everybody must refrain from trespassing on my land. In contrast, a right *in personam* is a right in the behaviour of some person, such as the right to the performance of a contract. Rights *in personam* bind only specific individuals; only the other party to the contract has any obligations which correlate to one's contractual rights. * * *

One may visualize the holder of a right *in rem* as standing at the hub of a spoked wheel, with the spokes representing relations to a multitude of duty-owers. Yet one may just as easily visualize the ower of a duty not to interfere with property, i.e. the ower of a duty *in rem*, in exactly the position, at the hub, so to speak, except that the spokes will represent relations to all those who hold property. These are lousy pictures, because a moment's notice will confirm that any trace of a *res*, like a bicycle or a pound note, is missing, which is something of a deficiency if we are trying to explain the normative relation which comprises property. * * * But if we pay attention to the fact that rights and duties *in rem* do not refer to persons, not in the sense that the property is not owned by persons, but in the sense that nothing to do with *any particular individual's personality* is involved in the normative guidance they offer, we may get somewhere. * * *

[I]n general, it is completely unknown to us whether any given amount of property is owned by one person or by several or many. * * * We are under one duty to the plurality of property holders however their property is distributed amongst themselves. It is a simple, single duty, and very easy to comply with.† * * * As I walk through a car park, my actual, practical duty is only capable of being understood as a duty which applies to the cars there, not to a series of owners. For all I know, the cars are owned by the same person. The content of my duty not to interfere is not structured in any way by the actual ownership relation of the cars' owners to their specific cars. By the same token, if one of the cars has just been sold, so that there is a new owner, or if one of the cars has been lent to the owner's sister-in-law, again, my duty has not changed one whit. Thus transactions between an owner and a specific other do not change the duties of everyone else not to interfere with the property. * * *

The concepts of exclusion and use are more complex than they first appear, because, in general, they are intertwined. One can, of course, have a right to use something without having a right to exclude others, and vice versa. One can have the right to use a library, but no right to exclude others from it. Similarly a guard may have the right to exclude others from the library but no right to use it himself.

Yet rights purely to exclude or purely to use interact naturally, as it were, in the sense that use almost always involves some exclusion of others. As a rightful user of a library, I may not have the right to exclude others, but I would certainly have the right to occupy a desk, or take a book from a shelf. In this sense I have a right *not to be excluded* from the library, since use implies non-exclusion. * * *

† [The balance of this paragraph has been relocated from the original.—eds.]

How do the right to use and the right to exclude explain the right to property? The right to property is grounded by the interest we have in using things in the broader sense. No one has any interest in merely excluding others from things, for any reason and no reason at all. The interest that underpins the right to property is the interest we have in purposefully dealing with things. Because we have long-term interests in respect of things, and interests in using them in many different ways the broad definition of use is the appropriate one. But because we are concerned with the right to property, we must be concerned with the correlative duties imposed on others. Because of the social setting in which we live, we see that any meaningful right to use is the opposite side of the coin to a right to exclude. Secondly, the right to use reflects our practical interest in exclusively using things, which correlates to duties *in rem* on everyone else not to interfere with our uses of things. Their not using the property is framed in terms of their duties to exclude themselves from it.

Thus at a theoretical level we understand the right to property equally as a right of exclusion or a right of use, since they are opposite sides of the same coin. Yet we can equally see that only one of these ways of looking at the right might drive the analysis in understanding the shape of the property norms in the legal system. It is my contention that the law of property is driven by an analysis which takes the perspective of exclusion, rather than one which elaborates a right to use. In other words, in order to understand property, we must look to the way that the law contours the duties it imposes on people to exclude themselves from the property of others, rather than regarding the law as instituting a series of positive liberties or power to use particular things. This can be expressed as follows, in what I will call the *exclusion thesis: the right to property is a right to exclude others from things which is grounded by the interest we have in the use of things.*

On this formulation use serves a justificatory role for the right, while exclusion is seen as the formal essence of the right. It is our interest in the use of property which grounds the right *in rem* to property and the correlative general duty *in rem*; yet exclusion is the practical means by which that interest is protected, and that makes all the difference to our understanding of property. * * *

NOTES AND QUESTIONS

1.   The distinction between rights *in rem* and *in personam* is fundamental to the law of property, and we will encounter it periodically throughout these materials. The distinction concerns who bears the duty to respect the right. An in rem right creates duties in a large and indefinite class of others ("all the world" is the expression often used with some exaggeration) to respect the right. An in personam right creates a duty in only a small and definitely ascertained number of others (e.g., B owes a duty to A). Not all in rem rights (as defined) are property rights. Rights of bodily security, reputation, and privacy are also in rem in the sense that

they create duties of noninterference in a large and indefinite class of others. These are basic duties created by tort law. What makes something an in rem right of property is the recognition of duties in a large and indefinite class of others not to interfere with some *thing* (as opposed to a duty not to interfere with a person). Clearly, one can also have in personam rights with respect to things, in the sense of rights that create duties on the part of only a small number of ascertained others. Contract rights are the clear example. Very roughly speaking—and we emphasize the "very"—the law of torts as it applies to persons and the core of the law of property establish in rem rights, whereas the law of contract establishes in personam rights. One interesting implication of this distinction is that in rem rights tend to be simple, easy-to-understand duties of noninterference (like "no hitting" or "no trespassing"). This is because the duty that corresponds to the right has to be observed by such a large and indefinite mass of people. Complicated rights that impose affirmative duties to take particular actions are more likely to be in personam and hence will be more likely to be imposed by contract or government regulation. For further discussion see Thomas W. Merrill & Henry E. Smith, The Property/Contract Interface, 101 Colum. L. Rev. 773 (2001); Wesley Newcomb Hohfeld, Fundamental Legal Conceptions as Applied in Judicial Reasoning, 26 Yale L.J. 710 (1917).

2.   Penner's emphasis on the right to exclude captures the attitude of the Wisconsin Supreme Court about the property rights of Harvey and Lois Jacque. The court justifies the punitive damages award as a way of vindicating the Jacques' right to exclude others from their land, which the court says is central to the understanding that the land is their property. But what about the dispute in *Hinman*? The *Hinman* court seems to view property more as a collection of rights, and the question whether this includes the right to exclude airplane overflights depends on a considerations of competing social interests, not any a priori conception of what ownership entails.

3.   Penner's conception of property as the right to exclude others from things grounded in our interest in the use of the thing seems to fit ownership of land and tangible personal property like cars—for most purposes at least. It may even fit certain intellectual property rights like patents and copyrights, which are said to create a right to exclude others from using certain inventions or forms of expression. But how does Penner's conception apply to other interests we commonly call property, like stocks or bonds or money? Money started out as a tangible form of personal property—gold and silver coins that have an intrinsic value. Then it turned into pieces of paper which promised to pay the bearer on demand a certain amount of gold or silver. Today it is just "fiat" currency—a piece of paper (or a digital entry in a computer operated by a bank) of no intrinsic value but which society recognizes as a unit of value that can be exchanged for goods and services that have intrinsic value. See James Willard Hurst, A Legal History of Money in the United States, 1774–1970 (1973). We commonly think of money as property. But what exactly is the "thing" that

the owner of money is empowered to exclude others from under Penner's exclusion model?

4. If property rights, being in rem, create duties on the part of all persons in a community to respect owned things, how do these generalized duties get started? Can it be said that everyone has agreed or consented to being bound to respect property? If so, when and where was this consent given? See, e.g., Geraint Parry, John Locke 51 (1978); Jeremy Waldron, The Right to Private Property 126–283 (1988).

5. For other analyses that emphasize the centrality of the right to exclude others to the understanding of the interests we call property, see J.W. Harris, Property and Justice 13 (1996); Waldron, supra, at 26–61; Thomas W. Merrill, Property and the Right to Exclude, 77 Neb. L. Rev. 730 (1998).

Tom Grey, *The Disintegration of Property*, in NOMOS XXII: PROPERTY 69–71 (J. Pennock & J. Chapman eds., 1980)

In the English-speaking countries today, the conception of property held by the specialist (the lawyer or economist) is quite different from that held by the ordinary person. Most people, including most specialists in their unprofessional moments, conceive of property as *things* that are *owned* by *persons*. To own property is to have exclusive control of something—to be able to use it as one wishes, to sell it, give it away, leave it idle, or destroy it. Legal restraints on the free use of one's property are conceived as departures from an ideal conception of full ownership.

By contrast, the theory of property rights held by the modern specialist tends both to dissolve the notion of ownership and to eliminate any necessary connection between property rights and things. Consider ownership first. The specialist fragments the robust unitary conception of ownership into a more shadowy "bundle of rights." Thus, a thing can be owned by more than one person, in which case it becomes necessary to focus on the particular limited rights each of the co-owners has with respect to the thing. Further, the notion that full ownership includes rights to do as you wish with what you own suggest that you might sell off particular aspects of your control—rights to certain uses, to profits from the thing, and so on. Finally, rights of use, profit, and the like can be parceled out along a temporal dimension as well—you might sell your control over your property for tomorrow to one person, for the next day to another, and so on. * * *

The same point can be made with respect to fragmentation of ownership generally. When a full owner of a thing begins to sell off various of his rights over it—the right to use it for this purpose tomorrow, for that purpose next year, and so on—at what point does he cease to be the owner, and who then owns the thing? You can say that each one of the many rights holders owns it to the extent of the right, or you can say that no one owns it. Or you can say, as we still tend to do, in the vestigial deference to the lay conception of property, that some conventionally designated rights constitute "ownership." The issue is seen as one of terminology: nothing significant turns on it.

What, then, of the idea that property rights must be rights in things? Perhaps we no longer need a notion of ownership, but surely property rights are a distinct category from other legal rights, in that they pertain to things. But this suggestion cannot withstand analysis either; most property in the modern capitalist economy is intangible. Consider the common forms of wealth: shares of stock in corporations, bonds, various kinds of commercial paper, bank accounts, insurance policies—not to mention more arcane intangibles such as trademarks, patents, copyrights, franchises, and business goodwill.

In our everyday language, we tend to speak of these rights as if they were attached to things. Thus we "deposit our money in the bank," as if we were putting a thing in a place; but really we are creating a complex set of abstract claims against an abstract legal institution. We are told that as insurance policy holders we "own a piece of the rock"; but we really have other abstract claims against another abstract institution. We think of our share of stock in Megabucks Corporation as part ownership in the Megabucks factory outside town; but really the Megabucks board of directors could sell the factory and go into another line of business and we would still have the same claims on the same abstract corporation.

Property rights can no longer be characterized as "rights of ownership" or as "rights in things" by specialists in property. What, then, *is* their special characteristic? How do property rights differ from rights generally—from human rights or personal rights or rights to life or liberty, say? Our specialists and theoreticians have no answer; or rather, they have a multiplicity of widely differing answers, related only in that they bear some association or analogy, more or less remote, to the common notion of property as ownership of things. * * *

The conclusion of all this is that discourse about property has fragmented into a set of discontinuous usages. The more fruitful and useful of these usages are those stipulated by theorists; but these depart drastically from each other and from common speech. Conversely, meanings of "property" in law that cling to their origin in the thing-ownership conception are integrated least successfully into the general doctrinal framework of law, legal theory, and economics. It seems fair to conclude from a glance at the range of current usages that the specialists who design and manipulate the legal structures of the advanced capitalist economies could easily do without using the term "property" at all. * * *

The substitution of the bundle-of-rights for a thing-ownership conception of property has the ultimate consequence that property ceases to be an important category in legal and political theory. This in turn has political implications * * * The legal realists who developed the bundle-of-rights notion were on the whole supportive of the regulatory and welfare state, and in the writings that develop the bundle-of-rights conception, a purpose to remove the sanctity that had traditionally attached to the rights of property can often be discerned. * * *

I would want to deny, however, that the account and explanation of the breakdown of the concept of property offered here is in the last analysis ideological, in the pejorative sense of a mystifying or false apologetic. The development of a largely capitalist market economy toward industrialism objectively demands formulation of its emergent system of economic entitlements in something like the bundle-of-rights form, which in turn must lead to the decline of property as a central category of legal and political thought.

NOTES AND QUESTIONS

1.   Grey's defense of property as a contingent bundle of rights seems to describe the inquiry in *Hinman* fairly accurately. The dispute is over whether property in land does or does not include, as one of the sticks in the bundle, the right to block airplane overflights. Before the suit, there is uncertainty about whether this is one of the features of property in land. After the decision, we know it is not. According to the bundle of rights view, this is how we determine what "property" means, by building up or cutting down the number of sticks in the bundle over time. But how does the bundle of sticks metaphor account for the great importance that the Wisconsin Supreme Court in *Jacques* and other courts attribute to the right to exclude others from things as a central feature of property?

2.   Do Penner and Grey fundamentally disagree about the nature of the concept of property, or do they simply emphasize different aspects of a single but complex phenomenon? Penner, in seeking to explicate the meaning of property, takes as his core case individual ownership of land or tangible personal property. When he moves beyond the core case later in his book and takes up questions such as whether stocks, bonds, and money are "property," the analysis becomes more convoluted. Grey, for his part, does not deny that most people, "including most specialists in their unprofessional moments," have an intuitive conception of property as the right to control things. His case for the "disintegration" of property rests on emphasizing specialized discourses that deal with issues at some remove from the core case of individual ownership of things. If this characterization of the two readings is correct, then the question becomes: Which part of the story we should emphasize—the messiness at the perimeter, or the clarity at the core? Can the decisions in *Jacque* and *Hinman* be reconciled the same way—one dealing with the "normal" rule, the other with an "exception"? For another analysis that contrasts the thing-like view of property held by "ordinary observers" with the bundle-of-sticks view employed by "scientific policymakers," see Bruce A. Ackerman, Private Property and the Constitution (1977); see generally Thomas W. Merrill & Henry E. Smith, What Happened to Property in Law and Economics?, 111 Yale L.J. 357 (2001).

B.   THE TRESPASS/NUISANCE DIVIDE

Jacque v. Steenberg Homes and *Hinman v. Pacific Air Transport* represent two different responses to intentional trespasses to land by strangers. Another contrast, which exposes additional questions about the nature of property rights, concerns the distinction between invasions of land by large objects (like house trailers or airplanes) and interferences with the use and enjoyment of land caused by some activity on neighboring land, like generating pollution or making excessive noise. The latter sort of interferences are governed by a different common-law doctrine—the law of nuisance—which has traits very different from the law of trespass (at least the version applied in *Jacque*).

1. NUISANCE

P   *D*

Hendricks v. Stalnaker

Supreme Court of Appeals of West Virginia, 1989.
380 S.E.2d 198.

■ NEELY, JUSTICE: Walter S. Stalnaker, defendant below, appeals from a decision by the Circuit Court of Lewis County declaring a water well drilled on his property to be a private nuisance to Harry L. Hendricks and Mary Hendricks, plaintiffs below. The Hendrickses, owners of the property adjacent to that of Mr. Stalnaker, were refused a Health Department permit for a septic system located within 100 feet of Mr. Stalnaker's water well. The Circuit Court of Lewis County, based on a jury verdict, found the water well to be a private nuisance and ordered its abatement. On appeal, Mr. Stalnaker argues that because his water well was not an unreasonable use of his land, he is not liable for the effects on the Hendrickses' property. We agree and, therefore, reverse the decision of the circuit court.

Mr. Stalnaker owns approximately 10 acres of land situated on Glady Fork Road, Lewis County. In 1985, Mr. Stalnaker constructed his home on a 2.493 acre portion of the tract, and had two water wells dowsed. One well was located behind his house and the other, near the Hendrickses' property. The rear well was near land disturbed by a former strip mine and, therefore, the well produced poor quality water. Except for a small section of land near the Hendrickses' property—the location of the second "dowsed" well—most of Mr. Stalnaker's home tract had been disturbed by a strip mine. In August 1985, Mr. Stalnaker spent approximately $3,000 in an unsuccessful attempt to treat the water from the rear well.

In 1984, the Hendrickses purchased approximately 2.95 acres adjacent to Mr. Stalnaker's property for a home site or a trailer development. On 31 December 1985, Mr. Hendricks met with the Lewis County sanitarian to determine locations for a water well and a septic system. The Health Department requires a distance of 100 feet between water wells and septic systems before it will issue permits.[2] Because the Hendrickses' land was too hilly or had been disturbed in order to build a pond, the only location for a

---

2. The county sanitarian testified that the purpose of the distance requirement was to protect not just an individual well but to prevent contamination of the ground streams of the aquifer.

septic system on the tract was near Mr. Stalnaker's property. On 13 January 1986, the Hendrickses contacted the county sanitarian to visit their property to complete the septic system permit application. The county sanitarian said because of snowy weather he would come out later in the week.

On 13 January 1986, Mr. Stalnaker called the sanitarian and was told about the Hendrickses' proposed septic system. Mr. Stalnaker was also told that the county sanitarian would be unavailable on 14 January 1986 but could meet with him on 15 January 1986. On 14 January 1986, Mr. Stalnaker contacted a well driller, who applied for and received a well drilling permit for the second well from the assistant sanitarian. The well was completed on 25 January 1986 but was not connected to Mr. Stalnaker's home until January 1987.

On 15 January 1986, the county sanitarian informed Mr. Hendricks that no permit for his proposed septic system could be issued because the absorption field for his septic system was within one hundred feet of Mr. Stalnaker's water well. Mr. Hendricks did install a septic system without a permit in January 1987; however, the system was left inoperative pending the outcome of this suit.

The Hendrickses filed suit in the Circuit Court of Lewis County on 29 January 1987 requesting (1) the water well be declared a private nuisance, (2) the nuisance be abated, and (3) damages. In a bifurcated trial, the jury found that the water well was a private nuisance and the trial judge ordered it to be abated. On the issue of damages the jury found for the defendant and awarded no damages.

I

In the past we have broadly described what constitutes a nuisance:

> A nuisance is anything which annoys or disturbs the free use of one's property, or which renders its ordinary use or physical occupation uncomfortable.... A nuisance is anything which interferes with the rights of a citizen, either in person, property, the enjoyment of his property, or his comfort.... A condition is a nuisance when it clearly appears that enjoyment of property is materially lessened, and physical comfort of persons in their homes is materially interfered with thereby. (Citations omitted).

Martin v. Williams, 93 S.E.2d 835, 844 (W. Va. 1956). * * * This definition of nuisance includes acts or conditions that affect either the general public or a limited number of persons. In *Hark v. Mountain Fork Lumber Co.*, 34 S.E.2d 348, 354 (W. Va. 1945) we defined a public nuisance as that which "affects the general public as public, and [a private nuisance as that which] injures one person or a limited number of persons only."

In order clearly to delineate between a public nuisance and a private nuisance, we define a private nuisance as a substantial and unreasonable interference with the private use and enjoyment of another's land. The definition of private nuisance includes conduct that is intentional and unreasonable, negligent or reckless, or that results in an abnormally dangerous conditions or activities in an inappropriate place. See W. Prosser, Handbook of the Law of Torts § 87 at 580, § 89 at 593 (4th ed. 1971); Restatement (Second) of Torts §§ 821D, 821F, 822 (1979); W. Keeton, Prosser and Keeton on the Law of Torts § 87 (5th ed. 1984). Recovery for a private nuisance is limited to plaintiffs who have suffered a significant harm to their property rights or privileges caused by the interference. Restatement (Second) of Torts §§ 821E, 821F (1979).

Early West Virginia cases indicate that the existence of a private nuisance was determined primarily by the harm caused. Medford v. Levy, 8 S.E. 302 (W. Va. 1888) (cooking odors); Flanagan v. Gregory and Poole, Inc., 67 S.E.2d 865 (W. Va. 1951) (inadequate culvert). Gradually the focus included an examination of the reasonableness of the property's use. See McGregor v. Camden, 34 S.E. 936 (W. Va. 1899) (required an examination of the location, capacity and management of oil and gas well); Pope v. Edward M. Rude Carrier Corp., 75 S.E.2d 584 (W. Va. 1953) (transportation of explosives); Martin, supra (used automobile lot); State ex rel. Ammerman v. City of Philippi, 65 S.E.2d 713 (W. Va. 1951) (tire recapping business); Ritz v. Woman's Club of Charleston, 173 S.E. 564 (W. Va. 1934) (noise); Harless v. Workman, 114 S.E.2d 548 (W. Va. 1960) (coal dust).

In the area of public nuisance, we have made explicit that an examination of the "reasonableness or unreasonableness of the use of property in relation to the particular locality" is a fair test to determine the existence of a public nuisance. Similarly, any determination of liability for a private nuisance must include an examination of the private use and enjoyment of the land seeking protection and the nature of the interference.[5]

Because the present case concerns conduct that is not a negligent, reckless, or abnormally dangerous activity, our discussion of private nuisance is limited to conduct that is intentional and unreasonable. An interference is intentional when the actor knows or should know that the conduct is causing a substantial and unreasonable interference. Restatement (Second) of Torts § 825 (1979). The unreasonableness of an intentional interference must be determined by a balancing of the landowners' interests. An interference is unreasonable when the gravity of the harm outweighs the social value of the activity alleged to cause the harm. See W. Prosser, supra § 87, at 581, § 89 at 596; Restatement (Second) of Torts § 826 (1979); W. Keeton, supra § 88, at 629. Restatement (Second) of Torts §§ 827 and 828 (1979) list some of the factors to be considered in determin-

---

5. The *Restatement (Second) of Torts* § 822 (1979) requires a consideration of unreasonableness as part of the determination of liability.

One is subject to liability for a private nuisance if, but only if, his conduct is a legal cause of an invasion of another's interest in the private use and enjoyment of land, and the invasion is either

(a) intentional and unreasonable, or

(b) unintentional and otherwise actionable under the rules controlling liability for negligent or reckless conduct, or for abnormally dangerous conditions or activities.

ing the gravity of the harm and the social value of the activity alleged to cause the harm.[6] However, this balancing to determine unreasonableness is not absolute. Additional consideration might include the malicious or indecent conduct of the actor. Restatement (Second) of Torts § 829. * * *

In the case before us, the Hendrickses' inability to operate a septic system on their property is clearly a substantial interference with the use and enjoyment of their land. The record indicates that the installation of the water well was intentional, but there was no evidence that the installation was done so as maliciously to deprive the Hendrickses of a septic system. Mr. Stalnaker wanted to insure himself of an adequate water supply and found no alternative to the well he dug.

The critical question is whether the interference, the installation of a water well, was unreasonable. Unreasonableness is determined by balancing the competing landholders' interests. We note that either use, well or septic system, burdens the adjacent property. Under Health Department regulations, a water well merely requires non-interference within 100 feet of its location. In the case of a septic system, however, the 100 foot safety zone, extending from the edge of the absorption field, may intrude on adjacent property. Thus, the septic system, with its potential for drainage, places a more invasive burden on adjacent property.[7] Clearly both uses present similar considerations of gravity of harm and social value of the activity alleged to cause the harm. Both a water well and a septic system are necessary to use this land for housing; together they constitute the in and out of many water systems. Neither party has an inexpensive and practical alternative. The site of the water well means quality water for Mr. Stalnaker, and the Hendrickses have only one location available for their septic system.

In the case before us, we are asked to determine if the water well is a private nuisance. But if the septic system were operational, the same question could be asked about the septic system. Because of the similar competing interests, the balancing of these landowners' interests is at least equal or, perhaps, slightly in favor of the water well. Thus, the Hendrickses have not shown that the balancing of interests favors their septic system.

6. The *Restatement (Second) of Torts* § 827 (1979) lists the following "gravity of harm" factors:

(a) The extent of the harm involved;

(b) the character of the harm involved;

(c) the social value that the law attaches to the type of use or enjoyment invaded;

(d) the suitability of the particular use or enjoyment invaded to the character of the locality; and

(e) the burden on the person harmed of avoiding the harm.

The *Restatement (Second) of Torts* § 828 lists the following "utility of conduct" factors:

(a) the social value that the law attaches to the primary purpose of the conduct;

(b) the suitability of the conduct to the character of the locality; and

(c) the impracticability of preventing or avoiding the invasion.

7. Rules and Regulations of the Health Department § 64–9–5.7 [1983] require a recorded easement or authorization for use of or crossing of adjacent property for off lot disposal of sewage or effluent.

We find that the evidence presented clearly does not demonstrate that the water well is an unreasonable use of land and, therefore, does not constitute a private nuisance. * * *

We find that because the evidence is not disputed and only one interference is reasonable, the trial court should have held as a matter of law that the water well was not a private nuisance. * * *

Reversed.

NOTES AND QUESTIONS

1. The law of nuisance, in contrast to the conventional (*Jacque*-style) law of trespass, is neither simple nor rigorous. In fact, commentators have described nuisance doctrine as so complex and uncertain that it amounts to an "impenetrable jungle." William L. Prosser, Torts 571 (4th ed. 1971). The *Restatement of Torts* valiantly seeks to bring some order to this complexity by providing that a nuisance is an interference with the use and enjoyment of land that causes "significant harm" and is "unreasonable." Restatement (Second) of Torts §§ 821F, 822. The primary definition of "unreasonable," according to the *Restatement*, is that "the gravity of the harms outweighs the utility of the actor's conduct." Id. § 826. The *Hendricks* court, which generally follows the *Restatement*, reads this to mean that nuisance liability turns on "balancing the competing landowners' interests."

Definitions
Nuisance
Unreasonable

2. How does the court here arrive at the conclusion of reasonableness? The court says that the value of the competing interests is "similar," or "perhaps" is "slightly in favor of the water well." Does the opinion give any reasons that might support this conclusion? Should the court, following the guidance of the *Restatement*, have conducted a more rigorous (and perhaps quantified) analysis of the costs and benefits of septic tanks and water wells before deciding the reasonableness issue? Why do you suppose the court did not do this? If a rigorous cost-benefit analysis is not required, should the question of reasonableness be regarded as one of fact? If so, why shouldn't the court accept as controlling the jury's determination that the well was a nuisance?

3. Although the *Restatement* is widely followed—or at least cited—in modern nuisance cases, it is by no means the only possible approach that courts could take to resolving nuisance disputes. We take up nuisance in greater detail in Chapter IX, but for now, consider these possibilities and ask yourself whether any of them may have carried weight with the court in *Hendricks*:

(1) Instead of balancing the interests of the parties, perhaps courts should simply ask whether the defendant has committed some kind of "invasion" of plaintiff's land that causes harm above a certain threshold level ("significant harm"). Richard Epstein has argued that under the English common law, a nuisance would be found only if the defendant's conduct had caused or threatened to cause some kind of invasion, such as

by air pollution particles, sewage added to a stream, or sound waves—a kind of mini-trespass if you will. Richard A. Epstein, Nuisance Law: Corrective Justice and Its Utilitarian Constraints, 8 J. Legal Stud. 49 (1979). Is the outcome in the instant case consistent with this principle? Would Stalnaker's well, which would draw water from an aquifer common to both parcels of land, have caused any "invasion" of the Hendrickses' subsurface land rights? Conversely, would the Hendrickses' septic tank, which would diffuse waste water into the surrounding soil, have caused any "invasion" of Stalnaker's subsurface rights?

(2) Another possibility would be to decide these disputes by enforcing the general understanding in the relevant community of what constitute "normal uses" of land. See Robert C. Ellickson, Alternatives to Zoning: Covenants, Nuisance Rules, and Fines as Land Use Controls, 40 U. Chi. L. Rev. 681 (1973). Although it is unclear from the facts as stated, it is likely that both water wells and septic tanks are common uses of land in rural West Virginia. Can it be said that either a water well or a septic tank is more "normal" or "natural" than the other? Water wells have been around since the dawn of civilization, whereas septic fields are a more recent contrivance of human ingenuity. Should this matter?

(3) Some cases and commentators have given weight to temporal priority, in the sense that the first use to be established is given a presumption of validity relative to a later, incompatible use. See Donald Wittman, First Come, First Served: An Economic Analysis of "Coming to the Nuisance," 9 J. Legal Stud. 557 (1980). Note that Stalnaker rushes to complete his well before the Hendrickses can obtain a permit for their septic system. Is this a legitimate reason to prefer Stalnaker's use to the Hendricks's use in determining whether the well is a nuisance? Or is this undesirable behavior? Might it be a legitimate consideration in other circumstances?

(4) A final approach that may explain some of the cases is to ask whether the defendant (or the plaintiff) has been acting in a way consonant with general norms of "neighborliness." See Stewart E. Sterk, Neighbors in American Land Law, 87 Colum. L. Rev. 55, 88–103 (1987). For example, many jurisdictions recognize that the erection of a "spite fence," meaning a fence that is built for the sole purpose of irritating a neighbor, is an actionable nuisance. Id. at 62–63. As between Stalnaker and the Hendrickses, who is behaving in the more "neighborly" fashion? Is this judgment too subjective to serve as the basis for a rule of property law?

Given all these theories or themes in nuisance law competing with the *Restatement*'s balancing test and with each other, can you see why Prosser threw up his hands and said it was an "impenetrable jungle?"

4.   Consider again the decision in *Hinman v. Pacific Air Transport* in light of *Hendricks* and the brief summary of nuisance law provided here. Does *Hinman* ultimately subject airplane overflights to a mode of analysis more commonly associated with nuisance than trespass? If there is a subset of trespass cases that should be resolved using nuisance principles, how could that subset be defined? Conversely, is there a subset of nuisance cases

that should be handled using a strict liability doctrine like trespass? If so, how could this subset of nuisance cases be defined?

5.   Given that trespass is typically clear and strict, and nuisance is typically neither clear nor strict, the boundary between interferences governed by trespass and those governed by nuisance would seem to be a matter of some importance. In principle, the boundary between trespass and nuisance is fixed by the nature of the interests these actions are said to protect: <u>Trespass is said to protect the interest in *possession* of land, while nuisance is said to protect the *use and enjoyment* of la</u>nd. See Restatement (Second) of Torts § 821D, cmt. d. From this, it has generally been assumed that trespass applies when the defendant intrudes upon the land with some object large and solid enough to physically displace the plaintiff from a portion of her land, such as an intrusion by another person, a vehicle, standing water—or a mobile home. Conversely, if the invasion is committed by small objects like particles of gas or sound or light waves, this will be governed by the law of nuisance. Similarly, noninvasive interferences with use and enjoyment of land, like the construction of a spite fence, will be governed by the law of nuisance rather than trespass. (We take up the distinction between trespass and nuisance further in Chapter IX.)

2.   EXCLUSION AND GOVERNANCE

Another way to consider the distinction between trespass and nuisance is to think of them as two different strategies for resolving disputes about how scarce resources are used: exclusion and governance. See Henry E. Smith, Exclusion versus Governance: Two Strategies for Delineating Property Rights, 31 J. Legal Stud. S453 (2002); Henry E. Smith, Exclusion and Property Rules in the Law of Nuisance, 90 Va. L. Rev. 965 (2004). Under an exclusion strategy, decisions about resource use are delegated to an owner who acts as the manager or gatekeeper of the resource. For example, the owner decides who gets to come onto the property, what it will be used for, and so forth. To implement this delegation of gatekeeper authority, the law allows the owner of the resource to repel any and all intrusions that do not have the owner's consent. A crude signal—whether an object is intruding on the land or not—is a simple basis for finding a violation. Exclusion is likely to be favored where particular resources like land have multiple potential uses, and when we think it desirable to give owners discretion to choose which use is most valuable. The only task of judges and other officials, under this approach, is to backstop the authority of the owner as manager of the resource. In particular, these officials have no need to monitor—or even to identify—the various permissible uses of the resource. The law of trespass, at least as applied in *Jacque v. Steenberg Homes*, appears to reflect this kind of strategy.

A second and different strategy for solving resource use disputes is governance. This strategy focuses on particular uses of resources, and prescribes particular rules about permitted and prohibited uses without regard to the other attributes of the resource. Governance rules can derive from many sources, including social norms, contracts, government regulations, and common-law judgments. Governance tends to be used in situations where the particular uses of property are of heightened significance, either because they are strongly favored or disfavored. Thus, in *Hendricks v. Stalnaker*, the parties perceive that their land can either be used for groundwater extraction or sewage disposal—but quite likely cannot be used for both. The answer to the question of which use has priority will have very substantial implications for the use and enjoyment of their respective parcels. Under a governance strategy, courts or other officials determine directly how the property will be used along one or more dimensions singled out as critical. The law of nuisance, at least as applied in *Hendricks v. Stalnaker*, appears to reflect this kind of strategy.

At various points in these materials we will see property law shifting from an exclusion strategy to a governance strategy (or somewhere in between), particularly as disputes over conflicting uses of property become more intense, or more persons are affected by decisions by how property is used, or both. The distinction between trespass and nuisance is one of the clearest examples of this, and serves to some extent as a model for similar shifts that occur elsewhere in property law.

3.   THE COASE THEOREM

Nuisance law has given rise to a rich literature about the role of private agreements—contracts—that reassign property rights in ways different from how they are originally assigned as a matter of law. Ronald Coase is an economist who was awarded the Nobel Memorial Prize in Economics in 1991 for his identification of the importance of transaction costs in assessing the economic effects of alternative institutional arrangements. His most famous article, part of which is excerpted below, contains an elaborate discussion of English nuisance cases and the role of private agreements in reassigning the rights established by nuisance law. This is also the article that lays out what has subsequently come to be known as "the Coase theorem," which plays an important role in the economic analysis of property rights and in law and economics more generally. Although Coase does not have a law degree, this article has become the most frequently cited work in all of legal scholarship.

Ronald H. Coase, *The Problem of Social Cost*, 3 J.L. & ECON. 1–3, 6–8, 13–19 (1960)

This paper is concerned with those actions of business firms which have harmful effects on others. * * *

The question is commonly thought of as one in which A inflicts harm on B and what has to be decided is: How should we restrain A? But this is wrong. We are dealing with a problem of a reciprocal nature. To avoid the harm to B would inflict harm on A. The real question that has to be decided is: Should A be allowed to harm B or should B be allowed to harm A? The problem is to avoid the more serious harm. I instanced in my previous article[1] the case of a confectioner the noise and vibrations from whose machinery disturbed a doctor in his work. To avoid harming the doctor would inflict harm on the confectioner. The problem posed by this case was essentially whether it was worth while, as a result of restricting the methods of production which could be used by the confectioner, to secure more doctoring at the cost of a reduced supply of confectionery products. Another example is afforded by the problem of straying cattle which destroy crops on neighboring land. If it is inevitable that some cattle will stray, an increase in the supply of meat can only be obtained at the expense of a decrease in the supply of crops. The nature of the choice is clear: meat or crops. What answer should be given is, of course, not clear unless we know the value of what is obtained as well as the value of what is sacrificed to obtain it. * * * It goes almost without saying that this problem has to be looked at in total *and* at the margin.

I propose to start my analysis by examining a case in which most economists would presumably agree that the problem would be solved in a completely satisfactory manner: when the damaging business has to pay for all damage caused and the pricing system works smoothly (strictly this means that the operation of a pricing system is without cost).

A good example of the problem under discussion is afforded by the case of straying cattle which destroy crops growing on neighboring land. Let us suppose that a farmer and a cattle-raiser are operating on neighboring properties. Let us further suppose that, without any fencing between the properties, an increase in the size of the cattle-raiser's herd increases the total damage to the farmer's crops. What happens to the marginal damage as the size of the herd increases is another matter. This depends on whether the cattle tend to follow one another or to roam side by side, on whether they tend to be more or less restless as the size of the herd increases and on other similar factors. For my immediate purpose, it is immaterial what assumption is made about marginal damage as the size of the herd increases.

To simplify the argument, I propose to use an arithmetical example. I shall assume that the annual cost of fencing the farmer's property is $9 and that the price of the crop is $1 per ton. Also, I assume that the relation between the number of cattle in the herd and the annual crop loss is as follows:

(handwritten: changes due to loss from crop cattle)

(handwritten: If Rancher Liable)

(handwritten: Fixed ↑   must be constant ↓)

(handwritten: (if Rancher was there)   Farmer's Revenue F's Costs   F's Profit)
(handwritten: 0   0   12 → - 10 = 2)

Number in Herd (Steers)	Annual Crop Loss (Tons)	Crop Loss per Additional Steer (Tons)					
1	1	1	11	-	10	+1	= 2
2	3	2	9	-	10	+3	= 2
3	6	3	6	-	10	+6	= 2
4	10	4	2	-	10	+10	= 2

(handwritten: what Rancher must pay)

(handwritten: better to buy $9 fence)

Given that the cattle-raiser is liable for the damage caused, this additional annual cost imposed on the cattle-raiser if he increased his herd

1. Coase, The Federal Communications Commission, 2 J.L. & Econ. 26–27 (1959).

from, say, 2 to 3 steers is $3 and in deciding on the size of the herd, he will take this into account along with his other costs. That is, he will not increase the size of the herd unless the value of the additional meat produced (assuming that the cattle-raiser slaughters the cattle), is greater than the additional costs that this will entail, including the value of the additional crops destroyed. Of course, if, by the employment of dogs, herdsmen, aeroplanes, mobile radio and other means, the amount of damage can be reduced, these means will be adopted when their cost is less the value of the crop which they prevent being lost. Given that the annual cost of fencing is $9, the cattle-raiser who wished to have a herd with 4 steers or more would pay for fencing to be erected and maintained, assuming that other means of attaining the same end would not do so more cheaply. When the fence is erected, the marginal cost due to the liability for damage becomes zero, except to the extent that an increase in the size of the herd necessitates a stronger and therefore more expensive fence because more steers are liable to lean against it at the same time. But, of course, it may be cheaper for the cattle-raiser not to fence and to pay for the damaged crops, as in my arithmetical example, with 3 or fewer steers. * * *

I now turn to the case in which, although the pricing system is assumed to work smoothly (that is, costlessly), the damaging business is not liable for any of the damage which it causes. This business does not have to make a payment to those damaged by its actions. I propose to show that the allocation of resources will be the same in this case as it was when the damaging business was liable for damage caused. * * *

I return to the case of the farmer and the cattle-raiser. The farmer would suffer increased damage to his crop as the size of the herd increased. Suppose that the size of the cattle-raiser's herd is 3 steers (and that this is the size of the herd that would be maintained if crop damage was not taken into account). Then the farmer would be willing to pay up to $3 if the cattle-raiser would reduce his herd to 2 steers, up to $5 if the herd were reduced to 1 steer and would pay up to $6 if cattle-raising was abandoned. The cattle-raiser would therefore receive $3 from the farmer if he kept 2 steers instead of 3. This $3 foregone is therefore part of the cost incurred in keeping the third steer. Whether the $3 is a payment which the cattle-raiser has to make if he adds the third steer to his herd (which it would be if the cattle-raiser was liable to the farmer for damage caused to the crop) or whether it is a sum of money which he would have received if he did not keep a third steer (which it would be if the cattle-raiser was not liable to the farmer for damage caused to the crop) does not affect the final result. In both cases $3 is part of the cost of adding a third steer, to be included along with the other costs. If the increase in the value of production in cattle-raising through increasing the size of the herd from 2 to 3 is greater than the additional costs that have to be incurred (including the $3 damage to crops), the size of the herd will be increased. Otherwise, it will not. The size of the herd will be the same whether the cattle-raiser is liable for the damage caused to the crop or not. * * *

It is necessary to know whether the damaging business is liable or not for damage caused since without the establishment of this initial delimitation of rights there can be no market transactions to transfer and recombine them. But the ultimate result (which maximizes the value of production) is independent of the legal position if the pricing system is assumed to work without cost.

Judges have to decide on legal liability but this should not confuse economists about the nature of the economic problem involved. In the case of the cattle and the crops, it is true that there would be no crop damage without the cattle. It is equally true that there would be no crop damage without the crops. The doctor's work would not have been disturbed if the confectioner had not worked his machinery; but the machinery would have disturbed no one if the doctor had not set up his consulting room in that particular place. * * * If we are to discuss the problem in terms of causation, both parties cause the damage. If we are to attain an optimum allocation of resources, it is therefore desirable that both parties should take the harmful effect (the nuisance) into account in deciding on their course of action. It is one of the beauties of a smoothly operating pricing system that, as has already been explained, the fall in the value of production due to the harmful effect would be a cost for both parties. * * *

[I]t has to be remembered that the immediate question faced by the courts is *not* what shall be done by whom *but* who has the legal right to do what. It is always possible to modify by transactions on the market the initial legal delimitation of rights. And, of course, if such market transactions are costless, such a rearrangement of rights will always take place if it would lead to an increase in the value of production.

The argument has proceeded up to this point on the assumption * * * that there were no costs involved in carrying out market transactions. This is, of course, a very unrealistic assumption. In order to carry out a market transaction it is necessary to discover who it is that one wishes to deal with, to inform people that one wishes to deal and on what terms, to conduct negotiations leading up to a bargain, to draw up the contract, to undertake the inspection needed to make sure that the terms of the contract are being observed, and so on. These operations are often extremely costly, sufficiently costly at any rate to prevent many transactions that would be carried out in a world in which the pricing system worked without cost.

In earlier sections, when dealing with the problem of the rearrangement of legal rights through the market, it was argued that such a rearrangement would be made through the market whenever this would lead to an increase in the value of production. But this assumed costless market transactions. Once the costs of carrying out market transactions are taken into account it is clear that such a rearrangement of rights will only be undertaken when the increase in the value of production consequent upon the rearrangement is greater than the costs which would be involved in bringing it about. When it is less, the granting of an injunction (or the knowledge that it would be granted) or the liability to pay damages may result in an activity being discontinued (or may prevent its being started) which would be undertaken if market transactions were costless. In these conditions the initial delimitation of legal rights does have an effect on the efficiency with which the economic system operates. One arrangement of rights may bring about a greater value of production than any other. But unless this is the arrangement of rights established by the legal system, the costs of reaching the same result by altering and combining rights through the market may be so great that this optimal arrangement of rights, and the greater value of production which it would bring, may never be achieved. * * *

The discussion of the problem of harmful effects in this section (when the costs of market transactions are taken into account) is extremely inadequate. But at least it has made clear that the problem is one of choosing the appropriate social arrangement for dealing with the harmful effects. All solutions have costs and there is no reason to suppose that government regulation is called for simply because the problem is not well handled by the market or the firm. Satisfactory views on policy can only come from a study of how, in practice, the market, firms and governments handle the problem of harmful effects. Economists need to study the work of the broker in bringing parties together, the effect of restrictive covenants, the problems of the large-scale real-estate development company, the operation of Government zoning and other regulating activities. It is my belief that economists, and policy-makers generally, have tended to overestimate the advantages which come from governmental regulation. But this belief, even if justified, does not do more than suggest that government regulation should be curtailed. It does not tell us where the boundary line should be drawn. This, it seems to me, has to come from a detailed investigation of the actual results of handling the problem in different ways. * * *

NOTES AND QUESTIONS

1.   The problem of cattle trampling crops, which Coase takes as his central example in the excerpt reproduced here, is usually thought to be governed by a branch of the law of trespass rather than nuisance law. Interestingly, however, the rules regarding cattle trespass have varied in different parts of the country with respect to who has the duty to put up a fence to prevent livestock from damaging crops. See Robert C. Ellickson Order without Law: How Neighbors Settle Disputes 42–43 (1991). In most parts of the United States, a "fencing in" rule prevails, whereby the owner of the cattle or other livestock has the duty to put up a fence in order to keep the cattle in. If they escape and trample unfenced crops, the owner of the cattle is liable for damages for trespass. In certain parts of the western United States, however, where grazing livestock on the open range was the historical practice, a rule of "fencing out" sometimes prevails, whereby the burden is on the owner of the crops to put up a fence to keep the cattle out. If the crop owner has failed to put up a fence or to keep it maintained, the cattle owner is not liable when cattle wander into the field and trample the

[handwritten margin note:] Does not advocate complete "de-regulation"— just enough research to make sure the regulations in place are working

crops. Does the Coase theorem provide a basis for explaining why most states would adopt a fencing in rule, but others a rule of fencing out? See Kenneth R. Vogel, The Coase Theorem and California's Animal Trespass Law, 16 J. Legal Stud. 149 (1987). Nevertheless, the fencing in/fencing out distinction only applies to cattle that wander of their own volition without human guidance. If an owner of livestock deliberately induces his animals to graze on land belonging to another, this is regarded as a trespass, whether the land is open range or not. See Light v. United States, 220 U.S. 523 (1911); Musselshell Cattle Co. v. Woolfolk, 85 P. 874 (Mont. 1906). Also, as Ellickson discovered in his empirical study of modern-day Shasta County, California, landowners there follow a norm requiring that cattle be fenced in, without regard to whether the formal rule on the books requires fencing in or fencing out. Ellickson, supra, at 52–64. Can the Coase theorem explain these features of cattle trespass law and norms that appear to carry forward the traditional exclusion model?

2.   Work your way carefully through Coase's example about the rancher and the farmer, and make sure you understand the logic behind his argument that if it is costless to enter into contracts (that is, if "transaction costs" are zero), then the same number of cattle will be raised by the rancher, whether or not the rancher is liable to the farmer for cattle trespass. The basic idea is that if contracting is costless, the parties will keep contracting to modify the initial assignment of property rights until they have exhausted all possible deals that would be to their mutual advantage. The final stopping point will always be the use of resources that creates the greatest joint wealth for the parties, because once this point is reached, neither party can offer the other one a deal that would make both of them better off. Of course, this does not mean that the rancher and the farmer will be indifferent to the initial assignment of property rights. If the rancher starts out with the right to let cattle trespass, then the farmer will have to "bribe" the rancher to cut back to the joint-maximizing number. The rancher will be richer because of the initial assignment of rights. Conversely, if the farmer starts out with the right to be free of cattle trespasses, then the rancher will have to "bribe" the farmer to let him increase the number of cattle. The farmer will be richer because of the initial assignment of rights. So you can be sure that the rancher and the farmer (and others similarly situated) will care about the assignment of rights, because it affects the distribution of wealth. Coase's point is that if we ignore the distributional impact, and focus only on the question of how resources in society are used, the result would be the same regardless of the initial allocation of rights, provided transaction costs are zero. A good text providing further introduction to the Coase theorem and some basic economics concepts is Richard A. Ippolito, Economics for Lawyers 228–46 (2005).

3.   What other assumptions are necessary for the invariance outcome of the Coase theorem to apply? Two assumptions that Coase does not make explicit are that individuals are rational maximizers and that all values are capable of being expressed in monetary terms. The assumption that persons are rational maximizers means that they prefer more rather than less

(of whatever it is they happen to prefer), and that, subject to information constraints, when presented with a choice, they will choose the option that yields more rather than less. Nearly all economists would agree, however, that the assumption that people are rational maximizers is at most a generalization about human behavior, not a postulate that all people act rationally in pursuit of their interests all the time. (Before you have finished this Chapter, you will have encountered some people who probably cannot be regarded as rational maximizers.) How much should the possibility of irrational behavior concern someone interested in the design of legal institutions? Most economists would also agree that there are certain values that people hold dear that cannot be readily translated into dollar terms. How much of a concern should this be to someone designing legal institutions? Are there still other assumptions about human behavior lurking behind the Coase theorem? Robert Cooter has suggested that for the Coase theorem to hold, one must also assume that people are natural cooperators rather than ruthless exploiters. See Robert Cooter, The Cost of Coase, 11 J. Legal Stud. 1 (1982) (comparing the Coase Theorem and the "Hobbes Theorem"). For other issues, such whether the parties' wealth would affect the allocation of resources in the hypothetical world of zero transaction costs, see, e.g., R.H. Coase, The Firm, the Market, and the Law 170–74 (1988); Harold Demsetz, When Does the Rule of Liability Matter?, 1 J. Legal Stud. 13 (1972); Stewart Schwab, Coase Defends Coase: Why Lawyers Listen and Economists Do Not, 87 Mich. L. Rev. 1171, 1178–84 (1989).

4.   Coase himself has written that the assumption that it is costless to engage in contracts is very unrealistic—"as strange as the physical world without friction." R.H. Coase, The Firm, the Market, and the Law 14 (1988). So the Coase theorem should not be taken to be a guide to understanding the real world. Instead, the theorem should be seen as a kind of thought experiment, which is intended to reveal the importance of transaction costs in the design of legal institutions. Coase in later writing expressed frustration that people mistook his thought experiment to mean that markets achieve efficient results when transaction costs are low. "The world of zero transaction costs has often been described as a Coasian world. Nothing could be further from the truth. It is the world of modern economic theory, one which I was hoping to persuade economists to leave." Id. at 174. His point was more nearly the opposite: that transaction costs are always positive, and hence we cannot assume that *any* institutional arrangement will necessarily generate efficient results. Coase thought that it is always important to compare alternative institutional arrangements, and to try to determine which one will deviate the least from the unattainable ideal of the (mythical) world of zero transaction costs. For more about the Coase theorem and its place in legal scholarship, see Daniel A. Farber, Parody Lost/Pragmatism Regained: The Ironic History of the Coase Theorem, 83 Va. L. Rev. 397 (1997).

5.   One of Coase's controversial claims is that any conflict over resource use (like the rancher and farmer, or a nuisance dispute) is a "reciprocal" one, meaning that each party to the dispute is imposing costs

on the other party. This is plausible if we consider a dispute like *Hendricks v. Stalnaker*, involving adjacent landowners who make incompatible demands on the use of the land. But is it equally plausible to say that there is a "reciprocal" relationship between a property owner who has an in rem right to exclude others from her land, and the rest of the world which is subject to a duty to desist from interfering with her land? If the rule were that anyone—not just neighbors—would be entitled to trespass on land, with whom would the present owner of the land have to bargain in order to be free of such trespasses? Everyone on the block? In the United States? The world? What about unborn future would-be trespassers? Or do all these cases just point once again to the importance of transaction costs in the real world? See Clifford G. Holderness, The Assignment of Rights, Entry Effects, and the Allocation of Resources, 18 J. Legal Stud. 181 (1989). Further, the default package of rights the law provides is not as symmetrical with respect to invasions as one would expect if causation of harm were fully reciprocal; people have the right to prevent invasions but robust rights to commit invasions must usually be specially added to this package. See Henry E. Smith, Self–Help and the Nature of Property, 1 J.L. Econ. & Pol'y 69, 70–80 (2005) and Chapter IX.

6. There is also an enormous literature describing various attempts to test the Coase theorem empirically. See generally Steven G. Medema & Richard O. Zerbe, The Coase Theorem, in The Encyclopedia of Law and Economics 836, 858–73 (2000). Although generalizations are hazardous, much of this literature suggests that bargaining over entitlements is influenced not only by joint wealth maximization, but also by a variety of factors, including the initial distributions of rights, the history of interaction between the parties, and perceptions of what outcomes are regarded as fair.

4. Resolving Property Disputes by Contract

What, you may be asking yourself, is the payoff to the law student from studying the Coase theorem? One very important lesson is that, as a lawyer assisting a client in a dispute over the use of property, you should always try to imagine various ways in which contracts might be used to resolve the problem. Litigation to clarify or enforce property rights may ultimately be unavoidable. But contractual modifications of property rights—"Coasean bargains" as they are sometimes called—should be explored as an alternative to litigation. A contractual rearrangement of rights may be cheaper and more satisfactory to all concerned.

Consider again in this light the dispute in *Hendricks v. Stalnaker*. Nothing in the law would have prevented the parties from bargaining, at any stage of the dispute, over the placement of the well and the septic field. For example, the parties could have agreed to build a well on one parcel and a septic field on the other parcel, and could have granted reciprocal rights to each other (easements) so that each would have had access to both facilities. Alternatively, one party could have bought out the other, and then built a single well and septic field for both parcels; they could then have rented half of the land to a tenant (perhaps the other party) with water and septic services included in the rent.

Another dimension of *Hendricks* concerns the role that land-use regulation plays in creating the dispute. The reason both Stalnaker and the Hendrickses cannot do what they want to do is because of the County Health Department regulation requiring that there be at least 100 feet of separation between the edge of a septic field and any water well. Perhaps the Health Department would consider a waiver or modification of this rule if other adjustments were agreed upon by the parties. For example, if the Hendrickses agreed to pretreat their waste water before it enters the septic field, or if Stalnaker agreed to extra monitoring of his well water, perhaps the Health Department could be persuaded to relax its 100–foot buffer zone requirement. This type of solution would entail a more complicated set of negotiations among three parties—Stalnaker, the Hendrickses, and the Health Department. And of course, the Health Department may take the position that it has no authority to grant a variance from the rules, and even if it has authority, there may be no (lawful) method of making a side payment to the Department to induce it to be flexible. But a conscientious lawyer looking for a solution to the problem would want to explore the regulatory side of the dispute as well.

Why didn't any of these "Coasean" solutions happen? One possibility is that the parties (or their lawyers) did not think about these kinds of solutions. Another possibility is that they thought about them, but concluded they were too costly or were technically infeasible. A third possibility is that they did not think about them until transaction costs became too high for any kind of Coasean bargain to take place. The last possibility highlights another point taught by the Coase theorem: It is important to be sensitive to the causes of high transaction costs in order to guide clients toward potential Coasean bargains before those options are foreclosed and litigation is the only recourse.

Many factors, some physical, some psychological, enter into creating high transaction costs. We will not make any attempt to catalogue them all here. You will gradually come to have a greater appreciation of the many impediments to contractual solutions to resource disputes as you go through these materials. We will highlight two factors that loom large throughout property law: assembly problems and bilateral monopoly.

Assembly problems arise when someone wants to assemble property rights from a large number of owners in order to undertake some project. This is an instance in a property setting of high transaction costs stemming from large numbers of contracting parties. *Hinman* is an example of an assembly problem. Suppose each surface owner had the power to block airplanes from entering into the airspace above the surface of his or her land, and suppose that some kind of technology (like advanced radar) is available so that both surface owners and airplanes can detect when airplanes enter the column of space above someone's land. Under these circumstances, persons who want to fly would have to assemble permissions from a huge number of surface owners. This would entail major difficulties in identifying all the affected surface owners, and getting them to communicate and agree on a solution. Even if all the affected surface owners could be identified and engaged in negotiations, some owners might hold out for a very generous payment (unless they could be easily avoided by choosing a different route). More mundane assembly problems arise when highways or utility lines are built or when developers want to acquire multiple contiguous parcels for some large-scale project (see Figure 1–3). Each of these projects typically entails the need to assemble a large number of property rights, and each presents high transaction costs as a consequence.

Figure 1–3
A Holdout

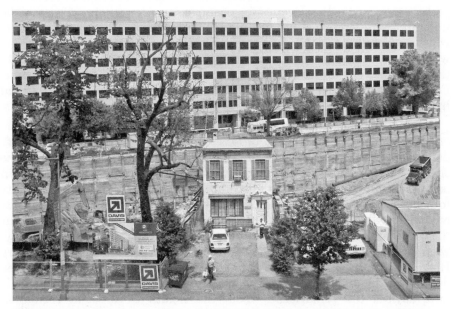

©2006, *The Washington Post*. Photo by Bill O'Leary. Reprinted with Permission.

This row house was owned by an architect who refused all entreaties to sell to the developer for many times its assessed value. The developer eventually decided to build around the house, at substantial additional expense. The holdout was reported to be planning to use the house to open a pizza parlor, which would yield much less revenue than if he had sold to the developer. Lyndsey Layton, A Solitary Stand at the Precipice, Washington Post, May 3, 2006, at A1.

Another cause of high transaction costs is bilateral monopoly. By this, we do not refer to large industrial monopolies, but rather to localized monopolies—situations in which an owner of property needs something that can be provided by only one other person or entity. In *Hendricks*, it would appear that the physical lay of the land caused each party to have only the other as a possible negotiating partner, as long as each wished to use the land for wells and/or septic systems. Similarly, in *Jacque*, Steenberg Homes had only one route to deliver the mobile home that it regarded as reasonable, but access to that route was controlled by the Jacques. Economists call these localized monopoly problems "bilateral monopolies," because there is a monopoly on each side: only one seller and one buyer for the contested resource. See Richard A. Posner, Economic Analysis of Law 60–61 (2003); Stewart E. Sterk, Neighbors in American Law, 87 Colum. L. Rev. 55, 57–58, 68–88 (1987).

These bilateral monopoly situations are also a source of high transaction costs, because each of the parties has nowhere else to turn in order to engage in an equivalent transaction. Thus, if the parties disagree about the price or terms for an exchange of resources, prolonged haggling can result. Perhaps one or both parties, perceiving that the other party has no good options, will bargain strategically to try to get an especially favorable deal. See Robert Cooter, The Cost of Coase, 11 J. Legal Stud. 1, 17–24 (1982). Or perhaps one party, the Jacques for example, may for whatever reasons be uninterested in entering into any kind of exchange. A further complication, which seems all too common, is that the parties may have gotten off on the wrong foot with each other, which has led to resentments or "bad blood" that make it very difficult to turn the relationship into a cooperative one. For whatever reasons, bilateral monopoly problems are extremely prevalent in property law.

The lesson for the lawyer advising clients is all too clear (but all too often ignored): It is important to look down the road in order to identify potential assembly problems and bilateral monopoly problems *before* the client gets trapped in a situation that precludes any kind of Coasean bargaining. If the client wants to acquire six contiguous parcels of property for a development, and the first five owners agree to sell but the sixth holds out, what will happen then? If the client wants to acquire a home site, but the only means of access for utility lines is across someone else's property, what will happen then? Ideally, someone should have advised Steenberg Homes about the difficult turn in the private road before it agreed to free delivery of the mobile home in the dead of winter. Ideally, someone should have advised the Hendrickses about the Health Department regulation requiring a 100–foot buffer zone around a septic field before they bought their property. Lawyers of course cannot foresee all problems, but they should be alert to the kinds of problems that can arise, and advise their clients to take all appropriate precautions to be able to acquire the resources they need before they fall into a high-transaction-cost trap.

C.   PROPERTY AND EQUITY

One development of great importance to property law was the emergence in England by the fifteenth century of a separate court known as the Court of Equity or Chancery. The Chancellor, who was the head of this court, was a learned counselor to the King. He heard petitions from persons who were frustrated by the rigidities or limitations of the common-law courts. The Court of Equity differentiated itself from the common-law courts on a number of dimensions. The procedures were different: Common-law courts traveled about the country and cases were tried to juries;

the Court of Equity sat in London and did not use juries. The style of decision making was different: The common-law courts followed a system of pleading in which the case had to be presented in terms of standardized writs; the Court of Equity was willing to consider a wider variety of factors bearing on the individual justice of the situation presented by the parties. These considerations of justice eventually coalesced into a series of equitable maxims that guided the discretion of the Chancellor. The remedies were different: The common law offered basically only awards of damages, whereas the Court of Equity resolved disputes by issuing mandatory decrees directing individuals to perform certain acts. These decrees "operated *in personam*; they were binding on the parties to the cause, but were not judgments of record binding on anyone else." J.H. Baker, An Introduction to English Legal History 89 (2d ed. 1979). Eventually, even the substantive law came to diverge: The Court of Equity, for example, was responsible for inventing the trust (studied in Chapter VI) and the equitable servitude (studied in Chapter IX), both of which were unknown at common law.

[handwritten margin note: "in personam" — individually, binding only to the particular case]

In America, the distinction between the common-law courts and the Court of Equity was never as sharply observed as in England. For example, in a number of colonies the same judges who sat as a court of common law would periodically sit as the court of equity. Lawrence M. Friedman, A History of American Law 47 (1973). Not all colonies were enthusiastic about equity, or at least about separate equity courts, associated as they were with royal prerogative. During the nineteenth century equity procedures started to converge with those of the common-law courts, even while the two courts, or modes of sitting as courts, were still kept distinct. Stanley N. Katz, The Politics of Law in Colonial America: Controversies over Chancery Courts and Equity Law in the Eighteenth Century, in 5 Perspectives in American History: Law in American History 259 (Donald Fleming & Bernard Bailyn eds., 1971); Amalia D. Kessler, Our Inquisitorial Tradition: Equity, Procedure, Due Process, and the Search for an Alternative to the Adversarial, 90 Cornell L. Rev. 1181 (2005). Starting in 1848, with the adoption of the Field Code in New York, many states formally abolished the distinction, declaring a "merger" of law and equity. In other states the distinction persisted, with some states preserving within a unitary judicial system a "law division" and an "equity division," and a few states, most prominently perhaps Delaware, preserving a separate "Court of Chancery." England formally abolished the distinction between law and equity courts in the Judicature Act of 1873.

Notwithstanding the formal elimination (in most places) of the two court systems, the different procedural, intellectual, and substantive traditions associated with the two systems continue to be important, especially in the law of property. In fact, one of the traditional maxims of equity is that property rights enjoy special protection in a court of equity. See 1 James L. High, A Treatise on the Law of Injunctions § 20b, at 34 (4th ed. 1905); Thomas C. Spelling & James Hamilton Lewis, A Treatise on the Law Governing Injunctions § 7, at 8-9 (1926). This maxim is reflected in the law in a number of ways, such as in the understanding that a court of *good example of difference ✳*

equity will generally grant specific performance to enforce a contract for the sale of real property, even though a breach of contract ordinarily results only in an award of damages. See Anthony T. Kronman, Specific Performance, 45 U. Chi. L. Rev. 351, 355–56 & n. 20 (1978). In general, however, if a plaintiff seeks an order compelling the defendant to perform a particular act—such as keeping off the plaintiff's land, or abating a nuisance that affects the plaintiff's land, or specifically performing a contract the defendant has entered into with respect to the land—then the plaintiff must satisfy the various traditions associated with equity in order to obtain such relief. This will become relevant at various points throughout the course.

We start our exploration of equity with a seemingly straightforward problem. At common law, the only remedy for trespass to land was an action for damages. Not surprisingly, however, landowners who got entangled in disputes over land boundaries or who were threatened with repeated trespasses went to the Court of Equity, seeking a mandatory order in the form of an injunction against their adversaries. At first the Chancellor refused to grant such relief, stating that equity was not available to enjoin a "mere trespass." But eventually, a variety of exceptions to this rule emerged. American courts of equity adopted these exceptions, which gradually became broader over time. The following decision illustrates the doctrine that eventually emerged.

1.   REPEATED TRESPASSES

Baker v. Howard County Hunt

Court of Appeals of Maryland, 1936.
188 A. 223.

■ OFFUTT, JUSTICE. In 1924 Dr. Laurence H. Baker and Rebekah W. Baker, his wife, acquired a small farm of about 65 acres located in the Fifth election district of Howard county on the Clarksville turnpike and the Patuxent river, a few miles from Ellicott City. For a time Dr. Baker used the farm as a "week end escape," but later he and his wife occupied it as a permanent home. From 1926 to 1929 he was the executive secretary of the Johns Hopkins Medical School. In connection with that work he became interested in the effect of well-balanced nutrition on stock, and began a series of experiments on rabbits to determine whether over a long period a well-balanced diet would result in improving the stock. He kept the rabbits used in those experiments on the farm. There he also raised hogs and chickens, kept a garden, and raised buckwheat and other crops. He and his wife lived there intermittently until about 1932, and from that time on he has resided there permanently.

Howard county is, and for many years has been, a foxhunting country, and it is no unusual thing for landowners to keep packs of foxhounds, but it does not appear that prior to 1930, when the Howard County Hunt was formed, there was any organized association of the followers of the sport.

That club is an unincorporated association of more than seven persons, which occupies a farm at the junction of the Triadelphia road and the Glenelg road, also in the Fifth election district of Howard county some six or seven miles from the Baker farm. The club itself owns no hounds, but employs as its huntsman Philip Bowen, who furnishes and hunts a pack of hounds for it.

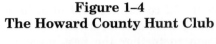

**Figure 1–4
The Howard County Hunt Club**

Courtesy Howard County Historical Society.

Weather permitting, the hounds are hunted three days a week throughout the hunting season from early in September to April over a territory which includes the Baker farm. In 1931 Dr. Baker, it was said, noticed foxhounds accompanied by riders in red hunting coats on his farm, and also heard "the horn carried by fox hunters." At that time he paid little attention to them, for he had then no "animals of any great quantity," and it made "very little difference." But by 1933 his stock of rabbits had greatly increased, and on January 14th of that year near sunset, while he was feeding the rabbits, he and his wife heard a great "hue and cry" at the back of the farm, and his wife said, "It looks as though the dogs were at our rabbits again." He "started off to one of the other points," and before he got back to her the dogs were swarming all around the place. Mrs. Baker attempted to drive them off, they "seemed to back right against her," she screamed that she was bitten, he "rushed and hollered at the dogs, and before we knew it they were in the woods." Following that incident, Mr. T. Stockton Matthews, president of the club, wrote Dr. Baker a letter in which in part he said:

> I was shocked to learn of the most unfortunate annoyance and damage caused you and Mrs. Baker last Saturday by hounds of the

Howard County Hunt. I immediately got in touch with Mrs. Clark and others whom I thought might know some more of the circumstances, with the concern particularly of the injury to Mrs. Baker and the hope of avoiding the possibility of any serious infection from the wound.

It is distressing to all of us that such an unprecedented and unfortunate accident should have happened. In the conduct of the Hunt and in the control of the hounds, we have endeavored always to merit the good-will and cordial interest of all those in the community who are in sympathy with good sport and with the aims and purposes of the organization to further the best interest of Howard County.

Notwithstanding the assurances in the letter, Dr. Baker complained that no real effort was made to keep the hounds off his property, that they trampled his crops, broke some hot frames, disturbed his rabbits and his chickens, and so annoyed Mrs. Baker that she left the place and that on one occasion in February, 1936, he had been compelled to shoot several of them to get them off his property where they were frightening his chickens. On March 9, 1936, he and Mrs. Baker filed the bill of complaint in this case against the Howard County Hunt and Philip Bowen, in which, after reciting these facts, he prayed: "That the said Howard County Hunt and Philip Bowen, their agents, servants and employees, they and each of them may be enjoined from hunting across your Complainants' property or permitting the pack of Fox Hounds owned by them or in their custody from hunting or overrunning the land of your Complainants or in any manner interfering with your Complainants enjoying the peaceful possession of their property."

In their answer the defendants averred that "members of the Howard County Hunt Club have only ridden through the Complainants' property on one occasion during the past five years; and the said pack of fox hounds have crossed the Complainants' property not more than four times during said period of five years." They further alleged that the injuries to Mrs. Baker "were suffered" more than three years before the suit, and that whatever rights she might have had "by reason" of those injuries "were barred by limitations and laches," and, while they admitted that "their pack of fox hounds" did cross the Baker property in February, 1936, they denied that they terrified the chickens or destroyed "freshly laid eggs," and as to that occasion they further said "that Laurence H. Baker, one of the above named Complainants, did wilfully and without any just cause whatsoever, deliberately shoot into the said pack of fox hounds, as a result of which one of them died shortly thereafter and another is seriously and permanently injured; and these respondents aver that the said pack of fox hounds at the time of the shooting as aforesaid in no way molested the Complainants or their property but were in the act of pursuing a fox."

The case was tried on the issues made by those pleadings, and at the conclusion of the case the court dismissed the bill.

The important questions presented by the appeal are whether equity may afford injunctive relief against a series of trespasses which, while not continuous, are nevertheless part of a single course of conduct which seriously interferes with the right of a landowner to the peaceful enjoyment of his property and, if it may, whether the appellants have made out a case for such relief. * * *

Without further elaboration of the evidence it is sufficient to say that it shows without any substantial doubt that the defendants' hounds have repeatedly overrun the Baker farm, have done substantial injury to their property, that defendants have made no serious effort to prevent the trespasses, and that the resulting damage is of such a character that the Bakers can obtain no adequate relief therefor in an action at law.

Summary of Decision / Facts leading to

Their property is their own; they have an unquestionable right to enjoy it in peace and quiet without molestation or hindrance and to use it for such purpose and pursuits as they will so long as their use of it does not harm others. On the other hand the defendants devote a part of their leisure to the pursuit of an ancient, exhilarating, and healthful sport which is not only lawful, but which for centuries has added to the health and to the pleasure of those who love to combine the freedom and the freshness of the open spaces with the thrills of the chase, the music of the hounds, the rushing air, the creaking of saddle leather, the dash of the thoroughbred, and the sights and sounds of the countryside in the crisp air of the fall and the early winter. They, too, have an unquestionable right to indulge that inclination but only so long as they do not permit it to interfere with the rights of others.

how

Much interesting learning and some space have been devoted by counsel for the parties to this appeal in tracing the origin, growth, and development of the relative rights of fox hunters and the owners of the land over which they hunt. Indeed, that search has extended from Bacon's Abridgement (1856) to Adkin's Law of Forestry and Law Relating to Trespass and Game (London 1914), but in the end there is no dispute as there can be no doubt that the rights of the fox hunter are subordinate to the rights of the landowner, and that, if the hunter himself goes on the lands of another against the owner's will, he is a trespasser. * * *

In respect to the liability of persons who either send dogs on the land of another in pursuit of game or of a fox which is not ordinarily classified as game, or hunt them in a neighborhood when they have reason to know that the chase will probably take them over land on which they have no right to go, the law is not so certain. It was said by some early commentator seeking a way out of the maze that "dog law is as hard to define as dog latin," Citizens' Rapid–Transit Co. v. Dew, 100 Tenn. 317, 45 S.W. 790, but since then much of the uncertainty as to the responsibility of the owners of dogs for their trespasses has disappeared. The difficulty of stating with certainty the status of a dog before the law is said to inhere in its nature and is inseparable from its known peculiarities, the difference in breeds, its diverse uses, the diseases to which it is subject, its infirmities of temper, and the impossibility of predicting when or how it will break through the artificial restraints of discipline and revert to its original and instinctive ferocity. 1 R.C.L. 1112.

But as with other branches of the law early doubts have disappeared, and others have succeeded them, in a natural process of evolution in which the law has changed to harmonize with changed conditions.

Thus it is broadly stated that at common law the owner of a dog is not liable for its mere trespass on land of its own volition, 3 C.J. 150, Read v. Edwards, 17 C.B.(N.S.) 245, 144, Reprint, 99, and that is probably still the law in many jurisdictions * * *

[I]n 1 R.C.L. 1118, it is said: "It seems that where a dog roams on another's land of its own accord and does damage or inflicts injury to persons, animals or property there, proof of the owner's knowledge of the dog's propensity to commit the evil complained of is necessary to a recovery. This distinction in the case of a dog is due to the fact that the common law, regarding the straying of a reputable dog as unlikely to cause an injury, did not impose on its master the duty of restraining it. But if, by the voluntary acts of the owner, the dog is unlawfully in the place where the injury was inflicted, as where a person takes his dog with him when trespassing on the premises of another, his liability does not depend on his previous knowledge that the dog was vicious."

From these cases and the statements of textwriters it may be said that, while the owner of a dog which he has no reason to believe is dangerous or likely to inflict harm upon the persons or property of others is not liable for its trespasses committed of its own volition while roaming abroad, he is liable if he either takes it himself where he knows that, because of its training, nature, and instinct, it will probably damage the property of others, or if with that knowledge he permits it to stray beyond his control.

Applying that rule to the facts of this case the conclusion seems inevitable that, after the defendants in this case had been warned in 1933 that their hounds while hunting in the neighborhood of the appellants' farm were likely to trespass thereon and inflict damage upon his property, they were under a duty to so control their hounds as to prevent further trespass. Nor is there any serious doubt that in violation of that duty they hunted their hounds in the neighborhood of appellants' farm knowing that under the impulse of their instincts and training in following the scent they might and probably would trespass thereon. Nor is there any doubt that, as a result of appellees' indifference to appellants' rights, their negligence in permitting their hounds to be beyond their control in the neighborhood of appellants' farm, appellees' hounds did overrun appellants' farm, disturbed and injured their poultry, rabbits and pigs, and annoyed both Dr. Baker and his wife.

The common law that the owner of a straying reputable dog is not liable for its trespasses because it was not likely to do much damage, 1 R.C.L. 1118, cannot well be applied to a pack or body of fifteen, twenty, or more hounds running as a pack on the same trail, for it is too obvious for comment that such a pack may do substantial damage even to crops.

The notion that a landowner is without remedy for damage or injury suffered as the result of such an invasion of his rights, or that the law affords him no protection against a repetition thereof, lacks substance and reality.

Appellants contend that their remedy is in equity, appellees say that appellants are not entitled to equitable relief, first because they have an adequate remedy at law, and, second, because they do not come into equity with clean hands. The second objection is based upon the fact that Dr. Baker shot several of the appellees' hounds while they were molesting his poultry. It is true that, apart from a statute conferring it, a landowner has no right to kill a dog which is merely trespassing, 3 C. J. 153, but even at common law he may kill it in defense of his person, his property, or of other persons, where circumstances justify a reasonable belief that so extreme and drastic a measure is necessary to protect himself, his family or his property from harm. Id. 153–158. * * * Baker testified that when he shot the hounds they were actually in his chicken yard, "swarming all through the yards," that "some of his" chickens were dead, others were frightened and dashed against the chicken house, and as a "result" he had to kill three of them. That testimony was not contradicted, but, on the other hand, was corroborated by the witness Johnson, who said that when they were shot the hounds were running through the chicken yard. Under such circumstances it cannot be said that Baker's act in shooting the dogs was so tortious as to place him beyond the pale of equitable relief. Assuming that the dogs were not interested in the chickens, but merely ran through or over them in their pursuit of the fox, Dr. Baker could not be expected to calmly analyze their motives in invading his chicken yards, when actually the chickens were flying in all directions before them.

Nor can it be said that appellants had an adequate remedy at law. Assuming that they could have recovered damages in an action at law against the appellees for the repeated invasions of their property, it does not follow that such damages as they might have recovered would have been adequate compensation for the injury done them.

First, because such injuries were in part intangible and incapable of measurement. Dr. Baker was conducting a series of experiments on rabbits. That work was interrupted and its value nullified by the trespassing hounds. The law affords no adequate measure of damages for such an injury. Appellants also attempted to use their farm as a refuge for birds and small animals. The repeated trespasses of the hounds interfered with that plan. The threat of the continued trespasses of the hounds, for those other reasons seriously interfered with their reasonable enjoyment of the property. Even though the hounds were, as appellees contended, "good and kind," that they never acted "mean," and were never known to bite anybody, the Bakers should not be expected to rely with complete confidence upon the mildness of their tempers in view of the fact that they had "scrambled up" on Mrs. Baker, tore her clothes, took the skin off the knuckles of both hands, and bit her in the left hand. For the actual physical injuries there may have been an adequate legal remedy, but for the interference with appellants' enjoyment of their property as affected by the threat of continued recurrences of such incidents the law affords no adequate relief.

Second, where it appears that the defendant manifests an intention of persisting in the perpetration of unlawful acts, the expense, annoyance, and trouble of prosecuting numerous actions at law to recover trifling damages render an action at law an inadequate remedy.

To justify refusal of equitable relief on the ground that the applicant therefor has a remedy at law, the legal remedy must be fully adequate and complete, Miller's Equity, p. 678, for, as stated in Fletcher, Equity Pleading and Practice, p. 246, "The remedy at law which precludes relief in equity must be as practical and efficient to the ends of justice and its prompt administration as the remedy in equity."

Early cases did hold that equity would not relieve against trespasses even though continuing, but it is long since settled that equity will relieve against continuing, Whalen v. Dalashmutt, 59 Md. 250, or repeated trespasses committed in pursuance of a single plan or purpose, Gilbert v. Arnold, 30 Md. 29, Georges Creek Coal & Iron Co.'s Lessee v. Detmold, 1 Md. 225. In Waring v. Stinchcomb, 119 A. 336, 340 (Md.), the court quoted with approval this statement found in Shipley v. Ritter, 7 Md. 408: "It is the settled law of this state, that although an injunction will not be granted to restrain a trespasser merely because he is a trespasser, yet equity will interfere where the injury is irreparable, or where full and adequate relief cannot be granted at law, or where the trespass goes to the destruction of the property as it had been held and enjoyed, or * * * to prevent multiplicity of suits."

In Spelling on Injunctions, etc. (2d Ed.) § 14 (1893), it is said: "An injunction lies to prevent threatened trespasses, though the damage be susceptible of compensation, where otherwise there is a probability of the wrong being often repeated. * * *"

Pomeroy in his work on Equitable Remedies (section 496) page 4338 et seq., after stating the minority view that equity will not intervene to prevent repeated trespasses by a single defendant, states that: "The jurisdiction of equity to restrain continuous or repeated trespasses rests on the ground of avoiding a repetition of similar actions. * * * When the trespasses complained of are caused by the separate acts of individuals, a multiplicity of suits may be caused to plaintiff either because the defendants are numerous or because a single defendant does the same or similar acts repeatedly. * * * The other view, and the one sustained alike by the weight of authority and by principle, is that if a defendant manifests a purpose to persist in perpetrating his unlawful acts, the vexation, expense and trouble of prosecuting the actions at law make the legal remedy inadequate, and justify a plaintiff in coming into equity for an injunction." * * *

It follows that equity had jurisdiction to grant relief to the appellants; that they made out a case justifying such relief; that the injunction prayed in their bill should have issued; and that there was error in refusing to grant the injunction and in dismissing this bill.

The decree appealed from must therefore be reversed.

NOTES AND QUESTIONS

1. This decision illustrates two important maxims of equity: that he who seeks equity must do equity (the clean hands requirement) and that equity will intercede only when the remedy at law is inadequate. Are you persuaded by the court's resolution of the clean hands issue? Suppose Dr. Baker did not shoot the dogs in the heat of the moment with chickens flying all about, but instead had lain in wait for them and fired as soon as they crossed the boundary into his farm. Should the court deny an injunction in these circumstances? Does the possibility of seeking punitive damages for intentional trespass, as authorized in *Jacque v. Steenberg Homes*, call into question the conclusion that the Bakers' remedy at law was inadequate? On the facts presented, would the Bakers be entitled to punitive damages had they sued for damages? Do punitive damages and injunctions serve somewhat interchangeable functions here? Which remedy is more likely to result in protecting the Bakers from future harassment by fox hunting parties?

2. According to the court, the first reason the remedy at law is inadequate is that the injuries sustained to the Bakers' property "were in part intangible and incapable of measurement." Will this be true in every case of threatened trespass to land? (In *Jacque v. Steenberg Homes*?) When one adds up all the exceptions to the rule that equity will not enjoin a mere trespass—if the injury is irreparable, or if the injury cannot be fully compensated by awards of damages, or if a series of trespasses have been repeated by the same person, or if multiple trespasses are being threatened by different persons—have the exceptions swallowed the rule? Would it be simpler and more accurate to say that equity will always enjoin a threatened trespass, as long as the risk of such an invasion is sufficiently great? (How great? More likely than not to occur?) Or would stating the rule in such an unequivocal fashion be undesirable, because it would deprive equity of its traditional discretion to grant or withhold mandatory relief in light of a wide range of factors that bear on the "justice" of the situation?

3. How do you suppose Coase would respond to the *Baker* case? Is this just like his example of the rancher and the farmer, or the various nuisance cases he discusses? Should the court have given more consideration to whether the Bakers' farm is more valuable (in terms of the parties' willingness to pay) if used for raising experimental rabbits or as a site for fox hunts? The transaction costs here do not seem to be too great; there are only two parties to the dispute and they have had some communication with each other before the lawsuit is filed. Why do you suppose they did not resolve their differences by contracting for some mutually satisfactory solution?

4. If the court had denied an injunction to the Bakers, and any damages award they received would be inadequate to deter future intrusions by the Hunt Club, would the Bakers have been able to purchase peace and quiet for their rabbits by entering into a contract with the Hunt Club? See Louis Kaplow & Steven Shavell, Property Rules Versus Liability Rules: An Economic Analysis, 109 Harv. L. Rev. 713, 722 (1996): "[E]ven though I

would be willing to pay Jack not to take my car if it were inadequately valued by the courts, there would be no point in paying him to desist—for Jill, or someone else, could come along and take it the next day. Consequently, I would not pay Jack to forbear, and not being paid, he would in fact take my car." Does this consideration provide a justification for awarding either injunctions or punitive damages against repeated trespasses, without regard to whether the trespassing activity is more valuable than the activity of the person trespassed upon?

2.   BUILDING ENCROACHMENTS

The question whether courts of equity should enjoin trespasses is particularly vexing in cases involving minor building encroachments. In the typical case, A builds a structure thinking it is on his own land, but it turns out that some portion of the building is actually on B's land. The portion of the building on B's land is a continuing trespass. Does this mean that B is entitled to an injunction that would require—in the extreme case—that the entire building be torn down? Consider the following decisions.

Pile v. Pedrick

Supreme Court of Pennsylvania, 1895.
31 A. 646.

■ WILLIAMS, J. The learned judge of the court below was right in holding that the wall in controversy was not a party wall. It was not intended to be. The defendants were building a factory, and, under the advice of their architect, decided to build within their own lines, in order to avoid the danger of injury to others from vibration which might result from the use of their machinery. They called upon the district surveyor to locate their line, and built within it, as so ascertained. Subsequent surveys by city surveyors have determined that the line was not accurately located at first, but was about 1 1/2 inches over on the plaintiffs'. This leaves the ends of the stones used in the foundation wall projecting into the plaintiffs' lands, below the surface, 1 3/8 inches. This unintentional intrusion into the plaintiffs' close is the narrow foundation on which this bill in equity rests. The wall resting on the stone foundation is conceded to be within the defendants' line. The defendants offered, nevertheless, to make it a party wall, by agreement, and give to plaintiffs the free use of it, as such, on condition that the windows on the third and fourth floors should remain open until the plaintiffs should desire to use the wall. This offer was declined. The trespass was then to be remedied in one of two ways: It could be treated, with the plaintiffs' consent, as a permanent trespass, and compensated for in damages, or the defendants could be compelled to remove the offending ends of the stones to the other side of the line. The plaintiffs insisted upon the latter course, and the court below has, by its decree, ordered that this should be done. The defendants then sought permission to go on the plaintiffs' side of the line and chip off the projecting ends, offering to pay for all inconvenience or injury the plaintiffs or their tenants might suffer by their so doing. This they refused. Nothing remained but to take down and rebuild the entire wall from the defendants' side, and with their building resting on it. This the decree requires, but in view of the course of the litigation the learned judge divided the costs. This is the chief ground of complaint on this appeal. Costs are not of course, in equity. They may be given or withheld as equity and good conscience require. It often happens that a chancellor is constrained to enforce a legal right under circumstances that involve hardship to the defendant, and in such cases it is, as it should be, common to dispose of the costs upon a consideration of all the circumstances, and the position and conduct of the parties. The costs in this case were within the power of the chancellor. They were disposed of in the exercise of his official discretion, and we see no reason to doubt that they were disposed of properly. The decree is affirmed; the costs of this appeal to be paid by the appellants.

Pile v. Pedrick

Supreme Court of Pennsylvania, 1895.
31 A. 647.

■ WILLIAMS, J. This is an appeal from the same decree just considered in *Pile v. Pedrick*, 31 Atl. 646. It is not denied that the foundation wall on which the appellant has built was located under a mistake made by the district surveyor, and does in fact project slightly into the plaintiffs' land. For one inch and three-eighths, the ends of the stones in the wall are said to project beyond the division line. The defendants have no right, at law or in equity, to occupy land that does not belong to them, and we do not see how the court below could have done otherwise than recognize and act upon this principle. They must remove their wall, so that it shall be upon their land. This the court directed should be done within a reasonable time. To avoid further controversy over this subject, we will so far modify the decree as to permit such removal to be made within one year from the date of filing hereof. In all other respects the decree is affirmed; the appellants to pay all costs made by them upon this appeal.

D P

Golden Press, Inc. v. Rylands

Supreme Court of Colorado, 1951.
235 P.2d 592.

■ STONE, JUSTICE. Plaintiffs Rylands and Reid owned a parcel of land fronting on West Colfax Avenue, Jefferson County, upon which were located their residence and garage and some rental cottages. Defendant Golden Press, Inc., constructed a one-story brick and cinder block business building on its property which adjoined plaintiffs' property on the east. According to plaintiffs' survey here unchallenged, the west wall of defendant's building is two inches clear of the lot line at the front or south end, is exactly on the line at the north end, and is approximately 160 feet in length.

In the action here involved, plaintiffs allege that in [constructing] the building defendant caused its foundation and footings to extend from two to three and a half inches upon plaintiffs' land. * * * Plaintiffs prayed for injunction requiring that defendant remove all footings and foundations upon their property * * * Upon issue raised by general denial the case was tried to a jury as to the issue of damages alleged by trespass, the court reserving the determination of the issue of injunction. On the issue of damages the jury returned a verdict in favor of the defendant. The court then found encroachment as alleged and granted mandatory injunction requiring that defendant's projecting footings be removed from plaintiffs' property * * *

Ordinarily, mandatory injunction will issue to compel removal of encroaching structures, but it is not to be issued as a matter of course. On appeal to the court for an equitable remedy, the court must consider the peculiar equities of the case. A study of many decisions discloses no specific and universally-accepted rule as to encroachments. Even in jurisdictions like Massachusetts, in which it has been declared that mandatory injunction for removal of encroachment can only be denied where estoppel or laches is shown, Beaudoin v. Sinodinos, 48 N.E.2d 19 (Mass.), there are numerous cases where injunction has been refused in the absence of those defenses. See cases cited as exceptional in Geragosian v. Un. Realty Co., 193 N.E. 726 (Mass.). Generally in other jurisdictions such harsh rule is not followed. Sometimes a slight and harmless encroachment is held to be within the rule "de minimis," as in Tramonte v. Colarusso, 152 N.E. 90 (Mass.), and McKean v. Alliance Land Co., 253 P. 134 (Cal.), and generally the courts require that he who seeks equity should do equity and come with clean hands. Tramonte v. Colarusso, supra; McKee v. Fields, 210 P.2d 115 (Or.)

"Clean Hands" Mandate for Equity

Where the encroachment is deliberate and constitutes a willful and intentional taking of another's land, equity may well require its restoration regardless of the expense of removal as compared with damage suffered therefrom; but where the encroachment was in good faith, we think the court should weigh the circumstances so that it shall not act oppressively. 5 Pomeroy' Equity Jurisprudence, page 852, § 508. While the mere balance of convenience is not the proper test, yet relative hardship may properly be considered and the court should not become a party to extortion. Restatement of the Law, Torts, § 941. Where defendant's encroachment is unintentional and slight, plaintiff's use not affected and his damage small and fairly compensable, while the cost of removal is so great as to cause grave hardship or otherwise make its removal unconscionable, mandatory injunction may properly be denied and plaintiff relegated to compensation in damages. Owenson v. Bradley, 197 N.W. 885 (N.D.); Nebel v. Guyer, 221 P.2d 337 (Cal. Dist. Ct. App.); Mary Jane Stevens Co. v. First Nat'l Bldg. Co., 57 P.2d 1099 (Utah).

In the case before us issue was raised in the argument as to whether or not the encroachment was intentional. There was no finding on this issue by the trial court and the decree is not necessarily predicated upon intent.

In the absence of proof to the contrary there is a presumption that men act in good faith and that they intend to do what they have the right to do. Prior to the building of the wall, plaintiffs and defendant each employed a surveyor, but neither was called as a witness and the results of their surveys are not disclosed * * *

There is disclosed continued argument by plaintiffs with representatives of defendant during construction of the wall as to trespassing on their lands, but we find no evidence from the record challenging the good faith of defendant's representative in locating the footings.

Again we note that while plaintiffs were continually complaining as to trespass of the workmen on their property, they took no steps for injunction or other legal determination of the disputed line until after both the foundation and upper wall were completed.

Further, we note that the encroachment here complained of is very slight. It is conceded that the wall above the foundation does not project over the property line and that the only encroachment consists of a projection of the footings a distance of two inches at the middle, increasing to three and a half inches at the north end. The top of these footings is about seven feet below the surface of the ground and they go down to nine feet below the surface. They constitute no interference whatever with plaintiffs' present use of the property as a driveway and iris bed, and the only testimony as to future damage was to the effect that if plaintiffs wished to build to their line with a basement, they would have to detour around this slight projection of defendant's footings.

The testimony indicates that the value of plaintiffs' lands is approximately $200 per front foot, so that if defendant had taken the entire strip of three and a half inches both at and below the surface, its value would have been only about $55, and the value of the portions extending from seven to nine feet below the surface and only along the rear eighty feet of wall would appear to be very small. Plaintiffs, at the trial, refused defendant permission to enter upon their property for the purpose of chipping off the encroaching footings with a jack hammer, and demanded that they be removed from defendant's side of the land, if necessary by tearing down the wall. The expense and hardship of such removal would be so great in comparison with any advantage of plaintiffs to be gained thereby that we think it would be unconscionable to require it, and that under all the circumstances disclosed mandatory injunction should have been denied by the trial court, with permission for plaintiffs to proceed, if desired, in damages.

Accordingly, the injunctive decree is reversed and the case remanded for further proceedings, if desired, consistent herewith.

NOTES AND QUESTIONS

1. The encroachments in *Pile* and *Golden Press* were extremely minimal—just a matter of a few inches underneath the soil in both cases.

Yet the courts in both cases accept that these intrusions are trespasses, and that some type of rectification is needed to vindicate the property rights of the encroached-upon landowner. This in itself is a testament to the hold of the *ad coelum* rule (discussed in connection with *Hinman*) on the judicial mind. But does rigid enforcement of property boundaries make sense in this context? Another approach, as noted in *Golden Press*, would declare that very small intrusions are "de minimis" and hence would entitle the plaintiff to only nominal damages. Would you favor this approach over the approaches of *Pile* and *Golden Press*? If so, what would be the point where the "de minimis" is passed, and the intrusion becomes subject to liability?

2. As the discussion in *Golden Press* suggests, courts in a number of jurisdictions have rejected the absolutist approach of *Pile*. Exactly how many jurisdictions would award injunctive relief against minor building encroachments is unclear, since some jurisdictions that purport to follow the automatic injunction rule nevertheless have recognized a number of exceptions to the rule (Massachusetts fits this description, see Peters v. Archambault, 278 N.E.2d 729 (Mass. 1972)). A safe generalization would be that, if faced with the facts of *Pile* or *Golden Press*—an unintentional encroachment, only slight damage to the plaintiff's interest, and grave hardship to the defendant if removal of the encroachment were required—most American courts today would probably deny injunctive relief and award only damages.

3. The doctrinal justification for awarding an injunction is relatively straightforward, although it is interesting that *Pile* sees no need to spell it out. The building encroachment started out as an unintentional trespass: The encroacher thought it was constructing the wall and footings on its own land. But once the true state of facts was revealed, the encroacher knew it had placed an unwanted structure on someone else's land. From this point on, the continuing presence of the encroaching structure is an *intentional* trespass. See Restatement (Second) of Torts § 158 ("One is subject to liability to another for trespass . . . if he intentionally . . . (c) fails to remove from the land a thing which he is under a duty to remove"); id. § 161(1) ("A trespass may be committed by the continued presence on the land of a structure . . . which the actor tortiously placed there whether or not the actor has the ability to remove it"). Intentional trespass, as we learned from *Jacque v. Steenberg Homes*, is forbidden without regard to any inquiry into the reasonableness of the intrusion or whether it causes any actual harm. Moreover, the building encroachment is a continuously repeated intentional trespass by the same party, and hence falls within one of the exceptions to the rule that equity will not enjoin a mere trespass (see *Baker*, supra). This line of reasoning, perhaps understood only intuitively, underlies the certitude with which the court in *Pile* states that it has no choice but to give the encroached-upon party the right to insist on removal of the subterranean encroachment.

4. The doctrinal justification for the outcome in *Golden Press* comes about from viewing the problem from a different angle within the traditions of equity. One of the maxims of equity is that an injunction will issue

only if a weighing of interests between the parties—generally called the "balance of the equities"—favors giving the victorious plaintiff the "extraordinary" relief of an injunction rather than damages. Thus, if the court balances the equities and finds they favor the plaintiff, it will issue an injunction; but if this exercise comes out in favor of the defendant, an injunction will be denied and the plaintiff will be limited to the relief it would be entitled to "at law," i.e., damages. This is the doctrinal path followed by *Golden Press* in deciding that the victorious plaintiff (the encroached-upon party) will get only damages, rather than an injunction requiring removal of the encroaching footings. Note that the court in *Pile* does not seem to disagree with the court in *Golden Press* about the balance of the equities. The only contested issue in *Pile* (at least on the first go around) is whether the trial court had authority to divide court costs between the parties rather than making the losing defendant pay all the costs. In exercising this limited discretion in this fashion, the court seems to signal its displeasure with the plaintiffs' extreme and unreasonable behavior in refusing a license to the defendant to enter onto the plaintiff's land to remove the footings. But because this is a continuing trespass the court in *Pile* does not perceive itself as having "equitable discretion" to go further and deny injunctive relief against the encroachment itself.

Clean Hands?

5. It bears emphasis that courts have employed the balancing-of-the-equities approach to deny injunctions against building encroachments only when the original encroachment is innocent—that is, when the encroaching party does not know that the building is encroaching on someone else's property at the time the building is constructed. Courts frequently refer to a person who violates another's property rights without knowing that he or she is doing so as a "good faith" violator. In contrast, someone who knowingly violates another's property rights is called a "bad faith" violator. (Be aware that "good faith" and "bad faith" may have slightly different meanings in other legal contexts, but in property law this is nearly always the meaning of these terms.) When an encroacher acts in bad faith at the time the building is constructed, then the courts universally agree that injunctive relief against the encroachment is appropriate. See, e.g., Warsaw v. Chicago Metallic Ceilings, Chapter IX (upholding injunction requiring destruction of a warehouse built with knowledge of a neighbor's claim that it would block an easement); Mark L. Share, Principles of Equity Will Not Protect Encroachers Who Have Knowingly Invaded Their Neighbors' Property, L.A. Law., Jan. 27, 2005, at 40. Does this exception to *Golden Press* (or perhaps limitation on the *Golden Press* exception to *Pile*) follow from the balancing-of-the-equities maxim, or does it reflect another maxim like the clean hands requirement? If the former, why not treat bad faith at the time the building was constructed as just another factor to weigh in the balance of interests?

6. Should courts that follow the approach of *Golden Press* focus only on the encroacher's actual knowledge at the time the encroaching structure was built, or should they also ask whether the encroacher acted negligently in failing to avoid the encroachment? California has adopted a Good Faith Improver Act that requires consideration not only of the good faith of the

encroacher, but also whether the encroacher was negligent, i.e., failed to procure a survey or ignored obvious warning signs. See Raab v. Casper, 124 Cal.Rptr. 590 (Cal. Ct. App. 1975) (discussing California Good Faith Improver Act as applied to encroaching cabin on adjacent foothill lot). Does this create better incentives for parties to take cost-justified precautions to avoid creating a building encroachment problem?

7. A dispute analogous to the issue in *Pile* and *Golden Press* recently reached the U.S. Supreme Court in the context of intellectual property rights (specifically patents). The question was whether the owner of a patent is automatically entitled to a permanent injunction against a defendant who has infringed the patent, or whether courts may sometimes deny an injunction and award only damages. In *eBay Inc. v. MercExchange, L.L.C.*, 126 S. Ct. 1837 (2006), the Court embraced the *Golden Press* position on this issue. Injunctive relief may issue, the Court said, only if the patent holder can show that such relief is required by "traditional standards of equity." This means the patent holder must satisfy a four-part test: "(1) that it has suffered an irreparable injury; (2) that remedies available at law, such as monetary damages, are inadequate to compensate for that injury; (3) that, considering the balance of hardships between the plaintiff and defendant, a remedy in equity is warranted; and (4) that the public interest would not be disserved by a permanent injunction." Id. at 1839. The Court did not apply this test, but remanded to the lower courts to determine whether an injunction was appropriate under the circumstances. A concurring opinion by Chief Justice Roberts, joined by two other Justices, emphasized that application of the traditional equitable test will usually result in issuing an injunction, "given the difficulty of protecting a right to *exclude* through monetary remedies that allow an infringer to *use* an invention against the patentee's wishes." Id. at 1841. Another concurring opinion by Justice Kennedy, joined by three other Justices, warned that courts should be wary of issuing injunctions in favor of firms that buy up patents to be "employed as a bargaining tool to charge exorbitant fees to companies that seek to buy licenses to practice the patent." Id. at 1842. The issue, clearly, is by no means fully settled.

3. Property Rules and Liability Rules

The question whether courts should issue injunctions or award damages for violations of property rights is often discussed in the scholarly literature in terms of the distinction between "property rules" and "liability rules." Credit for this distinction goes to Guido Calabresi, one of the early pioneers of law and economics who went on to become Dean of the Yale School and then a judge on the U.S. Court of Appeals for the Second Circuit, and one of his students, Douglas Melamed. As we shall see, property rules do not always equate with injunctions and damages do not always implement a liability rule. Nevertheless, property rights are strongly associated with "property rule" protection, while contract rights and rights protected by tort law are more closely associated with "liability rule" protection. In the hands of Calabresi and Melamed, however, all types of entitlements were merged together, and analyzed in terms of the degree of protection provided against takings by third parties or the state.

Guido Calabresi & A. Douglas Melamed, *Property Rules, Liability Rules, and Inalienability: One View of the Cathedral*, 85 HARV. L. REV. 1089, 1090, 1092–93 (1972)

* * * The first issue which must be faced by any legal system is one we call the problem of "entitlement." Whenever a state is presented with the conflicting interests of two or more people, or two or more groups of people, it must decide which side to favor. Absent such a decision, access to goods, services, and life itself will be decided on the basis of "might makes right"—whoever is stronger or shrewder will win. Hence the fundamental thing that law does is to decide which of the conflicting parties will be entitled to prevail. The entitlement to make noise versus the entitlement to have silence, the entitlement to pollute versus the entitlement to breathe clean air, the entitlement to have children versus the entitlement to forbid them—these are the first order of legal decisions. * * *

The state not only has to decide whom to entitle, but it must also simultaneously make a series of equally difficult second order decisions. These decisions go to the manner in which entitlements are protected and to whether an individual is allowed to sell or trade the entitlement. In any given dispute, for example, the state must decide not only which side wins but also the kind of protection to grant. * * * We shall consider three types of entitlements—entitlements protected by property rules, entitlements protected by liability rules, and inalienable entitlements. * * *

An entitlement is protected by a property rule to the extent that someone who wishes to remove the entitlement from its holder must buy it from him in a voluntary transaction in which the value of the entitlement is agreed upon by the seller. It is the form of entitlement which gives rise to the least amount of state intervention: once the original entitlement is decided upon, the state does not try to decide its value. It lets each of the parties say how much the entitlement is worth to him, and gives the seller a veto if the buyer does not offer enough. Property rules involve a collective decision as to who is to be given an initial entitlement but not as to the value of the entitlement.

Whenever someone may destroy the initial entitlement if he is willing to pay an objectively determined value for it, an entitlement is protected by a liability rule. This value may be what it is thought the original holder of the entitlement would have sold it for. But the holder's complaint that he would have demanded more will not avail him once the objectively determined value is set. Obviously, liability rules involve an additional stage of state intervention: not only are entitlements protected, but their transfer or destruction is allowed on the basis of a value determined by some organ of the state rather than by the parties themselves.

An entitlement is inalienable to the extent that its transfer is not permitted between a willing buyer and a willing seller. The state intervenes not only to determine who is initially entitled and to determine the compensation that must be paid if the entitlement is taken or destroyed, but also to forbid its sale under some or all circumstances. Inalienability rules are thus quite different from property and liability rules. Unlike those rules, rules of inalienability not only "protect" the entitlement; they may also be viewed as limiting or regulating the grant of the entitlement itself.

It should be clear that most entitlements to most goods are mixed. Taney's house may be protected by a property rule in situations where Marshall wishes to purchase it, by a liability rule where the government decides to take it by eminent domain, and by a rule of inalienability in situations where Taney is drunk or incompetent. * * *

NOTES

1.   Most of the scholarship that follows Calabresi and Melamed has focused on the distinction between property rules and liability rules and has assumed that "property rule" protection means mandatory relief (an injunction or no liability) and "liability rule" means payments of monetary compensation (usually from defendant to plaintiff but occasionally the other way around). This is an oversimplification. An entitlement is protected by a "property rule" when it cannot be taken without the holder's consent. An entitlement is protected by a "liability rule" when it can be taken by what amounts to a forced sale—the holder of the entitlement has no choice but to give it up in return for an award of monetary compensation. When we find that an entitlement is protected by a property rule, this understanding can be enforced in a variety of ways designed to preserve the principle that the entitlement cannot be taken without the holder's consent, including throwing violators of entitlements in jail or privileging entitlement holders to use self-help to deter violators. Recall that one purpose of the punitive damages award in *Jacque* was to make the point that entities like Steenberg Homes cannot enter real property without the owner's consent. Thus, it is inaccurate to suggest, as some of the literature does, that the court's decision to enter an injunction somehow "creates" a property rule. An injunction is an in personam order that binds a particular party to desist from certain acts or to perform certain acts. See J.H. Baker, An Introduction to English Legal History, quoted supra. An injunction thus will often *reflect* a judicial judgment that a certain entitlement is entitled to property rule protection. But the underlying understanding of what it means to protect an entitlement with a "property rule" is grounded in an anterior understanding about the nature of the rights that persons in the position of the entitlement holder have, and in particular in the perception that all other persons have a duty to respect these rights. Analogous points can be made about entitlements protected by liability rules. In general, whether a court decides to enter an injunction or award damages is *evidence* of the court's conception of the degree of protection the entitlement should be given, but these remedial orders do not themselves define the appropriate degree of protection. See Jules L. Coleman & Jody Kraus, Rethinking the Theory of Legal Rights, 95 Yale L. J. 1335, 1345 (1986);

Dale A. Nance, Guidance Rules and Enforcement Rules: A Better View of the Cathedral, 83 Va. L. Rev. 837 (1997).

2. The common starting point in the literature discussing property rules and liability rules is that courts have a "choice" along two dimensions. First, they can choose to assign "the entitlement" to either the plaintiff or the defendant. Second, they can choose to protect this entitlement with either a property rule or a liability rule. This yields four "rules," conventionally diagrammed as follows:

Figure 1–5
Calabresi & Melamed box

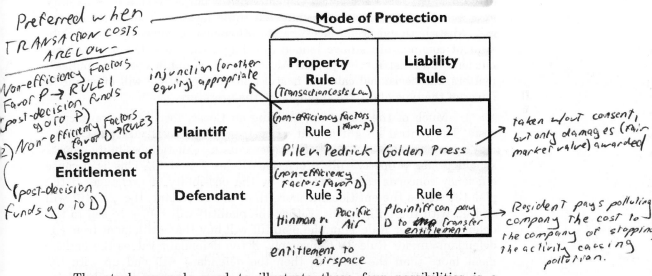

Handwritten annotations:

Preferred when TRANSACTION COSTS ARE LOW—

Non-efficiency Factors Favor P → RULE 1 (post-decision funds go to P)

2) Non-efficiency Factors favor D → RULE 3 (post-decision funds go to D)

injunction (or other equity) appropriate

taken w/out consent, but only damages (fair market value) awarded

Resident pays polluting company the cost to the company of stopping the activity causing pollution.

entitlement to airspace

Mode of Protection

Assignment of Entitlement

	Property Rule (Transaction Costs Low)	Liability Rule
Plaintiff	(non-efficiency factors favor P) Rule 1 — Pile v. Pedrick	Rule 2 — Golden Press
Defendant	(non-efficiency factors favor D) Rule 3 — Hinman v. Pacific Air	Rule 4 — Plaintiff can pay D to transfer entitlement

The stock example used to illustrate these four possibilities is a nuisance dispute, such as where the defendant is engaged in some polluting activity, and the plaintiff is a nearby resident who objects. But we can just as easily illustrate the possibilities in terms of a building encroachment problem, like the ones at issue in *Pile* and *Golden Press*. Thus, the plaintiff is the encroached-upon party, and the defendant is the encroacher. One possible choice the court can make (Rule 1) is to award the entitlement to the plaintiff and to protect this by a property rule. This means (among other things) that the plaintiff can insist on an injunction forcing the defendant to tear the building down. *Pile* is thus a Rule 1 decision. A second choice (Rule 2) is again to award the entitlement to the plaintiff, but this time to protect the entitlement with a liability rule. This means the defendant can take the plaintiff's entitlement without the plaintiff's consent, typically upon payment of court-determined damages, which here would probably be the fair market value of the land occupied by the encroachment. *Golden Press* is a Rule 2 decision. A third possibility (Rule 3) would be to award the entitlement to the defendant protected by a property rule. This means the building stays put, and the plaintiff can get it removed only by getting the *defendant's* consent to tear it down. Of the cases we have read so far, *Hinman* is a Rule 3 decision: The court holds that the airline companies have the entitlement to use the airspace, and the surface owner would have to get their consent to stop them from using it. Finally, a fourth possibility (Rule 4) is that the entitlement is awarded to the defendant, but the plaintiff can force the defendant to transfer the entitlement to the plaintiff in return for a payment of money compensation. We will encounter this possibility in a case in Chapter IX, *Spur Industries, Inc. v. Del E. Webb Development Co.*, where the court holds that the plaintiff can force the defendant to stop polluting but only upon paying compensation to the defendant for the cost that this would entail.

3.   In discussing how to assign the initial entitlement, and the choice of whether to protect that entitlement with a property rule or a liability rule, Calabresi and Melamed addressed three factors: "economic efficiency", "distributional preferences", and "other justice considerations." Subsequent commentators have tended to collapse the three factors into two: efficiency and distributive justice. Although this simplifies (oversimplifies?) matters, the decisional calculus is still quite complex. We will offer only a flavor of the type of discussion found in the literature.

4.   Much of the literature, building on Coase, focuses on transaction costs. The central insight is that when transaction costs are low, thereby making consensual exchange of entitlements a realistic possibility, courts should prefer property rule protection (Rules 1 and 3). This is because efficiency concerns can be satisfied by the possibility of exchange. If the plaintiff values the entitlement more than the defendant, the plaintiff will end up with the entitlement: Either the plaintiff will refuse to sell to the defendant (under Rule 1) or the plaintiff will buy the entitlement from the defendant (under Rule 3). Conversely, if the defendant values the entitlement more than the plaintiff, then the defendant will end up with the entitlement: Either the defendant will buy the entitlement from the plaintiff (under Rule 1) or the defendant will refuse to sell to the plaintiff (under Rule 3). Either way, the entitlement ends up in the hands of the party who values it the most, in terms of being willing to pay the most for it. And the parties themselves will have made the valuation of the entitlement, ensuring that no subjective or idiosyncratic values have been overlooked by the court. Thus, the court can concentrate on distributional concerns or other justice factors. If these non-efficiency factors favor the plaintiff, use Rule 1. Under this rule, any post-decisional flow of funds will go to the plaintiff. If the non-efficiency factors favor the defendant, use Rule 3. Any post-decisional flow of funds will then go to the defendant. Recently some scholars have argued that various more complicated liability rules can be tailored to solve these other problems, and controversy continues over the relative advantages of liability rules and property rules in the low transaction cost setting. See note 7 infra.

5.   Things get a good deal more complicated when transaction costs are high. Here, a variety of arguments about the relative merits of property rules and liability rules have been advanced, but one point of consensus is that when transaction costs are high there may be circumstances in which shifting to liability rules is preferred, at least on efficiency grounds. One

argument, which originated with Calabresi and Melamed themselves, focuses on assembly problems involving large numbers of parties on one side or another of a dispute. See 85 Harv. L. Rev. at 1106–08. Suppose we have one plaintiff and many defendants, or many plaintiffs and one defendant. If either Rule 1 or Rule 3 applies, then there is unlikely to be any exchange of entitlements. If the numerous side wants to buy out the singular side, it will be frustrated by free-rider problems: Some of the members of the numerous side will likely drag their feet about contributing to the buyout fund, making this option infeasible. Conversely, if the singular side wants to buyout the numerous side, it will be frustrated by holdout problems: Some of the members of the numerous side will stubbornly resist agreeing to a buyout price, making this option also infeasible. The only way to ensure a transfer of entitlements in these large-numbers situations, the argument goes, is to use liability rules. For example, a singular defendant can be made to compensate numerous plaintiffs for taking their entitlement under Rule 2. Or a singular plaintiff can force numerous defendants to give up an entitlement by using Rule 4. Note, however, that this argument for the superiority of these simple liability rules only works if the numerous side happens to be the side we want to receive payments in order to reach the "correct" result. The argument also assumes that the process of assessing damages is not fraught with the same problems that would be encountered in trying to negotiate the buyout of an entitlement. Damages must be calculated by the court, and if they vary from person to person or are difficult to measure, the assessment process may also encounter analogous difficulties that render the apparent advantage of liability rules illusory. See James E. Krier & Stewart J. Schwab, Property Rules and Liability Rules: The Cathedral in Another Light, 70 N.Y.U. L. Rev. 440, 453–64 (1995).

6. Another argument for liability rules under conditions of high transaction costs posits that courts may have more limited information than the parties about the benefits and costs of allocating entitlements. See, e.g., A. Mitchell Polinsky, Resolving Nuisance Disputes: The Simple Economics of Injunctive and Damage Remedies, 32 Stan. L. Rev. 1075 (1980). Suppose, for example, that the court has good information about the plaintiff's damages, but poor information about the defendant's costs of eliminating the harm. Let's say it's a building encroachment problem. The court is reasonably certain that the plaintiff's damages are $5,000, based on testimony about the value of the property before and after the encroachment. But the defendant claims that eliminating the encroachment will require demolition of the building, at a cost of tens of thousands of dollars. The court suspects that the defendant is bluffing, and that the actual cost of eliminating the encroachment may be much less. In these circumstances, the argument goes, the court can adopt Rule 2, in effect giving the defendant the option of paying the plaintiffs damages ($5,000) or eliminating the encroachment. Now the defendant no longer has any incentive to bluff. If she can figure out a way of eliminating the encroachment for less than $5,000, she will do so. If not, she will pay the plaintiff $5,000. The result will be efficient, in the sense that the defendant will choose the

lowest-cost solution for eliminating the plaintiff's injury, without any need for the court to dictate the solution or the parties to engage in exchanges of entitlements. This argument, like the previous one, only works if the incomplete information fortuitously lines up the way we would like the damage payments to flow in order to reach the "correct" result.

7.   The literature on property rules and liability rules, like the literature on the Coase theorem, is vast. For an overview, see Carol M. Rose, The Shadow of the Cathedral, 106 Yale L.J. 2175 (1996). The Krier and Schwab article cited above provides a particularly clear summary of the principal developments in the literature. See also, e.g., Ian Ayres, Optional Law: The Structure of Legal Entitlements (1995) (arguing for general superiority of various liability rules); Louis Kaplow & Steven Shavell, Property Rules Versus Liability Rules: An Economic Analysis, 109 Harv. L. Rev. 713 (1996) (arguing that liability rules are better when the parties assert incompatible demands on a resource, but property rules are better when the parties seek to make the same use of a resource); Henry E. Smith, Property and Property Rules, N.Y.U. L. Rev. 1719 (2004) (defending widespread use of property rules based on information costs).

8.   Calabresi and Melamed also have interesting things to say about inalienability rules, which prohibit the transfer of entitlements from the original holder. Inalienability rules usually apply to persons (e.g., you cannot sell yourself into slavery), body parts (e.g., sales of organs and tissue are either prohibited or tightly regulated), cultural patrimony (e.g., you cannot sell certain kinds of Native American cultural artifacts), and so forth. We take up these issues in Chapter III.

4.   THE EX ANTE/EX POST PROBLEM

Another important consideration in deciding between property rules or liability rules is whether we analyze the situation as it exists *before* the particular conflict over resources arises, or *after* that conflict arises. Economists often speak of "ex ante" analysis and "ex post" analysis (this locution has been picked up by courts in recent years). Ex ante analysis simply refers to an analysis of the situation before some critical event like an accident, or a contract, or a commitment to a particular use of resources, takes place. Ex post analysis refers to an analysis of the situation after such a critical event occurs. In the context of building encroachments, an ex ante analysis would consider the circumstances of two adjacent landowners, one contemplating a building to be placed near the boundary line between their properties, before the building is constructed. Ex post analysis would consider the circumstances of the two landowners after the building is constructed. The analysis of both efficiency and justice may differ dramatically, depending on whether we consider a particular situation from an ex ante or an ex post perspective.

Assume that A and B are neighboring landowners. A is planning to build a warehouse on her land. B has already built and is occupying a single-family residence on his land. From A's perspective, each additional foot that the warehouse extends in the direction of B's house will increase the value of her warehouse (because it will be bigger). From B's perspective, each additional foot that the warehouse comes closer to B's house will decrease the use and enjoyment of his house (because it will cut off the flow of air and sunlight to the house). The following table indicates the relative values to A and B at different degrees of separation between the warehouse and the home. The values to A are positive and grow larger as the warehouse gets closer to the house; the values to B are negative (and are shown in parentheses to indicate they are negative) and grow larger (in a negative direction) as the warehouse gets closer to the house.

Figure 1–6
Warehouse Encroachment—Ex Ante Analysis

Feet of Separation	Gain to A	Loss to B	
0	$20,000	($30,000)	−10k *Illegal (Trespassing)*
1	$18,000	($23,000)	−5k
2	$16,000	($18,000)	−2k
3	$14,000	($14,000)	−0−
4	$12,000	($11,000)	+1k *(Original Intended Location) Property Boundary*
5	$10,000	($8,000)	+2k
6	$8,000	($5,000)	+3k *Legal (within Property)*
7	$6,000	($2,000)	+4k*
8	$4,000	($1,000)	+3k
9	$2,000	($500)	+1.5k

B should be willing to offer more than $6k, less than $9k

Suppose A commissions a survey, and learns that the boundary is four feet from B's house. A informs B that she intends to build the warehouse to the edge of the property line. What happens next? The Table tells us that four feet of separation is not the efficient distance to place the warehouse. To be sure, at this distance A's gain—$12,000—is larger than B's loss—($11,000). But there is room to modify the initial assignment of property rights so as to make both parties better off. If A agrees to move the warehouse back to five feet of separation, A loses $2,000 (because A moves from a gain of $12,000 to a gain of only $10,000), but B gains $3,000 (because B's loss shrinks from $11,000 to $8,000). So B should be willing to offer A something more than $2,000, and something less than $3,000, and

To cover A's loss of profits

B's "profit" gained (through less losses) from A moving back

both parties would be better off. The same reasoning applies to a further dropback of the warehouse from five feet to six feet. A loses another $2,000, but B gains another $3,000, so there is again room for a mutually advantageous adjustment of rights. How far will the bargaining continue? A quick way to determine the joint-welfare maximizing result is to subtract the values in the Loss to B column from the values in the Gain to A column at each number of feet of separation, and determine which degree of separation produces the largest net positive gain for the two parties. We can see that a distance of seven feet between the warehouse and the house would produce an overall gain of $4,000 (a $6,000 gain to A offset by a $2,000 loss to B), which is the maximum joint benefit at any distance. Once the parties settle on this distance, there are no further trades to be made that would make them better off.

Of course, none of this may happen. A and B are in a bilateral monopoly situation before the warehouse is built. From B's perspective, A is the only source he can deal with in order to obtain more light and air for his house than would be provided if a warehouse is built four feet away. From A's perspective, B is the only source of cash side payments that may be worth more to her than expanding her warehouse up to the very edge of the property line. Given the bilateral monopoly, the parties may haggle endlessly, or bargain strategically, or may get off on the wrong foot with each other, and no deal may ever be reached. But note that in terms of property rules and liability rules (at least ones that are not systematically under- or over-compensatory), it does not seem to make much difference which mode of protection we select ex ante, before the warehouse goes up. A knows that if she builds the warehouse three feet from B's house, she may face an injunction requiring that the building be torn down. Alternatively, if she builds at three feet, she may have to pay damages equal to $3,000 (the difference between the harm to B at four feet, where the warehouse is legal, and three feet, where it is not), which is more than she stands to gain by building at three feet (another $2,000)—and this should also be enough to induce A to respect B's property rights.

Let us modify the problem by considering how the situation might be viewed *after* the warehouse is built. Let us assume now that A goes ahead with the construction and, based on a faulty assumption about where the boundary lies, constructs the warehouse three feet from B's house. Once the warehouse is built it will cost $50,000 to tear it down. Suppose that B sues A, and the court determines that the actual boundary is four feet from B's house. The ex post analysis of the situation is reflected in the following modified table (Figure 1–7).

Assume that *Pile v. Pedrick* describes the law in the relevant jurisdiction. The construction of the building, and the judicial determination that the building is encroaching on B's lot by one foot, mean that B is now entitled to an injunction ordering that the building be demolished (and if rebuilt, be one foot further from B's house). If B stands on his rights, A

Figure 1–7
Warehouse Encroachment—Ex Post Analysis

Feet of Separation	Gain to A	Demolition Cost to A	Loss to B	
0	$20,000	($50,000)	($30,000)	
1	$18,000	($50,000)	($23,000)	
2	$16,000	($50,000)	($18,000)	
3	$14,000	($50,000)	($14,000)	Building Location
4	$12,000	($0)	($11,000)	Actual Boundary
5	$10,000	$0	($8,000)	
6	$8,000	$0	($5,000)	
7	$6,000	$0	($2,000)	
8	$4,000	$0	($1,000)	
9	$2,000	$0	($500)	

Point is moving from 3 to 4 feet is no longer just the loss in value to A, but the cost of removing the building as well. — this makes courts favor liability rules.

stands to lose $52,000: $50,000 in costs to demolish the warehouse, and $2,000 in lost warehouse space if she builds a new warehouse. (For convenience, we will ignore the costs of the new warehouse.) For his part, the gain to B, again assuming A rebuilds the warehouse, is only $3,000: the difference between the (negative) value to B of having the warehouse four feet away ($11,000) as opposed to three feet away ($14,000). Given the large difference between the loss to A and the gain to B, what is likely to happen?

On the one hand, it might seem that transaction costs are still pretty low in this situation. There are only two parties to the dispute, who are clearly identified. There is no uncertainty about where the boundary line is. And if *Pile v. Pedrick* is the law, there is no uncertainty about whether B is entitled to an injunction. On the other hand, we have a bilateral monopoly situation, as we did before the warehouse went up. But now the potential difficulty created by the bilateral monopoly has been greatly aggravated by the construction of the warehouse. In contrast to the ex ante analysis, the stakes on the table are now very large. B will be better off accepting anything more than $3,000. A will be better off accepting anything less than $52,000. This is a $49,000 difference, which is much larger than the bargaining range that exists in the ex ante version of the problem ($1,000). Given the high stakes, it is much more likely now that A and B will haggle endlessly, or B will try to strategically bargain to "extort" a huge payment from A, or B may regard A with suspicion or contempt because of the encroachment that has occurred. This could result in an inefficient outcome if no agreement is reached to modify B's entitlement. It could also result in an outcome that many would regard as unjust, if A is required to pay an enormous sum like $45,000 in order to secure B's agreement to the modification of rights.

Suppose the dispute goes to litigation, and B obtains an injunction requiring that A tear down the warehouse. Is bargaining more or less likely to occur now that the court has intervened? One question you might reasonably ask here is whether A and B can enter into a contract to sell A's injunction right. Coase and his many follows have assumed that such contracts are possible. It is not entirely clear this is correct. There are few recorded instances of individuals literally selling judicial judgments as if they were a type of property right; indeed, most jurisdictions prohibit the assignment of legal claims. See Michael Abramowicz, On the Alienability of Legal Claims, 114 Yale L.J. 697 (2005). But there are ways to accomplish the same thing (lawyers get paid to figure these things out). The parties could settle the case, either before judgment is entered or even in a post-judgment settlement, and the settlement agreement could provide for a different outcome than the one specified in the court's injunction. The settlement could call for a money payment from A to B, as well as an agreement by A to a different injunction, which might then be entered by the court as a consent decree. Alternatively, B could agree to sell an additional one foot of land to A, in return for a payment of money by A, which would eliminate the encroachment. But even assuming we can devise a way to engage in post-injunction bargaining, how likely is that bargaining will take place once a dispute gets that far? One study of 20 litigated nuisance cases resulting in a "property rule" result (injunction or no liability) found that not one set of parties bargained around the final judgment. Ward Farnsworth, Do Parties to Nuisance Cases Bargain After Judgment? A Glimpse Inside the Cathedral, 66 U. Chi. L. Rev. 373 (1999). The lawyers interviewed attributed the lack of trades to mutual enmity. Although the sample of cases was small, it suggests that if the parties cannot agree on a negotiated solution before they go to court, they are unlikely to sit down and negotiate afterwards.

Given the bilateral monopoly problem that exists in the ex post situation, and the very real possibility that there will be no post-injunction modification of rights, can you see how courts might be drawn to a "liability rule" solution for handling building encroachment controversies? If the court shifts from *Pile v. Pedrick* to *Golden Press v. Rylands*—that is, from Rule 1 to Rule 2—what will be the measure of damages to which B, from our hypothetical, will be entitled? Will the joint wealth of the parties be greater under this solution than it would be under a Rule 1 solution, assuming no post-injunction modification of rights? Will the outcome be more just than the one that will likely result if the court sticks with *Pile*?

Courts are naturally drawn to ex post analysis because this is how controversies are presented to them. People typically go to court after an accident has happened, a contract has been breached, or a building encroachment has occurred. The court takes the situation as it is presented, and looks for the solution that makes the most sense (is both efficient and fair) given what has transpired and the circumstances in which the parties find themselves. But this does not necessarily mean that the ex post perspective is the correct perspective for thinking about such problems. Ex post analysis tends to focus on fairness and distributional concerns, whereas ex ante analysis is more likely to consider incentives for future conduct. Property rules might be inefficient from an ex post perspective, and yet still be the more efficient rule in the long run—that is, from an ex ante perspective that stresses incentives for future behavior. Can you think of an argument for adhering to property rules in building encroachment cases, even in cases where the encroachment has already occurred and we are certain the parties will not negotiate for a modification of the injunction? (Hint: Can the $50,000 cost of demolishing and rebuilding the warehouse be regarded as analogous to the award of $100,000 in punitive damages in *Jacque v. Steenberg Homes*?)

D. RESTITUTION

The common law of contracts is broadly concerned with bargained-for benefits and harms. The common law of torts is broadly concerned with non-bargained-for harms. This leaves a category of events unaccounted for: non-bargained-for benefits. Issues involving non-bargained-for benefits are often said to be covered by the law of restitution. Since liability for restitution is grounded neither in contract nor in tort, restitution is often classified as a property-based body of law. Restitution is another idea that has been bequeathed to us by equity, in the sense that the principles that form the body of the law of restitution derive from decisions invoking precepts of equity, most importantly the idea of "unjust enrichment."

The basic elements of an action for restitution are: (1) an "enrichment" of the defendant; (2) at the expense of the plaintiff; (3) under circumstances that are "unjust." See Warren A. Seavey & Austin W. Scott, Restitution, 54 L.Q. Rev. 29, 32 (1938). Note carefully the relational nature of the claim for restitution. There must be a particular defendant who has experienced some kind of windfall, but it must be a windfall "at the expense" of a particular identified plaintiff. Thus, severe misfortune by the plaintiff that does not enrich another particular person will not do. Nor does blind luck on the part of the defendant if this does not come at the expense of someone else. It takes two to make a claim for restitution, and this significantly cabins the scope of the action. Still, the general formulation of the principle raises a number of vexing questions—most obviously about what makes an enrichment of the defendant at the expense of the plaintiff "unjust." Nevertheless, principles of restitution or unjust enrichment enter into the formulation of many property doctrines and qualify many others.

1. THE MISTAKEN IMPROVER

Pile v. Pedrick and *Golden Press v. Rylands* were concerned with building encroachments that harm the encroached-upon party—or least provide no benefit to the encroached-upon party. But what if the encroacher makes a whopping big mistake, and constructs an entire new building on land belonging to someone else? Now the mistake cannot clearly be characterized as causing harm; if anything, it probably confers a benefit on the true owner. Under ordinary rules of property law, the building would be a fixture attached to the land, and hence ownership of the building would automatically pass to the true owner of the land by accession. (For more on fixtures, see Chapter II.) Does the mistaken improver nevertheless have any right to recover for the benefit conferred on the true owner? Does the mistaken improver have a privilege to enter the land to remove the building? What if the true owner does not like the building, and was planning to do something else with the land? These issues provide the background for the inquiry in the following case, which involves a mistaken improver with an unusual twist.

George R.   *Montgomery*   P   D   *H.P. Orts*

Producers Lumber & Supply Co. v. Olney Building Co.

Court of Civil Appeals of Texas, 1960.
333 S.W.2d 619.

■ MURRAY, CHIEF JUSTICE. This suit was instituted by Producers Lumber & Supply Company, Inc., against Olney Building Company, a corporation, seeking to recover damages resulting from the conduct of H. P. Orts, president of defendant, when he caused his construction superintendent and a large crew of men to go upon Lot 8, Block 9, New City Block 12459, Northeast Park, an addition situated in the corporate limits of the City of San Antonio, Bexar County, Texas, owned by plaintiff, and demolish a dwelling constructed thereon by Olney Building Company.

The trial was to a jury and, based partly upon the verdict of the jury, the trial court rendered judgment in favor of plaintiff against defendant in the sum of $600. Producers Lumber & Supply Company, Inc., has prosecuted this appeal, contending that the judgment should have been in the sum of $5,900.

The issues submitted to the jury and the answers thereto are as follows:

Question No. 1: Do you find from a preponderance of the evidence that H. P. Orts, as president of Olney Building Company, acted in good faith in erecting the building on the plaintiff's lot?

Answer "Yes" or "No."

We, the jury, answer: Yes.

Question No. 2: What do you find from a preponderance of the evidence would be the reasonable and necessary cost of restoring the lot in question to substantially the same condition that it was in immediately before the construction was commenced thereon?

Answer by stating the cost:

We, the jury, answer: $600.00.

Question No. 3: Do you find from a preponderance of the evidence that H. P. Orts, as president of Olney Building Company, acted maliciously in removing the building from the lot in question?

Answer "Yes" or "No."

We, the jury, answer: Yes.

Question No. 4: What sum of money, if any, do you find from a preponderance of the evidence is the plaintiff, Producers Supply & Lumber Company, entitled to receive as exemplary damages, if any, as that term is defined herein below?

Answer by stating the amount, if any:

We, the jury, answer: $300.00.

The parties stipulated that the dwelling on Lot 8 had a value of $5,000, and that the dwelling had enhanced the value of Lot 8 by $5,000.

After the verdict was returned, appellant moved that the jury's answer to Question No. 1 be disregarded, and for a judgment in its favor in the sum of $5,900, while appellee moved that the jury's answer to Questions Nos. 3 and 4 be disregarded and judgment for appellant be confined to the sum of $600. This latter motion was granted and judgment rendered accordingly.

Appellant assigns as error the trial court's action in sustaining appellee's motion to disregard the jury's answers to Special Issues Nos. 3 and 4. The jury's answers to these issues were well supported by the evidence, were very material and the court erred in setting them aside. Special Issue No. 3 inquired whether H. P. Orts, as president of appellee acted maliciously in removing the building from Lot No. 8. The jury very properly found that he did. It might be well here to make a rather complete statement of the evidence in the case. H. P. Orts owned several corporations and was the head and general manager of them all, including Olney Building Company. Prior to November 1, 1956, Elliott Construction Co., Inc., hereinafter referred to as Elliott, was the owner of Lot 8, Block 9, New City Block 12,459, involved herein. On that date H. P. Orts, executed a warranty deed, which was properly recorded, from Elliott Construction Co., Inc., as its Assistant Secretary and Agent and Attorney in Fact, to Producers Lumber & Supply Co., appellant herein, conveying Lot 8 for a consideration of $1,428. The lot was purchased by appellant with the intention that later its general manager, George R. Montgomery, and his wife would build a home for themselves thereon. Montgomery and wife had the lot graded and planted some trees and grass on it. On or about February 27, 1958, Orts and Elliott decided to construct nine dwellings, one on Lot 8, and eight on other nearby lots. Orts called A. L. Burden, secretary-treasurer of appellee, and asked him whether Lot 8 had been sold. Burden, after consulting a map on the wall, assured Orts it had not been sold. Orts inspected Lot 8 and noticed the trees planted there, he thought it was nice of someone to plant trees on this lot. Shortly thereafter the construction of the nine houses was begun[.] [O]n April 1, 1958, appellee ordered Stewart Title Company to issue a Title Binder covering all nine lots to Frost National

About 1 year, 3 months after sale

Bank in connection with appellee's interim financing. On April 14, 1958, Orts learned from the Title Company that Lot 8 had been sold to appellant. Orts then notified Mr. Montgomery of the circumstances, and this was the first notice to appellant that construction had been commenced on its lot. The dwelling on Lot 8 had been almost completed when the discovery was made. The house had been constructed without the knowledge or consent of appellant and against its wishes, and contrary to the plans that Montgomery and wife had for their own home. Orts began negotiations with Montgomery, trying to reach an amicable settlement of the matter. Orts told Montgomery that he, Montgomery, had him at his mercy. Various offers and counter-offers were made, but no settlement had been reached, when suddenly on April 22, 1958, Orts broke off negotiations and sent his construction superintendent with a large crew of men and heavy equipment to Lot 8, and demolished the dwelling constructed thereon, leaving nothing but a heap of crude building material and debris. With reference to the destruction of this dwelling, Orts testified as follows:

Q. Now, you did, on or about April 22, 1958, remove those improvements, did you not? A. That is correct, sir.

Q. Did you notify Mr. Montgomery or anyone from Producers Lumber and Supply Company that you were going to remove them? A. No, sir.

Q. How many men do you remember employing on the job of removal? A. Does this have to be exact, or will an approximation do?

Q. Well, if you know, tell me exactly; otherwise, it has to be approximately. A. I will say—I am going to say ten.

Q. Approximately ten? A. Yes.

Q. Isn't it a fact that you started the removal of these improvements about 2:00 o'clock in the afternoon? A. That is correct, sir.

Q. Isn't it a fact that by 6:00 o'clock in the afternoon, by the use of a bulldozer and a dozen or more men, you had completely removed everything but the slab? A. That's right.

Q. Isn't it a fact that you made no effort to salvage anything on the removal? A. No, sir.

Q. You say that is not true? A. No, sir.

Q. What did you salvage? A. All of the interior partitions, the exterior partitions, the siding, not the siding, but the exterior sheeting, the roof sheeting, electrical and plumbing.

Q. Well, now, actually what happened was that several of your men went out and tore the roof off, isn't that right? A. That's right.

Q. And then you, for lack of a better word I will say "unjointed", the corners and then you hooked on with a dozer and dragged the partitions and framing and roof trusses across the street, is that right? A. Partially, that is correct.

Q. You say that is not true? A. Not all of it.

Q. What is not true? A. The side walls were taken down piece by piece.

Q. The side walls were taken down piece by piece? A. Yes, sir. * * *

Q. You said that you salvaged the electrical? A. Yes. * * *

Q. Now, who did you employ to remove the slab? A. My superintendent.

Q. How did Crea Brothers get on the job? A. I hired their equipment.

Q. What equipment did you hire from Crea Brothers? A. A D–12 tractor, and I believe that slab was so good they couldn't get it up with a D–12 and finally they had to get a crane with a drop hammer, and I told my superintendent if Crea Brothers didn't have the—well, frankly, I don't know where I got the crane with the drop hammer.

Q. Isn't it a fact that they also used a couple of air hammers? A. Oh, yes.

Q. Air hammers, and they had to use torches to cut the steel? A. That is correct.

With reference to the destruction of the dwelling Orts further testified as follows:

Q. So the night you tore that house down, $2,768.00 went down the drain; is that right? A. Yes, sir. My money.

Q. Yes, sir. $2,768.00 went up just like that (slapping hands together)? A. That is right.

Q. As if you had set a match to it, didn't it? A. That is right.

It cost more than $1,300 to put the concrete foundation in, and, of course, it was worthless after the crane and drop hammer, cutting torches, etc., had been used upon it. This and other evidence clearly supports the finding of the jury that H. P. Orts, as president of appellee, acted maliciously in removing the building from Lot 8.

The finding of the jury that appellant was entitled to recover exemplary damages in the sum of $300 was also fully supported by the evidence.

The jury found in answer to Special Issue No. 1, that Orts had built the dwelling on Lot 8 in good faith. The evidence shows that at the time he began the construction of the dwelling there was a deed on record signed by Orts, conveying this lot to appellant. Orts simply forgot about signing this deed some eighteen months before. * * *

However, if the evidence may be regarded as sufficient to support the jury's answer to Issue No. 1, appellee cannot prevail upon his plea of improvement in good faith, because of his malicious destruction of the dwelling he had constructed on Lot 8.

The law at one time was quite clear that where a person erects a building upon the land of another without his knowledge and consent the building became a fixture and belonged to the owner of the land and the builder was without remedy. Foxworth–Galbraith Lumber Co. v. Thorp, 86

S.W.2d 644 (Tex. Civ. App. 1935); Rotan Grocery Co. v. Dowlin, 77 S.W. 430 (Tex. Civ. App. 1903). This rule was regarded as harsh, but was thought necessary to make people careful with reference to their examination of the title to the land upon which they place buildings and other permanent improvements. 14 R.C.L. 17–19, § 5.

It is only where a person places permanent improvements upon land belonging to another in a good faith belief that he is the owner of the land, that he has any remedy at all. Luker v. Luker, 226 S.W.2d 482 (Tex. Civ. App. 1949). Where he has built such improvements in good faith, he has a somewhat limited right to go into court, and upon proof of such good faith ask the court to grant him equitable relief. Bonner v. Wiggins, 52 Tex. 125 (1879); 27 Am.Jur. 261, § 3. Under such circumstances, a court of equity may grant relief in several ways. If the building can be removed without great injury to the building or to the land, the court may permit the improver to move the building. Salazar v. Garcia, 232 S.W.2d 685 (Tex. Civ. App. 1950). Where the building cannot well be removed the court or jury can find the market value of the land before and after the making of the improvement, and allow the improver to recover for the amount of this enhanced value, if any. The landowner will first be permitted to pay the enhanced value and keep the land, but if he is unable or unwilling to do so, then the improver may be permitted to pay the value of the land before the improvements were placed thereon, and thus become the owner of the land and the improvements. Rzeppa v. Seymour, 203 N.W. 62 (Mich. 1925). If the landowner is unable to pay for the improvements and the improver is unable to pay for the land, then the court may order the land and the improvements sold to the highest bidder and the money divided between the owner and the improver as their respective interests appear. Or the court may give the improver judgment for the amount the lot has been enhanced in value, together with a lien against the lot to secure the payment of the judgment. 27 Am.Jur. 282, §§ 29 and 30.

Under no circumstances is an improver authorized to go upon the land of another, without his knowledge and consent, and demolish the improvements that he has through mistake placed thereon, and if he does so he commits waste and can be required to pay the landowner for such waste. 1 Thompson on Real Property 262, § 174; 42 C.J.S., Improvements §§ 4a and 4c, pp. 425–427; 27 Am.Jur. 261, § 3.

When Orts went upon Lot 8 without the knowledge or consent of appellant and demolished the dwelling he had placed thereon, he committed waste and must pay appellant for the value of the dwelling he destroyed, which as stipulated by the parties is the sum of $5,000. And Orts will not be heard to claim, in equity, reimbursement for the amount he had enhanced the value of the lot by the erection of the dwelling thereon. He resorted to self-help and took the law into his own hands, and before a court of equity could determine the rights of the parties he went upon Lot 8, which at the time he well knew belonged to appellant, and demolished the dwelling stipulated to be worth $5,000, thereby causing great destruction of property. He cannot now come into court, with unclean hands, and seek the equitable remedy of reimbursement for the amount he had enhanced the value of Lot 8 by the erection of the dwelling thereon.

Appellee seems to contend that appellant has unclean hands because it did not offer to pay appellee what it contended the dwelling was worth. In this appellee is mistaken. Appellant was not required to pay appellee anything until appellee had secured a finding in a court of equity that Orts had constructed the dwelling in good faith and not as a result of his own negligence. Appellant had good reason to believe that such an issue might be decided in its favor, in which event it would owe appellee nothing, and, further, if it lost on this issue, appellant would have to pay only such sum as a jury, or other trier of the facts, might find appellee had enhanced the value of Lot 8 by the construction of the dwelling thereon. None of these matters had been decided or stipulated at the time Orts, as president of appellee, entered upon appellant's lot and demolished the dwelling he had built thereon, but which under the law belonged to appellant. Appellant is not here asserting an equitable remedy, it is suing in law for the damage that was wilfully done to its property by Orts, acting for appellee, but, even if appellant were seeking equitable relief, its failure to settle its claim upon Orts' terms, or any other terms, would not render its hands unclean. Commonwealth v. Filiatreau, 170 S.W. 1182 (Ky. 1914); Plenderleith v. Glos, 160 N.E. 745 (Ill. 1928).

The judgment of the trial court will be amended so as to permit appellant, Producers Lumber & Supply Company, Inc., to recover the sum of $5,000, the stipulated value of the dwelling demolished by Orts, and $300, found by the jury as exemplary damages, in addition to the sum of $600 awarded by the trial court, thus making the total amount of the judgment the sum of $5,900, and as thus amended the judgment will be affirmed. The cost of this appeal is adjudged against appellee.

[handwritten margin note: $5,000 = value of unfinished house (WASTE) $600 = damage to lot $300 = exemplary damages]

■ BARROW, JUSTICE (dissenting). I do not concur in the opinion of the majority. * * *

There is no doubt that appellant is entitled to recover such damages as it suffered to its lot, which is all that it had at the inception of this transaction. Producers is also entitled to recover exemplary damages under the jury finding that the house was torn down and removed maliciously, but I cannot agree that it is entitled to recover compensatory damages for the removal of the house.

[handwritten margin note: Issue of the Dissent]

Regardless of what the law may be in other jurisdictions, it is well settled in this State, that a person who has in good faith made improvements upon the lands of another may obtain relief either in a suit in trespass to try title in an independent action for the purpose, *or in defense of a suit for removing the improvement.* Long v. Cude, 12 S.W. 827 (Tex. 1889); Salazar v. Garcia, 232 S.W.2d 685 (Tex. Civ. App. 1950); Mulholland v. Jolly, 17 S.W.2d 1109 (Tex. Civ. App. 1929); Murphy v. Benson, 245 S.W. 249 (Tex. Civ. App. 1922); Mason v. Hood, 230 S.W. 468 (Tex. Civ. App. 1921); Dean v. Dean, 214 S.W. 505 (Tex. Civ. App. 1919); Wood v. Cahill, 50 S.W. 1071 (Tex. Civ. App. 1899). It has also been held that a defendant in an action of trespass to try title may recover on equitable grounds, independently of the statutes, should his pleadings and proof warrant it, even though the plaintiff does not need or seek the aid of equity. Pomeroy v. Pearce, 2 S.W.2d 431 (Tex. Com. App. 1928).

Appellant has cited no Texas authority which conflicts with the rules above stated, and no such case appears in the majority opinion. I have found no such authority in my own search. It is clear, under the authorities in this State, that such an improver does not lose his equitable rights by removing the improvements, but may urge in equity his defense in a suit for damages for the removal of the improvements. The right of the good faith improver to remove his property is also recognized. Authorities supra, also 1 Thompson on Real Property, 261, § 173. Section 174, on page 262, cited by the majority, has no application for the reason that the matter there discussed does not involve a good faith improver. * * *

The majority opinion holds that Olney is not entitled to reimbursement for the amount its improvements enhanced the value of Producers' land because it resorted to "self-help," and took the law into its own hands, and demolished the building, causing great destruction of property, and by reason thereof Olney does not come into equity with clean hands, and therefore cannot seek equitable relief. I cannot agree with such reasoning. First, it is common knowledge that if Olney had a right to remove the building, which the authorities hold that it did, then if it became necessary to tear down the building in order to do so, it had that right, subject to its responsibility to pay for any damages to Producers' lot. Second, Olney does not seek any reimbursement, but only interposes its right in defense of Producers' suit for damages for the removal of the property. Third, the property "demolished," belonged to Olney and not to Producers. Fourth, had the house remained on Producers' lot, before it could claim the same it would have had to pay Olney the amount of the enhancement in value of its property. Fifth, it appears from the record that immediately upon discovery of the mistake, Olney contacted Producers and sought to adjust the difficulty. It first offered to buy the lot, and Producers asked $3,600 or $3,700 for the lot, although it cost $1,428. Producers' manager and witness Montgomery, testified the lot was worth $1,700 or $1,800. Olney then offered to trade any lot in the subdivision for Producers' lot. Producers declined on the ground that none of the lots would fit the plan of house that had been planned for its manager's home, although it was admitted that several of the lots offered were more valuable than Producers' lot. In that connection, it appears that the manager's home was not built on the lot in question, but was built on Walzen Road. Olney offered to sell the house to Producers either in its incomplete condition, or to complete it according to F.H.A. specifications at its cost. Producers declined and finally made a counter offer that it would give $7,000 for the house as so completed. The evidence shows that when completed the house would cost Olney $10,400. Montgomery testified that the completed house with the lot would be of the value of $12,000 to $12,900. When Producers made the offer of $7,000 for the completed house, it notified Olney that it was its final offer, although, at the time Montgomery was instructed to make the offer, Producers' president told Montgomery that he would give $8,000 for the house. This was not communicated to Olney, they said: "Let's offer him $7,000.00." Producers never at any time offered to pay the amount of the stipulated enhancements of its lot. Thus the record shows that Producers, having Olney "at its mercy" attempted to drive an unconscionable bargain. It was at this point that Olney proceeded to tear down the house and remove it. In that connection, I have found no authority which makes any distinction between moving the improvements intact or tearing it down and removing it, so long as the land is not damaged. * * *

Keeping in mind that appellant seeks to recover as damages the value of a house that it did not build and has not one dollar invested in, and that it seeks to recover such damages against appellee, which at its own expense built the house in question, I cannot in good conscience agree to such an inequitable decision. Appellant has sustained no injury so far as the house is concerned. * * *

There is no sound reason to exact of appellee additional punitive damages in the sum of $5,000 and make the donation to appellant, as chastisement for appellee's alleged uncleanliness of hands, after full restitution has been made in awarding to appellant all damages which the jury found it suffered, as well as the exemplary damages found by the jury. Equity looks on that done which ought to be done.

As said by the Supreme Court in French v. Grenet, 57 Tex. 273, 279 (1881), in a situation similar to that involved here:

> In such case, the question is not whether a mistake of law shall vest title, but whether the penalty for that mistake, however innocently made and however diligently guarded against, shall be the forfeiture for a claim for improvements which enhanced the value of that property. To so decide would palpably violate that maxim, founded in the highest natural equity, that no one should be made richer to the damage and wrong of another.

$\longrightarrow$ *Main idea of RESTITUTION*

I respectfully dissent.

NOTES AND QUESTIONS

1. Consider how the case of the mistaken improver would be handled in a jurisdiction following a pure *Pile*-type approach to building encroachments. Presumably, such a jurisdiction would apply the law of trespass, and would give the true owner of the land an election: either an injunction ordering the encroacher to tear the building down, or a declaration that the building belongs to the true owner as a fixture incident to its ownership of the land (see Chapter II for a discussion of the law of fixtures). If the true owner chooses to treat the building as a fixture, the result would be a windfall for the true owner—a free building. Of course, from a social welfare perspective this may be a better result than requiring the encroacher to destroy the structure. The encroacher suffers a severe penalty either way, but at least the value of the building is preserved for the benefit of society.

2. As in the case of the small encroachments considered in *Pile* and *Golden Press*, courts in many jurisdictions have balanced the equities in mistaken improver cases, in effect adopting a principle of restitution. If they find the encroaching party acted in good faith at the time of construction, they may modify the severity of the *Pile*-type remedial regime. The principal case discusses three remedial options that a court of equity might adopt in a case of a good faith improver: (1) let the true owner keep the house and pay the encroacher its value (an equitable award of restitution); (2) transfer the lot to the encroacher in return for payment of its fair market value (effected by a common-law award of damages and motivated by considerations of unjust enrichment); (3) sell the property to a third party and apportion the proceeds between the true owner and the encroacher in accordance with their respective entitlements (a judicial award of partition, again reflecting principles of restitution or unjust enrichment—see Chapter V for details). As things stand today, some courts in mistaken improver cases continue to follow the *Pile* approach, and others balance the equities. The *Restatement (First) of Restitution* § 42(1) (1937) reaffirmed the *Pile* approach as a matter of common law (with certain qualifications), but noted that many jurisdictions have enacted "betterment" or "good faith improver" statutes that require something like a balancing of equities. (For a survey of betterment statutes, see Kelvin H. Dickinson, Mistaken Improvers of Real Estate, 64 N.C. L. Rev. 37, 42–49 (1985).) Recognizing that these statutes provide mistaken improvers relief only in certain limited circumstances, the tentative draft of the third *Restatement* adopts a more liberal rule, granting restitution "as necessary to prevent unjust enrichment" while avoiding "undue prejudice to the owner." Restatement (Third) of Restitution and Unjust Enrichment § 10 cmt. b (Tentative Draft No. 1, 2001).

3. Do you agree that mistaken-improver cases should necessarily be handled by denying the true owner the right to enjoin the continued intrusion of the structure? A key aspect of *Golden Press* was that the intrusion was very small, and hence did not subtract from the true owner's property rights very much. In the mistaken-improver cases, by contrast, the intrusion is typically quite large (like an entire house in the instant case). To be sure, the improvement is a windfall for the true owner. But doesn't it also largely negate the autonomy of the true owner to do what she wants with her property? In *Producers Lumber*, the Montgomerys—the true owners of Lot 8—did not want a house like the one Olney Building was constructing; they had their own design in mind. In another case involving a mistaken improver, a dissenting judge argued that in order to protect owner autonomy, the encroached-upon party should be given the option of requiring the encroacher to tear the house down. The true owner should not be allowed to keep the house as a fixture, since that would be unjust enrichment. But if the owner does not like the improvement, or has other plans for the property, she should be able to insist that the property be restored to its prior condition. Somerville v. Jacobs, 170 S.E.2d 805, 815–17 (W. Va. 1969) (Caplan, J., dissenting). Do you agree with this argument?

Does the answer depend in part on whether we conceive of property as entailing a right to exclude, as opposed to being a bundle of rights?

4. The principal case adds yet a further twist. According to the jury, H.P. Orts was an innocent improver when he built the house on Lot 8, but then acted maliciously when he ordered the work crew to enter Lot 8 to tear the house down. Given the finding of malice in tearing the house down, the majority departs from the ordinary analysis that would apply in a case of a mistaken improver, and requires that Orts pay the Montgomerys for the value of the house he destroys. How is it possible that Orts would be both entitled to restitution for building a house and liable for restitution for tearing it down? If Orts is entitled to the value of the house because it is really "his" house—only put in the wrong place by mistake—how can he be held liable for destroying his own property? Or is the outcome explainable by the way in which the jury perceives the "justness" of situation, depending on Orts's behavior at different times in the controversy?

5. The majority opinion seems intent on ordering Orts to pay restitution for the value of the destroyed home in part to deter persons in his position from engaging in inappropriate behavior. Exactly what is the behavior that the court is seeking to deter? Is it the use of self-help to recover improvements mistakenly built on someone else's land? Or is it the destruction of a valuable asset, thereby depriving society of its use? Suppose the improvement can be removed through self-help without destroying it, for example, suppose the improvement is a mobile home which can be retrieved from its pad with a tractor trailer without any damage to the underlying real estate. If a person like Orts can remove the mobile home using self-help, should he be required to pay the true owner the value of the mobile home? If self-help is still frowned upon even where the asset can be retrieved without harm, what is the appropriate relief to deter self-help in these circumstances? For more on self-help, see Chapter IV.

6. Did Orts behave irrationally in ordering the crew to tear the house down? The majority opinion emphasizes the suddenness with which Orts acted, and the violence of the crew in reducing the house to a pile of rubble in hours. This is designed to lead the reader to feel that Orts was acting impulsively and without adequate provocation. But the dissent offers more details about the negotiations between Producers Lumber/Montgomery and Olney Building/Orts, and concludes that Producers Lumber was behaving as if it had Olney "at its mercy" and was trying to exact an "unconscionable bargain." Is it irrational to react to someone trying to drive a hard bargain in a bilateral monopoly situation by destroying the principal source of value being disputed? Under what assumptions might this be rational behavior?

2. The Origins and Basis of Restitution

The common law contained no cause of action to recover non-bargained-for benefits. The matter was not governed by the law of contract, because there is no agreement between the two parties. Nor was it governed by the law of tort, since the defendant had committed no wrong of which the plaintiff could complain. Somewhat by default, the right of restitution has been assigned to the law of property. Perhaps this makes sense if we consider that one of the core attributes of property is that it cannot be taken away without consent (or some other established legal process like adverse possession or eminent domain). From this perspective, someone who loses property because of a mistake (like mistakenly building a house on property that belongs to some one else), should be able to get the value of the house back, since she never consented to give away the house. The action for restitution to recover property transferred to another by mistake (or other circumstances that make the transfer unjust) can therefore be viewed is an important action for vindicating rights in property. It is a reflection of the same preference for owner autonomy we see in the law of trespass (*Jacque, Baker*) and in the understanding that property is ordinarily given "property rule" protection.

As in the case of the development of the law of equity and the right to an injunction for trespasses to property, it took quite a long time for the common law to recognize a general right to restitution for property unjustly conveyed to another. The roots of the idea lie in the decisions of courts of many different jurisdictions struggling to find some way to provide relief in situations involving persons who have unintentionally transferred property or other value to another. For example, as the dissent notes in the principal case, the Texas courts had allowed an innocent improver of real property either to sue in trespass for a determination of title to the land, and obtain relief for the value of the improvement as part of that action, or to seek to remove the improvement from the land, and assert the right to removal or to compensation for the value of the improvements as a defense to a trespass action by the true owner.

Not until the twentieth century was any attempt made to gather together the many disparate circumstances in which the law would grant some relief for what has come to be called unjust enrichment. In 1937, two American law professors, Warren A. Seavey and Austin W. Scott, brought together a number of situations involving non-bargained-for benefits or unjust enrichment and gave them a name: the law of restitution. Their efforts were given legitimacy by the American Law Institute, which published the *Restatement (First) of Restitution* in 1937. The first *Restatement* identified equitable considerations as the normative foundation for the law of restitution, and cited as its justification the famous statement by Lord Mansfield: "In one word, the gist of this kind of action is that the defendant upon the circumstances of the case, is obliged by the ties of natural justice and equity to refund the money." Moses v. Macferlan, 2 Burr. 1005, 97 Eng. Rep. 676 (K.B. 1760). See Restatement (First) of Restitution § 42(1). The idea that unjust enrichment is inequitable can in fact be traced back to antiquity. The Roman jurist Pomponius of the second century A.D. is quoted as saying: "For it is by nature fair that nobody should enrich himself at the expense of another." Mark P. Gergen, What Renders Enrichment Unjust?, 79 Tex. L. Rev. 1927, 1927 & n.1 (2001).

In recent years the law of restitution has become a matter of theoretical interest among scholars in England, other commonwealth countries, Israel, and some civil-law countries. Although interest has lagged in the United States, the birthplace of restitution, it appears to be picking up here as well. The subject is fascinating, in part because it does not easily fit within the common-law trilogy of contracts-torts-property, and in part because it presents a challenge to explain the doctrine in terms of theoretical frameworks such as economic analysis or corrective justice. See Saul Levmore, Explaining Restitution, 71 Va. L. Rev. 65 (1985) (seeking to explain restitution in terms of wealth distribution effects and a desire to encourage participation in markets).

At a more practical level, the idea that unjust enrichment can form an independent basis for liability has been criticized on two grounds. One criticism is that the doctrine seems to rest solely on principles of morality, rather than on a more solid foundation in law. See Restatement (Third) of Restitution and Unjust Enrichment § 1 cmt. b (Discussion Draft, 2000). In an effort to address this criticism, the authors of the current draft *Restatement* propose to cabin restitution as falling within a set of circumstances they term *unjustified* enrichment—"enrichment that lacks an adequate legal basis" because "it results from a transfer that the law treats as ineffective to work a conclusive alteration in ownership rights." Id. at § 1 cmt. b. Under this approach, restitution may be appropriate for transfers of property "that cannot be justified by the terms of a valid and enforceable exchange transaction; by the intention of the transferor to make a gift; or by the existence of a legal duty to the transferee [such as a judgment in tort]." Id. Some examples include a transfer of property to another based on a good faith mistake of fact about the item being transferred or the identity of the transferee; the provision of emergency medical services to a person who is unconscious and cannot give her assent; or profits gained beyond ordinary rental value from intentionally trespassing on someone's land. See also Andrew Kull, Rationalizing Restitution, 83 Cal. L. Rev. 1191 (1995) (Kull is the Reporter for the *Restatement Third*).

Another criticism is that restitution does not embody any unitary principle, but merely reflects a miscellany of circumstances giving rise to the right to restitution. See Peter Birks, Unjust Enrichment and Wrongful Enrichment, 79 Tex. L. Rev. 1767 (2001). Emily Sherwin, for example, argues that unjust enrichment serves merely a descriptive and organizational function—"a common theme of the various doctrines grouped together as restitution"—rather than a unified doctrine complementing common-law rules of contract, tort, and property. Emily Sherwin, Restitution and Equity: An Analysis of the Principle of Unjust Enrichment, 79 Tex. L. Rev. 2083, 2108–12 (2001). Hanoch Dagan is less skeptical, and sees unjust enrichment as a loose framework that encompasses benefit-based liabilities that do not fit within the fields of tort, contract, or property law. He advocates using the principle of unjust enrichment as a launching point for a contextual normative analysis that weighs other values such as autonomy, utility, and community. See Hanoch Dagan, The Law and Ethics of Restitution 14–15 (2004). But Dagan also worries that the open-ended nature of this equitable principle may be criticized for allowing judges "unbridled discretion" to fashion remedies. This concern is not new: In the seventeenth century, John Selden complained that because equity was based on the Chancellor's conscience, it was a "roguish thing" and would vary from Chancellor to Chancellor with the length of "the Chancellor's foot." This has animated various attempts to constrain equitable discretion throughout its history. See also Gee v. Pritchard, 36 Eng. Rep. 670, 674 (Ch. 1818); William Holdsworth, Some Makers of English Law 198 (1938).

However these debates are eventually resolved, there is a widespread consensus that restitution is an appropriate remedy in certain circumstances. Be alert throughout these materials for situations in which principles of unjust enrichment or restitution are at work, either in name or in practice.

CHAPTER II

ORIGINAL ACQUISITION

Most of the property you own was probably acquired from someone else, by purchase or gift. The person from whom you acquired it probably got it from someone else, also by purchase or gift. That person, in turn, got it from someone else, and so on. But how do these chains of ownership get started? What sort of events qualify as establishing a root of title, from which a sequence of voluntary conveyances can then unfold? In this Chapter we consider various modes of original acquisition—ways in which ownership can be established other than through voluntary conveyance from a previous owner. We consider five general principles: first possession, discovery, creation, accession, and adverse possession. We also examine some problems that arise when a series of involuntary acquisition events occurs, and when different principles of establishing original acquisition come into conflict.

A. FIRST POSSESSION

Perhaps the most familiar principle for establishing a new root of title is simply being the first to possess something that is unclaimed by anyone else. "First in time" is deceptively simple, but what does it mean to "possess" something? What sorts of resources can be said to be "unclaimed" by anyone else? From where do we derive standards for resolving these sorts of issues?

1. WILD ANIMALS

Pierson v. Post

Supreme Court of New York, 1805.
3 Cai. R. 175, 2 Am. Dec. 264.

This was an action of trespass on the case commenced in a justice's court, by the present defendant against the now plaintiff.

The declaration stated that *Post,* being in possession of certain dogs and hounds under his command, did, "upon a certain wild and uninhabited, unpossessed and waste land, called the beach, find and start one of those noxious beasts called a fox," and whilst there hunting, chasing and pursuing the same with his dogs and hounds, and when in view thereof, Pierson, well knowing the fox was so hunted and pursued, did, in the sight of Post, to prevent his catching the same, kill and carry it off. A verdict having been rendered for the plaintiff below, the defendant there sued out a *certiorari,* and now assigned for error, that the declaration and the matters therein contained were not sufficient in law to maintain an action. * * *

■ Tompkins, J. delivered the opinion of the court. This cause comes before us on a return to a *certiorari* directed to one of the justices of Queens county.

The question submitted by the counsel in this cause for our determination is, whether Lodowick Post, by the pursuit with his hounds in the manner alleged in his declaration, acquired such a right to, or property in, the fox, as will sustain an action against Pierson for killing and taking him away?

The cause was argued with much ability by the counsel on both sides, and presents for our decision a novel and nice question. It is admitted that a fox is an animal *ferae naturae,** and that property in such animals is acquired by occupancy only. These admissions narrow the discussion to the simple question of what acts amount to occupancy, applied to acquiring right to wild animals?

If we have recourse to the ancient writers upon general principles of law, the judgment below is obviously erroneous. Justinian's Institutes, lib. 2. tit. 1. s. 13. and Fleta, lib. 3. c. 2. p. 175. adopt the principle, that pursuit alone vests no property or right in the huntsman; and that even pursuit, accompanied with wounding, is equally ineffectual for that purpose, unless the animal be actually taken. The same principle is recognised by Bracton, lib. 2. c. 1. p. 8.

Puffendorf, lib. 4. c. 6. s. 2. and 10. defines occupancy of beasts *ferae naturae,* to be the actual corporal possession of them, and Bynkershoek is cited as coinciding in this definition. It is indeed with hesitation that Puffendorf affirms that a wild beast mortally wounded, or greatly maimed, cannot be fairly intercepted by another, whilst the pursuit of the person inflicting the wound continues. The foregoing authorities are decisive to show that mere pursuit gave Post no legal right to the fox, but that he became the property of Pierson, who intercepted and killed him.

It therefore only remains to inquire whether there are any contrary principles, or authorities, to be found in other books, which ought to induce a different decision. Most of the cases which have occurred in England, relating to property in wild animals, have either been discussed and decided upon the principles of their positive statute regulations, or have arisen between the huntsman and the owner of the land upon which beasts *ferae naturae* have been apprehended; the former claiming them by title of occupancy, and the latter *ratione soli.*** Little satisfactory aid can, therefore, be derived from the *English* reporters.

---

* [Wild by nature, as opposed to domestic animals—eds.]   ** [By reason of the soil—eds.]

Barbeyrac, in his notes on Puffendorf, does not accede to the definition of occupancy by the latter, but, on the contrary, affirms, that actual bodily seizure is not, in all cases, necessary to constitute possession of wild animals. He does not, however, *describe* the acts which, according to his ideas, will amount to an appropriation of such animals to private use, so as to exclude the claims of all other persons, by title of occupancy, to the same animals; and he is far from averring that pursuit alone is sufficient for that purpose. To a certain extent, and as far as Barbeyrac appears to me to go, his objections to Puffendorf's definition of occupancy are reasonable and correct. That is to say, that actual bodily seizure is not indispensable to acquire right to, or possession of, wild beasts; but that, on the contrary, the mortal wounding of such beasts, by one not abandoning his pursuit, may, with the utmost propriety, be deemed possession of him; since, thereby, the pursuer manifests an unequivocal intention of appropriating the animal to his individual use, has deprived him of his natural liberty, and brought him within his certain control. So also, encompassing and securing such animals with nets and toils, or otherwise intercepting them in such a manner as to deprive them of their natural liberty, and render escape impossible, may justly be deemed to give possession of them to those persons who, by their industry and labour, have used such means of apprehending them. Barbeyrac seems to have adopted, and had in view in his notes, the more accurate opinion of Grotius, with respect to occupancy [requiring more than wounding but allowing possession by instruments such as nets]. * * * The case now under consideration is one of mere pursuit, and presents no circumstances or acts which can bring it within the definition of occupancy by Puffendorf, or Grotius, or the ideas of Barbeyrac upon that subject.

The case cited from 11 Mod. 74–130 [*Keeble v. Hickeringill*], I think clearly distinguishable from the present; inasmuch as there the action was for maliciously hindering and disturbing the plaintiff in the exercise and enjoyment of a private franchise; and in the report of the same case, 3 Salk. 9. Holt, Ch. J. states, that the ducks were in the plaintiff's decoy pond, and *so in his possession,* from which it is obvious the court laid much stress in their opinion upon the plaintiff's possession of the ducks, *ratione soli.*

We are the more readily inclined to confine possession or occupancy of beasts *ferae naturae,* within the limits prescribed by the learned authors above cited, for the sake of certainty, and preserving peace and order in society. If the first seeing, starting, or pursuing such animals, without having so wounded, circumvented or ensnared them, so as to deprive them of their natural liberty, and subject them to the control of their pursuer, should afford the basis of actions against others for intercepting and killing them, it would prove a fertile source of quarrels and litigation.

However uncourteous or unkind the conduct of Pierson towards Post, in this instance, may have been, yet his act was productive of no injury or damage for which a legal remedy can be applied. We are of opinion the judgment below was erroneous, and ought to be reversed.

■ LIVINGSTON, J. My opinion differs from that of the court. Of six exceptions, taken to the proceedings below, all are abandoned except the third, which reduces the controversy to a single question.

Whether a person who, with his own hounds, starts and hunts a fox on waste and uninhabited ground, and is on the point of seizing his prey, acquires such an interest in the animal, as to have a right of action against another, who in view of the huntsman and his dogs in full pursuit, and with knowledge of the chase, shall kill and carry him away?

This is a knotty point, and should have been submitted to the arbitration of sportsmen, without poring over Justinian, Fleta, Bracton, Puffendorf, Locke, Barbeyrac, or Blackstone, all of whom have been cited; they would have had no difficulty in coming to a prompt and correct conclusion. In a court thus constituted, the skin and carcass of poor *reynard* would have been properly disposed of, and a precedent set, interfering with no usage or custom which the experience of ages has sanctioned, and which must be so well known to every votary of Diana. But the parties have referred the question to our judgment, and we must dispose of it as well as we can, from the partial lights we possess, leaving to a higher tribunal, the correction of any mistake which we may be so unfortunate as to make. By the pleadings it is admitted that a fox is a "wild and noxious beast." Both parties have regarded him, as the law of nations does a pirate, "*hostem humani generis*,"* and although "*de mortuis nil nisi bonum*,"** be a maxim of our profession, the memory of the deceased has not been spared. His depredations on farmers and on barn yards, have not been forgotten; and to put him to death wherever found, is allowed to be meritorious, and of public benefit. Hence it follows, that our decision should have in view the greatest possible encouragement to the destruction of an animal, so cunning and ruthless in his career. But who would keep a pack of hounds; or what gentleman, at the sound of the horn, and at peep of day, would mount his steed, and for hours together, "*sub jove frigido*," or a vertical sun, pursue the windings of this wily quadruped, if, just as night came on, and his stratagems and strength were nearly exhausted, a saucy intruder, who had not shared in the honours or labours of the chase, were permitted to come in at the death, and bear away in triumph the object of pursuit? Whatever Justinian may have thought of the matter, it must be recollected that his code was compiled many hundred years ago, and it would be very hard indeed, at the distance of so many centuries, not to have a right to establish a rule for ourselves. In his day, we read of no order of men who made it a business, in the language of the declaration in this cause, "with hounds and dogs to find, start, pursue, hunt, and chase," these animals, and that, too, without any other motive than the preservation of Roman poultry; if this diversion had been then in fashion, the lawyers who composed his institutes, would have taken care not to pass it by, without suitable encouragement. If any thing, therefore, in the digests or pandects shall appear to militate against the defendant in error, who, on this

---

* [Enemy of the human race—eds.]   ** [Do not speak ill of the dead—eds.]

occasion, was the foxhunter, we have only to say *tempora mutantur*;*** and if men themselves change with the times, why should not laws also undergo an alteration?

— CARDOZO (Realist)

It may be expected, however, by the learned counsel, that more particular notice be taken of their authorities. I have examined them all, and feel great difficulty in determining, whether to acquire dominion over a thing, before in common, it be sufficient that we barely see it, or know where it is, or wish for it, or make a declaration of our will respecting it; or whether, in the case of wild beasts, setting a trap, or lying in wait, or starting, or pursuing, be enough; or if an actual wounding, or killing, or bodily tact and occupation be necessary. Writers on general law, who have favoured us with their speculations on these points, differ on them all; but, great as is the diversity of sentiment among them, some conclusion must be adopted on the question immediately before us. After mature deliberation, I embrace that of Barbeyrac, as the most rational, and least liable to objection. If at liberty, we might imitate the courtesy of a certain emperor, who, to avoid giving offence to the advocates of any of these different doctrines, adopted a middle course, and by ingenious distinctions, rendered it difficult to say (as often happens after a fierce and angry contest) to whom the palm of victory belonged. He ordained, that if a beast be followed with *large dogs and hounds*, he shall belong to the hunter, not to the chance occupant; and in like manner, if he be killed or wounded with a lance or sword; but if chased with *beagles only*, then he passed to the captor, not to the first pursuer. If slain with a dart, a sling, or a bow, he fell to the hunter, if still in chase, and not to him who might afterwards find and seize him.

— Barbeyrac gives range of possibilities

Now, as we are without any municipal regulations of our own, and the pursuit here, for aught that appears on the case, being with dogs and hounds of *imperial stature*, we are at liberty to adopt one of the provisions just cited, which comports also with the learned conclusion of Barbeyrac, that property in animals *ferae naturae* may be acquired without bodily touch or manucaption, provided the pursuer be within reach, or have a *reasonable* prospect (which certainly existed here) of taking, what he has *thus* discovered an intention of converting to his own use.

When we reflect also that the interest of our husbandmen, the most useful of men in any community, will be advanced by the destruction of a beast so pernicious and incorrigible, we cannot greatly err, in saying, that a pursuit like the present, through waste and unoccupied lands, and which must inevitably and speedily have terminated in corporal possession, or bodily *seisin*, confers such a right to the object of it, as to make any one a wrongdoer, who shall interfere and shoulder the spoil. The justice's judgment ought, therefore, in my opinion, to be affirmed.

Judgment of reversal.

*** [Times change—eds.]

NOTES AND QUESTIONS

1. *Pierson v. Post* is probably the most famous case in property law, but until recently little was known about Jesse Pierson and Lodowick Post, or the background to their dispute over the fox. Two property scholars have now added significantly to our knowledge about the case. See Bethany R. Berger, It's Not About the Fox: The Untold History of *Pierson v. Post* 55 Duke L.J. 1089 (2006); Andrea McDowell, Legal Fictions in *Pierson v. Post*, 105 Mich.L.Rev. 735 (2007). The episode on which the case is based occurred near Southampton, in eastern Long Island, not in Queens, where it was tried (perhaps for the convenience of the attorneys). According to Bethany Berger, Jesse Pierson, the defendant, was a schoolmaster who was descended from one of the families that founded Southampton. His father, David Pierson, was a farmer and a pillar of the community. As a "proprietor" of the town, David claimed special privileges in the areas treated as commons where the episode with the fox presumably took place. Lodowick Post, the plaintiff who organized the fox hunting party, was the son of Nathan Post, who had made large amounts of money as a privateer in the Revolutionary War and later through commercial ventures following the war. Although poorly educated, Nathan purchased a large home in the center of town, flaunted his wealth in various ways (including, presumably, by supporting fox hunting parties), and contested the rights of the proprietors to their special privileges in the use of the commons. Berger plausibly concludes that the litigation reflected a clash between a traditional elite and new wealth: Both sides perceived in the actions of the other a fundamental challenge to different visions of how the community should be organized and controlled.

Andrea McDowell focuses on the customs associated with fox hunting. We learn from her study that organized fox hunting with hounds was a social activity, not an efficient means of destroying foxes as predators. If one wanted to exterminate foxes in a cost-effective manner, trapping was the way to go. One of the conventions of organized fox hunting was that the fox should be killed by the hounds. This was to give the hounds a "taste of blood," which would make them more eager to chase down foxes in the future. So it is unlikely that Post had any expectation of capturing the fox as a trophy or obtaining any value from the fox pelt (which would be worth only a few dollars in any event). In England the principle of *ratione soli* (referred to in passing by Justice Tompkins in his majority opinion) applied only to animals hunted as game, such as deer and rabbits, not to predators like foxes. This principle conferred an exclusive privilege on the owner of land to hunt, or to license others to hunt game on his land. Until 1809, foxes and other beasts of prey were regarded as "outlaws" and could be pursued by any person even on private land owned by another. In *Essex v. Capel* (1809) (reported in: An account of the trial between George Earl of Essex, plaintiff, and the Hon. & Rev. Wm. Capel, defendant ... at the Summer Assizes holden at Hertford, July 20th, 1809 (London, Luke Hansard & Sons 1810)), this privilege was overturned, and the court held that a landowner could exclude a foxhunting party, although local mores operated to permit foxhunting on private property for many years afterwards.

2. *Pierson* was decided shortly after the American Revolution, and the court declines to follow English regulations and doctrines. Not surprisingly, there were no prominent American precedents on point. Faced with a dearth of authority, the judges (guided by the lawyers) not surprisingly turned to legal treatises for an answer to the question of who had a better claim to the fox. The treatises cited cover a vast range of time and space. Justinian's *Institutes* are a synthesis of Roman law compiled during the reign of the Emperor Justinian in the fifth century A.D. Bracton and Fleta were English legal writers of the thirteenth century. Grotius, Pufendorf, Bijnkershoek, and Barbeyrac were legal writers from the continent of Europe writing in the seventeenth and eighteenth centuries. Blackstone wrote his influential *Commentaries on the Laws of England* in the eighteenth century. What assumption about the nature of property rights are the lawyers and judges making when they consult these types of sources and implicitly give them equal weight in their quest to determine who has the better claim to the fox? When Justice Livingston's dissent suggests, perhaps semi-facetiously, that the dispute should have been submitted to "the arbitration of sportsmen," is he making a different assumption about the nature of property rights? Which premise strikes you as better? By what criteria should we decide which premise is better?

3. This is a suit between just two individuals, but the outcome will determine who owns the dead fox. If property rights are good against "all the world," or create duties of noninterference in all persons in the relevant legal community, how can such rights be established in a suit between A and B? Is it because the fox is assumed to be an "unowned" thing and hence up for grabs by the first person to "capture" it or reduce it to possession in some other way, such as by killing it? How do we know foxes are unowned things? What if the owner of the land on which the fox was hunted down (or the proprietors of Southampton, see Note 1 above) asserted a claim to the fox? What if the State of New York claimed ownership of all wild animals found within the state? See Geer v. Connecticut, 161 U.S. 519 (1896) (holding that state could prohibit transport of captured wild animals to another state because the state owned such animals before they were captured); Hughes v. Oklahoma, 441 U.S. 322 (1979) (overruling *Geer*).

4. First possession is a widespread device for establishing claims of ownership in a variety of contexts, not just wild-animal law. Why? One set of answers centers around Locke's famous defense of private property based on labor and individual desert. See John Locke, Two Treatises of Government, Second Treatise, §§ 25–51, at 285–302 (Peter Laslett ed., 1988) (1690). Locke argued that every person owns his own body and his own labor. Hence, when a person mixes his labor with some unclaimed thing (like a wild animal), that person can justly claim also to own the thing. Certainly, Locke argued, the person who has expended labor acquiring the object has a better claim to it than anyone else, as long as he leaves "enough and as good" for others to acquire, and does not overclaim things to the point that they spoil or go to waste. Which of the two opinions in *Pierson v. Post*—Justice Tompkins' opinion for the majority or Justice Livingston's dissent—seems to put the most weight on desert arising from

the expenditure of labor, in deciding when possession of a wild animal has been established? Why does mixing labor with a thing make the thing mine rather than constitute an abandonment of my labor—or merely give me the right to demand payment for my services? (See Wetherbee v. Green, infra, and the treatment of the common-law doctrine of accession.) For discussion of these and related questions, see Richard A. Epstein, Possession as the Root of Title, 13 Ga. L. Rev. 1221 (1979). Elsewhere in the same article Epstein also suggests that Livingston's position might have been correct because the custom of hunters would have given the fox to Post. Assuming that was indeed the custom of hunters, do you agree that custom should provide the basis for the legal rule?

In sport, yes

5.   One reason custom might play a role in resolving disputes over possession is the need to communicate claims of possession to others. Who are the others in *Pierson v. Post*? Post, of course. But should Pierson be taken as also communicating to other hunters? To the general public? On the communication problem in possession, see Carol M. Rose, Possession as the Origin of Property, 52 U. Chi. L. Rev. 73, 78 (1985); Henry E. Smith, The Language of Property: Form, Context, and Audience, 55 Stan. L. Rev. 1105, 115–25 (2003).

6.   *Pierson* is often viewed through the lens of incentives. See, e.g., Dhammika Dharmapala & Rohan Pitchford, An Economic Analysis of "Riding to Hounds": *Pierson v. Post* Revisited, 18 J.L. Econ. & Org. 39 (2002). Does the certain control rule provide less incentive for hunting foxes, as Livingston suggests, or does it encourage those in the position of Post to hurry up and catch the fox? Is protection of poultry really the object here? It would seem that huntsmen in England and their imitators in the United States actually paid farmers to tolerate—and sometimes even to raise—foxes in order to have the pleasure of hunting them. See McDowell, supra.

7.   Whatever the incentive effects in the context of fox hunting, a first-in-time rule can lead to wasteful competitions and races to be first. First-in-time seems to work best when a clear winner will emerge quickly because of that person's special skill or relationship to the resource. That person's advantage will forestall wasteful competition to be first. See, e.g., Dean Lueck, First Possession as the Basis of Property, in Terry L. Anderson & Fred S. McChesney, Property Rights: Cooperation, Conflict, and Law 200 (2003), and the Eggertsson excerpt, infra. It can also be helpful if some salient feature marks out the clear winner such that potential competitors will recognize the "winner" early and give up the contest. Does anything in the rule of first possession help ensure this result?

*Libellant
(Ship captain
that killed whale)*

Ghen v. Rich — *Respondent (bought whale + sold oil)*

United States District Court, District of Massachusetts, 1881.
8 F. 159.

■ NELSON, D.J. This is a libel to recover the value of a fin-back whale. The libellant lives in Provincetown and the respondent in Wellfleet. The facts, as they appeared at the hearing, are as follows:

In the early spring months the easterly part of Massachusetts bay is frequented by the species of whale known as the fin-back whale. Fishermen from Provincetown pursue them in open boats from the shore, and shoot them with bomb-lances fired from guns made expressly for the purpose. When killed they sink at once to the bottom, but in the course of from one to three days they rise and float on the surface. Some of them are picked up by vessels and towed into Provincetown. Some float ashore at high water and are left stranded on the beach as the tide recedes. Others float out to sea and are never recovered. The person who happens to find them on the beach usually sends word to Provincetown, and the owner comes to the spot and removes the blubber. The finder usually receives a small salvage for his services. Try-works are established in Provincetown for trying out the oil. The business is of considerable extent, but, since it requires skill and experience, as well as some outlay of capital, and is attended with great exposure and hardship, few persons engage in it. The average yield of oil is about 20 barrels to a whale. It swims with great swiftness, and for that reason cannot be taken by the harpoon and line. Each boat's crew engaged in the business has its peculiar mark or device on its lances, and in this way it is known by whom a whale is killed.

The usage on Cape Cod, for many years, has been that the person who kills a whale in the manner and under the circumstances described, owns it, and this right has never been disputed until this case. The libellant has been engaged in this business for ten years past. On the morning of April 9, 1880, in Massachusetts bay, near the end of Cape Cod, he shot and instantly killed with a bomb-lance the whale in question. It sunk immediately, and on the morning of the 12th was found stranded on the beach in Brewster, within the ebb and flow of the tide, by one Ellis, 17 Miles from the spot where it was killed. Instead of sending word to Provincetown, as is customary, Ellis advertised the whale for sale at auction, and sold it to the respondent, who shipped off the blubber and tried out the oil. The libellant heard of the finding of the whale on the morning of the 15th, and immediately sent one of his boat's crew to the place and claimed it. Neither the respondent nor Ellis knew the whale had been killed by the libellant, but they knew or might have known, if they had wished, that it had been shot and killed with a bomb-lance, by some person engaged in this species of business.

The libellant claims title to the whale under this usage. The respondent insists that this usage is invalid. It was decided by Judge Sprague, in Taber v. Jenny, 1 Sprague, 315, that when a whale has been killed, and is anchored and left with marks of appropriation, it is the property of the captors; and if it is afterwards found, still anchored, by another ship, there is no usage or principle of law by which the property of the original captors is diverted, even though the whale may have dragged from its anchorage. The learned judge says:

When the whale had been killed and taken possession of by the boat of the Hillman, (the first taker,) it became the property of the owners of that ship, and all was done which was then practicable in order to secure it. They left it anchored, with unequivocal marks of appropriation.

In Bartlett v. Budd, 1 Low. 223, the facts were these: The first officer of the libellant's ship killed a whale in the Okhotsk sea, anchored it, attached a waif to the body, and then left it and went ashore at some distance for the night. The next morning the boats of the respondent's ship found the whale adrift, the anchor not holding, the cable coiled round the body, and no waif or irons attached to it. Judge Lowell held that, as the libellants had killed and taken actual possession of the whale, the ownership vested in them. In his opinion the learned judge says:

> A whale, being ferae naturae, does not become property until a firm possession has been established by the taker. But when such possession has become firm and complete, the right of property is clear, and has all the characteristics of property.

He doubted whether a usage set up but not proved by the respondents, that a whale found adrift in the ocean is the property of the finder, unless the first taker should appear and claim it before it is cut in, would be valid, and remarked that "there would be great difficulty in upholding a custom that should take the property of A. and give it to B., under so very short and uncertain a substitute for the statute of limitations, and one so open to fraud and deceit." Both the cases cited were decided without reference to usage, upon the ground that the property had been acquired by the first taker by actual possession and appropriation.

In Swift v. Gifford, 2 Low, 110, Judge Lowell decided that a custom among whalemen in the Arctic seas, that the iron holds the whale was reasonable and valid. In that case a boat's crew from the respondent's ship pursued and struck a whale in the Arctic ocean, and the harpoon and the line attached to it remained in the whale, but did not remain fast to the boat. A boat's crew from the libellant's ship continued the pursuit and captured the whale, and the master of the respondent's ship claimed it on the spot. It was held by the learned judge that the whale belonged to the respondents. It was said by Judge Sprague, in Bourne v. Ashley, an unprinted case referred to by Judge Lowell in Swift v. Gifford, that the usage for the first iron, whether attached to the boat or not, to hold the whale was fully established; and he added that, although local usages of a particular port ought not to be allowed to set aside the general maritime law, this objection did not apply to a custom which embraced an entire business, and had been concurred in for a long time by every one engaged in the trade.

In Swift v. Gifford, Judge Lowell also said:

> The rule of law invoked in this case is one of very limited application. The whale fishery is the only branch of industry of any importance in which it is likely to be much used, and if a usage is

found to prevail generally in that business, it will not be open to the objection that it is likely to disturb the general understanding of mankind by the interposition of an arbitrary exception.

I see no reason why the usage proved in this case is not as reasonable as that sustained in the cases cited. Its application must necessarily be extremely limited, and can affect but a few persons. It has been recognized and acquiesced in for many years. It requires in the first taker the only act of appropriation that is possible in the nature of the case. Unless it is sustained, this branch of industry must necessarily cease, for no person would engage in it if the fruits of his labor could be appropriated by any chance finder. It gives reasonable salvage for securing or reporting the property. That the rule works well in practice is shown by the extent of the industry which has grown up under it, and the general acquiescence of a whole community interested to dispute it. It is by no means clear that without regard to usage the common law would not reach the same result. That seems to be the effect of the decisions in Taber v. Jenny and Bartlett v. Budd. If the fisherman does all that is possible to do to make the animal his own, that would seem to be sufficient. Such a rule might well be applied in the interest of trade, there being no usage or custom to the contrary. Holmes, Com. Law, 217. But be that as it may, I hold the usage to be valid, and that the property in the whale was in the libelant.

The rule of damages is the market value of the oil obtained from the whale, less the cost of trying it out and preparing it for the market, with interest on the amount so ascertained from the date of conversion. As the question is new and important, and the suit is contested on both sides, more for the purpose of having it settled than for the amount involved, I shall give no costs.

Decree for libellant for $71.05, without costs.

NOTES AND QUESTIONS

1. Most customary whaling rules are variants on first-in-time. As described by Robert Ellickson, the two major rules were the "fast-fish-loose-fish" rule and the "iron-holds-the-whale" rule. Under the fast-fish rule, a whale belonged to the first harpooner as long as whale was attached to his boat, in which case he got to keep the whole whale. This rule applied in particular to right whales, which are relatively slow-moving. Under the iron-holds-the-whale or first-iron rule, the first harpooner would get exclusive rights to the whale as long as he was in fresh pursuit. The first-iron rule tended to be adopted where sperm whales are predominant. Sperm whales were the most valuable and the most dangerous. Ellickson argues that these customs and the custom for finback whales in the *Ghen* case make sense in light of the different resources—types of whales—to which they apply. He also argues that their efficiency (from the point of view of whalers) confirms the hypothesis that close-knit groups will devise and enforce norms among themselves that maximize their wealth (but may cause uncompensated harm to those outside the group—or outgroup exter-

nalities). See Robert C. Ellickson, A Hypothesis of Wealth–Maximizing Norms: Evidence from the Whaling Industry, 5 J.L. Econ. & Org. 83 (1989). For a famous discussion of the concept of fast fish versus loose fish, see Herman Melville, Moby Dick, Chapter 89 (1851).

2. The finder in *Ghen* was not a whaler. But was he part of a close-knit whaling community? Was he likely to have known of the custom of notifying the owner? If not, should he have known that someone was making a claim to the whale? Does that matter?

3. Interestingly, the fast-fish rule seems to have been the "default" custom and the first-iron rule a departure from it only in those areas where sperm whales predominated. The fast-fish rule accords with the general norms of possession. Might this have made it easier to communicate to others?

P   *D*

Keeble v. Hickeringill

Queen's Bench, 1707.
11 East 574, 103 Eng. Rep. 1127 [report date 1809].

Action upon the case. Plaintiff declares that he was, 8th November in the second year of the Queen [1704], lawfully possessed of a close of land called Minott's Meadow, [in which was] a decoy pond, to which divers wildfowl used to resort and come: and the plaintiff had at his own costs and charges prepared and procured divers decoy ducks, nets, machines and other engines for the decoying and taking of the wildfowl, and enjoyed the benefit in taking them: the defendant, knowing which, and intending to damnify the plaintiff in his vivary, and to fright and drive away the wildfowl used to resort thither, and deprive him of his profit, did, on the 8th of November, resort to the head of the said pond and vivary, and did discharge six guns laden with gunpowder, and with the noise and stink of the gunpowder did drive away the wildfowl then being in the pond: and on the 11th and 12th days of November the defendant, with design to damnify the plaintiff, and fright away the wildfowl, did place himself with a gun near the vivary, and there did discharge the said gun several times that was then charged with the gunpowder against the said decoy pond, whereby the wildfowl were frighted away, and did forsake the said pond. Upon not guilty pleaded, a verdict was found for the plaintiff and 20£ damages.

■ HOLT C.J. I am of opinion that this action doth lie. It seems to be new in its instance, but is not new in the reason or principle of it. For, 1st, this using or making a decoy is lawful. 2dly, this employment of his ground to that use is profitable to the plaintiff, as is the skill and management of that employment. As to the first, every man that hath a property may employ it for his pleasure and profit, as for alluring and procuring decoy ducks to come to his pond. To learn the trade of seducing other ducks to come there in order to be taken is not prohibited either by the law of the land or the moral law; but it is as lawful to use art to seduce them, to catch them, and destroy them for the use of mankind, as to kill and destroy wildfowl or tame cattle. Then when a man useth his art or his skill to take them, to sell and dispose of for his profit; this is his trade; and he that hinders another in his trade or livelihood is liable to an action for so hindering him. * * * [W]here a violent or malicious act is done to a man's occupation, profession, or way of getting a livelihood; there an action lies in all cases. But if a man doth him damage by using the same employment; as if Mr. Hickeringill had set up another decoy on his own ground near the plaintiff's, and that had spoiled the custom of the plaintiff, no action would lie, because he had as much liberty to make and use a decoy as the plaintiff. This is like the case of 11 H. 4, 47. One schoolmaster sets up a new school to the damage of an antient school, and thereby the scholars are allured from the old school to come to his new. (The action was held there not to lie.) But suppose Mr. Hickeringill should lie in the way with his guns, and fright the boys from going to school, and their parents would not let them go thither; sure that schoolmaster might have an action for the loss of his scholars. 29 E. 3, 18. A man hath a market, to which he hath toll for horses sold: a man is bringing his horse to market to sell: a stranger hinders and obstructs him from going thither to the market: an action lies, because it imports damage.

Figure 2–1

Drawn by Author.   Vincent Brooks Day & Son, lith

ENTRANCE TO A DECOY PIPE, WITH DOG AT WORK AND WILD FOWL
FOLLOWING HIM UP THE PIPE.

Source: Sir Ralph Payne–Gallwey, The book of duck decoys, their construction, management, and history (London, J. Van Voorst, 1886).

Action upon the case lies against one that shall by threats fright away his tenants at will. 9 H. 7, 8. 21 H. 6,31. 9 H. 7, 7. 14 Ed. 4, 7. Vide Rastal. 662. 2 Cro. 423. * * * Now considering the nature of the case, it is not possible to declare of the number that were frighted away; because the plaintiff had not possession of them, to count them. Where a man brings trespass for taking his goods, he must declare of the quantity, because he, by having had the possession, may know what he had, and therefore must know what he lost. * * * The plaintiff in this case brings his action for the apparent injury done him in the use of that employment of his freehold, his art, and skill, that he uses thereby. * * * And when we do know that of long time in the kingdom these artificial contrivances of decoy ponds and decoy ducks have been used for enticing into those ponds wildfowl, in order to be taken for the profit of the owner of the pond, who is at the expence of servants, engines, and other management, whereby the markets of the nation may be furnished; there is great reason to give encouragement thereunto; that the people who are so instrumental by their skill and industry so to furnish the markets should reap the benefit and have their action. But, in short, that which is the true reason is that this action is not brought to recover damage for the loss of the fowl, but for the disturbance; as 2 Cro. 604, Dawney v Dee. So is the usual and common way of declaring.

NOTES AND QUESTIONS

1. Samuel Keeble was a yeoman who made a living from catching ducks. A duck decoy is an elaborate system of passages and nets. According to Brian Simpson, both Keeble and his neighbor, Hickeringill, had constructed duck decoys. Keeble's original decoy was far away from his neighbor's, but when Keeble built a new decoy much closer to Hickeringill's, the closeness and the resultant competition provoked a characteristically direct response from the latter. Edmund Hickeringill, for whom the term "eccentric" hardly does justice, has been called a "half crazy minister and controversial pamphleteer." (His last work is apparently "A Burlesque Poem in Praise of Ignorance," in which he has unkind things to say of lawyers.) He was an excommunicated Baptist, then a Quaker, then a Deist. After a military career at the end of the Commonwealth, he was ordained in the Church of England. His troubles and disputes, both inside and outside the courtroom, were epic—particularly with his bishop, who after Hickeringill's death is said to have ordered the complimentary remarks chiseled off Hickeringill's tombstone. Despite all this behavior, Hickeringill would be considered a gentleman landowner. A.W. Brian Simpson, Leading Cases in the Common Law 58–61 (1995); A.R. Solly, Edmund Hickeringill, Eccentric, 58 Essex Rev. 127 (1949).

2. This case is the subject of multiple, conflicting reports. The others are 11 Mod. 74, 130 (sub nom. Keble v. Hickringill); 3 Salk. 9 (sub nom. Keeble v. Hickeringhall). The one reproduced here, from the East report and reprinted in the English Reports, was taken from a manuscript by Chief Justice Holt and is thought to be the most reliable. Notice that the version of *Keeble* cited in *Pierson v. Post*, supra, characterizes the grounds of decision quite differently, as resting on *ratione soli*. The East version was not available until after the decision in *Pierson v. Post*. Does this change your view of *Pierson*?

3. The case is brought in trespass on the case rather than plain trespass, because Hickeringill did not physically invade Keeble's land. How would the court in *Hendricks v. Stalnaker*, Chapter I, have handled this type of dispute? How if at all would the newness of Keeble's second decoy and its proximity to Hickeringill's older decoy affect a balancing of the gravity of the harm versus the utility of the defendant's conduct?

4. The law is often called upon to regulate various forms of competition. Cases like *Pierson v. Post*, *Ghen v. Rich*, and other possession cases in the following materials involve competition to capture resources—sometimes but not always wild animals—and make them into private property. *Keeble v. Hickeringill* is about wild animals, but is it about property in animals? Property in land? About competition? Is this competition harmful? How can one tell whether a given type of competition is harmful or beneficial overall? See, e.g., Harold Demsetz, Wealth Distribution and the Ownership of Rights, 1 J. Legal Stud. 223, 231–32 (1972); Benjamin L. Fine, An Analysis of the Formation of Property Rights Underlying Tortious Interference with Contracts and Other Economic Relations, 50 U. Chi. L. Rev. 1116 (1983).

Consider in this regard that the East version of *Keeble* was reported as a note to a similar case from 1809, *Carrington v. Taylor*, 11 East 571, 103 Eng. Rep. 1126 (K.B. 1809). In that case, the defendant had shot at birds from a boat in a public river and drove them from plaintiff's "ancient decoy"—but he did not shoot into the decoy. The court held there was sufficient evidence of "willful disturbance" to support a jury verdict for the plaintiff.

2. OPEN ACCESS AND THE COMMONS

First possession is used to establish ownership when the thing being claimed is regarded as unowned—as being up for grabs. We need to form a clearer understanding of this state of affairs in order to have a better sense of the contexts in which things are eligible for claiming through first possession. That state of affairs is often returned to as a "commons," but this term is fraught with ambiguity.

[handwritten margin note: → when state of affairs is "commons," first possession is eligible]

Thráinn Eggertsson, *Open Access versus Common Property*, in Terry L. Anderson & Fred S. McChesney, Property Rights: Cooperation, Conflict, and Law, 74–82, 84–85 (2003)

The treatment of common property in the literature is engulfed in confusion. The confusion may be due to Garret Hardin's (1968) famous "The Tragedy of the Commons," which discusses open access and its consequences. Hardin's paper has created something of a tragedy in itself by triggering hundreds of empirical studies showing that, in various parts of the world, well-functioning common property regimes do not create open access outcomes. In retrospect, the confusion over the nature of common property probably was caused substantially by a mix-up of proper names and theoretical categories. In the field, resources that are governed by open access arrangements often are locally known as "the commons" (or have the word "commons" in their name) because previously they were exclusive common property. The confusion is facilitated by the proximity of open access and common property on the privatization scale. Relatively small changes in the economic environment can push a common property regime into open access or vice versa.

Let us consider more carefully how the structure of rules and enforcement mechanisms differ between open access and common property. If no one holds rights to exclude others from the using the asset, its use is open to all. Because the earth's scarce resources with the exception of the high seas or the outer atmosphere are controlled by nation states, however, access to resources, is never open to all. When we talk about open access, what we usually mean is that access is open to all members of a particular community or jurisdiction, but not to all outsiders, including people from other countries. Sometimes access is open also to outsiders, but then they often are excluded by transportation costs. People who withdraw units from open access resources almost always employ tools and other inputs that are exclusively owned, and the so-called rule of capture immediately establishes ownership of resource units once they are withdrawn. Fishers, for instance, own the fish they catch in an open access fishery. The utilization of open access resources, therefore, involves a complex bundle of rights, but entry is free and the users have neither the rights nor much incentive to manage the resource and invest in improving it.

Common property regimes are complex structures that involve rules and enforcement mechanisms, often located at several societal levels, that regulate exclusion and (internal) governance. When an asset is under a well-defined common property regime, an easily identifiable group of insiders controls the use and management of the resource and holds exclusive user rights, which outsiders do not enjoy. The rights of insiders often are formally recognized by the state, although in traditional societies, rights of isolated groups sometimes are based on local customary law and social norms. Ostrom (1997) observes that newly independent states in the Third World, because they were not always fully aware of these regimes or for other reasons, sometimes nationalized the assets without providing effective enforcement. In many cases, nationalization transformed common property regimes into open access regimes. * * *

Open access problems arise when independent actors (people or firms with independent goals) have both the incentive and the ability to withdraw, at will and on a large scale, resource units from an asset that they access together. When a resource is in high demand, open access has adverse consequences that include economic and sometimes biological overuse of the resource. Although the consequences tend to be complex and subtle, we can summarize the effects under two headings, the supply effects and the demand effects. * * *

We begin by examining adverse effects on the supply side. Rational actors who hold exclusive rights to some resource have an incentive to invest in maintaining or improving the asset, provided that they expect the marginal benefits to exceed the marginal costs of maintenance and improvement in quality. Under open access, rational actors have little or no incentive to make such investments. The net returns are likely to be negative because the investors cannot exclude other users from collecting some or all of the benefits. Under open access, therefore, users prefer to withdraw resources in their unimproved or natural form. Open access agricultural land is used for grazing rather than for planting fruit trees; those who seek shelter in open access housing units usually ignore maintenance until they somehow establish exclusive rights. In sum, open access is associated with depletion and disinvestment rather than with accumulation and economic growth.

On the demand side, undesirable results of open access include perverse timing and excessive withdrawal of resource units. When a valuable resource is in open access, actors have an incentive to enter a race to be first to appropriate resource units while they are abundant. Berries on open access land are picked before they are fully ripe, fishers in open access fisheries install large engines in their boats to win races to the fishing grounds. In effect, the now-or-never motive drives actors to deplete nonrenewable resources without due attention to optimal time preferences and patterns of demand. Renewable natural resources, such as fish stocks, can support various levels of sustainable yield (various permanent rates of withdrawal) but open access users do not systematically select the level of sustainable yield that maximizes joint wealth. In fact, if their needs are large relative to the resource stock and if their technology permits it, open access users have an incentive to deplete a renewable natural resource and lower its economically usable yield to zero.

Under open access, so-called external effects are important. External effects arise when some activities of actor A impose costs on or bring benefits to other actors, but A ignores these effects in her decisions because she neither is compensated for the incremental benefits nor charged for the incremental costs. The effects are external to her decisions. The theory also postulates that, in their decisions, people watch marginal effects and tend to make efficient decisions (maximize joint wealth), provided they are responsible for all costs and benefits that follow from their actions. But with open access, people are not fully accountable for their actions and therefore the outcomes are inefficient and reflect average values rather than marginal values.

Think of a driver who wants to go from X to Y as fast as possible and has the choice of narrow and slow secondary roads and potentially fast travel on a freeway. The secondary roads are uncrowded, but the freeway is crowded. The driver's only concern is how much time she will save by choosing the freeway. Access to the freeway is open, and being a rational maximizer, the driver ignores the fact that her entry on the freeway will slightly slow down other travelers. The driver gains six minutes by using the freeway rather than secondary roads, but slows down one hundred other freeway drivers, each by six seconds. Her personal opportunity cost of imposing delays on fellow travelers is zero, but the total opportunity cost is

> Highway Example (faster for you, but slightly slows all others, resulting in a net loss)

> Fisherman Example (new boat might catch enough fish for profit, but all others catch less, resulting in less total net profit)

the ten minutes (one hundred drivers at six seconds each) of total delay she causes for the other drivers. The ten minutes are external effects because they do not enter into the driver's calculations. In the aggregate, the driver's decision to use the freeway creates a net social loss of the value of four minutes.

The same reasoning explains a fisherman's decision to take his boat and gear into already crowded fishing grounds. It is possible, when the grounds are crowded, that a new boat may catch enough fish to make small profits, but also reduce the profits of all the other boats by an even larger amount and generate a net loss for the fishers as a whole. The new entrant, however, does not care about others' losses, only about his gains. * * *

How can dissipation of the rent be avoided?* One potential solution involves contracting among the fishers to limit excessive withdrawal. With open access, however, contracting is likely to face insurmountable problems because of pressures from a steady inflow of new actors. The more successful the insiders are in protecting the rent, the more attractive (profitable) it is for outsiders to enter, and outsiders are not bound by the contract. When a resource is scarce and the number of potential entrants is large, exclusive rights usually are a necessary condition for avoiding excessive use. Once the insiders have exclusive rights, an efficient solution may involve a single firm and hierarchical relations or some communal arrangement.

Yet another solution has a private owner or the state control the resource and use prices to regulate access. The upper limit for the total of such admission charges equals the entire rent from the resource, which would give the fishers only normal returns on their investments. When the license to enter is free, the license holders collect all the rent.   *no cost to maintain resource*

Most states take measures to prevent open access to their major resources, but fisheries outside national jurisdictions have suffered the ill effects of open access. The introduction in the early 1970s of a 200–mile economic zone in the ocean for coastal states did not immediately end open access fisheries because most fishing nations, after excluding foreigners, did not establish effective exclusion and internal governance regimes for domestic fishers. In recent years, individual transferable quotas have raised hopes for greater efficiency in coastal fisheries of countries such as Iceland and New Zealand which have pioneered these arrangements. Initially, transferable quotas were assigned to vessels on the basis of their fishing history in the years immediately prior to the introduction of the new system. * * *

The fact that access is not perfectly exclusive does not mean the institution is necessarily inefficient. Open access is efficient when there are no net benefits from establishing effective exclusive rights, and such conditions often emerge at the margins of complex property rights structures. Consider the structure of property rights that governs the operation

ITQs-Chapter X

---

* [Economic rent from a resource is the return from it that exceeds the cost of creat-   ing and maintaining the resource.—eds.]

of a restaurant. As Barzel (1997) emphasizes, it often is efficient for the owner of a restaurant not to enforce control at certain margins. Within limits, the time guests spend at their table is not priced, nor is the salt, sugar, and pepper they use. Similarly, many movie theaters sell all their seats at one price. With one price for all seats, people engage in races (use valuable time) to claim a good location in a theater, but we cannot refer to such behavior as inefficient if alternative seating arrangements (numbered seats) would involve greater additional costs (monitoring and enforcement) than benefits.

NOTES AND QUESTIONS

1. The potential problems with open access have long been apparent. Garrett Hardin, whose work is referred to by Eggertsson, coined the immensely influential phrase, "the tragedy of the commons," to describe the problems associated with an open-access resource in which there is an unrestricted privilege to capture some valued feature of the resource. See Garrett Hardin, The Tragedy of the Commons, 162 Science 1243 (1968). However, Hardin's treatment was anticipated years earlier in the academic literature by H. Scott Gordon, in his analysis of fisheries. See H.S. Gordon, The Economic Theory of a Common Property Resource: The Fishery, 62 J. Pol. Econ. 124 (1954). Gordon's analysis, in turn, had been anticipated many years earlier by Jens Warming, writing in Danish. See Om "Grun-drente" af Fiskegrunde, 49 Nationalökonomisk Tidsskrift 495 (1911), Jens Warming, Aalgaardsretten, 69 Nationalökonomisk Tidsskrift 151 (1931), transl. in P. Anderson, "On Rent of Fishing Grounds": A Translation of Jens Warming's 1911 Article, with an Introduction, 15 Hist. Pol. Econ. 391 (1983). And the nub of the idea can be found in Aristotle, who wrote: "[W]hat is common to the greatest number has the least care bestowed upon it. Everyone thinks chiefly of his own, hardly at all of the common interest." Aristotle, The Politics and the Constitution of Athens 33 (Steven Everson ed. & Benjamin Jowett trans., 1996). So who gets to claim to be the "first possessor" of the idea of the tragedy of the commons: Aristotle, Warming, Gordon, or Hardin? Does this example provide a clue as to why ideas are not subject to ownership through first possession?

2. Hardin was a biologist, and his big concern was with overpopula-tion. His work fits into a neo-Malthusian movement of the 1960s and 1970s that emphasized the finiteness of the earth and predicted imminent deple-tion of natural resources. That there is a potential tragedy in the use of natural resources is well understood. But in what sense is there an additional tragedy of the commons in "breeding," as Hardin believed?

3. Hardin's primary example, the traditional grazing commons, was hardly tragic. Grazing commons in traditional agricultural societies such as those of medieval and early modern Europe were not open access. A limited group had grazing rights and exercised the right to exclude noncommoners. Over centuries, those with access to common grazing areas governed their behavior with restrictions on the amount and manner of grazing. Some of

these grazing commons survive to this day and do not show obvious signs of tragedy. For an analysis of a range of case studies and discussion of factors leading toward and away from tragedy, see Elinor Ostrom, Governing the Commons (1990).

4. Solutions to the problem of the commons require some form of coercion or cooperation. For example, a group of herders might (as has often happened) institute rules to limit their use of the commons and achieve conservation. But how is such cooperation forthcoming? Isn't the provision of such rules a commons itself? See James E. Krier, The Tragedy of the Commons, Part Two, 15 Harv. J.L. & Pub. Pol'y 325, 336–38 (1992).

5. Eggertsson briefly mentions another possible solution to overuse of an open access resource like fisheries: creating a new type of property individual transferable quotas (ITQs) that restrict the overall level of access to the fishery and yet are transferable, so individuals can exit and enter from the fishing industry. For more on this potential solution, see Chapter X.

COMMONS, ANTICOMMONS, AND SEMICOMMONS

If an open access regime creates the "tragedy of the commons," in which no one has the right to exclude anyone else, is there a mirror image problem, in which everyone has the right to exclude everyone else? From a hypothetical proposed by Frank Michelman, Michael Heller developed the concept of the *anticommons*, where too many have the right to exclude and consequently no one is able to use a resource. Michael Heller, The Tragedy of the Anticommons: Property in the Transition from Marx to Markets, 111 Harv. L. Rev. 621 (1998); Michael A. Heller, The Boundaries of Private Property, 108 Yale L.J. 1163, 1176–78 (1999); see also Frank I. Michelman, Ethics, Economics, and the Law of Property, in NOMOS XXIV: Ethics, Economics, and the Law 3, 15 (1982). Heller's primary example was street kiosks in post-Soviet Moscow. Because too many stakeholders had rights in storefronts and could prevent their use, new businesses bypassed empty store buildings and set up shop in metal kiosks on the sidewalks in front of the stores. Traditional holdout problems can sometimes be characterized as an anticommons: If too many permissions are required, rights to a larger resource may never be assembled. Patents on gene fragments are a particular source of anticommons worries because research projects may require the collection of many permissions from many different patent holders. Michael A. Heller & Rebecca S. Eisenberg, Can Patents Deter Innovation? The Anticommons in Biomedical Research, 280 Science 698–701 (1998). Evidence is hard to come by, but surveys of industry participants have found that patents on research tools have not restricted access as much as anticommons theory might suggest; solutions to the problem of fragmented rights include licensing, inventing around, infringing, public disclosure, and litigation. See, e.g., John P. Walsh, Ashish Arora, & Wesley M. Cohen, Effects of Research Tool Patents and Licensing on Biomedical Innovation, in Patents in the Knowledge–Based Economy 285 (Wesley M. Cohen & Stephen A. Merrill eds., 2003).

Others have argued that in certain specialized contexts, an anticommons can be a good thing. For example, giving many people a veto over development of a resource like a park can help secure the commitment to preserve the park for future generations. Abraham Bell & Gideon Parchomovsky, Of Property and Antiproperty, 102 Mich. L. Rev. 1 (2003). Similarly, there is sometimes virtue to be found in multiple vetoes in the political arena. Political scientists and others have theorized that under some conditions multiple vetoes are beneficial in terms of producing stability (with some sacrifice of decisiveness in decisionmaking). See, e.g., Josephine T. Andrews & Gabriella R. Montinola, Veto Players and the Rule of Law in Emerging Democracies, 37 Comp. Pol. Stud. 55 (2004); George Tsebelis & Eric C. Chang, Veto Players and the Structure of Budgets in Advanced Industrialized Countries, 43 Eur. J. of Pol. Res. 449 (2004). The Framers of the U.S. Constitution may have had something like this in mind when setting up a system of federalism and separation of powers, which creates many checks and balances on political actors. See The Federalist No. 51 (James Madison).

[margin note: → Checks & Balances]

Note that the underlying dynamic that creates a tragedy of the anticommons is similar to that which gives rise to the tragedy of the commons. For each tragedy, the individual has an incentive to act in a way that imposes costs on others, either by exercising her right of access (to a commons) or her right to exclude others (from an anticommons). For each tragedy, overcoming the problem requires some kind of realignment of rights, and doing this requires dealing with holdouts and freeriders. So are there really mirror image problems, or is there only one underlying tragedy at work? For discussion, see James M. Buchanan & Yong J. Yoon, Symmetric Tragedies: Commons and Anticommons, 43 J.L. & Econ. 1 (2000); Lee Anne Fennell, Common Interest Tragedies, 98 Nw. U. L. Rev. 907 (2004); Francesco Parisi, Norbert Schulz & Ben Depoorter, Duality in Property: Commons and Anticommons, 25 Int'l Rev. L. & Econ. 578 (2006).

The commons and the anticommons are not the only common-property regimes in town. Others have identified the ~~semicommons~~, which occurs when a given resource is subject to private exclusion rights in some uses or along some dimensions, but is open access for other purposes or along other dimensions. Fish in the ocean are regarded as an open-access resource in their natural state, but once they have been reduced to possession under the rule of capture they are regarded as privately owned. In many traditional grazing commons farmers would have exclusive rights to particular strips of land to grow crops during part of the year, but then the strips would be thrown open for common grazing during other parts of the year. See Henry E. Smith, Semicommon Property Rights and Scattering in the Open Fields, 29 J. Legal Stud. 131 (2000). In such a system, individuals will have an incentive to favor their part of the semicommons (with goods like manure) and to trash other parts of the semicommons (with excessive trampling, etc.); elaborate governance rules and configurations of rights seem to have been developed to contain these problems. Intellectual property rights are particularly likely to be incomplete, leaving room for interaction between exclusion rights and the commons (the public domain). For

[margin note: → Intellectual Property a common example (protected by ownership, yet allowed to be quoted/cited in some instances)]

example, consider the doctrine of fair use in copyright, which permits copying of portions of copyrighted works for certain purposes, such as criticism, reporting, or scholarship. See 17 U.S.C. § 107. This effectively makes a work subject to the owner's exclusive control for some purposes, and yet in the public domain for other purposes. See, e.g., Ellen P. Goodman, Spectrum Rights in the Telecosm to Come, 41 San Diego L. Rev. 269, 379–403 (2004); Robert A. Heverly, The Information Semicommons, 18 Berkeley Tech. L.J. 1127 (2003); Henry E. Smith, Governing the Tele–Semicommons, 22 Yale J. on Reg. 289 (2005); Peter K. Yu, Intellectual Property and the Information Ecosystem, 2005 Mich. St. L. Rev. 1, 11–12. As with the anticommons, a full-blown semicommons with an effective governance structure can be quite stable, but may be hard to change because the interlocking private and commons rights are difficult to disentangle and negotiate over.

3. OTHER APPLICATIONS OF FIRST POSSESSION

The principle of first possession applies in contexts besides hunting and fishing. For example, abandoned or lost property is subject to the rule of first possession. Suppose you decide to dispose of your old computer monitor by setting it on the curb where the garbage gets picked up. You have in effect relinquished ownership of the monitor, and implicitly signaled that it can now be claimed by the first person who comes along and decides to take possession of it. Or, suppose you lose a ring that falls out of your pocket on the public sidewalk. Here, you have not relinquished ownership, but (subject to some qualifications considered later in the chapter) the first person who comes along and decides to take possession of the ring can claim a kind of qualified ownership of it: The finder has a superior right to the ring relative to everyone in the world, *except you*, the true owner.

D   *P*
Eads v. Brazelton

Supreme Court of Arkansas, 1861.
22 Ark. 499, 79 Am.Dec. 88.

■ FAIRCHILD, J. * * * The bill in this case is founded upon a right of occupancy which Brazelton, the plaintiff, insists was vested in him by his discovery of the wreck of the steamboat America, and by his intentions and acts relating thereto. Because this right was not respected by the defendants, partners and servants of a firm of wreckers doing business in the Mississippi river and its tributaries, under the style of Eads & Nelson, Brazelton filed his bill on the chancery side of the circuit court of Mississippi county, to obtain the protection of the court, to relieve him from the interference of the defendants in his own intended labors to recover the property in the wreck, and to obtain compensation for what they had taken therefrom.

From what is before us it may be taken as shown in the case that, in November, 1827, the boat named sank in the Mississippi river, within the limits of Mississippi county; that, of her cargo, shot and bundles of bar lead of an unascertained quantity, and lead in pigs to about the number of three thousand, remained in the river, wholly abandoned by the owners; that Brazelton, having information of the place where the boat sank, proceeded, in December, 1854, to ascertain its exact locality in the bed of the river, with the view of raising the sunken lead; that, in January, 1855, he arrived at the vicinity of the wreck, with his diving boat, to carry out his intention, and fastened a buoy to a weight that rested upon the wreck, with the expectation of putting his boat over it the next day, but that he was detained by other business, and by the difficulties and dangers of the work in the existing state of water, with boats like his, and by the necessity for making repairs upon his boat, and apparatus for raising the cargo, till the defendants, upon the 28th of September, 1855, caused one of their boats to stop at the shore near the wreck, to search for and find it, to place their boat over it, and to commence raising the lead.

Figure 2–2
Eads and Nelson's Steam Wreck Boat Sub–Marine No. 7, 1858

Courtesy Missouri Historical Society, St. Louis. Sub–Marine No. 7 is a later version of the type used to raise the lead from the *America*.

The quantity of lead raised by the defendants was stated in their answer, and applying the price thereto, as shown by the evidence, its value was found to be four thousand, five hundred and seven dollars and ninety-six cents, for which sum the court below gave a decree, perpetuated the preliminary injunction which was granted at the beginning of the suit, and which arrested the defendants in their labor upon the lead. * * *

But as the principal ground of controversy in the case, and one that may supersede all others, is Brazelton's right of occupancy of the wreck by finding, and as that may depend upon its possession, the pleadings which allege and deny the possession, and the facts relative to this issue may well be subjected to closer scrutiny.

When Brazelton found the wreck he traced lines to it from different points on the Arkansas side of the river, so that their intersection would show the situation of the wreck, and the lines were indicated by marks upon the trees. It was upon the return of Brazelton from St. Louis with his bell boat that a float or buoy was placed by Brazelton over the wreck, and this was done with the intention of signifying the place to which the diving boat was to be dropped the next morning. It was not to be expected that such objects would remain permanent fixtures, as the wreck was in the main channel of the river, and it is evident that Brazelton considered them as guides to the situation of the wreck, as the marked trees were, as he stated to Seth Daniel, in the presence of Reese Bowen, that it would make no difference if they should be washed away, as he could find the wreck from the ranges of his lines. Brazelton does not pretend to have put his boat over the wreck, or to have had any claim to the wreck but by occupancy, which depended upon his finding it, upon his providing means for easy approaches to it by landmarks, and floats upon water, and upon his being in the neighborhood of the wreck from January to the last of September, without any other appropriation of the wreck, but with a continual assertion of his claim, and with the intention of making it good by future action. This, doubtless, he would have done in the winter of 1855, had not the sinking of the steamboat Eliza afforded the opportunity of other work to which he confined himself till June. Then he would have applied himself to the America, but the periodical rise of the river at that season prevented him from so doing, and when he was nearly ready, with his boat and machinery in order for effective labor, with favorable water for work, safe from rafts and flat and coal boats, the Submarine, No. 4, belonging to the defendants, passed him on the 28th of September, and within two days was placed over the wreck, and thenceforward the defendants were its occupants in fact, and claimed to be so by right.

If Brazelton boat had been accompanied with steam power as was the Submarine, No. 4, the rise of the water in June, or the season of floating boats and rafts would not have been uncontrollable obstructions to his desire to save the lead of the America; and he could, while the boat of the defendants was hovering in the vicinity of the wreck, have placed his own boat over it and thereby acquired a possession which the custom of the river, as alluded to in this case, would have respected as a right. But it is for us to declare the legal effect of what he did, and not speculate upon the possible result of a different course of action, which he might have pursued had wind and water permitted, and if other business had not called him from the prosecution of his original purpose. * * *

It is not established that the defendants knew that Brazelton was about to work upon the America, although a witness so inferred from the conversation of the Captain and others of the boat, while there is no room for suspicion that they intended to interfere with any occupancy of the boat by Brazelton, and the whole case is, that they did not do so according to their understanding of Brazelton's right.

But what that right was remains to be determined.

Notwithstanding the point made by the defendant, that Brazelton had no right to the lead which the law would protect, it being the property of the original owners of the cargo, there is no room for doubt that the lead was abandoned by its owners; and even without the positive testimony of an owner of the boat and cargo in affirmation of the fact, the law would so imply from the term of the loss, and from the fact of its having been covered by an island formed upon it, which sustained trees grown to the height of thirty or forty feet. All reasonable hope of acquiring the property must have been given up from the nature of the case; and the evidence shows that during the two years that intervened between the sinking of the boat and its being covered by the tow head and island, no effort was made or design entertained to save the part of the cargo that was abandoned when the high water interrupted the labor of saving it, that was prosecuted for two weeks after the loss of the boat, save that an excluded deposition mentions that one hundred and sixteen pigs of lead were afterwards got out by residents of the neighborhood. Having saved the specie that was on board belonging to the United States, the furs and one-half of the six hundred pigs of lead, and a part of the shot, with which articles the boat was laden, and the boilers and machinery of the boat, the owners of the America seem to have contented themselves therewith; and to have wholly abandoned the remaining shot and lead. * * *

The occupation or possession of property lost, abandoned or without an owner, must depend upon an actual taking of the property and with the intent to reduce it to possession. The intent may not be that this possession shall be absolute or perpetual appropriation of the property to the use of the finder, it may be subject to the claim of the real owner, the possession may be taken for his exclusive good, or it may be taken as a means of subsistence or accumulation, according to the course of business of the parties to this suit. But in this case title by occupancy must rest upon intentional actual possession of the thing occupied. * * *

[W]e hold that Brazelton never attained to the possession of the wreck of the America, that he therefore had no title to it by occupancy, had no right upon which judicial protection could operate, none which the court below should have recognized. He had considered the wreck as his as its finder, but had not actually appropriated it to himself; his intention to possess was useless without detention of the property; he had not found the lead in the required sense of discovering it, and taking it up; he was not a finder, in that he had not moved the wrecked property, or secured it; he had the intention of possessing it as owner, but did not acquire its corporeal possession; to his desire to possess there was not joined a prehension of the thing.

Brazelton's act of possession need not have been manual, he was not obliged to take the wreck or the lead between his hands, he might take such possession of them as their nature and situation permitted; but that his circumstances should give a legal character to his acts, making that to be possession which the law declares not to be possession, assume more than a court can sanction. Marking trees that extended across the wreck, affixing temporary buoys to it were not acts of possession; they only indicated Brazelton's desire or intention to appropriate the property. Placing his boat over the wreck, with the means to raise its valuables, and with persistent efforts directed to raising the lead, would have been keeping the only effectual guard over it, would have been the only warning that intruders, that is, other longing occupants would be obliged to regard, would have been such acts of possession as the law would notice and protect. If Brazelton in the winter of 1855, deferred raising the lead to wreck the steamboat Eliza, he was free to do so, but must abide the legal consequences of his choice. If afterwards he could not work in the main channel of the river, owing to high water, strong wind, or to damaged boats and rigging, his ill fortune could not bend the law to his circumstances, nor could he with right warn off the defendants from the occupancy of the America, when they were as willing and more able than himself to raise the lead in her hold. * * *

The decree of the circuit court of Mississippi county sitting in chancery is reversed * * *

NOTES AND QUESTIONS

1.   James Eads' story has been the material for a Horatio Alger-style biography. See Louis How, James B. Eads (1900). He began his working life early selling apples in the street and later clerked in a dry goods store. There, with the encouragement of his employer, he studied engineering in his spare time. Later he served for 20 years on Mississippi steamboats, where he realized that many wrecks resided at the river bottom. Eads invented a diving bell, for which he received a patent, and started a ship salvage partnership at the age of 22. His constant improvements to his "submarines" gave him a technological edge reflected in the famous case of *Eads v. Brazelton*, decided on the eve of the Civil War. His other exploits included building ironclad gunboats for the Union in the war and supervising construction of the Eads Bridge over the Mississippi in Saint Louis, on which he employed some of his diving bell technology. See Barlow Burke, Jr., A Reprise of the Case of *Eads v. Brazelton*, 44 Ark. L. Rev. 425 (1991).

2.   Notice or communication of an intention to appropriate is important to the concept of possession, as Carol Rose has emphasized. See Carol M. Rose, Possession as the Origin of Property, 52 U. Chi. L. Rev. 73, 78 (1985). But given Brazelton's marking the blazes on the trees and floating a buoy above the wreck, there is not much doubt about Brazelton's notice

of an intention to appropriate the wreck, is there? *Eads v. Brazelton* seems to put more emphasis on another idea—that one must be diligently moving toward use, consumption, or other exploitation of a resource before one can be said to be "in possession" of it. The idea that first possession claims require a certain degree of due diligence plays an important role in mining law, especially in an intriguing doctrine called the *pedis possessio*. Under this rule, which arose out of the customs of the mining camps, someone who is exploring diligently and in good faith for minerals has the exclusive right to work a given spot even before he makes a discovery or acquires a mineral claim establishing formal rights against the government and third parties. See Union Oil v. Smith, 249 U.S. 337 (1919). Due diligence also enters into certain intellectual property regimes based on first possession, such as patent law, which requires that the patent application's disclosure must show that the inventor was in possession of the invention at the time of filing. 35 U.S.C. § 112.

3. *Eads* also suggests how the rules for possession can evolve in response to new technologies of discovery. For sunken ships consider *Columbus–America Discovery Group, Inc. v. The Unidentified, Wrecked and Abandoned Sailing Vessel, S.S. Central America*, 1989 A.M.C. 1955 (E.D. Va. 1989), in which the court allowed "telepossession," defined as "(1) locating the object searched; (2) real time imaging of the object; (3) placement or capability to place teleoperated or robotic manipulators on or near the object, capable of manipulating it as directed by human beings exercising control from the surface; and (4) present intent to control . . . the location of the object." Id. at 1958. Should one be able to claim possession of foxes or whales by videotaping them? Why not?

4. *Eads* indicates that one important variable in cases involving the search for sunken vessels is whether the vessel has been "abandoned." Property is abandoned when an owner manifests an intention to relinquish all future claims of possession or ownership. See Chapter IV. In maritime law, a distinction is drawn between one who finds a sunken vessel that has been abandoned and one who finds such a vessel that is still claimed by its owners (or their insurers). A finder who takes possession of an abandoned vessel becomes the owner. By contrast, if the vessel is not abandoned, a "salvor" (as such a person is called in this context) has a claim for a generous percentage of the value of the vessel and its cargo, but does not acquire ownership of the vessel or its full value. Perhaps not surprisingly, the standard for possession of a salvor is lower than that for finders of abandoned vessels. That is, acts that would be sufficient for salvage-possession might not be sufficient for a finder to establish possession. As one court put it:

> To enjoy the continued right to exclusive possession and protection from interference of rival salvors, a salvor must exercise due diligence and must be capable of actually saving the property. The salvor must intend to reduce the property to physical possession by dealing with the entire wreck site in such a manner as to warn other potential salvors of the claimed area.

MDM Salvage, Inc. v. Unidentified, Wrecked and Abandoned Sailing Vessel, 631 F.Supp. 308, 312 (S.D. Fla. 1986). These salvor-in-possession rights, however, do not extend to preventing others from visiting or photographing the wreck. See R.M.S. Titanic, Inc. v. Haver, 171 F.3d 943 (4th Cir. 1999).

HOME RUN BASEBALLS

In the late 1990s, major league baseball players, assisted (it now appears) by performance-enhancing drugs, began hitting record numbers of home runs. Milestone home run balls became important collector's items, commanding large sums of money. Not surprisingly, fans inside and some-times outside the ball parks engaged in intense competitions to snag one of these prize home run baseballs. These competitions, in turn, sometimes generated controversies about who had been the first to capture or reduce to possession a particular ball. The most famous of these controversies resulted in a litigated decision, *Popov v. Hayashi*, 2002 WL 31833731 (Sup. Ct. San Francisco 2002).

Baseballs used in professional baseball games are considered the property of the home team, but once they leave the playing field are regarded as abandoned property. Like other abandoned property, they can be claimed by the first person to take possession of them. The *Popov* case involved a dispute over who was the first to possess the record-setting 73rd home run ball hit by Barry Bonds of the San Francisco Giants at San Francisco's PacBell Park on October 7, 2001. A video tape recorded at the scene showed that after the ball sailed over the fence, it landed in the webbing of a softball glove worn by Alex Popov. It was unclear from the tape, however, whether Popov was still juggling the ball as he fell to the ground. Popov was immediately engulfed by a mob of fans, who grabbed and kicked at him trying to obtain the ball. At some point, the ball came loose from the scrum, and was picked up by Patrick Hayashi (who was standing to the side and was not part of the mob). Hayashi put the ball in his pocket and waited until he had the attention of the video camera operator, at which time he held the ball aloft, showing that he had the ball. Popov sued Hayashi, claiming that Popov was the first possessor and hence was entitled to the ball. At the time of trial, it was thought the ball might be worth as much as $1 million, although eventually it was sold for $450,000.

The trial featured, in addition to the video tape and the testimony of numerous eye witnesses, expert witness testimony of several law professors about the application of the rule of first possession to home run baseballs. Judge Patrick McCarthy, who presided over the trial, eventually reached a Solomonic judgment: He decreed that the ball should be sold, with half the proceeds given to Popov and half to Hayashi. He reasoned that although Popov could not prove that he had established possession of the baseball, once it landed in his mitt he had an exclusive "pre-possessory interest" in being allowed to complete the catch without interference. The mob had interfered with this interest. Hayashi, for his part, had not been part of the mob, and was the first unambiguously to establish possession of the ball. Judge McCarthy concluded: "Both men have a superior claim to the ball as against all the world. Each man has a claim of equal dignity as to the other.

* * * The court therefore declares that both plaintiff and defendant have an equal and undivided interest in the ball. * * * In order to effectuate this ruling, the ball must be sold and the proceeds divided equally between the parties." As authority for ordering the property sold and the proceeds divided, the judge cited a law review article, R.H. Helmholz, Equitable Division and the Law of Finders, 52 Fordham L. Rev. 313 (1983), which in turn built on a student note, Comment, Lost, Mislaid and Abandoned Property, 8 Fordham L. Rev. 222 (1939).

NOTES AND QUESTIONS

1. Decisions that divide an asset between two potential possessors are rare. Splitting entitlements—or their value—has been more popular with commentators than with courts. Why do you suppose division is not used more often? Would you recommend this as a solution to wild animal cases like *Pierson v. Post* or *Ghen v. Rich*? What about the right to raise a sunken vessel, at issue in *Eads v. Brazelton*?

2. What role should custom play in determining the rules for establishing ownership of home run baseballs? If custom is important, which customs should we look to? The rules of sports like baseball deal with questions about when a player controls a ball sufficiently to be deemed to have caught it. Are these rules relevant to determine whether a fan has possession of a ball hit out of the park?

3. The potential for violence among fans is yet another (vivid) example of wasteful and destructive racing behavior. These problems also face fishers and oil drillers. Observers of intellectual property rights have pointed out that too great a reward for being the first to invent can lead to wasteful races. Some scholars have hypothesized that first possession works best when a clear winner is declared at a stage when other competitors are unlikely to be able to compete effectively. Thus, first-in-time rules work best when potential appropriators have heterogeneous knowledge and abilities. Conversely, where multiple actors must share a resource under a governance scheme of rules of proper use, it is helpful if all those sharing the resource have similar abilities and knowledge. Homogeneity of appropriators conduces to well-functioning governance regimes. See Dean Lueck, The Rule of First Possession and the Design of the Law, 38 J.L. & Econ. 393 (1995); David D. Haddock, First Possession Versus Optimal Timing: Limiting the Dissipation of Economic Value, 64 Wash. U. L.Q. 775 (1986). What implications does this hypothesis have for determining how to allocate home run baseballs? Are the potential appropriators here relatively homogeneous in their knowledge and ability, or heterogeneous?

4. There has been an outpouring of scholarship on the question of ownership of milestone home run baseballs. See, e.g., Peter Adomeit, The Barry Bonds Baseball Case—An Empirical Approach—Is Fleeting Possession Five Tenths of the Ball?, 48 St. Louis U. L.J. 475 (2004); Paul Finkelman, Fugitive Baseballs and Abandoned Property: Who Owns the Home Run Ball?, 23 Cardozo L. Rev. 1609 (2002); Steven Semeraro, An

Essay on Property Rights in Milestone Home Run Baseballs, 56 SMU L. Rev. 2281 (2004).

B.   DISCOVERY

Closely associated with first possession or capture is the notion that original title to property can be established through discovery. Certainly, both doctrines rely heavily on being the first to claim something. But whereas first possession requires that one be the first *actually to possess* an unclaimed thing, discovery establishes a unique *right to possess* a thing. The most prominent decision to invoke discovery as a basis for ownership was far more controversial than *Pierson v. Post*, and undoubtedly far more consequential.

P   D

Johnson v. M'Intosh

Supreme Court of the United States, 1823.
21 U.S. (8 Wheat.) 543.

ERROR to the District Court of Illinois. This was an action of ejectment for lands in the State and District of Illinois, claimed by the plaintiffs under a purchase and conveyance from the Piankeshaw Indians, and by the defendant, under a grant from the United States. It came up on a case stated, upon which there was a judgment below for the defendant. * * *

[The statement of facts begins with an elaborate chronology of the colony of Virginia, founded by royal charter in 1609, which purported to grant to Virginia lands as far west as present day Illinois and Indiana. It traces the history of those lands, from a European perspective, up to the cession by Virginia to the federal government during the Revolutionary War. It notes that, "from time immemorial," the Illinois and Piankeshaw tribes had actually held and inhabited the lands in controversy in what is now central and southern Illinois and western Indiana.

On July 5, 1773, the chiefs of the Illinois sold certain lands inhabited by the tribe to William Murray and others, for the sum of $24,000. On October 18, 1775, the chiefs of the Pianekeshaw sold certain lands occupied by the tribe to Louis Viviat and others for $31,000. One of the grantees in this last transaction was Thomas Johnson, who died in 1819, leaving his interest to his son, Joshua Johnson, and his grandson, Thomas Graham, who were plaintiffs in the case.

In 1795, the Illinois and Piankeshaw tribes entered into treaties with the United States, retaining certain lands as reservations, but ceding to the federal government other of the lands they had previously occupied. On July 20, 1818, the United States sold to William M'Intosh, the defendant, some of the same lands granted by the Piankeshaw to Thomas Johnson, and subsequently inherited by Joshua Johnson and Thomas Graham. Johnson and Graham brought an action in ejectment against M'Intosh, in an effort to establish their superior claim of title to the lands in question. The lower courts ruled for the defendant, M'Intosh.].

■ MR. CHIEF JUSTICE MARSHALL delivered the opinion of the Court. The plaintiffs in this cause claim the land, in their declaration mentioned, under two grants, purporting to be made, the first in 1773, and the last in 1775, by the chiefs of certain Indian tribes, constituting the Illinois and the Piankeshaw nations; and the question is, whether this title can be recognised in the Courts of the United States?

The facts, as stated in the case agreed, show the authority of the chiefs who executed this conveyance, so far as it could be given by their own people; and likewise show, that the particular tribes for whom these chiefs acted were in rightful possession of the land they sold. The inquiry, therefore, is, in a great measure, confined to the power of Indians to give, and of private individuals to receive, a title which can be sustained in the Courts of this country.

As the right of society, to prescribe those rules by which property may be acquired and preserved is not, and cannot be drawn into question; as the title to lands, especially, is and must be admitted to depend entirely on the law of the nation in which they lie; it will be necessary, in pursuing this inquiry, to examine, not singly those principles of abstract justice, which the Creator of all things has impressed on the mind of his creature man, and which are admitted to regulate, in a great degree, the rights of civilized nations, whose perfect independence is acknowledged; but those principles also which our own government has adopted in the particular case, and given us as the rule for our decision.

On the discovery of this immense continent, the great nations of Europe were eager to appropriate to themselves so much of it as they could respectively acquire. Its vast extent offered an ample field to the ambition and enterprise of all; and the character and religion of its inhabitants afforded an apology for considering them as a people over whom the superior genius of Europe might claim an ascendency. The potentates of the old world found no difficulty in convincing themselves that they made ample compensation to the inhabitants of the new, by bestowing on them civilization and Christianity, in exchange for unlimited independence. But, as they were all in pursuit of nearly the same object, it was necessary, in order to avoid conflicting settlements, and consequent war with each other, to establish a principle, which all should acknowledge as the law by which the right of acquisition, which they all asserted, should be regulated as between themselves. This principle was, that discovery gave title to the government by whose subjects, or by whose authority, it was made, against all other European governments, which title might be consummated by possession.

The exclusion of all other Europeans, necessarily gave to the nation making the discovery the sole right of acquiring the soil from the natives, and establishing settlements upon it. It was a right with which no Europeans could interfere. It was a right which all asserted for themselves, and to the assertion of which, by others, all assented.

Those relations which were to exist between the discoverer and the natives, were to be regulated by themselves. The rights thus acquired being exclusive, no other power could interpose between them.

In the establishment of these relations, the rights of the original inhabitants were, in no instance, entirely disregarded; but were necessarily, to a considerable extent, impaired. They were admitted to be the rightful occupants of the soil, with a legal as well as just claim to retain possession of it, and to use it according to their own discretion; but their rights to complete sovereignty, as independent nations, were necessarily diminished, and their power to dispose of the soil at their own will, to whomsoever they pleased, was denied by the original fundamental principle, that discovery gave exclusive title to those who made it.

Thus, The lands no longer lie in an Indian "nation," but within The U.S., so no longer had power to transfer ownership of land.

While the different nations of Europe respected the right of the natives, as occupants, they asserted the ultimate dominion to be in themselves; and claimed and exercised, as a consequence of this ultimate dominion, a power to grant the soil, while yet in possession of the natives. These grants have been understood by all, to convey a title to the grantees, subject only to the Indian right of occupancy.

Must in order to legitimize claims of independence from Rev war

The history of America, from its discovery to the present day, proves, we think, the universal recognition of these principles. * * *

No one of the powers of Europe gave its full assent to this principle, more unequivocally than England. The documents upon this subject are ample and complete. So early as the year 1496, her monarch granted a commission to the Cabots, to discover countries then unknown to *Christian people*, and to take possession of them in the name of the king of England. Two years afterwards, Cabot proceeded on this voyage, and discovered the continent of North America, along which he sailed as far south as Virginia. To this discovery the English trace their title. * * *

Thus has our whole country been granted by the crown while in the occupation of the Indians. These grants purport to convey the soil as well as the right of dominion to the grantees. * * *

[C]onflicting claims produced a long and bloody war, which was terminated by the conquest of the whole country east of the Mississippi. In the treaty of 1763, France ceded and guaranteed to Great Britain, all Nova Scotia, or Acadie, and Canada, with their dependencies; and it was agreed, that the boundaries between the territories of the two nations, in America, should be irrevocably fixed by a line drawn from the source of the Mississippi, through the middle of that river and the lakes Maurepas and Ponchartrain, to the sea. This treaty expressly cedes, and has always been understood to cede, the whole country, on the English side of the dividing line, between the two nations, although a great and valuable part of it was occupied by the Indians. Great Britain, on her part, surrendered to France all her pretensions to the country west of the Mississippi. It has never been supposed that she surrendered nothing, although she was not in actual possession of a foot of land. She surrendered all right to acquire the country; and any after attempt to purchase it from the Indians, would have been considered and treated as an invasion of the territories of France.

By the 20th article of the same treaty, Spain ceded Florida, with its dependencies, and all the country she claimed east or southeast of the Mississippi, to Great Britain. Great part of this territory also was in possession of the Indians.

By a secret treaty, which was executed about the same time, France ceded Louisiana to Spain; and Spain has since retroceded the same country to France. At the time both of its cession and retrocession, it was occupied, chiefly, by the Indians.

Thus, all the nations of Europe, who have acquired territory on this continent, have asserted in themselves, and have recognised in others, the exclusive right of the discoverer to appropriate the lands occupied by the Indians. Have the American States rejected or adopted this principle?

By the treaty which concluded the war of our revolution, Great Britain relinquished all claim, not only to the government, but to the "propriety and territorial rights of the United States," whose boundaries were fixed in the second article. By this treaty, the powers of government, and the right to soil, which had previously been in Great Britain, passed definitively to these States. We had before taken possession of them, by declaring independence; but neither the declaration of independence, nor the treaty confirming it, could give us more than that which we before possessed, or to which Great Britain was before entitled. It has never been doubted, that either the United States, or the several States, had a clear title to all the lands within the boundary lines described in the treaty, subject only to the Indian right of occupancy, and that the exclusive power to extinguish that right, was vested in that government which might constitutionally exercise it. * * *

The States, having within their chartered limits different portions of territory covered by Indians, ceded that territory, generally, to the United States, on conditions expressed in their deeds of cession, which demonstrate the opinion, that they ceded the soil as well as jurisdiction, and that in doing so, they granted a productive fund to the government of the Union. The lands in controversy lay within the chartered limits of Virginia, and were ceded with the whole country northwest of the river Ohio. This grant contained reservations and stipulations, which could only be made by the owners of the soil; and concluded with a stipulation, that "all the lands in the ceded territory, not reserved, should be considered as a common fund, for the use and benefit of such of the United States as have become, or shall become, members of the confederation," &c. "according to their usual respective proportions in the general charge and expenditure, and shall be faithfully and *bona fide* disposed of for that purpose, and for no other use or purpose whatsoever."

The ceded territory was occupied by numerous and warlike tribes of Indians; but the exclusive right of the United States to extinguish their title, and to grant the soil, has never, we believe, been doubted. * * *

The United States, then, have unequivocally acceded to that great and broad rule by which its civilized inhabitants now hold this country. They hold, and assert in themselves, the title by which it was acquired. They maintain, as all others have maintained, that discovery gave an exclusive right to extinguish the Indian title of occupancy, either by purchase or by conquest; and gave also a right to such a degree of sovereignty, as the circumstances of the people would allow them to exercise.

The power now possessed by the government of the United States to grant lands, resided, while we were colonies, in the crown, or its grantees. The validity of the titles given by either has never been questioned in our Courts. It has been exercised uniformly over territory in possession of the Indians. The existence of this power must negative the existence of any right which may conflict with, and control it. An absolute title to lands cannot exist, at the same time, in different persons, or in different governments. An absolute, must be an exclusive title, or at least a title which excludes all others not compatible with it. All our institutions recognise the absolute title of the crown, subject only to the Indian right of occupancy, and recognise the absolute title of the crown to extinguish that right. This is incompatible with an absolute and complete title in the Indians.

We will not enter into the controversy, whether agriculturists, merchants, and manufacturers, have a right, on abstract principles, to expel hunters from the territory they possess, or to contract their limits. Conquest gives a title which the Courts of the conqueror cannot deny, whatever the private and speculative opinions of individuals may be, respecting the original justice of the claim which has been successfully asserted. The British government, which was then our government, and whose rights have passed to the United States, asserted title to all the lands occupied by Indians, within the chartered limits of the British colonies. It asserted also a limited sovereignty over them, and the exclusive right of extinguishing the title which occupancy gave to them. These claims have been maintained and established as far west as the river Mississippi, by the sword. The title to a vast portion of the lands we now hold, originates in them. It is not for the Courts of this country to question the validity of this title, or to sustain one which is incompatible with it.

Although we do not mean to engage in the defence of those principles which Europeans have applied to Indian title, they may, we think, find some excuse, if not justification, in the character and habits of the people whose rights have been wrested from them.

The title by conquest is acquired and maintained by force. The conqueror prescribes its limits. Humanity, however, acting on public opinion, has established, as a general rule, that the conquered shall not be wantonly oppressed, and that their condition shall remain as eligible as is compatible with the objects of the conquest. Most usually, they are incorporated with the victorious nation, and become subjects or citizens of the government with which they are connected. The new and old members of the society mingle with each other; the distinction between them is gradually lost, and they make one people. Where this incorporation is practicable, humanity demands, and a wise policy requires, that the rights of the conquered to property should remain unimpaired; that the new subjects should be governed as equitably as the old, and that confidence in their security should gradually banish the painful sense of being separated from their ancient connexions, and united by force to strangers.

When the conquest is complete, and the conquered inhabitants can be blended with the conquerors, or safely governed as a distinct people, public opinion, which not even the conqueror can disregard, imposes these restraints upon him; and he cannot neglect them without injury to his fame, and hazard to his power.

But the tribes of Indians inhabiting this country were fierce savages, whose occupation was war, and whose subsistence was drawn chiefly from the forest. To leave them in possession of their country, was to leave the country a wilderness; to govern them as a distinct people, was impossible, because they were as brave and as high spirited as they were fierce, and were ready to repel by arms every attempt on their independence.

What was the inevitable consequence of this state of things? The Europeans were under the necessity either of abandoning the country, and relinquishing their pompous claims to it, or of enforcing those claims by the sword, and by the adoption of principles adapted to the condition of a people with whom it was impossible to mix, and who could not be governed as a distinct society, or of remaining in their neighbourhood, and exposing themselves and their families to the perpetual hazard of being massacred.

Frequent and bloody wars, in which the whites were not always the aggressors, unavoidably ensued. European policy, numbers, and skill, prevailed. As the white population advanced, that of the Indians necessarily receded. The country in the immediate neighbourhood of agriculturists became unfit for them. The game fled into thicker and more unbroken forests, and the Indians followed. The soil, to which the crown originally claimed title, being no longer occupied by its ancient inhabitants, was parcelled out according to the will of the sovereign power, and taken possession of by persons who claimed immediately from the crown, or mediately, through its grantees or deputies.

Illustrates, in Marshall's view, that Indians had a different concept of 'property' than did the whites

That law which regulates, and ought to regulate in general, the relations between the conqueror and conquered, was incapable of application to a people under such circumstances. The resort to some new and different rule, better adapted to the actual state of things, was unavoidable. Every rule which can be suggested will be found to be attended with great difficulty.

However extravagant the pretension of converting the discovery of an inhabited country into conquest may appear; if the principle has been asserted in the first instance, and afterwards sustained; if a country has been acquired and held under it; if the property of the great mass of the community originates in it, it becomes the law of the land, and cannot be questioned. So, too, with respect to the concomitant principle, that the Indian inhabitants are to be considered merely as occupants, to be protected, indeed, while in peace, in the possession of their lands, but to be deemed incapable of transferring the absolute title to others. However this restriction may be opposed to natural right, and to the usages of civilized nations, yet, if it be indispensable to that system under which the country has been settled, and be adapted to the actual condition of the two people, it may, perhaps, be supported by reason, and certainly cannot be rejected by Courts of justice. * * *

After bestowing on this subject a degree of attention which was more required by the magnitude of the interest in litigation, and the able and elaborate arguments of the bar, than by its intrinsic difficulty, the Court is decidedly of opinion, that the plaintiffs do not exhibit a title which can be sustained in the Courts of the United States; and that there is no error in the judgment which was rendered against them in the District Court of Illinois. * * *

NOTES AND QUESTIONS

1.   This case illustrates the practice of courts when faced with conflicting claims to a single piece of property: They recreate the "chains of title" underlying the competing claims, in order to determine which of the parties has the stronger claim. Each claim is traced back a link at a time, until we arrive at the "root of title." Often this exercise will lead back to a single common grantor (e.g., the government or the first possessor), in which case the first transferee from the common grantor is deemed to have the better claim to title. If we assume the Illinois and Piankeshaw Tribes are the common grantor, who would prevail here—Joshua Johnson, who claims by inheritance from Thomas Johnson, who was an original grantee from the Piankeshaw in 1775, or M'Intosh, who purchases from the United States in 1818, which acquired the rights from the Illinois and Piankeshaw by treaty in 1795?

2.   In order to displace the conclusion that would be drawn from ordinary principles about transfers from a common grantor, Chief Justice Marshall draws a distinction between sovereign title ("dominion") based on discovery and Indian title ("occupancy") based on possession. He then traces the chain of title back in time, looking now to acts of discovery that establish dominion rather than occupancy. This takes him all the way back to 1609 when Virginia was established, or perhaps even to 1496 when Cabot discovered North America. Who wins under the tracing-back exercise once we recharacterize the relevant interests in this fashion?

3.   Eric Kades has recently called into question whether this case was really about competing chains of title to the same land. According to Kades, this was a fabricated suit based on false stipulated facts: The plaintiffs' and the defendant's land did not even overlap, as reflected in his map, reproduced here as Figure 2–3. Eric Kades, History and Interpretation of the Great Case of *Johnson v. M'Intosh*, 19 Law & Hist. Rev. 67, 68 (2001). The plaintiffs' predecessors (Murray, Viviat, etc.) had tried repeatedly to get the

Figure 2–3

Map of Land Claims in *Johnson v. M'Intosh*

Legend

▤ Tracts Purchased by Illinois Company (1773)

▦ Tracts Purchased by Wabash Company (1775)

■ Townships Containing McIntosh Purchases of 1815 (at issue in case)

▨ Township Containing McIntosh Purchase of 1819 (not at issue in case)

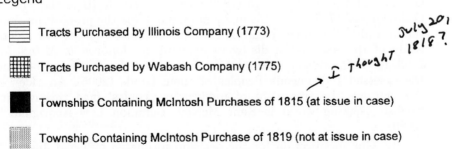

→ I thought July 20, 1818?

From the Law and History Review. Copyright 2001 by the Board of Trustees of the University of Illinois. Used with permission of the University of Illinois Press.

Virginia colonial governor and later Congress to recognize their titles, to no avail. Nor did the plaintiffs get "title" from all the Indians that had some claim to the land. Eric Kades, The Dark Side of Efficiency: *Johnson v. M'Intosh* and the Expropriation of American Indian Lands, 148 U. Pa. L. Rev. 1065, 1067, 1081–90 (2000). Such contrived lawsuits were not as uncommon in those days, though today we assume that "feigned" lawsuits do not satisfy the "case or controversy" requirement of Article III of the Constitution.

4.   Some of the selling tribes in *Johnson v. M'Intosh* were under great pressure because of declining population due to disease and surrounding enemy Indian tribes. The great Illinois confederation could not defend itself against other tribes and settlers. The first two parcels in the case, in South and Central Illinois, were purchased from three remaining Illinois tribes (the Kaskaskia, Peoria, and Cahokia tribes). Their numbers had recently been much reduced (Illinois tribes fell from 10,500 in 1680 to 2,500 in 1736 to 500 in 1800, because of disease and Indian enemies on all sides). The second two parcels, in Southern Illinois and Indiana, came from the Piankeshaw tribe, one of six Miami tribes (Miami population fell from 7,500 in 1682 to some 2,000 in 1736). Kades, supra, at 1081–82.

5.   What is the relationship between dominion and occupancy? How can the Indian right of occupancy be extinguished? Why should "conquest" be regarded as an acceptable method of extinguishing the right of occupancy? Does Marshall think that the result he reaches is consistent with what morality and international law would dictate? What do you make of the line in the opinion, "Conquest gives a title which the Courts of the conqueror cannot deny"? Does this concede too much to raw power? Or is the point rather that too many titles to too much land depend on the validity of discovery and conquest as means of establishing original title to land in North America—that the assumed validity of these methods of original acquisition has too much gravitational force for courts to ignore it? Either way, does this case validate the view that property is theft? Does it at least imply that all property ultimately flows from the state, with its monopoly on the legitimate use of force and coercion? Note that conquest was later limited by the Court to "defensive" or "just cause" wars. Worcester v. Georgia, 31 U.S. (6 Pet.) 515 (1832); see also Article III of the Northwest Ordinance of 1787. Does this make more palatable the proposition that the Indian right of occupancy can be extinguished by conquest? For a detailed study of the use of the discovery doctrine in *Johnson v. M'Intosh*, see Lindsay G. Robertson, Conquest by Law: How the Discovery of America Dispossessed Indigenous Peoples of their Lands (2005). An older study that surveys the treatment of indigenous peoples' land throughout the English-speaking world is Kent McNeil, Common Law Aboriginal Title (1989).

6.   One justification for the decision intimated by Chief Justice Marshall is that the Indians had no concept of property in land comparable to the understanding of the white settlers. He describes "the tribes of Indians inhabiting this country" as "fierce savages" "whose subsistence was drawn chiefly from the forest." They were hunter-gatherers, who had left the land "a wilderness." The white settlers, in contrast, were "agriculturists," who parceled out the land in private plots, causing game to flee "into thicker and more unbroken forests" and the Indians to follow. These views, which

[handwritten margin note: Necessary for the American Revolution to be recognized as legitimately establishing a new & independent nation]

were standard for the time in which Marshall lived and wrote, have recently been called into question. According to William Cronon, for example, New England Indians recognized the concept of territoriality, in the sense of areas subject to exclusive control and use by particular villages. William Cronon, Changes in the Land: Indians, Colonists, and the Ecology of New England 58–61 (1983). They also recognized individual property rights in utilitarian objects such as baskets, kettles, hoes, bows, arrows, and canoes. Id. at 61. With respect to land, southern New England Indians, who engaged in extensive agriculture, recognized something close to exclusive rights of particular families to fields planted with corn, although these fields were generally abandoned every eight years or so when soil nutrients were exhausted. Id. at 62. Other recognized land rights were similar to what the Romans called <u>usufructs</u>—rights to engage in particular uses of particular parcels of land. Thus, "different groups of people could have different claims on the same tract of land depending on how they used it. Any village member, for instance, had the right to collect edible wild plants, cut birchbark or chestnut for canoes, or gather sedges for mats, wherever these things could be found. . . . The same was not true, on the other hand, of hunting that involved the setting of snares or traps. . . . [Animals that had to be caught by using traps] were best hunted by spreading the village population over as broad a territory as possible, and so usufruct rights had to be designed to hold the overlap of trapped areas to a reasonable minimum." Id. at 63–64. See also Philip P. Frickey, Marshalling Past and Present: Colonialism, Constitutionalism, and Interpretation in Federal Indian Law, 107 Harv. L. Rev. 381 (1993); Charles F. Wilkinson, American Indians, Time, and the Law: Native Societies in a Modern Constitutional Democracy (1987). Similar conclusions about aboriginal understandings of property have been reached by other scholars. See, e.g., Stuart Banner, Two Properties, One Land: Law and Space in Nineteenth–Century New Zealand, 24 Law & Soc. Inquiry 807, 811–12 (1999); Robert Williams, The American Indian in Western Legal Thought (1990).

7.   One understanding that Indians almost surely did not originally share with the European settlers was that of land as a commercial commodity subject to bargain and sale. The question of the nature of sales by Indians to Europeans and later Americans has been the subject of much research and commentary. Many of the sales were fraught with misunderstanding in the very earliest times in the eastern United States, and with violence in later times in the West when Indians had fewer places to which they could retreat. See Terry L. Anderson & Peter J. Hill, The Not So Wild, Wild West: Property Rights on the Frontier (2004); Cronon, supra, at 67–81; Stuart Banner, How the Indians Lost Their Land: Law and Power on the Frontier (2005).

8.   What was the ultimate impact on Native Americans of the doctrine of discovery rationalized in *Johnson v. M'Intosh*? Commentators today tend to take an uncharitable view of the decision. Kades argues that the policy of only allowing non-Indians to purchase land from Indians with the permission of the United States government was disadvantageous to the Indians. Kades, supra, at 1103–31. This policy, recognized in *Johnson v. M'Intosh*,

was originally codified in the Indian Trade and Intercourse Act of 1790, ch. 33, 1 Stat. 137 (expired 1793). See also William C. Canby, Jr., The Status of Indian Tribes in American Law Today, 62 Wash. L. Rev. 1, 2–6 (1987). Indians could theoretically remain on the land but could not force potential buyers to compete with each other, thus depressing prices. A more charitable view of the decision might ask whether Indians were likely to get a better deal in the nineteenth century from Congress and the federal judiciary, or from state legislatures and state judiciaries. By distinguishing between dominion and occupancy, and asserting that only the federal government could extinguish native rights of occupancy, Chief Justice Marshall—at least in theory—inserted the federal government and its courts as a buffer between natives and their property interests and the land-hungry European settlers. The federal government, representing a more diffuse set of interests, was arguably more even-handed in its treatment of land disputes between natives and European settlers than state governments and state courts would have been. On the other hand, the further west land sales occurred, the less likely that the federal government could enforce its wishes. Also, Anderson and Hill point out that members of the U.S. Army, both privates and officers, had incentives to drum up business by fomenting conflicts with the Indians.

9.   The history of Indian land ownership after *Johnson v. M'Intosh* has been an unfortunate one. As the nineteenth century drew on, Indians were forced into reservations in the West. In the Dawes General Allotment Act of 1887, 24 Stat. 388, Congress allotted land to various tribes and imposed a version of an Anglo–American style property system, all with the purpose of Indian assimilation. Allotted lands were to be held in trust by the United States and then turned over to individual Indian owners, but placed under the jurisdiction of the state in which the land was located. Proponents and opponents of allotment both believed that Indians had only common property and systematically ignored the mix of private and common property and the diversity of Indian property systems and their development over time. After allotment, any changes in Indian property systems had to be effected by federal legislation. Various provisions of the allotment act caused Indian land ownership to decline by 80% by 1934 when Congress passed the Indian Reorganization Act. This statute promoted Indian governments but retained much federal control and proved rigidly bureaucratic. In *Tee–Hit–Ton Indians v. United States*, 348 U.S. 272 (1955), the Supreme Court held that Congress could take Indian land without compensation. The Court again downplayed Indian notions of property and Indian sovereignty. At one point the Court quoted from Justice Jackson in another case: "We agree . . . that no legal rights are today to be recognized in the Shoshones by reason of this treaty. We agree . . . as to their moral deserts. We do not mean to leave the impression that the two have any relation to each other." Northwestern Bands of Shoshone Indians v. United States, 324 U.S. 335, 358 (1945) (Jackson, J., concurring).

LAND GRANTS FROM THE FEDERAL PUBLIC DOMAIN*

When the original thirteen colonies broke free from Britain, a number of them—Massachusetts, Connecticut, New York, Virginia, North and South Carolina, and Georgia—had charters that included lands extending from the Atlantic seaboard to the Mississippi River. The remaining colonies had much more limited claims to territories along the Atlantic coast. After much political wrangling, the states with claims to western lands agreed to cede those lands to the newly formed federal government. This was the beginning of the federal public domain, a vast quantity of land held by the federal government for disposition and eventual formation of new states. The original federal public domain, which extended from the Allegheny Mountains to the Mississippi River, was soon enormously expanded. The largest augmentations were the Louisiana Purchase of 1803, which acquired most of the land from Louisiana to Montana; the Treaty with Spain in 1818, which added Florida and western Louisiana; the annexation of Texas in 1845; the Oregon Compromise with Britain in 1846, which secured what is now Washington, Oregon and Idaho; the concessions wrested from Mexico in 1848 after the Mexican–American War, which included California, Nevada, Utah, Arizona, New Mexico, and western Colorado; and the purchase of Alaska from Russia in 1867. The quantity of resources to be disposed of, once Indian title to the lands was extinguished by treaty or conquest, was staggering—approximately 1.4 billion acres of land.

When the western lands were ceded, the reigning idea was that the federal government would sell the lands at auction in order to raise money to pay off the Revolutionary War debts. To facilitate this process, Congress (during the waning days of the Articles of Confederation) adopted legislation known as the Land Ordinance of 1785. This statute probably had a more profound impact on the physical appearance of America than any other piece of legislation before or since. Influenced by the ideas of a committee headed by Thomas Jefferson, the Ordinance of 1785 mandated a system for surveying and disposing of public domain lands. Starting from the point where the Ohio River crosses the Pennsylvania border, "a north-south line—a principal meridian—was to be run and a base line westward—the geographer's line—was to be surveyed; parallel lines of longitude and latitude were to be surveyed, each to be 6 miles apart, making for townships of 36 square miles or 23,040 acres. Seven rows or ranges of townships running south from the base line and west of the principal meridian were to be surveyed. Each township was to be divided into lots of one mile square containing 640 acres." Paul W. Gates, History of Public Land Law Development 65 (1968). Nearly all the land in the federal public domain—the vast preponderance of the physical space of America—was eventually surveyed and disposed of using this system. This is why rural roads in most parts of the country run along straight lines (section lines), why most farms are square in shape, and why most lots in cities are rectangular.

---

* [The following account is primarily drawn from Paul W. Gates, History of Public Land Law Development (1968), a magisterial study of the history of public lands in the United States.—eds.]

The following diagram illustrates the system of surveying established by the Land Ordinance of 1785. It shows how you would identify a tract of

Figure 2–4
System of Land Description Established by the Land Ordinance of 1785

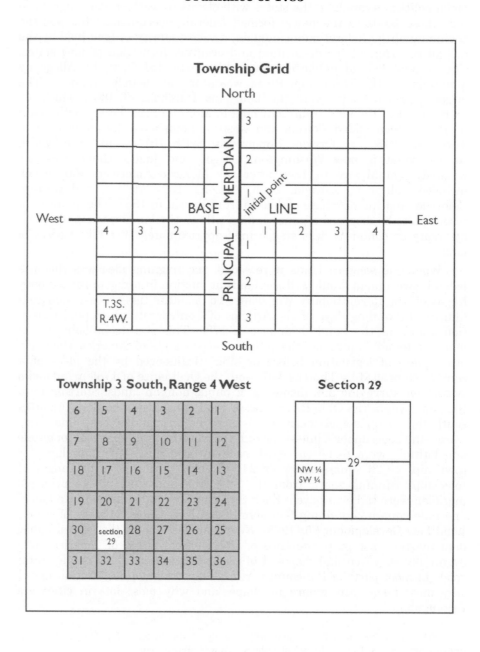

property with the following legal description: "the Northwest quarter of the Southwest quarter of Section 29, Township 3 South, Range 4 West, ____ Base and Meridian." Note that every section contains 640 acres, a quarter section 160 acres, and a quarter-quarter section (such as described here) 40 acres.

Another important provision of the Ordinance of 1785 was the reservation of section 16 in every township "for the maintenance of public schools within the said township." The idea was not that all 640 acres in Section 16 would be the playground for a one-room school house (although one can see the remains of one-room school houses on Section 16 in many rural areas today). Rather, the territorial governments, and then the states formed out of the territories, would be able to sell or lease the land in Section 16 in order to raise revenue for the support of public schools. Thus, the federal government, from the very beginning, was committed to heavily subsidizing public education through the disposition of the public lands. This was followed by other measures, most prominently the Morrill Act of 1862, which set aside large tracts of public lands for sales to support the creation of public universities—the so-called "land grant" colleges and universities that form the backbone of much of our system of higher education today.

Following the Ordinance of 1785, the official policy of the federal government continued to emphasize sales of land from the public domain. Once Indian claims were extinguished and the land was surveyed, it would be placed for sale at public auction. Congress set the initial minimum price at $2 an acre, with no limitation on the amount of land that could be purchased. Sales were disappointing, however, apparently because the minimum price was too high, and agitation for more liberal divestment policies quickly mounted. Congress responded by easing the conditions for sales on credit. Widespread defaults and forfeitures followed. Various relief acts were passed by Congress to benefit those who were unable to come up with cash to pay for the lands they had purchased. In 1821 further credit sales were prohibited, and the minimum price was reduced to $1.25 per acre. Forfeitures continued to plague those who had previously purchased on credit, and in 1832 Congress essentially gave up on further attempts to recover amounts still owed. Federal land prices were lowered further by the Graduation Act of 1854, which allowed for progressively lower prices for any land that did not sell at the minimum price.

While official federal policy continued to favor sales of land, the reality on the ground was different. During the colonial era, many states outside

New England had seen widespread claims of unsettled land by squatters who moved onto choice parcels without any pretense of legal title. As Paul W. Gates recounts:

> Squatters were a rough and sometimes unruly lot. They were contemptuous of the rights of large owners, contributed no taxes to the support of government, and caused conflicts for colonial administrations by their intrusions into areas claimed by the Indians. James Logan, agent for the Penn holdings, described the Scotch–Irish—the most restless and least law-abiding of the hordes of immigrants coming into Pennsylvania—as "bold and indigent strangers" who, when challenged for their titles, replied that the Penns "had solicited for colonists and they had come accordingly." They took up land in "an audacious manner," alleging that "it was against the laws of God and nature that so much land should be idle while so many Christians wanted it to labor on to raise their bread."

Gates, supra, at 66. These squatters became numerous and vociferous enough that even before the cession of western lands to the federal government, Virginia and North Carolina had enacted laws allowing squatters a right of "preemption," which essentially gave squatters an option to purchase the land they occupied, thereby trumping the rights of purchasers at subsequent public-land sales.

After 1785, the practice of squatting continued, notwithstanding the official policy of disposing of land by sale. Although the practice was frequently condemned, Congress received hundreds of petitions from squatter-settlers seeking preemption rights for their holdings. Often, but not always, Congress responded with ad hoc legislation granting these requests, effectively ratifying acts that had been illegal when the land was taken. As western interests' political representation in Congress increased, preemption acts became broader. The process culminated in the enactment of the Preemption Act of 1841, which granted a general prospective preemption right on federal land, provided Indian title had been extinguished and the land had been surveyed. Settlers could claim up to 160 acres of land before it went to public auction, provided they inhabited and improved the land, constructed some kind of dwelling on it, and agreed to pay the minimum price of $1.25 per acre. There is considerable evidence that the Preemption Act was often abused. For example, logging companies would use dummies, persons appearing independent but actually controlled by the company, to file preemption claims for timber land in Michigan, Wisconsin, and Minnesota, which provided the legal authority to enter the land. The companies would then clear cut the standing timber—often magnificent old-growth white pines—and the preemption claim would be abandoned before any funds were paid to the government. Nevertheless, preemption remained a significant avenue for disposal of public lands until 1891, when the Preemption Act was finally repealed.

Squatter-settlers adopted another tactic for securing legal title to the land they had occupied: They banded together to form claims associations. These were combinations designed to prevent competitive bidding at public land sales, in order to ensure that local settlers could purchase the land of their choosing at the minimum price. Little is known about exactly how these associations operated, since they did not keep written records of their activities. But it is widely surmised that they had an even greater impact on securing land for squatter-settlers than did the preemption laws. Gates relates the following account:

> Sandford C. Cox, an eye-witness of a government sale at the Crawfordsville, Indiana office, wrote of the town being full of strangers when the sales commenced [in 1825]. The eastern and southern portions of the state were strongly represented, as well as Ohio, Kentucky, Tennessee, and Pennsylvania. There was little competitive bidding as "the settlers, or 'squatters' as they are called by speculators, have arranged matters among themselves to their general satisfaction. If, upon comparing numbers, it appears that two are after the same tract of land, one asks the other what he will take not to bid against him. If neither will consent to be bought off, they then retire, and cast lots, and the lucky one enters the tract at Congress' price—$1.25 per acre—and the other enters the second choice on his list." If a speculator "showed a disposition to take a settler's claim from him, he sees the white of a score of eyes snapping at him, and at the first opportunity he crawfishes out of the crowd."

Gates, supra at 152.

The most interesting legislation disposing of federal land, in terms of its impact on the popular imagination, was the Homestead Act of 1862. This legislation grew out of a land reform movement of the 1830s and 1840s, spearheaded by the New York newspaper publisher Horace Greeley. Advocates argued that the government should grant free small homesteads to any citizen who relocated westward, in order to draw surplus labor from the cities in the East. This, they argued, would help raise wages for the poor who remained behind, and would act as a "safety valve" against urban unrest. The original Act of 1862 allowed any citizen to claim 160 acres of unsold surveyed land. If the homesteader inhabited the land and cultivated it for five years, he received title to the land without any payment (other than filing fees). Only one homestead could be acquired per family, but it was possible to obtain 160 acres by homestead and another 160 by preemption—although not at the same time, since actual inhabitation was required for each. Homesteaders could also get title to their homestead land before five years were up, by converting the claim to a preemption claim and paying $1.25 per acre. Congress eventually realized that 160 acres was too small to sustain productive agricultural operations in arid areas on the Great Plains, where there is not enough rainfall for crop production. Later homestead acts authorized larger claims of up to 640 acres.

Although granting individual plots of land to settlers was probably the largest single category of federal land disposal, the government granted lands for other purposes as well. Veterans of the Revolutionary War, the War of 1812, the Mexican–American War, and the Civil War were given "scrip" that could be exchanged for federal lands. As previously noted, states were given Section 16 of every township to support public education,

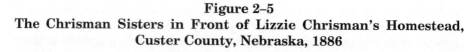

Figure 2–5
The Chrisman Sisters in Front of Lizzie Chrisman's Homestead,
Custer County, Nebraska, 1886

Courtesy Nebraska State Historical Society Photograph Collections. To help their family accumulate enough acreage in western Nebraska to graze livestock, each of the four Chrisman sisters took homestead, timber, and preemption claims, each having a sod house similar to the one in the picture. Two or more of the sisters would then take turns living with each other, in order to comply with the family-habitation requirements of the laws.

and were later given large grants for the support of state colleges. Generous grants of land were also given to companies formed to build turnpikes, canals, and railroads. Finally, special grants of land were made to settlers who agreed to plant trees on the prairies (the Timber Culture Act of 1873) or to irrigate desert areas (the Desert Land Act of 1877).

By the late nineteenth century, public attitudes toward disposition of the public domain began to change. The process of settlement began to run out of gas, as remaining tracts were too arid, mountainous, or remote to attract further private entry. The public also began to perceive that some of the federal land was simply too valuable to sell or give away. The area now occupied by Yellowstone National Park was reserved from further entry or homesteading in 1872, and reservations of Yosemite and other future national parks followed. Huge tracts of forested land in the West were reserved by presidential proclamation, followed by the creation of the National Forest System in 1897 and the National Park System in 1916. Finally, the Taylor Grazing Act of 1934 closed all of the remaining public domain from further private entry (other than entry by prospectors for mineral claims). Public sentiment since then has if anything hardened against further private disposition of federal lands. The result is that today almost 30 percent of the land mass of the United States—approximately 662 million acres—is controlled by the federal government. These lands are managed by large federal bureaucracies—the Bureau of Land Management, the Bureau of Indian Affairs, and the National Park Service in the Department of Interior, and the National Forest Service in the Department of Agriculture.

NOTES AND QUESTIONS

1.   In retrospect, congressional policy toward disposition of the public domain seems riddled with inconsistencies. Congress was at once too generous (making grants to veterans and railroads and favored insiders) and too stingy (setting the initial minimum price for sale at $2 per acre). Part of the problem was conflicting desires: to tap public lands as a source of revenue in order to pay off war debts; to promote rapid development of the interior of the continent; to avoid sanctioning either "speculators" or "squatters." Two relatively consistent policies, either of which would have promoted rapid development, would have been to auction the land to the highest bidder with no minimums, or to permit unlimited homesteading. Either policy, however, might have reduced federal revenues from initial land sales. And the first (unlimited sales) would have had the appearance of abetting "speculators," while the second (unlimited homesteading) would have appeared to sanction "squatters." So instead, Congress vacillated back and forth between promoting sales (subject to minimum prices) and promoting homesteading (subject to acreage restrictions and other limitations). Somehow, the country got developed, although the system of disposal produced enormous conflict and litigation along the way.

2.   Economists have pointed out that despite the appearance of free land, homesteading carried with it a steep price paid for by the hardships endured by the settlers and the concomitant premature cultivation of remote tracts. See Terry L. Anderson & P. J. Hill, The Race for Property Rights, 33 J.L. & Econ. 177, 195 (1990). Again, racing behavior if unconstrained can dissipate the value of a natural resource. On the other hand, it has also been argued that from the United States' point of view, homesteading provided collective defense of the frontier areas against Europeans, Mexicans, and Indians. See Douglas W. Allen, Homesteading and Property Rights; or, "How The West Was Really Won," 34 J.L. & Econ. 1, 22–23 (1991).

3.   Are preemption laws and homestead laws additional examples of acquisition of property by first possession? By discovery? Under both systems, claimants would scout around until they spotted a choice parcel of unclaimed land, which they would then occupy and claim for themselves upon payment of a fixed minimum price ($1.25 under the Preemption Act) or minimal filing fees (under the homestead acts). The law on the books— the Ordinance of 1785 and the system of land sales and registrations managed by the Land Office—would suggest that the public domain was divided into well-defined parcels and distributed in a very orderly fashion.

But would it be more accurate to characterize the situation on the ground, at least for the first hundred years or so, as a kind of open-access commons? If so, what does this tell us about the conditions that cause a resource to be regarded as a commons?

4.   What accounts for the great resistance today to further privatization of the public domain? Many national forests, for example, could be owned and managed by privately-owned lumber and paper companies, many of which already own and manage large tracts of forest lands. On one estimate, the National Forest System loses 25 cents on every dollar it spends managing the National Forests. Could it be that a variety of interest groups, including lumber and paper companies, are happy having their activities subsidized by federal taxpayers? See James L. Huffman, The Inevitability of Private Rights in Public Lands, 65 U. Colo. L. Rev. 241 (1994). Or have past abuses of federal lands, such as the clear cutting of old-growth forests in the upper Midwest, created pervasive distrust of private stewardship for resources like timber?

THE MINING CAMPS

Another type of discovery that has played a prominent role in American history involves the discovery of gold, silver, and other valuable minerals on federal public domain land. Many of the mining camps established in the Far West between 1848 and 1890 were remote from any sort of functioning government or judicial system. As a result, the miners had to devise their own rules for resolving conflicts over claims.

Gary D. Libecap, *Contracting for Property Rights*, 29–34, 36–37 (1989)

Competitive pressures for what were, effectively, open access mineral lands were intense. For example, within months of the first ore discoveries on Sutter Creek in 1848, the population of California rose from a few thousand to 107,000 and by 1860, to 380,000, with most people concentrated in the mining camps of the central Sierra Nevada foothills. In the absence of legal rules to assign ownership of the valuable mineral lands, there was the potential for violent contention for control. Uncertainty about ownership was a likely result, because none of the competing groups had a monopoly in the use of force to claim and hold mineral land. The historical record suggests that the first miners were concerned that this environment would not support extensive prospecting and mining to access the ore and that the promised bonanza might not be theirs.

In response to these concerns, miners quickly formed over 600 mining camp governments in the Far West to devise local rules for recognizing and enforcing private mineral rights. There was a common pattern for contracting across the mining camps as described by Shinn (1948, pp. 160–2):

> A few hours' labor convinced the discoverers that the royal metal was there in paying quantities . . . soon the news spread; and within a week there were fifteen or twenty men at work in the . . . bed or creek. At first the camp had no organization or government, and every man's

conduct conformed to his own ideas of right and justice. Each miner had chosen a "spot to work in," and no question of encroachment could possibly arise until in the widening circle their operations began to approach each other. About the close of the first week after the establishment of the camp, the near approach of two miners' operations caused a dispute about the size of the claims. One of the miners considered his rights infringed upon; and a few days later, after a good deal of talk, his friends circulated an informal oral request through the camp, whose population had by that time increased to fifty or more, asking for a miners' meeting in the evening.

Through these mining camp meetings the squatters' rights of the miners were recognized and local rules were devised for establishing, exchanging, and protecting private mineral claims. The mining camp regulations were incorporated subsequently in state legislation and judicial rulings throughout the West. Moreover, they were specifically recognized in the federal Mining Laws of 1866 and 1872, which allowed for the private patenting of federal mineral land. Within this legal framework private property rights were assigned, refined, and made secure.

* * * [A] number of reasons can be identified as to why mineral rights agreements were completed rapidly and were refined repeatedly to avoid some of the losses of an open access or common pool resource. First, the expected aggregate gains from the establishment of private property rights were large, and most of the contracting parties expected to share in those gains. In these circumstances, concessions could be made in bargaining within the mining camps and among politicians within the state legislatures to reach agreement without disruptive distributional conflicts.

The possible losses from the absence of any recognized ownership of the mineral lands provided the incentives for miners to agree on mineral rights arrangements. The gold and silver discoveries were made on federal lands in advance of general settlement, without any provisions in federal land law for the establishment of private mineral rights. The thousands of miners who were attracted to the ore deposits had no formal institutions for staking claims, receiving title, or arbitrating disputes. Given the value of the land, violent competition and uncertain control were recognized as likely outcomes.

The need for secure mineral rights to promote investment and the realization of the potential of both surface and, later, deep-vein mines was emphasized repeatedly as the mining region was settled. For example, the San Francisco *Alta California,* January 24, 1861, commented on the growing uncertainty over the control of mineral lands along the Comstock Lode in Nevada (Washoe): "Without some such step (a territorial government or annexation to California) it is becoming apparent that Washoe, with all its mineral resources, will fail to command the confidence of capitalists and thus, come short of that permanent and rapid progress that would otherwise be her lot."

These problems of insecure tenure became more critical as surface ore, which could be accessed with little capital, was depleted and mining turned to more capital-intensive activities. Deep-vein mining, which became common in most parts of the West, required tunnels to be sunk with elaborate structural supports; roads to be built to haul ore, overburden, and supplies; mills to be constructed to separate the ore from its surrounding elements; and extensive aqueducts to be developed to bring water to the mines. Once rights were made secure, equity was exchanged especially through use of the new San Francisco Stock Exchange, to raise capital for the development of the mines.

Besides having so much at stake, a second reason why early miners could reach agreement on mineral rights was because the number of contracting parties typically was small, perhaps 20 to 30 individuals in an early mining camp. Further, the groups were relatively homogeneous with respect to race, culture, skill, and technology so that they had similar experiences and expectations regarding legal institutions and private ownership (Umbeck, 1977b; Hallagan, 1978; Libecap, 1979). Additionally, there generally were no significant, competing vested interests in the mining regions whose claims had to be reconciled with those of the miners. This condition allowed later refinements in the mining camp rules to be made by politicians in the state and federal governments at the urging of the mining industry without serious distributional conflicts. The relative absence of nonmining vested interests was because gold and silver discoveries were made on previously unclaimed land well in advance of agricultural settlement in areas naturally unsuited for farming. In these circumstances, state legislatures and courts could devote attention to the demands of their major constituents, the mining industry, for the refinement and protection of private mineral rights and the overall promotion of the industry.

Table 3.1 illustrates the importance of the mining industry in the economies of selected far western states in the nineteenth century. Comparative data are available only from 1870, which unfortunately is well after the initial development of the industry and establishment of secure mineral rights through mining camp rules and legislative and judicial actions. Nevertheless, the data reveal that as late as 1870, mining of gold and silver dominated the value of agricultural output, the other major industry, in leading mining states except California. Given the singular early importance of mining and the lack of significant competing lobby groups, western state legislatures and courts could be responsive to the demands of the industry at low political cost. Only in California, where agriculture also developed relatively quickly, did the legislature and courts have to address the competing interests of agriculture when they came into conflict with mining (McCurdy, 1976).

A third reason why mineral rights agreements could be reached was because there were no known critical informational asymmetries among the contracting parties regarding the valuing and marking of individual claims. Initial mining camp agreements were made prior to extensive development, so that information regarding land values was more or less evenly spread among the contracting parties. Ore bodies were stationary, and procedures were adopted in the mining camps for adjusting the size of allowed claims according to expectations regarding their value. Smaller claims based on visible markers, such as trees or rock outcroppings, were allowed in stream beds where placer or surface ore was known to congregate. Larger individual claims were allowed on hillsides where ore locations were more problematical.

For subsurface ore, which was accessed later in development, the potential for disputes among claimants was greater because there was less information regarding the extent and direction of the underground ore vein. Because of this lack of information and the desire to promote excavation of veins, mining camp rules assigned ownership to portions of the known vein, separating it from ownership of surface land, and procedures were adopted *ex ante* for resolving conflicts and assigning ownership should subsurface veins merge and boundaries become confused. These rights to follow a vein below the surface lands of others were called *extralateral rights*.

Table 3.1 *Relative value[a] of gold and silver production and agricultural production for leading mining states*

	1870		1880		1890	
	Gold and silver	Agricultural production	Gold and silver	Agricultural production	Gold and silver	Agricultural production
California	$25,000	$49,900	$18,600	$59,700	$13,700	$87,000
Colorado	3,700	2,300	20,200	5,000	28,500	13,100
Montana	9,100	1,700	4,900	2,000	23,700	6,300
Nevada	16,000	1,700	15,700	2,900	8,600	2,700

[a] *Note:* In current thousands of dollars.
Source: U.S. House of Representatives, Statistics of Mines and Mining in the States and Territories West of the Rocky Mountains, Executive Document 177, 43d Congr., 2d Sess. (1874); U.S. Department of the Treasury, Report of the Director of the Mint (1881); id. (1891); and U.S. Department of the Interior, Abstract of the Eleventh Census, 1890, at 69 (1894).

The fourth reason for the rapid agreement on mineral rights was that most of the contracting parties expected a share in the aggregate gains from establishing property rights. This expectation appears to have been due to two factors. One was that the valuable ore deposits were believed to be extensive relative to the number of claimants. Second, * * * there was a political consensus in the United States that federal land should be distributed quickly and at low cost to individuals on an egalitarian basis (Gates, 1968). Although the federal laws focused on agriculture and did not specifically address mineral rights, in dividing mineral lands and assigning them to individual claimants, miners were following well-established practices in claiming a share of the federal estate. Not only did federal land policy establish a general right to claim land, but it set precedents for a relatively equal distribution of holdings.

The emphasis on an egalitarian distribution is reflected in mining camp restrictions on the size of individual claims and in the requirement that holdings could be maintained only with continued development. There was to be no hoarding or monopoly control of mining districts, at least in early development. Unworked claims were considered abandoned and open for other claimants. Further, the number of claims held by each individual prospector was limited to one, with multiple claims given as a reward only to the discoverer of the local mining district. As rights were formalized and exchanged in a district and as the scale of mining increased, particularly for deep-vein ore deposits, consolidation of private mineral claims occurred. Nevertheless, the staking of new claims in other areas remained subject to the egalitarian restrictions of the mining camp rules. * * *

[T]he lack of divisive conflict over the allocation of private mineral rights was due in part to the frontier environment and optimism which existed in the midnineteenth century. * * *

The miners who rushed to the Far West after 1848 were part of the general transfer of federal lands to private claimants that characterized American economic development in the eighteenth and nineteenth centuries. Until the late nineteenth century, federal land was seen as a source of great opportunity for individual advancement and the overall development of both the American society and its economy. The more or less piecemeal distribution of land to new farmers and the avoidance of large concentrations of ownership seem to have been viewed as critical for forming a cohesive society. The widespread distribution of federal land also offered important political benefits to members of Congress who could use land policy to fashion supportive constituents among groups of voters. The practices used in allocating agricultural land helped to form individual expectations for the later claiming of federal mineral land. * * *

The enormous extent of federal lands in the midnineteenth century and the optimism they helped to foster for projected individual and general economic advancement served to offset distributional concerns and conflicts. These conditions provided a political basis for the rapid assignment of private mineral rights on remote western lands. * * *

Miners established locally accepted rules for assigning private mineral rights, but until, 1866, there were no provisions for the federal government to recognize those rules. The policy of the federal government since 1785 had been to retain title to its mineral lands in order to extract rents from them. Congress required that the new states created in the West accept its ownership of mineral lands, and such lands were expressly not included in the General Preemption Act of 1841 and other laws designed to transfer agricultural land. Instead, Congress experimented with leasing mineral lands when copper and lead deposits were discovered in the Midwest. High enforcement costs, however, led to the abandonment of leasing and to the sale of land with lead and copper deposits in 1846 and 1847. Prior to the California gold discoveries beginning in 1848, there was no information to suggest that federal mineral lands were very extensive.

The reservation of ownership of mineral land by the federal government, however, was put to test with the California discoveries. As thousands of miners hurried to the region and staked private claims to the land, the new U.S. military governor at Monterey unsuccessfully attempted to evict them. Many of his soldiers deserted for the mines, and given the remoteness of ore strikes relative to the rest of the country, there was little the federal government could do at the time to maintain its claims. Under these conditions, miners were left to assign private squatters' rights within the mining camps in a manner similar to the division of federal agricultural lands through claims clubs and other arrangements (Gates, 1968). These mining camp rules became the basis for the subsequent development of both private placer (surface) and deep-vein mining. With the importance of mining in the economies of western territories and states and the political demand for security of tenure, legislatures and courts gave rapid legal support to the mining camp rules by incorporating them into statutes and judicial rulings. Although the statehood acts admitting California and Nevada to the Union in 1850 and 1864, respectively, reaffirmed federal ownership of the mineral lands, there was no interference by Congress with local mining arrangements.

After 1864, however, the position of Congress changed as it considered various bills to seize and to sell the western mineral lands as a means of raising funds to reduce the large Civil War debt. Various tax measures on bullion also were contemplated. These threats to the established mineral rights structure led to lobby activity by the mining industry and by western legislatures to block federal action. For example, on May 20, 1864, the San Francisco Chamber of Commerce sent a memorial to Congress voicing its "surprise and alarm" at the various proposals to seize or tax the mines (San Francisco *Alta California,* May 20, 1864). Other efforts were mounted to secure federal legislation to recognize mining camp allocations and to authorize private patenting of mineral lands.

In 1866, the first federal mineral rights law authorizing the transfer of title to private claimants was passed in Congress through the sponsorship of Senator William Stewart of Nevada. Section 1 of the law dropped any royalty requirements and opened federal mineral lands to private claiming, subject to local mining camp rules. Sections 2 and 3 specified the procedures by which an individual could obtain title. In this way, the 1866 law ratified the distribution of ownership authorized by local mining camp rules. The provisions of the law were kept intact in the Mining Law of 1872, which remains in effect for patenting private hard rock mineral claims on federal land.

NOTES AND QUESTIONS

1. Notice the complex sources of mining law. Discovery remains the core principle of the system. But custom, ideology, geography, patterns established in disposing of other resources, and interest group politics all interact to produce the rules for establishing claims and resolving disputes. Despite recurring efforts to achieve reform, the scheme reflected in the Mining Act of 1872 continues to govern mining on federal land to this day. For competing perspectives, see John D. Leshy, The Mining Law: A Study in Perpetual Motion (1987); Andrew P. Morriss et al., Homesteading Rock: A Defense of Free Access Under the General Mining Act of 1872, 34 Envtl. L. 745 (2004).

2.   Libecap at several points in the excerpt emphasizes the importance of relatively equal opportunities for acquiring claims, and relative equality in the size of shares, as variables that help to explain how the system of mining claims worked without undue violence or turmoil. Do you think this observation generalizes to other original acquisition schemes as well? Does the equality of opportunity here reflect the emergence of efficient norms in a close-knit community? Or is it an example of norms of fairness trumping efficiency considerations? For a variety of additional views, see, e.g., David D. Haddock, Force, Threat, Negotiation: The Private Enforcement of Rights, in Property Rights: Cooperation, Conflict, and Law (Terry L. Anderson & Fred. S. McChesney eds., 2003); Andrea G. McDowell, From Commons to Claims: Property Rights in the California Gold Rush, 14 Yale J.L. & Hum. 1 (2002); Richard O. Zerbe Jr. & C. Leigh Anderson, Culture and Fairness in the Development of Institutions in the California Gold Fields, 61 J. Econ. Hist. 114 (2001).

C.   CREATION

A third principle used to establish original ownership is <u>creation</u>. This principle applies primarily to property in the form of information. Persons who create new information are (sometimes) rewarded with a right to exclude others from using the information, and this exclusion right is called <u>intellectual property</u>. As technological innovation accelerates and is disseminated more quickly throughout the world, property rights in information are becoming increasingly important to the U.S. and world economies, and are commanding an increasing share of legal attention and resources, compared to tangible property.

Property rights in information are different from property rights in tangible goods in important ways. Perhaps most significantly, although information can be costly to produce, the marginal post-production cost of copying or reproducing it is zero (or close to it). Moreover, use of the information by one consumer does not diminish the use by another; in this sense, information is what economists call a "nonrival" good. Thus, the primary reason for creating property rights in information is to provide incentives for producing more of it, not to assure that it is allocated efficiently among potential users of it.

Information = "non-riva" good Use by one does diminish The use by another

Intellectual property rights are today governed primarily by complicated statutory regimes adopted by the U.S. Congress. The principal regimes are patent which applies to new, useful, and nonobvious inventions; copyright, which applies to original works of authorship; and trademark, which applies to words or symbols that identify commercial enterprises, goods, and services. It would take us too far afield to study any one of these statutory regimes, let alone all three, in any detail in an introductory course in property. Instead, we will include cases and materials that arise out of intellectual property controversies throughout the course where they illustrate or present problems that are characteristic of property rights more generally. In this section, which deals with the principle of establishing title by creation, we will concentrate primarily on rights in information that have a common-law basis.

1. MISAPPROPRIATION AND THE QUASI-PROPERTY RIGHT IN HOT NEWS

𝒟   𝓅

International News Service v. Associated Press

Supreme Court of the United States, 1918.
248 U.S. 215.

■ MR. JUSTICE PITNEY delivered the opinion of the Court. The parties are competitors in the gathering and distribution of news and its publication for profit in newspapers throughout the United States. The Associated Press, which was complainant in the District Court, is a co-operative organization, incorporated under the Membership Corporations Law of the state of New York, its members being individuals who are either proprietors or representatives of about 950 daily newspapers published in all parts of the United States. * * * Complainant gathers in all parts of the world, by means of various instrumentalities of its own, by exchange with its members, and by other appropriate means, news and intelligence of current and recent events of interest to newspaper readers and distributes it daily to its members for publication in their newspapers. The cost of the service, amounting approximately to $3,500,000 per annum, is assessed upon the members and becomes a part of their costs of operation, to be recouped, presumably with profit, through the publication of their several newspapers. Under complainant's by-laws each member agrees upon assuming membership that news received through complainant's service is received exclusively for publication in a particular newspaper, language, and place specified in the certificate of membership, that no other use of it shall be permitted, and that no member shall furnish or permit any one in his employ or connected with his newspaper to furnish any of complainant's news in advance of publication to any person not a member. And each member is required to gather the local news of his district and supply it to the Associated Press and to no one else.

Defendant is a corporation organized under the laws of the state of New Jersey, whose business is the gathering and selling of news to its customers and clients, consisting of newspapers published throughout the United States, under contracts by which they pay certain amounts at stated times for defendant's service. It has widespread news-gathering agencies; the cost of its operations amounts, it is said, to more than $2,000,000 per annum; and it serves about 400 newspapers located in the various cities of the United States and abroad, a few of which are represented, also, in the membership of the Associated Press.

The parties are in the keenest competition between themselves in the distribution of news throughout the United States; and so, as a rule, are the newspapers that they serve, in their several districts.

Complainant in its bill, defendant in its answer, have set forth in almost identical terms the rather obvious circumstances and conditions under which their business is conducted. The value of the service, and of the news furnished, depends upon the promptness of transmission, as well as upon the accuracy and impartiality of the news; it being essential that the news be transmitted to members or subscribers as early or earlier than similar information can be furnished to competing newspapers by other news services, and that the news furnished by each agency shall not be furnished to newspapers which do not contribute to the expense of gathering it. * * *

The bill was filed to restrain the pirating of complainant's news by defendant in three ways: First, by bribing employes of newspapers published by complainant's members to furnish Associated Press news to defendant before publication, for transmission by telegraph and telephone to defendant's clients for publication by them; second, by inducing Associated Press members to violate its by-laws and permit defendant to obtain news before publication; and, third, by copying news from bulletin boards and from early editions of complainant's newspapers and selling this, either bodily or after rewriting it, to defendant's customers.

Offense in question →

The District Court, upon consideration of the bill and answer, with voluminous affidavits on both sides, granted a preliminary injunction under the first and second heads, but refused at that stage to restrain the systematic practice admittedly pursued by defendant, of taking news bodily from the bulletin boards and early editions of complainant's newspapers and selling it as its own. * * *

The only matter that has been argued before us is whether defendant may lawfully be restrained from appropriating news taken from bulletins issued by complainant or any of its members, or from newspapers published by them, for the purpose of selling it to defendant's clients. Complainant asserts that defendant's admitted course of conduct in this regard both violates complainant's property right in the news and constitutes unfair competition in business. And notwithstanding the case has proceeded only to the stage of a preliminary injunction, we have deemed it proper to consider the underlying questions, since they go to the very merits of the action and are presented upon facts that are not in dispute. As presented in argument, these questions are: 1. Whether there is any property in news; 2. Whether, if there be property in news collected for the purpose of being published, it survives the instant of its publication in the first newspaper to which it is communicated by the news-gatherer; and 3. whether defendant's admitted course of conduct in appropriating for commercial use matter taken from bulletins or early editions of Associated Press publications constitutes unfair competition in trade.

The federal jurisdiction was invoked because of diversity of citizenship, not upon the ground that the suit arose under the copyright or other laws of the United States. Complainant's news matter is not copyrighted. It is said that it could not, in practice, be copyrighted, because of the large number of dispatches that are sent daily; and, according to complainant's contention, news is not within the operation of the copyright act. Defendant, while apparently conceding this, nevertheless invokes the analogies of the law of literary property and copyright, insisting as its principal contention that, assuming complainant has a right of property in its news, it can be maintained (unless the copyright act be complied with) only by being kept secret and confidential, and that upon the publication with complainant's consent of uncopyrighted news of any of complainant's members in a newspaper or upon a bulletin board, the right of property is lost, and the subsequent use of the news by the public or by defendant for any purpose whatever becomes lawful. * * *

In considering the general question of property in news matter, it is necessary to recognize its dual character, distinguishing between the substance of the information and the particular form or collocation of words in which the writer has communicated it.

No doubt news articles often possess a literary quality, and are the subject of literary property at the common law; nor do we question that such an article, as a literary production, is the subject of copyright by the terms of the act as it now stands. * * *

But the news element—the information respecting current events contained in the literary production—is not the creation of the writer, but is a report of matters that ordinarily are *publici juris*; it is the history of the day. It is not to be supposed that the framers of the Constitution, when they empowered Congress "to promote the progress of science and useful arts, by securing for limited times to authors and inventors the exclusive right to their respective writings and discoveries" (Const. art. 1, § 8, par. 8), intended to confer upon one who might happen to be the first to report a historic event the exclusive right for any period to spread the knowledge of it.

We need spend no time, however, upon the general question of property in news matter at common law, or the application of the copyright act, since it seems to us the case must turn upon the question of unfair competition in business. * * * We are dealing here not with restrictions upon publication but with the very facilities and processes of publication. The peculiar value of news is in the spreading of it while it is fresh; and it is evident that a valuable property interest in the news, as news, cannot be maintained by keeping it secret. Besides, except for matters improperly disclosed, or published in breach of trust or confidence, or in violation of law, none of which is involved in this branch of the case, the news of current events may be regarded as common property. What we are concerned with is the business of making it known to the world, in which both parties to the present suit are engaged. That business consists in maintaining a prompt, sure, steady, and reliable service designed to place the daily events of the world at the breakfast table of the millions at a price that, while of trifling moment to each reader, is sufficient in the aggregate to afford compensation for the cost of gathering and distributing it, with the added profit so necessary as an incentive to effective action in the commercial world. The service thus performed for newspaper readers is not only innocent but extremely useful in itself, and indubitably constitutes a legitimate business. The parties are competitors in this field; and, on fundamental principles, applicable here as elsewhere, when the rights or privileges of the one are liable to conflict with those of the other, each party is under a duty so to conduct its own business as not unnecessarily or unfairly to injure that of the other.

Obviously, the question of what is unfair competition in business must be determined with particular reference to the character and circumstances of the business. The question here is not so much the rights of either party as against the public but their rights as between themselves. And, although we may and do assume that neither party has any remaining property interest as against the public in uncopyrighted news matter after the moment of its first publication, it by no means follows that there is no remaining property interest in it as between themselves. For, to both of them alike, news matter, however little susceptible of ownership or dominion in the absolute sense, is stock in trade, to be gathered at the cost of enterprise, organization, skill, labor, and money, and to be distributed and sold to those who will pay money for it, as for any other merchandise. Regarding the news, therefore, as but the material out of which both parties are seeking to make profits at the same time and in the same field, we hardly can fail to recognize that for this purpose, and as between them, it must be regarded as *quasi* property, irrespective of the rights of either as against the public.

In order to sustain the jurisdiction of equity over the controversy, we need not affirm any general and absolute property in the news as such. The rule that a court of equity concerns itself only in the protection of property rights treats any civil right of a pecuniary nature as a property right (In re Sawyer, 124 U.S. 200, 210; In re Debs, 158 U.S. 564, 593); and the right to acquire property by honest labor or the conduct of a lawful business is as much entitled to protection as the right to guard property already acquired (Truax v. Raich, 239 U.S. 33, 37–38 (1916); Brennan v. United Hatters, 65 Atl. 165, 171–72 (N.J.); Barr v. Essex Trades Council, 30 Atl. 881 (N.J. Ch.)). It is this right that furnishes the basis of the jurisdiction in the ordinary case of unfair competition. * * *

The peculiar features of the case arise from the fact that, while novelty and freshness form so important an element in the success of the business, the very processes of distribution and publication necessarily occupy a good deal of time. Complainant's service, as well as defendant's, is a daily service to daily newspapers; most of the foreign news reaches this country at the Atlantic seaboard, principally at the city of New York, and because of this, and of time differentials due to the earth's rotation, the distribution of news matter throughout the country is principally from east to west; and, since in speed the telegraph and telephone easily outstrip the rotation of the earth, it is a simple matter for defendant to take complainant's news from bulletins or early editions of complainant's members in the eastern cities and at the mere cost of telegraphic transmission cause it to be published in western papers issued at least as early as those served by complainant. Besides this, and irrespective of time differentials, irregularities in telegraphic transmission on different lines, and the normal consumption of time in printing and distributing the newspaper, result in permitting pirated news to be placed in the hands of defendant's readers sometimes simultaneously with the service of competing Associated Press papers, occasionally even earlier.

Defendant insists that when, with the sanction and approval of complainant, and as the result of the use of its news for the very purpose for which it is distributed, a portion of complainant's members communicate it to the general public by posting it upon bulletin boards so that all may read, or by issuing it to newspapers and distributing it indiscriminately, complainant no longer has the right to control the use to be made of it; that when it thus reaches the light of day it becomes the common possession of all to whom it is accessible; and that any purchaser of a newspaper has the right to communicate the intelligence which it contains to anybody and for any purpose, even for the purpose of selling it for profit to newspapers published for profit in competition with complainant's members.

The fault in the reasoning lies in applying as a test the right of the complainant as against the public, instead of considering the rights of complainant and defendant, competitors in business, as between themselves. The right of the purchaser of a single newspaper to spread knowledge of its contents gratuitously, for any legitimate purpose not unreasonably interfering with complainant's right to make merchandise of it, may be admitted; but to transmit that news for commercial use, in competition with complainant—which is what defendant has done and seeks to justify—is a very different matter. In doing this defendant, by its very act, admits that it is taking material that has been acquired by complainant as the result of organization and the expenditure of labor, skill, and money, and which is salable by complainant for money, and that defendant in appropriating it and selling it as its own is endeavoring to reap where it has not sown, and by disposing of it to newspapers that are competitors of complainant's members is appropriating to itself the harvest of those who have sown. Stripped of all disguises, the process amounts to an unauthorized interference with the normal operation of complainant's legitimate business precisely at the point where the profit is to be reaped, in order to divert a material portion of the profit from those who have earned it to those who have not; with special advantage to defendant in the competition because of the fact that it is not burdened with any part of the expense of gathering the news. The transaction speaks for itself and a court of equity ought not to hesitate long in characterizing it as unfair competition in business. * * *

It is no answer to say that complainant spends its money for that which is too fugitive or evanescent to be the subject of property. That might, and for the purposes of the discussion we are assuming that it would furnish an answer in a common-law controversy. But in a court of equity, where the question is one of unfair competition, if that which complainant has acquired fairly at substantial cost may be sold fairly at substantial

RULE

RULE

The test in this sort of situation seems to be that, when taken to the extreme (or some far limit), if D's actions result in the loss of profitability for the industry in question (and thus, its collapse), the the actions can be considered "unfair competition"

How this will be applied in practice

Misappropriation — sells another's goods as one's own
Misrepresentation — sells one's own goods as those of another

profit, a competitor who is misappropriating it for the purpose of disposing of it to his own profit and to the disadvantage of complainant cannot be heard to say that it is too fugitive or evanescent to be regarded as property. It has all the attributes of property necessary for determining that a misappropriation of it by a competitor is unfair competition because contrary to good conscience. * * *

* * * Indeed, it is one of the most obvious results of defendant's theory that, by permitting indiscriminate publication by anybody and everybody for purposes of profit in competition with the news-gatherer, it would render publication profitless, or so little profitable as in effect to cut off the service by rendering the cost prohibitive in comparison with the return. * * *

It is to be observed that the view we adopt does not result in giving to complainant the right to monopolize either the gathering or the distribution of the news, or, without complying with the copyright act, to prevent the reproduction of its news articles, but only postpones participation by complainant's competitor in the processes of distribution and reproduction of news that it has not gathered, and only to the extent necessary to prevent that competitor from reaping the fruits of complainant's efforts and expenditure, to the partial exclusion of complainant, and in violation of the principle that underlies the maxim *sic utere tuo*, etc.

It is said that the elements of unfair competition are lacking because there is no attempt by defendant to palm off its goods as those of the complainant, characteristic of the most familiar, if not the most typical, cases of unfair competition. But we cannot concede that the right to equitable relief is confined to that class of cases. In the present case the fraud upon complainant's rights is more direct and obvious. Regarding news matter as the mere material from which these two competing parties are endeavoring to make money, and treating it, therefore, as *quasi* property for the purposes of their business because they are both selling it as such, defendant's conduct differs from the ordinary case of unfair competition in trade principally in this that, instead of selling its own goods as those of complainant, it substitutes misappropriation in the place of misrepresentation, and sells complainant's goods as its own.

Besides the misappropriation, there are elements of imitation, of false pretense, in defendant's practices. The device of rewriting complainant's news articles, frequently resorted to, carries its own comment. The habitual failure to give credit to complainant for that which is taken is significant. Indeed, the entire system of appropriating complainant's news and transmitting it as a commercial product to defendant's clients and patrons amounts to a false representation to them and to their newspaper readers that the news transmitted is the result of defendant's own investigation in the field. But these elements, although accentuating the wrong, are not the essence of it. It is something more than the advantage of celebrity of which complainant is being deprived. * * *

■ MR. JUSTICE HOLMES, dissenting. When an uncopyrighted combination of words is published there is no general right to forbid other people repeating them—in other words there is no property in the combination or in the thoughts or facts that the words express. Property, a creation of law, does not arise from value, although exchangeable—a matter of fact. Many exchangeable values may be destroyed intentionally without compensation. Property depends upon exclusion by law from interference, and a person is not excluded from using any combination of words merely because some one has used it before, even if it took labor and genius to make it. If a given person is to be prohibited from making the use of words that his neighbors are free to make[,] some other ground must be found. One such ground is vaguely expressed in the phrase fair trade. This means that the words are repeated by a competitor in business in such a way as to convey a misrepresentation that materially injures the person who first used them, by appropriating credit of some kind which the first user has earned. The ordinary case * * * is palming off the defendant's product as the plaintiff's but the same evil may follow from the opposite falsehood—from saying whether in words or by implication that the plaintiff's product is the defendant's, and that, it seems to me, is what has happened here. * * *

[I]n my view, the only ground of complaint that can be recognized without legislation is the implied misstatement[.] [I]t can be corrected by stating the truth; and a suitable acknowledgement of the source is all that the plaintiff can require. I think that within the limits recognized by the decision of the Court the defendant should be enjoined from publishing news obtained from the Associated Press for   hours after publication by the plaintiff unless it gives express credit to the Associated Press; the number of hours and the form of acknowledgment to be settled by the District Court.

■ MR. JUSTICE BRANDEIS, dissenting. * * * The sole question for our consideration is this: Was the International News Service properly enjoined from using, or causing to be used gainfully, news of which it acquired knowledge by lawful means (namely, by reading publicly posted bulletins or papers purchased by it in the open market) merely because the news had been originally gathered by the Associated Press and continued to be of value to some of its members, or because it did not reveal the source from which it was acquired? * * *

News is a report of recent occurrences. The business of the news agency is to gather systematically knowledge of such occurrences of interest and to distribute reports thereof. The Associated Press contended that knowledge so acquired is property, because it costs money and labor to produce and because it has value for which those who have it not are ready to pay; that it remains property and is entitled to protection as long as it has commercial value as news; and that to protect it effectively, the defendant must be enjoined from making, or causing to be made, any gainful use of it while it retains such value. An essential element of individual property is the legal right to exclude others from enjoying it. If the property is private, the right of exclusion may be absolute; if the property is affected with a public interest, the right of exclusion is qualified. But the fact that a product of the mind has cost its producer money

(on to next page)

and labor, and has a value for which others are willing to pay, is not sufficient to ensure to it this legal attribute of property. The general rule of law is, that the noblest of human productions—knowledge, truths ascertained, conceptions, and ideas—became, after voluntary communication to others, free as the air to common use. Upon these incorporeal productions the attribute of property is continued after such communication only in certain classes of cases where public policy has seemed to demand it. These exceptions are confined to productions which, in some degree, involve creation, invention, or discovery. But by no means all such are endowed with this attribute of property. The creations which are recognized as property by the common law are literary, dramatic, musical, and other artistic creations; and these have also protection under the copyright statutes. The inventions and discoveries upon which this attribute of property is conferred only by statute, are the few comprised within the patent law. There are also many other cases in which courts interfere to prevent curtailment of plaintiff's enjoyment of incorporeal productions; and in which the right to relief is often called a property right, but is such only in a special sense. In those cases, the plaintiff has no absolute right to the protection of his production; he has merely the qualified right to be protected as against the defendant's acts, because of the special relation in which the latter stands or the wrongful method or means employed in acquiring the knowledge or the manner in which it is used. Protection of this character is afforded where the suit is based upon breach of contract or of trust or upon unfair competition.

The knowledge for which protection is sought in the case at bar is not of a kind upon which the law has heretofore conferred the attributes of property; nor is the manner of its acquisition or use nor the purpose to which it is applied, such as has heretofore been recognized as entitling a plaintiff to relief. * * *

[T]he plaintiff does not contend that the posting was wrongful or that any papers were wrongfully issued by its subscribers. On the contrary it is conceded that both the bulletins and the papers were issued in accordance with the regulations of the plaintiff. Under such circumstances, for a reader of the papers purchased in the open market, or a reader of the bulletins publicly posted, to procure and use gainfully, information therein contained, does not involve inducing any one to commit a breach either of contract or of trust, or committing or in any way abetting a breach of confidence. * * *

Plaintiff further contended that defendant's practice constitutes unfair competition, because there is "appropriation without cost to itself of values created by" the plaintiff; and it is upon this ground that the decision of this court appears to be based. To appropriate and use for profit, knowledge and ideas produced by other men, without making compensation or even acknowledgment, may be inconsistent with a finer sense of propriety; but, with the exceptions indicated above, the law has heretofore sanctioned the practice. Thus it was held that one may ordinarily make and sell anything in any form, may copy with exactness that which another has produced, or may otherwise use his ideas without his consent and without the payment of compensation, and yet not inflict a legal injury; and that ordinarily one is at perfect liberty to find out, if he can by lawful means, trade secrets of another, however valuable, and then use the knowledge so acquired gainfully, although it cost the original owner much in effort and in money to collect or produce.

Such taking and gainful use of a product of another which, for reasons of public policy, the law has refused to endow with the attributes of property, does not become unlawful because the product happens to have been taken from a rival and is used in competition with him. The unfairness in competition which hitherto has been recognized by the law as a basis for relief, lay in the manner or means of conducting the business; and the manner or means held legally unfair, involves either fraud or force or the doing of acts otherwise prohibited by law. In the "passing off" cases (the typical and most common case of unfair competition), the wrong consists in fraudulently representing by word or act that defendant's goods are those of plaintiff. In the other cases, the diversion of trade was effected through physical or moral coercion, or by inducing breaches of contract or of trust or by enticing away employees. In some others, called cases of simulated competition, relief was granted because defendant's purpose was unlawful; namely, not competition but deliberate and wanton destruction of plaintiff's business.

That competition is not unfair in a legal sense, merely because the profits gained are unearned, even if made at the expense of a rival, is shown by many cases besides those referred to above. He who follows the pioneer into a new market, or who engages in the manufacture of an article newly introduced by another, seeks profits due largely to the labor and expense of the first adventurer; but the law sanctions, indeed encourages, the pursuit. * * *

[handwritten margin note: → Court has allowed "reaping" w/out "sowing"]

It is also suggested that the fact that defendant does not refer to the Associated Press as the source of the news may furnish a basis for the relief. But the defendant and its subscribers, unlike members of the Associated Press, were under no contractual obligation to disclose the source of the news; and there is no rule of law requiring acknowledgment to be made where uncopyrighted matter is reproduced. The International News Service is said to mislead its subscribers into believing that the news transmitted was originally gathered by it and that they in turn mislead their readers. There is, in fact, no representation by either of any kind. Sources of information are sometimes given because required by contract; sometimes because naming the source gives authority to an otherwise incredible statement; and sometimes the source is named because the agency does not wish to take the responsibility itself of giving currency to the news. But no representation can properly be implied from omission to mention the source of information except that the International News Service is transmitting news which it believes to be credible.

Nor is the use made by the International News Service of the information taken from papers or bulletins of Associated Press members legally objectionable by reason of the purpose for which it was employed. The acts here complained of were not done for the purpose of injuring the business of the Associated Press. Their purpose was not even to divert its trade, or to put it at a disadvantage by lessening defendant's necessary expenses. The purpose was merely to supply subscribers of the International News Service promptly with all available news. * * *

The great development of agencies now furnishing country-wide distribution of news, the vastness of our territory, and improvements in the means of transmitting intelligence, have made it possible for a news agency or newspapers to obtain, without paying compensation, the fruit of another's efforts and to use news so obtained gainfully in competition with the original collector. The injustice of such action is obvious. But to give relief against it would involve more than the application of existing rules of law to new facts. It would require the making of a new rule in analogy to existing ones. The unwritten law possesses capacity for growth; and has often satisfied new demands for justice by invoking analogies or by expanding a rule or principle. This process has been in the main wisely applied and should not be discontinued. Where the problem is relatively simple, as it is apt to be when private interests only are involved, it generally proves adequate. But with the increasing complexity of society, the public interest tends to become omnipresent; and the problems presented by new demands for justice cease to be simple. Then the creation or recognition by courts of a new private right may work serious injury to the general public, unless the boundaries of the right are definitely established and wisely guarded. In order to reconcile the new private right with the public interest, it may be necessary to prescribe limitations and rules for its enjoyment; and also to provide administrative machinery for enforcing the rules. It is largely for this reason that, in the effort to meet the many new demands for justice incident to a rapidly changing civilization, resort to legislation has latterly been had with increasing frequency.

The rule for which the plaintiff contends would effect an important extension of property rights and a corresponding curtailment of the free use of knowledge and of ideas; and the facts of this case admonish us of the danger involved in recognizing such a property right in news, without imposing upon news-gatherers corresponding obligations. A large majority of the newspapers and perhaps half the newspaper readers of the United States are dependent for their news of general interest upon agencies other than the Associated Press. The channel through which about 400 of these papers received, as the plaintiff alleges, "a large amount of news relating to the European war of the greatest importance and of intense interest to the newspaper reading public" was suddenly closed. The closing to the International News Service of these channels for foreign news (if they were closed) was due not to unwillingness on its part to pay the cost of collecting the news, but to the prohibitions imposed by foreign governments upon its securing news from their respective countries and from using cable or telegraph lines running therefrom. For aught that appears, this prohibition may have been wholly undeserved; and at all events the 400 papers and their readers may be assumed to have been innocent. For aught that appears, the International News Service may have sought then to secure temporarily by arrangement with the Associated Press the latter's foreign news service. For aught that appears, all of the 400 subscribers of the International News Service would gladly have then become members of the Associated Press, if they could have secured election thereto. It is possible, also, that a large part of the readers of these papers were so situated that they could not secure prompt access to papers served by the Associated Press. The prohibition of the foreign governments might as well have been extended to the channels through which news was supplied to the more than a thousand other daily papers in the United States not served by the Associated Press; and a large part of their readers may also be so located that they cannot procure prompt access to papers served by the Associated Press.

A Legislature, urged to enact a law by which one news agency or newspaper may prevent appropriation of the fruits of its labors by another, would consider such facts and possibilities and others which appropriate inquiry might disclose. Legislators might conclude that it was impossible to put an end to the obvious injustice involved in such appropriation of news, without opening the door to other evils, greater than that sought to be remedied. * * *

Courts are ill-equipped to make the investigations which should precede a determination of the limitations which should be set upon any property right in news or of the circumstances under which news gathered by a private agency should be deemed affected with a public interest. Courts would be powerless to prescribe the detailed regulations essential to full enjoyment of the rights conferred or to introduce the machinery required for enforcement of such regulations. Considerations such as these should lead us to decline to establish a new rule of law in the effort to redress a newly disclosed wrong, although the propriety of some remedy appears to be clear.

NOTES AND QUESTIONS

1. The majority says that in order to sustain the injunction, "we need not affirm any general and absolute property in the news as such." Do you agree? Does the principle that underlies the injunction establish an in personam right running against one entity (International News) in favor of another (Associated Press)? Or is it a more general right in rem that binds all the world? Whatever the Supreme Court thought it was doing, lower courts have relied on the decision to create what amounts to a common-law right to exclude others from time-sensitive information that the plaintiff has produced with some effort. See, e.g., National Basketball Association v. Motorola, Inc., 105 F.3d 841 (2d Cir. 1997); Board of Trade of Chicago v. Dow Jones & Co., 456 N.E.2d 84 (Ill. 1983).

2. *International News* is a leading judicial statement—perhaps *the* leading statement—of the idea that property rights should be based on desert, that one should not be allowed to reap where another has sown.

[handwritten margin note: Exactly what dissent was warning of — rules have been set even w/ possibility of judicial incompetence causing rules to be inefficient in practice.]

This is generally associated with John Locke's labor theory of property, briefly described in the first note after *Pierson v. Post*, as opposed to theories based on utility, autonomy, or personhood. Scholars and judges, however, are deeply divided over the foundational principle of intellectual property rights. Are such rights based on protection of the labor and desert of those who create such rights—artists, inventors, or gatherers of hot news? Or are they grounded in the social utility created by providing incentives designed to stimulate the production of new and valuable works, inventions, and information? Compare Douglas G. Baird, Common Law Intellectual Property and the Legacy of *International News Service v. Associated Press*, 50 U. Chi. L. Rev. 411 (1983) (arguing that the law provides for no general reap-what-you-sow principle) with Wendy J. Gordon, On Owning Information: Intellectual Property and the Restitutionary Impulse, 78 Va. L. Rev. 149 (1992) (arguing that intellectual property is consistent with principles behind the law of restitution).

3.   Is *International News* an application of the principle of unfair competition, recognized in *Keeble v. Hickeringill*, supra? Is it an application of the idea of restitution for unjust enrichment, considered in conjunction with *Producers Lumber & Supply v. Olney Building Co.*, reproduced in Chapter I?

4.   Why couldn't the Associated Press solve its problem by copyright? Under the 1909 Copyright Act in effect when the *International News* case arose, certain notice-giving formalities were required ("Copyright" or an abbreviation and the name of the copyright holder in prescribed places) as well as registration at the Copyright Office. The Associated Press could not comply with the registration requirements before the newspapers were distributed. Since U.S. ratification of the Berne Convention in 1988, no notice is required for protection of original works. Hence, at least insofar as the International News Service was copying the text of AP stories (as opposed to reporting on the information they contained), the problem in *International News* could be solved by copyright protection today. The formalities are still relevant, but only because they confer certain evidentiary advantages. See id. § 401(d). Registration is not required but likewise confers certain advantages. Id. § 412.

5.   Another cluster of issues in the *INS* case centers on the role of custom. What if it were true that news organizations had a custom of respecting each other's claims to hot news? Should a court then enforce this custom? For an argument in the affirmative, see Richard A. Epstein, *International News Service v. Associated Press*: Custom and Law as Sources of Property Rights in News, 78 Va. L. Rev. 85 (1992).

6.   A final issue of importance concerns which institution in society— the courts or the legislature—should decide whether to provide legal protection against misappropriation of hot news. The issue is especially important for intellectual property, but applies in principle to any question about whether to create a new type of property right. Justice Brandeis gives some reasons for preferring the legislature to make these sorts of decisions. What might be the arguments in favor of allowing courts to make

the decision (subject, presumably, to revision by the legislature)? For general discussion of the criteria for choosing between courts and legislatures in resolving social policy questions, see Neil K. Komesar, Imperfect Alternatives: Choosing Institutions in Law, Economics, and Public Policy (1994). For discussion focused on which institution should recognize new property rights, see Thomas W. Merrill & Henry E. Smith, Optimal Standardization in the Law of Property: The *Numerus Clausus* Principle, 110 Yale L.J. 1, 58–68 (2000).

2.   THE RIGHT OF PUBLICITY

Another area in which the courts have been unusually active in creating new property-like rights is the right of publicity.

P   *D*

Midler v. Ford Motor Company

United States Court of Appeal for the Ninth Circuit, 1988.
849 F.2d 460.

■ NOONAN, CIRCUIT JUDGE: This case centers on the protectibility of the voice of a celebrated chanteuse from commercial exploitation without her consent. Ford Motor Company and its advertising agency, Young & Rubicam, Inc., in 1985 advertised the Ford Lincoln Mercury with a series of nineteen 30 or 60 second television commercials in what the agency called "The Yuppie Campaign." The aim was to make an emotional connection with Yuppies, bringing back memories of when they were in college. Different popular songs of the seventies were sung on each commercial. The agency tried to get "the original people," that is, the singers who had popularized the songs, to sing them. Failing in that endeavor in ten cases the agency had the songs sung by "sound alikes." Bette Midler, the plaintiff and appellant here, was done by a sound alike.

Midler is a nationally known actress and singer. She won a Grammy as early as 1973 as the Best New Artist of that year. Records made by her since then have gone Platinum and Gold. She was nominated in 1979 for an Academy award for Best Female Actress in The Rose, in which she portrayed a pop singer. Newsweek in its June 30, 1986 issue described her as an "outrageously original singer/comedian." Time hailed her in its March 2, 1987 issue as "a legend" and "the most dynamic and poignant singer-actress of her time."

When Young & Rubicam was preparing the Yuppie Campaign it presented the commercial to its client by playing an edited version of Midler singing "Do You Want To Dance," taken from the 1973 Midler album, "The Divine Miss M." After the client accepted the idea and form of the commercial, the agency contacted Midler's manager, Jerry Edelstein. The conversation went as follows: "Hello, I am Craig Hazen from Young and Rubicam. I am calling you to find out if Bette Midler would be interested in doing ...?" Edelstein: "Is it a commercial?" "Yes." "We are not interested."

Undeterred, Young & Rubicam sought out Ula Hedwig whom it knew to have been one of "the Harlettes" a backup singer for Midler for ten years. Hedwig was told by Young & Rubicam that "they wanted someone who could sound like Bette Midler's recording of [Do You Want To Dance]." She was asked to make a "demo" tape of the song if she was interested. She made an a capella demo and got the job.

At the direction of Young & Rubicam, Hedwig then made a record for the commercial. The Midler record of "Do You Want To Dance" was first played to her. She was told to "sound as much as possible like the Bette Midler record," leaving out only a few "aahs" unsuitable for the commercial. Hedwig imitated Midler to the best of her ability.

After the commercial was aired Midler was told by "a number of people" that it "sounded exactly" like her record of "Do You Want To Dance." Hedwig was told by "many personal friends" that they thought it was Midler singing the commercial. Ken Fritz, a personal manager in the entertainment business not associated with Midler, declares by affidavit that he heard the commercial on more than one occasion and thought Midler was doing the singing.

Neither the name nor the picture of Midler was used in the commercial; Young & Rubicam had a license from the copyright holder to use the song. At issue in this case is only the protection of Midler's voice. The district court described the defendants' conduct as that "of the average thief." They decided, "If we can't buy it, we'll take it." The court nonetheless believed there was no legal principle preventing imitation of Midler's voice and so gave summary judgment for the defendants. Midler appeals.

The First Amendment protects much of what the media do in the reproduction of likenesses or sounds. A primary value is freedom of speech and press. Time, Inc. v. Hill, 385 U.S. 374, 388 (1967). The purpose of the media use of a person's identity is central. If the purpose is "informative or cultural" the use is immune; "if it serves no such function but merely exploits the individual portrayed, immunity will not be granted." Felcher and Rubin, Privacy, Publicity and the Portrayal of Real People by the Media, 88 Yale L.J. 1577, 1596 (1979). Moreover, federal copyright law preempts much of the area. "Mere imitation of a recorded performance would not constitute a copyright infringement even where one performer deliberately sets out to simulate another's performance as exactly as possible." Notes of Committee on the Judiciary, 17 U.S.C.A. § 114(b). It is in the context of these First Amendment and federal copyright distinctions that we address the present appeal.

Nancy Sinatra once sued Goodyear Tire and Rubber Company on the basis of an advertising campaign by Young & Rubicam featuring "These Boots Are Made For Walkin'," a song closely identified with her; the female singers of the commercial were alleged to have imitated her voice and style and to have dressed and looked like her. The basis of Nancy Sinatra's complaint was unfair competition; she claimed that the song and the arrangement had acquired "a secondary meaning" which, under California law, was protectible. This court noted that the defendants "had paid a very substantial sum to the copyright proprietor to obtain the license for the use of the song and all of its arrangements." To give Sinatra damages for their use of the song would clash with federal copyright law. Summary judgment for the defendants was affirmed. Sinatra v. Goodyear Tire & Rubber Co., 435 F.2d 711, 717–718 (9th Cir. 1970). If Midler were claiming a secondary meaning to "Do You Want To Dance," or seeking to prevent the defendants from using that song, she would fail like Sinatra. But that is not this case. Midler does not seek damages for Ford's use of "Do You Want To Dance," and thus her claim is not preempted by federal copyright law. Copyright protects "original works of authorship fixed in any tangible medium of expression." 17 U.S.C. § 102(a). A voice is not copyrightable. The sounds are not "fixed." What is put forward as protectible here is more personal than any work of authorship.

Bert Lahr once sued Adell Chemical Co. for selling Lestoil by means of a commercial in which an imitation of Lahr's voice accompanied a cartoon of a duck. Lahr alleged that his style of vocal delivery was distinctive in pitch, accent, inflection, and sounds. The First Circuit held that Lahr had stated a cause of action for unfair competition, that it could be found "that defendant's conduct saturated plaintiff's audience, curtailing his market." Lahr v. Adell Chemical Co., 300 F.2d 256, 259 (1st Cir. 1962). That case is more like this one. But we do not find unfair competition here. One-minute commercials of the sort the defendants put on would not have saturated Midler's audience and curtailed her market. Midler did not do television commercials. The defendants were not in competition with her. See Halicki v. United Artists Communications, Inc., 812 F.2d 1213 (9th Cir. 1987).

California Civil Code section 3344 is also of no aid to Midler. The statute affords damages to a person injured by another who uses the person's "name, voice, signature, photograph or likeness, in any manner." The defendants did not use Midler's name or anything else whose use is prohibited by the statute. The voice they used was Hedwig's, not hers. The term "likeness" refers to a visual image not a vocal imitation. The statute, however, does not preclude Midler from pursuing any cause of action she may have at common law; the statute itself implies that such common law causes of action do exist because it says its remedies are merely "cumulative." Id. § 3344(g).

The companion statute protecting the use of a deceased person's name, voice, signature, photograph or likeness states that the rights it recognizes are "property rights." Id. § 990(b). By analogy the common law rights are also property rights. Appropriation of such common law rights is a tort in California. Motschenbacher v. R.J. Reynolds Tobacco Co., 498 F.2d 821 (9th Cir. 1974). In that case what the defendants used in their television commercial for Winston cigarettes was a photograph of a famous professional racing driver's racing car. The number of the car was changed and a wing-like device known as a "spoiler" was attached to the car; the car's features of white pinpointing, an oval medallion, and solid red coloring were retained. The driver, Lothar Motschenbacher, was in the car but his features were not visible. Some persons, viewing the commercial, correctly inferred that the car was his and that he was in the car and was therefore endorsing the product. The defendants were held to have invaded a "proprietary interest" of Motschenbacher in his own identity. Id. at 825.

Midler's case is different from Motschenbacher's. He and his car were physically used by the tobacco company's ad; he made part of his living out of giving commercial endorsements. But, as Judge Koelsch expressed it in *Motschenbacher*, California will recognize an injury from "an appropriation of the attributes of one's identity." Id. at 824. It was irrelevant that Motschenbacher could not be identified in the ad. The ad suggested that it was he. The ad did so by emphasizing signs or symbols associated with him. In the same way the defendants here used an imitation to convey the impression that Midler was singing for them.

Why did the defendants ask Midler to sing if her voice was not of value to them? Why did they studiously acquire the services of a sound-alike and instruct her to imitate Midler if Midler's voice was not of value to them? What they sought was an attribute of Midler's identity. Its value was what the market would have paid for Midler to have sung the commercial in person.

A voice is more distinctive and more personal than the automobile accouterments protected in *Motschenbacher*. A voice is as distinctive and personal as a face. The human voice is one of the most palpable ways identity is manifested. We are all aware that a friend is at once known by a few words on the phone. At a philosophical level it has been observed that with the sound of a voice, "the other stands before me." D. Ihde, Listening and Voice 77 (1976). A fortiori, these observations hold true of singing, especially singing by a singer of renown. The singer manifests herself in the song. To impersonate her voice is to pirate her identity. See W. Keeton, D. Dobbs, R. Keeton, D. Owen, Prosser & Keeton on Torts 852 (5th ed. 1984).

We need not and do not go so far as to hold that every imitation of a voice to advertise merchandise is actionable. We hold only that when a distinctive voice of a professional singer is widely known and is deliberately imitated in order to sell a product, the sellers have appropriated what is not theirs and have committed a tort in California. Midler has made a showing, sufficient to defeat summary judgment, that the defendants here for their own profit in selling their product did appropriate part of her identity.

Reversed and remanded for trial.

NOTES AND QUESTIONS

1. Slightly more than half of the 27 states recognizing the right of publicity have done so at least initially as a matter of judicial lawmaking. For new types of property, this is unusual; legislatures typically take the lead in adding to, subtracting from, and making major modifications to the basic set of property rights under law. Which institution, legislatures or courts, is the better arena for deciding whether and to what extent to recognize rights of publicity?

2. Many have decried the expansive sweep of some states' right of publicity. In one notable example the Ninth Circuit overturned a grant of summary judgment against Vanna White, who had claimed that an ad based on attempted humor, which included a robot in a dress turning letters on a board made up to resemble the one in the television show *Wheel of Fortune*, violated her common-law right of publicity. In a vigorous dissent from a denial of rehearing en banc, Judge Kozinski had this to say:

* * * The majority isn't, in fact, preventing the "evisceration" of Vanna White's existing rights; it's creating a new and much broader property right, a right unknown in California law. It's replacing the existing balance between the interests of the celebrity and those of the public by a different balance, one substantially more favorable to the celebrity. Instead of having an exclusive right in her name, likeness, signature or voice, every famous person now has an exclusive right to anything that reminds the viewer of her. After all, that's all Samsung did: It used an inanimate object to remind people of White, to "evoke [her identity]." 971 F.2d at 1399.

Consider how sweeping this new right is. What is it about the ad that makes people think of White? It's not the robot's wig, clothes or jewelry; there must be ten million blond women (many of them quasi-famous) who wear dresses and jewelry like White's. It's that the robot is posed near the "Wheel of Fortune" game board. Remove the game board from the ad, and no one would think of Vanna White. But once you include the game board, anybody standing beside it—a brunette woman, a man wearing women's clothes, a monkey in a wig and gown—would evoke White's image, precisely the way the robot did. It's the "Wheel of Fortune" set, not the robot's face or dress or jewelry that evokes White's image. The panel is giving White an exclusive right not in what she looks like or who she is, but in what she does for a living.

This is entirely the wrong place to strike the balance. Intellectual property rights aren't free: They're imposed at the expense of future creators and of the public at large. Where would we be if Charles Lindbergh had an exclusive right in the concept of a heroic solo aviator? If Arthur Conan Doyle had gotten a copyright in the idea of the detective story, or Albert Einstein had patented the theory of relativity? If every author and celebrity had been given the right to keep people from mocking them or their work? Surely this would have made the world poorer, not richer, culturally as well as economically.

This is why intellectual property law is full of careful balances between what's set aside for the owner and what's left in the public domain for the rest of us: The relatively short life of patents; the longer, but finite, life of copyrights; copyright's idea-expression dichotomy; the fair use doctrine; the prohibition on copyrighting facts; the compulsory license of television broadcasts and musical compositions; federal preemption of overbroad state intellectual property laws; the nominative use doctrine in trademark law; the right to make sound-alike recordings. All of these diminish an intellectual property owner's rights. All let the public use something created by someone else. But all are necessary to maintain a free environment in which creative genius can flourish.

The intellectual property right created by the panel here has none of these essential limitations: No fair use exception; no right to parody; no idea-expression dichotomy. It impoverishes the public domain, to the detriment of future creators and the public at large. Instead of well-defined, limited characteristics such as name, likeness or voice, advertisers will now have to cope with vague claims of "appropriation of identity," claims often made by people with a wholly exaggerated sense of their own fame and significance. Future Vanna Whites might not get the chance to create their personae, because their employers may fear some celebrity will claim the persona is too similar to her own. The public will be robbed of parodies of celebrities, and our culture will be deprived of the valuable safety valve that parody and mockery create.

Moreover, consider the moral dimension, about which the panel majority seems to have gotten so exercised. Saying Samsung "appropriated" something of White's begs the question: Should White have the exclusive right to something as broad and amorphous as her "identity"? Samsung's ad didn't simply copy White's schtick—like all parody, it created something new. True, Samsung did it to make money, but White does whatever she does to make money, too; the majority talks of "the difference between fun and profit," 971 F.2d at 1401, but in the entertainment industry fun is profit. Why is Vanna White's right to exclusive for-profit use of her persona a persona—that might not even be her own creation, but that of a writer, director or producer— superior to Samsung's right to profit by creating its own inventions? Why should she have such absolute rights to control the conduct of others, unlimited by the idea-expression dichotomy or by the fair use doctrine?

To paraphrase only slightly *Feist Publications, Inc. v. Rural Telephone Service Co.*, 499 U.S. 340 (1991), it may seem unfair that much of the fruit of a creator's labor may be used by others without compensation. But this is not some unforeseen byproduct of our intellectual property system; it is the system's very essence. Intellectual property law assures authors the right to their original expression, but encourages others to build freely on the ideas that underlie it. This result is neither unfair nor unfortunate: It is the means by which intellectual property law advances the progress of science and art. We give authors certain exclusive rights, but in exchange we get a richer public domain. The majority ignores this wise teaching, and all of us are the poorer for it.

White v. Samsung Electronics America, Inc., 989 F.2d 1512, 1525–17 (9th Cir. 1993).

3. Has Midler appropriated anything in a Lockean sense? If so, has she left enough and as good for others?

4. Recent controversies provide mixed signals about the trajectory of the right of publicity. Tending in the direction of lesser protection is the opinion in a recent case in which Tiger Woods sued a company that had marketed copies of a painting by Rick Rush, "Masters of Augusta," commemorating the 1997 Masters golf tournament in Augusta, Georgia, at which Tiger Woods became the youngest player ever to win a Masters tournament. The painting featured a scene containing inter alia three large likenesses of Woods in the foreground, with pictures of the clubhouse and past masters in the background. The Sixth Circuit held that the artistic aspect of the painting gave it First Amendment protection against Woods' right of publicity claim. See ETW Corp. v. Jireh Pub., Inc., 332 F.3d 915 (6th Cir. 2003).

Tending in the direction of continued protection is a recent controversy in which Governor Arnold Schwarzenegger's film production company threatened to sue an Ohio company manufacturing bobbleheads, little caricature-like statuettes whose heads bob up and down. The company had a line of politician bobbleheads, including one of President Bush and of various 2004 presidential candidates. The company used the name and likeness of each of the politicians on the bobblehead itself and in advertisements. The Schwarzenegger bobblehead was wearing a suit and a bandolier and carrying an assault rifle. The governor's lawyers sent a blistering letter informing the company that the Governor was entitled to "substantial damages" from the "unauthorized commercial exploitation" of his image. The lawyers further explained that the governor never allows commercial exploitation of his image in the United States except for purposes of movie promotion. Todd D. Bosley, the president of the Ohio company, claims the dolls were meant as parody and are protected under the First Amendment. See John Broder, Schwarzenegger Files Suit Against Bobblehead Maker, N.Y. Times, at A16 (May 18, 2004). In August 2004, the two sides settled. Under the settlement, the company can continue to market the bobblehead but without the gun, and part of the profits will go to a charity sponsored by the Governor.

3. NOVELTY

Creation, like discovery, bears a degree of similarity to first possession, in that being *first* is important to all three general principles of original acquisition. What seems to distinguish creation is that some type of originality is required. In intellectual property law, for example, it is almost never sufficient just to be first; something more, some kind of novelty, is required. Different types of novelty are required for different forms of protection, and it is always difficult to specify exactly what distinguishes the novel from merely being the first of its kind. In the patent context, challenges to the novelty of a patented invention can be brought in litigation, in the following case as a defense of invalidity of the patent in response to the plaintiff's claim of infringement. The following case illustrates some of the difficulties involved.

Trenton Industries v. A. E. Peterson Manufacturing Co.

United States District Court, Southern District of California, 1958.
165 F.Supp. 523.

■ HOLTZOFF, DISTRICT JUDGE. This is the trial of an action to recover compensation for the use of a patented invention involving an improvement in high chairs intended for the use of infants. The complaint in its present form consists of two counts. The first count asserts a claim for infringement of the patent, and is in the customary form of complaints in patent infringement suits. The second count sounds in quasi-contract and seeks to recover compensation for the use of the patented device during the period prior to the issuance of the patent.

This claim is based on the contention that the plaintiff caused information concerning the invention to be communicated to the defendant with the view to authorizing the defendant to manufacture the invention on a royalty basis, or some other arrangement for compensation, and that the defendant appropriated and used the idea but declined to pay any compensation therefor. Recovery is sought under Count 2 on the theory of unjust enrichment.

Each of the two counts is entirely independent of the other. Each is based on different principles of law, and founded on different states of facts. Accordingly, the court will deal with each of them separately and decide each separately.

The first count deals with infringement of the patent issued to John Adler and Dale O. Adler on an application filed September 18, 1953, serial number 380,991. Patent No. 2,699,817 was granted on this application on January 18, 1955, and was assigned to the plaintiff corporation, which is a concern controlled by the inventor John Adler. The defenses are, first, that the patent is invalid; and, second, that if it is valid, it has not been infringed.

John Adler was active in the manufacture of furniture of various types, among them, high chairs intended for the use of babies. He endeavored to develop a high chair that would easily fold and collapse, and when so folded would make a compact and short package that could be easily shipped, as well as handled with facility by the customer who bought the chair. He experimented with high chairs for some time and finally developed the chair on which the patent claims involved in this case were granted.

In general, the plaintiff's chair is set on two pairs of legs, each rear leg crossing the corresponding front leg. The upper ends of the legs are pivotally attached to the underside of the seat. In view of the fact that the chair is intended for the use of infants, it has a tray that is usually attached to such chairs. A series of pivotal connections makes the chair easily collapsible, and when folded makes a very short package and thereby

Figure 2–6
Drawing from Adler Folding High Chair Patent

Jan. 18, 1955   J. ADLER ET AL   2,699,817
                       FOLDING HIGH CHAIR

Filed Sept. 18, 1953   2 Sheets–Sheet 2

reduces the difficulties and cost of shipment, as well as facilitating the handling of the chair by the customer. The particular advance over the prior art, for indeed collapsible high chairs were known previously to the plaintiff's development, consisted, according to the plaintiff, in pivotally attaching the tops of the legs to the under surface of the seat, instead of, as had been a frequent practice theretofore, attaching them to the sides of the seat. This change made it easier to fold the chair and also made a shorter and more compact package when folded.

The patent has five claims, only three of which, claims 1, 2, and 3, are asserted in this litigation. The principal claim is claim 1, and reads as follows:

> A collapsible high-chair comprising: a pair of supporting front legs and a pair of supporting rear legs, the front legs, intermediate their ends, extending across the rear legs intermediate their ends; a pivot member for pivotally connecting said front legs and said rear legs together at the point of crossing, a seat bottom pivotally connected from the underside thereof, forwardly of its transverse medial line, to the upper ends of said rear legs; a seat back pivotally connected, at its lower edge, to the rear edge of said seat bottom and pivotally connected, above its lower edge and below its transverse medial line, to the upper ends of said front legs; a pair, of spaced apart tray supporting-arms pivotally connected to said seat back above the point of connection of said seat back with said front legs and extending forwardly therefrom; and a brace bar pivotally connected, at its lower end, to said seat bottom and to the upper ends of said rear legs and at its upper end to said supporting-arms.

The carrying or inventive element of this combination is asserted to be, "a seat bottom pivotally connected from the underside thereof, forwardly of its transverse medial line, to the upper ends of said rear legs." That is claimed by the plaintiff to be the advance made by Adler.

35 U.S. Code § 112 requires a claim to point out particularly and distinctly the subject matter which the applicant regards as his invention. Strictly speaking, this claim does not do so. It merely enumerates the elements of the combination without indicating wherein it is claimed that the novelty of the invention is to be found. Nevertheless, it has been the practice of applicants for patents for many years to draw combination claims in this manner, and unfortunately many a patent fails, either in its claims or in its specifications, actually to point out wherein the real novelty of the invention is to be found. The Patent Office has acquiesced in this practice and in fact probably a majority of patents containing combination claims are phrased in this manner. It is a fact that one who reads the patent in this instance is unable to determine therefrom in what the novelty of the invention consists. The novelty was, however, pointed out by counsel at the trial, and the plaintiff is submitting the case on the basis of that contention.

There is no doubt that the plaintiff developed an improvement over similar articles that had been previously on the market, and that he contributed a product that has proved commercially useful. Naturally, one has sympathy for a person who develops an ingenious idea, embodies it in a product that he successfully places on the market, and finds that someone else is imitating it and making use of his brain child. The other person, of course, is trying to reap where he did not sow.

The philosophy of the patent law, however, does not contemplate that the 17–year monopoly, such as a patent confers, should be granted to every person who develops a commercially useful idea.* There is a sound basis for this view. If every new idea, no matter how minor or how narrow and short a step forward is involved, were subject to a 17–year monopoly, the public would be prevented from making use of ordinary routine improvements, and a person ordinarily skilled in his particular art might be impeded and hindered from making betterments in his work, because someone else might have patented them.

This feature has been emphasized in this Circuit in a recent case, Hycon Manufacturing Co. v. H. Koch & Sons, 219 F.2d 353, 355, in which the court stated:

> In a patent case there are three interested parties, the patent holder, the user of an accused device, and the public. The interest of the last is paramount.

Hence, the patent law has been developed in such a manner as to accord the protection of a 17–year monopoly only to a person who makes an invention, that is, whose idea and development is the product of the inventive faculty that rises to the dignity of an invention, rather than such an improvement or advance as would be within the ability of the average reasonable person familiar with the art in which he works and in which he is reasonably skilled. *Definition of "invention"*

A pungent summary of this doctrine in an early case in the Supreme Court is found in Atlantic Works v. Brady, 107 U.S. 192, 200. This statement has been often quoted, but stands repetition:

> The design of the patent laws is to reward those who make some substantial discovery or invention, which adds to our knowledge and makes a step in advance in the useful arts. Such inventors are worthy of all favor. It was never the object of those laws to grant a monopoly for every trifling device, every shadow of a shade of an idea, which would naturally and spontaneously occur to any skilled mechanic or operator in the ordinary progress of manufactures. Such an indiscriminate creation of exclusive privileges tends rather to obstruct than to stimulate invention. It creates a class of speculative schemers who make it their business to watch the advancing wave of improvement, and gather its foam in the form of patented monopolies, which enable them to lay a heavy tax upon the industry of the country, without

---

* [The patent term now runs from issuance until 20 years from the date of the filing of the application, rather than for 17 years after issuance.—eds.]

reaping w/out sowing

contributing anything to the real advancement of the art. It embarrasses the honest pursuit of business with fears and apprehensions of concealed liens and unknown liabilities to lawsuits and vexatious accountings for profits made in good faith.

A comparatively recent enunciation of the same idea, though differently phrased, is found in the opinion of Mr. Justice Jackson in Great Atlantic & Pacific Tea Co. v. Supermarket Equipment Corp., 340 U.S. 147, 152. He said:

> Courts should scrutinize combination patent claims with a care proportioned to the difficulty and improbability of finding invention in an assembly of old elements. The function of a patent is to add to the sum of useful knowledge. Patents cannot be sustained when, on the contrary, their effect is to subtract from former resources freely available to skilled artisans. A patent for a combination which only unites old elements with no change in their respective functions, such as is presented here, obviously withdraws what already is known into the field of its monopoly and diminishes the resources available to skillful men.

Then Mr. Justice Jackson goes on to add the following:

* * * commercial success without invention will not make patentability.

It is a fact well known to all those who are interested in the law of patents that during the past 25 or 30 years Supreme Court decisions have gradually raised the standard of patentability without actually changing the formula or test of what constitutes a patentable invention. Necessarily, few patents reach the Supreme Court, but of the comparatively small number that have been passed upon by that tribunal, very few have been sustained during the past quarter of a century, and some of those that were sustained were construed so narrowly as to be rendered of but little value.

The 1952 codification of the patent law formulated the tests of patentability as follows. 35 U.S. Code § 103 reads:

> A patent may not be obtained * * * if the differences between the subject matter sought to be patented and the prior art are such that the subject matter as a whole would have been obvious at the time the invention was made to a person having ordinary skill in the art to which said subject matter pertains. Patentability shall not be negatived by the manner in which the invention was made.

The test set forth in the first sentence of Section 103 is phrased substantially no differently than the test that had been evolved by the earlier decisions of the Supreme Court. It is a test that the later decisions have not actually changed in so many words. A question has arisen whether the intention of the Congress in enacting Section 103 was to lower the standard of patentability which had been raised, as has been stated, by the Supreme Court decisions.

The Second Circuit answered this question in the affirmative in a well considered opinion by Judge Learned Hand in Lyon v. Bausch & Lomb Optical Co., 224 F.2d 530. Judge Hand discusses this topic in his usual inimitable manner and reaches the conclusion that in fact it was intended by the Congress to lower the requirement of patentability. It is doubtful, however, whether this Circuit is of the same opinion, because in a later case, Bergman v. Aluminum Lock Shingle Corp., 251 F.2d 801, 802, the Court of Appeals for this Circuit stated:

> Twilight is falling upon "gadgets" as subjects of patents. The dusk commenced to gather half a dozen years ago when, in an epochal decision, the Supreme Court fixed its canon against dignifying combined "segments of prior art" with the title of "inventions."

The court cites with approval the opinion of the Supreme Court in Great Atlantic & Pacific Tea Co. v. Supermarket Equipment Corp., to which reference has already been made.

ie: lowering the requirement of patentability

As it is not quite clear whether the doctrine of the Bausch & Lomb case will be or has been accepted in this Circuit, the court will consider the question from both points of view. As heretofore indicated, there is no doubt that a certain amount of ingenuity and skill was required and was exercised by Adler in developing his chair, and that he made a contribution to the industry, which was to some degree accepted on the market, in that he created an easily collapsible chair that made a very short and compact package. The question necessarily is whether his contribution is the result of mechanical skill or should be deemed to rise to the dignity of a product of the inventive faculty.

In this connection, it must be indicated that the recent section, Section 103, to which reference has been made, did make two changes on the issue of patentability. The second sentence, to the effect, "Patentability shall not be negatived by the manner in which the invention was made" obviously was intended to do away with the requirement that in order to constitute invention the steps taken by the inventor must have been the result of a flash of genius, as some of the cases have said. They may be the consequence of prolonged toil and protracted experimentation in endeavoring to find a solution to a problem. So, too, the invention need not necessarily be made by the proverbial poor inventor experimenting in a garret, but may be the product of a group of scientists or technicians working in a laboratory conducted by a large corporation.

We are dealing in this case with a very narrow art in which a great deal of work had previously been done. Numerous prior patents have been introduced in evidence covering various aspects of collapsible chairs in general, and collapsible high chairs in particular. Collapsible and folding chairs have been known for years, and so have collapsible and folding high chairs. Room for invention in this field naturally is limited, and but short steps in advance are likely to be taken by a person seeking to improve high chairs, unless, indeed, someone should at some time develop an article of an entirely different type.

As has been stated, the steps that the inventor in this case claims constitute the novelty in his product, and on which he predicates the contention that he made an invention worthy of a patent, is the attachment of a pivotal kind between the tops of the legs and the underside of the seat, it having been the previous practice—or at least it is so contended—to attach the tops of the legs to the sides of the seat. It is further claimed that this was not a mere difference in design, but produced a more efficient result in creating a shorter and more compact package when the chair is folded. The difficulty with this contention is that the attachment of the tops of the legs to the underside of the seat was known and disclosed in earlier patents. * * *

Thus, he is not adding to "the sum of knowledge"

The conclusion necessarily follows that the alleged novel feature of the plaintiff's invention was known and disclosed by the prior art, and consequently the court is of the opinion that the combination as a whole, though it may indeed be an improvement over prior articles of a similar kind, is the product of mechanical skill rather than the result of the exercise of inventive faculty, and therefore under the law does not justify the issuance of a patent. * * *

The court reaches the conclusion that in the light of the foregoing discussion claim 1 of the patent is invalid. Claims 2 and 3 are repetitions of claim 1, with the addition of certain details. Consequently claims 2 and 3 must likewise fall, and all of the three claims are adjudged invalid. * * *

This brings the court to a consideration of the second count, namely, the count based on unjust enrichment, which seeks compensation for the use of the patented invention during the period that preceded the granting of the patent.

The facts pertaining to this cause of action are as follows. One Haugh, who apparently was a middleman or a broker who in part at least earned his living by trying to market new products and endeavored to interest manufacturers who might fabricate them, learned of the development by Adler of his new folding high chair. He was introduced to Adler by a mutual friend and asked Adler to give him a specimen chair which he would show to persons that he thought might be interested. Adler did so. Haugh then took the chair to Peterson and indicated in one way or another that he would be interested in endeavoring to negotiate an agreement between Peterson and Adler, or their respective corporations, whereby Peterson would undertake the manufacture of the chair on a royalty basis.

Peterson took the chair and kept it for two months. Admittedly, he examined it carefully, made a photograph of it, showed it to members of his staff who likewise scrutinized it, and then he returned the chair and indicated that he was not interested. Shortly thereafter, through the defendant corporation, he placed a chair on the market that embodied some of the features of the plaintiff's disclosure.

It would seem appropriate at this point to turn to the authorities governing the plaintiff's rights under this state of facts. One of the leading cases on this point is a decision of the Fourth Circuit in which Judge

Parker wrote the opinion, Hoeltke v. C. M. Kemp Manufacturing Co., 80 F.2d 912, 922–923. The court stated:

> The general rule, of course, is that the monopoly of a patent which entitles a patentee to damages for infringement commences only when the patent is granted; but where, in advance of the granting of a patent, an invention is disclosed to one who, in breach of the confidence thus reposed, manufactures and sells articles embodying the invention, such person should be held liable for the profits and damages resulting therefrom, not under the patent statutes, but upon the principle that equity will not permit one to unjustly enrich himself at the expense of another.

And, again, it continues to say:

> It would be a reproach to any system of jurisprudence to permit one who has received a disclosure in confidence to thus appropriate the ideas of another without liability for the wrong.

Judge Parker concludes this branch of his discussion as follows:

> While there was no express agreement that defendant was to hold the information so disclosed as a confidential matter and to make no use of it unless it should purchase the invention, we think that in equity and good conscience such an agreement was implied; and having obtained the disclosure under such circumstances, defendant ought not be heard to say that there was no obligation to respect the confidence thus reposed in it.

The court cites with approval a decision of the Seventh Circuit, Booth v. Stutz Motor Car Co., 56 F.2d 962. * * *

The general doctrine on which these rulings were based was summarized by Judge Charles E. Clark in Matarese v. Moore–McCormack Lines, 2 Cir., 158 F.2d 631, 634, as follows:

> The doctrine of unjust enrichment or recovery in quasi-contract obviously does not deal with situations in which the party to be charged has by word or deed legally consented to assume a duty toward the party seeking to charge him. Instead, it applies to situations where as a matter of fact there is no legal contract, but where the person sought to be charged is in possession of money or property which in good conscience and justice he should not retain, but should deliver to another. * * * Where this is true the courts impose a duty to refund the money or the use value of the property to the person to whom in good conscience it ought to belong. * * * The doctrine is applicable to a situation where, as here, the product of an inventor's brain is knowingly received and used by another to his own great benefit without compensating the inventor.

The most recent case on this point was decided in this Circuit, in which this doctrine was approved and applied. Filtex Corp. v. Amen Atiyeh, 216 F.2d 443.

The principles here involved may be summarized as follows. If a person communicates a novel idea to another with the intention that the latter may use the idea and compensate him for such use, the other party is liable for such use and must pay compensation if actually he appropriates the idea and employs it in connection with his own activities. It is immaterial whether the communication is expressly made in confidence, so long as it is made on an understanding either tacit or express that the person communicating the idea, or the owner of the idea, expected to be compensated if it was to be used by the person receiving it. This doctrine is not limited to patentable inventions, and has been extended to ideas of various kinds that were not subject either to patents or copyrights. An example is found in Belt v. Hamilton National Bank, D.C., 108 F.Supp. 689, affirmed in 210 F.2d 706.

The facts of this case bring the situation that confronts the court in the second count within these principles. The defendant, however, explained that after he received and examined the plaintiff's chair he happened to be in his church one time and saw that the chairs that were used in the church had a similar folding mechanism, or so he thought, as is found in the plaintiff's structure, and consequently he felt free to use that structure because his theory was that it was then in the public domain. It is significant, however, that he had seen these church chairs on numerous prior occasions, but he did not take any particular notice of them and did not derive the thought that it was possible to use a similar mechanism in manufacturing a high chair, until he received and scrutinized the plaintiff's disclosure. It would seem, therefore, to the court that he was using this other structure, which has been denominated throughout the case as the church chair, as an afterthought and as an excuse for using the idea that was communicated to him by the plaintiff through an intermediary.

It may well be that the defendant honestly and in good faith thought that he was entitled to do what he did. He is not being charged with fraud, actual or constructive. The issue is not one of good or bad faith. Good faith is immaterial. The question is whether the defendant has been unjustly enriched by using the plaintiff's idea, and should pay compensation therefor *ex aequo et bono*.*

So, too, the fact that apparently the defendant thought that the plaintiff's device had already been patented does not justify him in doing what he did. The existence or lack of a patent is immaterial because, as indicated, the principles of quasi-contract here applicable extend to both patentable and non-patentable structures and ideas. * * *

Moreover, the defendant has throughout maintained that the plaintiff's patent is invalid. He has done so successfully, because the court has adjudicated the patent to be invalid. He can hardly take advantage of the patent for one purpose and claim that it is invalid in another connection.

Under the circumstances, the court is of the opinion that the plaintiffs are entitled to recover a reasonable royalty on the chairs manufactured by

---

* [According to what is right and good.— eds.]

the defendant and embodying substantially elements of the plaintiff's structure during the period between the date on which Haugh made the disclosure to the defendant of the plaintiff's structure and the date on which the patent was issued. * * *

NOTES AND QUESTIONS

1. The holder of a patent has the right to exclude others from the patented invention because "whoever without authority makes, uses, offers to sell, or sells any patented invention, within the United States or imports into the United States any patented invention during the term of the patent therefor, infringes the patent." 35 U.S.C. § 271. It is important to understand what this does and does not give the patentee. The patentee has the right to prevent others from making, using, selling, etc. the invention. But nothing in the patent gives the patentee the affirmative right to *use* the invention. For example, if the invention is a drug, denial of an FDA application will mean that the patentee cannot use the invention as it might like.

2. The standard for nonobviousness (earlier "invention") has been among the most contested in patent law. In the early twentieth century the Supreme Court took an increasingly stringent view of what would satisfy the requirement of "invention" or "inventive step," culminating in the "flash of creative genius" test. Cuno Engineering Corp. v. Automatic Devices Corp., 314 U.S. 84 (1941). Towards the end of this era, Justice Jackson quipped that "the only patent that is valid is one which this Court has not been able to get its hands on." Jungersen v. Ostby & Barton Co., 335 U.S. 560, 572 (1949). The Supreme Court eventually acknowledged that the 1952 Act abolished the flash of creative genius test, and while stating that the 1952 Act did not lower the standard for patentable invention, the Court has largely interpreted its precedent in a more patent-friendly manner. See Graham v. John Deere Co., 383 U.S. 1 (1966). Importantly, the creation in 1982 of the Federal Circuit with exclusive jurisdiction to hear all patent appeals (not just those from the Patent and Trademark Office) has led to a more pro-patent approach. See generally Donald S. Chisum et al., Principles of Patent Law 532–734 (3d ed. 2004); but see Lee Petherbridge & R. Polk Wagner, The Federal Circuit and Patentability: An Empirical Assessment of the Law of Obviousness (August 9, 2006), available at http://ssrn.com/abstract=923309 (presenting empirical study of Federal Circuit cases suggesting relatively stable and consistent approach to obviousness that has not had a discernable effect on the results of obviousness cases).

3. In copyright law, the corresponding "newness" requirement is "originality." In the leading decision, the Supreme Court held that a list of names and telephone numbers arrayed alphabetically in a directory was not sufficiently "original" to be copyrighted. Feist Publications, Inc. v. Rural Telephone Service Co., 499 U.S. 340 (1991). Generally speaking, however, the requirement of originality is easy to satisfy in copyright. The most

tedious and uninspired law review article that has nothing new to say is entitled to copyright protection, as long as the form of expression does not duplicate that found in some other article. Why do you think a lesser degree of novelty is required to obtain a copyright than a patent?

4. In the misappropriation cases, some jurisdictions require that the information be novel in general, not just new to the defendant. Others permit a claim so long as the information is novel to the defendant. For a summary, see Mary LaFrance, Something Borrowed, Something New: The Changing Role of Novelty in Idea Protection Law, 34 Seton Hall L. Rev. 485 (2004). Recently New York has gravitated toward an intermediate approach: Novelty in general is required for a misappropriation claim, but only novelty to the defendant is required for an implied contract claim. Apfel v. Prudential–Bache Securities Inc., 81 N.Y.2d 470 (1993); see also Nadel v. Play–By–Play Toys & Novelties, Inc., 208 F.3d 368 (2d Cir. 2000). On this approach, an idea lacking in novelty is likely to be open to all and so cannot be misappropriated, unless the defendant is under some contractual obligation to the plaintiff not to use the information. Nadel, 208 F.3d at 378. Which of these various approaches makes the most sense?

5. In part of the opinion not reproduced here, the court discusses whether the patent, if it were valid, would have been infringed by the acts of the defendant. Infringement in patent law requires that the defendant be making, using, or selling etc. the invention without authority. In the case of a device, the defendant's device should contain all the elements set forth in the claims of the plaintiff's patent. If the defendant's device contains other elements besides, it may be an improvement. If so, then the improver may be able to acquire a patent to block the patentee from using the improvement. The earlier patentee can practice the invention without the improvement but must acquire permission from the improver to practice the patented improvement. Recall that a patent does not give the patentee an affirmative right to use anything: The improver cannot practice either version unless the improver obtains a license from the earlier patentee. In this situation of "blocking patents" what would one expect to happen in practice? See Robert Merges, Intellectual Property Rights and Bargaining Breakdown: The Case of Blocking Patents, 62 Tenn. L. Rev. 75 (1994).

6. A number of requirements of patent law are designed to furnish notice to the public of what is being claimed and to protect the public reliance on the appearance that material is in the public domain. How do these considerations figure in the court opinion? Further, it is worth noting that the United States is the only country in the world to have a first-to-invent patent system. The alternative is a first-to-file system, in which the first to file an application receives the patent (as long as the other requirements are met) even if the first applicant is not the actual first inventor. What impact does this choice have on racing behavior, incentives to invest and commercialize, and the furnishing of notice to third parties?

D.   THE PRINCIPLE OF ACCESSION

A fourth general principle that is used to establish title to property other than through voluntary conveyance is the principle of accession. We will distinguish between the *principle of accession* and the *doctrine of accession*. The principle of accession refers to a family of doctrines, each of which shares a common feature: Ownership of some unclaimed or contested resource is assigned to the owner of some *other* resource that has a particularly prominent relationship to the unclaimed or contested resource. In each case, the assignment of ownership occurs without regard to any voluntary conveyance of the unclaimed or contested resource, and without regard to whether the existing owner is in possession of the contested resource. As the philosopher David Hume wrote: "We acquire the property of objects by *accession*, when they are connected in an intimate manner with objects that are already our property, and at the same time are inferior to them. Thus the fruits of our garden, the offspring of our cattle, and the work of our slaves, are all of them esteem'd our property, even before possession." David Hume, A Treatise of Human Nature 327 (David Fate Norton & Mary J. Norton eds., 2000) (1739). The doctrine of accession refers to a narrower common-law doctrine that is part of this larger family of doctrines—the doctrine that applies when someone mistakenly takes up a physical object that belongs to someone else and transforms it through her labor into a fundamentally different object. More on the doctrine of accession momentarily.

1.   INCREASE

Our first example of the principle of accession, mentioned by Hume, is that "the offspring of our cattle * * * [are] esteem'd our property, even before possession." This is known as the doctrine of *increase*. As summarized in one opinion, "The general rule, in the absence of an agreement to the contrary, is that the offspring or increase of tame or domestic animals belongs to the owner of the dam or mother.... In this respect the common law follows the civil law and is founded on the maxim, *partus sequitur ventrem* [the offspring follows the mother—eds.].... Furthermore, the increase of the increase, ad infinitum, of domestic animals comes within the rule and belongs to the owner of the original stock." Carruth v. Easterling, 150 So.2d 852, 855 (Miss. 1963) (quoting 4 Am. Jur. 2d Animals § 10).

In *Carruth*, a herd of cattle owned by Easterling wandered onto a farm owned by Carruth. Most were eventually returned, but a dispute arose between the parties as to whether Easterling had promised Carruth that he could keep two cows as compensation for the inconvenience of the trespass. When Easterling sued for the return of the two cows, a further dispute arose about whether Easterling was also entitled to a calf that had been born to one of the cows while being kept in custody by Carruth. The

Mississippi Supreme Court held that the calf also belonged to Easterling, even though it had likely been conceived while on Carruth's land.

NOTES AND QUESTIONS

1. The doctrine of increase is apparently one of those legal rules recognized in every known legal system that addresses the issue. See Felix Cohen, Dialogue on Private Property, 9 Rutgers L. Rev. 357, 366 (1954). Moreover, it is a rule, not a standard: Courts have not carved out exceptions for calves sired by prize-winning bulls, or for calves raised at great expense by someone other than the owner of the mother. Id.

2. What is the explanation for the doctrine of increase? The doctrine makes sense if we assume that young animals are generally dependent on their mothers for nurture and upbringing. Assigning ownership of the offspring to the owner of the mother helps ensure that this maternal connection remains unbroken. It may also be easier to identify the mother of a young animal than the father or the owner of the land on which the offspring was sired or born. Thus, the doctrine has evidentiary advantages. But are these pragmatic considerations sufficient to explain the universal and deeply entrenched nature of the rule? Does it also rest on a psychological perception of the "closeness" of the relationship between the offspring and the mother? Can it be said that in some sense the mother is "in possession" of the offspring? Is the principle of accession another principle of ownership grounded in intuitions about possession? See 2 Blackstone, Commentaries *404 ("The doctrine of property arising from *accession* is also grounded on the right of occupancy.").

2. THE DOCTRINE OF ACCESSION

D　　*P*

Wetherbee v. Green

Supreme Court of Michigan, 1871.
22 Mich. 311.

[handwritten margin note: Law.com Dictionary]
[handwritten margin note: replevin (n) — under common law, the right to bring a lawsuit for recovery of goods improperly taken by another. In almost all states, the term ... is no longer used, since the states have adopted "one cause of action" for all civil wrongs.]

This was an action of replevin, brought by George Green, Charles H. Camp and George Brooks, in the circuit court for the county of Bay, against George Wetherbee, for one hundred and fifty-eight thousand black ash barrel-hoops, alleged to be of the value of eight hundred dollars. * * * [T]he jury found for plaintiffs. The judgment entered upon the verdict comes into this court by writ of error.

■ COOLEY J.: * * * Wetherbee claimed * * * that replevin could not be maintained for the hoops, because he had cut the timber in good faith, relying upon a permission which he supposed proceeded from the parties having lawful right to give it, and had, by the expenditure of his labor and money, converted the trees into chattels immensely more valuable than they were as they stood in the forest, and thereby he had made such chattels his own. And he offered to show that the standing timber was worth twenty-five dollars only, while the hoops replevied were shown by the evidence to be worth near seven hundred dollars * * * The evidence offered to establish these facts was rejected by the court, and the plaintiffs obtained judgment. * * *

The objections to allowing the owner of the trees to reclaim the property under such circumstances are, that it visits the involuntary wrong-doer too severely for his unintentional trespass, and at the same time compensates the owner beyond all reason for the injury he has sustained. In the redress of private injuries the law aims not so much to punish the wrongdoer as to compensate the sufferer for his injuries; and the cases in which it goes farther and inflicts punitory or vindictive penalties are those in which the wrong-doer has committed the wrong recklessly, willfully, or maliciously, and under circumstances presenting elements of aggravation. Where vicious motive or reckless disregard of right are not involved, to inflict upon a person who has taken the property of another, a penalty equal to twenty or thirty times its value, and to compensate the owner in a proportion equally enormous, is so opposed to all legal idea of justice and right and to the rules which regulate the recovery of damages generally, that if permitted by the law at all, it must stand out as an anomaly and must rest upon peculiar reasons.

As a general rule, one whose property has been appropriated by another without authority has a right to follow it and recover the possession from any one who may have received it; and if, in the mean time, it has been increased in value by the addition of labor or money, the owner may, nevertheless, reclaim it, provided there has been no destruction of substantial identity. So far the authorities are agreed. A man cannot generally be deprived of his property except by his own voluntary act or by operation of law; and if unauthorized parties have bestowed expense or labor upon it, that fact cannot constitute a bar to his reclaiming it, so long as identification is not impracticable. But there must, nevertheless, in reason be some limit to the right to follow and reclaim materials which have undergone a process of manufacture. Mr. Justice Blackstone lays down the rule very broadly, that if a thing is changed into a different species, as by making wine out of another's grapes, oil from his olives, or bread from his wheat, the product belongs to the new operator, who is only to make satisfaction to the former proprietor for the materials converted: 2 Bl. Com., 404. We do not understand this to be disputed as a general proposition, though there are some authorities which hold that, in the case of a willful appropriation, no extent of conversion can give to the willful trespasser a title to the property so long as the original materials can be traced in the improved article. The distinction thus made between the case of an appropriation in good faith and one based on intentional wrong, appears to have come from the civil law, which would not suffer a party to acquire a title by accession, founded on his own act, unless he had taken the materials in ignorance of the true owner, and given them a form which precluded their being restored to their original condition. 2 Kent, 363. While many cases have followed the rule as broadly stated by Blackstone, others have adopted the severe rule of the civil law where the conversion was in willful disregard of right. The New York cases of *Betts v. Lee,* 5

Johns. 348; *Curtis v. Groat*, 6 Johns. 168, and *Chandler v. Edson*, 9 Johns. 362, were all cases where the willful trespasser was held to have acquired no property by a very radical conversion * * * But we are not called upon in this case to express any opinion regarding the rule applicable in the case of a willful trespasser, since the authorities agree in holding that, when the wrong had been involuntary, the owner of the original materials is precluded, by the civil law and common law alike, from following and reclaiming the property after it has undergone a transformation which converts it into an article substantially different.

The cases of confusion of goods are closely analogous. It has always been held that he who, without fraud, intentional wrong, or reckless disregard of the rights of others, mingled his goods with those of another person, in such manner that they could not be distinguished, should, nevertheless, be protected in his ownership so far as the circumstances would permit. The question of motive here becomes of the highest importance; for, as Chancellor Kent says, if the commingling of property as willfully made without mutual consent, * * * the common law gave the entire property, without any account, to him whose property "was originally invaded, and its distinct character destroyed. Popham's Rep. 38, Pl. 2. If A will willfully intermix his corn or hay with that of B, or casts his gold into another's crucible, so that it becomes impossible to distinguish what belonged to A from what belonged to B, the whole belongs to B." But this rule only applies to wrongful or fraudulent intermixtures. There may be an intentional intermingling, and yet no wrong intended, as where a man mixes two parcels together, supposing both to be his own; or, that he was about to mingle his with his neighbor's, by agreement, and mistakes the parcel. In such cases, which may be deemed accidental intermixtures, it would be unreasonable and unjust that he should lose his own or be obliged to take and pay for his neighbor's * * * In many cases there will be difficulty in determining precisely how he can be protected with due regard to the rights of the other party; but it is clear that the law will not forfeit his property in consequence of the accident or inadvertence, unless a just measure of redress to the other party renders it inevitable.

The important question on this branch of the case appears to us to be, whether standing trees, when cut and manufactured into hoops, are to be regarded as so far changed in character that their identity can be said to be destroyed within the meaning of the authorities. And as we enter upon a discussion of this question, it is evident at once that it is difficult, if not impossible, to discover any invariable and satisfactory test which can be applied to all the cases which arise in such infinite variety. "If grain be taken and made into malt, or money taken and made into a cup, or timber taken and made into a house, it is held in the old English law that the property is so altered as to change the title." 2 Kent, 363. But cloth made into garments, leather into shoes, trees hewn or sawed into timber, and iron made into bars, it is said may be reclaimed by the owner in their new and original shape. Some of the cases place the right of the former owner to take the thing in its altered condition upon the question whether its identity could be made out by the senses. But this is obviously a very unsatisfactory test, and in many cases would wholly defeat the purpose which the law has in view in recognizing a change of title in any of these cases. That purpose is not to establish any arbitrary distinctions, based upon mere physical reasons, but to adjust the redress afforded to the one party and the penalty inflicted upon the other, as near as circumstances will permit, to the rules of substantial justice.

It may often happen that no difficulty will be experienced in determining the identity of a piece of timber which has been taken and built into a house; but no one disputes that the right of the original owner is gone in such a case. A particular piece of wood might, perhaps, be traced without trouble into a church organ, or other equally valuable article; but no one would defend a rule of law which, because the identity could be determined by the senses, would permit the owner of the wood to appropriate a musical instrument, a hundred or a thousand times the value of his original materials, when the party who, under like circumstances, has doubled the value of another man's corn by converting it into malt, is permitted to retain it, and held liable for the original value only. Such distinctions in the law would be without reason, and could not be tolerated. When the right to the improved article is the point in issue, the question, how much the property or labor of each has contributed to make it what it is, must always be one of first importance. The owner of a beam built into the house of another loses his property in it, because the beam is insignificant in value or importance as compared to that to which it has become attached, and the musical instrument belongs to the maker rather than to the man whose timber was used in making it—not because the timber cannot be identified, but because, in bringing it to its present condition the value of the labor has swallowed up and rendered insignificant the value of the original materials. The labor, in the case of the musical instrument, is just as much the principal thing as the house is in the other case instanced; the timber appropriated is in each case comparatively unimportant.

No test which satisfies the reason of the law can be applied in the adjustment of questions of title to chattels by accession, unless it keeps in view the circumstance of relative values. When we bear in mind the fact that what the law aims at is the accomplishment of substantial equity, we shall readily perceive that the fact of the value of the materials having been increased a hundred-fold, is of more importance in the adjustment than any chemical change or mechanical transformation, which, however radical, neither is expensive to the party making it, nor adds materially to the value. There may be complete changes with so little improvement in value, that there could be no hardship in giving the owner of the original materials the improved article; but in the present case, where the defendant's labor—if he shall succeed in sustaining his offer of testimony—will appear to have given the timber in its present condition nearly all its value, all the grounds of equity exist which influence the courts in recognizing a change of title under any circumstances.

We are of opinion that the court erred in rejecting the testimony offered. The defendant, we think, had a right to show that he had manufactured the hoops in good faith, and in the belief that he had the proper authority to do so; and if he should succeed in making that showing, he was entitled to have the jury instructed that the title to the timber was changed by a substantial change of identity, and that the remedy of the plaintiff was an action to recover damages for the unintentional trespass.

* * * For the reasons given the judgment must be reversed, with costs, and a new trial ordered.

NOTES AND QUESTIONS

1. The doctrine of accession is another illustration of the broader principle of accession, at least if we make the Lockean assumption that every person owns his or her own labor. On this assumption, the question in such cases is which "property right" is more prominent: the original object (the tree, the grapes, the wheat) or the labor expended by the improver in transforming the original object (making hoops, or wine, or bread). If the labor is "insignificant" and the original object "prominent," then title stays with the original owner of the object. If the labor is "prominent" and the original object "insignificant," then title passes to the improver (and the improver pays the original owner damages equal to the value of the original object).

2. Justice Cooley emphasizes the importance of the good faith/bad faith distinction, and indicates his agreement with cases that refuse to transfer title to the creator/improver who has acted in bad faith, i.e., with knowledge that someone else has superior title to the original object. Do you think that bad faith should be irrelevant (Blackstone's view, apparently), should automatically disqualify someone from obtaining title by accession (Cooley's view), or should be one factor to weigh against other factors, like the degree of transformation and the disparity in value added? Recall the contrast in Chapter I between *Pile v. Pedrick* (good faith or bad faith irrelevant to the right of the true owner to enjoin the encroachment) and *Golden Press v. Rylands* (good faith encroacher may be able to obtain additional land upon paying damages to the true owner).

3. Justice Cooley also seeks to downplay the significance of the degree of transformation of the object, and instead puts greater weight on the disparity in value. He had to do this in order to find title by accession in Wetherbee, since although the identity of the original logs could be traced in the hoops, the disparity in value was enormous: $700 for the hoops versus $25 for the trees, or a ratio of 28 to 1. Interestingly, just six years later, in *Isle Royale Mining Co. v. Hertin*, 37 Mich. 332 (1877), Cooley, by then Chief Justice, also wrote for the court in denying a claim seeking restitution for the value of labor expended in mistakenly cutting trees on land owned by someone else. The value of the cut timber was $2.87½ per cord, of which $1.87½ was attributable to labor of the improver, for a ratio of 1.875 to 1. Perhaps more importantly, the mistaken improver had not really transformed the trees at all, other than to cut them down. The opinion in *Isle Royale* placed considerably more emphasis on the absence of

transformation, noting that "[p]erhaps no case has gone further than *Wetherbee v. Green* ... [where] the identity of trees and hoops was perfectly capable of being traced and established."

4.   Why do you suppose the degree of transformation has been an important factor in the law of accession—perhaps more important than good faith or relative value—from Roman times down to the present? Does extensive transformation suggest that the laborer has taken "possession" of the object?

5.   Note that the doctrine of accession also incorporates the principle of restitution, discussed in Chapter I. If the improver is deemed to be the more prominent contributor of value to the transformed object, the improver gets title to the object, but must pay damages to the owner of the raw materials that have been transformed. The measure of damages is presumably the fair market value of the raw material in its pre-transformation state. Suppose the contrary conclusion is reached—that the owner of the raw materials is the more prominent contributor of final value, and hence gets title to the object. Must the owner of the raw material make restitution to the improver for the increased value to the object caused by the improvements? What if, say, the original owner of the timber did not want the trees cut down, but rather prefers that they remain standing as a forest?

6.   Most of the cases involving the doctrine of accession have a quaint quality: hoops being carved from logs, wine being pressed from grapes, and so forth. But issues involving improvements arise with considerable frequency in modern intellectual property law. Suppose A gets a patent on a new invention, and B then makes an improvement on the invention. Or suppose A writes a novel which is copyrighted, and B then turns it into a screenplay for a movie. What are the respective rights of A and B in these situations? Intellectual property law does not use accession doctrine in resolving these issues. Instead, Mark Lemley, a leading intellectual property scholar, summarizes patent law this way:

> The basic structure of the patent model is * * * quite simple. The treatment of improvements is a function of the value and significance of the improvement in relation to the original invention. Improvements which are minor in relation to the original invention are likely to be found to infringe * * * More significant improvements within the range of the original claims still infringe the original patent, but in such cases the improver is entitled to a patent of his own. This not only encourages the development of significant improvements, but gives improvers bargaining leverage in licensing negotiations in direct proportion to the relative value of their improvements. Finally, truly radical improvements are exempted from liability to the original patent owner, regardless of whether they fall within the literal scope of the original claims, in order to encourage such improvements and to ensure that they reach the market.

Mark A. Lemley, The Economics of Improvement in Intellectual Property Law, 75 Tex. L. Rev. 989, 1070 (1997). How would you characterize the differences between the intellectual property solution to the problem of improvements, and the doctrine of accession? Which do you think is better, and why?

3.   EXPLAINING THE PRINCIPLE OF ACCESSION

What accounts for the principle of accession? Certainly, one can think of various utilitarian arguments supporting various accession doctrines. But it has also been argued, starting with the philosopher David Hume, that accession is also—and perhaps more importantly—a function of human psychology, or what Hume called "the imagination."

David Hume, *A Treatise of Human Nature*, 327 n.75 (David Fate Norton & Mary J. Norton eds., 2000) (1739)

This source of property can never be explain'd but from the imagination * * * [F]rom an object, that is related to us, we acquire a relation to every other object which is related to it, and so on, till the thought loses the chain by too long a progress. However the relation may weaken by each remove, 'tis not immediately destroy'd; but frequently connects two objects by means of an intermediate one, which is related to both. And this principle is of such force as to give rise to the right of *accession*, and causes us to acquire the property not only of such objects as we are immediately posses'd of, but also of such as are closely connected with them. * * *

The empire of *Great Britain* seems to draw along with it the dominion of the *Orkneys,* the *Hebrides,* the isle of *Man,* and the isle of *Wight;* but the authority over those lesser islands does not naturally imply any title to *Great Britain*. In short, a small object naturally follows a great one as its accession; but a great one is never suppos'd to belong to the proprietor of a small one related to it, merely on account of that property and relation. * * * Suppose, therefore, a great and small object to be related together; if a person be strongly related to the great object, he will likewise be strongly related to both the objects, consider'd together, because he is related to the most considerable part. On the contrary, if he be only related to the small object, he will not be strongly related to both, consider'd together, since his relation lies only with the most trivial part, which is not apt to strike us in any great degree, when we consider the whole. And this is the reason, why small objects become accessions to great ones, and not great to small. * * *

Robert Sugden, *The Economics of Rights, Co-operation and Welfare*, 91–92, 101–03 (2d ed. Palgrave Macmillan 2004)

When oil and gas reserves were discovered under the North Sea the problem arose of who had the right to exploit them. The potential claimants were the nation states. Given the power of most nation states to inflict harm on most others, it was important to find some way of dividing up the reserves that would be generally acceptable. In effect, nations were involved in a variant of the division game, but with many players instead of just two.

The solution reached was to allocate each portion of the sea bed to the country whose coastline happened to be nearest. In terms of any abstract theory of justice, this seems completely arbitrary. The main beneficiaries from this arrangement were the United Kingdom and Norway. West Germany, despite its large population and considerable length of North Sea coastline, came out badly. Why did West Germany acquiesce in such an unfair partition? Why, for that matter, should the share-out have been restricted to countries with a North Sea coastline? The poor countries of Africa and Asia might have used arguments of distributive justice to support claims to North Sea oil. If it is replied that these countries lack the military power to support such claims, how much military power does Norway have? And the United States and the Soviet Union are overwhelmingly more powerful than any of the North Sea countries; yet they too got nothing.

One answer might be that this peculiar division of the sea bed was prescribed by international law. In 1958 an international conference in Geneva had drafted a convention which was to come into force when it had been ratified by 22 states; the 22nd state signed in 1964. According to this convention, each state has a right to exploit the continental shelf adjacent to its coastline. International boundaries on the continental shelf are to be fixed by agreement between the states concerned, but in case of dispute, median lines (i.e. lines equidistant from the coasts of two countries) are to be used. In fact, however, the agreement among the North Sea countries departed from this convention quite significantly. There is a deep trench between the Norwegian coast and the North Sea oilfields; according to the Geneva Convention these oilfields were all on the British continental shelf, even though in some cases the closest coastline was Norway. In the event the North Sea countries opted for the simpler rule of ignoring the depth of the sea bed and allocating every portion of the continental shelf to the country with the closest coastline. So the partition of the North Sea was not arrived at by applying international law. * * *

[After quoting from Hume's *Treatise*, including the passage above about accession, Sugden continues:]

[C]onventions may exploit two-step relations between persons and objects: if I am in possession of object X, and if there is some especially prominent relation between object X and some "inferior" object Y, then this may be enough to establish a prominent relation between me and object Y. This idea may help to explain the attraction of the median-line solution to the problem of partitioning the North Sea. Among geographical features, the relation of closeness seems to have an inescapable prominence, and in this sense it is natural to associate each portion of the sea bed with the closest land mass, and thus with the nation that is in possession of that land. * * *

I suspect that many readers will be inclined to object that there is another kind of prominent solution, at least for the division game: the solution of equal division. Perhaps, it might be added, this solution did not occur to Hume in the way that it does to us because we live in a more egalitarian age than he did. No doubt there would be some truth in saying this. Nevertheless, the equal-division solution is not as easily defined—and hence not so uniquely prominent—as it seems at first sight.

Consider the case of the North Sea. Why didn't the disputants agree to divide the sea bed equally between them? As soon as one begins to take this possibility seriously, all sort of difficulties start to emerge. The first is to decide who are the disputants, each of whom is to receive an equal share. Suppose we accept that only nation states can count as claimants—a presupposition that also underlies the median-line rule. Then which nations are to be allowed to claim? Unless we answer, "All the nations of the world", where is the line to be drawn? Nations with a North Sea coastline? European nations? Nations with *any* coastline? * * *

A second problem * * * is that the resource in dispute is far from homogeneous. The disputants knew that some areas of the North Sea were more likely to yield oil and gas than others; so an equal division of the *area* of the North Sea would not have been appropriate. But an equal division of the *value* of the sea bed would have required a unit of value—prior to the detailed exploration that would not be carried out until the division had been agreed. There does not seem to be any uniquely obvious way of defining an equal share. Contrast these difficulties with the simplicity of the rule that each piece of the sea bed goes to the nearest country. This latter rule may be arbitrary, in a way that a rule of equal division is not; but the arbitrariness of the median-line solution is, in a sense, part of its prominence. By this I mean that the arbitrariness of the solution provides few footholds for special pleading by aggrieved parties; there is much less scope for sophisticated argument around the question "Where are the median lines?" than around "What is an equal share?"

NOTES AND QUESTIONS

1. Elsewhere Sugden also discusses the convention that people will defend when they are in possession and defer to a prior possessor, which is sometimes termed the "bourgeois" strategy. Why don't we see the reverse strategy—challenging possessors but retreating from possession when challenged? The territorial behavior of many animals bears striking resemblance to human possessory conventions. Animals, especially nonhuman primates and birds, can also be shown to alter their territorial behavior according to the costs and benefits of the resource (e.g., a feeding ground). See, e.g., Jeffrey Evans Stake, The Property "Instinct," 359 Phil. Trans. Royal Soc'y Lond. B 1763 (2004); see also Elizabeth Cashdan, Spatial Organization and Habitat Use, in Evolutionary Ecology and Human Behavior 237, 262–63 (Eric Alden Smith & Bruce Winterhalder eds., 1992). Do these animals perform a cost-benefit analysis? Do people? Animals' territoriality has facilitated property: Dogs can be trained to defend humans' property boundaries making them quite cheap to defend, whereas enforcing

norms of good behavior requires judgment that is beyond a dog's capacity. See Robert C. Ellickson, Property in Land, 102 Yale L.J. 1315, 1329 (1993).

2.   What is the source of the convention of possession, or even ideas about what counts as possession? Sugden suggests that it is not simply a matter of might makes right. But how do expectations converge on the proximity rule? Some solutions are said to be "focal" in that people can guess each other's answers without communication. In a famous experiment, people were asked where they would go and when, if told to meet a friend the next day in New York City who had been given similar instructions but with whom no communication was possible. Despite the enormous number of possibilities, a majority picked Grand Central Station and almost all chose noon, exhibiting a high degree of what Thomas Schelling termed "tacit cooperation." Thomas C. Schelling, The Strategy of Conflict 54–56 (1963). Focal solutions to situations that can be modeled as cooperative games draw on common knowledge, but some have argued that these solutions can arise from hard-wired aspects of mind as well. More generally, can "focal" behavior based on either source be said to be rational? For a discussion of these issues and their relevance to law, see Richard H. McAdams, A Focal Point Theory of Expressive Law, 86 Va. L. Rev. 1649, 1659–63 (2000).

3.   What if possessory behavior were conclusively shown to reflect a hard-wired territorial psychology? Would this make property more legitimate, less legitimate, or neither?

4.   THE *AD COELUM* RULE

The <u>ad coelum rule</u> is short for the Latin maxim, *cujus est solum, ejus est usque ad coelum et ad inferos*. This has been translated as "To whomever the soil belongs, he owns also to the sky and to the depths." Black's Law Dictionary (6th ed. 1990). We encountered the doctrine in connection with *Hinman v. Pacific Air Transport*, the airplane overflight case in Chapter I. The doctrine also applies to resources discovered beneath the surface, such as minerals, oil and gas deposits, or, as in the next case, caves.

Edwards v. Sims

Court of Appeals of Kentucky, 1929.
232 Ky. 791, 24 S.W.2d 619.

Opinion by Commissioner Stanley. This case presents a novel question.*

[About [thirteen] years ago L. P. Edwards discovered a cave under land belonging to him and his wife, Sally Edwards. The entrance to the cave is on the Edwards land. Edwards named it the "Great Onyx Cave," no doubt because of the rock crystal formations within it which are known as onyx.

---

* [The next paragraph is taken from a subsequent opinion on remedies.—eds.]

This cave is located in the cavernous area of Kentucky, and is only about three miles distant from the world-famous Mammoth Cave. Its proximity to Mammoth Cave, which for many years has had an international reputation as an underground wonder, as well as its beautiful formations, led Edwards to embark upon a program of advertising and exploitation for the purpose of bringing visitors to his cave. Circulars were printed and distributed, signs were erected along the roads, persons were employed and stationed along the highways to solicit the patronage of passing travelers, and thus the fame of the Great Onyx Cave spread from year to year, until eventually, and before the beginning of the present litigation, it was a well-known and well-patronized cave. Edwards built a hotel near the mouth of the cave to care for travelers. He improved and widened the footpaths and avenues in the cave, and ultimately secured a stream of tourists who paid entrance fees sufficient not only to cover the cost of operation, but also to yield a substantial revenue in addition thereto. The authorities in charge of the development of the Mammoth Cave area as a national park undertook to secure the Great Onyx Cave through condemnation proceedings, and in that suit the value of the cave was fixed by a jury at $396,000. In April, 1928, F. P. Lee, an adjoining landowner, filed this suit against Edwards and the heirs of Sally Edwards, claiming that a portion of the cave was under his land, and praying for damages, for an accounting of the profits which resulted from the operation of the cave, and for an injunction prohibiting Edwards and his associates from further trespassing upon or exhibiting any part of the cave under Lee's land. At the inception of this litigation, Lee undertook to procure a survey of the cave in order that it might be determined what portion of it was on his land. The chancellor ordered that a survey be made, and Edwards prosecuted an appeal from that order to this court. The appeal was dismissed because it was not from a final judgment. Edwards v. Lee, 230 Ky. 375.] It was held that the order was interlocutory and consequently one from which no appeal would lie.

Following that decision, this original proceeding was filed in this court by the appellants in that case (who were defendants below) against Hon. N. P. Sims, judge of the Edmonson circuit court, seeking a writ of prohibition to prevent him enforcing the order and punishing the petitioners for contempt for any disobedience of it. It is alleged by the petitioners that the lower court was without jurisdiction or authority to make the order, and that their cave property and their right of possession and privacy will be wrongfully and illegally invaded, and that they will be greatly and irreparably injured and damaged without having an adequate remedy, since the damage will have been suffered before there can be an adjudication of their rights on a final appeal. * * *

There is but little authority of particular and special application to caves and cave rights. In few places, if any, can be found similar works of nature of such grandeur and of such unique and marvelous character as to

Figure 2–7

Postcard published by the Great Onyx Cave Hotel (L.P. Edwards, Proprietor).
Courtesy Kentucky Library, Western Kentucky University.

give to caves a commercial value sufficient to cause litigation as those peculiar to Edmonson and other counties in Kentucky. The reader will find of interest the address on "The Legal Story of Mammoth Cave" by Hon. John B. Rodes, of Bowling Green, before the 1929 Session of the Kentucky State Bar Association, published in its proceedings. In Cox v. Colossal Cavern Co., 276 S.W. 540 (Ky. 1925), the subject of cave rights was considered, and this court held there may be a severance of the estate in the property, that is, that one may own the surface and another the cave rights, the conditions being quite similar to but not exactly like those of mineral lands. But there is no such severance involved in this case, as it appears that the defendants are the owners of the land and have in it an absolute right.

Cujus est solum, ejus est usque ad coelum *[et] ad infernos* (to whomsoever the soil belongs, he owns also to the sky and to the depths), is an old maxim and rule. It is that the owner of realty, unless there has been a division of the estate, is entitled to the free and unfettered control of his own land above, upon, and beneath the surface. So whatever is in a direct line between the surface of the land and the center of the earth belongs to the owner of the surface. Ordinarily that ownership cannot be interfered with or infringed by third persons. There are, however, certain limitations on the right of enjoyment of possession of all property, such as its use to the detriment or interference with a neighbor and burdens which it must bear in common with property of a like kind.

With this doctrine of ownership in mind, we approach the question as to whether a court of equity has a transcendent power to invade that right through its agents for the purpose of ascertaining the truth of a matter before it, which fact thus disclosed will determine certainly whether or not the owner is trespassing upon his neighbor's property. Our attention has not been called to any domestic case, nor have we found one, in which the question was determined either directly or by analogy. It seems to the court, however, that there can be little differentiation, so far as the matter now before us is concerned, between caves and mines. And as declared in 40 C. J. 947:

> A court of equity, however, has the inherent power, independent of statute, to compel a mine owner to permit an inspection of his works at the suit of a party who can show reasonable ground for suspicion that his lands are being trespassed upon through them, and may issue an injunction to permit such inspection.

There is some limitation upon this inherent power, such as that the person applying for such an inspection must show a bona fide claim and allege facts showing a necessity for the inspection and examination of the adverse party's property; and, of course, the party whose property is to be inspected must have had an opportunity to be heard in relation thereto. In the instant case it appears that these conditions were met. The respondent cites several cases from other jurisdictions in which this power has been recognized and exercised. * * *

We can see no difference in principle between the invasion of a mine on adjoining property to ascertain whether or not the minerals are being extracted from under the applicant's property and an inspection of this respondent's property through his cave to ascertain whether or not he is trespassing under this applicant's property.

It appears that before making this order the court had before him surveys of the surface of both properties and the conflicting opinions of witnesses as to whether or not the Great Onyx Cave extended under the surface of the plaintiff's land. This opinion evidence was of comparatively little value, and as the chancellor (now respondent) suggested, the controversy can be quickly and accurately settled by surveying the cave; and "if defendants are correct in their contention this survey will establish it beyond all doubt and their title to this cave will be forever quieted. If the survey shows the Great Onyx Cave extends under the lands of plaintiffs, defendants should be glad to know this fact and should be just as glad to cease trespassing upon plaintiff's lands, if they are in fact doing so.'' The peculiar nature of these conditions, it seems to us, makes it imperative and necessary in the administration of justice that the survey should have been ordered and should be made.

It appearing that the circuit court is not exceeding its jurisdiction or proceeding erroneously, the claim of irreparable injury need not be given consideration. It is only when the inferior court is acting erroneously, *and* great or irreparable damage will result, *and* there is no adequate remedy by appeal, that a writ of prohibition will issue restraining the other tribunal, as held by authorities cited above.

[Handwritten margin note: Remaining issues not given consideration]

The writ of prohibition is therefore denied.

■ LOGAN, J. (dissenting). The majority opinion allows that to be done which will prove of incalculable injury to Edwards without benefiting Lee, who is asking that this injury be done. I must dissent from the majority opinion, confessing that I may not be able to show, by any legal precedent, that the opinion is wrong, yet having an abiding faith in my own judgment that it is wrong.

It deprives Edwards of rights which are valuable, and perhaps destroys the value of his property, upon the motion of one who may have no interest in that which it takes away, and who could not subject it to his dominion or make any use of it, if he should establish that which he seeks to establish in the new suit wherein the survey is sought.

It sounds well in the majority opinion to tritely say that he who owns the surface of real estate, without reservation, owns from the center of the earth to the outmost sentinel of the solar system. The age-old statement, adhered to in the majority opinion as the law, in truth and fact, is not true now and never has been. I can subscribe to no doctrine which makes the owner of the surface also the owner of the atmosphere filling illimitable space. Neither can I subscribe to the doctrine that he who owns the surface is also the owner of the vacant spaces in the bowels of the earth.

[Handwritten margin note: same wording as in "Hinman"]

The rule should be that he who owns the surface is the owner of everything that may be taken from the earth and used for his profit or happiness. Anything which he may take is thereby subjected to his dominion, and it may be well said that it belongs to him. I concede the soundness of that rule, which is supported by the cases cited in the majority opinion; but they have no application to the question before the court in this case. They relate mainly to mining rights; that is, to substances under the surface which the owner may subject to his dominion. But no man can bring up from the depths of the earth the Stygian darkness and make it serve his purposes; neither can he subject to his dominion the bottom of the ways in the caves on which visitors tread, and for these reasons the owner of the surface has no right in such a cave which the law should, or can, protect because he has nothing of value therein, unless, perchance, he owns an entrance into it and has subjected the subterranean passages to his dominion.

[Handwritten margin note: Caves w/ no material goods should be subject to the dominion of whomever holds the land with its entrance]

Rule proposed by the Dissent

A cave or cavern should belong absolutely to him who owns its entrance, and this ownership should extend even to its utmost reaches if he has explored and connected these reaches with the entrance. When the surface owner has discovered a cave and prepared it for purposes of exhibition, no one ought to be allowed to disturb him in his dominion over that which he has conquered and subjected to his uses.

It is well enough to hang to our theories and ideas, but when there is an effort to apply old principles to present-day conditions, and they will not fit, then it becomes necessary for a readjustment, and principles and facts as they exist in this age must be made conformable. For these reasons the old sophistry that the owner of the surface of land is the owner of everything from zenith to nadir must be reformed, and the reason why a reformation is necessary is because the theory was never true in the past, but no occasion arose that required the testing of it. Man had no dominion over the air until recently, and, prior to his conquering the air, no one had any occasion to question the claim of the surface owner that the air above him was subject to his dominion. Naturally the air above him should be subject to his dominion in so far as the use of the space is necessary for his proper enjoyment of the surface, but further than that he has no right in it separate from that of the public at large. The true principle should be announced to the effect that a man who owns the surface, without reservation, owns not only the land itself, but everything upon, above, or under it which he may use for his profit or pleasure, and which he may subject to his dominion and control. But further than this his ownership cannot extend. It should not be held that he owns that which he cannot use and which is of no benefit to him, and which may be of benefit to others.

The holding from 'Hinman'

Shall a man be allowed to stop airplanes flying above his land because he owns the surface? He cannot subject the atmosphere through which they fly to his profit or pleasure; therefore, so long as airplanes do not injure him, or interfere with the use of his property, he should be helpless to prevent their flying above his dominion. Should the waves that transmit intelligible sound through the atmosphere be allowed to pass over the lands of surface-owners? If they take nothing from him and in no way interfere with his profit or pleasure, he should be powerless to prevent their passage?

If it be a trespass to enter on the premises of the landowner, ownership meaning what the majority opinion holds that it means, the aviator who flies over the land of one who owns the surface, without his consent, is guilty of a trespass as defined by the common law and is subject to fine or imprisonment, or both, in the discretion of a jury.

If he who owns the surface does not own and control the atmosphere above him, he does not own and control vacuity beneath the surface. He owns everything beneath the surface that he can subject to his profit or pleasure, but he owns nothing more. Therefore, let it be written that a man who owns land does, in truth and in fact, own everything from zenith to nadir, but only for the use that he can make of it for his profit or pleasure. He owns nothing which he cannot subject to his dominion.

In the light of these unannounced principles which ought to be the law in this modern age, let us give thought to the petitioner Edwards, his rights and his predicament, if that is done to him which the circuit judge has directed to be done. Edwards owns this cave through right of discovery, exploration, development, advertising, exhibition, and conquest. Men fought their way through the eternal darkness, into the mysterious and abysmal depths of the bowels of a groaning world to discover the theretofore unseen splendors of unknown natural scenic wonders. They were conquerors of fear, although now and then one of them, as did Floyd Collins, paid with his life, for his hardihood in adventuring into the regions where Charon with his boat had never before seen any but the spirits of the departed. They let themselves down by flimsy ropes into pits that seemed bottomless; they clung to scanty handholds as they skirted the brinks of precipices while the flickering flare of their flaming flambeaux disclosed no bottom to the yawning gulf beneath them; they waded through rushing torrents, not knowing what awaited them on the farther side; they climbed slippery steeps to find other levels; they wounded their bodies on stalagmites and stalactites and other curious and weird formations; they found chambers, star-studded and filled with scintillating light reflected by a phantasmagoria revealing fancied phantoms, and tapestry woven by the toiling gods in the dominion of Erebus; hunger and thirst, danger and deprivation could not stop them. Through days, weeks, months, and years—ever linking chamber with chamber, disclosing an underground land of enchantment, they continued their explorations; through the years they toiled connecting these wonders with the outside world through the entrance on the land of Edwards which he had discovered; through the years they toiled finding safe ways for those who might come to view what they had found and placed their seal upon. They knew nothing, and cared less, of who owned the surface above; they were in another world where no law forbade their footsteps. They created an underground kingdom where Gulliver's people may have lived or where Ayesha may have found the revolving column of fire in which to bathe meant eternal youth.

When the wonders were unfolded and the ways were made safe, then Edwards patiently, and again through the years, commenced the advertisement of his cave. First came one to see, then another, then two together, then small groups, then small crowds, then large crowds, and then the multitudes. Edwards had seen his faith justified. The cave was his because he had made it what it was, and without what he had done it was nothing of value. The value is not in the black vacuum that the uninitiated call a cave. That which Edwards owns is something intangible and indefinable. It is his vision translated into a reality.

— Hume's idea "property comes from imagination"

Then came the horse leach's daughters crying: "Give me," "give me." Then came the "surface men" crying, "I think this cave may run under my lands." They do not know they only "guess," but they seek to discover the secrets of Edwards so that they may harass him and take from him that which he has made his own. They have come to a court of equity and have asked that Edwards be forced to open his doors and his ways to them so that they may go in and despoil him; that they may lay his secrets bare so that others may follow their example and dig into the wonders which Edwards has made his own. What may be the result if they stop his ways? They destroy the cave, because those who visit it are they who give it value, and none will visit it when the ways are barred so that it may not be exhibited as a whole.

It may be that the law is as stated in the majority opinion of the court, but equity, according to my judgment, should not destroy that which belongs to one man when he at whose behest the destruction is visited, although with some legal right, is not benefited thereby. Any ruling by a court which brings great and irreparable injury to a party is erroneous.

NOTES AND QUESTIONS

1. It is well established, at least in American jurisprudence, that the owner of the surface is entitled to any valuable minerals that may be discovered below the surface, and as *Edwards* holds, can exploit the value of a cave discovered below the surface. Rights to water below the surface and to "fugacious" minerals like oil and gas discovered below the surface are more complex, but the basic rule is that the surface owner has a presumptive right to drill for water or oil and gas below the surface, as long as the drilling apparatus stays within the "column of space" projected down from the surface. Slant drilling, i.e., drilling down at an angle that intersects a neighbor's column of space, is deemed a form of trespass.

2. In other legal systems, ownership of the surface does not entail ownership of minerals found beneath the surface. Many civil-law countries, including most Latin American countries, follow the rule that minerals below the surface are owned by the government. See Peter Bakewell, *Mining*, in Colonial Spanish America 203, 232 (Leslie Bethell ed., 1987).

3. Does the dissent in the principal case disagree with the *ad coelum* rule, or does it argue for a different interpretation of the rule than the one advocated by the majority? Under the dissent's proposed rule, what additional facts might have to be found before determining that Lee has no rights to the cave, assuming it occupies a portion of his column of space underground? — *that he has no entrance to the cave system on his land*

4. Can you see how the *ad coelum* rule represents another example of the general principle of accession? We start with ownership of the surface. Then, as new increments in value are discovered below the surface (minerals, caves, oil and gas) or above the surface (engineering capabilities to construct very tall buildings), these increments in value are automatically assigned to the owner of the surface—the most prominent pre-assigned property. Does the *ad coelum* rule also represent a generalization about who is assumed to be "in possession" of minerals or caves discovered beneath the surface? Is the problem in the present case that this generalization is difficult to justify on the particular facts presented?

5. After much litigation over the Great Onyx Cave, the state exercised its power of eminent domain and operated the cave itself. Edwards v. Lee's Administrator, 96 S.W.2d 1028, 1029 (Ky. 1936).

Different interpretation (though the same as the majority in Hinman) - ownership to anything above & below surface that one is using for enjoyment of land (or that one has established DOMINION over)

6. Suppose the Great Onyx Cave is a flop as a tourist attraction, and Edwards decides to use it as a giant storage tank for natural gas. The molecules of gas naturally migrate into the portion of the cave under Lee's property, as well as the portion under Edward's surface rights. Can Lee sue Edwards for trespass, and collect as damages the fair rental value of the portion of the cave under his surface rights? Would this sort of "invasion" be governed by the law of nuisance rather than trespass? What if Lee did not sue, but decided to drill down into the cave to extract the gas injected by Edwards for his own commercial purposes? Would this be a conversion? For consideration of some of these issues, see Hammonds v. Central Kentucky Natural Gas Co., 75 S.W.2d 204 (Ky. 1934). The court analogized natural gas to a wild animal previously captured and then released. How does this assumption affect your analysis of the issues?

5. ACCRETION

P   *D*

Nebraska v. Iowa

Supreme Court of the United States, 1892.
143 U.S. 359.

This is an original suit, brought in this court by the state of Nebraska against the state of Iowa, the object of which is to have the boundary line between the two states determined. Iowa was admitted into the Union in 1846, and its western boundary, as defined by the act of admission, was the middle of the main channel of the Missouri river. Nebraska was admitted in 1867, and its eastern boundary was likewise the middle of the channel of the Missouri river. Between 1851 and 1877, in the vicinity of Omaha, there were marked changes in the course of this channel, so that in the latter year it occupied a very different bed from that through which it flowed in the former year. Out of these changes has come this litigation, the respective states claiming jurisdiction over the same tract of land. * * *

■ MR. JUSTICE BREWER, after stating the facts in the foregoing language, delivered the opinion of the court. It is settled law that when grants of land border on running water, and the banks are changed by that gradual process known as "accretion," the riparian owner's boundary line still remains the stream, although, during the years, by this accretion, the actual area of his possessions may vary. In *New Orleans v. United States*, 10 Pet. 662, 717, this court said: "The question is well settled at common law, that the person whose land is bounded by a stream of water which changes its course gradually by alluvial formations shall still hold by the same boundary, including the accumulated soil. No other rule can be applied on just principles. Every proprietor whose land is thus bounded is subject to loss by the same means which may add to his territory; and, as he is without remedy for his loss in this way, he cannot be held accountable for his gain."

It is equally well settled that where a stream, which is a boundary, from any cause suddenly abandons its old and seeks a new bed, such change of channel works no change of boundary; and that the boundary remains as it was, in the center of the old channel, although no water may be flowing therein. This sudden and rapid change of channel is termed, in the law, "avulsion." In Gould on Waters, sec. 159, it is said: "But if the change is violent and visible, and arises from a known cause, such as a freshet, or a cut through which a new channel is formed, the original thread of the stream continues to mark the limits of the two estates."

These propositions, which are universally recognized as correct where the boundaries of private property touch on streams, are in like manner recognized where the boundaries between states or nations are, by prescription or treaty, found in running water. Accretion, no matter to which side it adds ground, leaves the boundary still the center of the channel. Avulsion has no effect on boundary, but leaves it in the center of the old channel. * * *

Summary of Rule

The result of these authorities puts it beyond doubt that accretion on an ordinary river would leave the boundary between two states the varying center of the channel, and that avulsion would establish a fixed boundary, to-wit, the center of the abandoned channel. It is contended, however, that the doctrine of accretion has no application to the Missouri river * * * because of the peculiar character of that stream, and of the soil through which it flows, the course of the river being tortuous, the current rapid, and the soil a soft, sandy loam, not protected from the action of water either by rocks or the roots of trees; the effect being that the river cuts away its banks, sometimes in a large body, and makes for itself a new course, while the earth thus removed is almost simultaneously deposited elsewhere, and new land is formed almost as rapidly as the former bank was carried away. * * * "The test as to what is gradual and imperceptible in the sense of the rule is that, though the witnesses may see from time to time that progress has been made, they could not perceive it while the process was going on." [quoting Jefferis v. East Omaha Land Co., 134 U.S. 178, 190 (1890), quoting in turn County of St. Clair v. Lovingston, 90 U.S. (23 Wall.) 46, 68 (1874)]. * * *

But what are the facts apparent from [the] testimony? The Missouri river is a winding stream, coursing through a valley of varying width, the substratum of whose soil, a deposit of distant centuries, is largely of quicksand. In building the bridge of the Union Pacific Railway Company across the Missouri river in the vicinity of the tracts in controversy, the builders went down to the solid rock, 65 feet below the surface, and there found a pine log a foot and a half in diameter—of course, a deposit made in the long ago. The current is rapid, far above the average of ordinary rivers; and by reason of the snows in the mountains there are two well-known rises in the volume of its waters, known as the April and June rises. The large volume of water pouring down at the time of these rises, with the rapidity of its current, has great and rapid action upon the loose soil of its banks. Whenever it impinges with direct attack upon the bank at a bend of the stream, and that bank is of the loose sand obtaining in the valley of the Missouri, it is not strange that the abrasion and washing away is rapid and great. Frequently, where above the loose substratum of sand there is a deposit of comparatively solid soil, the washing out of the underlying sand causes an instantaneous fall of quite a length and breadth of the superstratum of soil into the river; so that it may, in one sense of the term, be said, that the diminution of the banks is not gradual and imperceptible, but sudden and visible. Notwithstanding this, two things must be borne in mind, familiar to all dwellers on the banks of the Missouri river, and disclosed by the testimony: that, while there may be an instantaneous and obvious dropping into the river of quite a portion of its banks, such portion is not carried down the stream as a solid and compact mass, but disintegrates and separates into particles of earth borne onward by the flowing water, and giving to the stream that color, which, in the history of the country, has made it known as the "muddy" Missouri; and also that, while the disappearance, by reason of this process, of a mass of bank may be sudden and obvious, there is no transfer of such a solid body of earth to the opposite shore, or anything like an instantaneous and visible creation of a bank on that shore. The accretion, whatever may be the fact in respect to the diminution, is always gradual, and by the imperceptible deposit of floating particles of earth. There is, except in such cases of avulsion as may be noticed hereafter, in all matter of increase of bank, always a mere gradual and imperceptible process. There is no heaping up at an instant, and while the eye rests upon the stream, of acres or rods on the forming side of the river. No engineering skill is sufficient to say where the earth in the bank washed away and disintegrating into the river finds its rest and abiding place. The falling bank has passed into the floating mass of earth and water, and the particles of earth may rest one or fifty miles below, and upon either shore. There is, no matter how rapid the process of subtraction or addition, no detachment of earth from the one side and deposit of the same upon the other. The only thing which distinguishes this river from other streams, in the matter of accretion, is in the rapidity of the change, caused by the velocity of the current, and this in itself, in the very nature of things, works no change in the principle underlying the rule of law in respect thereto.

Our conclusions are that, notwithstanding the rapidity of the changes in the course of the channel, and the washing from the one side and onto the other, the law of accretion controls on the Missouri river as elsewhere; and that not only in respect to the rights of individual landowners, but also in respect to the boundary lines between states. The boundary, therefore, between Iowa and Nebraska is a varying line, so far as affected by these changes of diminution and accretion in the mere washing of the waters of the stream.

It appears, however, from the testimony, that in 1877 the river above Omaha, which had pursued a course in the nature of an ox-bow, suddenly cut through the neck of the bow and made for itself a new channel. This does not come within the law of accretion, but of that of avulsion. By this selection of a new channel the boundary was not changed, and it remained, as it was prior to the avulsion, the center line of the old channel; and that, unless the waters of the river returned to their former bed, became a fixed and unvarying boundary, no matter what might be the changes of the river in its new channel.

We think we have, by these observations, indicated as clearly as is possible the boundary between the two states, and upon these principles the parties may agree to a designation of such boundary, and such designation will pass into a final decree. If no agreement is possible, then the court will appoint a commission to survey and report in accordance with the views herein expressed.

Figure 2–8
Iowa–Nebraska Border

NOTES AND QUESTIONS

1. As the Court explains, *accretion* refers to the "gradual deposit by water of solid material, whether mud, sand, or sediment, producing dry

land which was before covered by water"; and *avulsion* "is the sudden change of the banks of a stream such as occurs when a river forms a new course by going through a bend, the sudden abandonment by a stream of its old channel and the creation of a new one, or a sudden washing away from one of its banks of a considerable quantity of land and its deposit on the opposite bank." 3 American Law of Property § 15.26, at 855–56 (A. Casner ed., 1952). Other terms sometimes encountered are *reliction*, which refers to "land that has been covered by water, but which has been uncovered by the imperceptible recession of the water;" and *erosion,* which "is the gradual and imperceptible wearing away of land (bordering on water) by the natural action of the elements." Id. Two other terms that arise in this context are *riparian*, which refers to "land bordering on any type of water—rivers, streams, lakes, ponds, and arms of the ocean," and *littoral,* which refers more properly to land bordering the ocean or a major inland sea. Id.

2.   Accretion, reliction, and erosion are all governed by the same rule. Owners of riparian land that grows through the operation of accretion or reliction automatically gain title to the new land. Owners of riparian land that shrinks due to erosion automatically lose title to the lost land. This is a rule of law, not just a rule of construction or a default rule. Avulsion, as explained in the principal case, results in no change of boundary lines. What do you suppose happens when the opposite of reliction occurs, that is, when dry land is gradually inundated by a new body of standing water?

3.   Like the rule of increase, the rules of accretion and avulsion are quite universally followed. They date from Roman law, and are apparently followed in virtually all civil-law and common-law jurisdictions. As the principal case suggests, they form part of the international law of boundaries as well as the law of property.

4.   Hume, supra, mentions the rule of accretion as an example of the principle of accession. One can see the logic of this. Deposits of sand and mud imperceptibly added to riparian land are imagined to belong to the riparian landowner, because the deposits are "small" and the existing riparian land is "large," and the deposits are directly attached to the existing land. So the riparian landowner is regarded as the most prominent existing source of property rights to which to assign ownership of the new deposits added by accretion. But can Hume's psychological theory also account for the exception to the rule that governs avulsions?

6.   FIXTURES

A fixture is defined as "a thing which, although originally a movable chattel, is by reason of its annexation to, or association in use with land, regarded as part of the land." Ray Andrews Brown, The Law of Personal Property 698 (1955).

P   *D* — seller of House

Buyer of House

Strain v. Green

Supreme Court of Washington, 1946.
172 P.2d 216.

■ ROBINSON, JUSTICE. On August 7, 1943, Jacob Green agreed to sell to William Strain his waterfront home on Mercer Island for thirty-five thousand dollars * * * On August 20, 1943, Green and wife executed a statutory warranty deed to Strain and wife, which they duly acknowledged and delivered to the purchasers on August 27th, receiving the purchase price in full. At some time thereafter, they left the premises, taking with them, from the basement, the hot water tank and enclosed electric heater, the Venetian blinds from the windows, certain lighting fixtures, and three mirrors, two of which were rather firmly attached to the walls. It was also claimed, in the ensuing lawsuit, that they unlawfully carried away a fireplace screen, a tool house, and certain chicken wire, with the posts which supported it. The total value of the articles removed was alleged to be $1,105.

On November 8, 1943, Mr. Hamley, as attorney for the Strains, demanded, in writing, that all of said property be returned to the premises. No part of the demand being complied with, this action was brought in March, 1944. The plaintiffs prayed for a judgment requiring the defendants to return the property, or, in case that that could not be done, for $1,105, and additional sums alleged to have been necessarily expended by the plaintiffs on account of the removal from the property, or which they would be required to expend to reinstall it.

It appears from the evidence that, when the defendants purchased the home, they found the hot water system inadequate, and put in a large, modern insulated tank, with an automatic electric control. When they left the house, they disconnected that tank from the plumbing and electric system, and reconnected the much smaller tank which was serving the house when they bought it. This the plaintiffs found wholly inadequate, and supplemented it, as far as, in view of war time scarcities, they were able to do so, by buying and hooking up two large tanks, and making certain other additions.

When the plaintiffs agreed to buy the house, and up until they had completed the payment on the purchase price, there was a large and beautiful crystal chandelier in the center of the dining room ceiling, and five other matching fixtures in that room and adjoining rooms. The distinctive feature of these articles was their ornamentation by a great number of pendants of imported crystal glass. These fixtures the Greens also disconnected and took with them. Before departing, however, they bought, and installed in place of the fixtures removed, some highly inferior plastic imitations.

When the plaintiffs purchased the house, there was a large plate glass mirror on one of the dining room walls. It had been installed in the following manner: A large piece of three-eighths-inch plywood was firmly nailed to the plastered wall, and the mirror was attached to this backing by screws. The mirror itself was, of course, readily removed. The Greens removed it, and left the plastered wall with the large square of plywood in the middle of it. The mirror having been removed, the plywood had no visible excuse for being there, and the Strains removed it. It still had twenty-six nails in it when introduced in evidence, and holes where there had been a dozen or so more. When the plywood was pried from the wall, each nail brought some of the plaster with it. The mirror over the living room fireplace was attached to the wall in the same manner, although fewer nails were used. This mirror the Greens also removed. The mirror in what was known as the powder room also had a plywood backing, but there is no very convincing testimony that the plywood was nailed, or attached, to the wall, and Mrs. Green's testimony was to the effect that the mirror merely rested upon a table and was held in place by a wire which ran to a hook above it, just as pictures are hung.

As for the other articles, the Venetian blinds were of odd sizes, cut and built especially for the windows of the house. The so-called tool house turned out to be a child's playhouse, and there was no evidence that chicken wire was ever taken from the premises.

The trial court held that the automatic hot water tank was a fixture, and must be returned. The Venetian blinds were also held to be fixtures, and ordered returned. Certain damages were awarded with respect to reinstallations. As the defendants have not cross-appealed, we are not concerned with that portion of the judgment. The court, however, held that the light fixtures and mirrors were personal property, which the defendants had a right to remove, and it is from that holding that this appeal is taken.

We will not undertake to write a treatise on the law of fixtures. Every lawyer knows that cases can be found in this field that will support any position that the facts of his particular case require him to take. As early as 1899, the court said, in Philadelphia Mortgage & Trust Co. v. Miller, 20 Wash. 607: "there is a wilderness of authority on this question of fixtures * * * cases, * * * are so conflicting that it would be profitless to undertake to review or harmonize them."

Throughout the trial, the trial judge repeatedly referred to that case as "the Miller case," and counsel, in his opening brief, refers to it as "the leading case in this jurisdiction." It held that four mantels, a bathtub, and a hot water heater connected with the plumbing were not fixtures. Since much reliance is placed upon that decision, we will quote rather freely from the opinion:

> Anciently, mantels were uniformly built as a part of the house, and therefore became a fixture to the realty. * * * But advancing mechanical science and taste have evolved an altogether differently constructed mantel, and mantels such as are described by the testimony in this case are now constructed without reference to any particular house or particular fireplace. They are what are called "stock" mantels, and are sold separately, and made adaptive to any kind of a house. They are, in fact, as much a separate article of merchandise as a bedstead or a table. * * * The same advancement has been made in bath tubs. The

old-fashioned bath tub, that was sealed in and actually made a part of the bath room, has largely given place to the more convenient bath tub, that rests upon legs, and can be attached to any heating system that happens to prevail in the house where it is used. And so with heaters or boilers. In this instance the boiler is in no way attached to the building, excepting by its plumbing connections. It could be detached without in any way injuring the realty; * * *. The testimony shows that the building back of the mantels, or that portion of it which was concealed by the mantels, was plastered and kalsomined; that for about three years the mantels were not fastened to the wall in any way, but supported themselves in the position they occupied, and that, after that time, they were fastened to the wall by screws, to render them more stable and keep them from toppling. The boiler and bath tub were not placed in the building for several years after the mortgage was given.

It would seem that the court could not very well have held otherwise than it did, without encroaching upon the province of the jury; for, it is further said:

> The question of whether or not the particular piece of furniture or machinery is a chattel or fixture has been held by a majority of the courts to be a mixed question of law and fact. In this case the court instructed the jury. These instructions were not excepted to, and must be presumed to have correctly stated the law; and, the jury having found the facts in favor of the respondent, we would be loath to disturb their findings, unless we were compelled to say that, as a matter of law, the property sued for was a part of the realty.

Respondents also strongly rely on Hall v. Law Guarantee & Trust Society, 22 Wash. 305. The first headnote to this case reads as follows:

> Gas and electric light fixtures and globes, a windmill, a hot water tank, curtains, window and door screens, when attached to a house, are not fixtures as between a mortgagor and a mortgagee.

Referring to these two cases, the first of which was decided in 1899, and the second in 1900, respondents say, in their brief, that they "have never been overruled in this state and are the law today." Although they may never have been expressly overruled, they at least have been outmoded. We think it highly improbable that it would now be held, even in a case between a mortgagor and a mortgagee, that a mantel, or a bathtub, or an electric hot water heater connected with both the plumbing and the electrical system is not a fixture. The law relating to fixtures has slowly and gradually changed as times have changed. Various household appliances, not formerly held to be fixtures, have become so in this "built-in" era. But the major changes are probably the result of an awareness of the fact that the luxuries of a given generation become the necessities of the next. It seems highly improbable that any present-day court would hold that a foreclosed mortgagor, on surrendering the premises, could lawfully disconnect, and take with him, the household bathtub. * * *

[B]oth Mr. and Mrs. Green categorically testified that they never had any intention that the chandelier, sidelights, and mirrors should ever become fixtures, and that they had removed them, as personal property, from the former houses in which they had lived. Furthermore, their testimony was in no way rebutted.

We do not wish it to be understood that we in any way question the veracity of the respondents, but we are here considering an alleged rule that may be involved in future cases, and, treating the matter wholly impersonally, if a witness testifies that, when he put a chandelier in a house, he intended to take it out if he should ever sell the house, in what possible way can his evidence be disputed? And, passing that, by what ex post facto system of mind reading could a purchaser determine the vendor's state of mind when he installed the chandelier? There is no evidence whatever in the instant case that the respondents told the appellants that they had ever had such an intention until after the appellants had bought, and paid for, the house. If it held in this case that the secret intention of the defendants is determinative of the question whether or not the articles involved are fixtures, that holding will encourage and invite persons less honest than the respondents to attempt to remove from premises sold every at-all-movable article that can be disconnected without breakage.

It has never been the law of this jurisdiction, nor, we think, of any other, that the secret intention of the owner who affixed the disputed *Rule* article, of itself, determines whether or not it was a fixture or a mere personal chattel.

[In] Ballard v. Alaska Theatre Co., 161 P. 478, 481 [this Court said]:

> The intent is not to be gathered from testimony of the actual state of the mind of the party making the annexation but is to be inferred, when not determined by an express agreement, from the nature of the article affixed, the relation and situation to the freehold of the party making the annexation, the manner of the annexation, and the purpose for which it is made.

The case cited in the above quotation [Washington National Bank v. Smith, 45 P. 736] was decided fifty years ago, in 1896. Turning to the opinion in the case, we find the following statement, 45 P. on page 739:

> That the intention with which machinery is placed upon the real estate is one of the elements to be taken into consideration in determining whether or not it remains a chattel, or becomes a part of such real estate, is conceded; but *it does not follow that such intention can be shown by testimony as to the actual state of the mind of the person who attached the machinery to the real estate at the time it was attached. On the contrary, his intention must be gathered from circumstances surrounding the transaction, and from what was said and done at the time, and cannot be affected by his state of mind retained as a secret.* (Italics ours.)

It is also said, in Ballard v. Alaska Theatre Co., supra:

RULE

Even when it is the same object attached in the same way

Based on presumptions above absent on express agreement.

When the annexation is made by a tenant or licensee the presumption is that he did not intend to enrich the freehold, but intended to reserve title to the chattel annexed in himself, while from an annexation by the owner of the property, the presumption is the other way. [Citing cases.] It therefore often happens that the same character of article annexed to the realty in the same way will be held to be a trade fixture and removable when annexed by a tenant, but real property and not removable when annexed by the owner of the property.

The opinion in Hall v. Dare, 252 P. 926, 928, by reference, approves the rule laid down in Filley v. Christopher, 39 Wash. 22, in which it is said:

The true criterion of a fixture is the united application of these requisites: (1) Actual annexation to the realty, or something appurtenant thereto; (2) application to the use or purpose to which that part of the realty with which it is connected is appropriated; and (3) the intention of the party making the annexation to make a permanent accession to the freehold.

Respondents in this case were owners when they installed the articles in question. The presumption, then, is (as held in the last of the quotations hitherto made from Ballard v. Alaska Theatre Co., supra) that it was their intention to enrich the freehold. This presumption is not overcome by evidence of secret intention, as is shown by the first of the quotations hitherto made from the same case, and then more plainly by the other quotation to the same effect from Washington National Bank v. Smith. Nor is the fact that the respondents successfully removed the articles from house to house of much, if any, probative value.

The chandelier and sidelights were actually annexed to the realty, and, clearly, for the use or purpose of that part of the realty (the house) with which they were connected. Their purpose, of course, was to make it livable. The fact that such articles are universally called "light fixtures," is, though not determinative, some evidence that they are fixtures. The fact that, after removing the chandelier and sidelights, the respondents replaced them with others, amounts to an implied admission on their part that a house without light fixtures would not be a complete house. In our opinion, the chandelier and sidelights were fixtures in law and in fact.

The mirrors—at least two of them—present a much closer question. We are satisfied that there is no adequate proof that the powder room mirror was physically annexed to the realty, and as to that mirror, which seems to have been the most valuable of the three, we need not inquire further. It was not a fixture. The others present a unique situation. Each of them could be taken down from the respective walls by removing a few screws, but in each case that would leave on the wall a large square of plywood which could not be removed, in the one case, without damaging the plaster, and, in the other, without leaving some damage by nail holes, and a portion of the wall of a different shade. We have arrived at the opinion that each of these mirrors and its plywood backing should be regarded as one article, and that in each case that article should be regarded as having been a portion of the house walls, and that, as such, they went with the house to the purchasers by the warranty deed which contained no reservations whatsoever.

Except as to the powder room mirror, the judgment, in so far as appealed from, is reversed, and the cause remanded to the trial court for the entry of judgment in accordance herewith.

NOTES AND QUESTIONS

1. Disputes over whether things are personal property or fixtures arise with some regularity and in several different contexts. One context, represented by the principal case, is when A sells real property to B, and a dispute arises as to whether particular things associated with the property are personal property belonging to A, or fixtures belonging to B. Another context is when C leases an apartment from D, and a dispute arises at the end of the lease over whether particular things C has added to the apartment are personal property belonging to C, or fixtures belonging to the landlord D. A third context is when E takes out a loan secured by a mortgage on real estate with bank F, and a dispute arises over whether certain things E has added to the property are included in F's security interest when E defaults on the loan.

2. Although the same doctrine nominally applies in each of these contexts, many observers believe that judges lean one way or another in close cases depending on the context. There is a hint of this in *Strain* when the court observes that mantels, bathtubs, and water heaters would most probably be regarded as fixtures "even in a case between a mortgagor and a mortgagee," suggesting that courts would be more likely to consider something as personal property in that context. If true, do you think this is because courts are more sympathetic to some classes of claimants (purchasers, tenants, and borrowers) and less sympathetic to others (sellers, landlords, lenders)? Or can the differences be explained, as the principal case suggests, by different presumptions about the likely intentions of persons in these different contexts?

3. Is fixtures doctrine just a default rule to be applied in determining the intentions of the parties to a bilateral contract? If so, can it really be said to be a doctrine about original acquisition of property rights? Or does the doctrine have certain applications that run counter to the parties' intentions, making it an example of how someone—an owner of land—can acquire objects that originally were personal property belonging to someone else, who had no intention to make a voluntary conveyance?

4. Although Hume does not mention the law of fixtures, the doctrine can be explained in terms of his theory of the principle of accession. In particular, psychological perceptions seem to play a substantial role in fixtures cases. Consider the different disposition the court reaches in *Strain* with regard to the mirrors in the dining room and living room, and the mirror in the powder room. The same intention and relationship among the parties exists with respect to each of the mirrors. The only difference is that the mirrors in the dining room and living room were attached to the

plywood by screws, whereas the mirror in the powder room was hung by wire from a hook. The greater connectedness or proximity between the attached mirrors and the real property causes the court to conclude they are fixtures, i.e., they belong to the owner of the real property, whereas the looser connection between the hung mirror and the realty causes the court to conclude it is personal property.

E.   ADVERSE POSSESSION

Our final principle of original acquisition is adverse possession. Courts have long held that when an owner sits on her right to exclude, and the statute of limitations for challenging the original unlawful entry expires, not only is the original owner barred from asserting the right to exclude but a new title also springs up in the adverse possessor. In effect, the adverse possessor becomes the new true owner, and can now exercise the right to exclude against all the world, including the original owner. Adverse possession applies to both real and personal property, and we provide cases illustrating both applications. If the owner fails to prevent someone from using the property for a particular purpose, as opposed to possessing it, and the statute of limitations runs, then this can give rise to a prescriptive easement. We take up this doctrine in Chapter IX.

Lessee of Ewing v. Burnet

Supreme Court of the United States, 1837.
36 U.S. (11 Pet.) 41.

■ BALDWIN, JUSTICE, delivered the opinion of the court. In the court below, this was an action of ejectment, brought in November 1834, by the lessor of the plaintiff, to recover possession of lot No. 209, in the city of Cincinnati; the legal title to which is admitted to have been in John Cleves Symmes, under whom both parties claimed; the plaintiff, by a deed dated 11th of June 1798, to Samuel Foreman, who, on the next day, conveyed to Samuel Williams, whose right, after his death, became vested in the plaintiff; the defendant claimed by a deed to himself, dated 21st of May 1803, and an adverse possession of twenty-one years before the bringing of the suit. It was in evidence, that the lot in controversy is situated on the corner of Third and Vine streets; fronting on the former 198, on the latter, 98 feet; the part on Third street is level for a short distance, but descends towards the south along a steep bank, from forty to fifty feet, to its south line; the side of it was washed in gullies, over and around which the people of the place passed and repassed at pleasure. The bed of the lot was principally sand and gravel, with but little loam or soil; the lot was not fenced, nor had any building or improvement been erected or made upon it, until within a few years before suit brought; a fence could have been kept up on the level ground on the top of the hill on Third street, but not on its declivity, on account of the deep gullies washed in the bank; and its principal use and value was in the convenience of digging sand and gravel for the inhabitants. Third street separated this lot from the one on which the defendant resided from 1804, for many years, his mansion fronting on that street; he paid the taxes upon this lot from 1810 until 1834, inclusive; and from the date of the deed from Symmes, until the trial, claimed it as his own. During this time, he also claimed the exclusive right of digging and removing sand and gravel from the lot; giving permission to some, refusing it to others; he brought actions of trespass against those who had done it, and at different times made leases to different persons, for the purpose of taking sand and gravel therefrom, besides taking it for his own use, as he pleased. This had been done by others, without his permission, but there was no evidence of his acquiescence in the claim of any person to take or remove the sand or gravel, or that he had ever intermitted his claim to the exclusive right of doing so; on the contrary, several witnesses testified to his continued assertion of right to the lot; their knowledge of his exclusive claim, and their ignorance of any adverse claim, for more than twenty-one years before the present suit was brought. They further stated, as their conclusion from these facts, that the defendant had, from 1806, or 1807, in the words of one witness, "had possession of the lot;" of another, that since 1804, "he was as perfectly and exclusively in possession as any person could possibly be of a lot not built on or inclosed;" and of a third, "that since 1811, he had always been in the most rigid possession of the lot in dispute; a similar possession to other possessions on the hill lot." It was further in evidence, that Samuel Williams, under whom the plaintiff claimed, lived in Cincinnati, from 1803, until his death in 1824; was informed of defendant having obtained a deed from Symmes, in 1803, soon after it was obtained, and knew of his claim to the lot; but there was no evidence that he ever made an entry upon it, demanded possession or exercised or assumed any exercise of ownership over it; though he declared to one witness, produced by plaintiff, that the lot was his, and he intended to claim and improve it, when he was able. This declaration was repeated often, from 1803, till the time of his death, and on his death-bed; and it appeared, that he was, during all this time, very poor; it also appeared in evidence, by the plaintiff's witness, that the defendant was informed, that Williams owned the lot, before the deed from Symmes, in 1803, and after he had made the purchase.

This is the substance of the evidence given at the trial, and returned with the record and a bill of exceptions, stating that it contains all the evidence offered in the cause; whereupon, the plaintiff's counsel moved the court to instruct the jury, that on this evidence the plaintiff was entitled to a verdict; also, that the evidence offered by the plaintiff and defendant was not sufficient, in law, to establish an adverse possession by the defendant; which motions the court overruled. This forms the first ground of exception by the plaintiff to the overruling his motions: 1. The refusal of the court to instruct the jury that he was entitled to recover: 2. That the defendant had made out an adverse possession. * * *

Now, as the jury might have refused credence to the only witness who testified to the notice given to the defendant of Williams's ownership of the lot in 1803, and of his subsequent assertion of claim, and intention to

Figure 2–9
Map of Cincinnati Wards, 1853

improve it; the testimony of this witness must be thrown out of the case, in testing the correctness of the court in overruling this motion; otherwise, we should hold the court below to have erred, in not instructing the jury on a matter exclusively for their consideration—the credibility of a witness, or how far his evidence tended to prove a fact, if they deemed him credible. This view of the case throws the plaintiff back to his deed, as the only evidence of title; on the legal effect of which, the court were bound to instruct the jury as a matter of law, which is the only question to be considered on this exception.

It is clear, that the plaintiff had the elder legal title to the lot in dispute, and that it gave him a right of possession, as well as the legal seisin and possession thereof, co-extensively with his right; which contin- ued till he was ousted by an actual adverse possession; or his right of possession had been in some other way barred. It cannot be doubted, that from the evidence adduced by the defendant, it was competent for the jury to infer these facts—that he had claimed this lot under color and claim of title, from 1804 until 1834; had exercised acts of ownership on and over it, during this whole period; that his claim was known to Williams and to the plaintiff; was visible, of public notoriety, for twenty years previous to the death of Williams. And if the jury did not credit the plaintiff's witness, they might also find that the defendant had no actual notice of Williams's claim; that it was unknown to the inhabitants of the place, while that of the defendants was known; and that Williams never did claim the lot, to assert a right to it, from 1803 until his death in 1824. The jury might also draw the same conclusion from these facts, as the witnesses did; that the defendant was, during the whole time, in possession of the lot, as strictly, perfectly and exclusively, as any person could be of a lot not inclosed or built upon; or as the situation of the lot would admit of. The plaintiff must, therefore, rely on a deed of which he had given no notice, and in opposition to all the evidence of the defendant, and every fact which a jury could find, that would show a right of possession in him, either by the presumption of a release or conveyance of the elder legal title, or by an adverse possession. * * *

On the next motion, the only question presented is on the legal sufficiency of the evidence to make out an ouster of the legal seisin and possession of Williams by the defendant; and a continued adverse possession for twenty-one years before suit brought. An entry by one man on the land of another, is an ouster of the legal possession arising from the title, or not, according to the intention with which it is done; if made under claim and color of right, it is an ouster, otherwise, it is a mere trespass; in legal language, the intention guides the entry and fixes its character. * * *

Must have intention to assert dominion

It is well settled, that to constitute an adverse possession, there need not be a fence, building or other improvement made; it suffices for this purpose, that visible and notorious acts of ownership are exercised over the premises in controversy, for twenty-one years, after an entry under claim and color of title. So much depends on the nature and situation of the property, the uses to which it can be applied, or to which the owner or claimant may choose to apply it, that it is difficult to lay down any precise rule, adapted to all cases. But it may with safety be said, that where acts of ownership have been done upon land, which, from their nature, indicate a notorious claim of property in it, and are continued for twenty-one years, with the knowledge of an adverse claimant, without interruption, or an adverse entry by him, for twenty-one years; such acts are evidence of an ouster of a former owner, and an actual adverse possession against him; if the jury shall think, that the property was not susceptible of a more strict or definite possession than had been so taken and held. Neither actual occupation, cultivation nor residence, are necessary to constitute actual possession, when the property is so situated as not to admit of any permanent useful improvement, and the continued claim of the party has been evidenced by public acts of ownership, such as he would exercise over property which he claimed in his own right, and would not exercise over property which he did not claim. Whether this was the situation of the lot in question, or such was the nature of the acts done, was the peculiar province of the jury; the evidence, in our opinion, was legally sufficient to draw the inference that such were the facts of the case, and if found

RULE

specially, would have entitled the defendant to the judgment of the court in his favor; they, of course, did not err in refusing to instruct the jury that the evidence was not sufficient to make out an adverse possession. * * *

It has also been urged, in argument, that as the defendant had notice of the claim of Williams, his possession was not fair and honest, and so not protected by the statute. This admits of two answers: 1. The jury were authorized to negative any notice; 2. Though there was such notice of a prior deed, as would make a subsequent one inoperative to pass any title, yet an adverse possession for twenty-one years, under claim and color of title, merely void, is a bar; the statutory protection being necessary, only where the defendant has no other title but possession, during the period prescribed. The judgment of the circuit court is, therefore, affirmed.

NOTES AND QUESTIONS

1.   John Cleve Symmes, a prominent land speculator, formed a private land company and eventually persuaded Congress to grant him 311,682 acres of land in the Northwest Territory north of the Ohio River, between the Great Miami and Little Miami rivers, including much of present-day Cincinnati. "Symmes was a poor businessman. His accounts were badly deranged and he sold land before he had title, and tracts to which he had no title." Paul W. Gates, History of Public Land Law Development 71 (1968). As *Ewing v. Burnet* reveals, he also sold some land twice.

2.   The doctrine of adverse possession evolved from judicial decisions resolving disputes over the application of the statute of limitations for recovery of possession of property. Assume the true owner of property (TO) is for some reason out of possession. She is, say, an absentee owner of land holding it for speculation, or has lost some personal property. Meanwhile, someone else, say a squatter or a finder or other type of adverse possessor (AP), has come into possession of the property. The TO has various causes of action allowing her to recover possession of property from an AP, such as trespass or ejectment in the case of land, and conversion or replevin in the case of personal property. See Chapter IV. But she cannot wait forever to bring such an action. The legislature (Parliament in England or the legislatures of the American states) typically will have enacted statutes of limitations that bar the bringing of such actions after a certain number of years have passed. The time for bringing an action to recover possession of real property varies widely from state to state, from a low of five years to a high of 40 years. See Joseph William Singer, Introduction to Property § 4.2.6 (2001). The time period for bringing an action in conversion or replevin to recover personal property is typically shorter (most commonly three to five years).

3.   In addition to the all-important running of the relevant statute of limitations, courts have said that adverse possession requires that other elements be satisfied as well. The typical hornbook lists five additional elements: the possession of the AP must have been (1) actual, (2) exclusive, (3) open and notorious, (4) continuous, and (5) adverse under a claim of

right. Each of these elements has a certain logic grounded in the cause of action to recover possession and/or the application of the statute of limitations. Three are elements that would have to be established to show that the TO had a cause of action. The *actual* possession requirement is necessary in order to bring an action for trespass, ejectment, conversion, or replevin, each of which is based on the premise that the AP has in fact deprived the TO of possession. Similarly, the *exclusive* element can be explained as designed to show that the AP is the one in possession of the property, to the exclusion of the TO. The *adverse under a claim of right* element is designed to show (at a minimum) that the possession was without permission of the TO—in other words that the TO had not granted the AP a license or lease. The *open and notorious* element, for its part, is designed to show that the TO had notice of the AP's possession; as stated in one early case, the AP must "keep his flag flying" so as to alert the TO of his "adverse pretensions." Stephens v. Leach, 19 Pa. 262, 264 (1852). The *continuous* element is designed to show that the cause of action accrued at the time of the original entry or taking of possession by the AP, and hence that the running of the statute of limitations on this claim encompasses all subsequent periods of possession as well, as opposed to there being a series of discrete periods of possession, each of which starts the statute running anew. Which of the foregoing five standard doctrinal elements does the court in *Ewing v. Burnet* make reference to? Which ones are ignored? Which ones does the court regard as being contested in the case?

4.   Probably the most contentious issue in the law of adverse possession is what it means to say that the AP's possession must be adverse under a claim of right. (Sometimes courts say "hostile under a claim of right" or just "adverse" or "hostile.") Commentators generally distinguish three positions: (1) Adverse under a claim of right means that the AP subjectively (but mistakenly) believes he is legally entitled to possession of the property, i.e., the AP is acting in good faith. (2) Adverse under a claim of right means that the AP subjectively believes he is not legally entitled to possession of the property, i.e., the AP is acting in bad faith. (3) The AP's subjective state of mind is irrelevant; all that matters is that the AP has not been given permission by the TO to use the property. The rule (our (2)) requiring bad faith has been called the "Maine Rule," after the decision in Preble v. Maine Cent. R. Co., 27 A. 149 (Me. 1893). It has always been the minority rule; indeed, Maine itself no longer follows it. See Maine Rev. Stat. § 810–A. Most commentators favor the so-called Connecticut Rule (our (3)), which makes state of mind irrelevant. But disagreement abounds as to whether good faith should be required or all that is required is lack of permission. Compare Lee Anne Fennell, Efficient Trespass: The Case for Bad Faith Adverse Possession, 100 Nw. U. L. Rev. 1037 (2006) with Jeffrey Evans Stake, The Uneasy Case for Adverse Possession, 89 Geo. L.J. 2419 (2001). Keep the issue of state of mind in mind when we turn to considering the purposes of adverse possession.

5.   What is the best characterization of the state of mind of Burnet (the adverse possessor) in *Ewing v. Burnet*: good faith, bad faith, or

Handwritten margin notes:

 5 Elements of Adverse Possession (in addition to the running of the statute of limitations) ① ② ③ ④ ⑤

3 Camps of "Adverse Under a Right of Claim"

└ assuming P's witness was not credible

unclear? What state of mind does the Court seem to require in order to establish a claim of title by adverse possession? Consider in this regard the second-to-last sentence in the opinion. Is the Court saying that bad faith (notice of Williams' prior deed) would not bar adverse possession? Consider also the Court's statement: "An entry by one man on the land of another, is an ouster of the legal possession arising from the title, or not, according to the intention with which it is done; if made under claim and color of right, it is an ouster, otherwise, it is a mere trespass; in legal language, the intention guides the entry and fixes its character." What is the distinction between "an ouster" and "a mere trespass"? Is the Court suggesting that an AP must enter the land with the intent *to possess* it, that is, to become the gatekeeper? See Stake, supra, at 2428 (arguing that adverse possession requires "physical occupation with the intent to exercise dominion"). Is this understanding also implicit in the meaning of "adverse under a claim of right"?

6.   If "claim of right" means, roughly, an intent to possess something as one's own, then what does "color of title" mean? A person enters under color of title when he or she has some document—usually a deed, will, or judicial decree—that purports to convey title but does not in fact do so because of some legal defect (e.g., the grantor did not own the land, or the instrument was improperly executed). A few states require "color of title" as an element of adverse possession, but most do not. Still, an adverse possessor with color of title has certain legal advantages. In some states the statute of limitations, which sets the requisite period of adverse possession, is shorter for possessors with color of title. In nearly all states, either by statute or under well-established doctrine, one who actually possesses part of a parcel of land under an instrument giving color of title to the whole parcel is deemed to "constructively possess" the whole. So *actual* adverse possession of part of the parcel described in a defective deed may give rise to *constructive* adverse possession of the whole parcel.

PURPOSES OF ADVERSE POSSESSION

Why do we permit longstanding adverse possession of property to ripen into a new title good against all the world, including the former owner? The general reasons for having a statute of limitations do not answer this question. There are, to be sure, justifications for having statutes of limitations. As time passes, witnesses die, memories fade, and evidence gets lost or destroyed. The costs of proving or disproving claims invariably increase over time. When these costs get too large, it is unfair to subject defendants to the risk of having to disprove them, and unduly burdensome to force courts to sort them out. But these costs could be avoided simply by interpreting the statute of limitations for actions to recover property to mean that the plaintiff cannot rely on events that happened before the period prescribed by the statute. Suppose the statute of limitations is ten years and the defendant constructed a building on plaintiff's land fifteen years ago. We could interpret the statute to mean that the plaintiff cannot allege or prove events occurring more than ten years ago, such as the original construction of the building. But this would not bar the plaintiff from proving that the building now sits on his land, that it is presently depriving him of possession, and that it should be torn down so as to permit him to recover possession. Such an interpretation would avoid any danger of having to rely on lost evidence or to call witnesses whose memories have faded. In order to justify the doctrine of adverse possession—which treats the passage of the statute not just as a rule that cuts off old claims but as an event that transfers ownership to the adverse possessor—we need some other reason or rationale.

Perhaps the most commonly cited rationale is couched in terms of the reliance interests that the possessor may have developed through longstanding possession of the property. Holmes expressed the idea in typically colorful fashion: "[M]an, like a tree in the cleft of a rock, gradually shapes his roots to his surroundings, and when the roots have grown up to a certain size, can't be displaced without cutting at his life." Letter from Oliver Wendell Holmes to William James (Apr. 1, 1907), in The Mind and Faith of Justice Holmes: His Speeches, Essays, Letters and Judicial Opinions 417, 417–18 (Max Lerner ed., 1943). Modern commentators have recast the argument in terms of loss aversion or the endowment effect. Psychological studies show that people tend to experience losses more acutely than gains. In other words, losing something one already has is relatively more painful than not getting something one does not yet have. If the AP is the person who "has" the property—which makes sense given that the AP is the one in possession—then taking it from the AP may be more demoralizing to the AP than denying it to the TO would be demoralizing to the TO. See Stake, supra, at 2459–71. An alternative way to make the point is that the AP may have more of her "personhood" wrapped up in the property than the TO. For the AP, the dispute involves some "thing" which the AP possesses; for the TO, what is at issue is more in the nature of a fungible asset interchangeable with other assets. See Margaret Jane Radin, Time, Possession, and Alienation, 64 Wash. U. L.Q. 739, 748 n.26 (1986).

Another longstanding rationale claims that adverse possession is a penalty designed to discourage TOs from "sleeping on their rights." This has been criticized as privileging active exploitation of land and resources and discouraging passive, preservationist uses. See John C. Sprankling, An Environmental Critique of Adverse Possession, 79 Cornell L. Rev. 816 (1994). But if we recast the point in terms of the gatekeeper idea perhaps it avoids this criticism. Private property can be seen as a system that delegates managerial authority over resources to private individuals who act as gatekeepers. If the gatekeeper falls down on the job, the resource may not be protected against abuse. Indeed, if the resource is a forest or a wetland, a sleeping gatekeeper may result in the resource being looted as an open access commons. Adverse possession can be seen from this perspective as a device for firing gatekeepers guilty of nonfeasance and replacing them with persons who have shown a greater aptitude and eagerness to play the gatekeeper role.

A third rationale is that adverse possession reduces the transaction costs of determining title to assets that last for a long time (like land). Over time, various potential claims to assets can accumulate: Perhaps the property was mortgaged at various times and it is unclear whether those security interests were released; perhaps a married couple owned the property and it is unclear whether both spouses released their claims; perhaps taxes due on the property were not paid in a given year. If all these claims had to be investigated, no matter how old they might be, the costs of establishing clear title to durable assets would be very large—large enough that they could impair the effective functioning of markets for durable assets. By systematically eliminating these old claims, like a broom that sweeps away old cobwebs, adverse possession reduces the costs of engaging in these transactions, and hence enhances the efficiency of property markets. Sometimes it is said that marketable title acts are equally or more effective in eliminating these old claims. See Stake, supra, at 2443–44. These statutes apply a conclusive presumption that claims more than a certain number of years old (e.g., 40 years) can be disregarded in establishing title to property. But marketable title acts can be regarded as a version of adverse possession law—a version with a longer statute of limitations and fewer additional elements. See Herbert Hovenkamp & Sheldon F. Kurtz, The Law of Property § 14.7, at 523–24 (5th ed. 2001). So the existence of these statutes only confirms the need for some mechanism like adverse possession to clear away old claims to property. For more on marketable title acts and land records generally, see Chapter VIII.

ADVERSE POSSESSION AGAINST THE GOVERNMENT

At common law one could not obtain title by adverse possession against the crown. This was pursuant to the maxim, *nullus tempus occurrit regi*, no time runs against the king. As Blackstone explained, the law presumes "the king is always busied for the public good, and therefore has not leisure to assert his right within the times limited to subjects." 1 Blackstone, Commentaries *240. This assumption carried over to the United States, with the people's elected representatives now enjoying the presumption formerly accorded the king. See, e.g., United States v. Thompson, 98 U.S. 486 (1878); United States v. Hoar, 26 F. Cas. 329 (C.C. Mass. 1821) (Story. J.). The courts concluded that "[i]n a representative government, where the people do not and cannot act in a body, where their power is delegated to others, and must of necessity be exercised by them, if exercised at all, the reason for applying these principles is equally cogent." Thompson, 98 U.S. at 489.

The presumption that adverse possession does not apply to the government took on special significance, given the widespread practice of squatting on the federal public lands, described earlier in this Chapter. Since the courts would not permit adverse possession as a matter of common law, this meant that Congress could determine, in its discretion, the terms and conditions for permitting squatters to obtain title to public land. Congress, through the preemption acts, generally treated the squatters more generously than they would have been treated under the law of adverse possession—but this judgment was for Congress to make. The common-law rule takes on special importance today, given the federal government's retention of millions of acres of National Parks, National Forests, Wilderness Areas, and other uninhabited lands. If adverse possession could be claimed against the federal government, these lands could be at risk, given the very high monitoring costs that would be involved. See Round Table Discussion, Time, Property Rights, and the Common Law, 64 Wash. U. L.Q. 793, 832–33 (1986) (comments of Robert Ellickson). The presumption that adverse possession does not apply against the government has been retained in some states, modified in others with longer statutes of limitations against the government than against private owners, and has been abolished in still others. See R. P. Davis, Acquisition by Adverse Possession or Use of Public Property Held by Municipal Corporation or Other Governmental Unit Otherwise than for Streets, Alleys, Parks, or Common, 55 A.L.R.2d 554 (1957).

Carpenter v. Ruperto

Supreme Court of Iowa, 1982.
315 N.W.2d 782.

■ McCormick, Justice. Plaintiff Virginia Carpenter appeals from an adverse decree in her action to quiet title to land adjacent to her residential premises based on a theory of adverse possession. * * * We affirm * * *

Plaintiff and her husband moved in 1951 to a home which they purchased in southeast Des Moines. Plaintiff's husband subsequently died, but plaintiff has lived on the premises continuously. Her lot has a frontage of 40 feet and is 125 feet long. * * *

A larger undeveloped lot bounded plaintiff's property to the north. * * *

Defendants and their predecessors have held record title to this lot at all material times.

The property which plaintiff claims to have acquired by adverse possession is the south 60 feet of defendants' lot. Thus, the property in dispute is a 60 by 125 foot parcel adjacent to the north boundary of plaintiff's lot.

When plaintiff and her husband moved into their home in July 1951, the lot north of their property was a cornfield. Although plaintiff was not certain of the location of the northern boundary of her lot, she knew her lot's dimensions, and she knew it did not include the cornfield. In 1952 the corn was not planted as far south on the adjacent lot. Concerned about rats and the threat of fire, and desiring additional yard for their children, plaintiff and her husband cleared several feet of the property to the north, graded it, and planted grass seed on it. Since that time plaintiff has used the land as an extension of her yard. She planted peony bushes on it during the 1950's, installed a propane tank on it approximately 30 feet north of her lot in 1964, constructed a dirt bank on the city right of way to divert water from that parcel in 1965, and put in a driveway infringing five feet onto the land in 1975.

The remainder of defendants' lot was planted in corn until approximately 1957. The lot was owned by Abraham and Beverly Rosenfeld from July 1960 until February 1978. During that period the only use Rosenfelds made of the property was to store junk and debris on it. Except for the strip used by plaintiff, the lot was overgrown with brush and weeds. The Rosenfelds paid all taxes and special assessments on the property. Plaintiff and her husband at one time obtained the Rosenfelds' permission to keep a horse on the lot. On one occasion in the 1960's plaintiff examined the plat of defendants' lot in the courthouse to see if it ran all the way to a street to the north.

When defendant McCormick purchased his interest in the lot in 1978, he was aware of the possibility of a boundary dispute because of the location of plaintiff's propane tank and driveway. He and the other defendants were unsuccessful in their efforts to settle the dispute with plaintiff, who subsequently brought this action.

In seeking to establish her ownership of the disputed parcel, plaintiff alleged she had "for more than thirty (30) years last past been in open, exclusive, hostile, adverse and actual possession under claim of right." The trial court held in part that she did not establish her possession was under a claim of right. The court reasoned that a claim of right must be made in good faith and that plaintiff was not in good faith because she knew someone else had title to the land. Although the court found plaintiff had not proved her claim of adverse possession, it ordered defendants to "do equity" by deeding to her the strip of land her driveway was on and to pay the costs of moving the propane tank to her lot. * * *

The doctrine of adverse possession is based on the ten-year statute of limitations for recovery of real property in section 614.1(5), The Code. One claiming title by adverse possession must establish hostile, actual, open, exclusive and continuous possession, under a claim of right or color of title, for at least ten years, by clear and positive proof. Because the law presumes possession under regular title, the doctrine is strictly construed. These and other governing principles are explained in *I–80 Associates, Inc. v. Chicago, Rock Island and Pacific Railroad*, 224 N.W.2d 8, 10–11 (Iowa 1974).

As permitted, plaintiff relied on claim of right rather than color of title. In contending the trial court erred in finding she failed in her proof of this element, she attacks the viability of the principal case relied on by the trial court, Goulding v. Shonquist, 141 N.W. 24 (Iowa 1913). Its facts are analogous to those here.

In *Goulding* the individual also cleared land adjacent to his house. The land was overrun with brush and willows and was frequented by hunters. After clearing it, the individual used the land as a pasture and garden. In finding he did not establish good faith claim of right, the court said:

When he moved into his present property, the lands in question were objectionable because they were frequented by hunters, and for that reason he and his wife thought they ought to clear them up. He says he supposed they were part of the old river bed or waste land upon which anyone could enter. No other facts are offered by defendant as a reason for entering into the possession of the land at that time. Whether the title to the land was in the state or some other person, the defendant knew that he had no title and that he had no claim of title, and no right whatever to enter into the possession, and his possession was not in good faith for that reason.

141 N.W. at 25. The court quoted a statement from Litchfield v. Sewell, 66 N.W. 104, 106 (Iowa 1896), * * * "that there can be no such thing as adverse possession where the party knows he has no title, and that, under the law, he can acquire none by his occupation."

Plaintiff argues that it is inconsistent to say ownership can be acquired by claim of right as an alternative to color of title and at the same time say ownership cannot be acquired by a person who knows he does not have title. She also argues that the good faith requirement was eliminated by the court decision in *I–80 Associates, Inc.* Although we agree it is an overstatement to say ownership cannot be acquired by a person who knows he does not have title, plaintiff is incorrect in her argument that good faith is not an essential component of claim of right. Moreover, we agree with the trial court that plaintiff did not prove this element of her adverse possession claim.

The overbreadth of the statement that title cannot be obtained through adverse possession by one who knows he has no title is demonstrated in *Litchfield*, *Goulding* and subsequent decisions. In *Litchfield* the court rejected the adverse possession claim of a person in possession of land under a quitclaim deed from a squatter. In finding an absence of good faith, the court noted the adverse possession doctrine "has no application to one who actually knows that he has no claim, or title, or right to a title." 66 N.W. at 106. Under this holding a mere squatter or one who claims under a squatter cannot have a good faith claim of right to the property, but mere knowledge by the person that he has no title is not preclusive. A claim of right by a squatter is a false claim. To permit a squatter to assert a claim of right would put a premium on dishonesty. See 4 H. Tiffany, Real Property § 1147 at 792 (3d ed. 1975). One of the main purposes of the claim of right requirement is "to bar mere squatters from the benefits of adverse possession." 7 R. Powell, Real Property ¶ 1015 (Rohan ed. 1981).

As in *Litchfield*, the possessor in *Goulding* not only knew that he had no title but that he had no claim of title or any right to enter into possession of the property. He was a mere squatter.

Knowledge of a defect in title is not alone sufficient to preclude proof of good faith:

One is not deprived of the benefit of the statute of limitations merely because his claim of right is unenforceable or his title is known to be defective. The doctrine of adverse possession presupposes a defective title. It is not based on, but is hostile to, the true title. If the statute were to run only in favor of a valid title, it would serve no purpose. The holder of such a title has no need to invoke the statute. Where bad faith is held to negative an alleged claim of right, it is only another way of saying that such claim has been disproved.

Creel v. Hammans, 13 N.W.2d 305, 307 (Iowa 1944).

RULE

Nevertheless, when knowledge of lack of title is accompanied by knowledge of no basis for claiming an interest in the property, a good faith claim of right cannot be established. * * *

We believe plaintiff failed to prove a good faith claim of right in the present case. She knew her lot did not include the cornfield north of it. She knew someone else had title to it and she had no interest in it or claim to it. This is not a case of confusion or mistake. At the time she entered possession of the disputed land, plaintiff knew she had no legal right to do so. To say that one can acquire a claim of right by merely entering possession would recognize squatter's rights. Possession for the statutory period cannot be bootstrapped into a basis for claiming a right to possession.

We hold that the trial court was right in rejecting plaintiff's claim. * * *

Figure 2–10
Land at Issue in *Carpenter v. Ruperto*, June 2006

(Note that the land is now surrounded by a fence.)

NOTES AND QUESTIONS

1. *Carpenter* is probably in the minority in explicitly requiring good faith as a condition of obtaining title by adverse possession. The English cases and most American legal commentators favor the objective non-permission interpretation of adverse under a claim of right. This position is logical if we think of adverse possession as being grounded in the application of the statute of limitations to a legal action in trespass, ejectment, conversion, or replevin to recover possession of property. None of these actions requires subjective good faith or bad faith on the part of the possessor—lack of permission from the TO is enough—so it stands to reason that the statute of limitations on these actions will run without regard to the subjective state of mind of the adverse possessor. In an important survey of the American appellate case law, however, Professor Helmholz concluded that courts generally grant adverse possession only to possessors who act in good faith. See Richard Helmholz, Adverse Possession and Subjective Intent, 61 Wash. U. L.Q. 65 (1983). His claim is controversial, and has elicited a vigorous rejoinder. See Roger Cunningham, Adverse Possession and Subjective Intent: A Reply to Professor Helmholz, 64 Wash. U. L.Q. 1 (1986); Richard Helmholz, More on Subjective Intent: A Response to Professor Cunningham, 64 Wash. U. L.Q. 65 (1986). Helmholz does not contend that most courts actually require good faith; his claim is that, as he reads the recitation of the facts in reported appellate opinions, when courts award title by adverse possession, the AP almost invariably is portrayed in the opinion as having acted in good faith.

2. In a recent decision, *J.A. Pye (Oxford) Ltd. v. The United Kingdom* (Nov. 15, 2005, application no. 44302/02), the European Court of Human Rights ruled that the law of adverse possession of the United Kingdom violates the European Convention on Human Rights. The case in question involved squatters on agricultural land acting in bad faith. The House of Lords, the highest appellate tribunal in the U.K., ruled that the squatters were entitled to judgment in their favor under English law. By a vote of 4–3, the European Court held that this judgment violated the Convention. It reasoned that the government was obliged either to provide some mechanism for compensating the true owner when property is taken through adverse possession, or for giving actual notice of a potential adverse possession claim to the registered owner and an opportunity for the owner to reassert ownership before it is lost. Does this judgment suggest that the Iowa Supreme Court's position that squatters cannot obtain title to land by adverse possession is the wave of the future?

3. Why do you suppose courts might be reluctant to award title by adverse possession when the original entry of possession was in bad faith? Consider in this regard the reluctance of many courts to dismiss on grounds of adverse possession claims by descendants of victims of Nazi persecution seeking to recover art work and other valuable assets looted by

the Nazis over 60 years ago. See, e.g., Howard J. Trienens, Landscape with Smokestacks: The Case of the Allegedly Plundered Degas (2000). Is there a limit to how far back we are willing to go to rectify the acquisition of property in bad faith? Should there be a two-tiered statute of limitations (and doctrine of adverse possession)—a relatively short period (say 10 years) for good faith misappropriations, and a much longer period (say 50 years or even 100 years) for bad faith misappropriations? See Richard A. Epstein, Past and Future: The Temporal Dimension in the Law of Property, 64 Wash. U. L.Q. 667, 685–89 (1986).

Howard v. Kunto

Court of Appeals of Washington, 1970.
477 P.2d 210.

■ PEARSON, JUDGE. Land surveying is an ancient art but not one free of the errors that often creep into the affairs of men. In this case, we are presented with the question of what happens when the descriptions in deeds do not fit the land the deed holders are occupying. Defendants appeal from a decree quieting title in the plaintiffs of a tract of land on the shore of Hood Canal in Mason County.

At least as long ago as 1932 the record tells us that one McCall resided in the house now occupied by the appellant-defendants, Kunto. McCall had a deed that described a 50–foot–wide parcel on the shore of Hood Canal. The error that brings this case before us is that the 50 feet described in the deed is not the same 50 feet upon which McCall's house stood. Rather, the described land is an adjacent 50–foot lot directly west of that upon which the house stood. In other words, McCall's house stood on one lot and his deed described the adjacent lot. Several property owners to the west of defendants, not parties to this action, are similarly situated.

Over the years since 1946, several conveyances occurred, using the same legal description and accompanied by a transfer of possession to the succeeding occupants. The Kuntos' immediate predecessors in interest, Millers, desired to build a dock. To this end, they had a survey performed which indicated that the deed description and the physical occupation were in conformity. Several boundary stakes were placed as a result of this survey and the dock was constructed, as well as other improvements. The house as well as the others in the area continued to be used as summer recreational retreats.

The Kuntos then took possession of the disputed property under a deed from the Millers in 1959. In 1960 the respondent-plaintiffs, Howard, who held land east of that of the Kuntos, determined to convey an undivided one-half interest in their land to the Yearlys. To this end, they undertook to have a survey of the entire area made. After expending considerable effort, the surveyor retained by the Howards discovered that according to the government survey, the deed descriptions and the land occupancy of the parties did not coincide. Between the Howards and the Kuntos lay the Moyers' property. When the Howards' survey was completed, they discovered that they were the record owners of the land occupied by the Moyers and that the Moyers held record title to the land occupied by the Kuntos. Howard approached Moyer and in return for a conveyance of the land upon which the Moyers' house stood, Moyer conveyed to the Howards record title to the land upon which the Kunto house stood. Until plaintiffs Howard obtained the conveyance from Moyer in April, 1960, neither Moyer nor any of his predecessors ever asserted any right to ownership of the property actually being possessed by Kunto and his predecessors. This action was then instituted to quiet title in the Howards and Yearlys. The Kuntos appeal from a trial court decision granting this remedy.

At the time this action was commenced on August 19, 1960, defendants had been in occupance of the disputed property less than a year. The trial court's reason for denying their claim of adverse possession is succinctly stated in its memorandum opinion: "In this instance, defendants have failed to prove, by a preponderance of the evidence, a continuity of possession or estate to permit tacking of the adverse possession of defendants to the possession of their predecessors."

Finding of fact 6,[4] which is challenged by defendants, incorporates the above concept and additionally finds defendant's possession not to have been "continuous" because it involved only "summer occupancy."

Two issues are presented by this appeal:

(1) Is a claim of adverse possession defeated because the physical use of the premises is restricted to summer occupancy?

(2) May a person who receives record title to tract A under the mistaken belief that he has title to tract B (immediately contiguous to tract A) and who subsequently occupies tract B, for the purpose of establishing title to tract B by adverse possession, use the periods of possession of tract B by his immediate predecessors who also had record title to tract A?

"Tacking"

---

4. "In the instant case the defendants' building was not simply over the line, but instead was built wholly upon the wrong piece of property, not the property of defendants, described in Paragraph Four (4) of the complaint herein, but on the property of plaintiffs, described in Paragraph Three of the complaint and herein. That the last three deeds in the chain of title, covering and embracing defendants' property, including defendants' deed, were executed in other states, specifically, California and Oregon. And there is no evidence of pointing out to the grantees in said three deeds, aforesaid, including defendants' deed, of any specific property, other than the property of defendants, described in their deed, and in Paragraph Four (4) of the complaint, and herein; nor of any immediate act of the grantees, including defendants, in said Three (3) deeds, aforesaid, of taking possession of any property, other than described in said three (3) deeds, aforesaid; and the testimony of husband, defendant, was unequivocally that he had no intention of possessing or holding anything other than what the deed called for; and, that there is no showing of any continuous possession by defendants or their immediate predecessors in interest, since the evidence indicates the property was in the nature, for [use], as a summer occupancy, and such occupancy and use was for rather limited periods of time during comparatively short portions of the year, and was far from continuous."

Figure 2–11

In approaching both of these questions, we point out that the evidence, largely undisputed in any material sense, established that defendant or his immediate predecessors did occupy the premises, which we have called tract B, as though it was their own for far more than the 10 years as prescribed in RCW 4.16.020.[5]

We also point out that finding of fact 6 is not challenged for its factual determinations but for the conclusions contained therein to the effect that the continuity of possession may not be established by summer occupancy,

5. This statute provides:

4.16.020 Actions to be commenced within ten years. The period prescribed in RCW 4.16.010 for the commencement of actions shall be as follows:

Within ten years;

Actions for the recovery of real property, or for the recovery of the possession thereof; and no action shall be maintained for such recovery unless it appears that the plaintiff, his ancestor, predecessor or grantor was seized or possessed of the premises in question within ten years before the commencement of the action.

and that a predecessor's possession may not be tacked because a legal "claim of right" did not exist under the circumstances.

We start with the oft-quoted rule that: "To constitute adverse possession, there must be actual possession which is *uninterrupted*, open and notorious, hostile and exclusive, and under a *claim of right* made in good faith for the statutory period." Butler v. Anderson, 426 P.2d 467, 470 (Wash. 1967) (emphasis added).

We reject the conclusion that summer occupancy only of a summer beach home destroys the continuity of possession required by the statute. It has become firmly established that the requisite possession requires such possession and dominion "as ordinarily marks the conduct of owners in general in holding, managing, and caring for property of like nature and condition." Whalen v. Smith, 167 N.W. 646, 647 (Iowa 1918).

We hold that occupancy of tract B during the summer months for more than the 10–year period by defendant and his predecessors, together with the continued existence of the improvements on the land and beach area, constituted "uninterrupted" possession within this rule. To hold otherwise is to completely ignore the nature and condition of the property.

We find such rule fully consonant with the legal writers on the subject. In F. Clark, Law of Surveying and Boundaries, § 561 (3d ed. 1959) at 565: "Continuity of possession may be established although the land is used regularly for only a certain period each year." Further, at 566:

> This rule * * * is one of substance and not of absolute mathematical continuity, provided there is no break so as to sever two possessions. It is not necessary that the occupant should be actually upon the premises continually. If the land is occupied during the period of time during the year it is capable of use, there is sufficient continuity.

We now reach the question of tacking. The precise issue before us is novel in that none of the property occupied by defendant or his predecessors coincided with the property described in their deeds, but was contiguous.

In the typical case, which has been subject to much litigation, the party seeking to establish title by adverse possession claims *more* land than that described in the deed. In such cases it is clear that tacking is permitted.

In Buchanan v. Cassell, 335 P.2d 600, 602 (Wash. 1959) the Supreme Court stated: "This state follows the rule that a purchaser may tack the adverse use of its predecessor in interest to that of his own where the land was intended to be included in the deed between them, but was mistakenly omitted from the description." El Cerrito, Inc. v. Ryndak, 376 P.2d 528 (Wash. 1962).

The general statement which appears in many of the cases is that tacking of adverse possession is permitted if the successive occupants are in "privity." See Faubion v. Elder, 301 P.2d 153 (Wash. 1956). The deed running between the parties purporting to transfer the land possessed traditionally furnishes the privity of estate which connects the possession of the successive occupants. Plaintiff contends, and the trial court ruled, that where the deed does not describe *any* of the land which was occupied, the actual transfer of possession is insufficient to establish privity.

To assess the cogency of this argument and ruling, we must turn to the historical reasons for requiring privity as a necessary prerequisite to tacking the possession of several occupants. Very few, if any, of the reasons appear in the cases, nor do the cases analyze the relationships that must exist between successive possessors for tacking to be allowed. See W. Stoebuck, The Law of Adverse Possession In Washington in 35 Wash.L.Rev. 53 (1960).

The requirement of privity had its roots in the notion that a succession of trespasses, even though there was no appreciable interval between them, should not, in equity, be allowed to defeat the record title. The "claim of right," "color of title" requirement of the statutes and cases was probably derived from the early American belief that the squatter should not be able to profit by his trespass.[6]

However, it appears to this court that there is a substantial difference between the squatter or trespasser and the property purchaser, who along with several of his neighbors, as a result of an inaccurate survey or subdivision, occupies and improves property exactly 50 feet to the east of that which a survey some 30 years later demonstrates that they in fact own. It seems to us that there is also a strong public policy favoring early certainty as to the location of land ownership which enters into a proper interpretation of privity.

On the irregular perimeters of Puget Sound exact determination of land locations and boundaries is difficult and expensive. This difficulty is convincingly demonstrated in this case by the problems plaintiff's engineer encountered in attempting to locate the corners. It cannot be expected that every purchaser will or should engage a surveyor to ascertain that the beach home he is purchasing lies within the boundaries described in his deed. Such a practice is neither reasonable nor customary. Of course, 50–foot errors in descriptions are [devastating] where a group of adjacent owners each hold 50 feet of waterfront property.

The technical requirement of "privity" should not, we think, be used to upset the long periods of occupancy of those who in good faith received an erroneous deed description. Their "claim of right" is no less persuasive than the purchaser who believes he is purchasing *more* land than his deed described.

In the final analysis, however, we believe the requirement of "privity" is no more than judicial recognition of the need for some reasonable connection between successive occupants of real property so as to raise their claim of right above the status of the wrongdoer or the trespasser. We think such reasonable connection exists in this case.

6. The English common law does not require privity as a prerequisite for tacking. See F. Clark, Law of Surveying and Boundaries, § 561 (3d ed. 1959) at 568.

Where, as here, several successive purchasers received record title to tract A under the mistaken belief that they were acquiring tract B, immediately contiguous thereto, and where possession of tract B is transferred and occupied in a continuous manner for more than 10 years by successive occupants, we hold there is sufficient privity of estate to permit tacking and thus establish adverse possession as a matter of law.

We see no reason in law or in equity for differentiating this case from *Faubion v. Elder*, 301 P.2d 153 (Wash. 1956) where the appellants were claiming *more* land than their deed described and where successive periods of occupation were allowed to be united to each other to make up the time of adverse holding. This application of the privity requirement should particularly pertain where the holder of record title to tract B acquired the same with knowledge of the discrepancy.

Judgment is reversed with directions to dismiss plaintiffs' action and to enter a decree quieting defendants' title to the disputed tract of land in accordance with the prayer of their cross-complaint.

NOTES AND QUESTIONS

1. A large number of adverse possession disputes seem to involve seasonal or vacation properties. Why do you suppose this might be the case?

2. Which of the five standard doctrinal elements is at issue in *Howard v. Kunto*? Why are the other issues ignored?

3. What is the best characterization of the state of mind of the Kuntos (adverse possessors): good faith, bad faith, or unclear? What state of mind does the State of Washington appear to require in order to establish title by adverse possession? *Good Faith*

4. By limiting tacking to situations in which successive APs are in "privity of estate," the court permits tacking when A enters adversely, and then sells to B, who then sells to C. But tacking would not be permitted where A enters adversely, and then B enters adversely (the very instant A leaves), and the then C enters adversely (the very instant B leaves). Why should these two situations be treated differently? *No continuity — all distinct entries rather than one continuous AP based on the transfer of the deed (the deed provides the "privity")*

5. Note that issues about tacking can arise on both the AP side of the dispute (as discussed in *Howard v. Kunto*) or on the TO side of the dispute. In fact, isn't there a tacking issue on both the AP side and the TO side in *Howard v. Kunto*? The Howards only just recently acquired from the Moyers the deed describing the land on which the Kuntos' house sits. In theory, therefore, the Kuntos must show that the transfer of the deed from the Moyers to the Howards did not start the statute of limitations running anew. Should privity of estate also be required before an AP can tack the current TO's period of ownership onto that of a prior owner in order to show that the period of the statute of limitations has elapsed?

6. Another wrinkle in the adverse possession timeline is the doctrine of "relation back." Once the AP has satisfied the requirements for acquisition of title by adverse possession, the AP is (now) deemed to have been the owner from the time that the AP first entered into (adverse) possession. Of course, during that time, if the TO had sued the AP in trespass or in a

quiet title action, the TO would (absent error) be declared the owner. Why might relation back matter?

DISABILITIES

Another issue that occasionally arises in determining whether the statute of limitations has run involves whether the TO's circumstances should excuse her from bringing suit or whether they should either slow down or stop the clock running on bringing suit. Typically, state statutes provide that the statute of limitations is tolled for owners suffering from certain narrow classes of disabilities, including being under age, insane, legally incompetent, or (sometimes) in prison, _at the time the AP entered_. Disabilities arising later usually do not affect the running of the statute, and disabilities in the same or successive owners cannot be tacked. Also, other hardships that might hinder the TO from bringing suit, such as poverty (as was claimed in _Ewing_ about Samuel Williams), do not affect the running of the statute.

The mechanisms for altering the statutory period vary. Under one common approach, a shorter period of time, say 10 years as opposed to 20 years, is provided as a minimum after the removal of the disability. See, e.g., N.D. Cen. Code §§ 28–01–08 & –14 (providing for special 10–year statute of limitations instead of 20 years in cases of disability); Ohio Rev. Code Ann. § 2305.04 (providing for 10 years after removal of disability if the regular 21–year statute of limitations would already have run). In other states, the disability tolls the statute. See, e.g., Mont. Code § 70–19–413. Usually, a successor of the landowner under the disability benefits from the same provision, but not all states allow for this.

Consider this example. The statutory period for adverse possession is 20 years. When the AP enters, TO is insane. Twenty-five years pass, and then TO regains his sanity. On the first "additional time" approach, the TO then has 10 years to bring an action to regain possession. (What if the regular statute of limitations is 20 years and the disability is removed in Year 19?) On the second, "tolling" approach, the TO would now have 20 years. If the TO had been a minor at the time of entry by the AP and in the meantime had become insane or gone to prison, the statutory clock would start ticking again when TO attains the age of majority.

It is easy to see how the disability might make us skeptical that the TO is being truly slothful. Do these rules about disabilities fit in with any of the other rationales for adverse possession? Why should only disabilities existing at the time of the AP's entry effect the length of the statutory period for adverse possession?

Songbyrd, Inc. v. Estate of Grossman

United States District Court, N.D. New York, 1998.
23 F. Supp. 2d 219.

■ HOMER, UNITED STATES MAGISTRATE JUDGE. Plaintiff Songbyrd, Inc. ("Songbyrd") brought this action seeking monetary damages and a declaration of rights in certain recorded music tracks. Presently pending is a motion by defendant Estate of Albert B. Grossman, doing business as Bearsville

Records, Inc. ("Bearsville") for summary judgment pursuant to Fed. R.Civ.P. 56 on the ground that the action is barred by the applicable statute of limitations. Songbyrd opposes the motion. For the reasons which follow, the motion is granted.

Figure 2–12
Professor Longhair, 1977

Courtesy Leni Sinclair.

I.   Facts

This case concerns the possession, ownership, and usage of several master recordings of musical performances made in the early 1970s by New Orleans musician Henry Roeland Byrd, who was professionally known as "Professor Longhair" ("Byrd").[2] The tapes were produced in a Baton Rouge, Louisiana recording studio and soon thereafter came into the possession of a predecessor in interest to Bearsville located in Woodstock, New York. Over time several requests have been made by representatives of Byrd to secure return of the tapes. It is unclear what if any response those requests received, but the tapes have remained in the physical custody of Bearsville continuously since the 1970s.

In August 1986, Bearsville licensed certain of the master recordings to Rounder Records Corporation, which in 1987 released an album of Byrd's music produced from the recordings. In 1991, another recording based on the disputed master recordings was released by Rhino Records. That release was made possible by a licensing agreement between Bearsville and the production company.

II.   Procedural Background

Originally filed in Louisiana state court in 1995, this action was removed by Bearsville to the United States District Court for the Eastern District of Louisiana. Bearsville then moved pursuant to Fed.R.Civ.P. 12(b) to dismiss the claim on the ground that the court lacked personal jurisdiction and the claim was barred by Louisiana's period of prescription.[3] The district court held that the action was barred by the applicable prescriptive period and granted the motion without addressing the jurisdictional question. Songbyrd, Inc. v. Bearsville Records, Inc., Civ.A. No. 95–3706, 1996 WL 337259 (E.D.La. June 18, 1996). Songbyrd appealed and the Fifth Circuit Court of Appeals reversed, holding that the claim was not prescribed under Louisiana law. 104 F.3d 773, 779 (5th Cir. 1997). On remand, the district court considered the question of personal jurisdiction, concluded that jurisdiction was lacking, and transferred the action to this district. The present motion followed. * * *

IV.   Discussion

A.   Choice of Law

* * * Both parties agree that * * * disposition of this case is governed by New York law.

---

2. Songbyrd incorporated in 1993 and conducts business as a successor in interest to Byrd.

3. The period of prescription in civil law jurisdictions like Louisiana is roughly synonymous with the common law concept of a statute of limitations. See FDIC v. Barton, 96 F.3d 128, 131 n. 2 (5th Cir. 1996).

B.   New York Statute of Limitations

This action is governed by the three year statute of limitations for recovery of chattel provided in N.Y. Civ. Prac. L. & R. § 214(3) (McKinney 1990); Johnson v. Smithsonian Inst., 9 F.Supp.2d 347, 354 (S.D.N.Y. 1998) (New York statute of limitations for conversion and replevin is three years). The issue presented here is when the claim accrued for statute of limitations purposes.

The statute of limitations for conversion begins to run at the time of the conversion. Sporn v. MCA Records, Inc., 448 N.E.2d 1324, 1327 (N.Y. 1983); see also Vigilant Ins. Co. of Am. v. Housing Auth. of the City of El Paso, Tex., 660 N.E.2d 1121, 1126 (N.Y. 1995). In *Sporn*, New York's Court of Appeals was presented with a case very similar to the case at bar. There, the plaintiff, the successor in interest to the purported owner of rights in certain master recordings, sued the defendant record company for commercially exploiting the master recordings contrary to the plaintiff's interests. Sporn, 448 N.E.2d at 1325–26. The record company defended on the ground that the three year limitations period had begun to run at the time it began using the master recordings contrary to the plaintiff's purported interest and had expired prior to the commencement of the action. Holding that the statute of limitations for conversion begins to run at the time of the conversion, the Court of Appeals affirmed the grant of summary judgment in favor of the record company. Id. at 1327.

Songbyrd contends that *Solomon R. Guggenheim Found. v. Lubell*, 569 N.E.2d 426 (N.Y. 1991) (*"Guggenheim"*), not *Sporn*, governs this action. In *Guggenheim*, the New York Court of Appeals held that "a cause of action for replevin against a good-faith purchaser of a stolen chattel accrues when the true owner makes demand for return of the chattel and the person in possession of the chattel refuses to return it." Id. at 429. Songbyrd argues that under *Guggenheim* the statute of limitations does not begin to run until after a demand for return has been refused, that such a demand has been made but not refused here and as a result the limitations period has not yet begun to run. *Guggenheim*, however, addresses the different circumstance of possession of a chattel by a bona fide purchaser for value and does not, therefore, provide the controlling rule of law here.

Guggenheim, in fact, recognized that a different rule applies when the stolen chattel remains in the possession of the thief. Citing *Sporn*, the court stated that in such a circumstance the statute of limitations begins to run from the time of the theft. Guggenheim, 569 N.E.2d at 429. Here, the chattel at issue has remained in the possession of Bearsville, the party alleged to have committed the wrongful taking. There is no evidence that Bearsville was ever a bona fide purchaser for value. Thus, the statute of limitations here began to run at the time Bearsville converted the master recordings. See Vigilant Ins. Co., 660 N.E.2d at 1126 (in a case not involving a bona fide purchaser, a conversion claim accrues at the time of the conversion). Thus, *Guggenheim* is limited to circumstances involving a bona fide purchaser possession of the chattel.

Having concluded that Songbyrd's conversion claim accrued at the time of the conversion, the question becomes when the master recordings were allegedly converted. "The tort of conversion is established when one who owns and has a right to possession of personal property proves that the property is in the unauthorized possession of another who has acted to exclude the rights of the owner." Key Bank of N.Y. v. Grossi, 642 N.Y.S.2d 403, 405 (App. Div. 3d Dep't 1996). A party acts to the exclusion of the rights of another by exercising dominion and control over the property that is inconsistent with the interests of the true owner. Shaw v. Rolex Watch, U.S.A., Inc., 673 F.Supp. 674, 682 (S.D.N.Y. 1987). Accepting this definition of conversion, the decisive issue is when Bearsville began unauthorized possession of the master recordings.

Bearsville undeniably had lawful and authorized possession of the master tapes when they were first transferred to its predecessor in 1972. In August 1986, the master recordings were licensed by Bearsville to Rounder Records. The result of this agreement was the 1987 release of an album of Byrd's music taken from the master recordings. This licensing agreement clearly demonstrated Bearsville's intent to exercise control over the Byrd recordings to the exclusion of Songbyrd. See Jaywyn Video Productions, Ltd. v. Servicing All Media, Inc., 577 N.Y.S.2d 847, 848 (App. Div. 1st Dep't 1992) (licensing of property rights demonstrates exercise of dominion and control). Any claim for conversion, therefore, accrued no later than August 1986 and was time barred at the time this action was filed in 1995.[4] That Songbyrd may not have known of the conversion at the time it occurred is of no moment. Two Clinton Square Corp. v. Friedler, 459 N.Y.S.2d 179 (App. Div. 4th Dep't 1983); Memorial Hosp. v. McGreevy, 574 N.Y.S.2d 923, 925 (Sup. Ct. 1991) (claim accrues at time of conversion "even though the plaintiff may have been unaware of the occurrence.").

Where, as here, "[t]he conduct of the defendant certainly constituted a denial of both the plaintiff's right to the master recording and a total usurping of plaintiff's right to possess the master recording," the claim is properly stated as one for conversion. Sporn, 448 N.E.2d at 1327. That claim is clearly untimely. The time bar arose in August 1989, three years following the licensing agreement with Rounder Records.[6] Conversion is not a continuing wrong for which every new act that might constitute conversion restarts a new limitations period. Tinker v. Abrams, 640

---

4. Songbyrd has not argued that any tolling provision applies here.

6. In the alternative the conversion occurred no later than August 1991 when Bearsville licensed the master recordings to Rhino Records. That agreement resulted in the 1991 Rhino Records release of an album containing seven tracks produced from the master recordings. The exact date of the Rhino Records licensing deal is not clear in the record but necessarily occurred in or before 1991. Thus, with 1991 as the date of conversion, Songbyrd's claim was time barred prior to the commencement of this action in 1995.

F.Supp. 229, 232 (S.D.N.Y. 1986) (citing Sporn, 448 N.E.2d at 1326–27). Here, Songbyrd simply failed to commence this action within the applicable statute of limitations. Bearsville's motion must, therefore, be granted.

NOTES AND QUESTIONS

1. The Fifth Circuit's decision holding that Songbyrd's claim was not subject to prescription under Louisiana law provides some additional details about Professor Longhair:

> The late Henry Roeland Byrd, also known as "Professor Longhair," was an influential New Orleans rhythm-and-blues pianist and composer, and is widely regarded as one of the primary inspirations for the renaissance of New Orleans popular music over the last thirty years. His numerous hits included original compositions such as "Tipitina" and "Go to the Mardi Gras," as well as his famous renditions of Earl King's "Big Chief." After achieving modest commercial success as a local performer and recording artist in the 1940's and 1950's, Byrd fell on hard times during the 1960's. His fortunes began to change for the better in 1970, however, when New Orleans music aficionado Arthur "Quint" Davis, along with others, founded the New Orleans Jazz and Heritage Festival ("JazzFest"). Needing talented performers for Jazz-Fest, Davis located Byrd in 1971 working in an obscure record store in New Orleans and transformed him into a perennial star attraction of the JazzFest and other venues from that time until his death in 1980.

Songbyrd, Inc. v. Bearsville Records, Inc., 104 F.3d 773, 774 (5th Cir. 1997). Albert Grossman, who died in 1986, was one of the founders of the Newport Folk Festival and promoted the careers of a number of musical stars, including Bob Dylan, Janis Joplin, and Gordon Lightfoot. Bearsville, New York, where he lived and worked, is a small town near Woodstock, New York.

2. If one were simply to weigh the equitable claims of the parties, one might expect that courts would give true owners more time to recover property taken by a person in bad faith, like a thief, and less time to recover property taken by someone who has acted in good faith, like a good faith purchaser. Yet New York law regarding adverse possession of personal property appears to do the opposite. Under the time-of-conversion rule applied in the principal case, the statute of limitations begins to run as soon as the property is converted, resulting in a short period to seek recovery. Under the demand rule of *Guggenheim*, the statute of limitations does not begin to run until the true owner makes a demand for the return of the property, and the demand is refused. This typically results in a longer period to seek recovery, since the demand and refusal will virtually always occur after the conversion. As a result, New York treats thieves more favorably than good faith purchasers. Is there any justification for this distinction that would explain what otherwise seems quite counterintuitive?

3. The New Jersey Supreme Court, in *O'Keeffe v. Snyder*, 416 A.2d 862 (N.J. 1980), adopted a third test for determining when the statute of

limitations starts to run for purposes of adverse possession of personal property: the discovery rule. Under this rule, "a cause of action will not accrue until the injured party discovers, or by exercise of reasonable diligence and intelligence should have discovered, facts which form the basis of a cause of action." Id. at 869. Generally speaking, the discovery rule would give the TO an intermediate period of time to recover personal property, somewhere in between the conversion rule and the demand rule. The conversion rule applied in *Songbyrd* will generally result in the shortest period because the statute starts to run at the moment of conversion; the discovery rule would provide more time, because it may take a while for a diligent TO to learn about the conversion or discover the whereabouts of the object; the demand rule would provide the longest time, because there is no requirement that the TO show reasonable diligence before asserting the demand for return of the property. What advantages and disadvantages do you see in adopting the discovery rule, as opposed to either the conversion rule or the demand rule?

4. What is the best characterization of the state of mind of the defendant in *Songbyrd*: good faith, bad faith, or unclear? What state of mind does the Court seem to require for establishing a claim of title by adverse possession?

5. One oddity of this case is that the parties are really concerned with what is on the tapes—the song recordings—rather than with the physical tapes themselves. Copyright law distinguishes between musical works (music and lyrics) and sound recordings. See 17 U.S.C. § 101. Musical works were brought into federal copyright in 1831, but sound recordings did not receive protection until 1972 and this protection is somewhat different from that for musical works. Can the copyright in a sound recording be adversely possessed? If not, why not?

F. SEQUENTIAL POSSESSION ISSUES

What happens if multiple persons serially claim property on some theory other than purchase or gift from the prior owner? This rarely happens, but when it does, it brings out a fundamental proposition about the system of property rights, sometimes called the relativity of title and sometimes referred to as the rejection of the *jus tertii* defense—i.e., a defense based on the rights of third parties. Property rights may be good against all the world, but disputes over property usually take the form A v. B, and courts usually ask only as between A and B who has the superior title.

Armory v. Delamirie

King's Bench, 1722.
1 Strange 505.

The plaintiff being a chimney sweeper's boy found a jewel and carried it to the defendant's shop (who was a goldsmith) to know what it was, and delivered it into the hands of the apprentice, who under the pretense of weighing it, took out the stones, and calling to the master to let him know it came to three halfpence, the master offered the boy the money, who refused to take it, and insisted to have the thing again; whereupon the apprentice delivered him back the socket without the stones. And now in trover against the master these points were ruled:

1. That the finder of a jewel, though he does not by such finding acquire an absolute property or ownership, yet he has such a property as will enable him to keep it against all but the rightful owner, and consequently may maintain trover.

2. That the action will lay against the master, who gives a credit to his apprentice, and is answerable for his neglect.

3. As to the value of the jewel several of the trade were examined to prove what a jewel of the finest water that would fit the socket would be worth; and the Chief Justice directed the jury, that unless the defendant did produce the jewel, and show it not to be of the finest water, they should presume the strongest against him, and make the value of the best jewels the measure of the damages; which they accordingly did.

NOTES AND QUESTIONS

1. As we shall see, courts are fond of reciting the rule of law announced in the first numbered paragraph of the opinion in *Armory v. Delamirie*. But notice that this rule of law is much broader than was needed to decide the case. The case was a dispute between someone assumed to be the "finder" of a jewel and the jewelry shop owner whose apprentice wrongfully converted the jewel when it was handed to the apprentice for purposes of valuation. So we have sequential possession of an object by a finder and a converter. All the court needed to decide to rule for Armory was "that the finder of a jewel, though he does not by such finding acquire an absolute property or ownership, yet he has such a property as will enable him to keep it against a subsequent converter or thief." This narrower rule of law is easy to justify, isn't it? On what possible theory could one defend a rule that allowed thieves to obtain good title to objects they steal from finders? On the other hand, as we shall see, the broad proposition enunciated by the court in support of its ruling, that the finder obtains "such a property as will enable him to keep it against all but the rightful owner," quickly descends into controversy when applied in other factual circumstances.

2. Suppose Armory stole the jewel from a dresser in a house in which he was cleaning a chimney. Later, the jewel falls through a hole in a pocket in Armory's trousers. Delamirie, the professional jeweler, spots it on the sidewalk and, recognizing its value, claims it as a found object. In a suit by Armory against Delamirie to recover the value of the jewel, what result under the rule of law announced in the principal case? Is this consistent with the outcome we would want to reach as a matter of policy?

3. A finder, such as Armory, differs from a pure first possessor, like Pierson in *Pierson v. Post*, in two respects. First, when a finder takes possession of an object, the finder does not thereby become the owner. The object is understood to belong to someone else, the true owner, who cannot be identified or located. Thus, whatever rights a finder like Armory has against a third party like Delamirie, the finder's rights are subordinate to those of the true owner (whoever that may be). Second, because the finder's rights remain subordinate to the true owner's, the finder has certain duties toward the true owner. Courts have frequently said in this context that a finder acts as a bailee for the true owner. (See Chapter IV for more on bailments.) In theory at least, this means the finder may be under a legal duty not to convert the object to the finder's own use, or not to deliver the object to anyone other than the true owner. In practice, since the true owner is the only one who could enforce these duties, as time passes and the true owner fails to appear, the finder may be able to treat the lost object as if it were not different from the finder's own property. But until the statute of limitations for recovery of personal property runs, and the finder can claim title by adverse possession, the finder's title is a qualified one.

4. Some commentators have advocated a system of rewards for finders. See, e.g., R.H. Helmholz, Equitable Division and the Law of Finders, 52 Fordham L. Rev. 313 (1983). Japan has such a system in its Law Concerning Lost Articles (Ishitsubutsuhō [Law Concerning Lost Articles], Law no. 40 (1899)). Mark West argues that Japan's reputation for getting lost property back to owners stems in large part from its elaborate legal regime of finders' duties to turn in lost property to the police (or to owners of the establishment at which it is found), and of owners' duties to pay rewards of between 5 and 20% of the value of the lost property; possession is awarded to the finder after six months. Much effort is put into teaching this system to schoolchildren. Mark D. West, Losers: Recovering Lost Property in Japan and the United States, 37 Law & Soc'y Rev. 369 (2003). West also reports on an empirical study in which cell phones and wallets were deliberately left at locations in a mixed business-shopping district of Tokyo, in midtown Manhattan, and in front of a New York grocery store catering to a Japanese expatriate clientele (with return rates highest in Tokyo and lowest in New York, and the New York Japanese location in between). Although less well-known, New York law provides that objects worth more than $20 must be turned into the police, and finders can claim the object after a period ranging from 3 months and 10 days to three years and 10 days, depending on the object's value. New York Personal Property Law §§ 252–253.

Clark v. Maloney

Superior Court of Delaware, 1840.
3 Del. 68.

Action of trover to recover the value of ten white pine logs. The logs in question were found by plaintiff floating in the Delaware bay after a great freshet, were taken up and moored with ropes in the mouth of Mispillion creek. They were afterwards in the possession of defendants, who refused to give them up, alleging that they had found them adrift and floating up the creek.

Bayard, Chief Justice, charged the jury.—

The plaintiff must show *first*, that the logs were his property; and *secondly*, that they were converted by the defendants to their own use. In support of his right of property, the plaintiff relies upon the fact of his possession of the logs. They were taken up by him, adrift in the Delaware bay, and secured by a stake at the mouth of Mispillion creek. Possession is certainly prima facie evidence of property. It is called *prima facie* evidence because it may be rebutted by evidence of better title, but in the absence of better title it is as effective a support of title as the most conclusive evidence could be. It is for this reason, that *the finder of a chattel, though he does not acquire an absolute property in it, yet has such a property, as will enable him to keep it against all but the rightful owner.* The defence consists, not in showing that the defendants are the rightful owners, or claim under the rightful owner; but that the logs were found by them adrift in Mispillion creek, having been loosened from their fastening either by accident or design, and they insist that their title is as good as that of the plaintiff. But it is a well settled rule of law that the loss of a chattel does not change the right of property; and for the same reason that the original loss of these logs by the rightful owner, did not change his absolute property in them, but he might have maintained trover against the plaintiff upon refusal to deliver them, so the subsequent loss did not divest the *special* property of the plaintiff. It follows, therefore, that as the plaintiff has shown a special property in these logs, which he never abandoned, and which enabled him to keep them against all the world but the rightful owner, he is entitled to a verdict.

Verdict for the plaintiff.

NOTES AND QUESTIONS

1. Although the facts are a bit cryptic, it appears that *Clark v. Maloney* involves sequential possession by two finders, Finder 1 (Clark) and Finder 2 (Maloney). The court paraphrases the broad rule of law laid down in *Armory v. Delamirie*, and rules for Finder 1. But couldn't the court cite the very same proposition in support of a ruling for Finder 2? If *Armory* would equally support a ruling for either plaintiff or defendant, obviously we need some other principle of law to decide the case. What is that principle?

2. Do you think the court in the principal case may have harbored suspicions about the defendants' claim that that they had found the logs "adrift and floating up the creek?" In general, if the rule in cases of Finder 1 versus Finder 2 were that the property goes to Finder 2, would this indirectly encourage theft? The current possessor (who might be a thief)

would always claim that he was a finder, and the burden would be on the first finder to disprove this claim. This might be difficult to do.

3.   Suppose we want to design the rules in these sequential possession cases so as to maximize the chances that the true owner will be able to recover the property. Which party is more likely to be located by the true owner—Finder 1 or Finder 2?

Anderson v. Gouldberg

Supreme Court of Minnesota, 1892.
53 N.W. 636.

This action was brought by the plaintiff, Sigfrid Anderson, against defendants, partners as Gouldberg & Anderson, to recover the possession of ninety-three pine logs, marked L S X, or the value thereof. Plaintiff claimed to have cut the logs on section 22, township 27, range 15, Isanti County, in the winter of 1889–1890, and to have hauled them to a mill on section 6, from which place defendants took them. The title to section 22 was in strangers, and plaintiff showed no authority from the owners to cut the logs thereon. Defendants claimed that the logs were cut on section 26, in the adjoining township, on land belonging to the Ann River Logging Company, and that they [the defendants] took the logs by direction of the Logging Company, who were the owners. The court charged that even if the plaintiff got possession of the logs as a trespasser, his title would be good as against any one except the real owner or some one who had authority from the owner to take them, and left the case to the jury on the question as to whether the logs were cut on the land of the Logging Company, and taken by defendants under its authority. The jury found a verdict for the plaintiff and assessed his damages at $153.45. From an order denying their motion for a new trial, defendants appeal * * *

■ MITCHELL, J. It is settled by the verdict of the jury that the logs in controversy were not cut upon the land of the defendants, and consequently that they were entire strangers to the property. For the purposes of this appeal, we must also assume the fact to be (as there was evidence from which the jury might have so found) that the plaintiffs obtained possession of the logs in the first instance by trespassing upon the land of some third party. Therefore the only question is whether bare possession of property, though wrongfully obtained, is sufficient title to enable the party enjoying it to maintain replevin against a mere stranger, who takes it from him. We had supposed that this was settled in the affirmative as long ago, at least, as the early case of Armory v. Delamirie, 1 Strange, 504, so often cited on that point. When it is said that to maintain replevin the plaintiff's possession must have been lawful, it means merely that it must have been lawful as against the person who deprived him of it; and possession is good title against all the world except those having a better title. Counsel says that possession only raises a presumption of title, which, however, may be rebutted. Rightly understood, this is correct; but counsel misapplies it. One who takes property from the possession of another can only rebut this presumption by showing a superior title in himself, or in some way connecting himself with one who has. One who has acquired the possession of property, whether by finding, bailment, or by mere tort, has a right to retain that possession as against a mere wrongdoer who is a stranger to the property. Any other rule would lead to an endless series of unlawful seizures and reprisals in every case where property had once passed out of the possession of the rightful owner.

Order affirmed.

NOTES AND QUESTIONS

1.   Given the jury's rejection of the defendants' story that they were acting on the authority of the true owners, *Anderson v. Gouldberg* becomes a case of Converter 1 (Anderson) versus Converter 2 (Gouldberg and partner). The court regards the rule of law in *Armory v. Delamirie* as resolving such a dispute. Do you agree? Doesn't the court substitute an even broader proposition of law for the one announced in *Armory*? Is this broader proposition justifiable as a matter of policy in all circumstances involving persons who acquire possession wrongfully? For example, does this broader proposition mean it would be improper for a Good Samaritan to chase down a purse snatcher who has stolen a purse from a third party?

2.   Even if we reject the idea that Converter 1 should prevail against subsequent possessors who do not act wrongfully (say a Good Samaritan who recovers the property or a finder), the question remains: Who should prevail in the case of Converter 1 versus Converter 2? Are you persuaded by the court's statement that Converter 1 should prevail because "[a]ny other rule would lead to an endless series of unlawful seizures and reprisals in every case where property had once passed out of the possession of the rightful owner?" Could it not be argued that a rule of "no property among thieves" would reduce the economic returns to thievery, and thus reduce the incidence of theft?

3.   As might be expected, there are relatively few reported decisions involving lawsuits between a Converter 1 and a Converter 2. But there is at least one other reported decision, *Russell v. Hill*, 34 S.E. 640 (N.C. 1899), which reaches the opposite result to the one in *Anderson v. Gouldberg*. This was yet another dispute about logs that had been wrongfully taken by A, and then were taken wrongfully from A by B. The court permitted B to defeat an action in trover by A by showing that the true owner of the logs was C. In support of this outcome, the court stated in part:

> [I]n some of the English books, and in some of the Reports of our sister states, cases might be found to the contrary, but * * * those cases were all founded upon a misapprehension of the principle laid down in the case of Armory v. Delamirie, 1 Strange, 505. There a chimney sweep found a lost jewel. He took it into his possession, as he had a right to do, and was the owner, because of having it in possession, unless the true owner should become known. That owner was not known, and it was properly decided that trover would lie in favor of the

finder against the defendant, to whom he had handed it for inspection. But the court said the case would have been very different if the owner had been known * * *

Id. at 640–41. Is this an accurate reading of *Armory v. Delamirie?*

4.   Suppose we want to design the rules in these sequential possession cases to maximize the chances that the true owner will be able to recover the property. Which party is more likely to be found by the true owner— Converter 1 or Converter 2? Is it easier or harder to answer this question than it is when the choice is between Finder 1 and Finder 2?

RELATIVITY OF TITLE AND REJECTION OF THE *JUS TERTII* DEFENSE

Armory v. Delamirie and cases like *Clark v. Maloney* and *Anderson v. Gouldberg* are often cited for the proposition that an action to protect possession of property cannot be defeated by setting up a superior title in a third party (the *jus tertii*). The leading case for this view is often said to be *Jeffries v. The Great Western Railway*, 119 Eng. Rep. 680 (Q.B. 1856). This was an action in trover to recover damages for wrongful taking of some railroad cars; the defendant sought to defeat the action by proving that title to the cars had been assigned to someone else. In rejecting the defense, Chief Justice Campbell said:

I am of the opinion that the law is that a person possessed of goods as his property has a good title as against every stranger, and that one who takes them from him, having no title in himself, is a wrongdoer, and cannot defend himself by showing that there was title in some third person; for against a wrongdoer possession is a title. The law is * * * essential for the interests of society, that peaceable possession should not be disturbed by wrongdoers. * * * It is not disputed that the jus tertii cannot be set up as a defense to an action of trespass for disturbing the possession. In this respect I see no difference between trespass and trover; for in truth the presumption of law is that the person who has possession has the property. Can that presumption be rebutted by evidence that the property was in a third person, when offered as a defense by one who admits that he himself had no title and was a wrongdoer when he converted the goods? I am of the opinion that this cannot be done * * *

The proposition that a defendant cannot invoke the *jus tertii* to defeat an action to protect possession can be defended on either a substantive or procedural theory. The excerpt from *Jeffries* invokes the substantive theory: One of the objects of the law is to protect peaceful possession; hence, someone who wrongfully interferes with peaceful possession should not be let off the hook by invoking the superior rights of some third party. The procedural theory invokes the bilateral nature of common-law litigation, and the availability of direct testimony by the two opposing parties in such litigation. A sues B; A testifies to what A knows, B testifies to what B knows; the jury decides which party is the more credible. To allow one of the parties to put in issue the rights of a third party not before the court would present potential difficulties of proof, particularly in a time before title registration acts when the best evidence of title would be deeds in the possession of the true owner.

G. COMPETING ORIGINAL ACQUISITION PRINCIPLES

Now that we have seen five principles for establishing original acquisition (first possession, discovery, creation, accession, adverse possession), we can also see that some of the more difficult problems of original acquisition in fact involve clashes between parties claiming under competing principles of original acquisition. Since the principles proceed from different premises, it is difficult to say that there is a "right answer" in any of these cases. The cases selected here all involve conflicts between first possession and accession, but in theory similar conflicts could arise between any of the five principles.

Fisher v. Steward

New Hampshire Supreme Court, 1804.
Smith 60.

Trover for a swarm of bees. There was a second count for two hundred pounds of honey in the comb.

The case was, the plaintiffs found a swarm of bees in a tree on the (defendant's) land in Claremont, marked the tree, and notified the defendant, who cut down the tree, September, 1803, and converted the honey to his own use. * * *

At the trial there was some dispute whether the plaintiffs or one of the defendant's family first discovered the bees, and whether the plaintiffs gave notice of the finding and marking the tree. The other parts of the case were proved.

The Court summed up, and observed that two questions had been made on the trial: first, whether the plaintiffs first discovered the bees; and, secondly, supposing they did, whether the property in the honey was in them.

The first is a question of evidence proper for the consideration of the jury.

The second is a question of law, and one about which the Court entertained no doubt. The plaintiffs do not pretend to have any property in the land or in the tree, nor had they any property in the bees. How then came they by a property in the honey? It must have been by occupancy. But how did they occupy, or appropriate the honey to themselves? They saw the bees enter the tree, they heard them make a noise near the tree, and they marked the tree. The two first gave no right; they do not amount to occupancy. The marking of the tree was a trespass, and consequently can avail the plaintiffs nothing. The doctrine contended for by plaintiffs is injurious to the rights of property. Till the bees occupied the tree in question, it is not pretended that plaintiffs had any right in it. What gave them a right? Having seen a swarm of bees, in which they had no property, occupying it? This circumstance, whether the effect of accident, or the result of labor and skill, cannot lessen the rights of the owner of the soil. Will it be pretended that plaintiffs thereby acquired a right to the tree? If they acquired a title to the honey, they must necessarily have a right to take it away, to cut down the tree, to pass over the defendant's land for the purpose, & c. Admitting the plaintiffs could acquire property in a swarm of bees, or in the honey, by finding, in some cases, they could not do so in the present case, because such right or property interferes with the rights and property clearly vested in defendant; it is inconsistent with it; it lessens its value at least. It is much more consonant to our ideas of property to say, that the bees and honey in the defendant's trees belong to him in the same manner and for the same reasons as all mines and minerals belong to the owner of the soil.

Will it be pretended by the plaintiffs that they could have put, without defendant's permission, a swarm of bees into defendant's tree, and there kept them till they had made honey; and then, in case he cut down the tree, maintained trespass for the cutting, or trover for the honey? One would suppose the present case was not stronger than that; here they had no right to the bees.

It has been said, that, by the usage of this part of the State, the person who finds bees acquires a property in them wherever found. We recognize no such usage. We have no local customs or usages which are binding in one part of the State and not in another. If this be the law here, it must be so in every other part of the State.

Verdict for defendant.

NOTES AND QUESTIONS

1.   The principle that captured wild animals belong to the owner of the land where they are captured, sometimes called *ratione loci* or *ratione soli*, is alluded to in *Pierson v. Post*, supra. Post (the huntsman) alleged in his complaint that the fox had been hunted on a "wild and uninhabited, unpossessed and waste land, called the beach." The court seized on this allegation to sidestep English precedent, observing that the English decisions "have either been discussed and decided upon the principles of their positive statute regulations, or have arisen between the huntsman and the owner of the land upon which beasts *ferae naturae* have been apprehended; the former claiming them by title of occupancy, and the latter *ratione soli.*" The *Pierson* court was therefore able to decide the dispute based solely on the principle of first possession, rather than having to sort out the competing claims of first possession and *ratione soli*, a species of accession doctrine.

2.   Could the court in *Fisher* have ruled for the defendant on the ground that the plaintiff had not performed acts sufficient to constitute

possession of the bees or the hive? Recall in this connection the discussion in *Pierson v. Post* and *Eads v. Brazelton* about what acts are required to establish possession.

3.   The tension between first possession and accession in wild animal law is nowhere greater than with respect to bees. *Ratione soli*—an instance of the principle of accession—may loom especially large with respect to bees because bees make hives in fixed locations, and the economic value of the bees (i.e., the honey they produce) inheres in this fixed location. Given this feature, it may be that American courts have been rather more sympathetic to the idea that ownership of bees goes with ownership of land than they have been to the notion that ownership of other types of wild animals killed or captured on private land goes with the land. See Dale D. Goble & Eric T. Freyfogle, Wildlife Law 133–145 (2002) (noting that early American courts were hostile to English doctrines about ownership of land giving rise to control over wildlife on the land, and were sympathetic with the idea of a general privilege to hunt on any unenclosed or uncultivated land). Another wild animal that builds elaborate homes in fixed locations is the beaver— something to bear in mind when considering Harold Demsetz's explanation in the next chapter of the way private property rights in beaver territories emerged among certain Native American tribes when the value of beaver pelts rose.

4.   The court in the principal case had a rather easy out in deciding between first possession and accession insofar as the plaintiff could not have marked the tree or harvested the honey without trespassing on the defendant's land. Generally speaking, first possessors have not fared well in disputes with landowners over things that the possessor has discovered while trespassing on the land. See, e.g., Favorite v. Miller, 407 A.2d 974 (Conn. 1978) (judgment for plaintiff landowner against defendant trespasser who, based on archival research and with the aid of a metal detector, found on plaintiff's land a fragment of an equestrian statue of George III toppled in the Revolutionary War).

Goddard v. Winchell

Supreme Court of Iowa, 1892.
52 N.W. 1124.

■ GRANGER, J. The district court found the following facts, with some others, not important on this trial: "That the plaintiff, John Goodard, is, and has been since about 1857, the owner in fee simple of the north half of section No. three, in township No. ninety-eight, range No. twenty-five, in Winnebago county, Iowa, and was such owner at the time of the fall of the meteorite hereinafter referred to. (2) That said land was prairie land, and that the grass privilege for the year 1890 was leased to one James Elickson. (3) That on the 2d day of May, 1890, an aerolite passed over northern and northwestern Iowa, and the aerolite, or fragment of the same, in question in this action, weighing, when replevied, and when produced in court on the trial of this cause, about 66 pounds, fell onto plaintiff's land, described above, and buried itself in the ground to a depth of three feet, and became imbedded therein at a point about 20 rods from the section line on the north. (4) That the day after the aerolite in question fell it was dug out of the ground with a spade by one Peter Hoagland, in the presence of the tenant, Elickson; that said Hoagland took it to his house, and claimed to own same, for the reason that he had found same and dug it up. (5) That on May 5, 1890, Hoagland sold the aerolite in suit to the defendant, H. V. Winchell, for $105, and the same was at once taken possession of by said defendant, and that the possession was held by him until same was taken under the writ of replevin herein; that defendant knew at the time of his purchase that it was an aerolite, and that it fell on the prairie south of Hoagland's land. * * * (10) I find the value of said aerolite to be one hundred and one dollars ($101) as verbally stipulated in open court by the parties to this action; that the same weighs about 66 pounds, is of a black, smoky color on the outside, showing the effects of heat, and of a lighter and darkish gray color on the inside; that it is an aerolite, and fell from the heavens on the 2d of May, 1890; that a member of Hoagland's family saw the aerolite fall, and directed him to it."

As conclusions of law, the district court found that the aerolite became a part of the soil on which it fell; that the plaintiff was the owner thereof; and that the act of Hoagland in removing it was wrongful. It is insisted by appellant that the conclusions of law are erroneous; that the enlightened demands of the time in which we live call for, if not a modification, a liberal construction, of the ancient rule, "that whatever is affixed to the soil belongs to the soil," or, the more modern statement of the rule, that "a permanent annexation to the soil, of a thing in itself personal, makes it a part of the realty." In behalf of appellant is invoked a rule alike ancient and of undoubted merit, "that of title by occupancy;" and we are cited to the language of Blackstone, as follows: "Occupancy is the taking possession of those things which before belonged to nobody;" and "whatever movables are found upon the surface of the earth, or in the sea, and are unclaimed by any owner, are supposed to be abandoned by the last proprietor, and as such are returned into the common stock and mass of things; and therefore they belong, as in a state of nature, to the first occupant or finder." * * *

If, from what we have said, we have in mind the facts giving rise to the rules cited, we may well look to the facts of this case to properly distinguish it. The subject of the dispute is an aerolite, of about 66 pounds' weight, that "fell from the heavens" on the land of the plaintiff, and was found three feet below the surface. It came to its position in the earth through natural causes. It was one of nature's deposits, with nothing in its material composition to make it foreign or unnatural to the soil. It was not a movable thing "on the earth." It was in the earth, and in a very significant sense immovable; that is, it was only movable as parts of earth are made movable by the hand of man. Except for the peculiar manner in which it came, its relation to the soil would be beyond dispute. It was in its substance, as we understand, a stone. It was not of a character to be thought of as "unclaimed by any owner," and, because unclaimed, "supposed to be abandoned by the last proprietor," as should be the case under the rule invoked by appellant. In fact, it has none of the characteristics of the property contemplated by such a rule.

We may properly note some of the particular claims of appellant. * * * The general rules of the law, by which the owners of riparian titles are made to lose or gain by the doctrine of accretions, are quite familiar. These rules are not, however, of exclusive application to such owners. Through the action of the elements, wind and water, the soil of one man is taken and deposited in the field of another; and thus all over the country, we may say, changes are constantly going on. By these natural causes the owners of the soil are giving and taking as the wisdom of the controlling forces shall determine. By these operations one may be affected with a substantial gain, and another by a similar loss. These gains are of accretion, and the deposit becomes the property of the owner of the soil on which it is made.

A scientist of note has said that from six to seven hundred of these stones fall to our earth annually. If they are, as indicated in argument, departures from other planets, and if among the planets of the solar system there is this interchange, bearing evidence of their material composition, upon what principle of reason or authority can we say that a deposit thus made shall not be of that class of property that it would be if originally of this planet and in the same situation? * * * It is not easy to understand why stones or balls of metallic iron, deposited as this was, should be governed by a different rule than obtains from the deposit of boulders, stones, and drift upon our prairies by glacier action; and who would contend that these deposits from floating bodies of ice belong, not to the owner of the soil, but to the finder? Their origin or source may be less mysterious, but they, too, are "telltale messengers" from far-off lands, and have value for historic and scientific investigation.

It is said that the aerolite is without adaptation to the soil, and only valuable for scientific purposes. Nothing in the facts of the case will warrant us in saying that it was not as well adapted for use by the owner of the soil as any stone, or, as appellant is pleased to denominate it, "ball of metallic iron." That it may be of greater value for scientific or other purposes may be admitted, but that fact has little weight in determining who should be its owner. We cannot say that the owner of the soil is not as interested in, and would not as readily contribute to, the great cause of scientific advancement, as the finder, by chance or otherwise, of these silent messengers. This aerolite is of the value of $101, and this fact, if no other, would remove it from uses where other and much less valuable materials would answer an equally good purpose, and place it in the sphere of its greater usefulness.

The rule is cited, with cases for its support, that the finder of lost articles, even where they are found on the property, in the building, or with the personal effects of third persons, is the owner thereof against all the world except the true owner. The correctness of the rule may be conceded, but its application to the case at bar is very doubtful. The subject of this controversy was never lost or abandoned. Whence it came is not known, but, under the natural law of its government, it became a part of this earth, and, we think, should be treated as such. * * *

The judgment of the district court is affirmed.

NOTES AND QUESTIONS

1.   Horace V. Winchell, the defendant in this action, was a geologist with the University of Minnesota and an avid collector of aerolites, or meteorites as they are more commonly called today. When Winchell heard about a large meteorite shower near Forest City, Iowa, he hastened to the site. He arrived at Peter Hoagland's farm at the same time as William Bradford, a local lawyer who evidently sought to acquire the aerolite to resell it for a profit, and a bidding war ensued. Bradford would not pay more than $100, so Winchell won. The lawyer later discovered that the aerolite had fallen on Goddard's land, not Hoagland's, and sued out a writ of replevin in Goddard's name, posting a bond for twice the value of the stone. (See Chapter IV for more on replevin.) This caused the sheriff to seize the aerolite at the train station, as Winchell was preparing to ship it to Minneapolis. Before the first replevin was tried, Winchell persuaded the University to bring a second replevin action, posting an even higher bond. This caused the sheriff to seize the stone again and turn it back over to Winchell, who spirited it out of the state in a mad dash. The decision reproduced here is the appeal from the first replevin action. Once the Iowa Supreme Court decided the question of title, the only issue in the second action was damages. The jury in this second action fixed the value at $480, which the University paid rather than give up the stone. See Horace V. Winchell, A Meteoric Career, A True Story, 131 Atlantic Monthly 779 (June 1923). According to Professor E. Calvin Alexander, Jr. of the University of Minnesota Department of Geology and Geophysics, the "Forest City Meteorite" remains the property of the University of Minnesota, although it has been on loan to the Smithsonian Institution in Washington, D.C. for several decades.

2.   The court here may have thought that it had no easy out based on trespass. Goddard, the owner of the pasture where the aerolite fell, had leased the land to Elickson as tenant. A tenant typically exercises full possessory rights over leased property, including the right to determine who may and may not enter the land and on what terms. Since Elickson had granted permission to Hoagland to enter the field and recover the aerolite, it would have been difficult to award the aerolite to Goddard on the simple ground that Hoagland was a trespasser. On the other hand, someone who exceeds the scope of an owner's consent (in the form of a license or easement, see Chapters IV and IX) becomes a trespasser even if his initial entry was lawful. In this case, the tenant Elickson had only the "grass privilege," probably meaning that Elickson had no right to dig for minerals. Would it have exceeded the scope of Elickson's rights if he had dug the aerolite out of the ground himself? If Elickson likewise had no actual authority to authorize digging by Hoagland, does that make Hoag-

land a trespasser? Would this depend on what Hoagland reasonably believed about the scope of Elickson's rights? How would we expect Hoagland to inform himself about such matters?

Figure 2–13
Mayor Ed J. Howard, Ann E. Hodges, and Chief W.D. Ashcraft, the afternoon of the fall

Courtesy Alabama Museum of Natural History, The University of Alabama. Note the hole in the ceiling and Ann Hodges' swollen hand.

3.   How important to the result is it that the aerolite was buried three feet into the ground? Suppose it came down and bounced off a piece of granite, and thus stayed on the surface of the land. Same result? Consider the famous Hodges meteorite. On November 30, 1954, a 8 ½ pound

fragment of a meteorite fell through the roof of a house in Sylacauga, Alabama, bounced off a console radio, and struck Ann Hodges who, not feeling well, had been napping on the living-room couch. (See Figure 2–13.) Hodges was painfully but not seriously injured in the arm and hip and was later hospitalized, partly to avoid the clamor of press and curiosity seekers who descended on the Hodges home. Hodges and her husband occupied the house under a lease, and later the Hodges and their landlord, Birdie Guy, got into a legal dispute over who was the owner of the meteorite. Guy's attorney believed that caselaw supported Mrs. Guy's position, based on her ownership of the real property. But public opinion was firmly behind Mrs. Hodges, in part because the meteorite had physically struck her. Should this affect the analysis of the rival claims of ownership? What would Hume and Sugden say? After preliminary sparring (including a threat by Mrs. Hodges to sue Mrs. Guy for her injuries if she was awarded ownership of the meteorite), the case was settled in September 1955, with Mrs. Hodges paying Mrs. Guy $500 to relinquish her claim. Mrs. Hodges donated the meteorite the next year to the Alabama Museum of Natural History, where it is on permanent display. For this information we are indebted to John Hall, retired assistant director of the museum. John C. Hall, The Day the Star Fell in Sylacauga (unpublished draft, October 2006).

Hannah v. Peel

King's Bench Division, 1945.
[1945] K.B. 509.

On December 13, 1938, the freehold of Gwernhaylod House, Overton-on-Dee, Shropshire, was conveyed to the defendant, Major Hugh Edward Ethelston Peel, who from that time to the end of 1940 never himself occupied the house and it remained unoccupied until October 5, 1939, when it was requisitioned, but after some months was released from requisition. Thereafter it remained unoccupied until July 18, 1940, when it was again requisitioned, the defendant being compensated by a payment at the rate of £250 a year. In August, 1940, the plaintiff, Duncan Hannah, a lance-corporal, serving in a battery of the Royal Artillery, was stationed at the house and on the 21st of that month, when in a bedroom, used as a sick-bay, he was adjusting the black-out curtains when his hand touched something on the top of a window-frame, loose in a crevice, which he thought was a piece of dirt or plaster. The plaintiff grasped it and dropped it on the outside window ledge. On the following morning he saw that it was a brooch covered with cobwebs and dirt. Later, he took it with him when he went home on leave and his wife having told him it might be of value, at the end of October, 1940, he informed his commanding officer of his find and, on his advice, handed it over to the police, receiving a receipt for it. In August, 1942, the owner not having been found the police handed the brooch to the defendant, who sold it in October, 1942, for £66, to Messrs. Spink & Son, Ltd., of London, who resold it in the following month for £88. There was no evidence that the defendant had any knowledge of the existence of the brooch before it was found by the plaintiff. The defendant had offered the plaintiff a reward for the brooch, but the plaintiff refused to accept this and maintained throughout his right to the possession of the brooch as against all persons other than the owner, who was unknown. By a letter, dated October 5, 1942, the plaintiff's solicitors demanded the return of the brooch from the defendant, but it was not returned and on October 21, 1943, the plaintiff issued his writ claiming the return of the brooch, or its value, and damages for its detention. By his defence, the defendant claimed the brooch on the ground that he was the owner of Gwernhaylod House and in possession thereof.

■ BIRKETT J. There is no issue of fact in this case between the parties. As to the issue in law, the rival claims of the parties can be stated in this way: The plaintiff says: "I claim the brooch as its finder and I have a good title against all the world, save only the true owner." The defendant says: "My claim is superior to yours inasmuch as I am the freeholder. The brooch was found on my property, although I was never in occupation, and my title, therefore, ousts yours and in the absence of the true owner I am entitled to the brooch or its value." Unhappily the law on this issue is in a very uncertain state and there is need of an authoritative decision of a higher court. Obviously if it could be said with certainty that this is the law, that the finder of a lost article, wherever found, has a good title against all the world save the true owner, then, of course, all my difficulties would be resolved; or again, if it could be said with equal certainty that this is the law, that the possessor of land is entitled as against the finder to all chattels found on the land, again my difficulties would be resolved. But, unfortunately, the authorities give some support to each of these conflicting propositions.

In the famous case of *Armory v. Delamirie*, 1 Str. 505, the plaintiff, who was a chimney sweeper's boy, found a jewel and carried it to the defendant's shop, who was a goldsmith, in order to know what it was, and he delivered it into the hands of the apprentice in the goldsmith's shop, who made a pretence of weighing it and took out the stones and called to the master to let him know that it came to three-halfpence. The master offered the boy the money who refused to take it and insisted on having the jewel again. Whereupon the apprentice handed him back the socket of the jewel without the stones, and an action was brought in trover against the master, and it was ruled "that the finder of a jewel, though he does not by such finding acquire an absolute property or ownership, yet he has such a property as will enable him to keep it against all but the rightful owner, and consequently may maintain trover." The case of *Bridges v. Hawkesworth*, 21 L. J. (Q. B.) 75, is in process of becoming almost equally as famous because of the disputation which has raged around it. The headnote in the Jurist is as follows: "The place in which a lost article is found does not constitute any exception to the general rule of law, that the finder is entitled to it as against all persons except the owner." * * * The facts appear to have been that in the year 1847 the plaintiff, who was a commercial traveller, called on a firm named Byfield & Hawkesworth on business, as he was in the habit of doing, and as he was leaving the shop he picked up a small parcel which was lying on the floor. He immediately showed it to the shopman, and opened it in his presence, when it was found to consist of a quantity of Bank of England notes, to the amount of £65. The defendant, who was a partner in the firm of Byfield & Hawkesworth, was then called, and the plaintiff told him he had found the notes, and asked the defendant to keep them until the owner appeared to claim them. Then various advertisements were put in the papers asking for the owner, but the true owner was never found. No person having appeared to claim them, and three years having elapsed since they were found, the plaintiff applied to the defendant to have the notes returned to him, and offered to pay the expenses of the advertisements, and to give an indemnity. The defendant refused to deliver them up to the plaintiff, and an action was brought in the county court of Westminster in consequence of that refusal. The county court judge decided that the defendant, the shopkeeper, was entitled to the custody of the notes as against the plaintiff, and gave judgment for the defendant. Thereupon the appeal was brought which came before the court composed of Patteson J. and Wightman J. Patteson J. said: "The notes which are the subject of this action were incidentally dropped, by mere accident, in the shop of the defendant, by the owner of them. The facts do not warrant the supposition that they had been deposited there intentionally, nor has the case been put at all upon that ground. The plaintiff found them on the floor, they being manifestly lost by someone. The general right of the finder to any article which has been lost, as against all the world, except the true owner, was established in the case of Armory v. Delamirie which has never been disputed. This right would clearly have accrued to the plaintiff had the notes been picked up by him outside the shop of the defendant and if he once had the right, the case finds that he did not intend, by delivering the notes to the defendant, to waive the title (if any) which he had to them, but they were handed to the defendant merely for the purpose of delivering them to the owner should he appear." Then a little later: "The case, therefore, resolves itself into the single point on which it appears that the learned judge decided it, namely, whether the circumstance of the notes being found inside the defendant's shop gives him, the defendant, the right to have them as against the plaintiff, who found them." After discussing the cases, and the argument, the learned judge said: "If the discovery had never been communicated to the defendant, could the real owner have had any cause of action against him because they were found in his house? Certainly not. The notes never were in the custody of the defendant, nor within the protection of his house, before they were found, as they would have been had they been intentionally deposited there; and the defendant has come under no responsibility, except from the communication made to him by the plaintiff, the finder, and the steps taken by way of advertisement. ... We find, therefore, no circumstances in this case to take it out of the general rule of law, that the finder of a lost article is entitled to it as against all persons except the real owner, and we think that that rule must prevail, and that the learned judge was mistaken in holding that the place in which they were found makes any legal difference. Our judgment, therefore, is that the plaintiff is entitled to these notes as against the defendant."

It is to be observed that in Bridges v. Hawkesworth which has been the subject of immense disputation, neither counsel put forward any argument on the fact that the notes were found in a shop. Counsel for the appellant assumed throughout that the position was the same as if the parcel had been found in a private house, and the learned judge spoke of "the protection of his" (the shopkeeper's) "house." The case for the appellant was that the shopkeeper never knew of the notes. Again, what is curious is that there was no suggestion that the place where the notes were found was in any way material; indeed, the judge in giving the judgment of the court expressly repudiates this and said in terms "The learned judge was mistaken in holding that the place in which they were found makes any legal difference." * * *

With regard to South Staffordshire Water Co. v. Sharman, [1896] 2 Q. B. 44, the first two lines of the headnote are: "The possessor of land is generally entitled, as against the finder, to chattels found on the land." I am not sure that this is accurate. The facts were that the defendant Sharman, while cleaning out, under the orders of the plaintiffs, the South Staffordshire Water Company, a pool of water on their land, found two rings embedded in the mud at the bottom of the pool. He declined to deliver them to the plaintiffs, but failed to discover the real owner. In an action brought by the company against Sharman in detinue it was held that the company were entitled to the rings. Lord Russell of Killowen C.J. said (id. at 46): "The plaintiffs are the freeholders of the locus in quo, and as such they have the right to forbid anybody coming on their land or in any way interfering with it. They had the right to say that their pool should be cleaned out in any way that they thought fit, and to direct what should be done with anything found in the pool in the course of such cleaning out. It is no doubt right, as the counsel for the defendant contended, to say that the plaintiffs must show that they had actual control over the locus in quo and the things in it; but under the circumstances, can it be said that the Minster Pool and whatever might be in that pool were not under the control of the plaintiffs? In my opinion they were.... The principle on which this case must be decided, and the distinction which must be drawn between this case and that of Bridges v. Hawkesworth, is to be found in a passage in Pollock and Wright's 'Essay on Possession in the Common Law,' p. 41: 'The possession of land carries with it in general, by our law, possession of everything which is attached to or under that land, and, in the absence of a better title elsewhere, the right to possess it also'." If that is right, it would clearly cover the case of the rings embedded in the mud of the pool, the words used being "attached to or under that land." Lord Russell continued: " 'And it makes no difference that the possessor is not aware of the thing's existence.... It is free to anyone who requires a specific intention as part of a de facto possession to treat this as a positive rule of law. But it seems preferable to say that the legal possession rests on a real de facto possession constituted by the occupier's general power and intent to exclude unauthorized interference.' That is the ground on which I prefer to base my judgment. There is a broad distinction between this case and those cited from Blackstone. Those were cases in which a thing was cast into a public place or into the sea—into a place, in fact, of which it could not be said that anyone had a real de facto possession, or a general power and intent to exclude unauthorized interference." Then Lord Russell cited the passage which I read earlier in this judgment and continued: "It is somewhat strange"—I venture to echo those words—"that there is no more direct authority on the question; but the general principle seems to me to be that where a person has possession of house or land, with a manifest intention to exercise control over it and the things which may be upon or in it, then, if something is found on that land, whether by an employee of the owner or by a stranger, the presumption is that the possession of that thing is in the owner of the locus in quo." It is to be observed that Lord Russell there is extending the meaning of the passage he had cited from Pollock and Wright's essay on "Possession in the Common Law," where the learned authors say that the possession of land carries with it possession of everything which is attached to or under that land. Then Lord Russell adds possession of everything which may be on or in that land. South Staffordshire Water Co. v. Sharman, which was relied on by counsel for the defendant, has also been the subject of some discussion. It has been said that it establishes that if a man finds a thing as the servant or agent of another, he finds it not for himself, but for that other, and indeed that seems to afford a sufficient explanation of the case. The rings found at the bottom of the pool were not in the possession of the company, but it seems that though Sharman was the first to obtain possession of them, he obtained them for his employers and could claim no title for himself.

The only other case to which I need refer is Elwes v. Brigg Gas Co., 33 Ch. D. 562, in which land had been demised to a gas company for ninety-nine years with a reservation to the lessor of all mines and minerals. A prehistoric boat embedded in the soil was discovered by the lessees when they were digging to make a gasholder. It was held that the boat, whether regarded as a mineral or as part of the soil in which it was embedded when discovered, or as a chattel, did not pass to the lessees by the demise, but was the property of the lessor though he was ignorant of its existence at the time of granting the lease. Chitty J. said (id. at 568): "The first question which does actually arise in this case is whether the boat belonged to the plaintiff at the time of the granting of the lease. I hold that it did, whether it ought to be regarded as a mineral, or as part of the soil within the maxim above cited, or as a chattel. If it was a mineral or part of the soil in the sense above indicated, then it clearly belonged to the owners of the inheritance as part of the inheritance itself. But if it ought to be regarded as a chattel, I hold the property in the chattel was vested in the plaintiff, for the following reasons." Then he gave the reasons, and continued: "The plaintiff then being thus in possession of the chattel, it follows that the property in the chattel was vested in him. Obviously the right of the original owner could not be established; it had for centuries been lost or barred, even supposing that the property had not been abandoned when the boat was first left on the spot where it was found. The plaintiff, then, had a lawful possession, good against all the world, and therefore the property in the boat. In my opinion it makes no difference, in these circumstances, that the plaintiff was not aware of the existence of the boat.''

A review of these judgments shows that the authorities are in an unsatisfactory state, and I observe that Sir John Salmond in his book on Jurisprudence (9th ed., at p. 383), after referring to the cases of Elwes v. Brigg Gas Co. and South Staffordshire Water Co. v. Sharman, said: ''Cases such as these, however, are capable of explanation on other grounds, and do not involve any necessary conflict either with the theory of possession or with the cases already cited, such as Bridges v. Hawkesworth. The general principle is that the first finder of a thing has a good title to it against all but the true owner, even though the thing is found on the property of another person,'' and he cites Armory v. Delamirie and Bridges v. Hawkesworth in support of that proposition. Then he continues: ''This principle, however, is subject to important exceptions, in which, owing to the special circumstances of the case, the better right is in him on whose property the thing is found,'' and he names three cases as the principal ones: ''When he on whose property the thing is found is already in possession not merely of the property, but of the thing itself; as in certain circumstances, even without specific knowledge, he undoubtedly may be.'' The second limitation Sir John Salmond puts is: ''If anyone finds a thing as the servant or agent of another he finds it not for himself, but for his employer.'' Then: ''A third case in which a finder obtains no title is that in which he gets possession only through a trespass or other act of wrongdoing.'' It is fairly clear from the authorities that a man possesses everything which is attached to or under his land. Secondly, it would appear to be the law from the authorities I have cited, and particularly from Bridges v. Hawkesworth, that a man does not necessarily possess a thing which is lying unattached on the surface of his land even though the thing is not possessed by someone else. A difficulty however, arises, because the rule which governs things an occupier possesses as against those which he does not, has never been very clearly formulated in our law. He may possess everything on the land from which he intends to exclude others, if Mr. Justice Holmes is right; or he may possess those things of which he has a de facto control, if Sir Frederick Pollock is right.

There is no doubt that in this case the brooch was lost in the ordinary meaning of that term, and I should imagine it had been lost for a very considerable time. Indeed, from this correspondence it appears that at one time the predecessors in title of the defendant were considering making some claim. But the moment the plaintiff discovered that the brooch might be of some value, he took the advice of his commanding officer and handed it to the police. His conduct was commendable and meritorious. The defendant was never physically in possession of these premises at any time. It is clear that the brooch was never his, in the ordinary acceptation of the term, in that he had the prior possession. He had no knowledge of it, until it was brought to his notice by the finder. A discussion of the merits does not seem to help, but it is clear on the facts that the brooch was ''lost'' in the ordinary meaning of that word; that it was "found" by the plaintiff in the ordinary meaning of that word, that its true owner has never been found, that the defendant was the owner of the premises and had his notice drawn to this matter by the plaintiff, who found the brooch. In those circumstances I propose to follow the decision in Bridges v. Hawkesworth, and to give judgment in this case for the plaintiff for £66.

NOTES AND QUESTIONS

1.   According to a local historian, the Peels were the "lords of the manor" of Overton and still live in the village today. The main house of the Peel estate is Bryn y Pys, located nearby; they purchased Gwernhaylod in 1934 primarily to add its farmland and woods to their existing holdings, and they leased the house to tenants. Consider some further history:

> I am afraid Gwernheylod suffered the same fate as many country houses in the U.K. They were requisitioned by the British army 1939–46 and after the war were left in such an awful state by the uncaring and unsupervised soldiers, that they had to be demolished. Windows smashed, lead stolen from roofs, led to the weather getting in and the houses starting to decay and getting into a state that would be too expensive to repair * * * It was also a time when men returning from the war had no desire to go back to be servants and the size of large houses was impractical to run without servants. The final blow was the death of Major Hugh Peel in 1950, leaving his heir, one very young granddaughter. The estate was for a time therefore managed by Trustees on her behalf who made the decision to demolish the old house. There is still a cottage there created from outbuildings of the old house and this is now lived in by the Peel estate's gamekeeper.

Email communication from Jill Burton, Royal Commission on the Ancient and Historical Monuments of Wales, July 29, 2006.

2.   Again, there is easy solution here based on trespass. Corporal Hannah had full permission to be where he was when he found the brooch. He was staying at Gwernhaylod on the orders of the British Army, which had requisitioned it during the War.

3.   The court appears to give reduced weight to Major Peel's interest as owner of the house, on the ground that he had never entered into actual possession of the house before the brooch was found. This seems to tilt the court away from accession towards first possession. Major Peel's lack of possession could hardly be a decisive factor, however, given the decision in *Elwes v. Brigg Gas Co.*, cited in the main case, which awarded a pre-historic boat found buried on the land to the landlord rather than the tenant gas company that discovered it while digging. One can hardly be more out of possession than a landlord under a 99–year lease. Would *Hannah v. Peel* have come out the other way if Gwernhaylod had been Major Peel's ancestral home where he had grown up as a boy?

Figure 2–14
Gwernhaylod House, Overton: West Elevation, 1956

© Crown copyright: Royal Commission on the Ancient and Historical Monuments of Wales.

4. Suppose the brooch had been discovered by Corporal Hannah buried under one inch of soil in the garden. Different result? English law recognizes a special rule for treasure trove, defined to mean gold, silver, bullion, or money concealed in a hidden place. If the treasure trove is buried under ground, it belongs to the Crown. See Barlow Burke, Personal Property 159–61 (3d ed. 2003). Should the court in *Hannah* have extended this doctrine to award the brooch to the British government? Absent any Crown and operating in a culture that puts a high premium on individualism, American courts have tended to reject any special rule for treasure trove and generally treat buried treasure like any other kind of lost or abandoned property.

5. American courts sometimes distinguish between lost and mislaid property in deciding who gets to keep a found object. See, e.g., McAvoy v. Medina, 93 Mass. 548 (1866). An object is said to be mislaid when the owner intentionally places it somewhere and then forgets it (for example, the owner places it on a counter in a store and then leaves without it). An object is said to be lost when the owner is unaware of losing possession of it (for example, it falls out of the owner's pocket). Courts that observe the distinction generally award lost property to the finder, and mislaid property to the owner of the land where it is found. Does this distinction make

sense? What policy or objective is being pursued by further subdividing the world of misplaced objects in this fashion? Was the brooch in *Hannah* lost or mislaid?

CONCLUDING NOTE AND QUESTIONS

Notice that the idea of possession appears repeatedly in all the material we have covered about original acquisition of property. First possession, obviously, is based on being the first to possess an unclaimed thing. Discovery is based on being the first to discover some thing, and hence having a unique claim to possess it. Creation involves being the first to possess some new or novel thing. Accession is more complicated, but in many of its applications appears to involve the perception that one thing bears such a prominent relationship to another thing that possession of the one thing is also possession of the other thing. And of course adverse possession is based on someone possessing a thing for such a long period of time that the rights of the original owner are extinguished. Moreover, the sequential possession issues seem to suggest that prior possession is privileged in the law, and the cases about competing acquisition principles can be read as turning on which of two rival claims of possession the court finds more compelling in any given context. Does all this suggest that there is only one principle of original acquisition, based on having a stronger claim of possession? Why should possession play such a pivotal role in assigning ownership to things? Can you think of some other principle, unrelated to possession, that might serve as an alternative basis for establishing original claims to ownership of things?

CHAPTER III

VALUES SUBJECT TO OWNERSHIP

What sorts of resources are eligible for claims of property rights? Clearly not every thing of value is or should be property. Human slavery was a system in which one human being claimed ownership of another. A Civil War was fought over this issue, and led to the adoption of the Thirteenth Amendment, which abolished all forms of slavery and involuntary servitude. This gives us one fixed point of reference as to what cannot be included in the system of property rights. Selling babies is also forbidden, although some economists have argued that this policy should be reconsidered. On the opposite side of the coin, other resources are thought to belong to the public at large—highways and waterways, and in the more intangible realm, ideas and perhaps the law itself. How do we determine the proper domain of the system of property rights? We start by considering several controversies about interests that may be thought to be too personal or private to be subject to property rights—human bodies and body parts, artists' moral rights, and cultural patrimony. We then consider certain academic perspectives that inform debates about the proper scope of the system of property rights. This is followed by a consideration of interests that may be thought to be too public to be subject to property rights—like harbors and beaches. We end with sections that examine more closely two resources that seem to call for some mixture of public and private rights—water and electronic communications, including cyberspace.

A. PERSONHOOD

One issue that confronts any system of property rights is whether there are certain interests that are inappropriate for treatment as property because they are too closely connected to personhood. There is a universal consensus today that people are not a permissible subject of property rights. Not only is formal slavery abolished, but the Supreme Court has long invalidated schemes that would permit peonage—systems of servitude based on unpaid debts. See, e.g., Bailey v. Alabama, 219 U.S. 219 (1911). The usual justification for this understanding is that people, as autonomous moral agents, should not be regarded as objects or commodities to be bought and sold by other people. But how far does this anti-commodification principle extend? As the cases in this section clearly reveal, modern medical technology is rapidly generating controversial questions about the boundary between persons and property. There is every reason to believe that these issues will multiply and become ever more vexing in the near future. As things presently stand, the law is deeply ambivalent about whether to apply the "property" template in resolving these issues. Controversy is also growing about whether unique forms of human expression—such as the creations of artists or objects that are of special importance to particular cultural groups—should be subject to treatment as property.

1.   PROPERTY AND THE HUMAN BODY

P   *D - Coroner*

Newman v. Sathyavaglswaran

United States Court of Appeals, Ninth Circuit, 2002.
287 F.3d 786.

■ FISHER, CIRCUIT JUDGE. Parents, whose deceased children's corneas were removed by the Los Angeles County Coroner's office without notice or consent, brought this 42 U.S.C. § 1983 action alleging a taking of their property without due process of law. The complaint was dismissed by the district court for a failure to state a claim upon which relief could be granted. We must decide whether the longstanding recognition in the law of California, paralleled by our national common law, that next of kin have the exclusive right to possess the bodies of their deceased family members creates a property interest, the deprivation of which must be accorded due process of law under the Fourteenth Amendment of the United States Constitution. We hold that it does. * * *

I.   FACTUAL AND PROCEDURAL BACKGROUND

* * * Robert Newman and Barbara Obarski (the parents) each had children, Richard Newman and Kenneth Obarski respectively, who died in Los Angeles County in October 1997. Following their deaths, the Office of the Coroner for the County of Los Angeles (the coroner) obtained possession of the bodies of the children and, under procedures adopted pursuant to California Government Code § 27491.47 as it then existed,[1] removed the corneas from those bodies without the knowledge of the parents and without an attempt to notify them and request consent. The parents became aware of the coroner's actions in September 1999 and subsequently filed this § 1983 action alleging a deprivation of their property without due process of law in violation of the Fourteenth Amendment. * * *

II.   PROPERTY INTERESTS IN DEAD BODIES

The Fourteenth Amendment prohibits states from "depriv[ing] any person of life, liberty, or property, without due process of law." U.S. Const. amend. XIV, § 1. At the threshold, a claim under § 1983 for an unconstitutional deprivation of property must show (1) a deprivation (2) of property (3) under color of state law. See Parratt v. Taylor, 451 U.S. 527, 536–37

---

1. California Government Code § 27491.47(a) stated:

Notwithstanding any other provision of law, the coroner may, in the course of an autopsy, remove and release or authorize the removal and release of corneal eye tissue from a body within the coroner's custody, if . . . [t]he coroner has no knowledge of objection to the removal. . . .

(1981), overruled on other grounds, Daniels v. Williams, 474 U.S. 327 (1986). If these elements are met, the question becomes whether the state afforded constitutionally adequate process for the deprivation. Id. at 537. Here, it is uncontested that the coroner's action was a deprivation under color of state law. The coroner argues, however, that the dismissal of the parents' complaint was proper because they could not have a property interest in their children's corneas. * * *

"[T]he property interests protected by procedural due process extend well beyond actual ownership of real estate, chattels, or money." Board of Regents v. Roth, 408 U.S. 564, 571–72 (1972). "The Fourteenth Amendment's procedural protection of property is a safeguard of the security of interests that a person has already acquired[.]" Id. at 576.[4] These property interests "are not created by the Constitution[,] . . . they are created and their dimensions are defined by existing rules or understandings that stem from an independent source such as state law[.]" Id. at 577. Thus, the first step of our analysis is to analyze the history of rules and understandings of our nation with respect to the possession and protection of the bodies of the dead.

A. History of Common Law Interests in Dead Bodies

Duties to protect the dignity of the human body after its death are deeply rooted in our nation's history. In a valuable history of the subject, the Supreme Court of Rhode Island recounted:

> By the civil law of ancient Rome, the charge of burial was first upon the person to whom it was delegated by the deceased; second, upon the *scripti haeredes* (to whom the property was given), and if none, then upon the *haeredes legitimi* or *cognati* in order. . . . The heirs might be compelled to comply with the provisions of the will in regard to burial. And the Pontifical College had the power of providing for the burial of those who had no place of burial in their own right.

Pierce v. Proprietors of Swan Point Cemetery, 10 R.I. 227, 235–36 (1872) (citations omitted).

In 17th century England, and in much of Europe, duties to bury the dead and protect the dignified disposition of the body, described as flowing from a *"right of burial, . . . a person's right to be buried,"* id. at 238–39 * * *[5] were borne primarily by churches, which had a duty to bury the

---

4. See Arthur Linton Corbin, Taxation of Seats on the Stock Exchange, 31 Yale L.J. 429, 429 (1922) ("Our concept of property has shifted. . . . '[P]roperty' has ceased to describe any res, or object of sense, at all, and has become merely a bundle of legal relations—rights, powers, privileges, immunities.")

5. The logical relationship between rights and duties has been the subject of considerable academic examination. Wesley

Hohfeld famously described rights and duties as "jural correlatives"—different aspects of the same legal relation. See Wesley Hohfeld, Some Fundamental Legal Conceptions as Applied in Judicial Reasoning, 23 Yale L.J. 16 (1913); see also Joseph William Singer, The Legal Rights Debate in Analytical Jurisprudence from Bentham to Hohfeld, 1982 Wis. L.Rev. 975; Arthur Corbin, Jural Relations and Their Classification, 30 Yale L.J. 226 (1921). Oliver Wendell Holmes described bodies of those residing in their parishes. Pierce, 10 R.I. at 236. These duties, and the explanation of their genesis in the rights of the dead, carried over into New England colonial practice where "[i]n many parts . . . the parish system prevailed, and every family was considered to have a right of burial in the churchyard of the parish in which they lived." Id. at 235.

The Roman practice of including duties to protect the body of the dead in civil law had no parallel in the early English common law because burials were matters of ecclesiastical cognizance. Id. Thus, Blackstone explained that "though the heir has a property [interest] in the monuments and escutcheons of his ancestors, yet he has none in their bodies or ashes; nor can he bring any suit or action against such as indecently, at least, if not injuriously, violate and disturb their remains, when dead and buried." 1 Blackstone, Commentaries *429. * * *

Many early American courts adopted Blackstone's description of the common law, holding that "a dead body is not the subject of property right." Bessemer Land & Improvement Co. v. Jenkins, 18 So. 565, 567 (Ala. 1895). The duty to protect the body by providing a burial was often described as flowing from the "universal . . . right of sepulture," rather than from a concept of property law. Wynkoop v. Wynkoop, 42 Pa. 293, 300–01 (1862). As cases involving unauthorized mutilation and disposition of bodies increased toward the end of the 19th century, paralleling the rise in demand for human cadavers in medical science and use of cremation as an alternative to burial, see In re Johnson's Estate, 7 N.Y.S.2d at 85–86 (describing "an outpouring" of such cases), courts began to recognize an exclusive right of the next of kin to possess and control the disposition of the bodies of their dead relatives, the violation of which was actionable at law. Thus, in holding that a city council could not "seize upon existing private burial grounds, make them public, and exclude the proprietors from their management," the Supreme Court of Indiana commented that "the burial of the dead can [not] . . . be taken out of the hands of the relatives thereof" because "we lay down the proposition, that the bodies of the dead belong to the surviving relations, in the order of inheritance, as property, and that they have the right to dispose of them as such, within restrictions analogous to those by which the disposition of other property may be regulated." Bogert v. City of Indianapolis, 13 Ind. 134, 136, 138 (1859). Over a decade later, the Rhode Island Supreme Court * * * described the nation's common law as bestowing upon next of kin "a duty [towards the dead], and we may also say a right, to protect from violation; and a duty on the part of others to abstain from violation"; a dead body "may therefore be considered as a sort of *quasi* property." Pierce, 10 R.I. at 238.

rights as "intellectual constructs used to describe the consequences of legal obligations. As he puts it [in *The Common Law* (1881)], 'legal duties are logically antecedent to legal rights.'" Horowitz, *supra* at 138. Holmes' description appears particularly apt in respect to the law regarding dead bodies where duties to provide burial were recognized as flowing from a right of the dead, even though "strictly speaking, . . . a dead man cannot be said to have rights." Pierce, 10 R.I. at 239.

B. Interests in Dead Bodies in California Law

In 1872, the same year *Pierce* was decided, California enacted Penal Code § 292, imposing a legal duty on next of kin to bury the deceased. In 1899, the California Supreme Court held that duty required recognition of exclusive rights of possession, control and disposition vesting in those with the duty. O'Donnell v. Slack, 55 P. 906, 907 (Cal. 1899). These rights, it explained, were by law "protected, and for a violation of which [next of kin] are entitled to indemnification." Id. * * *

* * * Following [*O'Donnell*] and *Pierce,* California courts commonly use the term "quasi property" to describe the rights of next of kin to the body of the deceased.

In 1931, the exclusive rights of possession, control and disposition of the corpse recognized in [*O'Donnell*], together with the duty previously contained in Penal Code § 292, were codified in Health and Safety Code § 7100.[7] California has at all times recognized these rights as exclusive of others. Thus civil litigants have no right to demand an autopsy, Walsh v. Caidin, 283 Cal.Rptr. 326, 328 (Cal. Ct. App. 1991); Holm v. Superior Court, 232 Cal.Rptr. 432, 437 (Cal. Ct. App. 1986), and friends of the deceased have no right to attend the burial, Ross v. Forest Lawn Mem'l Park, 203 Cal.Rptr. 468, 472 (Cal. Ct. App. 1984), over the objection of next of kin. Violation of the correlative duty of others to refrain from disturbing the body is subject to an action for "tortious interference with a right to dispose of a decedent's remains." Sinai Temple v. Kaplan, 127 Cal.Rptr. 80, 86 (Cal. Ct. App. 1976); cf. Christensen v. Superior Court, 820 P.2d 181, 196 (Cal. 1991) (permitting action for unauthorized harvesting of corneas and other organs by mortuary); Palmquist v. Standard Acc. Ins. Co., 3 F.Supp. 358, 359–360 (S.D. Cal. 1933) (permitting action for unauthorized retention of organs after an autopsy).

C. The Right to Transfer Body Parts

The first successful transplantation of a kidney in 1954 led to an expansion of the rights of next of kin to the bodies of the dead. In 1968, the National Conference of Commissioners on Uniform State Laws approved the Uniform Anatomical Gift Act (UAGA), adopted by California the same

---

7. At the time relevant to this case, the statute read:

> The right to control the disposition of the remains of a deceased person, unless other directions have been given by the decedent, vests in, and the duty of interment and the liability for the reasonable cost of interment of such remains devolves upon the following in the order named:
>
> (a) The surviving spouse.
>
> (b) The surviving child or children of the decedent.

(c) The surviving parent or parents of the decedent.

(d) The person or persons respectively in the next degrees of kindred in the order named by the laws of California as entitled to succeed to the estate of the decedent.

(e) The public administrator when the deceased has sufficient assets.

Id. (amended 1999).

year, which grants next of kin the right to transfer the parts of bodies in their possession to others for medical or research purposes. Cal. Health & Safety Code § 7150 et seq. The right to transfer is limited. The California UAGA prohibits any person from "knowingly, for valuable consideration, purchas[ing] or sell[ing] a part for transplantation, therapy, or reconditioning, if removal of the part is intended to occur after the death of the decedent," Cal. Health & Safety Code § 7155, as does federal law, 42 U.S.C. § 274e (prohibiting the "transfer [of] any human organ for valuable consideration") * * *

In the 1970s and 1980s, medical science improvements and the related demand for transplant organs prompted governments to search for new ways to increase the supply of organs for donation. * * * Many perceived as a hindrance to the supply of needed organs the rule implicit in the UAGA that donations could be effected only if consent was received from the decedent or next of kin. Erik S. Jaffe, "She's Got Bette Davis['s] Eyes": Assessing the Nonconsensual Removal of Cadaver Organs Under the Takings and Due Process Clauses, 90 Colum. L.Rev. 528, 535 (1990); cf. S. Rep. 98–382 at 2 (discussing estimates that "organs are ... recovered from fewer than 15 percent" of people who die under circumstances that make them suitable donors). In response, some states passed "presumed consent" laws that allow the taking and transfer of body parts by a coroner without the consent of next of kin as long as no objection to the removal is known. Jaffe, supra at 535–36. California Government Code § 27491.47, enacted in 1983, was such a law.[10]

III. DUE PROCESS ANALYSIS

"[T]o provide California non-profit eye banks with an adequate supply of corneal tissue," S. Com. Rep. SB 21 (Cal. 1983), § 27491.47(a) authorized the coroner to "remove and release or authorize the removal and release of corneal eye tissue from a body within the coroner's custody" without any effort to notify and obtain the consent of next of kin "if ... [t]he coroner has no knowledge of objection to the removal." The law also provided that the coroner or any person acting upon his or her request "shall [not] incur civil liability for such removal in an action brought by any person who did not object prior to the removal ... nor be subject to criminal prosecution." § 27491.47(b).[11]

---

10. In 1998, § 27491.47(a)(2) was amended to require that the coroner obtain written or telephonic consent of the next of kin prior to removing corneas. The Committee Report accompanying that change in law argued that "existing law governing corneal tissue removal does not adequately reflect the importance of obtaining the consent of a decedent's next-of-kin.... [A]natomical gifts are ... 'gifts' and ... the removal of corneal tissue without the consent of a decedent's next-of-kin violates the legally recognized principle that ... an individual's right to make or decline to make an anatomical gift [is] passed on to the next-of-kin." S. Com. Rep. S.B. 1403 (1998).

11. For body parts other than corneas, California adopted the 1987 version of the UAGA authorizing transfer when no knowledge of objection is known and after "[a] reasonable effort has been made to locate and inform [next of kin] of their option to make, or object to making, an anatomical gift." Cal. Health & Safety Code § 7151.5(a)(2).

In analyzing whether the implementation of that law by the coroner deprived the parents of property, we define property as "the group of rights inhering in the citizen's relation to the physical thing, as the right to possess, use and dispose of it. . . . In other words, it deals with what lawyers term the individual's 'interest' in the thing in question." United States v. General Motors Corp., 323 U.S. 373, 378 (1945); accord Phillips v. Washington Legal Found., 524 U.S. 156, 167–68 (1998); cf. Perry v. Sindermann, 408 U.S. 593, 601 (1972) (explaining that " 'property' denotes a broad range of interests"). "To have a property interest . . . a person clearly must have more than an abstract need or desire" for the thing in question, "[h]e must, instead, have a legitimate claim of entitlement to it. . . . It is a purpose of the constitutional right to a hearing to provide an opportunity for a person to vindicate those claims." Roth, 408 U.S. at 577.

In two decisions the Sixth Circuit, the only federal circuit to address the issue until now, held that the interests of next of kin in dead bodies recognized in Michigan and Ohio allowed next of kin to bring § 1983 actions challenging implementation of cornea removal statutes similar to California's. Whaley v. County of Tuscola, 58 F.3d 1111 (6th Cir. 1995) (Michigan); Brotherton v. Cleveland, 923 F.2d 477 (6th Cir. 1991) (Ohio). The Sixth Circuit noted that courts in each state had recognized a right of next of kin to possess the body for burial and a claim by next of kin against others who disturb the body. Whaley, 58 F.3d at 1116; Brotherton, 923 F.2d at 482. Those common law rights, combined with the statutory right to control the disposition of the body recognized in each state's adoption of the UAGA, was held to be sufficient to create in next of kin a property interest in the corneas of their deceased relatives that could not be taken without due process of law. Whaley, 58 F.3d at 1117; Brotherton, 923 F.2d at 482. * * *

We agree with the reasoning of the Sixth Circuit and believe that reasoning is applicable here. Under traditional common law principles, serving a duty to protect the dignity of the human body in its final disposition that is deeply rooted in our legal history and social traditions, the parents had exclusive and legitimate claims of entitlement to possess, control, dispose and prevent the violation of the corneas and other parts of the bodies of their deceased children. With California's adoption of the UAGA, Cal. Health and Safety Code § 7151.5, it statutorily recognized other important rights of the parents in relation to the bodies of their deceased children—the right to transfer body parts and refuse to allow their transfer. These are all important components of the group of rights by which property is defined, each of which carried with it the power to exclude others from its exercise, "traditionally . . . one of the most treasured strands in an owner's bundle of property rights." Loretto v. Teleprompter Manhattan CATV Corp., 458 U.S. 419, 435–436 (1982); see Thomas W. Merrill, Property and the Right To Exclude, 77 Neb. L.Rev. 730, 740–752 (1998) (discussing the "primacy of the right to exclude"); Jeremy Bentham, The Limits of Jurisprudence Defined 164 (Charles Warren Everett ed., 1945) (stating that "[t]o give a man a property" interest in a thing, there must be "a mandate prohibiting persons at large from meddling with it"). Thus, we hold that the parents had property interests in the corneas of their deceased children protected by the Due Process Clause of the Fourteenth Amendment.

Our holding is not affected by California's labeling of the interests of the next of kin as "quasi property," a term with little meaningful legal significance.[13] "Although the underlying substantive interest is created by 'an independent source such as state law,' federal constitutional law determines whether that interest rises to the level of a 'legitimate claim or entitlement' protected by the Due Process Clause." Memphis Light, Gas and Water Div. v. Craft, 436 U.S. 1, 9 (1978). * * * Our holding similarly turns on the substance of the rights California recognizes, not on the label given to them.

Nor does the fact that California forbids the trade of body parts for profit mean that next of kin lack a property interest in them. The Supreme Court has "never held that a physical item is not 'property' simply because it lacks a positive economic or market value." Phillips, 524 U.S. at 169; cf. International News Service v. Associated Press, 248 U.S. 215, 246 (1918) (Holmes, J. dissenting) ("Property, a creation of law, does not arise from value. . . .").

Because the property interests of next of kin to dead bodies are firmly entrenched in the "background principles of property law," based on values and understandings contained in our legal history dating from the Roman Empire, California may not be free to alter them with exceptions that lack "a firm basis in traditional property principles." Phillips, 524 U.S. at 165–68 * * * cf. PruneYard Shopping Center v. Robins, 447 U.S. 74, 93–94 (1980) (Marshall, J. concurring) ("[T]here are limits on governmental authority to abolish 'core' commonlaw rights."). We need not, however, decide whether California has transgressed basic property principles with enactment of § 27491.47 because that statute did not extinguish California's legal recognition of the property interests of the parents to the corneas of their deceased children. It allowed the removal of corneas only if "the coroner has no knowledge of objection," a provision that implicitly acknowledges the ongoing property interests of next of kin.[15]

13. The Supreme Court has used the term to identify a property interest only once. In *International News Service v. Associated Press*, 248 U.S. 215, 236–242 (1918) the majority held that news "must be regarded as quasi property," the taking of which without consent constitutes the basis for an unfair competition action. The Court's label did not affect the holding of the case. There is no entry for "quasi property" in Blacks Law Dictionary (6th ed. 1990) or Ballentine's Law Dictionary (3d ed. 1969), although each contains entries for "quasi contract." The only examples of "quasi property" listed under the entry in Words and Phrases are news, citing *International News Service,* and dead bodies. 35A Words and Phrases 487 (1965); see id. (2000 cumulative supp.).

15. In this respect, § 27491.47(a) differs from California law governing the state's duty to conduct autopsies to determine the cause of death which may be performed contrary to the wishes of the individual or next of kin. See Cal. Govt.Code § 27491; Huntly v. Zurich Gen. Accident & Liab. Ins. Co., 100 Cal.App. 201, 280 P. 163 (1929) (holding next of kin have no right to prohibit state from performing invasive autopsy to determine cause of death).

The effect of § 27491.47 was to remove a procedure—notice and request for consent prior to the deprivation—and a remedy—the opportunity to seek redress for the deprivation in California's courts. A state may not evade due process analysis by defining " '[p]roperty' ... by the procedures provided for its deprivation." Cleveland Bd. of Educ. v. Loudermill, 470 U.S. 532, 541 (1985). "While the legislature may elect not to confer a property interest ... it may not constitutionally authorize the deprivation of such an interest, once conferred, without appropriate procedural safeguards." Id. (citations omitted). With § 27491.47, California eliminated procedural safeguards but retained the interest.

When the coroner removed the corneas from the bodies of the parents' deceased children and transferred them to others, the parents could no longer possess, control, dispose or prevent the violation of those parts of their children's bodies. To borrow a metaphor used when the government physically occupies property, the coroner did not merely "take a single 'strand' from the 'bundle' of property rights: it chop[ped] through the bundle, taking a slice of every strand." Loretto, 458 U.S. at 435. This was a deprivation of the most certain variety.

At bottom, "[p]roperty rights serve human values. They are recognized to that end, and are limited by it." State v. Shack, 277 A.2d 369, 372 (N.J. 1971). The property rights that California affords to next of kin to the body of their deceased relatives serve the premium value our society has historically placed on protecting the dignity of the human body in its final disposition. California infringed the dignity of the bodies of the children when it extracted the corneas from those bodies without the consent of the parents. The process of law was due the parents for this deprivation of their rights. * * *

We do not hold that California lacks significant interests in obtaining corneas or other organs of the deceased in order to contribute to the lives of the living. Courts are required to evaluate carefully the state's interests in deciding what process must be due the holders of property interests for their deprivation. * * * But our Constitution requires the government to assert its interests and subject them to scrutiny when it invades the rights of its subjects. Accordingly, we reverse the district court's dismissal of the parents' complaint and remand for proceedings in which the government's justification for its deprivation of parents' interests may be fully aired and appropriately scrutinized.

The dismissal of the parents' § 1983 claim is REVERSED and REMANDED for further proceedings.

■ FERNANDEZ, CIRCUIT JUDGE, Dissenting: * * * [A]ny civilized state desires that the bodies of its deceased members be disposed of in an appropriate way, on grounds of decency, consideration for others, and pragmatism. And it should be done with reasonable haste and without undue acrimony.

California's statutory scheme reflects all of that. It decidedly does not confer a property right upon anyone. Assuming that a decedent has not made his own arrangements for disposal of his own earthly remains, the state makes sure that somebody else will both do so and pay for it. To that end, California has provided that "[t]he right to control the disposition of the remains of a deceased person . . . vests in, and the duty of disposition and the liability for the reasonable cost of disposition of the remains devolves upon," a list of individuals. Cal. Health & Safety Code § 7100(a). Thus, this so-called right is actually in the nature of a duty and expense designed to assure that the remains will not simply be left about, but will be quickly interred. And the state has created something like a table of intestate succession for the purpose of assuring that the right and duty land firmly on a defined group. First comes the person who has a power of attorney for healthcare. Cal. Health & Safety Code § 7100(a)(1). Then comes the spouse. Id. at (a)(2). Then adult children, then parents, then next of kin. Id. at (a)(3)–(5). At the end is the public administrator, but he only gets the so-called right if there are "sufficient assets" to allow him to discharge his duty. Id. at (a)(6). This somewhat remarkable list surely shows just how peculiar it is to dub what we are dealing with a constitutionally protected property right. Is not it interesting that the holder of a power of attorney comes before the closest relatives, and equally interesting to see that the public administrator may wind up with the "right?" Or is it essentially a duty?

I rather think that it is really a duty rather than a right, and because a duty in one person must mean that a right is lodged in someone else, it seems pellucid that the state holds the right to demand that someone on the list bear the burden of disposing of the deceased's remains; it then makes it possible for that person to do so by also giving him the right to do so. Again, that hardly looks like the kind of interest that United States Constitution was designed to protect. * * *

Nobody who has had the misfortune of having his loved ones die can fail to be moved by the prospect that somebody else will treat the loved one's former earthly vessel with disrespect. That feeling does not, however, demonstrate that California has conferred a constitutionally protected property right upon family members. In fact, it has not; it has merely given them enough of a right to allow them to fulfill their duty, and it has limited that in a number of ways. One of those ways has to do with corneal tissue. As to that, the duty may not devolve, and concomitantly the right will be neither necessary nor constitutionally protected.

NOTES AND QUESTIONS

1. Laws providing for involuntary organ donation are motivated by shortages under existing voluntary systems. As of July 23, 2004, there were 86,190 names on the United Network for Organ Sharing (UNOS) waiting list for donated organs. In the period January 1 to June 29, 2004, UNOS recorded 4,536 donors and 8,658 transplants. Another alternative is to legalize markets in body parts. Proposals abound, but are often met with

unease sounding in moral and personhood concerns. Do involuntary donations or markets have the greater tendency to make body parts into property? To commodify? Impair autonomy?

2. Questions about the proper methodology for determining whether "property" exists for purposes of federal constitutional challenges are addressed in Chapter XI. To anticipate, the Ninth Circuit is surely correct that the label attached by state law to an interest—"property," "quasi-property," or "not-property"—is not dispositive of whether that interest is property for purposes of federal constitutional law (although it may have some relevance). But beyond this, doesn't the Ninth Circuit need a clearer conception of what criteria constitute "property" before it can conclude that California does or does not recognize that next of kin have "property" in the bodies of deceased loved ones?

3. In procedural due process terms, there are at least two issues presented by the California presumed-consent statute. One is whether the state can dispense with giving individualized notice to the next of kin that corneas will be removed from cadavers unless they object. The second is whether the state can adopt an opt-out requirement, as opposed to an opt-in requirement—in other words, whether the state can place the burden of initiative on the next of kin to object, instead of requiring the state to ask them for their consent. Assuming there is a property right here, as the court finds, the requirement of individual notice seems to follow fairly readily. See Mullane v. Central Hanover Bank & Trust Co., 339 U.S. 306 (1950) (due process requires individualized notice whenever practicable before state can extinguish property rights). Once the state gives notice, the choice between an opt-out procedure and an opt-in procedure seems like a closer call. Can you articulate the arguments for and against opt-in or opt-out in this context?

4. Does contract law provide a possible answer to the problem of determining whether persons want their corneas removed for medical transplantation purposes after their death? Most estate planners today urge persons to execute "living wills" that describe what sort of medical interventions they would like to be undertaken on their behalf if they become incompetent. Similar documents can and do address questions about the possible donation of body parts for research or transplantation upon death. As of 2006, 43 states have adopted statutes providing for "first person consent" under which a person's expression of consent to donate reflected in a donor card or a registry of consent will after the person's death override objections from the next of kin. Amy Vandenbroucke, HIV and Organ Donation: Illinois' Solution to Organ Donation Shortages, 9 DePaul J. Health Care L. 1285 (2006). Would California be better advised to institute an aggressive program of encouraging persons to draft such documents while they are living, rather than to rely on presumed-consent statutes that apply once they are dead?

Figure 3–1
Organ Donor Card

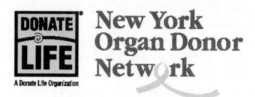

D O N O R   C A R D

New York
Organ Donor
Network

www.donatelifeny.org

PLEASE CARRY THIS CARD AND TELL YOUR NEXT OF KIN

In the hope that I may help others, I hereby make this anatomical gift, to take effect upon my death.

For the purpose of transplantation I give:
☐ Any needed organs and tissues
☐ Only the following organs and tissues _____

_____

_____

Signature of Donor   *Donor's Birthdate*

Date Signed _____ *City / State* _____

Courtesy New York Organ Donor Network.

5.   Some have suggested that donations of body parts are superior to sales because the quality of the material will be higher. In a famous study one author argued for the superiority of blood donations over market forms of transfer. Richard Titmuss, The Gift Relationship: From Human Body to Social Policy (1971). Blood from uncompensated donors was of higher quality (less infection) than blood from paid donors. This donor quality effect is especially important where tests of quality are not readily available. If altruistic transfers are important, might they be "crowded out" by sales? By involuntary seizures by the government? For more on gifts, see Chapter IV.

6.   Despite the federal ban on selling body parts for transplant (but not for other purposes such as research), commercial activity with respect to body parts exists. Donors may not be paid, but recipients pay to receive the body part, and various procurement organizations and specialists—as well as the operating doctor—are paid for their "services." What are the chances that these intermediaries are deriving monetary rewards from the

organ itself? Do such implicit sales raise personhood concerns? On existing commercial activity in body parts, see, e.g., Julia D. Mahoney, The Market for Human Tissue, 86 Va. L. Rev. 163, 165 (2000).

Property in and possible commercial exploitation of body parts are issues that involve material from living persons as well. Consider the following case.

Moore v. Regents of the University of California

Supreme Court of California, In Bank, 1990.
793 P.2d 479.

I. INTRODUCTION

■ PANELLI, JUSTICE. We granted review in this case to determine whether plaintiff has stated a cause of action against his physician and other defendants for using his cells in potentially lucrative medical research without his permission. Plaintiff alleges that his physician failed to disclose preexisting research and economic interests in the cells before obtaining consent to the medical procedures by which they were extracted. The superior court sustained all defendants' demurrers to the third amended complaint, and the Court of Appeal reversed. We hold that the complaint states a cause of action for breach of the physician's disclosure obligations, but not for conversion.

II. FACTS

[According to the complaint, John Moore, who lived in Seattle, was diagnosed as having hairy-cell leukemia. He traveled to Los Angeles to be treated by Dr. David Golde at the UCLA Medical Center. Golde recommended that Moore's spleen be removed in order to slow down the progress of the disease. Moore signed a written consent form authorizing the operation. Without informing Moore, Dr. Golde and his associates also developed plans to do research on certain white blood cells called T-lymphocytes taken from Moore's spleen. The objective was to produce certain lymphokines, or proteins that regulate the immune system. The genetic code for making these lymphokines is identical in all persons, but it is hard to locate the particular genes responsible for making each lymphokine. Because of his disease, the cells in Moore's spleen had overproduced certain lymphokines, making the process of identification easier.

In order to pursue this research, Dr. Golde and his associates established a new cell line from Moore's T-lymphocytes. They then sought on behalf of themselves and UCLA a patent on the new cell line. The patent was granted, and Golde negotiated a contract with Genetics Institute, Inc., granting the firm exclusive access to the materials and research based on the cell line, in return for $440,000 in salary and research support over three years. Biotech industry trade periodicals estimated that the total potential market for products based on lymphokines might eventually reach $3 billion per year.

When Moore learned the use to which his spleen cells had been put, he sued Dr. Golde, his associates, and UCLA. His complaint asserted a number of causes of action including conversion—the taking of property from someone without their consent and converting it to the use of the defendant. He also asserted a number of other causes of action, including lack of informed consent and unjust enrichment. The trial court held that the action for conversion could not be maintained because Moore had no property right in his spleen cells after they had been removed from his body, and that this defect meant that all the other asserted causes of action failed too. Moore appealed.]

III.   DISCUSSION

A.   Breach of Fiduciary Duty and Lack of Informed Consent

Moore repeatedly alleges that Golde failed to disclose the extent of his research and economic interests in Moore's cells before obtaining consent to the medical procedures by which the cells were extracted. These allegations, in our view, state a cause of action against Golde for invading a legally protected interest of his patient. This cause of action can properly be characterized either as the breach of a fiduciary duty to disclose facts material to the patient's consent or, alternatively, as the performance of medical procedures without first having obtained the patient's informed consent. * * *

Accordingly, we hold that a physician who is seeking a patient's consent for a medical procedure must, in order to satisfy his fiduciary duty and to obtain the patient's informed consent, disclose personal interests unrelated to the patient's health, whether research or economic, that may affect his medical judgment. * * *

B.   Conversion

Moore also attempts to characterize the invasion of his rights as a conversion—a tort that protects against interference with possessory and ownership interests in personal property. He theorizes that he continued to own his cells following their removal from his body, at least for the purpose of directing their use, and that he never consented to their use in potentially lucrative medical research. Thus, to complete Moore's argument, defendants' unauthorized use of his cells constitutes a conversion. As a result of the alleged conversion, Moore claims a proprietary interest in each of the products that any of the defendants might ever create from his cells or the patented cell line.

No court, however, has ever in a reported decision imposed conversion liability for the use of human cells in medical research. While that fact does not end our inquiry, it raises a flag of caution. In effect, what Moore is asking us to do is to impose a tort duty on scientists to investigate the consensual pedigree of each human cell sample used in research. To impose such a duty, which would affect medical research of importance to all of society, implicates policy concerns far removed from the traditional, two-party ownership disputes in which the law of conversion arose. Invoking a tort theory originally used to determine whether the loser or the finder of a horse had the better title, Moore claims ownership of the results of socially important medical research, including the genetic code for chemicals that regulate the functions of every human being's immune system.

We have recognized that, when the proposed application of a very general theory of liability in a new context raises important policy concerns, it is especially important to face those concerns and address them openly. * * * Moreover, we should be hesitant to "impose [new tort duties] when to do so would involve complex policy decisions" (Nally v. Grace Community Church, 763 P.2d 948, 960 (Cal. 1988)), especially when such decisions are more appropriately the subject of legislative deliberation and resolution. This certainly is not to say that the applicability of common law torts is limited to the historical or factual contexts of existing cases. But on occasions when we have opened or sanctioned new areas of tort liability, we "have noted that the 'wrongs and injuries involved were both comprehensible and assessable within the existing judicial framework.' " (Nally v. Grace Community Church, supra, at 960, quoting Peter W. v. San Francisco Unified Sch. Dist., 131 Cal.Rptr. 854, 860 (Cal. Ct. App. 1976).)

Numerous Clauses Principle

Accordingly, we first consider whether the tort of conversion clearly gives Moore a cause of action under existing law. We do not believe it does. Because of the novelty of Moore's claim to own the biological materials at issue, to apply the theory of conversion in this context would frankly have to be recognized as an extension of the theory. Therefore, we consider next whether it is advisable to extend the tort to this context.

1. Moore's Claim Under Existing Law

"To establish a conversion, plaintiff must establish an actual interference with his _ownership_ or _right of possession_.... Where plaintiff neither has title to the property alleged to have been converted, nor possession thereof, he cannot maintain an action for conversion." (Del E. Webb Corp. v. Structural Materials Co. 176 Cal. Rptr. 824, 833 (Cal. Ct. App. 1981), emphasis added.) * * *

Since Moore clearly did not expect to retain possession of his cells following their removal, to sue for their conversion he must have retained an ownership interest in them. But there are several reasons to doubt that he did retain any such interest. First, no reported judicial decision supports Moore's claim, either directly or by close analogy. Second, California statutory law drastically limits any continuing interest of a patient in excised cells. Third, the subject matters of the Regents' patent—the patented cell line and the products derived from it—cannot be Moore's property.

a) directly
b) by analogy

Neither the Court of Appeal's opinion, the parties' briefs, nor our research discloses a case holding that a person retains a sufficient interest in excised cells to support a cause of action for conversion. We do not find this surprising, since the laws governing such things as human tissues,

a) Directly

transplantable organs,[22] blood,[23] fetuses, pituitary glands, corneal tissue,[26] and dead bodies deal with human biological materials as objects sui generis, regulating their disposition to achieve policy goals rather than abandoning them to the general law of personal property. It is these specialized statutes, not the law of conversion, to which courts ordinarily should and do look for guidance on the disposition of human biological materials.

Lacking direct authority for importing the law of conversion into this context, Moore relies, as did the Court of Appeal, primarily on decisions addressing privacy rights. One line of cases involves unwanted publicity. (Lugosi v. Universal Pictures, 603 P.2d 425 (Cal. 1979); Motschenbacher v. R.J. Reynolds Tobacco Company 498 F.2d 821 (9th Cir. 1974) [interpreting Cal. law].) These opinions hold that every person has a proprietary interest in his own likeness and that unauthorized, business use of a likeness is redressible as a tort. But in neither opinion did the authoring court expressly base its holding on property law. Each court stated, following Prosser, that it was "pointless" to debate the proper characterization of the proprietary interest in a likeness. For purposes of determining whether the tort of conversion lies, however, the characterization of the right in question is far from pointless. Only property can be converted.

Not only are the wrongful-publicity cases irrelevant to the issue of conversion, but the analogy to them seriously misconceives the nature of the genetic materials and research involved in this case. Moore, adopting the analogy originally advanced by the Court of Appeal, argues that "[i]f the courts have found a sufficient proprietary interest in one's persona, how could one not have a right in one's own genetic material, something far more profoundly the essence of one's human uniqueness than a name or a face?" However, as the defendants' patent makes clear—and the complaint, too, if read with an understanding of the scientific terms which it has borrowed from the patent—the goal and result of defendants' efforts has been to manufacture lymphokines. Lymphokines, unlike a name or a face, have the same molecular structure in every human being and the same, important functions in every human being's immune system. Moreover, the particular genetic material which is responsible for the natural production of lymphokines, and which defendants use to manufacture lymphokines in the laboratory, is also the same in every person; it is no

22. See the Uniform Anatomical Gift Act, Health and Safety Code section 7150 et seq. The act permits a competent adult to "give all or part of [his] body" for certain designated purposes, including "transplantation, therapy, medical or dental education, research, or advancement of medical or dental science." (Health & Saf.Code, §§ 7151, 7153.) The act does not, however, permit the donor to receive "valuable consideration" for the transfer. (Health & Saf.Code, § 7155.)

23. See Health & Safety Code section 1601 et seq., which regulates the procurement, processing, and distribution of human blood. Health and Safety Code section 1606 declares that "[t]he procurement, processing, distribution, or use of whole blood, plasma, blood products, and blood derivatives for the purpose of injecting or transfusing the same ... is declared to be, for all purposes whatsoever, the rendition of a service ... and shall not be construed to be, and is declared not to be, a sale ... for any purpose or purposes whatsoever."

26. See Government Code section 27491.47: "The coroner may, in the course of an autopsy [and subject to specified conditions], remove ... corneal eye tissue from a body ..." (id., subd. (a)) for "transplant, therapeutic, or scientific purposes" (id., subd. (a)(5)).

more unique to Moore than the number of vertebrae in the spine or the chemical formula of hemoglobin. * * *

* * * [T]he Court of Appeal in this case concluded that "[a] patient must have the ultimate power to control what becomes of his or her tissues. To hold otherwise would open the door to a massive invasion of human privacy and dignity in the name of medical progress." Yet one may earnestly wish to protect privacy and dignity without accepting the extremely problematic conclusion that interference with those interests amounts to a conversion of personal property. Nor is it necessary to force the round pegs of "privacy" and "dignity" into the square hole of "property" in order to protect the patient, since the fiduciary-duty and informed-consent theories protect these interests directly by requiring full disclosure.

The next consideration that makes Moore's claim of ownership problematic is California statutory law, which drastically limits a patient's control over excised cells. Pursuant to Health and Safety Code section 7054.4, "[n]otwithstanding any other provision of law, recognizable anatomical parts, human tissues, anatomical human remains, or infectious waste following conclusion of scientific use shall be disposed of by interment, incineration, or any other method determined by the state department [of health services] to protect the public health and safety." Clearly the Legislature did not specifically intend this statute to resolve the question of whether a patient is entitled to compensation for the nonconsensual use of excised cells. A primary object of the statute is to ensure the safe handling of potentially hazardous biological waste materials. Yet one cannot escape the conclusion that the statute's practical effect is to limit, drastically, a patient's control over excised cells. By restricting how excised cells may be used and requiring their eventual destruction, the statute eliminates so many of the rights ordinarily attached to property that one cannot simply assume that what is left amounts to "property" or "ownership" for purposes of conversion law.

It may be that some limited right to control the use of excised cells does survive the operation of this statute. There is, for example, no need to read the statute to permit "scientific use" contrary to the patient's expressed wish. A fully informed patient may always withhold consent to treatment by a physician whose research plans the patient does not approve. That right, however, as already discussed, is protected by the fiduciary-duty and informed-consent theories.

Finally, the subject matter of the Regents' patent—the patented cell line and the products derived from it—cannot be Moore's property. This is because the patented cell line is both factually and legally distinct from the cells taken from Moore's body. Federal law permits the patenting of organisms that represent the product of "human ingenuity," but not naturally occurring organisms. (Diamond v. Chakrabarty (1980) 447 U.S. 303, 309–310.) Human cell lines are patentable because "[l]ong-term adaptation and growth of human tissues and cells in culture is difficult—often considered an art ...," and the probability of success is low. (U.S. Congress, Office of Technology Assessment, New Developments in Biotechnology: Ownership of Human Tissues and Cells (1987) at p. 33 (hereafter OTA Report).) It is this *inventive effort* that patent law rewards, not the discovery of naturally occurring raw materials. Thus, Moore's allegations that he owns the cell line and the products derived from it are inconsistent with the patent, which constitutes an authoritative determination that the cell line is the product of invention. * * *

2.   Should Conversion Liability Be Extended?

* * * There are three reasons why it is inappropriate to impose liability for conversion based upon the allegations of Moore's complaint. First, a fair balancing of the relevant policy considerations counsels against extending the tort. Second, problems in this area are better suited to legislative resolution. Third, the tort of conversion is not necessary to protect patients' rights. For these reasons, we conclude that the use of excised human cells in medical research does not amount to a conversion.

Of the relevant policy considerations, two are of overriding importance. The first is protection of a competent patient's right to make autonomous medical decisions. That right, as already discussed, is grounded in well-recognized and long-standing principles of fiduciary duty and informed consent. This policy weighs in favor of providing a remedy to patients when physicians act with undisclosed motives that may affect their professional judgment. The second important policy consideration is that we not threaten with disabling civil liability innocent parties who are engaged in socially useful activities, such as researchers who have no reason to believe that their use of a particular cell sample is, or may be, against a donor's wishes.

To reach an appropriate balance of these policy considerations is extremely important. * * *

Indeed, so significant is the potential obstacle to research stemming from uncertainty about legal title to biological materials that the Office of Technology Assessment reached this striking conclusion: "[R]egardless of the merit of claims by the different interested parties, resolving the current uncertainty may be more important to the future of biotechnology than resolving it in any particular way." (OTA Rep., supra, at p. 27.)

We need not, however, make an arbitrary choice between liability and nonliability. Instead, an examination of the relevant policy considerations suggests an appropriate balance: Liability based upon existing disclosure obligations, rather than an unprecedented extension of the conversion theory, protects patients' rights of privacy and autonomy without unnecessarily hindering research.

To be sure, the threat of liability for conversion might help to enforce patients' rights indirectly. This is because physicians might be able to avoid liability by obtaining patients' consent, in the broadest possible terms, to any conceivable subsequent research use of excised cells. Unfortunately, to extend the conversion theory would utterly sacrifice the other goal of protecting innocent parties. Since conversion is a strict liability tort,[38] it would impose liability on all those into whose hands the cells come, whether or not the particular defendant participated in, or knew of, the inadequate disclosures that violated the patient's right to make an informed decision. In contrast to the conversion theory, the fiduciary-duty and informed-consent theories protect the patient directly, without punishing innocent parties or creating disincentives to the conduct of socially beneficial research. * * *

[T]he theory of liability that Moore urges us to endorse threatens to destroy the economic incentive to conduct important medical research. If the use of cells in research is a conversion, then with every cell sample a researcher purchases a ticket in a litigation lottery. Because liability for conversion is predicated on a continuing ownership interest, "companies are unlikely to invest heavily in developing, manufacturing, or marketing a product when uncertainty about clear title exists." (OTA Rep., supra, at p. 27.) * * *[42]

* * * If the scientific users of human cells are to be held liable for failing to investigate the consensual pedigree of their raw materials, we believe the Legislature should make that decision. Complex policy choices affecting all society are involved, and "[l]egislatures, in making such policy decisions, have the ability to gather empirical evidence, solicit the advice of experts, and hold hearings at which all interested parties present evidence and express their views . . . ." (Foley v. Interactive Data Corp., 765 P.2d 373, 397, fn. 31 (Cal. 1988).) * * *

Finally, there is no pressing need to impose a judicially created rule of strict liability, since enforcement of physicians' disclosure obligations will protect patients against the very type of harm with which Moore was threatened. So long as a physician discloses research and economic interests that may affect his judgment, the patient is protected from conflicts of interest. Aware of any conflicts, the patient can make an informed decision to consent to treatment, or to withhold consent and look elsewhere for medical assistance. As already discussed, enforcement of physicians' disclo-

---

38. " 'The foundation for the action for conversion rests neither in the knowledge nor the intent of the defendant. . . . [Instead,] "the tort consists in the breach of what may be called an absolute duty; the act itself . . . is unlawful and redressible as a tort." ' [Citation.]" (Byer v. Canadian Bank of Commerce, 65 P.2d 67, 68 (Cal. 1937), quoting Poggi v. Scott, 139 P. 815, 816 (Cal. 1914). See also City of Los Angeles v. Superior Court, 149 Cal.Rptr. 320, 323 (Cal. Ct. App. 1978) ["'[c]onversion is a species of strict liability in which questions of good faith, lack of knowledge and motive are ordinarily immaterial."].)

42. In order to make conversion liability seem less of a threat to research, the dissent argues that researchers could avoid liability by using only cell lines accompanied by documentation of the source's consent. (Dis. opn. of Mosk, J., post.) But consent forms do not come with guarantees of validity. As medical malpractice litigation shows, challenges to the validity and sufficiency of consent are not uncommon. Moreover, it is sheer fantasy to hope that waivers might be obtained for the thousands of cell lines and tissue samples presently in cell repositories and, for that reason, already in wide use among researchers. The cell line derived from Moore's T-lymphocytes, for example, has been available since 1984 to any researcher from the American Type Culture Collection. (American Type Culture Collection, Catalogue of Cell Lines and Hybridomas, supra, at p. 176.) Other cell lines have been in wide use since as early as 1951. (OTA Rep., supra, at p. 34.)

sure obligations protects patients directly, without hindering the socially useful activities of innocent researchers.

For these reasons, we hold that the allegations of Moore's third amended complaint state a cause of action for breach of fiduciary duty or lack of informed consent, but not conversion. * * *

Moral Argument— ■ ARABIAN, JUSTICE, concurring. I join in the views cogently expounded by the majority. I write separately to give voice to a concern that I believe informs much of that opinion but finds little or no expression therein. I speak of the moral issue.

Plaintiff has asked us to recognize and enforce a right to sell one's own body tissue *for profit.* He entreats us to regard the human vessel—the single most venerated and protected subject in any civilized society—as equal with the basest commercial commodity. He urges us to commingle the sacred with the profane. He asks much. * * *

It is true, that this court has not often been deterred from deciding difficult legal issues simply because they require a choice between competing social or economic policies. The difference here, however, lies in the nature of the conflicting moral, philosophical and even religious values at stake, and in the profound implications of the position urged. The ramifications of recognizing and enforcing a property interest in body tissues are not known, but are greatly feared—the effect on human dignity of a marketplace in human body parts, the impact on research and development of competitive bidding for such materials, and the exposure of researchers to potentially limitless and uncharted tort liability.

Whether, as plaintiff urges, his cells should be treated as property susceptible to conversion is not, in my view, ours to decide. The question implicates choices which not only reflect, but which ultimately define our essence. A mark of wisdom for us as expositors of the law is the recognition that we cannot cure every ill, mediate every dispute, resolve every conundrum. Sometimes, as Justice Brandeis said, "the most important thing we do, is not doing."[1]

Where then shall a complete resolution be found? Clearly the Legislature, as the majority opinion suggests, is the proper deliberative forum. Indeed, a legislative response creating a licensing scheme, which establishes a fixed rate of profit sharing between researcher and subject, has already been suggested. Such an arrangement would not only avoid the moral and philosophical objections to a free market operation in body tissue, but would also address stated concerns by eliminating the inherently coercive effect of a waiver system and by compensating donors regardless of temporal circumstances. * * *

Patients right—
to determine use of
organ pre-removal
↳supports cause
of action for conversion
■ BROUSSARD, JUSTICE, concurring and dissenting. * * * I dissent from the majority's conclusion that the facts alleged in this case do not state a cause of action for conversion.

1. Bickel, The Least Dangerous Branch (1962) page 71.

The majority opinion fails to recognize * * * the pertinent inquiry is not whether a patient generally retains an ownership interest in a body part after its removal from his body, but rather whether a patient has a right to determine, before a body part is removed, the use to which the part will be put after removal. Although the majority opinion suggests that there are "reasons to doubt" that a patient retains "any" ownership interest in his organs or cells after removal the opinion fails to identify any statutory provision or common law authority that indicates that a patient does not generally have the right, before a body part is removed, to choose among the permissible uses to which the part may be put after removal. On the contrary, the most closely related statutory scheme—the Uniform Anatomical Gift Act (Health & Saf.Code, § 7150 et seq.)—makes it quite clear that a patient does have this right. * * *

It is also clear, under traditional common law principles, that this right of a patient to control the future use of his organ is protected by the law of conversion. As a general matter, the tort of conversion protects an individual not only against improper interference with the right of possession of his property but also against unauthorized use of his property or improper interference with his right to control the use of his property. Sections 227 and 228 of the Restatement Second of Torts specifically provide in this regard that "[o]ne who uses a chattel in a manner which is a serious violation of the right of another to control its use is subject to liability to the other for conversion" and that "[o]ne who is authorized to make a particular use of a chattel, and uses it in a manner exceeding the authorization, is subject to liability for conversion to another whose right to control the use of the chattel is thereby seriously violated." California cases have also long recognized that "unauthorized use" of property can give rise to a conversion action.

One of the majority's principal policy concerns is that "[t]he extension of conversion law into this area will hinder research by restricting access to the necessary raw materials"—the thousands of cell lines and tissues already in cell and tissue repositories. The majority suggests that the "exchange of scientific materials, which still is relatively free and efficient, will surely be compromised if each cell sample becomes the potential subject matter of a lawsuit."

This policy argument is flawed in a number of respects. First, the majority's stated concern does not provide any justification for barring plaintiff from bringing a conversion action against a party who does not obtain organs or cells from a cell bank but who directly interferes with or misappropriates a patient's right to control the use of his organs or cells. Although the majority opinion suggests that the availability of a breach-of-fiduciary-duty cause of action obviates any need for a conversion action against this category of defendants the existence of a breach-of-fiduciary-duty cause of action does not provide a complete answer. * * * For example, if a patient donated his removed cells to a medical center, reserving the right to approve or disapprove the research projects for which the cells would be used, and if another medical center or a drug manufacturer stole the cells after removal and used them in an unauthorized manner for its own economic gain, no breach-of-fiduciary-duty cause of action would be available and a conversion action would be necessary to vindicate the patient's rights. Under the majority's holding, however, the patient would have no right to bring a conversion action, even against such a thief. As this hypothetical illustrates, even if there were compelling policy reasons to limit the potential liability of innocent researchers who use cells obtained from an existing cell bank, those policy considerations would not justify the majority's broad abrogation of *all* conversion liability for the unauthorized use of body parts. * * *

■ MOSK, JUSTICE, dissenting. I dissent. * * *

The concepts of property and ownership in our law are extremely broad. (See Civ.Code, §§ 654, 655.) A leading decision of this court approved the following definition: " 'The term "property" is sufficiently comprehensive to include every species of estate, real and personal, and everything which one person can own and transfer to another. It extends to every species of right and interest capable of being enjoyed as such upon which it is practicable to place a money value.' " (Yuba River Power Co. v. Nevada Irr. Dist., 279 P. 128, 129 (Cal. 1929).)

Being broad, the concept of property is also abstract: rather than referring directly to a material object such as a parcel of land or the tractor that cultivates it, the concept of property is often said to refer to a "bundle of rights" that may be exercised with respect to that object—principally the rights to possess the property, to use the property, to exclude others from the property, and to dispose of the property by sale or by gift. "Ownership is not a single concrete entity but a bundle of rights and privileges as well as of obligations." (Union Oil Co. v. State Bd. of Equal., 386 P.2d 496, 500 (Cal. 1963).) But the same bundle of rights does not attach to all forms of property. For a variety of policy reasons, the law limits or even forbids the exercise of certain rights over certain forms of property. For example, both law and contract may limit the right of an owner of real property to use his parcel as he sees fit. Owners of various forms of personal property may likewise be subject to restrictions on the time, place, and manner of their use. Limitations on the disposition of real property, while less common, may also be imposed. Finally, some types of personal property may be sold but not given away,[9] while others may be given away but not sold,[10] and still others may neither be given away nor sold.[11]

In each of the foregoing instances, the limitation or prohibition diminishes the bundle of rights that would otherwise attach to the property, yet

---

9. A person contemplating bankruptcy may sell his property at its "reasonably equivalent value," but he may not make a gift of the same property. (See 11 U.S.C. § 548(a).)

10. A sportsman may give away wild fish or game that he has caught or killed

pursuant to his license, but he may not sell it. (Fish & Game Code, §§ 3039, 7121.)

The transfer of human organs and blood is a special case that I discuss below (pt. 5).

11. E.g., a license to practice a profession, or a prescription drug in the hands of the person for whom it is prescribed.

what remains is <u>still deemed in law to be a protectible property interest</u>. "Since property or title is a complex bundle of rights, duties, powers and immunities, the pruning away of some or a great many of these elements does not entirely destroy the title. . . ." (People v. Walker, 90 P.2d 854, 855 (Cal. Dist. Ct. App. 1939) [even the possessor of contraband has certain property rights in it against anyone other than the state].) The same rule applies to Moore's interest in his own body tissue: even if we assume that section 7054.4 limited the use and disposition of his excised tissue in the manner claimed by the majority, Moore nevertheless retained valuable rights in that tissue. Above all, at the time of its excision he at least had *the right to do with his own tissue whatever the defendants did with it:* i.e., he could have contracted with researchers and pharmaceutical companies to develop and exploit the vast commercial potential of his tissue and its products. Defendants certainly believe that *their* right to do the foregoing is not barred by section 7054.4 and is a significant property right, as they have demonstrated by their deliberate concealment from Moore of the true value of his tissue, their efforts to obtain a patent on the Mo cell line, their contractual agreements to exploit this material, their exclusion of Moore from any participation in the profits, and their vigorous defense of this lawsuit. The Court of Appeal summed up the point by observing that "Defendants' position that plaintiff cannot own his tissue, but that they can, is fraught with irony." It is also legally untenable. As noted above, the majority cite no case holding that an individual's right to develop and exploit the commercial potential of his own tissue is *not* a right of sufficient worth or dignity to be deemed a protectible property interest. In the absence of such authority—or of legislation to the same effect—the right falls within the traditionally broad concept of property in our law. * * *

[O]ur society acknowledges a profound ethical imperative to respect the human body as the physical and temporal expression of the unique human persona. One manifestation of that respect is our prohibition against direct abuse of the body by torture or other forms of cruel or unusual punishment. Another is our prohibition against indirect abuse of the body by its economic exploitation for the sole benefit of another person. The most abhorrent form of such exploitation, of course, was the institution of slavery. Lesser forms, such as indentured servitude or even debtor's prison, have also disappeared. Yet their specter haunts the laboratories and boardrooms of today's biotechnological research-industrial complex. It arises wherever scientists or industrialists claim, as defendants claim here, the right to appropriate and exploit a patient's tissue for their sole economic benefit—the right, in other words, to freely mine or harvest valuable physical properties of the patient's body: "Research with human cells that results in significant economic gain for the researcher and no gain for the patient offends the traditional mores of our society in a manner impossible to quantify. Such research tends to treat the human body as a commodity—a means to a profitable end. The dignity and sanctity with which we regard the human whole, body as well as mind and soul, are absent when we allow researchers to further their own interests without the patient's participation by using a patient's cells as the basis for a marketable product." (Danforth, Cells, Sales, and Royalties: The Patient's Right to a Portion of the Profits 6 Yale L. & Pol'y Rev. 179, 190 (1988).)

A second policy consideration adds notions of equity to those of ethics. Our society values fundamental fairness in dealings between its members, and condemns the unjust enrichment of any member at the expense of another. This is particularly true when, as here, the parties are not in equal bargaining positions. * * *

There will be * * * equitable sharing if the courts recognize that the patient has a legally protected property interest in his own body and its products: "property rights in one's own tissue would provide a morally acceptable result by giving effect to notions of fairness and preventing unjust enrichment.... [¶] Societal notions of equity and fairness demand recognition of property rights. There are bountiful benefits, monetary and otherwise, to be derived from human biologics. To deny the person contributing the raw material a fair share of these ample benefits is both unfair and morally wrong." (Note, Toward the Right of Commerciality: Recognizing Property Rights in the Commercial Value of Human Tissue, 34 UCLA L.Rev. 207, 229 (1986).) * * *

The inference I draw from the current statutory regulation of human biological materials, moreover, is the opposite of that drawn by the majority. By selective quotation of the statutes the majority seem to suggest that human organs and blood cannot legally be sold on the open market—thereby implying that if the Legislature were to act here it would impose a similar ban on monetary compensation for the use of human tissue in biotechnological research and development. But if that is the argument, the premise is unsound: contrary to popular misconception, it is not true that human organs and blood cannot legally be sold.

As to organs, the majority rely on the Uniform Anatomical Gift Act (Health & Saf.Code, § 7150 et seq., hereafter the UAGA) for the proposition that a competent adult may make a post mortem gift of any part of his body but may not receive "valuable consideration" for the transfer. But the prohibition of the UAGA against the sale of a body part is much more limited than the majority recognize: by its terms (Health & Saf.Code, § 7155, subd. (a)) the prohibition applies only to sales for "transplantation" or "therapy." Yet a different section of the UAGA authorizes the transfer and receipt of body parts for such additional purposes as "medical or dental education, research, or advancement of medical or dental science." (Health & Saf.Code, § 7153, subd. (a)(1).) No section of the UAGA prohibits anyone from selling body parts for any of those additional purposes; by clear implication, therefore, such sales are legal.[23] Indeed, the

---

23. "By their terms ... the statutes in question forbid only sales for transplantation and therapy. In light of the rather clear authorization for donation for research and education, one could conclude that sales for these non-therapeutic purposes are permitted. Scientists in practice have been buying and selling human tissues for research apparently without interference from these statutes." (Note, "She's Got Bette Davis['s] fact that the UAGA prohibits *no* sales of organs other than sales for "transportation" or "therapy" raises a further implication that it is also legal for anyone to sell human tissue to a biotechnology company for research and development purposes. * * *

It follows that the statutes regulating the transfers of human organs and blood do not support the majority's refusal to recognize a conversion cause of action for commercial exploitation of human blood cells without consent. On the contrary, because such statutes treat both organs and blood as property that can legally be sold in a variety of circumstances, they impliedly support Moore's contention that his blood cells are likewise property for which he can and should receive compensation, and hence are protected by the law of conversion. * * *

NOTES AND QUESTIONS

1. *Moore* is an unusual case, but has prompted a torrent of commentary. Personhood concerns loom large here. Does denying Moore a property interest in his spleen promote personhood? Or just deny him compensation that others are receiving?

2. Or *does* it deny him compensation? A fully informed patient could condition the doctors' right to perform the operation on their sharing the fruits of the spleen with him. If the UCLA doctors refuse, could Moore shop his proposal to USC and other hospitals? Or should this be illegal? If so, why? Does the right to refuse consent mean that a patient has some right to determine the use of the severed body part? Would that make it property?

3. What is at stake in calling Moore's entitlement with respect to his spleen "property?" Adopting the bundle-of-sticks metaphor, Justice Mosk points out that property need not include the right to transfer for consideration. So under this approach, what work does the notion of property do?

4. Why hasn't Moore abandoned any interest in his spleen cells? If you go to a salon to get a haircut, isn't the usual assumption that you have abandoned your hair cuttings, and the salon can dispose of them as it sees fit? What happens if you learn later that your hair is commercially valuable? Consider the recent threat by Neil Armstrong, the first man to walk on the moon, to sue his barber for gathering some of Armstrong's hair off the shop floor and selling it for $3,000. (In case you're wondering, the buyer was a Connecticut collector listed by Guinness World Records as having the world's largest collection of celebrity hair.) Terry Kinney, Neil Armstrong Threatens To Sue Barber Who Sold Hair, Akron Beacon Journal, June 1, 2005, at B1. Or is hair less personal than other body parts? Incidentally, if Armstrong claimed a violation of his right of publicity, see Chapter II, how would he likely fare? How should he?

Eyes": Assessing the Nonconsensual Removal of Cadaver Organs Under the Takings and Due Process Clauses (1990) 90 Colum.L.Rev. 528, 544, fn. 75.)

5.   One concern motivating both the majority opinion and some of the dissents relates to the in rem aspect of property. If Moore has property and can sue for conversion, the set of dutyholders is not limited to the doctors who operated on him. This is beneficial to Moore, but it puts scientists at risk of violating rights about which they may have difficulty informing themselves. Would a registry of cell lines with provenances help here? What about existing cell lines?

6.   As the majority points out, patent law is quite clear about who is and is not a joint inventor and hence the initial owner of a patent. But the patenting of living organisms has been controversial. Section 101 of the Patent Act, echoing language of Thomas Jefferson in the 1793 Patent Act, provides that "[w]hoever invents or discovers any new and useful process, machine, manufacture, or composition of matter, or any new and useful improvement thereof, may obtain a patent therefor, subject to the conditions and requirements of this title." 35 U.S.C. § 101. In the case of *Diamond v. Chakrabarty*, 447 U.S. 303 (1980), mentioned in the *Moore* opinion, the Supreme Court held that patentable subject matter "include[s] everything under the sun that is made by man," a phrase used by the drafters in the legislative history of the 1952 Act. Ideas and laws of nature are still not patentable subject matter, but this exception is in practice narrower than it once was. To be patentable, a living organism should be altered from any naturally existing form or at least distilled in a way not occurring in nature. Does this exhaust concerns one might have? How if at all is patenting a gene sequence different from patenting a life-saving pharmaceutical?

7.   How would Moore fare under the law of accession? (See Chapter II.D.) Could one say that the good doctors combined their labor with Moore's spleen to create a new asset—intentionally? Should the court have considered whether Moore was entitled to an award of restitution? Could the court have awarded restitution without determining that Moore had a property right in his spleen cells?

Hecht v. Superior Court

Court of Appeal, Second District, Division 7, California, 1993.
20 Cal.Rptr.2d 275, 16 Cal.App.4th 836.

■ LILLIE, PRESIDING JUSTICE. Petitioner, the girlfriend of decedent William E. Kane, seeks a peremptory writ of mandate/prohibition to vacate a January 4, 1993 order directing the personal representative of decedent's estate to destroy all of the decedent's sperm in the custody and control of California Cryobank, Inc. The real parties in interest are the administrator of the decedent's estate, (Robert L. Greene) and the decedent's adult son (William E. Kane, Jr.) and adult daughter (Katharine E. Kane). We issued an order to show cause and order staying execution of the January 4, 1993 order.

This proceeding presents several matters of first impression involving the disposition of cryogenically-preserved sperm of a deceased. We conclude that the trial court's order constituted an abuse of discretion in the procedural posture of this case which compels us to set aside such order.

FACTUAL AND PROCEDURAL BACKGROUND

At the age of 48, William E. Kane took his own life on October 30, 1991, in a Las Vegas hotel. For about five years prior to his death, he had been living with petitioner, 38–year–old Deborah Hecht. Kane was survived by two college-aged children of his former wife whom he had divorced in 1976.

In October 1991, decedent deposited 15 vials of his sperm in an account at California Cryobank, Inc., a Los Angeles sperm bank (hereinafter sperm bank). On September 24, 1991, he signed a "Specimen Storage Agreement" with sperm bank which provided in pertinent part that "In the event of the death of the client [William E. Kane], the client instructs the Cryobank to: ... [¶] Continue to store [the specimens] upon request of the executor of the estate [or] [r]elease the specimens to the executor of the estate." A provision captioned "Authorization to Release Specimens" states, "I, William Everett Kane, ... authorize the [sperm bank] to release my semen specimens (vials) to Deborah Ellen Hecht. I am also authorizing specimens to be released to recipient's physician Dr. Kathryn Moyer."

On September 27, 1991, decedent executed a will which was filed with the Los Angeles County Superior Court and admitted to probate. The will named Hecht as executor of the estate, and provides, "I bequeath all right, title, and interest that I may have in any specimens of my sperm stored with any sperm bank or similar facility for storage to Deborah Ellen Hecht." A portion of the will entitled "Statement of Wishes" provided, "It being my intention that samples of my sperm will be stored at a sperm bank for the use of Deborah Ellen Hecht, should she so desire, it is my wish that, should [Hecht] become impregnated with my sperm, before or after my death, she disregard the wishes expressed in Paragraph 3 above [pertaining to disposition of decedent's 'diplomas and framed mementoes,'] to the extent that she wishes to preserve any or all of my mementoes and diplomas and the like for our future child or children."

The will also bequeaths a home in Monterey County to Hecht and an adjoining seven-and-one-half-acre parcel of unimproved land to William E. Kane, Jr., and Katharine Kane, on condition that they deed and convey .4 acre of unimproved land adjacent to the home to Hecht. The residue of the estate was bequeathed to Hecht, the will stating, "I recognize that my children ... are financially secure and therefore leave them nothing other than the land included in this bequest, subject to the conditions as set forth above."

An October 21, 1991 letter signed by Kane and addressed to his children stated: "I address this to my children, because, although I have only two, Everett and Katy, it may be that Deborah will decide—as I hope she will—to have a child by me after my death. I've been assiduously generating frozen sperm samples for that eventuality. If she does, then this letter is for my posthumous offspring, as well, with the thought that I have loved you in my dreams, even though I never got to see you born. [¶] If you are receiving this letter, it means that I am dead—whether by my own hand or that of another makes very little difference. I feel that my time has come; and I wanted to leave you with something more than a dead enigma that was your father. [¶] ... I am inordinately proud of who I have been—what I made of me. I'm so proud of that that I would rather take my own life now than be ground into a mediocre existence by my enemies—who, because of my mistakes and bravado have gained the power to finish me."

After several pages of childhood memories and family history, the letter stated: "So why am I checking out now? Basically, betrayal, over and over again, has made me tired. I've picked up some heavyweight enemies along the way—ranging from the Kellys of the world, to crazies with guns, to insurance companies, to the lawyers that have sucked me dry.... I don't want to die as a tired, perhaps defeated and bitter old man. I'd rather end it like I have lived it—on my time, when and where I will, and while my life is still an object of self-sculpture—a personal creation with which I am still proud. In truth, death for me is not the opposite of life; it is a form of life's punctuation."

Kane committed suicide on October 30, 1991, in Las Vegas, Nevada. On November 18, 1991, Robert L. Greene was appointed special administrator of the estate of William Everett Kane. On December 3, 1991, William Kane, Jr., and Katharine Kane each filed separate will contests. * * *

Greene requested the court to select one of four alternative dispositions: (1) order destruction of the sperm; (2) order distribution of the sperm to decedent's children; (3) order distribution of 80 percent of the sperm to decedent's children and 20 percent to Hecht, and determine whether any children subsequently conceived by use of the sperm shall be entitled to distribution of estate assets; and (4) order distribution of the sperm to Hecht, but reserve one or two vials for future DNA/paternity testing, and determine to what extent any children subsequently conceived shall be entitled to estate assets.

Real parties Katharine Kane and William Kane, Jr., filed a statement of interested parties in which they argued that ordering destruction of decedent's sperm would "help guard the family unit in two different ways": First, such an order would prevent the birth of children who will never know their father and "never even have the slightest hope of being raised in a traditional family." Second, such an order would "prevent the disruption of existing families by after-born children," and would "prevent additional emotional, psychological and financial stress on those family members already in existence." They characterized the desire to father children after one's death as "egotistic and irresponsible," and stated that they "have lost their father to a tragic death which Hecht could easily have prevented; they do not wish to suffer any more at her hands. Further, they do not wish to be troubled for the rest of their lives with worries about the fate of their half-sibling(s)."[2] * * *

I

PROBATE PRINCIPLES

"All proceedings in the probate court are limited and special or limited and statutory. [Citation.] The power of the probate court extends only to the property of the decedent." (Estate of Lee, 124 Cal.App.3d 687, 692 (1981).) The right of inheritance, as well as the right of testamentary disposition, is entirely within the control of the state Legislature and is subject only to the conditions prescribed by such body. (Harkness v. Harkness, 205 Cal.App.2d 510, 516 (1962).) "Whether this accords with natural right and justice is a question upon which we cannot enter. The right of inheritance in this state does not depend upon the ideas of court or counsel as to justice and natural right. The entire matter is in the control of the legislature...." (Id. at pp. 515–516, internal quotation marks omitted.) * * *

In light of the foregoing principles, we conclude that we cannot uphold the trial court's order on the theory urged by real parties, that the trial court's order "was entirely proper under the authority of [*Moore v. Regents of University of California*, 793 P.2d 479 (Cal. 1990)] and Health and Safety Code section 7054.4."[4] It is self-defeating for real parties to argue, under the rationale of *Moore*, that decedent had no ownership or possessory interest in his sperm once it left his body, because the sperm then would not constitute part of Kane's estate and the probate court would not have jurisdiction over its disposition.

As we hereinafter explain, the decedent's interest in his frozen sperm vials, even if not governed by the general law of personal property, occupies "an interim category that entitles them to special respect because of their potential for human life" (See Davis v. Davis, 842 S.W.2d 588, 597 (Tenn. 1992)), and at the time of his death, decedent had an interest, in the nature of ownership, to the extent that he had decision making authority as to the sperm within the scope of policy set by law. (Ibid.) Thus, decedent had an interest in his sperm which falls within the broad definition of property in

---

2. On November 12, 1992, decedent's children filed against Hecht a first amended complaint for wrongful death and intentional infliction of emotional distress, wherein they alleged, inter alia, that their father, who had been unemployed for some time, became deeply depressed and began to seriously contemplate suicide about September 1, 1991; for six weeks before his death, Hecht was aware of decedent's "disturbed plan" to end his life; that Hecht convinced him to allow her to have his child after his death and to leave her a substantial amount of his property to raise and care for this child; in the week before his death, Hecht encouraged and assisted decedent in transferring property to her and decedent emptied his personal checking account by issuing a check to Hecht for $80,000; Hecht assisted decedent in purchas-

ing a one-way ticket to Las Vegas and took him to the airport.

4. * * * As will be apparent from the discussion below, *Moore* is distinguishable from the instant case both because of its facts and its procedural posture. Unlike the facts in *Moore,* a contract with the sperm bank purports to evidence decedent's intent and expectation that he would in fact retain control over the sperm following its deposit. Depending upon the resolution of other matters, *Moore* may ultimately be pertinent to the disposition of some or all of Kane's stored sperm; however at this point, the pertinence of *Moore* is *speculative* as the issue of the actual disposition of decedent's sperm is not before us.

Probate Code section 62, as "anything that may be the subject of ownership and includes both real and personal property and any interest therein."

II

NATURE OF RIGHTS IN SEMEN

"The present legal position toward property rights in the human body is unsettled and reflects no consistent philosophy or approach. Until recently, the common law either refused to recognize a property right in human bodies or recognized only a quasi-property right.... [The court in *Moore v. Regents of University of California*, supra] did not resolve the debate over the existence or extent of a property interest in one's body. Nor does the existing statutory scheme quiet the debate. The statutes that address individuals' control over their bodies delineate the extent of that control in specific situations, but do not establish a general principle." (Note, Personalizing Personalty: Toward a Property Right in Human Bodies (1990) 69 Tex.L.Rev. 209, 220, fns. omitted.)

As also recognized by the court in *Moore,* "the laws governing such things as human tissues, transplantable organs, blood, fetuses, pituitary glands, corneal tissue, and dead bodies deal with human biological materials as objects sui generis, regulating their disposition to achieve policy goals rather than abandoning them to the general law of personal property. It is these specialized statutes, not the law of conversion, to which courts ordinarily should and do look for guidance on the disposition of human biological materials." * * *

One commentator recently noted that although some sperm banks operate as commercial enterprises, they are virtually free from state licensing and other regulation. (Wadlington, Artificial Conception: The Challenge for Family Law, 69 Va.L.Rev. 465, 468 (1983).) The various state statutes modeled after the Uniform Parentage Act (see, e.g., Civ.Code, § 7000 et seq.) address the issue of the legal relationship between the sperm donor and the child born by artificial insemination. However, "[n]one of the statutes on artificial insemination indicate who owns the sperm donation, but sperm banks generally require those donors who are to be anonymous to sign a written waiver of any rights to the deposit and any paternity claims to children born from it. In return, the sperm bank guarantees the donor's anonymity. Thus, according to the contract between the parties, the donor no longer 'owns' the sperm. [¶] Men who use sperm banks to store their sperm for their own future use, however, do own their donation(s) of sperm and are required to pay for its maintenance and its later withdrawal. Upon notice of the death of the donor, however, many storage agreements authorize the sperm bank to dispose of the deposit. Requests from the widow of the donor to be inseminated with the sperm, as a matter of practice, are denied absent express instructions in the donor's will or a court order." (Shapiro & Sonnenblick, The Widow and the Sperm: The Law of Post–Mortem Insemination (1986) 1 J. Law & Health 229, 243–244, fns. omitted.) * * *

Although *Davis v. Davis*, supra, 842 S.W.2d 588, involved the disposition of frozen preembryos (four-to-eight-celled entities)[5] of a married couple who had attempted to bear a child through in vitro fertilization but divorced before they could do so, the court's discussion of the legal status of preembryos is informative. For various reasons, not pertinent to our discussion, the Supreme Court of Tennessee concluded that the preembryos could not be considered "persons" under Tennessee law. The court also refused to characterize the interest of the Davises in the preembryos as a property interest under general property law; rather they "occupy an interim category that entitles them to special respect because of their potential for human life. It follows that any interest that Mary Sue Davis and Junior Davis have in the preembryos in this case is not a true property interest. However, they do have an interest in the nature of ownership, to the extent that they have decision-making authority concerning disposition of the preembryos, within the scope of policy set by law." (842 S.W.2d at p. 597.)

The court in *Davis* found persuasive a report of the Ethics Committee of The American Fertility Society, which identified three major ethical positions that have been articulated in the debate over preembryo status. At one extreme is the view that the preembryo is a human subject after fertilization, which requires that it be accorded the rights of a person; the opposite extreme is the view that the preembryo has a status no different from any other human tissue; a third view, " 'one that is most widely held—takes an intermediate position between the other two. It holds that the preembryo deserves respect greater than that accorded to human tissue but not the respect accorded to actual persons. The preembryo is due greater respect than other human tissue because of its potential to become a person and because of its symbolic meaning for many people. Yet, it should not be treated as a person, because it has not yet developed the features of personhood, is not yet established as developmentally individu-

---

5. According to the scientific testimony in *Davis,* the process of fertilization of the egg with the sperm results in a one-cell zygote which contains a new hereditary constitution (genome) contributed to by both parents through the union of sperm and egg; the stage subsequent to the zygote is cleavage, during which the single cell undergoes successive equal divisions with little or no intervening growth; the resulting cells, (blastomeres) become smaller, while the size of the total aggregate of cells remains the same; after three such divisions, the aggregate contains eight cells in relatively loose association; each blastomere, if separated from the others, has the potential to develop into a complete adult; " '[s]tated another way, at the 8–cell stage, the developmental singleness of one person has not been established.' " (842 S.W.2d at p. 593.)

"Today, under federal law and all state statutory law except Louisiana, embryos [created by in vitro fertilization] do not possess rights or have legal status. In Louisiana, embryos have been given rights and limits have been imposed on how embryos may be treated." (Poole, Allocation of Decision–Making Rights to Frozen Embryos, 4 Amer.J. of Fam. Law 67, 84–85 (1990).) The Louisiana statute defines "human embryo" as "an in vitro fertilized human ovum" and prohibits its destruction unless it fails to develop further over a 36 hour period, except when the embryo is in a state of cryopreservation. (Id., at pp. 78–79.) In Poole's opinion, the Louisiana statute may be unconstitutional under federal law because "it infringes on individual's right of procreative choice at a stage where the state has no compelling interest in the embryo." (Id. at p. 85.)

al, and may never realize its biologic potential.' " (Davis v. Davis, supra, 842 S.W.2d at p. 596.)

The *Davis* court also notes that The American Fertility Society suggests that " 'Within the limits set by institutional policies, decision-making authority regarding preembryos should reside with the persons who have provided the gametes.... As a matter of law, it is reasonable to assume that the gamete providers have primary decision-making authority regarding preembryos in the absence of specific legislation on the subject. A person's liberty to procreate or to avoid procreation is directly involved in most decisions involving preembryos.' " (842 S.W.2d at p. 597.)

Sperm which is stored by its provider with the intent that it be used for artificial insemination is thus unlike other human tissue because it is "gametic material" (Davis v. Davis, supra, 842 S.W.2d 588, 597) that can be used for reproduction. Although it has not yet been joined with an egg to form a preembryo, as in *Davis,* the value of sperm lies in its potential to create a child after fertilization, growth, and birth. We conclude that at the time of his death, decedent had an interest, in the nature of ownership, to the extent that he had decision making authority as to the use of his sperm for reproduction. Such interest is sufficient to constitute "property" within the meaning of Probate Code section 62. Accordingly, the probate court had jurisdiction with respect to the vials of sperm.

In concluding that the sperm is properly part of decedent's estate, we do not address the issue of the validity or enforceability of any contract or will purporting to express decedent's intent with respect to the stored sperm. In view of the nature of sperm as reproductive material which is a unique type of "property," we also decline petitioner's invitation to apply to this case the general law relating to gifts of personal property or the statutory provisions for gifts in view of impending death. (See Prob.Code, § 5700 et seq.)

We now address the propriety of the trial court's order that the sperm be destroyed. In order to do so, we examine several theories proffered by the parties to explain or uphold the trial court's order.

In this case, the trial court could not have properly ordered the sperm destroyed by applying the provisions of the will; Hecht is not only the residual beneficiary specified therein, but the will evidences the decedent's intent that Hecht, should she so desire, is to receive his sperm stored in the sperm bank to bear his child posthumously. Moreover, there is no indication that the trial court itself purported to apply the terms of the will or was adjudicating the issue of the validity of the will. There is also no indication in our record that the trial court's order was based upon a theory the will was invalid or subject to revocation. Although real parties' answer to the instant petition asserts affirmative defenses that the will and the sperm bank contract are invalid on the grounds that decedent was of unsound mind, subject to Hecht's undue influence, and that decedent lacked testamentary and legal capacity at the time of execution of those documents, our record contains no evidentiary hearing as to these allegations and the order cannot be upheld on these grounds. * * *

Citing *Davis*, real parties also urge this court to uphold the trial court's order on the ground that Hecht "can easily procreate by a variety of other means," and she "cannot bear a child using [decedent's] sperm without encroaching upon the family integrity of [decedent's] existing children." As pointed out above, our record is inadequate to address the issue of real parties' "family integrity."

As to the issue of whether Hecht has other means to bear a child, the issue is a factual one which our record fails to address. Moreover, it must be pointed out that the court in *Davis* was called upon to resolve a dispute involving the disposition of preembryos where the gamete-providers *disagreed* as to their disposition and where there was no written agreement of the parties or state statute governing such disposition. Under those circumstances, the court held as follows: "[W]e hold that disputes involving the disposition of preembryos produced by *in vitro* fertilization should be resolved, first, by looking to the preferences of the progenitors. If their wishes cannot be ascertained, or if there is dispute, then their prior agreement concerning disposition should be carried out. If no prior agreement exists, then the relative interests of the parties in using or not using the preembryos must be weighed. Ordinarily, the party wishing to avoid procreation should prevail, assuming that the other party has a reasonable possibility of achieving parenthood by means other than use of the preembryos in question. If no other reasonable alternatives exist, then the argument in favor of using the preembryos to achieve pregnancy should be considered. However, if the party seeking control of the preembryos intends merely to donate them to another couple, the objecting party obviously has the greater interest and should prevail." (Davis v. Davis, supra, 842 S.W.2d 588, 604.) * * *

Real parties also intimate that the birth of a child by Hecht using decedent's sperm will create psychological burdens on them, decedent's surviving adult children, as well as financial burdens on society and on the estate.

In light of the UPA and Probate Code sections 6407 and 6408, it is unlikely that the estate would be subject to claims with respect to any such children. If the Second Settlement Agreement is enforceable against Hecht, the estate may also be protected from any claims with respect to such children. * * *

Decedent's adult children also fail to provide any legal or factual basis to support their contention that the birth of a child through the artificial insemination of Hecht with decedent's sperm implicates their "fundamental right to protection of their family integrity," and thus their psychological well-being.

At this point, it is also entirely speculative as to whether any child born to Hecht using decedent's sperm will be a burden on society. Real parties also offer no authority for their suggestion that if the sperm is to be distributed to Hecht, the probate court should first treat the matter as a surrogacy arrangement or adoption and appoint a guardian ad litem for the unborn child(ren) and conduct a fitness hearing as to Hecht's fitness to bear a child. We know of no authority which would authorize the probate court to proceed in the foregoing manner, much less provide it authority to address the issue of Hecht's fitness to bear a child.

As recently stated by our Supreme Court in a case involving a surrogacy contract: "It is not the role of the judiciary to inhibit the use of reproductive technology when the Legislature has not seen fit to do so; any such effort would raise serious questions in light of the fundamental nature of the rights of procreation and privacy." (Johnson v. Calvert (1993) 5 Cal.4th 84, 101, 851 P.2d 776.)

For the foregoing reasons we conclude that the trial court abused its discretion in ordering decedent's sperm destroyed.

We emphasize again that we are not adjudicating the issues of the validity of the will, the sperm bank contract, or the enforceability of the settlement agreements in this case or any other issue not before us. * * *

NOTES AND QUESTIONS

1. As we will see in Chapter V, the law sometimes places limits on dead hand control—the ability of a person to control resources after his or her death. Even if sperm is treated as property, none of these restrictions applies here directly. If men are allowed to sell sperm to sperm banks, why is it worse to leave sperm to someone by will? What does the personhood perspective have to say?

2. James E. Penner, whom we encountered briefly in Chapter I, has also advanced what he calls the "separation thesis": Only items that are thought of as separate from their owners can be "things" and hence objects of property—the right to a thing. Thus, spleens or sperm would not be property before separation from the person. Does this accord with the treatment in these cases? With your intuition? See J.E. Penner, The Idea of Property in Law 111–27 (1997).

3. In *Davis v. Davis*, discussed in the main case, the court engaged in balancing the interests of the husband and wife (after having overturned the trial court's finding that embryos themselves are persons). It found that the interest of the husband in not becoming a father outweighed the interest of the wife in donating the frozen embryos. What if the wife wanted to attempt a pregnancy herself? Might a husband in a bitter divorce wish to see frozen embryos destroyed knowing that this would be the wife's last chance (but not his) to be a biological parent? If there is any theme in the embryo cases, even ones in which there is a contract governing the disposition of the frozen embryos, it is that either party can back out and veto use of the embryos at any time before implantation. Is this equality? In light of all this, is the frozen embryo property? What if both biological contributors agreed to sell the frozen embryos? For a discussion of cases in this and other countries and a variety of academic perspectives, see, e.g., Ruth Colker, Pregnant Men Revisited or Sperm Is Cheap, Eggs Are Not, 47 Hastings L.J. 1063 (1996); John A. Robertson, Precommitment Strategies

for Disposition of Frozen Embryos, 50 Emory L.J. 989 (2001); Helene S. Shapo, Frozen Pre–Embryos and the Right to Change One's Mind, 12 Duke J. Comp. & Int'l L. 75 (2002).

4.   All three of the decisions excerpted in this section arose in California. Chronologically speaking, *Moore* was the first. It denies that a person has any property right in cells removed from his spleen during an operation. *Hecht* comes next. Distinguishing *Moore*, it holds that frozen sperm cells can be distributed as property through the probate system. *Newman* is the most recent. Although it applies federal constitutional law, it purports to be guided by California law insofar as the identification of property is concerned. *Moore* is not mentioned. In light of these precedents, how would you characterize the status of the *Moore* decision today?

[handwritten margin notes: No prop. rights to body parts — Moore (1990) ↓ Sperm can be prop — Hecht (1993) cites/distinguishes Moore ↓ Newman (2002) Had prop. rights (no mention of Moore)]

2.   ARTISTS' MORAL RIGHTS

Personhood rights are also implicated when individuals create things that are expressions of their beliefs and experiences. Should artists (or others) retain some control over the use to which such creations are put by future owners? The idea has considerable force in Europe, and is beginning to appear in the United States as well.

[handwritten: P   D — pastor of church]

Moakley v. Eastwick

Supreme Judicial Court of Massachusetts, 1996.
666 N.E.2d 505.

■ GREANEY, JUSTICE. We allowed the plaintiff's application for direct appellate review to resolve issues under the so-called Art Preservation Act, G.L. c. 231, § 85S (Act), inserted by St.1984, c. 488, § 1, effective April 7, 1985. By his complaint in the Superior Court, the plaintiff, John C. Moakley, an artist, brought a claim under the Act against the defendants, the Grace Bible Church Fellowship, Inc., Grace Bible Church (church), and Maurice T. Eastwick, the pastor of the church, and additional claims for intentional and negligent infliction of emotional distress. The plaintiff sought a declaration of his rights, injunctive relief, and the assessment of damages. The plaintiff appeals from a judgment entered in favor of the defendants after a bench trial before a judge in the Superior Court.

The dispute concerns a work of art, created by the plaintiff, which is located on the grounds of the former First Parish Unitarian Church in East Bridgewater, now owned by the church. * * *

The facts found by the judge are as follows. In 1971, the plaintiff, an established sculptor and potter, was commissioned by the pastor of the First Parish Unitarian Church in East Bridgewater to create and install a work of art on church property. The result of this commission consisted of a sixty-eight foot long concrete block wall to which the plaintiff affixed a mural composed of approximately 600 separate ceramic tiles, organized into

Figure 3–2
The Moakley Mural and the Grace Bible Church,
East Bridgewater, Massachusetts

Courtesy Craig Murray.

ten panels (work). The work constituted an historical "time line," in relief, of events and social trends in East Bridgewater from its earliest days to the time of the commission. The final panel of the work contained references to social issues in the 1960's and 1970's, including drug use, environmental pollution, nuclear war, and civil unrest. The judge found that the plaintiff had invested substantial time and emotional resources in the work, and that it was "an expression of [the plaintiff's] personality." The judge also accepted the testimony of two experts that the wall with the affixed mural "was a work of fine art of recognized quality."[3] Because of the method of its construction, the work cannot be moved intact from its present site.

In October, 1989, the property on which the work is located was acquired by the Grace Bible Church Fellowship, Inc., for use as a house of worship for members of the church. The property was dilapidated when the church acquired it. On October 21, 1989, shortly after the purchase was complete, approximately sixty members of the church joined in a "clean-up day." The church intended to remove the work in its entirety, and, at some

---

3. General Laws c. 231, § 85S (1994 ed.) (Act), protects "works of fine art," which are defined, in subsection (b), as "any original work of visual or graphic art of any media which shall include, but not limited to [*sic*], any painting, print, drawing, sculpture, craft object, photograph, audio or video tape, film, hologram, or any combination thereof, of recognized quality." In determining whether a work is one of "fine art" within the meaning of the Act, a judge is directed to rely "on the opinions of artist [*sic*], art dealers, collectors of fine art, curators of art museums, restorers and conservators of fine art and other persons involved with the creation or marketing of fine art." G.L. c. 231, § 85S(f).

point during the clean-up day, a substantial portion of the east end of the wall, constituting about one-seventh of the entire work, was demolished. The judge accepted as credible testimony by the pastor of the church that the work was objectionable to the church on religious grounds, and that it was for this reason that the church had decided to remove it.

The plaintiff was informed of the partial destruction of his work by the chairwoman of the East Bridgewater Historical Commission. On the basis of the Act, he obtained a preliminary injunction prohibiting the church from causing or permitting any further physical defacement or alteration of the work.[4] On appeal, the plaintiff argues that the judge erred in concluding that the Act, as applied, would violate the defendants' rights under art. 2 [of the Declaration of Rights of the Massachusetts Constitution, guaranteeing freedom of religion and worship]. We need not reach this constitutional issue, however, because we agree with the defendants' contention that the Act was not intended to apply retrospectively to works created before its enactment and owned by someone other than the artist.[5]

1. Because the plaintiff sought relief under the Act, which we have not previously had occasion to consider, we begin by discussing the Act's content and its relation to existing law. According to a commentator, the Act follows similar legislation in the States of California and New York "in attempting to graft onto a generally inhospitable common law tradition the civil law concept of *droit moral*, whereby a creative artist retains certain inalienable rights with respect to his or her creation before and after publication, display or sale" (footnote omitted). Koven, Observations on the Massachusetts Art Preservation Act, 71 Mass.L.Rev. 101, 101 (1986). The primary goal of the Act is to safeguard the professional reputations of Massachusetts's artists by protecting the work which forms the basis of the artists' reputations. See G.L. c. 231, § 85S(a). To this end, the Act protects what has been referred to as the "Right of Integrity," Koven, supra at 103, by prohibiting the physical defacement or alteration of a work of fine art, see note 4, supra, for the lifetime of the artist and for fifty years thereafter. G.L. c. 231, § 85S(g).[7] The Act also protects what has been referred to as the "Right of Paternity," see Koven, supra, that is, the right of the artist to claim authorship of his work, or "for just and valid reason, to disclaim

---

4. Subsection (c) of the Act provides, in part, that "[n]o person, except an artist who owns or possesses a work of fine art which the artist has created, shall intentionally commit, or authorize the intentional commission of any physical defacement, mutilation, alteration, or destruction of a work of fine art."

5. The plaintiff's claims are based on conduct by the defendants (the deliberate destruction of part of the work) that occurred after the effective date of the Act. The parties have discussed the question of the application of the Act's provisions to a work created prior to its enactment as one of retrospectivity, and

it is in this sense that we use the term in this opinion.

7. Because its provisions only apply for fifty years after an artist's death, much of what the general public would consider "fine art" clearly is not protected by the Act. Thus, it is somewhat misleading to refer to this legislation as an "Art Preservation Act." As has been previously noted, the legislation serves primarily to safeguard artists' professional reputations by preserving the integrity of the creative work which forms the basis for those reputations. The Act's preservation function is subsidiary to this main purpose.

authorship of his work of fine art."[8] G.L. c. 231, § 85S(d). The rights of integrity and paternity are enforceable by the artist, or his duly authorized representative, by an action in the Superior Court. G.L. c. 231, § 85S(e). The Act deals separately with "fine art [that] cannot be removed from a building without substantial physical defacement, mutilation, alteration, or destruction of such work." G.L. c. 231, § 85S(h). As to these works, the rights and duties created under the Act are forfeited, "unless expressly reserved by an instrument in writing signed by the owner of such building and properly recorded prior to the installation of such art." Id. The Act creates new rights for artists with respect to their work after it has left their hands, and it creates new duties for owners of fine art, who may not alter, destroy, or grossly neglect a work of fine art in their possession that is subject to the provisions of the Act. G.L. c. 231, § 85S(c).

2. The defendants contend that, in the absence of a legislative directive mandating retrospective application, the Act, which alters the relationship and expectations of artists and owners of art, should not be applied retrospectively to an owner of a work of fine art that was created and permanently left the artist's possession before the effective date of the Act. We agree with the defendants that the text of the Act and its legislative history compel the conclusion that it does not apply to a piece of fine art, like the work, whose creation preceded the enactment of the protective legislation.

Whether a new law applies retrospectively is a question of legislative intent. "In the absence of an express legislative directive, this court has usually applied '[t]he general rule of interpretation ... that all statutes are prospective in their operation, unless an intention that they shall be retrospective appears by necessary implication from their words, context or objects when considered in the light of the subject matter, the pre-existing state of the law and the effect upon existent rights, remedies and obligations. Doubtless all legislation commonly looks to the future, not to the past, and has no retroactive effect unless such effect manifestly is required by unequivocal terms. It is only statutes regulating practice, procedure and evidence, in short, those relating to remedies and not affecting substantive rights, that commonly are treated as operating retroactively....' " Fontaine v. Ebtec Corp., 613 N.E.2d 881 (Mass. 1993), quoting City Council of Waltham v. Vinciullo, 307 N.E.2d 316 (Mass. 1974).

As the judge noted, the Act does not expressly address whether its provisions should apply retrospectively to work created before its enactment. General Laws c. 231, § 85S(b), defines "[f]ine art" broadly, as "*any* original work of visual or graphic art of any media," (emphasis supplied), and the legislative purpose, the protection of fine art as an expression of an

---

8. Cognate Federal legislation, the Federal Visual Artists Rights Act of 1990, explicitly sets forth the circumstances in which an artist or his or her representative is entitled to disclaim authorship of a visual work of fine art. An artist has the right "to prevent the use of his or her name as the author of the work of visual art in the event of a distortion, mutilation, or other modification of the work which would be prejudicial to his or her honor or reputation." 17 U.S.C. § 106A(a)(2) (1994).

artist's personality and the basis for his reputation, logically could extend to art created prior to the legislation's enactment.

Nonetheless, the text of the Act poses barriers to its application to works created prior to its enactment. The Act exempts from its protections fine art attached to a building, which cannot be removed without defacement or destruction, unless the rights and duties created by the Act are "expressly reserved by an instrument in writing signed by the owner of such building and properly recorded, prior to the installation of such art." G.L. c. 231, § 85S(h). This condition obviously could not be satisfied with respect to a work of art created as an integral part of a building prior to the Act's effective date. Thus, at best, the Act could only apply selectively to some works of fine art created prior to its enactment, and it could not apply to most works of immovable art, which may, in fact, face the greatest risk of defacement or destruction because an owner cannot otherwise dispose of such a work.

In addition to the forward-looking nature of the reservation provision in § 85S(h), there are other compelling reasons to conclude that the Legislature's failure to provide for retrospective application of the Act represents a deliberate choice that should be respected by this court. A comparison of the texts indicates that the Act was modeled on the so-called California Art Preservation Act, Cal.Civ.Code § 987, enacted in 1979 (West 1982 & Supp. 1996) (California Act). See Koven, supra at 104. In most respects, the Act follows quite precisely the language of the California Act.[9] There is, however, one omission from, and one addition to, the Act, both bearing directly on the question of retrospective application. Where the California Act (§ 987[j]) provides that it shall "apply to claims based on proscribed acts occurring on or after [the effective date of the Act] to works of fine art *whenever created,*" (emphasis supplied), the Act is silent on this point. In addition, as noted above, the Act will not protect a work of fine art which is attached to a building and cannot be removed unless a preservation restriction applicable to the work has been recorded prior to the work's creation. The California Act also requires the recordation of a preservation restriction for works of fine art attached to a building, but does not require that the restriction be recorded before such a work is created and installed.

The legislative history of the Act strongly suggests that the changes just described were deliberate and, consequently, supports the view that the Legislature did not intend the Act to apply retrospectively to works created before its enactment. Prior to its enactment, a different version of the Act had been proposed. 1984 House Doc. No. 2576. That version included the language, found in the California Act, which would have made

---

9. There are differences between the Act and the California Art Preservation Act, Cal.Civ.Code § 987 (West 1982 & Supp. 1996), in addition to those discussed in the body of this opinion. Most significantly, the definition of "[f]ine art" in the Act is considerably more inclusive, extending to audiotapes, videotapes, and films, none of which is protected by the California Act. Compare G.L. c. 231, § 85S(b), with Cal.Civ.Code § 987(b)(2).

Court's main argument re: text of act prohibiting retroactive application

the Act applicable to "works of fine art whenever created." Id. at 4. In addition, the proposed legislation did not require that an appropriate preservation restriction on a work of fine art attached to a building be recorded prior to creation of the work. Id. at 3. These two provisions were eliminated from the Act before it became law. While there are other differences of import between the proposed and the final versions of the legislation,[10] these two changes demonstrate that the revisions made prior to passage included a purposeful determination to limit the applicability of the Act to works of fine art created after its enactment. See Green v. Wyman–Gordon Co., 664 N.E.2d 808 (Mass. 1996) (deletions prior to enactment normally assumed to be intentional).

Statutes in other jurisdictions, comparable to the Act in that they protect works of art from destruction, mutilation, or alteration, all address specifically whether their provisions apply to works of fine art created prior to enactment. See Visual Artists Rights Act of 1990, 17 U.S.C. § 106A(d)(1) & (2) (1994); Cal.Civ.Code § 987(j); Conn.Gen.Stat.Ann. § 42–116t(g) (1995); Fine Arts Preservation Act, Pa.Stat. Ann. tit. 73, § 2110(b) (1993). It is worth noting that the Legislatures responsible for these various laws have chosen differently on this point. The Federal Act applies to works created on or after the effective date of the statute and to works created prior to the statute's effective date "but title to which has not, as of such effective date, been transferred from the author." Connecticut's Act, enacted in 1988, applies only to works created on or after October 1, 1988. In contrast, as has been previously noted, the California Act applies to works of fine art whenever created, as does the Pennsylvania Act (although the Pennsylvania Act has the additional limitation that it applies only to works of fine art displayed in a place accessible to the public). We may infer from these diverging approaches that our Legislature is not alone in having concluded that the rights and duties created by legislation like the Act sufficiently alter the expectations and responsibilities of owners or possessors of fine art, that these duties should not be imposed on a person who acquired a work of fine art that was created before such duties were imposed by law. The Legislature also may have considered the obvious point that the author of a work created before the Act's effective date could not have acted in reliance on the rights created by the legislation. It is for the Legislature to pronounce the scope of the changes in rights and duties that it intends to effect by a new law. We agree with the defendants that the Legislature did not intend the Act to apply to preexisting works of fine art.

3. We also affirm the judgment on the plaintiff's claims of intentional and negligent infliction of emotional distress. While we do not doubt that the partial destruction of the work caused serious distress to the plaintiff, as matter of law, the defendants' conduct cannot be considered extreme

---

10. Most notably, the proposed legislation had provided for the availability of punitive damages, which the enacted legislation does not, and the enacted legislation includes a provision which permits the Attorney General to assert the rights under the Act of a deceased artist with respect to a work of fine art that is in public view.

and outrageous. An owner in fee of real property, such as the church, generally has the right to renovate or remove structures or objects on the property, and the exercise of that right, at least in the circumstances of this case, cannot be classified as extreme and outrageous behavior. As to the claim of negligent infliction of emotional distress, as finder of fact, faced with testimony about fairly amorphous symptoms of physical harm, the judge was entitled to conclude that the plaintiff had not satisfied his burden of proof, by a preponderance of the evidence, on this point.

The judgment is modified to add to it a provision declaring that the plaintiff's work of art is not subject to the protections contained in G.L. c. 231, § 85S, and, as so modified, the judgment is affirmed.

NOTES AND QUESTIONS

1. The court decides the case on the principle that a statute imposing new disabilities on property owners should apply retroactively only if this is the clear intention of the legislature. We give further consideration to this constructional principle as a device for protecting expectations of property owners in Chapter XI. Suppose the Massachusetts legislature had said that moral rights attach to previously created works of art, in other words, it had explicitly made the statute retroactive. How would you weigh the competing claims of Moakley and the church in these circumstances?

2. To what sorts of works of creation should the principle of "moral rights" be extended? Suppose M purchases a decrepit Victorian house and works for twenty years restoring it to its original splendor, complete with refinished woodwork and wallpaper made to order to match the original. M expends enormous labor and care in the process, and is extremely proud of the result. M then sells the house and lot (at a significant profit, even taking into account the thousands of hours of "sweat equity" she has invested) to L. A year later, M learns that L is planning to tear down the restored Victorian in order to build a McMansion on the lot. Should M have any right to object to the tear down? Should architects have moral rights claims in the buildings they have designed? Software engineers in the computer programs they have created?

3. In 1990, Congress passed the first federal moral rights legislation, the Visual Artists Rights Act, which added Section 106A to the Copyright Act of 1976. Section 106A(a) provides:

Rights of attribution and integrity.—Subject to section 107 and independent of the exclusive rights provided in section 106, the author of a work of visual art—

(1) shall have the right—

(A) to claim authorship of that work, and

(B) to prevent the use of his or her name as the author of any work of visual art which he or she did not create;

Rights seem to be waived by receiving compensation for the work.

↓

similar to "work for hire" (next page)

(2) shall have the right to prevent the use of his or her name as the author of the work of visual art in the event of a distortion, mutilation, or other modification of the work which would be prejudicial to his or her honor or reputation; and

(3) subject to the limitations set forth in section 113(d), shall have the right—

(A) to prevent any intentional distortion, mutilation, or other modification of that work which would be prejudicial to his or her honor or reputation, and any intentional distortion, mutilation, or modification of that work is a violation of that right, and

(B) to prevent any destruction of a work of recognized stature, and any intentional or grossly negligent destruction of that work is a violation of that right.

In *Carter v. Helmsley–Spear, Inc.*, 71 F.3d 77 (2d Cir. 1995), three sculptors sued to prevent the removal, modification, or destruction of a work of art that had been installed in a building lobby under a commission from a former tenant of the building. The Second Circuit reversed the grant of a permanent injunction on the grounds that the sculpture was a work for hire and hence outside the definition of "visual art." The Copyright Act defines "work made for hire" in part as "a work prepared by an employee within the scope of his or her employment." 17 U.S.C. § 101.

4.   European, and especially French, copyright laws provide for more extensive artists' moral rights. In France such rights extend to works not covered by the VARA and are often said to be inalienable and perpetual. Which approach is better?

3.   Cultural Patrimony

Personhood interests are also implicated when cultural artifacts are taken from the communities in which they have particular significance. One notable effort to address this problem is reflected in the Native American Graves Protection and Repatriation Act, considered in the following case.

United States v. Corrow

United States Court of Appeals, Tenth Circuit, 1997.
119 F.3d 796.

■ John C. Porfilio, Circuit Judge. This appeal raises issues of first impression in this Circuit under the Native American Graves Protection and Repatriation Act, 25 U.S.C. §§ 3001–3013 (NAGPRA) * * *. Richard Nelson Corrow challenges the constitutionality of 25 U.S.C. § 3001(3)(D) of NAGPRA which defines "cultural patrimony," the basis for his conviction of trafficking in protected Native American cultural items in violation of 18 U.S.C. § 1170(b). [He] contends the definition is unconstitutionally vague, an argument the district court rejected in denying his motion to dismiss that count of the indictment and to reverse his conviction. * * * We affirm.

I. Background

Until his death in 1991, Ray Winnie was a *hataali,* a Navajo religious singer. For more than twenty-five years Mr. Winnie chanted the Nightway and other Navajo ceremonies wearing Yei B'Chei originally owned by Hosteen Hataali Walker. Yei B'Chei or Yei B'Chei *jish* are ceremonial adornments, Native American artifacts whose English label, "masks," fails to connote the Navajo perception these cultural items embody living gods. Traditionally, a *hataali* passes the Yei B'Chei to a family or clan member who has studied the ceremonies or loans the Yei B'Chei to another Navajo clan, Mr. Winnie having acquired his Yei B'Chei from a different clan during his *hataali* apprenticeship. When Mr. Winnie died, he left no provision for the disposition of his Yei B'Chei, and no family or clan member requested them.

Richard Corrow, the owner of Artifacts Display Stands in Scottsdale, Arizona, is an afficionado of Navajo culture and religion, having, on occasion, participated in Navajo religious ceremonies. Some time after Mr. Winnie's death, Mr. Corrow traveled to Lukachukai, Arizona, to visit Mrs. Fannie Winnie, Mr. Winnie's 81–year–old widow, chatting with her; her granddaughter, Rose Bia; and other family members: a great granddaughter, Harriette Keyonnie; and a son-in-law. During one visit, Mrs. Winnie displayed some Navajo screens and robes, and Mr. Corrow inquired about the Yei B'Chei. By his third visit in August 1993, the Winnie family revealed the Yei B'Chei, twenty-two ceremonial masks, and permitted Mr. Corrow to photograph them. Mr. Corrow told Mrs. Winnie he wanted to buy them, suggesting he planned to deliver the Yei B'Chei to a young Navajo chanter in Utah to keep them sacred. Although Mr. Corrow initially offered $5,000, he readily agreed to the family's price of $10,000 for the Yei B'Chei, five headdresses, and other artifacts. Mr. Corrow drafted a receipt,[1] and Mrs. Winnie, who spoke no English, placed her thumbprint on the document after Ms. Bia read it to her in Navajo.

In November 1994, the owners of the East–West Trading Company in Santa Fe, New Mexico, contacted Mr. Corrow telling him that a wealthy Chicago surgeon was interested in purchasing a set of Yei B'Chei. In fact, the purported buyer was James Tanner, a National Park Service ranger operating undercover on information he had received about questionable trade at East–West. When Agent Tanner visited the business, its owners showed him photographs of seventeen of the twenty-two Yei B'Chei that

---

1. The receipt stated:

Sold to Richard N. Corrow on this date for cash paid in full, all of the medicine bundles for yei be chai [sic] and fire dance including masks owned by Hosteen Ray Winnie of Lukachucki [sic], AZ.

Selling these medicine bundles or jish is the wife of the late Mr. Winnie, Fanny [sic], and his granddaughter Rose, and his great granddaughter, Harriet, whose signatures are below.

The selling price is in cash of $10,000. Received by below this date.

Mr. Corrow purchased from Mrs. Winnie. In the photos, he noticed eagle and owl feathers in several of the large headdresses and ceremonial sticks bundled with small eagle feathers. After negotiations, Agent Tanner agreed to a purchase price of $70,000 for the Yei B'Chei, $50,000 for Mr. Corrow and a $20,000 commission to East–West's co-owners.

On December 9, 1994, Mr. Corrow arrived at the Albuquerque airport en route to Santa Fe carrying one large suitcase, one small suitcase, and a cardboard box. Yet once he was in Santa Fe, F.B.I. agents became worried East–West's owners had been alerted and abandoned their script for the planned buy, instead directly executing the search warrant. Agents found the two suitcases Mr. Corrow had carried to East–West, one holding Navajo religious objects, small bundles, herbs, mini prayer sticks, and other artifacts adorned with eagle feathers. Another suitcase contained eagle feathers rolled inside several cloth bundles, Yei B'Chei dance aprons, and five headdress pieces made of eagle and owl feathers. In the cardboard box was the set of twenty-two Yei B'Chei.

The government subsequently charged Mr. Corrow in a two-count indictment, Count one for trafficking in Native American cultural items in violation of 18 U.S.C. § 1170, 25 U.S.C. §§ 3001(3)(D), 3002(c), and 18 U.S.C. § 2; and Count two for selling Golden Eagle, Great Horned Owl, and Buteoine Hawk feathers protected by the [Migratory Bird Treaty Act, 16 U.S.C. §§ 701–712,] in violation of 16 U.S.C. § 703, 16 U.S.C. § 707(b)(2), and 18 U.S.C. § 2. The court rejected Mr. Corrow's pretrial motion to dismiss Count one based on its purported unconstitutional vagueness, and the trial proceeded comprised predominantly of the testimony of expert witnesses clashing over whether the Yei B'Chei constitute "cultural patrimony" protected by NAGPRA. Having concluded they do, the jury convicted Mr. Corrow of illegal trafficking in cultural items, Count one, but acquitted him of Count two, selling protected feathers, instead finding him guilty of committing the lesser included offense, possession of protected feathers. * * * The district court * * * sentenced him to two concurrent five-year probationary terms and one hundred hours of community service.

II. NAGPRA

Congress enacted NAGPRA in 1990 to achieve two [principal] objectives: to protect Native American human remains, funerary objects, sacred objects and objects of cultural patrimony presently on Federal or tribal lands; and to repatriate Native American human remains, associated funerary objects, sacred objects, and objects of cultural patrimony currently held or controlled by Federal agencies and museums. H.R.Rep. No. 101–877, 101st Cong., 2d Sess.1990, reprinted in 1990 U.S.C.C.A.N. 4367, 4368. The legislation and subsequent regulations, 43 C.F.R. §§ 10.1–10.17, provide a methodology for identifying objects; determining the rights of lineal descendants, Indian tribes and Native Hawaiian organizations; and retrieving and repatriating that property to Native American owners. NAGPRA's reach in protecting against further desecration of burial sites and restoring countless ancestral remains and cultural and sacred items to their tribal homes warrants its aspirational characterization as "human rights legislation." Jack F. Trope & Walter R. Echo–Hawk, The Native American Graves Protection and Repatriation Act: Background and Legislative History, 24 Ariz. St. L.J. 35, 37 (1992). Indeed, a Panel of National Dialogue on Museum–Native American Relations, which was convened to address the divergent interests of the museum and Native American communities, reported to Congress that "[r]espect for Native human rights is the paramount principle that should govern resolution of the issue when a claim is made." 1990 U.S.C.C.A.N. 4369–70.

Nonetheless to give teeth to this statutory mission, 18 U.S.C. § 1170 penalizes trafficking in Native American human remains and cultural items and creates a felony offense for a second or subsequent violation. Subsection 1170(b), the basis for prosecution here, states:

> Whoever <u>knowingly</u> sells, purchases, uses for profit, or transports for sale or profit any Native American cultural items obtained in violation of the Native American Grave Protection and Repatriation Act shall be fined in accordance with this title, imprisoned not more than one year, or both, and in the case of a second or subsequent violation, be fined in accordance with this title, imprisoned not more than 5 years, or both.

One must look to NAGPRA, 25 U.S.C. § 3001, for the definition of "cultural item." Section 3001(3) states:

> "cultural items" means human remains and—

> (D) "cultural patrimony" which shall mean an object having ongoing historical, traditional, or cultural importance central to the Native American group or culture itself, rather than property owned by an individual Native American, and which, therefore, cannot be alienated, appropriated, or conveyed by any individual regardless of whether or not the individual is a member of the Indian tribe or Native Hawaiian organization and such object shall have been considered inalienable by such Native American group at the time the object was separated from such group.

Cultural Patrimony

Thus, to be judged "cultural patrimony"[4] the object must have (1) ongoing historical, cultural or traditional <u>importance</u>; and (2) be considered <u>inalienable</u> by the tribe by virtue of the object's centrality in tribal culture. That is, the cultural item's essential function within the life and history of the tribe engenders its inalienability such that <u>the property cannot constitute the personal property of an individual tribal member</u>. "The key aspect of this definition is whether the property was of such central importance to the tribe or group that it was owned communally." Francis P. McManamon & Larry V. Nordby, Implementing the Native American Graves Protection and Repatriation Act, 24 Ariz. St. L.J. 217, 233–34 (1992). The regulations mirror this definition * * *

---

4. Webster's Third New International Dictionary defines "patrimony" as "anything derived from one's father or ancestors: HER-ITAGE; an inheritance from the past; an estate or property held by ancient right."

Just restating elements of "cultural patrimony"

In this prosecution, then, the definition of cultural patrimony divided into its three component parts required the government prove Mr. Corrow trafficked in an object that (1) was not owned by an individual Native American; (2) that could not be alienated, appropriated, or conveyed by an individual; and (3) had an ongoing historical, traditional, or cultural importance central to the Native American group. Mr. Corrow contends the first and second elements are unintelligible. Thus, he argues, relying upon *United States v. Agnew,* 931 F.2d 1397, 1403 (10th Cir. 1991), the definition does not comport with the due process clause of the Fourteenth Amendment because it fails to give ordinary people fair notice about what conduct is prohibited in such a manner that discourages arbitrary and discriminatory law enforcement.

In support, Mr. Corrow arrays the conflicting expert testimony, characterized by the *amicus curiae*[7] as a conflict between orthodox and moderate Navajo religious views. For the government, Alfred Yazzie, an ordained *hataali* and Navajo Nation Historic Preservation representative, testified the Yei B'Chei must remain within the four sacred mountains of the Navajo for they represented the "heartbeat" of the Navajo people. Also for the government, Harry Walters, a Navajo anthropologist, stated there is "no such thing as ownership of medicine bundles and that these are viewed as living entities." He equated ownership with use, knowing the rituals, but acknowledged often cultural items are sold because of economic pressures. For Mr. Corrow, Jackson Gillis, a medicine man from Monument Valley, testified that if no claim is made by a clan relative or other singer, the *jish* pass to the widow who must care for them. If the widow feels uncomfortable keeping the *jish,* Mr. Gillis stated she has the right to sell them. Harrison Begay, another of Mr. Corrow's expert witnesses, agreed, explaining that because the masks themselves are "alive," a widow, uneasy about their remaining unused, may sell them. Billy Yellow, another *hataali* testifying for Mr. Corrow, reiterated the traditional disposition of a *hataali*'s Yei B'Chei to a spouse, the children, and grandchildren, although he stated nobody really owns the *jish* because they are living gods.

Defense argument re: vagueness of "ownership" element

Given these conflicting views on the alienability of the Yei B'Chei, Mr. Corrow asks how an individual, even one educated in Navajo culture, indeed, one accepting the responsibility of inquiring further about the status of the item as the district court deduced from its reading of NAGPRA, can "ascertain ownership when the group itself cannot agree on that point?" The shadow cast by this question, he insists, sufficiently clouds the meaning of "cultural patrimony" to render it unconstitutional. Mr. Corrow's invocation of void-for-vagueness review, however, obfuscates both its doctrinal reach and its application to the facts of this case.

"[T]he void-for-vagueness doctrine requires that a penal statute define the criminal offense with sufficient definiteness that ordinary people can

---

7. The Antique Tribal Art Dealers Association, a trade organization promoting authenticity and ethical dealing in the sale of Native American artifacts, filed an amicus brief contending the government in this case "exploited a controversy between orthodox and moderate Navajo religious perspectives."

understand what conduct is prohibited and in a manner that does not encourage arbitrary and discriminatory enforcement." Kolender v. Lawson, 461 U.S. 352, 357 (1983). Although *Kolender* acknowledged a judicial shift from concern over deciding whether the statute provides actual notice to "the more important aspect of the vagueness doctrine ... the requirement that a legislature establish minimal guidelines to govern law enforcement," id. at 358, the legality principle, no crime or punishment without law, is the essence of a Fifth Amendment due process challenge. See 1 W. LaFave & A. Scott, Substantive Criminal Law § 3.1, at 271 (1986). That is, given the limitations of language and syntax, a statute must convey to those individuals within its purview what it purports to prohibit and how it will punish an infraction. * * *

Mr. Corrow cannot meet that burden. First, deciding whether the statute gave him fair notice, the district court found, after reviewing all of the expert testimony, Mr. Corrow is knowledgeable about Navajo traditions and culture and "would have been aware that various tribal members viewed ownership of property differently." The court cited the testimony of Ms. Charlotte Frisbie, author of *Navajo Medicine Bundles or Jish: Acquisition, Transmission and Disposition in the Past and Present* (1987). Ms. Frisbie related several calls from Mr. Corrow inquiring about the prices of certain Navajo artifacts. Although she stated he did not specifically ask her about these Yei B'Chei, she expressed her objection to dealers and commercial handlers selling Native American cultural objects in the open market. Ms. Frisbie also reminded him both of the Navajo Nation's implementing procedures to return cultural items and of the enactment of NAGPRA. Most damning, Ms. Bia, Mrs. Winnie's granddaughter, recounted Mr. Corrow's representation that he wanted to buy the Yei B'Chei to pass on to another young chanter in Utah. Reasonably, a jury could infer from that representation that Mr. Corrow appreciated some dimension of the Yei B'Chei's inherent inalienability in Navajo culture. Although Mrs. Winnie stated she believed the Yei B'Chei belonged to her, she testified, "[t]here was another man that knew the ways and he had asked of [the Yei B'Chei] but I was the one that was stalling and ended up selling it." Although this man trained with her husband, he had not offered her any money. This is not a case of an unsuspecting tourist happening upon Mrs. Winnie's hogan and innocently purchasing the set of Yei B'Chei. * * *

Surely, this evidence establishes Mr. Corrow had some notice the Yei B'Chei he purchased were powerfully connected to Navajo religion and culture. While it may be true that even the experts in that culture differed in their views on alienability, *no* expert testified it was acceptable to sell Yei B'Chei to non-Navajos who planned to resell them for a profit, the very conduct § 1170(b) penalizes. All experts testified the Yei B'Chei resided within the Four Corners of the Navajo people and acknowledged the ritual cleansing and restoration required were the Yei B'Chei to be defiled in any way. Thus, while the parameters of the designation "cultural patrimony" might be unclear in some of its applications and at its edges, there is no doubt, in this case as applied to Mr. Corrow, the Yei B'Chei were cultural items which could not be purchased for a quick $40,000 turn of profit.

* * * Consequently, even if the term cultural patrimony "might reflect some uncertainty as applied to extreme situations, the conduct for which [defendant] was prosecuted and convicted falls squarely within the core of the [Act]." United States v. Amer, 110 F.3d 873, 878 (2d Cir. 1997). * * *

Consequently, we believe Mr. Corrow had fair notice—if not of the precise words of NAGPRA—of their meaning that Native American objects "having ongoing historical, traditional, or cultural importance central to the Native American group ... rather than property owned by an individual Native American" could not be bought and sold absent criminal consequences. Moreover, contrary to Mr. Corrow's assertion, § 3001(3)(D) is not infirm because it fails to list examples of cultural items. "In short, due process does not require that citizens be provided actual notice of all criminal rules and their meanings. The Constitution is satisfied if the necessary information is reasonably obtainable by the public." United States v. Vasarajs, 908 F.2d 443, 449 (9th Cir. 1990). * * *

While not dispositive, we would add § 1170(b) includes scienter as an element of the offense ("Whoever knowingly sells, purchases, uses for profit. . . ."). "A statutory requirement that an act must be willful or purposeful may not render certain, for all purposes, a statutory definition of the crime which is in some respects uncertain. But it does relieve the statute of the objection that it punishes without warning an offense of which the accused was unaware." Screws v. United States, 325 U.S. 91, 101–02 (1945) (Douglas, J., concurring). Here, the government was required to prove Mr. Corrow knowingly used the Yei B'Chei for profit assuring his understanding of the prohibited zone of conduct. "[A] scienter requirement may mitigate a criminal law's vagueness by ensuring that it punishes only those who are aware their conduct is unlawful." Gaudreau, 860 F.2d at 360. * * *

We therefore AFFIRM the judgment of the district court.

NOTES AND QUESTIONS

1. The prohibition on individual ownership or sale of "cultural patrimony" in the Native American Graves Protection and Repatriation Act (NAGPRA) appears only in the definitional section of the Act, under the definition of "cultural patrimony" (quoted in the court's opinion). There is no separate prohibition, in the operative sections of the Act, of alienation, appropriation, or conveyance of cultural patrimony. Corrow was prosecuted under a separate provision of the federal criminal code making it a criminal offense to obtain any "cultural item" "in violation of the Native American Grave Protection and Repatriation Act." 18 U.S.C. § 1170. (Does this strike you as an overly-cryptic way to establish, as a matter of federal law, that cultural patrimony cannot be subject to conventional property rights?) Putting the two provisions together, federal law appears to require, first, a determination that items cannot be subject to private ownership or sale *as a matter of tribal law or tradition*, and then, second, a determination that

someone has attempted to acquire such an item in a manner prohibited by tribal law or tradition.

2. Under the interpretation of NAGPRA approved in the principal case, could Mrs. Fannie Winnie also be prosecuted for violating the Act? If one of the purposes of the Act is to prevent commodification of culturally significant objects, should federal prosecutors concentrate only on the demand for such objects from dealers and collectors, or should they also try to suppress the supply?

3. Another recent decision arising under NAGPRA concerned the status of the skeletal remains known as "Kennewick Man," discovered by some students on the banks of the Columbia River in Washington. Preliminary carbon dating indicated that the remains were 8,340 to 9,200 years old, predating the time when it is believed the ancestors of most of today's Native Americans migrated to the Americas. Some of the features of the skeleton were also inconsistent with most Native American skeletal remains. The Interior Department ordered that the skeletal remains be repatriated to area tribes under NAGPRA. When this decision was challenged by a group of scientists anxious to study the remains, the Ninth Circuit reversed. Bonnichsen v. United States, 357 F.3d 962 (9th Cir. 2004). The court held that the Act applies only to remains affiliated with presently existing tribes, peoples, or cultures, and there was no evidence that any presently existing tribe could trace its ancestry back 9,000 years.

4. The Supreme Court has been unsympathetic to claims seeking protection for culturally significant property as a matter of constitutional law. In *Lyng v. Northwest Indian Cemetery Protective Ass'n*, 485 U.S. 439 (1988), for example, the Court rejected the claim that building a road through an Indian burial ground would violate the Free Exercise rights of Native Americans. Can you explain why a majoritarian institution like Congress would be more solicitous of the rights of cultural minorities than a court, which is supposed to be more sensitive to minority rights? For a variety of views, see, e.g., Ellen Adair Page, The Scope of the Free Exercise Clause: *Lyng v. Northwest Indian Cemetery Protective Association*, 68 N.C. L. Rev. 410, 421 (1990) (arguing for stricter judicial test); Joseph William Singer, Property and Coercion in Federal Indian Law: The Conflict between Critical and Complacent Pragmatism, 63 S. Cal. L. Rev. 1821 (1990) (criticizing version of pragmatism in *Lyng* for being too complacent and majority-oriented); Marcia Yablon, Property Rights and Sacred Sites: Federal Regulatory Responses to American Indian Religious Claims on Public Land, 113 Yale L.J. 1623 (2004) (arguing for administrative rather than judicial protection).

5. Although NAGPRA is unusual in prohibiting any attempt to treat cultural patrimony as private property, restrictions on the use and development of culturally significant properties are more common. Many cities, for example, have enacted historic preservation laws that limit the ability of owners of properties of cultural or historical significance to make modifications to these properties. We will encounter a famous constitutional challenge to the New York City preservation ordinance in Chapter XII.

B.   ACADEMIC PERSPECTIVES ON THE DOMAIN OF PROPERTY

Before moving from personhood to public rights, we offer some academic perspectives on the general question of what values should be subject to ownership. The first excerpt, by a leading law-and-economics pioneer, offers a positive theory of the evolution of property rights. Harold Demsetz attempts to explain, in economic terms, when and why property rights emerge in resources that previously were regarded as not being subject to ownership. Margaret Jane Radin, our second author (with excerpts from two different articles), is concerned with normative rather than positive theory. In other words, she attempts to outline a moral basis for regarding certain things as inappropriate subjects for treatment as property.

Harold Demsetz, *Toward a Theory of Property Rights*, 57 AM. ECON. REV. 347–48, 350–58 (1967) (Papers & Proceedings)

* * * The Concept and Role of Property Rights

In the world of Robinson Crusoe property rights play no role. Property rights are an instrument of society and derive their significance from the fact that they help a man form those expectations which he can reasonably hold in his dealings with others. These expectations find expression in the laws, customs, and mores of a society. An owner of property rights possesses the consent of fellowmen to allow him to act in particular ways. An owner expects the community to prevent others from interfering with his actions, provided that these actions are not prohibited in the specifications of his rights.

It is important to note that property rights convey the right to benefit or harm oneself or others. Harming a competitor by producing superior products may be permitted, while shooting him may not. A man may be permitted to benefit himself by shooting an intruder but be prohibited from selling below a price floor. It is clear, then, that property rights specify how persons may be benefited and harmed, and, therefore, who must pay whom to modify the actions taken by persons. The recognition of this leads easily to the close relationship between property rights and externalities.

Externality is an ambiguous concept. For the purposes of this paper, the concept includes external costs, external benefits, and pecuniary as well as nonpecuniary externalities. No harmful or beneficial effect is external to the world. Some person or persons always suffer or enjoy these effects. What converts a harmful or beneficial effect into an externality is that the cost of bringing the effect to bear on the decisions of one or more of the interacting persons is too high to make it worthwhile, and this is what the term shall mean here. "Internalizing" such effects refers to a process, usually a change in property rights, that enables these effects to bear (in greater degree) on all interacting persons.

A primary function of property rights is that of guiding incentives to achieve a greater internalization of externalities. Every cost and benefit associated with social interdependencies is a potential externality. One condition is necessary to make costs and benefits externalities. The cost of a transaction in the rights between the parties (internalization) must exceed the gains from internalization. In general, transacting cost can be large relative to gains because of "natural" difficulties in trading or they can be large because of legal reasons. In a lawful society the prohibition of voluntary negotiations makes the cost of transacting infinite. Some costs and benefits are not taken into account by users of resources whenever externalities exist, but allowing transactions increases the degree to which internalization takes place. * * *

The element needed for Externality

The Emergence of Property Rights

If the main allocative function of property rights is the internalization of beneficial and harmful effects, then the emergence of property rights can be understood best by their association with the emergence of new or different beneficial and harmful effects. *(that will thus be internalized by the new rights)*

Changes in knowledge result in changes in production functions, market values, and aspirations. New techniques, new ways of doing the same things, and doing new things—all invoke harmful and beneficial effects to which society has not been accustomed. It is my thesis in this part of the paper that the emergence of new property rights takes place in response to the desires of the interacting persons for adjustment to new benefit-cost possibilities.

Thesis

re: cause of new prop. rights

The thesis can be restated in a slightly different fashion: property rights develop to internalize externalities when the gains of internalization become larger than the cost of internalization. Increased internalization, in the main, results from changes in economic values, changes which stem from the development of new technology and the opening of new markets, changes to which old property rights are poorly attuned. A proper interpretation of this assertion requires that account be taken of a community's preferences for private ownership. Some communities will have less well-developed private ownership systems and more highly developed state ownership systems. But, given a community's tastes in this regard, the emergence of new private or state owned property rights will be in response to changes in technology and relative prices.

I do not mean to assert or to deny that the adjustments in property rights which take place need be the result of a conscious endeavor to cope with new externality problems. These adjustments have arisen in Western societies largely as a result of gradual changes in social mores and in common law precedents. At each step of this adjustment process, it is unlikely that externalities per se were consciously related to the issue being resolved. These legal and moral experiments may be hit-and-miss procedures to some extent but in a society that weights the achievement of efficiency heavily, their viability in the long run will depend on how well they modify behavior to accommodate to the externalities associated with important changes in technology or market values.

A rigorous test of this assertion will require extensive and detailed empirical work. A broad range of examples can be cited that are consistent with it: the development of air rights, renters' rights, rules for liability in automobile accidents, etc. In this part of the discussion, I shall present one group of such examples in some detail. They deal with the development of private property rights in land among American Indians. These examples are broad ranging and come fairly close to what can be called convincing evidence in the field of anthropology.

The question of private ownership of land among aboriginals has held a fascination for anthropologists. It has been one of the intellectual battle-grounds in the attempt to assess the "true nature" of man unconstrained by the "artificialities" of civilization. In the process of carrying on this debate, information has been uncovered that bears directly on the thesis with which we are now concerned. What appears to be accepted as a classic treatment and a high point of this debate is Eleanor Leacock's memoir on *The Montagnais "Hunting Territory" and the Fur Trade*.[3] Leacock's research followed that of Frank G. Speck[4] who had discovered that the Indians of the Labrador Peninsula had a long-established tradition of property in land. This finding was at odds with what was known about the Indians of the American Southwest and it prompted Leacock's study of the Montagnes who inhabited large regions around Quebec.

Leacock clearly established the fact that a close relationship existed, both historically and geographically, between the development of private rights in land and the development of the commercial fur trade. The factual basis of this correlation has gone unchallenged. However, to my knowledge, no theory relating privacy of land to the fur trade has yet been articulated. The factual material uncovered by Speck and Leacock fits the thesis of this paper well, and in doing so, it reveals clearly the role played by property right adjustments in taking account of what economists have often cited as an example of an externality—the overhunting of game.

Because of the lack of control over hunting by others, it is in no person's interest to invest in increasing or [maintaining] the stock of game. Overly intensive hunting takes place. Thus a successful hunt is viewed as imposing external costs on subsequent hunters—costs that are not taken into account fully in the determination of the extent of hunting and of animal husbandry.

Before the fur trade became established, hunting was carried on primarily for purposes of food and the relatively few furs that were required for the hunter's family. The externality was clearly present. Hunting could be practiced freely and was carried on without assessing its

3. Eleanor Leacock, American Anthropologist (American Anthropological Asso.), Vol. 56, No. 5, Part 2, Memoir No. 78.

4. Cf., Frank G. Speck, "The Basis of American Indian Ownership of Land," Old Penn Weekly Rev. (Univ. of Pennsylvania), Jan. 16, 1915, pp. 491–95.

impact on other hunters. But these external effects were of such small significance that it did not pay for anyone to take them into account. There did not exist anything resembling private ownership in land. And in the *Jesuit Relations*, particularly Le Jeune's record of the winter he spent with the Montagnes in 1633–34 and in the brief account given by Father Druilletes in 1647–48, Leacock finds no evidence of private land holdings. Both accounts indicate a socioeconomic organization in which private rights to land are not well developed.

We may safely surmise that the advent of the fur trade had two immediate consequences. First, the value of furs to the Indians was increased considerably. Second, and as a result, the scale of hunting activity rose sharply. Both consequences must have increased considerably the importance of the externalities associated with free hunting. The property right system began to change, and it changed specifically in the direction required to take account of the economic effects made important by the fur trade. The geographical or distributional evidence collected by Leacock indicates an unmistakable correlation between early centers of fur trade and the oldest and most complete development of the private hunting territory.

> By the beginning of the eighteenth century, we begin to have clear evidence that territorial hunting and trapping arrangements by individual families were developing in the area around Quebec.... The earliest references to such arrangements in this region indicates a purely temporary allotment of hunting territories. They [Algonkians and Iroquois] divide themselves into several bands in order to hunt more efficiently. It was their custom to appropriate pieces of land about two leagues square for each group to hunt exclusively. Ownership of beaver houses, however, had already become established, and when discovered, they were marked. A starving Indian could kill and eat another's beaver if he left the fur and the tail.[5]

The next step toward the hunting territory was probably a seasonal allotment system. An anonymous account written in 1723 states that the "principle of the Indians is to mark off the hunting ground selected by them by blazing the trees with their crests so that they may never encroach on each other.... By the middle of the century these allotted territories were relatively stabilized."[6]

The principle that associates property right changes with the emergence of new and reevaluation of old harmful and beneficial effects suggests in this instance that the fur trade made it economic to encourage the husbanding of fur-bearing animals. Husbanding requires the ability to prevent poaching and this, in turn, suggests that socioeconomic changes in property in hunting land will take place. The chain of reasoning is consistent with the evidence cited above. Is it inconsistent with the absence of similar rights in property among the southwestern Indians?

5. Eleanor Leacock, op. cit., p. 15.   **6.** Eleanor Leacock, op. cit., p. 15.

Two factors suggest that the thesis is consistent with the absence of similar rights among the Indians of the southwestern plains. The first of these is that there were no plains animals of commercial importance comparable to the fur-bearing animals of the forest, at least not until cattle arrived with Europeans. The second factor is that animals of the plains are primarily grazing species whose habit is to wander over wide tracts of land. The value of establishing boundaries to private hunting territories is thus reduced by the relatively high cost of preventing the animals from moving to adjacent parcels. Hence both the value and cost of establishing private hunting lands in the Southwest are such that we would expect little development along these lines. The externality was just not worth taking into account.

The lands of the Labrador Peninsula shelter forest animals whose habits are considerably different from those of the plains. Forest animals confine their territories to relatively small areas, so that the cost of internalizing the effects of husbanding these animals is considerably reduced. This reduced cost, together with the higher commercial value of fur-bearing forest animals, made it productive to establish private hunting lands. Frank G. Speck finds that family proprietorship among the Indians of the Peninsula included retaliation against trespass. Animal resources were husbanded. Sometimes conservation practices were carried on extensively. Family hunting territories were divided into quarters. Each year the family hunted in a different quarter in rotation, leaving a tract in the center as a sort of bank, not to be hunted over unless forced to do so by a shortage in the regular tract. * * *

NOTES AND QUESTIONS

1. Demsetz's theory is built around the costs and benefits of property rights. One such cost is the cost of excluding others—marking boundary lines, putting up fences, suing trespassers. Robert Ellickson points out that one reason private ownership based on exclusion is cheaper than communal ownership and mutual monitoring is that the technologies for monitoring are cheaper in the case of exclusion:

> Because private property in land necessitates the policing of boundaries, advances in surveying and fencing techniques may enhance the comparative efficiency of the institution. Preliterate societies developed many simple technologies that a landowner could use to detect and deter trespassers. During Hammurabi's reign around 1750 B.C., pegs were used to mark borders. Cairns, dikes, and stone walls are even more graphic and immovable. In social environments in which neighbors are inclined to cooperate, physically marked boundaries, if uncontroversially placed, are largely self-enforcing. A four-year old can understand the convention that one does not cross a marked boundary. By contrast, the internal work rules that govern behavior within group-owned land are not nearly as plain to observers.

For millennia, absentee owners have employed simple technologies such as hedges, moats, and impregnable fencing to keep out persons and animals that do not respect boundaries. In addition, domesticated dogs, especially ones that instinctively bark at or attack strangers, are superb boundary defenders. By contrast, dogs are quite useless in enforcing a group's internal rules of conduct. Can a dog be trained to bark when a familiar person has shirked or pilfered? A modern-day landowner intent on detecting boundary violations can resort, in lieu of a dog, to an inexpensive electronic motion detector. "Shirking detectors"—devices that would sound an alarm when a worker was simply going through the motions—have yet to be invented.

Robert C. Ellickson, Property in Land, 102 Yale L.J. 1315, 1328–29 (1993). Is excluding others always cheaper than policing the behavior of those with permitted access? Ellickson notes that things tend to become less clear when the externalities involve larger rather than smaller events. Also, many (most?) assets are best used by more than one person. How is this achieved?

2.   If an increase in the value of an asset (and hence the stakes of a resource conflict) can lead to the emergence of property rights, the reverse should also be true: If an asset becomes less valuable, will less effort be expended on protecting property rights in the asset, and in extreme situations resulting in abandonment of the asset into the public domain? Such cases have been documented. In an interesting study of property rights in the nineteenth-century American West, Anderson and Hill show that as land and animals increased and then decreased in value, property rights to them became correspondingly more and less articulated. Terry L. Anderson & P.J. Hill, The Evolution of Property Rights: A Study of the American West, 18 J.L. & Econ. 163, 170–71, 172–76 (1975). Interestingly, Demsetz's example of property rights in beavers shows a similar pattern; as prices for beaver pelts have decreased in recent years, unclaimed beavers in Manitoba are proliferating to the point where they are often considered pests, with a government bounty on their heads. See Beavers' Dual Role: National Icon and Huge Pest, N.Y. Times, Mar. 31, 2001, at A4.

3.   Notwithstanding the confident tone of discussion in this article, the nature of property rights in beavers among the Naskapi and Montagne tribes in Labrador actually presents some interesting complexities. Although barely mentioned in Demsetz's article, the rights to beaver hunting territories were subject to important qualifications. Individuals had a right to take anyone's beavers as long as it was for the individual's own consumption. This may have served as an institutionalized kind of insurance against famine. But this reintroduces some of the common-pool incentives to overuse beavers, and the rule about leaving the pelt is not easy to enforce. According to John C. McManus, An Economic Analysis of Indian Behavior in the North American Fur Trade, 32 J. Econ. Hist. 36 (1972), the beaver population decreased after the rise of the fur trade, whereas with exclusive rights one would expect a stable or growing population. In addition, the Hudson Bay Company had to incur costs to conserve

the beavers, which should not have been necessary according to Demsetz's model. In a sense, the own-consumption exception made the beavers into a semicommons—a regime combining common and private property and in which the two elements interact. Here communal rights for use as food impacted the beavers as private property in the fur trade. Henry E. Smith, Semicommon Property Rights and Scattering in the Open Fields, 29 J. Legal Stud. 131, 143 (2000). For a more systematic study of property rights in traditional societies, see Martin J. Bailey, Approximate Optimality of Aboriginal Property Rights, 35 J.L. & Econ. 183 (1992).

4. How did the property rights among the Native Americans "evolve?" How do property rights ever evolve? Demsetz abstracts away from the processes that supply property rights and focuses only on the demand side: Where there is a need for property something emerges. Others have tried to explore the supply of property rights. Some of these accounts emphasize that property starts out as a social norm among the relevant actors, and then is embodied in a more official rule. Recall in this connection the materials in Chapter II about the possible efficiency of custom and its role in common-law adjudication. Other accounts suggest that certain key players or entrepreneurs who stand to gain disproportionately will lobby for the recognition of property rights. But if property comes into existence only if those who stand to benefit disproportionately seek it, what reason do we have for being optimistic that property will serve to internalize externalities? Why won't those seeking to establish property rights simply grab assets and impose costs on others? For some discussion of these issues, see Gary D. Libecap, Contracting for Property Rights (1989); Stuart Banner, Transitions between Property Regimes, 31 J. Legal Stud. S359 (2002); Saul Levmore, Two Stories about the Evolution of Property Rights, 31 J. Legal Stud. S421 (2002).

5. The Demsetzian approach would lead one to expect property rights to emerge as new resource conflicts arise. How if at all would Demsetz explain the decisions in Part A of this Chapter dealing with property rights in corneas, sperm, and human cell lines? Do these decisions, taken as a whole, suggest that property rights in body parts and materials are gradually emerging as technology develops new and more valuable uses for these things? Does the Demsetzian model shed any light on the emergence of artists' moral rights or prohibitions on sales of cultural patrimony? Or do these developments defy explanation in purely economic terms?

6. Are measurable costs and benefits all that the law of property responds to? Consider the following for a very different perspective.

Margaret Jane Radin, *Property and Personhood*, 34 STAN. L. REV. 957, 959–61, 965–66, 968–70, 986–87 (1982)

* * * Most people possess certain objects they feel are almost part of themselves. These objects are closely bound up with personhood because they are part of the way we constitute ourselves as continuing personal entities in the world. They may be as different as people are different, but some common examples might be a wedding ring, a portrait, an heirloom, or a house.

One may gauge the strength or significance of someone's relationship with an object by the kind of pain that would be occasioned by its loss. On this view, an object is closely related to one's personhood if its loss causes pain that cannot be relieved by the object's replacement. If so, that particular object is bound up with the holder. For instance, if a wedding ring is stolen from a jeweler, insurance proceeds can reimburse the jeweler, but if a wedding ring is stolen from a loving wearer, the price of a replacement will not restore the status quo—perhaps no amount of money can do so.

The opposite of holding an object that has become a part of oneself is holding an object that is perfectly replaceable with other goods of equal market value. One holds such an object for purely instrumental reasons. The archetype of such a good is, of course, money, which is almost always held only to buy other things. A dollar is worth no more than what one chooses to buy with it, and one dollar bill is as good as another. Other examples are the wedding ring in the hands of the jeweler, the automobile in the hands of the dealer, the land in the hands of the developer, or the apartment in the hands of the commercial landlord. I shall call these theoretical opposites—property that is bound up with a person and property that is held purely instrumentally—personal property and fungible property respectively. * * *

Once we admit that a person can be bound up with an external "thing" in some constitutive sense, we can argue that by virtue of this connection the person should be accorded broad liberty with respect to control over that "thing." But here liberty follows from property for personhood; personhood is the basic concept, not liberty. Of course, if liberty is viewed not as freedom from interference, or "negative freedom," but rather as some positive will that by acting on the external world is constitutive of the person, then liberty comes closer to capturing the idea of the self being intimately bound up with things in the external world.

It intuitively appears that there is such a thing as property for personhood because people become bound up with "things." But this intuitive view does not compel the conclusion that property for personhood deserves moral recognition or legal protection, because arguably there is bad as well as good in being bound up with external objects. If there is a traditional understanding that a well-developed person must invest herself to some extent in external objects, there is no less a traditional understanding that one should not invest oneself in the wrong way or to too great an extent in external objects. Property is damnation as well as salvation, object-fetishism as well as moral groundwork. In this view, the relationship between the shoe fetishist and his shoe will not be respected like that between the spouse and her wedding ring. At the extreme, anyone who lives only for material objects is considered not to be a well-developed person, but rather to be lacking some important attribute of humanity.

* * * [L]et us begin with the person conceived as bodily continuity. Locke says that "every Man has a Property in his own Person," from which it immediately follows that "[t]he Labour of his Body, and the Work of his

hands ... are properly his.''[28] Though * * * Locke elsewhere considers the person as reflective consciousness and memory, he may well mean here that one literally owns one's limbs and hence must own their product. If not, perhaps property in one's person should be understood to mean simply that an individual has an entitlement to be a person or to be treated as a person. This would probably include the right to self-preservation on which Locke bases the right to appropriate.

If it makes sense to say that one owns one's body, then, on the embodiment theory of personhood, the body is quintessentially personal property because it is literally constitutive of one's personhood. If the body is property, then objectively it is property for personhood. This line of thinking leads to a property theory for the tort of assault and battery: Interference with my body is interference with my personal property. Certain external things, for example, the shirt off my back, may also be considered personal property if they are closely enough connected with the body.

The idea of property in one's body presents some interesting paradoxes. In some cases, bodily parts can become fungible commodities, just as other personal property can become fungible with a change in its relationship with the owner: Blood can be withdrawn and used in a transfusion; hair can be cut off and used by a wigmaker; organs can be transplanted. On the other hand, bodily parts may be too "personal" to be property at all. We have an intuition that property necessarily refers to something in the outside world, separate from oneself. Though the general idea of property for personhood means that the boundary between person and thing cannot be a bright line, still the idea of property seems to require some perceptible boundary, at least insofar as property requires the notion of thing, and the notion of thing requires separation from self. This intuition makes it seem appropriate to call parts of the body property only after they have been removed from the system. * * *

Finally, let us consider the view that what is important in personhood is a continuing character structure encompassing future projects or plans, as well as past events and feelings. The general idea of expressing one's character through property is quite familiar. It is frequently remarked that dogs resemble their masters; the attributes of many material goods, such as cars and clothes, can proclaim character traits of their owners. Of course, many would say that becoming too enthralled with property takes away time and energy needed to develop other faculties constitutive of personhood. But, for example, if you express your generosity by giving away fruits that grow in your orchard, then if the orchard ceases to be your property, you are no longer able to express your character. This at least suggests that property may have an important relationship to certain character traits that partly constitute a person.

28. John Locke, Second Treatise of Government (New York 1952) (6th ed. London 1764), ch. V, § 27.

This view of personhood also gives us insight into why protecting people's "expectations" of continuing control over objects seems so important. If an object you now control is bound up in your future plans or in your anticipation of your future self, and it is partly these plans for your own continuity that make you a person, then your personhood depends on the realization of these expectations. * * *

We must construct sufficiently objective criteria to identify close object relations that should be excluded from recognition as personal property because the particular nature of the relationship works to hinder rather than to support healthy self-constitution. A key to distinguishing these cases is "healthy." We can tell the difference between personal property and fetishism the same way we can tell the difference between a healthy person and a sick person, or between a sane person and an insane person. In fact, the concepts of sanity and personhood are intertwined: At some point we question whether the insane person is a person at all. Using the word "we" here, however, implies that a consensus exists and can be discerned. Because I seek a source of objective judgments about property for personhood, but do not wish to rely on natural law or simple moral realism, consensus must be a sufficient source of objective moral criteria—and I believe it can be, sometimes, without destroying the meaning of objectivity. In the context of property for personhood, then, a "thing" that someone claims to be bound up with nevertheless should not be treated as personal vis-à-vis other people's claimed rights and interests when there is an objective moral consensus that to be bound up with that category of "thing" is inconsistent with personhood or healthy self-constitution. _____

as opposed to a fetish of the object

Judgments of insanity or fetishism are both made on the basis of the minimum indicia it takes to recognize an individual as one of us. There does not seem to be the same reason to restrain a private fetishist as there would be to restrain an insane person prone to violence against others. But the restraint of denying the fetishist's property special recognition as personal is less severe than that imposed on someone deemed violently insane. To refuse on moral grounds to call fetishist property personal is not to refuse to call it property at all. The immediate consequence of denying personal status to something is merely to treat that thing as fungible property, and hence to deny only those claims that might rely on a preferred status of personal property.

A broader aspect of the problem of fetishism is suggested by Marx's "fetishism of commodities."[47] Marx attributed power in a market society to the commodities that form the market. He believed that people become subordinate in their relations to these commodities. In other words, under capitalism property itself is anti-personhood.

Even if one does not accept that all capitalist market relations with objects destroy personhood, it is probably true that most people view the caricature capitalist with distaste. Most people might consider her lacking in some essential attribute of personhood, such as the capacity to respect

47. Karl Marx, Capital ch. I (S. Moore
& E. Aveling trans. 1889).

other people or the environment. If there is some moral cut-off point, beyond which one is attached too much or in the wrong way to property, the extent to which someone may emulate the caricature capitalist and still claim property for personhood is not clear, but is not unlimited. Although the caricature capitalist cannot express her nature without control over a vast quantity of things and other people, her need for this control to constitute herself the complete capitalist could not objectively be recognized as personal property because at some point there is an objective moral consensus that such control is destroying personhood rather than fostering it. * * *

The personhood dichotomy comes about in the following way: A general justification of property entitlements in terms of their relationship to personhood could hold that the rights that come within the general justification form a continuum from fungible to personal. It then might hold that those rights near one end of the continuum—fungible property rights—can be overridden in some cases in which those near the other—personal property rights—cannot be. This is to argue not that fungible property rights are unrelated to personhood, but simply that distinctions are sometimes warranted depending upon the character or strength of the connection. Thus, the personhood perspective generates a hierarchy of entitlements: The more closely connected with personhood, the stronger the entitlement.

Does it make sense to speak of two levels of property, personal and fungible? I think the answer is yes in many situations, no in many others. Since the personhood perspective depends partly on the subjective nature of the relationships between person and thing, it makes more sense to think of a continuum that ranges from a thing indispensable to someone's being to a thing wholly interchangeable with money. Many relationships between persons and things will fall somewhere in the middle of this continuum. Perhaps the entrepreneur factory owner has ownership of a particular factory and its machines bound up with her being to some degree. If a dichotomy telescoping this continuum to two end points is to be useful, it must be because within a given social context certain types of person-thing relationships are understood to fall close to one end or the other of the continuum, so that decisionmakers within that social context can use the dichotomy as a guide to determine which property is worthier of protection. For example, in our social context a house that is owned by someone who resides there is generally understood to be toward the personal end of the continuum. There is both a positive sense that people are bound up with their homes and a normative sense that this is not fetishistic. * * *

NOTES AND QUESTIONS

1. Radin introduces the distinction between property for personhood and fungible property in order to distinguish between the degrees of protection property should receive in different contexts. For example, she argues that the government should have a higher burden of justification to

take an occupied home by eminent domain (see Chapter XII) than to take industrial, commercial, or agricultural property. But as she briefly suggests, the personhood perspective can also be used to argue that certain kinds of objects that are intensely connected to personhood should not be considered property at all.

2.   Radin distinguishes good personhood relations from bad ones based on the idea of fetishism. Is this notion very clear? How much of a consensus on these matters is there? Should there be? Is Radin right that denying strong property protection is not coercive to those whose property relations are deemed to be fetishistic? What would Radin make of the PBS program "Antiques Roadshow," in which people typically bring in various family heirlooms, patiently endure a longwinded mini-lecture on the object's origins and significance, and then rejoice if the expert gives a higher-than-expected price estimate? There is no suggestion that the participants intend to sell the heirlooms. But does their intense interest in the monetary valuation of the objects at least suggest that the interplay between "personhood" values and "fungible" values is more complex than Radin's account implies?

3.   Which of the various things at issue in the cases in Part A, supra, should be regarded as property for personhood as opposed to being either fungible or fetishistic property: corneas taken from one's deceased children; cells taken from one's spleen; frozen sperm belonging to one's father; a work of art produced for and transferred to a client; and Yei B'Chei used in Navaho religious ceremonies? Even if all these things are plausibly regarded as closely linked to personhood, is it clear that personhood concerns are advanced by denying them some or all of the traditional attributes of ownership? Could one argue that the persons for whom these items are personally important are more likely to find their interests disregarded or abused if these things are *not* regarded as property?

4.   Radin has revised her views, situating them in philosophical pragmatism, and has offered a response to critics in Margaret Jane Radin, Reinterpreting Property 1–34 (1993).

ANTI–COMMODIFICATION AND INALIENABILITY RULES

Calabresi and Melamed, whom you met briefly in Chapter I, not only introduced the concepts of property rules and liability rules, but also the concept of "inalienability rules." Guido Calabresi & A. Douglas Melamed, Property Rules, Liability Rules, and Inalienability: One View of the Cathedral, 85 Harv. L. Rev. 1089, 1111–15, 1123–24 (1972). These they defined as rules that prohibit the transfer of an entitlement between a willing buyer and willing seller, in some or all circumstances. An alternative characterization of the rulings in many of the cases in this Chapter is not that they deny the existence of property in particular resources, but rather they conclude that the entitlements in question should be protected by an inalienability rule.

Why might it make sense to recognize property in certain things but make them inalienable? Calabresi and Melamed suggest that such an approach might be justified by a variety of rationales. Such a rule might reduce externalities in some contexts, for example if the transferee would likely use the thing in such a way as to impose harms on third parties. They also suggest that inalienability might be justified by what they called "moralisms": "If Taney is allowed to sell himself into slavery, or to take undue risks of becoming penniless, or to sell a kidney, Marshall may be harmed, simply because Marshall is a sensitive man who is made unhappy by seeing slaves, paupers or persons die because they have sold a kidney." Id. at 1112. Finally, they suggest that inalienability rules may be justified by paternalism, if we conclude that "a person may be better off if he is prohibited from bargaining." Id. at 1113–14.

Subsequent commentators have offered other rationales for inalienability rules. Susan Rose–Ackerman argues that such rules may be justified by imperfect information. For example, a rule that blood may be donated but not sold may generate better information about the quality of the blood supply. "If it is difficult for hospitals to judge whether blood contains the dangerous hepatitis virus, then ideally one would design a system that gives contributors an incentive to reveal any past cases of hepatitis." Susan Rose–Ackerman, Inalienability and the Theory of Property Rights, 85 Colum. L. Rev. 931, 945–46 (1985); see also Richard Titmuss, The Gift Relationship: From Human Body to Social Policy (1971). Richard Epstein emphasizes that inalienability rules may be a response to common-pool problems—"those contexts in which one person is not the exclusive owner of a single resource, but shares it in indefinite proportions with other claimants." Richard A. Epstein. Why Restrain Alienation?, 85 Colum. L. Rev. 970, 978 (1985). These sorts of situations create a danger of overconsumption or excessive withdrawal of resources from the common pool—often termed the "Tragedy of the Commons" (see Chapter II). Restraints on alienation can be one tool for minimizing these dangers.

Margaret Jane Radin, whom you encountered immediately above in the excerpt on "Property and Personhood," has also turned her sights more specifically on the problem of inalienability rules.

Margaret Jane Radin, *Market–Inalienability*, 100 HARV. L. REV. 1849, 1909–10, 1912, 1915–17 (1987)

* * * If some people wish to sell something that is identifiably personal, why not let them? In a market society, whatever some people wish to buy and others wish to sell is deemed alienable. Under these circumstances, we must formulate an affirmative case for market-inalienability, so that no one may choose to make fungible—commodify—a personal attribute, right, or thing. In this Section, I propose and evaluate three possible methods of justifying market-inalienability based on personhood: a prophylactic argument, assimilation to prohibition, and a domino theory.

The method of justification that correlates most readily with traditional liberal pluralism is a prophylactic argument. For the liberal it makes sense to countenance both selling and sharing of personal things as the holder freely chooses. If an item of property is personal, however, sometimes the circumstances under which the holder places it on the market might arouse suspicion that her act is coerced. Given that we cannot know whether anyone really intends to cut herself off from something personal by commodifying it, our suspicions might sometimes justify banning sales. The risk of harm to the seller's personhood in cases in which coerced transactions are permitted (especially if the thing sought to be commodified is normally very important to personhood), and the great difficulties involved in trying to scrutinize every transaction closely, may sometimes outweigh the harm that a ban would impose on would-be sellers who are in fact uncoerced. A prophylactic rule aims to ensure free choice—negative liberty—by the best possible coercion-avoidance mechanism under conditions of uncertainty. This prophylactic argument is one way for a liberal to justify, for example, the ban on selling oneself into slavery. We normally view such commodification as so destructive of personhood that we would readily presume all instances of it to be coerced. We would not wish, therefore, to have a rule creating a rebuttable presumption that such transactions are uncoerced (as with ordinary contracts), nor even a rule that would scrutinize such transactions case-by-case for voluntariness, because the risk of harm to personhood in the coerced transactions we might mistakenly see as voluntary is so great that we would rather risk constraining the exercise of choice by those (if any) who really wish to enslave themselves.

A liberal pluralist might use a prophylactic justification to prevent poor people from selling their children, sexual services, or body parts. The liberal would argue that an appropriate conception of coercion should, with respect to selling these things, include the desperation of poverty. Poor people should not be forced to give up personal things because the relinquishment diminishes them as persons, contrary to the liberal regime of respect for persons. We should presume that such transactions are not the result of free choice. * * *

A second method of justifying market-inalienability assimilates it to prohibition. If we accept that the commodified object is different from the "same" thing noncommodified and embedded in personal relationships, then market-inalienability is a prohibition of the commodified version, resting on some moral requirement that it not exist. What might be the basis of such a moral requirement? Something might be prohibited in its market form because it both creates and exposes wealth-and-class-based contingencies for obtaining things that are critical to life itself—for example, health care—and thus undermines a commitment to the sanctity of life. Another reason for prohibition might be that the use of market rhetoric, in conceiving of the "good" and understanding the interactions of people respecting it, creates and fosters an inferior conception of human flourishing. For example, we accept an inferior conception of personhood (one allied to the extreme view of negative freedom) if we suppose people may freely choose to commodify themselves. * * *

A third method of justifying market-inalienability, the domino theory, envisions a slippery slope leading to market domination. The domino theory assumes that for some things, the noncommodified version is morally preferable; it also assumes that the commodified and noncommodified versions of some interactions cannot coexist. To commodify some things is simply to preclude their noncommodified analogues from existing. Under this theory, the existence of some commodified sexual interactions will contaminate or infiltrate everyone's sexuality so that all sexual relationships will become commodified. If it is morally required that noncommodified sex be possible, market-inalienability of sexuality would be justified. This result can be conceived of as the opposite of a prohibition: there is assumed to exist some moral requirement that a certain "good" be socially available. The domino theory thus supplies an answer (as the prohibition theory does not) to the liberal question why people should not be permitted to choose both market and nonmarket interactions: the noncommodified version is morally preferable when we cannot have both.

We can now see how the prohibition and domino theories are connected. The prohibition theory focuses on the importance of excluding from social life commodified versions of certain "goods"—such as love, friendship, and sexuality—whereas the domino theory focuses on the importance for social life of maintaining the noncommodified versions. The prohibition theory stresses the wrongness of commodification—its alienation and degradation of the person—and the domino theory stresses the rightness of noncommodification in creating the social context for the proper expression and fostering of personhood. If one explicitly adopts both prongs of this commitment to personhood, the prohibition and domino theories merge.
* * *

Often commodification is put forward as a solution to powerlessness or oppression, as in the suggestion that women be permitted to sell sexual and reproductive services. * * * The argument that commodification empowers women is that recognition of these alienable entitlements will enable a needy group—poor women—to improve their relatively powerless, oppressed condition, an improvement that would be beneficial to personhood.
* * *

The rejoinder is that, on the contrary, commodification will harm personhood by powerfully symbolizing, legitimating, and enforcing class division and gender oppression. It will create the two forms of alienation that correlate with commodification of personal things. Women will partly internalize the notion that their persons and their attributes are separate, thus creating the pain of a divided self. To the extent that this self-conception is not internalized, women will be alienated from the dominant order that, by allowing commodification, sees them in this light. Moreover, commodification will exacerbate, not ameliorate, oppression and powerlessness, because of the social disapproval connected with marketing one's body. * * *

These conflicting arguments illuminate the problem with the prophylactic argument for market-inalienability. If we now permit commodification, we may exacerbate the oppression of women—the suppliers. If we now disallow commodification—without what I have called the welfare-rights corollary, or large-scale redistribution of social wealth and power—we force women to remain in circumstances that they themselves believe are worse than becoming sexual commodity-suppliers. Thus, the alternatives seem subsumed by a need for social progress, yet we must choose some regime now in order to make progress. This dilemma of transition is the double bind.

The double bind has two main consequences. First, if we cannot respect personhood either by permitting sales or by banning sales, justice requires that we consider changing the circumstances that create the dilemma. We must consider wealth and power redistribution. Second, we still must choose a regime for the meantime, the transition, in nonideal circumstances. To resolve the double bind, we have to investigate particular problems separately; decisions must be made (and remade) for each thing that some people desire to sell.

If we have reason to believe with respect to a particular thing that the domino theory might hold—commodification for some means commodification for all—we would have reason to choose market-inalienability. But the double bind means that if we choose market-inalienability, we might deprive a class of poor and oppressed people of the opportunity to have more money with which to buy adequate food, shelter, and health care in the market, and hence deprive them of a better chance to lead a humane life. Those who gain from the market-inalienability, on the other hand, might be primarily people whose wealth and power make them comfortable enough to be concerned about the inroads on the general quality of life that commodification would make. Yet, taking a slightly longer view, commodification threatens the personhood of everyone, not just those who can now afford to concern themselves about it. Whether this elitism in market-inalienability should make us risk the dangers of commodification will depend upon the dangers of each case.

NOTES AND QUESTIONS

1. Consider again the various things at issue in the cases in Part A of this Chapter: corneas taken from one's deceased children; cells taken from one's spleen; frozen sperm belonging to one's father; a work of art produced for and transferred to a client; and Yei B'Chei used in Navaho religious ceremonies. How would Radin, applying her personhood theory, resolve the questions about whether these items should be alienable? In which cases is the prophylactic theory most relevant? The prohibition theory? The domino theory? In the end, does the personhood perspective help decide whether to adopt an inalienability rule in each of the foregoing situations?

2. The one clear conclusion that seems to follow from Radin's article on market-inalienability is that minimum welfare rights are necessary to

prevent people from being treated like commodities. Do we need the personhood theory in order to reach this conclusion?

3. Most often to date, those concerned with freedom of contract and economic efficiency tend to favor expanding the domain of property rights in contested areas ("commodification" if you will), whereas those who give priority to other values such as equality and community often oppose treating body parts, intimate relations, and personal identity like property ("anti-commodification"). More recently, however, some feminists have argued that anti-commodification sometimes promotes subordination, especially in the context of the division of marital property on divorce. See Chapter V. More generally, many have argued that the boundary between market and nonmarket spheres is not a fixed and brightline one: Nonmarket relations often have market aspects and vice versa. For discussion of these and related issues, see Rethinking Commodification: Cases and Readings in Law and Culture (Martha M. Ertman & Joan C. Williams eds., 2005).

C. PUBLIC RIGHTS

In the previous section, we considered whether there are certain things that are too private or connected to personhood to be objects of ownership as property. In this section, we take up something of the opposite question—whether there are certain resources that are too "public" to be parceled out into private ownership. In other words, is there a category of resources that should be regarded as "inherently public," and hence should remain accessible only on equal terms to all members of the community?

1. THE NAVIGATION SERVITUDE

a. NAVIGABLE WATERS

The resource with the longest historical claim to being inherently public is navigable water. Under Roman law, according to Justinian's *Institutes*, "all of these things are by natural law common to all: air, flowing water, the sea and, consequently, the shores of the sea." Institutes 2.1.1–5 (J. Moyle trans., 5th ed. 1913). Bracton, writing in the mid-thirteenth century, borrowed from Justinian's *Institutes* and claimed that at common law the sea and seashore were common to all. 2 Henry de Bracton, On the Laws and Customs of England 39–40 (Samuel E. Thorne trans., 1968). Eventually, English law gave distinct treatment to "navigable waters" in four ways: (1) any member of the public had the right to travel by vessel on a body of water that was navigable; (2) any member of the public had the right to fish in a body of water that was navigable; (3) the land beneath navigable water was presumptively owned by the Crown; and (4) disputes arising out of incidents on navigable water were decided by the Royal Admiralty Courts rather than the common-law courts. See Daniel J. Hulsebosch, Writs to Rights: "Navigability" and the Transformation of the

Common Law in the Nineteenth Century, 23 Cardozo L. Rev. 1049, 1055, 1066–67 (2002); James R. Rasband, The Disregarded Common Parentage of the Equal Footing and Public Trust Doctrines, 32 Land & Water L. Rev. 1 (1997).

The decisional law within each of these categories was thin, and there was considerable uncertainty about how far a determination that a body of water was or was not "navigable" in one context would extend to another context, and if so what the consequences of that extension would be. Consequently, treatises took on an especially prominent importance in this area. The first and most important of these was written by Matthew Hale in the late seventeenth century, but not published until 1787. See Matthew Hale, De Jure Maris et Brachiorum eujusdem, in 1 A Collection of Tracts Relative to the Law of England 1–44 (Francis Hargrave ed., London, T. Wright 1787). Hale presented a tidier and more integrated view of the law than the case law perhaps justified. See Hulsebosch, supra. But it was Hale's version of English law that served as the starting point for American writers, most notably Joseph Angell and James Kent, who presented a vision of English water law as a baseline for introducing the American law on the subject. See Joseph K. Angell, A Treatise on the Common Law in Relation to Water–Courses: Intended More Particularly as an Illustration of the Rights and Duties of the Owners and Occupants of Water Privileges 14–20 (Boston, 1824); 3 James Kent, Commentaries on American Law 427–28 (New York, 1828).

As summarized by Kent and Angell, under English law the King as sovereign owned and controlled all navigable waters within the realm (as opposed to the high seas, which no one owned), and presumptively owned the land beneath navigable waters. Navigable waters, however, were narrowly defined to mean those waters subject to the ebb and flow of the tides. Consequently, submerged land under rivers and lakes not affected by the tides was subject to private ownership. Absent a grant to the contrary, the owner of land bordering on a nonnavigable body of water owned the submerged land to the thread of the current or center line of the river or lake on which the land abutted.

The sovereign's ownership and control of navigable waters was qualified by important public rights (*jus publicum*). All waters, whether tidal or not, were subject to a general public easement of free navigation. The King was powerless to interfere with this right. Moreover, private owners of waters that were nontidal but navigable in fact could not interfere with public navigation, provided those wishing to traverse such waters could obtain access without trespassing. The right to fish was also understood to be a public right that could not be defeated by the King as owner of tidal waters and the beds of tidal waters. Although the law was more poorly developed with respect to fishing rights, it was thought that nontidal waters owned by private persons were *not* subject to a general public easement for fishing. With respect to the King's ownership of the bed of tidal waters, this was characterized as a private right (*jus privatum*), and hence could be granted by the King to a private party. Over time, however, the law evolved a rule of strict construction that presumed against such a grant in cases of ambiguity. Moreover, any such grant, for example, to engage in shellfishing, had to be exercised in such a way that it would not interfere with the general right of the public to travel by vessel and fish in navigable waters. Finally, the jurisdiction of the Royal Admiralty Courts was confined to issues and disputes arising out of events on navigable— that is tidal—waters.

Adapting these understandings to the American context was complicated by the division of authority between the federal government and the states. The U.S. Constitution gave Congress authority to "regulate Commerce with foreign nations, and among the several States, and with the Indian Tribes." U.S. Const., art. I, § 8, cl. 3. "Commerce" in 1789 took place largely through vessels plying navigable waterways, and so the Constitution appeared to contemplate a federal role in preserving and enhancing navigation. The Constitution also extended the judicial power of the federal courts to "all Cases of admiralty and maritime Jurisdiction." Id. art. III, § 2. This too suggested that the federal courts were to assume the jurisdiction historically exercised by the Royal Courts of Admiralty over disputes arising on navigable waters.

These expectations were eventually vindicated. Congress conferred admiralty jurisdiction on the federal courts in the Judiciary Act of 1789. At first, this jurisdiction was understood to extend only to disputes arising out of navigable waters as defined by English law—that is, to disputes arising out of waters subject to the ebb and flow of the tides. See The Steamship Thomas Jefferson, 23 U.S. (10 Wheat.) 428 (1825). But in 1851, in a dramatic reversal, the Court overruled this decision and held that the admiralty jurisdiction of the federal courts was not limited to tidal waters but extended to all waters that are navigable in fact. The Propeller Genesee Chief v. Fitzhugh, 53 U.S. (12 How.) 443 (1851). The Court noted that in England, with its long coast line and short rivers, the equation of navigable waters with tidal waters did not do great violence to commercial realities. On the North American continent, by contrast, a large number of waterways are not tidal yet are navigable in fact, including the Great Lakes and rivers like the Ohio and the Mississippi. By 1851 it was clear that these waterways would play a vital role in the development of American commerce, and therefore a broader definition of navigable waters was needed.

The federal role in preserving free navigation under the Commerce Clause emerged more slowly. The first decisive step was the Supreme Court's decision in *Gibbons v. Ogden*, 22 U.S. (9 Wheat.) 1 (1824), where the Court invalidated a monopoly charter granted by the New York legislature to operate steamboats between New York City and New Jersey. Chief Justice Marshall wrote that the word "commerce" in the Constitution "comprehends, and has been always understood to comprehend, navigation within its meaning; and a power to regulate navigation, is as expressly granted, as if that term had been added to the word 'commerce.' " Id. at 193. *Gibbons* established that Congress has plenary authority to legislate on the subject of commercial navigation. Soon, the commerce power came to be understood as self-executing, even in the absence of legislation by Congress. Thus, for example, in *Pennsylvania v. Wheeling & Belmont Bridge Co.*, 54 U.S. (13 How.) 518 (1851), the Court held that the federal courts, on the authority of the Commerce Clause and without any implementing legislation, could issue an injunction directing that a low-lying bridge be raised in order to prevent undue interference with navigation on the Ohio River. Although Congress could intercede and revise such decisions (as it did with respect to the Wheeling Bridge, see Pennsylvania v. Wheeling & Belmont Bridge Co., 59 U.S. (18 How.) 421 (1855)), the Court deemed the principle of free navigation too important to await implementing legislation from Congress.

Decisions like those involving the Wheeling Bridge eventually crystallized into the notion that the Commerce Clause, of its own force, imposes a "navigation servitude" on all waters of the United States that are in fact navigable. Under this navigation servitude, no state government, and no individual or corporation acting under the authority of state law, has the power to obstruct or interfere with the public's right to free use of waterways for transportation. As the Supreme Court wrote in *United States v. Rands*, 389 U.S. 121, 122–23 (1967):

> The Commerce Clause confers a unique position upon the Government in connection with navigable waters. "The power to regulate commerce comprehends the control for that purpose, and to the extent necessary, of all the navigable waters of the United States.... For this purpose they are the public property of the nation, and subject to all the requisite legislation by Congress." *Gilman v. City of Philadelphia*, 3 Wall. 713, 724–725 (1865). This power to regulate navigation confers upon the United States a "dominant servitude," *FPC v. Niagara Mohawk Power Corp.*, 347 U.S. 239, 249 (1954), which extends to the entire stream and the stream bed below ordinary high-water mark. The proper exercise of this power is not an invasion of any private property rights in the stream or the lands underlying it, for the damage sustained does not result from taking property from riparian owners within the meaning of the Fifth Amendment but from the lawful exercise of a power to which the interests of riparian owners have always been subject. *United States v. Chicago, M., St. P & P.R. Co.*, 312 U.S. 592, 596–597 (1941); *Gibson v. United States*, 166 U.S. 269, 275–276 (1897). Thus, without being constitutionally obligated to pay compensation, the United States may change the course of a navigable stream, *State of South Carolina v. State of Georgia*, 93 U.S. 4 (1876), or otherwise impair or destroy a riparian owner's access to navigable waters, *Gibson v. United States*, 166 U.S. 269 (1897); *Scranton v. Wheeler*, 179 U.S. 141 (1900); *United States v. Commodore Park, Inc.*, 324 U.S. 386 (1945), even though the market value of the riparian owner's land is substantially diminished.

Today, it can be said that American law recognizes something similar to the *jus publicum* of English common law, but it is grounded in a conception of the self-executing power of the Commerce Clause more than in any conception of inherently public property rights. This federal navigation servitude trumps state laws as well as rights of private property. Congress, for its part, has consistently endorsed the idea that the navigable waters of the United States shall remain open to public navigation. For example, an early statute designed to regulate the sale of territorial land provided that "all navigable rivers, within the territory to be disposed of by virtue of this action, shall be deemed to be, and remain public highways...." 1 U.S. Stat. 468 (1796). And in the Submerged Lands Act, which confirmed states' title to the submerged lands under navigable waters within their borders, Congress reserved to the federal government "all its navigation servitude and rights in and powers of regulation and control of said lands and navigable waters for the constitutional purposes of commerce, navigation, national defense, and international affairs, all of which shall be paramount to, but shall not be deemed to include, proprietary rights of ownership...." 67 Stat. 32, 43 U.S.C. § 1314.

Yet, no authoritative decision has suggested that Congress itself is bound by the navigation servitude. There is thus a tantalizing question whether Congress could exercise its power under the Commerce Clause to *defeat* the public right of navigation. For example, could Congress, in the interest of environmental protection, direct that navigable rivers be allowed to return to their natural state (i.e., undredged and without locks to bypass hazards), thereby rendering public transportation impracticable? However intriguing, the question so far remains entirely hypothetical, since Congress has never questioned the imperative of public navigation.

The question of who has title to submerged land beneath navigable waters has followed a convoluted path in the United States. In England, the King as sovereign was presumptively the owner of the lands beneath tidal waters, but could convey private rights in these lands by a very clear and express grant. In *Martin v. Waddell*, 41 U.S. (16 Pet.) 367 (1842), the U.S. Supreme Court took the first important step in adapting this understanding to the American context, holding that the original colonies succeeded to the position of the English Crown with respect to ownership of submerged tidal lands. Thus, after the colonies gained independence, title to these lands vested in the state governments. Soon thereafter, in *Pollard v. Hagan*, 44 U.S. (3 How.) 212 (1845), the Court extended this reasoning to subsequently admitted states created out of federal territory. Given the "equal footing" language of these statehood grants, the Court reasoned that states carved out of federal territory inherited the same rights to submerged lands under tidal waters that the original states owned by direct inheritance from the British Crown.

These decisions addressed only lands under tidal waters, which Kent, Angell, and other early commentators understood to be the full extent of "navigable" waters under English law. After *Martin v. Waddell* and *Pollard v. Hagan*, the courts of the various states divided over how the principles of those decisions should apply to land under waters that were not tidal but navigable in fact. A majority of state courts adhered to the English common law, and held that state ownership was limited to land under tidal waters, while lands under other waters—including nontidal waters that are navigable in fact—were owned by adjacent riparian landowners (subject, of course, to a public easement of free navigation). A significant minority of state courts, however, concluded that English law was unsuited to conditions in North America. These courts adopted the view that submerged lands under all waters that are navigable in fact are owned by the state as sovereign. The Supreme Court eventually confirmed that state law controls on the question of ownership of the bed under navigable waters, although federal law governs as to whether the waters are navigable or not. See Packer v. Bird, 137 U.S. 661, 671 (1891); cf. Illinois Central Railroad Co. v. Illinois, infra.

Even if a state chooses to recognize or create private property rights in the bed of navigable waters, however, those rights remain subordinate to the federal navigation servitude. Thus, for example, in *United States v. Cherokee Nation of Oklahoma*, 480 U.S. 700 (1987), the Court held that the United States Army Corps of Engineers was free to dredge mineral deposits from the bed of a navigable river in order to improve public navigation— even if the mineral deposits were acknowledged to be private property. Moreover, the United States could not be charged with a duty to pay just compensation for destroying the mineral rights, because every one who acquires such land is on notice "that their very title to the submerged lands 'is acquired and held subject to the power of Congress to deepen the water over such lands or to use them for any structure which the interest of navigation, in its judgment, may require.'" Id. at 705 (quoting Lewis Blue Point Oyster Cultivation Co. v. Briggs, 229 U.S. 82, 88 (1913)).

b. NAVIGABLE AIRSPACE

In *United States v. Causby*, 328 U.S. 256 (1946), the Supreme Court held that the principles of federal control over navigable waterways extend to navigable airspace. Causby, a chicken farmer in Greensboro, North Carolina, had the misfortune of having a military airport next to his farm during the run up to World War II. The testimony showed that roaring military planes passed as low as 83 feet over his property, which so frightened the chickens that some of them flew into the walls and killed themselves, while others stopped laying eggs. Causby sued the United States, claiming that the overflights were a taking of his air rights under the *ad coelum* doctrine. In an opinion by Justice Douglas, the Court agreed that there had been a taking, but only because the overflights caused a direct injury to Causby's use and enjoyment of the land. The Court took pains to emphasize that the federal government has ample authority to assure that navigable airspace remains a public resource:

> The United States relies on the Air Commerce Act of 1926, 44 Stat. 568, 49 U.S.C. § 171 et seq., as amended by the Civil Aeronautics Act of 1938, 52 Stat. 973, 49 U.S.C. § 401 et seq. Under those statutes the United States has "complete and exclusive national sovereignty in the air space" over this country. 49 U.S.C. § 176(a). They grant any citizen of the United States "a public right of freedom of transit in air commerce through the navigable air space of the United States." 49 U.S.C. § 403. And "navigable air space" is defined as "airspace above the minimum safe altitudes of flight prescribed by the Civil Aeronau-

tics Authority." 49 U.S.C. § 180. And it is provided that "such navigable airspace shall be subject to a public right of freedom of interstate and foreign air navigation." Id. It is, therefore, argued that since these flights were within the minimum safe altitudes of flight which had been prescribed, they were an exercise of the declared right of travel through the airspace. The United States concludes that when flights are made within the navigable airspace without any physical invasion of the property of the landowners, there has been no taking of property. * * *

It is ancient doctrine that at common law ownership of the land extended to the periphery of the universe—*Cujus est solum ejus est usque ad coelum.* But that doctrine has no place in the modern world. The air is a public highway, as Congress has declared. Were that not true, every transcontinental flight would subject the operator to countless trespass suits. Common sense revolts at the idea. To recognize such private claims to the airspace would clog these highways, seriously interfere with their control and development in the public interest, and transfer into private ownership that to which only the public has a just claim. * * *

The airplane is part of the modern environment of life, and the inconveniences which it causes are normally not compensable under the Fifth Amendment. The airspace, apart from the immediate reaches above the land, is part of the public domain. We need not determine at this time what those precise limits are. Flights over private land are not a taking, unless they are so low and so frequent as to be a direct and immediate interference with the enjoyment and use of the land.

Id. at 260–61, 266. As noted in connection with the *Hinman* case (Chapter I), the Court's characterization of the *ad coelum* doctrine as obsolete is best viewed as a piece of rhetorical excess. But there remain significant questions of how to apply or modify *ad coelum* in light of the relatively recent possibility of overflights by aircraft.

After the *Causby* decision, navigable airspace in the United States has assumed roughly the same status as navigable waterways: Federal law trumps any attempt by the states or private property owners to interfere with free public navigation; federal law plays a paramount role in regulating the use of and access to the navigable airspace; and federal policy has been to encourage public access to navigable airspace; but there is no authoritative decision indicating that this policy of open access is binding on Congress.

2.   THE PUBLIC TRUST DOCTRINE

D   P

Illinois Central Railroad Co. v. Illinois

Supreme Court of the United States, 1892.
146 U.S. 387.

■ MR. JUSTICE FIELD delivered the opinion of the court. This suit was commenced on the 1st of March, 1883, in a circuit court of Illinois, by an information or bill in equity filed by the attorney general of the state, in the name of its people, against the Illinois Central Railroad Company, a corporation created under its laws, and against the city of Chicago. * * *

The object of the suit is to obtain a judicial determination of the title of certain lands on the east or lake front of the city of Chicago, situated between the Chicago river and Sixteenth street, which have been reclaimed

Figure 3–3
Chicago Lakefront, Late 1880s

from the waters of the lake, and are occupied by the tracks, depots, warehouses, piers, and other structures used by the railroad company in its business, and also of the title claimed by the company to the submerged lands, constituting the bed of the lake, lying east of its tracks, within the corporate limits of the city, for the distance of a mile, and between the south line of the south pier near Chicago river, extended eastwardly, and a line extended in the same direction from the south line of lot 21 near the company's roundhouse and machine shops. The determination of the title of the company will involve a consideration of its right to construct, for its own business, as well as for public convenience, wharves, piers, and docks in the harbor. * * *

The city of Chicago is situated upon the southwestern shore of Lake Michigan, and includes, with other territory, fractional sections 10 and 15, in township 39 north, range 14 east of the third principal meridian, bordering on the lake, which forms their eastern boundary. For a long time after the organization of the city, its harbor was the Chicago river, a small, narrow stream opening into the lake near the center of the east and west line of section 10; and in it the shipping arriving from other ports of the lake and navigable waters was moored or anchored, and along it were docks and wharves. The growth of the city in subsequent years, in population, business, and commerce, required a larger and more convenient harbor * * *

The case proceeds upon the theory and allegation that the defendant the Illinois Central Railroad Company has, without lawful authority, encroached, and continues to encroach, upon the domain of the state, and its original ownership and control of the waters of the harbor and of the lands thereunder, upon a claim of rights acquired under a grant from the state * * *

The state prays a decree establishing and confirming its title to the bed of Lake Michigan, and exclusive right to develop and improve the harbor of Chicago by the construction of docks, wharves, piers, and other improvements, against the claim of the railroad company that it has an absolute title to such submerged lands by the act of 1869 * * *

We proceed to consider the claim of the railroad company to the ownership of submerged lands in the harbor, and the right to construct such wharves, piers, docks, and other works therein as it may deem proper for its interest and business. The claim is founded upon the third section of the act of the legislature of the state passed on the 16th of April, 1869, the material part of which is as follows:

> Sec. 3. * * * [A]ll the right and title of the state of Illinois in and to the submerged lands constituting the bed of Lake Michigan, and lying east of the tracks and breakwater of the Illinois Central Railroad Company, for a distance of one mile, and between the south line of the south pier extended eastwardly and a line extended eastward from the south line of lot twenty-one, south of and near to the roundhouse and machine shops of said company, in the south division of the said city of Chicago, are hereby granted in fee to the said Illinois Central Railroad Company, its successors and assigns: provided, however, that the fee to said lands shall be held by said company in perpetuity, and that the

said company shall not have power to grant, sell, or convey the fee to the same, and that all gross receipts from use, profits, leases, or otherwise, of said lands, or the improvements thereon, or that may hereafter be made thereon, shall form a part of the gross proceeds, receipts, and income of the said Illinois Central Railroad Company, upon which said company shall forever pay into the state treasury, semiannually, the per centum provided for in its charter, in accordance with the requirements of said charter: and provided, also, that nothing herein contained shall authorize obstructions to the Chicago harbor, or impair the public right of navigation, nor shall this act be construed to exempt the Illinois Central Railroad Company, its lessees or assigns, from any act of the general assembly which may be hereafter passed, regulating the rates of wharfage and dockage to be charged in said harbor.

The act of which this section is a part was accepted by a resolution of the board of directors of the company at its office in the city of New York, July 6, 1870, but the acceptance was not communicated to the state until the 18th of November, 1870. A copy of the resolution was on that day forwarded to the secretary of state, and filed and recorded by him in the records of his office. On the 15th of April, 1873, the legislature of Illinois repealed the act. The questions presented relate to the validity of the section cited, of the act, and the effect of the repeal upon its operation. * * *

The act, if valid and operative to the extent claimed, placed under the control of the railroad company nearly the whole of the submerged lands of the harbor, subject only to the limitations that it should not authorize obstructions to the harbor, or impair the public right of navigation, or exclude the legislature from regulating the rates of wharfage or dockage to be charged. With these limitations, the act put it in the power of the company to delay indefinitely the improvement of the harbor, or to construct as many docks, piers, and wharves and other works as it might choose, and at such positions in the harbor as might suit its purposes, and permit any kind of business to be conducted thereon, and to lease them out on its own terms for indefinite periods. The inhibition against the technical transfer of the fee of any portion of the submerged lands was of little consequence when it could make a lease for any period, and renew it at its pleasure; and the inhibitions against authorizing obstructions to the harbor and impairing the public right of navigation placed no impediments upon the action of the railroad company which did not previously exist. A corporation created for one purpose, the construction and operation of a railroad between designated points, is by the act converted into a corporation to manage and practically control the harbor of Chicago, not simply for its own purpose as a railroad corporation, but for its own profit generally.

The circumstances attending the passage of the act through the legislature were on the hearing the subject of much criticism. As originally introduced, the purpose of the act was to enable the city of Chicago to enlarge its harbor, and to grant to it the title and interest of the state to certain lands adjacent to the shore of Lake Michigan, on the eastern front of the city, and place the harbor under its control; giving it all the necessary powers for its wise management. But during the passage of the act its purport was changed. Instead of providing for the cession of the submerged lands to the city, it provided for a cession of them to the railroad company. It was urged that the title of the act was not changed to correspond with its changed purpose, and an objection was taken to its validity on that account. But the majority of the court were of opinion that the evidence was insufficient to show that the requirement of the constitution of the state, in its passage, was not complied with.

The question, therefore, to be considered, is whether the legislature was competent to thus deprive the state of its ownership of the submerged lands in the harbor of Chicago, and of the consequent control of its waters; or, in other words, whether the railroad corporation can hold the lands and control the waters by the grant, against any future exercise of power over them by the state.

That the state holds the title to the lands under the navigable waters of Lake Michigan, within its limits, in the same manner that the state holds title to soils under tide water * * * we have already shown; and that title necessarily carries with it control over the waters above them, whenever the lands are subjected to use. But it is a title different in character from that which the state holds in lands intended for sale. It is different from the title which the United States hold in the public lands which are open to pre-emption and sale. It is a title held in trust for the people of the state, that they may enjoy the navigation of the waters, carry on commerce over them, and have liberty of fishing therein, freed from the obstruction or interference of private parties. The interest of the people in the navigation of the waters and in commerce over them may be improved in many instances by the erection of wharves, docks, and piers therein, for which purpose the state may grant parcels of the submerged lands; and, so long as their disposition is made for such purpose, no valid objections can be made to the grants. * * * But that is a very different doctrine from the one which would sanction the abdication of the general control of the state over lands under the navigable waters of an entire harbor or bay, or of a sea or lake. Such abdication is not consistent with the exercise of that trust which requires the government of the state to preserve such waters for the use of the public. The trust devolving upon the state for the public, and which can only be discharged by the management and control of property in which the public has an interest, cannot be relinquished by a transfer of the property. The control of the state for the purposes of the trust can never be lost, except as to such parcels as are used in promoting the interests of the public therein, or can be disposed of without any substantial impairment of the public interest in the lands and waters remaining. * * * A grant of all the lands under the navigable waters of a state has never been adjudged to be within the legislative power; and any attempted grant of the kind would be held, if not absolutely void on its face, as subject to revocation. The state can no more abdicate its trust over property in which the whole people are interested, like navigable waters and soils under them, so as to leave them entirely under the use and control of private parties, except in the instance of parcels mentioned for the improvement of the navigation and use of the waters, or when parcels can be disposed of without impairment of the public interest in what remains, than it can abdicate its police powers in the administration of government and the preservation of the peace. In the administration of government the use of such powers may for a limited period be delegated to a municipality or other body, but there always remains with the state the right to revoke those powers and exercise them in a more direct manner, and one more conformable to its wishes. So with trusts connected with public property, or property of a special character, like lands under navigable waters; they cannot be placed entirely beyond the direction and control of the state.

The harbor of Chicago is of immense value to the people of the state of Illinois, in the facilities it affords to its vast and constantly increasing commerce; and the idea that its legislature can deprive the state of control over its bed and waters, and place the same in the hands of a private corporation, created for a different purpose,—one limited to transportation of passengers and freight between distant points and the city,—is a proposition that cannot be defended.

The area of the submerged lands proposed to be ceded by the act in question to the railroad company embraces something more than 1,000 acres, being, as stated by counsel, more than three times the area of the outer harbor, and not only including all of that harbor, but embracing adjoining submerged lands, which will, in all probability, be hereafter included in the harbor. It is as large as that embraced by all the merchandise docks along the Thames at London; is much larger than that included in the famous docks and basins at Liverpool; is twice that of the port of Marseilles, and nearly, if not quite, equal to the pier area along the water front of the city of New York. And the arrivals and clearings of vessels at the port exceed in number those of New York, and are equal to those of New York and Boston combined. Chicago has nearly 25 per cent. of the lake carrying trade, as compared with the arrivals and clearings of all the leading ports of our great inland seas. In the year ending June 30, 1886, the joint arrivals and clearances of vessels at that port amounted to 22,096, with a tonnage of over 7,000,000; and in 1890 the tonnage of the vessels reached nearly 9,000,000. As stated by counsel, since the passage of the lake front act, in 1869, the population of the city has increased nearly 1,000,000 souls, and the increase of commerce has kept pace with it. It is hardly conceivable that the legislature can divest the state of the control and management of this harbor, and vest it absolutely in a private corporation. Surely an act of the legislature transferring the title to its submerged lands and the power claimed by the railroad company to a foreign state or nation would be repudiated, without hesitation, as a gross perversion of the trust over the property under which it is held. So would a similar transfer to a corporation of another state. It would not be listened to that the control and management of the harbor of that great city—a subject of concern to the whole people of the state—should thus be placed elsewhere than in the state itself. All the objections which can be urged to such attempted transfer may be urged to a transfer to a private corporation like the railroad company in this case.

Any grant of the kind is necessarily revocable, and the exercise of the trust by which the property was held by the state can be resumed at any time. Undoubtedly there may be expenses incurred in improvements made under such a grant, which the state ought to pay; but, be that as it may, the power to resume the trust whenever the state judges best is, we think, incontrovertible. The position advanced by the railroad company in support of its claim to the ownership of the submerged lands, and the right to the erection of wharves, piers, and docks at its pleasure, or for its business in the harbor of Chicago, would place every harbor in the country at the mercy of a majority of the legislature of the state in which the harbor is situated.

We cannot, it is true, cite any authority where a grant of this kind has been held invalid, for we believe that no instance exists where the harbor of a great city and its commerce have been allowed to pass into the control of any private corporation. But the decisions are numerous which declare that such property is held by the state, by virtue of its sovereignty, in trust for the public. The ownership of the navigable waters of the harbor, and of the lands under them, is a subject of public concern to the whole people of the state. The trust with which they are held, therefore, is governmental, and cannot be alienated, except in those instances mentioned, of parcels used in the improvement of the interest thus held, or when parcels can be disposed of without detriment to the public interest in the lands and waters remaining. * * *

■ MR. JUSTICE SHIRAS, with whom concurred MR. JUSTICE GRAY and MR. JUSTICE BROWN, dissenting. * * * [We agree that the State cannot part,] by contract, with her sovereign powers. The railroad company takes and holds these lands subject at all times to the same sovereign powers in the state as obtain in the case of other owners of property. Nor can the grant in this case be regarded as in any way hostile to the powers of the general government in the control of harbors and navigable waters.

The able and interesting statement, in the opinion of the majority, of the rights of the public in the navigable waters, and of the limitation of the powers of the state to part with its control over them, is not dissented from. But its pertinency in the present discussion is not clearly seen. It will be time enough to invoke the doctrine of the inviolability of public rights when and if the railroad company shall attempt to disregard them.

Should the state of Illinois see in the great and unforeseen growth of the city of Chicago and of the lake commerce reason to doubt the prudence of her legislature in entering into the contract created by the passage and acceptance of the act of 1869, she can take the rights and property of the railroad company in these lands by a constitutional condemnation of them. So, freed from the shackles of an undesirable contract, she can make, as she expresses in her bill a desire to do, a "more advantageous sale or disposition to other parties," without offense to the law of the land. * * *

NOTES AND QUESTIONS

1. Justice Field's opinion seems to imply that the Lake Front Act of 1869 conferred monopoly control over the Chicago harbor on a private railroad company. But this is not true, as is confirmed by Map C reproduced from the record in the case (see Figure 3–3). At the time of the grant, the harbor of Chicago was the Chicago River, which was entered from Lake Michigan in the center of the city. The grant of submerged land to the Illinois Central Railroad began at the south bank of the River and ran from there in a southerly direction. What the Lake Front Act in fact contemplated was that the Illinois Central would construct and operate a new "outer harbor" in the lake south of the river, which would supplement the existing facilities in the Chicago River. To be sure, this supplemental harbor would make the railroad the largest operator of piers and wharfs in the Chicago area, and its facilities would have had a favored position by being nearest the lake. But being the biggest and closest does not make one a monopolist, and it is likely that plenty of competition would have remained to constrain the pricing of the railroad for its harbor services. Justice Field was an ardent free-marketeer, but he was also a populist who was intensely suspicious of special privileges and charters for corporations. See The Slaughter–House Cases, 83 U.S. (16 Wall.) 36, 83 (1873) (Field, J. dissenting); Paul Kens, Justice Stephen Field: Shaping Liberty from the Gold Rush to the Gilded Age (1997); Charles W. McCurdy, Justice Field and the Jurisprudence of Government–Business Relations: Some Parameters of Laissez–Faire Constitutionalism, 1863–1897, J. Am. Hist. 960, 970, 973 (1975). The argument between Justice Field and Justice Shiras in *Illinois Central* has strong echoes of the debate in *Charles River Bridge v. Warren Bridge*, Chapter XI, where Chief Justice Taney argues that corporate chapters should be narrowly construed to avoid conferring monopoly privileges and Justice Story, in dissent, says that corporate charters are property that can be modified only by paying just compensation to the owners.

2. Further information about the background of the case may be found in Joseph D. Kearney & Thomas W. Merrill, The Origins of the American Public Trust Doctrine: What Really Happened in *Illinois Central*, 71 U. Chi. L. Rev. 799 (2004). Three points are especially noteworthy. First, the railroad's motivations in seeking a grant of the submerged land of the lake in 1869 were largely defensive—to fend off efforts by other groups to obtain a grant of these lands, which would have left the railroad's existing improvements isolated by unfriendly forces. The principal rival consortium was headed up by a Chicago lawyer named Melville Fuller, who by 1892 was Chief Justice of the U.S. Supreme Court. This lends additional significance to his recusal from the case, the stated ground for which was that he had served as counsel to the City of Chicago in the court below. Second, no one in 1869 imagined that the State of Illinois had the resources or expertise to construct an outer harbor for Chicago. Downstate legislators favored a grant to the Illinois Central, which did have the resources and expertise, because the revenues generated by a new harbor operated by the railroad would have been subject to the seven percent gross receipts tax

that was then applicable to all of the railroad's in-state operations, and this additional revenue could be spent by the legislature for projects throughout the state. Chicago-based legislators tended to favor a grant to the City of Chicago, which would have allowed the aldermen of the City Council to control construction contracts and leases of harbor facilities, and hence to enrich themselves and their friends. Third, the railroad was accused for many years of using corrupt means to procure the enactment of the Lake Front Act, as is perhaps alluded to in the paragraph in the opinion about alleged irregularities in the passage of the Act. Although there is no hard evidence of bribery of the legislature, the weight of the evidence suggests that some type of corruption did take place in 1869, although, as noted above, the motivation for the graft was largely defensive.

Figure 3–4
A View of Navy Pier from the Shoreline in Chicago

Author: David Bjorgen. This image is licensed under the Creative Commons Attribution ShareAlike License v. 2.5: http://creativecommons.org/licenses/by-sa/2.5/.

3.   The outer harbor contemplated by the Lake Front Act of 1869 was never built. Litigation over the grant and repeal kept the project tied up into the twentieth century, by which time commercial traffic on the Great Lakes had begun to decline. The U.S. Army Corps of Engineers eventually dredged a harbor in Lake Calumet at the southern boundary of Chicago, which soon supplanted the Chicago River as the area's principal port. The only commercial harbor facility of any significance ever built in Lake Michigan by the government was Navy Pier, which juts into the lake just north of the Chicago River (see Figure 3–4). This was never very successful as a harbor facility; it is today leased out to the commercial operator of a multi-use tourist attraction.

4. What is the source of law for the trust obligation that the Supreme Court identifies as constraining the disposition of public lands under navigable waters? Justice Field never says whether he is applying federal law or state law in *Illinois Central*. In subsequent public trust decisions, the Supreme Court has consistently maintained that the doctrine is grounded in state law. See, e.g., Shively v. Bowlby, 152 U.S. 1 (1894); Appleby v. City of New York, 271 U.S. 364 (1926). This means that the states are free to repudiate the trust, either by statute or by an amendment to their state constitutions. Commentators have been uneasy about this implication, and so there have been recurrent attempts to argue that the trust is in fact grounded in federal law. Perhaps the most plausible theory for a federal basis would be that the trust is an implication of the federal navigation servitude. But this theory would limit the public trust doctrine to navigable waters and dispositions of land that might interfere with public navigation, and most commentators have not been eager to embrace the implication that the public trust is so narrow.

5. One implication of the public trust doctrine, as extended by *Illinois Central* to waters that are nontidal but navigable in fact, is that privately-owned fishing streams such as are found in England and Scotland are difficult if not impossible to establish in the U.S. In *Collins v. Gerhardt*, 211 N.W. 115 (Mich. 1926), for example, the defendant was wading and fishing in the Pine River, a fast-moving trout stream accessible by no vessel larger than a canoe. The plaintiff, who owned the land on both sides and the bed of Pine River, sued the defendant for trespass. The court held for the defendant: "From this it follows that the common-law doctrine, viz., that the right of fishing in navigable waters follows the ownership of the soil, does not prevail in this state. It is immaterial who owns the soil in our navigable rivers. The trust remains. From the beginning the title was impressed with this trust for the preservation of the public right of fishing and other public rights which all citizens enjoyed in tidal waters under the common law." Id. at 116. Is this declaration of an inalienable public right of access to fishing streams a blessing or a bane for the protection of fish populations and habitats?

6. The public trust doctrine led a quiet existence until 1970. In that year, Professor Joseph Sax wrote a law review article arguing that the doctrine could be employed as an effective tool for environmental protection. See Joseph Sax, The Public Trust Doctrine: Effective Judicial Intervention, 68 Mich. L. Rev. 471 (1970). Sax did not advocate a rigid rule against privatization of public resources; he was more concerned with developing new forms of public participation and judicial oversight to act as a counterweight to capture of state and local legislatures by developers. The *Illinois Central* decision, which Sax characterized as involving a massive giveaway of public resources with no public interest justification, featured prominently in illustrating the dangers of capture. The article proved to be enormously influential. It transformed the public trust from a doctrine about public access to commercial navigation, into a doctrine about preservation of natural resources.

PURPESTURES

Closely related to the public trust doctrine is the problem of encroachments by private persons on navigable waterways or public highways. For example, someone owning land that abuts a navigable river may build a dock that makes it difficult for vessels to pass, or someone owning land next to a public street may construct a building with a cornice that overhangs the street and makes it difficult for tall vehicles to pass. These sorts of encroachments on public lands are called purpestures. At common law, purpestures were controlled by public nuisance actions, not by trespass law. This is probably because navigable rivers and public highways are inherently open to use by the public, so a bright line test based on boundary crossing as with trespass would not make sense (this would interfere with highly valuable multiple use). Instead, the law required a more discriminating doctrine that would distinguish between permissible and interfering uses, and the more flexible doctrine associated with nuisance was enlisted for these purposes. Nevertheless, not everything was given over to balancing. "Any permanent, fixed, or stationary object or impediment, as distinguished from a mere temporary obstruction incidental to a lawful use of the way, which unreasonably and unnecessarily interferes with public travel, or which endangers the safety of travelers, constitutes a public nuisance per se." 39 Am. Jur. 2d, Highways, Streets, and Bridges § 310 (2006). (For more on nuisance per se, see Chapter IX.A.) The elaborate landfilling of Lake Michigan by the Illinois Central was also challenged as a purpesture, but as we have seen the Court focused on the public title to the lakebed rather than the interference with public navigation.

Lake Michigan Federation v. United States Army Corps of Engineers

United States District Court, N.D. Illinois, Eastern Division, 1990.
742 F.Supp. 441.

■ ASPEN, DISTRICT JUDGE: The Lake Michigan Federation ("Federation") has filed this action for declaratory and injunctive relief against Loyola University of Chicago ("Loyola"), the United States Army Corps of Engineers, and various officials of the United States Army Corps of Engineers (collectively referred to as "the Corps"). The Federation seeks an injunction restraining Loyola from constructing a twenty acre lakefill on its Lake Shore campus in Chicago, Illinois. Because we find that the property to be used for this project was conveyed in violation of the public trust, we grant the Federation's motion for injunctive relief.

Loyola is a private educational institution organized as a not-for-profit corporation. Among Loyola's campuses in the Chicago area is its Lake Shore campus bordering Lake Michigan on the north side of the city. In 1988, Loyola decided to expand this campus. Loyola determined that it would not be feasible to expand onto adjacent land. Instead, it developed plans to construct a lakefill of approximately twenty acres in the waters of neighboring Lake Michigan. Because erosion had damaged the existing shoreline, Loyola viewed the lakefill both as a means for the expansion and protection of its campus.

The plans developed by Loyola called for a lakefill of about 18.5 acres. Along the perimeter of the lakefill, Loyola intended to construct a stone revetment, as well as bike and walking paths, a seatwall, and lawn areas. The public would have unrestricted access to these areas, which comprise about 2.1 acres of lakefill. In the interior portion of the lakefill, Loyola plans to build athletic facilities, including a running track, a women's softball field, and multi-purpose athletic fields. The public would have access to these areas, but subject to Loyola's right of ownership. In addition, Loyola proposed restoration and improvements to Hartigan Park Beach, which borders the proposed lakefill.

Loyola sought and received legislative and municipal approval of this project. In Public Act 85–1145, S.B. 1171, the Illinois Legislature conveyed approximately 18.5 acres of the lakebed to Loyola for the purpose of expansion. In this act, the legislature acknowledged that it holds the title of submerged lands in trust for the people of Illinois. However, because the public would benefit from the lakefill in various ways, the legislature reasoned that it had the power to convey the land to Loyola. In addition to obtaining approval from the Illinois legislature, Loyola also entered into a contract with the Park District of the City of Chicago allowing Loyola to proceed with the project.

After securing the approval of state and local governmental entities, Loyola also cleared federal statutory hurdles. Pursuant to § 404 of the Clean Water Act, 33 U.S.C. § 1344, and § 10 of the Rivers and Harbors Act, 33 U.S.C. § 403, Loyola had to obtain a permit from the Corps before proceeding with construction. Loyola submitted a permit application on December 9, 1988. In addition to its permit review under the Clean Water Act and the Rivers and Harbors Act, the Corps was also required to consider the potential environmental impact of the project [under] the National Environmental Policy Act ("NEPA"), 42 U.S.C. § 4321 et seq. The Corps received and considered information provided by Loyola and its consultants, state and federal agencies, citizens' groups and individuals. The Corps ultimately concluded that the project would have no adverse impact on the environment, and issued a Finding of No Significant Impact ("FONSI"), pursuant to 33 C.F.R. part 325. Because the Corps issued a FONSI, it was not required to prepare an Environmental Impact Statement ("EIS") under NEPA. The Corps also concluded that the project was permissible under the Clean Water Act and the Rivers and Harbors Act. Accordingly, on April 20, 1990, the Corps issued a permit to Loyola, which proceeded with its plans to begin construction of the project.

The Federation seeks to enjoin the construction of the lakefill. Its complaint for declaratory and injunctive relief recites several legal grounds upon which an injunction should issue. The Federation attacks both the Corp's decision to issue the permit and the validity of the legislative grant of property to Loyola. Because we find that the legislative conveyance of the lakebed to Loyola violated the public trust doctrine, we need not reach the issue of whether the Corp's review of the permit application was arbitrary or capricious.

The classic statement of the public trust doctrine was promulgated in *Illinois Central Railroad Company v. Illinois,* 146 U.S. 387 (1892). In this case, the Supreme Court invalidated the transfer of 1000 acres of submerged lands in Lake Michigan to the Illinois Central Railroad. The Court explained that dominion and sovereignty over submerged lands belong to the State in which the land is found. Id. at 435. However, the title to these submerged lands is "different in character from that which the State holds in lands intended for sale." Id. at 452. "It is a title held in trust for the people of the State that they may enjoy the navigation of the waters, carry on commerce over them, and have liberty of fishing therein freed from the obstruction or interference of private parties." Id. "The State can no more abdicate its trust over property in which the whole people are interested, like navigable waters and the soils under them, so as to leave them entirely under the use and control of private parties . . . than it can abdicate its police powers in the administration of government and the preservation of peace." Id. at 453.

Since the Supreme Court's decision in *Illinois Central Railroad Co. v. Illinois,* several attempts by the State of Illinois to transfer public lands have been scrutinized under the public trust doctrine. For example, in *Illinois Cent. R. Co. v. City of Chicago,* 50 N.E. 1104 (Ill. 1898), the Illinois Supreme Court, relying heavily on *Illinois Central Railroad Co. v. Illinois,* held that the Illinois legislature lacked the power to allow the Illinois Central Railroad to appropriate a parcel of the lakebed for private use. Similarly, in *People v. Kirk,* 45 N.E. 830 (Ill. 1896), the Illinois Supreme Court utilized the public trust doctrine to evaluate a transfer of the lakebed. In this case, a portion of the lakebed was transferred in order to construct an extension of Lake Shore Drive. The Court found that the transfer did not violate the public trust doctrine because the legislature had not attempted to relinquish its power over the land and because the project would directly benefit the public. Id. at 835. See also, Paepcke v. Public Building Commission of Chicago, 263 N.E.2d 11 (Ill. 1970) (Diversion of land previously used as a park to a new public use did not violate public trust doctrine).

The most recent and exhaustive analysis of the public trust doctrine was given in *People ex rel. Scott v. Chicago Park Dist.,* 360 N.E.2d 773 (Ill. 1976). The Illinois Attorney General challenged a bill which conveyed 194.6 acres of land submerged in the waters of Lake Michigan to the United States Steel Corporation ("U.S. Steel"). The Illinois Supreme Court observed that, "[i]t is obvious that Lake Michigan is a valuable resource belonging to the people of this State in perpetuity . . . and any attempted ceding of a portion of it in favor of a private interest has to withstand a most critical examination." Id. 360 N.E.2d at 780. The Court ultimately concluded that the conveyance of land to U.S. Steel could not withstand this critical examination.

In holding that the conveyance violated the public trust doctrine, the Court focused on the purpose behind the challenged legislation. Reviewing its prior public trust jurisprudence, the Court noted that it had never upheld a grant of governmental land where its primary purpose was to benefit a private interest. Id. 360 N.E.2d at 780. Indeed, the Court observed that in the only case in which a grant to a private entity had been sustained, *People ex rel. Moloney v. Kirk,* "the main purpose of the statute was to allow public officials to construct a needed extension of Lake Shore Drive for direct public benefit." Id. 360 N.E.2d at 779. Therefore, the Court concluded that in order to satisfy the public trust doctrine, the primary purpose of the challenged grant must be to benefit the public, rather than a private interest. Moreover, the Court held that the public purpose advanced by the grant must be direct. Thus, it found that benefits to the public through additional employment and economic improvement were "too indirect, intangible, and elusive to satisfy the requirement of a public purpose." Id.

RULE

Three basic principles can be distilled from this body of public trust case law. First, courts should be critical of attempts by the state to surrender valuable public resources to a private entity. Second, the public trust is violated when the primary purpose of a legislative grant is to benefit a private interest. Finally, any attempt by the state to relinquish its power over a public resource should be invalidated under the doctrine.

Applying these criteria to the legislative grant of the lakebed to Loyola, it is apparent that the transfer violates the public trust doctrine. First, while the project has some aspects which are beneficial to the public, the primary purpose of the grant is to satisfy a private interest. Loyola sought and received the grant in order to satisfy its desire for a larger campus. The improvement of Hartigan Park Beach, erosion protection and other measures may benefit the public, but these benefits are only incidental to the primary and private goal of enlarging the Loyola campus. While such improvements may have made the project more palatable to Illinois legislators, the inescapable truth is that the lakebed property will be sacrificed to satisfy Loyola's private needs. Under the public trust doctrine, such a sacrifice cannot be tolerated.

Not only does the challenged legislation give away public trust property to satisfy a private interest, but it also constitutes an attempt to relinquish state power over this property. Upon completion of the project, Loyola will become the owner of 18.5 acres of land which previously belonged to the state. Accordingly, the state will relinquish its control over the [land] and its corresponding ability to safeguard the interests of the public as to this land.

Loyola contends that the limitations placed on its ownership by the State are sufficient to constitute state control over the property. By the terms of the conveyance, Loyola is not allowed to construct buildings or parking areas on the lakefill. The state also has a right of reentry should Loyola attempt to transfer the property to any entity which does not operate as a nonprofit educational institution. In addition, the legislation provides "[s]ubject to Loyola University's rights and obligations of ownership, including but not limited to maintenance and security, public access to, and public use and enjoyment of, the lakefill shall not be unreasonably denied." Public Act 85–1145, S.B. 1171 § 1(e)(1)(iii).

It remains to be seen whether these restrictions are more than illusory. For example, subsequent legislation could be passed which lifts the restrictions placed on the conveyance. Alternatively, the State of Illinois could choose not to exercise its right of re-entry or otherwise enforce the restrictions which are to be placed on the quitclaim deed.

However, even if we accept the proposition that the conditions of conveyance constitute bonafide restrictions, we do not agree that these restrictions are sufficient to constitute retention of public control over the lakefill. Although Loyola would lack the complete discretion over the use of its property, it is undeniable that its rights would be superior to those of the public. The enabling legislation gives Loyola the power to control public access to the property. However, as the property currently exists, citizens have access to Lake Michigan, free "from the obstruction or interference of private parties." Illinois Central Railroad Company v. Illinois, 146 U.S. at 452. The discretion vested in Loyola by the legislature is precisely the type of restriction which the public trust doctrine is intended to proscribe.

Loyola suggests that we should not apply the public trust doctrine because the lakefill will increase the public's opportunity to enjoy that portion of the lakefront. Loyola observes that the existing shoreline is privately owned by Loyola, with no right of public access. In addition, this portion of the lake shore has been damaged by erosion. Therefore, Loyola reasons that if it is allowed to complete the lakefill, the public will be in a better position to enjoy the lake because of the aesthetic improvement to the coastline and the property on the whole.

This argument is seriously flawed. Loyola ignores the fact that the public will have to sacrifice 18.5 acres of publicly held land in order to obtain a coastline to which it has unlimited access. Moreover, it glosses over the fact that the public is actually gaining nothing. The public currently has unrestricted access to the submerged lands which will become the new coastline. In reality, the public is losing its right of access to the portion of the lake which would become the interior portion of the lakefill. In essence, Loyola's argument that the public will gain from the construction of the lakefill is merely a value dependent assessment of the best use of the property. This judgment is not only highly subjective, but also irrelevant to an analysis of the propriety of a grant of public land.

Loyola also argues that we should be deferent to the Illinois legislature's determination that the grant at issue did not violate the public trust. In both the debate before the law was passed and in the legislation itself, the legislature acknowledged that it held the lakebed in trust for the public and declared that the grant would not violate this trust because of the project's numerous public benefits. According to Loyola, we should yield to this specific legislative consideration of public interest.

However, this claim is incorrect both as a matter of logic and precedent. The very purpose of the public trust doctrine is to police the legislature's disposition of public lands. If courts were to rubber stamp legislative decisions, as Loyola advocates, the doctrine would have no teeth. The legislature would have unfettered discretion to breach the public trust as long as it was able to articulate some gain to the public. Moreover, Illinois courts have acknowledged that courts are not encumbered by legislative expressions of public interest. For example, in *People ex rel. Scott v. Chicago Park Dist.*, the Illinois Supreme Court stated that, "[w]hile courts certainly should consider the General Assembly's declaration that given legislation is to serve a described purpose ... the self-serving recitation of a public purpose within a legislative enactment is not conclusive of the existence of such purpose." Id., quoting People ex rel. City of Salem v. McMackin, 291 N.E.2d 807 (Ill. 1972). See also, Paepcke v. Public Building Comm. of Chicago, 263 N.E.2d at 16 (Court should be skeptical of governmental conduct allocating resource to the self interest of private parties). Therefore, we find that the legislative determination that the lakefill would serve the public is no obstacle to our conclusion that the grant was in breach of the public trust. * * *

Conclusion

What we have here is a transparent giveaway of public property to a private entity. The lakebed of Lake Michigan is held in trust for and belongs to the citizenry of the state. The conveyance of lakebed property to a private party—no matter how reputable and highly motivated that private party may be—violates this public trust doctrine. This improper conveyance is not made any more palatable by attaching cosmetic conditions to the conveyance which permit restricted public access to the private property. Because the conveyance of lakebed to Loyola violated the public trust doctrine, Loyola, its agents and contractors are, effective immediately, permanently enjoined from placing any fill material in the lake or proceeding, in any manner, with further construction of the lakefill. * * *

ON MOTION FOR RECONSIDERATION

On June 29, 1990, Loyola University of Chicago ("Loyola") filed a motion for reconsideration of this Court's order of June 22, 1990, granting a permanent injunction against the extension of its campus into Lake Michigan. * * * On July 11, 1990, before its reply brief in support of its motion for reconsideration was due, Loyola announced at a press conference the abandonment of its lakefill project. * * *

[T]he Court's ruling has been questioned on [the ground] that Northwestern University's early 1960's lakefill extension of its campus (an extension apparently never challenged in court) is "precedent" in favor of approving the Loyola project. Significantly, Loyola has not raised Northwestern's campus extension as precedent before this Court. This, of course, is because Northwestern's unchallenged lakefill expansion is not *legal* precedent. The law does not permit one entity to violate the law because another has successfully evaded the same law on another occasion. * * *

At its press conference, Loyola stated that it must now abandon its lakefill project solely because of the cost and time involved in any appeal. Whether or not to pursue this case further is, of course, a decision solely for Loyola. However, the abandonment of a multimillion dollar project which has been ongoing for years solely for this reason strains credulity. A prompt and relatively inexpensive review of this Court's ruling is available before the Seventh Circuit. The legal issues have been promptly decided and clearly drawn. They are important both from a legal and environmental standpoint. If Loyola believes that these issues have been incorrectly decided, it should pursue its appeal. Had Loyola won before this Court, certainly the Federation would have appealed from any such decision—resulting in the very same expected expense and delay which is purportedly the basis for Loyola going no further. Would Loyola have abandoned a successful decision before this Court because of the cost and time required to defend such decision on appeal? Could any litigant not anticipate the possibility of an appeal in a case of this importance, regardless of the outcome in the District Court? Given the amount of money that Loyola has invested and plans to invest in this project, the cost of appellate review is relatively negligible. Also, given the amount of time Loyola has already devoted to this project, the short time now required to effect its appeal is *de minimis*.

* * * The motion for reconsideration is denied.

Figure 3–5
Lake Michigan at Loyola University Chicago, 2006

NOTES AND QUESTIONS

1.   Most of the Chicago lakefront is parkland today, virtually all of which was created by landfilling conducted by public authorities (the City of Chicago and the Chicago Park District) in the years since *Illinois Central* was decided. An exception is the far north side of Chicago, where the Loyola campus at issue in this case is located. In this part of the city, known as Rogers Park, most of the lakeshore is privately owned, and high-rise condominiums directly abut the lake, severely restricting public access. The project invalidated by the court in the name of the public trust doctrine would have ameliorated this situation to a degree, by creating a new bicycle and jogging path open to the public along the lakefront in the area of the campus, and by expanding and improving the adjacent Hartigan Park. Does it make sense to invoke the public trust doctrine to invalidate a project that would improve public access to the lakefront, on the ground that title to the project would be held by a private university?

2.   The public trust doctrine is used in *Lake Michigan Federation* for preservationist ends—the plaintiffs seek and obtain a permanent injunction that keeps Lake Michigan closer to its "natural" condition than would be the case if the landfilling project were allowed to go forward. But is the underlying premise of the doctrine—that title to the bed of the lake must remain in governmental hands—necessarily well designed to achieve preservationist ends? The Illinois Supreme Court's most recent explication of the public trust doctrine rejects a challenge to a radical reconstruction of Soldier Field, located on landfill in an area that was once the bed of Lake Michigan. The reconstruction was undertaken to keep the Chicago Bears football team playing its home games at Soldier Field. The court reasoned that the public trust doctrine was not violated because fee simple title to Soldier Field remained in the Chicago Park District, even though the Park District had entered into a 40-year lease with the Bears. See Friends of the Parks v. Chicago Park District, 786 N.E.2d 161 (Ill. 2003).

3.   The area of the Chicago lakefront covered by the public trust doctrine is today adorned not only with the reconstructed Soldier Field, which looks something like a space ship, but also the huge McCormick Convention Center, the new Millennium Park with its "exploding" music pavilion designed by Frank Gehry and massive sculptural works sponsored by various corporate donors, and of course Navy Pier, which features, among other attractions, a giant Ferris wheel (see Figure 3–4). But, as always, the relevant question is a comparative one: Is a rule that insists that certain resources remain titled in the name of the government more likely to work to preserve these resources in a relatively unspoiled condition, compared to a rule that permits such resources to be transferred entirely into private hands? Absent the public trust doctrine, would the landfill area along the Chicago lakefront be one long wall of condominiums?

4.   Another irony of *Lake Michigan Federation* concerns the role of the public trust doctrine in preserving democratic control over state-owned resources. In *Illinois Central*, the public trust doctrine is used to uphold the

state legislature's most recent determination of the proper use of the bed of the lake. In 1873 the legislature repealed the 1869 grant to the railroad, restoring title to the lake bed in the State of Illinois; the Supreme Court rejected the railroad's claim of vested rights and upheld the repeal, reasoning that one legislature cannot tie the hands of another in determining the proper disposition of public resources. The decision seems to be a vindication of the principle of democratic control of public resources. In *Lake Michigan Federation*, all relevant publicly accountable governmental bodies—the state legislature, the City of Chicago, the U.S. Army Corps of Engineers—had signed off on the project, deeming it to be in the public interest. The court, however, nullifies this collective judgment of politically accountable bodies in the name of the public trust doctrine. The decision seems like a repudiation of democratic control over public resources. Courts of course invalidate democratically-adopted policies when those policies violate constitutions (though constitutions are also democratically-adopted instruments). But there is no obvious constitutional provision, either in the federal Constitution or in most state constitutions, that authorizes the public trust doctrine. Does the public trust doctrine suffer from a democracy deficit? See William D. Araiza, Democracy, Distrust, and the Public Trust: Process–Based Constitutional Theory, the Public Trust Doctrine, and the Search for a Substantive Environmental Value, 45 UCLA L. Rev. 385 (1997).

RESOURCES COVERED BY THE PUBLIC TRUST DOCTRINE

Most judicial decisions enforcing the public trust doctrine involve resources that have some connection with navigable water. This is true, of course, of *Illinois Central* and *Lake Michigan Federation*, both of which involved Lake Michigan, which the Court in *Illinois Central* determined to be navigable water. Many contemporary public trust controversies concern public rights to beaches adjacent to navigable waters. In one controversial case, the California Supreme Court used the public trust doctrine to abrogate appropriated water rights in nonnavigable streams in order to prevent ecological harms said to follow from a decline in the water level of a lake fed by the streams. National Audubon Society v. Superior Court, 658 P.2d 709 (Cal. 1983). But even here, the lake into which the streams flowed, Mono Lake, was a navigable body of water.

In a portion of the opinion we have omitted, the Court in *Illinois Central* cited with approval *Newton v. Commissioners*, 100 U.S. 548 (1879), a decision holding that one legislature cannot bind another on the question of which town is to be the seat of a county. This suggests that the scope of the public trust doctrine might extend far beyond navigable waters. Some court decisions have applied the public trust doctrine to public parks and state wilderness areas unconnected with navigable waters. Richard J. Lazarus, Changing Conceptions of Property and Sovereignty in Natural Resources: Questioning the Public Trust Doctrine, 71 Iowa L. Rev. 631, 649–50 (1986). Richard Epstein has recently suggested that the public trust doctrine should also apply to intellectual property rights whose period of protection has expired, allowing the material to enter the public domain.

Richard A. Epstein, Intellectual Property, Congressional Power, and the Constitution: The Dubious Constitutionality of the Copyright Term Extension Act, 36 Loyola L.A. L. Rev. 123 (2002). Epstein argues that this would discourage Congress from enacting retroactive extensions of intellectual property right protections, at the behest of interest groups that profit from these rights. (For more on copyright extensions and the public domain, see Chapter X.)

Nearly 30% of the land mass of the United States is owned by the federal government. Much of this land is "leftovers" that no one took during the era when the federal public domain was open to purchase and homestead claims. (With narrow exceptions, the Taylor Grazing Act of 1934 closed the federal public domain to further private appropriation.) But the federal public lands also include spectacular national parks and wilderness areas. The Supreme Court has occasionally spoken of the federal lands as being held by the United States in "trust" for the people. See, e.g., Light v. United States, 220 U.S. 523 (1911) (upholding the creation of the National Forest System). Many states also hold ordinary lands in trust—for example, for support of schools—which are not necessarily subject to the public trust doctrine. Jon A. Souder & Sally K. Fairfax, State Trust Lands: History, Management, and Sustainable Use (1996). Should the 30% of the national land mass held by the United States be subject to the public trust doctrine, as it is explicated in *Illinois Central* and *Lake Michigan Federation*? Although commentators have occasionally advanced this argument, see, e.g., Charles F. Wilkinson, The Public Trust Doctrine in Public Land Law, 14 U.C. Davis L. Rev. 269 (1980), to our knowledge no federal court has ever endorsed it. Why do you suppose the public trust doctrine has more vitality with respect to state-owned resources than it does with respect to federally-owned resources?

State of Oregon ex rel. Thornton v. Hay

Supreme Court of Oregon, 1969.
462 P.2d 671.

■ GOODWIN, JUSTICE. William and Georgianna Hay, the owners of a tourist facility at Cannon Beach, appeal from a decree which enjoins them from constructing fences or other improvements in the dry-sand area between the sixteen-foot elevation contour line and the ordinary high-tide line of the Pacific Ocean.

The issue is whether the state has the power to prevent the defendant landowners from enclosing the dry-sand area contained within the legal description of their ocean-front property. * * *

The defendant landowners concede that * * * all tideland lying seaward of the ordinary, or mean high-tide line is a state recreation area as defined in ORS 390.720.[1]

---

1.   ORS 390.720 provides:

Ownership of the shore of the Pacific Ocean between ordinary high tide and extreme low tide, and from the Oregon and Washington state line on the north to the Oregon and California state line on the south, excepting such portions as may have been disposed of by the state prior to July 5, 1947, is vested in the

From the trial record, applicable statutes, and court decisions, certain terms and definitions have been extracted and will appear in this opinion. A short glossary follows:

ORS 390.720 refers to the "ordinary" high-tide line, while other sources refer to the "mean" high-tide line. For the purposes of this case the two lines will be considered to be the same. * * *

The land area in dispute will be called the dry-sand area. This will be assumed to be the land lying between the line of mean high tide and the visible line of vegetation.

The vegetation line is the seaward edge of vegetation where the upland supports vegetation. It generally falls in the vicinity of the sixteen foot elevation contour line * * *

The extreme high-tide line and the highwater mark are mentioned in the record, but will be treated as identical with the vegetation line. * * *

Below, or seaward of, the mean high-tide line, is the state-owned foreshore, or wet-sand area, in which the landowners in this case concede the public's paramount right, and concerning which there is no justiciable controversy.

The only issue in this case, as noted, is the power of the state to limit the record owner's use and enjoyment of the dry-sand area, by whatever boundaries the area may be described.

The trial court found that the public had acquired, over the years, an easement for recreational purposes to go upon and enjoy the dry-sand area, and that this easement was appurtenant to the wet-sand portion of the beach which is admittedly owned by the state and designated as a "state recreation area."

Because we hold that the trial court correctly found in favor of the state on the rights of the public in the dry-sand area, it follows that the state has an equitable right to protect the public in the enjoyment of those rights by causing the removal of fences and other obstacles. * * *

In order to explain our reasons for affirming the trial court's decree, it is necessary to set out in some detail the historical facts which lead to our conclusion.

The dry-sand area in Oregon has been enjoyed by the general public as a recreational adjunct of the wet-sand or foreshore area since the beginning of the state's political history. The first European settlers on these shores found the aboriginal inhabitants using the foreshore for clam-digging and the dry-sand area for their cooking fires. The newcomers continued these customs after statehood. Thus, from the time of the earliest settlement to

State of Oregon, and is declared to be a state recreation area. No portion of such ocean shore shall be alienated by any of the agencies of the state except as provided by law.

the present day, the general public has assumed that the dry-sand area was a part of the public beach, and the public has used the dry-sand area for picnics, gathering wood, building warming fires, and generally as a head-quarters from which to supervise children or to range out over the foreshore as the tides advance and recede. In the Cannon Beach vicinity, state and local officers have policed the dry sand, and municipal sanitary crews have attempted to keep the area reasonably free from man-made litter.

Perhaps one explanation for the evolution of the custom of the public to use the dry-sand area for recreational purposes is that the area could not be used conveniently by its owners for any other purpose. The dry-sand area is unstable in its seaward boundaries, unsafe during winter storms, and for the most part unfit for the construction of permanent structures. While the vegetation line remains relatively fixed, the western edge of the dry-sand area is subject to dramatic moves eastward or westward in response to erosion and accretion. For example, evidence in the trial below indicated that between April 1966 and August 1967 the seaward edge of the dry-sand area involved in this litigation moved westward 180 feet. At other points along the shore, the evidence showed, the seaward edge of the dry-sand area could move an equal distance to the east in a similar period of time.

Until very recently, no question concerning the right of the public to enjoy the dry-sand area appears to have been brought before the courts of this state. The public's assumption that the dry sand as well as the foreshore was "public property" had been reinforced by early judicial decisions. See Shively v. Bowlby, 152 U.S. 1 (1894), which affirmed Bowlby v. Shively, 22 Or. 410, 30 P. 154 (1892). These cases held that landowners claiming under federal patents owned seaward only to the "high-water" line, a line that was then assumed to be the vegetation line.

In 1935, the United States Supreme Court held that a federal patent conveyed title to land farther seaward, to the mean hightide line. Borax Consolidated, Ltd. v. Los Angeles, 296 U.S. 10 (1935). While this decision may have expanded seaward the record ownership of upland landowners, it was apparently little noticed by Oregonians. In any event, the Borax decision had no discernible effect on the actual practices of Oregon beach-goers and upland property owners.

[handwritten margin note: Existing custom prevails ↓ Even though Borax' technically extends prop. rights to the high-tide mark (ie- includes dry-sand area)*]*

Recently, however, the scarcity of oceanfront building sites has attract-ed substantial private investments in resort facilities. Resort owners like these defendants now desire to reserve for their paying guests the recreational advantages that accrue to the dry-sand portions of their deeded property. Consequently, in 1967, public debate and political activity result-ed in legislative attempts to resolve conflicts between public and private interests in the dry-sand area:

ORS 390.610

(1) The Legislative Assembly hereby declares it is the public policy of the State of Oregon to forever preserve and maintain the sovereign-

ty of the state heretofore existing over the seashore and ocean beaches of the state from the Columbia River on the North to the Oregon–California line on the South so that the public may have the free and uninterrupted use thereof.

(2) The Legislative Assembly recognizes that over the years the public has made frequent and uninterrupted use of lands abutting, adjacent and contiguous to the public highways and state recreation areas and recognizes, further, that where such use has been sufficient to create easements in the public through dedication, prescription, grant or otherwise, that it is in the public interest to protect and preserve such public easements as a permanent part of Oregon's recreational resources.

(3) Accordingly, the Legislative Assembly hereby declares that all public rights and easements in those lands described in subsection (2) of this section are confirmed and declared vested exclusively in the State of Oregon and shall be held and administered in the same manner as those lands described in ORS 390.720. * * *

concessions from P + D — Essentially Statute vs Custom

The state concedes that such legislation cannot divest a person of his rights in land, Hughes v. Washington, 389 U.S. 290 (1967), and that the defendants' record title, which includes the dry-sand area, extends seaward to the ordinary or mean high-tide line. Borax Consolidated Ltd. v. Los Angeles, supra.

The landowners likewise concede that since 1899 the public's rights in the foreshore have been confirmed by law as well as by custom and usage. Oregon Laws 1899, p. 3, provided:

That the shore of the Pacific ocean, between ordinary high and extreme low tides, and from the Columbia river on the north to the south boundary line of Clatsop county on the south, is hereby declared a public highway, and shall forever remain open as such to the public.

"sui generis" one of a kind/unique

The disputed area is *sui generis*. While the foreshore is "owned" by the state, and the upland is "owned" by the patentee or record-title holder, neither can be said to "own" the full bundle of rights normally connoted by the term "estate in fee simple." 1 Powell, Real Property § 163, at 661 (1949).

In addition to the *sui generis* nature of the land itself, a multitude of complex and sometimes overlapping precedents in the law confronted the trial court. Several early Oregon decisions generally support the trial court's decision, i.e., that the public can acquire easements in private land by long-continued user that is inconsistent with the owner's exclusive possession and enjoyment of his land. A citation of the cases could end the discussion at this point. But because the early cases do not agree on the legal theories by which the results are reached, and because this is an important case affecting valuable rights in land, it is appropriate to review some of the law applicable to this case.

One group of precedents relied upon in part by the state and by the trial court can be called the "implied-dedication" cases. The doctrine of implied dedication is well known to the law in this state and elsewhere. See cases collected in Parks, The Law of Dedication in Oregon, 20 Or.L.Rev. 111 (1941). Dedication, however, whether express or implied, rests upon an intent to dedicate. In the case at bar, it is unlikely that the landowners thought they had anything to dedicate, until 1967, when the notoriety of legislative debates about the public's rights in the dry-sand area sent a number of ocean-front landowners to the offices of their legal advisers.

A second group of cases relied upon by the state, but rejected by the trial court, deals with the possibility of a landowner's losing the exclusive possession and enjoyment of his land through the development of prescriptive easements in the public.

In Oregon, as in most common-law jurisdictions, an easement can be created in favor of one person in the land of another by uninterrupted use and enjoyment of the land in a particular manner for the statutory period, so long as the user is open, adverse, under claim of right, but without authority of law or consent of the owner. Feldman et ux. v. Knapp et ux., 250 P.2d 92 (Or. 1952); Coventon v. Seufert, 32 P. 508 (Or. 1893). In Oregon, the prescriptive period is ten years. ORS 12.050. The public use of the disputed land in the case at bar is admitted to be continuous for more than sixty years. There is no suggestion in the record that anyone's permission was sought or given; rather, the public used the land under a claim of right. Therefore, if the public can acquire an easement by prescription, the requirements for such an acquisition have been met in connection with the specific tract of land involved in this case.

The owners argue, however, that the general public, not being subject to actions in trespass and ejectment, cannot acquire rights by prescription, because the statute of limitations is irrelevant when an action does not lie.

While it may not be feasible for a landowner to sue the general public, it is nonetheless possible by means of signs and fences to prevent or minimize public invasions of private land for recreational purposes. In Oregon, moreover, the courts and the Legislative Assembly have both recognized that the public can acquire prescriptive easements in private land, at least for roads and highways. See, e.g., Huggett et ux. v. Moran et ux., 266 P.2d 692 (Or. 1954), in which we observed that counties could acquire public roads by prescription. And see ORS 368.405, which provides for the manner in which counties may establish roads. The statute enumerates the formal governmental actions that can be employed, and then concludes: "This section does not preclude acquiring public ways by adverse user."

Another statute codifies a policy favoring the acquisition by prescription of public recreational easements in beach lands. See ORS 390.610. While such a statute cannot create public rights at the expense of a private landowner the statute can, and does, express legislative approval of the common-law doctrine of prescription where the facts justify its application. Consequently, we conclude that the law in Oregon, regardless of the generalizations that may apply elsewhere, does not preclude the creation of prescriptive easements in beach land for public recreational use.

Because many elements of prescription are present in this case, the state has relied upon the doctrine in support of the decree below. We believe, however, that there is a better legal basis for affirming the decree. The most cogent basis for the decision in this case is the English doctrine of custom. Strictly construed, prescription applies only to the specific tract of land before the court, and doubtful prescription cases could fill the courts for years with tract-by-tract litigation. An established custom, on the other hand, can be proven with reference to a larger region. Ocean-front lands from the northern to the southern border of the state ought to be treated uniformly.

The other reason which commends the doctrine of custom over that of prescription as the principal basis for the decision in this case is the unique nature of the lands in question. This case deals solely with the dry-sand area along the Pacific shore, and this land has been used by the public as public recreational land according to an unbroken custom running back in time as long as the land has been inhabited.

A custom is defined in 1 Bouv. Law Dict., Rawle's Third Revision, p. 742 as "such a usage as by common consent and uniform practice has become the law of the place, or of the subject matter to which it relates."

In 1 Blackstone, Commentaries *75–*78, Sir William Blackstone set out the requisites of a particular custom.

Paraphrasing Blackstone, the first requirement of a custom, to be recognized as law, is that it must be ancient. It must have been used so long "that the memory of man runneth not to the contrary." Professor Cooley footnotes his edition of Blackstone with the comment that "long and general" usage is sufficient. In any event, the record in the case at bar satisfies the requirement of antiquity. So long as there has been an institutionalized system of land tenure in Oregon, the public has freely exercised the right to use the dry-sand area up and down the Oregon coast for the recreational purposes noted earlier in this opinion.

The second requirement is that the right be exercised without interruption. A customary right need not be exercised continuously, but it must be exercised without an interruption caused by anyone possessing a paramount right. In the case at bar, there was evidence that the public's use and enjoyment of the dry-sand area had never been interrupted by private landowners.

Blackstone's third requirement, that the customary use be peaceable and free from dispute, is satisfied by the evidence which related to the second requirement.

The fourth requirement, that of reasonableness, is satisfied by the evidence that the public has always made use of the land in a manner appropriate to the land and to the usages of the community. There is evidence in the record that when inappropriate uses have been detected, municipal police officers have intervened to preserve order.

The fifth requirement, certainty, is satisfied by the visible boundaries of the dry-sand area and by the character of the land, which limits the use thereof to recreational uses connected with the foreshore.

The sixth requirement is that a custom must be obligatory; that is, in the case at bar, not left to the option of each landowner whether or not he will recognize the public's right to go upon the dry-sand area for recreational purposes. The record shows that the dry-sand area in question has been used, as of right, uniformly with similarly situated lands elsewhere, and that the public's use has never been questioned by an upland owner so long as the public remained on the dry sand and refrained from trespassing upon the lands above the vegetation line.

Finally, a custom must not be repugnant, or inconsistent, with other customs or with other law. The custom under consideration violates no law, and is not repugnant.

Two arguments have been arrayed against the doctrine of custom as a basis for decision in Oregon. The first argument is that custom is unprecedented in this state, and has only scant adherence elsewhere in the United States. The second argument is that because of the relative brevity of our political history it is inappropriate to rely upon an English doctrine that requires greater antiquity than a newly-settled land can muster. Neither of these arguments is persuasive.

The custom of the people of Oregon to use the dry-sand area of the beaches for public recreational purposes meets every one of Blackstone's requisites. While it is not necessary to rely upon precedent from other states, we are not the first state to recognize custom as a source of law. See Perley et ux'r v. Langley, 7 N.H. 233 (1834).

On the score of the brevity of our political history, it is true that the Anglo–American legal system on this continent is relatively new. Its newness has made it possible for government to provide for many of our institutions by written law rather than by customary law.[6] This truism does not, however, militate against the validity of a custom when the custom does in fact exist. If antiquity were the sole test of validity of a custom, Oregonians could satisfy that requirement by recalling that the European settlers were not the first people to use the dry-sand area as public land.

---

6.   The English law on customary rights grew up in a small island nation at a time when most inhabitants lived and died without traveling more than a day's walk from their birthplace. Most of the customary rights recorded in English cases are local in scope. The English had many cultural and language groups which eventually merged into a nation. After these groups developed their own unique customs, the unified nation recognized some of them as law. Some American scholars, looking at the vast geography of this continent and the freshness of its civilization, have concluded that there is no need to look to English customary rights as a source of legal rights in this country. See, e.g., 6 Powell, Real Property § 934, note 5, at 362 (1949). Some of the generalizations drawn by the text writers from English cases would tend to limit customary rights to specific usages in English towns and villages. See Gray, The Rule Against Perpetuities §§ 572–588 (1942). But it does not follow that a custom, established in fact, cannot have regional application and be enjoyed by a larger public than the inhabitants of a single village.

Finally, in support of custom, the record shows that the custom of the inhabitants of Oregon and of visitors in the state to use the dry sand as a public recreation area is so notorious that notice of the custom on the part of persons buying land along the shore must be presumed. In the case at bar, the landowners conceded their actual knowledge of the public's long-standing use of the dry-sand area, and argued that the elements of consent present in the relationship between the landowners and the public preclud-ed the application of the law of prescription. As noted, we are not resting this decision on prescription, and we leave open the effect upon prescrip-tion of the type of consent that may have been present in this case. Such elements of consent are, however, wholly consistent with the recognition of public rights derived from custom.

Because so much of our law is the product of legislation, we sometimes lose sight of the importance of custom as a source of law in our society. It seems particularly appropriate in the case at bar to look to an ancient and accepted custom in this state as the source of a rule of law. The rule in this case, based upon custom, is salutary in confirming a public right, and at the same time it takes from no man anything which he has had a legitimate reason to regard as exclusively his.

For the foregoing reasons, the decree of the trial court is affirmed.

NOTES AND QUESTIONS

1. The Oregon Supreme Court backed off from the full force of *Thornton* in McDonald v. Halvorson, 780 P.2d 714 (Or. 1989), holding that customary rights attach only to those beaches for which actual proof of public use can be shown. Does *McDonald* undercut *Thornton*'s rationale for preferring the doctrine of custom over the doctrine of public prescription?

2. Ownership of land in Oregon, like that of most other states west of the original thirteen, derives from patents or grants from the federal government. As the court notes in passing, the Supreme Court held in 1935 that federal patents naming the Pacific Ocean as their boundary should be construed as extending to the mean high tide line—that is, as including the dry sand area. Borax Consolidated Ltd. v. Los Angeles, 296 U.S. 10 (1935). Why weren't property owners in Oregon whose land borders on the Pacific Ocean entitled to rely on this decision as an authoritative expression of the extent of their property rights? Is it enough to say that the decision "was apparently little noticed by Oregonians" and "had no discernible effect on the actual practices of Oregon beachgoers and upland property owners?"

3. The court makes much of the fact that most upland property owners do not object when beachgoers use the dry sand area for picnics or supervising children at play. But why isn't this just neighborly behavior? Wouldn't it be reasonable for an upland owner to tacitly consent to such innocuous use, while reserving the right to evict the occasional raucous beer bash?

4.   Beaches are today without doubt the most contested ground for claims that property is inherently public and cannot be subject to private exclusion rights. The issue has been fought out state by state, and sometimes beach by beach. A number of states have used the public trust doctrine to hold that all or part of the dry sand beach is inherently public property. See, e.g., Glass v. Goeckel, 703 N.W.2d 58 (Mich. 2005) (Michigan public trust doctrine protects public right of access to beaches up to the mean high water mark); Matthews v. Bay Head Improvement Assn., 471 A.2d 355 (N.J. 1984) (New Jersey public trust doctrine protects public access to dry sand areas of a beach controlled by a homeowners' association). Florida, Texas, and Hawaii have joined Oregon in dusting off versions of the customary rights doctrine to declare public rights of access to dry sand beaches. Still others have rejected entreaties to declare beaches public property on any theory. See, e.g., State ex rel. Haman v. Fox, 594 P.2d 1093 (Idaho 1979). Given the plethora of theories and outcomes, it is difficult to say with much confidence in many states exactly what rights the public has to beaches. See, e.g., Sean D. Hamill, No Line in the Sand on Beach Rights: Confusion Reigns in State on Public Access to Shore, Chi. Trib., Aug. 9, 2005, Metro at 1 (surveying various experts and getting conflicting opinions as to the extent of public access to beaches in Illinois).

5.   Notwithstanding the confusion, the overall trend seems to be toward greater public rights or open access to beaches. How, if at all, would Demsetz explain the apparent evolution away from exclusion rights and private property in beaches toward a regime that is more like an open-access commons?

6.   One difference between customary rights and other theories for protecting public rights in beaches and other analogous resources concerns the ability of the legislature to revise the decision. The public trust doctrine may or may not be subject to legislative revision. It depends on how one conceives of the legal source of the doctrine (federal versus state law, constitutional law versus common law), and whether the doctrine is viewed as a rule of construction or a fixed qualification on title. In some states, like Illinois, the public trust doctrine is viewed as a fixed qualification on title and so cannot be revised by the legislature. See Lake Michigan Federation, supra. The doctrine of public prescription probably is subject to legislative revision, although since prescriptive easements are property rights (see Chapter IX), the government might have to condemn these rights and pay just compensation in order to eliminate them. (If the prescriptive easement belongs to the public, who would receive the compensation?) The doctrine of customary rights is clearly subject to legislative revision. Moreover, since it is unclear that a customary right is a property right, it is at least arguable that the government would not have to pay just compensation to anyone in abrogating customary rights. Customary rights thus are the easiest for the legislature to modify. Do you think this attribute of customary rights provides an additional reason to favor the approach of the Oregon Supreme Court, or does it count against the court's approach?

7. If the judiciary changes the status of a resource like dry sand beaches from private property to open access, as arguably happened in *Thornton*, does this give rise to a claim that the state has taken private property without just compensation? In *Nollan v. California Coastal Comm'n*, 483 U.S. 825, 831 (1987), the Court indicated that state laws or regulations requiring property owners to open their beachfront to public access are "takings" requiring the exercise of the power of eminent domain and payment of just compensation. Why should it make any difference if the same result is achieved by the courts employing doctrines like the public trust or custom? Is it because these sorts of decisions rest on a judicial declaration that the right to use the beach has belonged to the public all along? But why should the institution (legislature versus court) or the rationale (condemnation for public use versus declaration of public trust or custom) make any difference in deciding whether the owners are entitled to compensation? For discussion of these and related puzzles, see Barton H. Thompson, Jr., Judicial Takings, 76 Va. L. Rev. 1449 (1990).

Carol Rose, *The Comedy of the Commons: Custom, Commerce, and Inherently Public Property*, 53 U. Chi. L. Rev. 711, 713–21, 749–54, 757–58, 779–81 (1986)

[D]espite the power of the classical economic argument for private property, a curious cross-current has continually washed through American law. Our legal doctrine has strongly suggested that some kinds of property should not be held exclusively in private hands, but should be open to the public or at least subject to what Roman law called the "jus publicum": the "public right."

Moreover, this view is not merely a vestige of premodern thought; there is currently an extensive academic and judicial discussion of the possibility that certain kinds of property ought to be public. In recent years, the most striking version of this "inherent publicness" argument has appeared in a series of cases expanding public access to waterfront property. The land between the low and high tides has traditionally been considered "public property," or at least subject to a public easement for navigational and fishing purposes. But some modern courts have stretched this easement to include a new use—recreation—and have expanded its area from the tidelands to the dry sand areas landward of the high-tide mark.

These new cases extrapolate from older precedents in which the public acquired—or allegedly reasserted—claims to certain types of property, most notably roadways and lands under navigable waters. Like the older precedents, the new beach cases usually employ one of three theoretical bases: (1) a "public trust" theory, to the effect that the public has always rights of access to the property in question, and that any private rights are subordinate to the public's "trust" rights; (2) a prescriptive or dedicatory theory, by which a period of public usage gives rise to an implied grant or gift from private owners; and (3) a theory of "custom," where the public asserts ownership of property under some claim so ancient that it antedates any memory to the contrary.

Approaches

1) "Public Trust"
2) Usage leads to implied grant
3) Custom

These theories of increased public access to shores and waterways have garnered a vocal but decidedly mixed reaction. In discussing these theories, some commentators applaud what they regard as a proper recognition of public needs. The public trust idea in particular has spawned an enormous number of cases and articles, some urging extension of a public trust to a much wider range of property where public access or control should be vindicated. But there have also been several very sharp critiques of these cases and articles, and of the expansive doctrines of public control they propound. Some critics deny the underlying public trust and dedicatory theories, and deplore what they see as an unjust and disruptive destruction of private property rights. They argue that if the public wants or needs these waterfront lands so much, it should have to purchase them from the private owners. Moreover, they warn of the consequences of these uncompensated and unpredictable transfers of property rights: frustrated private owners may overreact in trying to protect their property from any implication of "dedication" by installing guard dogs or blowing up access paths to the beach.

More generally, these critics reiterate the basic arguments in favor of private ownership: uncertainty about property rights invites conflicts and squanders resources. The public access cases turn the waterfront into a "commons," where no one has any incentive to purchase the property, invest in it, or care for it, but only to consume as much as possible—all of which leads to deterioration and waste. * * *

Perhaps these doctrines are indeed easily explicable through classical economic thought, and can be subsumed under the well-recognized exceptions to the general principle favoring private and exclusive property rights: "plenteous" goods and "public goods." The first class of exception concerns things that are either so plentiful or so unbounded that it is not worth the effort to create a system of resource management for them, or—stated differently—things for which the difficulty of privatization outweighs the gains in careful resource management. Thus the oceans and air (it used to be said) are at once so plentiful and so difficult to reduce to property that they are left open to the public at large.

see Demsetz essay- Pg. 292

The "plenitude" or "boundlessness" exceptions, however, fail to explain the "publicness" of those properties that our traditional doctrines most strongly deemed public property. Roadways, waterways, and submerged lands—not to speak of open squares, which have also sometimes been presumed public—are hardly so copious or so unbounded that they are incapable of privatization. Riverbeds and shorelands can be staked out, roadways can be obstructed, waterways diverted, squares plowed up; in short, they can easily be "reduced to possession" in the classic common law manner of creating proprietary rights out of a "commons." Thus the "public" character of such lands, or even a public easement over them, must have some basis other than our incapacity to reduce them to private possession.

The second exception to the general rule favoring private property may be of more assistance. Since the mid-nineteenth century, economists have told us that there exist predictable instances of "market failure," where Adam Smith's invisible hand fails to guide privately owned resources to their socially optimal uses. These involve "public goods," "natural monopolies," "externalities," and the like. While some of these problems may be solved by collective agreements among the owners of the resources, such agreements are costly and, particularly where a large number of parties must be involved, private collective action is not always possible. Inefficiencies will remain.

Thus a governmental body might be the most useful manager where many persons desire access to or control over a given property, but they are too numerous and their individual stakes too small to express their preferences in market transactions; governmental ownership could broker those preferences. Similarly, a government might be a superior manager (or regulator) of a property whose use involves economies of scale—the railways, bridges, or grain elevators whose monopoly position classically justified governmental ownership or control. Or a government might be a superior manager of those "collective goods" like the broadcast spectrum, wherein some management structure is required to make individual users take account of other users' interests. In a sense, we rely on governmental management of our preeminent system of resource management—private property—and we might view the entire private property regime as a "public property" owned and managed by governmental bodies.

Conventional wisdom instructs that in such cases, the most productive solution would be for government to assume some or all of the rights of ownership and control over the property, and to use its powers to correct the market's misallocation. This conventional conclusion is subject to four conventional caveats: the state must be able correctly to identify instances of market failure; it must be clever enough to exercise its powers so as to reduce the inefficiency; it must avoid errors or political temptations to exercise its powers in ways that create new inefficiencies; and the costs of effective state intervention must not exceed the increase in production it brings about.

This standard paradigm of neoclassical economics and modern microeconomic theory recognizes only two property regimes: either ownership is vested in private parties or it resides with an organized state. The usual economic approach to property law suggests that productive efficiency will be enhanced when private property is the norm, but government intervenes in recognized instances of market failure.

Thus in the conventional lore, markets are based on private rights or, when markets fail, property may be governmentally managed in the interests of aggregate efficiency. Yet these two options do not logically exhaust all the possible solutions. Neither can they adequately describe all that one finds in the recorded history of property in the Anglo–American universe. In particular, there lies outside purely private property and government-controlled "public property" a distinct class of "inherently public property" which is fully controlled by neither government nor private agents. Since the Middle Ages this category of "inherently public property" has provided

[handwritten margin notes:]

Conditions where Gov't ownership is most productive

① Market Failure must be predicted accurately

② Must be capable of using powers to reduce inefficiency

③ Must not in turn create new inefficiencies (ie - too much red tape)

④ Cost of intervention must not be greater than increased production each member of some "public" with a bundle of rights, neither entirely alienable by state or other collective action, nor necessarily "managed" in any explicitly organized manner. Aside from individual private property, the nineteenth-century common law of property in both Britain and America, with surprising consistency, recognized two distinguishable types of public property. One of these was property "owned" and actively managed by a governmental body. The other, however, was property collectively "owned" and "managed" by society at large, with claims independent of and indeed superior to the claims of any purported governmental manager. It is this latter type that I call "inherently public property."

Implicit in these older doctrines is the notion that, even if a property should be open to the public, it does not follow that public rights should necessarily vest in an active governmental manager. Despite the well-known problems of unorganized collective access to a resource—the "tragedy of the commons"—equally difficult problems are posed by governmental management: the cost of instituting that management and, perhaps, the temptations of politically motivated redistribution. In some circumstances, then, nineteenth-century common law recognized collective public rights as the optimal alternative whether or not those rights were managed governmentally. * * *

What was so bad about private ownership of "inherently public properties"? * * *

Some nineteenth-century doctrinal controversies pointedly implied [an] anti-holdout rationale both for public prescription of roads and for public trust in waterways. * * *

One controversy of particular importance for nineteenth-century roadway prescription concerned the location of purported roads. The older cases often held that the public could acquire prescriptive rights of passage in a narrow path, but not in open and uncultivated fields. On open fields, public passage was presumed to be by permission of the owner, and could give rise to no inference of dedication or adverse use.

Courts gave several reasons for this limitation. One was the magnitude of the owner's possible loss: if the public could acquire access or a right-of-way by going anywhere across a tract, an owner could be entirely divested of his property. * * *

However, other rationales contradicted this loss-minimization policy. For example, it was said that public passage across open and uncultivated fields would not support a prescriptive right because such public use did not preclude any use by the owner himself, and so was not genuinely adverse. * * *

These reasons seem at best inconclusive. Open spaces could not be acquired by public prescription because the owner would lose too much to be fair to him—or contrariwise, because he would lose too little to presume genuine adversity. We must find other reasons for the narrow-passage rule; and the anti-holdout rationale is a very strong contender.

Insofar as the specific passage rule related to areas where much land was open and unused, the public had many potential pathways; hence there was little danger if one owner or another enclosed his land and blocked public crossing. Conversely, insofar as the rule permitted prescription of a narrow, defined path, it suggested that the public had singled out a particular passage that might be especially valuable. Without public prescription doctrine, each owner along the way might bar the passage at will and siphon off its public value, thus capturing the "rents" from that public usage. But this is precisely what the rule prevented.

As a general rule, then, * * * the exception for roadways applied only to specific passageways, not to open spaces. This exception prevented private holdout against public passage; but it only came into play upon a genuine threat of such behavior. Public meanderings anywhere across an open field suggested that the public had no focused need for a particular path and private owners felt no pronounced temptation for exploitation; therefore such meanderings would not raise a presumption of "dedication."

This anti-holdout rationale is strengthened by its similarity to other nineteenth-century American roadway doctrines. Roadways were the classic subject of eminent domain by the "organized" public. Prescriptive doctrines, by analogy to private law doctrines, assured that the "unorganized" public—which could not exercise eminent domain—was also protected from private holdout. A private party could sometimes own a toll road, but his potential power to capture all "rents" of travel was tempered by treatment as a public utility: the road was open to all members of the public, and the owner could charge tolls reflecting not what the market would bear, but only what would suffice to reimburse his expenses. * * *

Like roadway doctrine, waterway doctrine also reflected an antipathy to the possibility of private monopolization of public passage. This was hardly surprising; it was a commonplace of nineteenth-century jurisprudence that waterways were a "highway" for travel and commerce. Moreover, their location was largely fixed by nature, so that their use was even more subject to holdout than roadways, which are movable. Thus holdout potential explains several cases elevating the public right of water passage above all other uses, even bridges for land roads unless specifically authorized by legislatures. Land traffic might find some other route, whereas ships had no alternative and were especially susceptible to exploitation. * * *

Th[e] rejection of recreation as a public trust purpose, taken together with strong protection of commercial travel on waterways, suggests that the fear of private holdout was central to early nineteenth-century thinking about public access to waterways. * * * The uses of waterways most subject to monopolization or holdout were transportation and commerce, which involved movement from place to place over a relatively narrow "path." As one British court stated, the beach is "not to be regarded as in the full sense of the word a highway," open to recreational uses: no matter how ungenerous the act, beach owners were entitled to treat as trespassers "every bather, every nursemaid with a perambulator, every boy riding a donkey, and every preacher on the shore."[229]

Thus, it is difficult to fit into a "holdout" rationale such public trust uses as swimming, fishing, and hunting. Recreational uses might occur in numerous places, without requiring any great stretch of waterway; moreover, in any normal market, a variety of riparian owners might compete to provide swimming or other recreational facilities. This presents [a] problem * * *: why should we guarantee public access for recreational purposes when there seems to be no threat of private holdout?

[Professor Rose then argues that in addition to holdout prevention, a second rationale supports the publicness of certain spaces, namely increasing returns to scale of the activities practiced there. She notes that the traditional public trust doctrines for roads and waterways overwhelmingly focused on encouraging commerce, and that commerce itself has increasing returns as markets expand; those reasons would support doctrines of open lanes to encourage ever more members of the public to participate. She then returns to the subject of recreation.] * * *

Certainly the role of recreation is a striking example of historic change in public property doctrine. If recreation now seems to support the "publicness" of some property, this undoubtedly reflects a change in our attitudes toward recreation. We might suspect that this changed attitude relates to an increasing perception of recreation as having something analogous to scale returns, and as a socializing institution.

Recreation is often carried on in a social setting, and therefore it clearly improves with scale to some degree: one must have a partner for chess, two teams for baseball, etc. But in the mid-nineteenth century, Frederick Law Olmsted argued that recreation had scale returns in a much more expansive sense: recreation can be a socializing and educative influence, particularly helpful for democratic values.[320] Thus rich and poor would mingle in parks, and learn to treat each other as neighbors. Parks would enhance public mental health, with ultimate benefits to sociability; all could revive from the antisocial characteristics of urban life under the refining influence of the park's soothing landscape. Later recreation and park advocates, though moving away from Olmsted's more contemplative ethic, also stressed the democratic education that comes with sports and team play.

Insofar as recreation educates and socializes us, it acts as a "social glue" for everyone, not just those immediately engaged; and of course, the more people involved in any socializing activity, the better. Like commerce, then, recreation has social and political overtones. The contemplation of nature elevates our minds above the workaday world, and thus helps us to cope with that very world; recreational play trains us in the democratic

---

229. Llandudno Urban Dist. Council v. Woods, 2 Ch. 705, 709, [1899] All E.R. 895, 896, 81 L.T.R. 170, 171 (1899).

320. Frederick Law Olmsted, Civilizing American Cities: A Selection of Frederick Law Olmsted's Writings on City Landscapes 74–81 (S. Sutton ed. 1971).

give-and-take that makes our regime function. If these arguments are true, we should not worry that people engage in too much recreation, but too little. This again argues that recreation should be open to all at minimal costs, or at costs to be borne by the general public, since all of us benefit from the greater sociability of our fellow citizens. If we accept these arguments, we might believe that unique recreational sites ought not be private property; their greatest value lies in civilizing and socializing all members of the public, and this value should not be "held up" by private owners.

These arguments support the recent decisions defending public access to the beach. The public's recreational use arguably is the most valuable use of this property and requires an entire expanse of beach (for unobstructed walking, viewing, contemplation) which could otherwise be blocked and "held up" by private owners. But * * * [d]o people using the beach really become more civil, or acquire the mental habits of democracy? And even if they do, is there really a danger of holdout that necessitates inalienable public access?

Attractive as this Olmstedian view may seem, these are not always easy arguments to support, and are extraordinarily difficult to prove. The argument that recreation or the contemplation of nature makes us more civilized and sociable has a very long pedigree in Western thought. Moreover, it may seem particularly attractive as our confidence has waned (perhaps somewhat unjustifiably) in the socializing qualities of commerce. With respect to the holdout problem, one might be skeptical and think that where waterfront owners are numerous, they cannot really siphon off the value of expansive public uses. But whether or not one accepts these arguments in the modern beach debate, older doctrine suggests that the "scale returns" of socialization, taken together with the possibility of private holdout, will underlie any arguments for the inherent publicness of property.

Perhaps the chief lesson from the nineteenth-century doctrines of "inherently public property," then, is that while we may change our minds about which activities are socializing, we always accept that the public requires access to some physical locations for some of these activities. Our law consistently allocates that access to the public, because public access to those locations is as important as the general privatization of property in other spheres of our law. In the absence of the socializing activities that take place on "inherently public property," the public is a shapeless mob, whose members neither trade nor converse nor play, but only fight, in a setting where life is, in Hobbes' all too famous phrase, solitary, poor, nasty, brutish, and short.

NOTES AND QUESTIONS

1. Considering the material covered in this section—including that on navigable waters, navigable airspace, the public trust doctrine, customary rights, and the doctrine of public prescriptive rights mentioned in *Thornton*

and in the Rose excerpt—do you agree with Rose that there is a category of "inherently public property" separate and distinct from "government-owned property?" In other words, are there three categories of property—private, governmental, and inherently public—or just two categories—private and governmental?

2. One operational distinction between governmental property and inherently public property might be based on who has standing to enforce the property right. Governmental property would be property that can be enforced only by duly appointed officers of the state—such as the state Attorney General's office or the U.S. Department of Justice. Inherently public property would be property that any member of the public can seek to enforce. In this regard, it is interesting to note that many states, including Illinois, have moved toward recognizing very broad "citizen standing" to enforce the public trust doctrine. In *Illinois Central*, the action by the state against the railroad was brought by the State Attorney General. In *Lake Michigan Federation*, the action was bought by a citizens' group dedicated to environmental protection of Lake Michigan.

3. If we decide that certain types of resources, like beaches, are "inherently public," and if we confer standing on any member of the public to block privatization or perhaps even development of these resources, does this create a danger of a regulatory "anticommons"? See Chapter II. In other words, do we create too much exclusion?

D. WATER

Water is a particularly important resource with a wide variety of uses, including drinking and household consumption, farming and livestock raising, irrigation, mining, power, manufacturing, sewage, navigation, wild-life, and recreation. Water can also serve aesthetic and environmental values. These last include what are sometimes called "ecosystem services." Given a growing population with rising demand for water for consumptive uses, and the simultaneous rise in demand for preservation of lakes and streams for recreational and ecological purposes, clashes over water rights will likely intensify in the coming years.

Water is a unique resource different in many respects from land and the typical objects of personal property rights. Water is a fugitive resource with a flow that is only partly predictable. It is also a replenishable resource, as a result of the hydrologic cycle. Given its peculiar characteristics, water has always been treated differently from other kinds of resources. Water rights have aspects of both private rights and public rights; they are at once open to individual appropriation and subject to correlative duties to other users. Given the uniqueness of water rights, arguments for greater privatization of water—such as by making water rights freely transferable like other commodities—have long been, and continue to be, controversial.

In the United States, water law consists of a common-law base with state statutory and federal overlays. In these materials we will concentrate on the common law of water and how it relates to property law's treatment of other resources.

First, some terminology. The law distinguishes water along two axes: *surface* versus *underground*, and *diffuse* versus *in a defined channel (or body)*. We turn first to water in a surface stream, with a look at two different systems, riparian rights and first appropriation. Diffuse surface water is very different—it is considered undesirable and something to be warded off rather than "used." Next we take a look at groundwater, for which the distinction between diffuse and running in a defined channel has often been important, but also criticized.

1. WATERCOURSES

A riparian owner is one whose land abuts the watercourse, and riparian water rights are appurtenant to the land—the rights to the land and the right to use the water from the surface stream form a package that cannot be split up. (The "littoral" rights of owners whose land abuts a lake, sea, or ocean are similar to riparian rights.) English law developed a conception of riparian rights known as the natural flow theory, whereby each riparian owner could prevent any diversion of the natural flow of a river or stream by an upstream riparian owner. In effect, any disturbance of the natural flow required the consent of each downstream owner. This conception of riparian rights found little favor in the United States, on the grounds that it imposed too great a barrier to the use of water for economic development, such as diverting streams to power water mills. Early on, American courts began to reject the natural flow theory in favor of a more flexible conception of riparian rights that came to be known as the reasonable use theory. The next case is illustrative of the circumstances that gave rise to this American version of riparian rights doctrine.

Evans v. Merriweather

Supreme Court of Illinois, 1842.
4 Ill. 492, 38 Am. Dec. 106.

■ LOCKWOOD, JUSTICE, delivered the opinion of the court: This was an action on the *case*, brought in the Greene Circuit Court, by Merriweather against Evans, for obstructing and diverting a water course. The plaintiff obtained a verdict, and judgment was rendered thereon. On the trial the defendant excepted to the instructions asked for and given, at the instance of the plaintiff. The defendant also excepted, because instructions that were asked by him, were refused. After the cause was brought into this court, the parties agreed upon the following statement of facts, as having been proved on the trial, to wit:

> It is agreed between the parties to this suit, that the following is the statement of facts proved at the trial in this case, and that the

same shall be considered as part of the record by the court, in the adjudication of this cause. Smith and Baker, in 1834, bought of T. Carlin six acres of land, through which a branch ran, and erected a steam mill thereon. They depended upon a well and the branch for water in running their engine. About one or two years afterwards, John Evans bought of T. Carlin six acres of land, on the same branch, above and immediately adjoining the lot owned by Smith & Baker, and erected theron a steam mill, depending upon a well and the branch for water in running his engine.

Smith & Baker, after the erection of Evans' mill, in 1836 or 1837, sold the mill and appurtenances to Merriweather, for about $8,000. Evans' mill was supposed to be worth $12,000. Ordinarily there was an abundance of water for both mills; but in the fall of 1837, there being a drought, the branch failed, so far that it did not afford water sufficient to run the upper mill continually. Evans directed his hands not to stop, or divert the water, in the branch; but one of them employed about the mill did make a dam across the branch, just below Evans' mill, and thereby diverted all the water in the branch into Evans' well. Evans was at home, half a mile from the mill, and was frequently about his mill, and evidence was introduced conducing to prove that he might have known that the water of the branch was diverted into his well. After the diversion of the water into Evans' well, as aforesaid, the branch went dry below, and Merriweather's mill could not and did not run, in consequence of it, more than one day in a week, and was then supplied with water from his well. Merriweather then brought this suit, in three or four weeks after the putting of the dam across the branch for the diversion of the water, and obtained a verdict for $150. This suit, it is admitted, is the first between the parties litigating the right as to the use of the water. It is further agreed, that the branch afforded usually sufficient water for the supply of both mills, without materially affecting the size of the current, though the branch was not depended upon exclusively for that purpose. Furthermore, that at the time of the grievances complained of by the plaintiff below, the defendant had water hauled in part for the supply of his boilers. That the dam was made below the defendant's well, across the branch, which diverted as well the water hauled and poured out into the branch above the well, as the water of the branch, into the defendant's well. . . .

Upon this state of facts, the question is presented, as to what extent riparian proprietors, upon a stream not navigable, can use the water of such stream? The branch mentioned in the agreed statement of facts, is a small natural stream of water, not furnishing, at all seasons of the year, a supply of water sufficient for both mills. There are no facts in the case showing that the water is wanted for any other than milling purposes, and for those purposes to be converted into steam, and thus entirely consumed. In an early case decided in England,[1] it is laid down that "A water course

1. Bulstrode, 339.

begins '*ex jure naturae,*' and having taken a certain course naturally, can not be diverted." The language of all the authorities is, that water flows in its natural course, and should be permitted thus to flow, so that all through whose land it naturally flows, may enjoy the privilege of using it. The property in the water, therefore, by virtue of the riparian ownership, is in its nature usufructuary, and consists, in general, not so much of the fluid itself, as of the advantage of its impetus.[2] A riparian proprietor, therefore, though he has an undoubted right to use the water for hydraulic or manufacturing purposes, must so use it as to do no injury to any other riparian proprietor. Some decisions, in laying down the rights of riparian proprietors of water courses, have gone so far as to restrict their right in the use of water flowing over their land, so that there shall be no diminution in the quantity of the water, and no obstruction to its course. The decisions last referred to can not, however, be considered as furnishing the true doctrine on this subject. Mr. Justice Storey, in delivering the opinion of the court, in the case of Tyler v. Wilkinson,[3] says,

> I do not mean to be understood as holding the doctrine that there can be no diminution whatever, and no obstruction or impediment whatever, by a riparian proprietor in the use of water as it flows; for that would be to deny any valuable use of it. There may be, and there must be, of that which is common to all, a reasonable use. The true test of the principle and extent of the use is, whether it is to the injury of the other proprietors or not. There may be diminution in quantity, or a retardation or acceleration of the natural current, indispensable for the general and valuable use of the water, perfectly consistent with the use of the common right. The diminution, retardation, or acceleration, not positively and sensibly injurious, by diminishing the value of the common right, is an implied element in the right of using the stream at all. The law here, as in many other cases, acts with a reasonable reference to public convenience and general good, and is not betrayed into a narrow strictness, subversive of common use, nor into an extravagant looseness, which would destroy private rights.

The same learned judge further says, "That of a thing common by nature, there may be an appropriation by general consent or grant. Mere priority of appropriation of running water, without such consent or grant, confers no exclusive right." * * *

Each riparian proprietor is bound to make such a use of running water as to do as little injury to those below him as is consistent with a valuable benefit to himself. The use must be a reasonable one. Now the question fairly arises, is that a reasonable use of running water by the upper proprietor, by which the fluid itself is entirely consumed? To answer this question satisfactorily, it is proper to consider the wants of man in regard to the element of water. These wants are either natural or artificial. Natural are such as are absolutely necessary * * * to his existence.

---

2.   2 Barn & Cres., 510; Angell on Water Courses, 11.

3.   4 Mason, 400.

Artificial, such only as, by supplying them, his comfort and prosperity are increased. To quench thirst, and for household purposes, water is absolutely indispensable. In civilized life, water for cattle is also necessary. These wants must be supplied, or both man and beast will perish.

The supply of man's artificial wants is not essential to his existence; it is not indispensable; he could live if water was not employed in irrigating lands, or in propelling his machinery. In countries differently situated from ours, with a hot and arid climate, water doubtless is absolutely indispensable to the cultivation of the soil, and in them, water for irrigation would be a natural want. Here it might increase the products of the soil, but it is by no means essential, and can not, therefore, be considered a natural want of man. So of manufactures, they promote the prosperity and comfort of mankind, but can not be considered absolutely necessary to his existence; nor need the machinery which he employs be set in motion by steam.

From these premises would result this conclusion: that an individual owning a spring on his land, from which water flows in a current through his neighbor's land, would have the right to use the whole of it, if necessary to satisfy his natural wants. He may consume all the water for his domestic purposes, including water for his stock. If he desires to use it for irrigation or manufactures, and there be a lower proprietor to whom its use is essential to supply his natural wants, or for his stock, he must use the water so as to leave enough for such lower proprietor. Where the stream is small, and does not supply water more than sufficient to answer the natural wants of the different proprietors living on it, none of the proprietors can use the water for either irrigation or manufactures. So far, then, as natural wants are concerned, there is no difficulty in furnishing a rule by which riparian proprietors may use flowing water to supply such natural wants. Each proprietor in his turn may, if necessary, consume all the water for these purposes. But where the water is not wanted to supply natural wants and there is not sufficient for each proprietor living on the stream, to carry on his manufacturing purposes, how shall the water be divided? We have seen that, without a contract or grant, neither has a right to use all the water; all have a right to participate in its benefits. Where all have a right to participate in a common benefit, and none can have an exclusive enjoyment, no rule, from the very nature of the case, can be laid down, as to how much each may use without infringing upon the rights of others. In such cases, the question must be left to the judgment of the jury, whether the party complained of has used, under all the circumstances, more than his just proportion.

It appears, from the facts agreed on, that Evans obstructed the water by a dam, and diverted the whole into his well. This diversion, according to all the cases, both English and American, was clearly illegal. For this diversion, an action will lie. * * * Having availed himself of the illegal act of his servant, the law presumes he authorized it. Having arrived at the conclusion that an action will lie in behalf of Merriweather against Evans, for obstructing and diverting the water course mentioned in the plaintiff's declaration, I have not deemed it necessary to examine the instructions given by the court, to see if they accord with the principles above laid down. Having decided that the plaintiff below has a right to recover on the facts, whether the instructions were right or wrong would not vary that result. It is possible that if the true principles which govern this action had been correctly given to the jury, the damages might have been either less or more than the jury have given; but in this case, as the damages are small, the court ought not, where justice has upon the whole been done, to send the case back, to see if a jury, upon another trial, would not give less.

For these reasons I am of opinion that the judgment ought to be affirmed, with costs.

NOTES AND QUESTIONS

1. The English natural flow theory bears a resemblance to the law of trespass, in the sense that any material interference with downstream riparian rights is forbidden unless the downstream owner consents. The American reasonable use doctrine is more like the law of nuisance, in the sense that a wide variety of contextual factors are relevant in determining whether a diversion is actionable. According to the *Restatement (Second) of Torts* § 850(A) (1970), a court determining whether a use is reasonable should consider the purpose of the use, its suitability to the water course, the economic and social values at stake, the harm caused, possible accommodation techniques, the protection of existing investments, the ability of adversely affected riparians to bear the loss, and "justice." That would seem to cover just about everything. What accounts for the shift from a strict and predictable doctrine that emphasizes bargaining and consent to one that allows courts to arbitrate disputes among competing riparian claimants? Are the factors that explain the shift similar to the ones that might explain the shift from trespass to nuisance when we move from large invasions of land to small invasions or other interferences with use and enjoyment of land? The emergence of new technologies like water mills is clearly part of the explanation. See Morton J. Horwitz, The Transformation of American Law, 1780–1860, at 34–47 (1977); Carol Rose, Energy and Efficiency in the Realignment of Common–Law Water Rights, 19 J. Legal Stud. 261, 264–96 (1990). Does this suggest that the shift to reasonable use has a broadly Demsetzian explanation?

2. In at least one critical respect the analogy between the riparian doctrine of reasonable use and the law of nuisance is incomplete. As mentioned earlier, riparian rights run with the land and cannot be severed. Thus, riparian owner A could not sell his rights to nonriparian owner B. Courts have tended to enforce this rule quite strictly. What accounts for this refusal to treat water as a pure commodity that can be severed from use with respect to particular parcels of riparian land? Of course, people inevitably found room to maneuver around the rule against severance. What happens if A subdivides his parcel into two parcels, each with one half of the frontage on the water course? Why stop at two parcels? This is the so-called "bowling alley parcel" problem, in which a riparian landowner

sells narrow strips of land to nonriparians, who would then claim rights of reasonable use. Riparian law accordingly developed detailed doctrines to deal with subdivisions of the riparian parcels that threatened to impose too great a burden on other riparian owners.

3. *Evans v. Merriweather* also draws a sharp distinction between "natural" wants and "artificial" wants. A more common way of drawing the same distinction today is to distinguish between "domestic" and "other" (i.e., nondomestic) uses. The granting of an absolute priority for "natural" or "domestic" uses over "artificial" or "other" uses is also characteristic of reasonable use doctrine. Domestic uses include household uses (for cleaning and cooking) and small-scale livestock watering—the small farm or homestead is the model for "natural" or "domestic" needs. As employed by the *Evans* court, this distinction comes into play only during periods of drought, when there is too little water to satisfy the natural wants of all riparians. *Evans* seems to suggest that when drought strikes, the upstream riparian can fulfill all his domestic needs, even if this means downstream riparians get little or no water at all. Why privilege the upstream riparian in this fashion? Why not award the water to the first of the competing riparians to have appropriated water for domestic uses? Why not apportion the water among the competing riparians—equally, according to frontage, or on some other basis?

4. Do principles of adverse possession, considered in Chapter II, apply to riparian water rights? If so, how should adverse use be defined in this context? Is prior appropriation of water enough to establish adversity as against other riparians who seek to appropriate water at a later time? Or must the appropriation be sufficiently great to interfere with what would be classified as "natural" or domestic uses by other riparians?

5. *Evans* suggests that periods of drought will be relatively rare in a state like Illinois, which usually has adequate rainfall to replenish flowing streams. But what happens in a relatively more arid state where drought is more or less the perpetual state of affairs? Consider the following case.

Coffin v. The Left Hand Ditch Company

Supreme Court of Colorado, 1882.
6 Colo. 443.

■ HELM, J. Appellee, who was plaintiff below, claimed to be the owner of certain water by virtue of an appropriation thereof from the south fork of the St. Vrain creek. It appears that such water, after its diversion, is carried by means of a ditch to the James creek, and thence along the bed of the same to Left Hand creek, where it is again diverted by lateral ditches and used to irrigate lands adjacent to the last named stream. Appellants are the owners of lands lying on the margin and in the neighborhood of the St. Vrain below the mouth of said south fork thereof, and naturally irrigated therefrom.

In 1879 there was not a sufficient quantity of water in the St. Vrain to supply the ditch of appellee and also irrigate the said lands of appellant. A portion of appellee's dam was torn out, and its diversion of water thereby seriously interfered with by appellants. The action is brought for damages arising from the trespass, and for injunctive relief to prevent repetitions thereof in the future. * * *

It is contended by counsel for appellants that the common law principles of riparian proprietorship prevailed in Colorado until 1876, and that the doctrine of priority of right to water by priority of appropriation thereof was first recognized and adopted in the constitution. But we think the latter doctrine has existed from the date of the earliest appropriations of water within the boundaries of the state. The climate is dry, and the soil, when moistened only by the usual rainfall, is arid and unproductive; except in a few favored sections, artificial irrigation for agriculture is an absolute necessity. Water in the various streams thus acquires a value unknown in moister climates. Instead of being a mere incident to the soil, it rises, when appropriated, to the dignity of a distinct usufructuary estate, or right of property. It has always been the policy of the national, as well as the territorial and state governments, to encourage the diversion and use of water in this country for agriculture; and vast expenditures of time and money have been made in reclaiming and fertilizing by irrigation portions of our unproductive territory. Houses have been built, and permanent improvements made; the soil has been cultivated, and thousands of acres have been rendered immensely valuable, with the understanding that appropriations of water would be protected. Deny the doctrine of priority or superiority of right by priority of appropriation, and a great part of the value of all this property is at once destroyed. * * *

We conclude, then, that the common law doctrine giving the riparian owner a right to the flow of water in its natural channel upon and over his lands, even though he makes no beneficial use thereof, is inapplicable to Colorado. Imperative necessity, unknown to the countries which gave it birth, compels the recognition of another doctrine in conflict therewith. And we hold that, in the absence of express statutes to the contrary, the first appropriator of water from a natural stream for a beneficial purpose has, with the qualifications contained in the constitution, a prior right thereto, to the extent of such appropriation. See Schilling v. Rominger, 4 Colo. 100, 103 (1878).

The territorial legislature in 1864 expressly recognizes the doctrine. It says: "Nor shall the water of any stream be diverted from its original channel to the detriment of any miner, millmen or others along the line of said stream, *who may have a priority of right,* and there shall be at all times left sufficient water in said stream for the use of miners and agriculturists along said stream." Session Laws of 1864, p. 68, § 32.

The priority of right mentioned in this section is acquired by priority of appropriation, and the provision declares that appropriations of water shall be subordinate to the use thereof by prior appropriators. This provision remained in force until the adoption of the constitution; it was repealed in 1868, but the repealing act re-enacted it *verbatim*.

But the rights of appellee were acquired, in the first instance, under the acts of 1861 and 1862, and counsel for appellants urge, with no little skill and plausibility, that these statutes are in conflict with our conclusion that priority of right is acquired by priority of appropriation. The only provision, however, which can be construed as referring to this subject is § 4 on page 68, Session Laws of 1861. This section provides for the appointment of commissioners, in times of scarcity, to apportion the stream "in a just and equitable proportion," to the best interests of all parties, "with a due regard to the legal rights of all." What is meant by the concluding phrases of the foregoing statute? What are the legal rights for which the commissioners are enjoined to have a "due regard?" Why this additional limitation upon the powers of such commissioners?

It seems to us a reasonable inference that these phrases had reference to the rights acquired by priority of appropriation. This view is sustained by the universal respect shown at the time said statute was adopted, and subsequently by each person, for the prior appropriations of others, and the corresponding customs existing among settlers with reference thereto. This construction does not, in our judgment, detract from the force or effect of the statute. It was the duty of the commissioners under it to guard against extravagance and waste, and to so divide and distribute the water as most economically to supply all of the earlier appropriators thereof according to their respective appropriations and necessities, to the extent of the amount remaining in the stream.

It appears from the record that the patent under which appellant George W. Coffin holds title was issued prior to the act of congress of 1866, hereinbefore mentioned. That it contained no reservation or exception of vested water rights, and conveyed to Coffin through his grantor the absolute title in fee simple to his land, together with all incidents and appurtenances thereunto belonging; and it is claimed that therefore the doctrine of priority of right by appropriation cannot, at least, apply to him. We have already declared that water appropriated and diverted for a beneficial purpose is, in this country, not necessarily an appurtenance to the soil through which the stream supplying the same naturally flows. If appropriated by one prior to the patenting of such soil by another, it is a vested right entitled to protection, though not mentioned in the patent. But we are relieved from any extended consideration of this subject by the decision in Broder v. Notoma W. & M. Co., 101 U.S. (11 Otto) 274 (1879).

It is urged, however, that even if the doctrine of priority or superiority of right by priority of appropriation be conceded, appellee in this case is not benefited thereby. Appellants claim that they have a better right to the water because their lands lie along the margin and in the neighborhood of the St. Vrain. They assert that, as against them, appellee's diversion of said water to irrigate lands adjacent to Left Hand creek, though prior in time, is unlawful. In the absence of legislation to the contrary, we think that the right to water acquired by priority of appropriation thereof is not in any way dependent upon the locus of its application to the beneficial use designed. And the disastrous consequences of our adoption of the rule contended for, forbid our giving such a construction to the statutes as will concede the same, if they will properly bear a more reasonable and equitable one.

The doctrine of priority of right by priority of appropriation for agriculture is evoked, as we have seen, by the imperative necessity for artificial irrigation of the soil. And it would be an ungenerous and inequitable rule that would deprive one of its benefit simply because he has, by large expenditure of time and money, carried the water from one stream over an intervening watershed and cultivated land in the valley of another. It might be utterly impossible, owing to the topography of the country, to get water upon his farm from the adjacent stream; or if possible, it might be impracticable on account of the distance from the point where the diversion must take place and the attendant expense; or the quantity of water in such stream might be entirely insufficient to supply his wants. It sometimes happens that the most fertile soil is found along the margin or in the neighborhood of the small rivulet, and sandy and barren land beside the larger stream. To apply the rule contended for would prevent the useful and profitable cultivation of the productive soil, and sanction the waste of water upon the more sterile lands. It would have enabled a party to locate upon a stream in 1875, and destroy the value of thousands of acres, and the improvements thereon, in adjoining valleys, possessed and cultivated for the preceding decade. Under the principle contended for, a party owning land ten miles from the stream, but in the valley thereof, might deprive a prior appropriator of the water diverted therefrom whose lands are within a thousand yards, but just beyond an intervening divide.

We cannot believe that any legislative body within the territory or state of Colorado ever *intended* these consequences to flow from a statute enacted. Yet two sections are relied upon by counsel as practically producing them. These sections are as follows:

> All persons who claim, own or hold a possessory right or title to any land or parcel of land within the boundary of Colorado territory, . . . when those claims are on the bank, margin or neighborhood of any stream of water, creek or river, shall be entitled to the use of the water of said stream, creek or river for the purposes of irrigation, and making said claims available to the full extent of the soil, for agricultural purposes. Session Laws 1861, p. 67, § 1.

> Nor shall the water of any stream be diverted from its original channel to the detriment of any miner, millmen or others along the line of said stream, and there shall be at all times left sufficient water in said stream for the use of miners and farmers along said stream. Latter part of § 13, p. 48, Session Laws 1862.

The two statutory provisions above quoted must, for the purpose of this discussion, be construed together. The phrase "along said stream," in the latter, is equally comprehensive, as to the extent of territory, with the expression "on the bank, margin or neighborhood," used in the former, and

both include all lands in the immediate valley of the stream. The latter
provision sanctions the diversion of water from one stream to irrigate lands
adjacent to another, provided such diversion is not to the "detriment" of
parties along the line of the stream from which the water is taken. If there
is any conflict between the statutes in this respect, the latter, of course,
must prevail. We think that the "use" and "detriment" spoken of are a use
existing at the time of the diversion, and a detriment immediately resulting
therefrom. We do not believe that the legislature intended to prohibit the
diversion of water to the "detriment" of parties who might at some future
period conclude to settle upon the stream; nor do we think that they were
legislating with a view to preserving in such stream sufficient water for the
"use" of settlers who might never come, and consequently never have use
therefor.

But "detriment" at the time of diversion could only exist where the
water diverted had been previously appropriated or used; if there had been
no previous appropriation or use thereof, there could be no present injury
or "*detriment*."

Figure 3–6
The St. Vrain Creek

Courtesy Susan Thomas.

Our conclusion above as to the intent of the legislature is supported by the fact that the succeeding assembly, in 1864, hastened to insert into the latter statute, without other change or amendment, the clause, *"who have a priority of right,"* in connection with the idea of *"detriment'"* to adjacent owners. This amendment of the statute was simply the acknowledgment by the legislature of a doctrine already existing, under which rights had accrued that were entitled to protection. In the language of Mr. Justice Miller, above quoted, upon a different branch of the same subject, it "was rather a voluntary recognition of a pre-existing right constituting a valid claim, than the creation of a new one." * * *

But this is an action of trespass; the defendants below were, according to the verdict of the jury, and according to the view herein expressed, wrong-doers * * *

Affirmed.

NOTES AND QUESTIONS

1. Is the Colorado Supreme Court's exercise in statutory interpretation convincing? Do the legal principles laid down by the Colorado legislature sound all that different from those applied as a matter of common law in the *Evans* case?

2. The "Colorado doctrine," or prior appropriation, appears to move a long way toward recognizing water as a full-fledged private property right. Water rights are now based on a version of the first-in-time approach that is characteristic of original acquisition of other types of property rights, such as rights to wild animals or abandoned property. Moreover, in contrast to natural flow theory or the reasonable use doctrine, prior appropriation unambiguously permits the first appropriator to take all of the water in the stream. And of course, as *Coffin* holds, prior appropriation permits water to be severed from riparian land and even transported into another watershed. Yet notwithstanding these differences, it would be inaccurate to characterize prior appropriation as treating water like any other commodity. In addition to de facto and de jure restrictions on sales of water rights (see Note 6 infra), the prior appropriation doctrine incorporates notions of proper use: Generally speaking, only "beneficial uses" of appropriated water are permitted. As in the case of "reasonable use," it is difficult to state with certainty exactly what it means to be a beneficial use. The most famous example cited to show what is not beneficial is using water to flood gophers off one's land. See Tulare Irrigation Dist. v. Lindsay–Stratmore Irrigation Dist., 45 P.2d 972, 1007 (Cal. 1935). That helps.

3. In practice, prior appropriation systems are more of a governance regime than an exclusion regime, and with increased levels of regulation (of environmental quality issues, for example) may be becoming even more so. See Eric T. Freyfogle, Context and Accommodation in Modern Property Law, 41 Stan. L. Rev. 1529, 1530 (1989). Traditionally, prior appropriation rights gave a right to use water in a certain way for a certain period of time—rather than a right to a certain volume of water. This helps explain the often-decried doctrine that an appropriator who stops using the water or whose use becomes more efficient has no rights in the excess water. See

2 Waters and Water Rights § 12.03(c)(2) (Robert E. Beck ed., 1991 & Supp. 1995).

4. One limit on well-defined entitlements to water is the measurement technology available. In an earlier era the "miner's inch" was used, which involved forcing water through a one-inch square orifice under conditions that were neither easily controlled nor standardized. See George A. Gould & Douglas L. Grant, Cases and Materials on Water Law 11–12 (6th ed. 2000). The uncertainty associated with measurement technology probably helps explain the requirement of beneficial use: It was easier to monitor uses than to measure flows of water. Today, the official statutory measure in most western states is the cubic foot per second ("second foot" or "c.f.s."), which is measured with various meters and registers—and more recently with satellite monitors.

5. One frequent explanation of the tendency for western states to adopt some variant of prior appropriation is that in the arid West, water is more valuable and hence private property rights in water are more worthwhile. Eastern reasonable use doctrine and Western first appropriation then become a classic Demseztian story. See, e.g., Terry L. Anderson & P.J. Hill, The Evolution of Property Rights: A Study of the American West, 18 J.L. & Econ. 163, 176–78 (1975). Additionally, once the potential set of rightholders in the West was no longer limited to riparian owners or even to those whose lands were located in the same watershed, some limiting principle was needed in order to prevent water rights from becoming so finely subdivided as to be of little value. See Benjamin N. Cardozo, The Growth of the Law 117–20 (1924); David B. Schorr, Appropriation as Agrarianism: Distributive Justice in the Creation of Property Rights, 32 Ecology L.Q. 3 (2005). This was also a major concern in mining camps, out of which western water law grew (on mining camps, see Chapter II.B).

On the other hand, as Carol Rose has pointed out, the uses to which water was put in the two areas was different:

> Western water rights evolved from uses of water that were essentially consumptive. Some of these were power uses, such as forced-water hosing of offstream mining slopes, while other uses included such partial consumption as irrigation. * * * [W]estern water uses * * * consumed the water * * * because they took the water away from the stream and did not return it, or at least much of it. * * *
>
> But eastern riparian rights did not grow up around these consumptive uses of water, even though consumptive uses were sometimes at issue. Eastern riparian rights grew up around the use of water for power—that is—instream power—which is not necessarily a zero-sum game. * * * [I]f I have a mill on the river, and you do too, we can both use the water as it flows by—provided that we do so carefully and do not, for example, alternately interrupt and pour out the water in such a way as to disrupt the millworks downstream. * * *
>
> [T]he point of riparian law was to place boundaries on these necessarily consumptive aspects of water flow use, holding them within

"reasonable" and commonly accepted bounds so that the bulk of the water flow would be left intact. What I am suggesting, of course, is that eastern riparian law evolved from an aspect of water use, namely, power, that has aspects of a public good, quite unlike the individually consumptive uses of water that are characteristic of the West. * * *

Carol M. Rose, Energy and Efficiency in the Realignment of Common–Law Water Rights, 19 J. Legal Stud. 261, 290–92 (1990). Which of the foregoing explanations for the emergence of the Colorado doctrine or western appropriation theory is more convincing? Are they incompatible? Consider the conflict in *Evans v. Merriweather* again in the light of Rose's account.

6.   One of the most contentious issues these days is the marketing of water rights. Whether water rights can be sold has always been controversial, and the law on the subject has wavered over time. Today, prior appropriation regimes generally allow sales of water rights unless the sale would impose unwanted effects on third parties, such as downstream users of the return flow. The fact that water can fetch much higher prices in urban areas than in areas of longstanding agricultural use has led to posturing and bitter political conflict, most notoriously in Los Angeles's purchase of water rights from farmers in the Owens Valley. Compare William L. Kahrl, Water and Power: The Conflict over Los Angeles' Water Supply in the Owens Valley (1982) (arguing that transfers were coercive and devastated the Owens Valley) with Gary D. Libecap, Chinatown: Owens Valley and Western Water Reallocation—Getting the Record Straight and What It Means for Water Markets, 83 Tex. L. Rev. 2055 (2005) (arguing that transfers benefited Owens Valley owners but that owners received prices closer to value of land in agricultural rather than municipal use). There is a discernible trend now in the direction of market-alienability. What is the problem with commodifying water in the first place?

7.   Acquiring rights for instream uses, such as rafting or fishing is another live issue in western states today. If water is market-alienable, why not let those who would like to enjoy uninterrupted flow purchase the rights? Traditionally, under prior appropriation, a claim for instream use would not count as an appropriation for beneficial use, perhaps because of a lack of environmental concern or difficulty in delineating instream rights. More recently western states have been amending their water laws to provide for rights for instream users. In addition, the public trust doctrine (see supra Part C.2) can sometimes unexpectedly cause nonconsumptive uses to trump longstanding appropriative rights. What is the best way to integrate new-found demand for instream flows into the mosaic of water rights?

DIFFUSE SURFACE WATER

What about surface water that is not in a defined channel, or what is sometimes termed "casual water?" Under the "common enemy" doctrine, first adopted in *Luther v. Winnisimmet Co.*, 63 Mass. (9 Cush.) 171 (1851), each landowner has an absolute right to use self-help to repel inflows of these waters—that is, to combat the "common enemy" of surface water—

even if this causes damaging flooding to other landowners. 2 Waters and Water Rights § 10.03(b)(1) (Robert E. Berk ed., 1991 ed., 2000 replacement vol., 2001); 5 Waters and Water Rights § 59.02(b)(2). But if one landowner uses self-help to repel the water and causes the surface water to flow to a second owner's land, the second owner is similarly privileged to try to send the water back. Neither can sue the other. More recently, as conflicts have grown, the common enemy doctrine has been modified (or supplanted) by judicial policing for reasonableness. Again, we can discern a trend from a trespass-like doctrine (absolute privilege to repel invasions) to a more nuisance-like doctrine (arbitrating the rights of the parties under a broad context-sensitive reasonableness standard).

2. GROUNDWATER

Higday v. Nickolaus

Kansas City Court of Appeals, Missouri, 1971.
469 S.W.2d 859.

■ SHANGLER, PRESIDING JUDGE. This appeal is from a judgment dismissing plaintiffs' Petition for Declaratory Judgment and Injunction. The judgment of dismissal was entered upon defendant City's Motion to Dismiss which alleged that plaintiffs' petition failed to plead either a justiciable controversy or any claim upon which relief could be granted. The questions raised on this appeal are: whether the averments of the petition entitle plaintiffs, to a judicial declaration of their rights to the percolating waters underlying their lands, and if so, whether defendant City's threatened use of the percolating waters is such an infringement of those rights as will be enjoined by equity.

The facts alleged and in substance shown by the petition of plaintiffs, now appellants, are these: Appellants are the several owners of some 6000 acres of farm land overlying an alluvial water basin in Boone County known as the McBaine Bottom. These lands (projected on Exhibit "A" appended hereto [Figure 3–7 on the following page]) extend from Huntsdale at the north to Easley at the south; they are bordered by a line of limestone bluffs on the east and are enclosed by a sweeping bend of the Missouri River on the west. Underlying this entire plain are strata of porous rock, gravel and soil through which water, without apparent or definite channel, filtrates, oozes and percolates as it falls. This water (much of which has originated far upstream within the Missouri River Valley) has been trapped by an underlying stratum of impervious limestone so that the saturated soil has become a huge aquifer or underground reservoir.

Appellants have devoted the overlying lands to agricultural use with excellent resultant yields. They attribute the fertility of the soil to the continuing presence of a high subterranean water level which has unfailingly and directly supplied the moisture needs of the crops whatever the vagaries of the weather. Appellants also use the underground water for personal consumption, for their livestock, and in the near future will require it for the surface irrigation of their crops.

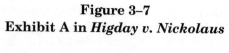

Figure 3–7
Exhibit A in *Higday v. Nickolaus*

Respondent City of Columbia is a burgeoning municipality of 50,000 inhabitants which has been, since 1948, in quest of a source of water to replenish a dwindling supply. Following the advice of consulting engineers, it settled on a plan for the withdrawal of water by shallow wells from beneath the McBaine Bottom where appellants' farms are located and thence to transport the water to the City some twelve miles away for sale to customers within and without the City. In December of 1966, the electorate approved a revenue bond issue for the development of a municipal water supply by such a system of shallow wells in the McBaine Bottom. Further scientific analysis and measurement of the basin's water resources followed. With the aid of a test well, it was determined that the underground percolating water table, when undisturbed, rises to an average of ten feet below the soil surface. These waters move laterally through the McBaine alluvium at the rate of two feet per day and in so doing displace 10.5 million gallons of water daily.

Respondent City, by threat of condemnation, has acquired from some of these appellants five well sites totalling 17.25 acres. The City now threatens to extract the groundwater at the rate of 11.5 million gallons daily for purposes wholly unrelated to any beneficial use of the overlying land, but instead, intends to transport the water to its corporate boundaries some miles away for purposes of sale. The mining of the water as contemplated will reduce the water table throughout the basin from the present average of ten feet to a new subsurface average of twenty feet. Appellants complain that this reduction of the water table will divert percolating waters normally available and enjoyed by appellants for their crops, livestock and their personal use and will eventually turn their land into an arid and sterile surface.

On the basis of these pleaded allegations, plaintiffs sought (1) a judicial declaration that defendant City is without right to extract the percolating waters for sale away from the premises or for other use not related with any beneficial ownership or enjoyment of the land from which they are taken when to do so will deprive them, the owners of the adjacent land, of the reasonable use of the underground water for the beneficial use of their own land, and (2) that defendant City be enjoined from undertaking to do so. * * *

In determining the sufficiency of plaintiffs' pleading as a petition for declaratory judgment, we accord it the benefit of every favorable and reasonable intendment the facts alleged will allow. So construed, the petition is sufficient as a statement of a claim for declaratory relief. Unquestionably, it pleads an actual, existing and real controversy between the parties, one which has put plaintiffs in grave uncertainty as to their rights. The petition describes the defendant City as having embarked upon a course of action, subscribed by the electorate, as will ultimately and inevitably culminate in damage to plaintiffs by the permanent lowering of the water table throughout the basin with the consequent impoverishment of plaintiffs' lands. The facts pleaded show the City's design to exploit the McBaine Bottom as the principal source of the municipal water supply has advanced to the point where well sites have been acquired on land adjacent to that held by plaintiffs. (The City acknowledges in its brief that it has committed almost $5,000,000 to this project, that it has acquired the sites for wells and a water treatment plant, and that the laying of water lines is virtually completed.) When the wells become operative, the City claims the right to withdraw groundwater in any quantity at will, for sale, even though damages may result to plaintiffs. Plaintiffs deny the City has such a right. They seek a declaration that the City has an obligation to conform to a standard of beneficial use of groundwater, a use that is related to the overlying land. * * *

Respondent maintains that since Springfield Waterworks Co. v. Jenkins, 62 Mo.App. 74, was decided by the St. Louis Court of Appeals in 1895, Missouri has recognized the common law rule that a landowner has absolute ownership to the waters under his land and, therefore, may without liability withdraw any quantity of water for any purpose even though the result is to drain all water from beneath his neighbors' lands. Therefore, contends respondent, since the threatened damage plaintiffs plead describes a consequence of the rightful use by respondent of its land, it is *damnum absque injuria* and not actionable. * * *

Simply stated, plaintiffs allege that defendant City claims [a] right to their groundwater and threatens to use it in such a manner as will injure plaintiffs. Plaintiffs ask if, under the circumstance, the City may do so lawfully. This aspect of plaintiffs' action is in the nature of a suit to quiet title to water rights (In re Bear River Drainage Area, 271 P.2d 846, 848 (Utah 1954)) and is a use to which the declaratory judgment remedy has been aptly applied. Applying the precepts we have examined, it is clear these averments invoke substantial principles of law which entitle plaintiffs to some relief. The issue raised affects the legal interest of plaintiffs, an interest which the trial court should have protected by an appropriate declaration, after an evidentiary hearing, thereby relieving plaintiffs of their uncertainty. It was error for the trial court to have denied plaintiffs an evidentiary hearing on their allegations for declaratory relief. * * *

It is fundamental that injunction will not be granted unless there is some substantial right to be protected. The indispensable basis for injunctive relief is the wrongful and injurious invasion of some legal right existing in plaintiff. The writ will issue also if invasion of that right is threatened by one having the power to do the wrong. Whether plaintiffs' allegations that the defendant municipality threatens to capture the percolating waters from their subjacent lands for purposes of sale in such quantities as will damage them describe an invasion of legal right which equity will enjoin depends upon whether plaintiffs have a right of property in these waters. The answer to that question, in turn, depends upon the rule to be applied to the ownership and use of subterranean percolating waters.

In legal contemplation, subterranean waters fall into two classifications, either underground streams or percolating waters.[2] An underground stream is defined as water that passes through or under the surface in a

---

2. These legal classifications have been roundly criticized by hydrologists and legal commentators as without scientific basis both as to the distinction attempted between percolating waters and underground streams and also because they ignore the essential interrelationship between surface and ground waters. See, e.g., Danielson, Ground Water in Nebraska, 35 Neb.L.Rev. 17 (1955); Clark, Groundwater Management: Law and Local Response, 6 Ariz.Law Rev. 188 (1965); 1 R. Clark, Waters and Water Rights, Sec. 3.1, p. 332 (1967). Also, Restatement, Torts, comment a to Sec. 858 (1939); Lauer, Reflections on Riparianism, 35 Mo.L.Rev. 1, 7 (1970).

definite channel or one that is reasonably ascertainable. Percolating waters include all waters which pass through the ground beneath the surface of the earth without a definite channel and not shown to be supplied by a definite flowing stream. They are waters which ooze, seep, filter and otherwise circulate through the interstices of the subsurface strata without definable channel, or in a course that is not discoverable from surface indications without excavation for that purpose. The rule is that all underground waters are presumed to be percolating and therefore the burden of proof is on the party claiming that a subterranean stream exists. Maricopa County Municipal Water Conservation Dist. No. 1 v. Southwest Cotton Co., 4 P.2d 369, 376 (Ariz. 1931); C & W Coal Corp. v. Salyer, 104 S.E.2d 50, 53 (Va. 1958); Wilkening v. State, 344 P.2d 204, 206 (Wash. 1959).

The law with respect to rights in percolating waters was not developed until a comparatively recent period.[3] Under the English common law rule, percolating waters constitute part and parcel of the land in which they are found and belong absolutely to the owner of such land who may without liability withdraw any quantity of water for any purpose even though the result is to drain all water from beneath the adjoining lands. Under this rule, a municipality [owning] land may collect the underlying percolating waters and use them to supply its inhabitants regardless of the effect on adjoining landowners.

The English rule relating to percolating groundwater was generally followed by American courts through the mid-nineteenth century, although not always with the full rigor of the absolute ownership doctrine. At an early day, the courts expressed dissatisfaction with the English common law rule and began applying what has come to be known variously, as the rule of "reasonable use", or of "correlative rights", or the "American rule."[4] By the turn of the century, a steady trend of decisions was discernible away from the English rule to a rule of reasonable use. The trend continues.[6]

Generally, the rule of reasonable use is an expression of the maxim that one must so use his own property as not to injure another—that each landowner is restricted to a reasonable exercise of his own rights and a reasonable use of his own property, in view of the similar rights of others. As it applies to percolating groundwater, the rule of reasonable use recognizes that the overlying owner has a proprietary interest in the water under his lands, but his incidents of ownership are restricted. It recognizes

---

3.   Acton v. Blundell, 12 Mees & W. 324, 152 Eng.Rep. 1223 (Exch. 1843), is generally cited as establishing the doctrine, but an earlier American decision, Greenleaf v. Francis, 35 Mass. (18 Pick) 177 (1836) had reached much the same result. See: Hutchins, Symposium on Water Law, 5 U.Kans.L.Rev. 533, 541 (1957).

4.   This rule originated in 1862 when the New Hampshire Supreme Court in Bassett v. Salisbury Mfg. Co., 43 N.H. 569, 573 (1862), rejected the doctrine of absolute ownership of percolating waters and adopted a rule of reciprocal reasonable use.

6.   Rothrauff v. Sinking Spring Water Co., 14 A.2d 87, 90 (Pa. 1940); City of Corpus Christi v. City of Pleasanton, 276 S.W.2d 798, 801 (Tex. 1955).

that the nature of the property right is usufructuary rather than absolute as under the English rule. Under the rule of reasonable use, the overlying owner may use the subjacent groundwater freely, and without liability to an adjoining owner, but only if his use is for purposes incident to the beneficial enjoyment of the land from which the water was taken. This rule does not prevent the consumption of such groundwater for agriculture, manufacturing, irrigation, mining or any purpose by which a landowner might legitimately use and enjoy his land, even though in doing so he may divert or drain the groundwater of his neighbor.

The principal difficulty in the application of the reasonable use doctrine is in determining what constitutes a reasonable use. What is a reasonable use must depend to a great extent upon many factors, such as the persons involved, their relative positions, the nature of their uses, the comparative value of their uses, the climatic conditions, and all facts and circumstances pertinent to the issues. Bristor v. Cheatham, 255 P.2d 173, 179 (Ariz. 1953); Bollinger v. Henry, 375 S.W.2d 161, 166 (Mo. 1964).[8] However, the modern decisions agree that under the rule of reasonable use *an overlying owner, including a municipality, may not withdraw percolating water and transport it for sale or other use away from the land from which it was taken if the result is to impair the supply of an adjoining landowner to his injury.* Such a use is unreasonable because non-beneficial and "is not for a 'lawful purpose within the general rule concerning percolating waters, but constitutes an actionable wrong for which damages are recoverable' ". Bristor v. Cheatham, supra, 255 P.2d at 178; Canada v. City of Shawnee, 64 P.2d 694 (Okla. 1936); Forbell v. City of New York, 58 N.E. 644, 646 (N.Y. 1900); Rothrauff v. Sinking Spring Water Co., 14 A.2d 87, 90 (Pa. 1940); Meeker v. City of East Orange, 74 A. 379, 385 (N.J. 1909); and cases listed in 55 A.L.R. 1404.

The "reasonable use" rule as developed in the law of ground waters must be distinguished from the "correlative rights" rule. In 1902, the California Supreme Court repudiated the English common law rule in favor of the distinctive correlative rights doctrine which is based on the theory of proportionate sharing of withdrawals among landowners overlying a common basin.[9] Under the doctrine, overlying owners have no proprietary interest in the water under their soil. California remains the only important correlative rights state; Utah has abandoned it, and only Nebraska also applies it to some extent.[10] The administration of such a system of rights has proved extremely difficult in times of water shortage and has tendered towards an "equalitarian rigidity" which does not take into account the relative value of the competing uses. However suitable this doctrine may be for California—the prime consumer of ground water in the

---

8. Bollinger v. Henry, supra, suggests certain factors in the determination of the reasonableness of a use of riparian waters. Secs. 852 and 861 of the Restatement of the Law of Torts (1939) state that the problem of determining a reasonable use is the same whether water is in a water course or lake or under the surface of the earth.

9. Katz v. Walkinshaw, 74 P. 766 (Cal. 1903).

10. 1 R. Clark, Water and Water Rights, Sec. 52.2(B), p. 331.

country—or any other state which may follow it, the reasonable use rule offers a more flexible legal standard for the just determination of beneficial uses of ground water, particularly under the climatic conditions of Missouri.

Respondent City contends that the English common law rule of absolute ownership of percolating waters governs in Missouri by virtue of statute and judicial decision. The City seems to suggest that since the Territorial Laws of 1816 adopted the common law as the rule of action and decision in this state and present Sec. 1.010 V.A.M.S. continues that legislative policy, we have no power to change or abrogate it. As we have already noted, Acton v. Blundell (marginal reference 3, supra), which is generally cited as having established the "English common law" rule of percolating waters, was decided in 1843 long after the Territorial Laws of 1816 were enacted. And not until 1860 was it decided that, without liability to an adjoining owner, an overlying owner might exhaust the groundwater to furnish a municipal water supply. Thus, there was no law of any kind on the subject at the time the common law was adopted by statute in this state. The subsequent English decisions declaring the common law on percolating waters are no more binding on us than the decisions of any court of another state. There is no impediment of inherited doctrine to our determination of the question presented according to the justice of the case.

The Missouri law of groundwater rests on a single case, Springfield Waterworks Company v. Jenkins, 62 Mo.App. 74, decided by the St. Louis Court of Appeals in 1895. Respondent City contends the holding in that case "reaffirms the English or Common Law Rule as to percolating waters and (that) this is the final word in Missouri on the subject." * * * We do not share respondent City's confidence that this decision either announces or follows the common law doctrine on the subject. * * *

The intervening three-quarters of a century since Springfield Waterworks Company v. Jenkins, supra, has seen for Missouri a significant urban, industrial and population increase and with it greater demands upon a relatively static water supply. In the past such water disputes as have been brought to our courts usually have arisen "from factual situations pertaining to the existence of too much rather than too little water". Bollinger v. Henry, supra, 375 S.W.2d at 165. The controversy between respondent City and plaintiffs over the McBaine Bottom groundwater, however, is prompted by a scarcity, not an excess, of water to supply the vital needs of both. It is a competition which is destined to recur between other municipalities and landowners as present sources of municipal water supplies diminish and the need for them increases. In such circumstances, appeals to a dogma of absolute ownership of groundwater without consideration of the rights of adjoining landowners seem unpersuasive.

Also, since Springfield Waterworks v. Jenkins, supra, the science of groundwater hydrology has come into existence and has proven the postulates of the common law rule to be unsound. The premise that the owner of the soil owns all that lies beneath the surface so that he may use the percolating water in any way he chooses without liability to an adjoining owner fails to recognize that the supply of groundwater is limited, and that the first inherent limitation on water rights is the availability of the supply.[14] Another postulate of the common law doctrine ascribes to percolating waters a movement so "secret, changeable and uncontrollable", that no attempt to subject them to fixed legal rules could be successfully made. Chatfield v. Wilson, 28 Vt. 49, 53 (1855); Frazier v. Brown, 12 Ohio St. 294 (1861). Modern knowledge and techniques have discredited this premise also. The movement, supply, rate of evaporation and many other physical characteristics of groundwater are now readily determinable. * * *

Recently, in Bollinger v. Henry, supra, 375 S.W.2d at 166, the Supreme Court of Missouri applied the rule of reasonable use to determine the rights of riparian owners. Subterranean streams are governed by the rules applying to natural watercourses on the surface, so the rule of reasonable use is now applicable to them also. 93 C.J.S. Waters § 89; 56 Am.Jur., Waters, Sec. 109; Springfield Waterworks Co. v. Jenkins, supra, 62 Mo.App. at 80. We believe the same rule should apply to subterranean percolating waters. Jones v. Oz–Ark–Val Poultry Company, 306 S.W.2d 111, 113 (Ark. 1957); Wrathall v. Johnson, 40 P.2d 755, 776 (Utah 1935). It is that legal standard, in absence of a statutory expression of a priority of uses, by which existing water resources may be allocated most equitably and beneficially among competing users, private and public. The application of such a uniform legal standard would also give recognition to the established interrelationship between surface and groundwater and would, therefore, bring into one classification all waters over the use of which controversy may arise.

Under the rule of reasonable use as we have stated it, the fundamental measure of the overlying owner's right to use the groundwater is whether it is for purposes incident to the beneficial enjoyment of the land from which it was taken. Thus, a private owner may not withdraw groundwater for purposes of sale if the adjoining landowner is thereby deprived of water necessary for the beneficial enjoyment of his land. Katz v. Walkinshaw, 74 P. 766 (Cal. 1902). Here, the municipality has acquired miniscule plots of earth and by the use of powerful pumps intends to draw into wells on its own land for merchandising groundwater stored in plaintiffs' land, thereby depriving plaintiffs of the beneficial use of the normal water table to their immediate injury and to the eventual impoverishment of their lands. "There is no apparent reason for saying that, because defendant is a municipal corporation, seeking water for the inhabitants of a city, it may therefore do what a private owner of land may not do. The city is a private owner of this land, and the furnishing of water to its inhabitants is its private business. It is imperative that the people of the city have water; it is not imperative that they secure it at the expense of those owning lands adjoining lands owned by the city." Schenk v. City of Ann Arbor, 163 N.W. 109, 114 (Mich. 1917). Under the rule we apply, however, plaintiffs could

---

14. 1 R. Clark, Waters and Water Rights, Secs. 2.1–2.5; 16 Rocky Mountain Mineral Law Institute 114 (1970); Lauer, Reflections in Riparianism, 35 Mo.L.Rev. 1, 2 (1970).

have no basis for complaint if the City of Columbia's withdrawals of groundwater for municipal purposes from the McBaine Bottom do not interfere with plaintiffs' beneficial use of such water. Under the facts pleaded, the water table could be maintained at its normal level and damage to plaintiffs avoided if the City were to limit its withdrawals to such quantity as would not exceed the daily recharge rate of 10.5 million gallons. If, on the other hand, the City perseveres in its declared intention to mine the water by at least one million gallons per day, it will become accountable to plaintiffs for [whatever] injury results from such diversion. * * *

This is not to suggest that should proof follow upon the pleadings, perforce injunction will issue. Injunctive relief is a matter of grace, not of right. "The writ of injunction is an extraordinary remedy. It does not issue as a matter of course, but somewhat at the discretion of the chancellor. It is his duty to consider its effect upon all parties in interest, and to issue it only in case it is necessary to protect a substantial right, *and even then not against great public interest*." (Emphasis supplied) Smith v. City of Sedalia, 149 S.W. 597, 601 (Mo. 1912); Johnson v. Independent School Dist. No. 1, 199 S.W.2d 421, 424 (Mo. Ct. App. 1947); 43 C.J.S. Injunctions § 31. It requires the application of the principles of equity under all the circumstances. * * *

The rule of comparative injury suggest that under the facts pleaded and concessions of counsel it may be more equitable to deny injunctive relief than to grant it. * * *

The City has resisted plaintiffs' requested declaratory and injunctive relief on the theory that the common law rule of absolute ownership of percolating waters has governed its relationship with plaintiffs and, therefore, any damage to them could not be a legal injury. It has not sought to exercise its power of eminent domain to acquire the right to withdraw water from beneath plaintiffs' lands doubtless on the premise that it was under no duty to do so. Should the trial court adjudge that plaintiffs are entitled to the declarations they seek, the rule of reasonable use will apply and defendant City will be answerable to plaintiffs for any damage from its unreasonable use of groundwater. Should the trial court adjudge injunctive relief for plaintiffs appropriate, it would be well within its discretion to condition the imposition of that restraint upon the exercise by the City within a reasonable time, of its power of eminent domain to acquire the water rights it has been violating. Failing that, plaintiffs would still have available to them a remedy in the nature of an inverse condemnation for any damage caused by the City's unreasonable use.

The judgment of the trial court is reversed and the cause is remanded for further proceedings consistent with the views we have expressed.

NOTES AND QUESTIONS

1. The English Rule of *Acton v. Blundell*, also termed the absolute ownership rule, gives the owner of land an absolute right to use as much

percolating groundwater as he pleases. The owner is privileged to pump within the space defined by the *ad coelum* rule. The American Rule of reasonable use (or correlative rights) can be seen as an application of the principle of another famous maxim, *sic utere tuo ut alienum non laedas*, "use your property in such a way as not to injure another's." Under this approach, what constitutes a harm (or conversely what is a proper use) must be defined. How would you characterize these approaches in terms of the distinction between trespass and nuisance, or exclusion and governance (see Chapter I)?

2.   The court here hints strongly that if the City is found to divert groundwater in excess of the natural recharge rate it will be liable for damages but not an injunction. Would the same conclusion follow in a future case when the applicable rule is clearer? What if the diversion had been for a privately owned manufacturing plant rather than a municipal water system?

3.   The problem of groundwater pumping is somewhat reminiscent of the common pool in oil and gas. Although oil and gas flow somewhat differently, there is still potential for a tragedy of the commons. Solutions to the common-pool problem with oil and gas have been late in coming and only partially successful. In particular, those owning lands over oil and gas fields typically have heterogeneous interests and asymmetric information, while at the same time the stakes are quite high, making bargaining very difficult. See Gary D. Libecap, Contracting for Property Rights 93–114 (1989); Gary D. Libecap & James L. Smith, The Economic Evolution of Petroleum Property Rights in the United States, 31 J. Legal Stud. S589 (2002).

E.   ELECTRONIC COMMUNICATIONS

Since the advent of radio, important resource conflicts have occurred between users of the electromagnetic spectrum for broadcast—and later other communicative—purposes. More recently, disputes have emerged over the principles for control of resources in cyberspace. Both electromagnetic waves and digital transmission of electrons support vast amounts of information communication: conventional and cellular telephone calls, paging services, television and radio programming, email, postings on and visits to websites, and so forth. Somewhat like water, the systems that sustain these electronic communications have both private rights and public rights aspects. They have private rights aspects in that the broadcast spectrum or cyberspace can feasibly be carved into zones of exclusion and these zones assigned to particular owner-gatekeepers. But also like water, these resources have peculiar features that give them a collective or correlative rights dimension, which may justify restrictions on how they are deployed in order to make them more valuable to the largest number of users. Consequently, we also find a blending of exclusion rights and open-access features in electronic communications media.

We begin with radio signals. Sending broadcast signals across someone's land has never been regarded as a violation of the landowner's property rights under the *ad coelum* rule. Can you see why? Instead, the spectrum has usually been regarded as a resource unto itself and has been the object of either private property rights or administrative regulation, depending partly on the intellectual fashions of the era.

The 1920s saw the rise of radio networks, with the National Broadcasting Corporation (NBC), a subsidiary of the Radio Corporation of America (RCA), in a dominant position. Increasing potential for interference between rival broadcasters led first to efforts by the U.S. Commerce Department to impose restrictions on radio broadcast licenses. Because license renewal and approvals of transfers were routine, in effect rights to airwaves were effectively bought and sold as part of a package of rights associated with ownership of particular radio stations. The Commerce Department also prevented crowding by denying some applications. Then in 1923, a federal court held that the Commerce Secretary had no authority to withhold licenses, but it upheld restrictions as to times and wavelengths for purposes of reducing interference. See Hoover v. Intercity Radio, 286 F. 1003 (D.C. 1923). This case did not much impact Commerce Department practice. But in *United Stated v. Zenith Radio Corp.*, 12 F.2d 614 (N.D. Ill. 1926), the court held that the Commerce Department lacked authority even to impose the license restrictions. The decision caused many observers to predict imminent "chaos" in the form of interference among broadcast signals, and led to calls for regulation by Commerce Secretary Herbert Hoover and by the sponsors of dozens of bills in Congress—as well as to the following case.

Tribune Co. v. Oak Leaves Broadcasting Station, Inc.

Circuit Court of Cook County, Illinois, 1926.
reprinted in 68 Cong. Rec. 215, 215–19, 69th Cong. (2d Sess. 1926).

The Court. This matter comes before me on a motion on bill and answer filed herein to dissolve a temporary restraining order granted October 9, 1926, restraining the defendants from broadcasting over the same wave length as that employed by the complainant, or from broadcasting over a wave length in such close proximity thereto as to cause interference with the broadcasting station of the complainant. * * *

The bill very briefly charges that the complainant is and has been for some time a corporation organized under the laws of the State of Illinois, with its principal place of business in the city of Chicago, and is engaged in the publication of a newspaper known as the Chicago Daily Tribune, and that it has an average daily paid circulation of several hundred thousand subscribers.

It further charges that since March 29, 1924, it has been engaged in broadcasting by radio of daily programs of information, amusement and entertainment to the general public, and particularly to that part of the general public residing in and in the vicinity of the city of Chicago, and for that purpose the complainant operates an apparatus generally known as a broadcasting station located on the Drake Hotel and another such broadcasting station operated near the city of Elgin.

Figure 3–8
Elliott Jenkins and Thorne Donnelley, Founders of WDAP,
Forerunner of WGN

Reprinted with permission from WGN Radio, Chicago, Illinois.

The bill further charges that it has been the custom for several years for persons engaged in broadcasting to designate their certain stations by certain combinations of letters known as call letters, and that these call letters serve to enable persons using radio receiving sets to identify the particular station, and in this instance the complainant has been using the letters WGN, which stand for the abbreviation of the World's Greatest Newspaper, which appears to have been adopted by the complainant as a sort of trade name indicating the Chicago Daily Tribune.

It is further charged in the bill that it is the custom for such newspapers owning and operating broadcasting stations to make announcements of their programs in the daily editions of the paper, and that the complainant has, since March 29, 1924, used the designation WGN, and further charges that its program is of a high-class character, and that by reason of its broadcasting it has built up a good will with the public, which is of great value to the complainant, in that it has enhanced the value of the newspaper and increased the profits.

Further charges, on information and belief, that the number of persons who listen in to the said broadcasting of the complainant is in excess of 500,000 and that these persons are educated to listen in or tune in on the wave length of the complainant for the purpose of hearing and enjoying the programs so broadcasted.

The bill further charges that, when two stations are broadcasting on the same or nearly the same wave length, the result will be that the users of the radio will either hear one of the stations to the exclusion of the other or hear both of the stations at the same time, which will cause confusion to the listener, or will hear one to the exclusion of the other but accompanied by a series of noises, such as whistles and roars, which render the program practically useless.

The bill further charges that for several years the broadcasting in the United States and Canada has been done on sending wave lengths varying from 201 meters to 550 meters, inclusive, the United States Government, by an enactment of Congress, having forbidden to private and commercial broadcasters the use of wave lengths from 601 meters to 1,600 meters, and the use of wave lengths under 200 meters because of the impracticability of the use of said wave lengths under 200 meters by reason of natural causes and because of the fact that this field is open to amateurs and used by a large number of the same.

Furthermore, that most of the radio receiving sets are so constructed as to be adapted to the receiving of broadcasting within this band of wave lengths included above the 200 meters and under 500 meters. * * *

The complainant further charges that on the 14th of December, 1925, it did, and ever since then has, broadcast on a sending wave length of 302.8 meters (the kilocycles characteristic of such wave length being 990) and that it broadcasts from both the Drake Hotel and from its Elgin broadcasting station and that, at that time, no other broadcasting station in the city of Chicago or in the entire State of Illinois was using said wave length or any wave length sufficiently near to interfere with the complainant's broadcasting and that this fact was generally known to the public and that the public had access by reason thereof to the programs of the complainant as broadcast over the same wave length from the two broadcasting stations and which programs were announced at different periods of time by arrangement of the complainant.

Further charges that the complainant has expended large sums of money during said period of time in building up and betterment of said broadcasting stations and in the furnishing of high-class talent for its programs and in the payment of salaries and expenses in its business of broadcasting.

The bill further charges that the complainant is, and has been since it first engaged in broadcasting, duly licensed by the Secretary of Commerce of the United States to operate and broadcast from said stations and has complied with the act of Congress of August 13, 1912, entitled "An act to regulate radio communication."

That the defendants, the Oak Leaves Broadcasting Station (Inc.), and the Coyne Electrical School (Inc.) are corporations existing under and by virtue of the laws of Illinois, and that the defendant, Guyon, is a resident of

Chicago, Ill., engaged in business in said city under the name of Guyon's Paradise Ball Room, and operates a dance hall in the city of Chicago.

The bill further charges that the broadcasting station, heretofore used and operated by the defendants, Oak Leaves Broadcasting Station (Inc.), and Coyne Electrical School (Inc.), which had been operated from Oak Park, a suburb of the city of Chicago, was moved to 124 North Crawford Avenue, where Guyon's Paradise Ball Room is located, and is being now operated from that point, and charges that the said defendant, Guyon, became the owner and operator of said broadcasting station and that the other defendants have some interest in said station which is unknown to the complainant, but which is charged to be true on information and belief.

The bill further charges that said station of the defendants had originally sent a wave length of 226 meters (1,330 kilocycles) and had a license issued by the Secretary of Commerce to use said wave length and that, later, it changed its wave length to 249.9 meters (1,200 kilocycles), which it continued to use until on or about September 7, 1926, and further charges that the defendants had never enjoyed any considerable degree of good will of the public, nor was it popular with the users of radio receiving sets, but was comparatively unknown in Chicago or its vicinity.

That on or about September 7, 1926, the said Guyon's Paradise Broadcasting Station, used and operated by the defendants, changed its sending wave length to a wave length either the same as that of the complainant (i.e., 302.8) or one having a frequency of considerably less than 50 kilocycles different than that of the complainant, and that it is now using said wave length and has from that time until the date of the filing of the bill herein, and that it has no special license or special authority, but has a general license, dated October 5, 1926, authorizing it to use and operate Guyon's Paradise Broadcasting Station, and that this license was issued to, and that the general license was issued to Oak Leaves Broadcasting Station, but that neither of the other defendants has any license to operate such a station.

The bill further charges that the defendants have, since September 7, 1926, used the said new wave length during the hours of the day when complainant is broadcasting, and that by reason thereof said broadcasting by the said defendants has interfered with and destroyed complainant's broadcasting to the public in the city of Chicago and throughout the region where complainant's newspaper circulates, and that by reason thereof radio receivers have been unable to hear the programs of the complainant and that if it is allowed to continue it will work incalculable damage and injury to the good will of the complainant's broadcasting, and consequently will injure the circulation of the complainant in so far as its newspaper is concerned and deprive it of great profits.

Further charges that there are other wave lengths which are usable by the defendants and that this wave length can be changed with practically no expense and within a short period of time.

The bill prays for an order restraining the defendants from broadcasting from said station in such a manner as to interfere with the broadcasting of the complainant, and more particularly from using any wave length within 100 miles of the city of Chicago having a frequency of less than 1,040 kilocycles per second, or more than 940 kilocycles per second, charging the effect, that any wave length within that designated number of kilocycles would necessarily cause an interference with the broadcasting of the complainant.

The answer filed in this case admits practically all the allegations of the bill as to the operation of a broadcasting station by the complainant and admits the allegations of the bill of the complainant in regard to the use of the letters WGN, and that they have become known to the users of radio receiving sets in the city of Chicago, but says they have no knowledge of any good will or popularity achieved by the complainant by reason of said broadcasting. * * *

The answer admits that on September 7, 1926, the said defendants' station changed its wave length, but denies that they are broadcasting over the same wave length as that of the complainant, but state that they are sending over a wave length which is removed 40 kilocycles from the wave length used by the complainant, and that said wave length used is 315.6 meters with a frequency of 950 kilocycles. * * *

It is a matter of general knowledge that in the last few years there has grown up in the United States, as well as abroad, a well recognized calling or business known as broadcasting which consists in sending from a central station, electrically equipped, programs of music and amusement, speeches by men of prominence, news of the day and items of interest taking place in the world, and that these various programs are received by the public over radio receiving sets which have been installed in homes, hotels, and various other places, and that a large industry has grown up and developed in the making and manufacturing of radio sets, so that in the United States, at this time, there are millions of dollars invested by the public at large, which has made the investment for the purpose of and with the knowledge that they could receive these programs, speeches, and items of interest from various broadcasting stations located in various parts of the United States and in other countries.

It might also be stated that, so far as broadcasting stations are concerned, there has almost grown up a custom which recognizes the rights of the various broadcasters, particularly in that certain broadcasters use certain hours of the day, while other broadcasters remain silent during that particular period of time. Again, in this particular locality, a certain night is set aside as silent night, when all local broadcasters cease broadcasting in order that the radio receivers may be able to tune in on outside distant stations.

Wave lengths may have been bought and sold and broadcasting stations have changed hands for a consideration. Broadcasting stations have contracted with each other so as to broadcast without conflicting and in this manner be able to present their different programs to the waiting

Custom exists in a new field & defines some of the laws

public. The public itself has become educated to the use of its receiving sets so as to be able to obtain certain particular items of news, speeches, or programs over its own particular sets.

The theory of the bill in this case is based upon the proposition that by usage of a particular wave length for a considerable length of time and by reason of the expenditure of a considerable amount of money in developing its broadcasting station and by usage of a particular wave length educating the public to know that that particular wave length is the wave length of the complainant and by furnishing programs which have been attractive and thereby cause a great number of people to listen in to their particular programs that the said complainant has created and carved out for itself a particular right or easement in and to the use of said wave length which should be recognized in a court of equity and that outsiders should not be allowed thereafter, except for good cause shown, to deprive them of that right and to make use of a field which had been built up by the complainant at a considerable cost in money and a considerable time in pioneering.

The defendants, in effect, rely upon the fact and claim that by the passage of the act of August 13, 1912, entitled "An act to regulate radio communication," passed by Congress, the United States Government has taken over the control of broadcasting stations and that, therefore, the questions herein involved become questions of interstate commerce and that a State court has no jurisdiction to pass upon said questions or to grant the relief prayed for in the bill.

The defendants further insist that a wave length can not be made the subject of private control and, further and lastly, that as a matter of fact they are not interfering with the complainant by the use of the present wave length employed by them from their broadcasting station. * * *

On July 8, 1926, Acting Attorney General Donovan rendered an opinion for the Department of Justice at Washington which in effect advised the Department of Commerce that from his construction of the act broadcasting stations coming within the prescribed band could not be regulated except for the purpose of designating normal wave lengths under regulation 1 and that the act conferred no general authority to fix hours of operation or to limit power: that any station might with impunity operate at hours and with powers other than those fixed in its license, subject only to regulations 12 and 13 and to the penalties against malicious interference contained in section 5. While this opinion is not a judicial interpretation of the act, it would appear to this court that it is a correct interpretation, and if true, there is nothing contained in the act of Congress of August 13, 1912, that would provide against such use of wave lengths, except as contained in said enactment and as so interpreted. * * *

This court is of the opinion, from its interpretation of the act of August 13, 1912, that Congress did not intend to undertake to assume the right to regulate broadcasting under its powers given it to regulate commerce and that until such time as it does, litigants may enforce such rights as they may have by reason of operating broadcasting stations in the State courts having jurisdiction of the person of the parties. Having arrived at this conclusion, it necessarily follows that the question to be determined is whether or not the complainant has such rights as would entitle it to the protection of a court of equity. * * *

In the first place, it is argued that there are no rights in the air and that the law has no right or authority to restrict the using of wave lengths or to exclude others from their use. In answer to this it might be said that Congress has already attempted to regulate the use of the air in its enactment of August 13, 1912, by providing that only certain strata of the air or ether may be used for broadcasting purposes and, further, requiring persons to take out a license before they are permitted to exercise the use of the air or ether. Moreover, it appears to this court that the situation is such from the past development of the industry of broadcasting and radio receiving and from the apparent future, as indicated by the past, that, unless some regulatory measures are provided for by Congress or rights recognized by State courts, the situation will result in chaos and a great detriment to the advancement of an industry which is only in its infancy. * * *

[asking Legislature for regulation]

[The court then considers by way of analogy situations in which courts have recognized property rights or rights to be free from interference in the areas of trademarks, water, and electrical interference with telephone lines.]

It is argued that the case is new and novel and uncertain in its final outcome after the hearing of all the proof, and that a court of equity should not issue a temporary restraining order because of the uncertainty. We can not concur in this because, in our view of the situation, we believe that the equities of the situation are in favor of the complainant on the facts as heretofore shown, particularly in that the complainant has been using said wave length for a considerable length of time and has built up a large clientage, whereas the defendants are but newly in the field and will not suffer as a result of an injunction in proportion to the damage that would be sustained by the complainant after having spent a much greater length of time in the education of the general radio-receiving public to the wave length in question.

We are of the opinion further, that, under the circumstances in this case, priority of time creates a superiority in right, and the fact of priority having been conceded by the answer it would seem to this court that it would be only just that the situation should be preserved in the status in which it was prior to the time that the defendants undertook to operate over or near the wave length of the complainant. * * *

It is difficult to determine at this time how a radio station should be properly run, but it is also true that the science of broadcasting and receiving is being subject every day to change and it is possible that within a short time this may be accomplished, although it is the opinion of the court from an examination of the affidavits and exhibits in the cause that 40 kilocycles is not at this time recognized as a safe limitation for the prevention of interference between stations located in the same locality. It is true that stations sufficiently removed from each other can broadcast even over the same wave length, but it necessarily follows that they must be so far apart that the wave lengths do not reach or come in contact with each other to the extent of creating interference.

In the case at bar the contestants are so located with reference to each other that the court does not feel that 40 kilocycles is sufficient. The court is of the opinion, however, that until there has been a final hearing of this cause no order prohibiting the defendants from the use of any particular wave length should be entered and to that extent the order heretofore entered will be modified so that it will read that the defendants are restrained and enjoined from broadcasting over a wave length sufficiently near to the one used by the complainant so as to cause any material interference with the programs or announcements of the complainant over and from its broadcasting station to the radio public within a radius of 100 miles, and in order that the defendants may be apprised of the feeling of the court in this regard, while the order is not expressly one of exact limitation, nevertheless, the court feels that a distance removed 50 kilocycles from the wave length of the complainant would be a safe distance and that if the defendants use a wave length in closer proximity than the one stated it must be at the risk of the defendants in this cause.

[handwritten margin note: Essentially asking for regulation]

NOTES AND QUESTIONS

1. *Tribune v. Oak Leaves* is cited by those who argue that a common-law system of property rights in spectrum would have been superior to regulation. See, e.g., Peter W. Huber, Law and Disorder in Cyberspace: Abolish the FCC and Let Common Law Rule the Telecosm (1997). But such was not to be. Congress passed the Radio Act of 1927, which prohibited property rights in spectrum and provided for Federal Radio Commission licensing of broadcast use of the spectrum under a standard of "public interest, convenience, or necessity." Congress later elaborated upon this scheme in the Federal Communications Act of 1934, which gave the licensing and regulatory functions to the Federal Communications Commission we have today. For an argument that the sponsors of regulation knew that the "chaos" could be solved by property rights to spectrum (as in *Oak Leaves* or with some version of historic practice), and that the primary motivation for the regulatory regime of the 1927 and 1934 Acts was its favorable distributive consequences for large broadcasters, regulators, and politicians in Congress, see Thomas W. Hazlett, The Rationality of U.S. Regulation of the Broadcast Spectrum, 33 J.L. & Econ. 133 (1990).

2. Ronald Coase, whose 1960 article introducing what came to be known as the Coase theorem was introduced in Chapter I, published an article one year earlier arguing against the then-prevailing wisdom behind government licensing. He advocated instead a system of private property rights that could be bought and sold in a secondary market, which he believed would produce a more efficient allocation of the broadcast spectrum. R.H. Coase, The Federal Communications Commission, 2 J.L. &

Econ. 1 (1959). In response to critics who claimed that property rights in this area would be too difficult to define and enforce, he responded:

> What does not seem to have been understood is that what is being allocated by the Federal Communications Commission, or, if there were a market, what would be sold, is the *right to use a piece of equipment to transmit signals in a particular way.* Once the question is looked at in this way, it is unnecessary to think in terms of ownership of frequencies or the ether.

Id. at 33 (emphasis added). Coase rejected analogies to air rights over land as "tend[ing] to obscure the question that is being decided." Id. at 34. He continued: "[W]hether we have the right to shoot over another man's land has been thought of as depending on who owns the airspace over the land. *It would be simpler to discuss what we should be allowed to do with a gun.*" Id. (emphasis added). Does this make Coase's vision more tort-like than property-like?

3.   Coase was far ahead of his time. Recently, the FCC has auctioned off segments of spectrum for a variety of uses. Thomas W. Hazlett, Assigning Property Rights to Radio Spectrum Users: Why Did FCC License Auctions Take 67 Years?, 41 J.L. & Econ. 529, 530, 538, 560–68 (1998) (noting influence of Coase's critique of licensing and his advocacy of auctions and discussing recent adoption of auctions). The set of potential uses is wide, and more so than when Coase was writing—especially with the advent of various wireless devices for personal communication—and likely to get wider. The question of whether property in spectrum should be based on simple trespass-like rights to exclude or on rights to engage in specific uses is still a live debate.

4.   The electromagnetic spectrum, like water, has been treated as a separate resource, subject to a mixture of public and private rights. Controversy rages over whether the spectrum should be sold off in chunks or kept as some type of commons or open access. Some of those advocating for open access (or a shift towards more use of open access) believe that various spectrum-sharing technologies will eliminate interference and so will remove the scarcity rationale for propertizing spectrum and will capture network benefits from open access; if so, spectrum would be "comedic" in Carol Rose's sense of the more the merrier. Lawrence Lessig, The Future of Ideas: The Fate of the Commons in a Connected World (2001); Yochai Benkler, Overcoming Agoraphobia: Building the Commons of the Digitally Networked Environment, 11 Harv. J.L. & Tech. 287 (1998); Eli Noam, Spectrum Auctions: Yesterday's Heresy, Today's Orthodoxy, Tomorrow's Anachronism. Taking the Next Step to Open Spectrum Access, 41 J.L. & Econ. 765 (1998). Remaining interference could be handled by a tort-like system that focuses on activities. Kevin Werbach, Supercommons: Toward a Unified Theory of Wireless Communication, 82 Tex. L. Rev. 863 (2004). On the other hand, those who emphasize the role of property do not share this technological optimism. They point out that greater supply of spectrum has historically called forth more demand (sometimes called "Say's Law") and that shifting from one use to another is easier if one need not

coordinate with other users of the same frequency. See Thomas W. Hazlett, The Wireless Craze, the Unlimited Bandwidth Myth, the Spectrum Auction Faux Pas, and the Punchline to Ronald Coase's "Big Joke": An Essay on Airwave Allocation Policy, 14 Harv. J.L. & Tech. 335 (2001); Pablo T. Spiller & Carlo Cardilli, Towards a Property Rights Approach to Communications Spectrum, 16 Yale J. on Reg. 53 (1999). Some of these arguments have close parallels in the controversies over market transfers of water rights. See, e.g., Dale B. Thompson, Of Rainbows and Rivers: Lessons for Telecommunications Spectrum Policy from Transitions in Property Rights and Commons in Water Law, 54 Buff. L. Rev. 157 (2006). Some have advocated public "parks"—islands of open access—in the midst of privatized spectrum. See Gerald R. Faulhaber & David Farber, Spectrum Management: Property Rights, Markets, and the Commons, in Rethinking Rights and Regulations: Institutional Responses to New Communication Technologies 193 (Lorrie Faith Cranor & Steven S. Wildman eds., 2003). Should the public trust doctrine apply in the area of spectrum resources? For the time being, spectrum is likely to be governed by both private and common property regimes, and the main questions will be the size of the parcels and the relative weight of the two (or more) types of regimes.

5. If sending electromagnetic signals over someone's land is not a trespass, what about receiving them? It has long been illegal to "steal" satellite television broadcasts. More recently, the first criminal charge for using someone's else Wi–Fi signal has been brought against a Florida man who used a resident's signal with his laptop while sitting in a car parked on the street. *Man Charged with Stealing Wi–Fi Signal*, Associated Press, July 6, 2005. What property exactly is being "stolen" here?

People for the Ethical Treatment of Animals v. Doughney

United States Court of Appeals, Fourth Circuit, 2001.
263 F.3d 359.

■ GREGORY, CIRCUIT JUDGE: People for the Ethical Treatment of Animals ("PETA") sued Michael Doughney ("Doughney") after he registered the domain name *peta.org* and created a website called "People Eating Tasty Animals." PETA alleged claims of service mark infringement under 15 U.S.C. § 1114 and Virginia common law, unfair competition under 15 U.S.C. § 1125(a) and Virginia common law, and service mark dilution and cybersquatting under 15 U.S.C. § 1123(c). Doughney appeals the district court's decision granting PETA's motion for summary judgment and PETA cross-appeals the district court's denial of its motion for attorney's fees and costs. Finding no error, we affirm.

not relevant →

I.

PETA is an animal rights organization with more than 600,000 members worldwide. PETA "is dedicated to promoting and heightening public awareness of animal protection issues and it opposes the exploitation of animals for food, clothing, entertainment and vivisection.''

Doughney is a former internet executive who has registered many domain names since 1995. For example, Doughney registered domain names such as *dubyadot.com, dubyadot.net, deathbush.com, RandallTerry.org* (Not Randall Terry for Congress), *bwtel.com* (Baltimore–Washington Telephone Company), *pmrc.org* ("People's Manic Repressive Church"), and *ex-cult.org* (Ex–Cult Archive). At the time the district court issued its summary judgment ruling, Doughney owned 50–60 domain names.

Doughney registered the domain name *peta.org* in 1995 with Network Solutions, Inc. ("NSI"). When registering the domain name, Doughney represented to NSI that the registration did "not interfere with or infringe upon the rights of any third party," and that a "non-profit educational organization" called "People Eating Tasty Animals" was registering the domain name. Doughney made these representations to NSI despite knowing that no corporation, partnership, organization or entity of any kind existed or traded under that name. Moreover, Doughney was familiar with PETA and its beliefs and had been for at least 15 years before registering the domain name.

After registering the *peta.org* domain name, Doughney used it to create a website purportedly on behalf of "People Eating Tasty Animals." Doughney claims he created the website as a parody of PETA. A viewer accessing the website would see the title "People Eating Tasty Animals" in large, bold type. Under the title, the viewer would see a statement that the website was a "resource for those who enjoy eating meat, wearing fur and leather, hunting, and the fruits of scientific research." The website contained links to various meat, fur, leather, hunting, animal research, and other organizations, all of which held views generally antithetical to PETA's views. Another statement on the website asked the viewer whether he/she was "Feeling lost? Offended? Perhaps you should, like, *exit immediately*." The phrase *"exit immediately"* contained a hyperlink to PETA's official website.

Doughney's website appeared at "www.peta.org" for only six months in 1995–96. In 1996, PETA asked Doughney to voluntarily transfer the *peta.org* domain name to PETA because PETA owned the "PETA" mark ("the Mark"), which it registered in 1992. See U.S. Trademark Registration No. 1705,510. When Doughney refused to transfer the domain name to PETA, PETA complained to NSI, whose rules then required it to place the domain name on "hold" pending resolution of Doughney's dispute with PETA. Consequently, Doughney moved the website to *www.mtd.com/tasty* and added a disclaimer stating that "People Eating Tasty Animals is in no way connected with, or endorsed by, People for the Ethical Treatment of Animals."

In response to Doughney's domain name dispute with PETA, *The Chronicle of Philanthropy* quoted Doughney as stating that, "[i]f they [PETA] want one of my domains, they should make me an offer." Non–Profit Groups Upset by Unauthorized Use of Their Names on the Internet,

The Chronicle of Philanthropy, Nov. 14, 1996. Doughney does not dispute making this statement. Additionally, Doughney posted the following message on his website on May 12, 1996:

"PeTa" has no legal grounds whatsoever to make even the slightest demands of me regarding this domain name registration. If they disagree, they can sue me. And if they don't, well, perhaps they can behave like the polite ladies and gentlemen that they evidently aren't and negotiate a settlement with me.... Otherwise, "PeTa" can wait until the significance and value of a domain name drops to nearly nothing, which is inevitable as each new web search engine comes online, because that's how long it's going to take for this dispute to play out.

PETA sued Doughney in 1999, asserting claims for service mark infringement, unfair competition, dilution and cybersquatting. PETA did not seek damages, but sought only to enjoin Doughney's use of the "PETA" Mark and an order requiring Doughney to transfer the *peta.org* domain name to PETA.

Doughney responded to the suit by arguing that the website was a constitutionally-protected parody of PETA. Nonetheless, the district court granted PETA's motion for summary judgment on June 12, 2000. * * *

II.

* * * A. *Trademark Infringement/Unfair Competition*

Not Issue
↳ANALYSIS

A plaintiff alleging causes of action for trademark infringement and unfair competition must prove (1) that it possesses a mark; (2) that the defendant used the mark; (3) that the defendant's use of the mark occurred "in commerce"; (4) that the defendant used the mark "in connection with the sale, offering for sale, distribution, or advertising" of goods or services; and (5) that the defendant used the mark in a manner likely to confuse consumers. 15 U.S.C. §§ 1114, 1125(a); Lone Star Steakhouse & Saloon v. Alpha of Virginia, 43 F.3d 922, 930 (4th Cir. 1995).

There is no dispute here that PETA owns the "PETA" Mark, that Doughney used it, and that Doughney used the Mark "in commerce." Doughney disputes the district court's findings that he used the Mark in connection with goods or services and that he used it in a manner engendering a likelihood of confusion.

1.

To use PETA's Mark "in connection with" goods or services, Doughney need not have actually sold or advertised goods or services on the *www. peta.org* website. Rather, Doughney need only have prevented users from obtaining or using PETA's goods or services, or need only have connected the website to other's goods or services.

While sparse, existing caselaw on infringement and unfair competition in the Internet context clearly weighs in favor of this conclusion. For example, in *OBH, Inc. v. Spotlight Magazine, Inc.*, the plaintiffs owned the

"The Buffalo News" registered trademark used by the newspaper of the same name. 86 F.Supp.2d 176 (W.D.N.Y. 2000). The defendants registered the domain name *thebuffalonews.com* and created a website parodying The Buffalo News and providing a public forum for criticism of the newspaper. Id. at 182. The site contained hyperlinks to other local news sources and a site owned by the defendants that advertised Buffalo-area apartments for rent. Id. at 183.

The court held that the defendants used the mark "in connection with" goods or services because the defendants' website was "likely to prevent or hinder Internet users from accessing plaintiffs' services on plaintiffs' own web site." Id.

> Prospective users of plaintiffs' services who mistakenly access defendants' web site may fail to continue to search for plaintiffs' web site due to confusion or frustration. Such users, who are presumably looking for the news services provided by the plaintiffs on their web site, may instead opt to select one of the several other news-related hyperlinks contained in defendants' web site. These news-related hyperlinks will directly link the user to other news-related web sites that are in direct competition with plaintiffs in providing news-related services over the Internet. Thus, defendants' action in appropriating plaintiff's mark has a connection to plaintiffs' distribution of its services.

Id. Moreover, the court explained that defendants' use of the plaintiffs' mark was in connection with goods or services because it contained a link to the defendants' apartment-guide website. Id.

Similarly, in *Planned Parenthood Federation of America, Inc. v. Bucci*, the plaintiff owned the "Planned Parenthood" mark, but the defendant registered the domain name *plannedparenthood.com*. 42 U.S.P.Q.2d 1430, 1997 WL 133313 (S.D.N.Y. 1997). Using the domain name, the defendant created a website containing information antithetical to the plaintiff's views. Id. at 1435. The court ruled that the defendant used the plaintiff's mark "in connection with" the distribution of services

> because it is likely to prevent some Internet users from reaching plaintiff's own Internet web site. Prospective users of plaintiff's services who mistakenly access defendant's web site may fail to continue to search for plaintiff's own home page, due to anger, frustration, or the belief that plaintiff's home page does not exist.

Id.

The same reasoning applies here. As the district court explained, Doughney's use of PETA's Mark in the domain name of his website

> is likely to prevent Internet users from reaching [PETA's] own Internet web site. The prospective users of [PETA's] services who mistakenly access Defendant's web site may fail to continue to search for [PETA's] own home page, due to anger, frustration, or the belief that [PETA's] home page does not exist.

Doughney, 113 F.Supp.2d at 919 (quoting Bucci, 42 U.S.P.Q.2d at 1435). Moreover, Doughney's web site provides links to more than 30 commercial operations offering goods and services. By providing links to these commercial operations, Doughney's use of PETA's Mark is "in connection with" the sale of goods or services.

2.

The unauthorized use of a trademark infringes the trademark holder's rights if it is likely to confuse an "ordinary consumer" as to the source or sponsorship of the goods. Anheuser–Busch, Inc. v. L & L Wings, Inc., 962 F.2d 316, 318 (4th Cir. 1992) (citing 2 J. McCarthy, Trademarks and Unfair Competition § 23:28 (2d ed. 1984)). To determine whether a likelihood of confusion exists, a court should not consider "how closely a fragment of a given use duplicates the trademark," but must instead consider "whether the use in its entirety creates a likelihood of confusion." Id. at 319.

Doughney does not dispute that the *peta.org* domain name engenders a likelihood of confusion between his web site and PETA. Doughney claims, though, that the inquiry should not end with his domain name. Rather, he urges the Court to consider his website in conjunction with the domain name because, together, they purportedly parody PETA and, thus, do not cause a likelihood of confusion.

A "parody" is defined as a "simple form of entertainment conveyed by juxtaposing the irreverent representation of the trademark with the idealized image created by the mark's owner." L.L. Bean, Inc. v. Drake Publishers, Inc., 811 F.2d 26, 34 (1st Cir. 1987). A parody must "convey two simultaneous—and contradictory—messages: that it is the original, but also that it is *not* the original and is instead a parody." Cliffs Notes, Inc. v. Bantam Doubleday Dell Publ. Group, Inc., 886 F.2d 490, 494 (2d Cir. 1989) (emphasis in original). To the extent that an alleged parody conveys only the first message, "it is not only a poor parody but also vulnerable under trademark law, since the customer will be confused." Id. While a parody necessarily must engender some initial confusion, an effective parody will diminish the risk of consumer confusion "by conveying [only] just enough of the original design to allow the consumer to appreciate the point of parody." Jordache Enterprises, Inc. v. Hogg Wyld, Ltd., 828 F.2d 1482, 1486 (10th Cir. 1987).

Looking at Doughney's domain name alone, there is no suggestion of a parody. The domain name *peta.org* simply copies PETA's Mark, conveying the message that it is related to PETA. The domain name does not convey the second, contradictory message needed to establish a parody—a message that the domain name is not related to PETA, but that it is a parody of PETA.

Doughney claims that this second message can be found in the content of his website. Indeed, the website's content makes it clear that it is not related to PETA. However, this second message is not conveyed *simultaneously* with the first message, as required to be considered a parody. The domain name conveys the first message; the second message is conveyed only when the viewer reads the content of the website. As the district court explained, "an internet user would not realize that they were not on an official PETA web site until after they had used PETA's Mark to access the web page 'www.peta.org.'" Doughney, 113 F.Supp.2d at 921. Thus, the messages are not conveyed simultaneously and do not constitute a parody. See also Morrison & Foerster LLP v. Wick, 94 F.Supp.2d 1125 (D. Co. 2000) (defendant's use of plaintiffs' mark in domain name "does not convey two simultaneous and contradictory messages" because "[o]nly by reading through the content of the sites could the user discover that the domain names are an attempt at parody"); Bucci, 42 U.S.P.Q.2d at 1435 (rejecting parody defense because "[s]eeing or typing the 'planned parenthood' mark and accessing the web site are two separate and nonsimultaneous activities"). The district court properly rejected Doughney's parody defense and found that Doughney's use of the *peta.org* domain name engenders a likelihood of confusion. Accordingly, Doughney failed to raise a genuine issue of material fact regarding PETA's infringement and unfair competition claims.

B.   *Anticybersquatting Consumer Protection Act*

The district court found Doughney liable under the Anticybersquatting Consumer Protection Act ("ACPA"), 15 U.S.C. § 1125(d)(1)(A). To establish an ACPA violation, PETA was required to (1) prove that Doughney had a bad faith intent to profit from using the *peta.org* domain name, and (2) that the *peta.org* domain name is identical or confusingly similar to, or dilutive of, the distinctive and famous PETA Mark. 15 U.S.C. § 1125(d)(1)(A).

Doughney makes several arguments relating to the district court's ACPA holding: (1) that PETA did not plead an ACPA claim, but raised it for the first time in its motion for summary judgment; (2) that the ACPA, which became effective in 1999, cannot be applied retroactively to events that occurred in 1995 and 1996; (3) that Doughney did not seek to financially profit from his use of PETA's Mark; and (4) that Doughney acted in good faith.

None of Doughney's arguments are availing. * * *

Doughney's second argument—that the ACPA may not be applied retroactively—also is unavailing. The ACPA expressly states that it "shall apply to all domain names registered before, on, or after the date of the enactment of this Act[.]" Pub.L. No. 106–113, § 3010, 113 Stat. 1536. See also Sporty's Farm L.L.C. v. Sportsman's Market, Inc., 202 F.3d 489, 496 (2d Cir. 2000) (same). Moreover, while the ACPA precludes the imposition of *damages* in cases in which domain names were registered, trafficked, or used before its enactment, Pub.L. No. 106–113, § 3010, 113 Stat. 1536 ("damages under subsection (a) or (d) of section 35 of the Trademark Act of 1946 (15 U.S.C. 1117), ... shall not be available with respect to the registration, trafficking, or use of a domain name that occurs before the date of the enactment of this Act"), it does not preclude the imposition of *equitable remedies*. See also Virtual Works, Inc. v. Volkswagen of America,

Inc., 238 F.3d 264, 268 (4th Cir. 2001). Here, the district court did not award PETA damages (nor did PETA request damages), but ordered Doughney to relinquish the domain name, transfer its registration to PETA, and limit his use of domain names to those that do not use PETA's Mark. *Doughney,* 113 F.Supp.2d at 922. Thus, the district court properly applied the ACPA to this case.

Doughney's third argument—that he did not seek to financially profit from registering a domain name using PETA's Mark—also offers him no relief. It is undisputed that Doughney made statements to the press and on his website recommending that PETA attempt to "settle" with him and "make him an offer." The undisputed evidence belies Doughney's argument.

Doughney's fourth argument—that he did not act in bad faith—also is unavailing. Under 15 U.S.C. § 1125(d)(1)(B)(i), a court may consider several factors to determine whether a defendant acted in bad faith, including

(I) the trademark or other intellectual property rights of the person, if any, in the domain name;

(II) the extent to which the domain name consists of the legal name of the person or a name that is otherwise commonly used to identify that person;

(III) the person's prior use, if any, of the domain name in connection with the bona fide offering of any goods or services;

(IV) the person's bona fide noncommercial or fair use of the mark in a site accessible under the domain name;

(V) the person's intent to divert consumers from the mark owner's online location to a site accessible under the domain name that could harm the goodwill represented by the mark, either for commercial gain or with the intent to tarnish or disparage the mark, by creating a likelihood of confusion as to the source, sponsorship, affiliation, or endorsement of the site;

(VI) the person's offer to transfer, sell, or otherwise assign the domain name to the mark owner or any third party for financial gain without having used, or having an intent to use, the domain name in the bona fide offering of any goods or services, or the person's prior conduct indicating a pattern of such conduct;

(VII) the person's provision of material and misleading false contact information when applying for the registration of the domain name, the person's intentional failure to maintain accurate contact information, or the person's prior conduct indicating a pattern of such conduct;

(VIII) the person's registration or acquisition of multiple domain names which the person knows are identical or confusingly similar to marks of others that are distinctive at the time of registration of such domain names, or dilutive of famous marks of others that are famous at the time of registration of such domain names, without regard to the goods or services of the parties; and

(IX) the extent to which the mark incorporated in the person's domain name registration is or is not distinctive and famous within the meaning of subsection (c)(1) of this section.

15 U.S.C. § 1125(d)(1)(B)(i). In addition to listing these nine factors, the ACPA contains a safe harbor provision stating that bad faith intent "shall not be found in any case in which the court determines that the person believed and had reasonable grounds to believe that the use of the domain name was fair use or otherwise lawful." 15 U.S.C. § 1225(d)(1)(B)(ii).

The district court reviewed the factors listed in the statute and properly concluded that Doughney (I) had no intellectual property right in *peta.org;* (II) *peta.org* is not Doughney's name or a name otherwise used to identify Doughney; (III) Doughney had no prior use of *peta.org* in connection with the bona fide offering of any goods or services; (IV) Doughney used the PETA Mark in a commercial manner; (V) Doughney "clearly intended to confuse, mislead and divert internet users into accessing his web site which contained information antithetical and therefore harmful to the goodwill represented by the PETA Mark"; (VI) Doughney made statements on his web site and in the press recommending that PETA attempt to "settle" with him and "make him an offer"; (VII) Doughney made false statements when registering the domain name; and (VIII) Doughney registered other domain names that are identical or similar to the marks or names of other famous people and organizations. People for the Ethical Treatment of Animals, 113 F.Supp.2d at 920. * * *

For the foregoing reasons, the judgment of the district court is affirmed.

Figure 3–9
PETA Bumper Sticker

Courtesy PETA.

NOTES AND QUESTIONS

1. A service mark is like a trademark but the mark is used in connection with services rather than goods. Trademarks are protected under state law (common and statutory) and federal legislation (the Lanham Act). Acquiring a trademark is based on first use, and registration makes one eligible for further federal protection. Recently, the Lanham Act, 15 U.S.C. §§ 1051–1129, which provides for federal registration and protection of marks, has been amended to allow for some registrations based on intent to use. As we asked in connection with the *Midler* case (see Chapter II supra), what did PETA appropriate and did it leave enough and as good for others? Consider in this regard the second statutory factor cited in the case, "the extent to which the domain name consists of the legal name of the person or a name that is otherwise commonly used to identify that person." 15 U.S.C. § 1125(d)(1)(B)(i)(II).

2. Trademark is very different from copyright, patent, and some other forms of intellectual property protection in that no novelty or originality is required. The Lanham Act was passed pursuant to Congress's power under the Commerce Clause, Art. I, § 8, cl. 3, not the Patent and Copyright Clause, Art. I, § 8, cl. 8., which gives Congress the power "to promote the Progress of Science and the useful Arts by securing for limited Times to Authors and Inventors the exclusive Right to their respective Writings and Discoveries." As interpreted by the U.S. Supreme Court, a writing requires originality, and thus the Patent and Copyright Clause cannot serve as the basis for Lanham Act-type trademark legislation. See Feist Publications v. Rural Telephone Service, 499 U.S. 340 (1991) (holding that data compilation in a telephone book cannot be copyrighted because it was lacking in constitutionally required originality). In the pre–1937 era of narrow Commerce Clause jurisprudence (making that source of authority unavailable), the Supreme Court held in *In re Trade–Mark Cases*, 100 U.S. 82, 94 (1879) that the first federal trademark legislation could not rest on the Patent and Copyright Clause because what it would protect was neither a "discovery" nor a "writing" under the Clause and the trademark acts "did not depend upon novelty, upon invention, upon discovery, or upon any work of the brain. It requires no fancy or imagination, no genius, no laborious thought. It is simply founded on priority of appropriation."

Although originality is not required, generic terms like "car" and "chair" cannot be trademarks. (Indeed, some everyday words like "aspirin" and "cellophane" were once trademarks but lost that status through use as a generic term, in a process known as "genericide.") Nongeneric but "descriptive" marks, such as "Dunkin' Donuts" must acquire "secondary meaning"—an association in the minds of consumers between the mark and the product—in order to be protectible. Fanciful marks like "Exxon" and "Kodak" and arbitrary marks like "Apple" for computers need only be used in commerce to be protected. (In between descriptive marks and arbitrary or fanciful marks are "suggestive marks" like "Jaguar" for cars and "Orange Crush" for a soft drink, which require some leap of imagination to see the association between the mark and the product; such marks also do not require a showing of secondary meaning.) See Abercrombie & Fitch Co. v. Hunting World, Inc., 537 F.2d 4 (2d Cir. 1976).

3.   Traditionally the test for infringement has been consumer "confusion," which reflects trademark's role in helping consumers identify the source of goods and lowering their search costs. Trademark protection allows suppliers to build up goodwill; others cannot freeride on, and possibly cause damage to, that goodwill by passing off their goods as coming from the source with the good reputation in the market. In recent decades state courts and legislatures have increasingly allowed trademark owners to sue for trademark "dilution," even where there is no likelihood of consumer confusion. For an early example, a court issued an injunction against Kodak bicycles even though there was little chance that a consumer would think that the bicycles had anything to do with the well-known camera company. See Eastman Photographic Materials Co. v. John Griffiths Cycle Corp., 15 R.P.C. 105 (Ch. 1898) (U.K.). As you can see from the *PETA v. Doughney* case, Congress in 1996 amended Section 43 of the Lanham Act to cover dilution as well. Should trademark owners be able to control the use of the mark in this way? Has trademark become more "propertized," as some are claiming? Is this desirable?

4.   In *Lamparello v. Falwell*, 420 F.3d 309 (4th Cir. 2005), reversing summary judgment for the trademark owner and granting it to the registrant of www.fallwell.com, a site critical of the Reverend Jerry Falwell's views on homosexuality, the Fourth Circuit backed away from some of the more expansive implications of *Doughney*. In *Lamparello*, the court held that to violate a trademark the use of a domain name as a whole must cause confusion; "initial interest" confusion is not enough. See also Bosley Med. Inst. v. Kremer, 403 F.3d 672 (9th Cir. 2005). On the issue of cybersquatting, the court in *Lamparello* contrasted Doughney's large inventory of domain names and invitations to "settle" with him and "make him an offer." Which approach to trademark and cybersquatting would you favor?

5.   Turning to domain names, dilution can play a role under the Anticybersquatting Consumer Protection Act. For famous marks, liability for commercial use of famous mark in the offending domain name need not involve a confusingly similar mark or one that would draw customers away, but can also be for registering and using a domain name that incorporates the famous mark in a way that is "dilutive of" the mark. 15 U.S.C.A. § 1125(d)(1)(A)(ii). While there is still some uncertainty, recent cases suggest that so-called "cybergriping" or "sucks" sites ([name]sucks.com) are protected as parody and generally do not violate the ACPA absent bad faith behavior of the registrant. J. Ryan Gilfoil, A Judicial Safe Harbor under the Anti–Cybersquatting Consumer Protection Act, 20 Berkeley Tech. L.J. 185 (2005). Under the Uniform Domain Name Dispute Resolution Policy (UDRP) of the Internet Corporation for Assigned Names and Numbers (ICANN), panels have been split on the question of dilution and cybergripe sites. See Jonathan Band & Matthew Schruers, Toward a

Bright–Line Approach to [Trademark]Sucks.Com, 20 Computer & Internet Law. 1 (July 2003).

6.   What if Doughney had not used "peta" in the domain name but only in the metatags for his website (which direct users of a search engine to that site)? Should the result be different? See Brookfield Communications, Inc. v. West Coast Entm't Corp., 174 F.3d 1036, 1061–64 (9th Cir. 1999) (holding that use of another's trademark in metatags can be actionable on grounds of initial interest confusion). In actual space, as opposed to cyberspace, one can, within certain restrictions protest or leaflet outside a place of business. Is there an equivalent for a web business? Should there be?

7.   As the stock of short and convenient domain names has been increasingly claimed, other top-level domains such as .biz and .info have been added. Trademark owners will want to control all domain names containing their trademarks regardless of which top-level domain they fall under. Is this a case of protecting owners of marks against confusion or dilution? If we allowed different entities to use the same name in different top-level domains, wouldn't people's expectations adjust so that confusion would be less likely?

CHAPTER IV

OWNER SOVEREIGNTY AND ITS LIMITS

As we saw in Chapter I, Blackstone referred to property with some hyperbole as "that sole and despotic dominion which one man claims and exercises over the external things of the world, in total exclusion of the right of any other individual in the universe." 2 William Blackstone, Commentaries on the Laws of England *2. In a famous essay written in the Legal Realist era, Morris Cohen agreed that property is a kind of delegated sovereignty over particular resources. Morris R. Cohen, Property and Sovereignty, 13 Cornell L.Q. 8 (1927). But while Blackstone celebrated owner sovereignty, Cohen warned against conferring too much power on individuals over resources, and argued that the general public, speaking through the sovereign government, should be able to make extensive modifications to owner sovereignty. In this Chapter, we consider in greater detail the extent to which property ownership conveys a type of sovereign authority over things. Those who embrace the sovereignty thesis (either affirmatively like Blackstone or critically like Cohen) invariably identify the right to exclude others as a key attribute of owner sovereignty. (Recall the excerpt from Penner in Chapter I.) Accordingly, we start by surveying the various ways in which the law recognizes and protects the right of an owner to exclude others from her "thing." We then consider various exceptions to the right to exclude, including necessity, custom, public accommodations laws, and anti-discrimination laws. This is followed by a consideration of other basic powers that are often associated with owner sovereignty, such as the right to include others (license), the right to transfer custody but not ownership (bailment), the right to abandon or destroy property, and the right to transfer ownership.

A. PROTECTING THE RIGHT TO EXCLUDE

If property entails, at least in its core signification, the right to exclude others from some thing, then it is important to consider the ways in which the law protects this exclusion right. Property owners are in fact given a considerable arsenal of weapons to vindicate their right to exclude others.

1. CRIMINAL LAWS

By convention the criminal laws that protect property are studied in criminal law courses, not property courses, so we will not attempt anything like comprehensive treatment here. Yet it is important not to lose sight of the fact that the criminal law provides extensive protection to property, and that these protections reinforce the civil remedies that traditionally have received attention in property courses. The criminal law "backstopping" of ownership rights is arguably critical to the maintenance of a system of private property. If property owners were left solely to their civil remedies, they might be easily overwhelmed or exhausted by the need to enforce those rights, particularly if violations became numerous or persistent. See Guido Calabresi & A. Douglas Melamed, Property Rules, Liability Rules, and Inalienability: One View of the Cathedral, 85 Harv. L. Rev. 1089 (1972) (explaining criminal law as a mechanism for preventing "property rules" from being unilaterally converted into "liability rules"); Alvin K. Klevorick, On the Economic Theory of Crime, in Criminal Justice: Nomos 27, 289, 301–04 (J. Roland Pennock & John W. Chapman eds., 1985) (explaining the function of criminal law in maintaining the "transaction structure" of legal entitlements including property rights). Another reason for providing criminal law protection of property rights is to utilize the police as an agency for enforcing exclusion rights in settings where costs and delays would make civil litigation ineffective, and hence the only realistic alternative would be self-help.

a.   CRIMINAL LAWS PROTECTING PERSONAL PROPERTY

We start with personal property. At common law, personal property was protected by the criminal law of larceny, which prohibited taking of personal property from the possession of another without legal authority. Possession, as you should be aware by now, can be tricky to define. The requirement of taking from possession poses a number of puzzles, one of which is the subject of the following case.

People v. Olivo

Court of Appeals of New York, 1981.
420 N.E.2d 40.

■ Cooke, Chief Judge. These cases present a recurring question in this era of the self-service store which has never been resolved by this court: may a person be convicted of larceny for shoplifting if the person is caught with goods while still inside the store? For reasons outlined below, it is concluded that a larceny conviction may be sustained, in certain situations, even though the shoplifter was apprehended before leaving the store.

I

In *People v. Olivo*, defendant was observed by a security guard in the hardware area of a department store. Initially conversing with another person, defendant began to look around furtively when his acquaintance departed. The security agent continued to observe and saw defendant assume a crouching position, take a set of wrenches and secret it in his clothes. After again looking around, defendant began walking toward an exit, passing a number of cash registers en route. When defendant did not stop to pay for the merchandise, the officer accosted him a few feet from the exit. In response to the guard's inquiry, [defendant] denied having the wrenches, but as he proceeded to the security office, defendant removed the wrenches and placed them under his jacket. At trial, defendant testified that he had placed the tools under his arm and was on line at a cashier when apprehended. The jury returned a verdict of guilty on the charge of petit larceny. The conviction was affirmed by Appellate Term.

II

In *People v. Gasparik*, defendant was in a department store trying on a leather jacket. Two store detectives observed him tear off the price tag and remove a "sensormatic" device designed to set off an alarm if the jacket were carried through a detection machine. There was at least one such machine at the exit of each floor. Defendant placed the tag and the device in the pocket of another jacket on the merchandise rack. He took his own jacket, which he had been carrying with him, and placed it on a table. Leaving his own jacket, defendant put on the leather jacket and walked through the store, still on the same floor, by passing several cash registers. When he headed for the exit from that floor, in the direction of the main floor, he was apprehended by security personnel. At trial, defendant denied removing the price tag and the sensormatic device from the jacket, and testified that he was looking for a cashier without a long line when he was stopped. The court, sitting without a jury, convicted defendant of petit larceny. Appellate Term affirmed.

III

In *People v. Spatzier*, defendant entered a bookstore on Fulton Street in Hempstead carrying an attaché case. The two co-owners of the store observed the defendant in a ceiling mirror as he browsed through the store. They watched defendant remove a book from the shelf, look up and down the aisle, and place the book in his case. He then placed the case at his feet and continued to [browse]. One of the owners approached defendant and accused him of stealing the book. An altercation [ensued] and when defendant allegedly struck the owner with the attaché case, the case opened and the book fell out. At trial, defendant denied secreting the book in his case and claimed that the owner had suddenly and unjustifiably accused him of stealing. The jury found defendant guilty of petit larceny, and the conviction was affirmed by the Appellate Term.

IV

The primary issue in each case is whether the evidence, viewed in the light most favorable to the prosecution, was sufficient to establish the elements of larceny as defined by the Penal Law. To resolve this common question, the development of the common-law crime of larceny and its evolution into modern statutory form must be briefly traced.

Larceny at common law was defined as a trespassory taking and carrying away of the property of another with intent to steal it (e.g., La Fave & Scott, Criminal Law, § 85, at p. 622; see 4 Blackstone's Commentaries, at pp. 229–250). The early common-law courts apparently viewed larceny as defending society against breach of the peace, rather than protecting individual property rights, and therefore placed heavy emphasis upon the requirement of a *trespassory taking* (e.g., Fletcher, Metamorphosis of Larceny, 89 Harv.L.Rev. 469; American Law Institute, Model Penal Code [Tent Draft No. 1], art. 206, app. A, at p. 101; La Fave & Scott, Criminal Law, § 85, at pp. 622–623). Thus, a person such as a bailee who had rightfully obtained possession of property from its owner could not be guilty of larceny (e.g., Glanvill, Treatise on the Laws and Customs of the Realm of England [Hall ed, 1965], pp. 128–130 [Book 10, at pp. 13–14]; see, e.g., Carrier's Case, Y B Pasch 13 Edw. IV, f.9, pl 5 [1473]). The result was that the crime of larceny was quite narrow in scope.

Gradually, the courts began to expand the reach of the offense, initially by subtle alterations in the common-law concept of possession (e.g., American Law Institute, Model Penal Code [Tent Draft No. 1], art 206, app. A, p. 101). Thus, for instance, it became a general rule that goods entrusted to an employee were not deemed to be in his possession, but were only considered to be in his custody, so long as he remained on the employer's premises (e.g., 3 Holdsworth, A History of English Law [3d ed, 1923], at p. 365). And, in the case of *Chisser* (Raym. Sir.T. 275, 83 Eng.Rep. 142), it was held that a shop owner retained legal possession of merchandise being examined by a prospective customer until the actual sale was made. In these situations, the employee and the customer would not have been guilty of larceny if they had first obtained lawful possession of the property from the owner. By holding that they had not acquired possession, but merely custody, the court was able to sustain a larceny conviction.

As the reach of larceny expanded, the intent element of the crime became of increasing importance, while the requirement of a trespassory taking became less significant. As a result, the bar against convicting a person who had initially obtained lawful possession of property faded. In *King v. Pear* (1 Leach 212, 168 Eng.Rep. 208), for instance, a defendant who had lied about his address and ultimate destination when renting a horse was found guilty of larceny for later converting the horse. Because of the fraudulent misrepresentation, the court reasoned, the defendant had never obtained legal possession (id., see King v. Semple, 1 Leach 420, 421–324, 168 Eng.Rep. 312, 313; 1 Hawkins, Pleas of the Crown [Leach 6th ed], 135, n. 1). Thus, "larceny by trick" was born (see Hall, Theft, Law and Society [2d ed], at p. 40).

Later cases went even further, often ignoring the fact that a defendant had initially obtained possession lawfully, and instead focused upon his later intent (e.g., Queen v. Middleton, LR 2 Cr.Cas.Res. 38 [1873]; Queen v. Ashwell, 16 QBD 190 [1885]). The crime of larceny then encompassed, not only situations where the defendant initially obtained property by a trespassory taking, but many situations where an individual, possessing the requisite intent, exercised control over property inconsistent with the continued rights of the owner.[3] During this evolutionary process, the purpose served by the crime of larceny obviously shifted from protecting society's peace to general protection of property rights (Fletcher, Metamorphosis of Larceny, 89 Harv.L.Rev. 469, 519–520, La Fave & Scott, Criminal Law, § 84, at pp. 618–619).[4]

Modern penal statutes generally have incorporated these developments under a unified definition of larceny (see, e.g., American Law Institute, Model Penal Code [Tent Draft No. 1], § 206.1 [theft is appropriation of property of another, which includes unauthorized exercise of control]). Case law, too, now tends to focus upon the actor's intent and the exercise of dominion and control over the property (see, e.g., People v. Alamo, 315 N.E.2d 446 (N.Y. 1974); People v. Baker, 365 Ill. 323 (1937); People v. Britto, 402 N.Y.S.2d 546 (N.Y. City Crim. Ct. 1978)). Indeed, this court has recognized, in construing the New York Penal Law,[5] that the *"ancient common-law concepts of larceny"* no longer strictly apply (People v. Alamo, supra, 315 N.E.2d at 450 [emphasis added]).

This evolution is particularly relevant to thefts occurring in modern self-service stores. In stores of that type, customers are impliedly invited to examine, try on, and carry about the merchandise on display. Thus in a sense, the owner has consented to the customer's possession of the goods for a limited purpose (see, e.g., Day v. Grand Union Co., 113 N.Y.S.2d 436, 437–38 (App. Div. 1952); Lasky v. Economy Grocery Stores, 65 N.E.2d 305 (Mass. 1946); Groomes v. United States, 155 A.2d 73 (D.C. 1959)). That the owner has consented to that possession does not, however, preclude a conviction for larceny. If the customer exercises dominion and control wholly inconsistent with the continued rights of the owner, and the other

---

3. Parliament also played a role in this development. Thus, for example, in 1857 a statute extended larceny to all conversions by bailees (20 & 21 Vict., ch. 54).

4. One commentator has argued that the concept of possessorial immunity—i.e., that one who obtains possession of property by delivery from the owner cannot be guilty of larceny—stems from a general reluctance of the early common law to criminalize acts arising out of private relationships (Fletcher, Metamorphosis of Larceny, 89 Harv.L.Rev. 469, 472–476). Thus, although an owner deprived of property by a bailee could seek a civil remedy in detinue and later trover (Maitland, Equity and the Forms of Action at Common Law, at pp. 356–357, 365), the harm was deemed private and not a matter for societal intervention. Over time, the public-private dichotomy waned and the criminal law increasingly was viewed as an instrument for protecting certain interests and control-

ling social behavior (Fletcher, at pp. 502–504). As a concomitant development, the criminal law changed its main focus from the objective behavior of the defendant to his subjective intent (id., at pp. 498–518).

5. Section 155.05 of the Penal Law defines larceny: "1. A person steals property and commits larceny when, with intent to deprive another of property or to appropriate the same to himself or to a third person, he wrongfully takes, obtains, or withholds such property from an owner thereof. 2. Larceny includes a wrongful taking, obtaining or withholding of another's property, with the intent prescribed in subdivision one of this section, committed in any of the following ways: (a) By conduct heretofore defined or known as common law larceny by trespassory taking, common law larceny by trick, embezzlement, or obtaining property by false pretenses."

elements of the crime are present, a larceny has occurred.[6] Such conduct on the part of a customer satisfies the "taking" element of the crime.

It is this element that forms the core of the controversy in these cases. The defendants argue, in essence, that the crime is not established, as a matter of law, unless there is evidence that the customer departed the shop without paying for the merchandise.

Although this court has not addressed the issue, case law from other jurisdictions seems unanimous in holding that a shoplifter need not leave the store to be guilty of larceny * * * It would be well-nigh impossible, and unwise, to attempt to delineate all the situations which would establish a taking. But it is possible to identify some of the factors used in determining whether the evidence is sufficient to be submitted to the fact finder.

In many cases, it will be particularly relevant that defendant concealed the goods under clothing or in a container. Such conduct is not generally expected in a self-service store and may in a proper case be deemed an exercise of dominion and control inconsistent with the store's continued rights. Other furtive or unusual behavior on the part of the defendant should also be weighed. Thus, if the defendant surveys the area while secreting the merchandise or abandoned his or her own property in exchange for the concealed goods, this may evince larcenous rather than innocent behavior. Relevant too is the customer's proximity to or movement towards one of the store's [exits]. Certainly it is highly probative of guilt that the customer was in possession of secreted goods just a few short steps from the door or moving in that direction. Finally, possession of a known shoplifting device actually used to conceal merchandise, such as a specially designed outer garment or false bottomed carrying case, would be all but decisive.

Of course, in a particular case, any one or any combination of these factors may take on special significance. And there may be other considerations, not now identified, which should be examined. So long as [it] bears upon the principal issue—whether the shopper exercised control wholly inconsistent with the owner's continued rights—any attending circumstance is relevant and may be taken into account.

V

Under these principles, there was ample evidence in each case to raise a factual question as to the defendants' guilt. In *People v. Olivo*, defendant not only concealed goods in his clothing, but he did so in a particularly

---

6. Also, required, of course, is the intent prescribed by subdivision 1 of section 155.05 of the Penal Law, and some movement when property other than an automobile is involved (see People v. Alamo, 315 N.E.2d 446, supra). As a practical matter in shoplifting cases the same evidence which proves the taking will usually involve movement.

The movement, or asportation requirement has traditionally been satisfied by a slight moving of the property (see Harrison v. People, 50 N.Y. 518 (1872)). This accords with the purpose of the asportation element which is to show that the thief had indeed gained possession and control of the property (People v. Alamo, supra, at 449–50; see Harrison v. People, supra).

suspicious manner. And, when defendant was stopped, he was moving towards the door, just three feet short of [exiting] the store. It cannot be said as [a] matter of law that these circumstances failed to establish a taking.

In *People v. Gasparik*, defendant removed the price tag and sensor device from a jacket, abandoned his own garment, put the jacket on and ultimately headed for the main floor of the store. Removal of the price tag and sensor device, and careful concealment of those items, is highly unusual and suspicious conduct for a shopper. Coupled with defendant's abandonment of his own coat and his attempt to leave the floor, those factors were sufficient to make out a prima facie case of a taking.

In *People v. Spatzier*, defendant concealed a book in an attaché case. Unaware that he was being observed in an overhead mirror, defendant looked furtively up and down [an] aisle before secreting the book. In these circumstances, given the manner in which defendant concealed the book and his suspicious behavior, the evidence was not insufficient as a matter of law. * * *

VII

In sum, in view of the modern definition of the crime of larceny, and its purpose of protecting individual property rights, a taking of property in the self-service store context can be established by evidence that a customer exercised control over merchandise wholly inconsistent with the store's continued rights. Quite simply, a customer who crosses the line between the limited right he or she has to deal with merchandise and the store owner's rights may be subject to prosecution for larceny. Such a rule should foster the legitimate interests and continued operation of self-service shops, a convenience which most members of the society enjoy.

Accordingly, in each case, the order of the Appellate Term should be affirmed.

NOTES AND QUESTIONS

1. As mentioned in the excerpted opinion, a conventional explanation for the "taking from possession" element of larceny is that the law was more concerned with protecting persons than ownership of things:

> The principal factor which limited the scope of larceny was the requirement that the thief must take it from the victim's possession; larceny requires a "trespass in the taking," as the matter is often stated. The judges who determined the scope of larceny (including its limitations) apparently considered larceny to be a crime designed to prevent breaches of the peace rather than protecting property from wrongful appropriation. The unauthorized taking of property, even by stealth, from the owner's possession is apt to produce an altercation if the owner discovers the property moving out of his possession in the hands

of the thief. But when the wrongdoer already has the owner's property in his possession at the time he misappropriates it (today's embezzlement) or when he obtains the property from the owner by telling him lies (now the crime of false pretenses) there is not the same danger of an immediate breach of the peace. Upon learning how he has been wronged the owner may be as angry at the wrongdoer in these two situations as he is at the thief caught in the act of taking his property by stealth, but the malefactor in these two cases is generally less available for retaliatory measures than when the owner discovers him in the process of taking the property out of his possession.

Wayne R. LaFave, Criminal Law § 19.1(a), at 919–20 (4th ed. 2003). Nevertheless, as *Olivo* recounts, courts and later legislatures kept adding to the inventory of property offenses, often through various "constructive possession" theories. Does this process of evolution tend to undermine the story about the primary concern of the criminal law being the protection of persons rather than ownership of things?

2.   The court describes a broad movement in the law of larceny from a focus on taking or asportation to "intent." What exactly is the relevant intent that must be shown to convict a person of larceny today? How would you draft an appropriate instruction for the jury? Do the behaviors that the court singles out as probative of criminal intent go to the defendant's intent to deprive the victim of her property, or to the defendant's guilty state of mind? Are these the same thing? Are these behaviors defined by law or by social norms and customs? Should criminal liability turn on something as ineffable as norms and customs? In footnote 6, the court reaffirms that some physical movement of the property is still required to establish larceny. Why is proof of movement required if intent is now all-important? If some movement is required, why not require movement that takes the property out of the possession and control of the victim?

3.   Despite what the court in *Olivo* says about modern "unified" larceny and the many calls and some attempts to achieve consolidation into a single "theft" crime, older distinctions—such as between larceny, embezzlement, larceny by trick, and so forth—tend to persist, even in jurisdictions that have attempted consolidation. This creates problems for prosecutors in choosing the right crime to charge. How relevant is this complexity to the potential defendant? How does a shopper know what is and is not allowed?

4.   Personal property is covered by a complex menu of criminal prohibitions. Takings of personal property that directly endanger persons are often punished under the rubric of *robbery*, which is the common-law crime of larceny with the added element that the property is taken from the possession of the victim using force or by putting the victim in fear of immediate serious bodily injury. See Model Penal Code § 222.1. Persons who damage, but do not take, personal property can be charged with the crime of *criminal mischief*. Id. § 220.3.

b. CRIMINAL LAWS PROTECTING REAL PROPERTY

D - lawyer for CRLS

State v. Shack

Supreme Court of New Jersey, 1971.
277 A.2d 369.

■ WEINTRAUB, C.J. Defendants entered upon private property to aid migrant farmworkers employed and housed there. Having refused to depart upon the demand of the owner, defendants were charged with violating N.J.S.A. 2A:170–31 which provides that "[a]ny person who trespasses on any lands * * * after being forbidden so to trespass by the owner * * * is a disorderly person and shall be punished by a fine of not more than $50." Defendants were convicted in the Municipal Court of Deerfield Township and again on appeal in the County Court of Cumberland County on a trial de novo. We certified their further appeal before argument in the Appellate Division.

Before us, no one seeks to sustain these convictions. The complaints were prosecuted in the Municipal Court and in the County Court by counsel engaged by the complaining landowner, Tedesco. However Tedesco did not respond to this appeal, and the county prosecutor, while defending abstractly the constitutionality of the trespass statute, expressly disclaimed any position as to whether the statute reached the activity of these defendants.

Complainant, Tedesco, a farmer, employs migrant workers for his seasonal needs. As part of their compensation, these workers are housed at a camp on his property.

Defendant Tejeras is a field worker for the Farm Workers Division of the Southwest Citizens Organization for Poverty Elimination, known by the acronym SCOPE, a nonprofit corporation funded by the Office of Economic Opportunity pursuant to an act of Congress, 42 U.S.C.A. §§ 2861–2864. The role of SCOPE includes providing for the "health services of the migrant farm worker."

Defendant Shack is a staff attorney with the Farm Workers Division of Camden Regional Legal Services, Inc., known as "CRLS," also a nonprofit corporation funded by the Office of Economic Opportunity pursuant to an act of Congress, 42 U.S.C.A. § 2809(a)(3). The mission of CRLS includes legal advice and representation for these workers.

Differences had developed between Tedesco and these defendants prior to the events which led to the trespass charges now before us. Hence when defendant Tejeras wanted to go upon Tedesco's farm to find a migrant worker who needed medical aid for the removal of 28 sutures, he called upon defendant Shack for his help with respect to the legalities involved. Shack, too, had a mission to perform on Tedesco's farm; he wanted to discuss a legal problem with another migrant worker there employed and housed. Defendants arranged to go to the farm together. Shack carried literature to inform the migrant farmworkers of the assistance available to them under federal statutes, but no mention seems to have been made of that literature when Shack was later confronted by Tedesco.

Defendants entered upon Tedesco's property and as they neared the camp site where the farmworkers were housed, they were confronted by Tedesco who inquired of their purpose. Tejeras and Shack stated their missions. In response, Tedesco offered to find the injured worker, and as to the worker who needed legal advice, Tedesco also offered to locate the man but insisted that the consultation would have to take place in Tedesco's office and in his presence. Defendants declined, saying they had the right to see the men in the privacy of their living quarters and without Tedesco's [supervision]. Tedesco thereupon summoned a State Trooper who, however, refused to remove defendants except upon Tedesco's written complaint. Tedesco then executed the formal complaints charging violations of the trespass statute.

I.

The constitutionality of the trespass statute, as applied here, is challenged on several scores. * * * These constitutional claims are not established by any definitive holding. We think it unnecessary to explore their validity. The reason is that we are satisfied that under our State law the ownership of real property does not include the right to bar access to governmental services available to migrant workers and hence there was no trespass within the meaning of the penal statute. The policy considerations which underlie that conclusion may be much the same as those which would be weighed with respect to one or more of the constitutional challenges, but a decision in nonconstitutional terms is more satisfactory, because the interests of migrant workers are more expansively served in that way than they would be if they had no more freedom than these constitutional concepts could be found to mandate if indeed they apply at all.

II.

Main Point ✳

Property rights serve human values. They are recognized to that end, and are limited by it. Title to real property cannot include dominion over the destiny of persons the owner permits to come upon the premises. Their well-being must remain the paramount concern of a system of law. Indeed the needs of the occupants may be so imperative and their strength so weak, that the law will deny the occupants the power to contract away what is deemed essential to their health, welfare, or dignity.

Here we are concerned with a highly disadvantaged segment of our society. We are told that every year farmworkers and their families numbering more than one million leave their home areas to fill the seasonal demand for farm labor in the United States. The Migratory Farm Labor Problem in the United States (1969 Report of Subcommittee on Migratory Labor of the United States Senate Committee on Labor and Public Welfare), p. 1. The migrant farmworkers come to New Jersey in substantial numbers. * * *

The migrant farmworkers are a community within but apart from the local scene. They are rootless and isolated. Although the need for their labors is evident, they are unorganized and without economic or political power. It is their plight alone that summoned government to their aid. In response, Congress provided under Title III–B of the Economic Opportunity Act of 1964 (42 U.S.C.A. § 2701 et seq.) for "assistance for migrant and other seasonally employed farmworkers and their families." Section 2861 states "the purpose of this part is to assist migrant and seasonal farmworkers and their families to improve their living conditions and develop skills necessary for a productive and self-sufficient life in an increasingly complex and technological society." * * *

These ends would not be gained if the intended beneficiaries could be insulated from efforts to reach them. It is in this framework that we must decide whether the camp operator's rights in his lands may stand between the migrant workers and those who would aid them. The key to that aid is communication. Since the migrant workers are outside the mainstream of the communities in which they are housed and are unaware of their rights and opportunities and of the services available to them, they can be reached only by positive efforts tailored to that end. The Report of the Governor's Task Force on Migrant Farm Labor (1968) noted that "One of the major problems related to seasonal farm labor is the lack of adequate direct information with regard to the availability of public services," and that "there is a dire need to provide the workers with basic educational and informational material in a language and style that can be readily understood by the migrant" (pp. 101–102). The report stressed the problem of access and deplored the notion that property rights may stand as a barrier, saying "In our judgment, 'no trespass' signs represent the last dying remnants of paternalistic behavior" (p. 63).

A man's right in his real property of course is not absolute. It was a maxim of the common law that one should so use his property as not to injure the rights of others. Broom, Legal Maxims (10th ed. Kersley 1939), p. 238; 39 Words and Phrases, "Sic Utere Tuo ut Alienum Non Laedas," p. 335. Although hardly a precise solvent of actual controversies, the maxim does express the inevitable proposition that rights are relative and there must be an accommodation when they meet. Hence it has long been true that necessity, private or public, may justify entry upon the lands of another. * * *

The subject is not static. As pointed out in 5 Powell, Real Property (Rohan 1970) § 745, pp. 493–494, while society will protect the owner in his permissible interests in land, yet

> * * * [s]uch an owner must expect to find the absoluteness of his property rights curtailed by the organs of society, for the promotion of the best interests of others for whom these organs also operate as protective agencies. The necessity for such curtailments is greater in a modern industrialized and urbanized society than it was in the relatively simple American society of fifty, 100, or 200 years ago. The current balance between individualism and dominance of the social

interest depends not only upon political and social ideologies, but also upon the physical and social facts of the time and place under discussion.

Professor Powell added in § 746, pp. 494–496:

As one looks back along the historic road traversed by the law of land in England and in America, one sees a change from the viewpoint that he who owns may do as he pleases with what he owns, to a position which hesitatingly embodies an ingredient of stewardship; which grudgingly, but steadily, broadens the recognized scope of social interests in the utilization of things. * * *

To one seeing history through the glasses of religion, these changes may seem to evidence increasing embodiments of the golden rule. To one thinking in terms of political and economic ideologies, they are likely to be labeled evidences of "social enlightenment," or of "creeping socialism" or even of "communistic infiltration," according to the individual's assumed definitions and retained or acquired prejudices. With slight attention to words or labels, time marches on toward new adjustments between individualism and the social interests.

The process involves not only the accommodation between the right of the owner and the interests of the general public in his use of this property, but involves also an accommodation between the right of the owner and the right of individuals who are parties with him in consensual transactions relating to the use of the property. Accordingly substantial alterations have been made as between a landlord and his tenant. See Reste Realty Corp. v. Cooper, 251 A.2d 268 (N.J. 1969); Marini v. Ireland, 265 A.2d 526 (N.J. 1970).

The argument in this case understandably included the question whether the migrant worker should be deemed to be a tenant and thus entitled to the tenant's right to receive visitors, or whether his residence on the employer's property should be deemed to be merely incidental and in aid of his employment, and hence to involve no possessory interest in the realty. * * *

We see no profit in trying to decide upon a conventional category and then forcing the present subject into it. That approach would be artificial and distorting. The quest is for a fair adjustment of the competing needs of the parties, in the light of the realities of the relationship between the migrant worker and the operator of the housing facility.

Thus approaching the case, we find it unthinkable that the farmer-employer can assert a right to isolate the migrant worker in any respect significant for the worker's well-being. The farmer, of course, is entitled to pursue his farming activities without interference, and this defendants readily concede. But we see no legitimate need for a right in the farmer to deny the worker the opportunity for aid available from federal, State, or local services, or from recognized charitable groups seeking to assist him. Hence representatives of these agencies and organizations may enter upon the premises to seek out the worker at his living quarters. So, too, the migrant worker must be allowed to receive visitors there of his own choice, so long as there is no behavior hurtful to others, and members of the press may not be denied reasonable access to workers who do not object to seeing them.

It is not our purpose to open the employer's premises to the general public if in fact the employer himself has not done so. We do not say, for example, that solicitors or peddlers of all kinds may enter on their own; we may assume for the present that the employer may regulate their entry or bar them, at least if the employer's purpose is not to gain a commercial advantage for himself or if the regulation does not deprive the migrant worker of practical access to things he needs.

And we are mindful of the employer's interest in his own and in his employees' security. Hence he may reasonably require a visitor to identify himself, and also to state his general purpose if the migrant worker has not already informed him that the visitor is expected. But the employer may not deny the worker his privacy or interfere with his opportunity to live with dignity and to enjoy associations customary among our citizens. These rights are too fundamental to be denied on the basis of an interest in real property and too fragile to be left to the unequal bargaining strength of the parties. See Henningsen v. Bloomfield Motors, Inc., 161 A.2d 69 (N.J. 1960); Ellsworth Dobbs, Inc. v. Johnson, 236 A.2d 843 (N.J. 1967).

It follows that defendants here invaded no possessory right of the farmer-employer. Their conduct was therefore beyond the reach of the trespass statute. The judgments are accordingly reversed and the matters remanded to the County Court with directions to enter judgments of acquittal.

NOTES AND QUESTIONS

1. Recall that the first case in Chapter I also involved a criminal trespass to real property. In *Jacque v. Steenberg Homes*, the issue was punitive damages, but Steenberg Homes had also been fined $30 for misdemeanor trespass. The *Jacque* court concluded that the criminal fine was insufficient to vindicate the owner's right to exclude. The *Shack* court, in contrast, finds that even a $50 criminal fine results in too much owner sovereignty. What accounts for the difference? The *Shack* court perceives a conflict between the rights of the property owner and the rights of persons. Is there no such conflict in *Jacque*? If not, why not?

2. One important difference between *Shack* and decisions such as *Jacque* is that the court implicitly treats the owner's right to exclude not as a rule but as a standard. Generally speaking, rules are simple decisional devices that take the form: If x (a particular fact or condition) then y (a particular legal result). For example, this is a rule: If a stranger crosses the boundary of an owner's property, then the owner can have the stranger evicted. Rules generate legal conclusions at low cost and without regard to whether the underlying purposes of the rule are satisfied in any particular case. A standard, in contrast, is a decisional device that directly invokes

some conception of the law's purposes or goals. Generally speaking, standards are more complex decisional devices and are more costly to apply, but they hold forth the promise of reaching results that are more consistent with the purposes or goals the law is seeking to achieve. *Shack* seems to invoke a standard something like this: If a stranger crosses the boundary of an owner's property, then the owner can have the stranger evicted—provided the owner's interest in protecting his autonomy is sufficiently great and the interests of other persons in abrogating the owner's right to exclude are not more important. Which approach generates a more satisfactory result in this particular case? Which approach provides a more practical basis for a system of property rights that governs the actions of millions of people interacting with millions of parcels of property on a daily basis? The question of rules versus standards pervades the law. See Frederick Schauer, Playing by the Rules 131 (1991). Some see the key difference between rules and standards in the timing of the decision: Standards, unlike rules, rely on ex post decisionmaking in which the decisionmaker has a greater degree of discretion, whereas rules spell out criteria beforehand. Others stress that rules are more costly to create but cheaper to apply. See Louis Kaplow, Rules Versus Standards: An Economic Analysis, 42 Duke L.J. 557, 608–17 (1992). How do these underlying considerations bear on the situation in *Shack*? On other issues of the extent of owner sovereignty?

3. Trespass was not a traditional common-law crime, unless the trespass involved tended to a breach of the peace. Only in the second half of the nineteenth century did criminal trespass statutes become common. See State v. Goduto, 174 N.E.2d 385 (Ill. 1961). Some of the early statutes were narrow. Texas's statute covered only hunting, camping, or fishing on enclosed land, and was only amended in 1971 to cover intrusions more generally:

> Whoever enters upon the land of another, after receiving, immediately before such entry, notice from the owner, or some person exercising possession for the owner, that such entry is forbidden, or remains upon the land of another, after receiving notice to depart from the owner, or some person exercising possession for the owner, shall be fined not exceeding $200.00.

Tex. Penal Code Ann. § 30.05(a); see also 720 Ill. Comp. Stat. § 5/21–3(a). Still, even under the modern statutes the penalties for criminal trespass remain quite modest—a maximum fine of $50 as in *Shack* is in no way unusual.

4. The modesty of the penalties for criminal trespass raises questions about the function of these laws. The small penalties for criminal trespass cannot be regarded as having any significant deterrent force. (Unless perhaps the social stigma of a misdemeanor trespass conviction is large. Is it?) How then does a landowner protect the right to exclude? One answer would seem to be civil actions (like the civil trespass action at issue in *Jacque v. Steenberg Homes*), but these are rare. Another answer, probably more important historically, is that landowners may use "self-help." In

other words, the landowner is privileged to use "reasonable force" to expel unwanted intruders from the land—but not deadly force, at least if the intrusion is onto land or an unoccupied building, see Katko v. Briney, 183 N.W.2d 657 (Iowa 1971) (spring gun cannot be used to defend unoccupied building against trespassers). Self-help has some obvious drawbacks—such as the possibility of violence or injury to either the landowner or the intruder—which we consider in greater detail below. This suggests that the principal function of criminal trespass statutes is to create an alternative to landowner self-help. The criminal trespass statutes substitute a police offer for agents of the landowner in enforcing the right to exclude. The police officer is less likely than the landowner to overreact to the situation, and less likely to encounter resistance from the intruder. If there is a genuine dispute between the owner and the intruder over the right of access, it can then be resolved—peacefully—in court. Does this cast the situation in *Shack* in a new light, and provide a possible justification for the outcome (dismissal of the charges), whatever you think of the court's implicit decision to treat the right to exclude as a standard rather than a rule?

5. Given the availability of the police to enforce the landowner's right to exclude in many situations, does this suggest that self-help should be prohibited as a means of enforcing the right when police intervention is feasible? See Berg v. Wiley, infra.

6. Many criminal trespass statutes make it a crime to refuse to leave property in possession of another only after being notified to do so. See the Texas statute quoted above. This imposes a small affirmative burden on the landowner—to notify the intruder to leave before calling the police. Statutes specify in more or less detail what counts as notice not to enter or when to leave. For example, the Texas statute provides for notice by oral or written communication; fencing or enclosure; signs indicating that entry is forbidden; "purple paint marks" on trees or posts that are "vertical lines of not less than eight inches in length and not less than one inch in width" and subject to elaborate spacing requirements; or the presence of standing crops. Tex. Penal Code Ann. § 30.05(b)(2). Why put the burden on the landowner to communicate the intent to exclude rather than put the burden on the intruder to obtain permission to enter? Is this necessary to establish the required scienter (mental state) on the part of the defendant before imposing criminal liability? What implications does the allocation of the burden of communication have for the development of norms of "neighborliness" within a community? Consider also the environmental consequences of the notification requirement. This is presumably responsible (at least in significant part) for the proliferation of "No Trespassing," "Private Property," and "Do Not Enter" signs one sees on walls, doors, and fences throughout the land. Would rural and urban landscapes be more attractive if the law simply imposed a duty not to trespass on any land enclosed by a fence, wall, or other obvious border, without requiring explicit "notification"?

7. Parallel to the question of who has the burden of notification that intrusions are either prohibited or permitted is the issue of who has the

burden to establish an exception to the right to exclude. For example, in *Shack*, the court adopts an exception to the owner's right to exclude that applies to aid workers. Should the owner be free to impose any conditions he wants on the public's right of access, unless and until someone shows that a higher legal authority (like a legislature) has adopted a supervening legal principle that requires him to grant access? Illinois for example has included in its criminal trespass statute an exception to cover the situations like that in *State v. Shack*. 720 Ill. Comp. Stat. § 5/21–3(c) ("This Section does not apply to any person . . . invited by [a] migrant worker or other person so living on such land to visit him at the place he is so living upon the land."). Or, by opening up its land to the migrant workers, should the owner be taken to have relinquished the right to exclude any person the migrant workers might invite? On the approach taken in *Shack*, is this presumption irrebutable?

8.   Real property is protected by criminal laws other than criminal trespass, often with considerably more firepower. Interestingly, however, the heavy artillery of the criminal law, insofar as property in land is concerned, is concentrated almost entirely on offenses that involve buildings or occupied structures. The crime of *arson*, for example, is defined as causing a fire or explosion that destroys "a building or occupied structure of another." Model Penal Code § 220.1(1). Arson is a felony subject to very severe penalties. The crime of *burglary* occurs when a person "enters a building or structure, or separately secured or occupied portion thereof, with purpose to commit a crime therein, unless the premises are at the time open to the public or the actor is licensed or privileged to enter." Id. § 221.1(1). Burglary is also a felony subject to severe penalties. The penalties for criminal trespass are also frequently more severe if the trespass involves a building or occupied structure. Does this overall pattern lend support to the claim that the criminal law is systematically more concerned with protection of persons than protection of property, since occupied structures by definition include persons, and persons are more likely to be found in buildings than in open fields? In any event, arson and burglary, which are the most severely punished crimes involving land, both pose obvious threats to the security of the person.

2.   CIVIL ACTIONS

Civil actions to protect and recover property have a long and complicated history. These actions started out as common-law "writs," which were a kind of standardized pleading that required certain kinds of proof and afforded certain prescribed remedies. Over time, especially with the adoption of the Field Codes in the mid-nineteenth century and then the emergence of modern "notice" or "fact" pleading, the rigidities associated with the writs have been much relaxed. See Rodolfo Batiza, Sources of the Field Civil Code: The Civil Law Influences on a Common Law Code, 60 Tul. L. Rev. 799 (1986).

Nevertheless, the elements associated with the individual writs continue to live on, in judicial understandings about what must be proved in order to establish a "cause of action." You may have already noticed this shift in some of the cases covered in this book. Older cases commonly begin with the court reciting the common-law writ that governs the action. See, e.g., Pierson v. Post, Chapter II ("This was an action of trespass on the case . . ."); Wetherbee v. Green, Chapter II ("This was an action in replevin . . ."); Clark v. Maloney, Chapter II ("Action of trover to recover the value of ten white pine logs."). More recent cases no longer follow this format, but they often contain elaborate discussions of whether the defendant's behavior gives rise to a particular cause of action. See, e.g., Producers Lumber & Supply v. Olney Building Co., Chapter I (whether defendant's actions gave rise to a claim for restitution); Moore v. Regents of the University of California, Chapter III (whether defendants' taking of plaintiff's body cells gave rise to an action for conversion). Thus, the features of the common-law writs live on in the law, but in a less direct and noticeable fashion. A good source for those seeking more detail about the common-law writs is Joseph H. Koffler & Alison Reppy, Common Law Pleading (1969).

a.   CIVIL ACTIONS PROTECTING REAL PROPERTY

We start here with actions to protect real property, which begin somewhat earlier in time than the actions that relate to personal property. By the thirteenth century, English courts would hear claims based on the so-called real actions, such as the writ of novel disseisin and the writ of mort d'ancestor. These actions protected seisin of land, a concept that started out meaning something like possession, but over time became encrusted with technicalities. See A.W.B. Simpson, A History of the Land Law 40–41 (2d ed. 1986). By the end of the sixteenth century, the real actions had fallen into disuse, and had been replaced by writs from the trespass family. Especially prominent were *trespass quare clausum fregit* (trespass "because he broke the close," often called simply "trespass q.c.f."), and trespass *de ejectione firmae*, which became known simply as *ejectment*. Both were originally actions for money damages, but by the sixteenth century, the common-law courts began to give specific recovery of land to certain parties who won an ejectment action. The real actions never were much used in the United States, where the actions of importance in protecting the right to land have always been trespass and ejectment.

Trespass protects possession. Thus, a party must be in possession of land to sue an intruder for trespass q.c.f. There was a longstanding debate, both in England and the United States, whether ejectment was an action that protected possession or title or both. See, e.g., Tapscott v. Cobbs, 52 Va. (11 Gratt.) 172 (1854). Whatever ambiguities existed historically, today it is relatively clear that trespass (the q.c.f. is usually dropped these days) is used to vindicate the interest that a person in actual possession has in exclusive possession of land, and ejectment is used to vindicate the interest of a person who has title to land against a person wrongfully in possession. For example, if land is under lease, and a trespass such as a building encroachment occurs, the tenant in possession is the only one who can bring an action in trespass. The landlord would have to sue in ejectment. See Prosser and Keeton, The Law of Torts § 13, at 78 (5th ed. 1984).

Although the remedy for trespass was originally damages, courts for several centuries have also awarded injunctions against trespasses. See discussion in Baker v. Hunt Club, Chapter I. Typically, the plaintiff/possessor can recover both in a single action: damages for injuries incurred in the past, and an injunction against recurring injury in the future. The plaintiff/owner suing in ejectment can also seek both damages and injunctive relief: damages in the form of so-called mesne profits—for example the rental value of the property during the period of wrongful possession—and an injunction that restores the owner to possession.

The other civil action of importance to landowners is *nuisance*. A quasi-criminal action known as the assize of nuisance existed as early as the thirteenth century. It was soon replaced by the action on the case for nuisance. Nuisance originally applied to injuries that originated outside the plaintiff's land, whereas trespass q.c.f. required a breaking of the close, and hence an injury that originated on the land itself. Today, nuisance is understood to protect the interest in use and enjoyment of land, as opposed to trespass, which protects the interest in exclusive possession of land. Damages were the original remedy for a nuisance, but as in the case of trespass q.c.f., injunctive relief became available along the way. (For more on trespass and nuisance, see Chapter IX.)

b.   CIVIL ACTIONS PROTECTING PERSONAL PROPERTY

At common law, a number of distinctive writs or rights of action developed to protect owners of personal property. One, which dates from the early fourteenth century and was probably quasi-criminal in its origins, was also a member of the trespass family, in this case the writ of *trespass de bonis asportatis* (or trespass d.b.a.), which applied to the forcible carrying off (asportation) of the plaintiff's goods. It was necessary to allege that the goods had been wrongfully taken from the plaintiff's possession, but was not necessary to allege that they had been converted to the defendant's own use. As with other early trespass actions, an award of money damages was the only remedy available under this writ. The plaintiff could not recover the goods themselves.

Another common-law writ, which emerged in the early fifteenth century and evolved out of the older action for debt, was *detinue*. In contrast to trespass d.b.a., which was based on an unlawful taking, detinue was based on the unlawful detention of goods. Detinue applied when the plaintiff alleged that the defendant had unjustly detained specific goods which remained in the defendant's possession, and which the plaintiff alleged should be returned to him. It was used mainly to recover lost property and in disputes over bailments (temporary possession, see Section C.2 below). If the defendant was found liable, he had the option of either returning the object to the plaintiff or paying its value in damages.

A third common-law writ that became important after the middle of the sixteenth century was *trover*. This action also evolved out of the trespass family, and in particular out of the action for trespass on the case, which was the general action for indirect rather than direct harms. Like detinue, trover did not require that the plaintiff prove an unlawful taking. Trover was used to allege that the defendant had wrongfully converted the plaintiff's goods to his own use. It was not necessary to allege that the goods remained in the defendant's possession as under detinue, only that they had been converted to the defendant's use. Damages were the only remedy until 1854, when Parliament passed a statute authorizing the judge to order return of the goods in appropriate cases.

A fourth common-law writ, and the only one which provided a mechanism for recovering the personal property itself, was *replevin*. Replevin was also an old action, dating from the fourteenth century, and it was originally used in the narrow context where a landlord seized personal property of the plaintiff as a distraint for unpaid rent. Like trespass d.b.a., it was based on a wrongful taking of goods (e.g., because the plaintiff claimed no rent was owed), rather than wrongful detention. Replevin had an unusual procedure. It began with the plaintiff posting a bond, usually for twice the value of the property, whereupon the plaintiff could immediately recover possession of the property. If the plaintiff won, the bond was returned. If the plaintiff lost, then the bond was used to satisfy the defendant's claim (e.g., for unpaid rent).

A fifth common-law writ, which also evolved from the trespass family, was *trespass to chattels*. This action applied when there had been no asportation of personal property, but the defendant had injured or interfered with the property, in some manner falling short of conversion, while it remained in the possession of the plaintiff. This action was invoked relatively rarely—at least until recently, when it has been dusted off and thrust into the limelight with the emergence of disputes over hacking into computer systems, spamming and other unwanted intrusions into internet websites and email systems. See Intel Corp. v. Hamidi, infra.

This was the basic menu of options for protecting personal property when the American colonies broke free of England in 1776. The newly independent states eventually adopted laws "receiving" the common law of England, including the writs of trespass d.b.a., detinue, trover, replevin, and trespass to chattels. Ford W. Hall, The Common Law: An Account of Its Reception in the United States, 4 Vand. L. Rev. 791 (1951). But the courts would often modify the common law to accommodate the different circumstances or needs of the fledgling nation.

Replevin was popular in America because it allowed the plaintiff to recover possession of goods rather than simply damages. Over time, the action expanded well beyond its original context of distraint for rent, and came to be used in a variety of circumstances involving the wrongful taking of personal property in which the plaintiff wanted to recover possession. By a variety of fictions and legislative changes, replevin was also expanded to include situations involving wrongful detention, as opposed to takings, of goods. Usually, the state courts retained some version of the original procedure calling for a posting of a bond by the plaintiff and recovery of possession at the outset of the litigation.

Trover became the favored action for plaintiffs seeking relief from wrongful conversion of personal property. Under the influence of the Field Codes popular in the mid-nineteenth century, trover came to be supplanted by the tort of conversion, although in substance it was largely the same. Today, one rarely sees reference to trover. The principal actions for protection of personal property today are replevin, conversion, and trespass to chattels.

Intel Corporation v. Hamidi

Supreme Court of California, 2003.
71 P.3d 296.

■ WERDEGAR, J. Intel Corporation (Intel) maintains an electronic mail system, connected to the Internet, through which messages between employees and those outside the company can be sent and received, and permits its employees to make reasonable nonbusiness use of this system. On six occasions over almost two years, Kourosh Kenneth Hamidi, a former Intel employee, sent e-mails criticizing Intel's employment practices to numerous current employees on Intel's electronic mail system. Hamidi breached no computer security barriers in order to communicate with Intel employees. He offered to, and did, remove from his mailing list any recipient who so wished. Hamidi's communications to individual Intel employees caused neither physical damage nor functional disruption to the company's computers, nor did they at any time deprive Intel of the use of its computers. The contents of the messages, however, caused discussion among employees and managers.

On these facts, Intel brought suit, claiming that by communicating with its employees over the company's e-mail system Hamidi committed the tort of trespass to chattels. The trial court granted Intel's motion for summary judgment and enjoined Hamidi from any further mailings. A divided Court of Appeal affirmed.

After reviewing the decisions analyzing unauthorized electronic contact with computer systems as potential trespasses to chattels, we conclude that under California law the tort does not encompass, and should not be extended to encompass, an electronic communication that neither damages the recipient computer system nor impairs its functioning. Such an electronic communication does not constitute an actionable trespass to personal property, i.e., the computer system, because it does not interfere with the possessor's use or possession of, or any other legally protected interest in, the personal property itself. The consequential economic damage Intel claims to have suffered, i.e., loss of productivity caused by employees reading and reacting to Hamidi's messages and company efforts to block the messages, is not an injury to the company's interest in its computers—

which worked as intended and were unharmed by the communications—any more than the personal distress caused by reading an unpleasant letter would be an injury to the recipient's mailbox, or the loss of privacy caused by an intrusive telephone call would be an injury to the recipient's telephone equipment.

Our conclusion does not rest on any special immunity for communications by electronic mail; we do not hold that messages transmitted through the Internet are exempt from the ordinary rules of tort liability. To the contrary, e-mail, like other forms of communication, may in some circumstances cause legally cognizable injury to the recipient or to third parties and may be actionable under various common-law or statutory theories. Indeed, on facts somewhat similar to those here, a company or its employees might be able to plead causes of action for interference with prospective economic relations, interference with contract or intentional infliction of emotional distress. And, of course, as with any other means of publication, third party subjects of e-mail communications may under appropriate facts make claims for defamation, publication of private facts, or other speech-based torts. Intel's claim fails not because e-mail transmitted through the Internet enjoys unique immunity, but because the trespass to chattels tort—unlike the causes of action just mentioned—may not, in California, be proved without evidence of an injury to the plaintiff's personal property or legal interest therein.

Nor does our holding affect the legal remedies of Internet service providers (ISP's) against senders of unsolicited commercial bulk e-mail (UCE), also known as "spam." A series of federal district court decisions, beginning with *CompuServe, Inc. v. Cyber Promotions, Inc.*, 962 F.Supp. 1015 (S.D.Ohio 1997), has approved the use of trespass to chattels as a theory of spammers' liability to ISP's, based upon evidence that the vast quantities of mail sent by spammers both overburdened the ISP's own computers and made the entire computer system harder to use for recipients, the ISP's customers. In those cases, discussed in greater detail below, the underlying complaint was that the extraordinary *quantity* of UCE impaired the computer system's functioning. In the present case, the claimed injury is located in the disruption or distraction caused to recipients by the *contents* of the e-mail messages, an injury entirely separate from, and not directly affecting, the possession or value of personal property. * * *

The pertinent undisputed facts are as follows.

Hamidi, a former Intel engineer, together with others, formed an organization named Former and Current Employees of Intel (FACE–Intel) to disseminate information and views critical of Intel's employment and personnel policies and practices. FACE–Intel maintained a Web site (which identified Hamidi as Webmaster and as the organization's spokesperson) containing such material. In addition, over a 21–month period Hamidi, on behalf of FACE–Intel, sent six mass e-mails to employee addresses on

Intel's electronic mail system. The messages criticized Intel's employment practices, warned employees of the dangers those practices posed to their careers, suggested employees consider moving to other companies, solicited employees' participation in FACE–Intel, and urged employees to inform themselves further by visiting FACE–Intel's Web site. The messages stated that recipients could, by notifying the sender of their wishes, be removed from FACE–Intel's mailing list; Hamidi did not subsequently send messages to anyone who requested removal.

Each message was sent to thousands of addresses (as many as 35,000 according to FACE–Intel's Web site), though some messages were blocked by Intel before reaching employees. Intel's attempt to block internal transmission of the messages succeeded only in part; Hamidi later admitted he evaded blocking efforts by using different sending computers. When Intel, in March 1998, demanded in writing that Hamidi and FACE–Intel stop sending e-mails to Intel's computer system, Hamidi asserted the organization had a right to communicate with willing Intel employees; he sent a new mass mailing in September 1998.

The summary judgment record contains no evidence Hamidi breached Intel's computer security in order to obtain the recipient addresses for his messages; indeed, internal Intel memoranda show the company's management concluded no security breach had occurred. Hamidi stated he created the recipient address list using an Intel directory on a floppy disk anonymously sent to him. Nor is there any evidence that the receipt or internal distribution of Hamidi's electronic messages damaged Intel's computer system or slowed or impaired its functioning. Intel did present uncontradicted evidence, however, that many employee recipients asked a company official to stop the messages and that staff time was consumed in attempts to block further messages from FACE–Intel. According to the FACE–Intel Web site, moreover, the messages had prompted discussions between "[e]xcited and nervous managers" and the company's human resources department.

Intel sued Hamidi and FACE–Intel, pleading causes of action for trespass to chattels and nuisance, and seeking both actual damages and an injunction against further e-mail messages. Intel later voluntarily dismissed its nuisance claim and waived its demand for damages. The trial court entered default against FACE–Intel upon that organization's failure to answer. The court then granted Intel's motion for summary judgment, permanently enjoining Hamidi, FACE–Intel, and their agents "from sending unsolicited e-mail to addresses on Intel's computer systems." Hamidi appealed; FACE–Intel did not.

The Court of Appeal, with one justice dissenting, affirmed the grant of injunctive relief. * * *

We granted Hamidi's petition for review.

Figure 4–1
Hamidi, left, and a supporter delivering a message to Intel employees on a floppy disk after the Superior Court had enjoined his emails

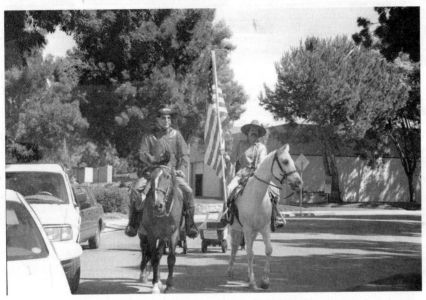

Source: Don Preisler/New York Times.

DISCUSSION

I. Current California Tort Law

Dubbed by Prosser the "little brother of conversion," the tort of trespass to chattels allows recovery for interferences with possession of personal property "not sufficiently important to be classed as conversion, and so to compel the defendant to pay the full value of the thing with which he has interfered." (Prosser & Keeton, Torts § 14, pp. 85–86 (5th ed. 1984).)

Though not amounting to conversion, the defendant's interference must, to be actionable, have caused some injury to the chattel or to the plaintiff's rights in it. Under California law, trespass to chattels "lies where an intentional interference with the possession of personal property *has proximately caused injury*." (Thrifty–Tel, Inc. v. Bezenek 54 Cal.Rptr.2d 468 (Cal. Ct. App. 1996), italics added.) In cases of interference with possession of personal property not amounting to conversion, "the owner has a cause of action for trespass or case, *and may recover only the actual damages suffered by reason of the impairment of the property or the loss of its use.*" (Zaslow v. Kroenert, 176 P.2d 1 (Cal. 1946) (italics added)). In modern American law generally, "[t]respass remains as an occasional remedy for minor interferences, *resulting in some damage,* but not sufficiently serious or sufficiently important to amount to the greater tort" of conversion. (Prosser & Keeton, Torts, supra, § 15, p. 90, italics added.)

The Restatement, too, makes clear that some actual injury must have occurred in order for a trespass to chattels to be actionable. Under section 218 of the Restatement Second of Torts, dispossession alone, without further damages, is actionable (see id., par. (a) & com. d, pp. 420–421), but other forms of interference require some additional harm to the personal property or the possessor's interests in it. (Id., pars. (b)–(d).) "The interest of a possessor of a chattel in its inviolability, unlike the similar interest of a possessor of land, is not given legal protection by an action for nominal damages for harmless intermeddlings with the chattel. In order that an actor who interferes with another's chattel may be liable, his conduct must affect some other and more important interest of the possessor. *Therefore, one who intentionally intermeddles with another's chattel is subject to liability only if his intermeddling is harmful to the possessor's materially valuable interest in the physical condition, quality, or value of the chattel, or if the possessor is deprived of the use of the chattel for a substantial time, or some other legally protected interest of the possessor is affected as stated in Clause (c).* Sufficient legal protection of the possessor's interest in the mere inviolability of his chattel is afforded by his privilege to use reasonable force to protect his possession against even harmless interference." (Id., com. e, pp. 421–422, italics added.) * * *

In this respect, as Prosser explains, modern day trespass to chattels differs both from the original English writ and from the action for trespass to land: "Another departure from the original rule of the old writ of trespass concerns the necessity of some actual damage to the chattel before the action can be maintained. Where the defendant merely interferes without doing any harm—as where, for example, he merely lays hands upon the plaintiff's horse, or sits in his car—there has been a division of opinion among the writers, and a surprising dearth of authority. *By analogy to trespass to land there might be a technical tort in such a case ..... Such scanty authority as there is, however, has considered that the dignitary interest in the inviolability of chattels, unlike that as to land, is not sufficiently important to require any greater defense than the privilege of using reasonable force when necessary to protect them. Accordingly it has been held that nominal damages will not be awarded, and that in the absence of any actual damage the action will not lie.*" (Prosser & Keeton, Torts, supra, § 14, p. 87, italics added, fns. omitted.) * * *

The dispositive issue in this case, therefore, is whether the undisputed facts demonstrate Hamidi's actions caused or threatened to cause damage to Intel's computer system, or injury to its rights in that personal property, such as to entitle Intel to judgment as a matter of law. [T]he undisputed evidence revealed no actual or threatened damage to Intel's computer hardware or software and no interference with its ordinary and intended operation. * * *

Relying on a line of decisions, most from federal district courts, applying the tort of trespass to chattels to various types of unwanted

[handwritten margin note: Elements for 'Trespass to Chattels']

electronic contact between computers, Intel contends that, while its computers were not damaged by receiving Hamidi's messages, its interest in the "physical condition, quality or value" (Rest.2d Torts, § 218, com. e, p. 422) of the computers was harmed. We disagree. The cited line of decisions does not persuade us that the mere sending of electronic communications that assertedly cause injury only because of their contents constitutes an actionable trespass to a computer system through which the messages are transmitted. Rather, the decisions finding electronic contact to be a trespass to computer systems have generally involved some actual or threatened interference with the computers' functioning. * * *

In each of these spamming cases, the plaintiff showed, or was prepared to show, some interference with the efficient functioning of its computer system. In *CompuServe,* the plaintiff ISP's mail equipment monitor stated that mass UCE [unsolicited commercial bulk e-mail] mailings, especially from nonexistent addresses such as those used by the defendant, placed "a tremendous burden" on the ISP's equipment, using "disk space and drain[ing] the processing power," making those resources unavailable to serve subscribers. (CompuServe, supra, 962 F.Supp. at p. 1022.) Similarly, in *Hotmail Corp. v. Van$Money Pie, Inc.,* supra, 1998 WL 388389 at page *7, the court found the evidence supported a finding that the defendant's mailings "fill[ed] up Hotmail's computer storage space and threaten[ed] to damage Hotmail's ability to service its legitimate customers." America Online, Inc. v. IMS, decided on summary judgment, was deemed factually indistinguishable from *CompuServe*; the court observed that in both cases the plaintiffs "alleged that processing the bulk e-mail cost them time and money and burdened their equipment." * * *

Though Hamidi sent thousands of copies of the same message on six occasions over 21 months, that number is minuscule compared to the amounts of mail sent by commercial operations. * * * The functional burden on Intel's computers, or the cost in time to individual recipients, of receiving Hamidi's occasional advocacy messages cannot be compared to the burdens and costs caused ISP's and their customers by the ever-rising deluge of commercial e-mail.

In addition to impairment of system functionality, *CompuServe* and its progeny also refer to the ISP's loss of business reputation and customer goodwill, resulting from the inconvenience and cost that spam causes to its members, as harm to the ISP's legally protected interests in its personal property. Intel argues that its own interest in employee productivity, assertedly disrupted by Hamidi's messages, is a comparable protected interest in its computer system. We disagree. * * *

CompuServe's customers were annoyed because the system was inundated with unsolicited commercial messages, making its use for personal communication more difficult and costly. Their complaint, which allegedly led some to cancel their CompuServe service, was about *the functioning of CompuServe's electronic mail service.* Intel's workers, in contrast, were allegedly distracted from their work not because of the frequency or quantity of Hamidi's messages, but because of assertions and opinions the messages conveyed. Intel's complaint is thus about *the contents of the messages* rather than the functioning of the company's e-mail system. Even accepting *CompuServe*'s economic injury rationale, therefore, Intel's position represents a further extension of the trespass to chattels tort, fictionally recharacterizing the allegedly injurious effect of a communication's *contents* on recipients as an impairment to the device which transmitted the message.

This theory of "impairment by content" (Burk, The Trouble with Trespass, [4 J. Small & Emerging Bus.L. 27, 37 (2000)]) threatens to stretch trespass law to cover injuries far afield from the harms to possession the tort evolved to protect. Intel's theory would expand the tort of trespass to chattels to cover virtually any unconsented-to communication that, solely because of its content, is unwelcome to the recipient or intermediate transmitter. * * * While unwelcome communications, electronic or otherwise, can cause a variety of injuries to economic relations, reputation and emotions, those interests are protected by other branches of tort law; in order to address them, we need not create a fiction of injury to the communication system.

Nor may Intel appropriately assert a *property* interest in its employees' time. "The Restatement test clearly speaks in the first instance to the impairment of the chattel.... But employees are not chattels (at least not in the legal sense of the term)." (Burk, The Trouble with Trespass, supra, 4 J. Small & Emerging Bus.L. at p. 36.) Whatever interest Intel may have in preventing its employees from receiving disruptive communications, it is not an interest in personal property, and trespass to chattels is therefore not an action that will lie to protect it. Nor, finally, can the fact Intel staff spent time attempting to block Hamidi's messages be bootstrapped into an injury to Intel's possessory interest in its computers. To quote * * * from the dissenting opinion in the Court of Appeal: "[I]t is circular to premise the damage element of a tort solely upon the steps taken to prevent the damage. Injury can only be established by the completed tort's consequences, not by the cost of the steps taken to avoid the injury and prevent the tort; otherwise, we can create injury for every supposed tort."

Intel connected its e-mail system to the Internet and permitted its employees to make use of this connection both for business and, to a reasonable extent, for their own purposes. In doing so, the company necessarily contemplated the employees' receipt of unsolicited as well as solicited communications from other companies and individuals. That some communications would, because of their contents, be unwelcome to Intel management was virtually inevitable. Hamidi did nothing but use the e-mail system for its intended purpose—to communicate with employees. The system worked as designed, delivering the messages without any physical or functional harm or disruption. These occasional transmissions cannot reasonably be viewed as impairing the quality or value of Intel's computer system. We conclude, therefore, that Intel has not presented undisputed facts demonstrating an injury to its personal property, or to its legal interest in that property, that support, under California tort law, an action for trespass to chattels.

II.   Proposed Extension of California Tort Law

We next consider whether California common law should be *extended* to cover, as a trespass to chattels, an otherwise harmless electronic communication whose contents are objectionable. * * *

Writing on behalf of several industry groups appearing as amici curiae, Professor Richard A. Epstein of the University of Chicago urges us to excuse the required showing of injury to personal property in cases of unauthorized electronic contact between computers, "extending the rules of trespass to real property to all interactive Web sites and servers." The court is thus urged to recognize, for owners of a particular species of personal property, computer servers, the same interest in inviolability as is generally accorded a possessor of land. In effect, Professor Epstein suggests that a company's server should be its castle, upon which any unauthorized intrusion, however harmless, is a trespass.

Epstein's argument derives, in part, from the familiar metaphor of the Internet as a physical space, reflected in much of the language that has been used to describe it: "cyberspace," "the information superhighway," e-mail "addresses," and the like. Of course, the Internet is also frequently called simply the "Net," a term, Hamidi points out, "evoking a fisherman's chattel." A major component of the Internet is the World Wide "Web," a descriptive term suggesting neither personal nor real property, and "cyberspace" itself has come to be known by the oxymoronic phrase "virtual reality," which would suggest that any real property "located" in "cyberspace" must be "virtually real" property. Metaphor is a two-edged sword.

Indeed, the metaphorical application of real property rules would not, by itself, transform a physically harmless electronic intrusion on a computer server into a trespass. That is because, under California law, intangible intrusions on land, including electromagnetic transmissions, are not actionable as trespasses (though they may be as nuisances) unless they cause physical damage to the real property. (San Diego Gas & Electric Co. v. Superior Court, 920 P.2d 669 (Cal. 1996).) Since Intel does not claim Hamidi's electronically transmitted messages physically damaged its servers, it could not prove a trespass to land even were we to treat the computers as a type of real property. Some further extension of the conceit would be required, under which the electronic signals Hamidi sent would be recast as tangible intruders, perhaps as tiny messengers rushing through the "hallways" of Intel's computers and bursting out of employees' computers to read them Hamidi's missives. But such fictions promise more confusion than clarity in the law.

The plain fact is that computers, even those making up the Internet, are—like such older communications equipment as telephones and fax machines—personal property, not realty. Professor Epstein observes that "[a]lthough servers may be moved in real space, they cannot be moved in cyberspace," because an Internet server must, to be useful, be accessible at a known address. But the same is true of the telephone: to be useful for incoming communication, the telephone must remain constantly linked to the same number (or, when the number is changed, the system must include some forwarding or notification capability, a qualification that also applies to computer addresses). Does this suggest that an unwelcome message delivered through a telephone or fax machine should be viewed as a trespass to a type of real property? We think not: As already discussed, the contents of a telephone communication may cause a variety of injuries and may be the basis for a variety of tort actions (e.g., defamation, intentional infliction of emotional distress, invasion of privacy), but the injuries are not to an interest in property, much less real property, and the appropriate tort is not trespass.

More substantively, Professor Epstein argues that a rule of computer server inviolability will, through the formation or extension of a market in computer-to-computer access, create "the right social result." In most circumstances, he predicts, companies with computers on the Internet will continue to authorize transmission of information through e-mail, Web site searching, and page linking because they benefit by that open access. When a Web site owner does deny access to a particular sending, searching, or linking computer, a system of "simple one-on-one negotiations" will arise to provide the necessary individual licenses.

Other scholars are less optimistic about such a complete propertization of the Internet. Professor Mark Lemley of the University of California, Berkeley, writing on behalf of an amici curiae group of professors of intellectual property and computer law, observes that under a property rule of server inviolability, "each of the hundreds of millions of [Internet] users must get permission in advance from anyone with whom they want to communicate and anyone who owns a server through which their message may travel." The consequence for e-mail could be a substantial reduction in the freedom of electronic communication, as the owner of each computer through which an electronic message passes could impose its own limitations on message content or source. As Professor Dan Hunter of the University of Pennsylvania asks rhetorically: "Does this mean that one must read the 'Terms of Acceptable Email Usage' of every email system that one emails in the course of an ordinary day? If the University of Pennsylvania had a policy that sending a joke by email would be an unauthorized use of their system, then under the logic of [the lower court decision in this case], you commit 'trespass' if you emailed me a ... cartoon." (Hunter, Cyberspace as Place, and the Tragedy of the Digital Anticommons 91 Cal. L. Rev. 439, 508–509 (2003).)

Web site linking, Professor Lemley further observes, "would exist at the sufferance of the linked-to party, because a Web user who followed a 'disapproved' link would be trespassing on the plaintiff's server, just as sending an e-mail is trespass under the [lower] court's theory." Another writer warns that "[c]yber-trespass theory will curtail the free flow of price and product information on the Internet by allowing website owners to tightly control who and what may enter and make use of the information housed on its Internet site." (Chang, Bidding on Trespass: *eBay, Inc. v. Bidder's Edge, Inc.* and the Abuse of Trespass Theory in Cyberspace Law, 29 AIPLA Q.J. 445, 459 (2001).) A leading scholar of Internet law and policy, Professor Lawrence Lessig of Stanford University, has criticized Professor Epstein's theory of the computer server as quasi-real property, previously put forward in the *eBay* case, on the ground that it ignores the costs to society in the loss of network benefits: "eBay benefits greatly from a network that is open and where access is free. It is this general feature of the Net that makes the Net so valuable to users and a source of great innovation. And to the extent that individual sites begin to impose their own rules of exclusion, the value of the network as a network declines. If machines must negotiate before entering any individual site, then the costs of using the network climb." (Lessig, The Future of Ideas: The Fate of the Commons in a Connected World (2001) p. 171; see also Hunter, Cyberspace as Place, and the Tragedy of the Digital Anticommons, supra, 91 Cal. L.Rev. at p. 512 ["If we continue to mark out anticommons claims in cyberspace, not only will we preclude better, more innovative uses of cyberspace resources, but we will lose sight of what might be possible"].)

We discuss this debate among the amici curiae and academic writers only to note its existence and contours, not to attempt its resolution. Creating an absolute property right to exclude undesired communications from one's e-mail and Web servers might help force spammers to internalize the costs they impose on ISP's and their customers. But such a property rule might also create substantial new costs, to e-mail and e-commerce users and to society generally, in lost ease and openness of communication and in lost network benefits. In light of the unresolved controversy, we would be acting rashly to adopt a rule treating computer servers as real property for purposes of trespass law.

The Legislature has already adopted detailed regulations governing UCE. (Bus. & Prof.Code, §§ 17538.4, 17538.45). It may see fit in the future also to regulate noncommercial e-mail, such as that sent by Hamidi, or other kinds of unwanted contact between computers on the Internet, such as that alleged in *eBay, supra,* 100 F.Supp.2d 1058. But we are not persuaded that these perceived problems call at present for judicial creation of a rigid property rule of computer server inviolability. * * *

Because we conclude no trespass to chattels was shown on the summary judgment record, making the injunction improper on common law grounds, we need not address at length the dissenters' constitutional arguments. A few clarifications are nonetheless in order. * * *

[T]he nonexistence of a "constitutional right to trespass" (dis. opn. of Mosk, J., *post)* [does not] make an injunction in this case per se valid. Unlike, for example, the trespasser-to-land defendant in *Church of Christ in Hollywood v. Superior Court,* 121 Cal.Rptr.2d 810 (Cal. Ct. App. 2002), Hamidi himself had no tangible presence on Intel property, instead speaking from his own home through his computer. He no more invaded Intel's property than does a protester holding a sign or shouting through a bullhorn outside corporate headquarters, posting a letter through the mail, or telephoning to complain of a corporate practice. (See *Madsen v. Women's Health Center*, 512 U.S. 753, 765 (1994) [injunctions restraining such speakers must "burden no more speech than necessary to serve a significant government interest"].)[8] * * *

The judgment of the Court of Appeal is reversed.

■ Concurring Opinion by Kennard, J. [omitted].

■ Dissenting Opinion of Brown, J. * * * Intel has invested millions of dollars to develop and maintain a computer system. It did this not to act as a public forum but to enhance the productivity of its employees. Kourosh Kenneth Hamidi sent as many as 200,000 e-mail messages to Intel employees. The time required to review and delete Hamidi's messages diverted employees from productive tasks and undermined the utility of the computer system. "There may ... be situations in which the value to the owner of a particular type of chattel may be impaired by dealing with it in a manner that does not affect its physical condition." (Rest.2d Torts, § 218, com. h, p. 422.) This is such a case.

Dissent's Issue [

The majority repeatedly asserts that Intel objected to the hundreds of thousands of messages solely due to their content, and proposes that Intel seek relief by pleading content-based speech torts. This proposal misses the point that Intel's objection is directed not toward Hamidi's message but his use of Intel's property to display his message. Intel has not sought to prevent Hamidi from expressing his ideas on his Web site, through private mail (paper or electronic) to employees' homes, or through any other means like picketing or billboards. But as counsel for Intel explained during oral argument, the company objects to Hamidi's using Intel's property to advance his message.

Of course, Intel deserves an injunction even if its objections are based entirely on the e-mail's content. Intel is entitled, for example, to allow employees use of the Internet to check stock market tables or weather forecasts without incurring any concomitant obligation to allow access to pornographic Web sites. (Loving v. Boren 956 F.Supp. 953, 955 (W.D.Okla. 1997).) A private property owner may choose to exclude unwanted mail for any reason, including its content. (Rowan v. U.S. Post Office Dept. 397 U.S. 728, 738 (1970).) * * *

Regardless of whether property is real or personal, it is beyond dispute that an individual has the right to have his personal property free from interference. There is some division among authorities regarding the available remedy, particularly whether a harmless trespass supports a claim for nominal damages. The North Carolina Court of Appeal has found there is

---

8. Justice Brown would distinguish *Madsen v. Women's Health Center*, supra, on the ground that the operators of the health center in that case would not have been entitled to "drive[ ] [the protesters] from the public streets," whereas Intel was entitled to block Hamidi's messages as best it could. (Dis. opn. of Brown, J., post.) But the health center operators *were* entitled to block protesters' messages—as best they could—by closing windows and pulling blinds. That a property owner may take physical measures to prevent the transmission of others' speech into or across the property does not imply that a court order enjoining the speech is not subject to constitutional limitations.

no damage requirement for a trespass to chattel. (See Hawkins v. Hawkins, 400 S.E.2d 472, 475 (N.C. 1991).) * * * Several authorities consider a harmless trespass to goods actionable per se only if it is intentional. (Winfield & Jolowicz on Torts, Trespass to Goods 403 (10th ed. 1975); Clerk & Lindsell on Torts ¶ 13–159, p. 703 (17th ed. 1995).) The Restatement Second of Torts, section 218, which is less inclined to favor liability, likewise forbids unauthorized use and recognizes the inviolability of personal property. * * * "The interest of a possessor of a chattel in its inviolability, unlike the similar interest of a possessor of land, is not given legal protection *by an action for nominal damages* for harmless intermeddlings with the chattel. . . . Sufficient legal protection of the possessor's interest in the mere *inviolability of his chattel* is afforded by his *privilege to use reasonable force* to protect his possession against *even harmless interference.*" (Rest.2d Torts, § 218, com. e, pp. 421–422, italics added.) Accordingly, the protection of land and chattels may differ on the question of nominal damages unrelated to actual injury. The authorities agree, however, that (1) the chattel is inviolable, (2) the trespassee need not tolerate even harmless interference, and (3) the possessor may use reasonable force to prevent it. Both California law and the Restatement authorize reasonable force regardless of whether the property in question is real or personal. (Civ.Code, § 51; Rest.2d Torts, § 77.) * * *

From the modest distinction holding that only victims of a trespass to land may profit in the form of damages exceeding actual harm, defendant offers the position that only trespasses to land may be *prevented.* The law is to the contrary; numerous cases have authorized injunctive relief to safeguard the inviolability of personal property. * * *

Notwithstanding the general rule that injunctive relief requires a showing of irreparable injury (5 Witkin, Cal. Procedure Pleading, § 782, p. 239 (4th ed. 1997)), Witkin also observes there are exceptions to this rule where injunctive relief is appropriate; these include repetitive trespasses. * * *

In 1996, the Appellate Division of the New York Supreme Court considered the claim of plaintiff Tillman, who sought to enjoin the unwanted delivery of a newspaper onto his property. (Tillman v. Distribution Systems of America Inc., 224 A.D.2d 79, 648 N.Y.S.2d 630 (1996).) He offered no specific critique of the newspaper's content, observing only " '[t]here is no reason that we have to clean up [defendant's] mess.' " (Id. at p. 632.) * * * [T]he court rejected the defendants' argument "that there is nothing a homeowner can do to stop the dumping on his or her property of pamphlets or newspapers, no matter how offensive they might be," and instead upheld Tillman's right to prevent the mail's delivery, regardless of whether his objection was due to the quantity (volume) or quality (content) of the messages. (Tillman, at p. 636.) In authorizing injunctive relief, the *Tillman* court found no need to quantify the actual damage created by the delivery; it merely noted that the homeowner should not be forced either "to allow such unwanted newspapers to accumulate, or to expend the time and energy necessary to gather and to dispose of them." (Ibid.) Subsequent courts have extended this policy to the delivery of e-mail as well. * * *

Hamidi concedes Intel's legal entitlement to block the unwanted messages. The problem is that although Intel has resorted to the cyberspace version of reasonable force, it has so far been unsuccessful in determining how to resist the unwanted use of its system. Thus, while Intel has the legal right to exclude Hamidi from its system, it does not have the physical ability. It *may* forbid Hamidi's use, but it *can* not prevent it.

To the majority, Hamidi's ability to outwit Intel's cyber defenses justifies denial of Intel's claim to exclusive use of its property. Under this reasoning, it is not right but might that determines the extent of a party's possessory interest. Although the world often works this way, the legal system should not. * * *

Those who have contempt for grubby commerce and reverence for the rarified heights of intellectual discourse may applaud today's decision, but even the flow of ideas will be curtailed if the right to exclude is denied. As the Napster controversy revealed, creative individuals will be less inclined to develop intellectual property if they cannot limit the terms of its transmission. Similarly, if online newspapers cannot charge for access, they will be unable to pay the journalists and editorialists who generate ideas for public consumption. * * *

The principles of both personal liberty and social utility should counsel us to usher the common law of property into the digital age.

■ Dissenting Opinion by MOSK, J.[††] * * * The majority fail to distinguish open communication in the public "commons" of the Internet from unauthorized intermeddling on a private, proprietary intranet. Hamidi is not communicating in the equivalent of a town square or of an unsolicited "junk" mailing through the United States Postal Service. His action, in crossing from the public Internet into a private intranet, is more like intruding into a private office mailroom, commandeering the mail cart, and dropping off unwanted broadsides on 30,000 desks. Because Intel's security measures have been circumvented by Hamidi, the majority leave Intel, which has exercised all reasonable self-help efforts, with no recourse unless he causes a malfunction or systems "crash." Hamidi's repeated intrusions did more than merely "prompt[ ] discussions between '[e]xcited and nervous managers' and the company's human resource department" (maj. opn., ante); they also constituted a misappropriation of Intel's private computer system contrary to its intended use and against Intel's wishes.

The law of trespass to chattels has not universally been limited to physical damage. I believe it is entirely consistent to apply that legal theory to these circumstances—that is, when a proprietary computer system is being used contrary to its owner's purposes and expressed desires, and self-help has been ineffective. Intel correctly expects protection from an intrud-

---

[††] Associate Justice, Court of Appeal, Second Appellate District, Division Five, assigned by the Chief Justice pursuant to article VI, section 6 of the California Constitution.

er who misuses its proprietary system, its nonpublic directories, and its supposedly controlled connection to the Internet to achieve his bulk mailing objectives—incidentally, without even having to pay postage. * * *

Here, Hamidi's deliberate and continued intermeddling, and threatened intermeddling, with Intel's proprietary computer system for his own purposes that were hostile to Intel, certainly impaired the quality and value of the system as an internal business device for Intel and forced Intel to incur costs to try to maintain the security and integrity of its server— efforts that proved ineffective. These included costs incurred to mitigate injuries that had already occurred. It is not a matter of "bootstrapp[ing]" (maj. opn., ante) to consider those costs a damage to Intel. Indeed, part of the value of the proprietary computer system is the ability to exclude intermeddlers from entering it for significant uses that are disruptive to its owner's business operations. * * *

The fact that, like most large businesses, Intel's intranet includes external e-mail access for essential business purposes does not logically mean, as the majority suggest, that Intel has forfeited the right to determine who has access to its system. Its intranet is not the equivalent of a common carrier or public communications licensee that would be subject to requirements to provide service and access. Just as Intel can, and does, regulate the use of its computer system by its employees, it should be entitled to control its use by outsiders and to seek injunctive relief when self-help fails. * * *

As the Court of Appeal observed, connecting one's driveway to the general system of roads does not invite demonstrators to use the property as a public forum. Not mindful of this precept, the majority blur the distinction between public and private computer networks in the interest of "ease and openness of communication." (Maj. opn., ante) By upholding Intel's right to exercise self-help to restrict Hamidi's bulk e-mails, they concede that he did not have a right to send them through Intel's proprietary system. Yet they conclude that injunctive relief is unavailable to Intel because it connected its e-mail system to the Internet and thus, "necessarily contemplated" unsolicited communications to its employees. (Maj. opn., ante.) Their exposition promotes unpredictability in a manner that could be as harmful to open communication as it is to property rights. It permits Intel to block Hamidi's e-mails entirely, but offers no recourse if he succeeds in breaking through its security barriers, unless he physically or functionally degrades the system.

By making more concrete damages a requirement for a remedy, the majority has rendered speech interests dependent on the impact of the e-mails. The sender will never know when or if the mass e-mails sent by him (and perhaps others) will use up too much space or cause a crash in the recipient system, so as to fulfill the majority's requirement of damages. Thus, the sender is exposed to the risk of liability because of the possibility of damages. If, as the majority suggest, such a risk will deter "ease and openness of communication" (maj. opn., ante), the majority's formulation does not eliminate such deterrence. Under the majority's position, the lost freedom of communication still exists. In addition, a business could never reliably invest in a private network that can only be kept private by constant vigilance and inventiveness, or by simply shutting off the Internet, thus limiting rather than expanding the flow of information. Moreover, Intel would have less incentive to allow employees reasonable use of its equipment to send and receive personal e-mails if such allowance is justification for preventing restrictions on unwanted intrusions into its computer system. I believe the best approach is to clearly delineate private from public networks and identify as a trespass to chattels the kind of intermeddling involved here. * * *

NOTES AND QUESTIONS

1.   Recall that in *Jacque v. Steenberg Homes*, the Wisconsin Supreme Court upheld a $100,000 punitive damages award to a couple for a trespass to land that did no injury to the land or any other tangible interest of the owners. Yet according to the majority in *Hamidi*, there is no legal remedy other than self-help for an intentional trespass to personal property that does no physical injury to the property. This means, for example, that if someone repeatedly sits in your car without your permission, and does no damage to it, you have no civil remedy, either for an injunction or damages. Does this strike you as sound? What is the justification for requiring actual injury to establish trespass to chattels but not requiring this to show trespass to land? You may want to reconsider the issue after considering the next set of materials, on self-help.

2.   The majority and dissenting opinions disagree as to whether Intel Corporation has shown that it suffered actual injury because of the unwanted mass emails from Hamidi. Does the majority's conclusion of no injury rest on a presumption that injury based on the content of a communication cannot count as injury, at least for trespass purposes? Do the dissents' contrary conclusions rest on a presumption that injury is always present when a proprietor must take measures to exclude an intruder? Which presumption is more appropriate?

3.   Given that Hamidi's invasion of Intel's intranet took the form of electrons, why was trespass to chattels the correct cause of action? If real property were the interest at stake, wouldn't an invasion by electrons be governed by nuisance rather than trespass? (See Chapters I and IX.) Why is there no analogue to nuisance among the actions that protect personal property? Should there be? Should nuisance law be extended to cover intangible invasions into "virtual" space, such as an intranet? See Adam Mossoff, Spam—Oy, What a Nuisance!, 19 Berkeley Tech. L.J. 625 (2004).

4.   The most far-reaching issue discussed in *Hamidi* reverts to the question raised at the end of Chapter III: whether "cyberspace" should be subject to parcelization, with individually-developed segments like intranets and web-sites protected by property-like exclusion rights, or whether it should be regarded as an open-access resource, like navigable waterways and public highways. The debate between the expert witnesses summarized

by the majority in Part II of its opinion, "Proposed Extension of California Tort Law," poses the question in terms of transaction costs. Richard Epstein, of the University of Chicago Law School, argues that parcelization would produce efficient outcomes, because owners of intranets would grant blanket consent to "visitations" by outsiders, and would single out for exclusion only those that are unwanted. Mark Lemley, then of Berkeley's Boalt Hall Law School (and now at Stanford), and Larry Lessig, of Stanford Law School, argue that parcelization would require some kind of individually negotiated license between the proprietor of the intranet and each outside "visitor," and that these negotiations would unduly burden the flow of information and possibly create a cyber-anticommons. (On the anticommons, see Chapter II.)

5. More disgruntled employees: In *School of Visual Arts v. Kuprewicz*, 771 N.Y.S.2d 804 (N.Y. Sup. 2003), the defendant, a former employee at the School of Visual Arts, posted false job advertisements on Craigslist.com for the job held by SVA's Director of Human Resources, and registered her email address on several pornographic websites, causing her to receive "large volumes" of both applications for her job and pornographic emails. On a motion to dismiss, the court found that the many-headed complaint only stated a cause of action in trespass to chattels. Asserting its agreement with *Hamidi*, the court declared that its decision to sustain the complaint was based on the allegations of physical detriment to the computer system from the volume of mail, not on the intrusive and unwanted character of the emails. What if the case had involved a smaller volume of emails (or a less vulnerable computer) than was alleged, but the emails were just as disturbing? What if, further, the plaintiff had told the defendant to stop, but the plaintiff refused? Should it matter if self-help had been tried and failed, as in *Hamidi*? See, e.g., Patricia L. Bellia, Defending Cyberproperty, 79 N.Y.U. L. Rev. 2164 (2004); Symposium, Property Rights on the Frontier: The Economics and Self–Help and Self–Defense in Cyberspace, 1 J.L. Econ. & Pol'y 1 (2005).

6. Like many other issues we canvass in this book, the debate between the majority and the dissents is at least in part a debate about the choice of the appropriate institution to resolve an issue. The majority believes that trespass to chattels should be defined narrowly in the context of cyber-invasions, leaving more aggressive regulation up to the legislature. The dissents argue that the courts should step in and provide a remedy based on analogical extension of the common law, leaving it to the legislature to make revisions if necessary. Which approach do you think generally better for adjusting the law to inevitable technological and social changes?

3. SELF-HELP

To what extent is an owner or possessor permitted to use self-help in vindicating her interest in property? To some degree, self-help has always been and continues to be permitted. A person in possession of property can generally use reasonable force "to prevent or terminate an unlawful entry or other trespass upon land or a trespass against or the unlawful carrying away of tangible, movable property." Model Penal Code § 3.06(1)(a). The Model Penal Code takes the position that in the case of burglary, reasonable force does not mean deadly force, unless there is a danger to persons. Id. § 3.06 (3)(d). But many jurisdictions disagree, and permit the use of deadly force to avert burglary, whether or not there is proof of a specific threat to persons. See N.Y. Penal Law § 35.20(3). In any event, prosecutions of persons who shoot home invaders are rare.

More controversial is the use of self-help to recover property once possession has been lost. As the following cases suggest, the current state of the law diverges between real and personal property.

Berg v. Wiley

Supreme Court of Minnesota, 1978.
264 N.W.2d 145.

■ ROGOSHESKE, JUSTICE. Defendant landlord, Wiley Enterprises, Inc., and defendant Rodney A. Wiley (hereafter collectively referred to as Wiley) appeal from a judgment upon a jury verdict awarding plaintiff tenant, A Family Affair Restaurant, Inc., damages for wrongful eviction from its leased premises. The issues for review are whether the evidence was sufficient to support the jury's finding that the tenant did not abandon or surrender the premises and whether the trial court erred in finding Wiley's reentry forcible and wrongful as a matter of law. We hold that the jury's verdict is supported by sufficient evidence and that the trial court's determination of unlawful entry was correct as a matter of law, and affirm the judgment.

On November 11, 1970, Wiley, as lessor and tenant's predecessor in interest as lessee, executed a written lease agreement letting land and a building in Osseo, Minnesota, for use as a restaurant. The lease provided a 5-year term beginning December 1, 1970, and specified that the tenant agreed to bear all costs of repairs and remodeling, to "make no changes in the building structure" without prior written authorization from Wiley, and to "operate the restaurant in a lawful and prudent manner." Wiley also reserved the right "at (his) option (to) retake possession" of the premises "(s)hould the Lessee fail to meet the conditions of this Lease."[1] In early 1971, plaintiff Kathleen Berg took assignment of the lease from the prior lessee, and on May 1, 1971, she opened "A Family Affair Restaurant"

---

1. The provisions of the lease pertinent to this case provide:

Item #5 The Lessee will make no changes to the building structure without first receiving written authorization from the Lessor. The Lessor will promptly reply in writing to each request and will cooperate with the Lessee on any reasonable request.

Item #6 The Lessee agrees to operate the restaurant in a lawful and prudent manner during the lease period.

Item #7 Should the Lessee fail to meet the conditions of this Lease the Lessor may at their option retake possession of said premises. In any such event such act will not relieve Lessee from liability for payment [of] the rental herein provided or from the conditions or obligations of this lease.

on the premises. In January 1973, Berg incorporated the restaurant and assigned her interest in the lease to "A Family Affair Restaurant, Inc." As sole shareholder of the corporation, she alone continued to act for the tenant.

The present dispute has arisen out of Wiley's objection to Berg's continued remodeling of the restaurant without procuring written permission and her consequent operation of the restaurant in a state of disrepair with alleged health code violations. Strained relations between the parties came to a head in June and July 1973. In a letter dated June 29, 1973, Wiley's attorney charged Berg with having breached lease items 5 and 6 by making changes in the building structure without written authorization and by operating an unclean kitchen in violation of health regulations. The letter demanded that a list of eight remodeling items be completed within 2 weeks from the date of the letter, by Friday, July 13, 1973, or Wiley would retake possession of the premises under lease item 7. Also, a June 13 inspection of the restaurant by the Minnesota Department of Health had produced an order that certain listed changes be completed within specified time limits in order to comply with the health code. The major items on the inspector's list, similar to those listed by Wiley's attorney, were to be completed by July 15, 1973.

During the 2–week deadline set by both Wiley and the health department, Berg continued to operate the restaurant without closing to complete the required items of remodeling. The evidence is in dispute as to whether she intended to permanently close the restaurant and vacate the premises at the end of the 2 weeks or simply close for about 1 month in order to remodel to comply with the health code. At the close of business on Friday, July 13, 1973, the last day of the 2–week period, Berg dismissed her employees, closed the restaurant, and placed a sign in the window saying "Closed for Remodeling." Earlier that day, Berg testified, Wiley came to the premises in her absence and attempted to change the locks. When she returned and asserted her right to continue in possession, he complied with her request to leave the locks unchanged. Berg also testified that at about 9:30 p. m. that evening, while she and four of her friends were in the restaurant, she observed Wiley hanging from the awning peering into the window. Shortly thereafter, she heard Wiley pounding on the back door demanding admittance. Berg called the county sheriff to come and preserve order. Wiley testified that he observed Berg and a group of her friends in the restaurant removing paneling from a wall. Allegedly fearing destruction of his property, Wiley called the city police, who, with the sheriff, mediated an agreement between the parties to preserve the status quo until each could consult with legal counsel on Monday, July 16, 1973.

Wiley testified that his then attorney advised him to take possession of the premises and lock the tenant out. Accompanied by a police officer and a locksmith, Wiley entered the premises in Berg's absence and without her knowledge on Monday, July 16, 1973, and changed the locks. Later in the day, Berg found herself locked out. The lease term was not due to expire until December 1, 1975. The premises were re-let to another tenant on or

about August 1, 1973. Berg brought this damage action against Wiley and three other named defendants, including the new tenant, on July 27, 1973.[2]
* * *

The jury * * * awarded Berg $31,000 for lost profits and $3,540 for loss of chattels resulting from the wrongful lockout. The jury also specifically found that Berg neither abandoned nor surrendered the premises.
* * *

The first issue before us concerns the sufficiency of evidence to support the jury's finding that Berg had not abandoned or surrendered the leasehold before being locked out by Wiley. Viewing the evidence to support the jury's special verdict in the light most favorable to Berg, as we must, we hold it amply supports the jury's finding of no abandonment or surrender of the premises. While the evidence bearing upon Berg's intent was strongly contradictory, the jury could reasonably have concluded, based on Berg's testimony and supporting circumstantial evidence, that she intended to retain possession, closing temporarily to remodel. Thus, the lockout cannot be excused on ground that Berg abandoned or surrendered the leasehold.

The second and more difficult issue is whether Wiley's self-help repossession of the premises by locking out Berg was correctly held wrongful as a matter of law.

Minnesota has historically followed the common-law rule that a landlord may rightfully use self-help to retake leased premises from a tenant in possession without incurring liability for wrongful eviction provided two conditions are met: (1) The landlord is legally entitled to possession, such as where a tenant holds over after the lease term or where a tenant breaches a lease containing a reentry clause; and (2) the landlord's means of reentry are peaceable. Mercil v. Broulette, 69 N.W. 218 (Minn. 1896). Under the common-law rule, a tenant who is evicted by his landlord may recover damages for wrongful eviction where the landlord either had no right to possession or where the means used to remove the tenant were forcible, or both. See, e.g., Poppen v. Wadleigh, 51 N.W.2d 75 (Minn. 1952); Sweeney v. Meyers, 270 N.W. 906 (Minn. 1937); Lobdell v. Keene, 88 N.W. 426 (Minn. 1901). See, also, Minn.St. 566.01 (statutory cause of action where entry is not "allowed by law" or, if allowed, is not made "in a peaceable manner").

Wiley contends that Berg had breached the provisions of the lease, thereby entitling Wiley, under the terms of the lease, to retake possession, and that his repossession by changing the locks in Berg's absence was

---

2. Proceedings in this damage action were suspended for the duration of a separate unlawful detainer action in which Berg sought to recover possession of the premises under Minn.St. c. 566. In that action, this court reversed a judgment awarding possession of the premises to Berg, holding that an unlawful detainer action under Minn.St. c. 566 was not available to a tenant against his landlord. Berg v. Wiley, 226 N.W.2d 904 (1975). An amended complaint in this damage action was served on May 6, 1974. A second amended complaint was served on December 12, 1975, and proceedings were resumed.

accomplished in a peaceful manner. * * * Whether Berg had in fact breached the lease and whether Wiley was hence entitled to possession was not judicially determined. That issue became irrelevant upon the trial court's finding that Wiley's reentry was forcible as a matter of law because even if Berg had breached the lease, this could not excuse Wiley's non-peaceable reentry. The finding that Wiley's reentry was forcible as a matter of law provided a sufficient ground for damages, and the issue of breach was not submitted to the jury. * * *

It has long been the policy of our law to discourage landlords from taking the law into their own hands, and our decisions and statutory law have looked with disfavor upon any use of self-help to dispossess a tenant in circumstances which are likely to result in breaches of the peace. We gave early recognition to this policy in *Lobdell v. Keene*, 88 N.W. 426, 430 (Minn. 1901), where we said:

> The object and purpose of the legislature in the enactment of the forcible entry and unlawful detainer statute was to prevent those claiming a right of entry or possession of lands from redressing their own wrongs by entering into possession in a violent and forcible manner. All such acts tend to a breach of the peace, and encourage high-handed oppression. The law does not permit the owner of land, be his title ever so good, to be the judge of his own rights with respect to a possession adversely held, but puts him to his remedy under the statutes.

To facilitate a resort to judicial process, the legislature has provided a summary procedure in Minn.St. 566.02 to 566.17 whereby a landlord may recover possession of leased premises upon proper notice and showing in court in as little as 3 to 10 days. As we recognized in *Mutual Trust Life Ins. Co. v. Berg*, 246 N.W. 9, 10 (Minn. 1932), "(t)he forcible entry and unlawful detainer statutes were intended to prevent parties from taking the law into their own hands when going into possession of lands and tenements * * *." To further discourage self-help, our legislature has provided treble damages for forcible evictions, §§ 557.08 and 557.09, and has provided additional criminal penalties for intentional and unlawful exclusion of a tenant. § 504.25. In *Sweeney v. Meyers*, supra, we allowed a business tenant not only damages for lost profits but also punitive damages against a landlord who, like Wiley, entered in the tenant's absence and locked the tenant out.

In the present case, as in *Sweeney*, the tenant was in possession, claiming a right to continue in possession adverse to the landlord's claim of breach of the lease, and had neither abandoned nor surrendered the premises. Wiley, well aware that Berg was asserting her right to possession, retook possession in her absence by picking the locks and locking her out. The record shows a history of vigorous dispute and keen animosity between the parties. Upon this record, we can only conclude that the singular reason why actual violence did not erupt at the moment of Wiley's changing of the locks was Berg's absence and her subsequent self-restraint and resort to judicial process. Upon these facts, we cannot find Wiley's means of reentry peaceable under the common-law rule. Our long-standing

Main Point—
not The result
That determines
"peaceable" or
"forcible", but
The means

policy to discourage self-help which tends to cause a breach of the peace compels us to disapprove the means used to dispossess Berg. To approve this lockout, as urged by Wiley, merely because in Berg's absence no actual violence erupted while the locks were being changed, would be to encourage all future tenants, in order to protect their possession, to be vigilant and thereby set the stage for the very kind of public disturbance which it must be our policy to discourage. * * *

We recognize that the growing modern trend departs completely from the common-law rule to hold that self-help is never available to dispossess a tenant who is in possession and has not abandoned or voluntarily surrendered the premises. Annotation, 6 A.L.R.3d 177, 186; 76 Dickinson L.Rev. 215, 227. This growing rule is founded on the recognition that the potential for violent breach of peace inheres in any situation where a landlord attempts by his own means to remove a tenant who is claiming possession adversely to the landlord. Courts adopting the rule reason that there is no cause to sanction such potentially disruptive self-help where adequate and speedy means are provided for removing a tenant peacefully through judicial process. At least 16 states[6] have adopted this modern rule, holding that judicial proceedings, including the summary procedures provided in those states' unlawful detainer statutes, are the exclusive remedy by which a landlord may remove a tenant claiming possession.

While we would be compelled to disapprove the lockout of Berg in her absence under the common-law rule as stated, we approve the trial court's reasoning and adopt as preferable the modern view represented by the cited cases. To make clear our departure from the common-law rule for the benefit of future landlords and tenants, we hold that, subsequent to our decision in this case, the only lawful means to dispossess a tenant who has not abandoned nor voluntarily surrendered but who claims possession adversely to a landlord's claim of breach of a written lease is by resort to judicial process. We find that Minn.St. 566.02 to 566.17 provide the landlord with an adequate remedy for regaining possession in every such case.[8] Where speedier action than provided in §§ 566.02 to 566.17 seems necessary because of threatened destruction of the property or other exigent circumstances, a temporary restraining order under Rule 65, Rules of Civil Procedure, and law enforcement protection are available to the landlord. Considered together, these statutory and judicial remedies provide a complete answer to the landlord. In our modern society, with the availability of prompt and sufficient legal remedies as described, there is no

---

6. Annotation, 6 A.L.R.3d 177, 186, Supp. 13, shows this modern rule to have been adopted in California, Connecticut, Delaware, Florida, Georgia, Illinois, Indiana, Louisiana, Nebraska, North Carolina, Ohio, Tennessee, Texas, Utah, Vermont, and Washington.

8. Under §§ 566.05 and 566.06, a landlord may regain possession in default proceedings against a tenant personally served with process in as little as 3 to 10 days.

Default judgment against a tenant not present and served by posting may be procured in a week to 10 days. §§ 566.05 and 566.06. Trial is by the court unless either party demands a jury trial. § 566.07. Proceedings are stayed on appeal except as against a holdover tenant. § 566.12. Upon execution of a writ of restitution, the tenant is allowed 24 hours to vacate the property.

place and no need for self-help against a tenant in claimed lawful possession of leased premises.

Applying our holding to the facts of this case, we conclude, as did the trial court, that because Wiley failed to resort to judicial remedies against Berg's holding possession adversely to Wiley's claim of breach of the lease, his lockout of Berg was wrongful as a matter of law. The rule we adopt in this decision is fairly applied against Wiley, for it is clear that, applying the older common-law rule to the facts and circumstances peculiar to this case, we would be compelled to find the lockout nonpeaceable for the reasons previously stated. The jury found that the lockout caused Berg damage and, as between Berg and Wiley, equity dictates that Wiley, who himself performed the act causing the damage, must bear the loss.

Affirmed.

NOTES AND QUESTIONS

1.   Forcible entry and detainer (FED) statutes are used most often in landlord-tenant disputes. The most common type of action, as in the principal case, is one brought by the landlord seeking to regain possession of leased premises from a tenant. In order to bring such an action, the landlord must show that he or she has the right to possession of the premises, which in turn typically requires that the lease contain a clause providing that the tenant forfeits the right of possession or that the landlord has the right to reenter and retake possession on the happening of certain conditions (such as nonpayment of rent or holding over after a lease has expired). Can you identify such a clause in the lease in this case? In some states (though not Minnesota), FED statutes can also be invoked by tenants, provided the tenant wants to be restored to possession following an allegedly wrongful ouster by the landlord. See, e.g., Lees v. Wardall, 554 P.2d 1076 (Wash. Ct. App. 1976). Litigated disputes involving FED statutes also arise in the context of land sale contracts, for example where a seller refuses to turn over possession to a purchaser or where a purchaser enters into possession without having fulfilled all the requirements of the contract. FED statutes are also available in the event that someone with a legal right to possession is forcibly dispossessed by someone without such a right, e.g., a squatter. See generally William Lindsley, Forcible Entry and Detainer, 35A Am. Jur. 2d § 7 (2005). Reported opinions involving the use of FED statutes in such situations are very rare, however. Either these sorts of depredations do not occur very often, or if they do, they are resolved by the police or by criminal trespass charges rather than by civil litigation.

2.   Suppose Berg closed the restaurant, put out a sign that said "Closed for Remodeling," disappeared, and failed to pay the rent when it was due at the beginning of the next month. Would Wiley be obliged to file a FED action to regain possession of the premises in these circumstances? If your answer is yes, what if two months have gone by with no Berg and

no rent? Is the holding of *Berg v. Wiley* limited to cases where the tenant is still in possession? If so, how do we define "possession" in this context?

3. *Berg v. Wiley* may have reflected the "emerging trend" when it was decided in 1978, but it is by no means the unanimous view today. Other courts have more recently held that, at least in the context of commercial landlord-tenant disputes, self-help is still permitted. See, e.g., Northfield Park Associates v. Northeast Ohio Harness, 521 N.E.2d 466 (Ohio Ct. App. 1987); 2 Milton R. Friedman, Friedman on Leases § 18.6 (Patrick A. Randolph, Jr. ed. & rev., 5th ed. 2005). What factors are relevant in deciding whether self-help should be prohibited as a matter of law? For example, would it be relevant if there is a severe backlog of cases in landlord-tenant court or if the sheriff's department is so understaffed that it takes an average of three months to carry out an eviction order?

4. In jurisdictions that still permit self-help, recovery of possession must be accomplished without a breach of the peace. Both the trial court and the state supreme court in *Berg v. Wiley* held that Wiley's actions were not peaceable. What should Wiley have done differently in order to satisfy the requirement that there be no breach of the peace? Presumably politely asking the party in possession to leave is okay. What about asking the party to leave on threat of litigation? What about demanding that the party leave or else the landlord will cut off utilities or other services? Provided the landlord takes care to assure the tenant is not at the premises, what is wrong with changing the locks in the presence of a police officer? Given that Wiley changed the locks in Berg's absence and in the presence of a police officer, is it plausible to say, as the court does, that "the singular reason why actual violence did not erupt at the moment of Wiley's changing of the locks was Berg's absence and her subsequent self-restraint and resort to judicial process"?

P   *D*

Williams v. Ford Motor Credit Company

United States Court of Appeals, Eighth Circuit, 1982.
674 F.2d 717.

■ BENSON, CHIEF JUDGE. In this diversity action brought by Cathy A. Williams to recover damages for conversion arising out of an alleged wrongful repossession of an automobile, Williams appeals from a judgment notwithstanding the verdict entered on motion of defendant Ford Motor Credit Company (FMCC). * * *

In July, 1975, David Williams, husband of plaintiff Cathy Williams, purchased a Ford Mustang from an Oklahoma Ford dealer. Although David Williams executed the sales contract, security agreement, and loan papers, title to the car was in the name of both David and Cathy Williams. The car was financed through the Ford dealer, who in turn assigned the paper to FMCC. Cathy and David Williams were divorced in 1977. The divorce court granted Cathy title to the automobile and required David to continue to make payments to FMCC for eighteen months. David defaulted on the payments and signed a voluntary repossession authorization for FMCC.

Cathy Williams was informed of the delinquency and responded that she was trying to get her former husband David to make the payments. There is no evidence of any agreement between her and FMCC. Pursuant to an agreement with FMCC, S & S was directed to repossess the automobile.

On December 1, 1977, at approximately 4:30 a. m., Cathy Williams was awakened by a noise outside her house trailer in Van Buren, Arkansas.[1] She saw that a wrecker truck with two men in it had hooked up to the Ford Mustang and started to tow it away. She went outside and hollered at them. The truck stopped. She then told them that the car was hers and asked them what they were doing. One of the men, later identified as Don Sappington, president of S & S Recovery, Inc., informed her that he was repossessing the vehicle on behalf of FMCC. Williams explained that she had been attempting to bring the past due payments up to date and informed Sappington that the car contained personal items which did not even belong to her. Sappington got out of the truck, retrieved the items from the car, and handed them to her. Without further complaint from Williams, Sappington returned to the truck and drove off, car in tow. At trial, Williams testified that Sappington was polite throughout their encounter and did not make any threats toward her or do anything which caused her to fear any physical harm. The automobile had been parked in an unenclosed driveway which plaintiff shared with a neighbor. The neighbor was awakened by the wrecker backing into the driveway, but did not come out. After the wrecker drove off, Williams returned to her house trailer and called the police, reporting her car as stolen. Later, Williams commenced this action.

The case was tried to a jury which awarded her $5,000.00 in damages. * * * The district court entered judgment notwithstanding the verdict for FMCC, and this appeal followed.

Article 9 of the Uniform Commercial Code (UCC), which Arkansas has adopted and codified as Ark.Stat.Ann. § 85–9–503 (Supp. 1981), provides in pertinent part:

> Unless otherwise agreed, a secured party has on default the right to take possession of the collateral. In taking possession, a secured party may proceed without judicial process if this can be done without breach of the peace. . . .[2]

In *Ford Motor Credit Co. v. Herring*, 589 S.W.2d 584, 586 (Ark. 1979), which involved an alleged conversion arising out of a repossession, the

---

1. Cathy Williams testified that the noise sounded like there was a car stuck in her yard.

2. It is generally considered that the objectives of this section are (1) to benefit creditors in permitting them to realize collateral without having to resort to judicial process; (2) to benefit debtors in general by making credit available at lower costs, see Griffith v. Valley of the Sun Recovery and Adjustment Bureau, Inc., 613 P.2d 1283 (Ariz. Ct. App. 1980); and (3) to support a public policy discouraging extrajudicial acts by citizens when those acts are fraught with the likelihood of resulting violence, see Morris v. First Nat'l. Bank & Trust Co., 254 N.E.2d 683 (Ohio 1970).

Supreme Court of Arkansas cited Section 85–9–503 and referred to its previous holdings as follows:

> In pre-code cases, we have sustained a finding of conversion only where force, or threats of force, or risk of invoking violence, accompanied the repossession. Manhattan Credit Co., Inc. v. Brewer, 341 S.W.2d 765 (Ark. 1961); Kensinger Acceptance Corp. v. Davis, 269 S.W.2d 792 (Ark. 1954).

The thrust of Williams' argument on appeal is that the repossession was accomplished by the risk of invoking violence. The district judge who presided at the trial commented on her theory in his memorandum opinion:

> Mrs. Williams herself admitted that the men who repossessed her automobile were very polite and complied with her requests. The evidence does not reveal that they performed any act which was oppressive, threatening or tended to cause physical violence. Unlike the situation presented in *Manhattan Credit Co. v. Brewer*, supra, it was not shown that Mrs. Williams would have been forced to resort to physical violence to stop the men from leaving with her automobile.

In the pre-Code case *Manhattan Credit Co. v. Brewer*, 341 S.W.2d 765 (Ark. 1961), the court held that a breach of peace occurred when the debtor and her husband confronted the creditor's agent during the act of repossession and clearly objected to the repossession, 341 S.W.2d at 767–68. In *Manhattan*, the court examined holdings of earlier cases in which repossessions were deemed to have been accomplished without any breach of the peace, id. In particular, the Supreme Court of Arkansas discussed the case of *Rutledge v. Universal C.I.T. Credit Corp.*, 237 S.W.2d 469 (Ark. 1951). In *Rutledge*, the court found no breach of the peace when the repossessor acquired keys to the automobile, confronted the debtor and his wife, informed them he was going to take the car, and immediately proceeded to do so. As the *Rutledge* court explained and the *Manhattan* court reiterated, a breach of the peace did not occur when the "Appellant (debtor-possessor) did not give his permission but he did not object." Manhattan, supra, 341 S.W.2d at 767–68; Rutledge, supra, 237 S.W.2d at 470.

For a breach of peace, a clear objection is needed [handwritten marginal note]

We have read the transcript of the trial. There is no material dispute in the evidence, and the district court has correctly summarized it. Cathy Williams did not raise an objection to the taking, and the repossession was accomplished without any incident which might tend to provoke violence. See also Teeter Motor Co., Inc. v. First Nat'l Bank, 543 S.W.2d 938 (Ark. 1976).

Appellees deserve something less than commendation for the taking during the night time sleeping hours, but it is clear that viewing the facts in the light most favorable to Williams, the taking was a legal repossession under the laws of the State of Arkansas. The evidence does not support the verdict of the jury. FMCC is entitled to judgment notwithstanding the verdict.

The judgment notwithstanding the verdict is affirmed.

■ HEANEY, CIRCUIT JUDGE, dissenting. The only issue is whether the repossession of appellant's automobile constituted a breach of the peace by creating a "risk of invoking violence." See Ford Motor Credit Co. v. Herring, 589 S.W.2d 584, 586 (Ark. 1979). The trial jury found that it did and awarded $5,000 for conversion. Because that determination was in my view a reasonable one, I dissent from the Court's decision to overturn it.

Cathy Williams was a single parent living with her two small children in a trailer home in Van Buren, Arkansas. On December 1, 1977, at approximately 4:30 a. m., she was awakened by noises in her driveway. She went into the night to investigate and discovered a wrecker and its crew in the process of towing away her car. According to the trial court, "she ran outside to stop them * * * but she made no *strenuous* protests to their actions." (Emphasis added.) In fact, the wrecker crew stepped between her and the car when she sought to retrieve personal items from inside it, although the men retrieved some of the items for her. The commotion created by the incident awakened neighbors in the vicinity.

Facing the wrecker crew in the dead of night, Cathy Williams did everything she could to stop them, short of introducing physical force to meet the presence of the crew. The confrontation did not result in violence only because Ms. Williams did not take such steps and was otherwise powerless to stop the crew.

The controlling law is the UCC, which authorizes self-help repossession only when such is done "without breach of the peace * * *." Ark.Stat.Ann. § 85–9–503 (Supp. 1981). The majority recognizes that one important policy consideration underlying this restriction is to discourage "extrajudicial acts by citizens when those acts are fraught with the likelihood of resulting violence." Despite this, the majority holds that no reasonable jury could find that the confrontation in Cathy Williams' driveway at 4:30 a. m. created a risk of violence. I cannot agree. At a minimum, the largely undisputed facts created a jury question. The jury found a breach of the peace and this Court has no sound, much less compelling, reason to overturn that determination.

Indeed, I would think that sound application of the self-help limitation might require a directed verdict in favor of Ms. Williams, but certainly not against her. If a "night raid" is conducted without detection and confrontation, then, of course, there could be no breach of the peace. But where the invasion is detected and a confrontation ensues, the repossessor should be under a duty to retreat and turn to judicial process. The alternative which the majority embraces is to allow a repossessor to proceed following confrontation unless and until violence results in fact. Such a rule invites tragic consequences which the law should seek to prevent, not to encourage. I would reverse the trial court and reinstate the jury's verdict.

NOTES AND QUESTIONS

1. In a series of decisions in the 1970s, the U.S. Supreme Court wavered back and forth as to whether statutory provisions authorizing

summary repossession or disposal of personal property without a prior hearing violate the Due Process Clause. See Fuentes v. Shevin, 407 U.S. 67 (1972) (due process violated by statute authorizing replevin of personal property upon application and posting of bond with no hearing before repossession takes place); Mitchell v. W.T. Grant Co., 416 U.S. 600 (1974) (due process not violated by state statute authorizing "sequestration" of personal property pursuant to ex parte order of judge); North Georgia Finishing, Inc. v. Di–Chem, Inc., 419 U.S. 601 (1975) (due process violated by state statute permitting garnishment of bank account based on conclusory allegations before nonjudicial officer); Flagg Brothers, Inc. v. Brooks, 436 U.S. 149 (1978) (due process not implicated by provision of Uniform Commercial Code authorizing warehouse to sell goods in its custody to satisfy unpaid debt for warehouse services). Some lower courts interpreted these decisions to mean that self-help repossession authorized by Article 9 of the Uniform Commercial Code triggers a due process hearing right. See, e.g., Watson v. Branch County Bank, 380 F.Supp. 945 (W.D. Mich. 1974). But especially after *Flagg Brothers* was decided in 1978, most courts concluded that procedural due process does not apply to self-help repossession under then UCC § 9–503 (for the current version, see Revised UCC § 9–609), because such a repossession does not entail any "state action." Given the widespread adoption of the UCC by the states, creditors have tended to rely on the UCC self-help remedy rather than statutory remedies that might trigger due process hearing requirements under *Fuentes* or *Di-Chem*. As a result, persons who own personal property subject to a lien covered by UCC Article 9 have only those rights available under state constitutional law or under interpretations of UCC § 9–609.

2.   There is considerable irony in the fact that the UCC's self-help repossession remedy has generally been held not to trigger due process, whereas replevin actions or garnishment proceedings require due process hearings. Replevin and garnishment statutes typically give owners of personal property significantly *greater* protection than they get in a self-help repossession. But by exempting self-help from due process constraints, the courts have created a powerful incentive for lending companies to use self-help, rather than more protective statutory mechanisms. Contrast the reasoning of decisions like *Berg v. Wiley*, which hold that the creation of summary statutory remedies for recovery of possession of real property eliminates common-law self-help remedies. Few if any courts have adopted this line of reasoning with respect to self-help repossession of personal property. As a result, most repossessions of personal property today use self-help.

3.   As a further irony, consider that if S & S Recovery, Inc. had towed away Ms. Williams's car by mistake, when it really intended to repossess her neighbor's car, Ms. Williams might be forced to use a replevin action to get her car back. She could not use Article 9's self-help remedy, because she has no security interest in the car, and Article 9 only covers security interests. If Williams were forced to use replevin to get her car back, S & S Recovery would be entitled to a due process hearing before it could be ordered to return the car to her.

4. Notwithstanding these ironies, does it make sense as a policy matter to permit self-help repossession of personal property (at least when the owner is in default on a loan secured by the property) but not to permit self-help repossession of commercial real estate (as held in *Berg v. Wiley*)? Which position do you think is best: no self-help repossession of either real or personal property; self-help possession of either real or personal property provided there is no breach of the peace; or self-help repossession of personal property without breach of the peace, but no self-help repossession of real property?

5. In footnote 6, the court observes that one policy justification for permitting self-help repossession of personal property subject to a security interest is that it benefits "debtors in general by making credit available at lower costs." Can you spell out the argument as to why self-help repossession would have this effect? If self-help repossession would lower the costs of borrowing to finance an automobile or other personal property, would permitting self-help repossession of real property reduce the amount of rent that tenants in general must pay?

6. Which do you think was probably more unsettling to the individual property holder's sense of personal security and autonomy: Wiley's locking out Berg while her restaurant was closed for remodeling, or S & S Recovery's showing up at 4:30 a.m. to tow Williams's Mustang from her driveway?

B. EXCEPTIONS TO THE RIGHT TO EXCLUDE

Although the property owner has an impressive arsenal of criminal, civil, and self-help remedies to vindicate the right to exclude others, the law has always recognized exceptions to the exclusion right. We consider here four categories of exceptions. As always when one has a basic rule (the right to exclude) subject to exceptions, there is a question whether the exceptions should be stated in a rule-like fashion, or whether the whole issue (right to exclude or not to exclude) should be resolved in a case-by-case fashion with more attention to the balance of interests in each case. Keep this underlying question of legal design in mind in considering the following materials.

1. NECESSITY

Ploof v. Putnam

Supreme Court of Vermont, 1908.
71 A. 188.

■ MUNSON, J. It is alleged as the ground of recovery that on the 13th day of November 1904, the defendant was the owner of a certain island in Lake Champlain, and of a certain dock attached thereto, which island and dock were then in charge of the defendant's servant; that the plaintiff was then possessed of and sailing upon said lake a certain loaded sloop, on which were the plaintiff and his wife and two minor children; that there then arose a sudden and violent tempest, whereby the sloop and the property and persons therein were placed in great danger of destruction; that, to save these from destruction or injury, the plaintiff was compelled to, and did, moor the sloop to defendant's dock; that the defendant, by his servant, unmoored the sloop, whereupon it was driven upon the shore by the tempest, without the plaintiff's fault; and that the sloop and its contents were thereby destroyed, and the plaintiff and his wife and children cast into the lake and upon the shore, receiving injuries. This claim is set forth in two counts—one in trespass, charging that the defendant by his servant with force and arms willfully and designedly unmoored the sloop; the other in case, alleging that it was the duty of the defendant by his servant to permit the plaintiff to moor his sloop to the dock, and to permit it to remain so moored during the continuance of the tempest, but that the defendant by his servant, in disregard of this duty, negligently, carelessly, and wrongfully unmoored the sloop. Both counts are demurred to generally.

There are many cases in the books which hold that necessity, and an inability to control movements inaugurated in the proper exercise of a strict right, will justify entries upon land and interferences with personal property that would otherwise have been trespasses. A reference to a few of these will be sufficient to illustrate the doctrine. In Miller v. Fandrye, Poph. 161, trespass was brought for chasing sheep, and the defendant pleaded that the sheep were trespassing upon his land, and that he with a little dog chased them out, and that, as soon as the sheep were off his land, he called in the dog. It was argued that, although the defendant might lawfully drive the sheep from his own ground with a dog, he had no right to pursue them into the next ground; but the court considered that the defendant might drive the sheep from his land with a dog, and that the nature of a dog is such that he cannot be withdrawn in an instant, and that, as the defendant had done his best to recall the dog, trespass would not lie. * * * If one have a way over the land of another for his beasts to pass, and the beasts, being properly driven, feed [on] the grass by morsels in passing, or run out of the way and are promptly pursued and brought back, trespass will not lie. See Vin. Ab. Trespass, K. a, pl. 1. A traveler on a highway who finds it obstructed from a sudden and temporary cause may pass upon the adjoining land without becoming a trespasser because of the necessity. Henn's Case, W. Jones, 296; Campbell v. Race, 7 Cush. (Mass.) 408; Hyde v. Jamaica, 27 Vt. 443 (459); Morey v. Fitzgerald, 56 Vt. 487. An entry upon land to save goods which are in danger of being lost or destroyed by water or fire is not a trespass. 21 Hen. VII, 27; Vin. Ab. Trespass, H. a, 4, pl. 24, K. a, pl. 3. In Proctor v. Adams, 113 Mass. 376, the defendant went upon the plaintiff's beach for the purpose of saving and restoring to the lawful owner a boat which had been driven ashore, and was in danger of being carried off by the sea; and it was held no trespass.

This doctrine of necessity applies with special force to the preservation of human life. One assaulted and in peril of his life may run through the close of another to escape from his assailant. 37 Hen. VII, pl. 26. One may sacrifice the personal property of another to save his life or the lives of his fellows. In Mouse's Case, 12 Co. 63, the defendant was sued for taking and carrying away the plaintiff's casket and its contents. It appeared that the ferryman of Gravesend took 47 passengers into his barge to pass to London, among whom were the plaintiff and defendant; and the barge being upon the water a great tempest happened, and a strong wind, so that the barge and all the passengers were in danger of being lost if certain ponderous things were not cast out, and the defendant thereupon cast out the plaintiff's casket. It was resolved that in case of necessity, to save the lives of the passengers, it was lawful for the defendant, being a passenger, to cast the plaintiff's casket out of the barge; that, if the ferryman surcharge the barge, the owner shall have his remedy upon the surcharge against the ferryman, but that if there be no surcharge, and the danger accrue only by the act of God, as by tempest, without fault of the ferryman, every one ought to bear his loss to safeguard the life of a man.

It is clear that an entry upon the land of another may be justified by necessity, and that the declaration before us discloses a necessity for mooring the sloop. But the defendant questions the sufficiency of the counts because they do not negative the existence of natural objects to which the plaintiff could have moored with equal safety. The allegations are, in substance, that the stress of a sudden and violent tempest compelled the plaintiff to moor to defendant's dock to save his sloop and the people in it. The averment of necessity is complete, for it covers not only the necessity of mooring to the dock; and the details of the situation which created this necessity, whatever the legal requirements regarding them, are matters of proof, and need not be alleged. It is certain that the rule suggested cannot be held applicable irrespective of circumstance, and the question must be left for adjudication upon proceedings had with reference to the evidence [on] the charge. * * *

Judgment affirmed and cause remanded.

NOTES AND QUESTIONS

1. Some of the incidents discussed by the court involve great forces of nature like storms, whereas others involve the behavior of animals like dogs and cattle, and still others involve a response to acts of third parties, like running from an assailant. What are the common elements in these examples that cause courts to treat them as overcoming the owner's right to exclude that otherwise would exist?

2. Could the moving company in *Jacque v. Steenberg Homes*, Chapter I, have raised a defense to trespass based on necessity? If not, why not?

3. In another famous necessity case, *Vincent v. Lake Erie Transp. Co.*, 124 N.W. 221 (Minn. 1910), the defendant kept its boat tied to a dock longer than the plaintiff wanted it to remain there, in order to keep the boat from being destroyed by a violent storm arising on Lake Superior. The wind and waves caused the boat to damage the dock. The court held that

the defendant was justified in keeping the boat tied to the dock, but that the defendant had to pay the plaintiff for the damage caused to the dock. Is this an application of the principle of restitution, considered in Chapter I? Note that both the mistaken improver and the shipowner tying up to the dock can be viewed as trespassers, and both claim that special circumstances make strict enforcement of exclusion rights by injunction inappropriate.

4.   Consider the issue in *Ploof* and *Vincent* in terms of the framework of Calabresi and Melamed (Chapter I). In light of the damages rule in *Vincent*, some commentators have suggested that the defense of necessity in the context of trespass entails a shift from a property rule to a liability rule. The owner of land still has the entitlement, but it is no longer protected by a rule of exclusion. Instead, the intruder who is subject to forces of necessity can "take" the entitlement without the owner's consent, but when he does so, the intruder must pay the owner just compensation. A different way of characterizing the effect of the defense, focusing on the decision in *Ploof*, might be that the defense of necessity shifts the property rule from the landowner to the intruder, who if resisted by the landowner, could use deadly force. The plaintiff "intruders" in *Ploof* did state a cause of action in trespass, which hints at some kind of property rule protection for those in necessity.

5.   Would you apply the rule of compensation recognized in *Vincent v. Lake Erie Transp. Co.* in all cases of necessity? Should it be extended to cases like *Ploof* or *Mouse's Case* (discussed in *Ploof*) where the intrusion is justified by the need to save human life? What about cases involving animals that eat morsels of grass on the side of a designated right of way?

2.   CUSTOM

McConico v. Singleton

Constitutional Court of Appeals of South Carolina, 1818.
9 S.C.L. 244.

This was an action of trespass, *quare clausum fregit*, and to support it the plaintiff proved, that he had warned and ordered the defendant not to hunt on his lands, and that the defendant had, notwithstanding, rode over, and hunted deer on his unenclosed and unimproved lands. The verdict of the jury was, that each party should pay their own costs; and the plaintiff now moves for a new trial on the grounds:

1st. Because the riding over the unenclosed and unimproved lands is in law a trespass, for which an action will lie, when it is contrary to the express orders of the owner. * * *

■ JOHNSON, J. delivered the opinion of the court. Until the bringing of this action, the right to hunt on unenclosed and uncultivated lands has never been disputed, and it is well known that it has been universally exercised from the first settlement of the country up to the present time; and the time has been, when, in all probability, obedient as our ancestors were to the laws of the country, a civil war would have been the consequence of an attempt, even by the legislature, to enforce a restraint on this privilege. It was the source from whence a great portion of them derived their food and raiment, and was, to the devoted huntsman, (disreputable as the life now is,) a source of considerable profit. The forest was regarded as a common, in which they entered at pleasure, and exercised the privilege; and it will not be denied that animals, *ferae naturae*, are common property, and belong to the first taker. If, therefore, usage can make law, none was ever better established. This usage is also clearly recognized as a right by the several acts of the legislature on the subject; particularly the act of 1769, (Pub. Laws, 276,) which restrains the right to hunt within seven miles of the residence of the hunter. Now if the right to hunt beyond that, did not before exist, this act was nugatory; and it cannot be believed that it was only intended to apply to such as owned a tract of land, the diameter of which would be fourteen miles.

It appears to me also, that there is no rule of the English common law, at variance with this principle; but, it is said, that every entry on the lands of another is a trespass, and the least injury, as treading down grass, and the like, will support it. (1 Esp. Dig. Tit. Trespass, 221.) But there must be some actual injury to support the action. Now it will not be pretended that riding over the soil is an injury; and the forest being the common, in which the cattle of all are used to range at large, the grass, if perchance there be any, may also be regarded as common property; and surely no action will lie against a commoner for barely riding over the common. The right to hunt on unenclosed lands, I think, therefore, clearly established; but if it were doubtful, I should be strongly inclined to support it. Large standing armies are, perhaps, wisely considered as dangerous to our free institutions; the militia, therefore, necessarily constitutes our greatest security against aggression; our forest is the great field in which, in the pursuit of game, they learn the dexterous use and consequent certainty of firearms, the great and decided advantages of which have been seen and felt on too many occasions to be forgotten, or to require a recurrence to.

Having come to the conclusion, that it is the right of the inhabitants to hunt on unenclosed lands, I need not attempt to prove that the dissent or disapprobation of the owner cannot deprive him of it; for I am sure it never yet entered the mind of any man, that a right which the law gives, can be defeated at the mere will and caprice of an individual. * * *

NOTES AND QUESTIONS

1.   The decision in *McConico*, recognizing a general right of hunters to enter unenclosed rural land in pursuit of game without first obtaining permission from the owner, is no anomaly. Even to this day a large number of states have so-called "posting laws," which permit anyone to hunt on rural land unless "No Hunting" or "No Trespassing" signs have been prominently posted. See, e.g., Fla.Stat. § 588.10, § 810.09; N.D. Cent. Code

§ 20.1–01–18 (2002); McKee v. Gratz, 260 U.S. 127, 136 (1922) (Holmes, J.) ("[There is a] common understanding with regard to the large expanses of unenclosed and uncultivated land in many parts at least of this country. Over these it is customary to wander, shoot and fish at will until the owner sees fit to prohibit it. A license may be implied from the habits of the country."); Mark R. Sigmon, Hunting and Posting on Private Land in America, 54 Duke L.J. 549 (2004) ("Twenty-nine states currently require private landowners to post their land to exclude hunters, twenty-seven of these states by statute."). These laws impose an affirmative burden of notification on the possessor of land in order to assert the right to exclude. If the owner does not make the required notification, then the right to exclude is subordinated to the customary right to hunt on land owned by another.

2. In the circumstances described by the court, where there are large numbers of subsistence hunters and the value of land for agricultural purposes is often low, is there an efficiency justification for abrogating the general right of landowners to exclude hunters from rural land? What would one predict for the future evolution of legal rules concerning the right to hunt as hunting becomes progressively more of a sport and less of a subsistence activity, and as alternative uses of rural land become more valuable? Recall the Demsetz reading in Chapter III.

3. As noted in Chapter I, the states have also disagreed about who has the burden of installing fences to prevent trespass by livestock. Broadly speaking, most states east of the 100th meridian regulate trespass by livestock with fencing-in laws. That is, the owner of the livestock is responsible for assuring that his livestock do not escape and trample the vegetables or eat the grass on a neighbor's land. Many states west of the 100th meridian regulate trespass by livestock with fencing-out laws. As the name suggests, these laws require that a landowner concerned about having her vegetables trampled or her grass consumed by wandering livestock must put up a fence to keep them out. Fencing-out laws are a legacy of the open-range grazing system in the West, in which cattle (primarily) were allowed to roam in search of nourishment over vast stretches of land belonging to various owners (including the federal government), and were then rounded up at the end of the season and identified by brands. Can the difference be explained in terms of the scale of operations required to raise livestock in the West as opposed to the East, and hence the relative costs of fencing in or out? See generally, Kenneth R. Vogel, The Coase Theorem and California Animal Trespass Law, 16 J. Legal Stud. 149 (1987). Nevertheless, even areas in the West formally governed by fencing-out laws exhibit an informal norm of fencing in. See Robert C. Ellickson, Order without Law: How Neighbors Settle Disputes 52–81 (1991). Can this also be explained in terms of the changes in costs and benefits of land use in the West in recent decades? (Ellickson notes that many of the areas governed by fencing-out laws are now populated by small "ranchettes" where people keep some livestock but also commute to jobs in nearby cities.) Would you expect norms to be more or less uniform than formal

law? In close cases, would you expect the norm to be fencing in or fencing out? Which accords more with general norms of possession?

4. In England and some other commonwealth countries like New Zealand, laws have been enacted that create a "right to roam" over rural land. These laws allow persons who like to "ramble" in open countryside to gain access to designated private property without first seeking permission from the owner. See Alan Cowell, Right-to-Roam Laws Let British Walk Over Class Lines, New York Times, Sept. 20, 2004, at A4. The land that may be accessed must first be identified by officials as "mountain, moor, heath or down or registered common land," and mapped after consultation with landowners. Id. Landowners are entitled to designate up to 28 days per year on which the land can be closed to ramblers. Id. What might explain the adoption of right-to-roam laws in the twenty-first century, after a long period in which rural landowners were understood to have the right to exclude such intrusions? Would it be a good idea to adopt such laws in the United States?

3. Public Accommodations Laws

Another important qualification on the right to exclude results from public accommodations laws. Broadly speaking, the law distinguishes between property not open to the public, like homes, factories, and business offices, and property that offers itself as a "public accommodation." Owners of property not open to the public have long enjoyed broad sovereign authority to exclude others. At common law, subject to the defense of necessity and exceptions based on local custom, the owner of property not open to the public was said to have the right to exclude others for "any reason or no reason at all." Owners of public accommodations, in contrast, have a much more qualified right to exclude. Specifically, they are subject to a general duty of nondiscrimination among customers, meaning they must provide services to customers on a first-come, first-served basis, and they must charge customers only reasonable rates for the services they provide.

The law of public accommodations can be traced to certain implied duties that the common law imposed on persons who held themselves forth to the public as being engaged in one of the "common callings." Thus Blackstone wrote:

> There is also in law always an implied contract with a common inn-keeper, to secure his guest's goods in his inn; with a common carrier or bargemaster, to be answerable for the goods he carries; with a common farrier, that he shoes a horse well, without laming him; with a common taylor, or other workman, that he performs his business in a workman-like manner: in which if they fail, an action on the case lies to recover damages for such breach of their general undertaking. But if I employ a person to transact any of these concerns, whose common profession and business it is not, the law implies no such *general* undertaking; but in order to charge him with damages, a *special* agreement is required. Also if an inn-keeper, or other victualler, hangs out a sign and opens

> his house for travelers, it is an implied engagement to entertain all persons who travel that way; and upon this universal *assumpsit* an action on the case will lie against him for damages, if he without good reason refuses to admit a traveller.

3 William Blackstone, Commentaries *164.

Over time, these implied duties came to be focused on a narrower list of businesses associated with travel, generally referred to as "inn keepers and common carriers." See, e.g., A.K. Sandoval–Strausz, Travelers, Strangers, and Jim Crow: Law, Public Accommodations, and Civil Rights in America, 23 Law & Hist. Rev. 53 (2005) (arguing that by mid-nineteenth century the common law imposed special duties to serve only on businesses that served travelers); cf. Joseph William Singer, No Right to Exclude: Public Accommodations and Private Property, 90 Nw. U. L. Rev. 1283 (1996) (contending that before the Civil War all businesses open to the public were subject to a duty to serve, but acknowledging that the duty narrowed afterwards).

There has long been a debate over the reasons that led to this narrowing:

> In a series of books and articles, [Bruce] Wyman explained this narrowing by arguing that common carrier duties were applied only to those occupations that continued to exhibit effective monopoly. These duties were applicable in earlier times because transportation was very limited and because each town's craftsmen, therefore, had monopolies in their own services. Later the duties of common calling focused on innkeepers and carriers because those occupations entailed legal or economic monopolies. By contrast to Wyman, Charles Burdick, also writing in the early 1900s, challenged this view, noting that common carrier duties were often imposed without a specific finding of monopoly power. Burdick argued that the callings could be identified by a number of indicators that the enterprise was considered "public." First, common carrier duties applied to those activities which historically had been provided by the king or under the king's writ. Second, common carrier duties applied when the public had assisted the enterprise in some manner—through public spending, a grant of eminent domain authority, the use of public property, or the establishment of a legal monopoly. When the legislature had acted in one of these manners, the courts drew on the law of common callings to require that the enterprise serve all.

James B. Speta, A Common Carrier Approach to Internet Connection, 54 Fed. Comm. L.J. 225, 255–56 (2002).

Joseph Singer has advanced a third theory: He argues that the narrowing of public accommodations duties to innkeepers and common carriers was a product of the Jim Crow era of the late nineteenth century when many states, especially in the South, sought to maintain the subordinated position of African–Americans. See Singer, supra, at 1390–1411. In order to achieve this discriminatory objective, the duty to serve was narrowed to innkeepers and common carriers, and the businesses which remained subject to this narrowed duty were deemed to satisfy it by providing "separate but equal" facilities to persons of different races. The Supreme Court facilitated this program by endorsing the narrowed conception of public accommodations in the *Civil Rights Cases*, 109 U.S. 3, 25 (1883), and upholding the separate-but-equal interpretation of the duty against an equal protection challenge in *Plessy v. Ferguson*, 163 U.S. 537 (1896). Notice, however, that Singer's theory that the narrowing was a product of racism presupposes that the common-law duty was significantly broader than innkeepers and common-carriers before the Jim Crow era—a revisionist claim that remains controversial. See, e.g., Sandoval–Strausz, supra; Note, The Antidiscrimination Principle in the Common Law, 102 Harv. L. Rev. 1993, 1996 (1989).

Whatever the underlying reason for restricting the category of public accommodations to innkeepers and common carriers, the duties imposed on these enterprises were relatively limited ones. As summarized by Professor Speta, there were two important duties. Speta, supra, at 257–58. The most fundamental obligation was the duty to serve any person who requested service, provided it was available. Thus, innkeepers and common carriers could not refuse service to persons for "any reason or no reason at all." They would have to have some good reason to refuse service, such as the firm's capacity was exhausted, or the customer would interfere with the quality of service provided to other customers. Second, innkeepers and common carriers had to charge prices that were "reasonable." This did not mean they had to charge exactly the same price to different persons provided the same service. Different customers could be charged different prices, as long as each fell within the zone of reasonable charges.

In a further mutation, the category of enterprises known as innkeepers and common carriers eventually came to be known as public accommodations. Modern public accommodations laws have been influenced by antidiscrimination laws, most prominently Title II of the Civil Rights Act of 1964, 42 U.S.C. § 2000a (2000). This landmark statute provides that all persons are "entitled to the full and equal enjoyment" of places of "public accommodation" without "discrimination or segregation on the ground of race, color, religion or national origin." Id. § 2000a(a). "Public accommodation," in turn, is defined to include (1) "any inn, hotel, motel, or other establishment which provides lodging to transient guests;" (2) "any restaurant, cafeteria, lunchroom, lunch counter, soda fountain, or other facility principally engaged in selling food for consumption on the premises;" and (3) "any motion picture house, theater, concert hall, sports arena, stadium or other place of exhibition or entertainment." Id. § 2000a(b). This definition is broader than the common-law definition (imprecise though it was). The Civil Rights Act only prohibits discrimination based on race or other forbidden categories. But will its broader definition of "public accommodation" filter back and influence the judicial understanding of the types of businesses subject to common-law duties of nondiscrimination and reasonableness? Consider the following case.

Uston v. Resorts International Hotel, Inc.

Appellee

Supreme Court of New Jersey, 1982.   *∟Appellant*
445 A.2d 370.

■ PASHMAN, J. Since January 30, 1979, appellant Resorts International Hotel, Inc. (Resorts) has excluded respondent, Kenneth Uston, from the blackjack tables in its casino because Uston's strategy increases his chances of winning money. Uston concedes that his strategy of card counting can tilt the odds in his favor under the current blackjack rules promulgated by the Casino Control Commission (Commission). However, Uston contends that Resorts has no common law or statutory right to exclude him because of his strategy for playing blackjack.

We hold that the Casino Control Act, N.J.S.A. 5:12–1 to–152 gives the Commission exclusive authority to set the rules of licensed casino games, which includes the methods for playing those games. The Casino Control Act therefore precludes Resorts from excluding Uston for card counting. Because the Commission has not exercised its exclusive authority to determine whether card counters should be excluded, we do not decide whether such an exclusion would be lawful.

ie — if the Casino Control Commision decided to ban card counters, That may be allowed (depending on whether the court finds That exclusion to be lawful), but The Casino can not take it upon itself to ban anyone based on a common-law right.

I

Kenneth Uston is a renowned teacher and practitioner of a complex strategy for playing blackjack known as card counting.[1] Card counters keep track of the playing cards as they are dealt and adjust their betting patterns when the odds are in their favor. When used over a period of time, this method allegedly ensures a profitable encounter with the casino.

Uston first played blackjack at Resorts' casino in November 1978. Resorts took no steps to bar Uston at that time, apparently because the Commission's blackjack rules then in operation minimized the advantages of card counting.

On January 5, 1979, however, a new Commission rule took effect that dramatically improved the card counter's odds. The new rule, which remains in effect, restricted the reshuffling of the deck in ways that benefited card counters. Resorts concedes that the Commission could promulgate blackjack rules that virtually eliminate the advantage of card counting. However, such rules would slow the game, diminishing the casino's "take" and consequently its profits from blackjack gaming.

By letter dated January 30, 1979, attorneys for Resorts wrote to Commission Chairman Lordi, asking the Commission's position on the legality of summarily removing card counters from its blackjack tables. That same day, Commissioner Lordi responded in writing that no statute or regulation barred Resorts from excluding professional card counters from its casino. Before the day had ended, Resorts terminated Uston's career at its blackjack tables, on the basis that in its opinion he was a

---

1. Uston has described his strategy and his alleged success at Atlantic City blackjack tables on broadcast media and in books. See Uston, Two Books on Blackjack.

professional card counter. Resorts subsequently formulated standards for identification of card counters and adopted a general policy to exclude such players.[2]

The Commission upheld Resorts' decision to exclude Uston. Relying on *Garifine v. Monmouth Park Jockey Club*, 148 A.2d 1 (N.J. 1959), the Commission held that Resorts enjoys a common law right to exclude anyone it chooses, as long as the exclusion does not violate state and federal civil rights laws. The Appellate Division reversed, 421 A.2d 173 (N.J. Super. 1981). Although we interpret the Casino Control Act somewhat differently than did the Appellate Division, we affirm that court's holding that the Casino Control Act precludes Resorts from excluding Uston. The Commission alone has the authority to exclude patrons based upon their strategies for playing licensed casino games. Any common law right Resorts may have had to exclude Uston for these reasons is abrogated by the act. We therefore need not decide the precise extent of Resorts' common law right to exclude patrons for reasons not covered by the act. Nonetheless, we feel constrained to refute any implication arising from the Commission's opinion that absent supervening statutes, the owners of places open to the public enjoy an absolute right to exclude patrons without good cause. We hold that the common law right to exclude is substantially limited by a competing common law right of reasonable access to public places.

II

This Court has recognized that "[t]he statutory and administrative controls over casino operations established by the [Casino Control] Act are extraordinarily pervasive and intensive." Knight v. Margate, 431 A.2d 833 (N.J. 1981). The almost 200 separate statutory provisions "cover virtually every facet of casino gambling and its potential impact upon the public." Id. at 833. * * *

Pursuant to these statutes, the Commission has promulgated exhaustive rules on the playing of blackjack. These rules cover every conceivable aspect of the game, from determining how the cards are to be shuffled and cut, to providing that certain cards shall not be dealt "until the dealer has first announced 'Dealer's Card' which shall be stated by the dealer in a tone of voice calculated to be heard by each person at the table." It is no exaggeration to state that the Commission's regulation of blackjack is more extensive than the entire administrative regulation of many industries.

These exhaustive statutes and regulations make clear that the Commission's control over the rules and conduct of licensed casino games is intended to be comprehensive. The ability of casino operators to determine how the games will be played would undermine this control and subvert the important policy of ensuring the "credibility and integrity of the regulatory process and of casino operations." The Commission has promulgated the blackjack rules that give Uston a comparative advantage, and it has sole

---

2. Since then an industry-wide policy has developed to ban card counters. Each casino maintains its own list of persons to be barred as card counters.

authority to change those rules. There is no indication that Uston has violated any Commission rule on the playing of blackjack. Put simply, Uston's gaming is "conducted according to rules promulgated by the Commission." Resorts has no right to exclude Uston on grounds that he successfully plays the game under existing rules.

III

"or no reason or all"
(pg. 445)

Resorts claimed that it could exclude Uston because it had a common law right to exclude anyone at all for any reason. While we hold that the Casino Control Act precludes Resorts from excluding Uston for the reasons stated, it is important for us to address the asserted common law right for two reasons. First, Resorts' contentions and the Commission's position concerning the common law right are incorrect. Second, the act has not completely divested Resorts of its common law right to exclude.

The right of an amusement place owner to exclude unwanted patrons and the patron's competing right of reasonable access both have deep roots in the common law. See Arterburn, The Origin and First Test of Public Callings, 75 U.Pa.L.Rev. 411 (1927); Wyman, The Law of Public Callings as a Solution of the Trust Problem, 17 Harv.L.Rev. 156 (1904). In this century, however, courts have disregarded the right of reasonable access in the common law of some jurisdictions at the time the Civil War Amendments and Civil Rights Act of 1866 were passed. * * * See, e.g., Ferguson v. Gies, 46 N.W. 718 (Mich. 1890) (after passage of the Fourteenth Amendment, both the civil rights statutes and the common law provided grounds for a non-white plaintiff to recover damages from a restaurant owner's refusal to serve him, because the common law as it existed before passage of the civil rights laws "gave to the white man a remedy against any unjust discrimination to the citizen in all public places"); Donnell v. State, 48 Miss. 661 (1873) (state's common law includes a right of reasonable access to all public places).

The current majority American rule has for many years disregarded the right of reasonable access,[4] granting to proprietors of amusement places an absolute right arbitrarily to eject or exclude any person consistent with state and federal civil rights laws. See Annot., Propriety of exclusion of persons from horseracing tracks for reasons other than color or race, 90 A.L.R.3d 1361 (1979); Turner & Kennedy, Exclusion, Ejection and Segregation of Theater Patrons, 32 Iowa L.Rev. 625 (1947). See also Garifine v. Monmouth Park Jockey Club, 148 A.2d 1.

At one time, an absolute right of exclusion prevailed in this state, though more for reasons of deference to the noted English precedent of *Wood v. Leadbitter*, 13 M & W 838, 153 Eng.Rep. 351, (Ex. 1845), than for reasons of policy. * * * It hardly bears mention that our common law has evolved in the intervening 70 years. * * * [T]he decisions of this Court

---

4. The denial of freedom of reasonable access in some States following passage of the Fourteenth Amendment, and the creation of a common law freedom to arbitrarily exclude following invalidation of segregation statutes, suggest that the current majority rule may have had less than dignified origins. See Bell v. Maryland, [378 U.S. 226 (1964)].

have recognized that "the more private property is devoted to public use, the more it must accommodate the rights which inhere in individual members of the general public who use that property." State v. Schmid, 423 A.2d 615 (N.J. 1980).

State v. Schmid involved the constitutional right to distribute literature on a private university campus. The Court's approach in that case balanced individual rights against property rights. It is therefore analogous to a description of the common law right of exclusion. Balancing the university's interest in controlling its property against plaintiff's interest in access to that property to express his views, the Court clearly refused to protect unreasonable exclusions. Justice Handler noted that

> Regulations ... devoid of reasonable standards designed to protect both the legitimate interests of the University as an institution of higher education and the individual exercise of expressional freedom cannot constitutionally be invoked to prohibit the otherwise noninjurious and reasonable exercise of [First Amendment] freedoms. [Id. at 632]

In *State v. Shack*, 277 A.2d 369 (N.J. 1971), the Court held that although an employer of migrant farm workers "may reasonably require" those visiting his employees to identify themselves, "the employer may not deny the worker his privacy or interfere with his opportunity to live with dignity and to enjoy associations customary among our citizens." Id. at 374. The Court reversed the trespass convictions of an attorney and a social services worker who had entered the property to assist farmworkers there.

Pg. 405

Schmid recognizes implicitly that when property owners open their premises to the general public in the pursuit of their own property interests, they have no right to exclude people unreasonably. On the contrary, they have a duty not to act in an arbitrary or discriminatory manner toward persons who come on their premises. That duty applies not only to common carriers, Messenger v. Pennsylvania Railroad Co., 37 N.J.L. 531 (E. & A. 1874), innkeepers, see Garifine, supra, owners of gasoline service stations, Streeter v. Brogan, 274 A.2d 312 (N.J. Ch. Div. 1971), or to private hospitals, Doe v. Bridgeton Hospital Ass'n, Inc., 366 A.2d 641 (N.J. 1976), but to all property owners who open their premises to the public. Property owners have no legitimate interest in unreasonably excluding particular members of the public when they open their premises for public use.

Disruption, security concerns, etc. are all sufficient

→ a "legitimate interest" is needed for exclusion.

No party in this appeal questions the right of property owners to exclude from their premises those whose actions "disrupt the regular and essential operations of the [premises]," State v. Schmid, 423 A.2d at 631 (quoting Princeton University Regulations on solicitation), or threaten the security of the premises and its occupants, see State v. Shack, 277 A.2d at 374. In some circumstances, proprietors have a duty to remove disorderly or otherwise dangerous persons from the premises. See Holly v. Meyers Hotel and Tavern, Inc., 89 A.2d 6 (N.J. 1952). These common law principles enable the casino to bar from its entire facility, for instance, the disorderly, the intoxicated, and the repetitive petty offender.

Whether a decision to exclude is reasonable must be determined from the facts of each case. Respondent Uston does not threaten the security of any casino occupant. Nor has he disrupted the functioning of any casino operations. Absent a valid contrary rule by the Commission, Uston possesses the usual right of reasonable access to Resorts International's blackjack tables. * * *

V

In sum, absent a valid Commission regulation excluding card counters, respondent Uston will be free to employ his card-counting strategy at Resorts' blackjack tables. There is currently no Commission rule banning Uston, and Resorts has no authority to exclude him for card counting. However, it is not clear whether the Commission would have adopted regulations involving card counters had it known that Resorts could not exclude Uston. The Court therefore continues the temporary order banning Uston from Resorts' blackjack tables for 90 days from the date of this opinion. After that time, respondent is free to play blackjack at Resorts' casino absent a valid Commission rule excluding him.

NOTES AND QUESTIONS

1. Ken Uston was a famous blackjack player. As noted in the opinion he authored leading books on blackjack. His litigation exploits were more controversial. Uston had arrived in New Jersey after having been treated rather roughly and excluded from casinos in Las Vegas. In New Jersey, some people felt he made things worse for card counters and spoiled the game by litigating against the exclusion of card counters, because the measures that casinos would take to counter the counters—such as adding decks and moving up the shuffle point—made the game of blackjack worse. For an interview with Uston, covering his take on the litigation and his exploits in Nevada and New Jersey as a card counter, see Arnold Snyder, Interview with Ken Uston, 3 Blackjack Forum (No. 2, June 1983), available at http://www.blackjackforumonline.com/content/ustonint.htm. Uston and his team were quite successful, but Uston claimed that the casinos exaggerated the counters' take by reporting all winning customers as card counters. Id. In the 1980s, Uston wrote several books about video games such as PAC–MAN. He died of a heart attack in 1987. See also Contemporary Authors Online, Gale, 2006. Reproduced in Biography Resource Center. Farmington Hills, Mich.: Thomson Gale. 2006. http://galenet.galegroup.com/servlet/BioRC.

2. One way to read the decision in *Uston* is that the New Jersey Supreme Court simply shifted the legal boundaries by moving casinos from the category of private property into the category of public accommodations. Owners of entertainment venues like casinos, theaters, movie theaters, bars, and sports arenas have long occupied a kind of gray area in between private property and public accommodations. At common law, entertainment venues were generally not regarded as public accommodations, and hence were allowed to exercise the broad "sovereign" power of

exclusion rather than the circumscribed power of exclusion that applied to inns and common carriers. But the boundary between these categories has always been somewhat fluid, and is subject to legislative revision over time. As a public accommodation, a casino would be subject to a duty to accept all customers on a nondiscriminatory basis, unless it could show that the customer would be disruptive to other customers. A card counter does not fall into the disruptive category, and hence presumably must be admitted along with all the dupes more likely to lose to the house.

3. Other courts have reached the opposite conclusion about the continued vitality of the common-law rule giving owners of entertainment venues absolute discretion to exclude persons from the premises. For example, in *Brooks v. Chicago Downs Assn., Inc.*, 791 F.2d 512 (7th Cir. 1986), the court, applying Illinois law, held that a horse racing park could exclude a group of "self-proclaimed expert handicappers" from the park for any reason or no reason at all, as long as there was no discrimination based on "race, color, creed, national origin, or sex." In explaining why it declined to follow *Uston*, the court wrote in part:

> As a policy matter, it is arguably unfair to allow a place of amusement to exclude for any reason or no reason, and to be free of accountability, except in cases of obvious discrimination. In this case, the general public is not only invited but, through advertising, is encouraged to come to the race track and wager on the races' outcome. But the common law allows the race track to exclude patrons, no matter if they come from near or far, or in reasonable reliance on representations of accessibility. We may ultimately believe that market forces would preclude any outrageous excesses—such as excluding anyone who has blond hair, or (like the plaintiffs) who is from Pennsylvania, or (even more outrageous) who has $250,000 to spend in one day of betting. * * * [T]he premise of the consumer protection laws that the New Jersey Supreme Court alluded to in *Uston* * * * recognizes that the reality of an imperfect market allows numerous consumer depredations. Excluding a patron simply because he is named Adam Smith arguably offends the very precepts of equality and fair dealing expressed in everything from the antitrust statutes to the Illinois Consumer Fraud and Deceptive Business Practice Act.

> But the market here is not so demonstrably imperfect that there is a monopoly or any allegation of consumer fraud. Consequently, there is no such explicit legislative directive in the context of patrons attending horse races in Illinois—so the common law rule, relic though it may be, still controls.

Id. at 518–19.

4. Another way of reading the decision in *Uston* is that the right to exclude others from property in New Jersey is subject to a general "good cause" requirement. Do you think this is what the court has in mind? How do you suppose the New Jersey Supreme Court would decide *Jacque v. Steenberg Homes* (Chapter I)? The Jacques appeared to have had no good cause for refusing to permit the defendants to move the mobile home across

the Jacques' farm field, given that their fear of adverse possession was objectively unreasonable. If you respond that the New Jersey court would distinguish between a commercial enterprise open to the public like Resorts' casino and a privately-owned farm, recall that *State v. Shack*, supra, which is one of the decisions relied upon in *Uston*, involved the right to exclude from a privately owned farm. The court held that the right to exclude had to give way to the weightier interests of the migrant workers.

5.   How weighty is the casino's interest in this case? At one point the court notes that the casino conceded that the Commission could largely eliminate the advantages of card counting through different rules for the game of blackjack, but that these rules would slow the game and thereby reduce the house's take. Consider in this regard a study by Lawrence Ritter, who has indirectly measured the transaction costs associated with a medium of exchange by showing the amount of advantage Las Vegas casinos forego in order to avoid time-consuming handling of chips in games of dice. Lawrence S. Ritter, On the Fundamental Role of Transactions Costs in Monetary Theory: Two Illustrations from Casino Gambling, 10 J. Money, Credit & Banking 522, 524–28 (1978). The casinos calculate that foregoing the advantage of making more exact change is outweighed by the greater return from faster bets in a context in which the house has a built-in advantage. Who is best at making these types of decisions? Owners of casinos? The Commission? Courts?

6.   A third way to read *Uston* is that the New Jersey Supreme Court has transferred the right to exclude card counters from owners of casino property to a state regulatory agency, the Casino Commission. Does such a partial abrogation of the right to exclude constitute a taking of the casino's property? Ruling on an analogous question in *PruneYard Shopping Center v. Robins*, 447 U.S. 74 (1980), the United States Supreme Court said "no." Under federal constitutional law, a privately owned shopping center is entitled to exclude those who wish to engage in political expression at the shopping center. See Lloyd Corp. v. Tanner, 407 U.S. 551 (1972). The California Supreme Court, ruling as a matter of California state constitutional law, took a different view, and held that a privately owned shopping center must permit political expression in the shopping center, provided those engaging in such expression adhere to reasonable time, place, and manner restrictions adopted by the owner and do not unduly disturb other patrons. A California shopping center appealed this decision to the U.S. Supreme Court, claiming that the new California right of political access was an unconstitutional taking under the federal constitution, because it eliminated their right to exclude unwanted persons from their property. The Court, speaking through then-Justice William Rehnquist, rejected this claim:

> It is true that one of the essential sticks in the bundle of property rights is the right to exclude others. Kaiser Aetna v. United States, 444 U.S. 164, 179–180 (1979). And here there has literally been a "taking" of that right to the extent that the California Supreme Court has interpreted the State Constitution to entitle its citizens to exercise free

expression and petition rights on shopping center property. But it is well established that "not every destruction or injury to property by governmental action has been held to be a 'taking' in the constitutional sense." Armstrong v. United States, 364 U.S. 40, 48 (1960). Rather, the determination whether a state law unlawfully infringes a landowner's property in violation of the Taking Clause requires an examination of whether the restriction on private property "forc[es] some people alone to bear public burdens which, in all fairness and justice, should be borne by the public as a whole." Id., at 49. This examination entails inquiry into such factors as the character of the governmental action, its economic impact, and its interference with reasonable investment-backed expectations. Kaiser Aetna v. United States, supra, at 175. When "regulation goes too far it will be recognized as a taking." Pennsylvania Coal Co. v. Mahon, 260 U.S. 393, 415 (1922).

Here the requirement that appellants permit appellees to exercise state-protected rights of free expression and petition on shopping center property clearly does not amount to an unconstitutional infringement of appellants' property rights under the Taking Clause. There is nothing to suggest that preventing appellants from prohibiting this sort of activity will unreasonably impair the value or use of their property as a shopping center. The PruneYard is a large commercial complex that covers several city blocks, contains numerous separate business establishments, and is open to the public at large. The decision of the California Supreme Court makes it clear that the PruneYard may restrict expressive activity by adopting time, place, and manner regulations that will minimize any interference with its commercial functions. Appellees were orderly, and they limited their activity to the common areas of the shopping center. In these circumstances, the fact that they may have "physically invaded" appellants' property cannot be viewed as determinative.

447 U.S. at 83–85 (footnotes omitted).

7. As suggested by *State v. Shack* and *Uston*, the New Jersey Supreme Court has been particularly inclined to find reasons to qualify the right to exclude, giving special weight to the impact of exclusion on political expression. Consider another pair of New Jersey cases. In *State v. Schmid*, 423 A.2d 615, 616 (N.J. 1980), also mentioned by the court in *Uston*, Princeton University was denied the right to use the law of trespass to prevent a non-student activist from distributing political literature in an orderly manner on campus, based on the activist's strong interest in disseminating ideas and the University's relatively weak interest in excluding such communications given its traditional open campus policy and its mission of spreading ideas. (The case was dismissed by the U.S. Supreme Court for mootness after Princeton changed its policy. Princeton University v. Schmid, 455 U.S. 100 (1982).) However, in a subsequent case involving a for-profit vocational school, *State v. Guice*, 621 A.2d 553 (N.J. Super. Ct. Law Div. 1993), the court upheld the trespass conviction of students who

distributed political literature on school grounds in defiance of a school ban.

4.   ANTIDISCRIMINATION LAWS

Perhaps the most important exception to the general right of a property owner to exclude others is grounded in antidiscrimination laws. As we have seen, owners of public accommodations were subject to antidiscrimination rules at common law. But the Supreme Court, in *Plessy v. Ferguson*, 163 U.S. 537 (1896), held that the Equal Protection Clause was not violated if a state required common carriers to fulfill the antidiscrimination requirement by providing "separate but equal" facilities for persons of different races. After *Plessy* was effectively overruled by *Brown v. Board of Education*, 347 U.S. 483 (1954), separate-but-equal was dismantled in the realm of public accommodations, most decisively under Title II of the Civil Rights Act of 1964. But discrimination in the realm of property not open to the public has presented a more difficult issue. Significant restrictions have been imposed on the right to exclude based on race, gender, religion, national origin, familial status, and disability—and in some jurisdictions, based on marital status and sexual orientation. For example, if you sell your home, you cannot exclude potential buyers based on one of these protected categories. But even to this day, there is no legal principle that prohibits a homeowner or tenant from announcing that persons of a particular race or other protected category will be systematically excluded from her home or apartment. To that extent, a significant degree of owner sovereignty remains immune from antidiscrimination duties.

The following case, decided before *Brown v. Board of Education* declared separate-but-equal to be unconstitutional, reflects a notable attempt by the Supreme Court to reconcile the principle of owner sovereignty with the goals of equal protection in the context of housing.

Shelley v. Kraemer

Supreme Court of the United States, 1948.
334 U.S. 1.

■ MR. CHIEF JUSTICE VINSON delivered the opinion of the Court. These cases present for our consideration questions relating to the validity of court enforcement of private agreements, generally described as restrictive covenants, which have as their purpose the exclusion of persons of designated race or color from the ownership or occupancy of real property. Basic constitutional issues of obvious importance have been raised.

The first of these cases comes to this Court on certiorari to the Supreme Court of Missouri. On February 16, 1911, thirty out of a total of thirty-nine owners of property fronting both sides of Labadie Avenue between Taylor Avenue and Cora Avenue in the city of St. Louis, signed an agreement, which was subsequently recorded, providing in part:

* * * the said property is hereby restricted to the use and occupancy for the term of Fifty (50) years from this date, so that * * * hereafter no part of said property or any portion thereof shall be, for said term of Fifty-years, occupied by any person not of the Caucasian race, it being intended hereby to restrict the use of said property for said period of time against the occupancy as owners or tenants of any portion of said property for resident or other purpose by people of the Negro or Mongolian Race.

The entire district described in the agreement included fifty-seven parcels of land. The thirty owners who signed the agreement held title to forty-seven parcels, including the particular parcel involved in this case. At the time the agreement was signed, five of the parcels in the district were owned by Negroes. * * *

On August 11, 1945, pursuant to a contract of sale, petitioners Shelley, who are Negroes, for valuable consideration received from one Fitzgerald a warranty deed to the parcel in question. The trial court found that petitioners had no actual knowledge of the restrictive agreement at the time of the purchase.

Figure 4–2
House in *Shelley v. Kraemer* with Commemorative Marker

Source: Saint Louis Post–Dispatch.

On October 9, 1945, respondents, as owners of other property subject to the terms of the restrictive covenant, brought suit in Circuit Court of the city of St. Louis praying that petitioners Shelley be restrained from taking possession of the property and that judgment be entered divesting title out of petitioners Shelley and revesting title in the immediate grantor or in such other person as the court should direct. The trial court denied the requested relief on the ground that the restrictive agreement, upon which respondents based their action, had never become final and complete because it was the intention of the parties to that agreement that it was not to become effective until signed by all property owners in the district, and signatures of all the owners had never been obtained.

The Supreme Court of Missouri sitting en banc reversed and directed the trial court to grant the relief for which respondents had prayed. That court held the agreement effective and concluded that enforcement of its provisions violated no rights guaranteed to petitioners by the Federal Constitution. At the time the court rendered its decision, petitioners were occupying the property in question. * * *

Petitioners have placed primary reliance on their contentions, first raised in the state courts, that judicial enforcement of the restrictive agreements in these cases has violated rights guaranteed to petitioners by the Fourteenth Amendment of the Federal Constitution and Acts of Congress passed pursuant to that Amendment.[3] Specifically, petitioners urge that they have been denied the equal protection of the laws, deprived of property without due process of law, and have been denied privileges and immunities of citizens of the United States. We pass to a consideration of those issues.

I.

Whether the equal protection clause of the Fourteenth Amendment inhibits judicial enforcement by state courts of restrictive covenants based on race or color is a question which this Court has not heretofore been called upon to consider. Only two cases have been decided by this Court which in any way have involved the enforcement of such agreements. The first of these was the case of Corrigan v. Buckley, 271 U.S. 323 (1926). There, * * * [the] only constitutional issue which the appellants had raised in the lower courts, and hence the only constitutional issue before this Court on appeal, was the validity of the covenant agreements as such. This Court concluded that since the inhibitions of the constitutional provisions invoked, apply only to governmental action, as contrasted to action of private individuals, there was no showing that the covenants, which were

---

3. The first section of the Fourteenth Amendment provides: "All persons born or naturalized in the United States, and subject to the jurisdiction thereof, are citizens of the United States and of the State wherein they reside. No State shall make or enforce any law which shall abridge the privileges or immunities of citizens of the United States; nor shall any State deprive any person of life, liberty, or property, without due process of law; nor deny to any person within its jurisdiction the equal protection of the laws."

simply agreements between private property owners, were invalid. Accordingly, the appeal was dismissed for want of a substantial question. Nothing in the opinion of this Court, therefore, may properly be regarded as an adjudication on the merits of the constitutional issues presented by these cases, which raise the question of the validity, not of the private agreements as such, but of the judicial enforcement of those agreements.

The second of the cases involving racial restrictive covenants was Hansberry v. Lee, 311 U.S. 32 (1940). In that case, petitioners, white property owners, were enjoined by the state courts from violating the terms of a restrictive agreement. The state Supreme Court had held petitioners bound by an earlier judicial determination, in litigation in which petitioners were not parties, upholding the validity of the restrictive agreement, although, in fact, the agreement had not been signed by the number of owners necessary to make it effective under state law. This Court reversed the judgment of the state Supreme Court upon the ground that petitioners had been denied due process of law in being held estopped to challenge the validity of the agreement on the theory, accepted by the state court, that the earlier litigation, in which petitioners did not participate, was in the nature of a class suit. In arriving at its result, this Court did not reach the issues presented by the cases now under consideration. * * *

It cannot be doubted that among the civil rights intended to be protected from discriminatory state action by the Fourteenth Amendment are the rights to acquire, enjoy, own and dispose of property. Equality in the enjoyment of property rights was regarded by the framers of that Amendment as an essential pre-condition to the realization of other basic civil rights and liberties which the Amendment was intended to guarantee. Thus, § 1978 of the Revised Statutes, derived from § 1 of the Civil Rights Act of 1866 which was enacted by Congress while the Fourteenth Amendment was also under consideration, provides:

> All citizens of the United States shall have the same right, in every State and Territory, as is enjoyed by white citizens thereof to inherit, purchase, lease, sell, hold, and convey real and personal property.

This Court has given specific recognition to the same principle. Buchanan v. Warley, 245 U.S. 60 (1917).

It is likewise clear that restrictions on the right of occupancy of the sort sought to be created by the private agreements in these cases could not be squared with the requirements of the Fourteenth Amendment if imposed by state statute or local ordinance. We do not understand respondents to urge the contrary. In the case of Buchanan v. Warley, supra, a unanimous Court declared unconstitutional the provisions of a city ordinance which denied to colored persons the right to occupy houses in blocks in which the greater number of houses were occupied by white persons, and imposed similar restrictions on white persons with respect to blocks in which the greater number of houses were occupied by colored persons. During the course of the opinion in that case, this Court stated: "The Fourteenth Amendment and these statutes enacted in furtherance of its purpose operate to qualify and entitle a colored man to acquire property

— and only if imposed by the state — i.e, if private citizens do it, it is ok.

without state legislation discriminating against him solely because of color.''

In Harmon v. Tyler, 273 U.S. 668 (1927), a unanimous court, on the authority of Buchanan v. Warley, supra, declared invalid an ordinance which forbade any Negro to establish a home on any property in a white community or any white person to establish a home in a Negro community, ''except on the written consent of a majority of the persons of the opposite race inhabiting such community or portion of the City to be affected.''

The precise question before this Court in both the Buchanan and Harmon cases, involved the rights of white sellers to dispose of their properties free from restrictions as to potential purchasers based on considerations of race or color. But that such legislation is also offensive to the rights of those desiring to acquire and occupy property and barred on grounds of race or color, is clear * * * from the language of the opinion in Buchanan v. Warley, supra. * * *

But the present cases, unlike those just discussed, do not involve action by state legislatures or city councils. Here the particular patterns of discrimination and the areas in which the restrictions are to operate, are determined, in the first instance, by the terms of agreements among private individuals. Participation of the State consists in the enforcement of the restrictions so defined. The crucial issue with which we are here confronted is whether this distinction removes these cases from the operation of the prohibitory provisions of the Fourteenth Amendment.

Since the decision of this Court in the Civil Rights Cases, 109 U.S. 3 (1883), the principle has become firmly embedded in our constitutional law that the action inhibited by the first section of the Fourteenth Amendment is only such action as may fairly be said to be that of the States. That Amendment erects no shield against merely private conduct, however discriminatory or wrongful.

We conclude, therefore, that the restrictive agreements standing alone cannot be regarded as a violation of any rights guaranteed to petitioners by the Fourteenth Amendment. So long as the purposes of those agreements are effectuated by voluntary adherence to their terms, it would appear clear that there has been no action by the State and the provisions of the Amendment have not been violated. Cf. Corrigan v. Buckley, supra.

But here there was more. These are cases in which the purposes of the agreements were secured only by judicial enforcement by state courts of the restrictive terms of the agreements. The respondents urge that judicial enforcement of private agreements does not amount to state action; or, in any event, the participation of the State is so attenuated in character as not to amount to state action within the meaning of the Fourteenth Amendment. Finally, it is suggested, even if the States in these cases may be deemed to have acted in the constitutional sense, their action did not deprive petitioners of rights guaranteed by the Fourteenth Amendment. We move to a consideration of these matters.

II.

That the action of state courts and of judicial officers in their official capacities is to be regarded as action of the State within the meaning of the Fourteenth Amendment, is a proposition which has long been established by decisions of this Court. * * *

One of the earliest applications of the prohibitions contained in the Fourteenth Amendment to action of state judicial officials occurred in cases in which Negroes had been excluded from jury service in criminal prosecutions by reason of their race or color. These cases demonstrate, also, the early recognition by this Court that state action in violation of the Amendment's provisions is equally repugnant to the constitutional commands whether directed by state statute or taken by a judicial official in the absence of statute. Thus, in Strauder v. West Virginia, 100 U.S. 303 (1880), this Court declared invalid a state statute restricting jury service to white persons as amounting to a denial of the equal protection of the laws to the colored defendant in that case. In the same volume of the reports, the Court in Ex parte Commonwealth of Virginia, 100 U.S. 339 (1879), held that a similar discrimination imposed by the action of a state judge denied rights protected by the Amendment, despite the fact that the language of the state statute relating to jury service contained no such restrictions. * * *

But the examples of state judicial action which have been held by this Court to violate the Amendment's commands are not restricted to situations in which the judicial proceedings were found in some manner to be procedurally unfair. It has been recognized that the action of state courts in enforcing a substantive common-law rule formulated by those courts, may result in the denial of rights guaranteed by the Fourteenth Amendment, even though the judicial proceedings in such cases may have been in complete accord with the most rigorous conceptions of procedural due process. Thus, in American Federation of Labor v. Swing, 312 U.S. 321 (1941), enforcement by state courts of the common-law policy of the State, which resulted in the restraining of peaceful picketing, was held to be state action of the sort prohibited by the Amendment's guaranties of freedom of discussion. In Cantwell v. Connecticut, 310 U.S. 296 (1940), a conviction in a state court of the common-law crime of breach of the peace was, under the circumstances of the case, found to be a violation of the Amendment's commands relating to freedom of religion. In Bridges v. California, 314 U.S. 252 (1941), enforcement of the state's common-law rule relating to contempts by publication was held to be state action inconsistent with the prohibitions of the Fourteenth Amendment. * * *

III.

Against this background of judicial construction, extending over a period of some three-quarters of a century, we are called upon to consider whether enforcement by state courts of the restrictive agreements in these cases may be deemed to be the acts of those States; and, if so, whether that action has denied these petitioners the equal protection of the laws which the Amendment was intended to insure.

We have no doubt that there has been state action in these cases in the full and complete sense of the phrase. The undisputed facts disclose that petitioners were willing purchasers of properties upon which they desired to establish homes. The owners of the properties were willing sellers; and contracts of sale were accordingly consummated. It is clear that but for the active intervention of the state courts, supported by the full panoply of state power, petitioners would have been free to occupy the properties in question without restraint.

These are not cases, as has been suggested, in which the States have merely abstained from action, leaving private individuals free to impose such discriminations as they see fit. Rather, these are cases in which the States have made available to such individuals the full coercive power of government to deny to petitioners, on the grounds of race or color, the enjoyment of property rights in premises which petitioners are willing and financially able to acquire and which the grantors are willing to sell. The difference between judicial enforcement and nonenforcement of the restrictive covenants is the difference to petitioners between being denied rights of property available to other members of the community and being accorded full enjoyment of those rights on an equal footing.

The enforcement of the restrictive agreements by the state courts in these cases was directed pursuant to the common-law policy of the States as formulated by those courts in earlier decisions. * * * State action, as that phrase is understood for the purposes of the Fourteenth Amendment, refers to exertions of state power in all forms. And when the effect of that action is to deny rights subject to the protection of the Fourteenth Amendment, it is the obligation of this Court to enforce the constitutional commands.

We hold that in granting judicial enforcement of the restrictive agreements in these cases, the States have denied petitioners the equal protection of the laws and that, therefore, the action of the state courts cannot stand. We have noted that freedom from discrimination by the States in the enjoyment of property rights was among the basic objectives sought to be effectuated by the framers of the Fourteenth Amendment. That such discrimination has occurred in these cases is clear. Because of the race or color of these petitioners they have been denied rights of ownership or occupancy enjoyed as a matter of course by other citizens of different race or color. * * *[26]

Respondents urge, however, that since the state courts stand ready to enforce restrictive covenants excluding white persons from the ownership or occupancy of property covered by such agreements, enforcement of

---

26. Restrictive agreements of the sort involved in these cases have been used to exclude other than Negroes from the ownership or occupancy of real property. We are informed that such agreements have been directed against Indians, Jews, Chinese, Japanese, Mexicans, Hawaiians, Puerto Ricans, and Filipinos, among others.

covenants excluding colored persons may not be deemed a denial of equal protection of the laws to the colored persons who are thereby affected. This contention does not bear scrutiny. The parties have directed our attention to no case in which a court, state or federal, has been called upon to enforce a covenant excluding members of the white majority from ownership or occupancy of real property on grounds of race or color. But there are more fundamental considerations. The rights created by the first section of the Fourteenth Amendment are, by its terms, guaranteed to the individual. The rights established are personal rights. It is, therefore, no answer to these petitioners to say that the courts may also be induced to deny white persons rights of ownership and occupancy on grounds of race or color. Equal protection of the laws is not achieved through indiscriminate imposition of inequalities.

Nor do we find merit in the suggestion that property owners who are parties to these agreements are denied equal protection of the laws if denied access to the courts to enforce the terms of restrictive covenants and to assert property rights which the state courts have held to be created by such agreements. The Constitution confers upon no individual the right to demand action by the State which results in the denial of equal protection of the laws to other individuals. And it would appear beyond question that the power of the State to create and enforce property interests must be exercised within the boundaries defined by the Fourteenth Amendment. Cf. Marsh v. Alabama, 326 U.S. 501 (1946). * * *

For the reasons stated, the judgment of the Supreme Court of Missouri * * * must be reversed.

■ MR. JUSTICE REED, MR. JUSTICE JACKSON, and MR. JUSTICE RUTLEDGE took no part in the consideration or decision of these cases.

NOTES AND QUESTIONS

1. For further background on *Shelley*, see Carol Rose, Property Stories: *Shelley v. Kraemer*, in Property Stories 169–200 (Gerald Korngold & Andrew P. Morriss eds., 2004); see also Clement E. Vose, Caucasians Only: The Supreme Court, the NAACP, and the Restrictive Covenant Cases (1959); R.W. Brooks, Covenants & Conventions (Draft, Yale Law School, July 2005). A few years after the decision in *Shelley*, the Court ruled that judicial judgments awarding damages for breach of a racial covenant are also state action forbidden under the Equal Protection Clause. Barrows v. Jackson, 346 U.S. 1049 (1953). This eliminated the possible argument that the prohibitory nature of a judicial injunction makes this type of judicial judgment "state action," whereas other types of judicial action such as awarding damages for breach of contract or enforcing a racially discriminatory bequest in a will, are not.

2. We have seen a number of devices or ideas for drawing the line between the sphere of owner sovereignty and the sphere of collective or public sovereignty, including common-law restrictions (e.g., the defense of necessity), custom (e.g., hunting rights), and public policy (e.g., public

accommodations requirements). *Shelley* calls upon yet another device: the state action doctrine. *Shelley* says that a mere "voluntary agreement" among neighbors not to sell to African–Americans would not be state action, and hence is a permissible incidence of owner sovereignty. But if someone calls upon the powers of the courts to enforce such an agreement, any resulting judicial judgment is state action, and hence is subject to the limitations of the Constitution, including the Equal Protection Clause. Recall too that in the context of attempts to recover personal property, the Supreme Court has held that replevin actions and judicial garnishment orders are state action, and hence are subject to the constitutional requirements of the Due Process Clause—but courts have generally assumed that self-help repossessions are not state action, and hence escape due process limitations. Does this suggest that the sphere of owner sovereignty is limited to efforts to exclude others through informal persuasion based on norms and customs, voluntary compliance with contracts, and self-help? Does this mean that any attempt to invoke the private law of property in a court is automatically transformed into a species of federal constitutional law? Or does this result in too small a sphere for owner sovereignty relative to public sovereignty? Trying to identify some limiting principle for *Shelley*'s conclusion that judicial enforcement of racial covenants is state action has vexed scholars ever since the decision was handed down. See, e.g., Louis Pollak, Racial Discrimination and Judicial Integrity: A Reply to Professor Wechsler, 108 U. Pa. L. Rev. 1 (1959) (*Shelley* correctly decided because judicial enforcement of the covenant required a person who did not wish to discriminate to engage in discriminatory action); Thomas P. Lewis, The Meaning of State Action, 60 Colum. L. Rev. 1083, 1115 (1960) (*Shelley* correctly decided because racial covenants are functionally equivalent to zoning laws); Louis Henkin, *Shelley v. Kraemer*: Notes for a Revised Opinion, 110 U. Pa. L. Rev. 473 (1962) (*Shelley* justified under a balancing test that compares impact of discrimination on blacks against liberty interest of white property owners); Robert J. Glennon & John E. Nowak, A Functional Analysis of the Fourteenth Amendment "State Action" Requirement, 1976 Sup. Ct. Rev. 221 (*Shelley* properly separated out for invalidation those nongovernmental activities whose existence impairs fundamental constitutional values); Laurence H. Tribe, Constitutional Choices 260 (1985) (*Shelley* correctly decided because enforcement of the covenant was an exception to the general rule followed by the state of prohibiting restraints on alienation); Mark D. Rosen, Was *Shelley v. Kraemer* Incorrectly Decided? Some New Answers, 94 Cal. L. Rev. ___ (forthcoming 2007) (*Shelley* should have been decided under the Thirteenth Amendment and statutes implementing it rather than the Fourteenth Amendment).

3.   One related but distinct approach to the specter of racially restrictive covenants is to invalidate them on grounds of public policy. For example, in *Re Drummond Wren*, [1945] O.R. 778, 4 D.L.R. 674, the Ontario High Court held that a covenant prohibiting sale of real estate to "Jews or persons of objectionable nationality" was void as against public policy. Courts have traditionally exercised a common-law power to invalidate contracts on grounds of public policy. Indeed, the Supreme Court held,

immediately after the decision in *Shelley*, that judicial enforcement of racial covenants in Washington, D.C. would violate public policy. Hurd v. Hodge, 334 U.S. 24, 34–35 (1948). Why didn't the Court take the same tack in *Shelley* itself? What is the source of law for covenants in Missouri?

USE OF TRESPASS ACTIONS TO EXCLUDE PERSONS BASED ON RACE

Shelley v. Kraemer holds that judicial enforcement of a racial covenant to block the sale of a home from a willing seller to a willing African–American buyer is "state action," and hence violates the Equal Protection Clause of the Fourteenth Amendment. What then about judicial enforcement of trespass law at the behest of a property owner to block an African–American from entering property, in circumstances where the owner permits entry by whites? In other words, does *Shelley* require that *any* state enforcement of private property rights is "state action" subject to the constitutional limitations that apply to government, at least when the enforcement action is motivated by racial animus? This issue came to the fore during the civil rights movement of the early 1960s. African–American demonstrators staged numerous sit-ins at segregated lunch counters, restaurants, and public transportation systems, in order to dramatize the injustice of racial segregation at these establishments. White owners, in response, would often call the police to have the demonstrators arrested for trespassing.

In states where segregation was required by law, the Supreme Court held that prosecutions for criminal trespass were state action, without regard to whether the owner's action in calling the police was motivated by a desire to comply with the law or by personal prejudice. See Peterson v. Greenville, 373 U.S. 244 (1963). Justice Harlan, concurring in the judgment, thought that state action could be found only where there was individualized proof that the owner was motivated by a desire to comply with the statute. Id. at 252–53. But what if there were no state or local statute requiring segregation, and blacks were excluded from the restaurant or lunch counter because of the personal prejudice of the owner, or because the owner imagined that this was what a majority of his customers wanted?

A number of cases fitting the latter pattern reached the Supreme Court in *Bell v. Maryland*, 378 U.S. 226 (1964). One of the arguments advanced by the demonstrators was that their convictions for trespass were unconstitutional under *Shelley v. Kraemer*. They argued that allowing a restaurant owner who wants to discriminate against blacks to call upon the police and courts to enforce these preferences transforms private discriminatory animus into state action, and is forbidden by the Fourteenth Amendment.

The Court ducked the state action question presented. The lead case involved a sit-in at a restaurant in Baltimore, Maryland. Shortly after the Court granted review, Maryland enacted a statute making racial segregation in public accommodations, including restaurants, unlawful. The majority vacated and remanded for the Maryland courts to determine whether this development would mean that the state courts would "abate" the convictions.

Justice Hugo Black, a former Alabama Senator named to the Court by Franklin Roosevelt, filed a vigorous dissent, joined by Justices Harlan and White. Black struggled without notable success to distinguish *Shelley v. Kraemer*. But he wrote at a time when mounting civil disturbances over race relations had given rise in many quarters to concern about a breakdown in law and order. Black defended trespass law as a necessary ingredient in the maintenance of social order:

> The experience of ages points to the inexorable fact that people are frequently stirred to violence when property which the law recognizes as theirs is forcibly invaded or occupied by others. Trespass laws are born of this experience. They have been, and doubtless still are, important features of any government dedicated, as this country is, to a rule of law. Whatever power it may allow the States or grant to the Congress to regulate the use of private property, the Constitution does not confer upon any group the right to substitute rule by force for rule by law. Force leads to violence, violence to mob conflicts, and these to rule by the strongest groups with control of the most deadly weapons. Our Constitution, noble work of wise men, was designed—all of it—to chart a quite different course: to "establish Justice, insure domestic Tranquility * * * and secure the Blessings of Liberty to ourselves and our Posterity." At times the rule of law seems too slow to some for the settlement of their grievances. But it is the plan our Nation has chosen to preserve both "Liberty" and equality for all. On that plan we have put our trust and staked our future. This constitutional rule of law has served us well. Maryland's trespass law does not depart from it. Nor shall we.

Id. at 346.

Justice Arthur Goldberg, joined by Chief Justice Warren and Justice Douglas, wrote a response to Justice Black's dissent, arguing that the convictions for trespass would have violated the Fourteenth Amendment, provided the state had not amended its law to prohibit segregation in public accommodations. Justice Goldberg did not endorse the theory that the trespass convictions were state action under *Shelley v. Kraemer*. Instead, he advanced an historical argument to the effect that the Framers of the Fourteenth Amendment intended to constitutionalize common-law rights of equal access to inns and common carriers as part of the civil rights enjoyed by all persons. These rights, he further argued, were inconsistent with discrimination by innkeepers or common carriers based on race. Finally, he maintained that these civil rights, as reasonably extrapolated to modern conditions, were broad enough to cover discrimination by restaurants and lunch counters. One virtue Justice Goldberg saw in this alternative theory was that it did not threaten to transform all judicial enforcement of trespass law into state action. His theory only proscribed judicial enforcement of trespass law that would deny African–Americans equal access to public accommodations. Id. at 288–312.

As it turned out, the Court never resolved the question whether enforcement of trespass law motivated by racial prejudice is state action. Shortly after *Bell v. Maryland* was decided, Congress passed the landmark Civil Rights Act of 1964. Title II of that Act prohibited racial discrimination in any public accommodation affected by interstate commerce. The Court quickly held that the Act abated convictions of sit-in protesters under state trespass law. See Jack Greenberg, The Supreme Court, Civil Rights and Civil Dissonance, 77 Yale L.J. 1520, 1532 (1968). The Act effectively ended the era of racial segregation in publication accommodations broadly defined, including restaurants, lunch counters, hotels, and common carriers. The fact that the Court had ducked the question whether enforcement of trespass law is state action, without more, meant that owners of property not open to the public can continue to call upon the power of the state to enforce their right to exclude, even when that right is exercised in a discriminatory manner.

A postscript: The named plaintiff in *Bell v. Maryland* was a high school student when he participated in the sit-in at the Baltimore restaurant. He later went on to college and law school. Today Robert M. Bell sits as the Chief Justice of the Maryland Court of Appeals. (Thanks to Jack Greenberg, who argued *Bell v. Maryland* in the U.S. Supreme Court, for supplying this information.)

THE FAIR HOUSING ACT

Congress soon enacted another major piece of civil rights legislation: the Fair Housing Act, as Title VIII of the Civil Rights Act of 1968 is usually known. After declaring "the policy of the United States [to be] to provide within constitutional limitations for fair housing throughout the United States," § 3601, the FHA goes on to prohibit a range of discriminatory behaviors against members of enumerated protected classes in the housing field, with certain exceptions. Over the years the FHA has been amended to add protected classes such as the disabled. Consider the following selected provisions of the FHA.

Fair Housing Act, 42 U.S.C. §§ 3601–3619

§ 3604. Discrimination in the sale or rental of housing and other prohibited practices

As made applicable by section 3603 of this title and except as exempted by sections 3603(b) and 3607 of this title, it shall be unlawful—

(a) To refuse to sell or rent after the making of a bona fide offer, or to refuse to negotiate for the sale or rental of, or otherwise make unavailable or deny, a dwelling to any person because of race, color, religion, sex, familial status, or national origin.

(b) To discriminate against any person in the terms, conditions, or privileges of sale or rental of a dwelling, or in the provision of services or facilities in connection therewith, because of race, color, religion, sex, familial status, or national origin.

(c) To make, print, or publish, or cause to be made, printed, or published any notice, statement, or advertisement, with respect to the sale or rental of a dwelling that indicates any preference, limitation, or discrimination based on race, color, religion, sex, handicap, familial status, or national origin, or an intention to make any such preference, limitation, or discrimination.

(d) To represent to any person because of race, color, religion, sex, handicap, familial status, or national origin that any dwelling is not available for inspection, sale, or rental when such dwelling is in fact so available.

(e) For profit, to induce or attempt to induce any person to sell or rent any dwelling by representations regarding the entry or prospective entry into the neighborhood of a person or persons of a particular race, color, religion, sex, handicap, familial status, or national origin.

(f)(1) To discriminate in the sale or rental, or to otherwise make unavailable or deny, a dwelling to any buyer or renter because of a handicap of—

    (A) that buyer or renter,

    (B) a person residing in or intending to reside in that dwelling after it is so sold, rented, or made available; or

    (C) any person associated with that buyer or renter.

(2) To discriminate against any person in the terms, conditions, or privileges of sale or rental of a dwelling, or in the provision of services or facilities in connection with such dwelling, because of a handicap of—

    (A) that person; or

    (B) a person residing in or intending to reside in that dwelling after it is so sold, rented, or made available; or

    (C) any person associated with that person.

    * * *

§ 3603(b). Exemptions

Nothing in section 3604 of this title (other than subsection (c)) shall apply to—

(1) any single-family house sold or rented by an owner: *Provided*, That such private individual owner does not own more than three such single-family houses at any one time: *Provided further*, That in the case of the sale of any such single-family house by a private individual owner not residing in such house at the time of such sale or who was not the most recent resident of such house prior to such sale, the exemption granted by this subsection shall apply only with respect to one such sale within any twenty-four month period: *Provided further*, That such bona fide private individual owner does not own any interest in, nor is there owned or reserved on his behalf, under any express or voluntary agreement, title to or any right to all or a portion of the proceeds from the sale or rental of, more than three such single-family houses at any one time: *Provided*

further, That after December 31, 1969, the sale or rental of any such single-family house shall be excepted from the application of this subchapter only if such house is sold or rented (A) without the use in any manner of the sales or rental facilities or the sales or rental services of any real estate broker, agent, or salesman, or of such facilities or services of any person in the business of selling or renting dwellings, or of any employee or agent of any such broker, agent, salesman, or person and (B) without the publication, posting or mailing, after notice, of any advertisement or written notice in violation of section 3604(c) of this title; but nothing in this proviso shall prohibit the use of attorneys, escrow agents, abstractors, title companies, and other such professional assistance as necessary to perfect or transfer the title, or

(2) rooms or units in dwellings containing living quarters occupied or intended to be occupied by no more than four families living independently of each other, if the owner actually maintains and occupies one of such living quarters as his residence.

"Mrs. Murphy" exception

§ 3607. Religious organization or private club exemption

(a) Nothing in this subchapter shall prohibit a religious organization, association, or society, or any nonprofit institution or organization operated, supervised or controlled by or in conjunction with a religious organization, association, or society, from limiting the sale, rental or occupancy of dwellings which it owns or operates for other than a commercial purpose to persons of the same religion, or from giving preference to such persons, unless membership in such religion is restricted on account of race, color, or national origin. Nor shall anything in this subchapter prohibit a private club not in fact open to the public, which as an incident to its primary purpose or purposes provides lodgings which it owns or operates for other than a commercial purpose, from limiting the rental or occupancy of such lodgings to its members or from giving preference to its members.

(b)(1) Nothing in this subchapter limits the applicability of any reasonable local, State, or Federal restrictions regarding the maximum number of occupants permitted to occupy a dwelling. Nor does any provision in this subchapter regarding familial status apply with respect to housing for older persons. * * *

NOTES AND QUESTIONS

1. Suppose an owner denies a single mother with children an apartment and says that he thinks children are too noisy. Does this violate the Act? What if the discrimination is more subtle? Plaintiffs under the FHA may not need to show discriminatory intent. For some courts, discriminatory *effect* suffices. Compare Betsey v. Turtle Creek Assocs., 736 F.2d 983, 986 (4th Cir. 1984) (holding that disparate impact is sufficient for a prima facie case under the FHA) with Brown v. Artery Org., Inc., 654 F.Supp. 1106, 1115–16 (D.D.C. 1987) (holding that prima facie case against a private actor requires proof of discriminatory intent, but effect is enough for prima facie case against government actors); see also Peter E. Mahoney,

The End(s) of Disparate Impact: Doctrinal Reconstruction, Fair Housing and Lending Law, and the Antidiscrimination Principle, 47 Emory L.J. 409 (1998). Some of the FHA cases involve towns disapproving developments, which plaintiffs have claimed caused a disparate impact on minorities. See the materials on exclusionary zoning in Chapter IX.

2.   Section 3603(b)(2) of the FHA is known as the "Mrs. Murphy" exception (presumably the name itself being an example of stereotyping), and is aimed at protecting the associational interests of a landlord living on the premises with three or fewer other apartments. Note that the exception does not apply to advertising. If a live-in owner in a building with four units refuses to rent to a single mother with a young child, is there a violation of the FHA? Suppose the owner places the following advertisement in a newspaper: "For rent: Furnished apartment. No children allowed." A single mother with two children applies and is rejected.

3.   What if the landlord places an advertisement saying that the premises would be "rented only to persons speaking Polish, German, or Swedish"? In one case, such an ad was found impermissibly to reflect a preference for certain nationalities even though the landlord contended that it fostered communication. See Holmgren v. Little Village Community Reporter, 342 F.Supp. 512 (N.D. Ill. 1971). Publications are potentially liable for carrying discriminatory advertisements, including those showing only white models in their pictures in such a way as to indicate a racial preference. In *Ragin v. New York Times Co.*, 923 F.2d 995 (2d Cir. 1991), this type of liability under the FHA was held not to violate the First Amendment. What about a recent Korean immigrant who advertises in Korean in a Korean-language newspaper in Los Angeles (but with no stated preference as to type of tenant)? Is there potential liability? How about a single woman who advertises for a female roommate to share an apartment?

4.   At the time the FHA was passed, the predominant vision of antidiscrimination law was an integrationist one, although the statute is framed in terms of individual rights. What if racial quotas are used to maintain integration? In the most famous such situation, Starrett City, a housing development in Brooklyn, used quotas to maintain a strict balance between blacks, Latinos, and whites. In the process black and Latino prospective tenants were turned away from apartments that were later rented to whites. Over a dissent by Judge Newman, the court held that racial ceiling quotas violated the FHA despite the owners' claim that they were being used to maintain integration and prevent "white flight." United States v. Starrett City Associates, 840 F.2d 1096 (2d Cir. 1988).

5.   It is important to remember that the Fair Housing Act is not the only antidiscrimination law that might apply to a given discriminatory act in the housing area. Notably, the Civil Rights Act of 1866 provides that "[a]ll citizens of the United States shall have the same right, in every State and Territory, as is enjoyed by white citizens thereof to inherit, purchase, lease, sell, hold, and convey real and personal property." 42 U.S.C. § 1982. This applies to race only, but the Supreme Court has held that the notion

of race here is the very broad one prevailing at the time the Act was passed. See Shaare Tefila Congregation v. Cobb, 481 U.S. 615, 617 (1987) (holding that with Civil Rights Act of 1866 Congress "intended to protect from discrimination identifiable classes of persons who are subjected to intentional discrimination solely because of their ancestry or ethnic characteristics" and that Jews are part of protected class) (quotation marks omitted). Based on contemporary Congressional debates, the Court has said that Section 1982 would include groups like Arabs, Chinese, Germans, and Anglo–Saxons. See Saint Francis College v. Al–Khazraji, 481 U.S. 604, 612 (1987). Also, Section 1982 contains no exceptions like those for small landlords and religious organizations in the FHA. When faced with a particular situation, state and local law may afford protections beyond those in federal law. Consider the following case.

Attorney General v. Desilets

Supreme Judicial Court of Massachusetts, 1994.
636 N.E.2d 233.

■ WILKINS, JUSTICE. This case involves the tension between a statutory mandate that a landlord not discriminate against unmarried couples in renting accommodations and a landlord's sincerely held religious belief that he should not facilitate what he regards as sinful cohabitation.

The defendants, who are brothers, own a four-unit apartment house in the Turners Falls section of the town of Montague. Paul and his wife jointly own two other apartment buildings in Turners Falls which have a total of twenty-one residential units. In August, 1989, Paul, acting for himself and his brother, declined to consider leasing an apartment in the four-unit building to Mark Lattanzi and Cynthia Tarail, an unmarried couple, because they would be cohabiting there.

The defendants have a policy of not leasing an apartment to any person who intends to engage in conduct that violates their religious principles. The defendants' sole reason for declining even to consider Lattanzi and Tarail as tenants was that religion-based policy. The defendants, who are Roman Catholics, believe that they should not facilitate sinful conduct, including fornication. Since developing the policy at least a decade earlier, the defendants have applied it ten or more times to deny tenancies to unmarried couples.

General Laws c. 151B, § 4(6), as in effect in August, 1989, provided, in part, that it shall be an unlawful practice for the owner of a multiple dwelling "to refuse to rent or lease ... or otherwise to deny to or withhold from any person or group of persons such accommodations because of the race, religious creed, color, national origin, sex, age, ancestry or *marital status* of such person or persons" (emphasis supplied). G.L. c. 151B, § 4(6) (1988 ed.).[3] We shall conclude that the defendants violated the provisions of

3. Statute 1989, c. 516, § 9, approved on November 15, 1989, inserted the category "sexual orientation, which shall not include persons whose sexual orientation involves minor children as the sex object" after the category "sex" in the quoted language.

this statute and that, therefore, we must consider the defendants' argument that enforcement of the statute against them violates their rights under the State and Federal Constitutions.

In September, 1989, Lattanzi and Tarail filed a housing discrimination complaint with the Massachusetts Commission Against Discrimination (MCAD), claiming that because of their marital status they were denied available housing in violation of G.L. c. 151B, § 4(6). After the MCAD had found probable cause, Lattanzi and Tarail filed a notice seeking a judicial determination of the matter in the Superior Court, pursuant to G.L. c. 151B, § 5 (1992 ed.). On October 4, 1990, the Attorney General, as was his obligation under G.L. c. 151B, § 5, commenced this action on behalf of the complainants in Superior Court in Franklin County.

A judge of the Superior Court decided the case on cross-motions for summary judgment. He allowed the defendants' motion for summary judgment and denied the Attorney General's. The motion judge correctly ruled that the defendants had violated G.L. c. 151B. He then ruled that, on the summary judgment record, application of the statute to the defendants in this case would be unconstitutional. We granted the Attorney General's application for direct appellate review. We conclude that, on the record before us, neither party was entitled to summary judgment and that the summary judgment for the defendants should be vacated.

1.   The defendants argue that they are not discriminating on the basis of marital status but rather on the basis of conduct and that consequently they are not discriminating in a way forbidden by G.L. c. 151B, § 4(6). There is no merit to this argument. This court's opinion in *Worcester Hous. Auth. v. Massachusetts Comm'n Against Discrimination,* 547 N.E.2d 43 (Mass. 1989), makes clear that the prohibition in G.L. c. 151B, § 4(6), against discrimination in leasing because of marital status applies to discrimination against an unmarried woman and an unmarried man seeking to rent an apartment for their joint occupancy. Moreover, analysis of the defendants' concerns shows that it is marital status and not sexual intercourse that lies at the heart of the defendants' objection. If married couple A wanted to cohabit in an apartment owned by the defendants, they would have no objection. If unmarried couple B wanted to cohabit in an apartment owned by the defendants, they would have great objection. The controlling and discriminating difference between the two situations is the difference in the marital status of the two couples.

2.   We consider first the protections provided by art. 46, § 1, of the Amendments to the State Constitution. Article 46, § 1 ("No law shall be passed prohibiting the free exercise of religion") parallels the First Amendment to the Constitution of the United States ("Congress shall make no law ... prohibiting the free exercise of religion"). See Commonwealth v. Nissenbaum, 536 N.E.2d 592 (Mass. 1989).

Despite the similarity of the two constitutional provisions, this court should reach its own conclusions on the scope of the protections of art. 46,

§ 1, and should not necessarily follow the reasoning adopted by the Supreme Court of the United States under the First Amendment. Indeed, after the release of our *Nissenbaum* opinion, the Supreme Court substantially altered its standard for determining whether conduct was protected under the free exercise of religion clause by its decision in *Employment Div., Dep't of Human Resources of Or. v. Smith,* 494 U.S. 872 (1990), a much criticized opinion that weakened First Amendment protections for religious conduct. See The Supreme Court, 1992 Term–Comment, The Resurrection of Religious Freedom?, 107 Harv.L.Rev. 118 & 118 n. 3 (1993).

In interpreting art. 46, § 1, we prefer to adhere to the standards of earlier First Amendment jurisprudence, such as we applied in *Alberts v. Devine,* 479 N.E.2d 113 (Mass. 1985), and *Attorney Gen. v. Bailey,* 436 N.E.2d 139 (Mass. 1982). In each opinion, we used the balancing test that the Supreme Court had established under the free exercise of religion clause in *Wisconsin v. Yoder,* 406 U.S. 205, 215–229 (1972), *Sherbert v. Verner,* 374 U.S. 398, 406–409 (1963), and subsequent opinions. * * * By applying the balancing test as we do, we extend protections to the defendants that are at least as great as those of the First Amendment. No further discussion of rights under the First Amendment is, therefore, necessary.

Our tasks are to determine whether the defendants have shown that the prohibition against housing discrimination based on marital status substantially burdens their free exercise of religion, and, if it does, whether the Commonwealth has shown that it has an interest sufficiently compelling to justify that burden. * * *

Because it is unchallenged on the summary judgment record, we must accept that the defendants sincerely believe that their behavior must in all respects conform to their religious beliefs and that, in their view, the operation of rental housing is not independent of those beliefs. Conduct motivated by sincerely held religious convictions will be recognized as the exercise of religion. * * *

The next question is whether the prohibition against discrimination based on marital status substantially burdens the defendants' exercise of their religion. * * * [T]he government has placed a burden on the defendants that makes their exercise of religion more difficult and more costly. The statute affirmatively obliges the defendants to enter into a contract contrary to their religious beliefs and provides significant sanctions for its violation. Moreover, both their nonconformity to the law and any related publicity may stigmatize the defendants in the eyes of many and thus burden the exercise of the defendants' religion. * * *

The fact that the defendants' free exercise of religion claim arises in a commercial context, although relevant when engaging in a balancing of interests, does not mean that their constitutional rights are not substantially burdened. This is not a case in which a claimant is seeking a financial advantage by asserting religious beliefs. * * *

We must, therefore, consider whether the record establishes that the Commonwealth has or does not have an important governmental interest that is sufficiently compelling that the granting of an exemption to people in the position of the defendants would unduly hinder that goal. The general objective of eliminating discrimination of all kinds referred to in the relevant version of § 4(6) ("race, religious creed, color, national origin, sex, age, ancestry or marital status") cannot alone provide a compelling State interest that justifies the application of that section in disregard of the defendants' right to free exercise of their religion. The analysis must be more focused. At the least, the Commonwealth must demonstrate that it has a compelling interest in the elimination of discrimination in housing against an unmarried man and an unmarried woman who have a sexual relationship and wish to rent accommodations to which § 4(6) applies.[8]
* * *

As the motion judge correctly ascertained, marital status discrimination is not as intense a state concern as is discrimination based on certain other classifications. Article 1 of the Massachusetts Declaration of Rights, as amended by art. 106, of the Amendments to the Massachusetts Constitution, states that "[e]quality under the law shall not be denied or abridged because of sex, race, color, creed or national origin." Because there is no constitutionally based prohibition against discriminating on the basis of marital status, marital status discrimination is of a lower order than those discriminations to which art. 1 refers. Moreover, in various ways, by statute[10] and judicial decision,[11] the law has not promoted cohabitation and

---

8. The Commonwealth concedes, and we therefore assume for the purposes of this case, that G.L. c. 151B, § 4, provides an exception from all its coverage for a religious institution and for an organization operated for charitable or educational purposes which is in turn operated by a religious organization. * * *

10. There are numerous statutes granting husbands and wives rights which do not extend to unmarried partners. See, e.g., G.L. c. 152, §§ 31–32 (1992 ed.) (workers' compensation law protecting interests of spouse of worker killed in industrial accident); G.L. c. 175, § 110I (1992 ed.) (providing for continued health insurance coverage for divorced or separated spouses); G.L. c. 175, § 111G (1992 ed.) (extent of family coverage under motor vehicle insurance policy limited to insured, insured's spouse, and unmarried dependent children under twenty-three years of age); G.L. c. 175, § 123 (1992 ed.) (for purposes of section dealing with restrictions on issuance of life insurance policies, "members of a family shall mean husband, wife, children, adopted children, or step-children"); G.L. c. 190, § 1 (1992 ed.) (spouse's right to share of

property not disposed of by will); G.L. c. 191, §§ 15, 16 (1992 ed.) (spouse's right to waiver of will and election of statutory share); G.L. c. 193, § 1 (1992 ed.) (surviving spouse listed first in schedule of persons entitled to appointment to administer intestate's estate); G.L. c. 229, § 1 (1992 ed.) (right of surviving spouse to bring wrongful death action); G.L. c. 233, § 20 (1992 ed.) (spouse's testimony ordinarily inadmissible as to contents of private husband-wife conversation; no marital communication privilege for conversations before marriage or between unmarried partners [see Reep v. Commissioner of the Dep't of Employment & Training, 593 N.E.2d 1297, 1303 (Mass. 1992) (Nolan, J., dissenting)]); G.L. c. 274, § 4 (1992 ed.) (spouse has defense against charge of being an accessory after the fact for harboring, concealing, or assisting spouse before or after spouse perpetrated a felony).

11. Our cases have made clear distinctions between the legal rights of marital and nonmarital partners. See, e.g., Collins v. Guggenheim, 631 N.E.2d 1016, 1017 (Mass. 1994) (long-term cohabitants not entitled to equitable distribution of property); Reep v.

has granted a married spouse rights not granted to a man or woman cohabiting with a member of the opposite sex.

The defendants argue further that G.L. c. 272, § 18 (1992 ed.), presents a public policy consideration that weighs against the interest stated in G.L. c. 151B against discrimination based on marital status. Section 18 makes fornication a crime. This statute is of doubtful constitutionality, at least as applied to the private, consensual conduct of persons over the age of consent. See Commonwealth v. Balthazar, 318 N.E.2d 478, 481 (Mass. 1974). It remains, however, as a criminal statute of the Commonwealth, which suggests some diminution in the strength of the Commonwealth's interest in the elimination of housing discrimination based on marital status.

Without supporting facts in the record or in legislative findings, we are unwilling to conclude that simple enactment of the prohibition against discrimination based on marital status establishes that the State has such a substantial interest in eliminating that form of housing discrimination that, on a balancing test, the substantial burden on the defendants' free exercise of religion must be disregarded. It is no doubt true that many men and women are cohabiting in the Commonwealth and that numbers have increased in the last twenty years. We have no sense, however, of the numbers of rental units that might be withheld from such people because of the religious beliefs of the owners of rental housing. Although the prohibition against discrimination based on marital status was enacted over twenty years ago (St.1973, c. 187), this is the first case of this character that has come to our attention.

We have no indication, beyond the facts of this case, whether the rental housing policies of people such as the defendants can be accommodated, at least in the Turners Falls (Montague) area, without significantly impeding the availability of rental housing for people who are cohabiting or wish to cohabit. Market forces often tend to discourage owners from restricting the class of people to whom they would rent. On the other hand, discrimination of the sort challenged here may present a significant housing problem if a large percentage of units are unavailable to cohabitants. * * *

We are not persuaded on the record that the Commonwealth's interests in the availability of rental housing for cohabiting couples must always prevail over the religion-based practices that people such as the defendants wish to pursue. On the other hand, we cannot say that it is certain that the

missioner of the Dep't of Employment & Training, supra, 593 N.E.2d at 1300–01 (married person who leaves work to join spouse is presumed to have satisfied statutory requirement for unemployment compensation eligibility; long-term nonmarital partner could offer proof toward meeting standard, but without benefit of same presumption); Feliciano v. Rosemar Silver Co., 514 N.E.2d 1095 (Mass. 1987) (nonmarital partners have no right to sue for loss of consortium); Heistand v. Heistand, 423 N.E.2d 313, 316 (Mass. 1981) ("Massachusetts does not recognize common-law marriage"); Davis v. Misiano, 366 N.E.2d 752, 754 (Mass. 1977) (nonmarital partners have no right to separate support and alimony).

Commonwealth could not prove in this case that it has some specific compelling interest that justifies overriding the defendants' interests.

The Commonwealth has the task of establishing that it has a compelling interest in eliminating housing discrimination against cohabiting couples that is strong enough to justify the burden placed on the defendants' exercise of their religion. * * *

The summary judgment record does not establish that there is no disputed material fact bearing on the compelling State interest question. In that circumstance summary judgment is inappropriate. There are factual circumstances that bear on the question, both as to the existence of a general State interest in the elimination of discrimination in housing based on marital status and as to the existence of a particularized State interest in the Turners Falls area. Uniformity of enforcement of the statute may be shown to be the least restrictive means for the practical and efficient operation of the antidiscrimination law. It should be remembered that the task is to balance the State's interests against the nature of the burden on the defendants and that we are concerned here with the business of leasing apartments, not with participation in a formal religious activity. * * *

The judgment for the defendants is vacated, and the case is remanded to the Superior Court for further consideration of the question whether art. 46, § 1, bars application of G.L. c. 151B, § 4, to the defendants in the circumstances of this case.

■ LIACOS, CHIEF JUSTICE (concurring) [omitted].

■ O'CONNOR, JUSTICE (dissenting, with whom NOLAN and LYNCH, JJ., join).

In keeping with their sincerely held religious beliefs, the defendants consider an unmarried couple's living together in a sexual relationship to be an offense against God. Also in keeping with their sincerely held religious beliefs, the defendants consider enabling or assisting another in the commission of an offense against God to be itself an offense against Him. Responding to those religious convictions, and out of respect for the will of God, the defendants refused to rent an apartment to an unmarried couple living in a sexual relationship (cohabiting couple). The court now concludes that an evidentiary hearing—a trial—is required before a determination can be made concerning whether the defendants may lawfully be forced to choose between violating their religiously informed consciences or withdrawing from their commercial endeavors. I disagree. No combination of facts that might be found after a trial would legally justify the imposition of such a choice. * * *

Because the defendants' right to the free exercise of their religion is substantially burdened by the operation of G.L. c. 151B, § 4(6), a matter about which none of the Justices seems to disagree, the Commonwealth would be required at trial to prove that "it has an interest sufficiently compelling to justify that burden." * * * In my view, the defendants have [already] succeeded in that regard. It is clear from the summary judgment materials that the Commonwealth can have no reasonable expectation of sustaining its burden of proving at trial an essential element of its case, which is that the Commonwealth has an interest in ensuring the availability of rental housing for unmarried couples with a sexual relationship—a relationship prohibited by G.L. c. 272, § 18 (1992 ed.)—that outweighs the defendants' interest in conforming their conduct to the will of God without State-imposed penalty.

"[M]arital status discrimination is not as intense a State concern as is discrimination based on certain other classifications." In contrast, the right to free exercise of religion is a fundamental right. Thus, the Commonwealth's interest in accommodating cohabitation cannot possibly outweigh the defendants' interest in conforming their conduct to their religious conviction without penalty * * *

The court states that "[t]here are factual circumstances that bear on the question [balancing of the State's and the defendants' interests], both as to the existence of a general State interest in the elimination of discrimination in housing based on marital status and as to the existence of a particularized State interest in the Turners Falls area." * * *. The court gives no hint of what circumstances could be shown that would permit a reasonable inference that the Commonwealth's interest in eliminating discrimination in housing based on marital status can only be served by punishing landlords for holding fast to the commitments dictated by their religious beliefs. I can envision no such circumstances. * * *

The court should affirm summary judgment for the defendants. If the Massachusetts Constitution is to be effectively amended by giving rights of cohabitation preferred status over an individual's right to live according to his or her religiously-informed conscience, a result I do not recommend, that amendment should be achieved by lawful procedures for constitutional amendment, not by judicial fiat.

NOTES AND QUESTIONS

1. Laws that prohibit discrimination in private (i.e., non-governmental) housing markets can be said to have three objectives or purposes. First, they are designed to increase housing opportunities for persons in the protected classes. If landlords and sellers are free to discriminate based on race, for example, African–Americans and members of other racial minority groups may find that much of the better-maintained units in more sought-after neighborhoods are foreclosed to them, without regard to their ability to pay. Prohibiting discrimination opens up these additional housing opportunities to members of the protected groups. Second, such laws are designed to eliminate the personal harm or indignity suffered by members of protected groups when they are rejected by a landlord or seller on the ground of their status as a member of the group. Third, these laws are designed to eliminate a social message of inferiority or subordination that is communicated to the community at large when landlords and sellers are permitted to discriminate against persons based on their membership in protected groups. The majority in the instant case says that "marital status discrimination is not as intense a state concern as is discrimination based

on certain other classifications." Which of the forgoing three purposes (if any) is less fully implicated by discrimination against unmarried couples relative to, say, discrimination against racial groups?

2.   The majority remands the case because there are "disputed material fact[s] bearing on the compelling State interest question." What exactly are the issues of fact that the majority contemplates will be examined at trial? How do they relate to the above-stated purposes of housing discrimination laws? Suppose the Commonwealth of Massachusetts hires an expert witness who testifies that approximately 10% of the rental housing in the Turner Falls area is owned by people who say, in response to a questionnaire, that they believe cohabitation by unmarried couples is a sin according to their religious beliefs. What follows? Suppose the Desilets hire an expert witness who testifies that 65% of unmarried couples who cohabit eventually get married (to someone, not necessarily their cohabitation partner). What follows? By remanding the issue for further factfinding, is the majority simply ducking a tough normative call, as suggested by the dissenting opinion?

3.   One of the difficulties confronting the court in the principal case is that the Massachusetts legislature has not exactly spoken in a uniform voice on the subject of married versus unmarried couples. The court notes that fornication (intercourse outside marriage) is still a crime in Massachusetts, and footnotes 10 and 11 describe various ways in which Massachusetts law distinguishes—and grants more favored treatment to—married couples. How should a court respond to such mixed signals? One response is to attempt to harmonize the law by construing the inclusion of marital status in the antidiscrimination law in light of this discordance. One such way to harmonize, reflected by the Minnesota Supreme Court in considering a similar dispute, would be to conclude that the legislature must have had something else in mind besides unmarried couples—such as discrimination against persons who are divorced or who are single—when it said discrimination based on marital status was prohibited. See State by Cooper v. French, 460 N.W.2d 2, 7 (Minn. 1990). The court in the principal case adopts a less extreme version of the harmonization strategy, by using the discordance as evidence that "marital status discrimination is not as intense a State concern as is discrimination based on certain other classifications." A third approach would be to conclude that the antidiscrimination measure, as the most recent pronouncement on the subject, represents the true measure of public policy in the state, and that the conflicting elements, as the product of an earlier time, are entitled to little weight as an expression of public policy. Swanner v. Anchorage Equal Rights Comm'n, 874 P.2d 274 (Alaska 1994); Foreman v. Anchorage Equal Rights Com'n, 779 P.2d 1199 (Alaska 1989). What are the strengths and weaknesses of these different approaches to sorting out conflicting signals in the law on an issue like this?

4.   Prior to the enactment of the Fair Housing Act in 1968, regulation of discrimination in housing markets was left largely to state and local governments. This resulted in considerable variation in antidiscrimination

law, enforcement practices, and social norms from one part of the country to another. The 1968 Act represented a major shift in antidiscrimination efforts to the federal level. This meant a movement toward greater uniformity throughout the country in terms of laws, enforcement, and (presumably at least to a degree) social norms. Recent years have seen at least a partial shift back toward more variety in laws and interpretations of laws among states and local governmental units, as the principal case illustrates. As the opinion recounts, Massachusetts prohibits discrimination in housing based on "marital status,"—something not found in the federal Fair Housing Act—but the federal Act does prohibit discrimination based on "familial status," which centers on the parent-child relationship. See Robert G. Schwemm, Housing Discrimination Law 378 (1983). As the opinion also notes, Massachusetts more recently amended its law to prohibit discrimination based on sexual orientation, also not covered by the federal law. In these respects, Massachusetts law enlarges the list of protected groups relative to the federal law—and relative to the law of other states, many of which also do not protect either of these groups. At the same time, the Massachusetts court, in the principal case, declines to follow the lead of the U.S. Supreme Court in limiting the protection of the Free Exercise Clause to laws that single out religious practices for adverse treatment, thereby exempting from constitutional challenge laws that apply in a neutral fashion to religiously-motivated and non-religiously motivated practices. Employment Div., Dep't of Human Resources of Oregon v. Smith, 494 U.S. 872 (1990). Under *Smith*, the landlords in the instant case would presumably lose. This interpretational move gives the version of the free exercise guarantee in the Massachusetts Constitutional a broader application than the Free Exercise Clause in the Federal Constitution, which in turn has the effect of creating a broader religious exercise defense than would be available under federal law, which in turn *reduces* the scope of protection afforded by the Massachusetts housing discrimination statute.

5.   To what extent do you think that this movement toward greater variety in antidiscrimination laws from one part of the country to another is desirable? Is this an example of states and local governments acting as "laboratories of experimentation" for the nation as a whole? Cf. New State Ice Co. v. Liebman, 285 U.S. 262, 311 (1932) (Brandeis, J. dissenting). Or does it simply reflect the reality that antidiscrimination laws have been overtaken by politics, with protections for new categories like disability or sexual orientation depending on the political clout of different groups at different levels of government?

6.   Implicit in the whole enterprise of enacting antidiscrimination laws is that a majority (or at least a dominant political coalition) in the enacting jurisdiction regards discrimination against a particular class or category of persons as wrongful. Thus, not every "discrete and insular" minority will be covered by these laws. For example, persons attempting to recover from drug dependency may qualify for protection under the three general purposes cited in Note 1 above—they could benefit from increased housing opportunities, they may suffer dignitary harm when excluded, and their exclusion is socially stigmatizing—but few if any antidiscrimination laws

explicitly include recovering drug addicts as a protected class (although there have been controversies about whether they are covered as disabled persons). Even more strikingly, persons who have been determined to be sexually dangerous (because of a history of predatory sex crimes) also might qualify under the three purposes listed in Note 1, but they are affirmatively discriminated *against* under so-called "Megan's Laws" that require notification of neighbors when such persons are in the process of considering moving into a community. (The notice presumably mobilizes pressure to keep such persons out of the neighborhood.) So the process of expanding or contracting the list of covered classes entails a collective moral judgment about what types of exclusion are wrongful.

7.   To return again to federalism. The collective moral judgment will differ from one part of the country to another, at least with respect to some contested classes, and the intensity of condemnation of discrimination will differ from one locality to another. In the instant case, it is likely that majorities in some communities in Massachusetts regard discrimination against unmarried couples as wrong, but majorities in other communities do not, and that the intensity of condemnation is relatively low even in areas where it is regarded as wrong. Does this suggest that a more localized approach would be better? For a general argument supporting greater local variation in accommodating different religious beliefs, see Richard C. Schragger, The Role of the Local in the Doctrine and Discourse of Religious Liberty, 117 Harv. L. Rev. 1810 (2004). But localized approaches unquestionably have their drawbacks. If the question whether to prohibit discrimination based on race had been left to state and local governments in the 1960s, as opposed to being federalized, this would have perpetuated racial segregation in the South. Today, laws prohibiting discrimination based on sexual orientation are highly localized, being confined in many states to municipal ordinances in major metropolitan areas. This has probably resulted in more protection for gays and lesbians than would have been possible if antidiscrimination laws could only be enacted at the national or even the state level. But it may also have had the effect of encouraging de facto segregation of gay people in certain urban communities, which may entrench discriminatory attitudes in more rural areas where gay people are less visible. So determining the right level of political jurisdiction at which to select groups for protection under antidiscrimination laws is complicated, to say the least.

C.   OTHER POWERS OF THE SOVEREIGN OWNER

If one thinks of property as a type of sovereignty over designated things, or perhaps as the power to act as the "gatekeeper" of a thing, then it is important not only to be able to exclude other persons from the thing, but also to be able to include other persons in the use and enjoyment of the thing—and perhaps to be able to exclude oneself from the thing as well. In this subchapter, we consider a number of basic powers of inclusion and exclusion that the sovereign owner or gatekeeper typically can exercise beyond the basic right to exclude others. These include: (1) the power to give permission to someone else to gain access to property, generally called a license; (2) the power to transfer temporary custody of property to someone else, known (at least in the context of personal property) as a bailment; (3) the powers to abandon and destroy property; and (4) the power to transfer property to someone else, either by sale or gift. These do not exhaust the elements of owner sovereignty, but we will postpone other attributes, such as the power to determine what happens to property after one's death, to later chapters.

1.   LICENSES

A license can be defined as a "permission slip" from an owner of an asset to another person allowing the latter to gain access to the asset on certain terms. It is, simply put, a waiver of the owner's right to exclude. In general, the term license refers to a waiver of the exclusion right that is temporary and revocable. A classic example of a license would be the owner's permission to a repair person to enter an apartment to fix a broken dishwasher. If the repair person fails to make the repairs properly, or otherwise misbehaves, the owner can revoke the license and ask him to leave. It is also possible to waive the exclusion right by granting someone an interest of greater permanence and security than a license, the most common examples being easements and leases. These more secure and permanent waivers are often called "property rights," and are distinguished from "mere licenses," but as always one must proceed with care in understanding what exactly is meant by these terms in this context.

Marrone v. Washington Jockey Club of the District of Columbia

Supreme Court of the United States, 1913.
227 U.S. 633.

■ MR. JUSTICE HOLMES delivered the opinion of the court: This is an action of trespass for forcibly preventing the plaintiff from entering the Bennings Race Track in this District after he had bought a ticket of admission, and for doing the same thing, or turning him out, on the following day, just after he had dropped his ticket into the box. There was also a count charging that the defendants conspired to destroy the plaintiff's reputation, and that they excluded him on the charge of having "doped" or drugged a horse entered by him for a race a few days before, in pursuance of such conspiracy. But as no evidence of a conspiracy was introduced, and as no more force was used than was necessary to prevent the plaintiff from entering upon the race track, the argument hardly went beyond an attempt to overthrow the rule commonly accepted in this country from the English cases, and adopted below, that such tickets do not create a right *in rem*. * * * Wood v. Leadbitter, 13 Mees. & W. 838, [153 Eng. Rep. 351 (Ex. 1845)]. * * *

We see no reason for declining to follow the commonly accepted rule. The fact that the purchase of the ticket made a contract is not enough. A contract binds the person of the maker, but does not create an interest in the property that it may concern, unless it also operates as a conveyance. The ticket was not a conveyance of an interest in the race track, not only because it was not under seal, but because by common understanding it did not purport to have that effect. There would be obvious inconveniences if it were construed otherwise. But if it did not create such an interest, that is to say, a right *in rem*, valid against the landowner and third persons, the holder had no right to enforce specific performance by self-help. His only right was to sue upon the contract for the breach. It is true that if the contract were incidental to a right of property either in the land or in goods upon the land, there might be an irrevocable right of entry; but when the contract stands by itself, it must be either a conveyance or a license, subject to be revoked.

Judgment affirmed.

NOTES AND QUESTIONS

1. As is often the case with Justice Oliver Wendell Holmes, Jr., there is a lot packed into this brief opinion. The basic point is that the ticket is not a right in rem, that is, a right to a particular thing good against the world. (What if Marrone had leased or purchased a skybox at the race track? Different result?) It is, rather, a contract or license from the owner of a thing. Holmes was a proponent of the view that contracts are promises to perform or else to pay damages. See Oliver Wendell Holmes, The Common Law 236 (Mark De Wolfe Howe ed., 1963) (1881). So he assumes that if the license-contract is breached, the remedy is an action for damages by the licensee against the owner-licensor; the holder of the ticket "had no right to enforce specific performance by self-help."

2. Holmes relies upon *Wood v. Leadbitter*, an influential—but controversial—English case. Wood, the plaintiff, purchased for one guinea a ticket admitting him to the grandstand to watch the Doncaster Races, held on the estate of the Earl of Eglintoun. Without any evidence in the record of misconduct on Wood's part, the Earl had his servant, Leadbitter, take hold of Wood and remove him from the grounds before the conclusion of the races. Wood sued for assault and false imprisonment. In a carefully considered opinion, Baron Alderson discoursed about the distinction between licenses and grants. A license, he said is "by its nature revocable." 153 Eng. Rep. at 354. A license can be made irrevocable only if it is coupled with a grant, and it does not matter whether the interest (license or grant) is given orally or by deed:

> Thus, a license by A. to hunt in his park, whether given by deed or parol, is revocable; it merely renders the act of hunting lawful, which, without the license, would have been unlawful. If the license be . . . a license not only to hunt, but also to take away the deer when killed to his own use, this is in truth a grant of the deer, with a license annexed

to come on the land; and supposing the grant of the deer to be good, then the license would be irrevocable by the party who had given it; he would be estopped from defeating his own grant, or act in the nature of a grant.

Id. at 355. Baron Alderson assumed that the ticket to view the Races was a mere license. As such, it was inherently revocable, and could be revoked by the Earl at any time for any reason. Once the license was rescinded, Wood became a mere trespasser. Thus, the Earl was not guilty of assault and false imprisonment for directing Leadbitter to eject Wood. It appears from the report that Wood did not get his guinea back; but since he did not sue for breach of contract, the question of his entitlement to get the money back or other damages was not discussed.

3.   Holmes goes beyond *Wood v. Leadbitter* in explicitly characterizing the license as a contract. If Marrone had sued for breach of contract, would he have won? If so, what relief would he be entitled to? Return of the price of admission? Lost profits from the bets he intended to place? Holmes says Marrone cannot obtain specific performance by self-help. But what if Marrone is very nimble and gets to court before the race starts? Is he entitled to specific performance of the contract from a judge, that is, to an injunction requiring that the defendant admit him to the park? If so, just what is the difference between a license and a grant?

P   D

Hurst v. Picture Theatres, Limited

Court of Appeal (U.K.), 1914.
[1915] 1 K.B. 1.

The plaintiff sued to recover damages for an alleged assault and false imprisonment.

The plaintiff stated in his evidence that, being attracted by an advertisement announcing that a picture of Lake Garda was being shewn at the defendants' cinema theatre at High Street, Kensington, he went to that theatre on March 17, 1913, for the purpose of seeing it. At the pay office he tendered a florin and asked for a sixpenny seat, and was given a metal check and the change; the check entitled him to an unreserved seat. He gave up his check at the door leading into the theatre, and was shown into a seat by a young woman with an electric torch. After the performance had proceeded for some little time, a girl came up and asked plaintiff if he had come in with a ticket, and, on his replying that he had, the girl went away. Shortly afterwards another girl came up and asked him to come out and see the manager, but he refused. Then a man in evening dress came up and asked him to come and see the manager, but he again refused. Then the manager himself came up and asked the plaintiff to come outside, and, on his refusing, said "Then we shall have to compel you." A porter or doorkeeper, who was sent by the manager, then asked the plaintiff to go out, which he refused to do. The porter went out and returned with a policeman, whom he asked to put the plaintiff out. This the policeman refused to do, suggesting that the porter should do it himself. The porter then made his way into the row of seats and, taking hold of the plaintiff under the arms, lifted him out of his seat. The plaintiff then walked quietly out. No unnecessary violence was used in thus ejecting the plaintiff.

The defendants justified their conduct on the ground that the plaintiff had not taken a ticket for that performance. They also contended that they were entitled, without assigning any reason, to call on the plaintiff to leave the theatre and, if he declined, to forcibly remove him, relying on the authority of *Wood v. Leadbitter*, 13 M. & W. 838 (Ex. 1845).

Channell J. was of opinion that *Wood v. Leadbitter* was no longer good law, and held that a visitor to a theatre who had paid for his seat had a right to retain his seat so long as the performance lasted, provided he behaved quietly and complied with the regulations laid down by the management. He left to the jury the question whether the plaintiff had paid for his seat, and the jury found that he had, and assessed the damages at 150 £.

[handwritten left margin: not relevant to main issue of law]

The defendants appealed. * * *

■ BUCKLEY L.J. We have listened in this case to a very ingenious and interesting argument from Mr. Mackinnon, but, if I may borrow the words of Lord Esher in *Butler v. Manchester, Sheffield and Lincolnshire Railway*, 21 Q. B. D. 207, 211 (Q.B. 1888), it may have been quite right for the appellants' counsel to suggest the point, but when considered it is contrary to good sense. I may add that I think it is not only contrary to good sense, but contrary also to good law as administered since the Judicature Act in this Court. The proposition which Mr. Mackinnon sets out to affirm is that if a man has paid for his seat at the opera, or the theatre, and has entered and taken his seat, and is behaving himself quite properly, it is competent to the proprietors of the theatre, merely because they choose so to do, to call upon him to withdraw before he has seen the performance for the enjoyment of which he has paid; that what he has obtained for his money is a mere revocable licence to come upon the land of the proprietor of the theatre, and that the proprietor may, simply because he chooses, say "I revoke your licence; go." If that proposition be true, it involves startling results. Kennedy L.J. has suggested one [at oral argument]. Suppose that there be sitting in the stalls a man who is a constant patron of the opera or the theatre, to whom the management pay great deference, whether from his rank or his habit of attendance: he goes to the management and says, "I do not like the person sitting in front of me or next to me; ask him to go." It would be competent to the management to go to that person and say, "Please go; you cannot have your money back, go." Further, if the proposition is right, it follows that, having let the seat to A., the management may come to A. at the end of the first act or before and say, "I revoke your licence, go," and he has to go. The management may let the seat to B. for the rest of the performance, and at the end of the second act or sooner they may come to B. and say, "I revoke your licence, go." He will have to go, and they may let the seat a third time to C. Those consequences ensue from this proposition if it be well founded. It was for that reason I said at the outset of my remarks that it seems to me, when the point comes to be considered, it is contrary to good sense.

Next it is to my mind contrary also to good law. The proposition is based upon the well-known decision in *Wood v. Leadbitter*. Let me at the outset say what *Wood v. Leadbitter* seems to me to have decided. It affirmed that a mere licence, whether or not it be under seal, by which I mean a licence not coupled with an interest or a grant whether it be under seal or not, is revocable. It affirmed also that if there be a licence coupled with an interest or coupled with a grant, it is not, or at any rate in general is not, revocable. * * * Those are propositions with which, as it seems to me, no one quarrels or can quarrel. *Wood v. Leadbitter* rested, I think, upon one of two grounds. * * * The first ground is that the man who bought his ticket for the race meeting had not obtained any grant of the right to come during the currency of the meeting to see any particular spectacle from its commencement to its termination. If that were the ground, it would, I think, be erroneous. I conceive he had the right to see what was to be seen during the days covered by his ticket. But I do not think that was the ground on which the Court decided it. They decided it upon the ground, which will be found at p. 842 and onwards, that no incorporeal inheritance affecting land can be created or transferred otherwise than by deed, a proposition which was discussed with some elaboration in the course of the judgment. What Alderson B. was saying there was: this man has got no deed; he has got nothing under seal; he has therefore not got a grant; he cannot in this Court be heard to say he is a grantee, and because he is not a grantee he is a mere licensee, and being a mere licensee (whether it is under seal or not under seal does not make any difference) the licence is revocable.

Let me for a moment discuss this present case upon the footing that *Wood v. Leadbitter* stands as good law at this date. I am going to say presently that to my mind it does not, but suppose it does stand as good law at this date. What is the grant in this case? The plaintiff in the present action paid his money to enjoy the sight of a particular spectacle. He was anxious to go into a picture theatre to see a series of views or pictures during, I suppose, an hour or a couple of hours. That which was granted to him was the right to enjoy looking at a spectacle, to attend a performance from its beginning to its end. That which was called the licence, the right to go upon the premises, was only something granted to him for the purpose of enabling him to have that which had been granted him, namely, the right to see. He could not see the performance unless he went into the building. His right to go into the building was something given to him in order to enable him to have the benefit of that which had been granted to him, namely, the right to hear the opera, or see the theatrical performance, or see the moving pictures as was the case here. So that here there was a licence coupled with a grant. If so, *Wood v. Leadbitter* does not stand in the way at all. A licence coupled with a grant is not revocable; *Wood v. Leadbitter* affirmed as much.

[handwritten margin notes:]

RULE

Similar to a movie or theatre show w/ a defined start-finish time (as opposed to an indefinite day of races)

Interest is in the access to the land, which a mere license w/out a deed, can not grant, thus license is revocable

— 1st ground from above

So far I have been treating it as if *Wood v. Leadbitter* were law as now administered in every Court. Let us see how that matter stands. *Wood v. Leadbitter* was a case decided in a Court of law before the Judicature Act; it was a case to be decided, therefore, simply upon the principles which are applicable in a Court of law as distinguished from a Court of Equity. * * * The position of matters now is that the Court is bound under the Judicature Act to give effect to equitable doctrines. The question we have to consider is whether, having regard to equitable considerations, *Wood v. Leadbitter* is now law, meaning that *Wood v. Leadbitter* is a decision which can be applied in its integrity in a Court which is bound to give effect to equitable considerations. In my opinion, it is not. * * * The present Lord Parker, then Parker J., in the case of *Jones v. Earl of Tankerville* says this ([1909] 2 Ch. 440, at p. 443.): "An injunction restraining the revocation of the licence, when it is revocable at law, may in a sense be called relief by way of specific performance, but it is not specific performance in the sense of compelling the vendor to do anything. It merely prevents him from breaking his contract, and protects a right in equity which but for the absence of a seal would be a right at law, and since the Judicature Act it may well be doubted whether the absence of a seal in such a case can be relied on in any Court." What was relied on in *Wood v. Leadbitter*, and rightly relied on at that date, was that there was not an instrument under seal, and therefore there was not a grant, and therefore the licensee could not say that he was not a mere licensee, but a licensee with a grant. That is now swept away. It cannot be said as against the plaintiff that he is a licensee with no grant merely because there is not an instrument under seal which gives him a right at law.

RULE (under equity)

There is another way in which the matter may be put. If there be a licence with an agreement not to revoke the licence, that, if given for value, is an enforceable right. If the facts here are, as I think they are, that the licence was a licence to enter the building and see the spectacle from its commencement until its termination, then there was included in that contract a contract not to revoke the licence until the play had run to its termination. It was then a breach of contract to revoke the obligation not to revoke the licence * * *

I will say a few words as to what were the facts in this case. The plaintiff entered this picture theatre and paid 6d. for his admission. The defendants denied that he had paid, and that was the question for the jury in the case. The jury have given the plaintiff a verdict; they have found that he did pay this 6d., and that fact is not now in contest before us. * * * The defendants had, I think, for value contracted that the plaintiff should see a certain spectacle from its commencement to its termination. They broke that contract and it was a tort on their part to remove him. They committed an assault upon him in law. It was not of a violent kind, because, like a wise man, the plaintiff gave way to superior force and left the theatre. They sought to justify the assault by saying that they were entitled to remove him because he had not paid. He had paid, the jury have so found. Failing on that question of fact, they say that they were entitled to remove him because his licence was revocable. In my opinion, it was not.

There was, I think, no justification for the assault here committed. Under the circumstances it was for the jury to give him such a sum as was right for the assault which was committed upon him, and for the serious indignity to a gentleman of being seized and treated in this way in a place of public resort. The jury have found that he was originally in the theatre as a spectator, that the assault was committed upon him, and that it was a wrongful act.

I think that the appeal which has been brought before us, and which is founded simply upon the question of law which I have discussed at the beginning of this judgment, fails and must be dismissed with costs.

■ KENNEDY L.J. I am of the same opinion. * * * [The balance of the opinion is omitted.]

■ PHILLIMORE L.J. All one's sympathy in this case must be for the plaintiff, and if he had failed in getting his judgment for the sum given to him by the jury for the unjustifiable assault, I should have thought at any rate he ought to have had judgment for his 6d., and very properly, as the issue which was raised reflected upon his character, with costs * * * But one must not allow one's sympathy for him to make one decide that which one does not think good law. Although I express my opinion with the very greatest diffidence, and put it as will be seen later in the nature of doubts, more as if the matter were non-proven than as a decision, I still feel bound to express those doubts. * * *

With regard to the results which are supposed to flow from an opposite conclusion, I can only say that if people are impracticable and unbusiness-like, very serious results would flow in either direction. Certainly I should advise the owners of places of entertainment, and still more the owners of picture theatres who have not the remedy of refusing to continue the performance if a person is impracticable, to put conditions upon their tickets in future.

DICTA
(Dissenting)

Now I start by saying that I think the circumstances in this case make it indistinguishable from *Wood v. Leadbitter* * * *

The equity cases—I am speaking of the equity cases before the Judicature Act—do not, in my opinion, detract in any way from *Wood v. Leadbitter*. All the cases which have been cited relate to an interest given in land, and the whole point of the decision in *Wood v. Leadbitter* was that the grant of the ticket there gives no interest in land, but only a licence,—it matters not whether by deed or otherwise—all licences, whether by deed or otherwise, being at law revocable. * * *

[H]as the Judicature Act made a difference? If it was a grant of an interest in land, yes. If it was not a grant of an interest in land, no. * * * Assume * * * that there was a contract, and assume that the purported revocation was a breach of the contract, and assume that of which I am not certain, that equity would give specific performance of such a contract, still specific performance does not necessarily put the man before he has got specific performance in the legal possession which he gets after he has got specific performance. It does in the case of interests in land because the interest in land now is the interest which he had in equity before. But it does not necessarily do so with regard to interests arising by reason of a contract. * * * Collins J. in *Kerrison v. Smith*, [1897] 2 Q. B. 445, puts it in this way: "It was conceded that the grantor has a right to revoke a licence, but the point set up by the plaintiff, that there was a contract, for the breach of which the plaintiff was entitled to recover damages, was never properly dealt with. There appears to be no case in which the point has been specifically raised and decided, as to whether there is a right to maintain an action for breach of contract, if a licence is revoked, although there is a right to revoke the licence, but on principle it seems to me that the two rights are compatible with one another." That is to say the licence can be revoked, in which case the man becomes a trespasser if he stays on, but nevertheless there may be a contract for which the man may recover damages. I do not say myself that is necessarily sound law; that is the view taken by Collins J. Then at the end of his judgment he quotes Clerk and Lindsell: "Such a licence, even though it may have been made by deed and for valuable consideration, is revocable at any time by the licensor; the licensee cannot after revocation justify entering upon the land for the purpose of using the privilege; his only remedy against his licensor, where the revocation is wrongful, is upon the contract." Sir Frederick Pollock is even more explicit at p. 390: "The revocation of a licence is in itself no less effectual, though it may be a breach of contract. If the owner of land or a building admits people thereto on payment, as spectators of an entertainment or the like, it may be a breach of contract to require a person who has duly paid his money and entered to go out, but a person so required has no title to stay, and if he persists in staying he is a trespasser. His only right is to sue on the contract, as he clearly may do where a contract exists: when, indeed, he may get an injunction and so be indirectly restored to the enjoyment of the licence." I just repeat some words for particular reasons: "but a person so required has no title to stay, and if he persists in staying, is a trespasser." That is the issue to be determined in this case. The action is for assault, and the defence is: "You were a trespasser; you had a warning to go, and I removed you, using no more force than necessary." The question is whether the man was a trespasser. Therefore it does not follow, because specific performance could be obtained of the contract, that till the contract has been specifically performed the man has the rights which he will get when the contract has been given specific performance.

However, there is a possible view of this case which may not make it necessary to take that view. I am not at all sure (here I think I differ from Collins J.) that the real construction of the case of *Wood v. Leadbitter* is not that the contract is not that which people think it was. I am not at all sure that the contract must not be said to be this: "I cannot grant you a licence because I cannot bind myself not to make it revocable, not even if I do so by deed; therefore I do not because the law does not allow me to do so. The real contract is this, in consideration of such a sum of pounds, shillings, and pence I give you a licence to enter my close and to remain there during a certain entertainment. If I revoke the licence for other than good cause, I will repay you the money you have paid." I put carefully "during the entertainment"; I think, unless the licensor lets the man stop until the end, he must return him all his money, and I throw out for consideration whether the real virtue of the decision in *Wood v. Leadbitter* is not that this is the nature of this contract. However that may be, not being able to distinguish this case from *Wood v. Leadbitter*, and thinking *Wood v. Leadbitter* was and remains good law, and thinking that the equity doctrines do not affect it, I am obliged to come to the conclusion, which I have tried to express with clearness, and I hope to be considered to express with diffidence, that my present view, unaided by further discussion, is that the appeal ought to be allowed.

Appeal dismissed.

NOTES AND QUESTIONS

1. The judges in *Hurst* can be said to disagree at several levels. First and most fundamentally, they appear to disagree about the nature of the rights conferred by the purchase of a ticket to see a motion picture. Judges Buckley and Kennedy seem to think that the ticket is itself a license, and hence the rights conferred by the ticket (explicitly or implicitly) define the terms of the license. Judge Phillimore, adhering to *Wood v. Leadbitter*, seems to think that a license is a kind of special interest in land—one that by its nature is always revocable—and that the ticket is a contract separate and distinct from the license. Second, Judges Buckley and Kennedy seem to think that the license/contract is a promise that the patron may enter the theater and remain there until the show is over. Judge Phillimore says that the contract, regarded as a promise distinct from the license, provides that the patron may enter the theater and remain there until the show is over, or get her money back. Third, the judges disagree about the implications of the merger of law and equity by the Judicature Act. Buckley and Kennedy think that *Wood v. Leadbitter* is no longer good law, because it was decided by a law court before the merger of law and equity. After the merger, a law court would be entitled to award specific performance of the license/contract reflected in a movie ticket. That being the case, the owner of the theater cannot evict a patron with a ticket without committing an assault. Phillimore is doubtful about whether specific performance is available in these circumstances. More fundamentally, he argues that until the patron gets the judgment of specific performance, he can still be removed. The license can always be revoked, and if the license is revoked the patron becomes a trespasser, and as such can be removed.

2. Is the path out of this confusion simply to start with the proposition that a license is a contract—an in personam agreement between the owner of a thing and the licensee granting permission to use the thing? Being contracts, licenses can be either oral or written. The default construction of the contract is that it is revocable at will. But, as in the case of other contracts, the parties can agree to modify the default understanding. (See Phillimore's comments advising theater owners to put "conditions upon their tickets in future.") One way the parties can modify the default

[handwritten margin note:] Good summary of Majority (Buckley & Kennedy) vs. Dissent (Phillimore)

understanding is by making the license irrevocable for a certain period of time. The key question in the case, from this perspective, is whether the contract reflected in the little metal disk given to Hurst in return for 6d. is implicitly irrevocable for the duration of the showing of the picture. (How should this question be resolved?) Once we think of a license as a contract, the remedies question also becomes easy. Hurst is entitled to whatever remedies he would be entitled to for breach of contract—including damages for assault and battery if it can be shown that he was contractually entitled to remain in the theater until the show was over. Specific performance of the contract might also be available (if this were practicable), provided Hurst could show that his damages remedies are inadequate and that he would suffer irreparable harm without an award of specific performance. See Baker v. Hunt Club, Chapter I. On this view, a license is not a property right, regardless whether it is oral, written, or embodied in a piece of paper called a deed, because it confers no rights on the licensee that are in rem, or good against the world. The only rights conferred by a license are personal as between the licensor and the licensee.

3.   If we think of licenses simply as in personam contracts, what is the correct way to think about a license coupled with an interest or a grant, such as the license to hunt deer discussed in *Wood v. Leadbitter*? What about a license that has been declared irrevocable by a court of equity because of the licensee's detrimental reliance on a misrepresentation by the licensor (see Holbrook v. Taylor, Chapter IX)?

Figure 4–3
Plaque in the Sidewalk at Rockefeller Center, New York City

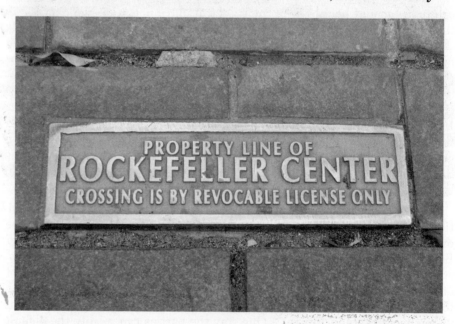

4.   Commentary about licenses in land is rather out of date. For older work that comes close to penetrating through the confusion, see Charles E. Clark, Licenses in Real Property Law, 21 Colum L. Rev. 757 (1921); Alfred F. Conard, An Analysis of Licenses in Land, 42 Colum. L. Rev. 809 (1942); Wesley Newcomb Hohfeld, Faulty Analysis in Easement and License Cases, 27 Yale L.J. 66 (1917).

ProCD, Inc. v. Zeidenberg

United States Court of Appeals, Seventh Circuit, 1996.
86 F.3d 1447.

■ EASTERBROOK, CIRCUIT JUDGE. Must buyers of computer software obey the terms of shrinkwrap licenses? The district court held not, for two reasons: first, they are not contracts because the licenses are inside the box rather than printed on the outside; second, federal law forbids enforcement even if the licenses are contracts. The parties and numerous amici curiae have briefed many other issues, but these are the only two that matter—and we disagree with the district judge's conclusion on each. Shrinkwrap licenses are enforceable unless their terms are objectionable on grounds applicable to contracts in general (for example, if they violate a rule of positive law, or if they are unconscionable). Because no one argues that the terms of the license at issue here are troublesome, we remand with instructions to enter judgment for the plaintiff.

I

ProCD, the plaintiff, has compiled information from more than 3,000 telephone directories into a computer database. We may assume that this database cannot be copyrighted, although it is more complex, contains more information (nine-digit zip codes and census industrial codes), is organized differently, and therefore is more original than the single alphabetical directory at issue in *Feist Publications, Inc. v. Rural Telephone Service Co.*, 499 U.S. 340 (1991). See Paul J. Heald, The Vices of Originality, 1991 Sup.Ct. Rev. 143, 160–68. ProCD sells a version of the database, called SelectPhone (trademark), on CD–ROM discs. (CD–ROM means "compact disc–read only memory." The "shrinkwrap license" gets its name from the fact that retail software packages are covered in plastic or cellophane "shrinkwrap," and some vendors, though not ProCD, have written licenses that become effective as soon as the customer tears the wrapping from the package. Vendors prefer "end user license," but we use the more common term.) A proprietary method of compressing the data serves as effective encryption too. Customers decrypt and use the data with the aid of an application program that ProCD has written. This program, which is copyrighted, searches the database in response to users' criteria (such as "find all people named Tatum in Tennessee, plus all firms with 'Door Systems' in the corporate name"). The resulting lists (or, as ProCD prefers, "listings") can be read and manipulated by other software, such as word processing programs.

The database in SelectPhone (trademark) cost more than $10 million to compile and is expensive to keep current. It is much more valuable to some users than to others. The combination of names, addresses, and SIC

[Standard Industrial Classification] codes enables manufacturers to compile lists of potential customers. Manufacturers and retailers pay high prices to specialized information intermediaries for such mailing lists; ProCD offers a potentially cheaper alternative. People with nothing to sell could use the database as a substitute for calling long distance information, or as a way to look up old friends who have moved to unknown towns, or just as an electronic substitute for the local phone book. ProCD decided to engage in price discrimination, selling its database to the general public for personal use at a low price (approximately $150 for the set of five discs) while selling information to the trade for a higher price. It has adopted some intermediate strategies too: access to the SelectPhone (trademark) database is available via the America Online service for the price America Online charges to its clients (approximately $3 per hour), but this service has been tailored to be useful only to the general public.

If ProCD had to recover all of its costs and make a profit by charging a single price—that is, if it could not charge more to commercial users than to the general public—it would have to raise the price substantially over $150. The ensuing reduction in sales would harm consumers who value the information at, say, $200. They get consumer surplus of $50 under the current arrangement but would cease to buy if the price rose substantially. If because of high elasticity of demand in the consumer segment of the market the only way to make a profit turned out to be a price attractive to commercial users alone, then all consumers would lose out—and so would the commercial clients, who would have to pay more for the listings because ProCD could not obtain any contribution toward costs from the consumer market.

To make price discrimination work, however, the seller must be able to control arbitrage. An air carrier sells tickets for less to vacationers than to business travelers, using advance purchase and Saturday-night-stay requirements to distinguish the categories. A producer of movies segments the market by time, releasing first to theaters, then to pay-per-view services, next to the videotape and laserdisc market, and finally to cable and commercial tv. Vendors of computer software have a harder task. Anyone can walk into a retail store and buy a box. Customers do not wear tags saying "commercial user" or "consumer user." Anyway, even a commercial-user-detector at the door would not work, because a consumer could buy the software and resell to a commercial user. That arbitrage would break down the price discrimination and drive up the minimum price at which ProCD would sell to anyone.

Instead of tinkering with the product and letting users sort themselves—for example, furnishing current data at a high price that would be attractive only to commercial customers, and two-year-old data at a low price—ProCD turned to the institution of contract. Every box containing its consumer product declares that the software comes with restrictions stated in an enclosed license. This license, which is encoded on the CD-ROM disks as well as printed in the manual, and which appears on a user's screen every time the software runs, limits use of the application program and listings to non-commercial purposes.

Matthew Zeidenberg bought a consumer package of SelectPhone (trademark) in 1994 from a retail outlet in Madison, Wisconsin, but decided to ignore the license. He formed Silken Mountain Web Services, Inc., to resell the information in the SelectPhone (trademark) database. The corporation makes the database available on the Internet to anyone willing to pay its price—which, needless to say, is less than ProCD charges its commercial customers. Zeidenberg has purchased two additional Select-Phone (trademark) packages, each with an updated version of the database, and made the latest information available over the World Wide Web, for a price, through his corporation. ProCD filed this suit seeking an injunction against further dissemination that exceeds the rights specified in the licenses (identical in each of the three packages Zeidenberg purchased). The district court held the licenses ineffectual because their terms do not appear on the outside of the packages. The court added that the second and third licenses stand no different from the first, even though they are identical, because they might have been different, and a purchaser does not agree to—and cannot be bound by—terms that were secret at the time of purchase.

II

Following the district court, we treat the licenses as ordinary contracts accompanying the sale of products, and therefore as governed by the common law of contracts and the Uniform Commercial Code. Whether there are legal differences between "contracts" and "licenses" (which may matter under the copyright doctrine of first sale) is a subject for another day. See Microsoft Corp. v. Harmony Computers & Electronics, Inc., 846 F.Supp. 208 (E.D.N.Y. 1994). * * * Zeidenberg [argues], and the district court held, that placing the package of software on the shelf is an "offer," which the customer "accepts" by paying the asking price and leaving the store with the goods. Peeters v. State, 142 N.W. 181 (Wis. 1913). In Wisconsin, as elsewhere, a contract includes only the terms on which the parties have agreed. One cannot agree to hidden terms, the judge concluded. So far, so good—but one of the terms to which Zeidenberg agreed by purchasing the software is that the transaction was subject to a license. Zeidenberg's position therefore must be that the printed terms on the outside of a box are the parties' contract—except for printed terms that refer to or incorporate other terms. But why would Wisconsin fetter the parties' choice in this way? Vendors can put the entire terms of a contract on the outside of a box only by using microscopic type, removing other information that buyers might find more useful (such as what the software does, and on which computers it works), or both. The "Read Me" file included with most software, describing system requirements and potential incompatibilities, may be equivalent to ten pages of type; warranties and license restrictions take still more space. Notice on the outside, terms on the inside, and a right to return the software for a refund if the terms are unacceptable (a right that the license expressly extends), may be a means of doing business valuable to buyers and sellers alike. See E. Allan Farnsworth, 1 Farnsworth on Contracts § 4.26 (1990); Restatement (2d) of Contracts § 211 comment a (1981) ("Standardization of agreements serves many of the same functions as standardization of goods and services; both are essential to a system of mass production and distribution. Scarce and costly time and skill can be devoted to a class of transactions rather than the details of individual transactions."). Doubtless a state could forbid the use of standard contracts in the software business, but we do not think that Wisconsin has done so.

Transactions in which the exchange of money precedes the communication of detailed terms are common. * * * [C]onsider the purchase of an airline ticket. The traveler calls the carrier or an agent, is quoted a price, reserves a seat, pays, and gets a ticket, in that order. The ticket contains elaborate terms, which the traveler can reject by canceling the reservation. To use the ticket is to accept the terms, even terms that in retrospect are disadvantageous. See Carnival Cruise Lines, Inc. v. Shute, 499 U.S. 585 (1991). Just so with a ticket to a concert. The back of the ticket states that the patron promises not to record the concert; to attend is to agree. A theater that detects a violation will confiscate the tape and escort the violator to the exit. One could arrange things so that every concertgoer signs this promise before forking over the money, but that cumbersome way of doing things not only would lengthen queues and raise prices but also would scotch the sale of tickets by phone or electronic data service. * * *

III

The district court held that, even if Wisconsin treats shrinkwrap licenses as contracts, § 301(a) of the Copyright Act, 17 U.S.C. § 301(a), prevents their enforcement. The relevant part of § 301(a) preempts any "legal or equitable rights [under state law] that are equivalent to any of the exclusive rights within the general scope of copyright as specified by section 106 in works of authorship that are fixed in a tangible medium of expression and come within the subject matter of copyright as specified by sections 102 and 103". ProCD's software and data are "fixed in a tangible medium of expression", and the district judge held that they are "within the subject matter of copyright". The latter conclusion is plainly right for the copyrighted application program, and the judge thought that the data likewise are "within the subject matter of copyright" even if, after *Feist*, they are not sufficiently original to be copyrighted. One function of § 301(a) is to prevent states from giving special protection to works of authorship that Congress has decided should be in the public domain, which it can accomplish only if "subject matter of copyright" includes all works of a type covered by sections 102 and 103, even if federal law does not afford protection to them. Cf. Bonito Boats, Inc. v. Thunder Craft Boats, Inc., 489 U.S. 141 (1989) (same principle under patent laws).

But are rights created by contract "equivalent to any of the exclusive rights within the general scope of copyright"? Three courts of appeals have answered "no." National Car Rental System, Inc. v. Computer Associates International, Inc., 991 F.2d 426, 433 (8th Cir. 1993); Taquino v. Teledyne Monarch Rubber, 893 F.2d 1488, 1501 (5th Cir. 1990); Acorn Structures, Inc. v. Swantz, 846 F.2d 923, 926 (4th Cir. 1988). The district court disagreed with these decisions, but we think them sound. Rights "equivalent to any of the exclusive rights within the general scope of copyright" are rights established by *law*—rights that restrict the options of persons who are strangers to the author. Copyright law forbids duplication, public performance, and so on, unless the person wishing to copy or perform the work gets permission; silence means a ban on copying. A copyright is a right against the world. Contracts, by contrast, generally affect only their parties; strangers may do as they please, so contracts do not create "exclusive rights." Someone who found a copy of SelectPhone (trademark) on the street would not be affected by the shrinkwrap license—though the federal copyright laws of their own force would limit the finder's ability to copy or transmit the application program.

Think for a moment about * * * everyday transactions in intellectual property. A customer visits a video store and rents a copy of *Night of the Lepus*. The customer's contract with the store limits use of the tape to home viewing and requires its return in two days. May the customer keep the tape, on the ground that § 301(a) makes the promise unenforceable?

A law student uses the LEXIS database, containing public-domain documents, under a contract limiting the results to educational endeavors; may the student resell his access to this database to a law firm from which LEXIS seeks to collect a much higher hourly rate? * * * Everyone remains free to copy and disseminate all 3,000 telephone books that have been incorporated into ProCD's database. Anyone can add SIC codes and zip codes. ProCD's rivals have done so. Enforcement of the shrinkwrap license may even make information more readily available, by reducing the price ProCD charges to consumer buyers. * * * Licenses may have other benefits for consumers: many licenses permit users to make extra copies, to use the software on multiple computers, even to incorporate the software into the user's products. But whether a particular license is generous or restrictive, a simple two-party contract is not "equivalent to any of the exclusive rights within the general scope of copyright" and therefore may be enforced.

REVERSED AND REMANDED.

NOTES AND QUESTIONS

1. As *ProCD* suggests, license agreements are extremely important in the world of intellectual property. Judge Easterbrook says that there may be some differences between licenses and contracts, but he leaves that for another day, and proceeds to treat a software license exactly like a contract. This is in keeping with the treatment of licenses in intellectual property law more generally. The use of licenses with intellectual property goes far beyond computer software. Consider, for example, the agreements by which firms like McDonald's or Coca–Cola license franchisees and distributors to

use their trademarks and trade names, or by which the producers of commercial movies license the distribution of videos and DVDs made from the movie, or by which the owners of patents license producing firms to use the patented inventions in furnishing various products and services.

2. Suppose the software is protected by a patent, having a term ending 20 years from the date of the filing of the patent application. The shrinkwrap license, which everyone who buys the software must agree to, provides that the purchaser promises not to allow anyone else to use the software, without the patent owner's express written permission, for 40 years. Has the device of the shrinkwrap license here been used effectively to amend the scope of monopoly protection given by the patent laws? The Supreme Court has made confusing pronouncements on this subject. Compare Brulotte v. Thys Co., 379 U.S. 29 (1964) (holding that the Patent Act preempts enforcement of contract providing for royalties that continue to accrue after the last of the patents incorporated into the machines in question expired) with Aronson v. Quick Point Pencil Co., 440 U.S. 257 (1979) (no preemption where agreement provided for reduced royalty in the event that inventor failed to get a patent). What is the difference between a property right to information, which binds the whole world, and a shrinkwrap license, which binds everyone who uses the information?

3. Some have expressed dismay at the degree of control that content providers can achieve through contractual restrictions and various technological measures, collectively known as Digital Rights Management, such as built-in software that automatically terminates access after a number of uses or after a set period of time. In what sense do these devices "propertize" information? Compare Julie E. Cohen, DRM and Privacy, 18 Berkeley Tech. L.J. 575 (2003); Dan Burk & Julie Cohen, Fair Use Infrastructure for Rights Management Systems, 15 Harv. J.L. & Tech. 41 (2001) with David Friedman, In Defense of Private Orderings: Comments on Julie Cohen's "Copyright and the Jurisprudence of Self–Help", 13 Berkeley Tech. L.J. 1151 (1998).

4. What if, in Judge Easterbrook's hypothetical about the software that someone dropped and another picked up off the sidewalk, one has to click past an agreement screen every time one launches the program? If consideration is the problem, assume that every time the agreement page is clicked a small payment is transferred via the Internet to the software provider. In what sense is the contract right in such a situation different from an in rem property right?

5. The rise of cyberspace has led to some creative uses of licenses. Consider "virtual worlds," in which people, through online characters called "avatars," can take various actions, interact with others, and acquire "virtual property." A Pennsylvania attorney has recently filed a complaint against the owners of one notable virtual world, Second Life (hosted at http://secondlife.com), for confiscating his virtual property after he had objected to their unwinding a virtual land transaction of his and not providing a refund of the $300 he had paid for the virtual land. The complaint alleges that the defendants then "stole" all of his virtual

belongings including $2000 of virtual cash. (Each day more than $250,000 of transfers are made in Second Life, among its population of more than 800,000.) The complaint sounds, inter alia, in fraud and breach of contract but also asserts that the virtual property has the features of property and draws parallels to the uniqueness of land in real property (making it virtual real property?). The defendants hold intellectual property rights in the game and claim to be merely licensing game participants. See Virtual Land Lawsuit Reveals Dark Side of Second Life, http://news.findlaw.com/prnewswire/20061006/06oct20061034.html. How would you characterize the legal relationship between game hosts and gamers? Should there be limits to what game owners can do with licenses?

2. BAILMENTS

A bailment arises when the owner of property (the bailor) temporarily transfers custody of the property to another (the bailee). Usually a bailment is created by a contract, express or implied, and the parties have some special purpose in mind that requires the transfer of possession of particular property; after this purpose is accomplished, it is understood that the property will be returned to the owner (the bailor). Familiar examples of bailments include the transfer of clothing to a dry cleaning shop for cleaning, the transfer of securities to a broker for safekeeping, or the transfer of an automobile to a valet for parking. Because the bailment relationship is usually created by contract, the respective rights and duties of the bailor and bailee have a strong contractual element, and can be modified by agreement of the parties. But because the essence of the bailment contract is the transfer of custody of property, some of the bailor's rights associated with ownership—most notably the right to exclude others from the owned thing—are also transferred to the bailee. Thus, insofar as third parties are concerned, the bailee's rights with respect to the thing are similar to those of an owner. This blending of contractual (in personam) and property (in rem) elements makes for some difficult and interesting complications in bailment law.

P, appellee   *D*

Allen v. Hyatt Regency—Nashville Hotel → *appellant*

Supreme Court of Tennessee, 1984.
668 S.W.2d 286.

■ HARBISON, JUSTICE. In this case the Court is asked to consider the nature and extent of the liability of the operator of a commercial parking garage for theft of a vehicle during the absence of the owner. Both courts below, on the basis of prior decisions from this state, held that a bailment was created when the owner parked and locked his vehicle in a modern, indoor, multi-story garage operated by appellant in conjunction with a large hotel in downtown Nashville. We affirm.

There is almost no dispute as to the relevant facts. Appellant is the owner and operator of a modern high-rise hotel in Nashville fronting on the south side of Union Street. Immediately to the rear, or south, of the main hotel building there is a multi-story parking garage with a single entrance and a single exit to the west, on Seventh Avenue, North. As one enters the parking garage at the street level, there is a large sign reading "Welcome to Hyatt Regency–Nashville." There is another Hyatt Regency sign inside the garage at street level, together with a sign marked "Parking." The garage is available for parking by members of the general public as well as guests of the hotel, and the public are invited to utilize it.

On the morning of February 12, 1981, appellee's husband, Edwin Allen, accompanied by two passengers, drove appellee's new 1981 automobile into the parking garage. Neither Mr. Allen nor his passengers intended to register at the hotel as a guest. Mr. Allen had parked in this particular garage on several occasions, however, testifying that he felt that the vehicle would be safer in an attended garage than in an unattended outside lot on the street.

The single entrance was controlled by a ticket machine. The single exit was controlled by an attendant in a booth just opposite to the entrance and in full view thereof. Appellee's husband entered the garage at the street level and took a ticket which was automatically dispensed by the machine. The machine activated a barrier gate which rose and permitted Mr. Allen to enter the garage. He drove to the fourth floor level, parked the vehicle, locked it, retained the ignition key, descended by elevator to the street level and left the garage. When he returned several hours later, the car was gone, and it has never been recovered. Mr. Allen reported the theft to the attendant at the exit booth, who stated, "Well, it didn't come out here." The attendant did not testify at the trial.

Mr. Allen then reported the theft to security personnel employed by appellant, and subsequently reported the loss to the police. Appellant regularly employed a number of security guards, who were dressed in a distinctive uniform, two of whom were on duty most of the time. These guards patrolled the hotel grounds and building as well as the garage and were instructed to make rounds through the garage, although not necessarily at specified intervals. One of the security guards told appellee's husband that earlier in the day he had received the following report:

> He said, "It's a funny thing here. On my report here a lady called me somewhere around nine-thirty or after and said that there was someone messing with a car."

The guard told Mr. Allen that he closed his office and went up into the garage to investigate, but reported that he did not find anything unusual or out of the ordinary.

Customers such as Mr. Allen, upon entering the garage, received a ticket from the dispensing machine. On one side of this ticket are instructions to overnight guests to present the ticket to the front desk of the hotel. The other side contains instructions to the parker to keep the ticket and that the ticket must be presented to the cashier upon leaving the parking area. The ticket states that charges are made for the use of parking space only and that appellant assumes no responsibility for loss through fire, theft, collision or otherwise to the car or its contents. The ticket states that cars are parked at the risk of the owner, and parkers are instructed to lock their vehicles.[1] The record indicates that these tickets are given solely for the purpose of measuring the time during which a vehicle is parked in order that the attendant may collect the proper charge, and that they are not given for the purpose of identifying particular vehicles.

The question of the legal relationship between the operator of a vehicle which is being parked and the operator of parking establishments has been the subject of frequent litigation in this state and elsewhere. The authorities are in conflict, and the results of the cases are varied.[2]

It is legally and theoretically possible, of course, for various legal relationships to be created by the parties, ranging from the traditional concepts of lessor-lessee, licensor-licensee, bailor-bailee, to that described in some jurisdictions as a "deposit."[3] Several courts have found difficulty with the traditional criteria of bailment in analyzing park-and-lock cases. One of the leading cases is *McGlynn v. Parking Authority of City of Newark*, 432 A.2d 99 (N.J. 1981). There the Supreme Court of New Jersey reviewed numerous decisions from within its own state and from other jurisdictions, and it concluded that it was more "useful and straightforward" to consider the possession and control elements in defining the duty of care of a garage operator to its customers than to consider them in the context of bailment. That Court concluded that the "realities" of the relationship between the parties gave rise to a duty of reasonable care on the part of operators of parking garages and parking lots. It further found that a garage owner is usually better situated to protect a parked car and to distribute the cost of protection through parking fees. It also emphasized that owners usually expect to receive their vehicles back in the same condition in which they left them and that the imposition of a duty to protect parked vehicles and their contents was consistent with that expectation. The Court went further and stated that since the owner is ordinarily absent when theft or damage occurs, the obligation to come forward with affirmative evidence of negligence could impose a difficult, if not insurmountable, burden upon him. After considering various policy considerations, which it acknowledged to be the same as those recognized by courts holding that a bailment is created, the New Jersey Court indulged or authorized a presumption of negligence from proof of damage to a car parked in an enclosed garage.

Although the New Jersey Court concluded that a more flexible and comprehensive approach could be achieved outside of traditional property concepts, Tennessee courts generally have analyzed cases such as this in terms of sufficiency of the evidence to create a bailment for hire by implication. We believe that this continues to be the majority view and the

---

1. It is not insisted that the language of the ticket is sufficient to exonerate appellant, since the customer is not shown to have read it or to have had it called to his attention. See Savoy Hotel Corp. v. Sparks, 421 S.W.2d 98 (Tenn. Ct. App. 1967).

2. See Annot. 13 A.L.R.4th 359 (1982); 7 A.L.R.3d 927 (1966).

3. See Gauthier v. Allright New Orleans, Inc., 417 So.2d 375 (La. Ct. App. 1982).

most satisfactory and realistic approach to the problem, unless the parties clearly by their conduct or by express contract create some other relationship.

The subject has been discussed in numerous previous decisions in this state. One of the leading cases is *Dispeker v. New Southern Hotel Co.*, 373 S.W.2d 904 (Tenn. 1963). In that case the guest at a hotel delivered his vehicle to a bellboy who took possession of it and parked it in a lot adjoining the hotel building. The owner kept the keys, but the car apparently was capable of being started without the ignition key. The owner apparently had told the attendant how to so operate it. Later the employee took the vehicle for his own purposes and damaged it. Under these circumstances the Court held that a bailment for hire had been created and that upon proof of misdelivery of the vehicle the bailee was liable to the customer.

In the subsequent case of *Scruggs v. Dennis*, 440 S.W.2d 20 (Tenn. 1969), upon facts practically identical to those of the instant case, the Court again held that an implied bailment contract had been created between a customer who parked and locked his vehicle in a garage. Upon entry he received a ticket dispensed by a machine, drove his automobile to the underground third level of the garage and parked. He retained his ignition key, but when he returned to retrieve the automobile in the afternoon it had disappeared. It was recovered more than two weeks later and returned to the owner in a damaged condition.

In that case the operator of the garage had several attendants on duty, but the attendants did not ordinarily operate the parked vehicles, as in the instant case.[5]

Although the Court recognized that there were some factual differences between the *Scruggs* case and that of *Dispeker v. New Southern Hotel Co.*, supra, it concluded that a bailment had been created when the owner parked his vehicle for custody and safe keeping in the parking garage, where there was limited access and where the patron had to present a ticket to an attendant upon leaving the premises. * * *

On the contrary, in the case of *Rhodes v. Pioneer Parking Lot, Inc.*, 501 S.W.2d 569 (Tenn. 1973), a bailment was found not to exist when the owner left his vehicle in an open parking lot which was wholly unattended and where he simply inserted coins into a meter, received a ticket, then parked the vehicle himself and locked it.

Denying recovery, the Court said:

In the case at bar, however, we find no evidence to justify a finding that the plaintiff delivered his car into the custody of the defendant, nor do we find any act or conduct upon the defendant's part which would justify a reasonable person believing that an obligation of bailment had been assumed by the defendant.

---

5. Appellant's employees occasionally parked the vehicles of patrons who were handicapped and under other unusual circumstances.

501 S.W.2d at 571.

In the instant case, appellee's vehicle was not driven into an unattended or open parking area. Rather it was driven into an enclosed, indoor, attended commercial garage which not only had an attendant controlling the exit but regular security personnel to patrol the premises for safety.

Under these facts we are of the opinion that the courts below correctly concluded that a bailment for hire had been created, and that upon proof of nondelivery appellee was entitled to the statutory presumption of negligence provided in T.C.A. § 24–5–111.

We recognize that there is always a question as to whether there has been sufficient delivery of possession and control to create a bailment when the owner locks a vehicle and keeps the keys. Nevertheless, the realities of the situation are that the operator of the garage is, in circumstances like those shown in this record, expected to provide attendants and protection. In practicality the operator does assume control and custody of the vehicles parked, limiting access thereto and requiring the presentation of a ticket upon exit. As stated previously, the attendant employed by appellant did not testify, but he told appellee's husband that the vehicle did not come out of the garage through the exit which he controlled. This testimony was not amplified, but the attendant obviously must have been in error or else must have been inattentive or away from his station. The record clearly shows that there was no other exit from which the vehicle could have been driven.

Appellant made no effort to rebut the presumption created by statute in this state (which is similar to presumptions indulged by courts in some other jurisdictions not having such statutes). While the plaintiff did not prove positive acts of negligence on the part of appellant, the record does show that some improper activity or tampering with vehicles had been called to the attention of security personnel earlier in the day of the theft in question, and that appellee's new vehicle had been removed from the garage by some person or persons unknown, either driving past an inattentive attendant or one who had absented himself from his post, there being simply no other way in which the vehicle could have been driven out of the garage.

→ presumption of negligence upon no delivery or mis-delivery of the car.

Under the facts and circumstances of this case, we are not inclined to depart from prior decisions or to place the risk of loss upon the consuming public as against the operators of commercial parking establishments such as that conducted by appellant. We recognize that park-and-lock situations arise under many and varied factual circumstances. It is difficult to lay down one rule of law which will apply to all cases. The expectations of the parties and their conduct can cause differing legal relationships to arise, with consequent different legal results. We do not find the facts of the present case, however, to be at variance with the legal requirements of the traditional concept of a bailment for hire. In our opinion it amounted to more than a mere license or hiring of a space to park a vehicle, unaccompanied by any expectation of protection or other obligation upon the operator of the establishment.

The judgment of the courts below is affirmed at the cost of appellant. The cause will be remanded to the trial court for any further proceedings which may be necessary.

DISSENT ■ DROWOTA, J., dissenting. * * * Even though some courts now suggest that the theory of bailment is an archaic and inappropriate theory upon which to base liability in modern park and lock cases, the majority opinion states that "Tennessee courts generally have analyzed cases such as this in terms of sufficiency of the evidence to create a bailment for hire by implication," and concludes that this is "the most satisfactory and realistic approach to the problem." I do not disagree with the longstanding use of the bailment analysis in this type of case. I do disagree, however, with the majority's conclusion that a bailment for hire has been created in this case.

The record shows that upon entering this parking garage a ticket, showing time of entry, is automatically dispensed by a machine. The ticket states that charges are made for the use of a parking space only and that the garage assumes no responsibility for loss to the car or its contents. The ticket further states that cars are parked at the risk of the owner, and parkers are instructed to lock their vehicles. The majority opinion points out that it is not insisted that this language on the ticket is sufficient to exonerate the garage, since the customer is not shown to have read it or to have had it called to his attention. Savoy Hotel Corp. v. Sparks, 421 S.W.2d 98 (Tenn. Ct. App. 1967). The ticket in no way identifies the vehicle, it is given solely for the purpose of measuring the length of time during which the vehicle is parked in order that a proper charge may be made.

In this case Mr. Allen, without any direction or supervision, parked his car, removed his keys, and locked the car and left the parking garage having retained his ignition key. The presentation of a ticket upon exit is for the sole purpose of allowing the cashier to collect the proper charge. The cashier is not required to be on duty at all times. When no cashier is present, the exit gate is opened and no payment is required.[1] As the majority opinion states, the ticket is "not given for the purpose of identifying particular vehicles." The ticket functioned solely as a source of fee computation, not of vehicle identification.

The majority opinion states: "[W]e do not find the facts of the present case to be at variance with the legal requirements of the concept of a bailment for hire." I must disagree, for I feel the facts of the present case are clearly at variance with what I consider to be the legal requirements of the traditional concept of a bailment for hire.

Bailment has been defined by this Court in the following manner:

The creation of a bailment in the absence of an express contract requires that possession and control over the subject matter pass from the bailor to the bailee. In order to constitute a sufficient delivery of the subject matter there must be a full transfer, either actual or

---

1. Between one or two in the morning and six or seven a.m., the garage is entirely open without a cashier to collect parking fees. During the day if the cashier leaves his or her post on a break, the exit gate is opened and the vehicle owner may exit without payment.

constructive, of the property to the bailee so as to exclude it from the possession of the owner and all other persons and give to the bailee, for the time being, the sole custody and control thereof. See Jackson v. Metropolitan Government of Nashville, supra, Scruggs v. Dennis, 440 S.W.2d 20 (Tenn. 1969); Old Hickory Parking Corp. v. Alloway, 177 S.W.2d 23 (Tenn. Ct. App. 1944). See generally, 8 Am.Jur.2d 960–61.

In parking lot and parking garage situations, a bailment is created where the operator of the lot or garage has knowingly and voluntarily assumed control, possession, or custody of the motor vehicle; if he has not done so, there may be a mere license to park or a lease of parking space. See, e.g., Lewis v. Ebersole, 12 So.2d 543 (Ala. 1943); Southeastern Fair Association v. Ford, 14 S.E.2d 139 (Ga. Ct. App. 1941).

Rhodes v. Pioneer Parking Lot, Inc., 501 S.W.2d 569, 570 (Tenn. 1973).

From its earliest origins, the most distinguishing factor identifying a bailment has been delivery. Our earliest decisions also recognize acceptance as a necessary factor, requiring that possession and control of the property pass from bailor to bailee, to the exclusion of control by others. The test thus becomes whether the operator of the vehicle has made such a delivery to the operator of the parking facility as to amount to a relinquishment of his exclusive possession, control, and dominion over the vehicle so that the latter can exclude it from the possession of all others. If so, a bailment has been created.

When the automobile began replacing the horse and buggy, our courts allowed bailment law to carry over and govern the parking of vehicles. * * * [C]ases involving parking attendants and personalized service have caused us no problems. The problem arises in this modern era of automated parking, when courts have attempted to expand the limits of existing areas of the law to encompass technological and commercial advances. Such is the case of *Scruggs v. Dennis*, 440 S.W.2d 20 (Tenn. 1969), relied upon in the majority opinion. In *Scruggs*, as in this case, the entire operation is automated, with the exception of payment upon departure. The operation bears little, if any, resemblance to the circumstances found in *Old Hickory Parking Corp.*, *Savoy Hotel*, and *Dispeker*. Yet the Court in *Scruggs*, in quoting extensively from the *Dispeker* opinion, states that "There are some minute differences of fact. . . ." Id., 440 S.W.2d at 22. As pointed out above, the differences of fact in *Dispeker* are not minute or so similar as the *Scruggs* court would suggest. Delivery, custody and control are clearly present in *Dispeker*. I fail to find such delivery, custody and control in *Scruggs* or in the case at bar. In *Dispeker*, the vehicle was actually taken from the owner by an attendant. I believe the *Scruggs* court and the majority opinion today attempt to apply bailment law in situations where there is not a true bailment relationship. * * *

The majority opinion, as did the *Scruggs* court, finds custody and control implied because of the limited access and because "the presentation of a ticket upon exit" is required. I cannot agree with this analysis as creating a bailment situation. I do not believe that based upon the fact that a ticket was required to be presented upon leaving, that this factor created a proper basis upon which to find a bailment relationship. The ticket did not identify the vehicle or the operator of the vehicle, as do most bailment receipts. The cashier was not performing the traditional bailee role or identifying and returning a particular article, but instead was merely computing the amount owed and accepting payment due for use of a parking space. I do not believe the Defendant exercised such possession and control over Plaintiff's automobile as is necessary in an implied bailment.

* * *

Plaintiff parked his car, locked it and retained the key. Certainly Defendant cannot be said to have sole custody of Plaintiff's vehicle, for Defendant could not move it, did not know to whom it belonged, and did not know when it would be reclaimed or by whom. Anyone who manually obtained a ticket from the dispenser could drive out with any vehicle he was capable of operating. Also, a cashier was not always on duty. When on duty, so long as the parking fee was paid—by what means could the Defendant reasonably exercise control? The necessary delivery and relinquishment of control by the Plaintiff, the very basis upon which the bailment theory was developed, is missing.

We should realize that the circumstances upon which the principles of bailment law were established and developed are not always applicable to the operation of the modern day automated parking facility. The element of delivery, of sole custody and control are lacking in this case.

NOTES AND QUESTIONS

1. As *Allen* illustrates, many activities in modern life involve more than one category of property relationship—in this case, the Allens and the hotel have entered into both a license agreement and (perhaps) a bailment agreement. As in the present case, selecting the proper category with which to analyze the case can have a pronounced influence on the outcome. There are no fixed rules for deciding which rubric is correct. It is mostly a matter of "fit," which is determined by looking at all the circumstances and the way similar cases have been categorized in the past. Did the court perform the classificatory analysis correctly in this case, based on the prior decisions the opinions discuss?

2. Why not resolve all these disputes by contract? Note that no one seems to take the language printed on the ticket in this case seriously—in contrast to the court in *ProCD*, which upholds the detailed provisions in the shrinkwrap license against various claims that it should not be binding. The problem with using contract to determine the rights and duties associated with various daily events like parking a car, checking a coat, dropping off clothing at the dry cleaners, and so forth is that few people have time to "shop around" to various bailees in order to compare the disclaimers or guarantees they are offering about risk of loss and other potential casualty events. A typical consumer will remain "rationally ignorant" of these details, because the value of the bailed item, discounted by the probability of a theft or accident occurring, does not warrant spending

much if any time comparing different standard-form-contract offerings. Of course, consumers may rely on other clues about the bailee, such as past experience with the bailee, the bailee's reputation in the community, or whether the bailee has a prominent brand name. But even so, there remains a case for imposing a degree of standardization on these relationships through "property" rules that are either nondisclaimable or that can be disclaimed only through very prominent disclosure. If you think standardization makes sense, who should do the standardizing? The courts, through episodic common-law rulings as in the present case? A regulatory agency established for this purpose? A trade association of bailees?

3.   If the Hyatt Regency in Nashville wants to modify the outcome in this case by contract, so that it does not face liability for auto theft in the future, what would you advise it to do?

THE BAILEE'S DUTY OF CARE

One longstanding matter of doctrinal controversy has been the duty of care that the bailee owes to the bailor. Suppose, for example, that the property is lost, stolen, or destroyed while in the custody of the bailee. By what standard do we determine whether the bailee is liable to the bailor for the value of the property that was the subject of the bailment?

The early common law apparently took the position that the bailee's liability to the bailor for lost, stolen, or destroyed goods was absolute. This was perhaps based on the understanding that the contract between the bailor and bailee called for the return of the goods when the purpose of the bailment was realized, and if the bailee failed to return the good, the bailee had violated the parties' understanding. But this rule seemed harsh in many circumstances, and so in *Coggs v. Bernard*, 2 Ld. Raym. 909 (K.B. 1703), Chief Justice Holt undertook to restate the law. His restatement, which was borrowed from the thirteenth-century writer Bracton, who in return borrowed from the Romans, consisted of a complicated six-fold classification of bailments, with different standards of care for each. Few traces of this effort remain today. More influential was Justice Story's effort in his treatise on bailments, which offered a more simplified set of rules:

> When the bailment is for the sole benefit of the bailor, the law requires only slight diligence on the part of the bailee, and of course makes him answerable only for gross neglect. When the bailment is for the sole benefit of the bailee, the law requires great diligence on the part of the bailee, and makes him responsible for slight neglect. When the bailment is reciprocally beneficial to both parties, the law requires ordinary diligence on the part of the bailee, and makes him responsible for ordinary neglect.

Joseph Story, Commentaries on the Law of Bailments § 3, at 27 (9th ed. 1878).

More recently, commentators have urged even greater simplification, advocating a universal standard of "reasonable care" for all bailments. See Kurt Philip Autor, Note, Bailment Liability: Toward a Standard of Reasonable Care, 61 S. Cal. L. Rev. 2117 (1988). In determining whether the bailee exercised reasonable care, such a standard would take into account all the circumstances surrounding the bailment relationship, including whether the bailee received compensation or whether the bailment was for the benefit of the bailee. A survey of modern bailment cases undertaken by Professor Helmholz, however, casts doubt on whether courts in fact apply such a uniform standard of reasonable care. R.H. Helmholz, Bailment Theories and the Liability of Bailees: The Elusive Uniform Standard of Reasonable Care, 41 Kan. L. Rev. 97 (1992).

One complication is that since the relationship between the bailor and bailee is a contractual one, the standard of care can be modified by agreement between the parties before the bailment commences. Attempts to do this are quite common, as when restaurants post signs in coat check rooms disclaiming any liability for items left there, or, as in the *Allen* case, a parking garage prints a disclaimer of liability on the back of the parking ticket dispensed by machine upon entry. Whether these efforts at modifying the standard of care are successful is open to question.

Another complication is that courts seem to be stricter about bailees who misdeliver goods—that is, when they turn the goods over to someone other than the true owner—than they are when the goods are lost, stolen, or destroyed while being held in the custody of the bailee for return to the true owner. Consider, in this light, the following case.

P   *D*
Cowen v. Pressprich

Supreme Court, Appellate Term, New York, 1922.
192 N.Y.S. 242.

■ MULLAN, J. Conversion, for the defendants' alleged wrongful delivery of a bond. The parties on both sides are stock exchange brokers. Plaintiffs had agreed to sell and deliver to defendants a bond of the Oregon Short Line Railroad of the par value of $1,000. To fill that order, plaintiffs ordered the bond from a third bond house, and the latter, by mistake, sent plaintiffs an Oregon & California Railroad bond, and plaintiffs, also by mistake, sent this Oregon & California bond to defendants. There is no controversy as to the manner of the sending. Plaintiffs handed the Oregon & California bond to Goldberg, a youth of 17 years, who was one of plaintiffs' two messengers, or "runners," as they seem to be called. With the bond was a memorandum (also called "slip" or "statement") briefly describing an Oregon Short Line bond. The bond and slip were inclosed together in an envelope. Goldberg took the envelope to defendants' place of business in a Wall Street office building. Defendants' suite of offices had two entrance doors from the office building hall, one for general use, and the other for persons, such as Goldberg, making deliveries. Goldberg entered at the latter door, and was then in a tiny outside room, described as about two feet by six feet. There was no door for passage between this small outside room and an inside, and presumably larger, room. Deliveries were made by dropping papers in a slot in one of the partitions partly forming this small outer room. Above the slot was a window of opaque glass that swung inwards. That window was kept closed unless or until the person acting for defendants at the delivery window should desire to talk to one making a delivery, when he would open the window. Next to the partition containing that slot and window, and in the inner room, was a desk at which was kept seated either a member of defendants' firm or a clerk. At the time here in question there were two persons at that desk, Mr. Quackenbush, of the defendants' firm, and an employee, one Campbell.

Goldberg dropped the envelope through the slot. His testimony was:

I waited until he [the person at the desk] took it in, and then I left. * * * I told him I will call back for a check. Q. Why didn't you ask for the receipt? A. Well, I was in a hurry; I had many deliveries that day, and I had to make them. * * * Q. How long would you say you were in that delivery room in front of that delivery window—from the time you put the bond in until you left? A. It was from a minute to a minute and a half.

Goldberg could not recall whether the person at the other side of the window said anything. He thought, but was not sure, that there was "somebody" else in the little outside room when he was there. It does not appear from Goldberg's testimony whether or not the delivery window was open during any part of his stay while making the delivery. Mr. Quackenbush testified as follows:

Q. Will you tell us what took place at the time of that delivery. A. It was about 10:30 in the morning. Mr. Campbell and myself stood there making up our loans, when a bond shoots through the window like a streak of lightning; it goes right down my desk—that was my desk about the width of this table (indicating stenographer's table)—right down in front of us. As it rolls over, I opened it up; just pulled the bond open that way instantly (indicating). The statement called for an Oregon Short Line five bond; I could see immediately that the bond was an Oregon & California, and we handle thousands of them. Q. What did you do then? A. I immediately opened the window. Q. Where was that; right in front of you? A. Right like that (indicating), and I yelled "Cowen." A young man steps right up, and I says, "Make your statement agree with the bond." The Court: Sir? The Witness: "Make your statement agree with the bond." He mumbled, "Alright," and takes the bond and goes out immediately like that. Q. And he took it? A. He took it. Q. When you say man—— A. A young boy 19 or 20 years old. Q. What did you do then; close the window? A. Closed the window; went about my work. Q. You were expecting from Cowen & Co. at that time a Short Line bond, were you not? A. Yes; we had purchased one, looking for it. Q. You were looking for it? A. Yes; some day. Q. And you say you instantly found it was not—— A. It was not more than 15 seconds. Q. And you were under no contract to purchase from Cowen & Co. a California bond? A. No, sir. Q. How long would you say it took between the time that bond came into your slot on to your desk and the time you opened the window and yelled "Cowen"? A. Not a second more than 15. Q. Fifteen seconds? A. Not a second more than that. Q. When you opened the window where did the boy come? A. To my left from the main door. Q. You heard the Goldberg boy testify, did you not, that when he put that bond into your window, he waited about a minute and a half; is that correct? A. I will say no. Q. Did you hear him say anything? A. Nothing. Q. The only thing you know is seeing the bond shoot into the window. A. Exactly. Q. Was there a receipt on that bond to be signed by you? A. No, sir; it was not. Q. It was merely a sale memorandum? A. Exactly. Q. Neither one of them is the young man to whom you delivered the bond? A. No, sir. Q. You delivered the bond to some one else? A. Neither one of those [plaintiffs'] boys.

Mr. Campbell substantially corroborated Mr. Quackenbush's version.

Concededly the boy to whom Quackenbush returned the bond delivered by Goldberg was not Goldberg, but some unidentified boy who made away with the bond. The bond was of the bearer type, fully negotiable.

The defendants have refused to make good the plaintiffs' loss, contending that they were chargeable only with due diligence, and that, accepting the version of the plaintiffs as given by Goldberg, it appears that they exercised all the care required of them. The plaintiffs contend that there was an absolute obligation on the part of the defendants to redeliver the bond to the plaintiffs, and that no question of negligence enters into the case. They also argue that, if the negligence question does enter, there was sufficient evidence to warrant a finding that the defendants did not, in fact, exercise due care. The learned trial judge did not state the ground of his decision in plaintiffs' favor.

A person who has been put, through no act or fault of his own, in such a situation as that in which the defendants were put upon the delivery to them of the wrong bond, has come to be known as "involuntary bailee" * * * or constructive or quasi bailee.

In the field of voluntary bailments, whether they be for hire or be otherwise coupled with an interest on the part of the bailee, or whether they be merely gratuitous, no rule is better settled than that it is the duty of the bailee to deliver the bailed article to the right person, and that delivery to the wrong person is not capable of being excused by any possible showing of care or good faith or innocence.

Such distinctions as have been drawn between the duties of voluntary bailees for compensation and voluntary gratuitous bailees relate solely to the degree of care the bailee should exercise in respect of the custody of the thing bailed. In respect of delivery to the proper person, no such distinction is drawn; the duty in both cases is absolute.

What, then, is the difference, if any, between the duty of a voluntary gratuitous bailee and that of a wholly involuntary bailee? There is an astonishing paucity of decision and text opinion upon the subject. I think, however, that all that can be found upon it points to the conclusion that the involuntary bailee, as long as his lack of volition continues, is not under the slightest duty to care for or guard the subject of the bailment, and cannot be held, in respect of custody, for what would even be the grossest negligence in the case of a voluntary bailment, but that, in case the involuntary bailee shall exercise any dominion over the thing so bailed, he becomes as responsible as if he were a voluntary bailee. * * *

I have reached the conclusion that while, at first blush, it may seem to be imposing upon the defendants an unduly severe rule of conduct to hold them to an absolute liability, the rule is no more severe than the occasion calls for. * * * The defendants could easily have protected themselves by telephoning the plaintiffs that the wrong bond had been delivered, or they could have sent the bond back to the plaintiffs by one of their own messengers. Instead, they chose to take chance of delivering it to the wrong messenger. As the delivery window was closed when the bond was dropped through the slot, and remained closed for an appreciable time, they could not have known what messenger had made the delivery. * * *

The plaintiffs, as has already been mentioned, urge that, if the defendants are not to be held in conversion, they are, at least, liable in negligence. The action, however, was brought in conversion, and both sides insist that it was tried as a conversion action. The judgment therefore may only be sustained, if at all, upon that theory. * * *

Judgment affirmed, with $25 costs, with leave to defendants to appeal to the Appellate Division.

■ BURR, J. (concurring). I concur in the conclusion reached by Mr. Justice MULLAN and vote to affirm. I believe that defendants, having received the bond and taken it into their possession, became liable even as gratuitous or involuntary bailees for its proper redelivery to the true owner.

■ LEHMAN, J. (dissenting). I agree in all material particulars with the statement of facts contained in the opinion of Mr. Justice MULLAN. * * *

It is unnecessary now to consider whether the complaint sufficiently sets forth any cause of action; for no motion was made by the defendants to dismiss the complaint on the ground of insufficiency, and no such point is raised on this appeal. It is to be noted, however, that the complaint does not allege any negligence on the part of the defendants, and I agree with Mr. Justice MULLAN that no such issue was litigated, and that the judgment can be sustained only if, as a matter of law, the defendants' mistake in returning the bond to the wrong messenger constituted a conversion of the bond or at least a breach of an implied agreement on their part to return the bond only to the plaintiffs.

While the slot in the window constituted an invitation to deliver at that place securities intended for the defendants, it is evident that it constituted an invitation only to deliver securities which the defendants were under some obligation to receive. Obviously no person could by slipping in other securities impose upon the defendants without their consent any affirmative obligation to care for these securities, to pay for them, or even to receive them. The plaintiffs never intended to deliver to the defendants an Oregon & California Railroad bond. By their mistake the plaintiffs divested themselves of possession of the bond, but they did not transfer to the defendants either title or right to possession if they demanded the return of the bond. The defendants had not consented to accept the bond as a deposit, they claimed no title to it, and they were not subject to any trust or obligation as bailees, for a bailment arises only through an express or implied contract. They were put in possession of the bond without any agreement on their part, express or implied, to accept the deposit of the bond; and, though persons who come into possession of the property of others without their consent are sometimes for convenience called "involuntary" or "quasi bailees," they incur no responsibility to the true owner in respect thereof. It is only where they commit some "overt act" of interference with the property that an implied contract of bailment is created. * * *

In the present case the defendants were put in possession of the bond by mistake; they discovered the mistake promptly, and thereafter they committed no "overt act" of interference with the bond except that they attempted to divest themselves of this possession by delivering the bond to a person whom they believed to be the messenger of the plaintiffs. That act was not only consistent with the continued title and right of dominion in the plaintiffs, but was an honest attempt to restore possession to the true owners. It certainly cannot be contended that the defendants were bound at their peril to wait until the plaintiffs came to their office and physically took away their property; they could take proper steps to divest themselves of the possession thrust upon them by mistake without thereby impliedly agreeing, contrary to their clear intention, to accept possession as bailees with the consequent obligations flowing from such relation. It is quite immaterial whether we call these defendants bailees or not if we keep in mind the fact that the possession of these goods was thrust upon them by mistake of the plaintiffs and without their invitation or consent, and that therefore any liability for failure to return the goods to the true owner upon demand must be the result of some act voluntarily done by the defendant thereafter. An attempt to return the bond to the true owner or to the person who delivered it cannot be considered as inconsistent with a recognition of the complete ownership and right of dominion by the true owner, and certainly shows no intent to accept the possession thrust upon the defendants by plaintiffs' mistake, and I fail to see how, in the absence of such elements, any implied contract of bailment can arise. If in making an attempt to return the goods, which was lawful and proper in itself, the defendants used means which were not reasonable and proper, and as a result thereof the goods were lost or misdelivered, then the defendants would be liable for negligence or possibly for conversion, for every man is responsible for his own acts; but, if the defendants had a right to divest themselves of possession and attempt to return the goods, then, in the absence of some obligation resting upon contract to deliver the goods only to the true owner or upon his order, I do not see how the mere fact that through innocent mistake the defendants handed the bond to the wrong messenger could constitute a conversion. The defendants could not properly disregard entirely the mistake in the delivery of the bonds. Common courtesy and prudence, if not the law, certainly placed upon them the duty to take some steps by which the plaintiffs would be apprised of their mistake and enabled to regain their property. The defendants might have placed the bond in a safe and telephoned to the plaintiffs to call for the bond, but they were under the impression that the messenger who delivered the bond was still present, and they gave the bond to him as a means of carrying out their evident duty to apprise the plaintiffs of their error and revest possession in them. * * *

Liability in law must in all cases be founded either on contract or on some wrongful act. The defendants in this case promptly evinced their intention not to accept the possession of the bond thrust upon them by mistake; they merely attempted to divest themselves of this possession, and certainly from such attempt no agreement to accept this possession can be implied. Until that time the defendants were under no obligation either to accept the bond as bailees or return it upon demand to the true owners unless at the time of the demand the bond was still in their possession; and it seems to me anomalous and illogical to say that an absolute obligation to return the bond to the plaintiffs, and not to deliver it to any other person, arises merely from the fact that the defendants did by mistake and through an honest disclaimer of any title or right of possession in the bond physically deliver it to another. They claimed no title and no right to possession in the bond; they attempted to transfer no title or right of possession of their own in the bond; they had physical possession of the bond through plaintiffs' mistake; and they transferred nothing but this physical possession. The plaintiffs could not compel them to retain physical possession, and their act of transferring physical possession even to a stranger under these circumstances shows no exercise of any dominion over the property, for it constitutes no denial of the complete and sole right of dominion in the plaintiffs. In my opinion plaintiffs have therefore no right of action against the defendants unless the means which the defendants used to rid themselves of their possession were not reasonable and proper. * * *

Even if under these pleadings we could consider the question of negligence, I find no evidence upon this question to sustain a judgment in favor of the plaintiffs. There is no doubt that the defendants acted in good faith and in the honest belief that they were handing back the bond to the messenger who delivered it. They had assumed no obligation of any kind to the plaintiffs; any act they performed was for the plaintiffs' benefit, and it was through plaintiffs' mistake that they were called upon to act at all in the premises. Doubtless, if they had foreseen the possibility of mistake, they would not have delivered the bond to the wrong messenger; but it was not unreasonable to suppose that the messenger might be waiting or that, if he had left, no thief would be in the office who would claim to represent the plaintiffs. They probably committed an error of judgment, but for such error they cannot be held liable. Since they owed no obligation to the plaintiffs and acted in good faith under the reasonable belief that they were returning the bond to the messenger who delivered it, I see no ground for imposing upon them liability for the loss of a bond which would never have been lost but for the plaintiffs' mistake, due apparently to the plaintiffs' negligence. * * *

For these reasons, it seems to me that the judgment should be reversed, with costs, and the complaint dismissed, with costs.

Cowen v. Pressprich — *Reverses and adopts dissenting opinion*

Supreme Court, Appellate Division, New York, 1922.
194 N.Y.S. 926.

Determination appealed from and judgment of the Municipal Court reversed, with costs to the appellants in this court and in the Appellate Term, and judgment ordered, for defendants, dismissing the complaint, with costs, upon the dissenting opinion of Lehman, J., at the Appellate Term. Order filed.

NOTES AND QUESTIONS

1. One general issue raised by *Cowen* is whether a bailment can ever be created when there is no contract—no meeting of the minds—between the bailor and the bailee. Esteemed commentators have long disagreed about this. Blackstone and Story both maintained that there could be no bailment without a contract. See 2 William Blackstone, Commentaries on the Laws of England *452–54; Joseph Story, Commentaries on the Law of Bailments § 2, at 5 (James Schouler ed., 9th ed. 1878). But other commentators have argued that bailment relationships can arise in contexts, like the finding of lost property, where no contract exists between the bailor and bailee. See 9 Samuel Williston, A Treatise on the Law of Contracts § 1030, at 875 (Walter H.E. Jaeger ed., 3d ed. 1967); William King Laidlaw, Principles of Bailment, 16 Cornell L. Q. 286, 287 (1931). To a certain extent this dispute is terminological. If different duties of care attach to someone who is a "true" bailee (based on contract) and an "involuntary" or "constructive" bailee (where there is no contract), then we can speak of Type I and Type II bailments, or of bailments and something else, like "custodial obligations." But if some duty of care attaches to a person who takes up custody of property he knows belongs to another, but with whom he has no contractual relationship, what is the source of this duty? Must these duties be grounded in some conception of the nature of property rights?

2. In *Cowen*, the court was required to sort out two issues. First, what sort of duty of care attaches to a firm that acquires temporary custody of a bond by mistake? Second, does the rule of strict liability that applies to a bailee who misdelivers a bailed good to a third party, as opposed to losing or damaging a good while it is in its custody, apply to such a firm? The categories the court has to work with—"bailee", "involuntary bailee," "stranger"—do not seem to be nuanced enough to allow the court to come up with a satisfactory resolution.

3. Does it make sense to treat a securities firm that receives the wrong bond by mistake from a firm with which it has regular dealings as being subject to the same standard of care as someone who finds a ring on the sidewalk? (Finders are typically regarded as "involuntary bailees.") Surely, given the relationship between the firms and their frequent interaction, one would expect the firm that receives the bond by mistake to take reasonable steps to secure the bond and ensure that it makes it back safely to the sending firm. It is not clear that one would expect the same degree of diligence on the part of a mere finder, who has no clue about the identity of the true owner.

4. Why are bailees subject to strict liability for misdelivery, but only subject to a duty of reasonable care for lost, stolen, or destroyed goods? The doctrinal answer is that bailors sued bailees for conversion in cases of misdelivery, and conversion is a strict liability tort. Bailors sued bailees for trespass on the case in instances involving lost, stolen, or destroyed goods, and this action came to require proof of negligence. Otherwise, commentators have found the distinction difficult to justify:

> The difference cannot be explained in terms of the degree of harm to the bailor. The bailor loses the property in either case. Indeed, the loss is if anything *less* severe in the case of misdelivery, because there is some chance that the property can be recovered from the third party who has erroneously received it.

> The higher standard of care that traditionally applies to misdelivery begins to make more sense, however, once we realize that misdelivery is a * * * situation that entails * * * the introduction of the * * * third party. The rule of strict liability seeks to correct for the unequal information between the bailor and the bailee about the risk of transfer to a third party.

Thomas W. Merrill & Henry E. Smith, The Property/Contract Interface, 101 Colum. L. Rev. 773, 816 (2001). The authors also note that "[b]ecause misdelivery confers a benefit on a third party, the bailee may be tempted to connive with a third party to 'misdeliver' the property, and it will be difficult for the bailor to prove that this has happened." Id. at 815.

The Winkfield

Court of Appeal (Eng.), 1901.
[1902] P. 42, [1900–1903] All E.R. 346.

On April 5, 1900, a collision occurred in a fog off Table Bay, on the coast of Cape Colony, South Africa, between the Government transport *Winkfield*, belonging to the Seafield Shipping Company, Limited, outward bound to the Cape with troops for service in South Africa, and the Union mail steam vessel *Mexican* from Cape Town, homeward bound to Southampton with mails, passengers, and cargo. The *Winkfield* was damaged and the *Mexican* sank, but not until all the passengers, crew, and some of the mails and luggage of the *Mexican* had been got on board the other vessel.

The owners, master, and crew of the *Mexican* and the owners of the *Winkfield* commenced cross-actions, which resulted in the owners of the *Winkfield* admitting liability for a moiety of the damage sustained by the *Mexican* * * *

■ COLLINS, MASTER OF THE ROLLS. This is an appeal from the order of Sir Francis Jeune dismissing a motion made on behalf of the Postmaster–General in the case of the *Winkfield*.

The question arises out of a collision which occurred on April 5, 1900, between the steamship *Mexican* and the steamship *Winkfield*, and which resulted in the loss of the former with a portion of the mails which she was carrying at the time.

The owners of the *Winkfield* under a decree limiting liability to 32,514£ 17s. 10d. paid that amount into court, and the claim in question was one by the Postmaster–General on behalf of himself and the Postmasters–General of Cape Colony and Natal to recover out of that sum the value of letters, parcels, & c., in his custody as bailee and lost on board the *Mexican*.

Figure 4–4
The *Mexican*

UNION R.M.S. *MEXICAN*, 1883
Sunk in collision near Capetown, 1900

Source: Marischal Murray, Ships and South Africa (1933).

The case was dealt with by all parties in the Court below as a claim by a bailee who was under no liability to his bailor for the loss in question, as to which it was admitted that the authority of *Claridge v. South Staffordshire Tramway Co.*, [1892] 1 Q. B. 422, was conclusive, and the President accordingly, without argument and in deference to that authority, dismissed the claim. The Postmaster–General now appeals.

The question for decision, therefore, is whether *Claridge's Case* was well decided. * * * For the reasons which I am about to state I am of opinion that *Claridge's Case* was wrongly decided, and that the law is that in an action against a stranger for loss of goods caused by his negligence, the bailee in possession can recover the value of the goods, although he would have had a good answer to an action by the bailor for damages for the loss of the thing bailed.

It seems to me that the position, that possession is good against a wrongdoer and that the latter cannot set up the jus tertii unless he claims under it, is well established in our law, and really concludes this case against the respondents. As I shall shew presently, a long series of authorities establishes this in actions of trover and trespass at the suit of a possessor. And the principle being the same, it follows that he can equally recover the whole value of the goods in an action on the case for their loss through the tortious conduct of the defendant. I think it involves this also, that the wrongdoer who is not defending under the title of the bailor is quite unconcerned with what the rights are between the bailor and bailee, and must treat the possessor as the owner of the goods for all purposes quite irrespective of the rights and obligations as between him and the bailor.

Wrongdoer can not use any relationship between bailor-bailee in his defense — as far as he is concerned, the possessor (bailee) has title to the goods (even if bailor in reality holds title)

I think this position is well established in our law, though it may be that reasons for its existence have been given in some of the cases which are not quite satisfactory. I think also that the obligation of the bailee to the bailor to account for what he has received in respect of the destruction or conversion of the thing bailed has been admitted so often in decided cases that it cannot now be questioned; and, further, I think it can be shewn that the right of the bailee to recover cannot be rested on the ground suggested in some of the cases, namely, that he was liable over to the bailor for the loss of the goods converted or destroyed.

Bailee will have to give the damages awarded to the Bailor

Bailee can sue even when he is not liable to Bailor for the value of goods lost

It cannot be denied that since the case of *Armory v. Delamirie*, 1 Stra. 504, not to mention earlier cases from the Year Books onward, a mere finder may recover against a wrongdoer the full value of the thing converted. That decision involves the principle that as between possessor and wrongdoer the presumption of law is, in the words of Lord Campbell in *Jeffries v. Great Western Ry. Co.*, 5 E. & B. 802, at p. 806, "that the person who has possession has the property." In the same case he says at p. 805: "I am of opinion that the law is that a person possessed of goods as his property has a good title as against every stranger, and that one who takes them from him, having no title in himself, is a wrongdoer, and cannot defend himself by shewing that there was title in some third person, for against a wrongdoer possession is title. * * * " Therefore it is not open to the defendant, being a wrongdoer, to inquire into the nature or limitation of the possessor's right, and unless it is competent for him to do so the question of his relation to, or liability towards, the true owner cannot come into the discussion at all; and, therefore, as between those two parties full damages have to be paid without any further inquiry. The extent of the liability of the finder to the true owner not being relevant to the discussion between him and the wrongdoer, the facts which would ascertain it would

Since evidence of the real relationship between the possessor and the bailor is irrelevant & inadmissible, the liability (or lack thereof) of the possessor to the bailor does not play a role when determining whether a possessor can sue a wrongdoer for damages.

not have been admissible in evidence, and therefore the right of the finder to recover full damages cannot be made to depend upon the extent of his liability over to the true owner. To hold otherwise would, it seems to me, be in effect to permit a wrongdoer to set up a jus tertii under which he cannot claim.

But, if this be the fact in the case of a finder, why should it not be equally the fact in the case of a bailee? Why, as against a wrongdoer, should the nature of the plaintiff's interest in the thing converted be any more relevant to the inquiry, and therefore admissible in evidence, than in the case of a finder? It seems to me that neither in one case nor the other ought it to be competent for the defendant to go into evidence on that matter. * * *

The ground of the decision in *Claridge's Case* was that the plaintiff in that case, being under no liability to his bailor, could recover no damages, and though for the reasons I have already given I think this position is untenable, it is necessary to follow it out a little further. There is no doubt that the reason given in *Heydon and Smith's Case*, 13 Rep. 69—and itself drawn from the Year Books—has been repeated in many subsequent cases. The words are these:

> Clearly, the bailee, or he who hath a special property, shall have a general action of trespass against a stranger, and shall recover all in damages because that he is chargeable over.

It is now well established that the bailee is accountable, as stated in the passage cited and repeated in many subsequent cases. But whether the obligation to account was a condition of his right to sue, or only an incident arising upon his recovery of damages, is a very different question, though it was easy to confound one view with the other.

Holmes C.J. in his admirable lectures on the Common Law, in the chapter devoted to bailments, traces the origin of the bailee's right to sue and recover the whole value of chattels converted, and arrives at the clear conclusion that the bailee's obligation to account arose from the fact that he was originally the only person who could sue, though afterwards by an extension, not perhaps quite logical, the right to sue was conceded to the bailor also. He says at p. 167: "At first the bailee was answerable to the owner because he was the only person who could sue; now it was said he could sue because he was answerable to the owner." * * * This inversion, as he points out, is traceable through the Year Books, and has survived into modern times, though, as he shews, it has not been acted upon. Pollock and Maitland's History of English Law, vol. 2, p. 170, puts the position thus:— "Perhaps we come nearest to historical truth if we say that between the two old rules there was no logical priority. The bailee had the action because he was liable, and was liable because he had the action." It may be that in early times the obligation of the bailee to the bailor was absolute, that is to say, he was an insurer. But long after the decision of *Coggs v. Bernard*, 2 Ld. Raym. 909 (1704), which classified the obligations of bailees, the bailee has, nevertheless, been allowed to recover full damages against a wrongdoer, where the facts would have afforded a complete answer for him against his bailor. The cases above cited are instances of this. In each of them the bailee would have had a good answer to an action by his bailor; for in none of them was it suggested that the act of the wrongdoer was traceable to negligence on the part of the bailee. I think, therefore, that the statement drawn, as I have said, from the Year Books may be explained, as Holmes C.J. explains it, but whether that be the true view of it or not, it is clear that it has not been treated as law in our Courts.

Upon this, before the decision in *Claridge's Case*, there was a strong body of opinion in text-books, English and American, in favour of the bailee's unqualified right to sue the wrongdoer * * * The bailee's right to recover has been affirmed in several American cases entirely without reference to the extent of the bailee's liability to the bailor for the tort, though his obligation to account is admitted * * * [T]he root principle of the whole discussion is that, as against a wrongdoer, possession is title. The chattel that has been converted or damaged is deemed to be the chattel of the possessor and of no other, and therefore its loss or deterioration is his loss, and to him, if he demands it, it must be recouped. His obligation to account to the bailor is really not ad rem in the discussion. It only comes in after he has carried his legal position to its logical consequence against a wrongdoer, and serves to soothe a mind disconcerted by the notion that a person who is not himself the complete owner should be entitled to receive back the full value of the chattel converted or destroyed. There is no inconsistency between the two positions; the one is the complement of the other. As between bailee and stranger possession gives title—that is, not a limited interest, but absolute and complete ownership, and he is entitled to receive back a complete equivalent for the whole loss or deterioration of the thing itself. As between bailor and bailee the real interests of each must be inquired into, and, as the bailee has to account for the thing bailed, so he must account for that which has become its equivalent and now represents it. What he has received above his own interest he has received to the use of his bailor. The wrongdoer, having once paid full damages to the bailee, has an answer to any action by the bailor.

[margin note: Summary Rule]

[margin note: Wrongdoer can only be sued once for the value of the converted goods]

The liability by the bailee to account is also well established—see the passage from Lord Coke, and the cases cited in the earlier part of this judgment—and therefore it seems to me that there is no such preponderance of convenience in favour of limiting the right of the bailee as to make it desirable, much less obligatory, upon us to modify the law as it rested upon the authorities antecedent to *Claridge's Case*. * * * *Claridge's Case* was treated as open to question by the late Master of the Rolls in *Meux v. Great Eastern Ry. Co.*, 2 Q. B. 387 (1895), and, with the greatest deference to the eminent judges who decided it, it seems to me that it cannot be supported. It seems to have been argued before them upon very scanty materials. Before us the whole subject has been elaborately discussed, and all, or nearly all, the authorities brought before us in historical sequence.

NOTES AND QUESTIONS

1. *The Winkfield* is significant in rejecting the *jus tertii* defense in the context of a bailment. The owners of the Winkfield are liable in tort. Tort damages are supposed to serve a deterrent as well as a compensatory

function. Should the immunity of the Postmaster have any effect on the level of care taken by the operators of the Winkfield? If the crew of the Winkfield had acted recklessly or even willfully, they should presumably be liable for punitive damages. To whom?

2. The court broadly hints that after this case, the Postmaster will hold the funds subject to claims by customers; there will be some way around the Postmaster's immunity. Would the Postmaster be liable to its customers in restitution (see Chapter I)? What if only 80% of the customers (the bailors) file claims? (In a similar vein, the postal customers theoretically could have sued the Mexican directly. W. Prosser, Handbook of The Law of Torts § 15, at 96 (4th ed. 1971). There are, however, significant practical obstacles where many customers have a small claim.) If fewer than all customers file claims, leaving some of the damages in the hands of the Postmaster, would such a windfall to the Postmaster call into question the result in the case?

3. What if the bailee is a private shipping company that is liable to the bailor for contract damages? According to the leading case of *Hadley v. Baxendale*, 156 Eng. Rep. 145 (Ex. 1854), the shipper is liable only for foreseeable damages, and if the customer would like damages for an especially valuable package the customer must reveal the value to the shipper. Tortfeasors like the Winkfield, on the other hand, are normally liable for any damage caused by a wrongful act whether foreseeable or not. See, e.g., Vosberg v. Putney, 50 N.W. 403 (Wis. 1891). Thus, the "eggshell skull" plaintiff can recover fully, or as is sometimes said, "you take your victim as you find him." So if a particularly valuable package were on the Mexican, would the Winkfield be liable for the full damages even though the shipping company would be liable only for reasonably foreseeable damages? Should the Winkfield be able to limit its liability under *Hadley*? Assuming that it cannot, should the shipper be able to keep the difference, or should it be liable in restitution to the less-than-forthcoming customer?

3. ABANDONMENT AND DESTRUCTION

Owner sovereignty is also commonly thought to include the right to abandon property (throw it away or relinquish all claim to title) and the right to destroy property (demolish, burn, or otherwise eliminate all or most of its value). This makes sense if we think of property as an individual right important to owner autonomy. If the sovereign owner concludes that the thing is more of a burden than a blessing, why shouldn't she be allowed to get rid of it? But from a broader social welfare perspective, it is not always so clear that abandonment and destruction should be permitted. Consider the following cases.

P

D

Pocono Springs Civic Association, Inc. v. MacKenzie

Superior Court of Pennsylvania, 1995.
667 A.2d 233.

(appellants)

■ ROWLEY, PRESIDENT JUDGE. The issue in this appeal is whether real property owned by appellants Joseph W. MacKenzie and Doris C. Mac-

Kenzie has been abandoned, as they claim. In an order entered January 5, 1995, the trial court granted summary judgment, in the amount of $1,739.82, in favor of appellee Pocono Springs Civic Association, Inc., which argued successfully to the trial court that appellants had not abandoned their property located in appellee's development, and, therefore appellants were still obligated to pay association fees.[1] * * *

We briefly outline the facts and procedural background of the case as follows: Appellants purchased a vacant lot at Pocono Springs Development, located in Wayne County, on October 14, 1969. In 1987, appellants decided to sell their still-vacant lot. A subsequent offer for the purchase of appellants' lot was conditioned upon the property being suitable for an on-lot sewage system. Upon inspection, the lot was determined to have inadequate soil for proper percolation, and appellants' sale was lost. Believing their investment to be worthless, appellants attempted to abandon their lot at Pocono Springs Development. Appellants claimed that because they successfully abandoned their lot, they are relieved from any duty to pay the association fees sought by appellee. The trial court held, however, that the appellant's abandonment defense is "not a valid defense." We agree with the trial court, and affirm. * * *

Appellants' argument, that they successfully abandoned their lot at Pocono Springs Development, is based upon several actions that they believe disassociate them from the land. First, appellants, after learning that the lot would not meet township sewage requirements, attempted to turn the lot over to appellee. Appellee declined to accept the property. Second, appellants tried to persuade appellee to accept the lot as a gift, to be used as a park-like area for the community. Appellee again declined. Third, in 1986 appellants ceased paying real estate taxes on their lot, and in 1988 the Wayne County Tax Claim Bureau offered the property for sale, due to delinquent tax payments. There were no purchasers. Fourth, in 1990, the lot was again offered for sale by the Tax Claim Bureau. The property again was not sold. The Bureau then placed the lot on its "repository" list. Fifth, appellants signed a notarized statement, mailed to "all interested parties," Brief for Appellants at 9, which expressed their desire to abandon the lot. Sixth, appellants do not accept mail regarding the property. These occurrences, together with appellants having neither visited the lot nor utilized the development's services since 1986, cause appellants to "assert that they do not have 'perfect' title to Lot #20, in Pocono Springs [Development,] [thus] they can and have abandoned said property back to the sovereign." Id. at 11. On the basis of the above, appellants argue that their conduct manifests an intent to abandon, and

---

1. The covenant upon which appellee relies reads as follows:

> An association of all property owners is to be formed by the Grantor and designated by such name as may be deemed appropriate, and when formed, the buyer covenants and agrees that he, his execu-

tors, heirs and assigns, shall be bound by the by-laws, rules and regulations as may be duly formulated and adopted by such association and that they shall be subject to the payment of annual dues and assessments of the same.

Deed, Covenant Number 11.

that their intent to abandon should be a question of fact which precludes summary judgment.

The law of abandonment in Pennsylvania does not support appellants' argument. This Court has held that abandoned property is that:

> ... to which an owner has voluntarily relinquished all right, title, claim and possession with the intention of terminating his ownership, but without vesting it in any other person and with the intention of not reclaiming further possession or resuming ownership, possession or enjoyment.

Commonwealth v. Wetmore, 447 A.2d 1012, 1014 (Pa. Super. 1982) (citations omitted). However, in the instant case, appellants have not relinquished their rights, title, claim and possession of their lots. They remain owners of real property in fee simple, with a recorded deed and "perfect" title. Absent proof to the contrary, possession is presumed to be in the party who has record title. Overly v. Hixson, 82 A.2d 573 (Pa. Super. 1951). As appellants themselves concede, with commendable candor, see Brief for Appellants at 15, no authority exists in Pennsylvania that allows for the abandonment of real property when owned in fee simple with perfect title.[3] Additionally, appellants properly admit that neither refusal to pay taxes nor non use of real property constitutes abandonment. Brief for Appellants at 16; see also Petition of Indiana County, 62 A.2d 3, 5 (Pa. 1948) ("It has frequently been held that abandonment of title is not to be presumed from a mere failure to possess the land or from neglect to pay the taxes thereon; inchoate rights may be abandoned but abandonment is not predictable of perfect titles[.]"). Yet, appellants nonetheless maintain that their non use, refusal to pay taxes, and offers to sell create an abandonment, because of a displayed intent to abandon.

But appellants simply do not accept that the record shows that they have retained "perfect" title to their lot. Neither title nor deed has been sold or transferred. * * * Perfect title, under Pennsylvania law, cannot be abandoned. O'Dwyer v. Ream, 136 A.2d 90 (Pa. 1957). In O'Dwyer, our Supreme Court held that once it is determined that good title exists, then the abandonment theory cannot succeed. See also A.D. Graham & Company, Inc. v. Pennsylvania Turnpike Commission, 33 A.2d 22, 29 (Pa. 1943) (which held that the doctrine of abandonment does not apply to perfect titles, only to imperfect titles). Appellants do not cite, and our own research has not discovered, any more recent cases that would cause us to question the authority of the cited decisions. Absent authority to support their

---

3. Most commonly, abandonment involves personal property or railway lines not owned in fee simple. See Quarry Office Park Associates v. Philadelphia Electric Company, 576 A.2d 358 (Pa. Super 1990) (Court reversed order granting summary judgment and remanded the case, holding that whether Conrail abandoned a rail line was a question for the factfinder, because Conrail owned a right of way, rather than a fee simple inter- est); Commonwealth v. Wetmore, 447 A.2d 1012 (Pa. Super. 1982) (Court affirmed order of trial court that arrested judgment following a jury trial; Court held that abandonment of shotgun occurred when father told chief of police to keep and dispose of weapon); In re Perlman's Estate, 35 A.2d 418 (Pa. 1944) (fiduciary abandoned interest in life insurance policies).

argument, therefore, the appeal cannot be successful for appellants. In short, as the trial court held, "[appellant's] 'Abandonment Authorization' [is] not a valid defense." Trial Court Opinion (Conway, P.J.), 1/5/95, at 6.

Appellants further claim that the trial court erred in granting summary judgment because whether they abandoned their lots should be a question of intent, for a jury to determine. * * * In the instant case, appellants' intent is irrelevant. What is controlling is our law, which states *RULE* that real property cannot be abandoned. The law, therefore, leaves nothing for a jury to decide on this claim, which amounts to a legal impossibility.

* * * [A]ppellee is entitled to judgment as a matter of law.

NOTES AND QUESTIONS

1. The MacKenzies' property was eventually purchased at a tax foreclosure sale for about $300 and was purchased again, presumably sight unseen, by a California land trust for about $500. The lot remains undeveloped to this day. Pocono Springs Estates is a gated residential community intended as a retreat for residents of New York City, New Jersey, and Philadelphia. To hold down prices, the lots were made narrow, the expectation being that a community sewer system would be installed. But sales of lots were disappointing, assessments lagged, and the sewer system was never installed. Most of the lots remain undeveloped today, and many like the MacKenzies' have been purchased by internet speculators who do not pay their assessments. The association web site contains the following disclaimer: "If you are looking to purchase a lot in Pocono Springs, whether it is from a private owner or the county itself, we advise that you do some research prior to purchasing. *There are some lots in Pocono Springs that do not perk. There are other lots that are not of buildable size.*" http://www.poconosprings.org/realestate/real_estate.htm. Perhaps because of the high rate of tax foreclosures, the community is intensely suspicious of outsiders. One of the editors was denied permission to enter the community to photograph the MacKenzies' lot.

2. Abandonment of personal property occurs all the time. Every time you take out the garbage, throw something in the waste basket, or haul something to the dump, you are abandoning personal property. Mineral rights are often subject to claims of abandonment when the owners have done nothing to exploit the rights for a period of time. Likewise, easements can be abandoned. Nevertheless the traditional rule, as the Pennsylvania Supreme Court reports, is that real property cannot be abandoned. See Restatement of Property § 504 cmt. a (1944). The original rationale for this rule probably related to the incidents and services that landowners were supposed to perform in feudal England, which meant that there could be no gap in "seisin" of real property. See Chapter V. In reality abandonment of real property was quite common during the settlement of the United States. Settlers would purchase land (often sight unseen) or file a claim for land under the Homestead Acts; if they discovered once they took up possession of the land that they could not make a go of it, they would

simply "pull up stakes" and move on. So in this sense the Pennsylvania court's ruling, although consistent with older doctrine, is a departure from actual practice.

3.   The notion that one cannot abandon real property is also a little odd given other powers (or liabilities) associated with ownership of land. If the owner of real property pays no attention to it, and another person enters onto the property, the owner can lose title to the occupant by adverse possession (see Chapter II). Isn't this a kind of abandonment by inattention or negligence? And of course gifts of real property are perfectly permissible. Isn't a gift of real property a decision by the owner to abandon any claim to the property, combined with designation of someone else as the new owner? Note however that in the adverse possession and gift situations, a new owner takes the place of the owner who has lost or abandoned any claim. The MacKenzies want to relinquish ownership without any substitute owner being designated to take their place.

4.   The MacKenzies' basic problem is that their lot in the Poconos has become a negative-value asset. The liabilities associated with the lot—the annual assessment fee imposed by the homeowners' association plus the property taxes—exceed the positive value anyone can obtain from the lot, given that local land-use regulations prohibit the installation of a septic field. So no one wants it—not the MacKenzies, not any potential purchaser, not the homeowners' association, not even the Commonwealth of Pennsylvania (which has the right to take and sell the land because of the unpaid property taxes). But doesn't this describe the condition that leads to abandonment of property in any context? The reason one throws a piece of paper in the wastebasket or an empty food container in the garbage is because it has become (for the owner) a negative-value asset. Provided the MacKenzies' action violates no environmental laws, why shouldn't they be allowed to toss the lot in the Poconos in the trash can, so to speak?

5.   Perhaps real property is different because of concern about externalities that might be created by abandonment of real property. The most obvious example would be real property that is a hazardous waste disposal site. Cleaning up the wastes (to protect against future releases affecting neighboring property or exposure of third parties) can often cost more than the property is worth in fair market value terms. Not surprisingly, therefore, environmental statutes like the Comprehensive Environmental Response, Compensation, and Liability Act (CERCLA) impose limits on an owner's ability to escape liability for cleanup costs through abandonment. See 42 U.S.C. § 101(20)(A) (providing that if a state or local government acquires property through abandonment "any person who owned, operated, or otherwise controlled activities at such facility immediately beforehand" is deemed to be the owner).

6.   Come to think of it, aren't there externality problems associated with abandonment of personal property too? What do you think about a strategy of reducing litter, and encouraging recycling, by declaring that personal property cannot be abandoned?

7. Whether property has been abandoned is a question of intent: The owner must intend to relinquish all claims to the property. Whether someone intends to abandon property is usually clear from context. An old chair placed just outside the front door is probably being moved in or out; the same chair placed on the curb is probably being abandoned. Nevertheless, problems are encountered. A German art museum discovered that custodial workers had thrown out a work of art by Berlin sculptor Michael Beutler made out of yellow plastic sheeting used to encase cement. The workers had assumed it was construction rubbish. After the episode, the museum announced that it was instituting "monthly Check Your Art Sense! classes, at which the city's garbage collectors can learn about understanding and appreciating art." See http://www.cbc.ca/story/arts/national/2005/01/11/Arts/trashedart050111.html (posted Jan. 11, 2005).

Eyerman v. Mercantile Trust Co.

Missouri Court of Appeals, St. Louis District, 1975.
524 S.W.2d 210.

■ RENDLEN, JUDGE. Plaintiffs appeal from denial of their petition seeking injunction to prevent demolition of a house at #4 Kingsbury Place in the City of St. Louis. The action is brought by individual neighboring property owners and certain trustees for the Kingsbury Place Subdivision. We reverse.

Louise Woodruff Johnston, owner of the property in question, died January 14, 1973, and by her will directed the executor "... to cause our home at 4 Kingsbury Place ... to be razed and to sell the land upon which it is located ... and to transfer the proceeds of the sale ... to the residue of my estate." Plaintiffs assert that razing the home will adversely affect their property rights, violate the terms of the subdivision trust indenture for Kingsbury Place, produce an actionable private nuisance and is contrary to public policy.

The area involved is a "private place" established in 1902 by trust indenture which provides that Kingsbury Place and Kingsbury Terrace will be so maintained, improved, protected and managed as to be desirable for private residences. The trustees are empowered to protect and preserve "Kingsbury Place" from encroachment, trespass, nuisance or injury, and it is "the intention of these presents, forming a general scheme of improving and maintaining said property as desirable residence property of the highest class." The covenants run with the land and the indenture empowers lot owners or the trustees to bring suit to enforce them.

Except for one vacant lot, the subdivision is occupied by handsome, spacious two and three-story homes, and all must be used exclusively as private residences. The indenture generally regulates location, costs and similar features for any structures in the subdivision, and limits construction of subsidiary structures except those that may beautify the property, for example, private stables, flower houses, conservatories, play houses or buildings of similar character.

On trial the temporary restraining order was dissolved and all issues found against the plaintiffs. * * *

The issues, simply stated, involve: (1) Private nuisance; (2) enforcement of restrictive covenants and (3) public policy. * * *

Whether #4 Kingsbury Place should be razed is an issue of public policy involving individual property rights and the community at large. The plaintiffs have pleaded and proved facts sufficient to show a personal, legally protectible interest.

Demolition of the dwelling will result in an unwarranted loss to this estate, the plaintiffs and the public. The uncontradicted testimony was that the current value of the house and land is $40,000.00; yet the estate could expect no more than $5,000.00 for the empty lot, less the cost of demolition at $4,350.00, making a grand loss of $39,350.33 if the unexplained and capricious direction to the executor is effected. Only $650.00 of the $40,000.00 asset would remain.

Kingsbury Place is an area of high architectural significance, representing excellence in urban space utilization. Razing the home will depreciate adjoining property values by an estimated $10,000.00 and effect corresponding losses for other neighborhood homes. The cost of constructing a house of comparable size and architectural exquisiteness would approach $200,000.00.

The importance of this house to its neighborhood and the community is reflected in the action of the St. Louis Commission on Landmarks and Urban Design designating Kingsbury Place as a landmark of the City of St. Louis. This designation, under consideration prior to the institution of this suit, points up the aesthetic and historical qualities of the area and assists in stabilizing Central West End St. Louis. It was testified by the Landmarks Commission chairman that the private place concept, once unique to St. Louis, fosters higher home maintenance standards and is among the most effective methods for stabilizing otherwise deteriorating neighborhoods. The executive director of Heritage St. Louis, an organization operating to preserve the architecture of the city, testified to the importance of preserving Kingsbury Place intact:

> The reasons (sic) for making Kingsbury Place a landmark is that it is a definite piece of urban design and architecture. It starts out with monumental gates on Union. There is a long corridor of space, furnished with a parkway in the center, with houses on either side of the street, ... The existence of this piece of architecture depends on the continuity of the (sic) both sides. Breaks in this continuity would be as holes in this wall, and would detract from the urban design qualities of the streets. And the richness of the street is this belt of green lot on either side, with rich tapestry of the individual houses along the sides. Many of these houses are landmarks in themselves, but they add up to much more ... I would say Kingsbury Place, as a whole, with its design, with its important houses ... is a most significant piece of urban design by any standard.

To remove #4 Kingsbury from the street was described as having the effect of a missing front tooth. The space created would permit direct access to Kingsbury Place from the adjacent alley, increasing the likelihood the lot will be subject to uses detrimental to the health, safety and beauty of the neighborhood. The mere possibility that a future owner might build a new home with the inherent architectural significance of the present dwelling offers little support to sustain the condition for destruction.

We are constrained to take judicial notice of the pressing need of the community for dwelling units as demonstrated by recent U.S. Census Bureau figures showing a decrease of more than 14% in St. Louis City housing units during the decade of the 60's. This decrease occurs in the face of housing growth in the remainder of the metropolitan area. It becomes apparent that no individual, group of individuals nor the community generally benefits from the senseless destruction of the house; instead, all are harmed and only the caprice of the dead testatrix is served. Destruction of the house harms the neighbors, detrimentally affects the community, causes monetary loss in excess of $39,000.00 to the estate and is without benefit to the dead woman. No reason, good or bad, is suggested by the will or record for the eccentric condition. This is not a living person who seeks to exercise a right to reshape or dispose of her property; instead, it is an attempt by will to confer the power to destroy upon an executor who is given no other interest in the property. To allow an executor to exercise such power stemming from apparent whim and caprice of the testatrix contravenes public policy.

Public Policy over individual will of the deceased

The Missouri Supreme Court held in State ex rel. McClintock v. Guinotte, 204 S.W. 806, 808 (Mo. 1918), that the taking of property by inheritance or will is not an absolute or natural right but one created by the laws of the sovereign power. The court points out the state "may foreclose the right absolutely, or it may grant the right upon conditions precedent, which conditions, if not otherwise violative of our Constitution, will have to be complied with before the right of descent and distribution (whether under the law or by will) can exist." Further, this power of the state is one of inherent sovereignty which allows the state to "say what becomes of the property of a person, when death forecloses his right to control it." McClintock v. Guinotte, supra, at 808, 809. While living, a person may manage, use or dispose of his money or property with fewer restraints than a decedent by will. One is generally restrained from wasteful expenditure or destructive inclinations by the natural desire to enjoy his property or to accumulate it during his lifetime. Such considerations however have not tempered the extravagance or eccentricity of the testamentary disposition here on which there is no check except the courts.

Normal restrictions or considerations that a living person has in regard to his property do not restrain the dead, thus courts must step in to control abuse of privileges.

see bottom of next page

In the early English case of Egerton v. Brownlow, 10 Eng.Rep. 359, 417 (H.L.C. 1853), it is stated: "The owner of an estate may himself do many things which he could not (by a condition) compel his successor to do. One example is sufficient. He may leave his land uncultivated, but he cannot by a condition compel his successor to do so. The law does not interfere with the owner and compel him to cultivate his land, (though it may be for the

RULE

public good that land should be cultivated) so far the law respects ownership; but when, by a condition, he attempts to compel his successor to do what is against the public good, the law steps in and pronounces the condition void and allows the devisee to enjoy the estate free from the condition." A more recent application of this principle is found in M'Caig's Trustees v. Kirk–Session of the United Free Church of Lismore, et al., 1915 Sess.Cas. 426 (Scot.). There, by codicil to her will, testatrix ordered certain statues erected to honor her family in a tower built in the form of an amphitheater on a hill. Balustrades were to be erected so that even the public would have no access inside the tower. Special provision was made for keeping out the public and the ground enclosed was expressly declared to be a private enclosure. There were no living descendants of any member of the family who might, if so permitted, take pleasure in contemplating the proposed statues. The court states at 434: "If a bequest such as in Miss M'Caig's codicil were held good, money would require to be expended in perpetuity merely gratifying an absurd whim which has neither reason nor public sentiment in its favor." In striking down the provisions of the codicil, the court further notes that there is indeed a "difference between what a man, uncognosed, may do at his own hand, and what the law will support under the provisions of his will ... therefore, without being illegal in the sense of being contrary to any express rule of the common law or contrary to any statute, the principle of public policy will prevent such post-mortem expenditure. Whether the act is sufficiently contrary to public policy to warrant the court's interference must depend on the degree to which it is against public policy." The court further observed that the erection of the eleven statues "would be of no benefit to anyone except those connected with the carrying out of the work, for whose interest she expresses no concern." M'Caig's Trustees v. Kirk–Session of the United Free Church of Lismore, et al., supra at 438. In the case sub judice, testatrix similarly expressed no such concern; nothing in the will or record indicates an intent to benefit any razing company called upon to destroy her beautiful home.

In the case of In re Scott's Will, Board of Commissioners of Rice County v. Scott et al., 93 N.W. 109 (Minn. 1903), the Supreme Court of Minnesota stated, when considering the provision of a will directing the executor to destroy money belonging to the estate: "We assume, for purpose of this decision, that the direction in the codicil to the executor to destroy all of the residue of the money or cash or evidences of credit belonging to the estate was void." In re Scott's Will, supra at 109. See also Restatement, Second, Trusts § 124, at 267: "Although a person may deal capriciously with his own property, his self interest ordinarily will restrain him from doing so. Where an attempt is made to confer such a power upon a person who is given no other interest in the property, there is no such restraint and it is against public policy to allow him to exercise the power if the purpose is merely capricious." The text is followed by this illustration: "A bequeaths $1,000.00 to B in trust to throw the money into the sea. B holds the money upon a resulting trust for the estate of A and is liable to

as pointed out on bottom of previous page

the estate of A if he throws the money into the sea." Restatement, supra at 267. * * *

It is important to note that the purposes of testatrix's trust will not be defeated by injunction; instead, the proceeds from the sale of the property will pass into the residual estate and thence to the trust estate as intended, and only the capricious destructive condition will be enjoined. * * *

The term "public policy" cannot be comprehensively defined in specific terms but the phrase "against public policy" has been characterized as that which conflicts with the morals of the time and contravenes any established interest of society. Acts are said to be against public policy "when the law refuses to enforce or recognize them, on the ground that they have a mischievous tendency, so as to be injurious to the interests of the state, apart from illegality or immorality." Dille v. St. Luke's Hospital, 196 S.W.2d 615, 620 (Mo. 1946); Brawner v. Brawner, 327 S.W.2d 808, 812 (Mo. banc 1959).

Public policy may be found in the Constitution, statutes and judicial decisions of this state or the nation. In re Rahn's Estate, 291 S.W. 120 (Mo. 1927). But in a case of first impression where there are no guiding statutes, judicial decisions or constitutional provisions, "a judicial determination of the question becomes an expression of public policy provided it is so plainly right as to be supported by the general will." In re Mohler's Estate, 22 A.2d 680, 683 (Pa. 1941). In the absence of guidance from authorities in its own jurisdiction, courts may look to the judicial decisions of sister states for assistance in discovering expressions of public policy.

Although public policy may evade precise, objective definition, it is evident from the authorities cited that this senseless destruction serving no apparent good purpose is to be held in disfavor. A well-ordered society cannot tolerate the waste and destruction of resources when such acts directly affect important interests of other members of that society. It is clear that property owners in the neighborhood of #4 Kingsbury, the St. Louis Community as a whole and the beneficiaries of testatrix's estate will be severely injured should the provisions of the will be followed. No benefits are present to balance against this injury and we hold that to allow the condition in the will would be in violation of the public policy of this state.

Having thus decided, we do not reach the plaintiffs' contentions regarding enforcement of the restrictions in the Kingsbury Place trust indenture and actionable private nuisance, though these contentions may have merit.

The judgment is reversed and the cause remanded to the Circuit Court to enter judgment as prayed.

■ CLEMENS, JUDGE (dissenting). * * * The simple issue in this case is whether the trial court erred by refusing to enjoin a trustee from carrying out an explicit testamentary directive. In an emotional opinion, the majority assumes a psychic knowledge of the testatrix' reasons for directing her home be razed; her testamentary disposition is characterized as "capricious," "unwarranted," "senseless," and "eccentric." But the record is utterly silent as to her motives.

The majority's reversal of the trial court here spawns bizarre and legally untenable results. By its decision, the court officiously confers a "benefit" upon testamentary beneficiaries who have never litigated or protested against the razing. The majority opinion further proclaims that public policy demands we enjoin the razing of this private residence in order to prevent land misuse in the City of St. Louis. But the City, like the beneficiaries, is not a party to this lawsuit. The fact is the majority's holding is based upon wispy, self-proclaimed public policy grounds that were only vaguely pleaded, were not in evidence, and were only sketchily briefed by the plaintiffs. * * *

Kingsbury Place is a "private place" established in 1902 by trust indenture. Except for one well-tended vacant lot (whose existence the majority ignores in saying the street minus #4 Kingsbury Place would be like "a missing front tooth") the trust indenture generally regulates size, constructions and cost of structures to be built on Kingsbury Place. It empowers the trustees to maintain vacant lots and to protect the street from "encroachment, trespass, nuisance and injury." The indenture's acknowledgment that vacant lots did and would exist shows that such lots were not to be considered an "injury." The fact the indenture empowers the trustees to maintain vacant lots is neither an express nor an implied ban against razing residences. The indenture simply recognizes that Kingsbury Place may have vacant lots from time to time—as it now has—and that the trustees may maintain them—as they now do. The indenture itself affords plaintiffs no basis for injunctive relief. * * *

The majority opinion bases its reversal on public policy. But plaintiffs themselves did not substantially rely upon this nebulous concept. Plaintiffs' brief contends merely that an "agency of the City of St. Louis has recently [?] designated Kingsbury Place as a landmark," citing § 24.070, Revised Code of the City of St. Louis. Plaintiffs argue removal of the Johnston home would be "intentional ... destruction of a landmark of historical interest." Neither the ordinance cited in the brief nor any action taken under it were in evidence. Indeed, the Chairman of the Landmarks and Urban Design Commission testified the Commission did not declare the street a landmark until after Mrs. Johnston died. A month after Mrs. Johnston's death, several residents of the street apparently sensed the impending razing of the Johnston home and applied to have the street declared a landmark. The Commissioner testified it was the Commission's "civic duty to help those people." * * *

The leading Missouri case on public policy as that doctrine applies to a testator's right to dispose of property is In re Rahn's Estate, 291 S.W. 120 (Mo. banc 1927). There, an executor refused to pay a bequest on the ground the beneficiary was an enemy alien, and the bequest was therefore against public policy. The court denied that contention: "We may say, at the outset, that the policy of the law favors freedom in the testamentary disposition of property and that it is the duty of the courts to give effect to the intention of the testator, as expressed in his will, provided such intention does not contravene an established rule of law." And the court wisely added, "it is not the function of the judiciary to create or announce a public policy of its own, but solely to determine and declare what is the public policy of the state or nation as such policy is found to be expressed in the Constitution, statutes, and judicial decisions of the state or nation, ... not by the varying opinions of laymen, lawyers, or judges as to the demands or the interests of the public." And, in cautioning against judges declaring public policy the court stated: "Judicial tribunals hold themselves bound to the observance of rules of extreme caution when invoked to declare a transaction void on grounds of public policy, and prejudice to the public interest must clearly appear before the court would be warranted in pronouncing a transaction void on this account." In resting its decision on public-policy grounds, the majority opinion has transgressed the limitations declared by our Supreme Court in Rahn's Estate. * * * It requires judicial imagination to hold, as the majority does, that the mere presence of a second vacant lot on Kingsbury Place violates public policy.

opposing the majority's view that it can define "Public Policy" when not explicitly found elsewhere

As much as our aesthetic sympathies might lie with neighbors near a house to be razed, those sympathies should not so interfere with our considered legal judgment as to create a questionable legal precedent. Mrs. Johnston had the right during her lifetime to have her house razed, and I

See bottom of pages 525 & 526

Figure 4–5
#4 Kingsbury Place, Saint Louis, 2006

find nothing which precludes her right to order her executor to raze the house upon her death. It is clear that "the law favors the free and untrammeled use of real property." Gibbs v. Cass, 431 S.W.2d 662 (Mo. Ct. App. 1968). This applies to testamentary dispositions. Mississippi Valley Trust Co. v. Ruhland, 222 S.W.2d 750 (Mo. 1949). An owner has exclusive control over the use of his property subject only to the limitation that such use may not substantially impair another's right to peaceably enjoy his property. City of Fredricktown v. Osborn, 429 S.W.2d 17 (Mo. Ct. App. 1968), Reutner v. Vouga, 367 S.W.2d 34 (Mo. Ct. App. 1963). Plaintiffs have not shown that such impairment will arise from the mere presence of another vacant lot on Kingsbury Place.

I find no plain error in the trial court's denial of injunctive relief, and on the merits I would affirm the trial court's judgment. * * *

NOTES AND QUESTIONS

1. The issue in *Eyerman* is complicated by the (belated) designation of the Johnston home as a historical and aesthetic landmark. Today, historical and architectural preservation laws are much more common than they were when the principal case was decided. In an important decision reproduced in Chapter XII, *Penn Central Transp. Co. v. New York City*, 438 U.S. 104 (1978), the Supreme Court upheld such a historical preservation law against a challenge that it caused a taking of the owner's property. After *Penn Central*, is it clear that St. Louis could prohibit the destruction of an architecturally significant home, before or after the owner's death, so long as the prohibition did not impose unduly harsh financial losses on the owner (or her estate)?

2. Suppose the owner of the Barry Bonds baseball at issue in *Popov* (discussed in Chapter II) decides for some idiosyncratic reason to destroy the baseball in a public ceremony. (Perhaps more understandably, such a thing occurred recently in Chicago with a certain notorious baseball caught by a Cubs fan.) This imposes no obvious loss on the community. The actual baseball is a fungible asset indistinguishable from tens of thousands of other baseballs, and is easily reproduced. But because this is understood to be the Barry Bonds record-breaking baseball, the stunt results in the destruction of an asset having at the time a market value among collectors of $450,000. On the authority of *Eyerman*, would a court be justified, perhaps at the instance of a suit brought by other baseball collectors, in enjoining such destruction as contrary to public policy?

[Handwritten margin note: But this is not a direct + actual loss for anyone, just a potential future asset no longer available for purchase (or sale)]

3. Interestingly, the legal philosopher John Austin uses the type of situation in *Eyerman* to illustrate his conception of ownership: "If I am the absolute owner of my house, I may destroy it if I will. But I must not destroy it in such a manner as would amount to an injury to any of my neighbors." 3 John Austin, Lectures on Jurisprudence 6 (1861–1863). Did that happen here? What if Mrs. Johnston's reason for directing that the house be razed was that she wanted to prevent members of a class protected under antidiscrimination law from ever living there?

4.   How much can we rely on the owner's incentives as a stand in for social benefits and costs? On the one hand, an owner who reduces value to future owners thereby reduces the price she might sell it for now, as long as the conditions for capitalization of future values into present market values holds (or, alternatively, the owner can hold the asset long enough for the market price to reflect these values). See, e.g., Harold Demsetz, Toward a Theory of Property Rights, 57 Am. Econ. Rev. 347, 355 (1967) (Papers & Proc.); Lior Jacob Strahilevitz, The Right to Destroy, 114 Yale L.J. 781 (2005). On the other hand, much commentary focuses on the defects in owners' decisionmaking processes and the need for collective intervention to prevent waste. See, e.g., Joseph L. Sax, Playing Darts with a Rembrandt: Public and Private Rights in Cultural Treasures (1999); Edward J. McCaffery, Must We Have the Right to Waste?, in New Essays in the Legal and Political Theory of Property 76 (Stephen R. Munzer ed., 2001); see also Michael Heller, The Boundaries of Private Property, 108 Yale L.J. 1163, 1165–66 (1999). We return to this issue in the materials on dead hand control in Chapters V and VI. Incidentally, according to the website zillow.com, the house at #4 Kingsbury Place is still intact and is estimated to be worth $1,265,787 as of December 29, 2006.

5.   From a social welfare perspective, is the right to destroy more problematic than the right to abandon? After all, abandonment leaves open the possibility that some other person will take up the property and put it to some productive use. Destruction eliminates any value for all time. But if individual owners are not allowed to make the decision whether to destroy property, who should make this decision? Does the value of the right to destroy depend on whether property is personal as opposed to fungible (see excerpts from Margaret Jane Radin, Chapter III)? Should people be allowed to leave valuable objects like wedding rings in caskets of loved ones when they are buried? Should famous people—political leaders, artists and writers, actors and actresses—be allowed to destroy their personal papers and diaries before they die? For further discussion of these issues, see Strahilevitz, supra.

4.   TRANSFER

The right to transfer is also considered a fundamental attribute of owner sovereignty. The right to transfer enhances owner autonomy, because it permits the owner to shed gatekeeper responsibility for things that no longer suit the owner's wants or needs, and at the same time to acquire other things that may be better suited to the owner's wants and needs. Moreover, the right to transfer confers a significant power on the owner, in that the owner is allowed in effect to appoint his or her successor as gatekeeper of the asset. The right to transfer also has powerful efficiency justifications. Free transferability permits things to be reallocated from one person to another so as to allow those who place a higher value on the asset to end up in control of it. If the process of transfer were costless (recall the Coase theorem, Chapter I) all things would end up in the hands of the persons who value them the most. In this happy state of affairs, society would be better off, in terms of the satisfaction of all persons' wants and needs, than it would be under any other allocation of things. Although this state of nirvana is unachievable in practice given positive transaction costs, it is quite likely that society will come closer to achieving such a state if assets are freely transferable, than it will if there are significant restrictions on the transfer of assets.

This is not to say that free transferability is always and everywhere desirable. We have seen in Chapter III that some kinds of things—human beings, body parts, and cultural patrimony—may be regarded as being inappropriate for treatment as "property." One reason for this is concern about permitting such things to be freely transferred from one person to another. Thus, one intermediate solution mentioned in those materials is to afford to certain things—like body parts—some of the attributes of property, such as the right to exclude, while denying these things the feature of full transferability.

Types of Transfers
① Exchanges
② Gifts

Transfers of property come in two basic types: exchanges (quid pro quos), in which an owner relinquishes title to some owned thing in exchange for a reciprocal transfer of some other thing (including money); and gifts, in which an owner relinquishes title to some owned thing in favor of another without explicitly receiving or expecting to receive something in return. The law of exchanges of property is bound up with the law of contracts and is primarily studied in courses on contracts. The law of gifts is bound up with the law of trusts and estates and is often studied in courses on these topics. Here we will consider only selected topics that bear on the sovereign owner's right to transfer her owned thing.

We begin with some rules designed to enhance the transferability of assets. These rules, paradoxically, limit the unrestricted freedom of owners to dispose of things in order to preserve the right of other persons, down the road, to engage in transfers of the same thing. We then consider another requirement imposed in several contexts in order to establish a valid transfer of some thing: namely, the requirement that the thing be delivered to the transferee.

a.   RULES DESIGNED TO ENHANCE TRANSFERABILITY

The law has long favored transferability of property. Nowhere is this more clearly seen than in the common-law rule against restraints on alienation. In its simplest form, this rule says that an owner may not transfer property to another on condition that the transferee will not retransfer the property. This rule, of course, limits the freedom of the original owner to transfer: The original owner is barred from engaging in a transfer that limits further transfers. Why might owners want to put restrictions on the right of future transfers? Consider the following case.

Lauderbaugh v. Williams
Supreme Court of Pennsylvania, 1962.
186 A.2d 39.

■ O'Brien, Justice. These appeals are from decrees entered in an action to Quiet Title and an Equity Action to set aside a deed of conveyance of land.

The cases involve the same questions and were tried together. In 1940, Mildred B. Lauderbaugh and her husband, Dayton S. Lauderbaugh, became the owners by purchase of land in Wayne and Monroe Counties which included a lake known as Watawga. The Lauderbaughs laid out some lots in a plan on the westerly shore and began the sale of lots in 1949. In June, 1951 the purchasers of the lots and the Lauderbaughs entered into an agreement whereby, as a condition precedent, future purchasers of land along the shore of the lake were required to be members of the Lake Watawga Association. The Association was formed to control the development along the shore of the lake. Many attractive homes representing a substantial investment had been erected. After the formation of the Association and Agreement other lots were sold to those who became members of the Association and homes were built. Mrs. Lauderbaugh instituted an action to quiet title in March, 1958, her husband being deceased, to remove a cloud on her title by seeking to have the agreement restricting the sale of property to members of the Association declared void. In February, 1960, Mrs. Lauderbaugh, together with Asher Seip, Jr., and Jacob Seip were named defendants in a complaint in Equity to set aside a deed of December 3, 1959, for land along the lake shore from Mrs. Lauderbaugh to Asher Seip, Jr.,—Jacob Seip being the partner of Asher Seip, Jr., grantee in the deed—as a violation of the agreement of June 1951, and to enjoin Mrs. Lauderbaugh from conveying land along the lake shore except to persons approved for membership in the Lake Watawga Association. The plaintiffs in the Equity case were mostly the persons named as defendants in Action to Quiet Title. The trial court entered a decree upholding the validity of the agreement but restricted its application to the westerly shore of the lake and entered a decree setting aside the deed from Mrs. Lauderbaugh to Asher Seip, Jr., and enjoining her from conveying land on the western shore of the lake except in accordance with the agreement of June, 1951, and in accordance with the rules, regulations and by-laws of the Lake Watawga Association. Both sides filed exceptions, which exceptions were dismissed, thereby giving rise to the instant appeals.

The agreement of June, 1951 provides that:

The First Parties [the Lauderbaughs], for themselves, their heirs and assigns, agree that membership in the Lake Watawga Association shall be a condition precedent for future purchasers of land along the shore of Lake Watawga; that in the event such prospective purchasers qualify as members as aforesaid, the First Parties will, upon payment of purchase price, execute and deliver to them deeds. * * *

The pertinent portions of the By–Laws of the Lake Watawga Association provide as follows:

Article V

Membership

Section 1. No person shall be eligible to membership in the Association who does not meet the requirements hereinafter specified. Such person shall be either the owner or a prospective owner of property along the shore of Lake Watawga, but such ownership or prospective ownership shall not in itself entitle such person or persons to become a member of this Association. This by-law can be amended only by a vote of three-fourths of the total membership of the Association.

Section 4. Application for membership shall be made to the Secretary, and by him referred to the Board of Directors, who shall act upon the same at their earliest convenience. Notice of the application for membership shall be given to every member at least 10 days prior to the time when such application shall be acted upon. The Board of Directors shall carefully consider any objections made to applicants. An Investigation Committee composed of three members of the Board of Directors shall be appointed by the President of the Board, which Committee shall report its findings to the Board of Directors before the application is acted upon. If written objections are filed by one member of the Association, when the membership is less than ten, the applicant shall be rejected. If written objections are filed by three or more members, when the membership of the Association is more than ten, the applicant shall be rejected. If written objections are filed by less than three members, when the membership is more than ten, the applicant may be elected by a two-thirds vote of the Directors present when such application is considered.

Essentially the question is the legality of the agreement restricting alienation of lake shore property to members of the Association only. This precise question has never before been decided by this court. However, while we do not have prior cases presenting similar factual conditions we are amply supplied with firmly established legal principles. Every restraint on alienation of real property is not necessarily void. True, such restraints are not favored in the law. Further, an absolute restraint is against public policy and, therefore, of no legal effect. However, a limited and reasonable restraint on the power of alienation may be valid. See, Restatement of Property, § 406, and 26 C.J.S. Deeds § 145.

Whether the agreement of June, 1951 is construed to create a condition precedent, a covenant not to convey or anything else, it is clear that its effect, when read in conjunction with the requirements of membership in the Association, is to limit unreasonably the free alienation of land bordering Lake Watawga, since conveyances may be made only to members of the Association. Control over the membership of the Association lies not with the grantor, but with others, the consent of all but two of whom must be obtained in order for any prospective alienee to be eligible for membership.

We do not seek to impugn the motives of the members of the Association and, for the purposes of deciding the issues presented, assume that their motives are of the purest, their sole concerns being the orderly development of the area and, quite properly, the protection of their investments. Be that as it may however, the fact remains that no standards for admission to the Association are set out in its by-laws and it is possible that three members by whim, caprice or for any reason, good or bad, or for no reason, could deny membership to any prospective alienee, thereby depriving Mrs. Lauderbaugh of her right to alienate her land. It must be further noted that the restriction is not limited in time and purports to be a perpetual one, a fact which militates strongly against its enforcement. * * *

NOTES AND QUESTIONS

1. The court notes that "an absolute restraint is against public policy and, therefore, of no legal effect." This is a settled proposition of property law. If an owner attempts to impose a direct and unconditional restraint on alienation, courts everywhere will strike this down as void. At one time, some distinction was made among restraints according to their form. Thus, courts would distinguish among *disabling restraints*, which deny the power of the transferee to alienate, *forfeiture restraints*, which provide that if the transferee tries to alienate, the property will be forfeited to someone else, and *promissory restraints*, in which the transferee enters into a contract with the transferor promising not to alienate. Disabling restraints were always void, forfeiture restraints usually void, and promissory restraints often void but sometimes upheld. (What might be the justification for these distinctions?) A more accurate statement of the law today would probably be that any absolute restraint on alienation, no matter what form it takes, will be invalidated. What is the justification for this unyielding rule? At first blush, the prohibition on absolute restraints on alienation would seem to promote free transferability of property. But does it? Recall the material on bailments. If one had a mandatory rule that bailees would always be able to sell property to a third party, would bailors think twice about "alienating" possession to the bailee?

2. The restriction at issue in *Lauderbaugh* is not an absolute restraint on alienation. It allows alienation, provided the Board of Directors of the Property Owners Association agrees to admit the transferee into the Association. Such partial restraints on alienation are evaluated under the understanding that they will be upheld only if they are "reasonable." The standards for distinguishing reasonable from unreasonable partial restraints on alienation are very muddled. Does it turn on the percentage of the potential market for the property that is foreclosed by the restraint? On how much discretion is given to the entity that decides whether to permit alienation? On whether the exercise of discretion is guided by standards that would permit courts to determine whether there has been an abuse of discretion? On the "weightiness" of what the court perceives to be the interests advanced by the restraint? On the degree of risk that the power to restrict alienation will be exercised to discriminate against minority groups or for other illegitimate purposes? Which of these factors, or combination of factors, do you think motivated the *Lauderbaugh* court to find the partial restraint entailed by the requirement of prior Board approval unreasonable?

3. Mrs. Lauderbaugh was instrumental in setting up the system of restraints on alienation at Lake Watawga, yet in this case she was seeking

to have them set aside. What accounts for her change in position? As we will see in Chapter IX, courts often take a dim view of real estate developers who put restrictions on the first lots in a subdivision, and then change their minds when they try to sell the remaining lots. Should the court adopt a similar skepticism about Mrs. Lauderbaugh's actions here?

4. In Chapter VI we take up cooperatives and condominiums. Requirements that members of these associations approve the sale of a unit are given more deference than similar requirements in a common-interest community like that in *Lauderbaugh*. Why the difference?

THE STATUTE OF FRAUDS

Other doctrines besides the rule against restraints on alienation also serve to promote transferability. Another such rule, which will poke its head up from time to time in these materials (although again it is primarily covered in the course in contracts) is the Statute of Frauds. Originally enacted by Parliament in 1677 under the title "An Act for Prevention of Frauds and Perjuryes," 29 Car. II, c. 3, some version of the Statute of Frauds is in force in all states except Louisiana. It contains several provisions of importance to the law of property. Section one provides that a wide range of interests in land, including leases, must be "putt in Writeing and signed by the parties soe making or creating the same" or else they "shall have the force and effect of Leases or Estates at Will onely." Section two excepts from this requirement "all Leases not exceeding the terme of three years." Section three provides that no interest in land may be "assigned granted or surrendered unlesse it be by Deed or Note in Writeing signed by the party soe assigning granting or surrendering the same." Section four provides, in part, that "noe Action shall be brought * * * upon any Contract or Sale of Lands * * * or any Interest in or concerning them * * * unlesse the Agreement upon which such Action shall be brought or some Memorandum or Note thereof shall be in Writeing and signed by the partie to be charged therewith." In short, any conveyance of a property right in land, (other than a short term lease) and any contract for the assignment, surrender, or sale of a property right in land must be in writing and signed by at least one of the parties.

There has been a longstanding debate whether the Statute of Frauds, especially as applied to contracts for sales of goods and services, prevents more frauds than it promotes. But there is not much doubt that, as applied to transfers of property rights in land, it has increased the overall security of property rights, and hence has enabled transfers of property to occur more frequently and at lower cost. Indeed, the original statute was passed as a substitute for a system of registration of rights in land, and was widely perceived as successfully promoting greater security in land markets. See Philip Hamburger, The Conveyancing Purposes of the Statute of Frauds, 27 Am. J. Legal Hist. 354 (1983). So here again we see an example of a restriction on alienation—a law that interferes with the ability of owners to dispose of property by oral agreement or in an unsigned writing—which nevertheless functions to enhance the overall transferability of property. See also Anthony T. Kronman & Richard A. Posner, The Economics of

Contract Law 253–67 (1979); Jason Scott Johnston, The Statute of Frauds, in The New Palgrave Dictionary of Economics and Law (Peter Newman ed., 1998).

b.   THE DELIVERY REQUIREMENT

In several contexts, the law requires that a transfer take place only if the thing being transferred or some evidence of title is delivered to the transferee. For example, whenever land or an interest in land (such as an easement) is transferred by deed (a formal writing evidencing a transfer), the transfer is deemed to have taken place only if the deed is delivered to the transferee. Thus, if the transferor makes out a deed to the transferee, informs the transferee that the deed has been signed and sealed, and then puts the deed in his safe, courts will hold that no valid transfer has occurred. As the expression goes, the deed must be "signed, sealed, and *delivered*" before the transaction is complete. The other prominent type of transfer that requires delivery is a gift. Here, the law requires either a deed of gift (which must be delivered) or actual delivery of the object given. What is the purpose of insisting on delivery to the recipient before the courts will recognize a valid gift?

Irons v. Smallpiece

Kings Bench, 1819.
106 Eng. Rep. 467.

Trover for two colts. Plea, not guilty. The defendant was the executrix and residuary legatee of the plaintiff's father, and the plaintiff claimed the colts, under the verbal gift made to him by the testator twelve months before his death. The colts however continued to remain in possession of the father until his death. It appeared further that about six months before the father's death, the son having been to a neighboring market for the purpose of purchasing hay for the colts, and finding the price of that article very high, mentioned the circumstance to his father; and that the latter agreed to furnish the colts any hay they might want at a stipulated price, to be paid by the son. None however was furnished to them till within three or four days before the testator's death. Upon these facts, Abbott, C.J., was of opinion, that the possession of the colts never having been delivered to the plaintiff, the property therein has not vested in him by the gift; but that it continued in the testator until at the time of his death, and consequently that it passed to his executrix under the will; and the plaintiff therefore was nonsuited.

■ ABBOTT, C.J. I am of opinion that by the law of England, in order to transfer property by gift there must either be a deed or instrument of gift, or there must be an actual delivery of the thing to the donee. Here the gift is merely verbal, and differs from a donation mortis causa only in this respect, that the latter is subject to a condition, that if the donor live the thing shall be restored to him. Now it is a well established rule of law, that a donation mortis causa does not transfer the property without an actual delivery. The possession must be transferred, in point of fact; and the late case of Bunn v. Markham, 2 Marsh. 532, where all the former authorities were considered, is a very strong authority upon that subject. There Sir G. Clifton had written upon the parcels containing the property the names of the parties for whom they were intended, and had requested his natural son to see the property should pass to the donees. It was therefore manifestly his intention that the property should pass to the donees; yet as there was no actual delivery, the Court of Common Pleas held that it was not a valid gift. I cannot distinguish that case from the present, and therefore think that this property in the colts did not pass to the son by the verbal gift; and I cannot agree that the son can be charged with the hay which was provided for these colts three or four days before the father's death; for I cannot think that that tardy supply can be referred to the contract which was made so many months before.

■ HOLROYD, J. I am also of the same opinion. In order to change the property by a gift of this description, there must be a change of possession: here there has been no change of possession. If indeed it could be made out that the son was chargeable for the hay provided for the colts, then the possession of the father might be considered as the possession of the son. Here however no hay is delivered during the long interval from the time of the contract, until within a few days of the father's death; and I cannot think that the hay so delivered is to be considered in execution of the contract made so long before, and consequently the son is not chargeable of the price of it. * * *

NOTES AND QUESTIONS

1. *Irons* is usually cited for the proposition that delivery is a requirement for a valid gift. If this is so, then why did the judges seem to think that the result might have been different if the father had charged the son for hay shortly after the son reported that prices for hay were too high in the market? At that time, the colts still remained in the custody of the father. Does this perhaps suggest that the judges in *Irons* regarded delivery as just one piece of evidence tending to show that a valid gift has been made? Is the delivery requirement here a functional substitute for the signed writing required in other contexts by the Statute of Frauds? If so, how well does it perform the "fraud preventing" function?

2. Why impose restrictions on gifts that do not apply to sales? In many cultures gift-giving involves an elaborate system of quid pro quo and is a major part of the economy. A classic study is Marcel Mauss, The Gift: Forms and Functions of Exchange in Archaic Societies (Ian Cunnison transl., 1954). Is a quid pro quo absent from gift-giving in our own culture? A related but not necessarily identical distinction between gifts and sales is important in tax law (because gifts are not includable in the donee's income and are not deductible to the donor). In the leading decision, the U.S. Supreme Court indicated that transferor intent was crucial—namely whether the donor made the transfer from a "detached and disinterested

generosity" or "out of affection, respect, admiration, charity or like impulses." Commissioner v. Duberstein, 363 U.S. 278, 285 (1960) (citations and internal quotations marks omitted). Factfinders were instructed to discover this by applying the "mainsprings of human conduct to the totality of the facts of each case." Id. at 289. Does the common law do any better? How distinct are gifts, exchanges, and thefts anyway? See Carol M. Rose, Giving, Trading, Thieving, and Trusting: How and Why Gifts Become Exchanges, and (More Importantly) Vice Versa, 44 Fla. L. Rev. 295 (1992).

3.   When we say that an asset is inalienable, what does this mean? Quite a number of assets can be given away but not sold. They are market-inalienable. Recall the discussion of body parts and personhood in Chapter III and the excerpt from Margaret Jane Radin. Other assets, like a vote or one's entire person, cannot be transferred at all. See, e.g., Richard A. Epstein, Why Restrain Alienation?, 85 Colum. L. Rev. 970 (1985); Susan Rose–Ackerman, Inalienability and the Theory of Property Rights, 85 Colum. L. Rev. 931 (1985).

4.   The opinions in *Irons* refer to gifts *causa mortis*, which means gifts in contemplation of death. Such gifts are will substitutes, and rules governing their validity developed even earlier than the law on ordinary gifts, like the one in *Irons*. A valid gift *causa mortis* requires, in addition to delivery, that the donor die after making the gift. If the donor recovers, the gift is nullified. Implementing the delivery requirement can be especially difficult when one is on her deathbed, as the following case illustrates.

P   *D*
Foster v. Reiss

Supreme Court of New Jersey, 1955.
112 A.2d 553.

■ VANDERBILT, C.J. On April 30, 1951 the decedent, Ethel Reiss, entered a hospital in New Brunswick where she was to undergo major surgery. Just prior to going to the operating room on May 4, 1951, she wrote the following note in her native Hungarian language to her husband, the defendant herein:

My Dearest Papa:

In the kitchen, in the bottom of the cabinet, where the blue frying pan is, under the wine bottle, there is one hundred dollars. Along side the bed in my bedroom, in the rear drawer of the small table in the corner of the drawer, where my stockings are, you will find about seventy-five dollars. In my purse there is six dollars, where the coats are. Where the coats are, in a round tin box, on the floor, where the shoes are, there is two hundred dollars. This is Dianna's. Please put it in the bank for her. This is for her schooling.

The Building Loan book is yours, and the Bank book, and also the money that is here. In the red book is my son's and sister's and my brothers address. In the letter box is also my bank book.

Give Margaret my sewing machine and anything else she may want; she deserves it as she was good to me.

God be with you. God shall watch your steps. Please look out for yourself that you do not go on a bad road. I cannot stay with you. My will is in the office of the former Lawyer Anekstein, and his successor has it. There you will find out everything.

Your Kissing, loving wife,

Ethel Reiss 1951–5–4.

She placed the note in the drawer of a table beside her bed, at the same time asking Mrs. Agnes Tekowitz, an old friend who was also confined in the hospital, to tell her husband or daughter about it—"In case my daughter come in or my husband come in, tell them they got a note over there and take the note." That afternoon, while the wife was in the operating room unconscious under the effects of ether, the defendant came to the hospital and was told about the note by the friend. He took the note from the drawer, went home, found the cash, the savings account passbook, and the building and loan book mentioned in the note, and has retained possession of them since that time.

The wife was admittedly in a coma for three days after the operation and the testimony is in dispute as to whether or not she recovered consciousness at all before her death on the ninth day. Her daughter, her son-in-law, Mrs. Waldner, an old friend and one of her executrices who visited her every day, and Mrs. Tekowitz, who was in the ward with her, said that they could not understand her and she could not understand them. The defendant, on the other hand, testified that while she was "awful poor from ether" after the operation, "the fourth, fifth and sixth days I thought she was going to get healthy again and come home. She talked just as good as I with you." The trial judge who saw the witnesses and heard the testimony found that

> After the operation and until the date of her death on May 13, 1951 she was in a coma most of the time; was unable to recognize members of her family; and unable to carry on intelligent conversation * * * Mrs. Reiss was never able to talk or converse after coming out of the operation until her death.

The decedent's will gave $1 to the defendant and the residue of her estate to her children and grandchildren. The decedent's personal representatives and her trustees under a separation agreement with the defendant, brought this action to recover the cash, the passbook, and the building and loan book from the defendant, who in turn claimed ownership of them based on an alleged gift *causa mortis* from his wife. The trial court granted judgment for the plaintiffs, concluding that there had been no such gift. The Appellate Division of the Superior Court reversed, and we granted the plaintiff's petition for certification to the Appellate Division.

The doctrine of *donatio causa mortis* was borrowed by the Roman law from the Greeks, 2 Bl.Com. 514, and ultimately became a part of English and then American common law. Blackstone has said that there is a gift *causa mortis* "when a person in his last sickness, apprehending his dissolution near, delivers or causes to be delivered to another the possession of any personal goods, to keep in case of his decease." 2 Bl.Com. 514. Justinian offered this definition:

> A gift *causa mortis* is one made in expectation of death; when a person gives upon condition that, if any fatality happen to him, the receiver shall keep the article, but that if the donor should survive, or if he should change his mind, or if the donee should die first, then the donor shall have it back again. These gifts *causa mortis* are in all respects put upon the same footing as legacies. * * * To put it briefly, a gift *causa mortis* is when a person wishes that he himself should have the gift in preference to the donee, but that the donee should have it in preference to the heir. Walker's Just., at 119.

* * * There is some doubt in the New Jersey cases as to whether as a result of a gift *causa mortis* the property remains in the donor until his death, or whether the transfer is considered absolute even though it is defeasible. In any event, a gift *causa mortis* is essentially of a testamentary nature and as a practical matter the doctrine, though well established, is an invasion into the province of the statute of wills * * *

In Ward v. Turner, supra, 2 Ves.Sr. 431, 28 E.R. 275, 279, Lord Chancellor Hardwicke said that "it was a pity that the Statute of Frauds did not set aside all these kinds of gifts." Lord Eldon expressed the opinion that it would be an improvement of the law to strike out altogether this peculiar form of gift, but since that had not been done, he felt obliged to "examine into the subject of it." Duffield v. Elwes, 1 Bligh (N.S.) 533, 4 E.R. 959, 972 (1827). Our own Vice–Chancellor Stevenson referred to it as "that ancient legal curiosity." Dunn v. Houghton, 51 A. 71, 78 (N.J. Ch. 1902), and then later said that such gifts are "dangerous things":

> These gifts *causa mortis* are dangerous things. The law requires, before Mr. Hitt can come into this court and claim $10,000 as an ordinary testamentary gift from Mrs. Thompson, that he should produce an instrument in writing signed by Mrs. Thompson, and also acknowledged with peculiar solemnity by her in the presence of two witnesses, who thereupon subscribed their names as witnesses. That is what Mr. Hitt would have to prove if he claimed a testamentary gift in the ordinary form of one-third of Mrs. Thompson's estate. And yet, in cases of these gifts *causa mortis*, it is possible that a fortune of a million dollars can be taken away from the heirs, the next of kin of a deceased person, by a stranger, who simply has possession of the fortune, claims that he received it by way of gift, and brings parol testimony to sustain that claim. Varick v. Hitt, 55 A. 139, 153 (N.J. Ch. 1903). * * *

The first question confronting us is whether there has been "actual, unequivocal, and complete delivery during the lifetime of the donor, wholly divesting him [her] of the possession, dominion, and control" of the property * * * [citations omitted]

Here there was no delivery of any kind whatsoever. We have already noted the requirement so amply established in our cases of "actual, unequivocal and complete delivery during the lifetime of the donor, wholly divesting her of the possession, dominion, and control" of the property. This requirement is satisfied only by delivery by the *donor*, which calls for an affirmative act on her part, not by the mere taking of possession of the property by the donee. * * *

Here we are concerned with three separate items of property—cash, a savings account represented by a bank passbook, and shares in a building and loan association represented by a book. There was no actual delivery of the cash and no delivery of the indicia of title to the savings account or the building and loan association shares. Rather, the donor set forth in an informal writing her desire to give these items to the defendant. Although the writing establishes her donative intent at the time it was written, it does not fulfill the requirement of delivery of the property, which is a separate and distinct requirement for a gift *causa mortis*. The cash, passbook, and stock book remained at the decedent's home and she made no effort to obtain them so as to effectuate a delivery to the defendant.

We disagree with the conclusion of the Appellate Division that the donee already had possession of the property, and therefore delivery was unnecessary. Assuming, but not deciding, the validity of this doctrine, we note that the house was the property of the deceased and, although defendant resided there with her, he had no knowledge of the presence of this property in the house, let alone its precise location therein; therefore it cannot be said that he had possession of the property. * * *

But it is argued that the decedent's note to her husband in the circumstances of the case was an authorization to him to take possession of the chattels mentioned therein which when coupled with his taking of possession thereof during her lifetime was in law the equivalent of the delivery required in the Roman and common law alike and by all the decisions in this State for a valid gift *causa mortis*. Without accepting this contention, it is to be noted that it has no application to the present case, because here at the time the defendant obtained her note the decedent was in the operating room under ether and, according to the finding of the trial court, supra,

> after the operation and until the date of her death on May 13, 1951 she was in a coma most of the time; was unable to recognize members of her family; and unable to carry on intelligent conversation * * * Mrs. Reiss was never able to talk or converse after coming out of the operation until her death.

In these circumstances the note clearly failed as an authorization to the defendant to take possession of the chattels mentioned therein, since at the time he took the note from the drawer the decedent was under ether and according to the findings of the trial court unable to transact business until the time of her death. * * *

The judgment of the Appellate Division of the Superior Court is reversed and the judgment of the Chancery Division of the Superior Court will be reinstated.

DISSENT

■ JACOBS, J. (with whom WACHENFELD and WILLIAM J. BRENNAN, JR., JJ., agree) dissenting. The decedent Ethel Reiss was fully competent when she freely wrote the longhand note which was intended to make a gift *causa mortis* to her husband Adam Reiss. On the day the note was written her husband duly received it, located the money and books in accordance with its directions, and took personal possession of them. Nine days later Mrs. Reiss died; in the meantime her husband retained his possession and there was never any suggestion of revocation of the gift. Although the honesty of the husband's claim is conceded and justice fairly cries out for the fulfillment of his wife's wishes, the majority opinion (while acknowledging that gifts *causa mortis* are valid in our State as elsewhere) holds that the absence of direct physical delivery of the donated articles requires that the gift be stricken down. I find neither reason nor persuasive authority anywhere which compels this untoward result. See Gulliver and Tilson, Classification of Gratuitous Transfers, 51 Yale L.J. 1, 2 (1941):

> One fundamental proposition is that, under a legal system recognizing the individualistic institution of private property and granting to the owner the power to determine his successors in ownership, the general philosophy of the courts should favor giving effect to an intentional exercise of that power. This is commonplace enough but it needs constant emphasis, for it may be obscured or neglected in inordinate preoccupation with detail or dialectic. A court absorbed in purely doctrinal arguments may lose sight of the important and desirable objective of sanctioning what the transferror wanted to do, even though it is convinced that he wanted to do it.

Harlan F. Stone in his discussion of Delivery in Gifts of Personal Property, 20 Col.L.Rev. 196 (1920), points out that the rule requiring delivery is traceable to early notions of seisin as an element in the ownership of chattels as well as well as land; and he expresses the view that as the technical significance of seisin fades into the background, courts should evidence a tendency to accept other evidence in lieu of delivery as corroborative of the donative intent. See Philip Mechem, The Requirement of Delivery in Gifts of Chattels, 21 Ill.L.Rev. 341, 345 (1926). Nevertheless, the artificial requirement of delivery is still widely entrenched and is defended for modern times by Mechem (supra, at 348) as a protective device to insure deliberate and unequivocal conduct by the donor and the elimination of questionable or fraudulent claims against him. But even that defense has no applicability where, as here, the donor's wishes were freely and clearly expressed in a written instrument and the donee's ensuing possession was admittedly bona fide; under these particular circumstances every consideration of public policy would seem to point towards upholding the gift. * * *

When Ethel Reiss signed the note and arranged to have her husband receive it, she did everything that could reasonably have been expected of her to effectuate the gift *causa mortis;* and while her husband might conceivably have attempted to return the donated articles to her at the hospital for immediate redelivery to him, it would have been unnatural for him to do so. It is difficult to believe that our law would require such wholly ritualistic ceremony and I find nothing in our decisions to suggest it. The majority opinion advances the suggestion that the husband's authority to take possession of the donated articles was terminated by the wife's incapacity in the operating room and thereafter. The very reason she wrote the longhand note when she did was because she knew she would be incapacitated and wished her husband to take immediate possession, as he did. Men who enter hospitals for major surgery often execute powers of attorney to enable others to continue their business affairs during their incapacity. Any judicial doctrine which would legally terminate such power as of the inception of the incapacity would be startling indeed—it would disrupt commercial affairs and entirely without reason or purpose. * * *

NOTES AND QUESTIONS

1. As implied by this case, gifts *causa mortis* potentially override other more formal methods of disposing of property upon death—here the will giving the husband $1. (The husband would probably be entitled to more than this under a forced share statute. See Chapter V.) What is the rationale for insisting on the delivery requirement in the context where the intentions of the deceased seem unequivocally clear? Is it because, as the majority's reference to the Statute of Frauds suggests, the court is worried about the possibility of fraud being perpetrated in some other case? Formalities like drawing up a new will can prevent self-interested parties from perpetrating frauds, but they can do so at the cost of defeating true transferor intent. Or, does the delivery requirement provide additional assurance that the donor adequately appreciates the potential finality of the decision she is making? Cf. Lon L. Fuller, Consideration and Form, 41 Colum. L. Rev. 799, 800–03 (1941) (describing the "cautionary" function of certain legal formalities). But why doesn't the carefully composed letter satisfy this concern?

2. Does one draw any comfort from the fact that the note was in Mrs. Reiss's own hand? About half the states accept a will unattested by witnesses if it is in the testator's own hand—a so-called holographic will. The Uniform Probate Code takes this approach as well. Uniform Probate Code § 2–502(b) (formerly § 2–503). Nevertheless, coercion would invalidate any such instrument.

3. What additional acts would have been required to establish delivery in this case? If Adam had retrieved the pass books and the cash, had handed them to Ethel, and she had immediately handed them back, would this be enough? What is the point of requiring such a ritual?

CHAPTER V

THE FORMS OF OWNERSHIP

"Out of ould fields must spring and grow the new Corne."
—Sir Edward Coke, Commentaries, Vol. 1, Preface (1600)

A. INTRODUCTION

Property law would hardly exist in a world of Robinson Crusoes, each owning an island and all it contains. Even in our world, if each identified thing had only a single owner, property law would be quite a bit simpler. But either way property law would fail to unlock much value from things. Resources are often put to best use if they can be shared in some fashion. If A and B can both have access to a resource, they can both bring their special skills to using it and can spread the risk involved in owning it.

Access to resources can be divided along a number of dimensions. We have already seen situations in which an owner's right to exclude gives way to other interests, and this reflects a kind of sharing of assets. We have also seen how ownership can be separated from possession, as in the case of bailments. In this Chapter we focus on divisions that are built into the title of property itself. The law has developed an elaborate menu of forms of ownership, which permit divisions both across time and among multiple persons at any one point in time. We will not consider all forms of ownership in this Chapter. Those covered here are forms of ownership that evolved over time for freehold interests in land (and some extensions to personal property). They are less important today than they were when land was the principal form of wealth and prestige in society. But it is still true that one cannot understand the system of property rights we have today without a basic grasp of these forms and the doctrines that govern their interpretation and implementation. Other forms of property that permit more elaborate governance of complexes of assets are covered in Chapter VI, including leaseholds (landlord-tenant), condominiums and co-operatives, and trusts. Security interests, another important type of division, are covered in Chapter VII. Limited use rights, including easements and servitudes, are treated in Chapter IX.

Any time an asset is shared among multiple owners, a collective action problem is created, which can be seen as a kind of miniature "tragedy of the commons" (Chapter II). Consider the situation in which two people share ownership of a common asset, say a house. If they are members of the same household, they could divide the burdens and benefits associated with ownership of the house in a variety of ways. One could own the house and charge the other rent, either monetary or in kind. Or both could own and share the responsibilities for taxes, repairs, etc. The house itself might be part of a larger complex of property rights such as a common-interest community. (See the next Chapter.) Problems would arise if one of the owners caused damage to the house or piled too much junk in it, leaving too little room for the other to share the space. Another problem, to which we turn momentarily, is presented by successive owners or users. Ownership can also be split across time, but current owners do not always have their successors' interests at heart, and vice versa. Another consideration: If people could split ownership of any asset in any way they please, might things start to get too complicated? In part to limit the collective action problems associated with having too many claimants, and in part to keep the information costs associated with complexity from spiraling out of control, the law limits the number and variety of ways in which co-ownership can be organized.

We focus in this Chapter on freehold interests in land, which (for purely historical reasons) exclude leases. The forms of ownership for freehold interests recognized today are the product of historical evolution over many centuries. The aspirations that motivated legal actors to develop certain forms, and to impose certain limitations on their use, have in many instances long since disappeared. Yet the sedimentary residue of their efforts remains. For example, the understanding that someone must "stand seized" of real property at all times is still reflected in contemporary decisions. Yet the original motivation for this rule was to assure that someone was always available to fulfill feudal services and incidents—and these were abolished in 1660! The good news is that the system of forms devised by common-law lawyers from the seventeenth century onward has a remarkable internal logic to it—more so than most of the common law, and enough so that it is possible to present the system as a body of rules. It will be useful to advert to the historical rationale for various rules from time to time, but the rules themselves largely stand on their own.

B.   DIVISIONS BY TIME

When dividing property rights to land over time, the pieces created must conform to a menu of possibilities called estates in land. An *estate* is a type of property right and measures a person's interest in the land in terms of duration. An interest may be either a present possessory estate or one that does not take possession until the happening of some future event—a future interest.

Developments in England and America since the late Middle Ages have had a major impact on the particular forms and vocabulary used in dividing up property rights, and on the system of estates in land in particular. Perhaps more importantly, some of the abiding controversies over this long span of history are at the heart of questions about what function, if any, some of the doctrines surrounding estates and future interests perform.

The estates themselves, or at least the vocabulary in which they are presented, have their roots in the Middle Ages. Under the feudal system, particularly as it emerged in the aftermath of the Norman Conquest of 1066, personal relations were very important. The King would grant tenure—something less than full ownership—over lands to lords who in turn would owe services, chief among them military services, to the King. These lords would then be able to turn around and subinfeudate to their underlings. At the bottom of this feudal property-holding hierarchy were freeholding peasants. Again, the landholding relation between lord and peasants centered around a flow of services in both directions—protection and adjudication in return for labor and other services. The obligations of the tenant were originally centered around military service and farm labor. The "feudal incidents" of the military tenures, for example, ranged from the duty to do the lord and the land no harm ("homage") to the duty to provide funds in exigent circumstances and on the marriage of the lord's daughter ("aids") to the duty to pay to allow the heir of the deceased tenant to assume the tenancy ("relief"). Some peasants would hold land in more informal arrangements called copyhold, which over time became more formalized. In the feudal relationship, the identity of the one holding beneath made a lot of difference. The emphasis was on ensuring service rather than making land alienable. Alienability threatened the securing of the feudal services.

As time went on and the military aspect of feudalism became less important, money transfers replaced some of these services, and land became correspondingly more alienable. The component of services became less important and perhaps more of a notice-giving device, in some cases fancifully so. See A.W.B. Simpson, A History of the Land Law 6 (2d ed. 1986) (noting grant from one William Earl Warren to be held subject to the service of providing one mad bull annually for his lordship's amusement and a grant of lands requiring the tenant each Christmas Day "to make a leap, a whistle and a fart coram domino rege.") Again, it is important to remember that in the more personal world of feudal obligation, the terms of the deal between grantor and grantee were far less standardized than the package of rights afforded to owners today. See Marc Bloch, Feudal Society 115–16, 143–54 (L. A. Manyon trans., 1961).

The conflict over alienation raged with much maneuvering until 1290 with the Statute Quia Emptores (so-called because these were its first two words, meaning "because purchasers") made what later became the fee simple fully alienable, without a fine, by permitting substitution of the grantee for the grantor as the lord's new tenant. The medieval land market thus created started out on a small-scale, mostly involving odd acres and plots between peasants of the same community. With the upheaval in the wake of the Black Death of the mid-fourteenth century, peasants became more mobile and began moving in and out of villages; land sales became significantly more active. Sir Frederick Pollock & Frederic William Maitland, The History of English Law Before the Time of Edward I (2d ed. 1898); Sir William Holdsworth, An Historical Introduction to the Land Law (1927); Donald N. McCloskey, The Open Fields of England: Rent, Risk and the Rate of Interest, 1300–1815, in Markets in History: Economic Studies of the Past 5, 31–32 (D.W. Galenson ed., 1989).

The problem of occasional payments called feudal incidents—particularly those due on the death of the owner before transfer to an heir—remained, and landowners came to employ a proto-trust device, recognized in Chancery, called a *use* to avoid the feudal incidents. By having legal title technically reside in a replaceable trustee and equitable title in the owner (and later his family successors), one could avoid payments and obligations that were due only on the death of the owner of a corresponding legal estate. In 1535, Henry VIII, in order to deal with various financial and other difficulties, made a deal with the common-law lawyers in Parliament that resulted in the Statute of Uses, effective the next year. The Statute converted many equitable interests into legal interests, thereby restoring feudal incidents and increasing the business of the common-law courts and the lawyers who practiced before them. The use soon returned, in the form of the trust, to which turn in Chapter VI. A century later, the parliamentary party undid the resurrection of the feudal tenures, which was confirmed by Parliament at the Restoration of the monarchy in 1660. This legislation prohibited the monarch from creating new feudal tenures, reinforcing the move towards a more strictly standardized property system, with legislatures as the main sources of change.

The early state legislatures in the United States carried these developments further, abolishing the remnants of feudal incidents. Notions we have today—such as that a payment of rent is inconsistent with a fee simple—emerged from conflicts between farmers and landowners, especially in states like New York with a history of founding by major proprietors. See Eric Kades, The End of the Hudson Valley's Peculiar Institution: The Anti–Rent Movement's Politics, Social Relations, and Economics, 27 Law & Soc. Inquiry 941 (2002). As you will see, the simplification of the system of property forms has been carried only so far, and has not been pushed as far as it has in England since 1925. American commentators have long called for further simplification. See, e.g., T.P. Gallanis, The Future of Future Interests, 60 Wash. & Lee L. Rev. (2003); Lawrence W. Waggoner, Reformulating the Structure of Estates: A Proposal for Legislative Action, 85 Harv. L. Rev. 729, 732 (1972).

ESTATES IN LAND

The so-called freehold interests include the undivided fee simple and two types of lesser property rights that leave room for future interests—the life estate and the defeasible fees. Freehold interests originally were those that, as noted above, involved feudal military service obligations, whereas the lease—a nonfreehold estate—did not. This distinction was reflected in the types of actions that could be brought to protect the interest, and in the formalities required to transfer them. In the case of freehold interests, livery of seisin was required to give publicity to the transfer, which was originally effected by transferring a clod of earth, a twig, or a key to the grantee in front of a crowd of people. (In a less than humane but psychologically insightful procedure, a young child would sometimes be beaten on the spot in order to make the memory of the occasion an indelible and long-lasting one.) Livery of seisin has its echoes in another notice-giving device we will study later: Freehold interests tend to be recorded in land registries, but short-term leases are not.

Figure 5–1
Present Possessory Estates

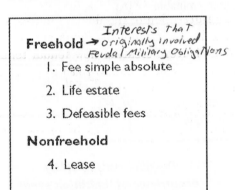

Note that the holders of a freehold interest as well as leaseholders are still sometimes called "tenants."

To understand the system as a whole it is important to keep in mind which future interests can follow which present possessory interests. As we consider present possessory interests, future interests retained by the grantor, and future interests created in a third party, the following diagrams may be helpful.

Figure 5–2
Diagram of Estates

To Grantor → "Reversion"

"Rest" (remaining interest)

To someone else → "Remainder"

③ Defeasible Fees (3 Types)

Only 2 FUTURE Interests subject to RAP
- contingent remainders
- executory interests

PRESENT POSSESSORY INTERESTS

1. **Fee Simple Absolute.** The fee simple absolute is the largest package of ownership rights, from which others are carved. It is indefinite in time, or, put differently, it has no natural end. No owner will live forever, but the owner can designate a successor owner, by gift, sale, or will. If the owner dies intestate—without a will—a state intestacy statute will designate certain others, typically spouse, children, or various blood relatives, as the person's heirs, who will then take the property in fee simple.

Example 1: O grants Blackacre "to Marge and her heirs" or "to Marge in fee simple," or "to Marge."

The fee simple is the largest package of rights, and in a transfer, a grantor is presumed to give all that she has, unless she indicates otherwise. Today this is reflected in the fact that if Owner grants Blackacre "to A," this creates a fee simple.

There was a time when to create a fee simple in a deed (but not in a will, where the search for testator's intent has always led to more leniency), one had to use the magic words "to A and his/her heirs." Saying simply "to A" or even "to A in fee simple" would result in a life estate and a reversion (see below). Lawyers tend to be cautious people, and in deeds conveying fees simple, they still often use "to A and his/her heirs" or "to A in fee simple" even though strictly speaking these locutions are no longer required.

Contrary to some popular usage, a person does not have heirs until her death (while alive, someone has at most *heirs apparent*). Marge Simpson has no heirs until she dies; her husband Homer, and her children, Bart, Lisa, and Maggie, are only heirs apparent. If a person dies intestate (without a will) and without heirs, then the property will escheat to the state in which the property is located.

Understanding the traditional formulation "and his heirs" is important not just because the phrase is still in common use. It can be misleading. The phrase does not mean that the heirs receive any interest. Recall that a person does not even have heirs until death. Thus, if Owner grants "to Marge and her heirs," Homer and her children receive nothing. (Depending on the state's marital laws, Homer might be entitled to something on divorce or at Marge's death, questions to which we return below.) Rather, "and her heirs" are words of *limitation*, as opposed to "to Marge," which are words of *purchase*. ("Words of limitation" is something of a misnomer in the case of the fee simple, which is not limited in the sense of the other estates.) Only words of purchase designate someone who is to receive an interest, and a purchaser in this context can be the recipient by sale, gift, or devise. Here that's Marge (only). Thus, if Marge sells Blackacre, Homer and the children lose their expectancy; they never had an interest to lose in the first place.

2. Life Estate. Unlike the fee simple, which is of unlimited duration, the life estate comes to a natural end with the death of a named person, usually the holder of the estate. Here is an example:

Example 2: O grants Blackacre "to Marge for life, and then to Lisa."

Here Marge has a life estate, followed by a remainder in fee simple in Lisa. We return to remainders and other future interests shortly. Note that the life estate ends with Marge's death; this is built in to the life estate.

The life estate is alienable by gift or sale (but not by will—can you see why?). What if Marge sells Blackacre during her life? Marge cannot sell more than she has; when Marge dies Lisa will take. If Marge sells, the purchaser will receive a life estate *pur autre vie*—a life estate according to Marge's, not the new owner's, lifespan. So the new owner will lose the property to Lisa when Marge dies. Keep in mind though that the life estate *pur autre vie* involves Marge's mortality risk—the duration of the right

[margin note: Because Marge's death ends her interest in the estate, thus she has no interest to grant upon her death through her will.]

depends on when Marge will die—and will be correspondingly less attractive to purchasers in the first place.

3. Defeasible Fees. The defeasible fees come in three closely related but for some purposes quite distinct varieties. These interests are like the fee simple absolute except that they may end on the happening of a named contingency. This leaves room for future interests to become possessory when such a contingency occurs.

a. Fee Simple Determinable. The fee simple determinable ends automatically upon the occurrence of a named event, whereupon the grantor or the grantor's successor takes the property. This event might never happen, in which case the fee simple determinable acts much like the fee simple absolute, except for the possibility of the contingency happening.

> *Example 3*: O grants Blackacre "to Springfield Law School as long as it is used for instruction in the law, then to O."

The fee simple determinable is created using language of duration, such as "as long as," "so long as," "while," "during," and "until." In traditional parlance, this is a "limitation" rather than a condition. (Here O has a possibility of reverter, to which we return.)

b. Fee Simple Subject to Condition Subsequent. This defeasible fee continues indefinitely except that, upon happening of the named event—the condition—the interest does *not* automatically end but *can* be ended by action (self-help or lawsuit) by the grantor or the grantor's successor (as we will see, called a right of entry or a power of termination).

> *Example 4*: O grants Blackacre "to Springfield Law School, but if it is not used for instruction in the law, then O has the right to reenter and take the premises."

Here Springfield Law School has a fee simple subject to condition subsequent and O has a right of entry (also called a "power of termination," see infra). If a condo is built instead, then the Law School only loses Blackacre if O (or his successor in interest) takes action to recover the property. With the fee simple subject to condition subsequent, the end of the interest and the transfer to the next interest holder is not automatic, as it was with the fee simple determinable. The fee simple subject to condition subsequent usually employs language such as "but if," "on condition that," "provided that," "provided however," and "if" (as opposed to the language of duration in the determinable fee, e.g., "as long as" as in Example 3), and the condition subsequent is often separated from the description of the interest by a comma. The condition is treated as something separate from the interest that it can cut short and this is often reflected in the condition being located in its own clause.

c. Fee Simple Subject to Executory Limitation. If the defeasible fee is followed by an interest not reserved to the grantor—i.e., granted to some third party at the time of conveyance of the present possessory estate—the defeasible fee is called a fee simple subject to executory limitation (and, as we will see, the following future interest is called an executory interest).

> *Example 5A*: O grants Blackacre "to Springfield Law School as long as it is used for instruction in the law, then to the Springfield Animal Hospital."

Example 5B: O grants Blackacre "to Springfield Law School, but if it is not used for instruction in law, then to the Springfield Animal Hospital."

Notice that here with the fee simple subject to executory limitation, the future interest is in a third party, Springfield Animal Hospital, rather than in the grantor (as was the case with future interests in O in Examples 3 and 4). Notice also that the fee simple subject to executory limitation conflates the nature of the two defeasible fees followed by an interest reserved in the grantor (the fee simple determinable and the fee simple subject to condition subsequent). One can use the "as long as" or "but if" ← *language used* style language interchangeably. The conventional wisdom seems to be that the interest is automatically cut short by the following executory interest upon the happening of the named event, regardless of whether durational or conditional language is used. See Thomas F. Bergin & Paul G. Haskell, Preface to Estates in Land and Future Interests 52 (1984). At least this is what the commentators say; there seems to be little law on this subject.

Although seldom used, the system of estates allows interests other than the fee simple to be determinable and subject to condition subsequent. For example, "to A for life so long as alcohol is not consumed on the premises" creates and grants a life estate determinable. As we will see, a lease too can be determinable.

As mentioned earlier, the history of the forms of ownership reflects an attempt by owners both to avoid feudal obligations and to tie up property in their families over the generations. These issues are reflected both in the catalogue of estates and in the doctrines, such as rules on alienability and the Rule against Perpetuities, that constrain the manipulation of estates. In the past this conflict played itself out over another type of fee, the fee tail, which was created by the statute *De Donis Conditionalibus*, 13 Edw., ch. 1, in 1285 and which acquired the feature of long-term inalienability by the fifteenth century. The fee tail has been abolished in most states and has at most a theoretical existence in the others. To create a fee tail, one would use the language "to A and the heirs of his/her body" or "to A and his/her issue." Such an interest would give something like a nontransferable life estate to be followed by a similar interest in the blood descendants (issue) of that person, and so on and on. Only when A's bloodline ends— when A "dies without issue" which can happen hundreds of years after A's death—does the fee tail end. The property would then revert to the grantor (or if the grantor has died, those who have received the grantor's reversion through a chain of transfers by will or under the intestacy statute). The fee tail is a lesser estate than the fee simple absolute; the difference is a reversion in the grantor, even if it is not terribly likely that this reversion will ever become possessory. Keep this in mind when we take up the principle of the conservation of estates. By statute, most states provide today that any attempt to create a fee tail shall be deemed to be another interest or interests, most commonly a fee simple in the immediate grantee.

FUTURE INTERESTS

As we have seen, other than the fee simple absolute, the other estates do not continue indefinitely but may end one way or another. This means that compared with the fee simple absolute, there is "something left," and that is a future interest. These future interests come in a surprisingly large number of varieties. A basic division, reflected in terminology and to a lesser extent in the rules that apply to them, is between interests retained by the grantor and interests created in a third party. These differences are less important than they once were, because interests retained by the grantor are now generally alienable. If they are alienated, though, they do not change their name or character. As we will see when we turn to the Rule against Perpetuities, interests retained by the grantor are treated as already "vested" and so they present no problem under the Rule.

Figure 5–3
Future Interests Retained by Grantors

1. Reversion (*NOT* "Remainder")

2. Possiblity of reverter

3. Right of entry (power of termination)

1. INTERESTS RETAINED BY THE GRANTOR

Not all interests give their owners a present right to possession. Some interests do not become possessory until sometime in the future, and the circumstances under which this may or may not happen help to define which interest a person has. If a person has a future interest, one also has to ask what present possessory interest one would have if the interest becomes possessory, or in other words what estate is in waiting. For example, if O grants "to A for life, and then to B," A has a present possessory interest in life estate and B has a remainder in fee simple. That is, when A dies, B will have a fee simple. B owns something now, but it is a remainder in fee simple, a future interest.

Future interests retained by the grantor are sometimes called "reversionary" interests, even though only one of the three such interests is called a "reversion." One of the pitfalls of the system of classifying estates is the many r-words describing a number of future interests.

a. Reversion. The reversion follows the natural end of a life estate and in other contexts in which an owner has not disposed of the entire fee (such as leaseholds, see Chapter VI).

Example 6: O grants Blackacre "to Marge for life, then to O."

O here retains a reversion. (O could also implicitly retain a reversion if the grant had been simply "to Marge for life.") O had a fee simple and carved out a life estate, retaining the rest of the original fee simple. The "rest" retained is a reversion. Don't call this "rest" a remainder. A reversion is to be contrasted with a remainder, the interest (also following a life estate) in someone other than the grantor (to which we return in subsection 2).

As we will see, in the landlord-tenant relationship the landlord retains a reversion, but the landlord also has a present interest—the fee simple subject to the lease—in addition to this reversion.

b. Possibility of Reverter. This is the interest reserved to the grantor that follows a fee simple determinable. That is, O will automatically get the property back if the limitation built into the fee simple determinable occurs (hence the explosion in the diagram, in Figure 5–2, supra). In Example 3 above, repeated here, there is an explicit possibility of reverter:

> *Example 3*: O grants Blackacre "to Springfield Law School as long as it is used for instruction in the law, then to O."

If O has died, then O's successor (by will, intestacy, or by sale, etc.) will take. The possibility of reverter can also be implicit:

> *Example 7*: O grants Blackacre to "to Springfield Law School as long as it is used for instruction in the law."

Here O is not mentioned but because O owned the entire fee simple and granted a fee simple determinable, O must retain a possibility of reverter, here implicitly. In either case, O need not do anything to regain ownership. If the condition occurs (here Blackacre ceases to be used for law instruction), then O (or O's successor owner of the future interest) becomes the fee simple owner again. Notice that if the holder of the fee simple determinable (here the Springfield Law School) does not quit possession, it can start a period of adverse possession. (See Chapter II.) Can you see why?

c. Right of Entry/Power of Termination. Like the possibility of reverter, this is an interest retained by the grantor that follows a defeasible fee, but here the preceding defeasible fee must be a fee simple subject to condition subsequent. Consider Example 4 again:

> *Example 4*: O grants Blackacre "to Springfield Law School, but if it is not used for instruction in the law, then O has the right to reenter and take the premises."

O has a right of entry (also called a power of termination). The condition is a condition subsequent for the preceding interest and a condition precedent for the future interest—the right of entry (represented by the lighting bolt in Figure 5–2, supra). If it occurs, nothing happens automatically, but it does give O the right (the power) to change legal relations by ousting the holder of the fee simple subject to condition subsequent. O can either attempt a physical entry (subject to the limits on self-help) or bring an action to recover possession of the land. If O does nothing, then the owner continues on as owner as before. If enough time passes, the right of entry may no longer be exercisable, through the doctrine of laches. The right of entry must be exercised within a reasonable time, which some courts take to be the period in the statute of limitations for bringing an action in ejectment. See, e.g., Jeffries v. State ex rel. Woodruff County, 226 S.W.2d 810 (Ark. 1950); Bredell v. Kerr, 147 S.W. 105 (Mo. 1912).

2. Interests Created in a Grantee

The present possessory interests need not be followed by an interest in the grantor. Instead the grantor can simultaneously create an interest in a third party. The set of such interests bears different names and has somewhat different features from the otherwise similar set of future interests created in the grantor herself.

Figure 5–4
Future Interests in Grantees

---

1. **Remainder** (*NOT "Reversion"*)

   Indefeasibly vested (*no other contingency, other than natural termination, needs to be fulfilled*).

   Contingent

   Vested subject to complete defeasance

   Vested subject to partial defeasance (or subject to open)

2. **Executory interest**

---

a. **Remainder.** Like the reversion, the remainder follows a life estate, never a fee simple, but unlike the reversion the remainder is in a party other than the grantor.

> *Example 8*: Marge grants Blackacre "to Homer for life, then to Bart, Lisa, and Maggie and their heirs."

Terminology can be confusing, because if instead of granting the "rest" of the fee to a third party, the owner retains it, this "rest" is not a remainder but a reversion. Remainders come in a number of varieties.

Indefeasibly vested

The remainder in Example 8 is *indefeasibly vested*, meaning that the identity of the takers—Bart, Lisa, and Maggie—is known and there is no other contingency that has to be fulfilled before the interest is ready to become possessory other than the natural termination of the preceding interest (Marge's death). Further, the remainder in Example 8 is indefeasibly vested because no condition subsequent can cut short the remainder (something to which we return shortly).

Other types of remainder have conditions. One common condition, a condition precedent, makes the remainder a *contingent* remainder. At their creation, remainders can be vested or contingent. These remainders are contingent:

> *Example 8A*: Marge grants Blackacre "to Homer for life, then to his children and their heirs."

> *Example 8B*: Marge grants Blackacre "to Homer for life, then to Bart if he graduates from high school by age 19."

Contingent

In each of these, some uncertainty remains as to the identity of the class of takers (Example 8A) or the occurrence of the condition (Example 8B, assuming Bart has not graduated yet). When this uncertainty is resolved, the remainders are said to *vest in interest*. We will come back to the distinction between vesting in interest and vesting in possession, but for now note that uncertainty about the identity of the taker or whether a condition for its happening will be fulfilled—vesting in interest—can occur without the person actually coming into possession—vesting in possession. For example, in Example 8B, suppose Homer is alive and Bart has just graduated from high school at an age under 19. Bart's remainder is vested in interest but has not yet vested in possession, which does not happen until Homer dies and his life estate ends. One might ask what would happen in Example 8B if Homer died before Bart had a chance to graduate from high school. It may not be immediately apparent but the life estate and the contingent remainder in Example 8B are supported by a reversion in Marge, which would take after Homer dies and can be divested by Bart's graduation from high school by age 19 (in which case Bart takes). However, if Bart reaches age 19 without having graduated from high school, Marge's reversion vests indefeasibly. Remember, there always has to be someone ready to take, and if the grantor has not given everything away, a (supporting) reversion is retained.

In situations like that in Example 8B, the grantor could also use alternative contingent remainders such that one vests if the other does not and vice versa:

> *Example 8C*: Marge grants Blackacre "to Homer for life, then to Bart if he graduates from high school by age 19, otherwise to Lisa and her heirs."

Do alternative contingent remainders add up to a vested remainder? One might think so, but for historical reasons courts held that they do not, and that there is an implied reversion in Marge in these circumstances, even though the chances of the reversion vesting in possession are extremely remote.[1]

Some remainders are vested but not indefeasibly so. A remainder is said to be vested "subject to complete divestment" if the occurrence of a condition can cause the interest to shift to someone else.

> *Example 8D*: Marge grants Blackacre "to Homer for life, then to Bart; but if Bart fails to graduate from high school by age 19, then to Lisa."

Unlike the indefeasibly vested remainder in the three named children in Example 8, Bart's remainder here, a remainder subject to complete divestment, can be cut short. But unlike the contingent remainder in Example 8B, the condition here is a condition subsequent not a condition precedent: Bart's remainder vests upon the natural termination of the preceding estate but then can be cut short for reasons other than the natural termination of his own interest. (As we will see, Lisa here has a shifting executory interest.)

[handwritten margin note: vested subject to Complete Defeasance]

---

1. Contingent remainders were historically regarded as "destructible" if the preceding estate terminated for a reason other than its natural termination through death. Thus, if Homer committed treason, and this led to the forfeiture of his life estate, the two alternative contingent remainders would both be destroyed. In this scenario, Blackacre would revert to Marge under her implied reversion.

Vested subject to Partial Defeasance (or subject to open)

As opposed to complete divestment in Example 8D, divestment can be partial. Consider a variant on Example 8A, with a little context added:

Example 8E: Marge grants Blackacre "to Homer for life, then to his children and their heirs." At the time of the grant, Homer is the father of Bart and Lisa (but not yet Maggie).

In such a situation, what, if anything, do Bart and Lisa have? They are part of a class "subject to open" because more members could enter the class (by being born as Homer's children). Thus, Bart and Lisa have vested remainders subject to partial divestment. The remainder is vested because there is no uncertainty as to their status as children of Homer and there is no condition precedent on their remainders. But the remainders in Bart and Lisa are subject to partial divestment because if more children are born to Homer they would diminish the interest of Bart and Lisa (e.g., from one-half to one-third, etc.). So when Maggie is born, the vesting of her remainder partially divests those of Bart and Lisa. Now all three children have remainders subject to partial divestment. When Homer dies, the remainders would vest and, assuming no more children have been born after Maggie, Bart, Lisa, and Maggie would own Blackacre in fee simple absolute.

The remainder is normally not in the grantee of the life estate—as in "to A for life, then to A" or "to A for life, then to A's heirs"—both because this would not be terribly useful and because traditional doctrines would merge the two interests to reassemble a fee simple in A. By contrast, in Example 8 above the language "and their heirs" simply emphasizes that this is a remainder in fee simple; when the interest becomes possessory it will become a fee simple in the three children.

b. Executory Interest. This is an interest in a transferee (not retained by the grantor) that divests or cuts short a previous interest (hence the ax in Figure 5–2). That is, the executory interest does not become possessory upon the natural end of the preceding interest (death) as in the case of a remainder following a life estate.

Example 9: Marge grants Blackacre "to Bart, but if alcohol is ever consumed on the premises, then to Ned Flanders."

Thus in Example 9, the defeasible fee (fee simple subject to an executory limitation) is cut off early by the happening of the condition subsequent, and the following interest in Ned Flanders is an executory interest. Because the executory interest divests the interest of a third party (here Bart), it is a "shifting" executory interest. If the executory interest divests an interest in the grantor, it is called a "springing" executory interest:

Example 9A: Marge grants Blackacre "to Bart for life, remainder to Lisa 5 years after his death."

Recall that there is a reversion in Marge here that would become possessory in the 5–year period after Bart's death. Lisa has a springing executory interest because it divests the reversion in the grantor (Marge).

An executory interest can cut short—bring to an unnaturally early end—an interest that would otherwise come to a natural end (by death) as in the following example:

Example 10: Homer grants Blackacre "to Marge for life, but if she remarries, then to Lisa."

Figure 5–5
Summary of Estates and Future Interests

Present Interest	Examples	Typical Future Interest
Fee Simple Absolute	*O grants Blackacre to M.* *O grants B to M in fee simple.* *O grants B to M and her heirs.*	None None None
Life Estate	*O grants B to M for life.*	Reversion (in O)
	O grants B to M for life, then to N.	Remainder; *indefeasibly vested*
	O grants B to M for life, then to her adult children.	Remainder; *contingent**
	O grants B to M for life, then to N if Condition (C) occurs.	Remainder; *contingent**
	O grants B to M for life, then to N, but if C occurs, then to K.	Remainder (in N); *vested subject to complete defeasance*
	O grants B to M for life, then to her children. *[N was the only child at the grant]*	Remainder (in N); *vested subject to open**
Fee Simple Determinable	*O grants B to M as long as C occurs, (then to O).*	Possiblity of reverter (in O)
Fee Simple Subject to Condition Subsequent	*O grants B to M, but if C occurs, then O has the right to reenter and take the premises.*	Right of entry/power of termination (in O)
Fee Simple Subject to Executory Limitation	*O grants B to M as long as C occurs, then to N.* *O grants B to M, but if C occurs, then to N.*	Executory interest (in N)*

* Subject to the Rule against Perpetuities

Incidentally, interests like this were allowed if they could be taken to be motivated by a concern to support a widowed spouse until remarriage, but not if they seemed to be motivated out of a desire to prevent someone's marriage (as in "to Marge for life but if she ever marries Ned Flanders, then to Lisa").

> *Example 11*: Marge grants Blackacre "to Bart as long as the premises are not used for consuming alcohol, then to Ned Flanders."

This is another fee simple subject to an executory limitation (using the "as long as" language) followed by an executory interest. Notice that because the interest in the third-party transferee becomes possessory automatically on the happening of the condition no matter how the triggering event is phrased (as a limitation in the preceding interest or as a condition subsequent to the interest), there is traditionally no future interest in a grantee that works like the right of entry. Again, there is little law dealing with this issue. Keep in mind, though, that even where the preceding interest ends without any affirmative act of the next interest-holder, some action on her part is likely to be necessary for a transfer, and further down the line, in order to avoid the effect of adverse possession.

We can summarize the discussion thus far in the chart in Figure 5–5 (we will return to the Rule against Perpetuities later in the Chapter).

VESTING

One source of confusion stems from the multiple senses of "vested." An interest *vests in possession* when the interest becomes a present possessory one. But an interest can vest *in interest* before it vests in possession. Vesting in interest means that various types of uncertainty about the interest have been resolved. This notion of vesting in interest is particularly important in the case of remainders. When created, a remainder is clearly not vested in possession; it is a future interest that will not become possessory until the interests preceding it have terminated. However, a remainder may or may not be vested in interest, and much may turn on this question. In this latter sense, "vested" means that a certain type of uncertainty about whether the interest will ever come to a particular individual has been resolved. This uncertainty can stem from two main sources. First, it may be unclear who will take the interest when it does become possessory.

> *Example 12*: To A for life, then to A's children.

If this is an inter vivos gift (one made while the grantor is still living) there is uncertainty as to who will be a child of A at A's death. (Notice that this not a problem in the remainder in Example 8, because there the children are listed by name. In Example 8, if more children come along, they do not take.) In Example 12, suppose A has children now. The remainder is vested as to them, but more children may be born. In this situation we would say that the remainder is vested subject to partial divestment (or vested subject to open, as it is sometimes called).

The second type of uncertainty that prevents vesting in interest relates to contingencies.

> *Example 13*: To any of my now living children who pass the bar.

Here there is no uncertainty as to who the children are but there is uncertainty as to whether they will pass the bar (until any such child actually passes it). As children pass the bar, the interest becomes vested as to that child. Now consider this future interest:

> *Example 14*: To A for life, then to the children of A alive at A's death who have by then reached the age of 21.

The contingent remainder here combines elements of uncertainty over both identity and reaching 21. Present children can die and others can be born, and any children under 21 have to reach that age. When a child reaches 21 that child has an interest subject to partial divestment (from other children reaching 21) and divestment from dying early. The supporting reversion in O is considered vested.

In contrast to remainders, reversionary interests and executory interests are much simpler as to when they vest in interest. A reversionary interest (a reversion, a possibility of reverter, or a right of entry) is considered vested in interest upon its creation, whether or not the interest ever becomes possessory. (Such an understanding has little to recommend it these days, particularly as interests created in the grantor have become more fully alienable, rendering the family connection to the grantor less distinctive in the case of reversionary interests.) The reality is that it is uncertain whether they will become possessory, and that uncertainty will not be resolved until the contingent event occurs. Nevertheless they are considered vested from the moment they are created. Executory interests present the opposite case; normally they must become possessory (vest in possession) in order to vest in interest.[2] As we will see, this aspect of executory interests will be very important because executory interests can easily vest too remotely, in violation of the Rule against Perpetuities.

PROBLEMS

What interests are created in the following?

1. O grants Blackacre "to A for life, then to B and his heirs."

2. Same as in Question 1. Then C enters adversely. Then thirty years later C is still on Blackacre and A, still alive, has never entered.

3. O grants Blackacre "to A for life, then to B and her heirs; but if B ever remarries, then to C and her heirs."

4. O grants Blackacre "to Huxley College, as long as it is used for instructional purposes."

5. O grants Blackacre "to A; but if marijuana is inhaled on the premises, then O shall have the right to reenter and take the premises."

2. The one exception to this generalization is for situations in which an executory interest can change into an indefeasibly vested remainder. For example, O transfers Blackacre "to A for life, remainder to B, but if B fails to survive A, then to C." If B predeceases A, then C's executory interest becomes an indefeasibly vested remainder.

[Handwritten margin notes, left side:]

6
A - Fee simple subject
to Executory Limitation
B - Executory Interest

7
A - Life Estate
B - Remainder in Life Estate
C - Remainder in Fee Simple
(B's interest is contingent)

8
A - Life Estate
B - Contingent Remainder in Life Estate
Children - Contingent Remainders in Fee Simple
O - Reversion (to grantor)

9
Spring Hosp. - Fee Simple subject to Exec. Limit.
Spring Animal - Exec. Int.

10
A - Life Estate
A Husband - Contingent Remainder in Fee Simple
O - Reversion

11
IMPORTANT
A - Life Estate — O has Reversion in case A dies before B passes bar
B - Contingent remainder in fee simple determinable
O - Possibility of Reverter

6. O grants Blackacre "to A; but if marijuana is inhaled on the premises during A's life, then to B and her heirs."

7. O conveys Blackacre "to A for life, then to B for life, then to C."

8. O grants Blackacre "to A for life, then to B for life, then to B's children who survive him." *→ This condition makes it CONTINGENT*

9. O grants Blackacre "to Springfield Hospital as long as it is used for the care of patients, then to Springfield Animal Clinic."

10. To A for life, then to A's husband if he survives her.

11. O conveys to A for life, then, if B passes the bar, to B and his heirs as long as he remains a member in good standing of the bar. B is a student in law school.

12. Bequest by O of "$100,000 to A, to be paid when A reaches age twenty-one." *→ just an example of the numerous clauses principle. Closest thing is O's heirs having a fee simple, and A having an executory interest.*

C. MAINTAINING THE SYSTEM

Knowing how to classify estates and interests and even how they combine is just the beginning. Many difficulties arise when property rights are divided, because those with a stake are not guaranteed to agree with each other. And in the case of future interests the person with the interest may not even be born, and is unavailable for negotiation. In this Section we consider a number of doctrines that are supposed to maintain the system, often by placing limits on what those dividing property rights or enjoying the resulting pieces may do.

1. CONSERVATION OF ESTATES

We have already seen how the system of estates and future interests acts as a sort of "grammar" of property rights. One feature of the system is that when a transfer is made all of what the grantor had must be accounted for, even if this means implying a reversion. That is, the fee simple (or other interest that O starts out with) must be conserved. The principle of conservation of estates ensures that all the pieces of the estate are accounted for.

The principle of conservation applies whenever a grantor might convey something less than her full interest. This usually happens when the grantor starts with a fee simple and conveys away some of that interest. We have already seen numerous examples in which the fee owner grants away a life estate or a defeasible fee and retains a reversionary interest, explicitly or implicitly. But the fee owner may retain something other than the "last" part of the fee simple.

Example: Marge conveys "to Bart when he reaches the age of 21."

Here Marge has conveyed an executory interest to Bart. It is called a springing executory interest because it follows an interest retained by the grantor—as opposed to a shifting executory interest, which takes after another interest created in a third party. Here Marge has retained what's left, but this is a present possessory interest, probably a fee simple subject to an executory limitation. The pieces add up to the fee simple Marge started out with. Marge could have retained the "middle" of the timeline as well:

> *Example*: Homer conveys "to Abe for life, then ten years later to Marge and her heirs."

Here Homer has conveyed a life estate to Abe and an executory interest in fee simple that springs from a reversionary interest retained by Homer. The reversionary interest would be a reversion in fee simple subject to executory limitation. The limitation event here is the tenth anniversary of Abe's death. (Notice that although this interest is for a stated number of years it is a reversion, not a "term of years," which would be a lease.) Again, the interests granted and retained must add up to the fee simple Homer has to begin with.

While the interest retained is either a reversion or a present possessory interest, notice that in a conveyance, the "last" interest, implicit or explicit, must be a fee simple when it becomes possessory. If the last interest is a reversion it must be a reversion in fee simple; if it is a remainder or an executory interest, it must be a remainder in fee simple or an executory interest in fee simple. If not, the chain of interests could come to an end with no one ready to take. Because the whole fee is of unlimited duration, this could never happen. If a holder in fee simple dies without heirs, the property escheats to the state. This is a slight echo of the feudal system, in which all owners ultimately held of the monarch. See In re O'Connor's Estate, 252 N.W. 826 (Neb. 1934).

Williams v. Estate of Williams

Supreme Court of Tennessee, 1993.
865 S.W.2d 3.

■ REID, CHIEF JUSTICE. This suit seeks the construction of the last will and testament of G.A. Williams, deceased, and the declaration of the rights of the parties in a tract of land described in the will.

The record does not contain all the information necessary for the Court to adjudicate the ownership of the land. * * *

The only facts alleged are that G.A. Williams died on November 17, 1944, the instrument attached to the complaint is a copy of his last will and testament, the farm mentioned in the will is located in McMinn County, and, inferentially, the farm was owned by the testator at the time of his death. These allegations are admitted by Rachel Couch, Curtis Williams, and Wayne Williams, the only defendants actually before the Court.

Additional facts, though not proven or stipulated but apparently not disputed by the parties before the Court, are relied upon in the briefs. The will was executed on July 18, 1933, and probated in the Probate Court of

McMinn County on November 24, 1944. The testator was survived by nine children, including the three daughters named in the will. The plaintiff, Ethel Williams, who was 92 years of age when the complaint was filed, is the only survivor of the three children named in the will. The defendant Etta Tallent is the only other surviving child of the testator, and the other defendants are lineal descendants of the testator. (There is no statement that the named defendants are all the heirs at law of the testator.) Ethel Williams has maintained possession of the farm since the death of the testator, jointly with Ida Williams and Mallie Williams until their deaths. Apparently none of the three-named daughters ever married, though that fact does not affirmatively appear.

The will is as follows:

I, G.A. WILLIAMS, being of sound mind make this my last will and Testament: At my death I want Ida Williams, Mallie Williams, and Ethel Williams, three of my daughters to have my home farm where I now live, consisting of one hundred and eighty-eight acres, to have and to hold during their lives, and not to be sold during their lifetime. If any of them marry their interest ceases and the ones that remain single have full control of same. I am making this will because they have stayed at home and taken care of the home and cared for their mother during her sickness, and I do not want them sold out of a home. If any one tries to contest this will I want them debarred from any interest in my estate. /s/ G.A. Williams, July the 18, 1933.

Issue: Fee Simple or Life Estate?

The complaint alleged that the interest received by Ethel Williams was a life estate under the will or, in the alternative, a life estate under the will and a "remainder interest" by intestate succession. The latter disposition was adopted by the Chancellor initially, but on rehearing was abandoned for the finding that the devise of a life estate without limitation over indicated an intention that the named daughters have the property in fee simple, which is the position asserted by Ethel Williams on appeal.

The Court of Appeals affirmed the holding of the trial court. It held, on the authority of *White v. Brown,* 559 S.W.2d 938 (Tenn. 1977), that each named daughter owned a one-third undivided interest in fee simple. The record does not support that decision.

Rule— intent of the testator will not be defeated by literal translations of the wording in a will

The function of a suit to construe a will is to ascertain and effect the intention of the testator. The determinative intention is the predominant purpose expressed by the testator in the will. Statements regarding the means whereby the predominant purpose of the will is to be accomplished will not be given literal effect if they would defeat the predominant intention. * * *

This Court stated the rule more concisely in *Moore v. Neely,* 370 S.W.2d 537 (Tenn. 1963):

Another rule of construction is that when a controlling or predominate purpose of the testator is expressed, it is the duty of the court to effectuate that purpose, and to construe all subsidiary clauses so as to bring them into subordination to such purpose. The language of a single sentence is not to control as against the evident purpose and intent shown by the whole will.

Id. 370 S.W.2d at 540.

In the case before the Court, the predominant intention of the testator is clear. Each of the testator's three daughters who had "stayed home" was to have the farm jointly with the other two daughters, so long as they were living and unmarried, as a residence and for their support; after the death or marriage of any of the three daughters, the remaining two daughters would hold jointly until the marriage or death of another; and the remaining unmarried daughter was to hold until she married or died. The statements that the farm was "not to be sold during their lifetime" and "I do not want them sold out of a home" emphasized and re-enforced the predominant intention that each of the three daughters have a residence and support during her life or until she should marry. The testator's statement that he was favoring those children above the others because they had "stayed at home and taken care of ... their mother" implicitly recognized that each had foregone the opportunity to become self-supporting or be supported by a husband, and limiting the duration of the devise to such time as a daughter should marry, indicates that the devise was intended to be a substitute for support that might otherwise have been available.

The intention of the testator was not to make an absolute gift to all or either of the daughters. The first statement in the will limits the devise "during their lives." The next statement limits the devise to the duration of their unmarried state. The testator devised to the daughters an interest not readily alienable and one that could not be defeated by a suit for partition or sale for partition. His reason for selecting the estate devised is indicated by the statements "not to be sold during their lifetime" and "I do not want them sold out of a home." Upon the death or marriage of the named daughters, the testator's purpose as to them would have been accomplished and the testator's heirs would inherit the property by intestate succession.

The testator recognized that his other heirs would acquire some interest in the property upon his death. The primary emphasis was that the daughters' limited interests not be disturbed by the owners of the interest not devised to the daughters. The severity of his admonition is shown by the provision that any person who should "contest" the will would be "debarred" from any interest, not just in the farm but in his estate.

This case is not controlled by *White v. Brown*, relied upon by the Court of Appeals. In that case, the following provision was found to constitute the devise of a fee simple:

> "... I wish Evelyn White to have my home to live in and *not* to be *sold*. I also leave my personal property to Sandra White Perry. My house is not to be sold."

559 S.W.2d at 938. The majority in *White* based its decision on that portion of what is now T.C.A. § 32–3–101 (1984) which provides:

> A will ... shall convey all the real estate belonging to [the testator], or in which he had any interest at his decease, unless a contrary intention appear by its words in context.

However, in language applicable to the case before the Court, Justice Harbison, dissenting, stated:

> I have serious doubt that the testatrix intended to create any illegal restraint on alienation or to violate any other rules of law. It seems to me that she rather emphatically intended to provide that her sister-in-law was not to be able to sell the house during the lifetime of the latter—a result which is both legal and consistent with the creation of a life estate.

Id. at 942. That statute does not control the disposition in the case before the Court because, as discussed above, a contrary intention appears from the will. The provision that each daughter's interest would terminate upon her marriage, as well as upon her death, is a further indication that the testator did not intend for the named daughters to have an absolute estate in the farm. As stated in *Page on Wills*,

> The gift to A may indicate quite clearly that it is a gift for the life of A, as where the gift is to A for life or until her marriage, or a gift to A for life or during her widowhood. In gifts of this sort, A takes a life estate, since the provision with reference to marriage or widowhood is, at least, not sufficient to overcome the effect of the provisions of the will which show that testator intends to give to A a life estate only.
>
> .....
>
> ... By what seems to be the weight of authority, a gift to A until her marriage or during widowhood gives a life estate to A. Such life estate would be defeasible or determinable upon the marriage of A.

4 William J. Bowe & Douglas H. Parker, Page on Wills, § 37.22, at 632–634 (4th ed. 1961) (footnotes omitted).

The will as a whole conveys a definite meaning. Though the author obviously was not a skilled legal draftsman, he, also obviously, had a good command of language and was familiar with legal phrases commonly used and understood beyond the legal profession. The testator accurately described the instrument he was writing as his "last will and testament," he asserted that he was "of sound mind," and he employed the traditional words of conveyance—"to have and to hold"—in devising an interest in real estate to the daughters. Even "contest," though perhaps not used accurately in its narrow, technical sense, may indicate an action designed to defeat a testamentary disposition. The conclusion is almost inescapable that, had the testator intended to devise the named beneficiaries an estate in fee, he would have expressed that intention quite clearly. Consequently, the estate devised to the named daughters was less than a fee simple.

Upon the death of the testator, each named daughter held a life estate, defeasible or determinable upon her marriage. See Id. Each daughter also had an executory interest in each of the other two daughters' one-third

[handwritten margin note: RULE – Gifts until marriage or during widowhood = life estate]

interest, which would vest in her possession if the other life tenant should die or marry while she remained unmarried. See Lewis M. Simes & Allan F. Smith, The Law of Future Interests, § 285 (2d ed. 1956). The heirs-at-law of the testator held a reversion in fee simple, subject to the determinable life estates and the executory interests in the named daughters, which reversion would vest in possession, at the latest, upon the death of the survivor of the named daughters. See Cornelius J. Moynihan, Introduction to the Law of Real Property, at 94–95 (1962).

The judgment of the Court of Appeals is reversed, and the case is remanded for further proceedings. * * *

NOTES AND QUESTIONS

1. One principle implicit in the reasoning of both the Tennessee Supreme Court and the appellate court is the *conservation of estates*. Grantors may break up their interests and transfer some or all of the pieces, but the pieces have to add up to what the grantor started out with. Where, as in the *Williams* case, someone is granting a fee simple, all of the pieces have to add up to a fee simple. Can you see why on the Tennessee Supreme Court's approach, but not on that of the appellate court, a reversion in the heirs is necessary?

2. The court believes that the will's mention of the heirs (and the possibility of their contesting the will) means that the testator intended that they would take some interest in the property under the will. Does this follow? By definition the heirs are those who would take under the intestacy statute. Wouldn't that furnish sufficient incentive for them to contest the will—and for the testator to worry about this possibility? Do you agree that the testator's use of legal terminology makes the court's conclusion "almost inescapable?" If not, why not?

3. The will here is apparently a holographic will, i.e., one handwritten by the testator. In some states, statutes provide that some of the requirements (such as witnesses) are dispensed with in the case of holographic wills. Courts also tend to take a less formalistic approach in interpreting holographic wills. In general, will interpretation is a curious blend of formalism and a search for testator's intent. See, e.g., Bruce H. Mann, Formalities and Formalism in the Uniform Probate Code, 142 U. Pa. L. Rev. 1033 (1994); John H. Langbein, Substantial Compliance with the Wills Act, 88 Harv. L. Rev. 489 (1975). Among the many rules of interpretation that courts employ is one that favors interpretations that avoid intestacy. This canon reflects an assumption that once a testator is expressing an intent, she is unlikely to be expressing a partial intent and deliberately invoking the intestacy laws. (Indeed, the intestacy laws are meant in part to specify a default intent where none is expressed.) Many wills include a residuary clause of this sort: "I give all the rest, residue, and remainder of my estate to...." From the absence of such a clause, do you think the testator wished to create a partial intestacy here?

4. The court asserts that the set of interests here is inalienable during the lives of the three sisters. Should the testator be able to prevent alienation in this way? Notice that if the testator had employed a trust, the testator could choose whether to give the trustee the power of alienation.

5. Most life estates these days are created in trust; they are equitable as opposed to legal life estates. The major source of legal life estates is holographic wills. Such was the case in *Williams*. Lawyers generally avoid legal life estates as cumbersome and litigation-prone, and will instead employ a trust with a lifetime beneficiary coupled with a gift over to the same or to a third party. In a trust arrangement, the various estates and interests serve as methods of carving up the value of the trust assets.

City of Klamath Falls v. Bell

Oregon Court of Appeals, 1971.
490 P.2d 515.

■ SCHWAB, CHIEF JUDGE. In 1925, a corporation conveyed certain land to the city of Klamath Falls as a gift for use as the site for a city library. The deed provided, among other things, that the city should hold the land "so long as" it complied with that condition with regard to its use.

In 1969, the city terminated the use of the land for a library, and the question presented by this appeal is, "Does the title to the land remain in the city or did the termination of use as a library cause title to pass to the descendants of the shareholders of the donor-corporation (now dissolved)?"

The issue was presented to the trial court in the form of an agreed narrative statement, pertinent portions of which, in addition to the facts set forth above, are: the donor-corporation was known as the Daggett–Schallock Investment Company; the corporate deed provided that if at any time the city ceased to use the land for library purposes, title to the land should pass to Fred Schallock and Floy R. Daggett, their heirs and assigns; on September 19, 1927, the corporation was voluntarily dissolved, all creditors paid, and all assets (which we interpret as including the rights of the corporation, if any, in the land in question) were distributed in accordance with law to the sole shareholders Schallock and Daggett.

The city of Klamath Falls built a library on the land in 1929 in compliance with the conditions set out in the deed. The library continued in use from that date until July 1, 1969, when the books were moved to the County Library Building. Since that time, the city library services have been provided by Klamath County on a contract basis. The City Library building has not been used for any other purpose and now stands vacant.

After the library closure, the city of Klamath Falls filed a complaint against all the heirs of Schallock and Daggett for declaratory judgment pursuant to ORS ch. 28, asking the court to adjudicate the respective rights of the parties under the deed. The city joined Constance F. Bell, the sole heir of Fred Schallock, and Marijane Flitcraft and Caroline Crapo, the sole heirs of Floy R. Daggett, along with George C. Flitcraft, the husband of Marijane Flitcraft, and Paul Crapo, the husband of Caroline Crapo, as all the necessary parties to the suit.

Figure 5–6
Klamath Falls City Library, ca. 1960

Courtesy Klamath County Museums. The building is now used as the Klamath Falls City Hall.

The defendants Constance F. Bell, Caroline Crapo, and Paul Crapo conveyed their interests in the real property to the defendant Marijane Flitcraft in May and June 1970.

The trial court found that title to the real property was vested in the city of Klamath Falls. Its decision was based on a finding that the gift over to Fred Schallock and Floy R. Daggett was void under the rule against perpetuities.

The deed, in pertinent part, is as follows:

KNOW ALL MEN BY THESE PRESENTS That Daggett–Schallock Investment Company, a corporation organized and existing under the laws of the State of Oregon, for and as a gift and without any consideration, does hereby give, grant and convey unto the City of Klamath Falls, Oregon, so long as it complies with the conditions hereinafter set forth, and thereafter unto Fred Schallock and Floy R. Daggett, their heirs and assigns, the following described parcel of real estate, in Klamath County Oregon, to-wit * * *

To have and to hold the same unto the said City of Klamath Falls, Oregon (and to any other municipal corporation which may lawfully succeed it) so long as it complies with the conditions above set forth, and thereafter unto Fred Schallock and Floy R. Daggett, their heirs and assigns forever. * * *

I

We conclude that the estate that passed to the city under this deed was a fee simple on a special limitation, which is also known as a fee simple determinable, or a base or qualified fee.* The "magic" words "so long as" have generally been held to create such an estate. Simes and Smith, The Law of Future Interests 345, § 287 (2d ed. 1956), states:

> * * * The words of duration "so long as" will almost certainly be judicially recognized as the distinctive insignia of such an estate, and, if coupled with a provision which clearly calls for an automatic termination of the estate granted, there is little room for construction. * * *

O'Connell, Estates on Condition Subsequent and Estates on Special Limitation in Oregon, 18 Or.L.Rev. 63, 73 (1939), stresses the use of words:

> [T]he creation of an estate on a special limitation is characterized generally by the use of certain words. Typical words are "so long as," "until," or "during." However, any language in the instrument indicating an intent that the estate shall automatically end upon the occurrence of a designated event will be sufficient.

See also Magness v. Kerr, 254 P. 1012 (Or. 1927).

One of the features of the fee simple on a special limitation thus created is that it terminates automatically upon breach of condition.[2] Fremont Lbr. Co. v. Starrell Pet. Co., 364 P.2d 773 (Or. 1961), and cases cited therein.

II

Upon breach of the condition, the deed provided for a gift over to Fred Schallock and Floy R. Daggett or their heirs and assigns. This gift over was an attempt to grant an executory interest since only an executory interest can follow an earlier grant in fee simple.

The rule against perpetuities applies to executory interests. * * * [T]he trial judge correctly found that the gift over to Fred Schallock and Floy R. Daggett, their heirs and assigns, was void ab initio under the rule against perpetuities.

---

* [This interest would be termed a "fee simple subject to executory limitation" on the more widely used terminology adopted in this book, with fee simple determinable being reserved for an interest followed by an interest reserved by the grantor (a possibility of reverter).—Eds.]

2. There would be a different result if the interests of the city of Klamath Falls were characterized as a fee simple on a condition subsequent, which is also known as a fee simple conditional. When such an estate is created, there is no forfeiture until the grantor exercises his right of re-entry.

III

The trial court's conclusion does not, however, dispose of the case at bar. Just because the gift over is invalid, it does not follow that the city of Klamath Falls now has an absolute interest in the property in question. There remains the question of whether under the deed a possibility of reverter remained in the grantor corporation.

When a deed reveals an unquestionable intent to limit the interest of the first grantee (here the city of Klamath Falls) to a fee simple on a special limitation, the courts of the United States do not create an indefeasible estate in the first grantee when a subsequent executory interest (here that of Schallock and Daggett) is void under the rule against perpetuities. Instead, the grantor (here the corporation) retains an interest known as a possibility of reverter.[3]

RULE

The general rule has been stated to be:

> [W]hen an executory interest, following a fee simple interest in land * * * is void under the rule against perpetuities, the prior interest becomes absolute unless the language of the creating instrument makes it very clear that the prior interest is to terminate whether the executors interest takes effect or not.

Simes and Smith, The Law of Future Interests 316, 318, § 827 (2d ed. 1956).

All the jurisdictions in the United States which have dealt with a determinable fee and an executory interest void under the rule against perpetuities have followed this rule. * * * This conclusion is favored by Restatement, 2 Property, app. 34–47, §§ 228, 229.

IV

However, before this conclusion can be reached, an unusual Oregon rule must be considered. Oregon is one of a small minority of states that holds that a possibility of reverter cannot be alienated, Magness v. Kerr, 254 P. 1012 (Or. 1927); see Annotation, 53 A.L.R.2d 224 (1957), but the Oregon Supreme Court has never held that an attempt to alienate a possibility of reverter destroys it. In the case at bar, the grantor-corporation did attempt to alienate the possibility of reverter with its abortive gift over to Schallock and Daggett.[4] Thus, the question of whether an attempt

which would mean the 'possibility of reverter' of the dissolved corporation could not have been granted to Schallock and Daggett when they dissolved it.

---

3. It is well settled that the rule against perpetuities does not apply to possibilities of reverter. Gray, The Rule Against Perpetuities 46, 348, 349, §§ 41, 313, 314 (4th ed. 1942); Simes and Smith, The Law of Future Interests 311, § 825 (2d ed. 1956); Tiffany, Real Property 167, § 404 (3d ed. 1939). This historical anomaly has been criticized for allowing "dead hand rule" and creating "appalling practical results" when a possibility of reverter does fall in many years after the original grant. Leach, Perpetuities in Perspective:

Ending the Rule's Reign of Terror, 65 Harv. L.Rev. 721, 739 (1952); Leach, Perpetuities: The Nutshell Revisited, 78 Harv.L.Rev. 973, 980 (1965). * * * Where the rule against perpetuities has been applied to possibilities of reverter, it has always been done by legislative action. See, 78 Harv.L.Rev. 973, supra, at 989; Sparks, A Decade of Transition in Future Interests, 45 Va.L.Rev. 339, 362 (1959).

4. ORS 93.120 provides:

to alienate a possibility of reverter destroys it is presented to an Oregon appellate court for the first time. * * *

In Pure Oil Co. v. Miller–McFarland Drilling Co., 34 N.E.2d 854 (Ill. 1941), the Illinois court held that a possibility of reverter is not destroyed when the grantor tries to transfer it, even though the possibility of reverter is not alienable under Illinois law. In Reichard v. Chicago, B. & Q. R. Co., 1 N.W.2d 721 (Iowa 1942), which involved a conveyance after termination of a fee simple subject to a special limitation, the same facts as in Magness v. Kerr, supra, the court said:

> It seems rather fantastic to us, that a conveyance which is ineffective to convey what it attempts to convey is nevertheless an effective means of destroying it.

1 N.W.2d at 729.

We hold that an attempt by a grantor to transfer his possibility of reverter does not destroy it.

V

The remaining issue is the city's contention that upon dissolution of the corporation in 1927, or at the latest, upon the post-dissolution, winding-up period, ORS 57.630(2),[5] the corporation was civilly dead and without a successor to whom the possibility of reverter could descend. As is pointed out in Addy v. Short, 89 A.2d 136, 139 (Del. 1952), the statutory provision for distribution of corporate assets upon dissolution,

> is in effect a statutory expansion of the equitable doctrine that upon dissolution of a corporation its property, notwithstanding the technical rules of the early common law, does not escheat to the sovereign or revert to the original grantor, and will be administered * * * for the purpose of winding up the corporate affairs and distributing the assets to those equitably entitled to them.

In *Addy*, the corporation owning a possibility of reverter was dissolved and five years later the event (the abandonment of the use upon which the

---

* * * Any conveyance of real estate passes all the estate of the grantor, unless the intent to pass a lesser estate appears by express terms, or is necessarily implied in the terms of the grant.

5. ORS 57.630(2) provides:

Whenever any such corporation is the owner of real or personal property, or claims any interest or lien whatsoever in any real or personal property, such corporation shall continue to exist during such five-year period for the purpose of conveying, transferring and releasing such real or personal property or interest or lien therein, and such corporation shall continue after the expiration of such five-year period to exist as a body corporate for the purpose of being made a party to, and being sued in any action, suit or proceeding against it involving the title to any such real or personal property or any interest therein, and not otherwise; and any such action, suit or proceeding may be instituted and maintained against any such corporation as might have been had prior to the expiration of said five-year period. This section shall not be construed as affecting or suspending any statute of limitations applicable to any suit, action or proceeding instituted hereunder.

deed was conditioned) occurred. Delaware had only a three-year corporate dissolution winding-up period. The Delaware statutes did contain a provision that even after the three-year period, upon application of creditors or shareholders of a dissolved corporation, the court could appoint a receiver to take charge of the estate of the corporation and to collect debts and property due and belonging to the company. *Addy* held that neither the dissolution of the corporation nor the expiration of the three-year dissolution period worked an extinguishment of the possibility of reverter retained by the deed in question, and that upon the abandonment of the land by the grantee, the possibility of reverter was enlarged to a fee simple title. It further held that as statutory successors to the rights and powers of the corporation the receivers were entitled to the land.

Oregon has no such receivership statute, but the Oregon statutes make it clear that corporate assets no longer escheat or revert to the original grantor upon dissolution. In this case, the parties agree that the corporation was lawfully dissolved, all the creditors paid, and that Daggett and Schallock, the sole shareholders of the corporation, were statutorily entitled to and did receive all of the remaining assets of the corporation. One such asset was the possibility of reverter of the land in question.

The parties further agree that the defendants in this case were all of the heirs of Daggett and Schallock. As is pointed out in 18 Or.L.Rev. 63, supra, there is no Oregon decision on the issue of the descendability of the possibility of reverter. However, the weight of authority recognizes that such an interest is descendable. Restatement, 2 Property 606, Comment A, § 164, and 3 Simes 144–45, § 707 (1936). We discern no sound policy considerations which lead us to a contrary conclusion.[6]

Marijane Flitcraft acquired all rights to the property when the other defendants conveyed their interests to her in 1970.

Reversed.

NOTES AND QUESTIONS

1. Do you see how this decision involves an application of the principle of conservation of estates? The Daggett–Schallock Investment Company started out with a fee simple absolute having an unlimited duration. It executed a deed that carved this fee simple up into two smaller interests: a fee simple subject to an executory limitation, which was donated to the City, and an executory interest, which was conveyed to the two principal shareholders of the Company, Daggett and Schallock. (The corporation is assumed to have a legal personality separate and distinct from its shareholders; they are, for legal purposes, regarded as separate "persons.") Many years later, the executory interest is declared void under the Rule against Perpetuities (more on this shortly; for now just take it on faith that this conclusion is correct.) This means that there is now something left

6. It is difficult to understand the reason for the rule that a future interest in the nature of a possibility of reverter should be inalienable.

over which has not been accounted for—the interest originally occupied by the executory interest—and the difficult question for the court is what sort of legal interest should be implied as a matter of law to fill the void. The perceived imperative that this gap must be filled in order to account for the unlimited duration of the original fee simple is the principle of conservation of estates.

2.   The court discusses two possibilities for filling the gap. First, as argued by the City, the interest originally given to the City—a fee simple subject to an executory limitation—could be expanded into a fee simple absolute. One could say that the City had a fee simple with a forfeiture cloud hanging over its head; the mechanism for enforcing the forfeiture has been declared void; ergo the cloud has now been lifted. Second, as argued by the heirs of Daggett and Shallock, the court invalidating the executory interest can imply a possibility of reverter in the grantor—the Investment Company—and then, given that the corporation has been dissolved, award the possibility of reverter to the shareholders of the corporation (Daggett and Schallock as it happens) and their heirs. In a subsequent decision, the court decided that a possibility of reverter is alienable in Oregon. State ex rel. Dept. of Transportation v. Tolke, 586 P.2d 791 (Or. Ct. App. 1978). Does it matter to the result in this case if the possibility of reverter is alienable?

Apparently not, since they use the concept of "descendability" (?) instead to get around it.

3.   Assuming the legal authorities were sufficiently balanced to permit the court to embrace either the City's view or the heirs' view, why do you suppose the court found the heirs' position more appealing? What was the purpose of imposing the executory limitation in the first place? If invalidated executory interests always result in the expansion of the underlying defeasible fee into a fee simple absolute, what effect might this have on the incentives of persons to make charitable donations of property?

4.   There was a third option for filling the gap in *City of Klamath Falls*: The court could have held that the possibility of reverter escheated to the State of Oregon. Can you articulate the argument that would support this outcome? What advantages and disadvantages would this solution have relative to the two options considered by the court? Should the court have notified the attorney general of Oregon and allowed him or her to enter an appearance to argue in support of escheat? (Note that the State of Oregon and the City of Klamath Falls are different political entities, and might put the land to different uses or spend the proceeds from selling the land in different ways.) Should courts adopt a presumption against escheat? In favor of escheat? Should it depend on the nature of the property? Suppose the corporation dissolved in 1927 and the city stops using the land as a library 100 years later. Suppose further that there are over one hundred descendants of the original stockholders, and, unlike the descendants in the *City of Klamath Falls* case, they cannot agree on a consolidation of their interests. Who is going to take responsibility for notifying all the heirs of their interests, and representing them in court? Will the transaction costs of identifying and adjudicating the claims of the heirs eat up most of the value of the property in dispute?

5. Interests less than a fee simple can be held void for reasons of public policy or constitutionality. In *Evans v. Newton*, 382 U.S. 296 (1966), the Supreme Court considered the will of Senator A.O. Bacon of Georgia, who died in 1911. The will left a tract of land, known as Baconsfield, to the city of Macon for use as a park restricted to white persons only. The Court held that Macon could not continue to operate the park on a segregated basis because this would violate the Equal Protection Clause. On remand, the Georgia courts considered whether to revise the will under the cy pres doctrine (see Chapter VI) by striking out the racial restriction, or to declare that the gift to the city had failed. Based on evidence in the will that Senator Bacon was adamant about wanting no mixing of the races in the park, the Georgia courts declared that the gift had failed. Although the will contained no residuary clause, the Georgia courts implied a reversion in the heirs of Senator Bacon. Thus, the park passed by operation of law back into the family's hands. On further review, a divided Supreme Court affirmed. Evans v. Abney, 396 U.S. 435 (1970). The court concluded that the result, although unfortunate, simply reflected a good faith application of state law rules for interpreting and administering wills: Senator Bacon lived and died in a racist era, and the Georgia courts were simply giving effect to his intent. Justices Douglas and Brennan dissented, arguing that the judgment, by perpetuating the discriminatory intentions of Senator Bacon, was state action in violation of the equal protection guarantee. Relying in part on *Shelley v. Kraemer*, Chapter IV, which invalidated judicial enforcement of private racial covenants, they would have reversed.

6. In considering the effect of an invalid condition in a defeasible fee, might it make a difference whether the grantor used a fee simple determinable or a fee simple subject to condition subsequent? If the executory limitation in *City of Klamath Falls* had been expressed using condition subsequent language ("but if" or "provided that") rather than durational language ("so long as"), the City might well have won. See Restatement of Property § (1936); see also Hermitage Methodist Homes of Virginia, Inc. v. Dominion Trust Co., 387 S.E.2d 740 (Va. 1990) (holding determinable nature of racially restrictive trust interests to cause entire interests to fail, as opposed to condition subsequent which would have avoided forfeiture from invalidity of condition); Jonathan L. Entin, Defeasible Fees, State Action, and the Legacy of Massive Resistance, 34 Wm. & Mary L. Rev. 769 (1993).

[margin handwritten note: → because the court could have simply removed the clause within the commas, thus giving the city a fee simple absolute.]

DISCLAIMER

Recall that one of the powers of the owner is to make a gift, but a valid gift requires acceptance by the donee. More generally, it takes two to transfer, and the potential transferee has a veto over the transfer; no one is obligated to accept a property interest. As one court put it, "[t]he law certainly is not so absurd as to force a man to take an estate against his will." Townson v. Tickell, 106 Eng. Rep. 575, 576–77 (K.B. 1819). These principles form the basis of the law of disclaimer, under which a potential recipient can refuse property. Disclaimer has roots in the common law but is now provided for by statute. States vary in terms of whether the statutory disclaimer is the exclusive method. Statutes typically require a clear and unequivocal expression, and accepting any benefit of the asset in question defeats any attempt at disclaimer. Many statutes require certain formalities such as a writing describing the property in order to disclaim interests in real property. A successful disclaimer results in the one disclaiming being treated as never having owned the disclaimed interest. Why might someone disclaim an interest? In the context of family wealth transmission, a beneficiary might prefer the property to go to the next taker but would like to avoid the tax consequences of a double transfer. A disclaimer may help avoid probate and may prevent the disclaimant's creditors from reaching the property. See Joan B. Ellsworth, On Disclaimers: Let's Renounce I.R.C. Section 2518, 38 Vill. L. Rev. 693 (1993). Recall also the material on abandonment; some property has a negative value because of liabilities such as for environmental clean-up.

2.   THE FLEXIBILITY OF THE ESTATE SYSTEM

As you read through the following materials ask yourself whether the system of estates and future interests can be used to achieve the goals of a system of property. Do we have enough devices to achieve the objectives of those wishing to split ownership over time? Or do we, as many argue, have too many interests? As we will see, one of the central features of the estate system is that the menu of forms of ownership is fixed, finite, and closed, a doctrine known (especially in the civil law) as the *numerus clausus* (closed number) of forms of property. One may not create a new form of ownership, in stark contrast to the approach in contract law, in which free customizability (within broad limits) is the norm. Before considering why property takes this very noncontractarian approach, one might ask how it is possible that a fixed system of estates could possibly be flexible enough to serve people's needs.

One reason that the system is more flexible than appears at first blush is something known in formal language theory as recursiveness. Consider the following example:

Example: O to A for life, then to B for life, then to C for life.

Here in effect what O has done is to carve out a life estate and a reversion and immediately carved out another life estate for B, pushing back the implied reversion still further, and then done so again for C. (If B dies before A or if C dies before either A or B, their respective remainders in life estate are extinguished.) One could think of the owner employing this set of rules (out of a larger set some of which would correspond to the diagrams above):

(i) Fee simple → Life estate + Reversion

(ii) Reversion → Life estate + Reversion

What is special about these rules is that rule (ii) can feed itself. Rules whose output can be fed back into the rule are called *recursive*, as reflected by the fact that Reversion appears on both sides of the arrow in (ii). The owner in the example can be considered to have used Rule (i) and then

Rule (ii), and then Rule (ii) again (i.e., twice). In principle there is no limit to how many times O could carve out life estates and push the reversion back yet further. As a result, any set of rules containing a recursive rule like (ii) generates an infinite set of potential outputs. Something similar is true in many computer programs and in the grammars of natural languages. Among the linguistic phenomena that call for a model including a recursive rule is the complement clause beginning with *that*: "Pat said/believed that Chris is sick," "Leslie said/believed that Pat said/believed that Chris is sick," etc. A sentence can consist of *that* plus another sentence (which can in turn consist of *that* plus another sentence, etc.), with no limit in principle. While it is certainly the case that people can make up new words, one cannot unilaterally make up a rule like the *that* rule. But the *that* rule (and rules like it) permit a finite grammar to capture an infinite set of possible sentences. So too with the basic building blocks of property and the rules for combining them.

USING THE ESTATE SYSTEM FOR ESTATE PLANNING

One reason flexibility is important is that it facilitates estate planning—determining the distribution of assets that occurs when an individual dies. The system of estates in land was primarily devised with estate planning in mind, and this continues to be one of its primary functions today. When the system was devised, land was all-important, and the family patriarch (land being controlled by the husband as head of the household) would often want to assure that Blackacre would remain in the family to provide a source of support (and social status) for a surviving spouse and his children, and he might hope to keep it in the family even longer (in his dreams perhaps forever). Today attitudes are different, but the estate system still provides the building blocks for estate planners. Now, however, rather than leaving Blackacre in a series of legal estates in land, virtually all estate planners will create a trust, either before an owner dies or as part of a will. The corpus of the trust is much more likely to consists of stocks, bonds, partnership interests, and other intangible assets than Blackacre; if there is a Blackacre, its disposition may be regarded as a detail. We take up trusts in greater detail in the next Chapter. For now, the important point is that the trust will give legal title to all the assets to a trustee (a trusted family member or friend or a professional financial institution) in fee simple, and will describe various beneficial interests in the earnings from the assets in a surviving spouse, children, etc., understood to be equitable interests, not legal interests. Importantly—and this is a primary reason you are studying these materials—the vocabulary for describing these beneficial equitable interests in trust is the *same* system of estates originally devised for freehold interests in land. Thus, lawyers and other estate planners will employ forms such as the life estate, the remainder, and the executory interest in formulating an estate plan that seeks to realize the goals of the individual for whom such a trust is being set up. Facility with these forms is therefore necessary to be an effective estate planner.

Another reason to use a will—with or without a trust—is to avoid the application of the intestacy statute. Each state has a statute that determines the decedent's heirs and how and when they inherit property. The intestacy statute reflects a default presumption about what a decedent would wish if there had been a valid will reflecting his or her intent. Sometimes a person's desires diverge very much from these defaults. Such persons have an extra reason to need a will, but studies suggest that many if not most people in the United States die intestate. Intestacy is a blunt instrument and the law does not favor this situation. Wills are construed to avoid intestacy. A partially invalid will can lead to partial intestacy.

Under the typical intestacy statute, the intestate's successors are the family, with priority going to the decedent's spouse and issue (lineal descendants). Traditionally, the spouse would get between one third and one half. The 1990 Uniform Probate Code Section 2–102 would increase this share to 100% under a wide variety of circumstances including no lineal descendants or no lineal descendants who are not also lineal descendants of the surviving spouse. Studies suggest that this better tracks the preferences of most people. In the absence of any surviving spouse or issue, other relatives are the successors. These are lineal ascendants (parents, grandparents, and so on) and collaterals, who are designated blood relatives who are neither lineal descendants or ascendants, i.e., siblings, uncles and aunts, nephews and nieces, cousins, and so on. Various systems exist for determining who among these non-spouse, non-issue people succeed. Generally speaking "nearer" blood relatives take precedence over more distant ones, but states vary as to whether this is based on degrees of *consanguinity* or on the *parentelic* system. Consanguinity counts distance in terms of the number of generations to a common ancestor (e.g., one between parent and child, two between grandparent and grandchild) and if necessary down to the collateral (so degree two for a sibling, i.e., up to the parent and down to the sibling; three for a nephew or niece, etc.). In the parentelic system, priority is given to those close by in terms of sharing a common ancestor even if the deceased and the person in question belong to very different generations. So under the parentelic system grandnieces (related in the fourth degree in terms of consanguinity) have priority over aunts (related in the third degree) because a grandniece is descended from the decedent's parents but an aunt is descended from the grandparents. For details, see Elias Clark et al., Cases and Materials on Gratuitous Transfers 49–54 (4th ed. 1999). As you can imagine, these differences and their technical nature can lead to undesired results for the uninformed.

What if a spouse does have a will but leaves the surviving spouse one dollar, or nothing at all? Generally states have a spousal elective share—typically one third, which the surviving spouse may (but need not) elect. Others designated under the will then take proportionately less. Such elective shares replaced earlier special marital property interests in surviving spouses, called dower and curtesy. We return to marital property rights in Part E of this Chapter.

[Handwritten margin notes:] See hand-out from class – Table of Consanguinity Majority Rule: Parentelic Minority Rule: Consanguinity

What if a child predeceases a parent who then dies intestate? The child cannot then be an heir. But intestacy statutes differ as to how any surviving descendants of the predeceased child will be treated. Under one system, such children (grandchildren of the intestate) will be allocated shares of the estate *per stirpes*: the estate is divided into equal shares based on the number of children, alive or deceased, who have descendants living at the intestate's death. Then any share corresponding to a predeceased child is divided in a similar fashion among his descendants. So if O dies with no surviving spouse and has two living children A and B and one predeceased child C who left children C1 and C2, then C1 and C2 each get one-sixth of the estate (A and B each get one-third). In a *per capita* system the estate is divided up equally among the members of the generations closest to the intestate with at least one living member (usually the children). In the example, A, B, C1, and C2 all get one fourth. Notice that in each system C is represented by C1 and C2. But any will C may have left generally has nothing to do with how the intestate scheme works with respect to allocating O's assets upon her death. These rules have evolved greatly from earlier notions of primogeniture favoring eldest sons, especially for real estate. Modern intestacy laws, particularly in states using a system based on consanguinity, look more like the traditional system for personal property, which called for equal shares among surviving children.

[Handwritten margin notes: See class notes (#23) from 10/16/09. Per stirpes: O — A 1/3, B 1/3, C pre-deceased; C1 1/6, C2 1/6. Per Capita: O — A 1/4, B 1/4, C pre-deceased; C1 1/4, C2 1/4.]

3. THE *NUMERUS CLAUSUS*

The catalog of estates is finite and closed, a principle sometimes called the *numerus clausus*. The term *numerus clausus* comes from the civil law, which in its various versions, exhibits a strong and explicit principle that property, unlike contract, is not freely customizable by parties but rather is standardized into a closed set of approved forms. In the common law, and U.S. law in particular, the *numerus clausus* is more implicit. As a matter of justification, in both the civil-law and common-law traditions the *numerus clausus* has been something of a puzzle.

Thomas W. Merrill & Henry E. Smith, *Optimal Standardization in the Law of Property: The* Numerus Clausus *Principle*, 110 Yale L.J. 1, 24–28, 31–35, 38, 40, 42 (2000)

III. Measurement Costs, Frustration Costs, and the Optimal Standardization of Property Rights

What accounts for the widespread adherence to the *numerus clausus*, not only in the common law but in postfeudal legal systems throughout the world? To the extent that an explanation can be found in the American legal literature, it focuses on a concern with undue restraints on alienation.

* * *

The problem with this argument is that the system of estates in land is sufficiently flexible that one can nearly always find a way to effectuate a complicated conveyance. * * *

The leading English case affirming what we call the *numerus clausus* principle, *Keppell v. Bailey*,[102] suggests a different rationale. *Keppell* involved the conveyance of an iron works, in which the purchasers covenanted on behalf of themselves and their successors and assigns to acquire all limestone required by the works from a particular quarry and to ship the limestone to the works on a particular railroad. The Court of Chancery held that this type of agreement, although enforceable as a contract between the original parties, did not fall within the recognized types of servitudes enforceable against subsequent purchasers as a property right running with the land. There was, however, no suggestion in the case that the covenants worked an undue restraint on alienation; indeed, the works had recently been conveyed from the original purchasers to another party. Instead, Lord Chancellor Brougham stressed the more systemic consequences of allowing such "fancies," as they have been called, to be enforced as property rights:

> There can be no harm to allowing the fullest latitude to men in binding themselves and their representatives, that is, their assets real and personal, to answer in damages for breach of their obligations. This tends to no mischief, and is a reasonable liberty to bestow; but great detriment would arise and much confusion of rights if parties were allowed to invent new modes of holding and enjoying real property, and to impress upon their lands and tenements a peculiar character, which should follow them into all hands, however remote. Every close, every messuage, might thus be held in several fashion; and it would hardly be possible to know what rights the acquisition of any parcel conferred, or what obligations it imposed.[105]

In modern terminology, the Lord Chancellor thought that permitting interests like the covenants in *Keppell* to be established as property rights would create unacceptable information costs to third parties.

In this Part, we develop Lord Chancellor Brougham's germ of an insight by presenting a theory of the *numerus clausus* based on optimal standardization of property rights.

A.   Measurement–Cost Externalities

When individuals encounter property rights, they face a measurement problem. In order to avoid violating another's property rights, they must ascertain what those rights are. In order to acquire property rights, they must measure various attributes, ranging from the physical boundaries of a parcel, to use rights, to the attendant liabilities of the owner to others (such as adjacent owners). Whether the objective is to avoid liability or to acquire rights, an individual will measure the property rights until the

---

102.   39 Eng. Rep. 1042 (Ch. 1834).   **105.**   Keppell, 39 Eng. Rep. at 1049.

marginal costs of additional measurement equal the marginal benefits. When seeking to avoid liability, the actor will seek to minimize the sum of the costs of liability for violations of rights and the costs of avoiding those violations through measurement. In the potential transfer situation, the individual will measure as long as the marginal benefit in reduced error costs exceeds the marginal cost of measurement.

The need for standardization in property law stems from an externality involving measurement costs: Parties who create new property rights will not take into account the full magnitude of the measurement costs they impose on strangers to the title. An example illustrates. Suppose one hundred people own watches. *A* is the sole owner of a watch and wants to transfer some or all of the rights to use the watch to *B*. The law of personal property allows the sale of *A*'s entire interest in the watch, or the sale of a life estate in the watch, or the sale of a joint tenancy or tenancy in common in the watch. But suppose *A* wants to create a "time-share" in the watch, which would allow *B* to use the watch on Mondays but only on Mondays (with *A* retaining for now the rights to the watch on all other days). As a matter of contract law, *A* and *B* are perfectly free to enter into such an idiosyncratic agreement. But *A* and *B* are not permitted by the law of personal property to create a *property right* in the use of the watch on Mondays only and to transfer this property right from *A* to *B*.[110]

MAIN POINT

Why might the law restrict the freedom of *A* and *B* to create such an unusual property right? Suppose, counterfactually, that such idiosyncratic property rights are permitted. Word spreads that someone has sold a Monday right in a watch, but not which of the one hundred owners did so. If *A* now decides to sell his watch, he will have to explain that it does not include Monday rights, and this will reduce the attractiveness of the watch to potential buyers. Presumably, however, A will foresee this when he sells the Monday rights, and is willing to bear the cost of that action in the form of a lower sales price. But consider what will happen now when any of the *other* ninety-nine watch owners try to sell their watches. Given the awareness that someone has created a Monday-only right, anyone else buying a watch must now also investigate whether any particular watch does not include Monday rights. Thus, by allowing even one person to create an idiosyncratic property right, the information processing costs of all persons who have existing or potential interests in this type of property go up. This external cost on other market participants forms the basis of our explanation of the *numerus clausus*.

At this point, it is useful to distinguish three classes of individuals who might be affected by the decision to create idiosyncratic property rights, or fancies, as illustrated by Figure 1. First are the *originating parties,* who are the participants to the transaction creating the fancy; this is *A* and *B* in Figure 1. Second are the *potential successors in interest* to the asset that is

---

110. Time shares are a creation of statute, and the various statutes appear to limit time shares to real estate. Ellen R. Peirce & Richard A. Mann, Time–Share Interests in Real Estate: A Critical Evaluation of the Regulatory Environment, 59 Notre Dame L. Rev. 9, 37–42 (1983).

being subjected to the fancy. This would be anyone who might purchase A's reserved rights (after the transfer to *B*) as well as anyone who succeeds to the interest acquired by *B*. Potential successors in interest are shown as *C*s and *D*s in Figure 1. Finally, there are the *other market participants*, people who will deal in or with watches other than the one over which *A* and *B* have transacted. Other market participants include those selling and acquiring rights in other watches such as *E* and *F* and *G* and *H* in Figure 1. They also include all who must avoid violating property rights in all watches, rights that are enforced against the world represented by *I* and *J* in Figure 1.[111] In the hypothetical example above, the other market participants are the other ninety-nine watch owners and their successors in title, as well as anyone who potentially might violate a property right in a watch.

Figure 1—The Classes of Affected Parties

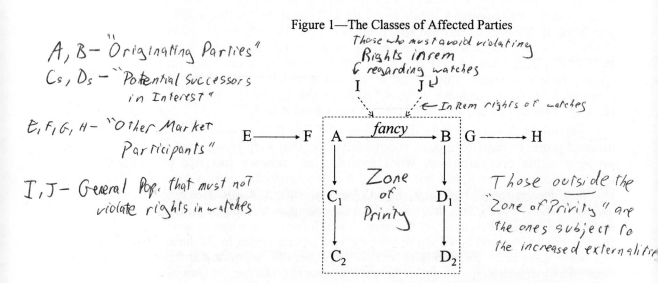

A, B — "Originating Parties"

Cs, Ds — "Potential Successors in Interest"

E, F, G, H — "Other Market Participants"

I, J — General Pop. that must not violate rights in watches

Those who must avoid violating Rights in rem regarding watches

← In Rem rights of watches

Zone of Privity

Those outside the "Zone of Privity" are the ones subject to the increased externalities

The difference between other possible explanations of the *numerus clausus* and our information-cost theory can be understood in terms of this three-way classification. Other explanations focus on the effect of novel property rights on the originating parties and potential successors in interest—the *A*s, *B*s, *C*s, and *D*s of the world. One may say that these classes of individuals fall within the "zone of privity" designated by the box with the dotted line in Figure 1. Our explanation, in contrast, focuses on the effect of unusual property rights on other market participants—the *E*s, *F*s, *G*s, *H*s, *I*s, and *J*s of the world—classes of individuals who fall outside the zone of privity. As we argue, explanations based on classes of individuals within the zone of privity have difficulty identifying costs that are not impounded into the price facing those who make the decision whether to create the fancy in the first place. An explanation based on costs incurred

111. Thus, other market participants include those whose actual dealings with watches occur by means other than consensual transactions.

by classes of individuals outside the zone of privity does not have this difficulty. * * *

When *A* creates the Monday right, this can raise the information costs of third parties. If the law allows *A* to create a Monday interest, individuals wishing to buy watches or bailees asked to repair watches will have to consider the possibility that any given watch is a Monday-only watch (or a watch for any other proper subset of days of the week) rather than a full-week watch. While *A* and *B* might be expected to take into account the market-value-lowering effect of undesirable idiosyncratic rights when third parties like *C* or *D* consider purchasing property in this watch, they will not take into account the more general effect on processing costs created by the existence of such rights when *F* is considering a purchase of rights in *E*'s watch, or *I* and *J* are worried about violating property rights.

A and B may have subjective reasons for creating property rights based on days of the week. But, the possible existence of such rights will cause information costs for others—such as *E*, *F*, *G*, *H*, *I*, and *J*—to rise. Those considering whether to purchase property rights in watches will have more to investigate: They will have to assure themselves that they are getting all the days of the week that they want. Furthermore, they will have to worry about dimensions of division and elaboration that perhaps no one has yet thought of, making the acquisition of any watch more uncertain as well as riskier. With an indefinite set of types of rights, these costs will be higher than where parties, especially unsophisticated ones, are restricted to the limited menu the law allows. Furthermore, because property rights are in rem, all those who might violate property rights, accidentally or not, must know what they are supposed to respect. An indefinite set of types of rights will raise the cost of preventing violations through investigation of rights.

To return to our hypothetical world of one-hundred watch owners, suppose the value of creating the Monday-only right to A is $10, but the existence of this idiosyncrasy increases processing costs by $1 for all watch owners. The net benefit to A is $9, but the social cost is $90. As this example suggests, idiosyncratic property rights create a common-pool problem. The marginal benefits of the idiosyncrasy are fully internalized to the owner of the property right, but the owner bears only a fraction of the general measurement costs thereby created. Overall, the creation of external costs associated with this common-pool problem is likely to proceed beyond the optimal level. The problem cannot be resolved by side payments from the remaining ninety-nine to A, because the transaction costs are virtually certain to be prohibitive. Consequently, since an individual's interest in creating the nonstandard right—the extra benefit from using it rather than the next best alternative—is less than the additional measurement costs imposed on the other market participants, there is a rationale for the law to prohibit the creation of this kind of idiosyncratic right.

One way to control the external costs of measurement to third parties is through compulsory standardization of property rights. Standardization reduces the costs of measuring the attributes of such rights. Limiting the number of basic property forms allows a market participant or a potential

(handwritten margin notes:)
For A:
Value of Fancy: $10
Processing Cost: −$1
Net Benefit to A: $9

For all watch owners (100):
Value of Fancy: $10
Processing Cost: −$100
Net Social Cost: $90

violator to limit his or her inquiry to whether the interest does or does not have the features of the forms on the menu. Fancies not on the closed list need not be considered because they will not be enforced. When it comes to the basic legal dimensions of property, limiting the number of forms thus makes the determination of their nature less costly. The "good" in question here might be considered to be the prevention of error in ascertaining the attributes of property rights. Standardization means less measurement is required to achieve a given amount of error prevention. Alternatively, one can say that standardization increases the productivity of any given level of measurement efforts.

One would expect standardization to have the most value in connection with the dimensions of property rights that are least visible, and hence the most difficult for ordinary observers to measure. The tangible attributes of property, such as its size, shape, color, or texture, are typically readily observable and hence can be relatively easily measured by third parties. In the watch example, the watch can be a Timex or a Rolex and can be any size or color, and so forth. These physical attributes, and of course the price, are relatively easy for third parties to process using their senses, and thus there is less to be gained from standardizing them. The legal dimensions of property are less visible and less easy to comprehend, especially when they deviate from the most familiar forms such as the undivided fee simple. Thus, one would expect the effort to lower third-party information costs through standardization to focus on the legal dimension of ownership.

B.   Frustration Costs and the Language of Property Rights

If the only concern were in reducing third-party measurement costs, then there should be only one mandatory package of property rights, presumably a simple usufruct or an undivided fee simple. But standardization imposes its own costs. Mandatory rules sometimes prevent the parties from achieving a legitimate goal cost-effectively. Enforcing standardization can therefore frustrate the parties' intentions.

Although the *numerus clausus* sometimes frustrates parties' objectives, often those objectives can be realized by a more complex combination of the standardized building blocks of property. For example, sophisticated parties with good legal advice can create the equivalent of a lease "for the duration of the war" by entering into a long-term lease determinable if the war ends. The fact that the *numerus clausus* is in this sense "avoidable" does not mean that it is trivial: Even if the standardization effected by the *numerus clausus* principle does not absolutely bar the parties from realizing their ends, this standardization comes at a price. The effect is roughly that of price discrimination: Parties willing to pay a great deal for an objective can achieve it by incurring higher planning and implementation costs. Furthermore, the design and implementation costs imposed by the *numerus clausus* function as a sort of "pollution tax" that should deter parties from insisting on overusing hard-to-process property forms, thereby placing higher processing burdens on market participants and especially courts. * * *

C. Optimal Standardization and the *Numerus Clausus*

We are now in a position to see how the *numerus clausus* functions to promote the optimal standardization of property rights. From a social point of view, the objective should be to minimize the sum of measurement (and error) costs, frustration costs, and administrative costs. In other words, what we want is not maximal standardization—or no standardization—but optimal standardization. Fortunately, standardization comes in degrees. There is a spectrum of possible approaches to property rights, ranging from total freedom of customization on the one hand to complete regimentation on the other. Neither of these endpoints on the spectrum is likely to minimize social costs. Extreme standardization would frustrate many of the purposes to which property rights are put. On the other hand, total freedom to customize rights would create large third-party measurement and error costs and high administrative costs. Attention should focus on the middle range of the spectrum. Starting from a position of complete regimentation, permitting additional forms of property rights should reduce frustration costs by more than it increases measurement and error costs to third parties and administrative costs. Conversely, if one starts from a position of complete customization of rights, increasing the degree of standardization should lower measurement and error costs and administrative costs by more than the attendant frustration costs will rise. * * *

The *numerus clausus* principle can be seen from this perspective as a device that moves the system of property rights in the direction of the optimal level of standardization * * * By creating a strong presumption against judicial recognition of new forms of property rights, the *numerus clausus* imposes a brake on efforts by parties to proliferate new forms of property rights. On the other hand, by grandfathering in existing forms of property, and permitting legislative creation of new forms, the *numerus clausus* permits some positive level of diversification in the recognized forms of property. We do not argue that any particular number of property forms is in fact optimal. Nor do we argue that the forms currently recognized by the common law are ideal and beyond improvement. We do submit, however, that the *numerus clausus* strikes a rough balance between the extremes of complete regimentation and complete freedom of customization, and thus leads to a system of property rights that is closer to being optimal than that which would be produced by either of the extreme positions.

D. Information Costs and the Dynamics of Property

Finally, our explanation of the *numerus clausus* generates some general predictions about the way in which property regimes will change over time: As the costs of standardization to the parties and the government shift, we expect the optimal degree of standardization to rise or fall. Consider the rise of registers of interests in real property, that is, recording acts. This device lowers the costs of notice; it is an alternative method of lowering information costs. * * *

Likewise, the more recent move toward increased use of contract principles in areas like electronic commerce fits in well with the information-cost theory of the *numerus clausus*. Notice is arguably easier to furnish (if not to process) when, for example, rights to digital content are being transferred, and notice of restrictions and other features of rights transferred are technologically not difficult to provide. * * * In general, to the extent that technological change allows cheaper notice of relevant interests, the need for standardization by the law will be somewhat diminished. Just as the rise of land registers allowed some loosening of the *numerus clausus*, so too technology that lowers information costs can be expected to weaken the *numerus clausus* further.

NOTES AND QUESTIONS

1. The *numerus clausus* is a mandatory rule that conflicts with the principle of freedom of contract. Why is free customizability of contract rights exempt from the problem of information costs? Do contracts ever present these problems? What makes contracts relevantly different from property? Is it some notion of privity? For one thing the average property right lasts a lot longer. Who is the "audience" for claims of a property sort? Claims under a contract? See, e.g., Thomas W. Merrill & Henry E. Smith, The Property/Contract Interface, 101 Colum. L. Rev. 773 (2001); Carol M. Rose, What Government Can Do for Property (and Vice Versa), in The Fundamental Interrelationships Between Government and Property 214–15 (Nicholas Mercuro & Warren J. Samuels eds. 1999); Bernard Rudden, Economic Theory v. Property Law: The *Numerus Clausus* Problem, in Oxford Essays in Jurisprudence 239, 241 (3d Series, John Eekelaar & John Bell eds., 1987); Henry E. Smith, The Language of Property: Form, Context, and Audience, 55 Stan. L. Rev. 1105 (2003).

2. One alternative explanation for the *numerus clausus* is that it prevents excessive fragmentation. If there are too many veto-wielding co-owners, holdout behavior will cause a resource to be underused. As we saw in Chapter II, this would be a mirror image of the situation with the tragedy of the commons, and has been termed the "tragedy of the anticommons." See Michael A. Heller, The Boundaries of Private Property, 108 Yale L.J. 1163, 1176–78 (1999). Ask yourself whether the *numerus clausus* and the other maintenance doctrines in this section serve to limit the number of claimants or the number of types of property rights, or both.

3. Another aspect of the *numerus clausus* relates to institutional choice. Innovation in property law does occur; for all its antiquarian flavor, even the estate system is quite different from what it was even 100 years ago. The *numerus clausus* directs judges to avoid creating or recognizing private efforts at creating new property forms. But legislatures have the power to do so, and the *numerus clausus* channels innovation into the legislative arena. Consider some examples. The abolition of the fee tail was accomplished by statute, not by judicial decision. As another example, the nineteenth century saw many innovations in marital property. The older

[handwritten margin note: Since contracts are 'in personam', all of the affected parties are aware of the conditions, thus there are no other participants to consider.]

interests were dower, which gave a surviving wife a life estate in one third of the real property held by the husband, and curtesy, which among other things gave a widower a life estate in the wife's land. Eventually, legislatures abolished these forms of property and replaced them with gender-neutral statutes creating a surviving spouse's forced share (usually one third) of the deceased spouse's estate. A surviving spouse of either gender can now elect to take either what the will provides or a fee simple ownership of one third of the estate. See, e.g., June R. Carbone & Margaret F. Brinig, Rethinking Marriage: Feminist Ideology, Economic Change, and Divorce Reform, 65 Tul. L. Rev. 953, 1010 (1991).

4. Is it a good idea to give legislatures primary responsibility for creating and destroying forms of property? Elsewhere in this excerpted article, Merrill and Smith argue that making legislatures rather than courts the source of legal change affords the benefits of clarity, universality, comprehensiveness, stability, prospectivity, and implicit compensation. See Merrill & Smith, *Numerus Clausus*, supra, at 58–68. Can you think of contrary arguments that might support giving courts a more active role here? Keep these questions of institutional choice in mind when we discuss developments in landlord-tenant law and condominiums in the next chapter.

5. Why does the *numerus clausus* remain a largely unacknowledged design principle in Anglo–American law? One can see the idea in operation in many ways. For example, one of the traditional maxims observed by the courts of equity was that equity will modify property rights less readily than contracts. See Charles Gray, The Boundaries of the Equitable Function, 20 Am. J. Legal Hist. 192 (1976). But European civil codes often contain express provisions acknowledging the *numerus clausus*. The principle is unquestionably weaker in the common law than in the civil law, and weaker in the United States than in most other common-law systems.

There was a time when the menu of property rights included the fee tail along with variants that would keep the property in a designated part of a family ("to A and his heirs by his wife B") or to issue of one gender ("to A and the heirs male of his/her body" or "to A and the heirs female of his/her body," etc., creating the fee tail male and fee tail female, respectively). Once these estates were abolished, some people might still want them. What is to prevent them from creating what they want?

Johnson v. Whiton

Supreme Judicial Court of Massachusetts, 1893.
34 N.E. 542.

■ Holmes, J. This is an action to recover a deposit paid under an agreement to purchase land. The land in question passed under the seventh clause of the will of Royal Whiton to his five grandchildren, and a deed executed by them was tendered to the plaintiff, but was refused, on the ground that one of the grandchildren, Sarah A. Whiton, could not convey a fee-simple absolute, and this action is brought to try the question. The clause of the will referred to is as follows: "After the decease of all my children, I give, devise, and bequeath to my granddaughter Sarah A. Whiton and her heirs on her father's side one-third part of all my estate, both real and personal, and to my other grandchildren and their heirs, respectively, the remainder, to be divided in equal parts between them."

We see no room for doubt that the legal title passed by the foregoing clause. We think it equally plain that the words "and her heirs on her father's side" are words of limitation, and not words of purchase. The only serious question is whether the effect of them was to give Sarah A. Whiton only a qualified fee, and whether, by reason of the qualification, she is unable to convey a fee simple. We do not think that it would be profitable to follow the decisions to be found in Preston on Estates, p. 449 et seq., and Challis on Real Property, c. 19. By the old law, to take land by descent a man must be of the blood of the first purchaser, (Co. Litt. 12a; 2 Bl.Comm. 220;) and by St. 3 & 4 Wm. IV. c. 106, § 2, descent is traced from the purchaser. For instance, if the land had been acquired in fee simple by Sarah A. Whiton's father, it could only have descended from her to her heirs on her father's side. It was no great stretch to allow a limitation in the first instance to Sarah of a fee with the same descendible quality that it would have had in the case supposed. Challis, Real. Prop. 216, 222, 224; Co. Littl. 220b; Blake v. Hynes, L.R. 11 Ir. 284; 1 Prest.Est. 474. See St. 22 & 23 Vict. c. 35, § 19. Especially is this true if, as Mr. Challis argues, the grantee under such a limitation could convey a fee simple, just as he or she could have done if the estate actually had descended from the father. But our statute of descent looks no further than the person himself who died seised of or entitled to the estate. Pub.St. c. 125. The analogy which lies at the foundation of the argument for the possibility of such limitations is wanting. A man cannot create a new kind of inheritance. Co. Litt. 27; Com. Dig. "Estates by Grant," A, 6. These and other authorities show, too, that, except in the case of a grant by the king, if the words "on her father's side" do not effect the purpose intended, they are to be rejected, leaving the estate a fee simple, which was Mr. Washburn's opinion. 1 Washb.Real.Prop. 61. Certainly, it would seem that in this commonwealth an estate descending only to heirs on the father's side was a new kind of inheritance.

What we have to consider, however, is not the question of descent, but that of alienability; and that question brings a further consideration into view. It would be most unfortunate and unexpected if it should be discovered at this late day that it was possible to impose such a qualification upon a fee, and to put it out of the power of the owners to give a clear title for generations. In the more familiar case of an estate tail, the legislature has acted, and the statute has been carried to the furthest verge by construction. Pub.St. c. 120, § 15; Coombs v. Anderson, 138 Mass. 376. It is not too much to say that it would be plainly contrary to the policy of the law of Massachusetts to deny the power of Sarah A. Whiton to convey an unqualified fee.

Judgment for defendant.

NOTES AND QUESTIONS

1.   As Justice Holmes notes, the fee tail had been abolished in Massachusetts. One way to read the decision is that it simply refuses to give effect to a testamentary devise that seems to create a kind of fee tail, in order to effectuate the legislative policy. If Massachusetts has determined that fees tail are to be converted into fees simple, then this odd devise should also be construed to be a fee simple. But Holmes also says that "A man cannot create a new kind of inheritance." And the opinion invokes concerns about alienability, an issue not unrelated to the *numerus clausus* principle and to which we return soon. So it is possible to read the decision more broadly as invoking the idea that the number of options in the system of estates is fixed or closed, at least insofar as courts are concerned.

2.   One issue that arises with mandatory rules like the *numerus clausus* is that they frustrate parties' intent. Yet as noted above, certain features of the estate system ensure that most objectives can be achieved using the limited set of building blocks allowed by the *numerus clausus*. Ask yourself whether Royal Whiton could have achieved most of his objectives without running afoul of the *numerus clausus*. Looking back over the list of possible interests, consider the fee simple determinable and the fee simple subject to condition subsequent. To help you think about this issue, notice that the interest created by Royal Whiton was of unclear import. On the one hand, we might take it to give Sarah a fee simple, but if she died intestate the property could be inherited only on her father's side. On the other hand, the interest might be interpreted as an attempt at something like the (abolished) fee tail, descending from generation to generation not to the issue of Sarah's body but the heirs on her father's side. If so, the class of potential claimants would not be known until Sarah's last heir on her father's side died without issue (which would be like the "indefinite failure of issue" in the old fee tail). Which interpretation does Holmes adopt? How closely might a well-advised Royal Whiton have come to achieving either objective?

P   D – tenant

Garner v. Gerrish

New York Court of Appeals, 1984.
473 N.E.2d 223.

■ WACHTLER, JUDGE. The question on this appeal is whether a lease which grants the tenant the right to terminate the agreement at a date of his choice creates a determinable life tenancy on behalf of the tenant or merely establishes a tenancy at will. The courts below held that the lease created a tenancy at will permitting the current landlord to evict the tenant. We granted the tenant's motion for leave to appeal and now reverse the order appealed from.

In 1977 Robert Donovan owned a house located in Potsdam, New York. On April 14 of that year he leased the premises to the tenant Lou Gerrish. The lease was executed on a printed form and it appears that neither side was represented by counsel. The blanks on the form were filled in by

Donovan who provided the names of the parties, described the property and fixed the rent at $100 a month. With respect to the duration of the tenancy the lease provides it shall continue "for and during the term of *quiet enjoyment* from the *first* day of *May,* 1977 which term will end—*Lou Gerrish has the privilege of termination [sic] this agreement at a date of his own choice*" (emphasis added to indicate handwritten and typewritten additions to the printed form). The lease also contains a standard reference to the landlord's right to reentry if the rent is not timely paid, which is qualified by the handwritten statement: "Lou has thirty days grace for payment".

Gerrish moved into the house and continued to reside there, apparently without incident, until Donovan died in November of 1981. At that point David Garner, executor of Donovan's estate, served Gerrish with a notice to quit the premises. When Gerrish refused, Garner commenced this summary proceeding to have him evicted. Petitioner contended that the lease created a tenancy at will because it failed to state a definite term. In his answering affidavit, the tenant alleged that he had always paid the rent specified in the lease. He also contended that the lease granted him a tenancy for life, unless he elects to surrender possession during his lifetime.

The County Court granted summary judgment to petitioner on the ground that the lease is "indefinite and uncertain . . . as regards the length of time accorded respondent to occupy the premises. Although the writing specifies the date of commencement of the term, it fails to set forth the duration of continuance, and the date or event of termination". The court concluded that the original landlord leased the premises to the tenant "for a month-to-month term and that petitioner was entitled to terminate the lease upon the death of the lessor effective upon the expiration of the next succeeding monthly term of occupancy". In support of its decision the court quoted the following statement from our opinion in *Western Transp. Co. v. Lansing,* 49 N.Y. 499, 508: "A lease . . . for so long as the lessee shall please, is said to be a lease at will of both lessor and lessee".

The Appellate Division affirmed for the same reasons in a brief memorandum.

On appeal to our court, the parties concede that the agreement creates a lease. The only question is whether it should be literally construed to grant to the tenant alone the right to terminate at will, or whether the landlord is accorded a similar right by operation of law.

At early common law according to Lord Coke, "when the lease is made to have and to hold at the will of the lessee, this must be also at the will of the lessor" (1 Co.Litt., § 55a). This rule was generally adopted in the United States during the 19th century and at one time was said to represent the majority view (see Ann., 137 A.L.R. 362, 367; 51C C.J.S., Landlord and Tenant, § 167, p. 475). However, it was not universally accepted (see, e.g., Effinger v. Lewis, 32 Pa. 367; Gunnison v. Evans, 18 P.2d 191 (Kan.); Thompson v. Baxter, 119 N.W. 797 (Minn.)) and has been widely criticized, particularly in this century, as an antiquated notion which violates the terms of the agreement and frustrates the intent of the parties (1 Tiffany, Real Property [3d ed.], § 159; 1 American Law of Real Property [Casner ed., 1952], § 3.30; Schoshinski, American Law of Landlord and Tenant, § 2:7; see, also, Restatement, Property 2d, Landlord and Tenant, § 1.6).

It has been noted that the rule has its origins in the doctrine of livery of seisin (Tiffany, op. cit., § 159; Effinger v. Lewis, supra), which required physical transfer of a clod of earth, twig, key or other symbol on the premises in the presence of witnesses, to effect a conveyance of land interest (2 Blackstone's Comm., pp. 315, 316; Black's Law Dictionary [Fourth ed.], p. 1084). Although this ceremony was not required for leases, which were generally limited to a specified term of years, it was necessary to create a life tenancy which was viewed as a freehold interest. Thus, if a lease granting a tenant a life estate was not accompanied by livery of seisin, the intended conveyance would fail and a mere tenancy at will would result. The corollary to Lord Coke's comment is that the grant of a life estate would be enforceable if accompanied by livery of seisin and the other requisites for a conveyance. Because such a tenancy was terminable at the will of the grantee, there was in fact no general objection at common law to a tenancy at the will of the tenant. The express terms of a lease granting a life tenancy would fail, and a tenancy at will would result, only when livery of seisin, or any other requirement for a conveyance, had not been met (see, generally, Tiffany, op. cit., § 159; Effinger v. Lewis, supra; Tennant v. Tennant Mem. Home, 167 Cal. 570, 140 P. 242; Myers v. East Ohio Gas Co., 364 N.E.2d 1369 (Ohio)).

Because livery of seisin, like the ancient requirement for a seal, has been abandoned, commentators generally urge that there is no longer any reason why a lease granting the tenant alone the right to terminate at will, should be converted into a tenancy at will terminable by either party (Tiffany, op. cit., § 159; 1 American Law of Property, op. cit., § 3.30; Schoshinski, op. cit., § 2:16, pp. 61, 62). The Restatement adopts this view and provides the following illustration: "L leases a farm to T 'for as long as T desires to stay on the land'. The lease creates a determinable life estate in T, terminable at T's will or on his death." (Restatement, Property 2d, Landlord and Tenant, § 1.6, Comment g, Illustration 6.) This rule has increasingly gained acceptance in courts which have closely examined the problem (Myers v. East Ohio Gas Co., supra; Collins v. Shanahan, 523 P.2d 999 (Colo. App.); Thompson v. Baxter, supra; Gunnison v. Evans, supra; Effinger v. Lewis, supra).

This court has never specifically addressed the issue. In 1872 we applied the Coke dictum by analogy, and without attribution, in *Western Transp. Co. v. Lansing,* 49 N.Y. 499, supra. The case did not deal with a tenant's right to terminate a lease, but with the right of a tenant to renew a lease beyond its initial term "for such further time, after the expiration of said term, as said party of the second part (the lessee) shall choose or elect" (Western Transp. Co. v. Lansing, supra, at p. 502). The initial term was for 15 years. At its expiration the original lessor had died and the lessee had assigned the lease to a corporate tenant which sought specific performance of the right to renew. Although on that occasion the assignor only requested renewal for an additional 15 years, we held that the renewal clause itself was indefinite and unenforceable. In the course of the opinion we observed (at p. 508) that the renewal clause "is similar to a provision for such time as both parties please ... or a lease giving a right to occupy as long as lessee pleases ... A lease for so long as both parties shall please, or for so long as the lessee shall please, is said to be a lease at the will of both lessor and lessee".

Several years later, however, in *Hoff v. Royal Metal Furniture Co.*, 103 N.Y.S. 371 (N.Y. App. Div.), where the initial term of the lease was for one year renewable "from year to year" by the tenant "its successors or assigns", our earlier *Western Transp.* case was held by the Appellate Division to pose no obstacle to enforcing the original tenant's request for a one-year renewal made during the life of the lessor who had signed the lease. On appeal to this court we affirmed without opinion (82 N.E. 1128). These cases illustrate that seemingly perpetual leases are not favored by the law, and will not be enforced unless the lease clearly grants to the tenant or his successors the right to extend beyond the initial term by renewing indefinitely.

In the case now before us the lease does not provide for renewal, and its duration cannot be said to be perpetual or indefinite. It simply grants a personal right to the named lessee, Lou Gerrish, to terminate at a date of his choice, which is a fairly typical means of creating a life tenancy terminable at the will of the tenant (Restatement, Property 2d, op. cit., Illustration 6; Collins v. Shanahan, supra). Thus the lease will terminate, at the latest, upon the death of the named lessee. The fact that it may be terminated at some earlier point, if the named tenant decides to quit the premises, does not render it indeterminate. Leases providing for termination upon the occurrence of a specified event prior to the completion of an otherwise fixed term, are routinely enforced even when the event is within the control of the lessee (Schoshinski, op. cit., § 2:7, pp. 41–42).

In sum, the lease expressly and unambiguously grants to the tenant the right to terminate, and does not reserve to the landlord a similar right. To hold that such a lease creates a tenancy terminable at the will of either party would violate the terms of the agreement and the express intent of the contracting parties.

Accordingly, the order of the Appellate Division should be reversed and the petition dismissed.

NOTES AND QUESTIONS

1.   Did the court allow a lease for life or not? The court seems to think that not much rides on the classification of the interest of Lou Gerrish as freehold (a life estate) or nonfreehold (a lease), now that seisin is no longer an important legal concept. In the next Chapter we will examine the many protections that the law now affords tenants under a lease, especially a

residential lease. Would such protections apply to a life estate? Should they?

2. The more common approach to the lease-for-life problem is to construe the interest as fitting in the closest of the boxes provided by the estate system through the *numerus clausus*. What would be closest to a lease for life? Compare Thompson v. Baxter, 119 N.W. 797 (Minn. 1909) (life estate) with Kajo Church Square, Inc. v. Walker, 2003 WL 1848555 (Tex. Ct. App.) (tenancy at will); Nitschke v. Doggett, 489 S.W.2d 335 (Tex. Civ. App. 1972), vacated on other grounds, 498 S.W.2d 339 (Tex. 1973) (same).

3. Professional drafters are a cautious lot, and attempts to create new estates or fancies are rare. One recurring problem comes from attempts during various wars to create a lease for the duration of the war. As we will see, leases come in four varieties, and a lease for the duration of the war is not one of them. Most courts will deem such leases to be a tenancy at will (a type of lease). See, e.g., National Bellas Hess v. Kalis, 191 F.2d 739 (8th Cir. 1951); Stanmeyer v. Davis, 53 N.E.2d 22 (Ill. App. Ct. 1944); Lace v. Chandler, 1 All E.R. 305 (K.B. 1944). The minority of courts that have upheld a lease purporting to be a lease for the duration of a war as being a lease for a term of years have generally done so by changing the definition of a term of years rather than by holding that the parties may freely contract for new types of leases. See, e.g., Smith's Transfer & Storage Co. v. Hawkins, 50 A.2d 267, 268 (D.C. App. 1946). What would be the harm in a lease "for the duration of the war"? → "*war*" defined by major combat? Signed truces/Declarations?

4. As reflected in the court's reference to seisin, the doctrine of fixed estates, an aspect of the *numerus clausus*, is sometimes associated with the feudalism out of which the estate system grew. Often arguments that some feature is "repugnant" to the nature of an estate (often the fee simple) are regarded as circular, formalistic, and dustily feudal. This type of argument is in fact quite ahistorical. In civil law the *numerus clausus* in its modern form arose in the efforts during and after the French Revolution to abolish the complex feudal property arrangements. In this country, repugnancy to the fee was the doctrinal battle cry of those who wanted to abolish the vestiges of feudalism in nineteenth-century New York, where large landowners had conveyed fees but reserved the right to perpetual ground rents. On rent-related strife in nineteenth-century New York, see Charles W. McCurdy, The Anti–Rent Era in New York Law and Politics, 1839–1865 (2001).

PERSONAL PROPERTY

The menu of forms of property for real estate is lengthy, very probably too lengthy. What about personal property? Does the system of estates, developed in the context of land, also apply to personal property? There is surprisingly little authority on the question of how far the system of estates applies to personal property. Some standard reference works state that personal property is subject to the same elaborate structure of forms that applies to estates in land (including future interests). See Restatement (First) of Property § 9 cmt. a, at 23 (1936); 2 William Blackstone, Commentaries *398. But case law does not fully support this broad proposition. One can find decisions upholding future interests in personal property. For example, in *Gruen v. Gruen*, 496 N.E.2d 869 (N.Y. 1986), the court upheld the inter vivos gift of a remainder in a painting following a retained life estate in the donor. But such decisions are rare. See generally John Chipman Gray, Future Interests in Personal Property, 14 Harv. L. Rev. 397 (1901).

In one respect, there is no doubt that the estate system applies to personal property. As has been mentioned, most trusts today consist of assets that would be described as personal rather than real property— stocks, bonds, money markets funds, and other investment vehicles. The beneficial interests in these trusts are described in terms of the estates in land, such as life estates, remainders, and executory interests. So the estate system unquestionably applies to equitable interests in personal property held in trust. To the extent one wishes to create divided ownership in a particularly valuable piece of personal property like a painting or other collectible, it would almost certainly be advisable to use a trust to do this, rather than attempt to create divided legal title using the forms of property recognized for freehold interests.

Our knowledge of the early history of the law of personal property is limited by the tendency for litigation over items like farm equipment, produce, and animals to take place in local courts with less record keeping. Likewise title in such items typically was less elaborate than in the case of land. Most personal property does not last as long as land does, so there is typically less incentive to specify who will take personal property in future generations. Thus, an additional source of indifference to future interests in personal property probably stemmed from their perishable nature and the high ratio of complication to benefit in such interests.

The analog of the fee simple absolute is "absolute ownership" of personal property. As best we know, the original understanding seems to have been that personal property could not be divided into lesser interests. To get around this rule, people would use bailments, because the bailor was considered to retain the fee-like ownership during the bailment. Beginning in the fifteenth century, gifts by will of the use and occupancy of personal property for the life of the grantee were allowed. In the nineteenth century some English courts treated such bequests as giving an absolute interest to the intended life recipient and an executory interest to the intended future interest holder. Only later did some courts in England and the United States treat inter vivos gifts with similar accommodation. For a more detailed treatment, see Thomas F. Bergin & Paul G. Haskell, Preface to Estates in Land and Future Interests (2d ed. 1984); Lewis M. Simes & Allan F. Smith, The Law of Future Interests (2d ed. 1956).

Even today, courts apply some restrictions on the creation of future interests in personal property. All courts follow the rule that a future interest cannot be created in a "consumable" chattel. This rule can have real bite when testators are setting up trusts. If the will creates a trust out of all the "rest and residue" of the testator's property, this is likely to include "not only securities or other assets that are appropriate for a trust, but also such egregiously inappropriate items as collar buttons, pet cats, and frying pans...." Ashbel Green Gulliver, Cases and Materials on the Law of Future Interests 68 (1959). Given that one cannot create a future interest in a consumable, this makes for entertaining line-drawing exercises, with food and current crops on one side, diamonds on the other, and conflicting views on farming implements and animals. The solution is to make specific grants of the personal property.

Another limitation involves attempts to create easements or analogous restrictions on the use of chattels that would follow ("run with") the chattel into remote hands. English courts have said this is impermissible, and this seems to be the tendency in the United States. See, e.g., Dr. Miles Medical Co. v. Park, 220 U.S. 373, 404 (1911); Zechariah Chafee, Jr., Equitable Servitudes on Chattels, 41 Harv. L. Rev. 945, 977–980 (1928); Zechariah Chafee, Jr., The Music Goes Round and Round: Equitable Servitudes and Chattels, 69 Harv. L. Rev. 1250 (1956) (commenting on a decision departing from the general understanding). This has been particularly contentious in the area of software licensing. Compare Glen O. Robinson, Personal Property Servitudes, 71 U. Chi. L. Rev. 1449 (2004) (arguing for enforceability) with Julie E. Cohen, *Lochner* in Cyberspace: The New Economic Orthodoxy of "Rights Management," 97 Mich. L. Rev. 462 (1998) (criticizing tendency to provide legal support for private efforts to enclose information).

A general concern raised by the possibility of creating nonpossessory property rights in chattels is the problem of notice. Such property rights are in rem, but how are dutyholders supposed to know the content of the right? As we will see, in the case of land the notice function is largely served by registries of documents evidencing rights in land. For most types of personal property, such registries are not available. The more valuable, durable, and immobile an asset, the more likely there will be a registry. Planes, automobiles, and increasingly valuable art works have registries that one can consult to learn about the various interests of other parties in the assets. But other types of personal property have no registries, making it especially perilous to impose in rem duties on persons with respect to such property when they have no way of knowing which items are restricted and which ones are not.

D. MEDIATING CONFLICTS OVER TIME

1. WASTE

When two of more persons hold interests in a single piece of property there is always potential for conflict. This is certainly true when a grantor divides a fee simple into a life estate and one or more remainders. The holder of the life estate will tend to favor current consumption and investments that produce a quick return. In contrast, the holders of remainders are likely to prefer conservation of the asset and longer-term investments. This conflict may be mitigated somewhat when, as is often the case, the parties are closely related; for example, the life tenant is the grantor's spouse and the holders of the remainders are the couple's children. But intra-familial conflict also occurs, as the following case demonstrates. Here one Isaac V. Brokaw built several adjacent mansions. By will, he left to each of his four children—three sons and a daughter—a life interest in one of four separate dwelling houses. Each life estate was followed by a remainder to the issue of the life tenant. The will provided that if any of the life tenants should die without issue, the remaining heirs of Isaac would get that house. Thus, in the following case, the plaintiff (Isaac's son George) had a life estate, followed by a contingent remainder in George's daughter, subject in turn to a contingent remainder in the three other children of testator Isaac and their issue living at the time of George's death if George should survive his daughter. It is these holders of the contingent remainders who object to the razing of the allegedly obsolete mansion.

[handwritten: Isaac's son George] *[handwritten: P]*

Brokaw v. Fairchild

[handwritten: D — Isaac's remaining children (or the holders of their original interests)]

Supreme Court, New York County, New York, 1929.
135 Misc. 70, 237 N.Y.S. 6.

■ HAMMER, J. This is an action under section 473 of the Civil Practice Act and Rules of Civil Practice 210 to 212, in which plaintiff asks that it be declared and adjudged that the plaintiff, upon giving such security as the court may direct, has the right and is authorized to remove the present structures and improvements on or affecting the real property No. 1 East Seventy–Ninth street, or any part thereof, except the party wall, and to erect new structures and improvements thereon in accordance with certain proposed plans and specifications. * * *

In the year 1886 the late Isaac V. Brokaw bought for $199,000 a plot of ground in the borough of Manhattan, city of New York, opposite Central Park, having a frontage of 102 feet 2 inches on the easterly side of Fifth avenue and a depth of 150 feet on the northerly side of Seventy–Ninth street. Opposite there is an entrance to the park and Seventy–Ninth street is a wide crosstown street running through the park. Upon the corner portion, a plot of ground 51 feet 2 inches on Fifth avenue and a depth of 110 feet on Seventy–Ninth street, Mr. Brokaw erected in the year 1887, for his own occupancy, a residence known as No. 1 East Seventy–Ninth street, at a cost of over $300,000. That residence and corner plot is the subject-matter of this action. The residence, a three-story, mansard and basement granite front building, occupies the entire width of the lot. The mansard roof is of tile. On the first floor are two large drawing rooms on the Fifth avenue side, and there are also a large hallway running through from south to north, a reception room, dining room, and pantry. The dining room is paneled with carved wood. The hallway is in Italian marble and mosaic. There are murals and ceiling panels. There is a small elevator to the upper portion of the house. On the second floor are a large library, a large bedroom with bath on the Fifth avenue side, and there are also four other bedrooms and baths. The third floor has bedrooms and baths. The fourth floor has servants' quarters, bath, and storage rooms. The building has steam heat installed by the plaintiff, electric light and current, hardwood floors, and all usual conveniences. It is an exceedingly fine house, in construction and general condition as fine as anything in New York. It is contended by plaintiff that the decorations are heavy, not of a type now required by similar residences, and did not appeal to the people to whom it was endeavored to rent the building. It is "a masonry house of the old-fashioned type with very thick walls and heavy reveals in the windows, very high ceilings, monumental staircase and large rooms." "Such as has not been built for probably twenty-five years." "Utterly impractical to remodel for occupancy by more than one family." It "was offered to a great many people for rental at $25,000 with the statement that a lower figure might be considered and no offer of rental was obtained. Mr. Brokaw (the plaintiff) directed that the asking rental be $30,000 to start and finally reduced to $20,000. There is no demand for rental of private houses. There is a sporadic demand for purchase and sale on Fifth avenue for use as private homes. Once in a while somebody will want a private house." The taxes are $16,881, upkeep for repairs $750, and watchman $300. The taxes for 1913 were $8,950.77.

Since 1913, the year of the death of Isaac V. Brokaw and the commencement of the life estate of plaintiff, there has been a change of circumstances and conditions in connection with Fifth avenue properties. Apartments were erected with great rapidity and the building of private residences has practically ceased. Forty-four apartments and only 2 private residences have been erected on Fifth avenue from Fifty–Ninth street to 110th street. There are to-day but 8 of these 51 blocks devoted exclusively to private residences. Plaintiff's expert testified: "It is not possible to get an adequate return on the value of that land by any type of improvement other than an apartment house. The structure proposed in the plans of plaintiff is proper and suitable for the site and show 172 rooms which would rent for $1,000 per room. There is an excellent demand for such apartments. * * * There is no corner in the City of New York as fine for an apartment house as that particular corner."

The plaintiff testified also that his expenses in operating the residence which is unproductive would be at least $70,542 greater than if he resided in an apartment. He claims such difference constitutes a loss and contends that the erected apartment house would change this loss into an income or profit of $30,000. Plaintiff claims that under the facts and changed conditions shown the demolition of the building and erection of the proposed apartment is for the best interests of himself as life tenant, the inheritance, and the remaindermen. The defendants deny these contentions and assert certain affirmative defenses: (1) That the proposed demolition of the residence is waste, which against the objection of the adult defendant remaindermen plaintiff cannot be permitted to accomplish. * * *

Coming, therefore, to plaintiff's claimed right to demolish the present residence and to erect in its place the proposed apartment, I am of the opinion that such demolition would result in such an injury to the inheritance as under the authorities would constitute waste. The life estate given to plaintiff under the terms of the will and codicil is not merely in the corner plot of ground with improvements thereon, but, without question, in the residence of the testator. Four times in the devising clause the testator used the words "my residence." This emphasis makes misunderstanding impossible. The identical building which was erected and occupied by the testator in his lifetime and the plot of ground upon which it was built constitute that residence. By no stretch of the imagination could "my residence" be in existence at the end of the life tenancy were the present building demolished and any other structure, even the proposed 13–story apartment, erected on the site.

RULE

General Rules of the rights of a holder of a life estate

It has been generally recognized that any act of the life tenant which does permanent injury to the inheritance is waste. The law intends that the life tenant shall enjoy his estate in such a reasonable manner that the land shall pass to the reversioner or remainderman as nearly as practicable unimpaired in its nature, character, and improvements. The general rule in this country is that the life tenant may do whatever is required for the general use and enjoyment of his estate as he received it. The use of the estate he received is contemplated, and not the exercise of an act of dominion or ownership. What the life tenant may do in the future in the way of improving or adding value to the estate is not the test of what constitutes waste. The act of the tenant in changing the estate, and whether or not such act is lawful or unlawful, *i. e.*, whether the estate is so changed as to be an injury to the inheritance, is the sole question involved. The tenant has no right to exercise an act of ownership. In the instant case the inheritance was the residence of the testator—"my residence"—consisting of the present building on a plot of ground 51 feet 2 inches on Fifth avenue by 110 feet on Seventy–Ninth street. "My residence," such is what the plaintiff under the testator's will has the use of for life. He is entitled to use the building and plot reasonably for his own convenience or profit. To demolish that building and erect upon the land another building, even one such as the contemplated 13–story apartment house, would be the exercise of an act of ownership and dominion. It would change the inheritance or thing, the use of which was given to the plaintiff as tenant for life, so that the inheritance or thing could not be delivered to the remaindermen or reversioners at the end of the life estate. The receipt by them at the end of the life estate of a 13–story $900,000 apartment house might be more beneficial to them. Financially, the objecting adults may be unwise in not consenting to the proposed change. They may be selfish and unmindful that in the normal course of time and events they probably will not receive the fee. With motives and purposes the court is not concerned. In *Matter of Brokaw's Will*, 219 N.Y.S. 734 (N.Y. App. Div. 1927); affd., 157 N. E. 880 (N.Y. 1927), their right to object to a proposed building loan and mortgage for the erection of the proposed apartment was established by decision. They have the same right of objection in this action. To tear down and demolish the present building, which cost at least $300,000 to erect and would cost at least as much to replace, under the facts in this case, is clearly and beyond question an act of waste. In *Winship v. Pitts*, 3 Paige, Ch. 259, Chancellor Walworth, although holding that an injunction was properly refused to restrict the erection of a building upon premises where the lease did not specifically limit the use thereof, nevertheless (at page 262 of 3 Paige Ch.) said: "I have no hesitation in saying, that by the law of this state, as now understood, it is not waste for the tenant to erect a new edifice upon the demised premises; *provided it can be done without destroying or materially injuring the buildings or other improvements already existing thereon. I admit he has no right to pull down valuable buildings, or to make improvements or alterations which will materially and permanently change the nature of the property, so as to render it impossible for him to restore the same premises, substantially, at the expiration of the term.*" (Italics mine.)

In *Agate v. Lowenbein*, 57 N.Y. 604, 607 (1874), the court said: "Had there been no license given to the defendants to do the acts of which the plaintiff complains, the injuries done to the property would have been, apparently, acts of waste, for which the plaintiff could, by the rules of the common law, have brought an action on the case in the nature of waste. *The right which the tenant has is to make use of the property.* The power of making an alteration does not arise out of a mere right of user; it is, therefore, incompatible with his interest for a tenant to make any alteration, unless he is justified by the express permission of his landlord. Holroyd, J., in Farrant v. Thompson (5 B. & Ald., 826) defines the extent of a lessee's rights. By a lease, *the use, not dominion of the property demised, is conferred.* If a tenant exercises an act of ownership, he is no longer protected by his tenancy."

And at page 614 of 57 N.Y., the court said: "It is, in general, no justification for an act of waste that a party will, at some future time, put the premises in the same condition as they were when the lease was made. The question is, whether the tenant, at the time the wrongful act was done, caused an injury which then affected the plaintiff as to his reversion. * * * The tenant has no right to exercise an act of ownership."

In *Kidd v. Dennison*, 6 Barb. 9, 13, the court said: "So if the tenant materially changes the nature and character of the buildings, it is waste, although the value of the property should be enhanced by the alteration. * * * The tenant has no authority to assume the right of judging what may be an improvement to the inheritance. He must confine himself to the conditions of his lease." * * *

The cases given by plaintiff are either cases where a prohibitory injunction against future waste has been sought and the parties have been refused the injunction and relegated to an action for damages for waste, or where, in condemnation proceedings or actions in equity, it appears that the equities between the parties are such that the technical waste committed has been ameliorated. The three cases upon which the plaintiff principally relies are *Melms v. Pabst Brewing Co.*, 79 N. W. 738 (Wis. 1899), and

[Handwritten margin note:] The focus is on retaining the nature & characteristic of the original property so as to be able to pass on the property to the ultimate holder in fee simple substantially in the same condition as original holder had it.

New York, O. & W. R. Co. v. Livingston, 144 N. E. 589 (N.Y. 1924), and *Doherty v. Allman*, 3 L. R. App. Cas. 709, 717, 721. These are readily distinguishable from the case at bar. In *Melms v. Pabst Brewing Co., supra*, there was a large expensive brick dwelling house build by one Melms in the year 1864. He also owned the adjoining real estate and a brewery upon part of the premises. He died in 1869. The brewery and dwelling were sold and conveyed to Pabst Brewing Company. The Pabst Company used the brewery part of the premises. About the year 1890 the neighborhood about the dwelling house had so changed in character that it was situated on an isolated lot standing from 20 to 30 feet above the level of the street, the balance of the property having been graded down to fit it for business purposes. It was surrounded by business property, factories, and railroad tracks with no other dwellings in the neighborhood. Pabst Brewing Company, in good faith regarding itself as the owner, tore down the building and graded down the ground for business purposes. Thereafter it was held, in the action of *Melms v. Pabst Brewing Co.*, 66 N. W. 244, that the brewing company had only acquired a life estate in the homestead, although in another action between the same parties (66 N. W. 518 (Wis. 1896)) it was held that as to the other property the brewing company had acquired full title in fee. The action for waste in which the [1899 decision] was delivered was brought and decided after the decisions in the other actions. We find it there said at 79 N. W. 738: "The action was tried before the court without a jury, and the court found, in addition to the facts above stated, that the removal of the building and the grading down of the earth was done by the defendant in 1891 and 1892, believing itself to be the owner in fee simple of the property, and that by the said acts the estate of the plaintiffs in the property was substantially increased, and that the plaintiffs have been in no way injured thereby."

Again, it was stated at 79 N. W. 740: "There are no contract relations in the present case. The defendants are the grantees of a life estate, and their rights may continue for a number of years. The evidence shows that the property became valueless for the purpose of residence property as the result of the growth and development of a great city. Business and manufacturing interests advanced and surrounded the once elegant mansion, until it stood isolated and alone, standing upon just enough ground to support it, and surrounded by factories and railroad tracks, <u>absolutely undesirable as a residence, and incapable of any use as business property.</u> Here was a complete change of conditions, not produced by the tenant, but resulting from causes which none could control. Can it be reasonably or logically said that this entire change of condition is to be completely ignored, and the ironclad rule applied that the tenant can make no change in the uses of the property because he will destroy its identity? Must the tenant stand by, and preserve the useless dwelling house, so that he may at some future time turn it over to the reversioner, equally useless?"

The facts in the above case are clearly not analogous to the facts here. Especially is this recognized from the fact that the plaintiff's dwelling house is far from being "isolated and alone, standing upon just enough ground to support it, surrounded by factories and railroad tracks, absolutely undesirable as a residence.'' It is located on the northeast corner of Fifth avenue and Seventy–Ninth street. Across the avenue to the west is Central Park. To the south across Seventy–Ninth street the block Seventy–Eighth to Seventy–Ninth streets is restricted to private dwellings. The residence itself is surrounded by the three other palatial Brokaw dwellings, forming a magnificent residential layout of the four plots. It may, of course, be that the situation will change in the future. The decision here is concerned only with the present. * * *

The facts, it is seen, in none of the cases cited are analogous to the case at bar. The law and procedure therein also contain no analogy. *Melms v. Pabst Brewing Co.* was a law action for waste claimed to have been committed prior to the action. Upon the existing facts proved at the trial it was found as fact and in equity that the claimed waste was ameliorated and the plaintiff not damaged. * * *

From the foregoing I am of the opinion, and it will accordingly be adjudged and declared, that upon the present facts, circumstances, and conditions as they exist and are shown in this case, regardless of the proposed security and the expressed purpose of erecting the proposed 13–story apartment, or any other structure, the plaintiff has no right and is not authorized to remove the present structures on or affecting the real estate in question. * * *

Figure 5–7
The Brokaw Mansion, 1 East 79th Street, New York City

The Irving Brokaw Mansion Fifth Avenue & 79th Street. Glass Plate Negative. Undated. Museum of the City of New York. The Underhill Collection. B.1642.

Figure 5–8
1 East 79th Street, New York City, in 2006

NOTES AND QUESTIONS

1. George Brokaw's repeated efforts to persuade the courts to permit him to tear the house down were all rebuffed. He lived in the house until his death in 1935, but neither he nor his wife liked it. The Brokaws divorced in 1929, and Mrs. Brokaw later remarried and went on to greater fame as Clare Boothe Luce. She acquired a half-interest in the house after George's death, which she sold to her second husband, Henry Luce, the publisher of *Time* magazine. In 1964, although the house had been designated a landmark by the city, new owners managed to raze the building along with two adjoining mansions, over the objections of the New York City Landmarks Preservation Commission. A large apartment building now

stands on the site. Thomas W. Ennis, Landmark Mansion on 79th St. To Be Razed, N.Y. Times (Sept. 17, 1964), at 1.

2.   Who should have standing to bring an action for waste? The original action for waste, following the Statute of Gloucester, 6 Edw. I, ch. 5 (1278), provided for forfeiture of the estate of one guilty of waste, plus the payment of treble damages to those holding affected nonpossessory interests. Perhaps because of the severity of the remedy, courts held that only those holding indefeasibly vested remainders or reversions had standing to bring an action for waste. Later, when the Chancery Court began to issue injunctions against the commission of waste by a tenant-in-possession, the standing rules were relaxed, and holders of contingent remainders, defeasible reversions, or executory interests were allowed to sue, provided they sued on behalf of all nonpossessory interest holders. See William B. Stoebuck & Dale A. Whitman, The Law of Property 159–64 (3d ed. 2000). This appears to be the understanding that permits the contingent remaindermen in *Brokaw* to bring an action to enjoin George Brokaw from committing waste. But suppose someone with only a possibility of reverter or an executory interest with a highly remote chance of ever becoming vested seeks to bring an action for waste? Where should the courts draw the line in granting standing to regulate the behavior of the tenant-in-possession?

3.   The action for waste is very old, dating from the twelfth century, and originally had its own writ—the writ of waste. It remains today perhaps the most important cause of action that can be brought by persons who hold nonpossessory interests in property against other owners currently in possession. Although the action for waste is probably invoked most often by holders of remainder interests against life tenants, it potentially applies in any situation of concurrent or sequential ownership. The action for waste can also be brought by a landlord against a tenant, although most landlords probably prefer to particularize the tenant's duty to repair or otherwise maintain property through appropriate lease provisions.

4.   Courts over time have developed different categories of waste. The basic distinction is between affirmative waste and permissive waste. *Affirmative waste* is a type of misfeasance. It occurs when the life tenant takes some affirmative action on the property that is unreasonable and causes "excess" damage to the reversionary or remainder interest. The actions that constitute affirmative waste are often defined in terms of what is regarded as "normal" use of the property. Thus, if the property contains minerals or trees, the life tenant is permitted to engage in normal extraction of minerals and normal tree-cutting, but anything beyond normal would be affirmative waste. One rule of thumb, the "open mines" doctrine, provided that any extraction of minerals was waste unless mining was already occurring on the land at the beginning of the life estate. *Permissive waste* is a type of nonfeasance. It occurs when the life tenant fails to take some action with regard to the property and the failure to act is unreasonable and causes excess damage to the reversionary or remainder interest. Again, rough conceptions of normal behavior serve to define the baseline against which liability is be determined. Prominent examples of permissive

waste include failing to repair a roof resulting in water damage, not paying taxes as they come due, or allowing an adverse possessor to remain on the land.

5. A more controversial type of waste—and the type at issue in *Brokaw*—is sometimes called *ameliorative waste*. This is a type of affirmative act by the life tenant that significantly changes the property, but results in an increase, rather than a diminution, in its market value. The traditional view, which is reflected in *Brokaw*, is that ameliorative waste is just another type of affirmative waste and is not permitted. Under this understanding, the holders of remainder interests are entitled to take possession of the property at the end of the life tenancy in substantially the same form it had when the life tenant first took possession. Significant change or transformation is ruled out. A minority view adopted in some American jurisdictions—of which *Melms v. Pabst Brewing Co.*, distinguished in *Brokaw*, is arguably an example—permits ameliorative waste, at least when it can be justified by changed circumstances. Here as elsewhere, the law of waste has become more flexible in the United States, and generally speaking, the greater one's interest, the more freedom one gets as owner. See generally, Jedediah Purdy, The American Transformation of Waste Doctrine: A Pluralist Interpretation, 91 Cornell L. Rev. 653 (2006).

6. Are the various rules about waste consistent with economic efficiency? Richard Posner has suggested that courts should apply a simple rule of wealth maximization: If the life tenant's action would maximize the present value of the property (including both the life tenant's interest and the reversion or remainder interests) then it is permissible; conversely, if the life tenant's action would not maximize the present value of the property, it should be condemned as waste. See Richard A. Posner, Economic Analysis of Law § 3.11, at 72–73 (6th ed. 2003). But the legal doctrine does not seem to require maximization of present value by the life tenant. Instead, it enforces "normal" behavior by the life tenant and the preservation of the status quo. Does this suggest the law is more concerned with protecting the autonomy of property owners than with promoting efficiency? Is it relevant here that the law of waste is a default rule, that is, a rule that applies only in the absence of a contrary agreement by the affected parties? Thus, for example, if the life tenant and the holders of remainders in *Brokaw* had all agreed, the mansion could be torn down. (What if Isaac Brokaw's will had stated that the house could be razed in the discretion of the life tenant?) Might concepts like "normal" behavior or use and preserving the status quo provide a better baseline for negotiating contractual modifications than a norm requiring present-value maximization? On the other hand, what if bargaining breaks down, as in *Brokaw*? Don't the ordinary rules of waste promote inefficient outcomes in these circumstances?

7. Should the law continue to prohibit ameliorative waste? How much should Isaac Brokaw's wishes govern future generations? Why should the holders of the remainders be able to trump the wishes of the life tenant as long as the life tenant is enhancing the value of the remainder? If the

remainder holders claim that they attach a high subjective value on preserving the mansion, how do we know whether to believe them? Were the holders of the remainders in *Brokaw* motivated by subjective attachments to the mansion, or by other concerns? Do changed circumstances call for judicial intervention? If so, why didn't the transformation of Fifth Avenue from a boulevard of single family residences to high-rise apartment buildings qualify as a changed circumstance? Compare the materials on cy pres in Chapter VI.

VALUATION OF INTERESTS

Whether legal or equitable, courts and others are sometimes called upon to value the various interests that have been carved out of a fee simple. For example, suppose land is divided between a life estate and a remainder, and both tenants decide to sell the property, or the state decides to take the property through eminent domain. The acquiring party will pay for the value of what it obtains—a fee simple—but then we have to decide how to divide the proceeds between the life tenant and the holder of the remainder. In such cases, resort is had to actuarial tables and discount rates.

An example will illustrate how this is done. Suppose Blackacre is worth $100,000 as a fee simple and (to make things less complicated) its value is not expected to change in the foreseeable future. A owns a life estate, and B owns the remainder. A is 98 years old and so has a life expectancy of three years (at least according to the actuarial tables used by the IRS, which does not distinguish male and female life expectancies). Thus, we can assume that A would get the use of the $100,000 asset for the next three years, and B would get the use of the asset thereafter. One way to determine the value of the respective interests is to ask what the remainder to B is worth today, given that B expects to receive Blackacre three years from now. Once we have the value of the remainder, when can then subtract this from $100,000, in order to determine the value of the life estate.

How do we determine the value of the remainder, assumed to be the equivalent of $100,000 received three years from today? If one had $100,000 today one could invest it in a safe investment and would wind up with more than $100,000 three years from now. What we want to find out is the amount today that is equivalent to what one would have to set aside in order to have $100,000 three years from now. To find this out, one would normally use spreadsheet software, but it is important to understand what is going on. First we need a discount rate, an amalgam of an interest rate and the expected rate of inflation.[3] Assume this is 7 percent. To have $1 one year from now, the amount P one has to set aside now is roughly 93 cents. $P \times (1 + .07) = \$1.00$ or $P = \$1.00 / (1.07) = \$.93$. That is, to find the present discounted value of a dollar amount one year from now, divide the future amount ($1.00) by the sum of one and the discount rate (here

---

3. The discount rate (r) is based on the real rate of interest and the expected rate of inflation:

$(1 + r) = (1 + m)(1 + i)$, where m is the market interest rate and i is the expected inflation rate.

1.07). One dollar two years from now is like one dollar one year from now, deferred an additional year. It is worth 87 cents now because $P \times (1 + .07) \times (1 + .07) = \$1.00$, or $P = \$1.00 / ((1.07) \times (1.07)) = \$.87$. A dollar deferred three years is worth $\$.82 = \$1.00 / (1.07)^3$, or more accurately 81.63 cents. Thus, the remainder that will be worth $100,000 three years from now is worth approximately $81,630 today ($100,000 / (1.07)^3$). This can be generalized.[4]

meaning A gets $18,370, and B gets $81,630 because that is the amount he would need to put into an interest accruing account for 3 years in order to get $100,000

What then is the life estate worth? The property itself is worth $100,000 now and the remainder is worth $81,630 now, leaving $18,370 ($100,000 − $81,630) for the life estate.

Another way to reach the same result is to determine what the life estate should be worth in terms of a stream of payments that $100,000 can earn over the three year period. Taking 7 percent to be the rate of return, the $100,000 investment will yield $7,000 each year. The $7,000 earned at the end of the first year is worth $6,542 today (= $7,000 / (1.07)$). (This can be thought of as 7,000 times the $.93 present value of each dollar a year from now). Similarly, year two's payment is $6,114 (= $7,000 / (1.07)^2$), and year three's payment is $5,714 (= $7,000 / (1.07)^3$). The three payments add to $18,370. If we calculate the value of the life estate this way, we can then subtract this from $100,000 to determine the value of the remainder ($81,630 as before).

The discount factor is crucial here. One interesting feature of the 7% discount rate is that an amount doubles roughly every 10 years at a 7% rate. For comparison, if the discount rate is 4%, the (expected three-year) life estate would be worth $11,100 and the remainder $88,900. But if the discount rate is 10%, then the life estate and remainder are worth $24,869 and $75,131, respectively, in present discounted value terms. The higher the discount rate, the less a future dollar is worth now (and the more valuable the life estate is because it is weighted more towards the present). And at any given discount rate, the further off in the future a dollar is, the less it is worth now. What (if any) discount rate should be applied to benefits obtained in the future from environmental regulation (especially future lives saved) has been the focal point of much controversy in environmental law. See, e.g., John J. Donohue III, Why We Should Discount the Views of Those Who Discount Discounting, 108 Yale L.J. 1901 (1999); Lisa Heinzerling, Regulatory Costs of Mythic Proportions, 107 Yale L.J. 1981 (1998); Richard L. Revesz, Environmental Regulation, Cost–Benefit Analysis, and the Discounting of Human Lives, 99 Colum. L. Rev. 941 (1999).

The present values of a life estate and the corresponding remainder also depend on the life expectancy of the life tenant. In our example this was assumed to be three years. Life estates, remainders, and other interests have to be valued for income tax purposes, and the methods there can

---

4. More generally, an amount C in the future equals the present value P times the discount factor r, applied for the requisite number n of time periods (here years), i.e., $C = P (1 + r)^n$. We can do this in reverse as well. From a future nominal amount we can calculate the present discounted value using the formula $P = C / (1 + r)^n$.

be taken as illustrative. See I.R.C. § 7520. Using a 7% interest rate, if the life tenant of the $100,000 property is 10 years old, the remainder would have present discounted value of $2,595. If the life tenant is 35, then the remainder is worth $9,155 now. And if the life tenant is 55, 70, or 90, the remainder would be valued at $24,604, $44,456, and $75,748, respectively. Of course, life expectancies are based only on averages over large groups of people. Psychologists have documented that most non-depressed people tend to be optimistic about their own abilities and prospects. (Depressed people are simply realistic in these matters.) Might this affect the negotiation between the holders of the life estate and the remainder?

2.   RESTRAINTS ON ALIENATION

We saw in Chapter IV that one of the normal incidents of owner sovereignty is transferability, and that courts consequently take a dim view of attempts to restrain the power of an owner to alienate. Thus, any attempt directly to restrain alienation will be held void as contrary to public policy. For example, if O grants Blackacre, which is otherwise generally alienable, "to A in fee simple, on the understanding that A has no power to alienate," the restraint on alienation will be struck down and the conveyance will be interpreted as if it said "to A in fee simple." It did not take courts long similarly to conclude that efforts to use defeasible fees or executory limitations to effectuate restraints on alienation are similarly void. For example, if O grants Blackacre "to A in fee simple so long as A does not alienate, then to O," this too will be struck down as an attempt to restrain alienation. But what about other conditions which have the effect of severely reducing the possibilities of alienation? Should courts also invalidate attempts to use the building blocks of the estate system in ways that, for practical purposes, impair free transferability? Or would this give courts too much power to interfere with an owner's ability to impose conditions on the future use of property?

P- Appellant

Mountain Brow Lodge No. 82, Independent Order of Odd Fellows v. Toscano— *D - Respondant*

Court of Appeal, Fifth District, California, 1967.
257 Cal.App.2d 22, 64 Cal.Rptr. 816.

■ GARGANO, ASSOCIATE JUSTICE. This action was instituted by appellant, a non-profit corporation, to quiet its title to a parcel of real property which it acquired on April 6, 1950, by gift deed from James V. Toscano and Maria Toscano, both deceased. Respondents are the trustees and administrators of the estates of the deceased grantors and appellant sought to quiet its title as to their interest in the land arising from certain conditions contained in the gift deed.

The matter was submitted to the court on stipulated facts and the court rendered judgment in favor of respondents. * * *

The controversy between the parties centers on the language contained in the habendum clause of the deed of conveyance which reads as follows: "Said property is restricted for the use and benefit of the second party, only; and in the event the same fails to be used by the second party or in the event of sale or transfer by the second party of all or any part of said lot, the same is to revert to the first parties herein, their successors, heirs or assigns." Respondents maintain that the language creates a fee simple subject to a condition subsequent and is valid and enforceable. On the other hand, appellant contends that the restrictive language amounts to an absolute restraint on its power of alienation and is void. It apparently asserts that, since the purpose for which the land must be used is not precisely defined, it may be used by appellant for any purpose and hence the restriction is not on the land use but on who uses it. Thus, appellant concludes that it is clear that the reversionary clause was intended by grantors to take effect only if appellant sells or transfers the land.

Admittedly, the condition of the habendum clause which prohibits appellant from selling or transferring the land under penalty of forfeiture is an absolute restraint against alienation and is void. The common law rule prohibiting restraint against alienation is embodied in Civil Code section 711 which provides: "Conditions restraining alienation, when repugnant to the interest created, are void." However, this condition and the condition relating to the use of the land are in the disjunctive and are clearly severable. In other words, under the plain language of the deed the grantors, their successors or assigns may exercise their power of termination "if the land is not used by the second party" or "in the event of sale or transfer by second party." Thus, the invalid restraint against alienation does not necessarily affect or nullify the condition on land use (Los Angeles Investment Company v. Gary, 186 P. 596 (Cal. 1919)).

RULE [in left margin]

The remaining question, therefore, is whether the use condition created a defeasible fee as respondents maintain or whether it is also a restraint against alienation and nothing more as appellant alleges. Significantly, appellant is a non-profit corporation organized for lodge, fraternal and similar purposes. Moreover, decedent, James V. Toscano, was an active member of the lodge at the time of his death. In addition, the term "use" as applied to real property can be construed to mean a "right which a person has to use or enjoy the property of another according to his necessities" (Mulford v. LeFranc, 26 Cal. 88, 102 (1864)). Under these circumstances it is reasonably clear that when the grantors stated that the land was conveyed in consideration of "love and affection" and added that it "is restricted for the *use* and benefit of the second party" they simply meant to say that the land was conveyed upon condition that it would be used for lodge, fraternal and other purposes for which the nonprofit corporation was formed. Thus, we conclude that the portion of the habendum clause relating to the land use, when construed as a whole and in light of the surrounding circumstances, created a fee subject to a condition subsequent with title to revert to the grantors, their successors or assigns if the land ceases to be used for lodge, fraternal and similar purposes for which the appellant is formed.[2] No formal language is necessary to create a fee simple subject to a condition subsequent as long as the intent of the grantor is clear. It is the rule that the object in construing a deed is to ascertain the intention of the grantor from words which have been employed and from surrounding circumstances.

RULE

It is of course arguable, as appellant suggests, that the condition in appellant's deed is not a restriction on land use but on who uses it. Be this as it may, the distinction between a covenant which restrains the alienation of a fee simple absolute and a condition which restricts land use and creates a defeasible estate was long recognized at common law and is recognized in this state. Thus, conditions restricting land use have been upheld by the California courts on numerous occasions even though they hamper, and often completely impede, alienation. A few examples follow: Mitchell v. Cheney Slough Irrigation Co., 134 P.2d 34 (Cal. Ct. App. 1943) (irrigation ditch); Aller v. Berkeley Hall School Foundation, 103 P.2d 1052 (Cal. Ct. App. 1940) (exclusively private dwellings); Rosecrans v. Pacific Electric Railway Co., 134 P.2d 245 (Cal. 1943) (to maintain a train schedule); Schultz v. Beers, 245 P.2d 334 (Cal. Ct. App. 1952) (road purposes); Firth v. Marovich, 116 P. 729 (Cal. 1911) (residence only).

Moreover, if appellant's suggestion is carried to its logical conclusion it would mean that real property could not be conveyed to a city to be used only for its own city purposes, or to a school district to be used only for its own school purposes, or to a church to be used only for its own church purposes. Such restrictions would also be restrictions upon who uses the land. And yet we do not understand this to be the rule of this state. For example, in *Los Angeles Investment Company v. Gary*, supra, land had been conveyed upon condition that it was not to be sold, leased, rented or occupied by persons other than those of Caucasian race. The court held that the condition against alienation of the land was void, but upheld the condition restricting the land use. Although a use restriction compelling racial discrimination is no longer consonant with constitutional principles under more recent decisions, the sharp distinction that the court drew between a restriction on land use and a restriction on alienation is still valid. For further example, in the leading and often cited case of *Johnston v. City of Los Angeles*, 168 P. 1047 (Cal. 1917), the land was conveyed to the City of Los Angeles on the express condition that the city would use it for the erection and maintenance of a dam, the land to revert if the city ceased to use it for such purposes. The Supreme Court held that the condition created a defeasible estate, apparently even though it was by necessity a restriction on who could use the land.

Our independent research indicates that the rule is the same in other jurisdictions. In *Regular Predestinarian Baptist Church of Pleasant Grove v. Parker*, 27 N.E.2d 522 (Ill. 1940), a condition " 'To have and to hold * * * as long as the same is used by the Regular Predestinarian Baptist

---

2. It is arguable that the gift deed created a fee simple determinable. However, in doubtful cases the preferred construction is in favor of an estate subject to a condition subsequent.

Church as a place of meeting * * * ' "was deemed to have created a defeasible estate by the Supreme Court of Illinois. * * *

For the reasons herein stated, the first paragraph of the judgment below is amended and revised to read:

1.　That at the time of the commencement of this action title to the parcel of real property situated in the City of Los Banos, County of Merced, State of California, being described as:

Lot 20 Block 72 according to the Map of the Town of Los Banos

was vested in the MOUNTAIN BROW LODGE NO. 82, INDEPENDENT ORDER OF ODD FELLOWS, subject to the condition that said property is restricted for the use and benefit of the second party only; and in the event the same fails to be used by the second party the same is to revert to the first parties herein, their successors, heirs or assigns.

As so modified the judgment is affirmed. Respondents to recover their costs on appeal.

STONE, ASSOCIATE JUSTICE. I dissent. I believe the entire habendum clause which purports to restrict the fee simple conveyed is invalid as a restraint upon alienation within the ambit of Civil Code section 711. It reads: "Said property is restricted for the use and benefit of the second party, only; and in the event the same fails to be used by the second party or in the event of sale or transfer by the second party of all or any part of said lot the same is to revert to the first parties herein, their successors, heirs or assigns."

If the words "sale or transfer," which the majority find to be a restraint upon alienation, are expunged, still the property cannot be sold or transferred by the grantee because the property may be used by only the I.O.O.F. Lodge No. 82, upon pain of reverter. This use restriction prevents the grantee from conveying the property just as effectively as the condition against "sale or transfer * * * of all or any part of said lot."

Certainly, if we are to have realism in the law, the effect of language must be judged according to what it does. When two different terms generate the same ultimate legal result, they should be treated alike in relation to that result.

Section 711 of the Civil Code expresses an ancient policy of English common law.* The wisdom of this proscription as applied to situations of

---

* "The conceptual argument is that the law defines the exact nature of every estate in land, that each has certain incidents which are provided by law, and that one of the principal incidents of a fee is alienability. Manning, The Development of Restraints on Alienation Since Gray, 48 Harv.L.Rev. 373 (1935).

"The first of the two reasons most often given for holding restraints void is that a restraint is repugnant to the nature of the fee. Murray v. Green, 28 P. 118 (Cal. 1883); Eastman Marble Co. v. Vermont Marble Co., 128 N.E. 177 (Mass. 1920); Andrews v. Hall, 58 N.W.2d 201 (Neb. 1963); 5 Tiffany, Real Property § 1343 (3d ed. 1939); Manning, supra, at 401. However, Lord Coke believed that restraints were void, not only because they were repugnant to the fee, but because "it is absurd and repugnant to reason" that a tenant in fee simple should be restrained "of all his power to alien." Co.Litt. 223a.

See page 611 for the continuation of this footnote.

this kind is manifest when we note that a number of fraternal, political and similar organizations of a century ago have disappeared, and others have ceased to junction in individual communities. Should an organization holding property under a deed similar to the one before us be disbanded one hundred years or so after the conveyance is made, the result may well be a title fragmented into the interests of heirs of the grantors numbering in the hundreds and scattered to the four corners of the earth. * * *

In any event, it seems to me that quite aside from section 782, the entire habendum clause is repugnant to the grant in fee simple that precedes it. I would hold the property free from restrictions, and reverse the judgment.

NOTES AND QUESTIONS

1.   Generally in cases in which an instrument's language is ambiguous as to whether it creates a fee simple determinable or a fee simple subject to condition subsequent courts tend to favor the latter because it will avoid automatic forfeiture. Does this construction also do more to promote free alienation of property? Recall that both types of interests can be extinguished if the condition is violated and the grantor (or his successor) fails to reclaim the property within the time established by the statute of limitations. If the interest is a possibility of reverter, and the grantor fails to sue to recover possession in an action in trespass or ejectment before the statute of limitations runs, then the owner of the fee simple determinable gets a fee simple absolute by adverse possession. If the interest is a right of entry, and the grantor fails to assert his right to re-enter within a reasonable period of time, then the owner of the fee simple subject to condition subsequent will be able to obtain an equitable judgment that re-entry is barred by the doctrine of laches, in effect creating a fee simple absolute. In determining what is a reasonable period of time for purposes of laches, courts generally look to the statute of limitations for adverse possession. So there is not a lot of room for distinguishing between the two types of defeasible fees on this ground. Is there some other ground for preferring the fee simple subject to condition subsequent construction on grounds of free alienation?

"The second and more practically oriented reason for holding restraints void is that a restraint, by taking land out of the flow of commerce, is detrimental to the economy. Gray, Restraints on Alienation § 21 (2d ed. 1895); 6 Powell, Real Property 1 (1958); 5 Tiffany, op. cit. supra, § 1343. Other reasons have been accepted on occasion by courts: to encourage improvement of property; hampering effect[ive] use of property if the buyer could put it to better use than the seller; removal from trade of increasing amounts of capital; not allowing an individual to appear more prosperous than he is, i.e., a borrower may appear to own property outright, thus able to sell it in payment of a debt, where in reality the property is restrained; balance of dead hand control, i.e., recognizing the right of the individual to control property after death by the proposition that life is for the living and should be controlled by the living and not by the extended hand of the dead. Bernhard, The Minority Doctrine Concerning Direct Restraints on Alienation, 57 Mich. L.Rev. 1173, 1177 (1959)." (12 U.C.L.A. Law Rev. No. 3, fn. p. 956.)

2. How far do you suppose the majority would be willing to extend its formal rule that restrictions on use do not violate the prohibition against restraints on alienation? Suppose only one member of the Odd Fellows Lodge, Local No. 82 is still alive, and he is on a respirator in a nursing home. Or, suppose all members of the Lodge have died, and the building stands vacant. Is the restriction still enforceable? How far do you suppose the dissent would be willing to extend its realistic test that would invalidate restrictions on use that have the practical effect of impairing alienation? Suppose it could be shown that any defeasible fee that restricts use to some specific charitable or nonprofit activity will severely impair the market value of the property. Would this be enough to justify a judgment invalidating the condition?

3. What exactly does it mean for property to be restricted to "the use and benefit" of some entity? Suppose there are only three elderly Odd Fellows still alive; they vote unanimously at a formal meeting of the Lodge to sell the building to a real estate developer and to use the proceeds for one final fling in Las Vegas. Is this for the "use and benefit" of the Lodge? Does your answer change if the proceeds are to be used to purchase adjacent rooms in a nursing home, where the three can continue to meet? If these sorts of transactions are permissible, does this significantly alleviate concerns about use restrictions impairing marketability?

4. If, following the majority, restrictions on use do not trigger the policy against restraints on alienation, should other doctrines be adjusted so as to provide a basis for setting aside conditions in defeasible fees that have outlived their usefulness? In Footnote 3 of the opinion (omitted above), the court notes:

> The distinction between defeasible estates and future interests which also curtail alienation was recognized at common law. In fact, the creation of future interests, through trusts and similar devises, whose vesting could be indefinitely postponed, resulted in the development of the rule against perpetuities. Significantly, the rule against perpetuities has no application to defeasible estates because reversions, possibilities of reverter and powers of termination are inherently vested in nature.

64 Cal.Rptr. at 818 n.3. Why should forfeiture rights retained by the grantor be exempt from rules designed to preserve free alienation, when other types of future interests are not?

3. THE RULE AGAINST PERPETUITIES

The Rule against Perpetuities (RAP) is a crystallization of older doctrines invalidating interests that gave too much remote control to the "dead hand." The RAP basically allows people to control the use of property for one generation into the future plus the next generation up to the traditional age of majority; it is sometimes thought that these are the only people that a testator can really have any knowledge of or benevolence towards. (Others might disagree.) Another policy sometimes invoked to justify the RAP is the breaking up of large, potentially overly aristocratic estates. We have seen that in earlier times elite families often regarded keeping property, especially landed property, within the family to be an overriding consideration.

These policies inform the RAP, but the RAP has evolved into a very formalistic rule, in the sense that it can be applied without direct reference to these policies, or much other contextual information, for that matter. The rule received its now-canonical form from Professor John Chipman Gray:

> No interest is good unless it must vest, if at all, not later than twenty-one years after some life in being at the creation of the interest.

"RULE AGAINST PERPETUITIES" (exact wording)

John Chipman Gray, Rule Against Perpetuities § 201 (Roland Gray ed., 4th ed. 1942). Gray sought in this formulation the brightest of bright-line rules that would receive "remorseless" application. Id. § 629. What the rule does is define a time period (lives in being plus 21 years) and ask whether within this time period we will know whether or not certain types of questions will be resolved. These questions have to do with uncertainty about vesting in interest, not necessarily vesting in possession. That is, we will be asking, whether within the "perpetuities period" contingencies about the identity of the takers and other named events will be removed. Moreover, the RAP is a rule against interests *vesting* (in interest) too remotely, and more precisely against interests *possibly* vesting too remotely, *not* a rule against interests lasting too long. Consider this example:

To Marge for life, then to Bart and his heirs.

The remainder here might last forever (and would if Bart turned out to be immortal), but this would be fine.

Vesting means the elimination of the "suspense" element. This can be of one or more of three types:

3 Types of the "Suspense" Element

(i) For a contingent remainder removing suspense means the ascertainment of the identity of the taker and the satisfaction of all conditions precedent:

1) Contingent Remainder
- *a) Identity of Taker*
- *b) Satisfaction of Conditions Precedent*

> Homer grants Blackacre "to Marge for life and to my first child who shall pass the bar, upon his or her marriage."

Here there is uncertainty as to who Homer's first child to pass the bar will be and whether and when he or she will marry.

2) Executory Interest
- *Occurrence that cuts short prior interest (whether it will happen)*

(ii) For an executory interest eliminating the relevant uncertainty means the taking of possession (the cutting short of the prior interest actually happens);[5]

3) Remainder Subject to Open ie—vested remainders subject to partial divestment
- *Closing of the class of possible takers (when this happens, total # of takers)*

> Marge grants Blackacre "to Bart as long as no alcohol is ever consumed on the premises, then to Lisa." Bart drinks a beer on Blackacre.

---

5. Or the conversion of the executory interest into a vested remainder, as in note 2 supra.

Here the uncertainty over whether the condition will occur has been resolved, because it has come to pass.

(iii) For a remainder subject to open (as in a class gift), it means the closing of the class:

> Abe grants Blackacre "to my children who shall reach the age of 21."

Lack of vesting can happen because the identity of a taker is not determined (for example, heirs are not determined yet) or there is a contingency that has not happened yet. Here we have both.

To summarize: Those future interests potentially subject to the RAP are contingent remainders, executory interests, and vested remainders subject to partial divestment (i.e., subject to open). All other future interests, including those retained by the grantor (reversions, possibilities of reverter, and rights of entry) and other types of vested remainders are not subject to the RAP. Vested remainders subject to complete divestment are not themselves subject to the RAP, although if the interests that divest these vested remainders are executory interests, they of course are subject to the RAP. See Figure 5–5 supra.

Note that for the RAP the measuring lives must exist at the time of the creation of the interest, and then comes the 21–year period (the 21–year period cannot come first). Why 21 years? The idea is that a testator or other grantor can legitimately care about and act paternalistically toward the next generation plus the next generation after that up to the age at which people become responsible, which courts assumed to be 21.

The RAP is tricky because some very similar sounding interests may fall on opposite sides of the line. Consider some more examples of a generic bequest of personal property:

> *Example 1*: T makes a bequest "to my grandchildren who shall reach the age of 21."

This is valid because all T's grandchildren must be born within the lives of T's children and these lives must be lives in being at T's death. This illustrates a couple of important points. First, a child who is born after T's death is deemed to be in being at conception if the child is later born alive. If the child was later born alive the common law would add the period of gestation to the perpetuities period. See Thellusson v. Woodford, 11 Ves. Jr. 112 (Ch. 1805); W. Barton Leach, Perpetuities in a Nutshell, 51 Harv. L. Rev. 638, 642 (1938). Second, the measuring lives do *not* have to be those of people mentioned in the instrument, need not be holders of previous estates, and need have no special connection to the property. They just need to be people who can affect the vesting (through the condition stated in the instrument or through the identity of the takers).

> *Example 2*: T sets up an inter vivos trust for "my grandchildren who shall reach the age of 21."

This is invalid. All the existing children of T may die. T might then have more children, one of whom has a grandchild who reaches 21 after the

Bequest goes into effect at death of T, thus at that moment, all of T's children are in being, and his grandchildren must be born within their lives (and thus, reach age 21 no later than 21 years after the death of the last of T's children).

This goes into effect during T's life, so the perpetuities clock starts at the death of T's last child and, assuming that T outlives them all as in the hypo, he could have another child, which could then have a child (which would be a grandchild of T) who reaches age 21 more than 21 years after the death of the last of T's previous batch of children.

perpetuities period. No other measuring lives can be found to make this interest satisfy the rule. Note that this illustrates the importance of considering the perpetuities issue from the standpoint of the time of the *creation of the interest*. This makes all the difference between this example and Example 1, where the interest comes into being when the testator dies and the death prevents the remote vesting scenario with the afterborn child.

> *Example 3*: T makes a bequest "to A's grandchildren who shall reach the age of 21." A is alive at the time of the testator's death.

This is invalid for reasons similar to those in Example 2. Because A can have more children, the children's lives cannot be taken as measuring lives. So the problem is not bequest versus inter vivos transfer but whether there can be more children or not. If so, they cannot be the measuring lives. One might ask what would happen if a bequest is made "to my children for their lives, remainder to my grandchildren who shall reach 21." Again, this is all right even if the testator has a child born several months after his death.

One of the enduring sports involving the RAP has been to maximize the perpetuities period by using a larger and younger set of measuring lives. Courts will invalidate such interests when the burden of keeping track of the measuring lives is too great. A time-honored technique is to create an interest that will vest 21 years after the death of the last of a list of a dozen or so healthy babies. Over the line are attempts to similarly use the list of everyone in the New York City phone directory ("to my descendants who shall be living 21 years after the death of everyone listed in the New York City phone book"). See also In re Moore, [1901] 1 Ch. 936, 938 (invalidating as void for uncertainty a gift in trust to endure until "twenty-one years from the death of the last survivor of all persons who shall be living at my death," and noting that "[i]t is impossible to ascertain when the last life will be extinguished.... Under these circumstances it is not, I think, necessary for me to consider whether the gift is void as transgressing the rule against perpetuity.") To take the most creative and successful example, in *In re Villar*, [1929] 1 Ch. 243 (C.A.) the court held that the RAP did not invalidate bequests in trust that were to vest "at the expiration of 20 years from the day of the death of the last survivor of all the lineal descendants of Her Late Majesty Queen Victoria who shall be living at the time of my death." [1929] 1 Ch. at 243. At the time of the testator's death in 1926 there were 120 or so such descendants then living. Although it has been suggested that an American court would not uphold such an interest (nor the one employing the city phone book formula), Restatement of Property § 374 cmt. l (1944), why are "royal lives" clauses more likely to be upheld in England than the city phone book approach?

Recall in this connection that future interests retained by the grantor are treated as vested on creation and so satisfy the RAP. Are such interests easier to keep track of than interests created in third parties?

As can be seen in the above examples, the RAP traditionally involved spinning out scenarios of what *might* happen based solely on information available at the time the interest was created. The common law pursued this approach relentlessly, and presumed that anyone, no matter how old, could marry or have children at any time, leading to invalidation on the possibility of "unborn widows" and "fertile octogenarians."

In the unborn widow scenario, a gift is made to A for life and then to A's widow for life, then to A's children then living. This seems fine at first blush, until one spins a story in which A's present wife dies or she and A divorce and A then marries a woman who was born after the creation of the interest. If so the interest in her children could vest outside the perpetuities period. As for the fertile octogenarian, suppose O conveys "to my wife A for life, then to my grandchildren who reach age 21." O and A, both age 80, have a child B, age 35, and B has a child C, age 10. Again this seems fine on cursory examination. But suppose, after the conveyance, that the octogenarian A has another child, D, who then produces a grandchild, E. There is no life in being at the time of the conveyance that can demonstrate, as a matter of what-might-happen logic, that the interest of E will vest or not within the perpetuities period. See Jee v. Audley, 1 Cox 324, 29 Eng. Rep. 1186 (Ch. 1787).

Not surprisingly, such results and the rule that produced them came in for heavy criticism, leading to limited reforms such as a presumption that the fertile octogenarian and unborn widow situations will not arise. Shortly we will take up more sweeping reforms, such as wait-and-see, which would also have saved these sorts of situations from invalidation.

More recently, assisted reproductive techniques have made postmenopausal births possible. More generally, techniques such as cryopreservation of sperm, eggs, and embryos present new challenges for the RAP, where the Rule still exists. Such techniques are sometimes said not to count for the common-law RAP. Can you see the problems posed? For a review of how various reforms do and do not address the challenges to the RAP and inheritance law raised by new reproductive technologies, see Sharona Hoffman & Andrew P. Morriss, Birth After Death: Perpetuities and the New Reproductive Technologies, 38 Ga. L. Rev. 575 (2004).

✳ A standard solution to the perpetuities problem is to insert a "perpetuities savings clause" into the relevant instrument. Such a clause refers explicitly to the possibility of invalidation under the RAP and specifies a backup plan. Consider the key part of one version of a savings clause:

> If any interest purported to be created in this instrument or in any instrument exercising a power created in this instrument is challenged under the Rule Against Perpetuities or any related rule, I direct the corporate donee (hereafter designated) to appoint the assets which the challenged interest purports to dispose of in such manner as will most closely approximate, within clearly permissible limits, the intention of the person who has executed the instrument purporting to create such interest.

W. Barton Leach & James K. Logan, Perpetuities: A Standard Saving Clause to Avoid Violations of the Rule, 74 Harv. L. Rev. 1141, 1141–42

(1961). Courts have upheld perpetuities savings clauses. See, e.g., Norton v. Georgia R.R. Bank & Trust, 322 S.E.2d 870 (Ga. 1984). The savings clause became a standard practice and made perpetuities problems relatively easy to avoid even before the judicial and statutory reforms discussed below.

Finally, courts have recently started using reinterpretation to save interests from invalidation under the RAP. The method here is in effect to rewrite the instrument so that it conforms with the grantor's intent as closely as possible, but consistently with the RAP. (Courts have had some experience in the doctrine of cy pres, which saves gifts to charity from impossibility, or more recently wastefulness, by substituting another close charity. See Chapter VI.) Even under older RAP doctrine, charities received somewhat favorable treatment. Consider the following example:

> *Example 4*: O grants Blackacre "to Springfield Law School so long as it is used for instruction in the law, but if it is not used for instruction in the law, then to Shelbyville Law School."

The Springfield Law School has a fee simple subject to executory limitation, and the Shelbyville Law School has an executory interest. The executory interest would normally violate the RAP because it is not guaranteed to vest within lives in being plus 21 years. Nevertheless, the executory interest would probably be all right under the rule of two charities: An interest does not violate the RAP if the interest involves a transfer from one charity to another, as here. Compare *City of Klamath Falls*, supra, where the executory interest was given to the stockholders of the donor corporation, and was therefore held to violate the RAP.

[handwritten margin note: 2 charities exception to RAP]

PROBLEMS

In the following, identify the interests O is trying to create, and if different, the interests actually created or resulting from the facts given. Assume that the common-law version of the Rule against Perpetuities is in force.   WORDS OF DURATION

1. O grants Blackacre "to Huxley College, as long as it is used for instructional purposes; then to my son A and his heirs."

[handwritten margin note: Huxley College – fee simple subject to executory limitation; A – executory interest]

2. O grants Blackacre "to A; but if marijuana is inhaled on the premises, then O has the right to reenter and take the premises."

[handwritten margin note: Interests reverting to grantor are ok under RAP]

3. O grants Blackacre "to A; but if marijuana is inhaled on the premises, then to B and her heirs."

4. O grants Blackacre "to A for life, then to B's grandchildren who reach the age of 21." Assume that B is dead at the time the interest is created, leaving children but no grandchildren.

5. O grants Blackacre "to A for life, then to my grandchildren who graduate from high school." O has children B and C, but no grandchildren at the time of the grant.

6. As in Problem 5, except the transfer is by devise (a grant of real estate in a will).

REFORMS

A growing number of states have abolished the common-law RAP. Much of the motivation for abolishing the RAP comes from the federal tax advantages to dynasty trusts, and there now seems to be a jurisdictional competition to attract trust business by abolishing the RAP (at least among states that do not tax income from trust funds). Max Schanzenbach & Robert Sitkoff, Jurisdictional Competition for Trust Funds: An Empirical Analysis of Perpetuities and Taxes, 114 Yale L.J. (2005). In addition to tax considerations, testators still do seem to want to exercise control over the future. Trust specialists seem to be advertising on that basis. Joshua C. Tate, Perpetual Trusts and the Settlor's Intent, 53 Kan. L. Rev. 595 (2005). Other reforms:

(i) *Wait and See for the common-law RAP period* (or some related period). Under this approach one would wait and see whether the interest vests remotely or not. Thus in Examples 2 and 3 (and in some of the Problems) above, one would wait and see whether additional children were born. If not, the interest would turn out to be valid. But notice that one would typically not know this for quite a while.

(ii) *Wait and See for the common-law period or 90 years.* This is like wait and see but allows for a 90–year alternative period. Like (i), this approach allows interests to satisfy the RAP the common-law way—ex ante, at the time the interest is created—as well. So if the interest satisfies the common-law RAP one can know it is valid right away. Also, one knows that one won't have to wait more than 90 years to find out either. Some commentators have heavily criticized the 90–year period on the grounds that interests that are only valid because of the 90–year wait-and-see period involve a high degree of uncertainty for this lengthy period of time. Keeping the RAP but adopting wait-and-see in general involves tolerating uncertainty.

(iii) *Interpretation and Implication.* Sometimes drafters and courts will insert a perpetuities savings clause or otherwise reform an interest (as by changing 25 years to 21 years). Courts will sometimes also refuse to invalidate a class gift if it fails to vest for the entire class within the perpetuities period. Thus in a gift to "A's children" the interest is held to vest even if a child might be born too remotely; the interest simply fails with respect to that child only, rejecting the all-or-nothing approach of the common-law RAP. See, e.g., In re Estate of Anderson, 541 So.2d 423 (Miss. 1989).

The Uniform Statutory Rule Against Perpetuities (USRAP) combines approaches (ii) and (iii). Among other things, the USRAP provides for a cy pres-like approach to saving ill-drafted instruments, under which an interested person can petition a court to "reform a disposition in the manner that most closely approximates the transferor's manifested plan of distribution and is within the 90 years allowed" as long as one of a number of conditions holds. As of 2003, the USRAP had been adopted in 24 states, and in an additional two (Alaska and New Jersey) which subsequently repealed it. Instead of a RAP these two states, like South Dakota and

Wisconsin, have a statute against suspending the power of alienation. Some 20 states allow for perpetual or nearly perpetual trusts. Delaware exempts personal property held in trust from the RAP, and Rhode Island has abolished the RAP altogether. See, e.g., Jesse Dukeminier & James E. Krier, The Rise of the Perpetual Trust, 50 UCLA L. Rev. 1303, 1308 & n.20 (2003).

THE PROBLEM OF DEAD HAND CONTROL

The intuition that there is something wrong with dead hand control is a longstanding and fairly robust one. For example, Adam Smith warned that "[t]o give a man power over his property after his death is very considerable, but it is nothing [compared] to an extension of this power to the end of the world." Adam Smith, Lectures on Jurisprudence 467 (R.L. Meek et al. eds., 1978) (ms. 1762–66). As in the case of rules against restraints on alienation, we can ask why we need mandatory rules against dead hand control.

What would testators do if given unlimited discretion? Many testators would like to give freedom to the recipient—often the testator's spouse or children—and here the issue does not arise. But sometimes testators will worry about unwise decisions by the donee, or the testator would like to condition or control the resources into the future. As we saw in Chapter IV, the law gives wide but not unlimited latitude to owners to destroy property, and at first glance controlling property into the future is a less sweeping use of the property. As in the right to destroy, keeping property and subjecting it to post mortem control is costly to the owner in that she cannot sell it (for a price that would reflect future use) or give it away in some other way. If the present discounted future benefits and liabilities of the property are reflected in current prices (known as "capitalization"), wouldn't the owner take these values into account? What, if anything does capitalization leave out of the picture?

Some have argued that dead people cannot experience utility, but even if so, people who are living may derive utility in anticipating such control and might even work harder to create wealth that they can subject to such control. Conversely, some focus on the needs of the members of the future generation who have to live with the dead hand conditions is appropriate. What do we owe future generations? Does the RAP serve these interests?

Others have argued that the future is full of uncertainty and a testator cannot be expected to foresee all the contingencies relevant to the testator's overall plan. We will take up such problems with the cy pres doctrine in Chapter VI. Property rights typically last a long time. Does dead hand control put too much of a burden on future owners and judges to figure out what the creator of the interest wanted? Why don't we have a menu of options for flexibility that the creator of the interest can choose from, ranging from wooden application of the testator's language to letting judges intervene according to their assessment of the future needs? If future people reach a consensus that some type of dead hand control is harmful, what is to stop them from simply doing as they wish? For discussion of these issues, see, e.g., Steven Shavell, Foundations of the Economic Analysis of Law 67–72 (2004); Lewis M. Simes, Public Policy and the Dead Hand (1955); Adam J. Hirsch & William K.S. Wang, A Qualitative Theory of the Dead Hand, 68 Ind. L.J. 1 (1992); Jeffrey E. Stake, Darwin, Donations, and the Illusion of Dead Hand Control, 64 Tul. L. Rev. 705 (1990); Symposium, Time, Property, Rights, and the Common Law, 64 Wash. U. L.Q. 661 (1986).

P   D

Symphony Space, Inc. v. Pergola Properties, Inc.

Court of Appeals of New York, 1996.
669 N.E.2d 799.

■ KAYE, CHIEF JUDGE. This case presents the novel question whether options to purchase commercial property are exempt from the prohibition against remote vesting embodied in New York's Rule against Perpetuities (EPTL 9–1.1[b]). Because an exception for commercial options finds no support in our law, we decline to exempt all commercial option agreements from the statutory Rule against Perpetuities.

Here, we agree with the trial court and Appellate Division that the option defendants seek to enforce violates the statutory prohibition against remote vesting and is therefore unenforceable.

I.   FACTS

The subject of this proceeding is a two-story building situated on the Broadway block between 94th and 95th Streets on Manhattan's Upper West Side. In 1978, Broadwest Realty Corporation owned this building, which housed a theater and commercial space. Broadwest had been unable to secure a permanent tenant for the theater—approximately 58% of the total square footage of the building's floor space. Broadwest also owned two adjacent properties, Pomander Walk (a residential complex) and the Healy Building (a commercial building). Broadwest had been operating its properties at a net loss.

Plaintiff Symphony Space, Inc., a not-for-profit entity devoted to the arts, had previously rented the theater for several one-night engagements. In 1978, Symphony and Broadwest engaged in a transaction whereby Broadwest sold the entire building to Symphony for the below-market price of $10,010 and leased back the income-producing commercial property, excluding the theater, for $1 per year. Broadwest maintained liability for the existing $243,000 mortgage on the property as well as certain maintenance obligations. As a condition of the sale, Symphony, for consideration of $10, also granted Broadwest an option to repurchase the entire building. Notably, the transaction did not involve Pomander Walk or the Healy Building.

The purpose of this arrangement was to enable Symphony, as a not-for-profit corporation, to seek a property tax exemption for the entire building—which constituted a single tax parcel—predicated on its use of the theater. The sale-and-leaseback would thereby reduce Broadwest's real estate taxes by $30,000 per year, while permitting Broadwest to retain the rental income from the leased commercial space in the building, which the trial court found produced $140,000 annually. The arrangement also furthered Broadwest's goal of selling all the properties, by allowing Broadwest to postpone any sale until property values in the area increased and until the commercial leases expired. Symphony, in turn, would have use of the theater at minimal cost, once it received a tax exemption.

Thus, on December 1, 1978, Symphony and Broadwest—both sides represented by counsel—executed a contract for sale of the property from Broadwest to Symphony for the purchase price of $10,010. The contract specified that $10 was to be paid at the closing and $10,000 was to be paid by means of a purchase-money mortgage.

The parties also signed several separate documents, each dated December 31, 1978: (1) a deed for the property from Broadwest to Symphony; (2) a lease from Symphony to Broadwest of the entire building except the theater for rent of $1 per year and for the term January 1, 1979 to May 31, 2003, unless terminated earlier; (3) a 25–year, $10,000 mortgage and mortgage note from Symphony as mortgagor to Broadwest as mortgagee, with full payment due on December 31, 2003; and (4) an option agreement by which Broadwest obtained from Symphony the exclusive right to repurchase all of the property, including the theater.

It is the option agreement that is at the heart of the present dispute. Section 3 of that agreement provides that Broadwest may exercise its option to purchase the property during any of the following "Exercise Periods":

    (a) at any time after July 1, 1979, so long as the Notice of Election specifies that the Closing is to occur during any of the calendar years 1987, 1993, 1998 and 2003;

    (b) at any time following the maturity of the indebtedness evidenced by the Note and secured by the Mortgage, whether by acceleration or otherwise;

    (c) during the ninety days immediately following any termination of the Lease by the lessor thereof other than for nonpayment of rent or any termination of the Lease by the lessee thereof * * *

    (d) during the ninety days immediately following the thirtieth day after Broadwest shall have sent Symphony a notice specifying a default by Symphony of any of its covenants or obligations under the Mortgage.

Section 1 states that "Broadwest may exercise its option at any time during any Exercise Period." That section further specifies that the notice of election must be sent at least 180 days prior to the closing date if the option is exercised pursuant to section 3(a) and at least 90 days prior to the closing date if exercised pursuant to any other subdivision.

[handwritten margin note:] ie — allows for purchase 24 years after interest rests (at time of signing) Seven w/ 180 days required notice

[handwritten margin note:] allows buy-back if Symphony Space defaults on Mortgage payments.

The following purchase prices of the property, contingent upon the closing date, are set forth in section 4: $15,000 if the closing date is on or before December 31, 1987; $20,000 if on or before December 31, 1993; $24,000 if on or before December 31, 1998; and $28,000 if on or before December 31, 2003.

Importantly, the option agreement specifies in section 5 that "Broadwest's right to exercise the option granted hereby is * * * unconditional and shall not be in any way affected or impaired by Broadwest's performance or nonperformance, actual or asserted, of any obligation to be performed under the Lease or any other agreement or instrument by or between Broadwest and Symphony," other than that Broadwest was required to pay Symphony any unpaid rent on the closing date. Finally, section 6 established that the option constituted "a covenant running with the land, inuring to the benefit of heirs, successors and assigns of Broadwest."

Symphony ultimately obtained a tax exemption for the theater. In the summer of 1981, Broadwest sold and assigned its interest under the lease, option agreement, mortgage and mortgage note, as well as its ownership interest in the contiguous Pomander Walk and Healy Building, to defendants' nominee for $4.8 million. The nominee contemporaneously transferred its rights under these agreements to defendants Pergola Properties, Inc., Bradford N. Swett, Casandium Limited and Darenth Consultants as tenants in common.

Subsequently, defendants initiated a cooperative conversion of Pomander Walk, which was designated a landmark in 1982, and the value of the properties increased substantially. An August 1988 appraisal of the entire blockfront, including the Healy Building and the unused air and other development rights available from Pomander Walk, valued the property at $27 million assuming the enforceability of the option. By contrast, the value of the leasehold interest plus the Healy Building without the option were appraised at $5.5 million.

Thus, actually exercised within the allowed period

Due to Symphony's alleged default on the mortgage note, defendant Swett served Symphony with notice in January 1985 that it was exercising the option on behalf of all defendants. The notice set a closing date of May 6, 1985. Symphony, however, disputed both that it was in default and Swett's authority to exercise the option for all of the defendants. According to Symphony, moreover, it then discovered that the option agreement was possibly invalid. Consequently, in March 1985, Symphony initiated this declaratory judgment action against defendants, arguing that the option agreement violated the New York statutory prohibition against remote vesting * * *

Defendant Pergola subsequently served Symphony with separate notice of default dated April 4, 1985, informing Symphony that it was exercising the option on behalf of all defendants pursuant to sections 1, 3(b) and 3(d) of the option agreement and setting the closing date for July 10, 1985. Pergola further notified Symphony that it was alternatively exercising the option under section 3(a) of the option agreement, which was not contingent upon Symphony's default, with the closing date scheduled for January 5, 1987. Symphony did not appear for any of the closing dates contained in Swett's or Pergola's notices. * * *

Thereafter, the parties cross-moved for summary judgment in the instant declaratory judgment proceeding. The trial court granted Symphony's motion while denying that of defendants. In particular, the court concluded that the Rule against Perpetuities applied to the commercial option contained in the parties' agreement, that the option violated the Rule and that Symphony was entitled to exercise its equitable right to redeem the mortgage. The trial court also dismissed defendants' counterclaim for rescission of the agreements underlying the transaction based on the parties' mutual mistake.

In a comprehensive writing by Justice Ellerin, the Appellate Division likewise determined that the commercial option was unenforceable under the Rule against Perpetuities and that rescission was inappropriate. The Appellate Division certified the following question to us: "Was the order of the Supreme Court, as affirmed by this Court, properly made?" We conclude that it was and now affirm.

II.   STATUTORY BACKGROUND

The Rule against Perpetuities evolved from judicial efforts during the 17th century to limit control of title to real property by the dead hand of landowners reaching into future generations. Underlying both early and modern rules restricting future dispositions of property is the principle that it is socially undesirable for property to be inalienable for an unreasonable period of time. These rules thus seek "to ensure the productive use and development of property by its current beneficial owners by simplifying ownership, facilitating exchange and freeing property from unknown or embarrassing impediments to alienability" (Metropolitan Transp. Auth. v. Bruken Realty Corp., 492 N.E.2d 379, 381 (N.Y. 1986), citing De Peyster v. Michael, 6 N.Y. 467, 494 (1852)).

> *Rationale & Reasons for R.A.P.*

The traditional statement of the common-law Rule against Perpetuities was set forth by Professor John Chipman Gray: "No interest is good unless it must vest, if at all, not later than twenty-one years after some life in being at the creation of the interest" (Gray, The Rule Against Perpetuities § 201, at 191 [4th ed. 1942]).

> *Black-letter wording in common-law of RAP*

In New York, the rules regarding suspension of the power of alienation and remoteness in vesting—the Rule against Perpetuities—have been statutory since 1830. Prior to 1958, the perpetuities period was two lives in being plus actual periods of minority (see, Real Property Law former § 42). Widely criticized as unduly complex and restrictive, the statutory period was revised in 1958 and 1960, restoring the common-law period of lives in being plus 21 years (see, L.1958, ch. 153; L.1960, ch. 448). * * *

New York's current statutory Rule against Perpetuities is found in EPTL 9–1.1. Subdivision (a) sets forth the suspension of alienation rule and deems void any estate in which the conveying instrument suspends the absolute power of alienation for longer than lives in being at the creation of

> *a) Restraints on Alienation*

b) Preventing Remote Vesting

the estate plus 21 years (see, EPTL 9–1.1[a][2]). The prohibition against remote vesting is contained in subdivision (b), which states that "[n]o estate in property shall be valid unless it must vest, if at all, not later than twenty-one years after one or more lives in being at the creation of the estate and any period of gestation involved" (EPTL 9–1.1[b]). This Court has described subdivision (b) as "a rigid formula that invalidates any interest that may not vest within the prescribed time period" and has "capricious consequences" (Wildenstein & Co. v. Wallis, 595 N.E.2d 828, 831–32 (N.Y. 1992)). Indeed, these rules are predicated upon the public policy of the State and constitute non-waivable, legal prohibitions (see, Metropolitan Transp. Auth. v. Bruken Realty Corp., 492 N.E.2d at 381).

Common-Law Rule for Unreasonable Restraints on Alienation

In addition to these statutory formulas, New York also retains the more flexible common-law rule against unreasonable restraints on alienation. Unlike the statutory Rule against Perpetuities, which is measured exclusively by the passage of time, the common-law rule evaluates the reasonableness of the restraint based on its duration, purpose and designated method for fixing the purchase price. (See, Wildenstein & Co. v. Wallis, 595 N.E.2d at 832; Metropolitan Transp. Auth. v. Bruken Realty Corp., 492 N.E.2d at 381–82).

Against this background, we consider the option agreement at issue.

III.   VALIDITY OF THE OPTION AGREEMENT

Defendants proffer three grounds for upholding the option: that the statutory prohibition against remote vesting does not apply to commercial options; that the option here cannot be exercised beyond the statutory period; and that this Court should adopt the "wait and see" approach to the Rule against Perpetuities. We consider each in turn.

A.   Applicability of the Rule to Commercial Options

Under the common law, options to purchase land are subject to the rule against remote vesting (see, Simes, Future Interests § 132 [2d ed 1966]; Simes and Smith, Future Interests § 1244 [2d ed]; Leach, Perpetuities in a Nutshell, 51 Harv.L.Rev. 638, 660; see also, London & S.W. Ry. Co. v. Gomm, 20 ChD 562). Such options are specifically enforceable and give the option holder a contingent, equitable interest in the land (Dukeminier, A Modern Guide to Perpetuities, 74 Cal.L.Rev. 1867, 1908; Leach, Perpetuities in Perspective: Ending the Rule's Reign of Terror, 65 Harv.L.Rev. 721, 736–737). This creates a disincentive for the landowner to develop the property and hinders its alienability, thereby defeating the policy objectives underlying the Rule against Perpetuities.

Typically, however, options to purchase are part of a commercial transaction. For this reason, subjecting them to the Rule against Perpetuities has been deemed "a step of doubtful wisdom" (Leach, Perpetuities in Perspective: Ending the Rule's Reign of Terror, 65 Harv.L.Rev. 737). As one vocal critic, Professor W. Barton Leach, has explained,

> [t]he Rule grew up as a limitation on family dispositions; and the period of lives in being plus twenty-one years is adapted to these gift

transactions. The pressures which created the Rule do not exist with reference to arms-length contractual transactions, and neither lives in being nor twenty-one years are periods which are relevant to business men and their affairs (Leach, Perpetuities: New Absurdity, Judicial and Statutory Correctives, 73 Harv.L.Rev. 1318, 1321–1322).

Professor Leach, however, went on to acknowledge that, under common law, "due to an overemphasis on concepts derived from the nineteenth century, we are stuck with the application of the Rule to options to purchase," urging that "this should not be extended to other commercial transactions" (id., at 1322).

It is now settled in New York that, generally, EPTL 9–1.1(b) applies to options. In Buffalo Seminary v. McCarthy, 86 A.D.2d 435, 440, 451 N.Y.S.2d 457, aff'd 447 N.E.2d 76 (N.Y. 1983), the court held that an unlimited option in gross to purchase real property was void under the statutory rule against remote vesting, and we affirmed the Appellate Division decision on the opinion of then-Justice Hancock. Since then, we have reiterated that options in real estate are subject to the statutory rule (see, e.g., Wildenstein & Co. v. Wallis, 595 N.E.2d at 832). * * *

While defendants offer compelling policy reasons—echoing those voiced by Professor Leach—for refusing to apply the traditional rule against remote vesting to these commercial option contracts, such statutory reformation would require legislative action similar to that undertaken by numerous other State lawmakers (see, e.g., Cal.Prob.Code § 21225; Fla.Stat.Annot. ch. 689.225; Ill.Stat.Annot. ch. 765, para. 305/4).

Applying RAP to land purchase options may not be ideal, but to change this policy would need legislative action.

Our decision in *Metropolitan Transp. Auth. v. Bruken Realty Corp.*, 492 N.E.2d 379, supra, is not to the contrary. In *Bruken,* we held that EPTL 9–1.1(b) did not apply to a preemptive right in a "commercial and governmental transaction" that lasted beyond the statutory perpetuities period. In doing so, we explained that, *unlike options,* preemptive rights (or rights of first refusal) only marginally affect transferability:

> An option grants to the holder the power to compel the owner of property to sell it whether the owner is willing to part with ownership or not. A preemptive right, or right of first refusal, does not give its holder the power to compel an unwilling owner to sell; it merely requires the owner, when and if he decides to sell, to offer the property first to the party holding the preemptive right so that he may meet a third-party offer or buy the property at some other price set by a previously stipulated method (id. at 382).

Enforcement of the preemptive right in the context of the governmental and commercial transaction, moreover, actually encouraged the use and development of the land, outweighing any minor impediment to alienability (id. at 383–84). * * *

Here, the option agreement creates precisely the sort of control over future disposition of the property that we have previously associated with purchase options and that the common-law rule against remote vesting—and thus EPTL 9–1.1(b)—seeks to prevent. As the Appellate Division explained, the option grants its holder absolute power to purchase the property at the holder's whim and at a token price set far below market value. This Sword of Damocles necessarily discourages the property owner from investing in improvements to the property. Furthermore, the option's existence significantly impedes the owner's ability to sell the property to a third party, as a practical matter rendering it inalienable.

That defendants, the holder of this option, are also the lessees of a portion of the premises does not lead to a different conclusion here.

Generally, an option to purchase land that originates in one of the lease provisions, is not exercisable after lease expiration, and is incapable of separation from the lease is valid even though the holder's interest may vest beyond the perpetuities period (see, Berg, Long–Term Options and the Rule Against Perpetuities, 37 Cal.L.Rev. 1, 21; Leach, Perpetuities: New Absurdity, Judicial and Statutory Correctives, 73 Harv.L.Rev. 1320; Simes and Smith, Future Interests § 1244). Such options—known as options "appendant" or "appurtenant" to leases—encourage the possessory holder to invest in maintaining and developing the property by guaranteeing the option holder the ultimate benefit of any such investment. Options appurtenant thus further the policy objectives underlying the rule against remote vesting and are not contemplated by EPTL 9–1.1(b) (see, Metropolitan Transp. Auth. v. Bruken Realty Corp., 492 N.E.2d at 383–84, supra).

To be sure, the option here arose within a larger transaction that included a lease. Nevertheless, not all of the property subject to the purchase option here is even occupied by defendants. The option encompasses the entire building—both the commercial space and the theater—yet defendants are leasing only the commercial space. With regard to the theater space, a disincentive exists for Symphony to improve the property, since it will eventually be claimed by the option holder at the predetermined purchase price. * * *

Put simply, the option here cannot qualify as an option appurtenant and significantly deters development of the property. If the option is exercisable beyond the statutory perpetuities period, refusing to enforce it would thus further the purpose and rationale underlying the statutory prohibition against remote vesting.

B. Duration of the Option Agreement

1. Duration Under Section 3(a) of the Agreement

Defendants alternatively claim that section 3(a) of the agreement does not permit exercise of the option after expiration of the statutory perpetuities period. According to defendants, only the possible closing dates fall outside the permissible time frame.

RULE [Where, as here, the parties to a transaction are corporations and no measuring lives are stated in the instruments, the perpetuities period is simply 21 years (see, Metropolitan Transp. Auth. v. Bruken Realty Corp., 492 N.E.2d at 381, supra). Section 1 of the parties' agreement allows the option holder to exercise the option "at any time during any Exercise

Period" set forth in section three. Section 3(a), moreover, expressly provides that the option may be exercised "*at any time* after July 1, 1979," so long as the closing date is scheduled during 1987, 1993, 1998 or 2003.

Even factoring in the requisite notice, then, the option could potentially be exercised as late as July 2003—more than 24 years after its creation in December 1978. Defendants' contention that section 3(a) does not permit exercise of the option beyond the 21–year period is thus contradicted by the plain language of the instrument.

Nor can EPTL 9–1.3—the "saving statute"—be invoked to shorten the duration of the exercise period under section 3(a) of the agreement. That statute mandates that, "[u]nless a contrary intention appears," certain rules of construction govern with respect to any matter affecting the Rule against Perpetuities (EPTL 9–1.3[a]). The specified canons of construction include that "[i]t shall be presumed that the creator intended the estate to be valid" (EPTL 9–1.3[b]) and "[w]here the duration or vesting of an estate is contingent upon * * * the occurrence of any specified contingency, it shall be presumed that the creator of such estate intended such contingency to occur, if at all, within twenty-one years from the effective date of the instrument creating such estate" (EPTL 9–1.3[d]).

By presuming that the creator intended the estate to be valid, the statute seeks to avoid annulling dispositions due to inadvertent violations of the Rule against Perpetuities. The provisions of EPTL 9–1.3, however, are merely rules of construction. While the statute obligates reviewing courts, where possible, to avoid constructions that frustrate the parties' intended purposes, it does not authorize courts to rewrite instruments that unequivocally allow interests to vest outside the perpetuities period (compare, EPTL 9–1.2 [reducing age contingency to 21 years, where interest is invalid because contingent on a person reaching an age in excess of 21 years]).

Indeed, by their terms, the rules of construction in EPTL 9–1.3 apply only if "a contrary intention" does not appear in the instrument. * * *

The unambiguous language of the agreement here expresses the parties' intent that the option be exercisable "at any time" during a 24–year period pursuant to section 3(a). The section thus does not permit a construction that the parties intended the option to last only 21 years.

Given the contrary intention manifested in the instrument itself, the saving statute is simply inapplicable. * * *

C.   *"Wait and See" Approach*

Defendants next urge that we adopt the "wait and see" approach to the Rule against Perpetuities: an interest is valid if it actually vests during the perpetuities period, irrespective of what might have happened (see, Dukeminier, A Modern Guide to Perpetuities, 74 Cal.L.Rev. 1867, 1880). The option here would survive under the "wait and see" approach since it was exercised by 1987, well within the 21–year limitation.

This Court, however, has long refused to "wait and see" whether a perpetuities violation in fact occurs. As explained in *Matter of Fischer*, 120 N.E.2d 688, 692 (N.Y. 1954), "[i]t is settled beyond dispute that in determining whether a will has illegally suspended the power of alienation, the courts will look to what might have happened under the terms of the will rather than to what has actually happened since the death of the testator."

The very language of EPTL 9–1.1, moreover, precludes us from determining the validity of an interest based upon what actually occurs during the perpetuities period. Under the statutory rule against remote vesting, an interest is invalid "unless it *must* vest, if at all, not later than twenty-one years after one or more lives in being" (EPTL 9–1.1[b] [emphasis added]). That is, an interest is void from the outset if it *may* vest too remotely * * * Because the option here could have vested after expiration of the 21–year perpetuities period, it offends the Rule.

We note that the desirability of the "wait and see" doctrine has been widely debated (see, 5A Powell, Real Property ¶ 827F[1], [3]; see also, Waggoner, Perpetuity Reform, 81 Mich.L.Rev. 1718 [describing "wait and see" as "(t)he most controversial of the reform methods"]). Its incorporation into EPTL 9–1.1, in any event, must be accomplished by the Legislature, not the courts.

We therefore conclude that the option agreement is invalid under EPTL 9–1.1(b). In light of this conclusion, we need not decide whether the option violated Symphony's equitable right to redeem the mortgage.

IV. REMEDY

As a final matter, defendants argue that, if the option fails, the contract of sale conveying the property from Broadwest to Symphony should be rescinded due to the mutual mistake of the parties. We conclude that rescission is inappropriate * * *

A contract entered into under mutual mistake of fact is generally subject to rescission (see, Matter of Gould v. Board of Educ., 616 N.E.2d 142, 145 (N.Y. 1993)). CPLR 3005 provides that when relief against mistake is sought, it shall not be denied merely because the mistake is one of law rather than fact. Relying on this provision, defendants maintain that neither Symphony nor Broadwest realized that the option violated the Rule against Perpetuities at the time they entered into the agreement and that both parties intended the option to be enforceable.

CPLR 3005, however, does not equate all mistakes of law with mistakes of fact * * *

Here, the parties' mistake amounts to nothing more than a misunderstanding as to the applicable law, and CPLR 3005 does not direct undoing of the transaction * * *

The remedy of rescission, moreover, lies in equity and is a matter of discretion (Rudman v. Cowles Communications, 280 N.E.2d 867, 874 (N.Y. 1972)). Defendants' plea that the unenforceability of the option is contrary to the intent of the original parties ignores that the effect of the Rule against Perpetuities—which is a statutory prohibition, not a rule of construction—is always to defeat the intent of parties who create a remotely vesting interest. As explained by the Appellate Division, there is "an irreconcilable conflict in applying a remedy which is designed to void a transaction because it fails to carry out the parties' true intent to a transaction in which the mistake made by the parties was the application of the Rule against Perpetuities, the purpose of which is to defeat the intent of the parties."

The Rule against Perpetuities reflects the public policy of the State. Granting the relief requested by defendants would thus be contrary to

Figure 5–9
Symphony Space, New York City, in 2006

public policy, since it would lead to the same result as enforcing the option and tend to compel performance of contracts violative of the Rule. Similarly, damages are not recoverable where options to acquire real property violate the Rule against Perpetuities, since that would amount to giving effect to the option (see, 5A Powell, Real Property ¶ 771[3]).

Accordingly, the order of the Appellate Division should be affirmed, with costs, and the certified question answered in the affirmative.

NOTES AND QUESTIONS

1. The RAP traditionally applies to options, and this can be a big problem especially because, as in *Symphony Space*, a corporation is not treated as a measuring life. See also Central Delaware County Authority v. Greyhound Corp., 588 A.2d 485 (Pa. 1991). Some states, especially those following the USRAP approach, exempt options from the Rule. (USRAP may leave the options subject to rules against unreasonable restraints on alienation.) Nevertheless, rights of first refusal such as those retained by a cooperative or condominium board to apply when a sitting occupant wants to sell, are not subject to the RAP. Likewise, options given to a lessee to renew the lease or purchase the land are not subject to the RAP, because it is thought that they do not inhibit but encourage improvement of the property. Why isn't this true more generally? Are we just surer here? Section 3.3 of the *Restatement (Third) of Property: Servitudes* would exempt all options from the RAP but subject them to the prohibitions on unreasonable restraints on alienation.

2. Courts often interpret ambiguous deeds or even those with contradictory phrases in order to pick the version under which the RAP is satisfied, but some courts will go further than others. The court in *Symphony Space* noted this possibility but saw the New York statute as forbidding the court from the extensive rewriting of an option agreement that would have been required to make the option conform to the RAP. Other courts are far more accommodating. See, e.g., In re Estate of Anderson, 541 So.2d 423 (Miss. 1989).

3. What if the option had been reserved in the grantor Broadwest Realty instead of granted back by Symphony Space after a conveyance of the entire estate from Broadwest to Symphony? Some courts would see the option as an interest that is immediately vested and so presenting no issue with the RAP. Others, like the New York courts, view the exercise of the option as a cutting-off event like that in an executory interest, thus making the RAP applicable even if the option is reserved in the grantor. Which view is better? Does this have anything to do with the wisdom of applying the RAP?

4. Why did the court strike the entire option under the RAP, rather than just striking the final closing date of 2003? If the option had provided that the last possible closing date was 1998, this would have been less than 21 years after the option contract was created, and hence would not have violated the rule. The court rejects the argument that the option agreement should be interpreted so as to provide an earlier date of execution of the

option. But isn't there also an issue as to how much of the option contract the RAP will be deemed to invalidate?

5. Interestingly, the RAP started out its career as a flexible and equitable standard. This is reflected in Lord Chancellor Nottingham's statement that future interests should be invalidated for remoteness "whereever any visible Inconvenience doth appear; for the just Bounds of a Fee-simple upon a Fee-simple are not yet determined." Duke of Norfolk's Case, 22 Eng. Rep. 931, 960 (Ch. 1682). Only later did the RAP crystallize into a hard rule. Hirsch & Wang, supra, at 55 n.223. Are rules or standards more appropriate here?

6. As mentioned earlier, one of the policies behind the RAP is the limiting of dead hand control. One area in which this concern about rigidity over time has been raised is conservation easements, in which an owner of land grants away (typically for all time) the right to develop the land. (See Chapter IX.) Power to enforce the restriction is typically given to a governmental or nonprofit body. What if it turns out years later that the land could be put to higher use, or that other land is more valuable in an undeveloped state, or even that notions of developed and undeveloped change? See Julia Mahoney, Perpetual Restrictions on Land and the Problem of the Future, 88 Va. L. Rev. 739 (2002).

VESTIGIAL MAINTENANCE DOCTRINES   *(WON'T BE ON FINAL)*

There are a number of doctrines that served at one time to clean up conveyances and make them more alienable than they otherwise might have been. In recent times, future interests have been made more fully alienable than they were at common law, thus alleviating some of the problems courts traditionally faced. In addition, as already mentioned, most future interests are now created in trust, where the trustee can be given powers of alienation and appointment, and the entire arrangement, as far as management and distribution of the proceeds is concerned, can be customized to a degree impossible within the catalog of legal estates and interests.

Four traditional maintenance rules are the Merger Rule, the Rule in Shelley's Case, the Doctrine of Worthier Title, and the Destructibility of Contingent Remainders. Probably only the first remains in full force and effect in most states today. The others have either been abolished, or live on only as rules of construction.

The Merger Rule. Before the feudal incidents were abolished by *✓ —still followed* Parliament in 1660, landowners would attempt various stratagems to avoid them, especially the requirement of paying relief in order to allow property to pass to descendants upon death (an early version of the estate tax). The common-law courts devised a number of doctrines to block these efforts at evasion of the feudal incidents. One stratagem would be for O, in one instrument, to convey "to A for life." This of course would create an implied reversion in O. O would then execute a second instrument, conveying his reversion to A. A now held both a life estate and the reversion at the end of the life estate—which together adds up to a fee simple absolute—but A would have acquired these interests by inter vivos conveyances, not by descent. Courts held that when this happened, the two separate conveyances were merged, and A would be treated as having a fee simple absolute. The same rule holds if A receives both a life estate and a vested remainder in fee simple, or if A conveys the life estate back to O who still holds the reversion, or any other combination of transfers that puts in the hands of a single person a series of interests that add up to a larger estate. Whatever its original motivation, the merger rule clearly promotes free alienation of property (can you see why?), and so it is still followed today.

The Rule in Shelley's Case. In another device to avoid having to pay relief, landowners would sometimes attempt to convey property while still alive in such a way that persons would take as purchasers rather than by descent. For example, O might convey in a single instrument "to A for life, then to A's heirs." In a rule first recognized in Abel's Case, Y.B. 18 Edw. 2, f.577 (1324), and given its definite form in Shelley's Case, 1 Co. Rep. 936 (1581), this stratagem was blocked. Under the rule, if someone uses a single instrument to create a life estate in land in A, and also to create a remainder in persons described as A's heirs (or the heirs of A's body), and the life estate and the remainder are both legal or both equitable, then the interest becomes a fee simple (or fee tail) *in A*. The Rule is a mandatory rule and is not overcome by manifestation of contrary grantor intent. Today, the Rule in Shelley's Case has been abolished in most states, but lives on in a few, primarily on the theory that it promotes alienability of land. (Again, can you see why the application of the rule would make land more alienable?)

X – mostly abolished

Doctrine of Worthier Title. Another scheme to avoid relief would be for a grantor to attempt to create a remainder or executory interest in his own (the grantor's) heirs. Thus, O would grant "to A for life, then to the heirs of O." This was blocked by the Doctrine of Worthier Title, which converted what was in form a remainder in the heirs of O into a reversion in the grantor. Thus, "to A for life, then to the heirs of O," would be treated as if it had said "to A for life, then to O." Again, whatever its original rationale, the rule marginally contributes to alienability. If O could make a grant to "the heirs of O," no one would be in a position to negotiate with anyone else as long as O is alive, because O's heirs have not yet been determined. If the grant is construed as creating a reversion in O, then O can negotiate for a transfer. To the extent the doctrine lives on today, it is as a rule of construction, not a fixed rule of law like the Rule in Shelley's Case. See Doctor v. Hughes, 122 N.E. 221 (N.Y. 1919). In theory, a grantor could overcome the presumption in the rule by using language exhibiting a contrary intent.

X – a rule of construction only – can be overcome by grantor's intent

Destructibility of Contingent Remainders. Traditionally, if a (legal, not equitable) contingent remainder in real property failed to take immediately on the termination of all the preceding estates, it would be destroyed. For example, if O conveyed Blackacre "to A for life, then to B if B passes the bar," and A died before B had passed the bar, the rule would destroy the contingent remainder. Who would take? O would, because of

X – because the intent of grantor would otherwise be frustrated, courts generally create an executory interest rather than destroy contingent remainder.

the supporting reversion retained by O. The destructibility rule seems to have come about because of a fixation on the definition of a remainder as an interest that takes effect upon the natural termination of a prior estate (death). See Thomas F. Bergin and Paul G. Haskell, Preface to Estates in Land and Future Interests 77–79 (2d ed. 1984). In the example, supposing A dies before B passes the bar, if B were subsequently to take the property this would cut short O's reversion; it would not follow the termination of a life estate like a well-behaved remainder should. Of course, by destroying the contingent remainder, the courts also frustrated O's intentions, all in the name of preserving the correct definition of a remainder. Today, the destructibility rule has largely vanished. Since the grantor could have accomplished the same result by creating an executory interest, courts treat a contingent remainder that does not become possessory upon the natural termination of the previous estate as if it were an executory interest. All states with clear law on the point, except Florida, have abolished the rule, although in a handful of additional states there are older precedents accepting the rule that have not been expressly overruled. In any event, since the doctrine never applied to equitable interests in trusts, and most contingent remainders today are created in trusts, the rule has little effect even in the rare state where it might be enforced.

E.   CO-OWNERSHIP AND MEDIATING CONFLICTS BETWEEN CO-OWNERS

There are many reasons for multiple people to wish to be co-owners, involving various types of multiple use and relationships based on sharing. But conflicts among co-owners can arise for a variety of reasons. The effects of the use by each co-owner are only partially internalized to that owner. That is why in many situations co-owners need some governance scheme, such as a contract or, more usually, a set of norms of proper use, to regulate their use and care of the property. In addition to these norms, the law itself sometimes provides off-the-rack solutions to the problems facing co-owners. These legal solutions tend to take two forms. One is to afford co-owners exit from the relationship; this is achieved primarily by the action for partition. The other is more detailed governance rules. These rules tend not to be as finegrained as the contractual and norm-based rules that co-owners devise for themselves, and the law's off-the-rack regime tends to protect co-owners mainly in situations of exit. In many American jurisdictions, holders of concurrent interests are not entitled to equitable remedies, and co-owners in some jurisdictions are not entitled to any remedy other than an accounting in a partition. 8 Thompson on Real Property § 70.09(h) (1994); 8 Powell on Real Property ch. 56 ¶ 643 (1998).

CONCURRENT AND MARITAL ESTATES

Property can be divided and shared among multiple simultaneous owners. This gives rise to divisions in two dimensions: "horizontal" divisions over time and "vertical" divisions at any given moment in time. The two types of division can be combined: Each of the estates in land defined in terms of temporal duration—fee simple, life estate, remainder, etc.—can also be divided among concurrent owners. Thus, one can create concurrent ownership in a fee simple, concurrent life estates (lasting until the last life tenant dies), and concurrent remainders or executory interests.

Some forms of co-ownership shade off into entity law, considered in Chapter VI. At one time, property could be owned by tenancy in partnership, in which the legal title to property was concurrently held by each of the partners. Today, most states provide by statute that the partnership as an entity holds title to the property, much the way corporations as entities hold title to property. Under this entity theory, there is only one owner of the property—the entity (partnership or corporation)—and issues about who manages and controls the property are resolved as a matter of partnership or corporation law, not property law. Nevertheless, keep in mind that forming a trust, partnership, or corporation is an alternative to the co-ownership arrangements considered here. For example, if A, B, and C want to share ownership of a summer cottage, they could either hold title to the cottage as concurrent owners, or they could form a partnership or corporation which would then hold title to the cottage.

The main forms of co-ownership today are the tenancy in common and the joint tenancy. Some states also have an older marital property arrangement, called the tenancy by the entirety, which is like the joint tenancy but more durable. All of the arrangements involve an equal right to possess whenever the interest in question is possessory. Not surprisingly and as we will see, this can lead to conflict.

Tenancy in Common. Each tenant in common has a separate but undivided interest. Each interest is *separate*, in the sense that it is independently descendible, conveyable, and devisable. Since either tenant can unilaterally convey her interest to a third party, property held as tenancy in common can be attached by creditors of each individual tenant. And since each share is independently descendible, there is no right of survivorship (as there would be in a joint tenancy, to which we turn next); the share of each tenant in common passes on death as part of his or her separate estate. Yet each interest in *undivided*, in the sense that each tenant in common has the right to possess the whole of the property (although they need not exercise that right). Moreover, there is no requirement that each cotenant hold an equal share. One can create a tenancy in common in which A owns a 60 percent interest, B a 30 percent interest, and C a 10 percent interest. Each tenant in such a tenancy in common has an equal right to possess the whole, but their respective share of rents or profits (or their respective obligations to contribute to the payment of taxes or mortgage obligations) will be determined by their respective percentage ownership.

Joint Tenancy. The joint tenancy is exactly like the tenancy in common, except for the treatment of survivorship. As in the tenancy in common, each joint tenant has a separate and undivided interest. Because the interest is undivided, each joint tenant has the right to possess the whole. The principal difference is that in a joint tenancy, a surviving joint tenant automatically acquires the interest of another joint tenant when the other tenant dies. Technically nothing passes; the deceased joint tenant's interest is simply extinguished. The joint tenancy requires four "unities" at the time of creation:

(i) Time. Each interest must be acquired or vest at the same time.

(ii) Title. Each must acquire title by the same instrument or by joint adverse possession, never by intestate succession or other act of law.

(iii) Interest. Each must have the same legal interest in the property, such as fee simple, life estate, lease, etc., although not necessarily identical fractional shares.

(iv) Possession. Each must have the *right* to possess the whole.

By contrast, the only unity required to create a tenancy in common is that of possession.

Traditionally, if any of the first three unities is destroyed in a joint tenancy, then we say the joint tenancy is severed and a tenancy in common is created. Each joint tenant has the power unilaterally to transfer his or her interest while they are living, and thus each may have his or her interest attached by creditors. When such a transfer or attachment occurs, this may have the effect of severing the unities (which ones?) and may convert the joint tenancy into a tenancy in common. In this sense, a joint tenancy comes with a partial exit right (through the possibility of severance), to supplement the more radical break up that can be achieved through partition. (For more on severance, see *Harms v. Sprague*, infra.) The joint tenancy is only appropriate for an intimate relationship such as a committed relationship or family business.

Tenancy by the Entirety. Only a minority of states have retained the tenancy by the entirety, which is only available for married couples. Like the tenancy in common and the joint tenancy, each co-owner has a separate and undivided interest, and each has the right to possession of the whole. Like the joint tenancy, there is a right of survivorship. But in some states that recognize the tenancy by the entirety, neither spouse can unilaterally transfer or encumber their share of the property without the consent of the other. See United States v. Craft, 535 U.S. 274 (2002) (discussing the law of one such state, Michigan, but declining to insulate property held in tenancy by the entirety from federal taxes owed by one spouse). In all states that recognize this tenancy, there is no *unilateral* exit option as long as the couple stays married. Both spouses can convey to a third person (a "straw") and then have the straw convey back to them as tenants in common, but neither spouse acting on his or her own can sever the tenancy, other than by getting a divorce. Thus, to the four unities required by the joint tenancy, a fifth, marriage, is added.

How do we know which type of concurrent tenancy is created when multiple persons acquire title to property, as when O conveys Blackacre "to

A and B" or when O devises Blackacre by will "to my Children, C, D, and F"? At common law, a joint tenancy was presumed in any conveyance that satisfied the four unities (time, title, interest, and possession). A tenancy by the entirety was presumed in any conveyance that satisfied the five unities (time, title, interest, possession, and marriage). Today, a tenancy in common is generally presumed unless there is some other manifestation of intent to create a joint tenancy or a tenancy by the entirety. Thus, if O conveys "to A and B" this will generally be presumed to be a tenancy in common. O would have to say something like "to and B as joint tenants with right of survivorship and not as tenants in common" to be sure to create a joint tenancy. Similarly one would have to specify "to A and B as tenants by the entirety" (and A and B would have to be married) to create a tenancy by the entirety. Nevertheless, some courts still presume a joint tenancy is intended in the case of an ambiguous transfer to a married couple, and some courts in some states that recognize the tenancy by the entirety will presume that this is intended in the case of an ambiguous transfer to a married couple, at least for interests in land.

How do potential co-owners choose which arrangement suits them best? Many factors may influence this decision. First, the survivorship feature in the joint tenancy or the tenancy by the entirety allows a remaining owner to avoid probate (which is costly, cumbersome, and time-consuming). The survivor can sell the property immediately if he or she so chooses. Second, depending on the rules in place in a given state, the joint tenancy (and even more so the tenancy by the entirety) may afford some protection of jointly owned assets from creditors of one of the co-owners. Finally, tax considerations may come into play. However, in the federal income tax, joint filing by married couples often but not always makes the form of ownership irrelevant for income tax purposes.

As we will see, the types of concurrent ownership arrangements are limited in number and have many mandatory features. Nevertheless, concurrent ownership has become somewhat more customizable in recent times. See, e.g., Jezo v. Jezo, 127 N.W.2d 246 (Wis. 1964) (holding that the presumption that joint tenants own equal shares is subject to rebuttal by evidence of contrary intent). Also, to the extent that partnership and other entity forms are a substitute for direct concurrent ownership of assets, it is worth noting that entity forms have a greater and increasing degree of customizability relative to the traditional forms of concurrent ownership.

Community Property. Some states of the South and West, especially those that have some Spanish or French law in their early histories, have community property for married couples. Under community property, all property acquired during the marriage (except in some states for gifts and bequests to one spouse) automatically becomes community property. Each spouse has a right to possess community property, but typically any alienation or encumbrance must have the consent of both spouses. Couples can transmute property from separate property to community property and vice versa, but there are often strong presumptions and formalities to overcome in order to prove that what would otherwise be community property is separate. Also, property acquired before the marriage is theoretically separate but may become community property through commingling with community property. On divorce, a spouse arguing that property is separate has the burden of proof and must be able to trace the property, i.e., to document its separate existence from community property, through time and possibly various transactions. Until recently, the community property system gave the husband sole management and control of the property during marriage. Now both spouses have such rights, and for certain important transactions to be valid both spouses must consent. This system never considered the wife's legal personality to merge with that of the husband, as was the case at common law (but not in equity). On divorce, community property is subject to equal division. We return below to the problem of defining property for purposes of division on divorce in the common-law (i.e., non-community-property) states.

1.   PARTITION

Partition is the most important legal remedy available to concurrent owners. Any cotenant can sue for partition for any reason or no reason at all, and the court will grant the request without further inquiry into the justness or reasonableness of the request. This in effect gives each cotenant an automatic right to terminate the cotenancy at any time. Partition is available to tenants in common and joint tenants. Tenants by the entirety must either convert the property into a tenancy in common or joint tenancy by mutual agreement, or sever the unity of marriage (by divorce), in order to obtain partition.

Delfino v. Vealencis

Supreme Court of Connecticut, 1980.
436 A.2d 27.

■ ARTHUR H. HEALEY, ASSOCIATE JUSTICE. The central issue in this appeal is whether the Superior Court properly ordered the sale, pursuant to General Statutes § 52–500,[1] of property owned by the plaintiffs and the defendant as tenants in common.

---

1.   General Statutes § 52–500 states:

Sale of Real or Personal Property Owned by Two or More. Any court of equitable jurisdiction may, upon the complaint of any person interested, order the sale of any estate, real or personal, owned by two or more persons, when, in the opinion of the court, a sale will better promote the interests of the owners. The provisions of this section shall extend to and include land owned by two or more persons, when the whole or a part of such land is vested in any person for life with remainder to his heirs, general or special, or, on failure of such heirs, to any other person, whether the same, or any part thereof, is held in trust or otherwise. A conveyance made in pursuance of a decree ordering a sale of such land shall vest the title in the purchaser thereof, and shall bind the person entitled to the life estate and his legal heirs and any other person having a remainder interest in the lands; but the court passing such decree shall make such order in relation to the investment of the avails of such sale as it deems necessary for the

The plaintiffs, Angelo and William Delfino, and the defendant, Helen C. Vealencis, own, as tenants in common, real property located in Bristol, Connecticut. The property consists of an approximately 20.5 acre parcel of land and the dwelling of the defendant thereon. The plaintiffs own an undivided 99/144 interest in the property, and the defendant owns a 45/144 interest. The defendant occupies the dwelling and a portion of the land, from which she operates a rubbish and garbage removal business.[3] Apparently, none of the parties is in actual possession of the remainder of the property. The plaintiffs, one of whom is a residential developer, propose to develop the property, upon partition, into forty-five residential building lots.

In 1978, the plaintiffs brought an action in the trial court seeking a partition of the property by sale with a division of the proceeds according to the parties' respective interests. The defendant moved for a judgment of in-kind partition[5] and the appointment of a committee to conduct said partition. The trial court, after a hearing, concluded that a partition in kind could not be had without "material injury" to the respective rights of the parties, and therefore ordered that the property be sold at auction by a committee and that the proceeds be paid into the court for distribution to the parties.

On appeal, the defendant claims essentially that the trial court's conclusion that the parties' interests would best be served by a partition by sale is not supported by the findings of subordinate facts, and that the court improperly considered certain factors in arriving at that conclusion. In addition, the defendant directs a claim of error to the court's failure to include in its findings of fact a paragraph of her draft findings.

General Statutes § 52–495 authorizes courts of equitable jurisdiction to order, upon the complaint of any interested person, the physical partition of any real estate held by tenants in common, and to appoint a committee for that purpose.[7] When, however, in the opinion of the court a sale of the jointly owned property "will better promote the interests of the owners," the court may order such a sale under § 52–500. See Kaiser v.

security of all persons having any interest in such land.

3. The defendant's business functions on the property consist of the overnight parking, repair and storage of trucks, including refuse trucks, the repair, storage and cleaning of dumpsters, the storage of tools, and general office work. No refuse is actually deposited on the property.

5. Such a partition is authorized by General Statutes § 52–495 which states:

Partition of Joint and Common Estates. Courts having jurisdiction of actions for equitable relief may, upon the complaint of any person interested, order partition of any real estate held in joint tenancy, tenancy in common or coparcenary, and may appoint a committee for that purpose, and may in like manner make partition of any real estate held by tenants in tail; and decrees aparting entailed estates shall bind the parties and all persons who thereafter claim title to such estate as heirs of their bodies.

7. If the physical partition results in unequal shares, a money award can be made from one tenant to another to equalize the shares. 4A Powell, Real Property ¶ 612, pp. 653–54; 2 American Law of Property, Partition § 6.26, p. 113.

Second National Bank, 193 A. 761, 764 (Conn. 1937); Johnson v. Olmsted, 49 Conn. 509, 517 (1882).

It has long been the policy of this court, as well as other courts, to favor a partition in kind over a partition by sale. The first Connecticut statute that provided for an absolute right to partition by physical division was enacted in 1720; Statutes, 1796, p. 258; the substance of which remains virtually unchanged today. Due to the possible impracticality of actual division, this state, like others, expanded the right to partition to allow a partition by sale under certain circumstances. See Penfield v. Jarvis, 399 A.2d 1280, 1283 (Conn. 1978); see also Restatement, 2 Property c. 11, pp. 658–61. The early decisions of this court that considered the partition-by-sale statute emphasized that "[t]he statute giving the power of sale introduces ... no new principles; it provides only for an emergency, when a division cannot be well made, in any other way. The Earl of Clarendon v. Hornby, 1 P.Wms., 446.4 Kent's Com., 365." Richardson v. Monson, 23 Conn. 94, 97 (1854). The court later expressed its reason for preferring partition in kind when it stated: "[A] sale of one's property without his consent is an extreme exercise of power warranted only in clear cases." Ford v. Kirk, 41 Conn. 9, 12 (1874). Although under General Statutes § 52–500 a court is no longer required to order a partition in kind even in cases of extreme difficulty or hardship; see Scovil v. Kennedy, 14 Conn. 349, 360–61 (1841); it is clear that a partition by sale should be ordered only when two conditions are satisfied: (1) the physical attributes of the land are such that a partition in kind is impracticable or inequitable; Johnson v. Olmsted, supra; and (2) the interests of the owners would better be promoted by a partition by sale. Kaiser v. Second National Bank, supra; see Gold v. Rosenfeld, Conn. (41 Conn.L.J., No. 4, p. 18) (1979). Since our law has for many years presumed that a partition in kind would be in the best interests of the owners, the burden is on the party requesting a partition by sale to demonstrate that such a sale would better promote the owners' interests.

RULE

The defendant claims in effect that the trial court's conclusion that the rights of the parties would best be promoted by a judicial sale is not supported by the findings of subordinate facts. We agree.

Under the test set out above, the court must first consider the practicability of physically partitioning the property in question. The trial court concluded that due to the situation and location of the parcel of land, the size and area of the property, the physical structure and appurtenances on the property, and other factors,[11] a physical partition of the property would not be feasible. An examination of the subordinate findings of facts and the exhibits, however, demonstrates that the court erred in this respect.

11. These other factors included the present use and the expected continued use by the defendant of the property, the property's zoning classification, and the plaintiffs' proposed subdivision plans. We consider these factors later in the opinion.

It is undisputed that the property in question consists of one 20.5 acre parcel, basically rectangular in shape, and one dwelling, located at the extreme western end of the property. Two roads, Dino Road and Lucien Court, abut the property and another, Birch Street, provides access through use of a right-of-way. Unlike cases where there are numerous fractional owners of the property to be partitioned, and the practicability of a physical division is therefore drastically reduced * * * in this case there are only two competing ownership interests: the plaintiffs' undivided 99/144 interest and the defendant's 45/144 interest. These facts, taken together, do not support the trial court's conclusion that a physical partition of the property would not be "feasible" in this case. Instead, the above facts demonstrate that the opposite is true: a partition in kind clearly would be practicable under the circumstances of this case.

Although a partition in kind is physically practicable, it remains to be considered whether a partition in kind would also promote the best interests of the parties. In order to resolve this issue, the consequences of a partition in kind must be compared with those of a partition by sale.

The trial court concluded that a partition in kind could not be had without great prejudice to the parties since the continuation of the defendant's business would hinder or preclude the development of the plaintiffs' parcel for residential purposes, which the trial court concluded was the highest and best use of the property. The court's concern over the possible adverse economic effect upon the plaintiffs' interest in the event of a partition in kind was based essentially on four findings: (1) approval by the city planning commission for subdivision of the parcel would be difficult to obtain if the defendant continued her garbage hauling business; (2) lots in a residential subdivision might not sell, or might sell at a lower price, if the defendant's business continued; (3) if the defendant were granted the one-acre parcel, on which her residence is situated and on which her business now operates, three of the lots proposed in the plaintiffs' plan to subdivide the property would have to be consolidated and would be lost; and (4) the proposed extension of one of the neighboring roads would have to be rerouted through one of the proposed building lots if a partition in kind were ordered. The trial court also found that the defendant's use of the portion of the property that she occupies is in violation of existing zoning regulations. The court presumably inferred from this finding that it is not likely that the defendant will be able to continue her rubbish hauling operations from this property in the future. The court also premised its forecast that the planning commission would reject the plaintiffs' subdivision plan for the remainder of the property on the finding that the defendant's use was invalid. These factors basically led the trial court to conclude that the interests of the parties would best be protected if the land were sold as a unified unit for residential subdivision development and the proceeds of such a sale were distributed to the parties. * * *

[A]ny inference that the defendant would probably be unable to continue her rubbish hauling activity on the property in the future is unfounded. We also conclude that the court erred in concluding that the city's planning

Possible Future actions of public bodies are generally not a strong factor

commission would probably not approve a subdivision plan relating to the remainder of the property. Any such forecast must be carefully scrutinized as it is difficult to project what a public body will decide in any given matter. See Rushchak v. West Haven, 356 A.2d 104, 107 (Conn. 1975). In this case, there was no substantial evidence to support a conclusion that it was reasonably probable that the planning commission would not approve a subdivision plan for the remainder of the property. Cf. Budney v. Ives, 239 A.2d 482, 485 (Conn. 1968). Moreover, there is no suggestion in the statute relating to subdivision approval; see General Statutes § 8–25; that the undeveloped portion of the parcel in issue, which is located in a residential neighborhood, could not be the subject of an approved subdivision plan notwithstanding the nearby operation of the defendant's business. The court's finding indicates that only garbage trucks and dumpsters are stored on the property; that no garbage is brought there; and that the defendant's business operations involve "mostly containerized ... dumpsters, a contemporary development in technology which has substantially reduced the odors previously associated with the rubbish and garbage hauling industry." These facts do not support the court's speculation that the city's planning commission would not approve a subdivision permit for the undeveloped portion of the parties' property.

The court's remaining observations relating to the effect of the defendant's business on the probable fair market value of the proposed residential lots, the possible loss of building lots to accommodate the defendant's business and the rerouting of a proposed subdivision road, which may have some validity, are not dispositive of the issue. It is the interests of all of the tenants in common that the court must consider; see Lyon v. Wilcox, 119 A. 361, 362–63 (Conn. 1923); 59 Am.Jur.2d, Partition § 118, p. 865; and not merely the economic gain of one tenant, or a group of tenants. The trial court failed to give due consideration to the fact that one of the tenants in common has been in actual and exclusive possession of a portion of the property for a substantial period of time; that the tenant has made her home on the property; and that she derives her livelihood from the operation of a business on this portion of the property, as her family before her has for many years. A partition by sale would force the defendant to surrender her home and, perhaps, would jeopardize her livelihood. It is under just such circumstances, which include the demonstrated practicability of a physical division of the property, that the wisdom of the law's preference for partition in kind is evident.

As this court has many times stated, conclusions that violate "law, logic or reason or are inconsistent with the subordinate facts" cannot stand. Russo v. East Hartford, 425 A.2d 1282, 1284 (Conn. 1979); Connecticut Coke Co. v. New Haven, 364 A.2d 178, 185 (Conn. 1975). Since the property in this case may practicably be physically divided, and since the interests of all owners will better be promoted if a partition in kind is ordered, we conclude that the trial court erred in ordering a partition by sale, and that, under the facts as found, the defendant is entitled to a partition of the property in kind.

There is error, the judgment is set aside and the case is remanded for further proceedings not inconsistent with this opinion.

Figure 5–10
Plat Showing Land at Issue in *Delfino v. Vealencis*

MAP 1. SUBDIVISION PLOT PLAN FOR THE 20.5 ACRE PARCEL

Source: Manel Baucells & Steven A. Lippman, Justice Delayed is Justice Denied: A Cooperative Game Theoretic Analysis of Hold–Up in Co–Ownership, 22 Cardozo L. Rev. 1191, 1222 (2001).

NOTES AND QUESTIONS

1. On remand, the court awarded Helen Vealencis approximately one acre, including the family homestead and dumpster operation, in the middle of the west end of the 20.5 acre plot (see Figure 5–10). The brothers were awarded the rest of the land, which they sold to a developer for $725,000, laid out in a plat of 42 lots. Based on this price, the market value

of the land awarded to Helen was about $72,000. Helen's acreage was separated from the new subdivision by a two-foot strip of land, running from lot 39 down to lot 40, which deprived her of any access to Dino Road in the subdivision. (Her only public access was to Birch Road, via an easement over lot 9C.) In addition, the court required Helen to make a payment of $26,000 to the brothers to compensate them for the adverse effect of the garbage dumpster operation on the value of subdivision. (Such a payment to correct imbalances in a partition in kind is called _owelty_.) So the final value of the award to Helen, in monetary terms, was $46,000; the brothers got $362,500 each. See Manel Baucells & Steven A. Lippman, Justice Delayed is Justice Denied: A Cooperative Game Theoretic Analysis of Hold–Up in Co–Ownership, 22 Cardozo L. Rev. 1191, 1220–43 (2001). Did the trial judge (who had originally ordered a partition sale, only to be reversed by the Connecticut Supreme Court) treat Helen fairly? Would she have been better off capitulating to the brothers at the outset and foregoing litigation?

Owelty – payment to balance out the court-determined equitable partitions

→ WTF!? NO!

2. Take a close look at the two-part test under Connecticut law for partition by sale (impracticability/inequitableness _and_ better promotion of the owners' interests). Once the court had satisfied itself that physical partition was practicable, why did it need to consider whether partition by sale would promote the best interests of the parties?

3. In theory, one co-owner can always buy out the other co-owners. What types of transaction costs are likely to impede some such sales? Why do you think bargaining broke down in _Delfino_, despite the surplus on the table?

4. Not all courts are as seemingly protective of the subjective value of one co-owner as the Connecticut Supreme Court in _Delfino_. Compare Johnson v. Hendrickson, 24 N.W.2d 914 (S.D. 1946) (ordering partition by sale despite some cotenants having a homestead on part of the property and a farm across the road from the homestead). Despite the traditional preference for partition in kind, courts have increasingly favored partition by sale. In a partition in kind, courts will try if possible to allow a cotenant living on the parcel to keep the portion on which she lives. See, e.g., Anderson v. Anderson, 560 N.W.2d 729 (Minn. Ct. App. 1997).

5. Partition affords each co-owner an avenue for _exit_, and the threat of exit can help a co-owner protect her interests. Her dealings with the co-owners occur under the shadow of the exit option. Another strategy for exercising leverage without exit is _voice_, expressing dissatisfaction and agitating for change within the group or organization. See Albert O. Hirschman, Exit, Voice, and Loyalty: Responses to Decline in Firms, Organizations and States (1970). A third strategy identified by Hirschman, _loyalty_, leads participants to avoid leaving and to leave quietly when they do. Hirschman explores the complex relationship between exit, voice, and loyalty and the circumstances under which each has advantages and where the two strategies of exit and voice reinforce or undermine each other. Exit places at least one co-owner on the "outside" of the property along with other dutyholders who must respect the exclusion rights of the owner.

3 Strategies for Exercising Leverage
1) Exit
2) Voice
3) Loyalty

Voice can be exercised in more or less formal ways within the structure of governance rules over uses of the resource. In the next chapter we take up condominiums and cooperatives, where these mechanisms are often explicitly incorporated into the bylaws of the relevant community. The notions of exit and voice have been applied to a wide range of public, commercial, and private organizations and groups.

6.   Partition by sale can cause a cash-strapped co-owner to lose subjective value. This is particularly likely in cases in which one of the co-owners is actually living on the property. Some have argued that the law of partition is to blame for the decline in African–American farming since the late nineteenth century, because African–Americans were less likely to have wills and land ownership passing by intestacy became fragmented among an ever-increasing number of descendants of the original owner. From 1920 to 1978, the number of farms operated by African–Americans declined 94%, from 925,710 to 57,271 (in the same period farms operated by Whites declined 56%, from about 5.4 million to about 2.4 million). U.S. Comm'n on Civil Rights, The Decline of Black Farming in America 2–3 (1982). For discussion see, e.g., John G. Casagrande Jr., Acquiring Property Through Forced Partitioning Sales: Abuses And Remedies, 27 B.C. L. Rev. 755 (1986); Thomas W. Mitchell, From Reconstruction to Deconstruction: Undermining Black Landownership, Political Independence, and Community Through Partition Sales of Tenancies in Common, 95 Nw. U. L. Rev. 505 (2001); see also Hanoch Dagan & Michael A. Heller, The Liberal Commons, 110 Yale L.J. 549, 602–09 (2001) (presenting partition sales involving African–American farmers as an example to suggest problems with partition). Other possible causes operating at various times include Jim Crow era discrimination in land markets for prime parcels, unequal access to credit and other government programs, and the general decline of the family farm (the latter assisted by agricultural subsidies and other programs favoring large farms). Pigford v. Glickman, 185 F.R.D. 82 (D.D.C. 1999) (approving proposed consent decree in class action brought by African–American farmers against U.S. Department of Agriculture for racial discrimination in violation of the Equal Credit Opportunity Act and discussing history of discrimination against African–American farmers in government agricultural programs); Loren Schweninger, Black Property Owners in the South, 1790–1915, at 143–84 (1990); Robert Higgs, Accumulation of Property by Southern Blacks Before World War I, 72 Am. Econ. Rev. 725, 728 (1982) (presenting econometric evidence of impact of public sector discrimination on black property ownership in Georgia).

7.   Would co-owners be better off if exit options were more limited? Some commentators have argued for an approach more like that in civil-law countries, which permit a greater degree of judicial intervention into co-owner relations, with a corresponding de-emphasis on easy partition; this, it has been suggested, might foster more communitarian relations. See Dagan & Heller, supra. But note that cotenants can agree by contract not to partition or can agree to limit the reasons for partition. Such contracts will be enforced, provided they are not an unreasonable restraint on alienation. See, e.g., Michalski v. Michalski, 142 A.2d 645 (N.J. Super. Ct.

App. Div. 1958). Also, those who want to provide for a more tailored relationship can form a partnership or a corporation to own the property, with provisions structuring their use of the property incorporated into the partnership agreement or the bylaws of the corporation. Do these sources of flexibility suggest that there is no need to modify the automatic exit right given by the common law?

2.   Contribution and Accounting

The law does provide some limited regulations of inputs and outputs as between co-owners. The degree to which courts will get involved is low when the parties continue in an ongoing relationship, but increases when one party seeks partition, or, as in the following case, when one party has "ousted" the other from possession.

Gillmor v. Gillmor

Supreme Court of Utah, 1984.
694 P.2d 1037.

■ Stewart, Justice: The defendant Edward Leslie Gillmor appeals from a $29,760 judgment awarded to Florence Gillmor, a cotenant, because defendant obstructed her from exercising her right to occupy land in which she owned an undivided interest with the defendant and C. Frank Gillmor. The property is made up of several large parcels amounting to some 33,000 acres located in Summit, Tooele, and Salt Lake counties.

Two brothers, the parties' fathers, Frank and Edward Lincoln Gillmor, had owned the land and used it for their ranching business. Upon the death of Frank Gillmor, his one-half interest in the property passed in equal shares to his sons, the defendant and C. Frank Gillmor. Edward Lincoln Gillmor continued the ranching business, and for several years grazed cattle and sheep on portions of the common properties. Upon the death of Edward Lincoln Gillmor, his one-half interest passed to his daughter, the plaintiff Florence Gillmor, and she, C. Frank, and the defendant became tenants in common.

In May 1979, the plaintiff filed the instant suit for an accounting and damages for the defendant's exclusive use of the property since January 1, 1979. She also filed a separate suit for partition of the common properties.

The trial was divided into two phases to determine first the damages from January 1, 1979, to May 31, 1980, and second the damages from June 1, 1980, to December 31, 1980. The trial court held that from January 1, 1979, to May 31, 1980, the defendant had grazed livestock on the common properties in such a manner as to constitute exclusive use of the properties and thereby exclude the plaintiff from grazing her livestock on those properties. The trial court awarded a $21,544.91 judgment for one-half the rental value of the properties in favor of Florence Gillmor and against defendant. Defendant did not appeal that decision.

In the second phase of the trial, the trial court found that "[b]etween June 1, 1980 and December 31, 1980, defendant Edward Gillmor continued to graze his sheep and cattle on the common properties in Salt Lake and Summit counties or to use said lands to produce feed for his cattle and sheep, and such use ... was to the exclusion of the plaintiff."

On appeal, the defendant argues with respect to the second judgment (1) that "there is no evidence or finding on the issue of ouster," and (2) that even if there were an ouster, the damages are excessive.

I.

RULE

The law is that a cotenant may sue for his share of rents and profits from common property if he has been ousted from possession of the common property. Roberts v. Roberts, 584 P.2d 378, 380 (Utah 1978). The defendant argues that the trial court did not find that the defendant ousted the plaintiff. The trial court did not specifically use that term in its findings of fact and conclusions of law, but it did find that the defendant had both exercised exclusive use and possession and had also excluded the plaintiff from use of the common properties.

Mere exclusive use of commonly held properties by one cotenant is not sufficient to establish an ouster. A tenant in common has the right to use and occupy the entire property held in cotenancy without liability to other cotenants. Each cotenant has the right to "free and unobstructed possession ... without liability for rents for the use and occupation thereof." Utah Oil Refining Co. v. Leigh, 96 P.2d 1100, 1102 (Utah 1939).

That one cotenant is not liable to his cotenant for rents for the occupancy of the common property is elemental. And this is true even though [the cotenant] uses it and derives income therefrom, as where he occupies ... or farms a piece and takes the crops; or uses it for storage purposes; as long as he does not interfere with the cotenant's right to likewise occupy, use and enjoy.

96 P.2d at 1103 (citations omitted).

However, a cotenant who ousts another cotenant or acts in such a fashion as to necessarily exclude a fellow cotenant, violates the rights of that cotenant. Roberts v. Roberts, 584 P.2d at 380; Utah Oil Refining v. Leigh, 96 P.2d at 1103. To establish a right to share in the rents and profits from the common property, it must be established that a cotenant has used the property so as to "necessarily exclude his cotenant." Utah Oil Refining Co., 96 P.2d at 1103.

Exclusive Use
1) Act of Exclusion, or
2) Use of a nature That necessarily excludes cotenant

Exclusive use means more than one cotenant using the entire property; it requires either an act of exclusion or use of such a nature that it necessarily prevents another cotenant from exercising his rights in the property.[2] Roberts v. Roberts, 584 P.2d at 380–81; Utah Oil Refinery Co. v. Leigh, 96 P.2d at 1103. * * *

---

2. It follows that the burden to establish ouster in a suit to recover rents and profits is less stringent than the burden to establish ouster in an adverse possession ac-

TAKE NOTE

The defendant contends that the trial court erred in finding that the defendant had exercised exclusive possession and use of the common properties in such a manner as to exclude the plaintiff from using the land. We disagree. The plaintiff sought to graze livestock on the land to the extent of her interest, but was effectively prevented from doing so. She sent defendant a letter expressing her intent to graze her livestock on the properties in proportion to her ownership and requested that the defendant accommodate her plans by altering his operations accordingly. The defendant refused to respond and continued to graze the lands to their maximum capacity. He even acknowledged that additional grazing would have damaged the range land. The defendant asserts that at various times he or his attorney invited the plaintiff onto the lands, but he never indicated any intention to alter his operations so as to accommodate the plaintiff's use of the land. Had the plaintiff grazed her livestock on the common properties while defendant's livestock was also there, the land would have been overgrazed. Indeed, the defendant admitted that if the plaintiff had attempted to put additional sheep on the land, he would have sought an injunction to prevent damage to the land.

We hold that when a cotenant out of possession makes a clear, unequivocal demand to use land that is in the exclusive possession of another cotenant, and that cotenant refuses to accommodate the other tenant's right to use the land, the tenant out of possession has established a claim for relief. It is not necessary that the out-of-possession cotenant resort to force or to means that would damage the common property to establish a right to legal redress.

]RULE

II.

The defendant argues that the damage award of $29,760 for seven months of grazing is excessive when contrasted with the award of $21,544.91 in the first phase of trial for seventeen months of grazing. * * * [The court goes on to uphold the damages award.]

The defendant also argues that the damages should not have been awarded for the time when he herded his livestock from one parcel of Gillmor land to another over land owned by a third party pursuant to trail or trespass rights, which include grazing along the way. See generally Anderson v. Osguthorpe, 504 P.2d 1000 (Utah 1972). Since the trail rights are appurtenant to the Gillmor land, there is no sound reason for distinguishing between them and the rights to the fee land. * * *

The defendant also argues that he is entitled to an offset for repairs made on the common property. Sometime after June 1, 1980, he repaired a range fence and a ditch on the common property. He asserts that the fence repairs directly benefited the plaintiff because she now owns land which borders the fence.

tion. Massey v. Prothero, 664 P.2d 1176 (Utah 1983); Olwell v. Clark, 658 P.2d 585 (Utah 1982); Memmott v. Bosh, 520 P.2d 1342 (Utah 1974); Holbrook v. Carter, 431 P.2d 123 (Utah 1967).

RULE

Where a cotenant in sole possession makes repairs or improvements to the common property without the consent of his fellow cotenants, he generally has no right of contribution. In *Heiselt v. Heiselt*, 349 P.2d 175, 178–79 (Utah 1960) (quoting 14 Am.Jur. Cotenancy § 49 at 115 (1938)), we stated:

> While contrary doctrines have been enunciated and the question is conceded to be one of great difficulty, it appears to be generally agreed that a cotenant who has made improvements upon the common property without the assent of his cotenants is not ordinarily entitled to contribution and cannot, as a matter of right, charge them with the value or costs thereof or maintain any action that would result in a personal judgment against them. * * * Compensation for improvements is allowed, however, where the other cotenants have stood by and permitted him to proceed to his detriment.

Exceptions to rule →

A cotenant may, however, be required to contribute his pro rata share of expenses if the cotenant in possession acted in good faith, with the bona fide belief that he was the sole owner of the property, or when the repairs were essential to preserve or protect the common estate. See *Zanzonico v. Zanzonico*, 2 A.2d 597 (N.J. Eq. 1938); 20 Am.Jur.2d Cotenancy and Joint Ownership § 62 (1965). Furthermore, where, as here, a cotenant out of possession seeks an accounting or damages, the cotenant in possession, who is held liable for the value of the use, occupancy, or rents collected, is entitled to recover reasonable expenditures made by him for necessary repairs and maintenance.[4] * * *

RULE

In the instant case, the evidence indicates that the repairs were a necessary cost of grazing the livestock and should have been deducted from the damages awarded. The case must therefore be remanded for a modification of the judgment. * * *

NOTES AND QUESTIONS

1. The right of a cotenant to obtain rental payments from another cotenant depends critically on whether the rental payments are based on a rental to a third party or are based on the rental value of the possession to an occupying cotenant. If one cotenant rents to a third party, then the renting cotenant is obliged to share the payments with other cotenants. In these circumstances the non-renting cotenant can bring an action for an accounting, and the court will apportion the rents in accordance with ownership shares. In contrast, there is in general no obligation for one cotenant to pay rent to other cotenants for the value of their possession. The exception is where the cotenant out of possession can prove an ouster. As to what constitutes an ouster, the cases are all over the lot. On the variety of approaches courts have taken, see Evelyn Alicia Lewis, Strug-

---

4. For example, cotenants have recovered their cost of painting buildings to make them suitable for sale or renting, Scott v. Staggs, 276 P.2d 605 (Cal. Ct. App. 1954); completing a partially finished house, Todd v. Stewart, 202 N.W. 844 (Iowa 1925); and making miscellaneous house repairs, Fassitt v. Seip, 95 A. 273 (Pa. 1915).

gling with Quicksand: The Ins and Outs of Cotenant Possession Value Liability and a Call for Default Rule Reform, 1994 Wis. L. Rev. 331. Acts of physical exclusion from the whole property are sufficient for ouster. But a letter telling a cotenant to vacate or pay rent may or may not be enough. What were the critical facts in *Gillmor* that led the court to find an ouster?

2. The requirement of complete ouster is sometimes "derived" from the unity of possession (each cotenant has a right to use and possess the whole) that is characteristic of the tenancy in common and other co-ownership arrangements. Is there any other reason? Some contracts scholars have invoked the difference between relatively hard-edged norms appropriate for endgame situations, and more accommodating "relationship preserving" norms often based on reciprocal trust. Enforcing relationship-preserving norms in an endgame scenario might undermine them. See Lisa Bernstein, Merchant Law in a Merchant Court: Rethinking the Code's Search for Immanent Business Norms, 144 U. Pa. L. Rev. 1765 (1996). Might something like this be going on here? As long as the relationship is continuing, should courts adjudicate who washes the car or mops the floor?

3. Once there is an ouster, the clock may also start ticking on adverse possession. As mentioned in Note 2 in the *Gillmor* case, the standard for ouster in the context of adverse possession is more stringent than for purposes of contribution and accounting. Illustrative of the difficulties is *McAllister v. Norville*, 514 So.2d 1270 (Ala. 1987), in which 14 boat pilots acquired property along Alabama's Gulf coast in 1872 as tenants in common but with an informal right as amongst themselves to "stake a claim" to a portion of the property and build a house on it. Over 100 years later the successors to the original pilots disputed title to parts of "Pilot Town." In a quiet title action, the trial court found an ouster for purposes of adverse possession, but the Supreme Court of Alabama reversed, holding that because the original pilots had wished to establish a selective community in which each owner would have an undivided one-fourteenth interest, the cotenants' acts of possession were permissive.

4. Whether courts will adjudicate claims by a cotenant for reimbursement from other cotenants also depends on whether the relationship is ongoing or has been terminated. If the relationship is ongoing, a cotenant can sue for contribution for expenditures that are necessary to preserve the property from being taken through forfeiture, such as the payment of property taxes or mortgage payments. But contribution is unlikely to be awarded for repairs and maintenance expenses, and certainly will not be awarded for improvements. When the relationship is at an end, however, either because one cotenant has sued for partition, or as in *Gillmor* one cotenant has proven ouster by another, courts are more willing to consider offsets for repair and maintenance expenses and may even take expenditures for improvements into account. Reimbursement for these expenditures may be reflected either as offsets from imputed rental payments (as in *Gillmor*) or may be awarded as owelty in a partition action.

3. SEVERANCE

The difference between a joint tenancy and tenancy in common is the right of survivorship. But either joint tenant can unilaterally "sever" the joint tenancy, which destroys the right of survivorship and converts the tenancy into a tenancy in common.

What actions lead to a severance? At common law, severance required the destruction of one of the four unities (time, title, interest, and possession). This was usually achieved through a conveyance to a third party (strawman or straw) who would then reconvey to the grantor. These days one can probably convey to oneself and effect a severance of the joint tenancy. Questions also arise as to whether a unilateral lease by one joint tenant, or as in the following case a unilateral mortgage, severs a joint tenancy.

P   D

Harms v. Sprague

Supreme Court of Illinois, 1984.
473 N.E.2d 930.

■ THOMAS J. MORAN, JUSTICE. Plaintiff, William H. Harms, filed a complaint to quiet title and for declaratory judgment in the circuit court of Greene County. Plaintiff had taken title to certain real estate with his brother John R. Harms, as a joint tenant, with full right of survivorship. The plaintiff named, as a defendant, Charles D. Sprague, the executor of the estate of John Harms and the devisee of all the real and personal property of John Harms. Also named as defendants were Carl T. and Mary E. Simmons, alleged mortgagees of the property in question. Defendant Sprague filed a counterclaim against plaintiff, challenging plaintiff's claim of ownership of the entire tract of property and asking the court to recognize his (Sprague's) interest as a tenant in common, subject to a mortgage lien. At issue was the effect the granting of a mortgage by John Harms had on the joint tenancy. Also at issue was whether the mortgage survived the death of John Harms as a lien against the property.

The trial court held that the mortgage given by John Harms to defendants Carl and Mary Simmons severed the joint tenancy. Further, the court found that the mortgage survived the death of John Harms as a lien against the undivided one-half interest in the property which passed to Sprague by and through the will of the deceased. The appellate court reversed, finding that the mortgage given by one joint tenant of his interest in the property does not sever the joint tenancy. Accordingly, the appellate court held that plaintiff, as the surviving joint tenant, owned the property in its entirety, unencumbered by the mortgage lien. * * *

Two issues are raised on appeal: (1) Is a joint tenancy severed when less than all of the joint tenants mortgage their interest in the property? and (2) Does such a mortgage survive the death of the mortgagor as a lien on the property?

A review of the stipulation of facts reveals the following. Plaintiff, William Harms, and his brother John Harms, took title to real estate located in Roodhouse, on June 26, 1973, as joint tenants. The warranty deed memorializing this transaction was recorded on June 29, 1973, in the office of the Greene County recorder of deeds.

Carl and Mary Simmons owned a lot and home in Roodhouse. Charles Sprague entered into an agreement with the Simmons whereby Sprague was to purchase their property for $25,000. Sprague tendered $18,000 in cash and signed a promissory note for the balance of $7,000. Because Sprague had no security for the $7,000, he asked his friend, John Harms, to co-sign the note and give a mortgage on his interest in the joint tenancy property. Harms agreed, and on June 12, 1981, John Harms and Charles Sprague, jointly and severally, executed a promissory note for $7,000 payable to Carl and Mary Simmons. The note states that the principal sum of $7,000 was to be paid from the proceeds of the sale of John Harms' interest in the joint tenancy property, but in any event no later than six months from the date the note was signed. The note reflects that five monthly interest payments had been made, with the last payment recorded November 6, 1981. In addition, John Harms executed a mortgage, in favor of the Simmonses, on his undivided one-half interest in the joint tenancy property, to secure payment of the note. William Harms was unaware of the mortgage given by his brother.

John Harms moved from his joint tenancy property to the Simmons property which had been purchased by Charles Sprague. On December 10, 1981, John Harms died. By the terms of John Harms' will, Charles Sprague was the devisee of his entire estate. The mortgage given by John Harms to the Simmonses was recorded on December 29, 1981.

Prior to the appellate court decision in the instant case no court of this State had directly addressed the principal question we are confronted with herein—the effect of a mortgage, executed by less than all of the joint tenants, on the joint tenancy. Nevertheless, there are numerous cases which have considered the severance issue in relation to other circumstances surrounding a joint tenancy. All have necessarily focused on the four unities which are fundamental to both the creation and the perpetuation of the joint tenancy. These are the unities of interest, title, time, and possession. (Jackson v. O'Connell, 177 N.E.2d 194 (Ill. 1961); Tindall v. Yeats, 64 N.E.2d 903 (Ill. 1946).) The voluntary or involuntary destruction of any of the unities by one of the joint tenants will sever the joint tenancy. Van Antwerp v. Horan, 61 N.E.2d 358 (Ill. 1945).

In a series of cases, this court has considered the effect that judgment liens upon the interest of one joint tenant have on the stability of the joint tenancy. In *Peoples Trust & Savings Bank v. Haas*, 160 N.E. 85 (Ill. 1927), the court found that a judgment lien secured against one joint tenant did not serve to extinguish the joint tenancy. As such, the surviving joint tenant "succeeded to the title in fee to the whole of the land by operation of law." 160 N.E. 85.

Citing to *Haas* for this general proposition, the court in *Van Antwerp v. Horan*, 61 N.E.2d 358 (Ill. 1945), extended the holding in *Haas* to the situation where a levy is made under execution upon the interest of the debtor joint tenant. The court found that the levy was "not such an act as can be said to have the effect of a divestiture of title * * * [so as to destroy the] identity of interest or of any other unity which must occur before * * * the estate of joint tenancy has been severed and destroyed." 61 N.E.2d 358.

In yet another case involving the attachment of a judgment lien upon the interest of a joint tenant, *Jackson v. Lacey*, 97 N.E.2d 839 (Ill. 1951), the court held that the estate of joint tenancy had not been destroyed. As in *Van Antwerp*, the judgment creditor had levied on the interest of the joint tenant debtor. In addition, that interest was sold by the bailiff of the municipal court to the other joint tenant, who died intestate before the time of redemption expired. While the court recognized that a conveyance, even if involuntary, destroys the unity of title and severs the joint tenancy, it held that there would be no conveyance until the redemption period had expired without a redemption. As such, title was not as yet divested and the estate in joint tenancy was unaltered.

Clearly, this court adheres to the rule that a lien on a joint tenant's interest in property will not effectuate a severance of the joint tenancy, absent the conveyance by a deed following the expiration of a redemption period. (See Johnson v. Muntz, 4 N.E.2d 826 (Ill. 1936).) It follows, therefore, that if Illinois perceives a mortgage as merely a lien on the mortgagor's interest in property rather than a conveyance of title from mortgagor to mortgagee, the execution of a mortgage by a joint tenant, on his interest in the property, would not destroy the unity of title and sever the joint tenancy.

Early cases in Illinois, however, followed the title theory of mortgages. In 1900, this court recognized the common law precept that a mortgage was a conveyance of a legal estate vesting title to the property in the mortgagee. (Lightcap v. Bradley, 58 N.E. 221 (Ill. 1900).) Consistent with this title theory of mortgages, therefore, there are many cases which state, in *dicta*, that a joint tenancy is severed by one of the joint tenants mortgaging his interest to a stranger. (Lawler v. Byrne, 96 N.E. 892 (Ill. 1911); Hardin v. Wolf, 148 N.E. 868 (Ill. 1925); Partridge v. Berliner, 156 N.E. 352 (Ill. 1927); Van Antwerp v. Horan, 61 N.E.2d 358 (Ill. 1945); Tindall v. Yeats, 64 N.E.2d 903 (Ill. 1946); Illinois Public Aid Com. v. Stille, 153 N.E.2d 59 (Ill. 1958) (personal property).) Yet even the early case of *Lightcap v. Bradley*, cited above, recognized that the title held by the mortgagee was for the limited purpose of protecting his interests. The court went on to say that "the mortgagor is the owner for every other purpose and against every other person. The title of the mortgagee is anomalous, and exists only between him and the mortgagor * * *." Lightcap v. Bradley, 58 N.E. 221.

Because our cases had early recognized the unique and narrow character of the title that passed to a mortgagee under the common law title theory, it was not a drastic departure when this court expressly characterized the execution of a mortgage as a mere lien in *Kling v. Ghilarducci,* 121 N.E.2d 752 (Ill. 1954). In *Kling,* the court was confronted with the question of when a separation of title, necessary to create an easement by implication, had occurred. The court found that title to the property was not separated with the execution of a trust deed but rather only upon execution and delivery of a master's deed. The court stated:

> In some jurisdictions the execution of a mortgage is a severance, in others, the execution of a mortgage is not a severance. In Illinois the giving of a mortgage is not a separation of title, for the holder of the mortgage takes only a lien thereunder. After foreclosure of a mortgage and until delivery of the master's deed under the foreclosure sale, purchaser acquires no title to the land either legal or equitable. Title to land sold under mortgage foreclosure remains in the mortgagor or his grantee until the expiration of the redemption period and conveyance by the master's deed.

121 N.E.2d 752.

Kling and later cases rejecting the title theory do not involve the severance of joint tenancies. As such, they have not expressly disavowed the *dicta* of joint tenancy cases which have stated that the act of mortgaging by one joint tenant results in the severance of the joint tenancy. We find, however, that implicit in *Kling* and our more recent cases which follow the lien theory of mortgages is the conclusion that a joint tenancy is not severed when one joint tenant executes a mortgage on his interest in the property, since the unity of title has been preserved. As the appellate court in the instant case correctly observed: "If giving a mortgage creates only a lien, then a mortgage should have the same effect on a joint tenancy as a lien created in other ways." Other jurisdictions following the lien theory of mortgages have reached the same result. People v. Nogarr, 330 P.2d 858 (Cal. Ct. App. 1958); D.A.D., Inc. v. Moring, 218 So.2d 451 (Fla. Dist. Ct. App. 1969); American National Bank & Trust Co. v. McGinnis, 571 P.2d 1198 (Okla. 1977); Brant v. Hargrove, 632 P.2d 978 (Ariz. Ct. App. 1981).

A joint tenancy has been defined as "a present estate in all the joint tenants, each being seized of the whole * * *." (Partridge v. Berliner, 156 N.E. 352 (Ill. 1927).) An inherent feature of the estate of joint tenancy is the right of survivorship, which is the right of the last survivor to take the whole of the estate. Because we find that a mortgage given by one joint tenant of his interest in the property does not sever the joint tenancy, we hold that the plaintiff's right of survivorship became operative upon the death of his brother. As such plaintiff is now the sole owner of the estate, in its entirety.

Further, we find that the mortgage executed by John Harms does not survive as a lien on plaintiff's property. A surviving joint tenant succeeds to the share of the deceased joint tenant by virtue of the conveyance which created the joint tenancy, not as the successor of the deceased. The property right of the mortgaging joint tenant is extinguished at the moment of his death. While John Harms was alive, the mortgage existed as a lien on his interest in the joint tenancy. Upon his death, his interest ceased to exist and along with it the lien of the mortgage. Under the circumstances of this case, we would note that the mortgage given by John Harms to the Simmonses was only valid as between the original parties during the lifetime of John Harms since it was unrecorded. (Ill.Rev.Stat. 1981, ch. 30, par. 29; 27 Ill.L. & Prac. Mortgages sec. 65 (1956).) In addition, recording the mortgage subsequent to the death of John Harms was a nullity. As we stated above, John Harms' property rights in the joint tenancy were extinguished when he died. Thus, he no longer had a property interest upon which the mortgage lien could attach.

In their petition to supplement defendant Sprague's petition for leave to appeal, the Simmonses argue that the application of section 20–19 of the Probate Act of 1975 (Ill.Rev.Stat.1981, ch. 110 1/2, par. 20–19) to the facts of this case would mandate a finding that their mortgage on the subject property remains as a valid encumbrance in the hands of the surviving joint tenant. Section 20–19 reads in relevant part:

> (a) When any real estate or leasehold estate in real estate subject to an encumbrance, or any beneficial interest under a trust of real estate or leasehold estate in real estate subject to an encumbrance, is specifically bequeathed or passes by joint tenancy with right of survivorship or by the terms of a trust agreement or other nontestamentary instrument, the legatee, surviving tenant or beneficiary to whom the real estate, leasehold estate or beneficial interest is given or passes, takes it subject to the encumbrance and is not entitled to have the indebtedness paid from other real or personal estate of the decedent.

(Ill.Rev.Stat.1981, ch. 110 1/2, par. 20–19.)

Dicta

While the Simmonses have maintained from the outset that their mortgage followed title to the property, they did not raise the applicability of section 20–19 of the Probate Act of 1975 at the trial level, and thus the issue is deemed waived. Moreover, because we have found that the lien of mortgage no longer exists against the property, section 20–19 is inapplicable, since plaintiff, as the surviving joint tenant, did not take the property subject to an encumbrance.

For the reasons stated herein, the judgment of the appellate court is affirmed.

NOTES AND QUESTIONS

1. If the Simmonses had dealt with both the Harms brothers, then the lien would have been unaffected by John Harms's death. A financial institution would likely require both of the joint tenants to sign, but the Simmonses were not sophisticated lenders. Should the rule be designed to protect informal lending, or should those involved in real estate sales be expected to hire a lawyer? Community property requires both spouses to consent for any alienation or encumbrance of land held as community property. See, e.g., La. Civ. Code art. 2347.

2.   Courts are all over the map on the issues raised in *Harms.* One might think that a court applying the title theory of mortgages would find severance. But as the court in Harms notes, the "title" here came to be viewed as given for limited purposes. Some courts still applying the title theory would find no severance by a mortgage given by only one of the joint tenants. With the lien theory, most courts would hold that the lien does not survive the death of the mortgagor joint tenant, but the opposite result under the lien theory can be reached. See Wilken v. Young, 41 N.E. 68 (Ind. 1895). One commentator maintains that the distinction between the "title theory" and the "lien theory" is very largely a formal one, and it becomes increasingly hard to defend it in an era when "the intention of the parties provides the touchstone for deciding most severance cases." R.H. Helmholz, Realism and Formalism in the Severance of Joint Tenancies, 77 Neb. L. Rev. 1, 28–29 (1998) (footnote omitted); see also Wesley A. Sturges & Samuel O. Clark, Legal Theory and Real Property Mortgages, 37 Yale L.J. 691, 709 (1928) (arguing that judges invoke title or lien theory "depending upon [their] sense of convenience and the matters which stimulate them in the particular case."). Should the parties' intent be the touchstone here? Who else has an interest in clarity and simplicity here? Is the Illinois Supreme Court's approach in *Harms v. Sprague* any less formalistic than the approach condemned by Helmholz? Should a court balance the hardship to the mortgagee and the surviving joint tenant on a case-by-case basis?

3.   What if William Harms had died first? If the mortgage lien did not sever the joint tenancy does this mean that the debt is now secured by the entire property?

4.   Although the Simmonses wished to add the argument that Section 20–19 of the Probate Act of 1975 mandates that the lien survive the death of John Harms, the court holds that this argument has been waived. But the court in dictum suggests that the result would be the same even if this provision did apply. Do you agree? How could the statute be clearer? Is the problem that the statute seems to presuppose that an interest "passes" upon the death of a joint tenant, whereas the court sees the survivorship under the joint tenancy as involving no passing of an interest, just the extinguishment of the deceased's interest? Or does the court simply disagree with the policy chosen by the Illinois legislature?

5.   On whether mortgages are liens, the Illinois legislature later adopted the Illinois Mortgage Foreclosure Law, which defines a "mortgage" as:

> any consensual lien created by a written instrument which grants or retains an interest in real estate to secure a debt or other obligation. The term "mortgage" includes, without limitation ... every deed conveying real estate, although an absolute conveyance in its terms, which shall have been intended only as a security in the nature of a mortgage.

735 ILCS ¶ 5/15–1207 (originally enacted on July 1, 1987, as amended). How would parties contract around this, by showing a contrary "intent"?

What about parties with mortgages from before 1987, in light of the provision also including within "mortgage" "instruments which would have been deemed instruments in the nature of a mortgage prior to the effective date of this amendatory Act of 1987"? Id. § 15–1207(e).

6. Another question that arises with some regularity is whether a lease by one joint tenant severs the joint tenancy. Again we find that courts have taken conflicting approaches. Compare Tenhet v. Boswell, 554 P.2d 330 (Cal. 1976) with Alexander v. Boyer, 253 A.2d 359 (Md. 1969). Also, courts will prevent one from profiting, including through inheritance, from one's own act of murder. In *Maine Savings Bank v. Bridges*, 431 A.2d 633 (Me. 1981), the court held that when the husband killed his wife, he severed the joint tenancy and held a one-half interest as a tenant in common with his wife's other heirs.

7. Not only may the joint tenancy be severed unilaterally, no notice is required. In *Riddle v. Harmon*, 162 Cal.Rptr. 530 (Cal. Ct. App. 1980), a married couple, Frances and Jack Riddle, owned real estate as joint tenants. Frances was distressed to learn from her lawyer about the survivorship feature of the joint tenancy and wanted to dispose of her share by will. At common law, to sever the joint tenancy would have required two conveyances, employing a straw: The joint tenant desiring severance would convey to the straw (often someone working in the lawyer's office) who would then reconvey back to the grantor, leaving the erstwhile joint tenants as tenants in common. In *Riddle*, Frances Riddle's attorney prepared a deed in which Frances granted to herself an undivided one-half interest in the property and a will in which she devised her share of the property to another. Twenty days later she died. Reversing the trial court, the appellate court held that a straw is not required to sever a joint tenancy. Do problems remain? Should the joint tenant be able to sever unilaterally without giving notice to anyone? Some statutes (currently including one in California) require recordation to sever a joint tenancy in some circumstances. Would this have helped here? What do you think Frances Riddle would have done with the above-described documents if her husband had suddenly predeceased her?

4. SPECIAL PROBLEMS OF JOINT BANK ACCOUNTS

Concurrent ownership is complicated enough in the case of real property. When two or more persons seek to share ownership of intangible property, the problems—and confusion—multiply. So-called joint tenancy bank accounts have been an especially fertile source of litigation. A major part of the problem is that people have different reasons for opening shared banks accounts, savings accounts, investment accounts, and the like. But the law in many jurisdictions provides a single "one-size-fits-all" form of account—the joint tenancy—that must be used in all situations.

Perhaps the most common situation is where two persons in an intimate relationship (such as a married couple) agree to pool their finances. Here the understanding may be that one or both will make deposits to the account and one or both will make withdrawals. If the two disagree about deposits and withdrawals, the solution may be to open separate accounts (or take more drastic action to end the relationship). There may or may not be an understanding about survivorship rights to the balance in the account if one tenant dies leaving the other as survivor. Another motivation for opening such an account is to create a will substitute. A wants to leave some money to B, but does not want to go to the trouble of writing a will and/or forcing B to go through the process of probate. Here the survivorship feature of the joint tenancy is the sole reason for opening the account. A third reason for opening such an account is to assist in managing the financial affairs of a dependent person, such as someone who is elderly or infirm. These are often called "convenience accounts." The dependent tenant typically makes the deposits, and the caretaker tenant typically makes the withdrawals, with the understanding (express or implied) that the caretaker is to use the withdrawals to pay for maintenance and support of the dependent tenant. Here there may or may not be any understanding about the survivorship feature of the joint tenancy.

If the motivations for using shared accounts vary widely among individual depositors, from the perspective of banks and other financial institutions it is imperative to have a clear set of rules that can be applied to thousands of small accounts without lots of individual fact finding. This, more than anything, explains why such accounts always take the form of joint tenancies. If one tenant dies, the bank can continue to do business with the survivor merely upon presentation of a death certificate. In contrast, if such accounts could be held as tenancies in common, the share of each tenant would pass by will or intestate succession. Thus, every time a tenant died, the bank would have to freeze the account or monitor activity until probate of the estate of the deceased tenant was completed. The costs and risks of doing business through shared accounts would rise significantly.

Each state has legislation that governs joint tenancy accounts. These laws have usually been drafted by financial institutions or at least with substantial input from them. In keeping with the interests of the financial institutions, they try to keep things simple and reduce to a minimum the grounds for dispute over the allocation of funds in accounts. The New York statute at issue in the following case provides as follows:

Joint deposits and shares; ownership and payment.

(a) When a deposit of cash, securities, or other property has been made or shall hereafter be made in or with any banking organization or foreign banking corporation transacting business in this state, * * * in the name of such depositor or shareholder and another person and in form to be paid or delivered to either, or the survivor of them, such deposit or shares and any additions thereto made, by either of such persons, after the making thereof, shall become the property of such persons as joint tenants and the same, together with all additions and accruals thereon, shall be held for the exclusive use of the persons so named, and may be paid or delivered to either during the lifetime of both or to the survivor after the death of one of them * * *

(b) The making of such deposit * * * in such form shall, in the absence of fraud or undue influence, be prima facie evidence, in any action or proceeding to which the banking organization, foreign banking corporation, surviving depositor or shareholder is a party, of the intention of both depositors or shareholders to create a joint tenancy and to vest title to such deposit or shares, and additions and accruals thereon, in such survivor. The burden of proof in refuting such prima facie evidence is upon the party or parties challenging the title of the survivor.

N.Y. Banking Law § 675 (2006).

In re Estate of Filfiley

Surrogate's Court, King's County, New York, 1970.
313 N.Y.S.2d 793.

■ NATHAN R. SOBEL, The trial of this discovery proceeding requires a determination of the rights of a surviving depositor of a joint savings account to the deposit. This surviving depositor had withdrawn the entire deposit one day before the death of her joint depositor. What are the respective rights of the estate of the deceased depositor and the surviving depositor? Many high court decisions discuss the problem. While the results reached are in each instance just and fair, these decisions provide very little in the way of a single rationale adequate to explain the results. This leaves the trial courts without any real guidance.

Some history is necessary to put the issue in proper perspective.

A statute governs such joint and survivorship accounts (Banking Law, § 675, formerly § 239, subd. 3). From the statute's inception in 1909, whether so purposed or not, it has authorized a reasonably reliable method of making a nontestamentary transfer of bank deposits at death. But it did more: it decided that upon the opening of such an account in proper form the deposit "shall become the property of such persons as joint tenants". The term "joint tenants" creates a special status carrying with it legal implications not particularly suited for any intangible personal property ownership but especially not for bank deposits. (See Hines, Personal Property Joint Tenancies, 54 Minn. L. Rev. 509 [1970].) A joint tenant of real property receives upon creation an undivided half, undivided in the sense that for purposes of tenure and user he may occupy the whole. But his undivided half is not readily alienable and he can under no circumstances convey the whole without his joint tenant joining in the deed. A joint tenant of a bank deposit also receives an undivided half. But one does not occupy a bank account. On the other hand either joint tenant of a bank deposit may withdraw, i.e. alienate his half or the whole by simply obtaining the possession of the bankbook. Only with respect to survivorship are both kinds of joint tenancies the same.

Another point. Joint tenants of real property usually intend joint tenure and user and survivorship. The average donor depositor usually intends survivorship but not always or even usually does he intend to transfer present ownership to any extent to his donee-depositor. Yet present ownership is a principal incident of a joint tenancy. * * *

[A] statutory joint deposit in New York results in a "joint tenancy", for it must be concluded that the Legislature used that term in the statute understandingly. * * *

Because of such problems the joint deposit statute has been amended several times.

It was held early in the statute's history, that the creation of a joint deposit in statutory form is presumed, in the absence of proof of contrary intent, to create a true joint tenancy (Clary v. Fitzgerald, 155 App. Div. 659, affd. 213 N.Y. 696). This presumption carried with it both incidents of a joint tenancy—(1) a present transfer of an undivided half and (2) a present transfer of a right to the whole to the ultimate survivor. Since the latter but not the former was usually intended, the courts in many cases understandably found that no true joint tenancy was intended. The presumption was not available to the parties. In order to establish a right of survivorship independent of the presumption of a joint tenancy, the agreement to such effect between the depositors had to be established. The "dead man's statute" stood in the way of such independent proof.[†] * * *

Under the new statute, the making of a joint deposit, in the absence of proof of contrary intent, is presumptive evidence of an intention to create a true joint tenancy and thus to effect a present transfer of both an alienable interest in one half of the deposit in both depositors and a right to the whole fund in the survivor after the death of one of them. In actions or proceedings in which one of the parties is a survivor, the new statute specifically places the burden of proof in rebutting such presumption on the party challenging the title of the survivor.

Today it is open to the parties to rebut the presumption by establishing that no true joint tenancy was intended. It may be established that the donor-depositor intended neither a transfer of a present right of withdrawal nor a right of survivorship; or that one but not the other was intended. * * *

[O]nce the evidence adduced or the prima facie presumption establishes that the bank account is a true joint tenancy, i.e. one uncomplicated by contrary agreement or intention, then the law governing a joint tenancy with all that the term entails becomes applicable. → *ie, survivorship + present* possession of the whole *

For one thing there is no longer any vestige of a donor-donee relationship, the law no longer being concerned with who created the account. For, upon creation, there is a *present* gift from the original donor to the joint

Dead Man's Statute

[†] [N.Y. C.P.L.R. § 4519. As summarized by a later decision, this statute prevents any person "interested in the event" from testifying to a "personal transaction" with the deceased "unless the representative of the deceased has waived the protection of the statute by testifying himself or introducing the testimony of the decedent into evidence at trial." In re Estate of Wood, 418 N.E. 2d 365 (N.Y. 1981).—eds.]

depositor of a moiety or one half of the account which each may alienate unilaterally while both are alive.

For a second thing there is a *present* transfer of a right to the whole fund to the survivor of the joint tenants. But this right is inchoate in both tenants until the contingency of the death of the other occurs. It would seem that unlike the rule applicable to real property, neither depositor by alienating his own moiety destroys the contingent survivorship right. No tenancy in common as is the case with real property occurs. This is by virtue of the deposit agreement.

Per my et per tout is the way our cases describe it—"by the half and the whole." A joint tenant has a present alienable interest in one half of the fund; he has a present inalienable and inchoate interest contingent on *his* survivorship in the whole (Matter of Tilley, 166 App. Div. 240, 242–243, affd. 215 N.Y. 702).

A joint tenant may unilaterally "sever" the joint tenancy to the extent of withdrawing his moiety or less than a moiety. When he does so he does not "terminate" the joint tenancy in the sense that he does not affect the right of survivorship. The survivor, whether the withdrawer or the other joint tenant will be entitled to the remainder upon the death of either joint tenant.

But a joint tenant may not unilaterally withdraw more than his moiety or, as usually happens, the whole fund. Such a withdrawal has no effect whatsoever. It is the same as if a joint tenant of real property unilaterally executed a deed to the whole property. The cases speak in terms of such withdrawals not "destroying" the joint tenancy. What is meant is that the whole fund withdrawn not just the excess over the moiety keeps its character as a joint tenancy no matter into what form it is converted. The ultimate survivor whether he be the withdrawer or the other joint tenant will be entitled to the whole fund withdrawn not just the excess over the moiety. In a sense therefore a joint tenant who withdraws more than his moiety "forfeits" his right to his own moiety and a few of the cases so hold. Technically, this is inaccurate because in law there is no "forfeiture"—the whole transaction is simply treated as a nullity.

This is the legal nature of the joint tenancy. In the main the cases follow the joint tenancy concept.

Before discussing the cases, two things should be noted.

First, the cases concerning depositor-bank relationships are not pertinent. The provision in the statute authorizing the bank to pay "to either during the lifetime of both" is for the protection of the bank and irrelevant to the rights of the depositors between themselves. Such a right to withdraw the whole fund is patently inconsistent with the incidents of a joint tenancy. Protection of the bank was a prime motivation for the legislation but the joint tenancy concept was probably the Legislature's with tax considerations in mind (*Matter of Tilley*, 116 App. Div. 240, affd. 215 N.Y. 702, supra).

Second, a true joint tenancy like any other status created by agreement may be altered, terminated or destroyed by agreement of both joint tenants. It is open to the parties to prove that there was prior consent or subsequent ratification of the acts of one by the other to withdrawals during the lifetime of both. Many cases concern such subsequent agreements; these are not pertinent to the discussion.

The cases are quite clear and in accord with a true joint tenancy concept in at least two respects:

1. In a true joint tenancy, uncomplicated by any issue of lifetime withdrawals, the whole fund will vest in the surviving joint tenant.

2. During the lifetime of both, each joint tenant has the right unilaterally to withdraw up to his moiety but not in excess of his moiety.

RULES governing "True joint tenancy" accounts

When one withdraws less than his moiety, the other should ordinarily withdraw his share. If he fails to do so he gambles that he and not the withdrawing joint tenant will be the survivor. As discussed heretofore, the survivor, whether the withdrawer or not is entitled to the remainder on deposit. The unilateral withdrawal of one joint tenant of less than his moiety severs the joint tenancy as to the portion withdrawn but it does not terminate the as yet inchoate right of survivorship.

RULE

However, if *during the lifetime of both*, one joint tenant without the consent or ratification of the other, unilaterally withdraws more than his moiety, the other joint tenant may recover the excess withdrawn. The joint tenancy is not destroyed. It is unaffected by the wrongful act. However since the right of survivorship has not as yet vested in one or the other, the "wronged" joint tenant is limited in his recovery to the *excess* withdrawn.

This much is clear and is consistent with the concept and legal consequences of a joint tenancy.

The cases are not clear however as to the consequences when one of the joint tenants has withdrawn more than his moiety and the right of survivorship has thereafter vested in one upon the death of the other. If the survivor is the one who has withdrawn the fund, the proceeding will be by the estate of the deceased joint tenant against the survivor; if the decedent joint tenant is the withdrawer, the proceeding will be by the survivor against the estate.

As has been discussed, under the joint tenancy concept the survivor necessarily takes all no matter what the circumstances. If the decedent joint tenant was the "wrongful" withdrawer, the survivor takes the whole fund by reason of the nullity of the transaction. If the survivor was the "wrongful" withdrawer, he takes the whole fund for the same reason. In short, there are no circumstances in which the survivor will be entitled to less than the whole fund where one of the tenants has withdrawn more than his moiety *and* the right of survivorship has vested in either one of them since a withdrawing joint tenant can only suffer a forfeiture to a survivor in whom that right has vested.

seems to be the absolute RULE

In short, after a right of survivorship has vested, there should in legal theory never be a recovery of half the fund or the excess over the moiety. *The survivor must take all.* Only while both joint tenants are still living may the recovery be for the excess over the moiety withdrawn. * * *

Obviously some confusion exists. It is suggested that there is no confusion with respect to the principles of law governing joint tenancies and the legal incidents thereof.

In a few cases where the appellate courts appear to depart from the accepted legal principles, it is from a desire to do justice in the given case. The remedy and probably a desirable remedy is not to depart from but to abolish the concept of joint tenancy and adopt a statutory "contract" concept for joint bank deposits.

From an examination of the factual patterns in the cases discussed, the obvious problem is the persistence of the donor-donee relationship. But when a true joint tenancy is created, the donor-donee relationship no longer exists. Yet courts have favored the donor-creator even when he was the "wrongdoer" decedent, as well as when he was the "victim"-decedent, by suggesting in dicta that his estate was entitled to half the fund from the survivor. This is the corollary to the rule already discussed that the withdrawal of the whole fund by the donor is evidence that no true joint tenancy was intended. Vestiges of his favored donor status continue to cling even after a true joint tenancy has been established.

In a true joint tenancy legally speaking there can be no such relationship as "wrongdoer"-"victim", terms sometimes employed by the courts. If one is a true joint tenant, like a member of a partnership, he cannot steal from his other joint tenant. He owns an *undivided* one half. He can withdraw all but must account for half during his lifetime. If he becomes the survivor he owns the whole fund; he cannot have been guilty of stealing from himself.

As a practical proposition few fact patterns in the cases indicate an intention to harm or defraud a joint tenant. In most cases withdrawals will be made under a claim of right, e.g. by a donor-creator on the theory that no true joint tenancy exists. Or by a donee joint tenant, who anticipating the expected death of the other joint tenant withdraws the fund to protect it from possible claims of other beneficiaries or distributees. The latter is the instant case. The facts are only briefly mentioned.

Before Mrs. Filfiley died she had converted what was theretofore a Totten trust account* for her daughter Alice into a joint account with her. The total deposit was $19,000. The day before her mother died, Alice withdrew the entire deposit and redeposited it in an account in her own name where it remains.

---

* [A Totten trust account is a trust in bank account form, revocable and modifiable during the life of the depositor, and is yet another will substitute. R (2003). For more on trusts, see Chapter VI.—eds.]

Alice is the executrix and a legatee under her mother's will. The husband of decedent has filed a notice of election to take against the will. He seeks to bring the joint account into the estate.

At the trial the husband sought to prove that this was not a true joint tenancy account but rather a "convenience" account; also that testatrix lacked mental capacity at the time she created the joint account. Alice sought to prove prior authorization for her withdrawal. Both sought to prove that they, not Mrs. Filfiley, were the source of the funds—proof hardly material since Mrs. Filfiley was on bank records the donor-creator.

Largely but not solely because of CPLR 4519 neither party proved any of their respective contentions. The statutory presumption therefore prevails. On the basis of the presumption and also other competent evidence, it is concluded that this was a true joint tenancy. Alice as the surviving joint tenant is entitled to the whole fund. Her withdrawal of the whole fund the day before her mother's death is a nullity—necessarily so since more than a moiety is unilaterally inalienable by either joint tenant.

Dead Man's statute

This last is the only single rationale adequate to explain the results of the high court cases discussed.

NOTES AND QUESTIONS

1. A later decision by New York's highest court appeared to reach a contrary result in a case that also involved lifetime withdrawals in excess of the moiety by the surviving tenant. Kleinberg v. Heller, 345 N.E.2d 592 (N.Y. 1976). The majority did not write an opinion. A concurring opinion, by Justice Fuchsberg, offered the following list of factors to be considered in deciding whether the surviving tenant could be forced to disgorge to the estate of the deceased tenant withdrawals beyond the moiety:

[T]he duration, nature and closeness of the business, social or familial relationship between the tenants; the presence or absence of a habit of freely commingling their funds; significant revelations, if any, in the tenants' testamentary dispositions; the generosity, or lack of it, manifested by the survivor in his other inter vivos dealings with the decedent; the amounts involved; the pattern of withdrawals; their purpose and timing; the age and physical and mental condition of each at the time of the withdrawal; the source of the funds; the circumstances in which possession of the bankbook came into the hands of the survivor at the time of the withdrawal; decedent's ignorance or knowledge of the withdrawal and, if the latter, the length of time during which it existed; the protest or lack of protest against the withdrawal; the efforts, if any, to effect its return, considering of course, the absence or presence of opportunity to do so; and, highly important, whether the survivor was the donor.

FACTORS

① Nature of Relationship
② Evidence of the comfort level of commingling funds
③ Decedent intentions (taken from will)
④ Level of generosity by survivor during decedents lifetime
⑤ Amounts involved
⑥ Prior pattern of withdrawals (+ the ones in question)
⑦ Purpose + timing of
⑧ Condition (phys/mental) of each person at time of withdrawal
⑨ Source of funds
⑩ How survivor got the bankbook
⑪ Decedent's knowledge of withdrawal. If ignorant, for how long?
⑫ Any protest against withdrawal
⑬ Efforts to force possible return of money

Id. at 844. Which approach do you prefer: the Surrogate's opinion in *Filfiley*, which would award all the funds to the survivor, unless the estate can prove fraud, undue influence, or a prior agreement that the funds were

✱ ⑭ Whether survivor was the donor

not held as a true joint tenancy? Or Justice Fuchberg's approach, which would have the court engage in a highly fact-specific inquiry in order to determine whether the surviving joint tenant must make restitution to the estate for funds previously withdrawn in excess of the moiety?

2. In the context of real estate, each cotenant has the right to equal and undivided possession of the whole of the property. Thus, in *Gillmor*, each cotenant had the right to graze cattle over the entire ranch. Translated to bank accounts, why doesn't this mean that each cotenant has an equal and undivided right to withdraw *all* the money at any time? Instead, courts universally hold, as suggested in *Filfiley*, that each cotenant is entitled to withdraw only a moiety, i.e., an equal share (typically half), of the account. What accounts for this understanding? Are joint tenancies in intangibles fundamentally different from joint tenancies in land? Consider in this regard that even in the context of land, when a cotenant in possession brings an action for contribution, or when an ousted cotenant brings an action for an accounting, the respective shares of the rents collected or due, or of taxes or mortgage payments made, are defined in terms of moieties. That is, in a two-person cotenancy, the tenant out of possession gets only half the rents collected, and is charged with only half the taxes owed, etc. Does this suggest that cotenancies are separate property as to values reducible to money, and undivided property as to physical assets that are capable of possession?

3. In trying to solve the dilemma of how to determine the respective rights of cotenants to a joint bank account, should we draw a distinction between the rights as between the cotenants and the financial institution, and the rights as between the cotenants (or their estates) themselves? In the former context, there is a strong argument for standardization and bright-line rules. Banks should not be required to engage in an all-things-considered inquiry before allowing a cotenant to make a withdrawal from an ATM. But when conflict erupts between cotenants, or a cotenant and the estate of a former cotenant, perhaps a more fine-grained examination of the course of dealing and expectations between the parties makes sense. If the fact-intensive inquiry is confined in this matter, would financial institutions have any quarrel with the test set forth by Justice Fuchberg in *Kleinberg*, quoted above?

F. MORE ON MARITAL INTERESTS

A special set of co-owners are married couples. While a marriage is ongoing the rules of co-ownership are largely the same for married people as for co-owners. (The main exception is the tenancy by the entirety, which is not available to nonmarried co-owners.) Special rules for marital interests emerge primarily in the context of divorce and inheritance. The spousal forced share, see Section C.2 supra, is currently the main constraint on testamentary freedom in the interest of a surviving spouse. We saw an intersection of family law, the law of wills, and the definition of property in the *Hecht* case, see Chapter III.

We focus here on the rules for property division on divorce. These are important in their own right, and because they define each spouse's exit option they can be expected to influence relations within an ongoing marriage. In community property states, the rules for division on divorce, as well as those for descent and concurrent use, are tightly connected to the definition of this form of co-ownership. In common-law states (common law for purposes of marital property), division on divorce is governed by principles of equitable division, to the extent they are not displaced by an antenuptial agreement. In recent years, courts have tended to bring equitable division somewhat closer to the approach under community property. One of the central issues in marital property law is how to define "property" for purposes of division on divorce, and in particular how to treat increases in human capital during the marriage.

O'Brien v. O'Brien

Court of Appeals of New York, 1985.
489 N.E.2d 712.

Plaintiff = Husband
Defendant = Wife

■ SIMONS, JUDGE. In this divorce action, the parties' only asset of any consequence is the husband's newly acquired license to practice medicine. The principal issue presented is whether that license, acquired during their marriage, is marital property subject to equitable distribution under Domestic Relations Law § 236(B)(5). Supreme Court held that it was and accordingly made a distributive award in defendant's favor.* It also granted defendant maintenance arrears, expert witness fees and attorneys' fees. On appeal to the Appellate Division, a majority of that court held that plaintiff's medical license is not marital property and that defendant was not entitled to an award for the expert witness fees. It modified the judgment and remitted the case to Supreme Court for further proceedings, specifically for a determination of maintenance and a rehabilitative award. The matter is before us by leave of the Appellate Division.

We now hold that plaintiff's medical license constitutes "marital property" within the meaning of Domestic Relations Law § 236(B)(1)(c) and that it is therefore subject to equitable distribution pursuant to subdivision 5 of that part. That being so, the Appellate Division erred in denying a fee, as a matter of law, to defendant's expert witness who evaluated the license.

I

Plaintiff and defendant married on April 3, 1971. At the time both were employed as teachers at the same private school. Defendant had a bachelor's degree and a temporary teaching certificate but required 18 months of postgraduate classes at an approximate cost of $3,000, excluding living expenses, to obtain permanent certification in New York. She claimed, and the trial court found, that she had relinquished the opportuni-

---

* The action was originally instituted by plaintiff husband and defendant wife asserted a counterclaim in her answer. Subsequently, the husband withdrew his complaint and reply to the counterclaim and the wife received an uncontested divorce.

ty to obtain permanent certification while plaintiff pursued his education. At the time of the marriage, plaintiff had completed only three and one-half years of college but shortly afterward he returned to school at night to earn his bachelor's degree and to complete sufficient premedical courses to enter medical school. In September 1973 the parties moved to Guadalajara, Mexico, where plaintiff became a full-time medical student. While he pursued his studies defendant held several teaching and tutorial positions and contributed her earnings to their joint expenses. The parties returned to New York in December 1976 so that plaintiff could complete the last two semesters of medical school and internship training here. After they returned, defendant resumed her former teaching position and she remained in it at the time this action was commenced. Plaintiff was licensed to practice medicine in October 1980. He commenced this action for divorce two months later. At the time of trial, he was a resident in general surgery.

During the marriage both parties contributed to paying the living and educational expenses and they received additional help from both of their families. They disagreed on the amounts of their respective contributions but it is undisputed that in addition to performing household work and managing the family finances defendant was gainfully employed throughout the marriage, that she contributed all of her earnings to their living and educational expenses and that her financial contributions exceeded those of plaintiff. The trial court found that she had contributed 76% of the parties' income exclusive of a $10,000 student loan obtained by defendant. Finding that plaintiff's medical degree and license are marital property, the court received evidence of its value and ordered a distributive award to defendant.

Defendant presented expert testimony that the present value of plaintiff's medical license was $472,000. Her expert testified that he arrived at this figure by comparing the average income of a college graduate and that of a general surgeon between 1985, when plaintiff's residency would end, and 2012, when he would reach age 65. After considering Federal income taxes, an inflation rate of 10% and a real interest rate of 3% he capitalized the difference in average earnings and reduced the amount to present value. He also gave his opinion that the present value of defendant's contribution to plaintiff's medical education was $103,390. Plaintiff offered no expert testimony on the subject.

The court, after considering the life-style that plaintiff would enjoy from the enhanced earning potential his medical license would bring and defendant's contributions and efforts toward attainment of it, made a distributive award to her of $188,800, representing 40% of the value of the license, and ordered it paid in 11 annual installments of various amounts beginning November 1, 1982 and ending November 1, 1992. The court also directed plaintiff to maintain a life insurance policy on his life for defendant's benefit for the unpaid balance of the award and it ordered plaintiff to pay defendant's counsel fees of $7,000 and her expert witness fee of $1,000. It did not award defendant maintenance. * * *

II

The Equitable Distribution Law contemplates only two classes of property: marital property and separate property (Domestic Relations Law § 236[B][1][c], [d]). The former, which is subject to equitable distribution, is defined broadly as "*all* property acquired by either or both spouses during the marriage and before the execution of a separation agreement or the commencement of a matrimonial action, *regardless of the form in which title is held*" (Domestic Relations Law § 236[B][1][c] [emphasis added]; see § 236[B][5][b], [c]). Plaintiff does not contend that his license is excluded from distribution because it is separate property; rather, he claims that it is not property at all but represents a personal attainment in acquiring knowledge. He rests his argument on decisions in similar cases from other jurisdictions and on his view that a license does not satisfy common-law concepts of property. Neither contention is controlling because decisions in other States rely principally on their own statutes, and the legislative history underlying them, and because the New York Legislature deliberately went beyond traditional property concepts when it formulated the Equitable Distribution Law (see generally, 2 Foster–Freed–Brandes, Law and the Family—New York ch. 33, at 917 et seq. [1985 Cum.Supp.]). Instead, our statute recognizes that spouses have an equitable claim to things of value arising out of the marital relationship and classifies them as subject to distribution by focusing on the marital status of the parties at the time of acquisition. Those things acquired during marriage and subject to distribution have been classified as "marital property" although, as one commentator has observed, they hardly fall within the traditional property concepts because there is no common-law property interest remotely resembling marital property. "It is a statutory creature, is of no meaning whatsoever during the normal course of a marriage and arises full-grown, like Athena, upon the signing of a separation agreement or the commencement of a matrimonial action. [Thus] [i]t is hardly surprising, and not at all relevant, that traditional common law property concepts do not fit in parsing the meaning of 'marital property' " (Florescue, "Market Value", Professional Licenses and Marital Property: A Dilemma in Search of a Horn, 1982 N.Y.St.Bar Assn.Fam.L.Rev. 13 [Dec.]). Having classified the "property" subject to distribution, the Legislature did not attempt to go further and define it but left it to the courts to determine what interests come within the terms of section 236(B)(1)(c).

We made such a determination in *Majauskas v. Majauskas*, 463 N.E.2d 15 (N.Y. 1984), holding there that vested but unmatured pension rights are marital property subject to equitable distribution. Because pension benefits are not specifically identified as marital property in the statute, we looked to the express reference to pension rights contained in section 236(B)(5)(d)(4), which deals with equitable distribution of marital property, to other provisions of the equitable distribution statute and to the legislative intent behind its enactment to determine whether pension rights are marital property or separate property. A similar analysis is appropriate here and leads to the conclusion that marital property encompasses a license to practice medicine to the extent that the license is acquired during marriage.

Section 236 provides that in making an equitable distribution of marital property, "the court shall consider: * * * (6) any equitable claim to, interest in, or direct or indirect contribution made to the acquisition of such marital property by the party not having title, including joint efforts or expenditures and contributions and services as a spouse, parent, wage earner and homemaker, and *to the career or career potential* of the other party [and] * * * (9) the impossibility or difficulty of evaluating any component asset or any interest in a business, corporation or *profession*" (Domestic Relations Law § 236[B][5][d][6], [9] [emphasis added]). Where equitable distribution of marital property is appropriate but "the distribution of an interest in a business, corporation or *profession* would be contrary to law" the court shall make a distributive award in lieu of an actual distribution of the property (Domestic Relations Law § 236[B][5][e] [emphasis added]). The words mean exactly what they say: that an interest in a profession or professional career potential is marital property which may be represented by direct or indirect contributions of the non-title-holding spouse, including financial contributions and nonfinancial contributions made by caring for the home and family.

The history which preceded enactment of the statute confirms this interpretation. Reform of section 236 was advocated because experience had proven that application of the traditional common-law title theory of property had caused inequities upon dissolution of a marriage. The Legislature replaced the existing system with equitable distribution of marital property, an entirely new theory which considered all the circumstances of the case and of the respective parties to the marriage (Assembly Memorandum, 1980 N.Y.Legis.Ann., at 129–130). Equitable distribution was based on the premise that a marriage is, among other things, an economic partnership to which both parties contribute as spouse, parent, wage earner or homemaker (id., at 130; see, Governor's Memorandum of Approval, 1980 McKinney's Session Laws of N.Y., at 1863). Consistent with this purpose, and implicit in the statutory scheme as a whole, is the view that upon dissolution of the marriage there should be a winding up of the parties' economic affairs and a severance of their economic ties by an equitable distribution of the marital assets. Thus, the concept of alimony, which often served as a means of lifetime support and dependence for one spouse upon the other long after the marriage was over, was replaced with the concept of maintenance which seeks to allow "the recipient spouse an opportunity to achieve [economic] independence" (Assembly Memorandum, 1980 N.Y.Legis.Ann., at 130).

The determination that a professional license is marital property is also consistent with the conceptual base upon which the statute rests. As this case demonstrates, few undertakings during a marriage better qualify as the type of joint effort that the statute's economic partnership theory is intended to address than contributions toward one spouse's acquisition of a professional license. Working spouses are often required to contribute substantial income as wage earners, sacrifice their own educational or career goals and opportunities for child rearing, perform the bulk of household duties and responsibilities and forego the acquisition of marital assets that could have been accumulated if the professional spouse had been employed rather than occupied with the study and training necessary to acquire a professional license. In this case, nearly all of the parties' nine-year marriage was devoted to the acquisition of plaintiff's medical license and defendant played a major role in that project. She worked continuously during the marriage and contributed all of her earnings to their joint effort, she sacrificed her own educational and career opportunities, and she traveled with plaintiff to Mexico for three and one-half years while he attended medical school there. The Legislature has decided, by its explicit reference in the statute to the contributions of one spouse to the other's profession or career (see, Domestic Relations Law § 236[B][5][d][6], [9]; [e]), that these contributions represent investments in the economic partnership of the marriage and that the product of the parties' joint efforts, the professional license, should be considered marital property.

The majority at the Appellate Division held that the cited statutory provisions do not refer to the license held by a professional who has yet to establish a practice but only to a going professional practice (see, e.g., Arvantides v. Arvantides, 478 N.E.2d 199 (N.Y. 1985); Litman v. Litman, 463 N.E.2d 34 (N.Y. 1984)). There is no reason in law or logic to restrict the plain language of the statute to existing practices, however, for it is of little consequence in making an award of marital property, except for the purpose of evaluation, whether the professional spouse has already established a practice or whether he or she has yet to do so. An established practice merely represents the exercise of the privileges conferred upon the professional spouse by the license and the income flowing from that practice represents the receipt of the enhanced earning capacity that licensure allows. That being so, it would be unfair not to consider the license a marital asset.

Plaintiff's principal argument, adopted by the majority below, is that a professional license is not marital property because it does not fit within the traditional view of property as something which has an exchange value on the open market and is capable of sale, assignment or transfer. The position does not withstand analysis for at least two reasons. First, as we have observed, it ignores the fact that whether a professional license constitutes marital property is to be judged by the language of the statute which created this new species of property previously unknown at common law or under prior statutes. Thus, whether the license fits within traditional property concepts is of no consequence. Second, it is an overstatement to assert that a professional license could not be considered property even outside the context of section 236(B). A professional license is a valuable property right, reflected in the money, effort and lost opportunity for employment expended in its acquisition, and also in the enhanced earning capacity it affords its holder, which may not be revoked without due process of law (see, Matter of Bender v. Board of Regents, 30 N.Y.S.2d 779, 784 (App. Div. 1941); People ex rel. Greenberg v. Reid, 136 N.Y.S. 428, 431

(App. Div. 1912)). That a professional license has no market value is irrelevant. Obviously, a license may not be alienated as may other property and for that reason the working spouse's interest in it is limited. The Legislature has recognized that limitation, however, and has provided for an award in lieu of its actual distribution (see, Domestic Relations Law § 236[B][5][e]).

Plaintiff also contends that alternative remedies should be employed, such as an award of rehabilitative maintenance or reimbursement for direct financial contributions. The statute does not expressly authorize retrospective maintenance or rehabilitative awards and we have no occasion to decide in this case whether the authority to do so may ever be implied from its provisions (but see, Cappiello v. Cappiello, 485 N.E.2d 983 (N.Y. 1985)). It is sufficient to observe that normally a working spouse should not be restricted to that relief because to do so frustrates the purposes underlying the Equitable Distribution Law. Limiting a working spouse to a maintenance award, either general or rehabilitative, not only is contrary to the economic partnership concept underlying the statute but also retains the uncertain and inequitable economic ties of dependence that the Legislature sought to extinguish by equitable distribution. Maintenance is subject to termination upon the recipient's remarriage and a working spouse may never receive adequate consideration for his or her contribution and may even be penalized for the decision to remarry if that is the only method of compensating the contribution. As one court said so well, "[t]he function of equitable distribution is to recognize that when a marriage ends, each of the spouses, based on the totality of the contributions made to it, has a stake in and right to a share of the marital assets accumulated while it endured, not because that share is needed, but because those assets represent the capital product of what was essentially a partnership entity" (Wood v. Wood, 465 N.Y.S. 2d 475, 477 (Sup. Ct. 1983)). The Legislature stated its intention to eliminate such inequities by providing that a supporting spouse's "direct or indirect contribution" be recognized, considered and rewarded (Domestic Relations Law § 236[B][5][d][6]).

Turning to the question of valuation, it has been suggested that even if a professional license is considered marital property, the working spouse is entitled only to reimbursement of his or her direct financial contributions (see, Note, Equitable Distribution of Degrees and Licenses: Two Theories Toward Compensating Spousal Contributions, 49 Brooklyn L.Rev. 301, 317–322). By parity of reasoning, a spouse's down payment on real estate or contribution to the purchase of securities would be limited to the money contributed, without any remuneration for any incremental value in the asset because of price appreciation. Such a result is completely at odds with the statute's requirement that the court give full consideration to both direct and indirect contributions "made to the acquisition of such marital property by the party not having title, including joint *efforts* or expenditures and *contributions and services as a spouse, parent,* wage earner *and homemaker*" (Domestic Relations Law § 236[B][5][d][6] [emphasis added]). If the license is marital property, then the working spouse is entitled to an equitable portion of it, not a return of funds advanced. Its value is the enhanced earning capacity it affords the holder and although fixing the present value of that enhanced earning capacity may present problems, the problems are not insurmountable. Certainly they are no more difficult than computing tort damages for wrongful death or diminished earning capacity resulting from injury and they differ only in degree from the problems presented when valuing a professional practice for purposes of a distributive award, something the courts have not hesitated to do. The trial court retains the flexibility and discretion to structure the distributive award equitably, taking into consideration factors such as the working spouse's need for immediate payment, the licensed spouse's current ability to pay and the income tax consequences of prolonging the period of payment (see, Internal Revenue Code [26 U.S.C.] § 71[a][1]; [c][2]; Treas Reg [26 CFR] § 1.71–1[d][4]) and, once it has received evidence of the present value of the license and the working spouse's contributions toward its acquisition and considered the remaining factors mandated by the statute (see, Domestic Relations Law § 236[B][5][d][1]–[10]), it may then make an appropriate distribution of the marital property including a distributive award for the professional license if such an award is warranted. When other marital assets are of sufficient value to provide for the supporting spouse's equitable portion of the marital property, including his or her contributions to the acquisition of the professional license, however, the court retains the discretion to distribute these other marital assets or to make a distributive award in lieu of an actual distribution of the value of the professional spouse's license. * * *

III

* * * Plaintiff also contends that the trial court erred in excluding evidence of defendant's marital fault on the question of equitable distribution. Arguably, the court may consider marital fault under factor 10, "any other factor which the court shall expressly find to be just and proper" (Domestic Relations Law § 236[B][5][d][10].). Except in egregious cases which shock the conscience of the court, however, it is not a "just and proper" factor for consideration in the equitable distribution of marital property (Blickstein v. Blickstein, 472 N.Y.S.2d 110, 113–14 (App. Div. 1984)). That is so because marital fault is inconsistent with the underlying assumption that a marriage is in part an economic partnership and upon its dissolution the parties are entitled to a fair share of the marital estate, because fault will usually be difficult to assign and because introduction of the issue may involve the courts in time-consuming procedural maneuvers relating to collateral issues. We have no occasion to consider the wife's fault in this action because there is no suggestion that she was guilty of fault sufficient to shock the conscience. * * *

Accordingly, in view of our holding that plaintiff's license to practice medicine is marital property, the order of the Appellate Division should be modified, with costs to defendant, by reinstating the judgment and the case remitted to the Appellate Division for determination of the facts, including the exercise of that court's discretion (CPLR 5613), and, as so modified, affirmed. Question certified answered in the negative.

■ MEYER, JUDGE (concurring). I concur in Judge Simons' opinion but write separately to point up for consideration by the Legislature the potential for unfairness involved in distributive awards based upon a license of a professional still in training.

An equity court normally has power to " 'change its decrees where there has been a change of circumstances' " (People v. Scanlon, 184 N.E.2d 302, 303 (N.Y. 1962), on second appeal, 194 N.E.2d 689 (N.Y. 1963)). The implication of Domestic Relations Law § 236(B)(9)(b), which deals with modification of an order or decree as to maintenance or child support, is, however, that a distributive award pursuant to section 236(B)(5)(e), once made, is not subject to change. Yet a professional in training who is not finally committed to a career choice when the distributive award is made may be locked into a particular kind of practice simply because the monetary obligations imposed by the distributive award made on the basis of the trial judge's conclusion (prophecy may be a better word) as to what the career choice will be leaves him or her no alternative.

The present case points up the problem. A medical license is but a step toward the practice ultimately engaged in by its holder, which follows after internship, residency and, for particular specialties, board certification. Here it is undisputed that plaintiff was in a residency for general surgery at the time of the trial, but had the previous year done a residency in internal medicine. Defendant's expert based his opinion on the difference between the average income of a general surgeon and that of a college graduate of plaintiff's age and life expectancy, which the trial judge utilized, impliedly finding that plaintiff would engage in a surgical practice despite plaintiff's testimony that he was dissatisfied with the general surgery program he was in and was attempting to return to the internal medicine training he had been in the previous year. The trial judge had the right, of course, to discredit that testimony, but the point is that equitable distribution was not intended to permit a judge to make a career decision for a licensed spouse still in training. Yet the degree of speculation involved in the award made is emphasized by the testimony of the expert on which it was based. Asked whether his assumptions and calculations were in any way speculative, he replied: "Yes. They're speculative to the extent of, will Dr. O'Brien practice medicine? Will Dr. O'Brien earn more or less than the average surgeon earns? Will Dr. O'Brien live to age sixty-five? Will Dr. O'Brien have a heart attack or will he be injured in an automobile accident? Will he be disabled? I mean, there is a degree of speculation. That speculative aspect is no more to be taken into account, cannot be taken into account, and it's a question, again, Mr. Emanuelli, not for the expert but for the courts to decide. It's not my function nor could it be."

The equitable distribution provisions of the Domestic Relations Law were intended to provide flexibility so that equity could be done. But if the assumption as to career choice on which a distributive award payable over a number of years is based turns out not to be the fact (as, for example, should a general surgery trainee accidentally lose the use of his hand), it should be possible for the court to revise the distributive award to conform to the fact. And there will be no unfairness in so doing if either spouse can seek reconsideration, for the licensed spouse is more likely to seek reconsideration based on real, rather than imagined, cause if he or she knows that the nonlicensed spouse can seek not only reinstatement of the original award, but counsel fees in addition, should the purported circumstance on which a change is made turn out to have been feigned or to be illusory.

NOTES AND QUESTIONS

1. What exactly is the property here? Is it the medical degree? How would the court treat increases in earning potential in a career that does not require a professional license? New York courts have decided that the increase in the extraordinary earning potential of an opera singer attributable in part to the domestic and voice coaching efforts of her husband were property subject to division. Elkus v. Elkus, 572 N.Y.S.2d 901 (App. Div. 1991). The court in *Elkus* held that "the enhanced skills of an artist such as the plaintiff, albeit growing from an innate talent, which have enabled her to become an exceptional earner, may be valued as marital property subject to equitable distribution." 572 N.Y.S.2d at 904. See also Piscopo v. Piscopo, 555 A.2d 1190, 1191 (N.J. Super. Ch. 1988). How should the role of innate talent be treated? By contrast, the court in *Bystricky v. Bystricky*, 677 N.Y.S.2d 443, 444 (N.Y. Sup. 1998) held that the increase in a husband's earning power from a promotion in a police department was not subject to equitable distribution. Does this make sense?

2. Does treating the degree as property improperly commodify some aspect of the degree spouse or the nondegree spouse's contribution to the marriage? On commodification, see Chapter III. Is this an arena in which fears of commodification tend to work inequity on the nondegree spouse? Is it possible to avoid such inequity and provide for a "clean break" in divorce? See, e.g., Margaret Jane Radin, Reinterpreting Property 32–24 (1993); Joan Williams, Unbending Gender: Why Family and Work Conflict and What to Do about It 118 (2000).

3. Property division can be agreed upon in an antenuptial agreement, but most couples do not take this route. What do you think most couples would agree on if presented ex ante with the question of how to divide assets on divorce? Is this the right question to be asking?

4. One question that arises where one spouse is to be compensated for investments made in the other spouse's human capital is what the nature of the interest is. Is the investment like a loan? Or an equity-like share? See, e.g., Daniel D. Polsby & Martin Zelder, Risk–Adjusted Valuation of Professional Degrees in Divorce, 23 J. Legal Stud. 273 (1994); Lloyd Cohen, Marriage, Divorce, and Quasi Rents; Or, "I Gave Him the Best Years of My Life," 16 J. Legal Stud. 267 (1987). Can the award of compensation to the supporting spouse be viewed as a type of restitution to compensate for what otherwise would be unjust enrichment?

5. Generally speaking, property division is not used to punish either spouse for behavior during the marriage and the trend has been towards

no-fault divorce. Consider the problem of the economically vulnerable spouse as in *O'Brien*. Does no-fault divorce improve or weaken her bargaining position?

Recently, the question has arisen over whether to extend marriage or marriage-like arrangements to gay couples. The courts also have been struggling for some time with the question of the rights of those exiting a cohabitating relationship. Consider the following case.

Marvin v. Marvin

Supreme Court of California, In Bank, 1976.
557 P.2d 106.

■ TOBRINER, JUSTICE. During the past 15 years, there has been a substantial increase in the number of couples living together without marrying. Such nonmarital relationships lead to legal controversy when one partner dies or the couple separates. Courts of Appeal, faced with the task of determining property rights in such cases, have arrived at conflicting positions: two cases (In re Marriage of Cary, 109 Cal.Rptr. 862 (Cal. Ct. App. 1973); Estate of Atherley, 119 Cal.Rptr. 41 (Cal. Ct. App. 1975)) have held that the Family Law Act (Civ.Code, § 4000 et seq.) requires division of the property according to community property principles, and one decision (Beckman v. Mayhew, 122 Cal.Rptr. 604 (Cal. Ct. App. 1975)) has rejected that holding. We take this opportunity to resolve that controversy and to declare the principles which should govern distribution of property acquired in a nonmarital relationship.

We conclude: (1) The provisions of the Family Law Act do not govern the distribution of property acquired during a nonmarital relationship; such a relationship remains subject solely to judicial decision. (2) The courts should enforce express contracts between nonmarital partners except to the extent that the contract is explicitly founded on the consideration of meretricious sexual services. (3) In the absence of an express contract, the courts should inquire into the conduct of the parties to determine whether that conduct demonstrates an implied contract, agreement of partnership or joint venture, or some other tacit understanding between the parties. The courts may also employ the doctrine of quantum meruit, or equitable remedies such as constructive or resulting trusts, when warranted by the facts of the case.

In the instant case plaintiff and defendant lived together for seven years without marrying; all property acquired during this period was taken in defendant's name. When plaintiff sued to enforce a contract under which she was entitled to half the property and to support payments, the trial court granted judgment on the pleadings for defendant, thus leaving him with all property accumulated by the couple during their relationship. Since the trial court denied plaintiff a trial on the merits of her claim, its decision conflicts with the principles stated above, and must be reversed.

1. The factual setting of this appeal.

Since the trial court rendered judgment for defendant on the pleadings, we must accept the allegations of plaintiff's complaint as true, determining whether such allegations state, or can be aménded to state, a cause of action. We turn therefore to the specific allegations of the complaint.

Plaintiff avers that in October of 1964 she and defendant "entered into an oral agreement" that while "the parties lived together they would combine their efforts and earnings and would share equally any and all property accumulated as a result of their efforts whether individual or combined." Furthermore, they agreed to "hold themselves out to the general public as husband and wife" and that "plaintiff would further render her services as a companion, homemaker, housekeeper and cook to ... defendant."

Shortly thereafter plaintiff agreed to "give up her lucrative career as an entertainer (and) singer" in order to "devote her full time to defendant ... as a companion, homemaker, housekeeper and cook;" in return defendant agreed to "provide for all of plaintiff's financial support and needs for the rest of her life."

Plaintiff alleges that she lived with defendant from October of 1964 through May of 1970 and fulfilled her obligations under the agreement. During this period the parties as a result of their efforts and earnings acquired in defendant's name substantial real and personal property, including motion picture rights worth over $1 million. In May of 1970, however, defendant compelled plaintiff to leave his household. He continued to support plaintiff until November of 1971, but thereafter refused to provide further support.

On the basis of these allegations plaintiff asserts two causes of action. The first, for declaratory relief, asks the court to determine her contract and property rights; the second seeks to impose a constructive trust upon one half of the property acquired during the course of the relationship.

Defendant demurred unsuccessfully, and then answered the complaint. Following extensive discovery and pretrial proceedings, the case came to trial. Defendant renewed his attack on the complaint by a motion to dismiss. * * *

After hearing argument the court granted defendant's motion and entered judgment for defendant. * * * Plaintiff * * * appealed from the judgment.

2. Plaintiff's complaint states a cause of action for breach of an express contract.

In *Trutalli v. Meraviglia*, 12 P.2d 430 (Cal. 1932) we established the principle that nonmarital partners may lawfully contract concerning the ownership of property acquired during the relationship. We reaffirmed this principle in *Vallera v. Vallera*, 134 P.2d 761, 763 (Cal. 1943), stating that "If a man and woman (who are not married) live together as husband and wife under an agreement to pool their earnings and share equally in their

RULE

joint accumulations, equity will protect the interests of each in such property.''

In the case before us plaintiff, basing her cause of action in contract upon these precedents, maintains that the trial court erred in denying her a trial on the merits of her contention. Although that court did not specify the ground for its conclusion that plaintiff's contractual allegations stated no cause of action, defendant offers some four theories to sustain the ruling; we proceed to examine them.

Defendant first and principally relies on the contention that the alleged contract is so closely related to the supposed ''immoral'' character of the relationship between plaintiff and himself that the enforcement of the contract would violate public policy. He points to cases asserting that a contract between nonmarital partners is unenforceable if it is ''involved in'' an illicit relationship, or made in ''contemplation'' of such a relationship. A review of the numerous California decisions concerning contracts between nonmarital partners, however, reveals that the courts have not employed such broad and uncertain standards to strike down contracts. The decisions instead disclose a narrower and more precise standard: a contract between nonmarital partners is unenforceable only *to the extent* that it *explicitly* rests upon the immoral and illicit consideration of meretricious sexual services. * * *

[A] standard which inquires whether an agreement is ''involved'' in or ''contemplates'' a nonmarital relationship is vague and unworkable. Virtually all agreements between nonmarital partners can be said to be ''involved'' in some sense in the fact of their mutual sexual relationship, or to ''contemplate'' the existence of that relationship. Thus defendant's proposed standards, if taken literally, might invalidate all agreements between nonmarital partners, a result no one favors. Moreover, those standards offer no basis to distinguish between valid and invalid agreements. By looking not to such uncertain tests, but only to the consideration underlying the agreement, we provide the parties and the courts with a practical guide to determine when an agreement between nonmarital partners should be enforced.

Defendant secondly relies upon the ground suggested by the trial court: that the 1964 contract violated public policy because it impaired the community property rights of Betty Marvin, defendant's lawful wife. Defendant points out that his earnings while living apart from his wife before rendition of the interlocutory decree were community property under 1964 statutory law (former Civ.Code, §§ 169, 169.2)[7] and that defendant's agreement with plaintiff purported to transfer to her a half interest in that community property. But whether or not defendant's contract with plaintiff exceeded his authority as manager of the community property (see former Civ.Code, § 172), defendant's argument fails for the reason that an improp-

---

7. Sections 169 and 169.2 were replaced in 1970 by Civil Code section 5118. In 1972 section 5118 was amended to provide that the earnings and accumulations of *both* spouses ''while living separate and apart from the other spouse, are the separate property of the spouse.''

er transfer of community property is not void *ab initio*, but merely voidable at the instance of the aggrieved spouse.

In the present case Betty Marvin, the aggrieved spouse, had the opportunity to assert her community property rights in the divorce action. The interlocutory and final decrees in that action fix and limit her interest. Enforcement of the contract between plaintiff and defendant against property awarded to defendant by the divorce decree will not impair any right of Betty's, and thus is not on that account violative of public policy. * * *

[A]dults who voluntarily live together and engage in sexual relations are nonetheless as competent as any other persons to contract respecting their earnings and property rights. Of course, they cannot lawfully contract to pay for the performance of sexual services, for such a contract is, in essence, an agreement for prostitution and unlawful for that reason. But they may agree to pool their earnings and to hold all property acquired during the relationship in accord with the law governing community property; conversely they may agree that each partner's earnings and the property acquired from those earnings remains the separate property of the earning partner.[10] So long as the agreement does not rest upon illicit meretricious consideration, the parties may order their economic affairs as they choose, and no policy precludes the courts from enforcing such agreements.

In the present instance, plaintiff alleges that the parties agreed to pool their earnings, that they contracted to share equally in all property acquired, and that defendant agreed to support plaintiff. The terms of the contract as alleged do not rest upon any unlawful consideration. We therefore conclude that the complaint furnishes a suitable basis upon which the trial court can render declaratory relief. The trial court consequently erred in granting defendant's motion for judgment on the pleadings.

3. Plaintiff's complaint can be amended to state a cause of action founded upon theories of implied contract or equitable relief.

* * * The parties have * * * briefed and discussed the issue of the property rights of a nonmarital partner in the absence of an express contract. Although our conclusion that plaintiff's complaint states a cause of action based on an express contract alone compels us to reverse the judgment for defendant, resolution of the *Cary* issue will serve both to guide the parties upon retrial and to resolve a conflict presently manifest in published Court of Appeal decisions.

Both plaintiff and defendant stand in broad agreement that the law should be fashioned to carry out the reasonable expectations of the parties. Plaintiff, however, presents the following contentions: that the decisions

---

10. A great variety of other arrangements are possible. The parties might keep their earnings and property separate, but agree to compensate one party for services which benefit the other. They may choose to pool only part of their earnings and property, to form a partnership or joint venture, or to hold property acquired as joint tenants or tenants in common, or agree to any other such arrangement. (See generally Weitzman, Legal Regulation of Marriage: Tradition and Change, 62 Cal.L.Rev. 1169 (1974).)

prior to *Cary* rest upon implicit and erroneous notions of punishing a party for his or her guilt in entering into a nonmarital relationship, that such decisions result in an inequitable distribution of property accumulated during the relationship, and that *Cary* correctly held that the enactment of the Family Law Act in 1970 overturned those prior decisions. Defendant in response maintains that the prior decisions merely applied common law principles of contract and property to persons who have deliberately elected to remain outside the bounds of the community property system. *Cary*, defendant contends, erred in holding that the Family Law Act vitiated the force of the prior precedents. * * *

[T]he truth lies somewhere between the positions of plaintiff and defendant. * * *

[T]he cases prior to *Cary* exhibited a schizophrenic inconsistency. By enforcing an express contract between nonmarital partners unless it rested upon an unlawful consideration, the courts applied a common law principle as to contracts. Yet the courts disregarded the common law principle that holds that implied contracts can arise from the conduct of the parties. Refusing to enforce such contracts, the courts spoke of leaving the parties "in the position in which they had placed themselves" (Oakley v. Oakley, 185 P.2d 848, 850 (Cal. Ct. App. 1947)), just as if they were guilty parties "in pari delicto." * * *

Still another inconsistency in the prior cases arises from their treatment of property accumulated through joint effort. To the extent that a partner had contributed *funds* or *property*, the cases held that the partner obtains a proportionate share in the acquisition, despite the lack of legal standing of the relationship. (Vallera v. Vallera, 134 P.2d 761; see Weak v. Weak, 21 Cal.Rptr. 9, 13 (Cal. Ct. App. 1962).) Yet courts have refused to recognize just such an interest based upon the contribution of *services*. As Justice Curtis points out "Unless it can be argued that a woman's services as cook, housekeeper, and homemaker are valueless, it would seem logical that if, when she contributes money to the purchase of property, her interest will be protected, then when she contributes her services in the home, her interest in property accumulated should be protected." (*Vallera v. Vallera, supra*, 134 P.2d 761, 764 (diss. opn.)) * * *

Thus as of 1973, the time of the filing of *In re Marriage of Cary*, supra, 109 Cal.Rptr. 862, the cases apparently held that a nonmarital partner who rendered services in the absence of express contract could assert no right to property acquired during the relationship. The facts of *Cary* demonstrated the unfairness of that rule.

Janet and Paul Cary had lived together, unmarried, for more than eight years. They held themselves out to friends and family as husband and wife, reared four children, purchased a home and other property, obtained credit, filed joint income tax returns, and otherwise conducted themselves as though they were married. Paul worked outside the home, and Janet generally cared for the house and children.

In 1971 Paul petitioned for "nullity of the marriage." Following a hearing on that petition, the trial court awarded Janet half the property acquired during the relationship, although all such property was traceable to Paul's earnings. The Court of Appeal affirmed the award.

Reviewing the prior decisions which had denied relief to the homemaking partner, the Court of Appeal reasoned that those decisions rested upon a policy of punishing persons guilty of cohabitation without marriage. The Family Law Act, the court observed, aimed to eliminate fault or guilt as a basis for dividing marital property. But once fault or guilt is excluded, the court reasoned, nothing distinguishes the property rights of a nonmarital "spouse" from those of a putative spouse. Since the latter is entitled to half the "quasi marital property" (Civ.Code, § 4452), the Court of Appeal concluded that, giving effect to the policy of the Family Law Act, a nonmarital cohabitator should also be entitled to half the property accumulated during an "actual family relationship." (109 Cal.Rptr. at 867.) * * *

"Cary" Findings

If *Cary* is interpreted as holding that the Family Law Act requires an equal division of property accumulated in nonmarital "actual family relationships," then we agree * * * that *Cary* distends the act. No language in the Family Law Act addresses the property rights of nonmarital partners, and nothing in the legislative history of the act suggests that the Legislature considered that subject. The delineation of the rights of nonmarital partners before 1970 had been fixed entirely by judicial decision; we see no reason to believe that the Legislature, by enacting the Family Law Act, intended to change that state of affairs.

But although we reject the reasoning of *Cary* and *Estate of Atherley*, 119 Cal.Rptr. 41 (Cal. Ct. App. 1975), we share the perception of the *Cary* and *Atherley* courts that the application of former precedent in the factual setting of those cases would work an unfair distribution of the property accumulated by the couple. * * *

The principal reason why the pre-*Cary* decisions result in an unfair distribution of property inheres in the court's refusal to permit a nonmarital partner to assert rights based upon accepted principles of implied contract or equity. We have examined the reasons advanced to justify this denial of relief, and find that none have merit.

First, we note that the cases denying relief do not rest their refusal upon any theory of "punishing" a "guilty" partner. Indeed, to the extent that denial of relief "punishes" one partner, it necessarily rewards the other by permitting him to retain a disproportionate amount of the property. Concepts of "guilt" thus cannot justify an unequal division of property between two equally "guilty" persons.

Other reasons advanced in the decisions fare no better. The principal argument seems to be that "(e)quitable considerations arising from the reasonable expectation of . . . benefits attending the status of marriage . . . are not present (in a nonmarital relationship)." (Vallera v. Vallera, supra, 134 P.2d at 763.) But, although parties to a nonmarital relationship obviously cannot have based any expectations upon the belief that they were married, other expectations and equitable considerations remain. The parties may well expect that property will be divided in accord with the parties' own tacit understanding and that in the absence of such understanding the courts will fairly apportion property accumulated through mutual effort. We need not treat nonmarital partners as putatively married persons in order to apply principles of implied contract, or extend equitable remedies; we need to treat them only as we do any other unmarried persons.[22]

The remaining arguments advanced from time to time to deny remedies to the nonmarital partners are of less moment. There is no more reason to presume that services are contributed as a gift than to presume that funds are contributed as a gift; in any event the better approach is to presume, as Justice Peters suggested, "that the parties intend to deal fairly with each other." (Keene v. Keene, 371 P.2d 329, 339 (Cal. 1962) (dissenting opn.).)

The argument that granting remedies to the nonmarital partners would discourage marriage must fail; as *Cary* pointed out, "with equal or greater force the point might be made that the pre–1970 rule was calculated to cause the income producing partner to avoid marriage and thus retain the benefit of all of his or her accumulated earnings." (109 Cal.Rptr. at 866.) Although we recognize the well-established public policy to foster and promote the institution of marriage (see Deyoe v. Superior Court, 74 P. 28 (Cal. 1903)), perpetuation of judicial rules which result in an inequitable distribution of property accumulated during a nonmarital relationship is neither a just nor an effective way of carrying out that policy.

In summary, we believe that the prevalence of nonmarital relationships in modern society and the social acceptance of them, marks this as a time when our courts should by no means apply the doctrine of the unlawfulness of the so-called meretricious relationship to the instant case. As we have explained, the nonenforceability of agreements expressly providing for meretricious conduct rested upon the fact that such conduct, as the word suggests, pertained to and encompassed prostitution. To equate the nonmarital relationship of today to such a subject matter is to do violence to an accepted and wholly different practice.

We are aware that many young couples live together without the solemnization of marriage, in order to make sure that they can successfully later undertake marriage. This trial period, preliminary to marriage, serves as some assurance that the marriage will not subsequently end in dissolution to the harm of both parties. We are aware, as we have stated, of the pervasiveness of nonmarital relationships in other situations.

The mores of the society have indeed changed so radically in regard to cohabitation that we cannot impose a standard based on alleged moral considerations that have apparently been so widely abandoned by so many.

---

22. In some instances a confidential relationship may arise between nonmarital partners, and economic transactions between them should be governed by the principles applicable to such relationships.

Lest we be misunderstood, however, we take this occasion to point out that the structure of society itself largely depends upon the institution of marriage, and nothing we have said in this opinion should be taken to derogate from that institution. The joining of the man and woman in marriage is at once the most socially productive and individually fulfilling relationship that one can enjoy in the course of a lifetime.

We conclude that the judicial barriers that may stand in the way of a policy based upon the fulfillment of the reasonable expectations of the parties to a nonmarital relationship should be removed. As we have explained, the courts now hold that express agreements will be enforced unless they rest on an unlawful meretricious consideration. We add that in the absence of an express agreement, the courts may look to a variety of other remedies in order to protect the parties' lawful expectations.[24]

The courts may inquire into the conduct of the parties to determine whether that conduct demonstrates an implied contract or implied agreement of partnership or joint venture, or some other tacit understanding between the parties. The courts may, when appropriate, employ principles of constructive trust or resulting trust. Finally, a nonmarital partner may recover in quantum meruit for the reasonable value of household services rendered less the reasonable value of support received if he can show that he rendered services with the expectation of monetary reward.

Since we have determined that plaintiff's complaint states a cause of action for breach of an express contract, and, as we have explained, can be amended to state a cause of action independent of allegations of express contract, we must conclude that the trial court erred in granting defendant a judgment on the pleadings.

The judgment is reversed and the cause remanded for further proceedings consistent with the views expressed herein.

■ CLARK, JUSTICE (concurring and dissenting). The majority opinion properly permits recovery on the basis of either express or implied in fact agreement between the parties. These being the issues presented, their resolution requires reversal of the judgment. Here, the opinion should stop.

This court should not attempt to determine all anticipated rights, duties and remedies within every meretricious relationship—particularly in vague terms. Rather, these complex issues should be determined as each arises in a concrete case. * * *

The general sweep of the majority opinion raises but fails to answer several questions. First, because the Legislature specifically excluded some parties to a meretricious relationship from the equal division rule of Civil

---

24. We do not seek to resurrect the doctrine of common law marriage, which was abolished in California by statute in 1895. (See Norman v. Thomson, 54 P. 143, 145–46 (Cal. 1898); Estate of Abate, 333 P.2d 200, 206 (Cal. Ct. App. 1958).) Thus we do not hold that plaintiff and defendant were "married," nor do we extend to plaintiff the rights which the Family Law Act grants valid or putative spouses; we hold only that she has the same rights to enforce contracts and to assert her equitable interest in property acquired through her effort as does any other unmarried person.

Code section 4452, is this court now free to create an equal division rule? Second, upon termination of the relationship, is it equitable to impose the economic obligations of lawful spouses on meretricious parties when the latter may have rejected matrimony to avoid such obligations? Third, does not application of equitable principles—necessitating examination of the conduct of the parties—violate the spirit of the Family Law Act of 1969, designed to eliminate the bitterness and acrimony resulting from the former fault system in divorce? Fourth, will not application of equitable principles reimpose upon trial courts the unmanageable burden of arbitrating domestic disputes? Fifth, will not a quantum meruit system of compensation for services—discounted by benefits received—place meretricious spouses in a better position than lawful spouses? Sixth, if a quantum meruit system is to be allowed, does fairness not require inclusion of all services and all benefits regardless of how difficult the evaluation? * * *

By judicial overreach, the majority perform a nunc pro tunc marriage, dissolve it, and distribute its property on terms never contemplated by the parties, case law or the Legislature.

NOTES AND QUESTIONS

1. Although the claim made famous by *Marvin v. Marvin* is often termed "palimony" (because it is a sort of alimony for pals), it is based on some kind of contract (or equitable contract substitute) rather than a dissolved status relationship, as would be the case with alimony and marriage. On remand, Michelle Marvin was awarded $104,000 as the type of equitable remedy mentioned in footnote 25 (omitted here) of the California Supreme Court's opinion. On appeal, the appeals court overturned the award on the grounds that the complaint did not ask for such relief. Marvin v. Marvin, 176 Cal.Rptr. 555 (Ct. App. 1981). In *Whorton v. Dillingham*, 248 Cal.Rptr. 405 (Ct. App. 1988), the court reversed a dismissal of a palimony suit by a gay man based on an unwritten cohabitors' agreement.

2. Most state courts have accepted palimony arising out of an explicit or implied contract. Some courts require an express contract, or have rejected the *Marvin* approach altogether. Ann Laquer Estin, Ordinary Cohabitation, 76 Notre Dame L. Rev. 1381 (2001); Milton C. Regan, Jr., Calibrated Commitment: The Legal Treatment of Marriage and Cohabitation, 76 Notre Dame L. Rev. 1435, 1435 (2001); see also Margaret F. Brinig & Steven L. Nock, Marry Me, Bill: Should Cohabitation Be The (Legal) Default Option?, 64 La. L. Rev. 403 (2004). Does the court in *Marvin* give adequate weight to the difficulty of determining the terms of an implied contract about financial sharing between two people who decide to live together? Given that the law provides two options—the "standard form" marriage contract, and an express contract between nonmarried cohabitants—why is it also necessary to offer a third option, in the form of the judicially-enforced implied contract?

3. Might cases like *Marvin* reflect a fundamentally contractarian view of marriage itself? Many observers, feminist and nonfeminist, treat mar-

riage as a contract, see, e.g., Katherine K. Baker, Comment, Contracting for Security: Paying Married Women What They've Earned, 55 U. Chi. L. Rev. 1193, 1206–13, 1220–27 (1988); Cohen, supra, but other models have their adherents. The law traditionally viewed marriage as a status with fixed attributes. Somewhere between status and contract is the partnership model, in which equal sharing and some degree of a partnership "entity" is assumed. Many feminist reformers argue that divorce and marital property law should be brought closer to the sharing ideal implicit in the partnership model. See, e.g., Marjorie E. Kornhauser, Theory Versus Reality: The Partnership Model of Marriage in Family and Income Tax Law, 69 Temp. L. Rev. 1413 (1996); see also Pepper Schwartz, Peer Marriages (1994) (documenting ideal of "peer marriage"—in which resources and responsibilities are shared—and deviation of practice from such ideal); cf. Martha Fineman, The Illusion of Equality: The Rhetoric and Reality of Divorce Reform 2–6, 29 (1991) (arguing that family patterns are currently so unequal that women are entitled to more than an equal share). Others find the notion of an entity separate from the individuals in the marriage to be problematic, with its overtones of the common-law merger of the wife's personality into the "unity" of the marriage. As we noted earlier, entity law, such as that governing partnerships, has become somewhat more contractarian and customizable in recent years. What is most appropriate for marriage? To what extent does marriage rely on informal third-party enforcement (for example, through gossip and the like)? Should it? Depending on your answer to this question, should marriage be subject to the *numerus clausus* with respect to some of its features?

4.   Even more than in co-ownership arrangements generally, courts are reluctant to afford remedies in property disputes between cohabitants other than division of assets upon exit from the relationship. What issues would legal enforcement of continuing obligations of support, for example, raise? Margaret F. Brinig, From Contract to Covenant: Beyond the Law and Economics of the Family (2000); Elizabeth S. Scott & Robert E. Scott, Marriage as Relational Contract, 84 Va. L. Rev. 1225 (1998).

CHAPTER VI

Entity Property

The forms of property considered in Chapter V are relatively few in number. To revert to a distinction introduced in Chapter I, they largely reflect an exclusion strategy for dealing with resources, rather than a governance strategy. That is, each of the traditional forms like the fee simple, the life estate, and even the tenancy in common operates on the assumption that, at any given point in time, one person or a small number of persons will function as the "gatekeeper" of the resource. The exclusion strategy, however, is too crude to serve as an effective basis for managing the resources used by complicated entities like high-rise apartment buildings, business firms, and pension plans. In order to provide for more effective management of resources in these complicated settings, the law has developed certain devices that effectively allow owners to switch to a governance strategy for the management of resources.

The key attribute of these entity property devices is that they permit the management of entity resources to be separated from their use and enjoyment. This separation allows the managerial or governance function to be concentrated in the hands of specialists, while the use and enjoyment is distributed over a larger and more diffuse group of individuals. Indeed, the principal difference between the traditional legal forms studied in Chapter V, and the entity property devices considered in this Chapter, is that the traditional forms do not permit specialization in the day-to-day management of assets (at least formally), whereas the entity property devices do permit such specialization. This specialization of functions, more than anything else, explains why entity property devices are so popular.

Although devices for separating management from use and enjoyment of resources can be categorized in different ways, we divide them here broadly in functional terms, based on the nature of the interests of those who use and enjoy the resources. Thus, we distinguish between devices whose function is to govern multiple *possessory* interests in the use of a single complex of assets, and devices whose function is to govern multiple *nonpossessory* interests in the enjoyment of assets (typically interests in the nature of a passive investment). The principal entity devices in the former category include leases, cooperatives, and condominiums. Each of these devices can be used to separate management of a complex of assets from regular actual use of some portion of the assets by various persons or family units. The principal entity devices in the latter category include trusts, corporations, nonprofit entities, and partnerships. Here, the organizational form is designed primarily to separate management of a complex of

684

assets from the enjoyment of financial or other intangible returns for various persons or family units.

Another broad distinction among these devices is legal rather than functional. Specifically, one can distinguish between devices that achieve a functional specialization between management and beneficial use of resources at the level of property rights, and devices that achieve this separation at the level of entity law. The lease, the condominium, and the trust all achieve this division of labor at the level of property rights. With leases, for example, both the tenant and the landlord are regarded as having a type of property right (the leasehold estate and the reversion, respectively), and the nature of these different property rights allows them to specialize their functions. Other devices that we briefly consider here, including the cooperative, the corporation, and the partnership, achieve a similar division of labor through provisions of entity law. With corporations, for example, the corporation is regarded as a legal persona that owns property in its own name, much the way individual persons own property, and the specialization of functions among shareholders, corporate managers, and corporate employees is achieved through the law of corporations, not through property law. This explains why we spend little time here on corporations and partnerships—the legal rules for these entities are covered in courses on business associations. But it is important to keep in mind that, functionally speaking, corporations and partnerships can often serve as substitutes for leases or trusts, so it is worth setting forth the full menu of options in considering entity property.

A.   ENTITY PROPERTY: POSSESSORY RIGHTS

We begin with a series of arrangements in which multiple persons have distinct possessory interests in a complex of assets. A preliminary question is why people would ever want to enter into such arrangements. An important part of the answer seems to be that they want to take advantage of the specialized skills of managers of assets, and in particular to concentrate managerial control over common areas or shared facilities that present potential collective action problems or commons tragedies. A key difference among these mechanisms concerns the participants' ability or willingness to commit capital to the enterprise. Leases are attractive to those who cannot or do not want to invest their own resources in the larger enterprise; condominiums and cooperatives are more attractive to those who do want to make such an investment (either for tax or investment reasons).

1.   LEASES

Leases, also known as leaseholds, tenancies, the term of years, or landlord-tenant interests—the terms are basically interchangeable—are very old. Roman law recognized an interest called the usufruct, which bears a similarity to the lease. At common law, leases of land were not recognized as a type of freehold interest, and the tenant was not regarded as being seised of the land. Consequently, leases were categorized as a type of personal property ("chattels real"), and passed upon death by rules for personal property. But by the thirteenth century, the common-law courts granted protection to the holder of a term of years. See A.W.B. Simpson, A History of The Land Law 74–75 (2d ed. 1986). Gradually—and with much confusion along the way—leases were assimilated to the system of estates in land created for freehold interests, and were given full protection as an interest in land. Once this assimilation occurred, leases could be thought of as another form of property, like the fee simple, life estate, and defeasible fees we studied in the last chapter. Yet leases have always been regarded as somehow different from these other forms. Perhaps this is just the lingering effects of history. But we suspect that it also reflects the fact that the landlord typically plays a much more active role in the governance of the underlying assets than do persons who hold nonpossessory interests under traditional freehold interests in property, such as those who hold reversions or remainders following a life estate or those who hold a possibility of reverter or right of entry following a defeasible fee simple.

In terms of the evolutionary struggle for survival among different property forms, leases are clearly one of the big winners. Other than the fee simple absolute (and its analog, "full" or "absolute" ownership in the case of personal property), leases are the most common form of property interest encountered today. Generalizing broadly, the three forms of legal ownership of greatest continuing importance are the fee simple (and full ownership), the lease, and the trust. (As noted earlier, ownership of property by corporations and partnerships, which is also very common, is not regarded as a separate form of property; thus, corporate or partnership property is nearly always held by these entities as a fee simple or lease.) There appear to be three aspects of leases that account for their enduring appeal.

First, leases are a type of de facto financing device. One can think of a lease as an arrangement in which the owner of the property lends possession to another, in return for periodic payments of money called rent. Indeed, it appears that the original function of leases was to avoid the medieval church's prohibition of usury: "A capitalist would give to an embarrassed landowner a sum of money down; in return he took a term of years sufficiently long to enable him to recover the capital, together with his profits, out of the revenues of the land." Theodore F.T. Plucknett, A Concise History of the Common Law 572–73 (5th ed. 1956). The close relationship between leases and loans is revealed today by the common practices of entering into a lease with an option to purchase at the end of the lease term (universally used with automobile leases, for example). Given that leases are a type of financing device, it is clear that the rent charge includes an interest component, reflecting the time value of money and the anticipated rate of inflation.

Once we see that leases are a type of financing device, we can understand part of their appeal. Persons who have not accumulated much in the way of assets and/or have poor credit will often prefer to lease assets rather than purchase them. This allows them to acquire shelter to live in, land to farm, or space in which to operate a business like a restaurant, without having to commit their scarce resources to purchasing real estate. Instead, the tenant can concentrate her limited resources on acquiring other inputs—like furniture for the apartment, or equipment to operate the farm, or tables and chairs for the restaurant. If the tenant prospers and accumulates more capital or develops a stronger credit rating, the tenant may eventually decide to own rather than lease the real estate in question. Or maybe not: Leases allow persons to "leverage" their limited resources in roughly the same way that borrowing allows persons to leverage limited resources, and so for any given level of resources some persons will prefer to continue to keep on leasing in order to leverage into larger apartments, bigger farms, more restaurants, etc. than they started out with.

Second, and related to the first point, leases operate as a risk-spreading device. See Steven N.S. Cheung, The Theory of Share Tenancy (1969). Consider this first from the tenant's perspective. Suppose you move to a new city to take up a new job. You are not sure you will like either the city or the job. You have accumulated enough in savings to purchase a home or apartment in the new city, but you are reluctant to tie up most of your funds in the purchase of one asset, when you may decide to pull up stakes and move elsewhere if things don't work out. Renting is a way of minimizing the risks of investing most of your savings in an asset that you may want to unload in fairly short order (and an asset whose risk may be tightly correlated with one's employment risk). The ability to minimize the risk from a new venture has been a powerful reason for leasing rather than owning over a wide range of activities for as long as leases have been around.

From the landlord's perspective, leasing can be a way of spreading risks of tenant default. If the tenant defaults on the rental obligation, it is usually easier to retake possession of the property than it is to foreclose on a mortgage and retake property held as security for a loan (see Chapter VII). Even greater risk spreading can be achieved if the landlord leases to multiple tenants. Some tenants may fail and default on payment of rent, but it is unlikely that all or even most will, and so the landlord can minimize the risk of nonpayment by spreading this risk over multiple tenants. The built-in security interest provided by leases and the ability to spread risks among multiple leaseholders have always made leasing of property a popular investment strategy.

Third, and relevant to the larger themes of this Chapter, leases operate as a form of entity property in which complexes of assets can be integrated and professionally managed. That is, they allow owners of resources to switch from a simple exclusion strategy to a governance strategy in overcoming various coordination problems. Not all leases fit this description. Some leases, like a lease of agricultural land, may function primarily as financing and/or risk-spreading devices. Here, simple possession is transferred from the landlord to the tenant, and the property continues to be managed using an exclusion strategy—with the tenant now exercising the right to exclude. Not surprisingly, agricultural leases are frequently oral or, if in writing, are very short. See Douglas W. Allen & Dean Lueck, The "Back Forty" on a Handshake: Specific Assets, Reputation, and the Structure of Farmland Contracts, 8 J.L. Econ. & Org. 366 (1992). But often leasing is used for highly complicated complexes of assets, like high-rise apartment buildings, office buildings, and shopping centers. Leases allow these complexes of assets to be managed using a governance strategy, characterized by a specialization of functions. One party (the landlord) specializes in constructing, maintaining, insuring, and coordinating assets common to the entire complex, while the other parties (the tenants) specialize in possession and operation of discrete units within the larger complex. In a shopping center, for example, the landlord can build, maintain, and insure the parking lot, the utility systems, the common walkways, and can even provide marketing for the complex as a whole. The tenants are thereby freed up to concentrate on the design, construction, and maintenance of their individual retail spaces. Both the common areas and the individual retail spaces are probably managed more effectively and with lower transaction costs because of this specialization of functions. A similar story can be told about apartment complexes and office buildings.

Although we usually think of leases in the context of interests in land, leasing is also very commonly used to acquire personal property like airplanes and automobiles. To some extent, the use of leasing in these contexts is driven by tax considerations, such as the ease of treating auto lease payments as a business expense. But we can also see the general economic rationale for leasing at work here too. Auto leasing, for example, is clearly a financing device, and functions as a substitute for purchasing an auto with a loan secured by a lien on the auto. Indeed, many banks and financing companies offer both auto leases and loans to consumers. Can you see how automobile leases might also function as risk-spreading devices and as a device allowing specialization of functions between automobile dealers and consumers?

One problem that has long vexed lease law is that it does not differentiate between leases in terms of the underlying functional reasons the parties have for entering into a lease. Instead, one body of legal doctrine has been developed that must accommodate both simple leases used as financing or risk-spreading devices, and complex leases used to provide governance structures for complicated enterprises serving multiple persons. To put the matter more concretely, the same law generally applies to long-term (or routinely renewed) leases of agricultural land and to short-term rentals of furnished apartments. Much of the tension in lease law is attributable to this one-size-fits-all aspect. Landlord-tenant law was formed during an era when leases were simple and were largely used as financing and risk-spreading devices, with the agricultural lease being the central example. Over time, the cases that came before the courts tended increasingly to involve complicated problems of governance, the multi-unit residential apartment building being the central example. The law has responded by moving at least part way from a "property" or exclusion model of leases to a ''contract'' or governance model, while continuing to strain to encompass both types of situations within a single body of doctrine.

a. LEASE TYPES

The common law generally recognized four types of leases: the term of years, the periodic tenancy, the tenancy at will, and the tenancy at sufferance.

Term of years. This refers to a lease that has a fixed time at which it terminates or ends. Usually this is for one or more years (hence the name), but it can be for a shorter time, like six months or even one day. Some jurisdictions impose an outer limit on the length of a term of years, like 99 years; but others do not, and some leases have been reported to exist that last for as long as 999 years. Although the original Statute of Frauds (Chapter IV) required that leases longer than three years had to be in writing in order to be enforceable, under the version of the Statute in effect in most states, leases for any term longer than one year must be in writing.

The unique legal aspect of the term of years is that neither the landlord nor the tenant is required to give notice to the other before terminating the relationship. On the stated day of termination, the lease simply ends. Usually, of course, the parties will communicate about what will happen upon termination, which in practice means they may negotiate a new term of years (or perhaps a periodic lease) to commence on the termination date. But this is not required. The tenant can just walk away, or the landlord can just reclaim possession, on the designated day of termination.

Periodic tenancy. This refers to a lease that automatically rolls over for a stated period of time, usually a year or a month. Thus, a lease from year to year is a periodic tenancy that automatically rolls over one year at a time, and a lease from month to month is a periodic tenancy that automatically rolls over one month at a time.

In contrast to the term of years, a periodic tenancy requires that each of the parties give notice to the other if they desire to terminate the lease. Usually, the notice period is the same as the period of recurring rollover. In a lease from month to month, the required notice is one month. In a lease from year to year, the required notice at common law was six months, although this has been modified by statute in many jurisdictions, especially for residential tenancies, with most statutes prescribing one month's notice for termination of a tenancy from year to year.

Tenancy at will. This refers to a tenancy that lasts only so long as both parties wish it to continue. Either party can terminate at any time for any reason.

At common law, no notice was required for termination of a tenancy at will. This has been changed in many jurisdictions to require notice equal to the period of time at which rent payments are made.

Tenancy at sufferance. This is sometimes not regarded as a true tenancy and refers to the situation that exists when an individual, who was once in rightful possession of property, holds over after this right has ended. A tenant at sufferance differs from a trespasser in that the tenant's original entry was not wrongful. In many jurisdictions, this difference may limit the landlord's ability to use self-help to evict the tenant at sufferance. See Berg v. Wiley, excerpted in Chapter IV. Otherwise, however, the landlord is free to evict the tenant at sufferance using forcible entry and detainer statutes, or by bringing an action in ejectment.

Suppose a tenant at sufferance mails the landlord a check equal to the rent specified under an expired lease, and the landlord cashes the check? Some courts have construed the tenant's proffer of the check and the landlord's cashing it to be an implied contract to create a new lease (typically a periodic tenancy). See, e.g., Crechale & Polles, Inc. v. Smith, 295 So. 2d 275 (Miss. 1974).

PROBLEMS

Term of Years ⟶
1. On January 23, L agrees to rent to T a furnished apartment until February 23 of the same year. What type of tenancy is created?

Periodic Tenancy ⟶
2. L agrees to lease a farm to T from year to year, starting on March 1. On November 1, L notifies T that the lease will terminate the following March 1. Under the common law, what type of tenancy does T have come March 1? ⟶ *ending next March 1 — a term of years because not enough notice was given.*

*↳ becomes
Tenancy at sufferance
under C.L. becomes
↳ under C.L.
Tenancy at will* ⟶
3. T is a defense contractor. War breaks out, and T needs additional warehouse space. L agrees to lease a warehouse to T "for the duration of the war." What type of tenancy is created? See Garner v. Gerrish, excerpted in Chapter V, and notes following.

NOTE AND QUESTIONS

The limited menu of lease types (term of years, periodic, at will, at sufferance) is another example of the *numerus clausus* principle, considered in Chapter V. Why do you suppose the common law recognized only four types of leases? The leasehold interest is primarily of significance to two parties—the landlord and the tenant—and they are permitted great flexibility in negotiating various terms and conditions in the written lease that typically governs their relationship (and must govern their relationship for leases of more than one year under the Statute of Frauds). Can one explain the standardization of lease types in terms of third-party interests in acquiring information about lease arrangements? Is it perhaps significant that most of the standardization serves to differentiate among leases that are short-term and often are not governed by a written lease agreement?

b. THE INDEPENDENT COVENANTS MODEL

It took some time before leases came to be used as an entity property device. Early leases functioned almost entirely as financing and risk-spreading devices. In that context, the courts developed certain assumptions about the nature of the reciprocal obligations between landlord and tenant. A central assumption was that the lease was at heart a conveyance of a possessory interest in property. The possessory right—including the right to exclude others from the asset—was transferred from the landlord to the tenant for the prescribed term of the lease. This assumption, in turn, led to certain critical conclusions about the allocation of risk of casualty losses as between the landlord and the tenant during the lease term.

Paradine v. Jane

King's Bench, 1647.
Aleyn 27, 82 Eng. Rep. 897.

In debt the plaintiff declares upon a lease for years rendering rent at the four usual feasts; and for rent behind for three years, ending at the Feast of the Annunciation, 21 Car. brings his action; the defendant pleads, that a certain German prince, by name Prince Rupert, an alien born, enemy to the King and kingdom, had invaded the realm with an hostile army of men; and with the same force did enter upon the defendant's possession, and him expelled, and held out of possession from the 19 of July 18 Car. till the Feast of the Annunciation, 21 Car. whereby he could not take the profits; whereupon the plaintiff demurred, and the plea was resolved insufficient * * *

It was resolved, that the matter of the plea was insufficient; for though the whole army had been alien enemies, yet he ought to pay his rent. And this difference was taken, that where the law creates a duty or charge, and the party is disabled to perform it without any default in him, and hath no remedy over, there the law will excuse him. * * * Now the rent is a duty created by the parties upon the reservation, and had there been a covenant to pay it, there had been no questions but the lessee must have made it good, notwithstanding the interruption by enemies, for the law would not protect him beyond his own agreement, no more than in the case of reparations; this reservation then being a covenant in law, and whereupon an action of covenant hath been maintained (as Roll said) it is all one as if there had been an actual covenant. Another reason was added, that as the lessee is to have the advantage of casual profits, so he must run the hazard of casual losses, and not lay the whole burthen of them upon his lessor; and *Dyer* 56.6 was cited for this purpose, that though the land be surrounded, or gained by the sea, or made barren by wildfire, yet the lessor shall have his whole rent: and judgment was given for the plaintiff.

Main Point

Figure 6–1
Prince Rupert

ILLVSTRISSIMVS PRINCEPS ROBBERTVS, COMES PALATINVS RHENI, EQVES
ORDINIS S^{ti} GEORGII HIPPARCHVS SVÆ MAI^{tis} MAGNÆ BRITANNIÆ ETC^a

Source: National Archives of Canada.

NOTES AND QUESTIONS

1. *Paradine v. Jane* is an extreme example of the artificiality of common-law pleading. Prince Rupert, described in the case report as "enemy to the King," was in fact King Charles I's nephew and best general. The "alien armies" were the armies for the King, composed almost exclusively of native Englishmen. The apparent explanation for this deliberate fabrication is that England was at Civil War. The courts were under control of Parliament, yet the common-law lawyers "had not yet imagined a basis for traditional common-law rights outside the old framework of royal authority." Hence the false pleading, in which the King's forces are described as "alien armies" and "enemies of the King," meaning, in reality,

enemies of Parliament. See Charles M. Haar & Lance Liebman, Property and Law 270–71 (2d ed. 1985).

2. *Paradine* reflects the view that a lease is a conveyance of an interest in land, but it also reflects the view that a lease is a contract—a bundle of covenants or promises, some running from landlord to tenant, others from tenant to landlord. The most important covenant by the landlord was (and is) the covenant of quiet enjoyment, meaning a promise not to interfere with the tenant's possession of the land during the term of the lease. This covenant is critical to the very conception of a lease—the transfer of possession of property from landlord to tenant—and hence is implied as a matter of law in all leases. The most important covenant by the tenant was (and is) the covenant to pay rent. As *Paradine* suggests, this too was regarded as sufficiently important that it is implied as a matter of law in all leases. Evidently the lease in *Paradine* specified the amount of rent, but did not expressly include a promise by the tenant to pay rent. But the court holds that such a covenant is implied as a matter of law in all leases.

3. *Paradine* is a leading example of what has been called the independent covenants model of the landlord-tenant relationship. The assumption of independent covenants provides that all covenants must be performed without regard to whether other covenants have been or can be performed. *Paradine* specifically holds that when Prince Rupert made it impossible for the tenant to plant and harvest crops and hence to enjoy the benefit of the lease, this did not excuse the tenant from performing the covenant to pay rent. Generalizing more broadly, even if the landlord fails to perform a covenant, such as a covenant to repair the premises, the tenant must continue to perform the covenant to pay rent. Alternatively, even if the tenant fails to perform the covenant to pay rent, the landlord must continue to perform the covenant of quiet possession. The remedy in all these events, under the independent covenants model, is for the aggrieved party to sue for breach of covenant. Thus, if the landlord fails to perform a covenant to repair, the tenant must continue to pay rent but may sue the landlord for breach of the covenant to repair. Or if the tenant fails to pay rent, the landlord must continue to perform the covenant of quiet possession, i.e., allow the tenant to stay in possession, but may sue the tenant for breach of the covenant to pay rent.

4. *Paradine* is also important because of its recognition of the allocation of risk under a lease. The court notes that windfall gains, such as high profits earned from high crop prices, would be captured by the tenant. By parity of reasoning, wipeout losses, such as the seizure of the farm by Prince Rupert, should also be born by the tenant. The general principle recognized by the court—that the tenant is the "residual claimant" with respect to economic gains and losses associated with the property during the term of the lease—continues to be sound. The typical lease for a fixed rent converts the landlord into a kind of bondholder who earns a fixed periodic payment from the property. The tenant performs a role akin to a stockholder, whose return from the property fluctuates with the vicissitudes of the weather and market conditions—and with the effort and skill the tenant puts into it. This allocation of risk is important to bear in mind and will come up later when we consider certain specific controversies about how gains and losses should be divided under leases.

5.   *Paradine*'s specific application of this understanding of the allocation of risk is that casualty losses associated with the rented property (such
as destruction of the premises by fire, earthquake, flood, or war) must be
borne by the tenant during the term of the lease, not the landlord. In other
words, when the property that is the subject of the lease is destroyed or
damaged, the tenant's obligation to pay rent continues uninterrupted. Over
time, this specific application of the allocation of risk has gradually been
changed by legislation. For example, if the lease involves residential housing, and the house or apartment burns down, this is deemed today in all
jurisdictions to be an event that terminates the lease and hence discharges
the tenant from any further obligation to pay rent. The rules with respect
to commercial property remain closer to the original understanding of
Paradine, but have also been modified in various ways in many jurisdictions. See 1 Milton R. Friedman on Leases § 9:2 (Patrick A. Randolph, Jr.,
ed. & rev., 5th ed. 2005). In a handful of jurisdictions, courts have held that
the contract doctrines of impossibility and frustration of purpose may apply
to relieve a tenant of further obligations when the premises are destroyed.
See, e.g., Albert M. Greenfield & Co. v. Kolea, 380 A.2d 758 (Pa. 1977).
Whatever rule is followed, the allocation of risk of casualty loss is generally
understood to be a default rule subject to modification by the parties in the
lease.

6.   There was no breach of the landlord's covenant of quiet enjoyment
in *Paradine*, because Prince Rupert was not acting as the agent of the
landlord. But suppose the landlord had breached the covenant of quiet
enjoyment, as by conveying the property to another tenant who has a
superior claim of title to the property, or by physically ousting the tenant?
Consider the following case.

Smith v. McEnany

Supreme Judicial Court of Massachusetts, 1897.
48 N.E. 781.

■ HOLMES, J. This is an action upon a lease for rent and for breach of a
covenant to repair. There also is a count on an account annexed, for use
and occupation, etc., but nothing turns on it. The defense is an eviction.
The land is a lot in the city of Boston, the part concerned being covered by
a shed which was used by the defendant to store wagons. The eviction
relied on was the building of a permanent brick wall for a building on
adjoining land belonging to the plaintiff's husband, which encroached 9
inches, by the plaintiff's admission, or, as his witness testified, from
measurements, 13 1/2 inches, or, as the defendant said, 2 feet, for 34 feet
along the back of the shed. The wall was built with the plaintiff's assent,
and with knowledge that it encroached on the demised premises. The judge
ruled that the defendant had a right to treat this as an eviction determining the lease. The plaintiff asked to have the ruling so qualified as to make
the question depend upon whether the wall made the premises "uninhabit-
able for the purpose for which they were hired, materially changing the

character and beneficial enjoyment thereof." This was refused, and the plaintiff excepted. The bill of exceptions is unnecessarily complicated by the insertion of evidence of waiver and other matters, but the only question before us is the one stated, and we have stated all the facts which are necessary for its decision.

The refusal was right. It is settled in this state, in accordance with the law of England, that a wrongful eviction of the tenant by the landlord from a part of the premises suspends the rent under the lease. The main reason which is given for the decisions is that the enjoyment of the whole consideration is the foundation of the debt and the condition of the covenant, and that the obligation to pay cannot be apportioned. Shumway v. Collins, 6 Gray, 227, 232; Leishman v. White, 1 Allen, 489; Royce v. Guggenheim, 106 Mass. 201, 202; Smith v. Raleigh, 3 Camp. 513; Watson v. Waud, 8 Exch. 335, 339. It also is said that the landlord shall not apportion his own wrong, following an expression in some of the older English books. Royce v. Guggenheim, supra; Colburn v. Morrill, 117 Mass. 262; Mirick v. Hoppin, 118 Mass. 582, 587. But this does not so much explain the rule as suggest the limitation that there may be an apportionment when the eviction is by title paramount or when the lessor's entry is rightful. It leaves open the question why the landlord may not show that his wrong extended only to a part of the premises. No doubt the question equally may be asked why the lease is construed to exclude apportionment, and it may be that this is partly due to the traditional doctrine that the rent issues out of the land, and that the whole rent is charged on every part of the land. Gilbert, Rents, 178, 179, gives this as one ground why the lessor shall not discharge any part from the burden and continue to charge the rest, coupled with considerations partly of a feudal nature. But the same view naturally would be taken if the question arose now for the first time. The land is hired as one whole. If by his own fault the landlord withdraws a part of it he cannot recover either on the lease or outside of it for the occupation of the residue.

It follows from the nature of the reason for the decisions which we have stated that, when the tenant proves a wrongful deforcement by the landlord from an appreciable part of the premises, no inquiry is open as to the greater or less importance of the parcel from which the tenant is deforced. Outside the rule de minimis, the degree of interference with the use and enjoyment of the premises is important only in the case of acts not physically excluding the tenant, but alleged to have an equally serious practical effect, just as the intent is important only in the case of acts not necessarily amounting to an entry and deforcement of the tenant. The inquiry is for the purpose of settling whether the landlord's acts had the alleged effect; that is, whether the tenant is evicted from any portion of the land. If that is admitted, the rent is suspended because, by the terms of the instrument as construed, the tenant has made it an absolute condition that he should have the whole of the demised premises, at least as against willful interference on the landlord's part. * * *

Only saying ✳ he does not have to pay the rent— still responsible for other obligations in the lease.

We must repeat that we do not understand any question, except the one which we have dealt with, to be before us. An eviction like the present does not necessarily end the lease, or other obligations of the tenant under it, such as the covenant to repair.

Exceptions overruled.

NOTES AND QUESTIONS

1. Courts from their earliest encounters with leases agreed that actual eviction or ouster (or "deforcement" in the words of the principal case) by the landlord was an exception to the rule of independent covenants recognized in *Paradine v. Jane*. If the landlord, or the landlord's agent, or someone claiming paramount title based on a prior conveyance from the landlord, evicts the tenant, then the tenant's covenant to pay rent is suspended as long as the eviction lasts. So at least one covenant—the covenant to pay rent—was recognized to be *dependent* on the performance of the covenant of quiet enjoyment.

2. The question in *Smith v. McEnany* is whether a partial ouster by the landlord completely absolves the tenant from performing the covenant to pay rent, or merely justifies a partial abatement in the rent. Do you see a parallel here to the building encroachment cases like *Pile v. Pedrick* considered in Chapter I? Are you persuaded by the court's reasons for concluding that a partial ouster completely absolves the tenant from paying rent? Can you think of other reasons that might support this result? Note that the court says the suspension of the duty to pay rent does not mean that the tenant is absolved from performing on other covenants, such as a covenant to repair. Do you see how this follows from the logic of the independent covenants model that the court is following (except for the covenant to pay rent)?

3. The court says that its rule would not apply to a de minimis encroachment. Why doesn't the case, involving a wall which encroaches at most two feet, and which apparently had no adverse effect on the tenant's use of the shed, fall within the de minimis category? Is de minimis defined by the number of feet or inches from which the tenant is ousted, the loss in value to the tenant from the ouster, or the mental state of the landlord in effecting the ouster?

Sutton v. Temple

Exchequer Division, 1843.
12 M. & W. 52, 152 Eng. Rep. 1108.

* * * At the trial, before Lord Abinger, C. B., at the last assizes at Lincoln, it appeared that the defendant took the eatage of a field in the parish of Skirbeck from the plaintiff, under the following agreement

"Boston, September 8, 1842.

"Memorandum, that Mr. Thomas Temple, of Boston West, agrees to take twenty-four acres of eddish of Anne Sutton, situate in Skirbeck parish, till the 6th of April, 1843, for £40; half the money to be paid at Boston mart, the other on the 6th of April.

"THOMAS TEMPLE."

The present action was brought to recover the first instalment of £20, due at the Boston Mart, which was held on the 12th of December. On the part of the defendant it was proved, that immediately on taking possession of the land, he stocked the eddish with fifteen beasts, four of which, on the 2nd of October, were found to have died. They were opened, and a veterinary surgeon who examined them stated his opinion that they had died from the poisonous effects of old refuse paint, a quantity of which was found in their stomachs. An examination was in consequence made of a manure heap which lay open in the field, and among the manure were discovered large quantities of refuse paint. The plaintiff was informed of what had occurred, but as she took no steps to remove the manure, the defendant fenced off the heap from the eddish, and again turned in a number of beasts. Four of these died about a fortnight afterwards, as it appeared, from the same cause. The eddish was then examined minutely all over, and amongst the grass were found particles of old paint, which had evidently been spread on the land with the manure in the preceding spring. The defendant thereupon declined any longer to stock the eddish, and told the plaintiff she might do what she pleased with it; she did not, however, resume possession of the land until after the 6th of April. There was no evidence to shew that the plaintiff was aware of the state of the eddish at the time of the letting.

Under these circumstances, it was contended for the defendant that he could not be made liable in this action, inasmuch as, the eddish being wholly unfit for the purpose for which it was taken, the food of beasts, the defendant could not be said to have had any beneficial use or enjoyment of it.

The Lord Chief Baron left it to the jury to say whether the cattle died in consequence of the eddish having been poisoned by the paint, and they found that they did. The verdict, under his Lordship's direction, was entered for the plaintiff for £12, that being a rateable proportion of the rent for the time the defendant actually occupied; leave being reserved to the defendant to move to enter a verdict for him, and to the plaintiff to move to increase the damages to £26. Cross rules were obtained accordingly * * *

■ LORD ABINGER, C. B. If this case involved the necessity of overruling the case of *Smith* v. *Marrable,* [11 M & W 6, 152 Eng. Rep. 693 (Exch. 1843),] I should hesitate long before I should acquiesce in doing so, for I entirely approve of the decision to which we came in that case. That was the case of a contract of a mixed nature—for the letting of a house and furniture at Brighton, and every one knows that the furniture, upon such occasions, forms the greater part of the value which the party renting it gives for the house and its contents. In such a case, the contract is for a house and furniture fit for immediate occupation; and can there be any doubt that, if a party lets a house, and the goods and chattels or the furniture it contains, to another, that must be such furniture as is fit for the use of the party who is to occupy the house? So it is in the case of other instances that may be supposed. For instance, if a carriage be let for hire, and it breaks down on the journey, the letter of it is liable, and not the party who hires it. So, if a party hire anything else of the nature of goods and chattels, can it be said that he is not to be furnished with the proper goods—such as are fit to be used for the purpose intended? Undoubtedly the party furnishing the goods is bound to furnish that which is fit to be used. In every point of view the nature of the contract is such, that an obligation is imposed upon the party letting for hire to furnish that which is proper for the hirer's accommodation. * * * On the same principle, if a party contract for the lease of a house ready furnished, it is to be furnished in a proper manner, and so as to be fit for immediate occupation. Suppose it turn out that there is not a bed in the house, surely the party is not bound to occupy it or to continue in it. So also in the case of a house infested with vermin; if bugs be found in the beds, even after entering into possession of a house, the lodger or occupier is not bound to stay in it. Suppose, again, the tenant discover that there are not sufficient chairs in the house, or that they are not of a sort fit for use, he may give up the possession of the house. The letting of the goods and chattels, as well as the house, implies that the party who lets it so furnished is under an obligation to supply the other contracting party with whatever goods and chattels may be fit for the use and occupation of such a house, according to its particular description, and suitable in every respect for his use. Where the party has had fair opportunity of personally inspecting a ready-furnished house by himself or his agent before entering on the occupation of it, perhaps the objection would not arise; but if a person take a ready-furnished house upon the faith of its being suitably furnished, surely the owner is under an obligation to let it in a habitable state. Common sense and common justice concur in that conclusion.

On this ground, I put the case of *Smith* v. *Marrable* out of the question in the present case, from which it is materially distinguishable. * * * [I]n this case the action is brought for the fulfilment of a certain contract applicable to land, viz, for the eddish or eatage of a field—that is, the use of the herbage to be eaten by cattle—for a certain time. It appears that the cattle were accordingly turned on the land, and that some of them were poisoned. A manure heap, in which were found quantities of poisonous matter, in the shape of refuse paint, is supposed to be the cause; the tenant accordingly divides this manure heap from the rest of the field, and puts in more beasts, and several of them also die from a similar cause. It is not suggested that the plaintiff had the least knowledge of the cause of this injury when she let the land. Now, it is said that there was, under these circumstances, an implied warranty on the part of the plaintiff, that the eatage was wholesome food for cattle. But I take the rule of law to be, that if a person contract for the use and occupation of land for a specified time, and at a specified rent, he is bound by that bargain, even though he took it for a particular purpose, and that purpose be not attained. Suppose, for instance, he took it with the object of making a handsome income out of it as a farm; if his object fail altogether, is it to be said that he is not liable for any rent? It might have been that the grass was wet and injurious at particular seasons of the year; is he not, therefore, to pay any rent for that period? The general rule must therefore be, that where a man undertakes to pay a specific rent for a piece of land, he is obliged to pay that rent, whether it answer the purpose for which he took it or not. Suppose the defendant had put into the field no cattle at all; he must have paid his rent, although, in one sense, he had no beneficial occupation. The right of the landlord to the rent does not depend upon that. Here the defendant is to pay £40 for a given portion of the year, and nothing is stipulated as to his getting any benefit by the occupation of the land. I think, therefore, that in this case the plaintiff is entitled to recover her whole rent. It is no doubt a case of considerable hardship on the defendant; but we must decide with reference to general principles of law, and not upon the hardship of any particular case. Upon these grounds, I am of opinion that the case of *Smith* v. *Marrable* is materially distinguishable from the present, and I think that the rule must be made absolute, to enter the verdict for the whole amount of the rent claimed in this action.

■ PARKE, B. I am of the same opinion. I think that the rule obtained to set aside the verdict ought to be discharged, and the other rule, for increasing it to the whole amount of £20 claimed in the action, ought to be made absolute.

* * * [The question is] whether a contract or condition is implied by law, on the demise of land, that it shall be reasonably fit for the purpose for which it is taken. If the question were res integra, I should entertain no doubt at all that no such contract or condition is implied in such a case. The word "demise" certainly does not carry with it any such implied undertaking; the law merely annexes to it a condition that the party demising has a good title to the premises, and that the lessee shall not be evicted during the term. If it included any such contract as is now contended for, then, in every farming lease, at a fixed rent, there would be an implied condition that the premises were fit for the purpose for which the tenant took them, and it is difficult to see where such a doctrine would stop. No authority has been cited to support such a doctrine. With respect to the leases which have been referred to, the law is clear enough on the subjects to which they relate. * * *

As to the case of *Smith* v. *Marrable*, it is sufficiently distinguished from the present, on the ground on which the Lord Chief Baron has put it; that there the contract was of a mixed nature, being a bargain for a house and furniture, which was necessarily to be such as was fit for the purpose for which it was to be used. It resembles the case of a ready-furnished room in an hotel, which is hired on the understanding that it shall be reasonably fit for immediate habitation. In such case the bargain is not so much for the house as the furniture, and it is well understood that the house is to be supplied with fit and proper furniture, and that, if it be defective, the landlord is bound to replace it. I think, therefore, that the present case may be decided without the necessity of saying that the decision in *Smith* v. *Marrable* was wrong. The rule obtained on the part of the defendant must therefore be discharged; and as he has had all that he was entitled to under the agreement, namely, a demise of the twenty-four acres from the 8th of September to the 6th of April, he is bound to pay the sum of £20 for each portion of that time which is mentioned in the agreement: the plaintiff's rule to increase the damages must therefore be made absolute. No doubt it is a hard case on the defendant, but we must not allow considerations of that kind to persuade us to introduce into the law an alteration of which we cannot foresee the consequences, by which the mere demise of a farm would carry with it an implied condition that the land was fit for the purpose for which the tenant took it.

■ GURNEY, B. I concur with my Lord and my Brother Parke, but I must say with some difficulty, for I think it is not easy to distinguish this case from that which has been cited and principally relied upon, of *Smith* v. *Marrable*: but as this relates to land, and not also to goods and chattels, it may admit of some distinction.

■ ROLFE, B. I also think that in this case the plaintiff is entitled to recover the whole amount of £20. The defence to this action is not founded on any supposed fraud of the plaintiff, who is, therefore, entitled to recover the rent stipulated for by the agreement, unless it can be made to appear that at the time of entering into the contract there was an implied warranty on her part, that the grass of this field was to be what might be denominated wholesome grass, reasonably fit for the food of cattle. It is clear there was no such express warranty; but it is contended that that is a warranty which the law itself implied. But I feel great difficulty in coming to that conclusion, unless we are to say that on every demise of property, whether of land or of houses, there is by law an implied condition that it shall answer a certain purpose contemplated by the lessee at the time of the letting. A great number of cases have already been put to shew the inconvenience of such a doctrine; I will put another. Suppose, for instance, a new sort of manure were used, which, although it might be beneficial for a time, and under certain circumstances, was afterwards found to be injurious, and to render the grass harsh and unwholesome. In this case the defence is set up against the party herself with whom the agreement was made; but the same rule would apply against a party who took by descent; so that, if a man took land on a building lease, and it were long afterwards discovered that there was a running sand underneath, which would make it impossible to build upon the spot intended, and which could not be removed but at a ruinous expense, it is nevertheless to be presumed in such a case, according to the argument, that there was to be an implied warranty that there was no running sand at that particular place, and the lessor must be held responsible. Another case may be supposed, where the party takes a house for the purpose of converting it into a hospital; if it should turn out to be in such an unwholesome situation as to render it unfit for that purpose, could it be said that the premises were let to him under an implied warranty that it should be fit to be converted into a hospital, and could this be any justification for his refusing to fulfil his contract by payment of the rent? The only difficulty in this case is, how to reconcile the decision in *Smith* v. *Marrable* with this. My Lord and my Brother Parke, however, have pointed out the ground upon which that case may be distinguished from the present. I think it is very probable that the two cases may be so distinguished; but if not, I should prefer at once to overrule that decision, than to follow it in the present case.

Rule for a nonsuit discharged; rule to increase the damages absolute.

NOTES AND QUESTIONS

1. *Sutton* illustrates the common-law rule of "caveat lessee" (tenant beware) in its pure and harsh form. There is no implied warranty that the leased premises will be fit for the tenant's intended purposes. To what extent does the rule follow from the understanding that the lease is a conveyance of a property right? To what extent does it follow from the general principle about the allocation of risk under a lease recognized in *Paradine v. Jane*? The rule, of course, was a default. Tenants like Thomas Temple were free to negotiate for express warranties of fitness as part of their lease, and such warranties would be enforced under standard rules of contract interpretation. But such express warranties were rare.

2. Suppose Anne Sutton knows that the eatage was contaminated by paint chips when the lease was entered into with Thomas Temple. Temple asks her if the eatage is healthy, and she responds: "As good as you will find in all of Skirbeck." Same result? Suppose Anne Sutton knows that the eatage was contaminated by paint chips when the lease was entered into, but Temple does not ask about the quality of the eatage, and she does not disclose the problem posed by the paint chips. Same result?

3. How important to the decision do you think it is that the lease here is for the use of raw pasture land and Temple is a farmer who is presumably familiar with the various qualities of pasture land? Is there any reason to think that, as a rule, landlords renting pasture land have a comparative advantage in inspecting the land and grass for suitability for the tenant's purposes, relative to the tenant? Here, of course, the defect in the grass was "latent," and not readily detectable upon inspection. But is it clear that the landlord, either as a rule or in this particular case, would be a better insurer against latent defects in eatage than the tenant?

4. The judges are at great pains to distinguish *Smith v. Marrable*, a then-recent decision which had held there is an implied warranty of habitability in a short term rental of a furnished vacation cottage. American courts later reached a similar result regarding furnished vacation rentals. See Ingalls v. Hobbs, 31 N.E. 286 (Mass. 1892). Are you persuaded by the argument that an implied warranty of habitability was appropriate in *Marrable*, but not in the instant case, because *Marrable* involved the lease of personal property as well as real property? Suppose A, a farmer, leases a team of workhorses (personal property) to B, another farmer. Would the courts imply a warranty of fitness in such a lease, on the ground that personal property is involved?

5.   One can see *Sutton* and *Marrable* as establishing two paradigms for whether the law should imply a warranty of habitability or fitness for purpose in a lease. In the first paradigm (*Sutton*), the tenant is presumed to be in as good or better position than the landlord to determine the fitness of the leased premises. In the second (*Marrable*), the landlord is presumed to be in a better position than the tenant to determine the fitness of the leased premises. How would you define the circumstances that demarcate the line between the two paradigms? Where would the rental of an unfurnished apartment in a multi-unit apartment building fall? Where would the rental of a space lease in a shopping center fall? If we think of leases in contractual terms, both paradigms would presumably function as default rules, subject to modification by the parties in the lease.

6.   Whatever the underlying distinction between *Sutton* and *Marrable*, one can imagine how the law might have gradually evolved, with the *Marrable* paradigm gradually expanding from furnished vacation rentals to encompass situations like rentals of apartments in multi-unit urban apartment complexes. But the law did not evolve in this way. Instead, courts tended to continue to assume that rentals of unfurnished apartments were governed by the rule of caveat lessee recognized in *Sutton*. Then, in the late 1960s and early 1970s, a sudden avulsion occurred, as one jurisdiction after another recognized an implied warranty of habitability in apartment rentals. See Javins v. First National Realty, infra.

c.   EXTENSIONS OF THE INDEPENDENT COVENANTS MODEL

As time marched on, a variety of exceptions and qualifications to the pure independent covenants model emerged. One of the most important was the development of *forfeiture clauses*. These were clauses in leases, invariably insisted upon by landlords, providing that upon the tenant's violation of enumerated covenants in the lease—most crucially the covenant to pay rent—the tenant's interest in the lease would be immediately forfeited. Forfeiture clauses take two forms, modeled after defeasible fees (see Chapter V). Under one form, analogous to the fee simple determinable, the lease forfeits automatically upon violation of specified covenants by the tenant. Under the other form, analogous to the fee simple subject to condition subsequent, the violation of specified covenants by the tenant authorizes the landlord to "reenter and retake" the premises. See David S. Hill, Landlord and Tenant Law 21–22 (4th ed. 2004). Which form would you prefer if a landlord? If a tenant? How do you suppose courts construe these clauses if it is ambiguous which form has been chosen?

Forfeiture clauses, which courts have generally upheld, in effect convert the specified tenant covenants covered by the forfeiture clause from independent covenants into dependent covenants. For example, under the model of independent covenants, the landlord's covenant of quiet possession was not extinguished by the tenant's failure to pay rent. The landlord's remedy was periodically to sue the tenant for damages equal to the unpaid rent. With the addition of an enforceable forfeiture clause, the situation is radically changed. Now, the tenant's failure to pay rent means that the tenant's interest in the leasehold estate is subject to forfeiture, in effect releasing the landlord from the covenant of quiet enjoyment. If the tenant remains in possession after forfeiture, he becomes a tenant at sufferance, liable to an action for eviction. If the tenant abandons after forfeiture, the landlord can immediately reenter and retake possession of the premises.

Forfeiture clauses had the effect of tilting the original independent covenants model in favor of the landlord, in that they transformed the lease into a bundle of covenants that were independent insofar as the promises ran to the tenant, and dependent insofar as the promises ran to the landlord. But the legal system responded by developing new doctrines that provided some relief for tenants. We consider here two such doctrines: constructive eviction and surrender.

Blackett v. Olanoff

Supreme Judicial Court of Massachusetts, 1977.
358 N.E.2d 817.

■ WILKINS, JUSTICE. The defendant in each of these consolidated actions for rent successfully raised constructive eviction as a defense against the landlords' claim. The judge found that the tenants were "very substantially deprived" of quiet enjoyment of their leased premises *"for a substantial time"* (emphasis original). He ruled that the tenants' implied warranty of quiet enjoyment was violated by late evening and early morning music and disturbances coming from nearby premises which the landlords leased to others for use as a bar or cocktail lounge (lounge). The judge further found that, although the landlords did not intend to create the conditions, the landlords "had it within their control to correct the conditions which . . . amounted to a constructive eviction of each (tenant)." He also found that the landlords promised each tenant to correct the situation, that the landlords made some attempt to remedy the problem, but they were unsuccessful, and that each tenant vacated his apartment within a reasonable time. Judgment was entered for each tenant; the landlords appealed; and we transferred the appeals here. We affirm the judgments.

The landlords argue that they did not violate the tenants' implied covenant of quiet enjoyment because they are not chargeable with the noise from the lounge. The landlords do not challenge the judge's conclusion that the noise emanating from the lounge was sufficient to constitute a constructive eviction, if that noise could be attributed to the landlords.[3] Nor do the landlords seriously argue that a constructive eviction could not be

---

3. There was evidence that the lounge had amplified music (electric musical instruments and singing, at various times) which started at 9:30 P.M. and continued until 1:30 A.M. or 2 A.M., generally on Tuesdays through Sundays. The music could be heard through the granite walls of the residential tenants' building, and was described variously as unbelievably loud, incessant, raucous, and penetrating. The noise interfered with conversation and prevented sleep. There was also evidence of noise from patrons' yelling and fighting.

found as matter of law because the lounge was not on the same premises as the tenants' apartments. See 1 American Law of Property § 3.51 at 281 (A. J. Casner ed. 1952). The landlords' principal contention, based on the denial of certain requests for rulings, is that they are not responsible for the conduct of the proprietors, employees, and patrons of the lounge.

Our opinions concerning a constructive eviction by an alleged breach of an implied covenant of quiet enjoyment sometimes have stated that the landlord must perform some act with the intent of depriving the tenant of the enjoyment and occupation of the whole or part of the leased premises. See Katz v. Duffy, 158 N.E. 264 (Mass. 1927), and cases cited. There are occasions, however, where a landlord has not intended to violate a tenant's rights, but there was nevertheless a breach of the landlord's covenant of quiet enjoyment which flowed as the natural and probable consequence of what the landlord did, what he failed to do, or what he permitted to be done. Charles E. Burt, Inc. v. Seven Grand Corp., 163 N.E.2d 4, 6 (Mass. 1959) (failure to supply light, heat, power, and elevator services). Westland Housing Corp. v. Scott, 44 N.E.2d 959, 962–63 (Mass. 1942) (intrusions of smoke and soot over a substantial period of time due to a defective boiler). Shindler v. Milden, 184 N.E. 673, 673–74 (Mass. 1933) (failure to install necessary heating system, as agreed). Case v. Minot, 33 N.E. 700, 701 (Mass. 1893) (landlord authorizing another lessee to obstruct the tenant's light and air, necessary for the beneficial enjoyment of the demised premises). Skally v. Shute, 132 Mass. 367, 370–371 (1882) (undermining of a leased building rendering it unfit for occupancy). Although some of our opinions have spoken of particular action or inaction by a landlord as showing a presumed intention to evict, the landlord's conduct, and not his intentions, is controlling.

The judge was warranted in ruling that the landlords had it within their control to correct the condition which caused the tenants to vacate their apartments. The landlords introduced a commercial activity into an area where they leased premises for residential purposes. The lease for the lounge expressly provided that entertainment in the lounge had to be conducted so that it could not be heard outside the building and would not disturb the residents of the leased apartments. The potential threat to the occupants of the nearby apartments was apparent in the circumstances. The landlords complained to the tenants of the lounge after receiving numerous objections from residential tenants. From time to time, the pervading noise would abate in response to the landlord's complaints. We conclude that, as matter of law, the landlords had a right to control the objectionable noise coming from the lounge and that the judge was warranted in finding as a fact that the landlords could control the objectionable conditions.

This situation is different from the usual annoyance of one residential tenant by another where traditionally the landlord has not been chargeable with the annoyance. See Katz v. Duffy, 158 N.E. 264 (Mass. 1927) (illegal sale of alcoholic beverages); DeWitt v. Pierson, 112 Mass. 8 (1873) (prostitution).[4] Here we have a case more like Case v. Minot, 33 N.E. 700 (Mass. 1893), where the landlord entered into a lease with one tenant which the landlord knew permitted that tenant to engage in activity which would interfere with the rights of another tenant. There, to be sure, the clash of tenants' rights was inevitable, if each pressed those rights. Here, although the clash of tenants' interests was only a known potentiality initially, experience demonstrated that a decibel level for the entertainment at the lounge, acoustically acceptable to its patrons and hence commercially desirable to its proprietors, was intolerable for the residential tenants.

Because the disturbing condition was the natural and probable consequence of the landlords' permitting the lounge to operate where it did and because the landlords could control the actions at the lounge, they should not be entitled to collect rent for residential premises which were not reasonably habitable. Tenants such as these should not be left only with a claim against the proprietors of the noisome lounge. To the extent that our opinions suggest a distinction between nonfeasance by the landlord, which has been said to create no liability (P. Hall, Massachusetts Law of Landlord and Tenant §§ 90–91 (4th ed. 1949)), and malfeasance by the landlord, we decline to perpetuate that distinction where the landlord creates a situation and has the right to control the objectionable conditions.

Judgments affirmed.

NOTES AND QUESTIONS

1. The theory of constructive eviction builds on the exception to independent covenants recognized for actual evictions by the landlord. See Smith v. McEnany, supra. Suppose the landlord commits some act that falls short of an actual eviction but so severely depresses the value of the tenancy that the tenant has no reasonable option but to vacate the premises. In these circumstances, is it not fair to say that the landlord has

---

4. The general, but not universal, rule, in this country is that a landlord is not chargeable because one tenant is causing annoyance to another (A. H. Woods Theatre v. North American Union, 246 Ill.App. 521, 526–527 (1927) (music from one commercial tenant annoying another commercial tenant's employees)), even where the annoying conduct would be a breach of the landlord's covenant of quiet enjoyment if the landlord were the miscreant. Contra Kesner v. Consumers Co., 255 Ill.App. 216, 228–229 (1929) (storage of flammables constituting a nuisance); Bruckner v. Helfaer, 222 N.W. 790, 791(Wis. 1929) (residential tenant not liable for rent where landlord, with ample notice, does not control another tenant's conduct).

The rule in New York appears to be that the landlord may not recover rent if he has had ample notice of the existence of conduct of one tenant which deprives another tenant of the beneficial enjoyment of his premises and the landlord does little or nothing to abate the nuisance. See Cohen v. Werner, 378 N.Y.S.2d 868 (N.Y. App. T. 1975); Rockrose Associates v. Peters, 366 N.Y.S.2d 567, 568 (N.Y. Civ. Ct. 1975) (office lease); Home Life Ins. Co. v. Breslerman, 5 N.Y.S.2d 272, 273 (N.Y. App. T. 1938). But see comments in Trustees of the Sailors' Snug Harbor in the City of New York v. Sugarman, 35 N.Y.S.2d 196, 197–98 (N.Y. App. Div. 1942) (no nuisance).

A tenant with sufficient bargaining power may be able to obtain an agreement from the landlord to insert and to enforce regulatory restrictions in the leases of other, potentially offending, tenants. See E. Schwartz, Lease Drafting in Massachusetts § 6.33 (1961).

constructively evicted the tenant? And if the covenant to pay rent is dependent rather than independent when the landlord actually evicts the tenant, shouldn't the covenant to pay rent also be dependent when the landlord constructively evicts the tenant? Upon this reasoning, courts concluded that landlord misfeasance sufficiently serious to cause a reasonable tenant to vacate was a constructive eviction, and excused the tenant from further payment of rent.

RULE [

2. *Blackett* involves the considerably trickier issue of landlord nonfeasance rather than misfeasance. The noise from the lounge is being caused by another tenant. The landlord is blamed for not stepping in and forcing the lounge-tenant to hold down the noise. One theory for holding a landlord responsible for constructive eviction based on nonfeasance turns on whether the landlord's inaction violates some specific clause in the tenant's lease. For example, suppose the landlord promises in the lease to provide a "waterproof" basement. The basement leaks, and the landlord does nothing. Courts have held in these circumstances that the landlord's failure to act may constitute a constructive eviction (if the landlord's breach otherwise causes effects that satisfy the severity requirements for constructive eviction and the tenant vacates because of those effects), because the failure to act was the breach of a specific duty outlined in the lease. See Reste Realty Corp. v. Cooper, 251 A.2d 268 (N.J. 1969). Is there a clause in the tenant's lease in *Blackett* that would justify a finding of constructive eviction under the breach-of-lease-clause theory?

3. How in fact does the court conclude that the landlord is liable for nonfeasance in *Blackett*? Under what circumstances should a landlord's tenant A be regarded as a third-party beneficiary of a clause in the lease between the landlord and tenant B? Many of the earliest constructive eviction cases involved nonfeasance in the form of a landlord who did nothing to evict prostitutes operating in a multi-unit building. See, e.g., Dyett v. Pendleton, 8 Cow. 727 (N.Y. 1826). Does the decision in the instant case rest on a pun on the term "quiet enjoyment"?

4. How critical is it to the theory of constructive eviction that the tenant actually vacates the premises? On the one hand, since the theory rests on an analogy to actual eviction, one could say that it is necessary that the tenant vacate the premises in order to establish constructive eviction. On the other hand, since the theory is designed to single out landlord breaches that "depriv[e] the tenant of the enjoyment and occupation of the whole or part of the leased premises," one could say that the tenant's decision to vacate is at most only evidence of the severity of the breach, but not a necessary element of the defense. Moreover, the requirement that the tenant vacate puts the tenant at extreme risk if the court agrees with the landlord that the conditions of the premises were not sufficiently dire to justify constructive eviction: The tenant could end up being liable for unpaid rent *and* would have given up whatever value was left in the premises. One possible solution would be to seek a declaratory judgment from a court before vacating, see Charles E. Burt, Inc. v. Seven Grand Corp., 163 N.E.2d 4 (Mass. 1959), although this would be expensive

and usually would take too long. The New Hampshire Supreme Court has recently held that it is not necessary that the tenant vacate the premises in order to establish constructive eviction. See Echo Consulting Servs., Inc. v. North Conway Bank, 669 A.2d 227 (N.H. 1995). Is this a wise decision? Can you see any functional justification for requiring that the tenant vacate before being allowed to invoke a defense that will eliminate all liability for payment of rent? Compare the discussion in Chapter V about courts being less willing to arbitrate relations between cotenants while the relationship is on-going than they are when one cotenant has been ousted or seeks partition.

5.   *Blackett* alludes to the possibility of proving a partial constructive eviction, meaning, presumably, that the tenant has been constructively evicted from one part of the premises but not from other parts. The law here is unsettled, but there are some precedents upholding claims for partial constructive eviction. See Dennison v. Marlowe, 744 P.2d 906 (N.M. 1987) (holding tenant could claim partial constructive eviction when landlord failed to make the second floor of restaurant habitable); East Haven Associates v. Gurian, 313 N.Y.S.2d 927 (Civ. Ct. of City of N.Y. 1970) (holding that landlord's failure to eliminate emission of green fluid from air conditioner and ash from incinerator constituted partial constructive eviction from terrace outside apartment). On the reasoning of *Smith v. McEnany*, supra, would a finding of partial constructive eviction authorize the tenant to withhold all of the rent until the partial constructive eviction is corrected?

In re Kerr

U.S. District Court, Southern District of New York, 1939.
29 F.Supp. 414.

■ GODDARD, DISTRICT JUDGE. Petition for review of an order of the [Bankruptcy] Referee allowing the claim of the Garment Center Capitol, Inc., against the estate of the bankrupts to rent in the amount of $3,622.57. The trustee objects to the allowance of the claim in this amount but concedes that the claimant has a claim for $689.42. The facts sufficient for determining the question now presented are as follows:

The bankrupts were tenants of the Garment Center Capitol, Inc., occupying a floor in a business building at 512 Seventh Avenue, New York City, under a lease for a term of two years commencing February 1, 1937 and ending January 30, 1939 at the annual rent of $5,820 payable $485 monthly in advance. The bankrupts paid the rent for two months but the rent due April 1, 1937 was not paid and on April 7th they made an assignment for the benefit of creditors; on May 13th an involuntary petition in bankruptcy was filed which was followed on June 2d by an adjudication; on May 6th the landlord entered into a lease of the premises in its own name with Tutbury, Inc., for a term ending January 30, 1941— that is two years beyond the term of the bankrupts' lease. The lease with Tutbury, Inc., provided that they were to have free rent from May 15 to

New lease has a period of free rent, and then cheap rent before increasing

August 1, 1937 and that the rent from August 1, 1937 to January 30, 1938 was to be at the rate of $2,875 per annum, and from February 1, 1938 to January 30, 1941 at the rate of $5,750 per annum. The pertinent part of paragraph Sixth of the bankrupts' lease reads "In any such case (default in the payment of rent) * * * the Landlord may, at the Landlord's option, and in the name of the Landlord or otherwise, relet the demised premises or any part or parts thereof, as the agent of the Tenant or otherwise, for the whole or any part of the term from time to time as it may deem best".

It is stipulated that the landlord did not give the bankrupts any notice of the termination of the lease or notice of reentry by the landlord, or notice of reletting the premises to Tutbury, Inc., and that no other agreement was entered into between them except the lease referred to above.

The trustee contends that any obligation of the bankrupts under their lease with Garment Center Capitol, Inc., was terminated by the new lease entered into by the landlord with Tutbury, Inc., for a term extending beyond the term of the bankrupts' lease; that this assertion of dominion over the premises by the landlord constituted an act of acceptance of the bankrupts' surrender and relieved the bankrupts of its obligations, and that at the time of the bankruptcy, either when the petition was filed on May 13, 1937 or on the day of the adjudication, June 2, 1937, the bankrupts were not obligated on the lease because of the surrender, and therefore the landlord has no claim against the bankrupts' estate except for the unpaid rent amounting to $689.42 which accrued prior to the surrender and acceptance of the lease.

The contention of the landlord is that under paragraph Sixth quoted above it was authorized to enter into a lease extending beyond the term of the bankrupts' lease. The landlord relies upon the portion of paragraph Sixth in the bankrupts' lease, which says that in case of default in payment of rent the landlord may, at its option "in the name of the Landlord or otherwise relet the demised premises or any part of parts thereof, as agent of the Tenant or otherwise, for the whole or any part of the term from time to time as it may deem best". The landlord and the referee construe "otherwise" to mean that the landlord is thus authorized to make a new lease for any length of time it deems best and to charge the tenant for its damages under the lease for the period up to the expiration of bankrupts' lease—January 30, 1939.

RULE

The courts of New York hold that in the absence of an express provision in the lease authorizing the landlord to relet the making of a new lease is an acceptance of surrender of a then existing lease. Gray v. Kaufman Dairy Co., 56 N.E. 903 (N.Y.). It is clear that under paragraph Sixth the landlord was given the right to relet for the balance of the term either as agent for the tenant or in its own name and hold the tenant for the difference between the rent reserved in the bankrupts' lease and the rent paid by the new tenant. However, in the case at bar the landlord entered into a lease extending beyond the term of the bankrupts' lease. In making such a lease the New York courts say that the landlord will be presumed to be acting for his own account and to have recognized a surrender of the premises in the absence of consent to such reletting. Brill v. Friedhoff, 183 N.Y.S. 463 (App. Div.); Matter of Adam's Estate, 267 N.Y.S. 910; Matter of Goldburg's Estate, 266 N.Y.S. 106; Bonsignore v. Koondel, 235 N.Y.S. 453.

I do not construe the words "or otherwise" as a consent by the bankrupts to the landlord entering into a lease extending beyond the term of the bankrupts' lease; therefore, when it did so the landlord was acting solely on its own account and recognized a surrender of the bankrupts' lease. It seems to me that the words "or otherwise" simply meant that the landlord might rent the premises in the landlord's own name or as agent for the tenant for the whole or any part or parts of the term.

The referee, in his opinion, says, "I should give effect to the words 'or otherwise' by holding that the legal effect of the lease to Tutbury is a renting for the account of the bankrupts up to the date of the expiration of the landlord's lease to the bankrupts, and a renting in the landlord's own right for the balance of the term of said lease". The referee expresses the view that it would be applying an over-technical and legalistic rule to hold that reletting by the landlord for a term extending two years beyond the term of the bankrupts' lease constituted an act of acceptance of the bankrupts' surrender. The bankrupts, I think, may well urge that the meaning or intent of paragraph Sixth cannot fairly be broadened or construed as authorizing the landlord to make a new lease covering the term of the bankrupts' lease and extending two years beyond the bankrupt's term at a yearly rental of $2,875 for the period of August 1, 1937 to January 30, 1938 and at a rental of $5,750 from February 1, 1938 to January 30, 1941; also to allow the new tenant, as an inducement for entering into such a lease, to occupy the premises free from May 1 to August 1, 1937. If the meaning of this paragraph is in doubt, it should, under the familiar rule, be resolved against the landlord who drew the lease. * * *

Accordingly the order of the referee is modified by reducing the claim allowed to $689.42, which is the amount of unpaid rent prior to surrender and acceptance of the lease.

[handwritten margin note: Cannot lesen as 2 separate leases (one to cover the term of original lease, + one to extend by 2 years) because it has inducements to enter the lease during the time frame of the original lease]

NOTES AND QUESTIONS

1.   The doctrine of surrender, applied in the principal case, is based on the idea of a contractual release of liability. The landlord and tenant create a leasehold interest by entering into a lease between themselves. They can extinguish such an interest by agreeing between themselves to release each other from the obligations of the lease. Ordinarily, such a release would require a written contract under the Statute of Frauds (if the lease were for more than one year). The surrender doctrine emerged as courts reasoned that the landlord and tenant could create a mutual release of further lease obligations by *implied contract*. This would happen if the tenant vacated the premises with the intention never to return, in effect making an

"offer" to surrender the leasehold estate, and the landlord responded by taking action inconsistent with the tenant's continuing right to the leasehold interest, in effect "accepting" the surrender of the leasehold estate. Although originally grounded in the idea of implied contract, the doctrine of surrender eventually came to be understood as a type of release implied as a matter of law. This means, among other things, that the "offer" and "acceptance" of the surrender do not have to be in writing, notwithstanding the Statute of Frauds.

longer than 1 year needs writing

2.   The doctrine of surrender, like the doctrine of constructive eviction, is pro-tenant. When a court finds that the landlord has accepted a surrender, the tenant is liable for the full amount of rent owed up to the moment of acceptance, but is off the hook thereafter. Landlords, naturally, did not like the doctrine of surrender, particularly when the leased premises might remain vacant for some time before a new tenant could be found. They sought to get around the doctrine by drafting lease provisions that would impose continuing liability on tenants who vacate the premises, even if the landlord has reentered and leased the premises to someone else. These clauses take various forms, but the clause at issue in *In re Kerr*, allowing the landlord to reenter and relet the premises as the "agent of" the tenant, is typical. Courts in most jurisdictions enforce these clauses against the abandoning tenant, at least insofar as the landlord cannot be made whole by reletting to another tenant. For example, if the landlord reenters and advertises the premises, but three months go by before a suitable substitute tenant is found, the original tenant will remain liable under a reenter and relet clause for an additional three months' rent (in addition to any unpaid rent up to the time of abandonment).

3.   The legal theory that makes such reenter and relet clauses enforceable against the original tenant is a little murky, given that the doctrine of surrender seems to say that the original lease has been extinguished as a matter of law by the landlord's re-entry. One idea offered in some decisions is that although the doctrine of surrender extinguishes "privity of estate" between landlord and tenant, it does not extinguish "privity of contract." (These concepts are explained more fully below in the context of transfers of tenant interests.) A further implication of this view is that, since the tenant's liability under a reenter and relet clause is purely contractual, the landlord is required to mitigate the tenant's damages. In other words, although at common law the landlord had no obligation to mitigate the tenant's damages merely because of the tenant's abandonment, once the landlord seeks to impose additional liability on the tenant under a reenter and relet clause, the landlord is under a contract-law-based duty to mitigate. Also, although the tenant under the surrender doctrine is absolved of any further liability for rent once the surrender is accepted, under a reenter and relet clause the tenant remains liable to the landlord for expectation damages if the landlord cannot with reasonable effort relet the premises at a rent equal to or higher than the original rent reserved.

4.   Although courts enforce renter and relet clauses (and similar clauses requiring tenants to indemnify landlords for losses caused by the

tenant's breach), they continue to show sympathy for tenants by strictly enforcing such clauses against the landlords (who are the ones who draft them and insist on putting them in leases). The principal case is a reflection of this attitude. Can you restate the steps in the court's reasoning that results in the tenants getting off the hook for any liability for rent after they abandon? (Hint: Start by considering how the case would be decided if there had been no reenter and relet clause in the lease.) Do you think the court was influenced by the fact that the landlord gave a substantial discount in rent to the new tenant, Tutbury, for the first year of the lease? Why might the existence of the reenter and relet clause have influenced the way the landlord structured the payments under the substitute lease?

5.   The doctrine of surrender requires that courts characterize both the actions of the tenant and the landlord as evidencing a particular state of mind. The tenant's state of mind must be to abandon the leasehold. This is usually pretty straightforward, although occasionally it can be disputed (see *Berg v. Wiley* in Chapter IV, for an example of a factual dispute over whether the tenant has abandoned). The landlord's state of mind must be to "accept" the abandonment, and reclaim the leasehold interest as an entitlement belonging to the landlord. This gives rise to many more disputes. Reasonably clear cases are when the landlord relets to a third person (unless this is authorized by a reenter and relet clause), or where the landlord changes the locks. But there is significant litigation over whether more equivocal actions, such as retaining the keys after they have been dropped off by the tenant or entering the premises to put up a "For Rent" sign, constitute an acceptance of surrender. See 2 Milton R. Friedman, Friedman on Leases § 16:3:2 (Patrick A. Randolph, Jr., ed. & rev., 5th ed. 2005). Landlords are routinely advised to communicate with tenants in writing stating unequivocally whether they are or are not accepting a surrender of the leasehold.

d.   THE MODEL OF DEPENDENT COVENANTS

The 1970s witnessed a "revolution" in landlord-tenant law, a revolution that was characterized at the time as entailing the repudiation of a "property" conception of leases in favor of a "contract" model of leases. There is reason to be somewhat skeptical of this characterization. As we have seen, landlord-tenant law has always had a strong contractual flavor, in the sense that leases are regarded as bundles of covenants. Moreover, some of the reforms of the 1970s are difficult to square with ordinary precepts of contract law, insofar as they entailed the adoption of mandatory rules of law rather than default rules (default rules are more typical in the law of contracts). See Roger A. Cunningham, The New and Statutory Warranties of Habitability in Residential Leases: From Contract to Status, 16 Urb. L. Ann. 3 (1979); Mary Ann Glendon, The Transformation of American Landlord–Tenant Law, 23 B.C. L. Rev. 503 (1982). A more accurate characterization might be that the contractual aspect of landlord-tenant law moved decisively away from the model of independent covenants toward the model of dependent covenants. Although this movement accelerated in the 1970s, it was clearly foreshadowed by earlier decisions, such as the following case, which anticipated in many respects what can be called modern landlord-tenant law.

Medico–Dental Building Company of Los Angles v. Horton and Converse ~ D - lessee

Supreme Court of California, 1942.
132 P.2d 457.

■ CURTIS, J. Plaintiff brought this suit for rent alleged to be due under a lease * * * A trial was had before the court without a jury, and findings were made in favor of the defendant pursuant to its claim that plaintiff's breach of a restrictive covenant in the lease, which violation was not waived by the defendant, prevented the maintenance of this action * * *. From the judgment rendered accordingly for defendant * * * plaintiff has taken this appeal.

On July 1, 1934, defendant, Horton & Converse, as lessee, entered into a written lease covering certain space on the ground floor of the Medico–Dental Building at Eighth and Francisco Streets, Los Angeles, for a term of sixteen years and four months, at a minimum monthly rental of $600 for the part of the term concerned herein, and a fixed percentage of the gross sales. At the time the lease was made, defendant was in possession of the premises, having occupied them since 1925 under a prior lease. As successor in interest by virtue of an assignment of the lease involved herein, plaintiff, Medico–Dental Building Company, stands in the position of the original lessor.

The lease provided that the premises should be "used and occupied by lessee as a drug store and for no other business or purpose, without the written consent of lessor." It also contained the following stipulation: "Lessor agrees not to lease or sublease any part or portion of the Medico–Dental Building to any other person, firm or corporation for the purpose of maintaining a drug store or selling drugs or ampoules, or for the purpose of maintaining a cafe, restaurant or lunch counter therein during the term of this lease."

On December 30, 1937, plaintiff leased the entire ninth floor of the same building to one Dr. Boonshaft, a physician, for a term of three years commencing April 15, 1938. This lease contained the following provisions: "The premises demised hereby are to be used solely as offices for the practice of medicine and dentistry, and lessee agrees that he will not maintain therein or thereon, nor permit to be maintained therein or thereon, a drug store or drug dispensary, nor will lessee compound or dispense, or permit to be compounded or dispensed, drugs or ampoules except in connection with the regular course of treatment of lessee's own patients. Lessee agrees not to display any sign or advertisement on the inside or outside of the demised premises, or the building of which the demised premises are a part embodying the words 'Pharmacy,' 'Drug

Store,' 'Dispensary' or words of like import. Lessee understands that lessor has heretofore executed a lease to Horton & Converse granting to said Horton & Converse the exclusive privilege of conducting a drug store business on the ground floor of said Medico–Dental Building, and lessee agrees that he will not do, or permit to be done, anything in connection with the premises demised hereby which would in any way conflict with or constitute a breach by the lessor therein of said Horton & Converse lease."

Dr. Boonshaft went into possession under his lease on April 15, 1938, and occupied the entire ninth floor of the building, where he had from thirty-two to thirty-six treatment rooms and had six to eight doctors associated with him in an organization known as the Boonshaft Medical Group. Independent of this staff but subject to frequent call to the premises in the course of the work of this enterprise were some thirty consultant doctors. The plan of operation of the medical organization was to register groups of employees and lodge members and their families for medical treatment on the basis of a monthly charge per family; registration and payment of the fixed sum entitled the patient to receive, among other things, certain drugs, but additional charges were made for other medicines. Dr. Boonshaft maintained a drug room wherein drugs were sold and prescriptions filled per the order of the regular staff or the consultant doctors in the treatment of patients of the Medical Group. He obtained a pharmacy license on May 10, 1938. Until June 25 of that year he bought his drugs from defendant's store *in the building*. However, he objected to the sales tax charged in connection with such purchases, and on June 25, 1938, he commenced buying wholesale from defendant's wholesale department *at another location*, which source of supply he continued to patronize to the time of trial. * * *

[T]he trial court found that plaintiff by executing the lease with Dr. Boonshaft did demise a part of the Medico–Dental Building to a tenant other than defendant for the purpose of maintaining a drug store and selling drugs on the premises, and that the making of the lease with Dr. Boonshaft was a breach of defendant's lease; that plaintiff in not taking immediate action to abate the drug store on the ninth floor of the building violated its lease with defendant; that plaintiff breached its lease with defendant on August 19, 1938, when it advised defendant that it could make no arrangements with Dr. Boonshaft and could not do anything with him regarding the selling of drugs and the maintaining of the drug store; and that such breaches of the lease were in material respects and were not waived by defendant.

The court also found that a material part of the consideration which induced defendant to enter into the lease with plaintiff was the right to be protected against competition, and that a material part of the consideration failed as the result of plaintiff's execution of the Boonshaft lease. * * *

On this appeal from the judgment rendered for defendant in consequence of the above findings, plaintiff advances the following propositions: (1) Covenants in leases are independent and performance of a covenant by the landlord is not a condition precedent to an action for rent against the

(2)

tenant; (2) a covenant "not to lease" for a restricted purpose is breached only by actual leasing for such purpose, or by acquiescence in the conduct of the second lessee which is in violation of the restriction, neither of which

(3)

appears in this case; (3) even if the covenants are dependent and there was a breach of the covenant involved herein, the breach was not so substantial as to go to the whole of the consideration; and (4) there was a waiver by the defendant of the alleged violation. Consideration of the legal aspect of these respective contentions in conjunction with the factual situation which confronted the trial court will demonstrate the propriety of the judgment entered.

(1)

The first controversial point is whether the covenants "not to lease" and "to pay rent" are mutually independent or dependent. It is plaintiff's position that a lease is a conveyance as distinguished from a contract, so that any covenant on the part of the lessor is independent of the lessee's obligation to pay rent and each party has his remedy for breach of covenant in an action for damages. While it is true that a lease is primarily a conveyance in that it transfers an estate to the lessee, it also presents the aspect of a contract. (Pollock on Contracts, Third Am. ed., p. 531.) This dual character serves to create two distinct sets of rights and obligations— "one comprising those growing out of the relation of landlord and tenant, and said to be based on the 'privity of estate,' and the other comprising those growing out of the express stipulations of the lease, and so said to be based on 'privity of contract.' " (Samuels v. Ottinger, 146 P. 638, 638–39 (Cal. 1915).) Those features of the lease which are strictly contractual in

RULE

their nature should be construed according to the rules for the interpretation of contracts generally and in conformity with the fundamental principle that the intentions of the parties should be given effect as far as possible. In line with this concept is the authoritative observation in 32 Am.Jur. § 144, p. 145, that "covenants and stipulations on the part of the lessor and lessee are to be construed to be dependent upon each other or independent of each other, according to the intention of the parties and the good sense of the case, and technical words should give way to such intention."

Noteworthy here are the several provisions of the lease itself plainly indicating the intention and understanding of the parties as to the interbalancing considerations existing between the respective covenants. The agreement by the lessor "not to lease" any other part of the building to any other person for the purpose of its use as a drug store or for the sale of drugs, and the agreement by the lessee "to pay rent" appear in a rider attached to and made a part of the lease, a circumstance of incorporation not to be overlooked in the measure of the parties' comprehension of the reciprocal nature of the specified promises. Moreover, the lessee was limited by the terms of the lease to maintaining a drug store, a restriction emphasizing the import of the lessor's duty in negotiating future demises of other portions of the building. Finally to be noted is the express language of the lease manifesting the conditional character of the stipulations therein contained: "Time is of the essence of this lease and all of the terms and covenants hereof are conditions, and upon the breach by lessee of any of the same lessor may, at lessor's option, terminate this lease...." Thus, the parties recognized in plain terms the essential interdependence of their obligations.

] RULE

It is an established rule that those covenants which run to the entire consideration of a contract are mutual and dependent. Undoubtedly the restrictive covenant in defendant's lease was of such a nature. The exclusive right to conduct a drug store in the building was vital to defendant's successful operation of its business under the circumstances which prevailed in this case. Defendant's pharmacy was of a distinctive type in that it catered principally to doctors and dentists for reference of prescription work, did not carry the general line of merchandise found in the ordinary drug store, and did not rely upon transient trade. Defendant was and had been maintaining a chain of exclusive prescription pharmacies in Los Angeles for eighteen years. The fact that the Medico–Dental Building was tenanted for the most part by practitioners of the medical and dental professions motivated defendant to select that location for the establishment of one of its retail units. Defendant had occupied the same premises since 1925, and depended upon the tenants of the building and their patients for the major portion of its business. In fact, when vacancies occurred defendant's income from the store suffered to such an extent that the rent was temporarily reduced, and restoration to the former monthly rental level was made contingent upon a material increase in the occupancy of the building. Thus plaintiff knew, as appears from its letter granting the rent concession to defendant, that the "chief source" of defendant's business on the premises was the tenants in the building, and that it was therefore of prime importance that no competitor be rented quarters there. The correlation of these facts with the express provisions of the lease above noted compels the conclusion that the restrictive covenant was not incidental or subordinate to the main object of the lease, but went to the whole of the consideration, and that as such it must be deemed a dependent covenant. * * *

The second question is whether the restrictive covenant was breached by leasing for the prohibited purpose or by the lessor's acquiescence in the conduct of the other lessee amounting to a violation of the restriction.

As to the first part of this question, relative to leasing for the forbidden purpose, the trial court found that plaintiff did lease *a portion of* the Medico–Dental Building to Dr. Boonshaft for the purpose of maintaining a drug store and selling drugs on the premises so demised; that, by executing such lease, plaintiff breached its agreement with defendant; and that, by virtue of one of the provisions of the lease with Dr. Boonshaft, plaintiff intended to and did give such tenant the right and privilege of maintaining a drug store, selling drugs and compounding prescriptions on the premises, and by so doing failed to protect the defendant against competition.

This finding, as to the purpose of plaintiff's demise to Dr. Boonshaft, was based undoubtedly upon inferences drawn from the provisions of that tenant's lease; inferences that plaintiff knew at the time such lease was executed that the Boonshaft Medical Group contemplated the conduct of a type of medical business which would require a large stock of drugs, and that a drug store would be operated in connection therewith; that Dr. Boonshaft regarded the privilege of maintaining a drug store as a material part of the consideration in support of his lease; and inferences drawn from the conduct of plaintiff and Dr. Boonshaft following the latter's entry into possession of the demised premises. * * *

b) As to the second part of the second question—whether the restrictive covenant was breached by the plaintiff's acquiescence in the conduct of Dr. Boonshaft amounting to a violation of the restriction—the trial court found that the plaintiff in not taking immediate action to abate the drug store on the ninth floor and in advising defendant that it could not do anything with Dr. Boonshaft with respect to the objectionable activity, breached its lease with defendant.

RULE
↓
Acquiescence to
the conduct of
another tenant that
violates the
conditions of a
lease is a breach
of the restrictive
covenant

Bearing on this feature of the case is the following evidence. The drug store on the ninth floor was opened in May, 1938. In the latter part of July, 1938, defendant learned that Dr. Boonshaft was maintaining a pharmacy on the premises, and on August 3, 1938, it wrote a letter to plaintiff protesting against the competing activity and demanding that plaintiff immediately put a stop to such objectionable practice. All of the parties concerned met in conference in defendant's office five days later, with the result that plaintiff promised to see what arrangements could be made and to advise defendant. Communications were thereupon had between plaintiff and Dr. Boonshaft, but defendant did not hear further from plaintiff until August 19, 1938, when plaintiff's attorney advised Mr. Horton, defendant's president, by telephone that he had been unable to do anything with Dr. Boonshaft, that "there could not be any arrangements made," and Mr. Horton then said that he thought the premises would be vacated, to which the attorney replied: "Use your own judgment about that."

From this summarization of the pertinent facts it appears that defendant did not precipitately vacate the premises upon learning in the latter part of July, 1938, that the competing drug store was being operated, but followed a reasonable and deliberate course of action designed to afford plaintiff an opportunity to adjust the controversy in a manner consistent with the rights and obligations of the parties. * * *

[T]he findings of the trial court relative to acquiescence have ample support in the evidence, and the conclusion is required that plaintiff concurred in Dr. Boonshaft's maintenance of his drug store in the building.

③ The third point, that even if there was a breach of the restrictive covenant, it was not so substantial as to go to the whole of the consideration, was discussed in part in connection with the treatment of the first proposition concerning the interdependence of the parties' covenants under the terms of the lease. As was there stated, various special circumstances such as the exclusive nature of defendant's pharmacy, the limited source of its patronage, and the many years of its tenancy in the building establish the materiality of plaintiff's breach of its obligation to protect defendant against a rival business. Another factor substantiating this view is the record's disclosure that the Horton & Converse lease here involved would not have been executed had it not been for the insertion of the restrictive covenant in accordance with the request of Mr. Horton, defendant's president, that plaintiff's assignor incorporate in the instrument the same rights as to freedom from competition that defendant enjoyed under its previous lease of the same quarters in the Medico–Dental Building. Thus, it is apparent that the exclusive right to engage in a specified business in a particular building was the essence of the consideration for defendant's payment of rent during its many years of occupancy of the premises. * * * [W]here, as here, the covenant of the lessor is of such character that its breach will defeat the entire object of the lessee in entering into the lease, such as rendering his further occupancy of the premises a source of continuing financial loss incapable of satisfactory measurement in damages, it must be held that the covenant goes to the root of the consideration for the lease upon the lessee's part. (University Club v. Deakin, 106 N.E. 790 (Ill. 1914); Hiatt Investment Co. v. Buehler 16 S.W.2d 219 (Mo. App. 1929).) Commensurate with this principle, it is plain that the defendant's loss of potential business on account of the competing drug store was not a matter easily susceptible of monetary estimate, and proof of this element was not required of defendant under its presentation of the rights and duties of the parties in the circumstances of this case. A contrary view would authorize plaintiff to execute instruments similar to the Boonshaft lease for every floor of its building and thus render the restrictive covenant in defendant's lease valueless insofar as the protection of its essential source of income was concerned.

> *RULE*

In the case of *Hiatt Investment Co. v. Buehler*, supra, where * * * the lessor's breach of a restrictive covenant similar to the one here involved did not permit its recovery in an action for rent, the court observed at pp. 163–164: "Defendant herein had a choice of several remedies: (1) He could rescind the lease, in which case he would not have been required to pay any further rent; (2) He could have continued under his lease and at the end of the term sued for loss of the profits suffered by reason of the competition of the Crown Drug Company; (3) He could have treated the violation of the covenant by the plaintiff as putting an end to the contract for purposes of the performance and sued for damages." Defendant elected to pursue the first course, and in this case the state of the record showing plaintiff's departure in substance from its contractual obligation establishes the propriety of defendant's position in accord with its choice of available relief. * * *

> *3 Possible remedies available for Defendant (Lessee)*

For the foregoing reasons the judgment is affirmed.

NOTES AND QUESTIONS

1. *Medico–Dental* is the clearest example we have seen yet of how leases can function as a mechanism for the governance of a complex of assets, as well as a financing or risk-spreading device. The Medico–Dental building is conceived of as a commercial office building devoted exclusively to offices for doctors and dentists. The retail space on the ground floor is

rented to a pharmacy. This arrangement is obviously to the benefit of the pharmacy-tenant, since many patients will stop by to fill prescriptions after leaving the doctors' and dentists' offices. But it is also of benefit to the doctors and dentists, insofar as the pharmacy serves the convenience of their patients and makes it more likely they will continue to patronize doctors and dentists in the building. The arrangement also poses a potential for conflict, as the case reveals. Such conflicts would ordinarily be resolved by the landlord, either through the landlord's drafting of appropriate lease provisions, or its enforcement of these provisions, or its attempt to negotiate compromises or solutions among tenants. When these efforts fail, one or more tenants may walk out, and litigation may result, as in the principal case. Given the complicated collective-governance questions involved, it is probably no accident that the court was drawn to the more flexible precepts of contract law, rather than simple exclusion postulates of property law, in resolving the dispute.

2.   *Medico–Dental* suggests that many disputes that arise under leases can be resolved by applying, in a fairly straightforward fashion, the general rules of contract law that apply to bilateral commercial contracts. A breach by one party, here the landlord, gives rise to a variety of remedial options for the other party, here the tenant. If the breach is sufficiently serious—if it goes to the essence of the consideration under the lease or is sufficiently material—then the options for the promisee (whether it be the landlord or the tenant) include rescission of the lease and termination of further performance by the promisee. If the breach involves a less serious covenant—one that does not go to the essence of the bargain or is not sufficiently material to justify rescission—then the promisee would be entitled to sue for damages only. The result would be, in effect, that major breaches would be treated under a model of dependent covenants, whereas minor breaches would continue to be handled under a model of independent covenants.

3.   Under the dependent covenants model of *Medico-Dental*, does the doctrine of constructive eviction have any continuing role to play? Consider in this regard *Wesson v. Leone Enterprises, Inc.*, 774 N.E.2d 611 (Mass. 2002). The tenant, a financial printing company, complained repeatedly to the landlord about roof leaks. The leaks caused the tenant to cover some of its machinery and supplies with plastic tarps to protect them from water damage, but did not cause any suspension of business activity. The tenant vacated the premises two years before the end of the lease term, citing the roof leaks as the reason. The landlord sued for unpaid rent. The Massachusetts Supreme Judicial Court held on these facts that the roof leaks were not a constructive eviction, because they did not make the property "untenantable for the purposes for which they were used." However, the court also concluded that under the lease, the landlord was responsible to maintain and repair the roof. Adopting the rule of mutually dependent covenants, the court held that the landlord's breach of the covenant to repair deprived the tenant of a "substantial benefit significant to the purpose of the lease" and hence justified the tenant in terminating the lease. The tenant was also awarded relocation costs. After this decision,

when if ever would a tenant need to invoke constructive eviction in Massachusetts?

4.   How would the dependent covenants model of *Medico–Dental* apply to a typical month-to-month residential tenancy, perhaps under an oral lease? Would the landlord's duties toward the tenant continue to be defined by the common-law rule of caveat lessee, as reflected in *Sutton v. Temple*? If so, then the new model would offer residential tenants little relief, unless they had the foresight (and the bargaining power) to insist on specific promises in the lease guaranteeing a minimal standard of quality. Perhaps for this reason, courts beginning in the late 1960s began to turn to a different contractual idea—that of the implied warranty of habitability—in addressing conditions of minimal quality standards in residential leases.

Javins v. First National Realty Corp.

United States Court of Appeals, District of Columbia Circuit, 1970.
428 F.2d 1071.

■ J. SKELLY WRIGHT, CIRCUIT JUDGE: These cases present the question whether housing code violations which arise during the term of a lease have any effect upon the tenant's obligation to pay rent. The Landlord and Tenant Branch of the District of Columbia Court of General Sessions ruled proof of such violations inadmissible when proffered as a defense to an eviction action for nonpayment of rent. The District of Columbia Court of Appeals upheld this ruling.

Because of the importance of the question presented, we granted appellants' petitions for leave to appeal. We now reverse and hold that a warranty of habitability, measured by the standards set out in the Housing Regulations for the District of Columbia, is implied by operation of law into leases of urban dwelling units covered by those Regulations and that breach of this warranty gives rise to the usual remedies for breach of contract.

I

The facts revealed by the record are simple. By separate written leases, each of the appellants rented an apartment in a three-building apartment complex in Northwest Washington known as Clifton Terrace. The landlord, First National Realty Corporation, filed separate actions in the Landlord and Tenant Branch of the Court of General Sessions on April 8, 1966, seeking possession on the ground that each of the appellants had defaulted in the payment of rent due for the month of April. The tenants, appellants here, admitted that they had not paid the landlord any rent for April. However, they alleged numerous violations of the Housing Regulations as "an equitable defense or (a) claim by way of recoupment or set-off in an amount equal to the rent claim," as provided in the rules of the Court of General Sessions. They offered to prove

> [t]hat there are approximately 1500 violations of the Housing Regulations of the District of Columbia in the building at Clifton Terrace,

where Defendant resides some affecting the premises of this Defendant directly, others indirectly, and all tending to establish a course of conduct of violation of the Housing Regulations to the damage of Defendants * * *

Appellants conceded at trial, however, that this offer of proof reached only violations which had arisen since the term of the lease had commenced. The Court of General Sessions refused appellants' offer of proof and entered judgment for the landlord. The District of Columbia Court of Appeals affirmed, rejecting the argument made by appellants that the landlord was under a contractual duty to maintain the premises in compliance with the Housing Regulations.

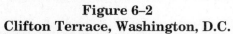

Figure 6–2
Clifton Terrace, Washington, D.C.

Courtesy Richard Chused.

II

Since, in traditional analysis, a lease was the conveyance of an interest in land, courts have usually utilized the special rules governing real property transactions to resolve controversies involving leases. However, as the Supreme Court has noted in another context, "the body of private property law * * *, more than almost any other branch of law, has been shaped by distinctions whose validity is largely historical." Courts have a duty to reappraise old doctrines in the light of the facts and values of contemporary life—particularly old common law doctrines which the courts themselves created and developed. As we have said before, "The continued vitality of the common law * * * depends upon its ability to reflect contemporary community values and ethics."

The assumption of landlord-tenant law, derived from feudal property law, that a lease primarily conveyed to the tenant an interest in land may have been reasonable in a rural, agrarian society; it may continue to be reasonable in some leases involving farming or commercial land. In these cases, the value of the lease to the tenant is the land itself. But in the case of the modern apartment dweller, the value of the lease is that it gives him a place to live. The city dweller who seeks to lease an apartment on the third floor of a tenement has little interest in the land 30 or 40 feet below, or even in the bare right to possession within the four walls of his apartment. When American city dwellers, both rich and poor, seek "shelter" today, they seek a well known package of goods and services—a package which includes not merely walls and ceilings, but also adequate heat, light and ventilation, serviceable plumbing facilities, secure windows and doors, proper sanitation, and proper maintenance. * * *

Some courts have realized that certain of the old rules of property law governing leases are inappropriate for today's transactions. In order to reach results more in accord with the legitimate expectations of the parties and the standards of the community, courts have been gradually introducing more modern precepts of contract law in interpreting leases.[11] Proceeding piecemeal has, however, led to confusion where "decisions are frequently conflicting, not because of a healthy disagreement on social policy, but because of the lingering impact of rules whose policies are long since dead."[12]

In our judgment the trend toward treating leases as contracts is wise and well considered. Our holding in this case reflects a belief that leases of urban dwelling units should be interpreted and construed like any other contract.

III

Modern contract law has recognized that the buyer of goods and services in an industrialized society must rely upon the skill and honesty of the supplier to assure that goods and services purchased are of adequate quality. In interpreting most contracts, courts have sought to protect the legitimate expectations of the buyer and have steadily widened the seller's responsibility for the quality of goods and services through implied warranties of fitness and merchantability. * * *

The rigid doctrines of real property law have tended to inhibit the application of implied warranties to transactions involving real estate. Now, however, courts have begun to hold sellers and developers of real property responsible for the quality of their product. For example, builders of new homes have recently been held liable to purchasers for improper construc-

---

11. E.g., Medico–Dental Building Co. v. Horton & Converse, 132 P.2d 457, 462 (Cal. 1942).

12. Kessler, The Protection of the Consumer Under Modern Sales Law, 74 Yale L.J. 262, 263 (1964).

tion on the ground that the builders had breached an implied warranty of fitness. In other cases courts have held builders of new homes liable for breach of an implied warranty that all local building regulations had been complied with. And following the developments in other areas, very recent decisions and commentary suggest the possible extension of liability to parties other than the immediate seller for improper construction of residential real estate.

Despite this trend in the sale of real estate, many courts have been unwilling to imply warranties of quality, specifically a warranty of habitability, into leases of apartments. Recent decisions have offered no convincing explanation for their refusal; rather they have relied without discussion upon the old common law rule that the lessor is not obligated to repair unless he covenants to do so in the written lease contract. However, the Supreme Courts of at least two states, in recent and well reasoned opinions, have held landlords to implied warranties of quality in housing leases. Lemle v. Breeden, 462 P.2d 470 (Haw. 1969); Reste Realty Corp. v. Cooper, 251 A.2d 268 (N.J. 1969). In our judgment, the old no-repair rule cannot coexist with the obligations imposed on the landlord by a typical modern housing code, and must be abandoned in favor of an implied warranty of habitability. In the District of Columbia, the standards of this warranty are set out in the Housing Regulations.

IV

A. In our judgment the common law itself must recognize the landlord's obligation to keep his premises in a habitable condition. This conclusion is compelled by three separate considerations. First, we believe that the old rule was based on certain factual assumptions which are no longer true; on its own terms, it can no longer be justified. Second, we believe that the consumer protection cases discussed above require that the old rule be abandoned in order to bring residential landlord-tenant law into harmony with the principles on which those cases rest. Third, we think that the nature of today's urban housing market also dictates abandonment of the old rule.

The common law rule absolving the lessor of all obligation to repair originated in the early Middle Ages.[30] Such a rule was perhaps well suited to an agrarian economy; the land was more important[31] than whatever small living structure was included in the leasehold, and the tenant farmer

30. The rule was "settled" by 1485. 3 W. Holdsworth, A History of English Law 122–123 (6th ed. 1934). The common law rule discussed in text originated in the even older rule prohibiting the tenant from committing waste. The writ of waste expanded as the tenant's right to possession grew stronger. Eventually, in order to protect the landowner's reversionary interest, the tenant became obligated to make repairs and liable to eviction and damages if he failed to do so. Ibid.

31. The land was so central to the original common law conception of a leasehold that rent was viewed as "issuing" from the land: "The governing idea is that the land is bound to pay the rent * * *. We may almost go to the length of saying that the land pays it through (the tenant's) hand." 2 F. Pollock & F. Maitland, The History of English Law 131 (2d ed. 1923).

was fully capable of making repairs himself. These historical facts were the basis on which the common law constructed its rule; they also provided the necessary prerequisites for its application.[33]

Court decisions in the late 1800's began to recognize that the factual assumptions of the common law were no longer accurate in some cases. For example, the common law, since it assumed that the land was the most important part of the leasehold, required a tenant to pay rent even if any building on the land was destroyed.[34] Faced with such a rule and the ludicrous results it produced, in 1863 the New York Court of Appeals declined to hold that an upper story tenant was obliged to continue paying rent after his apartment building burned down. The court simply pointed out that the urban tenant had no interest in the land, only in the attached building. * * *

Another line of cases created an exception to the no-repair rule for short term leases of furnished dwellings. The Massachusetts Supreme Judicial Court, a court not known for its willingness to depart from the common law, supported this exception, pointing out:

> * * * [A] different rule should apply to one who hires a furnished room, or a furnished house, for a few days, or a few weeks or months. Its fitness for immediate use of a particular kind, as indicated by its appointments, is a far more important element entering into the contract than when there is a mere lease of real estate. One who lets for a short term a house provided with all furnishings and appointments for immediate residence may be supposed to contract in reference to a well-understood purpose of the hirer to use it as a habitation. * * * It would be unreasonable to hold, under such circumstances, that the landlord does not impliedly agree that what he is letting is a house suitable for occupation in its condition at the time. * * *[37]

These as well as other similar cases demonstrate that some courts began some time ago to question the common law's assumptions that the land was the most important feature of a leasehold and that the tenant could feasibly make any necessary repairs himself. Where those assumptions no longer reflect contemporary housing patterns, the courts have created exceptions to the general rule that landlords have no duty to keep their premises in repair.

It is overdue for courts to admit that these assumptions are no longer true with regard to all urban housing. Today's urban tenants, the vast

---

33. Even the old common law courts responded with a different rule for a landlord-tenant relationship which did not conform to the model of the usual agrarian lease. Much more substantial obligations were placed upon the keepers of inns (the only multiple dwelling houses known to the common law). Their guests were interested solely in shelter and could not be expected to make their own repairs. "The modern apartment dweller more closely resembles the guest in an inn than he resembles an agrarian tenant, but the law has not generally recognized the similarity." J. Levi, P. Hablutzel, L. Rosenberg & J. White, Model Residential Landlord–Tenant Code 6–7 (Tent. Draft 1969).

34. Paradine v. Jane, Aleyn 26, 82 Eng. Rep. 897 (K.B. 1647) * * *

37. Ingalls v. Hobbs, 31 N.E. 286 (Mass. 1892).

majority of whom live in multiple dwelling houses, are interested, not in the land, but solely in "a house suitable for occupation." Furthermore, today's city dweller usually has a single, specialized skill unrelated to maintenance work; he is unable to make repairs like the "jack-of-all-trades" farmer who was the common law's model of the lessee. Further, unlike his agrarian predecessor who often remained on one piece of land for his entire life, urban tenants today are more mobile than ever before. A tenant's tenure in a specific apartment will often not be sufficient to justify efforts at repairs. In addition, the increasing complexity of today's dwellings renders them much more difficult to repair than the structures of earlier times. In a multiple dwelling repair may require access to equipment and areas in the control of the landlord. Low and middle income tenants, even if they were interested in making repairs, would be unable to obtain any financing for major repairs since they have no long-term interest in the property.

Our approach to the common law of landlord and tenant ought to be aided by principles derived from the consumer protection cases referred to above. In a lease contract, a tenant seeks to purchase from his landlord shelter for a specified period of time. The landlord sells housing as a commercial businessman and has much greater opportunity, incentive and capacity to inspect and maintain the condition of his building. Moreover, the tenant must rely upon the skill and bona fides of his landlord at least as much as a car buyer must rely upon the car manufacturer. In dealing with major problems, such as heating, plumbing, electrical or structural defects, the tenant's position corresponds precisely with "the ordinary consumer who cannot be expected to have the knowledge or capacity or even the opportunity to make adequate inspection of mechanical instrumentalities, like automobiles, and to decide for himself whether they are reasonably fit for the designed purpose." Henningsen v. Bloomfield Motors, Inc., 161 A.2d 69, 78 (N.J. 1960).

Since a lease contract specifies a particular period of time during which the tenant has a right to use his apartment for shelter, he may legitimately expect that the apartment will be fit for habitation for the time period for which it is rented. We point out that in the present cases there is no allegation that appellants' apartments were in poor condition or in violation of the housing code at the commencement of the leases. Since the lessees continue to pay the same rent, they were entitled to expect that the landlord would continue to keep the premises in their beginning condition during the lease term. It is precisely such expectations that the law now recognizes as deserving of formal, legal protection.

Even beyond the rationale of traditional products liability law, the relationship of landlord and tenant suggests further compelling reasons for the law's protection of the tenants' legitimate expectations of quality. The inequality in bargaining power between landlord and tenant has been well documented. Tenants have very little leverage to enforce demands for better housing. Various impediments to competition in the rental housing market, such as racial and class discrimination and standardized form leases, mean that landlords place tenants in a take it or leave it situation. The increasingly severe shortage of adequate housing further increases the landlord's bargaining power and escalates the need for maintaining and improving the existing stock. Finally, the findings by various studies of the social impact of bad housing has led to the realization that poor housing is detrimental to the whole society, not merely to the unlucky ones who must suffer the daily indignity of living in a slum.

Thus we are led by our inspection of the relevant legal principles and precedents to the conclusion that the old common law rule imposing an obligation upon the lessee to repair during the lease term was really never intended to apply to residential urban leaseholds. Contract principles established in other areas of the law provide a more rational framework for the apportionment of landlord-tenant responsibilities; they strongly suggest that a warranty of habitability be implied into all contracts[49] for urban dwellings.

RULE

B. We believe, in any event, that the District's housing code requires that a warranty of habitability be implied in the leases of all housing that it covers. The housing code—formally designated the Housing Regulations of the District of Columbia—was established and authorized by the Commissioners of the District of Columbia on August 11, 1955. Since that time, the code has been updated by numerous orders of the Commissioners. The 75 pages of the Regulations provide a comprehensive regulatory scheme setting forth in some detail: (a) the standards which housing in the District of Columbia must meet; (b) which party, the lessor or the lessee, must meet each standard; and (c) a system of inspections, notifications and criminal penalties. The Regulations themselves are silent on the question of private remedies.

→ see next page

Two previous decisions of this court, however, have held that the Housing Regulations create legal rights and duties enforceable in tort by private parties. * * *

The District of Columbia Court of Appeals gave further effect to the Housing Regulations in Brown v. Southall Realty Co., 237 A.2d 834 (D.C. App. 1968). There the landlord knew at the time the lease was signed that housing code violations existed which rendered the apartment "unsafe and unsanitary." Viewing the lease as a contract, the District of Columbia Court of Appeals held that the premises were let in violation of Sections 2304[53] and 2501 of the Regulations and that the lease, therefore, was void as an illegal contract. In the light of *Brown*, it is clear * * * that the basic validity of every housing contract depends upon substantial compliance with the housing code at the beginning of the lease term. The *Brown* court relied particularly upon Section 2501 of the Regulations which provides:

RULE

---

49. We need not consider the provisions of the written lease governing repairs since this implied warranty of the landlord could not be excluded.

53. "No person shall rent or offer to rent any habitation, or the furnishings thereof, unless such habitation and its furnishings are in a clean, safe and sanitary condition, in repair, and free from rodents or vermin."

Every premises accommodating one or more habitations shall be maintained and kept in repair so as to provide decent living accommodations for the occupants. This part of this Code contemplates more than mere basic repairs and maintenance to keep out the elements; its purpose is to include repairs and maintenance designed to make a premises or neighborhood healthy and safe.

By its terms, this section applies to maintenance and repair during the lease term. Under the *Brown* holding, serious failure to comply with this section before the lease term begins renders the contract void. We think it untenable to find that this section has no effect on the contract after it has been signed. To the contrary, by signing the lease the landlord has undertaken a continuing obligation to the tenant to maintain the premises in accordance with all applicable law.

RULE [

This principle of implied warranty is well established. Courts often imply relevant law into contracts to provide a remedy for any damage caused by one party's illegal conduct. * * * └→ *in the absence of provided remedies*

[T]he housing code must be read into housing contracts—a holding also required by the purposes and the structure of the code itself. The duties imposed by the Housing Regulations may not be waived or shifted by agreement if the Regulations specifically place the duty upon the lessor. Criminal penalties are provided if these duties are ignored. This regulatory structure was established by the Commissioners because, in their judgment, the grave conditions in the housing market required serious action. Yet official enforcement of the housing code has been far from uniformly effective. Innumerable studies have documented the desperate condition of rental housing in the District of Columbia and in the nation. * * *

RULE [

see previous page

We therefore hold that the Housing Regulations imply a warranty of habitability, measured by the standards which they set out, into leases of all housing that they cover.

V

In the present cases, the landlord sued for possession for nonpayment of rent. Under contract principles,[61] however, the tenant's obligation to pay rent is dependent upon the landlord's performance of his obligations, including his warranty to maintain the premises in habitable condition. In order to determine whether any rent is owed to the landlord, the tenants must be given an opportunity to prove the housing code violations alleged as breach of the landlord's warranty.[62]

RULE [

↓
Answers MAIN ISSUE

61. In extending all contract remedies for breach to the parties to a lease, we include an action for specific performance of the landlord's implied warranty of habitability.

62. To be relevant, of course, the violations must affect the tenant's apartment or common areas which the tenant uses. Moreover, the contract principle that no one may benefit from his own wrong will allow the landlord to defend by proving the damage was caused by the tenant's wrongful action. However, violations resulting from inadequate repairs or materials which disintegrate under normal use would not be assignable to the tenant. Also we agree with the District of Columbia Court of Appeals that the tenant's private rights do not depend on official in-

At trial, the finder of fact must make two findings: (1) whether the alleged violations[63] existed during the period for which past due rent is claimed, and (2) what portion, if any or all, of the tenant's obligation to pay rent was suspended by the landlord's breach. If no part of the tenant's rental obligation is found to have been suspended, then a judgment for possession may issue forthwith. On the other hand, if the jury determines that the entire rental obligation has been extinguished by the landlord's total breach, then the action for possession on the ground of nonpayment must fail.[64]

The jury may find that part of the tenant's rental obligation has been suspended but that part of the unpaid back rent is indeed owed to the landlord. In these circumstances, no judgment for possession should issue if the tenant agrees to pay the partial rent found to be due. If the tenant refuses to pay the partial amount, a judgment for possession may then be entered.

The judgment of the District of Columbia Court of Appeals is reversed and the cases are remanded for further proceedings consistent with this opinion.[67]

NOTES AND QUESTIONS

1. The implied warranty of habitability was one of several reforms to residential landlord-tenant law introduced by courts in the District of Columbia in the late 1960s and early 1970s. Two others of note are the doctrine of retaliatory eviction, see Edwards v. Habib, 397 F.2d 687 (D.C.

spection or official finding of violation by the city government. Diamond Housing Corp. v. Robinson, 257 A.2d 492, 494 (1969).

63. The jury should be instructed that one or two minor violations standing alone which do not affect habitability are de minimis and would not entitle the tenant to a reduction in rent.

64. As soon as the landlord made the necessary repairs rent would again become due. Our holding, of course, affects only eviction for nonpayment of rent. The landlord is free to seek eviction at the termination of the lease or on any other legal ground.

67. Appellants in the present cases offered to pay rent into the registry of the court during the present action. We think this is an excellent protective procedure. If the tenant defends against an action for possession on the basis of breach of the landlord's warranty of habitability, the trial court may require the tenant to make future rent payments into the registry of the court as they become due; such a procedure would be

appropriate only while the tenant remains in possession. The escrowed money will, however, represent rent for the period between the time the landlord files suit and the time the case comes to trial. In the normal course of litigation, the only factual question at trial would be the condition of the apartment during the time the landlord alleged rent was due and not paid.

→ and not whether rent was or was not paid.

As a general rule, the escrowed money should be apportioned between the landlord and the tenant after trial on the basis of the finding of rent actually due for the period at issue in the suit. To insure fair apportionment, however, we think either party should be permitted to amend its complaint or answer at any time before trial, to allege a change in the condition of the apartment. In this event, the finder of fact should make a separate finding as to the condition of the apartment at the time at which the amendment was filed. This new finding will have no effect upon the original action; it will only affect the distribution of the escrowed rent paid after the filing of the amendment.

Cir. 1968), and the illegal lease doctrine, see Brown v. Southall Realty Co., 237 A.2d 834 (D.C. 1968). All three doctrines built on the provisions of the local housing code establishing standards for safe and sanitary residential housing. The doctrine of retaliatory eviction posited that a landlord may not retaliate against a tenant for reporting code violations. Thus, even if the tenant is in a periodic tenancy that the landlord otherwise would be free to terminate at the end of the period (often month-to-month where low-income rental housing is concerned), the landlord cannot give notice to terminate if a court concludes that the termination was motivated by a desire to punish the tenant for asserting her rights under the code. The illegal lease doctrine posited that if the landlord leases property that is subject to one or more code violations, such that the premises are rendered unsafe and unsanitary, then the lease is void and of no legal effect. As a result, the landlord is precluded from suing for unpaid rent based on the lease.

Of the three doctrines, the implied warranty of habitability (IWH) has been the runaway success story. See Glendon, supra; Edward H. Rabin, The Revolution in Residential Landlord–Tenant Law: Causes and Consequences, 69 Cornell L. Rev. 517 (1984). According to a recent survey, only four states (Alabama, Arkansas, Colorado, and Wyoming) have not yet recognized an IWH for residential tenancies. 1 Milton R. Friedman, Friedman on Leases App. 10A (Patrick A. Randolph, Jr. ed. & rev., 5th ed. 2005). Interestingly, however, of the states that have adopted the IWH, most have done so by legislation, usually by adopting the relevant provisions of the Uniform Residential Landlord Tenant Act, rather than by judicial revision of the common law, as in *Javins*. Id. The doctrine of retaliatory eviction has been widely adopted to protect tenants who engage in protected activity, such as reporting housing code violations or attempting to organize a tenants' union. But this is a relatively small subset of tenants, relative to those affected by the conditions of the leased premises. The illegal lease doctrine suffers from the fact that if the lease is illegal, then it would seem that the tenant is not only released from the burdens of the lease but cannot claim the benefit of the lease either (such as the covenant of quiet enjoyment). Logically, the tenancy would become a tenancy at will or sufferance, which would allow the landlord to begin immediate eviction proceedings. The IWH, in contrast, gives the tenant additional rights under the lease without subjecting the tenant to immediate eviction. Not surprisingly, law reformers sympathetic to the plight of poor tenants quickly gravitated to the IWH rather than the illegal lease doctrine.

2.   How important was it to the outcome in *Javins* that the tenants alleged the violations of the housing code emerged after they had entered into the leases? What defenses might have been asserted if the allegation had been that the units were out of compliance with the code at the time the leases were signed? Is it plausible that there were no code violations at Clifton Terrace when the leases were signed, and 1,500 violations shortly thereafter?

3.   Note that the court only addresses the question whether there should be an implied warranty of habitability in leases of "urban residential housing." This leaves open the question whether a similar warranty of fitness for intended purpose should be implied in leases of commercial or agricultural property. To date, only a small minority of states have adopted an implied warranty of fitness in commercial cases. See, e.g., Barton Enters. v. Tsern, 928 P.2d 368 (Utah 1996). More commonly, courts have held, following *Medico-Dental*, that covenants in commercial leases are presumed to be mutually dependent. See, e.g., Teodori v. Werner, 415 A.2d 31 (Pa. 1980). What factors are responsible for courts limiting the implied warranty idea to residential leases?

4.   Should the implied warranty of habitability be a default rule or a mandatory rule of law? The *Restatement (Second) of Property: Landlord and Tenant* endorsed the IWH but provided that it could be waived for consideration (such as reduced rent), provided the agreement was not "unconscionable or significantly against public policy." Id. § 5.6. Most courts, however, have followed *Javins* (see footnote 49), in making the IWH a nonwaivable rule of law. This is seemingly at odds with the court's insistence that leases are contracts, since usually rules of contract law are defaults. The usual rationale for making the IWH a mandatory rule of law, following *Javins*, is the perception that tenants and landlords have "unequal bargaining power." What exactly does this mean in this context? That there is an imbalance between supply and demand in the market for low-income rental properties such that landlords can assume a "take it or leave it" attitude in lease negotiations? That there are asymmetries in the information available to landlords and tenants, such that tenants often would not understand the significance of a waiver of the IWH? That many tenants simply cannot afford the higher rents that landlords would charge for properties protected by a warranty of quality?

5.   The court in *Javins* puts great stress on the provisions of the housing code as defining the content of the IWH. But housing codes vary greatly in terms of the detail with which they regulate rental housing, as well as in the nature of the issues addressed. Should every violation of the housing code be deemed a violation of the IWH? Suppose, for example, that the code requires that all electrical outlets in the kitchen and bathrooms include circuit breakers to prevent shock or electrocution. Is an apartment that has only standard grounded outlets but no circuit breakers in violation of the IWH? Courts sometimes avoid this implication by holding that only those code provisions that implicate "health and safety" define the IWH. But don't circuit breakers implicate health and safety? Alternatively, can the conditions of the apartment violate the IWH even if there is no code violation? Suppose, for example, that the housing code does not require air conditioning. What if the air conditioning system in an apartment building is not working, but the landlord refuses to fix it even though the city is in the midst of a killer heat wave?

6.   Does the doctrine of constructive eviction (considered in *Blackett v. Olanoff*, supra) have any continuing role to play once a jurisdiction has

adopted the IWH? The answer is clearly yes, insofar as most jurisdictions have limited the IWH to residential leases and have not adopted an analogous implied warranty of fitness for purpose to commercial leases. Thus, insofar as issues arise about the adequacy of physical conditions and services under commercial leases, they continue to be addressed in most jurisdictions under specific lease provisions or the doctrine of constructive eviction. Constructive eviction may also be of continuing relevance under residential leases, insofar as the jurisdiction relies on its housing code to define the content of the IWH. For example, suppose the housing code does not address the permissible decibel level of noise that may emit from surrounding properties controlled by the landlord. Raucous noise from a bar leased by the landlord might not violate the IWH in these circumstances, requiring that the court turn to the doctrine of *Blackett v. Olanoff*, *supra*, to provide a remedy.

7.   What are the remedies for violation of the IWH? Courts, following *Medico-Dental* and *Javins*, have tended to say that all remedies are available that would apply in the case of a material breach of a bilateral commercial contract. These include: (1) rescission of the lease by the tenant, thereby allowing the tenant to vacate without further obligation to pay rent; (2) an order directing specific performance of the IWH; (3) an action for damages for breach of the IWH; (4) if the landlord has sued the tenant for unpaid rent, a set-off against rent liability reflecting the landlord's violation of the IWH; and (5) in some jurisdictions, withholding of all or a portion of the rent until the landlord corrects the violation of the IWH or permits the tenant to arrange for repair of the violation.

A particularly vexing question concerns how to determine the damages caused by a breach of the IWH for purposes of remedies (3)–(5) mentioned above—a tenant suit for damages, a setoff from a landlord action for unpaid rent, or rent withholding. The straightforward way to determine damages or set-offs would seem be to take the rent reserved under the lease and subtract the value of the premises in their noncompliant condition. The problem, as tenant advocates and courts quickly discovered, is that rental markets are not that inefficient: The rent reserved under the lease tends to be equal to the value of the premises in their actual (noncompliant) condition. So the standard formula often yields zero damages. This did not seem right to many advocates and courts, so two substitute formulas were developed. One asks, hypothetically, what the fair market rental value would be if the premises were in compliance with the IWH, and then subtracts the value of the premises in their noncompliant condition. This formula is open to the objection that it awards a windfall to the tenant if the rent reserved was less than the fair market value of the premises in compliance with the IWH: The tenant gets, through the damages formula, more than the tenant agreed to pay for. The other, "percentage reduction" formula develops a ratio between (i) the difference between the value of the premises if in compliance with the IWH and the value of the premises if not in compliance with the IWH over (ii) the value of the premises if in compliance with the IWH, and multiplies this ratio times the rent reserved, for the amount of the reduction (damages). Does this alternative avoid the charge of a windfall to the tenant, or is it open to the same objection? See generally, William B. Stoebuck & Dale A. Whitman, The Law of Property § 6.42 (3d ed. 2000).

8.   In a development probably not appreciated at the time, the IWH has had important implications for the scope of the landlord's duty to the tenant and the tenant's guests under tort law. See generally Olin L. Browder, The Taming of a Duty—The Tort Liability of Landlords, 81 Mich. L. Rev. 99 (1982). If we start with the common-law baseline, as reflected in *Paradine v. Jane*, we see that the risk of casualty losses under a lease is originally placed on the tenant. Accordingly, any tort liability for injuries incurred on the premises (slip and fall accidents, assaults by third parties, etc.) would lie with the tenant. This baseline can be modified by particular lease provisions. For example, if the landlord promises to keep the driveways and walkways clear of snow and ice, a slip and fall by a guest of a tenant may plausibly give rise to tort liability for the landlord, based on the landlord's specific undertaking in the lease. This narrow bridgehead of liability becomes potentially huge with the introduction of the implied warranty of habitability. Now, the landlord has a general legal obligation to maintain the premises in a manner consistent with the housing code, and otherwise to insure that it meets minimal standards of public safety and health. This legally-imposed duty can provide the foundation for a broad landlord duty in tort to the tenant and the tenant's guests, including a duty to protect these persons against assaults by intruders that could have been kept at bay with proper security cameras and locks. See, e.g., Sargent v. Ross, 308 A.2d 528 (N.H. 1973) (holding landlord liable for death of four-year-old girl who fell from outdoor stairway not part of a common area).

In California, the courts initially concluded, by analogy to products liability law, that the landlord would be strictly liable for tortious injuries caused by a breach of the IWH. Becker v. IRM Corp., 698 P.2d 116 (Cal. 1985). One decade later, the California Supreme Court changed its mind, overruled *Becker*, and decided that landlords would be liable only for negligent injuries caused by a breach of the IWH. Peterson v. Superior Court, 899 P.2d 905 (Cal. 1995). What do you suppose motivated the retreat? Another source of controversy has been landlord tort liability for crimes and intentional torts by third persons. If a landlord fails to keep the locks on doors in good repair, and a criminal exploits the situation to the injury of a tenant, should the landlord pay? See Kline v. 1500 Massachusetts Ave. Apartment Corp., 439 F.2d 477 (D.C. Cir. 1970) (holding landlord corporation liable in tort when tenant was criminally assaulted in apartment hallway).

THE CONSEQUENCES OF THE IMPLIED WARRANTY OF HABITABILITY

Without doubt the most controversial aspect of the IWH has been whether it improves the welfare of low-income tenants. Commentators have addressed this primarily from a theoretical perspective, although there is some empirical evidence bearing on the question.

Theory. In the early years after *Javins*, commentators divided into two camps about whether imposing a mandatory IWH would improve the welfare of low-income tenants. One camp, representing orthodox microeconomic assumptions, argued that the IWH, like any government-mandated minimal product quality standard, would increase both the demand for low-cost housing (because the product would be better) and increase the costs of supplying such housing (because strict code compliance by landlords costs money). Consequently, imposing the IWH would cause rents to rise and the supply of low-cost housing to fall. See Richard A. Posner, Economic Analysis of Law § 16.6 (6th ed. 2003); Lawrence Berger, The New Residential Tenancy Law—Are Landlords Public Utilities?, 60 Neb. L. Rev. 707 (1981); Charles J. Meyers, The Covenant of Habitability and the American Law Institute, 27 Stan. L. Rev. 879 (1975). Poor tenants would either have to dig deeper into their pockets to pay for housing, or would be forced to squeeze more people into smaller units by doubling up.

Another camp, representing legal scholars more sympathetic to the mandatory IWH, argued that the low-income rental market is different from other types of product markets, and that because of these differences, the IWH might improve the quality of housing without any significant increase in rents. Thus, Bruce Ackerman argued that low-income households could not afford to pay more in rent and would refuse to double up. At the same time, landlords, because of their large sunk investment, could not afford to exit from the market, and so the supply of low income housing was largely fixed. Ackerman accordingly argued that both the demand for and the supply of low income housing are largely inelastic, at least in the short run, permitting some redistribution from landlords to tenants through a mandatory IWH. Bruce A. Ackerman, Regulating Slum Housing Markets on Behalf of the Poor: Of Housing Codes, Housing Subsidies and Income Redistribution Policy, 80 Yale L.J. 1093 (1971). Duncan Kennedy argued that many slumlords recognize that their property is deteriorating and will have to be abandoned some years in the future; given this realization, such landlords may "milk" the property by forgoing even routine maintenance while continuing to collect as much rent as possible in the period before the end arrives. Imposing a mandatory IWH on such landlords, Kennedy argued, would not change their calculus about how long to remain in the market, but might result in significant improvements in quality for the tenants. Duncan Kennedy, The Effect of the Warranty of Habitability on Low Income Housing: "Milking" and Class Violence, 15 Fla. St. U. L. Rev. 485 (1987).

More recently, "second wave" treatments of the question suggest that the matter is more complex: Some tenants will benefit while others will lose from a mandatory IWH. See Richard Craswell, Passing on the Costs of Legal Rules: Efficiency and Distribution in Buyer–Seller Relationships, 43 Stan. L. Rev. 361 (1991). Craswell, for example, argues that it is critical to distinguish between "marginal" and "infra-marginal" tenants. In a competitive market, the price for a good like housing is determined by the intersection of demand and supply curves. Assuming landlords cannot discriminate among prospective tenants based on their demand for housing, the same rent will be charged to all tenants for housing of equivalent quality. The rent will be determined by the demand of the last or "marginal" tenant who is just willing to pay the price necessary to induce the last or "marginal" landlord to put the housing on the market. But this price does not reflect the value that other tenants place on housing of equivalent quality. The basic postulate of a downward sloping demand curve is that there are other tenants—fewer in number perhaps—who would be willing to pay even more for housing of equivalent quality. Economists refer to these other tenants as "infra-marginal." The marginal tenant pays a price for housing exactly equal to what that tenant is willing to pay. The infra-marginal tenant enjoys a "consumer surplus" equal to the difference between the price she would be willing to pay and the market price, which is determined by what the last or marginal tenant is willing to pay.

Craswell notes that when a mandatory warranty is introduced into a competitive market, the demand curve for the good will shift upward and to the right, because the good is now worth more to consumers than it was before. Similarly, the supply curve for the good will shift upward and to the left, because it is now more expensive to produce the good than it was before. Craswell argues, however, that the demand curve will not necessarily shift up and to the right parallel to the original demand curve. If marginal tenants place a low value on the warranty, perhaps because their budgets are already stretched to maximum and they cannot afford to pay even a few dollars more for housing, then it is possible that the demand curve will shift relatively little for the marginal tenants, but may shift further for the infra-marginal tenants. Conversely, the opposite might occur. Marginal tenants might place a higher value on the warranty than infra-marginal tenants do. These two possibilities are illustrated by the following graphic, taken from his article, id. at 378:

Figure 6–3
Low- and High-Valuing Marginal Customers

As Craswell explains, in the left hand side of the graphic:

[T]he vertical shift in the demand curve from *D1* to *D2* exceeds this price increase for most consumers of the product, especially those located toward the left of the graph. This implies that the price increase accompanying the warranty is less than the maximum these consumers are willing to pay for the warranty, so the warranty has made these consumers better off. The only consumers who lose from the introduction of the warranty are those located between the *Q1* and *Q2* lines, whose demand curve shifts upward by less than the price increase from *P1* to *P2*. These consumers are unwilling to buy the product/warranty combination at the higher price. Since these consumers were willing to buy the product before the introduction of the warranty, they are made worse off by having to give up this benefit.

By contrast, the graph on the right in [Figure 6–3] shows a market in which most consumers are made worse off by the warranty because the correlation of consumer preferences has been reversed. In this market, the infra-marginal consumers who are willing to pay the most for the product alone are willing to pay very little extra for the warranty. These consumers are located toward the left of the graph, where the *D1* curve (representing the demand for the product itself) is relatively high, but the *D2* curve (representing the additional demand for the warranty) is only slightly higher. These consumers value the warranty by less than the price increase from *P1* to *P2*, so these consumers will be made worse off by the warranty. Only the consumers located near the *Q1–Q2* margin place a large enough value on the warranty, so these are the only consumers who even come close to benefiting from the warranty.

Id. at 378–79.

Craswell suggests that insofar as the left side graphic is a more plausible depiction of the shift in the demand curve following the introduction of a mandatory warranty, infra-marginal consumers may well benefit from the warranty, whereas marginal consumers may well lose. "[T]he benefit to those consumers who continue to buy the product comes, at least partially, at the expense of the marginal consumers, who now find themselves priced out of the market." Id. at 395.

Craswell is only concerned with determining whether tenant welfare will be improved by imposing a mandatory IWH. What about landlord welfare? Can we presume that landlords will always be worse off, on the ground that if it were in their commercial interest to keep their rental units up to code, they would do so voluntarily? Suppose that in the aggregate the IWH makes infra-marginal tenants better off by, say $1,000, makes marginal tenants worse off by $500, and makes landlords worse off by $750. Are we justified in imposing the IWH on these facts? This outcome is inefficient under an aggregate wealth maximization (Kaldor–Hicks) standard for measuring social utility.

If we reject aggregate wealth maximization as the test, on the ground that it ignores distributional concerns, we still have a dilemma under Craswell's analysis. Suppose landlords are the best-off group affected by the IWH, infra-marginal tenants are the next best-off group, and marginal tenants are the worst-off group. Insofar as the IWH takes from the landlords and transfers to the infra-marginal tenants, it has egalitarian distributional consequences. But how do we weigh the fact that the IWH may also make the worst-off tenants (by assumption here the marginals) even worse off, while benefiting the less-worse-off tenants (here the infra-marginals)? John Rawls suggested in his *Theory of Justice* (1970) that deviations from equal treatment are justifiable if they can be shown to make the worst-off group in society better off. Does the IWH flunk the Rawlsian test under the hypothetical?

Empirical evidence. Most studies of the implied warranty of habitability have been theoretical and most of the empirical writing on this issue is casual at best. One early study found a statistically significant effect—an increase of approximately 12 percent—on rent in the early 1970s from receivership laws, in which a noncompliant landlord would lose control over a building to a receiver who would direct repairs. Werner Z. Hirsch, Joel G. Hirsch & Stephen Margolis, Regression Analysis of the Effects of Habitability Laws Upon Rent: An Empirical Observation on the Ackerman–Komesar Debate, 63 Cal. L. Rev. 1098 (1975). Other habitability laws, such as repair-and-deduct and withholding, showed a smaller effect on rents that was not statistically significant. Breaking the category of poor tenants down further, the authors found that the effect on elderly tenants was different from that on African–American tenants. Elderly indigent tenant demand for housing rose with receivership laws and shifted upward almost as much as supply, suggesting that receivership laws were not counterproductive for elderly indigent tenants. For African–American tenants the supply shift was three and one-half times as great as the shift in the demand function, suggesting that receivership laws were counterproductive for African–Americans. The authors speculate that landlords find aged tenants to be lower cost in part because they do not move much (many repairs must be done when apartments turn over) and possibly are perceived by landlords to cause less damage than other tenants. See also Werner Z. Hirsch, From "Food for Thought" to "Empirical Evidence" About Consequences Of Landlord–Tenant Laws, 69 Cornell L. Rev. 604 (1984). Whether the IWH has an effect on aggregate housing supply is difficult to disentangle from other trends in housing happening at the same time. One reason that the IWH has not had more of an effect is that enforcement levels have been low. Edward Rabin, The Revolution in Residential Landlord–Tenant Law: Causes and Consequences, 69 Cornell L. Rev. 517 (1984). More empirical work, of both the casual and more rigorous sort, has been done on the impact of rent control on housing supply and quality, a topic to which we return below.

- P - Landlord   D - Tenant

Sommer v. Kridel

New Jersey Supreme Court, 1977.
378 A.2d 767.

■ PASHMAN, J. We granted certification in these cases to consider whether a landlord seeking damages from a defaulting tenant is under a duty to mitigate damages by making reasonable efforts to re-let an apartment wrongfully vacated by the tenant. Separate parts of the Appellate Division held that, in accordance with their respective leases, the landlords in both cases could recover rents due under the leases regardless of whether they had attempted to re-let the vacated apartments. Although they were of different minds as to the fairness of this result, both parts agreed that it was dictated by *Joyce v. Bauman*, 174 A. 693 (N.J. 1934), a decision by the former Court of Errors and Appeals. We now reverse and hold that a landlord does have an obligation to make a reasonable effort to mitigate damages in such a situation. We therefore overrule *Joyce v. Bauman* to the extent that it is inconsistent with our decision today.

I

* * * This case was tried on stipulated facts. On March 10, 1972 the defendant, James Kridel, entered into a lease with the plaintiff, Abraham Sommer, owner of the "Pierre Apartments" in Hackensack, to rent apartment 6–L in that building.[1] The term of the lease was from May 1, 1972 until April 30, 1974, with a rent concession for the first six weeks, so that the first month's rent was not due until June 15, 1972.

One week after signing the agreement, Kridel paid Sommer $690. Half of that sum was used to satisfy the first month's rent. The remainder was paid under the lease provision requiring a security deposit of $345. Although defendant had expected to begin occupancy around May 1, his plans were changed. He wrote to Sommer on May 19, 1972, explaining

I was to be married on June 3, 1972. Unhappily the engagement was broken and the wedding plans cancelled. Both parents were to assume responsibility for the rent after our marriage. I was discharged from the U.S. Army in October 1971 and am now a student. I have no funds of my own, and am supported by my stepfather.

In view of the above, I cannot take possession of the apartment and am surrendering all rights to it. Never having received a key, I cannot return same to you.

I beg your understanding and compassion in releasing me from the lease, and will of course, in consideration thereof, forfeit the 2 month's rent already paid.

Please notify me at your earliest convenience.

Plaintiff did not answer the letter.

Subsequently, a third party went to the apartment house and inquired about renting apartment 6–L. Although the parties agreed that she was ready, willing and able to rent the apartment, the person in charge told her that the apartment was not being shown since it was already rented to

---

1. Among other provisions, the lease prohibited the tenant from assigning or transferring the lease without the consent of the landlord. If the tenant defaulted, the lease gave the landlord the option of re-entering or re-letting, but stipulated that failure to re-let or to recover the full rental would not discharge the tenant's liability for rent.

Kridel. In fact, the landlord did not re-enter the apartment or exhibit it to anyone until August 1, 1973. At that time it was rented to a new tenant for a term beginning on September 1, 1973. The new rental was for $345 per month with a six week concession similar to that granted Kridel.

Prior to re-letting the new premises, plaintiff sued Kridel in August 1972, demanding $7,590, the total amount due for the full two-year term of the lease. Following a mistrial, plaintiff filed an amended complaint asking for $5,865, the amount due between May 1, 1972 and September 1, 1973. The amended complaint included no reduction in the claim to reflect the six week concession provided for in the lease or the $690 payment made to plaintiff after signing the agreement. Defendant filed an amended answer to the complaint, alleging that plaintiff breached the contract, failed to mitigate damages and accepted defendant's surrender of the premises. He also counterclaimed to demand repayment of the $345 paid as a security deposit.

The trial judge ruled in favor of defendant. Despite his conclusion that the lease had been drawn to reflect "the 'settled law' of this state," he found that "justice and fair dealing" imposed upon the landlord the duty to attempt to re-let the premises and thereby mitigate damages. He also held that plaintiff's failure to make any response to defendant's unequivocal offer of surrender was tantamount to an acceptance, thereby terminating the tenancy and any obligation to pay rent. As a result, he dismissed both the complaint and the counterclaim. The Appellate Division reversed in a per curiam opinion, and we granted certification. * * *

II

As the lower courts in both appeals found, the weight of authority in this State supports the rule that a landlord is under no duty to mitigate damages caused by a defaulting tenant. This rule has been followed in a majority of states, Annot. 21 A.L.R.3d 534, § 2(a) at 541 (1968), and has been tentatively adopted in the American Law Institute's Restatement of Property. Restatement (Second) of Property, § 11.1(3) (Tent. Draft No. 3, 1975).

Nevertheless, while there is still a split of authority over this question, the trend among recent cases appears to be in favor of a mitigation requirement.

The majority rule is based on principles of property law which equate a lease with a transfer of a property interest in the owner's estate. Under this rationale the lease conveys to a tenant an interest in the property which forecloses any control by the landlord; thus, it would be anomalous to require the landlord to concern himself with the tenant's abandonment of his own property.

For instance, in *Muller v. Beck*, [110 A. 831 (N.J. 1920)], where essentially the same issue was posed, the court clearly treated the lease as governed by property, as opposed to contract, precepts.[3] The court there

---

3. It is well settled that a party claiming damages for a breach of contract has a duty to mitigate his loss.

observed that the "tenant had an estate for years, but it was an estate qualified by this right of the landlord to prevent its transfer," 110 A. at 832, and that "the tenant has an estate with which the landlord may not interfere." Id. Similarly, in *Heckel v. Griese*, [171 A. 148 (N.J. 1934)], the court noted the absolute nature of the tenant's interest in the property while the lease was in effect, stating that "when the tenant vacated, . . . no one, in the circumstances, had any right to interfere with the defendant's possession of the premises." 171 A. 148, 149. * * *

Yet the distinction between a lease for ordinary residential purposes and an ordinary contract can no longer be considered viable. As Professor Powell observed, evolving "social factors have exerted increasing influence on the law of estates for years." 2 Powell on Real Property (1977 ed.), § 221(1) at 180–81. The result has been that

> [t]he complexities of city life, and the proliferated problems of modern society in general, have created new problems for lessors and lessees and these have been commonly handled by specific clauses in leases. This growth in the number and detail of specific lease covenants has reintroduced into the law of estates for years a predominantly contractual ingredient. (Id. at 181)

Thus in 6 Williston on Contracts (3 ed. 1962), § 890A at 592, it is stated:

> There is a clearly discernible tendency on the part of courts to cast aside technicalities in the interpretation of leases and to concentrate their attention, as in the case of other contracts, on the intention of the parties * * *

See also Javins v. First National Realty Corp., 428 F.2d 1071, 1075 (D.C. Cir. 1970) ("the trend toward treating leases as contracts is wise and well considered") * * *

This Court has taken the lead in requiring that landlords provide housing services to tenants in accordance with implied duties which are hardly consistent with the property notions expressed in *Muller v. Beck*, supra, and *Heckel v. Griese*, supra. See Braitman v. Overlook Terrace Corp., 346 A.2d 76 (N.J. 1975) (liability for failure to repair defective apartment door lock); Berzito v. Gambino, 308 A.2d 17 (N.J. 1973) (construing implied warranty of habitability and covenant to pay rent as mutually dependent); Marini v. Ireland, 265 A.2d 526 (N.J. 1970) (implied covenant to repair); Reste Realty Corp. v. Cooper, 251 A.2d 268 (N.J. 1969) (implied warranty of fitness of premises for leased purpose). In fact, in *Reste Realty Corp. v. Cooper*, supra, we specifically noted that the rule which we announced there did not comport with the historical notion of a lease as an estate for years. And in *Marini v. Ireland*, supra, we found that the "guidelines employed to construe contracts have been modernly applied to the construction of leases." 265 A.2d at 532.

Application of the contract rule requiring mitigation of damages to a residential lease may be justified as a matter of basic fairness.[4] Professor McCormick first commented upon the inequity under the majority rule when he predicted in 1925 that eventually

> the logic, inescapable according to the standards of a "jurisprudence of conceptions" which permits the landlord to stand idly by the vacant, abandoned premises and treat them as the property of the tenant and recover full rent, will yield to the more realistic notions of social advantage which in other fields of the law have forbidden a recovery for damages which the plaintiff by reasonable efforts could have avoided. [McCormick, The Rights of the Landlord Upon Abandonment of the Premises by the Tenant, 23 Mich.L.Rev. 211, 221–22 (1925)]

Various courts have adopted this position. See Annot., supra, § 7(a) at 565, and ante at 770–771.

The pre-existing rule cannot be predicated upon the possibility that a landlord may lose the opportunity to rent another empty apartment because he must first rent the apartment vacated by the defaulting tenant. Even where the breach occurs in a multi-dwelling building, each apartment may have unique qualities which make it attractive to certain individuals. Significantly, in *Sommer v. Kridel*, there was a specific request to rent the apartment vacated by the defendant; there is no reason to believe that absent this vacancy the landlord could have succeeded in renting a different apartment to this individual.

We therefore hold that antiquated real property concepts which served as the basis for the pre-existing rule, shall no longer be controlling where there is a claim for damages under a residential lease. Such claims must be governed by more modern notions of fairness and equity. A landlord has a duty to mitigate damages where he seeks to recover rents due from a defaulting tenant.

If the landlord has other vacant apartments besides the one which the tenant has abandoned, the landlord's duty to mitigate consists of making reasonable efforts to re-let the apartment. In such cases he must treat the apartment in question as if it was one of his vacant stock.

As part of his cause of action, the landlord shall be required to carry the burden of proving that he used reasonable diligence in attempting to re-let the premises. We note that there has been a divergence of opinion concerning the allocation of the burden of proof on this issue. See Annot., supra, § 12 at 577. While generally in contract actions the breaching party has the burden of proving that damages are capable of mitigation, here the landlord will be in a better position to demonstrate whether he exercised reasonable diligence in attempting to re-let the premises. Cf. Kulm v. Coast

---

4. We see no distinction between the leases involved in the instant appeals and those which might arise in other types of residential housing. However, we reserve for another day the question of whether a landlord must mitigate damages in a commercial setting.

to Coast Stores Central Org., 432 P.2d 1006 (Or. 1967) (burden on lessor in contract to renew a lease).

III

The *Sommer v. Kridel* case presents a classic example of the unfairness which occurs when a landlord has no responsibility to minimize damages. Sommer waited 15 months and allowed $4658.50 in damages to accrue before attempting to re-let the apartment. Despite the availability of a tenant who was ready, willing and able to rent the apartment, the landlord needlessly increased the damages by turning her away. While a tenant will not necessarily be excused from his obligations under a lease simply by finding another person who is willing to rent the vacated premises, see, e.g., Reget v. Dempsey–Tegler & Co., 216 N.E.2d 500 (Ill. App. 1966) (new tenant insisted on leasing the premises under different terms); Edmands v. Rust & Richardson Drug Co., 77 N.E. 713 (Mass. 1906) (landlord need not accept insolvent tenant), here there has been no showing that the new tenant would not have been suitable. We therefore find that plaintiff could have avoided the damages which eventually accrued, and that the defendant was relieved of his duty to continue paying rent. Ordinarily we would require the tenant to bear the cost of any reasonable expenses incurred by a landlord in attempting to re-let the premises, but no such expenses were incurred in this case.[5] * * *

In assessing whether the landlord has satisfactorily carried his burden, the trial court shall consider, among other factors, whether the landlord, either personally or through an agency, offered or showed the apartment to any prospective tenants, or advertised it in local newspapers. Additionally, the tenant may attempt to rebut such evidence by showing that he proffered suitable tenants who were rejected. However, there is no standard formula for measuring whether the landlord has utilized satisfactory efforts in attempting to mitigate damages, and each case must be judged upon its own facts. Compare Hershorin v. La Vista, Inc., 138 S.E.2d 703 (Ga. App. 1964) ("reasonable effort" of landlord by showing the apartment to all prospective tenants); Carpenter v. Wisniewski, 215 N.E.2d 882 (Ind. App. 1966) (duty satisfied where landlord advertised the premises through a newspaper, placed a sign in the window, and employed a realtor); Re Garment Center Capitol, Inc., 93 F.2d 667 (2d Cir. 1938) (landlord's duty not breached where higher rental was asked since it was known that this was merely a basis for negotiations); Foggia v. Dix, 509 P.2d 412, 414 (Or. 1973) (in mitigating damages, landlord need not accept less than fair market value or "substantially alter his obligations as established in the pre-existing lease"); with Anderson v. Andy Darling Pontiac, Inc., 43 N.W.2d 362 (Wis. 1950) (reasonable diligence not established where newspaper advertisement placed in one issue of local paper by a broker); Scheinfeld v. Muntz T. V., Inc., 214 N.E.2d 506 (Ill. App. 1966) (duty

---

5. * * * Because we hold that plaintiff breached his duty to attempt to mitigate damages, we do not address defendant's argument that the landlord accepted a surrender of the premises.

breached where landlord refused to accept suitable subtenant); Consolidated Sun Ray, Inc. v. Oppenstein, 335 F.2d 801, 811 (8 Cir. 1964) (dictum) (demand for rent which is "far greater than the provisions of the lease called for" negates landlord's assertion that he acted in good faith in seeking a new tenant).

IV

The judgment in *Sommer v. Kridel* is reversed. * * *

Figure 6–4
Pierre Apartments, Hackensack, New Jersey

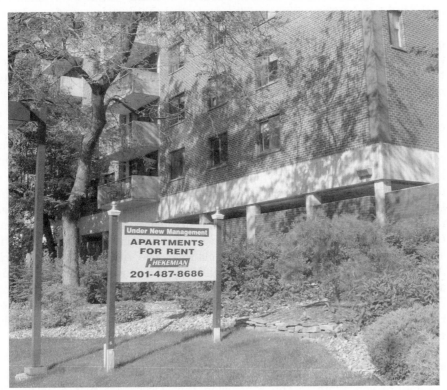

NOTES AND QUESTIONS

1. A recent decision reports that 42 states and the District of Columbia have adopted the duty to mitigate damages when the tenant abandons, at least for purposes of residential leases; six states continue to hold that the landlord has no duty to mitigate damages. See Austin Hill Country Realty, Inc. v. Palisades Plaza, Inc., 948 S.W.2d 293 (Tex. 1997) (adopting the duty to mitigate under Texas law). Thus, the duty-to-mitigate reform has been only slightly less successful than the IWH as a reform. As in the case of the IWH, the reform effort has focused on residential tenancies, and, as in the case of the IWH, has proceeded more by legislation than by

judicial reform. See 2 Milton R. Friedman, Friedman on Leases § 16:3:1 (Patrick A. Randolph, Jr. ed. & rev., 5th ed. 2005) (noting that in the commercial lease context "there has been very little change in the common-law rule, and in fact some major jurisdictions, including New York and Pennsylvania, have reiterated it"). The duty to mitigate, which is a pure contract doctrine, is in fact probably more unambiguously contractual than the IWH. Some decisions, including *Austin Hill*, recognize that the duty to mitigate is a default rule subject to modification by the parties in the lease; the IWH, in contrast, is generally regarded as a mandatory rule of law derived in part from the housing codes which is not subject to waiver.

2. Recall that the common-law courts, working within the framework of the independent covenants model, developed the doctrine of surrender to deal with tenants who abandon the premises. How would the instant cases have been decided under this doctrine? Are tenants always better off under the contractual duty to mitigate than they are under surrender? Are tenants free to invoke the old doctrine as an alternative to the duty to mitigate, or does the duty to mitigate overrule the doctrine of surrender?

3. Under the traditional view that a lease is (at least in part) a conveyance of land, rent is not owed until the period arrives in which the rent is due in exchange for the right to possession of the land. Courts sometimes refer to this idea by saying that "the rent issues out of the land." See Smith v. McEnany, supra. Courts influenced by this idea took a dim view of so-called "acceleration clauses," which provide that if the tenant breaches a covenant in the lease, the entire rental obligation under the lease is immediately due and owing. But if leases are viewed as bilateral contracts, and the landlord is under a duty to mitigate damages, what if anything is wrong with acceleration clauses? See Aurora Business Park Assoc. v. Michael Albert, Inc., 548 N.W.2d 153 (Iowa 1996) (upholding acceleration clause in conjunction with duty to mitigate as simply assuring that the landlord is made whole). Some jurisdictions, however, continue to refuse to enforce acceleration clauses, on the ground that they represent an excessive liquidated damages penalty.

e. TRANSFER OF INTERESTS

Before you jump to the conclusion that leases are just a branch of contract law, it is important to consider some issues where property-like notions continue to hold sway. One such issue involves the transfer of possession to the tenant. Under a lease, possession of the property (the land, the apartment, the car) shifts from the lessor to the lessee. Thus, during the term of the lease, the lessee acts as the general gatekeeper of the property, and can exercise the in rem rights of exclusion that we associate with possession of property. In this respect, leases are like bailments, which also entail a temporary transfer of possession (but not full ownership). Recall that in *The Winkfield*, in Chapter IV, the court held that a bailee has the right to bring actions against a third party tortfeasor for interfering with possession of property while in custody of the bailee. Similarly, the lessee has the right to bring actions like trespass or conversion against tortfeasors who interfere with leased land or chattels during the term of the lease.

Another set of issues that raise property-like notions involve transfers of either the landlord's reversion or the tenant's leasehold interest to some third party during the term of the lease. The general rule is that when the landlord transfers the reversion, the transferee takes subject to the tenant's leasehold interest, just as someone acquiring property in which another has a life estate would acquire subject to the life estate. But when this happens, is the new landlord bound by all the provisions of the original lease? Consider the following case.

] RULE

Mullendore Theatres, Inc. v. Growth Realty Investors Co.

Court of Appeals of Washington, 1984.
691 P.2d 970.

■ WORSWICK, JUDGE. Does a landlord's covenant to refund a tenant's security deposit run with the land, thus obligating a successor landlord to refund it? We hold it does not, where the lease permits but does not require that the deposit, if forfeited, be used for the benefit of the leased property.

In 1969, Conner Theatres Corporation became tenant of a part of the Jones Building in Tacoma under a lease that required a deposit of $22,500 as security for performance of the tenant's obligations. The lease provided in part:

> Should the Tenant default in the performance of said lease, the Landlord shall be entitled to apply said deposit on account of any damages which Landlord may sustain by reason of such default by the Tenant. In the event the Tenant shall not be in default under the provisions of said lease, the said deposit shall be returned and paid to the Tenant at the expiration of this lease, to wit, at the close of business on July 31, 1979. . . .

The lease also provided that all covenants in the lease would run with the land.

In 1974, Conner assigned its leasehold interest to Mullendore Theatres, Inc. At that time, the deposit was reduced to $6,000. Sometime before the assignment, the original landlord had transferred the property to North Pacific World Trade Center, Ltd. Growth Realty acquired it when North Pacific defaulted on a note and deed of trust in 1975. Growth ultimately sold it to the City of Tacoma. The City was concerned with the potential $6,000 liability, and wanted to reduce the purchase price by this amount. To avoid this, Growth agreed to indemnify the City for any liability it might have for the security deposit. In 1980, Mullendore negotiated a new lease with the City. To facilitate the transaction, it released any claims it might have against the City for return of the security deposit, but purported to reserve its claims against others who might be liable. Thereafter, it brought this action against Growth.

The trial court held that the covenant to refund the security deposit ran with the land and bound Growth through the indemnification clause in the sales contract between Growth and the City. Growth appeals, contending that the covenant did not run. In the alternative, Growth contends that any obligation it may have assumed was extinguished by Mullendore's release of the City. We agree with Growth's first contention.

RULE [

A lease covenant does not run with the land unless it touches or concerns the land. To do so, it must be so related to the land as to enhance its value and confer a benefit upon it. Otherwise, it is a collateral and personal obligation of the original lessor.

In order to be a running covenant, a promise to pay money must restrict the use of the funds to the benefit of the property. Rodruck v. Sand Point Maintenance Comm'n, 295 P.2d 714, 722 (Wash. 1956).[1]

There was no such restriction in this covenant. The landlord was not required to spend the money for repairs or maintenance, or in any other way related to the property. He was not even required to transfer it to his successors. The covenant was not directly related to, and did not touch and concern, the property.[2]

RULE [

Since it does not touch and concern the land, this covenant cannot run, despite the language in the lease which says it does. Intent is not enough to make a running covenant out of one which is by its nature personal.

The City had no obligation to return the security deposit. Growth agreed only to indemnify the City against potential liability. That agreement did not create any new liability. We need not consider further arguments concerning the effect of the transactions between the City and Growth or the City and Mullendore.

Reversed.

NOTES AND QUESTIONS

1. When the landlord transfers the reversion and the property is burdened by a lease that is still in effect, the ordinary rule is that new owner of the reversion takes subject to the ongoing leasehold interest. There is authority suggesting that the original parties can contract around this rule, and provide in the lease that the leasehold will terminate upon any transfer by the landlord—at least if the termination clause is very

---

1. In *Rodruck,* the court held a promise to pay assessments for maintenance to be a running covenant. It distinguished that covenant from one which provided for the payment of dues to a property owners association but did not specify how the money was to be spent.

2. This proposition is supported by the weight of authority from other jurisdictions. Almost all courts that have considered the question have held that a promise to return a security deposit does not run with the land. See Federated Mortgage Investors v. American S & L Ass'n, 121 Cal.Rptr. 137 (Cal App. 1975); McDonald's Corp. v. Blotnik, 328 N.E.2d 897 (Ill. App. 1975); Mauro v. Alvino, 152 N.Y.S. 963 (1915); Partington v. Miller, 5 A.2d 468 (N.J. 1939); Tuteur v. P. & F. Enterprises, Inc., 255 N.E.2d 284 (Ohio App. 1970).

prominently disclosed. See Robert S. Schoshinski, American Law of Landlord and Tenant § 8:3 (1980).

2.   However, it is also the ordinary rule that when the reversion is
sold the new landlord and the original tenant are not bound by all
provisions of the original lease, only by those that "run with the land." In
determining whether a lease covenant runs with the land, the ordinary
test, applied by the principal case, is to ask (1) whether the parties
intended the covenant to run, and (2) whether the covenant "touches and
concerns" the land. What is the purpose of imposing this additional
requirement beyond intent to run? What does it mean to say that a promise
"touches and concerns" the land? The court says that it means the promise
must be "so related to the land as to enhance its value and confer a benefit
upon it." This is not very helpful, but as we will see more fully when we
consider servitudes running with the land (where the "touch and concern"
test also applies), courts have not been able to do much better than this.
See Chapter IX. One would think that if the general rule about continuation of the leasehold when the reversion is sold is subject to modification by
contract (i.e., in the original lease), then the rule that only those lease
clauses that touch and concern the land would also be subject to modification by contract. (In other words, we would expect "touch and concern" to
be only a default rule.) But the court here holds that a provision in the
lease stating that all covenants run with the land will not be enforced if the
covenant does not in fact touch and concern the land. Can you think of any
justification for making the touch and concern test for running covenants
nonwaivable?

3.   The court says that in order for a promise to pay money to touch
and concern the land, the promise "must restrict the use of the funds to
the benefit of the property." Here, the promise is to return a security
deposit at the end of the lease. Broadly speaking, a security deposit can be
said to have one of two purposes. One is to provide a "damage deposit" that
the landlord can tap into to make any necessary repairs for which the
outgoing tenant is responsible under the lease. If this is the purpose of the
security deposit, why doesn't it touch and concern the land? Is the problem
that *keeping* the security deposit would "benefit the property," but *returning* it would not? But isn't the promise to return the deposit necessary
in order to get the money and have it on hand if it becomes necessary to
keep it? A second purpose is to provide a "security interest" to assure that
the landlord receives the final payment of rent. Why doesn't this purpose
also touch and concern the land? Consider the matter this way: Surely a
covenant to pay rent runs with the land and hence touches and concerns
the land. This is of the essence of the bargain between the landlord and the
tenant (recall that *Paradine v. Jane* holds that the covenant to pay rent is
implied in all leases). If the covenant to pay rent runs with the land, then
why doesn't a promise designed to assure that the tenant pays the rent also
run with the land? Is the problem again that the security deposit is not
being kept (to satisfy unpaid rent) but rather is sought to be returned? But
again, isn't the promise to return the deposit necessary to get the money in
the first place and hold it as security in the event of nonpayment of rent?

However questionable its reasoning might be, the principal case apparently reflects the majority view that a promise to return a security deposit does not run with the land.

Insane

4. Is the problem here that the original landlord, North Pacific World Trade Center, Ltd., very likely put the security deposit in its bank account, and is now bankrupt (and probably dissolved)? North Pacific received a windfall which cannot be recovered. But why, as between the tenant and the successor landlord, should the tenant be stuck with funding the windfall for the predecessor landlord?

ASSIGNMENT AND SUBLEASE

Although landlord-tenant law was not part of the original scheme of feudalism that gave rise to the system of estates in land studied in Chapter V, it contains analytical elements that are probably closer to feudalism than any other feature of property law. This emerges most clearly with respect to transfers of tenant interests. The law recognizes two types of transfers of tenant interests: sublease and assignment. A sublease operates very much like subinfeudation: The landlord starts with a fee simple; the landlord carves out a lease for the prime tenant from the fee simple; then the prime tenant carves out a sublease for the subtenant from the prime lease; then the subtenant carves out a sub-sublease for the sub-subtenant from the sublease, and so on. Each of the "carving outs" creates an interest of somewhat lesser extent than the interest from which it is taken. An assignment, in contrast, operates very much like alienation: The landlord starts with a fee simple; the landlord carves out a lease for the prime tenant from the fee simple; then the prime tenant alienates the prime lease to a first assignee; then the first assignee alienates the prime lease to a second assignee, and so forth. After the initial creation of the prime lease, there is no "carving out" here; rather the prime lease as a whole is transferred to successive assignees, each of which then steps into the shoes of her assignor. The distinction is illustrated in Figure 6–5.

The distinction between sublease and assignment is important because it affects who the landlord and the tenant in possession must deal with when problems arise in the ongoing relationship under the lease. A sublease is like a feudal hierarchy of lords and tenants; each lord deals with the tenant immediately below in the hierarchy, and each tenant deals with the lord immediately above. Thus, the original landlord would deal with the prime tenant, and the prime tenant with the subtenant. But the original landlord would not deal with the subtenant, nor the subtenant with the original landlord. At least in theory, each chain in the hierarchy has its own separate lease (sublease, sub-sublease, etc.) that defines the rights and obligations between the particular pair of parties to that instrument. With

Figure 6–5
Sublease and Assignment

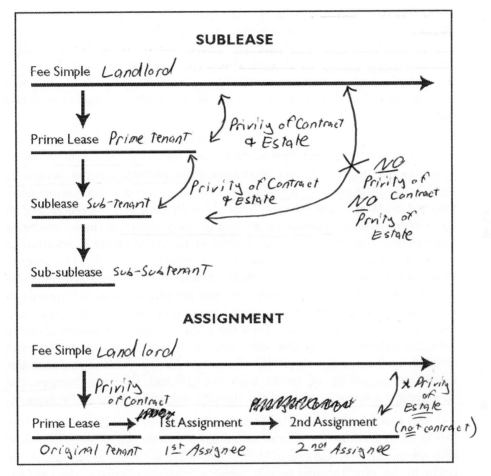

SUBLEASE

Fee Simple *Landlord*

Prime Lease *Prime Tenant*   *Privity of Contract*
                                     & Estate

Sublease *Sub-Tenant*   *Privity of Contract*   *NO*
                                & Estate   *Privity of*
                                                           Contract
                                                        NO
                                                        Privity or
                                                        Estate

Sub-sublease *Sub-Sub Tenant*

ASSIGNMENT

Fee Simple *Land lord*

                Privity
                of Contract   *★ Privity*
                                                           of
Prime Lease ⟶ *1st* Assignment ⟶ 2nd Assignment   *Estate*
                                                           (not contract)

Original Tenant   *1st Assignee*   *2nd Assignee*

an assignment, in contrast, the assignee steps into the shoes of the prime tenant, and as such enters into direct relations with the original landlord. After an assignment takes place, the original tenant drops out of the picture, as least insofar as having any direct responsibility for what happens on the property. So after a series of assignments, there are still only two parties who deal with the property: the original landlord and the latest assignee.

Things are slightly more complicated than this, especially on the assignment side, because lawyers over the years have said that there are two sources of landlord-tenant obligation: privity of estate and privity of contract. Privity of contract is easier to understand, so let's start there. The obligations that derive from privity of contract are simply the obligations that come from being a party to a binding bilateral contract, in this case, a written lease. So if the original landlord and the prime tenant enter into a lease, they are both bound by privity of contract. If the prime tenant and the subtenant enter into a sublease, they are both bound by privity of contract. But if the landlord and the subtenant have not entered into any contractual relationship with each other, they are not bound by privity of contract. One can identify the parties bound by privity of contract, and who they are bound with, simply by looking at the leases and seeing who has signed which lease.

The source of the obligations that derive from privity of estate are more mystical. Two conditions must be met for privity of estate to apply. First, the parties to be bound must have interests such that one is directly carved out of the interest of the other. One might say that the parties must have interests that are directly "nested" with each other. Second, one of the parties must be in actual possession of the property. If these conditions are satisfied, then the parties are bound by privity of estate in addition to privity of contract. So for example, in the sublease hierarchy, the original landlord is in privity of estate with the prime tenant as long as the prime tenant is in possession of the property, and the prime tenant is in privity of estate with the landlord. If the prime tenant subleases to a subtenant, and the subtenant is in possession, then the prime tenant is in privity of estate with the subtenant, and the subtenant with the prime tenant, but the original landlord is not in privity of estate with the subtenant, nor is the subtenant in privity of estate with the original landlord, because the subtenant's interest is not carved directly out of the landlord's interest.

"So what?," you are probably demanding to know. So far it sounds like privity of contract and privity of estate cover exactly the same people—and they do, on the sublease side of things. But when we get to assignments, we begin to see how the distinction becomes relevant. Suppose the original landlord enters into a lease with the prime tenant. They are in both privity of contract and privity of estate. Then the prime tenant enters into a contract to assign the lease to the first assignee. The assignment does not destroy the contractual relationship between the original landlord and the prime tenant—they are still in privity of contract. But there is no contractual relationship between the original landlord and the first assignee, and so there is no privity of contract between the original landlord and the first assignee. However, the first assignee has now stepped into the shoes of the prime tenant, and holds an interest—the prime leasehold interest—that is directly carved out of (is nested with) the landlord's interest, and the first assignee is now in possession of the property. So the original landlord and the first assignee *are* in privity of estate.

How do we know what sorts of obligations exist between two parties—like the original landlord and the first assignee in our example—who are in privity of estate but not privity of contract? Where is the document, analogous to the written lease we look to in determining the obligations entailed by privity of contract—that tells us what obligations are entailed by privity of estate? Answer: We look to the lease that defines the original leasehold interest, and we impose on the parties those covenants that run with the land. And which covenants run with the land? By now you should have guessed the answer: those covenants that "touch and concern" the land. In other words, we apply the same (rather mysterious) methodology that the *Mullendore Theatres* court used to determine which provisions of the lease bind a successor landlord, in order to determine which provisions of the lease bind a successor tenant in an assignment of the tenant's interest. Perfect symmetry!

Consider for a moment some of the practical implications of all this. If you are a landlord, and your prime tenant wants to exit from the relationship before the end of the lease, which is better: a sublease or an assignment? To some extent, it depends on how active you are in the management of the property. If you are inactive, you may prefer a sublease, because now the prime tenant will serve as the landlord to the subtenant, collecting rents, answering complaints about broken plumbing, and so forth. But if you are actively involved in management—say you are the landlord of a multi-unit apartment building—an assignment is probably better. With an assignment, the tenant in possession owes a duty to pay rent and perform other obligations that run with the land directly to you under privity of estate. And if for some reason the new tenant defaults, the prime tenant is still on the hook to you under privity of contract. The prime tenant acts as a surety for the performance of obligations by the assignee, as it were. If you are a tenant and you want to exit from the lease before the end of the term, somewhat similar considerations apply. You cannot escape from your obligations to the landlord; you will be stuck with privity of contract and estate under a sublease, and with privity of contract under an assignment. But an assignment may be preferable if you have no intention of returning to the property or otherwise remaining engaged in some aspect of its functioning, since under a sublease the new tenant must deal with you as landlord, whereas under an assignment the new tenant deals with the landlord, leaving you off the hook at least for management responsibilities.

If this were not complicated enough, there are two other concepts that are also relevant in the assignment context: assumption and novation. Assume that a landlord enters into a lease with a prime tenant, who then assigns the lease to the first assignee. An *assumption* would occur if the first assignee expressly agrees as part of an assignment agreement to be bound by the terms of the original lease. In effect, when an assignee makes an assumption, the assignee contractually agrees to be bound by privity of contract as well as by privity of estate. In the event of an assignment with an assumption, the prime tenant is still bound by privity of contract, meaning that there are now two parties bound by privity of contract with the landlord. A *novation* occurs when the parties agree to erase any privity of contract liability on the part of the prime tenant. Thus, if the prime tenant agrees to assign the lease to the first assignee, and the landlord agrees to a novation, then the prime tenant is off the hook altogether. The prime tenant is no longer in privity of estate, and the novation erases the prime tenant's privity of contract. The first assignee is bound by privity of estate, or if the first assignee has agreed to an assumption, by both privity of estate and privity of contract. Assumption and novation operate independently. One can have an assumption without a novation, or a novation without an assumption, or one can have both or neither. Careful drafting is critical to make sure that the right outcome is achieved by the parties involved.

Jaber v. Miller

Supreme Court of Arkansas, 1951.
239 S.W.2d 760.

■ GEORGE ROSE SMITH, JUSTICE. This is a suit brought by Miller to obtain cancellation of fourteen promissory notes, each in the sum of $175, held by the appellant, Jaber. The plaintiff's theory is that these notes represent monthly rent upon a certain business building in Fort Smith for the period beginning January 1, 1950, and ending March 1, 1951. The building was destroyed by fire on December 3, 1949, and the plaintiff contends that his obligation to pay rent then terminated. The defendant contends that the notes were given not for rent but as deferred payments for the assignment of a lease formerly held by Jaber. The chancellor, in an opinion reflecting a careful study of the matter, concluded that the notes were intended to be rental payments and therefore should be canceled.

In 1945 Jaber rented the building from its owner for a five-year term beginning March 1, 1946, and ending March 1, 1951. The lease reserved a monthly rent of $200 and provided that the lease would terminate if the premises were destroyed by fire. Jaber conducted a rug shop in the building until 1949, when he sold his stock of merchandise at public auction and transferred the lease to Norber & Son. Whether this instrument of transfer is an assignment or a sublease is the pivotal issue in this case.

In form the document is an assignment rather than a sublease. It is entitled "Contract and Assignment." After reciting the existence of the five-year lease the instrument provides that Jaber "hereby transfers and assigns" to Norber & Son "the aforesaid lease contract * * * for the remainder of the term of said lease." It also provides that "in consideration of the sale and assignment of said lease contract" Norber & Son have paid Jaber $700 in cash and have executed five promissory notes for $700 each, due serially at specified four-month intervals. Norber & Son agree to pay to the owner of the property the stipulated rental of $200 a month, and Jaber reserves the right to retake possession if Norber & Son fail to pay the rent or the notes. The instrument contains no provision governing the rights of the parties in case the building is destroyed by fire.

Later on the plaintiff, Miller, obtained a transfer of the lease from Norber & Son. Miller, being unable to pay the $700 notes as they came due, arranged with Jaber to divide the payments into monthly installments of $175 each. He and the Norbers accordingly executed the notes now in controversy, which Jaber accepted in substitution for those of the original notes that were still unpaid. When the premises burned Miller contended that Jaber's transfer to Norber & Son had been a sublease rather than an assignment and that the notes therefore represented rent. Miller now argues that, under the rule that a sublease terminates when the primary lease terminates, his sublease ended when the fire had the effect of terminating the original lease.

In most jurisdictions the question of whether an instrument is an assignment or a sublease is determined by principles applicable to feudal tenures. In a line of cases beginning in the year 1371 the English courts worked out the rules for distinguishing between an assignment and a sublease. See Ferrier, Can There be a Sublease for the Entire Term?, 18 Calif.L.Rev. 1. The doctrine established in England is quite simple: If the instrument purports to transfer the lessee's estate for the entire remainder of the term it is an assignment, regardless of its form or of the parties' intention. Conversely, if the instrument purports to transfer the lessee's estate for less than the entire term—even for a day less—it is a sublease, regardless of its form or of the parties' intention.

The arbitrary distinction drawn at common law is manifestly at variance with the usual conception of assignments and subleases. We think of an assignment as the outright transfer of all or part of an existing lease, the assignee stepping into the shoes of the assignor. A sublease, on the other hand, involves the creation of a new tenancy between the sublessor and the sublessee, so that the sublessor is both a tenant and a landlord. The common law distinction is logical only in the light of feudal property law.

In feudal times every one except the king held land by tenure from some one higher in the hierarchy of feudal ownership. "The king himself holds land which is in every sense his own; no one else has any proprietary right in it; but if we leave out of account this royal demesne, then every acre of land is 'held of' the king. The person whom we may call its owner, the person who has the right to use and abuse the land, to cultivate it or leave it uncultivated, to keep all others off it, holds the land of the king either immediately or mediately. In the simplest case he holds it immediately of the king; only the king and he have rights in it. But it well may happen that between him and the king there stand other persons; Z holds immediately of Y, who holds of X, who holds of V, who holds * * * of A, who holds of the king." Pollock and Maitland, History of English Law (2d Ed.), vol. I, p. 232. In feudal law each person owed duties, such as that of military service or the payment of rent, to his overlord. To enforce these duties the overlord had the remedy of distress, being the seizure of chattels found on the land.

It is evident that in feudal theory a person must himself have an estate in the land in order to maintain his place in the structure of ownership. Hence if a tenant transferred his entire term he parted with his interest in the property. The English courts therefore held that the transferee of the entire term held of the original lessor, that such a transferee was bound by the covenants in the original lease, and that he was entitled to enforce whatever duties that lease imposed upon the landlord. The intention of the parties had nothing to do with the matter; the sole question was whether the first lessee retained a reversion that enabled him to hold his place in the chain of ownership.

The injustice of these inflexible rules has often been pointed out. Suppose that *A* makes a lease to *B* for a certain rental. *B* then executes to *C* what both parties intend to be a sublease as that term is generally understood, but the sublease is for the entire term. If *C* in good faith pays his rent to *B*, as the contract requires, he does so at his peril. For the courts say that the contract is really an assignment, and therefore *C*'s primary obligation is to *A* if the latter elects to accept *C* as his tenant. Consequently *A* can collect the rent from the subtenant even though the sublessor has already been paid. For a fuller discussion of this possibility of double liability on the part of the subtenant see Darling, Is a Sublease for the Residue of a Lessee's Term in Effect an Assignment?, 16 Amer.L.Rev. 16, 21.

Not only may the common law rule operate with injustice to the subtenant; it can be equally harsh upon the sublessor. Again suppose that *A* makes a lease to *B* for a certain rental. *B* then makes to *C* what *B* considers a profitable sublease for twice the original rent. But *B* makes the mistake of attempting to sublet for the entire term instead of retaining a reversion of a day. The instrument is therefore an assignment, and if the original landlord acquires the subtenant's rights there is a merger which prevents *B* from being able to collect the increased rent. That was the situation in Webb v. Russell, 3 T.R. 393, 100 Eng.Rep. 639. The court felt compelled to recognize the merger, but in doing so Lord Kenyon said: "It seems to me, with all the inclination which we have to support the action (and we have hitherto delayed giving judgment in the hopes of being able to find some ground on which the plaintiff's demand might be sustained), that it cannot be supported. The defence which is made is made of a most unrighteous and unconscious nature; but unfortunately for the plaintiff the mode which she has taken to enforce her demand cannot be supported." Kent, in his Commentaries (14th Ed.), p. 105, refers to this case as reaching an "inequitable result"; Williams and Eastwood, in their work on Real Property, p. 206, call it an "unpleasant result." Yet when the identical question arose in California the court felt bound to hold that the same distasteful merger had taken place. Smiley v. Van Winkle, 6 Cal. 605.

A decided majority of the American courts have adopted the English doctrine in its entirety. Tiffany, Landlord & Tenant, § 151. A minority of our courts have made timid but praiseworthy attempts to soften the harshness of the common law rule. In several jurisdictions the courts follow the intention of the parties in controversies between the sublessor and the sublessee, thus preserving the inequities of feudal times only when the original landlord is concerned. Johnson v. Moxley, 113 S. 656 (Ala.); Saling v. Flesch, 277 P. 612 (Mont.); Mausert v. Feigenspan, 63 A. 610, 64 A. 801 (N.J. Eq.); Hobbs v. Cawley, 299 P. 1073 (N.M).

In other jurisdictions the courts have gone as far as possible to find something that might be said to constitute a reversion in what the parties intended to be a sublease. In some States, notably Massachusetts, it has been held that if the sublessor reserves a right of re-entry for nonpayment of rent this is a sufficient reversionary estate to make the instrument a sublease. Dunlap v. Bullard, 131 Mass. 161; Davis v. Vidal, 151 S.W. 290 (Tex.). But even these decisions have been criticized on the ground that at common law a right of re-entry was a mere chose in action instead of a reversionary estate. See, for example, Tiffany, supra, § 151.

The appellee urges us to follow the Massachusetts rule and to hold that since Jaber reserved rights of re-entry his transfer to Norber & Son was a sublease. We are not in sympathy with this view. It may be true that a right of re-entry for condition broken has now attained the status of an estate in Arkansas. See Moore v. Sharpe, 121 S.W. 341 (Ark.); Core, Transmissibility of Certain Contingent Future Interests, 5 Ark.L.Rev. 111. Even so, the Massachusetts rule was adopted to carry out the intention of parties who thought they were making a sublease rather than an assignment. Here the instrument is in form an assignment, and it would be an obvious perversion of the rule to apply it as a means of defeating intention.
* * *

In this state of the law we do not feel compelled to adhere to an unjust rule which was logical only in the days of feudalism. The execution of leases is a very practical matter that occurs a hundred times a day without legal assistance. The layman appreciates the common sense distinction between a sublease and an assignment, but he would not even suspect the existence of the common law distinction. As Darling, supra, puts it: "Every one knows that a tenant may in turn let to others, and the latter thereby assumes no obligations to the owner of the property; but who would guess that this could only be done for a time falling short by something—a day or an hour is sufficient—of the whole term? And who, not familiar with the subject of feudal tenures, could give a reason why it is held to be so?" It was of such a situation that Holmes was thinking when he said: "It is revolting to have no better reason for a rule than that so it was laid down in the time of Henry IV. It is still more revolting if the grounds upon which it was laid down have vanished long since, and the rule simply persists from blind imitation of the past." The Path of the Law, 10 Harv.L.Rev. 457, 469. The rule now in question was laid down some years before the reign of Henry IV.

The English distinction between an assignment and a sublease is not a rule of property in the sense that titles or property rights depend upon its continued existence. A lawyer trained in common law technicalities can prepare either instrument without fear that it will be construed to be the other. But for the less skilled lawyer or for the layman the common law rule is simply a trap that leads to hardship and injustice by refusing to permit the parties to accomplish the result they seek.

RULE [For these reasons we adopt as the rule in this State the principle that the intention of the parties is to govern in determining whether an instrument is an assignment or a sublease. If, for example, a tenant has leased an apartment for a year and is compelled to move to another city, we know of no reason why he should not be able to sublease it for a higher rent without needlessly retaining a reversion for the last day of the term. The duration of the primary term, as compared to the length of the sublease, may in some instances be a factor in arriving at the parties' intention, but we do not think it should be the sole consideration. The *Bailey* case, to the extent that it is contrary to this opinion, is overruled.

In the case at bar it cannot be doubted that the parties intended an assignment and not a sublease. The document is so entitled. All its language is that of an assignment rather than that of a sublease. The consideration is stated to be in payment for the lease and not in satisfaction of a tenant's debt to his landlord. The deferred payments are evidenced by promissory notes, which are not ordinarily given by one making a lease. From the appellee's point of view it is unfortunate that the assignment makes no provision for the contingency of a fire, but the appellant's position is certainly not without equity. Jaber sold his merchandise at public auction, and doubtless at reduced prices, in order to vacate the premises for his assignees. Whether he would have taken the same course had the contract provided for a cancellation of the deferred payments in case of a fire we have no way of knowing. A decision either way works a hardship on the losing party. In this situation we do not feel called upon to supply a provision in the assignment which might have been, but was not, demanded by the assignees.

Reversed.

NOTES AND QUESTIONS

1. The court makes several assumptions that might be challenged. First, it assumes that *Paradine v. Jane* still describes the risk of casualty loss as between landlord and tenant, unless the lease provides to the contrary. Second, it assumes that the provision in the original lease providing for termination in the event of destruction is not a covenant that runs with the leasehold upon assignment to a new tenant. Third, it assumes that if a prime lease is terminated, a sublease is also terminated. Which if any of these assumptions do you think is questionable? What would be the effect on the result in the case if any of these assumptions were reversed?

2. Although the court announces that it is foreswearing formalism and instead will enforce the intentions of the parties, it appears that the court still assumes that the inquiry into intent will reveal either that the parties intended an assignment or intended a sublease, one or the other.

The court does not contemplate the possibility that the analysis of intent might reveal some novel set of rights and duties between transferor and transferee that partake of characteristics different from the standard package of incidents one gets with either an assignment or a sublease. In this sense the anti-formalist inquiry into intentions is still broadly consistent with the *numerus clausus*.

3. The English rule described by the court, which categorizes transfers as being either an assignment or sublease based on whether the prime tenant retains a reversion (even if only of one day at the end of the prime lease), may have been derived from feudalism. But it also has the virtue of being very easy to apply, and hence to comply with. In opposition to the English rule, the court endorses "the common sense distinction between a sublease and an assignment." What is that? That a sublease occurs when the prime tenant acts as a landlord toward the new tenant, and an assignment occurs when the prime tenant just drops out of the picture? But what sorts of facts will be relevant in making this kind of "common sense" determination? An all-things-considered inquiry into the "common sense" of the situation will entail more uncertainty. The prospect of such uncertainty, and litigation caused by uncertainty, could result in much more elaborately drafted leases with lots of redundant declarations of intent superimposed on top of the old formalism. Are these additional drafting costs worth the benefits of avoiding the occasional injustices cited by the *Jaber* court? The court seems to imply that the old formalistic test would be okay if everyone had a competent lawyer; but this cannot be assumed, so we need to allow courts to engage in wide-ranging examinations of party intent. Yet if assignment and subletting occur primarily in commercial lease contexts, won't the parties nearly always be represented by counsel? Should legal rules be devised on the assumption that some significant percentage of parties advised by counsel will be advised incompetently?

4. Note that in the event of an assignment without an assumption by the new tenant of the original lease between the landlord and the original tenant, the test for which covenants in the original lease are binding as between the landlord and the new tenant is the same as the test for determining which lease covenants carry over upon the sale of the reversion by the original landlord—those covenants which touch and concern the land. Does this mean, on the reasoning of *Mullendore Theatres*, that the original landlord is not obliged to return a security deposit paid by the original tenant to the new tenant on the termination of the lease?

P   D — Respondent

Kendall v. Ernest Pestana, Inc.

Supreme Court of California, 1985.
709 P.2d 837.

■ BROUSSARD, JUSTICE. This case concerns the effect of a provision in a commercial lease[1] that the lessee may not assign the lease or sublet the premises without the lessor's prior written consent. The question we

---

1. We are presented only with a commercial lease and therefore do not address the question whether residential leases are controlled by the principles articulated in this opinion.

address is whether, in the absence of a provision that such consent will not be unreasonably withheld, a lessor may unreasonably and arbitrarily withhold his or her consent to an assignment.[2] This is a question of first impression in this court.

I.

* * * The allegations of the complaint may be summarized as follows. The lease at issue is for 14,400 square feet of hangar space at the San Jose Municipal Airport. The City of San Jose, as owner of the property, leased it to Irving and Janice Perlitch, who in turn assigned their interest to respondent Ernest Pestana, Inc. Prior to assigning their interest to respondent, the Perlitches entered into a 25–year sublease with one Robert Bixler commencing on January 1, 1970. The sublease covered an original five-year term plus four 5–year options to renew. The rental rate was to be increased every 10 years in the same proportion as rents increased on the master lease from the City of San Jose. The premises were to be used by Bixler for the purpose of conducting an airplane maintenance business.

Bixler conducted such a business under the name "Flight Services" until, in 1981, he agreed to sell the business to appellants Jack Kendall, Grady O'Hara and Vicki O'Hara. The proposed sale included the business and the equipment, inventory and improvements on the property, together with the existing lease. The proposed assignees had a stronger financial statement and greater net worth than the current lessee, Bixler, and they were willing to be bound by the terms of the lease.

The lease provided that written consent of the lessor was required before the lessee could assign his interest, and that failure to obtain such consent rendered the lease voidable at the option of the lessor.[5] Accordingly, Bixler requested consent from the Perlitches' successor-in-interest, respondent Ernest Pestana, Inc. Respondent refused to consent to the assignment and maintained that it had an absolute right arbitrarily to refuse any such request. The complaint recites that respondent demanded

---

2. Since the present case involves an assignment rather than a sublease, we will speak primarily in terms of assignments. However, our holding applies equally to subleases. * * *

5. Paragraph 13 of the sublease between the Perlitches and Bixler provides: "Lessee shall not assign this lease, or any interest therein, and shall not sublet the said premises or any part thereof, or any right or privilege appurtenant thereto, or suffer any other person (the agents and servants of Lessee excepted) to occupy or use said premises, or any portion thereof, without written consent of Lessor first had and obtained, and a consent to one assignment, subletting, occupation or use by any other person, shall not be deemed to be a consent to any subsequent assignment, subletting, occupation or use by another person. Any such assignment or subletting without this consent shall be void, and shall, at the option of Lessor, terminate this lease. This lease shall not, nor shall any interest therein, be assignable, as to the interest of lessee, by operation of alaw [sic], without the written consent of Lessor."

"increased rent and other more onerous terms" as a condition of consenting to Bixler's transfer of interest.

The proposed assignees brought suit for declaratory and injunctive relief and damages seeking, inter alia, a declaration "that the refusal of ERNEST PESTANA, INC. to consent to the assignment of the lease is unreasonable and is an unlawful restraint on the freedom of alienation...." The trial court sustained a demurrer to the complaint without leave to amend and this appeal followed.

II.

The law generally favors free alienability of property, and California follows the common law rule that a leasehold interest is freely alienable. Contractual restrictions on the alienability of leasehold interests are, however, permitted. "Such restrictions are justified as reasonable protection of the interests of the lessor as to who shall possess and manage property in which he has a reversionary interest and from which he is deriving income." (Schoshinski, American Law of Landlord and Tenant § 8:15, at pp. 578–579 (1980)).

The common law's hostility toward restraints on alienation has caused such restraints on leasehold interests to be strictly construed against the lessor. Thus, in *Chapman v. Great Western Gypsum Co.*, 14 P.2d 758 (Cal. 1932), where the lease contained a covenant against assignment without the consent of the lessor, this court stated: "It hardly needs citation of authority to the principle that covenants limiting the free alienation of property such as covenants against assignment are barely tolerated and must be strictly construed." Id. at 760. This is particularly true where the restraint in question is a "forfeiture restraint," under which the lessor has the option to terminate the lease if an assignment is made without his or her consent. (See Karbelnig v. Brothwell, 53 Cal.Rptr. 335, 340 (Cal. App. 1966); Civ.Code, § 1442 ["A condition involving a forfeiture must be strictly interpreted against the party for whose benefit it is created."]; 2 Powell on Real Property, ¶ 246[1], at pp. 372.100–372.101.)

Nevertheless, a majority of jurisdictions have long adhered to the rule that where a lease contains an approval clause (a clause stating that the lease cannot be assigned without the prior consent of the lessor), the lessor may arbitrarily refuse to approve a proposed assignee no matter how suitable the assignee appears to be and no matter how unreasonable the lessor's objection. The harsh consequences of this rule have often been avoided through application of the doctrines of waiver and estoppel, under which the lessor may be found to have waived (or be estopped from asserting) the right to refuse consent to assignment.

The traditional majority rule has come under steady attack in recent years. A growing minority of jurisdictions now hold that where a lease provides for assignment only with the prior consent of the lessor, such consent may be withheld *only where the lessor has a commercially reasonable objection to the assignment,* even in the absence of a provision in the lease stating that consent to assignment will not be unreasonably withheld.

For the reasons discussed below, we conclude that the minority rule is the preferable position. * * *

III.

The impetus for change in the majority rule has come from two directions, reflecting the dual nature of a lease as a conveyance of a leasehold interest and a contract. (See Medico–Dental etc. Co. v. Horton & Converse, 132 P.2d 457 (Cal. 1942).) The policy against restraints on alienation pertains to leases in their nature as *conveyances.* Numerous courts and commentators have recognized that "[i]n recent times the necessity of permitting reasonable alienation of commercial space has become paramount in our increasingly urban society." (Schweiso v. Williams, 198 Cal. Rptr. 238, 240 (Cal. App. 1984). See also Comment, The Approval Clause in a Lease: Toward a Standard of Reasonableness, 17 U.S.F.L.Rev. 681, 683, 689 (1983); Note, Landlord–Tenant–Lessor's Rejection of Sublease Agreement, Pursuant to a Consent Clause, Must be Judged Under a Reasonable Commercial Standard, 9 Cum.L.Rev. 309, 312 (1978).)

Civil Code section 711 provides: "Conditions restraining alienation, when repugnant to the interest created, are void." It is well settled that this rule is not absolute in its application, but forbids only *unreasonable* restraints on alienation. (Wellenkamp v. Bank of America, 582 P.2d 970, 973 (Cal. 1978).) Reasonableness is determined by comparing the justification for a particular restraint on alienation with the quantum of restraint actually imposed by it. "[T]he greater the quantum of restraint that results from enforcement of a given clause, the greater must be the justification for that enforcement." (Wellenkamp v. Bank of America, supra, at 973.). * * *

One commentator explains as follows: "The common-law hostility to restraints on alienation had a large exception with respect to estates for years. A lessor could prohibit the lessee from transferring the estate for years to whatever extent he might desire. It was believed that the objectives served by allowing such restraints outweighed the social evils implicit in the restraints, in that they gave to the lessor a needed control over the person entrusted with the lessor's property and to whom he must look for the performance of the covenants contained in the lease. Whether this reasoning retains full validity can well be doubted. Relationships between lessor and lessee have tended to become more and more impersonal. Courts have considerably lessened the effectiveness of restraint clauses by strict construction and liberal applications of the doctrine of waiver. With the shortage of housing and, in many places, of commercial space as well, the allowance of lease clauses forbidding assignments and subleases is beginning to be curtailed by statutes." (2 Powell, supra, ¶ 246[1], at pp. 372.97–372.98, fns. omitted.) * * *

The second impetus for change in the majority rule comes from the nature of a lease as a *contract.* As the Court of Appeal observed in *Cohen v. Ratinoff*, 195 Cal.Rptr. 84 (Cal. App. 1983), "[s]ince *Richard v. Degan & Brody, Inc.* [espousing the majority rule] was decided, . . . there has been an increased recognition of and emphasis on the duty of good faith and fair

* RULE

dealing inherent in every contract." (Id. at 88.) Thus, "[i]n every contract there is an implied covenant that neither party shall do anything which will have the effect of destroying or injuring the right of the other party to receive the fruits of the contract...." (Universal Sales Corp. v. Cal. etc. Mfg. Co.,128 P.2d 665, 677 (Cal. 1942)). * * * Here the lessor retains the discretionary power to approve or disapprove an assignee proposed by the other party to the contract; this discretionary power should therefore be exercised in accordance with <u>commercially reasonable standards.</u> "<u>Where a lessee is entitled to sublet under common law, but has agreed to limit that right by first acquiring the consent of the landlord, we believe the lessee has a right to expect that consent will not be unreasonably withheld.</u>" (Fernandez v. Vazquez, supra, 397 So.2d at 1174.)[15]

[handwritten margin note:] MAIN RULE

Under the minority rule, the determination whether a lessor's refusal to consent was reasonable is a question of fact. Some of the factors that the trier of fact may properly consider in applying the standards of good faith and commercial reasonableness are: financial responsibility of the proposed assignee; suitability of the use for the particular property; legality of the proposed use; need for alteration of the premises; and nature of the occupancy, i.e., office, factory, clinic, etc.

[handwritten margin note:] Factors to be considered by Trier of Fact for The "commercial reasonableness" of a refusal of assignment

Denying consent solely on the basis of personal taste, convenience or sensibility is not commercially reasonable. Nor is it reasonable to deny consent "in order that the landlord may charge a higher rent than originally contracted for." (Schweiso v. Williams, 198 Cal. Rptr. 238, 240 (Cal. App. 1984)). This is because the lessor's desire for a better bargain than contracted for has nothing to do with the permissible purposes of the restraint on alienation—to protect the lessor's interest in the preservation of the property and the performance of the lease covenants. " '[T]he clause is for the protection of the landlord *in its ownership and operation of the particular property*—not for its general economic protection.' " (Ringwood Associates, Ltd. v. Jack's of Route 23, Inc., 379 A.2d 508, 512 (N.J. Super. 1977), quoting Krieger v. Helmsley–Spear, Inc., 302 A.2d 129 (N.J. 1973), italics added.)

In contrast to the policy reasons advanced in favor of the minority rule, the majority rule has traditionally been justified on three grounds. Respondent raises a fourth argument in its favor as well. None of these do we find compelling.

First, it is said that a lease is a conveyance of an interest in real property, and that the lessor, having exercised a personal choice in the selection of a tenant and provided that no substitute shall be acceptable without prior consent, is under no obligation to look to anyone but the

---

15. Some commentators have drawn an analogy between this situation and the duties of good faith and reasonableness implied in all transactions under the Uniform Commercial Code. (U.Com.Code §§ 1–203, 2–103(b); see also U.Com.Code § 1–102, com. 1 [permitting application of the U.Com.Code to matters not expressly within its scope].) See Comment, The Approval Clause in a Lease: Toward a Standard of Reasonableness, supra, 17 U.S.F.L.Rev. 681, 695; see also Levin, Withholding Consent to Assignment: The Changing Rights of the Commercial Landlord, 30 De Paul L.Rev. 109, 136 (1980).

lessee for the rent. This argument is based on traditional rules of conveyancing and on concepts of freedom of ownership and control over one's property.

A lessor's freedom at common law to look to no one but the lessee for the rent has, however, been undermined by the adoption in California of a rule that lessors—like all other contracting parties—have a duty to mitigate damages upon the lessee's abandonment of the property by seeking a substitute lessee. (See Civ.Code, § 1951.2.) Furthermore, the values that go into the personal selection of a lessee are preserved under the minority rule in the lessor's right to refuse consent to assignment on any commercially reasonable grounds. Such grounds include not only the obvious objections to an assignee's financial stability or proposed use of the premises, but a variety of other commercially reasonable objections as well. (See, e.g., Arrington v. Walter E. Heller Int'l Corp., 333 N.E.2d 50 (Ill. App. 1975) [desire to have only one "lead tenant" in order to preserve "image of the building" as tenant's international headquarters]; Warmack v. Merchants Nat'l Bank of Fort Smith, 612 S.W.2d 733 (Ark. 1981) [desire for good "tenant mix" in shopping center]; List v. Dahnke 638 P.2d 824 (Colo. App. 1981) [lessor's refusal to consent to assignment of lease by one restaurateur to another was reasonable where lessor believed proposed specialty restaurant would not succeed at that location].) The lessor's interests are further protected by the fact that the original lessee remains a guarantor of the performance of the assignee.

The second justification advanced in support of the majority rule is that an approval clause is an unambiguous reservation of absolute discretion in the lessor over assignments of the lease. The lessee could have bargained for the addition of a reasonableness clause to the lease (i.e., "consent to assignment will not be unreasonably withheld"). The lessee having failed to do so, the law should not rewrite the parties' contract for them.

Numerous authorities have taken a different view of the meaning and effect of an approval clause in a lease, indicating that the clause is not "clear and unambiguous," as respondent suggests. As early as 1940, the court in *Granite Trust Bldg. Corp. v. Great Atlantic & Pacific Tea Co.*, supra, 36 F.Supp. 77, examined a standard approval clause and stated: "It would seem to be the better law that when a lease restricts a lessee's rights by requiring consent before these rights can be exercised, *it must have been in the contemplation of the parties that the lessor be required to give some reason for withholding consent.*" (Id., at 78, italics added.) * * * Again in 1963, the court in *Gamble v. New Orleans Housing Mart, Inc.*, 154 So.2d 625 (La. App. 1963), stated: "Here the lessee is simply not permitted to sublet without the written consent of the lessor. This does not *prohibit* or *interdict* subleasing. To the contrary, it permits subleasing provided only that the lessee first obtain the written consent of the lessor. *It suggests or connotes that, when the lessee obtains a subtenant acceptable or satisfactory to the lessor, he may sublet....* Otherwise the provision simply would prohibit subleasing." (Id., at 627, final italics added.) In *Shaker Bldg. Co. v.*

Federal Lime and Stone Co., supra, 277 N.E.2d 584, the court expressed the same view: "While the lease before the court clearly states that no assignment may take place without prior consent, inherent, however, in that provision is the representation that an assignment is possible. This court is of the opinion that *equally inherent in that provision is the representation that such prior consent will not be withheld under any and all circumstances, reasonable or unreasonable.*" (Id. at 587, italics added.)

RULE

In light of the interpretations given to approval clauses in the cases cited above, and in light of the increasing number of jurisdictions that have adopted the minority rule in the last 15 years, the assertion that an approval clause "clearly and unambiguously" grants the lessor absolute discretion over assignments is untenable. It is not a rewriting of a contract, as respondent suggests, to recognize the obligations imposed by the duty of good faith and fair dealing, which duty is implied by law in every contract.

The third justification advanced in support of the majority rule is essentially based on the doctrine of stare decisis. It is argued that the courts should not depart from the common law majority rule because "many leases now in effect covering a substantial amount of real property and creating valuable property rights were carefully prepared by competent counsel in reliance upon the majority viewpoint." (Gruman v. Investors Diversified Services, 78 N.W.2d 377 (Minn. 1956).) As pointed out above, however, the majority viewpoint has been far from universally held and has never been adopted by this court. Moreover, the trend in favor of the minority rule should come as no surprise to observers of the changing state of real property law in the 20th century. The minority rule is part of an increasing recognition of the contractual nature of leases and the implications in terms of contractual duties that flow therefrom. (See Green v. Superior Court, 517 P.2d 1168, 1172–73 (Cal. 1974).) We would be remiss in our duty if we declined to question a view held by the majority of jurisdictions simply because it is held by a majority. As we stated in *Rodriguez v. Bethlehem Steel Corp.*, 525 P.2d 669 (Cal. 1974), the "vitality [of the common law] can flourish only so long as the courts remain alert to their obligation and opportunity to change the common law when reason and equity demand it." (Id. at 676.)

A final argument in favor of the majority rule is advanced by respondent and stated as follows: "Both tradition and sound public policy dictate that the lessor has a right, under circumstances such as these, to realize the increased value of his property." Respondent essentially argues that any increase in the market value of real property during the term of a lease properly belongs to the lessor, not the lessee. We reject this assertion. One California commentator has written: "[W]hen the lessee executed the lease he acquired the contractual right for the exclusive use of the premises, and all of the benefits and detriment attendant to possession, for the term of the contract. He took the downside risk that he would be paying too much rent if there should be a depression in the rental market.... Why should he be deprived of the contractual benefits of the lease because of the fortuitous inflation in the marketplace[?] By reaping the benefits he does not deprive the landlord of anything to which the landlord was otherwise entitled. The landlord agreed to dispose of possession for the limited term and he could not reasonably anticipate any more than what was given to him by the terms of the lease. His reversionary estate will benefit from the increased value from the inflation in any event, at least upon the expiration of the lease." (Miller & Starr, Current Law of Cal. Real Estate 1984 Supp., § 27:92 at p. 321 (1977).)

Respondent here is trying to get *more* than it bargained for in the lease. A lessor is free to build periodic rent increases into a lease, as the lessor did here. Any increased value of the property beyond this "belongs" to the lessor only in the sense, as explained above, that the lessor's reversionary estate will benefit from it upon the expiration of the lease. We must therefore reject respondent's argument in this regard.[17] * * *

IV.

In conclusion, both the policy against restraints on alienation and the implied contractual duty of good faith and fair dealing militate in favor of adoption of the rule that where a commercial lease provides for assignment only with the prior consent of the lessor, such consent may be withheld only where the lessor has a commercially reasonable objection to the assignee or the proposed use. Under this rule, appellants have stated a cause of action against respondent Ernest Pestana, Inc.

■ LUCAS, JUSTICE, dissenting. I respectfully dissent. In my view we should follow the weight of authority which, as acknowledged by the majority herein, allows the commercial lessor to withhold his consent to an assignment or sublease arbitrarily or without reasonable cause. The majority's contrary ruling, requiring a "commercially reasonable objection" to the assignment, can only result in a proliferation of unnecessary litigation. * * *

NOTES AND QUESTIONS

1. The economic reality that underlies the dispute in the principal case is that market rents for hangar space at regional airports in California had undoubtedly risen significantly relative to the rent reserved under the prime lease. Leasing professionals refer to this as the "bonus value" of a lease. It is simply the difference between the rent reserved and the rent obtainable in the leasing market at any given point in time. There are two ways for the original transacting parties to try to capture a positive bonus value. If the landlord is permitted to terminate the original lease and enter into a new lease at market rents, the landlord can capture the bonus.

---

17. Amicus Pillsbury, Madison & Sutro request that we make clear that, "whatever principle governs in the absence of express lease provisions, nothing bars the parties to commercial lease transactions from making their own arrangements respecting the allo- cation of appreciated rentals if there is a transfer of the leasehold." This principle we affirm; we merely hold that the clause in the instant lease established no such arrangement.

Alternatively, if the tenant is permitted to assign or sublet the original lease, the tenant can assign the lease in return for a lump sum payment or can sublease at a higher rent and thereby capture the bonus. Economically speaking, the issue in the case is which party—landlord or tenant—is entitled to capture the bonus value under the terms of the prime lease. The landlord's position is that the lease entitles the landlord (under established California law) to block the tenant from assigning or subletting for any reason or no reason, so the landlord is entitled to capture the bonus as a condition of giving consent to assignment or subletting. The tenant's position is that as long as the prime lease remains in force, the landlord has no way unilaterally to capture the bonus; only the tenant can capture the bonus by assigning or subletting, so the bonus rightly belongs to the tenant. Do you agree with the court's analysis as to how the right to capture the "bonus" is allocated under the lease?

2.   Given that the court is addressing only commercial leases, and that the parties who enter into commercial leases like the one involved in the principal case usually act on advice of counsel, what is the justification for flipping the default rule and awarding the bonus to the tenant (unless the parties have explicitly allowed the landlord to refuse consent for any reason) rather than the landlord (unless the parties constrain the landlord's discretion by requiring a commercially reasonable ground for refusing consent)? Does the Coase theorem (Chapter I) suggest that the parties will bargain around whatever default rule is established to reach the rule that maximizes their joint welfare? If that is the case, does the decision constitute a one-time windfall for tenants under long-term commercial leases negotiated under the assumption that the old default rule would apply?

3.   Recall that leases often function as a mechanism for managing complexes of assets shared by multiple tenants. Does the decision here—requiring that landlords give judicially reviewable reasons for refusing to consent to subleases or assignments unless they expressly reserve the right to act unreasonably—enhance or undermine the landlord's ability to govern a multi-tenant complex?

f.   A FORM LEASE

Form leases may be obtained from a variety of sources. We reproduce below a form obtained from Gerry W. Beyer, 19A West's Legal Forms, Real Estate Transactions, Residential § 48.3 (3d ed. 2002).

Apartment Lease

[READ CAREFULLY]

THIS LEASE CONSTITUTES A BINDING CONTRACT

This [_____], 20__[_____] hereinafter called the ("Lessor") hereby lease to [_____], hereinafter called the ("Lessee") the following premises: Apartment No. [_____] ("the Apartment") Building No. [_____], located at [_____] [_____]. Rent per month $_____ Security Deposit $_____

TERM *[_____]* Commencement Date *[_____]* Termination Date
[_____]. Make rent checks payable to: *[_____]* (Tel. No. *___*) and remit
to: *[_____]*.

1. Term. This lease shall commence at 12 noon on the commencement date indicated above and shall terminate at 12 noon on the termination date indicated above at which time the Lessee shall return possession to the Lessor and return all keys to the Apartment, outside doors and mailbox to the Lessor.

2. Rent. The monthly rental to be paid by the Lessee for the Apartment shall be as indicated above to be paid on the first day of each and every month, in advance, so long as this lease is in force and effect.

3. Security Deposit. The Lessee will also pay over to the Lessor upon the execution of this lease the sum indicated above to be held by the Lessor during the term of this lease or any extension or renewal thereof, as a SECURITY DEPOSIT for the full, faithful and punctual performance by the Lessee of all lawful covenants and conditions of this lease. It is understood that this security deposit may be applied to damages caused by the Lessee. The Lessor will return the security deposit less the amount applied to damages with interest as required by law and make a full accounting to the Lessee for all damages applied within 30 days after the Apartment is vacated. It is further understood that the security deposit is not to be considered prepaid rent, [nor] shall damages be limited to the amount of this security deposit.

4. Notices and Complaints. Notices, bills and complaints to the Lessee shall be deemed sufficiently given if deposited in the Lessee's mailbox or sent by mail to the Lessee at his last known address. Notices and complaints by the Lessee to the Lessor shall be mailed to General Investment & Development Co. to the address indicated above or such other address as may be furnished in writing to the Lessee.

5. Utilities. All electricity charges to the Apartment, including electricity charges for lighting, appliances, heating, ventilating or air conditioning shall be paid for by the Lessee. The Lessor agrees that it will furnish reasonable hot and cold water and reasonable heat during the regular heating season in the Apartment, all in accordance with applicable laws, but the failure of the Lessor to provide any of the foregoing items to any specific degree, quantity, quality, or character due to any causes beyond the reasonable control of the Lessor, such as accident, acts of nature, restriction by City, State or Federal regulations, or during necessary repairs to the apparatus shall not form a basis of any claim for damages against the Lessor.

6. Mortgages. The Lessor shall have the right to mortgage and the Lessee's rights hereunder shall be subordinate to all mortgages now or hereafter of record affecting the real estate of which the Apartment forms a part.

7. Nuisance. The Lessee shall not cause any nuisance or act in an unreasonable manner either to the Lessor or to the other Lessees.

8. Assigning/Subletting. The Lessee will not assign this lease, nor sublet the Apartment, or any part thereof, nor make any alteration in the Apartment without the Lessor's prior consent in writing.

9. Fire and Casualty. The Lessee will, in the case of fire or other casualty, give immediate notice thereof to the Lessor, who shall thereupon cause the damage to be repaired as soon as it is reasonable and convenient for the Lessor, but if the Apartment be so damaged that the Lessor shall decide neither to rebuild nor to repair, the term of the lease shall cease.

10. Regulations. The Lessee hereby consents to and agrees to, observe any reasonable regulation that may be and as are in effect now or as may be promulgated from time to time. Notice of all current rules and regulations will be given to the Lessee by the Lessor and shall be made a part of this lease. The Lessor shall not, however, be responsible to the Lessee for any non-observance of rules, regulations or conditions on the part of the other Lessees.

11. Insurance. The Lessee understands and agrees that it shall be the Lessee's own obligation to insure his personal property located in the Apartment, and the lessee further understands that the Lessor will not reimburse the Lessee for damage to the Lessee's personal property.

12. Recreational Facilities. The Lessee agrees that he is renting only the Apartment. The monthly rent does not include use of any recreational facilities of the Lessor. The use of any recreational facilities of the Lessor may be allowed or revoked in the Lessor's sole discretion. The Lessor reserves the right to promulgate reasonable rules and regulations governing the use of recreational facilities and to establish and collect fees for the use thereof (and to amend such fees from time to time) and to impose other charges from time to time to cover the costs and expenses of operation, maintenance and ownership of all recreational facilities.

13. Condition of Apartment. It is agreed between the parties that the Apartment has been rented in good order and repair. The Lessee acknowledges that he has inspected the Apartment and the Apartment is in good order except as otherwise noted in writing to the Lessor. The Lessee further agrees that upon vacating the Apartment it will be returned to a similar condition as when it was rented, reasonable wear and tear excepted.

14. Attorney's Fees and Penalties. The Lessee agrees to pay all reasonable attorney's fees and expenses incurred as a result of any breach of this lease. The Lessee further agrees to pay as additional rent a late charge amounting to 10% of his rental obligation for any period of time that the Lessee's rent is more than thirty days late.

15. Complete Agreement. It is agreed, except as herein otherwise provided, that no amendment or change or addition to this lease shall be binding upon the Lessor or Lessee unless reduced to writing and signed by the parties hereto. It is hereby agreed that this is the entire agreement of the parties.

16. Joint and Several Obligations. If this lease is executed by more than one person or entity as Lessee, then and in that event all the obligations incurred by the Lessee under this lease shall be joint and several.

17. Severability. Unenforceability for any reason of any provision(s) of this lease shall not limit or impair the operation or validity of any other provision(s) of this lease.

18. Utility Rate Increases: [omitted]

19. Holdover. If the Lessee remains in possession without the written consent of the Lessor at the expiration of the term hereof or its termination, then the Lessor may recover, in addition to possession, the monthly rental stipulated above for each month, or portion thereof, during the Lessee's holdover plus either one and one-half (½) times the monthly rental or the actual damages sustained by the Lessor, whichever is greater, plus the Lessor's costs of recovering said amounts and possession, including reasonable attorney's fees.

20. Right of Entry. The Lessor may enter the Apartment at any time where such entry is made necessary by an extreme hazard involving the potential loss of life or severe property damage, and between 8:00 A.M. and 8:00 P.M. in order to inspect the Apartment, to make repairs thereto, to show the same to a prospective or actual purchaser or tenant, pursuant to court order, or if the Apartment appears to have been abandoned.

21. Delivery of Lease. The Lessor shall deliver a copy of this lease duly executed by the Lessor or his authorized agent, to the Lessee within thirty (30) days after the Lessee delivers an executed copy of this lease to the Lessor.

22. Renewal. It is understood that the Lessee, having received a renewal lease, shall execute and properly return the same to the Lessor or, alternatively, shall notify the Lessor of his intention not to so renew in either case within the time prescribed by the Lessor.

23. Trustees. No trustee nor any beneficiary of the trust shall be personally liable to anyone under any term, condition, covenant, obligation, or agreement expressed herein or implied hereunder or for any claim of damage arising out of the occupancy of the Apartment.

[signatures]

QUESTIONS

1. Assume you are advising a client who is interested in renting an apartment and who has been given this form to sign by her prospective landlord. The lease omits to mention certain covenants and provisions that, as we have seen, are critical from a tenant's perspective, such as the covenant of quiet enjoyment, the understanding that material covenants are dependent, a provision calling for termination of the lease upon destruction of the premises, the implied warranty of habitability, and the landlord's duty to mitigate damages. Are any of these omissions matters of serious concern for your client? If so, which ones?

2.   Consider the covenants that are included in the lease. Are there any provisions that you would advise your client to ask the landlord to delete? Are there any provisions that you would advise your client to ask the landlord to modify? If the landlord is willing to consider a short rider to the lease, what is the one thing you would be most anxious to add as an additional provision?

3.   Your client is otherwise happy with the apartment and the proposed rent. The landlord refuses to make any of your suggested deletions, modifications, or additions to the lease. Would you advise your client to go ahead a sign the lease, notwithstanding the reservations you might have about its deficiencies?

g.   RENT CONTROL

The United States is relatively unusual in that rents charged by landlords for both commercial and residential tenancies are today largely free of regulatory oversight by the government. Most other countries have some form of government controls on rents, at least for residential tenancies. Historically, the United States has also experienced significant episodes of rent control, such as during World War I and World War II and again during the period of high inflation in the 1970s and early 1980s. Today, only New York City, which has an usually high percentage of residents living in rental apartments, and a few cities in California (such as Berkeley and Santa Monica), still have significant rent control programs. But another major war or renewed inflation would predictably give rise to pressure for a reinstatement of rent controls, at least in urban areas.

One form of rent control is the rent freeze, which simply prohibits landlords from increasing the rents currently being charged. When rent controls are first imposed, as at the onset of a major war, they typically take the form of a rent freeze. Such regimes are adopted in response to an anticipated surge in demand for rental housing, and are designed to prevent unexpected hardships to tenants and windfall profits for landlords. See Franz Hubert, Rent Control: Academic Analysis and Public Sentiment, 10 Swedish Econ. Pol'y Rev. 61, 69 (2003). As time goes by, however, a rent freeze generates inequities and anomalies, especially if prices of inputs for which landlords must pay (such as for heating fuel) are not also controlled. Consequently, rent freezes are either suspended after a time, or they evolve into a more permanent form of regulation that allows for adjustments.

Rent control regimes that last for any appreciable period of time seek to stabilize rents rather than freeze them. Rent stabilization takes a variety of forms. Sometimes, as in post-War England up to the Thatcher regime or in communist China, a government authority sets a "fair rent" for each apartment. This can be based on a variety of factors, including landlord costs, tenant ability to pay, or the rents charged for comparable uncontrolled units. A more common system is called vacancy decontrol. This restricts rent increases while the tenant remains in possession of a unit, usually permitting annual percentage increases in accordance with some index established by a regulatory body. But when a tenant voluntarily vacates a unit, the landlord is allowed to adjust rents to market levels. Special exceptions may be made for increases in cases of landlord hardship or where a landlord has made significant improvements to the property. New York City has a complicated system in which rents are not decontrolled upon vacancy, but landlords find it much easier to obtain increases from regulators based on claims of hardship and improvements when a tenant vacates—primarily because there is no one to object to the increase. Hence a kind of de facto vacancy decontrol prevails.

Any system of rent stabilization tends to balloon into a system of comprehensive regulation of landlord-tenant relations, turning the rental housing industry into a kind of public utility. The principal reason for this is the vacancy decontrol feature. If landlords could insist that tenants take a one-year term of years, then the landlord could terminate each tenancy at the end of each year and reset rents to market levels. To prevent landlords from doing this, rent stabilization requires that the term of years be abolished, and that tenants be given what are in effect periodic tenancies for an indefinite term. But landlords still have an incentive to induce tenants to vacate, either by withholding services or otherwise engaging in belligerent behavior. To counteract this, landlord-tenant courts must be given authority to scrutinize the level of services landlords provide and to police other types of landlord behavior. Not surprisingly, landlord-tenant courts in New York City have enormous dockets, much larger than in any other major city without rent controls. Would going to a system in which a regulatory board establishes a fair rent (without regard to the tenure of the tenant) solve this problem? Or would it create other problems of equal or greater magnitude?

Economists have traditionally had nothing good to say about rent control. One survey taken in 1992 found that when economists were asked to respond to 40 statements related to economic policy the greatest recorded degree of consensus (93.5 percent) was to the proposition: "A ceiling on rents reduces the quantity and quality of housing available." Richard Arnott, Time for Revisionism in Rent Control? J. Econ. Perspectives, Winter 1995, at 100. The simple economic critique of rent control is as follows. If rents are fixed at levels below market clearing prices, then demand for rental housing will rise and the supply of rental housing will fall. This creates a gap between the quantity of housing demanded and the quantity supplied. In the short run, the gap will be closed by queuing: There will be waiting lists for housing, or units will be allocated based on favoritism or discrimination. In the long run, the supply will adjust to the controlled price, either because landlords allow the quality of housing to deteriorate, or they convert rental units to condominiums or otherwise take them off the market. So in the end, rent control simply gives tenants less housing or poorer-quality housing than they would have if government did not intervene in setting rents. See generally Edward L. Glaeser & Erzo F.P. Luttmer, The Misallocation of Housing Under Rent Control, 93 Am. Econ. Rev. 1027 (2003).

Defenders of rent control, such as Arnott, supra, point out that this traditional critique applies with greatest force to the rent freeze. A "well designed" rent stabilization program will have a less dramatic impact on landlords, because percentage increases are allowed each year. But even a "well designed" rent stabilization system can have serious distorting effects on the housing market. As other economists have pointed out, vacancy decontrol creates perverse distributional patterns, in which tenants who have lived in the same unit for many years pay substantially lower rents than tenants who have recently moved to the community or have just set up house on their own. See Kaushik Basu & Patrick Emerson, The Economics and Law of Rent Control, Policy Research Working Paper No. 1968 (World Bank, August 1998). The folklore of rent control contains many stories about wealthy dowagers living in spacious apartments at tiny rents, while recent college graduates pay half of their disposable income or more for studio apartments the size of a closet. There is also concern that vacancy decontrol can affect the mobility of the labor market, with workers who have scored a favorable rent control "deal" declining to move to another city to take up a better job because they would lose the subsidy they enjoy from rent control. Basu & Emerson, supra; Glaeser & Luttmer, supra.

Recently economists have offered additional arguments for rent control (of the rent stabilization variety). One argument points out that because each apartment is unique, and because search costs are high, each landlord enjoys a degree of localized monopoly power. Landlords may rationally attempt to exploit this quasi-monopoly by raising rents above levels that would prevail in a competitive market for fungible goods, like bushels of grain or shares of stock. Hence some tempering of rents, through rent stabilization, can improve the efficiency of the market by eliminating the premium the landlord can exact from their localized monopoly power. See Aaron S. Edlin, *The New Palgrave*: Surveying Two Waves of Economic Analysis of Law, 2 Am. L. & Econ. Rev. 407, 419–20 (2000). This argument, however, would seem to justify imposing price controls on virtually any nonfungible good. For example, freestanding homes are undoubtedly more unique than apartments, and the search costs of finding the right home are at least as high as those of finding the right apartment, yet few would argue that the prices of freestanding homes should be regulated. As Edlin suggests, the amount and quality of information required to use price controls to combat local monopoly may be too great.

Other commentators who reject the economic perspective have defended rent control on personhood and communitarian grounds. Most notably, Margaret Jane Radin has argued that rent control (of the vacancy decontrol variety) is justified precisely because it tends to lock people in to particular apartments and particular communities. See Margaret Jane Radin, Residential Rent Control, 25 Phil. & Pub. Affairs 350 (1986). People develop subjective attachments to their apartments, which become an important element in their personal identities. And they form networks of relationships in their communities, which would be disrupted if they—or the other members of the community—were continually moving out in response to rent increases. By providing an additional incentive for everyone to stay put, rent control thus enhances these personhood values. Note that this argument presents the flip side of the concerns of Basu & Emerson, supra, about how vacancy decontrol is unfair to newcomers and may create rigidities in labor markets. This is a theme we see often in property law— how to strike the right balance between stability and change (see Chapter XI in particular).

KEY CONCEPT

As is often the case, our capacity to theorize about a legal phenomenon, in this case rent control, exceeds our empirical knowledge. Nevertheless, a recent survey of empirical studies of rent control, drawing upon 27 different studies from around the world (with New York City being the most frequently studied), draws some qualified conclusions. See Bengt Turner & Stephen Malpezzi, A Review of Empirical Evidence on the Costs and Benefits of Rent Control, 10 Swedish Econ. Pol'y Rev. 11 (2003). The studies show that the "transfer efficiency"—the ratio of tenant benefits to landlord costs—is "less than 100 percent," although how much less varies depending on the market. Id. at 47. Translated, rent control reduces the aggregate wealth of society. The studies also show no consistent redistributive effects from rich to poor. Landlords tend to be somewhat better off than tenants, but not always, and some well-to-do tenants benefit from rent control. Id. Other findings, which are more qualified, are that rent control in one sector of the housing market tends to drive up rents in other uncontrolled sectors, id. at 46, and that the more stringent a country's system of rent controls, "the less housing investment is obtained" from the private sector, id. Do these findings, however qualified, vindicate the traditional hostility of economists to rent control?

CONSTITUTIONALITY OF RENT CONTROL

Rent control has been subject to repeated constitutional challenges ever since its initial introduction in the United States during World War I. In *Block v. Hirsh*, 256 U.S. 135 (1921), the Supreme Court rejected a due process challenge to controls established in Washington, D.C. to keep rents from rising with the influx of military and government workers during World War I. Speaking through Justice Holmes, the Court found that the rent controls satisfied a legitimate public purpose. He stressed that the controls were a temporary response to emergency conditions. "A limit in time, to tide over a passing trouble, well may justify a law that could not be upheld as a permanent change." Id. at 157. He noted further that "[m]achinery is provided to secure to the landlord a reasonable rent," and that on the question whether the rent was reasonable "the courts are given the last word." Id. at 157, 158. Justice McKenna, writing for four dissenters, asked: "If such exercise of government be legal, what exercise of government is illegal?" Id. at 161. He wondered whether "conditions come not only to the District of Columbia embarrassing the federal government, but to the world as well, that are not amenable to passing palliatives, and that Socialism, or some form of Socialism, is the only permanent corrective or accommodation?" Id. at 162.

More recently, the Supreme Court has considered several challenges to rent stabilization schemes. In *Pennell v. City of San Jose*, 485 U.S. 1 (1988), the Court held that it was not per se impermissible for a city to make "tenant hardship" one factor to be considered in determining whether to permit a landlord to impose a rent increase. The Court noted that balancing of producer and consumer interests had been held to be a "legitimate and rational goal" of price and rate regulation in the public utility context. Id. at 13. Justice Scalia, joined by Justice O'Connor, wrote a spirited dissent. He argued that unless the landlord could be shown to be the cause of the impecunious state of the tenant, it was simply unfair to make "one citizen pay, in some fashion other than taxes, to remedy a social problem that is none of his creation." Id. at 23.

In *Yee v. City of Escondido*, 503 U.S. 519 (1992), the Court considered the effect of two laws dealing with rentals of mobile home lots: a California state statute that allowed persons who lease mobile home pads to designate their successor tenant, and a local ordinance that sharply curtailed the level of rents that could be charged by the park owner for mobile home pads. The combined effect of the two laws was that

> the mobile home owner now owns, in addition to a mobile home, the right to occupy a pad at a rent below the value that would be set by the free market. Because * * * the park owner cannot evict a mobile home owner or easily convert the property to other uses, * * * the mobile home owner is effectively a perpetual tenant of the park, and the increase in the mobile home's value thus represents the right to occupy a pad at below-market rent indefinitely. And because the Mobilehome Residency Law permits the mobile home owner to sell the mobile home in place, the mobile home owner can receive a premium from the purchaser corresponding to this increase in value. * * * As a result, petitioners conclude, the rent control ordinance has transferred a discrete interest in land—the right to occupy the land indefinitely at a submarket rent—from the park owner to the mobile home owner.

Id. at 526–27. The court nevertheless held that this scheme did not effect a per se taking of property; the alternative question, whether there was a taking under an ad hoc balancing approach, had not been preserved for decision.

The Court's most recent rent control case, *Lingle v. Chevron USA Inc.*, 544 U.S. 528 (2005), presented the question whether a rent control scheme causes a taking of property if it fails substantially to advance a legitimate consumer-protection objective. The case involved a Hawaii statute that controls the rents that oil refining companies can charge to retail gasoline stations operating gas stations on property owned by the refiners. The stated objective of the statute was to restrain the prices of gasoline charged to consumers. The Ninth Circuit found that controlling the rents charged to dealers would not substantially advance the purpose of the statute—preventing consumer price increases—and hence that the scheme was a taking of the property of the oil refiners. The Supreme Court unanimously reversed, holding that the "substantially advances" requirement was not a proper element of regulatory takings law. *Lingle* preserves rent control's winning streak in the Supreme Court; the Court has never held a rent control scheme unconstitutional.

An interesting lower court opinion, which rejects a constitutional challenge to a Chicago ordinance adopting the implied warranty of habitability for both future and existing residential leases, is Chicago Bd. of Realtors v. City of Chicago, 819 F.2d 732 (7th Cir. 1987). A concurring opinion by Judge Posner, joined by Judge Easterbrook, rehearses the standard economist objections to rent control or imposing minimum quality standards for rental housing, predicting that the law will harm the poorest class of tenants and future tenants and largely benefits special interests. But Judge Posner concludes, based on Supreme Court precedent, that the ordinance is nevertheless constitutional.

2.   COOPERATIVES, CONDOMINIUMS, AND COMMON-INTEREST COMMUNITIES

Leases are the oldest form of entity property in which management is separated from interests in actual possession of the property, and they remain the most common form of entity property for these purposes. But recent decades have witnessed a surge in the use of alternative forms of entity property in which multiple persons enjoy possessory interests, namely cooperatives, condominiums, and other common-interest communities like gated private residential associations. These alternative forms all differ from leases in that, although common areas are owned collectively, the persons who obtain individual possessory rights in these complexes have ownership interests that can be described as equivalent to a fee simple.

Cooperatives, condominiums, and common-interest communities present governance issues that are more complicated than those presented by leases. In terms of the governance of common areas and shared facilities, the lease can be seen as a kind of dictatorship: The landlord rules as master over these aspects of the complex. The landlord is a constrained dictator, of course. The landlord must exercise her powers in such a way as to keep tenants paying their rent, convince tenants to renew their leases, and convince new tenants to enter into leases when old tenants vacate. Cooperatives, condominiums, and common-interest communities, in contrast, represent a kind of democracy. The unit owners must determine some way to organize themselves collectively in order to manage common areas and shared facilities. Usually this is done through some combination of a basic organizing document and an ongoing elected governing body. A number of commentators have observed that this amounts to a kind of "private government," complete with a constitution, a legislature, executive enforcement action, and a method for dispute resolution. See, e.g., Robert C. Ellickson, Cities and Homeowners Associations, 130 U. Pa. L. Rev. 1519 (1982).

a. INTRODUCTION

What accounts for the recent rise in the use of cooperatives, condominiums, and common-interest communities? The following excerpt explores some possible explanations.

Henry Hansmann, *Condominium and Cooperative Housing: Transactional Efficiency, Tax Subsidies, and Tenure Choice*, 20 J. LEGAL STUDIES 25, 25–30, 34–36, 39, 41, 43–44, 53–54, 60–65, 68 (1991)

TWENTY–FIVE years ago, cooperative apartment buildings were uncommon in the United States, and condominiums were virtually nonexistent. Since then, however, both forms, and particularly condominiums, have spread rapidly through the real estate market. This article explores the factors responsible for this development. In the process, it also assesses the relative transactional efficiency of consumer ownership and investor ownership in multiunit housing. * * *

In a housing cooperative, the occupants of the building lease their individual units. The arrangement is distinguished from an ordinary landlord-tenant relationship by the fact that the tenants collectively own the building by holding shares in a corporation that has title to the property. Thus, the tenants are collectively their own landlord. In a condominium, in contrast, the occupants each own the individual units they occupy. There remains an element of collective ownership in the condominium, but it is confined to the common elements of the property such as the hallways, elevators, exterior shell, roof, and grounds.

[handwritten margin note: Co-op — tenants lease apts from collectively owned corp. holding title. Condo — tenants own apts + share common ownership over common areas.]

One consequence of this distinction is that mortgage financing in a cooperative is generally obtained collectively by the cooperative corporation with a single blanket mortgage for the building as a whole, while in a condominium each unit owner obtains his own mortgage financing with only his individual unit pledged as security. In most other essential operational respects, the two forms are not notably different. In particular, the lease in a typical cooperative is a "proprietary lease" entitling the lessee to perpetual [occupancy] of the unit. The lease, and the associated shares of stock in the cooperative corporation, can be sold by the lessee at whatever price the market will bring. Thus a member of a cooperative, like the owner of a condominium, effectively has a perpetual, exclusive, and freely transferable property right in the physical unit he occupies. The term "owner-occupancy" will therefore be used here to encompass both forms.

In the United States, cooperatives long antedate condominiums. New York City's first cooperative apartment building, and perhaps the first in the United States, was built in 1876; by 1929 the city contained at least 125 cooperative apartment buildings, most of which were luxury buildings. Cooperative apartments also spread to other American cities during this period; Chicago, for example, had over 100 cooperative apartment buildings by 1930.

There are no accurate figures on the numbers of cooperatives in existence between 1930 and 1975. However, an estimate for 1960, which may be generous, suggests that there may have been as many as 150,000 cooperative units in existence then, amounting to roughly 1 percent of all multifamily dwellings; about one-third of these units were in New York City. Table 1 gives total housing stock data for cooperatives since 1975, when systematic data first became available; as shown there, the market share of cooperatives evidently reached its peak in 1976, when cooperatives accounted for 2.2 percent of all multiunit housing.

TABLE 1
COMPOSITION OF MULTIFAMILY HOUSING STOCK, 1975–83
(in Thousands of Units)

	Total Multifamily	Rental	Co-op	% Co-op	Condo	% Condo	% Co-op and Condo
1975	17,572	16,704	361	2.1	597	2.9	4.9
1976	18,022	16,983	405	2.2	634	3.5	5.8
1977	18,625	17,616	344	1.8	665	3.6	5.4
1978	19,162	17,949	348	1.8	865	4.5	6.3
1979	19,407	18,099	341	1.8	967	5.0	6.7
1980	19,672	18,269	313	1.6	1,090	5.5	7.1
1981	20,641	18,961	409	2.0	1,271	6.2	8.1
1983	21,331	19,582	360	1.7	1,389	6.5	8.2

Source.—U.S. Dept. of Housing and Urban Development. Annual Housing Survey: 1983, Part A, General Housing Characteristics (Current Housing Reports ser. H–150–83 (1984)).

As Table 1 also shows, in the 1970s the condominium form replaced the cooperative as the preferred device for owner-occupancy of apartment buildings in most of the country. New York City is the only significant jurisdiction where new cooperatives have remained an important part of the market.

Prior to 1961, no American state had enacted enabling legislation for housing condominiums. For this reason, and because condominiums were quite awkward (though not impossible) to fashion with the devices of common-law conveyancing, almost no condominium housing was created in the United States before then. Between 1961 and 1963, however, thirty-four states enacted enabling statutes for housing condominiums, and by 1967 all but one state had followed suit. * * *

Large-scale formation of condominiums did not immediately follow enactment of the statutes. In fact, relatively few condominium units were created prior to 1970. After that, however, condominiums began to be formed at an accelerating pace—both by new construction and by conversion from rental units—and quickly came to represent a substantial portion of the housing market. * * * Moreover, the spread of the condominium form has been nationwide; it now plays an important role in all large metropolitan areas. As Table 1 shows, cooperatives and condominiums combined accounted for 8.2 percent of all multifamily housing in 1983, compared to the market share of roughly 1 percent occupied by cooperatives in 1960. * * *

A potentially significant source of costs in residential cooperatives and condominiums, though one that is not often discussed, lies in the collective decision-making mechanisms that these forms require.

a) Inefficient Decisions. If the interests of all members of the cooperative or condominium were identical, the decisions they made collectively would presumably be efficient. In fact, however, their interests often diverge substantially. For one thing, members vary in their preferences: some will be satisfied with wood-grained vinyl for the elevator walls, while others will strongly prefer spending what is necessary to have real wood; some will want better laundry facilities in the basement, while those who take their laundry out or have their own machines will not. In addition, interests will diverge because the members' apartments differ in structure or location: those on the ground floor may be less eager than those on the top floor to refurbish the elevators. As a consequence, there will be substantial room for outcomes that do not maximize the aggregate surplus of the occupants. This might occur, for example, when the preferences of the median member are different from those of the mean, or when an unrepresentative coalition achieves dominance in collective decisions because their opportunity cost of time is low or because they are otherwise strategically positioned to dominate the decision-making process.

In contrast, the landlord of a rental building, in making decisions that affect the occupants of the building as a group, generally has an incentive to select policies that are efficient since that will maximize the aggregate rents she can charge. Moreover, the landlord, in contrast to the owner-occupants of a cooperative or condominium, is generally free to choose efficient outcomes since she contracts separately with each individual occupant, thus depriving them of the special opportunity that a voting mechanism gives them to act strategically. In short, market contracting is likely to be more efficient than voting in aggregating the preferences of a building's occupants.

b) Transaction Costs of Decision Making. Quite aside from the efficiency of the decisions ultimately made, there may be substantial transaction costs associated with the *process* of making collective decisions in a cooperative or condominium, such as the time that the occupants devote to meetings and other governance activities. A single individual acting as landlord can presumably collect information and make decisions with less expenditure of effort.

Moreover, the costs of collective decision making in a cooperative or condominium may be high even in comparison with *collective* ownership of the same building by a group of nonresident investors acting through a partnership or corporation. To be sure, the members of a cooperative or condominium have some distinct advantages in decision making that nonresident investor-owners lack. The members commonly occupy the building for a number of years and devote a substantial portion of their income to it; consequently, they have both the incentive and the opportunity to invest in information about the building. Moreover, much relevant information about the building is likely to come to the members without extra effort simply because they live there. And, because the members all reside in close proximity to each other, meetings are easy to arrange. In contrast, owners who are merely investors and not occupants will generally be located far from the building and from each other and, consequently, will be in a less advantageous position to exercise effective oversight or make collective decisions. Further, the investors' alternative is to delegate decision-making responsibility to a manager whom they will also have difficulty monitoring and who, lacking full ownership, will have interests that diverge from those of the investors.

On the other hand, investors differ from owner-occupants in having highly homogeneous interests. As a consequence, rental buildings, even when owned collectively by a numerous group of investors, may be spared the high transaction costs of decision making, as well as the potentially inefficient outcomes, that cooperatives and condominiums incur as a consequence of conflicts in preferences and interests among their members. And these savings may outweigh the economies that owner-occupants experience in gathering information and communicating with each other.

c) How Costly Is Collective Decision Making? Although it is difficult to obtain direct empirical observations on the costs of collective decisionmaking, substantial anecdotal and case-law evidence suggests that conflicts among members are, indeed, a serious problem in the governance of cooperatives and condominiums and that homogeneity of membership is an important aid to viability. Moreover, the success or failure of cooperative enterprise in a variety of industries other than housing seems strongly correlated with the degree of homogeneity of interest among the members.
* * *

The federal personal income tax, as presently structured, contains large subsidies for both rental and owner-occupied housing. The relative magnitude of these subsidies determines the net tax subsidy to owner-occupied as opposed to rental housing—that is, the bias in favor of owner-occupancy that is created by the current tax system, as compared to a world with no taxes or a world with a tax system that is neutral between the two forms of ownership. Surprisingly, the existing public finance literature contains no accurate estimate of this net subsidy. Such an estimate will consequently be presented here, together with an estimate of the changes in the magnitude of the net subsidy over the past fifty years.
* * *

Since 1942, tenant-stockholders in housing cooperatives have been permitted to deduct their proportionate share of the mortgage interest and property taxes paid by the cooperative. Prior to that time, no such deduction was permitted. This does not mean that cooperatives could not take advantage of the full tax subsidy to owner-occupied housing prior to 1942; rather, it means that, to get the full subsidy before that year, the building could not be financed with a mortgage but instead had to be owned outright by its members—which is probably the way that the luxury buildings that then accounted for most cooperatives were generally financed.

There is no special provision in the Internal Revenue Code that permits owner-occupants of condominium units to take deductions for property taxes and mortgage interest; rather, the deductions are allowed under the same provisions that apply to homeowners in general. Allowance for these deductions was first explicitly recognized by the Internal Revenue Service in 1964. It is not clear whether owners of condominium units prior to that time generally understood that these deductions were available, although some commentators have argued that the deductions were always implicit in the general provisions of the code. * * *

The federal tax code provides a subsidy to rental properties vis-à-vis other investments to the extent that it permits the owner of a rental building to take depreciation deductions that exceed the real rate of economic depreciation. In particular, between 1954 and 1986 the tax code made depreciation deductions extremely generous by permitting them to be computed according to the double declining balance method. Moreover, landlords were allowed to finance rental buildings through limited partnerships that permitted outside investors (serving as the limited partners) to shelter income they received from other sources by offsetting against it the large tax losses that the depreciation rules generated in the early years of the real estate investment. The result was that the depreciation deductions could effectively be sold to taxpayers in high tax brackets, thus permitting landlords to extract maximum value from the deductions. * * *

The Tax Reform Act of 1986 severely diminished the tax subsidy to rental housing. Depreciation deductions were substantially reduced and in many cases limited to the straight-line method. The minimum "useful life" over which a building could be depreciated was increased to 27.5 years. (It had been as low as 15 years from 1981 to 1984.) * * * Taxpayers were prohibited from offsetting ordinary earned income with "passive" losses from investments in real estate. And, finally, an "at-risk rule" was adopted to prevent investors from using nonrecourse debt as leverage to increase the value of depreciation deductions per dollar invested. * * *

Over the fifty-year period [from 1936 to 1985] there has been a clear progression toward stronger tax subsidies for owner-occupied as opposed to rental housing. In 1936, there was a net tax subsidy in favor of ownership only for housing occupants in the top 1 percent of the income distribution, regardless of the landlord's tax bracket, and that subsidy was substantial only for the small number of individuals in the very highest marginal brackets. By 1956, there was a net subsidy in favor of ownership in nearly all cases except when the landlord was in the top tax bracket. By 1966 and 1976 * * *, this net subsidy had broadened further to include all cases in which the potential landlord and occupant were in the same tax bracket. Finally, by 1988 there was a substantial net tax subsidy in favor of ownership in all cases. This pattern of development corresponds, in general terms, with the evolution of condominium and cooperative housing. In the 1930s, such housing was largely confined to the luxury market. The market share of cooperatives then grew, though at a modest pace, through the 1950s and was supplemented by the condominium form in the 1960s. Thereafter, the two forms together spread with increasing rapidity. * * *

Another possible explanation for the recent spread of condominiums is that the condominium form, when first introduced to American law in the early 1960s, constituted an organizational innovation that reduced the cost of owner-occupancy in multiunit dwellings significantly below that afforded by cooperatives and thus made owner-occupancy efficient for a much larger segment of the apartment market than it had been previously.

This explanation, which we can label the "organizational innovation theory," has some plausibility. By minimizing the common-property element in ownership and leaving each occupant to seek separate financing for her individual unit, a condominium, in contrast to a cooperative, reduces the extent to which the occupants of a building must serve as sureties for each other. Consequently, a condominium has better risk-sharing properties than a cooperative and is also less prone to the prospect that default by some of the building's occupants will lead to default and dislocation for the rest owing to the latter's limited liquidity. Moreover, in a cooperative as opposed to a condominium a member is (or was until recently) constrained to the same level of debt financing as the other members. If the collective mortgage represents only 40 percent of the current market value of the building, then a new tenant can in effect borrow no more or less than 40 percent of the cost of purchasing her unit.

On the other hand, occupants of a cooperative benefit from the savings that result from having only one large mortgage on a building rather than the many individual ones that must each be renegotiated each time a condominium unit changes hands. Furthermore, members of a cooperative may be less prone than members of a condominium to opportunistic default owing to their sense of obligation to their fellow tenants.

Consequently, it is not clear a priori that condominiums are markedly more efficient than cooperatives. Moreover, the process by which the condominium form has spread raises three objections to the organizational innovation theory.

A.   Why Was the Condominium Form Not Adopted Earlier?

The condominium form is an import from Europe, where it has been known for centuries. If condominiums are significantly more efficient than cooperatives, then why was the form not imported to the United States much earlier than the 1960s?

There may be a response to this objection. Arguably it is only recently—since the 1930s—that the European states have adopted condominium statutes that provide an adequate model for importation to the United States. Consequently, modern enabling statutes for condominiums may have come to the United States not much later than they did to Europe, constituting a more or less simultaneous legal innovation on the two continents. In any event, we know too little about the mechanics of legal transfers to infer that, simply because a legal form was slow in crossing the Atlantic, it did not represent an important improvement in efficiency.

The actual circumstances surrounding the enactment of condominium statutes in the United States shed little further light on this issue. In fact, the statutes were not directly imported from Europe but came to the mainland United States by a slow and circuitous path that led through Latin America and Puerto Rico and that appears to have been largely fortuitous. The critical event that stimulated the adoption of condominium statutes by the American states—namely the extension of FHA mortgage insurance to condominium units in 1961—was a response to lobbying by interests in Puerto Rico, which had long had the condominium form; it was not actively supported by housing developers, financers, or consumers in the continental United States, thus suggesting that the condominium form was not then perceived by the real estate community as offering important efficiency advantages—although this might, of course, have simply reflected their inexperience with the form. (It is, incidentally, clear that American legal scholarship played no important role in the condominium innovation; there appear to be *no* articles in U.S. legal periodicals dealing with condominiums between 1930 and 1960.)

B.   Why the Lag in Condominium Development?

A second objection to the organizational innovation theory is, If the condominium form constituted a conspicuous reduction in the cost of owner-occupancy for apartments, why did a decade elapse between the adoption of condominium statutes and the time when condominiums began to be developed in substantial numbers? This delay suggests that the efficiency advantages of condominiums over cooperatives may be relatively modest and that it was not until the 1970s, when the tax subsidy to owner-occupied apartments became exceptionally large, that widespread development of either cooperatives or condominiums became worthwhile. Then, owner-occupied apartments having finally become remunerative for a significant portion of the market, the condominium rather than the cooperative form was generally chosen because of the two it was marginally—but only marginally—more efficient.

But this objection, too, is not decisive. Even industrial process innovations, whose diffusion rates have been widely studied, commonly exhibit a lag of some years between introduction and widespread adoption. And an organizational innovation such as condominium housing, in contrast to industrial process innovations, requires not only that producers (in this case, developers) come to understand the advantages of the new form and the means of implementing it, but that lenders, brokers, and consumers also come to understand and trust it. Consumers, in particular, must come to believe that there will be a resale market for their units, which requires a substantial act of faith before that market has actually developed. A delay of a decade between the appearance of the innovation and its widespread adoption is therefore not necessarily evidence that the innovation did not represent a significant reduction in costs.

C. Why So Many Cooperatives in New York City?

The third and most telling objection to the organizational innovation theory is that in New York City there are still nearly five times as many cooperative units as there are condominium units; moreover, new cooperatives continue to be formed in New York City, through new construction and (primarily) conversion, in significantly larger numbers than condominiums. Presumably an important explanation for this is that New York consumers, lawyers, lenders, and real estate agents accumulated substantial experience with cooperatives through their relatively extensive development there—evidently as a response to rent control—between 1945 and 1965. This experience, which was lacking in other jurisdictions, apparently gave cooperatives a continuing transaction cost advantage over condominiums even after the latter form became available. If condominiums were significantly more efficient than cooperatives as an organizational form, it seems unlikely that such familiarity would in itself have been sufficient to cause cooperatives to continue to dominate the market for a quarter of a century after condominiums became available. * * *

These developments in New York City suggest that it is quite possible that, had condominium statutes never been adopted in the United States, many of the buildings organized as condominiums in the past two decades, not only in New York but throughout the country, would have been organized as cooperatives instead and that the total market share of owner-occupied apartments would still have grown roughly as it did. * * *

Even more persuasive evidence that the recent spread of cooperatives and condominiums is primarily a response to tax incentives, and not to other developments such as those just surveyed, comes from the remarkable paucity of commercial buildings organized as cooperatives or condominiums. * * *

Twenty years ago, when condominiums were still new, it was widely thought that they would see their greatest growth in the commercial sector. Yet this has not occurred. Commercial cooperatives and condominiums remain a rarity; multiunit commercial buildings are still almost universally organized on a rental basis. In New York City, for example, despite the extensive development of both cooperatives and condominiums in the residential sector, there was evidently only one office building organized as a condominium before 1978, and there were none organized as cooperatives. Since then, the rate of formation (primarily through conversion) of office cooperatives and condominiums has increased; nevertheless, as of December 1984 there were still only sixty such buildings in New York City in total, divided roughly equally between cooperatives and condominiums. And this was true despite the fact that office cooperatives and condominiums escape New York City's commercial rent tax. * * *

One reasonable overall interpretation of the data might be as follows: For all but a small fraction of the occupants of multiunit housing, neither the cooperative nor the condominium form would be competitive with rental in the absence of a tax subsidy. The condominium form, however, is somewhat more efficient than the cooperative form and requires a smaller subsidy to make it competitive with rental. By the mid–1950s, the net tax subsidy to owner-occupancy was sufficiently large to make cooperative housing less expensive than rental for a substantial segment of the population, and this is reflected in the gradually increasing share of the multiunit housing market represented by cooperatives in the 1950s and 1960s. Then, in the early 1960s, the condominium form was made available in the United States, largely fortuitously, though perhaps also in part as a response to the stronger demand for owner-occupied apartments generated by the tax subsidy. It subsequently took nearly a decade—until the early 1970s—to accumulate sufficient experience with the condominium form to make it acceptable to a broad segment of the market. After that, however, the existing tax subsidy sufficed to induce condominiums to spread rapidly through the housing market.

If this interpretation is roughly correct, it follows that, without a tax subsidy, cooperatives and condominiums might compete poorly with rental in the market for residential apartments and, at least outside of jurisdictions with rent control, might today have a relatively insignificant market share. This means, in turn, that the tax subsidy to owner-occupied housing may induce substantial inefficiency in the organization of apartment buildings and that a significant fraction of the value of the subsidy may be lost to this inefficiency. * * *

NOTES AND QUESTIONS

1. Since Hansmann wrote his article, changes in the federal income tax laws have arguably reduced the implicit subsidy for owner-occupation, at least for upper income taxpayers. The tax laws now provide for a partial "phaseout" of deductions for taxpayers who make more than about $150,000 per year, and impose (an increasingly important) Alternative Minimum Tax liability on taxpayers who take large deductions. Notwithstanding these changes, there has been no perceived shift back toward renting rather than owning on the part of high-income taxpayers. See Steven Siegel, The Constitution and Private Government: Toward the Recognition of Constitutional Rights in Private Residential Communities Fifty Years After *Marsh v. Alabama*, 6 Wm. & Mary Bill Rts. J. 461, 464–65 (1998) (reporting that one in eight Americans now lives in some type of residential community association, and that in many metropolitan areas units in such entities account for over fifty percent of new home sales). Does this call Hansmann's thesis into question?

2. Can you think of other explanations besides tax benefits or collective decision making efficiencies (or inefficiencies) for why persons might prefer to own rather than rent the personal living space they occupy? For example, who is more likely to have discretionary control over how to remodel a kitchen in an apartment: a renter or an owner of a cooperative or condominium unit? Is there any reason to think that preferences regarding these sorts of individual control variables may have changed in recent decades?

3. Hansmann focuses almost entirely on urban apartments. Does his thesis account for the surge in the popularity of community associations composed of freestanding homes, which are especially prevalent in the West

and Southwest? These include private gated communities created by developers in which the streets, sidewalks, other common areas like parks, and sometimes even the police force are privately owned and operated by a private homeowners' association organized along the lines of a condominium association. Presumably, persons who purchase freestanding homes in a gated community obtain no more in tax benefits than persons who purchase a freestanding home in an ordinary subdivision. What then accounts for the new popularity of this mode of living? Is the phenomenon entirely demand-driven, or is it possible that it is also in part supply-driven? In other words, can you think of reasons why, especially in rapidly-growing communities, developers might find it easier to obtain zoning and construction permits from local officials for gated communities as opposed to traditional subdivisions?

b. GOVERNANCE QUESTIONS

When multi-unit facilities like high-rise apartments or shopping centers are governed by leases, questions about governance of the complex are relatively straightforward: The landlord rules over the complex like a dictator. The landlord's dictatorship, as previously noted, is constrained by market forces and by the specific promises she makes in leases with tenants. But subject to these constraints, the landlord can make decisions about management of the common areas and shared facilities unilaterally. She can, for example, decide what color of wallpaper to put in the lobby, whether to convert the furnace from heating oil to natural gas, or whether the occupants of the individual units will be allowed to keep pets.

As Hansmann suggests, when multi-unit facilities are organized as cooperatives or condominiums, the governance questions are significantly more problematic. Now, the owners of the individual units are also, collectively, the body responsible for management of common areas and shared facilities. Two principal mechanisms are used in cooperatives and condominiums to solve ongoing governance problems. The first is contractual. The articles of incorporation or the deed establishing the cooperative or condominium will contain a number of rules and regulations that run with the ownership of the individual interests, and hence can be said to bind any person who acquires an ownership interest in one of the individual units. The other is to establish a board of directors, homeowners' association, or similar governing body that is charged with authority to establish rules and regulations—and bring enforcement actions—against individual unit owners. The following cases explore the role of the courts in overseeing both types of mechanisms.

Nahrstedt v. Lakeside Village Condominium Association, Inc.

Supreme Court of California, 1994.
878 P.2d 1275.

■ Kennard, Justice. A homeowner in a 530–unit condominium complex sued to prevent the homeowners association from enforcing a restriction against keeping cats, dogs, and other animals in the condominium development. The owner asserted that the restriction, which was contained in the project's declaration[1] recorded by the condominium project's developer, was "unreasonable" as applied to her because she kept her three cats indoors and because her cats were "noiseless" and "created no nuisance." Agreeing with the premise underlying the owner's complaint, the Court of Appeal concluded that the homeowners association could enforce the restriction only upon proof that plaintiff's cats would be likely to interfere with the right of other homeowners "to the peaceful and quiet enjoyment of their property."

Those of us who have cats or dogs can attest to their wonderful companionship and affection. But the issue before us is not whether in the

Figure 6–6
Lakeside Village, Culver City, California

Courtesy Jack and Ginny Sher.

1. The declaration is the operative document for a common interest development, setting forth, among other things, the restrictions on the use or enjoyment of any portion of the development. (Civ.Code, §§ 1351, 1353.) In some states, the declaration is also referred to as the "master deed." (See Dulaney Towers Maintenance v. O'Brey, 418 A.2d 1233, 1235 (Md.App. 1980).)

abstract pets can have a beneficial effect on humans. Rather, the narrow issue here is whether a pet restriction that is contained in the recorded declaration of a condominium complex is enforceable against the challenge of a homeowner. As we shall explain, the Legislature, in Civil Code section 1354, has required that courts enforce the covenants, conditions and restrictions contained in the recorded declaration of a common interest development "unless unreasonable."[2] * * *

I

Lakeside Village is a large condominium development in Culver City, Los Angeles County. It consists of 530 units spread throughout 12 separate 3–story buildings. The residents share common lobbies and hallways, in addition to laundry and trash facilities.

The Lakeside Village project is subject to certain covenants, conditions and restrictions (hereafter CC & R's) that were included in the developer's declaration recorded with the Los Angeles County Recorder on April 17, 1978, at the inception of the development project. Ownership of a unit includes membership in the project's homeowners association, the Lakeside Village Condominium Association (hereafter Association), the body that enforces the project's CC & R's, including the pet restriction, which provides in relevant part: "No animals (which shall mean dogs and cats), livestock, reptiles or poultry shall be kept in any unit."[3]

In January 1988, plaintiff Natore Nahrstedt purchased a Lakeside Village condominium and moved in with her three cats. When the Association learned of the cats' presence, it demanded their removal and assessed fines against Nahrstedt for each successive month that she remained in violation of the condominium project's pet restriction.

Nahrstedt then brought this lawsuit against the Association, its officers, and two of its employees, asking the trial court to * * * to declare the pet restriction "unreasonable" as applied to indoor cats (such as hers) that are not allowed free run of the project's common areas. Nahrstedt also alleged she did not know of the pet restriction when she bought her condominium. * * *

The Association demurred to the complaint. In its supporting points and authorities, the Association argued that the pet restriction furthers the collective "health, happiness and peace of mind" of persons living in close proximity within the Lakeside Village condominium development, and therefore is reasonable as a matter of law. The trial court sustained the demurrer as to each cause of action and dismissed Nahrstedt's complaint. Nahrstedt appealed.

A divided Court of Appeal reversed the trial court's judgment of dismissal. In the majority's view, the complaint stated a claim for declaratory relief based on its allegations that Nahrstedt's three cats are kept inside her condominium unit and do not bother her neighbors. According to the majority, whether a condominium use restriction is "unreasonable," as that term is used in section 1354, hinges on the facts of a particular

2. Under Civil Code section 1354, subdivision (a) such use restrictions are "enforceable equitable servitudes, unless unreasonable."

3. The CC & R's permit residents to keep "domestic fish and birds."

homeowner's case. Thus, the majority reasoned, Nahrstedt would be entitled to declaratory relief if application of the pet restriction in her case would not be reasonable. * * *

On the Association's petition, we granted review to decide when a condominium owner can prevent enforcement of a use restriction that the project's developer has included in the recorded declaration of CC & R's.

II

Today, condominiums, cooperatives, and planned-unit developments with homeowners associations have become a widely accepted form of real property ownership. These ownership arrangements are known as "common interest" developments. The owner not only enjoys many of the traditional advantages associated with individual ownership of real property, but also acquires an interest in common with others in the amenities and facilities included in the project. It is this hybrid nature of property rights that largely accounts for the popularity of these new and innovative forms of ownership in the 20th century. * * *

Use restrictions are an inherent part of any common interest development and are crucial to the stable, planned environment of any shared ownership arrangement. * * * The restrictions on the use of property in any common interest development may limit activities conducted in the common areas as well as in the confines of the home itself. Commonly, use restrictions preclude alteration of building exteriors, limit the number of persons that can occupy each unit, and place limitations on—or prohibit altogether—the keeping of pets.

Restrictions on property use are not the only characteristic of common interest ownership. Ordinarily, such ownership also entails mandatory membership in an owners association, which, through an elected board of directors, is empowered to enforce any use restrictions contained in the project's declaration or master deed and to enact new rules governing the use and occupancy of property within the project. * * *

In *Hidden Harbour Estates v. Basso,* 393 So.2d 637 (Fla. Dist. Ct. App. 1981), the Florida court distinguished two categories of use restrictions: use restrictions set forth in the declaration or master deed of the condominium project itself, and rules promulgated by the governing board of the condominium owners association or the board's interpretation of a rule. (Id. at p. 639.) The latter category of use restrictions, the court said, should be subject to a "reasonableness" test, so as to "somewhat fetter the discretion of the board of directors." (Id. at p. 640.) Such a standard, the court explained, best assures that governing boards will "enact rules and make decisions that are reasonably related to the promotion of the health, happiness and peace of mind" of the project owners, considered collectively. (Ibid.)

By contrast, restrictions contained in the declaration or master deed of the condominium complex, the Florida court concluded, should not be evaluated under a "reasonableness" standard. (Hidden Harbour Estates v.

Basso, supra, 393 So.2d at pp. 639–640.) Rather, such use restrictions are "clothed with a very strong presumption of validity" and should be upheld even if they exhibit some degree of unreasonableness. (Id. at pp. 639, 640.) Nonenforcement would be proper only if such restrictions were arbitrary or in violation of public policy or some fundamental constitutional right. (Id. at pp. 639–640.) * * *

Indeed, giving deference to use restrictions contained in a condominium project's originating documents protects the general expectations of condominium owners "that restrictions in place at the time they purchase their units will be enforceable." (Note, Judicial Review of Condominium Rulemaking, supra, 94 Harv.L.Rev. 647, 653; Ellickson, Cities and Homeowners' Associations, 130 U.Pa.L.Rev. 1519, 1526–1527 (1982) [stating that association members "unanimously consent to the provisions in the association's original documents" and courts therefore should not scrutinize such documents for "reasonableness."].) This in turn encourages the development of shared ownership housing—generally a less costly alternative to single-dwelling ownership—by attracting buyers who prefer a stable, planned environment. It also protects buyers who have paid a premium for condominium units in reliance on a particular restrictive scheme. * * *

III

In California, common interest developments are subject to the provisions of the Davis–Stirling Common Interest Development Act (hereafter Davis–Stirling Act or Act). (§ 1350 et seq.) The Act, passed into law in 1985, consolidated in one part of the Civil Code certain definitions and other substantive provisions pertaining to condominiums and other types of common interest developments. (Stats.1985, ch. 874, § 14, p. 2774.) * * *

Pertinent here is the Act's provision for the enforcement of use restrictions contained in the project's recorded declaration. That provision, subdivision (a) of section 1354, states in relevant part: "The covenants and restrictions in the declaration shall be enforceable equitable servitudes, unless unreasonable, and shall inure to the benefit of and bind all owners of separate interests in the development." (Italics added.)[9] To determine when a restrictive covenant included in the declaration of a common interest development cannot be enforced, we must construe section 1354. In doing so, our primary task is to ascertain legislative intent, giving the words of the statute their ordinary meaning. The words, however, must be read in context, considering the nature and purpose of the statutory enactment. * * *

As we discussed previously, recorded CC & R's are the primary means of achieving the stability and predictability so essential to the success of a shared ownership housing development. In general, then, enforcement of a common interest development's recorded CC & R's will both encourage the development of land and ensure that promises are kept, thereby fulfilling

---

9. Section 1354 also confers standing on owners of separate interests in a development and on the association to enforce the equitable servitudes, and it sets out requirements for commencing a civil action.

both of the policies identified by the Restatement. (See Rest., Property, § 539, com. f, p. 3230.)

When courts accord a presumption of validity to all such recorded use restrictions and measure them against deferential standards of equitable servitude law, it discourages lawsuits by owners of individual units seeking personal exemptions from the restrictions. This also promotes stability and predictability in two ways. It provides substantial assurance to prospective condominium purchasers that they may rely with confidence on the promises embodied in the project's recorded CC & R's. And it protects all owners in the planned development from unanticipated increases in association fees to fund the defense of legal challenges to recorded restrictions. * * *

Contrary to the dissent's accusations that the majority's decision "fray[s]" the "social fabric" (dis.opn., post), we are of the view that our social fabric is best preserved if courts uphold and enforce solemn written instruments that embody the expectations of the parties rather than treat them as "worthless paper" as the dissent would (dis.opn., post). Our social fabric is founded on the stability of expectation and obligation that arises from the consistent enforcement of the terms of deeds, contracts, wills, statutes, and other writings. To allow one person to escape obligations under a written instrument upsets the expectations of all the other parties governed by that instrument (here, the owners of the other 529 units) that the instrument will be uniformly and predictably enforced. * * *

Refusing to enforce the CC & R's contained in a recorded declaration, or enforcing them only after protracted litigation that would require justification of their application on a case-by-case basis, would impose great strain on the social fabric of the common interest development. It would frustrate owners who had purchased their units in reliance on the CC & R's. It would put the owners and the homeowners association in the difficult and divisive position of deciding whether particular CC & R's should be applied to a particular owner. Here, for example, deciding whether a particular animal is "confined to an owner's unit and create[s] no noise, odor, or nuisance" (dis. opn., post) is a fact-intensive determination that can only be made by examining in detail the behavior of the particular animal and the behavior of the particular owner. Homeowners associations are ill-equipped to make such investigations, and any decision they might make in a particular case could be divisive or subject to claims of partiality.

Enforcing the CC & R's contained in a recorded declaration only after protracted case-by-case litigation would impose substantial litigation costs on the owners through their homeowners association, which would have to defend not only against owners contesting the application of the CC & R's to them, but also against owners contesting any case-by-case exceptions the homeowners association might make. In short, it is difficult to imagine what could more disrupt the harmony of a common interest development than the course proposed by the dissent. * * *

V

RULE
↓

note: reasonableness standard still applies to restrictions voted on by board (re. Those not included in original deed).

Under the holding we adopt today, the reasonableness or unreasonableness of a condominium use restriction that the Legislature has made subject to section 1354 is to be determined *not* by reference to facts that are specific to the objecting homeowner, but by reference to the common interest development as a whole. As we have explained, when, as here, a restriction is contained in the declaration of the common interest development and is recorded with the county recorder, the restriction is presumed to be reasonable and will be enforced uniformly against all residents of the common interest development *unless* the restriction is arbitrary, imposes burdens on the use of lands it affects that substantially outweigh the restriction's benefits to the development's residents, or violates a fundamental public policy.

Accordingly, here Nahrstedt could prevent enforcement of the Lakeside Village pet restriction by proving that the restriction is arbitrary, that it is substantially more burdensome than beneficial to the affected properties, or that it violates a fundamental public policy. * * * We conclude, as a matter of law, that the recorded pet restriction of the Lakeside Village condominium development prohibiting cats or dogs but allowing some other pets is not arbitrary, but is rationally related to health, sanitation and noise concerns legitimately held by residents of a high-density condominium project such as Lakeside Village, which includes 530 units in 12 separate 3–story buildings.

Nahrstedt's complaint alleges no facts that could possibly support a finding that the burden of the restriction on the affected property is so disproportionate to its benefit that the restriction is unreasonable and should not be enforced. Also, the complaint's allegations center on Nahrstedt and her cats (that she keeps them inside her condominium unit and that they do not bother her neighbors), without any reference to the effect on the condominium development as a whole, thus rendering the allegations legally insufficient to overcome section 1354's presumption of the restriction's validity. * * *

[Reversed and remanded.]

↓ Dissent

■ ARABIAN, JUSTICE, dissenting.

"There are two means of refuge from the misery of life: music and cats."[1]

I respectfully dissent. While technical merit may commend the majority's analysis, its application to the facts presented reflects a narrow, indeed chary, view of the law that eschews the human spirit in favor of arbitrary efficiency. In my view, the resolution of this case well illustrates the conventional wisdom, and fundamental truth, of the Spanish proverb, "It is better to be a mouse in a cat's mouth than a man in a lawyer's hands."

As explained below, I find the provision known as the "pet restriction" contained in the covenants, conditions, and restrictions (CC & R's) govern-

---

1. Albert Schweitzer.

ing the Lakeside Village project patently arbitrary and unreasonable within the meaning of Civil Code section 1354. Beyond dispute, human beings have long enjoyed an abiding and cherished association with their household animals. Given the substantial benefits derived from pet ownership, the undue burden on the use of property imposed on condominium owners who can maintain pets within the confines of their units without creating a nuisance or disturbing the quiet enjoyment of others substantially outweighs whatever meager utility the restriction may serve in the abstract. It certainly does not promote "health, happiness [or] peace of mind" commensurate with its tariff on the quality of life for those who value the companionship of animals. Worse, it contributes to the fraying of our social fabric.

* * * [T]he value of pets in daily life is a matter of common knowledge and understanding as well as extensive documentation. People of all ages, but particularly the elderly and the young, enjoy their companionship. Those who suffer from serious disease or injury and are confined to their home or bed experience a therapeutic, even spiritual, benefit from their presence. Animals provide comfort at the death of a family member or dear friend, and for the lonely can offer a reason for living when life seems to have lost its meaning. In recognition of these benefits, both Congress and the state Legislature have expressly guaranteed that elderly and handicapped persons living in public-assistance housing cannot be deprived of their pets. (12 U.S.C. § 1701r–1; Health & Saf.Code, § 19901.) Not only have children and animals always been natural companions, children learn responsibility and discipline from pet ownership while developing an important sense of kindness and protection for animals. Single adults may find certain pets can afford a feeling of security. Families benefit from the experience of sharing that having a pet encourages. While pet ownership may not be a fundamental right as such, unquestionably it is an integral aspect of our daily existence, which cannot be lightly dismissed and should not suffer unwarranted intrusion into its circle of privacy. * * *

What is gained from an uncompromising prohibition against pets that are confined to an owner's unit and create no noise, odor, or nuisance?

To the extent such animals are not seen, heard, or smelled any more than if they were not kept in the first place, there is no corresponding or concomitant benefit. Pets that remain within the four corners of their owners' condominium space can have no deleterious or offensive effect on the project's common areas or any neighboring unit. Certainly, if other owners and residents are totally *unaware* of their presence, prohibiting pets does not in any respect foster the "health, happiness [or] peace of mind" of anyone except the homeowners association's board of directors, who are thereby able to promote a form of sophisticated bigotry. In light of the substantial and disproportionate burden imposed for those who must forego virtually any and all association with pets, this lack of benefit renders a categorical ban unreasonable under Civil Code section 1354. * * *

From the statement of the facts through the conclusion, the majority's analysis gives scant acknowledgment to any of the foregoing considerations but simply takes refuge behind the "presumption of validity" now accorded *all* CC & R's irrespective of subject matter. They never objectively scrutinize defendants' blandishments of protecting "health and happiness" or realistically assess the substantial impact on affected unit owners and *their* use of *their* property. * * *

Here, such inquiry should start with an evaluation of the interest that will suffer upon enforcement of the pet restriction. In determining the "burden on the use of land," due recognition must be given to the fact that this particular "use" transcends the impersonal and mundane matters typically regulated by condominium CC & R's, such as whether someone can place a doormat in the hallway or hang a towel on the patio rail or have food in the pool area, and reaches the very quality of life of hundreds of owners and residents. Nonetheless, the majority accept uncritically the proffered justification of preserving "health and happiness" and essentially consider only one criterion to determine enforceability: was the restriction recorded in the original declaration? If so, it is "presumptively valid," unless in violation of public policy. Given the application of the law to the facts alleged and by an inversion of relative interests, it is difficult to hypothesize any CC & R's that would not pass muster. Such sanctity has not been afforded any writing save the commandments delivered to Moses on Mount Sinai, and they were set in stone, not upon worthless paper.

Moreover, unlike most conduct controlled by CC & R's, the activity at issue here is strictly confined to the owner's interior space; it does not in any manner invade other units or the common areas. Owning a home of one's own has always epitomized the American dream. More than simply embodying the notion of having "one's castle," it represents the sense of freedom and self-determination emblematic of our national character. Granted, those who live in multi-unit developments cannot exercise this freedom to the same extent possible on a large estate. But owning pets that do not disturb the quiet enjoyment of others does not reasonably come within this compromise. Nevertheless, with no demonstrated or discernible benefit, the majority arbitrarily sacrifice the dream to the tyranny of the "commonality." * * *

[T]he majority's failure to consider the real burden imposed by the pet restriction unfortunately belittles and trivializes the interest at stake here. Pet ownership substantially enhances the quality of life for those who desire it. When others are not only undisturbed by, but *completely unaware of,* the presence of pets being enjoyed by their neighbors, the balance of benefit and burden is rendered disproportionate and unreasonable, rebutting any presumption of validity. Their view, shorn of grace and guiding philosophy, is devoid of the humanity that must temper the interpretation and application of all laws, for in a civilized society that is the source of their authority. As judicial architects of the rules of life, we better serve when we construct halls of harmony rather than walls of wrath.

I would affirm the judgment of the Court of Appeal.

NOTES AND QUESTIONS

1.   Natore Nahrstedt is said to "own" her condominium unit. But in what respects, if any, does she have more rights than a tenant would have under a lease of such a unit from a landlord (other than the convenient fact that she is allowed to deduct mortgage interest from her income for federal income tax purposes)? She is restricted by all kinds of rules and regulations, and has lost any power even to say whether she gets to keeps some harmless indoor cats. Apparently when she signed the deed to the property, she also signed away a good portion of the rights associated with the "Blackstonian bundle" of full ownership, including the right to keep a pet in the unit. Does this mean that she is an owner in only a qualified sense? Or is this just a reflection of the fact that part of what it means to be an owner is to be able to enter into contracts that waive or disclaim many of the traditional rights associated with being an owner?

2.   Is the majority opinion in *Nahrstedt* faithful to the controlling language of the statute that prescribes its role in reviewing covenants, conditions, and restrictions (CCRs)? The statute says such CCRs are to be enforced "unless unreasonable." The court seems to say that any restriction in the master deed is to be given a "presumption of validity" and upheld unless it produces a completely irrational result for everyone in the common interest community. Is the dissent's analysis, which seeks to show that the restriction is unreasonable as applied to Natore Nahrstedt, more faithful to what the statute says?

3.   Can *Nahrstedt*'s announced rule strictly enforcing CCRs in master deeds be reconciled with *Javins*' refusal to enforce certain provisions in leases such as the landlord's disclaimer of any implied warranty of habitability? Do prospective owners of condominium units have more choices in the marketplace than prospective residential tenants do? If so, why? Are prospective owners of condominium units more likely to be represented by counsel than are prospective residential tenants? If so, why?

4.   The California Supreme Court in *Nahrstedt* also specifically disapproved of two other California court of appeals decisions that had invalidated use restrictions in condominium complexes as unreasonable. One, *Bernardo Villas Management Corp. v. Black*, 235 Cal.Rptr. 509 (Cal. Ct. App. 1987), held that a restriction prohibiting residents from keeping any "truck, camper, trailer, boat . . . or other form of recreational vehicle" in a carport could not be applied to prevent a unit owner from keeping in the carport a clean new pickup truck with a camper shell that he used for personal transportation. The second, *Portola Hills Community Assn. v. James*, 5 Cal.Rptr.2d 580 (Cal. Ct. App. 1992), refused to enforce a planned community's restriction banning satellite dishes against a homeowner who had installed a satellite dish in his backyard that was not visible to other project residents or the public. Does *Nahrstedt*'s direction that both of these restrictions should have been upheld strike you as more problematic (in one case or in both) than upholding the restriction on pets at issue in *Nahrstedt*?

5.   Some law-and-economics influenced scholars, including Robert El-lickson in the article cited by the California Supreme Court, have argued that use restrictions contained in the master deed of a complex are presumptively efficient because the developer of the project (who writes the restrictions in the master deed) will have an incentive to include only those restrictions that cause the purchase price of units to go up. Thus, the developer of the Lakeside Village complex presumably included the restriction on pets because he or she concluded that prospective purchasers would be willing to pay more for units in a complex in which pets are prohibited. Or, perhaps more realistically, developers surmise that potential purchasers will separate into two groups—those that want to live in a pet-friendly complex and those who prefer a pet-free complex. Developers will accordingly either restrict all pets or permit pets, one way or another, in new projects depending on their perceptions of which way the market is tilting at any given pointing time. This process will continue so that, at any given moment, the condominium market is roughly in equilibrium with approximately the right balance of pet-friendly and pet-free options for prospective purchasers. Theoretical commentary on these issues is divided. Some authors express optimism about the ability of purchasers to get what they want. See, e.g., Ellickson, supra, 130 U. Pa. L. Rev. at 1543–44; Clayton P. Gillette, Mediating Institutions: Beyond the Public/Private Distinction: Courts, Covenants, and Communities, 61 U. Chi. L. Rev. 1375, 1363 (1994). Others are skeptical of the market's ability to deliver a large enough range of options or to protect democratic values. See, e.g., Lee Anne Fennell, Contracting Communities, 2004 U. Ill. L. Rev. 829; Gerald E. Frug, Cities and Homeowners Associations: A Reply, 130 U. Pa. L. Rev. 1589, 1592–96 (1982).

6.   For an interesting empirical study suggesting that developers are sensitive to the potential for later political conflict, see Yoram Barzel & Tim R. Sass, The Allocation of Resources by Voting, 105 Q. J. Econ. 745 (1990). Voting rules in common-interest communities tend to track economic stakes (i.e., by unit, floor area, or by value, and not one person one vote), and the authors argue that this is a market-driven efficient result. Barzel and Sass find that with increases in group heterogeneity and higher potential for wealth transfers, decision rules require larger supermajorities. Barzel and Sass argue that harmony is easier to achieve where pecuniary benefits are at stake, rather than direct consumption benefits. They also find that decisions over amenities that will have different impacts to different units tend to be constructed upfront rather than made subject to later decisions by the association. In some real estate markets, one positive selling point in advertisements for used condominium units is "No HOA!" What does this suggest about the efficiency of home owner association-imposed use rules?

7.   There is a growing segment of the housing market for common-interest communities that emphasizes the development of close-knit community. Particularly noteworthy is the co-housing movement, in which privately owned units (apartments or houses) are grouped around common facilities (such as for dining and child care), and participatory democracy is

emphasized. Co-housing communities vary in terms of how easily individuals can opt out of community activities. See, e.g., Kathryn McCamant & Charles Durrett, Cohousing: A Contemporary Approach to Housing Ourselves (2d ed. 1994); Mark Fenster, Community by Covenant, Process, and Design: Cohousing and the Contemporary Common Interest Community, 15 J. Land Use & Envtl. L. 3 (1999). Should courts give greater or lesser deference to rules produced by co-housing communities than those of the typical homeowners' association?

8. Six years after *Nahrstedt* was decided, the California legislature enacted a statute making it unlawful for a common-interest development like Lakeside Village to prohibit unit owners from keeping at least one pet. California Civil Code § 1360.5 (Supp. 2001, enacted 2000). Apparently pet lovers in California have more clout with the legislature than those who wish to live in a pet-free community. Does this strike you as an appropriate subject for legislative override of covenants, conditions, and restrictions in common-interest communities? How does this affect the living options of persons who have severe allergies to cats?

9. Recently a number of states have passed laws in response to complaints that homeowners' associations were enforcing aesthetic restrictions to prevent the flying of the American flag. For example, Illinois's recently enacted statute provides: "Notwithstanding any provision in the association's declaration, covenants, bylaws, rules, regulations, or other instruments ... a homeowners' association ... may not prohibit the outdoor display of the American flag or a military flag, or both, by a homeowner on that homeowner's property if the American flag is displayed in a manner consistent with ... Title 4 of the United States Code." Act of Aug. 8, 2003, 805 Ill. Comp. Stat. 105/103.30(a). The law allows associations to adopt "reasonable rules and regulations" regarding the display of these flags. Id. Does this legislation vindicate the freedom of the homeowner? Does it trench on the freedom of homeowners' associations? Does it promote a collective interest? Or is it impermissible viewpoint discrimination, as argued in Recent Legislation, 117 Harv. L. Rev. 2047 (2004)? Should homeowners' associations be able to ban all lawn signs, including those endorsing candidates or political positions? Should homeowners' rights to express themselves be inalienable? How would these situations be resolved under the test adopted in *Nahrstedt*?

40 West 67th Street v. Pullman

New York Court of Appeal, 2003.
790 N.E.2d 1174.

■ ROSENBLATT, J. In *Matter of Levandusky v. One Fifth Ave. Apt. Corp.*, 553 N.E.2d 1317 [N.Y. 1990], we held that the business judgment rule is the proper standard of judicial review when evaluating decisions made by residential cooperative corporations. In the case before us, defendant is a shareholder-tenant in the plaintiff cooperative building. The relationship between defendant and the cooperative, including the conditions under which a shareholder's tenancy may be terminated, is governed by the shareholder's lease agreement. The cooperative terminated defendant's tenancy in accordance with a provision in the lease that authorized it to do so based on a tenant's "objectionable" conduct.

Defendant has challenged the cooperative's action and asserts, in essence, that his tenancy may not be terminated by the court based on a

Figure 6–7
40 West 67th Street, New York City

review of the facts under the standard articulated in *Levandusky*. He argues that termination may rest only upon a court's independent evaluation of the reasonableness of the cooperative's action. We disagree. In reviewing the cooperative's actions, the business judgment standard governs a cooperative's decision to terminate a tenancy in accordance with the terms of the parties' agreement.

I.

Plaintiff cooperative owns the building located at 40 West 67th Street in Manhattan, which contains 38 apartments. In 1998, defendant bought into the cooperative and acquired 80 shares of stock appurtenant to his proprietary lease for apartment 7B.

Soon after moving in, defendant engaged in a course of behavior that, in the view of the cooperative, began as demanding, grew increasingly disruptive and ultimately became intolerable. After several points of friction between defendant and the cooperative,[1] defendant started complaining about his elderly upstairs neighbors, a retired college professor and his wife who had occupied apartment 8B for over two decades. In a stream of vituperative letters to the cooperative—16 letters in the month of October 1999 alone—he accused the couple of playing their television set and stereo at high volumes late into the night, and claimed they were running a loud and illegal bookbinding business in their apartment. Defendant further charged that the couple stored toxic chemicals in their apartment for use in their "dangerous and illegal" business. Upon investigation, the cooperative's Board determined that the couple did not possess a television set or stereo and that there was no evidence of a bookbinding business or any other commercial enterprise in their apartment.

Hostilities escalated, resulting in a physical altercation between defendant and the retired professor.[2] Following the altercation, defendant distributed flyers to the cooperative residents in which he referred to the professor, by name, as a potential "psychopath in our midst" and accused him of cutting defendant's telephone lines. In another flyer, defendant described the professor's wife and the wife of the Board president as having close "intimate personal relations." Defendant also claimed that the previous occupants of his apartment revealed that the upstairs couple have "historically made excessive noise." The former occupants, however, submitted an affidavit that denied making any complaints about noise from the upstairs apartment and proclaimed that defendant's assertions to the contrary were "completely false."

Furthermore, defendant made alterations to his apartment without Board approval, had construction work performed on the weekend in violation of house rules, and would not respond to Board requests to correct these conditions or to allow a mutual inspection of his apartment and the

1. Initially, defendant sought changes in the building services, such as the installation of video surveillance, 24–hour door service and replacement of the lobby mailboxes. After investigation, the Board deemed these proposed changes inadvisable or infeasible.

2. Defendant brought charges against the professor which resulted in the professor's arrest. Eventually, the charges were adjourned in contemplation of dismissal.

upstairs apartment belonging to the elderly couple. Finally, defendant commenced four lawsuits against the upstairs couple, the president of the cooperative and the cooperative management, and tried to commence three more.

In reaction to defendant's behavior, the cooperative called a special meeting pursuant to article III (First) (f) of the lease agreement, which provides for termination of the tenancy if the cooperative by a two-thirds vote determines that "because of objectionable conduct on the part of the Lessee * * * the tenancy of the Lessee is undesirable." The cooperative informed the share-holders that the purpose of the meeting was to determine whether defendant "engaged in repeated actions inimical to cooperative living and objectionable to the Corporation and its stockholders that make his continued tenancy undesirable."

Timely notice of the meeting was sent to all shareholders in the cooperative, including defendant. At the ensuing meeting, held in June 2000, owners of more than 75% of the outstanding shares in the cooperative were present. Defendant chose not attend. By a vote of 2,048 shares to 0, the share-holders in attendance passed a resolution declaring defendant's conduct "objectionable" and directing the Board to terminate his proprietary lease and cancel his shares. The resolution contained the findings upon which the shareholders concluded that defendant's behavior was inimical to cooperative living. Pursuant to the resolution, the Board sent defendant a notice of termination requiring him to vacate his apartment by August 31, 2000. Ignoring the notice, defendant remained in the apartment, prompting the cooperative to bring this suit for possession and ejectment, a declaratory judgment cancelling defendant's stock, and a money judgment for use and occupancy, along with attorneys' fees and costs.

The Supreme Court * * * declined to apply the business judgment rule to sustain the shareholders' vote and the Board's issuance of the notice of termination. Instead, the court invoked RPAPL 711(1) and held that to terminate a tenancy, a cooperative must prove its claim of objectionable conduct by competent evidence to the satisfaction of the court.

Disagreeing with Supreme Court, a divided Appellate Division * * * held that *Levandusky* prohibited judicial scrutiny of actions of cooperative boards "taken in good faith and in the exercise of honest judgment in the lawful and legitimate furtherance of corporate purposes" * * * We agree with the Appellate Division majority that the business judgment rule applies and therefore affirm.

II.   The *Levandusky* Business Judgment Rule

The heart of this dispute is the parties' disagreement over the proper standard of review to be applied when a cooperative exercises its agreed-upon right to terminate a tenancy based on a shareholder-tenant's objectionable conduct. In the agreement establishing the rights and duties of the parties, the cooperative reserved to itself the authority to determine whether a member's conduct was objectionable and to terminate the tenancy on that basis. The cooperative argues that its decision to do so should be reviewed in accordance with *Levandusky's* business judgment rule. Defendant contends that the business judgment rule has no application under these circumstances and that RPAPL 711 requires a court to make its own evaluation of the Board's conduct based on a judicial standard of reasonableness.

Levandusky established a standard of review analogous to the corporate business judgment rule for a shareholder-tenant challenge to a decision of a residential cooperative corporation. The business judgment rule is a common-law doctrine by which courts exercise restraint and defer to good faith decisions made by boards of directors in business settings * * * The rule has been long recognized in New York (see e.g., Flynn v. Brooklyn City R.R. Co., 53 N.E. 520 [N.Y. 1899]; Pollitz v. Wabash R.R. Co., 100 N.E. 721 [N.Y. 1912]). In *Levandusky,* the cooperative board issued a stop work order for a shareholder-tenant's renovations that violated the proprietary lease. The shareholder-tenant brought a * * * proceeding to set aside the stop work order. The Court upheld the Board's action, and concluded that the business judgment rule "best balances the individual and collective interests at stake" in the residential cooperative setting (Levandusky, 553 N.E.2d 1317).

In the context of cooperative dwellings, the business judgment rule provides that a court should defer to a cooperative board's determination "[s]o long as the board acts for the purposes of the cooperative, within the scope of its authority and in good faith" (553 N.E.2d 1317). In adopting this rule, we recognized that a cooperative board's broad powers could lead to abuse through arbitrary or malicious decision-making, unlawful discrimination or the like. However, we also aimed to avoid impairing "the purposes for which the residential community and its governing structure were formed: protection of the interest of the entire community of residents in an environment managed by the board for the common benefit" (553 N.E.2d 1317). The Court concluded that the business judgment rule best balances these competing interests and also noted that the limited judicial review afforded by the rule protects the cooperative's decisions against "undue court involvement and judicial second-guessing" (553 N.E.2d at 1323).

Although we applied the business judgment rule in *Levandusky,* we did not attempt to fix its boundaries, recognizing that this corporate concept may not necessarily comport with every situation encountered by a cooperative and its shareholder-tenants. Defendant argues that when it comes to terminations, the business judgment rule conflicts with RPAPL 711(1) and is therefore inoperative.[5] We see no such conflict. In the realm of cooperative governance and in the lease provision before us, the cooperative's

---

5. RPAPL 711(1), in pertinent part, states: "A proceeding seeking to recover possession of real property by reason of the termination of the term fixed in the lease pursuant to a provision contained therein giving the landlord the right to terminate the time fixed for occupancy under such agreement if he deem the tenant objectionable, shall not be maintainable unless the landlord shall by competent evidence establish to the satisfaction of the court that the tenant is objectionable."

[handwritten margin notes:]

✳ Requirements for Business Judgment Rule in Coops

1) Acts for the purpose of the co-op
2) Acts within scope of Authority
3) Acts in good faith

✳

determination as to the tenant's objectionable behavior stands as competent evidence necessary to sustain the cooperative's determination. If that were not so, the contract provision for termination of the lease—to which defendant agreed—would be meaningless.

We reject the cooperative's argument that RPAPL 711(1) is irrelevant to these proceedings, but conclude that the business judgment rule may be applied consistently with the statute. Procedurally, the business judgment standard will be applied across the cases, but the manner in which it presents itself varies with the form of the lawsuit. *Levandusky*, for example, was framed as a CPLR article 78 proceeding, but we applied the business judgment rule as a concurrent form of "rationality" and "reasonableness" to determine whether the decision was "arbitrary and capricious" pursuant to CPLR 7803(3) (553 N.E.2d at 1323 n.).

Similarly, the procedural vehicle driving this case is RPAPL 711(1), which requires "competent evidence" to show that a tenant is objectionable. Thus, in this context, the competent evidence that is the basis for the shareholder vote will be reviewed under the business judgment rule, which means courts will normally defer to that vote and the shareholders' stated findings as competent evidence that the tenant is indeed objectionable under the statute. As we stated in *Levandusky*, a single standard of review for cooperatives is preferable, and "we see no purpose in allowing the form of the action to dictate the substance of the standard by which the legitimacy of corporate action is to be measured" (553 N.E.2d 1317).

In addition, RPAPL 711 was derived from former Civil Practice Act § 1410(6), which was enacted in 1920 .... Before that, a landlord could evict a tenant based on the landlord's sole and unfettered determination that the tenant was objectionable (see e.g. Manhattan Life Ins. Co. v. Gosford, 23 N.Y.S. 7 [N.Y. 1893]; Waitt Constr. Co. v. Loraine, 179 N.Y.S. 167 [N.Y. 1919]). By enacting former Civil Practice Act § 1410(6), the Legislature imposed on the landlord the burden of proving that the tenant was objectionable. While RPAPL 711(1) applies to the termination before us, we are satisfied that the relationships among shareholders in cooperatives are sufficiently distinct from traditional landlord-tenant relationships that the statute's "competent evidence" standard is satisfied by the application of the business judgment rule.

Despite this deferential standard, there are instances when courts should undertake review of board decisions. To trigger further judicial scrutiny, an aggrieved shareholder-tenant must make a showing that the board acted (1) outside the scope of its authority, (2) in a way that did not legitimately further the corporate purpose or (3) in bad faith.

III.

A.   The Cooperative's Scope of Authority

Pursuant to its bylaws, the cooperative was authorized (through its Board) to adopt a form of proprietary lease to be used for all shareholder-tenants. Based on this authorization, defendant and other members of the

[handwritten margin notes:]

✳ Court quietly shifts the burden to the tenant to prove that he is not objectionable ✳

Must show that ← at least one of the elements of the "business judgment" rule was not satisfied cooperative voluntarily entered into lease agreements containing the termination provision before us. The cooperative does not contend that it has the power to terminate the lease absent the termination provision. * * *

The cooperative unfailingly followed the procedures contained in the lease when acting to terminate defendant's tenancy. In accordance with the bylaws, the Board called a special meeting, and notified all shareholder-tenants of its time, place and purpose. Defendant thus had notice and the opportunity to be heard. In accordance with the agreement, the cooperative acted on a super-majority vote after properly fashioning the issue and the question to be addressed by resolution. The resolution specified the basis for the action, setting forth a list of specific findings as to defendant's objectionable behavior. By not appearing or presenting evidence personally or by counsel, defendant failed to challenge the findings and has not otherwise satisfied us that the Board has in any way acted ultra vires. In all, defendant has failed to demonstrate that the cooperative acted outside the scope of its authority in terminating the tenancy.

B.   Furthering the Corporate Purpose

Levandusky also recognizes that the business judgment rule prohibits judicial inquiry into Board actions that, presupposing good faith, are taken in legitimate furtherance of corporate purposes. Specifically, there must be a legitimate relationship between the Board's action and the welfare of the cooperative. Here, by the unanimous vote of everyone present at the meeting, the cooperative resoundingly expressed its collective will, directing the Board to terminate defendant's tenancy after finding that his behavior was more than its shareholders could bear. The Board was under a fiduciary duty to further the collective interests of the cooperative. By terminating the tenancy, the Board's action thus bore an obvious and legitimate relation to the cooperative's avowed ends.

There is, however, an additional dimension to corporate purpose that *Levandusky* contemplates, notably, the legitimacy of purpose—a feature closely related to good faith. Put differently, all the shareholders of a cooperative may agree on an objective, and the Board may pursue that objective zealously, but that does not necessarily mean the objective is lawful or legitimate. Defendant, however, has not shown that the Board's purpose was anything other than furthering the overall welfare of a cooperative that found it could no longer abide defendant's behavior.

C.   Good Faith, in the Exercise of Honest Judgment

Finally, defendant has not shown the slightest indication of any bad faith, arbitrariness, favoritism, discrimination or malice on the cooperative's part, and the record reveals none. Though defendant contends that he raised sufficient facts in this regard, we agree with the Appellate Division majority that defendant has provided no factual support for his conclusory assertions that he was evicted based upon illegal or impermissible considerations. Moreover, as the Appellate Division noted, the cooperative emphasized that upon the sale of the apartment it "will 'turn over [to the defendant] all proceeds after deduction of unpaid use and occupancy, costs of sale and litigation expenses incurred in this dispute'" (742 N.Y.S.2d 264). Defendant does not contend otherwise.

Levandusky cautions that the broad powers of cooperative governance carry the potential for abuse when a board singles out a person for harmful treatment or engages in unlawful discrimination, vendetta, arbitrary decisionmaking or favoritism. We reaffirm that admonition and stress that those types of abuses are incompatible with good faith and the exercise of honest judgment. While deferential, the *Levandusky* standard should not serve as a rubber stamp for cooperative board actions, particularly those involving tenancy terminations. We note that since *Levandusky* was decided, the lower courts have in most instances deferred to the business judgment of cooperative boards but in a number of cases have withheld deference in the face of evidence that the board acted illegitimately.

The very concept of cooperative living entails a voluntary, shared control over rules, maintenance and the composition of the community. Indeed, as we observed in *Levandusky,* a shareholder-tenant voluntarily agrees to submit to the authority of a cooperative board, and consequently the board "may significantly restrict the bundle of rights a property owner normally enjoys" (553 N.E.2d 1317). When dealing, however, with termination, courts must exercise a heightened vigilance in examining whether the board's action meets the *Levandusky* test.

NOTES AND QUESTIONS

1. As mentioned in the excerpt by Hansmann, supra, housing cooperatives are an unusual legal animal. The building is owned by an entity (usually a corporation), in which the residents own shares, as in a corporation. The corporation then grants a perpetual lease in a particular unit to each resident, associated with the particular shares each owns. Since the cooperative is part-corporation, part-lease, you can see how the debate gets framed in *Pullman* over the standard of review of the shareholders' decision to expel Pullman. The corporation argues that the decision should be reviewed under the deferential business judgment rule that applies in shareholder suits against directors of corporations. Pullman argues that the review should be governed by the New York statute that applies to evictions of objectionable tenants under landlord-tenant law.

2. Given that residents in cooperatives are technically tenants, why isn't the standard that the New York legislature has prescribed for eviction of objectionable tenants fully applicable? Surely it cannot be the case that residents of cooperatives have a lesser interest in protecting their right to continue living in their home than do residents in rental apartments. Are commercial landlords more likely to act abusively or to seek to evict tenants for pretextual reasons? Under what circumstances might a commercial landlord have an incentive to try to terminate a lease before the end of the lease term? Does the fact that residents in a cooperative vote democratically provide additional protection against abusive eviction decisions? Or does

the possibility of mob prejudice make democratic voting a more feeble form of protection than the commercial self-interest of landlords?

3. Cooperatives, like commercial apartments, are subject to the Fair Housing Act and other antidiscrimination laws considered in Chapter IV. See Broome v. Biondi, 17 F. Supp. 2d 211 (S.D.N.Y. 1997) (awarding $640,000 judgment against cooperative apartment for turning down an application by a mixed race couple). But given that cooperative housing is subject to one blanket mortgage for which all residents are responsible, coops have traditionally managed to be very picky about who they agree to accept as shareholders, as long as they steer clear of violating the civil rights laws. This pickiness has carried over to rejecting applications from famous or otherwise notorious persons, including Barbara Streisand and Richard Nixon, perhaps on the ground that residents do not want publicity drawn to their building. Does this local custom or culture of pickiness justify relaxing the standard of review applied to eviction of a resident? Or does it justify applying a heightened standard of review?

B. ENTITY PROPERTY: NONPOSSESSORY INTERESTS

We now turn to entity property devices designed to promote nonpossessory beneficial enjoyment of assets. The principal entity devices in this category include trusts, corporations, nonprofit entities, and partnerships. Because the purpose of these organizational forms does not entail any right to possession of any particular assets, the manager is typically given greater discretion over the use and disposition of the assets than is the case with organizational forms designed for the management of a possessory interest, such as an apartment or space in a shopping center. This discretion, however, brings with it the potential for abuse. Consequently, a central concern in the design of this second category of entity property is what is sometimes called the "principal-agent" or "agency cost" problem. See, e.g., Michael C. Jensen & William H. Meckling, The Theory of the Firm: Managerial Behavior, Agency Costs, and Ownership Structure, 3 J. Fin. Econ. 305 (1976); see also, e.g., Stephen M. Bainbridge, Corporation Law and Economics § 1.5, at 26–38 (2002); Robert H. Sitkoff, An Agency Costs Theory of Trust Law, 89 Cornell L. Rev. 621 (2004). The manager (the trustee, the board of directors) is supposed to manage the property in the best interests of the beneficial owners (the trust beneficiaries, the stockholders). But it is often difficult to devise incentives that insure that the managers do not deviate from this ideal.

1. TRUSTS

Trusts have a long and complicated history. See generally George T. Bogert, Trusts ch. 1 (6th ed. 1987). The root idea of the modern trust is grounded in the division of authority between the common-law courts and the Chancery Court, or courts of law and equity. After the Statute of Uses of 1540, the law courts recognized only rights of ownership and possession.

But Chancery would recognize and enforce—by writs of injunction—certain equitable obligations to hold property for the benefit of a third person. The consequence was that certain assets came to have a dual personality. The legal title to the property was held in the name of one person (the "trustee"), and this person could call upon the law courts to enforce this title against third parties who entered into contracts pertaining to the property or committed torts against the property. But the beneficial use and enjoyment of the property would belong to someone else (the "beneficiary"), and Chancery would intervene to make sure that the legal title holder did not act in ways prejudicial to the equitable title of this beneficiary.

In its modern evolved form, every trust involves three legal personas plus at least one thing. See Restatement (Third) of Trusts § 3 (2003). The legal persona who creates the trust is known as the settlor. Typically, the settlor owns some property in fee simple or absolute title, and grants or conveys this property (without consideration, at least in return for the property so conveyed) to a trust. The legal persona who receives the property, and is responsible for its management and control, is known as the trustee. The trustee takes legal title to the property, and is responsible for managing it, investing in it, and protecting it against third-party intrusions. The legal persona for whose benefit the trustee manages the property is known as the beneficiary. The trustee is subject to a wide range of legal duties, known as fiduciary duties, which constrain the trustee to manage the property in the best interests of the beneficiary. The beneficiary, however, is not actively involved in managing the property nor, in most cases, does the beneficiary have any possessory interest in the property. Instead, the beneficiary typically receives periodic distributions of income from the trust. Finally, the whole arrangement revolves around some asset or collection of assets, known as the corpus of the trust or the trust *res*. This can include land, personal property, and intellectual property rights. But in the modern world, it increasingly has come to mean stocks, bonds, and other readily-marketable intangible assets with income-earning potential.

Although the trust involves three distinct legal personas (settlor, trustee, beneficiary), it is not necessary that distinct persons play each of these roles. For example, in 401(k) retirement plans, the settlor is an individual seeking to save for her retirement, but the same person is also usually the primary beneficiary. In the case of a living trust, or even a charitable trust, it is also possible for the settlor and the trustee to be the same person. Of course, where the settlor wants the trust to endure after her death, it is necessary that the settlor appoint someone else to serve as trustee after the settlor is gone. The one thing that traditionally has been prohibited is for one person to serve both as the sole trustee and the sole beneficiary of a trust. See Restatement (Third) of Trusts § 69 (2003).

Trusts can be created by will, by inter vivos transfer of assets from a settler to a trustee, or by a declaration of an owner that he holds property as trustee for one or more persons. Restatement (Third) of Trusts § 10

(2003). They can be created to manage the transfer of assets within a family from one generation to another, to establish instruments for charitable giving or the creation of charitable foundations, or for certain business purposes (such as where it is important to segregate assets from routine business transactions in the context of asset securitization). Putting aside its commercial applications, "[t]he normal private trust is essentially a gift, projected on the plane of time and so subjected to a management regime." John H. Langbein, Mandatory Rules in the Law of Trusts, 98 Nw. U. L. Rev. 1105, 1109 (2004) (citation omitted). Thus, trusts are interpreted on the assumption that the dominant purpose of the settler was to benefit the beneficiaries. Under the Statute of Frauds, trusts must be writing. See Bogert, supra, at 49–55.

Trusts are also one area of law where the common-law forms of ownership studied in Chapter V continue to play an important role. The legal title to trust assets is nearly always held as an undivided fee simple or absolute ownership. This permits the trustee to deal with these assets the way a full owner would—by buying, selling, leasing, or mortgaging the assets as market conditions dictate, in order to maximize the risk-appropriate return to the trust. The beneficial interest, however, is often carved up among several beneficiaries spread over multiple generations. In order to describe these interests, the law of trusts has borrowed the categories of the estate system. Thus, we commonly find that one beneficiary (a spouse for example) is given a life estate in trust, followed by one or more vested remainders in trust (in the children or grandchildren, for example). If children or grandchildren present more complicated contingencies, then contingent remainders or executory interests in trust can be used. This incorporation of the estate system to describe beneficial interests has no effect on the deployment of the underlying resources, since the trustee is free to deal with those resources without regard to the law of waste, the rules of contribution and accounting, or other rules that apply where legal interests are carved up using the categories of the estate system. The only function of the estate system in the law of trusts is in ascertaining which persons are to receive, in what amounts, periodic checks from the trustee as distributions of the earnings from the trust assets.

The fact that most of the exotic future interests studied in Chapter V exist today only as beneficial interests in trusts helps explain why these complications are tolerable from an information-gathering and enforcement perspective. If contingent remainders and executory interests were commonly encountered as in rem rights, they would greatly complicate the process of processing information about these rights, certainly for transactional and secured-lending purposes. But when these interests exist as beneficial interests in a trust, they do not complicate transactions in the underlying assets, which are typically held in fee simple by the trustee. Thus, the common use of trusts in the disposition of family wealth and pension plans permits the system of property rights to tolerate greater complexity than would be the case if all interests had to be held as legal estates.

To be sure, trusts afford settlors even greater flexibility through the use of powers of appointment. A power of appointment arises when a donor of property by will or trust creates or reserves a power in some other person to designate the recipient(s) of particular property or beneficial interests in property. The recipient of such a power can be either the trustee or one of the beneficiaries. This affords greater flexibility in carving up beneficial interests, but at the cost of greater discretion in the person exercising the power. This discretion comes in degrees because powers can be constrained by donor stipulation in various ways. See Restatement (Third) of Property: Wills and Other Donative Transfers (Tent. Draft No. 5, March 27, 2006).

a. SPENDTHRIFT TRUSTS

Scholars sometimes debate whether the trust is a distinctive form of property, or whether it is simply a type of third-party beneficiary contract in which the settlor contracts with the trustee to manage assets for the benefit of the beneficiary. Compare Henry Hansmann & Ugo Mattei, The Functions of Trust Law: A Comparative Legal and Economic Analysis, 73 N.Y.U. L. Rev. 434 (1998) with John H. Langbein, The Contractarian Basis of the Law of Trusts, 105 Yale L.J. 625 (1995). One critical point in favor of the "property" characterization is that trust assets are generally treated as being distinct from the assets of both the settlor and the trustee, and thus cannot be reached by individual creditors of either the settlor or the trustee. More controversially, in many jurisdictions the assets of some trusts cannot be reached by the individual creditors of the beneficiaries. In jurisdictions that permit these so-called "spendthrift trusts," trust assets are cordoned off from all but those who have dealt with the trust qua trust. At least in this sense, the trust can be regarded as a distinctive type of property right.

Broadway National Bank v. Adams

Supreme Judicial Court of Massachusetts, 1881.
133 Mass. 170.

■ MORTON, C. J. The object of this bill in equity is to reach and apply in payment of the plaintiff's debt due from the defendant Adams the income of a trust fund created for his benefit by the will of his brother. The eleventh article of the will is as follows: "I give the sum of seventy-five thousand dollars to my said executors and the survivors or survivor of them, in trust to invest the same in such manner as to them may seem prudent, and to pay the net income thereof, semiannually, to my said brother Charles W. Adams, during his natural life, such payments to be made to him personally when convenient, otherwise, upon his order or receipt in writing; in either case free from the interference or control of his creditors, my intention being that the use of said income shall not be anticipated by assignment. At the decease of my said brother Charles, my will is that the net income of said seventy-five thousand dollars shall be paid to his present wife, in case she survives him, for the benefit of herself and all the children of said Charles, in equal proportions, in the manner and upon the conditions the same as herein directed to be paid him during his life, so long as she shall remain single. And my will is, that, after the decease of said Charles and the decease or second marriage of his said wife, the said seventy-five thousand dollars, together with any accrued interest or income thereon which may remain unpaid, as herein above directed, shall be divided equally among all the children of my said brother Charles, by any and all his wives, and the representatives of any deceased child or children by right of representation."

Corpus of Trust never intended To go to Charles

There is no room for doubt as to the intention of the testator. It is clear that, if the trustee was to pay the income to the plaintiff under an order of the court, it would be in direct violation of the intention of the testator and of the provisions of his will. The court will not compel the trustee thus to do what the will forbids him to do, unless the provisions and intention of the testator are unlawful.

RULE

The question whether the founder of a trust can secure the income of it to the object of his bounty, by providing that it shall not be alienable by him or be subject to be taken by his creditors, has not been directly adjudicated in this Commonwealth. The tendency of our decisions, however, has been in favor of such a power in the founder.

It is true that the rule of the common law is, that a man cannot attach to a grant or transfer of property, otherwise absolute, the condition that it shall not be alienated; such condition being repugnant to the nature of the estate granted. Co. Lit. 223 a; Blackstone Bank v. Davis, 21 Pick. 42.

Lord Coke gives as the reason of the rule, that "it is absurd and repugnant to reason that he, that hath no possibility to have the land revert to him, should restrain his feoffee in fee simple of all his power to alien," and that this is "against the height and puritie of a fee simple." By such a condition, the grantor undertakes to deprive the property in the hands of the grantee of one of its legal incidents and attributes, namely, its alienability, which is deemed to be against public policy. But the reasons of the rule do not apply in the case of a transfer of property in trust. By the creation of a trust like the one before us, the trust property passes to the trustee with all its incidents and attributes unimpaired. He takes the whole legal title to the property, with the power of alienation; the *cestui que trust* [beneficiary] takes the whole legal title to the accrued income at the moment it is paid over to him. Neither the principal nor the income is at any time inalienable.

Everything involved in a trust is fully alienable by some person (principal + income)

The question whether the rule of the common law should be applied to equitable life estates created by will or deed, has been the subject of conflicting adjudications by different courts, as is fully shown in the able and exhaustive arguments of the counsel in this case. As is stated in *Sparhawk v. Cloon,* 125 Mass. 263, from the time of Lord Eldon the rule has prevailed in the English Court of Chancery, to the extent of holding that when the income of a trust estate is given to any person (other than a married woman) for life, the equitable estate for life is alienable by, and liable in equity to the debts of, the *cestui que trust,* and that this quality is so inseparable from the estate that no provision, however express, which does not operate as a cesser or limitation of the estate itself, can protect it from his debts.

The English rule has been adopted in several of the courts of this country.

Other courts have rejected it, and have held that the founder of a trust may secure the benefit of it to the object of his bounty, by providing that the income shall not be alienable by anticipation, nor subject to be taken for his debts.

RULE

The precise point involved in the case at bar has not been adjudicated in this Commonwealth; but the decisions of this court which we have before cited recognize the principle, that, if the intention of the founder of a trust, like the one before us, is to give to the equitable life tenant a qualified and limited, and not an absolute, estate in the income, such life tenant cannot alienate it by anticipation, and his creditors cannot reach it at law or in equity. It seems to us that this principle extends to and covers the case at bar. The founder of this trust was the absolute owner of his property. He had the entire right to dispose of it, either by an absolute gift to his brother, or by a gift with such restrictions or limitations, not repugnant to law, as he saw fit to impose. His clear intention, as shown in his will, was not to give his brother an absolute right to the income which might hereafter accrue upon the trust fund, with the power of alienating it in advance, but only the right to receive semiannually the income of the fund, which upon its payment to him, and not before, was to become his absolute property. His intentions ought to be carried out, unless they are against public policy. There is nothing in the nature or tenure of the estate given to the *cestui que trust* which should prevent this. The power of alienating in advance is not a necessary attribute or incident of such an estate or interest, so that the restraint of such alienation would introduce repugnant or inconsistent elements.

We are not able to see that it would violate any principles of sound public policy to permit a testator to give to the object of his bounty such a qualified interest in the income of a trust fund, and thus provide against the improvidence or misfortune of the beneficiary. The only ground upon which it can be held to be against public policy is, that it defrauds the creditors of the beneficiary.

It is argued that investing a man with apparent wealth tends to mislead creditors, and to induce them to give him credit. The answer is, that creditors have no right to rely upon property thus held, and to give him credit upon the basis of an estate which, by the instrument creating it, is declared to be inalienable by him, and not liable for his debts. By the exercise of proper diligence they can ascertain the nature and extent of his estate, especially in this Commonwealth, where all wills and most deeds are spread upon the public records. There is the same danger of their being misled by false appearances, and induced to give credit to the equitable life tenant when the will or deed of trust provides for a cesser or limitation over, in case of an attempted alienation, or of bankruptcy or attachment, and the argument would lead to the conclusion that the English rule is equally in violation of public policy. We do not see why the founder of a trust may not directly provide that his property shall go to his beneficiary with the restriction that it shall not be alienable by anticipation, and that his creditors shall not have the right to attach it in advance, instead of indirectly reaching the same result by a provision for a cesser or a limitation over, or by giving his trustees a discretion as to paying it. He has the entire *jus disponendi,* which imports that he may give it absolutely, or may impose any restrictions or fetters not repugnant to the nature of the estate which he gives. Under our system, creditors may reach all the property of the debtor not exempted by law, but they cannot enlarge the gift of the founder of a trust, and take more than he has given.

RULE

The rule of public policy which subjects a debtor's property to the payment of his debts, does not subject the property of a donor to the debts of his beneficiary, and does not give the creditor a right to complain that, in the exercise of his absolute right of disposition, the donor has not seen fit to give the property to the creditor, but has left it out of his reach.

Whether a man can settle his own property in trust for his own benefit, so as to exempt the income from alienation by him or attachment in advance by his creditors, is a different question, which we are not called upon to consider in this case. But we are of opinion that any other person, having the entire right to dispose of his property, may settle it in trust in favor of a beneficiary, and may provide that it shall not be alienated by him by anticipation, and shall not be subject to be seized by his creditors in advance of its payment to him.

MAIN RULE

It follows that, under the provisions of the will which we are considering, the income of the trust fund created for the benefit of the defendant Adams cannot be reached by attachment, either at law or in equity, before it is paid to him.

Bill dismissed.

NOTES AND QUESTIONS

1.   The purpose of a spendthrift trust is to provide financial support for persons who are regarded by the settlor as being less than fully capable of managing their own financial affairs. This could be because of the beneficiary's age (young or very old), or because the beneficiary is mentally incapacitated, or because the beneficiary simply lacks experience or judgment about worldly affairs. The spendthrift trust not only provides for specialized management of the assets dedicated to the beneficiary's support, but also assures that irresponsible actions by the beneficiary will not cause the size of the trust corpus to diminish below the level the settlor has deemed appropriate to set aside for the beneficiary's financial needs.

2.   A spendthrift trust, of course, does not shield money from creditors once it has been distributed to the beneficiary. What the instant decision

holds, and a majority of American jurisdictions concur in this, is that the settlor may provide in the trust agreement that the interest of the beneficiary cannot be attached or garnished by the beneficiary's creditors while it is still under the management and control of the trustee. Creditors therefore will have to periodically sue the beneficiary, when they calculate that the beneficiary has received a distribution from the trust, in an attempt to recover portions of the debt.

3. Not everyone has applauded these objectives. John Chipman Gray, a professor at Harvard Law School, thought that such trusts represented the triumph of paternalism over the ethic of individual responsibility. He wrote: "If there is one sentiment, therefore, which it would seem to be the part of all in authority, and particularly of all judges, to fortify, it is the duty of keeping one's promises and paying one's debts. [Judges approving spendthrift trusts were moved] by that spirit, in short, of paternalism, which is the fundamental essence alike of spendthrift trusts and of socialism." John Chipman Gray, Restraints on the Alienation of Property iii, ix (2d ed. 1895). Note that Gray did not object to large inheritances of wealth. His objection was to inheritances coupled with spendthrift clause protection. Can you articulate why someone like Gray might regard the ability to couple inheritance with spendthrift protection as presenting a much more troubling incursion on the ethic of individual responsibility than does large inheritance standing alone?

4. One of the objections to the creation of spendthrift trusts is that creditors of the beneficiary may not have notice that the assets which sustain the beneficiary cannot be reached to satisfy the beneficiary's personal debts. This is a version of the problem of "ostensible ownership," which we consider further in Chapter VII. The court says that this objection has little force in the context of spendthrift trusts, given that deeds to property are publicly recorded and wills are made public when they are probated. This does not cover all of the options, however, because it is also possible to create a trust while one is alive (called an inter vivos trust), and such a trust, including one having a spendthrift provision, could not be discovered by creditors by searching through records of deeds and probated wills. Also, how realistic is it to expect ordinary trade creditors (such as department stores and auto dealers) to engage in a search of property deeds and wills before extending credit to someone like Charles W. Adams?

5. The traditional understanding has been that spendthrift clauses can be imposed only on trusts created for the benefit of others; one cannot set up a trust for oneself protected by a spendthrift provision. See, e.g., Restatement (Third) of Trusts §§ 58(2) & 60, cmt. f (2003). This understanding is beginning to break down as several states, evidently in the interest of attracting trust business, have enacted statutes permitting the creation of self-settled "asset protection trusts." See Jesse Dukeminier et

al., Wills, Trusts, and Estates 557–60 (7th ed. 2005). If John Chipman Gray was so upset about spendthrift trusts for the benefit of others, what would he say about self-settled spendthrift trusts? If state legislatures cannot be counted on to reject such ideas, what remedy is there to stop their spread? See Stewart E. Sterk, Asset Protection Trusts: Trust Law's Race to the Bottom?, 85 Cornell L. Rev. 1035 (2000).

b. TRUST FIDUCIARY DUTIES

A pervasive difficulty created by the trust is making sure that the trustee follows the instructions of the settlor and exercises his managerial discretion in the interest of the beneficiaries. The settlor is often not around (indeed is often dead), and so cannot monitor the performance of the trustee. The beneficiaries may be very young, unsophisticated, or highly dispersed, making effective monitoring by the beneficiaries equally problematic. The law's solution to the monitoring problem has been to impose a series of duties on the trustee, called fiduciary duties, which are designed to insure that the trustee acts in the best interests of the trust and the beneficiaries, rather than using the trust *res* and powers given by the trust instrument for self-enrichment. Courts enforce these fiduciary duties quite strictly. We do not have the space here to provide a complete review of all trust fiduciary duties. For overviews, see John H. Langbein, Mandatory Rules in the Law of Trusts, 98 Nw. U. L. Rev. 1105 (2004); Restatement (Third) of Trusts: Prudent Investor Rule (1990); Bogert, supra, at 334–449. The following case is illustrative of the types of problems that can arise, and of the attitude of the courts when breaches of fiduciary duties are exposed.

Rothko v. Reis

Court of Appeals of New York, 1977.
372 N.E.2d 291.

■ COOKE, JUDGE. Mark Rothko, an abstract expressionist painter whose works through the years gained for him an international reputation of greatness, died testate on February 25, 1970. The principal asset of his estate consisted of 798 paintings of tremendous value, and the dispute underlying this appeal involves the conduct of his three executors in their disposition of these works of art. In sum, that conduct as portrayed in the record and sketched in the opinions was manifestly wrongful and indeed shocking.

[Rothko's] will was admitted to probate on April 27, 1970 and letters testamentary were issued to Bernard J. Reis, Theodoros Stamos and Morton Levine. Hastily and within a period of only about three weeks and by virtue of two contracts each dated May 21, 1970, the executors dealt with all 798 paintings.

Figure 6–8
Mark Rothko in his 69th Street Studio

Photograph by Hans Namuth. Courtesy Center for Creative Photography, University of Arizona. ©1991 Hans Namuth Estate.

By a contract of sale, the estate executors agreed to sell to Marlborough A.G., a Liechtenstein corporation (hereinafter MAG), 100 Rothko paintings as listed for $1,800,000, $200,000 to be paid on execution of the agreement and the balance of $1,600,000 in 12 equal interest-free installments over a 12–year period. Under the second agreement, the executors consigned to Marlborough Gallery, Inc., a domestic corporation (hereinafter MNY), "approximately 700 paintings listed on a Schedule to be prepared", the consignee to be responsible for costs covering items such as insurance, storage restoration and promotion. By its provisos, MNY could sell up to 35 paintings a year from each of two groups, pre–1947 and post–1947, for 12 years at the best price obtainable but not less than the appraised estate value, and it would receive a 50% Commission on each painting sold, except for a commission of 40% on those sold to or through other dealers.

Petitioner Kate Rothko, decedent's daughter and a person entitled to share in his estate by virtue of an election under EPTL 5–3.3, instituted this proceeding to remove the executors, to enjoin MNY and MAG from disposing of the paintings, to rescind the aforesaid agreements between the executors and said corporations, for a return of the paintings still in possession of those corporations, and for damages. She was joined by the guardian of her brother Christopher Rothko, likewise interested in the estate, who answered by adopting the allegations of his sister's petition and by demanding the same relief. The Attorney–General of the State, as the representative of the ultimate beneficiaries of the Mark Rothko Foundation, Inc., a charitable corporation and the residuary legatee under decedent's will, joined in requesting relief substantially similar to that prayed for by petitioner. * * *

Following a nonjury trial covering 89 days and in a thorough opinion, the Surrogate found: that Reis was a director, secretary and treasurer of MNY, the consignee art gallery, in addition to being a coexecutor of the estate; that the testator had a 1969 inter vivos contract with MNY to sell Rothko's work at a commission of only 10% and whether that agreement survived testator's death was a problem that a fiduciary in a dual position could not have impartially faced; that Reis was in a position of serious conflict of interest with respect to the contracts of May 21, 1970 and that his dual role and planned purpose benefited the Marlborough interests to the detriment of the estate; that it was to the advantage of coexecutor Stamos as a "not-too-successful artist, financially", to curry favor with Marlborough and that the contract made by him with MNY within months after signing the estate contracts placed him in a position where his personal interests conflicted with those of the estate, especially leading to lax contract enforcement efforts by Stamos; that Stamos acted negligently and improvidently in view of his own knowledge of the conflict of interest of Reis; that the third coexecutor, Levine, while not acting in self-interest or with bad faith, nonetheless failed to exercise ordinary prudence in the performance of his assumed fiduciary obligations since he was aware of Reis' divided loyalty, believed that Stamos was also seeking personal advantage, possessed personal opinions as to the value of the paintings and yet followed the leadership of his coexecutors without investigation of essential facts or consultation with competent and disinterested appraisers, and that the business transactions of the two Marlborough corporations were admittedly controlled and directed by Francis K. Lloyd. It was concluded that the acts and failures of the three executors were clearly improper to such a substantial extent as to mandate their removal under SCPA 711 as estate fiduciaries. The Surrogate also found that MNY, MAG and Lloyd were guilty of contempt in shipping, disposing of and selling 57 paintings in violation of the temporary restraining order dated June 26, 1972 and of the injunction dated September 26, 1972; that the contracts for sale and consignment of paintings between the executors and MNY and MAG provided inadequate value to the estate, amounting to a lack of mutuality and fairness resulting from conflicts on the part of Reis and Stamos and improvidence on the part of all executors; that said contracts were voidable and were set aside by reason of violation of the duty of loyalty and improvidence of the executors, knowingly participated in and induced by MNY and MAG; that the fact that these agreements were voidable did not revive the 1969 inter vivos agreements since the parties by their conduct evinced an intent to abandon and abrogate these compacts. The Surrogate held that the present value at the time of trial of the paintings sold is the proper measure of damages as to MNY, MAG, Lloyd, Reis and Stamos. He imposed a civil fine of $3,332,000 upon MNY, MAG and Lloyd, same being the appreciated value at the time of trial of the 57 paintings sold in violation of the temporary restraining order and injunction. It was held that Levine was liable for $6,464,880 in damages, as he was not in a dual position acting for his own interest and was thus liable only for the actual value of paintings sold MNY and MAG as of the dates of sale, and that Reis, Stamos, MNY and MAG, apart from being jointly and severally liable for the same damages as Levine for negligence, were liable for the greater sum of $9,252,000 "as appreciation damages less amounts previously paid to the estate with regard to sales of paintings." * * * The liabilities were held to be congruent so that payment of the highest sum would satisfy all lesser liabilities including the civil fines and the liabilities for damages were to be reduced by payment of the fine levied or by return of any of the 57 paintings disposed of, the new fiduciary to have the option in the first instance to specify which paintings the fiduciary would accept.

The Appellate Division * * * affirmed * * *

In seeking a reversal, it is urged that an improper legal standard was applied in voiding the estate contracts of May, 1970, that the "no further inquiry" rule applies only to self-dealing and that in case of a conflict of interest, absent self-dealing, a challenged transaction must be shown to be unfair. The subject of fairness of the contracts is intertwined with the issue of whether Reis and Stamos were guilty of conflicts of interest.[2] Scott is quoted to the effect that "[a] trustee does not necessarily incur liability merely because he has an individual interest in the transaction * * * In Bullivant v. First Nat. Bank (141 N.E. 41 (Mass.)) it was held that * * * the fact that the bank was also a creditor of the corporation did not make its assent invalid, if it acted in good faith and the plan was fair" (2 Scott, Trusts, § 170.24, p. 1384 (emphasis added)), and our attention has been called to the statement in Phelan v. Middle States Oil Corp., 220 F.2d 593, 603, (2d Cir.) where Judge Learned Hand found "no decisions that have applied (the no further inquiry rule) inflexibly to every occasion in which the fiduciary has been shown to have had a personal interest that might in fact have conflicted with his loyalty."

These contentions should be rejected. First, a review of the opinions of the Surrogate and the Appellate Division manifests that they did not rely solely on a "no further inquiry rule", and secondly, there is more than an adequate basis to conclude that the agreements between the Marlborough corporations and the estate were neither fair nor in the best interests of the estate. This is demonstrated, for example, by the comments of the Surrogate concerning the commissions on the consignment of the 698 paintings and those of the Appellate Division concerning the sale of the 100 paintings. The opinions under review demonstrate that neither the Surrogate nor the Appellate Division set aside the contracts by merely applying the no

---

2. In New York, an executor, as such, takes a qualified legal title to all personalty specifically bequeathed and an unqualified legal title to that not so bequeathed; he holds not in his own right but as a trustee for the benefit of creditors, those entitled to receive under the will and, if all is not bequeathed, those entitled to distribution under the EPTL (Blood v. Kane, 29 N.E. 994, 994–95 (N.Y); see Bischoff v. Yorkville Bank, 112 N.E. 759, 760 (N.Y.); Bankers Sur. Co. v. Meyer, 98 N.E. 399, 400 (N.Y.); but see Restatement, Trusts 2d, § 6; Bogert, Trusts (Hornbook Series 5th ed.), p. 31).

further inquiry rule without regard to fairness. Rather they determined, quite properly indeed, that these agreements were neither fair nor in the best interests of the estate.

To be sure, the assertions that there were no conflicts of interest on the part of Reis or Stamos indulge in sheer fantasy. Besides being a director and officer of MNY, for which there was financial remuneration, however slight, Reis, as noted by the Surrogate, had different inducements to favor the Marlborough interests, including his own aggrandizement of status and financial advantage through sales of almost one million dollars for items from his own and his family's extensive private art collection by the Marlborough interests. Similarly, Stamos benefited as an artist under contract with Marlborough and, interestingly, Marlborough purchased a Stamos painting from a third party for $4,000 during the week in May, 1970 when the estate contract negotiations were pending. The conflicts are manifest. Further, as noted in Bogert, Trusts and Trustees (2d ed.), "The duty of loyalty imposed on the fiduciary prevents him from accepting employment from a third party who is entering into a business transaction with the trust" (§ 543, subd. (S), p. 573). "While he [a trustee] is administering the trust he must refrain from placing himself in a position where his personal interest or that of a third person does or may conflict with the interest of the beneficiaries" (Bogert, Trusts (Hornbook Series 5th ed.), p. 343). Here, Reis was employed and Stamos benefited in a manner contemplated by Bogert. In short, one must strain the law rather than follow it to reach the result suggested on behalf of Reis and Stamos.

Levine contends that, having acted prudently and upon the advice of counsel, a complete defense was established. Suffice it to say, an executor who knows that his coexecutor is committing breaches of trust and not only fails to exert efforts directed towards prevention but accedes to them is legally accountable even though he was acting on the advice of counsel. When confronted with the question of whether to enter into the Marlborough contracts, Levine was acting in a business capacity, not a legal one, in which he was required as an executor primarily to employ such diligence and prudence to the care and management of the estate assets and affairs as would prudent persons of discretion and intelligence, accented by "[n]ot honesty alone, but the punctilio of an honor the most sensitive" (Meinhard v. Salmon, 164 N.E. 545, 546 (N.Y.)). Alleged good faith on the part of a fiduciary forgetful of his duty is not enough. He could not close his eyes, remain passive or move with unconcern in the face of the obvious loss to be visited upon the estate by participation in those business arrangements and then shelter himself behind the claimed counsel of an attorney.

Further, there is no merit to the argument that MNY and MAG lacked notice of the breach of trust. The record amply supports the determination that they are chargeable with notice of the executors' breach of duty.

The measure of damages was the issue that divided the Appellate Division. The contention of Reis, Stamos, MNY and MAG, that the award of appreciation damages was legally erroneous and impermissible, is based on a principle that an executor authorized to sell is not liable for an

RULE
re: measure of
damages

increase in value if the breach consists only in selling for a figure less than that for which the executor should have sold. For example, Scott states:

> The beneficiaries are not entitled to the value of the property at the time of the decree if it was not the duty of the trustee to retain the property in the trust and the breach of trust consisted merely in selling the property for too low a price. (3 Scott, Trusts (3d ed.), § 208.3, p. 1687 (emphasis added)).

> If the trustee is guilty of a breach of trust in selling trust property for an inadequate price, he is liable for the difference between the amount he should have received and the amount which he did receive. He is not liable, however, for any subsequent rise in value of the property sold. (Id., § 208.6, pp. 1689–1690.)

Restatement 2d

A recitation of similar import appears in Comment d under Restatement, Trusts 2d (§ 205): "d. Sale for less than value. If the trustee is authorized to sell trust property, but in breach of trust he sells it for less than he should receive, he is liable for the value of the property at the time of the sale less the amount which he received. If the breach of trust consists *only* in selling it for too little, he is not chargeable with the amount of any subsequent increase in value of the property under the rule stated in Clause (c), as he would be if he were not authorized to sell the property. See § 208." (Emphasis added.) However, employment of "merely" and "only" as limiting words suggests that where the breach consists of some misfeasance, other than solely for selling "for too low a price" or "for too little", appreciation damages may be appropriate. Under Scott (§ 208.3, pp. 1686–1687) and the Restatement (§ 208), the trustee may be held liable for appreciation damages if it was his or her duty to retain the property, the theory being that the beneficiaries are entitled to be placed in the same position they would have been in had the breach not consisted of a sale of property that should have been retained. The same rule should apply where the breach of trust consists of a serious conflict of interest which is more than merely selling for too little.

Public Policy
justification for
rule above

The reason for allowing appreciation damages, where there is a duty to retain, and only date of sale damages, where there is authorization to sell, is policy oriented. If a trustee authorized to sell were subjected to a greater measure of damages he might be reluctant to sell (in which event he might run a risk if depreciation ensued). On the other hand, if there is a duty to retain and the trustee sells there is no policy reason to protect the trustee; he has not simply acted imprudently, he has violated an integral condition of the trust.

"If a trustee in breach of trust transfers trust property to a person who takes with notice of the breach of trust, and the transferee has disposed of the property * * * (i)t seems proper to charge him with the value at the time of the decree, since if it had not been for the breach of trust the property would still have been a part of the trust estate" (4 Scott, Trusts (3d ed.)), § 291.2. This rule of law which applies to the transferees MNY and MAG also supports the imposition of appreciation damages against Reis and Stamos, since if the Marlborough corporations are liable for such damages either as purchaser or consignees with notice, from one in breach of trust, it is only logical to hold that said executors, as sellers and consignors, are liable also pro tanto.

Contrary to assertions of appellants and the dissenters at the Appellate Division, Menzel v. List, 246 N.E.2d 742, supra is authority for the allowance of appreciation damages. There, the damages involved a breach of warranty of title to a painting which at one time had been stolen from plaintiff and her husband and ultimately sold to defendant. Here, the executors, though authorized to sell, did not merely err in the amount they accepted but sold to one with whom Reis and Stamos had a self-interest. To make the injured party whole, in both instances the quantum of damages should be the same. In other words, since the paintings cannot be returned, the estate is therefore entitled to their value at the time of the decree, i. e., appreciation damages. These are not punitive damages in a true sense, rather they are damages intended to make the estate whole. Of course, as to Reis, Stamos, MNY and MAG, these damages might be considered by some to be exemplary in a sense, in that they serve as a warning to others, but their true character is ascertained when viewed in the light of over-riding policy considerations and in the realization that the sale and consignment were not merely sales below value but inherently wrongful transfers which should allow the owner to be made whole.

The decree of the Surrogate imposed appreciation damages against Reis, Stamos, MNY and MAG in the amount of $7,339,464.72 computed as $9,252,000 (86 works on canvas at $90,000 each and 54 works on paper at $28,000 each) less the aggregate amounts paid the estate under the two rescinded agreements and interest. Appellants chose not to offer evidence of "present value" and the only proof furnished on the subject was that of the expert Heller whose appraisal as of January, 1974 (the month previous to that when trial commenced) on a painting-by-painting basis totaled $15,100,000. There was also testimony as to bona fide sales of other Rothkos between 1971 and 1974. Under the circumstances, it was impossible to appraise the value of the unreturned works of art with an absolute certainty and, so long as the figure arrived at had a reasonable basis of computation and was not merely speculative, possible or imaginary, the Surrogate had the right to resort to reasonable conjectures and probable estimates and to make the best approximation possible through the exercise of good judgment and common sense in arriving at that amount. This is particularly so where the conduct of wrongdoers has rendered it difficult to ascertain the damages suffered with the precision otherwise possible. Significantly, the Surrogate's factual finding as to the present value of these unreturned paintings was affirmed by the Appellate Division and, since that finding had support in the record and was not legally erroneous, it should not now be subjected to our disturbance. * * *

We have considered the other alleged errors urged by the parties, and find those arguments to be without merit. In short, we find no basis for disturbing the result reached below.

NOTES AND QUESTIONS

1.   For further background, see Lee Seldes, The Legacy of Mark Rothko (1979). Seldes regards the case as "the greatest art scandal" of the century. Bernard Reis was a close confidant of Rothko and served as his principal advisor on financial and business matters. He drafted the will that named himself, Stamos, and Levine as the executors of Rothko's estate and as directors of the Rothko Foundation. The will left no paintings to Rothko's estranged widow or his two children, Kate and Christopher. Rothko's widow, Mell, died shortly after Rothko committed suicide, leaving the two children orphans. Through their guardians and lawyers, they elected to take a forced share, equal to one-half the estate under New York law, and brought suit to rescind the sweet-heart contract the executors had made with Marlborough. Seldes portrays Frank Lloyd, the director of Marlborough Gallery, as the mastermind who induced Reis and the other executors to breach their duties to the estate. He gave Reis and Stamos retainers that put them in a conflict of interest with the estate, and pushed successfully for the sweet-heart contract. After the New York Court of Appeals affirmed the judgment, Lloyd was indicted for tampering with evidence, and fled to the Bahamas to avoid extradition. Nevertheless, he returned the paintings that had been spirited out of the country in violation of the injunction, and paid off the judgment in full. Bernard Reis, his assets exhausted by the litigation, filed for bankruptcy.

2.   Although technically this decision involves the duties of the executors of an estate, as the court notes in footnote 2 executors act as trustees for the creditors and the beneficiaries of the estate. The court draws upon concepts of fiduciary duty developed in the context of trust management, and its conclusions would be equally applicable to the management of a family trust.

3.   Would the terms of the contract with Marlborough justify a finding of breach of fiduciary duty standing on their own? Notice that Rothko entered into a contract before his death giving Marlborough the exclusive right to sell his paintings at a 10% commission. This would tend to suggest that there was nothing inherently prejudicial to the estate in appointing Marlborough the exclusive sales agent. The executors also instructed the agent that after the initial batch of paintings were sold, sales were to be to limited to 35 paintings per year. This was designed to prevent flooding the market with Rothkos and driving down the price of the paintings. The principal bone of contention seems to be that the executors agreed to a higher commission—50% as opposed to 10% under the contract with Rothko. But is it clear that the 50% commission would result in a lower net value to the estate than a 10% commission? Presumably Marlborough has greater incentive under a 50% commission to work hard to sell the paintings at a high price. How is a court to decide whether agreeing to a 50% commission as opposed to a 10% commission is a breach of fiduciary duty? Suppose instead the estate agreed to sell all the paintings to Marlborough for $1 million dollars in cash, and several years later they are worth $5 million. Would the contract necessarily be suspect? Would anyone

complain if, instead of appreciating, the value of the paintings crashed in later years?

4. Here, of course, there was more than what appears to be a one-sided contract with Marlborough. Reis was a director and officer (and had an undisclosed retainer) with the gallery, and was eager to enlist Marlborough in selling art from his own collection. Stamos was also under contract with Marlborough and anxious to curry the gallery's favor. Levine was not charged with any conflict of interest, but was said to have acted imprudently by not objecting to the conflicts of Reis and Stamos. Would these conflicts be enough to remove the executors and charge them with millions of dollars in damages liability if they had negotiated a highly beneficial deal for the estate? Is there any claim that any of the executors stands to profit directly from the contract with Marlborough?

c. CHANGED CIRCUMSTANCES

One of the recurring problems with interests that persist over long periods of time is that conditions may change in ways that may not have been foreseeable to someone at the time the interest was created. Situations of this sort arise with particular frequency in the charitable trust context. The doctrine of cy pres operates where a settlor (who cannot be consulted) has expressed a specific charitable intent that, due to changed circumstances, is impossible or undesirable to fulfill, but where the settlor also expressed a related general charitable intent that could still be fulfilled with some judicial modification of the interests created. For example, a trust may provide that a house is to be used as a hospital in a particular town, but it turns out that the hospital in a neighboring village adequately serves the needs of the community. See In re Neher, 18 N.E.2d 625 (N.Y. 1939) (employing cy pres to allow the town to use the house for administrative purposes). The proper grounds and degree of judicial intervention remain controversial. Consider the following case.

Wilber v. Owens

Supreme Court of New Jersey, 1949.
65 A.2d 843.

■ HEHER, JUSTICE. The bill of complaint [by Charles P. Wilber, as sole acting executor of the last will of William Brokaw Bamford, deceased, against John Owens and Asbury Park National Bank & Trust Company, the Trustees of Princeton University, and others] seeks a construction of the will of William Brokaw Bamford, deceased.

The appeal is from the decretal findings that the testator had "a general charitable intent" (142 N.J.Eq. 99, 59 A.2d 570, 584) and the "trust created by" the tenth paragraph of the will "is a valid charitable trust," and also from the direction that the executor pay over the corpus of the trust to the Trustees of Princeton University "in trust to invest and reinvest the same, and to use the income in some fitting manner for scientific and philosophical research in its Department of Philosophy as said Trustees of Princeton may in their best judgment decide.''

Figure 6–9
Title Page of the First of the Bamford Manuscripts

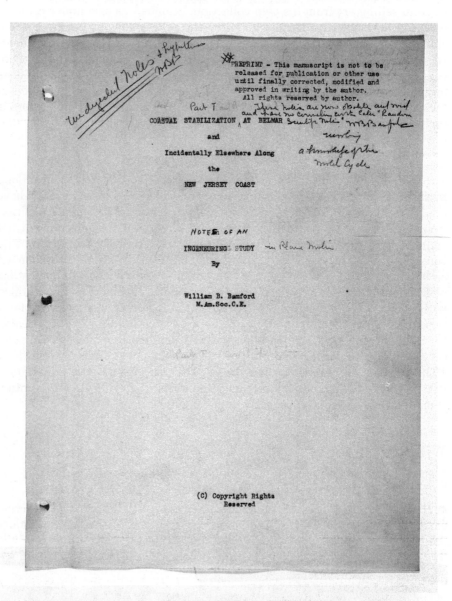

Courtesy Princeton University Library.

The avowed purpose of this provision of the will was the creation of a trust, to be known as the "Exton–Bamford Research Fund," and the use of "the income thereof in some fitting manner to continue and carry forward to a completion and to publish for popular understanding the results of the researches contained or outlined in" the testator's "manuscript entitled 'Random Scientific Notes seeking the Essentials in Place and Space' or by whatever future title" he "might designate them."

The learned Vice Chancellor found that the "Random Notes" are "irrational, unintelligible, and of no scientific or other value"; that "the express purpose of the trust created by" the cited paragraph of the will "is impossible of accomplishment;" that the testator had "a general charitable intent and the trust" so created "is a valid charitable trust;" and that under the doctrine of cy pres Chancery was empowered to direct the use of the trust fund "to carry out, as near as may be, the testator's general intent and purpose"; hence, the provision for the use of the income for "scientific and philosophical research" by Princeton University, who was named by the testator as the ultimate trustee for the execution of the trust if those given the prior option of service should decline to accept the trust on the terms and conditions laid down in the will.

First, the insistence is that the testator did not have a general charitable intent. It is said that the testator's "purpose" cannot be "disassociated from his Notes;" that while he indicated the "thought" that "his notes would be of world benefit," his "basic and fundamental purpose, desire and intent" was simply the "completion and publication for popular understanding of the results of his researches"; and that this was "paramount and vital," and not subordinate to a general charitable intent, and a construction "severing the decedent's intent from his Random Notes" would run counter to "the express terms of the will, the testimony and the evidence, all of which deny the existence of a general charitable intent."

The testamentary expression is not to be so narrowly read. It reveals a general charitable intent. The testator's dominant purpose was the devotion of his property to uses which are charitable. He gave what he considered was the bulk of his wealth to the charitable use provided in the tenth paragraph of the will. As it turned out, the bequest was far in excess of the value of his estate. The amount thus bequeathed was $150,000; and the bequest was conditioned upon the raising of a like sum by the trustee, the whole to constitute the principal of the trust in perpetuity. But the fulfillment of the trust was not made to depend upon the provision of the additional principal. In the event that the several trustees should refuse acceptance of the trust so conditioned, the same bequest was made, first to the League of Nations and, in case of a refusal, to Princeton University, in trust "for the same purposes, but upon any satisfactory terms and conditions by which" such accepting trustee "will agree to endeavor to carry out the purposes of this bequest and trust so that the results may be of benefit to the entire world." Such trustee was authorized to do the work attending the execution of the trust by its "own staff or by assignment to scientists or other qualified workers who believe that the common good of the worthy and meritorious of all mankind is greater than that of an isolated part."

Then came a series of specific and pecuniary legacies, the pecuniary legacies totalling $34,600, many of them charitable, but none to become effective until after "the provisions" of the tenth and other preceding paragraphs of the will "have been fully complied with." There was prior provision of $15,000 for the preservation of his "Random Notes" and for a scientific analysis and appraisal of the "researches" therein "outlined," to the end that such "researches" be made available "for the use and benefit of all mankind," if they "have any practical value." And, by the thirty-third paragraph of the will, the "residue" of the testator's estate was constituted a trust designated as the "Exton–Bamford Trust," to be administered by a "voluntary association" composed of designated "representative" second cousins.

This latter trust was to continue until the youngest of his second cousins attained the age of fifty years, when the corpus was to be divided equally among such of his second cousins therein mentioned as should then be living. Meanwhile, the income was to be "used and applied to promote the well being of mankind and more especially the social, physical and economic welfare and efficiency of any of my relatives who are worthy and deserving and are in special need of such assistance, or of any of my relatives who have * * * acquired special merit in their own lives through their efforts to help others beyond their ordinary duty or obligation." Authority was also given to apply such income "to the use and benefit of any worthy charitable, benevolent or educational purpose; or for the establishment and maintenance of any endowments or memorials" as may be found "to be appropriate following where reasonably possible the spirit of the various provisions of my will or of my Random Scientific Notes". In this paragraph the testator urged his kin to find "a fitting way" to "overcome the evil effects of direct inheritance of unearned property." In the event that such voluntary association should not for any reason be "set up or maintained," or if the income should not be spent by such association as provided in the will, or if all of the second cousins therein appointed to form and maintain the association should die "before the youngest one shall have attained the age of fifty years," then the residue of his estate would pass to the National Academy of Sciences at Washington, "in trust, as far as may be possible, as set forth to establish the 'Exton–Bamford Research Fund' for the purposes and under the same terms and conditions as provided" in the tenth paragraph of the will.

A general charitable intention is outstanding in these provisions. The design of the trust created by the tenth paragraph is the advancement of education and learning, and therefore it is a charitable trust. Trusts for the advancement of knowledge by research or otherwise are charitable. A gift for the benefit of an indefinite number of persons, by bringing their minds or hearts under the influence of education or religion, among other purposes, is a charity in the legal sense. A trust is charitable if the subject property is devoted to the accomplishment of purposes which are beneficial or may be supposed to be beneficial to the community. This is the prime distinction between private trusts and charitable trusts. The question is whether the accomplishment of the purpose is of such social interest to the community as to justify the dedication of the property to that purpose in perpetuity. Are the persons to benefit of a sufficiently large or indefinite class to give rise to community interest in the trust? Will the trust in operation advance the religious, educational, eleemosynary, governmental or other charitable interests of the community? Woodstown National Bank & Trust Co. v. Snelbaker, 40 A.2d 222 (N.J. Ch. 1944), affirmed, 44 A.2d 210 (N.J. 1945); Scott on Trusts, sections 348, 364, 368.

It was obviously not the testator's design to confine the trust created in paragraph ten to the mere publication of his "Random Scientific Notes" and the "results" of his "researches." He believed that the subject matter of the Notes provided the core for continued philosophic and metaphysical research that would be of inestimable benefit to mankind. The quantum of the trust fund, to run in perpetuity, is itself significant of this intention. He had evolved a social philosophy in which the economic "parasite" had no part. His worldly goods were largely inherited; and it was his belief that inherited wealth lays upon the possessor the solemn duty and responsibility of making "worthy use" of the inheritance. He had no kin nearer than first cousins; and he had determined to devote the major part of his property to the service and enrichment of his fellows. He sought to add "a small bit to the sum-total of desirable human knowledge, for the use and benefit of mankind." This we find in the "Introduction" to the first volume of his Notes. True, his Notes contributed nothing to the sum of human knowledge; and their development would not add to wisdom. Indeed, they have been termed "irrational and incoherent." Dr. Scoon said a part was understandable and a part not. Yet to the testator the text was real and vital and entirely reasonable and in keeping with his own meager understanding of the subject. No doubt, the testator's limited knowledge of the matter rendered him incapable of assessing the importance of his findings. Perhaps, he was not sufficiently tutored in the subject to voice with any degree of accuracy the thoughts that were striving for expression. But there can be no doubt of his ceaseless yearning to be of service to human kind and to use his property to that end. He conceived that his reflections and conclusions would provide the basis and the impetus for philosophic research that would in the end be socially constructive and otherwise serve the common good; but the charitable intent does not depend upon the scientific validity of his views or the depth of his understanding. We are not concerned with his philosophic or sociologic orthodoxy or rationality. Whatever the utility of his contribution, his undoubted aim was the use of his Notes as the beginning of an undertaking that would in scientific hands redound to the advantage of mankind. That was his avowed purpose. The will abounds in expressions to that effect. And in a summary or outline of his Notes, dictated shortly before his death, he declared that "The present world conditions and the critical post-war problems of world wide adjustments present a challenge to any thinking which offers promise of improved human relationships." This is an understandable commentary and a wholly rational aspiration, although the cynic would say an aspiration foredoomed. In a letter to Dr. Bowman, the President of Johns Hopkins College, written in 1935, he spoke of the trust as a means "to carry forward a research work in pure science at which I was then and still am active." And to Dr. Millikan he wrote, in the same year, of the execution of a will, still subsisting, bequeathing a trust fund of $150,000 "to carry forward a prosearch work in pure science at which I was then and still am active". But he realized that the content of his Notes might prove to be of little or no practical value. He knew the Notes were incomplete; his dominant purpose was continued research in the chosen field for the common benefit.

RULE

While the content of the Notes themselves may be wanting in scientific coherence and rationality, the ultimate aim of the testator was not irrational or absurd, and therefore the trust does not fail on this account. His was a "search for truth," not the propagation of nonsense or folly or the dissemination of absurd ideas. Even where the opinion sought to be propagated is "foolish or * * * devoid of foundation," the bequest is not necessarily void as a charitable use. Thorton v. Howe, 31 Beav. 14. In an early case in Massachusetts, the court upheld a trust to establish and maintain a school to be taught by females in which no books of instruction were to be used except spelling books and the Bible. Tainter v. Clark, 1862, 5 Allen, Mass., 66. If the general purposes for which the trust is created may reasonably be regarded as in the interest of the community, the mere fact that the members of the court and the vast majority of the people believe that the particular purpose is unwise does not serve to render the trust noncharitable. In an Irish case, upholding a trust to promote vegetarianism, Lord Justice Fitz Gibbon said that the test of beneficence is met if the "benefit" is "one which the founder believes to be of public advantage," and "his belief" is "at least rational, and not contrary either to the general law of the land, or the principles of morality." He continued: "A gift of such a character, dictated by benevolence, believed to be beneficent, devoted to an appreciably important object, and neither contra bonos mores nor contra legem, will, in my opinion, be charitable in the eye of the law, as settled by decisions which bind us. It is not for us to say that these have gone too far." In re Cranston (1898) 1 I.R. 431, 446–7.

The bequest here is for research in the sciences of philosophy and metaphysics for the ultimate good of mankind; and this is a charitable use wholly devoid of the element of illegality, immorality or absurdity, even though the matter provided by the testator as the basis for the inquiry is utterly without scientific or other value. The general purposes for which the trust was created are indubitably conducive to the common interest.

Cy Pres – "so near" or "as near"

The trust does not fail because it is impossible or impracticable to carry out the particular charitable purpose. The judicial power of cy pres is invocable to effectuate the more general intention to devote the property to charitable uses. The words "cy pres" are Norman French meaning "so near" or "as near;" and the term itself suggests the limitations of the principle. Cy pres is "the doctrine of nearness or approximation." MacKenzie v. Trustees of Presbytery of Jersey City, 61 A. 1027, 1035 (N.J. 1905); Crane v. Morristown School Foundation, 187 A. 632 (N.J. 1936). Where fulfillment of the specific charitable intent cannot be had, equity will in the exercise of the power apply the property to a similar charitable purpose in accordance with the more general charitable intent. This on the theory that the testator would have so ordained if he had realized that it

Application

would be impossible to carry out the particular purpose. By this process, the intention of the testator is fulfilled as nearly as it is possible to do. We find nothing to indicate a purpose to terminate the trust here if the specific intent failed of attainment. The special intent was but a means to an end. The particular purpose was subordinate to the general charitable intention; and the decree constitutes a proper exercise of the power of cy pres. It falls within the general charitable intention and approaches as nearly as may be the particular purpose of the settlor.

Even where it is possible to carry out the particular purpose, the principle of cy pres is applicable if the fulfillment of the more specific intention would frustrate the general charitable intention of the settlor. It is then "impracticable" to carry out the particular purpose. St. James Church v. Wilson, 89 A. 519 (N.J. Ch. 1913), affirmed on this point sub nom. West v. Rector, etc., of St. James' Episcopal Church, 91 A. 101 (N.J. 1914); Restatement, Trusts, section 399, Comment M.

Liberal application of cy pres

Where the principle is applicable, Chancery will give heed, in seeking for a charitable purpose falling within the general charitable intention, not only to the language of the trust instrument itself, but to all the circumstances tending to indicate the settlor's probable desires if he had realized that the particular purpose could not be carried out. This is according to the general canon of construction. In re Fisler's Estate, 30 A.2d 894 (N.J. 1943).

The decree is affirmed.

NOTES AND QUESTIONS

1. The materials that William B. Bamford referred to in his will as his "Random Scientific Notes seeking the Essentials in Place and Time" now reside in a box that can be accessed through the rare book room of the Princeton University Library. The notes in the box, collected in seven spiral binders (plus appendices), are not given the title mentioned in the will (or any other title). It is, however, reasonably accurate to characterize them as "random." The earliest material chronologically, which was compiled in 1927 and appears in the first binder, is devoted to problems of beach erosion on the New Jersey coast. (See Figure 6–9.) Later volumes, to the extent they are comprehensible, build upon observations about beach movements in an effort to develop more fundamental physical laws governing the universe. In the later volumes, composed toward the end of the author's life (he died in 1945), the notes are typed or scratched in pencil on the back of various letters, advertisements, and bank statements, and include speculations about the etymology of words and other thoughts that occurred to the author. Robert Scoon, the Stewart Professor of Philosophy at Princeton who reviewed the notes and filed an affidavit in the case with his assessment, remarked: "The author is evidently one of a class of people, that is unfortunately well known to University Professors, who ponder current problems in solitude, jump to some general solution without subjecting themselves to the disciplines of reading the authorities or facing

the criticism of other thinkers, and then appeal to us to validate their speculations." Renamed the "Exton–Bamford Fellowship Fund," the trust now "[s]upports fellowships in the Philosophy Department." Princeton University, Graduate School Announcement, 2005–06.

2.   What are the options of the court here in response to the request for construction of the will of William Brokaw Bamford? One, obviously, is to enforce paragraph ten as written, and to require that the trust "continue and carry forward" the tenets of the Random Scientific Notes. If Princeton refuses to act as trustee for this purpose, then the executor, with the court's approval, can probably designate a substitute trustee. Another option, as the decision holds, is to apply cy pres and modify the purposes of the trust created in paragraph ten so as to devote the money to something more sensible. A third option might be to declare that paragraph ten has failed because of the irrationality of the Random Notes, and that therefore the money should pass to the other pecuniary charities named in later paragraphs and ultimately to the second cousins under the residuary clause of the will, paragraph thirty-three. (Note that these residual takers apparently received nothing, because the estate ended up with less money than the decedent bequeathed in paragraph ten, which has priority over the later bequests.) If the objective is to fulfill the intentions of the donor, which of these three options do you think William Brokaw Bamford would have chosen if he were still alive? If the objective is to avoid irrationality while doing minimal violence to the provisions of the will, which would be the preferred option? Why might the court prefer the cy pres option rather than directing that the money pass under the residuary clause to the second cousins?

3.   One source of impossibility or impracticability is changed conditions. But how much do conditions have to change for a court to invoke cy pres? Bryan Mullanphy set up a trust by will in 1851, under which the income of one-third of the estate would be used "to furnish relief to all poor immigrants and travelers coming to St. Louis on their way, bona fide, to settle West." Repeated litigation beginning in 1902 sought to have cy pres applied because the number of eligible beneficiaries had dropped from an average of 1,500 per year in the period 1879 to 1896, to 387 per year by 1896, and the income far outstripped the expenses. Not until 1934 did a court apply cy pres. Even more dramatic is the story of the trusts set up by Benjamin Franklin to make start-up business loans of 60 pounds or less at 5% to young married artificers who had apprenticed in Boston or Philadelphia. Bonds in Spanish milled dollars were to be taken as security. Many aspects of the trust quickly became outmoded, including monetary amounts not indexed for inflation and the occupational paths taken by young people. Courts applied the cy pres doctrine slowly and piecemeal over decades. For a discussion of these cases, see Lewis M. Simes, Public Policy and the Dead Hand 127–31 (1955). In a recent and ongoing litigation saga, Dr. Albert C. Barnes established by his will a foundation to operate an art museum in Merion, Pennsylvania, a suburb of Philadelphia. The Barnes Foundation has argued for years that the museum should be allowed to relocate to Philadelphia, where it would be visited by more people. The trust indenture

[Handwritten margin note: RULE residual clauses of a trust only receive benefit when primary clause is completely satisfied]

also contained restrictions on how the works were to be displayed and forbidding them from being loaned out. Litigation has dragged out over the course of 50 years. Dr. Barnes was considered by some to be eccentric but he clearly did not trust the Philadelphia art world to display his collection properly. See Ilana H. Eisenstein, Keeping Charity in Charitable Trust Law: The Barnes Foundation and the Case for Consideration of Public Interest in Administration of Charitable Trusts, 151 U. Pa. L. Rev. 1747 (2003). In December 2004 a suburban Philadelphia orphans' court judge ruled that the Barnes Foundation could alter its charter and move the collection to Philadelphia.

4. Courts in the United States long harbored great suspicion of cy pres, stemming from abuses of related cy pres powers in England. U.S. courts are now more willing to apply cy pres to redirect property in cases in which the designated charitable purposes would be unlawful, impossible, impracticable, or wasteful. These days the courts feel increasingly free to select a substitute charitable purpose that is reasonably similar to the designated specific purpose, rather than necessarily the nearest possible one. See Uniform Trust Code § 413; 2 Restatement (Third) of the Law of Trusts § 67 (2003). The new *Restatement of Trusts* reflects the more expansive approach to cy pres under which courts can redirect the use of the property not just where the designated charitable purpose becomes unlawful, impossible, or impracticable, but also when applying all of the property to the original designated purpose would be wasteful. Not surprisingly, the new *Restatement* also would give courts freedom to select a "charitable purpose that reasonably approximates the designated purpose," rather than forcing a court to discern a general charitable intent.

5. Courts will also interpret trusts so as to account for changed circumstances without expressly invoking the cy pres doctrine. Joseph Pulitzer, the newspaper magnate, died in 1911 leaving his newspapers in a trust to be operated by his three sons. He gave the sons broad discretion to operate and dispose of the papers, including the *St. Louis Post–Dispatch*, except for his beloved *New York World*: "I particularly enjoin upon my sons and my descendants the duty of preserving, perfecting and perpetuating 'The World' newspaper (to the maintenance and upbuilding of which I have sacrificed my health and strength) in the same spirit in which I have striven to create and conduct it as a public institution, from motives higher than mere gain. . . ." Later, in the depths of the Great Depression, the sons petitioned the court for authority to sell the *World*. They showed that the paper had incurred heavy losses for five consecutive years, and was threatening to destroy the corpus of the trust. Without mentioning cy pres, the court agreed to permit the sale. The court noted that the law assumes that a settlor "had sufficient foresight to realize that securities bequeathed to a trustee may become so unproductive or so diminished in value as to authorize their sale where extraordinary circumstances develop or a crisis occurs. Such was the law in this state prior to the making of Mr. Pulitzer's Will. He is charged with knowledge of it." In re Pulitzer's Estate, 249 N.Y.S. 87, 93 (Surrogate's Court, N.Y. 1931). Ironically, although the *World* disappeared nineteen years after his death, the *Post–Dispatch*, which

Pulitzer "had several times tried to sell and to which he devoted much less attention," survives to this day. W.A. Swanberg, Pulitzer 417–18 (1967).

6.   Many trusts from earlier eras have provisions that discriminate on the basis of race, gender, or religion. Courts have often used cy pres to remove restrictions from gifts to schools for scholarships and other educational purposes. See, e.g., Trammell v. Elliott, 199 S.E.2d 194 (Ga. 1973) (applying cy pres to remove whites-only restriction from scholarship fund); Coffee v. William Marsh Rice University, 408 S.W.2d 269 (Tex. Civ. App. 1966) (use of cy pres to remove racial restriction from organic instruments by which university was created); but cf. Trustees of University of Delaware v. Gebelein, 420 A.2d 1191 (Del. Ch. 1980) (holding administration of women-only scholarship by state university to be state action but that remedial purpose of scholarship made discrimination permissible). Recall from Chapter IV that the U.S. Supreme Court has had difficulty articulating the boundaries of state action where courts give effect to claims of one private party against another. What if a court is asked to appoint trustees to a discriminatory trust? Courts are split over whether appointing private trustees is state action. Compare In re Wilson, 452 N.E.2d 1228 (N.Y. 1983) (no) with In re Certain Scholarship Funds, 575 A.2d 1325 (N.H. 1990) (yes).

7.   Although trusts are important in family wealth settlements and in transmitting property on death, they are also very important in commercial contexts. For example, trusts are commonly used in the administration of pension plans, and are used in creating separate entities to receive periodic payments like receivables or mortgage payments that can be "securitized" and sold in secondary securities markets. Overall, it has been estimated that 90% of all assets held in trust are held for commercial, rather than family, purposes. See John H. Langbein, The Secret Life of the Trust: The Trust as an Instrument of Commerce, 107 Yale L.J. 165, 177–78 (1997).

2.   CORPORATIONS AND PARTNERSHIPS

Corporations and partnerships are even more important than trusts as devices for separating the management and beneficial enjoyment of assets. You will very likely take an entire course in business associations, and we have no desire to duplicate such a course here, even in part. The point of bringing up corporations and partnerships is simply to highlight that they too serve as entity property devices, allowing large complexes of property to be effectively managed in ways that would be difficult if not impossible to achieve using only the common-law forms of property ownership. Placing ownership of property in a corporation or partnership is in effect an alternative to the lease, the condominium, or the trust as a mechanism for achieving integrated management of large complexes of assets.

The distinctive feature of corporations and partnerships, from a property rights perspective, is that an artificial entity is permitted to own property in its own name and right, as if it were a person. Thus, the assets of the corporation or the partnership are treated as separate and distinct from the assets of the owners or partners who form these entities. The corporation achieves this outcome by adopting a two-level ownership structure. The shareholders own the corporation. The corporation, in turn, holds title to various assets, including real and personal property, intangible property including intellectual property rights, and contract rights. The ownership interest of the shareholders gives them the right to receive dividends as periodically declared by the board of directors, and to a pro rata share of the assets upon dissolution of the corporation. Otherwise, the shareholders play only an episodic role in the management of the corporation and its assets. They elect a board of directors, and also vote on important amendments to the bylaws of the corporation and important corporate control transactions like mergers. But the day-to-day management and control of the various assets owned by the corporation is vested in the managers of the corporation, appointed by the directors. Thus, the various incidents of ownership we have studied—including the rights to exclude, to license, to destroy, and to transfer—are exercised by a large number of managers and employees, all acting in the name of the corporation. This separation of ownership and control has been familiar in corporate law since Berle and Means initially posed it as a problem. Adolf A. Berle & Gardiner C. Means, The Modern Corporation and Private Property 4–7 (1932). Their insight served as the starting point for the agency-cost theory of the firm. Berle and Means regarded separation of ownership and control as a challenge to traditional notions of property. But this separation of ownership and control can also be viewed as the way in which the exclusionary strategy traditionally associated with property is accommodated to the complexities of modern business organizations.

The relationships among the managers and employees are determined largely by contract (including the bylaws of the corporation and employment contracts). Hence corporations are often described as a "nexus of contracts." See, e.g., Frank Easterbrook & Daniel Fischel, The Economic Structure of Corporate Law 24–25 (1991); Michael C. Jensen & William H. Meckling, The Theory of the Firm: Managerial Behavior, Agency Costs, and Ownership Structure, 3 J. Fin. Econ. 305 (1976). But what gives the contracts a "nexus" is the understanding that the corporation as an entity owns the assets of the enterprise, and that the corporation as an entity is in turn owned by the shareholders. See Melvin A. Eisenberg, The Conception That the Corporation is a Nexus of Contracts, and the Dual Nature of the Firm, 24 J. Corp. L. 819 (1999).

For partnerships, the matter is more complicated, although practically speaking the result today is the same: entity ownership. It was not always so. Traditionally the formation of a partnership gave rise to ownership of the assets by tenancy in partnership. This operated something like a tenancy in common. Each partner was a direct owner of the assets (along with the other partners) and was entitled to a proportionate share of the earnings. Governance of the assets was by consent or by partnership agreement. Today, partnerships are everywhere regarded as having a two-level ownership structure, analogous to corporations. The partners own the partnership conceived of as an entity, and the partnership, as an entity, owns the underlying assets. This was achieved indirectly by the Uniform

Partnership Act, which defined a partnership as an association of co-owners, but then proceeded to give the partnership most of the attributes of ownership. See Uniform Partnership Act (1914). The Revised Uniform Partnership Act embraces this conclusion directly, providing in that "[a] partnership is an entity." Revised Uniform Partnership Act § 201 (1997).

What are the implications of recognizing corporations and partnerships as entities with ownership rights distinct from the rights of the shareholders and partners that own these entities? Henry Hansmann and Reinier Kraakman have argued that one very important implication is that corporations and partnerships are shielded from claims of creditors of the individual shareholders or partners. The entity itself is not liable for the personal debts of its owners. Thus, if shareholder A fails to pay his debts, A's creditors cannot come after the corporation's factory. Henry Hansmann & Reinier Kraakman, The Essential Role of Organizational Law, 110 Yale L.J. 387 (2000). Moreover, Hansmann and Kraakman argue that this aspect of entity law cannot be created by contract, because it would be prohibitively costly to do so; it must be authorized legislatively, and hence can be called a rule of property.

Another implication of the entity-ownership feature of corporations and partnerships is that it permits the specialization of functions we have emphasized throughout the chapter. By placing ownership of assets in an artificial legal entity like a corporation or a partnership, assets can be subjected to a sophisticated governance regime defined by the nexus of contracts that make up the legal entity. Thus, just as the trust permits a specialization of functions between the trustee as manager of assets and the beneficiaries as recipients of earnings, so corporations and partnerships permit a similar division. The officers and employees of the entity serve as the specialized managers of a complex of assets. The benefits of this asset management—typically in the form of profits earned—are then distributed among stakeholders, most prominently through dividends paid to shareholders or shares of earnings distributed to partners, in accordance with entity law and contractual understandings established for these purposes within the entity. This specialization of functions permits larger and more complicated collections of assets to be managed effectively than would be possible if the only tools available were simple exclusion rights and the common-law forms of property surveyed in Chapter V.

Also, as in the case of the trust, the corporation raises difficult problems about how to manage the managers. Like the trustees of a trust, the directors and officers of a corporation are subject to a variety of fiduciary duties. In particular, directors and officers are subject to a duty of loyalty to the corporation. This means, among other things, that they may not seek to benefit personally from business opportunities that by right belong to the corporation, nor may they take actions for their personal benefit that disadvantage the corporation. These doctrines apply to the management and acquisition of property by the corporation. See, e.g., Northeast Harbor Golf Club, Inc. v. Harris, 725 A.2d 1018 (Me. 1999) (president of golf course breached fiduciary duty by acquiring in her own name property surrounding the golf course for development). There is, needless to say, an enormous literature on whether the constraints corporate agents face are adequate. The constraints come from a variety of sources. The federal Securities and Exchange Commission regulates activities related to the issuance and transfer of corporate securities (shares of stock and bonds). Corporation law imposes various fiduciary duties on corporate directors and officers, and state courts entertain suits by shareholders for alleged violations of these duties. And the market provides a significant constraint, in that individual shareholders who do not approve of the conduct of the managers can sell their shares, and hence "exit" from the corporation at relatively low cost. If more shareholders exit than enter, the price of the stock falls, which may attract the attention of the board of directors or can even lead to a takeover of the corporation in order to replace the managers.

Note that business organizations come in a set list of forms somewhat reminiscent of the *numerus clausus* of forms of ownership. In addition to the sole proprietorship—where an individual owns the business assets in fee simple or absolute ownership—the principal options are the business corporation and the partnership. But there are variations, which have been expanding in number. For example, in a conventional partnership, the individual partners are liable for the debts of the partnership as an entity, in contrast to the corporation, where the shareholders have no liability for the debts of the corporation beyond the value of their shares. But recently, many states have recognized limited liability partnerships, which are like regular partnerships with the added feature of limited liability for the individual partners. This is why many law firms now sport the designation "LLP" after their name.

CHAPTER VII

SECURITY INTERESTS

One of the most important attributes of property, from both an economic and legal point of view, is its role in facilitating the flow of investment capital by providing a form of security for loans. Nearly all purchases of real property are made with borrowed money using the purchased property as security for the loan; most purchases of vehicles and other types of expensive personal property are also financed with security taken in the acquired property. In addition, owners of businesses, large and small, frequently borrow money to expand or improve their operations using existing, purchased, or after-acquired property as security. The total amount of secured debt in the United States has been conservatively estimated to be at least $2 trillion. See Ronald J. Mann, Explaining the Pattern of Secured Credit, 110 Harv. L. Rev. 625, 627 (1997). Secured lending has also been proclaimed as the key to greater and more equitably distributed economic growth in developing countries. Hernando de Soto among others has argued that if informal property rights of urban squatters and rural peasants were formalized, this would allow them to use these rights as collateral for secured loans, which could then be used to finance small start-up businesses. See Hernando de Soto, The Mystery of Capital (2000). Secured lending, on this view, is the secret of economic development in the West, and if emulated elsewhere could have a transformative effect on world poverty. Although these views have been contested, there is no doubt that secured lending is a central feature of mature economic systems, and a core contribution that private property makes to those systems.

A. INTRODUCTION

A security interest is a special type of property right in an asset called "collateral." The purpose of a security interest is to secure a loan; it makes an asset, the collateral, available as a source of value if the debtor defaults on the loan. Real estate mortgages are a familiar type of security interest, and the term "mortgage" is most commonly used today in the context of security interests in land. Beginning in the nineteenth century, most states by statute also provided for mortgages of personal property called chattel mortgages. These have now been superseded by Article 9 of the Uniform Commercial Code, which governs collateral in personal property, and uses the term "security interest" rather than "mortgage."

Consider a simple example of a real estate mortgage. P borrows $100,000 from Bank in order to finance the purchase of Blackacre from S.

830

In addition to the other transactional documents, P will sign a note promising to repay Bank according to a definite schedule. What if P defaults on the loan? Unless the loan is a nonrecourse loan, Bank could pursue a personal claim against P. But the fact that P is defaulting on the loan may mean that P is insolvent. Without more, Bank would have to share pro rata in a bankruptcy proceeding with the rest of P's creditors. Bank can gain greater assurance of being repaid—and hence offer a lower interest rate to P—if it also receives a mortgage as security from P. The mortgage gives Bank the right, upon default, to follow certain procedures to foreclose on the mortgage, force a judicially-supervised sale of the property, and pay off the balance of the loan from the proceeds. If those proceeds are insufficient to cover the balance on the loan and if the loan is a recourse loan (as residential mortgages usually are), Bank would in many states have a claim for the deficiency against P. But this claim would stand on the same footing as those of other creditors. If P files for bankruptcy, Bank will have to follow a different set of procedures and in some cases will find its security interest replaced with substitute rights in the bankruptcy.

Security interests can be seen as another form of divided ownership. Typically, the borrower holds a fee simple (or absolute title) and enjoys all rights associated with possession, including the right to exclude others. These rights are subject to the security interest, which is a nonpossessory interest that ripens into a possessory interest under certain conditions, namely, nonrepayment of the loan. In terms of the forms of property considered in Chapters V and VI, perhaps the closest analogue is a fee simple subject to an executory limitation, with the condition that leads to forfeiture being a default on the loan. In earlier times, this parallel was even closer, in that a mortgage was an actual transfer of title to the lender/mortgagee, which would be returned upon repayment of the loan. If the borrower/mortgagor defaulted, the title would remain with the lender. As we have seen in *Harms v. Sprague* (Chapter V), this "title" theory of mortgages at common law has largely given way to a lien theory; even those states in which mortgages are cast in the form of a land conveyance treat mortgages functionally as liens. Further, as we will discuss shortly, the harshness of the traditional conveyance approach to mortgages, under which the borrower/mortgagor would lose the property no matter how much of the loan had been paid at the time of default, has softened. After a great deal of maneuvering by parties, courts, and legislatures, a mortgagee seeking foreclosure these days must be very careful and must afford the mortgagor various opportunities to repair the situation and retain ownership of the property. In the case of personal property, the holder of the security interest can much more easily take possession of the collateral to satisfy the loan, often including by means of self-help, as we saw in *Williams v. Ford Motor Credit Co.* (Chapter IV).

The mortgage or other security interest is distinct from the debt it secures. In any mortgage of real estate the purchaser of the real estate (or someone borrowing on already-owned real estate) often signs and gives over two documents, a promissory note and the mortgage itself. The promissory note includes a promise to pay the principal with interest, a schedule of payment due dates, and conditions.[1] For example, the note may include a condition that upon a sale of the asset or failure to make timely payment the entire balance is due immediately. The second piece of paper, the mortgage, secures the debt embodied in the promissory note. It grants the lender (the obligee of the note) a conditional property interest in the asset. The mortgagor is thus the borrower (the obligor on the note) and the owner of the asset (for reasons we will see shortly, often the one with "equity" in the asset). The mortgagee is the one with the security interest and who is owed the balance of the loan plus interest. In the case of personal property, a security interest is often part of a financing statement, which tends to be a separate piece of paper in addition to the note itself.

For both real estate and personal property, mortgages and other security interests give their holders two rights, a "property right" and a "priority right," and it is useful to keep these distinct. Both rights relate to circumstances in which the debtor has trouble paying off the loan. In the event of a default on the loan or other breach, the *property right* gives the secured party the right to take over the property and sell it to satisfy the lien. Again, real and personal property security interests differ significantly in the level of procedural protections for the mortgagor. Process requirements often make security interests less attractive from the secured party's point of view; they can reduce the volume of lending and can lead to higher interest rates or evasions of such requirements by use of substitute devices. The history of security interests is littered with decisions over how to treat various installment sale contracts and special leases, as well as more modern "bankruptcy remote vehicles" used in asset securitizations.

The second right afforded by a security interest is the *priority right*. This means that where collateral is sold to satisfy the debt, the secured debt is satisfied out of the proceeds of the collateral in its order of seniority. Under the Uniform Commercial Code (UCC) as enacted in the states, a party with a security interest in personal property has priority over unsecured parties. Subject to exceptions, a secured party also has priority over other secured creditors according to the date on which it filed a financing statement or perfected its security interest, whichever is earlier. U.C.C. § 9–322. Perfection normally involves a filing of the financing statement in the prescribed place, or taking possession of the collateral. (Security interests given to finance the purchase of the property serving as security are governed by special rules. See U.C.C. §§ 9–309(1), 9–324). Interestingly the current (revised) Article 9 gives extra priority to possession or control, U.C.C. §§ 9–313, 9–314. Likewise, to preserve maximum

---

1. Many notes, such as those in the typical residential real estate transaction, provide for an "amortized" schedule of repayments. Amortization is a payment scheme for paying a predetermined sum plus interest over a fixed period of time so that the principal is eliminated at the end of the period. Usually the payments are equal in size, and each is comprised of principal and interest such that each payment's interest component is the rate-based amount of interest on the principal amount before that payment. The result is that early payments are weighted more towards interest and later ones more toward principal. As principal is paid off, the mortgagor builds up "equity" (short for "equity of redemption"), to which we turn in the next section.

priority, mortgages of real property are subject to the filing requirements of the state in which the property is located. These systems vary but all of them require some form of notice for the benefit of subsequent purchasers and lenders. Thus, debt secured by a first mortgage on real estate is paid before a debt secured by a second mortgage, and a second mortgage takes similar priority over a third mortgage. Here "first mortgage" and "second mortgage" refer to priority rights, and this usually follows the date of their creation (and filing, as required, see Chapter VIII), but parties can agree to subordinate their debt to other debt, usually in return for a higher interest rate. And all secured debt has priority over unsecured debt. If a loan is undersecured, then it is treated according to its priority up to the amount of the security and the rest is handled as unsecured debt. Thus, if a loan with an outstanding balance of $1,000 is secured by property worth only $800, the secured party is entitled to priority (within the hierarchy of secured debt if there is other secured debt) for $800 and has an unsecured claim for $200.

Security interests present a basic informational problem that is at the heart of property: How can people figure out which assets are subject to security interests? Without any limit on security interests or requirements to register them, one would always face the problem of the potential "secret lien," a problem that preoccupied people in earlier times, and is still a live issue today. For example, when should a purchaser of an asset take the asset subject to the seller's previously given security interest in favor of a third party? In earlier times, when registries were nonexistent and commerce was simpler, possession was usually taken as the best evidence of property rights. Thus, unless the lender took actual possession of the mortgaged property or collateral, the mortgagor would appear to the rest of the world as an owner. Accordingly, many security interests, especially in earlier times, involved the lender taking possession of the asset through a bailment, an arrangement which is called a "pledge." In some ancient societies such as in Mesopotamia, lenders would even take possession of land under a type of rent-free lease in order to secure loans, an arrangement that is almost unknown in modern economies. See Robert C. Ellickson & Charles DiA. Thorland, Ancient Land Law: Mesopotamia, Egypt, Israel, 71 Chi.-Kent L. Rev. 321, 395–96 (1995). Later in the ancient world, markers on the land itself would give notice of a mortgage, as with the engraved marker-stone (called a *horos*) in ancient Athens. Id. at 397. Pledges of personal property are still common, notably in pawn shops. Where the lender takes possession as security, the security interest does not present informational problems, although the lender as bailee might exceed its rights with respect to the collateral. Often, however, a borrower wants to give security in an asset that he will continue to use, such as business equipment.

Today, security interests in which the borrower keeps possession of the collateral are very common and well accepted. But this was not always so. Possession as evidence of ownership is both a historic approach and a departure point for the more complicated schemes we will study in this Chapter and the next. Particularly in the case of personal property, courts started from a basic suspicion of non-possessory security interests. These presented a problem of "ostensible ownership," in which third parties might deal with and lend further to the borrower in the belief that his assets would be available to back those further third-party claims. In real estate, mortgages could be recorded, thus diminishing but not extinguishing a similar concern about secret liens.

In the following case, the judges take the traditional skepticism about non-possessory security interests in personal property very seriously. The conflict is in part between different sets of creditors—George Poe, a former business partner of the debtor John Hancock, and two of John Hancock's secured creditors, Clow and Sharp. (Clow and Sharp did not lend directly to Hancock but, each in a slightly different way, agreed to guarantee his debt to others—debt which Hancock defaulted on, making Clow and Sharp liable and so creditors of Hancock.) In the case that follows, Clow and Sharp are suing the sheriff who executed an earlier judgment in favor of Poe. They are claiming in effect that they had better rights in the hides, tools, and goods, than did Poe.

Clow v. Woods

Supreme Court of Pennsylvania, 1819.
9 Am.Dec. 346, 5 Serg. & Rawle 275.

IN ERROR. [John Hancock], on the 19th September 1815, to secure two creditors, executed to them a mortgage of the bark and tools in his tanyard, of his skins and leather unfinished, in bark and vats for tanning, and provided that the mortgagor should continue in possession, for the purpose of working, tanning and finishing the same. The mortgage was not recorded, and the property remained in possession of [Hancock], who was a tanner, and he continued to work the leather in tanning, and to use, for that purpose, the tools and bark. No symbolical delivery took place, nor was there any schedule, inventory or appraisement of the property mortgaged * * *

Some time previously to the 19th September 1815, a George Poe entered into partnership with John Hancock, which was to continue for seven years. Before the expiration of this time, they dissolved the partnership by consent, and on the 20th November 1815, for the adjustment of their accounts, entered an amicable suit in the Court of Common Pleas of Allegheny county, and submitted it to arbitrators, who, on the 22d March 1816, reported in favor of George Poe the sum of $2252.73; judgment was entered thereon and a fieri facias was issued on the 22d March 1816, returnable to April term 1816, and directed to and put into the hands of the defendant, William Woods, the sheriff of the county. When the sheriff went to the house of John Hancock with the fieri facias to make a levy, and just before he made it, he received notice of the said mortgage, and not before. Nor had George Poe any notice of the said mortgage before the levy was made. The sheriff levied on the property contained in the said mortgage, removed, and sold the same for a sum more than sufficient to pay the mortgage. He refused, on request, to pay any part of the money arising from the said sale over to the said mortgagees, but paid the same to George Poe. * * *

■ GIBSON, J. The stat. 13 Eliz.* does not, in words, declare a conveyance of goods fraudulent, where the vendor retains possession; but in general terms renders void all conveyances made to the end, purpose and intent of defrauding creditors. Hence, it becomes incumbent on the courts to determine, from all the circumstances of the case, whether the conveyance be or be not made with a fraudulent intention; and in judging of that, it is held, that any neglect in leaving the vendor in possession, is fraudulent within the statute. The general rule is, that the possession must be transferred to the purchaser; and to this I propose to examine such exceptions as have been urged. It has been said, the rule does not apply to conditional sales; but that is altogether without foundation, for neither this statute nor the 27 Eliz., ch. 4, which provides for the securing of purchasers, makes any difference between absolute and conditional sales. The only question in any case is, whether the sale is fraudulent; and if it be, it is within the statute. Delivery of the subject-matter of the contract is as requisite in the case of a mortgage of goods, as it is in the case of an absolute sale. In Ryal v. Rowles, 1 Ves. 359; 1 Atk. 162 (S.C.), the cases on the point are ably examined, and it is conclusively shown to be immaterial whether the sale be conditional or not.

Again, it is said, wherever by the terms of the contract, it appears possession was not intended to follow immediately, the case is not within the purview of the statute. This, I apprehend, must be taken with great qualification. The contract, and the evidence of it, are secret matters between the parties themselves, and can afford no notice to creditors. What will it avail then, that a person intending to cover his property by a sham sale, has it expressed in the contract, that he is to retain indefinite possession? Such a conveyance would bear the stamp of dishonesty on its front. I take it to be necessary, not only that retention of possession be part of the contract, but that it also appear to be for a purpose fair, honest and absolutely necessary; or, at least, essentially conducive to some fair object the parties had in view, and which constituted the motive for entering into the contract. It is necessary, not only that appearances should agree with the real state of things, but also, that the real state of things should be honest and consistent with public policy, and that it afford no unnecessary facility to deception. * * * All the late cases in which the transfer has been sustained, have gone on the ground that the want of delivery was absolutely necessary to effect some fair purpose of the parties.

But I take it, where the motive of the sale is merely security to the vendee, and the owner is permitted to retain all the visible marks of ownership, for no other reason than the convenience of the parties, the contract will be void, although the reasons for the arrangement be inserted, and the possession be consistent with the deed. The law will not and ought

* [An Acte against fraudulent deedes, gifts, alienations, etc., 13 Eliz. C. 5, repealed, Law of Property 1925, ch. 20, § 207, sch. 7— eds.]

not to permit the owner of personal property to create an interest in another, either by mortgage or absolute sale, and still to continue to be the ostensible owner; and where the creating of such an interest is the sole object, the conveyance will be fraudulent, whether it contain a stipulation for retention of possession or not; for to indulge the motive that led to the arrangement would be against true policy. * * *

To come, however, to the case before us: I do not object to the transaction, altogether on the ground of the possession not having been immediately delivered. The hides, being in the process of tanning, could not be removed without great deterioration: and until finished, were unfit for market. The bark and tools were necessary to complete the process: and I think, the fair construction of the contract is, that all was to be delivered as soon as the leather should be in a fit state to be sold. Possession of the hides in the vats, to enable the mortgagor to complete the tanning would have been unavailing, without possession of the tanyard at the same time, which was not intended to be included in the mortgage. If the case stood clear of objection on another ground, I think a good reason might be assigned for the mortgagor continuing in possession as the agent of the mortgagee. I can see no objection to an absolute sale of an article undergoing a process of manufacture, to be delivered when finished; and if such a case would be good, a mortgage under the same circumstances would also be good. If, however, the intention were to conceal the lien thus created, and the transaction were industriously kept secret, it would amount to actual fraud.

But where, from the nature of the transaction, possession cannot be given, the parties ought in lieu, to do every thing in their power to secure the public from that deception which the possession of property without the ownership always enables a person to practice. When a ship at sea is sold, the grand bill of sale is delivered, and that divests the vendor of his last badge of ownership; and when goods are too bulky to admit of manual possession, the key of the room is handed over. In every case where possession is not given, the parties must leave nothing unperformed, within the compass of their power, to secure third persons from the consequences of the apparent ownership of the vendor. Here the defect is, that the articles conveyed are not described or particularized, either in a schedule or in the body of the instrument. This is fatal. In a case of this kind, the slightest neglect in any circumstance the nature of the case may admit of as an equivalent for actual possession, is unpardonable. Where there is to be delivery at the time of the sale, a schedule or description may be unnecessary, for it could not afterwards be alleged that an interest passed in anything not then delivered; but where the goods are to remain with the vendor, and nothing in particular is specified as the subject of the grant, there is imminent danger of fraud. The vendor continuing to treat the property as his own, it would be almost impossible for a third person to show, by evidence dehors the deed, what did or what did not pass. What was to prevent the plaintiffs here from covering any quantity of property of the kind expressed in the mortgage? The transaction being secret, John Hancock might have continued to carry on business, and purchase hides, bark and tools, as usual; and whether he should be able to shelter such property under the mortgage, would depend on the secrecy and adroitness with which the matter was managed. I do not suppose the parties had, in fact, a fraudulent view, but as such a transaction might be turned to a dishonest use, it was their duty, as far as in their power, to secure the public against it. * * *

I am of opinion, therefore, that judgment should be affirmed.

■ DUNCAN, J. The case stated is one in which the mortgage is not impeached on the ground of actual fraud. If it were so impeached, the common law, without the aid of statutes, would reach it and render it void.

The mortgage and the pledge or pawn of goods seem generally to have been confounded lately. A just discrimination has not been attended to and explained. The pawn or pledge is delivered to the pawnee, with the right to retain it, as a security for his debt. The legal property does not pass, as it does in the case of a mortgage with condition of defeasance. The general ownership remains with the pawner, and only a special property passes to the pawnee. * * * A mortgage is considered as an immediate disposition, to take effect immediately in possession, in contemplation of law. In a mortgage of lands, the possession usually remains with the mortgagor * * *; but not so of personal property. In Ryal v. Rowles, 1 Ves. 348, 1 Atk. 165, * * * Burnet, J., draws the true distinction between the mortgage of goods and lands. There is no way of coming at the knowledge of who is the owner of goods, but by seeing in whose possession they are; the title deeds give the information as to lands. * * *

It would be a proof of great improvidence in our laws, if a mortgage of goods unaccompanied by possession should be valid; * * * In chattels, possession is the strongest evidence of ownership. That a secret mortgage to secure a creditor, without any change of possession, the debtor in the daily and constant occupation of the goods, without valuation or inventory or specification accompanying the instrument, should be valid and bind the property against creditors, or sales made by the debtor without notice, would be a reproach to the law. It ought not, it cannot be so. If it were so, it would put an end to all credit. Credit is given on the possession, on the faith, that the man who was once the owner of goods continues the owner, until he parts with the possession. Indeed, if this instrument binds these goods, a parol executory agreement would equally bind them: an agreement to give the goods in security. I know not any doctrine that would tend to annihilate all credit, more than the establishment of such a principle. A contract such as this, where the possession of goods is to remain in one man, while the right remains in another, is, as to all third persons, fraudulent. The security by mortgage of lands, depends on the title and on the registry; of a mortgagee or pawnee of personal property, on the right of the mortgagor or pawnor, and on the delivery of the chattel, mortgaged or pledged; the custody and possession of which is to remain in him, be detained by him, as a security for his debt. It therefore appears to me, that by the principles of the common law, and the settled construction of the statutes of Elizabeth, to a mortgage of chattels, delivery is necessary; that every such mortgage, when the parties stand in the relation of debtor and creditor, unaccompanied with such possession as the subject-matter is capable of, is fraudulent and void against all other creditors, whether the debts were contracted antecedently or subsequently to the mortgage.

Judgment affirmed.

NOTES AND QUESTIONS

1.   The problem of ostensible ownership is a pervasive one. We have already considered bailments and leases in which the present possessor does not have full ownership, despite the fact that the bailee or the lessee largely exercises the right to exclude as a full owner would. One might say that any of these arrangements creates a problem of misleading appearances. On the other hand, such appearances are only misleading if people have an expectation that possessors are owners. Do they? Should they? How much should the law reflect or foster such generalizations? Laypeople probably cannot be expected to inform themselves of the debtor's total financial situation as could a bank or business partner. We will return in the next Chapter to the level of duty required for someone to prevail as a "bona fide purchaser." But note for now that not all ostensible ownership situations call for extensive inquiry into the rights and obligations of other actors. For example, commentators have suggested that the tort of inducing breach of contract can be thought of as protecting the contracting parties' "property" interest in performance. But the interfering third party in this context has very little duty of due diligence to make sure that a potential contracting partner would not be breaching an existing contract. See Richard A. Epstein, Inducement of Breach of Contract as a Problem of Ostensible Ownership, 16 J. Legal Stud. 1, 10–15 (1987); see also Lillian R. BeVier, Reconsidering Inducement, 76 Va. L. Rev. 877, 880 (1990); Fred S. McChesney, Tortious Interference with Contract Versus "Efficient" Breach: Theory and Empirical Evidence, 28 J. Legal Stud. 131, 133 (1999).

2.   As we will see in the next Chapter, the notice problem has been partially solved through recording systems for real estate and related filing systems for security interests in personal property. Some commentators see security interests as primarily a contractual problem with few or no third-party effects, see, e.g., Alan Schwartz, A Theory of Loan Priorities, 18 J. Legal Stud. 209, 220–22, 249–59 (1989), while others see them as presenting ostensible ownership problems for such third parties, see, e.g., Jonathan C. Lipson, Secrets and Liens: The End of Notice in Commercial Finance Law, 21 Emory Bankr. Dev. J. 421 (2005). Like bailments, leases, and trusts, security interests have both a contractual and property aspect. See Thomas W. Merrill & Henry E. Smith, The Property/Contract Interface, 101 Colum. L. Rev. 773, 833–43 (2001).

3.   The Uniform Commercial Code still allows taking a security interest by possession, known as a pledge. Indeed, this is the only way to create a security interest in money. As we will see in greater detail in the next Chapter, some instruments are negotiable, meaning that under a wide

variety of circumstances, the current holder is entitled to payment and is free from most defenses; money is the ultimate in negotiability in that one can get good title to cash even from a thief. Generally the more negotiable something is, the more a security interest in it has to be by possession. Can you see why? Negotiability and ostensible ownership rules (e.g., good faith purchaser) are in part about allocating information costs, the burdens of inquiry, and the costs of errors as between affected parties to a transaction.

4.   The result in *Clow* is that Poe gets the assets to satisfy his debt first, quite possibly leaving little or nothing for Clow and Woods. But did Poe do all he could to prevent unfair surprise to other creditors, such as Clow and Woods? One thing Poe did was get to the courthouse faster and obtain a judgment, thereby becoming a lien creditor. This does provide notice, and in general lien creditors are in a better position than general creditors. On the other hand, it is sometimes said that bankruptcy reflects a policy of trying to prevent creditors from racing to grab assets of a debtor on the brink of insolvency in an effort to satisfy themselves and leave other creditors empty-handed. See, e.g., Thomas H. Jackson, The Logic and Limits of Bankruptcy Law (1986). (Even receiving a voluntary payment from the debtor less than 90 days before the filing of a bankruptcy case generally will be deemed a voidable preference and the bankruptcy trustee can force its return to the estate. 11 U.S.C. § 547(b).) We don't know, but Hancock looks like a candidate for bankruptcy—at least he seems to be judgment-proof. We consider the priority of secured claims in bankruptcy later in this Chapter.

5.   Recall that one function of entity law is to designate a pool of assets to which business creditors can look without having to worry about the possible claims of the business-owner's personal creditors. What if instead of a former partner, someone who had been injured by Hancock and sued him to a judgment had gotten the sheriff to levy on Hancock's assets? Under current law, as long as they have met any filing requirements the UCC imposes for their kind of security interest, Clow and Woods would have priority over the tort creditor. Should they?

THE "PUZZLE" OF SECURED DEBT

Secured debt has been treated by commentators as something of a "puzzle" and has been regarded with a certain degree of suspicion. The central puzzle is this: Why would a borrower ever take on secured debt, instead of simply allowing all creditors to share pro rata in his or her assets? Thomas H. Jackson & Anthony T. Kronman, Secured Financing and Priority Among Creditors, 88 Yale L.J. 1143, 1146 (1979). True, the secured lender will offer a lower interest rate because of the decreased risk that it will not be repaid. But this simply *raises* the interest rate on whatever other debt the borrower will take on and lowers the value of the borrower's equity interest. At first blush, the total amount of risk remains the same, and manipulating the ratio of secured debt to unsecured debt (or debt to other equity-like interests) should not make any difference to total value under the control of a person or firm.

Some have gone further and argued that secured debt is pernicious: By taking out secured debt, the borrower gets a lower interest rate, but contrary to initial appearances not all other creditors adjust their interest rates to reflect the increased risk left over for them. The clearest case is tort creditors: Tort victims have no way of avoiding interactions with tortfeasors who are loaded up with secured debt, but the secured debt may make a judgment against the tortfeasor less valuable since it will have lower priority. Perhaps other creditors are also "nonadjusting" in this way; candidates would include trade creditors. See, e.g., Lucian Arye Bebchuk & Jesse M. Fried, The Uneasy Case for the Priority of Secured Claims in Bankruptcy, 105 Yale L.J. 857 (1996); Lynn M. LoPucki, The Unsecured Creditor's Bargain, 80 Va. L. Rev. 2021 (1994). A recent empirical study calls into question whether fraud on nonadjusting creditors actually occurs. See Yair Listokin, Is Secured Debt Used to Redistribute Value from Tort Claimants in Bankruptcy? An Empirical Analysis (Yale Law School Draft June 2006) (finding that firms facing high expected tort liability have unusually low amounts of secured debt).

More benign explanations for secured credit have also been offered. A secured creditor can specialize in monitoring a given asset, and this specialization can lower overall information costs. Debt holders must worry about the actions of the (equity) owners of the firm, because the latter will have an incentive to take risks with the firm's assets (including substituting them for riskier assets): The equity owners as holders of the residual claim will enjoy all of the upside, but will be able to force debt holders to take more downside risk. These "agency costs" can be addressed by security interests. The secured creditor specializes in monitoring the asset held as security. This reduces overall monitoring costs because it prevents duplicative monitoring of any given asset and prevents freeriding by other debt holders on these monitoring efforts. Moreover, each secured creditor can specialize in a class of asset (and a particular asset within the class as well), and need not worry about the interaction of risk from other assets with the risk from the asset in question. See, e.g., Jackson & Kronman, supra; Hideki Kanda & Saul Levmore, Explaining Creditor Priorities, 80 Va. L. Rev. 2103 (1994); Saul Levmore, Monitors and Freeriders in Commercial and Corporate Settings, 92 Yale L.J. 49 (1982); see also Henry Hansmann & Reinier Kraakman, The Essential Role of Organizational Law, 110 Yale L.J. 387, 406–23 (2000). In other words, the benefits of a security interest seem to be a special case of the internalization and information-cost benefits of property rights more generally. Bankruptcy, a subject for another course, has a slightly different effect on each of these rights. We return briefly to security interests in bankruptcy at the end of this Chapter.

B.   SECURITY INTERESTS IN LAND

Although we have seen that personal intangible property, especially intellectual property rights, are now more important than ever, land continues to be a convenient asset against which to borrow. The very features that make land a good candidate for centralized records—its value, fixed location, and permanence—make it a good candidate for an asset to use to secure loans, particularly long-term loans and even loans whose proceeds will be used to finance projects other than the acquisition of the real estate. The land records themselves make the functioning of mortgages smoother, although not without some bumpiness, as we will see in the next Chapter.

NOTE ON LAND TRANSACTIONS

To better understand the role of mortgages (and mortgage substitutes) and how courts have regulated them, it is necessary to locate the real estate mortgage within the larger context of a land transaction. (Sales of personal property tend to be more discrete events.) As noted earlier, in its form the mortgage itself sometimes resembles a sale of the real estate, particularly under the older "title" theory of the mortgage.

Some mortgages are taken on property already owned by the borrower, but many mortgages are purchase money mortgages, used to finance the acquisition of the land used as security for the loan. (Many personal property security interests likewise are purchase money security interests, and these receive special favorable treatment under the UCC. Think of security interests in consumer goods like cars or household furniture.) In transactions involving a purchase money mortgage, the source of the financing can be the seller of the asset or a financial institution. In the case of financial institutions, the mortgages are very often bought and sold, often in packages, to other institutions.

A land transaction is stretched out over time, and extends from negotiation, to contract execution, to closing and delivery, and finally recordation. Consider the purchase of residential real estate. The seller will usually employ a real estate agent and have the property listed. The buyer will often have a real estate agent during the search process. When the buyer is interested in a particular property, the buyer will ask her real estate agent, or possibly a lawyer, to make an offer in writing. This may be preceded or followed by negotiation. Once a written offer is accepted by the seller it is a contract, which will govern the dealings of the seller and the buyer until the closing. The Statute of Frauds requires any contract for the sale of real estate to be in writing (and signed by the person against whom it is being enforced). The real estate broker engaged by the seller will earn a commission, a percentage of the final sales price. States vary in terms of when the broker earns this commission. The law in many states provides a default rule that the broker earns the commission when the broker finds a buyer who is "ready, willing, and able" to buy the property. In such states, if the seller chooses not to sell, the seller is still liable to the broker for the commission (unless the seller and the broker have contracted for something else).

Once the contract is signed, the purchaser will seek credit to finance the purchase and will have the state of the title investigated. We will consider financing more in this Chapter and title in the next. Title examination will also be accompanied by an inspection of the premises for defects and facts, like possession by a third party, which might call the seller's title into question. As we will see in the next Chapter, the lawyer might check the land records and any other relevant records, or hire a title expert to conduct the search. Some of these title companies maintain their own set of records, called "title plants." Such companies will often insure title against the types of defects that a search should uncover, but not against facts like adverse possession that such a record search would not reveal.

The contract will state that the seller will provide marketable title at the closing. Marketable title is title that is free from defects and encumbrances but is not perfect title; rather some notion of reasonableness animates this standard, such that marketable title is sometimes said to be title that is free from reasonable doubt or title that a reasonable person would accept. Such a person is not expected to "purchase a lawsuit," though. For example, a claim of adverse possession or someone else's colorable claim to have title would make title unmarketable. An encroachment of a building like those we saw in Chapter I would make title unmarketable (and would involve the purchase of a lawsuit), but an overhanging awning or cornice probably would not render title unmarketable. A body of case law has built up around the notion of marketable title, in cases in which purchasers have tried to back out of the deal based on the failure to provide marketable title. 1 Milton R. Friedman, Contracts and Conveyances of Real Property ch. 4 (6th ed. 1998).

At the closing, the parties will execute the necessary documents and effect the transfers. The seller will execute and deliver the deed to the buyer. The buyer will make out a check to the seller for the rest of the purchase price (or will direct her attorney to disburse funds from an escrow account into which the purchase money was deposited prior to the closing), and will execute a note and mortgage for the lender. After the closing the contract is no longer operative but is said to "merge" with the deed. This means that any covenants that continue to bind the seller must be part of the deed if they are to bind at all. And if there is breach the buyer must sue on the deed, not the land sale contract. Deeds come in different varieties, depending on what sort of guarantee the seller makes to the buyer. A general warranty deed contains a covenant by the seller that he is able to, and does, convey good title to the buyer. It usually contains covenants that the seller has possession, the right to convey, that there are no encumbrances (easements, mortgages, etc.) other than those stated in the deed, that the seller will defend the buyer's title against attack, that the buyer will have quiet enjoyment, and that the seller will execute any further documents needed to provide clear title. By contrast, a quitclaim deed contains no covenant of title; such a deed conveys to the buyer whatever the seller had but contains no assurance as to what that is. A special warranty deed gives a covenant against title defects stemming from acts of the grantor and related parties, but not other defects. Again, deed covenants can be supplemented by title insurance.

Robert H. Skilton, *Developments in Mortgage Law and Practice*, 17 TEMP. U. L.Q. 315, 318–20, 321–31 (1943)

I. *Foreclosure by Court Action*

The type of foreclosure usually employed in England at the end of the seventeenth century was the old "strict foreclosure," whereby the mortgagee, without a sale of the premises, was decreed full owner of the property. Occasionally, where the mortgagor's interests seemed to demand it, a public sale was decreed, and in this case the mortgagee was not privileged to bid. He was, in case the property was sold for an amount less than his claim, entitled to a deficiency judgment. It was not possible, however, for him to acquire the property by strict foreclosure and thereafter claim a deficiency. He could have one but not both; either possession and title to the property, or the proceeds of sale of the property to a third party, and a claim for the balance due. * * *

The remedy of foreclosure, when imported into the colonies, naturally was subjected to modifications thought to be compatible with domestic needs. As time went on, strict foreclosure was supplanted in practically all states by foreclosure followed by public sale. This change was achieved sometimes simply by court practice, not re-enforced by statute; sometimes by statutes permitting courts to order a sale of mortgaged premises in their discretion; and, especially since codes of civil practice became current, frequently by statutory provision making public sale mandatory. * * *

By 1830, it would seem that strict foreclosure had been superseded in the great majority of states by foreclosure through public sale. In developing the device of public sale, American courts generally made these innovations[:] (1) they permitted the mortgagee to bid in the property himself; (2) they permitted him a claim for the difference between sale price and original claim, thus regarding the sale price as conclusively establishing value. Statutory formulae, developed for the administration of this new process of public sale, accounted, in part, for the growing tendency to treat public sale as finally cutting off the mortgagor's interest, with no succeeding period of redemption—contrary to the English practice in strict foreclosure. These innovations, apparently first appearing in New York cases in the early nineteenth century,[†] represented substantial concessions to the mortgagee: they made his remedies much more potent. * * *

III. *Foreclosure by Writ of Entry and by Peaceful Possession*

In Massachusetts, New Hampshire and Rhode Island, another type of remedy on the mortgage developed from colonial origins. The mortgagor's equity of redemption was barred by the running of a period of possession by the mortgagee after default. The remedy was achieved by a drastic shortening of the prescriptive period necessary to bar the equity of redemption by adverse possession. As early as 1698, a Massachusetts statute laid the

† [See, e.g., Mills v. Dennis, 3 Johns. Ch. 367 (N.Y. 1817) (Kent, Ch.).—eds.]

framework of present law, by shortening the period to three years. Since that time a series of statutes has clarified and developed the remedy. The former necessity of actual possession during the period has disappeared. Constructive possession by the mortgagee is now sufficient. The period runs from the time of notice of its commencement after default; either the written consent of the mortgagor to its commencement is necessary, or written notice must be served on the mortgagor, and a certificate to this effect filed of record. * * *

The remedy thus developed, of course, resembles strict foreclosure in that the final outcome is the conferment of full title upon the mortgagee, without public sale. But it seems to be a derivative of previous English rules relating to prescription. * * *

The remedy has been adopted in certain western states. Section 345 of the California Civil Code (enacted April I, 1872) provided:

> Action to Redeem. An action to redeem a mortgage of real property, with or without an account of rents and profits, may be brought by the mortgagor or those claiming under him, against the mortgagee in possession, or those claiming under him, unless he or they have continuously maintained an adverse possession of the mortgaged premises for five years after breach of some condition in the mortgage.[40]

Massachusetts, New Hampshire and Rhode Island, however, appear to be the only states where this method of acquiring title to mortgaged premises is frequent. An examination of case lists under this category revealed that extremely few cases arise from other jurisdictions. * * *

V. *Foreclosure by Power of Sale*

Not satisfied with the costly and complicated system of equitable foreclosure obtaining at the end of the eighteenth century, draftsmen representing mortgagees hit upon the idea of inserting in mortgage indentures an express authority to the mortgagee to sell the property without court action, freed of the equity of redemption. The legality of this device was at first questioned in England [but eventually won wide acceptance and approval, and even statutory authorization].

Powers of sale were recognized as valid in many states at an earlier date than in England. * * *

The growing popularity of this device was accompanied by statutes passed in most of the states, establishing conditions of advertisement and sale that had to be met in the valid exercise of the power. These statutes sometimes served to permit the sale out of court of mortgaged premises where no express power of sale was included. There is much statutory material on this point. Illustrative is the case of New York. In 1774 legislation specifically authorized the exercise of such power, thus clearing previous doubts as to its validity. Notice of sale was to be given by publication and posting. In 1844 the statute was amended to prescribe

---

40. Deering, Code of Civ. Proc. par. 346 (1923).

notice by personal service or mail, in addition to the previously stipulated methods. In 1857 it was provided that a copy of the notice should be delivered to the county clerk, and affixed to a book. In 1808 it was provided that the affidavit of the printer should be evidence of publication, posting and notice. In 1838 the mortgagee was permitted to buy the property himself. These and other statutes create a background for the exercise of the power, and their mandatory provisions must be fully complied with if a valid exercise is to be made, regardless of easier requirements in the mortgage.

Although recognized as lawful by the courts in many states, and in some cases reinforced by statutory authority, powers of sale continued to be viewed by courts with jealousy, as an invasion of their sphere. * * *

Restrictive judicial tendencies were carried to the extent in Virginia and other southern states that a power of sale given personally to the mortgagee was held to be invalid, and the practice developed of naming a third party as trustee to exercise the power. The result is that today in many southern states, and elsewhere, the deed of trust is the popular security device. * * *

Powers of sale out of court, either in mortgages or deeds of trust, have developed in popularity until they are in many states the chief method of foreclosure. They achieved such popularity because of the simplicity, speed and cheapness of their execution. There are but two steps necessary: notice and sale. * * *

By the time powers of sale received general acceptance, the tide of judicial and legislative interest in the problems of the mortgagee had spent itself. The United States was now beginning to experience a series of land and business depressions which resulted from its emergence as an industrial community. In the business downswings, the pressure of financially distressed classes of the community became too heavy to resist. From the early part of the nineteenth century to the present day, depression legislation has played a large part in shaping the mortgage into a legal cast designedly quite favorable to the interests of the mortgagor. [One influence of economic depressions was] the introduction of statutory periods of redemption in many states. . . .

VI. *The Development of Statutory Periods of Redemption*

A statutory period of redemption is to be distinguished from an equity of redemption in that the former is established by the legislature, the latter by adjudication. [T]he tendency has been to view foreclosure as finally terminating or barring the equity of redemption. On the other hand, the statutory period of redemption usually runs after foreclosure sale, being a period of grace which reminds us of a former practice of Chancery courts in allowing at least six months after foreclosure for the mortgagor to redeem. A summary of the growth and spread of this statutory period of redemption, now obtaining in a majority of the states, particularly western and central, may be interesting.

It seems clear that the first redemption period established by legislatures came as a consequence of early depressions, at a time when the courts had just abandoned their practice of granting the right to redeem after sale. This type of legislation may be traced back to 1820, when the country was sharing in the international economic disturbance following the Napoleonic Wars—in our country evidenced by the collapse of a land boom. The earliest redemptive legislation, however, did not specifically deal with mortgage sales: It referred to execution sales generally, and, as a matter of fact, was construed in two decisions not to include mortgage sales. But it may be viewed as the starting point from which mortgage redemptive legislation sprang.

New York legislation, passed April 12, 1820, provided that on execution sales of land, the sheriff should deliver to the purchaser a certificate, instead of a deed to the land itself: the certificate should recite the terms of the sale. The debtor could redeem within one year of sale. Apparently he kept possession of the property in the meantime. Specific reference was not made to the case of mortgage foreclosure sales. In *Tenbrook v. Lansing*,[58] the New York Act was declared inapplicable to foreclosures. * * *

Later legislatures were more specific. When the next depression came along, introduced by the panic of 1836, new redemption legislation was passed in some states; and now mortgage foreclosures are expressly included. From that time to this we may note the general tendency of legislation to give the mortgage debtors the same redemption rights as ordinary contract debtors. The New York Act of 1837 provided for redemption within one year after sale of real estate sold on foreclosure of a mortgage. The Illinois Act of 1841 specifically embraced mortgages. In 1842 Alabama authorized the redemption of mortgaged premises within two years after sale. In 1839 Michigan provided that the Chancellor shall not order the sale of mortgaged premises at a time less than two years and three months from the date of the filing of the bill. * * *

These early redemption statutes came as a result of depression periods, and may be associated with the general collapse of land values, the failure of governmental public land policy, and governmental relief and moratory measures in connection with the sale of public land. Other factors accounted for later developments. The next steps in the development of redemption periods, oddly enough, are associated with the spread of codes of civil practice: the movement for the simplification of civil procedure which began in 1848 with the adoption of the Field Code in New York. This movement, more legalistic than economic in motivation, accounts for the presence of redemption periods in the laws of most of the western states. * * *

The economic disturbances of the last decade of the nineteenth century contributed to the tendency to enlarge the period of redemption to one year. [Between the years 1886 and 1897, Washington, Idaho, Oregon, Montana and California all changed their period of redemption to a year.]

The reasons which led to the extension of redemption periods during the nineties appear to have been largely economic. * * *

---

58. 4 Johns. Ch. 601 (N.Y. 1820).

On the other hand, when business is on the upswing, there appears to be a tendency to shorten the redemption period, as an incentive to new investment. For example, the Michigan period was reduced by the Act of September 23, 1899, which provided that the court should not order a sale until six months after the filing of the bill, and that thereafter the debtor should have six months within which to redeem. Previously the mortgagor had two years and three months before sale. In 1889 Wisconsin, as part of a code amendment, reduced its previous two year period (established in 1849) to one year. * * *

Another tendency to weaken the effect of the redemption period developed in statutory or judicial approval of waiver of redemption rights. If validated by court or legislature, a waiver of a debtor's right to redeem virtually destroys the principle of redemption. It becomes a matter of form to include waiver provisions in all mortgages. For example, recognition of the power to waive debtor's exemption in Pennsylvania has resulted in the general inclusion of waiver clauses in all of the many form contracts used in that state. Courts frequently permit the destruction of a right by waiver by invoking the principle of "freedom of contract." In addition to some instances of judicial approval of waiver clauses in the present field, there is at least one case of legislative permission.

As they existed on the eve of the last depression, the redemption laws of the states were extremely varied. The laws of the states differed in many important respects. There were also gross inconsistencies. In California, for example, there was a redemptive period of twelve months if foreclosure was by court action, but none if foreclosure was by power of sale. Between the states, the laws differed extremely. Differences existed not only with respect to the length of the time of redemption, but also with respect to: (1) whether the redemption period preceded or succeeded the sale; (2) whether the debtor was allowed to retain possession of the mortgaged premises in the interim period; (3) the amount to be paid as the redemptive price. In Indiana, Nebraska, Oklahoma and Wisconsin, the redemptive period preceded the sale. In Washington, Oregon, California, Nevada, Montana, Idaho, Utah, Wyoming, Arizona, Colorado, New Mexico, North Dakota, South Dakota, Kansas, Minnesota, Iowa, Missouri, Arkansas, Illinois, Michigan, Indiana, Kentucky, Tennessee, Alabama, Vermont and Maine it followed sale. The remaining states, in the east and south, had no redemption periods. Nineteen states had redemption periods of one year; five states, of six months; two of nine months; two of two years; one of eighteen months. Nineteen states had no redemption periods. Of those with redemption periods, four allowed the mortgagee to take possession of the premises during the interim period.

Murphy v. Financial Development Corporation

Supreme Court of New Hampshire, 1985.
495 A.2d 1245.

■ Douglas, Justice. The plaintiffs brought this action seeking to set aside the foreclosure sale of their home, or, in the alternative, money damages.

The Superior Court (*Bean,* J.), adopting the recommendation of a Master (*R. Peter Shapiro,* Esq.), entered a judgment for the plaintiffs in the amount of $27,000 against two of the defendants, Financial Development Corporation and Colonial Deposit Company (the lenders).

The plaintiffs purchased a house in Nashua in 1966, financing it by means of a mortgage loan. They refinanced the loan in March of 1980, executing a new promissory note and a power of sale mortgage, with Financial Development Corporation as mortgagee. The note and mortgage were later assigned to Colonial Deposit Company.

In February of 1981, the plaintiff Richard Murphy became unemployed. By September of 1981, the plaintiffs were seven months in arrears on their mortgage payments, and had also failed to pay substantial amounts in utility assessments and real estate taxes. After discussing unsuccessfully with the plaintiffs proposals for revising the payment schedule, rewriting the note, and arranging alternative financing, the lenders gave notice on October 6, 1981, of their intent to foreclose.

During the following weeks, the plaintiffs made a concerted effort to avoid foreclosure. They paid the seven months' mortgage arrearage, but failed to pay some $643.18 in costs and legal fees associated with the foreclosure proceedings. The lenders scheduled the foreclosure sale for November 10, 1981, at the site of the subject property. They complied with all of the statutory requirements for notice. See RSA 479:25.

At the plaintiffs' request, the lenders agreed to postpone the sale until December 15, 1981. They advised the plaintiffs that this would entail an additional cost of $100, and that the sale would proceed unless the lenders received payment of $743.18, as well as all mortgage payments then due, by December 15. Notice of the postponement was posted on the subject property on November 10 at the originally scheduled time of the sale, and was also posted at the Nashua City Hall and Post Office. No prospective bidders were present for the scheduled sale.

In late November, the plaintiffs paid the mortgage payment which had been due in October, but made no further payments to the lenders. An attempt by the lenders to arrange new financing for the plaintiffs through a third party failed when the plaintiffs refused to agree to pay for a new appraisal of the property. Early on the morning of December 15, 1981, the plaintiffs tried to obtain a further postponement, but were advised by the lenders' attorney that it was impossible unless the costs and legal fees were paid.

At the plaintiffs' request, the attorney called the president of Financial Development Corporation, who also refused to postpone the sale. Further calls by the plaintiffs to the lenders' offices were equally unavailing.

The sale proceeded as scheduled at 10:00 a.m. on December 15, at the site of the property. Although it had snowed the previous night, the weather was clear and warm at the time of the sale, and the roads were clear. The only parties present were the plaintiffs, a representative of the lenders, and an attorney, Morgan Hollis, who had been engaged to conduct the sale because the lenders' attorney, who lived in Dover, had been apprehensive about the weather the night before. The lenders' representative made the only bid at the sale. That bid of $27,000, roughly the amount owed on the mortgage, plus costs and fees, was accepted and the sale concluded.

Later that same day, Attorney Hollis encountered one of his clients, William Dube, a representative of the defendant Southern New Hampshire Home Traders, Inc. (Southern). On being informed of the sale, Mr. Dube contacted the lenders and offered to buy the property for $27,000. The lenders rejected the offer and made a counter offer of $40,000. Within two days a purchase price of $38,000 was agreed upon by Mr. Dube and the lenders and the sale was subsequently completed.

The plaintiffs commenced this action on February 5, 1982. The lenders moved to dismiss, arguing that any action was barred because the plaintiffs had failed to petition for an injunction prior to the sale. The master denied the motion. After hearing the evidence, he ruled for the plaintiffs, finding that the lenders had "failed to exercise good faith and due diligence in obtaining a fair price for the subject property at the foreclosure sale...."

The master also ruled that Southern was a bona fide purchaser for value, and thus had acquired legal title to the house. That ruling is not at issue here. He assessed monetary damages against the lenders equal to "the difference between the fair market value of the subject property on the date of the foreclosure and the price obtained at said sale."

Having found the fair market value to be $54,000, he assessed damages accordingly at $27,000. He further ruled that "[t]he bad faith of the 'Lenders' warrants an award of legal fees." The lenders appealed.

The first issue before us is whether the master erred in denying the motion to dismiss. The lenders, in support of their argument, rely upon RSA 479:25, II, which gives a mortgagor the right to petition the superior court to enjoin a proposed foreclosure sale, and then provides: "Failure to institute such petition and complete service upon the foreclosing party, or his agent, conducting the sale prior to sale shall thereafter bar any action or right of action of the mortgagor based on the validity of the foreclosure."

If we were to construe this provision as the lenders urge us to do, it would prevent a mortgagor from challenging the validity of a sale in a case where the only claimed unfairness or illegality occurred during the sale itself—unless the mortgagor had petitioned for an injunction before any grounds existed on which the injunction could be granted. We will not construe a statute so as to produce such an illogical and unjust result.

The only reasonable construction of the language in RSA 479:25, II relied upon by the lenders is that it bars any action based on facts which the mortgagor knew or should have known soon enough to reasonably permit the filing of a petition prior to the sale.

The master could not have found that this was such an action, because the only unfairness referred to in his report involves the amount of the sale price. Thus, his denial of the lenders' motion to dismiss was proper.

The second issue before us is whether the master erred in concluding that the lenders had failed to comply with the often-repeated rule that a mortgagee executing a power of sale is bound both by the statutory procedural requirements *and* by a duty to protect the interests of the mortgagor through the exercise of good faith and due diligence. We will not overturn a master's findings and rulings "unless they are unsupported by the evidence or are erroneous as a matter of law." Summit Electric, Inc. v. Pepin Brothers Const., Inc., 427 A.2d 505, 507 (N.H. 1981).

The master found that the lenders, throughout the time prior to the sale, "did not mislead or deal unfairly with the plaintiffs." They engaged in serious efforts to avoid foreclosure through new financing, and agreed to one postponement of the sale. The basis for the master's decision was his conclusion that the lenders had failed to exercise good faith and due diligence in obtaining a fair price for the property.

This court's past decisions have not dealt consistently with the question whether the mortgagee's duty amounts to that of a fiduciary or trustee. Compare Pearson v. Gooch, 40 A. 390, 390–91 (N.H. 1897) and Merrimack Industrial Trust v. First Nat. Bank of Boston, 427 A.2d 500, 504 (N.H. 1981) (duty amounts to that of a fiduciary or trustee) with Silver v. First National Bank, 236 A.2d 493, 494–95 (N.H. 1967) and Proctor v. Bank of N.H., 464 A.2d 263, 266 (N.H. 1983) (duty does not amount to that of a fiduciary or trustee). This may be an inevitable result of the mortgagee's dual role as seller and potential buyer at the foreclosure sale, and of the conflicting interests involved.

We need not label a duty, however, in order to define it. In his role as a seller, the mortgagee's duty of good faith and due diligence is essentially that of a fiduciary. Such a view is in keeping with "[t]he 'trend . . . towards liberalizing the term [fiduciary] in order to prevent unjust enrichment.' " Lash v. Cheshire County Savings Bank, Inc., 474 A.2d 980, 981 (N.H. 1984) (quoting Cornwell v. Cornwell, 356 A.2d 683, 686 (N.H. 1976)).

A mortgagee, therefore, must exert every reasonable effort to obtain "a fair and reasonable price under the circumstances," Reconstruction &c. Corp. v. Faulkner, 143 A.2d 403, 410 (N.H. 1958), even to the extent, if necessary, of adjourning the sale or of establishing "an upset price below which he will not accept any offer." Lakes Region Fin. Corp. v. Goodhue Boat Yard, Inc., 382 A.2d 1108, 1111 (N.H. 1978).

What constitutes a fair price, or whether the mortgagee must establish an upset price, adjourn the sale, or make other reasonable efforts to assure a fair price, depends on the circumstances of each case. Inadequacy of price alone is not sufficient to demonstrate bad faith unless the price is so low as to shock the judicial conscience.

We must decide, in the present case, whether the evidence supports the finding of the master that the lenders failed to exercise good faith and due diligence in obtaining a fair price for the plaintiffs' property.

We first note that "[t]he duties of good faith and due diligence are distinct. . . . One may be observed and not the other, and any inquiry as to their breach calls for a separate consideration of each." Wheeler v. Slocinski, 131 A. 600, 600 (N.H. 1926). In order "to constitute bad faith there must be an intentional disregard of duty or a purpose to injure." Id. at 600–01.

There is insufficient evidence in the record to support the master's finding that the lenders acted in bad faith in failing to obtain a fair price for the plaintiffs' property. The lenders complied with the statutory requirements of notice and otherwise conducted the sale in compliance with statutory provisions. The lenders postponed the sale one time and did not bid with knowledge of any immediately available subsequent purchaser. Further, there is no evidence indicating an intent on the part of the lenders to injure the mortgagor by, for example, discouraging other buyers.

There is ample evidence in the record, however, to support the master's finding that the lenders failed to exercise due diligence in obtaining a fair price. "The issue of the lack of due diligence is whether a reasonable man in the [lenders'] place would have adjourned the sale," id. at 601, or taken other measures to receive a fair price.

In early 1980, the plaintiffs' home was appraised at $46,000. At the time of the foreclosure sale on December 15, 1981, the lenders had not had the house reappraised to take into account improvements and appreciation. The master found that a reasonable person in the place of the lenders would have realized that the plaintiffs' equity in the property was at least $19,000, the difference between the 1980 appraised value of $46,000 and the amount owed on the mortgage totaling approximately $27,000.

At the foreclosure sale, the lenders were the only bidders. The master found that their bid of $27,000 "was sufficient to cover all monies due and did not create a deficiency balance" but "did not provide for a return of any of the plaintiffs' equity."

Further, the master found that the lenders "had reason to know" that "they stood to make a substantial profit on a quick turnaround sale." On the day of the sale, the lenders offered to sell the foreclosed property to William Dube for $40,000. Within two days after the foreclosure sale, they did in fact agree to sell it to Dube for $38,000. It was not necessary for the master to find that the lenders knew of a specific potential buyer before the sale in order to show lack of good faith or due diligence as the lenders contend. The fact that the lenders offered the property for sale at a price sizably above that for which they had purchased it, only a few hours before, supports the master's finding that the lenders had reason to know, at the time of the foreclosure sale, that they could make a substantial profit on a quick turnaround sale. For this reason, they should have taken more measures to ensure receiving a higher price at the sale.

While a mortgagee may not always be required to secure a portion of the mortgagor's equity, such an obligation did exist in this case. The substantial amount of equity which the plaintiffs had in their property, the knowledge of the lenders as to the appraised value of the property, and the plaintiffs' efforts to forestall foreclosure by paying the mortgage arrearage within weeks of the sale, all support the master's conclusion that the lenders had a fiduciary duty to take more reasonable steps than they did to protect the plaintiffs' equity by attempting to obtain a fair price for the property. They could have established an appropriate upset price to assure a minimum bid. They also could have postponed the auction and advertised commercially by display advertising in order to assure that bidders other than themselves would be present.

Instead, as Theodore DiStefano, an officer of both lending institutions testified, the lenders made no attempt to obtain fair market value for the property but were concerned *only* with making themselves "whole." On the facts of this case, such disregard for the interests of the mortgagors was a breach of duty by the mortgagees.

Although the lenders *did* comply with the statutory requirements of notice of the foreclosure sale, these efforts were not sufficient in this case to demonstrate due diligence. At the time of the initially scheduled sale, the extent of the lenders' efforts to publicize the sale of the property was publication of a legal notice of the mortgagees' sale at public auction on November 10, published once a week for three weeks in the Nashua Telegraph, plus postings in public places. The lenders did not advertise, publish, or otherwise give notice to the general public of postponement of the sale to December 15, 1981, other than by posting notices at the plaintiffs' house, at the post office, and at city hall. That these efforts to advertise were ineffective is evidenced by the fact that no one, other than the lenders, appeared at the sale to bid on the property. This fact allowed the lenders to purchase the property at a minimal price and then to profit substantially in a quick turnaround sale.

We recognize a need to give guidance to a trial court which must determine whether a mortgagee who has complied with the strict letter of the statutory law has nevertheless violated his additional duties of good faith and due diligence. A finding that the mortgagee had, or should have had, knowledge of his ability to get a higher price at an adjourned sale is the most conclusive evidence of such a violation. See Lakes Region Fin. Corp. v. Goodhue Boat Yard, Inc., 382 A.2d at 1111.

More generally, we are in agreement with the official Commissioners' Comment to section 3–508 of the Uniform Land Transactions Act:

> The requirement that the sale be conducted in a reasonable manner, including the advertising aspects, requires that the person conducting the sale use the ordinary methods of making buyers aware that are used when an owner is voluntarily selling his land. Thus an advertisement in the portion of a daily newspaper where these ads are placed or, in appropriate cases such as the sale of an industrial plant, a display advertisement in the financial sections of the daily newspaper may be the most reasonable method. In other cases employment of a professional real estate agent may be the more reasonable method. It is unlikely that an advertisement in a legal publication among other legal notices would qualify as a commercially reasonable method of sale advertising.

13 Uniform Laws Annotated 704 (West 1980). As discussed above, the lenders met neither of these guidelines.

While agreeing with the master that the lenders failed to exercise due diligence in this case, we find that he erred as a matter of law in awarding damages equal to "the difference between the fair market value of the subject property . . . and the price obtained at [the] sale."

Such a formula may well be the appropriate measure where *bad faith* is found. In such a case, a mortgagee's conduct amounts to more than mere negligence. Damages based upon the *fair market value,* a figure in excess of a *fair* price, will more readily induce mortgagees to perform their duties properly. A "fair" price may or may not yield a figure close to fair market value; however, it will be that price arrived at as a result of due diligence by the mortgagee.

Where, as here, however, a mortgagee fails to exercise due diligence, the proper assessment of damages is the difference between a fair price for the property and the price obtained at the foreclosure sale. We have held, where lack of due diligence has been found, that "the test is not 'fair market value' as in eminent domain cases nor is the mortgagee bound to give credit for the highest possible amount which might be obtained under different circumstances, as at an owner's sale." Silver v. First National Bank, 236 A.2d 493, 495 (N.H. 1967) (quoting Reconstruction &c. Corp. v. Faulkner, 143 A.2d 403, 410 (N.H. 1958)) (citation omitted). Accordingly, we remand to the trial court for a reassessment of damages consistent with this opinion.

Because we concluded above that there was no "bad faith or obstinate, unjust, vexatious, wanton, or oppressive conduct," on the part of the lenders, we see no reason to stray from our general rule that the prevailing litigant is not entitled to collect attorney's fees from the loser. Therefore, we reverse this part of the master's decision.

Reversed in part; affirmed in part; remanded.

■ BROCK, JUSTICE, dissenting: I agree with the majority that a mortgagee, in its role as seller at a foreclosure sale, has a fiduciary duty to the mortgagor. I also agree with the majority's more specific analysis of that duty * * *, including its references to the commissioners' comment to the U.L.T.A., as well as those to *Wheeler* and other decisions of this court.

On the record presently before us, however, I cannot see any support for the master's finding that the lenders here failed to exercise due diligence as we have defined that term. I would remand the case to the superior court for further findings of fact.

Specifically, the master made no findings regarding what an "owner . . . voluntarily selling his land" would have done that the lenders here did not do, in order to obtain a fair price. * * *

Although the report nowhere states specifically *what* the lenders should have done, its clear implication is that they should have made a higher bid at the foreclosure sale.

There is no authority for such a conclusion. The mortgagee's fiduciary duty extends only to its role as a *seller*. Once the mortgagee has exerted every reasonable effort to obtain a fair price (which may sometimes include setting an upset price and adjourning the sale if no bidder meets that price), it has no further obligation in its role as a potential buyer.

As the majority notes, a low price is not of itself sufficient to invalidate a foreclosure sale, unless the price is "so low as to shock the judicial conscience." The price here was clearly not that low. Cf. Shipp Corp., Inc. v. Charpilloz, 414 So.2d 1122, 1124 (Fla. Dist. Ct. App. 1982) (bid of $1.1 million was not grossly inadequate compared to a market value of between $2.8 and $3.2 million).

Because it is unclear whether the master applied the correct standard regarding the mortgagee's duty, and because the record as presently constituted cannot support a determination that the lenders violated that standard, I respectfully dissent.

NOTES AND QUESTIONS

1. The duty of the mortgagee to obtain a fair price extends to the defaulting mortgagor. Might it extend to others? In DeLellis v. Burke, 598 A.2d 203 (N.H. 1991), the New Hampshire Supreme Court declined to extend the fiduciary duty of the mortgagee recognized in *Murphy* to other creditors of the mortgagor.

2. What is the minimum the mortgagee could have done to avoid liability here? Which is likely to be the better approach: A rule spelling out which procedures are sufficient (a safe harbor, if you will)? Or an ex post standard? Or some combination of the two? What exactly does it mean to obtain a "fair" price for property at a judicial sale? The concept of "fair market value" is well developed in the context of eminent domain: It is the value that a willing buyer would pay a willing seller for similar property in an arm's length transaction. See Chapter XII.A. The court indicates that a "fair" price can be less than fair market value, but exactly how close it must be is left pretty vague.

3. Even if a court sides with the mortgagor in a case like *Murphy*, mortgagors with substantial equity would be well-advised to try to sell the property themselves, if at all possible. The mortgagor is likely to get a much better price than the lender, even if spurred by the threat of *Murphy*-style litigation. Consider the Murphys. If they sell on their own, they can give clean title to the purchaser, and they should realize the fair market value. But if the property is sold by the lender through foreclosure, it will be subject to any common law or statutory rights of redemption that the Murphys have, which means it will sell at a substantial discount from its market value. The Murphys selling the house themselves thus looks like a win-win proposition: The lender gets its money back without incurring the costs of foreclosure, and the Murphys get to pocket the full amount of their equity in the house without having to spend time and money suing the lender. Given that the Murphys appear to have significant equity in the

house beyond the mortgage balance, why didn't they follow this course of action once it became clear that they would otherwise lose the house? They appear to be unwilling to take action themselves, preferring to sit and watch while the mortgagee sells their home at the foreclosure sale. How unusual do you suppose this response is for a family in financial crisis? If mortgagees have a fiduciary duty to try to get a "fair" price for the property through a judicial foreclosure sale, should mortgagors have a duty not to destroy value by doing nothing to prevent property with positive equity from going to foreclosure?

4.   There are substitutes to the mortgage for providing security in the transfer of real estate. Probably the most commonly encountered substitute is the land sale contract (or installment sale contract), considered in the next case. One reason to use a substitute like the land sale contract is to avoid the many restrictions on mortgages and mortgage foreclosures imposed by legislatures and courts over the years. As *Murphy* suggests, these restrictions add to the costs and risks of using mortgages. Another reason is to provide credit to persons who present an especially high risk of default. Land sale contracts are often used to finance a purchase of real estate when the prospective purchaser is unable to obtain financing from a bank or other professional lending institution, either because credit markets are tight or the purchaser is a very poor credit risk. In these circumstances, the seller may elect to finance the sale him or herself, by using a land sale contract.

Skendzel v. Marshall

Supreme Court of Indiana, 1973.
301 N.E.2d 641.

■ HUNTER, JUSTICE. Petitioners seek transfer to this Court as a result of an adverse ruling by the Court of Appeals. Plaintiff-respondents originally brought suit to obtain possession of certain real estate through the enforcement of a forfeiture clause in a land sale contract. Plaintiff-respondents suffered a negative judgment, from which they appealed. The Court of Appeals reversed, holding that the defendant-petitioners had breached the contract and that the plaintiff-respondents had not waived their right to [enforce] the forfeiture provisions of the contract.

In December of 1958, Mary Burkowski, as vendor, entered into a land sale contract with Charles P. Marshall and Agnes P. Marshall, as vendees. The contract provided for the sale of certain real estate for the sum of $36,000.00, payable as follows:

> $500.00, at the signing, execution and delivery of this contract, the receipt whereof is hereby acknowledged; $500.00 or more on or before the 25th day of December, 1958, and $2500.00 or more on or before the 15th day of January, 1960, and $2500.00 or more on or before the 15th day of January of each and every year thereafter until the balance of the contract has been fully paid, all without interest and all without relief from valuation and appraisement laws and with attorney fees.

The contract also contained a fairly standard section which provided for the treatment of prepayments—but which the Court of Appeals found to be of particular importance. It provided as follows:

> Should Vendees have made prepayments or paid in advance of the payments herein required, said prepayments, if any, shall at any time thereafter be applied in lieu of further principal payments required as herein stated, to the extent of such prepayments only.

The following is the forfeiture/liquidated damages provision of the land sale contract:

> It is further agreed that if any default shall be made in the payment of said purchase price or any of the covenants and/or conditions herein provided, and if any such default shall continue for 30 days, then, after the lapse of said 30 days' period, *all moneys and payments previously paid shall, at the option of the Vendor without notice or demand, be and become forfeited and be taken and retained by the Vendor as liquidated damages* and thereupon this contract shall terminate and be of no further force or effect; provided, however, that nothing herein contained shall be deemed or construed to prevent the Vendor from enforcing specific performance of this agreement in the event of any default on the part of the Vendees in complying, observing and performing any of the conditions, covenants and terms herein contained. * * *. (Emphasis added.)

The vendor, Mary Burkowski, died in 1963. The plaintiffs in this action are the assignees (under the vendor's will) of the decedent's interests in the contract. They received their assignment from the executrix of the estate of the vendor on June 27, 1968. One year after this assignment, several of the assignees filed their complaint in this action alleging that the defendants had defaulted through non-payment.

The schedule of payments made under this contract was shown by the evidence to be as follows:

Date	Amount Paid	Total of Paid Principal
12/1/1958	$ 500.00	$ 500.00
12/25/1958	500.00	1,000.00
3/26/1959	5,000.00	6,000.00
4/5/1960	2,500.00	8,500.00
5/23/1961	2,500.00	11,000.00
4/6/1962	2,500.00	13,500.00
1/15/1963	2,500.00	16,000.00
6/30/1964	2,500.00	18,500.00
2/15/1965	2,500.00	21,000.00

No payments have been made since the last one indicated above—$15,000.00 remains to be paid on the original contract price.

In response to the plaintiff's attempt to enforce the forfeiture provision, the defendants raised the affirmative defense of waiver. The applicable rule is well established and was stated by the Court of Appeals as follows:

> Where a contract for the sale and purchase of land contains provisions similar to those in the contract in the case at bar, *the vendor may waive strict compliance with the provisions of the contract by accepting overdue or irregular payments*, and having so done, equity requires the vendor give specific notice of his intent that he will no longer be indulgent and that he will insist on his right of forfeiture unless the default is paid within a reasonable and specified time. (Emphasis added.) * * *

It follows that where the vendor has not waived strict compliance by acceptance of late payments, no notice is required to enforce its provisions.

In essence, the Court of Appeals found that there was no waiver because the vendors were obligated to accept prepayment, and, "the payments made, although irregular in time and amount, were prepayments on the unpaid balance through and including the payment due on January 15, 1965." (289 N.E.2d at 771.) The Court concluded that up to January 15, 1966, "the vendors waived no rights under the contract, because they were obliged to accept prepayment." (Id.) and that, "(t)he vendors could not have insisted on forfeiture prior to January 15, 1966, the date of the first missed payment." (Id.) (We believe the Court of Appeals miscalculated here; the vendors could not have insisted on forfeiture until January 16, 1968.)

If forfeiture is enforced against the defendants, they will forfeit outright the sum of $21,000, or well over one-half the original contract price, as liquidated damages *plus possession*.

Forfeitures are generally disfavored by the law. In fact, ". . . (e)quity abhors forfeitures and beyond any question has jurisdiction, which it will exercise in a proper case to grant relief against their enforcement." 30 C.J.S. Equity § 56 (1965) and cases cited therein. This jurisdiction of equity to intercede is predicated upon the fact that "the loss or injury occasioned by the default must be susceptible of exact compensation." 30 C.J.S., supra. * * *

Paragraph 17 of the contract, supra, provides that all prior payments "become forfeited and be taken and retained by the Vendor as liquidated damages." "Reasonable" liquidated damage provisions are permitted by the law. See 22 Am.Jur., 2d Damages § 212 (1965). However, the issue before this Court, is whether a $21,000 forfeiture is a "reasonable" measure of damages. If the damages are unreasonable, i.e., if they are disproportionate to the loss actually suffered, they must be characterized as penal rather then compensatory. Under the facts of this case, a $21,000 forfeiture is clearly excessive. * * *

If we apply the specific equitable principle announced above—namely, that the amount paid be considered in relation to the total contract price— we are compelled to conclude that the $21,000 forfeiture as liquidated damages is inconsistent with generally accepted principles of fairness and equity. The vendee has acquired a substantial interest in the property, which, if forfeited, would result in substantial injustice.

Under a typical conditional land contract, the vendor retains legal title until the total contract price is paid by the vendee. Payments are generally made in periodic installments. *Legal* title does not vest in the vendee until the contract terms are satisfied, but equitable title vests in the vendee at the time the contract is consummated. When the parties enter into the contract, all incidents of ownership accrue to the vendee. The vendee assumes the risk of loss and is the recipient of all appreciation in value. The vendee, as equitable owner, is responsible for taxes. The vendee has a sufficient interest in land so that upon sale of that interest, he holds a vendor's lien.

This Court has held, consistent with the above notions of equitable ownership, that a land contract, once consummated constitutes a present sale and purchase. The vendor "has, in effect, exchanged his property for the unconditional obligation of the vendee, the performance of which is secured by the retention of the legal title." Stark v. Kreyling, 188 N.E. 680, 682 (Ind. 1934). The Court, in effect, views a conditional land contract as a sale with a security interest in the form of legal title reserved by the vendor. Conceptually, therefore, the retention of the title by the vendor is the same as reserving a lien or mortgage. Realistically, vendor-vendee should be viewed as mortgagee-mortgagor. To conceive of the relationship in different terms is to pay homage to form over substance. * * *

It is also interesting to note that the drafters of the Uniform Commercial Code abandoned the distinction between a conditional sale and a security interest. Section 1–201 of the UCC (IC 1971, 26–1–1–201) (Ind. Ann.Stat. § 19–1–201 (1964 Repl.)) defines "security interest" as "an interest in personal property or fixtures which secures payment or performance of an obligation . . . retention or reservation of title by a seller of goods notwithstanding shipment or delivery to the buyer is limited in effect to a reservation of 'security interest.' " We can conceive of no rational reason why conditional sales of real estate should be treated any differently.[1]

A conditional land contract in effect creates a vendor's lien in the property to secure the unpaid balance owed under the contract. This lien is closely analogous to a mortgage—in fact, the vendor is commonly referred to as an "equitable mortgagee." In view of this characterization of the vendor as a lienholder, it is only logical that such a lien be enforced through foreclosure proceedings. Such a lien "(has) all the incidents of a mortgage" D. S. B. Johnston Land Co. v. Whipple, 234 N.W. 59, 61 (N.D. 1930), one of which is the right to foreclose. * * *

---

1. In fact, the Commissioners on Uniform State Laws have recognized the transparency of any such distinctions. Section 3–102 of the Uniform Land Transactions Code (working draft of first tentative draft) reads as follows:

This Article applies to security interests created by contract, including mortgage . . . land sales contract . . . and any other lien or title retention contract intended as security.

We believe this position is entirely consistent with the evolving case law in the area.

The vendor's interest clearly constitutes a "lien upon real estate" and should, therefore, be treated as one. The basic foreclosure statute—that is for mortgages executed after July 1, 1957—provides for a six-month period of redemption, commencing with the filing of the complaint. Additionally, it establishes the procedures attendant to the foreclosure sale. * * *

Forfeiture is closely akin to strict foreclosure—a remedy developed by the English courts which did not contemplate the equity of redemption. American jurisdictions, including Indiana, have, for the most part, rejected strict foreclosure in favor of foreclosure by judicial sale:

> The doctrine of strict foreclosure developed in England at a time when real property had, to a great extent, a fixed value; the vastly different conditions in this country, in this respect, led our courts to introduce modifications to the English rules of foreclosure. Generally, in consonance with equity's treatment of a mortgage as essentially a security for the payment of the debt, foreclosure by judicial sale supplanted strict foreclosure as the more equitable mode of effectuating the mutual rights of the mortgagor and mortgagee; and there is at the present time, in the majority of the American states, no strict foreclosure as developed by the English courts—either at law or in equity—by which a mortgagee can be adjudged absolute owner of the mortgaged property. The remedy of the mortgagee is by an action for the sale of the mortgaged premises and an application of the proceeds of such sale to the mortgage debt, and although usually called an action to foreclose, it is totally different in its character and results from a strict foreclosure. The phrase "foreclosure of a mortgage" has acquired, in general, a different meaning from that which it originally bore under the English practice and the common law imported here from England. In this country, the modern meaning of the term "foreclosure" denotes an equitable proceeding for the enforcement of a lien against property in satisfaction of a debt.

55 Am.Jur.2d, Mortgages, § 549 (1971). Guided by the above principles we are compelled to conclude that judicial foreclosure of a land sale contract is in consonance with the notions of equity developed in American jurisprudence. A forfeiture—like a strict foreclosure at common law—is often offensive to our concepts of justice and inimical to the principles of equity. This is not to suggest that a forfeiture is an inappropriate remedy for the breach of all land contracts. In the case of an abandoning, absconding vendee, forfeiture is a logical and equitable remedy. Forfeiture would also be appropriate where the vendee has paid a minimal amount on the contract at the time of default and seeks to retain possession while the vendor is paying taxes, insurance, and other upkeep in order to preserve the premises. Of course, in this latter situation, the vendee will have acquired very little, if any, equity in the property. However, a court of equity must always approach forfeitures with great caution, being forever aware of the possibility of inequitable dispossession of property and exorbitant monetary loss. We are persuaded that forfeiture may only be appropri-

ate under circumstances in which it is found to be consonant with notions of fairness and justice under the law.

In other words, we are holding a conditional land sales contract to be in the nature of a secured transaction, the provisions of which are subject to all proper and just remedies at law and in equity.

Turning our attention to the case at hand, we find that the vendor-assignees were seeking forfeiture, including $21,000 already paid on said contract as liquidated damages and immediate possession. They were, in fact, asking for strict application of the contract terms at law which we believe would have led to unconscionable results requiring the intervention of equity. "Equity delights in justice, but that not by halves." (Story, Eq.Pl. § 72.) On the facts of this case, we are of the opinion that the trial court correctly refused the remedy sought by the vendor-assignees, but in so refusing it denied all remedial relief to the plaintiffs. Equity will "look upon that as done which ought to have been done." (Story, Eq.Jur. § 64(g)). Applying the foregoing maxims to the case at bar, where such parties seek unconscionable results in such an action, equity will treat the subject matter as if the final acts and relief contemplated by the parties were accomplished exactly as they should have been in the first instance. Where discretionary power is not exercised by a trial court, under the mistaken belief that it was without this power, a remand and direction by a court of review is necessary and proper. This is not an unwarranted interference with the trial court's function. Upon appeal to this Court, we have the judicial duty to *sua sponte* direct the trial court to apply appropriate equitable principles in such a case. Consistent with such above-stated rules, this Court has the undeniable authority to remand with guidelines which will give substantial relief to plaintiffs under their secured interests and will prevent the sacrifice of the vendees' equitable lien in the property.

For all of the foregoing reasons, transfer is granted and the cause is reversed and remanded with instructions to enter a judgment of foreclosure on the vendors' lien, pursuant to Trial Rule 69(C) and the mortgage foreclosure statute (IC 1971, 32–8–16–1 (Ind.Stat.Ann., § 3–1801 (1968 Repl.))) as modified by Trial Rule 69(C). Said judgment shall include an order for the payment of the unpaid principal balance due on said contract, together with interest at 8% per annum from the date of judgment. The order may also embrace any and all other proper and equitable relief that the court deems to be just, including the discretion to issue a stay of the judicial sale of the property, all pursuant to the provisions of Trial Rule 69(C). Such order shall be consistent with the principles and holdings developed within this opinion. * * *

■ PRENTICE, JUSTICE (concurring). I have some concern that our opinion herein might be viewed by some as indicating an attitude of indifference towards the rights of contract vendors. Such a view would not be a true reflection.

Because the installment sales contract, with forfeiture provisions, is a widely employed and generally accepted method of commerce in real estate in this state, it is appropriate that a vendee seeking to avoid the forfeiture, to which he agreed, be required to make a clear showing of the inequity of enforcement. In any given transaction anything short of enforcing the forfeiture provision may be a denial of equity to the vendor. It has been set forth in the majority opinion that if the vendee has little or no real equity in the premises, the court should have no hesitancy in declaring a forfeiture. It follows that if the vendee has indicated his willingness to forego his equity, if any, whether by mere abandonment of the premises, by release or deed or by a failure to make a timely assertion of his claim, he should be barred from thereafter claiming an equity.

If the court finds that forfeiture, although provided for by the terms of the contract, would be unjust, it should nevertheless grant the vendor the maximum relief consistent with equity against a defaulting vendee. In so doing, it should consider that, had the parties known that the forfeiture provision would not be enforceable, other provisions for the protection of the vendor doubtlessly would have been incorporated into the agreement. Generally, this would require that the transaction be treated as a note and mortgage with such provisions as are generally included in such documents customarily employed in the community by prudent investors. Terms customarily included in such notes and mortgages but frequently omitted from contracts include provisions for increased interest during periods of default, provision for the acceleration of the due date of the entire unpaid principal and interest upon a default continuing beyond a reasonable grace period, provisions for attorneys' fees and other expenses incidental to foreclosure, for the waiver of relief from valuation and appraisement laws and for receivers.

NOTES AND QUESTIONS

1.   Do you think the court's reaction to the suit to recover possession would be different if the $21,000 paid by the Marshalls had been characterized as rent? $21,000 is nearly 60 percent of the purchase price, which seems like a lot to forfeit. But another way of looking at the situation is that the $21,000 entitled the Marshalls to remain in possession for nine years, which works out to $194 per month. Could the contract be drafted in such a way as to convert the payments to rent rather than speak of forfeitures?

2.   By holding that the installment sales contract is a mortgage, *Skendzel* superimposes all the protections that legislatures and courts have afforded to mortgagors, plus any that the legislature might add later, onto the land sale contract. Is this outcome advantageous to purchasers of real estate with poor credit ratings? One way to look at the situation is to characterize mortgage foreclosure rules as a type of consumer protection law which legislatures and courts have determined should be afforded to all persons who finance the purchase of land. From this perspective, the land sale contract looks like a loophole that should be closed. Another way of looking at the situation is that the land sale contract is a type of financing device employed by sellers that comes into play primarily when purchasers

cannot obtain a mortgage from a bank or other professional lender. Sellers may be willing to finance the transaction themselves in these circumstances only if they have a very high degree of security in the event of default. If sellers under land sale contracts can get only the same heavily-regulated foreclosure rights that professional mortgagees get, then they may decline to engage in self-financing. This might leave potential purchasers with poor credit ratings with no option other than seeking financing from sub-prime mortgage lenders, where they will pay very high interest rates. (Note by the way that the land sale contract in *Skendzel* provides for no interest.)

3.   The court questions why a real estate mortgage should be treated any differently than a security interest in personal property. But the UCC does not prohibit the use of installment sales contracts; it merely recognizes that they are a type of security interest. See U.C.C. § 2–401. And there are differences between personal property and real estate as sources of collateral. For example, the extensive self-help available to the holder of a security interest in personal property (see Williams v. Ford Motor Credit Co., Chapter IV) does not apply to the holder of a real estate mortgage, who must bring a judicial foreclosure action. Also, there is nothing like the equity of redemption in the personal property context. Are there nevertheless reasons to welcome the court's effort to look to the UCC for guidance?

4.   Why should parties in effect be forbidden to contract around the protections afforded under judicial foreclosure? Why is following the parties' contract here to elevate form over substance: weren't the parties trying to achieve a different result, i.e., to bypass foreclosure? Here again the question of the parties' intent and its role is complicated. Under the UCC and the approach the court here takes toward real estate mortgages, parties will be taken to have created a security interest if that is their intent. But their intent is pigeonholed into the category of security interest. The parties are simply not allowed to contract for something like a security interest but with different features, such as a heftier remedy. This pigeonholing exercise can even crop up in a regulatory context. See FCC v. NextWave Pers. Commc'ns Inc., 537 U.S. 293 (2003) (holding that under the Bankruptcy Code the FCC could not achieve the effect of a security interest through cancellation of a broadband PCS license for failure to pay after a spectrum auction). Nevertheless, parties do sometimes, particularly with high-loan-to-value mortgages, contract for mortgage insurance, either with private companies, or one of two federal agencies, the Federal Housing Administration or the Veterans Administration. Federal regulation plays a major role in this market. See Quintin Johnstone, Private Mortgage Insurance, 39 Wake Forest L. Rev. 783 (2004).

5.   The court invokes the rule from contract law and equity that liquidated damages are enforceable only if they are a reasonable prediction of actual damages; anything in excess of this is a "penalty" and is unenforceable. This has long puzzled commentators. If the market is one in which even a small group of well-informed parties operates, why would they mutually agree to a clause that shrinks the size of the contractual pie?

One potential concern is that the parties might contract for penalties in order to deter entry by a third party, raising antitrust issues. See generally Aaron S. Edlin & Alan Schwartz, Optimal Penalties in Contracts, 78 Chi.-Kent L. Rev. 33 (2003); Alan Schwartz & Louis L. Wilde, Imperfect Information in Markets for Contract Terms: The Examples of Warranties and Security Interests, 69 Va. L. Rev. 1387 (1983). Others have argued that penalty clauses simply run counter to notions of fairness. See Arthur Allen Leff, Unconscionability and the Code—the Emperor's New Clause, 115 U. Pa. L. Rev. 485, 556–58 (1967); Todd D. Rakoff, Contracts of Adhesion: An Essay in Reconstruction, 96 Harv. L. Rev. 1174, 1225 (1983). One case commonly covered in contracts courses involved a lease-to-own arrangement that had the effect of an installment sales contract with a penalty plus a security interest in every item of furniture bought from the seller until the balance on the last item was paid. Williams v. Walker–Thomas Furniture Co., 350 F.2d 445 (D.C.Cir. 1965) (holding contract unconscionable). An alternative explanation for paternalism might be that we want to prevent people from taking risks that might increase the chance they will draw on public support programs. Eric A. Posner, Contract Law in the Welfare State: A Defense of the Unconscionability Doctrine, Usury Laws, and Related Limitations on the Freedom to Contract, 24 J. Legal Stud. 283 (1995).

6. For another case holding that a similar contractual arrangement (buyer transfers deed to lender and takes back a contract for deed that provides for a penalty-style forfeiture if there is a default) is subject to the state statute on mortgages, see Mid–State Investment Corp. v. O'Steen, 133 So.2d 455 (Fla. Dist. Ct. App. 1961). For the older approach upholding an installment land sale contract, see, e.g., Pease v. Baxter, 41 P. 899 (Wash. 1895).

Carol M. Rose, *Crystals and Mud in Property Law*, 40 STAN. L. REV. 577, 577–79, 583–85 (1988)

Property law, and especially the common law of property, has always been heavily laden with hard-edged doctrines that tell everyone exactly where they stand. Default on paying your loan installments? Too bad, you lose the thing you bought and your past payments as well. Forget to record your deed? Sorry, the next buyer can purchase free of your claim, and you are out on the street. Sell that house with the leak in the basement? Lucky you, you can unload the place without having to tell the buyer about such things at all.

In a sense, hard-edged rules like these—rules that I call "crystals"—are what property is all about. If, as Jeremy Bentham said long ago, property is "nothing but a basis of expectation," then crystal rules are the very stuff of property: their great advantage, or so it is commonly thought, is that they signal to all of us, in a clear and distinct language, precisely what our obligations are and how we may take care of our interests. Thus, I should inspect the property, record my deed, and make my payments if I don't want to lose my home to unexpected physical, legal, or financial impairments. I know where I stand and so does everyone else, and we can all strike bargains with each other if we want to stand somewhere else.

Economic thinkers have been telling us for at least two centuries that the more important a given kind of thing becomes for us, the more likely we are to have these hard-edged rules to manage it. We draw these ever-sharper lines around our entitlements so that we know who has what, and so that we can trade instead of getting into the confusions and disputes that would only escalate as the goods in question became scarcer and more highly valued.

At the root of these economic analyses lies the perception that it costs something to establish clear entitlements to things, and we won't bother to undertake the task of removing goods from an ownerless "commons" unless it is worth it to us to do so. What makes it worth it? Increasing scarcity of the resource, and the attendant conflicts over it. To use the example given by Harold Demsetz, one of the most notable of the modern economists telling this story, when the European demand for fur hats increased demand for (and scarcity of) fur-bearing animals among Indian hunters, the Indians developed a system of property entitlements to the animal habitat. Economic historians of the American West tell a similar story about the development of property rights in various minerals and natural resources. Easy-going, anything-goes patterns of appropriation at the outset came under pressure as competition for resources increased, and were finally superseded by much more sharply defined systems of entitle-ment. In effect, as our competition for a resource raises the costs of conflict about it, those conflict costs begin to outweigh the costs of taking it out of the commons and establishing clear property entitlements. We establish a system of clear entitlements so that we can barter and trade for what we want instead of fighting.

The trouble with this "scarcity story" is that things don't seem to work this way, or at least not all the time. Sometimes we seem to substitute fuzzy, ambiguous rules of decision for what seem to be perfectly clear, open and shut, demarcations of entitlements. I call this occurrence the substitution of "mud" rules for "crystal" ones.

Thus, in the examples with which I began, we find that, over time, the straightforward common law crystalline rules have been muddied repeated-ly by exceptions and equitable second-guessing, to the point that the various claimants under real estate contracts, mortgages, or recorded deeds don't know quite what their rights and obligations really are. * * *

B.   Of Mortgages and Mud

Early common law mortgages were very crystalline indeed. They had the look of pawnshop transactions and were at least sometimes structured as conveyances: I borrow money from you, and at the same time I convey my land to you as security for my loan. If all goes well, I pay back my debt on the agreed "law day," and you reconvey my land back to me. But if all does not go well and I cannot pay on the appointed day, then, no matter how heartrending my excuse, I lose my land to you and, presumably, any of the previous payments I might have made. As the fifteenth century commentator Littleton airily explained, the name "mortgage" derived from the rule that, if the debtor "doth not pay, then the land which he puts in pledge . . . is gone from him for ever, and so dead."

This system had the advantage of great clarity, but it sometimes must have seemed very hard on mortgage debtors to the advantage of scoundrelly creditors. Littleton's advice about the importance of specifying the precise place and time for repayment, for example, conjures up images of a wily creditor hiding in the woods on the repayment day to frustrate repayment; presumably, the unfound creditor could keep the property. But by the seventeenth century, the intervention of courts of equity had changed things. By the eighteenth and nineteenth centuries, the equity courts were regularly giving debtors as many as three or four "enlargements" of the time in which they might pay and redeem the property before the final "foreclosure," even when the excuse was lame. One judge explained that an equity court might well grant more time even after the "final" order of "foreclosure absolute," depending on the particular circumstances.

The muddiness of this emerging judicial remedy argued against its attractiveness. Chief Justice Hale complained in 1672 that, "[b]y the growth of Equity on Equity, the Heart of the Common Law is eaten out, and legal Settlements are destroyed; . . . as far as the Line is given, Man will go; and if an hundred Years are given, Man will go so far, and we know not whither we shall go."[40] Instead of a precise and clear allocation of entitlements between the parties, the "equity of redemption" and its unpredictable foreclosure opened up vexing questions and uncertainties: How much time should the debtor have for repayment before the equitable arguments shifted to favor the creditor? What sort of excuses did the debtor need? Did it matter that the property, instead of dropping in the lap of the creditor, was sold at a foreclosure sale?

But as the courts moved towards muddiness, private parties attempted to bargain their way out of these costly uncertainties and to reinstate a crystalline pattern whereby lenders could get the property immediately upon default without the costs of foreclosure. How about a separate deal with the borrower, for example, whereby he agrees to convey an equitable interest to the lender in case of default? Nothing doing, said the courts, including the United States Supreme Court, which in 1878 stated flatly that a mortgagor could not initially bargain away his "equity of redemption."[45] Well, then, how about an arrangement whereby it looks as if the lender already owns the land, and the "borrower" only gets title if he lives up to his agreement to pay for it by a certain time? This seemed more promising: In the 1890s California courts thought it perfectly correct to hold the buyer to his word in such an arrangement, and to give him neither an extension nor a refund of past payments. By the 1960s, however, they were changing their minds about these "installment land contracts." After

40. Roscarrick v. Barton, 22 Eng. Rep. 769, 770 (1672).

45. Peugh v. Davis, 96 U.S. 332, 337 (1878).

all, these deals really had exactly the same effect as the old-style mortgages—the defaulting buyer could lose everything if he missed a payment, even the very last payment. Human vice and error seemed to put the crystal rule in jeopardy: In a series of cases culminating with a default by a "willful but repentant" little old lady who had stopped paying when she mistakenly thought that she was being cheated, the California Supreme Court decided to treat these land contracts as mortgages in disguise.[48] It gave the borrower "relief from forfeiture"—a time to reinstate the installment contract or get back her past payments.

With mortgages first and mortgage substitutes later, we see a back-and-forth pattern: crisp definition of entitlements, made fuzzy by accretions of judicial decisions, crisped up again by the parties' contractual arrangements, and once again made fuzzy by the courts. Here we see private parties apparently following the "scarcity story" in their private law arrangements: when things matter, the parties define their respective entitlements with ever sharper precision. Yet the courts seem at times unwilling to follow this story or to permit these crystalline definitions, most particularly when the rules hurt one party very badly. The cycle thus alternates between crystal and mud. * * *

NOTES AND QUESTIONS

1.   Are we destined to cycle between crystals and mud in all areas? In the area of mortgages? Rose emphasizes the role that courts have played in "muddying up" mortgage law, especially because they see disputes arise individually and ex post. On the other hand according to some scholars, including Robert Skilton in the excerpt, supra, it has been legislatures responding to populist pressures during economic downturns that have provided relief from the stringency of mortgage law. See also, e.g., A.H. Feller, Moratory Legislation: A Comparative Study, 46 Harv. L. Rev. 1061 (1933); Sheldon Tefft, The Myth of Strict Foreclosure, 4 U. Chi. L. Rev. 575, 577–81, 588–90, 595 (1937). Interestingly, in the Colonial period and the early Republic, exemptions that had protected real property from creditors in England (in the interest of maintaining social position), were removed in favor of commercial interests, a development that led to lower interest rates, the rise of a market in land, and made capital available for economic development. Claire Priest, Creating an American Property Law: Alienability and Its Limits in American History, 120 Harv. L. Rev. 385 (2006).

2.   If some equilibrium between crystals and mud is possible, what is the optimal mix of the two? Does one's answer depend somewhat on who is expected to figure things out? What exactly does it mean for mortgage law to be "muddy?" Sometimes a contrast is drawn between rules in which decisions are made ex ante and standards which give discretion ex post. See, e.g., Louis Kaplow, Rules versus Standards: An Economic Analysis, 42

---

48. MacFadden v. Walker, 488 P.2d 1353 (Cal. 1971) * * *

Duke L.J. 557, 568–88 (1992). At other times, emphasis is placed on the amount of information required to make a decision under a rule (minimal) versus a standard (lots). See, e.g., Frederick Schauer, Playing by the Rules (1991); Henry E. Smith, The Language of Property: Form, Context, and Audience, 55 Stan. L. Rev. 1105 (2003). Recall the discussion of minor building encroachments in Chapter I, where one approach (*Pile v. Pedrick*) lays down a bright-line rule designed to provide clear incentives for future actors and another (*Golden Press v. Rylands*) assesses a wider range of contextual information in order to minimize the costs from mistakes committed in the past. Is the tension between these approaches the same as the dynamic described by Rose in the context of mortgage foreclosure?

3.   Recall the *numerus clausus* principle, which we explored in Chapter V. One aspect of the principle is that the legislature has primary responsibility for modifying the list of basic property forms. Does the history of foreclosure as described by Rose conform to this expectation? At least aspirationally, even old equity courts were supposed to exercise extra caution to avoid undoing the law and its attendant predictability where property rights are concerned. Charles Grey, The Boundaries of the Equitable Function, 20 Am. J. Legal Hist. 192 (1976). How much of the muddying here has consequences for third parties, through the in rem aspect of property? In her article, Rose finds the same cycle of crystals and mud with respect to land records, which, as we shall see in the next Chapter, present notice issues, often involving mortgages.

Figure 7–1
Walter Dendy Sadler, *A Little Mortgage*

C.   SECURITY INTERESTS IN BANKRUPTCY

Security interests give their owners a conditional property right (to seize the collateral in case of default on the loan it secures) and a priority right over other secured claims with less priority and over unsecured claims. These rights are most relevant for debtors in financial distress and it often happens that such debtors wind up in bankruptcy with the security interest in place. Bankruptcy law provides a procedure to collect the assets of the debtor and do a once-and-for-all division of these assets among the various claimants. Bankruptcy is closely related to insolvency, the state of having liabilities in excess of one's assets. Sometimes a solvent debtor can choose to enter bankruptcy to effect a reorganization, for a variety of reasons. Involuntary bankruptcies, in which a creditor can force a debtor into bankruptcy, are reserved for insolvent debtors. In the case of an individual debtor, the motivation is to provide a fresh start, subject to restraints on using the mechanism by certain debtors. Recent legislation, the Bankruptcy Abuse Prevention and Consumer Protection Act of 2005, Pub. L. No. 109–8, 119 Stat. 23 (codified at 11 U.S.C. § 101 et seq. (2005)), limits the use of personal bankruptcy by devices such as means testing, and great controversy has swirled around it. Compare Todd J. Zywicki, An Economic Analysis of the Consumer Bankruptcy Crisis, 99 Nw. U. L. Rev. 1463 (2005) (attributing bankruptcy crisis to poor incentives) with Elizabeth Warren, The Changing Politics of American Bankruptcy Reform, 37 Osgoode Hall L.J. 189 (1999) (criticizing legislation and attributing it to special interest influence). Many of the issues are empirical, including the reasons behind increased filings, and normative, including the proper role of stigma and the fresh start. See Michelle J. White, Economic Versus Sociological Approaches to Legal Research: The Case of Bankruptcy, 25 Law & Soc'y Rev. 685 (1991).

Business bankruptcy, which we concentrate on here, turns more on how best to preserve value in light of a company's insolvency or other misfortune, and can either result in liquidation, under Chapter 7, or reorganization under Chapter 11. While fairness plays a role in bankruptcy, bankruptcy is designed to make the best of a bad situation. Keep in mind that no business is without risk; reducing insolvency risk to zero would undoubtedly shrink the total size of the pie. In theory the choice between liquidation and reorganization should turn on whether the collection of assets (including business good will and human capital) embodied in the bankrupt firm is more valuable kept together and reorganized as a new firm shorn of its liabilities and owned by its current creditors, or as assets distributed to claimants or sold off (possibly as a group) and the proceeds distributed. A reorganization is in essence a sale of the firm as a whole to its creditors who exchange their claims for an interest in the earnings of the reorganized firm. Valuation of claims in bankruptcy is difficult and contested and is one of many sources of delay. In general, claimants (such as general creditors) with less to lose have an incentive to advocate reorganizations even if risky, and generally they have more to gain and less to lose from delay than do secured creditors. Chapter 11 has devices to protect secured creditors, but these do not provide full protection, and many secured creditors would have done better in a foreclosure outside bankruptcy or in a liquidation. If a reorganization plan is not accepted or turns out to be less desirable than expected, a Chapter 11 proceeding can be shifted to Chapter 7. Again, the choice between the two largely turns on how much going concern value there is and how feasible it is to protect it.

Bankruptcy is often thought of as procedural law, providing special federal courts and rules for rearranging the affairs of a debtor, as an alternative to state law. Particularly in the case of corporate bankruptcies, state law could be allowed to take its course, with secured creditors foreclosing and judgments being acquired, but it is thought that a collective proceeding can make all the claimants better off (with at least some better off and no one worse off) than they would be under state law. Nevertheless, it is fundamental to bankruptcy that the source of claimants' rights, including those of secured creditors, is state property and commercial law, and the Bankruptcy Code reflects a policy of respecting these rights, which largely prevails albeit with exceptions (as we will see in the next case). Thus, if an agreement with a debtor gives rise to a security interest under state law—consider in this regard the characterization of land sale contracts in *Skendzel*, supra—then it is a security interest in bankruptcy as well. Further, it is said that in bankruptcy "equality is equity," by which is meant that the relative positions of claimants outside bankruptcy should carry over into bankruptcy as well. One corollary of this is that the priority right of a secured creditor should mean that it either gets the collateral, or is paid before any junior creditor, or if any junior creditor is paid, the senior creditor should get as much in bankruptcy as it would outside. Things don't always work out this way, in part because the drafters of the Bankruptcy Code of 1978 and earlier bankruptcy legislation harbored some skepticism about the desirability and fairness of secured credit—concerns shared by numerous commentators as we saw earlier.

For all types of bankruptcy, the Bankruptcy Code provides for an automatic stay upon the filing of a bankruptcy petition. 11 U.S.C. § 362(a). This prevents creditors from foreclosing on their security interests and generally freezes debt collection, creditor lawsuits, and other efforts to obtain liens on the debtor's property. The procedural rights thus lost can either be restarted, sometimes at the election of the bankruptcy trustee or debtor in possession with the supervision of the bankruptcy court, or they are replaced with substitute procedural rights in bankruptcy. Put differently, in order to protect the debtor's equity in the collateral (which will ultimately belong to creditors), and to preserve property essential to a reorganization, the secured creditor may have the value of its security protected in place of its right to the asset itself. Meanwhile the secured creditor will have to deal with the trustee, or in a reorganization possibly the debtor in possession acting as a trustee. The trustee is elected by and mainly represents the unsecured creditors, and the trustee may be required to seek to invalidate property interests like security in order to maximize the pool available to unsecured creditors. The trustee acts as a hypothetical lien creditor, meaning that the trustee has all the powers to prevent priority and to avoid interests that someone with a valid execution lien would have at the time the petition was filed. This means that a secured creditor who has not perfected its security interests by whatever combination of possession and filing is required under the UCC or state mortgage law would in effect be treated as just another unsecured creditor. For secured creditors with perfected security interests, the Code protects the secured party's priority rights, to the extent of the value of the security. 11 U.S.C. § 1129(b)(2)(B). A secured creditor with a perfected interest can seek relief from the automatic stay if its interest is not being "adequately protected"—or if the asset in question is not subject to any debtor equity right and is not essential to reorganization. § 362(d). Nonetheless, a secured creditor may not do as well in bankruptcy as it would outside, as in the case that follows.

United Savings Association of Texas v. Timbers of Inwood Forest Associates, Ltd.

Supreme Court of the United States, 1988.
484 U.S. 365.

■ Justice Scalia delivered the opinion of the Court. Petitioner United Savings Association of Texas seeks review of an en banc decision of the United States Court of Appeals for the Fifth Circuit, holding that petitioner was not entitled to receive from respondent debtor, which is undergoing reorganization in bankruptcy, monthly payments for the use value of the loan collateral which the bankruptcy stay prevented it from possessing. We granted certiorari to resolve a conflict in the Courts of Appeals regarding application of §§ 361 and 362(d)(1) of the Bankruptcy Code, 11 U.S.C. §§ 361 and 362(d)(1) (1982 ed. and Supp. IV). * * *

I

On June 29, 1982, respondent Timbers of Inwood Forest Associates, Ltd., executed a note in the principal amount of $4,100,000. Petitioner is the holder of the note as well as of a security interest created the same day in an apartment project owned by respondent in Houston, Texas. The security interest included an assignment of rents from the project. On March 4, 1985, respondent filed a voluntary petition under Chapter 11 of the Bankruptcy Code, 11 U.S.C. § 101 et seq. (1982 ed. and Supp. IV), in the United States Bankruptcy Court for the Southern District of Texas.

On March 18, 1985, petitioner moved for relief from the automatic stay of enforcement of liens triggered by the petition, see 11 U.S.C. § 362(a), on the ground that there was lack of "adequate protection" of its interest within the meaning of 11 U.S.C. § 362(d)(1). At a hearing before the Bankruptcy Court, it was established that respondent owed petitioner $4,366,388.77, and evidence was presented that the value of the collateral was somewhere between $2,650,000 and $4,250,000. The collateral was appreciating in value, but only very slightly. It was therefore undisputed that petitioner was an undersecured creditor. Respondent had agreed to pay petitioner the postpetition rents from the apartment project (covered by the after-acquired property clause in the security agreement), minus operating expenses. Petitioner contended, however, that it was entitled to additional compensation. The Bankruptcy Court agreed and on April 19, 1985, it conditioned continuance of the stay on monthly payments by respondent, at the market rate of 12% per annum, on the estimated amount realizable on foreclosure, $4,250,000—commencing six months after the filing of the bankruptcy petition, to reflect the normal foreclosure delays. The court held that the postpetition rents could be applied to these payments. Respondent appealed to the District Court and petitioner cross-appealed on the amount of the adequate protection payments. The District Court affirmed but the Fifth Circuit en banc reversed.

We granted certiorari to determine whether undersecured creditors are entitled to compensation under 11 U.S.C. § 362(d)(1) for the delay caused by the automatic stay in foreclosing on their collateral.

II

When a bankruptcy petition is filed, § 362(a) of the Bankruptcy Code provides an automatic stay of, among other things, actions taken to realize the value of collateral given by the debtor. The provision of the Code central to the decision of this case is § 362(d), which reads as follows:

> On request of a party in interest and after notice and a hearing, the court shall grant relief from the stay provided under subsection (a) of this section, such as by terminating, annulling, modifying, or conditioning such stay—
>
> (1) for cause, including the lack of adequate protection of an interest in property of such party in interest; or
>
> (2) with respect to a stay of an act against property under subsection (a) of this section, if—
>
> (A) the debtor does not have an equity in such property; and
>
> (B) such property is not necessary to an effective reorganization.

The phrase "adequate protection" in paragraph (1) of the foregoing provision is given further content by § 361 of the Code, which reads in relevant part as follows:

> When adequate protection is required under section 362 ... of this title of an interest of an entity in property, such adequate protection may be provided by—
>
> (1) requiring the trustee to make a cash payment or periodic cash payments to such entity, to the extent that the stay under section 362 of this title ... results in a decrease in the value of such entity's interest in such property;

(2) providing to such entity an additional or replacement lien to the extent that such stay ... results in a decrease in the value of such entity's interest in such property; or

(3) granting such other relief ... as will result in the realization by such entity of the indubitable equivalent of such entity's interest in such property.

It is common ground that the "interest in property" referred to by § 362(d)(1) includes the right of a secured creditor to have the security applied in payment of the debt upon completion of the reorganization; and that that interest is not adequately protected if the security is depreciating during the term of the stay. Thus, it is agreed that if the apartment project in this case had been declining in value petitioner would have been entitled, under § 362(d)(1), to cash payments or additional security in the amount of the decline, as § 361 describes. The crux of the present dispute is that petitioner asserts, and respondent denies, that the phrase "interest in property" also includes the secured party's right (suspended by the stay) to take immediate possession of the defaulted security, and apply it in payment of the debt. If that right is embraced by the term, it is obviously not adequately protected unless the secured party is reimbursed for the use of the proceeds he is deprived of during the term of the stay.

The term "interest in property" certainly summons up such concepts as "fee ownership," "life estate," "co-ownership," and "security interest" more readily than it does the notion of "right to immediate foreclosure." Nonetheless, viewed in the isolated context of § 362(d)(1), the phrase could reasonably be given the meaning petitioner asserts. Statutory construction, however, is a holistic endeavor. A provision that may seem ambiguous in isolation is often clarified by the remainder of the statutory scheme— because the same terminology is used elsewhere in a context that makes its meaning clear, or because only one of the permissible meanings produces a substantive effect that is compatible with the rest of the law. That is the case here. Section 362(d)(1) is only one of a series of provisions in the Bankruptcy Code dealing with the rights of secured creditors. The language in those other provisions, and the substantive dispositions that they effect, persuade us that the "interest in property" protected by § 362(d)(1) does not include a secured party's right to immediate foreclosure.

Section 506 of the Code defines the amount of the secured creditor's allowed secured claim and the conditions of his receiving postpetition interest. In relevant part it reads as follows:

(a) An allowed claim of a creditor secured by a lien on property in which the estate has an interest ... is a secured claim to the extent of the value of such creditor's interest in the estate's interest in such property, ... and is an unsecured claim to the extent that the value of such creditor's interest ... is less than the amount of such allowed claim. . . .

(b) To the extent that an allowed secured claim is secured by property the value of which ... is greater than the amount of such claim, there shall be allowed to the holder of such claim, interest on such claim, and any reasonable fees, costs, or charges provided for under the agreement under which such claim arose.

In subsection (a) of this provision the creditor's "interest in property" obviously means his security interest without taking account of his right to immediate possession of the collateral on default. If the latter were included, the "value of such creditor's interest" would increase, and the proportions of the claim that are secured and unsecured would alter, as the stay continues—since the value of the entitlement to use the collateral from the date of bankruptcy would rise with the passage of time. No one suggests this was intended. The phrase "value of such creditor's interest" in § 506(a) means "the value of the collateral." H.R.Rep. No. 95–595, pp. 181, 356 (1977); see also S.Rep. No. 95–989, p. 68 (1978), U.S. Code Cong. & Admin. News 1978, pp. 5787, 5854, 6141, 6312. We think the phrase "value of such entity's interest" in § 361(1) and (2), when applied to secured creditors, means the same.

Even more important for our purposes than § 506's use of terminology is its substantive effect of denying undersecured creditors postpetition interest on their claims—just as it denies *over* secured creditors postpetition interest to the extent that such interest, when added to the principal amount of the claim, will exceed the value of the collateral. Section 506(b) provides that *"[t]o the extent that* an allowed secured claim is secured by property the value of which . . . is greater than the amount of such claim, there shall be allowed to the holder of such claim, interest on such claim." (Emphasis added.) Since this provision permits postpetition interest to be paid only out of the "security cushion," the undersecured creditor, who has no such cushion, falls within the general rule disallowing postpetition interest. See 11 U.S.C. § 502(b)(2). If the Code had meant to give the undersecured creditor, who is thus denied interest on his *claim,* interest on the value of his *collateral,* surely this is where that disposition would have been set forth, and not obscured within the "adequate protection" provision of § 362(d)(1). Instead of the intricate phraseology set forth above, § 506(b) would simply have said that the secured creditor is entitled to interest "on his allowed claim, or on the value of the property securing his allowed claim, whichever is lesser." Petitioner's interpretation of § 362(d)(1) must be regarded as contradicting the carefully drawn disposition of § 506(b).

Petitioner seeks to avoid this conclusion by characterizing § 506(b) as merely an alternative method for compensating oversecured creditors, which does not imply that no compensation is available to undersecured creditors. This theory of duplicate protection for oversecured creditors is implausible even in the abstract, but even more so in light of the historical principles of bankruptcy law. Section 506(b)'s denial of postpetition interest to undersecured creditors merely codified pre-Code bankruptcy law, in which that denial was part of the conscious allocation of reorganization benefits and losses between undersecured and unsecured creditors. "To allow a secured creditor interest where his security was worth less than the

value of his debt was thought to be inequitable to unsecured creditors."
Vanston Bondholders Protective Committee v. Green, 329 U.S. 156, 164
(1946). It was considered unfair to allow an undersecured creditor to
recover interest from the estate's unencumbered assets before unsecured
creditors had recovered any principal. See id., at 164, 166; Ticonic Nat.
Bank v. Sprague, 303 U.S. 406, 412 (1938). We think it unlikely that
§ 506(b) codified the pre-Code rule with the intent, not of achieving the
principal purpose and function of that rule, but of providing over-secured
creditors an alternative method of compensation. Moreover, it is incompre-
hensible why Congress would want to favor undersecured creditors with
interest if they move for it under § 362(d)(1) at the inception of the
reorganization process—thereby probably pushing the estate into liquidation—but not if they forbear and seek it only at the completion of the
reorganization. * * *

III

A

Petitioner contends * * * that failure to interpret § 362(d)(1) to require compensation of undersecured creditors for delay will create an
inconsistency in the Code in the (admittedly rare) case when the debtor
proves solvent. When that occurs, 11 U.S.C. § 726(a)(5) provides that
postpetition interest is allowed on unsecured claims. Petitioner contends it
would be absurd to allow postpetition interest on unsecured claims but not
on the secured portion of undersecured creditors' claims. It would be
disingenuous to deny that this is an apparent anomaly, but it will occur so
rarely that it is more likely the product of inadvertence than are the
blatant inconsistencies petitioner's interpretation would produce. Its inequitable effects, moreover, are entirely avoidable, since an undersecured
creditor is entitled to "surrender or waive his security and prove his entire
claim as an unsecured one." United States Nat. Bank v. Chase Nat. Bank,
331 U.S. 28, 34 (1947). Section 726(a)(5) therefore requires no more than
that undersecured creditors receive postpetition interest from a solvent
debtor on equal terms with unsecured creditors rather than ahead of
them—which, where the debtor is solvent, involves no hardship.

B

Petitioner contends that its interpretation is supported by the legislative history of §§ 361 and 362(d)(1), relying almost entirely on statements
that "[s]ecured creditors should not be deprived of the benefit of their
bargain." H.R.Rep. No. 95–595, at 339; S.Rep. No. 95–989, at 53, U.S. Code
Cong. & Admin. News 1978, pp. 5839, 6295. Such generalizations are
inadequate to overcome the plain textual indication in §§ 506 and 362(d)(2)
of the Code that Congress did not wish the undersecured creditor to receive
interest on his collateral during the term of the stay. If it is at all relevant,
the legislative history tends to subvert rather than support petitioner's
thesis, since it contains not a hint that § 362(d)(1) entitles the undersecured creditor to postpetition interest. Such a major change in the existing
rules would not likely have been made without specific provision in the text

of the statute, cf. Kelly v. Robinson, 479 U.S. 36, 47 (1986); it is most improbable that it would have been made without even any mention in the legislative history. * * *

The Fifth Circuit correctly held that the undersecured petitioner is not entitled to interest on its collateral during the stay to assure adequate protection under 11 U.S.C. § 362(d)(1). Petitioner has never sought relief from the stay under § 362(d)(2) or on any ground other than lack of adequate protection. Accordingly, the judgment of the Fifth Circuit is

Affirmed.

NOTES AND QUESTIONS

1. The principle that interest follows principal is an example of accession (see Chapter IV), but is overridden for undersecured creditors in bankruptcy. According to the majority opinion, the statute dictates the result. Are you convinced? One way to consider the issue is that the secured creditor should have the value of its rights determined by the value they would have had in a foreclosure, now made impossible by the bankruptcy. Under a foreclosure, the secured party would get the asset right away and would earn any return on it from that point on. Alternatively, if the secured party did not foreclose and the debtor kept making payments, the secured party would earn the contract interest. See Douglas G. Baird, Thomas H. Jackson & Barry E. Adler, Bankruptcy: Cases, Problems, and Materials 381 (3d ed. 2000). By contrast, in Associates Commercial Corp. v. Rash, 520 U.S. 953 (1997), the Supreme Court, per Justice Ginsburg, held that where secured creditors are entitled to the "value, as of the effective date of the plan" under Section 506(a) in plans over their objection ("cram downs"), the secured party's collateral must be valued for protection purposes at replacement value rather than foreclosure value. Again, the majority's result was said to be dictated by the statute, this time over a dissent by Justice Stevens who marshaled a number of policy reasons in favor of the foreclosure standard.

2. To make things more complex, it can happen that property rights in the return from an undersecured asset follow the property rights in the asset, *Timbers* notwithstanding. For example, if a security interest by its terms covers "proceeds, product, offspring, or profits," then if such returns are earned post-petition the security interest extends to them too. § 552(b). As we noted in our discussion of leases in Chapter VI, some of such returns will be the functional equivalent of interest.

3. The United States Bankruptcy Code provides less than full protection for the priority rights of secured creditors. Partly in response to this feature of the Code, some companies have engaged in "asset securitization." Unlike with a security interest, in an asset securitization a company holding a certain asset (say its claims to payment from customers) can transfer these assets to a separate entity. Then if the first company becomes insolvent the investors in the securitized assets need not deal with the bankruptcy because they simply own the stream of payments, rather

than just having a security interest in the corresponding asset in the hands of the (now insolvent) parent company. More complex arrangements involving leases of equipment are possible. In general these "bankruptcy remote" vehicles are designed to partition assets so as to shield them from the other creditors of a firm (secured and unsecured), and in particular to shield them from being included with the other assets of the firm should it file for bankruptcy.

National Peregrine, Inc. v. Capitol Federal Savings & Loan Association (In re Peregrine Entertainment, Ltd.)

United States District Court, Central District of California, 1990.
116 B.R. 194.

■ KOZINSKI, CIRCUIT JUDGE.* This appeal from a decision of the bankruptcy court raises an issue never before confronted by a federal court in a published opinion: Is a security interest in a copyright perfected by an appropriate filing with the United States Copyright Office or by a UCC–1 financing statement filed with the relevant secretary of state?

I

National Peregrine, Inc. (NPI) is a Chapter 11 debtor in possession whose principal assets are a library of copyrights, distribution rights and licenses to approximately 145 films, and accounts receivable arising from the licensing of these films to various programmers. NPI claims to have an outright assignment of some of the copyrights; as for the others, NPI claims it has an exclusive license to distribute in a certain territory, or for a certain period of time.

In June 1985, Capitol Federal Savings and Loan Association of Denver (Cap Fed) extended to American National Enterprises, Inc., NPI's predecessor by merger, a six million dollar line of credit secured by what is now NPI's film library. Both the security agreement and the UCC–1 financing statements[2] filed by Cap Fed describe the collateral as "[a]ll inventory consisting of films and all accounts, contract rights, chattel paper, general intangibles, instruments, equipment, and documents related to such inventory, now owned or hereafter acquired by the Debtor." Although Cap Fed filed its UCC–1 financing statements in California, Colorado and Utah,[4] it did not record its security interest in the United States Copyright Office.

---

* Sitting by designation pursuant to 28 U.S.C. § 291(b) (1982).

2. All references are to the California version of the Uniform Commercial Code.

4. Under UCC § 9103(3)(b), "[t]he law ... of the jurisdiction in which the debtor is located governs the perfection and the effect of perfection or nonperfection of the security interest" in a general intangible. "A debtor shall be deemed located at the debtor's place

of business ... [or] at the debtor's chief executive office if [it] has more than one place of business...." U.S.C. § 9103(3)(d). Because NPI is a Utah corporation that conducts much of its business in California, Cap Fed apparently deemed filing in both states prudent. Presumably, Cap Fed filed in Colorado because its own headquarters are located in Denver.

NPI filed a voluntary petition for bankruptcy on January 30, 1989. On April 6, 1989, NPI filed an amended complaint against Cap Fed, contending that the bank's security interest in the copyrights to the films in NPI's library and in the accounts receivable generated by their distribution were unperfected because Cap Fed failed to record its security interest with the Copyright Office. NPI claimed that, as a debtor in possession, it had a judicial lien on all assets in the bankruptcy estate, including the copyrights and receivables. Armed with this lien, it sought to avoid, recover and preserve Cap Fed's supposedly unperfected security interest for the benefit of the estate.

The parties filed cross-motions for partial summary judgment on the question of whether Cap Fed had a valid security interest in the NPI film library. The bankruptcy court held for Cap Fed. NPI appeals.

II

A.   *Where to File*

The Copyright Act provides that "[a]ny transfer of copyright ownership or other document pertaining to a copyright" may be recorded in the United States Copyright Office. 17 U.S.C. § 205(a); see Copyright Office Circular 12: Recordation of Transfers and Other Documents (reprinted in 1 Copyright L.Rep. (CCH) ¶ 15,015). A "transfer" under the Act includes any "mortgage" or "hypothecation of a copyright," whether "in whole or in part" and "by any means of conveyance or by operation of law." 17 U.S.C. §§ 101, 201(d)(1). The terms "mortgage" and "hypothecation" include a pledge of property as security or collateral for a debt. See Black's Law Dictionary 669 (5th ed. 1979). In addition, the Copyright Office has defined a "document pertaining to a copyright" as one that

> has a direct or indirect relationship to the existence, scope, duration, or identification of a copyright, or to the ownership, division, allocation, licensing, transfer, or exercise of rights under a copyright. That relationship may be past, present, future, or potential.

37 C.F.R. § 201.4(a)(2); see also Compendium of Copyright Office Practices II ¶¶ 1602–1603 (identifying which documents the Copyright Office will accept for filing).

It is clear from the preceding that an agreement granting a creditor a security interest in a copyright may be recorded in the Copyright Office. Likewise, because a copyright entitles the holder to receive all income derived from the display of the creative work, see 17 U.S.C. § 106, an agreement creating a security interest in the receivables generated by a copyright may also be recorded in the Copyright Office. Thus, Cap Fed's security interest *could* have been recorded in the Copyright Office; the parties seem to agree on this much. The question is, does the UCC provide a parallel method of perfecting a security interest in a copyright? One can answer this question by reference to either federal or state law; both inquiries lead to the same conclusion.

1. Even in the absence of express language, federal regulation will preempt state law if it is so pervasive as to indicate that "Congress left no room for supplementary state regulation," or if "the federal interest is so dominant that the federal system will be assumed to preclude enforcement of state laws on the same subject." Hillsborough County v. Automated Medical Laboratories, Inc., 471 U.S. 707, 713 (1985) (internal quotations omitted). Here, the comprehensive scope of the federal Copyright Act's recording provisions, along with the unique federal interests they implicate, support the view that federal law preempts state methods of perfecting security interests in copyrights and related accounts receivable.

The federal copyright laws ensure "predictability and certainty of copyright ownership," "promote national uniformity" and "avoid the practical difficulties of determining and enforcing an author's rights under the differing laws and in the separate courts of the various States." Community for Creative Non–Violence v. Reid, 490 U.S. 730 (1989); H.R.Rep. No. 1476, 94th Cong., 2d Sess. 129 (1976), U.S.Code Cong. & Admin.News 1976, p. 5659. As discussed above, section 205(a) of the Copyright Act establishes a uniform method for recording security interests in copyrights. A secured creditor need only file in the Copyright Office in order to give "all persons constructive notice of the facts stated in the recorded document." 17 U.S.C. § 205(c).[7] Likewise, an interested third party need only search the indices maintained by the Copyright Office to determine whether a particular copyright is encumbered.

A recording system works by virtue of the fact that interested parties have a specific place to look in order to discover with certainty whether a particular interest has been transferred or encumbered. To the extent there are competing recordation schemes, this lessens the utility of each; when records are scattered in several filing units, potential creditors must conduct several searches before they can be sure that the property is not encumbered. See Danning v. Pacific Propeller, Inc. (In re Holiday Airlines Corp.), 620 F.2d 731 (9th Cir.), cert. denied, 449 U.S. 900 (1980). It is for that reason that parallel recordation schemes for the same types of property are scarce as hens' teeth; the court is aware of no others, and the parties have cited none. No useful purposes would be served—indeed, much confusion would result—if creditors were permitted to perfect security interests by filing with either the Copyright Office or state offices. See G. Gilmore, Security Interests in Personal Property § 17.3, at 545 (1965); see also 3 Nimmer on Copyright § 10.05[A] at 10–44 (1989) ("a persuasive argument ... can be made to the effect that by reasons of Sections 201(d)(1), 204(a), 205(c) and 205(d) of the current Act ... Congress has preempted the field with respect to the form and recordation requirements applicable to copyright mortgages").

---

7. For a recordation under section 205 to be effective as against third parties, the copyrighted work must also have been registered pursuant to 17 U.S.C. §§ 408, 409, 410. See 17 U.S.C. § 205(c)(2). Of course, registration is also a prerequisite to judicial enforce- ment of a copyright, except for actions for infringement of copyrights in foreign works covered by the Berne Convention. 17 U.S.C. § 411; International Trade Management, Inc. v. United States, 553 F.Supp. 402, 402–03, 1 Cl.Ct. 39 (1982).

If state methods of perfection were valid, a third party (such as a potential purchaser of the copyright) who wanted to learn of any encumbrances thereon would have to check not merely the indices of the U.S. Copyright Office, but also the indices of any relevant secretary of state. Because copyrights are incorporeal—they have no fixed situs—a number of state authorities could be relevant. Thus, interested third parties could never be entirely sure that all relevant jurisdictions have been searched. This possibility, together with the expense and delay of conducting searches in a variety of jurisdictions, could hinder the purchase and sale of copyrights, frustrating Congress's policy that copyrights be readily transferable in commerce.

This is the reasoning adopted by the Ninth Circuit in *Danning v. Pacific Propeller. Danning* held that 49 U.S.C.App. § 1403(a), the Federal Aviation Act's provision for recording conveyances and the creation of liens and security interests in civil aircraft, preempts state filing provisions. 620 F.2d at 735–36.[8] According to *Danning,*

> [t]he predominant purpose of the statute was to provide one central place for the filing of [liens on aircraft] and thus eliminate the need, given the highly mobile nature of aircraft and their appurtenances, for the examination of State and County records.

620 F.2d at 735–36. Copyrights, even more than aircraft, lack a clear situs; tangible, movable goods such as airplanes must always exist at some physical location; they may have a home base from which they operate or where they receive regular maintenance. The same cannot be said of intangibles. As noted above, this lack of an identifiable situs militates against individual state filings and in favor of a single, national registration scheme.

Moreover, as discussed at greater length below, the Copyright Act establishes its own scheme for determining priority between conflicting transferees, one that differs in certain respects from that of Article Nine. Under Article Nine, priority between holders of conflicting security interests in intangibles is generally determined by who perfected his interest first. UCC § 9312(5). By contrast, section 205(d) of the Copyright Act provides:

---

8. Section 1403(a), which is similar in scope to section 205 of the Copyright Act, provides:

> The Secretary of Transportation shall establish and maintain a system for the recording of each and all of the following:
>
> (1) Any conveyance which affects the title to, or any interest in, any civil aircraft of the United States;
>
> (2) Any lease, and any mortgage, equipment trust, contract of conditional sale, or other instrument executed for security purposes, which lease or other instrument affects the title to, or any interest in [certain engines and propellers];
>
> (3) Any lease, and any mortgage, equipment trust, contract of conditional sale, or other instrument executed for security purposes, which lease or other instrument affects the title to, or any interest in, any aircraft engines, propellers, or appliances maintained by or on behalf of an air carrier....

49 U.S.C. App. § 1403(a).

> As between two conflicting transfers, the one executed first prevails if it is recorded, in the manner required to give constructive notice under subsection (c), *within one month after its execution in the United States or within two months after its execution outside the United States,* or at any time before recordation in such manner of the later transfer. . . .

17 U.S.C. § 205(d) (emphasis added). Thus, unlike Article Nine, the Copyright Act permits the effect of recording with the Copyright Office to relate back as far as two months.

Because the Copyright Act and Article Nine create different priority schemes, there will be occasions when different results will be reached depending on which scheme was employed. The availability of filing under the UCC would thus undermine the priority scheme established by Congress with respect to copyrights. This type of direct interference with the operation of federal law weighs heavily in favor of preemption. See generally Bonito Boats, Inc. v. Thunder Craft Boats, Inc., 489 U.S. 141 (1989).

The bankruptcy court below nevertheless concluded that security interests in copyrights could be perfected by filing either with the copyright office or with the secretary of state under the UCC, making a tongue-in-cheek analogy to the use of a belt and suspenders to hold up a pair of pants. According to the bankruptcy court, because either device is equally useful, one should be free to choose which one to wear. With all due respect, this court finds the analogy inapt. There is no legitimate reason why pants should be held up in only one particular manner: Individuals and public modesty are equally served by either device, or even by a safety pin or a piece of rope; all that really matters is that the job gets done. Registration schemes are different in that the *way* notice is given is precisely what matters. To the extent interested parties are confused as to which system is being employed, this increases the level of uncertainty and multiplies the risk of error, exposing creditors to the possibility that they might get caught with their pants down.

A recordation scheme best serves its purpose where interested parties can obtain notice of all encumbrances by referring to a single, precisely defined recordation system. The availability of parallel state recordation systems that could put parties on constructive notice as to encumbrances on copyrights would surely interfere with the effectiveness of the federal recordation scheme. Given the virtual absence of dual recordation schemes in our legal system, Congress cannot be presumed to have contemplated such a result. The court therefore concludes that any state recordation system pertaining to interests in copyrights would be preempted by the Copyright Act.

2.   State law leads to the same conclusion. Article Nine of the Uniform Commercial Code establishes a comprehensive scheme for the regulation of security interests in personal property and fixtures. By superseding a multitude of pre-Code security devices, it provides "a simple and unified structure within which the immense variety of present-day secured financing transactions can go forward with less cost and greater certainty." UCC

§ 9101, Official Comment. However, Article Nine is not all encompassing; under the "step back" provision of UCC § 9104, Article Nine does not apply "[t]o a security interest subject to any statute of the United States to the extent that such statute governs the rights of parties to and third parties affected by transactions in particular types of property."

For most items of personal property, Article Nine provides that security interests must be perfected by filing with the office of the secretary of state in which the debtor is located. See UCC §§ 9302(1), 9401(1)(c). Such filing, however, is not "necessary or effective to perfect a security interest in property subject to . . . [a] statute or treaty of the United States which provides for a national or international registration . . . or which specifies a place of filing different from that specified in [Article Nine] for filing of the security interest." UCC § 9302(3)(a). When a national system for recording security interests exists, the Code treats compliance with that system as "equivalent to the filing of a financing statement under [Article Nine,] and a security interest in property subject to the statute or treaty can be perfected only by compliance therewith. . . ." UCC § 9302(4).[9] * * *

Whether the federal statute also provides a priority scheme different from that in Article Nine is a separate issue, addressed below. Compliance with a national registration scheme is necessary for perfection regardless of whether federal law governs priorities.[13] Cap Fed's security interest in the copyrights of the films in NPI's library and the receivables they have generated therefore is unperfected.

B. *Effect of Failing to Record with the Copyright Office*

Having concluded that Cap Fed should have, but did not, record its security interest with the Copyright Office, the court must next determine whether NPI as a debtor in possession can subordinate Cap Fed's interest and recover it for the benefit of the bankruptcy estate. As a debtor in possession, NPI has nearly all of the powers of a bankruptcy trustee, see 11 U.S.C. § 1107(a), including the authority to set aside preferential or fraudulent transfers, as well as transfers otherwise voidable under applicable state or federal law. See 11 U.S.C. §§ 544, 547, 548.

---

9. According to the official commentary to section 9302:

> Subsection (3) exempts from the filing provisions of this Article transactions as to which an adequate system of filing, state or federal, has been set up outside this Article and subsection (4) makes clear that when such a system exists perfection of a relevant security interest can be had only through compliance with that system (i.e., filing under this Article is not a permissible alternative).
>
> . . . .
>
> Perfection of a security interest under a . . . federal statute of the type referred to in subsection (3) has all the consequences of perfection under the provisions of [Article Nine].

UCC § 9302, Official Comment ¶¶ 8, 9.

13. When a federal statute provides a system of national registration but fails to provide its own priority scheme, the priority scheme established by Article Nine—namely UCC § 9301—will generally govern the conflicting rights of creditors. Whether a creditor's interest is perfected, however, depends on whether the creditor recorded its interest in accordance with the federal statute. See UCC § 9302(4).

Particularly relevant is the "strong arm clause" of 11 U.S.C. § 544(a)(1), which, in respect to personal property in the bankruptcy estate, gives the debtor in possession every right and power state law confers upon one who has acquired a lien by legal or equitable proceedings.[15] If, under the applicable law, a judicial lien creditor would prevail over an adverse claimant, the debtor in possession prevails; if not, not. A lien creditor generally takes priority over unperfected security interests in estate property because, under Article Nine, "an unperfected security interest is subordinate to the rights of . . . [a] person who becomes a lien creditor before the security interest is perfected." UCC § 9301(1)(b). * * *

Because NPI meets all of the requirements for subsequent transferees to prevail under 17 U.S.C. § 205(d)—a transferee who took in good faith, for valuable consideration and without notice of the earlier transfer—Cap Fed's unperfected security interest in NPI's copyrights and the receivables they generated is trumped by NPI's hypothetical judicial lien. NPI may therefore avoid Cap Fed's interest and preserve it for the benefit of the bankruptcy estate.

CONCLUSION

The judgment of the bankruptcy court is reversed. The case is ordered remanded for a determination of which movies in NPI's library are the subject of valid copyrights. The court shall then determine the status of Cap Fed's security interest in the movies and the debtor's other property. To the extent that interest is unperfected, the court shall permit NPI to exercise its avoidance powers under the Bankruptcy Code.

NOTES AND QUESTIONS

1. Also holding that the Copyright Act preempts state commercial law on the question of filing to perfect a security interest in a copyright (on a film) is *Official Unsecured Creditors' Committee v. Zenith Prod.*, 127 B.R. 34 (Bankr.C.D. Cal. 1991), another case involving registered copyrights. The Ninth Circuit has not extended this preemption approach to unregistered copyrights, for which the UCC will control. In re World Auxiliary Power Co., 303 F.3d 1120 (9th Cir. 2002). Recall that since 1976, registration is not required for copyright to come into existence; copyright arises as soon as the work is fixed in a tangible medium of expression. 17 U.S.C. § 102(a). Why might perfection through filing be different for unregistered copyrights?

---

15. 11 U.S.C. § 544(a)(1) provides:

The [debtor in possession] shall have, as of the commencement of the case and without regard to any knowledge of the [debtor in possession] or of any creditor, the rights and powers of, or may avoid any transfer of property of the debtor or any obligation incurred by the debtor that is voidable by—

(1) a creditor that extends credit to the debtor at the time of the commencement of the case, and that obtains, at such time and with respect to such credit, a judicial lien on all property on which a creditor on a simple contract could have obtained such a judicial lien, whether or not such a creditor exists.

2. Notice and notice-giving are central to the operation of security interests. In the case of intellectual property, a national system sometimes preempts the system of filing under the states' commercial codes. One advantage of this is that personal property, and intellectual property in particular, is hard to locate, and can lead to complicated choice of law questions. (Where, for example, is a right of publicity located?) The effect of finding that the federal copyright scheme is so comprehensive as to preempt the filing provisions of the various states' commercial codes is that these complicated problems are solved in the case of registered copyrights. We consider registration systems in more detail in the next Chapter.

3. Personal property markets are increasingly national or at least regional in scope. Used automobiles, for example, are frequently auctioned and distributed to wholesalers who resell them, frequently in other states. Does this suggest that all personal property should be subject to a single, uniform system for filing security interests? The UCC in fact tolerates more diversity in filing systems than on virtually any other topic. What accounts for this?

CHAPTER VIII

TITLE RECORDS AND THE TRANSFER OF PROPERTY

We have seen in previous chapters how important it is for those who assert property rights to let others know what exactly is being asserted. The rules of first possession, for example, are designed to make clear to those who potentially would compete for the resource that it belongs to someone else. For ongoing ownership, markers like boundary stones and name tags serve to put others on notice of ownership claims. Starting with the ancient civilizations, records of various sorts have also served to evidence ownership. By collecting these records in a centralized location, those who might have some interest in the state of title to property need only look up the information.

Title records are deeply intertwined with transfers of property. Although persons other than potential purchasers might have reason to consult title records, purchasers—broadly conceived to include lenders—are the main users of title records. By investigating the state of title though the title records, a potential purchaser (usually having employed an expert) can gain assurance at reasonable cost that he or she is acquiring what the seller claims to have to transfer.

There is another sense in which transfer lies at the heart of a system of property records: It is the possibility of transfer that makes the state of title more difficult to establish. If each owned thing were assigned an owner who could not alienate it (with ownership going indefeasibly to the heirs or to the state upon death), property would be a lot less complicated—and a lot less useful. In the following materials we begin with the bedrock principle that an owner can only convey what the owner owns. We then turn to an important exception to this principle, in favor of good faith purchasers. Finally we survey some systems of records of ownership in various resources, including most prominently land.

A. NEMO DAT

The baseline principle of our system of property regarding transfers of ownership is *nemo dat quod non habet*—"no one can give that which he does not have." The phrase, in a closely related variant, traces back at least as far as the Digest of Justinian (Digest 50.54), which gives credit to the Roman jurist Ulpian (Ad Edictum 46). In other words, if I own something because someone transferred it to me—by sale, gift, bequest, etc.—I normally have only that which the previous owner had and nothing more. This is sometimes called the "derivation" principle: The transferee's rights derive from those of the transferor. See Douglas G. Baird & Thomas H. Jackson, Cases, Problems, and Materials on Security Interests in Personal Property 3–8 (2d ed. 1987). Willingness to buy the Brooklyn Bridge is considered a symbol of gullibility because we assume everyone knows about the principle of *nemo dat* and would have to be out of their mind to think that the offeror actually has the rights to sell. Jeanne L. Schroeder, Is Article 8 Finally Ready This Time? The Radical Reform of Secured Lending On Wall Street, 1994 Colum. Bus. L. Rev. 291, 296 & n.6.

Nemo dat is also related to the principle of "first in time is first in right." Here the classic problem is someone, A, who transfers his or her interest to B and then turns around, and out of mistake or worse, transfers to C. Who owns the property? According to the *nemo dat* principle, it would be B, because A had rights to transfer when A transferred to B. Now B has the rights. When A later transfers to C, A has no rights to transfer and hence by *nemo dat* C gets nothing. Of course C could sue A, but A in such situations will often (not coincidentally) have fled the jurisdiction or be judgment-proof. There are situations in which C could prevail over B, but *nemo dat* and its first-in-time implications are the baseline.

The *nemo dat* principle rests on a vision of a chain of transactions. Current owners must be able to trace their ownership back in time through a series of legitimate transfers (ideally) to an act of legitimate original acquisition. Later we consider ways in which the law cuts off the need for this tracing to an ultimate root of title. But the tracing itself can prove to be quite complicated, as illustrated by the following case.

Kunstsammlungen Zu Weimar v. Elicofon

United States District Court, Eastern District of New York, 1981.
536 F.Supp. 829, affirmed, 678 F.2d 1150 (2d Cir. 1982).

■ MISHLER, DISTRICT JUDGE. This action was commenced in 1969 by the Federal Republic of Germany, as the representative of the people of Germany, to recover possession from defendant Elicofon of two portraits painted by the renowned fifteenth century German artist Albrecht Duerer. The paintings disappeared from their place of safekeeping in Germany during the occupation of Germany by the Allied Forces in the summer of 1945. In 1966 the paintings were discovered in the possession of Elicofon, who had purchased them in Brooklyn, New York from an American serviceman in 1946.

By order dated March 25, 1969, this court granted the Grand Duchess of Saxony–Weimar leave to intervene as plaintiff. The Grand Duchess asserted ownership to the paintings by assignment from her husband, Grand Duke Carl August. And by order dated February 24, 1975, six years later, the Kunstsammlungen zu Weimar, a museum located in what is now the German Democratic Republic, the predecessor of which had possession of the paintings before their disappearance, and which claims to be entitled to recover them from Elicofon, was granted the right to intervene as plaintiff in this action.

Thereafter, on December 9, 1975, the original plaintiff, the Federal Republic of Germany, discontinued its claim with prejudice. And in a Memorandum of Decision and Order, dated August 24, 1978, this court dismissed the intervenor-complaint and cross-complaint of the Grand Duchess of Saxony–Weimar. Thus, the only parties remaining in the action are the plaintiff-intervenor Kunstsammlungen and the defendant Elicofon.

Presently before the court are the motions of plaintiff-intervenor Kunstsammlungen zu Weimar for summary judgment and the cross-motion of defendant Elicofon for summary judgment.

Figure 8–1
Albrecht Dürer, Portraits of Hans Tucher and Felicitas Tucher, née Rieter, 1499

(These are the portraits involved in *Kunstsammlungen zu Weimar v. Elicofon.*)

Each portrait: Oil on panel, 28 × 24 cm, Schlossmuseum, Weimar.

HISTORICAL SETTING & FACTS

Until 1927, the Duerer portraits which are the subject of this suit formed part of the private art collection of the Grand Duke of Saxe–Weimar–Eisenach. Under the terms of a Settlement Agreement of 1927 between the Land of Thuringia and the widow of Wilhelm Ernst, the then owner of the private collection, title to the Grand Ducal Art Collection had been transferred to the Land of Thuringia. Thuringia was created by Federal German Law of April 20, 1920 and was the legal successor to the territory of Weimar, which included as one of its seven subdivisions Saxe–Weimar–Eisenach, the territory over which the Grand Dukes formerly had presided before being ousted from power.

In 1933, Hitler assumed power in Germany. Throughout much of the period of the Third Reich, until 1943, the Duerer paintings remained on exhibit in a museum in Weimar, Thuringia, known as the Staatliche Kunstsammlungen zu Weimar, the predecessor to the Kunstsammlungen zu Weimar. But in 1943, after the commencement of World War II, Dr. Walter Scheidig, the then Director of the Staatliche, according to his account, anticipated the bombardment of Weimar and had the Duerers and other valuable items of the museum transferred to a storeroom in a wing of a nearby castle, the Schloss Schwarzburg, located in the District of Rudolstadt in the Land of Thuringia, where they remained until their disappearance in the summer of 1945.

On May 8, 1945, the Hitler Government surrendered. On June 5, 1945, the Allied Powers—the United Kingdom, the United States, the U.S.S.R. and the French Republic—issued a Declaration stating that the Allied Governments assumed supreme authority with respect to Germany, including all the powers possessed by the German Government. For the purposes of occupation, Germany was divided into four zones with one of the Four Powers assuming military authority over each zone to effect its own policy in regard to local matters and the policy of the Allied Control Council in regard to matters affecting Germany as a whole.

Under the June 1945 Declaration the Land of Thuringia was designated to be part of the Soviet Zone of Occupation. However, the American Military Forces had occupied Thuringia, with a regiment stationed at Schwarzburg Castle, since the defeat of Germany or some time before the official surrender in April or May of 1945. In accordance with the Allied plan, on July 1, 1945, the United States turned over control of Thuringia to the Soviet Armed Forces. According to Dr. Scheidig's account, the disappearance of the Duerer portraits from Schwarzburg Castle coincided in time with the departure of the American troops from the Castle.

Political differences and disagreement over the future of Germany developed between the Western Allies and the Soviet Union. Irreconcilable divisions prompted the Soviet Union's Commander in Chief to resign from the Allied Control Council on March 7, 1948 and the Council thereafter ceased meeting as the combined governing body of occupied Germany. On September 21, 1949, the Federal Republic of Germany was established in the former French, British and United States Zones; and on October 7, 1949, the German Democratic Republic was established in the former Soviet Zone.

On April 14, 1969, retroactive to January 1, 1969, the Minister of Culture of the German Democratic Republic, issued an order conferring juridical personality upon the former Staatliche Kunstsammlungen, which thereafter became known as the Kunstsammlungen zu Weimar, a status which under East German Law entitled the Kunstsammlungen to maintain suit for return of the Duerers. The Kunstsammlungen moved to intervene as a plaintiff in this action for return of the Duerer portraits in April 1969. In a Memorandum of Decision and Order dated September 25, 1972, we denied the motion to intervene on the ground that the Kunstsammlungen was an arm and instrumentality of the German Democratic Republic, a country not recognized by the United States at the time. On September 4, 1974, the United States extended formal recognition to the German Democratic Republic. Accordingly, by order of February 24, 1975, upon motion, we vacated our prior order and permitted the Kunstsammlungen to file its complaint. In its complaint, the Kunstsammlungen alleges that the Duerer paintings were stolen in 1945 from the Staatliche Kunstsammlungen zu Weimar and that Elicofon acquired them from the thief or his transferee and, therefore, has no right to them; and that as successor to the rights of the former Territory of Weimar and Land of Thuringia, the Kunstsammlungen is entitled to immediate possession. In his answer Elicofon denies that he holds the paintings wrongfully and on the basis of certain affirmative defenses, which are asserted in support of its motion for summary judgment, denies that the Kunstsammlungen is entitled to recover the paintings.

SUMMARY OF ARGUMENTS

In support of its motion for summary judgment, Kunstsammlungen argues:

There exists no genuine issue of material fact as to whether Elicofon could have acquired good title. The uncontradicted account of Dr. Scheidig, Director of the Kunstsammlungen at the time the paintings disappeared, creates the irrefutable inference that the paintings were stolen in 1945 from Schwarzburg Castle. Thus, Elicofon could not have acquired good title to the Duerers even if he purchased them without knowledge of their source. * * *

A.   The Kunstsammlungen's Motion for Summary Judgment

In moving for summary judgment the movant bears the burden of showing the absence of a genuine issue as to any material fact. The Kunstsammlungen argues that the irrefutable facts in this case indicate that Elicofon could not have acquired good title to the Duerers.

According to Elicofon, he acquired the Duerer portraits in 1946 when he bought them for $450 from a young American ex-serviceman, about 25 to 30 years old, who appeared at Elicofon's Brooklyn home with about eight paintings and who told Elicofon that he had purchased the paintings in Germany. Although Elicofon learned the name of the person he has since forgotten it. Elicofon had the paintings framed and hung them on a wall in his home with others. They remained there until 1966 when a friend, Stern, having seen a pamphlet containing lists of stolen artworks, informed Elicofon of their identity. At that time Elicofon made public his possession of the Duerers which precipitated a demand by the Kunstsammlungen for their return. Elicofon maintains that he purchased the paintings in good faith, without knowledge of their source or identity.

For the purpose of its motion for summary judgment, the Kunstsammlungen accepts the truth of Elicofon's version of the manner in which he acquired the Duerers. The Kunstsammlungen argues that good faith is irrelevant.

It is a fundamental rule of law in New York that a thief or someone who acquires possession of stolen property after a theft "cannot transfer a good title even to a bona fide purchaser for value [because] [o]nly the true owner's own conduct, or the operation of law . . . can act to divest that true owner of title in his property. . . ." 3 Williston, Sales § 23–12.

The Kunstsammlungen contends that the circumstances surrounding the disappearance of the Duerers leave no question that the paintings were stolen from Schwarzburg Castle where they had been stored, and that consequently Elicofon could not have acquired title to the paintings. Elicofon claims that there does exist a question as to those facts on which the Kunstsammlungen relies to establish a theft; alternatively, he claims, such a theft does not preclude a finding that Elicofon's transferor acquired good title to the paintings in Germany. Thus, the question on this motion is whether the facts about which there is no genuine dispute indicate that Elicofon bought the paintings from one who was incapable of conveying title.

1. The Occurrence of a Theft

On a motion for summary judgment, the moving party has the initial burden of presenting "evidence on which, taken by itself, it would be entitled to a directed verdict." Donnelly v. Guion, 467 F.2d 290, 293 (2d Cir. 1972). The facts about which the Kunstsammlungen contends there is no dispute were related by Dr. Walter Scheidig. Until 1940 Dr. Scheidig was the Deputy Director of the Kunstsammlungen zu Weimar, and from 1940 to 1967 was the Director of the museum. The facts were told by Dr. Scheidig at a deposition conducted by counsel for all parties to this action in May, 1971; in addition, various documents and letters are submitted as exhibits in support thereof. Dr. Scheidig died in 1974. [The court reviews the deposition testimony of Dr. Scheidig and concludes that there is no genuine issue of material fact as to the theft. The court then goes on to decide other issues of German law and of statutes of limitations and standing in favor of the East German art museum.] * * *

Plaintiff's motion for summary judgment is granted and defendant's cross motion for summary judgment denied. Defendant is directed to deliver the Duerers to plaintiff, the Kunstsammlungen.

NOTES AND QUESTIONS

1. In its opinion affirming the district court, the Second Circuit remarked: "The search for an answer to the deceptively simple question, 'Who owns the paintings?,' involves a labyrinthian journey through 19th century German dynastic law, contemporary German property law, Allied Military Law during the post-War occupation of Germany, New York State

law, and intricate conceptions of succession and sovereignty in international law." 678 F.2d at 1153. Other aspects of the dispute centered on whether the Grand Duchess of Saxony–Weimar had a claim to the paintings as being part of her ancestral private collection or whether the paintings were held as crown property. Because the court held them to be crown property, successor governments acquired all the rights of the predecessor governments; in other words, when old governments fell or one administrative unit was replaced by another, title passed from government to government under *nemo dat* as well. How does the *nemo dat* principle figure in Justice Marshall's opinion in *Johnson v. M'Intosh*, excerpted in Chapter II?

2.   This case also illustrates that the *nemo dat* baseline forms the backdrop not only to the common law but also German civil law. In German law, however, the good faith purchaser exception to *nemo dat* is wider than in American law, and in Germany a good faith purchaser could acquire good title from a thief. As stated in the case, the general rule in the United States is that one cannot acquire good title from a thief.

3.   The *Kunstsammlungen zu Weimar* case also involved unsuccessful claims of good faith purchase and something like adverse possession. As we shall see, these are the main exceptions to *nemo dat*.

B.   THE GOOD FAITH PURCHASER

The good faith purchaser doctrine represents an important exception to *nemo dat*, one that plays a central role in all the remaining materials that will be considered in this Chapter. Suppose A sells goods to B but for some reason the transaction is flawed. Let us suppose B paid for the goods with a check that bounces. B then turns around and sells the same goods to C. As long as C purchases the goods in good faith, that is, without knowledge of the flaw in the A-to-B transaction, and as long as C gives value—that is, the B-to-C transaction is not a gift—then the law will generally give C title to the goods as a good faith purchaser. The Uniform Commercial Code (UCC) recognizes both the *nemo dat* principle and the good faith purchaser exception in the following provision:

§ 2–403.

(1) A purchaser of goods acquires all title which his transferor had or had power to transfer except that a purchaser of a limited interest acquires rights only to the extent of the interest purchased. A person with voidable title has power to transfer a good title to a good faith purchaser for value. When goods have been delivered under a transaction of purchase the purchaser has such power even though

(a) the transferor was deceived as to the identity of the purchaser, or

(b) the delivery was in exchange for a check which is later dishonored, or or (c) it was agreed that the transaction was to be a "cash sale",

(d) the delivery was procured through fraud punishable as larcenous under the criminal law.

Notice that the UCC limits the good faith purchaser doctrine to circumstances in which the transferor (B in our hypothetical) has "voidable" title. This is to be distinguished from "void" title. Property acquired by theft is a primary example of void title. Void title gives no power to create rights in another (*nemo dat* continues to apply). But voidable title gives a power to transfer to a good faith purchaser for value. Subdivisions (a) through (d) of § 2–403 describe circumstances that the UCC considers to create "voidable" title. For example, acquiring goods with a check that bounces or by fraud creates "voidable" title. The UCC defines "purchase" broadly to mean "taking by sale, lease, discount, negotiation, mortgage, pledge, lien, security interest, issue or reissue, gift, or any other voluntary transaction creating an interest in property." § 1–201(29). Nevertheless, those who take by gift usually cannot claim the protections of the good faith purchaser rule, because they have not purchased "for value."

Kotis v. Nowlin Jewelry, Inc.

Court of Appeals of Texas, 1992.
844 S.W.2d 920.

■ DRAUGHN, JUSTICE. Eddie Kotis appeals from a judgment declaring appellee, Nowlin Jewelry, Inc., the sole owner of a Rolex watch, and awarding appellee attorney's fees. Kotis raises fourteen points of error. We affirm.

On June 11, 1990, Steve Sitton acquired a gold ladies Rolex watch, President model, with a diamond bezel from Nowlin Jewelry by forging a check belonging to his brother and misrepresenting to Nowlin that he had his brother's authorization for the purchase. The purchase price of the watch, and the amount of the forged check, was $9,438.50. The next day, Sitton telephoned Eddie Kotis, the owner of a used car dealership, and asked Kotis if he was interested in buying a Rolex watch. Kotis indicated interest and Sitton came to the car lot. Kotis purchased the watch for $3,550.00. Kotis also called Nowlin's Jewelry that same day and spoke with Cherie Nowlin.

Ms. Nowlin told Kotis that Sitton had purchased the watch the day before. Ms. Nowlin testified that Kotis would not immediately identify himself. Because she did not have the payment information available, Ms. Nowlin asked if she could call him back. Kotis then gave his name and number. Ms. Nowlin testified that she called Kotis and told him the amount of the check and that it had not yet cleared. Kotis told Ms. Nowlin that he did not have the watch and that he did not want the watch. Ms. Nowlin also testified that Kotis would not tell her how much Sitton was asking for the watch.

John Nowlin, the president of Nowlin's Jewelry, testified that, after this call from Kotis, Nowlin's bookkeeper began attempting to confirm whether the check had cleared. When they learned the check would not be honored by the bank, Nowlin called Kotis, but Kotis refused to talk to Nowlin. Kotis referred Nowlin to his attorney. On June 25, 1990, Kotis' attorney called Nowlin and suggested that Nowlin hire an attorney and allegedly indicated that Nowlin could buy the watch back from Kotis. Nowlin refused to repurchase the watch.

Figure 8–2
From the Nowlin Jewelry Website

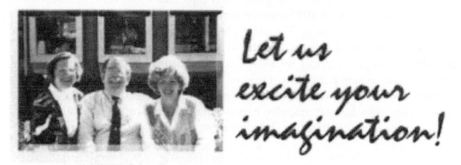

The Nowlin's - Marilyn John and Cherie   "The owner's always in."

With the values of integrity and knowledge we offer fine quality jewelry at appropriate prices and backup service.

Source: http://www.nowlinjewelry.com/body-pageintro2.htm
Courtesy John Nowlin.

After Sitton was indicted for forgery and theft, the district court ordered Nowlin's Jewelry to hold the watch until there was an adjudication of the ownership of the watch. Nowlin then filed suit seeking a declaratory judgment that Nowlin was the sole owner of the watch. Kotis filed a counterclaim for a declaration that Kotis was a good faith purchaser of the watch and was entitled to possession and title of the watch. After a bench trial, the trial court rendered judgment declaring Nowlin the sole owner of the watch. The trial court also filed Findings of Fact and Conclusions of Law.

In point of error one, Kotis claims the trial court erred in concluding that Sitton did not receive the watch through a transaction of purchase with Nowlin, within the meaning of Tex.Bus. & Com.Code Ann. § 2.403(a). Where a party challenges a trial court's conclusions of law, we may sustain the judgment on any legal theory supported by the evidence. Incorrect conclusions of law will not require reversal if the controlling findings of facts will support a correct legal theory.

Kotis contends there is evidence that the watch is a "good" under the UCC, there was a voluntary transfer of the watch, and there was physical delivery of the watch. Thus, Kotis maintains that the transaction between Sitton and Nowlin was a transaction of purchase such that Sitton acquired the ability to transfer good title to a good faith purchaser under § 2.403.

Section 2.403 provides:

A purchaser of goods acquires all title which his transferor had or had power to transfer except that a purchaser of a limited interest acquires rights only to the extent of the interest purchased. A person with voidable title has power to transfer good title to a good faith purchaser for value. When goods have been delivered under a transaction of purchase the purchaser has such power even though

(1) the transferor was deceived as to the identity of the purchaser, or

(2) the delivery was in exchange for a check which is later dishonored, or

(3) it was agreed that the transaction was to be a "cash sale", or

(4) the delivery was procured through fraud punishable as larcenous under the criminal law.

Tex.Bus. & Com.Code Ann. § 2.403(a) (Vernon 1968).

Neither the code nor case law defines the phrase "transaction of purchase." "Purchase" is defined by the code as a "taking by sale, discount, negotiation, mortgage, pledge, lien, issue or reissue, gift or any other voluntary transaction creating an interest in property." Tex.Bus. & Com.Code Ann. § 1.201(32) (Vernon 1968). Thus, only voluntary transactions can constitute transactions of purchase.

Having found no Texas case law concerning what constitutes a transaction of purchase under § 2.403(a), we have looked to case law from other states. Based on the code definition of a purchase as a voluntary transaction, these cases reason that a thief who wrongfully takes the goods against the will of the owner is not a purchaser. See Suburban Motors, Inc. v. State Farm Mut. Automobile Ins. Co., 268 Cal.Rptr. 16, 18 (Cal. Ct. App. 1990); Charles Evans BMW, Inc. v. Williams, 395 S.E.2d 650, 651–52 (Ga. Ct. App. 1990); Inmi–Etti v. Aluisi, 492 A.2d 917, 922 (Md. Ct. Spec. App. 1985). On the other hand, a swindler who fraudulently induces the victim to deliver the goods voluntarily is a purchaser under the code. Inmi–Etti, 492 A.2d at 922; Williams, 395 S.E.2d at 652.

In this case, Nowlin's Jewelry voluntarily delivered the watch to Sitton in return for payment by check that was later discovered to be forged. Sitton did not obtain the watch against the will of the owner. Rather, Sitton fraudulently induced Nowlin's Jewelry to deliver the watch voluntarily. Thus, we agree with appellant that the trial court erred in concluding that Sitton did not receive the watch through a transaction of purchase under § 2.403(a). We sustain point of error one.

In point of error two, Kotis contends the trial court erred in concluding that, at the time Sitton sold the watch to Kotis, Sitton did not have at least voidable title to the watch. In point of error nine, Kotis challenges the trial court's conclusion that Nowlin's Jewelry had legal and equitable title at all times relevant to the lawsuit. The lack of Texas case law addressing such issues under the code again requires us to look to case law from other states to assist in our analysis.

In *Suburban Motors, Inc. v. State Farm Mut. Automobile Ins. Co.*, the California court noted that § 2.403 provides for the creation of voidable title where there is a voluntary transfer of goods. 268 Cal.Rptr. at 18. Section 2.403(a)(1)–(4) set forth the types of voluntary transactions that can give the purchaser voidable title. Where goods are stolen such that there is no voluntary transfer, only void title results. Id. at 19; Inmi–Etti, 492 A.2d at 921. Subsection (4) provides that a purchaser can obtain voidable title to the goods even if "delivery was procured through fraud punishable as larcenous under the criminal law." Tex.Bus. & Com.Code Ann. § 2.403(a)(4) (Vernon 1968). This subsection applies to cases involving acts fraudulent to the seller such as where the seller delivers the goods in return for a forged check. See Inmi–Etti, 492 A.2d at 921. Although Sitton paid Nowlin's Jewelry with a forged check, he obtained possession of the watch through a voluntary transaction of purchase and received voidable, rather than void, title to the watch. Thus, the trial court erred in concluding that Sitton received no title to the watch and in concluding that Nowlin's retained title at all relevant times. We sustain points of error two and nine.

In point of error three, Kotis claims the trial court erred in concluding that Kotis did not give sufficient value for the watch to receive protection under § 2.403, that Kotis did not take good title to the watch as a good faith purchaser, that Kotis did not receive good title to the watch, and that Kotis is not entitled to the watch under § 2.403. In points of error four through eight, Kotis challenges the trial court's findings regarding his good faith, his honesty in fact, and his actual belief, and the reasonableness of the belief, that the watch had been received unlawfully.

Under § 2.403(a), a transferor with voidable title can transfer good title to a good faith purchaser. Tex.Bus. & Com.Code Ann. § 2.403(a) (Vernon 1968). Good faith means "honesty in fact in the conduct or transaction concerned." Tex.Bus. & Com.Code Ann. § 1.201(19) (Vernon 1968). The test for good faith is the actual belief of the party and not the reasonableness of that belief. La Sara Grain v. First Nat'l Bank, 673 S.W.2d 558, 563 (Tex. 1984).

Kotis was a dealer in used cars and testified that he had bought several cars from Sitton in the past and had no reason not to trust Sitton. He also testified that on June 12, 1990, Sitton called and asked Kotis if he was interested in buying a Ladies Rolex. Once Kotis indicated his interest in the watch, Sitton came to Kotis's place of business. According to Kotis, Sitton said that he had received $18,000.00 upon the sale of his house and that he had used this to purchase the watch for his girlfriend several months before. Kotis paid $3,550.00 for the watch. Kotis further testified that he then spoke to a friend, Gary Neal Martin, who also knew Sitton. Martin sagely advised Kotis to contact Nowlin's to check whether Sitton had financed the watch. Kotis testified that he called Nowlin's after buying the watch.

Cherie Nowlin testified that she received a phone call from Kotis on June 12, 1990, although Kotis did not immediately identify himself. Kotis asked if Nowlin's had sold a gold President model Rolex watch with a diamond bezel about a month before. When asked, Kotis told Ms. Nowlin that Sitton had come to Kotis' car lot and was trying to sell the watch. Ms. Nowlin testified that Kotis told her he did not want the watch because he already owned a Rolex. Ms. Nowlin told Kotis that Sitton had purchased the watch the day before. Kotis asked about the method of payment. Because Ms. Nowlin did not know, she agreed to check and call Kotis back. She called Kotis back and advised him that Sitton had paid for the watch with a check that had not yet cleared. When Ms. Nowlin asked if Kotis had the watch, Kotis said no and would not tell her how much Sitton was asking for the watch. Ms. Nowlin did advise Kotis of the amount of the check.

After these calls, the owner of Nowlin's asked his bookkeeper to call the bank regarding Sitton's check. They learned on June 15, 1990 that the check would be dishonored. John Nowlin called Kotis the next day and advised him about the dishonored check. Kotis refused to talk to Nowlin and told Nowlin to contact his attorney. Nowlin also testified that a reasonable amount to pay for a Ladies President Rolex watch with a diamond bezel in mint condition was $7,000.00–$8,000.00. Nowlin maintained that $3,500.00 was an exorbitantly low price for a watch like this.

The trier of fact is the sole judge of the credibility of the witnesses and the weight to be given their testimony. Kotis testified that he lied when he spoke with Cherie Nowlin and that he had already purchased the watch before he learned that Sitton's story was false. The judge, as the trier of fact, may not have believed Kotis when he said that he had already purchased the watch. If the judge disbelieved this part of Kotis' testimony, other facts tend to show that Kotis did not believe the transaction was lawful. For example, when Kotis spoke with Nowlin's, he initially refused to identify himself, he said that he did not have the watch and that he did not want the watch, he refused to divulge Sitton's asking price, and he later refused to talk with Nowlin and advised Nowlin to contact Kotis' attorney. Thus, there is evidence supporting the trial court's finding that Kotis did not act in good faith.

There are sufficient facts to uphold the trial court's findings even if the judge had accepted as true Kotis' testimony that, despite his statements to Nowlin's, he had already purchased the watch when he called Nowlin's. The testimony indicated that Kotis was familiar with the price of Rolex watches and that $3,550.00 was an extremely low price for a mint condition watch of this type. An unreasonably low price is evidence the buyer knows the goods are stolen. Although the test is what Kotis actually believed, we agree with appellee that we need not let this standard sanction willful disregard of suspicious facts that would lead a reasonable person to believe the transaction was unlawful. Thus, we find sufficient evidence to uphold the trial court's findings regarding Kotis' lack of status as a good faith purchaser. We overrule points of error three through eight. * * *

NOTES AND QUESTIONS

1.   If Sitton had broken into the Nowlins' shop and taken the watch or ripped it out of their hands and ran off with it, he would have been a thief. In such a case he would have no title at all in the watch (void title). But because he paid with a rubber check, he had voidable title, meaning that he had the power to give good title to a good faith purchaser for value. From the point of view of someone like Kotis, why does it matter whether Sitton is a thief or a fraudster? Or is the difference what we expect of the Nowlins in terms of guarding against theft versus fraud?

2.   In this case the appellate court was called upon to review the factual determination that Kotis did not satisfy the good faith requirement. It is likely that all the judges strongly suspected Kotis knew his seller's rights to the watch were problematic. However, precisely because no one can get inside Kotis's head, and Kotis adamantly claims to be a good faith purchaser, the question becomes in part what kind of notice Kotis had of the flaw in Sitton's title. Sometimes varieties of notice are distinguished. Someone with *actual notice* knows of the relevant fact, here the fraud in the prior sale. One can lack actual notice but have *inquiry notice*, which means that a reasonable person knowing what one does know would have engaged in further inquiry, and this further inquiry would likely have led to actual knowledge of the relevant fact. A registry, as in the case of land and a few types of personal property, is said to give *record notice* of the relevant fact. One who has a duty to search title records will be deemed to know relevant facts disclosed by the records even if that person does not in fact inspect the records. (Inquiry notice and record notice are sometimes called *constructive notice*.) What kind of notice, if any, did Kotis have?

3.   The proper scope of the good faith purchaser exception to *nemo dat* is a matter of controversy. The crux of the problem is that three parties are involved—the original owner, the bad actor who gains possession from the original owner in a wrongful fashion, and the innocent purchaser. Everyone agrees that the optimal solution is to force the bad actor to make everyone whole. But the problem is that the bad actor is usually gone or judgment-proof, and so we have to decide as between two comparatively innocent parties—the original owner and the innocent purchaser—who should bear the loss. One way to frame the question is to ask who as a general matter is in a better position to avoid the loss: the original owner or the potential good faith purchaser? Does the answer change depending on the situation, such that theft is covered by one rule, fraud by another, and purchases from an open street market by a third? Saul Levmore surveys a range of answers to these questions, in legal systems both ancient and modern. He hypothesizes that this is a case in which the question whether to impose the loss on the original owner or the innocent purchaser is a close one and evidence about who ought to bear the loss in any given case is hard to come by; hence we see a variety of approaches across time and space to the good faith purchaser. Saul Levmore, Variety and Uniformity in the Treatment of the Good–Faith Purchaser, 16 J. Legal Stud. 43 (1987). For example, U.S. law is less favorable to the good faith purchaser than is English or civil law.

4. Later we will consider how good faith purchasers of land are protected. But for now consider the related doctrine of estoppel by deed. Say A, who does not own Blackacre, gives B a deed for Blackacre. Then A acquires Blackacre. Can A prevail over B by claiming under *nemo dat* not to have conveyed anything to B? No: Under estoppel by deed, A is prevented from claiming superior title to his grantee. Under another version of the doctrine, title automatically passes to B when A finally acquires Blackacre.

Hauck v. Crawford

Supreme Court of South Dakota, 1953.
62 N.W.2d 92.

■ RUDOLPH, JUDGE. Although in form an action to quiet title, the real purpose of this action is to cancel and set aside a certain mineral deed admittedly signed by plaintiff and certain other deeds transferring the mineral rights by the grantee named in the original deed. No one has questioned the form of the action. The trial court entered judgment cancelling the deeds and defendants have appealed.

Cancellation was asked because of alleged fraud, and it was upon this basis that the trial court entered its judgment. The defendants contend, first, that there was no fraud and second, that the mineral rights were transferred to a bona fide purchaser for value and are not, therefore, subject to cancellation even though obtained by fraud in the first instance.

The facts most favorable in support of the judgment of the trial court are as follows: Plaintiff is a farmer owning and operating a farm located partly in South Dakota and partly in North Dakota. He lives on that part of the farm located in South Dakota in McPherson County. Plaintiff is 44 years old, has an 8th grade education, married and has a family. His farm consists of two sections of land which he purchased at three different times.

On May 23, 1951, while plaintiff was at a neighbor's place, three men approached him and discussed leasing plaintiff's land for oil and gas. A Mr. Crawford was the principal spokesman. Plaintiff testified that after some discussion Crawford offered 25¢ an acre for a lease. Plaintiff agreed, and one of the men apparently prepared the necessary papers on a typewriter while sitting in the back seat of the car. When the papers were prepared they were clamped to a board or pad and presented to plaintiff while in the car for signing. Printed forms were used which contained much fine print. The man who prepared the papers indicated where plaintiff should sign, and after signing in one place, partially turned the signed sheet and asked plaintiff to sign again, stating that this second sheet was a part of the lease, which plaintiff believed. Plaintiff testified that no mention was ever made of a mineral deed and to this extent is corroborated by Crawford who in response to the question, "Did you ever describe to Mr. Hauck one of the instruments as a mineral deed?", answered, "No, sir." Separate instruments were required for the land in each state. Plaintiff never received a copy of any of the instruments he signed.

It now appears that somehow plaintiff had signed a mineral deed conveying one-half the minerals in his land to D. W. Crawford. This deed was filed for record June 1, 1951, but on May 29, 1951, Crawford, the grantee, conveyed such mineral rights to the defendants White and Duncan at Gainsville, Texas. The trial court made no finding relating to the knowledge of White and Duncan concerning the conditions under which Duncan obtained the deed, but decided the case on the basis that they were in fact bona fide purchasers for value. This statement of the facts is sufficient for our present purpose.

We are concerned with a type of fraud which the trial court, texts and decided cases refer to as "fraud in the factum" or "fraud in the execution" as distinguished from "fraud in the inducement." This type of fraud relates to misrepresentation of the contents of a document by which one is induced to sign a paper thinking that it is other than it really is. It was this type of fraud with which this court was dealing in the case of Federal Land Bank v. Houck, 4 N.W.2d 213, 218 (S.D.). In this cited case we held that, as between the original parties, when a person is fraudulently induced to sign a paper believing that it is something other than it really is "the contractual knot was never tied" and such paper or instrument is not only voidable but actually void. In that case it was further held in conformity with prior holdings that "neither reason nor policy justifies the reception of a showing of negligence on the part of him who is overreached, as a countervailent or neutralizer of fraud." In other words, the perpetrator of the fraud cannot avoid his acts by a showing that the person upon whom the fraud was committed was negligent.

The Houck case, we are convinced, settles the issue of fraud. Accepting as a verity testimony of the plaintiff the misrepresentation and trickery of Crawford was complete. Crawford not only misrepresented the effect of the papers plaintiff signed, but by "manipulation of the papers" as found by the trial court tricked plaintiff into signing the deed thinking it was the lease. Under the rule of the Houck case plaintiff's negligence, if any, does not neutralize this fraud. As stated in the Houck case there was "no intention to do the act or say the words which manifest a volition to assent." It must therefore be held that as between Hauck, the grantor, and Crawford, the grantee, the deed was void.

The deed being void as distinguished from voidable it had no effect whatsoever, conveyed nothing to Crawford, and he in turn had nothing to convey to White and Duncan. As stated by Judge McCoy in the case of Highrock v. Gavin, 43 S.D. 315, 346, 179 N.W. 12, 23,

> The grantee under this void deed was as powerless to transmit title as would be the thief of stolen property. Said deed had no more force or effect than a forged deed, and, in principle, was legally analogous to a forged deed. The recording statutes furnish no protection to those who claim as innocent purchasers under a forged or otherwise void deed, where the true owner has been guilty of no negligence or acts sufficient to create an estoppel.

Throughout these proceedings appellant has contended that plaintiff is an intelligent farmer, operating a large farm, and that if he failed to detect the fact that he signed a deed such failure was due to his negligence and therefore he should not be permitted to prevail in these proceedings. We have pointed out above that plaintiff's negligence will not neutralize the fraud, or give validity to the deed, but we are convinced that this holding is not decisive as against a purchaser for value without notice. As indicated in the Highrock–Gavin case, supra, even though the deed is void if plaintiff were negligent or committed acts sufficient to create an estoppel he should bear the brunt of such negligence, rather than a bona fide purchaser.

> An "estoppel" arises when, by his conduct or acts, a party intentionally or through culpable neglect induces another to believe certain facts to exist, and such other party rightfully relies and acts on such belief so that he will be prejudiced if the former is permitted to deny the existence of such facts.

Lambert v. Bradley, 42 N.W.2d 606, 607 (S.D.).

As applied to civil actions the words "culpable negligence" mean the same as actionable negligence. The action being in form an action to quiet title there was no opportunity for appellants to plead an estoppel. There being no opportunity to plead it, the defense is not waived.

As we view this case, therefore, we must revert to the issue of whether plaintiff was negligent when he affixed his signature to this deed not knowing that it was a deed he signed. On this issue the trial court made no specific determination. Whether plaintiff was negligent under all the facts and circumstances presented by this record we believe to be a question of fact which should be determined by the trial court. The question is, did plaintiff act as a person of reasonable and ordinary care, endowed with plaintiff's capacity and intelligence, would usually act under like circumstances?

We are not inclined to accept the trial court's holding that the manner in which plaintiff's signature was obtained constituted a forgery. As disclosed by the notes in 14 A.L.R. 316 and 56 A.L.R. 582, such holding is a minority view, and seems to us unsound. We believe the rule we have announced in Federal Land Bank v. Houck, supra, and in this opinion will better sustain the ends of justice. Our holding, we believe, recognizes actualities. The signature was the real signature of the plaintiff. True, plaintiff was induced to sign by a false representation, but to hold a signature thus obtained a forgery seems artificial and out of harmony with the actual facts.

The judgment appealed from is reversed.

NOTES AND QUESTIONS

1.   This case illustrates the doctrinal variability that enters into good faith purchaser doctrine, especially in the context of real property, where the UCC does not apply. How would the case be analyzed if it were a

purchase of goods covered by the UCC? Should transactions tainted by "fraud in the factum" be treated differently than transactions tainted by "fraud in the inducement"? If so, why? Do you agree with the court's conclusion that the question of Hauck's negligence is critical to whether the Texas transferees (White and Duncan) should be able to keep the mineral rights as good faith purchasers? Why should the application of the doctrine turn on Hauck's behavior, rather than Crawford's?

2.   In the "eternal triangle" of original owner, wrongdoer, and good faith purchaser for value, the dilemma usually is that the wrongdoer is absent or judgment-proof, leaving two innocent parties as potential bearers of the loss. (This would have been the situation in the *Kotis* case if Kotis had been an innocent party; Sitton's check bounced and he was presumably not good for the damages.) Here Hauck managed to drag Crawford into court. Do you think Crawford's availability had an impact on the result? Assuming Crawford still has the proceeds from the sale and is not insolvent, how should Hauck's claim against Crawford for damages come out? How adequate are damages to farmer Hauck?

3.   We will consider land records in more detail later. But for now, consider how a subsequent purchaser is supposed to know that the deed from Hauck to Crawford was void. Forgeries and frauds are but some of the "off-record risks" in the land records.

C.   PROVING OWNERSHIP

In this Part we consider the system of records for a variety of types of property. Even under *nemo dat*, a purchaser would like to know if the title she is being offered is valid—whether the transferor really has the rights to transfer. To the extent we move away from *nemo dat* and allow good faith purchasers to establish title by routes other than the *nemo dat* principle, we also face the question of what constitutes notice and how to provide notice in a way that is generally cost-effective. In any event, for various resources the issue is what combination of possession, markings on the asset, and records (and of what type), is most cost-effective. Moreover, when things go wrong, courts will often be faced ex post with potential unfairness in the operation of some of these systems.

Douglas Baird & Thomas Jackson, *Information, Uncertainty, and the Transfer of Property*, 13 J. LEGAL STUD. 299, 302–04 (1984)

Anglo–American law assumes for the most part that an individual's interest in enjoying property that is acquired, in good faith, from someone else who appears to be the owner is not as important as recognizing the rights of the person who first owned it or who last owned it by wholly consensual transfers. Nevertheless, we shall want to ensure, even in a legal regime that conditions ownership on consensual transfer, that legal rules make it easy for prospective purchasers to investigate their chain of title. Consent, although usually a necessary condition, is rarely a sufficient one.

At one time, taking physical possession of real or tangible personal property was necessary before a person could be relatively certain that his claim was, and would remain, superior to that of others. This principle was affirmed in the case of personal property in 1601 in *Twyne's Case*. A person had purported to sell some sheep, but he had continued to take care of them, shear them, and treat them as his own. The court struck the transaction down as fraudulent, essentially on the ground that there was something wrong with selling goods but keeping possession of them. Since the transaction would have been valid had the property been physically transferred at the time of the sale, the sale itself was not at issue. Rather, the sticking point was the retention of possession. The problem with retention of possession—ostensible ownership—ultimately seems to return to a legal rule governing information as a means of reducing uncertainty. * * *

The system illustrated in *Twyne's Case* depended on a very simple legal rule and hence on minimal government intervention: to obtain priority in an asset over third-party claimants, an individual needed, in addition to the consent of the prior owner, to take physical possession of the asset. Under such a system, both *obtaining* information regarding prior claims and *disseminating* information regarding one's own claim were simple—one took possession. Between the parties to a transaction, such as a lender and the true owner, their private contract governed. But against most of the rest of the world, possession was also necessary.

Establishing ownership rights from possession, however, brings costs. A possession-based rule, for example, impedes temporal divisions of ownership of property. Under such a rule, one who acquires a remainder interest cannot easily take possession of the underlying property and ensure that his rights are superior to the rights of anyone else to whom his transferor might also try to convey the remainder interest. Moreover, a possession-based rule of title makes the tracing of claims for more than one generation difficult and hence increases the risks of a thief in the chain of title—a risk that one or the other party must bear. Certain attributes of particular kinds of property, in addition, may make such property more suitable to a system of filing claims to provide the relevant information.

Filing systems have evolved as the principal alternative to transfer rules based on possession. Public recording of interests in property may reduce the uncertainty concerning the transfer of property, because they contain virtually all relevant information, apart from that imparted by possession itself. Filing systems may also aid in the tracing of transfers over time and hence, compared to a possession-based system, reduce the risk of non-consensual transfers at the same time that they provide assurance to subsequent purchasers that they can in fact acquire good title. In short, rules of transfer that require public recordation can reduce the risks that a subsequent purchaser will not acquire good title without increasing the risk that a present owner will lose his property by theft.

Filing systems can be mixed in a variety of ways with possessory systems for determining rights to assets. * * *

Filing systems are not, however, equally suited to all kinds of property. The desirability of a particular kind of filing system turns on the type of property it is to cover. Filing systems are comparatively better than possessory systems when the property is valuable, when the property is not transferred often, and when it is important to share ownership of the property among several individuals, such as by creating a future interest or a security interest. Filing systems, moreover, are comparatively better when the property's physical use is important or when the underlying property right is abstract and unembodied. In such cases, requiring a transfer of possession as a condition of acquiring paramount rights to the asset brings with it substantial costs that do not outweigh the significant benefits of allowing one party to remain in possession despite his holding less than full ownership of the property. Filing systems, finally, will more easily accommodate *title* claims to an asset, and not just security claims, when describing the property identifies it more precisely than possessing it, when the asset has a long life, and when the property (or perhaps the debtor) is not likely to move. When these conditions hold, finding the property files and using them are comparatively easy and cost effective.

Some types of property seem better suited for one set of transfer rules than another. Real property is the paradigm of property for which a filing system of title claims is superior. One acquires ownership of Blackacre by engaging in certain public acts. This permits others who come later to discover the true owner easily, and hence facilitates consensual transfers by holders along the chain of title. As a first approximation, one has exclusive ownership of Blackacre to the extent that no one else, outside the chain of title, has engaged in those acts before, and one can lean about all such earlier acts, because notations in a filing system are both permanent and publicly accessible. * * *

The provisions requiring the recording of transfers of title to real property deal successfully with the need of potential purchasers of property for reliable information about who owns the land they wish to acquire. The recording system has the effect of reducing the uncertainty surrounding a transfer of real property without undermining the consensual nature of those transfers. And the more effective the set of rules governing the transfer of property is in increasing acquisitional certainty *and* dispositional certainty, the more valuable it is to own property in the first instance.

But not all types of property are equally suited to an informational system based on files. Money is the polar opposite of real property in that it is the best example of property that is *not* suitable for a filing system * * *

Other kinds of personal property provide intermediate cases. Recording systems that establish *title* of personal property are rare, at least when the owner is in possession of the property. The informational advantages that such a system provides do not, as a general matter, seem worth their costs. A piece of personal property is often less valuable than a piece of real property and is likely to be more frequently transferred. Moreover, a title-based recording system is much harder to organize for grain in a silo than it is for land. One has no easy way of knowing that this was the grain grown on Blackacre in one jurisdiction or on Whiteacre in another. Possession is often more reliable than description in sorting personal property. One also has no easy way of knowing in fact that the grain in the silo today was the grain that was there yesterday. Grain or its owner can easily move from one jurisdiction to another, and prospective purchasers may not know which file to check. * * *

NOTES AND QUESTIONS

1. How critical is the practice of secured lending (see Chapter VII) to the development of registration systems for property rights? Most of the types of property that are covered by registration systems are also used as security for loans. This includes land and associated real property interests, major forms of personal property like airplanes and automobiles, and patents. Indeed, many types of personal property (such as machinery) are registered only if they are used as security for loans. On the other hand, property interests that are not often used as security for loans, like works of art, have been slower to develop registration systems. Does the fact that security interests are invisible help explain why registration is necessary in order for secured lending to flourish? How important is taxation in explaining the development of registration of property rights? If the government were to rely heavily on personal property taxes on works of fine art, would you expect a system of registration to emerge for these works?

2. Possession and title records are meant to serve as notice to "all the world," but among that large class of persons some will need more information than others. Potential purchasers often need the most, and the title records are designed for their use—or for the experts they hire. How accessible do title records need to be? Does a potential trespasser need to look up the state of title? See, e.g., Mountain States Tel. & Tel. Co. v. Kelton, 285 P.2d 168 (Ariz. 1955) (holding that contractor is not deemed to have constructive notice of buried cable that was subject of recorded right of way because those with no interest in the title are not bound to search title to land); Statler Mfg., Inc. v. Brown, 691 S.W.2d 445 (Mo. Ct. App. 1985) (holding no constructive notice to contractor from properly recorded easement for aircraft right-of-way).

3. As you read the materials in the balance of this Chapter, ask yourself whether Baird and Jackson are too optimistic about the effectiveness of the recording system for property in land. See, e.g., D. Barlow Burke, Jr., American Conveyancing Patterns: Past Improvements and Current Debates 103–04 & n.2 (1978) (noting the many risks that American recording systems give rise to and how little protection a title search provides, and citing literature); Francis S. Philbrick, Limits of Record Search and Therefore of Notice: Part I, 93 U. Pa. L. Rev. 125 (1944).

1. Land

The keeping of land records is a practice both old and new. In the ancient Near East, records of land transactions and ownership were sometimes kept in the household—as, for example, attested by the story of Jeremiah's purchase in 587 B.C. of a field at Anathoth from his cousin Hanamel (Jer. 32:9–15)—and sometimes in central registries. In ancient Mesopotamia and Egypt, the centralized records were probably kept for purposes like tax collection rather than to bar the claims of third parties. Robert C. Ellickson & Charles DiA. Thorland, Ancient Land Law: Mesopotamia, Egypt, Israel, 71 Chi.-Kent L. Rev. 321 (1995).

Land records designed to cut off the contrary claims of third parties are a more recent development, which came earlier to the United States than to England. The first American recording act was the 1640 Massachusetts Bay recording statute, whose preamble states the act's purpose as "[f]or avoyding fraudulent conveyances, and that every man may know what estate or interest other men have." 6 Powell on Real Property ¶ 912 (1949) (quoting 1 Massachusetts Records at 306). In England, deeds were kept by owners and later by lawyers; concerns with privacy are thought to have delayed large-scale recording until the twentieth century. Even the major overhaul of English property in the English Land Registration Act of 1925 contained provisions for secrecy. C. Dent Bostick, Land Title Registration: An English Solution to an American Problem, 63 Ind. L.J. 55, 75–76 99–100 (1987) (arguing against these secrecy provisions for the United States).

Land records make notice by publicizing transactions—a method in evidence in the Hebrew Bible, the Middle Assyrian Laws, and medieval English sources—less necessary and increasingly vestigial. (Recall livery of seisin and the handing over of the twig or clod of dirt in the sale of a freehold estate, see Chapter V.) Nevertheless, notice by possession has not completely died out. Consider in the following materials the role of possession in furnishing notice to third-party potential purchasers.

Benito Arruñada, *Property Enforcement as Organized Consent*, 19 J. L. Econ & Org. 401, 405–07, 411, 414–16, 420–23 (2003)

 * * * [W]ithout the consent of affected right holders, transactions produce a mix of property and contractual rights: property—*in rem*—effects to the extent compatible with the surviving property rights held by others, and contractual rights for the difference. The proportion of property and contractual rights in the mix varies with the kind of conflicting right. In the extreme case of a fraudulent conveyance, the grantee gets only a contractual right against the grantor, who is not the true owner. More generally, any intended property right is in fact partially contractual if an affected right holder keeps a contradictory or concurrent right against it. This is also true of most disputes of title.[12] Let us assume A sells land to B, but C might be the true owner with some probability * * * Until C consents or the uncertainty is somehow resolved, C has a property right

---

12. The word "title" often refers to both a legal right, as here, and to the evidence of it. Established practice makes it impossible to avoid this ambiguity, which, for the most part, is easily clarified by context.

and *B*'s ownership is burdened with that title "cloud." (Depending on the specific circumstances, *B* will also have obtained a lower price or a contractual right against *A* and/or other participants in the transaction.)

Property rights thus face a trade-off with positive and negative effects. On the one hand, they facilitate specialization by ensuring enforcement, given that right-holders' consent is required to affect them. However, for the same reason, their survival after conveyance of the asset or any other transformation of rights requires costly institutions and resources in order to organize the process of searching, bargaining, and contracting for consent. An obvious cost is that the possibility of hidden property rights increases the information asymmetry between the conveying parties: in the absence of consent from the hidden right holder, the acquired asset is burdened with it and the acquirer has instead a contractual right against the seller. More generally, the need to know which conflicting property rights exist, of finding out who their right holders are, of bargaining with such right holders to obtain their consent, and of contracting or somehow formalizing an agreement with them all increase the costs of transforming and conveying rights. This may in turn hamper investment, trade, and specialization.

1.3   Privacy of Rights as a Benchmark

Under the Roman law tradition of private conveyance that was dominant in Europe until the 19th century, private contracts on land had *in rem* effects on third parties even if the parties kept them secret. In cases of conflict, courts "established title" (i.e., they allocated property and contractual rights) on the basis of evidence of possession and past transactions, whether or not these transactions had remained hidden. This potential enforcement of adverse hidden rights made full consent hard to reach ex ante, hindering trade and specialization. * * *

First, the use of physical possession as the basis for establishing property rights intrinsically limits specialization because it is not applicable to abstract rights like ownership and mortgages. For example, to the extent that possession is used to establish ownership, specialization of ownership and control is hindered—control requires possession, and this subjects owners to the risk of possessors using their position to acquire ownership or convey owners' rights. In such cases, owners will only hold a contractual right against the possessor committing the fraud. * * *

Second, some of the problems posed by possession are solved by embodying abstract rights such as ownership and liens, and even consent, in titles. Evidencing rights with the chain of title certainly facilitates the separation of ownership and control. However, acquirers remain fully unprotected against those hidden charges that are not voluntarily contracted, such as judgment and property tax liens. Furthermore, new possibilities for fraudulent conveyance appear (for instance, predating a sale or a mortgage in order to embezzle assets), which again give rise to contractual rights against the fraudulent grantor and the professionals involved in the transaction.[16] * * *

2.　Publicity Through Recording and Registration

Whatever the palliatives being applied, the costs of contracting property rights under a regime of pure privacy are such that most, if not all, modern systems of property law opt to reduce such costs by constraining contractual freedom in ways that depart substantially from the standards applied in other fields of law. In essence, the law induces or requires the publicity of contracts as a prerequisite for them to attain *in rem* effects. If they keep their rights private, right holders lose or risk losing *in rem* effects. Private contracts may create obligations among the parties, but do not bind third parties—all other right holders and especially potential future buyers and lenders. Publicity therefore facilitates the search for which property rights are alive, making it possible to reach consent ex ante, purging titles, and reducing information asymmetries between the parties.

Specific laws vary substantially, however, with respect to how and when any contradiction with other property rights must be purged by obtaining the consent of the holders of these affected rights. * * *

2.2　Recording of Deeds

In their current form, recorders of deeds have been used since the 19th century in most of the United States, part of Canada, France, and some other countries, most of them having a French legal background. They enroll and keep private contracts ("title deeds") and thus provide evidence on property claims. This evidence is used by the courts to allocate property rights ex post—after litigation. Furthermore, courts apply a nonstandard priority rule. When deciding on a conflict with third parties, they determine the priority of claims from the date of recording in the public office and not from the date of the contract.

This priority rule effectively motivates parties to record from fear of losing title through, for example, a wrongful second sale. If such a second sale were recorded first, it would gain priority over the first one. Consequently all relevant evidence on property rights is publicly available by inspecting both the public records and the land itself.[41] * * *

---

16. The pervasiveness of compulsory proof attests to the importance of restraining fraudulent conveyance. Ancient societies even treated deeds and land grants as sacred (Ellickson, 1993:1329, n. 49). In Egypt, land was transferred by conveying the full chain of titles, and deeds were "sealed" by a public official (Manning, 1995, 2003; Powelson, 1988:17–19; Silver, 1995:125). The use of titles might well have been even older. Practice among the Ewe people showed that titles do not need to be written, not even for using the chain of title as evidence of good title (Lowie, 1920:223–24). From early times, legal systems also required the presence of witnesses.

41. In most jurisdictions, it is also necessary to inspect the land to know about physical possession. This inspection provides actual notice as to the existence of a claim or right. The priority rule also varies substantially and is usually subject to good faith or qualified by buyer knowledge. See Baird and Jackson (1984) and Epstein (1987:7–19). In the present work, these complementary sources of evidence are sidelined to focus on the role of recorders and registers. * * *

It is therefore possible to produce information on the quality of title ("title reports") by having an expert examine all relevant deeds (those that have been recorded) and not only those deeds in the grantor's chain of title. If there is sufficient demand, a whole industry will develop to supply these title assurance services. This may take different forms: notaries public in France and abstractors, attorneys, title insurance agents, and title insurance underwriters in the United States. To motivate diligence and technological innovation, and to spread remaining risks, a standard of strict liability ("title insurance") tends to be applied to this activity. Title reports substantially reduce information asymmetry between the parties. Defects derived from title clouds of any kind can therefore be removed before contracting, obtaining the consent of the affected third parties. If not removed, the grantee will not transact or will insist on modifying the content of the private contract, reducing the price or including additional warranties, in compensation for the survival of property rights that are contradictory to those that figured in the preliminary contract.

Contractual and judicial procedures are also used to remove title defects. Compared to privacy, deed recording provides more possibilities for contracting the removal of defects, because defects are better known to buyers and insurers. The identification of right holders also makes more secure the functioning of summary judicial hearings that serve to reduce bargaining costs in complicated cases. These summary hearings continue to exist today in the judicial *purge* used in France and the U.S.'s "quiet title suit." The existence of such a court-ordered purging possibility also stimulates affected parties to reach an agreement privately.

Despite private incentives to purge rights ex ante, the public record *may*, however, contain evidence on potentially contradictory rights. The recording office is obliged by law to accept all deeds respecting certain formal requirements, whatever their legality. * * *

When public records are poorly organized, it has been useful to build privately owned, indexed databases (U.S. "title plants") that replicate public records in a more complete, reliable, and accessible manner. Fundamental improvements are tract indexes to locate the relevant information fast and safely, and a daily transfer and abstracting of relevant data. Computerization of land records, which allows searching by tract, might reduce this need in the future.

The analysis is consistent with the two main features of the law applied in jurisdictions with recording of deeds: adjudication using a rule of property, and greater freedom to structure property rights privately. First, disputes on title are solved using a property rule. If the seller's right is shown to be defective, the buyer loses the property right to the benefit of the true owner. The buyer is then left with contractual rights against the seller, the title examiner, and/or the title insurer. * * *

Second, the argument predicts that, under recording, enforcement of property rights will be comparatively unconstrained by the legal system— that is, parties will be relatively free to define the rights that they want to have enforced *in rem*. In terms more often used in civil law, the *numerus* *clausus* (closed number) of property rights will be larger.[46] This greater freedom makes sense when considering that this definition is only *in rem* to the extent that it does not conflict with other rights—any such conflicts will be resolved later, if ever. * * *

2.3   Registration of Rights

Registers of rights contain information not on claims but on the rights themselves. They thus require a previous, complete purge of property rights. Created within the German legal tradition, most of them were developed during the 19th century (Prussia, 1783; Austria, 1794; Spain, 1861; Australia, 1875; Germany, 1900) and are now used in most of the world, including the Australian "Torrens" variety, which has been introduced in some other common law jurisdictions. It is also the system being introduced in most former Socialist and developing countries.

Registers of rights also apply the priority rule. As in deed recording, private contracts gain priority when they are first filed or "presented" to the register. They are then subject, however, to substantive review by the registrar in order to detect any potential conflict which might damage other property rights * * * Possibilities here differ in the degree to which the law mandates the number and content of property rights and, correspondingly, reduces parties' freedom and registrars' discretion. Where property rights are narrowly defined by law, with stricter application of the *numerus clausus* principle, collision between rights is less likely and the affected parties are more easily identified by the registrar in order to check that the parties to the contract bring the consents of affected third parties. This is how the German *Grundbuch* functions. Conversely, when more attributes of property rights are defined by private contract, collision is more likely and it is more cumbersome for the registrar to identify who the affected third parties are. The Spanish *Registro de la Propiedad*, for example, works this way. The German solution is simpler but more rigid, while its alternative demands better incentives and qualification from registrars, in accordance with the greater scope and discretion of their work. By simplifying the custodian role of the register, a stricter *numerus clausus* thus indirectly serves to protect those right holders who might otherwise lose out from the stronger enforcement provided by registration in instances of registration failure.

46. On the rationale for this principle and its importance, even in common law jurisdictions, see Heller (1999), who points out the role it plays in solving the so-called anti-commons problems; Merrill and Smith (2000), who argue that it serves to reduce the information costs in transfers of property; and Hansmann and Kraakman (2002), who emphasize the verifiability costs faced by acquirers. These rationales, however, overlook the fact that a system of *numerus clausus* is needed to control the costs of organizing the consent of those holding potentially affected rights. Information costs and, in particular, verification costs are only part of the costs of consent. The core of real rights, however, is the relationship between both sellers and acquirers with holders of affected rights. A narrow focus on verification leads Hansmann and Kraakman, in particular, to underestimate the likely increase in the costs of consent caused when parties can freely multiply the type and number of individual rights once a verification system has been established.

In any case, rights are registered only when the registrar determines that they do not affect any other property right, or the holders of affected rights have consented. Otherwise registration is denied and the parties have to restructure their contract or obtain the relevant consents. Information on the register is simplified in parallel with the purge of rights. Rights defined in each new contract are registered together with all surviving rights on the same parcel of land. Extinguished rights are removed or deleted, however, which makes access to the register very simple. Effective identification of each parcel of land is necessary for the system to work, as is the use of a tract index to locate all rights in each parcel. Furthermore, rights are retroactively registered as of the date on which the deeds were first presented. A register of rights can thus be fruitfully seen as a double register: it is both a temporary record of deeds (the "presentment" book that dates titles) and a definitive register of rights.

This analysis is also consistent with the two main features of registration: the use of a liability rule for solving title disputes, and the enforcement of a more limited set of rights as property—*in rem*—rights. First, given that any contradictions are purged ex ante, the register is able to provide "conclusive," "indefeasible" title, meaning that a good faith buyer acquires a property right if the purchase is based on the information provided by the register. If the seller's right is later shown to be defective, the buyer keeps the property right and the true owner gets a contractual right against the seller and the register. The property right is allocated in these exceptional cases by applying a rule of liability, but this happens only when there has been a failure in the register. The standard property rule, based on right-holders' consent, is applied in normal circumstances. Registration thus interferes with private property much less than is often claimed, as its intervention focuses on the timing and the completeness of the private purging of rights. Registration is controlled by registrars or judges but ultimate decisions are made by right holders by giving consent.
* * *

The structure of records and registers further clarifies the role of adjudication rules in motivating the production of title information. Under registration, only an owner—the seller—is registered at any given moment. Incentives are concentrated to purge rights ex ante (at the time of a prior transaction) and to make sure that the registered owner is the true owner. The opposite happens under recording. Because the true owner and the seller are both potentially on record, the situation is propitious for motivating the production of information at the time of the subsequent conveyance, ex post. Exceptions confirm the argument. Even under registration, a rule of property is applied when the acquirer is assumed to know, or could have easily produced, the relevant information. This applies to the universal exclusion of donees and devisees, who remain unprotected but may reasonably be supposed to know the information. Similarly many laws either directly enforce adverse possessory rights or, indirectly, infer that the buyer acted in bad faith when he knew the seller was not in possession or the public record was wrong.[54]

The second key feature of registration is its stricter *numerus clausus*. In both systems, recording and registration, fewer property rights means that consent is easier to achieve ex ante because it facilitates the production of information as to which rights and right holders are affected and to what extent, and because it reduces bargaining costs. This effect is more valuable under registration, however, because registration aims to avoid any collision of rights ex ante. Registrars have to examine all transactions and parties have to cleanse even minor contradictory rights and title clouds ("fly specks") ex ante. In contrast, under recording, transactions are not necessarily examined ex ante, minor risks are often left alive and insured on a casualty basis, and the lapse of time probably plays a greater role in purging rights through the prescription of conflicting claims.

In addition to the econometric evidence presented in the preceding section that jurisdictions with registers of rights enforce a lower number of property rights, variety within registers of rights also supports this role of the *numerus clausus* principle. Registration systems with stricter *numerus clausus* are able to produce the strongest effects, with transactions concerning property rights being valid irrespective of the validity of the causal obligation * * *

NOTES AND QUESTIONS

1. One can perhaps summarize Arruñada's discussion of the differences between registration and recordation as follows. Registration resolves potential disputes about title ex ante, at the time of the transfer; recordation leaves disputes about title to be resolved ex post, once they arise. Registration confers rights in rem, in that the certificate of title is binding on third parties as well as on the parties to the transfer. Recordation by itself has no binding effect on third parties; recordation does no more than make available for public inspection copies of in personam transactions (contracts, deed, liens, etc.). Under recordation, however, ex post litigation in the form of a quiet title action may draw upon records of past transactions to render judgments that have an in rem effect.

2. In a sense, the registrar of deeds under the registration system stands in for the public of in rem duty holders. The property rights are given in rem effect precisely because the registrar has put in the ex ante effort to determine that such an effect is appropriate. Does this help explain why, according to an econometric study reported by Arruñada

---

54. This conjecture on the efficiency of the "knowledge requirement" is likely to depend on the value of the assets. As emphasized by Baird and Jackson (1984:312–318), this knowledge exception may produce more nuanced decisions but is costly to apply. To the extent that these costs are largely fixed, we should expect it to be applied more for valuable assets and security interests (also likely to be positively correlated to asset value) than for deciding title claims on standard movables. There is some indication of this in the treatment of commercial transactions, for which knowledge plays no role in most jurisdictions.

elsewhere in the article, the more definitive effect given to property rights by the registration system the fewer the forms of property the system will recognize (i.e., a stricter *numerus clausus* of property rights)? On one view, the *numerus clausus* is enforced in French law through the formalities required for recording interests in order to get *in rem* enforcement ex post. See Thomas W. Merrill & Henry E. Smith, Optimal Standardization in the Law of Property: The *Numerus Clausus* Principle, 110 Yale L.J. 1, 5 & n.8 (2000). Something similar may be true in Louisiana. See Alejandro M. Garro, The Louisiana Public Records Doctrine and the Civil Law Tradition 110–18, 150–82, 195–98 (1989).

3.   The registration system is thought to be more accurate than the recording system, but also more expensive. Among other things, it requires well-trained and non-corrupt officials to administer it. Debate about which system is better has raged for years. Compare Richard R. Powell, Registration of the Title to Land in the State of New York 69 (1938) (pro-recording); with Myres S. McDougal & John W. Brabner–Smith, Land Title Transfer: A Regression, 48 Yale L.J. 1125 (1939) (pro-registration). On the cost of title searches under various systems, see generally, Joseph T. Janczyk, An Economic Analysis of the Land Title Systems for Transferring Real Property, 6 J. Legal Stud. 213 (1977); see also Matthew Baker, Thomas J. Miceli, C. F. Sirmans & Geoffrey K. Turnbull, Optimal Title Search, 31 J. Legal Stud. 139 (2002). Note that many countries setting up land records for the first time opt for registration, but advanced countries with recordation face a somewhat different choice: whether the extra benefits of a registration system are worth the switching costs. See Joseph T. Janczyk, Land Title Systems, Scale of Operations, and Operating and Conversion Costs, 8 J. Legal Stud. 569 (1979). The benefits are likely to be less to the extent that a title insurance industry has emerged to furnish additional security of title to owners.

4.   Because registration systems rely heavily on state officials and uniform administrative procedures to certify title to land, they tend to be relatively inflexible, both in terms of how much effort officials put into any given title inquiry and in terms of the speed with which those officials generate registered deeds. Recording systems, which rely mostly on competing private actors (attorneys, title insurance companies) are more flexible, in the sense that the resources devoted to title questions and the speed with which title issues are resolved can be varied according to the value of the property and the urgency of completing any given transaction. Does this suggest that recording acts may have certain efficiencies overlooked in the traditional literature on tradeoffs between ex ante and ex post title determination?

5.   Land records are beginning to become available on the Internet. So far a few jurisdictions have put their indexes online. Orange County, California is an example. See, e.g., http://cr.ocgov.com/grantorgrantee/welcome.asp. Full document views are probably in the near future. Statutes will need to be passed in order to give online notice and searches legal effect. See Dale A. Whitman, Are We There Yet? The Case for a Uniform

Electronic Recording Act, 24 W. New Eng. L. Rev. 245 (2002). How might this lowering of information costs affect the strength of notice and the corresponding duty to search? Would you expect the availability of online records to lead to a tightening or loosening of the *numerus clausus* and related restrictions on property forms? How does the prospect of online land records affect the choice between registration and recordation? Digitized records should improve the efficiency of both registration and recordation, but insofar as recording systems rely on multiple sources of experts in competition with one another, would you expect recording systems to adopt new digitized technology more rapidly than registration systems?

2. AIRPLANES

Since the Civil Aeronautics Act of 1938, aviation law has been almost entirely federal, and requires the registration of civil aircraft (which in turn requires proof of ownership) and the recordation of transfers of aircraft ownership as well as instruments affecting title such as security interests and leases. 49 U.S.C. § 44102(a) (2004); id. § 44107 (2004); 14 C.F.R. § 11; id. § 47.31(a) (2004). Until the conveyance or encumbrance is recorded, it is good only against (1) the transferor, and (2) third parties with actual notice. Id. § 44108(a). After recordation, an interest is good against "all persons." Id. § 44108(b). In *Philko Aviation, Inc. v. Shacket*, 462 U.S. 406, 409–11 (1983), the Supreme Court interpreted this provision as creating something like a "race-notice" system (which we discuss further, infra), thereby preempting *nemo dat*-style state laws that would permit unrecorded transfers to be valid against innocent third persons. Interestingly, while the statute speaks of "actual notice," this has been taken to include "not only knowledge that one's seller lacks good title but also knowledge of facts that would lead a reasonable person to inquire further into the seller's title." Shacket v. Philko Aviation, Inc., 841 F.2d 166, 170 (7th Cir. 1988) (Posner, J.). So although the statute disavows any role for an FAA certificate of registration as evidence of ownership in judicial proceedings over title, 49 U.S.C. § 44103(c)(2) (2004), in the aftermath of the *Philko Aviation* litigation the FAA registry seems to have turned into a conventional recording system insofar as the rights of third parties are concerned.

Suppose that on December 1, 2004, A sells Blackcraft (the mythical prototypical airplane) to B, who then fails to file the bill of sale with the FAA. On January 15, 2005, A sells Blackcraft to C (who doesn't have notice of the earlier sale to B), who *does* file his bill of sale with the FAA. Though the statute suggests that B's failure to record won't prevent him from establishing ownership, the holding in *Philko Aviation* implies that C, because he recorded first and didn't have notice, will own Blackcraft. C can rely on the lack of recordation at the time he bought Blackcraft, and the FAA registry does indeed function as a recording system from C's point of view.

3. SHIPS

Starting with the Ship Mortgage Act of 1920, federal law has provided for enforcement of mortgages on documented vessels of greater than five tons. See 46 U.S.C. § 31301 et seq. (modified and recodified in 1988). Conveyances of ships, including mortgages, are given full in rem effect against third parties only if they have been filed with the Secretary of Transportation pursuant to 46 U.S.C. § 31321. Interests which have not been filed may still be enforced against the grantor/mortgagor or his heir or devisee, or against "a person having actual notice of the sale, conveyance, mortgage, assignment or related instrument." Id. § 31321(a)(1)(C). Thus, the Ship Mortgage Act, like the FAA's registration system for airplanes, operates in practice like a "race-notice" recording act. The Ship Mortgage Act was designed to bring greater certainty to ship ownership, because many liens on vessels are valid without filing or possession, leading one commentator, quoting a New Orleans attorney, to observe that " '[l]iens on ships, i.e. maritime liens, are often hidden and ships acquire liens like dogs get fleas.' " Matthew J. Bauer, Marine Title Insurance, 12 Conn. Ins. L.J. 17 (2005); see also Grant Gilmore & Charles L. Black, Jr., The Law of Admiralty 586–89 (2d ed. 1975). Because of these problems, a maritime title insurance industry, roughly analogous to its land-based counterpart, has arisen. See Bauer, supra.

Smaller vessels are subject to state registration schemes that operate much like automobile registration. See, e.g., Fla. Stat. Ann. § 328; Md. Code, Nat. Res., § 8–701 et seq. State vessel registration schemes vary in a fashion similar to those for auto registration. See 2 Benedict on Admiralty § 68b (7th ed. 2006).

4. AUTOMOBILES

In a way reminiscent of the federal regime for airplanes, state law provides for registration and certification of title to automobiles. Auto registration is a system under which owners have to pay a fee for the privilege of using the state's highways. Certification of title acts were passed later, at first to prevent theft. But they developed into a system for establishing the validity of ownership and security interests. To obtain a certificate of title, the owner submits an application with information including a statement of the applicant's title and each security interest in the automobile. When ownership is transferred, the owner must endorse and deliver the certificate of title to the transferee, and the transferee must then apply at the Department of Motor Vehicles for a new certificate of title within the prescribed time by presenting the endorsed certificate of title from the transferor.

States vary in what effect they give to the certification system. There are three varieties of statutes. First, "excepting" statutes provide that, when the statutory provisions on transfers of title aren't complied with, the transfer of title is invalid, except as between the two parties to the transaction. Second, "invalidating" statutes nullify a noncompliant transfer of title even as between the two parties to the transaction. Third, "nondirective" statutes provide for some penalty for noncompliance but do not affect the validity of the transfer of title. See Pamela Trimble, *Rudiger Charolais Ranches v. Van De Graaf Ranches*, and the Impact of Other State

Laws on the UCC Rights of a Good Faith Purchaser, 48 Consumer Fin. L.Q. Rep. 504, 507 (1994).

The last, nondirective type, is the easiest to integrate with the Uniform Commercial Code: The UCC applies in full. Interestingly, even excepting statutes have been held to give way to the UCC in allowing good faith purchasers in a noncomplying transaction to prevail. See, e.g., Island v. Warkenthien, 287 N.W.2d 487 (S.D. 1980); Heinrich v. Titus–Will Sales, 868 P.2d 169 (Wash. Ct. App. 1969). The net effect is to make what sound like systems analogous to Torrens-style (registration) systems for land into something like the recording systems, more equitable and oriented to the good faith purchaser. One major problem with any attempt at a definitive automobile title record is that cars can easily be taken to other jurisdictions. And a potential purchaser of an automobile has to worry that the vehicle is validly registered in another state.

Most states rely on state certificate of title acts for purposes of recording security interests in automobiles under Article 9 of the UCC (see Chapter VII). The lien is recorded on a state certificate of title, and potential transactors can ask the owner for a copy of the certificate in order to determine the status of the lien. The only potential problem arises before an application for a certificate of title is filed, but no actual case involving this gap seems to have come up. For details, see Lynn M. LoPucki & Elizabeth Warren, Secured Credit: A Systems Approach 406–19 (2006).

5. ART

Another type of personal property that might be considered a candidate for a registry is fine art. The ownership of art implicates two problems—theft and forgeries. Owners of well-known works want to establish that they have the best rights in the work and that the work really is what it purports to be.

At present there is no central registry for title to art works. Some owners feel nervous about publicizing their ownership—at least before a theft has occurred. There are partial registries of stolen works. Julian Radcliffe, The Work of the International Art and Antiques Loss Register, in The Recovery of Stolen Art: A Collection of Essays 189, 190 (Norman Palmer ed., 1998).

To establish ownership of a work of art—and thereby avoid the hazards of other claims and the possibility of fakery—one has to establish the provenance of the work. Sources used include museum catalogs and records of past exhibitions. Owners and transactors often rely on *catalogues raisonnés*, which are usually compiled by an acknowledged expert and contain information on every known piece by an individual artist, including a physical description and illustration of the work, and its provenance and exhibition history. Other documentary evidence (letters, memoirs, etc.) can also be used as evidence.

Researching a provenance is not only costly, but its reliability often cannot be compared to records in a central registry. A dramatic illustration of the problem is the famous recent forgery perpetrated by two Britons, John Drewe (*né* John Cockett) and John Myatt. Myatt forged over 200 paintings, many with acrylic paint and K–Y Jelly, and Drewe sold the works, mostly though London auction houses. But unlike most forgeries that rely on their resemblance to a master's style, Drewe forged the documents that would be used for the provenance of the works. After getting friends to sign letters attesting to their ownership of the paintings and their authenticity, he then forged and altered correspondence and catalogs in museum libraries. (The plot was discovered only when Drewe's girlfriend called the police.) Peter Landesmann, A 20th-Century Master Scam, N.Y. Times, July 18, 1999, at SM32; Eamonn O'Neil, The Art of Deception, Scotsman, July 6, 2002, at 12. Provenance is thus like recording in being based on a history of transactions, but unlike recording, the evidence is not kept in a systematic and secure fashion.

Figure 8–3
John Myatt in His Studio
(Motto: "In prison they called me Picasso")

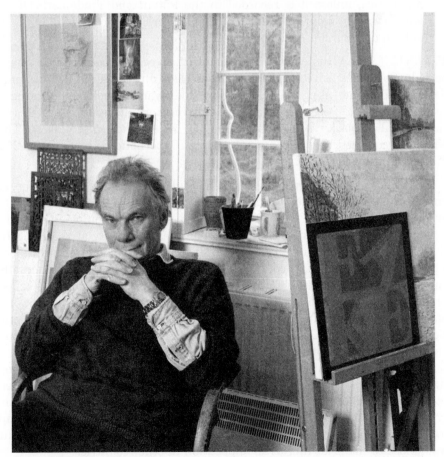

Photo: Jean–Philippe Defaut/The New York Times/Redux. Today Myatt runs a business called *Genuine Fakes*. See http://www.johnmyatt.com, "the official website of John Myatt, the artist behind the *'Greatest art fraud of the twentieth century'*."

Vintage violins, as aesthetically pleasing, valuable, and highly mobile objects, raise similar issues. Harvey Shapreau & Carla J. Shapreau, Violin Fraud: Deception, Forgery, Theft, and Lawsuits in England and America (2d ed. 1997).

6. INTELLECTUAL PROPERTY

Intellectual property is a form of personal property. But much of intellectual property law is federal law—unlike the law of personal property generally. We consider here the registration provisions for the major types of intellectual property: patent, trademark, and copyright.

In the case of patents, part of one section of the Patent Act deals with transfers and their effects against third parties:

> An assignment, grant, or conveyance shall be void as against any subsequent purchaser or mortgagee for a valuable consideration, without notice, unless it is recorded in the Patent and Trademark Office within three months from its date or prior to the date of such subsequent purchase or mortgage.

35 U.S.C. § 261. This system is like a notice recording act with a grace period. (For an explanation of the types of recording acts, see infra.) Some have argued that "assignment, grant, or conveyance" includes granting a security interest. See, e.g., Raymond T. Nimmer, Revised Article 9 and Intellectual Property Asset Financing, 53 Me. L. Rev. 287 (2001). The Ninth Circuit has held the opposite. In re Cybernetic Services, Inc., 252 F.3d 1039 (9th Cir. 2001).

Notice that the records kept by the patent office are like registration in another respect: the Patent and Trademark Office (PTO) is called upon to evaluate the application for the patent, and those questioning its validity can under some circumstances challenge a patent's validity at the PTO. In the early nineteenth century, a system of minimal examination prevailed, which relied more on the courts to sort out which patents were actually valid. Somewhat confusingly, this system of minimal examination is called "registration" (as opposed to "examination") in the patent context. Compare F. Scott Kieff, The Case for Registering Patents and the Law and Economics of Patent–Obtaining Rules, 45 B.C. L. Rev. 55 (2003) (proposing "soft-look" registration) with Jay P. Kesan, Carrots and Sticks to Create a Better Patent System, 17 Berkeley Tech. L.J. 763, 797 (2002) (advocating tightened standard for granting patents at the PTO). Relatedly, the United States is unique in having a first-to-invent system rather than a first-to-file system. 35 U.S.C. § 102. Thus, within limits, a first inventor who is second to file has a right to a patent under the system in the United States but would lose to the prior filer of an application in other countries.

For federal trademarks, the Lanham Act sets up a similar system for the "assignment" of trademarks:

An assignment shall be void against any subsequent purchaser for valuable consideration without notice, unless the prescribed information reporting the assignment is recorded in the United States Patent and Trademark Office within 3 months after the date of the assignment or prior to the subsequent purchase.

15 U.S.C. § 1060(a)(4). Again, this is comparable to the notice-plus-grace-period type of recording act. "Assignments" clearly include transfers of title but may not include security interests. For the complex interaction between federal intellectual property registration and (state law) Article 9, see, e.g., Nimmer, supra.

Copyrights are subject to a much looser regime. The history of copyright over the last century has been characterized by a move away from formalities. Registration is not required to claim copyright, but timely registration is advantageous for making statutory damages available when actual damages are hard to prove (and for being able to file certain infringement actions, for evidentiary purposes, etc.) But failure to register does not invalidate a copyright. 17 U.S.C. § 409–412. To comply with the Berne Convention, Congress eliminated the requirement of registration prior to suit for copyright owners from other Berne member countries.

7.   CASH AND NEGOTIABILITY

As mentioned by Baird and Jackson, cash illustrates the good faith purchaser rule at its widest. With cash there is no duty to inquire about where it came from and whether the holder has good title. This makes cash very liquid. A thief does not obtain title to stolen cash, but one can get good title to cash even from a thief. Cash is sometimes said to be the extreme of "negotiability." There is not only no registry of cash, but even an original owner who could prove by using serial numbers that certain cash was his cannot recover it from the present holder.

A written instrument is "negotiable" when it is "capable of being transferred by delivery or indorsement when the transferee takes the instrument for value, in good faith, and without notice of conflicting title claims or defenses." Black's Law Dictionary (8th ed. 2004). Cashier's checks and bearer bonds would be examples. Negotiability is useful where the issuer is more able to bear the risk of loss or there is some special value in avoiding inquiry on the part of transferees.

Negotiability takes the good faith purchaser exception to *nemo dat* the furthest. In U.S. law, an innocent holder can acquire good title to cash and negotiable instruments even with a thief in the chain back to the original owner.

D.   RECORDING ACTS

As explored in the excerpt by Arruñada, land records can be divided into recordation and registration. Nearly all localities in the United States use recordation. The key attribute of recording is that it generates, as a matter of law, constructive notice to all subsequent purchasers in the chain of title. Thus, recording acts create a powerful incentive for purchasers to file their deeds (and mortgagees their mortgages, etc.) in order to block possible good faith purchaser claims by subsequent transferees. Those interested in the state of title can examine the records, or more likely hire an expert to examine them (or a duplicate set maintained privately by the title company) and produce an "abstract" or report. From time to time, various jurisdictions in the United States have experimented with registration statutes, called Torrens Acts after the Australian law that inspired them. Most of these experiments failed, and today only the Minneapolis–St. Paul area is still covered by a Torrens title registration system. As Arruñada recounts, most of the rest of the world (including Germany, Great Britain, most of the other commonwealth countries, and most developing countries) uses registration.

The first recording acts were very simple and were what we would now call the "race" type, under which the first of two property claimants to file has the better claim. These acts in effect created an exception to the good faith purchaser rule, denying good faith purchaser status to anyone with respect to an interest that had been previously recorded. This led to great unfairness in certain circumstances, as where someone knowing of a prior transaction would "purchase" the land from the grantor—who would have nothing to transfer under *nemo dat*—and then would record first. The prior purchaser was out of luck. To avoid this result, courts held that subsequent purchasers with notice of a prior conveyance would not get the protection of the statute. Marshall v. Fisk, 6 Mass. (5 Tyng) 24 (1809); Farnsworth v. Childs, 4 Mass. (3 Tyng) 637 (1808). Courts also developed robust doctrines of constructive notice based on possession (especially open and notorious possession), M'Mechan v. Griffing, 20 Mass. (3 Pick.) 149 (1825), or even based on the publishing of the conveyance in the newspaper, Curtis v. Mundy, 44 Mass. (3 Met.) 405, 408 (1841).

In response to these developments, legislatures, with Massachusetts again in the lead, started to insert language in recording acts requiring good faith or lack of actual notice on the part of the subsequent purchaser. See 14 Powell on Real Property § 82.02[1][c][iii]. These "notice" statutes fundamentally altered the nature of the recording acts. Whereas a race statute in effect creates an exception to the good faith purchaser rule, a notice statute preserves the good faith purchaser rule in full force, with the modification that recordation provides constructive notice to subsequent purchasers. A third variation, the race-notice statutes, were adopted in the nineteenth century by several Middle Atlantic states (Maryland, New Jersey, New York, and Pennsylvania) in nearly identical language. These acts combined the features of the race statutes and the notice statutes, requiring in effect that persons be both good faith purchasers and be the first to record in order to prevail over other claimants. The Pennsylvania version spread to the Northwest Territory with the result that many of the states of the Old Northwest (e.g., Indiana, Ohio, Michigan, and Wisconsin, but not Illinois) have race-notice statutes.

Carol Rose has seen in the history of the recording acts a story of legislatures adopting "crystalline" rules followed by judicial decisions that soften the rules with various equitable defenses and qualifications, turning them into "mud." Carol Rose, Crystals and Mud in Property Law, 40 Stan. L. Rev. 577 (1988). (The portion of this article dealing with mortgage foreclosures and redemptions is excerpted in Chapter VII.) The early history certainly conforms to a pattern of crystals followed by mud. But it is less clear that any pattern of cycling between these poles has continued. Perhaps because the notice and race-notice statutes adopted in the nineteenth century had a built-in safety valve to prevent the worst abuses of the pure race statutes, courts were nowhere as aggressive in their construction of notice and race-notice statutes as they were of race statutes. Later in the nineteenth century, courts seem to have dropped the idea that possession by another (other than adverse possession) would itself cause subsequent purchasers to lose the protection of the recording act. To be sure, courts did make exceptions for situations of direct misrepresentation by the first purchaser to the second purchaser. See Guffey v. O'Reiley, 88 Mo. 418 (1885); Marling v. Milwaukee Realty Co., 106 N.W. 844 (Wis. 1906). Overall, however, it may be that we have achieved something of a stable equilibrium with respect to the understanding and application of recording acts today. (Which is not to say that application of the statutes is easy!)

Before we turn in more detail to the various types of recording acts, it is important to know how a title search does—and sometimes does not—work.

TITLE SEARCH AND "CHAIN OF TITLE"

Recording acts require that public officials, such as the county clerk or recorder of deeds, maintain an office in which deeds and other documents affecting title may be recorded. Typically there will be a recorder's office in every county in a state. The employees who run these offices do little if any screening of the documents submitted for recordation. Thus, not only deeds and mortgages, but also judicial judgments, letters, and memoranda may be recorded. Every recording office has at least two indexes: a grantee index and a grantor index. As their names suggest, the grantee index includes, by name, all grantees referenced in the documents that have been submitted for recordation; the grantor index includes, by name, all grantors referenced in the documents that have been submitted for recordation. Grantors and grantees are arranged alphabetically, although there may be a separate index for each year. Some recorder's offices—but not all—also keep something called a tract index, in which all documents submitted for recordation are listed by the legal description of the property established under the surveying system established by the Land Ordinance of 1785 (see Chapter II). This is extremely useful, either as a shortcut to doing a title search or as a check against the search results produced using the grantor and grantee indexes.

Performing a title search involves tracing the series of transactions from one's would-be transferor back to a "root of title" and then tracing forward. First one looks in the grantee index for one's transferor to find the deed by which he took from his predecessor. Then one looks for that name in the grantee index, and so on. In many states, marketable title acts (see below) allow the search to stop at some date in the past—say 30 or 40 years ago—rather than needing to trace all the way to the sovereign or some other "root." Second, once one has gone back far enough, then one repeats the process coming forward in time through the grantor index. Tracing forward involves investigating what each of the people discovered in the grantee index did with the title in the relevant period. One might think that this period is the time between execution of the deed to her and the date of execution of the deed from her to the next link in the chain, but this would be inadequate. Instead, for each of the people in the chain, one must look in the grantor index between (i) the date of execution of the deed to that person and (ii) the date that the deed from that person to the next person *was recorded*. One is responsible for knowing what each person might have granted from the time of execution of the deed to that person but before it is recorded, and one has to check for possible transactions after that person executed a deed to another but before that deed was recorded. Anything outside the period bounded by (i) and (ii)—the period before the execution of the deed to X and after the recording of the deed from X—is said to be outside the "chain of title" and as to such matters the land records do *not* furnish constructive notice. Consequently, if something is outside the chain of title (outside the legally defined reasonable search), the good faith purchaser exception to *nemo dat* applies.

The chain of title concept is a compromise between a more thorough but more expensive search and a less thorough but more manageable search. The mechanics are best appreciated though an example.

Example. On April 15, 2006 you are considering a purchase from D of a parcel known as Blackacre, located in the town of Springfield. You must perform a title search to ascertain the state of the title. Here is a sketch, assuming that the state only requires a title search going back 40 years. More might be required in other jurisdictions.

Running backwards in the Grantee Index:

1.   Look up D in the Grantee Index and find his grantor, C. The index refers to a deed from C to D on April 1, 1995, recorded that day.

2.   Search C backwards from April 1, 1995 until you find a reference to a deed from B, dated October 1, 1986 and recorded on April 15, 1991.

3.   Search under B backwards from October 1, 1986 and find a deed from A on January 30, 1968 and recorded that day.

4.   Search A backwards to 1966. A owned Blackacre on January 1, 1966.

Running forward in the Grantor Index:

1.   Search A forward in the Grantor Index from January 1, 1966 to January 30, 1968 (deed to B).

2. Search B forward from January 30, 1968 until *April 15, 1991* (recordation of deed to C).

3. Search C forward from *October 1, 1986* (date of deed to C) until April 1, 1995 (deed to D).

4. Search D forward from April 1, 1995 until the present.

<u>Chain of Title</u> (from the minimal search):

January 1, 1966—January 30, 1968: A owns and then conveys to B.

January 20, 1968—October 1, 1986: B owns and then conveys to C, but the deed is not recorded until April 15, 1991.

October 1, 1986—April 1, 1995: C owns and then conveys to D.

April 1, 1995—April 15, 2006: D owns.

In a recording system, the official keeping the records has a duty to accept and file records of the proper form, but has no duty to investigate the state of title. In this example, we assumed that all the recorded deeds were legitimate. This is not always so.

TYPES OF RECORDING ACTS

Today in the United States, there are three types of recording acts:

1. **Race.** The winner of the race to record prevails. This was the original type of statute, but now at most two states have the simple race statute. So if O sells to A and then sells to B, but B records before A, then B has title; A has only a claim against O. Race statutes create an exception to the *nemo dat* principle and a partial exception to the good faith purchaser doctrine, insofar as the first party to record wins even if she has actual notice of a prior conveyance. An example of a race statute:

> (a) No (i) conveyance of land, or (ii) contract to convey, or (iii) option to convey, or (iv) lease of land for more than three years shall be valid to pass any property interest as against lien creditors or purchasers for a valuable consideration from the donor, bargainor or lessor but from the time of registration thereof in the county where the land lies * * *

N.C. Stat. § 47–18. See Rowe v. Walker, 441 S.E.2d 156 (N.C. Ct. App. 1994), aff'd, 455 S.E.2d 160 (N.C. 1995).

2. **Notice.** A subsequent bona fide purchaser wins unless he has notice (actual, constructive, or inquiry), and a recorded interest gives constructive or "record" notice. Note the incentive to record immediately in order to be protected from subsequent good faith purchasers. An example of a notice statute:

> A conveyance of an estate in fee simple, fee tail or for life, or a lease for more than seven years from the making thereof, * * * shall not be valid as against any person, except the grantor or lessor, his heirs and devisees and persons having actual notice of it, unless it * * * is recorded in the registry of deeds for the county or district in which the land to which it relates lies.

Mass. Gen. Laws Ann. Ch. 183, § 4.

3. **Race–Notice.** A subsequent good faith purchaser wins only if he has no notice *and* records before the prior instrument is recorded. This is like the race statute but solves the problem of the unscrupulous subsequent buyer under the race approach. An example of a race-notice statute:

> Every conveyance of real property or an estate for years therein, other than a lease for a term not exceeding one year, is void as against any subsequent purchaser or mortgagee of the same property, or any part thereof, in good faith and for a valuable consideration, whose conveyance is first duly recorded * * *

Cal. Civ. Code § 1214.

4. **Mixed regimes.** Some states apply a race regime to mortgages but another type of recording act to conveyances in general. Compare the following two Arkansas statutes:

> Every mortgage of real estate shall be a lien on the mortgaged property from the time it is filed in the recorder's office for record, and not before. The filing shall be notice to all persons of the existence of the mortgage.

Ark. Code Ann. § 18–40–102.

> (a) Every deed, bond, or instrument of writing affecting the title, in law or equity, to any real or personal property, within this state which is, or may be, required by law to be acknowledged or proved and recorded shall be constructive notice to all persons from the time the instrument is filed for record in the office of the recorder of the proper county.
>
> (b) No deed, bond, or instrument of writing for the conveyance of any real estate, or by which the title thereto may be affected in law or equity, made or executed after December 21, 1846, shall be good or valid against a subsequent purchaser of the real estate for a valuable consideration without actual notice thereof or against any creditor of the person executing such an instrument obtaining a judgment or decree which by law may be a lien upon the real estate unless the deed, bond, or instrument, duly executed and acknowledged or proved as required by law, is filed for record in the office of the clerk and ex officio recorder of the county where the real estate is situated.

Ark. Code Ann. § 14–15–404. See also Pa. Stat. Ann. tit. 21, § 351 (race-notice statute for conveyances other than mortgages); id. § 622 (race statute for mortgages).

Some states allow a "grace period" for filing such that the bona fide purchaser prevails over the prior grantee only if the prior grantee fails to record within the grace period. See, e.g., Del. Code Ann. tit. 25, § 153 (providing for 15–day grace period).

THE SHELTER RULE

Finally, courts have interpreted recording acts to create an exception for certain transferees who otherwise would be barred from obtaining title because they are not good faith purchasers for value. Suppose O conveys to A, who does not record. Then O conveys to B who gives value and has no notice of the prior conveyance to A. B then records. Under a race, notice, or race-notice recording act, B should prevail over A. But what happens if B then gifts the land to C (so C is not a bona fide purchaser for *value* under the recording act), or B sells to C, even though C was aware of the prior deed to A? A literal reading of the statutes might lead one to think that C should lose to A under these circumstances, since C is not a good faith purchaser. But under what has been called the Shelter Rule, courts have held that C prevails against A. See, e.g., Hoggarth v. Somsen, 496 N.W.2d 35 (N.D. 1993). Once B prevails against A, they have reasoned, B should be given all the attributes of ownership, including the right to make normal *nemo-dat* style transfers of the property. If the rule were otherwise, then B would have less than full ownership, because he could not give away the property or sell it to those with notice of the transfer to A.

The Shelter Rule has limits of its own: If B in our hypothetical seeks to transfer the property back to O, the original owner, the Shelter Rule does not apply; under the "original owner exception" to the Shelter Rule, O cannot shelter under B's rights. See, e.g., Chergosky v. Crosstown Bell, Inc., 463 N.W.2d 522 (Minn. 1990). It is generally thought that the opportunities for collusion in such an arrangement are too great, and precluding B from conveying B's full rights to O does not significantly curtail B's market.

PROBLEMS

What is the result under each type of statute? [Hint: In working though the problems, begin with the last conveyance, chronologically speaking, and then work back toward conveyances earlier in time. Once you find a party that prevails under the recording act, that party will generally prevail against all earlier claimants.]

1.   O conveys to A. O then conveys to B, who is unaware of the conveyance to A. B records immediately. Then A records.

2.   O conveys to A. O then conveys to B, who is aware of the conveyance to A. B records immediately. Then A records.

3.   O conveys to A, who does not record. Then O conveys to B, who also does not record. Then O conveys to C, who does not record. First assume that B and C are each unaware of the previous grants from O. Then consider: What if each of them *is* aware?

4.   O conveys to A. O then conveys to B, who has no knowledge of A's deed. Then A records. B then records and sells to C.

5. O conveys to A. O then conveys to B, who has no knowledge of A's deed. Then A records. B then records and sells to O. (This is the same situation as in Problem 4, except C is replaced by O).

6. O conveys to A. O then conveys to B who has actual notice of the deed from O to A. B records, and then A records. Then B sells to C.

* * *

Given that most modern recordings acts are modifications of the good faith purchaser rule, elements of that rule continue to play an important role in the implementation of the recording acts. One important and recurring requirement that is drawn from good faith purchaser doctrine is that the recording acts only protect persons who are good faith purchasers "for value." Consider the following case.

Hood v. Webster

Court of Appeals of New York, 1936.
2 N.E.2d 43.

■ LOUGHRAN, JUDGE. Florence F. Hood owned a parcel of farm land in the town of Phelps, Ontario county. This property had been devised to her by her husband, whose will said that, should she predecease him, he wanted his estate to go to his brother, the plaintiff here. In 1913 Mrs. Hood executed a deed of the farm to the plaintiff and delivered it to his attorney as an escrow to take effect on her death. The Appellate Division has confirmed a finding of the Equity Term that this delivery was subject to no other condition. A majority of this court has come to the conclusion that the contrary of the fact so found may not be declared as matter of law on this record.

Having all along occupied the property, Mrs. Hood in 1928 granted it to the defendants (her brother and a nephew) by a deed then recorded. She died in 1933. The prior deed held as an escrow was thereupon delivered over to the plaintiff who had it recorded. In this action to annul the subsequent deed to the defendants, it has been held that on the foregoing facts the plaintiff was entitled to prevail.

On this appeal by the defendants, the parties concede that the case made by the findings depends for its solution upon the force and effect of section 291 of the Real Property Law (Consol.Laws, c. 50). It is thereby provided that every conveyance of real property not recorded "is void as against any subsequent purchaser in good faith and for a valuable consideration, from the same vendor, his heirs or devisees, of the same real property or any portion thereof, whose conveyance is first duly recorded."

Did the single circumstance that the subsequent deed to the defendants was first on record establish, in the absence of evidence to the contrary, the matters thus essential to avoid the prior deed to the plaintiff?

We think this question of burden of proof as fixed by the recording act is not for us an open one. The defendants were bound to make out by a fair preponderance of evidence the affirmative assertion of their status as purchasers in good faith and for a valuable consideration.

Brown v. Volkening, 64 N.Y. 76 (1876), and Constant v. University of Rochester, 19 N.E. 631 (N.Y. (1889)), Id., 31 N.E. 26, as read by us, are not authorities to the contrary. In those cases the court did say that the party who claimed under an unrecorded conveyance was required to prove that the subsequent record purchaser took with notice. But here, as elsewhere, it must be kept in mind that the phrase "burden of proof" may stand in one connection "for the never changing burden of establishing the proposition in issue," and in another "for the constantly changing burden of producing evidence." Thayer, Preliminary Treatise on Evidence, 353–389. In the Brown and Constant Cases the controlling factor was that substantial value had been paid for the subsequent conveyance. That fact was more than evidence of consideration. It was further the basis for the auxiliary inference that there was also good faith in the transaction, and what was said respecting the burden of proof had reference to the duty of adducing evidence to repel that inference. For the same reason, the burden of proof (in the same sense) is upon the holder of an unrecorded conveyance when a subsequent deed first recorded acknowledges receipt by the grantor of a consideration sufficient to satisfy the statute.

We have a different case here. Under their defense of purchase for value without notice the defendants offered no evidence of actual considerations given. The subsequent deed to them expressed their payment of "One Dollar and other good and valuable consideration." This recital was not enough to put them into the position of purchasers for a valuable consideration in the sense of the statute. Ten Eyck v. Witbeck, 31 N.E. 994 (N.Y. 1892); Lehrenkrauss v. Bonnell, 92 N.E. 637 (N.Y. 1910).

The duty of maintaining the affirmative of the issue, and in a primary sense the burden of proof, was cast upon the defendants by the recording act. They failed to discharge that burden.

The judgment should be affirmed, with costs.

■ CRANE, CHIEF JUDGE (dissenting). I cannot agree with Brother LOUGHRAN'S view of the law nor with his conclusion on the evidence in this case. * * *

It is conceded that the holder of a prior unrecorded deed has the burden of proving the lack of good faith in the holder of a subsequent recorded deed. The burden is upon him to prove notice or such circumstances as would give notice to a reasonable man. I can see no reason for complicating this rule by shifting the burden of proof when it comes to valuable consideration. It is just as easy to prove lack of consideration in this day when parties may be witnesses and examined before trial as it is to prove notice or bad faith. We should not impair the force and efficacy of the recording statutes upon which it has become a habit and custom to rely in the transfer of real property. A deed or mortgage on record is good as against prior unrecorded deeds or incumbrances until notice or bad faith or a lack of consideration is proven. The burden of proof should rest with the person who asserts the invalidity. * * *

Naturally this burden of proof readily shifts and where fraud is shown or circumstances which cast suspicion upon the transactions the defendant—subsequent vendee—may be called upon to show or prove his good faith and the consideration. * * *

I go still further, however, and hold that the plaintiff is not entitled to recover on the evidence. Florence F. Hood was a widow of about fifty-five years of age, living alone on a small farm, which is the subject of this action. The plaintiff, William J. Hood, is her brother-in-law. She married his brother. The defendant Almon B. Farwell is her brother, and the defendant Howard A. Webster her nephew. Mrs. Hood was left by her husband with this farm and no money with the exception of a mortgage of $1,200 upon property in Nebraska. She was desirous and anxious to get enough money to live on the farm and the plaintiff proposed to give it to her during her natural life in exchange for the farm. She was brought in January of 1913 to the office of the plaintiff's lawyer, at which time she executed a deed of the farm to the plaintiff and also an agreement, which was part and parcel of one transaction, wherein the plaintiff agreed to pay her $200 a year as long as she lived. The deed was not given to the plaintiff; it was given to the lawyer to hold in escrow for no other purpose that can be imagined except to insure the plaintiff's paying the $200 a year and keeping his agreement. The delivery of the deed in escrow and the promise of the plaintiff were all one and the same transaction, and the payment of the money by the plaintiff was clearly a condition precedent to be fulfilled before he was entitled to the deed. Florence Hood lived for twenty years thereafter and died on the 29th day of January, 1933. The plaintiff broke all his promises and agreements. He never paid her a dollar, so far as this record shows. He owed her at the time of her death $4,000, not counting simple interest, and the courts below, dealing in equity, have turned over to him the farm, without requiring the plaintiff to do equity and pay to the estate the money he owes.

The agreement drawn by the plaintiff's lawyer went so far as to require Florence Hood, during all the years that she lived, to work the farm and to pay out of its produce all the taxes and upkeep, and this she did. Florence Hood repudiated the plaintiff, no doubt because of his failure to pay her any money or to keep his agreement, and in 1928 executed and delivered a deed of the farm to Howard A. Webster, her nephew, who had come to live with her and help her on the farm. This deed has been recorded and is the one which the plaintiff seeks to set aside and which the courts below have set aside in the face of the plaintiff's default. In this I think the courts were clearly in error as there is no evidence to justify the conclusion that the farm was to be given or the deed to it turned over to the plaintiff without any consideration or regard whatever to his obligations, acts, or responsibilities. Even the $1,200 mortgage on the Nebraska property was given to the plaintiff in 1913 on the understanding and agreement that he was to support and care for his sister-in-law by paying $200 a year. This apparently he still keeps or has disposed of.

When we consider that this elderly widow had nothing but a farm which had to be worked, and was in fear and dread of financial distress, there is only one possible conclusion, in my judgment, to be drawn from the execution of these instruments. Florence Hood was to give the farm to William Hood at her death in consideration for his paying to her $200 a year for her to live on; and that it was never her intention or any part of the transaction that he should have the farm for nothing or in default of his obligation. The courts below have given him the farm for nothing, so far as this record shows, instead of to the nephew who helped his aunt work the farm in order to meet taxes, upkeep, and a living.

The record is none too full, so that the conclusions which I have drawn are based entirely upon the evidence or lack of evidence which appeared on the trial. As a matter of law, therefore, on this evidence, the plaintiff failed to make out a case entitling him to equitable relief and the removal of the defendants' deed from the record.

The judgment should be reversed and the complaint dismissed, with costs in all courts. * * *

Judgment affirmed.

NOTES AND QUESTIONS

1. What kind of recording act does New York have? Who should have the burden of proof on consideration and good faith? The burden of production?

2. What should qualify as "consideration" in order to make someone a purchaser "for value"? Why doesn't the nephew's agreement to move onto the farm to help his widowed aunt count as "consideration"? Suppose the widow's brother-in-law strongly encouraged the nephew to do this. Should his encouragement lead one to find "consideration"?

3. Is the majority expressing a preference for the *nemo dat* baseline? Does its decision undermine the policy of the recording act of allowing good faith purchasers to rely on the land records? As far as making the land records reliable here, who is the cheapest cost avoider? Does the fact that all of the parties here have some family connection influence the dissent? How about the majority?

E. THE LIMITS OF TITLE SEARCHES

Performing the prescribed title search and applying the recording act in effect in the jurisdiction do not necessarily resolve the question of who has title. We consider here two important qualifications to the recording acts. The first is for claims established by adverse possession. When adverse possession occurs, a new chain of title is started in the adverse possessor.

In the case of land, this can cause notice problems for those relying on land records, because claims based on adverse possession are not part of the land records. The second is for so-called "wild deeds" that are recorded but cannot be located in the transferor's chain of title.

Mugaas v. Smith

Supreme Court of Washington, 1949.
206 P.2d 332.

■ HILL, JUSTICE. This is an action by Dora B. Mugaas, a widow, to quiet title to a strip of land 135 feet in length and with a maximum width of 3 1/2 feet which she claims by adverse possession, and to compel Delmar C. Smith and his wife to remove therefrom any and all buildings and encroachments. From a judgment quieting title to the strip in Mrs. Mugaas and directing the removal of any and all buildings and encroachments, the Smiths appeal.

The appellants contend that the respondent has failed to establish adverse possession of the tract in question. The character of the respondent's possession over the statutory period is one of fact, and the trial court's finding in that regard is to be given great weight and will not be overturned unless this court is convinced that the evidence preponderates against that finding. We are of the opinion that the evidence was sufficient to sustain the trial court's findings, and the conclusions based thereon, that the respondent had acquired title to the strip in question by adverse possession. The evidence would have warranted a finding that her adverse possession dated back to 1910.

The only serious questions raised by this appeal are attributable to the fact that the fence which between 1910 and 1928 clearly marked the boundary line for which respondent contends, disappeared by a process of disintegration in the years which followed, and, when appellants purchased the property in 1941 by a legal description and with a record title which included the disputed strip, there was no fence and nothing to mark the dividing line between the property of appellants and respondent, or to indicate to the appellants that the respondent was claiming title to the strip in question.

We have on several occasions approved a statement which appears in Towles v. Hamilton, 143 N.W. 935, 936 (Neb. 1913), that:

> * * * It is elementary that, where the title has become fully vested by disseisin so long continued as to bar an action, it cannot be divested by parol abandonment or relinquishment or by verbal declarations of the disseizor, nor by any other act short of what would be required in a case where his title was by deed.

The fact that the respondent had ceased to use the strip in question in such a way that her claim of adverse possession was apparent did not divest her of the title she had acquired.

Appellants' principal contention is that we have held, in a long line of cases, that a bona fide purchaser of real property may rely upon the record title. The cases cited by appellants construe our recording statute, Rem. Rev.Stat. §§ 10596–1, 10596–2, and involve contests between those relying upon the record title and those relying upon a prior unrecorded conveyance as conveyances are defined by Rem.Rev.Stat. § 10596–1. The holdings in the cases cited give effect to that provision of § 10596–2 which states that any unrecorded conveyance "* * is void as against any subsequent purchaser or mortgagee in good faith and for a valuable consideration from the same vendor, his heirs or devisees, of the same real property or any portion thereof whose conveyance is first duly recorded. * * *"

Appellants cite no cases, and we have found none, supporting their contention that, under a recording statute such as Rem.Rev.Stat. §§ 10596–1, 10596–2, a conveyance of the record title to a bona fide purchaser will extinguish a title acquired by adverse possession. The trial judge, in his admirable memorandum decision, quoted the following from the opinion in Ridgeway v. Holiday, 59 Mo. 444, 454 (1875):

> * * * But it is contended by the defendant that he is a purchaser for value from Voteau who appeared from the record to be the owner, and was in possession, without any notice of the prior adverse possession which passed the title to Ridgeway, or of any claim on his part to the premises; and that as against him, the defendant, Ridgeway, cannot assert his title; that to permit him to do so, would be giving to an adverse possession greater force and efficacy than is given to an unrecorded conveyance. These objections, it must be admitted, are very forcible. The registry act, however, cannot, in the nature of things, apply to a transfer of the legal title by adverse possession, and such title does not stand on the footing of one acquired and held by an unrecorded deed, and of such title, the purchaser may not expect to find any evidence in the records.

He quoted, also, the following from Schall v. Williams Valley R. Co., 35 Pa. 191, 204 (1860):

> An unrecorded paper title does not affect a purchaser without actual notice, and the learned judge pronounced a title by the statute of limitations, if unaccompanied by a continued possession, as no more than an unrecorded paper title. If this be sound doctrine, then the claimant under the statute, however he may have perfected his right, must keep his flag flying for ever, and the statute ceases to be a statute of *limitations*.

> The first observation we have to make on his ruling is, that titles matured under the statute of limitations, are not within the recording acts. However expedient it might be to require some public record of such titles to be kept, and however inconvenient it may be to purchasers to ascertain what titles of that sort are outstanding, still we have not as yet any legislation on the subject, and it is not competent for judicial decision to force upon them consequences drawn from the recording acts. Those acts relate exclusively to written titles.

These cases seem to us to be directly in point, and to afford a complete answer to appellants' contention. However, appellants say that these and other cases are not applicable because legislation has been enacted, i.e., Rem.Rev.Stat. § 10577, to bring possessory titles within the recording act. That section reads as follows:

> Whenever any person, married or single, having in his or her name the legal title of record to any real estate, shall sell or dispose of the same to an actual bona fide purchaser, a deed of such real estate from the person holding such legal record title to such actual bona fide purchaser shall be sufficient to convey to and vest in such purchaser the full legal and equitable title to such real estate free and clear of any and all claims of any and all persons whatsoever not appearing of record in the auditor's office of the county in which such real estate is situated.

The appellants contend that, under this section of the statute, the full legal and equitable title is vested in them as bona fide purchasers from the record title holder, and that the title acquired by adverse possession is thereby extinguished. We again quote a sentence from the Pennsylvania decision:

> * * * If this be sound doctrine, then the claimant under the statute, however he may have perfected his right, must keep his flag flying for ever, and the statute ceases to be a statute of *limitations*.

If Rem.Rev.Stat. § 10577 has the effect claimed for it by the appellants, the only way in which a person who has acquired title by adverse possession could retain it against the purchaser of the record title is to make his possession and use of the property so continuous, so open, and so notorious as to prevent anyone from becoming a bona fide purchaser.

Immediately following this section in Rem.Rev.Stat., this statement appears in italics: "This section relates to community property only." It was § 1 of chapter 151 of the Laws of 1891, and the title of the act was "An Act to protect innocent purchasers of community real property." The other three sections of that act appear in Rem.Rev.Stat. as §§ 10578, 10579, and 10580; and the act in its entirety, in accordance with its title, is for the protection of innocent purchasers against undisclosed community interests. It is too clear for argument that the act never was intended to have, and could not have, constitutionally, in view of its restricted title, any such application as that for which appellants contend. * * *

Appellants have placed too great a weight on too frail a reed. * * *

The judgment is affirmed.

NOTES AND QUESTIONS

1. We encountered adverse possession in Chapter II as a mode of acquisition of property. Adverse possession can be seen as an exception to the *nemo dat* principle, in that it allows shifts in title other than by a chain of voluntary transfers. Nevertheless, recall that an adverse possessor only

holds adversely against the present possessor. Thus, for example, if the present possessor holds only a life estate, the adverse possessor acquires only a life estate at the end of the statutory period. This mimics *nemo dat* in that the forced transfer from the present title owner does not transfer rights greater than the owner had.

2.   The court seems to think that if adverse possession claims are subject to the recording act, then the adverse possessor (AP) would have to maintain adverse possession forever, which would run counter to its being based on a statute of limitations and its function to wipe away stale claims. How true is this? Couldn't the AP file a quiet title action and record the judgment, thus starting a new record chain of title? Wouldn't it be desirable for the AP to do so? Does this case give the AP much incentive to give notice? The U.S. Supreme Court has upheld statutes requiring owners of dormant mineral rights periodically to re-record their interest, on pain of having the interest lapse. See Texaco, Inc. v. Short, 454 U.S. 516 (1982). Would such a lapse statute be desirable for claims based on adverse possession?

3.   If adverse possession claims were trumped by interests memorialized in recording acts, wouldn't this greatly simplify the process of ascertaining whether the transferor of any particular piece of property has good title? Or would it in fact make the process of ascertaining title even more complicated, if an adverse possessor is currently on the property and there have also been multiple transfers and recordings of title in the recent past?

4.   Many states have adopted legislation that reflects something of a compromise between reliance on recording acts and allowing claims of title outside the record based on adverse possession. So-called *marketable title acts* set a period, often 30 or 40 years, beyond which claims are deemed extinguished and searchers need not inquire further in the official records. See, e.g., Fla. Stat. Ann. §§ 712.01–.10; Mich. Comp. L. § 565.101; N.C. Gen. Stat. § 47B–2; Utah Code Ann. §§ 57–9–1 to 57–9–10. The National Conference of Commissioners on Uniform State Laws proposed a Uniform Marketable Title Act in 1977 as one section of the Uniform Simplification of Land Transfers Act, which was then made into a stand-alone model act in 1990. This act was based on an influential Michigan act, which was modeled on legislation adopted in 1950 in Ontario, Canada. See Walter E. Barnett, Marketable Title Acts—Panacea or Pandemonium?, 53 Cornell L. Rev. 45, 47, 52–60 (1967). Such a statute makes most interests not enforceable after the specified time period unless something is put in the record within that time window. The idea is to allow people to stop title searches at a given point and not have to go all the way back to the sovereign. There are exceptions (allowing continued enforcement) for interests in the nature of easements that give notice by their physical existence and for other easements that were excepted or reserved by a recorded instrument and evidenced by something physical.

5.   Do marketable title acts represent a kind of adverse possession of claims based on adverse possession? Or do they have this function only for adverse possession claims that are no longer possessory? Suppose the

statute of limitations for adverse possession is 20 years and the marketable title act prescribes a period of 40 years for title examinations. B enters A's land in 1960 and remains on the land openly, notoriously, continuously, exclusively, and adversely under a claim of right for the next 45 years. B has made no attempt to record the right to the land based on adverse possession. In 2005, A transfers to C. Can C rely on the marketable title act to extinguish B's claim of title by adverse possession? See William B. Stoebuck & Dale A. Whitman, The Law of Property 901 (3d ed. 2000) (noting that "a person who is occupying the land may, under some of the acts, have possession treated as the equivalent of notice of his or her claim").

Zimmer v. Sundell

Supreme Court of Wisconsin, 1941.
296 N.W. 589.

■ WICKHEM, JUSTICE. Joseph McCann and his wife were the original owners of the land in question and both plaintiffs and defendants claim under them. On December 20, 1928, the McCanns conveyed to Peter P. Raab and wife. On December 28, Peter Raab died, and his wife Henrietta became owner of the land by right of survivorship. On February 4, 1932, Henrietta conveyed to defendants Carl, Viola J., Arthur and Carrie Raab. On August 1, 1933, the McCanns conveyed the same land by quitclaim deed to John Gage.* On December 13, 1933, John Gage quitclaimed the land to plaintiffs. The latter deed was recorded on the date of its execution. On September 3, 1935, a certificate of survivorship was issued to Henrietta Raab. On January 28, 1936, defendants recorded the deed from the McCanns to Peter Raab and wife, the certificate of survivorship to Henrietta Raab, and the deed from her to defendants. On April 2, 1936, the deed from McCann to Gage was recorded. The trial court found that when plaintiffs and defendants purchased and received conveyances they were unaware of any claim or interest in the land by the others, that they purchased in good faith, and that plaintiffs remained unaware of defendants' claim until in 1937 when they went to pay the taxes and discovered that defendants had paid them.

The conveyance under which plaintiffs claim was subsequent to those under which defendants claim. While plaintiffs' deed was recorded prior to defendants' conveyances, all of the latter were recorded before the deed from the McCanns to Gage, plaintiffs' grantor. Hence, when defendants recorded their conveyances plaintiffs' recorded deed had no apparent connection with or derivation from the McCanns' title—in other words, it was a mere fugitive deed, and plaintiffs were strangers to the title so far as the record disclosed.

* [A quitclaim deed transfers whatever rights the transferor has, without any war- ranty that there are any such rights. See Chapter VII.—eds.]

It is urged by defendants that in view of this, plaintiffs are not entitled to the protection of the recording statute. So far as important here, sec. 235.49, Stats., provides: "Every conveyance of real estate within this state hereafter made * * * which shall not be recorded as provided by law shall be void as against any subsequent purchaser in good faith and for a valuable consideration of the same real estate * * * whose conveyance shall first be duly recorded."

At the outset, it is important to note that since defendants' conveyances were all prior in time to that of plaintiffs, the latter, except for whatever protection is afforded them by section 235.49, have no title whatever—the title to the premises being entirely out of the McCanns when they conveyed to Gage, plaintiffs' immediate predecessor in title. Plaintiffs' sole standing is as subsequent purchasers in good faith and for valuable consideration who have recorded their deed before defendants' chain of title was recorded. Since in every other respect plaintiffs' situation answers to the calls of the statute, the precise question is whether the fact that plaintiffs' entire chain of title back to the common grantor was not recorded until after defendants' entire chain of title was recorded, deprived plaintiffs of the protection of the statute.

Both parties rely on the case of Fallass, Administrator v. Pierce et al., 30 Wis. 443 (1872). In that case the original owner was Pierce. On March 28, 1859, he mortgaged the premises to one Blanchard. This mortgage was recorded on the date of its execution. On April 2, 1859, Blanchard assigned the mortgage to one Rice. This assignment was recorded June 21, 1861. Thereafter, Rice assigned the mortgage to the plaintiff Fallass. Meantime, on August 10, 1859, Blanchard quitclaimed to the mortgagor Pierce and released the mortgage. These conveyances were recorded December 8, 1860. On September 19, 1860, Pierce, who took his release with notice of the assignment, conveyed by warranty deed to defendant Parks, who was an innocent purchaser for value but who neglected to put his deed on record until after the assignments of the mortgages to Rice and Fallass were made and recorded. The lower court found that the release to Pierce was void as to plaintiff, and that both Rice and plaintiff were bona fide purchasers of the mortgage and entitled to foreclose. The first opinion of this court was that the judgment must be reversed because the assignments had not been recorded at the time Parks purchased, and that being an innocent purchaser for value, Parks was entitled to rely upon the record and to purchase and hold the title against the assignments even though the latter were recorded prior to the time his deed was recorded. Upon rehearing, the court abandoned this position and held that the only person protected by the statute is an innocent purchaser who first records his instrument. The opinion of the court granting the rehearing (which is later by reference adopted as a part of the ultimate decision) states: "The only limitation which can be put upon the statute is, as suggested in Kennedy v. Northup [15 Ill. 148 (1853)], that which the manifest object of the law plainly indicates, namely, that it is to be so construed as to exclude from its protection those who may purchase from strangers to the title. Those persons only are affected with notice by the record, who deal with or on the credit of the title, in the line of which the recorded deed belongs."

This limitation is applicable here. Since plaintiffs purchased from a grantor who had no recorded title going back to the McCanns, and since the latter appeared upon the record to be the holders of the title, there was nothing in the record for plaintiffs to rely upon. Their grantor was a pure stranger to the title so far as the record disclosed.

In the Fallass case, in the course of holding that a person seeking protection of the statute must "put his deed first upon record" the court further said: "He is not required to put his deed first upon record in order to be protected as against prior conveyances from his grantor, but only to do so in order to protect himself against subsequent bona fide purchasers for value, from the same grantor or in the line of recorded conveyances from him."

The syllabus by the court in this case is as follows: "The protection of the recording act (R.S., ch. 86, sec. 25), which declares an unrecorded deed void, as against a subsequent purchaser in good faith, and for a valuable consideration, whose deed shall be first recorded, is not confined to a subsequent purchaser immediately from the same grantor, but applies to one who takes from him through mesne conveyances; and it protects him, if a purchaser in good faith, for value, in case the chain of title to him is first on record, although the intermediate grantees were chargeable with bad faith, or paid nothing." * * *

It is clear to us that the court in the Fallass case meant to and did hold that persons situated as are the plaintiffs are not entitled to the protection of the statute because their chain of title back to the common grantor was not first recorded. That this is in accord with the obvious purpose of the recording statute seems equally clear. If one who has no title under the laws governing conveyances is to have a superior one under the recording acts, it should be because he has relied upon the record, and when he purchases from one who is a stranger to the record title he has no grounds for such reliance. In Burns v. Berry, 3 N.W. 924, 925 (Mich. 1879), it was said: "The protection which this statute gives to a bona fide purchaser does not proceed upon the theory, and is not made to depend upon the fact, that the grantor at the time of such conveyance had any interest in the premises whatever, or that any passed from him by his conveyance to such subsequent purchaser. It is not by force of the conveyance, but by the terms of the statute, that such subsequent purchaser acquires title to the premises. His grantor having previously conveyed, has no title left to convey, and could therefore by his deed, unaided by the statute, pass none to any third person. Our registry laws, however, step in, and for the purpose of protecting an innocent purchaser give him what he supposed and from an examination of the records had a right to suppose, he was acquiring by his purchase, and to this extent cut off the previous purchaser, who negligently failed to record his conveyance."

Plaintiffs argue that the term "subsequent purchaser" is not confined to a subsequent purchaser immediately from the same grantor, but applies to one who takes from him through mesne conveyances. This is perfectly true in principle and authority, but we fail to see how it bears upon the facts of this case. The difficulty with plaintiffs' case is not that they did not take from the same grantor as did defendants. It is that their line of title to the common ancestor was not first recorded.

Judgment reversed and cause remanded with directions to dismiss plaintiffs' complaint, and to enter judgment for defendants upon their counterclaim.

NOTES AND QUESTIONS

1.   A deed like that from Gage to the plaintiffs is sometimes called a "wild deed." From the point of view of the defendants, this deed is outside the chain of title. The majority of courts agree that one cannot benefit from the recording act's exception to *nemo dat* if one traces one's ownership to a wild deed. For recent examples, see Salt Lake County v. Metro West Ready Mix, Inc., 89 P.3d 155 (Utah 2004); Holland v. Hattaway, 438 So.2d 456, 470 (Fla. Dist. Ct. App. 1983). Some courts simply deny that someone tracing their ownership back to a wild deed is a good faith purchaser.

2.   Note that if the holder of the "wild deed" would obtain title under *nemo dat*, nothing in *Zimmer* would prevent that title from being as good as any other *nemo dat* title. See Salt Lake County, supra, 89 P.3d at 159.

3.   The notions of chain of title and wild deed are relative. Thus, a deed with no connection to prior transactions is part of the chain of title of those tracing their claims back to that deed, and such successors to the wild-deed "owner" are on constructive notice of grants made by him. Cf. Lewis v. Gray, 201 S.W.2d 148 (Mo. 1947).

4.   A title search that turns up a clean title is not the end of the story. There are off-record matters that may still bind (or totally deprive) a subsequent bona fide purchaser. As we have seen, adverse possession is not reflected in the land records and no recording system cuts off adverse possession claims. This explains the need for surveying and physical inspection notwithstanding the cleanest of chains of titles as revealed by the recording system. As we have also seen, forgeries and frauds can lead to claims—especially if the fraud victim is wholly blameless—that a title search might not turn up. Similar problems can arise from the incapacity of a grantor, deficiencies in the formalities in the execution of an instrument, liens (such as those for taxes) that are not required to be recorded, and other matters. See Ralph L. Straw, Jr., Off–Record Risks for Bona Fide Purchasers of Interests in Real Property, 72 Dickinson L. Rev. 35 (1967). Sometimes officials at the records office accept documents (thereby making them recorded), but they fail to file or misfile them. Or multiple spellings of names can lead to confusion. States differ as to whom to hold responsible in such situations. Title insurance helps manage some of these risks. Other risks, like adverse possession, are not covered by title insurance policies. Probably prospective owners are more able to detect such problems than are title companies.

5. Recall the excerpt from Baird and Jackson, supra, in which the authors remark that "[r]eal property is the paradigm of property for which a filing system of title claims is superior." Given the many risks presented by American recording systems, and the many exceptions to the protection afforded by the recording acts, is this upbeat assessment justified? How might the system of title records be improved to provide a greater measure of security, without sacrificing our desire to achieve fair outcomes in individual cases?

CHAPTER IX

THE LAW OF NEIGHBORS

A world in which owners simply had the basic right to exclude is one in which many problems would be left unsolved. As we have seen, not all physical invasions are severe enough to warrant giving the owner any power of veto—think of high-altitude airplane overflights. Other invasions, while significant, are closer cases in terms of whether to permit owners to exclude, or not to exclude, or to force them to allow the invasion but at a judicially determined price. The uses to which neighboring property is put can also have an impact on the value and enjoyment of land even if there is nothing in the way of an invasion at all.

This Chapter will consider a range of legal devices to control conflicts among neighbors over incompatible uses of land. The principal devices considered are nuisance, servitudes (easements and covenants), and zoning. As solutions to land-use conflicts, these devices correspond roughly to tort, contract, and regulation. Each of these devices presents some special issues but they are often functional substitutes; for example, noise problems could be controlled by the law of nuisance, by covenants negotiated by neighbors or their predecessors, or by restrictions on commercial activities through the law of zoning. Sometimes more than one device may apply to the same problem, and sometimes they complement each other.

A. NUISANCE

Nuisance law has been termed a doctrinal "mess" and "mystery"—and even a "legal garbage can"—but the traditional starting point for nuisance is where trespass leaves off. Recall from Chapter I that relatively large intrusions of land are controlled by the law of trespass, which at least insofar as intentional intrusions are concerned, imposes a simple rule (no trespassing) subject to some exceptions (considered in Chapter IV, such as the defense of necessity and antidiscrimination laws). Lesser intrusions that go only to use and enjoyment are governed by the law of nuisance. In Chapter I, we encountered a nuisance case, *Hendricks v. Stalnaker*, which involved the court in a balancing of a water well and a septic system. The court found the defendant's well not to be a nuisance even though under local spacing regulations the plaintiff was no longer able to operate a septic system on his property.

Hendricks is not unusual in claiming that the law of nuisance requires the court to balance the utility of two conflicting uses. The *Restatement of*

Torts, which the court invoked, says that when a nontrespassory invasion of land is intentional, the question is whether the inference is substantial and unreasonable. Because an interference is intentional when the actor knows or should know that the conduct is causing harm, Restatement (Second) of Torts § 825 (1979), the reasonableness of the interference is often an issue. The reasonableness inquiry, according to the *Restatement*, calls for balancing the value of the competing landowners' activities: An activity is unreasonable if the social harm of the defendant's activity outweighs its social utility. W. Prosser, supra § 87, at 581, § 89 at 596; Restatement (Second) of Torts § 826–828 (1979). Not all courts subscribe to the *Restatement* approach, however, and where courts do not engage in explicit balancing one must ask whether some other approach better explains the result. As we will see, one of the reasons nuisance law appears so confused is that notions of invasion—who sent what where—continue to play a role in nuisance law.

On a doctrinal level, nuisance law literally picks up where trespass leaves off: A nuisance is commonly defined as a "nontrespassory" invasion of land of a certain sort. Restatement (Second) of Torts § 821D (1979). As you consider the relationship between trespass and nuisance and the many twists to nuisance law, consider what aspects of nuisance law help vindicate owners' rights to exclude and which go beyond exclusionary rights to prescribe a governance regime for particular use conflicts. Does nuisance law reinforce or challenge the view that the right to exclude is fundamental to property? To what extent does nuisance law serve to soften the hard edges of exclusion rights? Or does nuisance law exemplify the bundle-of-sticks picture of property?

Adams v. Cleveland–Cliffs Iron Company

Court of Appeals of Michigan, 1999.
602 N.W.2d 215.

■ O'CONNELL, J. Defendants appeal as of right from a jury verdict awarding damages in trespass for invasions of plaintiffs' property by intrusions of dust, noise, and vibrations. The gravamen of this appeal presents the question whether Michigan recognizes a cause of action in trespass stemming from invasions of these intangible agents. No published decision of an appellate court of this state is directly on point. Because of the importance of this issue of first impression, we will expound on it in some detail. Following a recitation of facts, we will examine the origins of the doctrines of trespass to land and nuisance, observe recent developments of those doctrines in this and other jurisdictions, and then reaffirm for this state the traditional requirements for a cause of action in trespass.

We conclude that the law of trespass in Michigan does not cover airborne particulate[s], noise, or vibrations, and that a complaint alleging damages resulting from these irritants normally sounds instead in nuisance.

I. Facts

Plaintiffs brought suit seeking damages in both trespass and nuisance, complaining of dust, noise, and vibrations emanating from the Empire Mine, which is operated by defendant Cleveland–Cliffs Iron Company and its subsidiary, defendant Empire Iron Mining Partnership.

The Empire Mine is one of the nation's largest mines, producing eight million tons of iron ore annually. The mine operates twenty-four hours a day, year round. At the time this action was commenced, all but three plaintiffs lived near the mine, in the village of Palmer in Marquette County. Cleveland–Cliffs, which also operates the nearby Tilden Mine, employs approximately 2,200 persons, making it the area's largest civilian employer.

Figure 9–1
The Empire Mine Today

Courtesy Cleveland–Cliffs Corporation.

The Empire Mine was originally dug in the 1870s, then expanded in the 1960s. A second pit was added in 1987, and a third in 1990–91.[2] The mine engages in blasting operations approximately three times a week, year round, and the extraction and processing of the iron ore generates a great deal of airborne dust. Plaintiffs complain that the blasting sends tremors through their property and that defendants' dust constantly accumulates inside and outside plaintiffs' homes. Plaintiffs assert that these emanations aggravate their need to clean and repaint their homes, replace carpets and drapes, repair cracks in all masonry, replace windows, and tend to cause plumbing leaks and broken sewer pipes.

According to the testimony, the dust from the mine is fine, gritty, oily, and difficult to clean. Some plaintiffs complained that they seldom opened their windows because of the dust, and virtually every plaintiff complained that the snow in Palmer tended to be gray or black. Evidence presented at trial indicates that the emissions from the mining operations have consistently remained within applicable air-quality standards and that the amount of particulate matter accumulating over Palmer each month amounts to less than the thickness of a sheet of paper, but that this amount is nonetheless four times greater than what normally settles onto surrounding communities.

In addition to concerns about the dust, many plaintiffs testified that the noise and vibrations from the blasts caused them to suffer shock, nervousness, and sleeplessness. Finally, several plaintiffs asserted that these conditions diminished the value of their homes, in some cases to the point of rendering them unmarketable.

At the close of proofs, the trial court instructed the jury concerning both trespass and nuisance. The jury found that three of the plaintiffs were not entitled to recover under either theory. Concerning the remaining fifty-two plaintiffs, however, the jury was unable to agree on a verdict regarding the nuisance claim, but returned a verdict in favor of these plaintiffs with regard to the trespass claim, awarding damages totaling $599,199. The court denied defendants' posttrial motions for a new trial or judgment notwithstanding the verdict.

The sole issue that defendants raise on appeal is the propriety of the trial court's jury instruction concerning plaintiffs' trespass claim:

> Every unauthorized intrusion onto the lands of another is a trespass upon those lands, and it gives rise to a right to recover damages for the trespass, if any damages were caused by the trespass. So a landowner who causes emissions, dust, vibration, noise from his property onto another [sic] property assumes the risk of trespass, if the dust, vibration, noise affects the neighbor's property, or if he causes by his actions, damages or invasion of his neighbor's land.

2. With each expansion, surface material, also called "overburden," consisting of soil, subsoil, and rock was blasted loose then stockpiled at the edge of the mine property. As the mine was dug deeper, waste rock was likewise blasted loose and stockpiled. The resulting mass of overburden and waste rock is unsightly and so large that residents of Palmer have nicknamed it "Mt. Palmer" and say that it causes their town to have early sunsets.

So again, to repeat. A trespass is an unauthorized intrusion into the lands of another.

* * *

II. Trespass and Nuisance

The general concept of "property" comprises various rights—a "bundle of sticks," as it is often called—which is usually understood to include "[t]he exclusive right of possessing, enjoying, and disposing of a thing." Black's Law Dictionary (6th ed., 1990), p. 1216. As this latter characterization suggests, the right to exclude others from one's land and the right to quiet enjoyment of one's land have customarily been regarded as separate sticks in the bundle. * * * Thus, possessory rights to real property include as distinct interests the right to exclude and the right to enjoy, violations of which give rise to the distinct causes of action respectively of trespass and nuisance. Prosser & Keeton, Torts (5th ed.), § 87, p. 622.

A. Historical Overview

"At common law, trespass was a form of action brought to recover damages for any injury to one's person or property or relationship with another." Black's Law Dictionary (6th ed.), p. 1502. This broad usage of the term "trespass" then gave way to a narrower usage, referring to intrusions upon a person's "tangible property, real or personal." Prosser & Keeton, supra at § 13, p. 67. Today, the general concept of "trespass" has been refined into several specific forms of trespass, see Black's Law Dictionary (6th ed.), pp. 1502–1504, and related doctrines known by various names. Landowners seeking damages or equitable relief in response to violations of their possessory rights to land now generally proceed under the common-law derivatives of strict liability, negligence, nuisance, or trespass to land. It is the latter two products of this evolution from the general concept of trespass that are at issue in the present case.

" '[T]respass is an invasion of the plaintiff's interest in the exclusive possession of his land, while nuisance is an interference with his use and enjoyment of it.' " Hadfield v. Oakland Co. Drain Comm'r, 422 N.W.2d 205 (Mich. 1988) (Brickley, J., joined by Riley, C.J., and Cavanagh, J.), quoting Prosser & Keeton, supra at § 87, p. 622. Historically, "[e]very unauthorized intrusion upon the private premises of another is a trespass...." Giddings v. Rogalewski, 158 N.W. 951 (Mich. 1916). Because a trespass violated a landholder's right to exclude others from the premises, the landholder could recover at least nominal damages even in the absence of proof of any other injury. Id. Recovery for nuisance, however, traditionally required proof of actual and substantial injury. Further, the doctrine of nuisance customarily called for balancing the disturbance complained of against the social utility of its cause.

Traditionally, trespass required that the invasion of the land be direct or immediate and in the form of a physical, tangible object. See, e.g., Williams v. Oeder, 659 N.E.2d 379, 382 n.2 (Ohio App. 1995) (noting then abandoning those traditional requirements); Davis v. Georgia–Pacific Corp., 445 P.2d 481, 483 (Or. 1968) (abandoning the traditional requirements); Norwood v. Eastern Oregon Land Co., 5 P.2d 1057, 1061 (Or. 1931), modified 7 P.2d 996 (Or. 1932) (wrongful diversion of water onto another's land does not constitute trespass to land). Under these principles, recovery in trespass for dust, smoke, noise, and vibrations was generally unavailable because they were not considered tangible or because they came to the land via some intervening force such as wind or water. Instead, claims concerning these irritants were generally pursued under a nuisance theory.

B. Recent Trends

Plaintiffs urge this Court to hold that they are entitled to recover in trespass for invasions of their premises by intangible things without regard for how these annoyances came to their land. Plaintiffs would have us follow the example of certain courts from other jurisdictions, which have eliminated the traditional requirements for trespass of a direct intrusion by a tangible object, directing the inquiry instead toward the nature of the interest harmed. These courts have permitted recovery in trespass for indirect, intangible invasions that nonetheless interfered with exclusive possessory interests in the land. See 75 Am. Jur. 2d, Trespass, § 33, p. 33 and cases cited. See also Mercer v. Rockwell Int'l Corp., 24 F.Supp.2d 735, 743 (W.D. Ky. 1998) (allowing an action in "negligent trespass" concerning intrusions of invisible polychlorinated biphenyls [PCBs] that actually harm the property); Williams, supra (airborne particulate matter from a sand and gravel processing facility, an asphalt plant, and a concrete plant constituted trespass); Martin v. Reynolds Metals Co., 342 P.2d 790 (Or. 1959) (trespass may stem from fluoride compounds in the form of gases and particles). We agree with the characterization of cases of this sort found in Prosser & Keeton as being "in reality, examples of the tort of private nuisance or liability for harm resulting from negligence," not proper trespass cases. Prosser & Keeton, supra at § 13, pp. 71–72 (concerning "decisions finding a trespass constituted by the entry of invisible gases and microscopic particles, but only if harm results"). Accordingly, we decline plaintiffs' invitation to strip the tort of trespass to land of its distinctive accouterments and commingle its identity with other causes of action.

As stated above, the traditional view of trespass required a direct entry onto the land by a tangible object. However, recent trends have led to an erosion of these requirements. Some courts have eliminated the requirement of a direct entry onto the land. E.g., Bradley v. American Smelting & Refining Co., 709 P.2d 782, 787–88 (Wash. 1985); Borland v. Sanders Lead Co., Inc., 369 So.2d 523, 527 (Ala. 1979); Martin, supra at 797 (observing the trend without deciding whether to join it), citing Prosser, Torts (2d ed.), p. 56; 1 Restatement, Torts, § 158, comment h. Some courts have likewise eliminated the requirement of a tangible object. E.g., Bradley, supra at 787–88; Borland, supra at 529. See also Martin, supra at 797 (trespass to land may be accomplished by "a ray of light, by an atomic particle, or by a particulate of fluoride"). In some cases the direct-and-tangible inquiry has been supplanted by an inquiry into the force and energy of the intruding agent. E.g., Bradley, supra at 788; Borland, supra at 527; Martin, supra at 793–94.

The courts that have deviated from the traditional requirements of trespass, however, have consequently found troublesome the traditional principle that at least nominal damages are presumed in cases of trespass. Thus, under the so-called modern view of trespass, in order to avoid subjecting manufacturing plants to potential liability to every landowner on whose parcel some incidental residue of industrial activity might come to rest, these courts have grafted onto the law of trespass a requirement of actual and substantial damages. Bradley, supra at 791; Borland, supra at 529. See also Martin, supra at 795 (observing that "[t]here are adjudicated cases which have refused to find a trespass where the intrusion is clearly established but where the court has felt that the possessor's interest should not be protected"). Logically following from a requirement of substantial damages is the weighing of those damages against the social utility of the activity causing them. Martin, supra at 795 (balancing "the intrusion ... against the socially desirable conduct of the defendant"). See also Bradley, supra at 787 ("While the strict liability origins of trespass encourage courts to eschew a balancing test in name, there is authority for denying injunctive relief if defendant has exhausted his technological opportunities for control.... Acknowledging technological or economic justifications for trespassory invasions does away with the historically harsh treatment of conduct interfering with another's possessory interests.").[11]

We do not welcome this redirection of trespass law toward nuisance law. The requirement that real and substantial damages be proved, and balanced against the usefulness of the offending activity, is appropriate where the issue is interference with one's use or enjoyment of one's land; applying it where a landowner has had to endure an unauthorized physical occupation of the landowner's land, however, offends traditional principles of ownership. The law should not require a property owner to justify exercising the right to exclude. To countenance the erosion of presumed damages in cases of trespass is to endanger the right of exclusion itself.

To summarize, the effects of recent trends in the law of trespass have included eliminating the requirements of a direct invasion by a tangible object, requiring proof of actual and substantial damages, and weighing the plaintiff's damages against the social utility of the operation causing them. This so-called "modern view of trespass" appears, with all its nuances and add-ons, merely to replicate traditional nuisance doctrine as recognized in Michigan. Indeed, the trends recognized or advanced by Bradley, Borland, Martin, and their kindred spirits have conflated nuisance with trespass to the point of rendering it difficult to delineate the difference between the two theories of recovery.

* * * We prefer to preserve the separate identities of trespass and nuisance. * * *

III.   Holding

Recovery for trespass to land in Michigan is available only upon proof of an unauthorized direct or immediate intrusion of a physical, tangible

---

11. We are of the opinion that this kind of analysis is generally only required in a nuisance case and that it is better to preserve that aspect of traditional trespass analysis requiring no proof of actual injury because the invasion of the plaintiff's right to exclude was regarded as tortious by itself.

object onto land over which the plaintiff has a right of exclusive possession. Once such an intrusion is proved, the tort has been established, and the plaintiff is presumptively entitled to at least nominal damages. Where the possessor of land is menaced by noise, vibrations, or ambient dust, smoke, soot, or fumes, the possessory interest implicated is that of use and enjoyment, not exclusion, and the vehicle through which a plaintiff normally should seek a remedy is the doctrine of nuisance. To prevail in nuisance, a possessor of land must prove *significant harm* resulting from the defendant's *unreasonable interference* with the use or enjoyment of the property. Cloverleaf Car Co. v. Phillips Petroleum Co., 540 N.W.2d 297, 301–02 (Mich.App. 1995), citing Adkins, supra at 720. Thus, in nuisance, the plaintiff must prove all damages, which may be awarded only to the extent that the defendant's conduct was "unreasonable" according to a public-policy assessment of its overall value. In the present case, because the intrusions of which plaintiffs complained were intangible things, the trial court erred in allowing the jury to award damages in trespass. Instead, any award of damages would have had to proceed from plaintiffs' alternative but (as yet) unsuccessful theory of nuisance. * * *

The trial court's instruction regarding trespass, as set forth above, recognized a right to recover in trespass "if any damages were caused by the trespass" and that the agents potentially causing the damages included "emissions, dust, vibration, noise." Thus the trial court seems to have mirrored (and indeed gone beyond) the so-called modern view of trespass according to which intangible irritants could constitute trespass. This instruction thus erroneously conflated trespass with nuisance and produced the anomalous result that the jury failed to reach agreement on the nuisance claim while awarding damages for intrusions of intangible things pursuant to the trespass claim.

A.   Tangible

Because noise or vibrations are clearly not tangible objects, we hold that they cannot give rise to an action in trespass in this state.[12] We further hold that dust must generally be considered intangible and thus not actionable in trespass.

We realize, of course, that dust particles are tangible objects in a strict sense that they can be touched and are comprised of physical elements. However, we agree with those authorities that have recognized, for practical purposes, that dust, along with other forms of airborne particulate, does not normally present itself as a significant physical intrusion. See anno: Recovery in trespass for injury to land caused by airborne pollutants, 2 A.L.R.4th 1054, 1055 ("[t]raditionally, an invasion of the exclusive

---

12. This holds even if the noise or vibrations are so intense as to shatter all glass and fell all masonry or otherwise so persistent as to drive all persons from the premises. Although such hazards would indeed infringe on a landowner's possessory interest, it is the interest in use and enjoyment of the premises, not in exclusion from them, and therefore the cause of action lies not in trespass, but in nuisance or the related doctrines of negligence or strict liability.

possession of land by intangible substances, such as an airborne pollutant, was usually held by the court not to constitute a trespass"); Williams, supra, 659 N.E.2d at 382 n.2 (observing that some courts have held that a " 'tangible invasion' or 'object' " must be "more substantial than dust, gas, or fumes"), citing Bradley, supra at 787.

Dust particles do not normally occupy the land on which they settle in any meaningful sense; instead they simply become a part of the ambient circumstances of that space. If the quantity and character of the dust are such as to disturb the ambiance in ways that interfere substantially with the plaintiff's use and enjoyment of the land, then recovery in nuisance is possible.

B.   Direct

"[S]ome courts have held that if an intervening force, such as wind or water, carries pollutants onto the plaintiff's land, then the entry is not 'direct.' " Williams, supra at 382, n. 2, citing Bradley, supra at 787. However, in order to avoid harsh results most courts have avoided an overly strict distinction between direct and indirect invasions, see Prosser & Keeton, supra at § 13, pp. 68–69. Still, "[t]he differentiation between direct and indirect results may not be absolutely dead." Id. at 71.

* * * We hold that the direct invasion requirement for an action in trespass to land is still alive in Michigan. The question then becomes, how strong must the connection between cause and effect be in order to satisfy this requirement?

We agree with the Restatement view that "[i]t is enough that an act is done with knowledge that it will to a substantial certainty result in the entry of the foreign matter." 1 Restatement Torts, 2d, § 158, comment i, p. 279. Thus, a "direct or immediate" invasion for purposes of trespass is one that is accomplished by any means that the offender knew or reasonably should have known would result in the physical invasion of the plaintiff's land.[15]

C.   Damages

* * * The trial court told the jury that "trespass ... gives rise to a right to recover damages for the trespass, if any damages were caused by the trespass." This instruction would be appropriate for nuisance, or negligence, under which theories the plaintiff must prove all damages, but

---

15. We note that the Restatement itself presents its rule as a departure from the traditional requirement of a direct or immediate invasion. 1 Restatement Torts, 2d, § 158, comment i, pp. 278–279 ("it is not necessary that the foreign matter should be thrown directly and immediately upon the other's land"). We would, however, adopt the Restatement's formulation as a liberalization, not a rejection, of the strictest sense of the traditional requirement for a direct or imme-diate invasion. Accordingly, rather than reject this traditional requirement, we preserve this requirement as something akin to proximate cause, meaning "that which, in a natural and continuous sequence, unbroken by any efficient intervening cause, produces the injury and without which the accident could not have happened, if the injury be one which might be reasonably anticipated or foreseen." Black's Law Dictionary (6th ed.), p. 1225.

not for trespass. A jury instruction with respect to the latter should announce that because the violation of the right to exclude causes cognizable injury in and of itself, a plaintiff proving that violation is presumptively entitled to at least nominal damages. The jury should be further instructed that beyond the presumed damages, the plaintiff may recover any additional, actual damages proved.

* * * We hold that recovery in trespass is appropriate for any *appreciable* intrusion onto land in violation of the plaintiff's right to exclude, while recovery in nuisance is appropriate for only *substantial* and *unreasonable* interference with the plaintiff's right to quiet enjoyment.

IV.   Conclusion

There is no need to reformulate the traditional law of trespass to accommodate the problems of airborne pollution, noise, or vibrations, because the doctrines of nuisance and related causes of action have always stood ready to provide remedies. Trespass in Michigan remains a distinct doctrine providing a remedy for violation of a distinct property right. A possessor of land proving a direct or immediate intrusion of a physical, tangible object onto the land is presumptively entitled to recover at least nominal damages even absent any proof of actual injury and may recover additional damages for any injuries actually proved. * * *

Reversed and remanded. We do not retain jurisdiction.

NOTES AND QUESTIONS

1.   At various times four tests have, singly or in combination, been used to demarcate the boundary of trespass and nuisance: (1) whether the defendant's action giving rise to the intrusion was committed on the plaintiff's land or outside the plaintiff's land; (2) whether the harm to the plaintiff's land was direct or indirect; (3) whether the invasion was committed by tangible matter or by some intangible substance; and (4) whether the intrusion deprives the plaintiff of possession of the land, or merely of use and enjoyment of the land. See generally Thomas W. Merrill, Trespass, Nuisance, and the Costs of Determining Property Rights, 14 J. Legal Stud. 13, 26–35 (1985). Although the *Adams* court was not willing to conflate trespass and nuisance, in some jurisdictions situations that would traditionally be treated as very serious nuisances can be charged as a basis for an action in trespass. One court has justified this move by observing that "the now famous equation $E = mc^2$ has taught us that mass and energy are equivalents and that our concept of 'things' must be reframed." See Martin v. Reynolds Metals Co., 342 P.2d 790, 793 (Or. 1959). Which approach makes more sense?

2.   The cases propounding what the *Adams* court calls the "modern view of trespass" may have been motivated less by the discoveries of modern physics than by sympathy for particular plaintiffs whose actions would be barred by the comparatively short statutes of limitations that generally apply to nuisance as opposed to trespass. See Martin v. Reynolds

Metals, supra (plaintiff's claim barred by statute of limitations if character-ized as a nuisance, but not if regarded as a trespass); Borland v. Sanders Lead Co., 369 So.2d 523 (Ala. 1979) (same). Why do you suppose trespass has a relatively long statute of limitations as compared to nuisance?

3. How do we tell whether an intrusion is "substantial"? The court states that a need to balance the plaintiff's damages against the social utility of the defendant's activity "[l]ogically follow[s]" from the require-ment of substantial damages. Do you agree? Is the court claiming that we can only know if damages are substantial if they outweigh the utility of the conduct that produces them? Would physical damage to the land ever be considered anything other than substantial? What if a plant producing a desperately needed drug moves next door to a modest residential communi-ty and causes deafening noise day and night? Is that substantial injury? Is the substantiality of the harm a question of fact? Despite the court's pronouncement, courts have taken a variety of approaches to figuring out what is substantial damage.

4. When should a "noninvasive" nuisance be actionable? Was the intrusion in *Hendricks v. Stalnaker*, excerpted in Chapter I, noninvasive? Many cases involve aesthetic blight along with noises and odors, but getting a court to recognize a purely aesthetic nuisance was once next to impossible and is still very difficult. Compare Foley v. Harris, 286 S.E.2d 186 (Va. 1982) (upholding injunction against storage of wrecked cars); Allison v. Smith, 695 P.2d 791 (Colo. Ct. App. 1984) (nuisance from storage of disused cars and other junk) with Carroll v. Hurst, 431 N.E.2d 1344, 1349 (Ill. App. Ct. 1982) (rejecting junkyard and salvage operation as nuisance because "[n]o testimony was given that defendant's use of his land created an unsightly view; indeed, under Illinois law, a landowner does not have a right to a pleasing view of his neighbor's land"); Ness v. Albert, 665 S.W.2d 1, 2 (Mo. Ct. App. 1983) (holding junk not to be a nuisance because aesthetic considerations are subjective); Mathewson v. Primeau, 395 P.2d 183 (Wash. 1964) (upholding injunction for odors from hog raising opera-tion but not for aesthetic harm from a pile of junk); see generally Prosser and Keeton on Torts § 87, at 626. In contrast, courts have been relatively receptive to noninvasive nuisance claims based on the depressing effect of funeral homes and graveyards. Does this make sense? Some commentators have urged a more expansive use of nuisance for noninvasive harms, on the ground that these harms are no less real than those flowing from noises and odors. See, e.g., John Copeland Nagle, Moral Nuisances, 50 Emory L.J. 265 (2001); George P. Smith & Griffin W. Fernandez, The Price of Beauty: An Economic Approach to Aesthetic Nuisance, 15 Harv. Envtl. L. Rev. 53, 53 (1991). Others would hew closer to the traditional invasion test, at least presumptively. See, e.g., Richard A. Epstein, Nuisance Law: Corrective Justice and Its Utilitarian Constraints, 8 J. Legal Stud. 49 (1979); J.E. Penner, Nuisance and the Character of the Neighbourhood, 5 J. Envtl. L. 1, 14–25 (1993); Henry E. Smith, Exclusion, Property Rules, and the Law of Nuisance, 90 Va. L. Rev. 965 (2004). Consider, in this regard, Mark v. State Department of Fish and Wildlife, 974 P.2d 716 (Or. App. 1999), in which the appeals court held the plaintiff stated a cause of action in private and

public nuisance against a state agency for failing to prevent public nudity in an adjacent wildlife area. Interestingly the court employed the term "invasive nudity" despite the fact that the nudists did not actually enter onto the plaintiff's land. Rather, what counted was the unavoidability of seeing the "full adult nudity" and "repeated acts of depravity, illegality and lewdness." Id. at 718. What are the grounds for considering naked adults a nuisance, but not junked cars?

5. Consider the role of location in trespass and nuisance. The essence of trespass is that someone has sent an object across the spatial boundary into the Blackstonian owner's column of space. What about nuisance? Many nuisances involve nonvisible "invasions," but there is another way that location is important in nuisance law. Unlike in trespass law, in which an invasion by an object would in theory be treated the same if it happened in a residential neighborhood or a factory district, the character of the surrounding area can matter a lot in nuisance. If nuisance is about proper use, it is inescapable that some uses will be offensive in some localities but not in others.

St. Helen's Smelting Company v. Tipping

House of Lords, 1865.
11 H.L.C. 642, 11 Eng. Rep. 1483.

This was an action brought by the Plaintiff to recover from the Defendants damages for injuries done, to his trees and crops, by their works. The Defendants are the directors and shareholders of the St. Helen's Copper Smelting Company (Limited). The Plaintiff, in 1860, purchased a large portion of the Bold Hall estate, consisting of the manor house and about 1300 acres of land, within a short distance of which stood the works of the Defendants. The declaration alleged that, "the Defendants erected, used, and continued to use, certain smelting works upon land near to the said dwelling house and lands of the Plaintiff and caused large quantities of noxious gases, vapours, and, other noxious matter, to issue from the said works, and diffuse themselves over the land and premises of the Plaintiff, whereby the hedges, trees, shrubs, fruit, and herbage, were greatly injured; the cattle were rendered unhealthy, and the Plaintiff was prevented from having so beneficial a use of the said land and premises as he would otherwise have enjoyed, and also the reversionary lands and premises were depreciated in value." The Defendants pleaded, Not guilty.

The cause was tried before Mr. Justice Mellor at Liverpool in August 1863, when the Plaintiff was examined and spoke distinctly to the damage done to his plantations, and to the very unpleasant nature of the vapour, which, when the wind was in a particular direction, affected persons as well as plants in his grounds. On cross examination, he said he had seen the Defendant's chimney before he purchased the estate, but he was not aware whether the works were then in operation. On the part of the Defendants, evidence was called to show that the whole neighbourhood was studded

Figure 9–2
New Bold Hall

Bold New Hall, late 19th Century

with manufactories and tall chimneys, that there were some alkali works close by the Defendants' works, that the smoke from one was quite as injurious as the smoke from the other, that the smoke of both sometimes united, and that it was impossible, to say to which of the two any particular injury was attributable. The fact that the Defendants' works existed before the Plaintiff bought the property was also relied on.

The learned Judge told the jury that an actionable injury was one producing sensible discomfort; that every man, unless enjoying rights obtained by prescription or agreement, was bound to use his own property in such a manner as not to injure the property of his neighbours; that there was no prescriptive right in this case; that the law did not regard trifling inconveniences; that everything must be looked at from a reasonable point of view; and therefore, in an action for nuisance to property, arising from noxious vapours, the injury to be actionable must be such as visibly to diminish the value of the property and the comfort and enjoyment of it. That when the jurors came to consider the facts, all the circumstances, including those of time, and locality, ought, to be taken into consideration; and that with respect to the latter it was clear that in counties where great works had been erected and carried on, persons must not stand on their extreme rights and bring actions in respect of every matter of annoyance, for if so, the business of the whole country would be seriously interfered with.

The Defendants' counsel submitted that the three questions which ought to be left to the jury were, "whether it was a necessary trade, whether the place was a suitable place, for such a trade, and whether it was carried on in a reasonable manner." The learned judge did not put the questions in this form, but did ask the jury whether the enjoyment of the Plaintiff's property was sensibly diminished, and the answer was in the affirmative. Whether the business there carried on was an ordinary business for smelting copper, and the answer was, "We consider it an ordinary business, and conducted in a proper manner, in as good a manner as possible." But to the question whether the jurors thought that it was carried on in a proper place, the answer was "We do not." The verdict was, therefore entered for the Plaintiff, and the damages were assessed at £361 18s. 4½d. A motion was made for a new trial, on the ground of misdirection, but the rule was refused (4 Best and Sm. 608). Leave was however given to appeal, and the case was carried to the Exchequer Chamber, where the judgment was affirmed, Lord Chief Baron Pollock there observing, "My opinion has not always been that which it is now. Acting upon what has been decided *in this Court*, my brother Mellor's direction is not open to a bill of exception" (4 Best and Sm. 616). This appeal was then brought.

The judges were, summoned, and Mr. Baron Martin, Mr. Justice Willes, Mr. Justice Blackburn, Mr. Justice Keating, Mr. Baron Pigott, and Mr. Justice Shee, attended. * * *

■ MR. BARON MARTIN.—My Lords, in answer to the questions proposed by your Lordships to the judges, I have to state their unanimous opinion that the directions given by the learned judge to the jury were correct, and that a new trial ought not to be granted. As far as the experience of all of us goes, the directions are such as we have given in these cases for the last twenty years.

■ THE LORD CHANCELLOR (5 July).—My Lords, I think your Lordships will be satisfied with the answer we have received from the learned judges to the questions put by this House. * * *

My Lords, * * * the jurors have found the existence of the injury; and the only ground upon which your Lordships are asked to set aside that verdict, and to direct a new trial, is this, that the whole neighbourhood where these copper smelting works were carried on, is a neighbourhood more or less devoted to manufacturing purposes of a similar kind, and therefore it is said, that inasmuch as this copper smelting is carried on in what the Appellant contends is a fit place, it may be carried on with impunity, although the result may be the utter destruction, or the very considerable diminution, of the value of the Plaintiff's property. My Lords, I apprehend that that is not the meaning of the word "suitable," or the meaning of the word "convenient," which has been used as applicable to the subject. The word "suitable" unquestionably cannot carry with it this consequence, that a trade may be carried on in a particular locality, the consequence of which trade may be injury and destruction to the neighbouring property. Of course, my Lords, I except cases where any prescriptive right has been acquired by a lengthened user of the place.

On these grounds, therefore, shortly, without dilating farther upon them (and they are sufficiently unfolded by the judgment of the learned judges in the Court below), I advise your Lordships to affirm the decision of the Court below, and to refuse the new trial, and to dismiss the appeal with costs.

■ Lord Cranworth.—My Lords, I entirely concur in opinion with my noble and learned friend on the Woolsack [the Lord Chancellor—eds.], and also in the opinion expressed by the learned Judges, that this has been considered to be the proper mode of directing a jury, as Mr. Baron Martin said, for at least twenty years; I believe I should have carried it back rather farther. * * *

I perfectly well remember, when I had the honour of being one of the Barons of the Court of Exchequer, trying a case in the county of Durham, where there was an action for injury arising from smoke, in the town of Shields. It was proved incontestably that smoke did come and in some degree interfere with a certain person; but, I said, "You must look at it not with a view to the question whether, abstractedly, that quantity of smoke was a nuisance, but whether it was a nuisance to a person living in the town of Shields;" because, if it only added in an infinitesimal degree to the quantity of smoke, I held that the state of the town rendered it altogether impossible to call that an actionable nuisance.

There is nothing of that sort, however, in the present case. It seems to me, that the distinction, in matters of fact, was most correctly pointed out by Mr. Justice Mellor, and I do not think he could possibly have stated the law, either abstractedly or with reference to the facts, better than he has done in this case.

■ Lord Wensleydale.—My Lords, I entirely agree in opinion with both my noble and learned friends in this case. In these few sentences I think everything is included: The Defendants say, "If you do not mind you will stop the progress of works of this description." I agree that it is so, because, no doubt, in the county of Lancaster above all other counties, where great works have been created and carried on, and are the means of developing the national wealth, you must not stand on extreme rights and allow a person to say, "I will bring an action against you for this and that, and so on." Business could not go on if that were so. Everything must be looked at from a reasonable point of view; therefore the law does not regard trifling and small inconveniences, but only regards sensible inconveniences, injuries which sensibly diminish the comfort, enjoyment or value of the property which is affected.

My Lords, I do not think the question could have been more correctly laid down by any one to the jury, and I entirely concur in the propriety of dismissing this appeal.

Judgment of the Exchequer Chamber affirming the judgment of the Court of Queen's Bench affirmed; and appeal dismissed with costs. Lords' Journals, 5th July, 1865.

NOTES AND QUESTIONS

1. William Whitacre Tipping's attempts at self-gentrification, of which the purchase of New Bold Hall, a princely Palladian mansion, was

but a part, are recounted in A.W. Brian Simpson, Leading Cases in the Common Law 163–94 (1995). Tipping was a wealthy cotton spinner, who was more than willing to finance extensive litigation out of his great wealth. Tipping lived out his days at New Bold Hall, "devoting himself to eccentric behaviour, litigation, and farming, at which he was apparently successful." Id. at 191. Simpson argues that *Tipping* demonstrates that a Coasean cost-benefit analysis simply requires too much information and that "the idea is wholly at odds with the sort of system of private property we have, in which idiots can be the beneficiaries of gifts, nincompoops can inherit, and chinless wonders can acquire title to pheasants by shooting them. In allocating property rights, private law treats economic efficiency as quite irrelevant." Id. at 194. Does Simpson's conclusion about the goals of property law follow from his brief summary of the leading cases? If property law is a blunt instrument, does that mean that efficiency is irrelevant? Or that judges are not asked to inquire into efficiency?

2.   Did Tipping prevail on appeal because of the locality rule, or in spite of the locality rule? What exactly is the function of the locality rule? How does the rule relate to the requirement of a threshold showing of substantial harm, which is thought not to depend on the neighborhood context? See Robert G. Bone, Normative Theory and Legal Doctrine in American Nuisance Law: 1850 to 1920, 59 S. Cal. L. Rev. 1101, 1159–60, 1160 n.126 (1986). One understanding is that the locality rule relaxes the Blackstonian exclusion regime, but only tolerates invasions that reflect mutually beneficial forbearance. As long as the uses in a given area are relatively uniform, each landowner gets what Richard Epstein calls "implicit in-kind compensation" in the form of an ability by the (unsuccessful) plaintiff to engage in the complained-of use as well. See, e.g., Richard A. Epstein, Nuisance Law: Corrective Justice and Its Utilitarian Constraints, 8 J. Legal Stud. 49, 88 (1979); see also J.E. Penner, Nuisance and the Character of the Neighbourhood, 5 J. Envtl. L. 1, 14–25 (1993). This live-and-let-live principle was very unlikely to extend to activities that cause physical damage to land. Why might that be? Another understanding, reflected in the reformulation of nuisance law in the *First Restatement*, subsumes the locality rule into a general utilitarian balancing test. Restatement (First) of Torts §§ 822, 826 (1939). Some commentators have proposed a compromise under which the locality would dictate the remedy available, with damages liability for activities deemed subnormal or unneighborly in light of community standards. See, e.g., Robert C. Ellickson, Alternatives to Zoning: Covenants, Nuisance Rules, and Fines as Land Use Controls, 40 U. Chi. L. Rev. 681, 728–33 (1973); Edward Rabin, Nuisance Law: Rethinking Fundamental Assumptions, 63 Va. L. Rev. 1299, 1317–21 (1977).

3.   One might say that more traditional approaches to nuisance, which make a defendant presumptively liable for invasions of a neighbor's land that exceed some threshold of injury, are more formalistic. Do they put nuisance closer to the exclusion end of the spectrum as opposed to governance-style balancing? Some have argued that nuisance should be more like negligence and that courts should apply a standard of reasonableness

across the board. See, e.g., Louise A. Halper, Untangling the Nuisance Knot, 26 B.C. Envtl. Aff. L. Rev. 89, 115–16 (1998).

4. Nuisance law denies recovery to hypersensitive plaintiffs for irritations that would not disturb an ordinary landowner. See, e.g., Amphitheaters, Inc. v. Portland Meadows, 198 P.2d 847, 853 (Or. 1948) (affirming directed verdict for defendant race track operator whose lights interfered with neighboring outdoor movie theater). To take another often-cited example, those who raise minks—very high-strung animals—cannot use nuisance law to maintain the level of peace and quiet required for their business. Why the different treatment for those deemed "hypersensitive?" What makes someone hypersensitive?

5. Is the result in *Tipping* simply a case of the wealthier litigant winning? (Is Tipping wealthier than the owners of the smelting works?) One piece of conventional wisdom is that nineteenth-century tort law softened liability for business as a "subsidy." See Lawrence M. Friedman, A History of American Law 475 (2d. ed. 1985); Morton J. Horwitz, The Transformation of American Law, 1780–1860, at 85–89 (1977) (setting forth the subsidy thesis). But this view has come in for heavy criticism. See Simpson, supra, at 163–94; Gary T. Schwartz, Tort Law and the Economy in Nineteenth–Century America: A Reinterpretation, 90 Yale L.J. 1717, 1735–58 (1981) (critiquing the subsidy thesis); Gary T. Schwartz, The Character of Early American Tort Law, 36 UCLA L. Rev. 641, 642–43 (1989) (arguing that courts in the nineteenth century were generous in upholding tort liability against defendants in emerging industry). We return to this issue with the *Boomer* case, infra.

Luensmann v. Zimmer–Zampese & Associates, Inc.

Court of Appeals of Texas, San Antonio, 2003.
103 S.W.3d 594.

■ CATHERINE STONE, JUSTICE. This appeal illustrates the tension that often arises when "modern development" occurs in what was once a quiet neighborhood. Anna Luensmann and her husband live in Guadalupe County in a home where Anna has lived since 1947. Edna Reininger lives nearby in a home she has occupied for the last twenty-six years. In May of 1999, Appellee Zimmer–Zampese & Associates, Inc. began constructing a drag racing strip approximately 700 feet from the Luensmann and Reininger homes. Appellants Anna and Roland Luensmann and Edna Reininger ("the Luensmanns") unsuccessfully sought to enjoin construction. River City Raceway now runs up to 200 races on Wednesday, Friday, Saturday, and Sunday nights. The Luensmanns claim that the races are loud and cause vibrations that shake their homes. They claim that lights from the track can be seen miles away and that smoke produced by the cars impedes visibility on the adjoining streets and blows onto their property. However, River City Raceway is not the only source of noise which affects the Luensmanns. Their homes are near a shooting range, railroad tracks, and Interstate 10. Their homes are also near the Zuehl Airport and in the flight path of Randolph Air Force Base. Adding to the noise, a moto-cross track recently opened in the neighborhood.

The Luensmanns sued on theories of nuisance, nuisance per se, and trespass, and obtained a temporary restraining order limiting Zimmer–Zampese's nocturnal operations. At trial, the court granted Zimmer–Zampese's motion for directed verdict on nuisance per se. The jury found that the racing strip was not a nuisance and Zimmer–Zampese did not trespass on the Luensmanns' land. The court entered judgment for Zimmer–Zampese and dissolved the temporary restraining order. On appeal, the Luensmanns claim that the trial court erred in excluding evidence of Penal Code violations, in instructing the jury on negligent nuisance, and in failing to grant their motion for judgment *non obstante verdicto*. We affirm the judgment of the trial court. * * *

The Luensmanns argue that they were entitled to judgment *non obstante verdicto* on the issue of nuisance per se. Zimmer–Zampese responds that the Luensmanns request relief to which they are not entitled because there was no jury verdict on nuisance per se for the court to set aside. Zimmer–Zampese also claims that the Luensmanns' failure to complain about the directed verdict entered in favor of Zimmer–Zampese waives any complaint relating to the nuisance per se claim. However, the Luensmanns' basic argument is that the trial court granted judgment as a matter of law to the wrong party. * * *

In reviewing a directed verdict, we decide whether there is any evidence of probative value to raise issues of fact on the material questions presented. We view the evidence in the light most favorable to the party suffering the adverse judgment. A directed verdict is proper if: (1) the opponent's pleadings are insufficient to support a judgment; (2) the evidence conclusively proves a fact that establishes a party's right to judgment as a matter of law; or (3) the evidence offered on a cause of action is insufficient to raise an issue of fact.

The parties disagree about the elements required to prove nuisance per se. The Luensmanns believe that nuisance and nuisance per se share the same relationship as negligence and negligence per se. However, a person does not commit nuisance per se simply by violating a statute and causing a nuisance. Instead, the Luensmanns can prove nuisance per se on one of two theories. Because there are no findings of fact and conclusions of law, and because the Luensmanns' pleadings and proof did not advance one theory over another, we will discuss both theories. First, the Luensmanns can prove nuisance per se by proving that the activity was a nuisance at all times, under any circumstances, and in any location. See Maranatha Temple, Inc. v. Enter. Prods. Co., 893 S.W.2d 92, 100 (Tex.App.–Houston [1st Dist.] 1994, writ denied). However, their own pleadings establish that racing is conducted only at night, and then only on certain nights. They have not alleged that the track is a nuisance when it is closed. Therefore, if the trial court based its directed verdict on the "at all times" theory, then the Luensmanns' own pleadings conclusively established Zimmer–Zampese's right to a directed verdict.

The second theory, most often applied in cases involving municipalities, permits a plaintiff to prove nuisance per se by proving a violation of law. See Newton v. Town of Highland Park, 282 S.W.2d 266, 277 (Tex. App.–Dallas 1955, writ ref'd n.r.e.). However, violation of a statute or ordinance, without additional evidence of nuisance, is insufficient to prove the claim. See Maranatha, 893 S.W.2d at 100. This type of nuisance per se case typically arises when the municipality categorizes a particular activity as a nuisance and forbids it within the jurisdiction. In such a case, the municipality's action is not valid unless the activity was a nuisance per se at common law. Id. This court addressed the "violation of law" theory of nuisance per se as it related to a horse racing track and held that the track was not a nuisance per se. See Otten v. Town of China Grove, 660 S.W.2d 565, 567 (Tex.App.–San Antonio 1983, writ dism'd).

In *Otten,* this court found that horse racing was not a nuisance per se at common law, even though the illegal gambling allegedly occurring at the track was, because horse racing had not been declared a nuisance by the Legislature and because it was not illegal to race horses. Id. Similarly, under the common law, Zimmer–Zampese's drag racing is not a nuisance per se. Drag racing has not been declared a nuisance by the Legislature, and no statute prohibits operation of a drag racing facility. The Luensmanns rely on the disorderly conduct statute to prove a violation of law, but they failed to allege that Zimmer–Zampese has been prosecuted for violating the disorderly conduct statute. Additionally, the statute requires that before a person can violate the disorderly conduct statute, they must be given a warning by a magistrate or peace officer. See Tex. Pen.Code Ann. 42.01(a)(5)(Vernon 2002). The record contains no evidence that such a warning has ever been given. Thus, even based on the "violation of law" theory of nuisance per se, the court correctly granted judgment as a matter of law. We therefore overrule the Luensmanns' second issue. * * *

The judgment of the trial court is affirmed in all respects.

NOTES AND QUESTIONS

1. One definition of a nuisance *per se*, as *Luensmann* reflects, is activity that constitutes a nuisance wherever and whenever it occurs. By contrast, a nuisance *per accidens* is otherwise permissible activity that constitutes a nuisance only because of where or when it takes place. See, e.g., Morgan v. High Penn Oil Co., 77 S.E.2d 682 (N.C. 1953). The court here makes much of the fact that the noisy drag racing only occurs at night. Is the periodic nature really to the point? What if the defendant were testing jet engines that would disturb any neighbor but defended on the grounds that the engines were tested only during the day?

2. In this case, the drag racing was not the only noisy activity in the neighborhood. If it is desirable that noisy activities cluster, can we expect that to happen under nuisance law? What about the first noisy use in an undeveloped area? Should neighboring holders of undeveloped land be able to sue to enjoin on a theory of nuisance? The problem of baselines is central

to the role that nuisance law and related ideas play in the law of takings. See Chapter XII.

Boomer v. Atlantic Cement Company, Inc.

Court of Appeals of New York, 1970.
257 N.E.2d 870.

■ BERGAN, JUDGE. Defendant operates a large cement plant near Albany. These are actions for injunction and damages by neighboring land owners alleging injury to property from dirt, smoke and vibration emanating from the plant. A nuisance has been found after trial, temporary damages have been allowed; but an injunction has been denied.

The public concern with air pollution arising from many sources in industry and in transportation is currently accorded ever wider recognition accompanied by a growing sense of responsibility in State and Federal Governments to control it. Cement plants are obvious sources of air pollution in the neighborhoods where they operate.

But there is now before the court private litigation in which individual property owners have sought specific relief from a single plant operation. The threshold question raised by the division of view on this appeal is whether the court should resolve the litigation between the parties now before it as equitably as seems possible; or whether, seeking promotion of the general public welfare, it should channel private litigation into broad public objectives.

A court performs its essential function when it decides the rights of parties before it. Its decision of private controversies may sometimes greatly affect public issues. Large questions of law are often resolved by the manner in which private litigation is decided. But this is normally an incident to the court's main function to settle controversy. It is a rare exercise of judicial power to use a decision in private litigation as a purposeful mechanism to achieve direct public objectives greatly beyond the rights and interests before the court.

Effective control of air pollution is a problem presently far from solution even with the full public and financial powers of government. In large measure adequate technical procedures are yet to be developed and some that appear possible may be economically impracticable.

It seems apparent that the amelioration of air pollution will depend on technical research in great depth; on a carefully balanced consideration of the economic impact of close regulation; and of the actual effect on public health. It is likely to require massive public expenditure and to demand more than any local community can accomplish and to depend on regional and interstate controls.

A court should not try to do this on its own as a by-product of private litigation and it seems manifest that the judicial establishment is neither equipped in the limited nature of any judgment it can pronounce nor prepared to lay down and implement an effective policy for the elimination of air pollution. This is an area beyond the circumference of one private lawsuit. It is a direct responsibility for government and should not thus be undertaken as an incident to solving a dispute between property owners and a single cement plant—one of many—in the Hudson River valley.

The cement making operations of defendant have been found by the court of Special Term to have damaged the nearby properties of plaintiffs in these two actions. That court, as it has been noted, accordingly found defendant maintained a nuisance and this has been affirmed at the Appellate Division. The total damage to plaintiffs' properties is, however, relatively small in comparison with the value of defendant's operation and with the consequences of the injunction which plaintiffs seek.

The ground for the denial of injunction, notwithstanding the finding both that there is a nuisance and that plaintiffs have been damaged substantially, is the large disparity in economic consequences of the nuisance and of the injunction. This theory cannot, however, be sustained without overruling a doctrine which has been consistently reaffirmed in several leading cases in this court and which has never been disavowed here, namely that where a nuisance has been found and where there has been any substantial damage shown by the party complaining an injunction will be granted.

The rule in New York has been that such a nuisance will be enjoined although marked disparity be shown in economic consequence between the effect of the injunction and the effect of the nuisance.

The problem of disparity in economic consequence was sharply in focus in Whalen v. Union Bag & Paper Co., 101 N.E. 805 (N.Y. 1913). A pulp mill entailing an investment of more than a million dollars polluted a stream in which plaintiff, who owned a farm, was "a lower riparian owner". The economic loss to plaintiff from this pollution was small. This court, reversing the Appellate Division, reinstated the injunction granted by the Special Term against the argument of the mill owner that in view of "the slight advantage to plaintiff and the great loss that will be inflicted on defendant" an injunction should not be granted (101 N.E. p. 805). "Such a balancing of injuries cannot be justified by the circumstances of this case", Judge Werner noted (101 N.E. p. 805). He continued: "Although the damage to the plaintiff may be slight as compared with the defendant's expense of abating the condition, that is not a good reason for refusing an injunction" (101 N.E. p. 806).

Thus the unconditional injunction granted at Special Term was reinstated. The rule laid down in that case, then, is that whenever the damage resulting from a nuisance is found not "unsubstantial", viz., $100 a year, injunction would follow. This states a rule that had been followed in this court with marked consistency (McCarty v. Natural Carbonic Gas Co., 81 N.E. 549 (N.Y.); Strobel v. Kerr Salt Co., 58 N.E. 142 (N.Y.); Campbell v. Seaman, 63 N.Y. 568).

There are cases where injunction has been denied. McCann v. Chasm Power Co., 105 N.E. 416 (N.Y.), is one of them. There, however, the damage shown by plaintiffs was not only unsubstantial, it was non-existent. Plaintiffs owned a rocky bank of the stream in which defendant had raised the level of the water. This had no economic or other adverse consequence to plaintiffs, and thus injunctive relief was denied. Similar is the basis for denial of injunction in Forstmann v. Joray Holding Co., 154 N.E. 652 (N.Y.), where no benefit to plaintiffs could be seen from the injunction sought (154 N.E. 655). Thus if, within Whalen v. Union Bag & Paper Co., supra which authoritatively states the rule in New York, the damage to plaintiffs in these present cases from defendant's cement plant is "not unsubstantial", an injunction should follow.

Although the court at Special Term and the Appellate Division held that injunction should be denied, it was found that plaintiffs had been damaged in various specific amounts up to the time of the trial and damages to the respective plaintiffs were awarded for those amounts. The effect of this was, injunction having been denied, plaintiffs could maintain successive actions at law for damages thereafter as further damage was incurred.

The court at Special Term also found the amount of permanent damage attributable to each plaintiff, for the guidance of the parties in the event both sides stipulated to the payment and acceptance of such permanent damage as a settlement of all the controversies among the parties. The total of permanent damages to all plaintiffs thus found was $185,000. This basis of adjustment has not resulted in any stipulation by the parties.

This result at Special Term and at the Appellate Division is a departure from a rule that has become settled; but to follow the rule literally in these cases would be to close down the plant at once. This court is fully agreed to avoid that immediately drastic remedy; the difference in view is how best to avoid it.*

One alternative is to grant the injunction but postpone its effect to a specified future date to give opportunity for technical advances to permit defendant to eliminate the nuisance; another is to grant the injunction conditioned on the payment of permanent damages to plaintiffs which would compensate them for the total economic loss to their property present and future caused by defendant's operations. For reasons which will be developed the court chooses the latter alternative.

If the injunction were to be granted unless within a short period—e.g., 18 months—the nuisance be abated by improved methods, there would be no assurance that any significant technical improvement would occur.

The parties could settle this private litigation at any time if defendant paid enough money and the imminent threat of closing the plant would build up the pressure on defendant. If there were no improved techniques found, there would inevitably be applications to the court at Special Term

---

* Respondent's investment in the plant is   people employed there.
in excess of $45,000,000. There are over 300

for extensions of time to perform on showing of good faith efforts to find such techniques.

Moreover, techniques to eliminate dust and other annoying by-products of cement making are unlikely to be developed by any research the defendant can undertake within any short period, but will depend on the total resources of the cement industry nationwide and throughout the world. The problem is universal wherever cement is made.

For obvious reasons the rate of the research is beyond control of defendant. If at the end of 18 months the whole industry has not found a technical solution a court would be hard put to close down this one cement plant if due regard be given to equitable principles.

On the other hand, to grant the injunction unless defendant pays plaintiffs such permanent damages as may be fixed by the court seems to do justice between the contending parties. All of the attributions of economic loss to the properties on which plaintiffs' complaints are based will have been redressed.

The nuisance complained of by these plaintiffs may have other public or private consequences, but these particular parties are the only ones who have sought remedies and the judgment proposed will fully redress them. The limitation of relief granted is a limitation only within the four corners of these actions and does not foreclose public health or other public agencies from seeking proper relief in a proper court.

It seems reasonable to think that the risk of being required to pay permanent damages to injured property owners by cement plant owners would itself be a reasonable effective spur to research for improved techniques to minimize nuisance.

The power of the court to condition on equitable grounds the continuance of an injunction on the payment of permanent damages seems undoubted. (See, e.g., the alternatives considered in McCarty v. Natural Carbonic Gas Co., supra, as well as Strobel v. Kerr Salt Co., supra.)

The damage base here suggested is consistent with the general rule in those nuisance cases where damages are allowed. "Where a nuisance is of such a permanent and unabatable character that a single recovery can be had, including the whole damage past and future resulting therefrom, there can be but one recovery" (66 C.J.S. Nuisances § 140, p. 947). It has been said that permanent damages are allowed where the loss recoverable would obviously be small as compared with the cost of removal of the nuisance (Kentucky–Ohio Gas Co. v. Bowling, 95 S.W.2d 1 (Ky.)). * * *

Thus it seems fair to both sides to grant permanent damages to plaintiffs which will terminate this private litigation. The theory of damage is the "servitude on land" of plaintiffs imposed by defendant's nuisance. (See United States v. Causby, 328 U.S. 256, 261, 262, 267, where the term "servitude" addressed to the land was used by Justice Douglas relating to the effect of airplane noise on property near an airport.)

The judgment, by allowance of permanent damages imposing a servitude on land, which is the basis of the actions, would preclude future recovery by plaintiffs or their grantees (see Northern Indiana Public Serv. Co. v. W. J. & M. S. Vesey, 200 N.E. 620).

This should be placed beyond debate by a provision of the judgment that the payment by defendant and the acceptance by plaintiffs of permanent damages found by the court shall be in compensation for a servitude on the land.

Although the Trial Term has found permanent damages as a possible basis of settlement of the litigation, on remission the court should be entirely free to ex-examine this subject. It may again find the permanent damage already found; or make new findings.

The orders should be reversed, without costs, and the cases remitted to Supreme Court, Albany County to grant an injunction which shall be vacated upon payment by defendant of such amounts of permanent damage to the respective plaintiffs as shall for this purpose be determined by the court.

■ JASEN, JUDGE (dissenting). I agree with the majority that a reversal is required here, but I do not subscribe to the newly enunciated doctrine of assessment of permanent damages, in lieu of an injunction, where substantial property rights have been impaired by the creation of a nuisance.

It has long been the rule in this State, as the majority acknowledges, that a nuisance which results in substantial continuing damage to neighbors must be enjoined. To now change the rule to permit the cement company to continue polluting the air indefinitely upon the payment of permanent damages is, in my opinion, compounding the magnitude of a very serious problem in our State and Nation today.

In recognition of this problem, the Legislature of this State has enacted the Air Pollution Control Act (Public Health Law, Consol.Laws, c. 45, §§ 1264 to 1299–m) declaring that it is the State policy to require the use of all available and reasonable methods to prevent and control air pollution (Public Health Law § 1265[1]).

The harmful nature and widespread occurrence of air pollution have been extensively documented. Congressional hearings have revealed that air pollution causes substantial property damage, as well as being a contributing factor to a rising incidence of lung cancer, emphysema, bronchitis and asthma.

The specific problem faced here is known as particulate contamination because of the fine dust particles emanating from defendant's cement plant. The particular type of nuisance is not new, having appeared in many cases for at least the past 60 years. (See Hulbert v. California Portland Cement Co., 118 P. 928 (Cal. 1911).) It is interesting to note that cement production has recently been identified as a significant source of particulate contamination in the Hudson Valley. This type of pollution, wherein very

---

1. See, also, Air Quality Act of 1967, 81 U.S. Stat. 485 (1967).

small particles escape and stay in the atmosphere, has been denominated as the type of air pollution which produces the greatest hazard to human health. We have thus a nuisance which not only is damaging to the plaintiffs, but also is decidedly harmful to the general public.

I see grave dangers in overruling our long-established rule of granting an injunction where a nuisance results in substantial continuing damage. In permitting the injunction to become inoperative upon the payment of permanent damages, the majority is, in effect, licensing a continuing wrong. It is the same as saying to the cement company, you may continue to do harm to your neighbors so long as you pay a fee for it. Furthermore, once such permanent damages are assessed and paid, the incentive to alleviate the wrong would be eliminated, thereby continuing air pollution of an area without abatement.

It is true that some courts have sanctioned the remedy here proposed by the majority in a number of cases, but none of the authorities relied upon by the majority are analogous to the situation before us. In those cases, the courts, in denying an injunction and awarding money damages, grounded their decision on a showing that the use to which the property was intended to be put was primarily for the public benefit. Here, on the other hand, it is clearly established that the cement company is creating a continuing air pollution nuisance primarily for its own private interest with no public benefit.

This kind of inverse condemnation may not be invoked by a private person or corporation for private gain or advantage. Inverse condemnation should only be permitted when the public is primarily served in the taking or impairment of property. The promotion of the interests of the polluting cement company has, in my opinion, no public use or benefit.

Nor is it constitutionally permissible to impose servitude on land, without consent of the owner, by payment of permanent damages where the continuing impairment of the land is for a private use. This is made clear by the State Constitution (art. I, § 7, subd. (a)) which provides that "[p]rivate property shall not be taken for *public use* without just compensation" (emphasis added). It is, of course, significant that the section makes no mention of taking for a Private use.

In sum, then, by constitutional mandate as well as by judicial pronouncement, the permanent impairment of private property for private purposes is not authorized in the absence of clearly demonstrated public benefit and use.

I would enjoin the defendant cement company from continuing the discharge of dust particles upon its neighbors' properties unless, within 18 months, the cement company abated this nuisance.

It is not my intention to cause the removal of the cement plant from the Albany area, but to recognize the urgency of the problem stemming from this stationary source of air pollution, and to allow the company a specified period of time to develop a means to alleviate this nuisance.

I am aware that the trial court found that the most modern dust control devices available have been installed in defendant's plant, but, I submit, this does not mean that *better* and more effective dust control devices could not be developed within the time allowed to abate the pollution.

Moreover, I believe it is incumbent upon the defendant to develop such devices, since the cement company, at the time the plant commenced production (1962), was well aware of the plaintiffs' presence in the area, as well as the probable consequences of its contemplated operation. Yet, it still chose to build and operate the plant at this site.

In a day when there is a growing concern for clean air, highly developed industry should not expect acquiescence by the courts, but should, instead, plan its operations to eliminate contamination of our air and damage to its neighbors. * * *

NOTES AND QUESTIONS

1. As a matter of history, the automatic injunction rule that *Boomer* ascribes to *Whalen v. Union Bag* may be overstated. The writ of nuisance, like other early common-law actions, provided only for damages. Eventually, landowners complaining of nuisances could also obtain injunctions from a court of equity, provided the harm was irreparable and the other conditions for equitable relief were met. Cf. Baker v. Hunt Club, Chapter I (describing the requirements for securing injunction against a trespass). But even after the merger of law and equity, New York courts never completely subscribed to the notion that injunctions were automatic. See Louise A. Halper, Nuisance, Courts and Markets in the New York Court of Appeals, 1850–1915, 54 Alb. L. Rev. 301 (1990). Still, the courts awarded injunctions in nuisance cases with some frequency. How does all this fit in with the "subsidy" thesis? Does the older preference for injunctions (absolute or not) protect landowners against industrialists? Some of the landowners in question were fairly wealthy and influential. Consider again *St. Helen's Smelting Company v. Tipping*, supra.

2. *Boomer* became a famous case, in part because when it was decided the then-nascent law-and-economics movement was concerned with problems of high transaction costs and holdouts when the number of affected parties is large. A conflict between a single polluter and multiple residents was the archetypal example of a high-transaction-cost dispute in this literature. Most commentators came to agree that in such a situation, damages (liability rules) are preferable to injunctions (property rules). The facts and the remedial outcome in *Boomer* seemed to confirm this analysis. See, e.g., Coase, The Problem of Social Cost, excerpted in Chapter I; see also Calabresi & Melamed, supra, Chapter I; A. Mitchell Polinsky, Resolving Nuisance Disputes: The Simple Economics of Injunctive and Damage Remedies, 32 Stan. L. Rev. 1075, 1076 (1980).

3. More recently, some have begun to voice doubts. See, e.g., Daniel A. Farber, Reassessing *Boomer*: Justice, Efficiency, and Nuisance Law, in

Property Law and Legal Education: Essays in Honor of John E. Cribbet 7, 8–9 (Peter Hay & Michael H. Hoeflich eds., 1988); Smith, 90 Va. L. Rev. at 1037–45. Consider again the building encroachment cases and the material on ex ante versus ex post perspectives in Chapter I. Do *Boomer* and the proponents of liability rule solutions to nuisance disputes look at the problem solely from an ex post perspective? What kinds of solutions might be available to polluters if they knew that courts would routinely enjoin nuisances that impose substantial injury on neighboring landowners? See Robert C. Ellickson & Vicki L. Been, Land Use Controls: Cases and Materials 845–54 (3d ed. 2005) (discussing the possibility of voluntary amassing of parcels using devices like a purchasing agent with an undisclosed principal); Victor P. Goldberg, The Relational Exchange, Contract Law, and the *Boomer* Problem, 141 J. Institutional & Theoretical Econ. 570 (1985). Might injunctions encourage those opening or expanding a plant to avoid the problem before it arises using these or other techniques? If they do not work and some relaxation of the injunctive approach is necessary, why is a move to damages called for? Would prior public hearings and a mandatory consideration of environmental impacts (as is required by the National Environmental Policy Act, for example) be superior? Would explicit use of eminent domain to acquire a pollution easement or a pollution buffer zone work better? In what sense was the cement plant a public use? For more on eminent domain and public use, see Chapter XII.A.

4. In *Boomer*, the plaintiffs did not ask for supracompensatory damages. Quite possibly this reflected the fact that their lawyers understood damages would be computed based on lost market value. W. Page Keeton et al., Prosser and Keeton on the Law of Torts, § 89, at 637–40 (5th ed. 1984) (discussing types of damages available to nuisance plaintiffs, including diminution in market value and under some circumstances special damages but not damages for subjective value); see also Boomer, 257 N.E.2d at 874–75 (discussing damages available and referring to diminution in objective value). One concern with market damages is they are undercompensatory: Landowners value their land at more than the market price, as evidenced by the fact that they were not selling in the first place. It is worth noting that on remand the trial court in *Boomer* found that the damages were far greater than in the conditional stipulation used by the Court of Appeals— around four times the $185,000 mentioned in the opinion you have here. See Farber, supra, at 8–11. How should the law respond to the problem of undercompensation under the market value formula? Would it be better to award nuisance victims some bonus above market value, as is sometimes proposed in the context of takings by eminent domain (see Chapter XII)? If polluters are relatively sure they will face liability, sometimes they will offer additional compensation to avoid litigation. For a recent episode in which an electric utility operating a coal-burning power plant offered to buy out an entire community at above-market prices, see Gideon Parchomovsky & Peter Siegelman, Selling Mayberry: Communities and Individuals in Law and Economics, 92 Cal. L. Rev. 75 (2004).

5. One argument in favor of loosening the automatic injunction rule—whether through damages or some other device—is that the harsh

results can lead courts to manipulate in the direction of finding no nuisance. Robert C. Ellickson, Alternatives to Zoning: Covenants, Nuisance Rules, and Fines as Land Use Controls, 40 U. Chi. L. Rev. 681, 720 (1973). Ellickson offers as an example another New York case, *Bove v. Donner-Hanna Coke Corp.*, 258 N.Y.S. 229 (App. Div. 1932), in which the court avoided finding a nuisance—which presumably would have resulted in an injunction—by doubtful reasoning that included the idea the plaintiffs had come to the nuisance and that the polluting factory was permitted under local zoning regulations.

6. Another argument for damages is that an injunction will feed into the "endowment effect," in which people come to place a higher value on existing entitlements than they are willing to pay to acquire an entitlement they do not have. See, e.g., Daniel Kahneman & Amos Tversky, Prospect Theory: An Analysis of Decision Under Risk, 47 Econometrica 263 (1979); see also Richard H. Thaler, The Winner's Curse: Paradoxes and Anomalies of Economic Life 63–78 (1992). If people are willing to pay less for the entitlement than they would have to be paid in order to give it up, is this a sign of irrationality? Or is it something that the law should accommodate? See Jeffrey J. Rachlinski & Forest Jourden, Remedies and the Psychology of Ownership, 51 Vand. L. Rev. 1541 (1998). In *Boomer*, the plaintiffs did not ask for supracompensatory damages. Is this evidence that they were suffering from a cognitive illusion rather than experiencing harm to subjective values? Id. at 1543–44. Or does it reflect the fact that the law will not give more than market damages? See Note 4 supra.

Spur Industries, Inc. v. Del E. Webb Development Co.

Supreme Court of Arizona, 1972.
494 P.2d 700.

■ CAMERON, VICE CHIEF JUSTICE. From a judgment permanently enjoining the defendant, Spur Industries, Inc., from operating a cattle feedlot near the plaintiff Del E. Webb Development Company's Sun City, Spur appeals. Webb cross-appeals. Although numerous issues are raised, we feel that it is necessary to answer only two questions. They are:

1. Where the operation of a business, such as a cattle feedlot is lawful in the first instance, but becomes a nuisance by reason of a nearby residential area, may the feedlot operation be enjoined in an action brought by the developer of the residential area?

2. Assuming that the nuisance may be enjoined, may the developer of a completely new town or urban area in a previously agricultural area be required to indemnify the operator of the feedlot who must move or cease operation because of the presence of the residential area created by the developer?

The facts necessary for a determination of this matter on appeal are as follows. The area in question is located in Maricopa County, Arizona, some 14 to 15 miles west of the urban area of Phoenix, on the Phoenix–Wickenburg Highway, also known as Grand Avenue. About two miles south of Grand Avenue is Olive Avenue which runs east and west. 111th Avenue runs north and south as does the Agua Fria River immediately to the west. See Exhibits A and B below.

Figure 9–3
Exhibits A and B

Farming started in this area about 1911. In 1929, with the completion of the Carl Pleasant Dam, gravity flow water became available to the property located to the west of the Agua Fria River, though land to the east remained dependent upon well water for irrigation. By 1950, the only urban areas in the vicinity were the agriculturally related communities of Peoria, El Mirage, and Surprise located along Grand Avenue. Along 111th Avenue, approximately one mile south of Grand Avenue and 1 1/2 miles north of Olive Avenue, the community of Youngtown was commenced in 1954. Youngtown is a retirement community appealing primarily to senior citizens.

In 1956, Spur's predecessors in interest, H. Marion Welborn and the Northside Hay Mill and Trading Company, developed feed-lots, about 1/2 mile south of Olive Avenue, in an area between the confluence of the usually dry Agua Fria and New Rivers. The area is well suited for cattle feeding and in 1959, there were 25 cattle feeding pens or dairy operations within a 7 mile radius of the location developed by Spur's predecessors. In April and May of 1959, the Northside Hay Mill was feeding between 6,000 and 7,000 head of cattle and Welborn approximately 1,500 head on a combined area of 35 acres.

In May of 1959, Del Webb began to plan the development of an urban area to be known as Sun City. For this purpose, the Marinette and the Santa Fe Ranches, some 20,000 acres of farmland, were purchased for $15,000,000 or $750.00 per acre. This price was considerably less than the price of land located near the urban area of Phoenix, and along with the success of Youngtown was a factor influencing the decision to purchase the property in question.

By September 1959, Del Webb had started construction of a golf course south of Grand Avenue and Spur's predecessors had started to level ground for more feedlot area. In 1960, Spur purchased the property in question and began a rebuilding and expansion program extending both to the north and south of the original facilities. By 1962, Spur's expansion program was completed and had expanded from approximately 35 acres to 114 acres. See Exhibit A above.

Accompanied by an extensive advertising campaign, homes were first offered by Del Webb in January 1960 and the first unit to be completed was south of Grand Avenue and approximately 2 1/2 miles north of Spur. By 2 May 1960, there were 450 to 500 houses completed or under construction. At this time, Del Webb did not consider odors from the Spur feed pens a problem and Del Webb continued to develop in a southerly direction, until sales resistance became so great that the parcels were difficult if not impossible to sell. * * *

By December 1967, Del Webb's property had extended south to Olive Avenue and Spur was within 500 feet of Olive Avenue to the north. See Exhibit B above. Del Webb filed its original complaint alleging that in excess of 1,300 lots in the southwest portion were unfit for development for sale as residential lots because of the operation of the Spur feedlot.

Del Webb's suit complained that the Spur feeding operation was a public nuisance because of the flies and the odor which were drifting or being blown by the prevailing south to north wind over the southern portion of Sun City. At the time of the suit, Spur was feeding between 20,000 and 30,000 head of cattle, and the facts amply support the finding of the trial court that the feed pens had become a nuisance to the people who resided in the southern part of Del Webb's development. The testimony indicated that cattle in a commercial feedlot will produce 35 to 40 pounds of wet manure per day, per head, or over a million pounds of wet manure per day for 30,000 head of cattle, and that despite the admittedly good feedlot management and good housekeeping practices by Spur, the resulting odor and flies produced an annoying if not unhealthy situation as far as the senior citizens of southern Sun City were concerned. There is no doubt that some of the citizens of Sun City were unable to enjoy the outdoor living which Del Webb had advertised and that Del Webb was faced with sales resistance from prospective purchasers as well as strong and persistent complaints from the people who had purchased homes in that area. * * *

[N]either the citizens of Sun City nor Youngtown are represented in this lawsuit and the suit is solely between Del E. Webb Development Company and Spur Industries, Inc.

MAY SPUR BE ENJOINED?

The difference between a private nuisance and a public nuisance is generally one of degree. A private nuisance is one affecting a single individual or a definite small number of persons in the enjoyment of private rights not common to the public, while a public nuisance is one affecting the rights enjoyed by citizens as a part of the public. To constitute a public nuisance, the nuisance must affect a considerable number of people or an entire community or neighborhood. City of Phoenix v. Johnson, 75 P.2d 30 (Ariz. 1938).

Where the injury is slight, the remedy for minor inconveniences lies in an action for damages rather than in one for an injunction. Kubby v. Hammond, 198 P.2d 134 (Ariz. 1948). Moreover, some courts have held, in the "balancing of conveniences" cases, that damages may be the sole remedy. See Boomer v. Atlantic Cement Co., 257 N.E.2d 870 (N.Y. 1970), and annotation comments, 40 A.L.R.3d 601.

Thus, it would appear from the admittedly incomplete record as developed in the trial court, that, at most, residents of Youngtown would be entitled to damages rather than injunctive relief.

We have no difficulty, however, in agreeing with the conclusion of the trial court that Spur's operation was an enjoinable public nuisance as far as the people in the southern portion of Del Webb's Sun City were concerned.

§ 36–601, subsec. A reads as follows:

§ 36–601. Public nuisances dangerous to public health

A. The following conditions are specifically declared public nuisances dangerous to the public health:

1. Any condition or place in populous areas which constitutes a breeding place for flies, rodents, mosquitoes and other insects which are capable of carrying and transmitting disease-causing organisms to any person or persons.

By this statute, before an otherwise lawful (and necessary) business may be declared a public nuisance, there must be a "populous" area in which people are injured:

[I]t hardly admits a doubt that, in determining the question as to whether a lawful occupation is so conducted as to constitute a nuisance as a matter of fact, the locality and surroundings are of the first importance. A business which is not per se a public nuisance may become such by being carried on at a place where the health, comfort, or convenience of a populous neighborhood is affected. * * * What might amount to a serious nuisance in one locality by reason of the density of the population, or character of the neighborhood affected, may in another place and under different surroundings be deemed proper and unobjectionable.

MacDonald v. Perry, 255 P. 494, 497 (Ariz. 1927).

It is clear that as to the citizens of Sun City, the operation of Spur's feedlot was both a public and a private nuisance. They could have successfully maintained an action to abate the nuisance. Del Webb, having shown a special injury in the loss of sales, had a standing to bring suit to enjoin the nuisance. Engle v. Clark, 90 P.2d 994 (Ariz. 1939); City of Phoenix v. Johnson, supra. The judgment of the trial court permanently enjoining the operation of the feedlot is affirmed.

MUST DEL WEBB INDEMNIFY SPUR?

A suit to enjoin a nuisance sounds in equity and the courts have long recognized a special responsibility to the public when acting as a court of equity:

§ 104. Where public interest is involved.

Courts of equity may, and frequently do, go much further both to give and withhold relief in furtherance of the public interest than they are accustomed to go when only private interests are involved. Accordingly, the granting or withholding of relief may properly be dependent upon considerations of public interest.

27 Am.Jur.2d, Equity, page 626.

In addition to protecting the public interest, however, courts of equity are concerned with protecting the operator of a lawfully, albeit noxious, business from the result of a knowing and willful encroachment by others near his business.

In the so-called "coming to the nuisance" cases, the courts have held that the residential landowner may not have relief if he knowingly came into a neighborhood reserved for industrial or agricultural endeavors and has been damaged thereby * * *

Were Webb the only party injured, we would feel justified in holding that the doctrine of "coming to the nuisance" would have been a bar to the relief asked by Webb, and, on the other hand, had Spur located the feedlot near the outskirts of a city and had the city grown toward the feedlot, Spur would have to suffer the cost of abating the nuisance as to those people locating within the growth pattern of the expanding city * * *

We agree, however, with the Massachusetts court that:

> The law of nuisance affords no rigid rule to be applied in all instances. It is elastic. It undertakes to require only that which is fair and reasonable under all the circumstances. In a commonwealth like this, which depends for its material prosperity so largely on the continued growth and enlargement of manufacturing of diverse varieties, "extreme rights" cannot be enforced.

Stevens v. Rockport Granite Co., 104 N.E. 371, 373 (Mass. 1914).

There was no indication in the instant case at the time Spur and its predecessors located in western Maricopa County that a new city would spring up, full-blown, alongside the feeding operation and that the developer of that city would ask the court to order Spur to move because of the new city. Spur is required to move not because of any wrongdoing on the part of Spur, but because of a proper and legitimate regard of the courts for the rights and interests of the public.

Del Webb, on the other hand, is entitled to the relief prayed for (a permanent injunction), not because Webb is blameless, but because of the damage to the people who have been encouraged to purchase homes in Sun City. It does not equitably or legally follow, however, that Webb, being entitled to the injunction, is then free of any liability to Spur if Webb has in fact been the cause of the damage Spur has sustained. It does not seem harsh to require a developer, who has taken advantage of the lesser land values in a rural area as well as the availability of large tracts of land on which to build and develop a new town or city in the area, to indemnify those who are forced to leave as a result.

Having brought people to the nuisance to the foreseeable detriment of Spur, Webb must indemnify Spur for a reasonable amount of the cost of moving or shutting down. It should be noted that this relief to Spur is limited to a case wherein a developer has, with foreseeability, brought into a previously agricultural or industrial area the population which makes necessary the granting of an injunction against a lawful business and for which the business has no adequate relief.

It is therefore the decision of this court that the matter be remanded to the trial court for a hearing upon the damages sustained by the defendant Spur as a reasonable and direct result of the granting of the permanent injunction. Since the result of the appeal may appear novel and both sides have obtained a measure of relief, it is ordered that each side will bear its own costs.

Affirmed in part, reversed in part, and remanded for further proceedings consistent with this opinion.

NOTES AND QUESTIONS

1. Note that *Spur* is brought as a public nuisance action, whereas the other cases we have considered were private nuisance actions. A public nuisance is not limited to conduct that interferes with the use and enjoyment of land. It encompasses a variety of threats and interferences to public health, safety, and comfort. These include obstructing a highway, keeping a vicious dog, and even putting on an opera that threatens to cause a riot. Star Opera Co. v. Hylan, 178 N.Y.S. 179 (N.Y. Sup. Ct. 1919) (refusing to enjoin officials from prohibiting performance of German-language opera until ratification of peace treaty with Germany, where company's past performances had led to riotous conduct and police intervention). Government officials always have standing and can seek an injunction against a public nuisance. Only those private parties suffering special injury from a public nuisance have standing. See generally, W. Page Keeton et al., Prosser and Keeton on the Law of Torts § 90 (5th ed. 1984). On what basis does the court here find that Del Webb satisfies the special injury requirement for standing?

2. Recall again the framework of property rules and liability rules developed by Calabresi and Melamed. Guido Calabresi & A. Douglas Melamed, Property Rules, Liability Rules, and Inalienability: One View of the Cathedral, 85 Harv. L. Rev. 1089, 1115–17 (1972) (excerpted and summarized in Chapter I). This framework suggests the existence of four rules for handling nuisance disputes, based on which party is given "the entitlement" and whether the entitlement is protected by a property rule or liability rule. The framework thus led to the "discovery" of Rule 4, in which the polluter would have the "entitlement" to pollute, but protected only by a liability rule. That is, one or more residents could sue to stop the pollution, but would have to pay the polluter's cost of abating or shutting down. The fact that the Arizona Supreme Court came up with something that looks very much like Rule 4 at roughly the same time Calabresi and Melamed wrote has been cited by subsequent commentators as vindicating the utility of their modeling exercise.

3. Indeed, a number of commentators have sought to build on the remedial innovation reflected in *Spur* and Calabresi and Melamed's Rule 4. See, e.g., Ellickson, Alternatives to Zoning, supra, at 744–46 (arguing for use of Rule 4 as a second stage option for the plaintiff when a nuisance defendant opts to pay Rule 2 damages and continues the nuisance); Jeff L. Lewin, Compensated Injunctions and the Evolution of Nuisance Law, 71 Iowa L. Rev. 775, 827–31 (1986) (arguing for limited use of compensated injunctions in the interest of fairness); Edward Rabin, Nuisance Law: Rethinking Fundamental Assumptions, 63 Va. L. Rev. 1299, 1339–46 (1977) (advocating compensated injunctions in cases of deserving plaintiffs only);

see also Ian Ayres & Paul M. Goldbart, Optimal Delegation and Decoupling in the Design of Liability Rules, 100 Mich. L. Rev. 1 (2001); Saul Levmore, Unifying Remedies: Property Rules, Liability Rules, and Startling Rules, 106 Yale L.J. 2149 (1997). Others have been less enthusiastic about the possibility of Rule 4. See, e.g., Richard A. Epstein, A Clear View of *The Cathedral*: The Dominance of Property Rules, 106 Yale L.J. 2091, 2103–05 (1997) (criticizing Rule 4 as destabilizing property); Jeanne L. Schroeder, Three's a Crowd: A Feminist Critique of Calabresi and Melamed's *One View of the Cathedral*, 84 Cornell L. Rev. 394, 438 (1999) (providing feminist critique of Rule 4); Henry E. Smith, Exclusion and Property Rules in the Law of Nuisance, 90 Va. L. Rev. 965, 1007–21 (2004) (portraying Rule 4 as inconsistent with system of basic entitlement that minimizes information costs).

4. In fact, it appears that *Spur* has received much more attention from law review articles than from courts. Andrew Morriss reports that "*Spur* has not had much direct influence" on the law of nuisance in Arizona, and that "[t]he only reported decision from outside Arizona to consider in detail the doctrinal developments in *Spur* came in an Ohio Common Pleas Court decision rejecting *Spur* as inapplicable because of the greater amount of open space in Arizona." Andrew P. Morriss, Cattle v. Retirees: Sun City and the Battle of *Spur Industries v. Del E. Webb Development Co.*, in Property Stories (Gerald Korngold & Andrew P. Morriss eds., 2004). What accounts for the paucity of judicial interest in the *Spur* remedy? Consider what would have happened if the conflict in *Spur* had simply been between the residents of Sun City and the feedlot. Does the court regard the senior citizens as innocent parties from whom it would not be appropriate to require payments to Spur? Would the residents have had much success in coming up with the money to purchase an injunction closing the feedlot? Given the collective-action difficulties this would have posed, how likely is it that a court would adopt such a remedy? See James E. Krier & Stewart J. Schwab, Property Rules and Liability Rules: The Cathedral in Another Light, 70 N.Y.U. L. Rev. 440, 470 (1995).

5. More fundamentally what is the nature of "the entitlement" under Rule 4? Does the Blackstonian package of rights ever come with a "right to pollute"? Would someone with such a "right to pollute" (in the sense of not being liable in nuisance) be able to enjoin the resident from blocking the pollution—as with fans or a wall? (Probably not.) As we will see, one might acquire an easement, by prescription or negotiation, to pollute and this would add to the polluter's default package of entitlements. See Henry E. Smith, Self–Help and the Nature of Property, 1 J.L. Econ. & Pol'y 69, 73–76 (2005). Does the Calabresi and Melamed framework rest on a flawed conception that whenever a court rules against a plaintiff the defendant has an entitlement that must either be purchased (Rule 3) or taken for just compensation (Rule 4) in order to achieve a different result?

B. SERVITUDES

Nuisance law is hardly the last word on land-use conflict. Conflicts among neighbors can also be resolved by contract. Any two neighbors or even a group of neighbors can enter into a contract that commits them to certain behavior regarding the use of their land, and this will be enforced like any other bilateral contract. But such contracts would be of limited usefulness if they were binding only on the initial parties to the agreement. If one of the parties sold her land and moved away, the original deal would no longer be of any use, and the remaining party might not be able to strike a new deal with the new owner. The important contribution of property law here has been the development of doctrines that allow parties to enter into contracts that "run with the land," meaning the terms and conditions of the agreement are binding not only on the original owners but on all future owners of both the benefited and the burdened parcels. Contracts that bind successors in ownership are generically called "servitudes."

The two principal types of servitudes are easements and covenants. Very roughly speaking, an easement is a contract in which an owner agrees to waive his or her right to exclude certain kinds of intrusions by another; a covenant is a contract in which an owner agrees to abide by certain restrictions on the use of his or her land for the benefit or one or more others. Covenants are thus more of a governance mechanism and more often than easements prescribe affirmative behavior on the part of the burdened landowner. Covenants against commercial use, for maximum building height, and even for door color have been used to control spillovers sometimes of a very subtle sort that would not fall under the law of nuisance. Easements always run with the land. Covenants sometimes run with the land if certain conditions are met, which we will consider in some detail. Easements have always been regarded as a type of property right, the exact significance of this appellation (beyond the understanding that easements run with the land) being somewhat unclear. Covenants, even when they run with the land, are less often described as a type of property; rather they are usually spoken of as "promises respecting the use of land." Although authority on this point is scant, it appears that easements have an in rem effect, in the sense that third parties may not interfere with the performance of rights under an easement. Covenants, however, generally do not give rise to any rights against third parties (other than successors to the burdened and benefited parcels), and in this sense are more accurately thought to be in personam.

1. EASEMENTS

a. INTRODUCTION

Baseball Publishing Co. v. Bruton

Supreme Judicial Court of Massachusetts, 1938.
18 N.E.2d 362.

■ LUMMUS, JUSTICE. The plaintiff, engaged in the business of controlling locations for billboards and signs and contracting with advertisers for the exhibition of their placards and posters, obtained from the defendant on October 9, 1934, a writing signed but not sealed by the defendant whereby the defendant "in consideration of twenty-five dollars * * * agrees to give" the plaintiff "the exclusive right and privilege to maintain advertising sign one ten feet by twenty-five feet on wall of building 3003 Washington Street" in Boston, owned by the defendant, "for a period of one year with the privilege of renewal from year to year for four years more at the same consideration." It was provided that "all signs placed on the premises remain the personal property" of the plaintiff. The writing was headed "Lease No. ___." It was not to be effective until accepted by the plaintiff.

It was accepted in writing on November 10, 1934, when the plaintiff sent the defendant a check for $25, the agreed consideration for the first year. The defendant returned the check. The plaintiff nevertheless erected the contemplated sign, and maintained it until February 23, 1937, sending the defendant early in November of the years 1935 and 1936 checks for $25 which were returned. On February 23, 1937, the defendant caused the sign to be removed. On February 26, 1937, the plaintiff brought this bill for specific performance, contending that the writing was a lease. The judge ruled that the writing was a contract to give a license, but on November 2, 1937, entered a final decree for specific performance, with damages and costs. The defendant appealed. It is stipulated that on November 3, 1937, the plaintiff tendered $25 for the renewal of its right for another year beginning November 10, 1937, but the defendant refused the money.

The distinction between a lease and a license is plain, although at times it is hard to classify a particular instrument. A lease of land conveys an interest in land, requires a writing to comply with the statute of frauds though not always a seal and transfers possession. A license merely excuses acts done by one on land in possession of another that without the license would be trespasses, conveys no interest in land, and may be contracted for or given orally. A lease of a roof or a wall for advertising purposes is possible. Alfano v. Donnelly, 189 N.E. 610 (Mass. 1934). The writing in question, however, giving the plaintiff the "exclusive right and privilege to maintain advertising sign * * * on wall of building," but leaving the wall in the possession of the owner with the right to use it for all purposes not forbidden by the contract and with all the responsibilities of ownership and control, is not a lease. Gaertner v. Donnelly, Mass., 5 N.E.2d 419 (Mass. 1936); and cases cited. The fact that in one corner of the writing are found the words, "Lease No. ___," does not convert it into a lease. Those words are merely a misdescription of the writing.

Subject to the right of a licensee to be on the land of another for a reasonable time after the revocation of a license, for the purpose of removing his chattels, it is of the essence of a license that it is revocable at the will of the possessor of the land. * * * Am.Law Inst. Restatement: Torts, §§ 167–171. The revocation of a license may constitute a breach of contract, and give rise to an action for damages. But it is none the less effective to deprive the licensee of all justification for entering or remaining upon the land. * * * Compare Hurst v. Picture Theatres, Ltd., [1915] 1 K.B. 1.

If what the plaintiff bargained for and received was a license, and nothing more, then specific performance that might compel the defendant to renew the license, leaving it revocable at will, would be futile and for that reason should not be granted. 5 Williston, Contracts (Rev.Ed.) § 1442; Am.Law.Inst.Restatement: Contracts, § 377. Specific performance that might render the license irrevocable for the term of the contract would convert it into an equitable estate in land, and give the plaintiff more than the contract gave. There can be no specific performance of a contract to give a license, at least in the absence of fraud or estoppel.

The writing in the present case, however, seems to us to go beyond a mere license. It purports to give "the exclusive right and privilege to maintain" a certain sign on the defendant's wall. So far as the law permits, it should be so construed as to vest in the plaintiff the right which it purports to give. That right is in the nature of an easement in gross, which, whatever may be the law elsewhere, is recognized in Massachusetts. Goodrich v. Burbank, 12 Allen 459; Carville v. Commonwealth, 78 N.E. 735 (Mass. 1906); American Telephone & Telegraph Co. of Massachusetts v. McDonald, 173 N.E. 502 (Mass. 1930); Jones v. Stevens, 177 N.E. 91 (Mass. 1931). We see no objection to treating the writing as a grant for one year and a contract to grant for four more years an easement in gross thus limited to five years. Similar writings have been so treated in other jurisdictions.

An easement, being inconsistent with seisin in the person owning it, always lay in grant and could not be created by livery of seisin. Randall v. Chase, 133 Mass. 210, 214 (1882). It is an interest in land within the statute of frauds and, apart from prescription, requires a writing for its creation. G.L.(Ter.Ed.) c. 183, § 3. Cook v. Stearns, 11 Mass. 533 (1814). Indeed, the creation of a legal freehold interest in an easement, apart from prescription, requires a deed. And differing from a lease of land for not more than seven years (Alfano v. Donnelly, 189 N.E. 610, 612 (Mass. 1934)), a grant of an easement for as short a term as five years apparently requires a deed in order to create a legal interest. Wood v. Leadbitter, 13 M. & W. 838; Chadwick v. Covell, 23 N.E. 1068 (Mass. 1890); Walker Ice Co. v. American Steel & Wire Co., 70 N.E. 937 (Mass. 1904), and especially Loring, J. at 70 N.E. 937. But in equity a seal is not necessary to the creation of an easement. Since equity treats an act as done where there is a duty to do it enforceable in equity, or, as more tersely phrased, equity treats that as done which ought to be done, an enforceable unsealed contract such as the writing in this case, providing for the creation of an easement, actually creates an easement in equity.

There is no error in the final decree granting specific performance. The affirmance of this decree will not prevent an assessment of the damages as of the date of the final decree after rescript.

Interlocutory decree overruling demurrer affirmed.

VARIETIES OF EASEMENTS

Easements are very common. They were recognized in Roman law and exist in some form in virtually all modern legal systems. What are the distinguishing features of an easement? On the one hand, an easement differs from other property rights such as a fee simple or a lease because an easement conveys the right to a particular *use* of land, as opposed to the right to *possession* of land. One can think of a possessory right as being a kind of gatekeeper right that allows the possessor to determine all of the uses to which the property will be devoted (out of a large and open-ended set of possibilities), and who will be allowed to engage in them. An easement, in contrast, is a conveyance of a right to engage in one particular use, ordinarily given to one particular person or set of persons. In terms of the bundle of sticks metaphor, a possessory right conveys a full bundle of sticks; an easement conveys just one stick out of the bundle. On the other hand, an easement differs from a mere license that permits someone to engage in a particular use of the land. A license is a contract right that is regarded (ordinarily) as being revocable. An easement, however, is regarded as an irrevocable conveyance of the right to engage in a particular use of land. (It need not be indefinitely irrevocable; it can be irrevocable for a term of years, as in *Baseball Publishing*.)

Easements have always been regarded as a type of property right, even though they convey only delimited use rights. One reason for regarding easements as property is purely formal—they are created by grant rather than by contract (see the next Section for more on what this means). But this is quite likely circular: One can argue just as easily that easements must be created by grant because they are property as that easements are property because they are created by grant. A more substantive reason is the feature of irrevocability. Easements have a "vested" quality that distinguishes them from licenses and other contract rights. A third possible reason is that easements do have in rem features. Although the relationship between the grantor and grantee of an easement looks much like a bilateral exchange of promises, a valid easement also gives rise to a general duty on the part of "all the world" not to interfere with the easement. Thus, for example, if B has an easement to cross the land of A, a third party—C—would be guilty of a wrong if C attempted to block B's passage across A's land.

Reasons Easements are Treated as Property Rights
1) Created by Grant
2) Irrevocable
3) In Rem Features

A basic distinction within the universe of easements is between *easements appurtenant* and *easements in gross*. An easement appurtenant is one that belongs to another parcel of land. So for example, assume Whiteacre and Blackacre are adjacent parcels of land. Whiteacre is owned by Sally and Blackacre is owned by Dan. Sally grants Dan an easement appurtenant to cross Whiteacre to reach Blackacre. Since the easement is appurtenant, it "belongs" to Blackacre, and is carved out of Whiteacre. This means that the benefit of the easement belongs to whoever happens to own Blackacre, and the burden of the easement belongs to whoever happens to own Whiteacre. The law speaks of Blackacre as being the *dominant* tract (the tract benefited or enhanced by the easement); and Whiteacre as being the *servient* tract (the tract burdened by or out of which is carved the easement). If Dan sells Blackacre to Daniella, Daniella as the owner of the dominant tract now has the right to use the right of way; Dan no longer has any rights in the easement. Similarly, if Sally sells Whiteacre to Saul, Saul is now the owner of the servient tract burdened by the easement; Sally is off the hook. An easement in gross is one that belongs to a particular grantee, as opposed to belonging to a particular tract of land. Suppose Sally grants Dan an easement in gross to fish in the pond on Whiteacre. Now, the benefit of the easement belongs to Dan personally, not to whoever happens to be the owner of Blackacre. If Dan sells Blackacre to Daniella, the easement in gross remains with Dan; Daniella has no rights to fish in the pond unless she gets her own easement.

English courts recognized only easements appurtenant. An attempt to create an easement in gross created only a license personal to the grantee. It was not inheritable, i.e., would not pass on death to the heirs of the grantee, and was not transferable to a third party. American courts have been more sympathetic to easements in gross. The usual explanation is the emergence of the railroad industry in nineteenth-century America. In order to build a railroad, it was necessary to acquire the right to operate along a long narrow strip of land cutting across hundreds of separately owned parcels of property. For various reasons, many owners were willing to grant easements to railroads (or were willing to allow railroads to condemn easements), but were more reluctant to convey a fee simple in a strip of land to a railroad. But such an easement, crossing many separate parcels, would not be appurtenant to any particular tract of land; it would be in gross to the railroad enterprise. So, in order to accommodate the growth of the railroad industry, many American courts concluded that easements in gross could be created that were inheritable and transferable—provided the grant was of a commercial character. Thus, most American states permitted easements in gross for railroad or utility purposes—or for the erection of billboards, as in the *Baseball Publishing* case—whereas in England one would have to use grants of a fee simple or leases to accomplish these purposes. Although courts have been increasingly liberal about permitting parties to create inheritable and transferable easements in gross, most courts continue to hold that easements in gross for purely recreational purposes such as hunting, camping, boating, or fishing are not inheritable or transferable. See Note, The Easement in Gross Revisited: Transferability and Divisibility Since 1945, 39 Vand. L. Rev. 109 (1986).

Closely related to an easement in gross, but narrower in purpose, is something called a *profit à prendre*, or "profit" for short. This is the right to enter on the land of another in order to extract something of value, such as timber, or fruit from trees, or fish or game from a lake or forest. It is also used to permit extraction of surface minerals, such as sand or gravel, although deep rock mining and oil and gas extraction are usually governed by mineral leases. Profits are very ancient and were recognized by the English common law. They are generally governed by the same rules as easements appurtenant. The grant of a profit carries with it an implied license to enter the land for purposes of carrying out the profit, and this license remains irrevocable as long as the profit continues to last.

Another basic distinction among easements is between *affirmative* easements and *negative* easements. Affirmative easements permit the easement holder to perform some affirmative action on the land of another. One can think of an affirmative easement as permitting action on the servient tract that otherwise would be a trespass or an invasive nuisance. A negative easement permits the easement holder to demand that the owner of the servient tract desist from certain actions that might harm the easement holder. Virtually all easements are affirmative easements. English common law recognized only four narrow categories of negative easements: blocking sunlight from falling on windows on the dominant tenement; interfering with the flow of air in a defined channel to the dominant tenement; removing lateral support to a building on the dominant tenement; and interfering with the flow of water in an artificial stream to the dominant tenement. English law also permitted easements to be established by prescription in these four narrow areas. (See Fontainebleau Hotel Corp. v. Forty–Five Twenty–Five, Inc., infra.) American courts have been somewhat more adventuresome about permitting express negative easements outside the traditional four categories. For example, the California Supreme Court once upheld a negative easement for an unobstructed view of San Francisco Bay over a neighboring property. Petersen v. Friedman, 328 P.2d 264 (Cal. Dist. Ct. App. 1958). As a rule, however, when someone wants to impose a negative duty on a servient landowner to desist from taking action that might harm the dominant tract, lawyers today will accomplish this by drafting a covenant that runs with the land. Once running covenants were recognized in *Tulk v. Moxhay*, infra, the logical thing to do would been to have restricted easements to affirmative easements (waivers of exclusion rights) and to have required that all negative duties imposed on servient landowners be embodied in written covenants. This is the general thrust of the way things are done, but the doctrine is not quite that tidy.

A final distinction that is sometimes of importance is between *private* easements and *public* easements. Private easements authorize specific named parties (individuals or enterprises) to use land for designated purposes. Public easements authorize the general public to use land for designated purposes. Public roads, highways, and navigable waterways are most often owned in fee simple by some governmental entity, subject to a trust obligation to the public (see Chapter III). But occasionally they are held as easements, in which case the public holds only a right to use the property, and the underlying owner of the fee retains all other rights. Public access rights for recreational purposes, such as beaches, bike trails, and portages, are more likely to be held as public easements than are roads and highways. Sometimes the public holds negative easements, such as scenic easements, conservation easements, or historic preservation easements. These, like public easements of access, can be acquired by condemnation as well as by gift or purchase.

NOTES AND QUESTIONS

1. Why was the common law so hostile to the creation of easements in gross? After the development of recording acts that permit the recording of property interests like easements, is there any continuing reason to disfavor easements in gross?

2. Easements ordinarily can be subdivided. For example, if Blackacre has an easement of way over Whiteacre, and Blackacre is subdivided into four lots, absent previous agreement to the contrary each of the new lot owners will have an easement over Whiteacre. Should parties be permitted to subdivide easements in gross? Suppose the Baseball Publishing Company wants to subdivide its easement in gross in order to allow three different firms to post billboards in the space initially designated for the Baseball Publishing Company. Do you foresee any problems in permitting this to happen?

3. Notice that *Baseball Publishing* is another illustration of the *numerus clausus* principle. The parties have an agreement that would allow the company to use the side of a building for a series of five renewable one-year terms for purposes of putting up an advertising sign. In order to ascertain the legal effect of this agreement, the court feels compelled to assign the agreement to one of several possible boxes: license, lease, or easement in gross. Should the court proceed this way, or should it just recognize a new interest ("advertising sign privileges on buildings for renewable terms") that corresponds with the apparent intentions of the parties?

b. CREATION OF EASEMENTS

Although easements are regarded as property rights, at common law they could not be created by the quaint ceremony of livery of seisin, only by grant. To create property by grant, including an easement, the grantor must deliver to the grantee a *deed* to the property. A deed, in turn, was originally understood to mean a writing under seal. The seal was a unique mark or symbol, impressed on paper with melted wax. Over the years, the requirement of melted wax was softened, to the point where today in most jurisdictions a deed is just a piece of paper that conveys a property right—although in some jurisdictions formalities such as attestation of signatures by notaries or witnesses are still required. Because an easement is an interest in land, the Statute of Frauds also requires that easements be in writing.

The common law imposed another limitation on the creation of easements that sometimes can provide a trap for the unwary. An easement could be created by grant, of the direct A-to-B variety. Alternatively, an easement could be created by reservation to the grantor, A, in a grant to B of a possessory interest in land. Thus, if A granted Blackacre to B, A could in the deed granting Blackacre reserve to himself an easement over Blackacre, perhaps to access other land retained by the grantor. But, at common law one could not create a grant by reservation in a third party.

For example, if A granted Blackacre to B, A could not in the deed to B reserve an easement in Blackacre running to C. Some modern American courts have disapproved of this rule. See, e.g., Willard v. First Church of Christ, Scientist, 498 P.2d 987 (Cal. 1972). They have reasoned that the original rationale for the rule was to prevent easements, which were created by grant rather than livery of seisin, from being used to do an end run around the rules of seisin important to the feudal system. Feudalism being dead, these courts have reasoned, the rule against creating easements in third parties by reservation should also be rejected. Can you think of other possible rationales for the rule against creating easements by reservation in third parties? If the recording system in the jurisdiction has only a grantor-grantee index, and does not have a tract index, might there be situations in which it would be hard to discover that someone like C holds an easement created by reservation in a deed between A and B?

All this sounds reasonably straightforward: If you want to create an easement, get a lawyer to put it in writing, follow whatever formalities are necessary to create a deed, and record the instrument in the local registry of deeds. Unfortunately, people seem more prone to ignore the need for writings and lawyers where easements are concerned, than they are when conveying possessory interests. There are a variety of possible reasons for this. Easements are generally of lower value (in the grand scheme of things) than possessory interests, and this may account for more rational ignorance about the requirements of the law. Also, norms of neighborly accommodation often serve as a substitute for, or a supplement to, explicit easements. People may rely on these norms, and may even feel that it is unneighborly to demand that informal understandings be formalized in legal agreements. In any event, the need for a writing is often ignored, and this has given rise to lots of litigation about issues of access to land. Courts have responded by creating a variety of doctrines that allow easements or easement-like rights to be recognized without any writing. Courts have held that when these doctrines apply, they constitute an implied exception to the requirements of the Statute of Frauds.

Schwab v. Timmons

Supreme Court of Wisconsin, 1999.
589 N.W.2d 1.

■ JON P. WILCOX, J. The petitioners, James and Katherine Schwab and Dorice McCormick (petitioners), seek review of a decision affirming the circuit court's dismissal of their declaratory judgment action requesting an easement by necessity or by implication for both ingress and egress and utilities over the properties owned by the respondents in order to gain access to their landlocked parcels located in Door County. The circuit court, as affirmed by the court of appeals, concluded that the historical circumstances in this case do not fit the typical situation from which ways of necessity are implied and that even if they did, the easement would not have survived because it was not recorded.

On appeal, the petitioners claim they are entitled to an easement by necessity or by implication over the respondents' properties; or in the alternative, they seek an expansion of the common law in this state to recognize an easement by necessity where property is landlocked due to geographical barriers and due to the actions of the common owner and grantor, in this case the United States. We conclude that the petitioners have failed to establish entitlement to an easement by implication or by necessity either because of actions by the federal government or by geographical barriers. Not only were the parcels at issue not landlocked at the time of conveyance, but the petitioners themselves created their landlocked parcels when they conveyed away their highway access. We refuse to turn 100–plus years of Wisconsin common law on its head to accommodate such actions. Accordingly, we affirm the court of appeals.

I.

The facts are not in dispute. The petitioners and the respondents all own property that is located on Green Bay in the Village of Ephraim in Door County. The properties are situated between the waters of Green Bay on the west and a bluff ranging in height from 37 to 60 feet on the east. [Figure 9–4] is a diagram of the properties (lots and parcels) involved.

Prior to 1854, the property involved was owned by the United States and was divided into three lots: Lot 2, the northernmost lot; Lot 3; and Lot 4, the southernmost lot. In 1854, the United States granted by patent Lot 4 to Ingebret Torgerson, but retained Lots 2 and 3. At the time that Lot 4 was severed from Lots 2 and 3, the United States did not retain a right-of-way through Lot 4 to get to Lots 2 and 3. At oral argument, it was explained that at the time of this conveyance by the United States, the eastern boundary of the lots extended to the east to what is now a public roadway. The lots were comprised of property both above and below the bluff with access to a public roadway from above. In 1882, the United States granted Lots 2 and 3 to Halvor Anderson.

At some point after the United States granted the lots, they were further subdivided into parcels. After 1854, Lots 2, 3, and 4 were never fully owned by one person or entity * * *

The petitioners' parcels are located in Lot 2, the northernmost lot. McCormick owns the northernmost parcel and the Schwabs own two adjacent parcels directly south of McCormick. Together the properties comprise over 1200 feet of frontage and over nine acres of property. Directly south of the Schwabs' parcels is a parcel owned by the Timmons within Lot 2, followed to the south by a parcel owned by the Lenzes, also in Lot 2; all of the remaining respondents' parcels follow sequentially to the south, located in Lots 3 and 4, with the parcel owned by Hobler being the southernmost parcel located at the southern boundary of Lot 4.

Figure 9–4
Map from *Schwab v. Timmons*

It was indicated at oral argument that the current eastern boundary line, the bluff line—which produced parcels above and below the bluff—was created at various unknown times. The Schwabs' parcels were originally purchased by James' parents in the 1940s and were later gifted to James in 1965 and 1974. At purchase, the Schwabs' parcels extended east from the waters of Green Bay to property above the bluff where there was access to a public roadway and a house. Some time after the 1974 inheritance, the Schwabs conveyed the property above the bluff to James' relatives and retained the parcel below. McCormick also inherited her parcel which originally included land above and below the bluff with highway access from above, and she conveyed the property above the bluff to a third party, retaining the parcel below.

As they currently stand, both of the petitioners' parcels are bordered by water on the east [sic] and the bluff on the west [sic]. Because their properties are between the lake and the bluff, the petitioners claim their only access is over the land to the south, owned by the respondents, for which they do not have a right-of-way.

A private road runs north from Hobler's parcel across all of the respondents' properties terminating on the Lenz parcel. Timmons also has the right to use the private road. This is the road that the petitioners are seeking to extend for their use. Negotiations for an agreement to extend the road have failed.

In 1988, the petitioners petitioned the Village of Ephraim, pursuant to Wis. Stat. § 80.13 (1985–86), to extend a public road—North Shore Drive—to the private road beginning at the Hobler property northward over all of the respondents' properties to McCormick's property. Section 80.13 allows a landowner to request the local government, in its discretion, to construct a public roadway at the petitioning landowners' expense. The Village of Ephraim board, however, declined the request finding that extending the road was not in the public's interest.

Consequently, the petitioners brought this declaratory judgment action seeking an easement by necessity or by implication to gain access to their land. The easement would include the perpetual right to travel, including the right for ingress, egress and for public utilities, over the now private road, which stretches over 15 of the respondents' parcels to the Lenz property, as well as the right to build a road over the Lenz and Timmons properties up to the McCormick property. The respondents filed motions to dismiss the amended complaint.[3] * * *

III.

The petitioners claim an easement by implication or by necessity over the respondents' properties. An easement is a "liberty, privilege, or advantage in lands, without profit, and existing distinct from the ownership of the land." Stoesser v. Shore Drive Partnership, 494 N.W.2d 204 (Wis. 1993). With an easement, there are two distinct property interests—the dominant estate, which enjoys the privileges granted by an easement and the servient estate, which permits the exercise of those privileges. An easement can be used only in connection with the real estate to which it belongs.

Easements by implication and by necessity are similar, but legally distinguishable concepts. Since the early 1900s, the public policy in Wisconsin has strongly opposed the implication of covenants of conveyance, i.e., easements. Backhausen v. Mayer, 234 N.W. 904 (Wis. 1931); Miller v. Hoeschler, 105 N.W. 790 (Wis. 1905).

An easement by implication arises when there has been a "separation of title, a use before separation took place which continued so long and was so obvious or manifest as to show that it was meant to be permanent, and it must appear that the easement is necessary to the beneficial enjoyment

---

3. Petitioners filed their initial complaint in May 1996. They then filed an   amended complaint in August 1996. * * *

of the land granted or retained." Bullis v. Schmidt, 93 N.W.2d 476, 478–79 (Wis. 1958) (quoting 1 THOMPSON, REAL PROPERTY § 390 at 630 (perm. ed.)).[4] Implied easements may only be created when the necessity for the easement is "so clear and absolute that without the easement the grantee cannot enjoy the use of the property granted to him for the purposes to which similar property is customarily devoted." Bullis, 93 N.W.2d at 480 (quoting Miller, 105 N.W. at 792).

The petitioners have failed to establish a claim for an easement by implication. While a landlocked parcel may satisfy the necessity element, it is apparent from the amended complaint that the private road the petitioners seek to extend does not and has never extended to the petitioners' properties. They have failed to allege that any use by the United States was so obvious, manifest or continuous as to show that it was meant to be permanent. * * *

An easement of necessity "arises where an owner severs a landlocked portion of his [or her] property by conveying such parcel to another." Ludke v. Egan, 274 N.W.2d 641 (Wis. 1979). To establish an easement by necessity, a party must show common ownership of the two parcels prior to severance of the landlocked parcel, and that the owner of the now landlocked parcel cannot access a public roadway from his or her own property, Ludke, 274 N.W.2d at 645. If this can be demonstrated, an easement by necessity will be implied over the land retained by the grantor. Id.

The petitioners argue that the United States ownership of all three lots prior to 1854 satisfies the common ownership requirement—a question never before addressed by this court. We conclude that we need not reach that issue because even if the United States' possession of the three lots could constitute common ownership, the petitioners have conceded that neither Lot 2, nor Lot 3 were landlocked when the United States conveyed Lot 4. Rather, at the time of conveyance, the eastern boundary of the lots was above and east of the bluff (the current boundary line). Access to a public roadway was possible above the bluff. A party may only avail himself or herself of an easement by necessity when the common owner severs *a landlocked portion* of the property and the owner of the landlocked portion cannot access a public roadway. Id. 274 N.W.2d 641. Because the United States never severed a landlocked portion of its property that was inaccessible from a public roadway, the petitioners have failed to establish the elements for an easement by necessity.

Nevertheless, petitioners insist that the property was effectively landlocked because of the geographical barriers inhibiting access. As the peti-

[handwritten margin note: RULE re- landlord must convey the landlocked portion... no easement if he retains it, as here]

---

4. The traditional elements of an implied easement are:

(1) common ownership followed by conveyance separating the unified ownership;

(2) before severance, the common owner used part of the property for the benefit of the other part, a use that was apparent, obvious, continuous and [permanent];

(3) and the claimed easement is necessary and beneficial to the enjoyment of the parcel previously benefitted.

7 THOMPSON, REAL PROPERTY § 60.03(b)(4)(i) at 426 (Thompson ed. 1994). Wisconsin courts have not specifically adopted these elements as the law of this state and we do not do so here.

tioners see it, their land was landlocked because the land to the south was owned by an individual, the land to the east and north was bordered by a cliff and rocky terrain, and the land to the west was bordered by the waters of Green Bay. * * *

Wisconsin courts have never before recognized geographical barriers alone as circumstances warranting an easement by necessity. In fact, case law suggests otherwise. This court stated in *Backhausen* that a way of necessity is not merely one of convenience, and "the law will not imply such a way where it has provided another method for obtaining the same at a reasonable expense to the landowner." Backhausen, 234 N.W. at 905.

While the petitioners have provided evidence that the cost of building a road over the bluff would cost approximately $700,000[,]an unreasonable expense, it is apparent that they consider other methods of access—a stairway, an elevator—unacceptable. Petitioners narrowly focus on vehicular access to the lake itself as the only possible way to enjoy this property. Certainly it may be more convenient for the petitioners to seek an extension of the private road to their parcels rather than travel across the property above the bluff and navigate the bluff, but that in itself does not create the right to an easement by necessity. A grantor is not landlocked when he or she has difficulty getting from his or her land to a public road as long as he or she can get from his or her land to a public road. See Ludke, 274 N.W.2d 641. See also Sicchio v. Alvey, 103 N.W.2d 544 (Wis. 1960) (Access to building at front, even though rear entry was used, does not allow for right-of-way by necessity to rear entry of store).

[RULE]

In this case, the petitioners had access to a public road, albeit not ideal or the most convenient access, which they sold off. Thus, the petitioners' current ownership of landlocked property resulted not from a grant of property to them but by their own acts in conveying away their highway access. They were not unwitting purchasers of landlocked property (stemming from the United States 1854 sale).

[RULE]

An easement by necessity only exists where an owner sells a *landlocked* parcel to another, in which case the law will recognize a way of necessity in the *grantee* over the land retained by the *grantor*. Rock Lake Estates Unit Owners Ass'n v. Township of Lake Mills, 536 N.W.2d 415, 424 (Wis. Ct. App. 1995) (citing Ludke, 274 N.W.2d at 645). The petitioners in this case are the grantors, not the grantees, and as in *Rock Lake Estates,* the conveyances which resulted in their landlocked property were made by the petitioners when they sold off the property above the bluff. We conclude that it would be contrary to this state's policy against encumbrances for this court to award an easement to the petitioners over parcels of unrelated third parties under these circumstances.

[it is key that they are unrelated 3rd parties to the conveyance that made the property landlocked]

Finally, the petitioners assert that without an easement their property will be virtually useless because they will have no way to get to it. Thus, the petitioners renew their request for a "drastic" expansion of the law arguing that there is no rational basis for landlocked property. The petitioners suggest that this court set forth a "reasonable use" test that balances the equities by weighing the competing interests of the need and benefit to allow access by easement to develop otherwise useless land versus the detriment such a burden may place on other property to use an existing road. The petitioners insist that the benefit and policy towards development far outweigh any anticipated costs to the burdened property.

In order to adopt the petitioners' proposal, we would have to ignore not only long-standing precedent in this state, but also well-established public policy as illustrated in our recording and conveyance statutes. Long ago this court recognized:

> It is so easy, in conveying a defined piece of land, to express either any limitations intended to be reserved over it, or to be conveyed with it over other land, that the necessity of raising any such grant or reservation by implication is hardly apparent. Courts of equity can afford relief where the grant is not of that understood by both parties to be conveyed, or so understood by one by inducement of the other. Such rights outside the limits of one's proper title seriously derogate from the policy of both our registry statutes and our statute against implication of [covenants] in conveyances. That policy is that a buyer of land may rely on the public records as information of all the conveyances, and upon the words of the instruments for all rights thereunder.

Miller, 105 N.W. at 792.

More recently in *Kordecki v. Rizzo*, 317 N.W.2d 479 (Wis. 1982), this court reiterated that a purchaser of real estate has three sources of information from which to learn of rights to the land he or she is about to purchase: (1) reviewing the chain of title; (2) searching other public records that may reveal other non-recorded rights, such as judgments or liens; and (3) inspecting the land itself. These sources may be irrelevant under the petitioners' proposal if someone with a landlocked piece of property desired a right-of-way through another person's property "in the interest of development."

3 sources of real estate information

The petitioners are effectively asking this court to sanction hidden easements. An easement which in this case was not created by, but was, according to petitioners, clearly intended by the United States at conveyance. * * *

The decision of the court of appeals is affirmed.

NOTES AND QUESTIONS

1. How do you suppose the Schwabs and Ms. McCormick got to their lakefront parcels between the 1940s and when the lawsuit was filed in 1996? Note that Timmons, their neighbor immediately to the south, is said to have the right to use the private road, even though it does not extend to his parcel.

2. Suppose the Schwab and McCormick parcels could be accessed from the lake by boat during the summer months, and suppose further that the principal use of property in Door County is for summer vacation homes.

Would this by itself suffice to defeat a claim for an easement by implication or by necessity?

3. The principal reason cited by the court for the hostility toward claims of easements by implication and by necessity is that this would "sanction hidden easements." In other words, prospective purchasers and other persons attempting to ascertain the nature and extent of property rights in the area would not be able to discover the existence of the easement by searching the public records. Why couldn't the court solve this problem by insisting that the petitioners, as a condition of obtaining the equitable relief they seek, record the judgment granting them an easement by implication or necessity along with the other deeds and instruments that pertain to the title to these lots? Can you think of reasons besides problems of notice why courts should be reluctant to recognize easements by implication or necessity?

Rule

4. Generally, in easements by necessity or easements by prior existing use, courts will hold *grantors* to a stricter requirement of necessity than in the case where the *grantee* is arguing for an easement—or will deny implied easements in favor of grantors altogether. Can you see why?

5. About half the states have adopted statutes that provide for condemnation of private easements for access to landlocked or inaccessible property. See, e.g., Sorenson v. Czinger, 852 P.2d 1124, 1127 (Wash. Ct. App. 1993), discussing Rev. Code Wash. § 8.24.010. Under these statutes, the landlocked owner can force the servient owner(s) to convey an easement, but must pay just compensation (fair market value) for the rights so obtained. (Typically, these statutes also require the landlocked owner to apply to a government official for permission and allow the owner of the proposed servient land to object.) Is this a better solution to the problem illustrated by the principal case than either forcing the parties to negotiate past a stalemate (as the Wisconsin Supreme Court's decision apparently contemplates) or granting an easement based on a balancing of costs and benefits (as the petitioners suggest in their last-ditch argument for a "drastic" expansion of easements by necessity)? Do rights of private condemnation for easements of access satisfy the "public use" requirement of the Fifth Amendment and parallel provisions of state constitutions (see Chapter XII)? If your answer is no, then why aren't the common-law doctrines of easements by implication or necessity also unconstitutional?

Warsaw v. Chicago Metallic Ceilings, Inc.

Supreme Court of California, 1984.
676 P.2d 584.

■ RICHARDSON, JUSTICE. We granted a hearing in this case to consider whether one who acquires a valid prescriptive easement over another's property nonetheless may be required to compensate that person for either (1) the fair market value of the easement, or (2) the cost of removing or relocating any encroaching structures which interfere with use of the easement. We conclude that the statutes which define and validate prescriptive easements neither authorize nor contemplate an award to the underlying property owner of compensation for the reasonable value of the easement, and that under the circumstances in this case it would be improper to charge the owner of the easement with any portion of the cost of removing encroachments.

Although we disagree with the Court of Appeal's resolution of the foregoing issues, its opinion (per Compton, J.) correctly determined the other issues on appeal from the trial court's judgment declaring that plaintiffs had acquired a prescriptive easement over defendant's property. 188 Cal.Rptr. 563. Accordingly, we adopt that portion of the opinion as follows:*

This is an appeal from an equitable decree which declared that plaintiffs had acquired an easement by prescription over the property of defendant. Defendant was ordered to dismantle and relocate a structure which had been erected on its own property but which interfered with plaintiffs' use of the easement. []

This action involves two contiguous parcels of real estate which front on [the west side of] Downey Road in the City of Vernon. Downey Road runs in a generally north-south direction. The two parcels are approximately 650 feet deep. Plaintiffs own the southerly parcel and defendant owns the northerly parcel. Both parcels were acquired in 1972 from a common owner.

At the time of acquisition both parcels were unimproved. Plaintiffs' arrangement with the seller was that the seller would construct on the parcel to be purchased by plaintiffs a large commercial building erected to plaintiffs' requirements. The building covered almost the entire parcel. A 40 foot wide paved driveway was laid out along the northern edge of plaintiffs' property to provide access to loading docks on the northern side of plaintiffs' building.

For its part defendant constructed on its property a substantially smaller building which ran only about one-half the depth of the northerly parcel and left vacant a strip of ground about 150 feet wide along the side of the parcel which abutted plaintiffs' property.

From the beginning it was apparent that plaintiff's 40 foot wide driveway was inadequate since the large trucks which carried material to and from plaintiffs' loading dock could not turn and position themselves at these docks without traveling onto the defendant's property. The inability of these trucks to make such use of defendant's property would destroy the commercial value of plaintiff's building.

The court found that because of the fact that the possibility of creating an easement over defendant's property was considered and rejected in the original negotiations between the seller, plaintiffs and defendant, no ease-

---

* Brackets together, in this manner [], are used to indicate deletions from the opinion of the Court of Appeal; brackets enclosing material * * * are, unless otherwise indicated, used to denote insertions or additions by this court.

ment by implication was created. The trial court further found that the existence of the driveway on plaintiffs' property militated against the creation of an easement by necessity.

7 years

From 1972 until 1979 trucks and other vehicles servicing plaintiffs' facility used a portion of the vacant ground on defendant's property to enter, turn, park and leave the area of plaintiffs' loading dock. On at least two occasions during that period plaintiffs sought, unsuccessfully, to acquire an easement from defendant or to create mutual easements over plaintiffs' and defendant's property.

In 1979 defendant developed plans to construct a warehouse on the southerly portion of the property including that portion of the property being used by plaintiffs. A pad of earth was raised along the southerly portion of defendant's property approximately five feet from the property line. This grading effectively blocked plaintiffs' use of the area and plaintiffs commenced this action for injunctive and declaratory relief.

When the trial court denied plaintiffs' request for a preliminary injunction to prevent further construction, defendant proceeded to erect a building on the contested area.

After a trial on the merits, the trial court found that plaintiffs had acquired a 25 foot wide prescriptive easement over and along the southern portion of defendant's property for the full depth of the property. As noted defendant was ordered to remove that portion of the building which interfered with the described easement. Further the trial court gave defendant 90 days to accomplish the removal and purported to reserve jurisdiction to award damages for failure of defendant to comply with the mandatory injunction. This appeal ensued.

Elements of a
Prescriptive Easement

1) *Open + Notorious*

2) *Continuous*

3) *Adverse*

4) *5 years (length can vary depending on statute)*

5) *Exclusive (no one else can use the land for the same purpose as adverse user)*
   ↳ must also be a certain/specific tract of land being used

The elements necessary to establish a prescriptive easement are well settled. The party claiming such an easement must show use of the property which has been open, notorious, continuous and adverse for an uninterrupted period of five years. Whether the elements of prescription are established is a question of fact for the trial court, and the findings of the court will not be disturbed where there is substantial evidence to support them.

Further, the existence of a prescriptive easement must be shown by a definite and certain line of travel for the statutory period. "The line of travel over a roadway which is claimed by prescription may not be a shifting course, but must be certain and definite. Slight deviations from the accustomed route will not defeat an easement, but substantial changes which break the continuity of the course of travel will destroy the claim to prescriptive rights.... [Citations.] [M]anifestly the distance to which a roadway may be changed without destroying an easement will be determined somewhat by the character of the land over which it passes, together with the value, improvements, and purposes to which the land is adapted." (Matthiessen v. Grand, 268 P. 675, 678 (Cal. Dist. Ct. App. 1928).)

The trial court found that "the truckers using [the disputed parcel] did, in fact, follow a definite course and pattern, and while admittedly, no two truck drivers followed the exact course . . . and the traffic situation . . . varied from day to day, the deviation taken by various drivers over the seven-year period was only slight."

The evidence revealed that truck drivers who were making deliveries to or receiving goods from plaintiffs used the parcel to approach the building, swing around and back into plaintiffs' loading dock. Since the drivers varied in their abilities, the space required to complete this [maneuver] was variable. No two drivers followed precisely the same course, but all used the parcel for the same purpose—to turn their vehicles so they could enter plaintiffs' loading docks. There was substantial evidence to support the findings on this issue.

Defendant contends that there was no evidence supporting use of several hundred feet of the westerly portion of the parcel. From the trial transcript, it is difficult to discern exactly to which portion of the parcel specific bits of testimony pertain. [] [Our review of the record, however, discloses substantial evidence supporting the establishment of a prescriptive easement over the westerly portion at issue.]

Defendant contends that there was no substantial evidence that plaintiffs' use of the property was hostile rather than permissive. Again, we find that this contention is without merit.

The issue as to which party has the burden of proving adverse or permissive use has been the subject of much debate. However, [] [we agree with the view, supported by numerous authorities,] that continuous use of an easement over a long period of time without the landowner's interference is presumptive evidence of its existence and in the absence of evidence of mere permissive use it will be sufficient to sustain a judgment. (MacDonald Properties, Inc. v. Bel–Air Country Club, [140 Cal.Rptr. 367 (Cal. Ct. App. 1977), and cases cited].)

Use is presumed to be adverse (Majority Rule)

Defendant relies on evidence that plaintiffs at one time attempted to purchase the disputed parcel from the seller and at various times attempted to negotiate for an express easement. Whether the use is hostile or is merely a matter of neighborly accommodation, however, is a question of fact to be determined in light of the surrounding circumstances and the relationship between the parties.

There was evidence adduced at trial that despite plaintiffs' unsuccessful attempts to negotiate an express easement, their use of the property continued uninterrupted for approximately seven years. There was no evidence that defendant had ever expressly permitted plaintiffs to use the parcel for truck and vehicular traffic. In fact defendant's adamant refusal to negotiate on the issue is evidence that no permission was given or contemplated.

Defendant's next assignment of error is addressed to the trial court's order to remove that part of the completed structure which interferes with plaintiffs' easement. Defendant argues that a mandatory injunction may not issue to enjoin a completed act. However, there is extensive authority standing for the proposition that a court of equity may, in a proper case, issue a mandatory injunction for protection and preservation of an ease-ment including, where appropriate, an order for removal of an obstruction already erected. The determination as to whether such remedy is appropri-ate is within the sound discretion of the trial court. A mandatory injunction may issue even if the cost of removal is great under certain circumstances, especially if the encroaching structure was wilfully erected with knowledge of the claimed easement. [citing cases]

As the court in *Morgan v. Veach*, 139 P.2d 976 (Cal. Dist. Ct. App. 1943), explained:

An appropriate statement relative to defendants' assertion that an injunction would work an inequitable burden is in 28 Am.Jur., section 56, page 253 as follows: "In view of the drastic character of mandatory injunctions, the rule under consideration as to balancing the relative conveniences of the parties applies with special force to a prayer for such mandatory relief. Where, therefore, by innocent mistake or over-sight, buildings erected ... slightly encroach ... and the damage to the owner of the buildings by their removal would be greatly dispropor-tionate to the injury ... the court may decline to order their remov-al. . . . But relief by way of a mandatory injunction will not be denied on the ground that the loss caused by it will be disproportionate to the good accomplished, where it appears that the defendant acted with a full knowledge of the complainant's rights and with an understanding of the consequences which might ensue. . . ."

In a note in 57 A.L.R., first column, page 343, it was said: "Wilfulness on the part of the defendant in proceeding with the violation of the restriction after warning by the complainant, especially after suit is brought, is a ground for equitable relief by mandatory injunction greatly stressed by the courts." (139 P.2d at 980.)

In the case at bench, the structure to be removed was not begun until after the underlying action was filed. It was completed while the litigation was still pending. Defendant gambled on the outcome of the action and lost. The fact that its decision may have been reasonable in light of the denial of the preliminary injunction does not change the result. * * * (End of Court of Appeal opinion.)

We next consider whether defendant is entitled to any offsetting monetary relief from plaintiffs. Defendant contends that the trial court's judgment is overly harsh because it both granted plaintiffs an easement over a 16,250-square-foot parcel of defendant's property free of charge and also required defendant to incur the entire cost of relocating or reconstruct-ing its building. Would application of equitable principles dictate that plaintiffs either pay to defendant the fair market value of the easement they acquired, or contribute a portion of the costs of relocating? We think not.

Initially, the statutory procedure for acquiring an easement by pre-scription quite clearly retains the traditional common law rule that such an easement may be obtained without incurring any liability to the underlying property owner. Civil Code section 1007, enacted in 1872, provides that "Occupancy for the period prescribed by the Code of Civil Procedure as sufficient to bar any action for the recovery of the property _confers a title thereto,_ denominated a title by prescription, _which is sufficient against all...._" (Italics added.) We have confirmed that if the requisite elements of a prescriptive use are shown, "Such use for the five-year statutory period of Code of Civil Procedure section 321 _confers a title by prescription._" (Taormino v. Denny, 463 P.2d 711, 716 (Cal. 1970) fns. omitted, italics added.)

Thus, plaintiffs herein have acquired a title by prescription which is "sufficient against all," including defendant. That being so, there is no basis in law or equity for requiring them to compensate defendant for the fair market value of the easement so acquired. To exact such a charge would entirely defeat the legitimate policies underlying the doctrines of adverse possession and prescription " 'to reduce litigation and preserve the peace by _protecting_ a possession that has been maintained for a statutorily deemed sufficient period of time.' " (Italics added, Gilardi v. Hallam, 636 P.2d 588, 592 (Cal. 1981), quoting from an earlier case; see also the Restatement of Property, intro. note at pp. 2922–2923; 3 Powell, The Law of Real Property (1981 ed.) ¶ 413, pp. 34–103—34–104.) As described by Professor Powell, "Historically, prescription has had the theoretical basis of a lost grant. Its continuance has been justified because of its functional utility in helping to cause prompt termination of controversies before the possible loss of evidence and in _stabilizing_ long continued property uses." (Ibid., fn. omitted, italics added.) If the doctrine of prescription is truly aimed at "protecting" and "stabilizing" a long and continuous use or possession as against the claims of an alleged "owner" of the property, then the latter's claim for damages or fair compensation for an alleged "taking" must be rejected.

The Court of Appeal recently described the rationale underlying the related adverse possession doctrine as follows: "[I]ts underlying philosophy is basically that land use has historically been favored over disuse, and that therefore he who uses land is preferred in the law to he who does not, even though the latter is the rightful owner. [Fn. omitted.] Hence our laws of real property have sanctioned certain types of otherwise unlawful taking of land belonging to someone else, while, at the same time, our laws with respect to other types of property have generally taken a contrary course. This is now largely justified on the theory that the intent is not to reward the taker or punish the person dispossessed, but to reduce litigation and preserve the peace by protecting a possession that has been maintained for a statutorily deemed sufficient period of time.... [¶] Quite naturally, however, dispossessing a person of his property is not easy under this theory, and it may even be asked whether the concept of adverse possession is as viable as it once was, or whether the concept always squares with modern ideals in a sophisticated, congested, peaceful society.... [¶] Yet _this method of obtaining land remains on the books,_ and if a party proves all five of the [requisite] elements [citation], he can claim title to another's land...." (Finley v. Yuba County Water Dist., 160 Cal.Rptr. 423, 427 (Cal. Ct. App. 1979), italics added.)

Similarly, the system of acquiring an interest in land by prescription "remains on the books," and any decision to alter that system by requiring the payment of compensation clearly would be a matter for the Legislature. Defendant cites no authorities indicating that the present system is unconstitutional in any respect.

Assuming that an award of compensation for the value of the easement is unavailable, may the courts nonetheless order the easement owner to contribute all or part of the cost of relocating or reconstructing an encroaching building? It is at least arguable that a court of equity could order, in an appropriate case, that the plaintiff contribute a portion of the cost of relocating an *innocent* encroachment, as a condition to an award of injunctive relief. As previously noted, it is well established that a court has discretion to balance the hardships and *deny* removal of an encroachment if it was innocently made and does not irreparably injure the plaintiff, and where the cost of removal would greatly exceed the inconvenience to the plaintiff by its continuance. If, as the foregoing cases establish, an outright denial of injunctive relief would be sustained under those circumstances, then no compelling reason exists for depriving the trial court of the *lesser* power of granting the injunction on condition that the plaintiff pay a reasonable portion of the cost of relocation. (See Collester v. Oftedahl, 120 Cal.Rptr. 710, 712–13 (Cal. Dist. Ct. App. 1941) [injunctive relief conditioned upon payment of costs]; cf. Farmers Ins. Exch. v. Ruiz, 59 Cal.Rptr. 13, 17–18 (Cal. Ct. App. 1967); 2 Witkin, Cal. Procedure (2d ed. 1970) Provisional Remedies, § 82, at p. 1520; 2 Pomeroy's Equity Jurisprudence (5th ed. 1941) § 385 et seq. ["He who seeks equity must do equity"].)

In the present case, however, it is apparent that it would be inequitable to charge plaintiffs, who lawfully perfected an easement by prescription, for the cost of removing an encroaching structure erected by defendant with prior notice of plaintiffs' claim. As previously noted, defendant's building was erected *after* plaintiffs' suit was filed and remained pending. Under similar circumstances, the courts have deemed an encroachment to be wilful and have ordered its removal despite a disproportionate hardship to the defendant. Likewise, plaintiffs should not be required to contribute to the cost of relocating encroaching structures which were erected by defendant with full knowledge of plaintiffs' claim.

The judgment is affirmed.

↓ Concurrence

■ GRODIN, JUSTICE, concurring. I cannot accept the majority's attempted justification for the current law of prescriptive easements. How, in today's urban society, litigation is reduced or the peace is preserved by allowing persons situated as are these plaintiffs to acquire rights in what is concededly the land of another without a cent of payment is beyond my comprehension. I therefore agree entirely with the policy criticisms contained in Justice Reynoso's dissenting opinion.

I am persuaded, however, that if change is to come to this arcane area of the law it should come through the Legislature rather than through the courts. It is not alone the existence of Civil Code section 1007 which persuades me, for as my dissenting colleague observes that section, adopted in 1872, was early interpreted as merely fixing the time within which a right by prescription may be acquired. But, in 1965 the Legislature modified the harsh application of the prescriptive easement doctrine by adding Civil Code section 1008, which permits a property owner to avoid acquisition of an easement by the simple expedient of posting a sign.[1] Given that modification, and that degree of legislative attention, I would leave the next move to Sacramento. I therefore join in affirming the trial court's judgment.

■ REYNOSO, JUSTICE, dissenting. I respectfully dissent from that portion of the majority opinion which denies compensation of fair market value for the easement. * * *

DISSENT

Plaintiffs called upon the power of the trial court, acting in equity, to declare and protect a prescriptive easement. The court agreed. Yet the practical result, as indicated by the Court of Appeal opinion (per Compton, J.), is that: "A simple affirmance of the judgment would result in plaintiffs, who are admittedly trespassers, acquiring practical possession of a sixteen thousand two hundred fifty (16,250) square foot parcel of defendant's valuable property free of charge...."

The majority argues that the result, unjust or not, is ordained by statute. I disagree. My review of the statutes cited by the majority convinces me that they have not removed from the courts the traditional power to invoke the equitable doctrines which deal with fairness. Those doctrines persuade me that plaintiffs should pay fair market value for the property interest acquired. * * *

The law of prescriptive easements and their enforcement enjoyed a long history at common law before 1872. In that year Civil Code section 1007 was enacted. It merely codified the general concept of prescriptive easement found at common law. We must look, therefore, to common law precepts to resolve the issue at hand.

At common law, the declaration of whether a prescriptive easement existed was considered an action at law. It remains so. However, the protection of the declared right was generally considered, and still is, an action in equity.

Mere citation to Civil Code section 1007 resolves nothing. The term "title by prescription," for example, describes the rights which a person acquires upon establishing a prescriptive easement. Nothing more. The case at bench assumes acquisition; the real issue deals with the conditions which the court may impose to protect that judicially declared easement. Thus, in *Taormino v. Denny*, 463 P.2d 711 (Cal. 1970), cited by the majority, our court did no more than affirm the prescriptive right over a private roadway. Not surprisingly, the parties have not cited the section

---

1. Civil Code section 1008 provides: "No use by any person or persons, no matter how long continued, of any land, shall ever ripen into an easement by prescription, if the owner of such property posts at each entrance to the property or at intervals of not more than 200 feet along the boundary a sign reading substantially as follows: 'Right to pass by permission, and subject to control, of owner: Section 1008, Civil Code.'"

before the trial court, the appellate court, or before us. Neither the trial court nor the Court of Appeal mentioned it. And no papers before us mention the code section. Yet, the section erroneously forms the basis for the majority opinion. * * *

The Court of Appeal correctly identified the nature of plaintiff's cause of action and the issue in this appeal when it wrote: "This is an appeal from an *equitable decree* which declared that plaintiffs had acquired an easement by prescription over the property of defendant." (Emphasis added.) Neither the parties nor the majority disagree with that characterization.

We come, therefore, to the power of the court in equity. Whether the trial court must order the plaintiffs to pay fair market value for the prescriptive easement, as the Court of Appeal concluded, depends on the breadth of discretion which the court in equity enjoys. Let us briefly explore the concept of equity.

Equity's origins lie in the King's extraordinary judicial power, exercised through the Chancery, to administer justice whenever "it was probable that a fair trial in the ordinary Courts would be impeded, and also whenever, . . ., the regular administration of justice was hindered." (5 Pomeroy's Equity Jurisprudence § 31 P. 37 (1941), hereinafter Pomeroy.) The Chancellor was obliged to look only to "Honesty, Equity, and Conscience [ ]" to decide conflicts. (Id., § 35, p. 40.) Today, it is only a matter of degree that separates the early Chancellors who decided "whether reason and conscience demanded special intervention. . . ." (Walsh on Equity, § 53, p. 282 (1930)) from the modern judges and their grants of equitable relief. (Id.) The modern judge remains the repositor of special relief; he stands in the states' stead "modifying the rigor of hard and fast rules at law where reason and conscience demand it." (Ibid.) * * *

Traditionally the courts have not imposed a condition that fair market value be paid before a prescriptive easement will be declared and protected. However, in my view, the courts do not [sic] have such power. In the case at bench that power should be exercised.

The role which the court in equity can play is seen in two disparate examples, one old and one new. First, we look to the traditional case wherein the building of one owner trespasses upon that of another. Where the law recognizes a legal wrong in such a trespass, and would normally order the removal of the encroaching building (as was done in the case at bench), the court in equity may instead order that money damages be paid by the encroaching party as a condition of protecting the encroachment, particularly where the encroachment was unintentional. (See Walsh, § 55, pp. 284–85.) Second, I cite a quite different example which does not deal with property. The courts, pursuant to their inherent equitable powers, have created several exceptions to the statutory rule (Code Civ.Proc., § 1021) which requires each party to pay his or her own attorney fees. (See Serrano v. Priest, 569 P.2d 1303, 1306–15 (Cal. 1977).) These examples simply illustrate the not too startling notion that courts of equity, in search of fairness, may (1) impose conditions before a decree protecting rights will issue, (2) grant monetary damages, and (3) extend statutory rights. I cite these only to stress that no reason abides in the history, concept or modern practice of equity which would so restrict the power of the court that it could not impose a requirement that fair market value be paid by the trespasser who is granted a prescriptive easement.

Finally, I turn to the fairness issue. By permitting the prescriptive easement in the case at bench the state, acting through the court, endorses a private action akin to eminent domain. Practically, it is the taking of property rights from defendant and giving them to plaintiff. Can it be fair to reward a wrongdoer and punish an innocent property owner?

The majority says "yes." It is fair, according to the majority, for several reasons including (1) reducing litigation, (2) protecting possession, and (3) preference for use over [disuse] of land. None of these reasons is convincing. First, no litigation was reduced. Society should not be in the business of forcing an owner of land to bring suit when a trespass has occurred. Such a policy increases litigation. Second, the possession of the easement has in fact been protected; plaintiffs are only required to pay for the easement. Third, modern society evidences a preference for planned use, not the ad hoc use of a trespasser. It is questionable that in the urban setting of the case at bench, such use by the trespasser is preferred by society.

I do not rely solely on my personal view of fairness. Rather, it is my role as a judge, as it was with the chancellor, to apply a "conception of justice in accordance with the prevailing reason and conscience of the time." (Walsh, § 53, p. 281.) (See also 5 Pomeroy, Equity Jurisprudence, § 67, p. 89; "[Equity] is so constructed ..., that it possesses an inherent capacity of expansion, so as to keep abreast of each succeeding generation and age.") The final decree of the trial court, approved by the majority, contravenes today's basic notions of fairness and justice. A requirement that plaintiffs pay fair market value for the land use given them is the least our society expects. * * *

The suggestion of the concurring opinion that the Legislature should study this area of law bears underscoring. The statutes need to reflect today's realities. Certainly—they should at least ameliorate the harsh consequences the majority feels compelled to enforce. However, I note that the recent legislative changes referred to in the concurrence only provide a landowner relief from the *creation* of a prescriptive easement. There remains the need for an equitable avenue by which the courts may relieve a landowner subject to a prescriptive easement of an otherwise inequitable burden.

I would affirm the judgment. However, I would remand to the trial court for further proceedings to fix an amount of reasonable compensation to be paid by plaintiffs to defendant. That compensation would be the fair market value of the property interest acquired. From that compensation damages, if any, sustained by plaintiff should be subtracted.

Figure 9–5
Land at Issue in *Warsaw v. Chicago Metallic Ceilings*

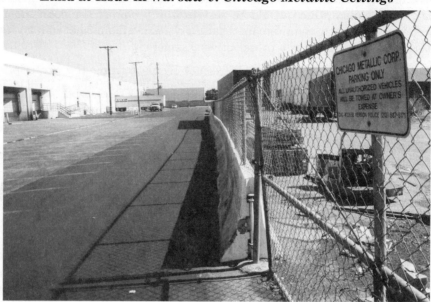

NOTES AND QUESTIONS

1.   Adverse possession involves the transfer of full possessory rights of ownership from the original true owner (TO) to the adverse possessor (AP), after the statute of limitations runs (provided the other elements of adverse possession are satisfied—see Chapter II). An easement by prescription involves the transfer of an easement over the land of the TO to the adverse user (AU), after the statute of limitations runs. How does one know whether the behavior of the adverse party constitutes adverse possession or adverse use? Suppose in *Warsaw* that the plaintiffs had not only permitted delivery trucks to drive onto the defendants' land in order to back up to the plaintiffs' loading dock, but had also suggested that the delivery trucks park on the defendants' land overnight. Would this transform a prescriptive easement case into an adverse possession case?

2.   Recall that the five standard elements for establishing adverse possession are that the possession must be (1) actual, (2) exclusive, (3) open and notorious, (4) continuous, and (5) adverse under a claim of right. Which of these elements are relaxed or modified in establishing an easement by prescription?

3.   What is the best characterization of the state of mind of the plaintiff in *Warsaw*: good faith, bad faith, or unclear? What state of mind does the California Supreme Court seem to require to establish an easement by prescription?

4.   What do you think of the idea of requiring the AU (or the AP) to pay the TO the fair market value of the easement (or the possessory rights)

obtained through prescription or adverse possession? The standard rules of prescription and adverse possession involve what Calabresi and Melamed call property rules. One day before the statute of limitations runs, the TO has the entitlement protected by a property rule. This means the TO can block the AU or AP from further using the property without the TO's consent. The day after the statute of limitations runs, the AU or AP has the entitlement, also protected by a property rule. This means that the AU or AP can now use self-help or otherwise stop the TO (or any other person) from interfering with her use right or possessory right without her consent. The innovation embraced by the California Court of Appeal, but rejected by a majority of the California Supreme Court, would mean that the passage of the statute of limitations would transform an entitlement in the TO protected by a property rule into an entitlement in the TO protected by a liability rule. In other words, the AU or AP could force a transfer of use rights or possessory rights by the TO, but only upon payment of just compensation to the TO.

5.   Like a number of other California cases we have considered (*Moore v. Regents of the University of California, Intel Corp. v. Hamidi, Marvin v. Marvin, Kendall v. Ernest Pestana, Nahrstedt v. Lakeside Village Condominium*) the debate among the Justices here centers on the question of institutional choice: Which institution, legislature or court, is primarily responsible for updating property law? Here all but one of the Justices thinks the legislature must do the updating. But is the proposal here really all that radical? Why isn't the defendant simply in the position of one seeking restitution for unjust enrichment (see Chapter I)?

6.   Under the liability rule regime endorsed by the Court of Appeal, what happens if the TO has abandoned the property or cannot be located to receive the payment of compensation? At what point in time would the property taken be valued—at the point of original entry or use, when the statute of limitations runs, or when the judgment awarding title to the AP (or ownership of an easement to the AU) becomes final? How would the shift from a property rule in the AU or AP to a liability rule in the TO affect the incentives of the parties to monitor for trespasses and negotiate written easements when appropriate? Would you allow compensation in all cases, or only in certain kinds of cases, e.g., where the original entry was in bad faith? For discussion of these issues, see Thomas W. Merrill, Property Rules, Liability Rules, and Adverse Possession, 79 Nw. U. L. Rev. 1123 (1985).

> Macey says at time of original trespass.

Holbrook v. Taylor

Supreme Court of Kentucky, 1976.
532 S.W.2d 763.

■ STERNBERG, JUSTICE. This is an action to establish a right to the use of a roadway, which is 10 to 12 feet wide and about 250 feet long, over the unenclosed, hilly woodlands of another. The claimed right to the use of the roadway is twofold: by prescription and by estoppel. Both issues are heatedly contested. The evidence is in conflict as to the nature and type of use that had been made of the roadway. The lower court determined that a right to the use of the roadway by prescription had not been established, but that it had been established by estoppel. The landowners, feeling themselves aggrieved, appeal. We will consider the two issues separately.

In *Grinestaff v. Grinestaff*, 318 S.W.2d 881 (Ky. 1958), we said that an easement may be created by express written grant, by implication, by prescription, or by estoppel. It has long been the law of this commonwealth that "(a)n easement, such as a right of way, is created when the owner of a tenement to which the right is claimed to be appurtenant, or those under whom he claims title, have openly, peaceably, continuously, and under a claim of right adverse to the owner of the soil, and with his knowledge and acquiescence, used a way over the lands of another for as much as 15 years." Flener v. Lawrence, 220 S.W. 1041 (Ky. 1920); Rominger v. City Realty Company, 324 S.W.2d 806 (Ky. 1959).

Requirements for a prescriptive easement [handwritten margin note]

In 1942 appellants purchased the subject property. In 1944 they gave permission for a haul road to be cut for the purpose of moving coal from a newly opened mine. The roadway was so used until 1949, when the mine closed. During that time the appellants were paid a royalty for the use of the road. In 1957 appellants built a tenant house on their property and the roadway was used by them and their tenant. The tenant house burned in 1961 and was not replaced. In 1964 the appellees bought their three-acre building site, which adjoins appellants, and the following year built their residence thereon. At all times prior to 1965, the use of the haul road was by permission of appellants. There is no evidence of any probative value which would indicate that the use of the haul road during that period of time was either adverse, continuous, or uninterrupted. The trial court was fully justified, therefore, in finding that the right to the use of this easement was not established by prescription.

As to the issue on estoppel, we have long recognized that a right to the use of a roadway over the lands of another may be established by estoppel. In *Lashley Telephone Co. v. Durbin*, 228 S.W. 423 (Ky. 1921), we said:

> Though many courts hold that a licensee is conclusively presumed as a matter of law to know that a license is revocable at the pleasure of the licensor, and if he expend money in connection with his entry upon the land of the latter, he does so at his peril * * *, yet it is the established rule in this state that where a license is not a bare, naked right of entry, but includes the right to erect structures and acquire an interest in the land in the nature of an easement by the construction of improvements thereon, the licensor may not revoke the license and restore his premises to their former condition after the licensee has exercised the privilege given by the license and erected the improvements at considerable expense; * * *

RULE to establish an easement by estoppel [handwritten margin note]

In *Gibbs v. Anderson*, 156 S.W.2d 876 (Ky. 1941), Gibbs claimed the right, by estoppel, to the use of a roadway over the lands of Anderson. The lower court denied the claim. We reversed. Anderson's immediate predecessor in title admitted that he had discussed the passway with Gibbs before it was constructed and had agreed that it might be built through his land. He stood by and saw Gibbs expend considerable money in this construction. We applied the rule announced in *Lashley Telephone Co. v. Durbin*, supra, and reversed with directions that a judgment be entered granting Gibbs the right to the use of the passway.

In *McCoy v. Hoffman*, 295 S.W.2d 560 (Ky. 1956), the facts are that Hoffman had acquired the verbal consent of the landowner to build a passway over the lands of the owner to the state highway. Subsequently, the owner of the servient estate sold the property to McCoy, who at the time of the purchase was fully aware of the existence of the roadway and the use to which it was being put. McCoy challenged Hoffman's right to use the road. The lower court found that a right had been gained by prescription. In this court's consideration of the case, we affirmed, not on the theory of prescriptive right but on the basis that the owner of the servient estate was estopped. After announcing the rule for establishing a right by prescription, we went on to say:

> * * * On the other hand, the right of revocation of the license is subject to the qualification that where the licensee has exercised the privilege given him and erected improvements or made substantial expenditures on the faith or strength of the license, it becomes irrevocable and continues for so long a time as the nature of the license calls for. In effect, under this condition the license becomes in reality a grant through estoppel. * * *.

In *Akers v. Moore*, 309 S.W.2d 758 (Ky. 1958), this court again considered the right to the use of a passway by estoppel. Akers and others had used the Moore branch as a public way of ingress and egress from their property. They sued Moore and others who owned property along the branch seeking to have the court recognize their right to the use of the roadway and to order the removal of obstructions which had been placed in the roadway. The trial court found that Akers and others had acquired a prescriptive right to the use of the portion of the road lying on the left side of the creek bed, but had not acquired the right to the use of so much of the road as lay on the right side of the creek bed. Consequently, an appeal and a cross-appeal were filed. Considering the right to the use of the strip of land between the right side of the creek bed and the highway, this court found that the evidence portrayed it very rough and apparently never improved, that it ran alongside the house in which one of the protestors lived, and that by acquiescence or by express consent of at least one of the protestors the right side of the roadway was opened up so as to change the roadway from its close proximity to the Moore residence. The relocated portion of the highway had only been used as a passway for about six years before the suit was filed. The trial court found that this section of the road had not been established as a public way by estoppel. We reversed. In doing so, we stated:

> We consider the fact that the appellees, Artie Moore, et al. had stood by and acquiesced in (if in fact they had not affirmatively consented) the change being made and permitted the appellants to spend money in

fixing it up to make it passable and use it for six years without objecting. Of course, the element of time was not sufficient for the acquisition of the right of way by adverse possession. But the law recognizes that one may acquire a license to use a passway or roadway where, with the knowledge of the licensor, he has in the exercise of the privilege spent money in improving the way or for other purposes connected with its use on the faith or strength of the license. Under such conditions the license becomes irrevocable and continues for so long a time as its nature calls for. This, in effect, becomes a grant through estoppel. Gibbs v. Anderson, 288 Ky. 488, 156 S.W.2d 876; McCoy v. Hoffman, Ky., 295 S.W.2d 560. It would be unconscionable to permit the owners of this strip of land of trivial value to revoke the license by obstructing and preventing its use.

In the present case the roadway had been used since 1944 by permission of the owners of the servient estate. The evidence is conflicting as to whether the use of the road subsequent to 1965 was by permission or by claim of right. Appellees contend that it had been used by them and others without the permission of appellants; on the other hand, it is contended by appellants that the use of the roadway at all times was by their permission. The evidence discloses that during the period of preparation for the construction of appellees' home and during the time the house was being built, appellees were permitted to use the roadway as ingress and egress for workmen, for hauling machinery and material to the building site, for construction of the dwelling, and for making improvements generally to the premises. Further, the evidence reflects that after construction of the residence, which cost $25,000, was completed, appellees continued to regularly use the roadway as they had been doing. Appellant J. S. Holbrook testified that in order for appellees to get up to their house he gave them permission to use and repair the roadway. They widened it, put in a culvert, and graveled part of it with "red dog", also known as cinders, at a cost of approximately $100. There is no other location over which a roadway could reasonably be built to provide an outlet for appellees.

No dispute had arisen between the parties at any time over the use of the roadway until the fall of 1970. Appellant J. S. Holbrook contends that he wanted to secure a writing from the appellees in order to relieve him from any responsibility for any damage that might happen to anyone on the subject road. On the other hand, Mrs. Holbrook testified that the writing was desired to avoid any claim which may be made by appellees of a right to the use of the roadway. Appellees testified that the writing was an effort to force them to purchase a small strip of land over which the roadway traversed, for the sum of $500. The dispute was not resolved and appellants erected a steel cable across the roadway to prevent its use and also constructed "no-trespassing" signs. Shortly thereafter, the suit was filed to require the removal of the obstruction and to declare the right of appellees to the use of the roadway without interference.

The use of the roadway by appellees to get to their home from the public highway, the use of the roadway to take in heavy equipment and material and supplies for construction of the residence, the general improvement of the premises, the maintenance of the roadway, and the construction by appellees of a $25,000 residence, all with the actual consent of appellants or at least with their tacit approval, clearly demonstrates the rule laid down in *Lashley Telephone Co. v. Durbin*, supra, that the license to use the subject roadway may not be revoked.

The evidence justifies the finding of the lower court that the right to the use of the roadway had been established by estoppel.

The judgment is affirmed.

NOTES AND QUESTIONS

1. If an encroaching user obtains an easement by prescription, this results in a perpetual easement in all respects equivalent to an easement by grant. What rights are established when the encroaching user obtains an irrevocable license by estoppel? Does an irrevocable license run with the land? Does it create rights enforceable against third parties? The court in the principal case quotes an earlier Kentucky decision which says the interest "continues for so long as its nature calls for." What does this mean?

2. Suppose landowner A, knowing where the lot line is, observes neighboring landowner B building a driveway over the land of owner A. Landowner B does not know he is trespassing and in fact thinks the driveway is on his own land. If landowner A simply watches the construction day after day without giving any permission, express or implied, to use his land for the driveway, and landowner B proceeds to complete the driveway, can landowner B claim an irrevocable license by estoppel?

3. Recall that the California Supreme Court in *Warsaw v. Chicago Metallic Ceilings* rejected the claim that the TO may seek indemnification from an AU who obtains an easement by prescription. Whether or not you agree with this result in the context of prescription (or adverse possession), do you think an indemnification requirement would make more sense, or less sense, in the context of an irrevocable license by estoppel? ⟶ *less sense - there is an element of some sort of permission by the owner of the land.*

4. Why does the law have so many different doctrines for bailing out owners of dominant tracts of land who fail to negotiate a written grant of an easement from the owner(s) of servient tracts? Can you think of ways of reducing the number of doctrines? Would you advocate replacing them all with something like the private condemnation statutes in use in about half the states?

_D (Appellant)   *_P (Appellee)*

Fontainebleau Hotel Corp. v. Forty–Five Twenty–Five, Inc.

District Court of Appeal of Florida, Third District, 1959.
114 So.2d 357.

■ PER CURIAM. This is an interlocutory appeal from an order temporarily enjoining the appellants from continuing with the construction of a fourteen-story addition to the Fontainebleau Hotel, owned and operated by the appellants. Appellee, plaintiff below, owns the Eden Roc Hotel, which was constructed in 1955, about a year after the Fontainebleau, and adjoins the Fontainebleau on the north. Both are luxury hotels, facing the Atlantic Ocean. The proposed addition to the Fontainebleau is being constructed twenty feet from its north property line, 130 feet from the mean high water mark of the Atlantic Ocean, and 76 feet 8 inches from the ocean bulkhead line. The 14–story tower will extend 160 feet above grade in height and is 416 feet long from east to west. During the winter months, from around two o'clock in the afternoon for the remainder of the day, the shadow of the addition will extend over the cabana, swimming pool, and sunbathing areas of the Eden Roc, which are located in the southern portion of its property.

In this action, plaintiff-appellee sought to enjoin the defendants-appellants from proceeding with the construction of the addition to the Fontainebleau (it appears to have been roughly eight stories high at the time suit was filed), alleging that the construction would interfere with the light and air on the beach in front of the Eden Roc and cast a shadow of such size as to render the beach wholly unfitted for the use and enjoyment of its guests, to the irreparable injury of the plaintiff; further, that the construction of such addition on the north side of defendants' property, rather than the south side, was actuated by malice and ill will on the part of the defendants' president toward the plaintiff's president; and that the construction was in violation of a building ordinance requiring a 100–foot setback from the ocean. It was also alleged that the construction would interfere with the easements of light and air enjoyed by plaintiff and its predecessors in title for more than twenty years and "impliedly granted by virtue of the acts of the plaintiff's predecessors in title, as well as under the common law and the express recognition of such rights by virtue of Chapter 9837, Laws of Florida 1923 * * *." Some attempt was also made to allege an easement by implication in favor of the plaintiff's property, as the dominant, and against the defendants' property, as the servient, tenement.

The defendants' answer denied the material allegations of the complaint, pleaded laches and estoppel by judgment.

The chancellor heard considerable testimony on the issues made by the complaint and the answer and, as noted, entered a temporary injunction restraining the defendants from continuing with the construction of the addition. His reason for so doing was stated by him, in a memorandum opinion, as follows:

> In granting the temporary injunction in this case the Court wishes to make several things very clear. The ruling is not based on any alleged presumptive title nor prescriptive right of the plaintiff to light and air nor is it based on any deed restrictions nor recorded plats in the title of the plaintiff nor of the defendant nor of any plat of record. It is not based on any zoning ordinance nor on any provision of the building code of the City of Miami Beach nor on the decision of any court, nisi prius or appellate. It is based solely on the proposition that no one has a right to use his property to the injury of another. In this

case it is clear from the evidence that the proposed use by the Fontainebleau will materially damage the Eden Roc. There is evidence indicating that the construction of the proposed annex by the Fontainebleau is malicious or deliberate for the purpose of injuring the Eden Roc, but it is scarcely sufficient, standing alone, to afford a basis for equitable relief.

This is indeed a novel application of the maxim *sic utere tuo ut alienum non laedas*. This maxim does not mean that one must never use his own property in such a way as to do any injury to his neighbor. Beckman v. Marshall, 85 So.2d 552 (Fla. 1956). It means only that one must use his property so as not to injure the lawful *rights* of another. Cason v. Florida Power Co., 76 So. 535 (Fla. 1918). In Reaver v. Martin Theatres, 52 So.2d 682, 683 (Fla. 1951), under this maxim, it was stated that "it is well settled that a property owner may put his own property to any reasonable and lawful use, so long as he does not thereby deprive the adjoining landowner of any right of enjoyment of his property *which is recognized and protected by law, and so long as his use is not such a one as the law will pronounce a nuisance*." [Emphasis supplied.]

RULE re: sic utere tuo ut alienum non laedas

No American decision has been cited, and independent research has revealed none, in which it has been held that—in the absence of some contractual or statutory obligation—a landowner has a legal right to the free flow of light and air across the adjoining land of his neighbor. Even at common law, the landowner had no legal right, in the absence of an easement or uninterrupted use and enjoyment for a period of 20 years, to unobstructed light and air from the adjoining land. Blumberg v. Weiss, 17 A.2d 823 (N.J. Eq. 1941); 1 Am.Jur., Adjoining Landowners, § 51. And the English doctrine of "ancient lights" has been unanimously repudiated in this country. 1 Am.Jur., Adjoining Landowners, § 49, p. 533; Lynch v. Hill, 6 A.2d 614 (Del. Ch. 1939), overruling Clawson v. Primrose, 4 Del.Ch. 643.

Application

There being, then, no legal right to the free flow of light and air from the adjoining land, it is universally held that where a structure serves a useful and beneficial purpose, it does not give rise to a cause of action, either for damages or for an injunction under the maxim *sic utere tuo ut alienum non laedas*, even though it causes injury to another by cutting off the light and air and interfering with the view that would otherwise be available over adjoining land in its natural state, regardless of the fact that the structure may have been erected partly for spite.

We see no reason for departing from this universal rule. If, as contended on behalf of plaintiff, public policy demands that a landowner in the Miami Beach area refrain from constructing buildings on his premises that will cast a shadow on the adjoining premises, an amendment of its comprehensive planning and zoning ordinance, applicable to the public as a whole, is the means by which such purpose should be achieved. (No opinion is expressed here as to the validity of such an ordinance, if one should be enacted pursuant to the requirements of law. Cf. City of Miami Beach v. State ex rel. Fontainebleau Hotel Corp., 108 So.2d 614, 619 (Fla. App. 1959).) But to change the universal rule—and the custom followed in this state since its inception—that adjoining landowners have an equal right under the law to build to the line of their respective tracts and to such a height as is desired by them (in the absence, of course, of building restrictions or regulations) amounts, in our opinion, to judicial legislation. As stated in Musumeci v. Leonardo, [75 A.2d 177 (R.I.)], "So use your own as not to injure another's property is, indeed, a sound and salutary principle for the promotion of justice, but it may not and should not be applied so as gratuitously to confer upon an adjacent property owner incorporeal rights incidental to his ownership of land which the law does not sanction."

We have also considered whether the order here reviewed may be sustained upon any other reasoning, conformable to and consistent with the pleadings, regardless of the erroneous reasoning upon which the order was actually based. We have concluded that it cannot.

The record affirmatively shows that no statutory basis for the right sought to be enforced by plaintiff exists. The so-called Shadow Ordinance enacted by the City of Miami Beach at plaintiff's behest was held invalid in City of Miami Beach v. State ex rel. Fontainebleau Hotel Corp., supra. It also affirmatively appears that there is no possible basis for holding that plaintiff has an easement for light and air, either express or implied, across defendants' property, nor any prescriptive right thereto—even if it be assumed, arguendo, that the common-law right of prescription as to "ancient lights" is in effect in this state. And from what we have said heretofore in this opinion, it is perhaps superfluous to add that we have no desire to dissent from the unanimous holding in this country repudiating the English doctrine of ancient lights.

The only other possible basis—and, in fact, the only one insisted upon by plaintiff in its brief filed here, other than its reliance upon the law of private nuisance as expressed in the maxim *sic utere tuo ut alienum non laedas*—for the order here reviewed is the alleged violation by defendants of the setback line prescribed by ordinance. The plaintiff argues that the ordinance applicable to the Use District in which plaintiff's and defendants' properties are located, prescribing "a front yard having a depth of not less than one hundred (100) feet, measured from the ocean, * * *," should be and has been interpreted by the City's zoning inspector as requiring a setback of 100 feet from an established ocean bulkhead line. As noted above, the addition to the Fontainebleau is set back only 76 feet 8 inches from the ocean bulkhead line, although it is 130 feet from the ocean measured from the mean high water mark.

While the chancellor did not decide the question of whether the setback ordinance had been violated, it is our view that, even if there was such a violation, the plaintiff would have no cause of action against the defendants based on such violation. The application of simple mathematics to the sun studies filed in evidence by plaintiff in support of its claim demonstrates conclusively that to move the existing structure back some 23 feet from the ocean would make no appreciable difference in the problem which is the subject of this controversy. The construction of the 14–story addition is proceeding under a permit issued by the city pursuant to the mandate of this court in City of Miami Beach v. State ex rel. Fontainebleau Hotel Corp., supra, which permit authorizes completion of the 14–story addition according to a plan showing a 76–foot setback from the ocean bulkhead line. Moreover, the plaintiff's objection to the distance of the structure from the ocean appears to have been made for the first time in the instant suit, which was filed almost a year after the beginning of the construction of the addition, at a time when it was roughly eight stories in height, representing the expenditure by defendants of several million dollars. In these circumstances, it is our view that the plaintiff has stated no cause of action for equitable relief based on the violation of the ordinance—assuming, arguendo, that there has been a violation.

Since it affirmatively appears that the plaintiff has not established a cause of action against the defendants by reason of the structure here in question, the order granting a temporary injunction should be and it is hereby reversed with directions to dismiss the complaint.

Reversed with directions.

NOTES AND QUESTIONS

1. The Fontainebleau, designed by architect Morris Lapidus, was the premier hotel of Miami Beach when it was constructed. It was originally owned by two partners, Ben Novack and Harry Mufson. When they had a falling out, Mufson proceeded to build the Eden Roc, immediately to the north of the Fontainebleau. Novack retaliated by ordering an addition, called the Fontainebleau Towers, on the site of the "kit kat" swimming pool, which was originally north of the main pool and hence abutted the Eden Roc property. This is the addition at issue in the principal case. When it was completed, the Towers nearly doubled the capacity of the Fontainebleau (to 1,000 rooms). Not only did the Towers cast a shadow on the Eden Roc swimming pool, Novack also ordered that the north wall of the addition, facing the Eden Roc, remain windowless and unpainted, thereby degrading the view of the Eden Roc patrons. However, after Mufson was defeated in his attempt to enjoin the addition, he was able to extend the deck of the Eden Roc, with a new pool, further to the east, thereby escaping the shadow cast in the winter months by the Towers. See Seth Bramson, Miami Beach 106, 108 (2005). According to a recent report, the owners of the Eden Roc have obtained zoning variances for remodeling their hotel. As part of the project, what the Eden Roc representative referred to as the Fontainebleau's "spite wall" will be incorporated into the renovation plan, thereby bringing the longstanding battle started by Novack and Mufson to an end. See Charlotte Libov, Beach panel OKs variances for Eden Roc renovation, Miami Today online, Jan. 12, 2006, at www.miamitodaynews.com/news/060112/story5.shtml.

Figure 9–6
The Fontainebleau and Eden Roc Hotels, Miami Beach, Florida

Courtesy The Bramson Archive, Miami, FL.

The Bramson Archive, Miami, FL. The top image shows the hotels before the wall, the bottom image after its construction.

2. Is there a simple explanation for the conclusion in *Fontainebleau Hotel* that one cannot create an easement by prescription in the flow of sunlight across land? A prescriptive easement arises when an AU repeatedly trespasses on the land of the TO, and the TO allows the statute of limitations for an action in trespass to run. Where is the trespass in *Fontainebleau Hotel*?

3. Can one obtain an easement by grant for the flow of sunlight across a neighbor's property? Some jurisdictions have said yes. See, e.g., Pacifica Homeowners' Ass'n v. Wesley Palms Retirement Community, 224 Cal.Rptr. 380 (Cal. Ct. App. 1986); Pierce v. Northeast Lake Washington Sewer and Water Dist., 870 P.2d 305 (Wash. 1994). But the most common way of providing for something like the flow of sunlight across land (other than through zoning ordinances) would be through negotiation of a restrictive covenant that limits the height of the neighboring building. Interestingly, one cannot obtain a restrictive covenant by prescription. The simple explanation, again, would be that the conduct required by the typical restrictive covenant does not involve any trespass by the benefited property owner on the land of the burdened property owner. Similarly, no state's common law provides for a right to acquire an easement of light by prescription. Comment, Solar Lights: Guaranteeing a Place in the Sun, 57 Or. L. Rev. 94, 112 (1977).

4. But here is a complication: In England and in most American jurisdictions, one can acquire by grant an easement to commit a nuisance on the land of another. For example, if A wants to construct a smelly smelter on his land, but anticipates that this will create a nuisance for B who lives next door, A can try to acquire an easement from B permitting A to cast smelly fumes on the land of B. (Of course, A will have to pay dearly for such an easement.) In England, and in some American states, one can also acquire an easement by prescription to commit a nuisance. Thus, if A builds a smelter which casts smelly fumes on the land of B, and the statute of limitations for B to bring a nuisance action against A runs, A can claim to have acquired an easement by prescription to create the nuisance. If one can acquire an easement by prescription to commit a nuisance on the land of a neighbor in the form of smelly fumes, why cannot one acquire an easement by prescription to be free of having the flow of sunlight blocked by a neighbor's building? Courts have generally rejected claims that blocking solar access is a nuisance. See Sher v. Leiderman, 226 Cal.Rptr. 698 (Cal. Ct. App. 1986); American Nat'l Bank & Trust Co. v. City of Chicago, 568 N.E.2d 25 (Ill. App. Ct. 1990). However, two jurisdictions have ruled to the contrary, holding that blocking sunlight can be a nuisance. See Tenn v. 889 Associates, Ltd., 500 A.2d 366 (N.H. 1985) (Souter, J.); Prah v. Maretti, 321 N.W.2d 182 (Wis. 1982). In such a jurisdiction, would *Fontainebleau Hotel* come out differently?

5.   In the case of the smelly fumes, the put-upon landowner has had its attention drawn to the adverse use. Can the same be said for someone whose neighbor claims later to have been relying on access to sunlight? If one accepted that blocking light could be a nuisance, how should a court resolve the conflict? Can any landowner with a worthy project acquire rights over adjacent land with no notice? If not, how should nuisance law evolve in response to changing conditions?

6.   As we saw in Chapter III, many Western states employ the doctrine of prior appropriation to allocate water, and some Western states have adopted legislation providing for prior appropriation rights in solar access, N.M. Stats. §§ 47–3–1 to 42–3–5; Wyoming Stat. § 34–22–101, et seq.; see also Note, The Allocation of Sunlight: Solar Rights and the Prior Appropriation Doctrine, 47 Colo. L. Rev. 421 (1976). Does a "me first" approach to solar collectors make sense? If the plaintiff had prevailed in *Fontainebleau Hotel*, would there be a potential for a wasteful race to build? If building and maintaining a swimming pool restricts the rights of the neighboring landowner, would each of the landowners be encouraged to build more quickly than they would otherwise? Is this a situation in which first-in-time should prevail, or one where its dangers of wasteful racing are prominent?

7.   The court in *Fontainebleau Hotel* states that it does not matter whether the addition to the Fontainebleau may have been constructed partly out of spite. But pure spite can sometimes lead to greater intervention. Particularly where one landowner erects a fence solely to block light and air from a neighbor, many courts have been willing to find a nuisance and issue an injunction. See, e.g., Flaherty v. Moran, 45 N.W. 381 (Mich. 1890). Mixed motives will usually lead to no liability. See, e.g., Kuzniak v. Kozminski, 65 N.W. 275 (Mich. 1895). Compare in this regard *Keeble v. Hickeringill*, in Chapter II. Might the spite fence doctrine be a solution to the problem of a landowner seeking to use the *ad coelum* rule to exclude highflying airplanes?

c.   TERMINATION OF EASEMENTS

Easements may be terminated in a number of ways. The most approved method is by deed, releasing or extinguishing the easement. Easements are also terminated as a matter of law when the dominant and servient tract come under common ownership. This is said to result in a merger of the easement into the larger fee simple. A third method of termination is adverse possession. If the owner of the servient tract blocks the easement, and the owner of the dominant tract fails to object before the statute of limitations runs, then the easement will be extinguished. Finally, easements may be extinguished if prolonged nonuse gives rise to an inference that the easement has been abandoned. However, changed circumstances are generally not considered a ground for modification or termination of an easement, unless the easement is stated in terms of a

[handwritten margin notes:]
Ways to terminate an Easement
1) Deed
2) Common Ownership
3) Adverse Possession
4) Abandonment
→ changed circumstances generally not sufficient

particular purpose that has become obsolete. See Jon W. Bruce & James W. Ely, Jr., The Law of Easements and Licenses in Land § 9.03 (1988).

d. MISUSE OF EASEMENTS

Appellant / P

Appellee / D

Penn Bowling Recreation Center, Inc. v. Hot Shoppes, Inc.

United States Court of Appeals, District of Columbia Circuit, 1949.
179 F.2d 64.

■ McALLISTER, CIRCUIT JUDGE. In 1938, the Norment Estate conveyed a portion of its real property to appellee, Hot Shoppes, Inc., and subjected a part thereof to a sixteen-foot right of way for ingress and egress. This resulted in an easement for the benefit of the balance of the unconveyed property, adjacent thereto, which was retained by the Estate, and which, by virtue of the easement, became the dominant tenement. A part of this dominant estate came into ownership of appellant, Penn Bowling Recreation Center, Inc., by mesne conveyances, in 1940, two years after the creation of the right of way.

On February 5, 1948, appellee, Hot Shoppes, erected a barrier of iron posts and cement concrete blocks within the right of way and alongside it, interfering with the full enjoyment of the easement by Penn Bowling; and shortly thereafter, appellant filed its complaint to enjoin appellee from maintaining the structure within the right of way and interfering with the use thereof. Appellee, in its answer denied that appellant was entitled to the use of the right of way, and asked for a permanent injunction against such use by appellant, as well as for a judgment declaring it to be permanently forfeited and extinguished by abandonment. Both parties filed motions for a preliminary injunction, but before a hearing was had on these motions, appellee filed a motion for summary judgment, asking dismissal of the complaint, a permanent injunction against the use by appellant of the right of way, and a declaratory judgment declaring that it had been permanently forfeited and extinguished by abandonment. The district court granted appellee's motion for summary judgment as prayed; and from such judgment, the Penn Bowling Recreation Center appeals.

The arguments that appellee addressed to the district court on the hearing on the motion for summary judgment embraced the contentions that appellant, as owner of the dominant tenement, had forfeited and extinguished the right of way by abandonment, as the result of subjecting the servient tenement to an additional and enlarged use or servitude in connection with other premises to which the easement was not appurtenant; that it had been guilty of the misuse of the easement of the right of way by reason of having used it for the parking of motor vehicles; and that, by certain masonry constructions, appellant had, in any event, made it impossible to use the right of way for egress and ingress.

Appellee (D) Arguments

With regard to the claim that appellant had subjected the servient tenement to a burden in excess of that imposed by the original easement, it appears that after the creation of the right of way for the benefit of the dominant tenement, appellant purchased not only that tenement but other real property adjacent thereto, the latter property not being entitled to the enjoyment of the easement. Appellant then constructed a building occupying a part of the dominant tenement, as well as the additional property adjacent thereto. Not all of the dominant tenement is occupied by the building. In fact, the total of the area of that portion of the dominant tenement, together with the non-dominant property over which the building is constructed, is a smaller area than the area of the original dominant tenement. The building, thus constructed, houses a large bowling alley and restaurant. Appellant in the past has been using the right of way to bring fuel oil, food, equipment, and supplies to the building, and removing trash, garbage, and other material therefrom.

It is contended by appellant that since the area of the dominant and non-dominant land served by the easement is less than the original area of the dominant tenement, the use made by appellant of the right of way to serve the building located on the lesser area is not materially increased or excessive. It is true that where the nature and extent of the use of an easement is, by its terms, unrestricted, the use by the dominant tenement may be increased or enlarged. McCullough et al. v. Broad Exchange Company et al., 92 N.Y.S. 533 (App. Div. N.Y.). But the owner of the dominant tenement may not subject the servient tenement to use or servitude in connection with other premises to which the easement is not appurtenant. See Williams v. James, Eng. Law. Rep. (1867), 2 C.P. 577. And when an easement is being used in such a manner, an injunction will be issued to prevent such use. Appellant, therefore, may not use the easement to serve both the dominant and non-dominant property, even though the area thereof is less than the original area of the dominant tenement.

The disposition of the foregoing issue brings us to the principal legal question in the case: whether appellant's use of the right of way resulted in the forfeiture and extinguishment of the easement by abandonment, and thereby entitled appellee, on a motion for summary judgment, to a decree permanently enjoining appellant from using the right of way.

Misuse of an easement right is not sufficient to constitute a forfeiture, waiver, or abandonment of such right. The right to an easement is not lost by using it in an unauthorized manner or to an unauthorized extent, unless it is impossible to sever the increased burden so as to preserve to the owner of the dominant tenement that to which he is entitled, and impose on the servient tenement only that burden which was originally imposed upon it.

From the record before us, we are unable to ascertain what the total additional burden is that has been cast upon the servient tenement as the result of appellant's use of the right of way for ingress to, and egress from, the building which was located on part of the dominant and the non-dominant property. As has been mentioned, the building houses a bowling alley and restaurant. From affidavits on file, it appears that a soda fountain and luncheonette used in connection with the restaurant are located in that

RULE

RULE
ie—only property on the dominant tenement can benefit from the easement

RULE
re: misuse of easement

part of the building situate on the non-dominant real estate, which, of course, is not entitled to enjoyment of the easement; and it further appears that the right of way is used for the purpose of bringing supplies for the fountain and luncheonette and removing trash and garbage therefrom. It is not disclosed whether other supplies or materials brought to, or removed from, the building over the right of way are required for the use of that part of the structure located on the dominant estate or on the non-dominant property, or both. Affidavits filed by appellant indicate, however, that oil for heating purposes is delivered to the loading platform over the right of way. Whether the oil furnace is located on the dominant or non-dominant property does not appear. But it is declared on the part of Penn Bowling that if the right of way were barred to appellant, a great hardship would result in the operation of the building housing the bowling alley and other facilities, and would necessitate large and expensive alterations of its building. Appellant may well be obliged to remodel its structure in order to operate, but it would appear that this can be done and, consequently, appellee is not entitled to a decree extinguishing the easement or to a permanent injunction on the pleadings and proofs before us. Furthermore, appellant's building fronts on a public thoroughfare and changes conceivably could be made so that the non-dominant property could be served from the street. In any event, appellant can use the right of way only to serve the dominant tenement.

An authorized use and an unauthorized use may be intermingled in such a way as to justify enjoining any use until the circumstances have so changed that the authorized use may be permitted without affording opportunity for the unauthorized use, which it would be difficult to discover or prove. In such a case, the issuance of an injunction may be justified restraining any use until the building is so altered or changed that that part of it which is on the dominant tenement may enjoy the easement without permitting its enjoyment by the other part of the building having no right thereto. So where it can not be ascertained whether the easement of a right of way is being used solely for the enjoyment of the dominant tenement, or for additional property also, an injunction may be granted against further use of the easement until such time as it may be shown that only the dominant tenement is served by the easement.

Appellee claims that appellant itself has made the use of the right of way for ingress and egress impossible, by constructing adjacent to its building a wall and loading platform which occupies the space between the building and the right of way, and that, therefore, appellant can not get onto its premises from the right of way but can only come up to them. To this contention, appellant replies that the platform, which occupies a space ten feet wide, can easily be demolished and leveled off even with the right of way, and thus afford ample space for any of its trucks to park on appellant's own land for purposes of loading or unloading. If the loading dock were removed so as to permit the use of the right of way for the dominant estate, appellee's contention that appellant has made it impossible to use the easement for ingress or egress could not be sustained. This is a question, however, to be determined by the trial court after the taking of proofs in regard thereto.

Moreover, it is asserted by appellant that, in any event, in using the right of way for ingress to and egress from the dominant tenement, appellant is not required to cross over the line separating its property from the right of way, but that ingress and egress not only mean passing over the easement onto appellant's property and going from such property back over the easement, but also comprehend the coming to, and going away from, the line of the dominant tenement. On this question, we here express no opinion, as the determination of such issue is, in the first instance, for the trial court.

Appellee further complains that appellant misused the easement by parking motor vehicles on the right of way. The use of the easement for purposes of ingress and egress does not include its use for parking purposes and an injunction may issue to prevent such a use. However, it is to be said that appellant is entitled to a reasonable use and enjoyment of the easement for purposes of ingress and egress. In determining what is a reasonable use, the easement is to be construed in the light of the situation of the property and the surrounding circumstances for the purpose of giving effect to the intention of the parties. The long continued use of the right of way for the purpose of loading or unloading supplies at appellant's premises may indicate an intention of the parties that the easement might be used for that purpose. But appellant would thereby acquire no right to make any use of the easement which would unreasonably interfere with its use by appellee. Appellee has located on the premises in question its central offices and commissary, which is engaged in supplying sixteen restaurants in Washington and vicinity, and requires almost constant use of the driveway by appellee. Appellant's parking of vehicles on the right of way at a time when appellee needs its use would constitute an unlawful interference with the latter's right. The determination of these questions largely depends upon the circumstances of the case and is properly for the district court.

In accordance with the foregoing, the judgment is set aside and the case remanded to the district court for further proceedings consonant with this opinion, with the reservation of right to the appellee to apply for a temporary injunction pending final decision of the court.

NOTES AND QUESTIONS

1. What is Hot Shoppes' real complaint here? Does the court's disposition promise to achieve a resolution of the dispute? Why did the parties resort to litigation rather than working out the conflict among themselves like good neighbors?

2. Suppose Penn Bowling does not use the easement for nonappurtenant property, but simply experiences a surge in patronage that requires more intensive use of the easement. What standard should a court employ in assessing a claim of "overuse" of an easement? See Hayes v. Aquia Marina, Inc., 414 S.E.2d 820 (Va. 1992) (applying a standard of reasonable-

ness in assessing such a claim). Does it make sense to apply a rule of strict liability to claims of nonappurtenant use, while assessing other claims of overuse under a standard of reasonableness?

3. The court in this case considers only injunctive relief (a property rule) rather than damages (a liability rule). Would a liability rule provide a better mechanism for mediating conflicts over misuse of an easement? In a widely noted case that also involved the use of an easement to serve after-acquired nonappurtenant property, the court decided to award damages rather than injunctive relief. Brown v. Voss, 715 P.2d 514 (Wash. 1986). But since no actual harm could be shown (the intensity of use did not increase), only $1 in nominal damages was awarded. Is such an award likely to achieve a resolution of the issues between the parties?

2. Covenants

Closely related to easements are covenants or promises respecting the use of land. Easements are paradigmatically about the right to go onto land; they are abrogations of the servient owner's right to exclude. Covenants are generally about the right to insist on the use or nonuse of land; as such, they typically prescribe a more or less elaborate system of governance rules. Easements are nearly always affirmative, but covenants can be either affirmative or negative.

There is little doubt that a contract between two neighbors, A and B, respecting the way they use their respective properties can be enforced by either one against the other. Thus, if A and B promise each other to plant only red geraniums in their window boxes, and A decides instead to plant white geraniums, B can sue A for breach of contract, assuming the usual contractual formalities (consideration, etc.) are met. The difficulties arise when one of the original parties, let's say A, has transferred her interest, and the question becomes whether the promise is enforceable against A's successor when A's successor decides to plant white geraniums. Over the years, courts have developed two theories that will allow promises respecting the use of the land to run with the land. One theory asks whether the promise is enforceable against successors as an "equitable servitude." The other asks whether the promise is enforceable against successors as a "real covenant." In a throwback to the old division between common-law courts and courts of equity, often the critical factor in determining which theory applies is the nature of the relief that the plaintiff seeks. If an injunction is sought, then the matter lies in equity, and courts will generally apply the equitable servitude theory. If damages are sought, then the matter falls on the common-law side of the old division, and courts will generally apply the real covenant theory. It is important to appreciate, however, that equitable servitudes and real covenants are not two different things. They are the same thing—promises respecting the use of land—and the label that attaches in deciding whether these promises run with the land is determined by the theory for enforcing the promise against successors, not by any thing intrinsic in the nature of the promise itself.

Notwithstanding the different theories for determining whether they run with the land, all covenants share certain features in common. Covenants are less "property like" than easements and lie closer to the contract end of the property-contract spectrum. Thus, it appears that covenants impose no duties of forbearance on third parties. Moreover, one cannot acquire a covenant by prescription, implication, necessity, or estoppel. The Statute of Frauds applies, and all covenants must be in writing. Generally speaking, covenants function like "add ons" to the basic package of rights and liabilities that landowners normally have, specific modifications that originate in written contractual undertakings that are specific to particular parcels of land.

a.   EQUITABLE SERVITUDES

English common law recognized only one circumstance in which covenants regarding the use of land would run to successors in interest: when either a landlord or a tenant transferred his interest in property subject to a lease (see Chapter VI). The common-law courts refused to enforce covenants between neighboring landowners as interests running with the land. This proved to be a major inconvenience in efforts to control incompatible land uses by contract. Eventually, the court of equity came to the rescue.

Tulk v. Moxhay

Court of Chancery, England, 1848.
2 Phillips 774, 41 ER 1143.

In the year 1808 the Plaintiff, being then the owner in fee of the vacant piece of ground in Leicester Square, as well as of several of the houses forming the Square, sold the piece of ground by the description of "Leicester Square garden or pleasure ground, with the equestrian statue then standing in the centre thereof, and the iron railing and stone work round the same," to one Elms in fee: and the deed of conveyance contained a covenant by Elms, for himself, his heirs, and assigns, with the Plaintiff, his heirs, executors, and administrators, "that Elms, his heirs, and assigns should, and would from time to time, and at all times thereafter at his and their own costs and charges, keep and maintain the said piece of ground and square garden, and the iron railing round the same in its then form, and in sufficient and proper repair as a square garden and pleasure ground, in an open state, uncovered with any buildings, in neat and ornamental order; and that it should be lawful for the inhabitants of Leicester Square, tenants of the Plaintiff, on payment of a reasonable rent for the same, to have keys at their own expense and the privilege of admission therewith at any time or times into the said square garden and pleasure ground."

The piece of land so conveyed passed by divers mesne conveyances into the hands of the Defendant, whose purchase deed contained no similar covenant with his vendor: but he admitted that he had purchased with notice of the covenant in the deed of 1808.

The Defendant having manifested an intention to alter the character of the square garden, and asserted a right, if he thought fit, to build upon it, the Plaintiff, who still remained owner of several houses in the square, filed this bill for an injunction; and an injunction was granted by the Master of the Rolls to restrain the Defendant from converting or using the piece of ground and square garden, and the iron railing round the same, to or for any other purpose than as a square garden and pleasure ground in an open state, and uncovered with buildings. * * *

■ THE LORD CHANCELLOR [Cottenham] * * * That this Court has jurisdiction to enforce a contract between the owner of land and his neighbour purchasing a part of it, that the latter shall either use or abstain from using the land purchased in a particular way, is, what I never knew disputed. Here there is no question about the contract: the owner of certain houses in the square sells the land adjoining, with a covenant from the purchaser not to use it for any other purpose than as a square garden. And it is now contended, not that the vendee could violate that contract, but that he might sell the piece of land, and that the purchaser from him may violate it without this Court having any power to interfere. If that were so, it would be impossible for an owner of land to sell part of it without incurring the risk of rendering what he retains worthless. It is said that, the covenant being one which does not run with the land, this Court cannot enforce it; but the question is, not whether the covenant runs with the land, but whether a party shall be permitted to use the land in a manner inconsistent with the contract entered into by his vendor, and with notice of which he purchased. Of course, the price would be affected by the covenant, and nothing could be more inequitable than that the original purchaser should be able to sell the property the next day for a greater price, in consideration of the assignee being allowed to escape from the liability which he had himself undertaken.

That the question does not depend upon whether the covenant runs with the land is evident from this, that if there was a mere agreement and no covenant, this Court would enforce it against a party purchasing with notice of it; for if an equity is attached to the property by the owner, no one purchasing with notice of that equity can stand in a different situation from the party from whom he purchased. * * *

With respect to the observations of Lord Brougham in *Keppell v. Bailey* (2 M. & K. 517), [39 Eng. Rep. 1042 (Ch. 1834),] he never could have meant to lay down that this Court would not enforce an equity attached to land by the owner, unless under such circumstances as would maintain an action at law. If that be the result of his observations, I can only say that I cannot coincide with it.

I think the cases cited before the Vice–Chancellor and this decision of the Master of the Rolls perfectly right, and, therefore, that this motion must be refused, with costs.

NOTES AND QUESTIONS

1. Leicester Square has had a long history that implicates many of the themes of this course:

In the middle of the seventeenth century the Earl of Leicester laid out Leicester Square and built Leicester House on its north side * * * The basin [in the center] was replaced in 1748 by a gilded equestrian statue, in metal, of George I by Van Nost. [The property descended to two married Sidney sisters, one of whose shares was sold to James S. Tulk in 1772. Later, partition was had.] Meanwhile, the social status of Leicester Square had declined, and since the division of ownership the central garden had fallen on evil days * * * The enclosure became a wilderness, a receptacle for rubbish, and a last resting place for dead cats. King George lost an arm and his horse a leg.

Both Tulk and Moxhay died in 1849. In 1851 (the year of the first International Exposition, at the Crystal Palace) Wyld, a geographer, purchased the garden from Moxhay's widow for the purpose of erecting thereon a building to contain a large model of the earth. As the Tulk family objected, Wyld made an agreement with them, which refers to the very ruinous and dilapidated condition of the garden and the iron railings, and in which Wyld was licensed to erect a globe for ten years in return for an option to the Tulks to purchase an undivided half of the garden at the end of that time for £500. The owners of the former Sidney houses on the north side of the Square refused to participate in this agreement. A vast domed structure known as "Wyld's Globe" was then erected and used for geographical and historical lectures and exhibits. In 1861 John A. Tulk, the grandson of Charles, exercised the option, so that he and Wyld became co-tenants of the garden. The Globe was taken down and the battered statue again set up, to be treated to the jokes of Punch and the pranks of idlers, who on October 17, 1866, painted the horse white with black spots and put a foolscap on the head of King George.

By this time the public authorities had become active. In 1863 a bill was introduced in Parliament for a public market in the Square, which was successfully opposed. In 1865 the Metropolitan Board of Works took possession of the garden under the Town Gardens Protection Act of 1863 (26 Vict. c.13), which empowered the Board to take charge of any grounds which had been set apart for the use of the inhabitants of a surrounding square, when the body appointed for the care of the same had neglected to keep it in proper order. John A. Tulk at once brought an action of trespass *quare clausum fregit* against the Board and won a decision that Leicester Square was not within the statute * * * Thus Tulk succeeded in keeping the Square in its desolate condition. Tulk hoped to convert the garden into building land, as Moxhay had formerly tried to do. The maintenance of billboards around the enclosure was prevented by another equity decree (unreported), probably at the suit of the north side owners. While an appeal was pending, the Metropolitan Board of Works obtained compulsory powers of acquisition by the Leicester Square Act, 1874 (27 & 38 Vict. c.10).

Before condemnation took place, Albert Grant, M.P., purchased Tulk's rights, opened negotiations with the other owners, took possession of the garden, and offered it free of cost to the Board of Works for public enjoyment. The unfortunate horse was removed in February, 1874 and replaced by a statue of Shakespeare, while the four corners of the garden were ornamented with statues of former residents of Leicester Square–Reynolds, Newton, Hogarth, and Dr. John Hunter. After Mr. Grant had laid out the park in its present form at a total expenditure of £28,000, it was handed over to the public on July 2, 1874.

Zechariah Chafee, Jr. & Sidney Post Simpson, Cases on Equity, Jurisdiction and Specific Performance 704–06, 710–11 (1934).

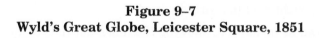

Figure 9–7
Wyld's Great Globe, Leicester Square, 1851

Source: Survey of London, Vol. 34, The Parish of St. Anne Soho (F.H.W. Sheppard ed., 1966) (illustration 43a, T.H. Shepherd).

2. Is the Chancellor's reasoning here circular? That one is bound to perform an obligation of which he has notice cannot be doubted, but just because one has notice does not mean that he has an obligation. Is the charge of circularity overcome by the observation that "the price would be affected by the covenant, and nothing could be more inequitable than that the original purchaser should be able to sell the property the next day for a greater price"? If the covenant is understood not to be binding on a subsequent purchaser, wouldn't this be reflected in the price?

3. Is *Tulk v. Moxhay* consistent with the *numerus clausus*? In order to meet the understandable demand for enforcement of covenants, the court in *Tulk* was well aware that it had to limit the holding in *Keppell v. Bailey*, 39 Eng. Rep. 1042 (Ch. 1834), the leading English case holding that courts lack authority to transform contract rights into new forms of property rights. In *Keppell*, the purchasers of an iron works covenanted on behalf of themselves and their successors and assigns to purchase all limestone required by the works from a particular quarry and to ship the limestone to the works on a particular railroad. In the court's view such an arrangement was enforceable as a contract between the original parties and would not work as an unreasonable restraint on alienation, but the Court of Chancery held that this type of agreement did not fall within the recognized types of servitudes enforceable against subsequent purchasers as a property right running with the land:

> There can be no harm to allowing the fullest latitude to men in binding themselves and their representatives, that is, their assets real and personal, to answer in damages for breach of their obligations. This tends to no mischief, and is a reasonable liberty to bestow; but great detriment would arise and much confusion of rights if parties were allowed to invent new modes of holding and enjoying real property, and to impress upon their lands and tenements a peculiar character, which should follow them into all hands, however remote. Every close, every messuage, might thus be held in several fashion; and it would hardly be possible to know what rights the acquisition of any parcel conferred, or what obligations it imposed.

39 Eng. Rep. at 1049. Lord Chancellor Brougham seemed to object to "fancies," as they have been called, on the grounds that they create excessive third-party information costs. For development of this idea, see Thomas W. Merrill & Henry E. Smith, Optimal Standardization in the Law of Property: The *Numerus Clausus* Principle, 110 Yale L.J. 1 (2000). Is *Tulk* inconsistent with this view? Who needs to look out for the content of covenants? Or does notice, such as that provided by modern land records, mean that any restriction should be able to run with the land? See, e.g., Richard A. Epstein, Notice and Freedom of Contract in the Law of Servitudes, 55 S. Cal. L. Rev. 1353 (1982); see also Alfred F. Conard, Easement Novelties, 30 Cal. L. Rev. 125, 131–33 (1942).

b. REAL COVENANTS

American courts did not consider themselves bound by the English view that covenants run to successors in interest only in the landlord-tenant context. Instead, they developed the concept of the real covenant—a covenant attached to fee simple property that, under certain circumstances analogous to the landlord-tenant doctrine of running covenants, will bind successors in an action at law. The following case applies this American invention to a subdivision that featured an early version of the common-interest communities so prevalent today (see Chapter VI).

Neponsit Property Owners' Association, Inc. v. Emigrant Industrial Savings Bank

Court of Appeals of New York, 1938.
15 N.E.2d 793.

■ Lehman, Judge. The plaintiff, as assignee of Neponsit Realty Company, has brought this action to foreclose a lien upon land which the defendant owns. The lien, it is alleged, arises from a covenant, condition or charge contained in a deed of conveyance of the land from Neponsit Realty Company to a predecessor in title of the defendant. The defendant purchased the land at a judicial sale. The referee's deed to the defendant and every deed in the defendant's chain of title since the conveyance of the land by Neponsit Realty Company purports to convey the property subject to the covenant, condition or charge contained in the original deed. * * *

It appears that in January, 1911, Neponsit Realty Company, as owner of a tract of land in Queens county, caused to be filed in the office of the clerk of the county a map of the land. The tract was developed for a strictly residential community, and Neponsit Realty Company conveyed lots in the tract to purchasers, describing such lots by reference to the filed map and to roads and streets shown thereon. In 1917, Neponsit Realty Company conveyed the land now owned by the defendant to Robert Oldner Deyer and his wife by deed which contained the covenant upon which the plaintiff's cause of action is based.

That covenant provides:

> And the party of the second part for the party of the second part and the heirs, successors and assigns of the party of the second part further covenants that the property conveyed by this deed shall be subject to an annual charge in such an amount as will be fixed by the party of the first part, its successors and assigns, not, however exceeding in any year the sum of four ($4.00) Dollars per lot 20x100 feet. The assigns of the party of the first part may include a Property Owners' Association which may hereafter be organized for the purposes referred to in this paragraph, and in case such association is organized the sums in this paragraph provided for shall be payable to such association. The party of the second part for the party of the second part and the heirs, successors and assigns of the party of the second part covenants that they will pay this charge to the party of the first part, its successors and assigns on the first day of May in each and every year, and further covenants that said charge shall on said date in each year become a lien on the land and shall continue to be such lien until fully paid. Such charge shall be payable to the party of the first part or its successors or assigns, and shall be devoted to the maintenance of the roads, paths, parks, beach, sewers and such other public purposes as shall from time to time be determined by the party of the first part, its successors or assigns. And the party of the second part by the acceptance of this deed hereby expressly vests in the party of the first part, its successors and assigns, the right and power to bring all actions

against the owner of the premises hereby conveyed or any part thereof for the collection of such charge and to enforce the aforesaid lien therefor.

These covenants shall run with the land and shall be construed as real covenants running with the land until January 31st, 1940, when they shall cease and determine.

Every subsequent deed of conveyance of the property in the defendant's chain of title, including the deed from the referee to the defendant, contained, as we have said, a provision that they were made subject to covenants and restrictions of former deeds of record.

Figure 9–8
Street Scene in Neponsit Subdivision, June 2006

There can be no doubt that Neponsit Realty Company intended that the covenant should run with the land and should be enforceable by a property owners association against every owner of property in the residential tract which the realty company was then developing. The language of the covenant admits of no other construction. Regardless of the intention of the parties, a covenant will run with the land and will be enforceable against a subsequent purchaser of the land at the suit of one who claims the benefit of the covenant, only if the covenant complies with certain legal requirements. These requirements rest upon ancient rules and precedents. The age-old essentials of a real covenant, aside from the form of the covenant, may be summarily formulated as follows: (1) It must appear that grantor and grantee intended that the covenant should run with the land; (2) it must appear that the covenant is one "touching" or "concerning" the land with which it runs; (3) it must appear that there is "privity of estate"

between the promisee or party claiming the benefit of the covenant and the right to enforce it, and the promisor or party who rests under the burden of the covenant. Clark on Covenants and Interests Running with Land, p. 74. Although the deeds of Neponsit Realty Company conveying lots in the tract it developed "contained a provision to the effect that the covenants ran with the land, such provision in the absence of the other legal requirements is insufficient to accomplish such a purpose." Morgan Lake Co. v. New York, N. H. & H. R. R. Co., 186 N.E. 685, 686 (N.Y.). In his opinion in that case, Judge Crane posed but found it unnecessary to decide many of the questions which the court must consider in this case.

The covenant in this case is intended to create a charge or obligation to pay a fixed sum of money to be "devoted to the maintenance of the roads, paths, parks, beach, sewers and such other public purposes as shall from time to time be determined by the party of the first part [the grantor], its successors or assigns." It is an affirmative covenant to pay money for use in connection with, but not upon, the land which it is said is subject to the burden of the covenant. Does such a covenant "touch" or "concern" the land? These terms are not part of a statutory definition, a limitation placed by the State upon the power of the courts to enforce covenants *intended* to run with the land by the parties who entered into the covenants. Rather they are words used by courts in England in old cases to describe a limitation which the courts themselves created or to formulate a test which the courts have devised and which the courts voluntarily apply. Cf. Spencer's Case, Coke, vol. 3, part 5, 16a; Mayor of Congleton v. Pattison, 10 East 130. In truth such a description or test so formulated is too vague to be of much assistance and judges and academic scholars alike have struggled, not with entire success, to formulate a test at once more satisfactory and more accurate. "It has been found impossible to state any absolute tests to determine what covenants touch and concern land and what do not. The question is one for the court to determine in the exercise of its best judgment upon the facts of each case." Clark, op. cit. p. 76.

Even though that be true, a determination by a court in one case upon particular facts will often serve to point the way to correct decision in other cases upon analogous facts. Such guideposts may not be disregarded. It has been often said that a covenant to pay a sum of money is a personal affirmative covenant which usually does not concern or touch the land. Such statements are based upon English decisions which hold in effect that only covenants, which compel the covenanter to submit to some *restriction on the use* of his property, touch or concern the land, and that the burden of a covenant which requires the covenanter to do an affirmative act, even on his own land, for the benefit of the owner of a "dominant" estate, does not run with his land. Miller v. Clary, 103 N.E. 1114 (N.Y.). In that case the court pointed out that in many jurisdictions of this country the narrow English rule has been criticized and a more liberal and flexible rule has been substituted. In this State the courts have not gone so far. We have not abandoned the historic distinction drawn by the English courts. So this court has recently said: "Subject to a few exceptions not important at this time, there is now in this state a settled rule of law that a covenant to do an affirmative act, as distinguished from a covenant merely negative in effect, does not run with the land so as to charge the burden of performance on a subsequent grantee [citing cases]. This is so though the burden of such a covenant is laid upon the very parcel which is the subject-matter of the conveyance." Guaranty Trust Co. of New York, v. New York & Queens County Ry. Co., 170 N.E. 887, 892 (N.Y.), opinion by Cardozo, Ch. J.

Both in that case and in the case of Miller v. Clary, supra, the court pointed out that there were some exceptions or limitations in the application of the general rule. Some promises to pay money have been enforced, as covenants running with the land, against subsequent holders of the land who took with notice of the covenant. Cf. Greenfarb v. R. S. K. Realty Corp., 175 N.E. 649 (N.Y.); Morgan Lake Co. v. New York, N. H. & H. R. R. Co., supra. It may be difficult to classify these exceptions or to formulate a test of whether a particular covenant to pay money or to perform some other act falls within the general rule that ordinarily an affirmative covenant is a personal and not a real covenant, or falls outside the limitations placed upon the general rule. At least it must "touch" or "concern" the land in a substantial degree, and though it may be inexpedient and perhaps impossible to formulate a rigid test or definition which will be entirely satisfactory or which can be applied mechanically in all cases, we should at least be able to state the problem and find a reasonable method of approach to it. It has been suggested that a covenant which runs with the land must affect the legal relations—the advantages and the burdens—of the parties to the covenant, as owners of particular parcels of land and not merely as members of the community in general, such as taxpayers or owners of other land. Clark, op. cit. p. 76. Cf. Professor Bigelow's article on The Contents of Covenants in Leases, 12 Mich.L.Rev. 639; 30 Law Quarterly Review, 319. That method of approach has the merit of realism. The test is based on the effect of the covenant rather than on technical distinctions. Does the covenant impose, on the one hand, a burden upon an interest in land, which on the other hand increases the value of a different interest in the same or related land?

Even though we accept that approach and test, it still remains true that whether a particular covenant is sufficiently connected with the use of land to run with the land, must be in many cases a question of degree. A promise to pay for something to be done in connection with the promisor's land does not differ essentially from a promise by the promisor to do the thing himself, and both promises constitute, in a substantial sense, a restriction upon the owner's right to use the land, and a burden upon the legal interest of the owner. On the other hand, a covenant to perform or pay for the performance of an affirmative act disconnected with the use of the land cannot ordinarily touch or concern the land in any substantial degree. Thus, unless we exalt technical form over substance, the distinction between covenants which run with land and covenants which are personal, must depend upon the effect of the covenant on the legal rights which otherwise would flow from ownership of land and which are connected with the land. The problem then is: Does the covenant in purpose and effect substantially alter these rights?

The opinion in Morgan Lake Co. v. New York, N. H. & H. R. R. Co., supra, foreshadowed a classification based upon substance rather than upon form. It was not the first case, however, in which this court has based its decision on the substantial effect of a covenant upon legal relations of the parties as owners of land. Perhaps the most illuminating illustration of such an approach to the problem may be drawn from the "party wall" cases in this State which are reviewed in the opinion of the court in Sebald v. Mulholland, 50 N.E. 260 (N.Y.). The court there pointed out that in cases, cited in the opinion, where by covenant between owners of adjoining parcels of land, "a designated party was authorized to build a party wall, the other agreeing to pay a portion of its value when it should be used by him," the court was constrained to hold that "the agreement was a present one. The party who was to build and the one who was to pay were expressly designated, and the covenant to pay was clearly a personal one" (50 N.E. page 263). At the same time, the court also pointed out that such covenants must be distinguished from the covenants (passed upon by the court in the earlier case of Mott v. Oppenheimer, 31 N.E. 1097 (N.Y.)), "by which the parties conferred, each upon the other, the authority to erect such [party] wall, and dedicated to that use a portion of each of their lots, with an agreement that, if either should build, the other might have the right to use it by paying his share of the expense" (50 N.E. page 262). In such a case, it was said by the court: "It was not and could not then be known who would build, or who was to pay when the wall was used. The agreement was wholly prospective, and its purpose was to impose upon the land of each, and not upon either personally, the burden of a future party wall, and to secure to the land, and thus to its subsequent owners, a corresponding right to the use of the wall by paying one-half of its value. * * * In that case the character of the agreement, its obvious purpose, its prospective provisions, and the situation of the lands when the agreement was made, all concurred in showing an intent that its covenants should run with the land, and clearly justified the court in so holding" (50 N.E. page 262).

Looking at the problem presented in this case from the same point of view and stressing the intent and substantial effect of the covenant rather than its form, it seems clear that the covenant may properly be said to touch and concern the land of the defendant and its burden should run with the land. True, it calls for payment of a sum of money to be expended for "public purposes" upon land other than the land conveyed by Neponsit Realty Company to plaintiff's predecessor in title. By that conveyance the grantee, however, obtained not only title to particular lots, but an easement or right of common enjoyment with other property owners in roads, beaches, public parks or spaces and improvements in the same tract. For full enjoyment in common by the defendant and other property owners of these easements or rights, the roads and public places must be maintained. In order that the burden of maintaining public improvements should rest upon the land benefited by the improvements, the grantor exacted from the grantee of the land with its appurtenant easement or right of enjoyment a covenant that the burden of paying the cost should be inseparably attached to the land which enjoys the benefit. It is plain that any distinction or definition which would exclude such a covenant from the classification of covenants which "touch" or "concern" the land would be based on form and not on substance.

Another difficulty remains. Though between the grantor and the grantee there was privity of estate, the covenant provides that its benefit shall run to the assigns of the grantor who "may include a Property Owners' Association which may hereafter be organized for the purposes referred to in this paragraph." The plaintiff has been organized to receive the sums payable by the property owners and to expend them for the benefit of such owners. Various definitions have been formulated of "privity of estate" in connection with covenants that run with the land, but none of such definitions seems to cover the relationship between the plaintiff and the defendant in this case. The plaintiff has not succeeded to the ownership of any property of the grantor. It does not appear that it ever had title to the streets or public places upon which charges which are payable to it must be expended. It does not appear that it owns any other property in the residential tract to which any easement or right of enjoyment in such property is appurtenant. It is created solely to act as the assignee of the benefit of the covenant, and it has no interest of its own in the enforcement of the covenant.

The arguments that under such circumstances the plaintiff has no right of action to enforce a covenant running with the land are all based upon a distinction between the corporate property owners association and the property owners for whose benefit the association has been formed. If that distinction may be ignored, then the basis of the arguments is destroyed. How far privity of estate in technical form is necessary to enforce in equity a restrictive covenant upon the use of land, presents an interesting question. Enforcement of such covenants rests upon equitable principles (Tulk v. Moxhay, 2 Phillips, 774; Trustees of Columbia College v. Lynch, 70 N.Y. 440; Korn v. Campbell, 85 N.E. 687 (N.Y.)), and at times, at least, the violation "of the restrictive covenant may be restrained at the suit of one who owns property or for whose benefit the restriction was established, irrespective of whether there were privity either of estate or of contract between the parties, or whether an action at law were maintainable." Chesebro v. Moers, 134 N.E. 842, 843 (N.Y.). The covenant in this case does not fall exactly within any classification of "restrictive" covenants, which have been enforced in this State, and no right to enforce even a restrictive covenant has been sustained in this State where the plaintiff did not own property which would benefit by such enforcement so that some of the elements of an equitable servitude are present. In some jurisdictions it has been held that no action may be maintained without such elements. But cf. VanSant v. Rose, 103 N.E. 194 (Ill.). We do not attempt to decide now how far the rule of Trustees of Columbia College v. Lynch, supra, will be carried, or to formulate a definite rule as to when, or

even whether, covenants in a deed will be enforced, upon equitable principles, against subsequent purchasers with notice, at the suit of a party
without privity of contract or estate. Cf. Equitable Rights and Liabilities of
Strangers to a Contract, by Harlan F. Stone, 18 Columbia Law Review, 291.
There is no need to resort to such a rule if the courts may look behind the
corporate form of the plaintiff.

The corporate plaintiff has been formed as a convenient instrument by
which the property owners may advance their common interests. We do not
ignore the corporate form when we recognize that the Neponsit Property
Owners' Association, Inc., is acting as the agent or representative of the
Neponsit property owners. As we have said in another case: when Neponsit
Property Owners' Association, Inc., "was formed, the property owners were
expected to, and have looked to that organization as the medium through
which enjoyment of their common right might be preserved equally for all."
Matter of City of New York, Public Beach, Borough of Queens, 199 N.E. 5,
9 (N.Y.). Under the conditions thus presented we said: "It may be difficult,
or even impossible to classify into recognized categories the nature of the
interest of the membership corporation and its members in the land. The
corporate entity cannot be disregarded, nor can the separate interests of
the members of the corporation" (199 N.E. page 8). Only blind adherence
to an ancient formula devised to meet entirely different conditions could
constrain the court to hold that a corporation formed as a medium for the
enjoyment of common rights of property owners owns no property which
would benefit by enforcement of common rights and has no cause of action
in equity to enforce the covenant upon which such common rights depend.
Every reason which in other circumstances may justify the ancient formula
may be urged in support of the conclusion that the formula should not be
applied in this case. In substance if not in form the covenant is a restrictive
covenant which touches and concerns the defendant's land, and in substance, if not in form, there is privity of estate between the plaintiff and the
defendant. * * *

The order should be affirmed, with costs, and the certified questions
answered in the affirmative.

NOTES AND QUESTIONS

1. The action here is to foreclose a lien on the property in order to
secure payment of a debt. Foreclosure was originally regarded as a proceeding in equity. Why then does the court apply the real covenant doctrine as
opposed to the equitable servitude theory of *Tulk v. Moxhay?*

2. Covenants in leases run to successors of the original landlord or
tenant if (1) the landlord and tenant intend that they will run; and (2) the
covenant is one that "touches and concerns" the land. The court here adds
a third requirement: that there be "privity of estate" between the party
claiming the benefit of the covenant and the party subject to the burden of

the covenant. This is obviously designed to mimic the privity of estate that exists in landlord-tenant law between the landlord and a tenant in possession (Chapter VI). But what function does the privity-of-estate requirement perform here? Would it be better to require that the party to be burdened must have notice of the covenant, as under the theory of equitable servitudes? Does privity of estate serve as a stand-in for a requirement that the benefit of the promise be appurtenant to a particular parcel of land? Does it make sense to restrict running covenants to those that benefit particular land? The English law of equitable servitudes, as it has developed since *Tulk*, limits running covenants to those appurtenant to particular interests in land. See Robert Megarry & William Wade, The Law of Real Property § 16–044, at 1018 (6th ed., Charles Harpum et al., eds., 2000).

3.   The court paraphrases with approval Professor Bigelow's definition of "touch and concern" as a promise that affects "the advantages and the burdens" of the owners of the parcels of land either benefited or burdened by the promise. How helpful is this in singling out those promises respecting land which should run? If the owner of Blackacre promises to cut the hair of the owner of Whiteacre, and the owner of Whiteacre promises in return to pay $10 a month to the owner of Blackacre, would not this affect "the advantages and the burdens" of owning either Blackacre or Whiteacre? Can you formulate a better test for giving content to what it means for a promise to touch and concern the land?

4.   Now that law and equity have merged, the distinction between equitable servitudes and real covenants grounded in the nature of the relief being sought no longer makes any sense. And indeed, there is authority suggesting that one can get damages under an equitable servitude theory and an injunction under a real covenant theory. See Joseph William Singer, Introduction to Property § 6.5 (2d ed. 2005). Most parties want specific performance—an injunction—anyway (*Neponsit* is something of an exceptional case in this regard). Having these two bodies of doctrine does give plaintiffs some flexibility in choosing which path to pursue in seeking enforcement. Let us then restate the elements that must be satisfied under the two approaches to running covenants.

c.   THE REQUIREMENTS FOR COVENANTS TO RUN

The major issue with covenants is whether the benefits and burdens of the deal between the original parties will extend to successors of those parties—whether the benefits and burdens "run with the land." The following diagram may be helpful, in which the original parties (A and B) stand in a relationship to be discussed shortly, called "horizontal" privity (denoted by horizontal arrows), and successors (C1, C2, etc., and D1, D2, etc.) stand in a relationship of "vertical" privity to the original parties, respectively.

Figure 9–9
Running Covenants

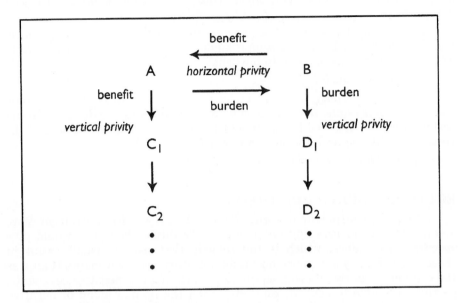

REAL COVENANT THEORY

At law (traditionally in a damages action), for the *burden* of a promise to run, one would have to establish:

(i) *Intent for the burden to run.* This can be by language or inferable from the context. So if A covenants with B, who is allergic to peanuts, that A will not eat peanuts in the backyard, the benefit probably won't run to B's successor unless the context indicates otherwise (for example, B is running an allergy clinic and sells to another allergy clinic).

(ii) *Horizontal privity.* Traditionally a landlord-tenant relationship was required. Later this was expanded to include some common interest, concurrent or successive—or perhaps some other relationship. Many have questioned whether this requirement has real content. This requirement (or lack of it) is illustrated in the following scenario: Two neighbors sign an agreement wherein they both agree to restrict their use of their parcels to residential use and they record. Because they are not in a grantor-grantee relationship (NB: they could have done this with a straw), there is no horizontal privity and so traditionally the burden does not run. Under the new *Restatement* (about which more later), which doesn't require horizontal privity, the burden would run.

(iii) *Vertical privity.* For the burden to run at law, the successor in interest to the person who covenanted for the *burden* must hold the entire durational interest held by the covenantor at the time she made the covenant. In landlord-tenant situations, vertical privity would be present in assignments (where these are determined by whether the whole interest is transferred, see Chapter VI), but not in a sublease.

(iv) *Touch and concern.* The covenant must touch and concern the land, as discussed in the cases. As we will see this requirement is abandoned in the new *Restatement*, but no court has yet followed this proposed approach.

At law, for the *benefit* of a promise to run, there are fewer requirements, presumably because a selling landowner would have an incentive to advertise benefits, as opposed to burdens:

(i) *Intent for the benefit to run.*

(ii) *Vertical privity.* For the benefit to run, the successor need only succeed to *some estate*, not necessarily an estate of the same duration as the covenantor's (so this is a less stringent requirement than in the case of the vertical privity required for burden to run).

(iii) *Touch and concern.*

EQUITABLE SERVITUDE THEORY

At equity, courts starting with *Tulk v. Moxhay,* infra, have been more accommodating in granting enforcement. Traditionally equity would give specific performance, which is the remedy that parties usually want in these cases. Equity was more hospitable to affirmative covenants than was the common law. By allowing equitable enforcement of negative covenants, parties were able to expand somewhat upon the limited menu of negative easements (light, air, subjacent/lateral support, flow of artificial stream).

For the *burden* of a promise to run at equity, there must be:

(i) *Intent.*

(ii) *Notice.* This is characteristic of equity. If the covenant is in the deed given to the grantee, there is no problem enforcing it against the grantee. If it is not in the deed, then actual or inquiry notice must be present. Inquiry notice is furnished by facts that would make a reasonable person inquire further and find the covenant. With the advent of recording acts, constructive notice through filing in the land records is another avenue for satisfying the notice requirement.

(iii) *Touch and concern.*

For the *benefit* of a promise to run at equity, there must be:

(i) *Intent.*

(ii) *Touch and concern.*

Can you see why notice would not be required for the benefit to run at equity?

THE *THIRD RESTATEMENT*

The American Law Institute's *Restatement (Third) of Property: Servitudes* (2000) (hereinafter "Restatement") relaxes some of these requirements. By and large, it takes a more contractarian approach to servitudes. The *Restatement* advocates abolishing the traditional property-law requirements for the running of servitudes, such as the touch and concern doctrine and the privity requirements. In place of the traditional requirements for enforcing servitudes against successors that made the running of a servitude exceptional, the *Restatement* makes enforceability the default, subject to limitations based on requirements of writing or violation of public policy. Broadly speaking, this would give servitudes a strongly contractarian flavor, with writing requirements and exceptions for violations of public policy, unconscionability, and the like. These exceptions are perhaps stronger than in current contract law but differ from them mostly in degree.

The *Restatement* provides for a baseline for the creation of servitudes that is grounded in contract and party intent: "A servitude is created (1) if the owner of the property to be burdened (a) enters into a contract or makes a conveyance intended to create a servitude that complies with § 2.7 (Statute of Frauds) or § 2.9 (exception to the Statute of Frauds) ..." Restatement (Third) of Property: Servitudes § 2.1 (2000). The associated commentary makes clear the motivation for this approach:

> This Chapter's [Chapter 2, Creation of Servitudes] treatment of servitude creation reflects the basic position that servitudes are useful devices that people ought to be able to use without artificial constraints. The primary function of the law is to ascertain and give effect to the intent of the parties, not to force them into arbitrary transactional forms. If they meet minimal formal requirements, their expressed intent is effective to create a servitude, unless the transaction violates a constitutional, statutory, or public-policy norm.

Id. Introductory Note at 49.

The *Restatement* is, if anything, clearer in making validity conform to a contract-like rather than a property-like vision of servitudes:

> A servitude created as provided in Chapter 2 is valid unless it is illegal or unconstitutional or violates public policy.
>
> Servitudes that are invalid because they violate public policy include, but are not limited to:
>
> (1) a servitude that is arbitrary, spiteful, or capricious;
>
> (2) a servitude that unreasonably burdens a fundamental constitutional right;
>
> (3) a servitude that imposes an unreasonable restraint on alienation under § 3.4 or § 3.5;
>
> (4) a servitude that imposes an unreasonable restraint on trade or competition under § 3.6; and
>
> (5) a servitude that is unconscionable under § 3.7.

Restatement (Third) of Property: Servitudes § 3.1 (2000). Comment a, entitled "Historical note and rationale" states:

> This section applies the modern principle of freedom of contract to creation of servitudes. The Restatement of Contracts explains the principle: "In general, parties may contract as they wish, and courts will enforce their agreements without passing on their substance.... The principle of freedom of contract is rooted in the notion that it is in the public interest to recognize that individuals have broad powers to order their own affairs."

Id. § 3.1 cmt. a. (footnote omitted, citing to Restatement Second, Contracts, Introductory Note to Chapter 8.). As noted earlier, this means that, as under contract law, servitudes are presumed valid. Id. ("The effect of the rule is to shift to the party claiming invalidity of a servitude the burden to establish that it is illegal or unconstitutional, or violates public policy.''). Id.

As of this writing no court has adopted this approach, to the annoyance of the Reporter. See Susan F. French, Symposium on Servitudes, Part II, Can Covenants Not to Sue, Covenants Against Competition and Spite Covenants Run with Land? Comparing Results Under the Touch or Concern Doctrine and the Restatement Third, Property (Servitudes), 38 Real Prop. Prob. & Tr. J. 267 (2003). Some commentators have argued that the older doctrines serve a useful purpose in allowing courts to police servitudes more closely. See, e.g., A. Dan Tarlock, Touch and Concern is Dead, Long Live the Doctrine, 77 Neb. L. Rev. 804 (1998); Jeffrey E. Stake, Toward an Economic Understanding of Touch and Concern, 1988 Duke L.J. 925.

Eagle Enterprises, Inc. v. Gross

Court of Appeals of New York, 1976.
349 N.E.2d 816.

■ GABRIELLI, JUSTICE. In 1951, Orchard Hill Realties, Inc., a subdivider and developer, conveyed certain property in the subdivision of Orchard Hill in Orange County to William and Pauline Baum. The deed to the Baums contained the following provision:

> The party of the first part shall supply to the party of the second part, seasonably from May 1st to October 1st, of each year, water for domestic use only, from the well located on other property of the party of the first part, and the party of the second part agrees to take said water and to pay the party of the first part, a fee of Thirty-five ($35.00) dollars per year, for said water so supplied.

In addition, the deed also contained the following:

> It is expressly provided that the covenants herein contained shall run with the land * * * and shall bind and shall enure to the benefit of the heirs, distributees, successors, legal representatives and assigns of the respective parties hereto.

Appellant is the successor in interest of Orchard Hill Realties, Inc., and respondent, after a series of intervening conveyances, is the successor in interest of the Baums. The deed conveying title to respondent does not contain the aforementioned covenant to purchase water and, in fact, none of the deeds following the original deed to the Baums contained the mutual promises regarding water supply. While some of the deeds in the chain of title from Baum contained a provision that they were made subject to the restrictions in the deed from Orchard Hill Realties to Baum, the deed to respondents contained no such covenants, restrictions or "subject to" clause.

According to the stipulated facts, respondent has refused to accept and pay for water offered by appellant since he has constructed his own well to service what is now a year-round dwelling. Appellant, therefore, instituted this action to collect the fee specified in the covenant (contained only in the original deed to Baum) for the supply of water which, appellant contends, respondent is bound to accept. The action was styled as one "for goods sold and delivered" even though respondent did not utilize any of appellant's water. Two of the lower courts found that the covenant "ran" with the land and, hence, was binding upon respondent as successor to the Baums, but the Appellate Division reversed and held that the covenant could not be enforced against respondent. We must now decide whether the promise of the original grantees to accept and make payment for a seasonal water supply from the well of their grantor is enforceable against subsequent grantees and may be said to "run with the land". We agree with the determination of the Appellate Division and affirm its order.

Regardless of the express recital in a deed that a covenant will run with the land, a promise to do an affirmative act contained in a deed is generally not binding upon subsequent grantees of the promisor unless certain well-defined and long-established legal requisites are satisfied (Nicholson v. 300 Broadway Realty Corp., 164 N.E.2d 832, 834 (N.Y.); Neponsit Prop. Owners' Assn. v. Emigrant Ind. Sav. Bank, 15 N.E.2d 793, 794–95 (N.Y.); see, also, Morgan Lake Co. v. New York, New Haven & Hartford R.R. Co., 186 N.E. 685, 687 (N.Y.); Miller v. Clary, 103 N.E. 1114 (N.Y.); Mygatt v. Coe, 42 N.E. 17 (N.Y.); 13 N.Y.Jur., Covenants and Restrictions, § 12, pp. 252–253). In the landmark Neponsit case (supra), we adopted and clarified the following test, originating in the early English decisions, for the enforceability of affirmative covenants (cf. Spencer's Case, 77 Eng.Rep. 72 (1583)), and reaffirmed the requirements that in order for a covenant to run with the land, it must be shown that:

> (1) The original grantee and grantor must have intended that the covenant run with the land.

> (2) There must exist "privity of estate" between the party claiming the benefit of the covenant and the right to enforce it and the party upon whom the burden of the covenant is to be imposed.

> (3) The covenant must be deemed to "touch and concern" the land with which it runs.

Even though the parties to the original deed expressly state in the instrument that the covenant will run with the land, such a recital is insufficient to render the covenant enforceable against subsequent grantees if the other requirements for the running of an affirmative covenant are not met. The rule is settled that "[r]egardless of the intention of the parties, a covenant will run with the land and will be enforceable against a subsequent purchaser of the land at the suit of one who claims the benefit of the covenant, only if the covenant complies with certain legal requirements" (Neponsit, supra, 15 N.E.2d p. 795; see, also, Morgan Lake Co. v. New York, New Haven & Hartford R.R. Co., supra, 262 186 N.E. p. 686). Thus, although the intention of the original parties here is clear and privity of estate exists, the covenant must still satisfy the requirement that it "touch and concern" the land.

It is this third prong of the tripartite rule which presents the obstacle to appellant's position and which was the focus of our decisions in *Neponsit* and *Nicholson v. 300 Broadway Realty Corp.* (164 N.E. 2d 832, 834, supra). *Neponsit* first sought to breathe substance and meaning into the ritualistic rubric that an affirmative covenant must "touch and concern" the land in order to be enforceable against subsequent grantees. Observing that it would be difficult to devise a rule which would operate mechanically to resolve all situations which might arise, Judge Lehman observed that "the distinction between covenants which run with land and covenants which are personal, must depend upon the effect of the covenant on the legal rights which otherwise would flow from the ownership of land and which are connected with the land" (Neponsit, 15 N.E.2d p. 796). Thus, he posed as the key question whether "the covenant in purpose and effect substantially alter[s] these rights" (15 N.E.2d p. 796). In *Nicholson*, this court reaffirmed the soundness of the reasoning in *Neponsit* as "a more realistic and pragmatic approach" (supra, 164 N.E.2d p. 835).

The covenants in issue in *Neponsit* required the owners of property in a development to pay an annual charge for the maintenance of roads, paths, parks, beaches, sewers and other public improvements. The court concluded that the covenant substantially affected the promisor's legal interest in his property since the latter received an easement in common and a right of enjoyment in the public improvements for which contribution was received by all the landowners in the subdivision (supra, 15 N.E.2d p. 797).

A close examination of the covenant in the case before us leads to the conclusion that it does not substantially affect the ownership interest of landowners in the Orchard Hill subdivision. The covenant provides for the supplying of water for only six months of the year; no claim has been advanced by appellant that the lands in the subdivision would be waterless without the water it supplies. Indeed, the facts here point to the converse conclusion since respondent has obtained his own source of water. The record, based on and consisting of an agreed stipulation of facts, does not demonstrate that other property owners in the subdivision would be deprived of water from appellant or that the price of water would become prohibitive for other property owners if respondent terminated appellant's service. Thus, the agreement for the seasonal supply of water does not seem to us to relate in any significant degree to the ownership rights of respondent and the other property owners in the subdivision of Orchard Hill. The landowners in *Neponsit* received an easement in common to utilize public areas in the subdivision; this interest was in the nature of a property right attached to their respective properties. The obligation to receive water from appellant resembles a personal, contractual promise to purchase water rather than a significant interest attaching to respondent's property. It should be emphasized that the question whether a covenant is so closely related to the use of the land that it should be deemed to "run" with the land is one of degree, dependent on the particular circumstances of a case (Neponsit, supra, 15 N.E.2d p. 796). Here, the meager record before us is lacking and woefully insufficient to establish that the covenant "touches and concerns" the land, as we have interpreted that requirement.

There is an additional reason why we are reluctant to enforce this covenant for the seasonal supply of water. The affirmative covenant is disfavored in the law because of the fear that this type of obligation imposes an "undue restriction on alienation or an onerous burden in perpetuity" (Nicholson v. 300 Broadway Realty Corp.,164 N.E.2d 832, 835, supra). In *Nicholson*, the covenant to supply heat was not interdicted by this concern because it was conditioned upon the continued existence of the buildings on both the promisor's and the promisee's properties. Similarly, in *Neponsit*, the original 1917 deed containing the covenant to pay an annual charge for the maintenance of public areas expressly provided for its own lapse in 1940. Here, no outside limitation has been placed on the obligation to purchase water from appellant. Thus, the covenant falls prey to the criticism that it creates a burden in perpetuity, and purports to bind all future owners, regardless of the use to which the land is put. Such a result militates strongly against its enforcement. On this ground also, we are of the opinion that the covenant should not be enforced as an exception to the general rule prohibiting the "running" of affirmative covenants. * * *

Order affirmed.

NOTES AND QUESTIONS

1. Does *Eagle Enterprises* clarify the legal meaning of "touch and concern" in any respect beyond the exposition in *Neponsit*? Why doesn't the promise to take water from the common well in return for a fee satisfy Professor Bigelow's definition—altering the advantages and burdens of owning particular tracts of land—endorsed in *Neponsit*?

2. Why did this covenant fail the touch and concern test? If there were visible pipes to bring the water to the land, would that serve as notice to successors? What if every house had a pipe leading to the central source? Is the problem that the later deeds did not contain the covenant? What if the developer had filed a plan for the entire subdivision containing the restrictions? Does *Eagle Enterprises* suggest that touch and concern functions as a kind of changed circumstances doctrine? For discussion, see Stake, supra.

3. What if each of the owners had also covenanted not to dig wells? Would the covenant to purchase water then touch and concern?

4. Should servitudes on personal property run to successive owners? The running of servitudes is more of an issue in the case of land because it lasts much longer than typical personal property. The law has had some suspicion of servitudes on personal property, often without a clear articulation for the reasons. See Zechariah Chafee, Jr., Equitable Servitudes on Chattels, 41 Harv. L. Rev. 945 (1928). Unlike land, where servitudes address spillovers that affect identifiable neighbors, personal property

servitudes often restrict use or the terms of resale of an item of personal property. Mostly the law has regulated these in terms of antitrust. See Dr. Miles Medical Co. v. Park, 220 U.S. 373 (1911). The issue of servitudes on personal property has gained more prominence recently with the increased importance of intellectual property. See Glen O. Robinson, Personal Property Servitudes, 71 U. Chi. L. Rev. 1449 (2004). The arrangement in *ProCD v. Zeidenberg*, see Chapter III, was in effect a sale of the software coupled with a servitude; the seller intended the restriction on the use of the software to bind any successor owner of the software as well. Patent owners sometimes impose single-use only restrictions that are meant to override a default license in the buyer to repair an item. Should holders of IP rights be able to contract for servitudes that will run with some property, tangible or intangible? An alternative to such servitudes would be to license the IP rights themselves and include the restrictions in the terms of the license. If so, should the result be any different?

d.   NOTICE AND THE COMMON PLAN

One of the requirements for covenants to run at equity is notice. If A personally deals with B, notice is an automatic by-product. In subdivisions, though, covenants trace back to a deal between the developer and the original purchasers, not directly between the purchasers themselves. Such a procedure saves greatly on transaction costs if what is desired is a set of interlocking identical mutual covenants. For a group of 100 parcels, the developer can substitute 100 similar covenants as part of the package on offer, as opposed to the 4,950 deals required for each parcel owner to covenant with each of the 99 others. Things can still go wrong, as in the following case.

Sanborn v. McLean

Supreme Court of Michigan, 1925.
206 N.W. 496.

■ WIEST, J. Defendant Christina McLean owns the west 35 feet of lot 86 of Green Lawn subdivision, at the northeast corner of Collingwood avenue and Second boulevard, in the city of Detroit, upon which there is a dwelling house, occupied by herself and her husband, defendant John A. McLean. The house fronts Collingwood avenue. At the rear of the lot is an alley. Mrs. McLean derived title from her husband, and, in the course of the opinion, we will speak of both as defendants. Mr. and Mrs. McLean started to erect a gasoline filling station at the rear end of their lot, and they and their contractor, William S. Weir, were enjoined by decree from doing so and bring the issues before us by appeal. Mr. Weir will not be further mentioned in the opinion.

Collingwood avenue is a high grade residence street between Woodward avenue and Hamilton boulevard, with single, double, and apartment houses, and plaintiffs, who are owners of land adjoining and in the vicinity of defendants' land, and who trace title, as do defendants, to the proprietors of the subdivision, claim that the proposed gasoline station will be a nuisance per se, is in violation of the general plan fixed for use of all lots on the street for residence purposes only, as evidenced by restrictions upon 53 of the 91 lots fronting on Collingwood avenue, and that defendants' lot is subject to a reciprocal negative easement barring a use so detrimental to the enjoyment and value of its neighbors. Defendants insist that no restrictions appear in their chain of title and they purchased without notice of any reciprocal negative easement, and deny that a gasoline station is a nuisance per se. We find no occasion to pass upon the question of nuisance, as the case can be decided under the rule of reciprocal negative easement.

This subdivision was planned strictly for residence purposes, except lots fronting Woodward avenue and Hamilton boulevard. The 91 lots on Collingwood avenue were platted in 1891, designed for and each one sold solely for residence purposes, and residences have been erected upon all of the lots. Is defendants' lot subject to a reciprocal negative easement? If the owner of two or more lots, so situated as to bear the relation, sells one with restrictions of benefit to the land retained, the servitude becomes mutual, and, during the period of restraint, the owner of the lot or lots retained can do nothing forbidden to the owner of the lot sold. For want of a better descriptive term this is styled a reciprocal negative easement. It runs with the land sold by virtue of express fastening and abides with the land retained until loosened by expiration of its period of service or by events working its destruction. It is not personal to owners, but operative upon use of the land by any owner having actual or constructive notice thereof. It is an easement passing its benefits and carrying its obligations to all purchasers of land, subject to its affirmative or negative mandates. It originates for mutual benefit and exists with vigor sufficient to work its ends. It must start with a common owner. Reciprocal negative easements are never retroactive; the very nature of their origin forbids. They arise, if at all, out of a benefit accorded land retained, by restrictions upon neighboring land sold by a common owner. Such a scheme of restriction must start with a common owner; it cannot arise and fasten upon one lot by reason of other lot owners conforming to a general plan. If a reciprocal negative easement attached to defendants' lot, it was fastened thereto while in the hands of the common owner of it and neighboring lots by way of sale of other lots with restrictions beneficial at that time to it. This leads to inquiry as to what lots, if any, were sold with restrictions by the common owner before the sale of defendants' lot. While the proofs cover another avenue, we need consider sales only on Collingwood.

Figure 9–10
Sanborn Fire Insurance Map of Area in *Sanborn v. McLean*

(note the structure marked "Filling Station" at the back of 158-162 Collingwood Avenue)

LAWRENCE   AV.

COLLINGWOOD   AV.

Source: 9 Sanborn Map Co., Insurance Maps of Detroit, Michigan, No.12 (1925)

Source: 9 Sanborn Map Co., Insurance Maps of Detroit, Michigan, No. 12 (1925).

December 28, 1892, Robert J. and Joseph R. McLaughlin, who were then evidently owners of the lots on Collingwood avenue, deeded lots 37 to 41 and 58 to 62, inclusive, with the following restrictions:

> No residence shall be erected upon said premises which shall cost less than $2,500, and nothing but residences shall be erected upon said premises. Said residences shall front on Helene (now Collingwood) avenue and be placed no nearer than 20 feet from the front street line.

July 24, 1893, the McLaughlins conveyed lots 17 to 21 and 78 to 82, both inclusive, and lot 98 with the same restrictions. Such restrictions were imposed for the benefit of the lands held by the grantors to carry out the scheme of a residential district, and a restrictive negative easement attached to the lots retained, and title to lot 86 was then in the McLaughlins. Defendants' title, through mesne conveyances, runs back to a deed by the McLaughlins dated September 7, 1893, without restrictions mentioned therein. Subsequent deeds to other lots were executed by the McLaughlins, some with restrictions and some without. Previous to September 7, 1893, a reciprocal negative easement had attached to lot 86 by acts of the owners, as before mentioned, and such easement is still attached and may now be enforced by plaintiffs, provided defendants, at the time of their purchase, had knowledge, actual or constructive, thereof. The plaintiffs run back with their title, as do defendants, to a common owner. This common owner, as before stated, by restrictions upon lots sold, had burdened all the lots retained with reciprocal restrictions. Defendants' lot and plaintiff Sanborn's lot, next thereto, were held by such common owner, burdened with a reciprocal negative easement, and, when later sold to separate parties, remained burdened therewith, and right to demand observance thereof passed to each purchaser with notice of the easement. The restrictions were upon defendants' lot while it was in the hands of the common owners, and abstract of title to defendants' lot showed the common owners, and the record showed deeds of lots in the plat restricted to perfect and carry out the general plan and resulting in a reciprocal negative easement upon defendants' lot and all lots within its scope, and defendants and their predecessors in title were bound by constructive notice under our recording acts. The original plan was repeatedly declared in subsequent sales of lots by restrictions in the deeds, and, while some lots sold were not so restricted, the purchasers thereof, in every instance, observed the general plan and purpose of the restrictions in building residences. For upward of 30 years the united efforts of all persons interested have carried out the common purpose of making and keeping all the lots strictly for residences, and defendants are the first to depart therefrom.

When Mr. McLean purchased on contract in 1910 or 1911, there was a partly built dwelling house on lot 86, which he completed and now occupies. He had an abstract of title which he examined and claims he was told by the grantor that the lot was unrestricted. Considering the character of use made of all the lots open to a view of Mr. McLean when he purchased, we think, he was put thereby to inquiry, beyond asking his grantor, whether there were restrictions. He had an abstract showing the subdivision and that lot 86 had 97 companions. He could not avoid noticing the strictly uniform residence character given the lots by the expensive dwellings thereon, and the least inquiry would have quickly developed the fact that lot 86 was subjected to a reciprocal negative easement, and he could finish his house, and, like the others, enjoy the benefits of the easement. We do not say Mr. McLean should have asked his neighbors about restrictions, but we do say that with the notice he had from a view of the premises on the street, clearly indicating the residences were built and the lots occupied in strict accordance with a general plan, he was put to inquiry, and, had he inquired, he would have found of record the reason for such general conformation, and the benefits thereof serving the owners of lot 86 and the obligations running with such service and available to adjacent lot owners to prevent a departure from the general plan by an owner of lot 86.

While no case appears to be on all fours with the one at bar, the principles we have stated, and the conclusions announced, are supported by Allen v. City of Detroit, 133 N. W. 317 (Mich.); McQuade v. Wilcox, 183 N. W. 771 (Mich.); French v. White Star Refining Co., 201 N. W. 444 (Mich.); Silberman v. Uhrlaub, 102 N. Y. S. 299 (N.Y. App. Div.); Boyden v. Roberts, 111 N. W. 701 (Wis.); Howland v. Andrus, 83 A. 982 (N.J. Eq.).

We notice the decree in the circuit directed that the work done on the building be torn down. If the portion of the building constructed can be utilized for any purpose within the restrictions, it need not be destroyed.

With this modification, the decree in the circuit is affirmed, with costs to plaintiffs.

NOTES AND QUESTIONS

1. The court here refers to the promises as "negative reciprocal easements," but what it is talking about would more commonly be called covenants or equitable servitudes today. You will find that the terminology used by courts has some variability here (as elsewhere).

2. Some courts do not go as far as the Michigan Supreme Court in recognizing the common plan doctrine. Some would not imply reciprocal negative easements at all, see, e.g., Riley v. Bear Creek Planning Comm., 551 P.2d 1213 (Cal. 1976), and others require a high proportion of the lots to have been sold with the restrictions, see, e.g., Whitton v. Clark, 151 A. 305 (Conn. 1930). The language in *Sanborn* if taken literally would imply a restriction based on the sale of one lot with the restriction. Another variable is the degree of uniformity of the restrictions required for a court to find a common scheme or plan. See Restatement (Third) of Property: Servitudes § 2.14 (2000), (allowing common plan to be found even with some variation in restrictions). Notice that the likelihood that a purchaser will have notice is greatly increased if her individual deed makes reference to a recorded subdivision map. Restrictions incorporated in this way will satisfy even the strictest courts' standards for notice.

3. Recall that restrictions not appearing in the land records make title searches more difficult. The restrictions on neighboring parcels here were not in the McLeans' chain of title. Instead, in the court's view, Mr. McLean had inquiry notice based on the uniformity of the neighborhood. If such uniformity could arise spontaneously, would there then be a need for covenants or for zoning (which did not exist at the time this case arose)? Should the subsequent rise of zoning affect a court's willingness to find inquiry notice in this scenario?

e.   CONSERVATION EASEMENTS

Perhaps the fastest growing type of covenant in the United States is the conservation easement. According to one recent estimate, the amount of land in the United States subject to conservation easements exploded from very little in 1980 to over 5 million acres by 2003. Land Trust Alliance, National Land Trust Census, Nov. 18, 2004 at http://www.land trustalliance.org/census/index.shtml. Conservation easements are servitudes that restrict the future development of land. The most common type of restriction prohibits subdivision and commercial development but permits existing agricultural and residential uses. Conservation easements come in a wide variety of forms, however, ranging from prohibitions on cutting timber to requiring the preservation of historic building facades.

The term "conservation easement" is something of a misnomer in that these restrictions are more accurately classified as negative covenants in gross. They are negative because they prohibit the servient landowner from engaging in certain kinds of activities; they are probably more accurately described as covenants rather than easements because they do not fit any of the traditional four categories of negative easements; and they are in gross because the power to enforce the restriction is typically given not to another landowner but to a unit of local government or a charitable land trust like the Nature Conservancy. A negative covenant in gross probably would not run with the land at common law. It could not be enforced as a real covenant, since the privity requirements would not be met. And courts generally refused to enforce covenants in gross as equitable servitudes; only appurtenant covenants were eligible for enforcement against successors with notice. See Gerald Korngold, Privately Held Conservation Servitudes: A Policy Analysis in the Context of In Gross Real Covenants and Easements, 63 Tex. L. Rev. 433, 470–79 (1984). Conservation easements therefore exist only because of legislation specifically authorizing them. Today virtually all states have enacted conservation easement laws, about half of which are based on the Uniform Conservation Easement Act promulgated in 1981. See Restatement (Third) of Property, Servitudes § 1.3, cmt. a & Statutory Note. In this sense, conservation easements are another example of a new form of property being created by legislation, consistent with the idea of the *numerus clausus*.

There appear to be multiple forces driving the rapid proliferation of conservation easements. First, many owners of land with significant aesthetic and environmental value worry about these lands succumbing to pressure for subdivision or commercial development. Of course, as long as the owners are living and hold the land in fee simple, they can reject the entreaties of developers. But many owners are apprehensive that the family farm, or woodlot, or waterfront retreat will be sold by their heirs or otherwise fall into the hands of developers after they die. A perpetual conservation easement is designed to "give peace-of-mind to current landowners worried about the future of a beloved property." The Nature Conservancy, Conservation Easements: All About Easements, at http://nature.org/aboutus/howwework/conservationmethods/privatelands/conservationeasements/about/allabout/html. In this sense, the impulse behind the movement for conservation easements is reminiscent of the aspirations of the English landed gentry to keep their country houses in the family in perpetuity.

Second, there are significant tax benefits to donating a conservation easement to a local unit of government or a charitable land trust. It is no accident that the boom in conservation easements started after the Internal Revenue Code was amended in 1976 specifically to permit tax-deductible donations of such interests. See IRC § 170(h). The instrument of donation must provide that the land is being restricted for one of several general purposes: outdoor recreation, wildlife habitat, scenic enjoyment, agricultural use, or historical importance. And the donation must be "perpetual." If these requirements are met, the landowner can deduct from her income taxes the difference between the appraised value of the land in an unrestricted state and the value of the land as restricted. Meanwhile, the landowner can continue to own the land in fee simple, pass it to heirs, or even sell it, subject to the restriction. Many states also provide that landowners are entitled to a reduction in property taxes to reflect the lower assessed value of the property after the restriction is in place. There are no reliable data on the total amount of deductions claimed for conservation easements, but according to one estimate "the charitable value of claimed donations nationwide was in the neighborhood of $20.7 billion from 2001 to 2003." Dominic P. Parker, Conservation Easements: A Closer Look at Federal Tax Policy 10 (PERC Policy Series, October 2005).

Third, many environmentalists, particularly those concerned about preserving local environmental values, have seen conservation easements as a potentially powerful tool in combating new commercial development. Traditional regulatory tools for fighting developers, such as restrictive zoning laws, encounter fierce resistance from particular landowners and developers and generate expensive litigation over regulatory takings claims (see Chapter XII). Conservation easements are the product of a voluntary agreement between a landowner and a unit of local government or a land trust, and hence encounter little or no opposition. Moreover, insofar as conservation easements are financed, at least in significant part, by off-budget tax benefits given to landowners, they do not encounter the same type of public scrutiny that would be given to direct government acquisition of new parkland or nature preserves.

The rapid emergence of conservation easements has not gone unnoticed, and is beginning to generate critical commentary. Julia Mahoney has written that the perpetual nature of conservation easements raises some of the same concerns about dead hand control we have seen in other contexts, such as the rule against restraints on alienation and the Rule against Perpetuities. See Julia D. Mahoney, Perpetual Restrictions on Land and the Problem of the Future, 88 Va. L. Rev. 739 (2002). She writes that conservation easements reflect a kind of hubris that "the ability of the present generation to predict the needs and preferences of future generations is so good that the present generation should save their descendents trouble and transaction costs by making a substantial number of land use decisions for them." Id. at 744. In addition, making easements perpetual presupposes that decisions about land use are irreversible, such that "the present generation represents nature's last or near-to-last chance, because once land is developed, it will never or almost never go back to being undeveloped." Id. at 745. This, she says, is contrary to historical experience, and reflects naiveté about "the instability of the categories of 'development' and 'preservation.'" Id.

The use of generous tax deductions to spur conservation easements has also encountered criticism as leading to abuses and poor planning. Despite safeguards in the tax code and regulations, many donors have overvalued conservation easements and taken deductions out of line with public benefits. See, e.g., Timothy Lindstrom, Income Tax Aspects of Conservation Easements, 5 Wyo. L. Rev. 1, 17–18 (2005). On the benefit side, an expose by two reporters for the *Washington Post* reported that conservation easements have been used to generate tax deductions for real estate developers in circumstances where it is doubtful that any public benefit is created. See Joe Stephens & David B. Ottaway, Developers Find Payoff in Preservation, Washington Post, Dec. 21, 2003, at A1. For example, some developers have built homes around a golf course and have then deducted the value of a donated conservation easement in the golf course fairways. Others have pointed out the tax deduction strategy results in a pattern of expenditures that favors horse farms, trophy ranches, Nantucket cottages, and other getaways of the wealthy, which may not be the best way to allocate resources for conservation of environmentally and historically significant resources. For example, preserving land for hiking or as habitat may require the preservation of multiple contiguous parcels of land, whereas conservation easements generate only a scattershot pattern of preserved lands.

Finally, some traditional environmentalists have objected to conservation easements on the ground that they deprive the public of any input into the development of conservation policy. See, e.g., John D. Echeverria, Revive the Legacy of Land Use Controls, 2 Open Space 12 (Summer 2004). Conservation easements represent a strategy of providing a type of public good (e.g., environmental amenities) by private contract. This largely eliminates any role for public input or oversight into decisions about what to preserve and what sorts of public access will be provided to the resources subject to preservation controls. Since the public is paying for the conservation, both directly through tax subsidies and indirectly through foregone development opportunities, the public should have some say into the process. Instead, conservation easements are created through private negotiations between landowners and land trusts, typically with no notice to the public even after they have been created.

NOTES AND QUESTIONS

1. Although conservation easements are becoming increasingly widespread, so far they have generated very little litigation. Why is this? What sorts of issues might you expect to arise in the future that could generate litigation?

2. Although the major objections to conservation easements relate to their perpetual nature, the use of tax subsidies, and the lack of public

oversight, these objections are interrelated. For example, the Internal Revenue Code provides that a donation will be deductible only if the easement is "perpetual." Why might Congress be reluctant to allow deductions for time-limited conservation easements? The IRS will allow an easement to be extinguished in the future if a change in conditions makes it "impractical or impossible" for the easement to serve its intended purpose, and if the funds acquired in extinguishing the easement are used for a conservation purpose similar to the one initially intended by the easement. Treas. Reg. § 1.170A–14(c)(2). Should a citizens' group have standing to intervene in a proceeding before the IRS to challenge either a finding that an easement had become "impractical or impossible" or the proposed use of the proceeds? See Carol Necole Brown, A Time to Preserve: A Call for Formal Private–Party Rights in Perpetual Conservation Easements, 40 Ga. L. Rev. 85 (2005) (advocating a broad right of private party standing).

3. Would you favor imposing some time limitation on conservation easements? What about subjecting such easements to the equitable doctrine of cy pres (Chapter VI)? See Nancy A. McLaughlin, Rethinking the Perpetual Nature of Conservation Easements, 29 Harv. Envtl. L. Rev. 421 (2005). Would these reforms reduce the incentives of persons to make donations of such easements?

f. TERMINATION OF COVENANTS

Bolotin v. Rindge

District Court of Appeal, Second District, Division 3, California, 1964.
41 Cal.Rptr. 376.

■ Files, Justice. This is an action for declaratory relief and to quiet title against tract-wide deed restrictions which limit the use of plaintiffs' property to single family residential purposes. The trial court gave judgment declaring the restrictions to be unenforceable in part. Defendants have appealed. It is necessary to reverse the judgment because of the absence of a finding of fact on an issue which must be resolved before the controversy can be decided.

Plaintiffs own an unimproved lot situated at the northeast corner of Wilshire Boulevard and Hudson Avenue in the City of Los Angeles. This lot is a part of a tract which was subdivided by G. Allen Hancock in 1923 in the area now known as Hancock Park. Defendants are owners of other lots in the same tract. All the lots in the tract are subject to deed restrictions imposed by the original subdivider. These restrictions require, among other things, that each lot shall be used solely for single, private residences and that each residence shall front on a northsouth street. These restrictions will expire January 1, 1970. All the lots in the tract except four have been improved with single family residences. The four lots which have never been improved are the northeast and northwest corners of Wilshire and

Hudson, and the two lots which are immediately north of the two corner lots.

Figure 9–11
Hudson Avenue Looking toward Wilshire Boulevard, 2006

As this photograph reveals, the undeveloped northeast corner lots at issue in *Bolotin* are now occupied by a substantial commercial building, as are the companion lots across the street.

There is no dispute that the Hancock Park area is one of the most desirable and expensive residential areas in the community. It is also undisputed that the character of Wilshire Boulevard has changed greatly since 1923. A stipulation of facts lists these changes in some detail. Plaintiffs' evidence also includes the testimony of a qualified real estate broker and appraiser who testified that in his opinion plaintiffs' lot was not suitable for single family residential use, that there was no commonsense use to which the property could be put so long as the deed restrictions remained, and that the highest and best use for the property would be a commercial building similar to others which have been built on Wilshire Boulevard, both east and west of the subject property. He expressed the opinion that such a development would have no adverse effect upon either the market values of the residences in the tract or upon the amenities of living there. In his opinion, a building on plaintiffs' lot would help to protect the residences from the noise of the Wilshire traffic. There is an office building on the south side of Wilshire whose parking lot is directly across the street from plaintiff's lot. The witness pointed out that the use of plaintiffs' property for a commercial building would bring the commercial influence only 100 feet closer to the defendants' residences.

Defendants produced the testimony of a real estate broker that an office building on plaintiffs' lot would make the residences in the tract much less desirable as homes. In his opinion, a commercial building would inevitably bring more traffic and more parking, and would shut out sunlight. Defendants' witness was also of the opinion that the market value of the residences would decrease if a commercial building were built on plaintiffs' lot.

The findings of fact made by the trial court consist of these two paragraphs:

The changes in the uses of property abutting Wilshire Boulevard in the vicinity of lot 212 of tract 6388 in the City of Los Angeles and the increase of vehicular traffic on said boulevard along said lot, have resulted in said lot having no substantial value solely for single family residential purposes, but said lot has a market value in excess of $200,000.00 for business uses.

The refusal to enforce the single family residence restriction and the prohibition of commercial use of said lot 212, contained in the deeds to said lot and adjacent lots issued in 1923 and subsequent thereto, will not have an adverse effect upon the market value of other lots in said tract or tract 7040.

The only formal conclusion of law made by the trial court was that plaintiffs are entitled to a judgment declaring that the deed restrictions are not enforceable in specified respects.

A court will declare deed restrictions to be unenforceable when, by reason of changed conditions, enforcement of the restrictions would be inequitable and oppressive, and would harass plaintiff without benefiting the adjoining owners. (Wolff v. Fallon, 284 P.2d 802 (Cal. 1955).) In that case there was a finding of fact, supported by expert testimony, that the use of the plaintiff's property for commercial purposes would not detrimentally affect the adjoining property or neighborhood. A judgment quieting title against the restrictions was affirmed.

In *Marra v. Aetna Construction Co.*, 101 P.2d 490 (Cal. 1940), at pages 492–493, the court said:

Also well recognized is the rule that a building restriction in the nature of a servitude will not be enforced where changed conditions in the neighborhood have rendered the purpose of the restrictions obsolete. [Citations.] But, if the original purpose of the covenant can still be realized, it will be enforced even though the unrestricted use of the property would be more profitable to its owner.

In that case the evidence showed that the lot for whose benefit the restriction had been imposed was no longer being used for residential purposes, and hence the Supreme Court concluded it was no longer equitable to restrict the servient lot to residential purposes.

The difficulty in the present case is that there is no finding that the purposes of the restrictions have become obsolete, or that the enforcement of the restrictions on the plaintiffs' property will no longer benefit the defendants. The trial court's finding as to the effect upon defendants is limited to the statement that there will be no adverse effect upon market value. This is not the test.

The purpose of the deed restrictions, it seems clear enough, was to preserve the tract as a fine residential area by excluding from the tract many of the activities which might be offensive to the residents or which would create noise, traffic, congestion, or other conditions which would lessen the comfort and enjoyment of the residents. Bringing the prohibited activities into the neighborhood might or might not depreciate the market value of the homes. If the restrictions should be broken, and a commercial building erected on the Wilshire frontage, speculators might be willing to pay more for the other parcels in anticipation of future expansion of the commercial development. Thus the intrusion of an office building might increase market values even though it offended the senses of the residents and destroyed the physical conditions which had made their neighborhood a desirable one for them.

In *Miles v. Clark*, 187 P. 167 (Cal. Dist. Ct. App. 1919), at p. 172, where a decree enjoining a breach of deed restrictions was affirmed, the court said:

> The fact that apart from and surrounding the tract some business has grown up, and that the land has become more valuable in consequence, in no manner entitles defendants to be relieved of the restrictions they have created. This condition is but the natural result of the improvement of the various tracts, and the fact that the property may have become more valuable thereby for business purposes is immaterial. [Citations.] Courts in such cases are not controlled exclusively by money value, but may protect a home.

Plaintiffs have not cited any cases in which deed restrictions have been held unenforceable upon findings which were limited to the economic consequences.[1] In *Hirsch v. Hancock*, 343 P.2d 959 (Cal. Dist. Ct. App. 1959), a case which plaintiffs characterize as "strikingly similar" to this one, the court granted relief against the deed restrictions on the property at the northeast corner of Wilshire Boulevard and Rossmore Avenue. The trial court in that case found that the enforcement of the restrictions would

---

1. We note in passing that the Restatement of Property, section 537, takes the position that a promise as to the use of land is binding upon successors of the promisor only if the performance will result in benefit "in the physical use or enjoyment of the land." Comment (f) states: "*Physical use or enjoyment*. For a promise to run with the land of the promisor it is not enough that the performance of the promise operates to benefit either the promisor or the beneficiary of the promise in the use of his land but it must operate to benefit him in the physical use of his land. It must in some way make the use or enjoyment more satisfactory to his physical senses. It is not enough that the income from it is increased by virtue of it." (Accord: Daniels v. Notor, 389 Pa. 510, 133 A.2d 520.)

Since the validity of the restrictions, as such, is not in issue in the present case, it is unnecessary to consider whether section 537 is the law of California. The section is mentioned as further recognition that deed restrictions have some legally protected purpose other than economic benefit.

be of no substantial benefit to the owners of the other lots in the tract. That finding of fact distinguishes that case from the present one. There is no suggestion in the *Hirsch* case that the courts are concerned only with economic benefits.

* * * It is for the trial court to resolve this issue of fact.

The judgment is reversed.

NOTES AND QUESTIONS

1. The problem of changed circumstances is a general one. What is special about the covenants here is that many have an interest in their enforcement. How does this situation compare to the cy pres cases discussed in Chapter VI?

2. How else might the problem of stability versus flexibility over time be handled? Some covenants contain sunset provisions. In some states such provisions are implied by law. See Robert C. Ellickson & Vicki L. Been, Land Use Controls: Cases and Materials 572–73, 575–76, 579–80 (3d ed. 2005). Would purchasers systematically make mistakes in this area?

3. If courts were more inclined to refuse enforcement of covenants at the edges of an area, what should happen when the owners on the new commercial-residential divide invoke changed circumstances? Might this explain the court's reluctance to intervene here?

Peckham v. Milroy

Court of Appeals of Washington, 2001.
17 P.3d 1256.

■ SWEENEY, J. A neighborhood covenant prohibits home businesses. So, the trial court enjoined Thomas Milroy's wife from operating a home day care after [a] neighbor complained.

The question before us is whether the trial court erred by enjoining the day-care business because the covenant was abandoned, or violated public policy. The trial court's findings are amply supported by the evidence here. And those findings amply support the court's conclusions of law that the covenant had not been abandoned through disuse. Nor does it violate public policy. We also agree that neither laches nor estoppel bars Mr. Peckham's claim here. We, therefore, affirm the court's summary dismissal.

FACTS

The material facts are not disputed. Spokane Terrace was platted in 1907. It includes the houses at issue here. The neighborhood is called the Spokane Terrace Addition (STA). The developer subjected some of the lots to restrictive covenants in 1955. One prohibited use of the property "for business purposes of any kind whatsoever...." Clerk's Papers at 38.

Gordon Peckham moved into the STA in 1958. Thomas Milroy's parents moved into the STA in 1992. The Milroy property is subject to the restriction.

Mr. Milroy's mother fell and broke her hip in 1994. She required assistance after that. Mr. Milroy, his wife, and family decided to move into his mother's home in the STA.

They remodeled the home to accommodate the Milroy family, which included five children. They began to remodel in August 1995 and completed in December 1995. Mr. Peckham watched and photographed the construction. He complained to the county about the construction in November 1995. And he filed zoning complaints in February 1996. The Milroys moved into the home in December 1995. Mrs. Milroy obtained a day-care license and began running a day care.

The children are noisy. Mr. Peckham can hear them from inside his home. Parents of the children parked in front of Mr. Peckham's house. They walk across his yard. And they park in the alley behind his house.

Mr. Milroy's mother passed away in July 1996. He inherited the home. Mr. Peckham told Mrs. Milroy she was violating the covenants in July 1996. Mr. Peckham sued to enjoin the day-care operation in November 1997.

Several home businesses operated in the STA in violation of the restrictive covenant. These include a drapery business, a painting business, a small construction business, and a TV repair service.

Following a trial the court concluded that Mrs. Milroy's day care was a business. And that Mr. Peckham had an equitable right to enforce the covenant. The court enjoined the Milroys from operating the day care.

ANALYSIS

ABANDONMENT.

Mr. Milroy first argues the covenant prohibiting home businesses has been abandoned.

Abandonment requires proof that prior violations have eroded the general plan and enforcement is therefore inequitable. Mountain Park Homeowners Ass'n v. Tydings, 883 P.2d 1383, 1386 (Wash. 1994). A covenant is abandoned when it has been "habitually and substantially violated...." Id. But a few violations do not constitute abandonment. White v. Wilhelm, 665 P.2d 407, 411 (Wash. App. 1983).

Mr. Milroy presented evidence of four home businesses in the STA. A drapery business has been run from a home in the STA since the late 1970s. A painting business was run from 1994 to 1997. A small construction and TV repair business was operated between 1963 and 1972. And a craft business has been operated from a home for the past five to six years.

The STA covers 41 blocks and includes approximately 38 to 40 lots each. The violations are neither habitual nor substantial. See Mountain

Park Homeowners, supra. They comprise a very small percentage of the subdivision. A few violations do not constitute abandonment. White, supra.

Substantial evidence supports the trial court's determination that the covenant has not been abandoned.

LACHES AND ESTOPPEL.

Mr. Milroy next contends that Mr. Peckham knew Mrs. Milroy intended to operate a home day care as early as August 1995. Yet Mr. Peckham waited until November 1997 to file this action. The delay caused injury to the Milroys and was therefore unreasonable.

Laches. Laches requires: "(1) knowledge or reasonable opportunity to discover on the part of a potential plaintiff that he has a cause of action against a defendant; (2) an unreasonable delay by the plaintiff in commencing that cause of action; (3) damage to defendant resulting from the unreasonable delay." Buell v. City of Bremerton, 495 P.2d 1358, 1361 (Wash. 1972); see Valley View Indus. Park v. City of Redmond, 733 P.2d 182, 191 (Wash. 1987).

Mr. Peckham saw the Milroys remodel. But he did not know they intended to build a day-care center until after the construction started. The Milroys incurred construction expenses before Mr. Peckham knew they intended to violate the covenant.

Mr. Peckham objected to the project through early 1996. Mr. Peckham tried to enlist the aid of the county to stop the day-care operation. He told Mrs. Milroy that she was violating the covenants in July 1996.

Mr. Milroy testified that the original purpose of remodeling was to provide room for his family, not a commercial day care. Mr. Milroy stated he and his wife did not originally plan to continue the day-care service. But then they decided they needed the money. He testified the decision to operate the day care was made in late 1995, after remodeling the home.

The defense of laches requires showing all three elements. See Buell, supra. The Milroys intended to remodel for reasons other than the day care. The cost of the remodel could not, then, result from Mr. Peckham's delay in bringing this action.

The court found that Mr. Peckham did not unreasonably delay the suit. That finding is amply supported by this record.

Equitable Estoppel. Equitable estoppel requires: "(1) an admission, statement or act inconsistent with the claim asserted afterward; (2) action by the other party in reasonable reliance on that admission, statement or act; and (3) injury to that party when the first party is allowed to contradict or repudiate its admission, statement or act." Wilhelm v. Beyersdorf, 999 P.2d 54, 62 (Wash. App. 2000). Each element must be proven by clear, cogent, and convincing evidence. Id. Equitable estoppel is not favored. Robinson v. City of Seattle, 830 P.2d 318, 345 (Wash. 1992).

Mr. Milroy has not established any of the elements of equitable estoppel. Mr. Peckham made no statements and he took no actions inconsistent with his current position—the day care violates the covenant.

Mr. Milroy argues that Mr. Peckham acquiesced to the day care through his silence. Silence can lead to equitable estoppel—"[w]here a party knows what is occurring and would be expected to speak, if he wished to protect his interest, his acquiescence manifests his tacit consent." Bd. of Regents v. City of Seattle, 741 P.2d 11, 16 (Wash. 1987). Mr. Peckham was not silent. He complained to the county. He complained to Mrs. Milroy.

Neither can the Milroys show that they relied on Mr. Peckham's acquiescence. Mrs. Milroy talked to representatives of the city, county, and state about the day-care operation. She did not rely on Mr. Peckham. * * * [The court then upholds the trial court's determination that the character of the neighborhood had not changed for purpose of the doctrine of changed neighborhood conditions.]

PUBLIC POLICY.

Mr. Milroy argues that Washington public policy makes quality child care a priority. And this public policy should override restrictive covenants preventing home day care.

Mr. Milroy cites statutes which prohibit cities, towns, and counties from prohibiting home day care in residentially zoned areas. RCW 35.63.185; RCW 36.70A.450. The regulations do not, however, limit private parties from restricting land use. Restrictive covenants in residential neighborhoods are enforceable. Metzner v. Wojdyla, 886 P.2d 154, 156–57 (Wash. 1994).

If restrictive covenants that incidentally prohibit home day care should be repealed on public policy grounds, the decision should come from the Legislature—not this court. See Mut. of Enumclaw Ins. Co. v. Wiscomb, 622 P.2d 1234, 1236–37 (Wash. 1980) (determining public policy is not the judiciary's function).

Affirmed.

NOTES AND QUESTIONS

1. We have seen abandonment and estoppel before. How are they similar or different in the context of covenants?

2. One might ask whether covenants can be *created* by estoppel. In general, there are no covenants by estoppel, implication, or prescription. Why? Do covenants typically deal with matters as serious as those involved in easements?

C. ZONING AND OTHER LAND-USE REGULATION

These days the main source of land-use control of a public character is zoning and related land-use regulation. Zoning in the United States arose in the early twentieth century in response to the perceived inadequacies of nuisance and covenants to secure a stable regime of residential land use in a rapidly urbanizing country.

Zoning is the regulation of land uses through a general regime permitting and forbidding particular uses of land in certain locations. In a proto-zoning period in the late nineteenth and early twentieth centuries, a number of municipalities adopted ordinances prohibiting a select few uses—for example, brick making in a residential area. Modern zoning ordinances, which are far more comprehensive, date from the landmark New York Zoning Ordinance of 1916. This prescribed three zones—residence, business, and unrestricted; today New York City's zoning ordinance provides for 176 use districts. Contemporary zoning also covers matters such as lot size and shape, and building bulk and placement. There are several types of zoning, including more recently zoning that involves a contract-like deal between developers and local government. When reading the following materials ask yourself to what extent zoning is public or private law or some mixture of the two. Related to this is the question of how great an impact zoning has on owner sovereignty—and how far it should.

Zoning of the type familiar today, which governs the types of uses to which parcels may be put, took off in the 1920s. Interestingly, zoning was heavily supported by some developers, particularly those of "high class" housing. Zoning originally targeted nuisances but now commonly zoning makes fine distinctions among uses and often also restricts height, bulk, area, and exterior design. As we will see, these measures can sometimes be used to keep out those who cannot afford large lots and large houses. The earliest zoning often explicitly targeted characteristics of the user (rather than just the use), and was used to enforce racial and economic segregation. In *Buchanan v. Warley*, 245 U.S. 60 (1917), the Supreme Court struck down such schemes as violating the Fourteenth Amendment's guarantee not to be deprived of the right to dispose of property without due process of law—in that case the white seller's right to dispose of the property by selling to blacks. (The lawsuit was a challenge by the local president of the NAACP, William Warley, and a white realtor friendly to the NAACP, Charles Buchanan, by having Buchanan sell to Warley on condition that Warley be able to occupy, and then having Warley breach and claim the condition as excusing performance.) The Louisville ordinance at issue in the case was designed to maintain segregation between whites and blacks and forbade any person from occupying a house on a block in which the majority of the other houses were occupied by members of the other race. See Benno C. Schmidt, Jr., Principle and Prejudice: The Supreme Court and Race in the Progressive Era, Part 1: The Heyday of Jim Crow, 82 Colum. L. Rev. 444, 498–523 (1982). We take up more subtle racial and class effects of zoning later in this Section.

Zoning ordinances and the apparatus for giving them effect are a matter of state and local law. Because local governments are creatures of their respective states, the authority to engage in zoning must come from the state. States can delegate the police power in the area of zoning to local governments. State constitutions or legislation, termed home rule provisions, can give some or all local governments sweeping powers to regulate, and zoning is within this broad authorization. Or the state can pass a zoning enabling act setting out the authority of local governments to act in this area.

Consider the typical zoning enabling act. Such legislation calls for a *comprehensive plan*. In many states, this requirement is in practice easy to meet, because the plan need not be in writing, or it is sometimes considered to be implicit in the *zoning ordinance*. Under the enabling act, relevant local governments—country commissions, city councils, etc.—are authorized to and expected to pass a zoning ordinance. Under such an ordinance, people can seek changes in zoning designations, but there is a danger that individually tailored adjustments will be attacked as unlawful "spot zoning." In general, it is fair to say that those envisioning the workings of zoning at the time it came into being seriously underestimated the dynamic aspect of land-use planning. Implementing change in a zoning scheme is not an easy process.

Under zoning, permits are commonly required for subdivisions, site plans, and building projects. A designated local official will be in charge of granting and denying requests for building permits, and the official will enforce the provisions of the zoning ordinance in the process of considering the request for a permit. Those dissatisfied with a denial of a permit as well as those aggrieved by the granting of a permit and certain other officials can appeal to a *Board of Zoning Appeals,* which can carry one of several similar sounding names and reviews these decisions but cannot make changes in basic zoning designations themselves. Consider who is likely to have enough of a stake and low enough organizing costs to be able to mount effective opposition to a zoning decision. Developers and neighbors often fit this description, but those who might become residents in the future are much less likely to have their voices heard directly.

The Board of Zoning Appeals not only hears appeals from denials of building permits but also hears requests for *variances* (which allow for relaxation of zoning requirements in cases of undue hardship), and hears requests for *special exceptions* (which go under various names and which permit uses only if conditions specified in the ordinance met). The difference between a variance and a special exception is that if one satisfies criteria set forth in the zoning ordinance, one has a right to a special exception, whereas a variance is given for special hardship as determined within a broad grant of discretion to the Board under the ordinance. Aggrieved landowners can seek judicial review of the Board's decision in the regular state courts.

Violators of zoning ordinances are theoretically liable for civil and criminal sanctions, although enforcement is sometimes spotty. Recall the ex ante versus ex post discussion in connection with building encroachments. Should those who have already built in violation of zoning be required to tear the offending structure down, even at great cost? Sometimes this happens. Examples include a Florida builder who was required to tear down apartments that violated a comprehensive plan and a New York City developer who claimed that he built 12 stories too high because of an error in a city map and who agreed after lengthy litigation to remove the 12 stories. See Ellickson & Been, supra, at 93.

In the courts, the Board of Zoning Appeals is treated like a quasi-judicial administrative agency in that principles of due process and administrative law apply. Principally challenges to zoning are based on due process (substantive and procedural), the takings clause (state and/or federal), equal protection, free speech, free association, and freedom of religion. We return to some of these issues later in this Section.

Zoning comes in a number of varieties, one of which is called "Euclidean" after the scheme in the following case.

Village of Euclid v. Ambler Realty Co.

Supreme Court of the United States, 1926.
272 U.S. 365.

■ MR. JUSTICE SUTHERLAND delivered the opinion of the Court. The village of Euclid is an Ohio municipal corporation. It adjoins and practically is a suburb of the city of Cleveland. Its estimated population is between 5,000 and 10,000, and its area from 12 to 14 square miles, the greater part of which is farm lands or unimproved acreage. It lies, roughly, in the form of a parallelogram measuring approximately three and one-half miles each way. East and west it is traversed by three principal highways: Euclid Avenue, through the southerly border, St. Clair Avenue, through the central portion, and Lake Shore Boulevard, through the northerly border, in close proximity to the shore of Lake Erie. The Nickel Plate Railroad lies from 1,500 to 1,800 feet north of Euclid Avenue, and the Lake Shore Railroad 1,600 feet farther to the north. The three highways and the two railroads are substantially parallel.

Appellee is the owner of a tract of land containing 68 acres, situated in the westerly end of the village, abutting on Euclid Avenue to the south and the Nickel Plate Railroad to the north. Adjoining this tract, both on the east and on the west, there have been laid out restricted residential plats upon which residences have been erected.

On November 13, 1922, an ordinance was adopted by the village council, establishing a comprehensive zoning plan for regulating and restricting the location of trades, industries, apartment houses, two-family houses, single family houses, etc., the lot area to be built upon, the size and height of buildings, etc.

The entire area of the village is divided by the ordinance into six classes of use districts, denominated U–1 to U–6, inclusive; three classes of height districts, denominated H–1 to H–3, inclusive; and four classes of area districts, denominated A–1 to A–4, inclusive. The use districts are classified in respect of the buildings which may be erected within their respective limits, as follows: U–1 is restricted to single family dwellings, public parks, water towers and reservoirs, suburban and interurban electric railway passenger stations and rights of way, and farming, non-commercial greenhouse nurseries, and truck gardening; U–2 is extended to include two-family dwellings; U–3 is further extended to include apartment houses, hotels, churches, schools, public libraries, museums, private clubs, community center buildings, hospitals, sanitariums, public playgrounds, and recreation buildings, and a city hall and courthouse; U–4 is further extended to include banks, offices, studios, telephone exchanges, fire and police stations, restaurants, theaters and moving picture shows, retail stores and shops, sales offices, sample rooms, wholesale stores for hardware, drugs, and groceries, stations for gasoline and oil (not exceeding 1,000 gallons storage) and for ice delivery, skating rinks and dance halls, electric substations, job and newspaper printing, public garages for motor vehicles, stables and wagon sheds (not exceeding five horses, wagons or motor trucks), and distributing stations for central store and commercial enterprises; U–5 is further extended to include billboards and advertising signs (if permitted), warehouses, ice and ice cream manufacturing and cold storage plants, bottling works, milk bottling and central distribution stations, laundries, carpet cleaning, dry cleaning, and dyeing establishments, blacksmith, horseshoeing, wagon and motor vehicle repair shops, freight stations, street car barns, stables and wagon sheds (for more than five horses, wagons or motor trucks), and wholesale produce markets and salesroom; U–6 is further extended to include plants for sewage disposal and for producing gas, garbage and refuse incineration, scrap iron, junk, scrap paper, and rag storage, aviation fields, cemeteries, crematories, penal and correctional institutions, insane and feeble-minded institutions, storage of oil and gasoline (not to exceed 25,000 gallons), and manufacturing and industrial operations of any kind other than, and any public utility not included in, a class U–1, U–2, U–3, U–4, or U–5 use. There is a seventh class of uses which is prohibited altogether.

Class U–1 is the only district in which buildings are restricted to those enumerated. In the other classes the uses are cumulative-that is to say, uses in class U–2 include those enumerated in the preceding class U–1; class U–3 includes uses enumerated in the preceding classes, U–2, and U–1; and so on. In addition to the enumerated uses, the ordinance provides for accessory uses; that is, for uses customarily incident to the principal use, such as private garages. Many regulations are provided in respect of such accessory uses.

The height districts are classified as follows: In class H–1, buildings are limited to a height of two and one-half stories, or thirty-five feet; in class H–2, to 4 stories, or fifty feet; in class H–3, to eighty feet. To all of these, certain exceptions are made, as in the case of church spires, water tanks, etc.

The classification of area districts is: In A–1 districts, dwellings or apartment houses to accommodate more than one family must have at least 5,000 square feet for interior lots and at least 4,000 square feet for corner lots; in A–2 districts, the area must be at least 2,500 square feet for interior lots, and 2,000 square feet for corner lots; in A–3 districts, the limits are 1,250 and 1,000 square feet, respectively; in A–4 districts, the limits are 900 and 700 square feet, respectively. The ordinance contains, in great variety and detail, provisions in respect of width of lots, front, side, and rear yards, and other matters, including restrictions and regulations as to the use of billboards, signboards, and advertising signs.

A single family dwelling consists of a basement and not less than three rooms and a bathroom. A two-family dwelling consists of a basement and not less than four living rooms and a bathroom for each family, and is further described as a detached dwelling for the occupation of two families, one having its principal living rooms on the first floor and the other on the second floor.

Appellee's tract of land comes under U–2, U–3 and U–6. The first strip of 620 feet immediately north of Euclid Avenue falls in class U–2, the next 130 feet to the north, in U–3, and the remainder in U–6. The uses of the first 620 feet, therefore, do not include apartment houses, hotels, churches, schools, or other public and semipublic buildings, or other uses enumerated in respect of U–3 to U–6, inclusive. The uses of the next 130 feet include all of these, but exclude industries, theaters, banks, shops, and the various other uses set forth in respect of U–4 to U–6, inclusive.

Annexed to the ordinance, and made a part of it, is a zone map, showing the location and limits of the various use, height, and area districts, from which it appears that the three classes overlap one another; that is to say, for example, both U–5 and U–6 use districts are in A–4 area district, but the former is in H–2 and the latter in H–3 height districts. The plan is a complicated one, and can be better understood by an inspection of the map * * *

Figure 9–12
Zoning of Properties near the Ambler Realty Tract

Source: Timothy Alan Fluck, *Euclid v. Ambler*: A Retrospective, 52 J. Am. Planning Ass'n 326, Map 2 (Summer 1986).

The lands lying between the two railroads for the entire length of the village area and extending some distance on either side to the north and south, having an average width of about 1,600 feet, are left open, with slight exceptions, for industrial and all other uses. This includes the larger part of appellee's tract. Approximately one-sixth of the area of the entire village is included in U–5 and U–6 use districts. That part of the village lying south of Euclid avenue is principally in U–1 districts. The lands lying north of Euclid Avenue and bordering on the long strip just described are included in U–1, U–2, U–3, and U–4 districts, principally in U–2.

The enforcement of the ordinance is entrusted to the inspector of buildings, under rules and regulations of the board of zoning appeals. Meetings of the board are public, and minutes of its proceedings are kept. It is authorized to adopt rules and regulations to carry into effect provisions of the ordinance. Decisions of the inspector of buildings may be appealed to the board by any person claiming to be adversely affected by any such decision. The board is given power in specific cases of practical difficulty or unnecessary hardship to interpret the ordinance in harmony with its general purpose and intent, so that the public health, safety and general welfare may be secure and substantial justice done. Penalties are prescribed for violations, and it is provided that the various provisions are to be regarded as independent and the holding of any provision to be unconstitutional, void or ineffective shall not affect any of the others.

The ordinance is assailed on the grounds that it is in derogation of § 1 of the Fourteenth Amendment to the Federal Constitution in that it deprives appellee of liberty and property without due process of law and denies it the equal protection of the law, and that it offends against certain provisions of the Constitution of the state of Ohio. The prayer of the bill is for an injunction restraining the enforcement of the ordinance and all attempts to impose or maintain as to appellee's property any of the restrictions, limitations or conditions. The court below held the ordinance to be unconstitutional and void, and enjoined its enforcement, 297 F. 307.

Before proceeding to a consideration of the case, it is necessary to determine the scope of the inquiry. The bill alleges that the tract of land in question is vacant and has been held for years for the purpose of selling and developing it for industrial uses, for which it is especially adapted, being immediately in the path or progressive industrial development; that for such uses it has a market value of about $10,000 per acre, but if the use be limited to residential purposes the market value is not in excess of $2,500 per acre; that the first 200 feet of the parcel back from Euclid Avenue, if unrestricted in respect of use, has a value of $150 per front foot, but if limited to residential uses, and ordinary mercantile business be excluded therefrom, its value is not in excess of $50 per front foot.

It is specifically averred that the ordinance attempts to restrict and control the lawful uses of appellee's land, so as to confiscate and destroy a great part of its value; that it is being enforced in accordance with its terms; that prospective buyers of land for industrial, commercial, and residential uses in the metropolitan district of Cleveland are deterred from buying any part of this land because of the existence of the ordinance and the necessity thereby entailed of conducting burdensome and expensive litigation in order to vindicate the right to use the land for lawful and legitimate purposes; that the ordinance constitutes a cloud upon the land, reduces and destroys its value, and has the effect of diverting the normal industrial, commercial, and residential development thereof to other and less favorable locations.

The record goes no farther than to show, as the lower court found, that the normal and reasonably to be expected use and development of that part of appellee's land adjoining Euclid Avenue is for general trade and commercial purposes, particularly retail stores and like establishments, and that the normal and reasonably to be expected use and development of the residue of the land is for industrial and trade purposes. Whatever injury is inflicted by the mere existence and threatened enforcement of the ordinance is due to restrictions in respect of these and similar uses, to which perhaps should be added—if not included in the foregoing—restrictions in respect of apartment houses. Specifically there is nothing in the record to suggest that any damage results from the presence in the ordinance of those restrictions relating to churches, schools, libraries, and other public and semipublic buildings. It is neither alleged nor proved that there is or may be a demand for any part of appellee's land for any of the last-named uses, and we cannot assume the existence of facts which would justify an injunction upon this record in respect to this class of restrictions. For present purposes the provisions of the ordinance in respect of these uses may therefore be put aside as unnecessary to be considered. It is also unnecessary to consider the effect of the restrictions in respect of U–1 districts, since none of appellee's land falls within that class. * * *

Building zone laws are of modern origin. They began in this country about twenty-five years ago. Until recent years, urban life was comparatively simple; but, with the great increase and concentration of population, problems have developed, and constantly are developing, which require, and will continue to require, additional restrictions in respect of the use and occupation of private lands in urban communities. Regulations, the wisdom, necessity, and validity of which, as applied to existing conditions, are so apparent that they are now uniformly sustained, a century ago, or even half a century ago, probably would have been rejected as arbitrary and oppressive. Such regulations are sustained, under the complex conditions of our day, for reasons analogous to those which justify traffic regulations, which, before the advent of automobiles and rapid transit street railways, would have been condemned as fatally arbitrary and unreasonable. And in this there is no inconsistency, for, while the meaning of constitutional guaranties never varies, the scope of their application must expand or contract to meet the new and different conditions which are constantly coming within the field of their operation. In a changing world it is impossible that it should be otherwise. But although a degree of elasticity is thus imparted, not to the *meaning*, but to the *application* of constitutional principles, statutes and ordinances, which, after giving due weight to the new conditions, are found clearly not to conform to the Constitution, of course, must fall.

The ordinance now under review, and all similar laws and regulations, must find their justification in some aspect of the police power, asserted for the public welfare. The line which in this field separates the legitimate from the illegitimate assumption of power is not capable of precise delimitation. It varies with circumstances and conditions. A regulatory zoning ordinance, which would be clearly valid as applied to the great cities, might be clearly invalid as applied to rural communities. In solving doubts, the maxim *sic utere tuo ut alienum non laedas*, which lies at the foundation of so much of the common law of nuisances, ordinarily will furnish a fairly helpful clew. And the law of nuisances, likewise, may be consulted, not for the purpose of controlling, but for the helpful aid of its analogies in the process of ascertaining the scope of, the power. Thus the question whether the power exists to forbid the erection of a building of a particular kind or for a particular use, like the question whether a particular thing is a nuisance, is to be determined, not by an abstract consideration of the building or of the thing considered apart, but by considering it in connection with the circumstances and the locality. A nuisance may be merely a right thing in the wrong place, like a pig in the parlor instead of the barnyard. If the validity of the legislative classification for zoning purposes be fairly debatable, the legislative judgment must be allowed to control.

There is no serious difference of opinion in respect of the validity of laws and regulations fixing the height of buildings within reasonable limits, the character of materials and methods of construction, and the adjoining area which must be left open, in order to minimize the danger of fire or collapse, the evils of overcrowding and the like, and excluding from residential sections offensive trades, industries and structures likely to create nuisances.

Here, however, the exclusion is in general terms of all industrial establishments, and it may thereby happen that not only offensive or dangerous industries will be excluded, but those which are neither offensive nor dangerous will share the same fate. But this is no more than happens in respect of many practice-forbidding laws which this court has upheld, although drawn in general terms so as to include individual cases that may turn out to be innocuous in themselves. The inclusion of a reasonable margin, to insure effective enforcement, will not put upon a law, otherwise valid, the stamp of invalidity. Such laws may also find their justification in the fact that, in some fields, the bad fades into the good by such insensible degrees that the two are not capable of being readily distinguished and separated in terms of legislation. In the light of these considerations, we are not prepared to say that the end in view was not sufficient to justify the general rule of the ordinance, although some industries of an innocent character might fall within the proscribed class. It cannot be said that the ordinance in this respect "passes the bounds of reason and assumes the character of a merely arbitrary fiat." Purity Extract Co. v. Lynch, 226 U. S. 192, 204. Moreover, the restrictive provisions of the ordinance in this particular may be sustained upon the principles applicable to the broader exclusion from residential districts of all business and trade structures, presently to be discussed.

It is said that the village of Euclid is a mere suburb of the city of Cleveland; that the industrial development of that city has now reached and in some degree extended into the village, and in the obvious course of things will soon absorb the entire area for industrial enterprises; that the effect of the ordinance is to divert this natural development elsewhere, with the consequent loss of increased values to the owners of the lands within the village borders. But the village, though physically a suburb of Cleveland, is politically a separate municipality, with powers of its own and authority to govern itself as it sees fit, within the limits of the organic law of its creation and the state and federal Constitutions. Its governing authorities, presumably representing a majority of its inhabitants and voicing their will, have determined, not that industrial development shall cease at its boundaries, but that the course of such development shall proceed within definitely fixed lines. If it be a proper exercise of the police power to relegate industrial establishments to localities separated from residential sections, it is not easy to find a sufficient reason for denying the power because the effect of its exercise is to divert an industrial flow from the course which it would follow, to the injury of the residential public, if left alone, to another course where such injury will be obviated. It is not meant by this, however, to exclude the possibility of cases where the general public interest would so far outweigh the interest of the municipality that the municipality would not be allowed to stand in the way.

We find no difficulty in sustaining restrictions of the kind thus far reviewed. The serious question in the case arises over the provisions of the ordinance excluding from residential districts apartment houses, business houses, retail stores and shops, and other like establishments. This question involves the validity of what is really the crux of the more recent zoning legislation, namely, the creation and maintenance of residential districts, from which business and trade of every sort, including hotels and apartment houses, are excluded. Upon that question this court has not thus far spoken. The decisions of the state courts are numerous and conflicting; but those which broadly sustain the power greatly outnumber those which deny it altogether or narrowly limit it, and it is very apparent that there is a constantly increasing tendency in the direction of the broader view. * * *

The matter of zoning has received much attention at the hands of commissions and experts, and the results of their investigations have been set forth in comprehensive reports. These reports which bear every evidence of painstaking consideration, concur in the view that the segregation of residential, business and industrial buildings will make it easier to provide fire apparatus suitable for the character and intensity of the development in each section; that it will increase the safety and security of home life, greatly tend to prevent street accidents, especially to children, by reducing the traffic and resulting confusion in residential sections, decrease noise and other conditions which produce or intensify nervous disorders, preserve a more favorable environment in which to rear children, etc. With particular reference to apartment houses, it is pointed out that the development of detached house sections is greatly retarded by the coming of apartment houses, which has sometimes resulted in destroying the entire section for private house purposes; that in such sections very often the apartment house is a mere parasite, constructed in order to take advantage of the open spaces and attractive surroundings created by the residential character of the district. Moreover, the coming of one apartment house is followed by others, interfering by their height and bulk with the free circulation of air and monopolizing the rays of the sun which otherwise would fall upon the smaller homes, and bringing, as their necessary accompaniments, the disturbing noises incident to increased traffic and business, and the occupation, by means of moving and parked automobiles, of larger portions of the streets, thus detracting from their safety and depriving children of the privilege of quiet and open spaces for play, enjoyed by those in more favored localities-until, finally, the residential character of the neighborhood and its desirability as a place of detached residences are utterly destroyed. Under these circumstances, apartment houses, which in a different environment would be not only entirely unobjectionable but highly desirable, come very near to being nuisances.

If these reasons, thus summarized, do not demonstrate the wisdom or sound policy in all respects of those restrictions which we have indicated as pertinent to the inquiry, at least, the reasons are sufficiently cogent to preclude us from saying, as it must be said before the ordinance can be declared unconstitutional, that such provisions are clearly arbitrary and unreasonable, having no substantial relation to the public health, safety, morals, or general welfare.

It is true that when, if ever, the provisions set forth in the ordinance in tedious and minute detail, come to be concretely applied to particular premises, including those of the appellee, or to particular conditions, or to be considered in connection with specific complaints, some of them, or even many of them, may be found to be clearly arbitrary and unreasonable. But where the equitable remedy of injunction is sought, as it is here, not upon the ground of a present infringement or denial of a specific right, or of a particular injury in process of actual execution, but upon the broad ground that the mere existence and threatened enforcement of the ordinance, by materially and adversely affecting values and curtailing the opportunities of the market, constitute a present and irreparable injury, the court will not scrutinize its provisions, sentence by sentence, to ascertain by a process of piecemeal dissection whether there may be, here and there, provisions of a minor character, or relating to matters of administration, or not shown to contribute to the injury complained of, which, if attacked separately, might not withstand the test of constitutionality. In respect of such provisions, of which specific complaint is not made, it cannot be said that the landowner has suffered or is threatened with an injury which entitles him to challenge their constitutionality. * * *

The relief sought here is of the same character, namely, an injunction against the enforcement of any of the restrictions, limitations, or conditions of the ordinance. And the gravamen of the complaint is that a portion of the land of the appellee cannot be sold for certain enumerated uses because of the general and broad restraints of the ordinance. What would be the effect of a restraint imposed by one or more or the innumerable provisions of the ordinance, considered apart, upon the value or marketability of the lands, is neither disclosed by the bill nor by the evidence, and we are afforded no basis, apart from mere speculation, upon which to rest a conclusion that it or they would have any appreciable effect upon those matters. Under these circumstances, therefore, it is enough for us to determine, as we do, that the ordinance in its general scope and dominant features, so far as its provisions are here involved, is a valid exercise of authority, leaving other provisions to be dealt with as cases arise directly involving them.

And this is in accordance with the traditional policy of this Court. In the realm of constitutional law, especially, this Court has perceived the embarrassment which is likely to result from an attempt to formulate rules or decide questions beyond the necessities of the immediate issue. It has preferred to follow the method of a gradual approach to the general by a systematically guarded application and extension of constitutional principles to particular cases as they arise, rather than by out of hand attempts to establish general rules to which future cases must be fitted. This process applies with peculiar force to the solution of questions arising under the due process clause of the Constitution as applied to the exercise of the flexible powers of police, with which we are here concerned.

Decree reversed.

■ MR. JUSTICE VAN DEVANTER, MR. JUSTICE McREYNOLDS, and MR. JUSTICE BUTLER dissent.

NOTES AND QUESTIONS

1. Euclid's scheme involved cumulative zoning; that is the ordinance defined a hierarchy of uses, roughly from most sensitive and least invasive to those that are least sensitive but most objectionable to others. In any zone of a given level one can have uses of that level or any "higher" use. Thus, as in Euclid, one could if one wished build a residence in an industrial zone but not vice versa. By contrast, in noncumulative zoning one can only have enumerated uses in any given zone. So unless it happened to be an allowable mixture, one would not be permitted to build a residence in an industrial zone. Which scheme is preferable in your view?

2. As with any scheme there is some limit as to how finegrained zoning can be, in an ex ante sense. As we saw in the case of area-wide covenants, borders between areas or zones tend to present problems. In *Euclid,* before the zoning, residences on the edge of the zone might be less desirable because of the prospect of nearby industry. In fact, the zoning is in some sense creating the reverse "externality" at the zoning border (the

actual border being within the tract that straddles the border), in the sense that the restriction to residences makes nearby valuable industrial use less viable. Ambler wanted to use the entire tract for industrial use, but the owners of the residential tracts wanted to see industrial development nearby blocked. What would a unitary owner of all the land in the area likely want to do? Incidentally, under the pressure of wartime industrial mobilization Euclid later rezoned the entire area for industrial use and a GM plant long occupied the site after World War II. Since 1999 a portion of the by then shut-down plant was converted into a sports facility, and the area now features a mixture of commercial, industrial, modest houses, and apartment buildings. See Ellickson & Been, supra, at 86.

3. When land-use regulations are analyzed—especially under the Takings Clause, as we will see—analogies are often drawn to nuisance. Although nuisance law itself is not the primary tool of externality-control these days, for better or worse, it forms a common vocabulary and possible baseline for evaluating the bads that stem from land use. *Euclid* is no exception. What do you think of Justice Sutherland's invocation of the notion of nuisance? Are apartment houses nuisances? Are duplexes (U-2) nuisances to owners of single-family homes (U-1)? For that matter, why do you think Justice Sutherland, one of the "Four Horsemen" of the pre-1937 Supreme Court, would uphold the zoning scheme here at issue in the face of the claims of a private property owner? See Barry Cushman, The Secret Lives of the Four Horsemen, 83 Va. L. Rev. 559 (1997) (arguing that the Four Horsemen were "closet liberals"). The other Horsemen (Justices Butler, McReynolds, and Van Devanter) were in dissent in *Euclid*. For a summary of views on Sutherland's reasons, see Ellickson & Been, supra, at 85.

4. Are apartment buildings "parasites," as Justice Sutherland would have it? By contrast, the trial court in *Euclid* had been highly critical of the exclusionary and class-segregating aspect of zoning. The ordinance here was innovative in keeping out apartment buildings, with the result of segregation by class and race. The result in this case made zoning an available tool for exclusion. On the background of racial zoning in the Cleveland area in this era and the attitudes of those involved in the *Euclid* case, see William M. Randle, Professors, Reformers, Bureaucrats, and Cronies: The Players in *Euclid v. Ambler*, in Zoning and the American Dream 31, 38–43 (Charles M. Haar & Jerrold S. Kayden eds., 1989).

5. After *Euclid* and *Nectow v. Cambridge*, 277 U.S. 183 (1928), the Supreme Court has had little to say about the constitutionality of zoning schemes under the Takings and Due Process Clauses. Much more happens at the state level, under state constitutions, and state courts vary greatly in how deferential they are to local zoning authorities. For example, Illinois and Pennsylvania are stricter than most about due process in the area of zoning.

6. Zoning is not the only public tool of land-use control. Also important are subdivision controls, which regulate new subdivisions, and prescribe features of streets, utility lines, and other public infrastructure and

amenities—and deal with more obvious externalities. Environmental laws and regulations can have major consequences for land use. Federal environmental laws like the Clean Water Act or Endangered Species Act can limit use of parcels. And some states require environmental impact statements for major new developments.

NONCONFORMING USES

Zoning ordinances typically grandfather nonconforming uses of property in existence when a zoning scheme is enacted. For example a commercial establishment in a residential area will be allowed to continue. Widespread intuition has it that once a use of property is established it becomes a "vested right." In contrast, an owner of undeveloped land has no vested right to any particular type of use, nor does the owner of property dedicated to a particular use have a vested right to switch to a different use. However poorly articulated and defended these assumptions may be, they have become established points of reference in zoning law.

The problem of nonconforming uses is more of an issue in older cities. The accommodation here is narrow; usually a zoning ordinance forbids a change of one nonconforming use to another. Some schemes allow a change to a "higher" nonconforming use. Originally it was thought that nonconforming uses would disappear fairly quickly as buildings aged and fell into disrepair. This did not always happen. One possible reason is that having the only use of a kind in an area is often valuable. Being the only bar in a neighborhood is advantageous to the bar owner. Eminent domain (taking the right to the specific use or taking ownership of the parcel) is a potential solution, but compensation must be paid. "Amortization" or phasing out the use is another solution that does not involve compensation. Some states do not allow it, and others do, using a multi-factor test. Uncertainty lingers, however, about whether amortization may be found to be a taking.

ZONING POLICY

Despite its prevalence, zoning has always been very controversial. The case for zoning rests on its potential to deal with land-use externalities. For those who see rampant market failure and collective-action problems, private solutions such as covenants cannot be the entire solution. The case for the inadequacy of covenants is greatest in older neighborhoods that lack covenants that would be desired now. The transaction costs of setting up covenants to govern micro-decisions like door color would be enormous and holdout problems loom large. (By contrast, in a new development, as we have seen, developers can insert whatever package of covenants that they think will maximize profits.) Furthermore, proponents of zoning view judicial efforts to control incompatible land uses through nuisance law as inadequate as well. Particularly where land-use controls involve specific targets—such as set-backs or lot coverage—or commercial uses like gas stations that may not rise to the level of a common-law nuisance, judges are ill-equipped to supply detailed governance regimes to prescribe proper use. This problem becomes more acute when zoning and land-use planning are regarded as involving choices on an area-wide or city-wide basis. Suburban growth controls can even involve regional planning.

Zoning also can play a role in the competition of localities for residents. If localities can offer different packages of taxes and public goods, residents can sort themselves into the places that most suit them. This sort of positive interjurisdictional competition is sometimes termed the Tiebout Hypothesis ("Tiebout" is pronounced "Tee–BOWE"). Charles M. Tiebout, A Pure Theory of Local Expenditures, 64 J. Pol. Econ. 416 (1956). Essential to this type of competition is that those who do not pay can be excluded from the benefits. Bruce W. Hamilton, Zoning and Property Taxation in a System of Local Governments, 12 Urb. Stud. 205 (1975). That is, only people paying taxes will enjoy the schools, parks, etc. that those taxes fund. For those who support this type of interjurisdictional competition, zoning is viewed as a tool to prevent "fiscal freeriding," by allowing municipalities to select the types of land uses they wish to attract or avoid. Moreover, the benefits and costs from the flow of municipal services and taxes in such a model seem to be capitalized into the price of houses, which would lead one to expect homeowners to support value-maximizing packages of public goods. Homeowners can be expected to care deeply about these values, because a home is most people's single largest investment. And because it is very difficult to diversify this investment (or to insure against drops in market value), one should expect to find risk-averse behavior among homeowners (with NIMBY-ism—the not-in-my-backyard phenomenon—being its most extreme form). William A. Fischel, The Homevoter Hypothesis: How Home Values Influence Local Government Taxation, School Finance, and Land–Use Policies (2001).

The case against zoning emphasizes the flip-side of the benefits of zoning. The notion of comprehensive planning itself has its skeptics. They point to the sorry record of planning and urban renewal in the mid-to-late twentieth century which emphasized largeness and rationalization and extreme separation of uses, leaving even the pro-planning side advocating new approaches emphasizing a greater mix of uses and consequently more vibrant street life. Zoning is subject to the limits of bureaucratic decision-making, including rigidity, high administrative costs, and blunt incentives, resulting in uniformity and lack of attention to widely dispersed knowledge. See Jane Jacobs, The Life and Death of Great American Cities (1961). Developers and homeowners may use the zoning process to engage in rent-seeking, restricting the supply of housing and creating local monopolies. Requirements of large lots cause urban sprawl, raise housing costs, and promote class and racial segregation. Basically, tools to exclude those who cannot afford prescribed types of housing can be used to prevent both fiscal freeriding and to keep out those undesired by current owners.

Most U.S. cities have zoning, and the only major city not to have zoning is Houston. This case has been much studied and opponents of zoning point to it as a relatively successful example of land use without zoning. Bernard H. Siegan, Land Use Without Zoning (1972). It should be remembered, though, that Houston is not devoid of land-use regulations. In addition to widespread use of covenants, Houston also has subdivision controls, which regulate matters like lot size. Nevertheless, Houston has a greater proximity of residential and commercial uses than other cities of its size. In an econometric study on Houston, Janet Spreyer finds that after controlling for a number of factors, zoning and covenants are equally and independently effective at raising home prices over a hypothetical nuisance-only regime. Janet Furman Spreyer, The Effect of Land Use Restrictions on the Market Value of Single Family Homes in Houston, 2 J. Real Estate Fin. & Econ. 117 (1989). Another jurisdiction that has attracted a lot of attention is New Haven. Compare Andrew J. Cappel, A Walk Along Willow: Patterns of Land Use Coordination in Pre–Zoning New Haven (1870–1926), 101 Yale L.J. 617 (1991) (finding large degree of land-use coordination in one pre-zoning New Haven neighborhood) with Stephen Clowney, A Walk Along Willard: A Revised Look at Land Use Coordination in Pre–Zoning New Haven, 115 Yale L.J. 116 (2005) (finding more mixed success and failure in four pre-zoning neighborhoods in New Haven).

Recently zoning has attracted additional interest of economists using advanced statistical techniques. One problem in drawing conclusions from studies of zoning based on housing prices is that zoning may increase prices (i) because it prevents negative externalities and thereby makes housing more valuable to its current and future owners or (ii) because it causes local monopolies in the market for housing and therefore decreases welfare. Or both. Even the original interest in zoning on the part of developers of high-grade housing in the early twentieth century is consistent with either the optimistic or the pessimistic story (or, again, both). Edward Glaeser and Joseph Gyourko manage to tease these effects apart by comparing housing prices and construction costs in localities across the United States. They find that the cost of housing in most places is quite close to the cost of construction except in a limited number of jurisdictions in California and some Eastern cities, where housing prices are significantly higher than construction costs. This suggests that zoning and other land-use controls are the major reason for the high cost of housing in those areas. Edward L. Glaeser & Joseph Gyourko, The Impact of Building Restrictions on Housing Affordability, 9 Econ. Pol'y Rev. 21 (2003). In a similar paper, these authors and Raven Saks isolate the contribution of increasingly difficult regulatory approval for new building to the increase in housing costs between 1950 and 1970. Edward L. Glaeser, Joseph E. Gyourko, & Raven E. Saks, Why Have Housing Prices Gone Up?, 95 Am. Econ. Rev. 329 (2005) (Pap. & Proc.); see also Bengte L. Evenson, Understanding House Price Volatility: Measuring and Explaining the Supply Side of Metropolitan Area Housing Markets (Illinois State University Department of Economics Working Paper 2002). Some argue that regulations may not prevent growth but affect the quality of the building that does happen. Kee Warner & Harvey Molotch, Building Rules. How Local Controls Shape Community Environments and Economies (2000).

On a worldwide scale, land-use regulation has had a major impact on the shape of cities with profound economic consequences. The strength of the regulatory regime tends to flatten and sometimes invert the usual sharply downward-sloping (negative exponential) population gradient. Alain Bertaud & Stephen Malpezzi, The Spatial Distribution of Population in 48 World Cities: Implications for Economies in Transition (working paper Dec. 17, 2003); Alain Bertaud & Bertrand Renaud, Socialist Cities without Land Markets, 41 J. Urban Econ. 137 (1997). These authors present a model and empirical results but consider some illustrative examples drawn from their papers. What the authors call "market cities" like Paris have the usual pattern (or one variant of it) with a low population density downtown, then rising steeply and then dropping density as one goes further out. In highly regulatory regimes housing supply is government-driven, leading sometimes to inverted density gradients; these cities include those shaped by socialism, like Moscow (see below) and cities with heavy planning like Brasilia.

Figure 9–13

Source: Institute of Master Plan of Moscow 1992

Source: Alain Bertaud & Bertrand Renaud, Socialist Cities without Land Markets, 41 J. Urban Econ. 137, 141 (1997).

High density far from the center makes development of transportation more difficult and commuting times greater, and can lead to eventual abandonment of such housing. In general, these patterns have major implications for economic development and for economies making the transition from socialism to capitalism, in particular.

EXCLUSIONARY ZONING

We now take a closer look at one aspect of the zoning controversy—exclusionary zoning. As noted above, some accuse zoning of promoting class and race segregation, while local officials will claim that the devices in question are designed to maintain a robust tax base. Consider the following case.

Southern Burlington County N.A.A.C.P. v. Township of Mount Laurel

Supreme Court of New Jersey, 1975.
336 A.2d 713.

■ HALL, J. This case attacks the system of land use regulation by defendant Township of Mount Laurel on the ground that low and moderate income families are thereby unlawfully excluded from the municipality. The trial court so found, 290 A.2d 465 (Law Div. 1972), and declared the township zoning ordinance totally invalid. * * *

Plaintiffs represent the minority group poor (black and Hispanic)[3] seeking such quarters. But they are not the only category of persons barred from so many municipalities by reason of restrictive land use regulations. We have reference to young and elderly couples, single persons and large, growing families not in the poverty class, but who still cannot afford the only kinds of housing realistically permitted in most places—relatively high-priced, single-family detached dwellings on sizeable lots and, in some municipalities, expensive apartments. We will, therefore, consider the case from the wider viewpoint that the effect of Mount Laurel's land use regulation has been to prevent various categories of persons from living in the township because of the limited extent of their income and resources. In this connection, we accept the representation of the municipality's counsel at oral argument that the regulatory scheme was not adopted with any desire or intent to exclude prospective residents on the obviously illegal bases of race, origin or believed social incompatibility. * * *

* * * [The township's] candid position is that, conceding its land use regulation was intended to result and has resulted in economic discrimination and exclusion of substantial segments of the area population, its policies and practices are in the best present and future fiscal interest of the municipality and its inhabitants and are legally permissible and justified. * * *

I

The Facts

Mount Laurel is a flat, sprawling township, 22 square miles, or about 14,000 acres, in area, on the west central edge of Burlington County. It is roughly triangular in shape, with its base, approximately eight miles long, extending in a northeasterly-southwesterly direction roughly parallel with

---

3. Plaintiffs fall into four categories: (1) present residents of the township residing in dilapidated or substandard housing; (2) former residents who were forced to move elsewhere because of the absence of suitable housing; (3) nonresidents living in central city substandard housing in the region who desire to secure decent housing and accompanying advantages within their means elsewhere; (4) three organizations representing the housing and other interests of racial minorities. * * *

and a few miles east of the Delaware River. Part of its southerly side abuts Cherry Hill in Camden County. That section of the township is about seven miles from the boundary line of the city of Camden and not more than 10 miles from the Benjamin Franklin Bridge crossing the river to Philadelphia.

In 1950, the township had a population of 2817, only about 600 more people than it had in 1940. It was then, as it had been for decades, primarily a rural agricultural area with no sizeable settlements or commercial or industrial enterprises. The populace generally lived in individual houses scattered along country roads. There were several pockets of poverty, with deteriorating or dilapidated housing (apparently 300 or so units of which remain today in equally poor condition). After 1950, as in so many other municipalities similarly situated, residential development and some commerce and industry began to come in. By 1960 the population had almost doubled to 5249 and by 1970 had more than doubled again to 11,221. These new residents were, of course, "outsiders" from the nearby central cities and older suburbs or from more distant places drawn here by reason of employment in the region. The township is now definitely a part of the outer ring of the South Jersey metropolitan area, which area we define as those portions of Camden, Burlington and Gloucester Counties within a semicircle having a radius of 20 miles or so from the heart of Camden city. And 65% of the township is still vacant land or in agricultural use.

The growth of the township has been spurred by the construction or improvement of main highways through or near it. * * * This highway network gives the township a most strategic location from the standpoint of transport of goods and people by truck and private car. There is no other means of transportation.

The location and nature of development has been, as usual, controlled by the local zoning enactments. The general ordinance presently in force, which was declared invalid by the trial court, was adopted in 1964. We understand that earlier enactments provided, however, basically the same scheme but were less restrictive as to residential development. The growth pattern dictated by the ordinance is typical.

Under the present ordinance, 29.2% of all the land in the township, or 4,121 acres, is zoned for industry. * * * Only industry meeting specified performance standards is permitted. The effect is to limit the use substantially to light manufacturing, research, distribution of goods, offices and the like. Some nonindustrial uses, such as agriculture, farm dwellings, motels, a harness racetrack, and certain retail sales and service establishments, are permitted in this zone. At the time of trial no more than 100 acres, mostly in the southwesterly corner along route 73 adjacent to the turnpike and I–295 interchanges, were actually occupied by industrial uses. * * * [I]t appeared clear that, as happens in the case of so many municipalities, much more land has been so zoned than the reasonable potential for industrial movement or expansion warrants. At the same time, however, the land cannot be used for residential development under the general ordinance.

The amount of land zoned for retail business use under the general ordinance is relatively small—169 acres, or 1.2% of the total. * * *

The balance of the land area, almost 10,000 acres, has been developed until recently in the conventional form of major subdivisions. The general ordinance provides for four residential zones, designated R–1, R–1D, R–2 and R–3. All permit only single-family, detached dwellings, one house per lot—the usual form of grid development. Attached townhouses, apartments (except on farms for agricultural workers) and mobile homes are not allowed anywhere in the township under the general ordinance. This dwelling development, resulting in the previously mentioned quadrupling of the population, has been largely confined to the R–1 and R–2 districts in two sections * * * The result has been quite intensive development of these sections, but at a low density. The dwellings are substantial * * *

A variation from conventional development has recently occurred in some parts of Mount Laurel, as in a number of other similar municipalities, by use of the land use regulation device known as "planned unit development" (PUD). This scheme differs from the traditional in that the type, density and placement of land uses and buildings, instead of being detailed and confined to specified districts by local legislation in advance, is determined by contract, or "deal," as to each development between the developer and the municipal administrative authority, under broad guidelines laid down by state enabling legislation and an implementing local ordinance. The stress is on regulation of density and permitted mixture of uses within the same area, including various kinds of living accommodations with or without commercial and industrial enterprises. The idea may be basically thought of as the creation of "new towns" in virgin territory, full-blown or in miniature, although most frequently the concept has been limited in practice, as in Mount Laurel, to residential developments of various sizes having some variety of housing and perhaps some retail establishments to serve the inhabitants. * * *

These projects, three in the southwesterly sector and one in the northeasterly sector, are very substantial and involve at least 10,000 sale and rental housing units of various types to be erected over a period of years. Their bounds were created by agreement rather than legislative specification on the zoning map, invading industrial, R–1, R–1D, R–3 and even flood plain zones. If completed as planned, they will in themselves ultimately quadruple the 1970 township population, but still leave a good part of the township undeveloped. (The record does not indicate how far development in each of the projects has progressed.) While multi-family housing in the form of rental garden, medium rise and high rise apartments and attached townhouses is for the first time provided for, as well as single-family detached dwellings for sale, it is not designed to accommodate and is beyond the financial reach of low and moderate income families, especially those with young children. The aim is quite the contrary; as with the single-family homes in the older conventional subdivisions, only persons of medium and upper income are sought as residents.

A few details will furnish sufficient documentation. Each of the resolutions of tentative approval of the projects contains a similar fact finding to the effect that the development will attract a highly educated and trained population base to support the nearby industrial parks in the township as well as the business and commercial facilities. The approvals also sharply limit the number of apartments having more than one bedroom. Further, they require that the developer must provide in its leases that no school-age children shall be permitted to occupy any one-bedroom apartment and that no more than two such children shall reside in any two-bedroom unit. The developer is also required, prior to the issuance of the first building permit, to record a covenant, running with all land on which multi-family housing is to be constructed, providing that in the event more than .3 school children per multi-family unit shall attend the township school system in any one year, the developer will pay the cost of tuition and other school expenses of all such excess numbers of children. In addition, low density, required amenities, such as central air conditioning, and specified developer contributions help to push rents and sales prices to high levels. These contributions include fire apparatus, ambulances, fire houses, and very large sums of money for educational facilities, a cultural center and the township library.

Still another restrictive land use regulation was adopted by the township through a supplement to the general zoning ordinance enacted in September 1972 creating a new zone, R–4, Planned Adult Retirement Community (PARC). * * * The extensive development requirements detailed in the ordinance make it apparent that the scheme was not designed for, and would be beyond the means of, low and moderate income retirees. * * *

All this affirmative action for the benefit of certain segments of the population is in sharp contrast to the lack of action, and indeed hostility, with respect to affording any opportunity for decent housing for the township's own poor living in substandard accommodations, found largely in the section known as Springville (R–3 zone). * * * In 1968 a private non-profit association sought to build subsidized, multi-family housing in the Springville section with funds to be granted by a higher level governmental agency. Advance municipal approval of the project was required. The Township Committee responded with a purportedly approving resolution, which found a need for "moderate" income housing in the area, but went on to specify that such housing must be constructed subject to all zoning, planning, building and other applicable ordinances and codes. This meant single-family detached dwellings on 20,000 square foot lots. (Fear was also expressed that such housing would attract low income families from outside the township.) Needless to say, such requirements killed realistic housing for this group of low and moderate income families.

The record thoroughly substantiates the findings of the trial court that over the years Mount Laurel "has acted affirmatively to control development and to attract a selective type of growth" and that "through its zoning ordinances has exhibited economic discrimination in that the poor have been deprived of adequate housing and the opportunity to secure the construction of subsidized housing, and has used federal, state, county and local finances and resources solely for the betterment of middle and upper-income persons.''

There cannot be the slightest doubt that the reason for this course of conduct has been to keep down local taxes on *property* (Mount Laurel is not a high tax municipality) and that the policy was carried out without regard for non-fiscal considerations with respect to *people*, either within or without its boundaries. * * *

This policy of land use regulation for a fiscal end derives from New Jersey's tax structure, which has imposed on local real estate most of the cost of municipal and county government and of the primary and secondary education of the municipality's children. The latter expense is much the largest, so, basically, the fewer the school children, the lower the tax rate. Sizeable industrial and commercial ratables are eagerly sought and homes and the lots on which they are situate are required to be large enough, through minimum lot sizes and minimum floor areas, to have substantial value in order to produce greater tax revenues to meet school costs. Large families who cannot afford to buy large houses and must live in cheaper rental accommodations are definitely not wanted, so we find drastic bedroom restrictions for, or complete prohibition of, multi-family or other feasible housing for those of lesser income.

This pattern of land use regulation has been adopted for the same purpose in developing municipality after developing municipality. Almost every one acts solely in its own selfish and parochial interest and in effect builds a wall around itself to keep out those people or entities not adding favorably to the tax base, despite the location of the municipality or the demand for varied kinds of housing. There has been no effective intermunicipal or area planning or land use regulation. * * * One incongruous result is the picture of developing municipalities rendering it impossible for lower paid employees of industries they have eagerly sought and welcomed with open arms (and, in Mount Laurel's case, even some of its own lower paid municipal employees) to live in the community where they work. * * *

II
The Legal Issue

The legal question before us, as earlier indicated, is whether a developing municipality like Mount Laurel may validly, by a system of land use regulation, make it physically and economically impossible to provide low and moderate income housing in the municipality for the various categories of persons who need and want it and thereby, as Mount Laurel has, exclude such people from living within its confines because of the limited extent of their income and resources. Necessarily implicated are the broader questions of the right of such municipalities to limit the kinds of available housing and of any obligation to make possible a variety and choice of types of living accommodations.

We conclude that every such municipality must, by its land use regulations, presumptively make realistically possible an appropriate variety and choice of housing. More specifically, presumptively it cannot foreclose the opportunity of the classes of people mentioned for low and moderate income housing and in its regulations must affirmatively afford that opportunity, at least to the extent of the municipality's fair share of the present and prospective regional need therefor. These obligations must be met unless the particular municipality can sustain the heavy burden of demonstrating peculiar circumstances which dictate that it should not be required so to do.[10]

We reach this conclusion under state law and so do not find it necessary to consider federal constitutional grounds urged by plaintiffs. We begin with some fundamental principles as applied to the scene before us.

Land use regulation is encompassed within the state's police power. * * *

It is elementary theory that all police power enactments, no matter at what level of government, must conform to the basic state constitutional requirements of substantive due process and equal protection of the laws. These are inherent in Art. I, par. 1 of our Constitution,[11] the requirements of which may be more demanding than those of the federal Constitution. It is required that, affirmatively, a zoning regulation, like any police power enactment, must promote public health, safety, morals or the general welfare. (The last term seems broad enough to encompass the others.) Conversely, a zoning enactment which is contrary to the general welfare is invalid. * * *

* * * Frequently the decisions in this state * * * have spoken only in terms of the interest of the enacting municipality, so that it has been thought, at least in some quarters, that such was the only welfare requiring consideration. It is, of course, true that many cases have dealt only with regulations having little, if any, outside impact where the local decision is ordinarily entitled to prevail. However, it is fundamental and not to be forgotten that the zoning power is a police power of the state and the local authority is acting only as a delegate of that power and is restricted in the same manner as is the state. So, when regulation does have a substantial external impact, the welfare of the state's citizens beyond the borders of the particular municipality cannot be disregarded and must be recognized and served. * * *

This essential was distinctly pointed out in Euclid, where Mr. Justice Sutherland specifically referred to " * * * the possibility of cases where the general public interest would so far outweigh the interest of the municipali-

---

10. While, as the trial court found, Mount Laurel's actions were deliberate, we are of the view that the identical conclusion follows even when municipal conduct is not shown to be intentional, but the effect is substantially the same as if it were.

11. The paragraph reads:

All persons are by nature free and independent, and have certain natural and unalienable rights, among which are those of enjoying and defending life and liberty, of acquiring, possessing, and protecting property, and of pursuing and obtaining safety and happiness.

ty that the municipality would not be allowed to stand in the way." (272 U.S. at 390). * * *

This brings us to the relation of housing to the concept of general welfare just discussed and the result in terms of land use regulation which that relationship mandates. There cannot be the slightest doubt that shelter, along with food, are the most basic human needs. * * *

It is plain beyond dispute that proper provision for adequate housing of all categories of people is certainly an absolute essential in promotion of the general welfare required in all local land use regulation. Further the universal and constant need for such housing is so important and of such broad public interest that the general welfare which developing municipalities like Mount Laurel must consider extends beyond their boundaries and cannot be parochially confined to the claimed good of the particular municipality. It has to follow that, broadly speaking, the presumptive obligation arises for each such municipality affirmatively to plan and provide, by its land use regulations, the reasonable opportunity for an appropriate variety and choice of housing, including, of course, low and moderate cost housing, to meet the needs, desires and resources of all categories of people who may desire to live within its boundaries. Negatively, it may not adopt regulations or policies which thwart or preclude that opportunity.

It is also entirely clear, as we pointed out earlier, that most developing municipalities, including Mount Laurel, have not met their affirmative or negative obligations, primarily for local fiscal reasons. * * *

We have spoken of this obligation of such municipalities as "presumptive." The term has two aspects, procedural and substantive. Procedurally, we think the basic importance of appropriate housing for all dictates that, when it is shown that a developing municipality in its land use regulations has not made realistically possible a variety and choice of housing, including adequate provision to afford the opportunity for low and moderate income housing or has expressly prescribed requirements or restrictions which preclude or substantially hinder it, a facial showing of violation of substantive due process or equal protection under the state constitution has been made out and the burden, and it is a heavy one, shifts to the municipality to establish a valid basis for its action or non-action. The substantive aspect of "presumptive" relates to the specifics, on the one hand, of what municipal land use regulation provisions, or the absence thereof, will evidence invalidity and shift the burden of proof and, on the other hand, of what bases and considerations will carry the municipality's burden and sustain what it has done or failed to do. Both kinds of specifics may well vary between municipalities according to peculiar circumstances.

We turn to application of these principles in appraisal of Mount Laurel's zoning ordinance, useful as well, we think, as guidelines for future application in other municipalities. * * *

[O]ur opinion is that Mount Laurel's zoning ordinance is presumptively contrary to the general welfare and outside the intended scope of the zoning power in the particulars mentioned. A facial showing of invalidity is thus established, shifting to the municipality the burden of establishing valid superseding reasons for its action and non-action. We now examine the reasons it advances.

The township's principal reason in support of its zoning plan and ordinance housing provisions, advanced especially strongly at oral argument, is the fiscal one previously adverted to, *i.e.*, that by reason of New Jersey's tax structure which substantially finances municipal governmental and educational costs from taxes on local real property, every municipality may, by the exercise of the zoning power, allow only such uses and to such extent as will be beneficial to the local tax rate. * * *

We have previously held that a developing municipality may properly zone for and seek industrial ratables to create a better economic balance for the community *vis-a-vis* educational and governmental costs engendered by residential development, provided that such was " * * * done reasonably as part of and in furtherance of a legitimate comprehensive plan for the zoning of the entire municipality." Gruber v. Mayor and Township Committee of Raritan Township, 186 A.2d 489, 493 (N.J. 1962). We adhere to that view today. But we were not there concerned with, and did not pass upon, the validity of municipal exclusion by zoning of types of housing and kinds of people for the same local financial end. We have no hesitancy in now saying, and do so emphatically, that, considering the basic importance of the opportunity for appropriate housing for all classes of our citizenry, no municipality may exclude or limit categories of housing for that reason or purpose. While we fully recognize the increasingly heavy burden of local taxes for municipal governmental and school costs on homeowners, relief from the consequences of this tax system will have to be furnished by other branches of government. It cannot legitimately be accomplished by restricting types of housing through the zoning process in developing municipalities. * * *

By way of summary, what we have said comes down to this. As a developing municipality, Mount Laurel must, by its land use regulations, make realistically possible the opportunity for an appropriate variety and choice of housing for all categories of people who may desire to live there, of course including those of low and moderate income. It must permit multi-family housing, without bedroom or similar restrictions, as well as small dwellings on very small lots, low cost housing of other types and, in general, high density zoning, without artificial and unjustifiable minimum requirements as to lot size, building size and the like, to meet the full panoply of these needs. Certainly when a municipality zones for industry and commerce for local tax benefit purposes, it without question must zone to permit adequate housing within the means of the employees involved in such uses. (If planned unit developments are authorized, one would assume that each must include a reasonable amount of low and moderate income housing in its residential "mix," unless opportunity for such housing has already been realistically provided for elsewhere in the municipality.) The amount of land removed from residential use by allocation to industrial and commercial purposes must be reasonably related to the present and future potential for such purposes. In other words, such municipalities must zone primarily for the living welfare of people and not for the benefit of the local tax rate.[20]

* * * Frequently it might be sounder to have more of such housing, like some specialized land uses, in one municipality in a region than in another, because of greater availability of suitable land, location of employment, accessibility of public transportation or some other significant reason. But, under present New Jersey legislation, zoning must be on an individual municipal basis, rather than regionally. So long as that situation persists under the present tax structure, or in the absence of some kind of binding agreement among all the municipalities of a region, we feel that every municipality therein must bear its fair share of the regional burden. (In this respect our holding is broader than that of the trial court, which was limited to Mount Laurel-related low and moderate income housing needs.)

The composition of the applicable "region" will necessarily vary from situation to situation and probably no hard and fast rule will serve to furnish the answer in every case. Confinement to or within a certain county appears not to be realistic, but restriction within the boundaries of the state seem practical and advisable. (This is not to say that a developing municipality can ignore a demand for housing within its boundaries on the part of people who commute to work in another state.) Here we have already defined the region at present as "those portions of Camden, Burlington and Gloucester Counties within a semicircle having a radius of 20 miles or so from the heart of Camden City." The concept of "fair share" is coming into more general use and, through the expertise of the municipal planning adviser, the county planning boards and the state planning agency, a reasonable figure for Mount Laurel can be determined, which can then be translated to the allocation of sufficient land therefor on the zoning map. * * *

There is no reason why developing municipalities like Mount Laurel, required by this opinion to afford the opportunity for all types of housing to meet the needs of various categories of people, may not become and remain attractive, viable communities providing good living and adequate services for all their residents in the kind of atmosphere which a democracy and free institutions demand. They can have industrial sections, commercial sections and sections for every kind of housing from low cost and multi-family to lots of more than an acre with very expensive homes. Proper planning and governmental cooperation can prevent over-intensive and too sudden development, insure against future suburban sprawl and slums and assure the preservation of open space and local beauty. We do not intend that developing municipalities shall be overwhelmed by voracious land speculators and developers if they use the powers which they have intelli-

---

20. This case does not properly present the question of whether a developing munici- pality may time its growth and, if so, how. * * *

gently and in the broad public interest. Under our holdings today, they can be better communities for all than they previously have been.

III
The Remedy

* * * We are of the view that the trial court's judgment should be modified in certain respects. We see no reason why the entire zoning ordinance should be nullified. Therefore we declare it to be invalid only to the extent and in the particulars set forth in this opinion. The township is granted 90 days from the date hereof, or such additional time as the trial court may find it reasonable and necessary to allow, to adopt amendments to correct the deficiencies herein specified. It is the local function and responsibility, in the first instance at least, rather than the court's, to decide on the details of the same within the guidelines we have laid down. If plaintiffs desire to attack such amendments, they may do so by supplemental complaint filed in this cause within 30 days of the final adoption of the amendments.

We are not at all sure what the trial judge had in mind as ultimate action with reference to the approval of a plan for affirmative public action concerning the satisfaction of indicated housing needs and the entry of a final order requiring implementation thereof. Courts do not build housing nor do municipalities. That function is performed by private builders, various kinds of associations, or, for public housing, by special agencies created for that purpose at various levels of government. The municipal function is initially to provide the opportunity through appropriate land use regulations and we have spelled out what Mount Laurel must do in that regard. It is not appropriate at this time, particularly in view of the advanced view of zoning law as applied to housing laid down by this opinion, to deal with the matter of the further extent of judicial power in the field or to exercise any such power. The municipality should first have full opportunity to itself act without judicial supervision. We trust it will do so in the spirit we have suggested, both by appropriate zoning ordinance amendments and whatever additional action encouraging the fulfillment of its fair share of the regional need for low and moderate income housing may be indicated as necessary and advisable. (We have in mind that there is at least a moral obligation in a municipality to establish a local housing agency pursuant to state law to provide housing for its resident poor now living in dilapidated, unhealthy quarters.) * * * Should Mount Laurel not perform as we expect, further judicial action may be sought by supplemental pleading in this cause.

The judgment of the Law Division is modified as set forth herein. No costs.

NOTES AND QUESTIONS

1. New Jersey's experience with judicial remedies for exclusionary zoning has been fairly unique. After this case, developers still found it

difficult to get approval for low- and moderate-income housing, in the face of the many obstacles towns could set up. In *Southern Burlington County NAACP v. Township of Mount Laurel* (*Mount Laurel II*), 456 A.2d 390 (N.J. 1983), the court sought to strengthen its approach with a "builder's remedy" (an injunction requiring a permit for a builder who has succeeded in *Mount Laurel*-type litigation) and the possibility that a court would order a revision in the zoning ordinance. The court also held that affirmative measures by municipalities, such as incentive zoning and set-asides, were within the constitutionally delegated power to zone and within the range of remedies that a court could order. More recently the New Jersey Supreme Court has upheld as constitutional New Jersey legislation that set up a Council on Affordable Housing that would decide what a municipality's fair share of low- and moderate-income housing would be, would pass on whether measures satisfy this obligation, and would approve regional agreements. Hills Development Co. v. Township of Bernards, 510 A.2d 621 (N.J. 1986) (sometimes known as "*Mount Laurel III*"). Other states have either not found any violation in exclusionary zoning or have adopted milder approaches than New Jersey's. For example, the Pennsylvania Supreme Court has adopted a "fair share" analysis but generally restricts remedies to cases in which localities try to impose blanket prohibitions on certain types of uses. See BAC, Inc. v. Board of Supervisors, 633 A.2d 144 (Pa. 1993) (holding that challenger had not met its burden where some mobile homes were allowed).

2. Many techniques have been alleged to be implicated in exclusionary zoning. These include minimum lot sizes and restrictions or prohibition on mobile homes. What if a town has never used any of these measures but still has little low- or moderate-income housing? According to the *Mount Laurel* line of decisions, would an already developed town have an affirmative obligation to provide low- and moderate-income housing? What about an older town that is gentrifying?

3. The court cites to the *Euclid* case. Recall Justice Sutherland's nuisance analogy and characterization of apartment houses as "parasites." Also, the scheme there even limited duplexes. Was Euclid's scheme an example of exclusionary zoning?

4. The *Mount Laurel* cases rested on the state constitution. Although the federal constitution has never been interpreted in a similar way, other federal law is relevant to the problem of exclusionary zoning. Consider the Fair Housing Act and the Civil Rights Act of 1866, supra Chapter IV. For some of the literature on racial and social exclusion, see, e.g., Charles M. Haar, Suburbs Under Siege: Race, Space, and Audacious Judges (1996); Richard Thompson Ford, The Boundaries of Race: Political Geography in Legal Action, 107 Harv. L. Rev. 1941 (1994).

5. The type of housing at issue in *Mount Laurel* was finally unanimously approved in 1997, despite protests by opponents. (Two earlier projects approved in 1984 turned out to be either more expensive or less diverse than envisioned by activists.) Ellickson & Been, supra, at 779–80. The evidence of how much *Mount Laurel* has contributed to the supply of

low- and moderate-income housing is mixed at best. For a discussion of the voluminous literature on this topic, see id. at 780–82.

THE RELIGIOUS LAND USE AND INSTITUTIONALIZED PERSONS ACT

Another arena in which claims of discrimination and exclusion contend with municipalities' stated desire to protect their tax bases and amenities comes from religious land use. Congress and the Supreme Court have been locked in a battle over free exercise and establishment of religion and the standard to be applied to laws of general application that are challenged on free exercise grounds. In 2000, Congress responded with the Religious Land Use and Institutionalized Persons Act (RLUIPA), which is at issue in the following case.

Sts. Constantine and Helen Greek Orthodox Church, Inc. v. City of New Berlin

United States Court of Appeals, Seventh Circuit, 2005.
396 F.3d 895.

■ POSNER, CIRCUIT JUDGE. This is a suit by a Greek Orthodox church (we'll call it the "Church") against a small town in Wisconsin (officially a "City") named New Berlin. There are additional parties on both sides, but there is no need to discuss them. The district court granted summary judgment for the defendants.

The suit is based on subsection (a)(1) of the cumbersomely titled Religious Land Use and Institutionalized Persons Act of 2000 (RLUIPA), 42 U.S.C. § 2000cc. That subsection forbids a government agency to "impose or implement a land use regulation in a manner that imposes a substantial burden on the religious exercise of a person, including a religious assembly or institution, unless the government demonstrates that imposition of the burden on that person, assembly or institution—(A) is in furtherance of a compelling governmental interest; and (B) is the least restrictive means of furthering that compelling governmental interest." 42 U.S.C. § 2000cc(a)(1). The Act was passed in the wake of the Supreme Court's decision in *City of Boerne v. Flores,* 521 U.S. 507 (1997), which invalidated the Religious Freedom Restoration Act of 1993 (RFRA), insofar as that Act regulated state as well as federal action, on the ground that it exceeded Congress's power under the enforcement clause (section 5) of the Fourteenth Amendment. The drafters of RLUIPA sought in 42 U.S.C. § 2000cc(a)(2) to avoid RFRA's fate by limiting the scope of the new Act to (1) state regulations (statutory or administrative) that affect commerce, (2) programs that receive federal financial assistance, and (3) programs under which the agency makes "individualized assessments of the proposed uses for the property involved." By these limitations, Congress avoided having to rely solely on section 5 of the Fourteenth Amendment: Applications (1) and (2) are supported by Congress's spending and commerce powers, and (3) codifies *Sherbert v. Verner,* 374 U.S. 398 (1963). *Boerne* reaffirmed *Sherbert* insofar as that case holds that a state that has a system for granting individual exemptions from a general rule must have a compelling reason to deny a religious group an exemption that is sought on the basis of hardship or, in the language of the present Act, of "a substantial burden on ... religious exercise." 521 U.S. at 512–14. *Sherbert* was an interpretation of the Constitution, and so the creation of a federal judicial remedy for conduct contrary to its doctrine is an uncontroversial use of section 5.

We held in *Charles v. Verhagen,* 348 F.3d 601, 610–11 (7th Cir.2003), that RLUIPA is not unconstitutional on its face, that is, in all possible applications. The Sixth Circuit disagrees, and its case is now in the Supreme Court. Cutter v. Wilkinson, 349 F.3d 257 (6th Cir.2003), cert. granted, 543 U.S. 924 (2004). No constitutional issue is raised in this appeal.

There is also no serious disagreement about the facts. By purchases made in 1995 and 1997 the Church acquired a 40–acre tract in a section of New Berlin zoned residential. It wanted to build a church on this land that would replace its existing church in the nearby city of Wauwatosa—a church that it was outgrowing because its congregation was getting larger. The tract it bought was bordered on one side by a Protestant church and on the other side by a parcel of land, belonging to another Protestant denomination, that the City had agreed to rezone to allow a church to be built on it.

In 2002 the Greek Orthodox Church applied to the City for permission to rezone a 14–acre chunk of its 40–acre property from residential to institutional so that it could build its church, which it estimated would cost $12 million. The New Berlin Planning Department, to which the application was first referred, expressed concern that should the parcel be rezoned for institutional use a school or other nonreligious facility might be built on it, instead of a church, were the Church unable to raise $12 million and as a result decided to stay put in Wauwatosa. To allay this concern the Church modified its application by coupling with the proposal for rezoning the 14–acre parcel a proposal that New Berlin promulgate a "planned unit development [PUD] overlay ordinance" that would limit the parcel to church-related uses. A specialized form of zoning ordinance, a PUD "differs from the traditional zoning in that the type, density and placement of land uses and buildings, instead of being detailed and confined to specified districts by local legislation in advance, is determined by contract, or deal, as to each development between the developer and the municipal administrative authority, under broad guidelines laid down by state enabling legislation and an implementing local ordinance." Old Tuckaway Associates Ltd. Partnership v. City of Greenfield, 509 N.W.2d 323, 326 n. 1 (Wis. 1993).

The City's Director of Planning was satisfied with the revised proposal and recommended that the Planning Commission approve it, but the Commission disagreed and on its recommendation the New Berlin City Council voted the proposal down, precipitating this suit. Concern was expressed in the Commission's deliberations that if the Church didn't build a church on the property but instead sold the land, the purchaser would not be bound by the PUD. That was wrong. Nothing in the text of the PUD proposed by the Church, in the provisions of the New Berlin Municipal Code, or in the general property law of Wisconsin or elsewhere, suggests that the ordinance would lapse with the sale of the property. If the PUD said it was just limiting what *the Greek Orthodox Church* could do with the property, then a subsequent purchaser would not be bound. But since the PUD would restrict the use of the property, rather than just the conduct of its present owner, the Church's successors would be bound.

It is true that zoning ordinances are not the same as restrictive covenants that run with the land and so bind subsequent purchasers. A covenant is a contract and an ordinance isn't—though a PUD is very close to being a covenant because, as the passage that we quoted from the *Tuckaway* case explains, it is the product of a deal between a developer and a municipality. No matter; a zoning ordinance has the same effect as a covenant because, unless worded to bind only the current owner, it limits the use of the land by whoever owns it, not just whoever owned it when the ordinance was enacted. Old Tuckaway Associates Ltd. Partnership v. City of Greenfield, supra, 509 N.W.2d at 325–26; Biblia Abierta v. Banks, 129 F.3d 899, 904 (7th Cir. 1997). In *Goldberg v. City of Milwaukee Board of Zoning Appeals*, 340 N.W.2d 558, 561 (Wis. 1983), the court was explicit that a zoning variance creates a restriction that runs with the land, just like a covenant; and there is no relevant difference between a variance and a PUD.

New Berlin's mayor suggested two possible courses of action that the Church might take. One was to apply for a conditional use permit, which would allow the building of the church without altering the zoning of the land. The problem was that the permit would lapse within a year unless construction began, New Berlin Municipal Code § 275–27(E), and it was infeasible for the Church to move that fast. If the Church waited to apply for the permit until it was within a year of starting construction, it would find it difficult to raise the necessary $12 million, since it could not assure donors that the church would actually be built. The statement in the City's brief that "it would not impose a substantial burden on the Church to wait to apply for a [conditional use permit] until it had its funds and plans in place" is unrealistic. Donors would be making contributions without any confidence that the contributions could be used for their intended purpose.

The City argues that the one-year deadline could be extended. Not true: "No extension shall be made to a conditional use permit." Id. The repeated legal errors by the City's officials casts doubt on their good faith.

The other alternative suggested by the mayor was that the Church apply for a PUD that would overlie not an institutional rezoning but instead the existing residential zoning, so that if the Church sold the parcel rather than building a church on it, and if the City were correct that such a sale would void the PUD, the buyer could not make an institutional use of the property because the property would revert to being zoned residential. The Church declined to follow this route too. It seemed obvious that the mayor, unless deeply confused about the law, was playing a delaying game. The PUD proposed by the Church would have had the same effect as the one proposed by the mayor, namely preventing a nonreligious institutional use of the property by either the Church or its successors.

To prevail in this suit, however, the Church has to show that the denial of its application for the rezoning with the PUD overlay has imposed a "substantial burden" on it. The district judge inferred from language in our *CLUB* decision (*Civil Liberties for Urban Believers v. City of Chicago*, 342 F.3d 752 (7th Cir.2003)) that to satisfy this requirement the Church would have to show that there was no other parcel of land on which it could build its church. But in *CLUB* the plaintiff churches were challenging Chicago's zoning ordinance, which—unlike New Berlin's—allows churches to build in areas zoned residential, though it requires them to obtain a permit to build in areas zoned commercial. The requirement of seeking a permit, given that churches don't need one to build in a residential zone, seemed to the panel majority in *CLUB* not to place a substantial burden on the churches. Id. at 761–62. The Church in our case doesn't argue that having to apply for what amounts to a zoning variance to be allowed to build in a residential area is a substantial burden. It complains instead about having either to sell the land that it bought in New Berlin and find a suitable alternative parcel or be subjected to unreasonable delay by having to restart the permit process to satisfy the Planning Commission about a contingency for which the Church has already provided complete satisfaction.

No doubt secular applicants for zoning variances often run into similar difficulties with zoning boards that, lacking legal sophistication and unwilling to take legal advice, may end up fearing legal chimeras. On that basis the City, flaunting as it were its own incompetence, suggests that the Church can't complain about being treated badly so long as it is treated no worse than other applicants for zoning variances. But that is a misreading of RLUIPA. A *separate* provision of the Act forbids government to "impose or implement a land use regulation in a manner that treats a religious assembly or institution on less than equal terms with a nonreligious assembly or institution." 42 U.S.C. § 2000cc(b)(1); see also id., § 2000cc(b)(2). The "substantial burden" provision under which this suit was brought must thus mean something different from "greater burden than imposed on secular institutions."

But if this provision is interpreted to place religious institutions in *too* favorable a position in relation to other land users, there is a danger that it will run afoul of the clause of the First Amendment that forbids Congress (and, by interpretation of the Fourteenth Amendment, state and local governments as well) to establish a church. Westchester Day School v. Village of Mamaroneck, 386 F.3d 183, 189–90 (2d Cir.2004). But that is not argued; and if it were argued a counterargument would be the vulnerability of religious institutions—especially those that are not affiliated with the mainstream Protestant sects or the Roman Catholic Church—to subtle forms of discrimination when, as in the case of the grant or denial of zoning variances, a state delegates essentially standardless discretion to nonprofessionals operating without procedural safeguards.

On this construal, the "substantial burden" provision backstops the explicit prohibition of religious discrimination in the later section of the Act, much as the disparate-impact theory of employment discrimination backstops the prohibition of intentional discrimination. If a land-use decision, in this case the denial of a zoning variance, imposes a substantial burden on religious exercise (the statute defines "religious exercise" to include the "use, building, or conversion of real property for the purpose of religious exercise," 42 U.S.C. § 2000cc–5(7)(B)), and the decision maker cannot justify it, the inference arises that hostility to religion, or more likely to a particular sect, influenced the decision.

The burden here was substantial. The Church could have searched around for other parcels of land (though a lot more effort would have been involved in such a search than, as the City would have it, calling up some real estate agents), or it could have continued filing applications with the City, but in either case there would have been delay, uncertainty, and expense. That the burden would not be insuperable would not make it insubstantial. The plaintiff in the *Sherbert* case, whose religion forbade her to work on Saturdays, could have found a job that didn't require her to work then had she kept looking rather than giving up after her third application for Saturday-less work was turned down. But the Supreme Court held that the fact that a longer search would probably have turned up something didn't make the denial of unemployment benefits to her an insubstantial burden on the exercise of her religion. 374 U.S. at 399 n. 2.
* * *

So the City was not entitled to summary judgment. Ordinarily the sequel to our ruling would be a trial. But as we said earlier, the facts are not in dispute. The only possible uncertainty is legal; and we acknowledge the possibility that some subtlety of the Wisconsin law of property has eluded us and that there is some danger after all that the 14–acre parcel may somehow end up with a school or hospital on it rather than a church. But since the Church is perfectly willing to bind itself by whatever means are necessary not to sell the land for a nonreligious institutional use, and the City has expressed no other concern about the use of the land, the only question is whether the Church's proposal may contain some loophole that might permit (though doubtless with low probability) the eventual putting of the property to a nonreligious institutional use. The closing of the loophole, if there is a loophole, does not require a trial in the district court or a further administrative proceeding of uncertain duration and, given the whiff of bad faith arising from the Planning Commission's rejection of a solution that would have eliminated the City's only legitimate concern, an uncertain outcome as well. All that is required is that we reverse, and instruct the district court to grant the relief requested by the plaintiffs but to stay its order for 90 days to give the City a chance to negotiate with the Church such arrangements as may be necessary to eliminate any possibility that the land might be put to a nonreligious institutional use without the City's consent. For example, if the City wants to substitute the mayor's second suggested alternative—the PUD ordinance overlaid on residential rather than institutional zoning—we assume that the Church would have no objection, at least no reasonable one, provided this is done promptly. Another alternative might be to make the institutional zoning with PUD overlay (the Church's proposal) conditional on the construction of a church on the property. We are sure that with the district judge's help the parties can work out a deal that will lift a substantial burden from the Church's shoulders without impairing any legitimate interest of the City.

REVERSED AND REMANDED, WITH DIRECTIONS.

NOTES AND QUESTIONS

1. In *Cutter v. Wilkinson*, 544 U.S. 709 (2005), referred to in the opinion, the Supreme Court unanimously held that RLUIPA's prisoner provisions do not violate the Establishment Clause of the First Amendment. The impact of this decision on other possible constitutional challenges, and to the land-use portions of RLUIPA, is unclear.

2. Courts have varied in their interpretation of the religious land-use portion of RLUIPA. For example, the Eleventh Circuit disagreed with the Seventh Circuit and reaffirmed its view that "substantial burden" requires that a regulation completely prevents someone from engaging in religiously mandated activity or requires participation in an activity banned by the person's religion. Midrash Sephardi, Inc. v. Town of Surfside, 366 F.3d 1214 (11th Cir. 2004). Traditionally many courts struck down zoning that prohibited all religious uses in a municipality and some went so far as to prevent zoning from banning houses of worship in residential areas. Compare Diocese of Rochester v. Planning Bd. of Brighton, 136 N.E.2d 827 (N.Y. 1956) (holding that zoning ordinance that wholly excludes houses of worship from residential areas bears no substantial relation to promotion of the public health, safety, morals, or general welfare of the community) with Milwaukie Co. of Jehovah's Witnesses v. Mullen, 330 P.2d 5 (Or. 1958) (upholding denial of permit for building of church). More recently, some courts have moved away from this approach, and some have contended that an assumption that religious land use is inherently beneficial would violate the Establishment Clause. See, e.g., Lakewood Ohio Congregation of Jehovah's Witnesses, Inc. v. City of Lakewood, 699 F.2d 303 (6th Cir. 1983). RLUIPA has generated a great deal of controversy among commentators, both with respect to how widespread discrimination against religious land uses is and as to whether RLUIPA goes too far in favoring religion or protects unpopular religious groups. Compare Mark Tushnet, Questioning the Value of Accommodating Religion, in Law and Religion: A Critical Anthology 245, 251–52 (Stephen M. Feldman ed., 2000) with Roman P. Storzer & Anthony R. Picarello, Jr., The Religious Land Use and Institutionalized Persons Act of 2000: A Constitutional Response to Unconstitutional Zoning Practices, 9 Geo. Mason L. Rev. 929, 977 (2001).

3. Recall that Judge Posner describes the contractual nature of the Planned Unit Development. The trend in zoning has been that the ordinance represents an "opening bid" for developers. How does RLUIPA apply to the ad hoc deals characteristic of much of modern zoning?

4. If discrimination against religion can be shown, other constitutional and statutory issues arise. If a zoning ordinance targets a religious practice for elimination, the ordinance would violate Free Exercise. See Church of the Lukumi Babalu Aye, Inc. v. City of Hialeah, 508 U.S. 520 (1993). What kinds of discrimination are covered by the Fair Housing Act? How should courts approach claims that a municipality is discriminating against a house of worship? Should this be a matter of federal law? State constitutional or statutory law? (Some states have passed their own Religious Freedom Restoration Acts, some modeled on the federal statute struck down in *City of Boerne v. Flores* and some even more stringent still.) Left entirely to localities? What if a locality explicitly disfavors religious land uses as not contributing to the tax base? If so, would eliminating houses of worship count as a public purpose under *Kelo v. City of New London*, excerpted in Chapter XII?

5. In the *Sts. Constantine and Helen Greek Orthodox Church* case, Judge Posner assumes that the restriction against institutional use other than for the church building would run to successors if the church sold the property. Does the restriction bind the City of New Berlin like a contractual provision? Does it run to successor officials? Does a specific promise to a developer or landowner derogate from the City's freedom to rezone? We take up questions like these in Chapters XI and XII on government forbearance.

CHAPTER X

PROPERTY AS AN INSTRUMENT OF SOCIAL POLICY

Most of the property rights we have studied in this book have emerged slowly over long periods of time. But property regimes—or perhaps more accurately "property-like regimes"—are also deliberately created in an effort to achieve certain social policy objectives. With a tip of the hat to Hayek, we can call the older property rights in land and personal property that have been around for so long no one remembers how they got started "spontaneous" or "grown" orders of property rights, and the newer, deliberately created schemes "made" orders of property rights. See F.A. Hayek, Law, Legislation, and Liberty: Rules and Order 35–54 (1973). One type of made property we have already encountered is intellectual property rights. Intellectual property rights have some common-law background. But today the existence and scope of such rights is strictly a function of legislation which is justified as advancing certain social policy objectives, such as stimulating the creation and development of new inventions and works of the imagination or reducing consumer confusion about goods and services. Made property orders have also been advocated as solutions to a variety of other social policy objectives. For example, we saw briefly in Chapter III that there has been some experimentation in making rights to portions of the broadcast spectrum more property-like, in the sense that such rights would not only give rise to rights of exclusion but would also be alienable subject to certain limitations. These proposals have been advanced in order to promote a more efficient use of the broadcast spectrum. Similar arguments have been advanced about creating transferable rights in natural resources like water and grazing privileges on public lands. Transferable permits, which share some features of property rights, have been proposed as solutions to a variety of environmental problems, ranging from congested roads to global warming. In fact, Congress in 1990 adopted a scheme of transferable permits to deal with the problem of acid rain, and permits that authorize emissions of the gases that are the precursors of acid rain can now be bought and sold on commodity exchanges. See 42 U.S.C. §§ 7651–7651a. There appears to be no limit other than the human imagination to the ways in which such property-mimicking regimes might be used to tackle social problems. See, e.g., Michael Abramowicz, The Law-and-Markets Movement, 49 Am. U. L. Rev. 327 (1999) (discussing range of market-mimicking proposals); A.C. Pritchard, Auctioning Justice: Legal and Market Mechanisms for Allocating Criminal Appellate Counsel, 34 Am.

Crim. L. Rev. 1161 (1997) (proposing auctioning rights to represent criminal defendants).

We make no attempt here to provide a comprehensive survey of made property (or "property-like") orders. Instead, we highlight two particular controversies arising out of such regimes that illustrate some of the issues they present. Our first example comes from the world of intellectual property, and concerns a recent controversy about a congressional extension of the term of copyrights. This controversy brought to the fore sharp disagreements about what portion of the world of creative expression should be subject to exclusion rights exercised by the creators of such expression, and what portion should be open to free use by the public. Our second example concerns a natural resources crisis—the rapid depletion of many species of fish in the world's oceans—and proposals to try to reverse this trend by adopting a kind of property-like device, individual transferable quotas (ITQs), that would limit the size of the catch permitted for each species. The American experience with attempts to implement ITQs reveals some of the difficult design problems inherent in efforts to overcome a tragedy of the commons by instituting property-like solutions.

A.   Copyright and Other Term-Limited Intellectual Property Rights

Unlike the fee simple or full ownership in the realm of tangible property, some types of intellectual property rights, most prominently patents and copyrights, are limited to fixed terms. (Other types of intellectual property, such as trademarks and rights of publicity are not time-limited.) The reason for limiting the term of patents and copyrights is that these made property orders entail a tradeoff: We want to provide an incentive to inventors and creators to discover new inventions and create new works of expression, but we do not want to interfere unduly with the flow of information available to the public. The result is a compromise: We give inventors and creators the right to exclude others from using or copying their innovations, but we put a time limit on how long these rights of exclusion can be exercised, after which the information can be used freely by anyone. The length of the term of intellectual property rights is thus critical in determining where we strike the balance between these conflicting objectives. Recent controversy over congressional extension of the term of copyright protection has helped to galvanize a movement skeptical about intellectual property rights in general, and has stimulated new debate about the nature and function of these made property regimes.

Lawrence Lessig, *Free Culture: The Nature and Future of Creativity*, 133–35 (2004)

When the first Congress enacted laws to protect creative property, it faced the same uncertainty about the status of creative property that the English had confronted in 1774. Many states had passed laws protecting creative property, and some believed that these laws simply supplemented common law rights that already protected creative authorship. This meant that there was no guaranteed public domain in the United States in 1790. If copyrights were protected by the common law, then there was no simple way to know whether a work published in the United States was controlled or free. Just as in England, this lingering uncertainty would make it hard for publishers to rely upon a public domain to reprint and distribute works.

That uncertainty ended after Congress passed legislation granting copyrights. Because federal law overrides any contrary state law, federal protections for copyrighted works displaced any state law protections. Just as in England the Statute of Anne eventually meant that the copyrights for all English works expired, a federal statute meant that any state copyrights expired as well.

In 1790, Congress enacted the first copyright law. It created a federal copyright and secured that copyright for fourteen years. If the author was alive at the end of that fourteen years, then he could opt to renew the copyright for another fourteen years. If he did not renew the copyright, his work passed into the public domain.

While there were many works created in the United States in the fist ten years of the Republic, only 5 percent of the works were actually registered under the federal copyright regime. Of all the work created in the United States both before 1790 and from 1790 through 1800, 95 percent immediately passed into the public domain; the balance would pass into the public domain within twenty-eight years at most, and more likely within fourteen years.

This system of renewal was a crucial part of the American system of copyright. It assured that the maximum terms of copyright would be granted only for works where they were wanted. After the initial term of fourteen years, if it wasn't worth it to an author to renew his copyright, then it wasn't worth it to society to insist on copyright, either.

Fourteen years may not seem long to us, but for the vast majority of copyright owners at that time, it was long enough: Only a small minority of them renewed their copyright after fourteen years; the balance allowed their work to pass into the public domain.

Even today, this structure would make sense. Most creative work has an actual commercial life of just a couple of years. Most books fall out of print after one year. When that happens, the used books are traded free of copyright regulation. Thus the books are no longer *effectively* controlled by copyright. The only practical commercial use of the books at that time is to sell the books as used books; that use—because it does not involve publication—is effectively free.

In the first hundred years of the Republic, the term of copyright was changed once. In 1831, the term was increased from a maximum of 28 years to a maximum of 42 by increasing the initial term of copyright from 14 years to 28 years. In the next fifty years of the Republic, the term increased once again. In 1909, Congress extended the renewal term of 14 years to 28 years, setting a maximum term of 56 years.

Then, beginning in 1962, Congress started a practice that has defined copyright law since. Eleven times in the last forty years, Congress has extended the terms of existing copyrights; twice in those forty years, Congress extended the term of future copyrights. Initially, the extensions of existing copyrights were short, a mere one to two years. In 1976, Congress extended all existing copyrights by nineteen years. And in 1998, in the Sonny Bono Copyright Term Extension Act, Congress extended the term of existing and future copyrights by twenty years.

The effect of these extensions is simply to toll, or delay, the passing of works into the public domain. This latest extension means that the public domain will have been tolled for thirty-nine out of fifty-five years, or 70 percent of the time since 1962. Thus, in the twenty years after the Sonny Bono Act, while one million patents will pass into the public domain, zero copyrights will pass into the public domain by virtue of the expiration of the copyright term.

The effect of these extensions has been exacerbated by another, little-noticed change in the copyright law. Remember I said that the framers established a two-part copyright regime, requiring a copyright owner to renew his copyright after an initial term. The requirement of renewal meant that works that no longer needed copyright protection would pass more quickly into the public domain. The works remaining under protection would be those that had some continuing commercial value.

The United States abandoned this sensible system in 1976. For all works created after 1978, there is only one copyright term—the maximum term. For "natural" authors, that term was life plus fifty years. For corporations, the term was seventy-five years. Then, in 1992, Congress abandoned the renewal requirement for all works created before 1978. All works still under copyright would be accorded the maximum term then available. After the Sonny Bono Act, that term was ninety-five years.

This change meant that American law no longer had an automatic way to assure that works that were no longer exploited passed into the public domain. And indeed, after these changes, it is unclear whether it is even possible to put works into the public domain. The public domain is orphaned by these changes in copyright law. Despite the requirement that terms be "limited," we have no evidence that anything will limit them.

The effect of theses changes on the average duration of copyright is dramatic. In 1973, more than 85 percent of copyright owners failed to renew their copyright. That meant that the average term of copyright in 1973 was just 32.2 years. Because of the elimination of the renewal requirement, the average term of copyright is now the maximum term. In thirty years, then, the average term has tripled, from 32.2 years to 95 years.

NOTES AND QUESTIONS

1. The term "free culture" is a play on the free labor movement of the nineteenth century, which sought to further human dignity through free as opposed to coercive exchange relationships. The Creative Commons is a project started by Lessig, which makes available licenses that promote access to works with the ultimate goal of transforming people's attitudes about the role of property in cultural production. See http://creativecom mons.org. See also Lawrence Lessig, The Creative Commons, 55 Fla. L. Rev. 763 (1994); Jedediah Purdy, A Freedom–Promoting Approach to Property: A Renewed Tradition for New Debates, 72 U. Chi. L. Rev. 1237, 1265 (2005).

2. For Lessig, intellectual property (and copyright in particular) derogates from the public domain. There is an economic argument at the foundation of this position. Because information is nonrival, it can be consumed at no extra marginal cost. Thus, if we are concerned only with the efficient allocation of information, as opposed to providing incentives for its production, the correct price for utilizing information should be zero. This aspect of information has been emphasized by proponents of the public domain and those skeptical of intellectual property rights in general. See, e.g., Yochai Benkler, Free as the Air to Common Use: First Amendment Constraints in Enclosure of the Public Domain, 74 N.Y.U. L. Rev. 354, 386–412 (1999) (arguing against expanding copyright at the expense of the public domain); James Boyle, The Second Enclosure Movement and the Construction of the Public Domain, 66 Law & Contemp. Probs. 33 (2003) (arguing against increased propertization of intellectual property law at the expense of the public domain); Mark A. Lemley, Romantic Authorship and the Rhetoric of Property, 75 Texas L. Rev. 873, 885–904 (1997) (criticizing trend of propertization of intellectual property law, including the coinage of the phrase "intellectual property"). Thus, the creation of property rights in information cannot be justified on the ground that this is necessary to internalize externalities or solve any allocation problem. But is this all that exclusion does in intellectual property? In property more generally?

3. Many issues in copyright interlock, in the sense that both the strength of the incentives and the impact on the public domain (positive and negative) stem from multiple features of copyright. Fair use is a defense to copyright infringement. See 17 U.S.C. 107. The statute defines fair use in terms of purposes—"purposes such as criticism, comment, news reporting, teaching (including multiple copies for classroom use), scholarship, or research"—and calls for evaluation of the use on the basis of mainly use-based factors, which include "(1) the purpose and character of the use, including whether such use is of a commercial nature or is for nonprofit educational purposes; (2) the nature of the copyrighted work; (3) the amount and substantiality of the portion used in relation to the copyrighted work as a whole; and (4) the effect of the use upon the potential market for or value of the copyrighted work." See also Metro–Goldwyn–Mayer Studios Inc. v. Grokster, Ltd., 545 U.S. 913 (2005); Sony Corporation of America v. Universal City Studios, Inc., 464 U.S. 417 (1984).

Without fair use, the degree of restriction on the use of copyrighted material would be far greater. For example, parodies and criticism might give rise to copyright infringement. (Such liability would raise serious First Amendment concerns, and many of the authors cited supra would argue that copyright already conflicts with the First Amendment.) Consider in the following how urgent some of the arguments advanced in *Eldred* and related litigation would be without the fair use doctrine, and consider whether the repeated extensions of the copyright term described by Lessig might warrant a broader fair use doctrine than we have today.

4. Another set of issues related to copyright's strength are the formalities such as registration (or lack thereof), mentioned in the Lessig excerpt. As Lessig points out, formalities can be used to prevent copyright from extending to works of little commercial value. This is because works of little commercial value will not be renewed. For a thorough exploration of these issues, see Christopher Sprigman, Reform(aliz)ing Copyright, 57 Stan. L. Rev. 485 (2004). Do you agree that many works with little commercial value still have cultural value as inputs to future creation?

5. Commentators hostile to the current copyright regime tend to argue that copyright law is not necessary to provide incentives to create or that the incentives are overdone in the current law. Unfortunately, the role that copyright does or does not play in providing incentives for creation rests largely on indirect evidence and empirical guesswork. See George L. Priest, What Economists Can Tell Lawyers About Intellectual Property: Comment on Cheung, 8 Res. in L. & Econ. 19, 19 (1986) ("[T]he ratio of empirical demonstration to assumption in this literature must be very close to zero...."). Closely related to the Creative Commons and the related movement was the litigation, largely conducted by Lessig himself, in the following case.

Eldred v. Ashcroft

Supreme Court of the United States, 2003.
537 U.S. 186.

■ Justice Ginsburg delivered the opinion of the Court. This case concerns the authority the Constitution assigns to Congress to prescribe the duration of copyrights. The Copyright and Patent Clause of the Constitution, Art. I, § 8, cl. 8, provides as to copyrights: "Congress shall have Power ... [t]o promote the Progress of Science ... by securing [to Authors] for limited Times ... the exclusive Right to their ... Writings." In 1998, in the measure here under inspection, Congress enlarged the duration of copyrights by 20 years. Copyright Term Extension Act (CTEA), Pub.L. 105–298, §§ 102(b) and (d), 112 Stat. 2827–2828 (amending 17 U.S.C. §§ 302, 304). As in the case of prior extensions, principally in 1831, 1909, and 1976, Congress provided for application of the enlarged terms to existing and future copyrights alike.

Petitioners are individuals and businesses whose products or services build on copyrighted works that have gone into the public domain. They seek a determination that the CTEA fails constitutional review under both the Copyright Clause's "limited Times" prescription and the First Amendment free speech guarantee. Under the 1976 Copyright Act, copyright protection generally lasted from the work's creation until 50 years after the author's death. Pub.L. 94–553, § 302(a), 90 Stat. 2572 (1976 Act). Under the CTEA, most copyrights now run from creation until 70 years after the author death. 17 U.S.C. 302(a). Petitioners do not challenge the "life-plus–70–years" timespan itself. "Whether 50 years is enough, or 70 years too much," they acknowledge, "is not a judgment meet for this Court."[1] Congress went awry, petitioners maintain, not with respect to newly created works, but in enlarging the term for published works with existing copyrights. The "limited Tim[e]" in effect when a copyright is secured, petitioners urge, becomes the constitutional boundary, a clear line beyond the power of Congress to extend. As to the First Amendment, petitioners contend that the CTEA is a content-neutral regulation of speech that fails inspection under the heightened judicial scrutiny appropriate for such regulations.

[W]e reject petitioners' challenges to the CTEA. * * *

A

We evaluate petitioners' challenge to the constitutionality of the CTEA against the backdrop of Congress' previous exercises of its authority under the Copyright Clause. * * * The measure at issue here, the CTEA, installed the fourth major duration extension of federal copyrights. Retaining the general structure of the 1976 Act, the CTEA enlarges the terms of all existing and future copyrights by 20 years. For works created by identified natural persons, the term now lasts from creation until 70 years after the author's death. 17 U.S.C. § 302(a). This standard harmonizes the baseline United States copyright term with the term adopted by the European Union in 1993. For anonymous works, pseudonymous works, and works made for hire, the term is 95 years from publication or 120 years from creation, whichever expires first. 17 U.S.C. § 302(c).

Paralleling the 1976 Act, the CTEA applies these new terms to all works not published by January 1, 1978. §§ 302(a), 303(a). For works published before 1978 with existing copyrights as of the CTEA's effective date, the CTEA extends the term to 95 years from publication. §§ 304(a) and (b). Thus, in common with the 1831, 1909, and 1976 Acts, the CTEA's new terms apply to both future and existing copyrights.

II

A

We address first the determination of the courts below that Congress has authority under the Copyright Clause to extend the terms of existing copyrights. * * *

---

1. Justice BREYER's dissent is not similarly restrained. He makes no effort meaningfully to distinguish existing copyrights from future grants. Under his reasoning, the CTEA's 20–year extension is globally unconstitutional.

The CTEA's baseline term of life plus 70 years, petitioners concede, qualifies as a "limited Tim[e]" as applied to future copyrights. Petitioners contend, however, that existing copyrights extended to endure for that same term are not "limited." Petitioners' argument essentially reads into the text of the Copyright Clause the command that a time prescription, once set, becomes forever "fixed" or "inalterable." The word "limited," however, does not convey a meaning so constricted. At the time of the Framing, that word meant what it means today: "confine[d] within certain bounds," "restrain[ed]," or "circumscribe[d]." S. Johnson, A Dictionary of the English Language (7th ed. 1785); see T. Sheridan, A Complete Dictionary of the English Language (6th ed. 1796) ("confine[d] within certain bounds"); Webster's Third New International Dictionary 1312 (1976) ("confined within limits"; "restricted in extent, number, or duration"). Thus understood, a timespan appropriately "limited" as applied to future copyrights does not automatically cease to be "limited" when applied to existing copyrights. * * *

To comprehend the scope of Congress' power under the Copyright Clause, "a page of history is worth a volume of logic." New York Trust Co. v. Eisner, 256 U.S. 345, 349 (1921) (Holmes, J.). History reveals an unbroken congressional practice of granting to authors of works with existing copyrights the benefit of term extensions so that all under copyright protection will be governed evenhandedly under the same regime. As earlier recounted, the First Congress accorded the protections of the Nation's first federal copyright statute to existing and future works alike. 1790 Act § 1. Since then, Congress has regularly applied duration extensions to both existing and future copyrights. 1831 Act §§ 1, 16; 1909 Act §§ 23–24; 1976 Act §§ 302–303; 17 U.S.C. §§ 302–304.

Because the Clause empowering Congress to confer copyrights also authorizes patents, congressional practice with respect to patents informs our inquiry. We count it significant that early Congresses extended the duration of numerous individual patents as well as copyrights. * * *

Further, although prior to the instant case this Court did not have occasion to decide whether extending the duration of existing copyrights complies with the "limited Times" prescription, the Court has found no constitutional barrier to the legislative expansion of existing patents. * * *

Congress' consistent historical practice of applying newly enacted copyright terms to future and existing copyrights reflects a judgment stated concisely by Representative Huntington at the time of the 1831 Act: "[J]ustice, policy, and equity alike forb[id]" that an "author who had sold his [work] a week ago, be placed in a worse situation than the author who should sell his work the day after the passing of [the] act." 7 Cong. Deb. 424 (1831) * * * The CTEA follows this historical practice by keeping the duration provisions of the 1976 Act largely in place and simply adding 20 years to each of them. Guided by text, history, and precedent, we cannot agree with petitioners' submission that extending the duration of existing copyrights is categorically beyond Congress' authority under the Copyright Clause.

Satisfied that the CTEA complies with the "limited Times" prescription, we turn now to whether it is a rational exercise of the legislative authority conferred by the Copyright Clause. On that point, we defer substantially to Congress. Sony, 464 U.S., at 429 ("[I]t is Congress that has been assigned the task of defining the scope of the limited monopoly that should be granted to authors ... in order to give the public appropriate access to their work product.").[10]

The CTEA reflects judgments of a kind Congress typically makes, judgments we cannot dismiss as outside the Legislature's domain. As respondent describes, a key factor in the CTEA's passage was a 1993 European Union (EU) directive instructing EU members to establish a copyright term of life plus 70 years. EU Council Directive 93/98, Art. 1(1), p. 11; see 144 Cong. Rec. S12377–S12378 (daily ed. Oct. 12, 1998) (statement of Sen. Hatch). Consistent with the Berne Convention, the EU directed its members to deny this longer term to the works of any non-EU country whose laws did not secure the same extended term. See Berne Conv. Art. 7(8); P. Goldstein, International Copyright § 5.3, p. 239 (2001). By extending the baseline United States copyright term to life plus 70 years, Congress sought to ensure that American authors would receive the same copyright protection in Europe as their European counterparts.[11] The CTEA may also provide greater incentive for American and other authors to create and disseminate their work in the United States. * * *

In addition to international concerns, Congress passed the CTEA in light of demographic, economic, and technological changes, and rationally credited projections that longer terms would encourage copyright holders to invest in the restoration and public distribution of their works; see

10. Justice BREYER would adopt a heightened, three-part test for the constitutionality of copyright enactments. He would invalidate the CTEA as irrational in part because, in his view, harmonizing the United States and European Union baseline copyright terms "apparent[ly]" fails to achieve "significant" uniformity. The novelty of the "rational basis" approach he presents is plain. Cf. Board of Trustees of Univ. of Ala. v. Garrett, 531 U.S. 356, 383 (2001) (BREYER, J., dissenting) ("Rational-basis review—with its presumptions favoring constitutionality—is 'a paradigm of *judicial* restraint.'" (quoting FCC v. Beach Communications, Inc., 508 U.S. 307, 314 (1993))). Rather than subjecting Congress' legislative choices in the copyright area to heightened judicial scrutiny, we have stressed that "it is not our role to alter the delicate balance Congress has labored to achieve." Stewart v. Abend, 495 U.S., at 230; see Sony Corp. of America v. Universal City Studios, Inc., 464 U.S. 417, 429 (1984). Congress' exercise of its Copyright Clause authority must be rational, but Justice BREYER's stringent version of rationality is unknown to our literary property jurisprudence.

11. Responding to an inquiry whether copyrights could be extended "forever," Register of Copyrights Marybeth Peters emphasized the dominant reason for the CTEA: "There certainly are proponents of perpetual copyright: We heard that in our proceeding on term extension. The Songwriters Guild suggested a perpetual term. However, our Constitution says limited times, but there really isn't a very good indication on what limited times is. The reason why you're going to life-plus–70 today is because Europe has gone that way...." Copyright Term, Film Labeling, and Film Preservation Legislation: Hearings on H.R. 989 et al. before the Subcommittee on Courts and Intellectual Property of the House Committee on the Judiciary, 104th Cong., 1st Sess., 230 (1995) (hereinafter House Hearings).

H.R.Rep. No. 105–452, p. 4 (1998) (term extension "provide[s] copyright owners generally with the incentive to restore older works and further disseminate them to the public").[15]

In sum, we find that the CTEA is a rational enactment; we are not at liberty to second-guess congressional determinations and policy judgments of this order, however debatable or arguably unwise they may be. Accordingly, we cannot conclude that the CTEA—which continues the unbroken congressional practice of treating future and existing copyrights in parity for term extension purposes—is an impermissible exercise of Congress' power under the Copyright Clause.

B

Petitioners' Copyright Clause arguments rely on several novel readings of the Clause. We next address these arguments and explain why we find them unpersuasive. * * *

[P]etitioners contend that the CTEA's extension of existing copyrights does not "promote the Progress of Science" as contemplated by the preambular language of the Copyright Clause. Art. I, § 8, cl. 8. To sustain this objection, petitioners do not argue that the Clause's preamble is an independently enforceable limit on Congress' power. Rather, they maintain that the preambular language identifies the sole end to which Congress may legislate; accordingly, they conclude, the meaning of "limited Times" must be "determined in light of that specified end." Brief for Petitioners 19. The CTEA's extension of existing copyrights categorically fails to "promote the Progress of Science," petitioners argue, because it does not stimulate the creation of new works but merely adds value to works already created.

15. Justice BREYER urges that the economic incentives accompanying copyright term extension are too insignificant to "mov[e]" any author with a "rational economic perspective." Post, at 808; see post, at 807–809. Calibrating rational economic incentives, however, like "fashion[ing] ... new rules [in light of] new technology," Sony, 464 U.S., at 431, is a task primarily for Congress, not the courts. Congress heard testimony from a number of prominent artists; each expressed the belief that the copyright system's assurance of fair compensation for themselves and their heirs was an incentive to create. See, e.g., House Hearings 233–239 (statement of Quincy Jones); Copyright Term Extension Act of 1995: Hearing before the Senate Committee on the Judiciary, 104th Cong., 1st Sess., 55–56 (1995) (statement of Bob Dylan); id., at 56–57 (statement of Don Henley); id., at 57 (statement of Carlos Santana). We would not take Congress to task for crediting this evidence which, as Justice

BREYER acknowledges, reflects general "propositions about the value of incentives" that are "undeniably true."

Congress also heard testimony from Register of Copyrights Marybeth Peters and others regarding the economic incentives created by the CTEA. According to the Register, extending the copyright for existing works "could ... provide additional income that would finance the production and publication of new works." House Hearings 158. "Authors would not be able to continue to create," the Register explained, "unless they earned income on their finished works. The public benefits not only from an author's original work but also from his or her further creations. Although this truism may be illustrated in many ways, one of the best examples is Noah Webster [,] who supported his entire family from the earnings on his speller and grammar during the twenty years he took to complete his dictionary." Id., at 165.

As petitioners point out, we have described the Copyright Clause as "both a grant of power and a limitation," *Graham v. John Deere Co. of Kansas City*, 383 U.S. 1, 5 (1966), and have said that "[t]he primary objective of copyright" is "[t]o promote the Progress of Science," *Feist*, 499 U.S., at 349. The "constitutional command," we have recognized, is that Congress, to the extent it enacts copyright laws at all, create a "system" that "promote[s] the Progress of Science." *Graham*, 383 U.S., at 6.[18]

We have also stressed, however, that it is generally for Congress, not the courts, to decide how best to pursue the Copyright Clause's objectives. * * *

Indeed, "[t]his Court has repeatedly laid down the principle that a contemporaneous legislative exposition of the Constitution when the founders of our Government and framers of our Constitution were actively participating in public affairs, acquiesced in for a long term of years, fixes the construction to be given [the Constitution's] provisions." *Myers v. United States*, 272 U.S. 52, 175 (1926). Congress' unbroken practice since the founding generation thus overwhelms petitioners' argument that the CTEA's extension of existing copyrights fails *per se* to "promote the Progress of Science."

Closely related to petitioners' preambular argument, or a variant of it, is their assertion that the Copyright Clause "imbeds a quid pro quo." They contend, in this regard, that Congress may grant to an "Autho[r]" an "exclusive Right" for a "limited Tim[e]," but only in exchange for a "Writin[g]." Congress' power to confer copyright protection, petitioners argue, is thus contingent upon an exchange: The author of an original work receives an "exclusive Right" for a "limited Tim[e]" in exchange for a dedication to the public thereafter. Extending an existing copyright without demanding additional consideration, petitioners maintain, bestows an unpaid-for benefit on copyright holders and their heirs, in violation of the *quid pro quo* requirement.

We can demur to petitioners' description of the Copyright Clause as a grant of legislative authority empowering Congress "to secure a bargain—

---

18. Justice STEVENS' characterization of reward to the author as "a secondary consideration" of copyright law, understates the relationship between such rewards and the "Progress of Science." As we have explained, "[t]he economic philosophy behind the [Copyright] [C]lause ... is the conviction that encouragement of individual effort by personal gain is the best way to advance public welfare through the talents of authors and inventors." *Mazer v. Stein*, 347 U.S. 201, 219 (1954). Accordingly, "copyright law *celebrates* the profit motive, recognizing that the incentive to profit from the exploitation of copyrights will redound to the public benefit by resulting in the proliferation of knowledge.... The profit motive is the engine that ensures the progress of science." *American Geophysical Union v. Texaco Inc.*, 802 F.Supp. 1, 27 (S.D.N.Y. 1992), aff'd, 60 F.3d 913 (C.A.2 1994). Rewarding authors for their creative labor and "promot[ing] ... Progress" are thus complementary; as James Madison observed, in copyright "[t]he public good fully coincides ... with the claims of individuals." The Federalist No. 43, p. 272 (C. Rossiter ed. 1961). Justice BREYER's assertion that "copyright statutes must serve public, not private, ends," similarly misses the mark. The two ends are not mutually exclusive; copyright law serves public ends by providing individuals with an incentive to pursue private ones.

this for that." [S]ee Mazer v. Stein, 347 U.S. 201, 219 (1954) ("The economic philosophy behind the clause empowering Congress to grant patents and copyrights is the conviction that encouragement of individual effort by personal gain is the best way to advance public welfare through the talents of authors and inventors in 'Science and useful Arts.' "). But the legislative evolution earlier recalled demonstrates what the bargain entails. Given the consistent placement of existing copyright holders in parity with future holders, the author of a work created in the last 170 years would reasonably comprehend, as the "this" offered her, a copyright not only for the time in place when protection is gained, but also for any renewal or extension legislated during that time.[21] Congress could rationally seek to "promote . . . Progress" by including in every copyright statute an express guarantee that authors would receive the benefit of any later legislative extension of the copyright term. Nothing in the Copyright Clause bars Congress from creating the same incentive by adopting the same position as a matter of unbroken practice. * * *

Further distinguishing the two kinds of intellectual property, copyright gives the holder no monopoly on any knowledge. A reader of an author's writing may make full use of any fact or idea she acquires from her reading. See § 102(b). The grant of a patent, on the other hand, does prevent full use by others of the inventor's knowledge. * * * Accordingly, we reject the proposition that a *quid pro quo* requirement stops Congress from expanding copyright's term in a manner that puts existing and future copyrights in parity.[22] * * *

III

Petitioners separately argue that the CTEA is a content-neutral regulation of speech that fails heightened judicial review under the First Amendment. We reject petitioners' plea for imposition of uncommonly strict scrutiny on a copyright scheme that incorporates its own speech-protective purposes and safeguards. The Copyright Clause and First

---

21. Standard copyright assignment agreements reflect this expectation. See, *e.g.,* A. Kohn & B. Kohn, Music Licensing 471 (3d ed. 1992–2002) (short form copyright assignment for musical composition, under which assignor conveys all rights to the work, "including the copyrights and proprietary rights therein and in any and all versions of said musical composition(s), and any renewals and extensions thereof (whether presently available *or subsequently available as a result of intervening legislation)*" (emphasis added)); 5 M. Nimmer & D. Nimmer, Copyright § 21.11[B], p. 21–305 (2002) (short form copyright assignment under which assignor conveys all assets relating to the work, "including without limitation, copyrights and renewals and/or extensions thereof"); 6 id., § 30.04[B][1], p. 30–325 (form composer-pro-

ducer agreement under which composer "assigns to Producer all rights (copyrights, rights under copyright and otherwise, whether now or hereafter known) and all renewals and extensions (as may now or hereafter exist)").

22. The fact that patent and copyright involve different exchanges does not, of course, mean that we may not be guided in our "limited Times" analysis by Congress' repeated extensions of existing patents. If patent's *quid pro quo* is more exacting than copyright's, then Congress' repeated extension of existing patents without constitutional objection suggests even more strongly that similar legislation with respect to copyrights is constitutionally permissible.

Amendment were adopted close in time. This proximity indicates that, in the Framers' view, copyright's limited monopolies are compatible with free speech principles. Indeed, copyright's purpose is to *promote* the creation and publication of free expression. As *Harper & Row* observed: "[T]he Framers intended copyright itself to be the engine of free expression. By establishing a marketable right to the use of one's expression, copyright supplies the economic incentive to create and disseminate ideas." 471 U.S., at 558.

In addition to spurring the creation and publication of new expression, copyright law contains built-in First Amendment accommodations. See id., at 560. First, it distinguishes between ideas and expression and makes only the latter eligible for copyright protection. Specifically, 17 U.S.C. § 102(b) provides: "In no case does copyright protection for an original work of authorship extend to any idea, procedure, process, system, method of operation, concept, principle, or discovery, regardless of the form in which it is described, explained, illustrated, or embodied in such work." As we said in *Harper & Row,* this "idea/expression dichotomy strike[s] a definitional balance between the First Amendment and the Copyright Act by permitting free communication of facts while still protecting an author's expression." 471 U.S., at 556 (internal quotation marks omitted). Due to this distinction, every idea, theory, and fact in a copyrighted work becomes instantly available for public exploitation at the moment of publication. See Feist, 499 U.S., at 349–350.

Second, the "fair use" defense allows the public to use not only facts and ideas contained in a copyrighted work, but also expression itself in certain circumstances. Codified at 17 U.S.C. § 107, the defense provides: "[T]he fair use of a copyrighted work, including such use by reproduction in copies ..., for purposes such as criticism, comment, news reporting, teaching (including multiple copies for classroom use), scholarship, or research, is not an infringement of copyright." The fair use defense affords considerable "latitude for scholarship and comment," Harper & Row, 471 U.S., at 560, and even for parody, see Campbell v. Acuff–Rose Music, Inc., 510 U.S. 569 (1994) (rap group's musical parody of Roy Orbison's "Oh, Pretty Woman" may be fair use). * * *

* * * We recognize that the D.C. Circuit spoke too broadly when it declared copyrights "categorically immune from challenges under the First Amendment." 239 F.3d, at 375. But when, as in this case, Congress has not altered the traditional contours of copyright protection, further First Amendment scrutiny is unnecessary. See Harper & Row, 471 U.S., at 560; cf. San Francisco Arts & Athletics, Inc. v. United States Olympic Comm., 483 U.S. 522 (1987).

IV

If petitioners' vision of the Copyright Clause held sway, it would do more than render the CTEA's duration extensions unconstitutional as to existing works. Indeed, petitioners' assertion that the provisions of the CTEA are not severable would make the CTEA's enlarged terms invalid even as to tomorrow's work. The 1976 Act's time extensions, which set the pattern that the CTEA followed, would be vulnerable as well.

As we read the Framers' instruction, the Copyright Clause empowers Congress to determine the intellectual property regimes that, overall, in that body's judgment, will serve the ends of the Clause. See *Graham,* 383 U.S., at 6 (Congress may "implement the stated purpose of the Framers by selecting the policy which *in its judgment* best effectuates the constitutional aim." (emphasis added)). Beneath the facade of their inventive constitutional interpretation, petitioners forcefully urge that Congress pursued very bad policy in prescribing the CTEA's long terms. The wisdom of Congress' action, however, is not within our province to second-guess. Satisfied that the legislation before us remains inside the domain the Constitution assigns to the First Branch, we affirm the judgment of the Court of Appeals.

It is so ordered.

■ JUSTICE STEVENS, dissenting. Writing for a unanimous Court in 1964, Justice Black stated that it is obvious that a State could not "extend the life of a patent beyond its expiration date," Sears, Roebuck & Co. v. Stiffel Co., 376 U.S. 225, 231 (1964). As I shall explain, the reasons why a State may not extend the life of a patent apply to Congress as well. If Congress may not expand the scope of a patent monopoly, it also may not extend the life of a copyright beyond its expiration date. Accordingly, insofar as the 1998 Sonny Bono Copyright Term Extension Act, 112 Stat. 2827, purported to extend the life of unexpired copyrights, it is invalid. Because the majority's contrary conclusion rests on the mistaken premise that this Court has virtually no role in reviewing congressional grants of monopoly privileges to authors, inventors, and their successors, I respectfully dissent. * * *

The federal Copyright Act was first amended in 1831. That amendment, like later amendments, not only authorized a longer term for new works, but also extended the terms of unexpired copyrights. Respondent argues that that historical practice effectively establishes the constitutionality of retroactive extensions of unexpired copyrights. * * *

The general presumption that historic practice illuminates the constitutionality of congressional action is not controlling in this case. That presumption is strongest when the earliest acts of Congress are considered, for the overlap of identity between those who created the Constitution and those who first constituted Congress provides "contemporaneous and weighty evidence" of the Constitution's "true meaning." *Wisconsin v. Pelican Ins. Co.,* 127 U.S. 265, 297 (1888). But that strong presumption does not attach to congressional action in 1831, because no member of the 1831 Congress had been a delegate to the framing convention 44 years earlier. * * *

The express grant of a perpetual copyright would unquestionably violate the textual requirement that the authors' exclusive rights be only "for limited Times." Whether the extraordinary length of the grants authorized by the 1998 Act are invalid because they are the functional equivalent of perpetual copyrights is a question that need not be answered in this case because the question presented by the certiorari petition merely challenges Congress' power to extend retroactively the terms of existing copyrights. Accordingly, there is no need to determine whether the deference that is normally given to congressional policy judgments may save from judicial review its decision respecting the appropriate length of the term. It is important to note, however, that a categorical rule prohibiting retroactive extensions would effectively preclude perpetual copyrights. More importantly, as the House of Lords recognized when it refused to amend the Statute of Anne in 1735, unless the Clause is construed to embody such a categorical rule, Congress may extend existing monopoly privileges *ad infinitum* under the majority's analysis. * * *

■ JUSTICE BREYER, dissenting. The Constitution's Copyright Clause grants Congress the power to *"promote* the *Progress* of Science . . . by securing for *limited* Times to *Authors* . . . the exclusive Right to their respective Writings." Art. I, § 8, cl. 8 (emphasis added). The statute before us, the 1998 Sonny Bono Copyright Term Extension Act, extends the term of most existing copyrights to 95 years and that of many new copyrights to 70 years after the author's death. The economic effect of this 20–year extension—the longest blanket extension since the Nation's founding—is to make the copyright term not limited, but virtually perpetual. Its primary legal effect is to grant the extended term not to authors, but to their heirs, estates, or corporate successors. And most importantly, its practical effect is not to promote, but to inhibit, the progress of "Science"—by which word the Framers meant learning or knowledge, E. Walterscheid, The Nature of the Intellectual Property Clause: A Study in Historical Perspective 125–126 (2002). * * *

The Copyright Clause and the First Amendment seek related objectives—the creation and dissemination of information. When working in tandem, these provisions mutually reinforce each other, the first serving as an "engine of free expression," Harper & Row, Publishers, Inc. v. Nation Enterprises, 471 U.S. 539, 558 (1985), the second assuring that government throws up no obstacle to its dissemination. At the same time, a particular statute that exceeds proper Copyright Clause bounds may set Clause and Amendment at cross-purposes, thereby depriving the public of the speech-related benefits that the Founders, through both, have promised.

Consequently, I would review plausible claims that a copyright statute seriously, and unjustifiably, restricts the dissemination of speech somewhat more carefully than reference to this Court's traditional Copyright Clause jurisprudence might suggest. *There is no need in this case to characterize that review as a search for " 'congruence and proportionality,' "* or as some other variation of what this Court has called "intermediate scrutiny," * * * Rather, it is necessary only to recognize that this statute involves not pure economic regulation, but regulation of expression, and what may count as rational where economic regulation is at issue is not necessarily rational where we focus on expression—in a Nation constitutionally dedicated to the free dissemination of speech, information, learning, and culture. In this sense only, and where line-drawing among constitutional interests is at issue, I would look harder than does the majority at the statute's rationality—though less hard than precedent might justify * * *

Thus, I would find that the statute lacks the constitutionally necessary rational support (1) if the significant benefits that it bestows are private, not public; (2) if it threatens seriously to undermine the expressive values that the Copyright Clause embodies; and (3) if it cannot find justification in any significant Clause-related objective. Where, after examination of the statute, it becomes difficult, if not impossible, even to dispute these characterizations, Congress' "choice is clearly wrong." Helvering v. Davis, 301 U.S. 619, 640 (1937). * * *

The Constitution itself describes the basic Clause objective as one of "promot[ing] the Progress of Science," *i.e.,* knowledge and learning. The Clause exists not to "provide a special private benefit," Sony, supra, at 429, but "to stimulate artistic creativity for the general public good," Twentieth Century Music Corp. v. Aiken, 422 U.S. 151, 156 (1975). It does so by "motivat[ing] the creative activity of authors" through "the provision of a special reward." Sony, supra, at 429. The "reward" is a means, not an end. And that is why the copyright term is limited. It is limited so that its beneficiaries—the public—"will not be permanently deprived of the fruits of an artist's labors." Stewart v. Abend, 495 U.S. 207, 228 (1990). * * *

Madison, like Jefferson and others in the founding generation, warned against the dangers of monopolies. See, e.g., Monopolies. Perpetuities. Corporations. Ecclesiastical Endowments. in J. Madison, Writings 756 (J. Rakove ed. 1999) (hereinafter Madison on Monopolies); Letter from Thomas Jefferson to James Madison (July 31, 1788), in 13 Papers of Thomas Jefferson 443 (J. Boyd ed. 1956) (hereinafter Papers of Thomas Jefferson) (arguing against even copyright monopolies); 2 Annals of Cong. 1917 (1791) (statement of Rep. Jackson in the First Congress, Feb. 1791) ("What was it drove our forefathers to this country? Was it not the ecclesiastical corporations and perpetual monopolies of England and Scotland?"). Madison noted that the Constitution had "limited them to two cases, the authors of Books, and of useful inventions." Madison on Monopolies 756. He thought that in those two cases monopoly is justified because it amounts to "compensation for" an actual community "benefit" and because the monopoly is "temporary"—the term originally being 14 years (once renewable). Ibid. Madison concluded that "under that limitation a sufficient recompence and encouragement may be given." Ibid. But he warned in general that monopolies must be "guarded with strictness agst abuse." Ibid. * * *

This statute, like virtually every copyright statute, imposes upon the public certain expression-related costs in the form of (1) royalties that may be higher than necessary to evoke creation of the relevant work, and (2) a requirement that one seeking to reproduce a copyrighted work must obtain the copyright holder's permission. The first of these costs translates into higher prices that will potentially restrict a work's dissemination. The second means search costs that themselves may prevent reproduction even where the author has no objection. Although these costs are, in a sense, inevitable concomitants of copyright protection, there are special reasons for thinking them especially serious here.

First, the present statute primarily benefits the holders of existing copyrights, *i.e.*, copyrights on works already created. And a Congressional Research Service (CRS) study prepared for Congress indicates that the added royalty-related sum that the law will transfer to existing copyright holders is large. E. Rappaport, CRS Report for Congress, Copyright Term Extension: Estimating the Economic Values (1998) (hereinafter CRS Report). In conjunction with official figures on copyright renewals, the CRS Report indicates that only about 2% of copyrights between 55 and 75 years old retain commercial value—*i.e.*, still generate royalties after that time. Brief for Petitioners 7 (estimate, uncontested by respondent, based on data from the CRS, Census Bureau, and Library of Congress). But books, songs, and movies of that vintage still earn about $400 million per year in royalties. CRS Report 8, 12, 15. Hence, (despite declining consumer interest in any given work over time) one might conservatively estimate that 20 extra years of copyright protection will mean the transfer of several billion extra royalty dollars to holders of existing copyrights—copyrights that, together, already will have earned many billions of dollars in royalty "reward." See id., at 16.

The extra royalty payments will not come from thin air. Rather, they ultimately come from those who wish to read or see or hear those classic books or films or recordings that have survived. Even the $500,000 that United Airlines has had to pay for the right to play George Gershwin's 1924 classic Rhapsody in Blue represents a cost of doing business, potentially reflected in the ticket prices of those who fly. * * *

A second, equally important, cause for concern arises out of the fact that copyright extension imposes a "permissions" requirement—not only upon potential users of "classic" works that still retain commercial value, but also upon potential users of *any other work* still in copyright. Again using CRS estimates, one can estimate that, by 2018, the number of such works 75 years of age or older will be about 350,000. Because the Copyright Act of 1976 abolished the requirement that an owner must renew a copyright, such still-in-copyright works (of little or no commercial value) will eventually number in the millions. * * *

The reason is that the permissions requirement can inhibit or prevent the use of old works (particularly those without commercial value): (1) because it may prove expensive to track down or to contract with the copyright holder, (2) because the holder may prove impossible to find, or (3) because the holder when found may deny permission either outright or through misinformed efforts to bargain. The CRS, for example, has found that the cost of seeking permission "can be prohibitive." CRS Report 4. And *amici*, along with petitioners, provide examples of the kinds of significant harm at issue. * * *

The majority also invokes the "fair use" exception, and it notes that copyright law itself is restricted to protection of a work's expression, not its substantive content. Neither the exception nor the restriction, however, would necessarily help those who wish to obtain from electronic databases material that is not there—say, teachers wishing their students to see albums of Depression Era photographs, to read the recorded words of those who actually lived under slavery, or to contrast, say, Gary Cooper's heroic portrayal of Sergeant York with filmed reality from the battlefield of Verdun. Such harm, and more, will occur despite the 1998 Act's exemptions and despite the other "First Amendment safeguards" in which the majority places its trust. * * *

What copyright-related benefits might justify the statute's extension of copyright protection? First, no one could reasonably conclude that copyright's traditional economic rationale applies here. The extension will not act as an economic spur encouraging authors to create new works. * * *

What potential Shakespeare, Wharton, or Hemingway would be moved by such a sum? What monetarily motivated Melville would not realize that he could do better for his grandchildren by putting a few dollars into an interest-bearing bank account? The Court itself finds no evidence to the contrary. It refers to testimony before Congress (1) that the copyright system's incentives encourage creation, and (2) (referring to Noah Webster) that income earned from one work can help support an artist who " 'continue[s] to create.' " But the first of these amounts to no more than a set of undeniably true propositions about the value of incentives *in general*. And the applicability of the second to *this* Act is mysterious. How will extension help today's Noah Webster create new works 50 years after his death? Or is that hypothetical Webster supposed to support himself with the extension's present discounted value, *i.e.*, a few pennies? Or (to change the metaphor) is the argument that Dumas *fils* would have written more books had Dumas *père*'s Three Musketeers earned more royalties?

Regardless, even if this cited testimony were meant more specifically to tell Congress that somehow, somewhere, some potential author might be moved by the thought of great-grandchildren receiving copyright royalties a century hence, so might some potential author also be moved by the thought of royalties being paid for two centuries, five centuries, 1,000 years, " 'til the End of Time." And from a rational economic perspective the time difference among these periods *makes no real difference*. The present extension will produce a copyright period of protection that, even under conservative assumptions, is worth more than *99.8% of protection in perpetuity* (more than *99.99%* for a songwriter like Irving Berlin and a song like Alexander's Ragtime Band). The lack of a practically meaningful distinction from an author's *ex ante* perspective between (a) the statute's extended terms and (b) an infinite term makes this latest extension difficult to square with the Constitution's insistence on "limited Times." * * *

In any event, the incentive-related numbers are far too small for Congress to have concluded rationally, even with respect to new works, that the extension's economic-incentive effect could justify the serious expression-related harms earlier described. And, of course, in respect to works already created—the source of many of the harms previously de-scribed—*the statute creates no economic incentive at all.*

Second, the Court relies heavily for justification upon international uniformity of terms. Although it can be helpful to look to international norms and legal experience in understanding American law, cf. Printz v. United States, 521 U.S. 898, 977 (BREYER, J., dissenting), in this case the justification based upon foreign rules is surprisingly weak. Those who claim that significant copyright-related benefits flow from greater international uniformity of terms point to the fact that the nations of the European Union have adopted a system of copyright terms uniform among them-selves. And the extension before this Court implements a term of life plus 70 years that appears to conform with the European standard. But how does "uniformity" help to justify this statute?

Despite appearances, the statute does *not* create a uniform American–European term with respect to the lion's share of the economically signifi-cant works that it affects—*all* works made "for hire" and *all* existing works created prior to 1978. * * *

The statute does produce uniformity with respect to copyrights in new, post–1977 works attributed to natural persons. Compare 17 U.S.C. § 302(a) with EU Council Directive 93/98, Art. 1(1), p. 11. But these works consti-tute only a subset (likely a minority) of works that retain commercial value after 75 years. And the fact that uniformity comes so late, if at all, means that bringing American law into conformity with this particular aspect of European law will neither encourage creation nor benefit the long-dead author in any other important way. * * *

Third, several publishers and filmmakers argue that the statute pro-vides incentives to *those who act as publishers* to republish and to redistrib-ute older copyrighted works. This claim cannot justify this statute, howev-er, because the rationale is inconsistent with the basic purpose of the Copyright Clause—as understood by the Framers and by this Court. The Clause assumes an initial grant of monopoly, designed primarily to encour-age creation, followed by termination of the monopoly grant in order to promote dissemination of already-created works. It assumes that it is the *disappearance* of the monopoly grant, not its *perpetuation,* that will, on balance, promote the dissemination of works already in existence. This view of the Clause does not deny the empirical possibility that grant of a copyright monopoly to the heirs or successors of a long-dead author could *on occasion* help publishers resurrect the work, say, of a long-lost Shake-speare. But it does deny Congress the Copyright Clause power to base its actions primarily upon that empirical possibility—lest copyright grants become perpetual, lest on balance they restrict dissemination, lest too often they seek to bestow benefits that are solely retroactive. * * *

This statute will cause serious expression-related harm. It will likely restrict traditional dissemination of copyrighted works. It will likely inhibit new forms of dissemination through the use of new technology. It threatens to interfere with efforts to preserve our Nation's historical and cultural heritage and efforts to use that heritage, say, to educate our Nation's children. It is easy to understand how the statute might benefit the private financial interests of corporations or heirs who own existing copyrights. But I cannot find any constitutionally legitimate, copyright-related way in which the statute will benefit the public. Indeed, in respect to existing works, the serious public harm and the virtually nonexistent public benefit could not be more clear. * * *

[Appendix to Opinion of BREYER, J. omitted]

NOTES AND QUESTIONS

1.   One of the characteristics of the debate over the scope of intellectual property is dueling accusations of Lochnerism, after the case, Lochner v. New York, 198 U.S. 45 (1905), that has come to symbolize the Supreme Court's aggressive substantive due process jurisprudence used to strike down economic legislation. Julie E. Cohen, *Lochner* in Cyberspace: The New Economic Orthodoxy of "Rights Management," 97 Mich. L. Rev. 462 (1998). In the context of *Eldred*, some authors have accused the "IP minimizers" of reading their policy preferences into the Constitution in such a way so as to constrain Congress from passing certain kinds of economic legislation. Paul M. Schwartz & William Michael Treanor, *Eldred* and *Lochner*: Copyright Term Extension and Intellectual Property as Constitutional Property, 112 Yale L.J. 2331 (2003). The relationship of the Copyright and Patent Clause to the First Amendment has generally been quite controversial. Compare Jed Rubenfeld, Freedom of Imagination: Copyright's Constitutionality, 112 Yale L.J. 1 (2002) with Thomas B. Nachbar, Intellectual Property and Constitutional Norms, 104 Colum. L. Rev. 272 (2004).

2.   As reflected especially in Justice Stevens's dissenting opinion, one of the primary battlegrounds in this fight is over history. Those leery of intellectual property point to the role of monopoly in early intellectual property rights and the antimonopoly thinking in the Statute of Anne, early cases such as *Darcy v. Allen*, 77 Eng. Rep. 1260 (K.B. 1603) ("The Case of Monopolies"), and the Statute of Monopolies (1624). For these skeptics, intellectual property was "born in sin," which was eventually overcome in the seventeenth and eighteenth century, which in turn influenced the Framers of the U.S. Constitution. See, e.g., Lessig, supra, at 88; Mark A. Lemley, Ex Ante versus Ex Post Justifications for Intellectual Property, 71 U. Chi. L. Rev. 129, 135 (2004). However, some of these early "antimonopoly" landmarks sound pro-competition but actually reflect victories in obtaining pro-guild mercantilist-inspired law, won by the Parliamentary party and the guilds against the Monarch (Elizabeth I and James I) and friends. The "liberty" protected by law like the Statute of Monopolies and *Darcy v. Allen* is the liberty of the producer to practice his trade without interference from interlopers, not the liberty of the consumer to purchase in a competitive market. See Thomas B. Nachbar, Monopoly, Mercantilism, and the Politics of Regulation, 91 Va. L. Rev. 1313 (2005).

3. One argument in the *Eldred* case that did not take center stage was based on the public trust, or at least an analogy to it. In what ways might withdrawing material from the informational public domain and subjecting it to private rights raise the types of concerns that motivate the public trust doctrine (see Chapter III)? For an argument against the Copyright Term Extension Act based on the public trust doctrine, see Richard A. Epstein, The Dubious Constitutionality of the Copyright Term Extension Act, 36 Loy. L.A. L. Rev. 123, 156–58 (2003).

4. What incentives does copyright promote? As in patent law, the idea that intellectual property rights are a reward for creation is widely cited and quite intuitive, even if many disagree on how much exclusion incentive is needed in addition to kudos, a head start in publishing, and so forth. In patent law, which affords stronger property rights than does copyright, commentators have offered a wider range of justificatory theories. A. Samuel Oddi, Un–Unified Economic Theories of Patents—The Not–Quite–Holy Grail, 71 Notre Dame L. Rev. 267 (1996). One of these theories is that patent law provides incentives for commercialization, i.e., the process of improving, developing, and marketing the invention. See, e.g., F. Scott Kieff, Property Rights and Property Rules for Commercializing Inventions, 85 Minn. L. Rev. 697 (2001) (arguing that commercialization function requires property rule protection for patents); Giles S. Rich, The Relation between Patent Practices and the Anti–Monopoly Laws, 24 J. Pat. Off. Soc'y 159, 177–80 (1942) (arguing that promoting commercialization of inventions is most important function of patent); see also Edmund W. Kitch, The Nature and Function of the Patent System, 20 J.L. & Econ. 265, 276–77, 284 (1977) (discussing role of patent in giving "the patent owner . . . an incentive to make investments to maximize the value of the patent" including investments in manufacture, distribution, and market development). The arguments about incentives to promote existing works raised in Justice Ginsburg's majority opinion and Justice Breyer's dissent are an echo of this part of patent theory. Generally speaking, the more one subscribes to a commercialization theory in patent law, the more broad and strong patent rights look attractive, and something similar may be true in copyright as well. Incentives and the copyright term are the subject of the following.

William M. Landes & Richard A. Posner, *Indefinitely Renewable Copyright*, 70 U. CHI. L. REV. 471, 471, 473–85, 487–89, 491, 493–95 (2003)

In this Article we raise questions concerning the widely accepted proposition that economic efficiency requires that copyright protection should be limited in its duration. * * * [W]e are interested in the economics of indefinitely renewing the copyright term and express no view on its legality.[9]

---

9. Compare Eldred v. Ashcroft, 537 U.S. 186 (2003) (upholding the constitutionality of the Sonny Bono Act).

In this Article, we use the term "indefinite renewal" rather than "perpetual" copyright because there is an important economic difference between granting perpetual copyrights and granting copyrights for a limited time with, however, a right to renew the copyright as many times as the owner (including the original owner's heirs and other successors) wants. * * *

Although a copyright that could be renewed indefinitely could turn out to be perpetual, this is unlikely for any but a tiny fraction of all copyrights. In the empirical part of this Article we show that fewer than 11 percent of the copyrights registered between 1883 and 1964 were renewed at the end of their twenty-eight-year term, even though the cost of renewal was small. And only a tiny fraction of the books ever published are still in print; for example, of 10,027 books published in the United States in 1930, only 174, or 1.7 percent, were still in print in 2001.[11] These data suggest that most copyrights depreciate rapidly and therefore few would be renewed if even a slight fee were required; the sheer bother of applying for renewal appears to be a significant deterrent. The in-print data are indeed merely suggestive, since it costs more to keep a book in print than to renew a copyright and since a copyrighted work's derivative works may have commercial value after the original work has lost it. Nevertheless, it is apparent that even with an unlimited right of renewal the public domain would remain a vast repository of intellectual "property" (in a legal sense, nonproperty) available for use without charge and also usable as free inputs into the creation of new intellectual property. Paradoxically, a system of unlimited renewals might, depending on the length of the initial term and on the fee structure, expand the number of works in the public domain, although the average (and conceivably the total) value of the works in the public domain might fall since copyright in the most valuable works would probably be renewed many times.

Furthermore, it is a mistake to treat the public domain as a fixed supply of works from which any enlargement of copyright protection subtracts. The size of the public domain is in part a positive function of the extent of copyright protection, since, as a first approximation, the more extensive copyright protection is, the greater the incentive to create intellectual property—some fraction of which will become a part of the public domain when the copyright expires or, under the system we are suggesting, is not renewed. * * *

I. The Economic Rationale of a Limited Copyright Term

Two propositions are widely believed by most economists; it is the unrecognized tension between them that makes the question of a limited versus indefinite copyright term an interesting and difficult one. The first proposition is that so far as is feasible, all valuable resources, including copyrightable works, should be owned, in order to create incentives for

---

11. We are indebted for this computation to Lawrence Lessig, who based it on data in library and book annuals. * * *

their efficient exploitation and to avoid overuse. The second proposition is that copyright should be limited in duration. The reasons for the second proposition are several: (1) tracing costs increase with the length of copyright protection; (2) transaction costs may be prohibitive if creators of new intellectual property must obtain licenses to use all the previous intellectual property they seek to incorporate; (3) because intellectual property is a public good, any positive price for its use will induce both consumers and creators of subsequent intellectual property to substitute inputs that cost society more to produce or are of lower quality, assuming (realistically however) that copyright holders cannot perfectly price discriminate; (4) because of discounting to present value, incentives to create intellectual property are not materially affected by cutting off intellectual-property rights after many years, just as those incentives would not be materially affected if, during the limited copyright term, lucrative new markets for the copyrighted work, unforeseen when the work was created, emerged; (5) in any event, retroactive extensions of copyright should not be granted, because such extensions do not affect the incentive to create works already in existence, but the possibility of such extensions invites rent-seeking.

These five points taken together imply that the optimal term of copyright protection is determined by balancing at the margin the incentive effects of a longer term against both the administrative and the access costs arising from the public goods aspect of intellectual property; by "access costs" we mean both the deadweight losses from limiting output and the transaction costs involved in obtaining a license from the copyright owner granting access to a copyrighted work. Since the incremental incentive to create new works as a function of a longer term is likely to be very small (given discounting and depreciation) beyond a term of twenty-five years or so, access costs will tend to dominate, implying an optimal copyright term considerably shorter than the current term of life plus seventy years. Thus, the second proposition (limited copyright terms) denies the first (valuable resources should be owned) and asserts that copyrightable intellectual property should be taken out of private ownership and placed in the public domain after a period of years no greater than necessary to induce the socially efficient incentives to create new works. But is the second proposition sound? It may be, for there undoubtedly are cases in which property rights cost more than they are worth (a homely example—a spatial counterpart to the temporal limitation of copyright—is shopping malls that do not charge for parking, thus treating their parking lot as a commons). It has seemed so to many students of copyright, but its soundness no longer seems obvious to us. * * *

Were a system of indefinitely renewable copyright to be instituted today but limited to works created after the system was in place, there need be no great difficulty in identifying copyright owners a century or for that matter a millennium hence if, for example, the law required copyright owners to reregister their copyrights every ten or even twenty-five years in some central registry under the name of the copyright holder and to notify the registry in the event the copyright was transferred. The owner would be required to provide the registry with his address and notify it of any changes of address; a transferee would likewise be required to furnish this information to the registry. Then a search of the registry under the name of the original owner would reveal the address of the copyright holder from whom a license would have to be sought. The analogy is to the registries in which titles to real estate are recorded and to the Uniform Commercial Code registries in which security interests in personal property are recorded. A fee would be charged for renewing a copyright registration in recognition of the costs imposed on the registry itself and on the searchers. The fee could exceed those costs if it were desired to expand the public domain by discouraging renewals of works unlikely to have much commercial value.

Tracing costs could be reduced further by requiring, when feasible, that a notice of copyright be placed on copyrighted works. * * *

We acknowledge a possible concern with joint ownership of copyrights; the more owners there are of a property, the greater will be the tracing and transaction costs. But these problems arise in the case of land and other physical property and are dealt with in a variety of ways, such as by forming a trust or corporation to own or operate the property, or by allowing partition. Problems of joint ownership of copyrights can be solved in similar ways. The counterpart to partition is the right of any joint owner of a copyright to license its use, subject to a duty to account for the profits to the other owners. Tracing and transaction costs reduce the value of property to its owner, thus giving them an incentive to reduce these costs by consolidating ownership or control. * * *

The transaction costs argument against indefinite renewal (compared to life plus seventy years or a single renewal term) is stronger than the argument from tracing costs but must not be exaggerated. Transaction costs, like tracing costs, might actually be lower under a system of indefinite renewal, though this would depend on how the system was configured, in particular on the length of the initial and renewal terms and on the renewal fee. Although transaction costs would be incurred each time a copyright was renewed, consisting mainly of the time costs of the copyright holder and the costs of administering the renewal system, these costs would be slight if most copyrights were not renewed—and the longer the initial term and the higher the renewal fee, the fewer would be renewed.

The transaction costs incurred in negotiating for the licensing of that minority of works on which the copyright has been renewed many times would often be higher. In many cases, it is true, a new work that potentially infringes the copyright on a very old one will infringe only on a single work, for example (if there had been indefinitely renewable copyright from the beginning of time) *Ulysses* and the *Odyssey*, the movie *Clueless* and the novel *Emma*, *West Side Story* and *Romeo and Juliet*, *Ragtime* and *Michael Kohlhaas*. And in that event transaction costs should not be very high, provided that copyright protection is narrow and excludes ideas, *mise en scène*, and other aspects of expressive works that go beyond the very specific, narrowly defined form or configuration of the copyrighted work;

and provided that there is a broad fair-use doctrine that protects, for example, parodies of copyrighted works from being treated as infringement. But these are settled and economically rational features of copyright law that we would not suggest be changed. * * *

The aggregate transaction costs of a system of indefinite copy-right renewals would depend on the number (and possibly the value) of licenses (holding tracing costs constant), the transaction costs per license, and the administrative costs of operating a renewal system (including the time and inconvenience costs that individuals incur in renewing copyrights). Since the number of licenses would depend in part on the total number of works renewed, aggregate transaction costs could actually fall compared to a system of automatic renewals or a single term of life plus seventy years.

We do not wish to be dogmatic about transaction costs, since their magnitude has not been estimated. If they are thought to be very great and especially if they are believed to increase exponentially with increases in copyright duration, this could be a compelling argument for placing an upper bound on the duration of copyright under a system of (finite) renewal. * * *

The public goods argument for limiting the copyright term is valid but overstated. The argument is best understood with the aid of an example. Suppose the marginal cost of manufacturing and distributing a copy of some novel is $1, there are no fixed production costs (typesetting and editing costs are zero), but the author incurs a cost of $1000 (mainly opportunity cost) to write the book—call this the cost of expression. This is a fixed cost, which, because it does not vary with output, does not influence output. As a result, in the absence of copyright, competition among publishers would expand output to the point at which the price of the book fell to $1, which would just cover the publisher's manufacturing and distribution costs and leave nothing with which to compensate the author for his efforts. The incentive of authors to write books would diminish, and with it the supply of new copyrightable works. Copyright protection enables the publisher to charge a price above $1 without worrying about competition from unauthorized copies. A price of, say, $2 would more than cover the publisher's costs and enable a financial return to the author, encouraging him to create new valuable works. But charging a $2 price generates an offsetting social cost. Potential users who value the copyrighted work at more than $1 but less than $2 substitute other goods. The result is a loss of value (deadweight loss) equal to the difference between these users' willingness to pay and the $1 marginal cost. Viewed as an institution for promoting economic efficiency, the copyright system seeks to balance the incentive gains from pricing expressive works above marginal cost against the deadweight loss and other costs. Protection beyond that point would yield additional benefits that were more than offset by the higher costs.

From this standpoint, however, it may seem puzzling that the copy-right term is so long today, let alone that we should be suggesting that it might be made even longer by being made renewable indefinitely. On the one hand, the present value of $1,000 in royalties to be received ninety-five years from now (life plus seventy years for a work written twenty-five years before the author's death) is trivial, given any plausible discount rate. On the other hand, such a long term of copyright protection can create access (deadweight plus transaction) costs by reducing the number of works that are in the public domain at any given time and can therefore be appropriated without need to obtain a license.

But this analysis is superficial in two respects. First, just as future revenues must be discounted to present value to determine their value, so future deadweight costs must be discounted to present value to determine their present cost. If the present value of some remote future benefit is trivial, so is the present cost of the equally remote future deadweight loss. Second, because the scope of copyright protection is, as noted earlier, very narrow, the size of the deadweight loss created by copyright protection is likely to be relatively small. The narrower the scope of a property right, the more good substitutes there are, the less the owner's monopoly power is, therefore, and so the smaller is the deadweight loss that the monopoly creates. It has even been argued that the optimal duration of a patent would be infinite if the scope of patent protection were narrowed appropriately. Conceivably the scope of copyright protection is already so narrow that an infinite copyright term would not be a source of significant deadweight loss. But this is merely a conjecture (are there good substitutes, for example, for Shakespeare's plays or Mozart's piano concertos?), and one reason the scope is narrow is that the public domain provides a source of free inputs into the creation of new copyrightable works. If valuable works are withheld from the public domain because the copyright term has been extended, there may be significantly fewer public domain works (weighting number by quality) upon which to draw, which will reduce competition with existing copyrightable works.

Our earlier point about the need to discount future deadweight costs loses most of its force, moreover, if the question is whether to extend the term of existing rather than future copyrights—at least existing copyrights that, unless extended, will soon expire. Suppose a copyright that was about to expire is extended another twenty years. The deadweight costs will begin to accrue immediately. They still must be discounted, but the present cost will be much greater than if the discounting were merely of deadweight costs that were to be incurred in a period beginning seventy-five years from now. * * *

The *composition* of the public domain might well differ under an indefinite-renewal system, because there would be better sorting of works into two categories: (1) valuable works, where the benefits of property rights may exceed the costs, and (2) works of little value, where the costs of administering copyright protection are very likely to exceed the benefits and a stiff renewal fee would discourage the owner from seeking continued copyright protection. We argue that this sorting might produce a more efficient system of copyright than the present system.

[Turning to rentseeking costs,] owners of copyrights on old but still commercially valuable works have an incentive to incur lobbying and related expenses to persuade Congress to extend the copyright term on these works. * * * Consider Disney's successful efforts to lobby for the Sonny Bono Act that extended its copyrights by twenty years in order to protect its soon-to-expire copyrights on Mickey Mouse and other cartoon characters. The costs of these efforts, and of the unsuccessful efforts of competing interests to oppose the extension, were incurred to obtain and limit economic rents, respectively, and if there are no offsetting social benefits these costs were wasted from a social standpoint.

Rent-seeking activities are a natural consequence of any fixed copyright term, since the Congress that enacts the term cannot prevent future Congresses from increasing the term retroactively. There will always be some copyright holders whose income will be diminished when their works fall into the public domain, and they have an incentive to seek retroactive extensions as the end of the copyright term draws near. The problem of rent-seeking that arises from the possibility of retroactive extensions of copyrights would be solved by indefinite renewals, though an alternative would be to interpret the Copyright Clause of the Constitution to forbid retroactive extensions. Since indefinite renewals would eliminate the prospect of losing the income produced by old but still valuable copyrights, there would be little incentive to lobby for copyright extensions. We say "little" rather than "no" because resources might still be spent lobbying for lower renewal fees and longer renewal terms. But normally it would be cheaper to pay the renewal fee than to try to change the law. Notice, however, that a system of indefinite renewals that was limited to future copyrights would fail to curb the incentive to seek retroactive extensions of existing copyrights. Notice, too, that fixing an upper bound to renewals would leave the rent-seeking problem unsolved, since, as the work approached expiration, if it retained commercial value the copyright holder would have an incentive to lobby for a right of further renewal. * * *

II.   Rationing and Maintaining Intellectual Property

* * * The public goods argument asserts, however, that whatever the case with regard to costs, there are no efficiency or social benefits from continuing indefinitely to protect even a small number of valuable works. It is this issue that we now take up. The argument assumes that the only justification for copyright protection is the incentives it produces to create new works. This may be wrong, or even anachronistic, since until the 1976 Copyright Act, and in the case of works for hire right up to the present day, federal copyright protection attached at dissemination or registration rather than at creation.

The economic theory of property rights emphasizes not only their incentive effects, that is, the investment that they encourage, but also their effect in optimizing current uses of property. Frank Knight made this argument many years ago, using the example of highway congestion. An example closer to intellectual property is a natural pasture. The purpose of assuming it to be natural rather than cultivated is to abstract from the incentive benefits of recognizing a property right. The natural pasture is not created by human effort and therefore there is no social value in encouraging investments in creating it. But in the absence of property rights the pasture would be overgrazed because none of the users would take account of the cost that his use imposed on the other users by making their cattle graze more to obtain the same amount of food. Thus, property rights would confer a social benefit but it would be unrelated to encouraging the creation of new property.

Analogous benefits of property rights are recognized in some areas of intellectual property. They are recognized in trademark law, which does not impose any fixed limitation on the duration of a trademark, since confusion would result if the same trademark denoted goods of different provenance and quality, and which, through the concept of "dilution," protects trademark owners from the loss of value resulting from nonconfusing duplication of their trademarks (as where a hot dog stand adopts the name "Tiffany's"). And increasingly they are recognized in the law of publicity rights as well, which prevents others from using one's name or likeness in advertising or other commercial uses without one's permission. The tendency is to make these rights inheritable. The motive is not to encourage greater investment in becoming a celebrity (the incremental encouragement would doubtless be minimal), but to prevent the premature exhaustion of the commercial value of the celebrity's name or likeness.

Recognition of an "overgrazing" problem in copyrightable works has lagged. * * *

But how far is the concern with technological externalities that has been flagged in reference to publicity rights actually applicable to copyright? A book or other copyrightable property is, as we noted earlier, a public good; its use by one consumer does not interfere with its use by any other. This point cannot be decisive, however; a celebrity's name or likeness has public good characteristics as well, yet unlimited reproduction of the name or the likeness could prematurely exhaust the celebrity's commercial value, just as unlimited drilling from a common pool of oil or gas would deplete the pool prematurely. The same could be true of a novel or a movie or a comic book character or a piece of music or a painting, particularly with regard to copyrights on components of completed works rather than on the completed works themselves. If because copyright had expired anyone were free to incorporate the Mickey Mouse character in a book, movie, song, etc., the value of the character might plummet. Not only would the public rapidly tire of Mickey Mouse, but his image would be blurred, as some authors portrayed him as a Casanova, others as catmeat, others as an animal-rights advocate, still others as the henpecked husband of Minnie. * * * To the extent that such appropriations of the Mickey Mouse character were classified as parodies, they would be sheltered by the fair-use doctrine. But not all would be so classified, and in that event the fair-use doctrine would not insulate them from liability under a regime of indefinitely renewable copyright.

We do not wish to press this argument too far. While examples can even be given of works of elite culture that may have been debased by unlimited reproduction (the *Mona Lisa*, the opening of Beethoven's *Fifth Symphony*, and several of Van Gogh's most popular paintings come immediately to mind), there are counterexamples, such as the works of Shakespeare, which seem undiminished by the proliferation of performances and derivative works, some of them kitsch, such as Shakespeare T-shirts and the movie *Shakespeare in Love*. * * *

A second economic argument against limiting the duration of copyright is unrelated to congestion or overuse externalities. It returns us to the question of incentives. The conventional economic criticism of unlimited duration draws too sharp a distinction between creation and copying. Imagine a novel published many years ago in which copyright has expired. The novelist is rediscovered and there is a surge in demand for his novels. Since no publisher could establish a property right in them, the incentives of publishers to publish and promote them might well be inadequate from a social standpoint. * * *

The essential points are illustrated by the copyright on Mickey Mouse. First, the character has changed in appearance over the years since it was first created, indicating continued investment after the initial creation of the copyrighted work. Second, should the copyright be fated to expire, Disney would have an incentive before expiration to change the character further so that, by copyrighting the changes, it might impede imitations. A further complication is that Mickey Mouse is a Disney trademark, and trademarks have no fixed expiration date. After the copyright expired, copiers would still need to disclaim a Disney origin in order to avoid trademark infringement; such disclaimers, like conspicuous notices on paintings, might in some instances impair the commercial value of the copy.

These examples, unlike the analysis of publicity rights and our extension of that analysis to copyright, show that a case against a definite time limit for copyrights can be based on the traditional incentive-based argument for property rights, though with a new twist. The new twist is recognition that the need to invest in intellectual property to maximize its value is not exhausted in the initial creation of the property. Investment is necessary to maintain the value of the property as well, and also to resurrect abandoned or otherwise unexploited intellectual property.

Magnitudes are critical, and in the absence of them only tentative conclusions are possible. * * *

[Consider] the case in which intellectual property that has fallen into the public domain by abandonment is sought to be revived. Suppose Tobias Smollett had copyrighted his books but after a few renewals his heirs had decided the books had no value and so declined to pay the renewal fee. Our analysis implies that a publisher who wants to publish Smollett's books today should be permitted to take out copyright on them, by analogy to the rule that allows finders to obtain title to abandoned (as distinct from merely misplaced) property. Unfortunately, the efficient implementation of such a rule is considerably more complicated in the case of intellectual than of physical property. In the latter case, allowing abandoned property to be withdrawn from the public domain unproblematically implements the policy that valuable property should be owned in order to create the correct incentives for its exploitation. But imagine a "finder" of intellectual property who claimed to have found, and who sought to obtain copyright in and register, all the books in the British Library on which copyright had expired. Such a claim, if honored, would be tantamount to "banking" trademarks by simply listing all possible combinations of the letters of the alphabet, and would create the rent-seeking and transaction-cost problems that we have elsewhere discussed in the trademark context.

The problem may not be insoluble. One way to deal with it would be to limit the acquisition of copyright in previously created works to works created after the law authorizing such acquisition was passed. Another would be to require the publication of such a work within a specified period of time after copyright was claimed in it. Another would be to charge a stiff fee for registering such a copyright. * * *

[T]here are at least three possible economic reasons for singling out the particular marketing expenditures in issue for protection by copyright law. First, the distinction between expressive works and the marketing of those works is overdrawn. Consider a record company that develops, promotes, and distributes new pop records. A few of them will be financial successes but the others will lose money. Which will be hits and which will be flops is not known in advance. In the absence of copyright protection—and here we are speaking just of protection against the copying of the sound recordings themselves—unauthorized copying of the hit records will drive their price down to their cost of manufacture and distribution and leave nothing for covering the costs incurred in developing and promoting recordings of new songs and new performers. Copyright protection enables the record company to earn enough money on the hits to cover both their costs and the production and marketing costs of the many failures. In effect, copyright indirectly prevents free riding on marketing and information expenditures that are similar to the expenditures incurred in rediscovering obscure public domain works and in maintaining interest in soon-to-expire copyrighted works. To state this another way, exploring the market for expressive works, the sort of exploration that the measures we are discussing would encourage, is a stage in the creation of intellectual property. * * *

NOTES AND QUESTIONS

1.   In another part of their article, Landes and Posner report on an empirical study of copyright renewals in the twentieth century. Through regression analysis they show that registrations and renewals are quite sensitive to modest changes in fees. From this they conclude that their proposal of indefinite renewals of copyright would expand the public domain and sort works into valuable and protected versus less valuable and unprotected by copyright. If so, where would Lessig disagree with their approach?

2.   Landes and Posner propose to alter the temporal scope of copyright, but in the process they put crucial emphasis on the system for registering rights. Without such a system, the tracing costs implied by indefinitely renewable copyright would be enormous. But are Landes and Posner too quick to assume that notice through registries essentially solves the tracing, or information-cost, problem? Based on what you have seen of registries in Chapter VIII, do you share their optimism in this regard?

3.   Landes and Posner also are not bothered by the possibility of fragmented rights—the "anticommons" problem. The possibility that multiple and especially overlapping rights would cause too many owners to be able to veto and hold out, thus preventing follow-on projects, has been explored as a theoretical possibility especially as applied to patenting in biotechnology. See Michael A. Heller & Rebecca S. Eisenberg, Can Patents Deter Innovation? The Anticommons in Biomedical Research, 280 Science 698–701 (1998). What little empirical evidence there is to date rests on surveys and indicates that anticommons problems can arise but usually do not pose major obstacles in the biotechnology industry. Methods used to overcome these problems range from licensing, to inventing around, to simple violation. See, e.g., John P. Walsh, Ashish Arora & Wesley M. Cohen, Effects of Research Tool Patents and Licensing on Biomedical Innovation, in Patents in the Knowledge–Based Economy 285 (Wesley M. Cohen & Stephen A. Merrill eds., 2003). Are anticommons problems likely to arise in copyright?

Hanoch Dagan, *Property and the Public Domain*, 18 Supp. YALE J.L. & HUMAN. 84, 84–86, 87, 91–93 (2006)

Friends of the public domain are typically suspicious of property-talk. Property is perceived as the foe, epitomizing the threat of a shrinking public domain. This common view is misguided; it is also unfortunate. It is misguided because the cleavage between property discourse and a thriving public domain is largely illusory. It is unfortunate because the concept of property has enormous rhetorical power in shaping people's expectations and therefore in the construction of what they deem normal, obvious, and thus clearly justified. For both reasons, friends of the public domain should embrace property, rather than fight it.

Lawrence Lessig's work epitomizes the suspicion of public domain advocates towards property. In *Re-crafting a Public Domain* Lessig laments the expanding rights of copyright holders to preclude others from using cultural artifacts and offers strategies for reversing the tide. Lessig claims that once classified as property, copyright is burdened by "the ordinary view about property" which is "binary at its core."[2] He believes that notwithstanding lawyers' understanding of property as a bundle of rights, the propertization of creative activity facilitates a social ecology in which you must secure permission before your use. This ecology (alongside the

---

2. Lawrence Lessig, Re-crafting a Public Domain, 17 Yale J.L. & Human. 56, 81 (2006).

powerful interest groups supporting it) accounts for Lessig's pessimism about the possibility of a happy legal reform. It also explains his apologetic response to critics of the attempt to encourage authors to opt into a system where only some of the rights copyright secures are typically reserved.[3]

Neither the pessimism nor the apologia is warranted. Nothing in the language of property necessarily invites the agenda of the content industry. Quite the contrary: the form, the substance, and the history of property convey lessons that are rather helpful to the goal, which I share, of re-crafting the public domain. By neglecting these lessons, guardians of the public domain allow copyright expansionists to capture the powerful brand-name of property, thus undermining their very own cause. * * *

The imagined war between property and the public domain begins with a dichotomy between lawyers' conception of property as a bundle of rights and its lay understanding as exclusion. The former view was never fully accepted in popular consciousness, so the argument goes, and therefore the latter must have won people's minds, entailing a set of devastating consequences for the increasingly propertized realm of creative activity. The validity of this argument depends on the plausibility of the conceptual choice it presents. Fortunately, this choice is as flawed as it is pervasive in property scholarship.

Neither the conception of property as exclusion nor that of property as a bundle bears any resemblance to the law of property as lawyers know it, or—even more importantly—as citizens experience it in everyday life. We should thus discard both of these conceptions of property and adopt one that is more in line with property's real life manifestations. Happily, as we will see, this understanding of property is hospitable to the purpose of reinvigorating a rich public domain.

Some measure of exclusion is, to be sure, part of what property usually entails. Yet, the conception of property *as* exclusion—understanding property law as the locus of a struggle between autonomous excluders, each cloaked in a Blackstonian armor of "sole and despotic dominion"[6]—is a great exaggeration. Exclusion can exhaust the field of property only if large parts of what is conventionally understood as the law of property are set aside. Numerous property rules, prescribing the rights and obligations of members of local communities, neighbors, co-owners, partners, and spouses cannot be fairly analyzed under the exclusion paradigm; the whole point of these elaborate doctrines, after all, is to provide structures for cooperative, rather than competitive, relationships. These doctrines are not marginal to the life of property. Rather, they deal with some of our most commonplace human interactions and thus tend to blend into our natural environment. Therefore, postulating exclusion as the lay understanding of property is not only condescending; it is also probably mistaken.

---

3. Id. at 74, 78–81. See also Lawrence Lessig, Free Culture 83–84, 117–19, 172 (2004).

6. William Blackstone, 2 Commentaries *2.

This failure of the exclusion conception of property does not mean that its "bundle of rights" counterpart is any more successful. Again, understanding property as a bundle has a grain of truth: property has no canonical composition, and therefore a reference to the concept of property can never entail an inevitable package of incidents. But property is not, as the bundle metaphor might suggest, a mere laundry list of rights with limitless permutations. Rather, as the *numerus clausus* principle prescribes, at any given time property law offers only a limited number of standardized forms of property. Not only do ordinary people not buy into the idea of open-ended bundles of rights; property law itself has never applied it either.

Rather than a uniform bulwark of exclusion or a formless bundle of rights, property should be thought of the way it actually is in both law and life: a set of institutions, each of which is constituted by a particular configuration of rights. * * *

Appreciating the multiple faces of property should relieve some of the concerns of public domain guardians and help direct their intellectual and public activity. Thus, rejecting property monism undermines the view, which Lessig takes seriously, that once creative activity is governed by a property regime—whatever its specific content may be—it necessarily becomes overly commercialized or carries overly individualistic connotations. In both law and life the repertoire of property institutions governs a wide array of types of social interactions, running from arm's length relationships guided by a competitive ideal, to familial relationships, where the ideal of equal sharing is the norm, with many intermediate categories along this spectrum. Indeed, the institutions of property are as diverse in their normative underpinnings as the categories of human interaction. The idea that the entitlements owners typically have in one type of property institution (governing, for example, commercial activity) necessarily apply with respect to others (such as those dealing with creative activity) is foreign to property law. It is also dramatically distant from the daily experience of property on the ground.

Therefore, instead of agonizing over the propertization of creativity, friends of the public domain should work toward a redefinition of the incidents of property rights in creative products, so that they properly respond to the normative concerns pertinent to the assignment of rights in information.[12] This is the usual story of property dynamism: existing property institutions are constantly evolving, and new institutions are added (while others are dropped). * * *

Lessig sketches three helpful suggestions for a legal reform that could support a permission-free culture: removing copying from the exclusive rights that copyright law grants, restoring formalities, and applying a modified [fair use] doctrine that would curtail the ability of copyright

---

12. As usual, this inquiry should take into account the nature of the resource at stake, in our case information. Thus, for example, the fact that the consumption of information is nonrivalrous is crucial insofar as the consideration of providing appropriate incentives is concerned.

holders to preclude others from using their work as part of a commentary or criticism in matters of public import. But he is rather pessimistic about the possibility of their adoption. I am not competent to assess the existing political clout of the rival camps in the copyright wars. But I believe that given the cultural power of property, this pessimism may be premature because friends of the public domain have not yet used the intellectual support they could extract from property discourse. * * *

To be sure, Lessig and others have demonstrated stronger links between a happy copyright reform and other values, such as facilitating efficiency, enriching our culture, and nourishing democratic political institutions.[36] But by situating these values outside property—let alone as counter-property concerns—they undermine the force of these claims, making them too easily dismissible or discounted given the cultural power of property. Here again the divorce of public domain advocates from property is not only unfortunate but also erroneous. Just like labor (or personhood), these important concerns are better conceptualized as property values because they are part of the reason why we have rights in intellectual property in the first place. While it is understandable that copyright expansionists would want to exclude these concerns from property discourse, public domain advocates have no good reason to follow suit.

A similarly promising convergence between property discourse and the agenda of public domain preservation emerges regarding Lessig's last doctrinal suggestion: making copyright more formal. Both aspects of this suggestion—utilizing more clear rules and less vague standards, and strengthening copyrights' registration system—are indeed desirable. Both are supported by property law and theory.

Property law has always been heavily-laden towards crystalline rules, as opposed to muddy standards.[40] This is not surprising given the important property values served by clear entitlements. The predictability of such entitlements does not only serve efficiency; it is also conducive to liberty as it limits the application of discretion following various types of interaction. Likewise, the increasing value of intellectual products and the decreasing value of the costs of copyright registration make Lessig's claim for copyright registry a casebook example of property theory. * * *

[T]he defense—or revival—of a robust public domain can benefit from drawing on the rich intellectual resources that the institutions, values, and doctrines of property provide. Therefore, Lessig and his many fellow travelers—I count myself as one—should positively engage in property-talk, rather than grudgingly concede its unfortunate presence.

---

36. On copyright and democracy see Neil Netanel, Copyright and a Democratic Civil Society, 106 Yale L.J. 283, 341–85 (1996). Cf. Niva Elkin–Koren, Cyberlaw and Social Change: A Democratic Approach to Copyright Law in Cyberspace, 14 Cardozo Arts & Ent. L.J. 215 (1996).

40. See Carol M. Rose, Crystals and Mud in Property Law, 40 Stan. L. Rev. 577 (1988).

NOTES AND QUESTIONS

1. Does Dagan's promotion of "property talk"—a phrase of Carol Rose's, in whose honor the symposium containing this article was held—really address Lessig's concern about the culture of propertization of culture? For an argument that even Lessig's Creative Commons, by offering a menu of access-promoting licenses, strengthens the tendency for creators to think of their creations as "theirs" and a source of value capture through property, see Niva Elkin–Koren, What Contracts Cannot Do: The Limits of Private Ordering in Facilitating a Creative Commons, 74 Fordham L. Rev. 375 (2005). Others, like Dagan, have argued that property can be used to enhance the public domain by creating public easements and other rights of access, a little like the streets and public ways in land law. See, e.g., Robert P. Merges, A New Dynamism in the Public Domain, 71 U. Chi. L. Rev. 183, 200–03 (2004); Carol M. Rose, Romans, Roads and Romantic Creators: Traditions of Public Property in the Information Age, 66 Law & Contemp. Probs. 89, 90 (2003); R. Polk Wagner, Information Wants to Be Free: Intellectual Property and the Mythologies of Control, 103 Colum. L. Rev. 995, 1032–33 (2003).

2. Do cultural concerns about property talk in this area really conflate all property with private property? Or is exclusion itself, even that involved in a commons, offensive to the public domain? In fact, efforts to promote access like the Creative Commons and the open-source software movement upon which it was based rest on a foundation of intellectual property and the exclusion rights it affords. What is unique about these efforts is that the basic exclusion rights associated with intellectual property are used to enforce adoption of licenses that promote access. Under some open-source licenses people wishing to use the information must not charge further users, and under so-called "infectious licenses" must require their licensees to include a similar access-promoting provision in their licenses, and so forth. See, e.g., Josh Lerner & Jean Tirole, The Scope of Open Source Licensing, 21 J.L. Econ. & Org. 20 (2005); Greg R. Vetter, "Infectious" Open Source Software: Spreading Incentives or Promoting Resistance?, 36 Rutgers L.J. 53 (2004). Do such licenses create excessive information costs, or does the Internet make such schemes easy to track? Are such licenses enforceable? To date, no court has squarely faced this question. Cf. Progress Software Corp. v. MySQL AB, 195 F. Supp. 2d 328 (D. Mass. 2002). A Linux programmer has successfully enforced a General Public License in a German case. Brian W. Carver, Share and Share Alike: Understanding and Enforcing Open Source and Free Software Licenses, 20 Berkeley Tech. L.J. 443, 468–72 (2005). Existing open source projects are a varying mix of proprietary and nonproprietary elements, see Lerner & Tirole, supra. In a sense, open source licensing creates a kind of "non-profit property," and can be viewed as an analogue to the entity property we studied in Chapter VI. Entity law includes various forms of cooperatives and nonprofits, in which producers, consumers, or some set of diffuse beneficiaries, "own" the residual claim on the organization. See Henry Hansmann, The Ownership of Enterprise (1996).

B.   INDIVIDUAL TRANSFERABLE QUOTAS (ITQs) AND THE DESTRUCTION OF OCEAN FISHERIES

Made property regimes vary widely in terms of how far or to what extent they confer exclusion rights on the holders of entitlements. In the environmental and natural resources context, transferable permits share some of the attributes associated with property, such as conferring widely dispersed authority, having monetary value, and being alienable. But in traditional property terms, transferable permits are closer to licenses— privileges to engage in particular activity—rather than in rem rights to exclude others from designated things. Nevertheless, such regimes are often characterized as property rights solutions, and they are certainly more property-like than top-down regulation (command and control), with which they are often contrasted. We consider here the prospects for using individual transferable quotas (ITQs) to save ocean fisheries from depletion and even prevent extinction of some of the world's most valuable resources.

Jonathan H. Adler, *Legal Obstacles to Private Ordering in Marine Fisheries*, 8 Roger Williams U. L. Rev. 9 (2002)

The overall state of the world's fisheries is much worse today than 45 years ago, even though most fisheries have come under government regulation in this period.

Fisheries worldwide are in decline. Overfishing and poor management have left numerous fish species in trouble. It is estimated that almost one-half of global fish stocks are fully exploited and approximately twenty-two percent are over-exploited. Even those who otherwise question tales of environmental ruin acknowledge the plight of the world's marine resources. The United States is no exception. The National Marine Fisheries Service (NMFS) identified sixty-five overfished species in its latest report to Congress. The status of an additional 589 species is unknown. While NMFS reports the number of healthy fish species has increased in recent years, such gains have come at tremendous cost to local fishing communities faced with fishery closings and other stringent conservation measures. Nearly three decades of federal regulation have failed to provide for the sustainable utilization of America's marine resources. * * *

Conservation of marine fisheries presents the archetypal "commons" problem * * * So long as there is open-access to the fishery, each fisher has an incentive to catch as much as possible, even beyond the point of sustainability. These incentives are strong in the fishery context as the marginal cost of increased fishing effort for an active fisher is often quite small compared to the potential economic reward. Fishers do not benefit from self-restraint because none has any assurance that other participants in the fishery will follow suit. * * *

The creation of property rights is the most obvious means of preventing the tragedy of the commons. As a general rule, where resources are owned, there is less concern about their overuse. Property owners have both the ability to protect the owned resource, and a substantial incentive to ensure that the value of their property—both to themselves and to others—is maintained. As Harold Demsetz explains, "[I]f a single person owns land, he will attempt to maximize its present value by taking into account alternative future time streams of benefits and costs and selecting that one which he believes will maximize the present value of his privately-owned land rights."[16] Conversely, the lack of property rights provides substantial incentives against resource conservation.

Not only do property rights provide incentives for better stewardship, they also foster private ordering by reducing the costs of negotiating over remaining externalities. Thus, it may not be necessary to establish property rights in all relevant resources to achieve a substantial amount of cost internalization. Conversely, the mere existence of externalities is often attributable to the absence of property rights and the consequent rights to contract.

The creation of property rights is not always an option, however. Property rights can be difficult to define, monitor, and enforce. In some cases the costs of establishing property rights will be greater than the benefits. There may also be political, cultural or social obstacles to their creation. In the context of fisheries, individuated private property rights in fisheries are generally lacking because many species are mobile across vast expanses and access is difficult to monitor. These factors, among others, make it particularly costly to define and enforce property rights in the marine context. Property rights in fisheries have also been disfavored in American law. Various legal doctrines, including that of the public trust, hold that fisheries are held in trust by the government for the common use of all citizens. For these reasons, most fishery conservation efforts of the past several decades have relied upon government regulation.

It is now generally accepted that traditional regulatory approaches to fishery conservation have been a "spectacular failure."[26] Regulatory controls have typically taken the form of limits on fishing seasons, boat size, fishing areas, equipment and the like. These measures are inefficient, in part, because they are all indirect means of conserving fish stocks. * * * License controls and other entry restrictions may limit the number of fishers, but they do not control the amount or intensity of fishing efforts. Mandates on the type of equipment that can be used, an effort to control total catch by mandating that fishers use less-efficient means of catching fish, encourage fishers to increase their investment in additional vessels or gear to compensate for the efficiency losses. Limits on the number of days fished encourage fishers to increase their effort on those days allowed. The

---

16. Harold Demsetz, Toward a Theory of Property Rights, 57 Am. Econ. Rev. 347, 355 (1967).

26. Alison Rieser, Property Rights and Ecosystem Management in U.S. Fisheries: Contracting for the Commons?, 24 Ecology L.Q. 813, 813 (1997).

results are rampant overcapitalization in fisheries and a destructive "derby" system in which each fisher races to catch as much as he or she can before the season closes. * * *

In Alaska's halibut fishery, for example, as the government shortened the fishing season to prevent overfishing, fishers responded by purchasing larger, more powerful boats and accelerating their catch. Eventually, the halibut season was compressed from several months to only a few days. Fishery regulations produced overcapitalization while reducing the value of the fish caught. The resulting "race to fish" also increased the occupational hazards faced by halibut fishers. Regrettably, this pattern has been repeated in many fisheries. Even where regulators set a total allowable catch (TAC) for the fishery, overcapitalization and the "race to fish" ensue. * * *

Figure 10–1
An Alaskan Fishing Boat

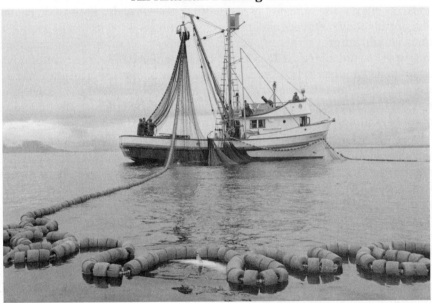

National Geographic Photograph courtesy of Getty Images.

There are numerous reasons for the failure of traditional regulatory controls. * * * Perhaps the greatest deficiency facing centralized regulatory authorities is the difficulty in centralizing sufficient knowledge to allocate resources in an efficient manner. * * * In other words, effective fishery management depends upon all manner of local and technical knowledge beyond the reach of any centralized management agency. As a result of this "knowledge problem," well-intentioned fishery management schemes have failed time and again. "The technological resourcefulness of fishermen has historically made a mockery of the most stringent and carefully crafted command and control regulations aimed at reducing fishing effort," note

Shi–Ling Hsu and James Wilen.[37] Even expert regulators fail to anticipate the unintended consequences and feedbacks their regulations can induce.

Politics also hampers the ability of regulators to safeguard fishery resources. Fishery management councils are often subject to political pressure to increase the total allowable catch in a given season. Where scientific assessments of sustainable catch levels are uncertain, as is typically the case, there is substantial pressure to adopt less conservative assessments. Without certain property rights in future catches, fishing interests have no incentive to endorse precautionary catch levels. This pressure can cause a "ratchet effect" that pushes fishing levels above sustainable levels. The problems of poor regulatory management have been combined by other government policies, such as subsidies, which further encourage overcapitalization and overfishing. * * *

The failure of traditional regulations, and the recent success of alternative management strategies, has renewed interest in the potential use of property rights for marine conservation. As already noted, there is a substantial body of academic research detailing why property rights regimes should improve the efficacy and efficiency of resource management. This work is not merely theoretical, however. There is a growing body of research documenting how various sorts of property institutions, particularly various common property regimes or de facto property rights regimes grounded in custom or contract, have evolved in various societies to address potential common pool resource concerns.

Comparative analyses of private and political resource management are instructive. Oyster beds in Maryland are managed by the state.[45] In neighboring Virginia, the beds are leased to private parties, while in Washington, oyster beds are privately owned in fee simple. As the theoretical literature would predict, privately managed oyster beds are healthier and more productive than those under state protection. Comparisons between privately leased and publicly managed oyster beds in Louisiana and Mississippi, respectively, yield similar results.

The effect of private ownership can also be seen in the explosion in aquaculture production, which more than tripled between 1985 and 1995. Aquaculture now accounts for approximately one-quarter of global fish harvests, and one-third of fish harvested for human consumption.[51] The explosion of aquaculture is relevant to the discussion of property rights in marine resources because the fundamental difference between aquaculture and traditional ocean fisheries is the "degree of control" which, "at its core, is largely defined by the strength of property rights."[52] Aquaculture

---

37. Shi–Ling Hsu & James E. Wilen, Ecosystem Management and the 1996 Sustainable Fisheries Act, 24 Ecology L.Q. 799, 806–07 (1997).

45. See Richard J. Agnello & Lawrence P. Donnelly, Prices and Property Rights in the Fisheries, 42 S. Econ. J. 253, 260 (1979).

51. James L. Anderson, Aquaculture and the Future: Why Fisheries Economists Should Care, 17 Marine Resource Econ. 133, 134 (2002).

52. Id. Of course, increased aquaculture production can contribute to other environmental concerns. * * *

operations are privately owned in their entirety. As a result, producers need not worry about the tragedy of the commons and, therefore, have the incentive "to tinker, to experiment, and to innovate" in order to increase the productivity of their facilities. Aquaculture production is not without problems, but the explosion in aquaculture production, when contrasted to the depletion of marine fisheries, illustrates the importance of property rights in conserving resources.

The interest in property rights is also buoyed by the practical experience in several countries with property-based management systems, such as individual transferable quotas (ITQs). Under an ITQ system, the government sets the total allowable catch for a given season, and then allocates shares of the catch—quota—to individuals, boats, or firms as a form of transferable right. ITQ programs have been implemented in several countries with substantial success at increasing fishing efficiency, reducing overcapitalization, and lessening the ecological impact of fishing operations. Particularly significant, ITQs have encouraged fishers to exercise greater stewardship. "It's the first group of fishers I've ever encountered who turned down the chance to take more fish," noted Philip Major of New Zealand's Ministry of Agriculture after the implementation of ITQs.[56] There have also been private initiatives to allocate annual harvests among firms in catch-limited fisheries so as to create quasi-property rights and capture the economic and ecological benefits that result. As discussed below, such cooperatives may develop where government resource managers have failed to implement ITQs or other property-based management regimes. * * *

As noted earlier, the mobility of many fish populations can make property rights in fish populations costly to define and enforce. These costs are, in part, a function of existing technology. Over time, human ability to define and mark territories or monitor given populations of a species improves, facilitating the application of property-based institutions. During the initial settlement of the American West, it was difficult to define and enforce property rights due to the vast expanses and relative lack of fencing materials. As populations increased, and the ability to assert control over water, grazing lands, and cattle herds became more important, the demand for technologies to define and enforce property rights increased. These pressures spurred the development of barbed wire and complex branding systems.[66] In much the same way, such branding and fencing technologies are beginning to emerge in the marine context, and may facilitate the further expansion of property rights in fisheries. Such innovations range from fish scale analysis, which approximates branding or fingerprinting and catch sampling technologies, to remote tracking of fishing vessels using satellites and autonomous underwater vehicles (e.g. "robo-tuna").

---

56. Michael DeAlessi, Fishing for Solutions: The State of the World's Fisheries, in Earth Report 2000 at 99 (Ronald Bailey, ed., 2000) (quoting Philip Major of New Zealand's Ministry of Agriculture after the implementation of ITQs).

66. Terry L. Anderson & Peter J. Hill, The Evolution of Property Rights: a Study of the American West, 18 J. L. & Econ. 163, 165–67 (1975).

The application of property rights to marine conservation does not only face economic and technical hurdles. The adoption of even modest property-based systems is politically controversial. ITQs can improve efficiency and facilitate conservation, but they may also lead to the redistribution of wealth or displacement of traditional fishing communities. Although ITQ systems have been implemented in a few U.S. fisheries, Congress enacted a moratorium on the adoption of ITQs in additional fisheries in 1996. The moratorium is due to expire, yet Congress is expected to impose new requirements on the adoption and operation of future ITQ systems in U.S. waters. Thus, while it is generally accepted that a move toward greater property rights in marine resources would be beneficial, such a move faces substantial obstacles. * * *

Property rights are often created by government action. Statutes or regulations may recognize or create rights in a previously unowned resource, such as radio spectrum, or expand the number of sticks in the bundle of rights associated with a particular resource. Examples of the latter would include the recognition of conservation easements in land or instream flow rights to water in the western United States. In each case, the resource in question—land, water—could be owned, but legislative action expanded the rights associated with the resource. In other cases, government entities may simply recognize rights that are observed and accepted within a local community. * * *

In recent years, modest fisher cooperatives have gained acceptance * * * One example of such a cooperative is the Pacific Whiting Conservation Cooperative (PWCC). Prior to creation of the PWCC, the U.S. Pacific Coast whiting fishery was subject to strict catch limits, fishing licenses were limited but transferable, and the total catch allowed was divided among several classes of fishing firms: on-shore processing plants, "mothership" processors, and catcher/processors. Within each class the fishery adopted an "olympic" system, whereby any licensed fishing firm was entitled to catch as much of the harvest allocated to its class as it was able. In practice, this encouraged a race to fish, as each fishing firm sought to harvest as many fish as it could within a short period of time so as to capture the greatest share of the harvest allocated to its class. While the total catch limit helped conserve the fishery, the competitive pressure of the "olympic" system fostered overcapitalization, inefficiency, and waste, including substantial by-catch—the incidental catching of non-target fish species. The race to fish was so intense that under the existing rules, the pressure to catch fish quickly was so great that the entire quota would be harvested in just fourteen days.

By 1996, there were only four catcher/processors left in the fishery. These firms recognized that the allocation of property rights to portions of the catch—ITQs or some other share allocation—would yield substantial benefits. Specifically, the firms recognized they could cut costs and increase product recovery by as much as twenty-five percent by allocating quota shares, thereby eliminating the race to fish. The formal creation of ITQs in the fishery was not an option, however, due to a Congressionally enacted ITQ moratorium.

To obtain the benefits of a property-based management system, the catcher/processors created the PWCC. Because there were so few firms involved, each sharing a common interest, the coordination costs were low enough to reach a quick agreement on how to divide the catch. They further agreed to make their allocations transferable among each other. The Antitrust Division of the Justice Department consented to the formation of the cooperative because the four firms agreed to continue processing, marketing, and selling their products on a competitive basis, and because the agreement would not further reduce fishery output. * * * To the contrary, due to increased efficiency, the cooperative would increase the volume of fish available to consumers from the same harvest level.

The results of the cooperative were impressive. As under ITQ programs, "more efficient operators leased shares from less efficient ones" and firms reduced the number of fishing vessels in the fishery. The recovery rate—the amount of saleable product recovered from fish—increased substantially. Indeed, the four firms produced over five million pounds more food from the same volume of fish caught—often of higher quality—while using fewer boats. At the same time, by-catch declined. To enforce the arrangement and prevent cheating, the cooperative contracted with a fishery harvest monitoring service, which also enabled federal regulators to increase the accuracy of the seasonal catch allocation. * * *

Congress could further facilitate private ordering in fisheries by providing explicit statutory authorization for the creation of fishing cooperatives or conservation associations. This could be achieved either by enacting a blanket antitrust exemption or by expanding the limited exemption provided by the Fisherman's Collective Marketing Act. An alternative would be to create a mechanism whereby NMFS or regional fishery management councils could authorize the creation and operation of a fishing cooperative. * * *

Conserving marine resources requires controlling access and reducing output. At issue is who, or what institution, should establish and enforce such controls. This is a question of institutional capacity as much as it is the inherent desirability of one institutional framework over another. The American legal tradition may disfavor property rights in wildlife, yet it may be the case that reliance upon government regulation to conserve some living marine resources is to condemn them to exhaustion. * * *

Environmental problems are typically characterized as resulting from "market failure"—a failure of private institutions to safeguard environmental resources. Yet the experience with marine resources suggests that "government failure" or "political failure" would be a more accurate diagnosis of the problem. It is not that private institutions have failed, it is that we have failed to have private institutions, and government policy is sometimes the cause. Moreover, the failure of private institutions to produce "optimal" results in some, even many, instances does not mean that political management will produce better outcomes; "the relevant question is whether private ordering reaches a result that is superior to the result public ordering reaches."[204] * * *

Private ordering will not solve every conservation concern—not even every fishery problem—but it could well supplement government efforts, if not replace them. Given the plight of marine fisheries, it would be folly to ignore a conservation tool as potentially powerful as private ordering.

NOTES AND QUESTIONS

1. We encountered the tragedy of the commons in Chapter II, in connection with the Thráinsson excerpt, where we had occasion to note that Hardin popularized earlier economic analyses of the problem. Interestingly these earlier, more rigorous treatments, were based on fisheries as the primary example. A resource like a fishery, unlike information, presents the potential for human exploitation in its natural form. Efforts to capture the return from such a resource—often called "rent" by economists—can lead to wasteful efforts at capture that can wind up dissipating some, all, or under certain conditions more than all the rent from the resource. See Terry L. Anderson & Peter J. Hill, Privatizing the Commons: An Improvement?, 50 Southern Econ. J. 438, 441, 447 (1983).

2. Three general justifications have been advanced for the superior efficiency of ITQs relative to traditional regulation of fisheries. See Katrina Miriam Wyman, From Fur to Fish: Reconsidering the Evolution of Private Property, 80 N.Y.U. L. Rev. 117, 160–62 (2005) (excerpted below). First, they reduce incentives to overinvest in fishing equipment and labor. In particular, the ability to transfer ITQs allows less productive vessels to sell out to more productive vessels, reducing the total amount of resources devoted to fishing. Second, ITQs increase the level of confidence that fishers will be able to meet their quotas, which allows each vessel to take more time to harvest a higher-value product, rather than rushing to harvest as many fish as possible in the shortest period of time. Third, ITQs may promote a greater sense of stewardship among fishers. For example, fishers who own ITQs have some incentive to insure the long-term sustainability of the stocks, such as returning immature fish to the ocean.

3. Property rights are costly to create and maintain and the question is whether their benefits outweigh those costs. In the case of ITQs, behavior of rights holders still has to be policed along multiple margins. For example, in a phenomenon called "highgrading," if one measures the ITQ by weight on shore, fishers may dump smaller, but already dead, fish, in order to fill the quota with higher-value big fish. Shi–Ling Hsu & James E. Wilen, Ecosystem Management and the Sustainable Fisheries Act, 24 Ecol. L.Q. 799, 809 (1997). Usually this is seen as a problem of "too much" property, but because it could theoretically be improved by closer monitoring it could also be regarded as a problem of "too little property." See Carol

---

204. Jonathan R. Macey, Public and Private Ordering and the Production of Legitimate and Illegitimate Legal Rules, 82 Cornell L. Rev. 1123, 1141 (1997).

M. Rose, The Several Futures of Property: Of Cyberspace and Folk Tales, Emission Trades and Ecosystems, 83 Minn. L. Rev. 129, 169–70 (1998). As far as efficiency is concerned, the question is whether such additional policing would be worth the additional costs.

4.   It might be thought that racing to appropriate the flows from a resource stock—a form of rentseeking—would be characteristic of natural resources but not of a nonrival resource like information. However, economists have explored the possibility that excessive rewards may induce people to race to invent—to expend rival resources to attain a patent, say— and that this might be wasteful from a social point of view. See Yoram Barzel, Optimal Timing of Innovations, 50 Rev. Econ. & Stat. 348 (1968); Jack Hirshleifer, The Private and Social Value of Information and the Reward to Inventive Activity, 61 Am. Econ. Rev. 561 (1971). Various theories of patent law in particular seek to explain the contours of the patent system as a response to the possibilities of rentseeking and related wasteful behavior. See, e.g., Mark F. Grady & Jay I. Alexander, Patent Law and Rent Dissipation, 78 Va. L. Rev. 305 (1992); Edmund W. Kitch, The Nature and Function of the Patent System, 20 J.L. & Econ. 265, 276–77, 284 (1977).

ITQs also raise distributional questions, as in the following case.

Alliance Against IFQs v. Brown

United States Court of Appeals, Ninth Circuit, 1996.
84 F.3d 343.

■ KLEINFELD, CIRCUIT JUDGE: The only issue in this case is whether regulations for implementing a fishery management plan in and near Alaska waters [were] arbitrary and capricious, or violative of the authorizing statute. We conclude that the regulations were a permissible exercise of authority by the Secretary of Commerce.

I.   FACTS AND REGULATORY FRAMEWORK

Commercial ocean fishing combines difficult and risky labor with large capital investments to make money from a resource owned by no one, the fish. Unlimited access tends to cause declining fisheries. The reason is that to get title to a fish, a fisherman has to catch it before someone else does. Pierson v. Post, 3 Caines 175 (N.Y. 1805). This gives each [fisherman] an incentive to invest in a fast, large boat and to fish as fast as possible. As boats and crews get more efficient, fewer fish escape the fishermen and live to reproduce. "The result is lower profits for the too many fishermen investing in too much capital to catch too few fish." Terry L. Anderson and Donald R. Leal, Free Market Environmentalism, 123 (1991).

Congress made findings in the Magnuson Fishery Conservation and Management Act ("Magnuson Act"), 16 U.S.C. § 1801 et seq., that "certain stocks of such fish have been overfished to the point where their survival is threatened," 16 U.S.C. § 1801(a)(2)(A), and that "[a] national program for the conservation and management of the fishery resources of the United

States is necessary to prevent overfishing, to rebuild overfished stocks, to ensure conservation, and to realize the full potential of the Nation's fishery resources." 16 U.S.C. § 1801(a)(6). Among the purposes of the Magnuson Act were providing for "fishery management plans which will achieve and maintain, on a continuing basis, the optimum yield from each fishery," 16 U.S.C. § 1801(b)(4), and "establish[ing] Regional Fishery Management Councils to ... prepar[e], monitor[ ] and revis[e] such plans." 16 U.S.C. § 1801(b)(5). The Secretary of Commerce, pursuant to the Magnuson Act and the Northern Pacific Halibut Act of 1982 ("Halibut Act"), 16 U.S.C. § 773 et seq., promulgated regulations to limit access to sablefish and halibut fisheries in the Gulf of Alaska and the Bering Sea and Aleutian Islands area. See 50 C.F.R., Part 676.

The Secretary of Commerce implemented by regulation a management plan for sablefish and pacific halibut fishing. 50 C.F.R. §§ 676.10–676.25. The basic scheme is that any boat that fishes commercially for the regulated fish in the regulated area must have an individual quota share (IFQ) permit on board, specifying the individual fishing quota allowed for the vessel, and anyone who receives the regulated fish must possess a "registered buyer permit." 50 C.F.R. § 676.13(a). * * *

The regional director of the National Marine Fisheries Service (NMFS) in the Department of Commerce assigns to each owner or lessee of a vessel which made legal landings of halibut or sablefish during 1988, 1989, or 1990, a quota share (QS) based on the person's highest total legal landings of halibut and sablefish during 1984 to 1990. 50 C.F.R. § 676.20(b). Each year, the regional director allocates individual fishing quotas (IFQs) by multiplying the person's quota share by the annual allowable catch. 50 C.F.R. § 676.20(f)(1). Subject to some restrictions, the quota shares and individual fishing quotas can be sold, leased and otherwise transferred. 50 C.F.R. § 676.21. If someone who did not fish in the regulated waters during 1988 to 1990 wants a quota share, he has to buy it from someone who did.

Like any governmental regulatory scheme, this one substitutes a governmental decision for myriad individual decisions to determine who shall be permitted to make money in the regulated industry. The plaintiffs are people who suffer from the economic impact of the regulation. Some have invested in fishing vessels and fished in the regulated waters for halibut or sablefish, but not during the critical three years which would give them a quota share. Some have consistently fished for the regulated fish in the regulated waters, but did not own or lease the boats. Of those who acquired quota shares under the scheme, some probably never fished, and just invested in fishing boats to get investment tax credits and depreciation. The regulatory scheme has the practical effect of transferring economic power over the fishery from those who fished to those who owned or leased fishing boats. For these reasons, among others, the case is troubling and difficult.

II. ANALYSIS

The district court granted summary judgment in favor of the government and dismissed the complaint. We review a grant of summary judgment *de novo*. Washington Crab Producers, Inc. v. Mosbacher, 924 F.2d 1438, 1440 (9th Cir. 1990). Where we review regulations promulgated by the Secretary of Commerce under the Magnuson Act, our only function is to determine whether the Secretary "has considered the relevant factors and articulated a rational connection between the facts found and the choice made." Id. at 1440–41 (quotation omitted). We determine only if the Secretary acted in an arbitrary and capricious manner in promulgating such regulations. Id. at 1441. See also 16 U.S.C. § 1855(b)(1)(B); 5 U.S.C. § 706(2)(A)–(D). We cannot substitute our judgment of what might be a better regulatory scheme, or overturn a regulation because we disagree with it, if the Secretary's reasons for adopting it were not arbitrary and capricious. * * *

A.   "Present Participation in the Fishery."

Congress erected various conditions on the Secretary's discretion to establish a limited access system for the fishery. Among the factors which the Council and Secretary must "take into account" is "present participation in the fishery." 16 U.S.C. § 1853(b)(6)(A):

(b) Discretionary provisions. Any fishery management plan which is prepared by any Council, or by the Secretary, with respect to any fishery, may—

. . .

(6) establish a system for limiting access to the fishery in order to achieve optimum yield if, in developing such system, the Council and the Secretary take into account—

(A) present participation in the fishery,

(B) historical fishing practices in, and dependence on, the fishery,

(C) the economics of the fishery,

(D) the capability of fishing vessels used in the fishery to engage in other fisheries,

(E) the cultural and social framework relevant to the fishery, and

(F) any other relevant considerations[.] * * *

The final rule was promulgated November 9, 1993. 58 Fed.Reg. 59,375 (1993). But the years during which people had to own or lease vessels and land halibut or sablefish, to obtain qualifying shares, were 1988, 1989 and 1990. 50 C.F.R. § 676.20(a)(1)(i). Plaintiffs argue that this violates the Congressional command to take into account "present" fishing. As they correctly observe, a person who last fished in 1988 would get a qualifying share, but someone who had fished only in 1991, 1992 and 1993 would not. Indeed, the complaint alleges that one of the plaintiffs fished for halibut in the regulated waters in 1975, 1977 through 1987, and 1992, but fished for salmon in Cook Inlet, not part of the regulated waters, during the three quota share years.

Substantial time was taken up between formulation of the plan and promulgation, by such activities as preparing environmental impact statements on the plan. In a 1992 environmental impact statement, the Council gave several reasons for using a 1990 cutoff. Perhaps the most persuasive was that if participation in the fishery while the rule was under consideration had been considered, then people would have fished and invested in boats in order to obtain quota shares, even though that would have exacerbated overcapacity and made no economic sense independently of the regulatory benefit. * * *

Congress left the Secretary some room for the exercise of discretion, by not defining "present participation," and by listing it as only one of many factors which the Council and the Secretary must "take into account." While the "participation" that the Council actually considered was admittedly in the "past" judged from the time when the final regulations were promulgated, it was roughly "present" with the time when the regulations were first proposed: The Council began its process on this plan in 1990, and considered participation in 1988, 1989, and 1990. The process required to issue a regulation necessarily caused substantial delay. The process of review, publication, public comments, review of public comments, and so forth, had to take a substantial amount of time, see 16 U.S.C. § 1854(a), and the environmental impact review also was lengthy, as it typically is, see 42 U.S.C. § 4332(2)(C). "Present" cannot therefore prudently be contemporaneous with the promulgation of the final regulations.

We further believe that the Secretary had a good reason for disregarding participation in the fishery during this lengthy process, because the alternative would encourage the speculative over-investment and overfishing which the regulatory scheme was meant to restrain. Under the regulations, eligibility for quota shares depends on fishing during the years 1988, 1989, and 1990. Whatever years are used necessarily recede into the distant past. Even in 2005, assuming the regulatory scheme lasts that long, the quota shares will be based on fishing prior to 1991. Future generations of fishermen will continue to be governed by these pre–1991 allocations. Had the Secretary extended the 1990 cutoff, the incentive to pour money and time into the fishery in order to get a bigger quota share, for those who could afford a long term speculation, would have been enormous.

Thus, while the length of time between the end of the participation period considered and the promulgation of the rule pushed the limits of reasonableness, we are unable to characterize use of a 1988 through 1990 period as so far from "present participation" when the regulation was promulgated in 1993 as to be "arbitrary or capricious." Washington Crab, 924 F.2d at 1441. * * *

B. The "Fair and Equitable Standard."

Plaintiffs argue that the allocation of quota shares to vessel owners and lessees violates the statutory requirement that allocation be "fair and equitable to all such fishermen." 16 U.S.C. § 1851(a)(4). The statute requires that a fishery management plan comply with a number of national standards:

> (a) In general. Any fishery management plan prepared, and any regulation promulgated to implement any such plan, pursuant to this subchapter [16 U.S.C. §§ 1851 et seq.] shall be consistent with the following national standards for fishery conservation and management.

> (1) Conservation and management measures shall prevent overfishing while achieving, on a continuing basis, the optimum yield from each fishery for the United States fishing industry.

> (2) Conservation and management measures shall be based upon the best scientific information available.

> (3) To the extent practicable, an individual stock of fish shall be managed as a unit throughout its range, and interrelated stocks of fish shall be managed as a unit or in close coordination.

> (4) Conservation and management measures shall not discriminate between residents of different States. If it becomes necessary to allocate or assign fishing privileges among various United States fishermen, such *allocation shall be (A) fair and equitable to all such fishermen;* (B) reasonably calculated to promote conservation; and (C) carried out in such manner that no particular individual, corporation, or other entity acquires an excessive share of such privileges.

> (5) Conservation and management measures shall, where practicable, promote efficiency in the utilization of fishery resources; except that no such measure shall have economic allocation as its sole purpose.

> (6) Conservation and management measures shall take into account and allow for variations among, and contingencies in, fisheries, fishery resources, and catches.

> (7) Conservation and management measures shall, where practicable, minimize costs and avoid unnecessary duplication.

16 U.S.C. § 1851(a) (emphasis added).

Plaintiffs make the sensible argument that a crew member is just as much of a fisherman as a vessel owner. If all the quota shares go to vessel owners and lessees during that period, and none to the crew, as the Secretary's approved plan provides, then this violates the statutory command of fairness and equity to "all" the fishermen.

As the quoted section of this statute shows, the Secretary's duty was not solely limited to allocating quota shares fairly and equitably among the fishermen. The plan also had to "prevent overfishing while achieving, on a continuing basis, the optimum yield," 16 U.S.C. § 1851(a)(1), be "reasonably calculated to promote conservation," 16 U.S.C. § 1851(a)(4), "promote efficiency," 16 U.S.C. § 1851(a)(5), "minimize costs and avoid unnecessary duplication," 16 U.S.C. § 1851(a)(7), and achieve several other criteria. There is a necessary tension, perhaps inconsistency, among these objectives. The tension, for example, between fairness among all fishermen, preventing overfishing, promoting efficiency, and avoiding unnecessary duplication, necessarily requires that each goal be sacrificed to some extent to meeting the others.

The Council and Secretary directed their attention to the fairness problem plaintiffs raise, but decided that the other standards imposed by the statute required allocation of quota shares to boat owners and lessees as opposed to all the fishermen. The Council thought that equity to people who had invested in boats, and the greater ease of ascertaining how much fish boats, as opposed to individual fishermen, had taken, favored allocating quota shares according to owner[s] and lessees of boats:

> There is no question that the IFQ program will restructure the current fixed gear fishery for halibut and sablefish. Some fishermen will be better off and some will be worse off under the IFQ program.... In brief, those persons benefited by receiving an initial allocation are vessel owners or lease holders.... The Council's rationale for this particular allocation is that vessel owners and lease holders are the participants who supply the means to harvest fish, suffer the financial and liability risks to do so, and direct the fishing operations.

> . . . .

> The advantaging of one group to the detriment of another is inherent in allocation.... The Council considered allocating [quota share] to crew members but decided against it because of the practical difficulties of documenting crew shares. Instead, the Council decided to give eligibility for initial allocations only to vessel owners and lease holders because they have a capital investment in the vessel and gear that continues as a cost after crew and vessel shares are paid from a fishing trip.

58 Fed.Reg. 59,375, 59,378, 59,386 (1993) (final rule, codified at 50 C.F.R. Parts 204, 672, 675, and 676). * * *

Congress required the Secretary to exercise discretion and judgment in balancing among the conflicting national standards in section 1851. "[U]nless the Secretary acts in an arbitrary and capricious manner promulgating such regulations, they may not be declared invalid." Alaska Factory Trawler Ass'n v. Baldridge, 831 F.2d 1456, 1460 (9th Cir. 1987). Although the Secretary's approval of the plan sacrificed the interest of nonowning crew members to boat owners and lessees, the Secretary had a reason for doing that which was consistent with the statutory standards. Controlling precedent requires that a plan not be deemed arbitrary and capricious, "[e]ven though there may be some discriminatory impact," if the regulations "are tailored to solve a gear conflict problem and to promote the conservation of sablefish." Id. The Secretary is allowed, under this authority, to sacrifice the interests of some groups of fishermen, for the benefit as the Secretary sees it of the fishery as a whole. Id.

The plan adopted will undoubtedly have an adverse impact on the lives of many fishermen who have done nothing wrong. Their entirely legitimate interest in making a living from the fishery has been sacrificed to an administrative judgment about conservation of fish and efficiency of the industry. That is, however, an unavoidable consequence of the statutory scheme. Despite the harshness to the fishermen who were left out, there is no way we can conclude on this record that the Secretary lacked a rational basis for leaving them out. The Secretary considered their interests, "considered the relevant factors and articulated a rational connection between the facts found and the choice made." Washington Crab, 924 F.2d at 1441. Because this standard was met, we do not have the authority to substitute our judgment for the Secretary's with regard to allocation of all the quota shares to boat owners and lessees. * * *

III. CONCLUSION

This is a troubling case. Perfectly innocent people going about their legitimate business in a productive industry have suffered great economic harm because the federal regulatory scheme changed. Alternative schemes can easily be imagined. The old way could have been left in place, where whoever caught the fish first, kept them, and seasons were shortened to allow enough fish to escape and reproduce. Allocation of quota shares could have been on a more current basis, so that fishermen in 1996 would not have their income based upon the fish they had caught before 1991. Quota shares could have been allocated to all fishermen, instead of to vessel owners and lessees, so that the nonowning fishermen would have something valuable to sell to vessel owners. But we are not the regulators of the north pacific halibut and sablefish industry. The Secretary of Commerce is. We cannot overturn the Secretary's decision on the ground that some parties' interests are injured. Government regulation of an industry necessarily transfers economic rewards from some who are more efficient and hardworking to others who are favored by the regulatory scheme. We have authority to overturn the Secretary's decisions only if they are arbitrary and capricious, or contrary to law. In this case, they are not.

AFFIRMED.

NOTES AND QUESTIONS

1.   Could the inequities discussed in *Alliance Against IFQs* be avoided by auctioning off ITQs rather than passing them out for free to a select group of incumbents? Under an auction system, those persons who have the capability of using the permits most efficiently would presumably bid the highest price for them. Thus, a highly efficient operator who happened to be working in a different market from 1988–90 might outbid operators who were in the market in 1988–90, or a talented fisher who has never owned or leased his own boat might be able to get financing to outbid less efficient boat operators. Apparently no regional counsel has ever proposed an auction of ITQs. Indeed, it appears that all schemes for using transferable permits to solve environmental problems begin by handing out permits free of charge to the incumbents in the industry who created the problem (overfishing, pollution, whatever) in the first place. Why do you suppose that is? See Thomas W. Merrill, Explaining Market Mechanisms, 2000 U. Ill. L. Rev. 275 (suggesting that free distribution to incumbents overcomes

political opposition to tradable permits by creating a kind of protectionist barrier against potential new entrants).

2. If ITQs are the best solution on the horizon for saving fish populations from potential extermination, as Adler, supra, and many others believe, then why doesn't the federal government just buy out the relatively small number of operators and fisher persons who object to their introduction? This would probably cost much less than many agricultural price support programs funded by federal taxpayers. Why is there no political support for such ideas? Where are the environmental groups in the *Alliance Against IFQs* case in other similar cases?

Katrina Miriam Wyman, *From Fur to Fish: Reconsidering the Evolution of Private Property*, 80 N.Y.U. L. REV. 117, 152–54, 167–72, 175–87, 197–200, 214–18, 224–26 (2005)

For over six decades, a movement has been underway around the world to enclose the oceans that cover at least seven-tenths of the earth. This enclosure movement has progressed in a series of waves, similar to the famous enclosures of common lands in England that began in the fifteenth century. Three waves of ocean enclosures in particular might be distinguished.

In the first wave, coastal countries began creating national property rights in parts of the oceans that historically had been accessible to all. * * * [T]he United States initiated the modern ocean enclosure movement in 1945 by unilaterally extending its jurisdiction over the continental shelf and proclaiming the right to establish conservation zones for fisheries. Other countries then followed suit, proclaiming national jurisdiction over ever-larger expanses of marine fisheries, either as part of, or independent of, broader claims to the oceans. The 1982 Convention on the Law of the Sea codified these extensions of national jurisdiction, establishing the right of countries to claim 200–mile Exclusive Economic Zones (EEZs) in which they could regulate fishing, as well as other activities.

In the second wave of enclosure, countries domestically began subdividing their expanded national rights over the oceans into communal regimes. In the United States and elsewhere, communal rights in fisheries have been established on several scales. The 1976 congressional legislation that expanded U.S. jurisdiction over fisheries out to 200 miles also established a domestic regulatory regime that assigned primary responsibility for managing marine fisheries in federal waters to eight regional councils. Each of these councils effectively has become the communal governor of the fisheries within a relatively wide geographically defined jurisdiction.

In many fisheries, the establishment of a collective regime at the regional level was followed by the creation of even smaller scale, species-specific communal regimes. For example, the regional fishery management councils have established numerous limited entry licensing regimes. A limited entry regime carves out a smaller community of fishers from a council's jurisdiction by excluding fishers from taking a particular species unless the fisher holds a valid license for the species. What keeps a limited entry license from being a full-fledged individual property right is that the license does not grant a fisher the right to a specific amount of fish. Instead, limited entry licensing delimits the group of fishers who can compete for a species without giving any of these fishers a right to a specific quantity of fish. In addition to—or instead of—limiting entry, councils have found other ways to protect fisheries, none of which create individual rights in specific quantities of fish. These other tools include a total allowable limit on the amount of fish that may be harvested or limits that resemble conventional command-and-control regulation used in other environmental policy areas, such as regulating the kind of gear, the size of boats, and the length of fishing seasons.

For over three decades, economists and others have been promoting, with limited success, a third wave of enclosure that would create individual property rights out of communal or national regimes: the establishment of individual transferable quotas. Individual transferable quotas are analogous to other property-based ideas for managing environmental resources, such as marketable pollution permits, transferable grazing rights, and tradable rights in habitat for endangered species, that come out of the growing interest in property rights theory in economics in the 1960s. Individual transferable quotas begin with a cap on the total amount of a particular fish species that can be harvested in a defined area: the total allowable catch. Under individual transferable quotas, rights adding up to this cap are distributed among harvesters, who may trade the rights. These rights typically are denominated as rights to a percentage of the harvest, which are translated annually into a specific volume of fish depending on the total amount of fish allowed to be caught that year. The transferability of the individual quota rights often is restricted to address distributional concerns in fishing communities, although the scale and content of restrictions on alienability differ considerably among programs. * * *

As of 2002, individual transferable quotas were used in few federal coastal fisheries. Only six federally regulated coastal fisheries were harvested under individual transferable quotas. Broadening the net, five other federally regulated coastal fisheries were caught under analogous instruments that share the same purpose and key features of individual transferable quotas. * * *

[T]he eleven fisheries with tradable rights together accounted for a small portion of fisheries in federal waters in 2002. I estimate that approximately six percent of coastal fish stocks under federal management were under tradable rights. Collectively, the eleven fisheries accounted for approximately twenty-four percent of the ex-vessel value of the fish caught in federal waters, and fifty-three percent of the volume. * * *

Why have U.S. fisheries been slow to adopt tradable rights, notwithstanding over thirty years of proselytizing by economists and others? The standard explanations for the evolution of property rights would suggest that the answer lies in underlying economic and social conditions. Consistent with my emphasis on the significance of political institutions, I begin instead by discussing the collective-choice rules for introducing tradable rights and then analyze the impact of underlying economic and social factors in light of these rules. * * *

Congress legislated a regulatory apparatus for managing the fisheries that came under federal jurisdiction when it was expanded to 200 miles in 1976. While the regulatory apparatus has been amended several times since, the standard initiators of federal fisheries regulation remain the eight regional fishery management councils created in 1976 to manage different parts of the U.S. EEZ. Under the Magnuson–Stevens Act, fishery-management measures, including individual transferable quotas, typically must originate in a recommendation from one of the councils to NMFS. * * *

Assigning the councils primary responsibility for proposing and initially allocating tradable rights in most fisheries increases the difficulty of introducing tradable rights. This is because the councils are collective decisionmaking bodies made up of representatives who are very susceptible to interest group pressures. The members of the councils are divided into voting and non-voting members. Most of the voting members are representatives of commercial and recreational fishing interests who are appointed by the U.S. Secretary of Commerce based on recommendations from state governors. The other voting members are primarily state marine fisheries regulators who acquire their voting seats by virtue of their positions. Finally, a senior NMFS administrator also has a voting seat on each of the councils. The appointed members of the councils tend to advocate for particular sectors of the fishing industry defined by geography, gear, or species fished, while the state regulatory officials tend to promote the interests of their home-state fisheries.

Since they are drawn predominantly from the fishing community, council members are cautious about recommending fishery-management measures such as individual transferable quotas that will affect fishers differentially. As a result, the councils are unwilling to proceed until they have crafted a proposal, including an initial allocation of tradable rights, that satisfies a broad range of the fishing interests represented on the councils. The councils' preference for consensus is indicated by council votes on proposals to recommend individual transferable quotas. Formally, the support of only a majority of the voting members is required in order to make such a recommendation. However, the councils' voting records suggest that council members will vote in favor of individual transferable quotas only if there is close to two-thirds support on the council.

Although the process seems to require a reasonably high degree of consensus among council members to introduce individual transferable quotas, it should be emphasized that the councils often are not representative of the various components of the industry. Consistent with the predictions of public choice theory, the councils tend to be more representative of the larger, better-capitalized segments of the fishing industry. This over-representation of the larger, better-capitalized interests likely helps to mitigate, although not eliminate, the otherwise high cost of bargaining a consensus on the introduction and initial allocation of individual transferable quotas. * * *

In addition to the difficulty of reaching agreement in the regional fishery management councils, another factor that increases the decision-making costs of establishing tradable rights is the existence of three veto players that may block council recommendations to proceed. NMFS, the courts, and Congress offer interest groups disgruntled with council recommendations opportunities to challenge those proposals. Moreover, there are indications that the existence of these veto players has feedback effects on the council process, as the councils appear to have internalized the possibility that these institutions may veto council proposals.

Under the Magnuson–Stevens Act, council recommendations cannot take effect unless they are approved by NMFS. An agency housed in the Department of Commerce, NMFS is limited to approving, disapproving, or partially approving council recommendations. NMFS rarely explicitly disapproves a fisheries management measure, and its reaction to individual transferable quota proposals transmitted by the councils is no exception. To my knowledge, it has never directly vetoed a suggestion to implement tradable rights.

Nonetheless, NMFS's history of approving individual transferable quotas should not be taken as an indication that agency approval is merely a formality in the process of implementing tradable rights. Combined with the voting seat of a NMFS regional administrator on each of the councils, NMFS's formal power of approval enables the agency to influence the development of individual transferable quota proposals before the councils. Indeed, the councils first considered using individual transferable quotas in the late 1980s and early 1990s partly because there were vocal proponents of tradable rights within NMFS in this period. Lacking the authority to introduce the quotas in most federal fisheries directly, these proponents promoted the use of individual transferable quotas indirectly, for example, by disseminating information about them.

In addition to NMFS, the federal courts are a potential veto player in the fisheries management process. In the early 1990s, disgruntled commercial fishing interests brought two suits challenging the rules implementing individual transferable quotas in four fisheries. Just as NMFS tended to approve individual transferable quota proposals submitted by the councils in the early 1990s, so the courts in these cases deferred to NMFS and the councils, upholding the individual transferable quota programs.[177] Even so,

---

177. See Alliance Against IFQs v. Brown, 84 F.3d 343 (9th Cir. 1996) (rejecting challenge to halibut and sablefish individual transferable quota programs brought by harvesters who did not receive initial allocations either because they did not fish in qualifying years, or because they did not own or lease boats and accordingly were ineligible as threshold matter); Sea Watch Int'l v. Mos-

bacher, 762 F.Supp. 370 (D.D.C. 1991) (rejecting challenges to individual fishing quotas implemented in Atlantic surfclam and ocean quahog fisheries).

For a constitutional rather than an administrative law challenge, see Arctic King Fisheries, Inc. v. United States, 59 Fed. Cl. 360 (Fed. Cl. 2004), which denied the plaintiff's challenge to the enactment of the Amer-the availability of judicial review provided a check on council arbitrariness in fashioning individual transferable quota programs. Moreover, the rise in litigation challenging fishery-management measures since the early 1990s and NMFS's deteriorating win-loss record suggest that the courts might become more active players in the establishment of tradable rights.

Of the three institutional actors who may block council recommendations to establish individual transferable quotas, members of Congress from coastal states, especially senators, have been the most visible veto players to date. The role of coastal-state senators in blocking the establishment of tradable rights was most evident between 1996 and 2002. During this period, a small group of coastal-state senators used the Senate's individualistic voting rules to significantly increase the costs of establishing tradable rights in many coastal fisheries.

Despite the fact that by 1995 individual transferable quotas had been established in a number of coastal fisheries and were under consideration for others, individual transferable quotas had attracted enough opposition from segments of the fishing industry and some environmentalists to inspire congressional opposition. When the Magnuson–Stevens Act was reauthorized in 1996, this opposition succeeded in obtaining a moratorium on the creation of new individual transferable quotas under the Act. Enacted against the wishes of NMFS and the councils, the moratorium prevented the councils from recommending, and NMFS from approving, individual transferable quotas for four years.

Ted Stevens, Republican senator from Alaska, took the lead in advocating for the moratorium, as well as on the final version of the entire 1996 reauthorization bill. The most powerful figure in U.S. fisheries politics, Stevens was joined in a bipartisan effort by two other senators from coastal states with fishing industries: Trent Lott, Republican senator from Mississippi and Majority Leader beginning in June 1996, and John Kerry, Democratic senator from Massachusetts. When initially enacted, the moratorium was characterized as a compromise between more extreme opponents of individual transferable quotas who were calling for an indefinite moratorium or other severe restrictions on individual quotas and proponents of tradable rights.

Notwithstanding the significance attached to the temporary nature of the moratorium by the supporters of individual transferable quotas in 1996, it was renewed in 2000 for two more years. The extension was instigated primarily by another coastal-state senator, Olympia Snowe, Republican from Maine, in response to concerns about individual transferable quotas among fishing communities in her home state. In extending the moratorium, Senator Snowe was assisted by Senator Stevens, then the Chairman of the powerful Senate Appropriations Committee. * * *

The cost of measuring and monitoring resources is another prominent theme in prevailing accounts of the evolution of private property. In

ican Fisheries Act and held that the exclusion of the plaintiff's vessel from the fishery in question was not a "taking" of the plaintiff's property.

particular, many scholars suggest that private property has been slow to develop in environmental resources such as fisheries, air, and water because of the higher aggregate cost of enforcing individual rights in resources that are often "fugitive."

Consistent with these theoretical arguments, there is empirical evidence that implementing tradable rights increases overall measuring and monitoring costs in fisheries. Under tradable rights, the amount of fish taken by individual users must be monitored to ensure that they hold rights for all of the fish they harvest. Such harvester-specific information typically is not required under the management approaches that predate tradable rights because these approaches do not include individual allotments.

Nonetheless, there are grounds for doubting that the higher aggregate costs of measuring and monitoring fisheries under tradable rights have been an important factor delaying their introduction since national jurisdiction was extended almost thirty years ago. Consider the following hypothesis: If measurement costs had been an important determinant of whether tradable rights were implemented in fisheries, then it might be expected that tradable rights would have developed first in the fisheries that are cheapest to measure and monitor. While fish often are migratory, certain species are comparatively sedentary. Since they do not roam far, sedentary species might be expected to be caught within a confined geographic area and sold at a relatively limited number of ports, which may facilitate monitoring of catches. If measurement costs had been a significant factor in implementing tradable rights, then relatively sedentary species might have been expected to be the first to shift to individual transferable quotas.

However, individual transferable quotas and analogous instruments were not introduced first in relatively sedentary species, and many of the stocks governed by tradable rights are migratory. This pattern of rights development casts doubt on the notion that aggregate increases in measurement and monitoring costs have been an important factor delaying the introduction of tradable rights. * * *

[I]n the standard accounts of the evolution of property rights, the characteristics of the users of a resource as well as the economic and physical attributes of the resource itself may be obstacles to change. More specifically, standard bottom-up explanations imply that individual tradable rights may have been slow to develop in U.S. fisheries because the fishing industry is too heterogeneous and includes too many fishers and processors. * * *

However, notwithstanding the presence of many heterogeneous interest groups in fisheries, it is not clear that heterogeneity consistently has been an obstacle to the introduction of tradable rights. On the contrary, there is evidence consistent with the argument * * * that heterogeneity may be conducive to private property rights formation in certain circumstances. In particular, there are indications that the presence of a distinct subgroup of wealthy and politically influential parties, such as large firms combining harvesting and processing operations, may facilitate the implementation of tradable rights. These firms may stand to gain disproportionately from tradable rights because they may allow the firms to reduce their harvesting costs, for example, by consolidating operations on fewer vessels. In addition, large vertically integrated harvesters and processors may be well positioned to pay the costs of lobbying for change, given the size of these costs relative to the magnitude of the benefits these firms stand to gain.

Consider, for instance, the history of harvesting cooperatives in the Alaskan pollock fishery, one of the most valuable commercial fisheries in the United States. An important impetus for establishing the cooperatives was a subset of the roughly ten large, mainly Washington State-based firms that operated combined harvesting and processing operations offshore in the 1990s. These catcher processors began arguing for individual transferable quotas for pollock in the early 1990s, when the catcher processor fleet harvested the vast majority of Alaska pollock. These firms promoted tradable rights because they believed that they would be more profitable if they held guaranteed rights to a portion of the harvest, enabling them to slow the pace of harvesting and reduce the number of vessels used in the fishery. To ease the acceptance of cooperatives, catcher processors not only assumed the initial cost of organizing for change in the Alaska pollock fishery, but also gave up part of the fleet's historical take from the pollock fishery and agreed not to increase the fleet's share of other Alaska fisheries. * * *

Heterogeneity may be conducive to institutional change in legislative and regulatory settings if it gives rise to a distinct subgroup motivated and well positioned to incur the costs of collective action. The history of property rights formation in the Alaska pollock fishery provides an example of this dynamic, with the catcher processors playing the role of the politically entrepreneurial subgroup. * * *

My findings about why tradable rights have been slow to develop in coastal fisheries in federal waters are necessarily tentative, given the limited number of fisheries that have shifted to tradable rights and that other factors have not been held constant while considering individual hypotheses. Nonetheless, two factors stand out as having contributed to the delay in introducing tradable rights in federal coastal fisheries.

First, the political institutions through which tradable rights typically must be established provide multiple veto points for interest groups to delay the pace of change. * * *

The second major cause of the delay in introducing tradable rights is the existence of conflicts among fishing interest groups over how to allocate the increased rents that tradable rights are expected to generate. The data about fish prices discussed in this Article provide only modest support for the proposition that fish prices must increase for tradable rights to be implemented. However, there is compelling evidence that conflicts over the distribution of expected rents have slowed the transition to tradable rights. While trends in fish prices may matter at the margin, distributional considerations seem to matter at the core.

Indeed, disputes about how tradable rights should be allocated when they first are implemented would seem to be the main reason that many of the veto points in the highly inclusive decisionmaking process have been exercised. Conflicts between interest groups in Alaska and Washington State about the initial allocation of rights provided an important initial impetus for the six-year moratorium on introducing individual transferable quotas through the council process. In addition, councils have taken a long time to develop proposals for individual transferable quotas, often because of disagreements among fishing interests seeking to maximize their share of the rights initially distributed for free. To be sure, the initial allocation of rights is not the sole determinant of who wins and loses under tradable rights, as parties who do not receive any or many rights at the outset still may benefit from more efficient fishing under tradable rights. Nonetheless, the initial allocation is an important determinant because the fishing industry's political clout has allowed it to ensure that rights are allocated for free at the outset, rather than sold. This means, in turn, that the parties who obtain large initial allocations will enjoy disproportionate gains should the rights increase in value.

Digging deeper, the role that allocation conflicts have played in delaying change raises the question of why distributional conflicts within fisheries have been vociferous, if not intractable. I hypothesize that two factors may have exacerbated these conflicts about the distribution of rents.

First, utilization levels in many fisheries may have contributed to the acrimoniousness of the conflicts. Experience to date suggests that full utilization may be the optimal level at which to introduce tradable rights, at least while they remain a relatively new concept in fisheries management. The costs of organizing the transition may be lower in fully utilized fisheries than overutilized fisheries where entrenched interests are competing for shares of a comparatively depleted resource. In addition, fully utilized fisheries may have a greater propensity to switch than underutilized fisheries because there are more fishers who would like to acquire property rights in a resource for which there is a well-developed market.

Second, the structure of the commercial fishing industry may have aggravated conflicts about the distribution of rents. My research suggests that heterogeneity along certain dimensions may be conducive to establishing tradable rights. In particular, the presence of a distinct subgroup of vertically integrated catcher processors, or other firms with access to capital, may facilitate rearranging rights. Since firms such as these stand to benefit from lower harvesting costs and more secure supplies of fish under tradable rights, these firms have an incentive (and the resources) to make compromises such as those made by the offshore pollock catcher processors in Alaska in the 1990s to obtain tradable rights. While more information about the industrial structure of individual U.S. fisheries is needed to make this argument conclusively, it is possible that distributional conflicts have been aggravated in fisheries by a lack of sufficient heterogeneity along economic dimensions. As discussed above, the prospect that heterogeneity is conducive to change runs counter to the prevailing hypothesis that private property is more likely to emerge when users are homogenous.

NOTES AND QUESTIONS

1.   Professor Wyman's study is part of an emerging literature on the evolution of property rights systems. See generally The Evolution of Property Rights, 31 J. Legal Stud. S331–S653 (2002) (Symposium). Broadly speaking, two hypotheses are prominent in that literature: a "bottom up" thesis that posits that legal property rights emerge out of informal social norms and practices, and a "top down" thesis that posits that legal property rights emerge when interest groups gain control of the state and impose property rights in order to enrich themselves. Where they differ concerns the distributional consequences of the introduction of property, and the role of those consequences in explaining exactly how new property systems come about. Wyman's careful study of the grudging introduction of ITQs into American offshore fishing industries is clearly aligned with the "top down" theories. But is it possible that "made" property orders like the ones studied in this Chapter are more likely to reflect the top down model than "spontaneous" or common-law property rights we have studied in other chapters?

2.   Wyman's finding that heterogeneity of interests in a fishing industry may facilitate the adoption of ITQs is in some tension with the experience in other countries where ITQs have been adopted. Iceland and New Zealand, for example, have adopted ITQ systems that by all accounts have been highly successful both in protecting fish populations and in enhancing the prosperity of the fishing industries in those countries. See, e.g., John Tierney, A Tale of Two Fisheries, N.Y. Times Mag., Aug. 27, 2000, at 38. But both Iceland and New Zealand are regarded as countries with very homogenous populations and fishing industries. Or is Wyman's point simply that when there are large numbers of "veto points" in a political system, as there are in the United States, then heterogeneity of interests in the industry becomes an advantage?

CHAPTER XI

GOVERNMENT FORBEARANCE

There is a longstanding debate about the relationship between government and property. Locke famously argued that property rights originate in the state of nature, and government was created to protect these rights. See John Locke, Two Treatises of Civil Government bk. II, ch. V (1690). Bentham responded bluntly that "[p]roperty and law are born together, and die together. Before laws were made there was no property; take away laws, and property ceases." Jeremy Bentham, The Theory of Legislation 113 (C.K. Ogden ed., 1931) (1802). The debate is largely philosophical; the historical record is too murky to provide a definite answer to the question whether property is "pre-political" or "post-political," at least insofar as most property rights that exist today are concerned. Whatever the role of the state in bringing property into being, there is no question that government action affects property rights in a great many important ways. As Blackstone observed, even if "[t]he original of private property is probably founded in nature" nevertheless "the method of conserving it in the present owner, and of translating it from man to man, are entirely derived from society." 1 Blackstone, Commentaries *134.

In this Chapter, we focus on the question of how much the government should forbear from interfering with, or frustrating, previously recognized property rights. This general inquiry entails several subsidiary questions: How explicit must the government's promise of forbearance be before property owners can justifiably rely upon it? What sort of public policy reasons suffice to permit the government to break its promise of forbearance? If the government breaks its promise, and has no adequate justification for doing so, what sort of remedies will the courts give to someone who has been injured by the government's lack of forbearance?

In the United States, these questions have commonly been addressed as a matter of constitutional law. During roughly the first century after the adoption of the Constitution, the clause invoked most frequently as a basis for adjudicating claims of inadequate forbearance was the Contracts Clause of Article I, § 10, which provides that no state shall pass any law "impairing the obligation of contract." The Supreme Court held in *Fletcher v. Peck*, 10 U.S. (6 Cranch) 87 (1810), that the obligation of contract includes grants of property in land, and then ruled in *Dartmouth College v. Woodward*, 17 U.S. (4 Wheat.) 518 (1819), that it also includes corporate charters. These decisions laid the groundwork for a jurisprudence in which the Court reviewed a wide range of claims of inadequate government forbearance under the Contracts Clause. Toward the end of the nineteenth century, the action shifted toward the Due Process Clauses of the Fifth and Fourteenth

Amendments, which the courts interpreted to impose certain substantive restraints on government action depriving individuals of private rights. *Lochner v. New York*, 198 U.S. 45 (1905), in which the Court invalidated a maximum hours regulation as interfering with liberty of contract, is the most famous decision of this era. But the Court also held that state interferences with the expectations of property owners could violate due process. See, e.g., Truax v. Corrigan, 257 U.S. 312 (1921); Missouri Pac. Ry. v. Nebraska, 164 U.S. 403 (1896); see Ronald J. Krotoszynski, Jr., Fundamental Property Rights, 85 Geo. L. J. 555, 561–67 (1997).

In recent decades, the dominant clause for addressing these issues has become the Takings Clause of the Fifth Amendment, which has been held to apply to the states through the Fourteenth Amendment. The Takings Clause provides: "nor shall private property be taken for public use without just compensation." This Clause functions in part to regulate the power of eminent domain. But the Court has also drawn upon the Clause for the understanding that certain regulations of property can go "too far," to the point where the government must proceed by eminent domain rather than by police power regulation. This understanding, which is called the "regulatory takings" doctrine, is taken up in Chapter XII.

Although constitutional constraints have been the focal point for discussion about the proper degree of government forbearance in interfering with property rights, government forbearance is also encouraged by nonconstitutional doctrines. In subpart C we consider some of these doctrines, including the rule of construction favoring vested rights, the doctrine favoring a strong version of stare decisis in matters involving property rights, the understanding that governments may be sued for breach of contract when they break specific regulatory promises, and foreign investment protection treaties. But first, we consider a classic Supreme Court decision that raises questions about government forbearance with a degree of explicitness that has rarely been matched in any subsequent decision.

A. THE GENERAL PROBLEM

Charles River Bridge v. Warren Bridge

Supreme Court of the United States, 1837.
36 U.S. (11 Pet.) 420.

■ TANEY, CH. J., delivered the opinion of the court. The questions involved in this case are of the gravest character, and the court have given to them the most anxious and deliberate consideration. The value of the right claimed by the plaintiffs is large in amount; and many persons may, no doubt, be seriously affected in their pecuniary interests, by any decision which the court may pronounce; and the questions which have been raised as to the power of the several states, in relation to the corporations they have chartered, are pregnant with important consequences; not only to the individuals who are concerned in the corporate franchises, but to the communities in which they exist. The court are fully sensible, that it is their duty, in exercising the high powers conferred on them by the constitution of the United States, to deal with these great and extensive interests, with the utmost caution; guarding, so far as they have the power to do so, the rights of property, and at the same time, carefully abstaining from any encroachment on the rights reserved to the states.

It appears, from the record, that in the year 1650, the legislature of Massachusetts granted to the president of Harvard College "the liberty and power," to dispose of the ferry from Charlestown to Boston, by lease or otherwise, in the behalf, and for the behoof, of the college; and that under that grant, the college continued to hold and keep the ferry, by its lessees or agents, and to receive the profits of it, until 1785. In the last-mentioned year, a petition was presented to the legislature, by Thomas Russell and others, stating the inconvenience of the transportation by ferries, over Charles river, and the public advantages that would result from a bridge; and praying to be incorporated, for the purpose of erecting a bridge in the place where the ferry between Boston and Charlestown was then kept. Pursuant to this petition, the legislature, on the 9th of March 1785, passed an act incorporating a company, by the name of "The Proprietors of the Charles River Bridge," for the purposes mentioned in the petition. Under this charter, the company were empowered to erect a bridge, in "the place where the ferry was then kept;" certain tolls were granted, and the charter was limited to forty years from the first opening of the bridge for passengers; and from the time the toll commenced, until the expiration of this term, the company were to pay £200, annually, to Harvard College; and at the expiration of the forty years, the bridge was to be the property of the commonwealth; "saving (as the law expresses it) to the said college or university, a reasonable annual compensation, for the annual income of the ferry, which they might have received, had not the said bridge been erected."

The bridge was accordingly built, and was opened for passengers on the 17th of June 1786. In 1792, the charter was extended to seventy years from the opening of the bridge; and at the expiration of that time, it was to belong to the commonwealth. The corporation have regularly paid to the college the annual sum of £200 and have performed all of the duties imposed on them by the terms of their charter.

In 1828, the legislature of Massachusetts incorporated a company by the name of "The Proprietors of the Warren Bridge," for the purpose of erecting another bridge over Charles river. This bridge is only sixteen rods, at its commencement, on the Charlestown side, from the commencement of the bridge of the plaintiffs; and they are about fifty rods apart, at their termination on the Boston side. The travellers who pass over either bridge, proceed from Charlestown square, which receives the travel of many great public roads leading from the country; and the passengers and travellers who go to and from Boston, used to pass over the Charles River bridge, from and through this square, before the erection of the Warren bridge.

Figure 11–1
Map of Boston and Environs
("1" denotes the Charles River Bridge and "2" the Warren Bridge.)

BOSTON AND ENVIRONS.

Source: Octavius Pickering, Case of the proprietors of Charles River bridge against the proprietors of Warren bridge: argued and determined in the Supreme Judicial Court of Massachusetts, 54 & plate (Boston, Hilliard, Gray, Little, and Wilkins 1830).
Courtesy of Special Collections Department, Harvard Law School Library.

The Warren bridge, by the terms of its charter, was to be surrendered to the state, as soon as the expenses of the proprietors in building and supporting it should be reimbursed; but this period was not, in any event, to exceed six years from the time the company commenced receiving toll.

When the original bill in this case was filed, the Warren bridge had not been built; and the bill was filed, after the passage of the law, in order to obtain an injunction to prevent its erection, and for general relief. The bill, among other things, charged as a ground for relief, that the act for the erection of the Warren bridge impaired the obligation of the contract between the commonwealth and the proprietors of the Charles River bridge; and was, therefore, repugnant to the constitution of the United States. Afterwards, a supplemental bill was filed, stating that the bridge had then been so far completed, that it had been opened for travel, and that divers persons had passed over, and thus avoided the payment of the toll, which would otherwise have been received by the plaintiffs. * * * In the argument here, it was admitted, that since the filing of the supplemental bill, a sufficient amount of toll had been reserved by the proprietors of the Warren bridge to reimburse all their expenses, and that the bridge is now the property of the state, and has been made a free bridge; and that the value of the franchise granted to the proprietors of the Charles River bridge, has by this means been entirely destroyed. * * *

A good deal of evidence has been offered, to show the nature and extent of the ferry-right granted to the college; and also to show the rights claimed by the proprietors of the bridge, at different times, by virtue of their charter; and the opinions entertained by committees of the legislature, and others, upon that subject. But as these circumstances do not affect the judgment of this court, it is unnecessary to recapitulate them.

The plaintiffs in error insist, mainly, upon two grounds: 1st. That by virtue of the grant of 1650, Harvard College was entitled, in perpetuity, to the right of keeping a ferry between Charlestown and Boston; that this right was exclusive; and that the legislature had not the power to establish another ferry on the same line of travel, because it would infringe the rights of the college; and that these rights, upon the erection of the bridge in the place of the ferry, under the charter of 1785, were transferred to, and became vested in "The Proprietors of the Charles River Bridge;" and that under, and by virtue of this transfer of the ferry-right, the rights of the bridge company were as exclusive in that line of travel, as the rights of the ferry. 2d. That independently of the ferry-right, the acts of the legislature of Massachusetts, of 1785 and 1792, by their true construction, necessarily implied, that the legislature would not authorize another bridge, and especially, a free one, by the side of this, and placed in the same line of travel, whereby the franchise granted to the "Proprietors of the Charles River Bridge" should be rendered of no value; and the plaintiffs in error contend, that the grant of the ferry to the college, and of the charter to the proprietors of the bridge, are both contracts on the part of the state; and that the law authorizing the erection of the Warren bridge in 1828, impairs the obligation of one or both of these contracts.

It is very clear, that in the form in which this case comes before us (being a writ of error to a state court), the plaintiffs, in claiming under either of these rights, must place themselves on the ground of contract, and cannot support themselves upon the principle, that the law divests vested rights. It is well settled, by the decisions of this court, that a state law may be retrospective in its character, and may divest vested rights, and yet not violate the constitution of the United States, unless it also impairs the obligation of a contract. [Satterlee v. Matthewson, 2 Pet. 413 (1829); Watson v. Mercer, 8 Pet. 88 (1834)]: * * * After these solemn decisions of this court, it is apparent, that the plaintiffs in error cannot sustain themselves here, either upon the ferry-right, or the charter to the bridge; upon the ground, that vested rights of property have been divested by the legislature. And whether they claim under the ferry-right, or the charter to the bridge, they must show that the title which they claim, was acquired by contract, and that the terms of that contract have been violated by the charter to the Warren bridge. In other words, they must show, that the state had entered into a contract with them, or those under whom they claim, not to establish a free bridge at the place where the Warren bridge is erected. Such, and such only, are the principles upon which the plaintiffs in error can claim relief in this case.

The nature and extent of the ferry right granted to Harvard College, in 1650, must depend upon the laws of Massachusetts; and the character and extent of this right has been elaborately discussed at the bar. But in the view which the court take of the case before them, it is not necessary to express any opinion on these questions. * * *

The fact that such a right was granted to the college, cannot, by any sound rule of construction, be used to extend the privileges of the bridge company, beyond what the words of the charter naturally and legally import. Increased population, longer experience in legislation, the different character of the corporations which owned the ferry from that which owned the bridge, might well have induced a change in the policy of the state in this respect * * *. The charter to the bridge is a written instrument which must speak for itself, and be interpreted by its own terms.

This brings us to the act of the legislature of Massachusetts, of 1785, by which the plaintiffs were incorporated by the name of "The Proprietors of the Charles River Bridge;" and it is here, and in the law of 1792, prolonging their charter, that we must look for the extent and nature of the franchise conferred upon the plaintiffs.

Much has been said in the argument of the principles of construction by which this law is to be expounded, and what undertakings, on the part of the state, may be implied. The court think there can be no serious difficulty on that head. It is the grant of certain franchises, by the public, to a private corporation, and in a matter where the public interest is concerned. The rule of construction in such cases is well settled, both in England, and by the decisions of our own tribunals. In the case of the *Proprietors of the Stourbridge Canal* v. *Wheeley and others*, 2 B. & Ad. 793, the court say, "the canal having been made under an act of parliament, the rights of the plaintiffs are derived entirely from that act. This, like many other cases, is a bargain between a company of adventurers and the public, the terms of which are expressed in the statute; and the rule of construction in all such cases, is now fully established to be this—that any ambiguity in the terms of the contract, must operate against the adventurers, and in favor of the public, and the plaintiffs can claim nothing that is not clearly given them by the act." And the doctrine thus laid down in abundantly sustained by the authorities referred to in this decision. * * *

Borrowing, as we have done, our system of jurisprudence from the English law; and having adopted, in every other case, civil and criminal, its rules for the construction of statutes; is there anything in our local situation, or in the nature of our political institutions, which should lead us to depart from the principle, where corporations are concerned? * * * We think not; and it would present a singular spectacle, if, while the courts in England are restraining, within the strictest limits, the spirit of monopoly, and exclusive privileges in nature of monopolies, and confining corporations to the privileges plainly given to them in their charter; the courts of this country should be found enlarging these privileges by implication; and construing a statute more unfavorably to the public, and to the rights of community, than would be done in a like case in an English court of justice.

But we are not now left to determine, for the first time, the rules by which public grants are to be construed in this country. * * * [T]he case most analogous to this, and in which the question came more directly before the court, is the case of the *Providence Bank* v. *Billings*, 4 Pet. 514, which was decided in 1830. In that case, it appeared, that the legislature of Rhode Island had chartered the bank, in the usual form of such acts of incorporation. The charter contained no stipulation on the part of the state, that it would not impose a tax on the bank, nor any reservation of the right to do so. It was silent on this point. Afterwards, a law was passed, imposing a tax on all banks in the state; and the right to impose this tax was resisted by the Providence Bank, upon the ground, that if the state could impose a tax, it might tax so heavily as to render the franchise of no value, and destroy the institution; that the charter was a contract, and that a power which may in effect destroy the charter is inconsistent with it, and is impliedly renounced by granting it. But the court said, that the taxing power was of vital importance, and essential to the existence of government; and that the relinquishment of such a power is never to be assumed. And in delivering the opinion of the court, the late chief justice states the principle, in the following clear and emphatic language. Speaking of the taxing power, he says, "as the whole community is interested in retaining it undiminished, that community has a right to insist that its abandonment ought not to be presumed, in a case in which the deliberate purpose of the state to abandon it does not appear." The case now before the court is, in principle, precisely the same. * * *

It may, perhaps, be said, that in the case of the Providence Bank, this court were speaking of the taxing power; which is of vital importance to the very existence of every government. But the object and end of all government is to promote the happiness and prosperity of the community by which it is established; and it can never be assumed, that the government intended to diminish its power of accomplishing the end for which it was created. And in a country like ours, free, active and enterprising, continually advancing in numbers and wealth, new channels of communication are daily found necessary, both for travel and trade, and are essential to the comfort, convenience and prosperity of the people. A state ought never to be presumed to surrender this power, because, like the taxing power, the whole community have an interest in preserving it undiminished. And when a corporation alleges, that a state has surrendered, for seventy years, its power of improvement and public accommodation, in a great and important line of travel, along which a vast number of its citizens must daily pass, the community have a right to insist, in the language of this court, above quoted, "that its abandonment ought not to be presumed, in a case, in which the deliberate purpose of the state to abandon it does not appear." The continued existence of a government would be of no great value, if, by implications and presumptions, it was disarmed of the powers necessary to accomplish the ends of its creation, and the functions it was designed to perform, transferred to the hands of privileged corporations.

The rule of construction announced by the court, was not confined to the taxing power, nor is it so limited, in the opinion delivered. * * * While the rights of private property are sacredly guarded, we must not forget, that the community also have rights, and that the happiness and well-being of every citizen depends on their faithful preservation.

Adopting the rule of construction above stated as the settled one, we proceed to apply it to the charter of 1785, to the proprietors of the Charles River bridge. This act of incorporation is in the usual form, and the privileges such as are commonly given to corporations of that kind. It confers on them the ordinary faculties of a corporation, for the purpose of building the bridge; and establishes certain rates of toll, which the company are authorized to take: this is the whole grant. There is no exclusive privilege given to them over the waters of Charles river, above or below their bridge; no right to erect another bridge themselves, nor to prevent other persons from erecting one, no engagement from the state, that another shall not be erected; and no undertaking not to sanction competition, nor to make improvements that may diminish the amount of its income. Upon all these subject, the charter is silent; and nothing is said in it about a line of travel, so much insisted on in the argument, in which they are to have exclusive privileges. No words are used, from which an intention to grant any of these rights can be inferred; if the plaintiff is entitled to them, it must be implied, simply, from the nature of the grant; and cannot be inferred, from the words by which the grant is made.

The relative position of the Warren bridge has already been described. It does not interrupt the passage over the Charles River bridge, nor make the way to it, or from it, less convenient. None of the faculties or franchises granted to that corporation, have been revoked by the legislature; and its right to take the tolls granted by the charter remains unaltered. In short, all the franchises and rights of property, enumerated in the charter, and there mentioned to have been granted to it, remain unimpaired. But its income is destroyed by the Warren bridge; which, being free, draws off the passengers and property which would have gone over it, and renders their franchise of no value. This is the gist of the complaint; for it is not pretended, that the erection of the Warren bridge would have done them any injury, or in any degree affected their right of property, if it had not diminished the amount of their tolls. In order, then, to entitle themselves to relief, it is necessary to show, that the legislature contracted not to do the act of which they complain; and that they impaired, or in other words, violated, that contract, by the erection of the Warren bridge.

The inquiry, then, is, does the charter contain such a contract on the part of the state? Is there any such stipulation to be found in that instrument? It must be admitted on all hands, that there is none; no words that even relate to another bridge, or to the diminution of their tolls, or to the line of travel. If a contract on that subject can be gathered from the charter, it must be by implication; and cannot be found in the words used. Can such an agreement be implied? The rule of construction before stated is an answer to the question: in charters of this description, no rights are taken from the public, or given to the corporation, beyond those which the words of the charter, by their natural and proper construction, purport to convey. There are no words which import such a contract as the plaintiffs in error contend for, and none can be implied; and the same answer must be given to them that was given by this court to Providence Bank. * * *

Indeed, the practice and usage of almost every state in the Union, old enough to have commenced the work of internal improvement, is opposed to the doctrine contended for on the part of the plaintiffs in error. Turnpike roads have been made in succession, on the same line of travel; the later ones interfering materially with the profits of the first. These corporations have, in some instances, been utterly ruined by the introduction of newer and better modes of transportation and travelling. In some cases, railroads have rendered the turnpike roads on the same line of travel so entirely useless, that the franchise of the turnpike corporation is not worth preserving. Yet in none of these cases have the corporation supposed that their privileges were invaded, or any contract violated on the part of the state. * * * The absence of any such controversy, when there must have been so many occasions to give rise to it, proves, that neither states, nor individuals, nor corporations, ever imagined that such a contract could be implied from such charters. * * *

And what would be the fruits of this doctrine of implied contracts, on the part of the states, and of property in a line of travel, by a corporation, if it would now be sanctioned by this court? To what results would it lead us? If it is to be found in the charter to this bridge, the same process of reasoning must discover it, in the various acts which have been passed, within the last forty years, for turnpike companies. And what is to be the extent of the privileges of exclusion on the different sides of the road? The counsel who have so ably argued this case, have not attempted to define it by any certain boundaries. How far must the new improvement be distant from the old one? How near may you approach, without invading its rights in the privileged line? If this court should establish the principles now contended for, what is to become of the numerous railroads established on the same line of travel with turnpike companies; and which have rendered the franchises of the turnpike corporations of no value? Let it once be understood, that such charters carry with them these implied contracts, and give this unknown and undefined property in a line of traveling; and you will soon find the old turnpike corporations awakening from their sleep, and calling upon this court to put down the improvements which have taken their place. The millions of property which have been invested in railroads and canals, upon lines of travel which had been before occupied by turnpike corporations, will be put in jeopardy. We shall be thrown back to the improvements of the last century, and obliged to stand still, until the claims of the old turnpike corporations shall be satisfied; and they shall consent to permit these states to avail themselves of the lights of modern science, and to partake of the benefit of those improvements which are now adding to the wealth and prosperity, and the convenience and comfort, of every other part of the civilized world. Nor is this all. This court will find itself compelled to fix, by some arbitrary rule, the width of this new kind of property in a line of travel; for if such a right of property exists, we have no lights to guide us in marking out its extent, unless, indeed, we resort to the old feudal grants, and to the exclusive rights of ferries, by prescription, between towns; and are prepared to decide that when a turnpike road from one town to another, had been made, no railroad or canal, between these two points, could afterwards be established. This court are not prepared to sanction principles which must lead to such results.

Many other questions, of the deepest importance, have been raised and elaborately discussed in the argument. It is not necessary, for the decision of this case, to express our opinion upon them; and the court deem it proper to avoid volunteering an opinion on any question, involving the construction of the constitution, where the case itself does not bring the question directly before them, and make it their duty to decide upon it. * * *

The judgment of the supreme judicial court of the commonwealth of Massachusetts, dismissing the plaintiffs' bill, must, therefore, be affirmed, with costs.

■ McLean, Justice. [omitted].

■ Story, Justice. (Dissenting.) * * * [B]efore we can properly enter upon the consideration of this subject, a preliminary inquiry is presented, as to the proper rules of interpretation applicable to the charter. Is the charter to receive a strict or a liberal construction? Are any implications to be made, beyond the express terms? And if so, to what extent are they justifiable, by the principles of law? No one doubts, that the charter is a contract and a grant; and that it is to receive such a construction as belong to contracts and grants, as contradistinguished from mere laws. But the argument has been pressed here, with unwonted earnestness (and it seems to have had an irresistible influence elsewhere); that this charter is to be construed as a royal grant, and that such grants are always construed with a stern and parsimonious strictness. * * * Under such circumstances, I feel myself constrained to go at large into the doctrine of the common law, in respect to royal grants, because I cannot help thinking, that, upon this point, very great errors of opinion have crept into the argument. A single insulated position seems to have been taken as a general axiom. In my own view of the case, I should not have attached so much importance to the inquiry; but it is now fit that it should be sifted to the bottom.

It is a well-known rule in the construction of private grants, if the meaning of the words be doubtful, to construe them most strongly against the grantor. But it is said, that an opposite rule prevails in cases of grants by the king; for, where there is any doubt, the construction is made most favorably for the king, and against the grantee. The rule is not disputed; but it is a rule of very limited application. To what cases does it apply? * * *

[T]his doctrine in relation to the king's prerogative of having a construction in his own favor, is exclusively confined to cases of mere *donation*, flowing from the bounty of the crown. Whenever the grant is upon a valuable consideration, the rule of construction ceases; and the grant is expounded exactly as it would be in the case of a private grant—favorably to the grantee. Why is this rule adopted? Plainly, because the grant is a contract, and is to be interpreted according to its fair meaning. It would be to the dishonor of the government, that it should pocket a fair consideration, and then quibble as to the obscurities and implications of its own contract. * * *

I admit, that where the terms of a grant are to impose burdens upon the public, or to create a restraint injurious to the public interest, there is sound reason for interpreting the terms, if ambiguous, in favor of the public. But at the same time, I insist, that there is not the slightest reason for saying, even in such a case, that the grant is not to be construed favorably to the grantee, so as to secure him in the enjoyment of what is actually granted. * * *

But it has been argued, and the argument has been pressed in every form which ingenuity could suggest, that if grants of this nature are to be construed liberally, as conferring any exclusive rights on the grantees, it will interpose an effectual barrier against all general improvements of the country. * * * For my own part, I can conceive of no surer plan to arrest all public improvements, founded on private capital and enterprise, than to make the outlay of that capital uncertain and questionable, both as to security and as to productiveness. No man will hazard his capital in any enterprise, in which, if there be a loss, it must be borne exclusively by himself; and if there be success, he has not the slightest security of enjoying the rewards of that success, for a single moment. If the government means to invite its citizens to enlarge the public comforts and conveniences, to establish bridges, or turnpikes, or canals, or railroads, there must be some pledge, that the property will be safe; that the enjoyment will be co-extensive with the grant; and that success will not be the signal of a general combination to overthrow its rights and to take away its profits. The very agitation of a question of this sort is sufficient to alarm every stockholder in every public enterprise of this sort, throughout the whole country. Already, in my native state, the legislature has found it necessary expressly to concede the exclusive privilege here contended against; in order to insure the accomplishment of a railroad for the benefit of the public. And yet, we are told, that all such exclusive grants are to the detriment of the public.

But if there were any foundation for the argument itself, in a general view, it would totally fail in its application to the present case. Here, the grant, however exclusive, is but for a short and limited period, more than two-thirds of which have already elapsed; and when it is gone, the whole property and franchise are to revert to the state. The legislature exercised a wholesome foresight on the subject; and within a reasonable period, it will have an unrestricted authority to do whatever it may choose, in the appropriation of the bridge and its tolls. There is not, then, under any fair aspect of the case, the slightest reason to presume that public improvements either can, or will, be injuriously retarded by a liberal construction of the present grant. * * *

I go further, and maintain, not only that it is not a case for strict construction; but that the charter, upon its very face, by its terms, and for its professed objects, demands from the court, upon undeniable principles of law, a favorable construction for the grantees. * * * [T]hey are to take upon themselves the chances of success; and if the enterprise fails, the loss is exclusively their own. Nor let any man imagine, that there was not, at the time when this charter was granted, much solid ground for doubting success. In order to entertain a just view of this subject, we must go back to that period of general bankruptcy, and distress and difficulty. The constitution of the United States was not only not then in existence, but it was not then even dreamed of. The union of the states was crumbling into ruins, under the old confederation. Agriculture, manufactures and commerce were at their lowest ebb. There was infinite danger to all the states, from local interests and jealousies, and from the apparent impossibility of a much longer adherence to that shadow of a government, the continental congress. And even four years afterwards, when every evil had been greatly aggravated, and civil war was added to other calamities, the constitution of the United States was all but shipwrecked, in passing through the state conventions; it was adopted by very slender majorities. These are historical facts, which required no coloring to give them effect, and admitted of no concealment, to seduce men into schemes of future aggrandizement. I would even now put it to the common sense of every man, whether, if the constitution of the United States had not been adopted, the charter would have been worth a forty years' purchase of the tolls.

This is not all. It is well known, historically, that this was the very first bridge ever constructed, in New England, over navigable tide-waters so near the sea. The rigors of our climate, the dangers from sudden thaws and freezing, and the obstructions from ice in a rapid current, were deemed by many persons to be insuperable obstacles to the success of such a project. It was believed, that the bridge would scarcely stand a single severe winter. And I myself am old enough to know, that in regard to other arms of the sea, at much later periods, the same doubts have had a strong and depressing influence upon public enterprises. If Charles River bridge had been carried away, during the first or second season after its erection, it is far from being certain, that up to this moment, another bridge, upon such an arm of the sea, would ever have been erected in Massachusetts. I state these things, which are of public notoriety, to repel the notion that the legislature was surprised into an incautious grant, or that the reward was more than adequate to the perils. There was a full and adequate consideration, in a pecuniary sense, for the charter. But, in a more general sense, the erection of the bridge, as a matter of accommodation, has been incalculably beneficial to the public. Unless, therefore, we are wholly to disregard the declarations of the legislature, and the objects of the charter, and the historical facts of the times; and indulge in mere private speculations of profit and loss, by our present lights and experience; it seems to me, that the court is bound to come to the interpretation of this charter, with a persuasion that it was granted in furtherance, and not in derogation, of the public good. * * *

The argument of the defendants is, that the plaintiffs are to take nothing by implication. Either (say they) the exclusive grant extends only to the local limits of the bridge; or it extends the whole length of the river, or, at least, up to old Cambridge bridge. The latter construction would be absurd and monstrous; and therefore, the former must be the true one. Now, I utterly deny the alternative involved in the dilemma. The right to build a bridge over a river, and to take toll, may well include an exclusive franchise, beyond the local limits of the bridge; and yet not extend through the whole course of the river, or even to any considerable distance on the river. There is no difficulty, in common sense, or in law, in maintaining such a doctrine. But then, it is asked, what limits can be assigned to such a franchise? The answer is obvious; the grant carries with it an exclusive franchise, to a reasonable distance on the river; so that the ordinary travel to the bridge shall not be diverted by any new bridge, to the injury or ruin of the franchise. A new bridge, which would be a nuisance to the old bridge, would be within the reach of its exclusive right. The question would not be so much as to the fact of distance, as it would be as to the fact of nuisance. There is nothing new in such expositions of incorporeal rights; and nothing new in thus administering, upon this foundation, remedies in regard thereto. The doctrine is coeval with the common law itself. Suppose, an action is brought for shutting up the ancient lights belonging to a messuage; or for diverting a water-course; or for flowing back a stream; or for erecting a nuisance near a dwelling-house; the question in such cases is not one of mere distance; of mere feet and inches, but of injury—permanent, real and substantial injury—to be decided upon all the circumstances of the case. But of this I shall speak again hereafter.

Let us see what is the result of the narrow construction contended for by the defendants. * * * Now, I put it to the common sense of every man, whether if, at the moment of granting the charter, the legislature had said to the proprietors; you shall build the bridge; you shall bear the burdens; you shall be bound by the charges; and your sole reimbursement shall be from the tolls of forty years: and yet we will not even guaranty you any certainty of receiving any tolls; on the contrary; we reserve to ourselves the full power and authority to erect other bridges, toll or free bridges, according to our own free will and pleasure, contiguous to yours, and having the same *termini* with yours; and if you are successful, we may thus supplant you, divide, destroy your profits, and annihilate your tolls, without annihilating your burdens: if, I say, such had been the language of the legislature, is there a man living, of ordinary discretion or prudence, who would have accepted such a charter, upon such terms? I fearlessly answer, no. There would have been such a gross inadequacy of consideration, and such a total insecurity of all the rights of property, under such circumstances, that the project would have dropped still-born. And I put the question further, whether any legislature, meaning to promote a project of permanent, public utility (such as this confessedly was), would ever have dreamed of such a qualification of its own grant, when it sought to enlist

private capital and private patronage to insure the accomplishment of it?
* * *

And yet it is conceded, that the legislature cannot revoke or resume
this grant. Why not, I pray to know? There is no negative covenant in the
charter; there is no express prohibition to be found there. The reason is
plain. The prohibition arises by natural, if not by necessary, implication. It
would be against the first principles of justice, to presume that the
legislature reserved a right to destroy its own grant. That was the doctrine
in *Fletcher* v. *Peck*, 6 Cranch 87, in this court; and in other cases turning
upon the same great principle of political and constitutional duty and right.
Can the legislature have power to do that indirectly, which it cannot do
directly? If it cannot take away, or resume, the franchise itself, can it take
away its whole substance and value? If the law will create an implication,
that the legislature shall not resume its own grant, is it not equally as
natural and as necessary an implication, that the legislature shall not do
any act directly to prejudice its own grant, or to destroy its value? * * *

It is upon this ground, and this ground only, that we can explain the
established doctrine in relation to ferries. When the crown grants a ferry
from A. to B., without using any words which import it to be an exclusive
ferry, why is it (as will be presently shown), that by the common law, the
grant is construed to be exclusive of all other ferries between the same
places or *termini;* at least, if such ferries are so near that they are injurious
to the first ferry, and tend to a direct diminution of its receipts? Plainly, it
must be, because from the nature of such a franchise, it can have no
permanent value, unless it is exclusive; and the circumstance that during
the existence of the grant, the grantee has public burdens imposed upon
him, raises the implication, that nothing shall be done to the prejudice of it,
while it is a subsisting franchise. * * *

In the case of a ferry, there is a public charge and duty. The owner
must keep the ferry in good repair, upon the peril of an indictment. He
must keep sufficient accommodations for all travellers, at all reasonable
times. He must content himself with a reasonable toll. Such is the *jus
publicum*. In return, the law will exclude all injurious competition, and
deem every new ferry a nuisance, which subtracts from him the ordinary
custom and toll. * * * The same principle applies, without a shadow of
difference that I am able to perceive, to the case of a bridge; for the duties
are *publici juris*, and pontage and passage are but different names for
exclusive toll for transportation. * * *

Wherever any other bridge or ferry is so near, that it injures the
franchise, or diminishes the toll, in a positive and essential decree, there it
is a nuisance, and is actionable. It invades the franchise, and ought to be
abated. But whether there be such an injury or not, is a matter, not of law,
but of fact. Distance is no otherwise important than as it bears on the
question of fact. All that is required, is, that there should be a sensible,
positive injury. In the present case, there is no room to doubt upon this
point, for the bridges are contiguous; and Warren bridge, after it was
opened, took away three-fourths of the profits of the travel from Charles

River bridge; and when it became free (as it now is), it necessarily took away all the tolls, or all except an unimportant and trivial amount. * * *

But it is said, if this is the law, what then is to become of turnpikes and canals? Is the legislature precluded from authorizing new turnpikes or new canals, simply because they cross the path of the old ones, and incidentally diminish their receipt of tolls? The answer is plain. Every turnpike has its local limits and local *termini;* its points of beginning and of end. No one ever imagined, that the legislature might grant a new turnpike, with exactly the same location and *termini.* That would be to rescind its first grant. The grant of a turnpike between A. and B., does not preclude the legislature from the grant of a turnpike between A. and C., even though it should incidentally intercept some of the travel; for it is not necessarily a nuisance to the former grant. The *termini* being different, the grants are or may be substantially different. But if the legislature should grant a second turnpike, substantially taking away the whole travel from the first turnpike, between the same local points; then, I say, it is a violation of the rights of the first turnpike. * * *

But then again, it is said, that all this rests upon implication, and not upon the words of the charter. I admit, that it does; but I again say, that the implication is natural and necessary. It is indispensable to the proper effect of the grant. The franchise cannot subsist without it, at least, for any valuable or practical purpose. What objection can there be to implications, if they arise from the very nature and objects of the grant? If it be indispensable to the full enjoyment of the right to take toll, that it should be exclusive within certain limits, is it not just and reasonable, that it should be so construed? * * *

To the answer already given to the objection, that, unless such a reservation of power exists, there will be a stop put to the progress of all public improvements; I wish, in this connection, to add, that there never can any such consequence follow upon the opposite doctrine. If the public exigencies and interests require that the franchise of Charles River bridge should be taken away, or impaired, it may be lawfully done, upon making due compensation to the proprietors. "Whenever," says the constitution of Massachusetts, "the public exigencies require that the property of any individual should be appropriated to public uses, he shall receive a reasonable compensation therefor;" and this franchise is property—is fixed determinate property. * * *

But it is said, that if the doctrine contended for be not true, then every grant to a corporation becomes, *ipso facto*, a monopoly or exclusive privilege. The grant of a bank, or of an insurance company, or of a manufacturing company, becomes a monopoly, and excludes all injurious competition. With the greatest deference and respect for those who press such an argument, I cannot but express my surprise that it should be urged. As long ago as the case in the Year Book, 22 Hen. VI. 14, the difference was pointed out in argument, between such grants as involve public duties and public matters for the common benefit of the people, and such as are for mere private benefit, involving no such consideration. If a bank, or insurance company, or manufacturing company, is established in any town, by an act of incorporation; no one ever imagined that the corporation was bound to do business, to employ its capital, to manufacture goods, to make insurance. The privilege is a mere private corporate privilege, for the benefit of the stockholders, to be used or not, at their own pleasure; to operate when they please; and to stop when they please. Did any man ever imagine, that he had a right to have a note discounted by a bank, or a policy underwritten by an insurance company? Such grants are always deemed *privati juris*. No indictment lies for a *non-user*. But in cases of ferries and bridges, and other franchises of a like nature (as has been shown), they are affected with a *jus publicum*. Such grants are made for the public accommodation; and pontage and passage are authorized to be levied upon travellers (which can only be by public authority); and in return, the proprietors are bound to keep up all suitable accommodations for travellers, under the penalty of indictment for their neglect. * * *

It has been further argued, that even if the charter of the Charles River bridge does imply such a contract on the part of the legislature, as is contended for, it is void for want of authority in the legislature to make it; because it is a surrender of the right of eminent domain, entrusted to the legislature and its successors, for the benefit of the public, which is not at liberty to alienate. If the argument means no more, than that the legislature, being entrusted with the power to grant franchises, cannot, by contract, agree to surrender or part with this power, generally, it would be unnecessary to consider the argument; for no one supposes that the legislature can rightfully surrender its legislative power. If the argument means no more, than that the legislature, having the right, by the constitution, to take private property (among which property are franchises) for public purposes, cannot divest itself of such a right, by contract, there would be as little reason to contest it. Neither of these cases is like that before the court. But the argument (if I do not misunderstand it) goes further, and denies the right of the legislature to make a contract granting the exclusive right to build a bridge between Charlestown and Boston, and thereby taking from itself the right to grant another bridge between Charlestown and Boston, at its pleasure; although the contract does not exclude the legislature from taking it for public use, upon making actual compensation; because it trenches upon the sovereign right of eminent domain. * * *

But let us see what the argument is, in relation to sovereignty in general. It admits, that the sovereign power has, among its prerogatives, the right to make grants, to build bridges, to erect ferries, to lay out highways; and to create franchises for public and private purposes. If it has a right to make such grants, it follows, that the grantees have a right to take, and to hold, these franchises. It would be a solecism, to declare that the sovereign power could grant, and yet no one could have a right to take. If it may grant such franchises, it may define and limit the nature and extent of such franchises; for, as the power is general, the limitations must depend upon the good pleasure and discretion of the sovereign power in making the particular grant. If it may prescribe the limits, it may contract that these limits shall not be invaded by itself or by others.

It follows, from this view of the subject, that if the sovereign power grants any franchise, it is good and irrevocable, within the limits granted, whatever they may be; or else, in every case, the grant will be held only during pleasure; and the identical franchise may be granted to any other person, or may be revoked at the will of the sovereign. This latter doctrine is not pretended; and, indeed, is unmaintainable in our systems of free government. * * * Thus, for example, if the sovereign power should expressly grant an exclusive right to build a bridge over navigable waters, between the towns of A. and B., and should expressly contract with the grantees, that no other bridge should be built between the same towns; the grant would, upon the principles of the argument, be equally void in regard to the franchise, within the planks of the bridge, as it would be in regard to the franchise, outside of the planks of the bridge; for, in each case, it would, *pro tanto*, abridge or surrender the right of the sovereign to grant a new bridge within the local limits. I am aware, that the argument is not pressed to this extent; but it seems to me a necessary consequence flowing from it. The grant of the franchise of a bridge, twenty feet wide, to be exclusive within those limits, is certainly, if obligatory, an abridgment or surrender of the sovereign power to grant another bridge within the same limits; if we mean to say, that every grant that diminishes the things upon which that power can rightfully act, is such an abridgment. Yet the argument admits, that within the limits and planks of the bridge itself, the grant is exclusive; and cannot be recalled. There is no doubt, that there is a necessary exception in every such grant, that if it is wanted for public use, it may be taken by the sovereign power for such use, upon making compensation. Such a taking is not a violation of the contract; but it is strictly an exception, resulting from the nature and attributes of sovereignty; implied from the very terms, or at least, acting upon the subject-matter of the grant, *suo jure.* * * *

Upon the whole, my judgment is, that the act of the legislature of Massachusetts granting the charter of Warren Bridge, is an act impairing the obligation of the prior contract and grant to the proprietors of Charles River bridge; and, by the constitution of the United States, it is, therefore, utterly void. I am for reversing the decree to the state court (dismissing the bill); and for remanding the cause to the state court for further proceedings, as to law and justice shall appertain.

■ THOMPSON, JUSTICE. [omitted]

NOTES AND QUESTIONS

1. For background on the case, see Stanley I. Kutler, Privilege and Creative Destruction: The Charles River Bridge Case (1971). Tolls on the Charles River Bridge were fixed by its legislative charter of 1785, and were never adjusted. Once the original construction costs were paid off, routine operating expenses were relatively low. As population and commercial

activity surged in the Boston area following the adoption of the Constitution, the bridge was soon generating enormous profits; shares in the corporation eventually increased to over 300% of their original value. Id. at 15. The perception that the bridge stockholders had profited handsomely contributed to agitation for construction of a new "free" bridge, and may also help account for the relatively unsympathetic attitude of the judiciary toward the claims of the Charles River Bridge proprietors. Kutler reports that as long as the Warren Bridge was charging tolls up through the early 1830s, the Charles River Bridge managed to remain profitable, although at a much reduced level. Once the Warren Bridge stopped charging tolls, in 1836, the Charles River Bridge could no longer cover its operating costs, and defaulted on the £200 annuity to Harvard (then worth $666). After the Supreme Court decision, the proprietors of the Charles River Bridge sold their franchise to the state for a mere $25,000. In 1847, the state eventually granted Harvard $3,333 in recognition of its lost annuities; this was the last revenue Harvard would see from its ferry monopoly. Ironically, both the buyout of the Charles River Bridge and the payment to Harvard were funded out of renewed tolls imposed by the state on both bridges.

2. Corporate charters and franchises were often viewed in the nineteenth century as a type of special privilege or monopoly that served to enrich a well-connected rentier class at the expense of the common people. The Second Bank of the United States, which Taney, serving as Attorney General, had shut down on orders from President Jackson, was a great symbol for those holding this political perspective. *Charles River Bridge* was also a contest over political symbols—the Proprietors of the Warren Bridge represented the anti-monopoly, anti-privilege views of the Jacksonian Democrats, whereas the Proprietors of the Charles River Bridge represented the pro-property rights, pro-internal improvement ideology of the Whigs like Joseph Story and Daniel Webster (who argued the cause for the Proprietors of the Charles River Bridge). Echoes of this debate reverberate down through American history, for example in struggles over the constitutionality of Progressive and New Deal era regulations of business, and modern debates over consumer and environmental regulation and the degree of progressivity of the tax system. Many of these issues surface in current debates over the "monopoly" rights of intellectual property.

3. The principal case involves a corporate charter or franchise, which all Justices agreed should be considered as a constitutionally protected right. But the doctrine of strict construction has also been applied to government grants of more conventional property rights. For example, in *Watt v. Western Nuclear, Inc.*, 462 U.S. 36 (1983), certain Homesteading Acts granting land to settlers had reserved to the government "all the coal and other minerals" in those lands. The question was whether the reservation of "other minerals" included gravel. The Court held that the gravel belonged to the United States, relying in part on "the established rule that land grants are construed favorably to the Government, that nothing passes except what is conveyed in clear language, and that if there are doubts they are resolved for the Government, not against it." Id. quoting United States v. Union Pac. R. Co., 353 U.S. 112, 116 (1957). (Recall also

that the public trust doctrine, discussed in Chapter III, sometimes functions as a rule of construction protecting public rights against alienation.)
Do you agree that the same considerations cited by Justice Taney for
construing corporate charters favorably to the government also require
that courts construe land grants to settlers favorably to the government?
For example, do considerations about the need to facilitate the development
of new technology and prevent monopoly apply with the same force to
grants of land to homesteaders? Another problem here is that the incidents
associated with conventional grants of property like land are typically not
spelled out in the grant, but are defined by common law (although in
Western Nuclear the reservation was written in the grant, albeit in ambiguous terms). How, if at all, does one apply the doctrine of strict construction
to property rights, the incidents of which are defined by common law?

4. Is Taney's proposed accommodation between change and reliance
only a temporary one? In effect, the principle of strict construction is just a
default rule, around which future charter promoters and legislatures are
free to contract. If the response to the decision is simply to require that all
charters be made explicitly exclusive, as Story suggests it will be, then what
exactly has been accomplished by the holding in the case? Will the new
generation of charters at least be clearer and less subject to disputes and
litigation? In *Bridge Proprietors v. Hoboken Co.*, 68 U.S. (1 Wall.) 116
(1863), the Court considered a 99–year charter that expressly barred "any
other bridge" from being built near the plaintiff's bridge. The Court held
that the charter was not impaired when the state permitted a railroad
bridge to be constructed nearby, because the word "bridge" did not clearly
encompass railroad bridge.

5. Taney and Story are acutely aware of the technological dynamism
of the American economy, discussing how ferries have been superseded by
bridges and turnpikes by railroads. But when an old-technology enterprise
that enjoys some kind of government charter is being displaced by a new-
technology enterprise that also enjoys some kind of government imprima-
tur, how does one distinguish between the impact of a change in government policy and a change in technology? In *Market Street Ry. Co. v.
Railroad Comm'n*, 324 U.S. 548 (1945), the Court was faced with the claim
by a street railway company that a state regulatory commission was driving
it out of business. But the Court concluded that the real problem was
competition from new technology, in the form of bus companies. Today,
local wire-line telephone companies are losing market share to wireless
telephony and, to some extent, to internet-based telephony. Their loss of
business is partly due to government policy and partly due to new technology. How can courts disentangle these causes?

6. A modern analogue of the dispute in *Charles River Bridge* is
provided by controversies over what have been called "deregulatory takings." Traditionally, public utility services like electric, gas, water, and
local telephony were thought to be natural monopolies, and so only one
firm was given a franchise to serve any given area. Advances in technology
and new thinking about the best method of utility regulation have led to

attempts to introduce competition into these industries (with mixed success). When the government sets policy so as to deliberately inject competition into a market that has previously been served by a monopoly, does the incumbent monopolist have a right to block the change or demand compensation for lost revenues? Should it matter if the utility franchise explicitly confers monopoly privileges on the incumbent carrier (most do not)? For a variety of perspectives on this problem see J. Gregory Sidak & Daniel F. Spulber, Deregulatory Takings and the Regulatory Contract (1997); William J. Baumol & Thomas W. Merrill, Deregulatory Takings, Breach of the Regulatory Contract, and the Telecommunications Act of 1996, 72 N.Y.U. L. Rev. 1037 (1997); Jim Chen, The Second Coming of *Smyth v. Ames*, 77 Tex. L. Rev. 1535 (1999); Susan Rose–Ackerman & Jim Rossi, Disentangling Deregulatory Takings, 86 Va. L. Rev. 1435 (2000).

FORBEARANCE VALUES

The dueling opinions in *Charles River Bridge* emphasize different values in trying to determine how strictly the government should be required to forbear from interfering with existing rights. Chief Justice Taney emphasizes the importance of accommodating change, so as to promote competition, encourage the development of new technologies like railroads, and free the present generation from the dead hand of old monopolies. Justice Story emphasizes the importance of protecting reliance interests, in order to encourage investors to put capital at risk in new projects. Both sets of values are still regarded today as being important in determining the optimal level of government forbearance. But there are other values to consider as well.

Chief Justice Taney emphasizes how over-protecting existing interests can stultify economic growth by stifling competition. Today, commentators would probably also consider distributive justice as a factor that might warrant government modification of property rights. Suppose, for example, that we conclude the extension of existing intellectual property rights confers a windfall on a lucky few at the expense of higher license costs and transaction costs for the many. (See Chapter X.A for discussion of the controversy over the Sonny Bono Act extending existing copyrights.) Should the government be allowed to rescind the legislation on the ground that the extension was distributively unjust? One general question here is how often it is necessary to interfere with specific property rights on distributive justice grounds, given the option of imposing progressive taxes which can be paid from a variety of sources. Expropriation or abolition of rights in specific property is an extreme measure that is deeply unsettling to owners and very likely discourages future investment. Ratcheting up tax rates, particularly when the increases apply only in future years, is arguably a less disruptive and more effective mechanism for achieving greater distributional equity. Still, there may be circumstances where interfering with specific property rights or expectations is the only course available to achieving what is regarded as a more just distribution of wealth.

Justice Story also invokes economic growth, but he takes the perspective of those who have investment capital available for new undertakings.

Is Justice Story's concern about protecting reliance interests focused on the level of return to investments, or on uncertainty regarding the level of return to investments? Both are obviously relevant to any entrepreneur thinking about making an investment in a new enterprise. But there is reason to think that uncertainty is a particular concern where government forbearance is at issue. If the government engages in random acts of expropriation, this may not change the expected level of return for other investments very much (on an ex ante basis). But it is likely to raise grave concerns about the future course of government behavior, and may have a disproportionate impact on discouraging new investment. (We consider at the end of the Chapter whether private insurance may be a solution to the problem of uncertainty about government behavior and policy.) Today, commentators would probably also emphasize another factor: A weak commitment on the part of government to forbear from interfering with property may encourage some people to spend time and money on efforts to secure legislation interfering with other people's property, and may in turn cause other people to spend time and money to head off such legislation in order to protect their property from interference. Economists often refer to this kind of jockeying for legislation as "rent-seeking," with the implication that this kind of competition for government favor is a dead-weight loss to society. The issue is extremely complicated, however, as sometimes competition for the recognition or modification of property rights can lead to policy changes that benefit society. Determining the optimal level of political agitation for change in policy regarding property is therefore an almost impossible task, although it may be possible to identify some measures— like laws that seize A's property and transfer it to B without any change in the anticipated use of the resources—as being presumptively unjustified.

Recently, a number of scholars have attempted to determine empirically what kind of impact government forbearance has on the general level of economic activity in different countries. See, e.g., Daron Acemoglu, Simon Johnson & James Robinson, The Colonial Origins of Comparative Development: An Empirical Investigation, 91 Am. Econ. Rev. 1369 (2001); Simon Johnson, John McMillan & Christopher Woodruff, Property Rights and Finance, 92 Am. Econ. Rev. 1335 (2002); Paul G. Mahoney, The Common Law and Economic Growth: Hayek Might Be Right, 30 J. Legal Stud. 503 (2001). These studies adopt a variety of measures of forbearance, although government commitment to pay just compensation when property is taken is one common yardstick. Whatever measures are used, virtually all these studies find a positive correlation between what we are calling forbearance and rates of aggregate economic growth. This provides some empirical support for Justice Story's concerns, if not for his particular application of those concerns in *Charles River Bridge*.

LEGISLATIVE ENTRENCHMENT

Another way to consider the problem in *Charles River Bridge* is to ask: To what extent should one legislature be able to tie the hands of a subsequent legislature? We live in a democracy, and a central tenet of democracy is majority rule. Ordinarily, majority rule is understood to mean rule by the current majority. Thus, if last year's duly-elected legislature enacts a particular measure, such as "no vehicles in the park," it is understood that this year's duly-elected legislature can adopt a different measure, such as "vehicles in the park are okay." We might think it incompatible with democracy for last year's legislature to enact a statute that says: "No vehicles in the park, and this rule cannot be repealed." If such a statute were enforced to block today's legislature from repealing the rule against vehicles in the park, this would seem like a type of dead hand control: A previous legislature, elected by a previous majority, is overriding the preferences of today's legislature, elected by today's majority, in violation of the general principle of majority rule. Commentators have taken a variety of positions on whether legislative entrenchment is permissible or desirable. For further discussion see David Dana & Susan P. Koniak, Bargaining in the Shadow of Democracy, 148 U. Pa. L. Rev. 473 (1999); Julian Eule, Temporal Limits on the Legislative Mandate: Entrenchment and Retroactivity, 1987 Am. B. Found. Res. J. 379; Michael J. Klarman, Majoritarian Judicial Review: The Entrenchment Problem, 85 Geo. L. J. 491 (1997); John O. McGinnis & Michael B. Rappaport, Symmetric Entrenchment: A Constitutional and Normative Theory, 89 Va. L. Rev. 385 (2003); Eric A. Posner & Adrian Vermeule, Legislative Entrenchment: A Reappraisal, 111 Yale L. J. 1665 (2002); John C. Roberts & Erwin Chemerinsky, Entrenchment of Ordinary Legislation: A Reply to Professors Posner and Vermeule, 91 Cal. L. Rev. 1773 (2003).

The proposition that government should be required to forbear from interfering with property presupposes that at least some legislative entrenchment is permissible. In particular, the hands of future legislatures must be tied insofar as they seek to repudiate promises, express or implied, to forbear from interfering with property rights. But while modern commentators often embrace extreme positions (never entrench, entrench whenever you like), notice that both Justice Taney and Justice Story adopt more nuanced views. Justice Taney is relatively hostile to legislative entrenchment, but even he believes that an express promise by the legislature to make a charter exclusive would be binding on a successor legislature and would be enforced under the Contracts Clause. Justice Story is more sympathetic to entrenchment, but even he acknowledges that a future legislature can get rid of a corporate charter using the power of eminent domain. So it is likely that in practice the legal system will take up a position between the polar extremes staked out by the commentators. The critical issues are what sort of doctrines will be used to impose a limited degree of entrenchment, and what kinds of circumstances will justify departures from entrenchment.

B.   DUE PROCESS

The Fifth Amendment to the Constitution provides that no person shall "be deprived of life, liberty, or property, without due process of law." U.S. Const. amend V. This language binds the federal government. In 1868 the Fourteenth Amendment was adopted, extending the same language to state governments (and local governmental authorities that derive their powers from the States). U.S. Const. amend. XIV. Commentators and (some) judges have pointed out that "due process of law" sounds like a requirement of procedural regularity only. See, e.g., Frank H. Easterbrook, Substance and Due Process, 1982 Sup. Ct. Rev. 85. Nevertheless, "due process of law" has long been understood as providing both procedural and substantive protection for property rights. The substantive protections include a requirement that courts give extra scrutiny of retroactive legislation affecting property, see, e.g., Usery v. Turner Elkhorn Mining Co., 428 U.S. 1, 16–18 (1976), as well as judicially-imposed limits on excessive penalties and civil damages awards, see, e.g., BMW of North Am. v. Gore, 517 U.S. 559 (1996). The core procedural protections are a requirement of notice and an opportunity to contest the legality of government deprivations of property before they occur. See, e.g., Jones v. Flowers, 126 S.Ct. 1708 (2006) (state must take measures reasonably designed to provide notice to owner before seizing home for nonpayment of taxes); United States v. James Daniel Good Real Property, 510 U.S. 43 (1993) (state must afford owner an opportunity to contest legality of forfeiture proceeding before seizing property).

Somewhat surprisingly, however, it was not until the 1970s that the Supreme Court began to attend to the question what sorts of interests are encompassed within the term "property" in the Due Process Clauses of the Fifth and Fourteenth Amendments. The decision that brought the question to the fore was *Goldberg v. Kelly*, 397 U.S. 254 (1970), where the Court— without explicitly so deciding—assumed that the right to receive welfare benefits was a form of "property" protected by procedural due process. *Goldberg* cited favorably to the work of Charles Reich, who had argued that government licenses, pension rights, contracts, grants, and jobs should all be characterized as forms of "new property" protected against abrogation or impairment by the government. See id. 262 n.8 (citing Charles Reich, Individual Rights and Social Welfare: The Emerging Legal Issues, 74 Yale L.J. 1245 (1965) and Charles Reich, The New Property, 73 Yale L.J. 733 (1964)). *Goldberg* unleashed a "due process revolution," as lower courts began requiring that claimants holding a variety of government "entitlements" critical to their wellbeing be given hearings before such entitlements were terminated. See Henry J. Friendly, "Some Kind of Hearing," 123 U. Pa. L. Rev. 1267, 1273 (1975). Perhaps taken aback, the Court quickly perceived that it was necessary to provide clearer guidance about when different forms of government entitlements should be regarded as "property" (or "liberty") sufficient to trigger due process protection. The effort to provide that guidance came in the following case.

Board of Regents v. Roth

Supreme Court of the United States, 1972.
408 U.S. 564.

■ MR. JUSTICE STEWART delivered the opinion of the Court. In 1968 the respondent, David Roth, was hired for his first teaching job as assistant professor of political science at Wisconsin State University–Oshkosh. He was hired for a fixed term of one academic year. The notice of his faculty appointment specified that his employment would begin on September 1, 1968, and would end on June 30, 1969.[1] The respondent completed that term. But he was informed that he would not be rehired for the next academic year.

The respondent had no tenure rights to continued employment. Under Wisconsin statutory law a state university teacher can acquire tenure as a "permanent" employee only after four years of year-to-year employment. Having acquired tenure, a teacher is entitled to continued employment "during efficiency and good behavior." A relatively new teacher without tenure, however, is under Wisconsin law entitled to nothing beyond his one-year appointment. There are no statutory or administrative standards defining eligibility for re-employment. State law thus clearly leaves the decision whether to rehire a nontenured teacher for another year to the unfettered discretion of university officials.

The procedural protection afforded a Wisconsin State University teacher before he is separated from the University corresponds to his job security. As a matter of statutory law, a tenured teacher cannot be "discharged except for cause upon written charges" and pursuant to certain procedures. A nontenured teacher, similarly, is protected to some extent during his one-year term. Rules promulgated by the Board of Regents provide that a nontenured teacher "dismissed" before the end of the year may have some opportunity for review of the "dismissal." But the Rules provide no real protection for a nontenured teacher who simply is not re-employed for the next year. He must be informed by February 1 "concerning retention or non-retention for the ensuing year." But "no reason for non-retention need be given. No review or appeal is provided in such case."

In conformance with these Rules, the President of Wisconsin State University–Oshkosh informed the respondent before February 1, 1969, that he would not be rehired for the 1969–1970 academic year. He gave the respondent no reason for the decision and no opportunity to challenge it at any sort of hearing.

The respondent then brought this action in Federal District Court alleging that the decision not to rehire him for the next year infringed his Fourteenth Amendment rights. He attacked the decision both in substance

---

1. The respondent had no contract of employment. Rather, his formal notice of appointment was the equivalent of an employment contract.

The notice of his appointment provided that: "David F. Roth is hereby appointed to the faculty of the Wisconsin State University Position number 0262. (Location:) Oshkosh as (Rank:) Assistant Professor of (Department:) Political Science this (Date:) first day of (Month:) September (Year:) 1968." The notice went on to specify that the respondent's "appointment basis" was for the "academic year." And it provided that "[r]egulations governing tenure are in accord with Chapter 37.31, Wisconsin Statutes. The employment of any staff member for an academic year shall not be for a term beyond June 30th of the fiscal year in which the appointment is made."

and procedure. First, he alleged that the true reason for the decision was to punish him for certain statements critical of the University administration, and that it therefore violated his right to freedom of speech.[5] Second, he alleged that the failure of University officials to give him notice of any reason for nonretention and an opportunity for a hearing violated his right to procedural due process of law.

The District Court granted summary judgment for the respondent on the procedural issue, ordering the University officials to provide him with reasons and a hearing. The Court of Appeals, with one judge dissenting, affirmed this partial summary judgment. We granted certiorari. The only question presented to us at this stage in the case is whether the respondent had a constitutional right to a statement of reasons and a hearing on the University's decision not to rehire him for another year. We hold that he did not.

I

The requirements of procedural due process apply only to the deprivation of interests encompassed by the Fourteenth Amendment's protection of liberty and property. When protected interests are implicated, the right to some kind of prior hearing is paramount.[7] But the range of interests protected by procedural due process is not infinite.

The District Court decided that procedural due process guarantees apply in this case by assessing and balancing the weights of the particular interests involved. It concluded that the respondent's interest in re-employment at Wisconsin State University–Oshkosh outweighed the University's interest in denying him re-employment summarily. Undeniably, the respondent's re-employment prospects were of major concern to him—concern that we surely cannot say was insignificant. And a weighing process has long been a part of any determination of the form of hearing required in particular situations by procedural due process.[8] But, to determine whether

5. While the respondent alleged that he was not rehired because of his exercise of free speech, the petitioners insisted that the non-retention decision was based on other, constitutionally valid grounds. The District Court came to no conclusion whatever regarding the true reason for the University President's decision. "In the present case," it stated, "it appears that a determination as to the actual bases of [the] decision must await amplification of the facts at trial.... Summary judgment is inappropriate." 310 F.Supp. 972, 982.

7. Before a person is deprived of a protected interest, he must be afforded opportunity for some kind of a hearing, "except for extraordinary situations where some valid governmental interest is at stake that justifies postponing the hearing until after the event." Boddie v. Connecticut, 401 U.S. 371, 379. "While '[m]any controversies have raged

about ... the Due Process Clause,' ... it is fundamental that except in emergency situations (and this is not one) due process requires that when a State seeks to terminate [a protected] interest ..., it must afford 'notice and opportunity for hearing appropriate to the nature of the case' before the termination becomes effective." Bell v. Burson, 402 U.S. 535, 542. For the rare and extraordinary situations in which we have held that deprivation of a protected interest need not be preceded by opportunity for some kind of hearing, see, e.g., Central Union Trust Co. v. Garvan, 254 U.S. 554, 566; Phillips v. Commissioner of Internal Revenue, 283 U.S. 589, 597; Ewing v. Mytinger & Casselberry, Inc., 339 U.S. 594.

8. "The formality and procedural requisites for the hearing can vary, depending upon the importance of the interests involved due process requirements apply in the first place, we must look not to the "weight" but to the nature of the interest at stake. We must look to see if the interest is within the Fourteenth Amendment's protection of liberty and property.

"Liberty" and "property" are broad and majestic terms. They are among the "[g]reat [constitutional] concepts ... purposely left to gather meaning from experience.... [T]hey relate to the whole domain of social and economic fact, and the statesmen who founded this Nation knew too well that only a stagnant society remains unchanged." National Mutual Ins. Co. v. Tidewater Transfer Co., 337 U.S. 582, 646 (Frankfurter, J., dissenting). For that reason, the Court has fully and finally rejected the wooden distinction between "rights" and "privileges" that once seemed to govern the applicability of procedural due process rights.[9] The Court has also made clear that the property interests protected by procedural due process extend well beyond actual ownership of real estate, chattels, or money. By the same token, the Court has required due process protection for deprivations of liberty beyond the sort of formal constraints imposed by the criminal process.

Yet, while the Court has eschewed rigid or formalistic limitations on the protection of procedural due process, it has at the same time observed certain boundaries. For the words "liberty" and "property" in the Due Process Clause of the Fourteenth Amendment must be given some meaning.

II

"While this court has not attempted to define with exactness the liberty ... guaranteed [by the Fourteenth Amendment], the term has received much consideration and some of the included things have been definitely stated. Without doubt, it denotes not merely freedom from bodily restraint but also the right of the individual to contract, to engage in any of the common occupations of life, to acquire useful knowledge, to marry, establish a home and bring up children, to worship God according to the dictates of his own conscience, and generally to enjoy those privileges long recognized ... as essential to the orderly pursuit of happiness by free men." Meyer v. Nebraska, 262 U.S. 390, 399. In a Constitution for a free

---

and the nature of the subsequent proceedings." Boddie v. Connecticut, 401 U.S. 371, 378 (1971). See, e.g., Goldberg v. Kelly, 397 U.S. 254, 263; Hannah v. Larche, 363 U.S. 420. The constitutional requirement of opportunity for some form of hearing before deprivation of a protected interest, of course, does not depend upon such a narrow balancing process. See n. 7, supra.

9. In a leading case decided many years ago, the Court of Appeals for the District of Columbia Circuit held that public employment in general was a "privilege," not a "right," and that procedural due process guarantees therefore were inapplicable. Bailey v. Richardson, 182 F.2d 46, aff'd by an equally divided Court, 341 U.S. 918. The basis of this holding has been thoroughly undermined in the ensuing years. For, as Mr. Justice Blackmun wrote for the Court only last year, "this Court now has rejected the concept that constitutional rights turn upon whether a governmental benefit is characterized as a 'right' or as a 'privilege.'" Graham v. Richardson, 403 U.S. 365, 374.

people, there can be no doubt that the meaning of "liberty" must be broad indeed. See, e.g., Bolling v. Sharpe, 347 U.S. 497, 499–500; Stanley v. Illinois, 405 U.S. 645.

There might be cases in which a State refused to re-employ a person under such circumstances that interests in liberty would be implicated. But this is not such a case.

The State, in declining to rehire the respondent, did not make any charge against him that might seriously damage his standing and associations in his community. It did not base the nonrenewal of his contract on a charge, for example, that he had been guilty of dishonesty, or immorality. Had it done so, this would be a different case. For "[w]here a person's good name, reputation, honor, or integrity is at stake because of what the government is doing to him, notice and an opportunity to be heard are essential." Wisconsin v. Constantineau, 400 U.S. 433, 437. In such a case, due process would accord an opportunity to refute the charge before University officials. In the present case, however, there is no suggestion whatever that the respondent's "good name, reputation, honor, or integrity" is at stake.

Similarly, there is no suggestion that the State, in declining to re-employ the respondent, imposed on him a stigma or other disability that foreclosed his freedom to take advantage of other employment opportunities. The State, for example, did not invoke any regulations to bar the respondent from all other public employment in state universities. Had it done so, this, again, would be a different case. * * *

To be sure, the respondent has alleged that the nonrenewal of his contract was based on his exercise of his right to freedom of speech. But this allegation is not now before us. The District Court stayed proceedings on this issue, and the respondent has yet to prove that the decision not to rehire him was, in fact, based on his free speech activities.

Hence, on the record before us, all that clearly appears is that the respondent was not rehired for one year at one university. It stretches the concept too far to suggest that a person is deprived of "liberty" when he simply is not rehired in one job but remains as free as before to seek another.

III

The Fourteenth Amendment's procedural protection of property is a safeguard of the security of interests that a person has already acquired in specific benefits. These interests—property interests—may take many forms.

Thus, the Court has held that a person receiving welfare benefits under statutory and administrative standards defining eligibility for them has an interest in continued receipt of those benefits that is safeguarded by procedural due process. Goldberg v. Kelly, 397 U.S. 254. See Flemming v. Nestor, 363 U.S. 603, 611. Similarly, in the area of public employment, the Court has held that a public college professor dismissed from an office held under tenure provisions, Slochower v. Board of Education, 350 U.S. 551, and college professors and staff members dismissed during the terms of their contracts, Wieman v. Updegraff, 344 U.S. 183, have interests in continued employment that are safeguarded by due process. Only last year, the Court held that this principle "proscribing summary dismissal from public employment without hearing or inquiry required by due process" also applied to a teacher recently hired without tenure or a formal contract, but nonetheless with a clearly implied promise of continued employment. Connell v. Higginbotham, 403 U.S. 207, 208.

Certain attributes of "property" interests protected by procedural due process emerge from these decisions. To have a property interest in a benefit, a person clearly must have more than an abstract need or desire for it. He must have more than a unilateral expectation of it. He must, instead, have a legitimate claim of entitlement to it. It is a purpose of the ancient institution of property to protect those claims upon which people rely in their daily lives, reliance that must not be arbitrarily undermined. It is a purpose of the constitutional right to a hearing to provide an opportunity for a person to vindicate those claims.

Property interests, of course, are not created by the Constitution. Rather they are created and their dimensions are defined by existing rules or understandings that stem from an independent source such as state law—rules or understandings that secure certain benefits and that support claims of entitlement to those benefits. Thus, the welfare recipients in *Goldberg v. Kelly*, supra, had a claim of entitlement to welfare payments that was grounded in the statute defining eligibility for them. The recipients had not yet shown that they were, in fact, within the statutory terms of eligibility. But we held that they had a right to a hearing at which they might attempt to do so.

Just as the welfare recipients' "property" interest in welfare payments was created and defined by statutory terms, so the respondent's "property" interest in employment at Wisconsin State University–Oshkosh was created and defined by the terms of his appointment. Those terms secured his interest in employment up to June 30, 1969. But the important fact in this case is that they specifically provided that the respondent's employment was to terminate on June 30. They did not provide for contract renewal absent "sufficient cause." Indeed, they made no provision for renewal whatsoever.

Thus, the terms of the respondent's appointment secured absolutely no interest in re-employment for the next year. They supported absolutely no possible claim of entitlement to re-employment. Nor, significantly, was there any state statute or University rule or policy that secured his interest in re-employment or that created any legitimate claim to it.[16] In these

16. To be sure, the respondent does suggest that most teachers hired on a year-to-year basis by Wisconsin State University–Oshkosh are, in fact, rehired. But the District Court has not found that there is anything approaching a "common law" of re-employ-ment, see Perry v. Sindermann, 408 U.S. 593, at 602, so strong as to require University officials to give the respondent a statement of reasons and a hearing on their decision not to rehire him.

circumstances, the respondent surely had an abstract concern in being rehired, but he did not have a property interest sufficient to require the University authorities to give him a hearing when they declined to renew his contract of employment.

IV

Our analysis of the respondent's constitutional rights in this case in no way indicates a view that an opportunity for a hearing or a statement of reasons for nonretention would, or would not, be appropriate or wise in public colleges and universities. For it is a written Constitution that we apply. Our role is confined to interpretation of that Constitution.

We must conclude that the summary judgment for the respondent should not have been granted, since the respondent has not shown that he was deprived of liberty or property protected by the Fourteenth Amendment. The judgment of the Court of Appeals, accordingly, is reversed and the case is remanded for further proceedings consistent with this opinion. It is so ordered. Reversed and remanded.

■ [Dissenting opinions by JUSTICE DOUGLAS and JUSTICE MARSHALL are omitted.]

NOTES AND QUESTIONS

1. On remand from the decision in the principal case, a jury concluded that Wisconsin State University–Oshkosh had declined to renew Roth's employment contract in retaliation for his exercise of First Amendment rights. He was awarded $6,746 in damages. The issue of reinstatement was not pressed, since Roth had found new employment teaching political science at Purdue. See Chronicle of Higher Education, Nov. 26, 1973, p. 3 col. 1.

2. *Roth* was apparently designed to legitimize the due process revolution, by reconciling it with the language of the Constitution and broad constitutional traditions, not to reign it in. In the years after *Roth*, the Court recognized due process "property" interests in a wide variety of government entitlements. These included rights to a public education, Goss v. Lopez, 419 U.S. 565 (1975); utility services, Memphis Light, Gas & Water Div. v. Craft, 436 U.S. 1 (1978); a horse trainer's license, Barry v. Barchi, 443 U.S. 55 (1979); and a cause of action against discrimination, Logan v. Zimmerman Brush Co., 455 U.S. 422, 430 (1982). More recently, the Court has adopted a more cautious attitude, and the expansion of due process rights appears to have halted. See generally Richard J. Pierce, Jr., The Due Process Counterrevolution of the 1990s?, 96 Colum. L. Rev. 1973 (1996). (See, for example, the next case, *Town of Castle Rock*).

3. Do you agree with the Court that the language of the Due Process Clauses requires a threshold determination that the claimant has an interest in either "liberty" or "property" (or presumably "life") at stake? This aspect of *Roth* reflects an important change in the law. "Prior to *Roth*, Supreme Court definitions of 'liberty' and 'property' had amounted to taking the words 'life, liberty, and property' as a unitary concept embracing all interests valued by sensible men. After *Roth*, however, each word of the clause must be examined separately; so examined, we find that they do not embrace the full range of state conduct having serious impact upon individual interests." Henry Paul Monaghan, Of "Liberty" and "Property," 62 Cornell L. Rev. 405, 409 (1977). Did the Framers of the Constitution intend this kind of careful parsing of each word as a threshold condition applying due process? Consider that words chosen by the Framers appear to describe the three types of punishment the state is likely to mete out for violation of a crime—execution (life), imprisonment (liberty), or fines and forfeitures (property)—and that the Clause appears in the Fifth Amendment, which is largely concerned with criminal procedure. (But not exclusively—it also contains the Takings Clause!) This might suggest the Framers understood these words collectively to embrace any action by the state that would constitute a "punishment" or "sanction" directed against an individual. Consider also the Declaration of Independence, which refers to "Life, Liberty and the pursuit of Happiness" as a general phrase descriptive of inalienable human rights. What are the pros and cons of having a very broad and general threshold trigger for due process protection ("all interests valued by sensible men") as opposed to three more narrowly defined triggers with strong common-law connotations?

4. Notice that the Court seems to prescribe different methodologies for ascertaining whether an interest is "liberty" as opposed to "property." The methodology for ascertaining liberty is not discussed in any detail, other than to quote a long list of rights from *Meyer v. Nebraska*, 262 U.S. 390, 399 (1923), a case holding that parents have a substantive due process right to teach their children German. In discussing the methodology for identifying property rights, however, the Court notes that property rights are "not created by the Constitution." Does this imply that the Court views liberty as being created by the Constitution, whereas property is created by statutes, common-law decisions, and other types of subconstitutional law? In later decisions, some Justices would quarrel with the notion that liberty is created by the Constitution, insisting that liberties are "inalienable rights" that are recognized by but not created by the Constitution. See Sandin v. Conner, 515 U.S. 472, 489 (1995) (Ginsburg, J. dissenting); Meachum v. Fano, 427 U.S. 215, 230 (1976) (Stevens, J. dissenting). On this view, liberty is a "natural right" that exists independently of the Constitution; the significance of the Due Process Clauses is that they recognize this right and provide that it may not be taken without due process. Why cannot "property" also be regarded as an inalienable or natural right? Is there something about property rights that would make it more problematic to attempt to develop a "list" of inalienable property rights, analogous to the list of liberties set forth in *Meyer* and endorsed in

Roth? In this regard, reconsider the material in Chapter III about different values subject to ownership, and how the scope of property rights has changed over time. By the way, what happened to "life" in the *Roth* discussion? What do you suppose the *Roth* Court would say about the proper method for ascertaining the meaning of "life"?

5. When the Court announces that property rights are "not created by the Constitution" but rather "are created and their dimensions are defined by existing rules and understandings" such as those grounded in state law, does the Court mean that courts should look to state law in order to determine what the state regards to be property? Or does it mean only that courts should look to state law to see what sorts of interests are recognized and protected, and should then independently determine as a matter of federal constitutional law whether these interest are property? See Monaghan, Of "Liberty" and "Property", supra; Thomas W. Merrill, The Landscape of Constitutional Property, 86 Va. L. Rev. 885, 916–42 (2000). The question is closely related to the more general issue, considered in Chapter I, whether "property" has some essentialist meaning, or should be considered as merely a contingent bundle of rights. If the Court understands that "property" has some distinctive federal constitutional meaning, did it provide adequate guidance in spelling out the elements or features of that meaning?

6. The Court proudly proclaims that it has rejected the "wooden distinction" between "rights" and "privileges" in determining the scope of the Due Process Clause. But how, if at all, does the rights/privileges distinction differ from the entitlements/unilateral expectancies distinction adopted by the Court in its place? Is it because "entitlements" are grounded in law? But aren't the "rights" that were juxtaposed to "privileges" also grounded in law, such as the common law? The Court doesn't seem to mean that entitlements must be grounded in written law; in a companion case, *Perry v. Sindermann*, 408 U.S. 593 (1972), as well as in footnote 16, the Court acknowledged that entitlements can also be grounded in common law. Is the shift in locution from rights/privileges to entitlements/expectancies merely a verbal cover for the fact that the Court has shifted the boundary of property for due process purposes to include various types of contractual or programmatic government benefits previously thought to be excluded?

7. Is the Court's approach to defining property—looking to settled expectations rooted in objective sources like state statutory and common law—broadly consistent with the understanding of "property" reflected in *Charles River Bridge*? Recall that all the Justices in that case appeared to accept the idea that a corporate franchise to operate a toll bridge is a type of "property" entitled to constitutional protection. A corporate franchise or charter is a type of "entitlement" that did not exist at common law, but is purely the creature of legislation. In this sense, it is not too fanciful to describe corporate charters as a kind of "new property," analogous to the new property rights given due process protection in *Goldberg* and *Roth*. See Kenneth J. Vandevelde, The New Property of the Nineteenth Century: The

Development of the Modern Concept of Property, 29 Buff. L. Rev. 325 (1980). Or does this overlook one potentially critical difference? Corporate charters and franchises, like common-law property, include the right to exclude others from certain assets; the government entitlements recognized to be property in *Goldberg* and *Roth* do not confer any right to exclude, but are more like contractual promises to a future stream of payments. Did the Court push the concept of "property" one step too far in *Roth*? Any further than the Court pushed the concept of the "obligation of contract" in holding that this includes a completed grant of property in *Fletcher v. Peck*?

8.   Consider procedural due process as yet another general strategy for resolving the government forbearance puzzle debated in *Charles River Bridge*. Implicit in the strategy is the principal of legality—that the government may deprive persons of property only in accordance with principles of law previously laid down. A central purpose of requiring notice and an opportunity for a hearing before any taking occurs is to give the owner a chance to show that the government lacks legal justification for its action. In effect, the government must forbear from interfering with previously recognized property rights unless it has a clear legal and factual justification for doing so. Of course, this strategy does not provide full protection against frustration of expectations. If the government recognizes property at T_1, then changes the law at T_2 in such a way as to authorize the property to be taken, and then gives the owner a hearing at T_3 in order to challenge the legality of the taking, the hearing will show that the government deprivation has been legally authorized at T_2. This is a point of time before the proposed taking, and thus satisfies the principle of legality, even though it is also a point in time after T_1, and thus may frustrate expectations formed at T_1. Still, if one of the lessons of *Charles River Bridge* is the need for some compromise between the need to accommodate change and the desirability of protecting expectations, doesn't the procedural due process strategy provide a kind of accommodation? As a compromise, does it lean too far toward accommodating change or toward protecting expectations? Does the answer depend on the nature of the government promise in question?

Town of Castle Rock, Colorado v. Gonzales

Supreme Court of the United States, 2005.
545 U.S. 748.

■ JUSTICE SCALIA delivered the opinion of the Court. We decide in this case whether an individual who has obtained a state-law restraining order has a constitutionally protected property interest in having the police enforce the restraining order when they have probable cause to believe it has been violated.

I

The horrible facts of this case are contained in the complaint that respondent Jessica Gonzales filed in Federal District Court. (Because the case comes to us on appeal from a dismissal of the complaint, we assume its allegations are true.) Respondent alleges that petitioner, the town of Castle Rock, Colorado, violated the Due Process Clause of the Fourteenth Amendment to the United States Constitution when its police officers, acting pursuant to official policy or custom, failed to respond properly to her repeated reports that her estranged husband was violating the terms of a restraining order.

The restraining order had been issued by a state trial court several weeks earlier in conjunction with respondent's divorce proceedings. The original form order, issued on May 21, 1999, and served on respondent's husband on June 4, 1999, commanded him not to "molest or disturb the peace of [respondent] or of any child," and to remain at least 100 yards from the family home at all times. The bottom of the pre-printed form noted that the reverse side contained "IMPORTANT NOTICES FOR RESTRAINED PARTIES AND LAW ENFORCEMENT OFFICIALS." (emphasis deleted). The preprinted text on the back of the form included the following "**WARNING**":

> **A KNOWING VIOLATION OF A RESTRAINING ORDER IS A CRIME**.... A VIOLATION WILL ALSO CONSTITUTE CONTEMPT OF COURT. **YOU MAY BE ARRESTED** WITHOUT NOTICE IF A LAW ENFORCEMENT OFFICER HAS PROBABLE CAUSE TO BELIEVE THAT YOU HAVE KNOWINGLY VIOLATED THIS ORDER.

The preprinted text on the back of the form also included a "**NOTICE TO LAW ENFORCEMENT OFFICIALS**," which read in part:

> YOU SHALL USE EVERY REASONABLE MEANS TO ENFORCE THIS RESTRAINING ORDER. YOU SHALL ARREST, OR, IF AN ARREST WOULD BE IMPRACTICAL UNDER THE CIRCUMSTANCES, SEEK A WARRANT FOR THE ARREST OF THE RESTRAINED PERSON WHEN YOU HAVE INFORMATION AMOUNTING TO PROBABLE CAUSE THAT THE RESTRAINED PERSON HAS VIOLATED OR ATTEMPTED TO VIOLATE ANY PROVISION OF THIS ORDER AND THE RESTRAINED PERSON HAS BEEN PROPERLY SERVED WITH A COPY OF THIS ORDER OR HAS RECEIVED ACTUAL NOTICE OF THE EXISTENCE OF THIS ORDER.

On June 4, 1999, the state trial court modified the terms of the restraining order and made it permanent. The modified order gave respondent's husband the right to spend time with his three daughters (ages 10, 9, and 7) on alternate weekends, for two weeks during the summer, and, " 'upon reasonable notice,' " for a mid-week dinner visit " 'arranged by the parties' "; the modified order also allowed him to visit the home to collect the children for such "parenting time."

According to the complaint, at about 5 or 5:30 p.m. on Tuesday, June 22, 1999, respondent's husband took the three daughters while they were playing outside the family home. No advance arrangements had been made for him to see the daughters that evening. When respondent noticed the children were missing, she suspected her husband had taken them. At about 7:30 p.m., she called the Castle Rock Police Department, which dispatched two officers. The complaint continues: "When [the officers] arrived ..., she showed them a copy of the TRO and requested that it be enforced and the three children be returned to her immediately. [The officers] stated that there was nothing they could do about the TRO and suggested that [respondent] call the Police Department again if the three children did not return home by 10:00 p.m."

At approximately 8:30 p.m., respondent talked to her husband on his cellular telephone. He told her "he had the three children [at an] amusement park in Denver." She called the police again and asked them to "have someone check for" her husband or his vehicle at the amusement park and "put out an [all points bulletin]" for her husband, but the officer with whom she spoke "refused to do so," again telling her to "wait until 10:00 p.m. and see if" her husband returned the girls.

At approximately 10:10 p.m., respondent called the police and said her children were still missing, but she was now told to wait until midnight. She called at midnight and told the dispatcher her children were still missing. She went to her husband's apartment and, finding nobody there, called the police at 12:10 a.m.; she was told to wait for an officer to arrive. When none came, she went to the police station at 12:50 a.m. and submitted an incident report. The officer who took the report "made no reasonable effort to enforce the TRO or locate the three children. Instead, he went to dinner."

At approximately 3:20 a.m., respondent's husband arrived at the police station and opened fire with a semiautomatic handgun he had purchased earlier that evening. Police shot back, killing him. Inside the cab of his pickup truck, they found the bodies of all three daughters, whom he had already murdered.

On the basis of the foregoing factual allegations, respondent brought an action under Rev. Stat. § 1979, 42 U.S.C. § 1983, claiming that the town violated the Due Process Clause because its police department had "an official policy or custom of failing to respond properly to complaints of restraining order violations" and "tolerate[d] the non-enforcement of restraining orders by its police officers." The complaint also alleged that the town's actions "were taken either willfully, recklessly or with such gross negligence as to indicate wanton disregard and deliberate indifference to" respondent's civil rights.

Before answering the complaint, the defendants filed a motion to dismiss under Federal Rule of Civil Procedure 12(b)(6). The District Court granted the motion, concluding that, whether construed as making a substantive due process or procedural due process claim, respondent's complaint failed to state a claim upon which relief could be granted.

A panel of the Court of Appeals affirmed the rejection of a substantive due process claim, but found that respondent had alleged a cognizable procedural due process claim. On rehearing en banc, a divided court reached the same disposition, concluding that respondent had a "protected property interest in the enforcement of the terms of her restraining order" and that the town had deprived her of due process because "the police never 'heard' nor seriously entertained her request to enforce and protect her interests in the restraining order." We granted certiorari.

II

The Fourteenth Amendment to the United States Constitution provides that a State shall not "deprive any person of life, liberty, or property, without due process of law." Amdt. 14, § 1. In 42 U.S.C. § 1983, Congress has created a federal cause of action for "the deprivation of any rights, privileges, or immunities secured by the Constitution and laws." Respondent claims the benefit of this provision on the ground that she had a property interest in police enforcement of the restraining order against her husband; and that the town deprived her of this property without due process by having a policy that tolerated nonenforcement of restraining orders.

As the Court of Appeals recognized, we left a similar question unanswered in *DeShaney v. Winnebago County Dept. of Social Servs.*, 489 U.S. 189 (1989), another case with "undeniably tragic" facts: Local child-protection officials had failed to protect a young boy from beatings by his father that left him severely brain damaged. Id., at 191–193. We held that the so-called "substantive" component of the Due Process Clause does not "requir[e] the State to protect the life, liberty, and property of its citizens against invasion by private actors." Id., at 195. We noted, however, that the petitioner had not properly preserved the argument that—and we thus "decline[d] to consider" whether—state "child protection statutes gave [him] an 'entitlement' to receive protective services in accordance with the terms of the statute, an entitlement which would enjoy due process protection." Id., at 195, n. 2.

The procedural component of the Due Process Clause does not protect everything that might be described as a "benefit": "To have a property interest in a benefit, a person clearly must have more than an abstract need or desire" and "more than a unilateral expectation of it. He must, instead, have a legitimate claim of entitlement to it." Board of Regents of State Colleges v. Roth, 408 U.S. 564, 577 (1972). Such entitlements are " 'of course, ... not created by the Constitution. Rather, they are created and their dimensions are defined by existing rules or understandings that stem from an independent source such as state law.' " Paul v. Davis, 424 U.S. 693, 709 (1976) (quoting Roth, supra, at 577); see also Phillips v. Washington Legal Foundation, 524 U.S. 156, 164 (1998).

A

Our cases recognize that a benefit is not a protected entitlement if government officials may grant or deny it in their discretion. See, e.g., Kentucky Dept. of Corrections v. Thompson, 490 U.S. 454, 462–463 (1989). The Court of Appeals in this case determined that Colorado law created an entitlement to enforcement of the restraining order because the "court-issued restraining order ... specifically dictated that its terms must be enforced" and a "state statute command[ed]" enforcement of the order when certain objective conditions were met (probable cause to believe that the order had been violated and that the object of the order had received notice of its existence). Respondent contends that we are obliged "to give deference to the Tenth Circuit's analysis of Colorado law on" whether she had an entitlement to enforcement of the restraining order.

We will not, of course, defer to the Tenth Circuit on the ultimate issue: whether what Colorado law has given respondent constitutes a property interest for purposes of the Fourteenth Amendment. That determination, despite its state-law underpinnings, is ultimately one of federal constitutional law. "Although the underlying substantive interest is created by 'an independent source such as state law,' *federal constitutional law* determines whether that interest rises to the level of a 'legitimate claim of entitlement' protected by the Due Process Clause." Memphis Light, Gas & Water Div. v. Craft, 436 U.S. 1, 9 (1978) (emphasis added) (quoting Roth, supra, at 577); cf. United States ex rel. TVA v. Powelson, 319 U.S. 266, 279 (1943). Resolution of the federal issue begins, however, with a determination of what it is that state law provides. In the context of the present case, the central state-law question is whether Colorado law gave respondent a right to police enforcement of the restraining order. It is on this point that respondent's call for deference to the Tenth Circuit is relevant.

We have said that a "presumption of deference [is] given the views of a federal court as to the law of a State within its jurisdiction." Phillips, supra, at 167. That presumption can be overcome, however, see Leavitt v. Jane L., 518 U.S. 137, 145 (1996) (per curiam), and we think deference inappropriate here. The Tenth Circuit's opinion, which reversed the Colorado District Judge, did not draw upon a deep well of state-specific expertise, but consisted primarily of quoting language from the restraining order, the statutory text, and a state-legislative-hearing transcript. These texts, moreover, say nothing distinctive to Colorado, but use mandatory language that (as we shall discuss) appears in many state and federal statutes. As for case law: the only state-law cases about restraining orders that the Court of Appeals relied upon were decisions of Federal District Courts in Ohio and Pennsylvania and state courts in New Jersey, Oregon, and Tennessee. Moreover, if we were simply to accept the Court of Appeals' conclusion, we would necessarily have to decide conclusively a federal constitutional question (*i.e.*, whether such an entitlement constituted property under the Due Process Clause and, if so, whether petitioner's customs or policies provided too little process to protect it). We proceed, then, to our own analysis of whether Colorado law gave respondent a right to enforcement of the restraining order.

B

The critical language in the restraining order came not from any part of the order itself (which was signed by the state-court trial judge and directed to the restrained party, respondent's husband), but from the preprinted notice to law-enforcement personnel that appeared on the back of the order. See *supra*. That notice effectively restated the statutory provision describing "peace officers' duties" related to the crime of violation of a restraining order. At the time of the conduct at issue in this case, that provision read as follows:

> (a) Whenever a restraining order is issued, the protected person shall be provided with a copy of such order. *A peace officer shall use every reasonable means to enforce a restraining order.*

> (b) *A peace officer shall arrest, or, if an arrest would be impractical under the circumstances, seek a warrant for the arrest of a restrained person* when the peace officer has information amounting to probable cause that:

>> (I) The restrained person has violated or attempted to violate any provision of a restraining order; and

>> (II) The restrained person has been properly served with a copy of the restraining order or the restrained person has received actual notice of the existence and substance of such order.

> (c) In making the probable cause determination described in paragraph (b) of this subsection (3), a peace officer shall assume that the information received from the registry is accurate. *A peace officer shall enforce a valid restraining order whether or not there is a record of the restraining order in the registry.* Colo.Rev.Stat. § 18–6–803.5(3) (emphases added).

The Court of Appeals concluded that this statutory provision—especially taken in conjunction with a statement from its legislative history, and with another statute restricting criminal and civil liability for officers making arrests—established the Colorado Legislature's clear intent "to alter the fact that the police were not enforcing domestic abuse retraining orders," and thus its intent "that the recipient of a domestic abuse restraining order have an entitlement to its enforcement." Any other result, it said, "would render domestic abuse restraining orders utterly valueless."

This last statement is sheer hyperbole. Whether or not respondent had a right to enforce the restraining order, it rendered certain otherwise lawful conduct by her husband both criminal and in contempt of court. See §§ 18–6–803.5(2)(a), (7). The creation of grounds on which he could be arrested, criminally prosecuted, and held in contempt was hardly "valueless"—even if the prospect of those sanctions ultimately failed to prevent him from committing three murders and a suicide.

We do not believe that these provisions of Colorado law truly made enforcement of restraining orders *mandatory.* A well established tradition of police discretion has long coexisted with apparently mandatory arrest statutes.

In each and every state there are long-standing statutes that, by their terms, seem to preclude nonenforcement by the police.... However, for a number of reasons, including their legislative history, insufficient resources, and sheer physical impossibility, it has been recognized that such statutes cannot be interpreted literally.... [T]hey clearly do not mean that a police officer may not lawfully decline to make an arrest. As to third parties in these states, the full-enforcement statutes simply have no effect, and their significance is further diminished. 1 ABA Standards for Criminal Justice 1–4.5, commentary, pp. 1–124 to 1–125 (2d ed. 1980) (footnotes omitted).

The deep-rooted nature of law-enforcement discretion, even in the presence of seemingly mandatory legislative commands, is illustrated by *Chicago v. Morales,* 527 U.S. 41 (1999), which involved an ordinance that said a police officer " 'shall order' " persons to disperse in certain circumstances, id., at 47, n. 2. This Court rejected out of hand the possibility that "the mandatory language of the ordinance ... afford[ed] the police *no* discretion." Id., at 62, n. 32. It is, the Court proclaimed, simply "common sense that *all* police officers must use some discretion in deciding when and where to enforce city ordinances." Ibid. (emphasis added).

Against that backdrop, a true mandate of police action would require some stronger indication from the Colorado Legislature than "shall use every reasonable means to enforce a restraining order" (or even "shall arrest ... or ... seek a warrant"), §§ 18–6–803.5(3)(a), (b). * * * It is hard to imagine that a Colorado peace officer would not have some discretion to determine that—despite probable cause to believe a restraining order has been violated—the circumstances of the violation or the competing duties of that officer or his agency counsel decisively against enforcement in a particular instance. The practical necessity for discretion is particularly apparent in a case such as this one, where the suspected violator is not actually present and his whereabouts are unknown.

The dissent correctly points out that, in the specific context of domestic violence, mandatory-arrest statutes have been found in some States to be more mandatory than traditional mandatory-arrest statutes. * * * Even in the domestic-violence context, however, it is unclear how the mandatory-arrest paradigm applies to cases in which the offender is not present to be arrested. As the dissent explains, much of the impetus for mandatory-arrest statutes and policies derived from the idea that it is better for police officers to arrest the aggressor in a domestic-violence incident than to attempt to mediate the dispute or merely to ask the offender to leave the scene. Those other options are only available, of course, when the offender is present at the scene. See Hanna, No Right to Choose: Mandated Victim Participation in Domestic Violence Prosecutions, 109 Harv. L.Rev. 1849, 1860 (1996) ("[T]he clear trend in police practice is to arrest the batterer *at the scene* ..." (emphasis added)). * * *

Respondent does not specify the precise means of enforcement that the Colorado restraining-order statute assertedly mandated—whether her interest lay in having police arrest her husband, having them seek a warrant for his arrest, or having them "use every reasonable means, up to and including arrest, to enforce the order's terms," Brief for Respondent 29–30. Such indeterminacy is not the hallmark of a duty that is mandatory. Nor can someone be safely deemed "entitled" to something when the identity of the alleged entitlement is vague. See Roth, 408 U.S., at 577 (considering whether "certain benefits" were "secure[d]" by rule or understandings). The dissent, after suggesting various formulations of the entitlement in question, ultimately contends that the obligations under the statute were quite precise: either make an arrest or (if that is impractical) seek an arrest warrant. The problem with this is that the seeking of an arrest warrant would be an entitlement to nothing but procedure—which we have held inadequate even to support standing, see Lujan v. Defenders of Wildlife, 504 U.S. 555 (1992); much less can it be the basis for a property interest. After the warrant is sought, it remains within the discretion of a judge whether to grant it, and after it is granted, it remains within the discretion of the police whether and when to execute it. Respondent would have been assured nothing but the seeking of a warrant. This is not the sort of "entitlement" out of which a property interest is created.

Even if the statute could be said to have made enforcement of restraining orders "mandatory" because of the domestic-violence context of the underlying statute, that would not necessarily mean that state law gave *respondent* an entitlement to *enforcement* of the mandate. Making the actions of government employees obligatory can serve various legitimate ends other than the conferral of a benefit on a specific class of people. * * *

Respondent's alleged interest stems only from a State's *statutory* scheme—from a restraining order that was authorized by and tracked precisely the statute on which the Court of Appeals relied. She does not assert that she has any common-law or contractual entitlement to enforcement. If she was given a statutory entitlement, we would expect to see some indication of that in the statute itself. * * *

The creation of a personal entitlement to something as vague and novel as enforcement of restraining orders cannot "simply g[o] without saying." We conclude that Colorado has not created such an entitlement.

C

Even if we were to think otherwise concerning the creation of an entitlement by Colorado, it is by no means clear that an individual entitlement to enforcement of a restraining order could constitute a "property" interest for purposes of the Due Process Clause. Such a right would not, of course, resemble any traditional conception of property. Although that alone does not disqualify it from due process protection, as *Roth* and its progeny show, the right to have a restraining order enforced does not "have some ascertainable monetary value," as even our "*Roth*-type property-as-entitlement" cases have implicitly required. Merrill, The Landscape of Constitutional Property, 86 Va. L.Rev. 885, 964 (2000).[12] Perhaps most

12. The dissent suggests that the interest in having a restraining order enforced does have an ascertainable monetary value, because one may "contract with a private radically, the alleged property interest here arises *incidentally,* not out of some new species of government benefit or service, but out of a function that government actors have always performed—to wit, arresting people who they have probable cause to believe have committed a criminal offense.

The indirect nature of a benefit was fatal to the due process claim of the nursing-home residents in *O'Bannon v. Town Court Nursing Center,* 447 U.S. 773 (1980). We held that, while the withdrawal of "direct benefits" (financial payments under Medicaid for certain medical services) triggered due process protections, id., at 786–787, the same was not true for the "indirect benefit[s]" conferred on Medicaid patients when the Government enforced "minimum standards of care" for nursing-home facilities, id., at 787. "[A]n indirect and incidental result of the Government's enforcement action ... does not amount to a deprivation of any interest in life, liberty, or property." Ibid. In this case, as in *O'Bannon,* "[t]he simple distinction between government action that directly affects a citizen's legal rights ... and action that is directed against a third party and affects the citizen only indirectly or incidentally, provides a sufficient answer to" respondent's reliance on cases that found government-provided services to be entitlements. Id., at 788. The *O'Bannon* Court expressly noted, ibid., that the distinction between direct and indirect benefits distinguished *Memphis Light, Gas & Water Div. v. Craft,* 436 U.S. 1 (1978), one of the government-services cases on which the dissent relies.

III

We conclude, therefore, that respondent did not, for purposes of the Due Process Clause, have a property interest in police enforcement of the restraining order against her husband. It is accordingly unnecessary to address the Court of Appeals' determination that the town's custom or policy prevented the police from giving her due process when they deprived her of that alleged interest. See American Mfrs. Mut. Ins. Co. v. Sullivan, 526 U.S. 40, 61 (1999).

In light of today's decision and that in *DeShaney,* the benefit that a third party may receive from having someone else arrested for a crime generally does not trigger protections under the Due Process Clause, neither in its procedural nor in its "substantive" manifestations. This result reflects our continuing reluctance to treat the Fourteenth Amend-

---

security firm ... to provide protection" for one's family. That is, of course, not as precise as the analogy between public and private schooling that the dissent invokes. Post, at n. 18. Respondent probably could have hired a private firm to guard her house, to prevent her husband from coming onto the property, and perhaps even to search for her husband after she discovered that her children were missing. Her alleged entitlement here, however, does not consist in an abstract right to

"protection," but (according to the dissent) in enforcement of her restraining order through the arrest of her husband, or the seeking of a warrant for his arrest, after she gave the police probable cause to believe the restraining order had been violated. A private person would not have the power to arrest under those circumstances because the crime would not have occurred in his presence. Colo.Rev.Stat. § 16–3–201. And, needless to say, a private person would not have the power to obtain an arrest warrant.

ment as " 'a font of tort law,' " Parratt v. Taylor, 451 U.S. 527, 544 (1984) (quoting Paul v. Davis, 424 U.S., at 701), but it does not mean States are powerless to provide victims with personally enforceable remedies. Although the framers of the Fourteenth Amendment and the Civil Rights Act of 1871, 17 Stat. 13 (the original source of § 1983), did not create a system by which police departments are generally held financially accountable for crimes that better policing might have prevented, the people of Colorado are free to craft such a system under state law. Cf. DeShaney, 489 U.S., at 203.[15]

The judgment of the Court of Appeals is *Reversed.*

■ Justice Stevens, with whom Justice Ginsburg joins, dissenting. * * * The central question in this case is * * * whether, as a matter of Colorado law, respondent had a right to police assistance comparable to the right she would have possessed to any other service the government or a private firm might have undertaken to provide. See Board of Regents of State Colleges v. Roth, 408 U.S. 564, 577 (1972) ("Property interests, of course, are not created by the Constitution. Rather, they are created and their dimensions are defined by existing rules or understandings that stem from an independent source such as state law—rules or understandings that secure certain benefits and that support claims of entitlement to those benefits").

There was a time when our tradition of judicial restraint would have led this Court to defer to the judgment of more qualified tribunals in seeking the correct answer to that difficult question of Colorado law. Unfortunately, although the majority properly identifies the "central state-law question" in this case as "whether Colorado law gave respondent a right to police enforcement of the restraining order," it has chosen to ignore our settled practice by providing its *own* answer to that question. [Justice Stevens argues that the Court should either have deferred to the court of appeals' construction of state law, or should have certified the questions about the nondiscretionary nature of state law to the state supreme court.]

III

Three flaws in the Court's rather superficial analysis of the merits highlight the unwisdom of its decision to answer the state-law question *de novo.* First, the Court places undue weight on the various statutes throughout the country that seemingly mandate police enforcement but are generally understood to preserve police discretion. As a result, the Court gives short shrift to the unique case of "mandatory arrest" statutes in the domestic violence context; States passed a wave of these statutes in the 1980's and 1990's with the unmistakable goal of eliminating police discretion in this area. Second, the Court's formalistic analysis fails to take

---

15. In Colorado, the general statutory immunity for government employees does not apply when "the act or omission causing ... injury was willful and wanton." Colo.Rev. Stat. § 24–10–118(2)(a). Respondent's complaint does allege that the police officers' actions "were taken either willfully, recklessly or with such gross negligence as to indicate wanton disregard and deliberate indifference to" her civil rights. * * *

seriously the fact that the Colorado statute at issue in this case was enacted for the benefit of the narrow class of persons who are beneficiaries of domestic restraining orders, and that the order at issue in this case was specifically intended to provide protection to respondent and her children. Finally, the Court is simply wrong to assert that a citizen's interest in the government's commitment to provide police enforcement in certain defined circumstances does not resemble any "traditional conception of property"; in fact, a citizen's property interest in such a commitment is just as concrete and worthy of protection as her interest in any other important service the government or a private firm has undertaken to provide.

In 1994, the Colorado General Assembly passed omnibus legislation targeting domestic violence. The part of the legislation at issue in this case mandates enforcement of a domestic restraining order upon probable cause of a violation, § 18–6–803.5(3), while another part directs that police officers "shall, without undue delay, arrest" a suspect upon "probable cause to believe that a crime or offense of domestic violence has been committed," § 18–6–803.6(1). In adopting this legislation, the Colorado General Assembly joined a nationwide movement of States that took aim at the crisis of police underenforcement in the domestic violence sphere by implementing "mandatory arrest" statutes. The crisis of underenforcement had various causes, not least of which was the perception by police departments and police officers that domestic violence was a private, "family" matter and that arrest was to be used as a last resort. Sack, Battered Women and the State: The Struggle for the Future of Domestic Violence Policy, 2004 Wis. L.Rev. 1657, 1662–1663 (hereinafter Sack). In response to these realities, and emboldened by a well-known 1984 experiment by the Minneapolis police department, "many states enacted mandatory arrest statutes under which a police officer must arrest an abuser when the officer has probable cause to believe that a domestic assault has occurred or that a protection order has been violated." Developments in the Law: Legal Responses to Domestic Violence, 106 Harv. L.Rev. 1498, 1537 (1993). The purpose of these statutes was precisely to "counter police resistance to arrests in domestic violence cases by removing or restricting police officer discretion; mandatory arrest policies would increase police response and reduce batterer recidivism." Sack 1670.

Thus, when Colorado passed its statute in 1994, it joined the ranks of 15 States that mandated arrest for domestic violence offenses and 19 States that mandated arrest for domestic restraining order violations. See Developments in the Law, 106 Harv. L.Rev., at 1537, n. 68 (noting statutes in 1993); N. Miller, Institute for Law and Justice, A Law Enforcement and Prosecution Perspective 7, and n. 74, 8, and n. 90 (2003), http://www.ilj.org/dv/dvvawa2000.htm (as visited June 24, 2005, and available in Clerk of Court's case file) (listing Colorado among the many States that currently have mandatory arrest statutes).

Given the specific purpose of these statutes, there can be no doubt that the Colorado Legislature used the term "shall" advisedly in its domestic restraining order statute. While "shall" is probably best read to mean "may" in other Colorado statutes that seemingly mandate enforcement, cf. Colo.Rev.Stat. § 31–4–112 (police *"shall suppress* all riots, disturbances or breaches of the peace, *shall apprehend* all disorderly persons in the city ..." (emphases added)), it is clear that the elimination of police discretion was integral to Colorado and its fellow States' solution to the problem of underenforcement in domestic violence cases.[10] Since the text of Colorado's statute perfectly captures this legislative purpose, it is hard to imagine what the Court has in mind when it insists on "some stronger indication from the Colorado Legislature."

While Colorado case law does not speak to the question, it is instructive that other state courts interpreting their analogous statutes have not only held that they eliminate the police's traditional discretion to refuse enforcement, but have also recognized that they create rights enforceable against the police under state law. * * * To what extent the Colorado Supreme Court would agree with the views of these courts is, of course, an open question, but it does seem rather brazen for the majority to assume that the Colorado Supreme Court would repudiate this consistent line of persuasive authority from other States.

Indeed, the Court fails to come to terms with the wave of domestic violence statutes that provides the crucial context for understanding Colorado's law. The Court concedes that, "in the specific context of domestic violence, mandatory-arrest statutes have been found in some States to be more mandatory than traditional mandatory-arrest statutes," but that is a serious understatement. The difference is not a matter of degree, but of kind. Before this wave of statutes, the legal rule was one of discretion; as the Court shows, the "traditional," general mandatory arrest statutes have always been understood to be "mandatory" in name only. The innovation of the domestic violence statutes was to make police enforcement, not "more mandatory," but simply *mandatory*. If, as the Court says, the existence of a protected "entitlement" turns on whether "government officials may grant or deny it in their discretion," the new mandatory

---

10. See Note, Mandatory Arrest: A Step Toward Eradicating Domestic Violence, But is It Enough? 1996 U. Ill. L.Rev. 533, 542, 544–546 (describing the problems that attend a discretionary arrest regime: "Even when probable clause is present, police officers still frequently try to calm the parties and act as mediators.... Three studies found the arrest rate to range between 3% and 10% when the decision to arrest is left to police discretion. Another study found that the police made arrests in only 13% of the cases where the victim had visible injuries.... Police officers often employ irrelevant criteria such as the 'reason' for the abuse or the severity of the victim's injuries in making their decision to arrest.... Some [officers] may feel strongly that police should not interfere in family

arguments or lovers' quarrels. Such attitudes make police much more likely to investigate intent and provocation, and consider them as mitigating factors, in responding to domestic violence calls than in other types of cases"); see also Walsh, The Mandatory Arrest Law: Police Reaction, 16 Pace L.Rev. 97, 98 (1995). Cf. Sack 1671–1672 ("Mandatory arrest policies have significantly increased the number of arrests of batterers for domestic violence crimes.... In New York City, from 1993, the time the mandatory arrest policy was instituted, to 1999, felony domestic violence arrests increased 33%, misdemeanor domestic violence arrests rose 114%, and arrests for violation of orders of protection were up 76%" (footnotes omitted)).

statutes undeniably create an entitlement to police enforcement of restraining orders.

Perhaps recognizing this point, the Court glosses over the dispositive question—whether the police enjoyed discretion to deny enforcement—and focuses on a different question—which "precise means of enforcement," were called for in this case. But that question is a red herring. The statute directs that, upon probable cause of a violation, "a peace officer shall arrest, or, if an arrest would be impractical under the circumstances, seek a warrant for the arrest of a restrained person." Colo.Rev.Stat. § 18–6–803.5(3)(b). Regardless of whether the enforcement called for in this case was arrest or the seeking of an arrest warrant (the answer to that question probably changed over the course of the night as the respondent gave the police more information about the husband's whereabouts), the crucial point is that, under the statute, the police were *required* to provide enforcement; *they lacked the discretion to do nothing.* The Court suggests that the fact that "enforcement" may encompass different acts infects any entitlement to enforcement with "indeterminacy." But this objection is also unfounded. Our cases have never required the object of an entitlement to be some mechanistic, unitary thing. Suppose a State entitled every citizen whose income was under a certain level to receive health care at a state clinic. The provision of health care is not a unitary thing—doctors and administrators must decide what tests are called for and what procedures are required, and these decisions often involve difficult applications of judgment. But it could not credibly be said that a citizen lacks an entitlement to health care simply because the content of that entitlement is not the same in every given situation. Similarly, the enforcement of a restraining order is not some amorphous, indeterminate thing. Under the statute, if the police have probable cause that a violation has occurred, enforcement consists of either making an immediate arrest or seeking a warrant and then executing an arrest—traditional, well-defined tasks that law enforcement officers perform every day. * * *

Because the statute's guarantee of police enforcement is triggered by, and operates only in reference to, a judge's granting of a restraining order in favor of an identified " 'protected person,' " there is simply no room to suggest that such a person has received merely an " 'incidental' " or " 'indirect' " benefit. As one state court put it, domestic restraining order statutes "identify with precision when, to whom, and under what circumstances police protection must be afforded. The legislative purpose in requiring the police to enforce individual restraining orders clearly is to protect the named persons for whose protection the order is issued, not to protect the community at large by general law enforcement activity." Not only does the Court's doubt about whether Colorado's statute created an entitlement in a protected person fail to take seriously the purpose and nature of restraining orders, but it fails to account for the decisions by other state courts that recognize that such statutes and restraining orders create individual rights to police action.

IV

Given that Colorado law has quite clearly eliminated the police's discretion to deny enforcement, respondent is correct that she had much more than a "unilateral expectation" that the restraining order would be enforced; rather, she had a "legitimate claim of entitlement" to enforcement. Roth, 408 U.S., at 577. Recognizing respondent's property interest in the enforcement of her restraining order is fully consistent with our precedent. This Court has "made clear that the property interests protected by procedural due process extend well beyond actual ownership of real estate, chattels, or money." Id., at 571–572. The "types of interests protected as 'property' are varied and, as often as not, intangible, 'relating to the whole domain of social and economic fact.'" Logan v. Zimmerman Brush Co., 455 U.S. 422, 430 (1982); see also Perry v. Sindermann, 408 U.S. 593, 601 (1972) ("'[P]roperty' interests subject to procedural due process protection are not limited by a few rigid, technical forms. Rather, 'property' denotes a broad range of interests that are secured by 'existing rules or understandings'"). Thus, our cases have found "property" interests in a number of state-conferred benefits and services, including welfare benefits, Goldberg v. Kelly, 397 U.S. 254 (1970); disability benefits, Mathews v. Eldridge, 424 U.S. 319 (1976); public education, Goss v. Lopez, 419 U.S. 565 (1975); utility services, Memphis Light, Gas & Water Div. v. Craft, 436 U.S. 1 (1978); government employment, Cleveland Bd. of Ed. v. Loudermill, 470 U.S. 532 (1985); as well as in other entitlements that defy easy categorization, see, e.g., Bell v. Burson, 402 U.S. 535 (1971) (due process requires fair procedures before a driver's license may be revoked pending the adjudication of an accident claim); Logan, 455 U.S., at 431 (due process prohibits the arbitrary denial of a person's interest in adjudicating a claim before a state commission).

Police enforcement of a restraining order is a government service that is no less concrete and no less valuable than other government services, such as education. The relative novelty of recognizing this type of property interest is explained by the relative novelty of the domestic violence statutes creating a mandatory arrest duty; before this innovation, the unfettered discretion that characterized police enforcement defeated any citizen's "legitimate claim of entitlement" to this service. Novel or not, respondent's claim finds strong support in the principles that underlie our due process jurisprudence. In this case, Colorado law *guaranteed* the provision of a certain service, in certain defined circumstances, to a certain class of beneficiaries, and respondent reasonably relied on that guarantee. As we observed in *Roth*, "[i]t is a purpose of the ancient institution of property to protect those claims upon which people rely in their daily lives, reliance that must not be arbitrarily undermined." 408 U.S., at 577. Surely, if respondent had contracted with a private security firm to provide her and her daughters with protection from her husband, it would be apparent that she possessed a property interest in such a contract. Here, Colorado undertook a comparable obligation, and respondent—with restraining order in hand—justifiably relied on that undertaking. Respondent's claim of entitlement to this promised service is no less legitimate than the other claims our cases have upheld, and no less concrete than a hypothetical agreement with a private firm.[19] The fact that it is based on a statutory enactment and a judicial order entered for her special protection, rather than on a formal contract, does not provide a principled basis for refusing to consider it "property" worthy of constitutional protection.

V

Because respondent had a property interest in the enforcement of the restraining order, state officials could not deprive her of that interest without observing fair procedures. Her description of the police behavior in this case and the department's callous policy of failing to respond properly to reports of restraining order violations clearly alleges a due process violation. At the very least, due process requires that the relevant state decisionmaker *listen* to the claimant and then *apply the relevant criteria* in reaching his decision. The failure to observe these minimal procedural safeguards creates an unacceptable risk of arbitrary and "erroneous deprivation[s]," Mathews, 424 U.S., at 335. According to respondent's complaint—which we must construe liberally at this early stage in the litigation—the process she was afforded by the police constituted nothing more than a " 'sham or a pretense.' " Joint Anti–Fascist Refugee Comm. v. McGrath, 341 U.S. 123, 164 (1951) (Frankfurter, J., concurring).

Accordingly, I respectfully dissent.

NOTES AND QUESTIONS

1. Does the decision in *Castle Rock* vindicate those critics of *Roth* who thought it a mistake to develop separate threshold definitions of "liberty" and "property," rather than treat the Due Process Clause as protecting "all interests valued by sensible men" (or women)? On what metric of values would protecting one's children from an unauthorized seizure by another person subject to a restraining order not qualify as important? Note that just because the interest is protected, it does not follow that the

---

19. As the analogy to a private security contract demonstrates, a person's interest in police enforcement has " 'some ascertainable monetary value.' " Cf. Merrill, The Landscape of Constitutional Property, 86 Va. L.Rev. 885, 964, n. 289 (2000) (remarking, with regard to the property interest recognized in *Goss v. Lopez*, 419 U.S. 565 (1975), that "any parent who has contemplated sending their children to private schools knows that public schooling has a monetary value"). And while the analogy to a private security contract need not be precise to be useful, I would point out that the Court is likely incorrect in stating that private security guards could not have arrested the husband under the circumstances, see ante n. 10. Because the husband's ongoing abduction of the daughters would constitute a knowing violation of the restraining order, and therefore a crime under the statute, see § 18–6–803.5(1), a private person who was at the scene and aware of the circumstances of the abduction would have authority to arrest. See § 16–3–201 ("A person who is not a peace officer may arrest another person when any crime has been or is being committed by the arrested person in the presence of the person making the arrest"). Our cases, of course, have never recognized any requirement that a property interest possess " 'some ascertainable monetary value.' " Regardless, I would assume that respondent would have paid the police to arrest her husband if that had been possible; at the very least, the entitlement has a monetary value in that sense.

procedure followed by the state necessarily violates due process. But on a unitary approach to the interests protected by due process, presumably the focus in a case like *Castle Rock* would shift from the threshold question whether the Clause applies to the question whether the procedures followed by the police were adequate.

2. In *Board of Regents v. Roth*, supra, the Court wrote: "It is a purpose of the ancient institution of property to protect those claims upon which people rely in their daily lives, reliance which must not be arbitrarily undermined." How could the State of Colorado have acted more clearly to try to induce reliance on the state in people's daily lives when it mandated the printing of the capitalized and bold face notices on the restraining order it gave to Jessica Gonzales? Is the Court being fundamentally unfaithful to the spirit of *Roth* when it declines to use the Due Process Clause as a vehicle for vindicating these kinds of specifically-induced forms of reliance on the government?

3. What do we learn about the meaning of "property," at least for procedural due process purposes, from the majority opinion in *Castle Rock*? Has the Court finally resolved the ambiguity in *Roth* about whether the definition of property is to be determined as a matter of state or federal law? If "property" is to be defined as a matter of federal law, what exactly are the elements of the definition, once we agree that statutory entitlements like welfare benefits or tenured employment are "property"? One element, obviously, is that the entitlement must be nondiscretionary. This is the principal ground on which the majority rejects Ms. Gonzales's claim that she has been deprived of property. But what do you make of the majority's suggestion (which appears to be dictum) that the entitlement must also have a monetary value? Is this restriction (or something like it) necessary to distinguish "property" from "liberty"? Does Justice Scalia have an adequate response to Justice Stevens' suggestion that the right to enforcement has a monetary value, because it is a substitute for hiring private security guards? Would adoption of this limitation mean that *Bell v. Burson*, 402 U.S. 535 (1971), which appears to hold (pre-*Roth*) that a state driver's license is property, was wrongly decided? Or could Justice Stevens argue that a driver's license has monetary value because it eliminates the need to hire a private chauffeur? Under Justice Stevens' substitute-value approach, would all government services, including the provision of the national defense and the enforcement of property rights, be themselves "property" rights (at least on this one dimension)?

4. The Court observes that the interest asserted by Ms. Gonzales does not, "of course, resemble any traditional conception of property." What features of the "traditional conception of property" are missing here? In another recent decision about the meaning of "property" for constitutional due process purposes, Justice Scalia wrote as follows:

> The hallmark of a protected property interest is the right to exclude others. That is "one of the most essential sticks in the bundle of rights that are commonly characterized as property." That is why the right that we all possess to use the public lands is not the "property" right

of anyone—hence the sardonic maxim, explaining what economists call the "tragedy of the commons," *res publica, res nullius*.

College Savings Bank v. Florida Prepaid Postsecondary Education Expense Bd., 527 U.S. 666, 673 (1999) (holding that a federal cause of action against false advertising by a competitor does not protect any constitutional property right because no one has the right to exclude others from future profits). It is difficult to see how a government guarantee of enforcement of a restraining order can be construed as a "right to exclude others" from some thing. Is this why Justice Scalia thinks a right to enforcement of a restraining order would not qualify as a traditional property right? Is the fundamental problem here that a restraining order confers an in personam right on the person protected by the order, rather than a right good against all the world? Is "property" for purposes of the Constitution limited to rights in rem? In what sense does the right to receive welfare benefits, or to remain in a government job protected against dismissal without cause, confer any kind of in rem right to exclude others? Do decisions like *Castle Rock* and *College Savings Bank* signal that the Court may reconsider the decisions in *Goldberg* and *Roth* extending due process protection to "new property" interests like government entitlements?

5. Why did Gonzales's lawyers not argue that she had a liberty interest in enforcement of the restraining order, rather than a property interest? Although *Roth* suggested that "liberty" is to be defined as a matter of direct interpretation of the Constitution, using historical understandings as a guide, the Court in several post-*Roth* decisions involving prison and parole conditions held that state statutes can also create "new liberty" interests. See, e.g., Meachum v. Fano, 427 U.S. 215 (1976). The Court has never expanded the concept of statutorily-created liberty beyond the prison and parole context, however, and its more recent decisions have cut back on the scope of liberty interests even in this context. See Sandin v. Conner, 515 U.S. 472, 484 (1995) (deprivation must cause "atypical and significant hardship" to qualify as statutory liberty interest). This may explain why Gonzales's lawyers focused on property rather than liberty. But putting aside tactical considerations, should the interest advanced by Gonzales fall more naturally on the liberty side of the constitutional trilogy of rights, or on the property side?

6. Suppose Ms. Gonzales had prevailed in her quest to establish that she had a property right in police enforcement of the restraining order, and that the repeated failures to respond to her pleas for action had deprived her of a fair hearing before being deprived of this right. What is her remedy? An award of damages? Would the damages be calculated on the basis of the expected cost of such a deprivation (what the average claimant would have suffered because of a failure to afford a proper hearing), or on the basis of the actual costs that Gonzales suffered (obviously incalculable, but including at a minimum the values of the lives of her three lost daughters plus an award for lost consortium and emotional distress)?

7.   If the Colorado legislature wants to amend the law to make sure that the police do not brush off persons like Gonzales in the future, what sorts of changes would you recommend they make?

8.   The opinions of Justices Scalia and Stevens in *Castle Rock* recapitulate the debate between Justices Taney and Story in *Charles River Bridge*, insofar as the principal question is whether the promises made by the state are sufficiently clear to qualify as property. Justice Scalia holds that Colorado has not spoken explicitly enough to establish that Jessica Gonzales had an unequivocal right to demand immediate police enforcement of the restraining order. Justice Stevens believes that the "fair implication" of the state law (to borrow Justice Story's expression), taking into account the highlighted statements printed on the restraining order and the general legislative purpose to promote police intervention in domestic violence cases, is that Ms. Gonzales was intended to have such a right. Do the divergent positions of the Justices in these cases suggest that there is no clear answer to the question of "how clear is clear"? Does the required degree of clarity always depend on the nature of the entitlement and the backdrop of traditional understandings surrounding it? If so, what exactly does the requirement of clarity add, other than a convenient rubric to allow judicial sorting among the promises as to which the government will be required to forbear from frustrating expectations, and those in which it will not?

C.   NONCONSTITUTIONAL MEANS OF ASSURING GOVERNMENT FORBEARANCE

Although constitutional provisions like the Contracts Clause, the Due Process Clauses, and the Takings Clause (taken up in the next Chapter) get the most attention as devices for assuring a degree of government forbearance from undermining property rights, various nonconstitutional doctrines and institutions play an important role in this regard as well. We consider briefly four such devices here: (1) canons of interpretation disfavoring retroactive laws; (2) stare decisis; (3) actions for breach of regulatory contracts; and (4) investor protections provided by international treaties.

1.   VESTED RIGHTS AND THE CANON DISFAVORING RETROACTIVE LAWS

Recall that Chief Justice Taney, in *Charles River Bridge*, remarks that "[i]t is well settled, by the decisions of this court, that a state law may be retrospective in its character, and may divest vested rights, and yet not violate the constitution of the United States, unless it also impairs the obligation of a contract." This was arguably accurate when it was written in 1837. There was no *federal* constitutional protection against impairment of "vested rights" by state governments other than the Contracts Clause of Article I, § 10; consequently, any federal constitutional claim that a state had impaired vested rights had to be characterized as an impairment of contract. The doctrine of substantive due process and the regulatory takings doctrine developed somewhat later, and there was no basis for applying either doctrine as a matter of federal constitutional law to the states until the Fourteenth Amendment was adopted in 1868. This does not mean that state courts applying state constitutional law were similarly limited in their efforts to protect vested rights. Protection of vested rights was arguably the single most important theme of American constitutional law in the early decades of the Republic. See Edward S. Corwin, The Basic Doctrine of American Constitutional Law, 12 Mich. L. Rev. 247 (1914). If federal courts were confined largely to the Contracts Clause, state courts applied a variety of doctrines to reinforce government forbearance from interfering with so-called vested rights, including the insistence that all legislation had to be prospective and general, restrictive definitions of the police power, and natural rights theories. Id. at 255–76.

What exactly was included in the concept of "vested rights"? We have encountered this concept before. Recall from Chapter V that the law distinguishes between vested and nonvested future interests and that certain consequences follow from this; for example, nonvested future interests are subject to the Rule against Perpetuities and vested interests are not. We note there that "vesting" is ambiguous because sometimes it means vested in interest and sometimes it means vested in possession. Recall too from Chapter IX that state courts in the context of zoning have treated established uses of property as vested, in the sense that a zoning law cannot be enacted that would have the effect of making an existing nonconforming use unlawful.

In constitutional law as it developed in the nineteenth century vested rights came to be understood as including, paradigmatically, private rights of property previously acquired. As Professor Woolhander has explained,

> That private rights [were] involved [was] understood to mean that legislatures [could] not make such laws retroactive. Thus, while state legislatures could relax the requirements for adverse possession in the future, they could not provide that past acts meeting the new requirements had already effected the transfer of property; likewise, while state legislatures could change their inheritance laws prospectively, they could not declare that property that had already descended to A now belonged instead to B. Retroactive laws of this sort were often said either to deprive people of property without "due process of laws" or to cross the line between "legislative" and "judicial" power. These two formulations drew on the same idea: the process that was considered "due" for an authoritative disposition of core private rights involved "judicial" application of the standing laws, and the separation of powers kept legislatures from supplying this process.

Ann Woolhander, Public Rights, Private Rights, and Statutory Retroactivity, 94 Geo. L. J. 1015, 1024–25 (2006). See also Corwin, supra at 275 (concluding that the core interest encompassed by the doctrine of vested rights was the right "of one who had *already* acquired some title of control over some particular piece of property, in the physical sense, to continue in that control.")

Over time, the concept of "vested rights" gradually lost its allure as a basis for constitutional protection of property rights. This was due in significant part to persistent academic criticism. The legal realists in particular savaged the vested rights doctrine in the early decades of the twentieth century. See generally James L. Kainen, The Historical Framework for Reviving Constitutional Protection for Property and Contract Rights, 79 Cornell L. Rev. 87, 103–11 (1993). Three especially telling points were advanced.

First, the vested rights doctrine assumed that interests were either vested or not vested, when in fact legal interests came with different degrees of expectation about how secure they were against legal change. The classic example was provided by the repeal of married womens' dower rights. (Dower was the right of a widow to a life estate in one-third of the real property of which her husband was seized during the marriage. Modification of dower rights was often a matter of controversy in the nineteenth century, see Kainen, supra, at 105–06. Dower has now been replaced in all states by some form of gender-neutral spousal share. See Chapter V.) A woman who was not married had some expectation that if she married, and if her husband acquired land, and if her husband died while married to her, she would have dower rights; a woman who was married had a stronger expectation that if her husband acquired land, and if he died while married to her, she would have dower rights; a woman who was married and whose husband had acquired land had an even stronger expectation that if her husband died married to her, she would have dower rights; a widow whose husband had acquired land while married had the strongest expectation of dower rights. At what point in time, as the various contingencies fall away, was a woman's expectation of receiving dower strong enough to be regarded as a "vested" right? Before marriage? After marriage? After the acquisition of real property during marriage? After the death of the husband? There is no clearly correct answer to this question, and it seemed artificial to insist that there was a single condition or set of circumstances that defined when the interest became vested.

Second, the vested rights doctrine was prone to circularity. This was because whether an interest was regarded as "vested" was in part a function of whether courts found legislative interference with the interest to be a violation of the Constitution. Thus, critics maintained that the identification of an interest as "vested" often simply begged the question; courts enjoined legislation interfering with vested rights or required the state to compensate for taking vested rights, but the right was regarded as vested—of high security—because the court deemed it to be immune from legislative abrogation or deemed its taking to require compensation.

Third, and perhaps most importantly, the concept of vested rights was not embodied in the language of the U.S. Constitution nor did it appear in most state constitutions. As courts were challenged to justify their authority to intercede to protect property rights against popularly-enacted legislation, they found it increasingly desirable to rest their decisions on specific constitutional clauses, like the Contracts Clause and the Takings Clause, rather than on the more amorphous concept of vested rights. The U.S. Supreme Court led the way. After a few early decisions that flirted with the idea of protecting vested rights as a matter of natural law, see Calder v. Bull, 3 U.S. (3 Dall.) 386 (1798); Fletcher v. Peck, 10 U.S. (6 Cranch) 87 (1810), the Court after the second decade of the nineteenth century consistently identified some specific textual authority for its interventions (recall again Chief Justice Taney's comments in *Charles River Bridge*). State supreme courts clung to the idea of vested rights much longer, but gradually followed the example of the U.S. Supreme Court.

Yet notwithstanding its general demise as a doctrine of constitutional law, the doctrine of vested rights reemerged as a canon of construction for interpreting legislation that arguably frustrates the expectations of owners of established property rights. The most complete modern discussion of the canon that statutes should be interpreted as applying only prospectively unless Congress clearly intends the contrary is found in the following decision.

Landgraf v. USI Film Products

U.S. Supreme Court, 1994.
511 U.S. 244.

■ JUSTICE STEVENS delivered the opinion of the Court. [The Civil Rights Act of 1991 imposed new types of liability on employers who engage in certain types of discrimination. At issue was whether the new Act applied to cases that were pending but not finally adjudicated on the effective date of the new Act. The Act said that it would "take effect upon enactment" and did not specifically address whether it would apply retroactively to conduct that took place or litigation that was commenced before enactment. The Court held that the Act should be interpreted to apply only to future conduct. Its decision includes the following discussion:]

[T]the presumption against retroactive legislation is deeply rooted in our jurisprudence, and embodies a legal doctrine centuries older than our Republic. Elementary considerations of fairness dictate that individuals should have an opportunity to know what the law is and to conform their conduct accordingly; settled expectations should not be lightly disrupted. For that reason, the "principle that the legal effect of conduct should ordinarily be assessed under the law that existed when the conduct took place has timeless and universal appeal." Kaiser Aluminum & Chem. Corp. v. Bonjorno, 494 U.S. 827, 855 (1990) (Scalia, J. concurring). In a free, dynamic society, creativity in both commercial and artistic endeavors is fostered by a rule of law that gives people confidence about the legal consequences of their actions.

It is therefore not surprising that the antiretroactivity principle finds expression in several provisions of our Constitution. [The Court briefly discusses the Ex Post Facto Clause, the Contracts Clause, the Takings

Clause, the Bill of Attainder Clause, and the Due Process Clause.] * * * These provisions demonstrate that retroactive statutes raise particular concerns. The Legislature's unmatched powers allow it to sweep away settled expectations suddenly and without individualized consideration. Its responsivity to political pressures poses a risk that it may be tempted to use retroactive legislation as a means of retribution against unpopular groups or individuals. * * *

The Constitution's restrictions, of course, are of limited scope. Absent a violation of one of those specific provisions, the potential unfairness of retroactive civil legislation is not a sufficient reason for a court to fail to give a statute its intended scope. Retroactivity provisions often serve entirely benign and legitimate purposes, whether to respond to emergencies, to correct mistakes, to prevent circumvention of a new statute in the interval immediately preceding its passage, or simply to give comprehensive effect to a new law Congress considers salutary. However, a requirement that Congress first make its intention clear helps ensure that Congress itself has determined that the benefits of retroactivity outweigh the potential for disruption or unfairness.

While statutory retroactivity has long been disfavored, deciding when a statute operates "retroactively" is not always a simple or mechanical task. Sitting on Circuit, Justice Story offered an influential definition in *Society for Propagation of the Gospel v. Wheeler,* 22 F.Cas. 756 (No. 13,156) (CCNH 1814), a case construing a provision of the New Hampshire Constitution that broadly prohibits "retrospective" laws both criminal and civil. Justice Story first rejected the notion that the provision bars only explicitly retroactive legislation, *i.e.,* "statutes ... enacted to take effect from a time anterior to their passage." Id., at 767. Such a construction, he concluded, would be "utterly subversive of all the objects" of the prohibition. Ibid. Instead, the ban on retrospective legislation embraced "all statutes, which, though operating only from their passage, affect vested rights and past transactions." Ibid. "Upon principle," Justice Story elaborated, "every statute, which takes away or impairs vested rights acquired under existing laws, or creates a new obligation, imposes a new duty, or attaches a new disability, in respect to transactions or considerations already past, must be deemed retrospective...."

Ibid. (citing Calder v. Bull, 3 Dall. 386 (1798), and Dash v. Van Kleeck, 7 Johns. 477 (N.Y. 1811)).

Though the formulas have varied, similar functional conceptions of legislative "retroactivity" have found voice in this Court's decisions and elsewhere.

A statute does not operate "retrospectively" merely because it is applied in a case arising from conduct antedating the statute's enactment, or upsets expectations based in prior law. Rather, the court must ask whether the new provision attaches new legal consequences to events completed before its enactment. The conclusion that a particular rule operates "retroactively" comes at the end of a process of judgment concerning the nature and extent of the change in the law and the degree of connection between the operation of the new rule and a relevant past event. Any test of retroactivity will leave room for disagreement in hard cases, and is unlikely to classify the enormous variety of legal changes with perfect philosophical clarity. However, retroactivity is a matter on which judges tend to have "sound ... instinct[s]," see Danforth v. Groton Water Co., 59 N.E. 1033, 1034 (Mass. 1901) (Holmes, J.), and familiar considerations of fair notice, reasonable reliance, and settled expectations offer sound guidance.

Since the early days of this Court, we have declined to give retroactive effect to statutes burdening private rights unless Congress had made clear its intent. * * * The largest category of cases in which we have applied the presumption against statutory retroactivity has involved new provisions affecting contractual or property rights, matters in which predictability and stability are of prime importance. The presumption has not, however, been limited to such cases. * * *

The presumption against statutory retroactivity had special force in the era in which courts tended to view legislative interference with property and contract rights circumspectly. In this century, legislation has come to supply the dominant means of legal ordering, and circumspection has given way to greater deference to legislative judgments. See Usery v. Turner Elkhorn Mining Co., 428 U.S., at 15–16; Home Building & Loan Assn. v. Blaisdell, 290 U.S. 398, 436–444 (1934). But while the *constitutional* impediments to retroactive civil legislation are now modest, prospectivity remains the appropriate default rule. Because it accords with widely held intuitions about how statutes ordinarily operate, a presumption against retroactivity will generally coincide with legislative and public expectations. Requiring clear intent assures that Congress itself has affirmatively considered the potential unfairness of retroactive application and determined that it is an acceptable price to pay for the countervailing benefits. Such a requirement allocates to Congress responsibility for fundamental policy judgments concerning the proper temporal reach of statutes, and has the additional virtue of giving legislators a predictable background rule against which to legislate. * * *

When a case implicates a federal statute enacted after the events in suit, the court's first task is to determine whether Congress has expressly prescribed the statute's proper reach. If Congress has done so, of course, there is no need to resort to judicial default rules. When, however, the statute contains no such express command, the court must determine whether the new statute would have retroactive effect, *i.e.,* whether it would impair rights a party possessed when he acted, increase a party's liability for past conduct, or impose new duties with respect to transactions already completed. If the statute would operate retroactively, our traditional presumption teaches that it does not govern absent clear congressional intent favoring such a result. * * *

[Concurring and dissenting opinions omitted.]

NOTES AND QUESTIONS

1. Recall from Chapter V that the common law also contains constructional rules favoring the protection of vested rights. For example, if a remainder can be interpreted as being either vested or contingent, courts favor the vested interpretation. This saves the remainder from possible invalidation under the Rule against Perpetuities, and from other doctrines like the Destructibility of Contingent Remainders. Similarly, courts developed rules for construing defeasible fees so as to make it less rather than more likely that the grantee would experience a forfeiture. Specifically, if a defeasible fee simple can be construed to be either a fee simple determinable or a fee simple subject to condition subsequent, courts prefer the latter interpretation, because it is somewhat less likely to result in forfeiture. A constructional rule similar to *Landgraf* also applies in the administrative law context. See Bowen v. Georgetown University Hospital, 488 U.S. 204 (1988) (holding that federal administrative agency may promulgate rules with retroactive effect only if clearly authorized to do so by Congress).

2. The clear intent rule of *Landgraf*, together with the various common-law rules favoring the preservation of vested rights, represents yet another strategy for reaching an accommodation between the forces of change and the need to protect reliance interests. What are the advantages and disadvantages of this strategy, relative to other strategies, such as the rule of strict construction of charters, the requirement of due process hearings before property is taken, and the requirement of compensation for takings of property? Suppose A owns Blackacre, and builds a waste recycling plant on it. At the time the plant is constructed, waste recycling is a lawful use. After the plant is up and running, the legislature adopts a statute that says: "All recycling plants are hereby prohibited. This statute takes effect upon enactment." Does the canon of interpretation in *Landgraf* provide any protection for A's investment in the recycling plant?

3. Is the clear intent rule of *Landgraf* consistent with the rule of strict construction of *Charles River Bridge*? The rule of strict construction is designed to minimize the creation of vested rights. The clear statement rule is designed to minimize the frustration of vested rights. So working in tandem, they do not directly conflict. But is the rationale for the clear statement rule, as set forth in *Landgraf*, more in keeping with the general position of Chief Justice Taney or Justice Story as to where the balance of accommodation should be struck between change and reliance?

ACADEMIC PERSPECTIVES ON RETROACTIVITY

Issues about the optimal policy toward legal retroactivity come up in many contexts, but nowhere more than in taxation, where the issue is often described in terms of "transition policy." A prototypical example of a change in tax law arguably requiring transition relief would be repealing the tax exemption from a previously tax-exempt class of bonds. Academic commentators have come to widely varying conclusions at different times about the wisdom of worrying about retroactivity and providing transition relief, such as paying damages or providing for some kind of grandfathering of existing arrangements (e.g., allowing existing tax-exempt bonds to continue to remain tax-exempt and applying the change only to newly issued bonds).

The idea with the longest history—extending back to Justice Story and beyond—is that the government should provide transition relief in order to internalize the harm of a taking or other new measure that defeats settled expectations. See Daniel E. Troy, Retroactive Legislation (1998); Richard A. Epstein, Beware of Legal Transitions: A Presumptive Voice for the Reliance Interest, 13 J. Contemp. Legal Issues 69 (2003). In the commentary on retroactivity, this "Old School" has been challenged by (what else?) a "New School," which argues that transition relief is inappropriate because of actions that owners can take to foresee and mitigate a taking or other retroactive law. See, e.g., Michael J. Graetz, Legal Transitions: The Case of Retroactivity in Income Tax Revision, 126 U. Pa. L. Rev. 47, 65 (1977); Louis Kaplow, An Economic Analysis of Legal Transitions, 99 Harv. L. Rev. 511 (1986). These scholars tend to emphasize the need for flexibility and the benefits of public-regarding projects. (Recall Chief Justice Taney's arguments about changed conditions and the need to accommodate new technology in *Charles River Bridge*.) They also analogize government-created risk to market-created risk, the latter of which we normally assume that parties can deal with on their own, through insurance or diversification.

More recently in what is sometimes termed a "New New School" (or is it "New Old School"?), some have proposed that transition relief may be appropriate when government is making a commitment upon which it is desirable for people to rely. Sometimes the government may want to make a specific commitment to forbear from change or to provide transition relief. It might want to do this in order to avoid having to pay a premium to induce persons to take certain actions (given the risk of future governmental changes in policy) or to obviate wasteful anticipatory private efforts at trying to avoid being bitten by change. See, e.g., Daniel Shaviro, When Rules Change: An Economic and Political Analysis of Transition Relief and Retroactivity (2000); Kyle D. Logue, Tax Transitions, Opportunistic Retroactivity, and the Benefits of Government Precommitment, 94 Mich. L. Rev. 1129 (1996). Other times, the government may want to avoid all transition relief in order to force people to anticipate desirable change. An example would be a polluter who may face new regulation restricting effluent about which the polluter has had good information. See Saul Levmore, Changes, Anticipations, and Reparations, 99 Colum. L. Rev. 1657, 1661–86 (1999); see also Saul Levmore, Retroactive Taxation, 3 New Palgrave Dictionary of Economics and the Law 340 (1998); Kyle D. Logue, If Taxpayers Can't Be Fooled, Maybe Congress Can: A Public Choice Perspective on the Tax Transition Debate, 67 U. Chi. L. Rev. 1507 (2000) (book review). The general issue then becomes: When if at all is it desirable for government to make general commitments to provide transition relief, or should government commitments of transition relief be channeled into formal contracts limited to specific situations?

2.   STARE DECISIS

Another general legal doctrine that promotes government forbearance is stare decisis—the practice of "standing by what has been decided." Courts have long said that the duty to follow precedent carries special force where property rights are involved. As the Court put it in *Payne v. Tennessee*, 501 U.S. 808, 828 (1991), "[c]onsiderations in favor of *stare decisis* are at their acme in cases involving property and contract rights, where reliance interests are involved." In contrast, the Court continued, "stare decisis carries comparatively less weight in cases 'involving procedural and evidentiary rules.'" Id. As the following excerpt suggests, this distinction is well supported by . . . precedent!

Thomas R. Lee, *Stare Decisis in Historical Perspective: From the Founding Era to the Rehnquist Court*, 52 VAND. L. REV. 647, 687–92, 694–96, 699, 702 (1999)

IV.   Rules of Property and Reliance Interests

Chief Justice Rehnquist's opinion for the Court in *Payne v. Tennessee* relied extensively on the notion of a sliding stare decisis scale on commercial reliance grounds. In abandoning the previously held view that the Eighth Amendment precluded victim-impact evidence in capital cases, Rehnquist asserted that "[c]onsiderations in favor of stare decisis are at their acme in cases involving property and contract rights, where reliance interests are involved." Because the question in *Payne* "involve[ed] procedural and evidentiary rules," Rehnquist concluded that considerations in favor of stare decisis were at a minimum, and error correction was more freely available. * * *

A.   Rules of Property in the Founding Era

History provides ample support for Chief Justice Rehnquist's side of the *Payne* debate. Blackstone's explication of error correction drew no express distinction between commercial cases and other decisions, but the distinction had already taken hold in the English courts. One early English statement appeared in *Morecock v. Dickins*, a 1768 case in the High Court of Chancery.[222] The issue in that case was whether Dickins, the holder of a legal mortgage on property, should be considered to have received constructive notice of a prior equitable mortgage held by Morecock, by virtue of Morecock's registration of the deed. Counsel for Morecock argued that registration should serve as constructive notice. Although Lord Camden indicated his inclination to agree with this argument on its merits, he refused to abandon settled precedent on the point:

> If this was a new point, it might admit of difficulty; but the determination in *Bedford v. Bacchus* seems to have settled it, and it would be mischievous to disturb it. . . . Much property has been settled, and conveyances have proceeded upon the ground of that determina-

---

222.   Morecock v. Dickins, 27 Eng. Rep. 440 (Ch. 1768).

tion. . . . A thousand neglects to search have been occasioned by that determination, and therefore I cannot take upon me to alter it. If this was a new case, I should have my doubts; but the point is closed by that determination, which has been acquiesced in ever since.

The commercial reliance interests in *Morecock* were unmistakable. "A thousand neglects to search" the registries had been premised on the proposition that registration of an equitable mortgage was not constructive notice to a legal mortgagee, and thus Lord Camden preserved the precedent despite his doubts about its merits.

The converse position was also recognized in the English courts of the founding era. In *Robinson v. Bland*, the court determined, among other things, to abandon the general rule limiting a prevailing plaintiff in a breach of contract suit to interest accruing to "the day that the writ is sued out."[227] The general rule was abandoned as certainly unreasonable, and replaced with a new standard awarding interest accruing "down to the time of the last act done by the Court, to liquidate the demand." Judge Wilmot's opinion offered a reliance-based justification for the court's correction of this error:

> Where an error is established and has taken root, upon which any rule of property depends, it ought to be adhered to by the Judges, till the Legislature thinks proper to alter it: lest the new determination should have a retrospect, and shake many questions already settled: but the reforming erroneous points of practice can have no such bad consequences; and therefore they may be altered at pleasure, when found to be absurd or inconvenient.

Thus, Judge Wilmot conceived of a bifurcated stare decisis standard that is reminiscent of that offered by Chief Justice Rehnquist in *Payne*. A decision establishing "any rule of property" must be retained, Wilmot says, even when in error. But error in "points of practice" is a different matter. A change of course on such issues does not affect reliance interests, and thus the courts may abandon precedents of this nature with fewer misgivings.

James Kent's conception of stare decisis similarly recognized the increased importance of stability as to rules of property. * * * He recognized that the policy of stability and certainty was more important in certain areas of the law than in others. When decisions "create a practical rule of property," Kent explained, they should be adhered to even when subsequent judges "may feel the hardship, or not perceive the reasonableness, of the rule."[232]

B.   Rules of Property in the Supreme Court

Although the dominant stare decisis question addressed by the Marshall Court was the extent of the Court's power to abandon precedent on the basis of its correctness, several Marshall Court decisions acknowledged

---

227. Robinson v. Bland, 96 Eng. Rep. 141, 142 (K.B. 1760).

232. 1 James Kent, Commentaries on American Law *478 (O.W. Holmes, Jr. ed., 14th ed., Boston, Little Brown 7 Co. 1896).

the notion of enhanced deference to property rules in the context of yielding to purportedly erroneous decisions of the state courts. In addition, the Marshall Court adverted to a similar approach in the context of suggesting that some deference was owed to a legislative construction of the Constitution, especially where property rights were implicated. Otherwise, the application and development of the rule of property standard in the Supreme Court occurred in the Taney era.

Indeed, the Taney Court's principal contribution to the stare decisis dialogue was to consider whether the Court's power of error correction varied depending on the extent of property and contract rights at stake.
* * *

Chief Justice Taney [emphasized] the rule of property theme in his opinion for the Court in *The Propeller Genesee Chief v. Fitzhugh*.[262] The *Genesee Chief* presented the question whether the federal courts' admiralty jurisdiction extended to a suit arising out of a collision on Lake Ontario. Presumably, the federal courts would have lacked jurisdiction under the Court's earlier pronouncement as to the scope of Article III's Admiralty Clause in *The Steam–Boat Thomas Jefferson*.[264] Justice Story's opinion for the Court in *The Thomas Jefferson* had held that admiralty under Article III extended only to cases where the voyage at issue "was substantially performed, or to be performed, upon the sea, or upon waters within the ebb and flow of the tide." Because the Missouri River voyage in *The Thomas Jefferson* "not only in its commencement and termination, but in all its intermediate progress, was several hundreds of miles above the ebb and flow of the tide," Story's opinion held that any exercise of admiralty jurisdiction in the case was beyond that authorized by Article III.

Chief Justice Taney's opinion in *The Genesee Chief* candidly overruled *The Thomas Jefferson* and adopted a new test for admiralty jurisdiction. Taney argued that the *Thomas Jefferson* test would undermine the goal of "a perfect equality in the rights and the privileges of the citizens of the different states," in that the benefits of "safety and convenience of commerce, and the speedy decision of controversies" presented by the admiralty courts would be reserved only for "states bordering on the Atlantic." Moreover, Taney asserted that the "ebb and flow" test was "arbitrary, without any foundation in reason" in that "there is certainly nothing in the ebb and flow of the tide that makes the waters peculiarly suitable for admiralty jurisdiction, nor any thing in the absence of a tide that renders it unfit." Thus, even though the ebb and flow test concededly was the prevailing standard in England at the time of the framing of the Constitution, Chief Justice Taney rejected it as "purely artificial and arbitrary as well as unjust." Accordingly, Taney concluded that the admiralty jurisdiction properly turned on whether the waters at issue are navigable, and not on whether they are within the ebb and flow of the tide.

---

262. The Propeller Genesee Chief v. Fitzhugh, 53 U.S. (12 How.) 443 (1851).

264. The Steam–Boat Thomas Jefferson, 23 U.S. (10 Wheat.) 428 (1825).

Despite the conviction of Taney's disdain for the rationale and correctness of *The Thomas Jefferson*, he expressly admitted to a certain degree of angst in overruling the case: "It is the decision in the case of the *Thomas Jefferson* which mainly embarrasses the court in the present inquiry. We are sensible of the great weight to which it is entitled." Having noted the general importance of adherence to precedent, however, Taney emphasized that "[t]he case of the *Thomas Jefferson* did not decide any question of property, or lay down any rule by which the right of property should be determined." Taney explained that if *The Thomas Jefferson* had established a rule of property, stare decisis would have demanded adherence to that decision:

> If it had, we should have felt ourselves bound to follow it notwithstanding the opinion we have expressed. For every one would suppose that after the decision of this court, in a matter of that kind, he might safely enter into contracts, upon the faith that rights thus acquired would not be disturbed. In such a case, stare decisis is the safe and established rule of judicial policy and should always be adhered to.... But the decision referred to has no relation to rights of property. It was a question of jurisdiction only, and the judgment we now give can disturb no rights of property nor interfere with any contracts heretofore made.... And as we are convinced that the former decision was founded in error, and that the error, if not corrected, must produce serious public as well as private inconvenience and loss, it becomes our duty not to perpetuate it.[273] * * *

C.   Rules of Property and Reliance Interests: A Comparative Analysis

By the founding era, English courts and American commentators had embraced the notion of an enhanced rule of stare decisis in cases involving rules of property. That principle also dominated the Court's treatment of precedent during the Taney era. Indeed, on closer scrutiny even the apparent anomalies noted above disappear. The extent of the Taney Court's willingness to correct apparently erroneous precedent turned entirely on whether a change of course would "disturb ... rights of property ... or interfere with any contracts heretofore made." * * *

By the Taney era, then, the Court had settled on a bifurcated stare decisis standard comparable to that advocated by Chief Justice Rehnquist in *Payne*.

NOTES AND QUESTIONS

1.   As Lee suggests, the idea that respect for precedent is especially important where property rights are concerned has very old roots. Note that before the merger of law and equity, one of the maxims of equity was to forbear from undoing the common law (and its predictability) with

---

273.   The Propeller Genesee Chief, at 458–59.

respect to property. See Charles Grey, The Boundaries of the Equitable Function, 20 Am. J. Legal Hist. 192 (1976).

2. Not withstanding its ancient roots, is the principle of respect for precedent honored more in the breach? We have considered a number of cases in this book where courts have either explicitly or implicitly overruled earlier decisions. Some examples: *Oregon ex rel. Thornton v. Hay*, Chapter III, recognizing for the first time a customary public right to use beach property in coastal Oregon; *Higday v. Nickolaus*, Chapter III, arguably departing from Missouri law in adopting a rule of reasonable use for groundwater rights; *Berg v. Wiley*, Chapter IV, adopting for the first time a rule prohibiting self-help in the recovery of real property; *Shelley v. Kraemer*, Chapter IV, disregarding prior decisional law suggesting that enforcement of racial covenants did not violate the Fourteenth Amendment; *Javins v. First National Realty*, Chapter VI, adopting an implied warranty of habitability for residential leases; *Sommer v. Kridel*, Chapter VI, adopting a duty to mitigate damages when a tenant abandons; *Kendall v. Ernest Pestana*, Chapter VI, overruling prior caselaw allowing a landlord to withhold consent to assignment of a lease for any or no reason at all; *Boomer v. Atlantic Cement Company*, Chapter IX, declining to follow prior New York decisions awarding injunctions against ongoing nuisances to property; *Tulk v. Moxhay*, Chapter IX, permitting equitable servitudes to run with the land, contrary to prior decisions limiting running covenants to landlord-tenant relations. Do these decisions support the proposition, reflected in the Lee excerpt and endorsed in *Payne*, that courts will generally avoid "disturbing rules of property" whereas they are more inclined to overrule rules of evidence and procedure? Do these cases suggest that a neat division of "property rules" and other kinds of rules is difficult or even infeasible? Or are cases reproduced in property casebooks likely to contain an unrepresentative sample of decisions in terms of stare decisis, insofar as they include a disproportionate percentage of controversial or pathbreaking decisions?

3. Note that the strong rule of stare decisis in property is designed to encourage forbearance by a different branch of government than the one usually of concern in this connection: the courts. Is unanticipated change in the rules a greater cause for concern when it comes from the courts, or a lesser concern? One factor here is that rule changes by courts are nearly always retroactive, in that they apply to the parties in the case where the change is announced. Another factor is that courts are usually regarded as more independent than legislatures, and hence less likely to succumb to pressure from the public or particular interest groups to interfere with established property rights. Which factor is more important in determining how much weight we should give to the need for forbearance by courts? See, e.g., Ronald A. Cass, Judging: Norms and Incentives of Retrospective Decisionmaking, 75 B.U. L. Rev. 941 (1995); Einer R. Elhauge, Does Interest Group Theory Justify More Intrusive Judicial Review?, 101 Yale L.J. 31 (1991); William N. Eskridge, Jr., Politics Without Romance: Implications of Public Choice Theory for Statutory Interpretation, 74 Va. L. Rev. 275 (1988).

3.   BREACH OF CONTRACT

Another device for reinforcing forbearance is to hold the government liable for damages when it changes the law in a way that defeats private expectations. One vehicle for forcing the government to pay is the Takings Clause, which we take up in the next chapter. But in recent decisions, the Supreme Court has also suggested that the government may be liable for breach of contract in some circumstances involving regulatory promises. In *United States v. Winstar*, 518 U.S. 839 (1996), the Court broadly held that certain savings and loan companies could sue the United States for breach of contract when the government promised they could compute loan reserve requirements a certain way, and Congress subsequently enacted legislation imposing different requirements. The decision produced a series of long and complicated opinions, none of which commanded a majority. *Winstar* was applied in the following decision.

Mobil Oil Exploration & Producing Southeast, Inc. v. United States

Supreme Court of the United States, 2000.
530 U.S. 604.

■ JUSTICE BREYER delivered the opinion of the Court. Two oil companies, petitioners here, seek restitution of $156 million they paid the Government in return for lease contracts giving them rights to explore for and develop oil off the North Carolina coast. The rights were not absolute, but were conditioned on the companies' obtaining a set of further governmental permissions. The companies claim that the Government repudiated the contracts when it denied them certain elements of the permission-seeking opportunities that the contracts had promised. We agree that the Government broke its promise; it repudiated the contracts; and it must give the companies their money back.

I

A

A description at the outset of the few basic contract law principles applicable to this action will help the reader understand the significance of the complex factual circumstances that follow. "When the United States enters into contract relations, its rights and duties therein are governed generally by the law applicable to contracts between private individuals." United States v. Winstar Corp., 518 U.S. 839, 895 (1996) (plurality opinion) (internal quotation marks omitted). The Restatement of Contracts reflects many of the principles of contract law that are applicable to this action. As set forth in the Restatement of Contracts, the relevant principles specify that, when one party to a contract repudiates that contract, the other party "is entitled to restitution for any benefit that he has conferred on" the repudiating party "by way of part performance or reliance." Restatement (Second) of Contracts § 373 (1979) (hereinafter Restatement). The Restatement explains that "repudiation" is a "statement by the obligor to the obligee indicating that the obligor will commit a breach that would of itself give the obligee a claim for damages for total breach." Id., § 250. And "total breach" is a breach that "so substantially impairs the value of the contract to the injured party at the time of the breach that it is just in the circumstances to allow him to recover damages based on all his remaining rights to performance." Id., § 243.

As applied to this action, these principles amount to the following: If the Government said it would break, or did break, an important contractual promise, thereby "substantially impair[ing] the value of the contract[s]" to the companies, *ibid.*, then (unless the companies waived their rights to restitution) the Government must give the companies their money back. And it must do so whether the contracts would, or would not, ultimately have proved financially beneficial to the companies. The Restatement illustrates this point as follows:

> A contracts to sell a tract of land to B for $100,000. After B has made a part payment of $20,000, A wrongfully refuses to transfer title. B can recover the $20,000 in restitution. The result is the same even if the market price of the land is only $70,000, so that performance would have been disadvantageous to B.

Id., § 373, Comment a, Illustration 1.

B

In 1981, in return for up-front "bonus" payments to the United States of about $156 million (plus annual rental payments), the companies received 10–year renewable lease contracts with the United States. In these contracts, the United States promised the companies, among other things, that they could explore for oil off the North Carolina coast and develop any oil that they found (subject to further royalty payments) provided that the companies received exploration and development permissions in accordance with various statutes and regulations to which the lease contracts were made "subject."

The statutes and regulations, the terms of which in effect were incorporated into the contracts, made clear that obtaining the necessary permissions might not be an easy matter. In particular, the Outer Continental Shelf Lands Act (OCSLA), 67 Stat. 462, as amended, 43 U.S.C. § 1331 et seq. (1994 ed. and Supp. III), and the Coastal Zone Management Act of 1972 (CZMA), 86 Stat. 1280, 16 U.S.C. § 1451 et seq., specify that leaseholding companies wishing to explore and drill must successfully complete the following four procedures.

First, a company must prepare and obtain Department of the Interior approval for a Plan of Exploration (Exploration Plan or Plan). 43 U.S.C. § 1340(c). Interior must approve a submitted Exploration Plan unless it finds, after "consider[ing] available relevant environmental information," § 1346(d), that the proposed exploration would probably cause serious harm or damage to life (including fish and other aquatic life), to property, to any mineral ..., to the national security or defense, or to the marine, coastal, or human environment. § 1334(a)(2)(A)(i).

Where approval is warranted, Interior must act quickly—within "thirty days" of the company's submission of a proposed Plan. § 1340(c)(1).

Second, the company must obtain an exploratory well drilling permit. To do so, it must certify (under CZMA) that its Exploration Plan is consistent with the coastal zone management program of each affected State. 16 U.S.C. § 1456(c)(3). If a State objects, the certification fails, unless the Secretary of Commerce overrides the State's objection. If Commerce rules against the State, then Interior may grant the permit. § 1456(c)(3)(A).

Third, where waste discharge into ocean waters is at issue, the company must obtain a National Pollutant Discharge Elimination System permit from the Environmental Protection Agency. 33 U.S.C. §§ 1311(a), 1342(a). It can obtain this permit only if affected States agree that its Exploration Plan is consistent with the state coastal zone management programs or (as just explained) the Secretary of Commerce overrides the state objections. 16 U.S.C. § 1456.

Fourth, if exploration is successful, the company must prepare, and obtain Interior approval for, a Development and Production Plan—a Plan that describes the proposed drilling and related environmental safeguards. 43 U.S.C. § 1351. Again, Interior's approval is conditioned upon certification that the Plan is consistent with state coastal zone management plans—a certification to which States can object, subject to Commerce Department override. § 1351(a)(3).

C

The events at issue here concern the first two steps of the process just described—Interior's consideration of a submitted Exploration Plan and the companies' submission of the CZMA "consistency certification" necessary to obtain an exploratory well drilling permit. The relevant circumstances are the following:

1. In 1981, the companies and the Government entered into the lease contracts. The companies paid the Government $156 million in up-front cash "bonus" payments.

2. In 1989, the companies, Interior, and North Carolina entered into a memorandum of understanding. * * *

3. In September 1989, the companies submitted their initial draft Exploration Plan to North Carolina. * * *

4. On August 20, 1990, the companies submitted both their final Exploration Plan and their CZMA "consistency certification" to Interior.

5. Just two days earlier, on August 18, 1990, a new law, the Outer Banks Protection Act (OBPA), § 6003, 104 Stat. 555, had come into effect.

That law prohibited the Secretary of the Interior from approving any Exploration Plan or Development and Production Plan or to award any drilling permit until (a) a new OBPA-created Environmental Sciences Review Panel had reported to the Secretary, (b) the Secretary had certified to Congress that he had sufficient information to make these OCSLA-required approval decisions, and (c) Congress had been in session an additional 45 days, but (d) in no event could he issue an approval or permit for the next 13 months (until October 1991). § 6003(c)(3). OBPA also required the Secretary, in his certification, to explain and justify in detail any differences between his own certified conclusions and the new Panel's recommendations. § 6003(c)(3)(A)(ii)(II).

6. About five weeks later, and in light of the new statute, Interior wrote a letter to the Governor of North Carolina with a copy to petitioner Mobil. It said that the final submitted Exploration Plan "is deemed to be approvable in all respects." * * * But, it noted, the new law, the "Outer Banks Protection Act (OBPA) of 1990 ... prohibits the approval of any Exploration Plan at this time." It concluded, "because we are currently prohibited from approving it, the Plan will remain on file until the requirements of the OBPA are met." In the meantime a "suspension has been granted to all leases offshore the State of North Carolina." * * *

9. In 1996, Congress repealed OBPA. § 109, 110 Stat. 1321–177.

D

In October 1992 * * * petitioners joined a breach-of-contract lawsuit brought in the Court of Federal Claims. On motions for summary judgment, the court found that the United States had broken its contractual promise to follow OCSLA's provisions, in particular the provision requiring Interior to approve an Exploration Plan that satisfied OCSLA's requirements within 30 days of its submission to Interior. The United States thereby repudiated the contracts. And that repudiation entitled the companies to restitution of the up-front cash "bonus" payments they had made.

A panel of the Court of Appeals for the Federal Circuit reversed, one judge dissenting. The panel held that the Government's refusal to consider the companies' final Exploration Plan was not the "operative cause" of any failure to carry out the contracts' terms because the State's objection to the companies' CZMA "consistency statement" would have prevented the companies from exploring regardless.

II

The record makes clear (1) that OCSLA required Interior to approve "within thirty days" a submitted Exploration Plan that satisfies OCSLA's requirements, (2) that Interior told Mobil the companies' submitted Plan met those requirements, (3) that Interior told Mobil it would not approve the companies' submitted Plan for at least 13 months, and likely longer, and (4) that Interior did not approve (or disapprove) the Plan, ever. The Government does not deny that the contracts, made "pursuant to" and "subject to" OCSLA, incorporated OCSLA provisions as promises. The

Government further concedes, as it must, that relevant contract law entitles a contracting party to restitution if the other party "substantially" breached a contract or communicated its intent to do so. See Restatement § 373(1); 11 W. Jaeger, Williston on Contracts § 1312, p. 109 (3d ed. 1968) (hereinafter Williston); 5 A. Corbin, Contracts § 1104, p. 560 (1964); see also Ankeny v. Clark, 148 U.S. 345, 353 (1893). Yet the Government denies that it must refund the companies' money.

This is because, in the Government's view, it did not breach the contracts or communicate its intent to do so; any breach was not "substantial"; and the companies waived their rights to restitution regardless. We shall consider each of these arguments in turn.

A

The Government's "no breach" arguments depend upon the contract provisions that "subject" the contracts to various statutes and regulations. Those provisions state that the contracts are "subject to" (1) OCSLA, (2) "Sections 302 and 303 of the Department of Energy Organization Act," (3) "all regulations issued pursuant to such statutes and in existence upon the effective date of" the contracts, (4) "all regulations issued pursuant to such statutes in the future which provide for the prevention of waste and the conservation" of Outer Continental Shelf resources, and (5) "all other applicable statutes and regulations." The Government says that these provisions incorporate into the contracts, not only the OCSLA provisions we have mentioned, but also certain other statutory provisions and regulations that, in the Government's view, granted Interior the legal authority to refuse to approve the submitted Exploration Plan, while suspending the leases instead. [The Court's discussion of the government's "no breach" arguments is omitted.] * * *

We conclude, for these reasons, that the Government violated the contracts. Indeed, as Interior pointed out in its letter to North Carolina, the new statute, OBPA, *required* Interior to impose the contract-violating delay. It therefore made clear to Interior and to the companies that the United States had to violate the contracts' terms and would continue to do so. * * *

We do not say that the changes made by the statute were unjustified. We say only that they were changes of a kind that the contracts did not foresee. They were changes in those approval procedures and standards that the contracts had incorporated through cross-reference. The Government has not convinced us that Interior's actions were authorized by any other contractually cross-referenced provision. Hence, in communicating to the companies its intent to follow OBPA, the United States was communicating its intent to violate the contracts.

B

The Government next argues that any violation of the contracts' terms was not significant; hence there was no "substantial" or "material" breach that could have amounted to a "repudiation." In particular, it says that

OCSLA's 30–day approval period "does not function as the 'essence' of these agreements." The Court of Claims concluded, however, that timely and fair consideration of a submitted Exploration Plan was a "necessary reciprocal obligation," indeed, that any "contrary interpretation would render the bargain illusory." We agree [discussion of materiality of breach omitted]. * * *

C

The Government argues that the companies waived their rights to restitution. It does not deny that the United States repudiated the contracts *if* (as we have found) OBPA's changes amounted to a substantial breach. The Government does not claim that the United States retracted its repudiation. Cf. Restatement § 256 (retraction will nullify the effects of repudiation if done before the other party either changes position in reliance on the retraction or communicates that it considers the repudiation to be final). It cannot claim that the companies waived their rights simply by urging performance. Id., § 257 (the injured party "does not change the effect of a repudiation by urging the repudiator to perform in spite of his repudiation"); see also 11 Williston § 1334, at 177–178. Nor has the Government convinced us that the companies' continued actions under the contracts amount to anything more than this urging of performance. Consequently the Government's waiver claim must come down to a claim that the companies *received* at least partial performance. Indeed, acceptance of performance under a once-repudiated contract can constitute a waiver of the right to restitution that repudiation would otherwise create. Restatement § 373, Comment a; cf. Restatement of Restitution § 68, Comment b (1936).

The United States points to three events that, in its view, amount to continued performance of the contracts. But it does not persuade us. [Discussion of the three events is omitted.] * * *

We conclude that the companies did not receive significant postrepudiation performance. We consequently find that they did not waive their right to restitution.

D

Finally, the Government argues that repudiation could not have hurt the companies. Since the companies could not have met the CZMA consistency requirements, they could not have explored (or ultimately drilled) for oil in any event. Hence, OBPA caused them no damage. As the Government puts it, the companies have already received "such damages as were actually caused by the [Exploration Plan approval] delay," namely, none. This argument, however, misses the basic legal point. The oil companies do not seek damages for breach of contract. They seek restitution of their initial payments. Because the Government repudiated the lease contracts, the law entitles the companies to that restitution whether the contracts would, or would not, ultimately have produced a financial gain or led them to obtain a definite right to explore. If a lottery operator fails to deliver a purchased ticket, the purchaser can get his money back—whether or not he eventually would have won the lottery. And if one party to a contract, whether oil company or ordinary citizen, advances the other party money, principles of restitution normally require the latter, upon repudiation, to refund that money. Restatement § 373.

III

Contract law expresses no view about the wisdom of OBPA. We have examined only that statute's consistency with the promises that the earlier contracts contained. We find that the oil companies gave the United States $156 million in return for a contractual promise to follow the terms of pre-existing statutes and regulations. The new statute prevented the Government from keeping that promise. The breach "substantially impair[ed] the value of the contract[s]." Id., § 243. And therefore the Government must give the companies their money back.

For these reasons, the judgment of the Federal Circuit is reversed. We remand the cases for further proceedings consistent with this opinion.

[The dissenting opinion by Justice Stevens is omitted]

NOTES AND QUESTIONS

1.   Note that the action that gives rise to a breach of contract in this case, and renders the United States liable for $156 million in restitution, is the enactment of a statute of general applicability by the U.S. Congress—the Outer Banks Protection Act of 1990. Presumably, the oil companies could have challenged this enactment as retroactive legislation violating the Due Process Clause. Such a challenge very likely would have failed. It is not entirely clear that the statute would be characterized as retroactive, since no permit to drill had yet been issued. Moreover, the relevant precedent requires only that Congress have a rational basis for adopting retroactive civil legislation. See, e.g., Usery v. Turner Elkhorn Mining Co., 428 U.S. 1 (1976). Alternatively, the companies could have challenged the statute as a regulatory taking (see Chapter XII). What result would courts reach in response to such a challenge? In *Tahoe–Sierra Preservation Council v. Tahoe Regional Planning Agency*, 535 U.S. 302 (2002), the Court held that statutes which temporarily deprive property owners of all economically beneficial use of their property should be assessed under an ad hoc balancing test rather than a test of strict liability. Moreover, insofar as the Outer Banks Protection Act was designed to reduce the risk of oil spills, it might qualify under the nuisance exception for takings liability (see *Lucas v. South Carolina Coastal Council*, in Chapter XII). In any event, the judgment in *Mobil Oil* suggests that persons who can characterize a lack of forbearance by the government as a breach of contract are more likely to gain relief from the courts than are persons who must characterize government action as a deprivation or a taking of their property. Does this simply invite persons frustrated by government action to repackage due process and takings claims as breach of contract actions? Or are there legitimate

reasons to provide greater assurances of government forbearance to persons whose expectations are grounded in commercial contracts rather than general property rights?

2.   In a parallel development, the Court has held state governments to a higher standard of punctiliousness when they are charged with impairing their own contracts under the Contracts Clause. See United States Trust Co. v. New Jersey, 431 U.S. 1 (1977). The Court has said that this is because "the State's self-interest is at stake." Id. at 26. Note that if governments were not obliged to perform their own contracts, parties who contract with the government would undoubtedly charge a premium to reflect the higher risk of not being compensated. Knowing this, wouldn't the "State's self interest" lead it to develop a reputation for faithful performance of its obligations, without any intervention by the courts? Or does experience suggest that one generation of government officials cannot always be counted on to consider the impact of its actions on future generations of taxpayers?

3.   What are the defining features of a case that will incline courts to characterize the enactment of a general statute like the Outer Banks Protection Act as a breach of contract by the government? A course of particularized negotiations between the claimant and officers of the government? The exchange of monetary consideration? The presence of a written agreement that sets forth reciprocal obligations? Were any of these features present in *Charles River Bridge*? In *Board of Regents v. Roth*?

4.   Historically speaking, courts have been reluctant to impose liability on the government for alleged contractual breaches caused by the enactment of general legislation. A number of doctrines have been interposed to filter out liability in these cases, including the doctrine that the government must "unmistakably" promise to do that which the subsequent statute forbids, and that "sovereign acts" unrelated to the subject of the contract provide the basis for a defense to liability. These doctrines were interpreted narrowly in *United States v. Winstar*, cited in the principal case, although no opinion commanded a majority of the Court on the critical issues. The government setback in *Winstar* probably explains why these doctrines were not pressed in *Mobil Oil*. The unmistakability doctrine in particular traces its lineage to the doctrine of strict construction advanced by Chief Justice Taney in *Charles River Bridge*. Can it be said that the lease options negotiated by the government in *Mobil Oil* "unmistakably" promised that they would not be frustrated by new legislation making offshore oil exploration more difficult? Does *Mobil Oil* give insufficient consideration to the need to strike a compromise between change and the protection of expectations? Or does it simply reflect the vindication of Justice Story's viewpoint that change should be accommodated by paying "just compensation" to those whose expectations have been dishonored by the government? For further discussion of the implications of *Winstar*, see Alan R. Burch, Purchasing the Right to Govern: *Winstar* and the Need to Reconceptualize the Law of Regulatory Agreements, 88 Ky. L.J. 245 (1999–2000); Gillian Hadfield, Of Sovereignty and Contract: Damages for Breach

of Contract by Government, 8 S. Cal. Interdisc. L.J. 467 (1999); Joshua I. Schwartz, Liability for Sovereign Acts: Congruence and Exceptionalism in Government Contracts Law, 64 Geo. Wash. L. Rev. 633 (1996).

5.   Should governments (federal, state, and local) seek to channel claims of forbearance into breach-of-contract actions by giving firms explicit contracts about what they can expect and not expect in terms of future regulatory action that affects the value of a proposed investment? Or are governments unlikely to do this, because if they over-promise, courts will not cut them any slack and they could face very large liability? Is there a general trend away from the use of "property" as a concept for assuring forbearance by government toward the use of "contract"? Recall in this connection that zoning practice in recent decades has moved away from Euclidian zoning toward a more flexible, contract-like approach in which local officials and developers negotiate a package of benefits and burden for each individual development. See Chapter IX.C.

4.   FOREIGN INVESTMENT TREATIES

Government forbearance is increasingly an issue in international law. Specifically, developed nations like the United States frequently negotiate foreign investment treaties which include among their provisions agreements by the host nation to forbear from interfering with capital projects owned or financed by firms in the developed nation. These treaties can be viewed as a version of the breach of contract model on display in *Mobil Oil*, with the twist that the contract is here a treaty negotiated among sovereign states on behalf of firms that choose to invest in another state. The most famous of the foreign investment protection regimes is contained in Chapter 11 of the North American Free Trade Agreement or NAFTA, entered into by the United States, Canada, and Mexico.

Metalclad Corp. v. United Mexican States

Arbitration Panel, International Centre for Settlement of Investment Disputes, 2000. Case No. ARB(AF)/97/1.
Available at http://naftaclaims.com/Disputes/Mexico/Metalclad/MetalcladFinalAward.pdf.

[Metalclad, a U.S. corporation, formed a Mexican subsidiary, COTE-RIN, to purchase land in Guadalcazar, Mexico, for the purpose of constructing a hazardous waste disposal site. Before it purchased the property, Metalclad was informed by the Federal Government of Mexico and the Mexican State of San Luis Potosi (SLP) that all necessary permits would be issued. Construction of the facility began in May 1994, and was completed in March 1995. A planned open house or "inauguration" of the site was disrupted by demonstrators. Later that year, Metalclad was informed that the Guadalcazar municipal authorities had, without notice to Metalclad, denied a construction permit for the facility. Subsequent efforts to resolve the impasse though litigation in the Mexican courts failed to achieve a resolution. Metalclad then initiated an arbitration proceeding against the Mexican government under Chapter 11 of NAFTA.

The arbitration panel began its decision by finding that the Mexican government, under international law, was responsible for the actions of SLP and Guadalcazar in blocking the opening of the hazardous waste facility. It continued:]

NAFTA Article 1105: Fair and Equitable Treatment

NAFTA Article 1105(1) provides that "each Party shall accord to investments of investors of another Party treatment in accordance with international law, including fair and equitable treatment and full protection and security". * * *

An underlying objective of NAFTA is to promote and increase cross-border investment opportunities and ensure the successful implementation of investment initiatives. (NAFTA Article 102(1)).

Prominent in the statement of principles and rules that introduces the Agreement is the reference to "transparency" (NAFTA Article 102(1)). The Tribunal understands this to include the idea that all relevant legal requirements for the purpose of initiating, completing and successfully operating investments made, or intended to be made, under the Agreement should be capable of being readily known to all affected investors of another Party. There should be no room for doubt or uncertainty on such matters. Once the authorities of the central government of any Party (whose international responsibility in such matters has been identified in the preceding section) become aware of any scope for misunderstanding or confusion in this connection, it is their duty to ensure that the correct position is promptly determined and clearly stated so that investors can proceed with all appropriate expedition in the confident belief that they are acting in accordance with all relevant laws.

Metalclad acquired COTERIN for the sole purpose of developing and operating a hazardous waste landfill in the valley of La Pedrera, in Guadalcazar, SLP.

The Government of Mexico issued federal construction and operating permits for the landfill prior to Metalclad's purchase of COTERIN, and the Government of SLP likewise issued a state operating permit which implied its political support for the landfill project.

A central point in this case has been whether, in addition to the above-mentioned permits, a municipal permit for the construction of a hazardous waste landfill was required.

When Metalclad inquired, prior to its purchase of COTERIN, as to the necessity for municipal permits, federal officials assured it that it had all that was needed to undertake the landfill project. * * *

Metalclad was led to believe, and did believe, that the federal and state permits allowed for the construction and operation of the landfill. Metalclad argues that in all hazardous waste matters, the Municipality has no authority. However, Mexico argues that constitutionally and lawfully the Municipality has the authority to issue construction permits.

Even if Mexico is correct that a municipal construction permit was required, the evidence also shows that, as to hazardous waste evaluations and assessments, the federal authority's jurisdiction was controlling and the authority of the municipality only extended to appropriate construction considerations. Consequently, the denial of the permit by the Municipality by reference to environmental impact considerations in the case of what was basically a hazardous waste disposal landfill, was improper, as was the municipality's denial of the permit for any reason other than those related to the physical construction or defects in the site. * * *

Moreover, the permit was denied at a meeting of the Municipal Town Council of which Metalclad received no notice, to which it received no invitation, and at which it was given no opportunity to appear.

The Town Council denied the permit for reasons which included, but may not have been limited to, the opposition of the local population, the fact that construction had already begun when the application was submitted, the denial of the permit to COTERIN in December 1991 and January 1992, and the ecological concerns regarding the environmental effect and impact on the site and surrounding communities. None of the reasons included a reference to any problems associated with the physical construction of the landfill or to any physical defects therein.

The Tribunal therefore finds that the construction permit was denied without any consideration of, or specific reference to, construction aspects or flaws of the physical facility. * * *

This conclusion is not affected by NAFTA Article 1114, which permits a Party to ensure that investment activity is undertaken in a manner sensitive to environmental concerns. The * * * issuance of the federal permits show clearly that Mexico was satisfied that this project was consistent with, and sensitive to, its environmental concerns.

Mexico failed to ensure a transparent and predictable framework for Metalclad's business planning and investment. The totality of these circumstances demonstrates a lack of orderly process and timely disposition in relation to an investor of a Party acting in the expectation that it would be treated fairly and justly in accordance with the NAFTA. * * *

The Tribunal therefore holds that Metalclad was not treated fairly or equitably under the NAFTA and succeeds on its claim under Article 1105.

NAFTA, Article 1110: Expropriation

NAFTA Article 1110 provides that "[n]o party shall directly or indirectly ... expropriate an investment ... or take a measure tantamount to ... expropriation ... except: (a) for a public purpose; (b) on a nondiscriminatory basis; (c) in accordance with due process of law and Article 1105(1); and (d) on payment of compensation...." "A measure" is defined in Article 201(1) as including "any law, regulation, procedure, requirement or practice".

Thus, expropriation under NAFTA includes not only open, deliberate and acknowledged takings of property, such as outright seizure or formal or obligatory transfer of title in favour of the host State, but also covert or incidental interference with the use of property which has the effect of depriving the owner, in whole or in significant part, of the use or reason-ably-to-be-expected economic benefit of property even if not necessarily to the obvious benefit of the host State.

By permitting or tolerating the conduct of Guadalcazar in relation to Metalclad which the Tribunal has already held amounts to unfair and inequitable treatment breaching Article 1105 and by thus participating or acquiescing in the denial to Metalclad of the right to operate the landfill, notwithstanding the fact that the project was fully approved and endorsed by the federal government, Mexico must be held to have taken a measure tantamount to expropriation in violation of NAFTA Article 1110(1). * * *

As determined earlier, the Municipality denied the local construction permit in part because of the Municipality's perception of the adverse environmental effects of the hazardous waste landfill and the geological unsuitability of the landfill site. In so doing, the Municipality acted outside its authority. * * *

These measures, taken together with the representations of the Mexican federal government, on which Metalclad relied, and the absence of a timely, orderly or substantive basis for the denial by the Municipality of the local construction permit, amount to an indirect expropriation.

The present case resembles in a number of pertinent respects that of *Biloune, et al. v. Ghana Investment Centre, et al.*, 95 I.L.R.183, 207–10 (1993) (Judge Schwebel, President; Wallace and Leigh, Arbitrators). In that case, a private investor was renovating and expanding a resort restaurant in Ghana. As with Metalclad, the investor, basing itself on the representations of a government affiliated entity, began construction before applying for a building permit. As with Metalclad, a stop work order was issued after a substantial amount of work had been completed. The order was based on the absence of a building permit. An application was submitted, but although it was not expressly denied, a permit was never issued. The Tribunal found that an indirect expropriation had taken place because the totality of the circumstances had the effect of causing the irreparable cessation of work on the project. The Tribunal paid particular regard to the investor's justified reliance on the government's representations regarding the permit, the fact that government authorities knew of the construction for more than one year before issuing the stop work order, the fact that permits had not been required for other projects and the fact that no procedure was in place for dealing with building permit applications. Although the decision in *Biloune* does not bind this Tribunal, it is a persuasive authority and the Tribunal is in agreement with its analysis and its conclusion. * * *

In conclusion, the Tribunal holds that Mexico has indirectly expropri-ated Metalclad's investment without providing compensation to Metalclad for the expropriation. Mexico has violated Article 1110 of the NAFTA.

VIII.   QUANTIFICATION OF DAMAGES OR COMPENSATION

In this instance, the damages arising under NAFTA, Article 1105 and the compensation due under NAFTA, Article 1110 would be the same since both situations involve the complete frustration of the operation of the landfill and negate the possibility of any meaningful return on Metalclad's investment. In other words, Metalclad has completely lost its investment. * * *

NAFTA, Article 1135(1)(a), provides for the award of monetary damages and applicable interest where a Party is found to have violated a Chapter Eleven provision. With respect to expropriation, NAFTA, Article 1110(2), specifically requires compensation to be equivalent to the fair market value of the expropriated investment immediately before the expropriation took place. This paragraph further states that "the valuation criteria shall include going concern value, asset value including declared tax value of tangible property, and other criteria, as appropriate, to determine fair market value".

Normally, the fair market value of a going concern which has a history of profitable operation may be based on an estimate of future profits subject to a discounted cash flow analysis. * * *

[T]he Tribunal agrees with the parties that fair market value is best arrived at in this case by reference to Metalclad's actual investment in the project. Thus, in *Phelps Dodge Corp. v. Iran* (10 Iran–U.S. C.T.R. 121 (1986)), the Iran–U.S. Claims Tribunal concluded that the value of the expropriated property was the value of claimant's investment in that property. In reaching this conclusion, the Tribunal considered that the property's future profits were so dependent on as yet unobtained preferential treatment from the government that any prediction of them would be entirely speculative. (Id. at 132–33). * * * The award to Metalclad of the cost of its investment in the landfill is consistent with the principles set forth in *Chorzow Factory (Claim for Indemnity) (Merits), Germany v. Poland*, P.C.I.J. Series A., No. 17 (1928) at p.47, namely, that where the state has acted contrary to its obligations, any award to the claimant should, as far as is possible, wipe out all the consequences of the illegal act and reestablish the situation which would in all probability have existed if that act had not been committed (the *status quo ante*). * * *

For the reasons stated above, the Tribunal hereby decides that, reflecting the amount of Metalclad's investment in the project, less the disallowance of expenses claimed for 1991 and 1992, less the amount claimed by way of bundling of certain expenses, and less the estimated amount allowed for remediation, plus interest at the rate of 6% compounded annually, the Respondent shall, within 45 days from the date on which this Award is rendered, pay to Metalclad the amount of $16,685,000.00. Following such period, interest shall accrue on the unpaid award or any unpaid part thereof at the rate of 6% compounded monthly.

NOTES AND QUESTIONS

1. NAFTA requires that investor-state disputes be submitted to arbitration. Arbitration panels consist of three members, one chosen by the investor, one by the defendant state, and the third picked by agreement between the disputing parties. The arbitrators are private individuals, typically international law practitioners, academics, or former government officials. They are not bound by stare decisis. Their decisions are final and are not subject to appeal to a higher level arbitration panel. The awards are enforceable like final judicial judgments in the courts of the state in which enforcement is sought. See Vicki Been & Joel C. Beauvais, The Global Fifth Amendment? NAFTA's Investment Protections and the Misguided Quest for an International "Regulatory Takings" Doctrine, 78 N.Y.U. L. Rev. 30, 45–46 (2003). Does this process afford sufficient procedural protections given the fundamental importance of the conflicting values at stake here? Although there is no right of appeal, arbitration decisions are subject to judicial review in the courts of the country where the arbitration takes place, to assure that the panel acted within the scope of its jurisdiction. The *Metalclad* decision was reviewed by a Canadian court. See United Mexican States v. Metalclad Corp., 89 B.C. L. R. 3d 359 (2001). The court held that the panel exceeded the scope of its jurisdiction in suggesting that Mexico was guilty of a lack of "transparency" in the way it handled the dispute over the building permit, but it otherwise upheld the award including the size of the judgment. Id. para. 70. (Mexico paid up.) Does the availability of judicial review, even if under a deferential standard, answer some of the procedural objections about the use of arbitration to enforce investor protection treaties?

2. Suppose the basic facts of *Metalclad* arose in one of the states of the United States, involving an American company seeking to develop a hazardous waste disposal site. The governor of the state, speaking on behalf of state officials, offers the same assurances given Metalclad by the federal authorities in Mexico. Municipal officials later deny permission for a building permit necessary to construct the site, citing local environmental concerns. What result if such a company brought an action for impairment of contract or a regulatory takings claim against the local officials who denied the construction permit (see Chapter XII)? What result if it brought an action for breach of contract? Compare Been & Beauvais, supra, 78 N.Y.U. L. Rev. at 59 (decrying *Metalclad* for suggesting "that Article 1110 may be interpreted to require compensation in several circumstances in which the Fifth Amendment has never before been applied."); with Guillermo Aguilar Alvarez & William W. Park, The New Face of Investment Arbitration: NAFTA Chapter 11, 28 Yale Int'l L. 365, 366 (2003) (arguing that "arbitration under investment treaties such as NAFTA will enhance the type of asset protection that facilitates wealth-creating cross-border capital flows, bringing net gains for both host state and foreign investor.").

3. What do you make of the NAFTA Chapter 11 provisions as a general strategy for assuring forbearance by governments? Should govern-

ments in the United States adopt similar provisions protecting domestic American investors from changes in U.S. regulatory policy?

4. What would Chief Justice Taney, author of the majority opinion in *Charles River Bridge*, say about the decision of the arbitration panel in this case? Did the Mexican government promise Metaclad with sufficient clarity that the company would be allowed to build a hazardous waste disposal facility without a local building permit?

POLITICAL RISK INSURANCE

One of the charges Been and Beauvais level against the *Metalclad* decision is that the need for compensation as ex post insurance for the risk of legal and regulatory change is obviated in part by the availability of ex ante insurance against political risk. 78 N.Y.U. L. Rev. at 38. This raises an important question about all the devices to encourage government forbearance we have considered: Can and should they be replaced by the purchase of insurance by persons anxious about the possible risk to their property from future changes in government policy? We expect property owners to purchase insurance against fires, floods, and theft. Why not require them to purchase insurance against government expropriation or other changes in government policy that destroy or devalue property rights?

The possibility of relying on insurance to compensate for takings of property or changes in government regulatory policy that adversely effect property has been recognized by some economists. See Lawrence Blume & Daniel Rubinfeld, Compensation for Takings: An Economic Analysis, 72 Cal. L. Rev. 569 (1984); see also Louis Kaplow, An Economic Analysis of Legal Transitions, 99 Harv. L. Rev. 511 (1986). As Blume and Rubinfeld see it, takings and other types of adverse government action are just another risk that property owners face. Consequently, what we are looking for is some mechanism to spread risks over time and across multiple owners. Political risk insurance is the most logical response to the problem. Blume and Rubinfeld recognize that private insurance faces two difficulties in this context. One is the problem of *adverse selection*: Those people who face the greatest likelihood of having their property taken or regulated may be ones most likely to purchase insurance, which would increase the costs of claims. Id. at 595–96. Another problem is *moral hazard*: Once persons have insurance, they may not put up much resistance to having their property taken or regulated, which would also increase the cost of claims. Id. at 594. Given these difficulties, Blume and Rubinfeld argue, the government probably has to step in and provide insurance (in the form of ex post compensation for takings) for persons unable to self-insure or purchase private insurance. But if these problems could somehow be overcome, private insurance would do the trick just fine.

The political risks faced by overseas investors provide an interesting test of the proposition that insurance can provide a substitute for government forbearance. Political risk insurance has been available to U.S. firms investing overseas since 1971, when Congress created the Overseas Private Investment Corporation (OPIC), a semi-public corporation capitalized by the federal government and backed by the full faith and credit of the federal government. For many years, political risk insurance was available only through OPIC and a similar agency of the World Bank. Commentators suggested that political risk insurance was not available without government subsidy, or perhaps that government-supported insurance has an inherent advantage over private insurers because the government-backed insurers can intervene with host countries to reduce the incidence of loss. See Maura B. Perry, A Model for Efficient Foreign Aid: The Case for the Political Risk Insurance Activities of the Overseas Private Investment Corporation, 36 Va. J. Int'l L. 511 (1996).

Interestingly, however, the private insurance industry has recently made significant major inroads into the political risk insurance market, to the point where private insurance now accounts for 48% of the market. See Jennifer M. DeLeonardo, Are Public and Private Political Risk Insurance Two of a Kind? Suggestions for a New Direction for Government Coverage, 45 Va. J. Int. L. 737, 745 (2005). DeLeonardo cites a number of factors that may account for the new viability of private political risk insurance, including improved information about political risks in developing countries and rising demand for such insurance after 9/11. But one of the most important reasons she cites is the emergence of bilateral investment treaties, with their prohibitions on expropriation and their provisions for mandatory dispute settlement through arbitration, as under NAFTA Chapter 11. Id. at 757–59. These treaty commitments, she argues, function as a warranty of forbearance by the host country, and offer a type of co-insurance (payable by the host country) for any investment losses. "By putting private source insurers more on par with public source insurers in terms of obtaining payments after settling claims, the U.S. government may have enabled private source insurers to offer products that more closely resemble public source [political risk insurance]." Id. at 759–60.

If DeLeonardo is correct that private, non-subsidized political risk insurance becomes viable only if host governments make credible commitments to forbear from interfering with property, then this suggests that private insurance cannot be a perfect substitute for other legal mechanisms to promote forbearance. To the contrary, it would seem that legal mechanisms (such as a right to compensation) may be a precondition to the development of a functioning insurance market—at least a private market not subsidized by taxpayers. Evidently, these other mechanisms reduce the risk of government expropriation or interference to the point where private insurance can handle the residual (uncompensated) risk. So perhaps insurance is not the complete answer to political risk after all. See also William A. Fischel & Perry Shapiro, Takings, Insurance, and Michelman: Comments on Economic Interpretations of Just Compensation Law, 17 J. Legal Stud. 269 (1988) (arguing that insurance only evens out the timing and variance of losses but does not eliminate the demoralization caused by expropriations and other government interferences).

CHAPTER XII

TAKINGS

"[N]or shall private property be taken for public use without just compensation."

—U.S. Const., amend. V.

The Takings Clause of the Fifth Amendment (quoted above) applies directly to the federal government, and has been held to apply to the state governments through the Due Process Clause of the Fourteenth Amendment. Chicago, Burlington & Quincy R.R. Co. v. Chicago, 166 U.S. 226, 238–39 (1897). Similarly worded clauses appear in the state constitutions of nearly all the states. These federal and state takings clauses directly constrain the use of eminent domain by the government. They have also been held to limit the power of government to adopt regulations of property that have an impact functionally equivalent to the exercise of eminent domain—the so-called regulatory takings doctrine. In both contexts, decisions of the United States Supreme Court have sought to define limits on the ability of government to rearrange property rights or to restrict the uses of property rights in the name of some public interest.

The Takings Clause is a fitting subject to conclude our study of property, because the Court, in applying the words of the Clause in different contexts, has drawn upon a number of themes and issues covered throughout the course. These include questions about how we define "property," how far property may be unbundled into discrete rights for purposes of legal analysis, how far claims of owner sovereignty should give way to concerns about public or community interests, the distinction between trespass and nuisance, the difference between possessory rights and servitudes, and—perhaps most centrally—how important it is that the government forbear from frustrating settled expectations about property.

A. EMINENT DOMAIN

Suppose the federal government wants to build a pipeline connecting a large underground oil depot that is part of the Strategic Petroleum Reserve with an oil shipping terminal many miles away. See Canova v. Shell Pipeline Company, 290 F.3d 753 (5th Cir. 2002). The pipeline has to run across hundreds of individual parcels of privately-owned land. Each owner, as a little mini-sovereign, has the right to exclude the pipeline, and can refuse to sell an easement to the government. Since the pipeline must run in a fairly straight line, and requires the assembly of many linked easements in a long horizontal line, each individual landowner and the government are locked in a bilateral monopoly situation. Each landowner has a monopoly on an easement needed by the government, and the government has a monopoly on payments for oil pipeline easements for each landowner. As we saw in Chapter I, bilateral monopolies can result in holdout problems: The parties may haggle endlessly, or engage in strategic behavior to capture a disproportionate share of the gain from the project, or can develop a strong dislike for each other if they get off on the wrong foot. One possible solution to this kind of holdout problem would be to say, "too bad for the government." If the government wants a pipeline, make the government pay whatever price it takes to buy the easements, or find some other route. But this would be expensive, and could be deeply prejudicial to the public interest in cases involving extreme holdouts. Another solution would be to allow the government to confiscate the needed easements without compensation. In effect, we would say, "too bad for the landowner who happens to be in the path of a government pipeline." But this would impose disproportionate losses on a few landowners for the benefit of the public at large, might encourage the government to engage in excessive confiscations of property, and might discourage investment in property that could be subject to uncompensated expropriations.

Instead of either of these extreme solutions, our legal system has adopted a compromise to resolve problems like the need for a government pipeline: Pursuant to the power of eminent domain, the government is allowed to compel a transfer of property rights in return for the payment of just compensation. This power of compulsory transfer is obviously an exception to the ordinary rules associated with property ownership. The ordinary rule is what Calabresi and Melamed called "property rule" protection: If B wants A's property, B must obtain A's consent to a transfer of property. See Chapter I. Eminent domain transforms property rule protection into what Calabresi and Melamed call "liability rule" protection: B can take A's property using the power of eminent domain in return for a payment of compensation determined by some official organ of the government like a court.

Eminent domain is an attribute of governmental power or sovereignty. Both the federal government and the 50 state governments have the power of eminent domain. The federal government has been held to have such power as an implied attribute of sovereignty. Kohl v. United States, 91 U.S. 367, 371–75 (1875). Some of the states have the power by express provisions in their state constitutions, and others have it as an implied attribute of sovereignty. The power of eminent domain, as an attribute of governmental sovereignty, is exercised in the first instance by the legislature. But the legislature can also delegate the power. The legislatures of all states have delegated the power of eminent domain to municipal governments and sometimes to other units of local government like counties. The federal government, and most states, have also delegated the power to certain administrative agencies. Most states have delegated the power to certain common carriers, like railroads, and to private utility companies that operate electric, natural gas, and telephone systems. In about half the states, the power of eminent domain has even been delegated to private landowners in circumstances where the landowner is landlocked and needs to obtain some kind of easement to gain access to her property. See Kirstin

Kanski, Case Note: Property Law—Minnesota's Lakeshore Property Owners without Road Access Find Themselves up A Creek without A Paddle— *In Re Daniel for the Establishment of a Cartway*, 30 Wm. Mitchell L. Rev. 725 (2003) (surveying statutes). But the important point is that eminent domain is a governmental power, and hence cannot be exercised by a private person unless there has been a valid delegation of eminent domain authority to that person.

Because eminent domain trumps ordinary property rights, the power has always been viewed with some suspicion in America. Exercises of eminent domain authority must satisfy both statutory and constitutional requirements. Statutory requirements vary, but typically the condemning authority must show that it has been delegated the power of eminent domain by the legislature, that the delegated power is broad enough to encompass the proposed project, that the exercise of eminent domain is "necessary" to complete the project, and that proper procedures have been followed for making these various statutory determinations. Some types of projects, such as urban renewal or economic development takings, may include additional statutory requirements, such as a finding that the property in question is "blighted." The principal constitutional requirements are that the project be a "public use" and that the condemning authority has offered the property owner "just compensation." The Due Process Clauses of the Fifth and Fourteenth Amendments also presumably require notice and an opportunity for a hearing on the issue of government authority before property is seized, although surprisingly there is some contrary authority in state courts. See Rhode Island Economic Development Corp. v. The Parking Company, 892 A.2d 87 (R.I. 2006) (reaffirming state precedent holding that due process does not require notice or a hearing before property is taken under expedited "quick take" eminent domain procedures).

1.   THE PUBLIC USE REQUIREMENT

One potentially significant constitutional limitation on the power of eminent domain is that it must be deployed for a "public use." There has been much debate about what this means. From the mid-nineteenth century through the early decades of the twentieth, a number of state courts (mostly applying state constitutional provisions) held that public use means actual "use by the public." See Philip Nichols, Jr., The Meaning of Public Use in the Law of Eminent Domain, 20 B.U. L. Rev. 615 (1940). Under this understanding, property could be taken for highways or parks or railroads which would be used by the public. But it could not be taken for a private home or factory. This restrictive view never gained favor with the U.S. Supreme Court, however, which always construed the public use requirement in the Fifth Amendment of the U.S. Constitution to mean public advantage or benefit. See Berman v. Parker, 348 U.S. 26 (1954); Rindge Co. v. Los Angeles County, 262 U.S. 700, 707 (1923). Under this broader interpretation, eminent domain can be used for any project that has some public interest rationale. The U.S. Supreme Court has also said that courts should give great deference to legislative bodies in their determinations of what sorts of projects satisfy the U.S. Constitution's public use requirement. Hawaii Housing Authority v. Midkiff, 467 U.S. 229, 241–43 (1984).

Given the Supreme Court's broad interpretation of the "public use" language in the Fifth Amendment and its deferential standard of review, federal courts throughout the last half of the twentieth century almost never invalidated a taking of property for failing the public use requirement. State courts applying takings clauses in state constitutions were somewhat more likely to say that some purposes—like a condemnation to create a private access road or to acquire a parking lot for a commercial enterprise—were not public uses. Surveys of appellate decisions in the fifty years after *Berman* have found that state courts presented with public use challenges (nearly always under state constitutions) invalidated about one of six takings challenged on this ground. See Thomas W. Merrill, The Economics of Public Use, 72 Cornell L. Rev. 61 (1986); Corey J. Wilk, The Struggle Over the Public Use Clause: Survey of Holdings and Trends, 1986–2003, 39 Real Prop. Prob. & Tr. J. 251 (2004). Still, eminent domain has been used in recent years for projects that many observers have found unsettling. Perhaps the most controversial decision was *Poletown Neighborhood Council v. City of Detroit*, 304 N.W.2d 455 (Mich. 1981), which upheld the condemnation of 465 acres of property in and near Detroit, Michigan for retransfer to General Motors Corp. for an auto assembly plant. The "public use" was said to be the preservation of jobs that would otherwise leave the city, contributing to a declining industrial and population base. In another case, the California Supreme Court said that eminent domain could be used to condemn the Oakland Raiders professional football team, in order to keep it from leaving the City of Oakland. See City of Oakland v. Oakland Raiders, 646 P.2d 835 (Cal. 1982).

At the beginning of the twenty-first century, criticisms of the use of eminent domain for economic development purposes began to mount. A number of lower court decisions invalidated exercises of eminent domain as a means of acquiring real estate for particular commercial entities. See, e.g., Southwestern Ill. Dev. Auth. v. National City Env., L.L.C., 768 N.E.2d 1 (Ill. 2002) (invalidating condemnation of recycling center for re-transfer to an auto race track for use as a parking lot); 99 Cents Only Stores v. Lancaster Redevelopment Agency, 237 F. Supp. 2d 1123 (C.D. Cal. 2001), appeal dismissed as moot, 60 Fed. Appx. 123 (9th Cir. 2003) (invalidating condemnation of lease in shopping center for retransfer to another store for expansion); Casino Reinvestment Development Authority v. Banin, 727 A.2d 102 (N.J. Super. 1998) (invalidating condemnation of land for future expansion of a commercial casino). Perhaps most dramatically, the Michigan Supreme Court overruled its decision in *Poletown*, holding that property cannot be condemned and retransferred to a commercial entity when the sole rationale is economic development. See County of Wayne v. Hathcock, 684 N.W.2d 765 (Mich. 2004). The Institute for Justice, a public interest law firm devoted to protecting private property rights, published a study collecting thousands of instances of property being condemned for retransfer to commercial entities throughout the nation. Dana Berliner, Public Power, Private Gain (2003). The Institute then convinced the U.S. Supreme Court to review one of the cases it had brought on behalf of objecting landowners in order to revisit the question of the meaning of public use. The upshot was the following intensely controversial decision.

Kelo v. City of New London, Connecticut

Supreme Court of the United States, 2005.
545 U.S. 469.

■ JUSTICE STEVENS delivered the opinion of the Court. In 2000, the city of New London approved a development plan that, in the words of the Supreme Court of Connecticut, was "projected to create in excess of 1,000 jobs, to increase tax and other revenues, and to revitalize an economically distressed city, including its downtown and waterfront areas." 843 A.2d 500, 507 (Conn. 2004). In assembling the land needed for this project, the city's development agent has purchased property from willing sellers and proposes to use the power of eminent domain to acquire the remainder of the property from unwilling owners in exchange for just compensation. The question presented is whether the city's proposed disposition of this property qualifies as a "public use" within the meaning of the Takings Clause of the Fifth Amendment to the Constitution.

I

The city of New London (hereinafter City) sits at the junction of the Thames River and the Long Island Sound in southeastern Connecticut. Decades of economic decline led a state agency in 1990 to designate the City a "distressed municipality." In 1996, the Federal Government closed the Naval Undersea Warfare Center, which had been located in the Fort Trumbull area of the City and had employed over 1,500 people. In 1998, the City's unemployment rate was nearly double that of the State, and its population of just under 24,000 residents was at its lowest since 1920.

These conditions prompted state and local officials to target New London, and particularly its Fort Trumbull area, for economic revitalization. To this end, respondent New London Development Corporation (NLDC), a private nonprofit entity established some years earlier to assist the City in planning economic development, was reactivated. In January 1998, the State authorized a $5.35 million bond issue to support the NLDC's planning activities and a $10 million bond issue toward the creation of a Fort Trumbull State Park. In February, the pharmaceutical company Pfizer Inc. announced that it would build a $300 million research facility on a site immediately adjacent to Fort Trumbull; local planners hoped that Pfizer would draw new business to the area, thereby serving as a catalyst to the area's rejuvenation. After receiving initial approval from the city council, the NLDC continued its planning activities and held a series of neighborhood meetings to educate the public about the process. In May, the city council authorized the NLDC to formally submit its plans to the relevant state agencies for review. Upon obtaining state-level approval, the NLDC finalized an integrated development plan focused on 90 acres of the Fort Trumbull area.

The Fort Trumbull area is situated on a peninsula that juts into the Thames River. The area comprises approximately 115 privately owned properties, as well as the 32 acres of land formerly occupied by the naval facility (Trumbull State Park now occupies 18 of those 32 acres). The development plan encompasses seven parcels. Parcel 1 is designated for a waterfront conference hotel at the center of a "small urban village" that will include restaurants and shopping. This parcel will also have marinas for both recreational and commercial uses. A pedestrian "riverwalk" will originate here and continue down the coast, connecting the waterfront areas of the development. Parcel 2 will be the site of approximately 80 new residences organized into an urban neighborhood and linked by public walkway to the remainder of the development, including the state park. This parcel also includes space reserved for a new U.S. Coast Guard Museum. Parcel 3, which is located immediately north of the Pfizer facility, will contain at least 90,000 square feet of research and development office space. Parcel 4A is a 2.4–acre site that will be used either to support the adjacent state park, by providing parking or retail services for visitors, or to support the nearby marina. Parcel 4B will include a renovated marina, as well as the final stretch of the riverwalk. Parcels 5, 6, and 7 will provide land for office and retail space, parking, and water-dependent commercial uses.

The NLDC intended the development plan to capitalize on the arrival of the Pfizer facility and the new commerce it was expected to attract. In addition to creating jobs, generating tax revenue, and helping to "build momentum for the revitalization of downtown New London," the plan was also designed to make the City more attractive and to create leisure and recreational opportunities on the waterfront and in the park.

The city council approved the plan in January 2000, and designated the NLDC as its development agent in charge of implementation. See Conn. Gen.Stat. § 8–188 (2005). The city council also authorized the NLDC to purchase property or to acquire property by exercising eminent domain in the City's name. § 8–193. The NLDC successfully negotiated the purchase of most of the real estate in the 90–acre area, but its negotiations with petitioners failed. As a consequence, in November 2000, the NLDC initiated the condemnation proceedings that gave rise to this case.

II

Petitioner Susette Kelo has lived in the Fort Trumbull area since 1997. She has made extensive improvements to her house, which she prizes for its water view. Petitioner Wilhelmina Dery was born in her Fort Trumbull house in 1918 and has lived there her entire life. Her husband Charles (also a petitioner) has lived in the house since they married some 60 years ago. In all, the nine petitioners own 15 properties in Fort Trumbull—4 in parcel 3 of the development plan and 11 in parcel 4A. Ten of the parcels are

Figure 12–1
Susette Kelo in Front of Her House

Photo by Isaac Reese, 2004 © Institute for Justice.

Figure 12–2
The Kelo House and Its Surroundings

Photograph by Tim Martin. Courtesy The Day Publishing Co., New London, Connecticut.

occupied by the owner or a family member; the other five are held as investment properties. There is no allegation that any of these properties is blighted or otherwise in poor condition; rather, they were condemned only because they happen to be located in the development area.

In December 2000, petitioners brought this action in the New London Superior Court. They claimed, among other things, that the taking of their properties would violate the "public use" restriction in the Fifth Amendment. After a 7–day bench trial, the Superior Court granted a permanent restraining order prohibiting the taking of the properties located in parcel 4A (park or marina support). It, however, denied petitioners relief as to the properties located in parcel 3 (office space).[4]

After the Superior Court ruled, both sides took appeals to the Supreme Court of Connecticut. That court held, over a dissent, that all of the City's proposed takings were valid. * * *

We granted certiorari to determine whether a city's decision to take property for the purpose of economic development satisfies the "public use" requirement of the Fifth Amendment.

III

Two polar propositions are perfectly clear. On the one hand, it has long been accepted that the sovereign may not take the property of *A* for the sole purpose of transferring it to another private party *B*, even though *A* is paid just compensation. On the other hand, it is equally clear that a State may transfer property from one private party to another if future "use by the public" is the purpose of the taking; the condemnation of land for a railroad with common-carrier duties is a familiar example. Neither of these propositions, however, determines the disposition of this case.

As for the first proposition, the City would no doubt be forbidden from taking petitioners' land for the purpose of conferring a private benefit on a particular private party. See Midkiff, 467 U.S., at 245 ("A purely private taking could not withstand the scrutiny of the public use requirement; it would serve no legitimate purpose of government and would thus be void"); Missouri Pacific R. Co. v. Nebraska, 164 U.S. 403 (1896). Nor would the City be allowed to take property under the mere pretext of a public purpose, when its actual purpose was to bestow a private benefit. The takings before us, however, would be executed pursuant to a "carefully

---

4. While this litigation was pending before the Superior Court, the NLDC announced that it would lease some of the parcels to private developers in exchange for their agreement to develop the land according to the terms of the development plan. Specifically, the NLDC was negotiating a 99-year ground lease with Corcoran Jennison, a developer selected from a group of applicants. The negotiations contemplated a nominal rent of $1 per year, but no agreement had yet been signed. See 843 A.2d 500, 509–10, 540 (Conn. 2004).

considered" development plan. The trial judge and all the members of the Supreme Court of Connecticut agreed that there was no evidence of an illegitimate purpose in this case.[6] Therefore, as was true of the statute challenged in *Midkiff,* 467 U.S., at 245, the City's development plan was not adopted "to benefit a particular class of identifiable individuals."

On the other hand, this is not a case in which the City is planning to open the condemned land—at least not in its entirety—to use by the general public. Nor will the private lessees of the land in any sense be required to operate like common carriers, making their services available to all comers. But although such a projected use would be sufficient to satisfy the public use requirement, this "Court long ago rejected any literal requirement that condemned property be put into use for the general public." Id., at 244. Indeed, while many state courts in the mid–19th century endorsed "use by the public" as the proper definition of public use, that narrow view steadily eroded over time. Not only was the "use by the public" test difficult to administer (*e.g.,* what proportion of the public need have access to the property? at what price?), but it proved to be impractical given the diverse and always evolving needs of society. Accordingly, when this Court began applying the Fifth Amendment to the States at the close of the 19th century, it embraced the broader and more natural interpretation of public use as "public purpose." See, e.g., Fallbrook Irrigation Dist. v. Bradley, 164 U.S. 112, 158–164 (1896). Thus, in a case upholding a mining company's use of an aerial bucket line to transport ore over property it did not own, Justice Holmes' opinion for the Court stressed "the inadequacy of use by the general public as a universal test." Strickley v. Highland Boy Gold Mining Co., 200 U.S. 527, 531 (1906). We have repeatedly and consistently rejected that narrow test ever since.

The disposition of this case therefore turns on the question whether the City's development plan serves a "public purpose." Without exception, our cases have defined that concept broadly, reflecting our longstanding policy of deference to legislative judgments in this field.

In *Berman v. Parker,* 348 U.S. 26 (1954), this Court upheld a redevelopment plan targeting a blighted area of Washington, D.C., in which most of the housing for the area's 5,000 inhabitants was beyond repair. Under the plan, the area would be condemned and part of it utilized for the construction of streets, schools, and other public facilities. The remainder of the land would be leased or sold to private parties for the purpose of redevelopment, including the construction of low-cost housing.

The owner of a department store located in the area challenged the condemnation, pointing out that his store was not itself blighted and arguing that the creation of a "better balanced, more attractive communi-

---

6. * * * [W]hile the City intends to transfer certain of the parcels to a private developer in a long-term lease—which developer, in turn, is expected to lease the office space and so forth to other private tenants—the identities of those private parties were not known when the plan was adopted. It is, of course, difficult to accuse the government of having taken *A*'s property to benefit the private interests of *B* when the identity of *B* was unknown.

ty" was not a valid public use. Id., at 31. Writing for a unanimous Court, Justice Douglas refused to evaluate this claim in isolation, deferring instead to the legislative and agency judgment that the area "must be planned as a whole" for the plan to be successful. Id., at 34. The Court explained that "community redevelopment programs need not, by force of the Constitution, be on a piecemeal basis—lot by lot, building by building." Id., at 35. The public use underlying the taking was unequivocally affirmed:

> We do not sit to determine whether a particular housing project is or is not desirable. The concept of the public welfare is broad and inclusive.... The values it represents are spiritual as well as physical, aesthetic as well as monetary. It is within the power of the legislature to determine that the community should be beautiful as well as healthy, spacious as well as clean, well-balanced as well as carefully patrolled. In the present case, the Congress and its authorized agencies have made determinations that take into account a wide variety of values. It is not for us to reappraise them. If those who govern the District of Columbia decide that the Nation's Capital should be beautiful as well as sanitary, there is nothing in the Fifth Amendment that stands in the way. Id., at 33.

In *Hawaii Housing Authority v. Midkiff,* 467 U.S. 229 (1984), the Court considered a Hawaii statute whereby fee title was taken from lessors and transferred to lessees (for just compensation) in order to reduce the concentration of land ownership. We unanimously upheld the statute and rejected the Ninth Circuit's view that it was "a naked attempt on the part of the state of Hawaii to take the property of A and transfer it to B solely for B's private use and benefit." Id., at 235 (internal quotation marks omitted). Reaffirming *Berman's* deferential approach to legislative judgments in this field, we concluded that the State's purpose of eliminating the "social and economic evils of a land oligopoly" qualified as a valid public use. 467 U.S., at 241–242. Our opinion also rejected the contention that the mere fact that the State immediately transferred the properties to private individuals upon condemnation somehow diminished the public character of the taking. "[I]t is only the taking's purpose, and not its mechanics," we explained, that matters in determining public use. Id., at 244. * * *

Viewed as a whole, our jurisprudence has recognized that the needs of society have varied between different parts of the Nation, just as they have evolved over time in response to changed circumstances. Our earliest cases in particular embodied a strong theme of federalism, emphasizing the "great respect" that we owe to state legislatures and state courts in discerning local public needs. See Hairston v. Danville & Western R. Co., 208 U.S. 598, 606–607 (1908) (noting that these needs were likely to vary depending on a State's "resources, the capacity of the soil, the relative importance of industries to the general public welfare, and the long-established methods and habits of the people"). For more than a century, our public use jurisprudence has wisely eschewed rigid formulas and intrusive scrutiny in favor of affording legislatures broad latitude in determining what public needs justify the use of the takings power.

IV

Those who govern the City were not confronted with the need to remove blight in the Fort Trumbull area, but their determination that the area was sufficiently distressed to justify a program of economic rejuvenation is entitled to our deference. The City has carefully formulated an economic development plan that it believes will provide appreciable benefits to the community, including—but by no means limited to—new jobs and increased tax revenue. As with other exercises in urban planning and development, the City is endeavoring to coordinate a variety of commercial, residential, and recreational uses of land, with the hope that they will form a whole greater than the sum of its parts. To effectuate this plan, the City has invoked a state statute that specifically authorizes the use of eminent domain to promote economic development. Given the comprehensive character of the plan, the thorough deliberation that preceded its adoption, and the limited scope of our review, it is appropriate for us, as it was in *Berman,* to resolve the challenges of the individual owners, not on a piecemeal basis, but rather in light of the entire plan. Because that plan unquestionably serves a public purpose, the takings challenged here satisfy the public use requirement of the Fifth Amendment.

To avoid this result, petitioners urge us to adopt a new bright-line rule that economic development does not qualify as a public use. Putting aside the unpersuasive suggestion that the City's plan will provide only purely economic benefits, neither precedent nor logic supports petitioners' proposal. Promoting economic development is a traditional and long accepted function of government. There is, moreover, no principled way of distinguishing economic development from the other public purposes that we have recognized. In our cases upholding takings that facilitated agriculture and mining, for example, we emphasized the importance of those industries to the welfare of the States in question, see, e.g., Strickley, 200 U.S. 527; in *Berman,* we endorsed the purpose of transforming a blighted area into a "well-balanced" community through redevelopment, 348 U.S., at 33;[13] in *Midkiff,* we upheld the interest in breaking up a land oligopoly that "created artificial deterrents to the normal functioning of the State's residential land market," 467 U.S., at 242; and in [Ruckelshaus v. Monsanto Co., 467 U.S. 986 (1984)], we accepted Congress' purpose of eliminating a "significant barrier to entry in the pesticide market," 467 U.S., at 1014–

---

13. It is a misreading of *Berman* to suggest that the only public use upheld in that case was the initial removal of blight. See Reply Brief for Petitioners 8. The public use described in *Berman* extended beyond that to encompass the purpose of *developing* that area to create conditions that would prevent a reversion to blight in the future. See 348 U.S., at 34–35 ("It was not enough, [the experts] believed, to remove existing buildings that were insanitary or unsightly. It was important to redesign the whole area so as to eliminate the conditions that cause slums.... The entire area needed redesigning so that a balanced, integrated plan could be developed for the region, including not only new homes, but also schools, churches, parks, streets, and shopping centers. In this way it was hoped that the cycle of decay of the area could be controlled and the birth of future slums prevented"). Had the public use in *Berman* been defined more narrowly, it would have been difficult to justify the taking of the plaintiff's nonblighted department store.

1015. It would be incongruous to hold that the City's interest in the economic benefits to be derived from the development of the Fort Trumbull area has less of a public character than any of those other interests. Clearly, there is no basis for exempting economic development from our traditionally broad understanding of public purpose.

Petitioners contend that using eminent domain for economic development impermissibly blurs the boundary between public and private takings. Again, our cases foreclose this objection. Quite simply, the government's pursuit of a public purpose will often benefit individual private parties. For example, in *Midkiff,* the forced transfer of property conferred a direct and significant benefit on those lessees who were previously unable to purchase their homes. In *Monsanto,* we recognized that the "most direct beneficiaries" of the data-sharing provisions were the subsequent pesticide applicants, but benefiting them in this way was necessary to promoting competition in the pesticide market. 467 U.S., at 1014. The owner of the department store in *Berman* objected to "taking from one businessman for the benefit of another businessman," 348 U.S., at 33, referring to the fact that under the redevelopment plan land would be leased or sold to private developers for redevelopment. Our rejection of that contention has particular relevance to the instant case: "The public end may be as well or better served through an agency of private enterprise than through a department of government—or so the Congress might conclude. We cannot say that public ownership is the sole method of promoting the public purposes of community redevelopment projects." Id., at 34.[16]

It is further argued that without a bright-line rule nothing would stop a city from transferring citizen *A*'s property to citizen *B* for the sole reason that citizen *B* will put the property to a more productive use and thus pay more taxes. Such a one-to-one transfer of property, executed outside the confines of an integrated development plan, is not presented in this case. While such an unusual exercise of government power would certainly raise a suspicion that a private purpose was afoot,[17] the hypothetical cases

16. Nor do our cases support Justice O'CONNOR's novel theory that the government may only take property and transfer it to private parties when the initial taking eliminates some "harmful property use." There was nothing "harmful" about the non-blighted department store at issue in Berman, 348 U.S. 26; see also n. 13, supra; nothing "harmful" about the lands at issue in the mining and agriculture cases, see, e.g., Strickley, 200 U.S. 527; and certainly nothing "harmful" about the trade secrets owned by the pesticide manufacturers in *Monsanto,* 467 U.S. 986. In each case, the public purpose we upheld depended on a private party's *future* use of the concededly nonharmful property that was taken. By focusing on a property's future use, as opposed to its past use, our cases are faithful to the text of the Takings Clause. See U.S. Const., Amdt. 5. ("[N]or shall private property be taken for public use, without just compensation"). * * *

17. Courts have viewed such aberrations with a skeptical eye. See, e.g., 99 Cents Only Stores v. Lancaster Redevelopment Agency, 237 F.Supp.2d 1123 (C.D. Cal. 2001); cf. Cincinnati v. Vester, 281 U.S. 439, 448 (1930) (taking invalid under state eminent domain statute for lack of a reasoned explanation). These types of takings may also implicate other constitutional guarantees. See Village of Willowbrook v. Olech, 528 U.S. 562 (2000) (per curiam).

posited by petitioners can be confronted if and when they arise.[18] They do not warrant the crafting of an artificial restriction on the concept of public use.

Alternatively, petitioners maintain that for takings of this kind we should require a "reasonable certainty" that the expected public benefits will actually accrue. Such a rule, however, would represent an even greater departure from our precedent. "When the legislature's purpose is legitimate and its means are not irrational, our cases make clear that empirical debates over the wisdom of takings—no less than debates over the wisdom of other kinds of socioeconomic legislation—are not to be carried out in the federal courts." Midkiff, 467 U.S., at 242. * * * The disadvantages of a heightened form of review are especially pronounced in this type of case. Orderly implementation of a comprehensive redevelopment plan obviously requires that the legal rights of all interested parties be established before new construction can be commenced. A constitutional rule that required postponement of the judicial approval of every condemnation until the likelihood of success of the plan had been assured would unquestionably impose a significant impediment to the successful consummation of many such plans.

Just as we decline to second-guess the City's considered judgments about the efficacy of its development plan, we also decline to second-guess the City's determinations as to what lands it needs to acquire in order to effectuate the project. "It is not for the courts to oversee the choice of the boundary line nor to sit in review on the size of a particular project area. Once the question of the public purpose has been decided, the amount and character of land to be taken for the project and the need for a particular tract to complete the integrated plan rests in the discretion of the legislative branch." Berman, 348 U.S., at 35–36.

In affirming the City's authority to take petitioners' properties, we do not minimize the hardship that condemnations may entail, notwithstanding the payment of just compensation.[21] We emphasize that nothing in our opinion precludes any State from placing further restrictions on its exercise of the takings power. Indeed, many States already impose "public use" requirements that are stricter than the federal baseline. Some of these requirements have been established as a matter of state constitutional law,[22] while others are expressed in state eminent domain statutes that carefully limit the grounds upon which takings may be exercised.[23] As the

---

18. Cf. Panhandle Oil Co. v. Mississippi ex rel. Knox, 277 U.S. 218, 223 (1928) (Holmes, J., dissenting) ("The power to tax is not the power to destroy while this Court sits").

21. The *amici* raise questions about the fairness of the measure of just compensation. See, e.g., Brief for American Planning Association et al. as *Amici Curiae* 26–30. While important, these questions are not before us in this litigation.

22. See, e.g., County of Wayne v. Hathcock, 684 N.W.2d 765 (Mich. 2004).

23. Under California law, for instance, a city may only take land for economic development purposes in blighted areas. Cal. Health & Safety Code Ann. §§ 33030–33037 (West 1997). See, e.g., Redevelopment Agency of Chula Vista v. Rados Bros., 115 Cal. Rptr.2d 234 (Cal. Ct. App. 2002).

submissions of the parties and their *amici* make clear, the necessity and wisdom of using eminent domain to promote economic development are certainly matters of legitimate public debate.[24] This Court's authority, however, extends only to determining whether the City's proposed condemnations are for a "public use" within the meaning of the Fifth Amendment to the Federal Constitution. Because over a century of our case law interpreting that provision dictates an affirmative answer to that question, we may not grant petitioners the relief that they seek.

The judgment of the Supreme Court of Connecticut is affirmed.

It is so ordered.

■ JUSTICE KENNEDY, concurring. I join the opinion for the Court and add these further observations. * * *

A court applying rational-basis review under the Public Use Clause should strike down a taking that, by a clear showing, is intended to favor a particular private party, with only incidental or pretextual public benefits, just as a court applying rational-basis review under the Equal Protection Clause must strike down a government classification that is clearly intended to injure a particular class of private parties, with only incidental or pretextual public justifications. See Cleburne v. Cleburne Living Center, Inc., 473 U.S. 432, 446–447, 450 (1985); Department of Agriculture v. Moreno, 413 U.S. 528, 533–536 (1973). * * *

A court confronted with a plausible accusation of impermissible favoritism to private parties should treat the objection as a serious one and review the record to see if it has merit, though with the presumption that the government's actions were reasonable and intended to serve a public purpose. Here, the trial court conducted a careful and extensive inquiry into "whether, in fact, the development plan is of primary benefit to ... the developer [*i.e.,* Corcoran Jennison], and private businesses which may eventually locate in the plan area [*e.g.,* Pfizer], and in that regard, only of incidental benefit to the city." The trial court considered testimony from government officials and corporate officers; documentary evidence of communications between these parties; respondents' awareness of New London's depressed economic condition and evidence corroborating the validity of this concern; the substantial commitment of public funds by the State to the development project before most of the private beneficiaries were known; evidence that respondents reviewed a variety of development plans and chose a private developer from a group of applicants rather than

---

24. For example, some argue that the need for eminent domain has been greatly exaggerated because private developers can use numerous techniques, including secret negotiations or precommitment strategies, to overcome holdout problems and assemble lands for genuinely profitable projects. See Brief for Jane Jacobs as *Amicus Curiae* 13–15; see also Brief for John Norquist as *Amicus Curiae.* Others argue to the contrary,

urging that the need for eminent domain is especially great with regard to older, small cities like New London, where centuries of development have created an extreme overdivision of land and thus a real market impediment to land assembly. See Brief for Connecticut Conference for Municipalities et al. as *Amici Curiae* 13, 21; see also Brief for National League of Cities et al. as *Amici Curiae.*

picking out a particular transferee beforehand; and the fact that the other private beneficiaries of the project are still unknown because the office space proposed to be built has not yet been rented.

The trial court concluded, based on these findings, that benefiting Pfizer was not "the primary motivation or effect of this development plan"; instead, "the primary motivation for [respondents] was to take advantage of Pfizer's presence." Likewise, the trial court concluded that "[t]here is nothing in the record to indicate that . . . [respondents] were motivated by a desire to aid [other] particular private entities." Even the dissenting justices on the Connecticut Supreme Court agreed that respondents' development plan was intended to revitalize the local economy, not to serve the interests of Pfizer, Corcoran Jennison, or any other private party. 843 A.2d 500, 595 (Conn. 2004) (Zarella, J., concurring in part and dissenting in part). This case, then, survives the meaningful rational basis review that in my view is required under the Public Use Clause. * * *

■ JUSTICE O'CONNOR, with whom THE CHIEF JUSTICE, JUSTICE SCALIA, and JUSTICE THOMAS join, dissenting. Over two centuries ago, just after the Bill of Rights was ratified, Justice Chase wrote:

> An ACT of the Legislature (for I cannot call it a law) contrary to the great first principles of the social compact, cannot be considered a rightful exercise of legislative authority. . . . A few instances will suffice to explain what I mean. . . . [A] law that takes property from A. and gives it to B: It is against all reason and justice, for a people to entrust a Legislature with SUCH powers; and, therefore, it cannot be presumed that they have done it. Calder v. Bull, 3 Dall. 386, 388 (1798) (emphasis deleted).

Today the Court abandons this long-held, basic limitation on government power. Under the banner of economic development, all private property is now vulnerable to being taken and transferred to another private owner, so long as it might be upgraded—*i.e.*, given to an owner who will use it in a way that the legislature deems more beneficial to the public—in the process. To reason, as the Court does, that the incidental public benefits resulting from the subsequent ordinary use of private property render economic development takings "for public use" is to wash out any distinction between private and public use of property—and thereby effectively to delete the words "for public use" from the Takings Clause of the Fifth Amendment. * * *

II

The Fifth Amendment to the Constitution, made applicable to the States by the Fourteenth Amendment, provides that "private property [shall not] be taken for public use, without just compensation." When interpreting the Constitution, we begin with the unremarkable presumption that every word in the document has independent meaning, "that no word was unnecessarily used, or needlessly added." Wright v. United States, 302 U.S. 583, 588 (1938). In keeping with that presumption, we have read the Fifth Amendment's language to impose two distinct conditions on the exercise of eminent domain: "the taking must be for a 'public use' and 'just compensation' must be paid to the owner." Brown v. Legal Foundation of Wash., 538 U.S. 216, 231–232 (2003).

These two limitations serve to protect "the security of Property," which Alexander Hamilton described to the Philadelphia Convention as one of the "great obj[ects] of Gov[ernment]." 1 Records of the Federal Convention of 1787, p. 302 (M. Farrand ed. 1934). Together they ensure stable property ownership by providing safeguards against excessive, unpredictable, or unfair use of the government's eminent domain power—particularly against those owners who, for whatever reasons, may be unable to protect themselves in the political process against the majority's will.

While the Takings Clause presupposes that government can take private property without the owner's consent, the just compensation requirement spreads the cost of condemnations and thus "prevents the public from loading upon one individual more than his just share of the burdens of government." Monongahela Nav. Co. v. United States, 148 U.S. 312, 325 (1893); see also Armstrong v. United States, 364 U.S. 40, 49 (1960). The public use requirement, in turn, imposes a more basic limitation, circumscribing the very scope of the eminent domain power: Government may compel an individual to forfeit her property for the *public's* use, but not for the benefit of another private person. This requirement promotes fairness as well as security.

Where is the line between "public" and "private" property use? We give considerable deference to legislatures' determinations about what governmental activities will advantage the public. But were the political branches the sole arbiters of the public-private distinction, the Public Use Clause would amount to little more than hortatory fluff. An external, judicial check on how the public use requirement is interpreted, however limited, is necessary if this constraint on government power is to retain any meaning. See Cincinnati v. Vester, 281 U.S. 439, 446 (1930) ("It is well established that ... the question [of] what is a public use is a judicial one").

Our cases have generally identified three categories of takings that comply with the public use requirement, though it is in the nature of things that the boundaries between these categories are not always firm. Two are relatively straightforward and uncontroversial. First, the sovereign may transfer private property to public ownership—such as for a road, a hospital, or a military base. See, e.g., Old Dominion Land Co. v. United States, 269 U.S. 55 (1925); Rindge Co. v. County of Los Angeles, 262 U.S. 700 (1923). Second, the sovereign may transfer private property to private parties, often common carriers, who make the property available for the public's use—such as with a railroad, a public utility, or a stadium. See, e.g., National Railroad Passenger Corporation v. Boston & Maine Corp., 503 U.S. 407 (1992); Mt. Vernon–Woodberry Cotton Duck Co. v. Alabama Interstate Power Co., 240 U.S. 30, 36 (1916). But "public ownership" and "use-by-the-public" are sometimes too constricting and impractical ways to define the scope of the Public Use Clause. Thus we have allowed that, in certain circumstances and to meet certain exigencies, takings that serve a public purpose also satisfy the Constitution even if the property is destined for subsequent private use. See, e.g., Berman v. Parker, 348 U.S. 26 (1954); Hawaii Housing Authority v. Midkiff, 467 U.S. 229 (1984).

This case returns us for the first time in over 20 years to the hard question of when a purportedly "public purpose" taking meets the public use requirement. It presents an issue of first impression: Are economic development takings constitutional? I would hold that they are not. * * *

In [*Berman* and *Midkiff*] we emphasized the importance of deferring to legislative judgments about public purpose. Because courts are ill-equipped to evaluate the efficacy of proposed legislative initiatives, we rejected as unworkable the idea of courts' " 'deciding on what is and is not a governmental function and ... invalidating legislation on the basis of their view on that question at the moment of decision, a practice which has proved impracticable in other fields.' " Id., at 240–241 (quoting United States ex rel. TVA v. Welch, 327 U.S. 546, 552 (1946)); see Berman, supra, at 32 ("[T]he legislature, not the judiciary, is the main guardian of the public needs to be served by social legislation"). Likewise, we recognized our inability to evaluate whether, in a given case, eminent domain is a necessary means by which to pursue the legislature's ends. Midkiff, supra, at 242; Berman, supra, at 103.

Yet for all the emphasis on deference, *Berman* and *Midkiff* hewed to a bedrock principle without which our public use jurisprudence would collapse: "A purely private taking could not withstand the scrutiny of the public use requirement; it would serve no legitimate purpose of government and would thus be void." Midkiff, supra, at 245. To protect that principle, those decisions reserved "a role for courts to play in reviewing a legislature's judgment of what constitutes a public use ... [though] the Court in *Berman* made clear that it is 'an extremely narrow' one." Midkiff, supra, at 240 (quoting Berman, supra, at 32).

The Court's holdings in *Berman* and *Midkiff* were true to the principle underlying the Public Use Clause. In both those cases, the extraordinary, precondemnation use of the targeted property inflicted affirmative harm on society—in *Berman* through blight resulting from extreme poverty and in *Midkiff* through oligopoly resulting from extreme wealth. And in both cases, the relevant legislative body had found that eliminating the existing property use was necessary to remedy the harm. Berman, supra, at 28–29; Midkiff, supra, at 232. Thus a public purpose was realized when the harmful use was eliminated. Because each taking *directly* achieved a public benefit, it did not matter that the property was turned over to private use. Here, in contrast, New London does not claim that Susette Kelo's and Wilhelmina Dery's well-maintained homes are the source of any social harm. Indeed, it could not so claim without adopting the absurd argument that any single-family home that might be razed to make way for an apartment building, or any church that might be replaced with a retail store, or any small business that might be more lucrative if it were instead part of a national franchise, is inherently harmful to society and thus within the government's power to condemn.

In moving away from our decisions sanctioning the condemnation of harmful property use, the Court today significantly expands the meaning of public use. It holds that the sovereign may take private property currently put to ordinary private use, and give it over for new, ordinary private use, so long as the new use is predicted to generate some secondary benefit for the public—such as increased tax revenue, more jobs, maybe even aesthetic pleasure. But nearly any lawful use of real private property can be said to generate some incidental benefit to the public. Thus, if predicted (or even guaranteed) positive side-effects are enough to render transfer from one private party to another constitutional, then the words "for public use" do not realistically exclude *any* takings, and thus do not exert any constraint on the eminent domain power.

There is a sense in which this troubling result follows from errant language in *Berman* and *Midkiff*. In discussing whether takings within a blighted neighborhood were for a public use, *Berman* began by observing: "We deal, in other words, with what traditionally has been known as the police power." 348 U.S., at 32. From there it declared that "[o]nce the object is within the authority of Congress, the right to realize it through the exercise of eminent domain is clear." *Id.,* at 33. Following up, we said in *Midkiff* that "[t]he 'public use' requirement is coterminous with the scope of a sovereign's police powers." 467 U.S., at 240. This language was unnecessary to the specific holdings of those decisions. *Berman* and *Midkiff* simply did not put such language to the constitutional test, because the takings in those cases were within the police power but also for "public use" for the reasons I have described. The case before us now demonstrates why, when deciding if a taking's purpose is constitutional, the police power and "public use" cannot always be equated. The Court protests that it does not sanction the bare transfer from A to B for B's benefit. It suggests two limitations on what can be taken after today's decision. First, it maintains a role for courts in ferreting out takings whose sole purpose is to bestow a benefit on the private transferee—without detailing how courts are to conduct that complicated inquiry. For his part, Justice KENNEDY suggests that courts may divine illicit purpose by a careful review of the record and the process by which a legislature arrived at the decision to take—without specifying what courts should look for in a case with different facts, how they will know if they have found it, and what to do if they do not. Whatever the details of Justice KENNEDY's as-yet-undisclosed test, it is difficult to envision anyone but the "stupid staff[er]" failing it. See Lucas v. South Carolina Coastal Council, 505 U.S. 1003, 1025–1026, n. 12 (1992). The trouble with economic development takings is that private benefit and incidental public benefit are, by definition, merged and mutually reinforcing. In this case, for example, any boon for Pfizer or the plan's developer is difficult to disaggregate from the promised public gains in taxes and jobs.

Even if there were a practical way to isolate the motives behind a given taking, the gesture toward a purpose test is theoretically flawed. If it is true that incidental public benefits from new private use are enough to ensure the "public purpose" in a taking, why should it matter, as far as the Fifth Amendment is concerned, what inspired the taking in the first place? How much the government does or does not desire to benefit a favored private party has no bearing on whether an economic development taking will or will not generate secondary benefit for the public. And whatever the reason for a given condemnation, the effect is the same from the constitutional perspective—private property is forcibly relinquished to new private ownership.

A second proposed limitation is implicit in the Court's opinion. The logic of today's decision is that eminent domain may only be used to upgrade—not downgrade—property. At best this makes the Public Use Clause redundant with the Due Process Clause, which already prohibits irrational government action. The Court rightfully admits, however, that the judiciary cannot get bogged down in predictive judgments about whether the public will actually be better off after a property transfer. In any event, this constraint has no realistic import. For who among us can say she already makes the most productive or attractive possible use of her property? The specter of condemnation hangs over all property. Nothing is to prevent the State from replacing any Motel 6 with a Ritz–Carlton, any home with a shopping mall, or any farm with a factory. Cf. Institute for Justice, D. Berliner, Public Power, Private Gain: A Five–Year, State-by-State Report Examining the Abuse of Eminent Domain (2003) (collecting accounts of economic development takings).

The Court also puts special emphasis on facts peculiar to this case: The NLDC's plan is the product of a relatively careful deliberative process; it proposes to use eminent domain for a multipart, integrated plan rather than for isolated property transfer; it promises an array of incidental benefits (even aesthetic ones), not just increased tax revenue; it comes on the heels of a legislative determination that New London is a depressed municipality. Justice KENNEDY, too, takes great comfort in these facts. But none has legal significance to blunt the force of today's holding. If legislative prognostications about the secondary public benefits of a new use can legitimate a taking, there is nothing in the Court's rule or in Justice KENNEDY's gloss on that rule to prohibit property transfers generated with less care, that are less comprehensive, that happen to result from less elaborate process, whose only projected advantage is the incidence of higher taxes, or that hope to transform an already prosperous city into an even more prosperous one.

Finally, in a coda, the Court suggests that property owners should turn to the States, who may or may not choose to impose appropriate limits on economic development takings. This is an abdication of our responsibility. States play many important functions in our system of dual sovereignty, but compensating for our refusal to enforce properly the Federal Constitution (and a provision meant to curtail state action, no less) is not among them.

* * *

It was possible after *Berman* and *Midkiff* to imagine unconstitutional transfers from A to B. Those decisions endorsed government intervention when private property use had veered to such an extreme that the public was suffering as a consequence. Today nearly all real property is susceptible to condemnation on the Court's theory. * * *

Any property may now be taken for the benefit of another private party, but the fallout from this decision will not be random. The beneficiaries are likely to be those citizens with disproportionate influence and power in the political process, including large corporations and development firms. As for the victims, the government now has license to transfer property from those with fewer resources to those with more. The Founders cannot have intended this perverse result. "[T]hat alone is a *just* government," wrote James Madison, "which *impartially* secures to every man, whatever is his *own*." For the National Gazette, Property, (Mar. 29, 1792), reprinted in 14 Papers of James Madison 266 (R. Rutland et al. eds. 1983).

I would hold that the takings in both Parcel 3 and Parcel 4A are unconstitutional, reverse the judgment of the Supreme Court of Connecticut, and remand for further proceedings.

■ JUSTICE THOMAS, dissenting. * * * Today's decision is simply the latest in a string of our cases construing the Public Use Clause to be a virtual nullity, without the slightest nod to its original meaning. In my view, the Public Use Clause, originally understood, is a meaningful limit on the government's eminent domain power. Our cases have strayed from the Clause's original meaning, and I would reconsider them.

I

* * * Though one component of the protection provided by the Takings Clause is that the government can take private property only if it provides "just compensation" for the taking, the Takings Clause also prohibits the government from taking property except "for public use." Were it otherwise, the Takings Clause would either be meaningless or empty. If the Public Use Clause served no function other than to state that the government may take property through its eminent domain power—for public or private uses—then it would be surplusage. * * * Alternatively, the Clause could distinguish those takings that require compensation from those that do not. That interpretation, however, "would permit private property to be taken or appropriated for private use without any compensation whatever." Cole v. La Grange, 113 U.S. 1, 8 (1885) (interpreting same language in the Missouri Public Use Clause). In other words, the Clause would require the government to compensate for takings done "for public use," leaving it free to take property for purely private uses without the payment of compensation. This would contradict a bedrock principle well established by the time of the founding: that all takings required the payment of compensation. 1 Blackstone 135; 2 J. Kent, Commentaries on American Law 275 (1827) (hereinafter Kent); J. Madison, for the National

Property Gazette, (Mar. 27, 1792), in 14 Papers of James Madison 266, 267 (R. Rutland et al. eds. 1983) (arguing that no property "shall be taken *directly* even for public use without indemnification to the owner"). The Public Use Clause, like the Just Compensation Clause, is therefore an express limit on the government's power of eminent domain.

The most natural reading of the Clause is that it allows the government to take property only if the government owns, or the public has a legal right to use, the property, as opposed to taking it for any public purpose or necessity whatsoever. At the time of the founding, dictionaries primarily defined the noun "use" as "[t]he act of employing any thing to any purpose." 2 S. Johnson, A Dictionary of the English Language 2194 (4th ed. 1773). The term "use," moreover, "is from the Latin *utor*, which means 'to use, make use of, avail one's self of, employ, apply, enjoy, etc.' " J. Lewis, Law of Eminent Domain § 165, p. 224, n. 4 (1888) (hereinafter Lewis). When the government takes property and gives it to a private individual, and the public has no right to use the property, it strains language to say that the public is "employing" the property, regardless of the incidental benefits that might accrue to the public from the private use. The term "public use," then, means that either the government or its citizens as a whole must actually "employ" the taken property. See id., at 223 (reviewing founding-era dictionaries). * * *

Tellingly, the phrase "public use" contrasts with the very different phrase "general Welfare" used elsewhere in the Constitution. See ibid. ("Congress shall have Power To ... provide for the common Defence and general Welfare of the United States"); preamble (Constitution established "to promote the general Welfare"). The Framers would have used some such broader term if they had meant the Public Use Clause to have a similarly sweeping scope. * * *

II

Early American eminent domain practice largely bears out this understanding of the Public Use Clause. This practice concerns state limits on eminent domain power, not the Fifth Amendment, since it was not until the late 19th century that the Federal Government began to use the power of eminent domain, and since the Takings Clause did not even arguably limit state power until after the passage of the Fourteenth Amendment. See Note, The Public Use Limitation on Eminent Domain: An Advance Requiem, 58 Yale L.J. 599, 599–600, and nn. 3–4 (1949); Barron ex rel. Tiernan v. Mayor of Baltimore, 7 Pet. 243, 250–251 (1833) (holding the Takings Clause inapplicable to the States of its own force). Nevertheless, several early state constitutions at the time of the founding likewise limited the power of eminent domain to "public uses." Their practices therefore shed light on the original meaning of the same words contained in the Public Use Clause.

States employed the eminent domain power to provide quintessentially public goods, such as public roads, toll roads, ferries, canals, railroads, and public parks. Lewis §§ 166, 168–171, 175, at 227–228, 234–241, 243.

Though use of the eminent domain power was sparse at the time of the founding, many States did have so-called Mill Acts, which authorized the owners of grist mills operated by water power to flood upstream lands with the payment of compensation to the upstream landowner. See, e.g., id., § 178, at 245–246; Head v. Amoskeag Mfg. Co., 113 U.S. 9, 16–19, and n. 2 (1885). Those early grist mills "were regulated by law and compelled to serve the public for a stipulated toll and in regular order," and therefore were actually used by the public. Lewis § 178, at 246, and n. 3; see also Head, supra, at 18–19. They were common carriers—quasi-public entities. These were "public uses" in the fullest sense of the word, because the public could legally use and benefit from them equally. See Public Use Limitations 903 (common-carrier status traditionally afforded to "private beneficiaries of a state franchise or another form of state monopoly, or to companies that operated in conditions of natural monopoly").

To be sure, some early state legislatures tested the limits of their state-law eminent domain power. Some States enacted statutes allowing the taking of property for the purpose of building private roads. See Lewis § 167, at 230. These statutes were mixed; some required the private landowner to keep the road open to the public, and others did not. *See id.,* § 167, at 230–234. Later in the 19th century, moreover, the Mill Acts were employed to grant rights to private manufacturing plants, in addition to grist mills that had common-carrier duties. See, e.g., M. Horwitz, The Transformation of American Law 1780–1860, pp. 51–52 (1977).

These early uses of the eminent domain power are often cited as evidence for the broad "public purpose" interpretation of the Public Use Clause, see, e.g., Brief for Respondents 30; Brief for American Planning Assn. et al. as *Amici Curiae* at 6–7, but in fact the constitutionality of these exercises of eminent domain power under state public use restrictions was a hotly contested question in state courts throughout the 19th and into the 20th century. Some courts construed those clauses to authorize takings for public purposes, but others adhered to the natural meaning of "public use." As noted above, the earliest Mill Acts were applied to entities with duties to remain open to the public, and their later extension is not deeply probative of whether that subsequent practice is consistent with the original meaning of the Public Use Clause. See McIntyre v. Ohio Elections Comm'n, 514 U.S. 334, 370 (1995) (THOMAS, J., concurring in judgment). At the time of the founding, "[b]usiness corporations were only beginning to upset the old corporate model, in which the raison d'être of chartered associations was their service to the public," Horwitz, supra, at 49–50, so it was natural to those who framed the first Public Use Clauses to think of mills as inherently public entities. The disagreement among state courts, and state legislatures' attempts to circumvent public use limits on their eminent domain power, cannot obscure that the Public Use Clause is most naturally read to authorize takings for public use only if the government or the public actually uses the taken property. * * *

IV

The consequences of today's decision are not difficult to predict, and promise to be harmful. So-called "urban renewal" programs provide some compensation for the properties they take, but no compensation is possible for the subjective value of these lands to the individuals displaced and the indignity inflicted by uprooting them from their homes. Allowing the government to take property solely for public purposes is bad enough, but extending the concept of public purpose to encompass any economically beneficial goal guarantees that these losses will fall disproportionately on poor communities. Those communities are not only systematically less likely to put their lands to the highest and best social use, but are also the least politically powerful. If ever there were justification for intrusive judicial review of constitutional provisions that protect "discrete and insular minorities," United States v. Carolene Products Co., 304 U.S. 144, 152, n. 4 (1938), surely that principle would apply with great force to the powerless groups and individuals the Public Use Clause protects. The deferential standard this Court has adopted for the Public Use Clause is therefore deeply perverse. It encourages "those citizens with disproportionate influence and power in the political process, including large corporations and development firms" to victimize the weak. Ante, (O'CONNOR, J., dissenting).

Those incentives have made the legacy of this Court's "public purpose" test an unhappy one. In the 1950's, no doubt emboldened in part by the expansive understanding of "public use" this Court adopted in *Berman*, cities "rushed to draw plans" for downtown development. B. Frieden & L. Sagalayn, Downtown, Inc. How America Rebuilds Cities 17 (1989). "Of all the families displaced by urban renewal from 1949 through 1963, 63 percent of those whose race was known were nonwhite, and of these families, 56 percent of nonwhites and 38 percent of whites had incomes low enough to qualify for public housing, which, however, was seldom available to them." Id., at 28. Public works projects in the 1950's and 1960's destroyed predominantly minority communities in St. Paul, Minnesota, and Baltimore, Maryland. Id., at 28–29. In 1981, urban planners in Detroit, Michigan, uprooted the largely "lower-income and elderly" Poletown neighborhood for the benefit of the General Motors Corporation. J. Wylie, Poletown: Community Betrayed 58 (1989). Urban renewal projects have long been associated with the displacement of blacks; "[i]n cities across the country, urban renewal came to be known as 'Negro removal.'" Pritchett, The "Public Menace" of Blight: Urban Renewal and the Private Uses of Eminent Domain, 21 Yale L. & Pol'y Rev. 1, 47 (2003). Over 97 percent of the individuals forcibly removed from their homes by the "slum-clearance" project upheld by this Court in *Berman* were black. 348 U.S., at 30. Regrettably, the predictable consequence of the Court's decision will be to exacerbate these effects. * * *

NOTES AND QUESTIONS

1. The decision in *Kelo* provoked a storm of protest, as internet bloggers, editorial writers, and politicians across the country condemned the decision as a threat to property rights. The U.S. House of Representatives passed a resolution expressing its "grave disapproval" of the decision,

and legislation was introduced in both Houses of Congress and in virtually every state to discourage or prohibit the use of eminent domain for economic development. By December, 2006, 34 states had adopted new laws or ballot measures in response to the *Kelo* decision. The responses are highly diverse, ranging from broad amendments to state constitutions prohibiting any use of eminent domain that yields a "private use" (New Hampshire) or a transfer to a "private party" (Nevada), to relatively minor adjustments in eminent domain procedures. Running tabulations of post-*Kelo* legislation are collected on the websites of the National Conference of State Legislatures (www.ncsl.org) and the Castle Coalition (www.castlecoali tion.org). What was it about the decision that accounts for this response? Was it the facts of the case, which were repeatedly reported in media accounts as suggesting that the petitioners' homes were being sacrificed to the whims of the Pfizer Corporation? Was it the rhetoric of Justice O'Connor's dissent, with its apocalyptic vision of a world in which every home is up for grabs if coveted by some real estate developer? Was it because the public has become increasingly skeptical of government efforts to intervene in the economy in order to promote economic growth or job creation? Whatever the explanation, the public repudiation of *Kelo* represents one of the most stunning instances of popular constitutionalism in our nation's history. Given this response, Justice O'Connor's dissent may offer a better guide to the future scope of eminent domain than does Justice Stevens' majority opinion. Indeed, in the first major state court decision after *Kelo*, *Norwood v. Horney*, 853 N.E.2d 1115 (Ohio 2006), the Ohio Supreme Court disavowed *Kelo*'s deferential approach to public use and held that, under the Ohio Constitution, property cannot be condemned solely for economic development.

2.   The aftermath in New London was also influenced by the public backlash against the Supreme Court's decision. Once the Court's mandate issued, the judgment of condemnation became final, and legal title to the properties passed to the City of New London. Nevertheless, a number of residents, including Susette Kelo and the Derys, refused to vacate their properties. In September 2005, the New London Development Corporation sought to force the issue by serving the former owners with eviction notices, and informing them that they would be held liable for rent for holding over in buildings now owned by the City. This triggered a new round of public outcry. Governor Jodi Rell ordered the Corporation to rescind the eviction notices, on pain of losing any further state redevelopment aid. The Governor then appointed a mediator to try to reach a compromise between the City and the former owners. Aided by a legal opinion from the state attorney general that the City could use redevelopment funds to negotiate settlements in amounts larger than the values set in the condemnation proceedings, the former owners gradually began to settle. In March 2006, Wilhelmina Dery died at the age of 89, in the same room in which she was born. Her family settled shortly thereafter. Finally, only two former owners, Susette Kelo and Michael Cristofaro, remained intransigent. The City Council voted in June 2006 to commence eviction proceedings against them. The Governor sought to broker a last minute

compromise, which the City rebuffed. The City combined its tough stance with sweetened settlement offers, which Kelo and Cristofaro accepted before any eviction could take place. The settlement with Kelo included an agreement by the City to pay to move her house to a new location, and forgive all claims of unpaid rents and taxes. One source reported the value of her settlement at $442,000, compared to the appraised value of her home of $123,000 in 2000. See Our View: Eminent Domain Ends Badly for Those Involved, Norwich Bulletin, August 29, 2006, at 7A. How, if at all, did the course of negotiations between the City and the former owners differ from what would have happened if the City had lost in the Supreme Court?

3.   In its most complete discussion of the public use requirement prior to *Kelo*, the Supreme Court had said that the public use requirement was "coterminous with the scope of the sovereign's police powers," and that courts should review exercises of eminent domain only to assure that they are "rationally related to a conceivable public purpose." Hawaii Housing Auth. v. Midkiff, 467 U.S. 229, 240, 242–43 (1984). (Interestingly, the Court's unanimous opinion in *Midkiff* was written by Justice O'Connor.) Courts understood this to mean that the Fifth Amendment's public use language required only the most deferential type of "rationality review," under which legislation is upheld as long as the court can conceive of a legitimate purpose the legislature might have harbored and a rational person might believe that the taking would achieve this purpose. Does *Kelo* reaffirm this highly deferential position, or does the Court suggest a more demanding standard of review?

4.   Note that the majority does not quote the line in *Berman* and *Midkiff* about eminent domain being coterminous with the police power, and Justice O'Connor, in her dissent, says "[t]his language was unnecessary to the specific holding" in *Midkiff* and "the police power and 'public use' cannot always be equated." The point the Court seemed to be making in *Berman* and *Midkiff* when it uttered these words was that the government could use the power of eminent domain to achieve any purpose within the permissible ends of government. Since government at all levels does all kinds of things to try to promote economic development, from regulating the money supply to providing tax incentives for new business investment to mandating that all children receive an education that allows them to be productive members of the workforce, the "coterminous powers" idea would seem to compel the conclusion that eminent domain can be used for economic development. Has the Court now embraced the notion that the power of eminent domain is narrower, in terms of the purposes for which it can be used, than the police power or the power to tax and spend? What is the justification for confining the power of eminent domain—which always requires the payment of just compensation—to a narrower sphere than the power to regulate or tax property—neither of which requires the payment of compensation?

5.   None of the opinions in *Kelo* discusses the holdout problem, which most commentators today regard as an important justification for the power of eminent domain. See Richard A. Posner, The Supreme Court 2004

Term, Foreword: A Political Court, 119 Harv. L. Rev. 31, 83–94 (2005). Did the New London redevelopment face a holdout problem? The NLRC acquired about 100 parcels in the 90–acre site through voluntary negotiations, but had reached an impasse with the nine owners of the last 15 parcels. Could it have built around these pockets of resistance? The answer is not clear, because it was not the focus of the judicial inquiry in the lower courts. One explanation for the need to acquire all parcels is that this would make the re-transfer to a developer more appealing, since the developer could then work on the equivalent of a greenfield site rather than have to make costly adjustments to accommodate existing structures. But this argument is just a matter of costs. As the Institute for Justice has noted in some of its public statements, the plan also called for the preservation of one structure—the Italian Dramatic Club—a private club patronized by many of the city's leading figures. So the project could have proceeded without the nonconsenting parcels, provided the City was prepared to offer additional subsidies to the developer. Another explanation is that much of the area is below the 100–year floodplain, and thus had to be re-graded in order to make it eligible for new development. Whether this could be accomplished without moving or at least jacking up existing structures is doubtful. Some type of coercion of the nonconsenting owners, whether through the use of eminent domain or the police power, may thus have been necessary to complete the project. Should courts pay more attention to the severity of the holdout problem in determining whether exercises in eminent domain are for a "public use"?

6. Does Justice O'Connor's dissenting opinion offer a normatively-justifiable theory of what "public use" means? Her opinion acknowledges that public use has been defined to mean public purpose, and that property can be condemned and retransferred to another private owner if there is a valid public purpose. But she insists that when public use is defined to mean public purpose, the purpose must be to rectify some "precondemnation use of the targeted property [that inflicts] affirmative harm on society." What is the constitutional theory that would justify restricting eminent domain to the rectification of undesirable conditions inherent in property or in the pattern of ownership of property, as opposed to the provision of public goods or positive externalities not attainable under the current pattern of ownership of property? What might Ronald Coase, see Chapter I, say about this distinction? Is this bad-prevention versus good-promotion distinction just a way to draw a line in the sand in order to avoid the slippery slopes Justice O'Connor perceives ahead if condemnation is permitted for economic development or other types of general public goods? If so, why draw the line at the bad/good distinction rather than some place else, such as the no-pretext formulation of the majority?

7. Would restricting eminent domain for economic development to cases involving blighted property protect minority and low-income neighborhoods, as Justices O'Connor implies? Or would minority and low-income neighborhoods be more likely to be targeted under a regime that requires a determination of "blight"? For evidence that traditional urban renewal programs, which typically begin with a determination that a neighborhood

is blighted, disproportionately affect poor and minority neighborhoods, see Wendell E. Pritchett, The Public Menace of Blight: Urban Renewal and the Private Uses of Eminent Domain, 21 Yale L. & Pol'y Rev. 1 (2003).

8. Many of the post-*Kelo* statutes and the Ohio Supreme Court's decision in *Norwood* prohibit the use of eminent domain for "economic development." What does this mean? Does it mean that economic development cannot be *a* purpose of condemnation? If so, then nearly all takings would be unconstitutional, since nearly all takings for highways or utility easements are motivated in part by a desire to encourage economic development. Does it mean that eminent domain cannot be the *sole* purpose of condemnation? But was economic development the sole purpose of the taking in New London? Would it be relatively easy to evade such a restriction, by tacking a public walkway or small park onto condemnation projects otherwise designed to further some commercial development?

9. Both Justice O'Connor and Justice Thomas argue that the words "for public use" would be meaningless unless they are understood to restrict the scope of the power of eminent domain. But why would these words be meaningless if they were understood to be a synonym for eminent domain? In other words, is it possible the Fifth Amendment can be read to say: Nor shall private property be taken *by eminent domain* without just compensation? This would not be a trivial provision: It would mandate just compensation whenever the government takes property by eminent domain (or by other processes tantamount to eminent domain), as opposed to in some other way, such as by committing a tort or by taxation. See Matthew P. Harrington, "Public Use" and the Original Understanding of the So–Called "Takings" Clause, 53 Hastings L.J. 1245 (2002). As long as we are looking closely at the language of the Fifth Amendment, why would the Framers put the word "without" before "just compensation," rather than before "public use," if public use were understood to be a restriction on the scope of the power of eminent domain? On the other hand, do such arguments mean that a taking from A to give to B would pass muster? Or are there some purpose-related limits implicit in "tak[ing] for public use"/eminent domain after all?

10. The actual drafting history of the Takings Clause is very thin. See David A. Dana & Thomas W. Merrill, Property: Takings ch. 2 (2002). Blackstone, on whom Justice Thomas relies, did not argue that eminent domain could be exercised only for public uses. Blackstone thought the power of condemnation required the constructive consent of the property owner, which could be obtained only through the approval of the legislature. 1 William Blackstone, Commentaries *135 (1768). The public use or public purpose requirement entered American law through the influence of natural rights jurists such as Grotius, Pufendorf, and Vattel. Dana & Merrill, supra at 19–22. These writers were the ones who first used the word "eminent domain," and this term, along with the movement to restrict eminent domain to actual public uses, entered American law in the 1830s. The debate over the original understanding of "for public use" thus may boil down to whether one thinks the Framers were more influenced by

Blackstone and Locke (who would require the consent of the legislature) or by continental thinkers like Grotius (who would require a public use or purpose).

11.   A federal statute, 28 U.S.C. § 1498, authorizes the federal government to use patented technology and copyrighted works without the owner's consent but upon payment of just compensation determined after the fact. The Supreme Court has analogized this statutory power to the exercise of the power of eminent domain. See Crozier v. Fried. Krupp Aktiengesellschaft, 224 U.S. 290, 307 (1912). Does this kind of blanket declaration that the federal government can take intellectual property rights for just compensation violate the requirement that each taking be justified by some public use? Or are intellectual property rights like patents and copyrights different, because they are in effect created by federal law? There is conflicting authority on this question. See generally Adam Mossoff, Patents as Constitutional Private Property: The Historical Protection of Patents under the Takings Clause (Draft, June 2006). Does it make a difference if the holder of the intellectual property right can still use the information himself? Or that the government takes only the right to use the information (for just compensation), but not the right to exclude others from using the information?

2.   JUST COMPENSATION

The other significant constitutional limitation on eminent domain is that the condemning authority must pay "just compensation." The following case discusses several difficult issues that arise in attempting to fix a "just" price on property when the owner and the condemning authority have not been able to negotiate a value acceptable to both sides.

United States v. Miller

Supreme Court of the United States, 1943.
317 U.S. 369.

■ MR. JUSTICE ROBERTS delivered the opinion of the Court. This case presents important questions respecting standards for valuing property taken for public use. * * *

The United States condemned a strip across the respondents' lands for tracks of the Central Pacific Railroad, relocation of which was necessary on account of the prospective flooding of the old right-of-way by waters to be impounded by the Central Valley Reclamation Project in California. * * *

In his report for the fiscal year ending June 30, 1937, the Secretary of the Interior stated that Shasta, California, had been selected for the site of the Sacramento River dam. Its construction involved relocation of some thirty miles of the line of the railroad.

Portions of respondents' lands were required for the relocated right-of-way. Alternate routes were surveyed by March 1936 and staked at intervals of 100 feet. Prior to the authorization of the project, the area of which respondents' tracts form a part was largely uncleared brush land. In the years 1936 and 1937 certain parcels were purchased with the intention of subdividing them and, in 1937, subdivisions were plotted and there grew up a settlement known as Boomtown, in which the respondents' lands lie. Two of the respondents were realtors interested in developing the neighborhood. By December 1938 the town had been built up for business and residential purposes.

December 14, 1938, the United States filed in the District Court for Northern California a complaint in eminent domain against the respondents and others whose lands were needed for the relocation of the railroad. On that day the Government also filed a declaration of taking. In this declaration the estimate of just compensation to be paid for a tract belonging to three of the respondents as co-tenants was estimated at $2,550 and that sum was deposited in court. On the application of these owners the court directed the Clerk to pay each of them one-third of the deposit, or $850, on account of the compensation they were entitled to receive.

The action in eminent domain was tried to a jury. The respondents offered opinion evidence as to the fair market value of the tracts involved and also as to severance damage to lots of which portions were taken. Each witness was asked to state his opinion as to market value of the land taken as at December 14, 1938, the date of the filing of the complaint. Government counsel objected to the form of the question on the ground that, as the United States was definitely committed to the project August 26, 1937, the respondents were not entitled to have included in an estimate of value, as of the date the lands were taken, any increment of value due to the Government's authorization of, and commitment to, the project. The trial court sustained the objection and required the question to be reframed so as to call for market value at the date of the taking, excluding therefrom any increment of value accruing after August 26, 1937, due to the authorization of the project. Under stress of the ruling, and over objection and exception, questions calling for opinion evidence were phrased to comply with the court's decision. The jury rendered verdicts in favor of various respondents.

The three respondents who had received $850 each on account of compensation were awarded less than the total paid them. The court entered judgment that title to the lands was in the United States and judgment in favor of respondents respectively for the amounts awarded them. Judgment was entered against the three respondents and in favor of the United States for the amounts they had received in excess of the verdicts with interest. They moved to set aside the money judgments against them on the ground that the court had no jurisdiction to enter them. The motions were overruled. All of the respondents appealed * * *

The Circuit Court of Appeals reversed the judgment holding, by a divided court, that the trial judge erred in his rulings and in his charge, and unanimously that the District Court was without jurisdiction to award the United States a judgment for amounts overpaid. A majority of the court were of opinion the witnesses should have been asked to state the fair market value of the lands as of the date of taking without qualification, and the judge should have charged that this value measured the compensation to which the respondents were entitled.

1.   The Fifth Amendment of the Constitution provides that private property shall not be taken for public use without just compensation. Such compensation means the full and perfect equivalent in money of the property taken. The owner is to be put in as good position pecuniarily as he would have occupied if his property had not been taken.

It is conceivable that an owner's indemnity should be measured in various ways depending upon the circumstances of each case and that no general formula should be used for the purpose. In an effort, however, to find some practical standard, the courts early adopted, and have retained, the concept of market value. The owner has been said to be entitled to the "value", the "market value", and the "fair market value" of what is taken. The term "fair" hardly adds anything to the phrase "market value", which denotes what "it fairly may be believed that a purchaser in fair market conditions would have given", or, more concisely, "market value fairly determined".

Respondents correctly say that value is to be ascertained as of the date of taking. But they insist that no element which goes to make up value as at that moment is to be discarded or eliminated. We think the proposition is too broadly stated. Where, for any reason, property has no market resort must be had to other data to ascertain its value; and, even in the ordinary case, assessment of market value involves the use of assumptions, which make it unlikely that the appraisal will reflect true value with nicety. It is usually said that market value is what a willing buyer would pay in cash to a willing seller. Where the property taken, and that in its vicinity, has not in fact been sold within recent times, or in significant amounts, the application of this concept involves, at best, a guess by informed persons.

Again, strict adherence to the criterion of market value may involve inclusion of elements which, though they affect such value, must in fairness by eliminated in a condemnation case, as where the formula is attempted to be applied as between an owner who may not want to part with his land because of its special adaptability to his own use, and a taker who needs the land because of its peculiar fitness for the taker's purposes. These elements must be disregarded by the fact finding body in arriving at "fair" market value.

Since the owner is to receive no more than indemnity for his loss, his award cannot be enhanced by any gain to the taker. Thus although the market value of the property is to be fixed with due consideration of all its available uses, its special value to the condemnor as distinguished from others who may or may not possess the power to condemn, must be excluded as an element of market value. The district judge so charged the jury and no question is made as to the correctness of the instruction.

There is, however, another possible element of market value, which is the bone of contention here. Should the owner have the benefit of any increment of value added to the property taken by the action of the public authority in previously condemning adjacent lands? If so, were the lands in question so situate as to entitle respondents to the benefit of this increment?

Courts have to adopt working rules in order to do substantial justice in eminent domain proceedings. One of these is that a parcel of land which has been used and treated as an entity shall be so considered in assessing compensation for the taking of part or all of it.

This has begotten subsidiary rules. If only a portion of a single tract is taken the owner's compensation for that taking includes any element of value arising out of the relation of the part taken to the entire tract. Such damage is often, though somewhat loosely, spoken of as severance damage. On the other hand, if the taking has in fact benefited the remainder the benefit may be set off against the value of the land taken.

As respect other property of the owner consisting of separate tracts adjoining that affected by the taking, the Constitution has never been construed as requiring payment of consequential damages; and unless the legislature so provides, as it may, benefits are not assessed against such neighboring tracts for increase in their value.

If a distinct tract is condemned, in whole or in part, other lands in the neighborhood may increase in market value due to the proximity of the public improvement erected on the land taken. Should the Government, at a later date, determine to take these other lands, it must pay their market value as enhanced by this factor of proximity. If, however, the public project from the beginning included the taking of certain tracts but only one of them is taken in the first instance, the owner of the other tracts should not be allowed an increased value for his lands which are ultimately to be taken any more than the owner of the tract first condemned is entitled to be allowed an increased market value because adjacent lands not immediately taken increased in value due to the projected improvement.

The question then is whether the respondents' lands were probably within the scope of the project from the time the Government was committed to it. If they were not, but were merely adjacent lands, the subsequent enlargement of the project to include them ought not to deprive the respondents of the value added in the meantime by the proximity of the improvement. If, on the other hand, they were, the Government ought not to pay any increase in value arising from the known fact that the lands probably would be condemned. The owners ought not to gain by speculating on probable increase in value due to the Government's activities.

In which category do the lands in question fall? The project, from the date of its final and definite authorization in August 1937, included the relocation of the railroad right-of-way, and one probable route was marked out over the respondents' lands. This being so, it was proper to tell the jury that the respondents were entitled to no increase in value arising after August 1937 because of the likelihood of the taking of their property. If their lands were probably to be taken for public use, in order to complete the project in its entirety, any increase in value due to that fact could only arise from speculation by them, or by possible purchasers from then, as to what the Government would be compelled to pay as compensation. * * *

2. We think the court below erred in holding the District Court without power to enter a judgment against three of the respondents to whom payments in excess of the jury's verdicts had been made out of the funds deposited with the Court.

Examination of the Act of February 26, 1931, discloses that the declaration of taking is to be filed in the proceeding for condemnation at its inception or at any later time. When the declaration is filed the amount of estimated compensation is to be deposited with the court to be paid as the court may order "for or on account" of the just compensation to be awarded the owners. Thus the acquisition by the Government of title and immediate right to possession, and the deposit of the estimated compensation, occur as steps in the main proceeding.

The purpose of the statute is twofold. First, to give the Government immediate possession of the property and to relieve it of the burden of interest accruing on the sum deposited from the date of taking to the date of judgment in the eminent domain proceeding. Secondly, to give the former owner, if his title is clear, immediate cash compensation to the extent of the Government's estimate of the value of the property. The Act recognizes that there may be an error in the estimate and appropriately provides that, if the judgment ultimately awarded shall be in excess of the amount deposited, the owner shall recover the excess with interest. But there is no correlative provision for repayment of any excess by the owner to the United States. The necessary result is, so the respondents say, that any sum paid them in excess of the jury's award is their property, which the United States may not recover.

All the provisions of the Act taken together require a contrary conclusion. The payment is of estimated compensation; it is intended as a provisional and not a final settlement with the owner; it is a payment "on account of" compensation and not a final settlement of the amount due. To hold otherwise would defeat the policy of the statute and work injustice; would be to encourage federal officials to underestimate the value of the property with the result that the Government would be saddled with interest on a larger sum from date of taking to final award, and would be to deny the owner the immediate use of cash approximating the value of his land.

Respondents assert that whatever the substantive right of the United States to repayment of the surplus, the District Court in rendering judgment against them deprived them of property without due process of law. We think the contention is unsound.

The District Court was dealing with money deposited in its chancery to be disbursed under its direction in connection with an action pending before it. The situation is like that in which litigants deposit money as security or to await the outcome of litigation. Notwithstanding the fact that the court released the fund to the respondents, the parties were still before it and it did not lose control of the fund but retained jurisdiction to deal with its retention or repayment as justice might require.

Denial of notice and hearing is asserted. But, while it is true that the court included the judgment of restitution in its general judgment in the condemnation proceedings without notice to the parties or hearing, the respondents made motions to set aside the judgment against them, and the court heard and acted on the motions. The respondents had full opportunity to urge any meritorious reasons why judgment of restitution should not be entered against them. We think they were entitled to no more. * * *

The judgment of the Circuit Court of Appeals is reversed and that of the District Court affirmed.

NOTES AND QUESTIONS

1. The idea of "fair market value" as the measure of just compensation is inherently paradoxical. Eminent domain is typically used when negotiations for a market transaction break down, so by definition there is no "market value" in the sense of an arm's length negotiated price for the property in question. Instead, fair market value refers to a hypothetical price—a guess about what the property would have fetched if it had followed the path of voluntary rather than compelled exchange. Real estate appraisers have developed a variety of approaches for estimating fair market value. The most common are (1) examining recent transactions in which the property in question was sold, and adjusting for general changes in market prices in the area since the date of those transactions; (2) examining recent transactions of other parcels of property in the area similar to the property in question, and adjusting for differences in size, location, and quality of improvements; (3) estimating the rental value of the property in question, and capitalizing this to reach a purchase price using a rate of return commonly used as a benchmark for real estate investments in the area; (4) determining the replacement cost of the land and improvements taken, and adjusting downward to reflect depreciation due to age and wear and tear. See 4 Julius L. Sackman, Nichols on Eminent Domain § 12.02 (3d ed. 2005); 1 Lewis Orgel, Valuation Under the Law of Eminent Domain §§ 136–38, 176–87 (James C. Bonbright ed., 2d ed. 1953); 2 id. §§ 188–89.

2. In economic terms, the *Miller* Court can be read as saying that the owner should be awarded the *opportunity cost* of having his land taken away. The opportunity cost is the highest and best use of the land *other than* the use proposed by the condemning authority. See, e.g., Armen A. Alchian, Cost, in 3 International Encyclopedia of the Social Sciences 404, 404 (David L. Sills ed., 1968) ("[T]he cost of an event is the highest-valued opportunity necessarily forsaken."). Thus, suppose the property is currently being used as a farm, the highest and best use would be as a suburban subdivision, and the government proposes to take the land for a highway. On condemnation, the government must pay the value the land would

obtain if sold for development as a subdivision, the highest and best use (other than as a highway). What might be the justification for basing compensation awards on opportunity costs, rather than on the existing use of the land?

3. The *Miller* Court also concludes that just compensation means that the owner is not entitled to an award based on the after-condemnation value of property in the area. Thus, for example, if the current use of the land is "uncleared brush land," and the government proposes to take the land for a reservoir project, the value should be based on the highest and best use of uncleared brush land, not the value of land next to a government reservoir. The intuition behind this is that awarding the condemnee the value of land next to a reservoir would confer a windfall on the condemnee. The condemnee has done nothing to create this enhanced value—it is a product of the capital, labor, and initiative that will be expended by the government in building the dam, which will be paid for by the taxpayers. Valuing condemned property on a post-condemnation basis would also be self-defeating, insofar as the public benefits of the taking would be capitalized in the land values and transferred to the condemnee.

4. The issue in *Miller* is trickier. Suppose the government builds the reservoir, paying for the land according to its pre-reservoir value. Then, one year later, the government decides to build a highway around the edge of the reservoir. What is the proper valuation of the land taken for the highway—uncleared brush land in the middle of nowhere or land in the vicinity of a reservoir? Here it seems clear that, under the opportunity-cost approach, the proper value is the value of land in the vicinity of a reservoir. See Christopher Serkin, The Meaning of Value: Assessing Just Compensation for Regulatory Takings, 99 Nw. U. L. Rev. 677, 688–89 (2005). But doesn't this also confer a windfall on the condemnee? Perhaps it does, if we focus on the original cost of the land to the condemnee, and the fact that the newly-enhanced value of the land is largely attributable to the capital and labor the government expended in creating the reservoir. Yet there is nevertheless a strong efficiency argument for awarding the condemnee the current value of the land: We want the government to select a route for the highway that takes into account all the costs of building the highway, including the costs of land. Perhaps there is a better route for the highway further away from the reservoir, one that goes through cheaper land that has fewer alternative uses. Pricing the land at its current opportunity cost sends the right signals on highway location to the government. Note too that if the condemnee had sold the land between the time the reservoir was built and the highway project was announced, the condemnee would have obtained a price that reflects the value of land in the vicinity of a reservoir, not the price of uncleared brush land in the middle of nowhere. So in this sense there is no windfall. Do you see now why the critical issue in *Miller* is whether the substitute right-of-way for the railroad was part of the original project, as opposed to being a separate project that arose after the reservoir was built?

5. Ordinarily, as the Court notes, the temporal reference point for determining fair market value is the date at which title transfers. Does the Court inject an element of indeterminacy into the rules for determining just compensation by departing from this reference point in determining whether the respondents' property was part of a single government project? For these purposes, the Court says that the temporal reference point is "the time the Government was committed to" the project. Isn't it likely that the government's "commitment" to a project like a major reservoir solidifies gradually over time, making the Court's test inherently problematic? Why was the Court willing to subject eminent domain to the added administrative costs of its "committed to the project" test? Was it simply a dislike of rewarding land speculators? Or is there a more substantive reason for moving the temporal reference point for the scope of the project to an earlier point in time than the transfer of title? See Serkin, The Meaning of Value, supra at 696–99.

6. Is it possible to distinguish between two types of value created by a project made possible by eminent domain? One is the value provided by the transformed use made possible by the project—such as the reservoir created in *Miller*. The other would be the value created by assembling a number of small parcels of land into a single large parcel, which can then be devoted to any number of possible uses, such as a reservoir, or a new town, or a corporate research park. The Supreme Court's cases strongly suggest that the "assembly gain" from the use of eminent domain is also an increment in value that belongs to the condemning authority. See City of New York v. Sage, 239 U.S. 57 (1915). But is this so clear? The transformed use value is clearly something created primarily by the efforts of the condemning authority. The assembly gain, by contrast, is created by the joint effort of the condemning authority and the individual owners of the parcels whose land is taken. Awarding 100 percent of the assembly gain to the condemning authority may constitute an implicit subsidy to the use of eminent domain, which may encourage overuse of the power (perhaps for condemn-and-retransfer schemes like those discussed in *Kelo*). Should the assembly value go to the condemnee rather than the condemnor, or should it be divided or apportioned in some way between the parties rather than awarded entirely to the condemnor?

7. Another objection to the fair-market-value formula is that it provides no recovery for the subjective value that owners attach to their property. Most people attach some premium above market value to property they own. Otherwise, they would sell for market value. The premium may be based on the fact that they are psychologically attached to the property, or they like the neighborhood, or they have made special modifications to the property to suit their particular needs, or simply because they want to avoid the inconvenience of moving. Under the fair-market-value standard, no compensation is given for this subjective premium above market value. Most commentators therefore have assumed that the fair market value measure results in systematic undercompensation of property owners, especially where the property is occupied by a residence or a functioning business. See Lee Anne Fennell, Taking Eminent Domain

Apart, 2004 Mich. St. L. Rev. 957, 960–79. Does the problem of uncompensated subjective value suggest that condemnation of certain kinds of property likely to have high subjective value should be off limits or subject to a higher standard of review under the public use requirement? See Margaret Jane Radin, Property and Personhood, 34 Stan L. Rev. 957 (1982) (excerpted in Chapter III). Would private residential homes be included in this category? What about a small family business or a family farm that has been in the same family for many years?

8. A less drastic proposal for dealing with the problem of subjective value would be to pay a bonus above fair market value at least in certain categories of takings. See, e.g., Robert C. Ellickson, Alternatives to Zoning: Covenants, Nuisance Rules, and Fines as Land Use Controls, 40 U. Chi. L. Rev. 681, 736–37 (1973). Some of the Mill Acts mentioned in *Kelo* (footnote 8, omitted in the excerpt) provided for such bonus compensation. See Head v. Amoskeag Mfg. Co., 113 U.S. 9 (1885) (quoting New Hampshire Mill Act, providing that compensation be set at 150% of appraised value). But would such a system of bonus compensation create a risk of overcompensating property owners who, for whatever reason, do not attach much subjective value to their holdings? The federal government and many states have partially responded to the undercompensation problem by enacting relocation acts, which give persons whose property is condemned additional monies for some transitional expenses like moving costs. See Uniform Relocation Assistance Act of 1970, 42 U.S.C. 4601 et seq. A recent study suggests that property owners, aided by generous interpretations of federal and state relocation acts, often receive substantial premiums above fair market value, especially where takings are politically controversial. See Nicole Stelle Garnett, The Neglected Political Economy of Eminent Domain, 105 Mich. L. Rev. 101 (2006). Does this suggest that caution is in order before mandating additional awards of bonus compensation?

9. The reasons for sticking to fair market value and denying any compensation for assembly gain or subjective values are several. The reason mentioned most often in the cases is the difficulty of valuing things like subjective value or consequential damages. Including such increments of value would therefore increase the administrative costs of eminent domain proceedings. See, e.g., United States v. 564.54 Acres of Land, 441 U.S. 506, 516–17 (1979) (declining to award replacement cost in condemnation of a summer camp). But a more important reason harkens back to the public use issue again. We presume eminent domain will be used only for public uses public projects like highways and schools that provide public goods that benefit everyone in the community. These sorts of projects arguably deserve public subsidies, and one form the subsidies can take is by providing less than full indemnification to those whose property is condemned to make way for the project. So there is a linkage between the public use limitation and incomplete compensation for takings. See Thomas W. Merrill, Incomplete Compensation for Takings, 11 N.Y.U. Envtl. L.J. 110 (2002). The stronger the public use limit, the stronger the case for incomplete compensation. Does it follow that a weak public use justification, like the one upheld in *Kelo*, should be coupled with a more complete

measure of just compensation? For an argument to this effect, see James E. Krier & Christopher Serkin, Public Ruses, 2004 Mich. St. L. Rev. 859.

10. *Miller* discusses another problem: how to determine just compensation when the government takes a *portion* of a parcel rather than the whole thing. Here, the established rule is that the landowner is entitled to the fair market value of what is taken plus so-called "severance damages" for any loss in value to the part that is not taken. 4A Julius L. Sackman, Nichols on Eminent Domain § 14A.03 (3d ed. 2005). As the Court observes, many jurisdictions, including the federal government, will also make adjustments for any offsetting benefits that the taking creates for the portion that is not taken. The easiest way to implement these partial takings rules is to compute the fair market value of the parcel before the taking, the fair market value of the parcel after the taking, and award the difference to the condemnee. See Merrill, Incomplete Compensation for Takings, supra, at 121–24. As *Miller* observes, the rules for partial takings apply only when a partial taking affects a single parcel. If a landowner owns two different parcels, any damage that a taking on one parcel does to the second parcel is not compensated (nor are offsetting benefits to the second parcel recouped). What is the rationale for the "single parcel" rule in applying the special rules for partial takings?

11. What happens if the government condemns land that is subject to divided ownership? The established rule here is that all owners of the condemned property are entitled to share in the just compensation. See Victor P. Goldberg et al., Bargaining in the Shadow of Eminent Domain: Valuing and Apportioning Condemnation Awards Between Landlord and Tenant, 34 UCLA L. Rev. 1083 (1987). Thus, for example, if the property is divided between a landlord and a tenant, the government will award the value of an undivided fee simple, and the landlord and tenant will then split this award in accordance with present value of their respective interests in the land. Note that this rule creates a type of "assembly gain" insofar as the value of an unrestricted fee simple may be greater than the sum of the fractional ownership interests in the property valued separately. Yet here, the assembly gain is awarded to the condemnees, not to the condemning authority. Is there a justification for awarding the assembly gain created by overcoming legal divisions in the ownership of the property to the condemnees, while awarding the assembly gain from overcoming the transaction costs of assembling multiple parcels of land into a single large parcel to the condemnor?

QUICK TAKE STATUTES

The condemnation in *Miller* occurred pursuant to the federal version of what are called "quick take" statutes. These statutes, which also exist in a majority of states, are designed to streamline eminent domain proceedings by transferring title to the condemning authority before all contested issues raised by the condemnation have been resolved. See Goodwill Community Chapel v. General Motors Corp., 503 N.W.2d 705, 707 (Mich. Ct. App. 1993); 6 Julius L. Sackman, Nichols on Eminent Domain 24.10 (3d ed. 2005). For many years, it was assumed that due process requires that persons whose property is taken are entitled to a hearing on issues like public use and the measure of compensation before title to the property passes to the condemning authority. This assumption gave property owners considerable leverage, since the more issues they raised in the pre-condemnation hearing, the longer the condemning authority would have to wait to get title to the property. The result was that condemned owners were able to negotiate relatively favorable settlements with the government about the value of their property.

Governments responded by enacting quick take statutes. These statutes generally provide that if the government deposits with the court the estimated value of the property, and the court is satisfied that the government has legal authority to condemn and that the project is for a public use, then the government can obtain title to the property before a final judgment fixing the amount of compensation is reached. As soon as the title transfers, the condemned party must move out. He collects the money deposited with the court, and then, as the respondents did in *Miller*, can continue to litigate the question of whether the compensation is adequate. If the government's estimate reflected in the money deposited with the court is too low, then the government must make up the difference (with interest) once a final judgment is entered. *Miller* holds that if the government's estimate turns out to be too high, the government is entitled to sue to get the money back. (Note that this is another example of the principle of restitution.)

When quick take statutes were initially adopted, the Supreme Court turned away due process challenges, reasoning that a post-deprivation remedy in the form of just compensation is all the Constitution requires. See, e.g., Bragg v. Weaver, 251 U.S. 57 (1919); Sweet v. Rechel, 159 U.S. 380, 395 (1895). Thus, it is settled that there is no due process violation when the government takes title before the amount of compensation is finally determined, provided it deposits a fair estimate of just compensation with the court and the taking is otherwise legally justified. But what if the condemnation is not legally justified, for example because the public use requirement is not met? Shouldn't property owners be entitled to a hearing to challenge the statutory authority for the condemnation and the government's assertion of a public use before title passes, even in the quick take situation? The Supreme Court has not addressed this question directly. See 6 Julius L. Sackman, Nichols on Eminent Domain 24.10[2] (3d ed. 2005); Nicole Stelle Garnett, The Public–Use Question as a Takings Problem, 71 Geo. Wash. L. Rev. 934, 970–74 (2003). Arguably, the scope of the public use requirement should be inversely related to the due process entitlement to a prior hearing. The broader the understanding of public use, the less the need for a prior hearing to determine if the taking is warranted. Thus, if state courts and legislatures respond to *Kelo* by narrowing the scope of permissible uses of eminent domain, this will increase the rationale for due process hearings before title transfers. In *Norwood v. Horney*, 853 N.E.2d 1115 (Ohio 2006), the Ohio Supreme Court, in the course of narrowing the meaning of public use as a matter of Ohio law, also held that an Ohio quick take statute prohibiting judicial stays pending appeal to challenge a public use determination violates state separation of powers doctrine. Could this be a harbinger of things to come?

Like other forms of American litigation, nearly all condemnation actions settle before trial. Curtis J. Berger & Patrick J. Rohan, The Nassau County Study: An Empirical Look Into the Practices of Condemnation, 67 Colum. L. Rev. 430, 458 n.60 (1967). Most persons whose property is slated for a taking agree to sell without the government having to file an eminent domain action. Of course, the amount they receive in the negotiated sale is affected by the shadow cast by a possible eminent domain action. Even if a voluntary transfer is not reached, and the government files a condemnation proceeding, most persons settle with the government, usually after some preliminary legal skirmishing, rather than going to trial. In most cases that go to trial, the amount of compensation will be fixed at some level between the government's figure and the owner's figure. Patricia Munch, An Economic Analysis of Eminent Domain, 84 J. Pol. Econ. 473 (1976) (finding that owners of high-valued properties received higher than market value but indigent owners received less than market value due to costs of litigation). Both sides know this, and can save legal fees by reaching a settlement that approximates what the court would determine after a trial. The main significance of quick take statutes is that they alter the relative bargaining power of the government and the individual property owner. In most condemnations, the amount of compensation is the only disputable issue. By allowing the government to take title to the property before this issue is resolved, the government's bargaining power relative to that of the owner is significantly enhanced. To the extent that due process concerns require modifications in quick take procedures, the balance of power will shift back somewhat to property owners.

B. REGULATORY TAKINGS—THE BASIC CONTOURS

The regulatory takings doctrine derives from the understanding that the government's power of eminent domain is distinct from its police power. When the power of eminent domain is exercised, the Fifth Amendment explicitly requires that the government pay "just compensation" for the property taken. But when the government regulates property under the police power—for example, when it adopts zoning or other regulations designed to reduce negative externalities associated with incompatible land uses—then it is understood that there is no constitutional requirement that the government compensate property owners for losses they may suffer due to the regulations. But where is the line that divides the exercise of eminent domain from the use of the police power? Basically, the regulatory takings doctrine says that if the government regulates property in an especially severe way, the regulation will be deemed to be a "taking" of private property, just as if the government had exercised the power of eminent domain. When this happens, the government must pay the owner just compensation for the value of the property taken, just as it would if the government had instituted a formal eminent domain proceeding. (For this reason, the regulatory takings doctrine is sometimes called the "inverse condemnation" doctrine.)

Virtually everything about the regulatory takings doctrine is controversial, including its origins. There is little evidence that regulations of the use of property—even quite severe ones—were thought to require compensation in the colonial era or at the time of the adoption of the Constitution. See John F. Hart, Colonial Land Use Law and its Significance for Modern Takings Doctrine, 109 Harv. L. Rev. 1252 (1996); William Michael Treanor, The Original Understanding of the Takings Clause and the Political Process, 95 Colum. L. Rev. 782 (1995). Some claim the regulatory takings doctrine can be traced in state court decisions decided in the middle of the nineteenth century. See Kris W. Kobach, The Origins of Regulatory Takings: Setting the Record Straight, 1996 Utah L. Rev. 1211. But most observers would agree that the Supreme Court's 1922 decision in *Mahon*, reproduced below, is where the modern doctrine began to take shape.

Pennsylvania Coal Co. v. Mahon

Supreme Court of the United States, 1922.
260 U.S. 393.

■ MR. JUSTICE HOLMES delivered the opinion of the Court. This is a bill in equity brought by the defendants in error to prevent the Pennsylvania Coal Company from mining under their property in such way as to remove the supports and cause a subsidence of the surface and of their house. The bill sets out a deed executed by the Coal Company in 1878, under which the plaintiffs claim. The deed conveys the surface but in express terms reserves the right to remove all the coal under the same and the grantee takes the premises with the risk and waives all claim for damages that may arise from mining out the coal. But the plaintiffs say that whatever may have been the Coal Company's rights, they were taken away by an Act of Pennsylvania, approved May 27, 1921 (P. L. 1198), commonly known there as the Kohler Act. * * *

The statute forbids the mining of anthracite coal in such way as to cause the subsidence of, among other things, any structure used as a human habitation, with certain exceptions, including among them land where the surface is owned by the owner of the underlying coal and is distant more than one hundred and fifty feet from any improved property belonging to any other person. As applied to this case the statute is admitted to destroy previously existing rights of property and contract. The question is whether the police power can be stretched so far.

Government hardly could go on if to some extent values incident to property could not be diminished without paying for every such change in the general law. As long recognized some values are enjoyed under an implied limitation and must yield to the police power. But obviously the implied limitation must have its limits or the contract and due process clauses are gone. One fact for consideration in determining such limits is the extent of the diminution. When it reaches a certain magnitude, in most if not in all cases there must be an exercise of eminent domain and compensation to sustain the act. So the question depends upon the particular facts. The greatest weight is given to the judgment of the legislature but it always is open to interested parties to contend that the legislature has gone beyond its constitutional power.

This is the case of a single private house. No doubt there is a public interest even in this * * *. But usually in ordinary private affairs the public interest does not warrant much of this kind of interference. A source of damage to such a house is not a public nuisance even if similar damage is inflicted on others in different places. The damage is not common or public. Wesson v. Washburn Iron Co., 13 Allen 96, 103 (Mass.). The extent of the public interest is shown by the statute to be limited, since the statute ordinarily does not apply to land when the surface is owned by the owner of the coal. Furthermore, it is not justified as a protection of personal safety. That could be provided for by notice. Indeed the very foundation of this bill is that the defendant gave timely notice of its intent to mine under the house. On the other hand the extent of the taking is great. It purports to abolish what is recognized in Pennsylvania as an estate in land—a very valuable estate—and what is declared by the Court below to be a contract hitherto binding the plaintiffs. If we were called upon to deal with the plaintiffs' position alone we should think it clear that the statute does not disclose a public interest sufficient to warrant so extensive a destruction of the defendant's constitutionally protected rights.

But the case has been treated as one in which the general validity of the act should be discussed. The Attorney General of the State, the City of Scranton and the representatives of other extensive interests were allowed to take part in the argument below and have submitted their contentions here. It seems, therefore, to be our duty to go farther in the statement of our opinion, in order that it may be known at once, and that further suits should not be brought in vain.

It is our opinion that the act cannot be sustained as an exercise of the police power, so far as it affects the mining of coal under streets or cities in places where the right to mine such coal has been reserved. As said in a Pennsylvania case, "For practical purposes, the right to coal consists in the right to mine it." Commonwealth v. Clearview Coal Co., 256 Pa. 328, 331. What makes the right to mine coal valuable is that it can be exercised with profit. To make it commercially impracticable to mine certain coal has very nearly the same effect for constitutional purposes as appropriating or destroying it. This we think that we are warranted in assuming that the statute does.

It is true that in Plymouth Coal Co. v. Pennsylvania, 232 U.S. 531, it was held competent for the legislature to require a pillar of coal to be left along the line of adjoining property, that with the pillar on the other side of the line would be a barrier sufficient for the safety of the employees of either mine in case the other should be abandoned and allowed to fill with water. But that was a requirement for the safety of employees invited into the mine, and secured an average reciprocity of advantage that has been recognized as a justification of various laws.

The rights of the public in a street purchased or laid out by eminent domain are those that it has paid for. If in any case its representatives have been so short sighted as to acquire only surface rights without the right of support we see no more authority for supplying the latter without compensation than there was for taking the right of way in the first place and refusing to pay for it because the public wanted it very much. The protection of private property in the Fifth Amendment presupposes that it is wanted for public use, but provides that it shall not be taken for such use without compensation. A similar assumption is made in the decisions upon the Fourteenth Amendment. Hairston v. Danville & Western Ry. Co., 208 U.S. 598, 605. When this seemingly absolute protection is found to be qualified by the police power, the natural tendency of human nature is to extend the qualification more and more until at last private property disappears. But that cannot be accomplished in this way under the Constitution of the United States.

The general rule at least is that while property may be regulated to a certain extent, if regulation goes too far it will be recognized as a taking. It may be doubted how far exceptional cases, like the blowing up of a house to stop a conflagration, go—and if they go beyond the general rule, whether they do not stand as much upon tradition as upon principle. Bowditch v. Boston, 101 U.S. 16. In general it is not plain that a man's misfortunes or necessities will justify his shifting the damages to his neighbor's shoulders. Spade v. Lynn & Boston Ry. Co., 172 Mass. 488, 489, 52 N.E. 747. We are in danger of forgetting that a strong public desire to improve the public condition is not enough to warrant achieving the desire by a shorter cut than the constitutional way of paying for the change. As we already have said this is a question of degree—and therefore cannot be disposed of by general propositions. But we regard this as going beyond any of the cases decided by this Court. The late decisions upon laws dealing with the congestion of Washington and New York, caused by the war, dealt with laws intended to meet a temporary emergency and providing for compensation determined to be reasonable by an impartial board. They were to the verge of the law but fell far short of the present act. Block & Hirsh, 256 U.S. 135; Marcus Brown Holding Co. v. Feldman, 256 U.S. 170; Levy Leasing Co. v. Siegel, 258 U.S. 242, March 20, 1922.

We assume, of course, that the statute was passed upon the conviction that an exigency existed that would warrant it, and we assume that an exigency exists that would warrant the exercise of eminent domain. But the question at bottom is upon whom the loss of the changes desired should fall. So far as private persons or communities have seen fit to take the risk of acquiring only surface rights, we cannot see that the fact that their risk has become a danger warrants the giving to them greater rights than they bought.

Decree reversed.

■ MR. JUSTICE BRANDEIS dissenting. The Kohler Act prohibits, under certain conditions, the mining of anthracite coal within the limits of a city in such a manner or to such an extent "as to cause the * * * subsidence of * * * any dwelling or other structure used as a human habitation, or any factory, store, or other industrial or mercantile establishment in which human labor is employed." Act Pa. May 27, 1921, § 1 (P. L. 1198). Coal in place is land, and the right of the owner to use his land is not absolute. He may not so use it as to create a public nuisance, and uses, once harmless, may, owing to changed conditions, seriously threaten the public welfare. Whenever they do, the Legislature has power to prohibit such uses without paying compensation; and the power to prohibit extends alike to the manner, the character and the purpose of the use. Are we justified in declaring that the Legislature of Pennsylvania has, in restricting the right to mine anthracite, exercised this power so arbitrarily as to violate the Fourteenth Amendment?

Every restriction upon the use of property imposed in the exercise of the police power deprives the owner of some right theretofore enjoyed, and is, in that sense, an abridgment by the state of rights in property without making compensation. But restriction imposed to protect the public health, safety or morals from dangers threatened is not a taking. The restriction here in question is merely the prohibition of a noxious use. The property so restricted remains in the possession of its owner. The state does not appropriate it or make any use of it. The state merely prevents the owner from making a use which interferes with paramount rights of the public. Whenever the use prohibited ceases to be noxious—as it may because of further change in local or social conditions—the restriction will have to be removed and the owner will again be free to enjoy his property as heretofore.

The restriction upon the use of this property cannot, of course, be lawfully imposed, unless its purpose is to protect the public. But the purpose of a restriction does not cease to be public, because incidentally some private persons may thereby receive gratuitously valuable special benefits. Thus, owners of low buildings may obtain, through statutory restrictions upon the height of neighboring structures, benefits equivalent to an easement of light and air. Welch v. Swasey, 214 U.S. 91. Compare Lindsley v. Natural Carbonic Gas Co., 220 U.S. 61; Walls v. Midland Carbon Co., 254 U.S. 300. Furthermore, a restriction, though imposed for a public purpose, will not be lawful, unless the restriction is an appropriate means to the public end. But to keep coal in place is surely an appropriate means of preventing subsidence of the surface; and ordinarily it is the only available means. Restriction upon use does not become inappropriate as a means, merely because it deprives the owner of the only use to which the property can then be profitably put. The liquor and the oleomargine cases settled that. Mugler v. Kansas, 123 U.S. 623, 668, 669; Powell v. Pennsylvania, 127 U.S. 678; see also Hadacheck v. Los Angeles, 239 U.S. 394; Pierce Oil Corporation v. City of Hope, 248 U.S. 498. Nor is a restriction imposed through exercise of the police power inappropriate as a means, merely because the same end might be effected through exercise of the power of eminent domain, or otherwise at public expense. Every restriction upon the height of buildings might be secured through acquiring by eminent domain the right of each owner to build above the limiting height; but it is settled that the state need not resort to that power. Compare Laurel Hill Cemetery v. San Francisco, 216 U.S. 358; Missouri Pacific Railway Co. v. Omaha, 235 U.S. 121. If by mining anthracite coal the owner would necessarily unloose poisonous gases, I suppose no one would doubt the power of the state to prevent the mining, without buying his coal fields. And why may not the state, likewise, without paying compensation, prohibit one from digging so deep or excavating so near the surface, as to expose the community to like dangers? In the latter case, as in the former, carrying on the business would be a public nuisance.

It is said that one fact for consideration in determining whether the limits of the police power have been exceeded is the extent of the resulting diminution in value, and that here the restriction destroys existing rights of property and contract. But values are relative. If we are to consider the value of the coal kept in place by the restriction, we should compare it with the value of all other parts of the land. That is, with the value not of the coal alone, but with the value of the whole property. The rights of an owner as against the public are not increased by dividing the interests in his property into surface and subsoil. The sum of the rights in the parts can not be greater than the rights in the whole. The estate of an owner in land is grandiloquently described as extending ab orco usque ad coelum. But I suppose no one would contend that by selling his interest above 100 feet from the surface he could prevent the state from limiting, by the police power, the height of structures in a city. And why should a sale of underground rights bar the state's power? For aught that appears the value of the coal kept in place by the restriction may be negligible as compared with the value of the whole property, or even as compared with that part of it which is represented by the coal remaining in place and which may be extracted despite the statute. * * *

Nor can existing contracts between private individuals preclude exercise of the police power. "One whose rights, such as they are, are subject to state restriction cannot remove them from the power of the state by making a contract about them." Hudson Water Co. v. McCarter, 209 U.S. 349, 357; Knoxville Water Co. v. Knoxville, 189 U.S. 434, 438; Rast v. Van Deman & Lewis Co., 240 U.S. 342. The fact that this suit is brought by a private person is, of course, immaterial. To protect the community through invoking the aid, as litigant, of interested private citizens is not a novelty in our law. That it may be done in Pennsylvania was decided by its Supreme Court in this case. And it is for a state to say how its public policy shall be enforced.

This case involves only mining which causes subsidence of a dwelling house. But the Kohler Act contains provisions in addition to that quoted above; and as to these, also, an opinion is expressed. These provisions deal with mining under cities to such an extent as to cause subsidence of—

(a) Any public building or any structure customarily used by the public as a place of resort, assemblage, or amusement, including, but not limited to, churches, schools, hospitals, theaters, hotels, and railroad stations.

(b) Any street, road, bridge, or other public passageway, dedicated to public use or habitually used by the public.

(c) Any track, roadbed, right of way, pipe, conduit, wire, or other facility, used in the service of the public by any municipal corporation or public service company as defined by the Public Service Law, section 1.

A prohibition of mining which causes subsidence of such structures and facilities is obviously enacted for a public purpose; and it seems, likewise, clear that mere notice of intention to mine would not in this connection secure the public safety. Yet it is said that these provisions of the act cannot be sustained as an exercise of the police power where the right to mine such coal has been reserved. The conclusion seems to rest upon the assumption that in order to justify such exercise of the police power there must be "an average reciprocity of advantage" as between the owner of the property restricted and the rest of the community; and that here such reciprocity is absent. Reciprocity of advantage is an important consideration, and may even be an essential, where the state's power is exercised for the purpose of conferring benefits upon the property of a neighborhood, as in drainage projects (Wurts v. Hoagland, 114 U.S. 606; Fallbrook Irrigation District v. Bradley, 164 U.S. 112,); or upon adjoining owners, as by party wall provisions (Jackman v. Rosenbaum Co., 260 U.S. 22). But where the police power is exercised, not to confer benefits upon property owners but to protect the public from detriment and danger, there is in my opinion, no room for considering reciprocity of advantage. There was no reciprocal advantage to the owner prohibited from using his oil tanks in 248 U.S. 498; his brickyard, in 239 U.S. 394, his livery stable, in 237 U.S. 171; his billiard hall, in 225 U.S. 623; his margarine factory, in 127 U.S. 678; his brewery, in 123 U.S. 623; unless it be the advantage of living and doing business in a civilized community. That reciprocal advantage is given by the act to the coal operators.

NOTES AND QUESTIONS

1. The factual circumstances underlying *Mahon* have been much investigated by scholars. See, e.g., William Fischel, Regulatory Takings: Law, Economics, and Politics 25–47 (1995); Carol M. Rose, *Mahon* Reconstructed: Why the Takings Issue is Still a Muddle, 57 S. Cal. L. Rev. 561 (1984); Robert Brauneis, "The Foundations of Our 'Regulatory Takings' Jurisprudence": The Myth and Meaning of Justice Holmes's Opinion in *Pennsylvania Coal Co. v. Mahon*, 106 Yale L.J. 613 (1996). Fischel reports that the practice among anthracite mining companies in eastern Pennsylvania was to provide compensation to surface owners if their property was damaged by subsidence, even if the surface owner (or her predecessor in

title) had waived the support right. The litigation in *Mahon* was motivated not by a design to end this practice, but by the objections of the companies to another statute, the Fowler Act, which required them to contribute to a fund to provide compensation to surface owners whose property was damaged by mining activity of *other* companies which had gone bankrupt. Even after their victory in the Supreme Court, the mining companies continued to pay compensation for subsidence damage caused by their own operations. Why do you suppose they did that?

2.   In a reprise of *Mahon*, the Supreme Court in *Keystone Bituminous Coal Assn. v. DeBenedictis*, 480 U.S. 470 (1987), considered a similar Pennsylvania statute that made coal companies responsible for subsidence damage caused by mining bituminous coal. Applying the approach initially adopted in *Penn Central Transportation Co. v. City of New York*, the next case you will read, the Court upheld this statute against a takings claim. Although the Court purported to distinguish *Mahon* rather than overrule it, there is little doubt that *Mahon* can no longer be considered good law with respect to the question whether anti-subsidence laws give rise to a takings claim.

3.   *Mahon* is still a very important decision, however, because it is generally regarded as the source of the regulatory takings doctrine—the idea that some exercises of the police power "go too far" and hence may be pursued only through an exercise of eminent domain. A proper exercise of the police power—the power to regulate crimes, public nuisances, and other activities that threaten the public health, safety, and welfare—does not require that compensation be paid to those who must comply with the relevant regulations. The exercise of the power of eminent domain, in contrast, can be exercised only if the government pays just compensation for property taken. *Mahon* can be read as recognizing that there must be some limit or boundary on the scope of the police power, or else the state could simply use the police power to acquire property for public use—but without having to pay just compensation. The regulatory takings doctrines recognized by the decision is, from this perspective, simply a boundary-maintenance or anti-evasion principle designed to preserve the basic distinction between two basic powers of sovereign government. Few would quarrel with the general proposition that as long as we recognize these two powers, and as long as they have very different consequences in terms of the government's duty of compensation, *some* kind of judicial policing is necessary in order to preserve the integrity of the boundary between them. (By the way, since only the states are thought to exercise a general police power, whereas the federal government is said to exercise only enumerated powers, what is it that the power of eminent domain is being juxtaposed against when the federal government is alleged to have engaged in a regulatory taking?)

4.   From this humble and rather uncontroversial foundation, however, the doctrine of *Pennsylvania Coal v. Mahon* has grown into something much more controversial. The regulatory takings doctrine today is the most frequently litigated constitutional constraint on governmental interference

with property rights. Other doctrines, such as the Contracts Clause and the doctrine of substantive due process, served this function in the past. With the passage of time, however, the Court has come to apply these other limits in a deferential fashion, at least insofar as they are used to protect property rights. The regulatory takings doctrine, especially after 1986 when William Rehnquist became Chief Justice of the United States, has emerged from the shadow of these other doctrines as the more powerful constraint on government.

5.   One highly significant difference among these doctrines is that the Contracts Clause and substantive due process mark boundaries beyond which the power of government may not extend. Hence, when these limits are violated, the proper remedy is to enjoin the government action in question. The regulatory takings doctrine, in contrast, requires only that the government pay "just compensation" when it adopts a regulation that goes too far and hence represents the kind of measure that should have been accomplished by eminent domain. The proper remedy for a violation of the regulatory takings doctrine, consequently, is an award of damages from the government equal to the "just compensation" that would have been paid if the government had condemned the property using the power of eminent domain. Regulatory takings, in other words, adopts a "liability rule" rather than a "property rule" approach to protecting property rights. See Calabresi & Melamed, in Chapter I. This distinction has important procedural consequences for raising regulatory takings issues. For example, it means that a claimant must exhaust possible procedures for obtaining compensation before challenging a regulation as being an unconstitutional regulatory taking. For an introduction to these complexities, see infra Section B.5.

6.   Note that the support right or "support estate" at issue in *Mahon* was, at least in functional terms, a covenant or servitude that ran with two other estates in land—the surface estate and the mineral estate. At common law, surface owners enjoy a right of subjacent support, which prohibits other persons (including owners of subjacent mineral rights) from excavating underneath the surface in such a way as to damage buildings or endanger persons and activities on the surface. (But if those buildings or activities require more support than the land in its natural state would provide, then one in need of extra support has to negotiate for a servitude for the extra support). In *Mahon*, the surface owners—the Mahons—had signed a deed conveying the mineral rights to the coal company that included a covenant *waiving* these common-law rights of subjacent support. The waiver was in effect a servitude running with the land. The Kohler Act, in functional terms, reinstated the common-law support rights, wiping out the covenant or servitude the parties had negotiated. How important is it to the Court's decision that this particular waiver or covenant has a property-like name: the "support estate" (sometimes referred to in Pennsylvania cases as the "third estate")? How important is it to the Court's decision that this particular covenant was explicitly negotiated and exchanged (presumably for consideration) between the parties?

7. In considering the broad run of cases, it seems reasonably clear that it is not considered a taking for the government to impose the functional equivalent of a servitude on parties who conceivably could have agreed to one as a matter of voluntary negotiation. See, e.g., Penn Central, infra (upholding historic preservation order); Gorieb v. Fox, 274 U.S. 603 (1927) (upholding open space restriction imposed by ordinance); Welch v. Swasey, 214 U.S. 91 (1909) (upholding height restriction on buildings imposed by ordinance). Why should it be permissible for the government to impose servitudes on property owners without compensation, but a taking for government to abrogate servitudes held by property owners without compensation? Should it be regarded as a regulatory taking for a court to abrogate restrictive covenants limiting houses in a subdivision to single-family occupancy under the changed circumstances doctrine (see Chapter IX)? Did the Supreme Court, when it declared racially restrictive covenants unenforceable in *Shelley v. Kraemer* (see Chapter IV), commit a regulatory taking? See generally Barton H. Thompson, Jr., Judicial Takings, 76 Va. L. Rev. 1449 (1990).

8. A careful reading of the opinions in *Mahon* will reveal that Justices Holmes and Brandeis (who more often agreed with each other on constitutional questions), did not really disagree about the three factors to be considering in deciding whether a police regulation "goes too far" and must be regarded as an exercise of eminent domain. Both agreed that the diminution in value caused by the regulation, the need to protect the public against nuisance-like harms, and reciprocity of advantage among property owners are relevant factors to be considered. See if you can articulate the reasons that caused the two Justices to disagree about how each of these factors should be applied to the Kohler Act. Are the disagreements based on differences about the characterization of the factor, about the proper institution to determine the relevance of the factor, or about the presumed importance of the factor in this case?

9. One specific ground for disagreement concerns the proper unit of property against which to measure the effect of the regulation. Justice Holmes appears to assume that the correct unit of analysis is the pillars of coal that must be left in place to support the surface. On this view, the regulation "takes" (or at least prevents the economic use of) the entire property right. Justice Brandeis, in contrast, argues that the appropriate unit of analysis is "the whole property" of the coal company. From this perspective, the regulation takes only a fraction of the property right. Which perspective is better? Under the Holmes approach, how narrowly should the "property" be defined? Can the conception of "property" be sliced finer and finer, until the definition of property coincides exactly with the interest affected by the regulation? Under the Brandeis approach, how far should the "whole property" of the company extend? To all its rights in the particular column of space in which the complaining surface owner resides? To all rights, mineral and surface, in the immediate area? To all assets on the company's balance sheet?

10. How would you explain the understanding that "blowing up a house to stop a conflagration" is not regarded as a taking requiring the payment of compensation? Is this understanding consistent with Justice Holmes's emphasis on diminution in value, reciprocity of advantage, and whether the government action has taken a recognized property right? The rule has been traced to the Great London Fire of 1666, where the Lord Mayor of London hesitated to order the destruction of the Inns of Court without the consent of the judges, with the result that the fire spread disastrously. See Respublica v. Sparhawk, 1 Dall. 357, 363 (Pa. 1788). Does this provide any hints about the rationale for the rule?

11. How well does the regulatory takings doctrine function as a device for determining the appropriate degree of government forbearance from interfering with established expectations about property? (See Chapter XI.) Commentators have been debating this question ever since *Mahon* was decided, and that debate will undoubtedly continue. One school of thought is that the doctrine imposes relatively little constraint on government regulation of property rights. From this perspective, the doctrine is not really about protecting expectations against unanticipated government regulation, but rather with preserving the boundary between the police power and eminent domain. The Supreme Court has sometimes endorsed this perspective, as in its recent observation that the touchstone of regulatory takings law is whether the challenged regulation is "functionally equivalent to the classic taking in which government directly appropriates private property or ousts the owner from his domain." Lingle v. Chevron U.S.A. Inc., 544 U.S. 528, 539 (2005). Professor Joseph Sax of Berkeley Law School, who has argued that the government should pay compensation when it acts in an "enterprise" capacity, but not when it is "mediating" between incompatible uses of property, is probably the academic most prominently associated with this view. See Joseph L. Sax, Takings and the Police Power, 74 Yale L.J. 36 (1964); Joseph L. Sax, Takings, Private Property and Public Rights, 81 Yale L.J. 149 (1971).

Another school of thought takes a more expansive and functionalist view of the purpose of the regulatory takings doctrine. This school, picking up on Justice Holmes's concern about regulations that go "too far," sees the doctrine as a device for softening the transition from one set of regulatory policies to another, by spreading the costs of legal change more equitably throughout society. The Supreme Court has given impetus to this view though its often-quoted observation that the Takings Clause is designed to bar the "Government from forcing some people alone to bear public burdens which, in all fairness and justice, should be borne by the public as a whole." Armstrong v. United States, 364 U.S. 40, 49 (1960). The work of Professor Frank Michelman of the Harvard Law School, who coined the phrase "demoralization costs" to describe the psychological disappointment and foregone investment activity that can follow from unanticipated shifts in government regulatory policy, is perhaps the foremost inspiration for this perspective. See Frank I. Michelman, Property, Utility, and Fairness: Comments on the Ethical Foundations of "Just Compensation" Law, 80 Harv. L. Rev. 1165 (1967). Both schools of thought are interwoven in the following case, where the Court restated the basic principles of the regulatory takings doctrine.

Penn Central Transportation Company v. City of New York

Supreme Court of the United States, 1978.
438 U.S. 104.

■ MR. JUSTICE BRENNAN delivered the opinion of the Court. The question presented is whether a city may, as part of a comprehensive program to preserve historic landmarks and historic districts, place restrictions on the development of individual historic landmarks—in addition to those imposed by applicable zoning ordinances—without effecting a "taking" requiring the payment of "just compensation." * * *

I

A

Over the past 50 years, all 50 States and over 500 municipalities have enacted laws to encourage or require the preservation of buildings and areas with historic or aesthetic importance. These nationwide legislative efforts have been precipitated by two concerns. The first is recognition that, in recent years, large numbers of historic structures, landmarks, and areas have been destroyed without adequate consideration of either the values represented therein or the possibility of preserving the destroyed properties for use in economically productive ways. The second is a widely shared belief that structures with special historic, cultural, or architectural significance enhance the quality of life for all. * * *

New York City, responding to similar concerns and acting pursuant to a New York State enabling Act, adopted its Landmarks Preservation Law in 1965. See N.Y.C. Admin. Code, ch. 8–A, § 205–1.0 et seq. (1976). * * *

The New York City law is typical of many urban landmark laws in that its primary method of achieving its goals is not by acquisitions of historic properties, but rather by involving public entities in land-use decisions affecting these properties * * * While the law does place special restrictions on landmark properties as a necessary feature to the attainment of its larger objectives, the major theme of the law is to ensure the owners of any such properties both a "reasonable return" on their investments and maximum latitude to use their parcels for purposes not inconsistent with the preservation goals.

The operation of the law can be briefly summarized. The primary responsibility for administering the law is vested in the Landmarks Preservation Commission (Commission), a broad based, 11–member agency assisted by a technical staff. The Commission first performs the function, critical to any landmark preservation effort, of identifying properties and areas that have "a special character or special historical or aesthetic interest or value as part of the development, heritage or cultural characteristics of the city, state or nation." § 207–1.0(n); see § 207–1.0(h). If the Commission determines, after giving all interested parties an opportunity to be heard, that a building or area satisfies the ordinance's criteria, it will designate a building to be a "landmark," § 207–1.0(n), situated on a particular "landmark site," § 207–1.0(o), or will designate an area to be a "historic district," § 207–1.0(h). After the Commission makes a designation, New York City's Board of Estimate, after considering the relationship of the designated property "to the master plan, the zoning resolution, projected public improvements and any plans for the renewal of the area involved," § 207–2.0(g)(1), may modify or disapprove the designation, and the owner may seek judicial review of the final designation decision. Thus far, 31 historic districts and over 400 individual landmarks have been finally designated, and the process is a continuing one.

Final designation as a landmark results in restrictions upon the property owner's options concerning use of the landmark site. First, the law imposes a duty upon the owner to keep the exterior features of the building "in good repair" to assure that the law's objectives not be defeated by the landmark's falling into a state of irremediable disrepair. See § 207–10.0(a). Second, the Commission must approve in advance any proposal to alter the exterior architectural features of the landmark or to construct any exterior improvement on the landmark site, thus ensuring that decisions concerning construction on the landmark site are made with due consideration of both the public interest in the maintenance of the structure and the landowner's interest in use of the property. See §§ 207–4.0 to 207–9.0.

In the event an owner wishes to alter a landmark site, three separate procedures are available through which administrative approval may be obtained. First, the owner may apply to the Commission for a "certificate of no effect on protected architectural features": that is, for an order approving the improvement or alteration on the ground that it will not change or affect any architectural feature of the landmark and will be in harmony therewith. See § 207–5.0. * * * Second, the owner may apply to the Commission for a certificate of "appropriateness." See § 207–6.0. Such certificates will be granted if the Commission concludes—focusing upon aesthetic, historical, and architectural values—that the proposed construction on the landmark site would not unduly hinder the protection, enhancement, perpetuation, and use of the landmark. * * * The final procedure—seeking a certificate of appropriateness on the ground of "insufficient return," see § 207–8.0—provides special mechanisms, which vary depending on whether or not the landmark enjoys a tax exemption, to ensure that designation does not cause economic hardship.

Although the designation of a landmark and landmark site restricts the owner's control over the parcel, designation also enhances the economic position of the landmark owner in one significant respect. Under New York City's zoning laws, owners of real property who have not developed their property to the full extent permitted by the applicable zoning laws are allowed to transfer development rights to contiguous parcels on the same city block. See New York City, Zoning Resolution Art. I, ch. 2, § 12–10

(1978) (definition of "zoning lot"). A 1968 ordinance gave the owners of landmark sites additional opportunities to transfer development rights to other parcels. Subject to a restriction that the floor area of the transferee lot may not be increased by more than 20% above its authorized level, the ordinance permitted transfers from a landmark parcel to property across the street or across a street intersection. In 1969, * * * [t]he class of recipient lots was expanded to include lots "across a street and opposite to another lot or lots which except for the intervention of streets or street intersections f[or]m a series extending to the lot occupied by the landmark building [, provided that] all lots [are] in the same ownership." New York City Zoning Resolution 74–79 (emphasis deleted). In addition, the 1969 amendment permits, in highly commercialized areas like midtown Manhattan, the transfer of all unused development rights to a single parcel. Ibid.

B

This case involves the application of New York City's Landmarks Preservation Law to Grand Central Terminal (Terminal). The Terminal, which is owned by the Penn Central Transportation Co. and its affiliates (Penn Central), is one of New York City's most famous buildings. Opened in 1913, it is regarded not only as providing an ingenious engineering solution to the problems presented by urban railroad stations, but also as a magnificent example of the French beaux-arts style.

The Terminal is located in midtown Manhattan. Its south facade faces 42d Street and that street's intersection with Park Avenue. At street level, the Terminal is bounded on the west by Vanderbilt Avenue, on the east by the Commodore Hotel, and on the north by the Pan–American Building. Although a 20–story office tower, to have been located above the Terminal, was part of the original design, the planned tower was never constructed. The Terminal itself is an eight-story structure which Penn Central uses as a railroad station and in which it rents space not needed for railroad purposes to a variety of commercial interests. The Terminal is one of a number of properties owned by appellant Penn Central in this area of midtown Manhattan. The others include the Barclay, Biltmore, Commodore, Roosevelt, and Waldorf–Astoria Hotels, the Pan–American Building and other office buildings along Park Avenue, and the Yale Club. At least eight of these are eligible to be recipients of development rights afforded the Terminal by virtue of landmark designation.

On August 2, 1967, following a public hearing, the Commission designated the Terminal a "landmark" and designated the "city tax block" it occupies a "landmark site." The Board of Estimate confirmed this action on September 21, 1967. Although appellant Penn Central had opposed the designation before the Commission, it did not seek judicial review of the final designation decision.

On January 22, 1968, appellant Penn Central, to increase its income, entered into a renewable 50–year lease and sublease agreement with appellant UGP Properties, Inc. (UGP), a wholly owned subsidiary of Union General Properties, Ltd., a United Kingdom corporation. Under the terms of the agreement, UGP was to construct a multistory office building above the Terminal. UGP promised to pay Penn Central $1 million annually during construction and at least $3 million annually thereafter. The rentals would be offset in part by a loss of some $700,000 to $1 million in net rentals presently received from concessionaires displaced by the new building.

Appellants UGP and Penn Central then applied to the Commission for permission to construct an office building atop the Terminal. Two separate plans, both designed by architect Marcel Breuer and both apparently satisfying the terms of the applicable zoning ordinance, were submitted to the Commission for approval. The first, Breuer I, provided for the construction of a 55–story office building, to be cantilevered above the existing facade and to rest on the roof of the Terminal. The second, Breuer II Revised, called for tearing down a portion of the Terminal that included the 42d Street facade, stripping off some of the remaining features of the Terminal's facade, and constructing a 53–story office building. The Commission denied a certificate of no exterior effect on September 20, 1968. Appellants then applied for a certificate of "appropriateness" as to both proposals. After four days of hearings at which over 80 witnesses testified, the Commission denied this application as to both proposals.

The Commission's reasons for rejecting certificates respecting Breuer II Revised are summarized in the following statement: "To protect a Landmark, one does not tear it down. To perpetuate its architectural features, one does not strip them off." Record 2255. Breuer I, which would have preserved the existing vertical facades of the present structure, received more sympathetic consideration. The Commission first focused on the effect that the proposed tower would have on one desirable feature created by the present structure and its surroundings: the dramatic view of the Terminal from Park Avenue South. Although appellants had contended that the Pan–American Building had already destroyed the silhouette of the south facade and that one additional tower could do no further damage and might even provide a better background for the facade, the Commission disagreed, stating that it found the majestic approach from the south to be still unique in the city and that a 55–story tower atop the Terminal would be far more detrimental to its south facade than the Pan–American Building 375 feet away. Moreover, the Commission found that from closer vantage points the Pan Am Building and the other towers were largely cut off from view, which would not be the case of the mass on top of the Terminal planned under Breuer I. * * *

Appellants did not seek judicial review of the denial of either certificate. * * * Instead, appellants filed suit in New York Supreme Court, Trial Term, claiming, *inter alia*, that the application of the Landmarks Preservation Law had "taken" their property without just compensation in violation of the Fifth and Fourteenth Amendments and arbitrarily deprived them of their property without due process of law in violation of the Fourteenth Amendment.

* * * The trial court granted * * * injunctive and declaratory relief, but severed the question of damages for a "temporary taking." * * * [The] Appellate Division, reversed. * * * The Appellate Division concluded that all appellants had succeeded in showing was that they had been deprived of the property's most profitable use, and that this showing did not establish that appellants had been unconstitutionally deprived of their property.

* * * The New York Court of Appeals affirmed. * * * We affirm.

II

The issues presented by appellants are (1) whether the restrictions imposed by New York City's law upon appellants' exploitation of the Terminal site effect a "taking" of appellants' property for a public use within the meaning of the Fifth Amendment, which of course is made applicable to the States through the Fourteenth Amendment, see Chicago, B. & Q. R. Co. v. Chicago, 166 U.S. 226, 239 (1897), and, (2), if so, whether the transferable development rights afforded appellants constitute "just compensation" within the meaning of the Fifth Amendment. We need only address the question whether a "taking" has occurred.

A

Before considering appellants' specific contentions, it will be useful to review the factors that have shaped the jurisprudence of the Fifth Amendment injunction "nor shall private property be taken for public use, without just compensation." The question of what constitutes a "taking" for purposes of the Fifth Amendment has proved to be a problem of considerable difficulty. While this Court has recognized that the "Fifth Amendment's guarantee ... [is] designed to bar Government from forcing some people alone to bear public burdens which, in all fairness and justice, should be borne by the public as a whole," Armstrong v. United States, 364 U.S. 40, 49 (1960), this Court, quite simply, has been unable to develop any "set formula" for determining when "justice and fairness" require that economic injuries caused by public action be compensated by the government, rather than remain disproportionately concentrated on a few persons. See Goldblatt v. Hempstead, 369 U.S. 590, 594 (1962). Indeed, we have frequently observed that whether a particular restriction will be rendered invalid by the government's failure to pay for any losses proximately caused by it depends largely "upon the particular circumstances [in that] case." United States v. Central Eureka Mining Co., 357 U.S. 155, 168 (1958).

In engaging in these essentially ad hoc, factual inquiries, the Court's decisions have identified several factors that have particular significance. The economic impact of the regulation on the claimant and, particularly, the extent to which the regulation has interfered with distinct investment-backed expectations are, of course, relevant considerations. See Goldblatt v. Hempstead, supra, 369 U.S., at 594. So, too, is the character of the governmental action. A "taking" may more readily be found when the interference with property can be characterized as a physical invasion by government, see, e. g., United States v. Causby, 328 U.S. 256 (1946), than when interference arises from some public program adjusting the benefits and burdens of economic life to promote the common good.

"Government hardly could go on if to some extent values incident to property could not be diminished without paying for every such change in the general law," Pennsylvania Coal Co. v. Mahon, 260 U.S. 393, 413 (1922), and this Court has accordingly recognized, in a wide variety of contexts, that government may execute laws or programs that adversely affect recognized economic values. Exercises of the taxing power are one obvious example. A second are the decisions in which this Court has dismissed "taking" challenges on the ground that, while the challenged government action caused economic harm, it did not interfere with interests that were sufficiently bound up with the reasonable expectations of the claimant to constitute "property" for Fifth Amendment purposes. See, e. g., United States v. Willow River Power Co., 324 U.S. 499 (1945) (interest in high-water level of river for runoff for tailwaters to maintain power head is not property); United States v. Chandler–Dunbar Water Power Co., 229 U.S. 53 (1913) (no property interest can exist in navigable waters); see also Sax, Takings and the Police Power, 74 Yale L.J. 36, 61–62 (1964).

More importantly for the present case, in instances in which a state tribunal reasonably concluded that "the health, safety, morals, or general welfare" would be promoted by prohibiting particular contemplated uses of land, this Court has upheld land-use regulations that destroyed or adversely affected recognized real property interests. See Nectow v. Cambridge, 277 U.S. 183, 188 (1928). Zoning laws are, of course, the classic example, see Euclid v. Ambler Realty Co., 272 U.S. 365 (1926) (prohibition of industrial use). * * *

B

In contending that the New York City law has "taken" their property in violation of the Fifth and Fourteenth Amendments, appellants make a series of arguments, which, while tailored to the facts of this case, essentially urge that any substantial restriction imposed pursuant to a landmark law must be accompanied by just compensation if it is to be constitutional. * * *

They first observe that the airspace above the Terminal is a valuable property interest, citing *United States v. Causby,* supra. They urge that the Landmarks Law has deprived them of any gainful use of their "air rights" above the Terminal and that, irrespective of the value of the remainder of their parcel, the city has "taken" their right to this superadjacent airspace, thus entitling them to "just compensation" measured by the fair market value of these air rights.

Apart from our own disagreement with appellants' characterization of the effect of the New York City law, see infra, the submission that appellants may establish a "taking" simply by showing that they have been denied the ability to exploit a property interest that they heretofore had believed was available for development is quite simply untenable. * * *

"Taking" jurisprudence does not divide a single parcel into discrete segments and attempt to determine whether rights in a particular segment have been entirely abrogated. In deciding whether a particular governmental action has effected a taking, this Court focuses rather both on the character of the action and on the nature and extent of the interference with rights in the parcel as a whole—here, the city tax block designated as the "landmark site."

Secondly, appellants, focusing on the character and impact of the New York City law, argue that it effects a "taking" because its operation has significantly diminished the value of the Terminal site. Appellants concede that the decisions sustaining other land-use regulations, which, like the New York City law, are reasonably related to the promotion of the general welfare, uniformly reject the proposition that diminution in property value, standing alone, can establish a "taking," see Euclid v. Ambler Realty Co., 272 U.S. 365 (1926) (75% diminution in value caused by zoning law); Hadacheck v. Sebastian, 239 U.S. 394 (1915) (87½% diminution in value), and that the "taking" issue in these contexts is resolved by focusing on the uses the regulations permit. Appellants, moreover, also do not dispute that a showing of diminution in property value would not establish a taking if the restriction had been imposed as a result of historic-district legislation, but appellants argue that New York City's regulation of individual landmarks is fundamentally different from zoning or from historic-district legislation because the controls imposed by New York City's law apply only to individuals who own selected properties. * * *

It is true, as appellants emphasize, that both historic-district legislation and zoning laws regulate all properties within given physical communities whereas landmark laws apply only to selected parcels. But, contrary to appellants' suggestions, landmark laws are not like discriminatory, or "reverse spot," zoning: that is, a land-use decision which arbitrarily singles out a particular parcel for different, less favorable treatment than the neighboring ones. In contrast to discriminatory zoning, which is the antithesis of land-use control as part of some comprehensive plan, the New York City law embodies a comprehensive plan to preserve structures of historic or aesthetic interest wherever they might be found in the city, and as noted, over 400 landmarks and 31 historic districts have been designated pursuant to this plan.* * *

Next, appellants observe that New York City's law differs from zoning laws and historic-district ordinances in that the Landmarks Law does not impose identical or similar restrictions on all structures located in particular physical communities. It follows, they argue, that New York City's law is inherently incapable of producing the fair and equitable distribution of benefits and burdens of governmental action which is characteristic of zoning laws and historic-district legislation and which they maintain is a constitutional requirement if "just compensation" is not to be afforded. It is, of course, true that the Landmarks Law has a more severe impact on some landowners than on others, but that in itself does not mean that the law effects a "taking." Legislation designed to promote the general welfare commonly burdens some more than others. The owners of the brickyard in *Hadacheck*, of the cedar trees in *Miller v. Schoene*, [276 U.S. 272 (1928),] and of the gravel and sand mine in *Goldblatt v. Hempstead*, were uniquely burdened by the legislation sustained in those cases. Similarly, zoning laws often affect some property owners more severely than others but have not been held to be invalid on that account. For example, the property owner in *Euclid* who wished to use its property for industrial purposes was affected far more severely by the ordinance than its neighbors who wished to use their land for residences.

In any event, appellants' repeated suggestions that they are solely burdened and unbenefited is factually inaccurate. This contention overlooks the fact that the New York City law applies to vast numbers of structures in the city in addition to the Terminal—all the structures contained in the 31 historic districts and over 400 individual landmarks, many of which are close to the Terminal. Unless we are to reject the judgment of the New York City Council that the preservation of landmarks benefits all New York citizens and all structures, both economically and by improving the quality of life in the city as a whole—which we are unwilling to do—we cannot conclude that the owners of the Terminal have in no sense been benefited by the Landmarks Law. Doubtless appellants believe they are more burdened than benefited by the law, but that must have been true, too, of the property owners in *Miller, Hadacheck, Euclid*, and *Goldblatt*.

Appellants' final broad-based attack would have us treat the law as an instance, like that in *United States v. Causby*, in which government, acting in an enterprise capacity, has appropriated part of their property for some strictly governmental purpose. Apart from the fact that *Causby* was a case of invasion of airspace that destroyed the use of the farm beneath and this New York City law has in nowise impaired the present use of the Terminal, the Landmarks Law neither exploits appellants' parcel for city purposes nor facilitates nor arises from any entrepreneurial operations of the city. The situation is not remotely like that in *Causby* where the airspace above the property was in the flight pattern for military aircraft. The Landmarks Law's effect is simply to prohibit appellants or anyone else from occupying portions of the airspace above the Terminal, while permitting appellants to use the remainder of the parcel in a gainful fashion. * * *

C

Rejection of appellants' broad arguments is not, however, the end of our inquiry, for all we thus far have established is that the New York City law is not rendered invalid by its failure to provide "just compensation" whenever a landmark owner is restricted in the exploitation of property interests, such as air rights, to a greater extent than provided for under applicable zoning laws. We now must consider whether the interference with appellants' property is of such a magnitude that "there must be an exercise of eminent domain and compensation to sustain [it]." *Pennsylvania Coal Co. v. Mahon*, 260 U.S., at 413. That inquiry may be narrowed to the question of the severity of the impact of the law on appellants' parcel, and its resolution in turn requires a careful assessment of the impact of the regulation on the Terminal site.

Unlike the governmental acts in *Goldblatt, Miller, Causby, Griggs,* [369 U.S. 84 (1962),] and *Hadacheck,* the New York City law does not interfere in any way with the present uses of the Terminal. Its designation as a landmark not only permits but contemplates that appellants may continue to use the property precisely as it has been used for the past 65 years: as a railroad terminal containing office space and concessions. So the law does not interfere with what must be regarded as Penn Central's primary expectation concerning the use of the parcel. More importantly, on this record, we must regard the New York City law as permitting Penn Central not only to profit from the Terminal but also to obtain a "reasonable return" on its investment.

Appellants, moreover, exaggerate the effect of the law on their ability to make use of the air rights above the Terminal in two respects. First, it simply cannot be maintained, on this record, that appellants have been prohibited from occupying *any* portion of the airspace above the Terminal. While the Commission's actions in denying applications to construct an office building in excess of 50 stories above the Terminal may indicate that it will refuse to issue a certificate of appropriateness for any comparably sized structure, nothing the Commission has said or done suggests an intention to prohibit *any* construction above the Terminal. * * *

Second, to the extent appellants have been denied the right to build above the Terminal, it is not literally accurate to say that they have been denied *all* use of even those pre-existing air rights. Their ability to use these rights has not been abrogated; they are made transferable to at least eight parcels in the vicinity of the Terminal, one or two of which have been found suitable for the construction of new office buildings. Although appellants and others have argued that New York City's transferable development-rights program is far from ideal, the New York courts here supportably found that, at least in the case of the Terminal, the rights afforded are valuable. While these rights may well not have constituted "just compensation" if a "taking" had occurred, the rights nevertheless undoubtedly mitigate whatever financial burdens the law has imposed on appellants and, for that reason, are to be taken into account in considering the impact of regulation.

On this record, we conclude that the application of New York City's Landmarks Law has not effected a "taking" of appellants' property. The restrictions imposed are substantially related to the promotion of the general welfare and not only permit reasonable beneficial use of the landmark site but also afford appellants opportunities further to enhance not only the Terminal site proper but also other properties.

Affirmed.

■ MR. JUSTICE REHNQUIST, with whom THE CHIEF JUSTICE and MR. JUSTICE STEVENS join, dissenting. Of the over one million buildings and structures in the city of New York, appellees have singled out 400 for designation as official landmarks. The owner of a building might initially be pleased that his property has been chosen by a distinguished committee of architects, historians, and city planners for such a singular distinction. But he may well discover, as appellant Penn Central Transportation Co. did here, that the landmark designation imposes upon him a substantial cost, with little or no offsetting benefit except for the honor of the designation. The question in this case is whether the cost associated with the city of New York's desire to preserve a limited number of "landmarks" within its borders must be borne by all of its taxpayers or whether it can instead be imposed entirely on the owners of the individual properties. * * *

I

The Fifth Amendment provides in part: "nor shall private property be taken for public use, without just compensation." In a very literal sense, the actions of appellees violated this constitutional prohibition. Before the city of New York declared Grand Central Terminal to be a landmark, Penn Central could have used its "air rights" over the Terminal to build a multistory office building, at an apparent value of several million dollars per year. Today, the Terminal cannot be modified in *any* form, including the erection of additional stories, without the permission of the Landmark Preservation Commission, a permission which appellants, despite good-faith attempts, have so far been unable to obtain. Because the Taking Clause of the Fifth Amendment has not always been read literally, however, the constitutionality of appellees' actions requires a closer scrutiny of this Court's interpretation of the three key words in the Taking Clause— "property," "taken," and "just compensation."

A

Appellees do not dispute that valuable property rights have been destroyed. And the Court has frequently emphasized that the term "property" as used in the Taking Clause includes the entire "group of rights inhering in the citizen's [ownership]." United States v. General Motors Corp., 323 U.S. 373 (1945). The term is not used in the

> vulgar and untechnical sense of the physical thing with respect to which the citizen exercises rights recognized by law. [Instead, it] ... denote[s] the *group of rights* inhering in the citizen's relation to the physical thing, as the right to possess, use and dispose of it ... the constitutional provision is addressed to *every sort of interest* the citizen may possess. Id., at 377–378 (emphasis added).

While neighboring landowners are free to use their land and "air rights" in any way consistent with the broad boundaries of New York zoning, Penn Central, absent the permission of appellees, must forever maintain its property in its present state. The property has been thus subjected to a nonconsensual servitude not borne by any neighboring or similar properties.

B

Appellees have thus destroyed—in a literal sense, "taken"—substantial property rights of Penn Central. While the term "taken" might have been narrowly interpreted to include only physical seizures of property rights, "the construction of the phrase has not been so narrow. The courts have held that the deprivation of the former owner rather than the accretion of a right or interest to the sovereign constitutes the taking." Id., at 378. Because "not every destruction or injury to property by governmental action has been held to be a 'taking' in the constitutional sense," Armstrong v. United States, 364 U.S., at 48, however, this does not end our inquiry. But an examination of the two exceptions where the destruction of property does *not* constitute a taking demonstrates that a compensable taking has occurred here.

1

As early as 1887, the Court recognized that the government can prevent a property owner from using his property to injure others without having to compensate the owner for the value of the forbidden use.

> A prohibition simply upon the use of property for purposes that are declared, by valid legislation, to be *injurious to the health, morals, or safety of the community*, cannot, in any just sense, be deemed a taking or an appropriation of property for the public benefit. Such legislation does not disturb the owner in the control or use of his property for lawful purposes, nor restrict his right to dispose of it, but is only a declaration by the State that its use by any one, for certain forbidden purposes, is prejudicial to the public interests. . . . The power which the States have of prohibiting such use by individuals of their property as will be prejudicial to the health, the morals, or the safety of the public, is not—and, consistently with the existence and safety of organized society, cannot be—burdened with the condition that the State must compensate such individual owners for pecuniary losses they may sustain, *by reason of their not being permitted, by a noxious use of their property, to inflict injury upon the community*.

Mugler v. Kansas, 123 U.S. 623, 668–669 (1887).

Thus, there is no "taking" where a city prohibits the operation of a brickyard within a residential area, see Hadacheck v. Sebastian, 239 U.S. 394 (1915), or forbids excavation for sand and gravel below the water line, see Goldblatt v. Hempstead, 369 U.S. 590 (1962). Nor is it relevant, where the government is merely prohibiting a noxious use of property, that the government would seem to be singling out a particular property owner. Hadacheck, supra, at 413. Each of the cases cited by the Court for the proposition that legislation which severely affects some landowners but not others does not effect a "taking" involved noxious uses of property. See Hadacheck; Miller v. Schoene, 276 U.S. 272 (1928); Goldblatt.

The nuisance exception to the taking guarantee is not coterminous with the police power itself. The question is whether the forbidden use is dangerous to the safety, health, or welfare of others. * * *

Appellees are not prohibiting a nuisance. The record is clear that the proposed addition to the Grand Central Terminal would be in full compliance with zoning, height limitations, and other health and safety requirements. Instead, appellees are seeking to preserve what they believe to be an outstanding example of beaux-arts architecture. Penn Central is prevented from further developing its property basically because *too good* a job was done in designing and building it. The city of New York, because of its unadorned admiration for the design, has decided that the owners of the building must preserve it unchanged for the benefit of sightseeing New Yorkers and tourists.

Unlike land-use regulations, appellees' actions do not merely *prohibit* Penn Central from using its property in a narrow set of noxious ways. Instead, appellees have placed an *affirmative* duty on Penn Central to maintain the Terminal in its present state and in "good repair." Appellants are not free to use their property as they see fit within broad outer boundaries but must strictly adhere to their past use except where appellees conclude that alternative uses would not detract from the landmark. While Penn Central may continue to use the Terminal as it is presently designed, appellees otherwise "exercise complete dominion and control over the surface of the land," United States v. Causby, 328 U.S. 256, 262 (1946), and must compensate the owner for his loss. Ibid. "Property is taken in the constitutional sense when inroads are made upon an owner's use of it to an extent that, as between private parties, a servitude has been acquired." United States v. Dickinson, 331 U.S. 745, 748 (1947).

2

Even where the government prohibits a noninjurious use, the Court has ruled that a taking does not take place if the prohibition applies over a broad cross section of land and thereby "secure[s] an average reciprocity of advantage." Pennsylvania Coal Co. v. Mahon, 260 U.S., at 415. It is for this reason that zoning does not constitute a "taking." While zoning at times reduces *individual* property values, the burden is shared relatively evenly and it is reasonable to conclude that on the whole an individual who is harmed by one aspect of the zoning will be benefited by another.

Here, however, a multimillion dollar loss has been imposed on appellants; it is uniquely felt and is not offset by any benefits flowing from the preservation of some 400 other "landmarks" in New York City. Appellees have imposed a substantial cost on less than one one-tenth of one percent of the buildings in New York City for the general benefit of all its people. It is exactly this imposition of general costs on a few individuals at which the "taking" protection is directed. * * * Less than 20 years ago, this Court reiterated that the

Fifth Amendment's guarantee that private property shall not be taken for a public use without just compensation was designed to bar Government from forcing some people alone to bear public burdens which, in all fairness and justice, should be borne by the public as a whole.

Armstrong v. United States, 364 U.S., at 49.

As Mr. Justice Holmes pointed out in *Pennsylvania Coal Co. v. Mahon,* "the question at bottom" in an eminent domain case "is upon whom the loss of the changes desired should fall." 260 U.S., at 416. The benefits that appellees believe will flow from preservation of the Grand Central Terminal will accrue to all the citizens of New York City. There is no reason to believe that appellants will enjoy a substantially greater share of these benefits. If the cost of preserving Grand Central Terminal were spread evenly across the entire population of the city of New York, the burden per person would be in cents per year—a minor cost appellees would surely concede for the benefit accrued. Instead, however, appellees would impose the entire cost of several million dollars per year on Penn Central. But it is precisely this sort of discrimination that the Fifth Amendment prohibits. * * *

C

Appellees, apparently recognizing that the constraints imposed on a landmark site constitute a taking for Fifth Amendment purposes, do not leave the property owner empty-handed. As the Court notes, the property owner may theoretically "transfer" his previous right to develop the landmark property to adjacent properties if they are under his control. Appellees have coined this system "Transfer Development Rights," or TDR's.

Of all the terms used in the Taking Clause, "just compensation" has the strictest meaning. The Fifth Amendment does not allow simply an approximate compensation but requires "a full and perfect equivalent for the property taken." Monongahela Navigation Co. v. United States, 148 U.S., at 326.

> [I]f the adjective "just" had been omitted, and the provision was simply that property should not be taken without compensation, the natural import of the language would be that the compensation should be the equivalent of the property. And this is made emphatic by the adjective "just." There can, in view of the combination of those two words, be no doubt that the compensation must be a full and perfect equivalent for the property taken. Ibid.

And the determination of whether a "full and perfect equivalent" has been awarded is a "judicial function." United States v. New River Collieries Co., 262 U.S. 341, 343–344 (1923). * * *

Appellees contend that, even if they have "taken" appellants' property, TDR's constitute "just compensation." Appellants, of course, argue that TDR's are highly imperfect compensation. Because the lower courts held that there was no "taking," they did not have to reach the question of whether or not just compensation has already been awarded. * * *

[I]n other cases the Court of Appeals has noted that TDR's have an "uncertain and contingent market value" and do "not adequately preserve" the value lost when a building is declared to be a landmark. French Investing Co. v. City of New York, 350 N.E.2d 381, 383 (N.Y. 1976). On the other hand, there is evidence in the record that Penn Central has been offered substantial amounts for its TDR's. Because the record on appeal is relatively slim, I would remand to the Court of Appeals for a determination of whether TDR's constitute a "full and perfect equivalent for the property taken."

II

Over 50 years ago, Mr. Justice Holmes, speaking for the Court, warned that the courts were "in danger of forgetting that a strong public desire to improve the public condition is not enough to warrant achieving the desire by a shorter cut than the constitutional way of paying for the change." Pennsylvania Coal Co. v. Mahon, 260 U.S., at 416. The Court's opinion in this case demonstrates that the danger thus foreseen has not abated. The city of New York is in a precarious financial state, and some may believe that the costs of landmark preservation will be more easily borne by corporations such as Penn Central than the overburdened individual taxpayers of New York. But these concerns do not allow us to ignore past precedents construing the Eminent Domain Clause to the end that the desire to improve the public condition is, indeed, achieved by a shorter cut than the constitutional way of paying for the change.

NOTES AND QUESTIONS

1. New York City's historic preservation ordinance was motivated in significant part by public outcry over the demolition of Penn Station at

Figure 12–3
Pennsylvania Railroad Station, New York City

Pennsylvania Railroad Station. Undated. Museum of the City of New York.

34th Street between Seventh and Eighth Avenues, a grand structure with a classical colonnade matching the appearance of the Post Office building across the street. Penn Station was replaced by a nondescript structure housing a relocated Madison Square Garden, with the railroad terminal moved underground. Given this background, it is not surprising that the Landmarks Commission took a dim view of the proposal to build a modern tower on top of Grand Central Station, the only remaining grand historic rail terminal building in Manhattan.

Figure 12–4
Madison Square Garden, New York City, 2006

2. On the occasion of the 25th anniversary of *Penn Central*, a conference was held at Fordham Law School that included a panel discussion by the lawyers who argued the case and the law clerks who assisted the Justices who wrote the opinions. See Looking Back at Penn Central: A Panel Discussion with the Supreme Court Litigators, 15 Fordham Envt'l L. Rev. 287 (2004). Among the interesting revelations are that Justice Stewart advised Justice Brennan's law clerk (David Carpenter) the opinion should say as little as possible; that Justice Brennan spent one day editing the draft opinion; and that Justice Rehnquist's dissent was already written before the majority opinion circulated.

3. Recall that both Justice Holmes and Justice Brandeis in *Mahon* seemed to believe that three factors were of primary importance in distin-

guishing between a police power measure and an exercise of the power of eminent domain: diminution in value, whether the measure is designed to regulate a nuisance, and reciprocity of advantage. Which of the dueling opinions in *Penn Central* is more faithful to this doctrinal framework: Justice Brennan's majority opinion, or Justice Rehnquist's dissent?

4. Justice Brennan's opinion stresses the "ad hoc" nature of regulatory takings inquiries, and does not appear to lay down any definitive test for determining whether a regulation "goes too far." Shortly after it was decided, however, *Penn Central* was recast as having prescribed a "three-part" inquiry, looking to "the economic impact of the regulation, its interference with reasonable investment backed expectations, and the character of the government action." Kaiser Aetna v. United States, 444 U.S. 164, 175 (1979). This made the inquiry seem more formulaic than it was in *Penn Central*, and probably more so than it is in practice today. Note that two of the factors considered key in *Mahon*—whether the regulation seeks to prevent a nuisance and whether it provides a reciprocity of advantage—disappear from the formulaic restatement. Yet it would be wrong to think that these factors have disappeared from the thinking of judges. For example, in *Keystone Bituminous Coal Assn. v. DeBenedictis*, 480 U.S. 470 (1987), the Court relied on the fact that the Pennsylvania anti-subsidence statute sought to regulate a nuisance-like harm in determining that the statute did not constitute a regulatory taking. And reciprocity of advantage has also been invoked as part of the inquiry into the "character of the government action." See, e.g., Lucas v. South Carolina Coastal Council, infra.

5. Consider the exchange between the majority and the dissent over whether New York's Landmarks Preservation Law is or is not like zoning. The Supreme Court had held in the *Euclid* case, excerpted in Chapter IX, that zoning is not a taking on its face, but might be a taking in particular applications. Given the discretionary and site-specific nature of the landmark designation process, does the Landmarks Preservation Law create a danger that it will be used in an oppressive or retaliatory fashion? In another prominent case involving New York's Landmarks Preservation Law, which upheld a landmark designation of a church on Park Avenue in the face of takings and free exercise of religion claims, the Second Circuit, speaking through Judge Winter, dropped the following footnote: "The Landmarks Law made a cameo appearance in a recent best-selling novel as a vehicle for political retaliation against a clerical official seeking to develop Church property. *See* T. Wolfe, *Bonfire of the Vanities* 569 (1987) ('Mort? You know that church, St. Timothy's? ... Right ... LANDMARK THE SON OF A BITCH!')." Rector of St. Bartholomew's Church v. City of New York, 914 F.2d 348, 355 n.3 (2d Cir. 1990).

6. One way of reading *Penn Central* is that the government can abrogate an owner's right to destroy property without incurring any takings liability, at least when the financial burden is not too extreme. How important is the right to destroy in the traditional "bundle of sticks" that makes up full ownership of property? See Lior Jacob Strahilevitz, The

Right to Destroy, 114 Yale L. J. 781, 794–96 (2005). Is abrogation of the right to destroy a more serious intrusion upon owner sovereignty than regulating the uses to which property can be put? The Court has also held that abrogation of the right to sell is not a taking, Andrus v. Allard, 444 U.S. 51, 67–68 (1979) (Congress can abrogate right to sell eagle feathers without creating takings liability). However, the Court has suggested that elimination of the right to transmit property upon death will presumptively be regarded as a taking, Hodel v. Irving, 481 U.S. 704, 717 (1987), and has stressed in a number of cases that abrogation of the right to exclude is regarded as particularly serious for takings purposes. See, e.g., Loretto v. Teleprompter Manhattan CATV Corp., 458 U.S. 419, 433–34 (1982) (excerpted infra); Dolan v. City of Tigard, 512 U.S. 374, 384 (1994) (excerpted infra); Nollan v. California Coastal Commission, 483 U.S. 825, 831 (1987); Kaiser Aetna v. United States, 444 U.S. 164, 176, 179–80 (1979); cf. PruneYard Shopping Center v. Robins, 447 U.S. 74, 84 (1980). Does the Court have a principled basis for deciding which incidents of property are more central to ownership than others, such that abrogation of the right is or is not regarded as likely to trigger takings liability? Or is the key point of *Penn Central* that generalizations about these things are not possible, and it all depends on context?

7. Was it appropriate for the Court to toss in the transfer development rights or TDRs awarded to Penn Central as one factor to balance in deciding whether the regulation was a taking? Or is Justice Rehnquist correct in assuming that the TDRs should be considered only on the question whether the company was given just compensation? In a later decision, Justice Scalia argued that "[p]utting TDRs on the taking rather than the just compensation side of the equation ... is a clever, albeit transparent, device that seeks to take advantage of a peculiarity of our Takings Clause jurisprudence: Whereas once there *is* a taking, the Constitution requires just (*i.e.*, full) compensation.... [a] regulatory taking generally does not *occur* so long as land retains substantial (albeit not its full) value." Suitum v. Tahoe Regional Planning Agency, 520 U.S. 725, 747–48 (1997) (concurring opinion). Building on this critique, could a political jurisdiction like New York avoid all takings liability by providing that just enough partial compensation will be awarded in each case to permit the court to conclude, on balance, that no taking has been committed?

8. At one point, *Penn Central* says that "a use restriction on real property may constitute a 'taking' if not reasonably necessary to the effectuation of a substantial public purpose, see Nectow v. Cambridge, supra." Two years later, in *Agins v. City of Tiburon*, 447 U.S. 255, 260 (1980), the Court repeated this dictum, stating that "[t]he application of a general zoning law to particular property effects a taking if the ordinance does not substantially advance legitimate state interests." After the Court repeated this line in a few more cases, eventually a doctrine grew up in the lower courts to the effect that a regulation can be a taking if it does not "substantially advance a legitimate state interest." The Court, however, never invoked this test standing alone to invalidate a regulation, and in *Lingle v. Chevron U.S.A. Inc.*, 544 U.S. 528 (2005), it reconsidered the

matter and decided that the "substantially advances" test has no place under the Takings Clause. The Court concluded that such a means-ends inquiry into the effectiveness of a regulation might make sense under the Due Process Clause, but had no place in a regulatory takings inquiry:

> [T]he "substantially advances" inquiry reveals nothing about the *magnitude or character of the burden* a particular regulation imposes upon private property rights. Nor does it provide any information about how any regulatory burden is *distributed* among property owners. In consequence, this test does not help to identify those regulations whose effects are functionally comparable to government appropriation or invasion of private property; it is tethered neither to the text of the Takings Clause nor to the basic justification for allowing regulatory actions to be challenged under the Clause.

544 U.S. at 542. Does this passage put too much emphasis on the distributional implications of specific regulations, and not enough on the "character of the government action," such as whether it is invasive or destroys a traditional property right?

9.   Whatever you think of *Penn Central* as a matter of constitutional law, do you think the practice of denying compensation for historic preservation orders makes sense as a matter of policy? Some commentators have worried that "freezing" the exterior design of notable buildings, without providing any compensation for lost development rights, may have two unintended consequences: (1) persons who own buildings that are potential targets for historic preservation designation may rush to demolish them before they are protected; and (2) persons who are contemplating commissioning the construction of new buildings may turn down dramatic or innovative designs out of fear that they will be "rewarded" with a historic preservation designation, and hence will be locked into the building for all time. See Mendes Hershman, Critical Legal Issues in Historic Preservation, 12 Urb. Law. 19, 28 (1980); Carol M. Rose, Preservation and Community: New Directions in the Law of Historic Preservation, 33 Stan. L. Rev. 473, 500–01 (1981); see also Strahilevitz, The Right to Destroy, supra, at 817–18; David A. Dana, Natural Preservation and the Race to Develop, 143 U. Pa. L. Rev. 655 (1995) (considering a similar critique in the context of natural preservation law). Either or both of these incentive effects could work to impoverish the overall architectural quality of the community. Providing compensation for lost development rights would presumably eliminate these incentive effects (at least in part). But of course, it would also mean that there would probably be many fewer historic designations, because of the expense to the community of paying for lost development rights.

Loretto v. Teleprompter Manhattan CATV Corp.

Supreme Court of the United States, 1982.
458 U.S. 419.

■ JUSTICE MARSHALL delivered the opinion of the Court. This case presents the question whether a minor but permanent physical occupation of an owner's property authorized by government constitutes a "taking" of property for which just compensation is due under the Fifth and Fourteenth Amendments of the Constitution. * * * The New York Court of Appeals ruled that this appropriation does not amount to a taking. Because we conclude that such a physical occupation of property is a taking, we reverse.

I

Appellant Jean Loretto purchased a five-story apartment building located at 303 West 105th Street, New York City, in 1971. The previous owner had granted appellees Teleprompter Corp. and Teleprompter Manhattan CATV (collectively Teleprompter) permission to install a cable on the building and the exclusive privilege of furnishing cable television (CATV) services to the tenants. The New York Court of Appeals described the installation as follows:

> On June 1, 1970 TelePrompter installed a cable slightly less than one-half inch in diameter and of approximately 30 feet in length along the length of the building about 18 inches above the roof top, and directional taps, approximately 4 inches by 4 inches by 4 inches, on the front and rear of the roof. By June 8, 1970 the cable had been extended another 4 to 6 feet and cable had been run from the directional taps to the adjoining building at 305 West 105th Street.

> Teleprompter also installed two large silver boxes along the roof cables. The cables are attached by screws or nails penetrating the masonry at approximately two-foot intervals, and other equipment is installed by bolts.

Initially, Teleprompter's roof cables did not service appellant's building. They were part of what could be described as a cable "highway" circumnavigating the city block, with service cables periodically dropped over the front or back of a building in which a tenant desired service. Crucial to such a network is the use of so-called "crossovers"—cable lines extending from one building to another in order to reach a new group of tenants. Two years after appellant purchased the building, Teleprompter connected a "noncrossover" line—*i.e.*, one that provided CATV service to appellant's own tenants—by dropping a line to the first floor down the front of appellant's building.

Prior to 1973, Teleprompter routinely obtained authorization for its installations from property owners along the cable's route, compensating the owners at the standard rate of 5% of the gross revenues that Teleprompter realized from the particular property. To facilitate tenant access to CATV, the State of New York enacted § 828 of the Executive Law, effective January 1, 1973. Section 828 provides that a landlord may not "interfere with the installation of cable television facilities upon his property or premises," and may not demand payment from any tenant for permitting CATV, or demand payment from any CATV company "in excess of any amount which the [State Commission on Cable Television] shall, by

Figure 12–5
303 West 105th Street, New York City, in 2006

regulation, determine to be reasonable." The landlord may, however, require the CATV company or the tenant to bear the cost of installation and to indemnify for any damage caused by the installation. Pursuant to § 828(1)(b), the State Commission has ruled that a one-time $1 payment is the normal fee to which a landlord is entitled. In the Matter of Implementation of Section 828 of the Executive Law, No. 90004, Statement of General Policy (New York State Commission on Cable Television, Jan. 15, 1976) (Statement of General Policy), App. 51–52; Clarification of General Policy (Aug. 27, 1976), App. 68–69. The Commission ruled that this nominal fee, which the Commission concluded was equivalent to what the landlord would receive if the property were condemned pursuant to New York's Transportation Corporations Law, satisfied constitutional requirements "in the absence of a special showing of greater damages attributable to the taking." Statement of General Policy, App. 52.

Appellant did not discover the existence of the cable until after she had purchased the building. She brought a class action against Teleprompter in 1976 on behalf of all owners of real property in the State on which Teleprompter has placed CATV components, alleging that Teleprompter's installation was a trespass and, insofar as it relied on § 828, a taking without just compensation. She requested damages and injunctive relief. Appellee City of New York, which has granted Teleprompter an exclusive franchise to provide CATV within certain areas of Manhattan, intervened. The Supreme Court, Special Term, granted summary judgment to Teleprompter and the city, upholding the constitutionality of § 828 in both crossover and noncrossover situations. The Appellate Division affirmed without opinion.

On appeal, the Court of Appeals, over dissent, upheld the statute. * * * We noted probable jurisdiction.

II

The Court of Appeals determined that § 828 serves the legitimate public purpose of "rapid development of and maximum penetration by a means of communication which has important educational and community aspects," and thus is within the State's police power. We have no reason to question that determination. It is a separate question, however, whether an otherwise valid regulation so frustrates property rights that compensation must be paid. See Penn Central Transportation Co. v. New York City, 438 U.S. 104, 127–128 (1978). We conclude that a permanent physical occupation authorized by government is a taking without regard to the public interests that it may serve. Our constitutional history confirms the rule, recent cases do not question it, and the purposes of the Takings Clause compel its retention.

A

In *Penn Central Transportation Co. v. New York City*, supra, the Court surveyed some of the general principles governing the Takings Clause. The Court noted that no "set formula" existed to determine, in all cases, whether compensation is constitutionally due for a government restriction of property. Ordinarily, the Court must engage in "essentially ad hoc, factual inquiries." Id., at 124. But the inquiry is not standardless. The economic impact of the regulation, especially the degree of interference with investment-backed expectations, is of particular significance. "So, too, is the character of the governmental action. A 'taking' may more readily be found when the interference with property can be characterized as a physical invasion by government, than when interference arises from some public program adjusting the benefits and burdens of economic life to promote the common good." Ibid. (citation omitted).

As *Penn Central* affirms, the Court has often upheld substantial regulation of an owner's use of his own property where deemed necessary to promote the public interest. At the same time, we have long considered a physical intrusion by government to be a property restriction of an unusually serious character for purposes of the Takings Clause. Our cases further establish that when the physical intrusion reaches the extreme form of a permanent physical occupation, a taking has occurred. In such a case, "the character of the government action" not only is an important factor in resolving whether the action works a taking but also is determinative.

When faced with a constitutional challenge to a permanent physical occupation of real property, this Court has invariably found a taking. As early as 1872, in *Pumpelly v. Green Bay Co.*, 13 Wall. (80 U.S.) 166, this Court held that the defendant's construction, pursuant to state authority, of a dam which permanently flooded plaintiff's property constituted a taking. A unanimous Court stated, without qualification, that "where real estate is actually invaded by superinduced additions of water, earth, sand, or other material, or by having any artificial structure placed on it, so as to effectually destroy or impair its usefulness, it is a taking, within the meaning of the Constitution." Id., 13 Wall. (80 U.S.) at 181. Seven years later, the Court reemphasized the importance of a physical occupation by distinguishing a regulation that merely restricted the use of private property. In *Northern Transportation Co. v. Chicago*, 99 U.S. 635 (1879), the Court held that the city's construction of a temporary dam in a river to permit construction of a tunnel was not a taking, even though the plaintiffs were thereby denied access to their premises, because the obstruction only impaired the use of plaintiffs' property. The Court distinguished earlier cases in which permanent flooding of private property was regarded as a taking, e.g., Pumpelly, supra, as involving "a physical invasion of the real estate of the private owner, and a practical ouster of his possession." In this case, by contrast, "[n]o entry was made upon the plaintiffs' lot." 99 U.S., at 642.

Since these early cases, this Court has consistently distinguished between flooding cases involving a permanent physical occupation, on the one hand, and cases involving a more temporary invasion, or government action outside the owner's property that causes consequential damages within, on the other. A taking has always been found only in the former situation. * * *

More recent cases confirm the distinction between a permanent physical occupation, a physical invasion short of an occupation, and a regulation that merely restricts the use of property. In United States v. Causby, 328 U.S. 256 (1946), the Court ruled that frequent flights immediately above a landowner's property constituted a taking, comparing such overflights to the quintessential form of a taking:

> If, by reason of the frequency and altitude of the flights, respondents could not use this land for any purpose, their loss would be complete. It would be as complete as if the United States had entered upon the surface of the land and taken exclusive possession of it. Id., at 261 (footnote omitted).

As the Court further explained,

We would not doubt that, if the United States erected an elevated railway over respondents' land at the precise altitude where its planes now fly, there would be a partial taking, even though none of the supports of the structure rested on the land. The reason is that there would be an intrusion so immediate and direct as to subtract from the owner's full enjoyment of the property and to limit his exploitation of it. Id., at 264–265.

The Court concluded that the damages to the respondents "were not merely consequential. They were the product of a direct invasion of respondents' domain." Id., at 265–266. See also Griggs v. Allegheny County, 369 U.S. 84 (1962). * * *

Although this Court's most recent cases have not addressed the precise issue before us, they have emphasized that physical *invasion* cases are special and have not repudiated the rule that any permanent physical *occupation* is a taking. The cases state or imply that a physical invasion is subject to a balancing process, but they do not suggest that a permanent physical occupation would ever be exempt from the Takings Clause. * * *

In short, when the "character of the governmental action," Penn Central, 438 U.S., at 124, is a permanent physical occupation of property, our cases uniformly have found a taking to the extent of the occupation, without regard to whether the action achieves an important public benefit or has only minimal economic impact on the owner.

B

The historical rule that a permanent physical occupation of another's property is a taking has more than tradition to commend it. Such an appropriation is perhaps the most serious form of invasion of an owner's property interests. To borrow a metaphor, cf. Andrus v. Allard, 444 U.S. 51, 65–66 (1979), the government does not simply take a single "strand" from the "bundle" of property rights: it chops through the bundle, taking a slice of every strand.

Property rights in a physical thing have been described as the rights "to possess, use and dispose of it." United States v. General Motors Corp., 323 U.S. 373, 378 (1945). To the extent that the government permanently occupies physical property, it effectively destroys *each* of these rights. First, the owner has no right to possess the occupied space himself, and also has no power to exclude the occupier from possession and use of the space. The power to exclude has traditionally been considered one of the most treasured strands in an owner's bundle of property rights.[12] See Kaiser Aetna,

---

12. The permanence and absolute exclusivity of a physical occupation distinguish it from temporary limitations on the right to exclude. Not every physical *invasion* is a taking. As *PruneYard Shopping Center v. Robins*, 447 U.S. 74 (1980); *Kaiser Aetna v. United States*, 444 U.S. 164 (1979), and the intermittent flooding cases reveal, such temporary limitations are subject to a more complex balancing process to determine whether they are a taking. The rationale is evident: they do not absolutely dispossess the owner of his rights to use, and exclude others from, his property.

444 U.S., at 179–180; see also Restatement of Property § 7 (1936). Second, the permanent physical occupation of property forever denies the owner any power to control the use of the property; he not only cannot exclude others, but can make no nonpossessory use of the property. Although deprivation of the right to use and obtain a profit from property is not, in every case, independently sufficient to establish a taking, see Andrus v. Allard, supra, at 66, it is clearly relevant. Finally, even though the owner may retain the bare legal right to dispose of the occupied space by transfer or sale, the permanent occupation of that space by a stranger will ordinarily empty the right of any value, since the purchaser will also be unable to make any use of the property.

Moreover, an owner suffers a special kind of injury when a *stranger* directly invades and occupies the owner's property. As Part II–A, supra, indicates, property law has long protected an owner's expectation that he will be relatively undisturbed at least in the possession of his property. To require, as well, that the owner permit another to exercise complete dominion literally adds insult to injury. See Michelman, Property, Utility, and Fairness: Comments on the Ethical Foundations of "Just Compensation" Law, 80 Harv.L.Rev. 1165, 1228, and n. 110 (1967). Furthermore, such an occupation is qualitatively more severe than a regulation of the *use* of property, even a regulation that imposes affirmative duties on the owner, since the owner may have no control over the timing, extent, or nature of the invasion. See n. 19, infra.

The traditional rule also avoids otherwise difficult line-drawing problems. Few would disagree that if the State required landlords to permit third parties to install swimming pools on the landlords' rooftops for the convenience of the tenants, the requirement would be a taking. If the cable installation here occupied as much space, again, few would disagree that the occupation would be a taking. But constitutional protection for the rights of private property cannot be made to depend on the size of the area permanently occupied. Indeed, it is possible that in the future, additional cable installations that more significantly restrict a landlord's use of the roof of his building will be made. Section 828 requires a landlord to permit such multiple installations.

Finally, whether a permanent physical occupation has occurred presents relatively few problems of proof. The placement of a fixed structure on land or real property is an obvious fact that will rarely be subject to dispute. Once the fact of occupation is shown, of course, a court should consider the *extent* of the occupation as one relevant factor in determining the compensation due. For that reason, moreover, there is less need to

---

The dissent objects that the distinction between a permanent physical occupation and a temporary invasion will not always be clear. This objection is overstated, and in any event is irrelevant to the critical point that a permanent physical occupation *is* unques-tionably a taking. In the antitrust area, similarly, this Court has not declined to apply a *per se* rule simply because a court must, at the boundary of the rule, apply the rule of reason and engage in a more complex balancing analysis.

consider the extent of the occupation in determining whether there is a taking in the first instance.

C

Teleprompter's cable installation on appellant's building constitutes a taking under the traditional test. The installation involved a direct physical attachment of plates, boxes, wires, bolts, and screws to the building, completely occupying space immediately above and upon the roof and along the building's exterior wall.[16]

In light of our analysis, we find no constitutional difference between a crossover and a noncrossover installation. The portions of the installation necessary for both crossovers and noncrossovers permanently appropriate appellant's property. Accordingly, each type of installation is a taking.

Appellees raise a series of objections to application of the traditional rule here. Teleprompter notes that the law applies only to buildings used as rental property, and draws the conclusion that the law is simply a permissible regulation of the use of real property. We fail to see, however, why a physical occupation of one type of property but not another type is any less a physical occupation. Insofar as Teleprompter means to suggest that this is not a permanent physical invasion, we must differ. So long as the property remains residential and a CATV company wishes to retain the installation, the landlord must permit it.[17]

Teleprompter also asserts the related argument that the State has effectively granted a tenant the property right to have a CATV installation placed on the roof of his building, as an appurtenance to the tenant's leasehold. The short answer is that § 828(1)(a) does not purport to give the *tenant* any enforceable property rights with respect to CATV installation, and the lower courts did not rest their decisions on this ground. Of course, Teleprompter, not appellant's tenants, actually owns the installation. Moreover, the government does not have unlimited power to redefine property rights. See Webb's Fabulous Pharmacies, Inc. v. Beckwith, 449 U.S. 155, 164 (1980) ("a State, by *ipse dixit*, may not transform private property into public property without compensation").

---

16. It is constitutionally irrelevant whether appellant (or her predecessor in title) had previously occupied this space, since a "landowner owns at least as much of the space above the ground as he can occupy or use in connection with the land." United States v. Causby, supra, at 264.

The dissent asserts that a taking of about one-eighth of a cubic foot of space is not of constitutional significance. The assertion appears to be factually incorrect, since it ignores the two large silver boxes that appellant identified as part of the installation. Although the record does not reveal their size, appellant states that they are approximately 18″ x 12″ x 6″, Brief for Appellant 6 n.*, and appellees do not dispute this statement. The displaced volume, then, is in excess of 1 ½ cubic feet. In any event, these facts are not critical: whether the installation is a taking does not depend on whether the volume of space it occupies is bigger than a breadbox.

17. It is true that the landlord could avoid the requirements of § 828 by ceasing to rent the building to tenants. But a landlord's ability to rent his property may not be conditioned on his forfeiting the right to compensation for a physical occupation.

Finally, we do not agree with appellees that application of the physical occupation rule will have dire consequences for the government's power to adjust landlord-tenant relationships. This Court has consistently affirmed that States have broad power to regulate housing conditions in general and the landlord-tenant relationship in particular without paying compensation for all economic injuries that such regulation entails. See, e.g., Heart of Atlanta Motel, Inc. v. United States, 379 U.S. 241 (1964) (discrimination in places of public accommodation); Queenside Hills Realty Co. v. Saxl, 328 U.S. 80 (1946) (fire regulation); Bowles v. Willingham, 321 U.S. 503 (1944) (rent control); Home Building & Loan Assn. v. Blaisdell, 290 U.S. 398 (1934) (mortgage moratorium); Edgar A. Levy Leasing Co. v. Siegel, 258 U.S. 242 (1922) (emergency housing law); Block v. Hirsh, 256 U.S. 135 (1921) (rent control). In none of these cases, however, did the government authorize the permanent occupation of the landlord's property by a third party. Consequently, our holding today in no way alters the analysis governing the State's power to require landlords to comply with building codes and provide utility connections, mailboxes, smoke detectors, fire extinguishers, and the like in the common area of a building. So long as these regulations do not require the landlord to suffer the physical occupation of a portion of his building by a third party, they will be analyzed under the multifactor inquiry generally applicable to nonpossessory governmental activity. See Penn Central Transportation Co. v. New York City, 438 U.S. 104 (1978).[19]

III

Our holding today is very narrow. We affirm the traditional rule that a permanent physical occupation of property is a taking. In such a case, the property owner entertains a historically rooted expectation of compensation, and the character of the invasion is qualitatively more intrusive than perhaps any other category of property regulation. We do not, however,

---

19. If § 828 required landlords to provide cable installation if a tenant so desires, the statute might present a different question from the question before us, since the landlord would own the installation. Ownership would give the landlord rights to the placement, manner, use, and possibly the disposition of the installation. The fact of ownership is, contrary to the dissent, not simply "incidental"; it would give a landlord (rather than a CATV company) full authority over the installation except only as government specifically limited that authority. The *landlord* would decide how to comply with applicable government regulations concerning CATV and therefore could minimize the physical, esthetic, and other effects of the installation. Moreover, if the landlord wished to repair, demolish, or construct in the area of the building where the installation is located, he need not incur the burden of obtaining the CATV company's cooperation in moving the cable. In this case, by contrast, appellant suffered injury that might have been obviated if she had owned the cable and could exercise control over its installation. The drilling and stapling that accompanied installation apparently caused physical damage to appellant's building. App. 83, 95–96, 104. Appellant, who resides in her building, further testified that the cable installation is "ugly." Id., at 99. Although § 828 provides that a landlord may require "reasonable" conditions that are "necessary" to protect the appearance of the premises and may seek indemnity for damage, these provisions are somewhat limited. Even if the provisions are effective, the inconvenience to the landlord of initiating the repairs remains a cognizable burden.

question the equally substantial authority upholding a State's broad power to impose appropriate restrictions upon an owner's *use* of his property.

Furthermore, our conclusion that § 828 works a taking of a portion of appellant's property does not presuppose that the fee which many landlords had obtained from Teleprompter prior to the law's enactment is a proper measure of the value of the property taken. The issue of the amount of compensation that is due, on which we express no opinion, is a matter for the state courts to consider on remand. * * *

■ JUSTICE BLACKMUN, with whom JUSTICE BRENNAN and JUSTICE WHITE join, dissenting. * * * In a curiously anachronistic decision, the Court today acknowledges its historical disavowal of set formulae in almost the same breath as it constructs a rigid *per se* takings rule: "a permanent physical occupation authorized by government is a taking without regard to the public interests that it may serve." To sustain its rule against our recent precedents, the Court erects a strained and untenable distinction between "temporary physical invasions," whose constitutionality concededly "is subject to a balancing process," and "permanent physical occupations," which are "taking[s] without regard to other factors that a court might ordinarily examine." * * *

[T]he Court * * * states that the permanent physical occupation authorized by § 828 is a *per se* taking because it uniquely impairs appellant's powers to dispose of, use, and exclude others from, her property. In fact, the Court's discussion nowhere demonstrates how § 828 impairs these private rights in a manner *qualitatively* different from other garden-variety landlord-tenant legislation. * * *

[Section] 828 differs little from the numerous other New York statutory provisions that require landlords to install physical facilities "permanently occupying" common spaces in or on their buildings. As the Court acknowledges, the States traditionally—and constitutionally—have exercised their police power "to require landlords to ... provide utility connections, mailboxes, smoke detectors, fire extinguishers, and the like in the common area of a building." Like § 828, these provisions merely ensure tenants access to services the legislature deems important, such as water, electricity, natural light, telephones, intercommunication systems, and mail service. A landlord's dispositional rights are affected no more adversely when he sells a building to another landlord subject to § 828, than when he sells that building subject only to these other New York statutory provisions.

The Court also suggests that § 828 unconstitutionally alters appellant's right to control the *use* of her one-eighth cubic foot of roof space. But other New York multiple dwelling statutes not only oblige landlords to surrender significantly larger portions of common space for their tenants' use, but also compel the *landlord*—rather than the tenants or the private installers—to pay for and to maintain the equipment. For example, New York landlords are required by law to provide and pay for mailboxes that occupy more than five times the volume that Teleprompter's cable occupies on appellant's building. See Tr. of Oral Arg. 42–43, citing N.Y.Mult.Dwell.Law § 57 (McKinney 1974). If the State constitutionally can insist that appellant make this sacrifice so that her tenants may receive mail, it is hard to understand why the State may not require her to surrender less space, *filled at another's expense*, so that those same tenants can receive television signals.

For constitutional purposes, the relevant question cannot be solely *whether* the State has interfered in some minimal way with an owner's use of space on her building. Any intelligible takings inquiry must also ask whether the *extent* of the State's interference is so severe as to constitute a compensable taking in light of the owner's alternative uses for the property. Appellant freely admitted that she would have had no other use for the cable-occupied space, were Teleprompter's equipment not on her building.

The Court's third and final argument is that § 828 has deprived appellant of her "power to exclude the occupier from possession and use of the space" occupied by the cable. This argument has two flaws. First, it unjustifiably assumes that appellant's tenants have no countervailing property interest in permitting Teleprompter to use that space.[11] Second, it suggests that the New York Legislature may not exercise its police power to affect appellant's common-law right to exclude Teleprompter even from one-eighth cubic foot of roof space. But this Court long ago recognized that new social circumstances can justify legislative modification of a property owner's common-law rights, without compensation, if the legislative action serves sufficiently important public interests. See Munn v. Illinois, 94 U.S. 113, 134 (1877) ("A person has no property, no vested interest, in any rule of the common law.... Indeed, the great office of statutes is to remedy defects in the common law as they are developed, and to adapt it to the changes of time and circumstance"); United States v. Causby, 328 U.S., at 260–261 (In the modern world, "[c]ommon sense revolts at the idea" that legislatures cannot alter common-law ownership rights).

As the Court of Appeals recognized, § 828 merely deprives appellant of a common-law trespass action against Teleprompter, but only for as long as she uses her building for rental purposes, and as long as Teleprompter maintains its equipment in compliance with the statute. * * *

This Court now reaches back in time for a *per se* rule that disrupts that legislative determination. Like Justice Black, I believe that "the solution of the problems precipitated by ... technological advances and new ways of living cannot come about through the application of rigid constitutional restraints formulated and enforced by the courts." United

---

11. It is far from clear that, under New York law, appellant's tenants would lack all property interests in the few square inches on the exterior of the building to which Teleprompter's cable and hardware attach. Under modern landlord-tenant law, a residential tenancy is not merely a possessory interest in specified space, but also a contract for the provision of a package of services and facili- ties necessary and appurtenant to that space. See R. Schoshinski, American Law of Landlord and Tenant § 3:14 (1980). A modern urban tenant's leasehold often includes not only contractual, but also statutory rights, including the rights to an implied warranty of habitability, rent control, and such services as the landlord is obliged by statute to provide.

States v. Causby, 328 U.S., at 274 (dissenting opinion). I would affirm the judgment and uphold the reasoning of the New York Court of Appeals.

NOTES AND QUESTIONS

1.   On remand from the decision here, the New York courts concluded that $1 was all the compensation Jean Loretto was entitled to receive. The courts reasoned that the introduction of cable service increased the rental value of apartments and hence of apartment buildings by more than the value of the tiny amount of roof space taken. Consequently, the award of $1 was more than "just" compensation. Loretto v. Teleprompter Manhattan CATV Corp., 446 N.E.2d 428 (N.Y. 1983). If the New York courts had simply ruled the first time around that the statute was a taking, but the loss in value to landlords was more than offset by the benefits from higher rental value, would the whole episode have been avoided?

2.   Do you think Jean Loretto was motivated to sue out of some dignitary concern about unwanted invasions of her property, or aesthetic revulsion at the cable draped on top of her building (and running down the side)? Note that the cable company originally offered landlords 5% of gross revenues derived from selling cable service to the building and then apparently got the State Cable Commission to reduce the compensation to $1. Note too that Loretto filed her suit as a class action, seeking damages equal to the difference between the original 5% fee and the $1 nominal compensation on behalf of all affected landlords. Case Note, 25 B.C. L. Rev. 459, 460–62 (1984). Whatever her motivation, Ms. Loretto was determined. After eleven years of litigation, in which she recovered $1, the New York Appellate Division denied her request for $500,000 in attorney's fees from the cable company. Loretto v. Group W Cable, Inc., 522 N.Y.S.2d 543 (N.Y. App. Div. 1987).

3.   Many commentators were surprised that the Supreme Court, only four years after comprehensively restating regulatory takings doctrine in *Penn Central*, and seemingly endorsing an ad hoc approach for all purposes, carved out an exception for permanent physical invasions in *Loretto*. The fact that Justice Marshall, ordinarily a staunch ally of Justice Brennan, was the author of the opinion, made it even more surprising. However, viewed from the perspective of eminent domain law, and in particular from the perspective of the use of eminent domain by public utilities, the decision seems quite unsurprising. All kinds of public utility companies—electric distribution companies, telephone companies, natural gas distribution companies—need to acquire easements to lay down their distribution lines. The established method of acquiring such easements is to use eminent domain. Thus, when a new type of distribution company comes along—cable television—it seems only natural that these newcomers should also use eminent domain to acquire rights to run their wires from building to building. A holding contrary to the one reached by the Court, suggesting that easements acquired by some utilities that impose only minor costs on servient landowners can proceed by police power regulation rather than eminent

domain, would have opened a big can of worms in an area of the law that had previously been regarded as settled.

4.   In terms of doctrinal development, *Loretto* was significant far beyond its holding. As suggested by footnote 12 in the Court's opinion, the combination of *Penn Central* and *Loretto* suggests that regulatory takings doctrine partakes of a general "ad hoc" test, supplemented by narrow rules of "per se" liability that apply in particular circumstances. This is similar to the approach of antitrust law, which follows a general "rule of reason" in determining whether particular restraints on trade violate the law, supplemented by narrow "per se" rules that apply to conduct that seems to warrant liability without regard to the circumstances. See, e.g., Broadcast Music, Inc. v. Columbia Broadcasting System, Inc., 441 U.S. 1 (1979). This two-tiered structure of decisional rules was to blossom into a more complete form in *Lucas*, the next case you will read. For overviews of the relationship between categorical and ad hoc takings tests, see Lingle v. Chevron U.S.A. Inc., 544 U.S. 528, 538–40 (2005); David A. Dana & Thomas W. Merrill, Property: Takings 86–168 (2002).

5.   Is the contrast between Justice Marshall's opinion in *Loretto* and Justice Brennan's opinion in *Penn Central* another example of the great divide in property law between trespass and nuisance, exclusion and governance? Or of the great divide between theories of property that stress the centrality of exclusion rights, and those that characterize property as a bundle of rights? Is *Loretto* just a reflexive transposition of a private law rule into a public law context, where it makes little sense? Or is it possible to justify the Court's rule by drawing upon some of the same reasons that justify strict liability for trespasses in the private law context?

6.   The right to exclude trespassory invasions, which is given such prominence in *Loretto*, also played a role in other takings controversies decided around the same time, with mixed results. In *Kaiser Aetna v. United States*, 444 U.S. 164 (1979), the Court considered whether a federal directive to open a privately-constructed marina to the general public as part of the navigable waters of the United States was a taking. Distinguishing cases holding that regulations designed to preserve the public "navigation servitude" are not takings, and stressing the importance of the right to exclude others in preserving investment-backed expectations, the Court found that the regulation was a taking. In *PruneYard Shopping Center v. Robins*, 447 U.S. 74 (1980), in contrast, the Court held that a state directive allowing persons to distribute political leaflets and information in a privately-owned shopping center was not a taking. The Court acknowledged the importance of the right to exclude, but noted that the shopping center had opened its doors to the general public (for shopping purposes), and concluded that the regulation had only a minor impact on any investment-backed expectations. Both decisions applied *Penn Central*'s ad hoc test, and did not suggest any per se rule for permanent invasions or occupations.

7.   After *Loretto*, the Court generally interpreted the exception for permanent occupations narrowly. For example, in *Yee v. City of Escondido*, 503 U.S. 519 (1992), the Court held that an ordinance that took away a

landlord's right to determine the identity of a replacement tenant in a mobile home park did not result in a permanent occupation, because the landlord had voluntarily chosen to lease the property in the first place. Similarly, in *FCC v. Florida Power Corp.*, 480 U.S. 245 (1987), the Court rejected the claim that a federal directive requiring utility companies to lease space on poles to cable companies at regulated rates was a permanent occupation, because the original lease arrangement had been voluntary. In two other decisions involving exactions imposed as a condition of developing property, however, the Court arguably expanded the per se rule in a significant fashion. See Nollan v. California Coastal Comm., 483 U.S. 825 (1987); Dolan v. City of Tigard, 512 U.S. 374 (1994), excerpted infra Section B.3. In both decisions, the Court indicated that regulations requiring property owners to dedicate a permanent easement of public access would be per se takings under *Loretto*. See Nollan, 483 U.S. at 832 ("We think a 'permanent physical occupation' has occurred . . . where individuals are given a permanent and continuous right to pass to and fro, so that the real property may continuously be traversed, even though no particular individual is permitted to station himself permanently on the premises.") Is this extension nevertheless consistent with the reasoning of the majority in *Loretto*?

8. Did *Loretto* mark a turn in regulatory takings law toward greater protection of property? Certainly, the 1980s saw a turn in scholarship toward greater solicitude for property, and greater skepticism about government regulation. Most notably, Richard Epstein, of the University of Chicago Law School, published a widely-discussed book that argued for strict scrutiny of all regulations of property under the Takings Cause. See Richard A. Epstein, Takings: Private Property and the Power of Eminent Domain (1985). Epstein argued, among other things, that the state's power to regulate property is no greater than the power of individual owners to object to uses of property by others, principally under the common law of nuisance. Any regulation that goes beyond the common law of nuisance, Epstein argued, should be regarded a taking, unless the regulation provides implicit in-kind compensation to all owners. After William H. Rehnquist was named Chief Justice and Antonin Scalia became an Associate Justice in 1986, the Supreme Court began to show increased interest in regulatory takings issues. See Frank Michelman, Takings, 1987, 88 Colum. L. Rev. 1600 (1988). The Rehnquist Court's takings jurisprudence reached its high water mark in the following case, in which many observers thought they detected the influence of Professor Epstein's theory.

Lucas v. South Carolina Coastal Council

Supreme Court of the United States, 1992.
505 U.S. 1003.

■ JUSTICE SCALIA delivered the opinion of the Court. In 1986, petitioner David H. Lucas paid $975,000 for two residential lots on the Isle of Palms in Charleston County, South Carolina, on which he intended to build single-family homes. In 1988, however, the South Carolina Legislature enacted the Beachfront Management Act, S.C.Code Ann. § 48–39–250 et seq. (Supp. 1990), which had the direct effect of barring petitioner from erecting any permanent habitable structures on his two parcels. See § 48–39–290(A). A state trial court found that this prohibition rendered Lucas's parcels "valueless." This case requires us to decide whether the Act's dramatic effect on the economic value of Lucas's lots accomplished a taking of private property under the Fifth and Fourteenth Amendments requiring the payment of "just compensation." U.S. Const., Amdt. 5.

I

A

South Carolina's expressed interest in intensively managing development activities in the so-called "coastal zone" dates from 1977 when, in the aftermath of Congress's passage of the federal Coastal Zone Management Act of 1972, 86 Stat. 1280, as amended, 16 U.S.C. § 1451 et seq., the legislature enacted a Coastal Zone Management Act of its own. See S.C.Code Ann. § 48–39–10 et seq. (1987). In its original form, the South Carolina Act required owners of coastal zone land that qualified as a "critical area" (defined in the legislation to include beaches and immediately adjacent sand dunes, § 48–39–10(J)) to obtain a permit from the newly created South Carolina Coastal Council (Council) (respondent here) prior to committing the land to a "use other than the use the critical area was devoted to on [September 28, 1977]." § 48–39–130(A).

In the late 1970's, Lucas and others began extensive residential development of the Isle of Palms, a barrier island situated eastward of the city of Charleston. Toward the close of the development cycle for one residential subdivision known as "Beachwood East," Lucas in 1986 purchased the two lots at issue in this litigation for his own account. No portion of the lots, which were located approximately 300 feet from the beach, qualified as a "critical area" under the 1977 Act; accordingly, at the time Lucas acquired these parcels, he was not legally obliged to obtain a permit from the Council in advance of any development activity. His intention with respect to the lots was to do what the owners of the immediately adjacent parcels had already done: erect single-family residences. He commissioned architectural drawings for this purpose.

The Beachfront Management Act brought Lucas's plans to an abrupt end. Under that 1988 legislation, the Council was directed to establish a "baseline" connecting the landward-most "point[s] of erosion ... during the past forty years" in the region of the Isle of Palms that includes Lucas's lots. S.C.Code Ann. § 48–39–280(A)(2) (Supp. 1988). In action not challenged here, the Council fixed this baseline landward of Lucas's parcels. That was significant, for under the Act construction of occupiable improvements was flatly prohibited seaward of a line drawn 20 feet landward of, and parallel to, the baseline. § 48–39–290(A). The Act provided no exceptions.

Figure 12–6
Map of the Area Involved in *Lucas*

Source: Douglas R. Porter, The *Lucas* Case, Urban Land, Sept. 1992, at 27, 29. Lucas's two lots are 22 and 24 (shaded). The lines indicate the shoreline in various years and the erosion in the years immediately prior to the case.

B

Lucas promptly filed suit in the South Carolina Court of Common Pleas, contending that the Beachfront Management Act's construction bar effected a taking of his property without just compensation. Lucas did not take issue with the validity of the Act as a lawful exercise of South Carolina's police power, but contended that the Act's complete extinguishment of his property's value entitled him to compensation regardless of whether the legislature had acted in furtherance of legitimate police power objectives. Following a bench trial, the court agreed. Among its factual determinations was the finding that "at the time Lucas purchased the two lots, both were zoned for single-family residential construction and ... there were no restrictions imposed upon such use of the property by either the State of South Carolina, the County of Charleston, or the Town of the Isle of Palms." The trial court further found that the Beachfront Management Act decreed a permanent ban on construction insofar as Lucas's lots were concerned, and that this prohibition "deprive[d] Lucas of any reasonable economic use of the lots, ... eliminated the unrestricted right of use, and render[ed] them valueless." The court thus concluded that Lucas's properties had been "taken" by operation of the Act, and it ordered respondent to pay "just compensation" in the amount of $1,232,387.50.

The Supreme Court of South Carolina reversed. It found dispositive what it described as Lucas's concession "that the Beachfront Management Act [was] properly and validly designed to preserve ... South Carolina's beaches." Failing an attack on the validity of the statute as such, the court believed itself bound to accept the "uncontested ... findings" of the South Carolina Legislature that new construction in the coastal zone—such as petitioner intended—threatened this public resource. The court ruled that when a regulation respecting the use of property is designed "to prevent serious public harm," (citing, *inter alia*, Mugler v. Kansas, 123 U.S. 623 (1887)), no compensation is owing under the Takings Clause regardless of the regulation's effect on the property's value. * * *

II

As a threshold matter, we must briefly address the Council's suggestion that this case is inappropriate for plenary review. [The Court held that the case was ripe for decision, had not been rendered moot by recent legislation, and otherwise presented a justiciable controversy.]

III

A

Prior to Justice Holmes's exposition in *Pennsylvania Coal Co. v. Mahon,* 260 U.S. 393 (1922), it was generally thought that the Takings Clause reached only a "direct appropriation" of property, Legal Tender Cases, 12 Wall. 457, 551 (1871), or the functional equivalent of a "practical ouster of [the owner's] possession," Transportation Co. v. Chicago, 99 U.S. 635, 642 (1879). Justice Holmes recognized in *Mahon,* however, that if the protection against physical appropriations of private property was to be meaningfully enforced, the government's power to redefine the range of interests included in the ownership of property was necessarily constrained by constitutional limits. 260 U.S., at 414–415. If, instead, the uses of private property were subject to unbridled, uncompensated qualification under the police power, "the natural tendency of human nature [would be] to extend the qualification more and more until at last private property disappear[ed]." Id., at 415. These considerations gave birth in that case to the oft-cited maxim that, "while property may be regulated to a certain extent, if regulation goes too far it will be recognized as a taking." Ibid.

Nevertheless, our decision in *Mahon* offered little insight into when, and under what circumstances, a given regulation would be seen as going "too far" for purposes of the Fifth Amendment. In 70–odd years of succeeding "regulatory takings" jurisprudence, we have generally eschewed any " 'set formula' " for determining how far is too far, preferring to "engag[e] in ... essentially ad hoc, factual inquiries." Penn Central Transportation Co. v. New York City, 438 U.S. 104, 124 (1978) (quoting Goldblatt v. Hempstead, 369 U.S. 590, 594 (1962)). See Epstein, Takings: Descent and Resurrection, 1987 S.Ct. Rev. 1, 4. We have, however, described at least two discrete categories of regulatory action as compensable without case-specific inquiry into the public interest advanced in support of the restraint. The first encompasses regulations that compel the property owner to suffer a physical "invasion" of his property. In general (at least with regard to permanent invasions), no matter how minute the intrusion, and no matter how weighty the public purpose behind it, we have required compensation. [Loretto v. Teleprompter Manhattan CATV Corp., 458 U.S. 419 (1982).] * * *

The second situation in which we have found categorical treatment appropriate is where regulation denies all economically beneficial or productive use of land. See Agins v. City of Tibuson, 447 U.S. 255, 260 (1980); see also Nollan v. California Coastal Comm'n, 483 U.S. 825, 834 (1987); Keystone Bituminous Coal Assn. v. DeBenedictis, 480 U.S. 470, 491–492 (1987); Hodel v. Virginia Surface Mining & Reclamation Assn., Inc., 452 U.S. 264, 295–296 (1981). As we have said on numerous occasions, the Fifth Amendment is violated when land-use regulation "does not substantially advance legitimate state interests *or denies an owner economically viable use of his land.*" Agins, supra, 447 U.S., at 260 (citations omitted) (emphasis added).[7]

We have never set forth the justification for this rule. Perhaps it is simply, as Justice Brennan suggested, that total deprivation of beneficial use is, from the landowner's point of view, the equivalent of a physical appropriation. See San Diego Gas & Electric Co. v. San Diego, 450 U.S. 621, 652 (1981) (dissenting opinion). "[F]or what is the land but the profits thereof[?]" 1 E. Coke, Institutes, ch. 1, § 1 (1st Am. ed. 1812). Surely, at least, in the extraordinary circumstance when *no* productive or economical-

---

7. Regrettably, the rhetorical force of our "deprivation of all economically feasible use" rule is greater than its precision, since the rule does not make clear the "property interest" against which the loss of value is to be measured. When, for example, a regulation requires a developer to leave 90% of a rural tract in its natural state, it is unclear whether we would analyze the situation as one in which the owner has been deprived of all economically beneficial use of the burdened portion of the tract, or as one in which the owner has suffered a mere diminution in value of the tract as a whole. (For an extreme—and, we think, unsupportable—view of the relevant calculus, see Penn Central Transportation Co. v. New York City, 366 N.E.2d 1271, 1276–1277 (N.Y. 1977), aff'd, 438 U.S. 104 (1978), where the state court examined the diminution in a particular parcel's value produced by a municipal ordinance in light of total value of the takings claimant's other holdings in the vicinity.) Unsurprisingly, this uncertainty regarding the composition of the denominator in our "deprivation" fraction has produced inconsistent pronouncements by the Court. Compare Pennsylvania Coal Co. v. Mahon, 260 U.S. 393, 414 (1922) (law restricting subsurface extraction of coal held to effect a taking), with Keystone Bituminous Coal Assn. v. DeBenedictis, 480 U.S. 470, 497–502 (1987) (nearly identical law held not to effect a taking); see also id., at 515–520 (REHNQUIST, C.J., dissenting); Rose, *Mahon* Reconstructed: Why the Takings Issue is Still a Muddle, 57 S.Cal.L.Rev. 561, 566–569 (1984). The answer to this difficult question may lie in how the owner's reasonable expectations have been shaped by the State's law of property—*i.e.*, whether and to what degree the State's law has accorded legal recognition and protection to the particular interest in land with respect to which the takings claimant alleges a diminution in (or elimination of) value. In any event, we avoid this difficulty in the present case, since the "interest in land" that Lucas has pleaded (a fee simple interest) is an estate with a rich tradition of protection at common law, and since the South Carolina Court of Common Pleas found that the Beachfront Management Act left each of Lucas's beachfront lots without economic value.

ly beneficial use of land is permitted, it is less realistic to indulge our usual assumption that the legislature is simply "adjusting the benefits and burdens of economic life," Penn Central Transportation Co., 438 U.S., at 124, in a manner that secures an "average reciprocity of advantage" to everyone concerned, Pennsylvania Coal Co. v. Mahon, 260 U.S., at 415. And the *functional* basis for permitting the government, by regulation, to affect property values without compensation—that "Government hardly could go on if to some extent values incident to property could not be diminished without paying for every such change in the general law," id., at 413—does not apply to the relatively rare situations where the government has deprived a landowner of all economically beneficial uses.

On the other side of the balance, affirmatively supporting a compensation requirement, is the fact that regulations that leave the owner of land without economically beneficial or productive options for its use—typically, as here, by requiring land to be left substantially in its natural state—carry with them a heightened risk that private property is being pressed into some form of public service under the guise of mitigating serious public harm. See, e.g., Annicelli v. South Kingstown, 463 A.2d 133, 140–141 (R.I. 1983) (prohibition on construction adjacent to beach justified on twin grounds of safety and "conservation of open space"); Morris County Land Improvement Co. v. Parsippany–Troy Hills Township, 193 A.2d 232, 240 (N.J. 1963) (prohibition on filling marshlands imposed in order to preserve region as water detention basin and create wildlife refuge). As Justice Brennan explained: "From the government's point of view, the benefits flowing to the public from preservation of open space through regulation may be equally great as from creating a wildlife refuge through formal condemnation or increasing electricity production through a dam project that floods private property." San Diego Gas & Elec. Co., supra, 450 U.S., at 652 (dissenting opinion). The many statutes on the books, both state and federal, that provide for the use of eminent domain to impose servitudes on private scenic lands preventing developmental uses, or to acquire such lands altogether, suggest the practical equivalence in this setting of negative regulation and appropriation. See, e.g., 16 U.S.C. § 410ff–1(a) (authorizing acquisition of "lands, waters, or interests [within Channel Islands National Park] (including but not limited to scenic easements)"); § 460aa–2(a) (authorizing acquisition of "any lands, or lesser interests therein, including mineral interests and scenic easements" within Sawtooth National Recreation Area); §§ 3921–3923 (authorizing acquisition of wetlands); N.C. Gen.Stat. § 113A–38 (1990) (authorizing acquisition of, *inter alia*, " 'scenic easements' " within the North Carolina natural and scenic rivers system); Tenn.Code Ann. §§ 11–15–101 to 11–15–108 (1987) (authorizing acquisition of "protective easements" and other rights in real property adjacent to State's historic, architectural, archaeological, or cultural resources).

We think, in short, that there are good reasons for our frequently expressed belief that when the owner of real property has been called upon to sacrifice *all* economically beneficial uses in the name of the common good, that is, to leave his property economically idle, he has suffered a taking.[8]

B

The trial court found Lucas's two beachfront lots to have been rendered valueless by respondent's enforcement of the coastal-zone construction ban. Under Lucas's theory of the case, which rested upon our "no economically viable use" statements, that finding entitled him to compensation. Lucas believed it unnecessary to take issue with either the purposes behind the Beachfront Management Act, or the means chosen by the South Carolina Legislature to effectuate those purposes. The South Carolina Supreme Court, however, thought otherwise. In its view, the Beachfront Management Act was no ordinary enactment, but involved an exercise of South Carolina's "police powers" to mitigate the harm to the public interest that petitioner's use of his land might occasion. By neglecting to dispute the findings enumerated in the Act or otherwise to challenge the legislature's purposes, petitioner "concede[d] that the beach/dune area of South Carolina's shores is an extremely valuable public resource; that the erection of new construction, *inter alia*, contributes to the erosion and destruction of this public resource; and that discouraging new construction in close proximity to the beach/dune area is necessary to prevent a great public harm." In the court's view, these concessions brought petitioner's challenge within a long line of this Court's cases sustaining against Due Process and Takings Clause challenges the State's use of its "police powers" to enjoin a property owner from activities akin to public nuisances. See Mugler v. Kansas, 123 U.S. 623 (1887) (law prohibiting manufacture of alcoholic beverages); Hadacheck v. Sebastian, 239 U.S. 394 (1915) (law barring operation of brick mill in residential area); Miller v. Schoene, 276

---

8. Justice STEVENS criticizes the "deprivation of all economically beneficial use" rule as "wholly arbitrary," in that "[the] landowner whose property is diminished in value 95% recovers nothing," while the landowner who suffers a complete elimination of value "recovers the land's full value." This analysis errs in its assumption that the landowner whose deprivation is one step short of complete is not entitled to compensation. Such an owner might not be able to claim the benefit of our categorical formulation, but, as we have acknowledged time and again, "[t]he economic impact of the regulation on the claimant and ... the extent to which the regulation has interfered with distinct investment-backed expectations" are keenly relevant to takings analysis generally. Penn Central Transportation Co. v. New York City, 438 U.S. 104, 124 (1978). It is true that in at least *some* cases the landowner with 95% loss will get nothing, while the landowner with total loss will recover in full. But that occa-

sional result is no more strange than the gross disparity between the landowner whose premises are taken for a highway (who recovers in full) and the landowner whose property is reduced to 5% of its former value by the highway (who recovers nothing). Takings law is full of these "all-or-nothing" situations. Justice STEVENS similarly misinterprets our focus on "developmental" uses of property (the uses proscribed by the Beachfront Management Act) as betraying an "assumption that the only uses of property cognizable under the Constitution are *developmental* uses." We make no such assumption. Though our prior takings cases evince an abiding concern for the productive use of, and economic investment in, land, there are plainly a number of noneconomic interests in land whose impairment will invite exceedingly close scrutiny under the Takings Clause. See, e.g., Loretto v. Teleprompter Manhattan CATV Corp., 458 U.S. 419, 436 (1982) (interest in excluding strangers from one's land).

U.S. 272 (1928) (order to destroy diseased cedar trees to prevent infection of nearby orchards); Goldblatt v. Hempstead, 369 U.S. 590 (1962) (law effectively preventing continued operation of quarry in residential area).

It is correct that many of our prior opinions have suggested that "harmful or noxious uses" of property may be proscribed by government regulation without the requirement of compensation. For a number of reasons, however, we think the South Carolina Supreme Court was too quick to conclude that that principle decides the present case. The "harmful or noxious uses" principle was the Court's early attempt to describe in theoretical terms why government may, consistent with the Takings Clause, affect property values by regulation without incurring an obligation to compensate—a reality we nowadays acknowledge explicitly with respect to the full scope of the State's police power. * * * "Harmful or noxious use" analysis was, in other words, simply the progenitor of our more contemporary statements that "land-use regulation does not effect a taking if it 'substantially advance[s] legitimate state interests'...." Nollan, supra, 483 U.S., at 834 (quoting Agins v. Tiburon, 447 U.S., at 260); see also Penn Central Transportation Co., supra, 438 U.S., at 127; Euclid v. Ambler Realty Co., 272 U.S. 365, 387–388 (1926).

The transition from our early focus on control of "noxious" uses to our contemporary understanding of the broad realm within which government may regulate without compensation was an easy one, since the distinction between "harm-preventing" and "benefit-conferring" regulation is often in the eye of the beholder. It is quite possible, for example, to describe in *either* fashion the ecological, economic, and esthetic concerns that inspired the South Carolina Legislature in the present case. One could say that imposing a servitude on Lucas's land is necessary in order to prevent his use of it from "harming" South Carolina's ecological resources; or, instead, in order to achieve the "benefits" of an ecological preserve. Compare, e.g., Claridge v. New Hampshire Wetlands Board, 485 A.2d 287, 292 (N.H. 1984) (owner may, without compensation, be barred from filling wetlands because landfilling would deprive adjacent coastal habitats and marine fisheries of ecological support), with, e.g., Bartlett v. Zoning Comm'n of Old Lyme, 282 A.2d 907, 910 (Conn. 1971) (owner barred from filling tidal marshland must be compensated, despite municipality's "laudable" goal of "preserv[ing] marshlands from encroachment or destruction"). Whether one or the other of the competing characterizations will come to one's lips in a particular case depends primarily upon one's evaluation of the worth of competing uses of real estate. See Restatement (Second) of Torts § 822, Comment g, p. 112 (1979) ("Practically all human activities unless carried on in a wilderness interfere to some extent with others or involve some risk of interference"). A given restraint will be seen as mitigating "harm" to the adjacent parcels or securing a "benefit" for them, depending upon the observer's evaluation of the relative importance of the use that the restraint favors. See Sax, Takings and the Police Power, 74 Yale L.J. 36, 49 (1964) ("[T]he problem [in this area] is not one of noxiousness or harm-creating activity at all; rather it is a problem of inconsistency between perfectly innocent and independently desirable uses"). Whether Lucas's construction of single-family residences on his parcels should be described as bringing "harm" to South Carolina's adjacent ecological resources thus depends principally upon whether the describer believes that the State's use interest in nurturing those resources is so important that *any* competing adjacent use must yield.

When it is understood that "prevention of harmful use" was merely our early formulation of the police power justification necessary to sustain (without compensation) *any* regulatory diminution in value; and that the distinction between regulation that "prevents harmful use" and that which "confers benefits" is difficult, if not impossible, to discern on an objective, value-free basis; it becomes self-evident that noxious-use logic cannot serve as a touchstone to distinguish regulatory "takings"—which require compensation—from regulatory deprivations that do not require compensation. A *fortiori* the legislature's recitation of a noxious-use justification cannot be the basis for departing from our categorical rule that total regulatory takings must be compensated. If it were, departure would virtually always be allowed. The South Carolina Supreme Court's approach would essentially nullify *Mahon*'s affirmation of limits to the noncompensable exercise of the police power. Our cases provide no support for this: None of them that employed the logic of "harmful use" prevention to sustain a regulation involved an allegation that the regulation wholly eliminated the value of the claimant's land. See Keystone Bituminous Coal Assn., 480 U.S., at 513–514 (Rehnquist, C.J., dissenting).

Where the State seeks to sustain regulation that deprives land of all economically beneficial use, we think it may resist compensation only if the logically antecedent inquiry into the nature of the owner's estate shows that the proscribed use interests were not part of his title to begin with. This accords, we think, with our "takings" jurisprudence, which has traditionally been guided by the understandings of our citizens regarding the content of, and the State's power over, the "bundle of rights" that they acquire when they obtain title to property. It seems to us that the property owner necessarily expects the uses of his property to be restricted, from time to time, by various measures newly enacted by the State in legitimate exercise of its police powers; "[a]s long recognized, some values are enjoyed under an implied limitation and must yield to the police power." Pennsylvania Coal Co. v. Mahon, 260 U.S., at 413. And in the case of personal property, by reason of the State's traditionally high degree of control over commercial dealings, he ought to be aware of the possibility that new regulation might even render his property economically worthless (at least if the property's only economically productive use is sale or manufacture for sale). See Andrus v. Allard, 444 U.S. 51, 66–67 (1979) (prohibition on sale of eagle feathers). In the case of land, however, we think the notion pressed by the Council that title is somehow held subject to the "implied limitation" that the State may subsequently eliminate all economically valuable use is inconsistent with the historical compact recorded in the Takings Clause that has become part of our constitutional culture.

Where "permanent physical occupation" of land is concerned, we have refused to allow the government to decree it anew (without compensation), no matter how weighty the asserted "public interests" involved, Loretto v. Teleprompter Manhattan CATV Corp., 458 U.S., at 426—though we assuredly *would* permit the government to assert a permanent easement that was a pre-existing limitation upon the landowner's title. * * * We believe similar treatment must be accorded confiscatory regulations, *i.e.*, regulations that prohibit all economically beneficial use of land: Any limitation so severe cannot be newly legislated or decreed (without compensation), but must inhere in the title itself, in the restrictions that background principles of the State's law of property and nuisance already place upon land ownership. A law or decree with such an effect must, in other words, do no more than duplicate the result that could have been achieved in the courts—by adjacent landowners (or other uniquely affected persons) under the State's law of private nuisance, or by the State under its complementary power to abate nuisances that affect the public generally, or otherwise.[16]

On this analysis, the owner of a lake-bed, for example, would not be entitled to compensation when he is denied the requisite permit to engage in a landfilling operation that would have the effect of flooding others' land. Nor the corporate owner of a nuclear generating plant, when it is directed to remove all improvements from its land upon discovery that the plant sits astride an earthquake fault. Such regulatory action may well have the effect of eliminating the land's only economically productive use, but it does not proscribe a productive use that was previously permissible under relevant property and nuisance principles. The use of these properties for what are now expressly prohibited purposes was *always* unlawful, and (subject to other constitutional limitations) it was open to the State at any point to make the implication of those background principles of nuisance and property law explicit. See Michelman, Property, Utility, and Fairness, Comments on the Ethical Foundations of "Just Compensation" Law, 80 Harv.L.Rev. 1165, 1239–1241 (1967). In light of our traditional resort to "existing rules or understandings that stem from an independent source such as state law" to define the range of interests that qualify for protection as "property" under the Fifth and Fourteenth Amendments, Board of Regents of State Colleges v. Roth, 408 U.S. 564, 577 (1972); see, e.g., Ruckelshaus v. Monsanto Co., 467 U.S. 986, 1011–1012 (1984); Hughes v. Washington, 389 U.S. 290, 295 (1967) (Stewart, J., concurring), this recognition that the Takings Clause does not require compensation when an owner is barred from putting land to a use that is proscribed by those "existing rules or understandings" is surely unexceptional. When, however, a regulation that declares "off-limits" all economically productive or beneficial uses of land goes beyond what the relevant background principles would dictate, compensation must be paid to sustain it.

---

16. The principal "otherwise" that we have in mind is litigation absolving the State (or private parties) of liability for the destruction of "real and personal property, in cases of actual necessity, to prevent the spreading of a fire" or to forestall other grave threats to the lives and property of others. Bowditch v. Boston, 101 U.S. 16, 18–19 (1880); see United States v. Pacific R., Co., 120 U.S. 227, 238–239 (1887).

The "total taking" inquiry we require today will ordinarily entail (as the application of state nuisance law ordinarily entails) analysis of, among other things, the degree of harm to public lands and resources, or adjacent private property, posed by the claimant's proposed activities, see, e.g., Restatement (Second) of Torts §§ 826, 827, the social value of the claimant's activities and their suitability to the locality in question, see, e.g., id., §§ 828(a) and (b), 831, and the relative ease with which the alleged harm can be avoided through measures taken by the claimant and the government (or adjacent private landowners) alike, see, e.g., id., §§ 827(e), 828(c), 830. The fact that a particular use has long been engaged in by similarly situated owners ordinarily imports a lack of any common-law prohibition (though changed circumstances or new knowledge may make what was previously permissible no longer so, see id., § 827, Comment g.) So also does the fact that other landowners, similarly situated, are permitted to continue the use denied to the claimant.

It seems unlikely that common-law principles would have prevented the erection of any habitable or productive improvements on petitioner's land; they rarely support prohibition of the "essential use" of land, Curtin v. Benson, 222 U.S. 78, 86 (1911). The question, however, is one of state law to be dealt with on remand. We emphasize that to win its case South Carolina must do more than proffer the legislature's declaration that the uses Lucas desires are inconsistent with the public interest, or the conclusory assertion that they violate a common-law maxim such as *sic utere tuo ut alienum non laedas.* As we have said, a "State, by *ipse dixit,* may not transform private property into public property without compensation...." Webb's Fabulous Pharmacies, Inc. v. Beckwith, 449 U.S. 155, 164 (1980). Instead, as it would be required to do if it sought to restrain Lucas in a common-law action for public nuisance, South Carolina must identify background principles of nuisance and property law that prohibit the uses he now intends in the circumstances in which the property is presently found. Only on this showing can the State fairly claim that, in proscribing all such beneficial uses, the Beachfront Management Act is taking nothing.[18]

* * *

The judgment is reversed, and the case is remanded for proceedings not inconsistent with this opinion.

■ JUSTICE KENNEDY, concurring in the judgment.

* * * In my view, reasonable expectations must be understood in light of the whole of our legal tradition. The common law of nuisance is too

---

18. Justice BLACKMUN decries our reliance on background nuisance principles at least in part because he believes those principles to be as manipulable as we find the "harm prevention"/"benefit conferral" dichotomy. There is no doubt some leeway in a court's interpretation of what existing state law permits—but not remotely as much, we think, as in a legislative crafting of the reasons for its confiscatory regulation. We stress that an affirmative decree eliminating all economically beneficial uses may be defended only if an *objectively reasonable application* of relevant precedents would exclude those beneficial uses in the circumstances in which the land is presently found.

narrow a confine for the exercise of regulatory power in a complex and interdependent society. Goldblatt v. Hempstead, 369 U.S. 590, 593 (1962). The State should not be prevented from enacting new regulatory initiatives in response to changing conditions, and courts must consider all reasonable expectations whatever their source. The Takings Clause does not require a static body of state property law; it protects private expectations to ensure private investment. I agree with the Court that nuisance prevention accords with the most common expectations of property owners who face regulation, but I do not believe this can be the sole source of state authority to impose severe restrictions. Coastal property may present such unique concerns for a fragile land system that the State can go further in regulating its development and use than the common law of nuisance might otherwise permit. * * *

■ JUSTICE BLACKMUN, dissenting. Today the Court launches a missile to kill a mouse. * * *

[T]he Court justifies its new rule that the legislature may not deprive a property owner of the only economically valuable use of his land, even if the legislature finds it to be a harmful use, because such action is not part of the " 'long recognized' " "understandings of our citizens." These "understandings" permit such regulation only if the use is a nuisance under the common law. Any other course is "inconsistent with the historical compact recorded in the Takings Clause." It is not clear from the Court's opinion where our "historical compact" or "citizens' understanding" comes from, but it does not appear to be history.

The principle that the State should compensate individuals for property taken for public use was not widely established in America at the time of the Revolution.

> The colonists ... inherited ... a concept of property which permitted extensive regulation of the use of that property for the public benefit— regulation that could even go so far as to deny all productive use of the property to the owner if, as Coke himself stated, the regulation "extends to the public benefit ... for this is for the public, and every one hath benefit by it." F. Bosselman, D. Callies, & J. Banta, The Taking Issue 80–81 (1973), quoting The Case of the King's Prerogative in Saltpetre, 12 Co.Rep. 12–13 (1606).

See also Treanor, The Origins and Original Significance of the Just Compensation Clause of the Fifth Amendment, 94 Yale L.J. 694, 697, n. 9 (1985).

Even into the 19th century, state governments often felt free to take property for roads and other public projects without paying compensation to the owners. See M. Horwitz, The Transformation of American Law, 1780–1860, pp. 63–64 (1977) (hereinafter Horwitz); Treanor, 94 Yale L.J., at 695. As one court declared in 1802, citizens "were bound to contribute as much of [land], as by the laws of the country, were deemed necessary for the public convenience." M'Clenachan v. Curwin, 3 Yeates 362, 373 (Pa. 1802). There was an obvious movement toward establishing the just compensation principle during the 19th century, but "there continued to be a strong current in American legal thought that regarded compensation simply as a 'bounty given . . . by the State' out of 'kindness' and not out of justice." Horwitz 65, quoting Commonwealth v. Fisher, 1 Pen. & W. 462, 465 (Pa. 1830). See also State v. Dawson, 3 Hill 100, 103 (S.C. 1836). * * *

In addition, state courts historically have been less likely to find that a government action constitutes a taking when the affected land is undeveloped. According to the South Carolina court, the power of the legislature to take unimproved land without providing compensation was sanctioned by "ancient rights and principles." Lindsay v. Commissioners, 2 S.C.L. 38, 57 (1796). "Except for Massachusetts, no colony appears to have paid compensation when it built a state-owned road across unimproved land. Legislatures provided compensation only for enclosed or improved land." Treanor, 94 Yale L.J., at 695 (footnotes omitted). This rule was followed by some States into the 1800's. See Horwitz 63–65. * * *

Nor does history indicate any common-law limit on the State's power to regulate harmful uses even to the point of destroying all economic value. Nothing in the discussions in Congress concerning the Takings Clause indicates that the Clause was limited by the common-law nuisance doctrine. Common-law courts themselves rejected such an understanding. They regularly recognized that it is "for the legislature to interpose, and by positive enactment to prohibit a use of property which would be injurious to the public." Tewksbury, 11 Metc., at 57. Chief Justice Shaw explained in upholding a regulation prohibiting construction of wharves, the existence of a taking did not depend on "whether a certain erection in tide water is a nuisance at common law or not." Alger, 7 Cush., at 104; see also State v. Paul, 5 R.I. 185, 193 (1858); Commonwealth v. Parks, 30 N.E. 174 (Mass. 1892) (Holmes, J.) ("[T]he legislature may change the common law as to nuisances, and may move the line either way, so as to make things nuisances which were not so, or to make things lawful which were nuisances").

In short, I find no clear and accepted "historical compact" or "understanding of our citizens" justifying the Court's new takings doctrine. Instead, the Court seems to treat history as a grab bag of principles, to be adopted where they support the Court's theory, and ignored where they do not. If the Court decided that the early common law provides the background principles for interpreting the Takings Clause, then regulation, as opposed to physical confiscation, would not be compensable. If the Court decided that the law of a later period provides the background principles, then regulation might be compensable, but the Court would have to confront the fact that legislatures regularly determined which uses were prohibited, independent of the common law, and independent of whether the uses were lawful when the owner purchased. What makes the Court's analysis unworkable is its attempt to package the law of two incompatible eras and peddle it as historical fact. * * *

■ JUSTICE STEVENS, dissenting. * * *

[T]he Court's new rule is wholly arbitrary. A landowner whose property is diminished in value 95% recovers nothing, while an owner whose property is diminished 100% recovers the land's full value. * * *

Moreover, because of the elastic nature of property rights, the Court's new rule will also prove unsound in practice. In response to the rule, courts may define "property" broadly and only rarely find regulations to effect total takings. This is the approach the Court itself adopts in its revisionist reading of venerable precedents. We are told that—notwithstanding the Court's findings to the contrary in each case—the brewery in *Mugler,* the brickyard in *Hadacheck,* and the gravel pit in *Goldblatt* all could be put to "other uses" and that, therefore, those cases did not involve total regulatory takings.[3]

On the other hand, developers and investors may market specialized estates to take advantage of the Court's new rule. The smaller the estate, the more likely that a regulatory change will effect a total taking. Thus, an investor may, for example, purchase the right to build a multifamily home on a specific lot, with the result that a zoning regulation that allows only single-family homes would render the investor's property interest "valueless." In short, the categorical rule will likely have one of two effects: Either courts will alter the definition of the "denominator" in the takings "fraction," rendering the Court's categorical rule meaningless, or investors will manipulate the relevant property interests, giving the Court's rule sweeping effect. To my mind, neither of these results is desirable or appropriate, and both are distortions of our takings jurisprudence.

Finally, the * * * Court suggests that "total deprivation of feasible use is, from the landowner's point of view, the equivalent of a physical appropriation." This argument proves too much. From the "landowner's point of view," a regulation that diminishes a lot's value by 50% is as well "the equivalent" of the condemnation of half of the lot. Yet, it is well established that a 50% diminution in value does not by itself constitute a taking. See Euclid v. Ambler Realty Co., 272 U.S. 365, 384 (1926) (75% diminution in value). Thus, the landowner's perception of the regulation cannot justify the Court's new rule. * * *

Like many bright-line rules, the categorical rule established in this case is only "categorical" for a page or two in the U.S. Reports. No sooner does the Court state that "total regulatory takings must be compensated," than it quickly establishes an exception to that rule. * * *

3. Of course, the same could easily be said in this case: Lucas may put his land to "other uses"—fishing or camping, for example—or may sell his land to his neighbors as a buffer. In either event, his land is far from "valueless."

This highlights a fundamental weakness in the Court's analysis: its failure to explain why only the impairment of *"economically beneficial or productive use,"* (emphasis added), of property is relevant in takings analysis. I should think that a regulation arbitrarily prohibiting an owner from continuing to use her property for bird watching or sunbathing might constitute a taking under some circumstances; and, conversely, that such uses are of value to the owner. Yet the Court offers no basis for its assumption that the only uses of property cognizable under the Constitution are *developmental* uses.

The Court's holding today effectively freezes the State's common law, denying the legislature much of its traditional power to revise the law governing the rights and uses of property. Until today, I had thought that we had long abandoned this approach to constitutional law. More than a century ago we recognized that "the great office of statutes is to remedy defects in the common law as they are developed, and to adapt it to the changes of time and circumstances." Munn v. Illinois, 94 U.S. 113, 134 (1877). * * *

Arresting the development of the common law is not only a departure from our prior decisions; it is also profoundly unwise. The human condition is one of constant learning and evolution—both moral and practical. Legislatures implement that new learning; in doing so they must often revise the definition of property and the rights of property owners. Thus, when the Nation came to understand that slavery was morally wrong and mandated the emancipation of all slaves, it, in effect, redefined "property." On a lesser scale, our ongoing self-education produces similar changes in the rights of property owners: New appreciation of the significance of endangered species, see, e.g., Andrus v. Allard, 444 U.S. 51 (1979); the importance of wetlands, see, e.g., 16 U.S.C. § 3801 et seq.; and the vulnerability of coastal lands, see, e.g., 16 U.S.C. § 1451 et seq., shapes our evolving understandings of property rights.

Of course, some legislative redefinitions of property will effect a taking and must be compensated—but it certainly cannot be the case that every movement away from common law does so. There is no reason, and less sense, in such an absolute rule. We live in a world in which changes in the economy and the environment occur with increasing frequency and importance. If it was wise a century ago to allow government " 'the largest legislative discretion' " to deal with " 'the special exigencies of the moment,' " Mugler, 123 U.S., at 669, it is imperative to do so today. The rule that should govern a decision in a case of this kind should focus on the future, not the past.[5] * * *

The Just Compensation Clause "was designed to bar Government from forcing some people alone to bear public burdens which, in all fairness and justice, should be borne by the public as a whole." Armstrong v. United States, 364 U.S. 40, 49 (1960). Accordingly, one of the central concerns of our takings jurisprudence is "prevent[ing] the public from loading upon one individual more than his just share of the burdens of government." Monongahela Navigation Co. v. United States, 148 U.S. 312, 325 (1893). We have, therefore, in our takings law frequently looked to the *generality* of a regulation of property. * * *

---

5. Even measured in terms of efficiency, the Court's rule is unsound. The Court today effectively establishes a form of insurance against certain changes in land-use regulations. Like other forms of insurance, the Court's rule creates a "moral hazard" and inefficiencies: In the face of uncertainty about changes in the law, developers will overinvest, safe in the knowledge that if the law changes adversely, they will be entitled to compensation. See generally Farber, Economic Analysis and Just Compensation, 12 Int'l Rev. of Law & Econ. 125 (1992).

In considering Lucas' claim, the generality of the Beachfront Management Act is significant. The Act does not target particular landowners, but rather regulates the use of the coastline of the entire State. See S.C. Code Ann. § 48–39–10 (Supp. 1990). Indeed, South Carolina's Act is best understood as part of a national effort to protect the coastline, one initiated by the federal Coastal Zone Management Act of 1972. Pub.L. 92–583, 86 Stat. 1280, codified as amended at 16 U.S.C. § 1451 et seq. Pursuant to the federal Act, every coastal State has implemented coastline regulations. Moreover, the Act did not single out owners of undeveloped land. The Act also prohibited owners of developed land from rebuilding if their structures were destroyed, see 1988 S.C. Acts 634, § 3, and what is equally significant, from repairing erosion control devices, such as seawalls, see S.C. Code Ann. § 48–39–290(B)(2) (Supp. 1990). In addition, in some situations, owners of developed land were required to "renouris[h] the beach ... on a yearly basis with an amount ... of sand ... not ... less than one and one-half times the yearly volume of sand lost due to erosion." 1988 S.C. Acts 634, § 3, p. 5140. In short, the South Carolina Act imposed substantial burdens on owners of developed and undeveloped land alike. This generality indicates that the Act is not an effort to expropriate owners of undeveloped land.

Admittedly, the economic impact of this regulation is dramatic and petitioner's investment-backed expectations are substantial. Yet, if anything, the costs to and expectations of the owners of developed land are even greater: I doubt, however, that the cost to owners of developed land of renourishing the beach and allowing their seawalls to deteriorate effects a taking. The costs imposed on the owners of undeveloped land, such as petitioner, differ from these costs only in degree, not in kind.

The impact of the ban on developmental uses must also be viewed in light of the purposes of the Act. The legislature stated the purposes of the Act as "protect[ing], preserv[ing], restor[ing] and enhanc[ing] the beach/dune system" of the State not only for recreational and ecological purposes, but also to "protec[t] life and property." S.C. Code Ann. § 48–39–260(1)(a) (Supp. 1990). The State, with much science on its side, believes that the "beach/dune system [acts] as a buffer from high tides, storm surge, [and] hurricanes." Ibid. This is a traditional and important exercise of the State's police power, as demonstrated by Hurricane Hugo, which in 1989, caused 29 deaths and more than $6 billion in property damage in South Carolina alone.

In view of all of these factors, even assuming that petitioner's property was rendered valueless, the risk inherent in investments of the sort made by petitioner, the generality of the Act, and the compelling purpose motivating the South Carolina Legislature persuade me that the Act did not effect a taking of petitioner's property. * * *

NOTES AND QUESTIONS

1. On remand, the South Carolina Supreme Court held that the restrictions imposed by the Beachfront Management Act would not have

been authorized under the South Carolina law of nuisance. Accordingly, the Act imposed a taking. The court held that the state could either abandon the law or could proceed to purchase or condemn the property. In either event, it would be liable to Mr. Lucas for having imposed a temporary taking during the time the ordinance blocked any development. Lucas v. South Carolina Coastal Council, 424 S.E.2d 484 (S.C. 1992). The case was settled when the state agreed to pay Lucas $850,000 for the two lots, plus $725,000 in interest, attorney's fees, and costs, for a total of $1,575,000. The state then turned around and sold the lots to another private developer, in order to recoup some of these expenses. See Oliver A. Houck, More Unfinished Stories: *Lucas, Atlanta Coalition*, and *Palila/SweetHome*, 75 U. Colo. L. Rev. 331, 366 (2004). Does the decision to sell the lots for private development suggest, as proponents of strong takings protection might argue, that the regulation imposed an extreme burden on the landowner, and that once the state was forced to internalize this burden, it realized the regulation was not worth it? Or does the sale for private development

Figure 12–7
Lucas's Two Lots, November 1994

"View of Lucas's two lots, on either side of large square house in the center, from the edge of the ocean (looking towards northwest). Note that Lucas's lots are the only vacant lots in sight along the beach." http://www.dartmouth.edu/~wfischel/lucasessay.html.

Courtesy William A. Fischel, Department of Economics, Dartmouth College.

suggest, as opponents of takings liability might argue, that states have no way to recoup the external benefits of land-use regulations, and if they have to compensate landowners for losses this will result in underregulation of environmental harms? For a variety of views, see, e.g., Fischel, Regulatory Takings, supra, at 59–63; Vicki Been, Lucas vs. The Green Machine: Using the Takings Clause to Promote More Efficient Regulation?, in Property Stories 221 (Gerald Korngold & Andrew P. Morriss eds., 2004); Carol M. Rose, The Story of *Lucas*: Environmental Land Use Regulations between Developers and the Deep Blue Sea, in Environmental Law Stories 237 (Oliver A. Houck & Richard James Lazarus eds., 2005).

Figure 12–8
One of the Former Lucas Lots after Construction, March 2000

"A closer view of the new, salmon-pink house. Jerry Finkel, who handled the sale of the lot for Lucas after he won his case, indicated that state officials had urged him to apply for a permit for the maximum-size house so that the state could get the highest possible price for the lot when it was sold. The house is about 5,000 square feet." http://www.dartmouth.edu/~wfischel/lucasupdate.html.

Courtesy William A. Fischel, Department of Economics, Dartmouth College.

2. Additional light on the question of how expanded liability for regulatory takings would affect government behavior is provided by experience with Oregon's Ballot Measure 37, adopted by voter initiative in 2004. Measure 37 requires that if a property owner can show that a "land use regulation" has caused a "reduction" in the fair market value of the property, then the government must either compensate the owner for the reduction in value, or modify the regulation to permit the owner to engage in any use that was permitted at the time the owner acquired the property. See ORS 197.352. The Measure also provides for awards of attorney's fees

to property owners who successfully challenge a land use regulation in court (obtaining either compensation or a waiver of regulation). Id. Initial experience suggests that municipalities and other local government entities are reluctant to defend regulations against Measure 37 claims, perhaps because of the one-way fee-shifting provision, which could expose them to large liability for attorney's fees. Instead, local authorities have tended to waive the application of regulations when they are challenged. Very few if any payments of compensation have been made, at least in part because the Oregon legislature has made no appropriations for this purpose. See Edward J. Sullivan, Year Zero: The Aftermath of Measure 37, 38 Urb. Law. 237 (2006). Does this experience imply that the regulations were unwise or does it tend to suggest that full cost internalization for regulatory changes would produce too little regulation? Or does the Oregon measure contain features that stack the deck against compensation in such a way as to make any such conclusion premature?

3. *Lucas* obviously fills out the structure of categorical rules and ad hoc review that the Court began to develop in *Loretto*. We now have at least two per se rules of liability: for permanent physical occupations and for regulations that deprive owners of "all economically beneficial or productive use of land." What exactly is the definition of this latter category? It depends in significant part on whether one focuses on "economically beneficial" or "productive." Is an owner deprived of all "economically beneficial" use of land only when the land has a fair market value of zero? If this is what *Lucas* means, then relatively few regulations would qualify (including the regulation in *Lucas* itself if the record had been properly developed on this point; surely the land could have been sold for some positive sum of money, if only for recreational use by neighboring property owners). The principal type of regulation that would meet this definition would probably be rules requiring the remediation of hazardous wastes deposited on the land, which can render land unmarketable (this is called the "Brownfields" problem). But these rules may also fall within the nuisance exception. Alternatively, all "productive" use of land could mean that the government has denied the owner the right to build on or otherwise economically extract value from land, as by farming. If this is what *Lucas* means, then many more regulations would fall afoul of such an understanding. For example, governments not infrequently deny development rights when development would entail destroying wetlands, or when it would eliminate the habitat of an endangered species. In a more recent dissenting opinion, Justices Thomas and Scalia have indicated that they understand *Lucas* to incorporate the second, prohibition-on-productive-use definition. See Tahoe–Sierra Preservation Council v. Tahoe Regional Planning Agency, 535 U.S. 302, 356 (2002) (Thomas, J., dissenting). It does not necessarily follow, of course, that the other Justices who joined the *Lucas* majority shared this understanding, or that the Court will embrace this understanding if and when it resolves the ambiguity.

4. Are there other candidates for rules of per se takings liability? Formal exercises of eminent domain clearly qualify as one. See Tahoe–Sierra, 535 U.S. at 322 ("When the government physically takes possession of an interest in property for some public purpose, it has a categorical duty

to compensate the former owner, *United States v. Pewee Coal Co.*, 341 U.S. 114, 115 (1951), regardless of whether the interest that is taken constitutes an entire parcel or merely a part thereof."). There is language in *Hodel v. Irving*, 481 U.S. 704, 717 (1987), suggesting that a complete abrogation of the right to transmit interests in land upon death might be regarded as a per se taking, although the opinion is not clear about this. In *Tahoe–Sierra Preservation Council*, supra, the Court rejected the argument that regulations that temporarily deprive owners of all economically beneficial use should receive per se treatment, and held instead that such regulations should be assessed under the ad hoc test of *Penn Central*. Does the ruling in *Tahoe–Sierra* mean that the South Carolina Supreme Court erred on remand in assuming that the Beachfront Management Act was a taking? What exactly does "temporary" and "permanent" mean in this context? If the government adopts an open-ended regulation that denies all economically beneficial use of land, the regulation is challenged as a taking, and the government then drops the regulation, does *Tahoe–Sierra* mean the landowner is automatically deprived of the benefits of the *Lucas* rule?

5. If there are per se rules of takings liability, are there per se rules of nonliability? Does the nuisance regulation exception that *Lucas* recognizes for what would otherwise be per se liability for total takings constitute a per se rule of nonliability for all purposes? What if the government permanently occupies private property in order to abate what would be a common-law nuisance? At least one court has suggested that government occupation of property for purposes of monitoring groundwater pollution from a hazardous waste site is a permanent physical occupation that requires compensation. See Hendler v. United States, 952 F.2d 1364, 13765 (Fed. Cir. 1991). Do you agree? Other candidates for rules of per se nonliability include forfeitures of property used in the commission of a crime, see Bennis v. Michigan, 516 U.S. 442 (1996); regulations that implement the navigation servitude, mentioned in Chapter III, see United States v. Cherokee Nation of Oklahoma, 480 U.S. 700 (1987); and government destruction of property in order to stop the spread of fire, mentioned in *Mahon* and in footnote 16 of the Court's opinion in *Lucas*. See David A. Dana & Thomas W. Merrill, Property: Takings 110–20 (2002).

6. More generally, what should be the standard for recognizing per se rules of takings liability or nonliability, as opposed to treating claims under *Penn Central*'s ad hoc test? Both *Lucas* and *Palazzolo v. Rhode Island*, 533 U.S. 606 (2001) (see note 8 below), seem to suggest that common-law rules enter into and restrict the title to property when it is acquired, but statutory rules do not, or do so only in a more qualified fashion. What might justify privileging common-law rules over statutory rules in this fashion? Does this provide any clue as to the standard the Court may be implicitly relying upon in recognizing per se rules of liability and nonliability?

7. The majority opinion at one point justifies its categorical rule treating all economic wipeouts as takings on the ground that such regulations "carry with them a heightened risk that private property is being

pressed into some form of public service under the guise of mitigating serious public harm." Later in the opinion, however, in justifying the need to confine the police power exception to regulations that track the common law of nuisance, the majority remarks that "the distinction between 'harm-preventing' and 'benefit-conferring' regulation is often in the eye of the beholder." Are these observations inconsistent? The first seems to presuppose that the benefit/harm distinction is intelligible, and that impressments of property to provide public benefits presumptively require use of eminent domain. The second seems to say that the benefit/harm distinction is not intelligible, and hence cannot be used as a basis for defining the class of regulations that can be imposed under the police power. Or is the point not that the harm/benefit distinction is unintelligible, but simply that the distinction is too manipulable to serve as a basis for legal doctrine?

8.   Justice Scalia often seeks to define constitutional rights in terms of rules rather than broad standards, see Antonin Scalia, The Rule of Law as the Law of Rules, 56 U. Chi. L. Rev. 1175 (1989), and often argues that such rules should be grounded in an objective source like the original understanding of the Framers or in well established traditions and practices. See Antonin Scalia, A Matter of Interpretation (1997). His effort in *Lucas* to define the police power exception in terms of established principles of nuisance law is plausibly regarded as being the product of similar impulses. If this is his objective, however, what do you make of his heavy reliance on the *Restatement of Torts* as a source for identifying existing rules of nuisance law? Recall from *Hendricks v. Stalnaker* and the notes following it in Chapter I that the *Restatement* essentially would define a nuisance in terms of a case-by-case balancing test. Such balancing tests are usually the last thing Justice Scalia wants to see adopted in constitutional law. What then accounts for Justice Scalia's willingness to endorse the *Restatement* for purposes of defining the nuisance exception to the new per se rule of liability for total takings? For criticism of this aspect of the decision, see Lynn E. Blais, Takings, Statutes, and the Common Law: Considering Inherent Limitation on Title, 70 S. Cal. L. Rev. 1 (1996); Louise A. Halper, Why the Nuisance Knot Can't Undo the Takings Muddle, 28 Ind. L. Rev. 329 (1995).

9.   Suppose A purchases two beachfront lots for $100,000, intending to build houses on them. The government then imposes a regulation that makes it impossible to build houses on the lots. Rather than filing a lawsuit, A sells the lots to B, for $10,000. (B may want the lots for purposes of sunbathing, or may hold them on speculation that the government may change its mind someday and permit them to be built on.) Can B now file a lawsuit challenging the no-construction regulation as a regulatory taking? A problem of this form arose in *Palazzolo v. Rhode Island*, 533 U.S. 606 (2001). The Court held that B was not barred from challenging the regulation by a per se rule of nonliability. Instead, the preexisting regulation, and its impact on "reasonable investment backed expectations," was just another factor to be considered under the *Penn Central* test. Does this ignore the fact that B paid a much reduced price for the property, in light of the prohibition reflected in the regulation? Or does focusing on B's

expectations look at the problem at the wrong moment in time? See William A. Fischel & Perry Shapiro, Takings, Insurance, and Michelman: Comments on Economic Interpretations of "Just Compensation" Law, 17 J. Legal Stud. 269 (1988) (arguing that if a regulatory taking arguably occurred when A owned the land, then B should be regarded as having purchased both the land and A's cause of action for a regulatory taking). Presumably the statute of limitations for A bringing a regulatory takings claim starts to run when the regulation is first imposed. Once the statute runs on any claim by A, does this mean the government has acquired the right to regulate by prescription, barring any subsequent takings clam by B? Or does the statute start to run again each time the land is transferred?

10.   Justice Blackmun's dissent marshals considerable evidence suggesting that regulations of the use of property were not thought to be "takings" at the time the Fifth Amendment was adopted. Does this mean that *Lucas*'s interpretation of the Takings Clause is contrary to the original understanding of the Framers? This would be ironic, because Justice Scalia, and some of the Justices who joined his opinion (most notably Justice Thomas) frequently criticize the Court for deviating from the original understanding in its interpretation of the Constitution. See Kelo v. City of New London, supra (Thomas, J., dissenting). Or does the question of original understanding depend on the level of generality with which one describes the views of the Framers? There is no question the members of the framing generation venerated private property, and regarded the protection of property to be a central task of government. See Jennifer Nedelsky, Private Property and the Limits of American Constitutionalism (1990). If the important "understanding" was that private property should be protected against harsh and oppressive government action, would it be contrary to the original understanding to hold that regulations that go beyond traditional nuisance regulation and deny owners all economically beneficial use of property are takings?

11.   There is a substantial scientific consensus that the earth is gradually but perceptibly warming. Climate Change Science Program & Subcommittee on Global Change, Temperature Trends in the Lower Atmosphere: Steps for Understanding and Reconciling Differences (Thomas R. Karl et al. eds., 2006), available at http://www.climatescience.gov/Library/sap/sap1–1/finalreport/sap1–1–final-all.pdf. The effects of this are uncertain, but two commonly cited predictions are that oceans will rise and violent storms will become more frequent. See Jonathan T. Overpeck et al., Paleoclimatic Evidence for Future Ice-sheet Instability and Rapid Sea-level Rise, 311 Science 1747 (2006); Thomas R. Knutson & Robert E. Tuleya, Impact of CO_2—Induced Warming on Simulated Hurricane Intensity and Precipitation: Sensitivity to the Choice of Climate Model and Convective Parameterization, 17 J. of Climate 3477 (2004), available at http://www.gfdl.noaa.gov/reference/bibliography/2004/tk0401.pdf. If it becomes necessary to evacuate barrier islands like the Isle of Palms and other low-lying coastal areas because of repeated devastation by storms and flooding, should the government be required to pay compensation to all persons whose property values are wiped out in the process? How do we distinguish

between property destroyed by acts of God or nature and those wiped out by acts of government in response to these phenomena? Consider again in this connection the conflagration rule mentioned in *Mahon* and in footnote 16 of Justice Scalia's opinion in *Lucas*. Does the debate between Justice Scalia and Justice Stevens about the generality of the Beachfront Management Act—whether or not it unfairly singles out David Lucas for harsh treatment—also have a bearing on this question?

12.   *Lucas* has generated much critical scholarship in its aftermath. Some, most notably Richard Epstein, criticized the Court for not going far enough, having declined to find that a partial infringement of a property interest could also be a taking. See Richard A. Epstein, *Lucas v. South Carolina Coastal Council*: A Tangled Web of Expectations, 45 Stan. L. Rev. 1369 (1993). Others criticized the Court's backwards-looking approach as going too far in handcuffing modern legislatures who might want to adopt regulations protecting sensitive environmental areas. See Eric T. Freyfogle, The Owning and Taking of Sensitive Lands, 43 UCLA L. Rev. 77, 191-21 (1995). Still others questioned the precedential value of the case in light of subsequent decisions and the idiosyncratic nature of the facts (rarely is all the economic value of a property destroyed). See Richard Lazarus, Putting the Correct "Spin" on *Lucas*, 45 Stan. L. Rev. 1411, 1425 (1993); Joseph L. Sax, Property Rights and the Economy of Nature: Understanding *Lucas v. South Carolina Coastal Council*, 45 Stan. L. Rev. 1433 (1993).

THE MEANING OF "PROPERTY" FOR REGULATORY TAKINGS PURPOSES

Most regulatory takings cases, like most eminent domain proceedings, involve property in land. Consequently, in most cases there is no dispute about whether the interest allegedly taken is "property." On occasion, however, regulatory takings claims are raised with respect to more novel types of interests, requiring the courts to determine whether the interest is "private property" protected by the Takings Clause. For the most part, the Supreme Court has sought to resolve "Is it property?" questions in the regulatory takings context by following the general precepts laid down in *Board of Regents v. Roth*, 408 U.S. 564 (1972), a procedural due process case excerpted in Chapter XI, supra. That is, the Court has said that whether a claimant has "private property" is to be determined by looking to independent sources, such as state law. As in the procedural due process context, the Court has not been very clear about whether one looks to state law for the definition of property, or only to determine the nature of the claimant's interest, with the characterization whether it is "private property" being a matter of federal constitutional law. See generally David A. Dana & Thomas W. Merrill, Property: Takings ch. IV (2002). Whatever methodology it has followed, the Court for the most part has reached what appear to be defensible conclusions about what is and is not "private property" for takings purposes. Thus, the Court has concluded that leases, trade secrets, and flowage easements are "private property," see id. at 59-60 n. 89, but that the head of water in a river, a delegated power of eminent domain, and the right to receive future social security benefits are not, id. at 60 n. 90.

One recent and especially contentious issue has involved Interest on Lawyer Trust Accounts or IOLTAs. Lawyers often hold client funds for various purposes, such as advances on anticipated expenses. Under banking regulations, these funds usually cannot be deposited in interest-earning bank accounts. But they can be combined and placed in trust accounts that pay interest, provided the interest is dedicated to a charitable purpose. Many state bar associations therefore have required that attorneys place such client funds in trust accounts, with the interest payable to a fund that underwrites legal services to the poor. In *Phillips v. Washington Legal Foundation*, 524 U.S. 156, 163 (1998), excerpted in Section B.2 infra, the Court ruled 5–4 that interest earned on sums deposited in IOLTA accounts is the "private property" of the client for Takings Clause purposes, even though the interest would not exist but for the IOLTA account. In reaching this decision, the Court majority purported to follow the methodology for identifying "property" developed in *Roth*, which focuses on whether independent sources of state law recognize an interest in property. In applying this methodology, however, the Court ignored the state rules requiring the deposit of such funds in IOLTA accounts, and instead emphasized that "interest follows principal" as a matter of common law. Phillips, supra, at 165–66. In this sense, the decision is consistent with *Lucas*, which insists that an owner's title is qualified by common-law nuisance rules in effect when the property is acquired, but not by statutory rules in effect when the property is acquired. Is it plausible to think that "property" is defined solely by judge-made rules of decision, and not also by state statutory law? Many forms of property, like the condominium, have been made possible only by legislation. Some kinds of property rights, like intellectual property, are almost entirely of statutory creation.

Another potentially significant decision, *Eastern Enterprises v. Apfel*, 524 U.S. 498 (1998), raised the question whether a statute that imposed a general liability on employers in the coal mining industry to fund health care benefits for retirees could be challenged under the Takings Clause. Justice O'Connor, writing for a plurality of four, assumed that the answer was yes; she and the Justices who joined her opinion would have invalidated the provision, which applied retroactively, as an uncompensated taking of property. Justice Kennedy concurred only in the judgment. He argued that the law did not affect any identifiable assets of the employers, and hence could not be challenged as a taking. Nevertheless, he provided the fifth vote to invalidate the law, on the ground that it violated substantive due process. Justice Breyer, writing for four dissenters, also agreed that the Takings Clause did not apply, because the law imposed only a general liability, and did not purport to take or regulate any discrete assets. Given that five Justices rejected the application of the Takings Clause, *Eastern Enterprises* suggests that "private property" for purposes of the Takings Clause refers to identifiable things or discrete assets taken by the government, but does not apply when the government simply imposes a general liability or tax that can be satisfied out of any source of wealth. This could be a significant limitation on the scope of the Clause, but the Court has yet to spell out its implications. See Thomas W. Merrill, The Landscape of Constitutional Property, 86 Va. L. Rev. 885, 974–78 (2000); Laura S. Underkuffler, *Tahoe*'s Requiem: The Death of the Scalian View of Property and Justice, 21 Const. Comment. 727, 740–46 (2004).

An even more recent case that bears on the meaning of property for constitutional purposes is *College Savings Bank v. Florida Prepaid Postsecondary Education*, 527 U.S. 666 (1999). This was not a takings case. The issue was whether Congress could subject the states to suits for false advertising under the Lanham Act under its power to enact appropriate legislation to enforce the Due Process Clause of the Fourteenth Amendment. College Savings Bank, the plaintiff, argued that the Lanham Act could be adopted under this power, since it was designed to protect the plaintiff's "property" against deprivations by the state without due process. The Court rejected this argument on the ground that the plaintiff had no "property right" in being free from false advertising by the state. Writing for a bare majority of five, Justice Scalia wrote in part as follows:

> The hallmark of a protected property interest is the right to exclude others. That is "one of the most essential sticks in the bundle of rights that are commonly characterized as property." That is why the right that we all possess to use the public lands is not the "property" right of anyone—hence the sardonic maxim, explaining what economists call the "tragedy of the commons," *res publica, res nullius*. The Lanham Act may well contain provisions that protect constitutionally cognizable property interests—notably, its provisions dealing with infringement of trademarks, which are the "property" of the owner because he can exclude others from using them. The Lanham Act's false advertising provisions, however, bear no relationship to any right to exclude; and Florida Prepaid's [the state agency's] alleged misrepresentations concerning its own products intruded upon no interest over which petitioner had exclusive dominion.

Id. at 673 (citations omitted).

Does this passage suggest that the Court is prepared to endorse an essentialist conception of property centered on the right to exclude others as the definition of property for federal constitutional purposes? Interestingly, the Court made no mention of *Roth* and the importance of independent sources like state law in either *Eastern Enterprises* or *College Savings Bank*. Does this mean the Court is prepared to abandon the *Roth* approach to defining property for constitutional purposes, at least insofar as it now sees the need to develop a general federal conception of what kinds of state-created interests might qualify as property? For further discussion, see Merrill, Landscape, supra.

C. REGULATORY TAKINGS—EXTENSIONS AND APPLICATIONS

1. THE SCOPE OF THE POLICE POWER

Regulatory takings law has always acknowledged that the state has broad police powers—powers to regulate in the interest of protecting the health, safety, and welfare of the public. The issue in regulatory takings cases has been when such an exercise of power interferes with property to such an extent that the government must pay just compensation. One sub-theme in the cases has been that certain types of regulations are so central to the police power that they should never be regarded as "takings." Thus, Justice Brandeis argues in *Mahon* that regulations of "noxious uses" of property are not takings, and Justice Scalia in *Lucas* acknowledges that a regulation which tracks the common law of nuisance is not a taking—even if it deprives an owner of all economic value of the property. One question left open by *Lucas* is whether the common law of nuisance should serve as a benchmark for all purposes for the type of police regulation exempt from takings claims, or whether a broader harm-prevention conception of the exemption should prevail when a regulation has a less severe financial impact on the owner than it did in *Lucas*. When we move beyond the benchmark of the common law of nuisance, however, is the distinction between harm-preventing and benefit-conferring regulation coherent? Consider the following case.

Miller v. Schoene

Supreme Court of the United States, 1928.
276 U.S. 272.

■ MR. JUSTICE STONE delivered the opinion of the Court. Acting under the Cedar Rust Act of Virginia, Acts Va. 1914, c. 36, as amended by Acts Va. 1920, c. 260, now embodied in Va. Code (1924) as sections 885 to 893, defendant in error, the state entomologist, ordered the plaintiffs in error to cut down a large number of ornamental red cedar trees growing on their property, as a means of preventing the communication of a rust or plant disease with which they were infected to the apple orchards in the vicinity. The plaintiffs in error appealed from the order to the circuit court of Shenandoah county which, after a hearing and a consideration of evidence, affirmed the order and allowed to plaintiffs in error $100 to cover the expense of removal of the cedars. Neither the judgment of the court nor the statute as interpreted allows compensation for the value of the standing cedars or the decrease in the market value of the realty caused by their destruction whether considered as ornamental trees or otherwise. But they save to plaintiffs in error the privilege of using the trees when felled. On appeal the Supreme Court of Appeals of Virginia affirmed the judgment. Miller v. State Entomologist, 135 S. E. 813 (Va.). Both in the circuit court and the Supreme Court of Appeals plaintiffs in error challenged the constitutionality of the statute under the due process clause of the Fourteenth Amendment and the case is properly here on writ of error.

The Virginia statute presents a comprehensive scheme for the condemnation and destruction of red cedar trees infected by cedar rust. By section 1 it is declared to be unlawful for any person to "own, plant or keep alive and standing" on his premises any red cedar tree which is or may be the source or "host plant" of the communicable plant disease known as cedar rust, and any such tree growing within a certain radius of any apple orchard is declared to be a public nuisance, subject to destruction. Section 2 makes it the duty of the state entomologist, "upon the request in writing of ten or more reputable freeholders of any county or magisterial district, to make a preliminary investigation of the locality * * * to ascertain if any cedar tree or trees * * * are the source of, harbor or constitute the host plant for the said disease * * * and constitute a menace to the health of any apple orchard in said locality, and that said cedar tree or trees exist within a radius of two miles of any apple orchard in said locality." If affirmative findings are so made, he is required to direct the owner in writing to destroy the trees and, in his notice, to furnish a statement of the "fact found to exist whereby it is deemed necessary or proper to destroy" the trees and to call attention to the law under which it is proposed to destroy them. Section 5 authorizes the state entomologist to destroy the trees if the owner, after being notified, fails to do so. Section 7 furnishes a mode of appealing from the order of the entomologist to the circuit court of the county, which is authorized to "hear the objections" and "pass upon all questions involved," the procedure followed in the present case.

As shown by the evidence and as recognized in other cases involving the validity of this statute, Bowman v. Virginia State Entomologist, 105 S. E. 141 (Va.); Kelleher v. Schoene 14 F. 2d 341 (D.C. Cir.), cedar rust is an infectious plant disease in the form of a fungoid organism which is destructive of the fruit and foliage of the apple, but without effect on the value of the cedar. Its life cycle has two phases which are passed alternately as a growth on red cedar and on apple trees. It is communicated by spores from one to the other over a radius of at least two miles. It appears not to be communicable between trees of the same species, but only from one species to the other, and other plants seem not to be appreciably affected by it. The only practicable method of controlling the disease and protecting apple trees from its ravages is the destruction of all red cedar trees, subject to the infection, located within two miles of apple orchards.

The red cedar, aside from its ornamental use, has occasional use and value as lumber. It is indigenous to Virginia, is not cultivated or dealt in commercially on any substantial scale, and its value throughout the state is shown to be small as compared with that of the apple orchards of the state. Apple growing is one of the principal agricultural pursuits in Virginia. The apple is used there and exported in large quantities. Many millions of dollars are invested in the orchards, which furnish employment for a large portion of the population, and have induced the development of attendant railroad and cold storage facilities.

On the evidence we may accept the conclusion of the Supreme Court of Appeals that the state was under the necessity of making a choice between the preservation of one class of property and that of the other wherever both existed in dangerous proximity. It would have been none the less a choice if, instead of enacting the present statute, the state, by doing nothing, had permitted serious injury to the apple orchards within its borders to go on unchecked. When forced to such a choice the state does not exceed its constitutional powers by deciding upon the destruction of one class of property in order to save another which, in the judgment of the legislature, is of greater value to the public. It will not do to say that the case is merely one of a conflict of two private interests and that the misfortune of apple growers may not be shifted to cedar owners by ordering the destruction of their property; for it is obvious that there may be, and that here there is, a preponderant public concern in the preservation of the one interest over the other. Compare Bacon v. Walker, 204 U.S. 311; Missouri, Kansas & Texas R. Co. v. May, 194 U.S. 267; Chicago, Terre Haute & Southeastern R. Co. v. Anderson, 242 U.S. 283; Perley v. North Carolina, 249 U.S. 510. And where the public interest is involved preferment of that interest over the property interest of the individual, to the extent even of its destruction, is one of the distinguishing characteristics of every exercise of the police power which affects property. Mugler v. Kansas, 123 U.S. 623; Hadacheck v. Los Angeles, 239 U.S. 394; Village of Euclid v. Ambler Realty Co., 272 U.S. 365; Northwestern Fertilizer Co. v. Hyde Park, 97 U.S. 659; Northwestern Laundry v. Des Moines, 239 U.S. 486; Lawton v. Steele, 152 U.S. 133; Sligh v. Kirkwood, 237 U.S. 52; Reinman v. Little Rock, 237 U.S. 171.

We need not weigh with nicety the question whether the infected cedars constitute a nuisance according to the common law; or whether they may be so declared by statute. See Hadacheck v. Los Angeles, supra, 411. For where, as here, the choice is unavoidable, we cannot say that its exercise, controlled by considerations of social policy which are not unreasonable, involves any denial of due process. The injury to property here is no more serious, nor the public interest less, than in Hadacheck v. Los Angeles, supra, Northwestern Laundry v. Des Moines, supra, Reinman v. Little Rock, supra, or Sligh v. Kirkwood, supra.

[The Court also rejected the contention that the right of "ten or more reputable freeholders" to trigger an investigation was fatal. The freeholders] do not determine the action of the state entomologist. They merely request him to conduct an investigation. In him is vested the discretion to decide, after investigation, whether or not conditions are such that the other provisions of the statute shall be brought into action; and his determination is subject to judicial review. The property of plaintiffs in error is not subjected to the possibly arbitrary and irresponsible action of a group of private citizens. * * *

Affirmed.

NOTES AND QUESTIONS

1. Recall the excerpt in Chapter I where Ronald Coase claims that in cases of incompatible land uses we should not ask which use is inflicting harm on the other. Rather, he says, the problem is a "reciprocal" one: "The real question that has to be decided is: Should A be allowed to harm B or should B be allowed to harm A? The problem is to avoid the more serious harm." Whatever you think about this claim in the context of

classic nuisances like air or water pollution, is this an apt characterization of the situation in *Miller v. Schoene*, where rust spores spread by leaping alternatively from cedar trees to apple trees? Does it follow that the legislature would have been equally justified in ordering the destruction of apple trees in order to halt the spread of the disease? Several authors have argued that *Miller v. Schoene* undermines the notion of state action (versus inaction) and the whole public/private distinction, because, in Justice Stone's words, a decision by Virginia not to have cedars cut would have been "none the less a choice." See, e.g., Louis M. Seidman & Mark V. Tushnet, Remnants of Belief: Contemporary Constitutional Issues 27 (1996); Warren Samuels, Interrelations Between Legal and Economic Processes, 14 J.L. & Econ. 435 (1971); see also Barbara H. Fried, The Progressive Assault on Laissez–Faire: Robert Hale and the First Law and Economics Movement (1998).

2. Recent research by William Fischel on the *Miller* case casts doubt on the "reciprocal" view of *Miller v. Schoene*, but raises some new questions. Fischel finds that there was a widespread and well-accepted custom that in situations where a fungus leaps from species to species of plant in its life cycle, the more commercially significant plant always prevails. He terms this norm "prices make rights." The custom clearly applied to parasite-ridden trees and other crops. Would it be a good idea to apply this notion more generally? (Does this notion in fact apply more generally?) This would be the shortest of short cuts to the result in *Kelo*, supra, since presumably it would allow any taking of property that would increase the size of the social pie. But wouldn't it also confirm Justice O'Connor's warnings about every Motel 6 being vulnerable to replacement by a Ritz–Carlton? At any rate, the more-valuable-plant-wins norm was a firm background principle when *Miller* was decided. The 1914 legislation in question in *Miller* passed the Virginia House of Delegates 88 to 0 with one Dr. Caspar Otto Miller, the cedar-owning plaintiff in this case, casting a yes vote. It also turns out that apple growers, who procured the legislation after a nasty bout of cedar-apple rust, had no objection to compensating cedar owners. But because the initial version of the law provided for compensation, some owners of cedar trees which were more valuable as cut wood than as standing trees made spurious claims for compensation. For more on the case and the ins and outs of cedar-apple rust, see William A. Fischel, The Law and Economics of Cedar–Apple Rust: State Action and Just Compensation in *Miller v. Schoene* (Dartmouth College Economics Department Working Paper, draft of April 23, 2004).

3. The Court defers to the judgment of the Virginia legislature that apple trees are of greater significance to the state economy than cedar trees, because apples are an important commercial product whereas cedar trees are used mostly for ornamental purposes. It would seem to follow that the legislature had a rational reason for ordering the destruction of infected cedar trees in order to spare the apple trees. This kind of reason is enough to save the statute from condemnation on substantive due process or equal protection grounds. See, e.g., Williamson v. Lee Optical Co., 348 U.S. 483 (1955). But does this answer the question whether the owners of cedar

trees should be compensated in full for their losses? Compare James Buchanan, Politics, Property, and the Law: An Alternative Interpretation of *Miller et al. v. Schoene*, 15 J.L. & Econ. 439 (1972) (arguing in favor of compensation in *Miller* on political economy grounds); with Samuels, supra at 439 (arguing against compensation on the ground that this allocates (ex post) a new stick to the apple tree owner's bundle of rights). Recall that in accession cases (Chapter II), courts award the thing to the party who has supplied greater value to the final good, but award damages to the other party. Does this suggest that although the apple tree owners have a better claim to keep their trees, they (or the state) should be required to compensate the owners of cedar trees?

4. The Court in *Miller* cites a number of decisions upholding regulations of "noxious uses," including *Mugler v. Kansas*, 123 U.S. 623 (1887) (distillery); *Northwestern Fertilizing Co. v. Hyde Park*, 97 U.S. 659 (1878) (fertilizer plant); *Reinman v. Little Rock*, 237 U.S. 171 (1915) (livery stable); and *Hadacheck v. Sebastian*, 239 U.S. 394 (1915) (brick yard). The owners of the offending properties in each of these cases could claim that at the time the facilities were constructed, the uses were entirely lawful and did not cause any appreciable harm to surrounding properties. It was only later, when social norms changed (as in *Mugler*, when the state enacted a prohibition law) or when the surrounding properties were developed for residential use (as in *Northwestern Fertilizer, Reinman*, and *Hadacheck*) that it was possible to say that the uses had become "noxious." The Court nevertheless steadfastly refused to require compensation in these situations, perhaps on the ground that the conflict was foreseeable at the time the facilities were built. Is the result in *Miller* similarly justified, or was the emergence of cedar rust and the danger it posed to apple trees less foreseeable than the harms caused by distilleries, livery stables, fertilizer plants, or brick yards? If the problem of cedar rust was entirely unforeseeable, are the owners of such trees like Miller innocent of wrongdoing in a way that the owners of the offending facilities in the noxious use cases are not?

5. If *Miller v. Schoene* arose today, would it be governed by the per se rule of *Lucas v. South Carolina Coastal Council*, on the ground that the economic value of the cedar trees is completely destroyed by the state order? Or would this rule not apply, because the owner gets to keep the wood after the trees are cut down? Is *Lucas* inapplicable because the total wipeout rule is limited to real property as opposed to personal property? (Are standing trees personal property or part of the realty?) Note that the Court declines to get drawn into the question whether cedar rust would be a nuisance at common law. Could the court avoid deciding this question after *Lucas*? Or does *Lucas*'s limitation of the police power exception to rules that track the common law of nuisance apply only to regulations that trigger the categorical rule against complete wipeouts? Does the "prices make rights" principle for parasites in plants, unearthed by Fischel, see above, supply the relevant background principle under *Lucas*? Does this raise anew the question whether courts are good at incorporating custom into their decisionmaking?

2. The Denominator Problem

Two of the tests the Court has adopted for identifying regulatory takings require that courts calculate the extent to which a regulation has diminished the value of property. First, diminution in value is an important variable under the *Penn Central* ad hoc takings test (indeed, this was also one of the factors mentioned in *Mahon*). Second, diminution in value is critical under the *Lucas* total takings test, at least if we interpret that test to mean that the regulation has deprived the owner of 100 per cent of the value of the property. (An alternative interpretation, which may be the one actually intended by Justice Scalia, is that the regulation has deprived the owner of all opportunity to engage in productive use of the land. This would be more of a qualitative inquiry, which would not necessarily entail an assessment of diminution in value.) For either purpose, courts must do a before-and-after comparison of values. More precisely, they must compare the "numerator"—the value of the property taken by the regulation—to the "denominator"—the value of the property before the regulation.

As suggested by the dueling opinions of Justices Holmes and Brandeis in *Pennsylvania Coal*, a critical issue here concerns the definition of the "denominator." Recall that in that case, Justice Holmes appeared to assume that the denominator was the pillars of coal that had to remain in place under the regulation, but which could have been mined in the absence of the regulation. Justice Brandeis, in contrast, argued that the denominator should be the "whole property" of the coal company. In more recent opinions, the Court has cautioned against slicing and dicing the property into smaller units for purposes of takings analysis. Thus, in *Penn Central*, the Court wrote:

> "Takings" jurisprudence does not divide a single parcel into discrete segments and attempt to determine whether rights in a particular segment have been entirely abrogated. In deciding whether a particular governmental action has effected a taking, this Court focuses rather both on the character of the action and on the nature and extent of the interference with rights in the parcel as a whole—here, the city tax block designated as the "landmark site." 438 U.S. at 130–31.

Similarly, in *Keystone Bituminous Coal Ass'n v. DeBenedictis*, 480 U.S. 470, 498 (1987), the Court rejected the claim that an anti-subsidence act that required an additional 27 million tons of coal to be left in the ground had effected a regulatory taking to this extent:

> The 27 million tons of coal do not constitute a separate segment of property for takings law purposes. Many zoning ordinances place limits on the property owner's right to make profitable use of some segments of his property. A requirement that a building occupy no more than a specified percentage of the lot on which it is located could be characterized as a taking of the vacant area as readily as the requirement that coal pillars be left in place. Similarly, under petitioners' theory one could always argue that a setback ordinance requiring that no structure be built within a certain distance from the property line consti-

tutes a taking because the footage represents a distinct segment of property for takings law purposes. Cf. Gorieb v. Fox, 274 U.S. 603 (1927) (upholding validity of setback ordinance) (Sutherland, J.). There is no basis for treating the less than 2% of petitioners' coal as a separate parcel of property.

Recall that in *Lucas v. South Carolina Coastal Council*, supra, Justice Scalia in footnote 7 addressed this issue in a way that suggested significant doubt remains about how to define the denominator: "Regrettably, the rhetorical force of our 'deprivation of all economically feasible use' rule is greater than its precision, since the rule does not make clear the 'property interest' against which the loss of value is to be measured." Justice Scalia went on to express confidence that the New York Court of Appeals, in the decision affirmed by the Supreme Court in *Penn Central*, supra, had gone too far when it suggested that the denominator should be expressed in terms of the "total value of the takings claimant's other holdings in the vicinity." But he concluded it was unnecessary to resolve the denominator question in *Lucas* because Lucas had a fee simple interest in real estate, and there was no question but that this was the interest that was claimed to have been taken. The only hint Justice Scalia provided about how the denominator should be identified in contested cases was that "[t]he answer to this difficult question may lie in how the owner's reasonable expectations have been shaped by the state's law of property—i.e., whether and to what degree the state's law has accorded legal recognition and protection to the particular interest in land with respect to which the takings claimant alleges a diminution in (or elimination of) value." What do you think Justice Scalia had in mind by this? Was he suggesting perhaps that "denominators" be limited to pre-packaged bundles of rights that are recognized by the relevant legal community as discrete property interests? Under this theory, who was right about the denominator in *Mahon*— Justice Holmes or Justice Brandeis?

In any event, considerable uncertainty remains about identifying denominators. One source of ambiguity goes by the name "conceptual severance." See John E. Fee, Of Parcels and Property, in Taking Sides on Taking Issues: Public and Private Perspectives 101 (Thomas E. Roberts ed., 2002); Marc R. Lisker, Regulatory Takings and the Denominator Problem, 27 Rutgers L.J. 663, 664–68 (1996); Margaret Jane Radin, The Liberal Conception of Property: Cross Currents in the Jurisprudence of Takings, 88 Colum. L. Rev. 1667, 1674–78 (1988); Leif Wenar, The Concept of Property and the Takings Clause, 97 Colum. L. Rev. 1923 (1997); see also Daryl J. Levinson, Framing Transactions in Constitutional Law, 111 Yale L.J. 1311, 1338–45 (2002). This refers to the practice of disaggregating an asset into separate rights of property—different sticks in the bundle of rights—and treating each separate entitlement as in itself a property right. If conceptual severance is permitted, then the denominator can be shrunk to the point where a takings claim becomes plausible. Another source of ambiguity concerns the exact dimensions of the "whole parcel" in any given situation. Suppose, for example, a developer owns a tract of 20 acres, which has been subdivided into 40 lots which have not yet been developed or sold. Is the "whole parcel" the 20 acres, or is it each individual lot? Does the answer change the minute one of the lots is sold? See Gregory M. Stein, Takings in the 21st Century: Reasonable Investment–Backed Expectations after *Palazzolo* and *Tahoe–Sierra*, 69 Tenn. L. Rev. 891, 934–37 (2002).

Potential issues of conceptual severance and controversies about the scope of the whole parcel continued to arise—at least implicitly—in the Court's post-*Lucas* decisions. Is progress being made toward solving these problems?

Phillips v. Washington Legal Foundation

Supreme Court of the United States, 1998.
524 U.S. 156.

■ CHIEF JUSTICE REHNQUIST delivered the opinion of the Court. Texas, like 48 other States and the District of Columbia, has adopted an Interest on Lawyers Trust Account (IOLTA) program. Under these programs, certain client funds held by an attorney in connection with his practice of law are deposited in bank accounts. The interest income generated by the funds is paid to foundations that finance legal services for low-income individuals. The question presented by this case is whether interest earned on client funds held in IOLTA accounts is "private property" of either the client or the attorney for purposes of the Takings Clause of the Fifth Amendment. We hold that it is the property of the client. * * *

II

The Fifth Amendment, made applicable to the States through the Fourteenth Amendment, Chicago, B. & Q.R. Co. v. Chicago, 166 U.S. 226, 239 (1897), provides that "private property" shall not "be taken for public use, without just compensation." Because the Constitution protects rather than creates property interests, the existence of a property interest is determined by reference to "existing rules or understandings that stem from an independent source such as state law." Board of Regents of State Colleges v. Roth, 408 U.S. 564, 577 (1972).

All agree that under Texas law the principal held in IOLTA trust accounts is the "private property" of the client. * * * When deposited in an IOLTA account, these funds remain in the control of a private attorney and are freely available to the client upon demand. As to the principal, then, the IOLTA rules at most "regulate the use of [the] property." Yee v. Escondido, 503 U.S. 519, 522 (1992). Respondents do not contend that the State's regulation of the manner in which attorneys hold and manage client funds amounts to a taking of private property. The question in this case is whether the interest on an IOLTA account is "private property" of the client for whom the principal is being held.

The rule that "interest follows principal" has been established under English common law since at least the mid–1700's. Beckford v. Tobin, 1 Ves.Sen. 308, 310, 27 Eng.Rep. 1049, 1051 (Ch. 1749) ("[I]nterest shall follow the principal, as the shadow the body"). Not surprisingly, this rule has become firmly embedded in the common law of the various States. The Court of Appeals in this case, two of the three judges of which are Texans, held that Texas also follows this rule, citing *Sellers v. Harris County,* 483 S.W.2d 242, 243 (Tex. 1972) ("The interest earned by deposit of money owned by the parties to the lawsuit is an increment that accrues to that money and to its owners.") Indeed, in *Webb's Fabulous Pharmacies, Inc. v. Beckwith,* 449 U.S. 155, 162 (1980), we cited the *Sellers* opinion as demonstrative of the general rule that "any interest ... follows the principal." * * *

We have never held that a physical item is not "property" simply because it lacks a positive economic or market value. For example, in *Loretto v. Teleprompter Manhattan CATV Corp.,* 458 U.S. 419 (1982), we held that a property right was taken even when infringement of that right arguably *increased* the market value of the property at issue. Id., at 437, n. 15. Our conclusion in this regard was premised on our longstanding recognition that property is more than economic value, see id., at 435; it also consists of "the group of rights which the so-called owner exercises in his dominion of the physical thing," such "as the right to possess, use and dispose of it," General Motors, supra, at 378. While the interest income at issue here may have no economically realizable value to its owner, possession, control, and disposition are nonetheless valuable rights that inhere in the property. See Hodel v. Irving, 481 U.S. 704, 715 (1987) (noting that "the right to pass on" property "is itself a valuable right"). The government may not seize rents received by the owner of a building simply because it can prove that the costs incurred in collecting the rents exceed the amount collected. * * *

This would be a different case if the interest income generated by IOLTA accounts was transferred to the State as payment "for services rendered" by the State. [Webb's Fabulous Pharmacies, supra,] at 157. Our holding does not prohibit a State from imposing reasonable fees it incurs in generating and allocating interest income. See id., at 162; cf. United States v. Sperry Corp., 493 U.S. 52, 60 (1989) (upholding the imposition of a "reasonable 'user fee'" on those utilizing the Iran–United States Claims Tribunal). But here the State does not, indeed cannot, argue that its confiscation of respondents' interest income amounts to a fee for services performed. * * *

In sum, we hold that the interest income generated by funds held in IOLTA accounts is the "private property" of the owner of the principal. We express no view as to whether these funds have been "taken" by the State; nor do we express an opinion as to the amount of "just compensation," if any, due respondents. We leave these issues to be addressed on remand. The judgment of the Court of Appeals is

Affirmed.

■ JUSTICE SOUTER, with whom JUSTICE STEVENS, JUSTICE GINSBURG, and JUSTICE BREYER join, dissenting [omitted].

NOTES AND QUESTIONS

1. Is the court guilty of conceptual severance here? In what sense are dollars of interest a separate "property" right from dollars of principal in a single account balance, like a savings account or NOW account? Does the principle of accession (see Chapter II) lie behind the conclusion that interest should follow principle, and if so, through what source of law, state or federal, does accession come into the analysis? Do policy considerations make accession superfluous? Or does policy point in the direction of incorporating widespread intuitions about accession into the (federal) definition of property?

2. In a subsequent decision, *Brown v. Legal Found. of Washington*, 538 U.S. 216 (2003), the Court held that the IOLTA program was a taking, because it deprived the clients of all the interest earned on funds deposited with their lawyers. However, the Court also held that the clients had not been deprived of just compensation, because they would have earned no interest on the principal in the absence of the IOLTA program. Thus, the program did not violate the Takings Clause. Does this outcome confirm that the Court was guilty of conceptual severance in the initial decision? How is the ultimate outcome here any different from that in *Loretto*, supra, where the New York courts on remand concluded that the landlord was entitled to $1 in nominal compensation for the permanent physical occupation by a cable wire on the roof of her building? Was the Court also guilty of conceptual severance in *Loretto*? If not, why not? If interest is a separate property right from principal, why weren't the air rights in *Penn Central* (or the support rights in *Keystone Bituminous Coal*) a separate property right from the column of space as a whole?

3. Can the Texas rule about interest on lawyer trust accounts be justified as a species of taxation? Is the rule any different than a law saying that any funds deposited by clients with lawyers will be subject to a tax equal to 100 percent of any interest earned? Courts have always assumed that taxes are immune from challenge under the Takings Clause. See, e.g., Penn Central, supra ("[G]overnment may execute laws or programs that adversely affect recognized economic values. Exercises of the taxing power are one obvious example.") The doctrinal explanation for this goes back to the foundations of the regulatory takings doctrine in the power of the eminent domain. Eminent domain is distinct not only from the police power, but also from the power of taxation. Just as exercises of the police power do not require compensation, neither do exercises of the power of taxation. Indeed, it would obviously be self-defeating to require the government to pay compensation for collecting taxes. But many commentators have thought this explanation is not satisfactory from a functional perspective that starts with the *Armstrong* principle that the just compensation requirement is "designed to bar Government from forcing some people alone to bear public burdens which, in all fairness and justice, should be borne by the public as a whole." Armstrong v. United States, 364 U.S. 40, 49 (1960). See, e.g., Eric Kades, Drawing the Line Between Taxes and Takings: The Continuous Burdens Principle, and its Broader Applications,

97 Nw. U. L. Rev. 189 (2002); Eduardo Moisés Peñalver, Regulatory Taxings, 104 Colum. L. Rev. 2182 (2004).

Palazzolo v. Rhode Island

United States Supreme Court, 2001.
533 U.S. 606.

■ JUSTICE KENNEDY delivered the opinion of the Court. [Petitioner challenged as a taking a decision by the Rhode Island Coastal Resources Management Council denying his application to fill 18 acres of coastal wetlands to construct a beach club. The evidence indicated that a portion of the parcel was uplands, and hence could be developed as a residence consistent with the wetlands regulations.]

[The Rhode Island Supreme Court] held that all economically beneficial use was not deprived because the uplands portion of the property can still be improved. On this point, we agree with the court's decision. Petitioner accepts the Council's contention and the state trial court's finding that his parcel retains $200,000 in development value under the State's wetlands regulations. He asserts, nonetheless, that he has suffered a total taking and contends the Council cannot sidestep the holding in *Lucas* "by the simple expedient of leaving a landowner a few crumbs of value."

Assuming a taking is otherwise established, a State may not evade the duty to compensate on the premise that the landowner is left with a token interest. This is not the situation of the landowner in this case, however. A regulation permitting a landowner to build a substantial residence on an 18-acre parcel does not leave the property "economically idle." Lucas, supra, at 1019.

In his brief submitted to us petitioner attempts to revive this part of his claim by reframing it. He argues, for the first time, that the upland parcel is distinct from the wetlands portions, so he should be permitted to assert a deprivation limited to the latter. This contention asks us to examine the difficult, persisting question of what is the proper denominator in the takings fraction. See Michelman, Property, Utility, and Fairness: Comments on the Ethical Foundations of "Just Compensation Law," 80 Harv. L.Rev. 1165, 1192 (1967). Some of our cases indicate that the extent of deprivation effected by a regulatory action is measured against the value of the parcel as a whole, see, e.g., Keystone Bituminous Coal Assn. v. DeBenedictis, 480 U.S. 470, 497 (1987); but we have at times expressed discomfort with the logic of this rule, see *Lucas, supra,* at 1016–1017, n. 7, a sentiment echoed by some commentators, see, e.g., Epstein, Takings: Descent and Resurrection, 1987 S.Ct. Rev. 1, 16–17 (1987); Fee, Unearthing the Denominator in Regulatory Takings Claims, 61 U. Chi. L.Rev. 1535 (1994). Whatever the merits of these criticisms, we will not explore the point here. Petitioner did not press the argument in the state courts, and the issue was not presented in the petition for certiorari. The case comes to us on the premise that petitioner's entire parcel serves as the basis for his takings claim, and, so framed, the total deprivation argument fails.

Tahoe–Sierra Preservation Council, Inc. v. Tahoe Regional Planning Agency

Supreme Court of the United States, 2002.
535 U.S. 302.

■ JUSTICE STEVENS delivered the opinion of the Court. The question presented is whether a moratorium on development imposed during the process of devising a comprehensive land-use plan constitutes a *per se* taking of property requiring compensation under the Takings Clause of the United States Constitution. [Lake Tahoe is a uniquely beautiful lake that straddles the border between California and Nevada. Rapid development of property on its shores threatened to damage the environmental quality of the lake and the areas surrounding it. The Tahoe Regional Planning Agency adopted two moratoriums on development, which together lasted 32 months, in order to preserve the environmental status quo while it attempted to draft a plan that would control future development.]

Petitioners make only a facial attack on [the moratoria]. They contend that the mere enactment of a temporary regulation that, while in effect, denies a property owner all viable economic use of her property gives rise to an unqualified constitutional obligation to compensate her for the value of its use during that period. * * *

[T]hey rely principally on our decision in *Lucas v. South Carolina Coastal Council,* 505 U.S. 1003 (1992)—a regulatory takings case that, nevertheless, applied a categorical rule—to argue that the *Penn Central* framework is inapplicable here. * * *

[The] requirement that "the aggregate must be viewed in its entirety" explains why * * * a regulation that prohibited commercial transactions in eagle feathers, but did not bar other uses or impose any physical invasion or restraint upon them, was not a taking. Andrus v. Allard, 444 U.S. 51, 66 (1979). It also clarifies why restrictions on the use of only limited portions of the parcel, such as setback ordinances, Gorieb v. Fox, 274 U.S. 603 (1927), or a requirement that coal pillars be left in place to prevent mine subsidence, Keystone Bituminous Coal Assn. v. DeBenedictis, 480 U.S., at 498, were not considered regulatory takings. In each of these cases, we affirmed that "where an owner possesses a full 'bundle' of property rights, the destruction of one 'strand' of the bundle is not a taking." *Andrus,* 444 U.S., at 65–66. * * *

Petitioners seek to bring this case under the rule announced in *Lucas* by arguing that we can effectively sever a 32–month segment from the remainder of each landowner's fee simple estate, and then ask whether that segment has been taken in its entirety by the moratoria. Of course, defining the property interest taken in terms of the very regulation being challenged is circular. With property so divided, every delay would become a total ban; the moratorium and the normal permit process alike would constitute categorical takings. Petitioners' "conceptual severance" argument is unavailing because it ignores *Penn Central's* admonition that in regulatory takings cases we must focus on "the parcel as a whole." 438 U.S., at 130–131. We have consistently rejected such an approach to the "denominator" question. See Keystone, 480 U.S., at 497. See also Concrete Pipe & Products of Cal., Inc. v. Construction Laborers Pension Trust for Southern Cal., 508 U.S. 602, 644 (1993) ("To the extent that any portion of property is taken, that portion is always taken in its entirety; the relevant question, however, is whether the property taken is all, or only a portion of, the parcel in question"). Thus, the District Court erred when it disaggregated petitioners' property into temporal segments corresponding to the regulations at issue and then analyzed whether petitioners were deprived of all economically viable use during each period. 34 F.Supp.2d, at 1242–1245. The starting point for the court's analysis should have been to ask whether there was a total taking of the entire parcel; if not, then *Penn Central* was the proper framework.

An interest in real property is defined by the metes and bounds that describe its geographic dimensions and the term of years that describes the temporal aspect of the owner's interest. See Restatement of Property §§ 7–9 (1936). Both dimensions must be considered if the interest is to be viewed in its entirety. Hence, a permanent deprivation of the owner's use of the entire area is a taking of "the parcel as a whole," whereas a temporary restriction that merely causes a diminution in value is not. Logically, a fee simple estate cannot be rendered valueless by a temporary prohibition on economic use, because the property will recover value as soon as the prohibition is lifted. Cf. Agins v. City of Tiburon, 447 U.S., at 263, n. 9 ("Even if the appellants' ability to sell their property was limited during the pendency of the condemnation proceeding, the appellants were free to sell or develop their property when the proceedings ended. Mere fluctuations in value during the process of governmental decisionmaking, absent extraordinary delay, are 'incidents of ownership. They cannot be considered as a "taking" in the constitutional sense' " (quoting Danforth v. United States, 308 U.S. 271, 285 (1939))). * * *

■ CHIEF JUSTICE REHNQUIST, with whom JUSTICE SCALIA and JUSTICE THOMAS join, dissenting. [omitted]

■ JUSTICE THOMAS, with whom JUSTICE SCALIA joins, dissenting. * * * I write separately to address the majority's conclusion that the temporary moratorium at issue here was not a taking because it was not a "taking of 'the parcel as a whole.' " While this questionable rule* has been applied to

---

* The majority's decision to embrace the "parcel as a whole" doctrine as settled is puzzling. See, e.g., Palazzolo v. Rhode Island, 533 U.S. 606, 631 (2001) (noting that the Court has "at times expressed discomfort with the logic of [the parcel as a whole] rule"); Lucas v. South Carolina Coastal Council, 505 U.S. 1003, 1017, n. 7 (1992) (recognizing that "uncertainty regarding the composition of the denominator in [the Court's] 'deprivation' fraction has produced inconsistent pronouncements by the Court," and that the relevant calculus is a "difficult question").

various alleged regulatory takings, it was, in my view, rejected in the context of *temporal* deprivations of property by *First English Evangelical Lutheran Church of Glendale v. County of Los Angeles,* 482 U.S. 304, 318 (1987), which held that temporary and permanent takings "are not different in kind" when a landowner is deprived of all beneficial use of his land. I had thought that *First English* put to rest the notion that the "relevant denominator" is land's infinite life. Consequently, a regulation effecting a total deprivation of the use of a so-called "temporal slice" of property is compensable under the Takings Clause unless background principles of state property law prevent it from being deemed a taking; "total deprivation of use is, from the landowner's point of view, the equivalent of a physical appropriation." Lucas v. South Carolina Coastal Council, 505 U.S. 1003, 1017 (1992).

A taking is exactly what occurred in this case. No one seriously doubts that the land-use regulations at issue rendered petitioners' land unsusceptible of *any* economically beneficial use. This was true at the inception of the moratorium, and it remains true today. These individuals and families were deprived of the opportunity to build single-family homes as permanent, retirement, or vacation residences on land upon which such construction was authorized when purchased. The Court assures them that "a temporary prohibition on economic use" cannot be a taking because "[l]ogically ... the property will recover value as soon as the prohibition is lifted." But the "logical" assurance that a "temporary restriction ... merely causes a diminution in value," is cold comfort to the property owners in this case or any other. After all, *"[i]n the long run* we are all dead." J. Keynes, Monetary Reform 88 (1924).

I would hold that regulations prohibiting all productive uses of property are subject to *Lucas' per se* rule, regardless of whether the property so burdened retains theoretical useful life and value if, and when, the "temporary" moratorium is lifted. To my mind, such potential future value bears on the amount of compensation due and has nothing to do with the question whether there was a taking in the first place. It is regrettable that the Court has charted a markedly different path today.

NOTE AND QUESTIONS

The Court says: "An interest in real property is defined by the metes and bounds that describe its geographic dimensions and the term of years that describes the temporal aspect of the owner's interest." Does this mean that if one of the petitioners was leasing the property for a term of five years, and the moratorium on development lasted five years, that particular petitioner would be able to advance a *Lucas* total takings challenge to a development moratorium? If this is what the Court's language means, then should all owners of property in areas subject to development moratoria engage in sale and lease back arrangements (perhaps with an option to repurchase and the end of the lease term), in order to make themselves eligible for just compensation for the period of the lease?

3. THE PROBLEM OF EXACTIONS

One of the features of modern zoning and land-use planning is that developers must submit their plans for new subdivisions, shopping centers, and other significant real estate developments to local planning authorities for their approval before construction may begin. Under the original conception of zoning, the purpose of requiring advance approval was to assure that the proposed development was consistent with the local zoning ordinance. As we saw in Chapter IX, in recent decades the approval process has evolved into complex negotiations between the developer and local authorities over the scope, uses, and density of the proposed project. See generally Vicki Been, "Exit" as a Constraint on Land Use Exactions: Rethinking the Unconstitutional Conditions Doctrine, 91 Colum. L. Rev. 473 (1991); Carol M. Rose, Planning and Dealing: Piecemeal Land Controls as a Problem of Local Legitimacy, 71 Cal. L. Rev. 837 (1983). These negotiations often include what are called exactions—an agreement by the developer to donate certain property or money to the local community—as a condition of obtaining approval from authorities to proceed with the development. The justification for these exactions is that they provide resources that the community can use for public goods like new parks or schools that offset, at least in part, the burdens imposed on the community by the new development. See generally Alan A. Altschuler et al., Regulation for Revenue: The Political Economy of Land Use Exactions (1993).

State courts have reviewed challenges to exactions for many years, typically under state constitutional doctrines like substantive due process. In 1987, the U.S. Supreme Court took up the issue under the Takings Clause, in *Nollan v. California Coastal Comm'n*, 483 U.S. 825 (1987). The Nollans owned a dilapidated beach front bungalow, which they wanted to replace with a larger house. The California Coastal Commission informed them that permission to undertake the development would not be granted unless they agreed to convey a lateral easement of public access along the beach behind their house. In a 5–4 decision authored by Justice Scalia, the Court declared that this exaction violated the Takings Clause. The Court assumed that the Commission could have denied the building permit outright, in the interest of assuring "visual access" to the ocean and preventing overcrowding of beaches. But it found no nexus between these asserted public justifications and the condition the Commission wanted to impose—a lateral easement facilitating the movement of the public up and down the beach. The Court suggested that "unless the permit condition serves the same governmental purpose as the development ban, the building restriction is not a valid regulation of land but 'an out-and-out plan of extortion.' " Id. at 837 (citation omitted).

Nollan was a confusing decision because it was unclear whether the Court was advancing a general requirement that all property regulations satisfy some level of means-ends rationality, or whether it was asserting a rule unique to exactions. The following decision restated the *Nollan* holding, and provided a clearer exposition of why exactions are a matter of heightened concern under the Takings Clause.

Dolan v. City of Tigard

Supreme Court of the United States, 1994.
512 U.S. 374.

■ CHIEF JUSTICE REHNQUIST delivered the opinion of the Court. Petitioner challenges the decision of the Oregon Supreme Court which held that the city of Tigard could condition the approval of her building permit on the dedication of a portion of her property for flood control and traffic improvements. We granted certiorari to resolve a question left open by our decision in *Nollan v. California Coastal Comm'n*, 483 U.S. 825 (1987), of what is the required degree of connection between the exactions imposed by the city and the projected impacts of the proposed development.

I

The State of Oregon enacted a comprehensive land use management program in 1973. Ore.Rev.Stat. §§ 197.005–197.860 (1991). * * * Pursuant to the State's requirements, the city of Tigard, a community of some 30,000 residents on the southwest edge of Portland, developed a comprehensive plan and codified it in its Community Development Code (CDC). * * * After the completion of a transportation study that identified congestion in the Central Business District as a particular problem, the city adopted a plan for a pedestrian/bicycle pathway intended to encourage alternatives to automobile transportation for short trips. The CDC requires that new development facilitate this plan by dedicating land for pedestrian pathways where provided for in the pedestrian/bicycle pathway plan.

The city also adopted a Master Drainage Plan (Drainage Plan). The Drainage Plan noted that flooding occurred in several areas along Fanno Creek, including areas near petitioner's property. The Drainage Plan also established that the increase in impervious surfaces associated with continued urbanization would exacerbate these flooding problems. * * * [The Plan recommended] ensuring that the floodplain remains free of structures and that it be preserved as greenways to minimize flood damage to structures. * * *

Petitioner Florence Dolan owns a plumbing and electric supply store located on Main Street in the Central Business District of the city. The store covers approximately 9,700 square feet on the eastern side of a 1.67–acre parcel, which includes a gravel parking lot. Fanno Creek flows through the southwestern corner of the lot and along its western boundary. The year-round flow of the creek renders the area within the creek's 100–year floodplain virtually unusable for commercial development. The city's comprehensive plan includes the Fanno Creek floodplain as part of the city's greenway system.

Figure 12–9
Plaque and Bicycle Path at the Site Involved in *Dolan v. City of*
Tigard

Courtesy Dan Dolan.

Petitioner applied to the city for a permit to redevelop the site. Her proposed plans called for nearly doubling the size of the store to 17,600 square feet and paving a 39–space parking lot. The existing store, located on the opposite side of the parcel, would be razed in sections as construction progressed on the new building. In the second phase of the project, petitioner proposed to build an additional structure on the northeast side of the site for complementary businesses and to provide more parking. The proposed expansion and intensified use are consistent with the city's zoning scheme in the Central Business District.

The City Planning Commission (Commission) granted petitioner's permit application subject to conditions imposed by the city's CDC. * * * [T]he Commission required that petitioner dedicate the portion of her property lying within the 100–year floodplain for improvement of a storm drainage system along Fanno Creek and that she dedicate an additional 15–foot strip of land adjacent to the floodplain as a pedestrian/bicycle pathway. The dedication required by that condition encompasses approximately 7,000 square feet, or roughly 10% of the property. * * *

Petitioner requested variances from the CDC standards. * * * The Commission denied the request. * * * The Oregon Court of Appeals affirmed * * *

II

* * * Without question, had the city simply required petitioner to dedicate a strip of land along Fanno Creek for public use, rather than conditioning the grant of her permit to redevelop her property on such a dedication, a taking would have occurred. Nollan, supra, 483 U.S., at 831. Such public access would deprive petitioner of the right to exclude others, "one of the most essential sticks in the bundle of rights that are commonly characterized as property." Kaiser Aetna v. United States, 444 U.S. 164, 176 (1979).

On the other side of the ledger, the authority of state and local governments to engage in land use planning has been sustained against constitutional challenge as long ago as our decision in *Village of Euclid v. Ambler Realty Co.*, 272 U.S. 365 (1926). "Government hardly could go on if to some extent values incident to property could not be diminished without paying for every such change in the general law." Pennsylvania Coal Co. v. Mahon, 260 U.S. 393, 413 (1922). A land use regulation does not effect a taking if it "substantially advance[s] legitimate state interests" and does not "den[y] an owner economically viable use of his land." Agins v. City of Tiburon, 447 U.S. 255, 260 (1980).[6] * * *

---

6. There can be no argument that the permit conditions would deprive petitioner of "economically beneficial us[e]" of her property as she currently operates a retail store on the lot. Petitioner assuredly is able to derive *some* economic use from her property. See, e.g., Lucas v. South Carolina Coastal Council, 505 U.S. 1003, 1019 (1992); Kaiser Aetna v. United States, 444 U.S. 164, 175 (1979); Penn Central Transp. Co. v. New York City, supra, 438 U.S., at 124.

Under the well-settled doctrine of "unconstitutional conditions," the government may not require a person to give up a constitutional right— here the right to receive just compensation when property is taken for a public use—in exchange for a discretionary benefit conferred by the government where the benefit sought has little or no relationship to the property. See Perry v. Sindermann, 408 U.S. 593 (1972); Pickering v. Board of Ed. of Township High School Dist. 205, Will Cty., 391 U.S. 563, 568 (1968).

Petitioner contends that the city has forced her to choose between the building permit and her right under the Fifth Amendment to just compensation for the public easements. Petitioner does not quarrel with the city's authority to exact some forms of dedication as a condition for the grant of a building permit, but challenges the showing made by the city to justify these exactions. She argues that the city has identified "no special benefits" conferred on her, and has not identified any "special quantifiable burdens" created by her new store that would justify the particular dedications required from her which are not required from the public at large.

III

In evaluating petitioner's claim, we must first determine whether the "essential nexus" exists between the "legitimate state interest" and the permit condition exacted by the city. *Nollan,* 483 U.S., at 837. If we find that a nexus exists, we must then decide the required degree of connection between the exactions and the projected impact of the proposed development. We were not required to reach this question in *Nollan,* because we concluded that the connection did not meet even the loosest standard. Id., at 838. Here, however, we must decide this question.

A

We addressed the essential nexus question in *Nollan.* The California Coastal Commission demanded a lateral public easement across the Nollans' beachfront lot in exchange for a permit to demolish an existing bungalow and replace it with a three-bedroom house. Id., at 828. The public easement was designed to connect two public beaches that were separated by the [Nollans'] property. The Coastal Commission had asserted that the public easement condition was imposed to promote the legitimate state interest of diminishing the "blockage of the view of the ocean" caused by construction of the larger house.

We agreed that the Coastal Commission's concern with protecting visual access to the ocean constituted a legitimate public interest. Id., at 835. We also agreed that the permit condition would have been constitutional "even if it consisted of the requirement that the Nollans provide a viewing spot on their property for passersby with whose sighting of the ocean their new house would interfere." Id., at 836. We resolved, however, that the Coastal Commission's regulatory authority was set completely adrift from its constitutional moorings when it claimed that a nexus existed between visual access to the ocean and a permit condition requiring lateral public access along the Nollans' beachfront lot. Id., at 837. How enhancing the public's ability to "traverse to and along the shorefront" served the same governmental purpose of "visual access to the ocean" from the roadway was beyond our ability to countenance. The absence of a nexus left the Coastal Commission in the position of simply trying to obtain an easement through gimmickry, which converted a valid regulation of land use into " 'an out-and-out plan of extortion.' " Ibid., quoting J.E.D. Associates, Inc. v. Atkinson, 584, 432 A.2d 12, 14–15 (N.H. 1981).

No such gimmicks are associated with the permit conditions imposed by the city in this case. Undoubtedly, the prevention of flooding along Fanno Creek and the reduction of traffic congestion in the Central Business District qualify as the type of legitimate public purposes we have upheld. Agins, 447 U.S., at 260–262. It seems equally obvious that a nexus exists between preventing flooding along Fanno Creek and limiting development within the creek's 100–year floodplain. Petitioner proposes to double the size of her retail store and to pave her now-gravel parking lot, thereby expanding the impervious surface on the property and increasing the amount of storm water runoff into Fanno Creek.

The same may be said for the city's attempt to reduce traffic congestion by providing for alternative means of transportation. In theory, a pedestrian/bicycle pathway provides a useful alternative means of transportation for workers and shoppers: "Pedestrians and bicyclists occupying dedicated spaces for walking and/or bicycling . . . remove potential vehicles from streets, resulting in an overall improvement in total transportation system flow." A. Nelson, Public Provision of Pedestrian and Bicycle Access Ways: Public Policy Rationale and the Nature of Private Benefits 11, Center for Planning Development, Georgia Institute of Technology, Working Paper Series (Jan. 1994). See also Intermodal Surface Transportation Efficiency Act of 1991, Pub.L. 102–240, 105 Stat.1914 (recognizing pedestrian and bicycle facilities as necessary components of any strategy to reduce traffic congestion).

B

The second part of our analysis requires us to determine whether the degree of the exactions demanded by the city's permit conditions bears the required relationship to the projected impact of petitioner's proposed development. Nollan, supra, 483 U.S., at 834, quoting Penn Central Transp. Co. v. New York City, 438 U.S. 104, 127 (1978) (" '[A] use restriction may constitute a "taking" if not reasonably necessary to the effectuation of a substantial government purpose' "). Here the Oregon Supreme Court deferred to what it termed the "city's unchallenged factual findings" supporting the dedication conditions and found them to be reasonably related to the impact of the expansion of petitioner's business. * * *

In some States, very generalized statements as to the necessary connection between the required dedication and the proposed development seem to suffice. See, e.g., Billings Properties, Inc. v. Yellowstone County, 394 P.2d 182 (Mont. 1964); Jenad, Inc. v. Scarsdale, 218 N.E.2d 673 (N.Y. 1966). We think this standard is too lax to adequately protect petitioner's right to just compensation if her property is taken for a public purpose.

Other state courts require a very exacting correspondence, described as the "specifi[c] and uniquely attributable" test. The Supreme Court of Illinois first developed this test in *Pioneer Trust & Savings Bank v. Mount Prospect*, 176 N.E.2d 799, 802 (Ill. 1961). Under this standard, if the local government cannot demonstrate that its exaction is directly proportional to the specifically created need, the exaction becomes "a veiled exercise of the power of eminent domain and a confiscation of private property behind the defense of police regulations." Id. at 802. We do not think the Federal Constitution requires such exacting scrutiny, given the nature of the interests involved.

A number of state courts have taken an intermediate position, requiring the municipality to show a "reasonable relationship" between the required dedication and the impact of the proposed development. Typical is the Supreme Court of Nebraska's opinion in *Simpson v. North Platte*, 292 N.W.2d 297, 301 (Neb. 1980), where that court stated:

> The distinction, therefore, which must be made between an appropriate exercise of the police power and an improper exercise of eminent domain is whether the requirement has some reasonable relationship or nexus to the use to which the property is being made or is merely being used as an excuse for taking property simply because at that particular moment the landowner is asking the city for some license or permit.

Thus, the court held that a city may not require a property owner to dedicate private property for some future public use as a condition of obtaining a building permit when such future use is not "occasioned by the construction sought to be permitted." Id. at 302.

Some form of the reasonable relationship test has been adopted in many other jurisdictions. See, e.g., Jordan v. Menomonee Falls, 137 N.W.2d 442 (Wis. 1965); Collis v. Bloomington, 246 N.W.2d 19 (Minn. 1976) (requiring a showing of a reasonable relationship between the planned subdivision and the municipality's need for land); College Station v. Turtle Rock Corp., 680 S.W.2d 802, 807 (Tex. 1984); Call v. West Jordan, 606 P.2d 217, 220 (Utah 1979) (affirming use of the reasonable relation test). Despite any semantical differences, general agreement exists among the courts "that the dedication should have some reasonable relationship to the needs created by the [development]." Ibid. See generally Note " 'Take' My Beach Please!": *Nollan v. California Coastal Commission* and a Rational–Nexus Constitutional Analysis of Development Exactions, 69 B.U.L.Rev. 823 (1989); see also Parks v. Watson, 716 F.2d 646, 651–653 (CA9 1983).

We think the "reasonable relationship" test adopted by a majority of the state courts is closer to the federal constitutional norm than either of those previously discussed. But we do not adopt it as such, partly because the term "reasonable relationship" seems confusingly similar to the term "rational basis" which describes the minimal level of scrutiny under the Equal Protection Clause of the Fourteenth Amendment. We think a term such as "rough proportionality" best encapsulates what we hold to be the requirement of the Fifth Amendment. No precise mathematical calculation is required, but the city must make some sort of individualized determination that the required dedication is related both in nature and extent to the impact of the proposed development.[8]

JUSTICE STEVENS' dissent relies upon a law review article for the proposition that the city's conditional demands for part of petitioner's property are "a species of business regulation that heretofore warranted a strong presumption of constitutional validity." But simply denominating a governmental measure as a "business regulation" does not immunize it from constitutional challenge on the ground that it violates a provision of the Bill of Rights. * * * We see no reason why the Takings Clause of the Fifth Amendment, as much a part of the Bill of Rights as the First Amendment or Fourth Amendment, should be relegated to the status of a poor relation in these comparable circumstances. We turn now to analysis of whether the findings relied upon by the city here, first with respect to the floodplain easement, and second with respect to the pedestrian/bicycle path, satisfied these requirements.

It is axiomatic that increasing the amount of impervious surface will increase the quantity and rate of storm water flow from petitioner's property. Therefore, keeping the floodplain open and free from development would likely confine the pressures on Fanno Creek created by petitioner's development. In fact, because petitioner's property lies within the Central Business District, the CDC already required that petitioner leave 15% of it as open space and the undeveloped floodplain would have nearly satisfied that requirement. But the city demanded more—it not only wanted petitioner not to build in the floodplain, but it also wanted petitioner's property along Fanno Creek for its greenway system. The city has never said why a public greenway, as opposed to a private one, was required in the interest of flood control.

---

8. Justice STEVENS' dissent takes us to task for placing the burden on the city to justify the required dedication. He is correct in arguing that in evaluating most generally applicable zoning regulations, the burden properly rests on the party challenging the regulation to prove that it constitutes an arbitrary regulation of property *rights. See, e.g.,* Village of Euclid v. Ambler Realty Co., 272 U.S. 365 (1926). Here, by contrast, the city made an adjudicative decision to condition petitioner's application for a building permit on an individual parcel. In this situa-

tion, the burden properly rests on the city. See Nollan, 483 U.S., at 836. This conclusion is not, as he suggests, undermined by our decision in *Moore v. East Cleveland,* 431 U.S. 494 (1977), in which we struck down a housing ordinance that limited occupancy of a dwelling unit to members of a single family as violating the Due Process Clause of the Fourteenth Amendment. The ordinance at issue in *Moore* intruded on choices concerning family living arrangements, an area in which the usual deference to the legislature was found to be inappropriate. Id., at 499.

The difference to petitioner, of course, is the loss of her ability to exclude others. As we have noted, this right to exclude others is "one of the most essential sticks in the bundle of rights that are commonly characterized as property." Kaiser Aetna, 444 U.S., at 176. It is difficult to see why recreational visitors trampling along petitioner's floodplain easement are sufficiently related to the city's legitimate interest in reducing flooding problems along Fanno Creek, and the city has not attempted to make any individualized determination to support this part of its request.

The city contends that the recreational easement along the greenway is only ancillary to the city's chief purpose in controlling flood hazards. It further asserts that unlike the residential property at issue in *Nollan*, petitioner's property is commercial in character, and therefore, her right to exclude others is compromised. The city maintains that "[t]here is nothing to suggest that preventing [petitioner] from prohibiting [the easements] will unreasonably impair the value of [her] property as a [retail store]." PruneYard Shopping Center v. Robins, 447 U.S. 74, 83 (1980).

Admittedly, petitioner wants to build a bigger store to attract members of the public to her property. She also wants, however, to be able to control the time and manner in which they enter. The recreational easement on the greenway is different in character from the exercise of state-protected rights of free expression and petition that we permitted in *PruneYard*. In *PruneYard*, we held that a major private shopping center that attracted more than 25,000 daily patrons had to provide access to persons exercising their state constitutional rights to distribute pamphlets and ask passers-by to sign their petitions. Id., at 85. We based our decision, in part, on the fact that the shopping center "may restrict expressive activity by adopting time, place, and manner regulations that will minimize any interference with its commercial functions." Id., at 83. By contrast, the city wants to impose a permanent recreational easement upon petitioner's property that borders Fanno Creek. Petitioner would lose all rights to regulate the time in which the public entered onto the greenway, regardless of any interference it might pose with her retail store. Her right to exclude would not be regulated, it would be eviscerated. * * *

With respect to the pedestrian/bicycle pathway, we have no doubt that the city was correct in finding that the larger retail sales facility proposed by petitioner will increase traffic on the streets of the Central Business District. The city estimates that the proposed development would generate roughly 435 additional trips per day. Dedications for streets, sidewalks, and other public ways are generally reasonable exactions to avoid excessive congestion from a proposed property use. But on the record before us, the city has not met its burden of demonstrating that the additional number of vehicle and bicycle trips generated by petitioner's development reasonably relate to the city's requirement for a dedication of the pedestrian/bicycle pathway easement. The city simply found that the creation of the pathway "could offset some of the traffic demand ... and lessen the increase in traffic congestion."

As Justice Peterson of the Supreme Court of Oregon explained in his dissenting opinion, however, "[t]he findings of fact that the bicycle pathway system '*could* offset some of the traffic demand' is a far cry from a finding that the bicycle pathway system *will*, or is *likely to*, offset some of the traffic demand." 854 P.2d, at 447 (emphasis in original). No precise mathematical calculation is required, but the city must make some effort to quantify its findings in support of the dedication for the pedestrian/bicycle pathway beyond the conclusory statement that it could offset some of the traffic demand generated.

IV

Cities have long engaged in the commendable task of land use planning, made necessary by increasing urbanization, particularly in metropolitan areas such as Portland. The city's goals of reducing flooding hazards and traffic congestion, and providing for public greenways, are laudable, but there are outer limits to how this may be done. "A strong public desire to improve the public condition [will not] warrant achieving the desire by a shorter cut than the constitutional way of paying for the change." Pennsylvania Coal, 260 U.S., at 416.

The judgment of the Supreme Court of Oregon is reversed, and the case is remanded for further proceedings not inconsistent with this opinion.

■ JUSTICE STEVENS, with whom JUSTICE BLACKMUN and JUSTICE GINSBURG join, dissenting [omitted].

■ JUSTICE SOUTER, dissenting [omitted].

NOTES AND QUESTIONS

1. The unconstitutional conditions doctrine imposes limits on the enforceability of waivers of constitutional rights. See generally Mitchell N. Berman, Coercion Without Baselines: Conditions in Three Dimensions, 90 Geo. L. J. 1, 36–40 (2001); Kathleen M. Sullivan, Unconstitutional Conditions, 102 Harv. L. Rev. 1413 (1989). The doctrine has been applied with the most rigor in the First Amendment context. With respect to other constitutional rights, such as the right to trial by jury in criminal cases, the right is enforced only to the extent that courts seek to assure that waivers are "knowing and intelligent." Was the Court justified in extending a moderately robust version of the doctrine to the Taking Clause? Property is bought and sold all the time. Why not let owners in effect sell property to the government in return for some benefit they value more, such as a permit to develop the property they retain? See Douglas T. Kendall & James E. Ryan, "Paying" for the Change: Using Eminent Domain to Secure Exactions and Sidestep *Nollan* and *Dolan*, 81 Va. L. Rev. 1801 (1995).

2. As is implicit in *Dolan*, the unconstitutional conditions analysis used in assessing exactions applies only where owners are asked to waive their rights to just compensation under clearly established protections under the Takings Clause. The Court later made this explicit. See City of Monterey v. Del Monte Dunes, 526 U.S. 687, 702–03 (1999) ("[W]e have

not extended the rough-proportionality test beyond the special context of exactions"); Lingle v. Chevron U.S.A. Inc., 544 U.S. 528, 547 (2005) ("*Nollan* and *Dolan* both involved dedications of property so onerous that, outside the exactions context, they would be deemed *per se* physical takings."). Efforts to extend the "nexus" or "rough proportionality" ideas to assess ordinary land-use regulations are therefore likely to be rejected.

3.   The Court requires that the exaction be "roughly proportionate" to the impact of the development. Does "impact of the development" refer to the harm the development would cause to the community absent the exaction, or to the benefit that the community will receive from the development with the exaction? The Court's language seems to suggest the former—requiring a focus on the harm that would be produced by a development (more traffic, more runoff into the creek) and comparing it to how much harm would be avoided by the exaction (fewer car trips, more absorption of water in the greenway). But from a social efficiency standpoint, isn't it better to compare the value of the exaction in the hands of the private owner (more parking places), with the value of the exaction in the hands of the community (more bike trails and greenways)? One reason for requiring the government to pay just compensation when it takes property is to induce the government to make these kinds of value comparisons, taking property only when the public willingness to pay exceeds the fair market value of the property. Should the exactions calculus try to mimic the same relevant comparisons?

4.   In *Kelo v. City of New London*, supra, the Court observes that the states have adopted different approaches to the "public use" question, and concludes that the federal constitutional standard should be a deferential one in order to permit the states to adopt different approaches to how the power of eminent domain is used. In *Dolan*, the Court also observes that the states have adopted different approaches to the degree of nexus required between exactions of property and the effects of a proposed development. But now, the Court takes this variation among the states as a kind of menu of options from which to select a federal standard, which will then be imposed on all other states. Is there a justification for this difference in the assumed relationship between federal and state law with respect to these two questions about local land-use issues? Or should the Court have consistently opted in both contexts either for state variation or minimum federal standards?

4.   TEMPORARY TAKINGS

For many years the Takings Clause was tangled up with the Due Process Clause. See Gregory M. Stein, Regulatory Takings and Ripeness in the Federal Courts, 48 Vand. L. Rev. 1, 66–92 (1995). Part of the reason for this is that the Takings Clause, which appears in the Fifth Amendment, originally applied only to the federal government. See Barron v. Mayor & City Council of Baltimore, 32 U.S. (7 Pet.) 243 (1833). Not until the Fourteenth Amendment was adopted in 1868 was there any basis for applying the principles of the Takings Clause to state and local governments through the Due Process Clause. Today the Court regularly says that the Takings Clause was "made applicable to the States through the Fourteenth Amendment" in *Chicago, B. & Q. R. Co. v. Chicago*, 166 U.S. 226, 239 (1897), see, e.g., Phillips, supra, but even this is a bit of an oversimplification. For many years after *Chicago, B. & Q. R. Co.* takings claims were litigated as due process claims, for which the usual remedy is an injunction against unconstitutional state action. Recall, for example, that in *Mahon* the mining companies asserted that the Kohler Act was invalid under the Due Process Clause of the Fourteenth Amendment. The Court referred to the principles of the Takings Clause, but did not say it was literally applying that Clause in adjudicating the dispute.

Given that takings claims brought against state and local governments were technically due process claims, some state courts took the position that the only remedy for a judgment that a state or local government had committed a regulatory taking was prospective in nature—an injunction, declaratory judgment, or decree in mandamus. The California Supreme Court was the most prominent state tribunal to take this position. See *Agins v. Tiburon*, 598 P.2d 25 (Cal. 1979), aff'd on other grounds, 447 U.S. 255 (1980). The problem with this theory, from the perspective of property owners, was that takings claims could drag on in state courts for many years, and if the property owner eventually prevailed on the takings claims, the owner would receive no compensation for the lost use of the property during the interim. The lack of any remedy for delay gave local governments little incentive to resolve such disputes expeditiously. Real estate interests mounted a vigorous campaign seeking a determination by the U.S. Supreme Court that incorporation of the Takings Clause through the Fourteenth Amendment required that state courts afford property owners complete just compensation for any taking, including compensation for the "temporary taking" that occurred during the time the regulation was being challenged in litigation. The issue was of considerable practical importance to the groups involved in real estate development, especially in California. But it was also of considerable theoretical significance, in terms of clarifying exactly what it means to say that the Takings Clause applies to the states through the Fourteenth Amendment. On four separate occasions starting in 1980, the Supreme Court granted review to consider this issue. See MacDonald, Sommer & Frates v. Yolo County, 477 U.S. 340 (1986); Williamson County Regional Planning Comm'n v. Hamilton Bank, 473 U.S. 172 (1985); San Diego Gas & Electric Co. v. City of San Diego, 450 U.S. 621 (1981); Agins v. Tiburon, supra. But each time, the majority found reasons why it was improper to reach the question given the procedural posture of the case. Finally, the Court found a case where it felt the issue was properly presented.

First English Evangelical Lutheran Church v. County of Los Angeles

Supreme Court of the United States, 1987.
482 U.S. 304.

■ CHIEF JUSTICE REHNQUIST delivered the opinion of the Court. In this case the California Court of Appeal held that a landowner who claims that his property has been "taken" by a land-use regulation may not recover damages for the time before it is finally determined that the regulation constitutes a "taking" of his property. We disagree, and conclude that in these circumstances the Fifth and Fourteenth Amendments to the United States Constitution would require compensation for that period.

In 1957, appellant First English Evangelical Lutheran Church purchased a 21-acre parcel of land in a canyon along the banks of the Middle Fork of Mill Creek in the Angeles National Forest. The Middle Fork is the natural drainage channel for a watershed area owned by the National Forest Service. Twelve of the acres owned by the church are flat land, and contained a dining hall, two bunkhouses, a caretaker's lodge, an outdoor chapel, and a footbridge across the creek. The church operated on the site a campground, known as "Lutherglen," as a retreat center and a recreational area for handicapped children.

In July 1977, a forest fire denuded the hills upstream from Lutherglen, destroying approximately 3,860 acres of the watershed area and creating a serious flood hazard. Such flooding occurred on February 9 and 10, 1978, when a storm dropped 11 inches of rain in the watershed. The runoff from the storm overflowed the banks of the Mill Creek, flooding Lutherglen and destroying its buildings.

In response to the flooding of the canyon, appellee County of Los Angeles adopted Interim Ordinance No. 11,855 in January 1979. The ordinance provided that "[a] person shall not construct, reconstruct, place or enlarge any building or structure, any portion of which is, or will be, located within the outer boundary lines of the interim flood protection area located in Mill Creek Canyon. . . ." The ordinance was effective immediately because the county determined that it was "required for the immediate preservation of the public health and safety. . . ." The interim flood protection area described by the ordinance included the flat areas on either side of Mill Creek on which Lutherglen had stood.

The church filed a complaint in the Superior Court of California a little more than a month after the ordinance was adopted. As subsequently amended, the complaint alleged two claims against the county and the Los Angeles County Flood Control District. * * * Appellant sought damages under each count for loss of use of Lutherglen. The defendants moved to strike the portions of the complaint alleging that the county's ordinance denied all use of Lutherglen, on the view that the California Supreme Court's decision in *Agins v. Tiburon*, 598 P.2d 25 (Cal. 1979), aff'd on other grounds, 447 U.S. 255 (1980), rendered the allegation "entirely immaterial and irrelevant[, with] no bearing upon any conceivable cause of action herein." * * *

In *Agins v. Tiburon, supra,* the California Supreme Court decided that a landowner may not maintain an inverse condemnation suit in the courts of that State based upon a "regulatory" taking. In the court's view, maintenance of such a suit would allow a landowner to force the legislature to exercise its power of eminent domain. Under this decision, then, compensation is not required until the challenged regulation or ordinance has been held excessive in an action for declaratory relief or a writ of mandamus and the government has nevertheless decided to continue the regulation in effect. Based on this decision, the trial court in the present case granted the motion to strike the allegation that the church had been denied all use of Lutherglen. * * *

On appeal, the California Court of Appeal [affirmed]. * * * The California Supreme Court denied review.

This appeal followed, and we noted probable jurisdiction. Appellant asks us to hold that the California Supreme Court erred in *Agins v. Tiburon* in determining that the Fifth Amendment, as made applicable to the States through the Fourteenth Amendment, does not require compensation as a remedy for "temporary" regulatory takings—those regulatory takings which are ultimately invalidated by the courts. * * * [W]e find the constitutional claim properly presented in this case, and hold that on these facts the California courts have decided the compensation question inconsistently with the requirements of the Fifth Amendment.

I

Concerns with finality left us unable to reach the remedial question in the earlier cases where we have been asked to consider the rule of *Agins.* See MacDonald, Sommer & Frates v. Yolo County, 477 U.S. 340, 351 (1986) (summerizing cases). * * *

The posture of the present case is quite different. Appellant's complaint alleged that "Ordinance No. 11,855 denies [it] all use of Lutherglen," and sought damages for this deprivation. In affirming the decision to strike this allegation, the Court of Appeal assumed that the complaint sought "damages for the uncompensated *taking* of all use of Lutherglen by County Ordinance No. 11,855." It relied on the California Supreme Court's *Agins* decision for the conclusion that "the remedy for a *taking* [is limited] to nonmonetary relief. . . ." The disposition of the case on these grounds isolates the remedial question for our consideration. * * *

We reject appellee's suggestion that, regardless of the state court's treatment of the question, we must independently evaluate the adequacy of the complaint and resolve the takings claim on the merits before we can reach the remedial question. However "cryptic"—to use appellee's description—the allegations with respect to the taking were, the California courts deemed them sufficient to present the issue. We accordingly have no occasion to decide whether the ordinance at issue actually denied appellant all use of its property or whether the county might avoid the conclusion that a compensable taking had occurred by establishing that the denial of all use was insulated as a part of the State's authority to enact safety regulations. See, e.g., Goldblatt v. Hempstead, 369 U.S. 590 (1962); Hadacheck v. Sebastian, 239 U.S. 394 (1915); Mugler v. Kansas, 123 U.S. 623 (1887). These questions, of course, remain open for decision on the remand we direct today. We now turn to the question whether the Just Compensation Clause requires the government to pay for "temporary" regulatory takings.

II

Consideration of the compensation question must begin with direct reference to the language of the Fifth Amendment, which provides in relevant part that "private property [shall not] be taken for public use, without just compensation." As its language indicates, and as the Court has frequently noted, this provision does not prohibit the taking of private property, but instead places a condition on the exercise of that power. See Williamson County Regional Planning Comm'n v. Hamilton Bank, 473 U.S. 172, 194 (1985), Hodel v. Virginia Surface Mining & Reclamation Assn., Inc., 452 U.S. 264, 297, n. 40 (1981); Hurley v. Kincaid, 285 U.S. 95, 104 (1932); Monongahela Navigation Co. v. United States, 148 U.S. 312, 336 (1893); United States v. Jones, 109 U.S. 513, 518 (1883). This basic understanding of the Amendment makes clear that it is designed not to limit the governmental interference with property rights *per se,* but rather to secure *compensation* in the event of otherwise proper interference amounting to a taking. Thus, government action that works a taking of property rights necessarily implicates the "constitutional obligation to pay just compensation." Armstrong v. United States, 364 U.S. 40, 49 (1960).

We have recognized that a landowner is entitled to bring an action in inverse condemnation as a result of " 'the self-executing character of the constitutional provision with respect to compensation. . . .' " United States v. Clarke, 445 U.S. 253, 257 (1980), quoting 6 P. Nichols, Eminent Domain § 25.41 (3d rev. ed. 1972). As noted in Justice BRENNAN's dissent in *San Diego Gas & Electric Co.,* 450 U.S., at 654–655, it has been established at least since *Jacobs v. United States,* 290 U.S. 13 (1933), that claims for just compensation are grounded in the Constitution itself * * * *Jacobs,* moreover, does not stand alone, for the Court has frequently repeated the view that, in the event of a taking, the compensation remedy is required by the Constitution. See, e.g., Kirby Forest Industries, Inc. v. United States, 467 U.S. 1, 5 (1984); United States v. Causby, 328 U.S. 256, 267 (1946); Seaboard Air Line R. Co. v. United States, 261 U.S. 299, 304–306 (1923); Monongahela Navigation, supra, 148 U.S., at 327.

It also been established doctrine at least since Justice Holmes' opinion for the Court in *Pennsylvania Coal Co. v. Mahon,* 260 U.S. 393 (1922) that "[t]he general rule at least is, that while property may be regulated to a certain extent, if regulation goes too far it will be recognized as a taking." Id., at 415. While the typical taking occurs when the government acts to condemn property in the exercise of its power of eminent domain, the entire doctrine of inverse condemnation is predicated on the proposition that a taking may occur without such formal proceedings. * * *

While the California Supreme Court may not have actually disavowed this general rule in *Agins,* we believe that it has truncated the rule by disallowing damages that occurred prior to the ultimate invalidation of the challenged regulation. * * *

In considering this question, we find substantial guidance in cases where the government has only temporarily exercised its right to use private property. In *United States v. Dow,* [357 U.S. 17, 26 (1958)], though rejecting a claim that the Government may not abandon condemnation proceedings, the Court observed that abandonment "results in an alteration in the property interest taken—from [one of] full ownership to one of temporary use and occupation. . . . In such cases compensation would be measured by the principles normally governing the taking of a right to use property temporarily. See Kimball Laundry Co. v. United States, 338 U.S. 1 [1949]; United States v. Petty Motor Co., 327 U.S. 372 [1946]; United States v. General Motors Corp., 323 U.S. 373 [1945]." Each of the cases cited by the *Dow* Court involved appropriation of private property by the United States for use during World War II. Though the takings were in fact "temporary," see United States v. Petty Motor Co., 327 U.S. 372, 375 (1946), there was no question that compensation would be required for the Government's interference with the use of the property; the Court was concerned in each case with determining the proper measure of the monetary relief to which the property holders were entitled. See Kimball Laundry Co. v. United States, 338 U.S. 1, 4–21 (1949); Petty Motor Co., supra, 327 U.S., at 377–381; United States v. General Motors Corp., supra, 323 U.S. 373, at 379–384 (1945).

These cases reflect the fact that "temporary" takings which, as here, deny a landowner all use of his property, are not different in kind from permanent takings, for which the Constitution clearly requires compensation. Cf. San Diego Gas & Electric Co., 450 U.S., at 657 (BRENNAN, J., dissenting) ("Nothing in the Just Compensation Clause suggests that 'takings' must be permanent and irrevocable"). It is axiomatic that the Fifth Amendment's just compensation provision is "designed to bar Government from forcing some people alone to bear public burdens which, in all fairness and justice, should be borne by the public as a whole." Armstrong v. United States, 364 U.S., at 49. See also Penn Central Transportation Co. v. New York City, 438 U.S. 104, 123–125 (1978); Monongahela Navigation Co. v. United States, 148 U.S., at 325. In the present case the interim ordinance was adopted by the County of Los Angeles in January 1979, and became effective immediately. Appellant filed suit within a month after the effective date of the ordinance and yet when the California Supreme Court denied a hearing in the case on October 17, 1985, the merits of appellant's claim had yet to be determined. The United States has been required to pay compensation for leasehold interests of shorter duration than this. The value of a leasehold interest in property for a period of years may be substantial, and the burden on the property owner in extinguishing such an interest for a period of years may be great indeed. See, e.g., United States v. General Motors, supra. Where this burden results from governmental action that amounted to a taking, the Just Compensation Clause of the Fifth Amendment requires that the government pay the landowner for the value of the use of the land during this period. Cf. United States v. Causby, 328 U.S., at 261 ("It is the owner's loss, not the taker's gain, which is the measure of the value of the property taken"). Invalidation of the ordinance or its successor ordinance after this period of time, though converting the taking into a "temporary" one, is not

a sufficient remedy to meet the demands of the Just Compensation Clause.
* * *

Nothing we say today is intended to abrogate the principle that the decision to exercise the power of eminent domain is a legislative function " 'for Congress and Congress alone to determine.' " Hawaii Housing Authority v. Midkiff, 467 U.S. 229, 240 (1984), quoting Berman v. Parker, 348 U.S. 26, 33 (1954). Once a court determines that a taking has occurred, the government retains the whole range of options already available—amendment of the regulation, withdrawal of the invalidated regulation, or exercise of eminent domain. Thus we do not, as the Solicitor General suggests, "permit a court, at the behest of a private person, to require the ... Government to exercise the power of eminent domain...." Brief for United States as *Amicus Curiae* 22. We merely hold that where the government's activities have already worked a taking of all use of property, no subsequent action by the government can relieve it of the duty to provide compensation for the period during which the taking was effective.

We also point out that the allegation of the complaint which we treat as true for purposes of our decision was that the ordinance in question denied appellant all use of its property. We limit our holding to the facts presented, and of course do not deal with the quite different questions that would arise in the case of normal delays in obtaining building permits, changes in zoning ordinances, variances, and the like which are not before us. We realize that even our present holding will undoubtedly lessen to some extent the freedom and flexibility of land-use planners and governing bodies of municipal corporations when enacting land-use regulations. But such consequences necessarily flow from any decision upholding a claim of constitutional right; many of the provisions of the Constitution are designed to limit the flexibility and freedom of governmental authorities, and the Just Compensation Clause of the Fifth Amendment is one of them. As Justice Holmes aptly noted more than 50 years ago, "a strong public desire to improve the public condition is not enough to warrant achieving the desire by a shorter cut than the constitutional way of paying for the change." Pennsylvania Coal Co. v. Mahon, 260 U.S., at 416.

Here we must assume that the Los Angeles County ordinance has denied appellant all use of its property for a considerable period of years, and we hold that invalidation of the ordinance without payment of fair value for the use of the property during this period of time would be a constitutionally insufficient remedy. The judgment of the California Court of Appeal is therefore reversed, and the case is remanded for further proceedings not inconsistent with this opinion.

■ JUSTICE STEVENS, with whom JUSTICE BLACKMUN and JUSTICE O'CONNOR join as to Parts I and III, dissenting [omitted].

NOTE AND QUESTIONS

The Supreme Court in recent years has held that a robust principle of state sovereign immunity is implicit in the design of the Constitution. See, e.g., Seminole Tribe of Fla. v. Florida, 517 U.S. 44 (1996); Alden v. Maine, 527 U.S. 706 (1999). The principle bars suits by private parties based on federal law against the states seeking money damages. It applies only to suits against the states themselves or their agencies; it does not apply to suits based on federal law against county and municipal governments. Is a regulatory takings suit against a state or state agency for temporary taking damages barred by this principle of sovereign immunity? Or does such a suit come within an exception to this principle, based on the "self-executing" nature of the Takings Clause, as stressed by the Court in *First English*? For discussion see Eric Berger, The Collision of the Takings and State Sovereign Immunity Doctrines, 63 Wash. & L. L. Rev. 493 (2006).

Tahoe–Sierra Preservation Council, Inc. v. Tahoe Regional Planning Agency

Supreme Court of the United States, 2002.
535 U.S. 302.

■ JUSTICE STEVENS delivered the opinion of the Court. * * *

IV

The text of the Fifth Amendment itself provides a basis for drawing a distinction between physical takings and regulatory takings. Its plain language requires the payment of compensation whenever the government acquires private property for a public purpose, whether the acquisition is the result of a condemnation proceeding or a physical appropriation. But the Constitution contains no comparable reference to regulations that prohibit a property owner from making certain uses of her private property.[17] Our jurisprudence involving condemnations and physical takings is as old as the Republic and, for the most part, involves the straightforward application of *per se* rules. Our regulatory takings jurisprudence, in contrast, is of more recent vintage and is characterized by "essentially ad hoc, factual inquiries," Penn Central, 438 U.S., at 124, designed to allow "careful examination and weighing of all the relevant circumstances." Palazzolo, 533 U.S., at 636 (O'CONNOR, J., concurring).

When the government physically takes possession of an interest in property for some public purpose, it has a categorical duty to compensate the former owner, United States v. Pewee Coal Co., 341 U.S. 114, 115 (1951), regardless of whether the interest that is taken constitutes an entire parcel or merely a part thereof. Thus, compensation is mandated when a leasehold is taken and the government occupies the property for its

---

17. In determining whether government action affecting property is an unconstitutional deprivation of ownership rights under the Just Compensation Clause, a court must interpret the word "taken." When the government condemns or physically appropriates the property, the fact of a taking is typically obvious and undisputed. When, however, the owner contends a taking has occurred because a law or regulation imposes restrictions so severe that they are tantamount to a condemnation or appropriation, the predicate of a taking is not self-evident, and the analysis is more complex.

own purposes, even though that use is temporary. United States v. General Motors Corp., 323 U.S. 373 (1945); United States v. Petty Motor Co., 327 U.S. 372 (1946). Similarly, when the government appropriates part of a rooftop in order to provide cable TV access for apartment tenants, Loretto v. Teleprompter Manhattan CATV Corp., 458 U.S. 419 (1982); or when its planes use private airspace to approach a government airport, United States v. Causby, 328 U.S. 256 (1946), it is required to pay for that share no matter how small. But a government regulation that merely prohibits landlords from evicting tenants unwilling to pay a higher rent, Block v. Hirsh, 256 U.S. 135 (1921); that bans certain private uses of a portion of an owner's property, Village of Euclid v. Ambler Realty Co., 272 U.S. 365 (1926); Keystone Bituminous Coal Assn. v. DeBenedictis, 480 U.S. 470 (1987); or that forbids the private use of certain airspace, Penn Central Transp. Co. v. New York City, 438 U.S. 104 (1978), does not constitute a categorical taking. "The first category of cases requires courts to apply a clear rule; the second necessarily entails complex factual assessments of the purposes and economic effects of government actions." Yee v. Escondido, 503 U.S. 519, 523 (1992). See also Loretto, 458 U.S., at 440; Keystone, 480 U.S., at 489, n. 18.

This longstanding distinction between acquisitions of property for public use, on the one hand, and regulations prohibiting private uses, on the other, makes it inappropriate to treat cases involving physical takings as controlling precedents for the evaluation of a claim that there has been a "regulatory taking," and vice versa. For the same reason that we do not ask whether a physical appropriation advances a substantial government interest or whether it deprives the owner of all economically valuable use, we do not apply our precedent from the physical takings context to regulatory takings claims. Land-use regulations are ubiquitous and most of them impact property values in some tangential way—often in completely unanticipated ways. Treating them all as *per se* takings would transform government regulation into a luxury few governments could afford. By contrast, physical appropriations are relatively rare, easily identified, and usually represent a greater affront to individual property rights. "This case does not present the 'classi[c] taking' in which the government directly appropriates private property for its own use," Eastern Enterprises v. Apfel, 524 U.S. 498, 522 (1998); instead the interference with property rights "arises from some public program adjusting the benefits and burdens of economic life to promote the common good," Penn Central, 438 U.S., at 124. * * *

First English was certainly a significant decision, and nothing that we say today qualifies its holding. Nonetheless, it is important to recognize that we did not address in that case the quite different and logically prior question whether the temporary regulation at issue had in fact constituted a taking.

In *First English,* the Court unambiguously and repeatedly characterized the issue to be decided as a "compensation question" or a "remedial question." Id., at 311 ("The disposition of the case on these grounds isolates the remedial question for our consideration"); see also id., at 313, 318. And the Court's statement of its holding was equally unambiguous: "We merely hold that where the government's activities *have already worked a taking* of all use of property, no subsequent action by the government can relieve it of the duty to provide compensation for the period during which the taking was effective." Id., at 321 (emphasis added). In fact, *First English* expressly disavowed any ruling on the merits of the takings issue because the California courts had decided the remedial question on the assumption that a taking had been alleged. Id., at 312–313 ("We reject appellee's suggestion that . . . we must independently evaluate the adequacy of the complaint and resolve the takings claim on the merits before we can reach the remedial question"). After our remand, the California courts concluded that there had not been a taking, First English Evangelical Church of Glendale v. County of Los Angeles, 210 Cal.App.3d 1353, 258 Cal.Rptr. 893 (1989), and we declined review of that decision, 493 U.S. 1056 (1990).

To the extent that the Court in *First English* referenced the antecedent takings question, we identified two reasons why a regulation temporarily denying an owner all use of her property might not constitute a taking. First, we recognized that "the county might avoid the conclusion that a compensable taking had occurred by establishing that the denial of all use was insulated as a part of the State's authority to enact safety regulations." 482 U.S., at 313. Second, we limited our holding "to the facts presented" and recognized "the quite different questions that would arise in the case of normal delays in obtaining building permits, changes in zoning ordinances, variances, and the like which [were] not before us." Id., at 321. Thus, our decision in *First English* surely did not approve, and implicitly rejected, the categorical submission that petitioners are now advocating.

Similarly, our decision in *Lucas* is not dispositive of the question presented. Although *Lucas* endorsed and applied a categorical rule, it was not the one that petitioners propose. * * * The categorical rule that we applied in *Lucas* states that compensation is required when a regulation deprives an owner of "*all* economically beneficial uses" of his land. Id., at 1019. Under that rule, a statute that "wholly eliminated the value" of Lucas' fee simple title clearly qualified as a taking. But our holding was limited to "the extraordinary circumstance when *no* productive or economically beneficial use of land is permitted." Id., at 1017. The emphasis on the word "no" in the text of the opinion was, in effect, reiterated in a footnote explaining that the categorical rule would not apply if the diminution in value were 95% instead of 100%. Id., at 1019, n. 8. Anything less than a "complete elimination of value," or a "total loss," the Court acknowledged, would require the kind of analysis applied in *Penn Central*. Lucas, 505 U.S., at 1019–1020, n. 8. * * *

Neither *Lucas,* nor *First English,* nor any of our other regulatory takings cases compels us to accept petitioners' categorical submission. In fact, these cases make clear that the categorical rule in *Lucas* was carved out for the "extraordinary case" in which a regulation permanently deprives property of all value; the default rule remains that, in the regulatory taking context, we require a more fact specific inquiry. Nevertheless, we will consider whether the interest in protecting individual property owners from bearing public burdens "which, in all fairness and justice, should be borne by the public as a whole," Armstrong v. United States, 364 U.S., at 49, justifies creating a new rule for these circumstances.

V

* * * [T]he ultimate constitutional question is whether the concepts of "fairness and justice" that underlie the Takings Clause will be better served by [a categorical rule] or by a *Penn Central* inquiry into all of the relevant circumstances in particular cases. From that perspective, the extreme categorical rule that any deprivation of all economic use, no matter how brief, constitutes a compensable taking surely cannot be sustained. Petitioners' broad submission would apply to numerous "normal delays in obtaining building permits, changes in zoning ordinances, variances, and the like," First English, 482 U.S., at 321, as well as to orders temporarily prohibiting access to crime scenes, businesses that violate health codes, fire-damaged buildings, or other areas that we cannot now foresee. Such a rule would undoubtedly require changes in numerous practices that have long been considered permissible exercises of the police power. As Justice Holmes warned in *Mahon,* "[g]overnment hardly could go on if to some extent values incident to property could not be diminished without paying for every such change in the general law." 260 U.S., at 413. A rule that required compensation for every delay in the use of property would render routine government processes prohibitively expensive or encourage hasty decisionmaking. Such an important change in the law should be the product of legislative rulemaking rather than adjudication.

* * * In rejecting petitioners' *per se* rule, we do not hold that the temporary nature of a land-use restriction precludes finding that it effects a taking; we simply recognize that it should not be given exclusive significance one way or the other.

A narrower rule that excluded the normal delays associated with processing permits, or that covered only delays of more than a year, would certainly have a less severe impact on prevailing practices, but it would still impose serious financial constraints on the planning process. Unlike the "extraordinary circumstance" in which the government deprives a property owner of all economic use, Lucas, 505 U.S., at 1017, moratoria like Ordinance 81–5 and Resolution 83–21 are used widely among land-use planners to preserve the status quo while formulating a more permanent development strategy. In fact, the consensus in the planning community appears to be that moratoria, or "interim development controls" as they are often called, are an essential tool of successful development. Yet even the weak version of petitioners' categorical rule would treat these interim measures as takings regardless of the good faith of the planners, the reasonable expectations of the landowners, or the actual impact of the moratorium on property values.

The interest in facilitating informed decisionmaking by regulatory agencies counsels against adopting a *per se* rule that would impose such severe costs on their deliberations. Otherwise, the financial constraints of compensating property owners during a moratorium may force officials to rush through the planning process or to abandon the practice altogether. To the extent that communities are forced to abandon using moratoria, landowners will have incentives to develop their property quickly before a comprehensive plan can be enacted, thereby fostering inefficient and ill-conceived growth. * * *

It may well be true that any moratorium that lasts for more than one year should be viewed with special skepticism. But given the fact that the District Court found that the 32 months required by TRPA to formulate the 1984 Regional Plan was not unreasonable, we could not possibly conclude that every delay of over one year is constitutionally unacceptable. Formulating a general rule of this kind is a suitable task for state legislatures. In our view, the duration of the restriction is one of the important factors that a court must consider in the appraisal of a regulatory takings claim, but with respect to that factor as with respect to other factors, the "temptation to adopt what amount to *per se* rules in either direction must be resisted." Palazzolo, 533 U.S., at 636 (O'CONNOR, J., concurring). There may be moratoria that last longer than one year which interfere with reasonable investment-backed expectations, but as the District Court's opinion illustrates, petitioners' proposed rule is simply "too blunt an instrument" for identifying those cases. Id., at 628. We conclude, therefore, that the interest in "fairness and justice" will be best served by relying on the familiar *Penn Central* approach when deciding cases like this, rather than by attempting to craft a new categorical rule.

■ CHIEF JUSTICE REHNQUIST, with whom JUSTICE SCALIA and JUSTICE THOMAS join, dissenting. [omitted]

■ JUSTICE THOMAS, with whom JUSTICE SCALIA joins, dissenting. [omitted]

QUESTIONS

1. Given the difficulty of establishing that a regulation is a taking under the *Penn Central* test, does *Tahoe–Sierra* mean that virtually any regulation of the use of property, as long as it either leaves some economic value in the land or, if it leaves no economic value is not made perpetual, is now effectively immune from takings liability?

2. After *Tahoe–Sierra*, what is the enduring significance of the great victory real estate interests won in *First English*? Does *Tahoe–Sierra* mean that even if a permanent regulation is invalidated as a taking on a per se theory of liability (*Loretto* or *Lucas*), the question whether the regulation was a taking for the period up to its invalidation will always be assessed under *Penn Central*?

3. After *Tahoe–Sierra*, what is the enduring significance of *Lucas*? Can a regulation of the use of land ever be said to permanently deprive an owner of all economic value, given that regulations can always be repealed?

5.   LITIGATING TAKINGS CASES

Litigation of regulatory takings claims is greatly complicated by the fact that the constitutional right in question is the right to compensation, not a right to a certain degree of protection from government interference. Thus, the Fifth Amendment is not violated until it is established both that the government has "taken" property, and that the government will not pay "just compensation" for this taking. This has led the Supreme Court to require that property owners exhaust available remedies under state law before they may turn to federal courts to assert takings claims. This is of great significance for two reasons. First, the requirement that claimants exhaust state law remedies means that regulatory takings cases drag on for interminably long periods of time. Exhaustion of remedies often means exhaustion of the patience and the pocketbooks of the contending parties. Second, once claimants have been sent packing to state courts, can they ever get back into federal court again to have their federal constitutional claim heard, or will they be barred from doing so by preclusion doctrines? Many observers (although not all) think that federal courts would be more sympathetic than state courts to regulatory takings claims brought against local governments. The exhaustion rules, coupled with preclusion doctrines, could therefore have outcome-determinative significance. Consider the following two cases.

Williamson County Regional Planning Comm. v. Hamilton Bank of Johnson City

Supreme Court of the United States, 1985.
473 U.S. 172.

■ JUSTICE BLACKMUN delivered the opinion of the Court. Respondent, the owner of a tract of land it was developing as a residential subdivision, sued petitioners, the Williamson County (Tennessee) Regional Planning Commission and its members and staff, in United States District Court, alleging that petitioners' application of various zoning laws and regulations to respondent's property amounted to a "taking" of that property. At trial, the jury agreed and awarded respondent $350,000 as just compensation for the "taking." Although the jury's verdict was rejected by the District Court, which granted a judgment notwithstanding the verdict to petitioners, the verdict was reinstated on appeal. * * *

I

A

Under Tennessee law, responsibility for land-use planning is divided between the legislative body of each of the State's counties and regional and municipal "planning commissions." The county legislative body is responsible for zoning ordinances to regulate the uses to which particular land and buildings may be put, and to control the density of population and the location and dimensions of buildings. Tenn.Code Ann. § 13–7–101

(1980). The planning commissions are responsible for more specific regulations governing the subdivision of land within their region or municipality for residential development. §§ 13–3–403, 13–4–303. Enforcement of both the zoning ordinances and the subdivision regulations is accomplished in part through a requirement that the planning commission approve the plat of a subdivision before the plat may be recorded. §§ 13–3–402, 13–4–302 (1980 and Supp. 1984). * * *

As required by § 13–3–402, respondent's predecessor-in-interest (developer) in 1973 submitted a preliminary plat for the cluster development of its tract, the Temple Hills Country Club Estates (Temple Hills), to the Williamson County Regional Planning Commission for approval. * * *

On May 3, 1973, the Commission approved the developer's preliminary plat for Temple Hills. The plat indicated that the development was to include 676 acres, of which 260 acres would be open space, primarily in the form of a golf course. * * *

Upon approval of the preliminary plat, the developer conveyed to the county a permanent open space easement for the golf course, and began building roads and installing utility lines for the project. The developer spent approximately $3 million building the golf course, and another $500,000 installing sewer and water facilities. Before housing construction was to begin on a particular section, a final plat of that section was submitted for approval. Several sections, containing a total of 212 units, were given final approval by 1979. The preliminary plat, as well, was reapproved four times during that period.

In 1977, the county changed its zoning ordinance to require that calculations of allowable density exclude 10% of the total acreage to account for roads and utilities. In addition, the number of allowable units was changed to one per acre from the 1.089 per acre allowed in 1973. The Commission continued to apply the zoning ordinance and subdivision regulations in effect in 1973 to Temple Hills, however, and reapproved the preliminary plat in 1978. In August 1979, the Commission reversed its position and decided that plats submitted for renewal should be evaluated under the zoning ordinance and subdivision regulations in effect when the renewal was sought. The Commission then renewed the Temple Hills plat under the ordinances and regulations in effect at that time.

In January 1980, the Commission asked the developer to submit a revised preliminary plat before it sought final approval for the remaining sections of the subdivision. * * *

The developer submitted a revised preliminary plat for approval in October 1980. Upon review, the Commission's staff and the Temple Hills Committee noted several problems with the revised plat. * * * [T]he Commission disapproved the plat * * *

The developer then appealed to the County Board of Zoning Appeals for an "interpretation of the Residential Cluster zoning [ordinance] as it relates to Temple Hills." On November 11, 1980, the Board determined that the Commission should apply the zoning ordinance and subdivision regulations that were in effect in 1973 in evaluating the density of Temple Hills. * * *

On November 26, respondent, Hamilton Bank of Johnson City, acquired through foreclosure the property in the Temple Hills subdivision that had not yet been developed, a total of 257.65 acres. * * * In June 1981, respondent submitted two preliminary plats to the Commission—the plat that had been approved in 1973 and subsequently reapproved several times, and a plat indicating respondent's plans for the undeveloped areas, which was similar to the plat submitted by the developer in 1980. The new plat proposed the development of 688 units; the reduction from 736 units represented respondent's concession that 18.5 acres should be removed from the acreage because that land had been taken for the parkway.

On June 18, the Commission disapproved the plat for eight reasons * * * The Commission declined to follow the decision of the Board of Zoning Appeals that the plat should be evaluated by the 1973 zoning ordinance and subdivision regulations, stating that the Board lacked jurisdiction to hear appeals from the Commission.

B

Respondent then filed this suit in the United States District Court for the Middle District of Tennessee, pursuant to 42 U.S.C. § 1983, alleging that the Commission had taken its property without just compensation and asserting that the Commission should be estopped under state law from denying approval of the project. * * *

After a 3–week trial, the jury found that respondent had been denied the "economically viable" use of its property in violation of the Just Compensation Clause, and that the Commission was estopped under state law from requiring respondent to comply with the current zoning ordinance and subdivision regulations rather than those in effect in 1973. The jury awarded damages of $350,000 for the temporary taking of respondent's property. The court entered a permanent injunction requiring the Commission to apply the zoning ordinance and subdivision regulations in effect in 1973 to Temple Hills, and to approve the plat submitted in 1981.

The court then granted judgment notwithstanding the verdict in favor of the Commission on the taking claim, reasoning in part that respondent was unable to derive economic benefit from its property on a temporary basis only, and that such a temporary deprivation, as a matter of law, cannot constitute a taking. In addition, the court modified its permanent injunction to require the Commission merely to apply the zoning ordinance and subdivision regulations in effect in 1973 to the project, rather than requiring approval of the plat, in order to allow the parties to resolve "legitimate technical questions of whether plaintiff meets the requirements of the 1973 regulations," through the applicable state and local appeals procedures.

A divided panel of the United States Court of Appeals for the Sixth Circuit reversed. 729 F.2d 402 (CA6 1984). The court held that application of government regulations affecting an owner's use of property may constitute a taking if the regulation denies the owner all "economically viable" use of the land, and that the evidence supported the jury's finding that the property had no economically feasible use during the time between the Commission's refusal to approve the preliminary plat and the jury's verdict. Rejecting petitioners' argument that respondent never had submitted a plat that complied with the 1973 regulations, and thus never had acquired rights that could be taken, the court held that the jury's estoppel verdict indicates that the jury must have found that respondent had acquired a "vested right" under state law to develop the subdivision according to the plat submitted in 1973. Even if respondent had no vested right under state law to finish the development, the jury was entitled to find that respondent had a reasonable investment-backed expectation that the development could be completed, and that the actions of the Commission interfered with that expectation. * * *

III

We examine the posture of respondent's cause of action first by viewing it as stating a claim under the Just Compensation Clause. This Court often has referred to regulation that "goes too far," Pennsylvania Coal Co. v. Mahon, 260 U.S. 393, 415 (1922), as a "taking." * * * [But] even assuming * * * that the Fifth Amendment requires the payment of money damages to compensate for such a taking, the jury verdict in this case cannot be upheld. Because respondent has not yet obtained a final decision regarding the application of the zoning ordinance and subdivision regulations to its property, nor utilized the procedures Tennessee provides for obtaining just compensation, respondent's claim is not ripe.

A

As the Court has made clear in several recent decisions, a claim that the application of government regulations effects a taking of a property interest is not ripe until the government entity charged with implementing the regulations has reached a final decision regarding the application of the regulations to the property at issue. In *Hodel v. Virginia Surface Mining & Reclamation Assn., Inc.*, 452 U.S. 264 (1981), for example, the Court rejected a claim that the Surface Mining Control and Reclamation Act of 1977, 91 Stat. 447, 30 U.S.C. § 1201 et seq., effected a taking because:

> There is no indication in the record that appellees have availed themselves of the opportunities provided by the Act to obtain administrative relief by requesting either a variance from the approximate-original-contour requirement of § 515(d) or a waiver from the surface mining restrictions in § 522(e). If [the property owners] were to seek administrative relief under these procedures, a mutually acceptable solution might well be reached with regard to individual properties, thereby obviating any need to address the constitutional questions. The potential for such administrative solutions confirms the conclusion that the taking issue decided by the District Court simply is not ripe for judicial resolution. 452 U.S., at 297 (footnote omitted).

Similarly, in * * * *Penn Central Transp. Co. v. New York City*, supra, the Court declined to find that the application of New York City's Landmarks Preservation Law to Grand Central Terminal effected a taking because, although the Landmarks Preservation Commission had disapproved a plan for a 50–story office building above the terminal, the property owners had not sought approval for any other plan, and it therefore was not clear whether the Commission would deny approval for all uses that would enable the plaintiffs to derive economic benefit from the property. 438 U.S., at 136–137.

Respondent's claim is in a posture similar to the claims the Court held premature in *Hodel.* * * * It appears that variances could have been granted to resolve at least five of the Commission's eight objections to the plat. The Board of Zoning Appeals had the power to grant certain variances from the zoning ordinance, including the ordinance's density requirements and its restriction on placing units on land with slopes having a grade in excess of 25%. The Commission had the power to grant variances from the subdivision regulations, including the cul-de-sac, road-grade, and frontage requirements. Indeed, the Temple Hills Committee had recommended that the Commission grant variances from those regulations. Nevertheless, respondent did not seek variances from either the Board or the Commission.

Respondent argues that it "did everything possible to resolve the conflict with the commission," and that the Commission's denial of approval for respondent's plat was equivalent to a denial of variances. The record does not support respondent claim, however. There is no evidence that respondent applied to the Board of Zoning Appeals for variances from the zoning ordinance. As noted, the developer sought a ruling that the ordinance in effect in 1973 should be applied, but neither respondent nor the developer sought a variance from the requirements of either the 1973 or 1980 ordinances. Further, although the subdivision regulations in effect in 1981 required that applications to the Commission for variances be in writing, and that notice of the application be given to owners of adjacent property, the record contains no evidence that respondent ever filed a written request for variances from the cul-de-sac, road-grade, or frontage requirements of the subdivision regulations, or that respondent ever gave the required notice. * * *

* * * Our reluctance to examine taking claims until such a final decision has been made is compelled by the very nature of the inquiry required by the Just Compensation Clause. Although "[t]he question of what constitutes a 'taking' for purposes of the Fifth Amendment has proved to be a problem of considerable difficulty," Penn Central Transp. Co. v. New York City, 438 U.S., at 123, this Court consistently has indicated that among the factors of particular significance in the inquiry are the economic impact of the challenged action and the extent to which it interferes with reasonable investment-backed expectations. Id., at 124. * * * Those factors simply cannot be evaluated until the administrative

agency has arrived at a final, definitive position regarding how it will apply the regulations at issue to the particular land in question.

Here, for example, the jury's verdict indicates only that it found that respondent would be denied the economically feasible use of its property if it were forced to develop the subdivision in a manner that would meet each of the Commission's eight objections. It is not clear whether the jury would have found that the respondent had been denied all reasonable beneficial use of the property had any of the eight objections been met through the grant of a variance. Indeed, the expert witness who testified regarding the economic impact of the Commission's actions did not itemize the effect of each of the eight objections, so the jury would have been unable to discern how a grant of a variance from any one of the regulations at issue would have affected the profitability of the development. Accordingly, until the Commission determines that no variances will be granted, it is impossible for the jury to find, on this record, whether respondent "will be unable to derive economic benefit" from the land.

Respondent asserts that it should not be required to seek variances from the regulations because its suit is predicated upon 42 U.S.C. § 1983, and there is no requirement that a plaintiff exhaust administrative remedies before bringing a § 1983 action. *Patsy v. Florida Board of Regents,* 457 U.S. 496 (1982). The question whether administrative remedies must be exhausted is conceptually distinct, however, from the question whether an administrative action must be final before it is judicially reviewable. See FTC v. Standard Oil Co., 449 U.S. 232, 243 (1980); Bethlehem Steel Corp. v. EPA, 669 F.2d 903, 908 (CA3 1982). See generally, 13A C. Wright, A. Miller & E. Cooper, Federal Practice and Procedure § 3532.6 (1984). While the policies underlying the two concepts often overlap, the finality requirement is concerned with whether the initial decisionmaker has arrived at a definitive position on the issue that inflicts an actual, concrete injury; the exhaustion requirement generally refers to administrative and judicial procedures by which an injured party may seek review of an adverse decision and obtain a remedy if the decision is found to be unlawful or otherwise inappropriate. *Patsy* concerned the latter, not the former.

The difference is best illustrated by comparing the procedure for seeking a variance with the procedures that, under *Patsy,* respondent would not be required to exhaust. While it appears that the State provides procedures by which an aggrieved property owner may seek a declaratory judgment regarding the validity of zoning and planning actions taken by county authorities, see Fallin v. Knox County Bd. of Comm's, 656 S.W.2d 338 (Tenn. 1983); Tenn.Code Ann. §§ 27–8–101, 27–9–101 to 27–9–113, and 29–14–101 to 29–14–113 (1980 and Supp. 1984), respondent would not be required to resort to those procedures before bringing its § 1983 action, because those procedures clearly are remedial. Similarly, respondent would not be required to appeal the Commission's rejection of the preliminary plat to the Board of Zoning Appeals, because the Board was empowered, at most, to review that rejection, not to participate in the Commission's decisionmaking.

Resort to those procedures would result in a judgment whether the Commission's actions violated any of respondent rights. In contrast, resort to the procedure for obtaining variances would result in a conclusive determination by the Commission whether it would allow respondent to develop the subdivision in the manner respondent proposed. The Commission's refusal to approve the preliminary plat does not determine that issue; it prevents respondent from developing its subdivision without obtaining the necessary variances, but leaves open the possibility that respondent may develop the subdivision according to its plat after obtaining the variances. In short, the Commission's denial of approval does not conclusively determine whether respondent will be denied all reasonable beneficial use of its property, and therefore is not a final, reviewable decision.

B

A second reason the taking claim is not yet ripe is that respondent did not seek compensation through the procedures the State has provided for doing so. The Fifth Amendment does not proscribe the taking of property; it proscribes taking without just compensation. Hodel v. Virginia Surface Mining & Reclamation Assn., Inc., 452 U.S., at 297, n. 40. Nor does the Fifth Amendment require that just compensation be paid in advance of, or contemporaneously with, the taking; all that is required is that a " 'reasonable, certain and adequate provision for obtaining compensation' " exist at the time of the taking. Regional Rail Reorganization Act Cases, 419 U.S. 102, 124–125 (1974) (quoting Cherokee Nation v. Southern Kansas R. Co., 135 U.S. 641, 659 (1890)). * * * If the government has provided an adequate process for obtaining compensation, and if resort to that process "yield[s] just compensation," then the property owner "has no claim against the Government" for a taking. [Ruckelshaus v. Monsanto Co., 467 U.S. 986, at 1013, 1018 n. 21 (1984)]. Thus, we have held that taking claims against the Federal Government are premature until the property owner has availed itself of the process provided by the Tucker Act, 28 U.S.C. § 1491. Monsanto, 467 U.S., at 1016–1020. Similarly, if a State provides an adequate procedure for seeking just compensation, the property owner cannot claim a violation of the Just Compensation Clause until it has used the procedure and been denied just compensation. * * *

Under Tennessee law, a property owner may bring an inverse condemnation action to obtain just compensation for an alleged taking of property under certain circumstances. Tenn.Code Ann. § 29–16–123 (1980). The statutory scheme for eminent domain proceedings outlines the procedures by which government entities must exercise the right of eminent domain. §§ 29–16–101 to 29–16–121. The State is prohibited from "enter[ing] upon [condemned] land" until these procedures have been utilized and compensation has been paid the owner, § 29–16–122, but if a government entity does take possession of the land without following the required procedures,

the owner of such land may petition for a jury of inquest, in which case the same proceedings may be had, as near as may be, as hereinbefore provided; or he may sue for damages in the ordinary way.... § 29–16–123.

The Tennessee state courts have interpreted § 29–16–123 to allow recovery through inverse condemnation where the "taking" is effected by restrictive zoning laws or development regulations. See Davis v. Metropolitan Govt. of Nashville, 620 S.W.2d 532, 533–534 (Tenn. Ct. App. 1981); Speight v. Lockhart, 524 S.W.2d 249 (Tenn. Ct. App. 1975). Respondent has not shown that the inverse condemnation procedure is unavailable or inadequate, and until it has utilized that procedure, its taking claim is premature.

* * * We therefore reverse the judgment of the Court of Appeals and remand the case for further proceedings consistent with this opinion.

[The dissenting opinion of Justice White and the concurring opinions of Justices Brennan and Stevens are omitted.]

NOTES AND QUESTIONS

1.   The first half of the *Williamson County* ripeness test—requiring a final decision by regulators about the scope of the permitted project—has proven to be rather malleable, at least in the hands of the Supreme Court. See, e.g., Lucas, supra (finding controversy ripe under *Williamson County* even though statute had been amended to permit special circumstances permits and landowner had not sought such a permit); Palazzolo, supra (finding controversy ripe under *Williamson County* even though landowner had made no attempt to secure approval of a less drastic proposal than the one rejected by the planning authority). A major difficulty in drawing up any firm rules about when a land-use decision is "final" is that local zoning and land-use permitting schemes typically allow limitless numbers of amendments and petitions for variances. So it is hard to say when enough is enough so as to allow a property owner to go to court under a regulatory takings theory.

2.   The Court holds that the developer is required to exhaust state administrative remedies but not state judicial remedies in order to establish that the regulation is final. But it then goes on to hold that the developer is required to exhaust state *judicial* remedies in order to determine whether it has been denied just compensation. Is the Court being inconsistent here? Does it depend on whether the state affords administrative remedies for obtaining just compensation, as opposed to providing solely judicial remedies? Is exhaustion under the compensation branch of *Williamson County* required if the state courts have made clear in previous decisions that they will deny compensation in the circumstances presented? Is the claimant required to file an appeal all the way to the state supreme court under this branch of *Williamson*, or is it enough to seek and be denied compensation by one level of state tribunals? For further discussion see Barry Friedman, Under the Law of Federal Jurisdiction: Allocating Cases between Federal and State Courts, 104 Colum. L. Rev. 1211, 1256–59, 1264–71 (2004);

Gregory M. Stein, Regulatory Takings and Ripeness in the Federal Courts, 48 Vand. L. Rev. 1, 34–41 (1995).

San Remo Hotel v. City and County of San Francisco

Supreme Court of the United States, 2005.
545 U.S. 323.

■ JUSTICE STEVENS delivered the opinion of the Court. This case presents the question whether federal courts may craft an exception to the full faith and credit statute, 28 U.S.C. § 1738, for claims brought under the Takings Clause of the Fifth Amendment.

Petitioners, who own and operate a hotel in San Francisco, California (hereinafter City), initiated this litigation in response to the application of a city ordinance that required them to pay a $567,000 "conversion fee" in 1996. After the California courts rejected petitioners' various state-law takings claims, they advanced in the Federal District Court a series of federal takings claims that depended on issues identical to those that had previously been resolved in the state-court action. In order to avoid the bar of issue preclusion, petitioners asked the District Court to exempt from § 1738's reach claims brought under the Takings Clause of the Fifth Amendment.

Petitioners' argument is predicated on *Williamson County Regional Planning Comm'n v. Hamilton Bank of Johnson City,* 473 U.S. 172 (1985), which held that takings claims are not ripe until a State fails "to provide adequate compensation for the taking." Id., at 195. Unless courts disregard § 1738 in takings cases, petitioners argue, plaintiffs will be forced to litigate their claims in state court without any realistic possibility of ever obtaining review in a federal forum. * * *

II

Article IV, § 1, of the United States Constitution demands that "Full Faith and Credit shall be given in each State to the public Acts, Records, and judicial Proceedings of every other State. And the Congress may by general Laws prescribe the Manner in which such Acts, Records and Proceedings shall be proved, and the Effect thereof." In 1790, Congress responded to the Constitution's invitation by enacting the first version of the full faith and credit statute. See Act of May 26, 1790, ch. 11, 1 Stat. 122. The modern version of the statute, 28 U.S.C. § 1738, provides that "judicial proceedings ... shall have the same full faith and credit in every court within the United States and its Territories and Possessions as they have by law or usage in the courts of such State...." This statute has long been understood to encompass the doctrines of res judicata, or "claim preclusion," and collateral estoppel, or "issue preclusion." See Allen v. McCurry, 449 U.S. 90, 94–96 (1980).[16] * * *

---

16. "Under res judicata, a final judgment on the merits of an action precludes the parties or their privies from relitigating issues that were or could have been raised in

The essence of petitioners' argument is as follows: because no claim that a state agency has violated the federal Takings Clause can be heard in federal court until the property owner has "been denied just compensation" through an available state compensation procedure, [Williamson County, supra,] at 195, "federal courts [should be] required to disregard the decision of the state court" in order to ensure that federal takings claims can be "considered on the merits in ... federal court." Therefore, the argument goes, whenever plaintiffs reserve their claims * * *, federal courts should review the reserved federal claims *de novo,* regardless of what issues the state court may have decided or how it may have decided them. * * *

We reject petitioners' contention. * * *

IV

[Petitioners] * * * argue that federal courts simply should not apply ordinary preclusion rules to state-court judgments when a case is forced into state court by the ripeness rule of *Williamson County.* For support, petitioners rely on the Court of Appeals for the Second Circuit's decision in *Santini* [*v. Connecticut Hazardous Waste Management Service,* 342 F.3d 118, 130 (2d Cir. 2003)].

In *Santini,* the Second Circuit held that parties "who litigate state-law takings claims in state court involuntarily" pursuant to *Williamson County* cannot be precluded from having those very claims resolved "by a federal court." 342 F.3d, at 130. The court did not rest its decision on any provision of the federal full faith and credit statute or our cases construing that law. Instead, the court reasoned that "[i]t would be both ironic and unfair if the very procedure that the Supreme Court required [plaintiffs] to follow before bringing a Fifth Amendment takings claim ... also precluded [them] from ever bringing a Fifth Amendment takings claim." *Ibid.* We find this reasoning unpersuasive for several reasons.

First, both petitioners and *Santini* ultimately depend on an assumption that plaintiffs have a right to vindicate their federal claims in a federal forum. We have repeatedly held, to the contrary, that issues actually decided in valid state-court judgments may well deprive plaintiffs of the "right" to have their federal claims relitigated in federal court. See, e.g., Migra v. Warren City School Dist. Bd. of Ed., 465 U.S. 75, 84 (1984); Allen, 449 U.S., at 103–104. This is so even when the plaintiff would have preferred not to litigate in state court, but was required to do so by statute or prudential rules. See id., at 104. The relevant question in such cases is not whether the plaintiff has been afforded access to a federal forum; rather, the question is whether the state court actually decided an issue of fact or law that was necessary to its judgment.

that action. Under collateral estoppel, once a court has decided an issue of fact or law necessary to its judgment, that decision may preclude relitigation of the issue in a suit on a different cause of action involving a party to the first case." Id., at 94 (citations omitted).

In *Allen,* the plaintiff, Willie McCurry, invoked the Fourth and Fourteenth Amendments in an unsuccessful attempt to suppress evidence in a state criminal trial. After he was convicted, he sought to remedy his alleged constitutional violation by bringing a suit for damages under 42 U.S.C. § 1983 against the officers who had entered his home. Relying on " 'the special role of federal courts in protecting civil rights' " and the fact that § 1983 provided the "only route to a federal forum," the court of appeals held that McCurry was entitled to a federal trial unencumbered by collateral estoppel. 449 U.S., at 93. We rejected that argument emphatically.

> The actual basis of the Court of Appeals' holding appears to be a generally framed principle that every person asserting a federal right is entitled to one unencumbered opportunity to litigate that right in a federal district court, regardless of the legal posture in which the federal claim arises. But the authority for this principle is difficult to discern. It cannot lie in the Constitution, which makes no such guarantee, but leaves the scope of the jurisdiction of the federal district courts to the wisdom of Congress. And no such authority is to be found in § 1983 itself.... There is, in short, no reason to believe that Congress intended to provide a person claiming a federal right an unrestricted opportunity to relitigate an issue already decided in state court simply because the issue arose in a state proceeding in which he would rather not have been engaged at all." Id., at 103–104.

As in *Allen,* we are presently concerned only with issues *actually decided* by the state court that are dispositive of federal claims raised under § 1983. And, also as in *Allen,* it is clear that petitioners would have preferred not to have been forced to have their federal claims resolved by issues decided in state court. Unfortunately for petitioners, it is entirely *unclear* why their preference for a federal forum should matter for constitutional or statutory purposes. * * *

The second reason we find petitioners' argument unpersuasive is that it assumes that courts may simply create exceptions to 28 U.S.C. § 1738 wherever courts deem them appropriate. Even conceding, *arguendo,* the laudable policy goal of making federal forums available to deserving litigants, we have expressly rejected petitioners' view. "Such a fundamental departure from traditional rules of preclusion, enacted into federal law, can be justified only if plainly stated by Congress." Kremer v. Chemical Constr. Corp., 456 U.S. 461, 485 (1982). Our cases have therefore made plain that "an exception to § 1738 will not be recognized unless a later statute contains an express or implied partial repeal." Id., at 468 (citing Allen, 449 U.S., at 99). Even when the plaintiff's resort to state court is involuntary and the federal interest in denying finality is robust, we have held that Congress "must 'clearly manifest' its intent to depart from § 1738." 456 U.S., at 477.

The same concerns animate our decision here. Congress has not expressed any intent to exempt from the full faith and credit statute federal takings claims. Consequently, we apply our normal assumption that the weighty interests in finality and comity trump the interest in giving losing litigants access to an additional appellate tribunal. * * *

Third, petitioners have overstated the reach of *Williamson County* throughout this litigation. Petitioners were never required to ripen the heart of their complaint—the claim that the [state regulation] was facially invalid because it failed to substantially advance a legitimate state interest—in state court. See Yee v. Escondido, 503 U.S. 519, 534 (1992). Petitioners therefore could have raised most of their facial takings challenges, which by their nature requested relief distinct from the provision of "just compensation," directly in federal court. Alternatively, petitioners had the option of reserving their facial claims while pursuing their as-applied claims along with their petition for writ of administrative mandamus. Petitioners did not have the right, however, to seek state review of the same substantive issues they sought to reserve. * * *

With respect to those federal claims that did require ripening, we reject petitioners' contention that *Williamson County* forbids plaintiffs from advancing their federal claims in state courts. The requirement that aggrieved property owners must seek "compensation through the procedures the State has provided for doing so," 473 U.S., at 194, does not preclude state courts from hearing simultaneously a plaintiff's request for compensation under state law and the claim that, in the alternative, the denial of compensation would violate the Fifth Amendment of the Federal Constitution. Reading *Williamson County* to preclude plaintiffs from raising such claims in the alternative would erroneously interpret our cases as requiring property owners to "resort to piecemeal litigation or otherwise unfair procedures." MacDonald, Sommer & Frates v. Yolo County, 477 U.S. 340, 350, n. 7 (1986).

It is hardly a radical notion to recognize that, as a practical matter, a significant number of plaintiffs will necessarily litigate their federal takings claims in state courts. It was settled well before *Williamson County* that "a claim that the application of government regulations effects a taking of a property interest is not ripe until the government entity charged with implementing the regulations has reached a final decision regarding the application of the regulations to the property at issue." 473 U.S., at 186. As a consequence, there is scant precedent for the litigation in federal district court of claims that a state agency has taken property in violation of the Fifth Amendment's takings clause. To the contrary, most of the cases in our takings jurisprudence, including nearly all of the cases on which petitioners rely, came to us on writs of certiorari from state courts of last resort. * * *

At base, petitioners' claim amounts to little more than the concern that it is unfair to give preclusive effect to state-court proceedings that are not chosen, but are instead *required* in order to ripen federal takings claims. Whatever the merits of that concern may be, we are not free to disregard the full faith and credit statute solely to preserve the availability of a federal forum. The Court of Appeals was correct to decline petitioners' invitation to ignore the requirements of 28 U.S.C. § 1738. The judgment of the Court of Appeals is therefore affirmed.

■ CHIEF JUSTICE REHNQUIST, with whom JUSTICE O'CONNOR, JUSTICE KENNEDY, and JUSTICE THOMAS join, concurring in the judgment. I agree that the judgment of the Court of Appeals should be affirmed. Whatever the reasons for petitioners' chosen course of litigation in the state courts, it is quite clear that they are now precluded by the full faith and credit statute, 28 U.S.C. § 1738, from relitigating in their 42 U.S.C. § 1983 action those issues which were adjudicated by the California courts. * * * I write separately to explain why I think part of our decision in *Williamson County Regional Planning Comm'n v. Hamilton Bank of Johnson City*, 473 U.S. 172 (1985), may have been mistaken. * * *

It is not clear to me that *Williamson County* was correct in demanding that, once a government entity has reached a final decision with respect to a claimant's property, the claimant must seek compensation in state court before bringing a federal takings claim in federal court. The Court in *Williamson County* purported to interpret the Fifth Amendment in divining this state-litigation requirement. * * * More recently, we have referred to it as merely a prudential requirement. Suitum v. Tahoe Regional Planning Agency, 520 U.S. 725, 733–734 (1997). It is not obvious that either constitutional or prudential principles require claimants to utilize all state compensation procedures before they can bring a federal takings claim. Cf. Patsy v. Board of Regents of Fla., 457 U.S. 496, 516 (1982) (holding that plaintiffs suing under § 1983 are not required to have exhausted state administrative remedies). * * *

The Court today [remarks] that state courts are more familiar with the issues involved in local land-use and zoning regulations, and it suggests that this makes it proper to relegate federal takings claims to state court. But * * * the Court has not explained why we should hand authority over federal takings claims to state courts, based simply on their relative familiarity with local land-use decisions and proceedings, while allowing plaintiffs to proceed directly to federal court in cases involving, for example, challenges to municipal land-use regulations based on the First Amendment, see, e.g., Renton v. Playtime Theatres, Inc., 475 U.S. 41 (1986); Young v. American Mini Theatres, Inc., 427 U.S. 50 (1976), or the Equal Protection Clause, see, e.g., Cleburne v. Cleburne Living Center, Inc., 473 U.S. 432 (1985); Village of Belle Terre v. Boraas, 416 U.S. 1 (1974). In short, the affirmative case for the state-litigation requirement has yet to be made.

Finally, *Williamson County*'s state-litigation rule has created some real anomalies, justifying our revisiting the issue. For example, our holding today ensures that litigants who go to state court to seek compensation will likely be unable later to assert their federal takings claims in federal court. * * * As the Court recognizes, *Williamson County* all but guarantees that claimants will be unable to utilize the federal courts to enforce the Fifth Amendment's just compensation guarantee. The basic principle that state courts are competent to enforce federal rights and to adjudicate federal takings claims is sound and would apply to any number of federal claims. Cf. 28 U.S.C. § 2254 (providing for limited federal habeas review of state-court adjudications of alleged violations of the Constitution). But that principle does not explain why federal takings claims in particular should be singled out to be confined to state court, in the absence of any asserted justification or congressional directive.

* * *

I joined the opinion of the Court in *Williamson County*. But further reflection and experience lead me to think that the justifications for its state-litigation requirement are suspect, while its impact on takings plaintiffs is dramatic. Here, no court below has addressed the correctness of *Williamson County*, neither party has asked us to reconsider it, and resolving the issue could not benefit petitioners. In an appropriate case, I believe the Court should reconsider whether plaintiffs asserting a Fifth Amendment takings claim based on the final decision of a state or local government entity must first seek compensation in state courts.

NOTES AND QUESTIONS

1. Suppose a property owner simply wants to make an as-applied challenge to a regulation under the ad hoc test of *Penn Central*. (For the distinction between as-applied and facial challenges, see Michael C. Dorf, Facial Challenges to State and Federal Statutes, 46 Stan. L. Rev. 235, 236 (1994).) If the state permits regulatory takings challenges in state court under state constitutional law, but follows *Penn Central* in assessing such claims, is there any way for the owner to have the claim heard by *any* federal court after *Williamson County* and *San Remo*? Note that if the state courts refuse to hear the federal takings claim, the final state court judgment will be insulated from review by the U.S. Supreme Court, because the judgment will rest solely on state law, and state law questions are not reviewable by the Supreme Court. Nevertheless, the issues resolved by the state courts, assuming they are identical to the issues that would have to be decided under federal law, will be given collateral estoppel effect under *San Remo* if the owner tries later to bring those issues to federal district court. Is there something wrong with a federal constitutional doctrine that can never be heard by any federal court?

2. After *Lingle v. Chevron U.S.A. Inc.*, 544 U.S. 528 (2005), which overturned the notion that a regulation which fails to substantially advance a legitimate state interest is a taking, how many facial challenges are left for property owners to preserve for federal court review? The categorical rule for permanent government occupations, recognized in *Loretto*, is one. Are there any others? Is the *Lucas* test a facial test or an as-applied test?

3. It appears that the petitioners in *San Remo* were largely to blame for injecting their facial claims (as opposed to the as-applied claim) into the state court litigation. (Their principal facial claim was that the regulation did not substantially advance a legitimate state interest, a theory that was

overturned by the Court in *Lingle* in the same Term as *San Remo*.) But suppose petitioners had assiduously avoided making any reference to their facial takings claims under the federal Constitution, and yet the state courts had *sua sponte* ruled on those claims anyway? Under the Full Faith and Credit Act, would this judgment be res judicata as to the federal claims? Would this mean that a state court could unilaterally block any further litigation of facial takings issues in the lower federal courts? (The property owner could still file a petition for certiorari from the final state court judgment with the Supreme Court, but these are rarely granted.)

4.   Recall that in *Dolan v. City of Tigard*, supra, Chief Justice Rehnquist wrote that the Takings Clause is "as much a part of the Bill of Rights as the First Amendment or Fourth Amendment," and that it should not "be relegated to the status of a poor relation in these comparable circumstances." This comment was offered by way of justifying the application of the unconstitutional conditions doctrine to the Takings Clause. Does *Williamson County* violate this precept? Or does *San Remo* merely stand for the proposition that the Takings Clause is not entitled to favored treatment relative to other constitutional claims, insofar as any constitutional claim is subject to preclusion if it happens to be litigated in state court before a claimant reaches federal court?

5.   *San Remo*, together with *Lingle v. Chevron U.S.A. Inc.*, supra, and *Tahoe–Sierra Preservation Council, Inc. v. Tahoe Regional Planning Agency*, 535 U.S. 302 (2002), appears to mark a broad retreat by the Court on regulatory takings, eliminating much of the expansion that occurred in the early years of the Rehnquist Court in decisions like *First English*, *Nollan*, and *Lucas*. Thus, for example, the threat of *First English* liability for temporary takings was significantly reduced by *Tahoe–Sierra*; *Lucas*'s per se rule for total takings was narrowed greatly by *Tahoe–Sierra*; liability for regulations that do not substantially advance governmental interests was eliminated by *Lingle*; the nexus and rough proportionality tests were confined to exactions by decisions like *Lingle*; and *San Remo* promises to keep nearly all regulatory takings out of federal court altogether. What accounts for this "self correction" by the Court, during a period when there was little turnover in Court personnel? What are the most important unresolved issues under the Court's regulatory takings doctrine? How do you predict those issues will be decided?

INDEX

References are to pages.

†